D1072552

DOUGLAS A. CAMPBELL is associate professor of New Testament at Duke Divinity School. His other books include *The Quest for Paul's Gospel: A Suggested Strategy.*

οὐαὶ μοί ἐστιν ἐὰν μὴ εὐαγγελίσωμαι

THE DELIVERANCE OF GOD

An Apocalyptic Rereading of Justification in Paul

Douglas A. Campbell

WILLIAM B. EERDMANS PUBLISHING COMPANY

GRAND RAPIDS, MICHIGAN / CAMBRIDGE, U.K.

© 2009 Douglas A. Campbell
All rights reserved

Published 2009 by
Wm. B. Eerdmans Publishing Co.
2140 Oak Industrial Drive N.E., Grand Rapids, Michigan 49505 /
P.O. Box 163, Cambridge CB3 9PU U.K.

Printed in the United States of America

15 14 13 12 11 10 09   7 6 5 4 3 2 1

ISBN 978-0-8028-3126-2

JKM Library
1100 East 55th Street
Chicago, IL 60615

www.eerdmans.com

To Rachel, Rupert, and Georgia,

whose sacrifices are inscribed unseen on every page

Contents

Part Five — Rereading the Heartland

Table of Chapters and Sections

Acknowledgments

The following material has been reprinted or substantially reproduced by the kind permission of Continuum International Publishing Ltd.: pages 146-64 and 253-56 from *The Quest for Paul's Gospel: A Suggested Strategy* (London: T&T Clark International [Continuum], 2005) — excerpts from chapter eight, "The Contractual (JF) Construal of Paul's Gospel, and Its Problems," and chapter eleven, "Rereading Romans 1.18–3:20," respectively; and pages 375-87 from "Towards a New, Rhetorically Assisted Reading of Romans 3.27–4.25," in *Rhetorical Criticism and the Bible,* ed. Stanley E. Porter and Dennis L. Stamps, JSNTSup 195 (Sheffield: Sheffield Academic Press [Continuum], 2002). Permission is also gratefully acknowledged from the Society of Biblical Literature to draw significantly from "2 Corinthians 4:13: Evidence in Paul That Christ Believes." *Journal of Biblical Literature* 128.2 (2009): 337-56. The bibliography supplied for part five, chapter twenty-one, §3.2, should also be updated in relation to this article.

Most of the English Scripture quotations herein (other than my own translations) are from the New Revised Standard Version Bible, copyright 1989, Division of Christian Education of the National Council of Churches of Christ in the U.S.A. Used by Permission. All rights reserved. Occasionally Scripture quotations are drawn from the Holy Bible, New International Version, copyright 1973, 1984, by the International Bible Society. Used by permission of Zondervan. All rights reserved.

Use is also gratefully acknowledged of the 27th critical edition of the New Testament edited by Eberhard and Erwin Nestle, Barbara and Kurt Aland, Johannes Karavidopoulos, Carlo M. Martini, and Bruce M. Metzger (Stuttgart: Deutsche Bibelgesellschaft, 1993), and of the critical edition of the Septuagint edited by Alfred Rahlfs, revised by Robert Hanhart (Stuttgart: Deutsche Bibelgesellschaft, 2006).

Most of the significant intellectual debts incurred during the course of this project are acknowledged plainly in what follows — in particular, those owed to the guidance and wisdom of Richard Longenecker, James and Alan Torrance, and Robert Jewett. But an earlier debt to an esteemed mentor is not so obvious — that is, to my teacher at the University of Toronto, Abraham Rotstein. It is a pleasure to acknowledge his importance to me here. I have also been greatly encouraged since my arrival at the Divinity School at Duke University in 2003 by students from every program — M.Div., M.T.S., Th.M., Ph.D., and Th.D. To put things at their plainest: their enthusiasm has been critical. Tommy Givens, Timothy "TJ" Lang, Colin Miller, Dan Rhodes, Scott Ryan, Robert Moses, and Celia Wolff deserve special mention. The School itself has also been right behind me, from the Dean downward! I have greatly appreciated this — especially the kindness and encouragement of Stanley Hauerwas. The "coffee-shop group" has also been critical — especially Jeff McSwain, Alan Koeneke, and Chris Smith. I am grateful to Ann Weston for her editorial help during the final push to delivery. Peter Lampe's support from Heidelberg has been much appreciated, as has the ongoing support of the Von Humboldt Foundation. Many from the United Kingdom and New Zealand have also been faithful — my parents in particular, Graeme and Leigh. And I owe an incalculable debt to Carol Shoun, whose editorial work is so meticulously diligent and deeply insightful.

Abbreviations

AB	Anchor Bible
ABD	*Anchor Bible Dictionary,* ed. D. N. Freedman. 6 vols. (New York: Doubleday, 1992)
ANE	Ancient Near East
ANRW	*Aufstieg und Niedergang der römischen Welt: Geschichte und Kultur Roms im Spiegel der neueren Forschung,* ed. H. Temporini and W. Haase. (Berlin: De Gruyter, 1978-)
ANTC	Abingdon New Testament Commentaries
BDAG	Bauer, W., F. W. Danker, W. Arndt, and F. W. Gingrich, eds., *A Greek-English Lexicon of the New Testament and Other Early Christian Literature,* 3rd ed. (Chicago: University of Chicago Press, 1999)
BDF	Blass, F., A. Debrunner, and R. W. Funk, eds., *A Greek Grammar of the New Testament.* (Chicago: University of Chicago Press, 1961)
BECNT	Baker Exegetical Commentaries on the New Testament
BNTC	Black's New Testament Commentaries
BZNW	Beihefte zur Zeitschrift für die neutestamentliche Wissenschaft
CD	Karl Barth, *Church Dogmatics,* ed. and tr. G. W. Bromiley. 13 vols. (Edinburgh: T&T Clark, 1936-69)
CSEL	Corpus scriptorum ecclesiasticorum latinorum
DC	my translation
DP&L	*Dictionary of Paul and His Letters,* ed. G. F. Hawthorne et al. (Downers Grove, Ill.: InterVarsity, 1993)
FRLANT	Forschungen zur Religion und Literatur des Alten und Neuen Testaments
HDR	Harvard Dissertations in Religion
HTKNT	Herders theologischer Kommentar zum neuen Testament
HTKNTSup	Herders theologischer Kommentar zum neuen Testament Supplement Series
ICC	International Critical Commentary

JSJSup	Journal for the Study of Judaism in the Persian, Hellenistic, and Roman Periods Supplement Series
JSNTSup	Journal for the Study of the New Testament: Supplement Series
LCC	Library of Christian Classics
LCL	Loeb Classical Library
LNSM	Louw, J. P., E. A. Nida, R. B. Smith, and K. A. Munson, eds., *Greek-English Lexicon of the New Testament Based on Semantic Domains*, 2nd ed. 2 vols. (New York: United Bible Societies, 1988, 1989)
LSJ	Liddell, H. G., R. Scott, and H. S. Jones, eds., *A Greek-English Lexicon*, rev. ed. (Oxford: Clarendon, 1968)
LXX	Septuagint
MT	Masoretic Text
NICNT	New International Commentary on the New Testament
NIGTC	New International Greek Testament Commentary
NIV	New International Version
NRSV	New Revised Standard Version
NovTSup	Novum Testamentum Supplements
SBL	Society of Biblical Literature
SBLDS	Society of Biblical Literature Dissertation Series
SBLSBS	Society of Biblical Literature Sources for Biblical Study
SBLSP	Society of Biblical Literature Seminar Papers
SJLA	Studies in Judaism in Late Antiquity
SNTSMS	Society for New Testament Studies Monograph Series
SNTW	Studies of the New Testament and Its World
TDNT	*Theological Dictionary of the New Testament,* ed. G. Kittel and G. Friedrich, trans. G. W. Bromiley. 10 vols. (Grand Rapids: Eerdmans, 1964-76)
THKNT	Theologischer Handkommentar zum Neuen Testament
WBC	Word Biblical Commentary
WMANT	Wissenschaftliche Monographien zum Alten und Neuen Testament
WUNT	Wissenschaftliche Untersuchungen zum Neuen Testament

Preface

It is sobering to think that as I write these final words in 2007, the origin of this project lies back in the early 1990s, in my years at the University of Otago in Dunedin, New Zealand. So over fifteen years of reflection and research is embodied in these pages (not the sort of book that tends to get written much these days in the modern university!). Its origin lies in a proverbial flash of inspiration caused by some essays written by the father of a colleague and close friend of mine — James B. Torrance. One auspicious day his son, Alan Torrance, gave me these pieces and suggested that I read them, and they turned out to be something of an epiphany. I sensed straightaway that their theological and methodological insights concerning theological foundationalism — in the form specifically of contractualism — had revolutionary implications for my discipline of Pauline studies, suggesting an immediate reordering of many of our most pressing questions, and an implicit resolution to most of them as well. (These questions were with me in particular because of my wonderful doctoral education at the University of Toronto, which was influenced in its final stages especially by Richard Longenecker, an astute placer of questions.) I intuited that most Pauline interpreters — including me — were caught up in contractual frameworks, struggling to resolve certain localized issues dictated by those frameworks, but without recognizing how those broader settings were both controlling and constraining our more focal discussions of Paul's texts and thinking. We needed first to recognize and break out of our contractual mental structures, at which point stunning new interpretative vistas would open up. But these implications were so wide and profound that I had no idea even how to articulate them at first. (Michael Polanyi never spoke truer words for me than "we know more than we can say.") I look back, then, on my seven years at the University of Otago as the project's inception and early development — rapid in some respects but also inchoate.

Certainly, I began to try to read Paul in a rather new way at this time — as if he was not a foundationalist or a contractual thinker. And some of the central

exegetical insights into the construal of Romans 1–4 that would later prove critical to the entire project's plausibility began to take shape during this period. But I
could not yet construct a conceptual and hence pedagogical and rhetorical bridge
from the methodological insights of Torrance to my exegetical work that was beginning to unfold on the ground in Paul's texts. The overarching articulation of
my intuitions remained rather confused, and this was not helped by my intellectual isolation at Otago.

In part to redress this difficulty, in 1996 I took up a post at the Department
of Theology and Religious Studies at King's College London — a vibrant (and at
first rather intimidating) research environment compared with what I was used
to! I began to acquire there some of the skills that would be necessary if my imaginative exegetical suggestions were ever to reach the important thresholds of
scholarly rigor and credibility; they could survive at King's — as I served them up
piecemeal on various exciting but also potentially excoriating occasions — only if
they were articulated in a reasonably rigorous fashion. The project therefore began to move forward. Teaching at a major London university of course places
challenges in the path of any large research program, however, so progress was
also sporadic. But in 2000 I received an enormous boost, courtesy of an Alexander von Humboldt award, which allowed me a year of uninterrupted study at
Heidelberg. And even the very process of application for that scholarship forced
me to take the articulation of my concerns to a new level. (That articulation developed ultimately into the introduction to this book.) Things seemed to be gaining momentum (and I am deeply grateful to the intercessions of Robert Jewett
and Peter Lampe at this point). I traveled optimistically to Heidelberg in 2000,
certain that a year of solitude, musing by the banks of the Neckar, would allow me
to write the book that I had been trying to write for some time. But my expectations were sorely disappointed, for all sorts of reasons.

I realized rapidly how short a time a year really was, and especially for a
project of this magnitude. And as I began to try to write, a frustrating experience
began to unfold — repeatedly. I would begin to articulate my concerns as best I
could, painfully compose a chapter or two of prose, and then the argument would
break down. It was as if a wave would run each time a little further up the beach
before it would break — which it always did — and run back to the sea. I seemed
to end up caught every time in circularity, needing to affirm a set of points in order to move on that had not yet been established, but that could not be established without affirming in some way what I was presently trying to say. Things
were just not lining up properly; indeed, the issues did not seem to fall into a
"line" at all. Furthermore, I had expected to build my research on Stendahl's classic essays, using them as a sort of methodological foundation. But when I worked
through them closely, their arguments began to dissolve in my hands. I realized
that I was reading a collection of brilliant intuitions with no real internal order
and very different levels of plausibility. Stendahl could not serve me as a guide for
a detailed critical project on the contractual reading of Paul — and neither could
anyone else. It seemed that I was on my own, in largely uncharted academic terri-

tory. I thought for a time that this might be fun, and even exhilarating. But in reality it was lonely and made for very hard work, along with a dubious sense of progress and no real way of measuring it.

As the year unfolded — all too rapidly — I began to sense that in order to travel from Torrance's theology and methodology to a radical, noncontractual rereading of Paul's texts, I had to navigate through a significant hermeneutical discussion as well; I had to account somehow for the potentially distorting effect of prior frameworks on detailed exegesis — in particular, the possible influences of Western theology, church history, politics, and culture on our construction of Paul — but in a way that did not lose a degree of objectivity in the process of exegesis itself. And I felt this concern for entirely practical reasons. Whenever I presented my exegetical suggestions in an academic setting by themselves — cold, as it were — I found that they were frequently opposed and rejected *for presuppositional, not exegetical, reasons.* It became increasingly clear that I could not simply present my own new rereadings without analyzing this dynamic first. (That is, I could not simply write parts four and five of this book and expect to get a fair hearing.) I did not yet know how to address these issues, however, or even where to place this discussion in the context of the broader project.

I was able in my year in Heidelberg to articulate the critical theoretical framework that I thought was in play (now chapter one), and to begin to outline a workable approach to these hermeneutical issues (now chapter seven — leaning here heavily on the basic epistemology of Michael Polanyi, which seemed to explain my hermeneutical experiences with deep insight). I was also able to assemble some of the key church-historical and Western cultural evidence (now chapters eight and nine). But I returned from Heidelberg deeply frustrated that I had not been able to finish the book, or even to bring the various phases of the project into a clear, sustainable order — and this after a year of generous funding, and the sacrifices of my wife and children. Indeed, on returning to a struggling department and a mounting administrative load in London, it seemed to me that my one real chance to finish the project might have passed.

However, I was able to address many of these difficulties by moving to a post at Duke Divinity School in Durham, North Carolina, in 2003. Duke was much better geared to support research of this nature, and I was able to return to it in due course with renewed energy — buoyed up in part by the enthusiasm of many of the students there for my work and the encouragement and support of the staff more broadly. Duke provided unmatched library and research resources, and even editorial support (the incomparable Carol Shoun). As a friend put it at the time, "this has been too big for you to carry by yourself," and at Duke I finally found people who could help me with the load (Gal. 6:2!). But they also enriched the project as well.

Surrounded by the ongoing integration at Duke of theology, ethics, and interpretation — and the broader context of the United States, with its unique, complicated, vigorous church and its distinctive politics, currently enmeshed and embroiled in military adventurism — I was finally able to grasp with clarity the powerful political and ethical dimensions within the exegetical situation that I was describing. In certain respects, the project became much more real. I saw, so to speak, the explicit link between exegesis and execution — the connections between the construal of Paul in this fundamentally contractual manner, along with the rigorous (and I think ultimately unchristian) God that this presupposed, and the execution of the supposedly delinquent that took place with depressing regularity a few miles down the road from where I was writing, often in the name of the Christian God. I was also finally able to achieve complete clarity concerning the project's basic structure.

If writing a big book is like journeying down a long road, then some people need to see the way right through to the end of the road before they can walk on it, and for better or worse, I am one of them. And I had not yet been able to see through to the end of this particular road. But the reasons for this finally became apparent: the principal argumentative problem that had been holding me up for so long was the difficulty of breaking down and criticizing in a linear fashion — as one has to for an argument in a book — a fundamentally multidimensional interpretative situation that was, furthermore, locked in a vicious circle, each phase presupposing a previous phase, which presupposed in turn a prior one, and this often with more than one dimension adding its particular spin to the circle. Working out how to break into this situation methodologically was what had been impeding much of my forward movement. Finally, however, I stumbled on the solution: I would enter the circle with a set of preliminary characterizations that were largely incontestable and could serve to establish and initiate the principal issues. I could then articulate their consequences in more detail — the other side of the circle — and then return to consider those initial formulations more clearly. In more practical terms, this meant beginning counterintuitively, with the theological and theoretical dimensions (and not with the texts and their exegesis), in order to learn how to neutralize any inappropriate hermeneutical influences from those dimensions, and only then to treat the texts themselves in detail. It seemed that I had worked out one way of making an interpretative circle into a line, and of doing so in a way that would allow me to walk an indifferent or even hostile reader through the process. So there were many reasons for struggling so hard to resolve this basic set of "architectonic" issues.

With this final conceptual breakthrough — a mere fifteen years or so after the initial flash of insight — I was able to move ahead rapidly with writing up the rest of the argument, from mid-2005 through mid-2007 (also encouraged generously now by Eerdmans, who contracted the manuscript in 2006). And this book is the result — a project that has finally reached its destination (and admittedly at times I can scarcely believe it). It would seem that the only thing left to do is to read it, but before beginning the detailed discussion, two sets of caveats should be noted about its rather distinctive nature and mode.

The Structure of the Project

It is clearly a long book, and yet my worry is of course that it is far too short. It is an overview of a complicated situation that has several interlocking interpretative dimensions — textual or exegetical, argumentative, theological, hermeneutical, church-historical, and ideocultural. My argument needs initially to treat this whole problematic dynamic — along with its solution — in one basic sweep. However, because of this breadth, each component does not receive the attention that it really deserves (which would make things impossibly long, and stretch well beyond my competence). Each of these dimensions merits at least a book in its own right (and I nurse the hope that people will yet write them). And yet it seems to me that those cannot be written before the entire problem has been presented in an integrated fashion; we need to know the basic topography of the situation before its specific features can be navigated in detail.

At the same time — having read what is said about other, rather milder proposals than mine — I am aware that some Pauline interpreters might not be favourably disposed toward my suggestions. So I am aware of the need to try to present a fully rounded, defensible argument — one that has covered all the obvious points of criticism. And certainly, the seriousness of the subject merits this care; a powerful and important conception of the gospel is at stake (and in fact two conceptions — the one I am challenging, and the one lying behind it that I am suggesting is authentic).

The basic mode of the book is also rather distinctive for a contribution to New Testament studies, and a word should be said about that as well. This book is trying to break new ground, and in a comprehensive fashion, addressing a very complicated set of interpretative dynamics (in fact, discarding one set and trying to introduce another). Given, then, that its subject matter is both unexplored and difficult, I have tried to place the emphasis in what follows on my text, letting the engagement with the primary sources and the manipulation of the critical argumentative and theoretical levels do the bulk of the work. Above all, the book is itself an argument — which is rather unusual for New Testament scholars, who tend to treat their subjects atomistically, supported by a great deal of tradition and argument from authority (i.e., annotation). Of course, these methods have their due place, but in my judgment, this discussion is not that place. There is very little detailed tradition to interact with in the areas that I engage here. And extremely detailed interactions with the vast New Testament literature more distantly related to the many dimensions that I mobilize would, I fear, make the book completely unmanageable. Things are difficult enough as they are! So I have tried to avoid inflicting on the reader an account of everything that I have read, and this means that quite a bit of material I have given some thought to is not discussed in detail. (In a sense, I am happy to trust my readers to make the relevant applications in studies that are related but not central to my developing argument.) In addition, by a great stroke of good fortune, one of my mentors, Robert Jewett, has just published his magisterial analysis of Romans in the Hermeneia commentary series (Minneapolis: Fortress, 2007). Jewett has done an astonishing job of collating and analyzing the relevant secondary literature on Romans — it is the work of a lifetime — so I lean heavily on his erudition in what follows. There is no need to duplicate his intricate accounts in my footnotes; interested readers should simply consult Jewett directly. (I will of course indicate which discussions of his are especially pertinent for my argument.)

One final aspect of the book's organization should be noted. Because the internal argumentative and theological dynamics functioning in different readings of Paul's texts are so important to this project, I have chosen to adopt a "horizontal" rather than a "vertical" approach to any textual analysis. (This pertains to most of parts three through five — so chapters ten through twenty-one.)

Traditional New Testament exegesis tends to be more vertical. That is, it breaks the primary text up into manageable pieces and then treats several levels of debate in relation to that text before moving on to treat the next piece of text in the same fashion (and so on). The different lines of interpretation therefore tend to play out immediately after the text in question, usually extending through complex footnotes — vertically. In what follows, however, I place a great deal of emphasis on the overarching construal of Paul's rhetoric and argumentation in his key Justification texts (which of course contain a great deal of theological reasoning as well), that is, on the way that these pieces function together as an integrated, unfolding semantic and rhetorical event. It is one of my central contentions that maintaining a tight grip on Paul's supposed moves and countermoves — which are often very subtle — is critical to an appreciation of what we have been misunderstanding in his Justification texts in the past, and of how to correct it. A vertical approach tends to place too much pressure on the reader in these vital respects. Few if any can carry the multiple threads of the overarching arguments, as those are dictated by different basic construals, from pericope to pericope (in effect, holding several different arguments in mind at any given moment, while also navigating the other complex analytical questions that are usually in view). To facilitate clarity, then, in matters of argumentation and theology I have adopted a more horizontal approach, supplying a series of comprehensive construals in turn, one after the other. So, for example, instead of reading the key text, Romans 1–4, only once, comparing four or five different lines of construal simultaneously as we go, we will read it repeatedly (although not always at the same level of detail), in a different way on each occasion, and then look back to see which reading has worked best. (This also tends to "bunch" the secondary literature in relation to the more traditional reading — here especially in chapters ten and eleven. As my analysis becomes more radical, it tends to leave the secondary discussion behind and drive itself in terms of the primary evidence and argumentative considerations alone — so chapters fourteen through eighteen.) Thus, from part three onward, we will read Romans 1–4 first in conventional terms, rather generously (in chapter ten), then more critically, discerning the numerous problems present within that reading (chapter eleven), then from the perspectives of several well-known revisionists — notably Watson, Sanders, Dunn, and Stowers (although not all of these actually offer a new reading; see chapter twelve) — and then from my alternative perspective that emphasizes a rhetorical quality in Paul's discussion and an apocalyptic understanding of his positive contributions to this (chapters fourteen through eighteen).[1] A similar, although rather briefer approach will then be taken to Paul's other Justification texts in part five (chapters nineteen through twenty-one). And with these final observations about my project's structure — that it is not only a linear account of a multidimensional, circular, interpretative construct but for the key texts a horizontally organized one at that — we can turn to its detailed exposition, beginning with a brief, strategic consideration of why contractual categories might be so much more significant for the analysis of Paul, and especially of his Justification texts, than we have hitherto suspected. Hence, we return here to my attempt to articulate in nuce just why James B. Torrance's essays were an interpretative epiphany for me so long ago, in New Zealand, in the early 1990s.

Douglas A. Campbell
Durham, North Carolina
September 22 (Yom Kippur), 2007

Common Problems and a Complex Culprit

Three classic interpretative conundrums in relation to Paul provide a useful starting point for the following investigation.

In the late nineteenth century various predominantly German scholars
raised a protest against the usual construal of Paul's gospel in "Lutheran" terms,[1]
namely, in terms of "justification not by works of law but by faith."[2] This was probably in part a reaction against the powerful influence of Ritschl, but it was also fed
positively in due course by a new-found enthusiasm for Greco-Roman sources.
The conventional "Lutheran" and essentially forensic construal they criticized was
rooted primarily in the terminology and argumentation of Romans 1–4, assisted in
the main by Romans 10, Galatians 2–3, and half a chapter in Philippians — the
other references in Paul being quite vestigial. The nineteenth- and early-
twentieth-century protesters argued that the rather different mystical, participatory account evidenced in detail by, for example, Romans 5–8 in fact constituted
Paul's true theological center over against the forensic approach found in the texts
just noted. The most well known German proponents of this mystical view were
probably G. Adolf Deissmann and Albert Schweitzer, although the protest was
made by many others, most perspicuously perhaps by William Wrede.[3] However,
these revisionist[4] scholars *offered no satisfactory explanation of how the two discourses, forensic and mystical, might fit together,* either in Romans, with its transition from the argumentation of chapters 1–4 to that of 5–8, or in Paul's thinking
about salvation as a whole. In short, convinced of the centrality of the apostle's
mystical, participatory account, they attempted to marginalize his use of an apparently forensic model — a use they nevertheless could not satisfactorily explain.

But conversely, neither could proponents of the conventional view of justification by faith, unconvinced by these protests, explain the relationship between
their anthropocentric construal of Paul's gospel and Paul's christocentric mysticism. The most popular counterexplanation used an old theological distinction
between justification and sanctification, but, as we will see in due course, this

1

claim quickly proved inadequate. So the result of the debate was essentially an interpretative standoff, with the forensic advocates probably achieving the upper
hand in a long battle of attrition. Post–World War I Germany was not a conducive
environment for the optimistic Christ-mysticism of Deissmann and his like, and
the immensely influential Bultmann was firmly in the opposing camp, although
the mystical view has arguably lived on in exile in various English-speaking advocates.[5] What resolution is apparent is really due more to broader historical factors
shaping the modern interpretative community than to any decisive exegetical solution. Hence, although this tension has been with Pauline studies for some time,
I still know of no effective interpretative solution to the conundrum — merely
different ways of living with it that are delivered in the main by the broader flow
of events. We turn now to our second conundrum.

It is widely acknowledged that the publication in 1977 of E. P. Sanders's *Paul
and Palestinian Judaism*[6] effected a seismic shift in Pauline scholarship, especially
in North America. Among other things, Sanders highlighted the problems present within any description of Judaism as legalistic in both structure and outlook,
which is to say, as characterized by attempted "justification through works of law"
in an especially negative sense.[7] Yet this view animates the standard "Lutheran"
preamble to the state of justification by faith in Paul, in which the ethically sensitive realize that their first legalistic efforts to achieve salvation fail. Hence, Judaism is, in and of itself, a soteriological *cul-de-sac*. But such an essentially negative
characterization of Judaism simply seems false as a general rule when Judaism's
own sources are read carefully — even granting that it remains true of certain
pockets of piety (something Sanders denied).

This protest, too, stretches back to the nineteenth century, but Sanders established it in the academy's broader consciousness especially successfully, to the extent that the conundrum is now widely acknowledged. In part this is because he
stated the case so comprehensively. But his publication coincided with an upsurge
of post-Holocaust sensitivities in the seventies, a radical and questioning time in
more general terms. Hence, since Sanders's seminal 1977 publication the protest
voiced from the margins of the Pauline interpretative community about the nature
of late Second Temple Judaism has moved to the center of many of its deliberations.
It would seem that the "legalistic" rubric "a Jew is (not) justified through works of
law" delivered by the conventional construal of Paul's forensic texts is something of
a caricature of Judaism in Paul's day. And thus a second major problem has been
identified in the "Lutheran" construal of Paul's justification discussions as a whole.
That construal's first phase, apparently centered on a commercial and ultimately
negative description of Judaism, simply seems descriptively pernicious.

Unlike the enduring difficulties raised by the *Religionsgeschichtliche Schule*
and others about Paul's participatory language, this conundrum has elicited a
widespread scholarly response in the last thirty years to the point of dominating
publication in the field. However, like the preceding conundrum, arguably no cogent solution yet seems apparent — certainly none has won wide acceptance from
the modern interpretative community. Thus a second major interpretative scan-

dal seems to hold for the conventional construal of Paul's justification texts — its distorted account of Judaism. We turn now to our third.

Also in the mid-1970s, Karl Donfried precipitated — probably unintentionally — a sharp dispute over the provenance of Romans. New Testament scholars are accustomed to giving judicious accounts of the origins of New Testament documents in terms of their circumstances of composition and their purposes, even though many now rightly urge increased caution concerning the reliability and interpretative value of such reconstructions. Donfried, in debate initially with R. J. Karris, catalyzed a widespread discussion that revealed, somewhat disturbingly, a plethora of hypotheses but no firm consensus behind any one theory. The reasons for the composition of Romans, the letter that freights Paul's most important discussions of justification, were, it seemed, essentially a mystery.[8] And while there is less general uncertainty about the circumstances that elicited Galatians — although there is some! — there remain important and unresolved debates over its precise temporal location and its position in Paul's letter sequence. Most agree that this letter is a response to anti-Pauline agitators circulating among the Galatian Christian communities, but scholars disagree over when exactly this episode occurred in Paul's life — this could be Paul's first letter, we are told, but it could also be one of his last. And there are numerous disputes over the exact nature of the opponents.

Thus, not only are Paul's justification discussions somewhat baffling in relation to his participatory arguments, but they open with a descriptive phase that may well be fundamentally vulgar. Further, we do not know *why* he wrote his major deployment of this material in Romans, and neither are we certain exactly *when* he wrote his important ancillary discussion in Galatians, or in relation *to whom*. Clearly then the field of Pauline studies is significantly disordered. Like an ice shelf feeling the effects of global warming, it seems cracked and eroded in several directions, and in danger of collapse.

The following study has been developing over the last ten years or so in relation to these — and other — conundrums. I would suggest that all three of these apparently unrelated problems are in fact generated by a common underlying cause, at which point it begins to become apparent that many past attempts to resolve them may have suffered from explanatory superficiality. A single culprit seems to generate our difficulties, namely, a particular *individualist* — and so possibly also rather modern — reading of Paul's justification terminology and argumentation that devolves into a *conditional* understanding of salvation (that is, salvation is granted in relation to individual actions). It therefore also construes Paul's soteriology — at least as it is articulated in these texts — in fundamentally *contractual* terms. Hence, like the six proverbial blind scholars of "Indostan" describing an elephant, Pauline interpreters in the past may have been grasping partial explanations of a much more substantial beast, which really needs to be identified in a clear and integrated way if it is ever to be addressed satisfactorily.[9] This reading is of course often laid at the feet of Luther; hence, it is referred to most frequently in New Testament circles as "the Lutheran reading," but this is in many ways a rather unhappy designation that I will revisit shortly and suggest abandoning. The reading's exegetical assumptions and soteriological dynamics will be investigated in great detail later on as well.[10] For now, it suffices to consider quickly how such a reading and its accompanying model of salvation could generate the three conundrums we have just noted (so, in fact, how the side, ear, and tusk all belong to the same animal, which will also by no means exhaust its description).

The conditionality of this model of salvation involves a sustained focus on the individual. *Rational decision* is at the center of its soteriological progress,[11] and that decision must be actively upheld over time (something that necessitates the maintenance of individuals themselves in some sort of continuity over time). The system is thus highly anthropocentric, and tension is largely unavoidable when it is juxtaposed with a system that emphasizes divine initiative over against human choice and couples that with a liberative and transformational view of salvation. Paul seems to suggest at some length in Romans 5–8 that people — treated in a more collective sense as well — are overshadowed and enslaved in their pre-Christian state and so overtly incapable of good decision making. They must consequently be set free by an outside agency, who must initiate that liberation. Moreover, that liberation must coincide with the inauguration of a process of transformation, since to save from ontological slavery is automatically to change. Hence, the mind of the saved will not necessarily correspond to the mind of the unsaved, the latter being largely unreliable and soteriologically irrelevant.

It may be suggested that these two systems could follow on one another tidily, as sanctification on justification or some such, but at first glance it seems more likely that directly contradictory views of salvation are in play. On the one hand, reasonably rational individuals make a crucial choice and move thereby from the unsaved to the saved condition, while on the other, a more collective mass of decidedly irrational people are set free by divine choice and transformed through that liberation — both models leading to salvation. However, the first model requires ontological continuity and proceeds prospectively, while the second presupposes discontinuity and operates retrospectively. Hence, it seems a reasonable prima facie conclusion that a contractual reading of Paul's justification texts will *inevitably* generate acute conceptual tensions over against his participatory discussions. Moreover, to let one system follow the other would be either to subordinate it to, or to redefine, the preceding material, which is of course not to resolve the basic problem of how such arguments fit together as they stand. It would seem, then, that understood in the preceding basic senses, the two systems deploy fundamental soteriological principles that are just contradictory.[12]

If the first conundrum comes from the placing of the conventional anthropocentric "Lutheran" reading and its corresponding forensic model next to another, more transformational model, the second derives from the internal dynamics of the "Lutheran" reading itself. An emphasis on individual decision making necessitates a prior phase of persuasive pressure designed to lead to that decision. Put simply, if an important decision is required, then a rational individual must be given good reasons for making it, and those reasons must of course come from the state *prior to* that decision — an elementary but most important point. The "Lutheran" configuration of this prior phase is consequently not flexible but sits like a template on human reality, delivering nothing less than its correct configuration; since this system claims to supply a true decision, its initial configuration must also be incontestably accurate. But while this supplies a reassuring certainty as well as a useful common strategy to its proponents, the claim that all of pre-Christian reality conforms to a particular scenario is vulnerable to falsification in empirical terms. Basically, if this preliminary template does not match reality or some aspect of it when it is independently examined, one might be forced to conclude that the preliminary phase's characterizations are false, a conclusion that then ought to follow, somewhat embarrassingly, for the model's subsequent phase of salvation as well. Moreover, as we have already noted, Paul's texts supply at these points a largely *negative* preliminary situation focused on the failure of legalism, a discussion focused, moreover, on Judaism. And this therefore leads directly to the possible descriptive falsification of this phase in relation to Judaism's own sources and piety, which may be both different from the model's characterizations and rather more positive, as suggested by the early work of Sanders and now acknowledged frequently by New Testament scholars. But this is to note only one of several possible criticisms at this point. Philosophers, theologians, scholars attuned to gender issues, and post-Holocaust critics can all make equivalent charges against the accuracy of other aspects of the first phase in the model (and these will be noted in due course[13]). Hence, our second conundrum really represents a set of vulnerabilities automatically built into the objective assertiveness of the opening phase of Paul's justification arguments as they are conventionally understood. The model's account of the pre-Christian state possesses certain strengths, but it would seem that these are purchased at the price of acute vulnerabilities. To assert the conventional construal is automatically to run an empirical gauntlet — and there is more than one gauntlet to run.

If the "Lutheran" reading configures the pre-Christian state assertively in order ultimately to generate the right Christian decision, it also largely removes its chosen Pauline texts from any contingency. So construed, the arguments in the apostle's justification texts do not speak of particular circumstances in the early Roman, Galatian, or Philippian Christian communities but address, in a rather totalizing way, reality and salvation per se. They are emphatically universal discussions. And if it is granted initially that Paul's participatory discussions are similarly generic, it now seems small wonder that scholars have struggled to give an account of the specific circumstances that called forth Romans in particular. This letter now carries a great weight of highly generalized material and relatively little information about local circumstances; further, that abstract information is often preoccupied with Judaism, and the meager specific information positioned largely in the letter's epistolary frame is overtly Gentile,[14] in the sense of being oriented toward converts from paganism.[15] Hence, to read Paul's justification discussions in the conventional manner is automatically to generate, or at least considerably to exacerbate, the parameters of "the Romans debate," where an explanation for the specific provenance of this particular letter is sought. In essence, to read abstractly and generally if not universally is *necessarily* to read noncircumstantially, so it seems no coincidence that such doubt over the exact circumstances surrounding the composition of Romans exists.

Now it may simply be the case that Paul composed Romans in this fashion. But if the conventional construal is incorrect in perceiving a universal soteriological discourse where Paul did not intend one,[16] this approach may instead have masked a considerable amount of highly contextualized information, information that, once recovered, might resolve the delicate equations of the Romans debate. This resolution might, furthermore, prove helpful for the polarized discussion currently running in relation to the timing of Galatians: contingency that helps us *explain the rationale* for Romans may also simultaneously help us *place* Galatians. We may, in short, be able to approach these letters in more historical-critical terms.

As we will eventually see, we are far from exhausting the unpalatable implications of the conventional construal of Paul's justification texts with these three well-known difficulties. But hopefully enough has been said to indicate the strategic location of this construct. It is the conventional "Lutheran" construal of the arguments of these distinctive texts, leading to an individualist, conditional, and contractual account of the whole notion of salvation, that arguably lies behind some of the most intractable interpretative conundrums in modern Pauline scholarship.

But to note the causality of these difficulties is by no means to have solved them. Indeed, it is possible at this point merely to accept the fact, however awkward, that Paul has bequeathed us some difficult and perhaps even badly conceptualized texts, and the scandal of the reading really translates thereby into the scandal of a fundamentally clumsy, if not confused, apostle. However, in the light of these difficulties, it at least ought to be considered whether this reading is wrong.

Let us consider this supposition for a moment. It might be that scholars have misunderstood some of the key arguments and terms in these texts while generating the "Lutheran" reading and its accompanying model of salvation, and consequently only *artificially generated* the conundrums we have just noted; our problems at these points would therefore be self-inflicted! In such a case the reading and its reverberating difficulties would constitute an essentially alien interpretative construct within our description of Paul. It would function rather like a computer virus that, having infiltrated a system, overwrites some of its key commands with a foreign code from another programmer and then goes on to execute a series of embarrassing and even destructive actions, often losing original material in the process. Now admittedly it is rather shocking to claim that the standard "Lutheran" reading of Paul's justification texts is the interpretative equivalent of a computer virus, but our three conundrums have already suggested that this reading may contain virulent dimensions. Indeed, such tensions, running in several different directions, ought to suggest that all is not right with this construct. And further reflection indicates that there is something deeply plausible about this entire proposal.

At the heart of the conventional "Lutheran" approach to these texts, as we have seen, are powerful commitments to individualism, to rationalism, and to consent, these being organized in turn by an overarching contractual structure. And all these elements are also fundamental components within Western history and culture, specifically, within the distinctive society that has evolved from Latin-speaking Christendom in Europe, and especially from its Protestant regions — a society that, allied with its extraordinary North American progeny, is progressively dominating global culture today. Hence, it seems no coincidence that the individualist, contractual reading of Paul's justification texts arrived and then spread rapidly in the aftermath of the first stirrings of this distinctive society during the Renaissance and its strong commitments to humanism and individualism. And European and post-European society has since, in a variety of ways, generally only strengthened its commitments to individualism, to consent, and to the practice of regulating human relationships through conditionality and contract.[17] So the individualist, contractual reading of Paul's gospel affirmed by a "Lutheran" approach has become only increasingly compatible with a global context that is itself increasingly being constructed in such terms.

But it is this very cultural compatibility that creates the possibility of error. In view of the intimate relationship between the construal and our distinctive and essentially modern culture, the suspicion is almost unavoidable that preceding treatment of the reading might have been overly generous — and from both uncritical *and* critical perspectives, if these particular Western presuppositions have not been clearly recognized by the reading's critics. Could it be that the reading relies too heavily on perhaps largely unacknowledged cultural commitments, and that it consequently overrides delicate textual signals that imply that such an interpretative structure is not entirely appropriate? — that its basic concerns, although self-evident to us, are essentially far too modern for Paul and his first readers? Indeed, in a supreme irony, could it be that a reading that lays claim to being a construal of the Pauline gospel is in fact a projection of essentially modern European cultural values into the Pauline texts and into their ostensible construal of salvation itself, and is therefore at bottom an idolatrous exercise — a mere pandering to the Western *Zeitgeist?* Have such interpreters constructed Paul at these points — and through him God's relationship with humanity — in their own image?! This is the scandalous possibility that the following study explores.

I know, however, not merely from theoretical reflection but also from hard experience that any attempt to demonstrate such theses must negotiate a series of peculiar difficulties in addition to the normal problems accompanying the interpretation of an ancient text. We have already noted that an alliance between the construal and European and post-European culture is possibly operative. We should also recall that a great deal is at stake theologically. The conventional individualist reading claims to deliver — often under the weighty authority of church tradition — the apostle's definitive soteriological program — that is, nothing less than the gospel itself. And the resulting quite distinctive power and status in the construal that is the focus of our critical attention tends to create an additional set of difficult interpretative dynamics. Unless these are appreciated clearly and then negotiated, any expectations of forward interpretative movement will be sorely disappointed.

Hence, in my view it will be largely pointless, despite our suspicions and the interpretative problems that seem evident in Paul, to proceed directly to exegesis; this would be to advance blindly into thoroughly prepared positions — a suicidal interpretative prospect. The various potentially distorting interpretative dynamics functioning at theoretical, church-historical, paradigmatic, ideological, and cultural levels must first be detected and carefully articulated, after which point the question of the reading's exegetical underpinnings can be addressed, the elaboration of these dynamics being the principal burden of part two (chapters seven through nine). In my view, only after these hermeneutical explorations are complete will any alternative exegetical approach be possible, which is to say that we should then be able to consider with a degree of fairness whether another reading can deliver a better account of the key texts, the principal burden of parts three through five (chapters ten through twenty-one). Part one, however, must first elaborate some of the concerns just expressed here, supplying a comprehensive account of the "Lutheran" reading's many problems. That account will provide much of the leverage for the hermeneutical and exegetical discussions that follow.

When all is said and done, we may find that if our reading of Paul's forensic texts can be freed from essentially European individualist, rationalist, and conditional presuppositions, they may yet speak in a more radical and liberating way to the conundrums of our own time: to *free* our reading (to a degree) *from* our modern culture is also to allow the apostle *to address* our culture more effectively. Hence, the end result of this process could be a clearer, simpler, and more theologically constructive Paul, along with a rather more christocentric apostolic gospel, and this even if we do not hear that gospel proclaimed so clearly by certain well-known texts. (Surely these are clarifications of which Luther himself would have approved!)

We turn, then, to a detailed pursuit of the foregoing claims, beginning with a more comprehensive account of the problem in part one. If we do not grasp the problem itself in all its complexity, it is unlikely that we will ultimately be able to offer any effective solutions. Indeed, we may not even realize that such solutions are vitally necessary. And these realizations must then be followed by a careful consideration of the problematic hermeneutical dimension informing Justification, undertaken through part two. These preliminary methodological discussions are in fact a sine qua non both for any clear grasp of our difficulties, and any effective resolutions. Indeed, it is precisely the absence of *these* discussions that has arguably led in the past to the current inability of many Pauline interpreters to fight free of their besetting problems in this relation. I cannot therefore stress strongly enough how integral and important they are to the arguments — and ultimately to the rereadings — that follow. To overlook their importance would be like trying to fight global warming without reference to the sun. We would be unlikely to succeed.

PART ONE

Justification Theory, and Its Implications

CHAPTER ONE

The Heart of the Matter:
The Justification Theory of Salvation

§1. Preamble

In this chapter we describe at some length a particular theory of salvation. This description seems to be the best point from which to begin our detailed analysis for a number of reasons (although, like most points of entry into complex situations, it is not perfect, leaving certain matters unresolved for the time being).[1] The description will allow us to go on to supply a more economic, albeit revisionist, explanation of a whole spectrum of problems within the interpretation of Paul through the rest of part one — and this spectrum turns out to be much larger than has previously been suspected. This in turn will establish the basic stakes of our discussion, and they are high. By the end of part one, then, on the one hand, we should be highly motivated to go on to find some solution to our difficulties — no matter how radical that solution proves in localized terms — or it will be apparent that Paul's theological description is destined for incoherence. On the other hand, we should already be sensing what the contours of that solution might be, one linked irreducibly to the theoretical cause of all the problems. Indeed, the fundamental role played in all the difficulties by a theory, now plainly apparent, will give us grounds for hope that a solution can ultimately be found, as we begin to consider in part two the illegitimate hermeneutical functions that the theory might be playing within the exegesis of Paul. For all these reasons, pursuing a crystal-clear grasp of the soteriological theory in question at the outset of our discussion could hardly be more important. It is this methodological imperative that we address here.

But some preliminary objections might be made to this whole approach before it even begins. First, might this theoretical description be a straw man? What is its status in relation to Paul? Has it simply been invented? Similarly, could the theory not simply be modified at certain points in order to avoid its awkward difficulties? Why must it take this particular form? And finally, is the following analysis not overly formal and rigorous? Paul is not necessarily a systematic or even a highly rigorous thinker, it might be objected, so any analysis of his thought in such terms is otiose.

If they proved sustainable, these objections would hamstring our inquiry from the start, and so we ought to pause here to consider whether they have merit. We will address them briefly in turn.

1.1. Basis

Objectors might be asking where my theoretical account has come from, especially in textual terms. And this is an entirely fair query.

The account will turn out to be an amalgam of a particular *reading* of various Pauline texts (but whose explicit identification and close analysis are best postponed for the moment) and a *theory* of salvation that, given certain key elements, simply must develop in certain directions as a matter of sheer rationality. In the latter relation, basic metaphors for humanity and for God, especially when combined with certain additional concerns and/or premises, have only a limited number of directions in which to develop coherently *as* an account of salvation. In the former relation, the connection between the methodologically distinguishable planes of text and theory ought to be as tight as possible, because ultimately the reading of certain sacred texts will underpin this theory.[2] So although the following discussion is primarily theoretical, taking that dimension with the most seriousness in this chapter, one eye is nevertheless always on the key texts as well.[3]

This looming textual constraint is also the principal reason why the theory cannot always be modified, even when that seems desirable in order to deal with pressing difficulties (and these begin to be noted from chapter two). This theory cannot lose touch with its key texts; it *must* ultimately be able to lay claim to a plausible reading of at least *some* of Paul's statements because it claims ultimately to be rooted in Scripture. A defensive theoretical adjustment purchased at the cost of losing Paul is therefore far too high a price to pay, because it would lead to the collapse of the entire system.

Two important qualifications of this theoretical construct may at least partially allay the further concerns of any objectors at this point.

First, the construct is generic, or radial; it represents, to a degree, a set or family of closely related theories.[4] It is an attempt to state the theoretically irreducible. Hence, small variations can be introduced at a number of points without affecting the overarching argument or results. Not all accounts of this theory have to be *exactly* the same, but they will all share certain fundamental commitments and ensuing argumentative developments (or else, at some point, either their theory will unravel or their textual justification will collapse — or both).

Second, the construct contains flaws. I cannot give a completely coherent account of the theory because, in my view, this is not possible; the theory itself has serious internal flaws, not to mention a number of exegetical difficulties that will become apparent in due course. It does not follow from the presence of these imperfections, however, that the construct is a straw man — far from it. In my view *it is the most formidable account of the data that we yet possess,* and this despite a great number of detractors.[5] It is a powerful theory, but not a perfect one.

Moreover, this construct does possess a provisional status at this point in my argument. Indeed, I am quite happy for my account to be viewed hypothetically through parts one and two until its textual basis in Paul is introduced (or, alternatively, until a superior theoretical account is supplied). There is a sense, then, in which this is something of a thought experiment: *if* Paul is interpreted ultimately at certain points in the following fashion, *then* all these consequences follow. Of course, if this thought experiment turns out to be well grounded in textual terms, then it will be an important one, and various significant issues will have been clarified en route (and I am confident that we will shortly find numerous interpreters attributing just this construct to Paul: see especially chapter ten). But now a different objection might be made to our unfolding conceptual experiment.

1.2. *Rigor*

Is a rigorous account of a theoretical dimension within the interpretation of Paul even appropriate if he was not in fact an especially systematic thinker — or, as a pastor and missionary, perhaps not even attempting to write systematically? Indeed, are realities, both in Paul and in church history, rather more untidy than this proposal's highly rigorous account allows, to the point that it can be safely ignored?

I suggest, however, that this is not an especially coherent claim to make *in advance of* an analysis. Most importantly, it is incorrect to exclude a given thinker from the quality of rigor *before* any attempt has been made to prove or to disprove that claim. Paul must be given the benefit of the doubt. He might of course ultimately prove to be lacking in rigor — but he might not. Hence, to insist on an absence of rigor as a prior methodological principle seems deeply self-contradictory.[6]

Further, it does not follow from the occasional nature of Paul's pastoral and missionary concerns and texts that they do not therefore contain systematic thinking. Rigorous thinking is not limited to professionals.[7] This sort of objection may betray a certain amount of hermeneutical incoherence as well, with exegetical, argumentative, and theoretical claims being played off against one another rather than being treated as mutually reinforcing and integrated considerations. However, this strategy will be clarified further in part two, chapter seven, when hermeneutical matters are treated in detail. For now it suffices to note that such maneuvers are not valid.

Finally, this objection seems to lack tactical foresight. Coherence has generally been regarded as one of the theory's strengths, not one of its weaknesses. Hence, the decision to trade away Paul's coherence in advance of any discussion leaves such critics defenseless against a reading of Paul that can demonstrate a reasonable degree of theoretical rigor while maintaining its exegetical integrity.[8] (And if this point is nevertheless insisted on, then we return to the self-contradictory conundrum just noted.)

In view of all these difficulties, any preclusive insistence on a lack of rigor in Paul that would also foreclose the description and arguments that follow seems unwise. Our description of a particular theory of salvation that we will ultimately link to a reading of some of the apostle's key texts should be as rigorous as we can make it.

1.3. The Question of Nomenclature

In the light of this theoretical emphasis, it will shortly become clear that the key to much of the debate is not some church-historical dimension or figure like Luther or Augustine — who will probably prove rather more complex (especially over time) than the relatively neat lines and commitments of a single theory. So it would be both descriptively inaccurate and needlessly inflammatory to discuss our difficulties in tradition-specific terms such as "Lutheran" — and hence my consistent use to this point of quotation marks. This designation is simply unfair, both to Luther and to many Lutherans.[9] Rather, the key to much of what follows is a particular theory of salvation — an essentially individualist, contractual construct — that is grounded in certain critical metaphors and reinforced by certain ideological and cultural positions, many of them distinctively modern. This theory, along with all its reinforcements, can in turn powerfully shape the way its advocates read certain texts in Paul. Hence, the entire situation is most helpfully designated in theoretical rather than church-historical terms. It is, in brief, both more accurate and more responsible to refer to the theory in terms of "Justification." (And other appropriate theoretical designations may be used from time to time — e.g., individualist, conditional, contractual, Western, or European.) We will see momentarily that this theory has a penchant for caricaturing its opposition, so it seems especially appropriate not to enter into this particular form of untruth. One outcome from the following investigation ought to be a more nuanced sense of description, both of Paul and by him. The replacement of the terminology of "Lutheran" with "Justification" is therefore an excellent place for us to begin our detailed analysis.

1.4. The Contribution of Federal Calvinism

Finally, we should register at the outset that the following concerns have been articulated quite precisely by certain theological descendants of Calvin — notably, in the debate over Federal Calvinism (from the Latin *foedus* for "contract"). J. B. Torrance has provided classic analyses of this debate, examining not just the history of its major controversies but the critical pastoral and theological dynamics that led to them.[10] Torrance points out the fundamentally contractual structure of this system's soteriology and the consequent theological difficulties and cultural alliances that such a model can generate.[11] Those observations underlie my detailed description of the inner workings of the Justification model here, along with its possible problems and cultural affinities, because the theory of salvation as it is adumbrated by some of Paul's texts is essentially contractual as well. Indeed, Federal Calvinism and Justification share the same basic model. (And thus we can see immediately at least one respect in which the name "Lutheran" is misleading.)

This model has a pronounced binary structure: one is supposed to move from an unsaved, "unjustified" condition to a saved, "justified" condition by means of the exercise of "faith."[12] It is very much a tale of two phases within a basic, overarching progression. And so our detailed discussion follows this arrangement.

§2. The First Phase: The Rigorous Contract

2.1. The Opening Progression

The theory of Justification supplies a particular model of salvation — an account of its nature, its presuppositions, and its appropriation. The model begins with the unsaved, non-Christian condition, but it is important to note that the potential movements and discoveries within that condition are not open ended. Non-Christians exist in a state that suggests, in this construct, that they ought to become Christians. Hence, there is a generally propulsive quality to the model's first phase, coupled with a fundamental assertiveness and rigidity in its characterizations of the human situation — which also leads to one of the important features of the explanation of salvation that follows. The Justification model will achieve a "law-free" result, something correlated in addition with justification sola fide, through faith alone. So the first phase will drive a journey from extensive law observance to the necessity for faith alone, and in a thoroughly rational progression. And it is this progression that will give the model its special purchase on the Pauline discussions of justification that contrast "works of law" and "faith"; the model — if it is accurate at these points — should enjoy a formidable exegetical base.

The Justification model presupposes a rational, self-interested individual. The model derives both its general negative pressure toward the individual's conversion and its distinctive judgments about the law from the same basic premise: that a God of justice is known to everyone. This premise is extremely important. God's existence and power are deduced from the cosmos without; God's ethical concerns, from the promptings of the conscience within. God is thus perceived not only as omnipotent *but also as a cosmic lawgiver and judge*. Equally important, this justice is understood in a specifically *retributive* sense, namely, in terms of process and strict desert-based requital. So the justice of God that undergirds the created cosmos is not "distributive" — based on a just final state, along with any reallocation necessary to produce it. Rather, it is retributive — bound to reward the righteous inevitably and punish the guilty implacably, irrespective of the final collective outcomes of any accumulation of such judgments.[13]

In short, the Justification model achieves its soteriological pressure on individuals largely by arguing for the necessary prior perception of a forensically retributive God; this is the (in)famous *iustitia Dei*, which ostensibly caused Luther such trouble (see especially his account of his struggle with the interpretation of Rom. 1:17, noted further in part two, chapter eight). The basic premise of divine *iustitia*, universally and innately comprehended, will allow a powerful, essentially rational dynamic to be played out in the model's first, non-Christian phase, as well as significant reinforcement for the theory to be derived in the end from sociopolitical quarters. Indeed, the basicality of this premise can hardly be underestimated. It remains in force as the model's fundamental axiom. If all else fails or is repudiated, the model still asserts that everyone, without exception, knows God in moral terms, as an arbiter who will reward righteous activity and punish transgression and thus is analogous primarily to a judge (hence the apparently appropriate translations of Paul's *dikaio-* terms using the English stem "just"). Note that this is a rigorous, even harsh premise that will generate in turn an equally rigorous contract. Justice conceived in these terms is potentially quite grim. But its proponents can accurately claim that it is, in terms of its own definition, fair, and not merely oppressive, arbitrary, or tyrannical. One must do no less than it requires. And so on occasion, for example, one will be compelled to put out an eye. But at the same time, one must do no *more,* and go on to put out two.

Now in order to perform the necessary righteous deeds, and avoid transgressions, one must have instructions as to what constitutes righteousness, and the Justification model is quite practical here. Jews possess extensive written legislation detailing righteous actions in the light of God's will, so they will be "without excuse" if they do not perform them. That is, the Jewish Scriptures are, in the main, a written codification of God's ethical demands, hence the functional appropriateness within the model of the translation of *nomos* as "law" and not "teaching," which would fail to carry the sense of potential punishment for infractions.

But the universal scope of the model at this point — not to mention the justice of God — dictates that an identical dynamic must hold for non-Jews as well. So the Justification model argues that the same demands are written, if a little more faintly, into everyone's consciences; all have access to God's ethical demands, even if they do not have direct access to the definitive written codification, at which point the much-debated role of natural theology and, in particular, of any ethical premises derived thereby is introduced. These assumptions are an irreducible constituent of the model. Consequently, if non-Jews fail to perform righteous deeds, they will be "without excuse" as well, since "the demands of God have been made plain to them" (Rom. 1:19, 20 DC). Jews, however, will be particularly culpable, since not only do they possess a clear written edition but even boast about their possession of and expertise in it, demonstrating beyond doubt that they have it and supposedly know it. Hence, Jews are the archetypal occupants of phase one, knowing God, knowing God's demands, and presumably also desiring to follow them (and so achieve reward and avoid punishment). But since the model necessarily applies to "all," Jews are technically representative of Everyman. All are in a sense Jews before they become Christians, and those who remain non-Christian therefore remain analogous to unconverted Jews.

Significantly, this approach gives any statement of the model a characteristic conditionality and, as a result, an essentially contractual structure: "*If* you do *x* (which is good), *then* you will be rewarded. Concomitantly, *if* you do *y* (which is bad) — or perhaps if you fail to do *x* — *then* you will be punished." The conditional grammar departing from God's ethical demands and followed by a consequence estimated in relation to individual fulfillment or lack thereof conveys the rational, conditional, and voluntarist dimensions in the model nicely, along with its basic ethical dynamic. There is also clearly an individual dimension here, although it is not yet a *radically* individualist model, as we will see shortly.

The description thus far can be summarized in simple propositional form:

1a. Humans are rational.
1b. Humans are self-interested.
1c. Humans are therefore ethical, in order to be saved (and this largely in relation to 1b).
2a. God is omnipotent (and presumably also omniscient and omnipresent).
2b. God is just.
2c. 2a is known to everyone from the cosmos without.
2d. 2b is known to everyone from the conscience within.
3a. The content of righteousness derives from God's nature (see 2b).
3b. God's ethical demands are revealed to Jews through written legislation.
3c. God's ethical demands are known to everyone else innately (2b via 2d).
4. Reward and punishment will be apportioned by God (so 2a) in relation to individuals' fulfillment or not of God's ethical demands (so 2b), that is, in accordance with righteous actions, which constitute righteousness, or their converse, and hence *on the basis of desert.* "If you do *x*, then you will be rewarded; if you do not, and/or do *y*, then you will be punished."

Note the salience of proposition 2b in the foregoing followed by 4. In a very real sense, *ethical legislation* based on *retributive justice* is the fundamental structure of the universe, as well as of the divine nature. But we must now address an important complication in this model.

2.2. The Future Eschatological Caveat

Late contributors to the Old Testament, and many occupants of intertestamental Judaism, were well aware that the imposition of this meritocratic calculus during earthly existence was problematic. As the book of Job points out at some length, the wicked appear to prosper and the righteous at times to suffer and die in pain, penniless and friendless. Appearances seem to contradict the truth of the calculus. But one solution hinted at by Job seems to have received widespread, although not universal, adoption in Paul's time — that is, the insertion of a future eschatological caveat. God will raise the dead and judge all at the end of present history, apportioning reward and punishment in the form of future positive and negative states, namely, heaven and hell. This will allow the apparent injustices of the present age to be eliminated and the equations of desert to hold, despite contrary appearances. God's omnipotence and omniscience, buttressed by omnipresence, will facilitate this process — indeed, without these attributes, the calculus would prove difficult to sustain. But God's perceived sovereignty translates easily into such terms, as do numerous biblical statements. Everything tends toward a future eschatological climax, when history will be unraveled into its dual constituents — the righteous and the wicked.[14]

5a. The injustices of life on earth will be rectified by a final judgment at the end of the present age.
5b. Those dead will be resurrected in order to take part in the judgment (through 2a).
5c. The future age will be constituted in positive and negative states (again through 2a).
5d. God will determine on this "day" (through 2a) which state each individual will enter on the basis of desert (see 4, effected at 5a through 5b).

So *ultimately* reward or punishment will be based on desert, desert itself being measured out as we would expect in relation to the performance of righteous actions in the light of their specification, or their converse. As one supposedly definitive exponent puts it: "For he will repay according to each one's deeds: to those who by patiently doing good seek for glory and honor and immortality, he will give eternal life; while for those who are self-seeking and who obey not the truth but wickedness, there will be wrath and fury. There will be anguish and distress for everyone who does evil . . . but glory and honor and peace for everyone who does good" (Rom. 2:6-10). Good cosmic citizens will be saved and cosmic criminals condemned. This is at bottom simply a strictly meritocratic approach; no positive discrimination here (see 2:11)! It is usually known in the New Testament trade as legalism, works righteousness, or justification by works of law.[15]

2.3. The Introspective Twist

If we left the model at this stage, it would hardly be very distinctive. Other theological models share these basic premises, and perhaps even more importantly, there is considerable overlap with numerous ethical and political systems, not to mention with other religions. Most approaches to ethics posit a degree of individual capacity for rational self-reflection and for ethical action, along with at least *some* constant principles that are held to be universally valid; the process of ethical analysis and reflection is then supposed to discover these and attempt to apply them. Hence, arguably, the foregoing premises are shared in large measure by Kant's *Critique of Practical Reason*. Similarly, most modern political systems — along with many ancient ones — elaborate detailed structures of laws and assume that people are capable of understanding and obeying them and that if not, sanction is appropriate. So the foregoing assumptions are largely shared by Aristotle's *Politics*, as well as much current government,[16] except that the *ephapax* eschatological scenario has been collapsed into immanent and ongoing systems (and often there is more than one god). So what makes the Justification model different? We come face-to-face here with one of the most distinctive features of this particular soteriology, the feature that creates its unusual two-phase structure: the initial, non-Christian condition — the "works" phase — is not meant to be stable in and of itself; it is meant to drive its occupants inevitably into a second, Christian condition. How it achieves this pressure is quite ingenious, involving, first, the rigor with which the law is upheld and, second, a principal of introversion. Both of these aspects must now be examined in more detail.

We can begin by considering the difference between what we might dub the 100 percent, or "perfectionist," demand and the 51 percent, or "pragmatic" (and more realistic), demand. As we have seen, many soteriologies share the Justification model's assumptions up to this point, but they vary in terms of what quantity of merit they hold to define true righteousness and therefore to warrant the appropriate reward.[17] (Of course there are also disputes over its precise content — for example, with respect to diet — but these questions can be set aside for the moment.) Perfectionists would argue that full law observance is necessary, so that one slip or fault entails punishment, much as a single breach of civil law induces guilt. All the law is righteous, and humans are capable of observing it; therefore, the fulfillment of all is required for righteousness to exist. So, for example, the Westminster Confession of 1647 states in chapter seven: "Life was promised to Adam, and in him to his Posterity; upon Condition of perfect and personal Obedience." And in chapter nineteen: "God gave to Adam a Law as a Covenant of Works, by which he bound him and all his Posterity to personal, entire, exact and perpetual Obedience; promised Life upon the fulfilling, and threatened Death upon the Breach of it; and indued him with Power and Ability to keep it." (The latter is a good example not just of the perfectionist position, but of the necessary optimism about human capacity that must undergird it.) Indeed, these represent the position of the Reformers for much of the time. As we will see shortly, the perfectionist variant enjoys, among other things, certain rhetorical advantages.

Pragmatists tend to regard this standard as unrealistic, however, and so soften the requirements. Here images of scales or balances that reflect quantification — and have an ancient religious and eschatological pedigree (although Egyptian!) — can be deployed, the argument being that the good deeds must *outweigh* the bad. (Jewish metaphors seem to have been more textual, in terms of accounting and books.)[18] Strictly speaking, this breaks with the model's premises, although it does still seem to be able to lay claim to a basic notion of justice, in that condemnation of someone more good than bad seems itself unfair and not based on desert.

Condemnation, however — dictated by the letter of the overarching contract — is usually held to be the essential point. Hence, the opening phase of the Justification model tends to reject the softer, pragmatic option, even if only implicitly: 100 percent righteousness is demanded of everyone at this stage, without exception.[19] And given the supposed rhetorical objective of this argument, many interpreters have not balked at the perfectionist requirement. The higher the initial standard, the more likely it is that everyone listening will feel the force of his or her failure and so be prepared to accept the ensuing offer of salvation through the Christian gospel. Indeed, there will be no embarrassing exceptions to the need for people to become Christian. Thus, there are good reasons for accepting such stringency.

We may turn now to the second aspect of the opening phase's distinctive dynamic. A clue to its operation is given by the fact that the initial endorsement of "justification [of all] through works informed by law" (cf. Rom. 3:20) is always followed by scathing condemnation (and often not just of the transgressors but also *of the attempt itself,* especially if it is continued). It would seem that in fact *no one* will be saved in this fashion; actually, such an assumption is the height of *im* piety! Probably more than anyone else in recent times, Krister Stendahl has illuminated the additional critical assumptions here (at least in a preliminary way). Only with the inclusion of what he characterizes as an introspective premise does this reversal of expectation and subsequent condemnation make any sense.[20] Indeed, it is at precisely this point that the Justification model's distinctive approach begins to unfold in tandem with its expectation of perfect obedience.

People are supposed to reflect on their own condition in the light of the demands of the law and to realize that they fall short of the requisite obedience. Luther is often cited as an example of this process (although the particular theological location of these reflections, not to mention the important question of his precise relationship with the model, will be considered later on). As he put it on one occasion:

> When I was a monk, I made a great effort to live according to the requirements of the monastic rule. . . . *Nevertheless, my conscience could never achieve certainty but was always in doubt and said: "You have not done this correctly. You were not contrite enough. You omitted this in your confession."* Therefore the longer I tried to heal my uncertain, weak, and troubled conscience with human traditions, the more uncertain, weak, and troubled I continually made it.[21]

If these particular introspective reflections are positioned in the non-Christian phase, then the resulting rhetorical force within the broader context of the model is considerable. Instead of a comfortable production of good deeds, the sensitive introvert faces an awful accumulation of bad ones, and the entire situation in the vestibule of desert is not an open-ended arrangement offering salvation but a terrifying *cul-de-sac*. Moreover, the salvific contract that initially appeared rigorous but fair now appears oppressive and impossible.

Lying behind this realization of course is the perception that people are not perfect. We sin — and sometimes fairly frequently. Moreover, it is assumed that if we look at ourselves honestly enough, we will *all* realize this (and Augustine's dark and passionate self-reflections can be cited at this point as well). In short, honest self-reflection in the light of a *strict* commitment to desert, along with a precise delineation of the *content* of desert, should end up recapitulating Luther's apparent journey to despair, or at least to an equivalent soteriological position. As our first famous exponent put it: "Whatever the law says, it speaks . . . so that every mouth may be silenced, and the whole world may be held accountable to God. . . . '[N]o human being* will be justified in his [that is, God's] sight by deeds prescribed by the law,' for through the law comes the knowledge of sin" (Rom. 3:19-20). This conclusion should hold if its supporting premises do as well, namely, (a) humans' ethical *in*capacity (possibly quite severe, although not necessarily) and (b) our ability to recognize that incapacity through honest self-examination, a recognition that unfolds as we attempt — but fail (and that possibly repeatedly, although, again, not necessarily) — to fulfill God's ethical demands. So a further chain of propositions ought now to unfold:

6a. Humans are inherently sinful; that is, everyone violates God's ethical demands (and probably often, in which case see also the supplementary "loop" immediately following).

6b. Honest self-reflection notes the consistent production of unethical deeds (6a, apparent in the light of 3a through 3c).

6c. Such self-reflection concludes — in an accurate anticipation — that God's final judgment will be negative (see 4, 5c, and 5d).

6d. Rational individuals are now afraid and desire somehow to avoid this inevitable consequence.

2.4. *The Loop of Despair*

But note a possible supplementary rational loop at this point, a "loop of despair":

1′. Accordingly, individuals might undertake a renewed attempt to be righteous.

2′. This attempt, however, will also fail, as 6a continues, noted by 6b, and so the conclusion of 6c will be reiterated, *leading to a strengthened 6d!*

A steady sinking into point 6d denotes the correct unfolding of the rational progression; despair is the correct conclusion to draw from this ethical and legal calculus. But people are not *forced* to conclude this, and many in fact seem not to. We should pause, then, to note how the unfolding model views these people, because this is an important point.

2.5. The Loop of Foolishness

Those who resist the conclusion of despair are fundamentally self-deluded. They are also probably ethically insensitive, overestimating their own ethical ability and possibly deliberately overlooking their transgressions while exaggerating the value of their good deeds, no doubt speaking of them and hence also *boasting*. Such boasting is not necessarily wrong in isolated instances, but it tends to be judged harshly because it denotes a refusal to accept the general thrust of the rational progression — *that all are ultimately doomed*. If they baptize their actions under the guise of piety, claiming the approval of God (which is absent), they are doubly despicable, bringing the names of both God and religion into disrepute. If they go on to compare their supposedly good records with the inferior records of obvious sinners around them, they are judgmental. And insofar as they encourage others to adopt this approach, they are fools and hypocrites, exhorting others to do what they themselves in fact cannot. These people are obstinate, refusing to accept the truth about their condition and its simple calculus. In short, they deserve to be punished — and they will be, at the end of the age.

Hence, the introspective set of possibilities can also generate a false or irrational calculus that reinforces the conclusion established above. It is a slightly longer feedback loop within the argument, a "loop of foolishness," which can supplement the short loop of despair that we have already noted.

1a″. Resistant individuals perceive and claim themselves to be righteous.
1b″. They are in fact not righteous (no one is free from all sin: so 6a).
2a″. Therefore, they are being dishonest with themselves, specifically, by underestimating their sinfulness and/or overestimating their rectitude.
2b″. Their judgment is ethically deficient (see 2a″).
2c″. This holds the more, the more ethical information they have (so Jews).
3a″. If they boast of their righteousness, they are liars and fakes.
3b″. If they invoke the names of God and religion, they are religious charlatans.
3c″. If they upbraid others and exhort others to imitate them, they are judgmental hypocrites.
3d″. If they continue this calculus and its behavior, they are irrational and obstinate, courting hell.
4″. The correct conclusion (obvious to the outsider): they doubly deserve the negative judgment awaiting them in 4-5d.

Thus, complementing the humble admission of a despairing Luther who has drawn the correct inferences from the law in view of his own ethical shortcomings is the foolish overconfidence of the "religious" who trust in their own ability to do good deeds in defiance of the introspective evidence, and this before God! Indeed, the failure to take the correct self-reflective journey seems to have dire consequences.

An inverted quality is also discernible in this rhetoric, and it is often a very useful argumentative resource. The most pious people are in fact now liable to the most guilt, and the least religious to the least guilt, because the pious probably prove the most resistant to the correct progression of the argument, while "sinners," recognizing their own shortcomings, presumably do not bother promulgating the loop of foolishness. In an apparent paradox, then, the religious or ethically upright — but also resistant — will be the most scathingly condemned, whereas honest sinners are at least on the right track, realizing their own shortcomings and refraining from any inappropriate boasting. And the progression as a whole consequently has a particular edge vis-à-vis religiosity and piety (although this is not really a complete inversion of these constituencies so much as a powerful flattening of them into one unhappy category within which there are more and less accurate degrees of self-knowledge).

Up to this point it should be apparent that the developing argument is assertive, quite aggressive (especially in a religious setting), and deeply pessimistic. An initially agreeable set of premises, when coupled with the self-evident fact of human incapacity, turns out to lead only to a ghastly dead end. Thus, it is not a positive system in its own right so much as a journey to a point of personal hopelessness, and any religious or ethical people caught up in its premises are particularly liable to feel its force: their efforts are futile, and the more they undertake them, the more obvious this becomes.

However, this apparent *cul-de-sac* is of course held by its advocates merely to be setting the stage for another argumentative progression. This threatening argumentative end point, correctly perceived, merely disposes its occupants to make a further correct move, namely, to appropriate the Christian gospel. Without this further offer, the Justification model's analysis of the non-Christian condition would be incomprehensibly bleak, leaving the rational and ethical person cycling within a state of despair fostered by cosmic terror: *there would be no way out.* But God in Christ provides a way out, so there is in effect a door at the end of the alley that the despairing will be powerfully motivated to open. The entire phase is consequently an open vestibule rather than a dead end.

Note, however, that the premises already in place will also dictate to a large degree the nature of the solution that is being offered. If the solution does not correspond to the problem, then either the solution will fail, because it cannot open the door, or the entire model will fail, because the vestibule is faulty. But we will return to these issues at a later point in our analysis.

The second phase of the model will be far more generous than the first. But because, like the first, it is appropriated by acting on certain stipulated criteria after reflection, it too may be accurately characterized as a contract, with a corresponding element of individualism. And accordingly, it too is conditional.[22] An initial harsh, or rigorous, contract is now being followed by a contrasting soft, or generous, one. Both contracts, as contracts, presuppose justice, especially in the sense of enforcement of stipulated outcomes in relation to fulfillment of stipulated conditions: you must do what you say you will — that is, follow the basic law of contract — hence, the system doubly reinforces the importance of this notion. The Justification model of salvation can be seen at bottom then as a tale of two salvific contracts in which only a fool clings to the first in defiance of the arrival of the second.

§3. The Second Phase: The Generous Contract

There are two main components in the new, generous contract being offered by God to humanity, which will resolve the problem of the old: (1) the satisfaction of God's justice (a critical axiom, as we have already seen), generally held to be accomplished with reference to the death of Christ, but also often accompanied by some positive transfer of righteousness, at least in certain variants of this model; and (2) the appropriation of that solution by the despairing sinner through some action, usually held of course to be "faith."

3.1. The Satisfaction of God's Justice

The Father graciously sends the Son to accept the despairing individual's deserved punishment through his death on the cross. The demands of justice from the cosmic ruler for the punishment of wrongdoing have thereby been met, as that punishment has rather cunningly been redirected, and this of course is the origin of the model's theology of the atonement. God's justice is neither relaxed nor compromised but *satisfied* by the payment, at least at some point, of *the penalty* due for wrongdoing; hence, the model is a punitive and satisfactory theory of the atonement — something often freighted in sacrificial language but not to be merely identified with it. And Christ's satisfactory sacrificial death is held to be definitive and *ephapax*. His sinlessness and divine status in effect provide limitless atoning value. Indeed, Christ in a sense has a monopoly on the atonement; this is his outstanding contribution to salvation. The result of the process for sinners is basically acquittal from the charges of wrongdoing awaiting them at the end of the age. They have been "justified," although the charges have not been removed or quashed so much as their requisite punishment fulfilled, so a more appropriate designation here might be "discharged."

Luther himself articulated some famous paradoxes at this point that we will have to consider carefully in due course, but they are consistent with the implications of the system. He argued that sinners are not actually transformed, or changed. They remain in and of themselves sinful and therefore constantly producing sins. In this way the reality of transgression in the New Testament and in one's personal life receives a continuing acknowledgement, and the model's opening calculus also remains essential (tending to be ceaselessly recapitulated). However, God does not view the sinner in these terms but rather via what amounts to a "legal fiction."

Some have thought, however, that Christ has an additional, more positive role to play at this point. Just as the sinner's punishment is redirected to the cross, so too Christ's own perfect righteousness can be redirected to the sinner (a process that again requires Christ to be sinless). It seems a little odd to leave sinners in an ethically "neutral" condition, with their sins forgiven but no positive state to occupy. Hence, as Melanchthon argued especially strongly,[23] the sinner can be viewed as if clothed in Christ's righteousness.

The standard theological terms for this divine "view" of the sinner — whether it includes only the forgiveness of sins or the attribution of positive righteousness as well — are "imputed" or "reckoned" or "credited" (drawing here especially on Paul's terminology in Rom. 3:28 and 4:2-8). God in effect does not "count" the sinner as a sinner. An alternative metaphor sees the sinner married to Christ and receiving a transfer, or *communicatio,* of his righteousness even as the sinner's sins are transferred to Christ, although the force and nature of these transfers should not be pressed. Indeed, the whole process has a difficult quality in its apparent function as an accounting or legal fiction, although it does retain its own rational force. Sinners remain a slightly contradictory construction — reckoned righteous in God's eyes as well as delivered from punishment, that is, acquitted, justified, or discharged, hence presumably delighted by this reckoning but also unchanged in substance, so to speak, and therefore repeatedly sinful and presumably somewhat depressed by this experience — *simul iustus et peccator.*

But alongside this mechanism for resolving sinners' hopeless condition, there is of course another critical component in the model's second phase. These benefits are not applied automatically but require the fulfillment of a contractual criterion. And it will be clearest at this point to return briefly to a common reading of Luther's desperate "pre-Protestant" condition.

3.2. The Appropriation of Salvation

In view of Luther's first judgments, formed largely from ethical introspection, he should hardly hesitate before grasping any alternative salvific offer from God; indeed, this is the primary purpose of the argumentative progressions in the model's first phase. To hesitate, then, would be positively irrational — it would be to court the fires of hell — and hence one would have to be wicked or deluded to tarry before accepting this offer. So Luther himself seems impatient with those who dally in this first phase.[24] But crucially, given his largely incapacitated (that is, sinful) condition, Luther cannot be asked to do too much when actually grasping this generous offer. Any new criterion of salvation must be *appropriately manageable.*

The saving action now required of Luther is of course "faith." Grasping the new contract effected by Christ in faith — whatever the precise meaning of that[25] — Luther feels that the portals of heaven have been opened, and he now loves his heavenly ruler instead of hating him. So "faith" is the critical action that provides access to the relief of the new Christian offer. It is of course a much less arduous criterion than the rigorous demand under the law for ethical perfection (or even for 51 percent righteousness), *but it is a criterion nevertheless*. It is Luther's own incapacity, now ruthlessly exposed, that demands this significantly reduced criterion, but the need for a criterion per se is grounded in the model's opening assumptions. Justification is a voluntarist model throughout, focused on the deliberations of a rational individual, so any such individual must at the crucial moment do something!

The rational progression of this new, much softer and more generous saving contract can be represented in summary propositions quite succinctly:

7a. God redirects, generously, the punishment due sinners to Christ (who dies).

(7b. Christ, being sinless and divine, can offer limitless satisfaction through dying.)

7c. God redirects, generously, the perfect righteousness of Christ to sinners, who are now viewed as if it were theirs.

(7d. Christ, being sinless, supplies perfect righteousness.)

8a. God, again generously, stipulates a manageable criterion (see 6a) for accessing or appropriating these redirections, namely, "faith."

8b. Individuals who have "faith," and thereby access 7a (and perhaps 7c), technically fulfill the criteria of requisite punishment and perfect righteousness and will receive a positive evaluation (via 4) on the day of judgment (5a, 5b, and 5d), proceeding to the state of blessed eternal life (5c).

As we have already seen, the Justification model leaves proposition 8b open as a choice. Strong reasons have been supplied for grasping it, but it is emphatically uncoerced. Indeed, *if the saving criterion were coerced, then the preceding progress of the rational individual would be pointless.* The model clearly places a great deal of emphasis on this archetypal progression to salvation. If it were lacking, then we would not really be dealing with this model at all.[26] And its presence necessitates a corresponding emphasis on soteriological voluntarism.

The actual nature of the saving criterion, "faith," will be examined carefully in due course, along with several aspects of its function. Here it suffices to note that the claim that faith *alone* saves is cradled by the logic of the first phase. By this is meant only that one should not try to do anything *more* than have faith, since this would mean slipping back into the hopeless cycles of attempted works within the first phase. Because of innate and repeated sinfulness, one simply cannot be saved through an accumulation of good works. Indeed, any attempt to add a criterion to the minimal one stipulated almost certainly betrays a fleshly and illegitimate desire to return to that earlier field of human endeavor; it denotes a false understanding of one's own piety. The constant repudiation of additional criteria and of the need for good works (along, presumably, with those who advocate them) consequently demonstrates that the lessons of the first phase have been well learned. It is in this sense particularly that the model's advocates rest on faith alone. In so doing, they rest in fact on the model's account of the unsaved state as the only correct one, from which the soteriological function of faith follows. Without the prior state and its difficulties, this emphasis would have no cogent rationale.

And this leads us to a brief consideration of the role of the law. In strictly soteriological terms, any role for the law has clearly been repudiated as fundamentally hopeless and impious (initial appearances notwithstanding). The law cannot save, although one must live through this experience in order to appreciate the real and rather easier criterion of salvation. One must live under the law for a time and then one must leave it behind — at which point one will also be motivated to do so! Hence, there is a legitimate law-free claim at the heart of the Justification model. It provides extensive argumentation for the proposition that *salvation* is not through law. But presumably other functions for the law are still possible (although the rational individual, once saved, may not need to pay a lot of attention to them).

We should note here as well that the second phase of saving action by God establishes a set of important possible continuities with New Testament language. In the first place, this supremely generous and forgiving action can be viewed as the content of the Pauline notion of divine "grace" — and there *is* something *undeserved* about sinners saved by faith: *they are not being treated strictly in accordance with their merits.* But grace, so defined, does not and cannot denote *unconditional* divine action or salvific initiative. This would be to overthrow some of the model's central elements — especially the acting subject (the rational individual). Grace, on this Justification reading, denotes the divine *generosity* displayed in the unmerited aspect of salvation by faith alone; it is no less than this and no more. It is "unmerited," or "undeserved," rather than "unconditional" (at which point one wonders whether it really is "grace" in the way that that signifier is usually defined theologically). However, saved individuals will doubtless respond to this salvation with a degree of joy, peace, and thanksgiving. They have, after all, been relieved of a mortal burden of anxiety. So the themes of joyful or contented responsiveness, peace, and gratitude that sound through Paul's texts can also be usefully integrated with the model at the appropriate points.

Finally, we should emphasize once again the contractual nature of the new soteriological arrangement. After a series of important realizations, the generic subject has to do something in order to be saved, namely, to exercise the criterion of faith (and he or she must continue to exercise it). *If* faith is exercised, *then* salvation takes place. If not, however, then this contract is not activated and its obligations not honored by God. And at this point one is left under the previous, harsher contract, which is premised on much more difficult stipulations and will inevitably end in divine punishment. Hence, the Justification model is a tale of two contracts that corresponds to its tale of two phases, although the first contract is held to be inherently unstable and to lead inexorably, for the rational person, to an embrace of the second. The contrast in their stipulations, between rigorous and generous conditions, is quite deliberate and generates much of the pressure that encourages the transfer of appropriately reflective individuals between them.

The foregoing should suffice as a preliminary — and largely positive — statement of the account of salvation offered by Justification theory. For ease of reference, the entire model's chains of argument are repeated here in sequence.

§4. Summary of the Argumentative Progressions in Propositional Form

The First Phase: The Rigorous Contract

1a. Humans are rational.

1b. Humans are self-interested.

1c. Humans are therefore ethical, in order to be saved (and this largely in relation to 1b).

2a. God is omnipotent (and presumably also omniscient and omnipresent).

2b. God is just.

2c. 2a is known to everyone from the cosmos without.

2d. 2b is known to everyone from the conscience within.

3a. The content of righteousness derives from God's nature (see 2b).

3b. God's ethical demands are revealed to Jews through written legislation.

3c. God's ethical demands are known to everyone else innately (2b via 2d).

4. Reward and punishment will be apportioned by God (so 2a) in relation to individuals' fulfillment or not of God's ethical demands (so 2b), that is, in accordance with righteous actions, which constitute righteousness, or their converse, and hence *on the basis of desert*. "If you do *x*, then you will be rewarded; if you do not, and/or do *y*, then you will be punished."

The Future Eschatological Caveat

5a. The injustices of life on earth will be rectified by a final judgment at the end of the present age.

5b. Those dead will be resurrected in order to take part in the judgment (through 2a).

5c. The future age will be constituted in positive and negative states (again through 2a).

5d. God will determine on this "day" (through 2a) which state each individual will enter on the basis of desert (see 4, effected at 5a through 5b).

The Introspective Twist

6a. Humans are inherently sinful; that is, everyone violates God's ethical demands (and probably often, in which case see also the supplementary "loop" immediately following).

6b. Honest self-reflection notes the consistent production of unethical deeds (6a, apparent in the light of 3a through 3c).

6c. Such self-reflection concludes — in an accurate anticipation — that God's final judgment will be negative (see 4, 5c, and 5d).

6d. Rational individuals are now afraid and desire somehow to avoid this inevitable consequence.

The Loop of Despair (Correct)

1′. Accordingly, individuals might undertake a renewed attempt to be righteous.

2′. This attempt, however, will also fail, as 6a continues, noted by 6b, and so the conclusion of 6c will be reiterated, *leading to a strengthened 6d!*

The Loop of Foolishness (Incorrect)

1a″. Resistant individuals perceive and claim themselves to be righteous.

1b″. They are in fact not righteous (no one is free from all sin: so 6a).

2a″. Therefore, they are being dishonest with themselves, specifically, by underestimating their sinfulness and/or overestimating their rectitude.

2b″. Their judgment is ethically deficient (see 2a″).

2c″. This holds the more, the more ethical information they have (so Jews).

3a″. If they boast of their righteousness, they are liars and fakes.

3b″. If they invoke the names of God and religion, they are religious charlatans.

3c″. If they upbraid others and exhort others to imitate them, they are judgmental hypocrites.

3d″. If they continue this calculus and its behavior, they are irrational and obstinate, courting hell.

4″. The correct conclusion (obvious to the outsider): they doubly deserve the negative judgment awaiting them in 4-5d.

The Satisfaction of God's Justice

7a. God redirects, generously, the punishment due sinners to Christ (who dies).

(7b. Christ, being sinless and divine, can offer limitless satisfaction through dying.)

7c. God redirects, generously, the perfect righteousness of Christ to sinners, who are now viewed as if it were theirs.

(7d. Christ, being sinless, supplies perfect righteousness.)

The Appropriation of Salvation

8a. God, again generously, stipulates a manageable criterion (see 6a) for accessing or appropriating these redirections, namely, "faith."

8b. Individuals who have "faith," and thereby access 7a (and perhaps 7c), technically fulfill the criteria of requisite punishment and perfect righteousness and will receive a positive evaluation (via 4) on the day of judgment (5a, 5b, and 5d), proceeding to the state of blessed eternal life (5c).

§5. "Root Metaphors"

While this chapter's account of Justification has emphasized its highly rational argumentative progressions, it is helpful to note that such arguments are often intimately related to the deployment of key images and metaphors.[27] Arguments tend to draw out more precisely the relationships and inferences inherent in a juxtaposition of premises — and premises often have a strong image-based or metaphorical dimension.[28] The Justification model is no exception. Its progressions are actually generated in part by the juxtaposition of certain fundamental images, or "root metaphors." Furthermore, its advocates can deploy the model in an indirect or even tacit fashion *by merely alluding to these basic semantic clusters*. It is therefore vital to isolate them as precisely as we can — and then to be alert to their abbreviated activation.

It should be evident from our previous description of its inner argumentative workings that Justification theory is launched by two fundamental images. Once the model is up and running, so to speak, additional images respond to this representation, essentially supplying further, explanatory layers to these two root metaphors. Specifically, Justification theory begins with a particular image of humanity and a particular image of God. Intriguingly, it is the person who appropriates this God in the first instance, and not the other way around; hence, the model's anthropology is especially fundamental.

Anthropology

At the heart of the Justification model is a particular conception of what a person is. This root anthropological metaphor comprises several important aspects. As we have already seen, humans are viewed primarily in *individual* terms; they are considered largely in and of themselves, in isolation from others. They are highly *rational* and *self-interested*; they think, perceive, deduce, reflect, and act in accordance with the dictates of "the will." They are, to a significant degree, a thinking construction. Hence, layered upon the model's image of humanity, and necessarily shaped by it, is a vision of knowledge and how it is acquired. The model's rational individuals acquire knowledge by reflecting on the world,[29] a process that therefore largely equates knowledge with the acquisition of a body of correct concepts or beliefs — with information.[30]

Significantly, then, in the Justification model an image of humanity dictates in turn a vision of knowledge and its acquisition: anthropology dictates epistemology. And this epistemology is irreducibly a priori, or prospective. It moves forward in a linear fashion, following the self-impelled acquisition and accumulation of information by individuals as they explore the surrounding world, adding to their base of knowledge step by step. We are dealing here with "philosophical man"[31] — an individualist and rationalistic depiction of the human condition in its most essential aspects. Humanity is primarily cognitive.

It follows in turn that this basic mode of knowledge must include the knowledge of God, and this is clearly an important point. Because knowledge depends on the exploration of the world by rational individuals who acquire correct information about it, knowledge of the divine must depend, at least initially, on these basic categories as well. The knowledge of God is, at first, nothing more than information; it consists of correct concepts or beliefs amassed by the individual concerning God but derived (somehow) from the world. Hence, the model's anthropology also dictates its *theological* epistemology. And this epistemology is also irreducibly a priori, that is, innate, universal, and prior to all other theological premises. It takes place as the first theological step, as natural theology.

However, the Justification model does not entertain many doubts at this point (being formulated long in advance of the European age of skepticism). It confidently asserts the existence of the divine at an early point in its system, as the majority of premodern systems did. God *can* be known from the world, from which realization further important points then unfold.

The knowledge of God includes the knowledge of God's ethical demands. So humans are *ethical*, although in a somewhat limited sense. Their activity is focused primarily on the discernment of God's ethical demands and on fulfilling — or not fulfilling — them in accordance with self-interest. These demands seem to comprise a social as well as a divine-human dimension and often refer in particular to sexual practices, although this specification can rapidly broaden to include a stereotypical series of sins including murder, greed, abuse, disrespect, and so on. Each person must take responsibility for these demands, and so the model presupposes just this degree of individualism. But there seems to be a certain ambiguity in this ethical dimension. Individuals are not disposed to act ethically because this is right or even because this is how they are constructed but largely because it is in their best interests so to act — an enduring conundrum for this approach to ethics.

Theology

We can now introduce our second root metaphor. The model's rational individuals detect a particular God who undergirds this activity. First, they detect *one* God and, second, one that cannot be imaged (something that sets this model apart from the bulk of ancient pagan religion; this God's worship must be aniconic). However, it is the fundamental character of this God, as we have already seen, that is most important: these rational individuals detect, third, a God who is just. The single and transcendant God is committed above all else to the promulgation of retributive justice, publishing its dictates and enforcing its observance. And it is this third attribute that generates most of the argumentative leverage in the model.

God is being conceived here in terms of a "strict" authority figure, to use Lakoff's term — whether, in more specific terms, the figure is functioning as a ruler, a judge, or a parent. Such a figure rules, judges, or parents in terms of retributive justice, rewarding good behavior and punishing wrongdoing appropriately. Indeed, the failure to punish wrongdoing would be inexcusable on several counts. It would violate God's basic nature, as well as the basic nature of the universe, and it would send the wrong signals to the wrongdoer, as well as to the rest of humanity. It is bad government and bad parenting to signal that punishment is not ultimately delivered justly to the perpetrators of immoral and unethical acts (and here the model's root theological image links hands with its root rationalistic anthropology; people can and must learn that punishment ought to follow crime as inevitably as night follows day).

We should also note a useful historical clarification at this point. In the modern period, the roles of governing official and judicial arbiter — and usually also of parent — are clearly separate. But in the premodern period, these separations did not exist, and so the metaphor of rule in terms of strict justice applied more broadly. In premodern societies, it was the monarch's duty to uphold the judiciary, and indeed to run it (and the retributive dimension within justice was largely unquestioned). Hence, when this God promulgates his will in the form of ethical decrees and then punishes ensuing infractions, he is acting in premodern settings like a king (or his equivalent) in his judicial role rather than merely as a judge per se — although, significantly, as one bound to an ethical and even a legislative dimension.[32] All of which is to say that a premodern political analogy can lie behind the Justification model, although not as an "absolute" monarchy. This monarch is still bound to a basic ethical code organized in terms of retributive justice.

In sum, a particular type of person — essentially individual, rational, and self-interested — grasps early on in his or her cognitive pilgrimage through the world that a particular type of God exists — a somewhat imperious one. And here we encounter another important aspect of the model's epistemology.

We have already seen in our account of Justification that a just God generates little or no leverage on the individual until the perception of this God is combined with one of internal sinfulness. So the further specification of *perceived ethical incapacity* must now be added to our unfolding image of the person. The rationalistic individuals envisaged here are, as it turns out, deeply sinful, since their honest self-reflection reveals — among other things — the committing of numerous transgressions. This perception necessarily places them in a problematic position vis-à-vis the divine monarch and his decrees, thereby generating much of the forward movement in the model.

And thus we have arrived at the model's second, salvific phase. As we already know, this phase comprises two basic components, a satisfactory one and an appropriative one, and their metaphorical dimensions can also be treated briefly in turn.

The model must supply some mechanism of *satisfaction* if it is to provide a way out for the individuals who have provoked God's retribution — some means whereby the anger of God against their accumulating sin can be assuaged and its penalty paid. And the Justification model focuses this notion, as we know, on Christ's death. But this event is also helpfully illuminated by an appreciation of its metaphorical dimension, which is layered on the model's root metaphor of God. At one level, there is the notion drawn directly from widespread legal and political practice that serious transgression is punishable by death. But this notion — a fundamentally gruesome image perhaps — does not entirely explain the function of Christ, who within the model both substitutes for the death of the individual and does so for the many (that is, for whosoever chooses to appropriate the offer). He does not die for his own sins, as this metaphor would dictate. So further metaphorical assistance is usually introduced here, drawing on other legal generalities and thereby reinforcing very exactly the overarching theistic image of a judging monarch. In general sociolegal terms, wrongdoing can be dealt with by a form of *compensation,* rather than solely by equivalence, so the metaphorical expansion at this point is *monetary.* It is assumed that wrongdoing can be amended by some sort of payment considered proportional, whether that specifically comprises gifts, money, service, time in confinement or something else deemed appropriate. This notion includes within it the connotation of *substitution,* since a compensation deliberately substitutes for a directly corresponding punishment, the latter being seen most famously perhaps in the adage "an eye for an eye." Hence, layered upon the image of God as a royal judge in an aggrieved state can be discerned a complementary sociolegal metaphor of substitutionary compensation, essentially analogous to the payment of money, which is applied by the Justification model specifically to account for Christ's death. And some notion of quantification is implicit here as well. Sin can be treated as a currency and dealt with by a legally valid act of compensation that encompasses transfer as well as costliness.

Just as the model deploys a vision of satisfaction that complements its image of God, so it deploys a vision of appropriation that complements its image of humanity, and this again via its epistemology. The individuals at the heart of the model ultimately do things for themselves; in the first, unsaved phase they ratiocinate and reflect and then go on to undertake further actions in the light of these initial actions. And the model simply continues this anthropological commitment in its salvific phase, asserting that the individuals must *do* something in order to access Christ's satisfactory function and in turn stipulating a mode of appropriation. That the model stipulates "faith" is, moreover, not only exegetically useful but supremely consistent with its unfolding image of humanity. Above all, the model's conception of anthropology is rationalist and thus oriented toward the acquisition of beliefs. Hence, that the criterion for appropriating salvation is really just the absorption and affirmation of further information could hardly be better. Just as these thinking individuals have thought their way through to the realization of a chronic need for salvation, so too they now think their way through to its appropriation. We should note that some of the model's advocates have an uneasy conscience about the impersonal nature of this action and assert instead a more personal action of "trust" that must be vested in God (and the difficulties implicit in this position will be registered subsequently). In terms of the model's structure, however, there is nothing embarrassing here. Individuals are saved by a mental action — a cognitive appropriation — and this is simply how they have behaved throughout. So the initial anthropological image has, once again, simply been layered metaphorically in quite consistent terms in phase two.[33]

By this point in our description, then, it should be clear that the driving force for the Justification model really comes from its two opening images — namely, its anthropology and its theology — and the latter in its conception of God in terms of strict authority. The anthropology is then layered in terms of epistemology, culminating in the first phase with a perception of internal sinfulness, or ethical incapacity. In the second, salvific phase, the conception of God is layered with a metaphor of satisfactory compensation in relation to Christ, and a further and quite consistent (again, epistemological) layer is added to the conception of humans in terms of the acquisition of new beliefs, which action constitutes the criterion for salvation.

Most importantly, the fundamental thrust of the model is consequently forward, prospective, or a priori. The system proceeds in essentially linear temporal terms from an account of the initial, unsaved state — the problem — to an account of the Christian, saved state — the solution. The initial state, assumed to be temporally prior, is also *conceptually determinative* for the rest of the model. Clearly, the solution then corresponds to the problem, nuancing it but by no means revising it. The initial root metaphors in play in the first phase consequently have a "ruling function" that governs any further theological development. Moreover, they must necessarily be posited in advance of the reception of any special Christian information; they occupy the preceding "state of nature." Christian information, which is more particular, really then just responds to an account already in place and deemed to be universally true and innately perceived, an account that turns out to possess both strengths and weaknesses.

The key metaphors and their additional metaphorical layers can be summarized in propositional form as follows:

I. *A conception of humanity as individual, rationalistic and self-interested.* We begin our analysis with "philosophical man" — humans as fundamentally cognitive. *I* discerns first *II*.

II. *A conception of God as an authority figure of strict justice.* Philosophical man discerns the existence of God as a strict authority figure — his basic divine attribute is retributive justice. *II* is discerned by *I*.

I'. *Humanity's self-perceived ethical incapacity.* Humans attempt to be ethical in the light of *II*, but only repeatedly transgress, and realize this: *I'* layers *I* in the light of *II*.

II'. *A compensatory mechanism of satisfaction, namely, Christ's atonement.* Christ's death pays the appropriate compensation for all these transgressions, and any more that may or do occur: *II'* responds to *I'* on behalf of *I* and the standards of *II*.

I''. *A stipulated criterion of salvation's appropriation, namely, faith.* Salvation is
grasped by individuals through an act of belief that takes place in some relation to Christ: I'', possible for anyone within I but constrained by I', activates II' for anyone so inclined. (As an action, it also corresponds to other
actions taking place within I and I'.)

In overall conclusion to this discussion it should be emphasized that the preceding description is primarily theoretical. Wherever possible I have tried to trace
the Justification model's approach to salvation in terms of the most coherent conceptual route to that end — what arguments make the most sense *simply in argumentative terms* given the opening assumptions and basic metaphorical commitments of the model (although various Pauline texts and ecclesial interpretative
traditions do tend to lie just out of sight behind this description). My principal intention here has been to emphasize the internal theoretical integrity of the model
— although, because it speaks of God, this must also in some sense be a theological integrity as well. That we have been able to articulate such a comprehensive
and integrated structure is testimony to the model's inherent explanatory
strength. We will see shortly that this structure is not perfect, yet it still possesses
an impressive rational integration. Our task from this point, however, is to examine the model's besetting problems and difficult implications.

CHAPTER TWO

Intrinsic Difficulties

§1. Preamble

This book is ultimately critical of Justification theory. That theory, I will argue, although it is seductive and powerful, is in fact bad theology. But in the first instance any opinion of this theological structure within Paul matters little. It may just be the case that the apostle was committed to theological positions that some of us now find unpalatable, and if so, then we must be honest about this and learn to live with it. However, if those commitments are not supported by his actual argumentation, or if they cause difficulties for Paul as he seems to reason elsewhere, or if they do not fit with relevant aspects of observable reality, then this ought to be noted. Such evidence might ultimately provide leverage for constructive interpretative alternatives. We might say that if what seems like bad theology to us is also incoherent or contradictory or empirically false theology in relation to the apostle himself, then options will be created. This could be the origins of a case that this is not in fact what he was writing about. And it is one of my central claims in what follows that the Justification theory of salvation described in chapter one does generate such difficulties.

Justification theory unleashes something of a shockwave of inconsistencies through the broader context of Paul's thought as a whole. Hence, when we try to give a comprehensive description of the apostle's thought, it is always riven with contradictions (which may often be intuited even if they are not articulated overtly). I dub these tensions difficulties at the "systematic" frame,[1] and they are discussed in detail in chapter three.

But it is also important to note the tensions caused by the theory's contractual soteriology in relation to the reality it purports to describe. Justification theory, *as* a theory, is necessarily committed to making claims about reality — but those claims need to be empirically accurate, that is, consistent with the reality we can observe. If they are not, then further interpretative leverage is created. I dub these tensions difficulties at the "empirical" frame, and they include in the main the much-discussed issues of Judaism and of Paul's own "conversion" (although the question of Paul's "conversion" could arguably be treated at the systematic frame). These tensions are discussed in chapters four and five respectively.

Finally, I would suggest that a clear-sighted scrutiny of contractual soteriology in Paul reveals a number of points where the theory itself breaks down *internally*, that is, *in strictly theoretical terms*. The theory seems to contain unexplained gaps within its all-important argumentative progressions or, worse, to rely on arguments that turn out on closer examination to be incoherent. Such difficulties contribute to the growing number of problems associated with a commitment to Justification theory within Paul's theology — and hence in due course to still more interpretative leverage.[2] This set of difficulties — of "intrinsic" theoretical tensions — is examined in the present chapter.

It might be argued immediately (again) that my representation of the various difficulties will be biased or unfair. My account, however, will give full consideration to rejoinders by the theory's defenders — where they have been offered — as we work through the difficulties systematically in turn, although, admittedly, we will conclude eventually that little or no effective defense against them is in fact ultimately possible; it seems that they are intrinsic to the theory.[3]

§2. Intrinsic Difficulties

We begin our more detailed critical analysis by examining the Justification model's internal theoretical difficulties, problems that it seems to face by virtue of its very construction.[4] We can identify seven points of tension or outright incoherence within Justification theory itself:

1. epistemology
2. natural revelation
3. law
4. anthropology
5. theodicy
6. Christology and atonement
7. faith

2.1. *Epistemology*

> *Justification theory argues in terms of two incompatible epistemologies: a general, atemporal, philosophical, and rational conception of knowledge — "objective" philosophical reasoning; and a particular, historical, revelatory, and interpersonal conception — notably, the witness of Scripture, but also the voice of God.*

The theory of Justification begins quite clearly with a universal scope and set of definitions and arguments. It applies to all people everywhere, irrespective of their place in history, walk of life, and so on. And this universality through time, culture, and space is achieved by an epistemology that is oriented toward the essentially philosophical contemplation of the cosmos by a rational individual. Anyone can undertake this activity, and in fact ought to. However, when the saving phase of the model begins, its parameters change to the particular and to the essentially historical. The focal point for salvation is the crucifixion and, more broadly, the sinless life of Christ. And from this point information about him and his achievements is carried by the church, and especially evangelists, out to the rest of the world and is then transmitted on through those who receive that message. This is particular, historical, contextualized activity. In addition, this message is attested in the Jewish Scriptures and eventually corroborated by its own Scripture, the writing, reading, and discussion of which are also entirely particular, albeit nicely transferable. Indeed, the point is obvious. Christianity, like historical Judaism, is particular. It is immersed in and spreads through history, and its texts reflect this. It unfolds through time and in relation to specific people who must come into contact with one another. But this means that Justification theory actually contains a significant epistemological difference between its two phases. Two radically different conceptions of knowledge are operative. And this is bound to cause difficulties.

The most obvious is that conclusions delivered by the second approach are not necessarily valid in terms of the first (and vice versa, but this is not so important; the model moves forward). The generic, philosophical individual has no way of verifying the truth of particular, revelatory claims; these have not been derived from the rational contemplation of the cosmos but are presented by a person as received truths. Hence, there is no way of objectively assessing them. Further, the philosophical argumentation within Justification has no real need of scriptural corroboration. Such support for the former is redundant if not opaque. These are serious problems.

Added to these difficulties, there are underlying temporal tensions that must be negotiated. The first phase of Justification is essentially atemporal and ahistorical; it can take place anytime, not to mention anywhere. However, once this phase has been negotiated, then the Christian solution, presented by the theory's second phase, is irreducibly temporal and historical. How is a generic and atemporal vestibule to lead on to an emphatically historical continuation? This is awkward. (Strictly speaking, only those fortunate enough to have been reached by bearers of the particularized information can progress from the vestibule at all.)

We could preserve the epistemological integrity of the theory by eliminating its difficult move to a particularized epistemology, and there is nothing theoretically offensive about such a modification. The general, philosophical epistemology of the first phase could simply be extended into the second, salvific phase. Consider Abraham in generic terms. Not only does he draw the appropriate conclusions from his contemplation of the cosmos about God's ethical concerns and his own sinfulness, but he goes on to deduce that salvation must therefore be through faith alone in the divinity behind creation. Furthermore, that divinity can clearly be trusted to provide some means of atonement for his transgressions, although it is not necessary for Abraham to know specifically what this is in order to benefit from the arrangement. God simply needs to have his just requirements satisfied. And thus our awkward epistemological shift has disappeared.[5]

But this possible solution illustrates well the limitations under which our entire analysis of Justification theory labors. Although the modified version is inoffensive theoretically — and in fact much improved by that measure — it would be ludicrous to suggest that a Pauline construct actually exists in such terms. We would have to find texts in Paul that actually argue for this approach, and none spring to mind. Here, both Judaism *and* the early church would have to be eliminated. Indeed, Paul's own extraordinary ministry would have to be jettisoned. *History* would have to disappear. Put slightly more technically, the framing tensions raised by this proposal are so extensive and acute, and any direct textual corroboration so obviously absent, that it is instantly rendered absurd. We must ultimately somehow accommodate Paul's apparent shift within Justification theory from a universal anthropocentric epistemology to a particularized revelational epistemology, and that as coherently as we can.

The difficulties caused by this epistemological cohabitation will recur at many points in our subsequent critical analysis. Suffice it to say at this point that such a dual epistemology, with one mode of knowledge leading to the other,[6] looks basically incoherent.

2.2. *Natural Revelation*

> *Justification theory builds from the objective discernment and linkage of certain propositions within creation — a universal recognition and derivation that, in strictly rational terms, is impossible.*

The first phase in Justification theory depends on individuals' detection within the cosmos of a series of propositions; this then establishes the conditions for any further progress toward salvation. Individuals must first grasp certain truths about God and then attempt to act on them (cf. Rom. 1:18-23). Specifically, they must grasp the truth of *theism*, of *monotheism*, of divine *transcendence* (that is, that this single God cannot be imaged, and so should not be), and the truth of this God's *retributive justice*. They must then grasp the specific concerns of this strictly just God with respect to human *heterosexuality* and *monogamy*,[7] as well as, beyond these, *a fuller ethical system* (no envy, murder, deceit, and so on; cf. Rom. 1:29-31).

theism
↓
monotheism
↓
divine transcendence/unimageability
↓
divine retributive justice
↓
divine concern for human heterosexuality
↓
and monogamy
↓
divine concern for a fuller ethical system

We can detect a cluster of problems in relation to these notions. Fundamentally, the rational derivation of this set of propositions seems to be impossible. A reflective individual in the modern world contemplating the cosmos would probably not detect any of them. And if it is replied — not entirely correctly[8] — that the argument should be contextualized to the first century, it remains the fact that philosophers contemporary to Paul detected wide variations on these themes as well, something a comparative religious perspective makes especially clear, although, admittedly, the first proposition in the series, namely, the existence of divine realities, would have been conceded by the majority. Thus, not one of these propositions is "apparent" in the cosmos, with the possible exception in the Principate of the existence of divinities (allowing that this is a relevant rejoinder). Moreover, *not one follows from another,* so neither are they mutually derivable. The directly ethical concerns of God in terms of heterosexuality and so on do not derive obviously from any philosophical grasp of transcendent monotheism, which itself is difficult if not impossible to derive from theism, and so on. I know of no adequate reply to the complaints of philosophers for some time that this progression lacks any basic rational plausibility. That is, I am persuaded by the validity of the skeptical philosophical response to the various attempted proofs of God's existence.[9] The latter are invalid, and hence the progression as a whole fails.

But even granting the truth of one or two steps in the progression, the further derivation of the divine characteristics needed by Justification theory is just not possible, and obviously this strengthens my confidence. So we could grant that "the god of the philosophers" had been rationally demonstrated, so that all right-thinking philosophers endorsed "his" existence, omnipotence, omniscience, and omnipresence. A case can be made here for God's singularity and transcendence, although perhaps the latter more plausibly than the former. But it now looks next to impossible to demonstrate that such a God is characterized by retributive justice and then in turn by specific commitments in terms of sexual relations and interpersonal relations as the theory enumerates those here. Such attributes and concerns cannot be shown to derive in strictly rational terms from the bland god of the philosophers. How do we deduce, by contemplating the cosmos, that a single transcendent god is offended by homosexuality? The philosophically astute Greeks never made this connection. (Indeed, it is reasonably obvious, given its frequent countercultural posture, that this concern is known only from special revelation.) And shortly we will touch on the still more acute question whether this god is offended by the consumption of meat with blood in it. Many ancient Jews seem to have thought that this divine concern was entirely obvious (cf. Gen. 9:4), but presumably few now would share that confidence.

Hence, it ought to be concluded that the theory's claims at these points are simply argumentatively false; its all-important progression that establishes human culpability in relation to certain divine realities and concerns is rationally invalid, something that becomes increasingly clear the further down the chain of propositions one attempts to progress.[10]

2.3. Law

Justification theory asserts two sets of law within one soteriology committed to a just God and perfect obedience — a dual system that is incoherent in terms of both content and desert.

Another nasty conundrum lurks within this broader argument (and it is linked to problem one — epistemology — that has just been noted). Either the model must claim that the Jewish law, in all its details, is derivable from the cosmos through natural revelation or it must work with two different ethical systems — one a more general set of ethical principles applicable to all and discernible in the cosmos, and the other a more extensive set with additional distinctive practices incumbent only on Jews and accessible primarily through revelation and texts.

The impossibility of the first strategy can be noted here rapidly; that the Jewish law in all its particulars can be derived merely through reflection on the cosmos is patently absurd. One simply cannot infer practices such as circumcision, abstention from consuming blood, the Jubilee, and a temple cultus from the contemplation of nature. As their textual settings suggest, these practices are bound up with specific historical events, cultures, and even with revelation. And no Jewish literature really expects *full* Mosaic law observance of pagans independently of direct access to the books of Moses. (Perhaps *Jubilees* comes the closest to this expectation, but only with respect to the patriarchs, and they also seem to receive a degree of direct assistance.) This approach is fundamentally unworkable.

Hence, the usual strategy has been to overlook the need for a strict equation in the theory at this point and to assume some difference between the Mosaic law and natural law. Pagans are held accountable to some trimmed-down version of the Mosaic law; the whole of that legislation is not binding on them. And this distinction can also find support contemporary to Paul, since some Jewish texts do distinguish in these terms between Jewish law and a much-reduced, generalized set of commandments applicable to all — the Noahide commandments (see Gen. 9:1-7, and possibly visible in Acts 15:29 as well).

However, at this point the key question is not so much whether the approach possesses a plausible historical setting (which, arguably, it seems to) as whether this distinction is *theoretically coherent*. Paul's contemporaries could have suffered from the same degree of incoherence as he did. But is this distinction plausible in purely rational terms when it operates within the broader parameters of Justification theory? On two grounds I would suggest that it is not.

First, it is hard to understand how this dual system could be coherent in terms of content. The criteria discerned in the Justification model's first phase ostensibly set forth the ethical concerns of God. They are rightly observed, because they reflect the concerns of the divine nature, and infractions are rightly punished. But it is hard to understand how two different sets of ethical instruction from God can then actually exist. (It is of course not difficult to imagine different sets of instruction on the human plane.) Clearly, a significant amount of ethical direction is not included in one of these sets — presumably, the shorter pagan version. And either the additional material in the longer Jewish set is a genuine reflection of God's ethical concerns, in which case the shorter pagan version is inadequate, or this extra material is not a genuine reflection of God's concerns, in which case we must question why it is present in the Jewish set at all. So, for example, the prohibition on cutting forelocks (Deut. 14:1) is either something that God does regard as important and that therefore should be included in any judgment of pagans, or it is not a matter of particular concern to God, in which case it should not be binding upon Jews. As a matter of strict justice, a prohibition (or a positive commandment) cannot be valid for one group but simultaneously invalid for another. Such a dual system is incoherent *in terms of content*. There is really no such thing as an *optional* right action prescribed by God.

Second, it is hard to understand how such a system could be coherent in terms of desert. People, it seems, will be judged strictly in accordance with deeds, but in relation to two very different sets of criteria (and recall that the theory expects perfect obedience).[11] One of these systems will presumably be more difficult than the other, so its deeds will be more difficult, and its constituents will be at a distinct disadvantage.[12] And this simply does not look just. A system of desert that functions in relation to two quite different sets of criteria seems to be fundamentally flawed *in terms of desert!*

These obvious problems have almost certainly been obscured in the past by the intrusion of various interpretative strategies that have allowed much of the specific Jewish legislation to be overlooked and marginalized — essentially a supersessionist perspective. Interpreters have then effectively endorsed a minimalist level of ethical content, thereby partially resolving these tensions. At bottom, only one integrated ethical code has been in play — the briefer pagan one. It is often said, for example, that Christ has fulfilled the temple, so any temple-related regulations are now superfluous. (This hermeneutical strategy has clearly benefited from the destruction of the actual temple in Jerusalem in 70 CE; God was arguably putting an end to such matters directly.) This approach may then be parlayed into a broader claim that the "ceremonial" law has been fulfilled, and hence only the "moral," or ethical, law remains in force with respect to both Jews and pagans.

But this strategy is rather dubious, and on numerous counts. It is unconvincing in terms of the Jewish law itself, which recognizes no such distinction between secondary, temple-related material and more important, ethical commandments. (And of course to assume the destruction of the temple is anachronistic for the early church; it was still standing when Paul's texts were penned.) Similarly, the fully extended strategy does not work at crucial points. It is not always clear what commandments fall into the marginalized category of "ceremonial." For example, the ten commandments are often invoked as the heart of the moral law, but the Sabbath tends to be discarded as a peculiarly Jewish ceremonial ordinance, although it is only arguably ceremonial and is certainly not temple related.[13] Similar difficulties exist for dietary issues, especially in relation to blood. Indeed, it is interesting to note that Jewish authors would include the prohibition on the eating of blood, and hence also of improperly prepared meats, in the most basic set of ethical prescriptions incumbent on all humanity (cf. Gen. 9:4), but later pagan Christian interpreters generally would not (cf. Acts 15:29, including the textual history!; also 1 Cor. 10:23-30).

It is evident, then, that the distinction between "ceremonial" and "moral" law is by no means unambiguous. And even to the extent that those categories might be discerned, they do not correspond neatly to the original categories of Jewish law and natural law. That is, much peculiarly Jewish material that only with great difficulty might be derived from the observation of the cosmos nevertheless seems to fall clearly outside the boundaries of ceremony — and hence within those of the general, moral law. (And some things that have traditionally been included in that general, moral code are arguably only ceremonial.)[14] So the cultic strategy falters.

In sum, it would seem that the precise content of the behavior that God requires of everyone cannot be clearly derived from the contemplation of nature; if it could, then these disputes would not have taken place. Furthermore, the hermeneutical strategies employed to deal with the troubling differences between the extensive and highly particular requirements of Jewish law and the minimal requirements supposedly in force for pagans simply don't hold up — that is, even if their validity is initially granted, which it should not be. Thus, the conundrums present in Justification theory at this point seem to persist. In positing two different sets of ethical instruction, the theory courts charges of incoherence on two counts: God reveals two different definitions of ethics — a blow in terms of content — and God judges humanity by two different sets of criteria — a blow in terms of desert.[15]

2.4. Anthropology

> *Justification theory presupposes in humans an inherent ability to deduce and appropriately fulfill the truth of certain axioms and, at the same time, a profound universal sinfulness — that is, fundamental and simultaneous capacity and incapacity.*

It was arguably one of Luther's most brilliant tactical moves to combine an essentially ethical scenario that presupposes human capacity with the confessional dimension of late medieval Catholicism, which asserts extensive individual sinfulness. This combination did not seem ultimately hopeless as long as a further, much easier route to salvation lay to hand. And it allowed a particular and quite fearsome rhetorical pressure to be built up on the individual within the unsaved state — and especially on the religious individual. Luther thereby achieved apparent success in merging two theological themes customarily held apart (while also fashioning a powerful and politically highly useful critique of "religion").

Optimistic commitments to human capacity, and to consequent ethical demands and behavior, are common both inside and outside the Christian tradition (as seen most overtly perhaps in Pelagius). Conversely, rather more pessimistic commitments to human *incapacity* are also quite prevalent within the Christian tradition, as well as within certain strands of Judaism (and the post-396 CE Augustine illustrates this nicely; he is discussed in more detail in part two, chapter eight). But the latter commitments are not usually concluded with a strong exhortation to act responsibly in the appropriate way. That is, these two perspectives are usually seen to be at cross-purposes. Luther, however, seems to have brought them together (and certainly Justification theory tries to). But there is in fact a problem at this point. Closer scrutiny would suggest that the mutual assertion of these two anthropological perspectives within the same construction of the individual is fundamentally incoherent.

The Justification model clearly presupposes individuals who can discern ethical dictates from God within the structure of the cosmos, if they do not possess a written account of them from Judaism. Moreover, these individuals can act in order to fulfill such commands, and they will be rewarded for doing so, suggesting that any such actions are somehow meritorious and hence presumably also uncoerced and autonomous. So clearly, these individuals possess a basic rational and ethical capacity. However, advocates of Justification theory hold of course that any optimism regarding this required level of ethical performance is misplaced. People are deeply sinful and constantly transgressing, as a modicum of self-examination suggests. So clearly, they also possess a basic *incapacity*: "*All have sinned and fall short of the glory of God,*" they might suggest (Rom. 3:23).

But how do these contradictory tendencies coexist within the same account of humanity? — the capacity to discern the good, to do it, and to be held accountable for it, combined with an inevitable and repeated sinfulness. Defenders of the theory's claims might try to employ dualistic metaphors. If humanity is composed of "spirit" and "flesh," the former aspect contains the upright ethical propensity to discern the good and to act accordingly, and the latter the evil propensity to transgress. Alternatively, the "mind" contains the good propensity and the "body" the wicked, or we can speak of the "inner" and the "outer" man, or of two "impulses" (see Rom. 7:22-23, 25b).

However, these essentially metaphorical explanations all rely on a sense of spatiality within their references that enables in turn the separation of the two conflicting anthropological propensities into two different "spaces" within the human being. From this point they can then be seen to coexist much as neighbors occupy adjacent properties, essentially apart but immediately alongside one another and perhaps squabbling from time to time. How convincing is this explanation? In my view, not very.

Although the explanation lays initial claim to spatiality, this notion is hardly applicable to the ethical construction of the human being in any real sense. It is *metaphorical*. Space is functioning here not literally but analogically to denote differentiation and difference. But space is necessary in *real* terms for this account of humanity to hold good. And when we turn to consider the underlying anthropological realities, we find that any sense of real space evaporates. All the individual's evaluations, propensities, and decisions, are operative in the mind, that is, in the *same* place. These all pertain to thought processes (at least to some degree). And the notion of separateness cannot really now be applied. Can we posit significantly separate ethical thought processes within the same basic human faculty, one pure and uncorrupted, the other impure and corrupted? Can we claim that one part of this faculty, along with its activity, is pristine but one part deeply flawed? This seems incoherent and consequently unsustainable.[16]

Hence, the claim that in the first phase of Justification individuals possess both capacity and incapacity seems fundamentally incoherent. The model's all-important anthropology is essentially garbled. (It is also worth emphasizing that this conundrum will be the deeper, the more any "depravity" or "original sin" is emphasized within the ontology of the non-Christian.)[17]

2.5. Theodicy

Justification theory posits a God of strict justice who holds all people accountable to a standard they are intrinsically unable to attain, and this seems unjust.

In close relation to the foregoing, it must be asked in what sense it is just for God to hold individuals accountable for failing to deliver ethical perfection when they are, by their very constitution, unable to do so. This would seem to be a game of impossible odds (or, as we say Down Under, little more than a kangaroo court). It simply does not seem fundamentally just to hold people accountable, on pain of dire punishment, for actions that they are predisposed to commit. Rather, true justice would seem to require that the criterion of ethical perfection be at least slightly relaxed.

This obvious problem of theodicy within Justification theory has been largely masked in the past by three important strategies: the orientation of the theory's initial phase toward a culpable, unlikable, and hence truly damnable constituency (i.e., a group who deserve hell anyway); the introduction of a deeply confessional dimension within this phase, related not infrequently to assertions about original sin and total depravity; and the immediate offer of a generous way out. We will treat these important gambits briefly in turn.

First, the acute issue of divine justice may be overlooked because the theory's initial accusations are almost invariably accompanied by a judgment of ethical opprobrium concerning the constituency being so accused. In Luther's case this constituency was (adopting his viewpoint for the moment) a deeply corrupt Catholic Church; Luther misses few opportunities to lambaste its perceived excesses. And the reader of his model feels a certain consequent justness in any final verdict of punishment. Wicked people do — at least arguably — deserve to be punished. In Paul's texts it is of course *Jews* who are primarily targeted. However, this constituency too could be viewed by many of Luther's contemporary readers as deserving their punishment at the end of the age; a negative valence of this constituency would have been standard until what is really a very recent historical moment. The Jews were implicated in the rejection of God's Son, continued to refuse opportunities to repent, and so on; there would be little distinction in the minds of most of the passionate Reformers between corrupt Catholics and recalcitrant Jews. And similar rhetorical ploys are apparent in many modern presentations of the model (as we will see in more detail in due course), perhaps most famously in Käsemann's stirring attacks on "the religious man," that is, on the complacent bourgeois Christian. (An analogous viewpoint is powerfully argued in Barth's famous commentary.)[18]

However, we must grasp that Justification's indictment in no sense relies on this common accompanying judgment, which merely tends to make the verdict more rhetorically palatable by bringing into focus a truly damnable constituency. The theory's vestibule targets "all," "without exception," and so must apply as well to the very inverse of this category of justly damned reprobates! Humble or saintly people too will be included within its indictment, at which point the theory's actual ground becomes plainly apparent. Indeed, it is only when we focus this calculus on good people that we comprehend its real dynamic. Truly humble saints, who have devoted their lives to the service of others — perhaps at great personal risk — *and who disclaim any pretense to perfect virtue*, will also be condemned at the end of the age as insufficiently righteous. What are we to make of such a verdict in relation to these inspirationally good people, that is, to the inverse of the normal target — those who are very good, although not perfect, and yet who humbly do not claim to be?

It now becomes apparent that the primary problem established by the theory's vestibule is not that individuals are self-inflated or hypocritical (although it will deal severely with those who are) but that they are not perfect. And no amount of rhetorical screening in terms of powerful indictments of the deservedly damnable can cover up this fundamental demand. In fact, Luther himself was presumably not a self-satisfied critic of medieval Catholic excesses but a serious-minded and idealistic reformer, yet he too felt deeply condemned. At bottom, the judgment in Justification's first phase is not related essentially to the unrepentant, corrupt religious person. It applies equally to the repentant and essentially pious person. Hence, *it bears no relation to the degree of recognition that individuals accord to their sinful state.* The judgment depends fundamentally on God's demand (at this point) *for ethical perfection,* in relation to which "all . . . fall short." And herein lies the problem.

This stringent demand by God for ethical perfection from essentially flawed human beings does not seem reasonable or just. Judgment is not pending merely for wicked and hypocritical people but also for kind, despairing, and even saintly folk, *and this seems fundamentally unjust in terms of proportionality.* (Other framing tensions will inevitably arise shortly at this point too.)

A second strategy that can mask the theory's problem of divine justice is the deployment of stronger notions of personal sinfulness, whether in a confessional mode or in explicit relation to original sin and putative total depravity. It is apparently entirely legitimate and even necessary for Christians to confess their sins and ongoing sinfulness and to acknowledge their parlous and darkened state before God. Many of Luther's statements are an excellent instance of this confessional piety, as are many of Augustine's. The general correctness of this activity and posture — especially for certain traditions — seems to overshadow any difficulties at this point within the theory: it is right for people to acknowledge their own sinfulness before God; hence, the argument seems true.

However, in so reasoning, Justification advocates have essentially repositioned a legitimate Christian activity in a location that renders that activity incoherent and, moreover, calls God's character radically into question. The correctness of Christian confession does not allow the theory's *non-Christian* confession to escape charges of incoherence and injustice. Indeed, those conundrums are deepened! The darker the depraved non-Christian mind, the more incoherent the divine expectation that important conclusions will be drawn rationally from the construction of the cosmos. By the same token, the fairness of a God who makes these demands is called still more seriously into question — the whole scenario is now profoundly unjust.

Hence, any appeal to "original sin" or some such at this point in the model is a rhetorically effective but theoretically bankrupt strategy. Such confessional actions feel right to Christian advocates who know that at some point they must embrace their own fallen and sinful condition. But any such appeals at a pre-Christian point within the developing account imperil it still more significantly as a theory.[19]

One could perhaps respond, then, third, that at least some way out is about to be provided, namely, the gospel. But neither does this respond to the problem at hand. Providing an escape route does not, strictly speaking, make the initial scenario any more just; it does not change the terms of that first situation. Some people will now simply escape from it and so will presumably no longer be concerned about its unfairness. But *that escape will be available only in a limited sense,* to those presented with the relevant saving information, and capable of accepting it. Hence, only those individuals at the age of rational assent who are fortunate enough to hear the gospel preached will possibly escape this dire initial state, which otherwise remains in force for the rest of humanity! The majority then simply endure a fundamentally unjust system — but this is not immediately apparent: the formulators, readers, and advocates of Justification almost certainly view themselves as occupying the smaller, saved constituency that has experienced God's generosity.

In short, the claims of retributive justice, which are basic to the theory's first phase and are strictly applied throughout the Justification model, do not seem compatible with the claim that human nature is in some sense seriously flawed and thus incapable of meeting God's high demands. It is not just to hold individuals accountable for acts that they cannot help committing.[20]

We could of course do much to alleviate the stress of the initial situation by lowering the bar. Justification theory requires perfect obedience of its generic individuals, and being fallen, they struggle to deliver this. But if God's final judgment were softened to a mere balancing of the good against the bad, or at least to a point where the difficulties that humans face in doing good deeds were taken into account, then the entire conundrum would be significantly mitigated.

However, this criterion cannot really be relaxed, because that would overthrow the basic argumentative function of the theory's first phase, which is *not* to effect a just final judgment so much as to drive everyone to the point where they are eager to embrace the Christian gospel. There can be no exceptions to this progression, because any exceptions would then open the theoretical door to the heinous prospect of non-Christian salvation. In a sense, only the depressed can be saved by Justification, and since everyone should be saved, then everyone must first be depressed. Hence, the perfectionist criterion fulfills exactly the task for which it was designed; it vanquishes all humanity. No softening of this criterion is possible.[21]

It would seem, then, that Justification theory must court the charge of injustice when it accuses everyone, without exception, of imperfect behavior, because the modifications required to avoid this problem would destroy its very rationale.

And it is also worth noting that this difficulty is exacerbated by another element that lies just ahead within the theory as a whole. Justification theory saves individuals who grasp its offer of salvation by transferring their deserved punishment onto the undeserving Christ on the cross. His painful death carries that burden, paying off the penalty they owe to God, so to speak. And this transfer can be accessed by a relatively simple action, namely, faith.

But this too is actually a fundamentally *un*just action, and on two counts.

Retributive justice requires malfeasants to pay the appropriate price for their wrongdoing; it is absolutely fundamental to this notion that wrongdoers are *themselves* punished. Justification theory, however, transfers that punishment to someone else. Wrongdoers are thereby separated from the appropriate desert for their action, and the innocent Christ, in a supremely unjust action, is punished in their place.

Now Justification advocates could explain this in terms of God's mercy and generosity. But a sudden change of approach at this point in the theory would be arbitrary and thus incoherent.[22] Similarly, the theory generally holds that God's justice is never overruled or compromised but *satisfied* by its construal of Calvary; God's justice is constant throughout. Clearly, however, that is not the case here. That a penalty is paid at some point for wrongs committed by someone else — a central tenet of retributive justice and of the Justification model — obscures the difficulties that the penalty is not paid by the right person, namely, the perpetrator, but by the wrong one, namely, an innocent.

Thus, Justification theory is not just, even though it claims to be. Indeed, its initial configuration is unjust, to a crushing degree, and its solution, focused on the atonement, is also unjust. At its heart the entire model seems deeply unfair (which might suggest in turn that it courts a further charge of hypocrisy on the part of its advocates; at this point the tables seem to have been well and truly turned).

2.6. Christology and Atonement

Justification theory does not explain why Christ must atone as against other people or things, and especially, in place of the established temple cultus.

The principal problem at this point is simple. Although Justification theory arguably establishes the need for an atonement of some sort — the punishment due sinful individuals must somehow be undergone — it supplies no specifications for the exact mechanism of that atonement beyond its punitive nature. We have just noted that there is something unjust about any transfer of punishment — and nothing within the first phase of the theory leads us to expect such a transfer. But granting the validity of some transfer here for the sake of argument, the theory provides no explanation for why *Christ* has to atone. In like measure, it does not explain why either someone or something else (like a temple cultus) could not atone and, furthermore, why existing modes of atonement (like the temple cultus in Jerusalem, still standing when Paul wrote his letters) now fail. With no such explanations, there is no evident need for Christ to fulfill the function of atonement within the model.

God could have stipulated any number of different options. He could presumably have sent a very large bull to atone for the sins of the world. Or he could have stipulated that such a bull be sacrificed repeatedly — daily or weekly — to make atonement. There is no need to make this payment a "one-off" affair. The point is to make atonement possible and then to provide it. Moreover, to send an especially costly or expensive means of atonement, like a son, is essentially otiose. It even seems slightly cruel.

Defenders of Justification would almost certainly turn to a particular reading of Anselm at this point or to a closely equivalent argument, who reprises this query exactly.[23] Indeed, Anselm's famous case in *Cur Deus Homo* could kill several birds with one stone: it could explain why Christ himself had to atone and, accordingly, why existing modes of atonement had proved inadequate and hence had to be superseded. (It could also explain why Christ had to be divine or the Son of God in the full Chalcedonian sense and so why he had to be incarnate, answers that may speak to framing tensions that arise shortly.) If this argument in fact held good, then a number of key vulnerabilities within Justification theory would be eliminated.[24]

We will set aside as irrelevant to our present concerns the question whether the following is a fair reading of Anselm's treatise; it is the cogency of this reading as an argumentative rejoinder in relation to these particular issues that matters for our present purposes.[25] The basic case is well known and so need be reprised only briefly.

Anselm — on a certain reading — argues that an offering of unlimited value was required in order to atone for, in the sense of compensating quantifiably for, a mass of sins of such enormous dimensions, namely, the ever-increasing sins of humanity.[26] Only the death of God himself could provide sufficient compensation for the sins of the world, and so the Father sent the Son to die. Certainly, no single innocent person could compensate proportionally for the sins of more than one other guilty person (while all owed God their lives in any case, and were already in debt because of sin). But the death of God — and the death of God alone — is presumably of limitless value, and God in Christ owes nothing at the outset. Moreover, it is reasonably easy to see how this argument allows a connection to be forged between Christ's identity and his atoning function. God incarnate must die — and must become incarnate in order to die. And Christ also thereby provides a convenient "once-and-for-all" solution.[27]

This explanation speaks to our questions about the alternative Jewish methods of atonement that seem already to have been in place. Apparently, these alternatives just could not cope with the sheer amount of atonement required; in view of new global conditions, so to speak, the scope and extent of the actual atonement on offer had to be massively upgraded. (And although one could argue that the previous methods of sacrifice could have been repeated until enough had been done, the quantitative defense should still work against this contention eventually as well.) In essence, only God was of sufficient value to pay for the sins of the world; his death was therefore necessary for full atonement to take place.[28] "[I]f the recompense of which we have spoken is not paid, which no one can pay except God, and no one ought to pay except man: it is necessary that a God-Man should pay it" (*Why God Became Man*, Bk 2, §6, 320). And this is a powerful and popular argument. However, despite its strengths, I am not convinced that it is sustainable in the present context.

For the argument to work, certain critical metaphorical transitions must be sustained. These transitions are in such wide use culturally that they may not even be generally remarked upon, let alone scrutinized. However, they are important, and when they are exposed their basis seems ultimately inadequate, as a result of which the overarching argument, in my opinion, collapses.[29]

The critical metaphorical transitions lie in the claims that notions like wrongdoing and punishment can be conceived of quite literally in terms of a financial system and that punishment can consequently be construed and effected in terms of a payment.[30] Anselm's argument depends on fundamentally quantitative and hence mutually comparable and transferable aspects within sinfulness and its atonement — "recompense ought to be proportional to the magnitude of the sin. . . . Tell me, then: what payment will you give to God in recompense for your sin?" (*Why God Became Man,* Bk 1, §20, 303). Given the truth of this basic analogy, Christ's death can function as a punishment that *pays* for an unlimited number of sins and is transferable to the accounts of those needing this payment. His value as God clearly outstrips the accumulating price of humanity's sins, no matter how large the latter might be: whereas sins must be finite, God is infinite — and good — and God's death therefore presumably of limitless value (cf. Bk 2, §14, 333-35). And it must be acknowledged that there is something quite plausible about this analysis. But is it actually appropriate?

Admittedly, the notion of wrongdoing as a sort of negative currency is ubiquitous.[31] Wrongdoing is viewed in this conception as an unfair or unlawful deprivation of goods or services caused by someone to someone else. The rightful results of economic activity have been wrongfully curtailed — whether through injury or theft. Hence, such wrongdoing is essentially some impediment to work and its results — property, money, and so on. The obvious response to such wrongdoing — which is also directly appropriate in terms of equivalence — is to pay money. We pay back either what we have unlawfully gained or what we have prevented from being gained. Wrongdoing is defined here as a loss of money or its equivalent *because in this realm that is what it is,* and hence punishment is appropriately understood in terms of the same.

Much wrongdoing within human society is of course economic, and such wrongs are clearly susceptible to an essentially economic analysis, with payment as an appropriate response. But violations that are not overtly economic are also common, and these *can* be assessed in economic terms, leading to an entire ancillary dimension within the law of compensation. It is not always desirable to impose a penalty of strict equivalence for a given wrong, and so an economic compensation might be accepted in lieu. For example, the crime of rape may not be held to have obvious economic consequences, but it could be compensated for in economic terms to avoid the imposition of a penalty of strict equivalence (namely, that the raper in turn be raped). In order for this mechanism to work, some "price" must be negotiated for the crime. And some cultures are accustomed to using quantitative metaphors to analyze various ethical situations. Indeed, various cultures articulate detailed schedules of monetary payment in compensation for strictly noneconomic crimes. (However, as such the notion of punishment begins to move away from a notion of strict equivalence and toward one of exacting from the offender some sort of economic penalty.)

The widespread cultural and legal interpenetration of these different conceptions of crime and punishment leads to a corresponding intermingling of metaphors when forensic issues are being described in real life. We speak of people who have been executed for murder as having paid for their crimes, and so on. This is clearly not strictly correct: no payment has been made but rather a punishment of strict equivalence exacted. Hence, the crucial question we must ask is whether it is valid to apply such an intermingled economic-equivalence view of punishment to *all* wrongdoing — and, most importantly, to offenses against God. Several reasons suggest that it is not.

Anselm's theory seems to demand a transfer of all wrongdoing to an economic plane, so that all sin can be "paid for" *in a quite literal sense*. And while this view's appropriateness can be acknowledged in relation to economic matters, and a degree of convenience can be allowed in relation to some other forms of wrongdoing (perhaps where equivalent punishment is actually impossible), it simply seems false to allow *all* instances of wrongdoing to be seen in fundamentally economic terms. In order for this view to hold good, the underlying premise would have to be granted that all human action is essentially economic — that society is at bottom a collocation of property-acquiring individuals concerned above all with material accumulation and its impediment. It would follow from the truth of this view that any interference with the activity of such individuals could always be construed in terms of a violation of economic accumulation. But not all wrongs do directly deprive people of money, hence not all wrongs can be reduced to a loss of money. And people are not fundamentally economic units (and the church struggled long and hard to establish this truth). While there is a certain overlap between the economic view of humanity and the anthropology implicit in Justification, not even Justification theory views reality in terms this reductionist, materialist, and individualist — and this principally because a God is involved.

Moreover, it simply seems ludicrous to imagine that human wrongdoing is essentially economic in any sense with respect to God — that human sins are a violation of God's rights to certain goods and services. God is both transcendent and the Creator! Nothing a person can do could deprive God of something, and certainly not of anything material. God can create material, but God is not bound up with materiality (being transcendent). The only thing that God can be deprived of is the honor and respect due him and his decrees. Hence, the economic view of wrongdoing makes little sense in relation to the God posited by the theory of Justification.

We may note further that the notion of payment tends to collapse under closer scrutiny as well. For Christ to effect a payment for the sins of the world, some sort of pricing arrangement would have to exist. But prices are simply a cultural contract that vary enormously over time and seem difficult if not impossible to apply to God. A price is an intersection of given supply and demand — what someone is willing to accept for a good or service and what someone is willing to offer for the same. For God to receive a payment from Christ's death sufficient to pay for the sins of the world, we must then in effect posit a marketplace *within God,* where a buyer and a seller agree on the price that these sins will cost (both parties being God) and then agree that Christ's death will more than pay for them (again, both parties being God). Hence, if pressed literally, it is clear that the entire conception is ludicrous (while it also raises an acute question of theodicy). We must posit a fundamentally economic view, not merely of reality, but of God Himself! — something, furthermore, that Justification theory gives us little cause to expect and little material to support.

Justification theory begins with a clear emphasis on the notion of wrongdoing as an offense to the divine honor, while its further development seems both to reinforce that emphasis and to resist any movement to another metaphor. God is rightly angered when his subjects violate his decrees and so he acts accordingly to punish them severely (although only as they deserve). This punishment assuages his wrath. Moreover, Jesus' death in ostensible satisfaction of that wrath is clearly a punishment in terms of strict equivalence, not substituted payment; he dies in place of others because their appropriate punishment is death. These themes within Justification consequently stand against the economic view. Indeed, they specifically oppose any translation into an alternative mode. The model is based on equivalence. Moreover, an offence against God's honor *has no economic implications whatsoever* (if it ever does, even in a human context).

A further difficulty implicit here is that Anselm and his advocates move from the notion that Christ has *value* (and that his death therefore deprives God — and us — of something of value) to the notion that he and his death have a *price* and can therefore *pay* for things. (This movement is complemented, as we have seen, by the perception that some transgressions can be dealt with effectively within human society by monetary payments, i.e., when one person deprives another unfairly of goods and services, and the further inference that all wrongs can therefore be so recompensed.) But these subtle metaphorical transitions from value to price and from compensation for some crimes to compensation for all — which enjoy so much cultural reinforcement — turn out to be unsupported and unwise in relation to matters divine (as human analogies so often do). Value is not actually equivalent directly to price (something that is often held to be the fundamental difficulty in Marxist economics). Prices can be paid not merely by individuals who want something — and so presumably attach value to it — but by individuals who themselves possess sufficient money to purchase something that they do in fact value. Hence individuals can in fact purchase things that they do not value (or that others do not value) and, more importantly, fail to purchase things they value highly. There is no simple relationship of equivalence operative here; purchase price and value are not the same. Yet Anselm's theory requires this if it is to function properly. That Christ and his death have *value* does not therefore entail that they have a *price,* or can in fact even function as a price. Only things that can be exchanged can function as payments and in relation to a price. (We value a stable global climate highly, but cannot pay anyone with it.)

In short, the literal application of these key metaphors to Christ and the atonement proves unwarranted and awkward if not ludicrous. And unfortunately, literal applications are necessary if Anselm's apology is to hold good. Without them his rejoinder founders. Before we move on, however, we should note an important caveat.

Monetary imagery can still be *employed* in relation to Justification theory — or indeed in relation to other theories. The semantic potential of commercial imagery gives rise to strong analogies with everyday life, as well as numerous notions that can color theories being argued on other grounds. However, it must be understood at all times that the imagery's application is essentially metaphorical, not literal. Thus, theorists can claim that sin has consequences that will "cost" us dearly at some point, but we will not literally pay God a sum of money. We may have to give something up — and possibly something very valuable — but we are, again, not literally paying God. Christ's "payment" on our behalf implies the costly and generous contribution of Christ to our salvation, but it is unlikely that he is actually transferring a sum of money to God's depleted account on our behalf. And so on.

This metaphorical — not literal — use of monetary imagery is discernible in Paul. He speaks overtly at one point of Christians as having been bought by God for a price, presumably like slaves. Because of God's costly and generous gift of salvation, the Corinthian Christians ought now to "glorify God in your body" (1 Cor. 6:20). But this is clearly metaphorical. Indeed, arguably, it does not make sense if viewed literally, in rationalist, commercial terms. That view would lead to the conclusion that "now you belong to God — so he can do with you whatever he wants." However, Paul has crafted an exhortation here indicating that the setting for the metaphor is fundamentally interpersonal and free. Because God has undertaken such a generous and costly act, the Corinthians (who do in some deep sense now belong to God) ought to respond with gratitude and respect.[32]

Similarly, in Romans itself Paul states famously in 6:23 that "the wages of sin is death." However, equally clearly, he does not mean to suggest that death is a sum of money, agreed upon in advance — and dictated in part by market forces in relation to labor — paid to Sin in response to work done (cf. Rom. 4:4!). This statement is a resonant metaphor suggesting that the inevitable and eventual accompaniment of sin and sinning is death, death arriving in due course after sin is committed much as wages arrive in due course after work is done. And here some of the force of the statement comes from its irony. A wage would ordinarily be looked forward to (although its size might be viewed unhappily); however, the coming payment of death is a dreaded reward — something we have "earned" unwillingly and stupidly.

Monetary metaphors can be both helpful and powerful. But pressed too far, to a strictly literal application, they tend to collapse because they are complex cultural analogies that fail to map accurately the relationship between humanity and God at its deepest levels. This is the fate that Anselm's famous apology suffers at this stage in our argument; hence, we judge the overarching conundrums in our critical analysis to remain: Justification theory provides no cogent rationale for Christ's role in atonement and thereby also fails to explain why alternative systems — whether existing or merely theoretical — could not atone equally well if not rather more humanely. In addition, the theory also fails to offer any obvious rationale for Christ's elevated or even divine identity, or his incarnation. For these theoretical demands to be met, his death would have to pay for sins in a literal sense, as their price, but this is clearly to press financial imagery too far. So the theory's strong assertion that Christ's death *is* the definitive atonement for sin is actually unjustified; a gap yawns here in the schema's basic integrity as a theoretical system.

2.7. Faith

Justification theory harbors a cluster of complex problems with respect to faith, in two main variations. The "Arminian" variant struggles to explain faith fully and, in particular, how individuals can actually exercise faith in order to be saved. The "Calvinist" variant can get beyond these difficulties by introducing revelation and election at the point of faith but then runs into further problems in relation to the privileging of faith and its gifting to individuals who have negotiated phase one. Ultimately, both variants collapse.

It is clear to most of its advocates that Justification theory requires the fulfillment of some criterion for the appropriation of salvation, and this largely because the entire schema presupposes the centrality of individual action; it is an essentially voluntarist model. Indeed, without this emphasis, the long progression through the first phase looks pointless. Individuals must do something in order to be saved, and they have learned this. Now they must exercise some saving criterion. And this criterion should fulfill certain conditions that have been established by the experiences of the first phase. The new saving criterion ought to be *clear* or *understandable;* otherwise, suitably positioned individuals will not be able to exercise it. In close relation to this, the criterion should be *based on information.* This might seem surprising at first. But the initial phase of the model contains no indications that the saving phase will pivot to a degree on a positive attitude found within a personal relationship or by means of revelation; what it does contain are information-based relationships. There are in fact no central personal relationships in the model's first phase, only ethical stipulations to perform correctly accompanied by numerous failures to do so. These maxims may involve relationships, but any personal qualities are not a necessary part of the journey through the first phase to hopelessness, which can be quite isolated. Individuals in this phase are oriented, rather, toward information and performance. This is what they will be assessed on.[33] Hence, at least initially, we would expect the saving criterion to continue within these parameters and be defined in terms of information.

Furthermore, the criterion ought to be *manageable*. This last characteristic derives from the ethical failures that individuals have already experienced. It seems that people cannot live perfect lives, and many seem to fail, doing the wrong thing repeatedly, so any further contract that hopes to be successful cannot ask too much of those it intends to save. The saving criterion will almost certainly be *particular* as well; it will be distinctively Christian and therefore freighted by Christian messengers who are related to communities, and so on (or, as we have noted, the immediate consequences at various frames will be absurd).

In short, the first, rigorous contract of Justification theory dictates that some saving criterion should be offered to individuals that is clear, information-based, manageable, and in some sense particular. (We would also expect something that is appropriate in terms of Paul's and his converts' general cultural background.) But beyond these parameters, *there is no determination from the first phase of the theory concerning the actual content of the all-important saving criterion*. Within the limits of clarity, informativeness, manageability, and particularity, God can stipulate anything as the act that accesses the benefits of the second, saving contract; like any sign-function, the correlation can be arbitrary. Hence, the claim that faith is *necessarily* the appropriate content of the saving criterion is false! Nothing in the first contract dictates in theoretical terms that the criterion for the second contract will be faith, although there will be beliefs concerning something, because of the role of information. So God could stipulate circumcision, and that alone, as the criterion necessary for the second contract (hopefully, along with some parallel ritual for women), provided that it was understood in some Christian way (see Col. 2:11, and note that various beliefs are also involved here). We would of course have to grasp this, that is, believe it, and also to do it. But then we would be saved. Alternatively, God could stipulate wearing a red T-shirt with "Jesus Saves" written on it (or the ancient equivalent), an appropriately clear, manageable, and particular act. We could be saved by eating certain foods with Christian symbolism, that is, by celebrating the Eucharist once a day, perhaps at a set time; by being baptized, whether once, a certain number of times, or daily; or by resting on Sundays. Or, we could be saved by believing certain sets of propositions — the Ten Commandments perhaps, or an early version of the Nicene Creed? God can stipulate whatever he wants, in theoretical terms, as long as it falls within the foregoing parameters, and quite a bit does.[34]

The obvious problem is that the theory provides no specific reasons for the function of faith in this role. Faith is clearly privileged in this position by all the key Pauline texts, but, strictly speaking, *Justification theory cannot explain it*. To be sure, faith basically fills the bill, but we do not know why it has been selected over so many other potentially effective candidates.[35] So why not stipulate "love" as the principal Christian condition, and/or "hope," and/or "humility," and/or "justice"?

But let us assume for the sake of argument that faith is the stipulated criterion for salvation through Justification's second, Christian phase. It should now be possible to bring some much-needed clarification to this principle's definition and discussion.

We should note initially that this criterion really contains *two* elements. First is the requirement that certain propositions be *believed,* this action constituting the satisfactory appropriation of the new, saving contract (something that creates obvious creedal analogies). Second, however, is the *content* of what must be believed, since belief per se is too general. Do we have to believe in the existence of Coca-Cola in order to be saved or, indeed, merely to believe that we have to believe? If it is the latter, then presumably most people are saved, and that without necessarily having endured a tortured prior journey that establishes the importance of grasping the gospel! Hence, it is clear that we must believe in something specific, and it has already been suggested that this will probably be information bound up with Christ, because this will satisfy the criterion of particularity (whereas information merely about "God" would not). In essence, then, Justification theory seems to suggest, in theoretical terms, that the appropriately anxious individual is saved through *believing in Christ.*[36]

We should note now that some problems are lurking here. The language of *choice* is almost universally deployed in relation to the gospel and faith. Individuals are motivated to make the right decision, but they must still *choose* to make it. Their response is uncoerced. Their allegiance to Christianity is free. We expect rational individuals to choose salvation through faith, because it offers them relief from the future prospect of hell and from the present anxiety and fear of considering that prospect. But anxiety and fear do not themselves constitute the critical decision; they merely provide a powerful motivation for making it.

Here we run squarely into the problem of "belief voluntarism," an issue rooted ultimately in certain observations by David Hume.[37] Although popular discourse uses the language of choice and free will ubiquitously in relation to matters of belief, *beliefs cannot in fact simply be chosen.* As Hume pointed out, we cannot alter a jot or tittle of our beliefs merely by an act of will. If we really hold something to be true, then we cannot alter that simply by choice, even if our lives depend on it, and the same goes for things we hold to be untrue. (We could say otherwise in order to save our lives, but we would of course be lying!) So by presenting anxious individuals with the prospect of salvation through faith and then exhorting them to choose this by an act of will, Justification theory is in fact asking people to do something they cannot do by virtue of their very construction. In some respects, this is the same as asking prospective converts to flap their arms and fly in order to be saved.

But the situation is not completely hopeless, because individuals might still be *convinced* to believe a saving criterion through various persuasive arguments and stratagems — in a word, through rhetoric. (And the audience on which it would act would be a willing one, so half the rhetorical battle would already be won.) However, what rhetorical resources can the Justification model supply that could, properly deployed, lead a willing individual eventually to saving belief? Here we run into further difficulties. Indeed, the difficult epistemological cohabitation that we noted earlier comes back to haunt the theory at this point (see §2.1).

Individuals operating in terms of the general epistemology that informs the model's first phase will not be able to assent to any propositions that are not either derived somehow from the structure of the cosmos or verified analogously. And this creates an insurmountable hurdle in relation to most propositions involving theological claims, because these are essentially unverifiable by such methods. So, for example, advocates of Justification will often urge their potential converts to believe that "Jesus died for their sins," and Paul clearly considers this an important proposition for Christians to believe (see 1 Cor. 15:3). But it is not verifiable by generic individuals as they operate in phase one; they have no way of knowing whether this is true, because it is not information that is rationally deducible from the cosmos. Hence, prospective converts cannot believe it. Only God knows if Jesus' death has really dealt with the sins of the world, and presumably that knowledge could be imparted only by direct disclosure. So given the approach to knowledge supplied initially by Justification theory — which has served so well up to this point — any such theological propositions must remain opaque. Similarly, how can prospective converts know that Jesus is Lord, that is, enthroned on high in heaven and coming again to judge the living and the dead? They have no access either to heaven or to the future.

Arguably, this difficulty can be mitigated in part if the propositions that individuals must believe in order to be saved are appropriately accessible.[38] For example, people could be asked to believe that Jesus rose from the dead because a chain of Christian witnesses could attest to it and/or the gospels could be corroborated as sufficiently reliable historical records to vouchsafe this claim (and so on).[39] These demonstrations might constitute the persuasive phase of Justification advocates' appeals. But we have still fallen well short of many of the beliefs that Paul's texts will clearly assert are basic to Christian cognition and salvation — Jesus' lordship, for example.

At bottom, taking the epistemology of the Justification model seriously means either minimizing the information that individuals must affirm in order to be saved or finding that certain important theological beliefs cannot actually be confirmed in such terms. Hence it would seem that we are caught in a circular dilemma — in fact, a dilemma following a dilemma. We cannot simply choose to believe what the Christian gospel exhorts us to believe in order to be saved, and neither can we verify as true what that gospel presents to us to believe in order to be saved! (Or, if we are presented with appropriately verifiable information, this seems in tension with the actual confessional material found in the NT — for example, resurrection!) We are trapped in phase one of the theory and hence doomed, and presumably also not a little anxious.

In the light of these difficulties with the voluntarist construal of faith — a construal we can dub the "Arminian" variant — we should consider a common apologetic move. We can abandon the language of choice and the notion of voluntarism within the broader process of Justification, attributing the saving event of faith directly to the work of God. The agency of faith can be divine. So God produces faith within prospective converts unconditionally, presumably simply through revelation and election — what we can dub the "Calvinist" variant.[40] And now affirming broad theological claims will not be a problem. Indeed, this is a classic Lutheran construal of the theory: faith is a gift.[41] But does the Calvinist variant ultimately fare any better than its Arminian rival? I suspect not. Two principal problems are detectable in this variant.

First, there is an *unaccountable privileging of faith.* We have already seen that the Arminian variant contains a small explanatory gap between its need for some saving criterion and faith. But faith — understood primarily in terms of believing — fills the role of saving criterion reasonably well: it seems to be based on information, it is manageable, and so on. The notion runs into severe difficulties only at a subsequent point, that is, when people try to exercise it. Hence, the Arminian variant retains a certain, if rather broad, theoretical justification for faith. The Calvinist variant, however, has effectively eliminated the saving criterion in view of its practical difficulties, attributing salvation instead directly to God. But if God unconditionally saves individuals who have undergone the depressing pedagogy of phase one in the Justification model, then *no saving criterion is now necessary at all;* God simply saves individuals at the requisite point. Indeed, this is the whole point of the modification of the theory. As God elects such individuals, revealing salvation to them directly, they enter upon the fullness of Christian existence and their complete transformation begins. From this point they are new creations (at least in part). Now, however, *the theory's continued privileging of faith is completely inexplicable.* Since there is no condition for salvation, what is faith doing in the argument? To be sure, saved individuals will have faith, but only as part of their overall transformation;[42] they will also possess love, not to mention joy, peace, patience, kindness, generosity, gentleness, and self-control. Yet Paul's texts massively privilege faith.[43] And the Calvinist variant has no explanation for this peculiar role.

Indeed, it tends to lapse back into the Arminian variant at such stages — a psychologically plausible but theoretically incoherent move! At least the Arminian variant knows why the argument focuses on faith, even if exercising it eventually proves impossible; it is better than trying to be justified by "works." But the Calvinist variant cannot even supply this initial enthusiasm. The individual's exercise of saving faith has been traded away because of the difficulties that became apparent in that claim. Nevertheless, if, as a result, the Calvinist variant's construal of Justification cannot give a plausible account of the role of faith in Paul's argument, then its prospects are hopeless. Ultimately, it will not possess any key corroborative texts in Paul (and will be embarrassed by many of the texts that he actually writes).

The second principal problem in the Calvinist variant of the theory is the *unaccountable lack of correlation between the two phases*. It is important to appreciate that phase one of Justification theory is significantly reoriented by the Calvinist variant. The first phase is no longer an essentially pedagogical journey that prepares individuals to grasp the gospel, because that journey no longer actually culminates in an individual's own decision or further realization. Indeed, the learning process undergone by individuals no longer has any purpose in and of itself, since God acts unconditionally at the journey's end — *unless that journey becomes the condition for salvation,* and God elects to salvation those who have undertaken it! But it would follow from this arrangement that God ought to elect to salvation all who have completed it. *Everyone* who negotiates the realizations of phase one in Justification ought to be saved by direct revelation in some relation to faith, because all those individuals have now fulfilled the principal condition for salvation.[44] And at this point the Calvinist variant again has serious difficulties.

It expects all such individuals to be elected to faith and then to ongoing Christian existence. But whereas the initial, philosophical phase of the theory is universal and generic, conceivably allowing anyone from any time or place to undertake its journey, the second, salvific phase is bound up irreducibly with particularity — with explicit Christian claims and the church, and with their particular epistemology. Thus, it seems unlikely if not impossible that the particular fulfillment of salvation will marry directly onto the general constituency destined for salvation by their negotiation of the prior philosophical journey, as it ought to. The two parts of the theory that ought to correlate exactly do not, and the Calvinist variant consequently seems to fracture at a crucial point. (And the alternative, namely, the claim that God *does* elect to salvation all those negotiating phase one's progressions, hence possibly independently of the church and its messengers, encounters irreconcilable framing tensions and corroborative difficulties in Paul and so can be discarded immediately.) Hence, the Calvinist variant's modification of Justification theory has actually driven it into the universal-particular dilemma within that theory with peculiar force. By making salvation correlate tightly with the theory's universal phase, the subsequent shift to particularity within the theory — which is nonnegotiable on other grounds — has been rendered incoherent.[45]

I nurse other suspicions about the Calvinist variant but feel that they are not as powerful as the two just mentioned. The foregoing conundrums — the inexplicable privileging of faith and the incoherent transition within the theory to particularity — are points of fairly devastating incoherence that prompt the variant's immediate abandonment. The following concerns are not quite so debilitating but still seem worth mentioning.

As is the case with many elective schemas, there is a nagging sense of arbitrariness about several aspects of the theory produced by the Calvinist variant. Why has God appointed a generic journey of self-understanding that culminates in a recognition of his justice as the necessary precondition of salvation? If it is replied that individuals need to know why they are being saved before they can be saved, then it must be retorted that in the Calvinist variant that is not the case; salvation is through election. (This would be an invalid appeal back to the Arminian account.) Furthermore, a great deal of important information will be learned unconditionally at the point of salvation; why could the information learned in phase one not be imparted then as well, or even later on in the process of salvation? As a *pedagogy,* then, the philosophical journey is unnecessary; as a *condition,* it simply seems arbitrary.[46] Also apparently arbitrary is the limitation of God's election to those who have negotiated this journey. In strictly theoretical terms, God could choose to so limit himself. But this seems odd. Elsewhere Paul seems to speak of a God whose benevolence is not so constrained. Indeed, from a biblical viewpoint such a limitation on the freedom of God is puzzling if not offensive.

The desire to incorporate Paul's language of divine initiative and unconditionality — and especially where that overlaps with "faith" terminology — into his account of salvation is ultimately, in my view, entirely healthy; in due course I will try to do this myself. However, the attempt to do so merely by modifying certain elements within Justification theory is profoundly misconceived. It preserves a fundamentally problematic schema, while nevertheless corroding some of its key advantages in terms of coherence *and* failing to take the elements introduced into it with sufficient seriousness — all in all, a poorly thought out and inadequate solution. It is a tinkering with an old, inherently flawed engine — with perhaps the attempted addition of one or two exciting new components from another model — when an entirely new design is needed. In more traditional terms, it is a pouring of new wine into old wineskins.

At bottom, then, the Calvinist variant has paid too high a price for its modifications. In so doing — and this is a consequence that apologetic modifications of Justification theory will repeatedly encounter — it has lost more than it has gained. Its modifications have eliminated important elements within Justification theory that it needs in order to continue to make sense simply as a theory. And the alert critic will detect any such debilitating concessions.

With this judgment, our broader account of the intrinsic difficulties within Justification is complete. We turn now to consider the theory's difficulties at the systematic frame.

CHAPTER THREE

Systematic Difficulties

§1. Preamble

If the essentially contractual theory of Justification is inserted into Paul's thought, then almost every aspect generates tension in relation to something the apostle says elsewhere — a complaint with a long pedigree within Pauline scholarship. However, tracing the various tensions coherently is a difficult matter. As we set out to examine them in this chapter, it will in fact be easiest to proceed backward. I will describe briefly an alternative Pauline theory drawn largely from Romans 5–8, from which description a soteriology that functions retrospectively will in turn become clear.[1] And from this point a whole cluster of closely related contradictions vis-à-vis Justification theory will become apparent. Proceeding in this fashion will have the signal virtue, then, of demonstrating the coherence *between* many of the criticisms made of Paul in this relation. At the end of this analysis we will have identified a set of systematic difficulties that Justification theory generates when it is assumed to be present within Paul's thought. So we embark now on (another) thought experiment.[2]

§2. An Alternative Pauline Theory

Let us assume that by a twist of canonical fate only Romans 5–8 — along with the odd paragraph from later chapters — had been preserved from Paul's writings within the New Testament. What would we conclude about the apostle's view of salvation on the basis of just these texts?[3] Perhaps surprisingly, the various assertions and arguments we encountered would be quite coherent.[4]

2.1. The Soteriology Apparent in Romans 5–8

First, it is worth noting that we would infer reasonably quickly that a theory of salvation was present. These texts speak repeatedly of "life," meaning primarily the life of the age to come, and of some sort of mysterious present involvement of "the brothers" in that life (7:1; 8:29). Present peace is complemented by "hope of sharing the glory of God" (5:1-2, 4-5, 17, 21). Similarly, the text speaks repeatedly of a certain "rule" or "reign" or "dominion" by God through Christ, as against another reign by more sinister figures (5:14, 17, 21), and this reign is both benevolent and reconciling (5:5, 6, 8, 10-11). But the implicit soteriological theory is complex. A number of different things are clearly bound up inextricably within that event — the nature of God, the work of Christ, the operation of the Spirit, the nature of Christian existence, both personally and interpersonally, and various ontological and epistemological realities. Unraveling this conception will be easiest if we begin with the state from which humanity is rescued, returning at a later point to consider its epistemological status.

Non-Christian reality, denoted in some sense by 7:7-25, is obviously a gloomy state of affairs. (It doesn't matter for the purposes of this claim whether that chapter describes pre-Christian existence, post-Christian fleshly existence in Paul's life, or a more general, "gnomic" view; this passage is assessed in more detail in chapter five.) The person of flesh (σάρξ) is enslaved by certain powerful forces, Sin and Death, the result being an oppressed and somewhat agonized condition — a "wretched" state in "a body of death," in which the will to do good seems powerless and the desire to do evil overwhelming. Such humans are, somewhat incredibly, fundamentally God's enemies (5:10; 8:5-8): "the sinful mind is hostile to God" (8:7a DC). But a close reading of Romans 7 hints at Paul's explanation of this enslaved and hostile condition.

All those descended from Adam have naturally inherited that progenitor's being, or "flesh," and Adam's being is oppressed by forces that were unleashed within the garden of Eden (see 7:7-11) and now rule over a sinister human kingdom of enslaved subjects (so 5:12-21; 8:10-11, 18-25, 38-39). People who exist in this dire condition — and we all do according to Paul here — are obviously incapable of accurate theological reflection or of any positive action, ethical or salvific. They need to be rescued first and then taught to think about God and to behave correctly, hence the text's repeated emphasis on deliverance (7:24b; 8:2; 12:2). And this rescue is apparently the result of interlocking actions by God the Father; his only, beloved Son, whom he sends into the enslaved Adamic condition; and the Holy Spirit.

The Father initiates these saving actions (8:28-30; see also the hint in 5:14b), and the initiative is revealed thereby to be fundamentally loving (so 5:5, 8; 8:32; note also that it is precisely a "revelation" or apocalypse). It is a deep concern for the plight of humanity that motivates the Father to send the Son, and the depth of that concern is proved by the fact that the Father does indeed send his only, beloved Son, much as Abraham was prepared to offer up Isaac.[5]

The Son is sent into this condition and assumes it — a "martyrological" narrative and journey of "descent"; he comes "in the precise likeness of sinful flesh" (8:3 DC).[6] But his singular act of obedience (see 5:18-19) seems to come to a climax in his death, which is presumably a crucifixion (so 6:6, "we are co-crucified with him" DC), although the theory does not seem to require a particular sort of death. Nevertheless, the death itself has a precise rationale. The old, en-slaved, Adamic being is terminated by this death (8:3). The Son is then raised to new life and to a new existence as no less than the template of a new humanity "that he might be the firstborn of many brothers" (8:29 DC). Hence, this death seems appropriately described at one point in atoning terms that resonate with Old Testament sacrificial idiom (περὶ ἁμαρτίας in 8:3), but Christ's saving work clearly extends beyond his death to his resurrected and glorified existence, which is the image, or εἰκών, of the new age. The text basically suggests that Christ en-tered the human condition, assumed it, terminated it, and is now reconstituted and enthroned on high as Messiah or King of Israel, humanity, and the entire cos-mos, where he continues to intercede for those still mired within it (8:34) — all actions that also speak powerfully of his deep love for humanity alongside the Fa-ther's (v. 35).

The Spirit is spoken of within these chapters primarily in relation to en-slaved humanity, inaugurating its rescue from the clutches of Sin and Death (8:2, 5-11; see 6:1-11; 7:6). Christians know the love of God through this intervention (5:5), which also engenders perseverance and hope (5:2-5; 8:23-25); a spirit of fear is displaced by a spirit of adoption (8:14-17). However, this is a process that has only begun. Its consummation lies in the future (8:11-39), and the Spirit accompa-nies laboring humanity through its somewhat agonized period of waiting, enter-ing into its deepest, most inexpressible utterances (8:23-27). Hence, although not articulated in such terms directly, the Spirit's benevolence toward humanity is im-plicit. The Spirit's activity in relation to Christ's entry into the human condition and reconstitution through resurrection can also be inferred from analogous ac-tivity in relation to humanity.

In view of this activity by divine or apparently divine actors, the nature of Christian salvation can be posited. Clearly, it is fundamentally transformational. Those people involved in it pass through a dramatic termination and an equally dramatic reconstitution. The imagery of complete immersion in and rising from the water in the ritual of baptism beautifully conveys its two aspects (6:1-11), while the analogy of marriage, first to one husband and then, after his death, to another, captures something of the deep and potentially intimate relationships involved, along with the displacement of the one for the other through death (7:1-4).[7] But the importance of the Spirit, evident especially in chapter 8, although prefigured in chapter 5, suggests that baptism is an essentially symbolic ritual and not a free-standing or efficacious event in its own right. It is the divine Spirit who actually ef-fects this transformation with reference to Christ. Moreover, Paul often seems to summarize his discussions of this process with the phrase "in Christ" or its close equivalent (6:4, 8, 11, 23; 8:1, 9-11, 39, and, perhaps in the opposite sense, 7:5; 8:8, 9).

There is an important ethical dimension to this transformation. A slavery to evil desires and to Sin — and thereby to the rule of Death — has been displaced by a new slavery "so to speak" (6:19a) to God that leads to holiness and to eternal life (6:19, 22-23). That is, a transformation of the ethical capacity of humanity seems intrinsic to the entire salvific process; it is part of the event of grace (6:15, 23). However, any use of the notion of freedom — and it is used in some sense — must be carefully qualified (6:18, 20, 22; 8:2, 20-21). Paul seems to be speaking here primarily of negative liberty, to borrow Isaiah Berlin's useful distinction.[8] The saved have been rescued *from* an oppressive slavery. They now stand under a new ruler. As chapter 6 emphasizes at length, they do not now enjoy unlimited freedom to direct their own lives but stand within a new, benevolent slavery. It is important to note, moreover, that the basic orientation of this account of salvation is a posteriori; it works backward. And it has to. A number of dimensions within this orientation now need to be articulated.

It becomes apparent only by way of involvement within this extraordinary process of salvation just how desperate the prior condition of humanity was "in Adam." In the light of the later process it can be seen that humanity is trapped, enslaved under hostile forces, and clearly powerless to do anything about it (see Paul's repeated exclamations of 7:14-24). Hence, the perception of human incapacity is grounded not in itself but in this event of transformation, and this stands to reason. If it were grounded in an analysis of human incapacity per se, then its conclusions would be self-contradictory; a corrupt human condition could not derive accurate conclusions about itself. But Paul does not seem to fall prey to this conundrum in Romans 5-8. Probably in part because of bitter experience, he seems overtly committed to the blindness of Adamic humanity in and of itself, and to the retrospective basis of any analysis of its incapacity: "the mind that is set on the flesh is hostile to God; it does not submit to God's law — indeed it cannot" (8:7 NRSV; see 2 Cor. 4:7). This humanity, as we have already noted, is actually *hostile* to the reconciling God! — which is to say that it is profoundly mistaken and disoriented. Thus, any knowledge of "the problem" for Paul, as attested by this text, is grounded in the revelation of the solution — in an apocalyptic moment and process.[9]

Having grasped both the incapacity of the human condition in Adam and the basis for that claim in the event of salvation (i.e., that it is a retrospective claim), we can recognize that the only appropriate solution to this sort of problem is one of deliverance, or rescue. And it is no coincidence that the text repeatedly characterizes God's saving intervention in terms of just this type of action. The agonized "I" of chapter 7 even cries out for such a solution: "Wretched man that I am! Who will *rescue* me from this body of death?" ("Thanks be to God . . . Jesus Christ our Lord": Rom. 7:24-25; see also 8:21, 23). Moreover, this event of rescue is clearly unconditional. A pessimistic anthropology dictates an unconditional solution. And no criteria for its activation, appropriation, or reception by humans are apparent in this text, while what causality or agency is apparent is attributed to God: "those whom he foreknew he also predestined . . . those whom he predestined he also called" (8:29-30; see also 5:6-8, 10). But this pessimistic anthropology — and consequently unconditional soteriology — is reinforced by the radically transformational nature of the salvation that is being experienced: human beings, however capable, can scarcely draw themselves into the death and reconstitution of another!

By this point it can be seen reasonably clearly then that a number of critical features within this soteriology stand (or fall) together. Its saving intervention reveals the depth of human incapacity prior to the transformation; and this, coupled with the radical nature of that transformation, affirms the unconditionality of the transformation itself. God must initiate this salvation, and he does so in love. It is a rescue. Moreover, epistemology is merely one aspect of the process, although an important one. It participates in all these movements, essentially thinking backward. The possession of criteria or expectations prior to the event of transformation is therefore irrelevant. Only in the light of this event is the truth about the pre-Christian situation actually revealed, along with the truth of the nature of its solution. (Doubtless, any such account will have important continuities with pre-Christian life, but these must be controlled by the event itself — note, for example, Paul's use of Jewish stories in relation to figures like Adam, Abraham and Isaac, and David.) The unconditional, revelatory, transformational, and liberational aspects of this event mean that it is appropriately described as "apocalyptic."

Moreover, this soteriology is a holistic process that extends far beyond mere corroboration. Its intrinsic ethical dimension has already been noted. But the text alludes to its *liturgical* quality. Those involved within its startling shifts cry, "Abba! Father!" essentially in doxology (8:15). The rescued wretch of 7:24 cries, "Thanks be to God!" in v. 25. The transformed also cry in suffering, even when it cannot be articulated, but they are supported in such extremity by the prayers of both the Spirit and the Son (8:26-27, 34). Hence, the participation of the Son and of the Spirit in the suffering of the human condition seems to call forth human participation in the liturgical communion of the divine condition.

It is of course repeatedly stated that this participation is yet only partial and must endure many trials and struggles. Patience, perseverance, and hope, not to mention character, are necessary to reach the final goal of complete transformation (5:2-5; 8:23-25), which will take place in relation to all of present creation (8:19-21). But these virtues of endurance are profoundly participatory. The Spirit is present in and through them, sustaining "the brothers" through sufferings that derive from "the one who subjected [creation]" to futility (which is presumably Adam: see 8:20; also 5:12-14 and 7:7-11). Moreover, these are also *Christ's* sufferings. Humans are "heirs of God and joint heirs with Christ" only "if, in fact, we suffer with him" (8:17). It is this sense of participation that guarantees future transformation and glorification, and here the text is quite explicit: "if the Spirit of him who raised Jesus from the dead dwells in you, he who raised Christ from the dead will give life to your mortal bodies also through his Spirit that dwells in you" (8:11). Furthermore, now having the Spirit *of* Christ (8:9), humans experience any sufferings as a participation in the first phase of Christ's own trajectory. To participate in the Son's suffering and death is to be guaranteed participation in his resurrection and glorification. And this sense of participation can be further assured by the proof that Christ's intervention provides of God the Father's limitless benevolence: "He who did not withhold his own Son, but gave him up for all of us, will he not with him also give us everything else?" (8:32). These interlocking warrants provide ample assurance in the face of any extremity, whether deep beyond articulation (8:26) or derived from human or even superhuman powers (8:35, 38-39).

Two loose ends — so to speak — should now be addressed.

"Faith" seems at first to be a rather marginal notion within this schema, receiving explicit mention only *once,* in 6:8 (εἰ δὲ ἀπεθάνομεν σὺν Χριστῷ, πιστεύομεν ὅτι καὶ συζήσομεν αὐτῷ . . .). Certainly, we would not dream of privileging it as the Christian virtue par excellence on the basis of these texts (and we have already noted that there is no explicit Christian criterion here for salvation — only a set of warrants). But it is more important than this single statistical occurrence might suggest. In fact, two distinguishable notions of "faith" are discernible within the text.

First, as 6:8 suggests, "faith" refers to the correct beliefs about God and salvation that follow, hopefully in increasing measure, upon the arrival of the event of salvation itself. Once people have died with Christ, it says, they can now "believe" or "understand" that they will also live with him, both now in a life of real transformation and in the future in a state of complete transformation. Indeed, we have just noted numerous warrants for these convictions. And in fact all of our chapters extant from Paul are really bound up with this struggle for cognitive clarification; they are a sustained appeal for various beliefs to be held in the Christian life as against other, apparently unhelpful ones (see, e.g., 6:1a, 15a; 7:7a; 8:33a!). Moreover, this whole journey seems to have begun in some relation to a certain act of *submission* to a form of teaching (6:17), although we would doubtless be unwise to separate this event from the work of the Spirit (see 5:5; 8:9-11, 14-17, 28-30). "Faith" in this sense, then, really refers to *the theological journey that Christians are meant to undertake in the light of the Christ event* — a journey that begins in the life of the Christian as that event does.

Clearly, it is rather difficult to respond appropriately to the Christ event, and indeed to communicate about it to others, if the wrong beliefs are in place. Correct understanding will be vital. (And while that understanding may never be perfect, obviously, the more accurate the understanding, the better.) Thus, the painstakingly crafted argument of Romans 5-8 is simply extended evidence that Paul is passionately committed to the formation of correct beliefs within his congregations. The struggle for right thinking and speaking about God is obviously very important to him, and faith is involved with this. But it is important to recall that any such beliefs also seem to be shaped by the retrospective process of salvation, along with its implicit epistemology, as that is explicated in these chapters. Beliefs, in a sense, look back on an event of revelation (which is both holistic and ongoing) and attempt to articulate it — and hence, perhaps, much of the struggle! This transformation of the mind seems to be difficult. The fleshly mind *resists* it. Nevertheless, according to these chapters, that difficult process is the origin of true belief.

But "faith" occurs in another distinguishable sense in these texts, even if not explicitly. The reader of Koiné Greek knows that πίστις often indicates an activity of faithfulness or fidelity. And this quality has already been much remarked on within Paul's argument here. Suffering, patience, perseverance, endurance, and hope are an unavoidable cluster within Paul's account of present Christian existence, occurring throughout these texts. In fact, the apostle articulates several dimensions within this semantic complex: the patient, persevering endurance of suffering in hope is to be expected (5:2-5; 8:9-25); it is necessary if final life or salvation is to be reached (5:1-5; 6:17; 8:18, 23-25, 35-39); it is aided by the presence of the Spirit (5:5; 8:9-17, 23, 26-27); it is a sharing in the sufferings of creation (8:19-21); it is also a sharing in the sufferings of Christ (8:17); and, perhaps most importantly, as a participation in Christ's trajectory toward death, which was followed for him by transformation and glorification, it is a guarantee of future transformation (8:9-11).

Hence, "faith" occurs in two distinguishable senses within Paul's discussion, denoting two important aspects of Christian existence — right beliefs about God acting in Christ, and faithfulness through suffering, in the sense of patient, hopeful endurance — although it should be noted that the fundamental rationale for both seems to be pneumatological and participatory.

It remains only to ask what sort of life "the brothers" of 8:29 have been introduced into. Devout readers might expect Paul to speak of the church, but he does not (at least not in these chapters). Nevertheless, certain critical indications are supplied concerning the nature of this redeemed existence.

The conclusion is largely unavoidable that this existence is fundamentally communal and interpersonal. It has been constituted by the closest interlinking of actions by God the Father, his beloved Son, and the Spirit of both the Father and the Son. They now rule this new reality, in love (5:5-8, 17, 21; 8:31-39). And this has established relationships that are *inseparable,* not to be broken by even the most fearsome apocalyptic forces (8:38-39). Furthermore, these relationships with the Father and Son follow adoption into the family categories of "children" and "brothers" (7:1; 8:12-17, 19, 21, 23, 29). A diverse conversation ensues encompassing doxology, petition (to the point of wordless petition), accurate description, rebuke, and worship. So it is hard to avoid the further implications that these relationships are intimate and affectionate, and this correlates with the explicit references by the text to the love of the divine actors for humanity, as well as implicit indications of the same.

It is important to grasp these indications precisely. This depiction of redeemed humanity *is neither individualist nor corporate.* The identity of the people involved is not defined fundamentally by way of reference to themselves; other key relationships constitute that identity. So the conception of the person is not individualist. The saved are "brothers" because they are all shaped by the image of the Son and are all beholden to the one Father, crying "Abba Father" by the shared Spirit. However, a degree of individuation is not erased by this process of "imaging," which is clearly metaphorical. Although the ontology of human beings is dictated to a large degree by their images, Adam and Christ, they are still distinguishable from these progenitors and from the mere fact of their ontology. So neither is the conception of the person simply corporate. This (redeemed!) anthropology is best described as fundamentally *relational,* and the new reality as communal and interpersonal (and even as networked). Further testimony to the relational nature of this reality is the diverse speech that characterizes it, flowing between its participants.

With these clarifications — of "faith," and of the nature of the redeemed community — we must turn to consider two of this schema's important implications in relation to the overarching argument of this book. First, what is the implicit view of Israel? And second, what is the view of coercive violence when that is viewed as the legitimate punishment of wrongdoing? (and here we may have to assume that one or two other paragraphs of Pauline text have fortuitously been preserved, in addition to Romans 5-8!).

We may extrapolate certain principles in relation to the characterization of Israel, turning occasionally to key texts elsewhere in Paul for confirmation.

The very categories that Paul uses to explain the saving intervention of Christ into humanity's enslaved condition at the behest of his Father, along with the complementary involvement of the Holy Spirit, are drawn from the Jewish Scriptures. These notions have been redeployed in a rather surprising, new way to articulate something unanticipated. But their origins are within the Scriptures and traditions of Israel. Implicit within their extensive usage, then, are the further claims that this salvation climatically fulfills those writings and presumably also the distinctive human group who transmits and venerates them. Indeed, Christ's very name is drawn from this tradition and denotes the fulfillment of certain Jewish expectations. A particular human history is therefore implicit in this account of salvation — a *Jewish* one.

The a posteriori function of the account entails, however, that only those involved within these fulfilling events will be able to discern them as such. To those on the outside — Jew or Greek — they must remain opaque. But for those like Paul, on the inside, the coming of Christ is doubtless the climax of Israel, her focal and highest point.

There is a hint, moreover, that this climax fulfills the patriarchs in some sense. In 8:32 Paul draws a text from Genesis 22. It is a brief citation, but the notion that it attests to functions in a significant way within his broader argument. God's action in sending Christ to redeem humanity is likened directly to Abraham's readiness to offer up Isaac. Hence, the purview of Israel within which Paul is working is apparently patriarchal: the Christ event fulfills the constitutive events of Israel in relation to her founding fathers (and mothers).[10]

But there is also the overt claim that only Christ can deal with the radical slavery of the Adamic condition. We have already seen that this state must be terminated and humanity reconstituted on the basis of an entirely new image or template. And consequently the Mosaic law, and indeed any law, cannot function effectively to resolve the situation. It lacks the essentially divine capacity to create or to re-create. Indeed, any commandment merely provides an opportunity for Sin to exploit (7:7-23), thereby adding to, not resolving, the basic human problem of enslavement to evil desires in the flesh, and thereby only augmenting the hegemony of Sin and of Death. The law itself, in whatever form it takes, is technically blameless within this situation (7:7, 12). It is the inherently manipulative propensity of Adamic human nature that causes the difficulty (7:5) — and for Jews as well as for pagans. But it does follow from this that Paul's suggested solution to the human condition must be independent of the law; it is a reconstitutive and transformational solution, not a directive one. Moreover, once it has arrived, humanity's new redeemed existence continues this disposition that is independent of the law (8:2-4). Christ is the template of the new humanity, and the Holy Spirit indwells it (7:6). So the law is displaced. It now possesses no independent ethical function at all; its only legitimate function is one of attestation. As we have already seen, the arrival of Christ in the life of humanity in general and the person in particular is and must be unconditional. No preparation is possible. And after the arrival of Christ and the Spirit, no additional ethical guidance is necessary — indeed, such guidance would only provide an opportunity for the flesh to exploit. But this arrival was *anticipated* in the Jewish Scriptures, and so presumably can continue to be illuminated by those in retrospect.

These are dramatic redefinitions of Israel and of the function of the law. In fact, it is now clear that the arrival of Christ is something of a *krisis* for the law as that was traditionally understood by Judaism. But there is nothing theoretically offensive about this. Furthermore, there is no intrinsic need for Paul to abandon either the existence or the importance of Israel — far from it. Israel was a light in a dark place; she pointed forward from her origins in Abraham to the dawning of the new creation in the Christ event, and her Scriptures attest to this and explain it. Indeed, given that Christ comes from within the heritage of Israel and also constitutes its crowning moment, there could hardly be a more important or a more positive heritage within human history (so 9:4-5). Anyone in Christ is "grafted into" the historical lineage of Israel (see 11:17-24). Israel's history is the only Adamic history that really matters. Moreover, Jesus Christ the Jew, and now the Jewish King, is the template of the new, eschatological reality. So heavenly existence is Jewish, and in a way that is far more programmatic even than humanity's original Adamic existence! But of course everything depends here on the legitimacy of the Christ event itself, in the light of which these stunning continuities are perceived.

In short, Paul's account of salvation as that is suggested largely by Romans 5-8 is inconceivable except as, simultaneously, an account of Israel (using that term in its broadest sense to include Israel's history, people, Scriptures, and traditions). But it is also a *redefinition* of Israel, in the light of the Christ event. All the apostle's claims here consequently stand or fall in relation to this central reality. And Israel, in turn, is a profoundly historical but reoriented and teleological construct — within Adam, in fulfillment of Abraham (and Isaac), and beyond Moses.

We turn now to consider the second of this developing theory's important implications for the overarching argument of this book — its view of violent punishment.

We have had cause to note repeatedly in the foregoing that God's fundamental posture toward humanity, evident in Father, Son, and Spirit, is unconditionally benevolent. Despite human hostility, a costly intervention is initiated in order to save those chosen for glory from the depredations of the Adamic condition. The death of Christ is a critical transformational event within this process that eliminates or terminates Adamic ontology; those mapped onto Christ's trajectory can thereby escape its clutches and be reconstituted in the Son's risen image beyond the evil rule of Sin and Death. And presumably those now involved in the ongoing mission of God to humanity — like Paul — share (or they *ought* to share) this basic disposition of benevolence toward humanity. In their case, moreover, this may be strengthened by the experience of having been part of hostile humanity originally and then saved by grace. In George Whitefield's famous phrase, "There but for the grace of God go I." Romans 5–8 shares this perspective.

However, the text gives little indication beyond this of the ultimate outcome of the process. It speaks from its midpoint. Certainly, it affirms strongly that those currently involved within salvation need have no fear of any accusation or conflict, whether human or superhuman. "The brothers" are destined for glory despite the suggestions of any present difficulties and irrespective of how extreme those might be. But we do not know how many people are involved within this process. We can infer that at present various people are not, because presumably they lie behind some of the trials that the brothers now face — "distress, . . . persecution, . . . peril, . . . sword" (8:35). Some are still hostile to God, living in the flesh (8:5-8). But beyond this only two points seem clear.

First, Christ's intervention is a superior imaging of humanity to Adam's; indeed, Adam was a mere foreshadowing of Christ, "a type of the one who was to come" (5:14). Christ's achievement is superior in many respects (this is the principal argumentative burden of 5:15-17). Hence, the universal thrust of God's work in Christ is unmistakable. In fact, Christ's work will ultimately redeem the entire groaning cosmos (8:19-21). *Nothing* can stand in its path (8:38-39). And God's call to unsaved humanity presumably ought to be integrated with this earlier material (see 8:28-30). Hence, there is no reason to separate the Father's universal intentions revealed in Christ over against Adam, as spoken of in chapter 5, from his saving intentions present from eternity in relation to Christ, as spoken of in chapter 8 (and his unconditional love is in any case a motif common to both these discussions). God's intentions and God's love are coterminous and hence universal.

But, second, there does seem to be a coming moment of wrath (5:9, and probably implicitly also in v. 10; see further the "justification" of 8:30 and the eschatological lawsuit of vv. 31-34). And presumably evil powers, such as Sin and

Death, will not be included in the glorious future kingdom of grace and life. They must therefore be eliminated at some point, most probably in this moment of wrath. The text thus anticipates some sort of final judgment, and at that point those things evil and hostile to God will be overthrown.

So our text leaves certain questions unresolved. It is confident about the destiny of Christians on the basis of their present participation in the lives of the Son and the Spirit. It is unambiguous about the universal and unconditional love of God for humanity. But it does not seem to ask explicitly, and hence to answer, whether God's universal designs in Christ are "irresistible" in relation to humanity as a whole. (Perhaps Paul felt that he did not need to ask this question.)[11]

2.2. Summary of the Soteriology Apparent in Romans 5–8 in Propositional Form

The First Phase: Unconditional Deliverance

1a. Salvation has arrived for the "brothers" unconditionally, at the behest of the Father, through the Son, bringing a spectrum of blessings — life, peace, hope, glory, dominion, reconciliation, atonement, ethical capacity, and so on.

1b. It is a dramatic, apocalyptic deliverance, inaugurating certain fundamental changes, and thereby prompting a reevaluation of the human problem in its light.

The Second Phase: A Retrospective Characterization of the Problem

2a. The powers of Sin and Death have entered the world by way of the original transgression of God's commandment by humanity — an Adamic narrative.

2b. These hostile powers have taken up residence in human flesh.

2c. Humanity, powerless ultimately to resist, is effectively enslaved — ruled and oppressed by way of "sinful passions," and hence oriented by and toward Sin and Death.

2d. The existence of humanity is consequently wretched, and its destiny is death.

2e. Any ongoing presence of a divine commandment exacerbates the problem, as Sin manipulates such instructions to create more transgressions!

2f. Unredeemed humanity now cannot comprehend either the problem or the solution.

The Saving Phase: The Father Sends the Son

3a. The Father views enslaved humanity with benevolence, desiring to help them.

3b. He sends his only beloved Son into this situation, to assume its distorted, Adamic ontology — its flesh. (3a is proved by 3b.)

3c. The Son consents to enter this existence, to suffer, and to die, thereby demonstrating his benevolence. In this act, Adamic ontology, or the flesh, as it is present in him, is also executed — an event that can be described in some sense as "atoning."

3d. The Son is raised from the dead to new life, thereby entering the new age — the age to come — as its firstborn and "image."

3e. The Son is glorified and enthroned on high; his eternal messiahship and inheritance are thereby affirmed.

The Saving Phase: The Spirit Incorporates Humanity in Christ

4a. The Spirit now "maps" humanity onto Christ's trajectory.

4b. Humans participate first in his martyrological journey, thereby dying; in so doing, their Adamic ontology is executed.

4c. Humans participate also in his messianic and eschatological journey, thereby living; in so doing, they receive a new ontology — a new flesh — free from the powers of Sin and Death, and a new inheritance.

4d. This salvation is fundamentally liberative (in an instance of negative liberty); it is a deliverance from slavery!

4e. The salvific process is best symbolized by immersion, that ritual being interpreted as a dying and rising with Christ.

4f. The new situation for Christians is typically summarized by Paul with the phrase "in Christ," or its close equivalent — a metaphor of location.

4g. This new situation is fundamentally communal and interpersonal: Christians join a community rooted in a divine communion.

4h. Implicit in this is a new conception *of* personhood, as precisely relational — within a communion.

With this alternative theory of salvation from Romans 5–8 in place,[12] we can turn to consider the tensions that arise when it is juxtaposed with Justification theory. The various conceptual difficulties caused by Justification theory throughout Paul should now be much easier to comprehend.

§3. The Resulting Tensions

Almost every feature of the alternative theory that has just been described in §2 creates tension when it is juxtaposed with the soteriological approach of Justification theory. I will note ten points of difficulty here — although some can be dealt with far more briefly than others:

1. epistemology
2. anthropology
3. theology
4. Christology and atonement

  5. soteriology
  6. faith
  7. ethics
  8. ecclesiology
  9. Judaism
 10. coercion and violent punishment

3.1. Epistemology

The basic conception of knowledge, especially in terms of its overall direction, is different elsewhere in Paul.

Justification theory begins with an essentially philosophical conception of knowledge. Knowledge is initially universal and largely ahistorical. God is known indirectly, by reasoning in relation to the created cosmos. This knowledge is primarily in terms of information. Justification theory arguably makes an awkward transition to more particular information around the point of salvation although, strictly speaking, any further realizations must build on the theory's initial conclusions in order to be both valid and recognizable. (Conclusions derived from the first, philosophical phase of the theory form the basis for any later conclusions or judgments that may be more particular, and, if necessary, should overrule them.) But the entire thrust of the theory is a priori, or "forward," and its tenor rationalistic.

The alternative theory is quite different. It proceeds a posteriori, or "backward." Rationality is realized by this process rather than presupposed. In the light of its revelation of salvation, people perceive that their initial condition was dire indeed. Therefore, knowledge must be disclosed initially from outside the human realm, and unconditionally (although the mediation of revelation by elements within this realm is possible, if not likely). Such knowledge is disclosed as one aspect of a broader salvific process that essentially brings different personal agents into relation with one another. Oppressed people are transformed and incorporated into an interpersonal communion of Father, Son, and Spirit, so the process of revelation is fundamentally personal. As a result, knowledge is necessarily particular and historical; interpersonal relations exist within history. This theory is consequently *rational*, but not in the reductive sense that Justification theory is (and hence my use in the latter relation of "rationalistic").

Clearly, then, utterly different epistemologies are in play within the two theories, diametrically opposed in direction and nature. And it is arguably far easier to document the particular, historical, revelatory, and interpersonal conception from elsewhere in Paul than its competitor.[13]

3.2. Anthropology

The presupposed conception of the person is different elsewhere in Paul.

Justification theory assumes that people are rational, self-interested, ethical individuals. They possess a fundamental capacity; they are capable of reasoning accurately about God in relation to the cosmos and acting accordingly. Their sinfulness entails that their reasoning necessarily ends in despair. However, it is not extensive enough to overpower their basic capacity.

The alternative theory presupposes a very different notion of the person. Non-Christians are fundamentally *in*capable of any such reasoning or activity. They are hostile to God, incapable of pleasing God or of submitting to the law because of their domination by the forces of Sin and Death at large within their flesh. Only after deliverance from this condition are they capable of the beginnings of accurate thought about God and the divine will, and of obedience. And at this point they enter a communal, interpersonal reality.

These two views are irreconcilable; they are contradictory conceptions of the human person. The one point of overlap is their agreement that human beings are deeply sinful. But the alternative theory puts this claim in more radical terms than Justification theory and derives it differently (and we have already seen that Justification theory courts a charge of outright argumentative incoherence in this regard). The more radical view of human sinfulness is — again — arguably the dominant opinion of Paul's other texts.[14]

3.3. Theology

The basic conception of God is different elsewhere in Paul.

In Justification theory the critical attribute of God is retributive justice, and this dictates in turn that any wrongdoing be appropriately punished. The divine attribute of justice is perceived universally by individuals within the theory's first phase (even if they do not acknowledge it), and a great deal flows from this basic commitment. It creates considerable pressure on individuals in the first phase to convert, and it justifies judgment of them if they do not. It then goes on to dictate the shape of Christ's work on behalf of sinners. (We will revisit each of these points shortly.)

Hence, the God who presides over the Justification model's first phase is not essentially personal, although it is customary to speak of him in those terms. Moreover, he is inherently only monotheistic. Christ is divine only if Anselm's account of the atonement as infinite, *ephapax* payment succeeds, and I suggested in the preceding chapter it does not.

The alternative theory — and this can hardly be overstated — has a fundamentally different view of God. God is inherently benevolent, and this attribute is visible in Father, Son, and Spirit. These actors are tightly coordinated but also distinguishable. The "presiding" God, who in this theory initiates salvation, is known as "the Father." He sends "the Son" into the oppressed human condition in order to transform it. But this transformation cannot be completed without the resurrecting or "ingrafting" actions of the Spirit (see Rom. 11:17-24). Hence, the alternative model's theology is inherently personal and Trinitarian.

These are actually two quite different conceptions of God. The divinity of Christ is not overtly attested in Paul much if at all; it must be inferred (although, arguably, some of the inferences are strong).[15] Christ's sonship is mentioned, but not commonly. The Spirit never receives as much emphasis elsewhere in Paul as in the arguments of Romans 8, but is not infrequently important in Paul's texts elsewhere. The motif of God the Father, however, is ubiquitous in Paul.[16] Moreover, there is a sense in which these two different conceptions of God become evident historically at different points. The God of justice will be perceived definitively at the *eschaton,* when all the peoples of the earth will be judged for their wrongdoing — many being sentenced, presumably, to the appropriate punishment. God is a just future judge. And if this is not especially apparent now, it will be then. However, the God of the alternative system — a God characterized fundamentally by benevolence — will be associated most tightly with salvation, and seen as involved in a historical sweep that begins with the sending of the Son in the incarnation, and extends through the present. This is not to exclude judging from that God's future actions, but to redefine this activity's criteria *and* possible role.[17]

3.4. Christology and Atonement

The role of Jesus Christ in the atonement is different elsewhere in Paul.

Justification theory orients the work of Christ entirely toward God's justice, and focuses significantly if not exclusively on his death. This is interpreted as dealing with the punishment necessitated by the sins of humanity; it is punitive, satisfactory, and substitutionary. (If Anselm's explanation of Christ's role here holds, then certain other functions become important; however, a truncated account is still produced.)[18] Christ came to die, and to do so paying a penalty.

The alternative theory understands Christ's atoning work as transformational, and this work consequently encompasses his incarnation, life, death, resurrection, and glorification. We have already noted that Jesus' death does not function as a punishment for sin so much as a termination of a sinful condition — a termination that then, by the work of the Spirit, can be universalized. (Indeed, a statement of some notion of universality is implicit within the incarnation itself: see 5:15-21.) But Jesus' death is part of a broader process of assumption, elimination, and reconstitution, all of which could be said to constitute "atonement" in the broad sense of that term.[19]

Clearly, then, very different views of the atonement are in view. And, as a result, Justification theory struggles to account for the soteriological value that Paul ascribes elsewhere to aspects of Christ in addition to his death — such as his resurrection. Furthermore, Justification is faced with the paucity if not absence of motifs analyzing that death in punitive terms.

3.5. Soteriology

The nature of salvation, including the basis and depth of Christian assurance, is different elsewhere in Paul.

Salvation in Justification theory is individual and conditional. It moves from a generic, universal situation to a degree of particularity as the gospel is preached. Agency throughout is primarily human. Individuals first learn about God from the cosmos, then realize their own condition, and then make a decision to embrace Christ's atoning work on the cross and to be saved. They relate to God primarily in terms of information. Indeed, it is a moot point whether the knowledge of Christ's atoning work on the cross is even necessary in order for salvation to take place. (Strictly speaking, it is not; moreover, the model provides no way of judging whether claims about Christ are actually true. But these implications are clearly troublesome and so are often avoided.) Hence, in terms of the theory, individual converts do not know God personally or intimately and have only a distant relationship with Christ, if they have one at all. No relationship with the Spirit is necessary at any point (a conundrum to which we will return momentarily).

Such converts will understand the sacraments in terms of these fundamental principles. Baptism is best undertaken at the moment of conversion, itself dependent in turn on belief; it ought to be "believer's baptism." Those below the age of rational consent (i.e., infants) must therefore wait (while other categories of people may have to wait indefinitely). Baptism symbolizes the forgiveness of sins that takes place through the appropriation of the work of the cross, although sins are not actually forgiven so much as their consequences redirected. As Christ's vicarious punishment is appropriated, God is no longer offended or justly angered by the converts' behavior and so can restore his relationship with them. The Eucharist is also oriented toward a satisfactory understanding of the atonement. But since the elements do focus on Christ's death, this is not overly difficult.

The mirror image of this view of salvation is also important. Because of its conditionality, there is a distinctly limited aspect to Christian salvation conceived of in these terms. Those who do not exercise the appropriate conditions for salvation — whether through ignorance or recalcitrance — are not saved, remaining under the just wrath of God, and destined for individual punishment. Moreover, the entire model will break down if this feature is relaxed. (Hence, a little paradoxically, the defense of God's punitive actions at the eschaton is a leitmotif for the Justification advocate, along with an emphasis on the limited nature of the atonement; ultimately Jesus came to die only for those who consciously accept that — "for all who believe" — the participle of belief functioning here in a limiting, rather than an inclusive way.)

The alternative theory of salvation suggested by Romans 5-8 is quite different. Salvation is of course unconditional, partly because human beings do not possess the capacity to analyze their own situation or to save themselves; they cannot undertake any action conditional for salvation even if that is necessary, and certainly they cannot transform their oppressed ontology by themselves. Hence, the alternative theory is characterized by grace and involves strong senses of election and assurance.[20] In addition, salvation is highly particular and historical. And it is personal and intimate throughout. The convert knows God the Father, crying "Abba! Father!"; God the Son, who is now "the firstborn of many brothers"; and the Holy Spirit, who joins in the wordless groans of suffering creation.

The sacraments are understood differently in the light of all this; they signify salvation through participation. Baptism evokes the immersion of people in Christ's death and their reconstitution or resurrection in his new life. Similarly, the eating of bread and drinking of wine in the Eucharist indicate the participation of the assembled people in Christ's Passion. But they make an ecclesial statement as well: those who participate in these events are profoundly unified by them.[21]

Moreover, because of its fundamentally elective and incursive dynamic, it is difficult to speak of limits on God's saving love, which is effected through the work of Christ and the Spirit. Hence, the atonement of Christ is, in this alternative system, more emphatically universal, reaching out to all who are lost: "just as one man's trespass led to condemnation for all, so one man's act of righteousness leads to justification for all" (Rom. 5:18). It is probably wise not to second guess the eschaton and pronounce definitively — not to mention, without warrant — on the future salvation of the human race. Neither is it necessary in the alternative system to affirm the lostness of anyone ex definitione; the system will not break down if the converse is the case. So any sense of soteriological limitation is conceptually curtailed by the alternative system, and the universality of the atonement is unconditioned and consequently more inherently dynamic and inclusive (that is, without being automatic).

The tensions here are both widespread and obvious. But it is worth emphasizing that only the alternative theory supplies an intimate relationship with Christ, along with a necessary and equally intimate role for the Holy Spirit. And only that theory knows God as a Father. In addition, while the implications of Justification theory are strangely scarce in Paul's writings, the personal and participatory dimensions of the alternative theory are discernible almost everywhere[22] (not to mention, a scandalously *inclusive* dynamic expressed in mission to those thought to be irredeemable; indeed, a pressure on limitation seems discernible[23]). But before laboring this point, we ought to move on immediately to consider further, closely linked aspects of this comparison.

3.6. Faith

The nature and role of faith are different elsewhere in Paul.

We have already noted that faith is a more awkward action within Justification theory than it first appears. But let us assume for the sake of argument that Justification supplies a coherent and manageable account of it. As we know well by now, faith is a choice — endorsing for the moment the Arminian variant as marginally more plausible — through which individuals appropriate salvation. It follows a period of introspection and probable despair in relation to ethical activity; this last is exposed as merely creating culpability. Hence, individuals ought to be motivated to choose salvation, and they are presumably capable of exercising "faith alone." Faith is the climactic action in this philosophical and ethical journey, although it must itself take place in relation to preaching.

It is understandable, as a result of these commitments, that advocates of Justification balk at the suggestion that Christ "believes." He alone of all humanity has no need to undergo this journey; Christ has no need to be justified. Indeed, if he did, then his peculiar contribution to salvation might even be jeopardized. Christ must be sinless in order to provide a perfect sacrificial payment that satisfies the offended Father and compensates for the sins of humanity. But his belief would presumably imply a prior journey through sinfulness like that of the rest of humanity, and this would destroy both his work and the theory. Alternatively, his faith is simply functionless. Without such a prior journey through sinfulness, the very point of justification by faith alone seems lost. So it is difficult to understand why it is worth mentioning. Jesus' faith has no rationale (and this is also a nice illustration of the degree to which faith within Justification depends for its role on the argument of the prior phase of attempted ethical performance and introspection; we might say, then, that "without works faith is dead").

As we have already seen, the alternative theory has a very different view of faith. First, its "faith" is a complex rather than a simple notion, denoting both Christian belief and Christian endurance. (Christ's fidelity could also denote, in broader narrative terms, the downward trajectory of Christ that culminated in crucifixion.)

Second, it tends to understand both those qualities retrospectively and unconditionally but without undue emphasis. The accurate understanding of God and any persistent fidelity to his calling are merely two aspects of salvation as that is being worked out within the life of the Christian. And Christian salvation as a whole is viewed in fundamentally revelatory and unconditional terms, as initiated by God. We would therefore expect belief and endurance to be part of a broader process of Christian transformation, and to possess a quality of giftedness. Faith, like everything else in Christian life, is a product of grace.

Third, the alternative theory would expect the Christian to share these attributes with Christ himself. Like any aspect of salvation, these virtues are generated as the Spirit transforms human ontology in relation to Christ, the template of the new eschatological humanity. A correct understanding of God and a steadfast endurance to his call are therefore exactly what Christians would hope to begin to share through their participation in Christ. But it follows from this that Christ himself possesses faith, and in all the relevant senses; he is in fact the "the architect and perfecter of Christian faith."[24] Conversely, to possess an important Christian virtue independently of Christ makes little or no sense. It is, strictly speaking, impossible. (The transformational work of the Spirit cannot plausibly be separated from Christ in Paul's thinking.)

We will address Paul's principal discussions of faith in detail in due course. It will suffice for now to point out that the alternative theory gives a good account of much of Paul's discussion of faith outside the classic Justification texts. In those texts faith has a gifted, unconditional quality that Justification theorists have often struggled to explain.

The semantic range of "faith" — denoting at times the content of belief and at times the quality of human loyalty or fidelity — is problematic for Justification theory.[25] Moreover, in the former sense there is a focus on resurrection,[26] and in the latter sense an almost superhuman strength — both at variance with the Justification account.[27] But these nuances are exactly what the alternative theory expects. Furthermore, faith is not privileged elsewhere in Paul as it is in Justification discussions; as the alternative theory expects, it is merely one of a spectrum of Christian virtues, all of which seem rooted in the character of Christ himself.[28] Indeed, if one virtue were to be privileged, that would be love, not faith[29] (and certain texts even seem to speak of the generative role of love in relation to faith, which is quite difficult for Justification theory to explain but which the alternative theory accounts for well[30]).

Finally, it is important to note that certain discussions of faith in Paul seem inexplicable unless they are referred to Christ himself; it is incoherent to read these texts in a sustained, anthropocentric fashion.[31] And we have already seen that Justification theory finds it extremely difficult to explain this reference; it is either theoretically fatal or otiose. But clearly the alternative theory has no difficulty at such points. Since as a theory it is fundamentally christocentric, such christocentric readings are exactly what we would expect.[32] Somewhat ironically, then, a careful consideration of the relevant data suggests that Justification theory struggles to supply a convincing account of faith in Paul — one of its leitmotifs — whereas the alternative theory embraces that data smoothly and plausibly.

3.7. Ethics

The conception of ethics is different elsewhere in Paul.

The differences between the two theories are never more apparent than in their contrasting conceptions of ethics. Justification theory famously struggles in relation to this whole area of Christian existence, but the alternative theory found in Romans 5–8 is *intrinsically* ethical.

A number of difficulties within Justification theory at this point need to be addressed. First is the well-known fact that Justification theory cannot, in strictly theoretical terms, generate a responsible ethical state within the Christian at all. From a very early point, the theory launches a scathing attack *on* ethical behavior. This attack, which provides such effective leverage on the unsaved individual, also condemns empty "religion" and potentially oppressive ecclesial institutions. But its initial rhetorical advantages come at a price. After reducing the condition of salvation from ethical perfection to faith alone, the theory cannot then consistently expect self-interested individuals to undertake further ethical behavior! Their sins are forgiven and they are saved, so no further leverage on them can be generated through self-interest (which previously came principally from the prospect of hell, but that problem has now been resolved). Moreover, such individuals are accustomed to *condemning* ethical performance *and* to perceiving repeated failure in relation to it as a healthy thing. Indeed, to deny this is to be hypocritical — one of the worst sins.

Most of the theory's advocates have shrunk from this rigorous application of its claims. But it is in fact difficult to generate ethical leverage within the parameters of Justification, even with a generous reading. Its occupants could be expected to respond to their salvation with joy, peace, and thanksgiving; they have after all been relieved of a great deal of anxiety. However, gratitude will get such converts only so far. They are already sensitive introverts, so they will doubtless simply continue to sin and to recognize that, although at least it will no longer cause mortal pangs. But nothing fundamental about their ethical situation has changed. And little reason to behave ethically has been supplied.

Perhaps aware of this dangerous shortfall, advocates of Justification have often appealed to an additional salvific phase at this point — "sanctification," which generally invokes the help of the Holy Spirit. The arrival of the Spirit transforms, motivates, and empowers individuals for ethical behavior. In effect, Justification takes care of salvation, and then sanctification addresses the problems of ongoing Christian existence, especially in its ethical aspect. But this appeal is problematic on a number of counts (and in fact has long been abandoned in academic argumentation, as we will see in more detail in chapter six, and part three, chapter eleven).

First, it is simply unmotivated in theoretical terms. Justification theory *itself* contains no obvious need for such assistance. The problem of sin in the sense of its ultimate punishment has already been dealt with. Second, any such introduction clashes with some of the theory's most fundamental axioms. By gifting the Spirit to Christians in order to transform their incapacity so that they can go on to behave ethically, God has acted in a fundamentally benevolent manner without consideration for matters of retribution. And the situation of the Christian has thereby been recognized as one of imprisonment and slavery rather than capacity, self-reflection, transgression, and the appropriate conclusions. We have, in short, *shifted to the alternative theory,* which contradicts the anthropology and soteriology of Justification. And these contradictions have now been introduced into Justification itself. But at this point we should ask, third, whether this is not only unmotivated and contradictory but also arbitrary. Why shift to a new set of axioms only at the point of ethical difficulty? Why not begin with those axioms? It also worth noting, fourth, that the pneumatology so posited is fundamentally inadequate *as* pneumatology. When the Spirit operates to transform human ethical incapacity, it is functioning essentially as a power (hence "it") and not either relationally or as a person. And this is not really the Spirit as we know her[33] from elsewhere in Paul, not to mention from much of the rest of the Bible. Any restrictions of the work of the Spirit to this limited role and this temporal location are unacceptable. The Spirit is free and sovereign.

We conclude, then, Justification theory has a serious ethical crisis. It has no convincing way of generating significant ethical behavior from its converts and consequently encounters a massive framing problem at this juncture, since we know from almost all of Paul's texts that he has high ethical expectations of his converts. A theory that cannot justify or even generate these expectations is clearly in serious difficulties on this front. But its ethical problems are far from over.

Let us grant for the moment that converts do want to try to behave ethically in a sustained fashion after conversion. What will now guide them? We would expect the firm response from Justification advocates — whatever they say positively — that this will not be by means of the law. But a close scrutiny of the theory suggests that it should be! It is an often unnoticed but entirely necessary corollary that the *full* Mosaic law actually remains in force ethically for the convert within Justification theory.[34]

Justification merely deals with the unpleasant *consequences* of attempting to live under law prior to the gospel. Consistent failure will lead to condemnation on the day of judgment. However, those consequences have now been dealt with. The actual revelation of God's ethical concerns within the pre-Christian condition has in no way been altered by the arrival of salvation. Those concerns remain in force as inviolable principles written into the very structure of the cosmos. And although we have noted a difficulty at this point, the theory itself holds that the revelations of nature and the written revelation in Scripture are essentially the same. Both reveal the will of God in ethical terms and result in complete accountability. Hence, Justification theory does not dispense with the law; it merely dispenses with its unpleasant outcome for the non-Christian. And some of its framing difficulties have now been considerably deepened. Obviously, Paul does not expect his pagan converts to observe the Mosaic law once they have converted — although they can undertake some observances in certain circumstances. (Indeed, even Jews can now exhibit a strange degree of flexibility with respect to its provisions.)

We have already briefly noted some hermeneutical strategies that attempt to soften the difficulties of the model at the epistemological point of difference between the general and the specific ethical codes. The troublesome difference between them is partly erased by suggestions that the temple is no longer in force and/or neither is the ceremonial part of the code. This draws the general and the written codes together in terms of content, blurring the awkward disparity between them. And these strategies may also function at the present point of difficulty, although with a slightly different effect. Such strategies suggest that some of the law is now superseded and so the gospel is law-free, at least in these respects. If Christ's death transcends the temple and/or the ceremonial part of the law, then much has been left behind. (Late Second Temple Judaism in Judea was, after all, in large measure a temple cult.) Hence, to a degree they mask the difficulty.

But we have also already seen that these strategies are invalid. And even were they to be granted, the basic difficulty remains that much of the law is still in force. Doing *these* works of law ought to be entirely legitimate. (Certainly, Justification theory supplies no reason why they should not be done.) In short, although justification is by faith, Christian life is still by works of law — which is to say, strictly speaking, by observing the whole law. And of course this is not what Paul seems stridently to affirm in most of his extant letters![35]

The alternative theory possesses none of these difficulties. As we have already seen, it is inherently ethical. The saving transformation of the human being through participation in Christ in the Spirit *is* simultaneously an ethical transformation. Ethics merely denotes the behavioral aspect of this overarching process. The involvement of people within the interpersonal communion of Life, as against the oppressive kingdom of Death, is, moreover, an ethical rationale in and of itself. To be involved in this communion is be ethical automatically. Moreover, people involved in the kingdom of Life essentially indwell their ethical criteria as they participate in the Son through the Spirit. Hence, there is a more intimate relationship with those criteria, so to speak, than was previously the case. And we would consequently expect ethical behavior as evidence of this involvement, although we would not expect perfection in view of its mere inauguration. The content of ethics is clearly supplied by this participation; consequently the Mosaic law is necessarily displaced.

With the coming of the Son and the Spirit, alternative disclosures of God's ethical concerns are redundant. They could presumably still contribute to the new dispensation, but only under the control of the new ruling criteria, which are personal. Doubtless, certain things will be taken up in the new community, but other things will be released. And it would seem that this redundancy includes — at least to a degree — the Mosaic law. In this light, Paul's freedom toward the law seems readily comprehensible.

Clearly, then, two very different ethical situations are presupposed by the two theories. Justification struggles in relation to ethics. It has difficulty motivating its converts to be ethical and, if they choose to act uprightly, it actually supplies them with the law as a guide. The alternative theory is much better positioned at this point (to put things mildly). It transforms its participants and so expects a qualitatively superior ethical reality within the redeemed community. But its fundamentally personal constitution also controls its ethical guidance. It is free to leave the law behind or to endorse aspects of it should it seem appropriate to do so. And this strong commitment to ethics but flexible attitude toward its content is arguably the dominant trend throughout most of Paul's extant texts.[36]

3.8. Ecclesiology

The nature of the church is different elsewhere in Paul.

Somewhat incredibly, Justification theory has no real need for a church! The basic Christian reality is an individual who exercises certain beliefs. Consequently, the church will consist only of an assembly of such individuals bound together by consent or convenience in something of a free association. Presumably, that assembly — if it takes place (and it may do so on nonrational or inconsistent grounds) — will have certain emphases implicit in the terms of its association. There will probably be an emphasis on information and hence on confession,[37] on scriptural warrant (although this raises certain awkward problems),[38] and on evangelism, understanding this practice in a certain way. Indeed, since the central moment of the model is conversion, the central task of the church will probably be evangelism, something that may well result in both crosscultural mission and church growth. Somewhat oddly, then, conversion — that is, entry into the church — will be the church's high point. Meanwhile, the church remains a discrete and "bounded" entity.

The alternative theory, by contrast, is inherently ecclesial. However, this last dimension must be understood appropriately. Those who are overtly involved within salvation are necessarily involved with one another; they are ontologically connected by virtue of their participation in the same Lord through the same Spirit. But "church" does not overshadow this new situation (or institutionalize it!); rather, it seems merely to name the interpersonal communion that now exists, with an emphasis on its human dimension.[39] It names the community of the called that results from the call of God. So presumably, other terms and metaphors could be employed to denote this dimension within salvation. Most importantly, being constituted by an elective and incarnating deity, the ontology of the church is relational and dynamic. It is not fundamentally a bounded entity so much as a pervasive phenomenon qualitatively different from its environment.

Once again, then, two very different conceptions are apparent. And they are fundamentally different conceptions. On the one hand, the church consists of a compact of rational individuals who emphasize purity of information and the moment of conversion with a principal demarcation between this group and those as yet undecided or unreached; on the other, it consists of an unconditional interpersonal communion, established by the divine trifold action — a dynamically centrifugal entity. The former establishes itself and remains essentially individualist; the latter is established and remains essentially interrelated. It is of course the latter notion that more obviously permeates the other writings of Paul.[40]

3.9. *Judaism*

The depiction of Judaism, including various accounts of the Torah, is different elsewhere in Paul.

We will discuss the question of Judaism in detail in the following chapter as difficulties become apparent at Justification theory's empirical frame. But some preliminary observations at the systematic frame will be useful here.

Justification theory views Judaism as a more specific version of the generic human condition. All individuals perceive that a just God will eventually judge them for their ethical performance by the terms of an eminently just but exacting "contract." Because of their repeated wrongdoing, however, they conclude (or ought to) that they fall well short of the requisite standard for salvation, which is very high, and are destined for eventual damnation. The stage is then set for the proclamation of the gospel and its second, generous contract. Jews' perception of this just God is augmented by a definitive written edition of God's ethical demands, which has been delivered — somewhat inconsistently — via revelation, but otherwise the basic dynamic is identical. Because they inevitably fail to meet the terms of the first, rigorous contract, Jews too are destined for damnation. Oppressed by their repeated sinfulness and fearful of the approaching judgment, pious Jews spiral downward in a "loop of despair." Or alternatively, rejecting this calculus and claiming themselves to be righteous — irrationally or hypocritically, or both — resistant Jews circle endlessly in a "loop of foolishness." And at this point the stage is set for the proclamation of the gospel and its second, saving contract (although this must of course wait until the coming of Christ and the preaching associated with the Christian dispensation). At bottom, this is a generic human condition. It holds independently of time and space, and hence also of history.

Thus, Justification theory defines Judaism in its first phase, and in largely generic terms. It is the critical, penultimate stage of the Christian progression. If things proceed appropriately, then all people will reach the position of the pious Jew, although this is meant to devolve immediately, through preaching, into the Christian condition. Consequently, Judaism is not a stable or final position in and of itself; it is anything but, consisting — correctly conceived — of anxiety and despair and — incorrectly conceived — of moralizing hypocrisy.

The alternative theory views Judaism very differently. The theory supplies a retrospective account and so presupposes the Christian condition. (Justification theory does not, so its account of Judaism stands independently of the arrival of Christ. Indeed, the arrival of Christ is premised upon its prior failure.) In addition, this alternative view is fundamentally historical and particular, just as was the arrival of Christ. Here Judaism journeys through time. In that specific journey, it is guided by particular revelations, notably the Scriptures. Of course, it journeys toward Christ himself, and so there is a sense in which this account of Judaism cannot even be placed on the table, so to speak, until the first century CE. (In this view,

Jesus Christ — not merely a Christ or Messiah, although he is this — is Judaism's fulfillment.) Thus, according to this explicitly christological account, Judaism's intrinsic structure is promissory and anticipatory. And its anticipations tend to be located in the primordial and the patriarchal narratives, as against in the Mosaic traditions, although various prophetic anticipations are also important.

In addition, the alternative theory tends not to ask a question that modern interpreters and Justification advocates regard as almost self-evident, namely, how were Jews saved prior to Christ? Since Christ has come, the critical issue for the alternative theory is how they ought to respond now! (Indeed, the query concerning how they ought to respond to God prior to Christ's arrival might be dismissed in view of this later, more urgent concern as something of an armchair question.) Modern scholars, with their historical concerns, want to know what was happening prior to the arrival of Christ, and Justification advocates regard this question as an essential prerequisite to the appropriation of Christ. But it is important to grasp that alternative theorists are under no such constraints. Salvation is simply not at stake in this question as it is for the advocates of Justification, because salvation is not at stake for them in any prior definition of Judaism.

Hence, there is clearly room within the alternative theory for a more nuanced description of Judaism, and this is what we tend to find elsewhere in Paul: Israel is historical, not generic; is not defined by law observance or failure thereof; is elective and teleological in structure; and may possess various privileges and blessings provided that those never overshadow the climactic blessing that is Christ. So, for example, in Romans 9:4-5a Paul lists various overt historical privileges for Judaism: "to them belong the adoption, the glory, the covenants, the giving of the law, the worship, and the promises; to them belong the patriarchs, and from them, according to the flesh, comes the Messiah."[41] The theme of God's initiative is also very much to the fore in the discussions of election, namely, Romans 9:6-29 and 11:5-10, 25-32, which are focused largely on Israel. (Indeed, these have occasionally been thought sufficient to ground an entire theological system!)[42]

Such brief indications suffice to show that acute tensions hold between these two definitions of Judaism in Paul, and especially as he expresses himself within Romans. The account undergirded by the alternative theory seems the more sensitive to Paul's views as they are expressed outside the classic Justification texts. Still, there are some apparent points of overlap between the two. Perhaps most importantly, both accounts of Judaism conceive it as deeply sinful.[43] But it is absolutely crucial to appreciate the different epistemological modes that underpin this judgment.

In the Justification account, Jews should learn themselves that they are sinful; if they resist this process, they are vulnerable to the strongest condemnation, and on supposedly objective grounds. This lesson is inherent to the very structure of Judaism. (Without it, the internal progression of the model is disrupted and Christian salvation itself imperiled.) Hence, the Jews' sinfulness is not sufficiently dire to overshadow a basic human capacity. People can discern the good and do it. It is just that everyone seems to choose not to, and it is this that establishes culpability. Furthermore, this sinfulness is revealed through repeated transgression of the law, whether that is general and internal or particular and more specific. Sinfulness is basically the perception by individuals that when they try to do the good they repeatedly fail.

In the alternative account, although the judgment is the same — that Jews are sinful — this is subtly different in content and profoundly different in mode. The perception of sinfulness is more radical. Human beings, including Jews, are incapable of doing the good because they are oppressed by evil forces that are too strong for them to resist. Judaism is in Adam, so its ontological plight is very serious; it shares this plight with the rest of humanity. However, Judaism is not for this reason strongly culpable, or even especially self-conscious about its dire condition. Such a judgment is reached only retrospectively, "in Christ." Hence, the principal stance of the alternative theory vis-à-vis non-Christian Israel is not one of judgment but, in a degree of solidarity, one that desires mercy and further disclosure — a stance presently of respect, and ultimately of hope.

And, once again, this stance seems closer to Paul's views when they occur elsewhere: "I have great sorrow and unceasing anguish in my heart. For I could wish that I myself were accursed and cut off from Christ for the sake of my own people, my kindred according to the flesh. They are Israelites . . ." (Rom. 9:2-4a). "[T]hey have now been disobedient in order that, by the mercy shown to you, they too may now receive mercy. For God has imprisoned all in disobedience so that he may be merciful to all" (Rom. 11:31-32; see also Gal. 6:16b — correctly interpreted!).[44]

We will revisit these issues in much more detail shortly. What we can say for now is that as Paul discusses Judaism outside the classic Justification texts, his descriptions seem both significantly different from the expectations of Justification theory (which are themselves both fixed and basic) and closer to the expectations of the alternative theory.[45]

3.10. *Coercion and Violent Punishment*

The endorsement of coercive violence for the punishment of wrongdoing is arguably rare elsewhere in Paul.

It is a central axiom within Justification theory, as we have seen repeatedly, that wrongdoing is appropriately dealt with by punishment. And punishment, which presupposes a relationship of power between the punisher and the wrongdoer, is by nature coercive. The correct response to wrongdoing is to inflict on the transgressor an equivalent punishment, which necessarily may — and, in ultimate terms, will — be violent. And this is consistent with the theory's basic commitment to God's retributive justice. Furthermore, this commitment is implemented at several points within Justification theory as a whole.

The most prominent point at which it is enacted is of course the cross; indeed, the notion of retributive justice lies at the center of the theory's understanding of Christ's death. Jesus' death on the cross is a punishment of sufficient weight to "pay" or "compensate" for the sins of whoever lays hold of it. But many apparently do not lay hold of it — whether because, not having heard the gospel and its offer of redirected punishment, they *can*not, or because, having heard the gospel and resisted it, they *will* not. Irrespective of the precise cause, the principle of retribution must now be applied to them directly. They will be condemned on the day of judgment and punished accordingly. So coercive or punitive violence is central and indeed definitive at two climactic points in the Justification model. But partial outworkings of the principle of retribution are in evidence throughout.

Earthly government is a dim reflection of the heavenly arrangement; it attempts to apply God's ethical dictates in the interim. Thus, government too may legitimately undertake the punishment of wrongdoing (and implicit here is an eventual theological endorsement of Constantinianism). Furthermore, the orientation of the Christian toward the non-Christian will be shaped strongly by this dynamic.

Those who have refused the gospel's offer of redirected punishment have betrayed a high degree of irrationality and/or willful disobedience. Any misfortune they might experience prior to the day of judgment is therefore appropriately construed as a proleptic experience of the punishment that awaits them, although it may also double as a pedagogical prompt. And perhaps these two dynamics may be fused when non-Christians experience awful punishments at the hands of a given government (although the forces of nature, including disease, can also function at this point). Essentially, non-Christians are a category that is fundamentally appointed for violent punishment. Hence, Christians' most important responsibility toward such unfortunates is to preach, or continue to preach, the gospel's opening scenario with as much conviction and clarity as can be mustered; the unredeemed must learn to interpret their own difficult situation more accurately. But until they do so, they are only getting what they deserve.[46]

Of course the alternative theory views things rather differently. Its conception of the problem facing humanity is bound up with an ontological conundrum rather than the dictates of retributive justice. The appropriate solution to that conundrum is transformational rather than satisfactory; hence, the death of Christ functions as a critical transitional moment for humanity rather than a payment or equivalent punishment in response to the demands of offended justice. Moreover, God the Father is motivated throughout by a near limitless benevolence. So this theory possesses no axiomatic commitment to coercive violence as the only appropriate response to wrongdoing. On the contrary, its axiomatic commitment is to resolving a situation of wrongdoing radically and unconditionally in transformational terms — a situation that is evil in part *because of* its own internal violence.

The alternative theory is indifferent if not hostile toward any notion of Christian government, that is, to the exercise of coercive power as a legitimate Christian activity. And its attitude toward the unredeemed is correspondingly different. Although non-Christians are deeply wrong, they need rescue, not condemnation. Moreover, the rescued retain a sense of solidarity with them, because the former have done nothing to deserve their rescue; God has acted unconditionally in order to save them. Hence, rather than recapitulating God's righteous judgment within their preaching, they are more likely to appeal in the wrongdoers' behalf for further mercy. In short, the alternative theory rooted in Romans 5–8 and analogous texts *provides no theological justification for coercive and violent punishment as the appropriate response to sinfulness.* Moreover, there seems to be good theological reason within the theory itself — or, more precisely, within the revealed events that it speaks of — *for the explicit repudiation of coercion and violence* as aspects of the evil regime that God is seeking to transform through the missions of the Son and the Spirit (a repudiation that *could* arguably apply to the notion of "government" as well, at least in some of its aspects). Hence, the theory not only suggests that coercive violence is not part of the divinely endorsed response to wrongdoing but implies that it may itself be an evil, which is to say that a key axiom within Justification theory must actually be repudiated as evil. At this point, then, the two theories collide visibly. What one theory calls divine the other calls sin.

The following claim may not in the end be completely probative, but it is still worth considering. As we might expect on the basis of the alternative theory, a case can be made for the rareness if not absence of any endorsement of coercive violence by Paul outside the classic Justification texts (the given reading of which will eventually be challenged). This absence is complemented by the endorsement of its converse, namely, noncoercive, nonviolent action. If this set of claims proves true, then it will of course be extremely troublesome for Justification theory. If it proves even half true — as seems likely — then this will still constitute a framing tension at the relevant points, although not necessarily a decisive one.

Excursus: The Case — Briefly — against Coercive Violence in Paul

There are several steps in the positive case, and then in any attempted rebuttal.

i. The central defining dimension in Paul's soteriology — the cross — is emphatically noncoercive and nonviolent. (Coercion and violence are of course received by Jesus at this point.) And according to Paul, Christians are saved by their participation in it. At the heart of the alternative account of Paul's soteriology is Christ's martyrdom, in which he refused to respond coercively or violently to an unjust and violent action — his crucifixion — despite his innocence. To the contrary, he submitted to it, enduring its shame, its suffering, and eventual death. Paul's soteriology, moreover, suggests the participation of people by means of the Spirit within this programmatic reality. To participate somehow in this death is to experience concretely a guarantee of the future resurrection and eschatological life beyond it that Christ is already experiencing. Hence, the steadfast endurance of suffering and violence without retaliation seems to be inherent within the most basic commitments of this theory and the reality of which it tries to speak. *There is no other route to salvation!* And this is probably why Paul writes at times of the ability of such participatory endurance to witness to outsiders.

This cluster of points is perhaps most clearly attested in Philippians. Christ, Paul famously states, "humbled himself and became obedient to the point of death — even death on a cross! Therefore God also highly exalted him" (Phil. 2:8-9a). Thus, Paul can go on to say, "I regard [all things] as rubbish, in order that I may gain Christ and be found in him. . . . I want to know Christ and the power of his resurrection and the sharing of his sufferings by becoming like him in his death, if somehow I may attain the resurrection from the dead" (3:8b-9a, 10-11).[47] So standing firm and being "in no way intimidated by your opponents" is for them "evidence of their destruction, but of your salvation. And this is God's doing" (1:28).[48] And in view of this, Paul also rejoices that his present trial may end in his death! (while suggesting no coercive or violent techniques for avoiding its outcome, despite the malice of his accusers: see 1:12-26; also 2:17-18).

Strong reasons will now have to be provided for any interruption of this participation by Christians in the noncoercive, nonviolent life of Christ. On what grounds could it be urged that this ontology be abandoned?

ii. In close relation to this, Paul views non-Christians essentially benevolently, despite their sinful situation. We will assess Paul's wrath and judgment statements shortly. For now it suffices to note that Paul often seems to view non-Christians as people who are in a desperate situation. This clearly involves sinful activity that is not pleasing to God, but outside the classic Justification texts, there is little suggestion either that such people can help this or that they deserve some punishment because of it. Above all, they seem to deserve pity and help. Mercy and election are the obvious concomitants to non-Christian sinfulness as the alternative theory conceives it, and numerous statements from other parts of the Pauline corpus attest to this. Romans 5 puts the matter especially succinctly: "God proves his love for us in that while we still were sinners Christ died for us. . . . For if while we were enemies, we were reconciled to God through the death of his Son, much more surely, having been reconciled, will we be saved by his life!" (Rom. 5:8, 10). There is also little indication of desert in the blunt observations of chapter 8: "The mind that is set on the flesh is hostile to God; it does not submit to God's law — indeed it cannot, and those who are in the flesh cannot please God" (8:7-8). And accordingly, the soteriological correlates to this observation are not repentance or faith, that is, acts grounded in human capacity, but divine rescue grounded in a benevolent divine election: "For the law of the Spirit of life in Christ Jesus has set you free from the law of sin and of death" (8:2), because "those whom he predestined he also called; and those whom he called he also justified; and those whom he justified he also glorified" (8:30 — and if the verb δικαιόω is rendered in a more liberative direction, analogous to "is freed" in 6:7, then the point is even more obvious: see more in this relation in part four, chapter sixteen [§§3 & 5], and part five, chapter nineteen [§9]). Hence, the principle that we have already noted in relation to Israel is explicitly said to hold in relation to all of humanity: "God has imprisoned all in disobedience so that he may be merciful to all" (11:32).

Paul's life is extended evidence of the concrete outworking of this principle of initiative, a dynamic of which he is quite self-conscious. So he attests at the very outset of his letter to the Romans that he received "grace and apostleship [or, arguably, the grace of apostleship] to bring about the obedience of faith among all the Gentiles. . . . [Thus] I am a debtor both to Greeks and to barbarians, both to the wise and to the foolish — hence my eagerness to proclaim the gospel to you also who are in Rome" (Rom. 1:5a, 14-15). The evidence for this could of course be broadened considerably, but it hardly seems necessary.

The origin of much of this conceptuality is probably the Adamic analysis of humanity's plight that we have already noted. According to Paul, humanity has been trapped within an enslaved ontology since the first transgression in the garden of Eden opened the door to the infiltration and oppression of human flesh by the powers of Sin and Death. The descendants of Adam sin repeatedly and horrifically, as 7:13-25 makes quite clear, but they also do so somewhat helplessly. Consequently, deliverance and not punishment is the obvious response — something Paul articulates immediately in the context of chapter 7: "Who will rescue me from this body of death? Thanks be to God through Jesus Christ our Lord!" (7:24-25).

In short, Paul's view of the unsaved — outside certain contested texts — does not seem to suggest that they occupy a situation framed fundamentally by retributive justice and hence necessarily in terms of a pending punishment. On the contrary, they are oppressed and incapacitated and so require deliverance through transformation (and we have already noted that neither is this process fundamentally coercive or violent).

iii. This is especially significant given Paul's coercive, violent past. Paul admits that prior to his call he violently attacked Christians in the name of God (see Gal. 1:13, 23; also 1 Cor. 15:9). This zealotry is listed as a positive religious virtue alongside his enthusiasm for "the traditions of my ancestors" (see Gal. 1:14). Yet now clearly this activity has been repudiated as shockingly sinful, in part because it was violent (and this narrative is treated in more detail in chapter five).

iv. Paul does not use coercion in the service of evangelism. Indeed, Paul suffers punishments without asking for a coercive or violent response, even when he is suffering unjustly. Similarly, although at times so angry that he is abusive, he never calls for coercive or violent actions against his opponents. Paul's approach to evangelism betrays no use of coercion. Paul seems to talk, to pray, to attempt miracles, to write letters, and to lead by example. There is not a hint from his letters, or from other sources, of more aggressive activity while evangelizing.

Moreover, Paul has clearly endured a great deal of violence during his mission work, but he never counsels response in like measure. He has suffered Roman civic chastisement three times, a Jewish synagogue lashing five times, a stoning, numerous imprisonments, and various other predations (see esp. 2 Cor. 11:23-26). It is really quite extraordinary, then, that he does not suggest some sort of retaliation. Furthermore, he never counsels a coercive or violent approach to his opponents, even when the stakes are extraordinarily high (see Gal. 1:7-9); even a curse does not now entail a coercive action like a stoning![49] The most that ever seems to be meant in terms of community discipline is social exclusion ("Do not even eat with such a one" [1 Cor. 5:11]).[50]

v. Paul explicitly repudiates a vengeful ethic by Christians. Hence, it is no surprise to read in Romans 12:17-21 — probably alluding to traditions stemming historically from Jesus — that Paul explicitly repudiates vengeful behavior by Christians. "Do not repay anyone evil for evil. . . . Never avenge yourselves, but leave room for the wrath of God; for it is written, 'Vengeance is mine, I will repay, says the Lord' [Deut. 32:35]. . . . Do not be overcome by evil, but overcome evil with good." Irrespective of the role of God in this quotation (which is addressed momentarily), the role of the Christian is quite clear.

vi. Paul systematically reinterprets military imagery metaphorically. He also relocates any conflict within the human sphere to a war with oppressive heavenly powers. The last statement in the preceding quotation is a useful illustration of the first claim here. The verb translated "overcome" in the NRSV is νικάω, which often carried a military connotation and/or an agonistic sense. It was frequently an aggressive signifier (see BDAG 673).

Yet Paul applies this word to a battle or struggle between Christian humanity and evil superhumanity. This achieves two things. First, any aggression is thereby relocated from intrahuman relationships to the relationship between saved humanity and the evil super-human forces that currently enslave the cosmos. And, second, the nature of the conflict it-self is reinterpreted. It is emptied of any coercive, violent sense because the notion of straightforward physical struggle or conquest is obviously inappropriate in relation to heavenly powers. Thus, "we do not wage war according to human standards; for the weap-ons of our warfare are not merely human, but they have divine power to destroy strong-holds. We destroy arguments and every proud obstacle raised up against the knowledge of God, and we take every thought captive to obey Christ" (2 Cor. 10:3-5). This relocation and reinterpretation is in fact standard practice for Paul;[51] it is coterminous with his concep-tion of the world in apocalyptic terms.[52]

This is an impressive array of evidence within Paul. It seems grounded coherently and consistently in some of his most central theological convictions and spread through a large number of different contingent applications. Clearly, any commitment by Paul to co-ercive violence or punishment elsewhere is now going to clash with this body of evidence.

However, Paul is arguably equivocal about punishment. It might be objected by Jus-tification advocates that, in addition to the foregoing emphases, Paul does leave room for God's wrath and for divine judgment (which of course can overlap) and that these are overtly punitive notions. We must pause, then, to consider these rejoinders.

Paul does speak at times of the wrath of God, even outside the classic Justification texts. Furthermore, non-Christians seem destined for it. (See Paul's use of "wrath," Greek ὀργή, in Rom. 1:18; 2:5, 8 [see also θυμός here]; 3:5; 4:15; 5:9; 9:22 [2x]; 12:19; 13:4, 5; 1 Thess. 1:10; 2:16 [this, a noneschatological and very controversial instance]; 5:9; all these texts be-ing roughly comparable to Eph. 2:3; 5:6; and Col. 3:6.) The motif is by no means wide-spread and seems heavily concentrated in Romans. But it is undeniably present. We will discuss its exact sense momentarily.

Paul also speaks at times outside the standard Justification texts of a final judgment (i.e., in addition to Rom. 2:6-16: Rom. 14:10-12; 1 Cor. 3:10-15; probably also 1:7-8; 5:5; 15:22-28; 2 Cor. 1:14; 5:10; Phil. 1:6, 10, 28; 2:16; 1 Thess. 5:2-4; see Eph. 2:1-3; 4:30; 2 Thess. 1:10; 2:2). Unfortunately, different aspects of this anticipated event are in view in different texts, and some of the references are quite brief. It could also be argued that the details are not always consistent. There are, however, obvious emphases on Christian accountability and vindica-tion. The former will be made possible in part by the fiery elimination of falsehood and shoddiness; things will be revealed as they really are.[53] And in order to benefit from the lat-ter, it is important to stand firm until the last and so be counted "blameless" (presumably "in Christ," since Paul is addressing the Corinthians at this point!). Hence, Paul's principal contingent concerns in speaking of the judgment are Christian. Furthermore, the antici-pated scenario is not necessarily punitive in fundamental terms; the accountability in view is clearly not absolute (i.e., strictly proportional), because salvation does not rest on it. Rather, it presupposes salvation.[54] And non-Christians are seldom even mentioned.

But when they are, the relevant texts suggest that the wrathful aspect of the final day will destroy or annihilate them (Gk ὄλεθρος or ἀπωλεία; Phil. 1:28; 1 Thess. 1:10; 5:3, 9). The "softer" reading of 1 Corinthians 5:3-5 certainly accords with this, as does v. 13a. Evidence from the disputed letters, however, is much more specific.

It is indeed just of God to repay with affliction those who afflict you, and to give re-lief to the afflicted as well as to us, when the Lord Jesus is revealed from heaven with his mighty angels in flaming fire, inflicting vengeance on those who do not know God and on those who do not obey the gospel of our Lord Jesus. Such people will be paid the penalty of eternal destruction from the appearance of the Lord and from his glorious strength when he comes to be glorified. (2 Thess. 1:6-10a; literal translation of v. 9 DC)

The complementary information from Ephesians is striking:

You were dead through the trespasses and sins in which you once lived, following the course of this world, following the ruler of the power of the air, the spirit that is now at work among those who are disobedient. All of us once lived among them in the passions of our flesh, following the desires of flesh and senses, and we were by nature children of wrath, like everyone else. (2:1-3)

Here the author of Ephesians — whether Paul or an early and rather sophisticated disciple of his teachings — connects the wrath of God with the enslaved Adamic ontology that the alternative theory has already described. And clearly it is God who must act eventually to eliminate this evil situation (2:4-10).

But arguably, it is appropriate for a benevolent God — and not just a retributive God — to do this. And thus the fundamental point of such wrath and destruction, which will be carried out definitively on the last day, may not necessarily be punishment. In view of an ontologically depraved situation, it could be more akin to a surgical action — the wrath of aggrieved love, not the anger of affronted justice. Paul could, in short, be viewing evil more in terms of purity and impurity than of human capacity and accountability (the latter arguably being a perspective much more congenial to a modern, post-Constantinian situation). Indeed, that the divine love would act in anger at some point to eliminate evil is almost to be expected.

The enslaved human condition notwithstanding, however, these texts still seem to view humans as *complicit* in their evil actions to some degree; they still do the will of the flesh and so must take *some* responsibility for their wrongdoing — hence the occasional language of punishment and accountability (see Rom. 10:3, 16-21!, treated more extensively in part five, chapter nineteen). Moreover, these explanations from disputed letters are to my mind authentically Pauline in tenor and partly confirmatory of accountability by the apostle's notorious discussion of imperial government in Romans 13.[55] Paul recognizes a degree of divine authorization within the Roman government to the point that an experience of "the sword" by wrongdoers is an appropriate experience of God's wrath and punishment (Rom. 13:3-4: Gk ἔκδικος εἰς ὀργήν[56]).[57] This perspective also explains Paul's quotation of Deuteronomy 32:35 in Romans 12:19. Paul seems to believe that one reason for Christians to refrain from revenge is that God reserves that right for himself! Not only does the nonretaliation of Christians heap burning coals on the heads of hostile non-Christians, but the endurance of ongoing hostility might simultaneously increase their future punishment (so v. 20).[58]

First Thessalonians 2:14-16 — another notorious text — also seems to fall into this category.[59] Here something explicitly as against only potentially negative within the historical realm (and a famine is often assumed) is explained as an instance of divine wrath punishing extreme disobedience by certain people, here Judeans. This prospect may be unpleasant, but it accords directly with Romans 12:19-21, 13:1-7, and the short explanations from the disputed letters. Hence, it seems clear that a punitive dimension within Paul's thought cannot be denied.

It is of course questionable how consistent these commitments within Paul are with the basic insights of his gospel. Even in Romans 12:21 Paul commands, "Do not be overcome by evil, but overcome evil with good" — injunctions that accord exactly with his central christological and soteriological convictions. Hence, Paul's eschatological vision of God the Father, dimly replicated in the Roman imperium or in possible natural catastrophes, does not always seem to accord with those instructions.

Such concerns might be reinforced by the more universalistic tendencies apparent in Paul that run counter to his gloomier vision of the eschaton — for example, his emphasis on Christ as the last Adam, and his expectation that "all things" will submit to God at the end in an inclusive fashion. Paul's language at times seems to feel the impress of his unconditional and benevolent soteriology, not to mention his necessarily triumphant Christology (see esp. Rom. 8:31-39; also Rom. 11:32; 1 Cor. 15:20-28; 2 Cor. 5:14; Phil. 2:10-11; see Eph. 1:9-10, 22-23; 4:10; Col. 1:16-20).[60] But this never becomes programmatic. Hence, such implications do not help us at this point in our argument decisively, although they counterbalance the evidence of a punitive eschaton with an alternative vision; they indicate some ambivalence on Paul's part about these future events.

In sum, in view of the scattered eschatological statements to the contrary — which are found largely in disputed texts but are corroborated by texts in uncontested letters — it cannot be claimed that Paul *never* endorses coercive or violent action in some sort of punitive sense by God against wrongdoing outside his classic Justification discussions. That *much* of what Paul said and did runs counter to any notion of coercive violence remains true; however, this is not sufficient to eliminate the countervailing evidence. Paul does occasionally endorse punitive action by God, and this even if his vision of the eschaton is not always consistent. This is a small vein of evidence in his texts, but I concede that it is there; Paul's thinking at this point is not unalloyed. As a result, this particular theoretical tension will not, it seems, run neatly along the border of Justification theory. It is instead a slightly more extensive tension within Paul's thought as a whole that can be either further exacerbated or mitigated by our approach to Justification. This tension is certainly in play within our broader argument, but it is not as decisive a claim as our previous nine observations. We might say then that the notion of divine punishment that is so fundamental to Justification theory is a distinctly muted theme in the rest of Paul's corpus — although it is there.[61]

This concludes our analysis of the various clusters of difficulties apparent when Paul's thought is considered as a whole, essentially systematically (although via the conceptual prism of Romans 5–8), and is juxtaposed with Justification theory. And they are extensive! We will go on to explore in chapter six how this formal account covers some of the protests raised against Justification theory by various significant traditions of critical scholarship in the past. Indeed, an astonishing amount of previous Pauline debate is explained by this particular conceptual dynamic — the clashing together of these two, very different soteriologies within Paul's thinking. We will also observe at that point (as well as later on in part three) how these criticisms have never received a plausible refutation by Justification's apologists. It turns out that this massive theoretical divide within the apostle's interpretation remains unbridged in any cogent sense. But for the time being we will continue to pursue our formal critical inquiry, and from this point specifically in terms of Justification's empirical claims. (The links with most of these critical debates in Pauline scholarship are best drawn only after the entire formal analysis premised on my theoretical account is complete.[62]) In the Introduction and chapter one we noted how Justification theory works forward, and so is committed to making strong truth claims about certain aspects of non-Christian reality. It then builds up from these to its distinctive, Christian solution to a problem that now seems to be obvious. But serious difficulties are apparent at these early conceptual points as well and we turn now to their detailed explication, beginning first in chapter four with a reconsideration of the well-known conundrum of Paul's description of Judaism.

CHAPTER FOUR

The Question of Judaism

§1. Preamble

Theories make claims about reality; this is one of their principal functions. And although Justification theory, unlike most theories, is not verified fundamentally with respect to objective claims — it is verified exegetically, not empirically — it does make such claims. Clearly, any such empirical claims ought to be accurate, and a theory whose claims prove problematic at the empirical frame is necessarily vulnerable. But Justification's objective opening claims — as we will see in more detail shortly[1] — are widely held to be one of its strengths.[2] The model begins with a universally verifiable account of reality in the light of which certain obvious argumentative progressions unfold. Indeed, if the basic nature of reality is grasped accurately — as it ought to be[3] — then everyone will become a Christian.[4] But this perceived strength conceals a deep vulnerability (apart from any question of what we might call "definitional imperialism").

It is clearly fundamental to the integrity of the entire system that its initial account of reality is correct. If Justification theory is to impose a quite particular framework upon reality, thereby "acquiring" its target audience and reducing them to an appropriately receptive state, it is strongly committed to the accuracy of that framework. Its account of reality *must* be true! If it is not, its audience will simply laugh and walk away. Hence, the strength of its claims of objectivity, along with all their supposedly useful argumentative consequences, is necessarily matched by an equal measure of empirical vulnerability. And many interpreters have challenged the theory in this sense — although without defining their criticisms in quite this fashion.

Two types of empirical criticisms have generally been made. First, Justification theory's account of Judaism has been widely challenged (although it has also been defended). Second, the theory's account of Paul's conversion has been challenged, although I will argue that this critical front should be significantly broadened.[5] The two clusters of criticisms that we are considering here — the nature of Judaism and of conversion (usually meaning here principally Paul's conversion) — are complex and require fairly extensive discussion, so each merits a chapter in its own right. In the present chapter we will treat the complicated question of Judaism, in five further stages (§§2-6).

§2. E. P. Sanders's Critique of Conventional Jewish Description in Paul

The origins of the widespread perception that Justification's claims about Judaism are inadequate lie of course in E. P. Sanders's famous study *Paul and Palestinian Judaism: A Comparison of Patterns of Religion,* published in 1977.[6] So our assessment can in the first instance orient itself toward this classic analysis. We must, however, go on to sift the debate that has developed from this point concerning "Paul and Judaism," because not all of it will prove relevant, and even the relevant aspects may not be presented in a way that is helpful for our current concerns. We are certainly beyond Sanders at this point. But I will suggest ultimately that even if Sanders needs significant reformulation, and many of the concerns of his subsequent critics are valid, the result is still a nasty empirical conundrum for Justification theory in this whole area. (We are not beyond Sanders then in the sense of being back before him.) We begin our more detailed analysis with a careful consideration of Sanders's original protest — although his seminal study must still itself be placed in a broader context — before going on to consider its ongoing plausibility.

As he freely admits, Sanders's study was not without precedent. A distinguished although minority tradition of interpreters had long protested that Paul's account of Judaism was somehow "unfair" (a claim that could then result in considerable reinterpretation of the apostle himself as well). The great Harvard rabbinic scholar George Foot Moore had made this case eloquently as early as 1921. E. P. Sanders's distinguished forebear, W. D. Davies, had argued the same case extensively in his classic *Paul and Rabbinic Judaism,* first published in 1948, and my Doktorvater, Richard N. Longenecker, had made much the same point in his *Paul, Apostle of Liberty,* first published in 1964. This tradition of protest included Jewish and Christian scholars.[7] But Sanders made the case especially powerfully.

Sanders took aim at a particular construction of Judaism — "Rabbinic Judaism as a religion of legalistic works-righteousness" (*P&PJ*, 54) — and it is worth noting that this is not quite the same target as Justification theory. According to Sanders, the principal culprit in the perpetration of the "legalistic" stereotype was Weber (although this view has much deeper and more complex antecedents within the interpretation of Paul and of Judaism by largely Christian scholars). From Weber's work the view passed into the work of Bousset, which has remained standard within New Testament scholarship, but also thereby into the immensely influential Bultmann and much of the *Theological Dictionary of the New*

Testament besides. In addition, it influenced the interpretation of Billerbeck's much-used orchestration of rabbinic sources. Despite learned protests to the contrary, the view persisted.[8]

The "legalistic" rubric actually alludes, according to Sanders, to a more extensive system.

> The principal element is the theory that works *earn* salvation; that one's fate is determined by *weighing* fulfilments against transgressions. Maintaining this view necessarily involves *denying* or getting around in some other way *the grace of God in the election*. . . . A third aspect of Weber's view, which is also tied to the theory of salvation by works, is that of establishment of *merit* and the possibility of a *transfer of merit* at the final judgment. The fourth element has to do with the attitude supposedly reflected in Rabbinic literature: *uncertainty* of salvation mixed with the self-righteous feeling of accomplishment. This too depends on the view that a man is saved by works. He will either be uncertain that he has done enough or proud of having been so righteous. Besides these main elements of Weber's soteriology, his view that God was *inaccessible* has also been maintained to the present day. (*P&PJ*, 54, emphases original)

Over against this complex and largely negative stereotype Sanders claimed that a fair consideration of the sources relevant to late Second Temple Judaism and beyond showed that it was a religion characterized almost uniformly by "covenantal nomism," although just what this "pattern of religion" represented was carefully qualified.[9] "Briefly put, covenantal nomism is the view that one's place in God's plan is established on the basis of the covenant and that the covenant requires as the proper *response* of man his obedience to its commandments, while providing means of atonement for transgression" (*P&PJ*, 75, emphasis added). Sanders undertook an impressively detailed analysis of the relevant Tannaitic sources, the Dead Sea Scrolls, and various Apocrypha and Pseudepigrapha, concluding that the negative Weberian stereotype of "petty" legalism was everywhere absent — except perhaps a few awkward texts like parts of Ben Sirach and *4 Ezra*. Conversely, the more positive "noble" and "gracious" system of covenantal nomism was essentially discernible everywhere (*P&PJ*, 419). Three elements within this complex description should be emphasized here in particular: Sanders's emphasis on the important role that the covenant plays in relation to Jewish salvation; his emphasis on the extensive means of "covenant restoration" within Jewish tradition, especially on means of atonement (sacrifices et cetera); and his plausible characterizations of Jewish motivations within this arrangement in positive terms — "noble" and "accepting" (et cetera).

But Sanders had further issues to raise. In an audacious move he reintroduced Schweitzer into the debate, claiming in turn that Paul's religion was characterized by "a transfer of lordship" rather than a movement from either legalism or covenantal nomism to Christianity. This may make the modern appropriation of

Paul more difficult, but it is nevertheless what the apostle thought and said: "that Christ was appointed Lord by God for the salvation of all who believe, that those who believe belong to the Lord and become one with him, and that in virtue of their incorporation in the Lord they will be saved on the Day of the Lord" (*P&PJ*, 523), a system that Sanders summarized as "participationist eschatology" (*P&PJ*, 549). The basic structure of Paul's thought was consequently retrospective; he thought "backward." Hence, the apostle's principal reason for rejecting the Judaism of his youth was that — in a much-quoted claim — "it is not Christianity" (*P&PJ*, 552). As a result of this, "Paul presents an *essentially different type of religiousness from any found in Palestinian Jewish literature*" (*P&PJ*, 543, emphasis original), whether the former is characterized in terms of legalism *or* of covenantal nomism.

Contradictions were thereby driven deep into Paul's construal along several axes. The apostle's apparently legalistic characterizations of Judaism in terms of "works of law" were problematized over against a more accurate understanding of Judaism, "covenantal nomism," *and* his own pattern of religion was said to be fundamentally different from *both* of the foregoing!

There was a propitious aspect to the timing of Sanders's work. His study's appearance in 1977 coincided with a wave of attention directed by many within Western societies and their academies toward previously oppressed minorities — African Americans, women, the poor in the third world, and so on.[10] Jews fit this category nicely, not to mention deservedly. Post-Holocaust studies were gaining momentum, as was the discipline of religious studies, within the boundaries of which many conversations were occurring — not least interreligious dialogues between Jews and Christians of various persuasions. The result was a seismic impact by Sanders's book on the entire field of Pauline interpretation. To accept Sanders's descriptive case, as many did, was to plunge into a creative but contradictory interpretative universe in relation to Paul, which was for some a refreshing but for others a deeply disturbing experience. The discussion of Paul's relationship to Judaism began to grow exponentially and became increasingly controversial. And from this point we can discern something of a parting of the ways within Pauline scholarship.

On the one hand, having largely accepted Sanders's analysis, many scholars attempted to build on his conclusions and insights. A recovery of enthusiasm for the Jewish sources is obvious, although this was assisted by other, simultaneous developments such as the rediscovery of apocalyptic and a renewed interest in Qumran. A considerable number of studies have since appeared that discuss aspects of late Second Temple Judaism with much greater sensitivity to the particularities of its sources, and often irrespective of the implications for Paul. Others have attempted to reorient the interpretation of Paul within this brave new Jewish world.[11]

On the other hand, many scholars have rejected Sanders's case as misleading and even destructive. Indeed, a great wave of such critical studies seems to have crested around the turn of the millennium.[12] And it is reasonably significant

that such interpreters are usually — although not invariably — of more conservative temperament and hence committed strongly to Justification as the correct
understanding of Paul's gospel. And this barrage of remonstrations raises the critical question: does the clock really need to be set back to a pre-Sanders understanding, as some of his critics suggest, or does his critique — either in whole or
in part — remain relevant and pointed, in which case it should be factored into
this unfolding analysis? *Is* there a problem for Justification theory in relation to
its implicit description of Judaism? And, if so, what is it?

In order to answer these questions adequately we will have to trace through
the post-Sanders debate in more detail. And I am going to suggest in particular
that certain aspects of Sanders's position can now be stated a little more precisely
— and this is hardly surprising, with some thirty years' hindsight! But I will claim
ultimately that the usual effect of these clarifications is a sharpening of the difficulties facing Sanders's critics. To reformulate Sanders's case is then — despite its
widespread criticism — to grasp that the present situation of the Justification advocate is as bad as, if not worse than it was when Sanders first unleashed his formidable broadside in 1977. We have not learned *nothing* from thirty years of critical
engagement with Sanders's theses and evidence. But neither has the basic situation
actually changed that significantly for the defender of Paul's conventional
construal in terms of Justification. There are three principal areas of reformulation
that have important implications for our overarching question, and they are now
treated in turn — the clarifications of certain key terms and motifs (undertaken in
§3), the drawing of a key methodological distinction between theory and psychology (in §4), and the rejection of monolithic and rigid descriptive parameters (in
§5). Following these discussions the empirical implications in this particular relation should be clear, although a further caveat will be introduced in §6.

§3. Clarifying Some Key Terms[13]

Four terminological ambiguities that derive from Sanders's original analysis
cloud much subsequent discussion and should now be clarified: the use of the
terms "benevolence," "mercy," and "grace" in relation to God, and of the term "response" for any corresponding human activity. Following the redefinition of
these terms, we then need to rehabilitate some notions that Sanders rejected —
namely, commercial or mercantile motifs.

Much confusion can be sown by characterizing God's actions within a "reasonable" or even kind contractual soteriological arrangement like covenantal
nomism as "benevolent" and "merciful," and hence also "gracious," or a product
of "grace." The language of "grace" commonly refers to *unconditional* actions by
God that deliver salvation to a given constituency with no strings attached, as
pure gift.[14] Within such a system, salvation is not conditional or contractual at all.
And such divine actions can also clearly be described as benevolent and merciful.
But in Sanders's construct, "grace" refers to benevolent and merciful actions that

are nevertheless at the same time conditional. Jews can lose their covenantal status by committing heinous sins or by failing to atone appropriately for sins, as the history of the covenant people sometimes suggests. The episode of the golden calf is a particular locus for such reflections (see Exodus 32). Indeed, Sanders argues against any of the relevant sources being construed in completely unconditional terms. Hence, unless carefully qualified, the language of "grace" can be profoundly ambiguous, denoting two salvific arrangements that are fundamentally and radically different.

It follows that any characterizations of God in terms of "benevolence" or "mercy" can be deeply ambiguous as well. The divine mercy evident in an unconditional salvation is of a different order from the divine mercy apparent within covenantal nomism. The former can operate outside the boundaries associated with a divine contract while the latter cannot. So any talk of divine "benevolence" or "mercy" in relation to an essentially conditional arrangement must be overtly qualified as limited and *not* fundamental to the character of God, since the operation is strictly constrained by the conditions of contract. (Recall that within any essentially contractual system the justice of God remains paramount, enforcing the terms of the contract; such a just God can then be *conditioned* into behaving with more mercy or benevolence.)

The terminology of "response" is likewise unhelpfully ambiguous. It can refer to human activity that merely "responds" to an unconditional gift of salvation and so possesses no saving efficacy in its own right *and* to activity that "responds" to a generous — but not "gracious" — offer of salvation by fulfilling easy contractual conditions and thereby grasping salvation. (It can also refer to supernumerary activity that "responds" to the establishment of a covenant by undertaking additional, nonessential actions within the covenant, even if the covenant retains a conditional dimension.)[15]

In view of all this, a temporary moratorium ought to be pronounced on any talk in the following of the divine "benevolence," "mercy," or "graciousness" in relation to conditional soteriological arrangements, and on any references to a countervailing human or Jewish "response" within the same contractual framework. This restraint will greatly clarify our further deliberations. These descriptors should be reserved — at this point purely in the interests of conceptual clarity — for *unconditional* soteriologies (that is, unless they are explicitly qualified).

With these clarifications in place, we turn now to some important notions Sanders rejected that — suitably qualified — need to be reintroduced into the debate: notions of "earning," "obligation," "desert," "merit," and "self-interest," together with analogies drawn from commerce and money.

Sanders, as we have already seen, launched his main attack against "legalism." It is not always easy to see just what within this construction he objects to as so deeply unfair, apart from its ostensibly negative motivations (and these are worthy of objection!). But at least in part it seems to be the elements within it that cast salvation in essentially monetary terms — "earning" it and the like. Sanders also dislikes its linkage with notions of self-interest. But significant ambiguities surround some of these notions, which should now be clarified.

I suspect that Sanders reacts negatively to pecuniary characterizations of Jews and Judaism often associated with legalism because of the long association within European history of Jews with negative mercantile stereotypes — that Jews were shylocks, given to extortionate usurious practices, and so on.[16] Of course, these stereotypes derived in large measure from the hypocritical construction of a Christian society that condemned "usury" (i.e., the charging of interest, and especially in the post-Cluniac period) but nevertheless needed a reliable banking system and so in effect pressed Jews into this service. Jews were conveniently forbidden from owning land and undertaking various other occupations and so needed such "unethical" employment.

But there is in fact no *necessary* association with such stereotypes. A metaphor of "earning" with respect to salvation need not be inherently exploitative and negative because of the prior European history of Jewish-Christian relations — although that association should be borne constantly in mind. In the modern period the association might linger, but the powerful social conditions for it have long since dissolved (although regrettably, perhaps not completely). Hence, soteriological statements in terms of "earning" may denote little more than an element of conditionality and so be inherently inoffensive. It is common to characterize ethical systems and soteriologies at some point with metaphors drawn from currency, as we have already seen in relation to Anselm, and these basically denote little more than notions of human agency, degree, or self-interest. Anselm's justification of the atonement is not generally viewed as inherently vulgar and flawed because of its mercantile metaphors (although they do in my view prove ultimately problematic in theological terms).

Moreover, closely related metaphors of "obligation" are largely unavoidable and relatively inoffensive. If the fulfillment of conditions is fundamental to salvation, and if this presumably depends on the individuals involved (doubtless at times with suitable communal support), then a metaphor of obligation in terms of currency seems appropriate to describe that situation. Fulfillment of the conditions within a stipulated contract places God in turn under an obligation to fulfill the divine part of the compact. God "owes" salvation to the individuals involved, who can also be said to have "earned" it by undertaking the specified actions. (And clearly this metaphor applies to actions of negative reward as well; the wicked have "earned" their punishment!) But this is *not* to suggest that such a person has placed God under an obligation in the first instance. God freely created this obligation by initiating a contract with humanity that stipulates certain conditions — the covenantal moment — and further, as Sanders rightly emphasizes, *that* moment was unconditional and collective.

This cluster of metaphors should be carefully distinguished from the notion of deserving the owed salvation on the basis of merit alone. All that is meant in the more inoffensive conception is that the individuals have fulfilled the terms of a contract and therefore ought to be paid the reward that the contract stipulates

— language that is ubiquitous in relation to contracts. It is a separate question whether the individuals "deserve," or "merit," the reward *fully* (that is, whether they have earned the contract's reward *through actions of equivalent value* so that to withhold it would be unjust).[17] There is no need to link the contractual language of "desert" or "merit" with the latter, stronger claim.

It should be clear by now that an element of self-interest is unavoidable within any characterization of Judaism — or, for that matter, Christianity — that is conditional and hence contractual in structure. But this is nothing to be ashamed of, at least in the first instance.[18] Contracts presuppose a degree of individual agency and rational prospective action: if certain actions are undertaken, then certain benefits are realized; if the actions are not undertaken, then the benefits are not realized. Those benefits are almost invariably *personally* beneficial, hence self-interested motivations are usually involved with such systems.[19] Consequently, *both* legalism *and* covenantal nomism, as soteriological contracts, seem to contain self-interested dimensions, *and legitimately and unavoidably so.*[20] Self-interest cannot be criticized within these basic soteriological arrangements without engaging in acute self-contradiction.[21] In short, talk of "earning," "obligation," "desert," "merit," and "self-interest" is an inoffensive and appropriate way of representing certain aspects of a conditional arrangement. The extreme and intrinsically negative deployment of such terminology is not appropriate, but such usage is itself not inevitably the case.

What then are the implications of these clarifications and reintroductions for Sanders's broader critique of Jewish description in terms of "legalism"?

It is now apparent that not a great deal actually separates Sanders's covenantal nomism from legalism *in strictly theoretical terms* — a claim that requires a little more elaboration. The motivational and emotional correlates of these two systems will be considered in more detail shortly; for now we are interested only in the way the soteriologies function qua soteriologies. But both systems are conditional and hence contractual characterizations of salvation, so much now depends on the terms within the respective contracts. And a, if not the, primary axis of disagreement within the debate concerning the contracts, now seems to concern a temporal distinction that turns out on closer analysis to be rather inoffensive.

Covenantal nomism emphasizes the initial giving of the contract, at Sinai — that is, in the past — at which point the possibility of salvation is firmly established.[22] And this seems to be a moment of divine, if contractually limited generosity. Legalism then emphasizes the evaluation of individual performance in relation to the terms of the contract, which must take place, if not during the actual life of the individual concerned, on the day of judgment — that is, in the present and the future.[23] But neither arrangement can function at all without fully functioning past, present, and future moments. The contract must at some point be given (and this is unconditional, for a divine-human arrangement), must at some present point be fulfilled (which is conditional), and must at some future point be evaluated.[24] So both covenantal nomism and legalism necessarily contain past, present, and future dimensions. Any quarrels at this point then seem to be largely a matter of emphasis, something presumably related in turn to any rhetorical concerns in the relevant texts (i.e., to localized, persuasive goals), and hence arguably not overly important! That is, texts will emphasize one or another of these temporal and theoretical aspects as their authors deem it appropriate for the constituencies that they are addressing, and not because of fundamental theoretical and theological differences.

The respective presumptions of the rigor of the two systems are also far from obvious — namely, that covenantal nomism is clearly more reasonable and benevolent than legalism. This all depends on the contractual conditions, *and these seem remarkably similar.* The conditions for remaining in the covenant for Sanders are law observance and the utilization, when necessary, of the means of atonement. But presumably, most "legalistic" characterizations of Judaism are roughly the same — after all, both systems are based on the same books! In historical terms, the means of atonement change dramatically after the destruction of the temple, but this unfortunate eventuality holds in equal measure for both systems. And they seem to have varied in any case. Hence, it is not at all obvious that Sanders's system of covenantal nomism is more reasonable than legalism, although it does not follow that covenantal nomism is therefore unreasonable; legalism might now simply be reasonable as well (but it is important to consider the issue discussed in the following subsection before pronouncing on this question definitively).

In short, it seems that the essential theoretical differences between covenantal nomism and legalism have effectively collapsed. Both these designations are really just different characterizations of the same basic saving arrangement — a contractual one. And certain further important implications now seem to flow from this strange convergence between earlier poles in the debate.

In the first instance we should note that a far more radical distinction seems to have been greatly neglected by much previous discussion — between conditional and unconditional soteriologies. Qumran represents the most fundamental challenge to the general soteriological description developed by Sanders, because it arguably breaks with the conditional approach to salvation entirely (although it should be appreciated that a move to unconditionality per se by no means solves all our difficulties; unconditional soteriologies can be as oppressive and abhorrent as conditional systems, if not more so).

In the second instance, we should note that many of Sanders's critics seem to operate in the space created by this unrecognized interpretative convergence, ostensibly recovering elements of legalism from at least some of the Jewish sources against his characterization of Judaism in terms of covenantal nomism. And so it might seem, at first blush, that these recoveries are a positive development for advocates of Justification theory, prompting the abandonment of Sanders's entire line of thinking. Judaism was legalistic after all, such critics suggest. Sanders was wrong, and we can put the clock back to pre-1977. However, I will suggest in due course that nothing is actually farther from the truth. But in order to grasp this point, we must press harder on another aspect of Sanders's critique and see where that leads us — the task of the next subsection. If covenantal nomism and legalism are essentially the same *theoretical* description, where does Sanders's critique of previous characterizations of Jewish description in Paul come from? Is it chimerical? Or, does it actually focus on something valid?

§4. Distinguishing between Theory and Psychology

When we return to consider Sanders's critique of "legalism" in the light of the previous clarification (along with those of the scholars who follow him in this general respect), it seems that a great deal of its success derives from the moral outrage he directs at the entire system's usual *psychological* characterizations. Sanders presents this situation in a fairly straightforward way (as we have already seen in part). On the one hand, the characterization of Judaism in terms of "legalism" is said to involve a petty, mercantile, detached, uncertain, and hypocritical cluster of motivations (et cetera). On the other hand, characterization in terms of "covenantal nomism" involves noble, accepting, and responsive motivations (et cetera). Sanders comprehensively rejects the descriptive accuracy of the former account as "unfair." But we must ask first how Sanders reached these judgments. And this question seems to require a more complex answer than first meets the eye.

In part Sanders seems simply to have followed the previous contours of the debate that attributed negative motivations to "legalistic" Judaism automatically *merely because it consisted of Jews.* And he goes on to reject these anti-Jewish characterizations, which were basically rooted in anti-Semitic stereotypes — for example, "usurious" Jews who "earned" their way to salvation *in a mercantile and calculatingly heartless fashion.* And there were an embarrassingly large number of such caricatures present within the previous debate, portrayals that he was able to dismiss immediately on grounds of overt and rather unreflective prejudice. (In addition, it is worth noting that many characterizations of "the Jew" in Paul in such terms were deliberate anachronisms, aimed ultimately more at nineteenth- and early-twentieth-century bourgeois European Christianity than at Jews per se — at "religious man," as in the work of (i.a.) Barth and Käsemann[25] — and this where they did not simply spring from covert anti-Catholic animus that had its roots in the polemics of the sixteenth century. However, as such, the basic rationale underlying them remained prejudicial.) Furthermore, such rejections were doubtless assisted by the great hermeneutical inversions associated with much liberational work in the seventies, which have been such a feature of the work of the humanities since then (and as was earlier noted). Hermeneutics of suspicion directed against marginalized groups were inverted into hermeneutics of generosity, and in the case of the Jews this was doubtless reinforced by post-Holocaust sympathies and reflections. It is now clearer than ever that it is utterly wrong to calumniate Jews in negative terms as "other" merely out of hand. Such negative stereotypes must be abandoned.

However, Sanders was doubtless reacting here as well to the pious tone of the Jewish sources (which may not be a completely reliable guide concerning Jewish motives but do presumably offer *some* indications). The sources just seemed to be free of the anxiety and/or calculations that ought to have characterized them. Sanders may in addition have been responding to the basic tenor of the soteriological contract underlying Judaism as he saw it. Covenantal nomism was apparently not a fearsome and oppressive contract like phase one in Justification, but quite the converse — an apparently reasonable arrangement — so there was no need to endorse accompanying emotional configurations that were negative, whether those were self-deceptive or agonized. Such motivations simply seemed inappropriate, if not a little neurotic (as Stendahl had also earlier averred).

The much-quoted James D. G. Dunn is an excellent example of this dynamic. In his seminal essay, he characterizes the old view of Judaism as "coldly and calculatingly legalistic . . . where salvation is *earned* by the *merit* of good works."[26] Later, he suggests (continuing to describe the old view) "the Judaism of Paul's time, was a *degenerate religion* . . . precisely because it was legalistic, dependent on human effort, and self-satisfied with the results. And the Pharisees were the worst of all — narrow-minded, legalistic bigots."[27]

It is easy to understand then why Sanders, Dunn, and those like them rejected this prevailing description of Judaism; apparently it equated a "legalistic" theoretical posture *with an essentially negative psychological state* — usually "hypocritical," "cold," selfish, and calculating (if not "degenerate"!) — the very antithesis of "pious." And this description seems to have rested on an underlying prejudicial equation between legalism as a system and the Jews as a religious group. Of course, this description seemed "unfair," and in many respects — especially when it was viewed with generous, not suspicious eyes. But some problems are now perceptible within this rejection.

We should note first that Sanders has on one level actually accepted the stereotypical analysis of Jewish soteriology in terms of legalism *and* an unvarying emotional accompaniment in unattractive and negative terms. And in so doing he has accepted a marriage more broadly between the theoretical and psychological levels within the basic task of historical description — here of late Second Temple Judaism. And this is problematic. But what happens if we scrutinize, expose, and reject this unholy methodological alliance?

The theoretical dimension refers to the actual principles and mechanisms being employed in *rational* terms — here to the saving contract as specified by God, to the appropriate fulfillment of its conditions by human actions, to the necessary rational sequences, and so on. Such notions tend to be embodied in the linguistic claims of texts and arguments. But the psychological dimension refers to the inner dispositions and motivations of the individuals and groups involved — factors that exert some ill-defined force over actions undertaken in fulfillment of theoretical directives. So we encounter here an essentially *causal* dimension (and one that is notoriously difficult to read out of texts, or chart in relation to them).

It is not uncommon for scholars to combine these two dimensions within one overarching explanation, but it is wiser to resist any such association *because their modes of operation are qualitatively distinct* and *they are not ultimately reducible to one another*. Indeed, these dimensions can operate at cross-purposes. A causal, psychological explanation of a theory actually denies that theory's efficacy *as* a theory; this is a supremely irrational explanation (although its broader framework is rational). The conclusions of a theory derive, it suggests, not from the progression of the theory itself — not from its own inherent rationality — but from the prior operation of psychological motives within the theory's propounder (to note but one point of possible psychological causality).[28] Conversely, a theoretical account can deny that any psychological motives currently operative are fundamentally significant. Actions are undertaken because of principles, mechanisms, and reasons, which are basically rational and cognitive; psychological disposition is largely irrelevant. Hence, it is not uncommon to encounter stringent protests against each of these modes of explanation from its counterpart where the two are not simply (and — necessarily — somewhat awkwardly) combined. Those who emphasize rational explanation and argument find the emotional reductionism of the psychologizers offensive, not to mention invalid ("poisoning the well") — and may be assisted here in New Testament circles by those who find the text to be largely self-sufficient. Those who find psychological, not to mention sociological, explanations profitable, however, find this resistance to such explanations puzzling and ahistorical (and so on).

We will take up a clear stance on this question in due course, discussing it in detail in part two, chapter seven. It will suffice for now to state that the rational and argumentative claims of Paul's texts must be placed centrally — and certainly so in the first instance — because the theory found there is so important. Theoretical claims must initially be treated seriously *as* components of any broader explanation. But we by no means exclude the possible causal analysis of theoretical texts. (Ultimately, we will treat such issues in terms of a framing requirement: a circumstantial framing explanation is still accorded value even when a rational explanation of a text is accorded full efficacy, although at first only *as* a framing explanation — that is, as an explanation of the text's genesis that can assist its reading.) And in due course we will consider even larger roles for such causal explanations, especially if the theory in question is held to collapse. However, at that later point — to anticipate the argument a little here — the fragility of such claims will also be evident, and especially when they are made in strong terms. Psychological claims that are strongly reductionist encounter a number of problems that in my view they have not yet fully resolved. We should not dissolve texts into the putative motives that produced them without strong grounds for doing so. And it follows from this that Sanders's claims about textual arguments and theories *must be carefully distinguished from his psychological claims*, except where those overlap explicitly. This important methodological principle can be illustrated by the following hypothetical example.

A group of Jewish legalists observes the Sabbath. One member of the group does so with an attitude of consistent joy, responding to God's generous gift of a saving contract in the law; one with indifference, as a matter on this particular day of religious routine; the third with an attitude of constant resentment and frustration. A fourth then does so expecting that it will in due course help him or her to be saved, while a fifth does so experiencing all four of these attitudes at different points during the day!

Now it would be difficult if not impossible to know just what was going on here in motivational terms, if only texts from the lives of these five figures were preserved (especially the authoritative texts that they were reading). If they all read and wrote conditional texts, we would nevertheless have learned next to nothing about the psychological and emotional states that accompanied their observance. Conversely, if we did fortuitously possess detailed information — presumably from interviews and participant observation — about their motivations (and this was all), this knowledge would tell us next to nothing about which soteriology was in play. All five of these Sabbath observers might be legalists *or* covenantal nomists, and the first three could be something else altogether! Perhaps Essenes are present, and everything is attributed in theoretical terms to the Spirit of Light, unconditionally! It follows from this realization that legalism *could* be reasonably positive in psychological terms — "the happy legalist" — and covenantal nomism *could* be negative — "the insecure" or "proud covenantal nomist." Or the legalist could be negative and the covenantal nomist positive. Or both theories could have mixed psychological correlates, and so on. *There are few fixed correlations between theory and emotion in Jewish description,* because such states do not need to correlate, and usually do not in fact. Texts are not reducible to the psychological states that produced them or read them. Moreover, motivational analyses are highly problematic in methodological terms, and arguably also related in quite complex ways to theoretical questions. *Motivational and theoretical or theological descriptions are distinguishable, and sometimes entirely detachable from one another.*

But if we detect the fragility of the methodological marriage between theory and psychology that is operative within Sanders and many of his critics, where does that leave both the broader debate, and Sanders's case in particular?

We can note in the first instance that the failure to draw this distinction explains a few of the vulnerabilities in Sanders's own position that have been detected and exploited by some of his critics, but also why the debate itself has not actually ended up where those critics think it ought to have.

It seems that Sanders really accepts the dangerous equation already present in much of the discussion between theory and psychology, and argues accordingly, thereby generating and pursuing an extremely bold strategy, but also a vulnerable one. Over against the fixed correlation between legalism and a negative psychological state he argues that the Jewish sources consistently reveal — and we will return to the issue of consistency momentarily in §5 below — a different equation as a whole, between covenantal nomism and a positive psychology. So, in order to refute a ghastly legalism, he undertakes a redescription of the entirety of late Second Temple Jewish piety! In effect, he argues for the validity of a second fundamental Jewish equation:

NOT legalism & negative psychological states everywhere
(self-interested, hypocritical, despairing, et cetera)

BUT covenantal nomism & positive psychological states everywhere
(noble, accepting, responsive, et cetera)

Now clearly Sanders has adopted a high-risk strategy here — an exhaustive redescription of late Second Temple Judaism, apparently in both theoretical and psychological terms. And in such terms he is open to descriptive attack. Reality seldom conforms to such neat equations. Hence, Philip Alexander (among others) suggests that "legalism" should actually be reconstrued in essentially positive terms. He argues — with some cause — that the attribution of negative psychological states to legalism depends more on accompanying Christian axioms than on Jewish sources and their intrinsic rationales, so the recognition of this dubious justification leads to a different description of Judaism — although in terms really of "the happy legalist." (So he switches theories without shifting motivations.) Conversely, Dunn suggests that "covenantal nomism" should be reconstrued in more negative terms, as somehow arrogant and boastful (at least in relation to some of its practices). (So he switches motivations, without switching theories.) Consequently the debate's initial set of two equations is thereby expanded immediately to four with the addition of the following two alternative constructs:[29]

Alexander et al.: legalism & positive psychological states
in most rabbinic sources
(i.e., reasonable, not especially sinful, et cetera)

Dunn: covenantal nomism & negative psychological states everywhere
(i.e., hoarding, privileged, boastful, et cetera)

Theory in play:	Covenantal	Legalistic
Motivations in play:		
Positive and noble (etc.)	Attractive covenantal nomism (Sanders)	Attractive legalism (Alexander)
Selfish and boastful (etc.)	Unattractive covenantal nomism (Dunn)	Unattractive legalism (the majority)

But several difficulties are now evident in the debate from this point.

First, we should note the frequent suggestion that Sanders's entire position has been falsified when it stumbles at just one of these points, and so ostensibly all disputants should now return to the standard legalistic description of Judaism familiar to Pauline interpreters for centuries. Essentially, if Sanders's uniform description of late Second Temple Judaism in terms of covenantal nomism is falsified at one point, his case supposedly collapses. (Part of Judaism might be exposed as legalistic, or legalism might be equated with a positive psychology, or covenantal nomism might be linked with a negative psychology, and so on.)

Now I concede that Sanders has chosen to argue in comprehensive terms, and so a falsification of his supposed portrait at one point does cause his positive descriptive task difficulties; his claim that Judaism is everywhere characterized by a noble covenantal nomism could well prove exaggerated. However, it does not follow from the falsification of his positive description, that his complaint concerning the previous, negative description of Judaism is also wrong. That is, any refutation of Sanders's positive case does not *automatically* rehabilitate the negative description that he protested against. This is simply a false inference (although it is psychologically plausible). If an American politician proposes a stunning reform of the tax system, her positive proposals might have loopholes or even be deeply flawed, but it does not follow from these that the existing system is perfect! And the relevance of this false inference is only enhanced when the more complex underlying situation is brought into view.

If the equation between theory and psychology is wrong, then Sanders's critics encounter just as many problems in this relation as he does, if not more. If his counter-proposal is based on this false equation, then any supposed falsification of that proposal that presupposes this equation as well is equally flawed. Indeed, his critics may well have been relying on this equation *for* their falsifications. If such equations hold good then any holes punctured in the equation of covenantal nomism and a positive psychological posture at a single point suggest defaulting back to the other comprehensive equation on the table — legalism and negativity. The debate remains in an "either-or" situation. However, we have already seen that these equations are oversimplified and various possible theoretical and psychological characterizations exist. And, while this suggests a nuancing of Sanders's position, it greatly complicates the task facing his critics. Sanders's falsification will now clearly *not* entail any corresponding endorsement of a negative legalism. Indeed, when the theoretical distinction between legalism and covenantal nomism is collapsed, as it ought to be, the entire descriptive situation is subtly reconfigured. We seem to have generated a pluralized motivational and psychological situation, orbiting around a widely assumed theoretical stance (although I am not conceding its universal accuracy, for reasons to be noted shortly).

So, where does this leave Sanders's critique, especially in relation to our overarching questions here? Although it is not completely intact in its own terms, once the relevant clarifications have been made it seems to me that Justification remains deeply problematized by the interpretative trajectory associated with Sanders, and on a number of counts.

We should recall at this point that Justification needs a strikingly negative experience in phase one of its saving progression, where Judaism is located, in order to justify Christ's provision of a solution to that problem *and* to propel that phase's occupants through to an appropriation of that solution. But the hard-nosed description of Judaism unfolding in relation to Sanders's contentions seems to suggest that few if any fixed correlations exist between Judaism as a theoretical system and any such negative psychological state. One or two possibilities exist at this point but, as we will see momentarily, these quickly prove inadequate. Hence, the post-Sanders debate seems to have radically undermined the cogency of Justification's first phase in descriptive terms. But not only has the fundamental constitution of Judaism in Justification theory been challenged: Sanders's basic complaint must also be conceded that a negative disposition cannot simply be attributed without evidence to a Jewish situation *because it is Jewish*. This essentially prejudicial action is no longer acceptable. Overt evidence must be supplied for any such claims — evidence that we have just noted is difficult to locate because it concerns psychological states. To make matters worse, Sanders and his supporters have made a detailed case that *positive* motivations and dispositions are frequently discernible in late Second Temple Judaism, even if only at points (although Sanders himself would not concede this last qualification). Such happy Jews would presumably have no need to grasp the Christian offer of salvation, since they feel no threat or disquiet in phase one. Hence, they explicitly falsify the claims of Justification theory in empirical terms.

Potentially, however, *some* carefully defined equations do provide a marriage between theory and motivation, so we must turn to consider if they can rescue Justification theory. Unfortunately, however, only two states have such a fixed correlation. And one is insufficient (as we have in fact already seen), while it is highly unlikely that the other one even exists.

We should recall briefly in the first instance that contractual theories appeal to self-interest, at least in part, and hence to that motivational state (one of the realizations of §3 above). However, self-interest alone will not drive a generic Jew to Christ. Self-interest needs some reason in order to function (and both legalistic and covenantal nomist Judaism provide reasons for remaining Jewish). Neither is it necessarily and inherently negative. A multitude of human actions involve self-interest and it is difficult to accuse all of them of ethical inadequacy. Moreover, self-interest seems able to co-exist with other motivational and psychological states. So this particular equation between a theory and psychology seems both too innocuous and ubiquitous to rescue Justification theory. More important is the potential equation between a "perfectionist" contract and the probable resulting psychological state of the individual — a question we must consider carefully.

We are concerned with a very specific question at this point within our broader inquiry — *whether a perfectionist soteriology is present within late Second Temple Judaism*. But it needs to be recalled just why our descriptive agenda has now become so specific.

It is a particular account of Judaism that functions within the theory's first and critical phase of salvation. Justification theory holds this description to be written into the fabric of the universe; it corresponds precisely to the revelation of the divine that takes place through nature. It follows from the specific axioms that are revealed there, and it then grounds the all-important argumentative progressions that flow from them and lead to the second, Christian offer of salvation that follows. Consequently, it creates the correct context for the gospel's proclamation. We might say, then, that Judaism as conceived by Justification leads to Christianity. And Judaism needs to work in just this fashion for the entire theory to unfold properly. If even one of its axioms is relaxed, *then Justification theory no longer actually works!* Hence, the description must be true, and in this particular sense. Moreover, we already know what this particularity consists of in some detail.

Justification expects that Judaism will be:

(1) fundamentally rational (if not rationalistic) and evidencing a "system" or "pattern," which will be largely uniform through both time and space;[30]
(2) fundamentally self-interested, focused ultimately on salvation;
(3) strictly just in retributive terms and hence conditional, with no obvious means of restoration once a transgression has been committed;
(4) closely linked to the law and law observance, so that the law necessarily functions (at least for some of the time) in terms of self-interest and soteriologically; and
(5) perfectionist, requiring 100 percent observance and not merely "adequacy" or "preponderance" in the sense of a greater number of good deeds than bad.

We return in this last claim to an absolutely critical element within our unfolding argument that needs to be fully appreciated.

It is difficult if not impossible for Justification theory to work properly if God does not require ethical perfection from those living within its first phase — from all non-Christians. As we know well by now, phase one is not supposed to be self-sufficient but intends to propel its occupants toward Christianity, holding them fully accountable if they resist this pressure. It ought to do this, furthermore, "without exception"; otherwise, the theory would be forced to admit the existence of two quite different routes to salvation, one of them bearing no relation to Christ.[31] *A situation of universal accountability can be guaranteed only through an insistence on ethical perfection in relation to the initial offer of salvation within phase one.* And "all" will almost certainly fail to fulfill this criterion, since "no one" is perfect. Consequently, there will ultimately be only one effective route to salvation, and it will be through Christ.

Many interpreters fail to grasp the theoretical necessity of this principle, however. And the severity of the initial situation — which seems deeply unattractive in certain respects — can be mitigated in a number of ways. God can be viewed as more benevolent and merciful, perhaps simply forgiving individuals a certain number of their sins (seven times, or seventy times seven?). God might alternatively — or additionally — provide various means of atonement, stipulating that the performance of certain especially meritorious or admirable acts leads to the "cancellation" of any previous sins and the effective restoration of ethical perfection. So, for example, perfection might be restored through contrition, repentance, material restitution, the offering of particular sacrifices, almsgiving, suffering, some form of cleansing, or some combination of the foregoing. And the Jewish Bible, not to mention Jewish tradition, does seem to articulate many of these practices — often at length![32]

However, from the point of view of Justification theory, such initial concessions on the part of God are rather unwise. Occupants could then legitimately circle within phase one indefinitely, so long as they performed the appropriate acts of cancellation. Hence, the very reasonableness of the arrangement is in fact its downfall. Individuals are, at bottom, no longer fearful and desperate; indeed, they may be the converse, quietly self-confident and so no longer motivated to be saved by some alternative system. Thus, mitigating the severity of the situation within phase one of Justification theory in order to deal with the empirical difficulty *undermines its actual function as a vestibule within that theory.* A reasonable vestibule is no longer actually a vestibule at all; it is itself now a main building within which people may comfortably live. We have embraced — perhaps without realizing it — a different soteriology altogether (and in fact a reasonable one!).

An alternative theoretical recourse at this point would be to assert such thoroughgoing corruption and sinfulness on the part of humanity that not even a reasonable arrangement could be fulfilled. Corrupt humanity fails even an easy contractualism without exception, it might be claimed (perhaps quoting Rom. 3:10-20 in support). However, we have already noted at some length that this adjustment runs a number of ultimately unacceptable risks — acute problems of epistemological incoherence and theodicy, to mention but two (see chapter two)[33] — and so in actuality it looks untenable.

In short, the "reasonable" account of phase one of Justification leads to the breakdown of that theory. People never move on to phase two! Only perfectionism results in the correct universal pressure being applied within the theory's opening progressions. Hence, in order for a correlation to hold good between the precise and largely rigid expectations of Justification theory and the empirical reality of Judaism in Paul's day, an independent investigation of late Second Temple Judaism would have to find there the basic description that has just been laid out — an expectation of perfect law observance, and so on.

Of course, it does not take a specialist in Judaism to realize immediately that this description cannot be found within Judaism in such terms. *The particular definition of Judaism prescribed by Justification theory is simply not found in the extant Jewish sources.*[34] Indeed, hardly a jot or tittle in the entire Old Testament, the Dead Sea Scrolls, the Apocrypha and Pseudepigrapha, other Jewish corpora such as the writings of Philo and Josephus, or the extant rabbinic writings arguably supplies explicit evidence for this particular soteriology.[35] So, put bluntly, *that this account of Judaism is absent from the Jewish sources roughly contemporary to Paul is self-evident.*[36] And although there is a shockingly summary aspect to this judgment, this should not really be surprising.

The account of Judaism in Justification theory is clearly a theological construct derived, on the one hand, from certain basic theological and philosophical axioms — a rational, self-interested individual, a retributive God, and so on — and, on the other hand, from certain Christian expectations that are tightly correlated with those axioms — salvation through faith alone, the atoning role of Christ, and so on.[37] It is consequently not at all surprising that this highly deductive and theoretical construct does not map onto the historical realities of Judaism very well. The surprising thing is that it was ever thought to, but this is testimony to the astonishing hermeneutical power of Justification theory, and perhaps also to a pervasive Christian ignorance of Judaism.[38]

In sum, it seems doubtful that a harsh perfectionism of the sort prescribed by Justification can be found in the Jewish sources at all. And the theory now faces a descriptive crisis in this regard. The challenge posed by Judaism at its empirical frame is therefore a serious one. It is, moreover, one of the great merits of the post-Sanders debate to have exposed this feature of the interpretative discussion vis-à-vis Paul. The progress that we have made in relation to Sanders's original proposals, including their later, more rigorous reformulations, has exposed that much of the debate — at least in relation to our present concerns — has been misdirected. Legalism per se is not the key question (which as a theory, is essentially indistinguishably from covenantal nomism). Justification needs so much more than this in order to function; it needs a characterization of Judaism in terms of legalistic perfection that thereby marries theory with an intensely negative — and hence propulsive — psychology. And — not surprisingly — this is just what neither Sanders nor his critics (generally!) find in the sources. Even Sanders's harshest critics have succeeded only in demonstrating the possible presence of a conditional mentality among many Jews in the late Second Temple period, and this is neither to establish a perfectionist theory of salvation *nor* to link any theory with a deeply negative psychological state. The Jew, as articulated by Justification theory, is a phantom, although the theory claims that that Jew characterizes all of pre-Christian humanity — a problem, to be sure.

But things are about to get worse for Justification's advocates as we turn to address a further set of issues in his critique — its basic descriptive parameters in monolithic, soteriological, and contractual terms.

§5. Qualifying the Descriptive Paradigm

Like much of his opposition, Sanders describes Judaism monolithically and soteriologically — although in suitably nuanced terms.[39] We have already seen that he detects a "pattern of religion" within the relevant sources; indeed, he is critical of those who track mere "motifs."[40] The particular pattern that he detects — covenantal nomism — is, moreover, although carefully qualified, overtly soteriological. In Sanders this approach seems in part an a priori claim about religions and their description generally and so is almost certainly — at least in part — a legacy from the liberal Protestant origins of much religious studies methodology. Schleiermacher argued that Christianity was reducible to a basic soteriological "essence," a claim that the discipline of religious studies has often since pressed.[41] This claim, however, is possibly now a little fragile.[42] Thus, in and of itself, Sanders's claim that Judaism was necessarily characterized uniformly — if only at bottom — by the soteriological pattern of covenantal nomism, looks vulnerable.[43] These assertions court a charge of anachronism. *Nevertheless, these are precisely the claims to which Justification theory is also committed.*

By virtue of its own theoretical commitments and claims, Justification theory must find a saving pattern *uniformly* throughout Judaism. Without the presence of this prior structure, Justification cannot develop as a Christian theological program at all. There would be significant exceptions to it in time and space. Hence, Justification theory expects a monolithic and soteriological characterization of Judaism, just as Sanders and most of his opponents do. Of course the vulnerability of this claim is now readily apparent, and Sanders's classic account serves to emphasize this dimension within our debate. His work highlights clearly that advocates of Justification must give a monolithic *and* soteriological account of late Second Temple Judaism if their theory is to prove sustainable — further descriptive demands that it will almost certainly fail to meet.

Further, Sanders highlights a useful specification. As a corollary to his emphasis on patterns, Sanders argues firmly that talk of motifs alone will not suffice. This point holds again in relation to our current concern with Justification (although it would not hold more broadly). It follows directly from an acceptance of the importance of patterns that any claims made simply on the basis of motifs will be insufficient. Motifs by their very nature cannot establish the presence of an entire pattern of religion; they are inherently ambiguous. The same motifs can function in completely different ways if they are framed within different systems, rather as similarly colored tiles can be positioned within different mosaics to create completely different pictures. This is an important corrective, because advocates of Justification, who tend to be deeply immersed in their own system, often make paradigmatic assumptions. They tend to assume that the reintroduction of mere motifs from the Jewish sources that fit Justification's broader description of Judaism suffices to establish that *theory* as a description of Judaism, thereby begging this crucial question that Sanders nicely elucidates. Motifs, no matter how useful their initial appearance, do not establish patterns.

For example, consider the motif "perfection of way," which is found at Qumran.[44] This might at first glance look like a significant endorsement of the key principle within phase one of Justification theory — that all the law should be observed "perfectly" or "blamelessly." But while the principle is the same in limited terms, further investigation reveals that its function at Qumran is very different. There it is part of a self-consciously historical analysis of salvation (the rest of Israel is essentially apostate), and it is *not* tightly correlated with a conviction of sinfulness in the manner that Justification advocates expect. To be sure, the Qumran covenanters are aware of their sin, and in this awareness arguably share another axiom with Justification theory. But the two principles never function together in the argumentative relation that Justification dictates; it is not a persistent failure to do the law perfectly *that leads to* a persistent awareness of sin. Rather, *despite* an ongoing consciousness of sin, the Spirit of Light will assist the covenanters to fulfill the demands of the law perfectly (at which point the covenanters are closer to the ethical rationale of our alternative theory); indeed, they are arguably predestined to keep the law, while the possession, study, and observance of the law defeat the evil impulse that leads to sin.[45] Perfect law observance at Qumran is fully responsive, directly assisted, and overwhelmingly nomistic; hence, it serves neither the preparatory *nor* the temporary functions that it fulfills in Justification theory. Thus, any appeal to this motif in support of a pattern of perfectionist soteriology in Judaism fails.[46]

Confirming this suspicion that a different system is in place at Qumran is a different view of God, who is hymned for fundamentally compassionate qualities,[47] and while the salvation that issues from this benevolence of course justifies, it does not do so "through faith alone"! Even the notion of "the works of the law," mentioned once in the extant sources, seems positioned within a different set of concerns from those of Justification. These works are encouraged neither to save through perfect observance nor to convict of sin but apparently in relation to more cultic and ritual concerns.[48]

Despite a plethora of similar motifs, Qumran and Justification theory evidence quite different patterns of religion. Hence, the most that can be said is that Qumran could provide many of the basic conceptual elements necessary for the construction of a theory of Justification. But these would have to be sifted out from the surrounding extraneous and contradictory material and significantly recombined. (We would need the advent of a Teacher of Justification!) So motifs alone do not suffice to establish the pattern of religion that Justification theory needs to find in Judaism if it is to prove successful. Justification must find a uniform saving system in Judaism tending toward negative or self-deceptive emotions if it is to survive in theoretical terms, and this looks increasingly unlikely. Sanders challenges these expectations by arguing for an alternative uniform saving pattern — covenantal nomism. But once again the same conclusion can be established, and still more radically: the detection of *any* uniform and saving pattern within Judaism at the time looks increasingly unrealistic, at which point Justification itself looks increasingly unrealistic as well.

It is helpful to link hands at this point with the second broad trajectory of scholarship that we earlier noted, in §2, characterizes much of the post-Sanders situation — the trend more positively disposed toward his work. It seems that this trajectory has greatly deepened the empirical difficulty facing Justification theory (while we have already seen that the negative trajectory has encountered deepening difficulties of its own on a number of fronts). Fortunately, we do not have to settle all the descriptive issues in order for the broad conclusion to hold with still greater force that whatever late Second Temple Judaism was, it was *not* the perfectionist soteriology that Justification theory needs, whether deluded or despairing. Underlying this judgment is the strengthening perception that Judaism in the time of Paul was characterized incorrigibly by *diversity,* a point that presses on the need for soteriological uniformity especially powerfully.

First, we should note the now commonplace observation that Judaism varied significantly through time. Although overtly critical of Sanders in relation to Paul and Justification, Martin Hengel's famous study *Judaism and Hellenism* has actually contributed to this confirmation of the theory's difficulties.[49] As is well known, Hengel's work here overthrows any strong distinction between "Hebraic Judean Judaism" and "Hellenized Diaspora Judaism" and in so doing emphasizes the powerful Hellenistic developments within all forms of Judaism. But if the regional variations within Judaism were thereby somewhat muted, the sense of change within Judaism through time was greatly strengthened. Hellenistic Judaism was in some respects emphatically different from its biblical forebears. It was a different "pattern of religion."[50]

Second, we should note the extent to which regional variation was also significant in late Second Temple Judaism because of the Diaspora. John Barclay's well-known study of Diaspora Judaism illuminates indirectly the narrow "Judaeocentric" focus that much discussion of Judaism has maintained.[51] But the Diaspora during the time of Paul — which is so difficult to reconstruct either fully or precisely — represented the majority of Jews and comprised extensive regional and local variations. There was, moreover, no system of centralized control that could either impose or simply enhance uniformity; Judaism had no Gregorian papacy. The network of Jewish communities was — as now — unified largely by modes of persuasion (see 4QMMT!). Hence, to take the Diaspora fully into account is to increase dramatically late Second Temple Judaism's diversity. Indeed, from a strictly descriptive point of view, the Samaritans should be included in any such account. And this is even to embrace phenomena such as alternative temple sites and temples to Jerusalem!

Third, we should note the diversity within Judaism in terms of goal or purpose, and some of Jacob Neusner's studies contribute to this confirmation from a variety of angles. Neusner edited a collection of studies that was famously titled *Judaisms and Their Messiahs.*[52] From a strictly descriptive point of view this volume suggests, largely undeniably, that Judaism is best viewed as a coalition of different Judaisms, *many of which denied the name "Judaism" (or its appropriate equivalent) to one another!* In terms of self-definition, then, there were many Judaisms in existence at the time of Paul.[53]

For some varieties of Judaism we can perhaps detect that soteriological conceptions were fundamental; they are therefore best described in soteriological terms. This was an important axis of difference for them. However, for other groups soteriology may have been less significant than alternative commitments, or it may have coexisted with other theories in no obvious priority — or even perhaps in flexible and partly contingent prioritizations. For them multiple and shifting axes of difference were in play. For still other forms of Judaism — perhaps quite extensive — there may have been little or no such soteriological speculation, so it was not an overt or valued axis at all. Hence, Judaisms that were entirely unselfconscious in soteriological terms must be admitted — Judaisms best explained by different theoretical agendas, and for much of the time by completely *non*theoretical agendas.

Neusner points out at length that the rabbinic sources are not necessarily best understood as oriented by soteriology at all (although Neusner points out many things about the rabbinic sources, and it is not always easy to reduce these to a coherent underlying explanation). He suggests (at times) that their discussions are framed by a vision of an alternative, essentially symbolic universe taking shape on earth, informed by Torah.[54] This is not to exclude soteriological issues as completely foreign or illegitimate, *but it is to claim that rabbinic law observance is not necessarily best comprehended within a soteriological or an individually self-interested framework.* At least on occasion, and arguably, it has a completely different rationale and intention.[55]

Philip Alexander offers a similar challenge from a different perspective. Alexander notes the difficulty in reducing the rabbis' complex legal corpus to a single soteriological position.[56] It is certainly plausible to suggest such a project in relation to an individual, although even that is difficult in relation to Paul (surely an ominous fact). But to assume that the rabbis, along with the rest of Second Temple Judaism, can be so described seems naive. It is simply implausible that one "party" within Judaism, developing over several centuries and preserving the opinions of hundreds of members, could be so reduced.[57] Indeed, this point seems self-evident in the light of the bulk of modern history and sociology.

Moreover, it must simply be recalled that human behavior in elite and semi-elite groups like the rabbis and their forebears is not necessarily best comprehended in terms that are fundamentally rationalist and self-interested. Law observance may be motivated primarily by cultural and interpersonal factors such as status, upward mobility, religiopolitical aspirations, and/or tradition and ancestry (all of which can be rational motivations without being rationalistic).[58] And the histories of such groups are likely to be extremely complex — accounts of shifting coalitions, negotiations, agendas, and loyalties, none of which link up in a straightforward fashion with soteriology.

We should also note, fourth, that the character of different Judaisms' soteriologies — where it is granted that a soteriology is active — is by no means uniform. First, these soteriologies are significantly distinguished by their conceptions of future benefits — whether they are this-worldly, eschatological, or some combination of the two. Also significant is the conditional spectrum, which probably ranges from difficult to easier salvific contracts. Various Judaisms are clearly positioned at different points on this continuum. *But some are positioned on a qualitatively different, unconditional spectrum.* Philip Alexander suggests that the Dead Sea Scrolls evidence an unconditional soteriology; their pattern of religion is thereby qualitatively different from either legalism or covenantal nomism.[59] This breaks any monolithically conditional account of the soteriology of late Second Temple Judaism[60] and also offers us more radical soteriological alternatives when we come to the reinterpretation of Paul.

Indeed, we should simply note the basic naivety of attempting to reduce late Second Temple Judaism's complex and subtle variations to a uniform description. And it is important to realize, fifth, that such variations are further complicated by issues of social location. We can identify three significant aspects within this broader category. First, Judith Lieu's work consistently suggests that the very attempt to describe "Judaism" as an entity entirely distinct from and hence *definable* over against its surroundings is much more difficult than it seems at first sight, and this includes the definition of "Judaism" over against "Christianity"![61] Theories too easily presuppose rigid boundaries around groups; the tendency, then, is to envision neat partitions between different "religions." But many of these theoretical parameters possess no actual correlation with the complex interlaced networks of people that they seek to map. Borderline groups demonstrate these difficulties clearly. Should synergizing Jews or partial converts like "God-fearers" be included within the description of "Judaism," or excluded? Posed in relation to discrete boundaries between different groups of people, such questions have no easy answer. Indeed, the analysis of human society in terms of bounded entities and groups has long been superseded in the humanities by work in terms of "difference," a notion rooted in perception and applicable to multiple axes and continua that are not necessarily consistently related to one another in a mutual fashion. One cluster of people may be self-consciously differentiated from other clusters in terms of some axes, identified with some clusters but not others in terms of different axes, and internally differentiated in multiple ways with reference to still more continua! The whole question of identification has been enormously complicated by this methodological development, which is nevertheless welcome in its ability to map social phenomena more accurately.[62] Unfortunately, such an approach renders a great deal of the older descriptive work concerning late Second Temple Judaism out of date.

Lieu's work implies, second, that much ostensibly descriptive work on (and by!) these ancient religious groups really presupposes a covert theological agenda. If a particular normative set of criteria is presupposed in relation to the identity of a given group, then the relevant empirical data can be manipulated to reflect those criteria. But the resulting portrait is clearly not a fundamentally descriptive one; normativity is masquerading as impartial empiricism.[63] The Jewish texts written during the NT period certainly reflect these biases, but so does much modern historiography of the period. To "define" either Judaism or Christianity is usually to be involved in politics, polemics, and normative theological agendas, *not* description. Behind the clarity of these definitions, much more complex realities lurk. (Indeed, such polemical definitions are often precisely an attempt to affect and to shape those scandalously plastic realities.)

Third, we should be aware of issues of social stratification. The bulk of the evidence preserved in relation to Judaism in the time of Paul — which consequently tends to dominate any subsequent reconstruction — is elite evidence. It was produced by a small fraction of the population and reflects their interests and religiosity. (This is a standard problem for the analysis of ancient societies.) Thus, our descriptions are biased in terms of gender, status, and class. The majority of ancient Jews are known to us only through occasional graffiti and the views of their despisers, because even epigraphic, papyrological, and archaeological evidence of ancient Judaism tends to presuppose wealth. So, in terms of numbers, the Jews involved in the production and reception of the sources analyzed by Sanders's early work and most of his critics — the Old Testament, the rabbinic texts, the Dead Sea Scrolls, and the Apocrypha and Pseudepigrapha — would have been extremely small. The synagogue may have partly alleviated this problem, but assessing its impact in Paul's day is difficult. Hence, it is even arguable that a different, popular religiosity occasionally seeps through the cracks of the elite sources and the pages of the NT — a point where Sanders has once again made a contribution to debate, with his notion of "common Judaism."[64] The social biases in our evidence must significantly qualify any descriptive claims vis-à-vis late Second Temple Judaism. This was a highly stratified, variegated phenomenon, and we possess incomplete and highly slanted information about most of it. Moreover, there is no immediately apparent reason why the representations of the dominant minority should be preferred.

In sum, the picture of late Second Temple Judaism emerging from these studies is a nuanced one. It is above all diverse, and this diversity can be accurately mapped only in terms of various interrelated principles, axes, and continua. The soteriological variations are important, to be sure, but we must also take into account the variations through time and space, as well as those in terms of social location. Finally, we must keep in mind that the question concerning precisely how Judaism effected a degree of integration on such matters — to the extent that it did — is an important one, since this was not achieved bureaucratically (as we moderns perhaps tend to assume[65]).[66]

All this escalating descriptive caution is really just what we would expect. Any strictly empirical claim for uniformity in relation to an entity as differentiated in historical terms as late Second Temple Judaism is almost certain to be false. Conversely, a growing appreciation for differences with respect to region, nuance, outlook, definition, politics, notions of difference, gender, status, and class is what we would expect to emerge from its ongoing analysis. The increasingly complex picture of Judaism that is emerging from its continuing scholarly investigation is merely a sign of the methodological maturation of the discipline of its investigation. And all of this interpretative work produces *at this point* a massively strengthened empirical conundrum for Justification theory. Sensitive description reveals a diverse Jewish mosaic through time and space — where it is revealed at all[67] — instead of the highly rationalistic soteriological uniformity demanded by Justification. And this only increasingly exposes the impossibility of the definition of Judaism that Justification theory demands.

What are the main implications flowing then from the three recalibrations of Sanders's classic critique that have just been undertaken in §§3-5 — the clarification of potentially ambiguous terms such as "grace" and "response," and the reintroductions of the notions of self-interest and related commercial metaphors, suitably qualified; the differentiation between theoretical and psychological types of explanation; and the qualification of the requirement for a monolithic and soteriological description of Judaism? There are several.

Sanders can now be seen — in part — to occupy an earlier phase in the debate that saw a directly antithetical response to the status quo. His powerful countervailing reaction actually accepts many of the grounds of the prior discussion — the assumption that self-interested and mercantile metaphors are inherently negative, the marriage of theory and psychology within the description of Judaism, the specific equation of legalism and a negative emotional state, the requirement of a uniform soteriological description of Judaism, and so on. In view of this it is all the more remarkable that most of his judgments still remain pertinent once the acceptance of these implicit positions has been exposed as unnecessary. His description of Judaism in terms of covenantal nomism will doubtless be an enduring characterization of at least some of that constituency (and doubtless scholars will continue to debate whether it characterizes a greater or a lesser part of it as well). But it can also be seen that the grounds of the debate have shifted.

It seems at first blush that the rehabilitation of legalism to something almost indistinguishable from covenantal nomism is a positive development for advocates of Justification theory. However, nothing could be further from the truth. The reshaped legalism emerging increasingly from our analysis is a thoroughly reasonable construct that is ultimately as problematic for Justification theory as covenantal nomism is. It has been detached from its automatically negative emotional accompaniments. Hence, there is as little reason for a Jew to abandon legalism and the law as there is for a well-disposed covenantal nomist to do the same. Hence, the rehabilitation of "legalism" by way of criticizing limited aspects of Sanders's descriptive project does not ultimately assist his critics on the decisive question being treated by this study. What they need is the rehabilitation of perfectionist Judaism or its equivalent, and the debate as a whole is moving increasingly away from such an eventuality.

Moreover, it is increasingly clear that the mere criticism of Sanders and his positions piecemeal does not rescue Justification. To be sure, if Sanders succeeds, then Justification is in serious difficulties; if all Jews were covenantal nomists as he describes them, then Judaism cannot function as the negative vestibule to Christianity's alternative system of salvation through faith alone. But merely to correct or to trim Sanders's description is not necessarily to rescue Justification, as we have just seen. A mere refutation or reversal at this point will not suffice. That theory requires the rehabilitation of an extreme form of legalism, with both its theoretical and psychological dimensions left intact. And as we have nuanced Sanders's project in relation to a spectrum of notions, carefully prizing its theoretical and psychological dimensions apart, the possibility of achieving this account of Judaism has begun to look next to impossible. "Legalism" is no longer a problem, and so *the* problem, in this relation.

In sum, although most would now acknowledge the need to qualify Sanders's classic critique — even if only a little — invariably in the qualification itself the difficulties of Justification advocates are simply deepened. There has been no real blunting of the force of Sanders's critique over the years in this regard. Indeed, if anything, it has become more powerful (although the debate has arguably become increasingly misdirected as well). It ought to be concluded then overall that Justification is falsified at its empirical frame in specific relation to its claims about Judaism. While the terms in which Sanders made this criticism may have changed, the criticism itself has not; rather, in this particular relation the difficulties that Justification advocates face have significantly deepened. There seems no cogent way out of them.

§6. The Option of Denial

The acute difficulties of Justification theory at its empirical frame in relation to Judaism may prompt its advocates to try simply to abandon the point. Does it matter that the vast majority of Jews historically — if not all of them! — have *not* shared the definition of Judaism offered by Justification theory? Perhaps this is not as serious a problem as we first thought.

This possible rejoinder forces us to ask a further question: on what basis does Justification theory hold its definition of Judaism to be true? And this throws us back in turn onto the argumentative progression that we dealt with earlier. Justification theory holds that both general and special revelation speak essentially with one voice about the same God and the same soteriological system — salvation through perfect performance of works. And this then should be accompanied by a perception of deep internal sinfulness (although, strictly speaking, one transgression will do), if that perception is not obscured by a rather foolish self-confidence. (And any scriptural statements or Jewish historical privileges that do not conform to these principles will ultimately be overruled by them.) Hence, the validity of the definition of Judaism offered by Justification theory depends on the validity of this argument. But we have learned that the argument is riddled with difficulties (and we will revisit some of these problems later on, when some of Paul's ostensible exegetical claims about Judaism are examined in parts three through five). Indeed, the empirical deviation of most if not all of contemporary Judaism from the definition of Judaism supplied by Justification theory functions primarily to indicate these underlying problems. The opening phase of the model is deeply flawed; its distorted argumentation seems to have led it way off course. By implication, the *foundational* dimension within the theory is completely wrong.

Furthermore, this problem must contribute to the theory's ineffectiveness as an evangelistic rhetoric. All those Jews who do not share the theory's basic axioms or its derivative definition of Judaism will not feel constrained by its arguments. So when the theory imposes its particular definition on them, along with its supposedly inevitable consequences, such Jews will simply "walk away"; they will move to their own definition of Judaism, which will almost certainly avoid these conundrums. And this can happen at almost every stage of the argument.

The basal definition of God as retributively just might be rejected in favor of a definition in terms of benevolence and mercy; the contractual coordination between law observance and salvation might be loosened so that law observance is not directly salvific and thus self-interested; the presence of deep sinfulness might well be conceded but the Jewish means of atonement (or God's merciful qualities, or the merits of the patriarchs, and so on) be mobilized to deal with it; the law might in fact be retained, with all its "ceremonial" aspects, because nothing leads Jews to suppose that it ought to be abandoned; et cetera.[68]

This may seem to be a problem limited to interreligious dialogue, but the interpretation of the Old Testament is at stake here as well. A canonical crisis for Christians is implicit in these difficulties. Whenever pious Jews walk away from the argumentative progressions of Justification because the claims of the latter are incomprehensibly and/or laughably inaccurate, any interpreters of Jewish tradition, including interpreters of the Old Testament, may feel pressed to do so at such points as well. And this creates a further crisis of continuity. For such interpreters there is no obvious way now to progress to Christianity from its Old Testament antecedents in terms of Justification theory, even if they wish to do so! The model has broken down almost completely.

In view of these failures, Justification theory's only hope may be to deny the relevance of the empirical evidence concerning Judaism in a still more radical way. Its advocates must accuse those Jews who do not share the first phase of Justification theory of being wrong and hence dismiss much of this evidence as irrelevant. (That is, they are not "true Jews," or they are essentially "misguided" or even "stupid Jews," or some such, and presumably the same judgment would apply to those interpreters of the Old Testament who are also having difficulties.) So anti-Jewish and anticanonical tendencies become especially overt within Justification theory at this rather desperate point.

Admittedly, many construals of Christianity do argue for some deviation between God's purposes and Judaism after the coming of Christ, because they feel that they have to — and this is awkward enough. The historical people of God seem to reject their fulfillment while various other peoples external to this sacred history accept it (or, better, are accepted by it: see Rom. 9:30-33, discussed in part five, chapter nineteen). But Justification theory has gone beyond this assertion. While certainly endorsing the shift at the turn of the ages with its various emphases on definitive atonement in Christ, a new saving criterion of faith in the gospel, and a law-free ethic, it pushes this shocking redefinition back into the pre-Christian phase as well! According to Justification theory, it would seem that most Jews *never* grasped God's purposes, even under the old covenant.[69] That is, Justification theory is committed to defining Judaism aggressively, in defiance of any Jewish self-definition, *before* the coming of Christ, thereby effectively overruling Jewish self-understanding at all points through history. Similarly, it overrules any alternative construal of the Old Testament. So Justification theory is inherently supersessionist *and not just at the point of Christ;* it involves a *comprehensive* and *radical* supersessionism.

These are rather appalling claims — undertaken on supposedly objective grounds, with no reference to Christian premises. But that all Jews would objectively misunderstand their nature and their history seems fairly unlikely, and the same point holds for interpreters of the Old Testament. Hence, we are forced back to the preceding conundrum, namely, that the reasoning underlying the definition of Judaism by Justification seems only to have led the theory drastically astray. Indeed, it has emphatically been called into question, and to deny this point is to court still more absurd consequences.

In sum, the yawning gap between Justification theory's description of Judaism and the actual nature of surrounding Judaism (insofar as we can describe that) suggests that the theory's foundational arguments are corrupt. But this gap also entails the argumentative ineffectiveness of the theory in relation to those Jews who do not share its definitions, that is, most if not all of them. There seems to be no cogent way for the people of God within the Old Testament, accompanied by those Scriptures, to proceed intelligibly to the new Christian dispensation. In view of this, there is arguably also no way to proceed *interpretatively* from the Old Testament to the New. Moreover, one of the only ways the theory can deal with this problem is to assert — rather unreasonably — that Jews (or Old Testament interpreters) who deny Justification's perspectives are not true Jews (or true interpreters); they are comprehensively wrong about their own religion or subject matter. In essence, then, the theory seems to be collapsing under the weight of its extreme descriptive claims. Pushed by them to more and more absurd extrapolations, the theory itself is looking increasingly invalid.

Hence, we conclude at this point that *the prospective, monolithic, and perfectionist account of Judaism supplied by Justification theory is in acute tension with the self-depiction of Judaism contemporary to Paul, thereby calling the theory's cogency into question.* Very few if any Jewish sources in Paul's day reflect this demanding view of salvation. (And this is not really surprising, because it is not ultimately a salvific system in its own right; it is a reflex of Christian theological commitments and, furthermore, it is meant to fail.)

This judgment is in marked contrast to some of the broad claims within much recent post-Sanders discussion of the relationship between Judaism and Paul. However, it is important to grasp how focused our concerns are relative to much of that debate. We have been looking for something quite specific — an empirical correlation between the theoretical expectations of Justification theory and late Second Temple Judaism, without which the theory cannot function. (Hence, to be untrue here is to risk being untrue everywhere.) We have found this correlation not to hold, and not remotely. But with this realization, the difficulties of Justification theory at its empirical frame are far from over.

CHAPTER FIVE

The Question of Conversion

§1. Preamble — the Question of Conversion

It has seemed important since Stendahl to debate the nature of Paul's "conversion"[1] in relation to wider questions concerning his theological interpretation. Indeed, the issue has generated a considerable body of discussion. Yet, although Stendahl was absolutely correct to target this issue, the exact reasons for the debate have not always been especially clear, nor have its broader implications been widely appreciated (for example, its links with the subject of the preceding chapter).

Stendahl's concern with the nature of Paul's conversion stemmed from his conviction that introspection was a key issue within the interpretation of Paul. He felt that while a tortured introspection was characteristic of much Western spirituality, as classically apparent in — not to mention endorsed by — the lives of Augustine and Luther, it was a rather negative phenomenon within the life of the church and so ought to be critically challenged. A strategic point at which to do so was to query whether Paul evidenced a similar attitude. So Stendahl briefly introduced certain positive and negative reasons to suggest that Paul did not possess a troubled introspective mind or undertake any such journey to salvation despite his previous characterization in such terms. Stendahl went on to claim famously that Paul possessed "a robust conscience" before he became a Christian. He also problematized the very use of the word "conversion," suggesting instead that the language of "call" was a more accurate description of the apostle's own statements. Paul, Stendahl claimed, never spoke of "converting" in the sense of leaving one religion and joining another. Rather, he spoke of a divine call to mission with language redolent of prophetic commissions in the Old Testament. The point of this challenge was then pressed into Stendahl's basic interpretative foe: the "Lutheran" reading of Paul.

Predictably, various Lutherans — along with those who shared certain convictions with them — reacted strongly to this challenge, producing a number of biographical studies of Paul. Not surprisingly, these claimed that the introspective "Lutheran" reading of the relevant data was still the correct one. But others were unconvinced by these apologies. (These exchanges are analyzed in more detail later in the chapter.) Meanwhile, the study of Paul's conversion was receiving considerable impetus in general terms from all this attention, both diversifying and overlapping with the consideration of other questions within his interpretation.

We will have to reach a judgment about the relevant aspects of this debate in due course, but at this point it is more important to recontextualize it. Here we are interested specifically in the problematic claims of Justification theory about broader reality — in difficulties at its empirical frame — and the theory clearly makes important claims about conversion. *Justification theory is almost entirely focused on the process of conversion,* and in fact claims to give a *universally valid* account of conversion. It is because of this universal purview that the critical front at this point within our discussion must be broadened significantly from Stendahl's original attack. As a *general* account of conversion, Justification theory ought to be true.

If it is not, then the consequences are fairly dire. The absurdity of a theory being unable to account for one of its principal concerns calls the validity of the theory immediately into question. But more than this is at stake. If Justification theory is employed by the church as its normative account of conversion and yet proves invalid, then it is likely that the process of conversion itself will be distorted. Appropriate approaches to conversion will be ignored if not opposed, and evangelism will be hindered by what is arguably a highly alienating procedure. Ironically, then, reliance on this theory dedicated to conversion will lead to the corruption of that process in genuine terms.[2] These seem to be good reasons for examining the entire area carefully.

We have already noted some lurking difficulties in this regard. During our consideration of the intrinsic problems, it became apparent that Justification theory's assumption that individuals can merely choose to believe things in order to be saved was naive; it ran squarely into the conundrum of "belief voluntarism." Here the critical theoretical fulcrum within the theory — the point of conversion — began to be problematized. Individuals cannot, it seems, simply decide to believe that certain things are true. In a slightly broader sense, the theory's confidence that human behavior can be explained essentially rationalistically, in terms of self-interest and so also individualistically, began to be exposed as well. Our investigation of Judaism began to uncover the considerable explanatory shortfall of any account of human behavior constructed in these terms. *Where Justification theory attempts to describe human behavior, it seems rationalistic and, to that degree, inaccurate vis-à-vis that (important!) aspect of reality.*

Our study of conversion in empirical terms integrates precisely with these earlier suspicions. We can suspect that here specifically Justification does not describe the process of conversion accurately. Furthermore, our doubts in this relation can be investigated rather more powerfully than was previously the case.

Social scientists have been evaluating the phenomenon of conversion for some time.[3] The particular usefulness of this material is that it allows a reasonably precise empirical check on the accounts of conversion supplied by converts themselves, which may already have been influenced by inappropriate theoretical constructs like Justification — ideology meets reality. Although this data is generally drawn from modern Western societies, it can probably still be deployed — with due caution — in relation to conversion within ancient societies. The culture of societies has changed greatly, but the essentially biological, emotional, and rational constitution of humanity that underpins human behavior has not. If conversion draws on such basic constituents, then modern observations may still be applicable in a carefully controlled sense to ancient phenomena (and certain historical controls can be introduced at this point as well). So this body of research is well worth considering here as long as its claims and relevance are not overstated.

However, one of the pitfalls in any general theory of social behavior is trying to predict the particular. Social theory is often not precise enough to allow this sort of confidence. It may still be the case that Paul himself does not follow a general pattern of conversion observable within history. Hence, it is doubly worth considering Paul's own experience of conversion: a look at this event in Paul's life, insofar as that is revealed by the available sources, will allow us to see whether general conversion theory is applicable to Paul's so-called conversion *and* whether Paul's supposed theoretical account of conversion is matched by his actual experience. It would of course be very troublesome if the latter two did not match, as Stendahl first intuited. ("He explains others but he cannot explain himself.") Indeed, ideally all three explanatory levels here should correlate if Justification is to hold good — a general account of conversion (i.e., the basic empirical correlation), Paul's theory of conversion, and Paul's actual conversion. Hence, Paul's experience of conversion will be the second of our main lines of inquiry within this newly broadened critical front — a more traditional one, although it will again be important to let Justification theory guide our discussion; Stendahl's original characterization of the issue, while prescient, is not always helpful, and the secondary discussion is voluminous but not always pertinent.[4]

It is, moreover, now also possible to see a third front emerging within this whole area — Paul's *method* of converting. This is a large question in its own right, so we will concentrate on his preaching. This should be a sufficiently limited and decisive issue. Justification theory expects conversion as a relatively immediate response to preaching, as prospective converts are first convinced of their desperate need for conversion, and then offered the lifeline of salvation through faith alone — "turn or burn" teaching, as it is sometimes denoted somewhat irreverently. So we can ask here simply if the relevant sources bear this expectation out — insofar as they allow us to reconstruct Paul's preaching at all (and if they did not, this would surely itself be significant). If they do not — or, even worse, attest to some other schema — then the implications for Justification advocates are again dire: Paul would not apparently *himself* attest to the practice of Justification theory as *he* sought converts, suggesting rather directly that Justification theory does not therefore supply an accurate account of his practice of conversion. So this seems an additional question well worth briefly exploring here.

We begin, then, with a more general consideration of conversion in §2. Does Justification theory's account of conversion match a more empirical account informed by social science? This will be followed in §3 by a critical survey of Paul's conversion and then, in §4, by an investigation of his preaching that ostensibly converted others.

§2. Conversion in General

The exact mechanism and nature of conversion are difficult and contentious matters. Fortunately, we are interested here only in investigating whether the expectations of Justification theory are met in relation to broader reality on this front, so that theory's definition can guide us in the first instance.

As we have seen, an account of sinful life and its struggles under the law before Christ is very significant if not cardinal for an individual's movement through the process of Justification. Ideally, a climactic moment of realization will characterize the end of this progression — the moment of conversion based on justification through belief alone! Here individuals reach an essentially rational conclusion through reflection and certain key recognitions. This moment should then result in an important cognitive shift to an essentially Christian perspective ("Jesus died *for me*" or some such), although an ongoing experience of some of the difficulties of sinfulness is not completely precluded. Hence, the entire progression is — as we well know by now — a prospective, individual, rational (if not rationalistic), largely cognitive, and even philosophical process, although its critical moment of transition ought to take place in relation to preaching. We can ask at this point then how this account of conversion compares with modern descriptions of the nature of conversion. But in order to pursue this inquiry further we must of course ask how we know what we currently think we know about conversion — or, in other words, ask which discipline is most helpful to us in answering this focused descriptive question.

It is in the first instance entirely fair to suggest that the analysis of conversion ought to take place in dialogue with many disciplines. Originally largely the preserve of psychologists of religion and Evangelicals, the modern conversation now includes anthropologists, sociologists, historians (including historians of Christianity), literary scholars, missiologists, and theologians.[5] Nevertheless, a quick review of many of these contributions — and especially of the frequently dominant perspectives of psychologists and Evangelicals (on which see more just below) — suggests that the sociologists (and the North American empirical sociologists in particular) have issued a fundamental challenge to the validity of much of this material as an accurate description of the *process* of conversion. The conversation about conversion is much broader than the strictly empirical question concerned with how it happens. Much of the discussion of that more limited question, however, is anecdotal, is shaped by prior agendas — often theological — dictating normative rather than descriptive accounts (and often argued in relation to Paul!), and is insensitive to the different aspects of the entire process, perhaps privileging one or another component such as "seeking." My inclination is to privilege in what follows material that is explicitly grounded by testable theories, empirical research, and extensive participant observation — that of the sociologists (notwithstanding their own peculiar difficulties). The many contributions of other disciplines will certainly be noted, but they will not be taken as normative, and this judgment applies in particular to psychological explanations that have long dominated the discussion. I have strong reservations about the cogency of much of this material, in part because of its deep-seated origins in much individualist European introspection, along with the subsequent dominance of the question by William James, whose views should now be viewed as brilliant but deeply problematic.[6] (James was not himself really intending to write theology, but the application of his approach to an event like Paul's conversion *assumes* this.[7]) The sociologists have, in my view, rather definitively exposed the normative and narrative distortions within the introspective evidence. This is not to deny its usefulness in other relations. Moreover, we do need to ask what converts were *thinking* as they were converting.[8] But as an accurate account of the *nature* or *mode* of conversion, such approaches are problematic, and remain usefully corrected in my view by a more sociological approach.

John Lofland and Rodney Stark pioneered the social scientific study of conversion in the early 1960s in the United States by observing at close hand the founding of a Unification church (i.e., a "Moonie" community) in the San Francisco Bay area.[9] From their observations they developed a famous seven-step model of conversion.[10] Lofland and Stark hypothesized that converts possessed three "predisposing conditions": acutely felt tension or deprivation, a religious problem-solving perspective, and an overall self-definition as a religious seeker. Four further conditions — "situational contingencies" — depended upon a concrete encounter with a cult: a self-perceived "turning point" (near the time of the encounter), a strong affective bond with one or more cult members, reduced or eliminated extra-cult attachments, and further intensive interaction with other cult members. An individual who met these four further conditions experienced full-fledged conversion and became a "deployable agent" of the new cult.

The development of this theory allowed a process of ongoing discussion and empirical testing to begin. The model itself has been strongly criticized, at times in every respect.[11] In particular, it is now clear that the theory does not describe a strictly sequential, integrated and "cumulative" model of conversion so much as a more general map of some of the key conditions of conversion (indeed, hopefully of most of them). These conditions may vary in relation to one another and in relation to different religions.[12] However, the model — suitably reformulated — seems more true than false and remains at the heart of ongoing research into conversion. Clearly, some of the factors that it isolates do need to be present for conversion to take place, and the presence of more factors seems to correlate with a greater likelihood and endurance of resulting conversion. Meanwhile, the theory's insights have garnered enough empirical support to constitute "the body of what we can confidently say about why people become involved with NRMs [new religious movements]."[13]

As is common in the social sciences, it is not possible to claim that everything in relation to conversion has now been explained for every convert to the point that reliable predictions can be made; we can claim only to have explained many of the most important factors in relation to many converts (and hence we will still fail to generate detailed predictions, possibly thankfully). However, there is a significant body of knowledge about conversion that can be usefully considered here. It may be helpful to distinguish three streams of partly separate theoretical development from Lofland and Stark's original point of investigation and theorizing:

(1) the "network" aspect of the theory, emphasized in particular within the subsequent work of Stark and his collaborators (and explained by Stark at times quite rationalistically in terms of the theory of social control and deviance[14]);[15]

(2) the role of rational choice, applied to the model by Stark in his analysis of religions as "firms" offering "products"; and

(3) the role of predisposing conditions, further emphasized in Lofland's work on converts as seekers, and further specified by accumulating empirical evidence suggesting that converts are often young, educated, and relatively unattached socially and ideologically.

Each of these theoretical developments is important and merits closer consideration in relation to our overarching concern with the portrait of conversion offered by Justification theory.

(1) Network Theory

The most important and well-attested dimension of conversion theory is its emphasis on networks. Stark and his collaborators perceived that conversion takes place in a fundamentally interpersonal fashion. "Converts" essentially "convert" when they begin to behave in a manner that is aligned with a given religious group rather than with their own previous affiliations and its different patterns, and they do this, Stark and Lofland assert, because their personal relationships with group members — their "attachments" — become more significant than their relational attachments outside the group. As a result, such shifts tend to take place along existing networks of personal relationships, which are principally those of close friends and family. So, for example, Mormons convert 50 percent of prospects whose first "mission" contact is in the home of a Mormon family member or friend[16] (a point where the important research collaboration between Stark and William Sims Bainbridge becomes apparent).

Stark and his more recent coworkers have continued to emphasize the final three steps of conversion within the original model, which can easily be viewed as a strengthening continuum rather than three separate factors. Converts must form (or already have) a significant attachment to a person within a religion or cult, must weaken any significant attachments outside the group, and must subsequently broaden such attachments within the group. (Without this third stage, conversions tend to lapse.) These "attachments" are often described in highly positive emotional terms — "vibrancy, warmth, openness, joy . . . , positive outlook."[17] The "network" facet of the theory has been validated by much empirical work: "studies of conversion and of specific groups have found that recruitment to NRMs happens primarily through pre-existing social networks and interpersonal bonds. Friends recruit friends, family members each other and neighbours recruit neighbours. . . . [T]he majority of recruits to the majority of NRMs come into contact with the groups they join because they personally know one or more members of the movement" (119). Furthermore, such claims seem to be corroborated by other bodies of evidence within the social sciences concerning the significance of personal attachments in religion[18] (while presumably, given space, such behavior could also be documented in relation to non-religious activities).

Stark points out that the origins of Islam, Christianity, and Mormonism conform to network theory. Muhammad's first followers were his wife, Khadijah, his cousin Ali, his servant Zeyd, and his old friend Abu Bakr. Jesus seems to have drawn his first supporters from the followers of John the Baptist — ironically, a deviant religious group to which he already belonged. Hence, he drew from people he had known for some time — his friends Peter, James, John, and so on. Later on, at least some of his family members seem to have become supportive — his mother, Mary, some of his brothers (at least James and Jude), and certain women involved in and through these relationships (see Mark 15:40-41; Luke 24:10). Joseph Smith's first followers were his two brothers, Hyrum and Samuel, and his close friends Oliver Cowdery and David and Peter Whitmer.[19] We could easily add to this list — most notably in terms of the origins of Buddhism and of many modern NRMs.[20]

The discovery by Stark and Lofland that conversion takes place along a continuum of concrete interpersonal relationships thus seems both important and well grounded. Moreover, these observations are a useful corroboration of their theory's historical value: it does seem, with due caution, to be transferable across time.[21] Four important developments from this particular theoretical strand are now worth noting:

(i) the influence of prior "network density" (which links up with predisposing conditions, our third major theoretical strand);

(ii) the reduction and reorientation of the role of formal and rational conversion techniques;

(iii) Stark's explanation of this in terms of the theory of social control and deviance; and

(iv) the consequent function of "the conversion narrative."

(i) As we might by now expect, the prior location of converts seems to have a significant influence on the ease and ultimate success of their development of the interpersonal attachments that underlie conversion. Dislocated individuals with weak prior attachments are more likely to convert to religious groups, because their current experience of relationships is less restrictive (although it follows that their position within a network that can then be exploited for further converts will be correspondingly weak).[22] Conversely, individuals already embedded in groups with a high level of personal attachment are least likely to convert to another one. And finally, the strength of the convert's prior networks will probably be a factor in the creation of the important further attachments within the cult. This causal connection, however — like most such connections grounded in human relationships and contexts — is not simple and invariable.

(ii) It follows from the importance of personal networking that more traditional and formal techniques of evangelism oriented in terms of doctrine, public presentations, or rationalistic decision making should be largely ineffective. And Lofland and Stark's early observations bore this important theoretical implication out. When the Unification Church was established in San Francisco by Young Oon Kim, numerous public meetings, radio spots, and so on yielded no converts at all. The founding members of the group were actually three housewives, already friends themselves, who came to know Miss Kim when she was a lodger with one of them. Their husbands subsequently joined, followed by several friends from their work. Stark notes that "[a]t the time Lofland and I arrived to study them, the group had never succeeded in attracting a stranger."[23] Further converts came from old friends or relatives of members of the group who visited from out of state and chose to stay on with the church. (These observations were actually the origins of the network theory of conversion.)

(iii) Stark goes on to suggest that network theory can itself be explained by the theory of social control and deviance. Joining a marginalized religious group is an act of deviance that people would ordinarily avoid. However, if a person's relationships with group members outweigh his or her relationships with outsiders, then the situation of deviance is reversed; it is an act of deviance to resist joining that group, and the deviants are in fact those outside the group.[24] (This may then generate further advantages for that community in turn, for example, through the elimination of "free riders."[25])

(iv) Lofland and Stark also suggested that self-conscious cognitive development in relation to a new religion was distinctly secondary (here complementing point *ii* above). Joining a group was clearly not a rationalistic decision based on the acquisition and analysis of information (although it is of course a *rational* decision to join a group with its higher level of personal attachments). The social scientists found that allegiance to a group's doctrine tended to develop well after conversion. It was at this later point that converts learned to narrate a correct account of their conversion experience, so — a little ironically — the ability to supply such an account of conversion is often taken to be a principal sign that a "genuine" conversion has taken place.[26] But this makes sense in terms of the theory's underlying principle. Converts are oriented primarily by the desire to enhance their new relationships with cult members. So they say what they ought to say and indeed what they have been taught to say. Consequently, conversion narratives do not really function as reports of conversion so much as public actions that affirm community identity; they indicate acceptance of the group's perceptions — including of its definitions of deviance! Clearly, this theoretical development has very important implications for any evaluation of personal conversion narratives as evidence of how those conversions actually took place.[27]

We turn now to consider the other two major theoretical developments from the original classic analysis.

(2) Product and Firm Theory

A further aspect of Stark's work is the application of rational choice theory and the characterization of religions as "firms" relative to the phenomena of religious conversion and growth, with which it is helpful also to link the notion of "product."[28] This aspect of Stark's theorizing serves to emphasize that conversion does not simply take place through networks of friends and families *tout court;* people are generally converting *to* something distinctive, and this behavior might be usefully comprehended as the selection of a particular "product" produced by a religious "firm." So while network theory emphasizes that such conversion is not merely in terms of some abstract market — and neither is the "product" strongly separable from the relationships within which the person is embedded (high quality relationships are in part a product) — product and firm theory suggests, by way of balance, that some consideration ought to be given to the perceived benefits of conversion and especially as those operate in relation to any potential competitors. Networks do things that certain people seem to find either interesting or enjoyable, an aspect of the process partly captured by the model of products and firms.

It is at this point that notions of rationality within conversion can be further developed, although any emphasis on this aspect of conversion should be carefully contextualized in historical terms as well.[29] New religious "firms" survive by competing with older, established "firms," presumably by offering the same products more cheaply. Alternatively, they can try to offer a new product that the older firms cannot actually produce. The latter would in effect create an entirely new market — if people wanted to "buy" the new product — which should in turn establish the new religion.[30]

Unfortunately, consideration of the Pauline mission's distinctive "product" would take us too far afield at this point (even assuming that such a comparison would be both legitimate and useful). Nevertheless, it is already clear that this highly rational model of conversion — which is not uncontested — is quite different from the rationalistic model adumbrated by Justification theory, and this is an important realization. Stark's product and firm model could hardly be more rationalist in terms of social theory. It operates in part in terms of perceived benefits, markets, and choices, *but these combine into a rather different progression from that relied upon by Justification theory.* Where the latter operates invariably in terms of an escape from a negative situation, the former, as its terminology suggests, views conversion more as the positive selection of a product or products from an array of competing alternatives — and those products will vary considerably depending on the historical setting of the firms producing the products and their prospective consumers. It is a much more diverse and historically contextualized *rational* model of conversion. As such, it seems to pose especially troublesome problems for Justification theory.[31]

We turn now to the third major strand of theoretical development from the original classic analysis of conversion.

(3) *Predisposing Conditions — "Seekers" et Cetera*

Lofland has developed the earlier rather than the later stages of the original theory of conversion in his subsequent work, and in a slightly less rationalist manner than Stark.[32] He emphasizes the predisposing conditions for converts and hence a degree of activity on their part, in particular, the quality of "seeking." (Any links with some recent church praxis that uses the same terminology are fortuitous.[33]) However, this concern is quite compatible with the earlier observations of network theory and the development of interpersonal attachments between a convert and existing cult members. It simply seems to follow from this emphasis that prospective converts should generally be located in unsatisfying contexts, or at least in less satisfying contexts than the cults that they are joining. The original theory posited some sort of social and ideological deprivation coupled with a questing religious mentality as a necessary preliminary stage for conversion. These claims are now viewed as overly rigid, but the fact remains that many converts do attest to conversion from a "seeking" phase within a generally negative context.[34] (To Lofland's emphasis on seeking we can now add impressive empirical evidence for youth in converts, along with the usual presence of a relatively high level of education.[35])

It is important to note in addition that the quest of the "seeker" — when this is a factor in conversion — is not necessarily well defined in rational or theoretical terms: "People inclined to be interested in even the possibility of joining an NRM have been reading related religious and philosophical literature and giving some serious thought to the so-called 'big questions' (e.g., What is the meaning of life? Is there a God? Is there life after death?)."[36] But there may be little more than that going on. Alternatively, such "seekers" may have been involved in another religious group. It is therefore quite fair to characterize the previous lives of *some* of these figures as "negative"; however, it is unfair to press a rigid descriptive schema onto that process. Seeking seems to take many forms, and this is clearly an extremely important observation, because it encompasses the "journeys" of so many Christian and non-Christian religious leaders. Augustine and Luther, not to mention Apuleius and Muhammad, all seem to fall within this category of "seeker," although in subtly different ways. Moreover, such seeking seems to be important for a significant percentage of converts, and certainly converts to modern NRMs. But it is also uncharacteristic of a significant percentage of converts who may convert merely through effective networking, *and neither is the seeking itself remotely uniform in terms of its specific content.* Hence, the key questions remain: whether Paul was in fact such a seeker, and if he was, what form his seeking took.

The body of research on conversion raises all sorts of interesting questions.[37] Our further pursuit here, however, will have to be limited to their immediate implications for Justification theory. There are two.

(1) Our most important finding is that most if not all aspects of the sociological description of conversion — even in its most rationalist moments — disconfirm Justification as a general account of conversion, and this confirms the suspicions that have already been gathering at the theoretical level in terms of belief voluntarism and at the empirical frame in more general historical terms, in relation to the nature of late Second Temple Judaism. Once again Justification theory seems to be running into acute difficulties when it abuts reality, and this calls the overarching cogency of the theory into question.

More specifically, the discovery by sociologists of the importance of concrete interpersonal networks for conversion, and this often irrespective of the substantive content of the cult or religion to which the convert converted, contradicts the individualist, rationalist, impersonal account offered by Justification theory, along with any climactic moment experienced in relation to preaching. The subordinate implications of network theory are equally problematic — the possible role of prior social and ideological dislocations, the consequent ineffectiveness of formal rational appeals, the possible influence of factors of deviance and social control, and the shaping of conversion narratives by community expectations. Similarly, the construal of conversion as the selection of a particular "product" produced by one religious "firm" in competition with others, while rationalist, is a quite different rational model from the one offered by Justification. And it is to my mind very significant that even granting the rationalist analysis of conversion, we find it nevertheless to disconfirm the rationalizations of Justification theory. Finally, the lack of uniformity among potential converts in possessing (or not) a "seeker" mentality, not to mention its specific form and content, is at odds with Justification's overly rationalist and rigid account of the "seeker" — which it holds to be mandatory.

It is important to appreciate, however, that Justification theory is by no means a complete failure in its description of conversion. Indeed, some of its emphases are quite prescient. (It is, after all, a premodern theory and is not simply attempting to model conversion.) Justification is clearly aware of the importance of a response by a convert to an offer made by someone specific and personal, such as a preacher or evangelist (although it struggles to accommodate this emphasis consistently in theoretical and epistemological terms); of a degree of rational choice by at least some converts in relation to perceived benefits (although its account of this dynamic is too negative and constricted); and of the resolution that the gospel frequently provides to the difficulties, negativity, and anxieties that might be suffered by a seeker (although it tends to define those anxieties overly restrictively, and to insist on finding them in *every* convert!). These emphases are accurate. But at every turn they are significantly misrepresented, while the overarching theory, as an explanation of conversion, is profoundly reductionist. For these reasons, Justification, although insightful, is nevertheless falsified as a general account of conversion by a more nuanced sociological description of that phenomenon.

(2) When the abandonment of Justification theory is suggested, one often encounters the claim that the notion of God's wrath (meaning the pending divine punishment of wrongdoing) must be maintained at all costs. Without this notion, it is said, conversion will be impossible and ethical behavior problematized — two entirely legitimate concerns. But of course this claim is mired in the particular rationalism of Justification theory, assuming that people will behave in a certain way only if they have been given a combination of strong incentives and disincentives that operate — in the case of evangelism — in the non- or pre-Christian condition. In this system, behavior is essentially a matter of individual rational choice in strict relation to positive and negative motivations.

It is now possible to see, however, in the light of how conversion arguably takes place through personal networks and their attachments (et cetera), that evangelism will not necessarily be negatively affected by the abandonment of a preliminary emphasis on the wrath of God. To the contrary, it may be greatly assisted by that abandonment, since the pursuit of evangelism in the formal and essentially disapproving terms encouraged by Justification probably inhibits the creation of the positive relationships and experiences actually necessary for effective conversion to occur. In place of the more intimate and satisfying personal relationships best undertaken within informal contexts, Justification theory tends to introduce more formal discourses that emphasize negative situations and depressing or anxious emotional states. If "the wrath of God" is placed appropriately within the broader theological pedagogy of the converted — and no longer pressed inappropriately on the prospective convert — then the consequences for the church's evangelism could be astonishingly positive.

We turn now to consider the question of Paul's own conversion.

§3. Paul's Conversion

3.1. Preamble

To my knowledge, network theory has not yet been applied thoroughly to Paul's mission,[38] although his communities have been analyzed periodically from a variety of sociological perspectives. Such work is not especially common — but when it does take place, it seems to be very good.[39] Sociological analyses of conversion in relation to Paul or his churches are still rarer.[40] This is not to say that Paul's *conversion* has not been studied; that has received a great deal of attention.[41] But our principal task at this point is not a conversation with sociology per se. We are asking primarily whether the sources suggest a conversion by Paul that accords with the expectations of Justification theory, because it will of course be quite troublesome if the propounder of a general theory of conversion does not fit his own model. At the same time, however, Paul's account can be usefully compared with the more general account of conversion offered by the sociologists. (Here we might find that conversion is best understood differently from its prevailing conceptualization — allowing for the possibility as well that Paul's conversion might not be best viewed *as* a conversion.) Do we find the individualist and rationalistic choices of Justification theory in the relevant sources concerning Paul's conversion? Do we find the conditions and dynamics described by the sociologists? (Or do we find something else?)

Putting matters in more visual terms for clarification, we might say that the following relationships ought to align with one another if Justification theory is to hold good. Unfortunately, the previous subsection has already cast doubt on the alignment of one of these relationships, and this subsection is about to problematize the second (possibly also thereby creating an alignment between Paul and the sociologists *over against* the expectations of Justification theory — the worst of all outcomes for Justification advocates)!

Paul ----------------------- the evidence of conversion in relation to him
Justification theory -------- its expectations of conversion
Sociology ------------------ its analytic description of conversion in general

3.2. Paul's Conversion in His Own Terms

It goes without saying that the apostle's letters provide invaluable primary evidence and so must be our point of departure and principal source.[42] However, even here we must of course be careful. Paul is reshaping the story of his conversion for specific rhetorical purposes within the broader setting of particular epistolary events, some of which are quite polemical. Hence, information that is less contingently relevant will possibly be more accurate than information that Paul wants to supply to his audiences overtly; similarly, silences at certain points will not necessarily denote absences. (We have already seen that postconversion narrations by converts are less reliable than they may at first appear — how much more, then, does this apply to public letters!)

In fact, Paul supplies very little information about his conversion in his extant letters, which may in itself be significant.[43] The best text with which to begin to develop a description of the event is Galatians 1:12-16, a mere five verses. Largely by implication, these verses supply a rough circumstantial frame for the apostle's famous encounter with Christ. We know that Paul was in the region of Damascus when his call took place — he uses the language of "call" here, καλέσας, in v. 15b — because he tells us that after his call and his subsequent trip to "Arabia," "he returned back" to that city (v. 17b: πάλιν ὑπέστρεψα εἰς Δαμασκόν). After three years he did visit Jerusalem briefly (vv. 18-24), and we know from 2 Corinthians 11:32-33 that he was forced to escape from Damascus at the start of this journey by being lowered in a basket from an opening in the city's walls — not an especially glorious departure. Following his visit to Jerusalem, where he met only Cephas and James (vv. 18-19), Paul went to the regions of Syria and Cilicia (v. 21), visiting Jerusalem again only many years later (2:1). Prior to this call he was of course persecuting "God's assembly" (ἐκκλησία; 1:13).

Paul discloses several important component features of his conversion in this compact account. First, he received the gospel by means of a revelation — an ἀποκάλυψις — "of Jesus Christ" (v. 12). Significantly, this statement *precedes any account of his previous life.* We do not know at first whether the genitive suggests that Jesus was the origin of the revelation or its content. But other Pauline statements suggest that both senses are ultimately appropriate and hence need not be distinguished here too strongly. Verses 15-16 immediately following denote God as the agent of this revelation and "his Son," Jesus, as its content. However, elsewhere Paul clearly claims to have seen the Lord Jesus himself (1 Cor. 9:1), so both the Father and the Son must have been directly involved in this event.[44] It is vital to note in addition that this disclosure has a specific element of commission; it takes place "so that [Paul] . . . might proclaim [literally, 'gospel'] him [God's Son] among the Gentiles," and this element is again reinforced by other texts, not to mention the allusion to Jeremiah 1:5. This is of course Paul's *apostolic commission.* He has been given a particular job to do — and arguably a rather strange one.[45]

It is often observed that this statement alludes to Isaiah 49:1 and Jeremiah 1:5 (at the least),[46] Paul describing his experience as a foreordained "call" analogous to the calls of the Servant in Isaiah 49 and of Jeremiah. However, this is Paul's subsequent, scripturally assisted *interpretation* of the event and one with clear rhetorical implications.[47] Hence, the information is pertinent but not empirically determinative. God presumably did not tell Paul at the time that he had been set apart from his mother's womb and was now being called by means of God's grace; this is Paul's qualification of God's action in context through later reflection upon certain scriptural texts (and Paul's use of the word "grace" here should not be overlooked; see v. 15).

Between the announcement of this revelation and its more nuanced description in Galatians lies a brief characterization of Paul's "way of life then in Judaism" (τὴν ἐμὴν ἀναστροφήν ποτε ἐν τῷ Ἰουδαϊσμῷ), which consisted of two elements: persecuting and destroying God's ἐκκλησία (i.e., the Christian community) and advancing well beyond his peers in zeal for the traditions of his fathers.

Intriguingly, Philippians 3:5-6 recapitulates these elements almost exactly (and this text is examined in detail in its broader context later in part five, chapter twenty-one). Paul's Jewish ancestry is enumerated by a stereotypical list in v. 5. It is here that the implicit claim in Galatians 1:14 that he was a Pharisee becomes explicit. We also learn that Paul was not a convert, that he was a Benjaminite, and that he was probably an Aramaic speaker (see 2 Cor. 11:22). Verse 6 describes his zeal in the two principal ways already noted in Galatians 1:13-14: he persecuted the ἐκκλησία and, in terms of the δικαιοσύνη available by means of the law, he was "blameless" (ἄμεμπτος). Unfortunately, his conversion is not then described, merely his current existence "in Christ" in relation to which all these former privileges or "gains" are now considered "loss" if not "excrement" (3:7-8), although ultimately this proves highly significant (see part five, chapter twenty-one).

It is at precisely this point that Stendahl made one of his most famous claims, namely, that the word ἄμεμπτος used here by Paul to describe his law observance suggests his possession prior to his conversion of a robust conscience. So the apostle did not suffer from the agonized progressions of Justification theory, Augustine, or Luther. (He was not then a "seeker," sorely afflicted or otherwise.) I am not sure, however, that Stendahl's case is sustainable.

Ἄμεμπτος, which means "blameless" or "faultless," *could* be read as suggesting this confidence. The signifier generally applies to people of exceptional merit and hence appears in association with qualities such as δίκαιος or ἀκέραιος (see Phil. 2:15; Job 1:1 LXX). But we can identify at least five qualifications in its use here that seem to work against Stendahl's claim. First, Paul is writing in a highly polemical situation within which he is unlikely to admit to imperfections. Second, the setting concerns reasons why someone might possess a boast in relation to "the flesh," that is, some sort of historically derived and measurable qualification in terms of ancestry or religious behavior that might convey advantage within an argument. Paul is therefore laying claim to faultlessness only in that respect (much, presumably, as a Christian citizen on trial in a court might claim to have a "perfect" record as a citizen without meaning by this that he or she was actually perfect). Third, it is a very brief claim — one word! — that seems, fourth, to recapitulate Paul's slightly longer statement in Galatians 1:14, which would reinforce the sense in which it refers to "externals" only. Paul was faultless in his law observance in all *observable* respects, but it does not follow that he was a faultless person in *all* respects. Corroborating this suspicion, fifth, the use at Qumran of "faultless law observance" seems compatible with a sense of deep sinfulness (as just noted in chapter four). Indeed, the incidence of the word in relation to Job should also give us pause. Job was technically faultless, as Job 1:1 suggests, but he did not deny either a sense of sinfulness or even various sins before God; he did not claim to be perfect (see Job 7:20-21; 13:26; 14:16-17; 19:4).

Lying behind these qualifications is the widespread and largely self-evident distinction between the act of thinking, and acting, beyond thought in relation to the surrounding environment. (I am not endorsing a thought-act dualism here but distinguishing between two types of actions.) Thoughts cannot be directly observed and are very complex, so they easily take a metaphor of interiority — "internal" or some such. Different acts, however, are more easily monitored by both the self and others; they are more "external." In the foregoing text, then, it is not necessarily being claimed that Paul's thought life — the "internal" life — is pure and faultless with not even a hint of a sinful impulse or idea. But his further action in relation to the environment — the "external" life — is entirely proper and without fault. If this creates a difficulty for the use of Philippians 3:6 as evidence of Paul's robust thought life or conscience prior to his conversion, then it also points ineluctably to the crucial debate over Romans 7.

In Romans 7:7-25 we find a long and complex account of sinful thought — of "interiority" — that would dominate any reconstruction of Paul if it proved to be biographically relevant. The question of its exact reference is consequently crucial. But it is also widely debated, although fortunately not all aspects of this debate concern us here. Justification advocates need to prove that Romans 7 is a psychological account of Paul's pre-Christian life. If they cannot, then the text can be excluded from our current description and we can move on in our broader discussion.

In fact, many scholars have asserted, against the suggestions of Justification advocates and their allies, either that Romans 7 is an account of post-Christian existence or that it describes a universal condition not peculiar to Paul in general or to his preconversion situation in particular; it is a generic account of life "in the flesh." This second view, associated with the classic analysis of W. G. Kümmel, is probably the dominant one at present, and with good reason. (Significantly, it can also be connected with a highly contingent reading of this passage as well.) A brief summary of the key contentions must suffice here.[48]

(1) This account was written by Paul as a Christian and an apostle some considerable time after his conversion. It is, therefore, in terms of its actual circumstances, a *retrospective* account. In order to suggest that it is nevertheless an accurate recollection of Paul's preconversion thinking, we need some explicit markers — which we do not find. *Paul nowhere in this text explicitly states that he is giving an account of his preconversion state of mind.* Moreover, we find no other statements or even hints in Paul that seem to affirm this extended and rather tortured account as a reference to his pre-Christian mentality. (Phil. 3:6 does stand against this claim rather more strongly than it can affirm positively a sin-free mental state at that time.) In short, we have no good reasons for thinking that this account is a report of Paul's state of mind prior to his conversion (that is, other than a priori theoretical ones supplied — i.a. — by Justification theory).

(2) There are good reasons for thinking that this is not a psychological report

of the apostle's pre-Christian condition. It is essentially unparalleled in the Jewish sources as an account of life under the law. Moreover, the terminology of movement from freedom and life to enslavement and death does not seem to describe appropriately the dawning awareness of sin through violation of a transgression (it seems closer to the Adamic narrative, as we will note just below). Even Justification theory does not assume that individuals are "alive" until they have violated the tenth commandment (or some such), at which point they die; the *realization* of sinfulness and hence of death might occur at this point, but this is not the same thing.[49]

(3) The account is marked instead by generic thematology: references to "the flesh" in vv. 5, 14 (σάρκινος), and 25b (see also 8:3); allusions to Adam and the narrative of Genesis 3 ("desire" in vv. 7 and 8; "commandment" in vv. 8, 10, 13; passage from life to death in vv. 8-11; and "deceived" in v. 11); and a possible evocation of "the Medea paradox" (vv. 15-23).[50] The motifs apparently drawn from Genesis 3 certainly seem to make better sense positioned within a generic account of fleshly human nature. Just these concerns are also signaled in the broader setting by Romans 5:12-21. Hence, these markers all converge on a broadly generic interpretation.

(4) In epistemological terms, it is essentially incoherent to claim to supply an accurate account of a condition within which the human mind is corrupted or distorted, as is evidently the case throughout Romans 7:7-25. Hence, Rom. 8:5-8 seems to supply an alternative account of the fleshly mind that is slightly different from 7:7-25 but reflects this epistemological conundrum more accurately: those "in the flesh" are *unaware* of how debilitating their condition is and hence are incapable of pleasing God. Conversely, Romans 7:24 portrays the necessary tortured and divided self, who can perceive this sinfulness but do nothing about it. (However, where does this dualist figure derive from in coherent terms?!) The assumption that 7:7-25 is a *retrospective* account of the flesh in general, however — that seems nevertheless (and therefore) still to be some dreadful possibility — deals with the epistemological conundrum in Romans 7 and removes any argumentative contradiction between the two descriptions (if it is assumed that 8:5-8 is a more phenomenological account). Furthermore, we should extend Paul the benefit of the doubt on both these counts — epistemological and argumentative coherence — as a matter of methodological necessity.

It is important to appreciate that a generic reading of Romans 7:7-25 does overlap with Paul's pre-Christian existence. He would regard it as a true account of his existence outside of Christ. However, he would not for those reasons necessarily regard it as an accurate psychological report of how he was thinking prior to his conversion. Far from it! It is a broader and more highly structured account than a mere psychological report. Essentially, it supplies a theological analysis of non-Christian ontology, whether that is present in the non-Christian (as seems obvious to the Christian) or in the Christian (as seems at least partly to be the

case on this side of the end of the age). Hence, it is fundamentally retrospective —
the result of a vantage point available only in Christ, which supplies the key theological categories and insights for constructing it.[51] So we should not expect either Paul as a non-Christian or any other non-Christian to share it self-
consciously. This profound analysis of the human condition in the flesh is the *result of,* not the *preparation for,* conversion — and therefore must be excluded
from any investigation of Paul's conversion.

The data with which we are concerned, then, has been rather curtailed. On
the basis of an examination of Galatians 1:12-16 and Philippians 3:5-6[-11], we
have isolated the following schema.

Prior to his conversion Paul was a Jew (and was born one, of the tribe of
Benjamin; he was also possibly raised an Aramaic speaker, although this does not
matter a great deal for our present purposes), and he was a *zealous* Jew as evidenced by two things in particular: first, his persecution of the early Christians;
and second, his progress in observance of Jewish law and tradition, which was
rigorous in the Pharisaic tradition, and "faultless." Paul's conversion — which
rather interrupted this lifestyle — seems to have contained four distinguishable
(although not separable) components: (i) God ("the Father") (ii) disclosed unconditionally (iii) "his Son," Jesus Christ, to Paul (and this was at least in part visual; i.e., Jesus "appeared" to Paul), but God also (iv) commissioned Paul, in a
manner analogous to the call of some of the prophets of old, *to proclaim Christ to
the pagans* (and this was presumably verbal).[52]

I am not sure that any of Paul's other allusions to his conversion and its immediate antecedents add significantly to this picture, with one possible exception.
First Corinthians 15:8-10 in its broader setting shows that Paul subsequently received some sort of personal catechesis, however troublesome that might prove for
his claims in Galatians 1:11–2:10. But this is entirely what we would expect from
Stark's network theory. Important new relationships were established by Paul's
conversion — if they were not already in place in some sense — and important information about the new movement was transmitted by means of those relationships. Paul learned some basic traditions about Christ and his significance and
then passed them on,[53] although, strictly speaking, Paul *could* exclude his apostolic calling from that information. Paul therefore conforms to the highly educated
— and possibly rather young — convert who is grafted into a set of new relationships, and in his case this was doubtless assisted by the fact that any return to his
old relationships might well have been fatal. His first community was based in Damascus (see Gal. 1:17b). Some of his catechesis, however, could have taken place
during his first visit as a Christian to Jerusalem, where he spent two weeks and met
both Cephas and James, before leaving for Syria (Gal. 1:21). These concrete relationships with other Christians should not be obscured by Paul's rhetorical emphasis within Galatians on his apostolic autonomy. His silence on such relationships in that context should be considered insignificant (that is, insignificant for
our present inquiry).

Paul's other allusions to his conversion add little to this portrait. First Corinthians 9:1, which we have already noted in passing, confirms nicely two of the key elements within that event — that Paul saw Jesus and that this encounter involved a commission. Romans 1:1 confirms what we already know about Paul's apostolic calling, as does 15:16(-22). Furthermore, 2 Corinthians 5:16, although both controversial and important for the broader theological interpretation of the apostle, adds little to our present concerns; that Paul had some knowledge of Jesus — enough to outrage him, presumably — prior to his conversion is obvious, because he was persecuting Christians before he became one himself.

However, these texts do at least provide some confidence that the foregoing schema is not a product merely of rhetorical circumstances or contingency. The key elements within Paul's pre-Christian life and his conversion appear in several of his letters; hence, it is very unlikely that the elements held in common are merely rhetorical. (If they were, then a case would have to be made that either the same contingency held in relation to each of these separate letters at these points, or a fortuitously similar one, which seems difficult if not impossible.)

Disputed evidence from Ephesians 3:2-12 and Colossians 1:25-27 enriches this picture but again adds nothing essentially new. These texts explicitly coordinate the language of mystery with Paul's apostleship, but this is by no means inappropriate; μυστήριον is standard Pauline parlance and fits smoothly with this particular question.[54] The language of mystery emphasizes both the unconditional nature of Paul's call and its particularity, two points that are themselves closely related. But our schema already contains these emphases, at which point we should note the possible implications of another contested text.

Just as the precise contributions of Philippians 3:6 and Romans 7:7-25 to the description of Paul's pre-Christian life had to be carefully considered and suitably parsed, so too the suggestion by some that 2 Corinthians 4:1-6 supplies precise information about Paul's conversion and so should broaden the foregoing portrait must be critically examined.[55] Indeed, I do not find this claim persuasive, and so exclude those verses from my description.[56] In essence, I would suggest that 2 Corinthians 4:4-6 is *highly* metaphorical, and obviously so. There is a pervasive use of wisdom material in this passage (hardly surprising within a missive to the Corinthians), and Paul is no more claiming here that he has actually seen the radiant face of Christ, as some suggest, than he is stating that God has actually, physically glowed in his heart, that the minds of non-Christians are actually, physically dark and blind, and that his body is a clay vessel! To press beyond these metaphors to a literal application to Paul's conversion seems to me to be inconsistent and hence tenuous.[57]

We turn now to the famous accounts of Paul's conversion supplied by Acts.

3.3. *Paul's Conversion according to Acts*

Acts emphasizes Paul's conversion, supplying three separate and reasonably lengthy accounts (9:1-19; 22:4-16; 26:9-18). But although these typically dramatic stories from the hand of Luke have greatly shaped most understandings of Paul's conversion, it is imperative to control them with Paul's own statements. Certainly, some difficulties become apparent when they are addressed in detail, both in relation to one another and against the information that Paul gives us himself.

First, the instructions that Paul receives from the risen Jesus are rather different in the third vision. In the first account Jesus says: "Saul, Saul, why do you persecute me? . . . I am Jesus, whom you are persecuting. But get up and enter the city, and you will be told what you are to do" (9:4-6). Ananias then supplies much of the specific content of Paul's commission (9:15-16). The second account adds the words "of Nazareth" after "Jesus" (22:7-8, 10).[58] Otherwise, Jesus' words are essentially identical, although Ananias's role is rather expanded and Paul's call is completed later on, during a trance in the temple at Jerusalem (22:17-21). In the third account, however, the risen Jesus says more:

> Saul, Saul, why are you persecuting me? It hurts you to kick against the goads. . . . I am Jesus whom you are persecuting. But get up and stand on your feet; for I have appeared to you for this purpose, to appoint you to serve and testify to the things in which you have seen me and to those in which I will appear to you. I will rescue you from your people and from the Gentiles — to whom I am sending you to open their eyes so that they may turn from darkness to light and from the power of Satan to God, so that they may receive forgiveness of sins and a place among those who are sanctified by faith in me. (26:14-18)

Much of the rest of the story has been stripped away. Ananias's role has been eliminated, as have Paul's blindness and his later trance in the Jerusalem temple. That is, most of the additional revelatory information that occurs earlier on in relation to these elements now occurs immediately, in Jesus' address to Paul.

There is also a minor but frequently noted discrepancy between the first two accounts concerning the bystanders. In 9:7 we are told that they heard a voice but saw no one, while in 22:9 the statement is reversed: they saw the light but heard nothing.[59]

Clearly, the three accounts are similar, but they are not exactly commensurate. On the one hand, they seem to display occasional embellishment in accordance with the needs of the story at the moment. So, for example, the Jewish piety of Ananias is emphasized when Paul speaks to the hostile crowd in the temple court in Jerusalem (22:12), and distinctly Jewish terminology is used, such as "the righteous one" (22:14; see 7:52). But the direct visionary nature of the experience is emphasized in front of the pagan Festus (and Ananias consequently disappears). A translation note is supplied (26:14a), and helpful explanatory glosses are even added, like the Hellenistic aphorism Paul quotes in 26:14: "It hurts you to kick against the goads." (This denoted an unequal struggle by a mortal against God or the gods.)[60]

On the other hand, the accounts show significant historical compression. From Paul's writings we can confirm that his call did take place in or around Damascus (Gal. 1:17), although it is difficult to tell whether he was on his first journey to that city. Paul's first journey to Jerusalem as a Christian took place three years later. In the intervening time he was in "Arabia." While earlier generations of scholars rather romanticized this statement, imagining Paul undergoing a long period of reflection in the desert, it is much more likely to be a reference principally to missionary activity in the region of Arabia, which included the kingdom of Nabataea and the independent principality of the Decapolis. And even Acts notes that Paul obeyed the divine command to preach Jesus immediately. But Acts omits all reference to the Arabian mission and refers to this three-year period as "many days."

The accounts in Acts are thus considerably reshaped — having been augmented as the narrative occasions demanded and highly compressed (as the narrative occasions really demanded as well). Yet Paul's statements do confirm the basic claims of Acts that a dramatic call to Paul took place in the vicinity of Damascus,[61] involving a vision of the risen Jesus *and* an apostolic commission.[62] This is also unquestionably an encounter with God. Moreover, Paul later left Damascus in ignominious circumstances (see Acts 9:24-25; 2 Cor. 11:32-33), and it should not be overlooked that Paul is described in Acts prior to this event as zealously persecuting the church, so the experience was clearly unexpected, which is also to say, unconditional. (Certain participants in the story emphasize this through their surprise — principally Ananias — thereby playing an analogous role to the surprised Christians in Judea in Gal. 1:23-24.) Paul's Jewish learning is also recognized frequently (see 26:24; earlier in the same speech, he is denoted as a Pharisee — see 26:5). Furthermore, having visited Jerusalem briefly,[63] he went first to the regions of Cilicia and Syria.

This is actually quite an impressive degree of correspondence — that is, *everything* from the letters is also attested by Acts. But we would be unwise to press much beyond Acts' correlation with Paul's account to supply additional information to our description on the basis of its further suggestions. There are narrative embellishments in Acts and (at the least) small imperfections. It is in any case a little hard to know exactly what those supplements might be![64] Further attacks on the accuracy of Acts' account from this point are in my view indecisive, and now largely irrelevant, although they are worth considering in passing, because the question of Acts' integrity will be so important for the claims of certain Justification advocates that we must consider momentarily.

Excursus: Possible Discrepancies between Acts and the Pauline Data concerning Paul's Conversion

Most of the criticisms of Acts in this relation derive from the immediate prelude to Paul's conversion in Acts, about which Paul is largely silent. We will look briefly at the two main concerns often expressed at this point.

(1) Was Paul only a young man at the time, as Acts suggests?

This is a complex issue. Acts 7:58 — at a most artful point! — calls Paul a νεανίας, or "young man." This probably denotes an age of around twenty, although the reference could be stretched beyond this: see Diogenes Laertius 8.10 and Philo, *On the Cherubim*, 114. In the latter it denotes the last stage of growth before perfect manhood or maturity, falling after puberty, after another stage, and after the growth of the beard! (ποῦ τὸ βρέφος, ποῦ ὁ παῖς, ποῦ [ὁ] ἀντίπαις, ποῦ ὁ ἄρτι ἡβῶν, ποῦ τὸ μειράκιον, ὁ πρωτογένειος, ὁ νεανίας, ὁ τέλειος ἀνήρ;). See also perhaps Phrynicus (ed. C. A. Lobeck) 218 (BDAG 667). We have only one possible reference to Paul's age from his own writings. He calls himself a πρεσβύτης in Philemon 9 — an "old man" — and this would probably contradict the suggestion of Acts.[65] However, this evidence is not clear-cut. Bentley early conjectured that scribes substituted this signifier for πρεσβευτής, an "ambassador," perhaps on the assumption that Paul wrote this letter at the end of his life in a long Roman incarceration. And many have followed this emendation. Diplomatic self-designation is common for Paul and is present in the possibly parallel text Ephesians 6:20 (πρεσβεύω ἐν ἁλύσει). Still more significantly, Paul's language of exhortation in 2 Corinthians 5:20 is closely linked to diplomatic imagery: πρεσβεύομεν ὡς τοῦ θεοῦ παρακαλοῦντος δι' ἡμῶν, the very word he uses in relation to Philemon here (διὰ τὴν ἀγάπην μᾶλλον παρακαλῶ). To make matters worse, the two nouns are found as variants in Polyaenus 8.9.1 (BDAG 863). Reluctantly, then, because it is vital to accord primacy to Paul's own evidence, I conclude that Acts' suggestion here concerning Paul's relatively young age — that of a young man — at the time of his conversion is not without merit (and at least this fits with some of the suggestions of the sociological conversion theorists that we noted earlier, although this correlation should not be given primacy).[66]

(2) Was Paul really present at the stoning of Stephen and hence persecuting the church in Jerusalem prior to making the journey to Damascus?

The author of Acts has a strong tendency to link his key characters, so it is entirely plausible to suggest that Paul's presence at the stoning of Stephen has been crafted artificially, and several further contentions may support this claim. Paul states that he was "unknown by sight to the assemblies of Judea in Christ" (Gal. 1:22 DC). It seems a little strange at first blush that the Christian communities in Judea would not actually know what their chief persecutor looked like. Nor does Paul include himself in his reference to their persecution by Judeans in 1 Thessalonians 2:14-16 (assuming the latter's authenticity). After his conversion Paul clearly uses Damascus as his base of operations, evangelizing in and around that city for three years. This, coupled with a complete lack of reference to any journey to Damascus at the time, seems to imply that he was actually living there. Adding to this suspicion is the dubious legal basis for Paul's mission to Damascus. Acts claims that Paul had letters from the high priest authorizing him to arrest Christian Jews in Damascus and bring them "bound" to Jerusalem (9:1-2). But it is correctly questioned whether the high priest in Jerusalem had the right to authorize the arrest of Jews who lived in a Roman province. Moreover, Luke tends to move characters around in accordance with legal protocols, some of which are either fictional or exaggerated (see Luke 2:1-5!; also Acts 25:11-12, 21; 26:32). This all seems like a reasonably powerful cumulative case that the story leading up to Paul's conversion in Acts is largely fabricated. However, each one of these contentions can be countered.

   That Paul would be unknown by sight to the Judean Christians that he had been persecuting is conceivable in an age when figures were known largely by reputation and not visually. If some of the Christians he had persecuted had fled (perhaps those in Greek-speaking synagogues), if the early church had also been partly divided and Paul had attacked only one part of it (Acts 6:1-6; 8:1), and if the persecution had been limited to Jerusalem at least as far as Paul was concerned, then this is the more comprehensible. The rest of the *Judeans* may well not have known their persecutor *by sight*. Further, Paul may omit reference to himself as a persecutor of Judeans in 1 Thessalonians 2:14-16 because the point of that statement is a reference to persecution *by their own countrymen,* and Paul was not a Judean. He of course repeatedly corroborates the basic claim of Acts that he had persecuted Christians.

That Paul, a Pharisee, would be living in Jerusalem as a young man is entirely plausible. We have little evidence of Pharisees at this time being resident outside Judea (and there may arguably have been good reasons for them to reside in Judea; see also Acts 23:16). And that after his conversion Paul would remain in Damascus is again entirely plausible. He had received a divine commission to evangelize pagans, so it would have made sense for him to begin in that pagan city and then to work in the surrounding pagan areas, that is, the Decapolis and Nabataea. Indeed, for him to have returned to Jerusalem would have been effectively to disobey his call. (He also needed to join a Christian community and to leave his former life situation, which was presumably hostile to Christians.)

It is not overly surprising that Paul never mentions his aggressive pre-conversion mission to Damascus. He supplies very few details about his turbulent life. (But Acts is correct about his dramatic escape from Damascus, which, it should be noted, is not mentioned in Galatians; that is, Galatians too is a selective account.) Furthermore, a case can be made for the legal rectitude of such a mission. The government of Jerusalem at times regarded Jewish communities in other regions as colonies, and Roman recognition seems periodically to have been accorded this view (see esp. 1 Macc. 15:21; also Josephus, *Antiquities,* 14.192-95). With the permission of the local authorities, the Jerusalem authorities could have claimed jurisdiction over Jews in other regions who were causing trouble in relation to their ostensible Jewish citizenship. So Paul's mission to Damascus does seem possible. Moreover, the "letters" in question may have been "requests" rather than "orders" and Luke a little hyperbolic at this point. That local Jewish authorities — in collaboration with local government — would respond to a written request from the high priest in Jerusalem seems quite plausible. (And so Luke would have slightly exaggerated the actual jurisdiction of these requests, which would hardly be out of character!: see 9:2.)

In sum, Acts does contain blemishes. Its accounts of Paul's conversion are different, and at certain points contradictory. The narrative drastically foreshortens the apostle's time in Damascus and then exaggerates some of the details of his later visit to Jerusalem, perhaps along with the exact basis of his initial journey to Damascus. But these might be reasonably construed as slips or literary flourishes. Beyond these difficulties it does not seem to be decisively proven that the overarching story is *extensively* fabricated. Rather, the correlations are more impressive than the divergences.

In view of this I suggest that we need not go beyond the account of Paul's conversion as I have articulated that in this chapter. Some might object that this account is rather minimalist. Others might suggest that I have given too much credence to Acts — but I can see little point in discarding information in Acts when nothing stands against it, and we have in any case used little if any evidence found there that is not directly corroborated by evidence from Paul's own hand.

With our description of Paul's conversion thus in place, we can turn to consider its implications for Justification theory. Does it match the progressions that Justification lays down as normative? (Or, does it conform more to the opinions of the sociologists?!) And while I do not see a direct and simple contradiction here — and hence falsification — as Stendahl did, I do see *three* difficulties that amount to a further acute tension at the theory's empirical frame: (1) there is an absence of direct corroborative evidence in Paul's writings for the theory of conversion endorsed by Justification theory, and this despite the claims by various scholars that it is there — "Paul's silences" (the subject of §3.4 following); (2) there are subtle but repeated indications that Justification theory does not account for Paul's actual development as a missionary, in particular that he did not immediately abandon the law in his pagan mission (i.e., as Justification theory both expects and demands) — "the case for Paul's *later* abandonment of mandatory law-observance — at Antioch" (§3.5); and (3) that his actual missionary preaching, insofar as we can reconstruct it, did not conform to the expectations of Justification theory (i.e., "turn or burn") — "Paul's scandalous proclamation" (§3.6).

3.4. Paul's Silences

Paul's biographical silence in relation to Justification theory is significant. Of course not all silences in our sources are significant, but this one seems pregnant.[67] Justification theory is tightly linked to biography, as is evident in many of its modern practitioners. It is a true account of the journey to salvation. So we would expect Paul to recapitulate at least some of its key realizations in any references that he makes to his own conversion; we would expect him to use its terms and moves to explain his own journey. Moreover, we would expect that journey to play a theologically significant role when he articulates and attempts to defend or to apply Justification theory to his recalcitrant readers. But we find almost no explicit deployment of Justification themes in Paul's discussions of his conversion, and there is a similar poverty in the overt deployment of biographical material in support of his Justification texts and arguments.

In Galatians, *none of the key terms within Justification occurs in Paul's account of his conversion* in 1:12-16.[68] Certainly, Paul observes the law as a Jew, and zealously. But he does not describe this in terms of "works of law," nor does he articulate any introspective realizations at this point. He does not even orient this activity salvifically. Law observance functions in parallel with persecution of the church, and hence merely as an illustration of his zeal for God (which presumably could itself have been motivated by various considerations). Similarly, the language of "faith" is not used in direct association with his conversion, and δικαιο-terms are completely absent throughout. Both these word groups achieve prominence in Galatians only from 2:15 onward. And this highlights precisely the ensuing difficulty that just when Paul's biographical argumentation ceases his Justification argumentation begins. (His conversion is long past.) The key terms within Justification theory are evident within Paul's argument, albeit a little irregularly, from 2:15 through 3:26, and some of them recur suddenly in the compact summary statements of 5:4-6. Hence, *just where the theory seems most prominent in Galatians, Paul's conversion narrative is entirely absent.* Paul returns to biographical argumentation in 4:11-20 (although not to his conversion), but this is one of the barren sections in the letter in terms of Justification terminology. The two themes seem to have no relation to one another.

Some Justification advocates have attempted to introduce a biographical dimension to Paul's quotations of covenantal curse language in 3:10 and 3:13 (citing Deut. 27:26 and 21:23 respectively), and this would pull references to his life into the middle of one of his most intense Justification discussions. We will examine this subsection in more detail in due course (in both part three, chapter twelve and part five, chapter twenty). For now it suffices to note that Paul makes no explicit biographical claims in relation to these quotations, nor does any biographical evidence from elsewhere in his texts support an analysis of his conversion in terms of curse. To the contrary, he never again uses curse texts in *any* capacity, which strongly confirms the suspicion that their deployment here is entirely contingent. Indeed, there are good reasons for relating these quotations in a purely rhetorical way to the Galatian situation. Hence, with an absence of any overt evidence in support, and the presence of good reasons to the contrary, it seems right to deny the biographical relevance of these statements for the moment.

To the substantial difficulty of these silences in Galatians we must now add the utter embarrassment of Paul's argumentation in Romans. Romans contains no explicit biographical analysis of Paul's conversion at all.[69] His apostolic office is affirmed on occasion, but without biographical elaboration or support (see 1:1, 5; 15:15-21), and what biographical information is present is in the main highly contingent (i.e., recent). Moreover, despite containing an ostensibly comprehensive articulation of Justification theory beginning in 1:16, not a jot or tittle of the argument is autobiographical. (And to the difficulty of reading 7:7-25 as an account of the pre-Christian Paul, we could add here the problem of its placement: the explication of Justification theory is in chapters 1–4, so the obvious point at which to include it would be chapter 2. Why the readers should wait until chapter 7 — presumably returning mentally to insert this material at the appropriate point in the earlier argument — is very difficult to explain.) A less concentrated use of Justification terms beginning in 9:30 also fails to draw on Paul's conversion. In short, the silence of Romans in terms of Paul's conversion is positively thunderous.

The same dislocated pattern is evident elsewhere in Paul. In 1 Corinthians, the references to Paul's conversion in 9:1 and 15:7-10 are devoid of Justification terminology or argumentation.[70] Philippians 3:2-11 is arguably the only exception to this trend; only in this fiery excursus do we find Justification terms and Paul's biography in close proximity. (πίστις occurs twice, in v. 9, and δικαιοσύνη three times, with one further probable elided instance, in vv. 6 and 9.) But even in this text any mutual support between conversion and Justification theory is arguably more apparent than real. This text will be examined in detail in due course (in part five, chapter twenty-one), so here we should simply note that although Paul introduces his pre-Christian background into the broader discussion, he does not characterize it in a helpful way for the theory of Justification. "Works," insofar as they are present, characterize certain specific people — the opponents of Paul, "the dogs." The motif is never applied to Paul himself. Furthermore, Paul's life as a Jew is at first a highly particular account of his Jewish ancestry — "qualifications" over which he himself had no control and hence could not work for! When he briefly characterizes his law observance, it is, as we have already noted, as an instance of zeal and is described as "faultless." There is no hint of an introspective journey here, as Stendahl well knew. Then, at just the point where we would most expect it, Paul's biographical account stops! There is no actual account of his conversion. We jump straight to an account of Paul's *present* existence "in Christ." Moreover, no judgment of "justification" is ever rendered in relation to these two phases. Instead, the orientation of the entire passage is toward resurrection (i.e., toward eschatological existence)! To make matters worse, the epistemological structure of the account is stated quite explicitly to be *retrospective*. Paul says clearly that *previously he accounted his well-qualified background to be a matter of "gain," but now, in the light of the knowledge of Christ, he considers it "loss" if not "dung."* This perspective is a complete reversal of the epistemological structure of Justification theory.[71]

For all these reasons, I am not sure that Philippians 3:2-11 really constitutes an exception to the trend we have established through the rest of Paul's texts. Although it is the best hope for Justification advocates in terms of its possible integration of Paul's conversion and his soteriological theory, it falls short of complete or convincing demonstration (and my later discussion will suggest that it is in fact profoundly awkward for that theory). And — in sum overall — it is hard to avoid the impression that Paul is much less interested in his conversion in terms of Justification theory than are some of his later interpreters. Indeed, his silences seem highly significant. If Paul talks about Justification so much in theoretical terms *and* if there is an organic relation of Justification with biographical issues, that Paul seldom — and arguably never — uses such terms in discussing his own journey is highly troublesome, as is his corresponding failure to support his theory with the appropriate stories drawn from his own life. We do not yet have a direct falsification of the expectations of Justification theory, as Stendahl attempted with his appeal to ἄμεμπτος (that is, a datum that directly contradicts the expectations of Justification theory in biographical terms). But we do seem to have an *indirect* falsification in the form of a complete absence of any causality or argumentative relationship between the two discourses of Justification and conversion in Paul's extant texts.

We should observe in this relation as well, however, that although a reasonably detailed portrait has emerged of Paul's famous shift in perspective, there is no endorsement *in* that description as yet of any of the key elements within Justification theory, and, in particular, of the critical journey that ostensibly takes place *prior* to conversion through faith, as the individual struggles with law, transgression, conscience, and the pending wrath of God. And this must be troubling for the Justification advocate. That is, not only is the linkage *between* Paul's Justification discussions and his references to his conversion absent, but the latter texts contain no explicit mention *of* Justification, which means in turn that *there is no direct evidence that the apostle's conversion took place in accordance with that theory's expectations.* We expect a journey through a long struggle with sin illuminated by the law before the bar of God's stern justice, to the relief of justification by faith alone (and as certain texts from Luther arguably suggest). *But we never get these.* (I am aware that an important scholarly trajectory has denied this, so I include some interaction with their — and related — arguments just below in an excursus. In a sense, this trajectory pushes beyond the evidence both in Paul and in Acts.)

Excursus: The "Lutheran" Biography of Paul

The largely conservative — but highly scholarly — interpretative tradition advocating the "Lutheran" biography of Paul features formidable studies by U. Wilckens, P. Stuhlmacher, S. Kim, C. Dietzfelbinger, and M. Hengel, among others.[72] (It can also link up with certain distinctive approaches to conversion in general mediated through the normative appropriation of Paul's.[73]) The "Lutheran" biography of Paul seeks a more maximalist reading of the data and argues that the workings of the Justification model are apparent in Paul's own conversion. This basic claim has three subordinate arguments, which we will consider here in turn, pausing to note their associated problems.[74] My protests here, however, can merely be added to those that have already been made — figures such as H. Räisänen and J. D. G. Dunn, who have earlier rejected these suggestions and, as far as I can tell, cogently.[75]

(1) The early Christians — that is, "the Stephen circle" — had a law-free gospel. Paul persecuted them because of his "zeal for the law." He then converted to the religion he had once opposed.

The problems. There is almost no evidence concerning the radical pre-Pauline Christians. But what evidence we do have does not suggest that they were "law-free" (see esp. Acts 6–8)! They were possibly critical of the temple, and perhaps also of the sacred status of the land of Israel, and these positions would almost certainly have been sufficiently deviant to arouse Paul's ire. They are not sufficient, however, to establish a law-free gospel, which is quite another thing. (So, e.g., Stephen does not attack the law, in Acts 7, *but bases his attacks of sacred τόπος on the law.*) Corroborating this initial difficulty — and as we will see in more detail shortly — the Jerusalem church does not seem to have been aware of a law-free mission until some years after Paul's conversion. This suggests that all the original variants of Jewish Christianity in Jerusalem were not law-free. (Paul's later difficulties with the early church leaders corroborate this protest.)[76]

(2) Christ appeared to Paul as "the end of the law" (Rom. 10:4). And so salvation could now no longer be restricted to Jews — that is, now that it was on the basis of faith alone. Thus, Paul became the apostle to the pagans.

The problem. Romans 10:4 cannot with surety be attributed to the Damascus road. It is more likely to stem from the contingent controversy in Rome. This text is discussed in detail in part five, chapter nineteen, at which point any links with Damascus look very tenuous. Certainly nothing in the text actually indicates this. Moreover, such a relocation can point to no explicit evidence in Paul concerning his conversion *or* from Acts. At bottom then this claim is rather extraordinary. (Presumably it rests on more programmatic claims, but their difficulties will be addressed shortly.)

(3) Paul may have persecuted Christians under the view that Christ was accursed (see Gal. 3:10, 13) and later, reflecting on the death of an innocent man, concluded that — rather — the law was accursed.

The problems. We should note this argument contains, first, significant non sequiturs, and, second, evidential falsifications. If Christ redeems "us" from the curse of the law, then the curse is valid for us and must remain so. Moreover, the law is not wrong to inflict it in these instances and thus not thereby called into question.[77] That Christ died as an innocent person, who should not have been accursed, is not the fault *of* the law, but of those who falsely accused and executed him — in fact, the Romans. Hence, no Jews up to this general point in history (or subsequently) seem to have drawn this conclusion from the fact of innocent crucified Jews.[78] So, for example, the fall of Jerusalem was not followed by a wave of law-free Jewish expressions as the crucifixion of hundreds of innocent Jews led to the survivors' perception that the law was now accursed. Indeed, not even Paul's Jewish Christian opponents seem to have concluded this.[79]

In the second instance, Galatians 3:13 and its citation of Deuteronomy 21:23 cannot with surety be attributed to self-reflection on the law stemming from the Damascus road. It is more likely to stem from the contingent argument in Galatia (as is Gal. 3:10 and its citation of Deut. 27:26), a point that we will address in more detail in part four, chapter thirteen, and part five, chapter twenty. Let it suffice for now to note then that Paul does not really explain his use of the Deuteronomy 21 text in its immediate setting; its deployment is *very* abbreviated. But a satisfactory account of its operation in contingent terms can be given, shifting the burden of proof for any more extensive implications onto those who would argue for them. However, fueling doubt at such points is the absence of any widespread or fully articulated use of the argument elsewhere by Paul. Its absence from the rest of Galatians, and from Romans in its entirety, is especially troubling.

At bottom then, the argument itself is not especially coherent or plausible, while the exegetical case is fragile (to say the least). We need a stronger foundation than this for Paul's controversial and radical movement past the law.

In short, a critical reading of the relevant texts simply cannot find the "Lutheran" biography there, although ideally we would spend rather more time demonstrating this claim. Such assertions tend to beg the question.

It seems that explicit biographical attestation in Paul to Justification theory is lacking — and despite its ardent attempted demonstration. Paul's conversion revolves around vigorous Jewish activity in relation to which no psychological data is supplied, an unexpected disclosure by God, and a set of particular revelations and instructions — in particular, to preach the son of God, the risen Christ, to the pagans. And while these activities and events are compatible with Justification theory, none of them amount *to* Justification theory (or one of its distinctive components). There is, in short, *no* explicit attestation to Justification in Paul's life. But this awkward observation has a reverse side as well.

Just as when Paul speaks of his conversion, he is silent in relation to Justification concerns, some of the key elements that he recounts in that conversion are not related intrinsically *to* Justification because of their particularity and unexpectedness. And this generates a further cluster of difficulties.

Justification can admittedly account for the *evangelism* of *everybody* (because sinful individuals can be saved only if they hear about the second, saving contract — salvation through faith alone). But an *apostolic commission to proclaim the son of God specifically to the pagans* is *not* what the theory builds toward. These are actually quite particular revelations. It is clear from Paul's writings that he regards his apostolicity as an unusual task and privilege; not all are called to this.[80] Moreover, a particular revelation is bound up with this — the proclamation of the good news of God's son, the risen Jesus, now enthroned on high and lord of all (see Rom. 10:9-10). And the generic realizations of Justification theory do not and cannot deliver this sort of information to a prospective convert; these specific realizations could, indeed, *only be achieved by way of revelation.* Indeed, not only is a disjunction apparent at this point, but Justification also cannot offer any criteria to the individual that could evaluate the truth of these particular claims cogently. If Paul was converted in terms of Justification theory then, he had no way of authenticating his apostolic commission or his gospel's content!

As if this was not enough, the two sets of difficulties that we have just noted — namely, the silence of Paul's conversion narratives concerning the realizations of Justification (especially in its first phase), and the disjunction between the main elements in Paul's conversion (of apostolicity and the like) and the realizations and ratifications achievable by Justification theory — now combine into a third problem. Justification theory is actually redundant as an explanation of Paul's conversion. It is not necessary in order to explain what Paul *does* tell us about the content of his conversion — which was quite particular — (i.e., problem two, just noted), and there are no indications in his texts that it was *otherwise* present (problem one). And this is quite an important realization.

It is possible to suggest the presence of Justification theory in Paul's life and thinking largely on the basis of theological inference. It *can* fit into his conversion and his gospel — at least at first glance — and perhaps then *ought* to because at least it explains that conversion, and Paul's subsequent law-free mission to the pagans. He is an apostle because Justification supplies such strong impetus for evangelism and preaching, and his mission is controversially but quite correctly law-free because Paul has undergone the harrowing journey through Justification's first phase and initial contract to faith alone, and realized that the law can only prepare for that Christian posture and must now be left behind (at least in its soteriological aspects). But we have just seen that things are not really this simple.

Paul's conversion is in part an overt call to apostolicity in relation to the risen Christ. And Justification does not correlate with these notions directly *and neither can it* (because of their particularity). So it does not really explain his conversion (while neither does it ever seem to overtly). Moreover, an alternative explanation for Paul's law-free gospel can be supplied (see especially the alternative soteriology sketched in chapter three, on the basis of Romans 5–8) — a more eschatological rationale. So any broadly inferential and theological case for the presence of Justification theory in relation to Paul's conversion has been undermined.[81] That hypothesis can only now be proved through the production of explicit evidence, but we have already seen that this too seems to be absent. We can turn then at this point to bang some final nails into Justification's biographical coffin — evidence that seems to contradict directly the biographical claims of Justification theory: specifically, that the law was abandoned by Paul on the road to Damascus, and that his subsequent preaching was essentially of Justification theory. Subtle but important evidence in Paul's letters seems to contradict both these two important inferences, thereby suggesting that Justification theory ought *not* to be mobilized as an explanation of Paul's conversion, apostolic call, and subsequent mission work.

3.5. The Case for Paul's Later Abandonment of Mandatory Law Observance — at Antioch

I am not convinced that Paul abandoned law observance immediately after his call — that he relinquished it immediately as a requirement for pagan conversion.[82] Clearly, he kept it himself on occasion, although not in any "necessary" sense (see 1 Cor. 9:19-23). The evidence suggests that this important transition actually took place several years later. If so, this would be extremely troublesome for Justification advocates. The arguments for a biography of Paul in terms of Justification would be instantly undercut.

The theory of Justification expects its converts to abandon the law as soon as they become Christians "by faith." Indeed, the abandonment of law must be prepared for before the moment of salvation by faith arrives. This abandonment is prompted largely by the frustration of repeated attempts to observe the law along with the inevitable failure to do so (although perseverance is nevertheless required as long as Christ's saving benefits are not accessed by faith). Without this experience (as we well know by now) individuals are not ready to receive the offer of the gospel; they do not yet know that they need it and are not yet motivated to accept it to escape an experience of terror and despair. It is consequently *impossible* to become a Christian without abandoning the law. A critical rational progression within the journey to conversion would have to be omitted, which would eliminate the opportunity for conversion itself. Hence, according to Justification, Paul almost certainly wanted to abandon the law before he encountered Christ near Damascus (perhaps having thought that way for some time). And he must have abandoned it in strict relation to that encounter, during which he realized that he was now justified by faith alone.[83] Indeed, his encounter is largely reducible to this realization of salvation sola fide.

It will be extremely troublesome for Justification theory then if it can be shown that Paul and his pagan converts were law observant *after* his conversion

— and possibly well after it (i.e., for several years) — in the sense that Paul's mission to the pagans did *not* at first allow converts to abandon the law. The evidence for this claim is admittedly not overwhelming, but it does exist, which immediately gives it certain advantages over the main competing accounts. There are three intersecting components underlying this claim, drawn from three separate texts:[84]

(1) Galatians 1:18–2:14

In this text Paul supplies an important account of his relationship with Jerusalem that presumably runs roughly up to the point at which he wrote that letter. It includes two visits to Jerusalem and a confrontation with Peter in Antioch (the latter episode being of less importance here). Paul dates these two visits carefully, supplying intervals of three and fourteen years respectively. On the second visit, fourteen years after either his call or his first visit, the nature of Paul and Barnabas's pagan mission is debated (2:1-10). Paul presents this meeting as concluding satisfactorily. The "pillars" in Jerusalem — James, Cephas, and John — offer their right hands to Paul and Barnabas in recognition of a pact (possibly sworn on oath or made in relation to some pledge), also recognizing thereby their divine authorization in evangelizing pagans. Furthermore, they do not curtail the "freedom" of any pagan converts, asking only for continued almsgiving. Conspicuously, Titus is not compelled to be circumcised. Hence, the momentous question of law observance by converts to the Christian movement from paganism has clearly been at stake, at least in part, at this meeting; and — rather incredibly — the pillars in Jerusalem have not insisted on it.[85]

That this was a highly controversial issue is emphasized by the short account that immediately follows. In 2:11-14 Paul recounts an ugly incident at Antioch that included Cephas and Barnabas. It is not necessary to decide here whether this incident occurred just before or just after the Jerusalem conference of 2:1-10. It is enough to say that there was a split in fellowship between Jewish and formerly pagan Christians at some time very close to that critical meeting. The Jewish Christians have separated themselves from pagan converts at mealtimes, presumably because of Jewish purity regulations related to food and hence, ultimately, the entire question of law observance.[86] Paul is greatly angered by what he takes to be an instance of hypocrisy that fails to accord with the straightforward truth of the gospel, and he claims to have rebuked Cephas publicly about it.

However, the first visit to Jerusalem by Paul, described before these rather dramatic encounters, is notable largely for its innocuousness (see 1:18-19). Somewhat curiously, Paul makes a strident claim that he met only two apostles then, Cephas and James (1:18-19). The visit lasted for two weeks and resulted in considerable glorification of God by the local Christians in Judea when they heard that the one who had formerly persecuted them was now vigorously engaged in preaching the gospel.[87]

The implications of all this for our current question are quite straightforward. The conclave in Jerusalem recounted in 2:1-10 was concerned in large measure with the question of law observance by pagan converts to Christianity. That this was a controversial question is indicated clearly by the difficulties that Paul notes with Cephas and Barnabas in Antioch, not to mention the problems he is currently occupied with at Galatia. In view of this, it seems almost certain then that this question was *not* discussed during Paul's first visit to Jerusalem, which took place only three years after his call. If it had been, then the second visit would have been redundant, as would the conflict at Antioch, both of which took place much later.

There could perhaps be another reason for this absence of earlier conversation. Paul might have already reached his radical position on law observance by the time he first visited Jerusalem but not explicitly communicated it to James and Cephas during his relatively brief stay. The issue didn't arise. But a moment's consideration suggests that this explanation is rather unlikely. Paul had been called by God to evangelize the pagans, and it seems rather implausible that an extraordinarily radical missionary praxis on his part went unmentioned to his senior colleagues in the church during a two-week stay with them. (Indeed, if he had tried to evangelize any pagans in Jerusalem, then it would have become quite obvious.) If Paul had been prosecuting a law-free gospel to the pagans at the time, then it seems almost certain that the Jerusalem conference would have taken place "three years," not "fourteen years," after his call.

The most likely explanation for the initial silence about this issue, then — and, consequently, the apparently tranquil first stay — along with the disruptive and controversial events that followed much later, is that Paul had not yet begun his law-free mission. But we are not left with merely an argument from silence (albeit a powerful one). One of Paul's texts arguably confirms this claim.

(2) Galatians 5:11

This is a brief appeal that occurs within a highly personal section of argument: "But my friends, why am I still being persecuted if I am still preaching circumcision? In that case the offense of the cross has [also] been removed" ('Εγὼ δέ, ἀδελφοί, εἰ περιτομὴν ἔτι κηρύσσω, τί ἔτι διώκομαι; ἄρα κατήργηται τὸ σκάνδαλον τοῦ σταυροῦ). This compressed argument is not especially easy to unravel; in fact, two claims seem to be involved (i.e., Paul has supplied two apodoses for one protasis). But we are interested here in only the first — and clearest — one.

The first half of the verse makes a point in terms of a compact hypothetical conditional (although its form is first class). At the most obvious level it falsifies the truth of the protasis. If Paul were still preaching circumcision then his opponents would not still be persecuting him (because presumably they would not find this offensive). However, they *are* still persecuting him — doubtless in part at Galatia — so he clearly is *not* still preaching circumcision. Paul does not spell out this entire argument, but it is the direct implication of his statement.[88] The crucial point here is of course Paul's use of the word "still" (ἔτι), which is so easily over-looked. This implies that at a previous point he *had* been preaching circumcision, assuming a temporal reading, as seems most likely.[89] Some interpreters have ex-plained this with reference to pre-Christian missionary work by Paul, but this is very unlikely, because such work would have no rhetorical value for the present situation. It is simply not an effective argument for Paul's opponents to claim at Galatia that Paul preached circumcision before he became a Christian. Paul could then claim that this was obviously irrelevant — compare 1:13-14! It is an effective charge only if Paul really did preach circumcision at some previous point in his life as an apostle to the pagans, and there is no reason to suppose that early on he did not (barring of course the programmatic influence of Justification theory!).

(3) Acts 11:26c

In view of these delicate inferences from Paul's own hand, Acts 11:26c is some-thing of a historical triumph. Here the author observes — almost in passing — that "the disciples were first called 'Christians' [lit. Χριστιανούς]" in Antioch. The historical significance of this comment is considerable. The surrounding pagans seem to have felt the need to designate the disciples at Antioch with a new name. Prior to this point, such a need had not been felt, for the obvious reason that to outsiders, Christians still looked very much like Jews. Their differences from mainstream Judaism were arguably subtle "internal" matters (as Gallio correctly observes: see Acts 18:14-16). Self-designations and perhaps also Jewish designa-tions might have been in circulation, but to the uninterested pagan world the usual umbrella terms would almost certainly have sufficed.[90] However, at Antioch something made this designation inappropriate to the point that a new name was called for, and a typical Roman name then seems to have been sup-plied: "a follower of Christ."[91] The obvious explanation for this phenomenon was that these "Jews" had stopped practicing the law at some crucial point or points — or never started — and so become unrecognizable to outsiders *as* Jews. A re-laxation of the need to be circumcised seems likely, but some relaxation of dietary and Sabbath regulations also seems possible.[92]

This church was a considerable distance from Jerusalem — approximately three hundred miles, making a six-hundred-mile round trip, or roughly thirty days of hard walking if the trip was made by road[93] — so contact between the two centers may not have been that common. Paul's further missionary work, more-over, would be still further to the west and northwest. Hence, that Jerusalem would have remained unaware of Antioch's radical missionary developments on the fringes of its purview is not that implausible. (Certainly, it is far less implausi-ble than the supposition that the law-free gospel was in place during Paul's first visit to Jerusalem!) Most importantly, this innocuous statement in Acts confirms precisely the scenario that we have been developing from hints within Paul's let-ters. Paul's gospel did not become explicitly law free in its missionary praxis until he reached Antioch.

Paul's mission in Antioch was of course *after* his first visit to Jerusalem but before his second. Either he found there a pagan Christian church that was already acting in this fashion, or a pagan church made the transition to a law-free existence while he was there. He then presumably concluded that this transition was theologically legitimate. And all of Paul's extant letters, written to churches founded west of this location and after this event, seem then to presuppose a law-free pagan Christian ethic. None suggest a "postfounding reorientation" on the matter.

In sum, this evidence points to a considerable difficulty for Justification theory. It would seem that Paul did not abandon law observance either theologically or practically on the road to Damascus. At least another three years would elapse before this momentous transition took place — a body blow for the biographical explanation offered by Justification theory, which, if true, expects Paul to abandon the law on the road to Damascus.[94] The available evidence points toward a very different biography, implying directly that Justification theory simply does not map what was going on in Paul's life and thinking. But another embarrassing line of evidence points in the same direction — away from Justification and toward a more apocalyptic construal of the apostle's gospel and mission.

3.6. Paul's Proclamation

I suggest for several reasons that a brief consideration of Paul's proclamation is not encouraging for Justification advocates. But because a detailed review of this activity in Paul must ultimately engage with several complex scholarly debates, the following observations will be more indicative than programmatic.[95]

The data on Paul's proclamation, or preaching, is notoriously difficult, and even defining this activity — in contradistinction, for example, to teaching — can be awkward. Nevertheless it is appropriate to consider here what Paul probably *said* when he *first* arrived in a Greco-Roman town or city to gather converts, because Justification advocates believe that he pursued conversions by proclaiming Justification theory! The preaching of this set of arguments would supposedly have attracted some rational individuals, and led them from their struggles with sin and the law — whether God's commands were known innately or via the Jewish written version — through to the decision of faith, at which point they were converted. So it seems fair to ask if the evidence supports this reconstruction. Unfortunately, direct discussion of preaching is rare and vestigial in Paul's extant letters, and even the indirect evidence is interwoven with many other contingent matters — especially at Corinth!

The most helpful discussions occur in the letter frame of Romans (esp. 1:1-16; 15:15-24; 16:4, 17-20 [and possibly 25-27]), and in the body, in Romans 10 (esp. vv. 6-18; but see also 2:16b, 29b; 3:8; 6:17); 1 Corinthians 1:17b-2:16; 9 (esp. vv. 1-2, 12, 14, 16-23, 27); and 15:1-17; in small snippets throughout 2 Corinthians (1:18-22; 2:12, 17; 3:3-6; 4:1-6, 13; 5:11, 14–6:3; 10:14–11:6, 12-15; 12:12, 14), and Galatians (1:1, 4,

6-12, 15-16; 2:2-9, 14; 3:1-5; 4:13, 19 [and probably also 6:14-16]); in Philippians 1 (esp. vv. 5-7, 12-18, 27-30; see also brief comments in 2:16, 22; 4:3); and in First Thessalonians 1 and 2 (see 1:4-10; 2:2, 4, 12-13; see also 3:2; and Phlm. 13).[96] I suggest that a satisfyingly coherent picture does eventually emerge from this data, although it remains incomplete. It is tempting to organize this material in terms of a form-content distinction, but that would be methodologically dubious. So in what follows we will first address the more easily recognizable theological loci of Christ, the Spirit, and soteriology, and then, beyond this, Paul's communication of these exciting new realities, along with the closely-related issue of epistemology (an issue that relates directly to the manner of his involvement).[97]

This theological locus will receive much greater elaboration later in my analysis (specifically in part four, chapter fifteen), hence, suffice it for now to point out that a narrative of Christ's passion is clearly discernible within much of the evidence of Paul's preaching.[98] Paul repeatedly emphasizes Jesus' death, burial, resurrection, heavenly enthronement as Lord, and future return, and not infrequently in rather shocking terms, speaking of Jesus' humiliating execution through torture. (These claims also often seem counterpoised to reliance on trained speech or rhetoric during proclamation, that is, Paul's struggling appearance and speech are in accordance with a message of crucifixion.) So we can speak with some accuracy of an initial narrative trajectory of descent, culminating in Christ's crucifixion and subsequent burial, and a trajectory of ascent, culminating in his future acclamation as Lord by the entire cosmos — the stories of Good Friday (and Saturday), and Easter Sunday respectively. It is not necessary to decide here whether this narrative began with some notion of pre-existence or not.[99] It would be universally conceded, however, that atonement is associated with his death, and that ascension is implicit in the narrative of heavenly glorification and inheritance. Moreover, the narrative of Jesus' death seems to have included an emphasis on his submission and obedience, and probably also some account of Maundy Thursday — that is, of the Last Supper and its establishment of the Eucharist, since Paul expects this ritual's observance in his communities of pagan converts (see 1 Cor. 11:23-26, esp. v. 23b: ὁ κύριος Ἰησοῦς ἐν τῇ νυκτὶ παρεδίδετο ἔλαβεν ἄρτον . . .).[100]

The Spirit is also a prominent element in the data concerning Paul's preaching. Paul speaks repeatedly of "signs and wonders" attesting to his apostolicity, and of God's presence in his proclamation, although he also moderates the importance of this phenomenon at one point, subordinating it to the cross (see 1 Cor. 1:22-23). Nevertheless, he almost immediately again affirms the "demonstration" or "proof" afforded by the Spirit that elicits human belief (2:4-5: ὁ λόγος μου καὶ τὸ κήρυγμά μου . . . ἐν ἀποδείξει πνεύματος καὶ δυνάμεως, ἵνα ἡ πίστις ὑμῶν μὴ ᾖ ἐν σοφίᾳ ἀνθρώπων ἀλλ᾽ ἐν δυνάμει θεοῦ). Furthermore, the presence of the Spirit in the lives of his converts is a critical attestation to the coming eschatological fulfillment of their initial salvation; the Spirit is a "downpayment" and "guarantee" of later events (2 Cor. 1:22; 5:5; see also Eph. 1:14; the closely-related notion of redemption is also mentioned in 1 Thess. 5:9; see also Eph. 1:14; 2 Thess.

2:14). Various charismatic gifts also seem to have functioned at this point, *both* missiologically and didactically (see esp. 1 Cor. 14:21-25). The presence of the Spirit is one of the most obvious associations with Paul's preaching — a sine qua non of its authenticity and effectiveness (see esp. Gal. 3:1-5).

The third standard theological locus discernible in Paul's preaching is a basic, three-part soteriological schema covering the definition of the particular problem facing humanity, some transition (where baptism seems to be involved), and a contrasting, saved state (see Romans 5–8; Gal. 3:26-28). Different details are supplied by different texts for this basic tripartite schema. At one point the problem is idolatry (see 1 Thess. 1:9-10), and at others, sexual immorality, drunkenness, and similar heinous sins (see 1 Cor. 5:11-12; 6:9-11; 1 Thess. 4:2-8). These practices must be left behind. The solution in some texts clearly involves the return of Christ, and in others the bodily transformation and resurrection of Paul's converts (1 Cor. 15:20-28, 35-58; 1 Thess. 1:10; 4:14-17). Hence the contrasting, saved state seems ultimately to be an eschatological event arriving in all its fullness (Gal. 6:14-15).

Somewhat frustratingly, however, Paul gives few explicit details about the way his original proclamation articulated this schema more specifically. So, without reconstructing his entire theological posture, and then somehow establishing that construct's connections with his initial preaching, it is not possible as yet to press beyond these programmatic claims. And at this point we consequently cannot say with certainty that Paul's preaching attached a condition to the transition from the problem to the solution, placing an imperative prior to the indicative of salvation, thereby echoing Justification theory. Or whether, rather, he placed the indicative *before* the imperative, characterizing salvation unconditionally, and so articulating Christian ethical activity in condition*ed* (not condition*al*) and responsive terms — an echo of the soteriological schema discernible in Romans 5–8. (If it is suggested that Rom. 10:9-10 and Gal. 3:1-5 provide explicit evidence of such a condition of "faith," I must point to my detailed analysis of these passages later on that finds no such attestation in them: see part five, chapters nineteen and twenty.) But while the explicit evidence might seem at this point to be fundamentally indecisive, a consideration of the apostolic and epistemological data will lead us indirectly to the probability of the latter, unconditional reconstruction, over against the conditional approach more supportive of Justification.

There are six interwoven emphases in the data that link epistemological claims and Paul's self-conception: (1) his constant emphasis on a fundamentally revelatory epistemology; (2) his consequent diplomatic persona; (3) the similarly consequent mediating role of his speech; (4) the elected, unconditional nature of human response; (5) his complementary disavowal of rhetorical technique; and (6) his complementary disavowal of "natural theology."

(1)   Underlying much of what Paul says in relation to his preaching is an emphasis on the knowledge of God in Christ as fundamentally revelatory. He grounds his repudiation of formal rhetoric vis-à-vis the Corinthians in

pneumatological disclosure (1 Cor. 1:17b–2:16), and his defense of his apostolic office in Galatians in much the same way (although here the agency of God is more obvious: see esp. 1:1, 4, 8-9, 12, 15-16). This emphasis is tightly interwoven with the next.

(2) Paul's apostolic office is, at least in part, simply a commission by God to proclaim a particular event to the pagans — their salvation through Christ; this exciting news is precisely the gospel that he announces, hence, its usual accompaniments of grace, peace, and joy (see esp. Rom. 1:1-16; 10:15; Phil. 1). Consequently, it is imperative that he proves trustworthy and reliable in discharging this trust (and the patient endurance of suffering and weakness can provide markers of that authenticity: so in particular 2 Cor. 2:14-17; 3:4-6; 4:7–6:10; 11:5-6, 23-33). Moreover, he is beholden to this task, in effect, enslaved to it and the God who authorizes it (Rom. 1:1). But this also explains much of the diplomatic imagery that surrounds this notion: he is God's appointed representative ("making a diplomatic overture" in 2 Cor. 5:20; see also Eph. 6:20; Paul might describe himself directly as an ambassador in Phlm. 9 as well). The disclosure of this particular calling is therefore part of the broader revelation spreading outward from the Christ event itself: Paul is an ambassador to the pagan nations from the newly enthroned king. (See a more detailed exposition of this dynamic in part four, chapter seventeen.)

(3) Consequently, Paul's proclamation *mediates* God's own word, as against reproducing or eliciting it; his speech is a vehicle through which God speaks and begins to rule (see esp. 1 Thess. 2:13; also Rom. 10:6-10, 14-17; 1 Cor. 2:4-6, 13-16), rather than an autonomous, self-directed, or self-grounded activity.

(4) And, as a further consequence of this, the word of God — mediated by the apostolic word — seems to *create* or *constitute* its appropriate response in its recipients. Those who are blind are enabled to see; those who are hostile in their understanding are reconciled (see 2 Cor. 4:4, 6; Rom. 5:10; 8:7-8). (As far as I can tell, however, this cognitive reconciliation should not be construed as overriding human dignity. As we will see in more detail in part five, chapter nineteen when discussing Romans 10, Paul continually creates room for the human rejection of God's constitutive initiative — although he views this as disobedient, sinful, and tragic.[101]) This realization concerning the constitutive dimension mediated by Paul's appointed proclamation also links up with — and explains — the strangely gestational language that the apostle uses on occasion to describe the origin of his communities. He is in birth pangs until Christ is formed (again) in the Galatians (4:19: οὓς πάλιν ὠδίνω μέχρις οὗ μορφωθῇ Χριστὸς ἐν ὑμῖν). Similarly, he is the Corinthians' "father," as against their pedagogue, and thereby "gave birth" to them (1 Cor. 4:15: ἐγέννησα) — the same image he uses for Onesimus's conversion (Phlm. 10; see also Gal. 4:29)![102] These are fundamentally ontological and constitutive metaphors (see Rom. 4:17b).

(5) It is a further predictable corollary that Paul, when pressed, also disavows human technique as the fundamental element supporting the effectiveness and authenticity of his proclamation (a theme especially in 1 Cor. 2:1-16, and 1 Thess. 2:1-13; see also Gal. 1:10; 4:13-20; 5:7-8). It would be unwise to press beyond Paul's contingent rejection of trained rhetoric, however, to a complete repudiation of all human planning and linguistic technique; his letters stand against this implication immediately. Nevertheless, in his disavowal of formal rhetoric we do see a strong reiteration of points one through four above — namely, that the fundamental epistemological and hence linguistic dynamic within his speaking is revelatory, and therefore his own speech must be a mediation of divine disclosure, that is itself unconditional and unconditioned and must be received through a constitutive act of God. No human techniques can ultimately create or manipulate this process. (And although they can presumably serve it, its success is not dependent on such techniques.) This is an important implication with significant consequences for Justification theory.

(6) It is a further and final corollary of this developing epistemological and apostolic portrait that Paul disavows any fundamental or foundationalist role for natural theology (with the possible exception of Rom. 1:19-20, but this text and its setting are treated in detail through part four, esp. chapters thirteen and fourteen, construed there consistently with the revelatory posture that is emerging here). Such a technique would contradict everything that has just been said, so it is not surprising to find Paul repudiating the effectiveness of human educated "wisdom" in favor of pneumatic revelation in 1 Corinthians 1–2 (see esp. 1:21, 22; 2:10, 12-13). It is important to appreciate at this point, however (in an analogous caveat to the one just noted in terms of human freedom under point 4), that the repudiation of a *foundationalist* theological role for natural theology does *not* exclude the *rhetorical* (i.e., persuasive) manipulation of an audience's presuppositions that might create an *Anknüpfungspunkt,* or "point-of-contact," for the gospel's announcement. At stake here is not the epistemological grounding of the gospel's truth in human assumptions and arguments, but the creation of a communicative situation of intelligibility if not of curiosity — precisely the dynamic that seems to underlie Paul's speeches in Acts 13 and 17. These two rhetorics can look very similar, but the underlying epistemological differences are worlds apart, and so must be carefully identified and distinguished.[103]

It is worth observing at this point that the alternative soteriology drawn from Romans 5–8 can coordinate all this data well. It suggests construing the brief soteriological schema apparent in Paul's preaching in fundamentally participatory terms, but such a construal encompasses all Paul's subsequent apostolic and epistemological emphases smoothly — largely because it is a creative and unconditional model. Paul could not *effect* this process; however, he could certainly be involved in it, summoned to proclaim it, and therefore to mediate it. But if this is a fair description of Paul's preaching, then it generates some serious tensions in relation to Justification theory. We will note five in particular:

(1) Justification theory is fundamentally rationalistic, not revelatory. So the picture of Paul's proclamation emerging from the sources contradicts Justification theory at a fundamental level. These two theories of proclamation actually operate on completely different planes. Justification theory does not mediate God's activity but is oriented toward individuals, asking them to make important decisions about God (doubtless with some assistance from the preacher). The argument *is* God's work (i.e., the two are identified), while the grasping of key pieces of information about God by the individualized audience is the theory's intended consequence and ontological climax. Consequently, this theory and Paul's apparent practice could hardly be more different in focus and mode.

(2) As we have already had occasion to note (in chapter three), Paul places a much stronger emphasis elsewhere on the Holy Spirit than Justification theory does, and here that tension becomes overt. Paul's apocalyptic proclamation is unintelligible without the intrinsic operation of the Spirit mediating divine truth and relationship. Justification theory, meanwhile, has no obvious role for the Spirit at all. Clearly then the two conceptions are utterly contradictory at this point.

(3) Justification theory depends on an *epistemologically,* and not merely a *rhetorically* prior phase. However, the former is not overtly attested in the Pauline evidence, nor does the evidence suggest any need for such a vestibule; in a revelational model it is unnecessary and inappropriate. (I am assuming my later construal of Rom. 1:19-20 in part four, chapter fourteen; I am also assuming at this point my more detailed reading of 1 Thess. 1:9-10 in part five, chapter twenty-one.) Hence, at its most critical point, the positive evidence in Paul is lacking, while the evidence we do have is discouraging.

(4) Again we strike here in an overt fashion one of the more generic, theoretical tensions noted earlier on — in this case, the redundancy of many parts of the christological narrative that Paul proclaims. Justification theory has no need for most of the elements that Paul is attested as proclaiming, although the alternative construal of his soteriology makes full use of them. In particular, Christ's resurrection is essentially redundant in Justification theory, while it is overtly salvific in the more participatory approach. But really *any* emphases outside Christ's death and shed blood are redundant for the Justification advocate. Paul's actual preaching seems far too focused on Christ, and then to dwell on him in a strangely extended fashion!

(5) Just as Justification theory lacks an overt and decisive statement of Paul's practice of beginning his account of the solution with his account of the problem — that is, in epistemological as well as rhetorical terms — so too it lacks a decisive statement of soteriological conditionality — that individu-

als *must* do X in order to be saved (and the usual suggestion involves "faith," although some might want to add a need for repentance, contrition, confession, or some combination of these). Rather, Paul's preaching seems to contain only repeated statements of, and indications toward the unconditional nature of the salvation he proclaims (this last therefore being a mediation). Justification advocates can appeal at this point to some texts (e.g., Rom. 10:9-10), but I will offer alternative construals of such statements later on (as already noted), and deny that any decisive attestation to soteriological conditionality can be found in them. It is, after all, right to insist on the unambiguous attestation of such an important theological claim, and to repudiate support generated merely by possible readings — that is, where alternative, unconditional readings of the key texts seem equally possible. If Paul's preaching emphasized the exercise of a particular condition by his prospective converts at some point *in order to be saved,* it is fair to expect an explicit statement of that at least once.

For all these reasons, then, Justification theory seems to struggle once again in relation to the notion of conversion in Paul — in this case, as it attempts to explain the content of Paul's initial proclamation, which ought to have been in terms *of* Justification theory. Justification advocates have certainly grasped Paul's emphasis on preaching per se — on its authority, importance, and central role in Christian growth; this is an important achievement. However, the nature of that preaching seems to have been fundamentally misconstrued when it is pressed for details and for its basic theological dynamic. I conclude then that a consideration of Paul's preaching practices — insofar as we can reconstruct those here briefly from the perhaps surprisingly vestigial evidence — leads to another important falsification of Justification theory on this broad empirical front. Where Justification theory abuts the Pauline reality of proclamation, just as when it abuts his actual conversion, it is found wanting: Paul's scandalous preaching of the crucified Messiah *also* scandalizes later attempts to conceive of that preaching in terms of Justification.

§4. The Implications

In sum, our consideration of conversion has revealed the following:

(1) Justification theory largely presupposes that conversion takes place as individuals reason in relation to the nature of their unsaved state and then decide to accept the offer of Christian salvation made through preaching. But widespread analysis of conversion, largely by social scientists, suggests that this is not in fact how conversion usually takes place; it is a relational, not a rationalistic, process, and thus also communal rather than individual. Hence, Justification theory seems to give a false account of conversion.

(2) The scant evidence concerning Paul's own conversion does not really accord with the Justification view. The dynamics of Justification cannot be found in the extant evidence. And positive evidence stands against this explanation — in particular, that Paul did not abandon the law on the road to Damascus (as Justification expects), but three years later, during the mission in Syrian Antioch.

(3) The scant evidence concerning Paul's proclamation does not accord with Justification theory. He ought to have preached Justification theory when trying to convert pagans. But the available evidence fails to corroborate that he did, and much of it is in tension with the theory's assumptions and dynamics.

Justification theory is thus once more compromised by its claims when it touches broader reality — here at the point of conversion, whether it attempts to explain that phenomenon in general, Paul's ostensible conversion in particular, or his attempts to convert others by way of preaching. I conclude that as an explanation of reality at this particular point — one for which it claims to give a definitive account — the theory of Justification has again been called into serious question. But before turning to our next phase of argument, it is worth noting that the portrait of conversion that has emerged from the sources has converged on the social scientific description, even as it has diverged away from the contours of Justification theory. A more communal, networked, and relational process is usually detectable, mediating key theological truths and disclosures. And this prompts a reconsideration of Stendahl's classic criticisms. Is it still necessary to insist that Paul's revelation of Christ near Damascus was a "call" and not a "conversion"? I suggest that everything now depends on what we bring to the signifier "conversion."

If we are still influenced — whether consciously or subliminally — by Justification theory (or something like it), then an insistence on this distinction is still useful if not important. It does not capture everything that is relevant in the debate, but the notion of call points quickly to certain things that remain problematic for the overarching construction of the situation in terms of Justification — that Paul's experience was quite particular and positive (being a commission to evangelize pagans), and lacks key markers of Justification's anxious introversion, and so on. This distinction points, in short, to the inadequacy of the categories of Justification for comprehending what actually happened to Paul near Damascus, and then, in turn, to the undesirability of extrapolating this narrative to all Christians normatively (because clearly not all are called to be apostles). I would want ultimately to say rather more than this in this relation, but such a distinction is a useful initial wedge into the position of those who are resisting the evidence. In short, if "conversion" is being defined in terms of Justification, then to insist rather on Paul's "call" is probably still a useful initial thing to say because it points quickly to the inadequacy of the former construction, and to some of the evidence underlying that criticism.

But if we have moved on from the debilitating — and fundamentally false — categories of Justification theory, to a new, more nuanced understanding of conversion informed by sociological theory, then it seems to me that little is to be gained by insisting on such a distinction. If conversion is now understood to be a relational process characterized by great variations, and the interaction of a number of different variables — a process operative, moreover, in relation to different communities and networks — then it seems fair to call Paul's Damascus encounter a "conversion." That Paul basically weakened his adherence to one network and became firmly committed to another seems clear — all that is needed for the sociologists to speak of a "conversion." It still remains an open question exactly what happened and how, and no implications are thereby generated for any other conversions; recall that only Justification theory prescribes tightly *how* individuals must convert. It is also no longer necessary to insist that all Paul's key theological notions were vitally reformulated at the moment when he joined a new religion. Paul's Christian theological position no longer depends on a prior theological journey and its categories. Most likely, in fact, is some ongoing process of theological reflection that took place later as Paul absorbed and assimilated the ideas of his new network — just what we have found to be the case in relation to pagan law-observance! (And that intellectual trajectory also need not progress at a steady rate; like many such journeys, it could be difficult to predict and somewhat variable.)

In sum, Paul was not a convert in terms of Justification, but he was a convert in reality.[104] And with these clarifications, we can draw together the discussion of our first five chapters, and assess Justification theory's difficulties as a whole — the task of chapter six.

CHAPTER SIX

Beyond Old and New Perspectives

§1. Preamble

We have reached an important stage in the overarching argument of this book —
where we grasp that our wise but blind scholars of "Indostan" have been touching
different parts of the same great beast.[1] My central contention through part one,
building toward this point, has been that the general description of Paul will be
greatly complicated if not disordered by the presence there of a fundamentally
contractual theory of salvation that we have dubbed Justification; my analysis has
therefore been theory driven and rather formal. We have seen how the endorsement of this construct as a valid description of part of Paul's thinking could generate an entire spectrum of difficulties through various levels within his broader
thinking — within his actual argumentation in this particular respect (i.e., intrinsically), within the wider frame of his more systematic theological thinking as a
whole, and in terms of implicit empirical claims about the realities of Judaism,
and of conversion (including here the phenomenon of conversion in general,
Paul's own momentous volte-face near Damascus, and his missiological praxis).
Furthermore, we have seen that these difficulties seem to be largely unavoidable
— that defenders of Paul's integrity in terms of Justification do not seem to be
able to explain them away satisfactorily *because they are largely inherent within
the dynamics of the theory itself.*[2]

Articulating these various difficulties, however, has taken us through
some quite diverse theoretical terrain and into the consideration of distant interpretative boundaries. So it should now be helpful to draw all these disparate difficulties together under one head — to summarize the entire spread of problems
— and then to show how various critical debates taking place elsewhere in isolation can be integrated by this unified characterization of our difficulties in terms
of Justification theory. In fact, from this point we will — first — be able to appreciate that while many past interpreters of Paul have been familiar with one or

more of these problems, few if any have grasped *the* problem: that a single construct, Justification theory, may underlie an entire spread of difficulties. (And thus previous characterizations of "the problem" in Paul have — somewhat ironically — tended to lack coherence.[3]) Hence, just as we have moved beyond the "Lutheran" reading of Paul to a more precise characterization in terms of Justification theory, we will now be able to move beyond the protests of "the new perspective" as well, to a more compact and coherent analysis.[4] But our clarifications will not stop at the boundaries of specialized Pauline debate. We will be able, second, to draw connections between our theory-driven analysis of certain difficulties in Paul and many broader theological and ecclesial debates. So the difficulties inaugurated by a commitment to Justification theory within Paul will be shown to reverberate far beyond the overt borders of the apostle's interpretation. Much more is at stake than the limited concerns articulated by New Testament scholarship.

After this web of linkages has been articulated, we will be able, third, to turn to the various highly significant implications that flow from it. And we will find that something of a methodological springboard has been created for us to launch our argument into the hermeneutical and exegetical challenges of parts two and three respectively.

For ease of reference the main difficulties that we have isolated formally up to this point are summarized here. Following this summary, we will consider the debates that they illuminate in more detail, beginning with the discussions peculiar to Pauline studies.

Intrinsic Difficulties (IDs)

ID 1: *Epistemology.* Justification theory argues two incompatible epistemologies: a general, atemporal, philosophical, and rational conception of knowledge — "objective" philosophical reasoning; and a particular, historical, revelatory, and interpersonal conception — notably, the witness of Scripture, but also the voice of God.

ID 2: *Natural revelation.* The theory builds from the objective discernment and linkage of certain propositions within creation — a universal recognition and derivation that, in strictly rational terms, is impossible.

ID 3: *Law.* The theory asserts two sets of law within one soteriology committed to a just God and perfect obedience — a dual system that is incoherent in terms of both content and desert.

ID 4: *Anthropology.* The theory presupposes in humans an inherent ability to deduce and appropriately act on the truth of certain axioms and, at the same time, a profound universal sinfulness — that is, fundamental capacity and incapacity.

ID 5: *Theodicy.* The theory posits a God of strict justice who seems rather unjustly to hold all people accountable to a standard they are intrinsically unable to attain — a God who by nature is both just and unjust.

ID 6: *Christology and atonement.* The theory does not explain why Christ must atone as against other people or things, and especially, in place of the established temple cultus.

ID 7: *Faith.* The theory harbors a cluster of complex problems with respect to faith, in two main variations. The "Arminian" variant struggles to explain faith fully and, in particular, how individuals can actually exercise faith in order to be saved. The "Calvinist" variant can get beyond these difficulties by introducing revelation and election at the point of faith but then runs into further problems in relation to the privileging of faith and its gifting to individuals who have negotiated phase one. Ultimately, both variants collapse.

Difficulties at the Systematic Frame (SDs)

SD 1: *Epistemology.* The basic conception of knowledge, especially in terms of its overall direction, is different elsewhere in Paul.

SD 2: *Anthropology.* The presupposed conception of the person is different elsewhere in Paul.

SD 3: *Theology.* The basal conception of God is different elsewhere in Paul.

SD 4: *Christology and atonement.* The role of Jesus Christ in the atonement is different elsewhere in Paul.

SD 5: *Soteriology.* The nature of salvation, including the basis and depth of Christian assurance, is different elsewhere in Paul.

SD 6: *Faith.* The nature and role of "faith" are different elsewhere in Paul.

SD 7: *Ethics.* The conception of ethics is different elsewhere in Paul.

SD 8: *Ecclesiology.* The nature of the church is different elsewhere in Paul.

SD 9: *Judaism.* The depiction of Judaism, including various accounts of the Torah, is different elsewhere in Paul.

SD 10: *Coercion and violence.* The endorsement of coercive violence for the punishment of wrongdoing is arguably rare elsewhere in Paul.

Difficulties at the Empirical Frame (EDs)

ED 1: *Judaism.* The prospective, monolithic, and perfectionist account of Judaism supplied by Justification theory is in acute tension with the self-depiction of Judaism contemporary to Paul.

ED 2: *Conversion.* Justification theory largely presupposes that conversion takes place as individuals reason in relation to the nature of their unsaved state and then decide to accept the offer of Christian salvation made through preaching. But widespread analysis of conversion, largely by social scientists, suggests that this is not in fact how conversion usually takes place; it is a relational, not a rationalistic, process, and thus also communal rather than individual. Hence, Justification theory seems to give a false account of conversion.

ED 3: *Paul's "conversion."* The scant evidence concerning Paul's own "conversion" does not really accord with the Justification view. The dynamics of Justification cannot be found in the extant evidence. And positive evi-

dence stands against this explanation — in particular, that Paul did not
abandon the law on the road to Damascus (as Justification expects), but
three years later, during the mission in Syrian Antioch.

ED 4: *Paul's proclamation.* The scant evidence concerning Paul's proclamation does not accord with Justification theory. He ought to have
preached Justification theory when trying to convert pagans. But the
available evidence fails to corroborate that he did, and much of it is in
tension with the theory's assumptions and dynamics.

It should now be marked carefully that this systematic enumeration of the difficulties caused by Justification theory for the broader interpretation of Paul overlaps rather significantly with many critical debates currently unfolding in relation
to Paul, and beyond him in the church more widely, and these points of contact
are also usefully highlighted here. We can identify nineteen existing clusters of
interpretative concern in relation to Paul that are explicable in terms of difficulties arising from Justification's contractual soteriology. It is true that the following
criticisms are not necessarily *completely* explained in this way; some of them
point to other difficulties as well. But we are interested for now in any difficulties
that are explicable in such terms, whether in whole or in part. As we will note in
more detail shortly, we cannot really move on to deal effectively with other problems in Paul while this complex web of distortions is still in place.

We begin with familiar criticisms from within the world of Pauline scholarship — our first six sets of concerns[5] — but then broaden our scope to note the
various concerns that have found expression in disparate historical and ecclesial
settings. Justification theory causes difficulties that ripple far beyond the rather
limited domain of the Pauline specialist. Those broader concerns can in turn be
divided into concerns with the implications of Justification's strong characterization of the pre-Christian state — six concerns about the characterization of the
"vestibule" — and seven concerns with the resulting characterization of Christianity, and here usually in relation to one of its more specific aspects — problematic
implications for theology, Christology, ecclesiology, and so on. There is of course
not a perfect one-to-one match between all these lists (i.e., my earlier intrinsic and
systematic concerns and these diverse critical debates drawn from different fields),
because those alert to various difficulties in Paul have not been working systematically from the underlying template of Justification theory, and neither have some
of our theological critics been concerned principally with Paul. (Nor — it should
be reiterated — are all the difficulties in and caused by Paul's interpretation reducible to Justification.) My earlier systematic enumeration should nevertheless prove
more comprehensive and definitive than the following list of Pauline debates, at
which point some of the explanatory power of our formal, theory-driven analysis
should become apparent. Indeed, this is arguably an important preliminary check
on its underlying cogency; we can suddenly grasp many of our difficulties in relation to Paul rather more clearly and comprehensively.

After all these connections have been detected, we can move on to consider their important implications (see §5). At the end of this comparison it will be apparent that we can kill several difficult birds with one stone if Justification theory is eventually dealt with effectively.[6]

Again, it should be helpful to introduce here in summary form the concerns of various different debates — whether narrowly Pauline or more broadly ecclesial — before enumerating their content in more detail in what follows.

Six Concerns of Pauline Interpreters

(1) The various concerns of Krister Stendahl (postponing for the moment a detailed account of his hermeneutical and church-historical suspicions)

(2) The concern that "mystical" or participatory and transformational aspects of Paul's soteriology are not being acknowledged or emphasized (and recall especially chapter three at this point, which discussed systematic difficulties in relation to an alternative soteriological schema)

(3) Certain "apocalyptic" concerns as represented by Ernst Käsemann and J. Louis (Lou) Martyn (recalling again some concerns voiced by chapter three)

(4) The concern, represented especially by Heikki Räisänen, that Paul is contradictory (implicit in chapter three again)

(5) The concern that various aspects of Paul's biography have been distorted — the nature and description of his Jewish background (so chapter four — and this is of course the principal point of departure for the new perspective), of his conversion (so chapter five), but also of other aspects of his biography (i.e., the use of Acts as a source for reconstructing his life and thought, his letter sequence, and even canonical decisions)

(6) The concern that "faith" terminology in Paul often seems oriented more toward the Christian than toward Christ; it is "my" faith and seldom if ever "his" fidelity — a concern often discussed specifically in terms of "the πίστις Χριστοῦ debate"

Six Broader Concerns with the Characterization
of the Pre-Christian Vestibule

(1) Barthian concerns with the endorsement of natural theology encompassing its specific form, its political ramifications, and its general endorsement of theological foundationalism (and linking hands here — to a degree — with the modern critique of the philosophical demonstration of God's existence)

(2) Post-Holocaust concerns with the condemnation and punishment of Jews as a specific instance of the treatment of the broader category of non-Christians/outsiders

(3) The concern of Queer theorists with the a priori condemnation and punishment of those practicing — or presumably simply endorsing — ostensibly deviant sexual activities

(4) Pacifist (et cetera) concerns with the endorsement of Constantinianism (and thereby also of certain aspects of the modern liberal nation-state, pos-

sibly linking hands at this point with what we might call — perhaps a little polemically — "Christian fascism")

(5) Certain postmodern concerns with the imposition upon reality of overly rigid, totalizing metanarratives and metaexplanations

(6) Concerns with the inaccurate and unhelpful depiction of conversion as expressed by certain sociologists and evangelists

Seven Broader Concerns with the Consequent Construal of Christianity

(1) Nicene and Chalcedonian concerns that this reading of Paul is not inherently or even possibly Trinitarian

(2) Revivalist concerns that the reading does not sufficiently emphasize the Spirit

(3) Calvinist concerns that the reading does not sufficiently emphasize the active role and obedience of Christ

(4) Reformed concerns that such a reading entails an insecure and anxious Christian existence (and here we note especially some of the concerns of John McLeod Campbell as elaborated by James Torrance)

(5) Catholic and Orthodox concerns that the reading underemphasizes the sacraments

(6) Concerns within various traditions that the reading does not sufficiently emphasize a vigorous ethics and a vital ecclesiology

(7) Ecumenical concerns that the Catholic-Protestant divide is being exacerbated by — if not premised upon! — the ostensible dichotomy between "justification by faith" and "justification through works" that Justification theory supplies

We will now consider each of these clusters of concern in more detail: the concerns of many specifically Pauline interpreters in §2; broader concerns with the pre-Christian vestibule in §3; and with the consequent construal of Christianity in §4.

§2. Concerns of Pauline Interpreters

It will be helpful to begin our account of the relevant Pauline debates with a consideration of Krister Stendahl's classic essay, "Paul and the Introspective Conscience of the West."[7] This is an excellent example of just the issues I am trying to clarify throughout my analysis by approaching our difficulties in the first instance from the theoretical point of view.

2.1. Krister Stendahl

I include here a brief reprise of Stendahl's arguments, although it is not my intention to interact with his work in detail so much as to try to distill the key issues from it.

Stendahl's principal problem, as his title suggests, arises from an introspective anthropology, something he views as distinctively Western and contemporary (79; see also 87, 88, 93-94, 95) — although rooted in late medieval piety and particularly in Luther (82-83), with an important antecedent in Augustine (85). This construct has led, in his view, to the misinterpretation of Paul's arguments, now read through a modernizing and psychologizing framework (which culminates in secular terms with Freud: 94-95). Early on in his argument Stendahl offers Philippians 3:2-11 as decisive evidence that Paul's conscience was in fact "robust," especially in the light of the claim in v. 6 that his previous Jewish behavior was "flawless" (ἄμεμπτος: 80-81). And this is further corroborated by a lack of any evidence of a troubled consciousness in Paul's later Christian life, as well as a parallel absence of the notion of forgiveness (81-82; also 90-91). Paul's preferred self-description is, rather, "weakness," which is not the same thing as guilt but in large measure a concrete experience of suffering.

Paul's arguments about the impossibility of fulfilling the law belong *not* to his own troubled experience but to an argument about the relation between Jews and Gentiles (81). That is, he arrived at his view of the law not in an introspective fashion but by grappling with the questions concerning the place of Gentiles in the church in relation to Jews and Jewish Christians (84), a reading that makes Romans 9–11 the climax of that letter rather than an appendix (85). Consequently, we must also view Paul's Damascus experience not as a conversion but as a call, something corroborated by the sources (84-85). Stendahl goes on to make an important programmatic statement: "Where Paul was concerned about the possibility for Gentiles to be included in the messianic community, his statements are now read as answers to the quest for assurance about man's salvation from a common human predicament" (86).

Stendahl also cites Galatians 3:24, Paul's famous metaphor of the law as pedagogue — and the first point where "faith" is mentioned in his study (see also 95) — contending that this metaphor functions salvation-historically rather than psychologically and individually. To fail to grasp this is to miss the "framework" within which Paul is arguing (86-87).[8] The famous struggles of Romans 7 are "a defense for the holiness and goodness of the Law" (92, 93), "based on the rather trivial observation that every man knows that there is a difference between what he ought to do and what he does. This distinction makes it possible for Paul to blame Sin and Flesh, and to rescue the Law as a good gift of God" (93).

Finally, Stendahl observes that "[t]he framework of 'Sacred History' . . . opens up a new perspective. . . . We find ourselves in the new situation where the faith in the Messiah Jesus gives us the right to be called Children of God" (95), a framework that is more authentic and less anachronistic than the modernizing preoccupation with "a trembling and introspective conscience" (94).

I find Stendahl's classic critique both brilliant and frustrating. I, along with many others, can affirm that there is something deeply insightful about his complaints. Stendahl has sensed a profound difficulty within the interpretation of Paul — if not a cluster of interlinked difficulties of great moment. But to search here for explicit guidance for a sustained project of criticism and reinterpretation is to be generally disappointed. Stendahl's criticisms are too brief and scattered to offer such guidance. His concerns are not actually linked and explained comprehensively, nor are his solutions. But the realization that Justification theory is operative within Paul's broader interpretation allows us to begin to coordinate Stendahl's concerns and thereby both to explain them more clearly and to indicate the necessary methodological route to their resolution. Indeed, the basic brilliance of Stendahl's work is apparent in his anticipation of the main phases within any cogent solution to these difficulties. We do not yet need to enter into a detailed discussion of all those anticipations. We do, however, need to note them briefly.

Many of Stendahl's concerns are fundamentally hermeneutical. He accuses modern scholars of construing Paul more in their own image than in terms of the apostle's ancient context, thereby distorting him. (This is of course a common charge in historical-critical circles, although Stendahl has specific figures and anachronisms in mind.) Stendahl thus points to an important task within the reinterpretative project: some way must be found to recognize and to compensate for anachronistic influences on Paul's construal. And this task will in fact be the principal burden of part two in this study.

Stendahl also intuits that the recovery of Paul necessitates some sort of fundamental reinterpretative strategy. He opts for what we will later discuss in detail as a reframing, and more specifically a causal or circumstantial strategy;[9] he offers a very different reading of *when* and *why* Paul wrote the texts that he now finds problematic (that is, rather than an alternative reading *of* those texts — a strategy of explicit *re*reading). And again his intuitions are basically correct. It is not enough merely to heap up criticisms of a particular approach to Paul. Some plausible alternative to the construal in question must also be supplied, and this will be the principal burden of part four here.

But most importantly for our present purposes, Stendahl also begins to compile a list of current interpretative difficulties with what he asserts is the common way of reading Paul. And this list of difficulties really functions to give weight to his programmatic alternative construal; indeed, without these difficulties there would be no need to entertain his sweeping alternative. And all these difficulties turn out to be problems caused by the presence of Justification theory (and Stendahl is led particularly to difficulties generated in systematic and circumstantial terms).

(1) Stendahl is clearly concerned with individualism within Paul's theological description. He points out that Paul's main anthropological categories actually arise from the broad ethnic distinction between those who are Jewish and those who are not — between Jews and Gentiles — that is, between peoples, not individuals. But Justification theory is of course a fundamentally individualist schema within which an isolated person rationalizes and hopefully chooses salvation.

(2) In close relation to the foregoing, Stendahl is concerned with the agonized introversion that individuals supposedly experience according to this reading of Paul. And again, this is an aspect of Justification theory: individuals must experience the "introspective twist" and so reach the "loop of despair"

if they are to be saved. (However, Justification theory also provides a useful precision to Stendahl's rather generalized charge of introspection at this point. It is a fundamentally rational introspection related to the commitment of transgressions and a resulting anxiety if not terror about future judgment experienced prior to conversion. Hence, it is not introspection per se.) Stendahl places pressure on this interpretative trend — which he dislikes — by pointing to what are effectively further framing tensions. He observes that there is an absence of attestation elsewhere in Paul to the notion that he was in fact this agonized and self-reflective.[10]

(3) Stendahl is concerned about any universalizing of Paul's discussions, especially with respect to soteriology, that overrides the apostle's overt and highly particular missionary and salvation-historical concerns. So, for example, the contributions of Romans 9–11 to his thought have tended to be marginalized. And here again we can point to the influence of Justification theory, whose timeless and ahistorical features override Paul's apparent commitments elsewhere to history in general, and to the history of Israel in particular — this last an especially acute systematic tension for Paul as a Jew, but generating deep tensions at the contextual frame as well, especially in Romans 3:1-9 and 9–11.

(4) In like manner, Stendahl is concerned with the quite particular early church settings of many of Paul's discussions, and especially the vigorous debate of the mission to the Gentiles that seems to have been overridden.[11] Justification theory is emphatically universal and also rather timeless and generic and so explains these oversights as well. Moreover — and as we will see in more detail shortly — Stendahl is again placing pressure on the frames of the reading that he dislikes, which is a useful tactic, although arguably not ultimately sufficient. That is, he is asking for a detailed contingent explanation of just why Paul penned these famous arguments when he did to those he did, something that advocates of Justification theory can struggle to supply (as we noted briefly in the Introduction). However, there is possibly an implicit substantive point here as well: Paul's main discussion of Justification theory spends most of its time attacking Jews (or, more accurately, "the Jew"); Stendahl seems, then, to be querying why this is the case when the principal concern of the apostle to the Gentiles was presumably Gentiles.

(5) Stendahl is concerned that Paul's biography has been distorted. Both his introspection and his conversion have been exaggerated and reoriented. Stendahl is well known for emphasizing Philippians 3:6 in this relation, a statement that may suggest Paul's "robust" as against Luther's agonized conscience. We have already seen that this text is not as decisive as Stendahl avers; however, the more general point about Paul's biography is well made. And Justification theory is of course again the principal culprit, since it is intrinsically committed to a particular Pauline biography, including a quite specific and rather agonized mental journey culminating in conversion,

which can then be equated with the dramatic events that took place on the road to Damascus — and indeed really must be by Justification's advocates.

A number of implications within the foregoing critical analysis should now be drawn together. First, it seems that most of Stendahl's direct substantive criticisms of the "Lutheran" reading of Paul are actually concerns with particular implications that flow from reading the apostle in terms of Justification theory. Second, those criticisms tend to manifest principally at the systematic and circumstantial frames (although hints in other directions can also be detected on occasion). Consequently, third, although Stendahl is one of the broadest critics of Paul in these terms, supplying the largest spread of actual criticisms, it is now apparent that his concerns delineate only a relatively small part of the actual underlying problem. Stendahl's famous critique is insufficiently radical! There is so much more to say in this relation than he averred.[12] But, fourth, he implied that there were at least two further major methodological tasks in any resolution of these difficulties: hermeneutical and reinterpretative.

We will turn to pursue these imperatives in detail at the appropriate time. But we must first complete the task of substantive identification and criticism. Only then will effective hermeneutical clarifications and reinterpretations prove possible. And we have just seen that, despite his concerns, Stendahl himself never really supplies such an articulation of "the problem"; he contents himself with broad ascriptions and aspersions in terms of Luther, Augustine, and introversion. His characterization of the problem consequently lacks precision, and two immediate results are a corresponding lack of comprehensiveness and an inadequate solution. Hence, Stendahl's classic critique indirectly confirms for us the importance of the clear theoretical articulation of the problem that has been supplied here. This articulation explains all of his substantive difficulties — but there are many more substantive difficulties caused by Justification theory than he himself supplied. Hence, we turn now to some of those additional problems as they have been voiced by other interpreters of Paul.

2.2. Participatory and Transformational Emphases

The exposure of this set of tensions remains in my view one of Sanders's most important contributions to our current understanding of Paul. Much of his work illustrates very clearly the tensions between different soteriological systems in the apostle's thinking.[13] But Sanders is by no means the first person to make this observation. Here he is ultimately dependent on a set of similar observations by Albert Schweitzer, who himself merely stood within an earlier German tradition that was fully conscious of these difficulties.[14] The Germans tended to describe the alternative system to Justification, rather unfortunately, as "mystical," as is apparent in such classic interpreters of Paul as W. Wrede and G. Adolf Deissmann. This characterization subsequently fell on hard times in Germany, probably because of a conjunction of factors — the deep pessimism generated by World War I, the rise of a powerful scholarly trajectory of Kantian Lutheranism with roots in Ritschl (et al.), and the growing dominance of Rudolf Bultmann (himself strongly influenced by Kant), who was opposed to the mystical reading. So, as the twentieth century progressed, commitments within German scholarship to this approach were increasingly rare. However, the mystical construal of Paul's gospel had in effect been exported to Scotland (as is apparent, for example, in James Stewart's widely read *A Man in Christ*[15]), and from there to the rest of Great Britain, so the approach lived on in exile, so to speak, long after it faded to the scholarly margins in Germany.[16] Important English scholars — often associated with Cambridge — then continued to endorse the reading, notably, C. F. D. Moule and Morna Hooker (successive occupants of the Lady Margaret chair of Divinity).[17] This ensured a major presence for the perspective within British scholarship. And from this point some penetration of North American circles was natural.[18] Moreover, Schweitzer's views have been enjoying renewed prominence in America since the last quarter of the twentieth century, thanks largely to Sanders's repristination of this earlier, classic case.[19] Hence, even some of Justification's recent apologists openly acknowledge the presence of this alternative system when discussing Paul — for example (with typical candor) Troels Engberg-Pedersen, in *Paul and the Stoics*.[20]

The crucial point to grasp is that this alternative approach to Paul's soteriology recapitulates most if not all of the tensions that were noted in formal terms in chapter three by way of a comparison between a putative soteriological system drawn from Romans 5–8 and one based on Justification. The "mystical" or "participatory" approach to Paul *is* an alternative soteriological account that then predictably collides with his construal in terms of Justification, just as Romans 5–8 did *and in much the same way*.[21] The collision is apparent within any of this interpretative trajectory's main representatives, although it is perhaps clearest in the classic work of Wrede.

Excursus: Wrede's Construal of Paul's Gospel

Indeed, it may be helpful to articulate here in detail this mystical system as it is characterized in his classic treatment *Paul*.[22]

Wrede's touch in this introductory treatment is astonishingly deft. He begins his account of Paul's thought by emphasizing its occasional development and expression and its important intertextual dimension in relation to Jewish Scripture, thereby anticipating two of the main methodological emphases of the last twenty-five years of Pauline interpretation in North America (74-75). He does not overemphasize its theoretical coherence, but neither does he trade that "structure of thought" away (76 — thereby addressing one of the principal debates of the Pauline Theology Group of the Society of Biblical Literature through the 1980s); to separate Paul's cognized theology and his felt religion is to embrace a false dichotomy. Wrede is alert to, and honest about, overt contradictions (77). Indeed, he allows that "strange ways of thinking penetrate even into the fundamental conceptions of the apostle" (81). This too has of course been much discussed in recent Pauline interpretation, as we will see momentarily in §2.4. For Paul, history "proceeds by hard oppositions and cleavages; for God's ways are by no means even and clear; it is incidental to their very nature that they should be paradoxical and should confound the wit of man" (83). So here Wrede correctly emphasizes the revelatory and antithetical dimensions to Paul's thought.

In his fuller description Wrede begins with the astounding claims that although "the Pauline world of thought stands in unmistakable contrast to Judaism," "this antago- nism governs no more than a definite circle of ideas" — a circle that excludes Paul's doc- trine of redemption, which is "a complete whole in itself" (84). So the separation of Paul's thought into two distinct systems could hardly be clearer, although Wrede quickly denies that the two systems are utterly separate. There are connections — a common rootedness in Christ — but the fact remains that the doctrine of "redemption" can be articulated fully with little or no reference to Judaism and Justification!

Wrede's account of Paul's doctrine of redemption is then exquisitely balanced. He begins by refusing a theocentric point of entry, affirming instead the need to begin with Christ and soteriology: "[T]he whole Pauline doctrine is a doctrine of Christ and his work; that is its essence" (86). Christology is clearly central, but Wrede goes on to note immedi- ately — and quite correctly — that "[t]he ordinary conception of a Messiah does not suf- fice to characterize the Christ of Paul" (86). Jesus is the Son of God for Paul and his origins lie in God. He is a "celestial being" who "took part as agent in the creation of the world" (87). But he resigned this heavenly life, becoming impoverished in his human condition, before returning to an even higher state (87-88). From this point on Wrede emphasizes Christ's concrete humanity: "Very much depends for him [Paul] on the reality of the hu- manity of Christ — so much that without it Christ could not be the redeemer of men" (89).[23] Indeed, this embodiment is simply for salvation, at which point "it becomes clear how this doctrine flows into the doctrine of redemption, and cannot be understood with- out it" (91). Wrede now describes in more detail (i) the source of the misery from which Christ's coming redeems humanity (92-97); (ii) the means whereby he does this (97-102); and (iii) the benefit of this redemption (102-9); also providing (iv) a "review," with four further emphases (109-15).

i. Redemption consists of "release from the misery of this whole present world," a world "under the domination of dark and evil powers" — chief among them "'flesh,' sin, the law, and death" (92). These are not abstractions but real, active agents. Man "through his mere earthly and bodily existence" is "subject to the power of sin." The Law then "embitter[s] this servitude" (94), while other beings contribute to the oppression — "mighty spirits, de- mons, and angelic powers" (95). Hence, "[t]he whole conception of the misery of mankind is . . . transferred . . . into the supersensual region," where "[e]ven the Jew has no advantage" (96-97). More recently, many scholars have called this depiction of "the problem" — argu- ably, a little imprecisely — "apocalyptic" (and see more on this in §2.3 just below).

ii. Wrede begins his analysis of the redemption wrought by Christ auspiciously: "Two experiences of one single being bring in the change for all mankind" (97). Again he stresses — a little inconsistently — Christ's solidarity with humanity. Christ assumes all under which mankind currently labors. (Wrede treads delicately around Christ's assump- tion of sin, claiming — "of course" [98] — that Christ did not actually sin.) Last of all, Christ assumes death, at which point its "necessity" for him becomes clear: "[H]e has taken upon himself that which, in the case of all men, leads to death, especially sin" (99). But now "the thought turns suddenly and completely about. Death is at the same time the liberation of Christ from all these powers of perdition" (99). And "what happened to

Christ, happened to all" (100). So "[f]rom the moment of his death all men are redeemed, as fully as he himself, from the hostile powers . . . [and] are transferred into indestructible life" (100). And Wrede goes on immediately to point out that this account of redemption, which is vicarious although not in any penal sense, includes a vigorous saving function for the resurrection as well as the cross. "It [the resurrection] is not merely the divine Amen to the death of the son of God, not merely its legitimation; it is in a truer sense the reverse side of that death itself" (101).

iii. In view of this central mechanism, Wrede goes on to repudiate the ethical and exemplary reading of Christ's death. Paul's expressions in this relation, he asserts, are "intended *actually and literally*" (103, emphasis original). "Paul is thinking of a real death, such a death as Christ has undergone, a *participation* in his death" (103, emphasis added). But Wrede is immediately concerned to note that a contradictory experience still remains for humankind. He ascribes this to the difference between the "already" and the "not yet" (103-4). So "[t]he whole Pauline conception of salvation is characterized by suspense . . . which strains forwards towards the final release, the actual death" (105). Moreover, Wrede adds that we must bear in mind the fact that Paul "believed with all his might in the speedy coming of Christ and the approaching end of the world. . . . This makes the suspense, the forward outlook, especially intelligible" (105). At the same time, "something real is already here — the spirit of God," in Paul's mind "an extraordinarily important element" (107). In short, Wrede now emphasizes four aspects of his soteriological account of Paul: the concrete reality of the Christian's participation in Christ; the inaugurated nature of this participation; the imminence of Christ's return for Paul; and the present reality and guarantee of the Spirit — four emphases that can only be regarded as prescient.

iv. In reviewing this doctrine, Wrede insists that it is "intrinsically . . . very simple" (110). Indeed, "it can be expressed by quite short sentences" (110): "Christ becomes what we are, that we through his death may become what he is" (110). But "certain elucidations are none the less necessary" (110). First, the "personal love of God . . . [and] the self-denying love of Christ" lie behind the entire process (110). Hence, Paul responds warmly and joyfully to it despite its unconditional character. Moreover, it is not fundamentally a subjective experience but an objective change in reality (111-12). Further, the ethical change involved is dependent on a change in the "nature of humanity," to which it is secondary although clearly itself also real (112). And finally, the appropriation of salvation — in what is arguably Wrede's first false step — is by "faith and baptism" (113). "Faith is simply an obedient acceptance of and assent to the preaching of redemption" (113, alluding to Rom. 1:5 and 16:26). This faith "*effects* at once that mystic union with Christ by dint of which his death and resurrection are automatically transferred to the believer, so that he also is dead and has risen again" (113, emphasis added).[24] However, Wrede goes on immediately to repudiate overly individualist and psychologizing characterizations of this event: "Death with Christ is a general fact, . . . not an event transacted in the individual soul" (114). Paul's thinking is actually highly historical, especially in relation to two ages: "Christ stands as the turning-point between an old and a new age" (115). Wrede describes this as "the salvation history" (115).

He then briefly considers how Paul's doctrine of redemption informs the apostle's broader thinking (115-22). Paul's ethic for the now-transformed community exhibits only a few "original features"; most important is his emphasis on love (117). The notion of life in Christ and possession of the Spirit generates an obligation to fight against sensuality and to "walk 'after the spirit'" (118). The church is "much more to the apostle than a community in worship or a religious society with a special constitution; fundamentally the church is to him the new humanity itself" (119). The sacraments also now receive a vigorous emphasis and definition. These are not "purely spiritual or symbolic" but "acts which are intrinsically operative" (120). Hence, there is "the closest connexion" between the sacraments and Paul's doctrine of redemption (121).

Wrede's encapsulation of Paul's soteriology thus emphasizes its simplicity, its unconditionality, its origins in divine benevolence (of both the Father and the Son), and its transformational character, which gives rise to a vigorous ethics. "Faith" makes its sole appearance here, functioning in parallel with baptism to effect entry into salvation. And it is interesting to note that this inclusion is formally unnecessary, because just previously Wrede emphasizes a benevolent unconditionality and just afterward — as he notes the system's implications for Paul's broader thinking — the inherent efficacy of the sacraments, including baptism. It is also interesting to note the dominance of Romans 5-8 in Wrede's cited support of the foregoing account. (The classic Justification texts are of course almost never in evidence.) He deploys just over 125 texts, and of these approximately 47 citations are drawn from Romans 5-8 (i.e., well over one-third).

Only now does Wrede turn to the doctrine of Justification, beginning his brief analysis with a further extraordinary claim:

> The best known of Paul's ideas, the so-called doctrine of justification by faith, has not yet been mentioned. Our silence in itself implies a judgment. The Reformation has accustomed us to look upon this as the central point of Pauline doctrine: but it is not so. In fact the whole Pauline religion can be expounded without a word being said about this doctrine, unless it be in the part devoted to the Law. (122-23)

Part of the basis for this claim is then revealed: "It would be extraordinary if what was intended to be the chief doctrine were referred to only in a minority of the epistles. That is the case with this doctrine: it only appears where Paul is dealing with the strife against Judaism [citing Galatians, Romans, and Phil. 3:6-9]. And this fact indicates the real significance of the doctrine. It is the *polemical doctrine* of Paul" (123, emphasis original). This observation allows the preliminary development of an explanatory strategy, although a fundamental causal, or "circumstantial," one.[25] Wrede holds that Justification appears in Paul only when a certain argument is being made, and here once again he is well ahead of the game: "[Justification] is only made intelligible by the struggle of his life, his controversy with Judaism and Jewish Christianity, and is only intended for this" (123). Stendahl will be hailed for making much the same assertions in 1963.

Wrede asserts that this argument is superficially artificial and weak but conveys powerful and important inner meanings. The "motives and aims" of the argument are paramount (124). At the outset of his more detailed discussion he declares with customary foresight: "One point seems to be particularly clear. As a missionary Paul could not endure that Jewish customs, circumcision and all the rest, should be made a condition of Christianity for the Gentiles" (124). But demonstrating "the superfluity, perhaps harmfulness of the Mosaic ceremonial" necessitated in turn defining "the real condition for entering into Christianity," namely, "belief in Jesus Christ" (124-25). Hence the formula *"not the Law with its works, but faith"* — and Wrede notes correctly that "[t]he negative part of this task was the chief part" (125, emphasis original). But Paul "does not attack simply the Jewish institutions; he attacks the whole Law" — a function, Wrede asserts, of his second argumentative motive (125). Paul must show "the Jewish way of salvation as a way of error, and Judaism itself as a superseded and false religion; and . . . grace . . . as the compendium of the true religion." Hence *"not the works of men, but grace"* — and Wrede notes that "[t]he positive part of this task was the chief part" (126, emphasis original).[26]

So, significantly, Wrede identifies two motives in Paul's conception of justification: "(1) the mission must be free from the burden of Jewish national custom; [and] (2) the superiority of the Christian faith in redemption over Judaism as a whole must be assured. *The doctrine of justification is nothing more than the weapon with which these purposes were to be won*" (127, emphasis original). And he sees the two as inevitably "intertwining and fusing together" (128).

A quite conventional and clear account of Justification theory then ensues, although it culminates — not surprisingly — in a claim closer to Schleiermacher than to Luther: "[T]he truly religious element in religion, such as corresponds to the consciousness of every pious man, is that man stands over against God simply as the receiver, and God alone is the giver" (131). Wrede also allows that it is at this point "wherein Luther really coincides with Paul. Otherwise Luther's doctrine is by no means coterminous with this Pauline theory" (131). Wrede locates Luther's struggles *in the church*: "Luther asks, how does the individual man, who stands in the church . . . , overcome the tormenting uncertainty whether salvation and the forgiveness of sins holds good personally for him?" (131-32). (The answer he found, according to Wrede, is that "it depends absolutely on grace, which God has unconditionally promised" [132].) Paul, Wrede claims, is not interested in such individualist and psychological reflections but in the condition for entry into the church — faith. Salvation in Christ holds good for all; it is more the declaration of God than the act of an individual (132).

Wrede refrains, however, from pressing this account through to a propitiatory account of the atonement. He allows that Christ's propitiatory death is a possible interpretation of Romans 3:24ff., "the weightiest instance" of this view, but asserts that "another interpretation is possible" (134, n. 1). Moreover, "Paul never says that God *could not forgive* until his justice was satisfied" (134, emphasis original). Indeed, "Paul, again, never speaks of a reconciliation *of God;* it is God's own *love* which, after the time of enmity, *brings about* reconciliation and peace" (134, emphasis original, and citing Rom. 5:8ff.). Moreover, this discussion clearly leads back "into the old thoughts on the redemption" in Romans 5-6 (134).

Wrede then concedes that there is something artificial about this rejection of the law. The thought of the law, if only in a more general, ethical sense, "is continually forcing its way in" (136; see Gal. 6:2; and Gal. 5:14; Rom. 13:8-9). Moreover, Paul also speaks of God's judgment according to works. Hence, "the chief point remains that this doctrine protects Christianity from institutions, and that it expresses the distinction between Christianity and Judaism, and therewith, for the first time, the full consciousness of the unique character of the Christian religion" (136). Still, "[t]he release from Judaism is not . . . perfect" (137). Paul still acts at times like a Jewish patriot, although Wrede concludes rather curiously that this is nevertheless consistent because Paul "expects that Judaism will one day cease to be Jewish" (137). Wrede now addresses the origins and development of Paul's theology — *not* as "Athene sprang armed in full power from the head of Zeus" (137)!

The constituents of Paul's thinking, Wrede asserts, bear the clear stamp of "a great Jewish heritage" (138): monotheism, providence and even election; the contrast between two ages, one eschatological; the evil heart of man "known to the Jewish apocalyptic books"; "the devastating effects of the sin of Adam," namely, death; the roles of angels and demons; and the importance of the Scriptures (139-41). Although "[n]o doubt Paul's experience had a share in the formation of his doctrine, . . . the concrete thoughts of the apostle can only in a small degree be explained as simply the reflex of his experiences" (142-43). Wrede is skeptical of the attribution of much of Paul's system to the Damascus event and also of the application of Romans 7 to Paul's biography. (Paul can supply statements of general validity using "I"; the gloom of the picture denotes that Paul is speaking retrospectively; "[t]he passage certainly deals with a type"; the continuation in chapter 8 speaks of those in Christ and so, in 8:2, uses a "you"; and 7:9 "hardly admits of being taken as a description of experience" [144-45, 145 n. 1].) Moreover, Philippians 3:6 "does not support this notion" (145)! "The truth is, the soul-strivings of Luther have stood as model for the portrait of Paul. And so disappears every inducement to derive the doctrine of justification and the rejection of the works of the Law directly from the conversion. To experience grace is not by any means the same thing as to set it up in contrast to human conduct. Belief in the death and resurrection of Christ is far from implying the necessity of doing away with circumcision and other rites, especially as Christ, in Paul's belief, had himself kept the Law" (146, this last statement citing Gal. 4:4 and Rom. 15:8). Hence, "this doctrine had its immediate origin in the exigencies of Paul's mission to the Gentiles. It furnished theoretical support for emancipation from Jewish institutions. In this case theory was the child, not the parent, of practice. . . . His rejection of the *whole Law,* as the embodiment of the principle of works, was no doubt a later development" (146-47).

Wrede's account of Paul's thought concludes with an alternative explanation for the genesis of Paul's doctrine of redemption, focusing in particular on the origins of his elevated understanding of Christ as the Son of God. He asserts programmatically — and probably quite rightly — that *"[t]he picture of Christ did not originate in an impression of the personality of Jesus"* (147, emphasis original). Paul's discussion of Jesus is focused heavily on his death, an event of "redeeming power," without which "it is nothing" (148). It is an "impossibility" that his view of Jesus as the Son of God who laid aside his divinity in order to accomplish this salvation was "a product of Paul's mind, a work of his imagination" (150). Perhaps a little unfortunately, Wrede then asserts that the only alternative explanation is that Paul already believed in some saving celestial being — a Christ — before he believed in Jesus. Apocalyptic apparently also confirms this, and here Wrede's account clearly links up with his more famous skeptical work on Jesus. (An alternative explanation at this point could have employed the revelatory categories to which Paul himself appeals.) At Damascus Paul identified this Christ with Jesus when the latter appeared to him "in the shining glory of his risen existence" (151) — an early version of "glory Christology"! Indeed, this identification was assisted by the fact that he had not known "the historical Jesus" (152); there were no practical impediments, then, to this identification. And "[p]robably these thoughts [of the redeeming Christ] had long been definitely formulated in his mind before he was led by polemical exigencies to mint the doctrine of justification" (154) — a bold but consistent note for Wrede to end on.

I suspect that neither Wrede's predecessors nor his followers (whether conscious or not that they stand in his tradition) improve in many respects on the compact account that he supplies of the alternative soteriological theory set forth earlier on here in chapter three. Moreover, most of the key moves that underpin some ultimate solution to the resulting bifocal characterization of Paul's soteriology are also present in his discussion — especially the perceptive emphases on contingent factors. However, Wrede himself never develops these into a consistent and coherent alternative explanation; he never shows us *how* the reading of Justification as a polemical doctrine actually generates an argument consistent with Paul's more basic doctrine of redemption as he describes that elsewhere. We are still waiting for this further contribution to the discussion.

It would be unwise to impose too high a degree of coherence on this trajectory, represented here in detail by Wrede,[27] and, to a lesser extent, by Schweitzer and Sanders. However, it does seem fair to suggest that most if not all of its more specific concerns are comprehensible as part of the broader and simpler claim that an alternative soteriological system to Justification is apparent in Paul, a system that is quite neatly summarized by a schema drawn from Romans 5–8 and that functions in participatory and transformational terms.

Excursus: Traditional but Problematic Solutions to This Dilemma

It is also not uncommon to encounter denials that the set of difficulties I have just outlined is especially serious; that the two soteriologies are inconsistent and so denote deep contradictions in Paul's thinking are said to be exaggerated charges. While Paul might not be fully "systematic," he is nevertheless — conceived in these terms — "coherent," and so we need not press further for some alternative explanation of this data over against its customary construal. Clearly, then, this rebuttal needs to be addressed because, if it is true, then much of the impetus for my overarching project will be dissipated. I would be making a mountain out of a mole hill, and suggesting that we all need to be equipped with alpine gear to move onward — clearly an unnecessary if not absurd proposition. But perhaps we *do* face a mountain rather than a mole hill, and the assurances that we do *not* need alpine gear in order to attempt a dangerous climb are false comfort. Where does the truth lie?

I suggest here that the situation remains contradictory and deeply so, as chapter three presented it, and any claims to the contrary of "coherence" are themselves incoherent (if not at times a little deceptive). Moreover, I will go on to suggest that the main explanations usually offered to resolve this incoherence — that tend to betray immediately in that act the existence of the problem! — are themselves inadequate. An alternative way through our difficulties must therefore still be sought; this mountain must yet be climbed (along with one or two others).

We will begin our more detailed consideration in this relation by addressing first the nature of our problem, following this with some well known attempted solutions. Does the presence of these competing discourses in Paul render him coherent or incoherent?

1. Coherent or Incoherent?

Chapters one and three have already offered characterizations of different approaches to soteriology within Paul. Chapter one is, strictly speaking, hypothetical at this point in my overarching argument, but will be linked tightly to texts and readings from part three, chapter ten onward, and especially to Romans 1–4. Chapter three was grounded directly on Romans 5–8, and annotated through Paul's extant texts much more broadly. So it is difficult to deny the basic plausibility of these two systems as descriptions of Paul's thought at these well-attested points, and to my knowledge, few if any interpreters do. Moreover, that they are different soteriologies is apparent at a glance. But just how different are they?

I would suggest initially that they are different in relation to nearly every significant theological question, whether in terms of theology, Christology, pneumatology, epistemology, soteriology, anthropology, ecclesiology, implicit politics, or ethics. The two systems offer different answers to all these questions.

In a little more detail (and as we have already seen), Justification posits a God characterized fundamentally by retributive justice, and then struggles to articulate commitments to Christ's divinity, incarnation, and resurrection — although it is strongly committed to his sinless life and death, has no role for the Spirit, and so is not recognizably Trinitarian. Its theological epistemology begins in the unsaved state, thereby attributing a fundamental capacity to humanity — the abilities to know God, to recognize the good and to do it (because humanity is culpable for not doing so). So at all these key points it works *forward*. It is also generic and universal at this critical first stage; it holds good irrespective of particularities or history. Consequently, its ecclesiology is fundamentally contractual or conditional and individualistic, its implicit politics is coercive, and its ethic is voluntarist (i.e., the individual can choose to act ethically, and should do so).

Conversely, the alternative theory articulated by Romans 5–8 posits a God characterized fundamentally by benevolence, and is innately committed to an incarnate and resurrected Christ. Further, only the Spirit can reconstitute humanity in relation to this paradigmatic trajectory, so the model is inherently elective and Trinitarian. It is also historical and particular in that God enters history at a specific point. Consequently, the model's theological epistemology is revelatory and retrospective; it works *backward*. Its anthropology is also fundamentally incapacitated, and its ecclesiology and ethics therefore irreducibly elective and so reconstitutive and liberative. Its implicit politics is not coercive.

In the light of these capsule summaries of earlier discussions, we must ask now if these *different* answers are *incommensurate*. Can these two contrasting systems still be folded together neatly, perhaps in the way that different mathematical descriptions of string theory can point to the same underlying reality? Unfortunately, the two systems offer directly opposing or contradictory responses to the same questions, so they do not and cannot integrate smoothly on any level — note especially the issues of epistemology, theology (broadly speaking), anthropology, and ethics.

The two systems reason theologically in diametrically opposed directions: one thinks forward, and the other backward. This entails that the presuppositions brought to any theological analysis also differ fundamentally as well: the God of Justification is just but the God of the alternative theory is benevolent. *Fundamentally different notions of God are in play.* Moreover, the subsequent roles of these presuppositions in any thinking are also contradictory (i.e., the two models have different starting points that tend to overrule one another). In Justification, the first premises introduced (i.e., in the non-Christian stage) are determinative; they overrule and govern all subsequent theological reflection, because the model works forward from its initial assumptions. In the alternative schema, the later, Christian premises are primary and govern any reconstruction of ostensible stages and history prior to Christ, because the model works backward. Hence, these systems are not merely different: properly understood, *they will override one another!*

Justification theory's opening premises will constrain and control the theological, christological, and pneumatological information introduced later on, from the saved state (because not to do so would undermine its own coherence and function as a prospective theory). Conversely, the alternative theory, reasoning backward from the saved situation, will override all the opening premises of Justification theory (because they are not confirmed by that revealed information, but are revealed to be a false account of matters). Justification theory will cancel out or redefine what follows, while the alternative theory will redefine what precedes it. Consequently any simultaneous affirmation of these two theories will only end up in an incurably contradictory situation.

As if these difficulties were not enough, the resulting anthropologies and ecclesiologies differ fundamentally in accord with the outworking of the initial principles in the two theories. Justification remains — in continuity with its determinative opening assumptions — voluntarist and individualistic. People can know the good and be held to account for failing to do it, and so, after salvation, with the terrors of eschatological justice averted, they should press on with this knowledge and activity. They are incapacitated — and arguably a little contradictorily so — but not *completely.* The alternative schema views this entire approach as futile, however, because humanity *is completely incapacitated,* being enslaved by powerful evil forces — Sin and Death. Only after a liberation and ontological reconstitution can appropriate ethical action even begin to take place. So, once again, both models criticize one another in ecclesiological and ethical terms and at a fundamental level. Justification regards the alternative approach as according insufficient dignity and accountability to humanity, whereas the alternative approach holds Justification to be oppressive and futile; it makes strong demands on a suffering and dominated humanity, but does not lift a finger to help. (So both approaches — in their own terms — view the other as "soft on sin.")

In the light of these differences, it is hard to avoid the conclusion that any broader approach to Paul that simply allows both systems to co-exist, releases confusion at almost every conceivable level through the description of his thinking. *Not a single topic of major theological importance ultimately receives a clear answer.* It is always possible to offer two diametrically opposed responses to any significant question.

To place only a few questions: How does Paul view the appropriation of salvation? It is both something individuals grasp for themselves, in an uncoerced decision (presumably of faith), *and* something that is simply introduced, unconditionally, by God working through Christ and the Spirit. Agency is both human and divine, in a strong (i.e., contradictory) sense. What features of Christ are the most important in salvific terms? Apparently his sinless life and death in penal substitutionary terms, *and* his enactment of the Father's limitless benevolence that inaugurates a saving process completed through his resurrection and ascension. So he reveals God's punitive anger *and* his limitless and unconditional love. What is the church? It is a compact of believing individuals bound by consent (and presumably dissolved when this shared confession is breached), *and* a new family, functioning as a beachhead of a new reality and undeterred by *any* conflict. How should Christians act? They should fulfill the dictates of the state of nature, because not to do so elicits God's wrath, *and* they should act as creatures of the new cosmos, which lies *beyond* current creaturely realities (at least in certain senses). What is the role of the law? It convicts justly of transgression, guides the Christian in terms of right and wrong, *and* oppresses intrinsically and inevitably, cannot be fulfilled, is temporary, and is not binding on non-Jews (and so on!). What is God's attitude to non-Christians? They are under his just wrath and will be punished in due course with suffering and death *and* he loves them extravagantly to the point that he is prepared to sacrifice his son in order to save them. What is the nature of Judaism? It is a sad striving after righteousness through works, intrinsically doomed, and individualistically self-centered, *and* a blessed ethnic trajectory through history, founded in heroic piety, blessed by God with many gifts — including the law! — and destined ultimately for salvation, in spite of any grievous sin.

It is a sad commentary on the state of theological description in relation to Paul that we tend to find these extraordinary tensions so easy to live with. But we need to recover the fact that they *are* tensions, and mere repetition does not eliminate them. The interpretation of Paul's theology becomes a scandalously contradictory enterprise when these two systems are allowed to roam unchecked (placing me at this point very much in sympathy with the views of scholars like Räisänen: see §2.4 below; there is a refreshing honesty about his characterization of the situation). It does not really help *anyone* — and certainly not the apostle's advocates — when these difficulties are not plainly acknowledged.[28] And this is to note only a superficial layer within the general problem. We have mentioned here very briefly some clashing answers to the same issues. But we have not emphasized the degree to which the entire theological process of reflection on the reality that is Christian salvation is shaped in fundamentally different ways by these two competing systems.

On the one hand, Justification works foundationally and forward; it builds up from reflection by a rational creature on the cosmos. These reflections then drive any ensuing reflections, effectively grounding them on a prior metaphysics. On the other hand, the alternative theory builds from the disclosures internal to the Christ event that are essentially gifted and ecclesially received, seeking to ground further reflection (whether prior or posterior to it in time) on those central divine realities. The two procedures are therefore irreducibly different approaches to the theological task.

But there may be an additional reason why these tensions are often not felt as acutely by Pauline interpreters as they perhaps should be. For much of his interpretative history, Paul has had an explanation applied at this point that mitigates some of these problems, and we need now to subject that explanation to closer scrutiny.

2. The Traditional Solution, and Its Problems

The foregoing tensions are frequently explained by way of a distinction in Paul's thinking between "justification" and "sanctification." The former process ostensibly explains how salvation initially takes place, and the latter how it continues. One is, in a sense, justified in order to be saved and become a Christian and then, once a Christian in the church, one gets on with sanctification (which is of course more ethically robust). As the Westminster Larger Catechism puts it: "Question: 'Wherein do justification and sanctification differ?' Answer: 'Although sanctification be inseparably joined with justification, yet they differ, in that God in justification imputeth the righteousness of Christ; in sanctification his Spirit infuseth grace, and enableth to the exercise thereof; in the former, sin is pardoned; in the other, it is subdued.'"[29]

Another way of utilizing this distinction is to say that Christians should "become what they (already) are" — become, that is, through sanctification, what they already are through justification, which is righteous. God *views* Christians as righteous after justification, *declaring* them as such, and perhaps even "imputing" a righteousness to them, but these are essentially legal fictions, and so Christians presumably ought to try to become righteous *in fact* (if not in substance) as well! And this explanation can arguably lay claim to the initial argumentative structure of Romans, an account of justification in chapters 1–4 being followed by an emphasis on sanctification in chapters 5–8, as well as to the basic structure of many of the apostle's letters, which seem to lay out substantive, doctrinal, declarative matters first, before moving on to ethical concerns in a parenetic section.

It is not especially common, however, to encounter this solution in modern scholarly treatments of Paul — or at least not as baldly stated as this! — and with good reason.

First, it is a "distinction" that Paul himself never seems to make. Certainly, he never articulates it as such. Second, a disconcerting amount of data in his texts deploys justification and sanctification language in *parallel*, and not in *sequence* (a sequence being what this explanation needs).[30] That is, "sanctification" language is really just any reference to an ethical process that tends to utilize purity metaphors. And this language is common in Paul, and is frequently interwoven with his justification material. But, third — and perhaps most importantly — this distinction does not really work in conceptual terms, *and for reasons that have just been articulated*. None of the contradictions that exist between the two soteriologies have been eliminated through simply placing them in a psychological sequence; Christians are merely being asked to shift conceptualities mid-stream, and from one conception to a completely different alternative! However, the explanation is seldom experienced in these stark terms. And this is probably because, fourth, it is not just a resequencing of conceptualities: the ordering of the two systems one after the other actually conceals a covert move whereby justification *marginalizes* sanctification and so subordinates it conceptually, eliminating at least some of the difficulties in the process. And we must now consider this phenomenon a little more closely.

If this explanation is adopted, then Justification is uncontested as far as being saved initially is concerned — the first stage in Christianity. And it will then be difficult to remove it in relation to any further Christian deliberations. Its key assumptions must of course remain in force or the notion of salvation will collapse. So the insights of "sanctification" will only be *added* to those already supplied by Justification, leading to many of the conceptual tensions that have already been exemplified. That is, any questions rooted in ongoing Christian existence will tend to receive confused or synergistic answers from Paul — at such points from both systems — *but those that occur prior to this point will simply be explained in terms of Justification*. So at least some clarity will be possible at this early stage of reflection. Furthermore, when conditional and unconditional conceptualities are later combined, *the result is usually a conditional characterization*, perhaps freighted with strikingly generous language that can also at times be a little confusing. If conditional and unconditional systems are combined, an irreducibly conditional element always remains that overrides the unconditionality contributed by the opposing approach. One cannot have a conditional unconditionality that is not in effect simply conditional!

So this solution, which seems to merge the two discourses, actually does so by subordinating the second one to the concerns of the first, and unleashing a degree of cognitive dissonance through Paul's interpretation — that is nevertheless not experienced as long as issues surrounding conversion are discussed. It is therefore an ingenious but ultimately unworkable and even a slightly deceptive solution that is justifiably abandoned by many modern scholars. At its deepest level, to assert this resolution is in fact to beg the question; the victory of Justification has already been assumed (and arbitrarily)! While purporting to smoothly join two discourses, one has quietly been marginalized.

For all these reasons then, I suggest rejecting this traditional explanation to our difficulties. A clear appreciation of the alternative theory's claims ought to lead to the *abandonment* of the key principles of Justification (which are *redefined* by the central disclosures of "sanctification"), *and to an entirely different conception of the problem and the solution*. As we have just seen, different answers are offered to *all* the key theological questions, *including to salvation*. That is — and in nuce — "sanctification" *is* a theory of salvation, which is entirely self-sufficient. It requires no supplementation, and makes claims in its own right to all the main theological questions.[31] Furthermore, it is arguably a *superior* theological explanation of salvation to Justification, because it is not foundationalist but is based on the self-disclosure of God in Christ. From its point of view, then, Justification is poor theology, if it can lay claim to that honored title at all. Adopting the traditional justification-sanctification distinction overrides the potentially independent if not self-sufficient status of sanctification, and so ought to be resisted (that is, unless we receive good reasons for adopting it).

It can probably be seen by this point then how insidious the application of a justification-sanctification distinction to the explanation of Paul really is; to accept it is to affirm the ongoing hegemony of Justification, *and* to fail to eliminate all the conceptual tensions generated in Paul by this decision![32] Consequently we conclude at this point in our discussion that the traditional justification-sanctification explanation of this set of tensions has really failed. And we can now press on fairly — here to the interpretative trajectory that characterizes Paul's thinking at times in overtly contradictory terms.

It is important to bear in mind then that these critical concerns, extensive as they are, have never been effectively resolved or rebutted, merely observed. The main explanation usually offered — a purported distinction between justification and sanctification — is plausible only at a popular level and has long been abandoned (by most!) for the purposes of academic discussion. So these tensions remain intact and unresolved — and they are far-reaching!

In closing we should recall that Wrede also touches on "apocalyptic" in his account, attributing Paul's anthropological pessimism concerning humanity — in his transformational soteriology — to Jewish commitments attested by certain apocalyptic texts, a move made much more aggressively by Schweitzer. And this claim points us to a tradition of critical interpretation slightly divergent from the one discussed here in terms of mysticism or participation, but nevertheless closely related to it — a tradition of "apocalyptic" protest.

2.3. The Apocalyptic Protest

As was the case for Sanders and the salience of Jewish descriptive questions, this distinct critical trajectory has older origins but a more recent climactic statement. In 1961 Ernst Käsemann gave a famous lecture to a New Testament congress in Oxford subsequently published (in its English version) as "'The Righteousness of God' in Paul."[33] There he urged a recovery of the more subjective sense of this critical phrase in Paul — and hence of the causality of God — along with a more "apocalyptic" interpretation of its meaning in terms of the "eschatological saving action of God," which thereby infused the notion of righteousness as a gift *from* God with the power *of* God. This suggestion was made in overt opposition to the more anthropocentric and conventional reading championed by Bultmann — who duly responded (being met in turn by Käsemann's further resistance).[34] Käsemann's more apocalyptic reading of this phrase, and through it of Paul's thought in general, was then subsequently embodied in one of the greatest

Romans commentaries ever written, published in various editions through the 1970s. We will examine Käsemann's particular solutions to various perceived plights within Paul's theology carefully in due course (most especially through parts three and four), so it can suffice for now merely to note the main outlines of his protests and where they overlap with the alternative theory we have already discerned in Romans 5–8.[35] Why did Käsemann fight so hard for a curiously bipolar construal of the phrase δικαιοσύνη Θεοῦ in Paul — in terms of a gift that nevertheless retained also the character of a power ("der Machtcharakter der Gabe")?

Käsemann emphasized through this set of reconstruals the sovereignty of God, the unconditional nature of the divine action within the world, the robust ethical commitment of God's resulting community called into being by the Christ event, and the reality of eschatology, in relation both to God's present divine intervention and to the coming consummation. Only these emphases, he asserted, provide the resources the church needs for opposing the evil that stalks the world. They also allow Christians to avoid the insipid optimism of Paul's liberal interpreters who reduce the apostle's ethics to an imitative voluntary effort grounded in the realities of individuals and their altered self-understandings, generating thereby a correspondingly individualist and impoverished church incapable of recognizing, let alone resisting tyranny and its demonic variants. Käsemann felt that he had experienced unequivocally the ethical and ecclesial failings of a liberal, individualist church in Germany prior to and during the Second World War. In his view, the theological and exegetical problems that underlay those failings were to be repudiated emphatically, and he chose the apocalyptic route to that end. His emphasis on eschatology also allowed him to circumvent many of the exemplary and merely ethical readings of Paul then fashionable — for example, in relation to Philippians 2:5-11 — and to speak rather of a coming hope for both the church and the world, further strengthening his distinctive ethical and ecclesial concerns. (These emphases allowed him, in the manner of Schweitzer, to draw much stronger connections back to a more vigorous Jesus as well. Links with Jewish apocalyptic sources added further support to his claims.) But strong emphases on present unconditional saving action by God in Christ and on its dramatic future consummation are at bottom simply consistent complementary theological and exegetical accents; to emphasize one of these poles generally allows emphasis simultaneously in some sense on the other as well. God's present and future lordship are intimately related.

Many of these concerns are now discernible in some of the towering interpretative figures of Paul in the last generation in North America — J.-C. Beker, Leander E. Keck, and J. Louis (Lou) Martyn.[36] Perhaps it is in this last named figure, however, that they receive their most widely circulated and well known expression.[37] Not all of Martyn's interpretative moves in relation to Paul concern us at this stage of our discussion, but some of his most consistent protests certainly do.

When Martyn speaks of Paul's apocalyptic gospel, he generally means to signal certain interrelated concerns: the gospel is visited upon Paul and his churches essentially unconditionally, by grace and by revelation. All Paul's reasoning is conditioned in the light of this initial disclosure and hence proceeds "backward" (although this particular characterization is Sanders's[38]); the apostle's *epistemology* is emphatically *retrospective*. This includes the apostle's views on Judaism, on the law, and on Scripture (and indeed on most things). This is, moreover, the disclosure of a new reality — the new age. Nothing can be the same again. Both Paul and his fellow Christians are living in a new reality that, in a sense, only they can understand. In the light of this new reality they understand that Christ has rescued them from a tortured previous reality within which they were oppressed by evil powers.[39] Christ and his followers are presently at war with that evil dominion, and to a degree the war extends through the middle of each Christian community and each Christian person in the form of an ongoing conflict between the flesh and the Spirit. Nevertheless, Christ has effected the decisive act of deliverance and victory. Christians are saved, and dramatically! They have been set free and must now resist the temptation to lapse back into the old, evil, but strangely comfortable reality from which they have been delivered.

This is a woefully incomplete account of Martyn's richly textured interpretation of Paul, but it will suffice for our present purposes. Clearly, this cluster of emphases bears an intimate relationship to the alternative soteriological theory based on Romans 5–8 (and this is encouraging, since Martyn bases much of his interpretation of Paul on Galatians). We do not yet need to entertain Martyn's solutions to the difficulties posed for this alternative apocalyptic system by Justification, and vice versa.[40] It suffices to note for now the presence of such tensions. Martyn, and the tradition within which he stands, shares the alternative theory's emphases on unconditionality and grace, on revelation, and on a fundamentally liberative soteriology, and this in terms of an inaugurated eschatological existence in relation to the entire cosmos. And in the light of these emphases he struggles with Justification's countervailing accents on conditionality and individuality, and on prospective, quasi-philosophical natural theology — not to mention a God of retributive justice rather than benevolence. Lying behind many of these concerns is a perceived impoverishment of the relationship between the church and her Lord, with a corresponding evisceration of ethics. It is thus apparent that the apocalyptic tradition of Pauline interpretation, with all its characteristic protests against prevailing interpretative emphases, raises a set of difficulties encompassed by the alternative soteriological construal of Paul; this tradition merely emphasizes certain of its aspects especially strongly — principally unconditionality, divine lordship, divine saving intervention, ecclesiology (to a degree), and ethics. Apocalyptic concerns with the interpretation of Paul are essentially an eloquent and passionate subset of the group of concerns generated formally by a juxtaposition of Justification with the alternative soteriological theory.

Before moving on, we ought to note one caveat. Barry Matlock has pointed out — at length — that various ambiguities attend the signifier "apocalyptic," potentially giving rise to a question-begging dimension within any discussion that deploys this term. "Apocalyptic" can denote a genre of literature or a particular worldview associated with that literature. Occasionally, it even carries fixed sociological connotations. And the interpreters of Paul just noted tend to use it in an even more strictly delimited sense. For them it denotes certain positions within the more diverse, Jewish apocalyptic corpus and worldview that are held to characterize Paul's gospel (e.g., theocentric rather than anthropocentric, and revelational versus philosophical emphases). It also points to the influence of Käsemann, to the importance of his agenda, and often even more specifically to his famous rereading of δικαιοσύνη Θεοῦ in Romans 1:17 (where the verb ἀποκαλύπτω is used). In view of all these semantic possibilities — and the further possibilities of confusion and corrupt argumentation — it might seem wise to abandon the term's use.

However, it seems to me that this is a little too severe. The signifier "apocalyptic" is a useful label at an introductory level of discussion when broad loyalties and orientations are being sketched in relation to different basic approaches to Paul; it denotes fairly that an approach to Paul is being pursued that ultimately aligns with the concerns and readings of — in this context in particular — Lou Martyn, and that therefore is in sympathy with the alternative texts and soteriological paradigm that he endorses, and sensitive to the tensions that he detects between that paradigm and Justification concerns. Certainly this term should not carry any heavier *argumentative* weight, however, as Matlock rightly notes. As we press on into a deeper analysis of Paul, it cannot be used *to base exegetical or interpretative conclusions on a priori*, neither can it simply be assumed to characterize the heart of Paul's thinking; such claims must be established in the usual fashion — with painstaking, integrated exegesis. Moreover, the ἀποκαλύπτ- word group, and the passages in which it occurs in Paul, do not automatically possess a special interpretative status (Lutheran fondness for Rom. 1:17 notwithstanding). But these legitimate caveats do not disqualify the term from serving a useful denotative purpose in relation to the history of Paul's interpretation — its function here.[41] Ultimately, I will urge an "apocalyptic" reading of Paul, and hence — if he is to be consistent — an apocalyptic *re*reading of his Justification texts. And I contend that this project, if it is successful, will solve a lot of difficulties in the field. It will not be successful simply because I call it apocalyptic. But that signifier does — suitably defined — indicate where my discussion is heading.

It should be admitted, in closing this discussion, that Käsemann and some of his followers deny shifting to an entirely different paradigm from Justification. However, those persuaded by him perceive greater and lesser degrees of tension at this point. Martyn in particular is alert to the difficulties in relation to Justification that derive from a strong commitment to Paul's apocalyptic construal. The strong endorsement of God's sovereignty and eschatological action in apocalyptic readings leads inevitably to an essentially unconditional conception of salvation. This unconditionality then imparts a retrospective character to epistemology. Salvation itself is also cosmic in breadth, and thus its recipients tend to be spoken of in collective and corporate terms. And all these concomitants then clash with

Justification's individualist, prospective, and emphatically conditional construction. So if Paul is to be delivered from them, it is necessary — among other things — to construe Galatians in a consistently apocalyptic fashion, and this Martyn proceeds to do with virtuosity and insight.

Martyn then perceives in the light of this saving apocalyptic intervention that humanity's prior condition was hopelessly fallen, and here he links hands with the soteriological concerns noted earlier on in chapter three, as well as with much of the imagery of superhuman warfare and oppression in apocalyptic literature. Salvation is fundamentally liberative and takes place in the face of evil powers, from whom humanity is freed. God, therefore, is not fundamentally just and the atonement designed to assuage God's righteous anger at transgression; God is fundamentally benevolent and the atonement intended to deliver humanity from bondage to evil powers and to reconstitute it in the age to come.

So it seems that Martyn is correct to perceive a high degree of tension between apocalyptic readings of Paul and his construal in terms of Justification (bearing in mind that many interpreters hold both systems to be operative at roughly the same time!). These tensions ought to be explained — at least initially — in terms of contradiction, and not of mere complementarity. Furthermore, by this point the soteriological tensions that we have already noted in relation to mystical or participatory concerns have been recapitulated almost exactly. It would seem that the apocalyptic Paul ultimately encounters as many difficulties in relation to Justification as does the Paul construed in terms of our alternative soteriology and the mystical (initially German) interpretative tradition. The route to these realizations is slightly different, as are the emphases made en route, but the destination is largely the same — and so is the basic problem. The "participatory" and the "apocalyptic" Paul are both posited in large measure in opposition to the same underlying problem: the construal of Paul's gospel in terms of Justification.

2.4. Contradictoriness

In a typically witty characterization, Stephen Westerholm identifies a particular trajectory of Pauline interpreters as raising "the hobgoblin of inconsistency" within Paul's thought — that (as Räisänen puts it) "contradictions and tensions have to be *accepted* as *constant* features of Paul's theology of the law."[42] Westerholm is concerned with the challenge that this poses to "Lutheranism" (which he defines slightly differently from Justification, although our two projects clearly overlap), and he aligns the work of John Drane, Hans Hübner, and Heikki Räisänen in this relation. I wish only to add E. P. Sanders to the list, at least in part, and to shift the focus of the ghoulish metaphor from the actual charge to its representatives, since much of their subsequent treatment — especially of Räisänen — suggests that this is in any case where the metaphor has operated.[43]

The crucial question to ask of this interpretative protest is how much of its case that Paul is contradictory derives from the construal of part of Paul's thought in terms of Justification (this then leading in the main to the juxtaposition of two different soteriologies in his thinking, as noted by chapter three, but also to various other problems) — the concomitant of this being, how much of the case would collapse if Paul's contradictions in this regard were resolved?[44] To put it slightly differently, we should inquire to what extent this tradition of protest is a restatement from a different angle of the protests that have just been noted in participatory and apocalyptic terms. And the short answer is that a considerable portion of this broad stream of criticism does seem to be generated by the presence of Justification in Paul's description alongside participatory and/or apocalyptic emphases. However, because this particular interpretative trajectory tends to focus on the fact of contradiction in Paul in specific relation to issues surrounding the law, it follows that data outside the Justification texts at times and considers other problems at such points.[45] So not everything is resolved in this relation if Justification is isolated and treated — merely a significant amount.[46] We might say then that the debates over Paul's ostensible contradictoriness will be greatly clarified if the issues generated by Justification are identified, although those debates will not then cease. (There is more work yet to be done!)

Excursus: Räisänen's View of Paul and the Law

It may be helpful to engage with Räisänen's case in a little more detail, since it is one of the most extensive and penetrating. Räisänen develops his case for contradiction in five broad stages, after which he probes other New Testament texts (including Deuteropauline letters), along with Jewish sources, for similar difficulties and then investigates possible historical explanations and solutions. We can identify six clusters of specific concern through this critique.[47]

i. Räisänen often notes that Paul's statements concerning the law tend to head in two directions. On the one hand, his commitment to its total, "radical" abolition is clear at times (42-56). On the other hand, at other times, it still seems to be in force, albeit usually partially (62-73). (He also thinks it "oscillates": 18-28.) And although our two critiques are by no means completely synchronized, it is possible to detect the disordering force of Justification theory in many of these concerns. In particular, Räisänen notes that many of the arguments ostensibly supplied for the abolition of the law by Paul are weak — the texts and arguments framed by Justification theory, since that theory, strictly speaking, does not supply a rationale for the law's *ethical* abolition! So, for example, discussing Gal. 3:13 specifically, he observes that "[i]t is not clear . . . that the thesis about the abolition of the law follows logically from the notion of a vicarious curse. If the requirement of the law is met, why should it follow that the law is to be rejected after that? There is hardly any reason to doubt that Paul's Jewish Christian opponents shared the notion of Christ's death ὑπὲρ ἡμῶν; yet they did not draw the conclusion that the law had come to an end" (*P&L*, 59). But these are problems generated, at least in part, by Justification theory. Paul seems to want to abolish the law, but his arguments for this, when framed in terms of Justification theory (as Räisänen assumes here), are invalid. Furthermore, that Paul then *does* go on to abolish it — at least at times — is inexplicable!

ii. Moreover, Räisänen points repeatedly to Paul's characterizations of the law in temporal and temporary terms (*P&L*, 60) — as a pedagogue (see Gal. 3:19-25) and a fading glory (2 Cor. 3). This is apparently one set of arguments that the apostle uses to support the thesis that the law should be superseded. But *these* statements concerning the function and status of the law are impossible to harmonize with any characterizations supplied else-where in terms of Justification theory, and not merely in terms of abolition! In Justification the law has a permanent and ongoing function in relation to every sinful individual within history, convicting of sin and pending just judgment. The notion of a temporary historical role — and largely in relation to Jews — is therefore utterly different and incommensura-ble, a set of systematic tensions generated again by Justification theory.

iii. Räisänen correctly detects that Paul at times demands 100 percent fulfillment of the law, and that this then generates a spectrum of related difficulties (see Gal. 3:10; 5:3; Rom. 1:18–3:20; *P&L*, 94-109, 118). This seems unreasonable, and also unhistorical in rela-tion to both what Paul says elsewhere about Judaism, and what Judaism actually was (*P&L*, 164-68). Räisänen asserts here that Paul "misconstrues Jewish 'soteriology'" (*P&L*, 200; and here he leans especially on Sanders). But it is now apparent that these are all dif-ficulties either exacerbated or generated by Justification theory. The issue of unreason-ableness was described earlier as the difficulty intrinsic to Justification theory of theodicy (problem 5; see chapter two: see *P&L*, 153), while the unhistorical description of Judaism that results is apparent both in what Paul says about Judaism elsewhere (problem 16; see chapter three), and what the Jewish sources contemporary to Paul also attest to (problem 18, noted in detail in chapter four). (Räisänen also notes in this relation that some people seem nevertheless to fulfill the law, thereby contradicting the important conclusion just registered — note especially Romans 2. [See *P&L*, 25-26, and 101-9, discussing esp. 2:12-16 and 26-27.] Paul also makes some rather unreasonable arguments about Jews [*P&L*, 97-101]. But, strictly speaking, this is not a theoretical problem within or along the borders of Justification theory but a textual embarrassment; so it is addressed in detail later on — see especially part three, chapter eleven, and part four, chapter fourteen.) So all of Räisänen's overlapping criticisms here turn out to be related to a reading of Paul in terms of Justification.

iv. Räisänen observes that Paul's accounts of the origins of sin are multiple and in tension with one another. In some texts, Paul asserts that the law exposes sin in every indi-vidual; in other texts, he seems to suggest that sin originated with Adam's fall (see *P&L*, 140-54). Here we should emphasize that the former explanation is a timeless, generic one and the latter deeply historicized, so they are contradictory in their entire orientation and not merely in point of detail. But clearly this criticism isolates an important element in the clash between Justification and the alternative theory as we have already detailed that in chapter three — namely, fundamentally different conceptions of "the problem." The indi-vidualized notion of sin "exposed" by the law is the view suggested by Justification (and ar-guably by the Justification texts alone). Different conceptions of the function of the law then correspond to these different conceptions of the problem — as "in principle" leading to salvation (as Justification suggests), over against "never" having any salvific purpose, as the alternative, more apocalyptic account of Paul suggests (*P&L*, 150-52).

v. In tandem with the foregoing, Räisänen asks if "Paul's critical attitude to the To-rah [is] rooted in *anthropology* or *Christology*?" (168; see more broadly 168-77) — a pithy expression of the differences discussed earlier here in chapter three between a prospective and a retrospective account of the problem. Clearly the majority of any tensions discerned in Paul in this relation are generated by the presence of the prospective system of Justification alongside Paul's otherwise retrospective explanations (which Räisänen can slip between a little too quickly: see *P&L,* 162).

vi. Räisänen problematizes Justification's account of the origin of many of these insights in Paul's life — most notably, in some relation to his "conversion" on the road to Damascus (*P&L,* 229-36, 249-56). Räisänen surveys this case and finds it generally wanting, thereby touching on some of the biographical issues that were addressed in detail in chapter five.[48] Justification is committed to a certain biography of Paul, and Räisänen is quite right to detect the difficulties in the evidence relating to this — essentially, failing to establish it.

In sum, six sets of difficulties within the contradictory description of Paul generated by Räisänen in specific relation to his views of the law are caused by the presence within that description of Justification theory. This seems a significant degree of overlap.

Ultimately, Räisänen views Paul's thinking on the law as profoundly ambiguous and vacillating and hence, in his view, probably a secondary rationalization of a deeper set of rather agonized commitments (so in a sense his view is quite Lutheran!). Räisänen merges a wide spectrum of difficulties and texts in support of this basic thesis, not all of which immediately convince. He consistently fails to supply a reasonable "apocalyptic" and retrospective account of some of Paul's arguments (e.g., of Gal. 3:15–4:10) and equally consistently fails to consider the possibility that Paul's Christian ethic is hermeneutically influenced — consistently! — by a Christian (and even christological) criterion that could generate legitimate selectivity in relation to preceding traditions. (Räisänen confesses at the outset that he "long held a rather standard Lutheran view," which only began to fracture on reading H.-J. Schoeps's *Paulus* in 1974.[49] So his familiarity with alternative theological readings of Paul may be quite limited.) In addition, one can simply disagree with his exegesis of particular texts.[50] The result of these potential rejoinders is that a certain number of Räisänen's criticisms can arguably be defused at the outset, although this cannot be demonstrated in detail here. However, several of his most important charges of inconsistency are positioned directly in relation to Justification, and it is of course those that interest us at this point.

In short, it seems that if Justification can be banished from Paul's thinking, then many of the hobgoblins of inconsistency will be disarmed as well, while our ability to address those that remain will also be greatly assisted. Perhaps the *real* demons of contradiction will then emerge into full clarity, while our own, countervailing capacities will be greatly enhanced (because Paul's conceptual clarity will have been both improved and simplified).

2.5. *Various Biographical Concerns*

A set of complex and important issues is generated when Justification theory is introduced into Paul's biography; however, we have already explored two of these in detail — the question of Paul's Jewish background, investigated in chapter four, and of conversion, analyzed in chapter five. So those discussions only need to be summarized here (in sections 1 and 2 respectively), while the remaining biographical issues can receive a more detailed treatment (in section 3).

(1) Paul's Jewish Background

Paul's relationship with Judaism encompasses a whole set of difficult issues including his understanding of the Jewish law, his interpretation of the Jewish Scriptures, and his view of the status of the Jewish people — all questions that seem, furthermore, to invite different answers before and after the coming of Christ. This set of questions has been important for the analysis of Paul from the inception of his critical interpretation and central to his scholarly discussion for the last quarter century (the principal impetus here being given, as we have seen, by Sanders in 1977). And it is largely self-evident that much of the content of this broad debate has been supplied by a construal of parts of Paul's corpus in terms of the theory of Justification, although not all of it, because the apostle discusses Jewish issues outside the traditional Justification texts (and this will prove important in due course). Nevertheless, Justification supplies a particular set of responses to this entire set of questions — a block of answers that are coordinated in a quite specific way.

We know well by now that law observance and pre-Christian Judaism are construed together by the theory of Justification in a fundamental and primarily negative soteriological relationship, which also largely subsumes broader historical construals of Israel. Furthermore, notions of "legalism" and "works righteousness" that have been so hotly debated of late are generated almost exclusively by texts interpreted in terms of Justification theory and hence within this framework — and this even if the debate proves on closer analysis to be less decisive than many of its participants think. (We will revisit much of this debate through parts three and four.) It is not then necessary to labor the point; clearly, Justification theory lies behind a great deal of the discussion of Paul in relation to various important Jewish questions, especially law observance, Scripture, and salvation. And we have already seen at some length in chapters three and four that its role in relation to those questions is highly problematic. The answers supplied by Justification theory to the key Jewish questions do not merely contradict much of what Paul says on these subjects elsewhere; they are empirically embarrassing and sometimes even morally repugnant — although at least they possess the virtue of simplicity.

(2) Paul's Conversion

The approach to Paul's apostolic call suggested by Justification theory has already been discussed in some detail in chapter five. Suffice it to summarize here, then, that Justification imparts a strong shape to any characterization of Paul's call, often beginning with its categorization as a paradigmatic "conversion." Paul must proceed from a state of anxious legalism to one of joyous, law-free Christian existence by way of a realization that justification is through faith alone. Numerous accounts of Paul's call — often by figures who elsewhere endorse Justification as the content of Paul's gospel — claim as much. And it is inevitable that the evidence in Acts will be drawn into this description, because Paul himself supplies so little information concerning his call in his extant letters. But there are ongoing and widespread suspicions on the part of many scholars as to whether Paul's Damascus experience in fact fits the Justification paradigm and, if not, what paradigm it does fit — along with what argumentative goals he is trying to achieve when he alludes to it. These suspicions then join with concerns about the veracity and construal of the relevant portions of Acts. Hence, much of the debate currently swirling around discussions of Paul's Damascus experience is intimately linked with the deeper question of the credibility of Justification theory. Furthermore, key elements in Paul's missionary praxis — especially the content and manner of his preaching — are shaped by expectations generated by Justification theory as well. Once again, many interpreters holds that the actual data does not fit these theoretical expectations especially well, if at all.

(3) Other Biographical Implications

Justification also lies behind some of the most important debates of Paul's subsequent biography, a claim that we have yet to treat in detail. (Theology and biography are almost invariably linked throughout the apostle's interpretation.) We have already seen that Justification imposes a particular shape on Paul's call to evangelize the pagans, characterizing this as a conversion. And it will often go on to shape any description of Paul's subsequent missionary practice rather programmatically. Somewhat intriguingly, it will also affect the roles of various sources within the reconstruction of Paul's life, as well as judgments concerning the placement and authenticity of some of his letters. The problems that any biographer of Paul faces are by no means reducible to Justification, but the involvement of that agenda within Pauline biography greatly complicates an already complex situation and does affect directly many of the biographical issues that are currently most debated. We should now address these issues in a little more detail — assuming here that Paul's Jewish background, call, and preaching have already received enough treatment.[51]

Justification theory is arguably bound up with the broader description of Paul's missionary career, where the role of Acts is once again significant. If Acts is read as *episodically* trustworthy, then Paul's mission praxis as it is depicted there arguably conforms reasonably well to the expectations of Justification theory. The apostle visits a number of ancient Greco-Roman towns and cities, scattered in the main around the littoral of the northeast Mediterranean, he preaches in them, and various individuals respond to that proclamation and are saved essentially by faith.[52] Moreover, if Acts is read as *sequentially* and not merely episodically trustworthy, then Galatians must be the first letter that Paul composed within his extant corpus and Romans one of the last, and this is clearly useful to the theory's advocates.

Galatians must appear shortly after Paul's first missionary journey (Acts 13–14), because Paul is about to make his third visit to Jerusalem at this point in the

Acts narrative, and Galatians — essentially under oath (see 1:20) — knows of only two visits to Jerusalem by this point in Paul's life (see 1:17-19; 2:1-10). The churches in Macedonia, Achaia, and Asia, then, have not yet been founded and so cannot be written to; hence, Galatians seems to be Paul's first extant letter. And this decision has the useful result that Paul seems to articulate the theory of Justification very clearly, in a bitter controversy, well before most of his successful mission work. Although it is not especially early in absolute terms — because Galatians still speaks of the lapse of fourteen if not seventeen years from his original call — the theory is positioned early *relative to* the rest of Paul's extant writings, and possibly also relative to the geographical spread of the Pauline mission, which by this point has reached only "Syria and Cilicia" (1:21).

Romans, however, inevitably holds its place in Paul's life and developing letter sequence just before his final fateful visit to Jerusalem. It was composed in Corinth and only slightly less obviously on the eve of Paul's final "collection" visit to the Jewish capital. (This evidence will be discussed in more detail in part four, chapter thirteen.) So it looks back on his most important years as a missionary. Justification is of course arguably quite central to Romans; hence, it would seem that Paul's *last* major letter — or at least his last major letter during his active missionary work — is in large measure a sustained account of Justification theory.

The common articulation of the theory of Justification by both these letters, one early and the other late and mature, now seems to lend considerable support to any claim that the theory is fundamental for Paul and not a mere creature of circumstance and even of polemic. Because Galatians is positioned relatively early, a gap of some time — perhaps around five years — along with a great deal of missionary work — Acts 15 through 20:3 — now intervenes before Romans. That the theory of Justification has its primary expression in these disparate locations undermines any reduction of Paul's distinctive Justification arguments to contingency — the suggestion that they are momentary tactical moves and not something deeper and more fundamental. The theory seems, rather, to be something he formulated before this missionary work and held constantly throughout it, in what was probably the most important period of his career.

Thus, an emphasis on the sequential trustworthiness of Acts lends considerable support to a biography of Paul in terms of Justification; it allows Justification advocates to repudiate with integrity certain troublesome biographical challenges (and we have already seen that it underwrites an appropriate view of Paul's call).[53] But it also facilitates a further defensive biographical move.

Although more conservative advocates of Justification tend to balk at skeptical decisions about pseudonymity within the Pauline corpus, (relatively!) more liberal advocates of Justification such as Käsemann, unencumbered by such qualms, can introduce one further defensive measure. The presence of Justification can actually be used as a yardstick for Pauline authorship, so that certain ostensibly Pauline letters can — at least partly on this basis — be excluded from Paul's authentic corpus. This tends to reduce a ten-letter canon to a slimmer seven-letter version that excludes Ephesians, Colossians, and 2 Thessalonians, and the defense of Justification again greatly benefits. Two further acute biographical difficulties are thereby foreclosed.

The closely related Ephesians and Colossians are widely held, if genuine, to be later than the rest of Paul's corpus and hence probably composed in one of the long captivities mentioned by Acts.[54] But the theory of Justification is barely mentioned in Ephesians — and even then is stated in a potentially troublesome form (see 2:8-10) — while it is simply absent from Colossians. And this poverty allows the critical biographer to suggest that Paul reconsidered his commitment to Justification in his later years, when he had rather more time to reflect on matters during his long imprisonments. Indeed, Ephesians may represent a more systematic statement of his theology than Romans, and yet it barely attests to Justification. The more mature Paul that seems to emerge from these texts is also a more "catholic" Paul.[55] But this scandalous potential development is neatly removed by the relegation of Ephesians and Colossians to pseudonymous status.

In like measure, 2 Thessalonians is largely devoid of reflection in terms of Justification. This is again troublesome in and of itself, but if a very early provenance for 2 Thessalonians proved likely, then it could be catastrophic.[56] Second Thessalonians would displace Galatians from the important position of Paul's first extant letter and would push Paul's silence concerning Justification into his early missionary career and, by implication, back as far as his call. A vigorous law-free gospel would clearly be in place by the time of the Macedonian mission, but Paul breathes not a word of Justification theory in this relation.[57]

For these reasons, excluding Ephesians, Colossians, and 2 Thessalonians from Paul's corpus is a further useful defensive move by advocates of Justification (although at bottom of course the argument — if it is made merely in these terms — is circular). These moves eliminate the possibilities of damaging counterattacks from both later and earlier points in Paul's life.

Despite the apparent strength of these integrated biographical claims — concerning the nature of Paul's call, the role of Acts in his biography, the positions of Galatians and Romans in relation to his most active missionary work, and the provenance of some of the disputed letters — many Pauline biographers have felt that the evidence points in other directions and have argued accordingly.

We have already noted the debate concerning the characterization of Paul's call. Here, then, we can add that the use of Acts in a foundational, primary manner to articulate Paul's biography and, further, the stringent defense of its sequential reliability have been much questioned. The former is simply incorrect from a methodological standpoint, while the latter encounters a series of difficulties in practical terms.[58]

As confidence in Acts erodes (that is, in these specific terms in relation to Paul's biography!), so too many reject the interval implied by Acts between Galatians and Romans. Various scholars question whether Galatians is separated from Romans by a long period of time and/or activity,[59] raising the possibility in turn that their similarities are in fact generated by similar circumstances peculiar to these letters. A more occasional account of the texts that underpin the theory of Justification then becomes possible (while the absence of Justification terms and arguments from most of Paul's other letters becomes still more troublesome). Similarly, various scholars question the widely accepted relegation of Ephesians, Colossians, and 2 Thessalonians to a marginal, disputed status and ask correspondingly whether their traditional points of composition are sustainable. Earlier provenances for any of these letters (coupled with authenticity) would increase the biographical pressure gathering against a comprehensive explanation of Paul in terms of Justification.[60]

Not all the questions circulating within the complex area of Pauline biography are in play by this point in our discussion, but it cannot be denied that many are, and some of the most central and hotly debated issues at that. All these points in the apostle's life — his conversion, his missionary practice, and the placement and authenticity of many of his letters — ought to reflect the theory of Justification fairly directly if the latter is actually true, so clearly a great deal of the biographical discussion of Paul is tightly bound up with Justification (and presumably might greatly benefit if this relationship is loosened). A quite different "shape" might be discernible in Paul's mission and closely related thinking, along with a rather different canon of authentic data.

2.6. "Faith" Terminology

A debate that we have not yet had cause to discuss a great deal is also deeply involved with the theory of Justification — the meaning of Paul's "faith" terminology. "Faith" plays a critical but, as we have already seen, an arguably problematic role within Justification theory. And it is no coincidence that the meaning of "faith" in Paul has been extensively discussed in recent times. That debate has focused specifically on a set of ambiguous genitive constructions in Paul that combine the substantive πίστις in some relation with Christ (i.e., with "Christ," "Jesus," "Christ Jesus," "Jesus Christ," and so on: see Rom. 3:22, 26; Gal. 2:16 [2x], 20; 3:22 [and see 3:26 in 𝔓[46]]; Phil. 3:9 [perhaps also 2x]; see also Eph. 3:12; 4:13).[61] These half dozen or so πίστις Χριστοῦ genitives occur in the middle of many of Paul's most important Justification texts and so draw more isolated instances of πίστις and πιστεύω into their orbit. Naturally, Justification theory expects these genitives to be translated with Christ as the object of πίστις, hence "faith *in* Christ." It would seem that they speak of the all-important condition of salvation within the model. But it is entirely possible merely on grammatical grounds to read these constructions subjectively, with the πίστις in question as Christ's own, hence the "fidelity" or "steadfastness" *of* Christ. And of course this reading opens up new avenues of interpretation within some of Paul's most important Justification texts.

The πίστις Χριστοῦ debate, along with its further implicit questions, is best considered when we turn to a detailed consideration of the key Justification texts in parts four and five (and see especially chapters fifteen and nineteen through twenty-one); however, it should certainly be noted that it arises in large measure in relation to the expectations of Justification, and the ongoing conduct of the debate is intimately bound up with this theory. Indeed, an understanding of the competing construals of the evidence, of the various arguments set forth by both sides, and of the overarching dynamic of the debate is simply impossible apart from a firm grasp of Justification theory.

2.7. Some Immediate Implications

At this point it is worth stepping back to consider the relationship between the spectrum of six Pauline debates that we have just noted and the more formal, systematic enumeration of problems caused in Paul's interpretation by Justification theory that was described from chapter one onward. One of my central claims thus far has been that a theory-driven analysis provides a more systematic account of many of the difficulties that Pauline interpreters face, and it can now be seen that this is the case. It is evident that the six Pauline debates just noted are linked by the role the Justification theory plays in relation to each one. These relationships are not necessarily exhaustive — as for example when contradictions ostensibly arise in Paul's thinking — but they are all significant, while in some cases they are exhaustive (i.e., the entire cluster of difficulties is caused by Justification theory, as in the various concerns of Stendahl). We do seem, then, to have usefully coordinated many debates that are often held apart within Pauline interpretation, the further important implication being that it is difficult to solve them if they continue to be held apart. If an underlying causality is in play, then *that* must be addressed in a single explanatory conception. This more fundamental dimension within our debates seems to have been revealed by the systematic approach that I have been using. But I have also suggested that such an approach is more comprehensive as well.

We have identified twenty-one difficulties by investigating Justification systematically. And it can now be seen that previous Pauline debates have tended to focus on single issues within this spectrum, or on particular clusters of related difficulties, thereby failing to enumerate *all* the problems that Pauline analysts face in this relation. So our problems are actually more extensive than we previously realized, even as they are also interconnected. Previous debates have certainly not done badly; *most* of the problematic issues have been isolated at some point. But not all. Counting generously, I would suggest the following correlations:

1. Krister Stendahl — perhaps the most diverse and extensive critic — raises issues SD 2, 9 and ED 3 in this relation. (His prescient hermeneutical and church-historical concerns will be addressed momentarily, in part two.)
2. Participatory interpreters tend to raise the difficulties I have analyzed at the systematic frame, although usually the last issue — of coercion and violence — is overlooked, so difficulties SD 1-9. (SD 6 — concerning faith —

and 9 — concerning the depiction of Judaism elsewhere in Paul — can be underplayed, but are raised by certain key interpreters.)

3. Apocalyptic interpreters tend to raise the same set of issues as participatory interpreters, although with different emphases, so difficulties SD 1-9 again (and with similar oversights — so, for example, Käsemann does not emphasize SD 6 or 9 much either).

4. Advocates of contradictoriness like Räisänen, where they do not raise the systematic tensions just noted, raise ED 1 and 3 — the empirical difficulties in relation to Judaism and Paul's own conversion. Alone of all the interpreters he tends to raise an intrinsic difficulty as well — specifically 5, the question of theodicy.

5. Biographical issues were noted here but play out in relation to the theory's circumstantial frame, and so are addressed in more detail in parts three through five. Nevertheless the two key issues of Paul's Jewish background and his conversion have been noted repeatedly — difficulties ED 1 and 3 that arise at the empirical frame.

6. The interpretation of "the faith of Christ" overlaps with intrinsic difficulty 7.

It seems then that past debate of Paul, suitably coordinated, has raised ID 5, 7, SD 1-9, ED 1 and 3. But ID 1-4, 6, SD 10, ED 2 and 4 ought to be added to our ongoing discussions — a significant broadening of our concerns. It seems that we have finally described the elephant! Furthermore, there is a sense in which our previous discrete debates can be subsumed within this systematic analysis, which articulates their concerns more accurately, fundamentally, and comprehensively (although overlapping debates must also retain their own integrity where their concerns fall outside Justification theory and its associated texts). We must from this point on, so to speak, address an elephant, and not a tusk, a trunk, or something similarly partial. In addition, it is clear by this point why we must move analysis beyond both "old" and "new" perspectives on Paul, although some further reasons for this will be given shortly.

On the one hand, the old perspective on Paul that I am articulating in terms of Justification theory is clearly a deeply problematic one; we have just broadened the thirteen previous specific concerns of various Pauline interpreters to a systematic list of twenty-one difficulties. And while these are severe, their enumeration is far from complete! The old perspective is a paradigm with multiple flaws.

On the other hand, the enumeration of difficulties generally supplied by advocates of the new perspective is also inadequate. Advocates of this interpretative trajectory rightly sense that something is wrong with current ways of explaining Paul; this is to their credit. But they tend to limit their concerns far too tightly, even rejecting valid concerns at times. Our interpretative difficulties are more fundamental and comprehensive than the new perspective generally suggests — and much more so! — consequently we must now push well past any articulations of "the problem" in Pauline interpretation in such terms. We are dealing with an elephant, and not a mere leg or tail. We are at this point in our discussion rapidly moving beyond both old and new perspectives on Paul, as we must.

With these clarifications in place, we can consider various programmatic theological and ecclesial difficulties that either arise from, or are significantly exacerbated by, Justification theory — a further deepening of our difficulties (i.e., an enlarging of the elephant, if that still seems possible). And we begin this further enumeration with six concerns expressed about the pre-Christian vestibule, as Justification theory articulates it.

§3. Broader Concerns with the Pre-Christian Vestibule

3.1. Natural Theology

Certain Barthian concerns with Paul's theology can be seen to rest primarily in Paul's construal in terms of Justification. These comprise both narrow and rather broader criticisms.

Romans 1:19-20, a key text for the launch of Justification theory in Paul, supplies the most explicit attestation in him — and arguably in all of Scripture — to natural theology, or general revelation. The text states that the essential facts about God — his eternity, power, divinity, transcendence, and singularity — are plainly evident in creation. The generic individual necessarily knows God in this sense, at any time or any place. But Barthians object to any such claim on two main grounds. First, it offers hostages to political fortune, and second, it is a grievous error in terms of theological epistemology — it is fundamentally foundationalist. To these problems we can add the third contention that the claim creates the very situation it seeks to avoid, namely, the a priori rejection of God, or atheism.[62] These are serious difficulties.

We should recall, first, that Barth's celebrated protest against natural theology — directed specifically at Brunner — was oriented more broadly against the rise of National Socialism in Germany in the 1930s. One of Barth's main points within this debate was that a strong commitment to natural theology has potentially sinister political consequences, allowing the emergence of an unchecked nationalism — indeed, even underwriting that emergence theologically. And subsequent events proved him profoundly right, even though at the time of his protest this was far from evident. Any theological agenda incapable of recognizing and opposing fascism ought to be treated with caution. And one that can lend positive support to such a program ought to be doubly scrutinized.

Second, it is important to grasp Barth's contention that these political failures were intrinsically connected to deeper failures in theological epistemology. Natural theology is merely one instance of theological foundationalism — here, the attempt to ground Christian theology and the articulation of the gospel in positions established independently of and prior to them. But such a program always runs the risk of introducing human concerns into that prior phase and thereby subordinating the gospel to those concerns rather than vice versa. It can be a particularly vicious situation, because the gospel itself is subverted while the gospel's capacity to correct is simultaneously obstructed.[63]

Intriguingly, Barth protested that there was something fundamentally disobedient about such a program in that it revolved around a failure to submit to the central defining revelation of Christ himself (effected in an essentially Trinitarian manner). So he did not protest primarily that *as a theological program* foundationalism was innately wrong or would inevitably fail; this prior judgment would have constituted another form of foundationalism! He observed that in the light of the gospel and the revelation of Christ, all other positions must be subordinated to that moment. And after such subordination it becomes apparent that other, foundational theological systems do in fact generally domesticate the Christian gospel to the concerns of theologians and their contexts, and often with disastrous consequences for the church and profoundly oppressive implications for those contexts. For that reason, Barth and those persuaded by him are bound to protest against any a priori, foundational schema as inherently flawed, disobedient, and vulnerable, whether it rests on natural theology, an analysis of human existence, a conception of Israel, or something else altogether.

At this point it is well worth recalling the irony we touched on earlier that is inherent within this epistemological situation. The attempted repudiation of atheism tends to generate the very possibility that it tries to exclude. This lends still further theological import to the developing conundrum.

If it is argued that the existence and the essential nature of God must be grasped as a necessary precursor to any encounter with special revelation, then a great deal turns on the success of this prior philosophical venture. If it fails in objective terms — and we have already suggested that it does — and honest but critical inquirers are not convinced that God exists, or that a certain sort of God exists, then such inquirers are entitled to dismiss the entire theological project as unproven if not false in terms that the project itself acknowledges are valid. The failure of this God's philosophical demonstration consequently leads to the legitimate repudiation of the gospel! Such inquirers have not merely failed to find God; they now have no way of finding God in the terms that have been set before them by theologians. And atheism has now been granted an objective status by these representatives of the church, who also possess no alternative resources themselves for refuting it. The attempt to force all people to Christ through rational persuasion results in the self-confident repudiation of the church. This process is in fact an endorsement *of* atheism!

Again, it is worth noting that the foregoing concerns of Barthians and their like overlap significantly with the alternative understanding of Paul's soteriology drawn primarily from Romans 5–8. That schema is a posteriori, revelatory, and christocentric; hence, not only does it avoid the criticisms that Barth and his supporters direct at Paul in terms of natural theology and foundationalism, but it can be construed as implicitly sharing those criticisms. In stark contrast, Paul's construal in terms of Justification can now be seen as the principal culprit in relation to the foregoing concerns. Certainly, it is the conventional reading of Romans 1:19-20 within the broader unfolding progressions of Justification that attributes natural theology to Paul, and in a foundationalist role[64] (and this dynamic is articulated in more detail in part three, chapter ten). Any construal of Paul in terms of Justification also attributes a fundamentally prospective, a priori theological epistemology to the apostle (although other readings of the Pauline gospel could be susceptible to this charge as well — for example, a strongly salvation-historical reading). The theory of Justification is overtly foundationalist. It goes without saying that Justification thereby raises the possibility of atheism and hence of its own complete cultural defeat. It would seem, then, that several extremely serious theological dangers are inherent in the construal of Paul in terms of Justification — dangers that Barth was especially sensitive to, although by no means alone in articulating.

3.2. Post-Holocaust Perspectives

Post-Holocaust perspectives have added a further important dimension to this discussion. Since Auschwitz it has been incumbent on Christian interpreters to consider the possible consequences of their readings of Paul, and Justification faces a peculiar challenge at this point.[65]

We have already seen that Justification theory conceives of Jews primarily as quintessential non-Christians, or "outsiders." And it largely reduces the pre-Christian condition of all humans to a particular conception of Judaism. So all individuals, without exception, are supposed to realize innately that their situation is fundamentally Jewish — bound up in the attempt to be justified through good deeds, which must, moreover, inevitably fail and consequently be punished. But the theory of Justification reserves especially harsh judgment for Jews who remain non-Christian. They are culpable in a strong sense for refusing to embrace Christ; indeed, in that refusal they inevitably involve themselves in various heinous sins. The typical pagan sins — with which Jews may be involved, although not necessarily — are idolatry and sexual immorality. But individuals who have actively resisted the offer of saving faith are also caught up in the "loop of foolishness," at which point they draw judgments of hypocrisy and of ethical and intellectual recalcitrance (and so on). Non-Christian Jews are objectively sinful and culpable, and Justification theory holds that such people will ultimately and deservedly be punished. Because of their failure to achieve perfection in good deeds, God will rightly condemn recalcitrant Jews on the day of judgment.

It follows from these dynamics that *Justification theory offers no constraints on the punishment or suffering of non-Christians and, moreover, regards any such experiences in relation to Jews as especially fitting.* Their light of revelation is greater, principally through their possession of the Scriptures; their responsibility is therefore greater and their repudiation of the Christian gospel more willful and disobedient. Hence, "their condemnation is deserved." Should history then visit suffering upon Jews in some morally neutral sense (i.e., through plague or natural disaster), Justification can construe it as legitimate punishment, and perhaps even pedagogically useful as well. Furthermore, Justification endorses human government, which can then mete out these consequences actively and without compunction (presumably on grounds of justice). At such a point Justification again offers no constraints. To be fair, the theory offers no constraints on such activity in relation to any non-Christians. But the visibility of Jews, their supposed "greater light of revelation," and the focus of the Justification texts on Jews make these dynamics hold in their case with peculiar force.

In short, when viewed in a post-Holocaust light, the theory of Justification is revealed to be fundamentally sinister. Strictly speaking, *Justification can offer no coherent protest in relation to the Holocaust,* while — it is chilling to think — *it might even be able to endorse those events.* The Holocaust is merely an anticipation of a verdict that God himself will deliver at the end of the age and, as such, is unexceptionable. And it *may* even serve the useful pedagogical purpose of jolting Jews into repentance and conversion (not that this actually proved to be the case). These are sobering considerations — while an important, and equally sinister interaction with race issues is also potentially operative at this point.[66]

We need now to explore the implications of Justification theory for government's relationship with other issues of alterity a little more deeply, at which point further new angles of protest emerge.

3.3. Homosexual Relations

Queer theorists[67] encounter in Romans 1:24-27 perhaps the most explicit articulation and condemnation of homosexual activity in all of Scripture.[68] Certainly, if this passage is read in the standard fashion dictated by Justification, then the reprehensibility of homosexual sex is unavoidable. Paul must himself be overtly and strongly committed to this stance. Furthermore, it is written into the natural order, within phase one of Justification, prior to any special Christian revelation. And this location generates several rather sinister concomitants. First, correct theology at all points now presupposes this stance, so to tamper with it is to risk undermining the later Christian dispensation that unfolds from it. Strong paradigmatic reasons now exist for the stance's maintenance. Second, the stance is attributed to all humanity on the basis of innate knowledge and hence independently of special revelation. So, third, it is insulated from correction by special revelation. (Indeed, as we have already seen, special revelation can now unfold only in these terms.) Fourth, since everyone can be expected to know that such behavior is deeply offensive to God, everyone so offending is liable entirely justly to punishment. Romans 1:18-32 — read in a certain way — tends to describe such punishment rather passively in terms of the divine deliverance of humanity up to the consequences of its twisted and chaotic desires, but Romans 2 will articulate almost immediately a more active and coercive response to sin (i.e., punishment).

And it is a short step from divine government and retribution to such action by human governments. Hence, not only is the condemnation of homosexual sex written into the foundation of the Christian gospel, but that condemnation legitimizes coercive state reaction against such apparent wrongdoing.[69]

If Romans 1:24-27 is set to one side momentarily, it is still possible that Paul's view of sexual relations was reasonably conventional in terms of ancient Judaism. He seems to endorse heterosexual monogamy as the main alternative to celibacy, and he occasionally condemns homosexual relations in the context of vice lists (see perhaps 1 Cor. 6:9). But the setting of that opinion is rather more flexible, as his conditional endorsement of divorce in 1 Corinthians 7 indicates. Moreover, the *foundational* theological function of sexual relations and their legitimate punishment is displaced by relocations both into the future eschatologically and a present ecclesial frame. So the stakes are fairly high for Queer theorists who find Paul's ostensible position on homosexual relations problematic. But it is the reading of Romans 1:24-27 in the broader context of 1:18-32 if not 1:18–3:20 in terms of Justification theory that generates the bulk of these difficulties. If Justification is removed from the situation, such difficulties are not eliminated, but their most severe implications are significantly mitigated. The foundational reprehensibility of homosexual relations and their punishment — if necessary by the state — are eliminated, while the resources of special revelation can rapidly be mobilized in relation to that stance, if Paul is not construed in terms of the theory of Justification. The terms of this significant debate are significantly altered.

3.4. Constantinianism

A tradition of protest against Constantinianism can now be seen to unfold in partial relation to Paul's interpretation in terms of Justification.[70] Such protestors question whether committed Christian discipleship can ever accept coercion or violence as legitimate Christian activity, thereby problematizing several potential actions by government — punishment, warfare, interrogation, and even binding legislation. Furthermore, some theologians influenced by this tradition ask whether the European liberal state is not a peculiarly problematic extension of this conundrum for Christians. As we will see in more detail shortly (see part two, chapter nine), not only does the modern liberal state continue to act coercively — as states presumably have always acted — but it confines religion to an individualized, "internal," and arguably largely irrelevant private sphere, thereby significantly reducing accountability by state action to the Christian tradition. Moreover, the modern state's astonishing mastery of technologies allows it to extend its enforcement far further than was the case for other states within history, while also increasing the stakes when actions like wars are actually undertaken (that is, they will probably prove bloodier, and often also longer).

It would be too much to claim that these implications are limited within Paul to Justification texts and arguments, but it can be suggested that the bulk of any putative endorsement of such a coercive state — liberal or otherwise — by the apostle derives from that theory.[71] We are already familiar with Justification's reinforcement of a coercive state based on retributive justice. God functions in a just fashion at a basal level, and this is evident in the theory's conceptions of the pre-Christian vestibule, the atonement, and eschatology. So the theory actually endorses a notion of the state on multiple levels. But as the discussion of this issue in relation to the alternative theory has shown, the presence of justified coercion in Paul outside the classic Justification texts and arguments is difficult to establish. Even if it is present, it is a distinctly muted motif. So the critique of Constantinianism in Paul, which is so pointed in the era of the modern liberal state, does pertain *primarily* — although not exclusively — to his construal in terms of Justification.

Essentially the same difficulty is apparent when it is asked what resources Paul supplies to Christians to challenge (if necessary) coercive actions undertaken in the name of patriotism (i.e., the support of a *particular* nation-state). It is difficult to find much endorsement of patriotism outside a reading of Paul in terms of Justification, but that theory seems positively to endorse certain coercive actions by a given state — and hence presumably also in some relation to patriotism — provided that they fulfill certain basic criteria. And those criteria are easy to fulfill. The right to rectify injustice actually creates constant opportunities for forcible interventions, domestic and international (while such "rectifications" may in turn create many more).[72] In this relation, it is then not inappropriate to speak at times of "Christian Fascism," because the full might of the state is appropriately deployed in support of certain key Christian decisions — many pertaining, moreover, to definitions found in the pre-Christian vestibule, and so vulnerable to distortions in terms of alterity (et cetera) at that point. Such a politics is merely a consistent extrapolation and application of Justification theory — a frightening prospect, but one that apparently needs to be confronted, and with increasing seriousness.[73] There is arguably nothing inherently democratic in a politics based on Justification theory, although a politics is directly implicit, and in unguardedly coercive terms.

In short, Justification seems to be the principal cause of Paul's apparent endorsement of Constantinianism and, by implication, of the modern liberal state, with all its peculiar dangers for Christianity, and extending, in certain circumstances, to a fascist project. Justification also seems largely to underlie the inability of Paul's theology to resist coercive actions undertaken in the name of patriotism, that is, in the name of a particular state. Paul's thought at such points seems both insufficiently critical and weak, qualities that are not normally associated with him.[74]

3.5. Totalizing Metanarratives

It is probably worth noting in passing that those who advocate a more postmodern approach to Paul — if not simply in general — also overlap significantly with our concerns here.[75] A particularly useful criticism emanating from postmodern readers is the challenge to descriptions that overreach themselves. A great deal of theorizing attempts to impose uniform and universal patterns upon reality — to supply totalizing metanarratives (an activity often dubbed — in ultimate dependence on Derrida — "logocentrism").[76] Postmodernists are quick to point to the arrogance and the frequent inaccuracy of such claims, echoing Jean-François Lyotard's (programmatic!) ". . . incredulity toward metanarratives."[77] Reality almost invariably squeezes out of the categories that are applied to it; it is a more complex, subtle, difficult thing than much theorizing admits. (Furthermore, such theorizing often masks unacknowledged ethical and political agendas. Reality in such templates is then not being explained so much as conformed to what it should be like in the view of the theorizer, who often, furthermore, occupies some privileged social location.[78]) When such challenges are applied to Paul, although not limited to questions related to Justification, they are certainly especially pointed in that relation. Justification is heavily dependent on just such an oversimplified totalizing metanarrative that purports to grasp non-Christian reality. There, among other things, it enfolds Judaism happily within its universal, highly reductionist, and fundamentally sinister embrace. So this specific concern of postmodernism intersects exactly with our broader suspicion that phase one within Justification theory is highly insensitive to reality per se and indeed projects onto reality a fundamentally banal and politically rather dangerous construct. And it is worth noting in passing that there are also solid theological grounds for concern in this relation — that Justification, like many other unhelpful theological programs, utilizes rather typical post-Enlightenment universalizing categories, rather than remaining attentive to particularities.[79]

3.6. Conversion

Missionaries and evangelists have periodically voiced concerns that Paul does not helpfully map the actual process of conversion. And the principal problem here is of course Justification.

As we have already seen in chapter five, many theorists and practitioners of conversion have argued that this process is in fact very different both from the accounts that converts often give of it and from the theory of Justification (and these two phenomena frequently overlap).[80] Justification supplies a highly individualist and rationalist model of conversion that struggles to account for how people actually convert. Indeed, it interposes a false model of that process and so actually interferes with it as conversion is attempted rationalistically, through a process of argument and aggressive preaching. The boredom and/or intimidation of this process is not merely fundamentally ineffective; it presumably not infrequently inhibits the formation of the intimate friendships that lie at the heart of actual conversion. (And hence people converting within processes structured by this model probably convert in spite of it!)

The dominance of Justification in relation to the topic of conversion can also override Paul's more accurate and positive contributions to the church's practice. A more sociologically sensitive approach to the interpretation of Paul's writings reveals a practice far closer to the modern observations of conversion. But this information can be anesthetized by the countervailing suggestions of Justification theory.

Hence, the theory of Justification seems to be the main problem behind an insensitive understanding of conversion within Paul's original mission, and often, by extension, within modern pursuits of the same.

§4. Broader Concerns with the Consequent Construal of Christianity

Many theological and ecclesial representatives and traditions have identified problems with certain elements in Paul's theology. However, many of these problems turn out to be difficulties with certain elements in Justification (and these often overlap with tensions that we find elsewhere within Paul in systematic descriptive terms). The range of ecclesial difficulties with various aspects of the reading of Paul in terms of Justification is quite astonishing. The following list is by no means exhaustive.

4.1. The Trinity and Atonement

Orthodox theologians — meaning those theologians dependent principally on Nicene and Chalcedonian affirmations — have problems with the indifference if not hostility of Paul's theology to the Trinity, and many of these difficulties can be traced to Justification.[81]

With the failure of a version of Anselm's argument for the incarnation and atonement of God, Justification theory contains no intrinsic commitment to Christ's divinity. Neither is it committed to the work of the Spirit. Indeed, it *excludes* the agency of the latter from any significant role within the unfolding process of Justification, because that would undermine the model's entire rationale in relation to individual agency and God's justice. Hence, at bottom, Justification theory is merely monotheistic. (And even if Anselm's argument succeeds, the model becomes only bitheistic, since there is no intrinsic commitment to either pneumatology or the *homoousion*.) Allied with this are concerns over the mechanism of salvation and atonement in relation to Christ if these are not conceived in Trinitarian terms.

We have already noted the conceptual difficulty with Anselm's suggestion — at least as Justification theory construes it — that the monetary metaphor be applied literally to Christ's atonement for all human transgressions. And we will note momentarily that Christ's life and obedience must somehow be taken into account as well, emphases that Justification struggles to accommodate. But there are various alternative understandings of the atonement with deep roots in various traditions within the church, and these are often at radical variance with the mechanism posited by Justification. So a Trinitarian understanding of the atonement, as seen most clearly perhaps in certain Orthodox expressions, strongly emphasizes participation, denoting this often by salvation conceived as *theosis*.[82]

Justification theory tends to bifurcate the work of the Father and the Son, characterizing their relationship in terms of the latter's acceptance of the former's (just) rage against sin. Certainly, there is no intrinsic and necessary connection between them, nor is their relationship fundamentally benevolent or even filial. The Holy Spirit's saving work, meanwhile, is extraneous if not unacceptable (because it would ostensibly override the human contribution to salvation). A *perichoretic* understanding of salvation is diametrically opposed to all these emphases in Justification; it will protest against the characterizations of each person within the divine unity *and* the implicit understanding of their interrelationships. Hence, not only is Justification theory problematic for Trinitarian concerns, but a Trinitarian — or allied — understanding of the atonement is in stark tension with Justification's conception of that process. At this point ontological and soteriological concerns mingle.

4.2. Pneumatology

Needless to say, any ecclesial traditions that emphasize the role of the Holy Spirit find Justification awkward. Those that have developed within Revivalist traditions have often accommodated their ecclesial experience of the Spirit to the theological strictures of Justification. They then may produce two- and three-stage soteriologies, as the saving conditions within Justification are simply multiplied to reflect mandatory emphases on various manifestations of the Spirit — speaking in tongues, and so on. But this addition of critical steps in relation to the Spirit is really evidence of a fundamental challenge to Justification's conditional understanding of salvation. Such expansions do not integrate smoothly with the model's actual workings. Can Justification itself contemplate any saving condition in addition to faith alone?! Clearly not. Deeper reflection on these traditions' emphases on the Spirit suggests, rather, that they challenge Justification's individualist, rationalist, and voluntarist understanding of salvation and that present accommodations are fragile.[83]

4.3. Christology

Any Calvinist emphasis on the vicarious function of Christ, perhaps by way of the *triplex munus,* jars with the role accorded Christ by Justification. James Torrance suggests, during his engagements with Federal Calvinism in the history of Scottish Presbyterianism, that much of Calvin's *Institutes* explicates the work of Christ in terms of his active representation of humanity to God, especially in his priestly office, with humanity incorporated in that representation. Just as Christ is God's movement toward humanity, so too Christ recapitulates and represents humanity to God. Hence, this theological tradition emphasizes (among other things!) Christ's identification with humanity and his life as the fulfillment of a priestly office of obedience, service, and supplication. (The exegesis of Hebrews is often prominent in support of these points.)[84] In these emphases, however, it finds little encouragement from Justification.

Justification theory accords very little significance to Christ's life. Christ's main human task seems to have been the avoidance of sin so that his sacrificial death might be unblemished and perfect.[85] Any notions of representation and participation are absent if not incomprehensible; certainly, they are superfluous.[86] The mechanism of participation within Christ is also opaque, as it must be if the Holy Spirit is not vitally involved. In short, those endorsing Calvin's emphases on Christ's representative human work as a definitive priest by whom we are represented to God and within whom we are involved will be vexed by Justification at just those points where our alternative soteriology encountered puzzling tensions in terms of participation.

4.4. Election and Assurance

John McLeod Campbell supplied a classic account of the insecurity of Christians, asserting that true Christian involvement should not be fundamentally anxious.[87] He located the origin of this insecurity in a conditional soteriology that led Christians to look to their own capacity to fulfill certain critical conditions for salvation (or in an inscrutable prior double decree in God concerning election that amounted to the same thing). Doubts inevitably ensued, because no human capacity was fundamentally and constantly reliable. Campbell's particular concern was Federal Calvinism, but the point is transferable to all conditional soteriologies. And clearly it finds its primary point of purchase within Pauline interpretation in the theory of Justification, which is explicitly conditional. Individuals can never be entirely certain that they have fulfilled the requisite conditions for salvation and will go on attempting to fulfill them indefinitely. And this, of course, is in stark contrast to the alternative soteriology rooted in Romans 5–8, which is explicitly oriented toward assurance.

The perceived difficulty with assurance links hands at this point with the broader concerns of certain Calvinists with election. Whatever the degree of emphasis and divine motivation, *any* emphasis on election encounters difficulties in Paul when he is read in terms of Justification. These difficulties are compounded by any commitment within Paul to divine initiative (which is plentiful). A primary emphasis on divine initiative is simply not compatible with Justification's commitment to the primacy of individual agency. Those who endorse the former therefore struggle with any readings of Paul in terms of the latter.

4.5. The Sacraments

The Catholic and Orthodox churches find the conception of the sacraments underwritten by Justification to be deeply impoverished. For Justification, the sacraments are symbolic of the two key principles within the saving contract — Christ's atonement and the individual's saving belief. They are involved in broader ecclesial practice then, but mean little if anything in their own right.[88] The alternative theory envisages a richer theology of the sacraments, as both baptism and the Eucharist point to the miraculous *involvement* of Christians in the death and resurrection of Christ himself. Many Catholic and Orthodox theologians would of course assert even more of the sacraments than this (and would add to their number).[89] Suffice it to say, then, that even a minimalist conception of the sacraments as asserted by the alternative theory — in principal dependence on Romans 6 — finds Justification theory's account of the sacraments inadequate and misleading.

4.6. Ethics and Ecclesiology

Many church traditions encounter vexations in relation to the ethical condition of Christians (while perhaps various representatives of the so-called Radical Reformation illustrate this most clearly). Advocates of what we might dub a "strong" approach to Christian ethics tend to emphasize devoted Christian discipleship — if necessary, to the point of death.[90] And these expectations make little sense outside a conception of Christian community that is equally committed. Hence, the ethical condition and the Christian polity produced by Justification are not merely puzzling; they are scandalous. Justification theory seems unable to ask its converts to do more than trust and believe; meanwhile, its ecclesiology is consensual, confessional, and correspondingly tepid.

These concerns might also become apparent in those church traditions concerned deeply with holiness.[91] A concern for holiness is often developed in terms of the sanctification of the individual believer and of the community, that is, in ethical and ecclesial terms.[92] It is unthinkable for such traditions that Christian disciples would need only to believe, with no further implications for their conduct. And the church is often involved as a setting for ethical exhortation, confession, and discipline. But such concerns are extrinsic to if not flatly contradicted by Justification theory, which establishes an ethical Christian only with great difficulty — if at all — and struggles in like measure to establish a vigorous polity.

In short, for any Christian traditions committed strongly to extensive ethical expectations on the part of Christians and a correspondingly intense and supportive ecclesia, Justification is deeply problematic and requires considerable supplementation if not reorientation. So here we encounter yet another element of tension between Justification and our alternative theory, which was powerfully ethical and ecclesial.

4.7. Ecumenism

Finally, it should be noted in this general relation that many of the supposedly irreducible differences between Catholicism and Protestantism are generated by Justification theory. Aspects of Justification — or the theory as a whole — are often said to be non-negotiable for Protestants, and thus to contribute to a permanent division between these different traditions if they cannot be accepted by Catholics — it is "the crux of all the disputes."[93] Hence, as Luther put things once rather famously, Justification is "articulus stantis et cadentis ecclesiae" (*The Smalcald Articles*[94] — and this statement will be considered in more detail, along with other aspects of his thought, in part two, chapter eight). It has, furthermore, proved difficult — if not impossible — to craft a mutually acceptable statement concerning Justification, as seen in the convolutions building up to, and following the "Joint Declaration on the Doctrine of Justification" (signed at Augsburg on October 31, 1999).[95] Clearly, then, if Justification as I have construed that here is eliminated from Paul, a major impediment to dialogue between Protestantism and Catholicism would be removed, and the ecumenical task could be correspondingly refashioned. This is not to exaggerate the contribution that such a reformulation might make to the complex issues of rapprochement and ecumenism more broadly, or to suggest that *other* differences would not also have to be negotiated (e.g., critical questions concerning the nature of analogy), *but this particular bone of contention could in my view safely be set to one side as a false problem!*

This is a fairly long list of difficulties. It is sobering to see how many concerns from a full spectrum of church traditions, not to mention various debates within Pauline studies, are arguably generated by the theory of Justification. These difficulties also invariably interconnect with the particular set of soteriological tensions within Paul's description that we have already noted; seldom if ever is a difficulty voiced about Paul by a given church tradition — or by Pauline analysts — that is not related to a particular tension between Justification and the alternative soteriology rooted in Romans 5–8. Admittedly, the debates from elsewhere within the church do not always overlap precisely with Justification theory. Some concern more general questions that have been greatly complicated by the need to take into account positions generated by Justification. Nevertheless, Justification, in the basic sense of the construal of much of Paul in terms of a fundamentally contractual and hence also individualist and rationalist soteriology, is implicated significantly in all these difficulties. So Paul's construal in terms of Justification clearly occupies a highly strategic position. Many roads within the apostle's interpretation as a whole lead to and from this highly problematic construct, and things will change greatly in terms of his broader description if that construct stands or falls.

We turn now to consider some of the implications that flow from this impressive array of problems (recalling as well that it is not exhaustive, in various respects[96]).

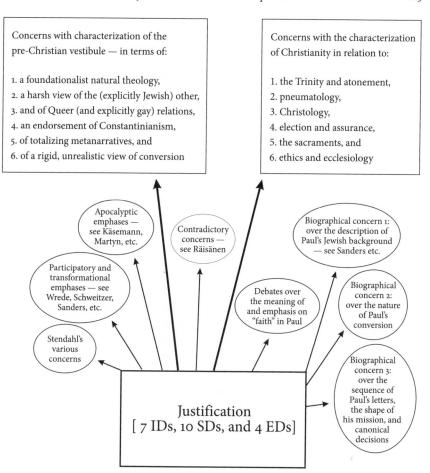

Concerns with characterization of the pre-Christian vestibule — in terms of:

1. a foundationalist natural theology,
2. a harsh view of the (explicitly Jewish) other,
3. and of Queer (and explicitly gay) relations,
4. an endorsement of Constantinianism,
5. of totalizing metanarratives, and
6. of a rigid, unrealistic view of conversion

Concerns with the characterization of Christianity in relation to:

1. the Trinity and atonement,
2. pneumatology,
3. Christology,
4. election and assurance,
5. the sacraments, and
6. ethics and ecclesiology

Apocalyptic emphases — see Käsemann, Martyn, etc.

Contradictory concerns — see Räisänen

Biographical concern 1: over the description of Paul's Jewish background — see Sanders etc.

Participatory and transformational emphases — see Wrede, Schweitzer, Sanders, etc.

Debates over the meaning of and emphasis on "faith" in Paul

Biographical concern 2: over the nature of Paul's conversion

Stendahl's various concerns

Biographical concern 3: over the sequence of Paul's letters, the shape of his mission, and canonical decisions

Justification
[7 IDs, 10 SDs, and 4 EDs]

§5. The Implications

A number of important implications lie within the preceding realizations. First, it is clear that our problems are much more *extensive* than was previously thought. We have seen that a score of difficulties is generated within the interpretation of Paul by his construal at times in terms of Justification theory — in internal, argumentative terms, and at the systematic and empirical frames — and these link hands helpfully with a half dozen or so discrete critical debates within Pauline studies, and with a dozen theological and ecclesial debates that range beyond the borders of Pauline scholarship. We should note further that these are serious difficulties. The Paul that results from this interpretative juxtaposition is a mass of contradictions at a significant level — the presumably central level of his soteriology.[97] Indeed, it is hard to avoid the judgment that a thinker so construed is fundamentally incoherent. Hence, our interpretative difficulties seem to extend past the point of basic cogency. In short, the difficulties caused by Justification theory for the interpretation of Paul are, in both breadth and depth, extensive.

Second, these difficulties can nevertheless be drawn together within the orbit of one explanation. There is a single, if complicated, cause underlying them. And this clarification may perhaps serve as a preliminary confirmation of the cogency of our developing analysis; such a simplification seems to suggest that we are grasping something that is both real and valid within a generally difficult interpretative situation. Hence, while the front of interpretative difficulties we are facing has been significantly broadened and deepened, the forces lying behind that front have been greatly concentrated. That is to say, our account of the difficulties is both *comprehensive* and *economic*.

Third, it looks as though these difficulties possess no effective rejoinder(s). They seem to be *intrinsic* to the function of Justification theory itself and so are generated automatically when that theory is juxtaposed with any alternative understanding of salvation in Paul (for example, as might be suggested by Romans 5–8).[98] To endorse Justification theory in any sense in Paul is therefore necessarily to generate these difficulties within his broader interpretation and, beyond him, within many of the more general theological debates of the church. Such difficulties are the automatic concomitants of this particular soteriological theory. They will stand or fall with the presence of the theory within the interpretation of Paul. Consequently, the boundaries of our difficulties correspond largely to the boundaries of Justification theory itself. They are coterminous.

Fourth, it follows that these problems constitute (in the main) "the stakes" when Justification theory is critically discussed through the rest of this analysis.[99] We stand to gain or to lose precisely this particular set of difficulties in relation to Paul, and clearly it is a far higher set of stakes than has usually been realized (as, for example, by many advocates of the new perspective). Although our basic problem is singular — the presence of a given theory within Paul — we have already noted that its resulting difficulties are widespread and deep. And this creates several further important realizations.

Denial of these difficulties does not seem to be a useful strategic option. That is, it would be a great relief to be able to lower the stakes by just denying that things are this serious — but if such a denial were actually to be true, it would have to be made demonstrably. It cannot simply be asserted. It would have to be shown that Justification does not *in fact* generate the particular problems in Paul and the broader theological deliberations of the church that we have identified. And prima facie, this looks difficult if not impossible. In the absence of any detailed demonstrations, this argumentative denial will devolve into a psychological denial. And such a denial will simply leave this dire conceptual description of Paul in place, because to avoid its resolution by failing to acknowledge that it exists *is actually to concede its basic correctness*. The claims of contradictoriness by Räisänen et al., although exaggerated in some respects, will thus be fundamentally vindicated. Paul's thinking *is* a mass of tensions, if not outright contradictions (and so on). Hence, this further set of realizations should lead to a reversal of some of the usual perceptions of the tactical situation. *It is an evangelical neces-sity to find some solution to this basic problem,* because simply to deny it is to de-liver Paul up to his detractors, and to concede at the outset that Paul's gospel is a creature of contradiction.[100]

It follows, moreover, that those committed to an ultimately coherent inter-pretation of Paul's soteriology should be prepared for challenging localized solu-tions if those prove possible. Certainly, such interpreters should be prepared to search vigorously for some solution. But a dire predicament may well necessitate some dramatic local responses, since the alternative is to concede permanently the claim that Paul is an incoherent thinker in terms of salvation, and on a fairly massive scale.

It is important to realize further that this search for some solution really needs to take place immediately. It is an urgent inquiry. As long as all these diffi-culties remain in place, Paul's thought is really too disordered to allow cogent so-lutions for other problems to present themselves — and this is a particular danger for discussions of Paul's relationship with any aspect of Judaism. If the disorder-ing positions unleashed by Justification theory are endorsed at the outset, then one wonders how any effective solution to "the Jewish questions" in Paul could even be contemplated. The inherent contradictoriness of any such investigation in terms of its results *has already been conceded!*

We noted above that it may be necessary to consider radical solutions in lo-calized terms. However, we should recall, further, that our economic analysis of the problem at least offers the possibility of an economic solution, however radi-cal. It is Justification theory itself that lies behind all these disparate difficulties; Justification is the principal culprit — as far as these particular difficulties are concerned. Hence, a solution that could plausibly eliminate Justification theory from Paul would resolve our difficulties. And in fact nothing less than this will re-solve them, because of their intrinsic nature. Any purported solution *must* be this comprehensive; it must be this radical. Thus, the contours of Justification theory, as the problem, point precisely to the contours of any truly effective solution. Our preceding analysis therefore holds out the promise of an ultimately coherent construal of Paul's soteriology; to have analyzed our problem this precisely is al-ready to have grasped much of its solution as well.[101]

In sum, interpreters of Paul concerned about his ultimate soteriological co-herence (and as a matter of methodological coherence, all interpreters should in the first instance be so concerned) *cannot avoid addressing the difficulties caused by Justification theory.* These difficulties should not be denied, bypassed, or pre-maturely explained. Furthermore, it is now apparent that if Paul's coherence is to be saved, *then Justification theory must somehow be eliminated.* The interpretative alternatives are not usually cast in this stark fashion, but this is actually how the underlying argumentative and theological situation is configured. *The elimina-tion of Justification theory from Paul's interpretation is vital to his fundamental evangelical integrity* — either this, or some alternative solution to our catalog of difficulties must be presented. But I know of no such solution, nor does one really seem possible. (This would be to deny a causality within these difficulties that is largely self-evident.)

In view of all this — the extensive and pressing nature of our difficulties and the dim if challenging contours of an apparent solution — do we turn now to the relevant texts to examine them critically in the light of Justification theory, hoping in fear and trembling to find some way of eliminating it? In an ideal world we would of course do just that. However, in the present instance it would be ill advised. Constructive discussion of the texts in relation to all these issues requires a level interpretative playing field. And in my experience, discussion of the Justification texts takes place more on the hermeneutical equivalent of a killing field. Powerful and largely unacknowledged interpretative forces are operative that tend to stifle effective debate and cut down any alternative suggestions as soon as they step timidly from their revisionist trenches. (This often manifests as question-begging argumentation, which is deeply detrimental to constructive discussion.)[102] As Stendahl perceptively grasped, something highly distorting is going on in this particular interpretative arena, and this phenomenon must be addressed and compensated for if any effective discussion of the texts is ultimately to take place. A truly level interpretative playing field is of course impossible, but we must approximate this situation as best we can in order to facilitate our later exegetical discussions. And this necessitates a prior exploration of the hermeneutical dimension in this whole area of discussion, to which we now turn in part two — something of a narrow and hard path to our ultimate objective.

Some Hermeneutical Clarifications

CHAPTER SEVEN

The Recognition of a Discourse

§1. Preamble — Preliminary Remarks on the Nature of Reading

By this point in our analysis it is apparent that Justification theory causes serious problems for the interpretation of Paul if it is included in any broader description of his thinking. So the question now arises *whether* in fact it is present there or not — and in precisely this form. This question must of course be answered ultimately in relation to the apostle's texts and their construal: do they actually suggest that Justification theory characterized his thinking at times? But it would in fact be naive and self-defeating to turn straight to Paul's texts at this point. We do not even know yet what the relevant texts are! Arguably, the recent history of Pauline scholarship is littered with the debris of premature attempts to analyze the texts and resolve these difficulties.[1] And the cause of many of our difficulties at this precise juncture is actually hermeneutical. An important, and possibly quite insidious, set of interpretative dynamics is operative that can distort any naive or merely unselfconscious approach to the texts. Hence, these dynamics must be grasped and neutralized — insofar as they can be — before we simply "read" Paul. For this reason — perhaps counterintuitively — it is only after an analysis of the hermeneutical situation is complete that we will be in a position to inquire whether Paul himself was committed to Justification theory in his texts, and to what degree and in what sense (at which stage cogent alternative readings might also become apparent). Thus, this inquiry constitutes a second major preparatory methodological task in our overarching analysis, although its discussion will not need to be as extensive as our elaboration of the first, which took place through part one (i.e., the establishment of the nature and extent of our problem). But how does one even begin to analyze such notoriously slippery methodological issues — here, the hermeneutical dynamics operative in relation to Paul's putative construal in terms of the theory of Justification?

I suggest that the best way forward from this point will be — as is often the case — to try to grasp the object of our critical inquiry more precisely. A clear grasp of the object that we are analyzing — here, an interpretative situation — should generate in turn a clear analysis of its dynamics, of all its possible problems, of the necessary hermeneutical responses, and also of the precise contours of any potentially effective exegetical solution(s). And this means in the present instance beginning with a brief consideration of certain aspects of the nature of reading,[2] since our object is fundamentally a way of reading Paul, along with its particular implications.[3]

The raw data of reading, a string of signifiers, is composed with essentially overlapping, or "fuzzy," components that are often also deliberately multiply coded. This intrinsic ambiguity gives rise, within many texts, to an enormous array of possible meanings. Moreover, the rules that readers bring to bear upon a text are complex and, in the case of ancient texts, almost certainly only partially understood. Readers nevertheless actively configure the data to create meaning, crafting a plausible semantic trajectory through a given text. In the process, a great deal of potential information is necessarily "narcotized," to adopt Eco's term.[4] And given the complexity of the whole operation, a great deal of the process takes place out of conscious purview, in the "tacit dimension." Indeed, perhaps only a small part of the text and its semantic possibilities are held in view — "in focus" — at any given moment.

The readers undertaking this operation — perhaps after many years of training in the case of written texts, and especially in the case of ancient ones — are also socially located. And in a social setting, reasons exist for a reading's correctness in addition to its accuracy, so that readers may function not merely as readers but in effect as advocates of their readings. Moreover, all readings have a social location of one sort or another. Consider a sophisticate giving her opinion of a novel in a book club, a politician defending his execution of manifesto promises in a party meeting, an academic presenting her reading of one of the past greats to a graduate seminar, a bus conductor pointing out why a given ticket is invalid. For each there is a complex of social considerations in relation to the correctness of the reading taking place, influenced by status, allegiance, fear of embarrassment or shame, authority, interest, and so on. And it is often difficult to distinguish such considerations — also frequently tacit — from those that are more strictly exegetical. In short, socially derived considerations functioning in relation to reading are endemic, numerous, and have a great deal of interpretative room to hide in.

As if to make matters worse, there seems to be a rough rule of proportionality at work: the more important a reading, the more complex and powerful the socially generated considerations in support of it are as well. In the case of very important readings that possess a significant interplay between construal and culture over time, we tend to speak of discourses. And discourses, because of their powerful social locations, are notoriously difficult to evaluate. We do not stand outside discourses but tend rather to be positioned within them to the point that they may be part of our perceptual apparatus, that is, part of the structure through which we view the rest of reality, or at least a significant part of it. *It is hard to view the way that we view.*[5]

A first step then toward the clarification of this complex and important situation in relation to Paul and Justification is (nevertheless!) to attempt a precise description of the entire interpretative situation. In particular, the hidden dimensions of the reading underlying Justification must be brought into conscious purview; its partly submerged interpretative architecture must be flushed out, so to speak — something we saw beginning in Stendahl's essay.[6] Following this, we will at least be able to scrutinize the reading clearly as a whole. Furthermore, Stendahl has already intimated that several interpretative dimensions are probably operative whenever Paul's texts are read in a "Lutheran" way, and few would dispute this suggestion. Hence, we must from the outset be sensitive to the different *types* of interpretative claims that are being made as well, and so to the different hermeneutical dimensions that are operative. Such dimensions are clearly distinguishable, each different in kind from the other dimensions surrounding it.[7] And recalling Einstein's useful dictum that "everything should be made as simple as possible but not simpler," the dimensions identified within the entire situation need to be simple enough to yield descriptive clarity yet comprehensive enough to provide real explanatory leverage. These dimensions should become apparent to us as they unfold largely necessarily from within this particular interpretative situation when it is examined more closely.[8]

§2. Recognizing a Discourse

2.1. The Data

The first irreducible interpretative level we can distinguish comprises the raw *data,* that is, the occurrence of signifiers or lexemes in sequences, and preserved in the case of Paul in a reasonably fixed canonical state disturbed only by text-critical decisions. Although this data does not exist meaningfully without interpretation, it still exists fundamentally in the form of a certain givenness that stands over against the reader and will admit only of certain interpretative possibilities. Moreover, it is widely acknowledged that Justification theory is related to certain distinctively defined texts in Paul — texts with characteristic incidences of lexemes and sequences that consequently comprise a well-defined cluster (and these are specified precisely at a more appropriate point in the argument — part three, chapter ten). Hence, the theory's underlying textual data is reasonably discrete. But we cannot pursue the actual definition of this data further without introducing additional levels within the process of reading, because some meaning must have been attributed to the raw data for them to be categorized.

2.2. The Exegetical Level

The second irreducible interpretative level we can distinguish is *exegesis,* that is — in the present project — the configuration of the raw data through interpretation into a meaningful entity. As much recent theory has emphasized, this must be done by a reader or an interpretative group — for example, the original Christian recipients of the letter — because uninterpreted textual data is almost completely inert. Exegesis, in the sense in which I use that term here, is undertaken on the basis of a complex of rules that correlates concepts with signifiers (in Paul's case, the vocabulary and grammar of Koiné Greek) and is shared, at least in part, by the sender and a receiver within their overarching social networks. The result is a semantic construct that claims to account accurately, or at least better than its competitors, for the textual data. In essence, as the "fit" between the hard data — the sequence of uninterpreted signifiers — and exegesis improves, we speak of a better exegesis. A worse exegesis, conversely, has a "fit" that is less adequate — by failing to account for all of the data, or failing to integrate it into a semantic entity with the same degree of coherence or plausibility as a competitor.

It is worth noting at this point that underlying Justification theory is the claim that its exegesis of certain key texts in Paul has a superior fit to all the alternatives. It is the "correct" exegesis, ultimately yielding a complete soteriology in terms of Justification, but at this stage in our analysis claiming merely to give the most accurate construal of the raw data through conscientious and accurate correlations in lexical and grammatical terms.

2.3. The Argumentative Level

Readings, however, seldom function in this simple generic state. As is well known, a whole arsenal of further interpretative techniques can be introduced, such as argumentative considerations, genre expectations, intertextuality, referential claims, and so on. Indeed, many further semantic signals are usually built into texts in addition to mere sequences of words coordinated by grammar. Texts are multilayered interpretative constructs, and the determination of the appropriate signals being sent is an important part of accurate construal, something often embedded in turn in particular histories, cultures, and locations. It would be widely conceded that Paul is not telling a story or reporting how he feels or remarking on local historical events when he discusses Justification (assuming for the moment that he does at some point). He is primarily making an *argumentative* case in a sequence of partly self-contained proofs or rational progressions. Hence, a third level is discernible within our interpretation that is not wholly separate from the preceding level but rather intertwined with it. The larger reading lays claim to argumentative shape and coherence — in essence, to logical consistency between rationally plausible premises and conclusions.[9]

Argumentative texts tend to follow their own specialized sets of additional rules; we do not read Plato's *Republic* as we might read a novel. Thus, in any consideration of a reading taking place in some relation to Justification theory, in addition to asking whether a particular construal looks like an accurate account of the given data — *good exegesis* — we must also ask whether that correlation possesses its own rational coherence — *good argumentation*. This complicates analysis but also allows a greater degree of interpretative control over suggested readings, as we will see.

There is a widespread tendency to assume that we are operating in a two-category "either-or" or "zero-sum" situation with respect to these two dimensions (+/- or -/+), but in fact we are operating with *four* alternatives — and it is vital to appreciate this clearly.

		Argumentation	
		Good (+)	Bad (-)
Exegesis	Good (+)	+/+	+/-
	Bad (-)	-/+	-/-

As interpreters, we would generally prefer +/- to -/+ (that is, a better account of the textual data that nevertheless ends up making a poor argument over against a poor account of the data that offers a better argument); however, what we *ought* to prefer — over all the other alternatives — is +/+ (a better exegesis that also renders a better argument), and it will be surprisingly important at times to point this out.[10] It is worth noting in addition that these two interpretative levels tend to be intertwined, so a better argumentative account of a given piece of data often turns out to be a better exegetical account as well. This correlation is not hard and fast, but a good argument *is* often a good account of the textual data *tout court*, especially when an essentially argumentative text is being discussed. Moreover, all other things being equal, we ought to prefer the superior argumentative account to a less cogent alternative *as a matter of methodological necessity* (that is, to prefer +/+ to +/-).[11]

2.4. Framing Requirements

We should now note that this data and its double-faceted construal automatically generate certain *framing requirements*. At various points the data with which we are centrally concerned makes transitions into other data, transitions that are noticeable at the textual level because, for example, certain characteristic lexemes diminish or disappear although the data field itself continues. We might think of these points of transition as the data's borders — a useful metaphor because it conveys a sense of distinction allied with senses of permeability and movement across a line of demarcation. In fact, there are often no actual separations or cleavages in the relevant data but only shifts in density.[12]

We have already intimated that the shifts in Paul's texts are significant enough to ultimately create certain specific foci for any analysis of Justification theory, although we have yet to argue for those shifts in precise terms.[13] But the important methodological consequences of the existence of these foci within more continuous data fields must also be grasped. Any account of the distinctive data at the center of the investigator's concern — here, the texts underlying Justification — *should also be capable of integrating with plausible accounts of its adjacent data,* an interpretative necessity dubbed in what follows a "framing requirement." The generally preferred word for this among New Testament interpreters is "context," but that term's value- and interpretation-neutral connotations are rather misleading.[14] The metaphor of framing emphasizes that situating the data with which we are primarily concerned within these surrounding, interrelated fields can only be done through further conscious interpretative reconstruction on our part — an *act* of framing, which is itself also a reading.

An account of a given pool or subfield of data that is incapable of integrating satisfactorily with some account of that pool's adjacent data is quite probably invalid. Hence, framing requirements are a useful additional check on interpretative validity, although it must be emphasized that there is an important distinction between actually *accounting for* that surrounding data and simply *integrating with* an account of that data. The former would lead to an infinite interpretative regress, among other things; the latter is the requirement being suggested here.

To focus for a moment on Romans: if we hold that Paul writes about Justification theory at length in 1:16–4:25, then we also need to account for why he seems to have followed that discussion with a rather different argument in 5:1–8:39 but then returns to Justification (or closely related material) in 9:30–10:17 in the context of the otherwise distinct 9:1–11:36, and so on. In other words, how we purport to read chapters 1–4 should be capable of integrating with a plausible account of chapters 5–8, as well as with a partial resumption of the discussion in chapter 10 — and this does not, of course, exhaust the relevant framing requirements in Romans.

Framing requirements emphasize that failure at any of these transitional points jeopardizes the whole interpretative venture. What use is a reading of Romans 1–4 that cannot integrate with a reasonable account of why Paul went on to write the rest of that letter? In view of its inability to satisfy plausibly its necessary framing requirements, any such reading — however satisfactory on internal grounds alone — *ought to be abandoned in favor of another reading that can do better on this additional ground.* (Note that I do not suggest abandoning it without the presence of a better alternative.) Similarly, how credible is a reading of Galatians 2:15-16 that cannot progress comprehensibly into v. 17 and on into the participatory language of vv. 18-20, over against one that can?

Such framing requirements, although considerably broadening the data we have to deal with, cannot be avoided. If the data is positioned within various broader fields, then those *must* be comprehended reasonably by framing accounts. Interpreters then have no choice but to face these requirements, and participants in the relevant debates should be held to them. But these same requirements may ultimately help us narrow our task in interpretative terms, since various initially plausible options in relation to the central data can often be discarded as they fail at the apparent points of transition.

We may now begin to distinguish more precisely the *types* of frames within which our data must fit (recalling again Einstein's useful principle concerning simplicity). In the first instance, New Testament scholars expect their accounts to satisfy a criterion of *general* historical plausibility. They ask, in essentially phenomenological terms, whether it is reasonable to suggest that the posited readings of a text could have arisen from their general cultural and symbolic frame. Could readers of the day have conceptualized — and read — in such terms?[15] Readings judged anachronistic in this sense tend to be discarded, and certainly they ought to be from a strictly historical-critical perspective.[16]

Second, as we have seen in the example from Romans just adduced, a reading should satisfy what can be further described as a *proximate* framing requirement. All frames unfold through time, and a proximate requirement merely refers in what follows to the need for a reading to integrate coherently with an account of the immediately adjacent textual data. The first Roman Christians heard chapters 5–8 being read immediately after they had heard the arguments of chapters 1–4, which had in turn followed the letter's introduction, a sequence presumably experienced as often as the letter was read. A reading that can accommodate a plausible account of these proximate transitions will be judged superior to one that cannot.

Third, and somewhat distinctively, New Testament scholars have especially strong expectations concerning a more distant frame (although it overlaps at times with the foregoing). They tend to ask whether their account of a text's *generation* or *production* is plausible — in what follows, a *circumstantial* framing requirement. That is, New Testament scholars expect any interpretation of a text — and especially of a genuine Pauline letter — to be able to integrate with a reasonable account of its composition: When was it written? To whom? And why?[17] And this last question (assuming the ease of answering the first few in relation to Romans and Galatians) is particularly important. Pauline scholars expect a plausible account of the motivation(s) in Paul at the time of writing that actually prompted the relatively expensive composition and dispatch of the letter in question.[18]

Expectations in terms of such generative accounts have admittedly at times been overly inflated. The meaning of a Pauline letter, that is, the construal of its text, is certainly not reducible to some account of the apostle's motives — "the intentional fallacy" — and a considerable degree of information can still be offered for texts that allow little if any generative accounting (in the New Testament, see especially Hebrews, but the Gospels also fall largely into this category). Further, the difficulty of giving such an account should not be underestimated; we are not mind readers, and especially not of ancient psyches.[19] Nevertheless, such specific framing requirements do enhance our interpretative purchase on a text if they can be responsibly achieved.[20]

In sum, framing requirements may provide a useful check on readings in what follows, even if they do not prove decisive. They do not themselves produce a reading of the central data; hence, a good reading with poor framing accounts might still surpass a poor reading with better framing accounts (although we will cross this particular evaluative bridge when we come to it). And three types of framing requirements have been identified:

> general: concerning the broad cultural and linguistic context, synonymous with the author's encyclopedia;
> proximate: concerning the immediately adjacent text; and
> circumstantial: concerning the text's generation or production.

We should observe now that the four distinguishable interpretative dimensions we have identified — data, exegesis, argumentation, and the appropriate framing requirements — really combine into one overarching interpretative process of reading, or construal, that simply purports to configure accurately a given sequence of lexical data in its original setting(s) — here Pauline data. The first level, the data, cannot exist in any meaningful sense without the second level, exegesis, which is in turn inextricably intertwined with the third level, argumentation — of central importance in the texts in which we are interested. But this construct is inevitably surrounded by certain frames, dictating the need for further interpretative requirements at its borders. All these distinguishable hermeneutical dimensions belong together as vital aspects of one ultimately unified interpretative operation.

The reading, or construal

Framing requirements:	The argumentative level	General Proximate Circumstantial
	The exegetical level	
	The data	

But our preliminary description of "reading" in this relation is not yet complete — although the relevant Pauline debates have paid little or no attention thus far to the crucial interpretative distinction that follows, and to its implications.

2.5. The Theoretical or Explanatory Level

The arguments in certain texts reach out beyond their own strings of signifiers and adjacent frames and purport to grasp features of broader reality — what a long European tradition tends to speak of as "the object."[21] Such texts attempt to communicate to others about this object, giving an accurate account of it. They are fundamentally referential. So, for example, Einstein's texts on relativity — texts that supply readings in terms of arguments and proofs, although often in mathematical language — communicate a grand *theory*, or *explanation*, of space-time reality premised on the speed of light as a universal constant. These texts were intended to give an account of the basic structure of the universe, the latter being the object of Einstein's explanation as well as the focus of his attention and so also the telos, so to speak, of the texts. Similarly, Keynes's carefully developed proofs concerning rates of saving and interest were meant to explain certain important features of modern economies, the economy being both the object of his inquiry and the problem he sought to resolve. These classic argumentative texts reach beyond themselves in an explanatory fashion to try to grasp reality and to communicate that supposedly successful feat to others. They are clearly more powerful texts as a result, since they allow reality to be understood and even manipulated;[22] thus, in an important sense, these particular texts are tools.

We can speak of "fit" again at this point, but in another sense, namely, the fit between a theory, or explanation, and the object it purports to describe (without claiming either that this is ever completely possible or that this exhausts the notion of truth). To have a good fit in this sense is to be truer than alternative explanations of an object.[23] (We can also speak of "fit" in purely internal terms: does the explanation itself fit together in a coherent fashion — that is, does it possess internal argumentative integrity?[24] — since good explanations should.)[25]

Now although many argumentative texts are ultimately *related* to explanation, certainly not all *are* actual explanations. Arguments — in very basic terms — merely connect premises and extrapolate their implications in accordance with certain rules (or some such). Hence, there is no inherent necessity for such texts to reach out and attempt to grasp a previously undisclosed object. That is not their only possible function. Argumentation can be used rhetorically, for example, for persuasion. Indeed, the use of argumentative texts in this last manner is widespread. Some argumentative texts merely attack other explanations, pointing out their problems, and these need not necessarily presuppose their own theories (although some will). Clearly, then, argumentation often *relates to* explanation, but this is not the same thing as *being* an explanation.[26]

It is largely overlooked but nevertheless absolutely vital to grasp that advocates of Justification theory in Paul claim that some of his argumentative texts supply an account in the foregoing powerful sense: they supply a theory, or explanation, of salvation. Moreover, the account is a universal one, applying to everyone throughout human time-space reality, so neither is it modest. And this set of claims generates certain very important consequences that will have to be taken into account by any complete description of this particular interpretative endeavor.

2.6. *Additional Framing Requirements*

We can begin our account of these further dimensions by identifying two additional framing requirements.

In the first instance, a theory operative at one point in Paul ought to be compatible with the apostle's discussions of the same or similar questions elsewhere. Paul's thinking at the theoretical/explanatory level *in general* ought to possess a degree of coherence. Otherwise, he risks being judged a muddled or confused thinker — and, with respect to Justification theory, in relation to supremely important matters. Hence, there is now a broader, *systematic* framing requirement in place:[27] how does this theory square with the apostle's thinking as it is evidenced elsewhere?[28]

Second — and as we have already seen at some length — Justification theory, like all theories, makes assertive claims as it seeks to grasp broader *reality;* hence, a new and very important framing consideration becomes operative. There is a need now to supply an accurate account of that part of reality that the theory purports to grasp or describe. We have called this an *empirical* framing requirement.[29] A reading that makes explanatory claims is potentially quite powerful. However, it is in equal measure vulnerable, because its broader claims may be proved false. The theory can be discredited — as a theory — at its broad, empirical frame if it fails to grasp aspects of that frame satisfactorily.[30] Theories and explanations are simply necessarily involved in these higher stakes. They trade off power against vulnerability through falsification. Other readings, however, that do not purport to supply theories or explanations are not involved in these higher stakes; they are neither this powerful nor this vulnerable.

A theoretical/explanatory reading

Additional framing requirements:	The theoretical/explanatory level	Systematic Empirical

Framing requirements:	The argumentative level	General Proximate Circumstantial
	The exegetical level	
	The data	

Finally, we should note that the presence of a theoretical dimension creates a peculiarly important set of dynamics for a *scripturally based* explanation. These dynamics relate to the central question concerning the entire reading's truth or validity. A scriptural constitution imparts quite distinctive dynamics to a theoretical reading's epistemological mode and integrity that need to be appreciated clearly at the appropriate point.

Having made these brief observations on various aspects of the theoretical level, we may now consider a number of additional interpretative dimensions in the broader sense that have almost certainly been put into play. One could view these as further frames, since a degree of reconstruction is involved in their characterization. But they function rather differently from the frames already noted and lead to different consequences within the whole debate, so that designation would be ultimately unhelpful. The critical difference from the five frames just recognized is that, whereas those frames place *integrative demands* on a reading at the specified points of transition, or borders, the dimensions that I am about to enumerate often exert *an active influence* on the actual process of interpretation — although this is not their only function. Hence, we do not have to explain these new dimensions, or "settings," so much as to recognize their dynamic contribution to the process of interpretation, and then to proceed accordingly. The first such setting develops from the great importance that can be attached to an explanatory reading — in this case, to its preoccupation with a theory of salvation.

2.7. The Paradigmatic Setting

Theories vary widely in significance, often in relation to the perceived importance of the object they purport to explain. Because Einstein's theory addresses the basic nature of the universe, it is often accorded tremendous significance. Theories of organic pork production in South Australia would generally be accorded less weight, even though their epistemological role in the foregoing sense is identical (acknowledging of course that to pig farmers in Victoria, Australia, their interest might well exceed that of Einstein's theory — at which point we return to the issue of social settings). Explanations that correlate with particularly important objects, and hence that are deemed themselves to be important, are dubbed in what follows *paradigms*. To be specific, by this is meant only that they function epistemologically in a central or even a "properly basic" fashion. They are axiomatic — the "hard core" of a wider theory or worldview.[31]

Such paradigmatic explanations tend to undergird more localized, specific, and less important explanations; indeed, this is one of the most critical functions of a paradigm as that concept is here defined. The theory of relativity allows us to calculate local planetary movement and to generate more accurate astronomical predictions involving light (and so on), so in terms of astrophysics, it is fundamental.[32] Analogously, an explanation of salvation in terms of Justification theory may allow us to comprehend the rest of Paul's writings and even the Bible as a whole, as well as the essential structure of Christian proclamation (and so on). Consequently, paradigmatic explanations are often associated with architectural metaphors of a fundamental nature such as foundation, bedrock, and basis. Alternatively, they are represented by spatial metaphors of centrality such as center, core, and heart (the latter clearly also drawing on biological metaphors of centrality and importance).

As we have already noted, it is widely assumed that some of Paul's texts and arguments constitute an explanation of salvation. But the further ramifications of this assumption tend to be passed over, namely, that to explain salvation is almost automatically to become paradigmatic for ecclesial groups. We might say that a reading of Paul in terms of Justification theory is not just an *explanation* of salvation but is also an explanation *of salvation!* And a cluster of additional interpretive dynamics is set in motion by this perception of importance that we will describe in due course. In essence, we tend to want our paradigms to be true. And any paradigm rooted in reading offers a host of insidious techniques for fulfilling that desire that we will have to identify carefully and guard against in what follows.

Most of our analysis to this point has been able to concentrate, partly for simplicity's sake, on synchronic perspectives. But we must now begin to address explicitly the diachronic influences on interpretation. Readings exist through time, especially important ones, and they tend to gather additional contexts as they go. The people and traditions who hold to a paradigmatic reading through time accompany it "like a great cloud of witnesses."[33]

2.8. The Church-Historical Setting

The diachronic life of a paradigmatic reading is evident in its *historical* settings — and in particular relation to the reading with which we are concerned, this can be specified first as its *church-historical* setting.

Almost all discussions of Justification in Paul appeal at some point to connections with the Protestant Reformation or, more specifically, with Luther, thereby linking the question of the theory's truth as a reading of the apostle to the resonant notions of the Reformation or one of its great champions — and raising the diachronic question concerning the history of this particular reading.[34] There is clearly something to be gained by considering the first formulations of the reading. And it may well be helpful to consider, in addition, the circumstances that gave rise to it, along with the explanations given by its first formulators. But these considerations should all function as part of the reading per se — how the Reformers (assuming for the moment that it was they) actually made sense of Paul's texts and argued for a certain construal of them. These are all textual, exegetical, argumentative, and even theoretical considerations.

Within the church-historical dimension, however, they can also function in an additional sense. They can be deployed as an argument in their own right for the validity of the reading: *because* Luther (or some such) said this, *then* it is almost certainly right (and so on). They can operate, in short, as an argument from authority. Hence, they function analogously to the paradigmatic influences that we have already noted. Such claims must of course be scrutinized carefully; the underlying realities turn out to be both less useful and more complicated than is often claimed. But they are certainly in play and so need to be accurately grasped.

2.9. The Ideocultural Setting

Beyond the overt church-historical influences often associated with a paradigmatic reading, there are further, less obvious — yet potentially far stronger — diachronic factors that must be taken into account. We must consider the possibility that central commitments within an interpreter's *ideology* and *culture* could legitimize central aspects of an explanatory reading. If a particular paradigm, rooted in a certain reading, supports some of our most cherished commitments, perhaps endorsing fundamental elements in our worldview, it is possible that our culture has at just those points not merely affirmed but in fact created that reading. And we are then trapped in a powerful spiral of hermeneutical reinforcement driven by our culture and its accompanying ideologies. Perhaps another reading is more accurate in historical-critical terms but lacks these culturally resonant elements, and so advocates of the reigning paradigm simply override it. ("It just doesn't feel right.") Hence, we must at least consider the possibility that the construal of Paul in terms of Justification theory could be caught up in these dynamics. And they are very difficult to control. Cultural influences are often unacknowledged by exegetes and thus largely divorced from critical evaluation (because they are not supposed to be operative). They tend in any case to operate out of conscious purview within the tacit dimension. Indeed, it is difficult at times even to recognize our own deepest ideological and cultural commitments. And yet we certainly act on them.

Thus we must try to recognize this distinctive interpretative setting as best we can — and go on to consider whether exegetes have deemed a particular reading of Paul's texts to be true essentially because it is like "us" (that is, in its affirmation of Western values). We must try to articulate explicitly any such factors and place them on the table, so to speak, during the process of exegetical evaluation, so that any inappropriate influence on the adjudication of susceptible readings can be consciously resisted. But a particular line of inquiry may guide us during this process. As we have already intimated in chapter one, it is often useful to ask what metaphors seem to be functioning at a fundamental level within a construct. For example, in the case of Paul's theories, what basic conception of God is operative — what root metaphor? Is he a King? a Judge? a Father? (And if so, what sort of King or Judge or Father?) Answers to this question may well supply useful controls on our broader consideration of the ideocultural dimension within the reading.[35]

2.10. A Discourse

It should be apparent by this point in our sketch that we are dealing with a complex multidimensional interpretative construct, something therefore perhaps most easily referred to in toto as a discourse, without making grandiose or metatheoretical claims for that notion.[36] Hence, we can speak from this point on of "the Justification *discourse*."[37]

The Justification discourse

	The ideocultural setting	
	The church-historical setting	
	The paradigmatic setting	
Additional framing requirements:	The theoretical/explanatory level	Systematic Empirical
Framing requirements:	The argumentative level	General Proximate Circumstantial
	The exegetical level	
	The data	

Our preliminary account of this discourse is meant merely to give a clarification and a statement of the obvious. I would hope that little or nothing can be found in this description that was not already either explicit or implicit in earlier Pauline debates — for example, in Stendahl's classic essays.

It ought also to be appreciated that I am not claiming that the foregoing is a universal account of reading. These various interpretative dimensions have been identified specifically in relation to the construal of Paul with respect ultimately to Justification theory, and with the origins and history of that construal in mind.[38] Hence, they do not always function together in relation to other texts (which is to say, in spatial terms, that they are often only overlapping dimensions). And with this preliminary description in place, we can now turn to consider the crucial question of the discourse's truth, along with its frequent collision with hermeneutical naivety. How *ought* this discourse to function in epistemological terms — and how *can* it and *does* it?!

§3. Beyond Interpretative Naïvety

3.1. Normative Function

The Justification discourse is a *scriptural* discourse, something with critical consequences for its ideal and ostensible function (and this position does not have to be shared personally in order for its recognition to remain methodologically central). In a scriptural discourse, put at its simplest, *the underlying reading sustains the higher theoretical complex in terms of its truthfulness.* The higher dimensions of Justification theory *must* arise out of the lower dimensions oriented around the reading — data, exegesis, argumentation, and immediate frames — and build on them; its legitimacy is entirely dependent on those underlying layers. The theory must be the correct reading of the relevant data. And this central dynamic is both a strength and a weakness.

Explanations (especially in modernity) do not normally depend on readings of particular texts, although they do tend to be communicated or mediated by them — an important distinction. Their truth tends to be assessed in relation to the object of which they seek to give an account. Are they an accurate account as measurable by other relevant means? But the delivery of an explanation via a reading, as is the case in a scriptural discourse, *eliminates this process,* making the truth of a given theory dependent only on correct exegesis — ultimately, an obvious point. Here to take and read is, as Augustine found, also to understand. And this can be quite convenient.

Interpretation of a text that is preserved and venerated by a community can thereby deliver explanatory truth to that community reasonably directly, without the added work of grasping and analyzing an object, which may be very difficult in cultural, technical, and economic terms. It is quite hard to analyze the cosmos in its entirety and one's place within it, especially in relation to God or gods, by examining it as an object. (If one wishes, for example, to understand the stars, it might be helpful to own powerful telescopes, but very few societies in historical terms have had the expertise and resources to do so.) Having all these explanations supplied by a text is therefore very convenient.

However, just as this different process of verification possesses a certain fundamental economy, it also possesses in equal measure a certain fundamental vulnerability.[39] Any correct *alternative* reading of such an explanation's texts must overthrow the legitimacy of that explanation *as* an explanation, from which point any further functions are interrupted (and especially paradigmatic functions). If the reading that undergirds the higher theoretical complex of the discourse turns out to be incorrect, then that complex automatically becomes untrue and falls, except as an item in the history of interpretation. (The lower levels still live on in a sense, although in a different form.) Moreover, such an explanation is vulnerable to "direct," empirical falsification. That is, even if the *reading* of the text is shown to be correct, the object described may overtly disprove the text's suggestions. The *reading* — and presumably also the *text itself* — may be wrong. In sum, it is both a strength and a weakness for an explanation — and especially an important, paradigmatic one — to have a scriptural constitution (and clearly here, once again, I am not stating anything remarkable).

In view of this peculiar dynamic with respect to explanatory legitimacy, as well as to any further relationships or functions premised on the theoretical/explanatory level, it will be useful to make a basic distinction within the Justification discourse. The three "lower" levels of interpretation that were identified in the preceding description, namely, data, exegesis, and argumentation, along with the framing requirements appropriate to those levels, *are ultimately responsible for the validity of Justification theory, along with any related interpretative dimensions "higher" up in the discourse's structure.*[40] Hence, borrowing some useful notions from Marx, we can dub this reading operation at its vital lower levels the discourse's "base." These lower levels constitute the critical underlying element, the phenomenon from which everything else arises and on which everything else depends. The four remaining interpretative dimensions — the theoretical/explanatory level, and the paradigmatic, church-historical (in the sense of appeals rooted in certain figures and traditions), and ideocultural settings — constitute the discourse's "superstructure." *The superstructure's truthfulness is entirely dependent on the correct function of the base.*[41]

The Justification discourse's normative scriptural function

The Superstructure

	The ideocultural setting	
	The church-historical setting	
	The paradigmatic setting	
Additional framing requirements:	The theoretical/explanatory level	Systematic Empirical

The base

	The argumentative level	General Proximate Circumstantial
Framing requirements:	The exegetical level	
	The data	

We have noted two important implications that flow from the discourse's normative scriptural function.

1. Falsification of this discourse must take place primarily in terms of reading, or construal; only an alternative reading of the key texts underlying Justification theory will eliminate the truth of that theory — at which point the theory itself might even disappear (except as a historical phenomenon).[42] Certainly, it will lose its status as truthful.

2. Falsification may occur secondarily in terms of empirical reality. Although the principal verification of the discourse is textual, if the resulting theory fails to grasp those objects within broader reality that it purports to explain with sufficient accuracy and rigor, then a degree of dissonance will be un-

leashed.[43] Advocates of the discourse will find themselves pulled in two directions. Scriptural interpretation will suggest the discourse's truth, while empirical checks might suggest the discourse's falsehood, perhaps shaking the confidence of the discourse's advocates.[44]

There is a further implication, however, that may not be as apparent.

3. Falsification of the discourse may occur through distortion of the normative function. If the superstructure of the discourse interferes with the process of construal taking place in the base, it may create a vicious self-legitimizing interpretative spiral. And this is such an important possibility — it is potentially so destructive, and yet so difficult to detect and compensate for — that it requires more extended treatment. Indeed, grasping and neutralizing this dynamic is the key to much of what follows.

3.2. Distorted Function

We have just seen that in the case of a scripturally constructed and authenticated explanation the reading is prior and fundamental; it generates and then supports the explanation as base to superstructure. But the resulting theory, once established, possesses its own integrity and coherence (or, at least, it ought to), to the point that it is largely detachable from its underlying texts. Hence, it can circulate independently from them. (Justification theory, for example, can be articulated with no mention of Paul or his letters.) And in the case of a particularly important reading, the theory's subsequent history and consequences can live on in some independence from the reading itself.

The principal cause of our potential problem at this point, then, is that the theory, with its own powerful claims of rational integration and coherence — not to mention further appeals grounded in its later church-historical and ideo-cultural history — *can intrude prematurely into the act of reading that supposedly undergirds it.* And this is quite understandable, although it is epistemologically disastrous. Such considerations generated by the superstructure are psychologically and sociologically simultaneous to the reading, if not prior to it, even though they are epistemologically dependent on it. Thus, we might learn about Justification *theory* first — perhaps from parents or in Sunday school — and then later find it (perhaps not surprisingly) corroborated by Paul in the Bible when we learn to do detailed exegesis of his texts (or some variation on this pattern). In essence, here the subsequent history and consequences of the reading can interfere with its present creation and assessment *as* a reading. And this is the more understandable given that we tend to structure our analyses of data in accordance with our theories — and our paradigms especially! This is how we seem to be mentally configured.

However, for a scriptural discourse any such structuring would clearly be

The assumed "normative" relationship
between Base and Superstructure

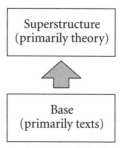

The potential distorted relationship
between Base and Superstructure

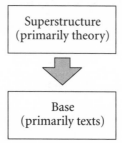

inappropriate, because it would disrupt the discourse's correct unfolding from the textual up to the explanatory level. (In fact, it would basically reverse it.) The superstructure would be supporting the base, and not vice versa. And we would not then know whether the sacred texts actually supplied this theory. The epistemological integrity of the entire system would be compromised. We cannot attribute the results of a reading to the reading itself! But this is precisely the danger that the resonant Justification discourse faces — and especially for those not alert to it.

In sum, it is to a degree the peculiarities of the Justification discourse as a scriptural discourse, combined with the natural psychological function of explanations, that have generated this interpretative pitfall for the unwary, a situation perhaps further reinforced by the great importance of the explanation in question. And it is a fatal trap, *for both the critics and the advocates of the discourse!* Those concerned about Justification's difficulties will be unable to challenge it fairly, while those confident about the theory's truthfulness will be unable to confirm it fairly.

It is worth noting that if this basic distortion *is* taking place, then it may be even more difficult to detect and defuse than a simple characterization of reversed influence might suggest. Any illegitimate epistemological causality flowing from the superstructure to the base may be cloaked in a variety of ways. In particular, enough material from the most useful texts in Paul may well be incorporated within the discourse's theory and broader superstructure to lend them a basic exegetical persuasiveness; its readings may not be *completely* flawed but perhaps only partly and subtly so, and at only the critical points.[45] Thus, the relationship between the textual base and the largely theoretical superstructure may in fact be merely circular. But circularity is quite sufficient to disrupt the normative function of the discourse, which ought to be unidirectional — the reading must give rise to the theory, with no prior interference, or that theory is not scripturally constituted. The presence of any circularity amounts to the introduction into the discourse of a vicious feedback loop.[46]

It should be apparent by now why any attempt simply to scrutinize Paul's texts and their exegesis in relation to the various difficulties generated by their ostensible commitment to Justification theory will probably fail. Such an attempt is fundamentally naive about the process of reading, and especially when the interpretation of extremely important texts like these is involved — when the stakes are so high. Simple scrutiny will be largely unguarded against the potentially problematic insinuation of the discourse's superstructure into that exegesis. It is this hermeneutical phenomenon that causes such difficulty whenever a critical inquiry is attempted, translating the ostensibly level exegetical playing field into something of an interpretative ambuscade. The presence of the superstructure is usually sufficient — in a variety of ways that we will document shortly — to overwhelm any alternative reading suggestions when they are made in relation to the base. But we are now alert to this general hermeneutical possibility. How, then, can we facilitate a more accurate scrutiny of the discourse's base in detailed terms, given that it must eventually take place, and especially in view of the extensive slate of difficulties that we identified through part one?

3.3. Strategy

In my view, the only way to guard against such illegitimate insinuations will be to introduce quite deliberately a reading strategy characterized by *articulation, recognition,* and then either *resistance* or *recovery.*[47]

Ultimately, we must *resist* the voice of the superstructure when it makes inappropriate suggestions during the process of reading as the latter unfolds within the base, and furthermore, we must *recover* the voice of the base when the superstructure operates inappropriately to suppress it. In order to do so, however, we must *recognize* the superstructure's suggestions and suppressions as they arrive, and so we must be familiar with them in advance of that moment. We must become fully aware of any potential subconscious interpretative moves (whether simply unacknowledged or repressed or tacit) so that they can be deliberately neutralized. And that means, in turn, that we must *articulate* the superstructure in full, in all its details, so that these moves can be anticipated. Such a strategy should allow us to read the relevant texts in Paul accurately in relation to Justification theory, scrutinizing whether that theory is in fact present without allowing the purported outcome of the reading to affect our evaluation of it *as* a reading. A reasonably fair evaluation of the basic interpretative situation should then be an option.

We can now consider what specific strategies might be expected to emanate from the superstructure as it tries to instill its particular concerns within the base.

3.4. Specifics

It is most likely that the superstructure treats its underlying reading in the base with the proverbial hermeneutic of generosity (and hostile alternative construals with a corresponding hermeneutic of suspicion, but that broad hermeneutical area will not concern us so much at this point). And a generous hermeneutic will probably in the main simply try to maximize the theory's advantages and minimize its difficulties. So, on the one hand, the superstructure will probably discover its own concerns in the relevant Pauline texts a little too easily, while, on the other hand, it will not be equally sensitive to difficulties in those texts. We have already seen that the process of reading necessarily involves readers attributing a great deal of information to a text, simultaneously narcotizing information that does not integrate with their developing construal. So the concerns of the superstructure could easily be insinuated into the legitimate processes of attribution and narcotization already taking place. Our task, in essence, is to detect and reverse any inappropriate claims in these two primary modes.

First, then, we should articulate, recognize, and *resist* any suggestions from outside the textual data and its historical-critical construal that endorse key elements within the theory of Justification without overt textual corroboration. Such illegitimate suggestions may attribute certainty to a text that is fundamentally ambiguous, or may actively attribute meaning where the text supplies no signals at all. Any such overly generous suggestions with respect to Justification theory thus constitute overdeterminations from the superstructure, corresponding — perhaps more importantly — to *underdeterminations* — that is, a lack of corroboration — in the text itself. At such points the text does not in fact supply what the superstructure and its theory require. A less generous if not suspicious reading might reveal that the text is silent at such junctures, whereas previously it has been held to speak.

Second, we should articulate, recognize, and *recover* elements within the text that supply something the superstructure does not need and so previously may have narcotized. Such *overdeterminations* from the text may be matters of mere redundancy or inconvenience; however, they may be more troublesome. That is, the relevant texts may at times deliver information that is awkward and even contradictory for Justification theory, information that past reading — intentionally or not — has minimized or overlooked.

Over- and underdeterminations

the ideal relationship:
textual base and superstructure correspond

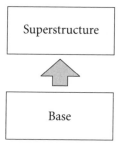

the possible relationship:
overdeterminations from
the superstructure and the base

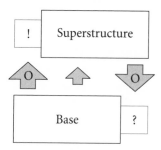

I am concerned in my broader argument first of all with overdeterminations from the superstructure. It will probably be most constructive to clear the textual ground of these types of potential difficulties first, and then to let potential difficulties in the texts themselves emerge. Indeed, it is only after these positive pressures have been neutralized that we can clearly discern what the key texts are. (One of the predictable overdeterminative moves by the superstructure is to lay claim to more texts than, strictly speaking, it should; it claims that its theory can be found explicitly in various texts where nothing of the sort is in fact apparent. Such positive interpretative pressures can be delivered by the theory, as well as all of its later major settings — paradigmatic, church-historical, and ideocultural.) In view of their complexity and depth, two of these potentially overdeterminative settings must be addressed in considerable detail. So chapter eight is devoted to the question of church-historical overdeterminations, and chapter nine to the less well known but arguably even more important ideocultural pressures. (From chapter ten onward we will be able to consider the texts themselves in more detail, beginning to *recover* their narcotized features — that is, finding *textual* overdeterminations from chapter eleven onward.) But overdeterminations from the superstructure's theoretical level and its paradigmatic setting, while extremely important, can be dealt with relatively briefly; hence, we will take them up here directly. Both tend to deliver the same type of interpretative dynamics, differing only in strength.

§4. Theoretical and Paradigmatic Overdeterminations

What additional overdeterminative dynamics are set in motion if a reading is also held to be a theory, and a particularly important one — in our terminology, a paradigm? In my view there are two especially significant interpretative consequences: (1) a methodological tendency toward etymologism, exacerbated by sloganizing, and of a peculiarly powerful sort; and (2) an argumentative tendency toward *petitio principii,* or question begging. These dynamics can be superficially impressive but are in fact deeply debilitating. If present — and they often are — they greatly handicap if not preclude effective debate. Hence, their detection and neutralization (here, through *resistance*) is vital.

4.1. Etymologism and Sloganizing

Etymologism is a pernicious and pervasive methodology that misinterprets single words or phrases by assuming that a fundamental core of meaning inheres in a root or stem over time, a fallacious understanding of language exposed in relation to New Testament studies in a classic work by James Barr.[48] A word does not really exist over time as such, nor does it have an essence or kernel of meaning that necessarily remains immutable. A word is in fact an arbitrary correlation of a "signifier" with a "signified" that communicating communities agree to treat as a rule. It is this agreement that allows communication to take place. The rule exists, but it changes, as most aspects of culture do. A word itself is no more than a "sign function" — an instance that passes immediately in time. Unfortunately, Barr's methodological strictures, although widely acknowledged, are not so widely practiced.[49]

Allied to this basic error of etymologism is the danger peculiar to important words of having an unacceptably extended meaning attributed to them as well. Their central unit of meaning is thus assumed not only to be diachronically static but to comprise a veritable theological program; such terms are not merely *mis*interpreted but *over*interpreted. And it is here that the influence of paradigms can often be detected, since such structures tend to lie behind heavily interpreted signifiers.

Paradigms are reducible in much of their discussion to key phrases and slogans that signal their presence, and this is simply a function of linguistic economy. Theologians, like all language users, develop and use shorthand. But this deliberate reduction for the purposes of summary and allusion makes the signifiers so used especially prone to theological overinterpretation.[50] Hence, historical-critical questions can usefully be asked of their earlier meaning, prior to their deliberate investment with an extended allusive sense.[51] An example from modern politics may be instructive. "Right (wing)" and "left (wing)" are standard summary signifiers in much political commentary in our day. To state that someone is "right wing" is to communicate instantly an entire cluster of policy positions (although a degree of oversimplification is almost certainly immediately involved). This is a highly resonant phrase in semantic terms. But modern political discourse has invested it with these connotations quite deliberately. Outside such a setting, even today, the phrase "right wing" does not necessarily evoke this extensive conceptual package. It may simply be a reference to part of the airplane one is flying in, or to a position in a game of football (whether rugby, rugby league, or soccer!). Moreover, this investment took place at a certain point in time. Hence, texts using the phrase two hundred years ago, even in a political setting, should clearly not be interpreted in the modern, heavily laden sense. But this is in fact what seems to happen with many New Testament signifiers.

If any New Testament signifiers were to be invested and defined largely in accordance with a programmatic theological significance today, we would expect them to be the key Protestant signifiers. And those of Justification — a self-consciously scriptural discourse, and one now, moreover, that dominates tracts of modern scholarly New Testament interpretation — are indeed candidates, perhaps along with the traditional Chalcedonian terms, for the dubious title of the most overinterpreted signifiers in all of biblical interpretation. Hence, in what follows we must ask not only whether the meaning of signifiers changes or spreads over time but also whether the significant meaning attached to important signifiers by New Testament interpreters would have been recognized by early non-Christian contemporaries. Any failure in this second test and we are probably in the presence of theological and lexical overinterpretation prompted by later, paradigmatically motivated function. A related test is to ask whether the suggested meaning of a signifier is close to an entire sentence. Complex meanings, including programmatic summaries, are generally carried by sentences and not by individual words.

It might immediately be replied of course that the early Christians, and Paul in particular, could have deliberately invested a more complex, theologically significant meaning in a particular signifier, thereby *creating* an early allusive or summary motif for a certain paradigm; they were therefore merely Protestants before their time, or some such (and the Reformation was consequently only a *re*discovery).

This can certainly be granted as a linguistic possibility (and even a theological necessity). However, *it must be demonstrated that this is in fact what took place* — that, for example, the early Christians' key words and slogans were also those selected and emphasized by later Protestantism. And *in the absence of any such demonstration we ought to assume that the use of language by early Christians was basically the same as that of their contemporaries*, with whom they interacted on a daily basis and also wished to communicate theologically. To fail to appreciate and apply this point is to lose interpretative control over any language used by the first Christians that has also become heavily interpreted by a later Christian tradition convinced of paradigmatic status in relation to it.[52]

An obvious example at this point is New Testament deployment of the phrase "Son of God" in relation to Jesus. No modern New Testament scholar would allow that this phrase *automatically* carries a fully Chalcedonian sense in the New Testament itself. That claim has to be demonstrated, and the burden of proof clearly lies on anyone who would demonstrate that the Chalcedonian sense is early. But why is the same point not appreciated in relation to other signifiers?[53] And why is the burden of proof so often seen to lie on the other party in relation to Justification concerns, namely, on those who see these later theological concerns — and they are *far* later than Chalcedon — as problematic within early Christian discourse? This is to get things precisely the wrong way around. If a protest against lexical overinterpretation on the basis of fifth-century concerns is valid, then protests based on sixteenth-century concerns should presumably also hold good.

If a signifier is assumed to carry the kernel of an entire theological program — which is what a paradigmatically prompted recoding would generate — then any further historical-critical exegesis will find it almost impossible to remove that interpretation. Any such retrojected information has been incorporated at the level of the signifier *before any consideration of syntactically coordinated information in the ancient texts takes place.* The insinuation of the program has therefore taken place as the first breath of exegesis has been drawn and certainly before the hard syntactical yards have been attempted. This particular overdetermination can resist exegesis itself; hence, it is especially difficult to detect and to control. Clearly, however, Paul's theological program should be carried by his sentences and arguments, and not by certain signifiers alone.

One of the primary dangers in this regard lies of course in Paul's phrase "justification by faith," this phrase or one of its components often carrying a great weight of theological interpretation. ("The righteousness of God" and "works of law" are similarly burdened phrases.) But to speak of "faith" or "justification" in a letter written to Rome during the early Principate is clearly not necessarily to have been evoking the passionate and powerful theological program of Luther (or some such) in its entirety. That it *might* have evoked such a system needs to be demonstrated, and demonstrated clearly, not merely assumed — an observation that leads us directly on to our next type of potential overdetermination from the theoretical level and the later paradigmatic setting of Justification theory.

4.2. Petitio Principii *and Complementary Misconstrual*

If a particular explanation is held to be especially important or paradigmatic, perhaps undergirding numerous other explanations and activities in addition to coding certain words as especially significant, it becomes largely unthinkable for its advocates that this structure could itself be wrong (something perhaps assisted in turn as that construct moves out of direct interpretative view and into the tacit dimension). The focus of its advocates will usually be on its application and not on its veracity. The unthinkability that a position could be wrong, however, issues directly in the corollary that it often does not have to do much to prove that it is right. A perception of importance here seems to translate easily into a method- ological and epistemological relaxation, to the point that a position feels true even if it is largely groundless.[54] This psychological self-confidence — especially characteristic of the occupants of powerful paradigms — can issue in turn in a su- perficially impressive but ultimately bankrupt and debilitating mode of argumen- tation, namely, *petitio principii,* or question begging. Technically, appeals in this vein are automatically false and the positions they undergird (if unsupported by anything else) overtly invalid.[55] But these corollaries often seem to slip past New Testament interpreters, so some careful explication here is necessary.

"Begging the question" basically assumes that the position at issue or in dis- pute is already true. It consists essentially in *repeating* the position, *without ever justifying it;* hence, the existence of the argument itself, along with any opposing point of view, is really just being denied.[56] At bottom, begging the question is a refusal to recognize that a particular position *is* being called into question.[57]

Such a procedure, viewed soberly, seems like complete argumentative mad- ness, but it is often plausible in debate because other factors are operative that make the mere repetition of a position seem like its justification. Principal among these of course is paradigmatic status. If something is so important that its incor- rectness is unthinkable, then a question-begging response to any criticism can seem quite reasonable. Also significant is the invalid stance that a paradigm is subject only to negative proof, *in the absence of which it can be assumed to be true!*[58] — an especially vicious suggestion when it is allied with paradigmatic etymologism. Because of the great importance of a paradigm, it might be asserted (and not infrequently is) that a great weight of evidence would need to be pre- sented in order to overthrow it; if only a small amount of evidence is presented, the paradigm, with its preponderance of support, continues to stand. But the New Testament, as a short compilation of rather ancient texts, often does not present a great deal of explicit evidence in relation to a given question. Hence, using this approach, it is possible to dismiss almost any accumulation of evidence in rela- tion to any question. But our difficulties with *petitio principii* do not stop here.

An important variation on this fallacy occurs in New Testament studies when it is stated that "the gospel" is at stake — what we might dub "evangelical" question begging. It is of course unthinkable for many that the gospel should be overthrown (I myself share such misgivings), a position one might view as a properly basic defense. But when certain readings are challenged, the gospel *itself* is not necessarily at stake; one need not rush to reject such challenges by any means possible. *One construal* of the gospel is at stake, which is rather a different thing. Indeed, such challenges may be issuing *from* "the gospel" — a gospel differ- ently construed of course! This equation between a particular construal of the gospel and the gospel itself is possible only in a highly paradigmatic situation, one that admits of no competitors or alternatives, and the rhetoric it then permits is extremely powerful. But this is again at bottom a question-begging strategy: *it assumes that the gospel is to be identified with one explanatory position, when this is precisely the point in contention.* (Advocates of Justification theory in Paul tend to make this claim not infrequently: if Justification is challenged, then the gospel itself is at issue, we are often told, but this is begging the evangelical question.)

The presence of this fallacy in relation to any position is peculiarly destructive for debate. In fact, if the claim is unchecked, then no genuine debate can occur. On the one hand, such a posture generally offers no account of its own cogency or plausibility. Its truth is simply assumed — and there may be little or no evidence supporting it! An opponent, then, has no real position to respond to. On the other hand, any opposing claim is from the outset denied or marginalized, irrespective of its cogency, using the sliding scale of evidence that we noted earlier. The question-begging advocate then marches on as if no doubts had been raised and no counterevidence deployed! In short, when advocates on one side of the dispute beg the question and get away with it, no playing field is in operation, and no sides are actually playing out an argumentative contest — *and so no one can win.*[59]

Finally, it is important to note briefly that these two critical — but false — dynamics can operate together in a peculiarly vicious alliance. *Petitio principii* at the broad level — strategic question begging — can rest on *petitio principii* at the etymological level — tactical question begging. So, for example, the theory of Justification is true, and it remains the only account of the Pauline gospel, because the words in the relevant texts that underlie it denote the theory ("justification," "faith," et cetera). This can be quite an impressive edifice, yet, in methodological and argumentative terms, it is a proverbial house of cards, built largely on the phenomenon of overdetermination from the superstructure, here specifically from the theoretical and paradigmatic dimensions. We must strongly resist this construct if we encounter it during our later discussions.

In sum, even though higher dimensions within the discourse might suggest it, certain of Paul's words are not necessarily to be interpreted as if they alone carried the heart of Justification theory through his texts and arguments. And neither ought it to be merely assumed that we are receiving in these texts an account of the gospel (which then ought to be defended against all comers). Both such suggestions, at the broadest and narrowest interpretative levels, are overdeterminations, manifesting in particular as *petitio principii,* which ought to be recognized and resisted. Resistance is the correct stance to deploy against all such overdeterminations, whether they are suggested by the theoretical level or by its paradigmatic, church-historical, or ideocultural settings. Without such recognition and resistance, the illegitimate overdetermination of Paul's texts will simply run on unchecked; we will never know what they actually may have meant to their original auditors. And with this danger in mind, we turn to consider in more detail just how those texts might be overdetermined by considerations from church history.

CHAPTER EIGHT

Distortions — The Church-Historical Pedigree

§1. Preamble

Important connections with church history in general, and with Luther and the Protestant Reformation in particular, have long been recognized as part of the broader interpretative situation. Indeed, since Stendahl this dimension has tended to name the entire problem; we are concerned supposedly with the "Lutheran" reading of Paul (although this is a rather unhappy characterization, as we have already seen and will see in much more detail momentarily). So clearly, we need to consider carefully what roles the church-historical dimension plays and ought to play within the Justification discourse.

Many assert that Justification theory is continuous with important moments and figures within church history. Luther and the Protestant Reformation are of course the primary loci for such assertions. Justification is correct, it is often suggested, because this is what Luther discovered and what the Protestant Reformation affirmed.[1] But there are some problems implicit in any such assertions that we must now try to unravel.

First, it might be claimed that Luther's *reading* of Paul is right and that any construal of the gospel simply emerges from that exegesis. However, if that is the case, we do not then need to know — except as an interesting item in the reading's historical pedigree — that *Luther* read Paul in this fashion. The reading will stand or fall on its own exegetical merits, that is, in relation to the evidence in Paul's text that supports it. That Luther or anyone else mobilized these considerations is largely irrelevant to the cogency of the reading itself simply as a reading. Hence, the historical exegetical claim seems redundant (other than, as we have just said, an item in exegetical history and attribution; we ought to acknowledge that Luther was the first person to formulate this reading — if he was).[2] So church history theoretically requires no special treatment in this sense. But the claim that Luther read Paul in a certain way — in *this* way — tends nevertheless to be repeated, at which point we begin to suspect that more than a merely exegetical assertion is being made. We face here in addition an argument from authority, and this argument ought now to be scrutinized. "Because *Luther* formulated this reading, it *ought* to be true," the argument goes.

However, as a claim concerning a fundamentally scriptural discourse, the correction that we just noted in fact continues to apply. Strictly speaking, it does not matter whether Luther himself made certain exegetical claims. Those claims must still be judged in relation to the discernible voice of Scripture itself. It is precisely the point of Scripture (and the Reformation often asserted this) to overrule inappropriate claims made merely on the basis of authority, so it would be supremely ironic if the authority of one of the Reformation's leading exegetes and churchmen were used to overrule later readings of Paul.[3] In its own terms, then, Justification ought not to recognize such claims, and we could possibly simply leave our discussion here.

However, we must address this argument from authority more comprehensively than in terms of a mere dismissal on methodological grounds, however fair that dismissal might prove. This is especially the case since an interpretative dynamic may at times be operating unacknowledged at this point, perhaps principally in the tacit dimension. It will be helpful if this dynamic can be further arrested. And it can be, in strictly descriptive terms.

There are two principal points at which exegetical claims in relation to Justification have tended to be reinforced by church-historical claims on the basis of authority. As we have just seen, much tends to be made of the reading of Paul in terms of Justification by the leading figures in the Reformation, and especially by Luther. But Stendahl also pushed this claim deep into the pre-Reformational period by making a set of negative assertions about Augustine. And although it is fair, as we have just noted, to deny the initial relevance of these claims, it will be useful to describe in more detail how such claims are oversimplifications as well. That demonstration should serve to break down further any psychological attachments by Pauline interpreters to false claims emanating from this dimension. Our principal focus will be on Luther and the other leading Reformers. Following this discussion we will turn to consider Augustine and the pre-Reformational situation more briefly.

My thesis throughout this analysis is essentially just a countervailing complaint of complexity: any assertion that Luther and/or Augustine (or others) *univocally* support a reading of some of Paul's key texts in terms of Justification theory, and hence underwrite a corresponding construal of his theology in those terms, is a distortion of the evidence. It is true that their support can be garnered for this theory *at times*. I concede this. However, it is also true that much of what they wrote at other times *is either explicitly or implicitly critical of this theory.* The picture is, in short, much more complex — not to mention conflicted — than Justification advocates tend to paint it. Hence, any claim by Justification advocates of a monochromatic or simple situation is false and ought to be rejected. The witness of Augustine, of Luther, and of the Reformation more broadly is far more ambiguous and contradictory than such assertions aver.[4]

If my countervailing claim proves sustainable, several important implications will follow.

i. The characterization of the entire interpretative situation in church-historical terms — as "Lutheran" or some such — is unhelpful and ought to be abandoned. Luther can be found on both sides of this debate! He can be deployed in support of Justification, but he can also be arraigned as its severest critic. Hence, any unqualified claims made in terms of Luther himself are bound to sow confusion. In and of themselves, they solve next to nothing.

ii. Since Luther is a more diverse exegete and theologian than the parameters of Justification theory suggest, other readings of Paul may well prove to be faithful to attested concerns of Luther that fall outside the boundaries drawn by Justification. Readings offered in criticism of the "Lutheran" reading of Paul may nevertheless be quite "Lutheran"! (and this will ultimately prove to be the case).

iii. Attacks on the "Lutheran" reading of Paul are needlessly inflammatory in denominational terms and ought to be abandoned. Lutherans do not have a monopoly on misreading Paul. They are no more in the hermeneutical dock — and probably no less — than most other denominations. Meanwhile, they have many exegetical alternatives in this relation that are quite faithful to their traditions. Lutherans may be as much a part of the answer as they are a part of the problem (as Stendahl's work intimates).[5]

iv. It follows that the legacy of the Reformation is *not* at stake in this whole debate. That "legacy" is a far more complex thing than Justification theory might suggest. Similarly, the broader debate in relation to the meaning of Paul's Justification texts and their implications is in many respects an in-house Protestant debate (not that other broad church traditions should be excluded from it).

v. It also follows from this more complex underlying reality that *merely reversing the situation does not solve it*. In response to the repeated charge that Luther misread Paul in terms of Justification theory, some apologists for Luther point to those texts where he seems to criticize the basic premises of Justification theory, if only by implication, and thereby come closer to an implicitly healthier reading of Paul as well. In a sense then it might be suggested here that (at least at these points), Luther read Paul in ways more akin to the new perspective. But this reversal does not supply a complete account. Luther is both supportive *and* unsupportive of the theory (and at times, of course, he is occupied with other matters altogether). This correction is consequently as oversimplified as the thesis it seeks to correct.

vi. The question of which reading of Paul is correct is also left dangerously ambiguous if not unresolved with such a strategy. That is, reorienting *Luther's*

role in all of this — insofar as we can — does not thereby remove the underlying interpretative problems in Paul to which Stendahl pointed using the
designation "Lutheran" — i.e. his Justification texts (interpreted in that
sense).[6] We might correct Stendahl's clumsy attributions here, desisting
from using the name "Lutheran" (as in fact we have in this volume), but in
so doing we have not necessarily resolved the interpretative issues themselves. Indeed, they tend to live on, presumably under a different name
(here, "Justification theory"). Clarifying Luther's role in all of this is therefore just one preliminary step within a broader solution.

In view of these important implications, a consideration of the church-
historical dimension within this debate is extremely important, if only to clear
the ground further of a number of unhelpful assumptions. We turn, then, to consider Luther and the Protestant Reformation in more detail, perhaps more aware
of just what is at stake in the discussion. The main thesis in what follows is reasonably easy to defend — the claim that Luther and the Reformation's other leading figures were rather more complex than Justification advocates tend to suggest. They can be deployed on *both* sides of most of the questions that we are
considering here in relation to Paul. So, in keeping with the basic thesis the
church-historical causalities are rather more complex than previous Pauline analysts seem to have recognized, I will present "positive" and "negative" evidence —
texts suggesting that the main Reformers did endorse Justification, and then texts
that challenge that support.[7]

§2. Justification and Protestantism in Positive Relation

2.1. Luther[8]

Irrespective of his own final or deepest positions the conclusion is basically unavoidable that Luther did release the theory of Justification, married to various
key Pauline texts, into the interpretative tradition. He is clearly a transmitter, and
almost certainly the origin, of this reading. It is not necessary to survey all of Luther's work in order to prove this assertion. A representative sample, which I have
drawn largely from his early lectures and pamphlets, supplemented by some later
key works, suffices to establish it.

(1) The Early Biblical Commentary

Luther began lecturing on the Bible in Wittenberg in October 1512, beginning,
most significantly, with the Psalms. In the summer of 1515 he began teaching on
Romans, the course running until the summer of 1516. From this point he turned
to Galatians and then to an explication of Hebrews, returning to the Psalms in
1517-18.[9] Indeed, it is clear that the Psalms are very much on Luther's mind at this

point. He quotes them throughout the Romans lectures, especially Psalm 51, the first few verses of which appear at times in almost every paragraph. Luther's commentary on Romans begins with some instructive summary comments:[10]

> The sum and substance of this letter is: to pull down, to pluck up, and to destroy all wisdom and righteousness of the flesh (i.e., of whatever importance they may be in the sight of men and even in our own eyes), no matter how heartily and sincerely they may be practiced, and to implant [or affirm], establish, and make large *the reality of sin (however unconscious we may be of its existence)*. (*LLR*, 3, emphasis added)

The a priori nature of Justification seems plainly apparent here, along with its fundamentally, aggressively, and radically negative initial thrust. These preliminary realizations will establish the gospel to the extent that the former and *not* the latter are said by Luther — accurately — to be the heart of Paul's argument so construed.[11] This negative premise is a primary theme in all that follows. Luther goes on to say:

> For God does not want to save us by our own but by an extraneous righteousness which does not originate in ourselves but comes to us from beyond ourselves, which does not arise on our earth but comes from heaven. Therefore, we must come to know this righteousness which is utterly external and foreign to us. That is why our own personal righteousness must be uprooted. (*LLR*, 4)

The two progressions in Justification are evident here, along with the powerful motif of inversion and the important genitive of authorship[12] that exegetically facilitated Luther's view of salvation. As we read on through the key texts in Paul,[13] these points are frequently repeated in a rich interweaving of personal piety, the Psalms, and the apostle's argument.[14] The lectures are preoccupied with sinfulness and a right understanding of it. Paul's text speaks to "me," and my inner reality is deeply iniquitous. This must be recognized, that is, confessed, just as David acknowledged his iniquity in relation to Bathsheba (traditionally) in Psalm 51. To resist this realization or to underplay its depth is heinous. But from this despair and terror salvation issues as God graciously gifts me with righteousness — as long as I grasp it by faith. Luther's understanding of the progression between these two states is therefore already overtly conditional, at least at times. See, for example, his gloss on Romans 4:17:

> If God gives his promise and there is none who believes him as he gives it, then certainly God's promise will not amount to anything and it cannot be fulfilled, for inasmuch as there is none to receive it, it cannot be a promise to anyone. Therefore, faith must be there to ratify the promise, and the promise needs the faith on the part of him to whom it is given. (Cited in *LLR*, lxvi)[15]

And:

> [I]ntrinsically, God and his words are just and true. But they do not become so in us until our wisdom and knowledge yield to them and through faith make room for them and accept them. This is why Ps 51:4 says: "Against thee have I sinned," i.e., I give up my righteousness and my understanding that resist and condemn thy words, and I confess that I am sinful and unrighteous and untruthful in order that thy words may dwell in me and be regarded as true and be and become true. (*LLR*, 77)

The point is made repeatedly. An especially compact enumeration is given in relation to Romans 10:15:

> Law-sin: the law uncovers sin; it makes the sinner guilty and sick; indeed, it proves him to be under condemnation.

> Gospel-grace: the gospel offers grace and forgives sin; it cures the sickness and leads to salvation. (*LLR*, 301)

But Luther uses more accessible illustrations as well:

> This is as if (to quote the story of Persius) a physician, intent on curing a patient, came upon a man who denies that he is sick and calls the doctor a fool who is much sicker than he because he presumes to promise health to a healthy man. This resistance makes it impossible for the physician to prove the effectiveness of his medical art. But he would succeed if this sick man, admitting that he is sick, would submit to the cure and say: I am indeed sick and you will be acclaimed as a healthy man, i.e., when you have restored my health. (*LLR*, 69)

A complete account of the commentary's concerns would range well beyond our present purposes.[16] Suffice it to say that the conditional and contractual soteriology that lies at the heart of the Justification discourse is clearly present in its pages. Consequently, Luther seems to have consciously articulated this model by 1515, although his understanding was in its early stages. Its incendiary application would follow shortly.

(2) The Early Pamphlets

The Ninety-Five Theses, posted on October 31, 1517, do not describe the Justification schema particularly clearly, being primarily concerned with the nature of true repentance and the related question of papal authority, although Luther's extreme sensitivity to sin is again readily apparent (see especially theses 1, 3, 4, and 7).[17] However, *The Heidelberg Disputation,* which took place on April 26, 1518, describes Justification clearly, if succinctly. Theses 1-16 speak of how works and law depress the individual. Thesis 17 states: "Nor does speaking in this manner give cause for despair, but for arousing the desire to humble oneself and seek the grace of Christ"; thesis 18 continues: "It is certain that man must utterly despair of his own ability before he is prepared to receive the grace of Christ." Hence, thesis 23 states: "The law brings the wrath of God, kills, reviles, accuses, judges, and condemns everything that is not in Christ (Rom. 4:15)"; thesis 25: "He is not righteous who does much, but he who, without work, believes much in Christ"; and thesis 26: "The law says, 'do this,' and it is never done. Grace says, 'believe in this,' and everything is already done" (*LW* 31:40-41). The powerful and elegant inversions of this pamphlet therefore seem to presuppose the distinctive argumentation of Justification, and that system seems to be clearly in place for Luther in a public and controversial sense by the middle of 1518. (This conclusion is reinforced by a consideration of *The Explanations,* finished in August of that year.)[18]

Later in 1518 Luther produced *The Proceedings at Augsburg,* following his celebrated hearing before Cajetan (*LW* 31:259-92). Intimations of Justification theory can be found here as well, for example: "it is clearly necessary that a man must believe with firm faith that he is justified and in no way doubt that he will obtain grace. For if he doubts and is uncertain, he is not justified but rejects grace. . . . [T]he justification and life of the righteous person are dependent upon his faith" (270). A conditional understanding of grace is then elaborated (270-74), along with an important set of statements on faith.

After this, either late in 1518 or early in 1519, Luther preached on Philippians 2:5-6, publishing the sermon as *Two Kinds of Righteousness* (*LW* 31:297-306). An emphasis on the key role of faith is again apparent,[19] amid an interesting discussion of different kinds of righteousness. Informed by texts from Isaiah and the Psalms (especially 31:1), Luther further articulates his view that righteousness comes *from* God *to* us as God's "alien" righteousness — a process that follows our abasement before God's stern righteousness. Luther goes on to exhort his listeners to "proper" (ethical, just, and devout) righteousness, which exists in contradistinction to false, boastful righteousness. He concludes with a significant affirmation of government and order, in relation to which it is not surprising to find that he cites Romans 13 (*LW* 31:304-6; and perhaps as a result the tract should be called "*Five* Kinds of Righteousness" — stern, alien, ethical, false, and governmental).

The year 1520 was dramatic.[20] The papal bull condemning Luther, *Exsurge Domine,* was promulgated on June 15. It made its way slowly across Europe to Wittenberg, where Luther publicly burned it on December 10. Between these dates — among other things — Luther penned three justly famous tracts: *The Address to the German Nobility,* published August 18, *The Babylonian Captivity of the Church,* published October 6, and *The Freedom of a Christian,* published in early November. The last of these is the most relevant to our concerns here.

The Freedom of a Christian (*LW* 31:333-77), one of Luther's most famous and widely read pieces, reproduces Justification neatly. After various preliminaries

Luther emphasizes the importance of faith[21] and then draws an important distinction between commandment and promise: "the commandments show us what we ought to do but do not give us the power to do it. They are intended to teach man to know himself, that through them he may recognize his inability to do good and may despair of his own ability" (348). This is then followed by such statements as, "If you believe, you shall have all things; if you do not believe, you shall lack all things" and "what greater wickedness" than the sin of unbelief, that is, rejecting God's generosity (*LW* 31:348-49, 350). The presence of Justification could hardly be clearer.

It is thus apparent that the early Luther did at times adumbrate an a priori, individualist, and conditional, hence also contractual account of salvation, basing that often in scriptural terms on Pauline terminology and texts, and deploying it quite self-consciously in his more general assault on the perceived excesses of Roman Catholicism. The widespread influence of these early, controversial pamphlets, allied with Luther's importance, therefore constitutes a pivotal moment in the apostle's interpretative history. It cannot be doubted that a significant impetus to install Justification as a paradigmatic explanation of salvation stems from this moment. The theory is already richly bedecked with ideological functions yet is freighted in fundamentally Pauline terminology drawn from the apostle's antithetical texts that contrast works of law and faith. But did the later Luther remain committed to these arguments?

(3) The Galatians Commentary

We can next consider the famous Galatians commentary based on lectures given in 1531 and published, after revision, in 1535. (Luther had lectured on Galatians much earlier, in 1516-17, publishing the scholia in 1519; he did not lecture on Romans after Melanchthon's arrival in Wittenberg in 1518.) Luther's later Galatians commentary is regarded as one of his masterpieces, and in it Justification theory is clearly apparent (*LW* 26[22]).

In the commentary Luther reprises one of his characteristic antitheses — that all of Scripture divides into law and gospel, or command and promise. The former categories lead to the latter. Hence, the "proper and absolute use" of the law (*LW* 26:310)[23] is as "a mighty hammer" (*LW* 26:336):

> If someone is not a murderer, adulterer, or thief, and abstains from external sins, . . . he develops the presumption of righteousness and relies on his good works. . . . The proclamation of free grace and the forgiveness of sins does not enter his heart and understanding. . . . Therefore this presumption of righteousness is a huge and a horrible monster. To break and crush it, God needs a large and powerful hammer, that is, the Law. (*LW* 26:310)

> Therefore the Law is a minister and a preparation for grace. For God is the God of the humble, . . . of those who have been brought down to nothing at

all. . . . When the Law drives you this way, so that you despair of everything that is your own and seek help and solace from Christ, then it is being used correctly. (*LW* 26:314, 316)

The preliminary rhetorical operation of the Justification system's vestibule, and the characteristically aggressive function of the law in its demand for ethical rectitude so as to break down any self-confidence, could hardly be more apparent. Luther goes on to suggest that this salutary function continues throughout the life of the Christian (and this is a variation with potentially highly significant theological and interpretative implications):

[A]s long as we live in a flesh that is not free of sin, so long the Law keeps coming back and performing its function. . . . [T]here is still need for a custodian to discipline and torment the flesh, that powerful jackass, so that by this discipline sins may be diminished and the way prepared for Christ. (*LW* 26:350)

And further:

It is extremely beneficial to the faithful to be aware of the uncleanness of their flesh; for it will keep them from being puffed up by a vain and wicked notion about the righteousness of works, as though they were acceptable to God on its account. . . . [W]e are not in a position to trust in our own righteousness, for we are aware of the uncleanness of the flesh. (*LW* 27:85-86)

An emphasis on faith, which is usually understood as a condition for salvation, is quite clear as well. For example, commenting on 2:16, Luther states:

To give a short definition of a Christian: A Christian is not somebody who has no sin, but somebody against whom God no longer chalks sin, because of his faith in Christ. This doctrine brings comfort to consciences in serious trouble. When a person is a Christian he is above law and sin. When the Law accuses him, and sin wants to drive the wits out of him, a Christian looks to Christ. . . . The true way of becoming a Christian is to be justified by faith in Jesus Christ, and not by the works of the Law. We know that we must also teach good works, but they must be taught in their proper turn, when the discussion is concerning works and not the article of justification. Here the question arises, by what means are we justified? We answer with Paul, "By faith only in Christ are we pronounced righteous, and not by works." Not that we reject good works. Far from it. But we will not allow ourselves to be removed from the anchorage of our salvation.[24]

Hence, the individualist, contractual system of Justification is still in place for Luther in relation to these texts when he comments on them later in his career.

(4) The Smalcald Articles

Another useful later point of reference is *The Smalcald Articles,* something of a theological "last will and testament" by Luther in response to the papal announcement of a church council in 1536[25] and his own serious illness at the time.

Luther summarizes accepted and then disputed but nonnegotiable principles briefly at the beginning of his discussion. The Hauptartikel in the text is a concise statement concerning justification largely constructed of scriptural quotations: Romans 3:23-25, 26-28; 4:25; John 1:29; Isaiah 53:5, 6; and Acts 4:12. Of it Luther states famously: "We cannot yield or concede anything in this article, even if heaven and earth, or whatever, do not remain. . . . On this article stands all that we teach and practice against the pope, the devil, and the world."[26] He then applies it in short order to various aspects of late medieval Catholicism that are, in his view, especially corrupt (*SA,* 6-16). More doctrinal exposition follows, beginning with an analysis of human sinfulness that is quickly supplemented by the law and an account of its "foremost office or power" — "that it reveals original sin and its fruits" (*SA,* 18):

> It shows human beings how deeply they have fallen and how their nature is completely corrupt. The law must say to them that they have no God. They honor or worship strange gods. This is something that they would not have believed before without the law. Thus they are terrified, humbled, despondent, and despairing. They anxiously desire help but do not know where to find it. . . . This is what is meant by Romans [4:15]: "The law brings wrath." (*SA,* 18)

A discussion of penance gives way to a digression on false penance, after which Luther returns to his main theme. In one of the final articles Luther asserts that good works do and must follow on faith, although he also confesses to a degree of uncertainty about how exactly this all fits together. He may emphasize the imputed nature of righteousness at this point: "God wants to regard and does regard us as completely righteous and holy, for the sake of Christ our mediator. Although sin in the flesh is still not completely gone or dead, God will still not count it or consider it" (*SA,* 32).

In short, while at times highly abbreviated and even structurally a little disjointed, the individualist, contractual schema of Justification is still clearly discernible at the heart of *The Smalcald Articles.* It is not elaborated in a sustained fashion, but many of its key motifs and themes are present, and some of them are briefly expanded. Furthermore, the aggressive, reforming aspect of the model is especially evident; a slate of ecclesial practices is redefined quickly by the model's application, and often without great subtlety!

(5) Luther in the Context of Late Medieval Piety and Exegesis

It is certainly fair to claim that Luther's work had several important Catholic antecedents. But did he inherit this actual theory, with its distinctive argumentative progressions and its grip on Paul's terminology in Romans and Galatians, directly from those antecedents, or was it his own creation? Here much scholarly analysis has been handicapped by the methodological vice of theological and lexical overinterpretation: that the key *words* were already in play within the Catholic tradition *does not prove that the entire system was.*[27] That commentary from this period on the Pauline letters, and any other dependent analyses, frequently used these terms is not overly surprising, since they are present in the apostle's texts. It is the presence of the distinctive argumentative progressions that is critical. And without claiming to supply a definitive solution, I would suggest that they are not in play — a suggestion that will be clarified when we turn to consider Augustine. The particular exegetical and theological emphases on faith *alone,* which are prefaced by the failures of life lived under the harsh tutelage of the law and which emphatically supersede it, seem unanticipated within the tradition — and especially when they are then applied more rigorously and consistently in the lives of individual believers and their communities to attack rituals, perceived hypocrisy, and other religious practices.

Marginally reinforcing this claim is the observation that Justification's opening premises and concerns seem particularly close to those that Luther himself enunciates biographically: an extremely stern view of God at times — one so stern as to provoke horror and even terror if he is offended; an *acute* consciousness of sinfulness (the frequent cause of offense); a critical concern with overelaborate religiosity; and a sudden breakthrough to some point of relief and gratitude that is explicitly grounded for much of the time in sola fide. It indeed seems likely, then, in view of these resonances, that Luther was responsible for the development of this distinctive soteriological system comprising two successive contracts, along with its marriage to certain of Paul's texts. This interpretative creation seems to have been facilitated by his work on the Psalms in combination with his lecturing on Romans and Galatians (and also on Hebrews). The Psalms seem to have delivered several important constituents for Luther's theological breakthrough: theological insights concerning God's benevolent activity that could be transferred to Paul's use of the same terminology; the possibility for a slightly naive, self-centered approach to Scripture; and this allied with an explicit engagement with individual sinfulness and a pronounced confessional dimension. Like his contemporaries, Luther read the Bible as applying to himself. Hence, when he turned to Romans, accompanied by his own acute concerns and his discovery of their articulation and treatment in the Psalms, *it seems that he read Paul in that manner as well,* something the text's apparent focus on individual sinfulness and associated elaborations seemed to allow.[28] The outcome was an essentially new reading and resulting theological model — one that could generate a significant degree of psychological relief as well as an equally significant rhetorical leverage against religious piety. In further corroboration of this suggestion we can observe that the system is not especially obvious in Catholic theology of the time or indeed subsequently (that is, until very recently). So it seems fair to call this reading, together with its resulting model, Luther's.[29] And at this point we can turn to consider the presence of the reading and the model in some of the other Reformers.

2.2. Melanchthon

(1) The Romans Commentary

Philip Melanchthon began teaching on Romans in 1519, the year after his arrival in Wittenberg. His famous *Loci Communes Theologici* was published in 1521, a reworking of themes and topics from his lectures originally published by his students in 1520. Luther published some of Melanchthon's lectures on Romans (along with some Corinthian material) in 1522. But Melanchthon himself published a commentary on Romans only in 1532, the year after his scripting of *The Apology* and two years after *The Augsburg Confession*. He revised and expanded the work significantly for republication in 1540. This commentary is often viewed as the quintessential example of a systematic theological understanding of Romans, the letter being read in abstraction from all circumstantial concerns; it is held to be a *christianae religionis compendium* (although Luther's reading differs little from this approach). Indeed, one could hardly wish for a clearer explication of Luther's distinctive theory of Justification than the one Melanchthon supplies in his extended introduction and elaborates in his ensuing exegesis. All the key assumptions, progressions, and caveats are present — and little else besides. That is, Luther's presentations (and Calvin's) tend to coexist with a certain amount of other material (as we will see shortly in §3). In Melanchthon, however, the model stands largely alone. It is essentially coterminous with a correct understanding of both Paul and the gospel.[30]

Excursus: Melanchthon's Commentary on Romans

Melanchthon begins his commentary with a lengthy introduction that simply explicates the soteriology of justification not by works but by faith. He starts by emphasizing the first, doctrinal part of the letter over against the latter, ethical part, commending it as "most necessary for every age and for the entire church. It contains the foremost and enduring topics of Christian doctrine, distinguishes the Gospel from the Law and from philosophy. . . . It proclaims these great things" (*MCR*, 11). He refers the reader to his *Loci*, which explained "simply and clearly . . . the doctrine of justification taught in the prophetic and apostolic writings." His mind has not changed on these matters (15); however, since they are the particular concern of this Pauline letter, he will repeat them to a degree here. A short summary is followed by a section on "the little word *gratis*" (*MCR*, 18). Melanchthon defines this overtly as God's generosity, which is related directly to Christ and hence focused on him; but it is *not* unconditional. To say that we are justified "*gratis* by faith," "solely by faith," and simply "by faith" is to say "*precisely the same thing*" (*MCR*, 19, emphasis added). Significantly, he also states that "disputes about predestination are to be laid aside for quite a while" (*MCR*, 20).

In the next section Melanchthon distinguishes between law and gospel in terms now familiar: "God wanted some knowledge to be in man which would judge sin. Sin has always been accused at all times by the voices of the Law in the preaching of repentance. Therefore Paul says: 'By the law is the knowledge of sin' [Rom. 3:20]" — and he is talking not just about "ceremonies" but chiefly about the Decalogue, or the moral law (*MCR*, 21). Moreover, "since human nature, vitiated by original sin, is not able to furnish perfect obedience, the Law shows the wrath of God against sin" (*MCR*, 21). But "[t]he Gospel proclaims repentance and the promise of grace and eternal life"; hence, "[t]he promise should be diligently distinguished from the Law" (*MCR*, 22). And this, unlike the law, is only divinely revealed, since "[h]uman reason by itself by no means sees this will of God — that God would send His Son that He might become a sacrificial victim for the church, that God wants to remit sins *gratis*" (*MCR*, 22). So the gospel is not a law, nor Christ merely a teacher. Moreover, the benefits of Christ "must be accepted by faith" (a claim supported by Rom. 1:16; *MCR*, 24). "And through this Gospel God is truly efficacious, gives the Holy Spirit, and begins in us a new light and eternal life" (*MCR*, 24).

Next is a short section on sin — which is not to be taken lightly. On account of it "God subjected the human race to death, and punishes and coerces them with immense calamities" (*MCR*, 25). And "[s]ince God was not willing to be placated by any sacrificial victim, only by the death of his Son, it must be an immense evil which had to be redeemed at so great a price" (*MCR*, 25). Therefore, we ought not to "minimize the sickness" (*MCR*, 25).

A brief account of justification follows. Romans 4 "defines justification as the forgiveness of sins," in continuity with ancient Hebrew usage, thus attesting with certainty that "justification signifies the remission of sins and acceptance to eternal life" (*MCR*, 25). By faith, justice is imputed and the Holy Spirit given, the latter supplying other virtues in turn. A short section on grace defines that as "gratuitous acceptance" (*MCR*, 26), a thesis Melanchthon then documents extensively. He emphasizes the necessity "that the gift be accepted by faith" (*MCR*, 28), a topic he then turns to in more detail.

Faith is "assent in the intellect . . . and relational" (*MCR*, 29).

> [I]t is necessary that mention be made of faith because it is necessary that there be some impulse by which we accept the gift and apply it to ourselves. And when we mention faith, let the mind look upon Christ and think of the gratuitous mercy promised because of him. . . . This impulse of faith in our minds is not an idle cogitation, but it wrestles with the terrors of sin and death. It fights with the devil, who attacks weak minds in dreadful ways in order to drive them either to contempt of God or to despair, like Cain, Saul, Judas and innumerable others who decided that they had been rejected by God and so hated God furiously. Others become atheists or Epicureans. . . . They do not sustain themselves by faith, but broken in mind they yield to the devil. (*MCR*, 29)

Further scriptural testimonies to this principle follow (Romans 4, especially 4:3 in relation to Gen. 15:6; Eph. 3:12; Rom. 5:1; Col. 2:12; 1 John 5:10; Rom. 4:18; Mark 9:24; Heb. 11:1; Acts 15:9; Rom. 10:11; and 2 Chron. 20:20 — as well as the dicta of ancient writers such as Augustine, Chrysostom, and Bernard).

Melanchthon then moves to consider good works in the life of the justified. The Word of God, especially the Decalogue, is our principal guide to what sort of works should be done, and the power to do them is given by the Holy Spirit, who comes "when hearts are raised up by faith, . . . in order that he may kindle a new light in the minds and excite pious impulses" (*MCR*, 37). However, Scripture and theology suggest that sin remains in the regenerate (*MCR*, 40-42). Obedience at this point does not achieve salvation, but it can receive rewards. Conversely, disobedience can result in the loss of salvation; it must be resisted by means of watchfulness, prayer, and discipline (*MCR*, 48). (Melanchthon then finishes his introduction by offering refutations of his opponents' arguments from difficult scriptural texts, such as Jas. 2:14, and their more scholastic rejoinders: *MCR*, 51-58).

We have spent some time on the Reformer's introduction because it is such a pristine statement of Justification. Melanchthon's actual commentary on Romans reiterates this system to an almost extraordinary degree. The approach is at least mentioned, but more often briefly adumbrated, *on almost every page that treats Paul's Justification texts* (and there is little else besides).[31] Hence, for Melanchthon Paul is almost entirely reducible to this schema. Pauline points of tension with this construal's individualist and contractual emphases — such as election — tend to be either overtly countered or overlooked.

(2) The Augsburg Confession

This statement was presented to Charles V in 1530 by various German princes and electors, but it was drafted by Melanchthon.

Article 4 of the *Confession* affirms justification by faith largely in the manner outlined earlier.[32] Article 13 insists that the sacraments be joined to faith in order to be efficacious. Article 20, the dominant article in the *Confession's* "Chief Articles of Faith," expounds faith at length in relation to good works in specific reliance on Pauline texts (Eph. 2:8-9 and Rom. 5:1), supported by appeals to Augustine and to Ambrose's *De Vocatione Gentium*. Indeed, a reliance on Paul is evident throughout the *Confession*: "Paul teaches everywhere that righteousness is not to be sought from our own observances and acts of worship, devised by men, but that it comes by faith to those who believe that they are received by God into grace for Christ's sake" (article 27).[33] This doctrine of faith is said to bring consolation to the terrified and anxious conscience.

Article 5 attributes faith to the working of the Holy Spirit: "through the Word and Sacraments, as through instruments, the Holy Ghost is given, who works faith; where and when it pleases God, in them that hear the Gospel, to wit, that God, not for our own merits, but for Christ's sake, justifies those who believe that they are received into grace for Christ's sake." Article 18 also circumscribes the effectiveness of free will. But then article 20 seems to reverse this order.

[B]ecause through faith the Holy Ghost is received, hearts are renewed and endowed with new affections, so as to be able to bring forth good works. For Ambrose says: Faith is the mother of a good will and right doing. For man's powers without the Holy Ghost are full of ungodly affections, and are too weak to do works which are good in God's sight. Besides, they are in the power of the devil who impels men to divers sins, to ungodly opinions, to open crimes. This we may see in the philosophers, who, although they endeavored to live an honest life could not succeed, but were defiled with many open crimes. Such is the feebleness of man when he is without faith and without the Holy Ghost, and governs himself only by human strength.

So an overt conditionality is present in the *Confession,* along with an account of Justification as a whole, although this is contradicted to a degree by article 5.[34] And indeed, it is apparent that Melanchthon is a faithful tradent of Luther's initial insights, in certain senses greatly clarifying the position of his theological master. He is a significant link in the interpretative chain. We turn now to one of the most important if not dominant links — Calvin.

2.3. Calvin

Calvin worked on successive editions of his magisterial *Institutes* from 1536 to 1559.[35] His treatment of faith appears at the beginning of book 3, the section dedicated as a whole to explicating the Holy Spirit, and so we might expect the entire model of justification by faith to appear at this point as well. But Calvin's treatment of faith is complex, and a full consideration of it is best postponed. He does provide, however, an isolated but clear hint concerning the model at the outset of this discussion. Calvin summarizes it with characteristic clarity and concision:

> Here it is of importance to call to mind what was formerly taught, first, That since God by his Law prescribes what we ought to do, failure in any one respect subjects us to the dreadful judgment of eternal death, which it denounces. Secondly, Because it is not only difficult, but altogether beyond our strength and ability, to fulfil the demands of the Law, if we look only to ourselves and consider what is due to our merits, no ground of hope remains, but we lie forsaken of God under eternal death. Thirdly, That there is only one method of deliverance which can rescue us from this miserable calamity — viz. when Christ the Redeemer appears, by whose hand our heavenly Father, out of his infinite goodness and mercy, has been pleased to succour us, if we with true faith embrace this mercy, and with firm hope rest in it. (*CI* 3.2.1; 1:469)

It is worth emphasizing that faith must be voluntary for this argument to function as a whole. If it is a gift, then the first two chains of self-discovery are redundant, and clearly Calvin did not intend them to function in this fashion. (Otherwise, presumably, he would not have included them.)

This summary receives no development for the best part of eight chapters, but in chapter 11 Calvin takes up the model of justification by faith in detail, devoting a further eight chapters to its account (*CI* 3.11–18; 2:36-129). (And after a consideration of Christian liberty and prayer, book 3 then concludes with a discussion of election in chapters 21 through 24, and of the resurrection in chapter 25.) Needless to say, Calvin gives an excellent account of the system. The power of Luther and the clarity of Melanchthon receive additional development, depth, and subtlety — something assisted by Calvin's more discursive format, although he can also be accused at times of a less elevated and even contradictory polemicism — for example, against Osiander (*CI* 3.11.5-12; 2:40-51).[36] But the system is still essentially the same and premised primarily on Paul's Justification texts. There is little point in citing the corroborating strings of citations; this section of *The Institutes* should simply be read. However, some of Calvin's particular emphases are worth noting.

(1) Calvin equates justification with reconciliation in the sense that the latter is semantically defined by the former. God is "reconciled" to us when our sins, which have rightly offended God and excited God's wrath and pending punishment, are dealt with.[37] To be "justified" is, moreover, to be deemed righteous and innocent of all transgression (*CI* 3.11.2-4; 2:37-40), which also entails acceptance.

(2) Calvin is emphatic that justification is simultaneous with the beginning of sanctification, or regeneration.[38] However, the latter process is the work of the Holy Spirit; the former, the result of our faith. This is the principal means by which Calvin asserts that good works flow from the believer (although he also uses an interesting argument from the indivisibility of Christ to prove the point). And this distinction allows him to face the reality of ongoing sinfulness in the life of the Christian in two modes: justification is in a sense a legal fiction that does not change the believer, and sanctification is merely inaugurated and never complete.

(3) Calvin emphasizes that complete or perfect obedience to the law is necessary if one is to be justified by works. This makes the depiction of God vulnerable to criticism in view of its apparent harshness; however, this can be partly mitigated by the immediate offer of the generous contract, and it has the added virtue of increasing the pressure on the individual in the first, pre-Christian phase. The claim also stands in its own right.[39]

> The righteousness of works consists in perfect obedience to the law. Hence you cannot be justified by works unless you follow this straight line (if I may so call it) during the whole course of your life. The moment you decline from it you have fallen into unrighteousness. Hence it appears, that righteousness is not obtained by a few works, but by an indefatigable and inflexible observance of the divine will. But the rule with regard to unrighteousness is very different. The adulterer or the thief is by one act guilty of death, because he offends against the majesty of God. [Calvin cites Jas. 2:10, 11 and comments on it.] Therefore, it should not seem absurd when we say that death is the just recompense of every sin, because each sin merits the just indignation and vengeance of God. (*CI* 3.18.10; 2:129)[40]

Lying behind the perfectionist view, then, is the notion that God is angry or wrathful with wrongdoing and takes vengeance against it no matter how minor it might be; indeed, there is really no such thing as "minor" transgression (see *CI* 3.11.2; 2:38).

(4) Calvin frequently emphasizes that a firm grasp of justification by faith gives Christians a sense of security. By this he seems to mean particularly that the pangs of conscience, excited by sinfulness and an anticipation of God's sternness toward wrongdoing, can be allayed.[41] Hence, to disturb this teaching is to disturb the peace of mind of believers and to deliver them over to anxiety.

(5) In order to cope with the rebuttal of opponents in relation to certain passages from Scripture, Calvin often argues for distinctions in the meaning of faith. Some passages and senses are attributed to the process of sanctification, where faith functions analogously to love, hope, and the other fruits of the Spirit. But this quality of fidelity is not the same as the justifying faith that initially grasps salvation.[42]

(6) Calvin also emphasizes two aspects of forgiveness in justification by Christ — the forgiveness of sins through Christ's death and the imputation of righteousness through Christ's perfect obedience.[43] Both are necessary for full acceptance and reconciliation.

(7) Calvin explicitly includes all works of the law in the rejection of the pre-Christian phase and not merely ceremonial works (against Origen).[44]

Hence, Calvin has clearly worked through many of the model's ramifications in some detail, prompted in large measure by criticism and controversy. The result is a very complete account. He understands the theory's workings intimately and defends it vigorously against its detractors.[45]

These conclusions are confirmed elsewhere in *The Institutes,* in particular, in a long analysis of the role of the law at the end of book 2.

As we have seen, Justification presupposes human capacity, and within this schema the law can — and indeed must — inform those outside Christ and drive them toward the gospel. Hence, the law functions primarily in the non-Christian condition, and Calvin overtly affirms this traditional role in terms of conviction (*CI* 2.7.6-9; 1:304-7). However, Calvin's darker view of non-Christian humanity elaborated in book 2 ought to entail that this function is largely useless. Yet intriguingly, he argues here that the law renders the reprobate "without excuse," this assertion seemingly a vestige of Justification theory retained somewhat inconsistently. (Alternatively, it signals the perception that human reprobation does retain an element of responsibility.) Calvin asserts in addition the law's role in keeping the recalcitrant in check — a governmental or civil use — however much they may rage against it and hate it (a point explicitly addressed to "his Majesty"!: see *CI* 2.7.10-11; 1:307-9).

Calvin also discusses the role of the law for the elect *after* their salvation, where it functions primarily as a guide — the ethical use of the law, "also the principal use, and more closely connected with its proper end" (*CI* 2.7.1-2, 12-15; 1:300-302, 309-11, quotation from 309). "The Law acts like a whip to the flesh, urging it on as men do a lazy sluggish ass" (*CI* 2.7. 12; 1:309). He then tries to deal with one of the glaring problems in the foregoing schema by distinguishing immediately (here!) between the moral and the ceremonial law. The latter is abrogated because its original function was merely typological — a claim greatly assisted by texts drawn from Hebrews.[46] With the arrival of the ceremonies' symbolic fulfillment, their continuance would only be misleading (see, e.g., *CI* 2.7.16; 1:311-12), although Christ's coming in an important sense seals their eternal value. (Calvin is an accurate and honest enough exegete, however, to recognize a semantic shortfall here when he attempts to apply this principle to Col. 2:13-14 and Eph. 2:14: see *CI* 2.7.17; 1:312-13.)

This typological argument is especially relevant to the temple service, which through its representations and intimations was designed to raise the Jews' minds to "higher" things (see, e.g., *CI* 2.7.1; 1:300). In and of themselves the rituals are clearly ludicrous. Hence, Calvin argues that Christ was present to Judaism throughout her history, principally in this fashion: "the law was not a stranger to Christ" (*CI* 2.7.1; 1:301). Rather, the law in historical terms led the Jews *to* Christ through its multiple typological attestations — priestly, prophetic, and royal.[47] Indeed, from Levi and from David, Calvin can develop some of the central principles of his christological exposition.

At this point Calvin offers an extended analysis of the ten commandments (*CI* 2.8; 1:316-62). He begins by asserting the importance of the convicting function of the law, but in fact his account is primarily directed toward Christians and hence falls under its ethical use. Clearly, the commandments all still hold good for Christians, if in certain somewhat redefined senses (notably, the Sabbath).[48] So Calvin states at the end of his exposition: "It will not now be difficult to ascertain the general end contemplated by the whole Law — viz. the fulfilment of righteousness, that man may form his life on the model of the divine purity" (*CI* 2.8.51; 1:356); and, slightly more fully: "That Christians are under the law of grace, means not that they are to wander unrestrained without law, but that they are engrafted into Christ, by whose grace they are freed from the curse of the Law, and by whose Spirit they have the Law written in their hearts" (*CI* 2.8.57; 1:360-61).

In sum, then, it is quite fair to claim that Luther's fundamentally individualist and conditional construal of salvation — that is, Justification theory — based in large measure on Paul's texts, can also be found in Calvin. It is clearly attested in his *Institutes* in an extended systematic exposition — book 3, chapters 11 to 18 — as well as figuring noticeably in other contexts, such as book 2, chapters 7 and 8. It follows from this, in tandem with our earlier demonstrations, that Justification is fundamentally a Protestant model.[49] But this is certainly not the whole story in relation to Protestantism — or even in relation to these particular figures — as we will now see.

§3. Justification and Protestantism in Negative Relation

3.1. Luther

(1) Preliminary Considerations

Unfortunately, there is insufficient space here to document the following claims as they deserve. This study is ultimately concerned with reading Paul, not with reading Luther or the other Reformers, and hence considers the latter only as they impinge on the interpretative operations that unfold in relation to the former. And this limits the relevance of some of the extensive and detailed debates surrounding the following issues, especially those that have run long within Luther studies. However, we should note here at the outset one current that has been running of late within modern Luther studies.

Much ecumenical discussion between Lutheran churches and other traditions since the last quarter of the twentieth century has emphasized increasingly the theme of deification (along with related material) that can be found in Luther's thought. In close relation to these discussions — and especially with respect to various Orthodoxies — a Finnish school of Luther interpretation has developed, inspired primarily by Tuomo Mannermaa. This approach argues for a non-traditional center for Luther's thought in categories similar to those that I will emphasize in what follows — in relation to Christ-intimacy, participation, transformation, and even some notion of deification or theosis. The Finns argue vigorously that Luther's justification language and argumentation presuppose this more fundamental, intimate, participatory, and even deificatory stratum.[50] But it is not necessary for their thesis to hold good in its entirety for my own contentions here to stand. I am happy to concede that Luther at times endorses an individualist, contractual, and nonparticipatory model. Indeed, I find the subsequent history of exegesis in relation to some of Paul's texts almost impossible to explain without this. However, my weaker suggestion that Luther *at times* speaks unequivocally of an intimate, participatory, and transformational soteriology as well is, it seems to me, substantially corroborated by the Finns' claims that Luther can be explained in these terms as a whole. Clearly, that they can even mount such a challenge indicates a formidable reservoir of such ideas in Luther's corpus — one that they expound with considerable expertise and detail, which the following sample faintly represents. My concession here, however, does lead me to the admission of fundamental contradictions in Luther's corpus, as well as in Calvin's *Institutes* (although this is something I conclude reluctantly as against presupposing, an order that will be especially important to recall in relation to Paul's interpretation later on).

Luther's support for Justification has already been described, drawing often on his early works, corroborated by certain later key treatments. But we can now note that the early works contain intimations of a different theological program as well. And these hints seem later to harden at times into a model directly contradictory to the individualist view — a tendency especially apparent in a different cluster of Luther's writings, namely, his antihumanist texts. Three specific theological motifs apparent in Luther from an early date are potentially in tension with Justification: first, an extremely pessimistic view of human capacity outside of Christ; second — perhaps complementing the foregoing — an emphasis on divine election within the salvific process, and this often in dependence on certain Pauline texts; and third, spiritual marriage with Christ, where an intimate union effects a transformation in the Christian and hence also increased ethical capacity. But why are these three particular motifs or themes important given our present critical purposes? As we have already seen in purely internal, argumentative terms in chapter two and in the broader setting of the discourse's systematic frame in chapter three, these theological commitments operate in acute tension with Justification theory, contradicting its most basic assumptions and progressions.

Justification assumes a significant degree of human capacity. Individuals must be capable of thinking and acting for themselves reasonably effectively. Hence, any sustained commitment to anthropological incapacity renders the model's entire starting point problematic. In essence, such people are too stupid or too sinful to attain to the correct realizations or to make the right decisions. And whereas Justification can place pressure on struggling and guilt-ridden individuals, the model has little purchase on those who are fundamentally hostile to God (although perhaps "their condemnation is deserved").[51]

A pessimistic view of human capacity tends to issue in a complementary affirmation of an elective view of soteriology, since humans so constructed clearly cannot be relied upon to achieve salvation for themselves. But an emphasis on divine election effectively reverses Justification's pattern of a passive God and an active individual, largely obviating the need for any fixed rational progression by the individual. (He or she can still navigate progressions, but their form is not prescribed and God's influence throughout is primary.)

An emphasis on personal transformation — often said to be through the Spirit — is then in continuity with these two countervailing themes but sits awkwardly alongside Justification theory.[52] This emphasis can be harmonized with an overarching contractual framework by being positioned after the correct progressions and decisions that lead to Justification have taken place. But, as we have already seen, this is a rather difficult if not impossible conceptual reconciliation: if God later transforms individuals, then the basic parameters of the initial conception of salvation have been altered (put more colloquially, the goalposts have been moved). By contrast, the notion of ethical transformation integrates effortlessly with a soteriological conception in which God's benevolent rescue of the fallen creates an intimate union with them through the Spirit.

We turn at this point, then, to ask whether Luther evidences strong commitments to these countervailing themes that are ultimately contradictory to Justification.

(2) The Early Works

The three awkward themes just noted are apparent already in Luther's commentary on Romans (1515-16). A transformational ethical view is suggested by such comments as, "We must understand that this doing or not doing must be freely accomplished by the love of God with all one's heart and not from a slavish fear of punishment or from a childish desire for advantage, and that this is impossible without the love that is shed abroad by the Holy Spirit" (*LLR*, 197, a corollary on Rom. 7:5-6).[53] Luther's pessimism about human capacity is also obvious throughout the discussion, for example:

[T]he Scripture . . . describes man as curved in upon himself to such an extent that he bends not only physical but also spiritual goods toward himself, seeking himself in all things. Now this curvedness is natural; it is a natural defect and a natural evil. Hence, man gets no help from the powers of his nature, but he is in need of some more effective help from the outside. And this is love. Without it he constantly sins against the commandment: "You shall not covet." (*LLR*, 218-19)

Luther subsequently notes that "it follows irrefutably: one does not become a son of God and an heir of the promise by descent but by the gracious election of God" (*LLR*, 266, commenting on 9:6); and states further that "[a] man owes his ability to will and to run, not to his own power, but to the mercy of God who gave him this power to will and to run. Without it, man could neither will nor run" (*LLR*, 269, commenting on 9:16 and citing immediately Phil. 2:13 in support).

So it seems fair to claim that intimations of alternative if not ultimately contradictory soteriological principles can be found in Luther's early but important commentary on Romans. And there are similar echoes in *The Heidelberg Disputation* (1518) and Luther's published sermon *Two Kinds of Righteousness* (1519).

Thesis 28 in the former states: "The love of God does not find, but creates, that which is pleasing to it. The love of man comes into being through that which is pleasing to it" (*LW* 31:57). Hence, although *The Heidelberg Disputation* is highly contractual, this small concession to election is clear.[54] Similarly, a strong theme of identification is present in the sermon on different types of righteousness published shortly after this, with Christ presented as the bridegroom to "us" as bride (*LW* 31:300-301). This intimacy is then the basis for Luther's following exhortations to righteousness — the righteousness of good living. Where strong ethical claims are made in relation to the Christian state, a transformational view of salvation based on intimacy with Christ, and often freighted in nuptial imagery, tends also to be present. This theme of intimacy with Christ is further echoed in *The Freedom of a Christian* (1520).

In this famous pamphlet Luther speaks at one point of the "third incomparable benefit" of faith: "that it unites the soul with Christ as a bride is united with her bridegroom. By this mystery, as the Apostle teaches, Christ and the soul become one flesh [Eph. 5:31-32]. And if they are one flesh and there is between them a true marriage . . . it follows that everything they have they hold in common, the good as well as the evil. Accordingly the believing soul can boast of and glory in whatever Christ has as though it were its own" (*LW* 31:351; see also 352). Although premised on faith — note "the believing soul" — this is clearly an intimate and transformational soteriological model and not the imputational and explicitly nontransformational juridical approach that otherwise dominates much of the treatise. Indeed, strictly speaking, "faith" cannot *effect* such an ontological transformation, but is better read as important evidence *of* such a change.

Do some of Luther's later key writings bear these early tendencies out?

(3) Later Works

Although we have already suggested that the individualist and contractual soteriology of Justification is in evidence — if not sharpened — in some of the famous later works, countervailing material also definitely remains present, while an awareness of some of the former model's problems seems to surface at times as well. There are various comments in Luther's benchmark commentary on Galatians (1531/1535) that suggest the alternative motifs.

For example: "we teach that to know Christ and to believe in Him is no achievement of man, but the gift of God. God alone can create and preserve faith in us. God creates faith in us through the Word. He increases, strengthens and confirms faith in us through His Word."[55] Similarly, Luther begins *The Smalcald Articles* (1537)[56] by affirming the standard trinitarian creeds — "the lofty articles of the divine majesty" (4). He does not elaborate these but, suitably expanded, they suggest a nonindividualist soteriology! More overtly, Luther is committed throughout the treatise to upright ethical conduct by Christians. He complains in the preface that Lutherans are being misrepresented as bestial and libertine: "A doctor, sent here to Wittenberg from France, told us openly that his king was persuaded beyond the shadow of a doubt that there was no church, no government, no marriage among us, but rather everything went on in public as with cattle, and all did what they want" (*SA*, 3). Similarly, many of Luther's main concerns remain with the frequent ethical lapses that he perceives in the church and in wider society — "disunity among the princes and the estates . . . [g]reed and charging interest . . . [r]ecklessness; lewdness; extravagant dress; gluttony; gambling; pompousness; all kinds of vice and wickedness; disobedience of subjects, servants, workers, all the artisans; extortion by the peasants" (*SA*, 3-4).

Luther also attacks "the scholastic theologians" for their overly optimistic view of human nature. He himself affirms that "original sin has caused such a deep, evil corruption of nature that reason does not comprehend it; rather, it must be believed on the basis of revelation from the Scriptures" (*SA*, 16). The view he attacks, however, is close if not identical to the anthropological starting point of his contractual theology, while the view he affirms here must, if pressed consistently, hamstring that model. But Luther really has in mind the revelation of the law concerning human transgression, which "shows human beings how deeply they have fallen and how their nature is completely corrupt" (*SA*, 18). As the pamphlet continues, and despite sounding the usual individualist and contractual themes, Luther affirms at one point, in relation to Romans 7:23, that "he [the Christian] wars with the law in his members, etc., and he does this not by using his own powers but with the gift of the Holy Spirit which follows the forgiveness of sins. This same gift daily cleanses and expels the sins that remain and works to make people truly pure and holy" (*SA*, 25 — a good example of the "subordinationist" strategy that makes sanctification, assisted by pneumatology, follow on justification in order to explain ethical transformation but thereby also preserve the initial terms *of* justification).[57] Luther suggests further that children be baptized, arguably in defiance of the implications of the contractual model (3.5.4; *SA*, 27). Finally we should note that Luther seems almost to confess to a theological shortfall when he states toward the end of the treatise in relation specifically to the connection between justification and good works:

> [1] I have no idea how to change what I have consistently taught about this until now, namely, that we receive a different, new, clean heart through faith. . . . God wants to regard and does regard us as completely righteous and holy, for the sake of Christ our mediator. Although sin in the flesh is still not completely gone or dead, God will still not count it or consider it. [2] After such faith, renewal, and forgiveness of sin, *good works follow,* and whatever in these works is still sinful or imperfect should not be even counted as sin or imperfection, for the sake of Christ. The human being should be called *and should be* completely righteous and holy, according to both the person and his or her works *from the pure grace and mercy that have been poured and spread over us in Christ.* . . . [4] If one has a gracious God, then everything is good. Furthermore, we say also that *if good works do not follow, then the faith is false* and not true. (3.13; *SA,* 32-33, emphasis added.)

Clearly, Luther is committed to a real and renewed ethical capacity in the Christian, a concern so interwoven with an individualist and contractual framework that the absence of such renewal renders faith itself false![58]

Even more emphatic are Luther's slightly earlier, antihumanist writings regarded by some as his theological high point. *The Bondage of the Will* is a sustained attack on Erasmus for his strong and typically humanist commitment to human capacity, including a significant role for this within the process of salvation. Luther's work is an aggressive polemic, well fortified with scriptural citation and analysis, that argues trenchantly against Erasmus for a fundamental human incapacity.[59] Here Luther seems to affirm at length an utter and complete depravity, one that contains no essential self-knowledge or any ability to will the good in any way, and this claim is emphatically grounded in the correct reading of Scripture: "If . . . we submit the case to the judgment of Scripture, I shall win on all counts, and there will not be a jot or a tittle left that will not damn the dogma of free choice" (*LW* 33:287).[60] It is difficult to select material from the work since almost the entire text is apposite, but perhaps see especially the following:

> [T]he ungodly does not come even when he hears the Word, unless the Father draws and teaches him inwardly, which He does by pouring out the Spirit. There is then another "drawing" than the one that takes place outwardly; for then Christ is set forth by the light of the Spirit, so that a man is rapt away to Christ with the sweetest rapture, and rather yields passively to God's speaking, teaching, and drawing than seeks and runs himself. (*LW* 33:286)

[I]t is evident that in the sight of God free choice, with its will and its reason alike, is reckoned as a captive of this sin and as damned by it. (*LW* 33:286)

He [Satan] holds captive to his will all who are not snatched away from him by the Spirit of Christ, . . . nor does he allow them to be snatched away by any powers other than the Spirit of God. . . . Into this Kingdom [viz., the Kingdom in which "Christ reigns"] we are transferred, not by our own power but by the grace of God, by which we are set free from the present evil age and delivered from the dominion of darkness. (*LW* 33:287)

The metaphors of bondage and liberation that Luther uses centrally in the foregoing passage are especially significant, connecting overtly with our identification of the same metaphors and issues at the systematic frame in Paul himself. Also noteworthy is Luther's testimony in the following statement to the fundamental insecurity of any soteriology that rests in a degree of human capacity:

[S]ince God has taken my salvation out of my hands into his, making it depend on his choice and not mine, and has promised to save me, not by my own work or exertion but by his grace and mercy, I am assured and certain both that he is faithful and will not lie to me, and also that he is too great and powerful for any demons or any adversities to be able to break him or to snatch me from him. (*LW* 33:289)

Luther seems to betray little cognizance of the fact that this position causes acute difficulty for his endorsement of Justification elsewhere. If the anthropology he elaborates here is correct, then such people cannot be expected to rationalize and to appropriate salvation as that model recommends. The contradiction is absolute. (And if the tension is relaxed through the adoption of synergism, then Luther's arguments against Erasmus still collapse.) That Luther felt no such tension either reduces our estimation of his own powers of rationality and coherence or suggests that the individualist, contractual model ought to be redeployed in relation to his own thinking (as in fact the Finnish school argues). We turn now to Calvin.[61]

3.2. Calvin

By the end of chapter 18 in book 3 of *The Institutes* Calvin has finished his extended account of justification (*CI*, 2:129). After chapters on liberty and prayer, he offers an extended account of election that runs from chapter 21 through chapter 24 (*CI*, 2:202-58). The discussion of faith and the life of the Christian in general that precedes the account of justification in book 3 is also instructive for our present purposes; it unfolds in chapters 1 through 10 (*CI*, 1:462–2:35). The extended treatment of human sinfulness as the preparation for an analysis of the work of

Christ, undertaken in book 2, chapters 1 through 11 — a discussion that progresses into a treatment of the law — is significant as well (*CI*, 1:209-399; Christ is discussed in chapters 12 through 17, *CI*, 1:400-459).

A great deal of complex material is present in these sections; however, we do not need to analyze it completely. For our purposes we need merely to know whether it is compatible with or in tension with Justification theory. And the short answer would have to be that for much of the time this material creates various relationships of tension. In these sections Calvin articulates at length theological commitments to utter human depravity outside of Christ, to election, and to regeneration in Christ by means of the Spirit, all positions that ultimately clash with the assumptions of Justification.

(1) *The Human Condition (Book 2).* In chapter 1 at the start of book 2 — book 2 being the major subsection in *The Institutes* that treats the second statement in the creed, Christ — Calvin undertakes what he holds to be an appropriate contextualization of this subject: a description of the human plight to which Christ stands as the solution (*CI* 2.1-11; 1:209-399). Significantly, however, he does not at this point introduce Justification theory, with its attempted conviction of humanity by the law and so on. Instead, he attributes the origin of humanity's problems to a particular historical figure and moment, namely, Adam and his fall, from which the rest of humanity inherits a depraved nature. Such an analysis of the human plight does not integrate especially well with the needs of Justification.

As we have seen, the latter requires a degree of rationality and autonomy in the pre-Christian state — in essence, human capacity — so that the correct conclusions can be drawn by the individual and the appropriate saving actions then undertaken. The tortured journey through the realm of the law must take place. However, Calvin's Adamic approach is rather different. It suggests a deeply corrupted rationality to the point of *imprisonment in corruption,* for which one is not entirely responsible and from which one is not capable of escaping: "everything which is in man, from the intellect to the will, from the soul even to the flesh, is defiled" (*CI* 2.1.8; 1:218). Such individuals *will not be capable of undertaking the requisite pre-Christian calculations and actions.* They are too distorted in their thinking and behavior; they are not free enough to act as Justification requires. Hence, this Adamic account of fallenness leads directly to a denial of free will and to a corresponding elective soteriology, within which God intervenes to assist, since pre-Christian sinners cannot really help themselves — something Calvin proceeds directly to develop.[62] (And so the perception of tension in Calvin's account at this point corresponds almost directly to the tension perceptible at the frame of Romans 1–4 over against the argument of Romans 5 following.)[63] It would seem, then, that a strong commitment to pre-Christian depravity will complement an elective soteriology but that this will sit awkwardly beside the demands of Justification. Depraved Calvinist non-Christians will be too darkened and corrupt actually to undertake that model's journey to salvation. These subjects are too fallen to help themselves; they need help from outside their condition, a condition traced — in defiance again of Justification — to a particular historical moment.

Furthermore, Calvin's commitment to this depraved pre-Christian subject is sustained, extending through four more chapters. Chapter 2 focuses directly on the question of free will, Calvin denying at some length that humans possess it. Every aspect of fallen humanity, he claims, is distorted. And despite knowledge — at times most ingenious — of secular things, when it comes to the things of God, men are "blinder than moles"; hence, "none can enter the kingdom of God save those whose minds have been renewed by the enlightening of the Holy Spirit." Furthermore, "[o]n this subject the clearest exposition is given by Paul" (*CI* 2.2.18, 20; 1:238, 240), although Calvin also frequently repairs to Augustine and to the Fourth Gospel. He goes on to argue — in dependence here on prophetic texts — that far from being merely assisted to do good, the will must be *re-created* by the Spirit if the appropriate cure for human corruption is to take place: "How can it be said that the weakness of the human will is aided so as to enable it to aspire effectually to the choice of good, when the fact is, that it must be wholly transformed and renovated?" (*CI* 2.3.6; 1:255). The corrupt will is as malleable as a stone (see Ezek. 36:26, 27; see also 11:19). "It always follows, both that nothing good can proceed from our will until it be formed again, and that after it is formed again, in so far as it is good, it is of God, and not of us" (*CI* 2.3.8; 1:258).[64]

In chapter 4 Calvin embraces the position that God is involved in blinding and hardening the reprobate and therefore also acts through Satan (*CI* 2.4.2, 3; 1:267). This argument then continues through a discussion of various scriptural texts in chapter 5, where discussion begins to spill over into a consideration of the role of the law (*CI* 2.5.5; 1:276-77; and 2.5.6; 1:278). After some preliminary flourishes, however, Calvin's analysis of the law moves back within more traditional parameters (beginning in *CI* 2.7.3; 1:302), as we have already noted.[65]

We turn now to the second important countervailing theme in *The Institutes* — election.

(2) *Election (Book 3).* Chapter 21 is principally taken up with cautionary material — a repeated theme — but Calvin articulates his position on election concisely toward the end of the chapter before offering a fuller exposition in chapters 22 through 24 (see *CI*, 2:202-58):

> The predestination by which God adopts some to the hope of life, and adjudges others to eternal death, no man who would be thought pious ventures simply to deny; but it is greatly cavilled at, especially by those who make prescience its cause. We, indeed, ascribe both prescience and predestination to God; but we say that it is absurd to make the latter subordinate to the former. . . . By predestination we mean the eternal decree of God, by which he determined with himself whatever he wished to happen with regard to every man. All are not created on equal terms, but some are preordained to eternal life, others to eternal damnation; and, accordingly, as each has been created for one or other of these ends, we say that he has been predestinated to life or to death. (*CI* 3.21.5; 2:206)

Significantly, the influence of Paul's discussion in Romans 9 (assisted by much of Romans 11) is plainly evident in much of what follows. Hence, partly encouraged by Romans 9:11 and 16, Calvin explicitly rejects any grounding of election in divine foreknowledge (as might perhaps be argued in accordance with Romans 8:29: see *CI* 3.22.4; 2:216), because this seems to open the door to works and further, more positively, would obscure the point that nothing good comes from humanity except that which God has bestowed (*CI* 3.22.5; 2:217). Hence, both faith and justification are explicitly subordinated to election (*CI* 3.22.10; 2:223), as is universality. The later Augustine — that is, "after he had made greater progress in the knowledge of Scripture" (*CI* 3.22.8; 2:220) — is also cited frequently here over against other, less insightful Fathers like Origen, Jerome, Bernard, and "the subtle Thomas." In chapter 23 Calvin famously affirms at some length that the election of the saints necessitates a converse reprobation of the damned — something he admits is "dreadful" (*CI* 3.23.7; 2:232; this theme is taken up in more detail in chapter 24). In fact, Calvin tends to rely heavily on a defense in terms of divine inscrutability from this point. But, significantly, this claim is grounded in divine omnipotence as well, which is pressed even in relation to Adam's fall: "The first man fell because the Lord deemed it meet that he should" (*CI* 3.23.8; 2:232-33; see also 231). At several points Calvin simply seems to affirm that divine election is properly basic:

> Foolish men . . . ask why God is offended with his creatures, who have not provoked him by any previous offence; for to devote to destruction whomsoever he pleases, more resembles the caprice of a tyrant than the legal sentence of a judge; and, therefore, there is reason to expostulate with God, if at his mere pleasure men are, without any desert of their own, predestinated to eternal death. If at any time thoughts of this kind come into the minds of the pious, they will be sufficiently armed to repress them, by considering how sinful it is to insist on knowing the causes of the divine will, *since it is itself,* and justly ought to be, *the cause of all that exists.* For if his will has any cause, there must be something antecedent to it, and to which it is annexed; *this it were impious to imagine.* The will of God is the supreme rule of righteousness, so that everything which he wills must be held to be righteous by the mere fact of his willing it. Therefore, when it is asked why the Lord did so, we must answer, Because he pleased. But if you proceed farther to ask why he pleased, you ask for something greater and more sublime than the will of God, *and nothing such can be found.* (*CI* 3.23.2; 2:227, emphasis added; see also 228.)

In view of this position, the New Testament's occasional claim that God shows no partiality must also be redefined (*CI* 3.23.10; 2:233-34: see Acts 10:34; Rom. 2:10; Gal. 3:28 [see 2:6]; Jas. 2:5). Calvin then states that Scripture "does not remind us of predestination to increase our audacity, and tempt us to pry with impious presumption into the inscrutable counsels of God, but rather to humble and abase us, that we may tremble at his judgment, and learn to look up to his mercy" (note, an a posteriori function; *CI* 3.23.12; 2:235). Chapter 24 goes on to link election with calling and the Holy Spirit. Here Calvin reiterates that one ought not to inquire into the cause behind or within the divine cause of one's election; to do so leads only to despair (a highly christocentric account of the divine choice is truncated within this broader discussion: see *CI* 3.24.5; 2:244-45). Just as it began, so in its closing exposition the broader discussion leans heavily on Romans 9, supplemented by selections from Romans 11. (Johannine texts are also much cited, in addition to certain key Old Testament texts[66] and supplementary New Testament material.)

That Calvin is clearly committed at times to a strong view of divine election — and often explicitly informed by Paul — is, hardly surprisingly, incontestable. Moreover, here the doctrine of election *overrules* Justification theory explicitly. Faith itself is a gift, as is perseverance, and justification is a consequence of election; no consideration of merit is allowed into the elective decision itself, which remains *inscrutably* just. Hence, if only these four chapters from *The Institutes* had survived from Calvin's corpus, no New Testament scholar would have dreamed of positing his support for Justification. He would have been inscribed in the history of interpretation instead as its overt opponent, endorsing — in a widely attested route of protest — Paul's argumentation in Romans 9-11. So although we might not know from these texts how Calvin actually resolves the tensions between the two soteriologies in Paul, we would have few doubts about where he actually stood.

In view of the foregoing, it would seem that Calvin — like Luther — cannot be cited unequivocally in support of a conditional view of soteriology in terms of the justification of the individual. His strong commitment to election is in direct contradiction to that model (irrespective of what he says elsewhere), *and this contradiction is grounded primarily on Pauline texts.*

We turn now to a brief characterization of the third main countervailing theme vis-à-vis Justification in *The Institutes* — a soteriology conceived in terms of an unconditional regeneration by the Holy Spirit.

(3) *The Life of the Christian (Book 3).* Just as Calvin often describes human depravity as a prelude to salvation, he repeatedly intimates the corresponding unconditional regeneration of humanity by the Spirit — and at times the latter seems to ground the former.[67] At the outset of his extended discussion of the Christian life in book 3 (see *CI* 3.1-10; 1:462–2:35), Calvin states:

> [W]e are said to be ingrafted into him and clothed with him, all which he possesses being, as I have said, nothing to us until we become one with him. And although it is true that we obtain this by faith, yet since we see that all do not indiscriminately embrace the offer of Christ which is made by the gospel, the very nature of the case teaches us to ascend higher, and inquire into the secret efficacy of the Spirit, to which it is owing that we enjoy Christ and all his blessings. . . . The whole comes to this, that the Holy Spirit is the bond by which Christ effectually binds us to himself. (*CI* 3.1.1; 1:463)

This is in effect an alternative soteriological principle to Justification — as Calvin intimates. Its dynamic is not grounded in individuals' ratiocinations but in the divine persons — Christ, God the Father, and the Spirit himself. Moreover, Christians are clearly ontologically affected by salvation, as the use of concrete metaphors of connection suggests. They are changed by this process, and this again is in important contrast to the legal fictions of Justification and its ongoing experience of transgression (which leads thereby to a constant grasping of faith but does not assist with respect to ethics). Indeed, at this point Calvin explicitly subordinates faith to the working of the Spirit:

> [F]aith is his principal work. . . . [It is] a supernatural gift, that those who would otherwise remain in unbelief receive Christ by faith. . . . [The] Holy Spirit . . . is the internal teacher, by whose agency the promise of salvation, which would otherwise only strike the air or our ears, penetrates into our minds. . . . [F]aith itself is produced only by the Spirit . . . so that he himself may be properly termed the key by which the treasures of the heavenly kingdom are unlocked, and his illumination, the eye of the mind by which we are enabled to see. (*CI* 3.1.4; 1:465-66)

It is interesting to note the way this definition of faith is linked to Calvin's conviction that human nature unassisted by the Spirit is too darkened to respond to God positively. Divine regeneration rather than human appropriation is the necessary concomitant of human depravity.[68] And Calvin effectively pauses here in his account to consider how his developing soteriological commitment to divine regeneration affects the question of salvific criteria — an analysis that should prove of great interest to us.

In these chapters Calvin analyzes the content of the various criteria suggested for salvation, focusing especially on the late medieval requirements that could be highly conditional — repentance, comprising contrition, confession, and satisfaction. His angle of engagement here is very significant. Calvin argues throughout essentially that, soberly considered, people cannot fulfill these criteria, whatever they are. Therefore, unless unending despair is to result, God must intervene more directly in soteriology. *But Calvin begins this discussion with an analysis of the cardinal Protestant principle of faith (CI 3.2; 1:467-507); hence, his negative case subsumes faith within it.*

In a little more detail: Calvin is initially conscious of the need for clear information about God in Christ that, although selective, is preferably unwavering. But faced with human realities, he appeals (once again) to the work of the Spirit:

> [T]he human mind, when blinded and darkened, is very far from being able to rise to a proper knowledge of the divine will; nor can the heart, fluctuating with perpetual doubt, rest secure in such knowledge. Hence, in order that the word of God may gain full credit, the mind must be enlightened, and the heart confirmed, from some other quarter. We shall now have a full definition of faith if we say that it is a firm and sure knowledge of the divine favour toward us, founded on the truth of a free promise in Christ, and revealed to our minds, and sealed on our hearts, by the Holy Spirit. (*CI* 3.2.7; 1:475)

This connection with the Spirit produces an affectionate dimension in faith (*CI* 3.2.8; 1:476). Calvin goes on to make some further interesting observations. Not only must faith exceed the assurance and fidelity normally inherent in human actions, but it must grasp the incomprehensible, a knowledge that "far surpasses understanding" (*CI* 3.2.14; 1:482, in dependence on Eph. 3:18, 19), and the assistance of the Spirit is therefore additionally required. Calvin now begins to address the Christian condition, which he sees as beset by human weakness. Here there is a need for constancy and not merely for understanding. Hence, the same argument applies, if not more so:

> So deeply rooted in our hearts is unbelief, so prone are we to it, that while all confess with the lips that God is faithful, no man ever believes it without an arduous struggle. Especially when brought to the test, we by our wavering betray the vice which lurked within. Nor is it without cause that the Holy Spirit bears such distinguished testimony to the authority of God, in order that it may cure the disease of which I have spoken, and induce us to give full credit to the divine promises. (*CI* 3.2.15; 1:482)

So at this point faith elides into confidence, or πληροφορία (*CI* 3.2.15; 1:483; see also 3.2.16; 1:484), although Calvin hastens also to discuss anxiety (et cetera) at length: "there is nothing inconsistent in believers being afraid, and at the same time possessing secure consolation as they alternately behold their own vanity, and direct their thoughts to the truth of God" (*CI* 3.2.23; 1:489). Shortly after this the argument becomes explicitly unconditional:

> [T]his promise must be gratuitous; for a conditional promise, which throws us back upon our works, promises life only in so far as we find it existing in ourselves. Therefore, if we would not have faith to waver and tremble, we must support it with the promise of salvation, which is offered by the Lord spontaneously and freely, from a regard to our misery, rather than our worth. (*CI* 3.2.29; 1:494)

In short, the dullness of the human mind, the difficulty of the material believed, *and* the need for an underlying unwavering security all prompt Calvin to affirm the primacy of the work of the Holy Spirit in relation to faith (see *CI* 3.2.33; 1:498-99). Moreover, it is the

Spirit's activity within faith that allows a smooth transition to the ingrafting of the Christian into Christ as well, so that regeneration may proceed (*CI* 3.2.35; 1:501).

The same argument is then rehearsed with respect to repentance and penitence in chapters 3 and 4. These requirements are difficult, and unredeemed human nature must despair of ever fulfilling them. The correct position for such ordinances is therefore *after* conversion, where, assisted by the Spirit, better attempts can be made and overwhelming anxiety avoided.[69] (Calvin also urges their simplification.)[70]

This sustained scrutiny of conditionality by Calvin is extremely suggestive, especially since it is pursued from a number of angles. Each condition is unpacked critically, usually revealing a far more demanding criterion than is otherwise appreciated. This difficulty is then exacerbated by a pessimistic anthropology, retained through the Christian state where that is considered apart from pneumatology. However, correctly understood, pneumatology allows all these problems to be addressed, including a smooth transition to ethical concerns. Divine regeneration, in some connection with a fully efficacious atonement, speaks to both non-Christian and Christian incapacity and in relation to any particular demands; apart from these, humanity is lost, trapped, and despairing.

Calvin then analyzes the Christian condition further — notably, its need for perseverance, self-denial, and costly obedience, and this basic focus again seems quite consistent. An unconditional model need be little concerned with the pre-Christian state but will likely be more concerned with the Christian's ongoing response to the divine intervention once it has taken place. Moreover, Calvin reads this situation not merely pneumatologically but christocentrically. Viewed broadly, then, it would seem that in the first half of book 3 Calvin is less concerned with soteriological conditionality — which he views as inherently problematic if not futile — than with Christian responsiveness, which he views as difficult and so analyzes in relation to the work of the Spirit and of Christ. (And in so doing he really provides all the argumentative and theological resources necessary for a thorough critical scrutiny of Justification!)

Viewed as a whole then, Calvin's support for Justification theory within *The Institutes* is highly problematic. Three themes in particular seem to generate quite astonishing theological tensions with that theory — commitments to depravity, to election, and to Christian regeneration by the Spirit.

While it is apparent from this basic survey of Luther and Calvin that their endorsements of the individualist, conditional, and contractual elements within Justification are at times clear, so too their commitments to this model, viewed as a whole, are rather more ambiguous. Indeed, various elements in their writings — and often in their leading texts — directly contradict some of the model's most important principles. It is therefore simply not accurate to claim their unequivocal support for the Justification discourse (at least, not without a complex biographical case that somehow subordinates this countervailing evidence, and I know of nothing approaching this, especially not for Calvin[71]). The support of Luther and Calvin for the Justification discourse can therefore only be described as mixed if not decidedly ambivalent.

3.3. Subsequent Protestantism

That the presence of the foregoing tensions in the writings of the Reformers is no chimera is amply attested by the subsequent history of Protestantism, especially in theological terms. Protestantism almost immediately experienced a series of sharp internal debates, often pitting one of these motifs against another. Two features of this history are worth noting briefly.

First, as David Steinmetz suggests, brief considerations of twenty different "lesser" Reformers from (broadly speaking) four different ecclesial traditions — Catholic, Lutheran, Reformed, and Radical — suggest only the diversity of the Protestant chapter in European history. "The Reformation was never monochromatic . . . [but] polychromatic."[72] So here, once again — that is, as in part one, chapters four and five, in relation to Judaism and conversion respectively — a detailed consideration of the untidy empirical realities contradicts the monolithic explanatory expectations of Justification theory awkwardly.

But, second — and to make matters worse — many of these subsequent debates juxtaposed Justification against election, the latter a motif that Calvin had emphasized in particular, although it was often combined in discussion with an emphasis on the depravity of human nature. In other words, Protestantism began to struggle immediately with some of the key tensions that we have already seen Justification theory generates in relation to Paul immediately.[73] Broadly speaking, the various historical traditions of Protestantism solved many of these problems essentially politically, by producing creedal statements that were fundamentally synergist — the English confessions in the Westminster tradition being a good example.[74] Hence, the underlying interpretative issues, both exegetical and theological, were never really resolved. However, Protestantism was at least able to move forward in practical terms (and there were, after all, a number of pressing issues to address). The important point for our purposes is to mark that the tensions within the leading Reformers generated in part by their commitments to both Justification and countervailing theological motifs were overtly noted by their subsequent traditions, while they also remained, at least to a degree, conceptually unresolved.

With the Justification discourse's relationship to Protestantism appropriately nuanced, we can turn now to consider the question of its possible church-historical antecedents — and here, perhaps not surprisingly, a similarly ambivalent situation becomes evident.

§4. Augustine and the Pre-Reformation Period

Krister Stendahl famously accused the "Lutheran" reading of Paul of borrowing not merely from anachronistic modern Freudian commitments but of retrieving an introspective Augustinian approach as well, leading to persistent assertions about Augustine within the broader discussion. Building on the well-known appeals by many of the Reformers to Augustine, Stendahl posited an introspective interpretative axis running from Augustine through Luther into particularly neurotic aspects of modernity, an axis that he accused of inappropriate projection in relation to Paul. But we must now assess the cogency of this claim. And although we may be grateful to Stendahl for introducing the important interpretative dimension of church history into the general debate, I suggest that his further assertions here in terms of an introspective axis have at times been unhelpful.

We have seen at some length that any claims that Justification is overtly Protestant or indeed strictly Lutheran (in the sense of conforming to Luther himself) are greatly oversimplified. There is a measure of truth but an equal measure of untruth and hence a deceptive quality within such assertions. Luther and the other Reformers (especially Calvin) are by no means reducible to Justification theory, although at times they do endorse it. We have also seen that it is not merely, or perhaps even primarily, a concern with introspection that is critical.[75] And when we come to the question of Augustine — and thereby raise the possibility of Justification's pre-Reformational historical pedigree — Stendahl's implications must again be carefully recalibrated.

Augustine (354-430 CE) was a brilliant and in many ways admirably honest thinker. He was also a classic instance of what one might call a developmental mind; Augustine constantly explored issues, new as well as old, from various angles, generating modified if not radically revised opinions as a result. His first major transition was his conversion from paganism to Christianity — the only "real" conversion among our central figures.[76] It took place toward the end of August in 386 CE, when Augustine was thirty-two, apparently the culmination of a long and twisting journey. En route, Augustine had moved from Manichaeanism to the very different system of neo-Platonism, and this pattern of intellectual discovery and movement continued well into if not throughout his Christian life.[77] Augustine was ordained — rather against his own inclinations — in 391 CE, from which point he began to engage more extensively with the Scriptures, and with the writings of Paul in particular. He was immediately involved in ecclesial polemics — in a difficult dispute with a North African reform movement, Donatism, and also against his former allegiance, Manichaeanism. Much use of neo-Platonic categories is evident in his rhetoric at this time. Around 396 CE another particularly important intellectual watershed seems to have occurred, marked by a letter to his old guide, Simplician.[78] From this moment (at least) Augustine seems to have begun to enunciate a more pessimistic view of human nature that ultimately developed into a highly sophisticated account of human incapacity.[79] This bleaker view of human nature, combined with a corresponding view of salvation in terms of divine initiative and election, eventually yielded a soteriology that was quite predestinarian: Augustine became an advocate of radical grace. Indeed, Augustine's developing anthropological pessimism, complemented by a God of overwhelming grace, overshadowed his immensely — and justly — famous *Confessions,* composed in 397-98 CE, and ultimately informed his *pièce de la resistance, The City of God,* composed in 413-26 CE. This viewpoint was also mobilized in his campaign against Pelagianism from 411 CE, in almost direct contrast to his early polemics (as Pelagius himself pointed out). It was the Pelagian controversy, prolonged through an extended engagement into Augustine's later years with the Pelagian *enfant terrible,* Julian of Eclanum, that really established Augustine's international reputation.

With these general observations in mind, we can now ask whether Stendahl's assertion of a significant causal relationship between Augustine and the later "Lutheran" reading still holds — as Luther's reasonably frequent citation of Augustine might suggest. I would caution, however, that any claims made in relation to Augustine must be qualified, just as I have argued is the case for Luther and Calvin. Moreover, precisely in view of Augustine's highly developmental intellectual biography, simple generalizations about his position on almost anything are deceptive. The key issues for our present purposes are illumined principally in relation to his developing views on the nature and extent of human free will, views that pivoted around his intellectual watershed in 396 CE. Hence, it will be important to locate any claim of support from Augustine in terms of his biography — in particular, to denote whether the early or the late Augustine (i.e., pre- or post-396 CE) is in play.[80]

Human capacity and divine election tend to play correlative roles in Augustine's thinking on the question of human freedom, along with prospective, foundationalist versus retrospective purviews. Where Augustine is optimistic about human capacity, commitments to a prospective (ergo foundationalist) theological structure — to some progression toward salvation, or *ordo salutis* — are in evidence. However, when he abandons all effective human capacity prior to the promptings of grace, any concomitant commitments to a prospective theological schema and a soteriological progression tend to evaporate.

As we have already noted, this development in Augustine's thinking seems to coincide with his Pauline exegesis. After his ordination, Augustine began to engage with the Scriptures, and especially with Paul (like many church leaders during the 390s). Over the period 394-96 CE, a gradual shift occurred from a conditional to a completely unconditional understanding of grace. Before this shift, Augustine can be viewed as a sympathetic forebear of Justification theory (although not, I would argue, as a precise prototype); after this shift he can only be viewed as highly problematic. The late, unconditional Augustine would have attacked Justification theory for being (semi-)Pelagian.

Two of Augustine's works directly concerned with Romans were composed just prior to his shift in 396 CE — his *Propositions from the Epistle to the Romans* and *Unfinished Commentary on the Epistle to the Romans.*[81] It is therefore especially significant that they do not evidence a complete soteriological schema. Like all soteriologies that presuppose human capacity or free will, they do assume a progression of sorts — an *ordo salutis.* Augustine articulates a four-stage schema in *Propositions* in theses 13-18 (out of a list ultimately of eighty-four): "prior to the Law; under the Law; under grace; and in peace" (4-5). The crucial transition, from stage two to stage three, is always spoken of here in terms of grace, "gratia," with no mention of faith. Faith is introduced in thesis 19, citing Romans 3:31 (6-7), and elaborated on briefly in relation to Abraham and Romans 4:1-23 (theses 20-25, 6-9), but plays a relatively minor role throughout the theses. Stage four, "in peace," is eschatological. It is also worth noting that Augustine pays no attention to Romans 1:16-17 and 3:21-26! The basic notion of justification, variously defined, is more prominent in his *Unfinished Commentary,* occurring twice in section 1.1, as well as in 8.6 and 10.13 (52-53, 62-63, 64-65).[82] But Augustine concludes the opening section by speaking of justification by "the discipline of humility," and there is no full development of the notion. (The commentary rapidly collapses under the weight of its own expectations; it only reaches 1:7 in Paul's text.) Babcock suggests that the exegesis of Romans 7:24-25 is an especially important indicator of the shift in Augustine's thinking that took place from this point onward.[83] The one earlier work that engages with Paul's texts is *The Way of Life of the Catholic Church* (388 CE).[84]

It is not entirely fair, however, to claim even that the early Augustine is a pristine advocate of Justification theory. Some of his statements are close to the full schema and, given strong convictions about the later appearance of the theory and its centrality to Paul, are understandably cited in its support. Nevertheless, I would suggest that this basic claim is incorrect; Justification really requires a *full* and *reasonably sustained* articulation if its attribution is to be granted — something the early Augustine does not provide.[85] But he is certainly an authentic *antecedent* of Justification theory in his commitment to a prospective salvific progression from an experience of the law to grace, the crucial transition being made by certain human actions (faith, humility, et cetera). Indeed, in this respect Augustine is perhaps broadly representative of many commentators and theologians within the Western church who anticipated Justification theory (arguably including Pelagius!).[86]

However, the anti-Pelagian Augustine, developing from 396 CE — if not earlier — and quite overt from 411 onward, is really one further witness directly against Justification in his dual emphases on human depravity and divine election. Indeed, arguably, although the Reformers' use of Augustine was frequent, they tended to use this anti-Pelagian material. Hence, the connections between Augustine and the Reformers (especially Luther and Calvin), although real, can be highly problematic for the endorsement of Justification. And the claim that Augustine directly anticipates the latter approach in this precise relation is really the antithesis of the truth. Like significant parts of Luther and much of Calvin, the anti-Pelagian Augustine contradicts the premises of Justification directly.[87]

Two further judgments can be added to this general set of conclusions:

1. The charge of tortured "introspection," made originally by Stendahl and echoed in more recent debate by many others, should be heavily qualified if not abandoned, and on two substantial grounds.

Introspection is present in both the early and the late Augustine, *but it functions theologically in completely different ways within those two settings.* We have already seen that introspection functions in a specific fashion within Justification theory (although it does function there, and Stendahl was quite right to point to that). But Justification theory relies heavily if not primarily on several other axioms in addition to "introspection." Hence, on the one hand, a criticism merely in terms of introspection risks missing the actual problem that underlies many of Stendahl's concerns with Paul's ostensible commitment to Justification. On the other hand, it risks confusing Paul's commitment to this model with his commitment to an alternative schema that is constructed in a fundamentally different fashion — the retrospective and unconditional schema we have identified in Romans 5–8, which uses introspection in an entirely different way. The case affirming the anachronistic use of introspection would have to be very strong in order to eliminate both soteriological schemas at one blow, while the significant differences within the schemas make it difficult to believe that the same argument would apply to both.

For these reasons, then, it seems that any charge of introspection per se must now be deployed much more cautiously in relation to the interpretation of Paul. Failing a comprehensive case that all such thinking prior to Augustine is an overt anachronism, it must be redeployed within our contractual theory and thereby focused more precisely, at which point this form of introspection — being rather mild and rational — does *not* seem anachronistic. Its problems are more philosophical (i.e., it does not seem capable of drawing the conclusions that it is supposed to draw within the pre-Christian human condition, nor are those conclusions evident within the cosmos). The searing, incapacitated, somewhat tortured introspection that troubled Stendahl is a more overt component within our alternative schema, being attested most clearly in Paul by Romans 7. Presumably, then, that is where the anachronistic charge must be fought out. It seems that only certain confusions — of little relevance — will be lost if we desist from accusations of "introspection" in the present relation.[88] Hence, it will probably be wise to do so.

2. The assumption that Augustine's *Confessions* is a straightforward account of his journey to salvation, challenged now by much scholarly work, should probably be abandoned.[89] This suggestion is reinforced by social scientific observations that converts seldom give an unmediated and accurate account of their actual conversions; such accounts tend to be learned narratives shaped as much by present community perceptions and needs as by what actually happened. Hence, insofar as it reproduces the progressions of Justification theory, *Confessions* may not necessarily be reliably claimed as empirical validation. But *Confessions* raises two further problems for Justification theory.

First, even as a theological account of conversion, it *contradicts* the account of Justification theory. Augustine's account of his 386 CE conversion in *Confessions* — written in 397 — is overtly unconditional. It is the gripping story of how the grace of God overcomes an incapacitated human being. Hence, it is as if Augustine is rewriting the narrative of his conversion in the light of the shift to theological unconditionality he has just made, at least in part on exegetical grounds. And this seems to be corroborated by the reflections on Genesis with which it concludes.[90]

Second, if *Confessions* is sifted with a more social-scientific eye, it arguably provides reasonably good evidence of the basic plausibility of network theory. Clearly, Augustine was not writing in order to endorse network theory. Hence, it seems significant that his account reveals that he was converted in part — apparently like so many Christians in the Roman Empire — through the influence of his pious mother, not to mention the complementary influence of high-status friends and acquaintances (such as Ambrose, whom he knew personally).

So Augustine, like Luther and Calvin, can be deployed on both sides of this question. The early, rather optimistic, and philosophically influenced Augustine can be seen to endorse Justification's anthropology, although not its distinctively individualist soteriological developments. The late Augustine, however, is a direct critic of some of that schema's most important assumptions. And, in sum, Justification is Augustinian only in a heavily qualified sense. The theory is in fact closer to Pelagius, as well as to Tertullian (at least, it shares a strong family resemblance with the latter figures because of their emphases on human capacity). It is fair then to claim that the early Augustine — who should also be characterized as neo-Platonic and even semi-Pelagian — supports Justification's initial premises, but the later or mature Augustine, evident from at least 396 CE onward, certainly does not, and would doubtless be appalled at any such suggestion! Similarly, any assertions of Augustinian "introspection" are overly vague and often misdirected. More precision and caution are in order. Further, Augustine continues to reinforce our growing suspicions in relation to any depiction of conversion; arguing from theology to sociological reality is difficult. And even *as* theology, Augustine's famous *Confessions* are deeply problematic for Justification theory. They are far closer to the alternative soteriological schema rooted in Romans 5–8 than to Justification. Hence, it would seem that Stendahl has been misleading in this relation. Augustine is largely on the critical side of the debate (i.e., Stendahl's side). He is part of the solution far more than he is part of the problem.

Similarly, Luther and Calvin are only ambiguously associated with Justification theory. *Much in their writings is in acute tension with that model's presuppositions* and arguably adumbrates an alternative soteriology — one closer to the mature Augustine as well as to various alternative biblical emphases. That these figures describe and defend Justification at times is not being denied. *But they are by no means reducible to this position*, as perhaps more plausibly Melanchthon is, as well as other lesser Reformers.

Hence, it is an important oversimplification — i.e. a distortion — to speak of "the Lutheran reading of Paul," thereby implying any univocity or its equivalent in Luther's or his tradition's historical attestations. We have consequently tended to speak throughout this treatment of "Justification theory" and the "Justification discourse," largely in anticipation of this discovery. The Justification discourse now stands over against the unconditional, christocentric, or elective Luther or Calvin, who suggest for much of the time a radically different understanding of Paul's gospel and consequently may imply a different construal of his Justification texts as well — something we will make full use of eventually. (Alternatively, they may imply a different estimate of their theological importance.) This does not foreclose the relevance of the church-historical dimension to our overarching discussion; Luther and his great interpretative contemporaries and forebears are not to be summarily dismissed from further consideration. But their exegetical concerns will take their place alongside those of others at the appropriate moment, enjoying no significant inherent authority simply because of their origin. These figures are capable of construing the Pauline texts as skillfully — or as woodenly — as the next reader.

But in reaching these conclusions we have yet to exhaust all the historical factors that may be playing upon the unselfconscious reader. We have considered here merely the overt church-historical influences. A great deal more could be involved in this general relation than only those figures that have been virtuous enough — or fortunate enough — actually to be named.[91] It is to the consideration of these silent factors — the possible *unnamed* but highly powerful diachronic influences operating within the Justification discourse — that we now turn.

CHAPTER NINE

Dangers — The Modern European Pedigree

§1. Preamble

In this chapter we begin to explore the peculiarly resonant relationship between the Justification discourse and modernity. Although the theory's Reformational and pre-Reformational lineage is usually presented as central — and it is important — I suggest that Justification's affinities with various aspects of modernity are in fact far stronger and more significant. Indeed, here we move from distortions — that is, from partial misrepresentations and exaggerations of the paradigm's historical pedigree — to dangers. There is a pervasive nexus of reinforcement running between the interpretation of Paul in terms of Justification and European modernity, one potentially activated in a whole variety of ways, and with potentially sinister consequences. And arguably, by hiding behind its ostensible church-historical pedigree, this underlying set of connections that is far less reputable in theological terms has insinuated itself into the interpretation of Paul.

In our detailed investigation we will consider first of all, in rather abstract terms, how Justification theory can function paradigmatically; that is the point at which this particular interpretative dimension within the discourse tends to emerge with special force. We will then trace the paradigm's prevalence in both conservative and liberal theological traditions to an underlying common affinity with many of the key assumptions of modern philosophical individualism. Here we will briefly consider the programs of certain especially indicative figures such as Immanuel Kant, Friedrich Schleiermacher, and Rudolf Bultmann, along with those of more popular conservative icons such as Billy Graham. The slightly frightening point of this analysis is to elucidate their similarities rather than their differences. Following the tracing of these affinities we will track the underlying liberal intellectual tradition further into its extremely important political, ideological, and cultural developments, where John Locke will emerge as especially significant. This further stage of investigation will reveal a set of strong affinities between Justification theory and the modern liberal *political* project — an important element within the discourse's history that is generally overlooked. The investigation will raise in turn the question of a relationship between Justification and capitalism, overlapping here with a standard question within sociological analysis since Weber's classic treatment of the relationship between Protestantism and capitalism. Following these investigations it will be apparent that the historical pedigree of the discourse is far more complex, and potentially rather more troubling, than the Justification discourse itself would have us believe. It is a distinctly *modern* discourse that enjoys a subtle but extensive network of reinforcements from post-European culture.

My intention throughout is not to supply a definitive account of Justification theory's perilous journey from the sixteenth century to the twenty-first, as desirable in many respects as that would be. Such a task is simply too large for the present study. I do hope, however, to supply strategically indicative evidence in support of certain key realizations — that the relationships between Justification and various aspects of modernity, both intellectual and concretely social, are real. Those relationships, which I speak of frequently in what follows as "affinities," ultimately have important hermeneutical implications for the discourse as a whole. They may encourage modern readers who share them to find the discourse in the ancient texts produced by Paul without realizing that in so doing they are shaping the texts' interpretation in their own image. But besides a potentially distorting role within interpretation, these affinities also reorient our understanding of the discourse's pedigree. Justification is not merely a Reformational construct, or even primarily a church-historical construct. It is these things, but it is much more: it is a discourse that has developed in an intimate relationship with modernity (meaning by this post-European, liberal, capitalist modernity). No accurate account of the discourse can overlook this potent history, because, among other things, it reaches out to include most of the current readers of Paul. Hence, readers who endorse the discourse are in large part endorsing certain aspects of themselves and their distinctively modern setting, and such readers will be naturally inclined to undertake interpretative operations in the opposite direction as well, endorsing readings of Paul under the impress of their prior modern commitments. In this way a silent but vicious interpretative circle will be set up — and its strength will be roughly equivalent to the commitments of its protagonists to their modern locations.[1]

§2. Justification as Paradigm

We begin our detailed analysis by considering Justification in a somewhat abstract sense, building our case from its all-important theoretical dimension. The theory of Justification gives explanations for an entire series of significant Christian concerns, prompting those persuaded by its claims to install it as an important and even a primary explanatory structure, that is, as a paradigm. This in turn allows the construal to lay claim to complete centrality within Paul, if not the canon as a whole.

Justification plausibly addresses eleven issues or sets of issues.

(1) Salvation

The model speaks to various aspects of the whole notion of salvation. It supplies an apparently effective strategy for evangelism, which tends to be a central emphasis. It describes what individuals must do in order to be saved (and, in the same breath, what they must do to stay saved), as well as — most importantly — why they should choose to be saved. Indeed, it can exert a near-overwhelming pressure on people positioned in the pre-Christian condition, driving them toward the model's climactic moment — conversion (defining this in a particular way).

(2) Truth

In so doing, the model lays claim to the objective truth of certain principles. And although we may question the theological value and philosophical cogency of these principles, the allure of apparently impartial, universal objectivity is quite powerful. The Justification model, with its declarations of Good and Evil, claims to be true for everyone, and demonstrably so.

(3) Civil Society

Implicit in this claim, as we have already seen, is the endorsement of government and codified ethics, along with their coercive enforcement if that proves necessary. The state is based on justice, and its retributive role is not challenged. At bottom, the universe, along with any political regulation of human society, possesses a divine ethical and legal order. This set of implications will be discussed in more detail shortly; here it suffices to observe that the model provides a binding account of civil society (while church attendance, conversely, is now fundamentally voluntarist!). The model is thus potentially quite conservative politically.

Intrinsic to the basic politico-ethical framework, and reinforced by the gospel's voluntarism, is the notion of contract. The principal of agreement by consent on the basis of stipulated criteria creates a potentially anti-tyrannical function for the model, although this would be a rather modern regulation of political reality.

(4) Theodicy

A powerful theodicy accompanies the model's endorsement of legitimate punishment. Justification explains evil and justifies hell. Underlying the explanations of evil and its consequences are assumptions concerning human free will and responsibility. Defenses of hell's existence and legitimacy therefore tend to function as leitmotifs for the model as a whole, since these are consistent with God's justice and are largely necessitated by that premise. Indeed, Justification is committed to the death penalty, in the sense of its legitimacy and its essential fairness; the appropriate retribution for evil is death.

(5) Christ's Death

Accordingly, the model gives a dramatic account of the function of Christ — in particular, his death — which is tied consistently to God's omnipotence and justice. The favored metaphors here are usually sacrificial, but these necessarily involve a penal meaning. Christ's "positive" work may also be in view, although this is not emphasized within much modern interpretation. (It is arguable just how necessary it is in theoretical terms.) Nevertheless, Christ has a critical mediatory role, and in some reasonably direct relation to the Christian. And this work also allows God to be spoken of as loving, generous, and gracious — although only in suitably defined terms — thereby creating important connections with other significant biblical themes. The divine generosity is particularly apparent when it stands over against the retributive part of God's personality. Instead of a very great punishment there is a very great forgiveness.

(6) Conscience and Performance

Justification assuages the genuinely afflicted or terrified conscience. For those already convinced of the existence of an omnipotent and sternly just God, and of their own repeated transgression or innate sinfulness, Justification's progressions should provide a degree of rest from anxiety — something Luther and Calvin both evidence and emphasize. Justified Christians, provided that they remain confident of their fulfillment of the human conditions of justification, should be able to leave the complaints of conscience behind.

In close relation to this, Justification contains a critical account of activity, or "performance," and there is almost certainly a useful psychological dimension here. Those addicted to performance (and it is an especially prominent issue in certain strata of modern society — perhaps especially in the middle class, with its frequently anxious emphasis on educational achievement) can have their value and destiny affirmed independently of, and in a sense beyond, that activity. Such affirmation may supply a sense of relief or liberation, simultaneously delivering a critical and even countercultural agenda to those so convinced — powerful attractions for individuals in certain mental states.[2] Note that the point here is not so much the exact theological and rational mapping of the theory's progressions as the broader characterization of the various states and the stark transition between them from "performance" to "faith [or some such] *alone*," the latter being a much easier religious mode. (Tensions with point three may become noticeable in this relation in due course.)

(7) Judaism

The Justification model offers a relatively simple explanation for why the first Christians apparently left the Jewish law behind and why they got into so much conflict over the issue, both internally and externally. (In external terms, it seems that many Jews resisted the movement into the second, salvific phase, recapitulating instead the "loop of foolishness.") It offers parallel explanations of the relationship between the Testaments and between Judaism and Christianity, that is, of law versus gospel (the former arguably interwoven with promise, the latter with fulfillment).

Hence, the model seems to explain why Christianity is *not* Judaism, as well as (perhaps) why many Jews did not become Christians and so the church is not congruent with Israel. Of course there is a harsh side to this explanation. But at least it supplies clear and cogent accounts for these critical points of development and transition that were so often apparently accompanied by conflict.

(8) Alternative Programs

The model supplies a powerful critique of alternative religious programs that do not share its definition of salvation. Essentially, occupants of *any* tradition will necessarily share the same position as recalcitrant Jews if they fail to convert. As we have already seen, the model inexorably conforms all extra-Christian reality to its own opening premises, then runs that freshly reconfigured reality through its well-trodden rational progressions to the appropriate conclusions. As a result, it is *intrinsically combative,* labeling any alternative programs as hypocritical and so on if they prove recalcitrant. Indeed, in a very real sense *the model reforms everything it encounters.* And this function of constant challenge and revision arguably creates further links with New Testament texts, most notably with some of Jesus' critical teaching.[3]

The innate critique generated by Justification theory is especially effective in an ongoing fashion against tradition and bureaucracy. Any demands issuing from those loci are subject to the scathing condemnation of attempted justification through works. The individual's faith alone ultimately serves to save; *neither tradition nor institution can do so.* Presumably, this critique is especially significant in relation to ecclesial traditions, but it could be focused on any traditional or institutionalized claims (including, presumably, traditional Reformation claims!).

(9) Progress and Growth

One further implication of this rolling critique is that the model is innately committed to growth. It aggrandizes. This means that in all likelihood the model's proponents will increase in demographic terms (even if their model does not always help them convert people directly). Justification thus presumably has an innate affinity with cultures of progress and growth.

(10) Universality

A related point is that the model is extremely portable in historical and cultural terms. Somewhat paradoxically, the fixed and universal nature of its opening premises allows it to address particular individuals from any time or culture and attempt to propel them through the same rational progressions — clearly an advantage in prosecuting point one noted earlier (although again arguably creating certain disadvantages[4]).

(11) Scripture

At all these points Justification theory claims to derive directly from the Scriptures — although most clearly from certain parts, here of Paul — and thereby affirms their fundamental importance as well. The model is based on the Bible and arises out of the Bible, merely by way of fair and accurate exegesis, thereby according both the Scriptures and exegesis fundamental roles in subsequent Christian behaviour.

Thus, Justification theory provides plausible explanations for an entire series of fundamental theological concerns, as well as some beyond the merely theological. It is reasonably coherent, well integrated, and relatively simple, grounded in assumptions with obvious analogies with key aspects of human society. Hence, Justification can plausibly serve as the nucleus for a complete theological program. It is small wonder that many have been persuaded by it. We turn now to consider its conservative advocates.

§3. Justification as a Widespread Conservative Theological Paradigm

It is well beyond the scope of this study to survey exhaustively the presence of the Justification discourse within Christianity from the Reformation to the present day.[5] But few would dispute its current widespread distribution within conservative Christian circles.[6] We can begin a representative sampling in support of this claim by noting some suggestive etymological indicators.

The signifier "the gospel" and the closely related "Christian," important and much-used terms, tend to receive considerable stylistic variation.[7] The following cannot be demonstrated here exhaustively but probably few would deny that in European and post-European church traditions the most common alternatives for "the gospel" and "Christian" are "the faith" and "believer." This usage is simply ubiquitous. Hence, the following equations are self-evident to many.

$$\text{the gospel} = \text{the faith}$$
$$\text{Christian(s)} = \text{Believer(s)}$$

But every occurrence of these equations is evidence that Justification theory has achieved the status of a paradigm. To assume that the center of the gospel is "faith" is to assume that this is the criterion of the new salvific contract; indeed, merely to speak of "faith" is to mobilize that entire soteriological arrangement paradigmatically. Moreover, the most important thing about Christians is now their "belief," namely, their fulfillment of that criterion. Hence, Justification is endorsed by every such utterance.

In exegetical terms the equation of "the gospel" with "the faith" is dependent (perhaps!) on one Pauline text, Galatians 1:23, read of course in terms of Justification.[8] It is true that "believers" is a reasonably frequent denotation of Christians in Paul's texts, because the latter name was not yet widespread or perhaps even coined, occurring in the New Testament only three times and never in Paul.[9] But other denotations are considerably more common in Paul, namely, ἅγιοι, which is usually translated a little awkwardly as "the saints," and, even more commonly, ἀδελφοί, "brothers" (although this is now perhaps more appropriately translated gender inclusively). These two terms enjoy an overwhelming statistical superiority over "believers."[10] So why has the latter passed into common Christian parlance as the largely ubiquitous verbal equivalent for "Christians"? Almost certainly, I would assert, because of the pressure exerted by the Justification paradigm. The word "believers" points to the essential characteristic of converts.

Some rapid surveys may further confirm these essentially obvious claims. In the first instance, two soundings into conservative Christianity — although of a more "mainstream" temperament — will prove indicative.

(1) Billy Graham

Perhaps the most famous conservative evangelist in the modern era in predominantly Western countries (and not a few others) is Billy Graham.[11]

Graham's preaching and publications reflect Justification theory very closely when he discusses soteriology, as seen especially in his book *How to Be Born Again*, first published in 1977.[12] Graham's argument here is structured in three parts, whose titles and content are instructive: "Man's Problem," "God's Answer," and "Man's Response" — that is, discussions of phase one and the two key principles in phase two of the Justification model. Certain chapter titles are equally suggestive, for example, "What Is This Thing Called Sin?" and "The King's Courtroom."

To be fair to Graham, his bestseller is by no means merely an account of Justification theory. It strongly emphasizes what many have dubbed "sanctification," and there is widespread reference to divine agency. But Justification theory is nevertheless reinforced throughout, however inconsistently in terms of surrounding material (and this is not the first time that we have encountered synergism). Indeed, Graham is aware of such disputes and reserves a degree of mystery for the process of being "born again" (preface, iv-v). But he goes on to assert: "However much the theologians may disagree about fine points of doctrine, the central truth of the new birth is clear. . . . Only by God's grace through faith in Christ can this new birth take place" (preface, v).[13]

(2) Campus Crusade for Christ

Campus Crusade for Christ is an international, interdenominational organization for Christian evangelism and discipleship founded in 1951 by Bill Bright. Bright's famous tract, "Have You Heard of the Four Spiritual Laws?" is thought to be the most widely distributed religious pamphlet in history, with more than 2.5 billion printed in some 200 languages since 1956. The soteriology articulated with matchless clarity by this tiny tract basically reflects Justification theory.[14]

Although Law One states that "God LOVES you and offers a wonderful PLAN for your life," that plan is accessed only by the Justification model, as the next three laws and the prayer of conversion clearly attest. Law Two, quoting Romans 3:23 and 6:23 for support, is that "Man is SINFUL and SEPARATED from God. Therefore, he cannot know and experience God's love and plan for his life" — phase one of Justification. The brief discussion here ends with the assurance that "[t]he third law explains the way to bridge this gulf." Quoting Romans 5:8, 1 Corinthians 15:3-6, and John 14:6, Law Three states: "Jesus Christ is God's ONLY provision for man's sin. Through Him you can know and experience God's love and plan for your life" — the first key principle in the second, salvific phase of Justification (the satisfaction of God's justice through Christ's atoning death). However, "[i]t is not enough just to know these three laws." Law Four explains: "We must individually RECEIVE Jesus Christ as Savior and Lord; then we can know and experience God's love and plan for our lives" — the second key principle in the second, saving phase, namely, the appropriation of salvation by faith. This law is glossed by further statements: "We Must Receive Christ"; "We Receive Christ Through Faith," and "We Receive Christ by Personal Invitation" (and these are supported by John 1:12; Eph. 2:8-9; and Rev. 3:20 — as well as, on occasion, by John 3:1-8[15]). Thus, despite its economy, the pamphlet takes time to emphasize that this invitation is more than mere intellectual assent; it is an act of "will" and a relationship of "trust" by individuals.[16]

Justification is clearly the basic model in operation throughout this enormously influential tract. Indeed, one could hardly wish for a crisper account of the theory's dynamics.

These soundings into conservative and mainstream Western Christian culture confirm the impression that Justification theory is in an extremely powerful position. It enjoys a virtual monopoly on the conception of soteriology within these highly motivated and mobilized constituencies. A largely unquestioning legion of supporters is carrying Justification determinedly to a status of global soteriological hegemony, at least within Western-dominated Christian traditions. It would seem that Justification is not *a* paradigm within conservative and mainstream Christianity; it is *the* paradigm.[17]

§4. Justification as a Widespread Liberal Theological Paradigm

It is widely overlooked but ultimately unsurprising that the theological paradigm of Justification is as widespread among theological "liberals" as it is within more conservative traditions — although the mode and manner of its presentation may well differ. A prime example is the enormously influential Rudolf Bultmann. It is important to appreciate immediately that this great figure is not reducible to the Justification paradigm, but its overt presence in much of his work is incontrovertible. This phenomenon is at its clearest in his famous *Theology of the New Testament*.[18] In this elegant treatment Bultmann reduces Pauline theology entirely to a two-stage contractual schema commensurate with Justification: "Man Prior to the Revelation of Faith" (1:190-269) and "Man under Faith" (1:270-352). The first main category is preoccupied with anthropology, and the second arranged in terms of "The Righteousness of God," "Grace," "Faith," and "Freedom" — clearly, themes that further reflect Justification's contractual schema along with its subsequent developments. All the relevant textual data — sometimes in most ingenious ways — is put directly into one of these categories, redefined so as to fit within them, or marginalized. We will not labor the documentation of these points in what follows, since they are widely known and just as widely granted.

The first category in Bultmann's exposition elaborates "man prior to the revelation of faith" largely by tracing Paul's key anthropological terms. And here it is significant that Bultmann stresses humans' will, their individuality, and their ethical nature, although not their inherent relationality or sociality. The universal sense of ethics is then also inextricably bound up with some notion of "law," mediated for most through the key phenomenon of "conscience" (συνείδησις); indeed, Bultmann's view of the role of the law is a classic instance of Justification.[19] Another important dimension in humans is the knowledge of God as Creator and themselves in turn as creatures, although they are sinfully inclined to deny this. Humans' basic state, "in the flesh," is characterized by false "moral and religious activity," and hence by "boasting," a desire to achieve righteousness that is itself fundamentally false, ignoring the appropriate situation of creature before Creator (§23; 1:239, 241,

242). In short, and at times in most ingenious ways, Bultmann articulates in this major subsection the progress of rational individuals to a situation of conviction, although he repeatedly denies the emotional side to this situation. The depiction is "objective" or "real," not merely a state of the heart, so to speak.[20] Humanity outside of or before Christ, asserts Bultmann, consisting of a certain sort of individual, knows God (as Creator), ethics, and law, and rejects these in various ways, despite humanity's possession of an effective will. The situation is bad, and Bultmann's description of it is also clearly quite traditional in most respects.

The forensic dimension is introduced in relation to Paul's use of δικαιο- terminology as Bultmann turns to describe the process of salvation (§§28-31). Bultmann's fundamental view of this terminology is meritocratic or retributive; righteousness is ultimately ethical and is also "the condition for receiving salvation or 'life'" (1:270). He goes on to describe further the classic Protestant view that righteousness is only imputed to the Christian, citing Romans 4:1-25 as the "Scripture proof" of this (§30; 1:280). The theme of reconciliation in Paul is subsumed within this description as well (§31). (Bultmann does sit lightly here, however, to the classic emphasis on atonement terminology.)

In a section entitled "Grace" (§§32-34), Bultmann especially emphasizes that grace — understood as a divine *"deed"* (1:289) — "constantly takes place anew" in the "event" of proclamation. The proclaimer brings the Word of God into the present, while the incarnation is really just a motif of weakness, seen now also in the lives of Paul and other preachers of the word (§33; 1:302).[21] The two sacraments of baptism and Eucharist are also subsumed within this scenario; so, for example, baptism makes the preached word real to the individual in an analogous way (§34). Bultmann seems to concede at this point that Christ's death does achieve a payment for guilt — a forensic cultic metaphor drawn, he asserts, primarily from tradition. (The resurrection, meanwhile, is elaborated in terminology echoing the Gnostics and Redeemer cults, since it had no place in the traditional forensic and cultic thinking [300]).

The obvious further thematic emphasis from this point is therefore "Faith" (§§35-37), which is the *condition* for receiving righteousness (1:316). And although faith is a theme inherited from the Hellenists, Paul gives it special clarity and emphasis. Faith is not a work but a "deed": "a waiver of any accomplishment whatever and thereby . . . radical obedience" (1:317). It involves confession and knowledge rather than remorse and (or) repentance. It is at once hopeful, confident, and insecure, and it results in the receipt of the Spirit (1:330; see Gal. 3:2, 5, 14). And Christians — now primarily believers — are after its exercise "free," at which point Bultmann can move to a discussion of ethics and related matters ("Freedom," §§38-40). The believer is free from sin, the law, and death — although much of this is "dialectic[al] or paradoxical" (1:341; characteristics to which we will return).

In sum, Bultmann's articulation of the soteriological schema of Justification in relation to Paul is both clear and helpful. That schema's emphasis on the appropriation of the gospel in the sense of accepting certain propositions as true (propositions presumably introduced by someone) is quite clear, as is the retributive underpinning of the entire arrangement in relation to divine justice, something that also affects the atonement. The extensive a priori vestibule oriented primarily toward the individual, within whom prior notions of God, divine justice, ethics, and sinfulness circulate, is also very clear. There are certain points where

Bultmann is apparently embarrassed by traditional emphases, and his ability to reduce all of Paul's theological argumentation to the foregoing categories is instructive if a little strained (something we will address in due course), but in essence he masterfully repristinates the model. It is also significant that Bultmann places Paul centrally in his theological characterization of the entire New Testament. So the paradigmatic pretensions of Justification theory have their canonical ambitions realized quite clearly and directly in his program.

There are two phases in Bultmann's elevation of the Justification model from theory to paradigm. First, he argues that Paul is largely reducible to the approach. Then, second, he places Paul in a pivotal position vis-à-vis the rest of New Testament theology.

These arguments need only be noted briefly here; we will examine their cogency in much more detail shortly.

The first set of claims is presented initially in the short preamble to chapter 4, "Preliminary Remarks," then reflected in the structure of Paul's fuller description in chapters 4 and 5 (§§17-40). The second set of claims is presented in §16, "The Historical Position of Paul," which prefaces the entire treatment of the apostle. The two arguments are best treated in this sequence (reversing Bultmann's order).

(i) Bultmann's remarks in the compact preamble to chapter 4 are very important. After some commonplace opening caveats Bultmann goes on to argue more significantly that because Paul is not "speculative," he "deals with God not as He is in Himself but only with God as He is significant for man, for man's responsibility and man's salvation. . . . Every assertion about God is simultaneously an assertion about man and vice versa. For this reason and in this sense Paul's theology is, at the same time, anthropology" (1:190-91). This claim is echoed by the further argument that "since God's relation to the world and man is not regarded by Paul as a cosmic process oscillating in eternally even rhythm, but is regarded as constituted by God's acting in history and by man's reaction to God's doing, therefore every assertion about God speaks of what He does with man and what He demands of him" (1:191). Consequently, and most significantly, "[t]he christology of Paul likewise is governed by this point of view. In it, Paul . . . speaks of him as the one through whom God is working for the salvation of the world and man. Thus, every assertion about Christ is also an assertion about man and vice versa; and Paul's christology is simultaneously soteriology" (1:191). Hence the crucial conclusion: "Therefore, Paul's theology can best be treated as his doctrine of man" (1:191).

Neither the deductive claims in the foregoing (which are really non sequiturs: it does not follow from the denial of "speculation" or of "cosmic system" and a corresponding assertion of incarnation that theology is *therefore* individualizing and anthropological) nor the claims of reversibility should be taken too seriously (these are not really in evidence either here or later on). More significant is the essentially dogmatic claim that theology is fundamentally characterized by anthropology, which is to say *by man in relation to God*, which is further to say by God's "demand" and man's "reaction." The other traditional theological loci are then reduced to this dimension, now suitably defined. So anthropology, Christology, and soteriology are all explicitly equated. And Bultmann's two broad descriptive categories flow from this.

Within these two categories the traditional Justification texts are of course relied on quite heavily. Bultmann tends to introduce competing conceptual material under the rubrics of Gnosticism, redeemer mythology, mystery-religious categories, or primitive magical thinking, thereby effectively marginalizing it as mythological and nonessential. Alternatively, he marginalizes terminology and notions from mere early church "tradition." His final theme, "Freedom" (§§38-40), assimilates large amounts of alternative material to the system that has by now been established. (We will note the presence of other ingenious assimilative techniques shortly.) The point here is not so much to scrutinize the plausibility of Bultmann's description as merely to note its dominance — indeed, even the final, "rag-bag" theme of "freedom" is a traditional Justification topos closely related to anthropology. The result is a neat reduction of Pauline theology to a classical Justification axiom, suitably elaborated, and to its two primary categories.

(ii) And this model has already been asserted by Bultmann, in his preface to the treatment of Paul (§16), to occupy a pivotal role in the early church and the development of the New Testament as a whole. The minimal role of the Jesus tradition in Bultmann's system is well known — something corroborated briefly in relation to Paul by the data, supplied by the apostle himself, that distances him from Jerusalem (found principally in Gal. 1:11–2:14; see 1:188-89). Far more important for Bultmann is the phenomenon of Hellenistic Christianity.[22] And "[s]tanding within the frame of Hellenistic Christianity he [Paul] raised the theological motifs that were at work in the proclamation of the Hellenistic Church to the clarity of theological thinking" (187). As a result, Paul "became the founder of Christian theology" (187). Bultmann immediately follows his treatment of Paul with a description of Johannine theology, at the beginning of volume 2,[23] by which point his program is largely in place.[24] The pivotal role of Paul's system — as Bultmann reconstructs it — is therefore clear.

Bultmann's posture remains representative of a position widely shared by many modern interpreters of Paul, and especially those located within the academy — those grouped here under the rubric of theological liberalism.[25] The liberal reading of Paul is strongly indebted to Justification, just as the conservative reading is.

§5. Justification and Modern Philosophical Individualism

The similarity between theologically liberal and theologically conservative readings of Paul in terms of Justification should not really occasion surprise. Both readings share strong affinities with certain characteristically modern epistemological concerns, although they develop in different directions depending in large measure on their underlying confidence — or lack thereof — in some of those concerns. We might say that modern liberal interpreters like Bultmann incline toward the Cartesian pole within the broad, basic dualism that tends to characterize post-Enlightenment philosophical individualism, feeling that a posture of doubt toward "external" reality is often necessary.[26] Modern theological conservatives tend to be more robust empiricists, entertaining fewer doubts about what lies concretely beyond the individual's mind and hence feeling free to build on supposed facts detected in that realm through sense experience and inquiry. This gives their approach to Paul in terms of Justification a slightly more traditional shape; such interpreters have more confidence in the discoveries of "phase one." Nevertheless, the two trajectories remain mere variations on a common underlying tradition of modern philosophical thought, which possesses a striking compatibility with the central emphases of Justification.[27]

5.1. The Cartesian Tradition and Theological Liberalism

The following sketch is necessarily oversimplified; however, it is still probably fair to suggest that, with the collapse of the ancient, essentially Platonic doctrine of essences in the face of forces like nominalism, the intelligibility and reliability of the broader world were increasingly problematized for late medieval and early modern thinkers. Moreover, the perceived epistemological center began to shift from God to the person, with notions of divine certitude (omniscience, etc.) often being transferred to this new locus in the form of a quest for certainty. For some thinkers, mathematics and logic held promise of such certainty, leading inevitably to the disparagement or marginalization of other forms of knowledge. And the result was a frequent collapse into the internal mental world of the individual as seen quintessentially in the analysis of Descartes (1596-1650). He began (in)famously with the ostensibly undeniable proposition rooted in the mental world of the individual: "I think, therefore I am." At least this was certain and hence "true," but almost everything else was doubtful.

Of course, it was difficult to remain in this world, and so bridges of various sorts had to be constructed into "external reality," that is, into the world of the body and of sense experience, although those could prove a little unreliable. Kant's system is perhaps the most significant in this regard (1724-1804). Kant retained Descartes's judgment that the internal, mental world of the individual was especially certain, not to mention "free," and he included there largely self-evident moral maxims — the categorical imperative, and so on. But he also attempted to grasp external reality as that was presented to the individual's mental world through sense experience, although he was forced to posit various basic structuring categories that could not themselves be justified in order to appropriate that information — most notably, the dimensions of space and time and the notion of causality. So the external world could be appropriated, but only under particular inevitable conditions of doubt.

The Cartesian influence of Kant on New Testament interpretation, and especially on the reading of Paul, is both significant and obvious. Kant was a particularly influential figure for many important German interpreters of Paul. His views, including his important understanding of ethics, influenced seminal Christian thinkers such as Gotthold Ephraim Lessing (1729-81) and Friedrich Schleiermacher (1768-1834).

Lessing summarizes with particular clarity the hermeneutical consequences of a Kantian view of reality in his essay "On the Proof of the Spirit and of Power" (1777).[28] A "broad ugly ditch" now intervenes between the external world, where the historical method forages in search of uncertain factual truths, and the internal world, where reside the "necessary truths of reason" that cannot be doubted. And much within the subsequent academic interpretation of the New Testament is comprehensible from this point. The historical reconstruction of Jesus is clearly an undesirable place to attempt to ground Christianity (and this conviction can link hands with Socinianism). Paul, however, seems to have a remarkably mature grasp of matters. He disparages "works of law," which seem irreducibly connected to bodily action within the external world, and bases salvation on faith alone, which is clearly operating in the internal and mental realm of absolute certainty. His ethics operates within this necessary realm as well, and he might even on one occasion, especially far-sightedly, disparage work on "the historical Jesus" (see 2 Cor. 5:16). Moreover, the transition from particularistic external Judaism to universal internal Christianity is now readily comprehensible. And arguably, the Fourth Gospel can be rapidly mobilized in support of these emphases within Paul.

Schleiermacher perhaps represents the classic statement of this theological program. The questing self-consciousness of the individual characterized by faith is the starting point, the essential dynamic, and in a real sense the climax of Christian theology.[29] The centrality of a certain reading of Paul to this modernizing redefinition of theology is obvious in the very title of Schleiermacher's masterpiece, *The Christian Faith*, which was published originally in 1821-22.[30]

It can now be seen that Bultmann merely represents a more exegetically detailed application of this entire approach — although an application largely unparalleled in its elegance and interpretative plausibility. Admittedly, Bultmann also looked to Martin Heidegger (1889-1976) and hence to existentialism, but those programs too are readily comprehensible as variations on the post-Cartesian philosophical project.[31] Indeed, it is fascinating to observe how easily the more traditional schema of Justification in Bultmann elides at times into modern philosophical discourse. This is generally a matter of emphasis, and at times a very subtle one, and hence not usually a qualitative transition — all of which suggests the basic compatibility between Justification and certain developments within modern philosophy.

In a little more detail: Bultmann's characterization of "man prior to the revelation of faith" contains numerous modern touches. His analysis begins with a quasi-Cartesian emphasis on individuals in isolation, "as subjects," establishing something of their own essential nature or existence: "having a relationship to one's self belongs essentially to being a man" (202). Ψυχή and πνεῦμα both suggest, in part, that man is "the *subject* of his own willing and doing" (§18; 1:203, emphasis original). Indeed, "in the statement of I Cor. 2.11 . . . πνεῦμα approaches the modern idea of consciousness" (1:207). He summarizes:

> [Man] is a person who can become an object to himself. He is a person having a relationship to himself (σῶμα). He is a person who lives in his intentionality, his pur-

suit of some purpose, his willing and knowing (ψυχή, πνεῦμα). This state of living toward some goal, having some attitude, willing something and knowing something, belongs to man's very nature and in itself is neither good nor bad. The goal toward which one's life is oriented is left still undetermined in the mere ontological structure of having some orientation or other; but this structure (which for Paul is, of course, the gift of the life-giving Creator) offers the possibility of choosing one's goal, of deciding for good or evil, for or against God. (1:209)

[Man] factually lives only by constantly moving on, as it were, from himself, by projecting himself into a possibility that lies before him. He sees himself confronted with the future, facing the possibilities in which he can gain his self or lose it. . . . Life is lived in some sphere and that sphere gives it its direction . . . , and just such statements show that a man's life can go astray in the illusion that he can live "for or to himself" instead of in dedication or self-surrender, renouncing the possibility of holding onto himself. (1:210)

We are of course some way from ancient anthropology, including Paul, in much of this, *but we are not that far from the presuppositions of the contractual theory of Justification.* In the foregoing, the acting, willing individual as "subject" and "object to himself" is teleological, then ethically teleological, then teleological in relation to an innately revealed Creator, by which point we have traveled from modern existentialism (if not Cartesianism) via neo-Kantianism to a stripped-down version of Justification.[32] But none of these transitions is especially painful. Bultmann's conception of sin — which he views, in typical Justification fashion, as integral to this a priori anthropology — is also nuanced in modern directions.

[M]an's effort to achieve his salvation by keeping the Law only leads him into sin, indeed this effort itself *is already sin.* It is the insight which Paul has achieved into the nature of sin that determines his teaching on the Law. This embraces two insights. One is the insight that sin is *man's self-powered striving to undergird his own existence* in forgetfulness of his creaturely existence, to procure his salvation by his own strength . . . , that striving which finds its extreme expression in "boasting" and "trusting in the 'flesh.'" . . . The other is the insight that man is always already a sinner, that, fallen into the power of sin . . . , *he is always already involved in a falsely oriented understanding of his existence.* . . . The reason, then, that man shall not, must not, be "rightwised" by works of the Law is that he must not be allowed to imagine that he is able to procure his salvation by his own strength; for he can find his salvation only *when he understands himself in his dependence* upon God the Creator. (1:264).

Here the traditional contractual claim of Justification vis-à-vis the pre-Christian's failure to fulfill the law's demands segues into a basic failure with respect to "self-understanding" and "existence." But it needs to be appreciated that both these notions are present within the classic theory of Justification; we simply do not find them so emphasized and defined in Luther himself or in older classic representatives of the approach. Clearly, however, it is not unfaithful to the theory to do so.

These modern compatibilities are also evident in the ensuing Christian soteriological schema. The way out of the foregoing dilemma is a "decision" or "realization" or "appropriation," which, although a "break" in one sense, is not a disjunction in the sense of a magical transformation of humanity's "substance": "[man's] new existence stands in historical continuity with the old" (1:269), as indeed it must if its basis is a decision and an ongoing understanding.

> A new *understanding of one's self* takes the place of the old — it does so, nevertheless, in such a manner that historical continuity is preserved; indeed, it thereby becomes one's own true history, for the transition from the old existence to the new does not take place as a mental development[33] from sin to faith; rather, faith is *decision* in regard to the grace which encounters a man in the proclaimed word. However much Paul's view of the history of salvation is oriented toward mankind, and not the individual . . . , it still is true that *the situation of mankind is also that of the individual.* He, the sinner who is in death, is confronted by the gospel when it reaches him with *the decision whether or not he is willing to understand himself anew* and to receive his life from the hand of God. *The possibility of understanding* is given him in the very fact that he is a sinner, that he is in death. . . . Salvation is naught else than . . . [a] *realization.* (1:269, emphasis added)

The fundamental compatibility between the individualism, mentalism, and voluntarism of the traditional theory of Justification and Bultmann's more contemporary concerns is apparent here.

Bultmann also famously detaches the gospel proclamation from history. The risen Christ is present in the proclamation of the word itself: "only so can it be believed" (305).[34] But, again, this is not necessarily unfaithful to implicit aspects of the classical model. Faith is only a criterion of appropriation. Although an objective atonement must lie behind the gospel in order for sins to be forgiven and righteousness imputed, the believers need not necessarily investigate these in order to appropriate the gospel. They must simply do what God dictates that they ought to do — here, "believe" (i.e., believe something). This, admittedly, is not Bultmann's exact concern — that autonomous modern individuals cannot find either certainty or immediacy in historical facts. But the immediacy of the preached word within the classic model and its potential dislocation from historical demonstration allow Bultmann's concern at these points to be accommodated with little ultimate structural damage to the soteriology as a whole. So, once again, modern concerns and nuances prove quite compatible with the older approach of Justification.

In sum, it seems that theological liberalism can espouse a Paul shaped in the interests of a modern philosophical, essentially neo-Kantian epistemological agenda (looking back to Descartes and proceeding by way of Schleiermacher and more modern philosophical variations). And it manages to achieve this version of the gospel principally in relation to the Justification discourse. In so doing, it does make certain important interpretative sacrifices, and we will revisit these in detail in due course. Because of its nervousness about empirical reality, the origins of Justification in natural revelation, and thereby in rigid, externally observable reality, must be renegotiated. However, the critical transition point of the individual's saving belief receives due attention, as does the Christian individual's dramatic progress beyond both works and a particularistic, historical Judaism.

Hence, the basic affinity between a modern philosophical individualism that looks back principally to Descartes and the construal of Paul (and the rest of the New Testament) in terms of a particular version of the Justification discourse seems clear. But the conservative construal of Paul in terms of Justification shares this affinity with the modern, rather dualistic philosophical project as well, although it tends to emphasize its other primary emphasis.

5.2. The Empiricist Tradition and Theological Conservatism

Not all modern philosophers began like Descartes with the individual's mind. Some thinkers were convinced, conversely, that sense experience, the body, and the external empirical world were primary, and hence that the mind's ability to map this external reality was the potentially doubtful dimension within knowledge. Like the Chinese philosopher who dreamed that he was a butterfly and then could never be certain that he was not a butterfly dreaming that he was a Chinese philosopher, such thinkers worried that their mental events were illusory. They would still attempt to build bridges to those mental events — because to fail to do so would be overtly self-contradictory — but those bridges began in the external, empirical world (and they too often proved unreliable).

This broad philosophical trajectory was basically Anglo-American, looking to founding figures such as Thomas Hobbes (1588-1679), John Locke (1632-1704), David Hume (1711-1776), and John Stuart Mill (1806-1873). And it found ready allies in the accelerating technologies of capitalism and the achievements of science. In the light of these ostensible advances, such thinkers were confident that the exploration of the world, which was ultimately verifiable through sense experience, yielded certain truths. Indeed, as the extraordinary systems of (i.a.) Isaac Newton (1643-1727) and Pierre-Simon Laplace (1749-1827) suggested, reality tended to reveal itself as a marvelous mechanism of wondrous complexity and reliability. Truth was available in this sense to industrious questing individuals, provided that they possessed the correct technologies *and* were free to pursue their inquiries wherever they led, unconstrained by preexisting dogmas or prejudices or by any institutional interference.

Hence, if theological liberals felt vindicated by Paul's emphasis on individual faith that seemed to pass such a radical judgment on unreliable external deeds, theological conservatives raised in the Anglo-American traditions of empiricism felt anchored by the incontestable epistemological truths that underlay the apostle's entire discourse of Justification. This discourse mapped reality accurately and responsibly from its first assumptions, when it claimed that rational individuals could explore the world and discover obvious evidence there of God's existence and his concerns. The apostle seemed to begin his argument as they did, with a certain form of philosophical Deism,[35] and the rest of his system simply unfolded consistently from this preliminary position. Presumably it still helped, however, that these questing individuals were supposed to turn their backs on any tradition-bound dogmas and institutions and to bind themselves to the church merely through their own consent.

At the root of this interpretative tradition, then, is the conviction that truth is susceptible to essentially "scientific" and rational individuals, who can discover it through their own efforts as they explore external reality for themselves. Such activity yields hard factual data on which other positions can be built, while no preconditions for this knowledge are necessary — no guiding traditions or institutions. Our questing individuals' minds are a *tabula rasa* (or, in Locke's system, an empty white box). And this epistemological stance is of course as characteristically modern as any tacit endorsement of Descartes and Kant. Many heroes of scientific inquiry such as Bacon (1561-1626) and Galileo (1564-1642) had fought long and hard to establish this approach to knowledge, and some had paid a high price for doing so (which is not to concede that the historical narrative supplied by this tradition is always fair).[36] The more conservative construal of Paul in terms of Justification clearly shares a strong affinity with this modern philosophical trajectory that is fundamentally individualist and rationalist, but also optimistic about individuals' capacity to discover incorrigible order and truths within the external world.[37]

By this point, then, the perhaps initially puzzling claim that both liberal and conservative readings of Paul share powerful affinities with modern individualist epistemologies is not so opaque. While those readings tend to build on different emphases within that interpretative tradition, both ultimately endorse the strangely bifurcated individual who stands at the heart of so much post-Enlightenment thinking, straddling the worlds of the mind and the body — as Gilbert Ryle famously put it, "the ghost in the machine."[38]

§6. Justification and Liberal Political Individualism

The mention of John Locke and John Stuart Mill within a largely Anglo-American and empiricist philosophical tradition raises a further possible set of affinities that is now worth exploring. The tradition of modern philosophical individualism is essentially an elite interpretative phenomenon. This is a discourse largely of the academy. As such, it will probably prove very important for Paul's elite interpreters, and it may from such points trickle down to other interpretative communities, although this secondary influence is presumably rather limited. However, we have already seen that the Justification paradigm in its conservative variant is widely distributed. And the roles of Locke and Mill raise the possibility that this distribution may have been mediated by an academic tradition ancillary to philosophy and epistemology per se, namely, *political* philosophy, a tradition with a very different ultimate impact on broader society. Hence, any affinities between Justification and this vastly more influential intellectual tradition focused on questions of politics, society, and property are well worth pursuing in more detail.[39] Fortunately, one figure suggests himself as especially critical (rather as

Kant was in our previous discussion, followed closely by Descartes): John Locke (1632-1704).

Locke wrote five works of signal importance within a relatively short time just after the "Glorious Revolution" of 1688 (i.e., the sudden accession of William and Mary to the British throne after James II): *A Letter Concerning Toleration* (the Latin edition was available in Holland in 1689, the English in 1690), *Two Treatises of Government* (1690), *An Essay Concerning Human Understanding* (1690), *Some Thoughts Concerning Education* (1690-95) and *The Reasonableness of Christianity* (1690-95).[40] Few corpuses in human history have been so widely influential. In these works Locke reveals himself to be — among other things — a theologian, a philosopher, a political philosopher, and an interpreter of Paul. But a thumbnail sketch of Locke's political system at this point should suffice for our present purposes.

At the heart of Locke's position are individuals in the "state of nature," who by their own self-willed actions establish claims or rights to the products or consequences of those actions over against any other person or group or set of claims. Locke speaks famously at this point of individuals "mixing" their labor with things in the natural, "common" state, thereby appropriating them as personal property. C. B. Macpherson suggests insightfully that the entire tradition is consequently characterized by "possessive individualism."[41] A notion of private property is inherent in its anthropology, and this is invariably developed in terms of "rights" (using here a much older discourse, although not in violation of its original formulations). This notion is deliberately defended at a fundamental conceptual level, and especially against any attempted tyrannical appropriation by a figure like a monarch. Consequently, individuals in the liberal political vision are less mentalist and isolated than the Cartesian or the Kantian subjects in that they stand in the world, act upon it, and thereby establish a fundamental claim to some aspect of it when it has been suitably worked on. But they are still emphatically alone. They can enter into agreements with other individuals but are bound only by their consent. No prior claims or obligations are recognized. Society develops from a flexible and individualist type of contract (a *Gesellschaftsvertrag*). And technically, a further contract — the specific terms of which can vary quite widely — then establishes a government (a *Herrschaftsvertrag*). The basic features of the system are thus empiricist, proprietary, individualist, and contractual.

Religion is positioned in the individual's realm of consent as well, being a matter essentially of beliefs and individual choices; it resides in the "private" sphere. The government is positioned in the state of nature on the basis of the contracts undertaken there and hence in the "public" sphere. It can no more encroach on the consensual religious sphere of individuals than it can appropriate the property for which they have labored. Meanwhile, the government's executive and legislative operations are guided by the immutable principles and laws of reality that are obvious to all rational individuals irrespective of their religious stance. That is, the state of nature is powerfully influenced by natural law, which is evident in turn to any rational person. Hence, the government rules over everyone within the jurisdiction of its contract but (usually) in a limited way. Beliefs and religion, along with all else in the private sphere, are "free" from the government's intrusion and control.

In the light of this it can be seen that the Justification discourse possesses an even stronger set of affinities with Locke's distinctively modern political theory than it does either with ancient and medieval systems or with modern philosophy. I detect in particular four positive affinities and one more general, negative affinity.

(1) *Contracts as individual (as against collective or no contract at all).* Both Justification and Locke's political system are oriented in terms of myriad individual contracts. (These can take place at the same time, but they are not for that reason the same contract.) Salvation within Justification is attempted first in relation to the contract of works and then in relation to the contract appropriated by faith. As each individual makes that saving decision, another contract is in effect established with God. Hence, Justification is a thoroughly individualist system with different contracts in play in relation to each individual. Similarly, Locke's political theory reflects a developing capitalist economy within which individuals are free to contract business with whomever they please. Locke's understanding of religion is individualistically contractual as well. Consequently, there are no dramatic moments in either system when a large group of people effects a collective contract, such as in a constitutional system. Nor does either system abandon human agency, perhaps in the manner that Qumran covenanters did when they ascribed everything unconditionally to the will of God (the contemporary political equivalent of whom might be Charles I). The two systems match each other nicely here, and in this way Justification proves itself highly compatible with the widespread individual contractualism of modernity.

(2) *Consent as limiting (divine) tyranny and underwriting a corresponding freedom.* Locke's system repudiates human tyranny by arguing that only a freely consenting subject is rightfully ruled by another human. If this consent is withdrawn fairly because the ruler has violated the terms of instatement, then that rule — if continued — is now illegitimate and tyrannical and can be rejected, if necessary by regicide and certainly by force. A free offer of consent by subjects, however, creates legitimate rule ("free" here meaning principally "uncoerced"). Justification is susceptible to a liberal interpretation in just these terms as well in relation to freedom, consent, and the repudiation of divine tyranny. It would seem that any unacceptable coercion of humanity by God is legitimately constrained by the role of consent within salvation; the fact that non-Christians may freely choose to believe — or not to believe — relieves God of any suspicion of such tyranny. Indeed, to deny the role of free choice within salvation would be to invite a charge of divine tyranny or, in what is much the same thing, to impose an unacceptable constraint on human freedom. For this reason the retention of freedom in relation to salvation is absolutely crucial. It is an indispensable apologetic (and a useful theodicy can be developed from this point as well). And the two discourses again clearly echo one another at these interrelated points.

(3) Genuine religion as individual and oriented fundamentally by beliefs, hence "internal" and "private." Justification mimics liberal politics' confinement of religion to the private sphere, although it does not necessarily speak of it in those terms. However, the focus of Christian salvation on an individual decision of faith relocates all true or genuine religion to the realm of individuals' beliefs, which are necessarily "internal" and hence "private." Here they must be free from traditional and institutional interference; these influences are secondary if not irreligious. Moreover, true religion does not progress significantly beyond such individual beliefs. To do so is to run the risk of lapsing back into the almost unforgivable condition of attempted justification by works. The beliefs of individuals cannot and should not interfere with the ostensibly objective situation of phase one, which is true but universally discernible irrespective of correct religious belief. That sphere is the realm of government and public policy. Hence, the liberal privatization of religion is intrinsic to Justification.

(4) Currency as universal to the human experience and structuring that experience. We have already had cause to note Justification theory's account of the atonement. In part one, chapter one, the satisfaction of the penalty required for human wrongdoing by God's retributive justice through Christ's death was described. And then, in chapter two, the problematic use of an essentially financial metaphor — a currency trope — within the actual mechanism suggested here was exposed. Despite these theoretical shortcomings, however, the model has persisted, and one reason is probably the way Locke's liberal political and social discourse deploys currency as a metaphor for almost all "civilized" human society (with scant consideration for an equivalent set of problems in its broader and literal application). Locke tends to reduce all human relationships to exchanges regulated by currency, and so provides just the universalizing discourse that Justification theory needs in order to flourish at this point — in terms of an uncontested, intuitively true, but in fact deeply problematic financial trope for the atonement that turns out to function literally in terms of a payment.[42]

(5) Few controls on liberal politics. In addition to its enjoyment of four significant affinities with liberal politics — individual contracts, the notion of consent, the privatization of religion, and the characterization of all human relationships in terms of a discourse of currency — Justification is unable to protest very vigorously against liberal politics. Several of the theory's features make it incapable of doing so.

The principal content of Justification theory's ethics is delivered in phase one of the schema, during the non-Christian stage. For non-Jewish individuals the mode of delivery is general revelation, or natural law. We have seen that this law is intended primarily to reduce potential converts to a state of eschatological anxiety. However, it is also the theory's only significant ethical contribution to any notion of government, since the laws dictating government must be universally discernible within the theory's first phase. Furthermore, we have seen that the natural law endorsed by Justification is characterized by a basic concern with retributive justice and by hostility to overt idolatry and violations of heterosexual monogamy (presumably other than celibacy). These prescriptions amount to a highly coercive and minimalist definition of government except in relation to matters of sexual ethics, since for almost all modern nations overt idolatry (i.e., the worship of statues of gods in temples) is no longer an issue. Little more than a night-watchman state is implicit in Justification theory, although this state does intrude into the bedroom! Furthermore, phase one of Justification is oriented fundamentally toward desert and works. So a notion of property if not of private property, while not necessarily innate to the theory, can certainly be integrated into it with minimal effort.[43]

In addition to these emphases, Justification theory resists any means whereby ethical (or unethical) practices set in motion by the opening assumptions could be corrected. Special revelation associated with either the Scriptures or the Christian dispensation is limited to the private sphere and constrained by the individual's need for faith alone. And tradition and institutional control are repudiated as not genuinely religious. Moreover, Justification finds it notoriously difficult to generate any significant ethical observance from its converts (indeed, it arguably *cannot* generate this). The theory is hostile to any religious activity beyond faith, labeling it derisively as "works." The ecclesia constituted by the theory remains similarly weak; it is fundamentally individualist, confessional, and voluntarist, rooted in consent. It can ask very little from its converts. And these limitations raise a frightening prospect.

If a government authorized by phase one of Justification were to prove overtly nationalistic, coercive, or materialistic, the theory would have no way of recognizing this as inappropriate *or* of challenging it! Justification's only real ethical concerns within the public sphere revolve around questions of appropriate punishment for crime and for violations of heterosexual monogamy, since offenses of this nature elicit the wrath of God. Beyond these ethical concerns — which are not themselves subject either to scrutiny or to correction — occupants of the paradigm are blind and silent. At least in the traditional Constantinian situation a government had to reckon with the full weight of the church and its traditions, which usually included a great deal of scriptural and christological guidance, even if those contributions were not unalloyed. But Justification theory *eliminates even those constraints on government, because it removes the church and its traditions from universal validity and guides the government only in terms of natural law, which is itself insulated from significant Christian correction.* Consequently, Christians, already positioned within a significantly diluted ecclesial polity, are beholden in politics only to their own perceptions and consciences, which supposedly allow them to discern enduring basic principles of justice within the cosmos that are shared in turn with non-Christians. A better theological recipe for the capture of the church by culture could hardly be imagined — a capture *by distinctively modern, liberal political culture.*

In sum, Justification theory fits liberal politics like a glove. Where it does not strongly endorse key elements within political liberalism, such as individual contracts and private religion, it offers no resistance to its political program, a conclusion made the more sinister by the following observations about the history of liberal politics.

Locke's views — or something similar to them — became that very strange thing: a successful philosophy in broad political, social, and even cultural terms. That is, unlike its strictly philosophical counterpart, the liberal political tradition enjoyed an astonishing historical success, and one that still continues, to the point that it is now one of history's dominant ideologies and arguably *the* dominant ideology of modernity.

The story of this success really begins in the eighteenth century, as various important European and post-European states made a transition into some form of liberal democracy. Locke's ideas, or ideas like his, were placed at the heart of various emerging states' new political and legal arrangements. Especially significant at this time were two auspicious moments: the independence of the United States, in 1776, and the French revolution that created the modern French nation-state, in 1789. (We will note the role of Great Britain in more detail shortly, picking up another story that ran through much of the eighteenth century.)

Both the newly independent United States and post-revolutionary France situated Locke's liberal vision at the heart of their defining constitutional moments, and hence in their political procedures as well as in much of their legal theory. This would lead in turn to pervasive emphases on the notion of consent and on the mechanism of contract within their societies and those they influenced. Furthermore, the articulation of the individual's basic claims in terms of "rights" would introduce a specific rights discourse into much political and legal theory, as well as into popular thinking, and the language of rights consequently remains a useful barometer for judging the penetration of this ideology. (We have already pointed out that the notion of individual rights is closely related to the notion of private property.)

French revolutionary zeal would shortly spread liberal reforms all over Europe in the wake of Napoleon's conquests and reorganizations, from Spain to the borders of Russia. Great Britain was in the process of acquiring a global empire, thereby spreading European practices around the world. And the United States would become the dominant power of the latter part of the twentieth century. Hence, the specific political philosophy represented by Locke seemed to "catch the wave" historically speaking when the post-revolutionary democracies emerged, passing quickly into a socially entrenched position, and through those primarily European powers progressively dominating the globe. Few intellectual traditions have enjoyed such influence.[44]

We have already noted that the colony of America was directly influenced by liberalism. However, the colonial movement itself would soon accelerate, bringing much of the globe into direct contact with these concerns.

During the late nineteenth century the largest European states consolidated and expanded worldwide empires. Technological superiority was a key ingredient in this, allowing both the establishment and the more effective maintenance of these far-flung organizations. And where the colonizers traveled, their views traveled with them. Furthermore, when these empires disintegrated after the two world wars, the newly emancipated colonies adopted liberal democratic constitutions almost without exception. (The application of these has sometimes left something to be desired, but this is arguably, at least in part, related to the unsuitability of the liberal political vision for many of these non-European countries.) The contrasting East European pursuit of totalitarian communism from 1945 proved relatively short-lived, the constitutions newly emerged since the late nineties also uniformly adopting liberal democratic constructions.[45] All of which is simply to say that the European liberal democratic model seems to have proved overpoweringly attractive within the important worldwide political developments that have taken place during the twentieth century. It has basically dominated the postcolonial and postcommunist eras in ideological terms.

This thumbnail sketch is meant only to indicate how, as the result of a certain rather fascinating period of historical development, liberal political concerns — those of "possessive individualism" — have become deeply rooted in our world. In them "we live and move and have our being." Moreover, we have seen that they possess a peculiarly strong set of affinities with the Justification discourse. Through that discourse Paul can be construed in a way that resonates strongly with the distinctive political vision of John Locke. And a particularly important feature of this political tradition is now worth noting in a little more detail — namely, its patriotism.

The ideology of political liberalism unleashed the liberal nation-state in a way that was arguably a little unexpected — in terms of nationalism. There are two important facets within this observation. First, patriotism was a new but very strong type of loyalty. Second, it was focused on entities of unparalleled historical power. And these two facets taken together make the ethical weakness of Justification theory in this regard all the more acute.

As seen most clearly in postrevolutionary France and America, liberal states engendered a new sort of loyalty. Having relegated religion to the private sphere, political liberalism nevertheless expected the allegiance of its occupants within the public sphere. Theoretically, the liberal states requested only a partial loyalty. Private matters need not be declared or taken into account. Only public matters in the public sphere were at issue, and people with such reduced loyalties were known as "citizens." But citizens were still expected to kill as part of their public commitment (that is, if the state deemed it necessary), and were treated punitively if they refused. The result seems to have been a new type of identity. However, it proved to be an extraordinarily strong one.[46]

The birth of the modern liberal nation-states was by no means an easy or a natural process. The fiction of the "nation-state" was widely disseminated — the idea that each nation had one state and vice versa — when almost all modern nation-states were created only as one region or "nation" imposed a political dominance on surrounding areas by force. (Great Britain was created by the dominance of England; France by the dominance of Paris and the northern regions; Italy by the triumph of Piedmont; and so on. Indeed, the American Civil

War is an excellent example of the forcible creation and maintenance of a modern nation-state.) Nation-states are almost invariably at bottom a colonial venture. A vast symbolic mobilization that rather obscures this then tends to follow — flags, anthems, capitals, language, and so on.

But these ventures succeeded to a degree because modern states were so much more powerful than their forebears. The modern liberal states possessed sharply defined and often very extensive territories, large bureaucracies with (relatively) efficient records,[47] and powerful, specialized armed forces resting on an industrial base. They dominated all the central processes of government — financial, executive, judicial, and so on. Resistance was futile, as most third-world countries were shortly to find out.

My point here is simply that political liberalism as an ideology facilitated the rise of the liberal nation-state and its patriotism. Modern post-European individuals do not tend to endorse strongly Locke's political vision per se, although they do tend to believe in it. *They endorse their particular liberal nation-state.* Hence, any attack on liberal institutions is easily construed as an attack on one's homeland — on one's "way of life." Powerful if conspicuously modern forces are clearly in play, and these are mobilized by the Justification discourse.

A final fascinating but very complex question lurks here: what is the relationship between the religious ideology of Justification, in association with the political ideology of liberalism, and the phenomenon of capitalism, which has arguably driven liberalism, at least to some degree, to such global dominance? It was in large measure the extraordinary economic acceleration and strength of Europe and North America from the eighteenth century onward — led by Great Britain — that generated widespread colonial empires until the postwar period, and still wider economic and cultural penetrations that are ongoing.[48] The various constitutional movements that we just noted can be explained largely in terms of emerging political units copying the European model. Furthermore, only very recently have non-European and Europe-derived economic centers arisen that can rival this initial conglomerate (if they can even now). And it is the claim of certain classic sociological studies that Protestantism somehow *facilitated* this! Weber, and later Tawney, argued that Protestantism was a necessary if not a sufficient cause of capitalism (a question revisited more recently by Giddens).[49] If some sort of relationship does hold at this point, then enormously powerful hermeneutical forces may well be operative, so we need to try to clarify this question, however provisionally.

But I am not inclined to trust the Protestant biases of much of this case, or indeed its intellectualist pretensions. Rather, I lean ultimately toward a more materialist explanation of history as a whole and of capitalism in particular.[50] That rise was arguably almost inevitable given various environmental factors. Liberalism did, however, *justify a certain distribution of the fruits of capitalist growth.* It was the perfect theory for the new capitalist class of managers and stockholders to use in order to defend themselves against appropriations by traditional ruling groups such as the aristocracy and the monarchy — a role illustrated nicely by

Locke himself, but obvious in many other analyses (see in the modern period perhaps especially Nozick). Political liberalism possessed, in short, a classic derivative ideological function. Like Mary's little lamb, wherever capitalism spread political liberalism tended to follow, as newly wealthy and hence increasingly powerful groups demanded increased status and influence. And so if capitalism had not developed political liberalism from the hand of Locke and his forebears, it would have had to invent it.

Moreover, the basic affinity between Justification and modernity seems to be even stronger than it first appeared. Not only does Justification share a close compatibility with modernity's two central philosophical variants, that seem to underpin in turn the two main traditions within the church today (i.e. "liberal" and "conservative") — a frightening enough alliance. But it seems to resonate even more powerfully with the world's regnant *political* philosophy, and so even arguably modulates in terms of its underlying economic system as well. Certainly it is deeply implicated in the modern nation state project, along with all its formidable loyalties. In short, Justification theory resonates with the very identity of the modern liberal individual. In something of an irony then, to challenge Justification is to challenge simultaneously that individual's very self-understanding (but usually without the individual registering this in these terms) — an apparently Quixotic action.

Irrespective of its prospects, we ought nevertheless to affirm that any reader endorsing Justification inevitably endorses certain central aspects of modernity, while — more importantly for this project — any reader positioned within modernity will be susceptible to its multiple endorsements of those overlapping commitments found within Justification theory.[51] Both of these temptations are clearly dangers for the unwary contractual advocate, while the theory itself is a rather more dangerous thing — especially in political terms — than initially it purports to be. No advocacy of Justification is politically innocent. And every modern advocate of Justification ought to interrogate the self-ratification — hermeneutical, political, and ethical — that is potentially implicit within that advocacy.

PART THREE

The Conventional Reading, and Its Problems

CHAPTER TEN

A Mighty Fortress: Justification Theory's Textual Base

§1. Preamble — Some Programmatic Issues

1.1. The Basic Thesis — Romans 1–4 as the Textual "Citadel"

My account of the textual situation begins with a significant claim — *that the Justification discourse's theoretical superstructure is based primarily on its construal of Romans 1:16–4:25.* It is the set of arguments perceived to be operative in this section of Paul's letter to the Roman Christians that establishes Justification theory in exegetical terms — at least in the first instance. So we can view this construal and its corresponding stretch of text in what follows as the discourse's textual "citadel" (a metaphor that will become more lucid in due course as it is extended in relation to other texts; see especially part five).

The basic rationale undergirding this claim is relatively simple: Justification theory — as we saw in detail in chapter one — is a complex set of interlocking arguments. A series of initial realizations about the construction of the cosmos and its theistic underpinnings unfolds through either a loop of despair or a loop of foolishness to create a particular situation that ought ideally then to lead to the embrace of the Christian gospel. A problem must be grasped and then traversed, leading to the possibility of a particular solution. It is obvious that for a biblical text to establish this theory, it must actually articulate, either implicitly or overtly, the theory's various premises and progressions. And it is equally obvious that a considerable amount of explication and argumentation will have to take place, because this is a relatively complex theory. (Our preceding discussion of it took over fourteen thousand words — although including a preamble and annotations in this total.) In short, if the Bible is at some point to attest to a soteriology conceived in terms of Justification theory, then at some point a text will have to articulate that theory, and because the theory is reasonably complex and extensive, we would expect its attestation to share similar degrees of complexity and extent. I would argue that, at first glance, only Romans 1:16–4:25 offers this complexity and extent — *and yet it does seem to offer it!* The conventional construal of Romans 1:16–4:25 seems to lay out at some length just the complex combinations of premises and progressions that Justification theory requires. Meanwhile, no other text in Paul remotely approaches this passage's degrees of detail and systematization, not even elsewhere in Romans (that is, in apparent relation to this theory), and neither is any text elsewhere in the Scriptures similarly detailed.[1] If this claim can be granted for the moment, then certain significant implications become apparent.

A careful investigation of this particular construal of Romans 1–4 is clearly paramount; much will stand or fall in relation to its plausibility. On the one hand, Justification theory might be vindicated exegetically, at which point quite different options would have to be explored in relation to any ultimate resolution of the problems that the theory causes for Pauline interpreters in broader terms. Indeed, in a certain sense those problems would now be unresolvable. On the other hand, if the reading falters at this critical point, then exegetical options may well be created for the other texts in Paul that are usually cited in the theory's support. Those could now be approached in rather different ways, freed from any undue influence from the theory's textual "citadel." A new hermeneutical space would be created for discussion.[2]

Our critical task at this point, then, is to consider carefully the exegesis of Romans 1–4 that serves to launch Justification theory within Paul — what we will call the "conventional" reading. After a generalized characterization of the reading's main features (see §§2-5) we will survey its astonishingly widespread distribution in secondary discussions of Paul (see §6). We will then be in a position to assess it more critically and to pose exegetical alternatives where those seem apposite, a process that begins in chapter eleven (and in fact dominates the majority of our ensuing argument).

1.2. The General Structure of the Conventional Reading of Romans 1–4

The conventional reading of Romans 1:16–4:25 generally divides this stretch of text into four subsections that associate in turn into three mutually related arguments.

Romans 1:16-17 is considered to be separate from what immediately follows (and also often from what precedes) and, because of close verbal and syntactical similarities, is associated with a second paragraph that is held to begin in 3:21. The conclusion of the later paragraph is a little unclear, occurring perhaps as early as v. 26 or perhaps as late as v. 31, but not a great deal yet turns on this point. These two sections — for the sake of argument, 1:16-17 and 3:21-31 — are held by most readers to constitute the central thesis of Paul's entire argument. Romans 1:16-17, often spoken of as "the theme of the letter," announces the thesis in advance of Paul's detailed argumentation, and 3:21-31 stands as the fulcrum on which the argument's broader progressions pivot. Of course, the latter elaborates the theme in more detail as well, but much critical material is held to precede this pivotal thesis in argumentative terms.

Romans 1:18–3:20 is almost invariably viewed as the argument that prepares for the thesis just identified; it is a complete articulation of a problem that sets the stage for the announcement of an appropriate solution. This judgment concerning the preparatory function of 1:18–3:20 is of course a crucial interpretative decision, but it is widely assumed in the passage's exegesis and is by no means without reason. A plausible reading of this extended argument seems very much to build toward the acknowledgement of a "plight" to which the proclamation of the Christian gospel is then the welcome solution. The argument itself seems to move through some half dozen or so steps that will be specified shortly in more detail.

The problem having been elaborated by 3:20 and its response pithily deployed by 3:31, Paul is usually held to turn in 4:1 to a detailed scriptural attestation to his thesis concerning salvation, because it is controversial in traditional Jewish terms. He focuses on the venerable and authoritative figure of Abraham and especially on his life as revealed by Genesis 15:6. Several steps are again apparent within the discussion — probably three or four. This corroborative discussion then seems to end around 4:22 and a transition to slightly different terminology and argumentation begins, culminating in a third brief statement of the argument's thesis in 4:25.[3]

In sum, the conventional construal of Romans 1:16–4:25 views the overarching structure of the argument as follows:

(1) a statement of the problem: 1:18–3:20;
(2) a description of the solution in thesis form: 1:16-17; 3:21-31 (and perhaps also 4:25); and
(3) an authoritative scriptural attestation to that solution: 4:1-25.

It is intriguing to note that the first of these major argumentative phases is by far the longest, comprising some sixty-four verses. The theses comprise only fourteen verses, and their scriptural corroboration another twenty-four, for a grand total of thirty-eight. In terms of lines — which are probably more indicative — the ratios are approximately 120:25(-26.5):49, or roughly 5:1:2. Hence, the articulation of "the solution" (statement plus corroboration) takes just over half as much space as that of "the problem." Even more precisely, we can say that the actual solution takes only 20 percent as much space as the problem, and its scriptural corroboration a further 40 percent. Clearly, then, the articulation of the problem is dominant, and this would conform to the expectations of Justification theory, where the statement of the initial problem in argumentative terms is also dominant.

We will now address the conventional reading of these three sets of texts in more detail, beginning with "the problem."

§2. The Problem — Romans 1:18–3:20

Even interpretative virtuosos such as the early Barth or Ernst Käsemann tend to reproduce, with superficial variations, a consensus concerning Romans 1:18–3:20. Paul's argument here is supposedly characterized by a single overarching function — "indictment."[4] The apostle is assumed to be establishing the incontrovertible and universally recognizable fact of humanity's eschatological culpability, a rhetorical objective supposedly stated overtly in 3:19: "whatever the law [and, we might add, Paul in the preceding argument] says, it speaks . . . so that every mouth may be silenced, and the whole world may be held accountable to God."[5] The vast majority of interpreters of Romans hold that the entire discussion from 1:18 builds toward this conclusion; they tend to differ only as to whether Paul's argument is entirely cogent or fair. Of course if the argument does succeed, then this conclusion is also a problem from which rational people would want to escape.

As is well known, Paul builds his specific case in this preparatory phase from the reality of divine retributive justice, which undergirds a soteriology in strict accordance with desert. This is then complemented by a claim of pervasive and universal sinfulness, which, in combination with the foregoing principles, yields an eventual verdict of condemnation. The recognition of these axioms — by and for both Jew and Greek — leaves all humanity "without excuse." The scene has now been well and truly set.

There are actually three specific stages in the argument so construed, the last being rather shorter than the first two: (1) 1:18–2:8; (2) 2:9–3:9; and (3) 3:9-20.

Stage one, 1:18–2:8, establishes the key principle that divine judgment will take place ultimately in accordance with works of law and desert, a principle based in turn, as we have already noted, on a divine nature defined in terms of retributive justice. Moreover, these principles are viewed as necessary, universal perceptions — whether rational and reflective or simply innate. This feature of the argument establishes universal culpability. Stage two, 2:9–3:9, overrides in four successive subordinate discussions any special pleading by Jews that might negate the implacable operation of this principle of desert, so that things like circumcision are brushed aside. Put colloquially, this stage levels the playing field between Jews and pagans, so that Jews as well as pagans seem to be in this sorry pass. Stage three, 3:9-20, then establishes the sinfulness of all humanity through massed scriptural quotation. Hence, although potentially positive, the divine eschatological assize will in fact necessarily reach only a negative verdict for every individual — Jew and Greek — an outcome of which all are innately aware in advance. So at this point every mouth is indeed stopped and the whole world held accountable to God. Everyone waits in breathless anticipation — and not a little anxiously — for some alternative, which, as it turns out, is soon presented.

This reading is well known, but we ought nevertheless to rehearse it here in slightly more detail, since its stages and specific argumentative dynamics are so important.

2.1. Stage One: Romans 1:18–2:8

As we have just noted, the fundamental premise in the conventional construal of Paul's argument is a coming judgment in accordance with desert assessed in relation to deeds, a principle elaborated particularly clearly in 2:6: "[God] will repay according to each one's deeds." It would seem that God will eventually judge humanity on the basis of performance with respect to an ethical law. Good deeds will merit salvation and bad deeds condemnation, and it is the burden of the argument's first phase to establish this basic axiom.

However, the principle is not stated baldly at the outset of the discussion. It is in fact elicited rather than asserted, the origins of its acknowledgement lying in the vivid proclamation of 1:18-32, which is possibly a vignette of standard Jewish propaganda. (Paul's argument seems clearly analogous to, or even dependent on, the Wisdom of Solomon, especially chs. 12–14.) For this basic premise of judgment by desert to be universally binding, all humanity must have access to some sort of ethical code by which they can actually be assessed; otherwise, the coming judgment in accordance with deeds would not be fair. Indeed, it would be impossible. The principle of a universal impartial judgment in terms of desert presupposes the presence of a universal ethical criterion enabling that judgment, as well as a degree of human capacity. So Paul needs to introduce the notion of natural revelation into his discussion — which he seems to do.

He states first, in 1:19-21a, that pagans perceive God's eternal divinity and power; he immediately castigates them, however, for idolatry and aberrant sexual behavior, so clearly the content of the naturally revealed ethical code is more extensive than the mere knowledge of these two divine attributes (as well as presumably their inherence in a single God). Those initial theological realizations do not obviously preclude the latter activities, not to mention much of the vice list in vv. 29-31; hence, it is not surprising to be told shortly that God's ethical demands are appreciated innately as well (in their "hearts" and "consciences"; see 2:14-15). At this point, then, two conduits for natural revelation seem to be in place — for want of better terms, external and internal — and their combined content comprises both metaphysical and ethical information. Universal disclosure of this information is an irreducible precondition for the argument's subsequent function.

The information actually revealed is God's concern for certain deeds over against others. God will condemn pagans — in somewhat stereotypical Jewish terms — for any idolatry or sexual immorality, the latter being defined by a norm of heterosexuality. But these principal sinful trends are soon expanded by a long list of obviously wicked if rather generic actions and dispositions — "envy, murder, strife, deceit, craftiness . . . ; [being] gossips, slanderers, God-haters, insolent, haughty, boastful . . . [and] foolish, faithless, heartless, ruthless" (1:29b-31).

Hence, the point of this revelation is not to convey specific information so much as to establish culpability when it is ignored. Having argued a sense of appropriate behavior for everyone, Paul goes on to state that the pagans are consequently "without excuse" when they sin, as they invariably do (1:20). The premises of natural revelation are rapidly combined with typical assertions of universal pagan abuses. And these violations, coupled with the criterion of divine judgment in accordance with desert, now establish the unsurprising conclusion that all pagans will ultimately be condemned; they are, in Paul's words, "worthy of death" — and they know it! (v. 32 DC).

It is well known that the argument turns in 2:1. But although New Testament scholars have hotly debated of late just what the identity of Paul's implied audience is at this point — whether Jewish or pagan — I am not sure that much ultimately depends on this decision in argumentative terms at this juncture in our description. The argument itself functions relatively simply as a universalization of the principle of judgment in accordance with desert, which is *implicit* within the preceding critique of pagan transgression. *Anyone either making or endorsing criticisms of pagan sinfulness like those expressed in 1:18-32 is now forced to submit personally to its central principle of judgment.* To claim otherwise would be inconsistent — preaching something to others that one did not personally follow — and therefore also hypocritical. Perhaps more importantly, however, viewed theologically, it would be futile. If God really does function in this fashion, then — absent special pleading — the accusers too, if they sin, "will [not] escape."

The principle itself, toward which we have been working all along, is now spelled out explicitly, and in scripturally resonant phraseology: "[God] 'will repay according to each one's deeds'" (2:6).[6] And for the conventional reader of Romans 1:18–3:20, everyone is now subjected to it, meaning future reward from the hand of God for consistently pursued acts of righteousness but future punishment from the same hand for consistently pursued acts of wickedness: "To those who by patiently doing good seek for glory and honor and immortality, he will give eternal life; while for those who are self-seeking and who obey not the truth but wickedness, there will be wrath and fury . . . ; anguish and distress for everyone who does evil . . . , but glory and honor and peace for everyone who does good" (2:7-10). This is a universally recognized and valid scenario whether for the clearly depraved (1:18, 20b-32) or the somewhat moralistic observer (2:1-5). It is a truth imprinted on the cosmos and on the minds of those who dwell in it — that judgment by the all-powerful God will take place on the basis of desert, and hence also in accordance with divine retributive justice, on "the day of wrath, when God's righteous judgment will be revealed" (2:5). The principle of future judgment in strict accordance with desert, having been independently established, is now formally laid out. The point is further reinforced by the citation of a Jewish *theologoumenon* in 2:11, "God shows no partiality" (see Deut. 10:17; also Gal. 2:6), although that saying may also play a role in the new argumentative contention that is just beginning to develop and that was in fact inaugurated from v. 9b.

2.2. Stage Two: Romans 2:9–3:9

Romans 2:9–3:9 is usually understood to apply this principle of judgment by desert consistently to Jews and Judaism, and Paul is supposed to have various good reasons for doing so. Most importantly, it creates equality between Jews and pagans in relation to Christian salvation, at the same time eliminating the need for law observance. (If such equality were not established at this point, Paul would perhaps have to explain later on why Jews also need the gospel he is about to offer to pagans.) Explanations of the widespread Jewish rejection of the Christian gospel, of the basis for Paul's law-free pagan mission, and perhaps also of his own journey to salvation are implicit here as well. This important argumentative reduction is actually pursued through four subordinate stages: (i) 2:9-16 claims that salvation is equally attainable for Jew and pagan, partly on the basis of the universal knowledge of God's law but also witnessed to by conscience, as we have already noted; (ii) 2:17-24 challenges Jews knowledgeable in terms of Torah, specifically for the somewhat lurid sins of stealing, adultery, and temple robbery; (iii) 2:25-29 denies the importance of circumcision in relation to the more basic principle of general desert, exposing a circumcised but unrighteous person to the mockery of an uncircumcised but righteous person at the judgment — someone for whom "circumcision is a matter of the heart . . . spiritual and not literal" (v. 29); and (iv) 3:1-9a presses the point home against the "faithfulness" and "righteousness" of God.

In more formal terms we might say, then, that this section pursues the consequences — at some length — of *the incompatibility of the principle of divine eschatological judgment in accordance with desert with any notion of Jewish privilege.* The section suggests seriatim that the principle will override the privilege, whatever the latter's specific manifestation — knowledge of God's will in the Torah, perhaps extending even to great insight (so 2:17-24); circumcision (so 2:25-29); or any appeal to the more benevolent divine attributes (so 3:1-9a). The first subsection, however, seems to press the inverse point, namely, that pagans *can* presumably be saved in accordance with desert and hence independently of Jewish privilege, and one supposes that this observation — in a notoriously difficult part of the argument — is intended to embarrass any notion of Jewish privilege as well. We will now discuss these points in more detail.

(i) Romans 2:9-16

This subsection begins with what is really just a bald statement of the central dynamic in the argument that follows, namely, that the categories of Jew and pagan are overruled by the principle of desert. These are now redistributed within the constituencies of humanity that really matter in ultimate terms — the righteous and the unrighteous (vv. 9-10; also vv. 12-13): "those persevering in good works . . . [will be given] eternal life; those through selfish ambition and disobedience to the truth being persuaded of unrighteousness [will be given] wrath and anger"

(vv. 7-8 DC). And both these categories may of course now include "Jews and Greeks" (so vv. 9-10): "[t]here will be anguish and distress for everyone who does evil, the Jew first and also the Greek, but glory and honor and peace for everyone who does good, the Jew first and also the Greek." Hence, "it is not the hearers of the law who are righteous in God's sight, but the doers of the law . . ." (v. 13). All this is then supported by the quotation of a Jewish saying in v. 11: "[f]or God shows no partiality." The more detailed premises concerning natural revelation necessary to sustain this rather shocking set of claims (especially with respect to pagans) are now redeployed (vv. 14-15). Even the pagans know "the work of the law" (v. 15 DC) in their hearts and so could qualify for the divine verdict of righteousness and the consequent reward of eternal life. The subsection concludes in v. 16a with an appropriate reiteration of the eschatological timing and causality of this scenario — "the day when . . . God . . . will judge the secret thoughts of all."

The actual status of the pagans here, who seem prominent especially in vv. 14-15, is much debated. A strong commitment to the reality of righteous pagans would be quite troublesome for Justification theory, which does not anticipate any exceptions ultimately to God's condemnation. Moreover, they seem to reemerge in the third subsection of Paul's argument (2:25-29), which follows shortly. Some interpreters suggest that these figures are merely a hypothetical category that does not exist; others, that they are an argumentative slip; and still others, that they are in fact Christians. None of these suggestions is wholly satisfactory. We will consider carefully the subsection and its implications in chapter eleven, and again in part four, chapter fourteen. Suffice it for now to note that this is an anomalous and unresolved element within the conventional reading, but one that does not seem to be an especially significant argumentative emphasis. Certainly, it is not generally accorded sufficient attention by commentators to deflect the overarching construal of the argument. This subsection does have the singular virtue, however, of emphasizing that pagans have some sort of ethical guidance apart from any possession of a written guide like the Jewish Scriptures. This is an essential presupposition for Justification theory's universal claims.

(ii) Romans 2:17-24

The key to much of what follows is the realization that the two principles of Jewish privilege and a final judgment functioning strictly in accordance with desert are not necessarily compatible. Hence, if Jews actually sin, they thereby run afoul of that judgment in accordance with desert, their special status notwithstanding. Having reiterated these issues in 2:9-16 and begun to direct them toward unrighteous Jews — see especially 2:12b — Paul now seems to argue more aggressively for the placement of Jews on the negative side of the eschatological evaluation. It can be seen that they belong there in toto. Just as intuitively law-observant pagans could theoretically be saved (see 2:27-29), although one suspects on the basis of 1:18-32 that most if not all will be found guilty and so condemned, so too intentionally law-observant Jews could theoretically be saved — but in fact all will be found guilty and so condemned. Jews must practice what they preach and there must be no contradiction between hearing, speaking, and doing (see vv. 21-23; also 2:13). The specific sins that Paul mentions are rather sensational, namely, stealing, adultery, and temple robbery, but this is perhaps consistent with the exaggerated nature of ancient polemic. Moreover, the point can easily be extrapolated, as it seems to be in 7:7-25, where the sin is covetousness. The privilege of "a Jew" with respect to the law is expounded at some length in this subsection (vv. 17-20), although the conventional reading tends to explain this in terms of such privilege generating greater culpability. Those calling themselves Jews here even end up — by way of overt and heinous sinfulness — calling the name of God into disrepute: "The name of God is blasphemed among the Gentiles because of you" (2:24, quoting Isa. 52:5; see also Ezek. 36:22).

So this section seems to be Paul's first attempt to supply an argument explicitly suggesting that the Jews will fail the final judgment by committing bad deeds. In particular, if one steals, commits adultery, or violates temples, then one is in trouble. Certainly, mere possession and knowledge of the law seems to be little decisive advantage in and of itself: good deeds must be *done!*

(iii) Romans 2:25-29

Paul seems to point out in this short subsection that the traditional badge of the covenant, circumcision — the sign that Jews enjoy a special arrangement with God (see esp. Gen. 17:1-14) — will not actually count for much if the criterion of judgment in accordance with works is to hold. The latter criterion overrules and effectively redefines the former sign. Hence, somewhat scandalously, a righteous pagan could end up condemning an unrighteous Jew on the day of judgment (v. 27). The true Jew is one in "heart" and in "spirit," a state that doubtless leads to good deeds (so v. 29). Here, then, in argumentative terms, Paul merely reasserts his original premise of judgment by desert, pointing out that *if it is accepted consistently* it will invalidate the mere possession of circumcision. Additional reasons for the abandonment of Jewish privilege have not been supplied, so doubtless some circumcised protesters would not necessarily be silenced by this contention. But Paul could presumably respond to such protestors that if privilege were accorded definitive weight, "how then could God judge the world?!" — that is, what would happen to the basicality of the judgment scenario that has just been described in terms of desert? And hence, apparently, the diatribe of 3:1-9a.

(iv) Romans 3:1-9a

Read in conventional terms, this subsection seems to elicit the admission from the mouth of an interlocutor that the faithlessness and unrighteousness of Jews, to which God ordinarily might respond with mercy and redemption, cannot undermine God's right to judge the cosmos in terms of desert: "Although everyone is a liar, let God be proved true" (v. 4). Indeed, if God were to act leniently be-

cause "our injustice serves to confirm the justice of God," "how could God judge
the world?" (vv. 5-6) — an appalling thought. Hence, the only "advantage" identified here for Jews is possession of "the oracles of God," that is, the Scriptures —
and presumably especially the Torah (see 2:17-20) — which of course only enhances their culpability.

Paul also seems to suggest in this subsection that any appeal to God's merciful qualities in the light of persistent sinfulness is perilously close to advocating
libertinism in the name of glorifying God, and the condemnation of such is deserved! Intriguingly, Paul himself seems to have been accused of this at some
point (". . . as some people slander us by saying that we say," v. 8).

In short, the approach of this diatribal subsection as a whole still seems to
be basically that of the previous subsections — here, countering possible ripostes
in terms of election or Jewish privilege against the argument in terms of desert
that Paul seems to be strongly endorsing. By the end of the discussion, it would
seem that all such protests have been effectively silenced.[7] Sinful Jews have no
further grounds for appeal. And with this victory, the argument turns to make its
final, deadly application.

2.3. Stage Three: Romans 3:9-20

The next major stage in the discussion as it is conventionally conceived consists
largely of the deployment of a carefully crafted set of scriptural texts that falls into
two slightly different clusters. The first cluster asserts that every person is in fact a
transgressor, without exception; it makes a claim to complete inclusiveness
within transgression through an artfully repeated "no one" or its close equivalent:
"there is *no one* [οὐκ ἔστιν] who is righteous . . . *no one* who has understanding . . .
no one who seeks God. *All* [πάντες] have turned aside, *together* [ἅμα] they have
become worthless; there is *no one* who shows kindness, there is *not even one* [οὐκ
ἔστιν ἕως ἑνός]" (see 3:10-12; see Pss. 14:1-3/53:1-3 [13:1-3/52:2-4 LXX]; Eccl. 7:20).
The second cluster of texts, running on immediately from the first, characterizes
different aspects of human anatomy to emphasize that humans are wholly sinful.
That is, sin is not merely universal but deeply embedded within humanity, taint-
ing "throats . . . tongues . . . lips . . . mouths . . . feet . . . [and] eyes" (see Pss. 5:9
[5:10 LXX]; 140:3 [139:4 LXX]; 10:7 [9:28 LXX]; Isa. 59:7, 8; Ps. 36:1 [35:2 LXX]).
The result of this twofold accusation is a powerful scriptural statement of utterly
universal culpability. And it would seem at this point in Paul's argument that the
Jewish Scriptures assert unequivocally what earlier stages in the argument merely
advanced as possibilities. Neither Jews nor pagans in fact do good works (or at
least enough of them), and both Jews and pagans in fact do evil works; "all" will
ultimately be judged negatively.

In short, in this subsection the Jewish Scriptures pronounce the failure of
humanity in relation to the principle of desert. Every single person, whether Jew
or pagan, is sinful and thus liable to the dire consequences of sin. The emphatic

introduction of this further premise — which seems largely undeniable — now establishes the conclusions of 3:19-20: "'no human being will be justified in his sight' by deeds prescribed by the law" (v. 20; actually a modification of Ps. 143:2 [142:2 LXX]). Moreover, the law has therefore provided a knowledge of sinfulness and nothing more. As a result, "every mouth is closed and all the cosmos . . . submitted to God" (v. 19 DC).

At the end of the entire section, then, Jews as well as pagans, and law observance in turn, have been crushed by this progression — and that seems to be precisely its point. The scene seems to have been well and truly set for the proclamation of the gospel, which follows in the letter immediately (3:21–4:25). In view of their indictment, *all non-Christians ought now to be rationally motivated to accept the generous offer of salvation through belief.* It is difficult to find interpreters of Romans — subtle nuances aside — who depart significantly from this basic reading of 1:18–3:20. (The suggestions of those who do will be considered carefully in due course, in chapter twelve.)

§3. The Solution — Romans 1:16-17 and 3:21-31 (and 4:23-25)

The deployment of "the solution" by Paul is generally held to be accomplished textually by the two paragraphs 1:16-17 and 3:21-31, these sections comprising just two and eleven verses respectively, although they should eventually be complemented by 4:25 (perhaps along with its two preceding verses), expanding the total of programmatic soteriological verses to fourteen (or sixteen). The economy of these statements is partly explained by the fact that much of the hard conceptual work seems to have been done by the time the gospel offering salvation is reached. Justification simply responds to a problem whose difficulties and parameters have already been established. Such is the brevity of these statements that they can be included here in their entirety.

> [1:16]For I am not ashamed of the gospel; it is the power of God for salvation to everyone who has faith, to the Jew first and also to the Greek. [17]For in it the righteousness of God is revealed through faith for faith; as it is written, "The one who is righteous will live by faith."[8]

> [3:21]But now, apart from law, the righteousness of God has been disclosed, and is attested by the law and the prophets, [22]the righteousness of God through faith in Jesus Christ for all who believe. For there is no distinction, [23]since all have sinned and fall short of the glory of God; [24]they are now justified by his grace as a gift, through the redemption that is in Christ Jesus, [25]whom God put forward as a sacrifice of atonement by his blood, effective through faith. He did this to show his righteousness, because in his divine forbearance he had passed over the sins previously committed; [26]it was to prove at the present time that he himself is righteous and that he justifies the one who has faith in Jesus.

[27]Then what becomes of boasting? It is excluded. By what law? By that of works? No, but by the law of faith. [28]For we hold that a person is justified by faith apart from works prescribed by the law. [29]Or is God the God of Jews only? Is he not the God of Gentiles also? Yes, of Gentiles also, [30]since God is one; and he will justify the circumcised on the ground of faith and the uncircumcised through that same faith. [31]Do we then overthrow the law by this faith? By no means! On the contrary, we uphold the law.

[4:23]Now the words, "it was reckoned to him," were written not for his sake alone, [24]but for ours also. It will be reckoned to us who believe in him who raised Jesus our Lord from the dead, [25]who was handed over to death for our trespasses and was raised for our justification.

These "thesis" statements are notoriously compact. They place on the table a panoply of motifs that readers have usually configured in relation to the progression that has just been developed in 1:18–3:20, thereby articulating a complete theory of salvation as well as a smoothly continuous argument and reading. Ten such motifs are initially apparent.[9]

  i. *righteousness* from God,[10] associated in chapter 4 with *reckoning* or *crediting* (4:24, 25);
 ii. *faith*, where we should also introduce Paul's *universal*, or *all-encompassing*, motif and terminology ("faith" or "belief" occurs in 1:16, 17; 3:22, 25, 26, 27, 28, 30, 31; 4:24; "all" or its equivalent in 1:16; 3:22, 23);
iii. *atonement*, expressed also in terminology such as *redemption* and *blood* (3:24, 25; and to a lesser degree, 4:25);
 iv. the resulting *justification* of the individual (3:24, 26, 28, 30; 4:25);
  v. various short summary references to *the problem*, whether *works of law* or *sin* and *trespasses* (et cetera) (3:21, 22b-23, 25, 27, 28; 4:25);[11]
 vi. God's *justice*, which is confirmed and attested or even "proved" by the foregoing motifs;[12]
vii. the additional divine attributes of *saving power, graciousness, forbearance,* and *unity* (1:16; 3:24, 25, 26, 29-30);
viii. the *gospel* (and, by implication, Paul's apostolate: 1:16; implicit throughout);
 ix. *scriptural attestation* (explicit in 3:21, probably in 31; implicit in 1:17); and
  x. *temporal references* to *the present* — literally, *"now"* (3:21, 26).[13]

The conventional construal of these motifs is as follows. God has made both righteousness (i) and atonement (iii) available in relation to Christ to those who appropriate them by faith (ii): "the gospel . . . is the power of God for salvation to everyone who has faith. . . . For in it the righteousness of God is revealed through faith for faith." This process forgives the believers' transgressions and arguably imputes to them Christ's perfect righteousness,[14] resulting in a divine verdict on the day of judgment of innocence (or, alternatively, of acquittal), a situation appropriately referred to as "justification" (iv): God "justifies the one who has faith in Jesus" (3:26).[15] The problem of transgression and pending judgment has thereby been resolved; the agonized conscience of the sinful individual has been quieted. And so a hopeless situation exposed or clarified by sinners' attempts to perform "works of law" has now been infused with hope: although "all have sinned and fall short of the glory of God; they are now justified by his grace as a gift" (3:23-24). All attempted deeds in relation to the law have been left behind: "we hold that a person is justified by faith apart from works prescribed by the law" (3:28).

This applies to everyone who believes, or to "all" who have faith. Hence, a centrifugal and even universal thrust is discernible in the gospel: "Is God the God of Jews only? Is he not the God of Gentiles also? Yes, of Gentiles also, since God is one; and he will justify the circumcised on the ground of faith and the uncircumcised through that same faith" (3:29-30). The need for belief alone flattens out the traditional distinction between these historically resonant categories.[16]

In so justifying believing individuals, God does not compromise God's perfect retributive justice but rather *affirms* it (vi), also displaying graciousness, a will to save, the power to do so, and patient forbearance (vii): "He did this to demonstrate his justice, because in his forbearance he had left the sins committed beforehand unpunished — he did it to demonstrate his justice at the present time, so as to be just and the one who justifies those who have faith in Jesus" (3:25-26 NIV).[17] This apparently contradictory activity is facilitated primarily by Christ's atonement (3:24-25), which we have already noted (iii). Christ's death satisfies God's wrath against human transgressions, accepting the penalty due those sinful deeds in a substitutionary and vicarious action that is profoundly benevolent: he "was handed over to death for our trespasses" (4:25a). In some sense he pays the price to God for human sins on humanity's behalf. So we "are now justified by his grace as a gift, through the redemption that is in Christ Jesus, whom God put forward as a sacrifice of atonement by his blood" (3:24-25a).[18] The demand of divine justice for punishment is met by Christ's vicarious acceptance of the penalty due for sins, in effect allowing God to act generously toward believing individuals in order to save them. In this way, God's integrity is not damaged but his generosity facilitated. Moreover, evil is thereby explained, being attributed ultimately to sinful humanity and not an inscrutable action of the sovereign God.[19]

The foregoing soteriological complex constitutes the gospel (1:16-17), which Paul has been commissioned to proclaim as apostle to the pagans and has also definitively understood (viii).[20] It is anticipated in and hence attested to by the Jewish Scripture, in both its major divisions (ix): "the righteousness of God has been disclosed, and is attested by the law and the prophets" (3:21).[21] And the first compact announcement of this gospel concludes with a scriptural quotation — Paul's first in the letter: "in it [i.e., the gospel] the righteousness of God is revealed through faith for faith; as it is written, 'The one who is righteous will live by faith'" (1:17, famously quoting Hab. 2:4).

The proclamation of this gospel is taking place in the present, "now" (x), following its recent establishment by Christ's life, although there it was apparent especially in relation to his crucifixion, which facilitated the element of atonement: "But *now*, apart from law, the righteousness of God has been disclosed" (3:21). Furthermore, God did it (i.e., put forth Christ) "to prove *at the present time* that he himself is righteous" (3:26). And we have already noted that this gospel opposes but also follows on from the failure of justification by works of law and the previous dispensation and so deals with the sinfulness and repeated transgressions exposed by that process (v), along with the inadequacy of law observance: "But now, *apart from law*, the righteousness of God has been disclosed" (3:21a). Indeed, "[t]hen what becomes of boasting? It is excluded. By what law? By that of works? No . . ." (3:27).

All the key soteriological elements, then, have been articulated repeatedly by these paragraphs. Moreover, these elements *are* a solution that corresponds precisely to the articulated problem (although some elements are arguably more awkwardly integrated into that solution than others[22]). So it is understandable that conventional readers characterize these sections as "theses."

And this brief characterization of Paul's thesis paragraphs in Romans should suffice for our present purposes. However, Paul's argument does not really pause at this point, as perhaps it could have. A longer discussion ensues that we must now address. In that discussion — somewhat intriguingly — Paul does not seem interested in all of the motifs that his theses have articulated. Some seem to drop from sight, and a few new motifs are introduced.

§4. Scriptural Attestation — Romans 4:1-25

The discussion that follows the thesis paragraph of 3:21-31 focuses on Abraham and extends for twenty-five verses. It modulates fairly distinctly after vv. 8 and 12, concluding with the resonant summary statements of v. 25 about Christ that we have already noted (the transition to that summary beginning in v. 23). So interpreters generally follow these subdivisions, or some close variation on them, when articulating the entire argument in detail, namely:

(1) 4:1-8: a scriptural (viz., pentateuchal) corroboration of the gospel's key soteriological principles in relation to Abraham as attested by Genesis 15:6;

(2) 4:9-12: an application of the argument specifically to circumcision;

(3) 4:13-22: a further, somewhat opaque analysis in terms of "the nature of faith" or some such;[23] and

(4) 4:23-25: a transition to a more christological focus and a final summary (hence, this subsection arguably belongs more to the overarching argument's thesis statements, 1:16-17 and 3:21-31, than to further articulation of the foregoing concerns).

The conventional reader views this argument principally as a more comprehensive address of the question of scriptural witness, a concern signaled by 3:21, 27, and 30, not to mention implemented by 1:17. Indeed, if Habakkuk 2:4 constitutes a witness from the Prophets, then the figure of Abraham, as suggested especially by Genesis 15:6, constitutes a witness from the Torah (so 3:21). As such, it can undergird a teaching concerning "faith" based on the Torah (as suggested by v. 27), which also "upholds" or "establishes" the Torah, provided it is properly applied (so v. 30). Hence, this discussion is usually understood to fulfill the expectations of scriptural attestation (motif ix) in the foregoing schema.

But in so doing it further describes some of the unfolding schema's key soteriological elements (it must attest *to* something) — specifically, the saving virtue of faith (motif ii), perhaps the imputation of righteousness (i), and the forgiveness of sins (iii), all of which result in justification (iv). This discussion also functions as a corroboration of "the problem," a condition generated by "works of law" but resulting in "ungodliness" (motif v). The scriptural analysis that unfolds from 4:1 thus verifies the essentially mechanical side to Justification soteriology, affirming the appropriation of salvation by the individual and most of its immediate aspects and results (motifs i-v and ix). Most of these elements have in fact been affirmed by the end of the first argumentative subsection, that is, by the end of v. 8. God's justice, God's other divine attributes, the gospel, and the gospel's occurrence and proclamation "now" (motifs vi-viii and x) are not so much in evidence (although a partial attestation to God's graciousness is arguably apparent in v. 5, corroborated by vv. 6-8).

We will now expand on these observations a little more fully.

4.1. Subsection One, 4:1-8:
Scriptural Corroboration of Key Soteriological Principles

It is difficult to construe Romans 4:1 precisely in the Greek; it is hard to tell whether Abraham is the subject of the discovery being spoken of or in some sense its object.[24] But perhaps not a lot turns on that alternative at this point. Regardless of whether it is the readers' or Abraham's understanding that is in view, readers will discover something about Abraham — as Paul wants to present him — in the following verses: "What . . . shall we say that Abraham, our forefather, discovered in this matter?" (v. 1).[25] This query also introduces the new motif of Abraham's fatherhood.

The seven verses that follow focus on the motif of "works of law" (v), defining it explicitly and associating it with boasting; the motif of crediting in relation to righteousness (i); and the interweaving of most of the motifs within two important scriptural citations, Genesis 15:6 and Psalm 32:1-2 [31:1-2 LXX]. Emerging from all this is a simple argument, although Paul shifts his terms rather awkwardly at times.

If Abraham "was justified by works" (v. 2), then "righteousness" was credited to him as a matter of obligation, just as workers receive wages: "when a man works, his wages are not credited to him as a gift, but as an obligation" (v. 4).[26]

This, it seems, in the case of religious work, could even result in a legitimate "boast" of work well done: "he had something to boast about" (v. 2). However, Paul denies this whole dynamic in relation to Abraham, largely on the basis of Genesis 15:6. The Genesis text speaks only of Abraham's believing, or faith, as present and therefore presumably activating the credit of righteousness: "to the man who does not work but trusts God who justifies the wicked, his faith is credited as righteousness" (v. 5). This claim explicates the point implicit in the statement from Scripture that has just been quoted in v. 3: "Abraham believed God, and it was credited to him as righteousness."

Psalm 32, quoted in vv. 7-8, most probably because of its analogous use of the verb λογίζομαι, reinforces this claim. In that Psalm, Paul asserts, "David . . . speaks of the blessedness of the man to whom God credits righteousness apart from works" (v. 6), although, as the Psalm casts it, the crediting actually refers to God's *not* crediting sins: "Blessed are they whose transgressions are forgiven. . . . Blessed is the man whose sin the Lord will never count against him." Still, the more basic point holds that God does not credit things to humanity strictly in relation to equity, whether righteousness positively or sins negatively. God's crediting (or not) is indeed a gift.

Thus, this compact discussion serves essentially as a scriptural corroboration (motif ix) of the central claim from the thesis statements that God justifies on the basis of belief, or faith, alone (ii); God seems to have acted in this fashion in relation to both Abraham and the person of whom David speaks (if that is not David himself). It is also possible to argue that an overt crediting of righteousness to the believing individual is evident as well (i). The receipt of "righteousness" seems, moreover, to be tied closely to the act of justification (iv; so v. 2). And the criterion of faith is quite explicitly contrasted with any justification in relation to works (v), which would apparently place God under an obligation and allow the recipient of that justification to boast. Scripture, it seems, simply rules this out. Paul even uses a phrase in passing that emphasizes God's saving attributes (vii) — "God who justifies the wicked" (v. 5). Indeed, this subsection seems to be an important corroboration of most of the claims that Paul has made in his thesis statements. Motifs i, ii, iv, v, vii, and ix all arguably receive explication and reinforcement here.

4.2. Subsection Two, 4:9-12:
Application to the Specific Issue of Circumcision

The correlation between justification and belief, or faith, now seems to be pressed home against the distinction between Jew and non-Jew in vv. 9-12 through the introduction of the new motifs of circumcision and uncircumcision. The ethnic differentiation between Jew and pagan, a preoccupation of Paul's through much of the discussion of the problem in 1:18–3:20, is evident in the thesis statements only implicitly, within the claims of universality, freighted by the words "all" and "everyone" (and those, in relation to the principle of believing). In the present short argument these concerns seem to reemerge. Here Paul leans again primarily — as he does through almost all of chapter 4 — on Genesis 15:6, although the angle of its application shifts from that in vv. 1-8. The argument is now temporal, still building on the basic claim that "Abraham's faith was credited to him as righteousness" (v. 9b), but now asking *when* this "blessedness" arrived: "Was it before or after he had been circumcised [i.e., in Genesis 17]?"[27] Of course "[i]t was not after, but before" (v. 10), because Genesis 15:6 occurs two chapters earlier in the story. Paul goes on to make the apparently reasonable application that Abraham's ancestry — literally, "fatherhood"; τὸν προπάτορα — can now be applied to both the uncircumcised and the circumcised, provided that they believe: he is "the ancestor of all who believe without being circumcised . . . and likewise the ancestor of the circumcised, . . . who also follow the example of the faith that our ancestor Abraham had" (vv. 11-12; literally, τοῖς στοιχοῦσιν τοῖς ἴχνεσιν τῆς ἐν ἀκροβυστίᾳ πίστεως τοῦ πατρὸς ἡμῶν Ἀβραάμ).[28] Indeed, the important Jewish motif of circumcision is rather redefined by this realization, being accorded the status of a "sign" and a "seal" of believing (v. 11; the word "seal" arguably carries on the commercial analogy already used in vv. 1-8; the word "sign" is more likely to have been drawn from Genesis 17 — see Gen. 17:11 LXX).

In this subsection, then, Paul's argumentative interests seem to narrow. The motif of scriptural corroboration (ix) is again apparent, operating in relation to the motif of faith (ii), here especially in relation to that motif's implicit universality. No further motifs from the thesis paragraphs seem to be strongly endorsed beyond these two. The new motif of Abraham's ancestry or fatherhood recurs from v. 1, here in a much stronger argumentative role, and it is interesting to note that this notion seems to displace justification (iv). Instead of being justified, as is conventional in the other texts, believers — whether uncircumcised or circumcised — are now children of one ancestor, Abraham.

4.3. Subsection Three, 4:13-22: Discussion of the Nature of Faith

Verses 13-21 are perhaps best viewed as an extended articulation of the motifs of faith and scriptural attestation (ii and ix) before Paul returns to an important christological summary that launches from v. 22. It is becoming increasingly clear that the correlation of these motifs is at the center of Paul's current argumentative concern.

In v. 13 "the law" is again introduced in a probable reprise of motif v. Paul claims — at times a little cryptically — that "the promise that he [Abraham and his descendants] would inherit the world" does not come through the law but through faith. If it did come through the law, then faith and the promise, he suggests, would have been "null and . . . void" (v. 14); moreover, the law functions to bring "wrath" and hence not inheritance of the world. Only "where there is no law, neither is there violation" (v. 15). Certainly, the argument here is very compact, and it reprises the relatively new motif of "promise."[29]

Paul then makes a transition — mentioning grace in passing — to a longer discussion of the nature of faith that extends from v. 18 to the end of v. 21. Abraham has faith in the resurrecting God, "the God . . . who gives life to the dead" (v. 17). Accordingly, Abraham believed in hope (v. 18), in defiance of bodily realities — both his and Sarah's (v. 19) — without wavering, glorifying God (v. 20), "being fully convinced that God was able to do what he had promised" (v. 21). Indeed, "this is why 'it was credited to him as righteousness'" (v. 22 NIV). So this dramatic if convoluted subsection seems to be an extended portrait of faith (motif ii) informed by justification (iv). After this heroic but perhaps also rather intimidating depiction of Abraham's faith, Paul fashions a transition back to more overtly Christian material.

4.4. Subsection Four, 4:23-25: Christologically Focused Summary

Paul claims that these words "were written not for his sake alone, but for ours also" (vv. 23b-24a), meaning the words of Genesis 15:6, which are liberally cited in the preceding subsection. Those who believe "in him who raised Jesus our Lord from the dead" will, like Abraham, have righteousness credited to them (v. 24b). Paul thus sets up some sort of analogy between Christians and the believing Abraham. A fairly straightforward way of construing this is to assume that Christians, in their believing, copy Abraham, who would consequently be their ancestor in the sense of being their prototypical example. Both believe primarily in the same object, the resurrecting God. But Christian believers must in addition affirm certain key theological statements that are apparently based in part on the notion of atonement (motif iii): they must believe that Jesus "was handed over to death for our trespasses" as well as being "raised [to life] for our justification" (v. 25; a final allusion to motif iv).[30]

So here christological material reenters the discussion after rather a long absence — since 3:25 — within a broader analogy between Christians and their believing father, Abraham. This final, climactic subsection functions to reestablish the importance of Christ. The main emphases, however, remain on faith and scriptural attestation (motifs ii and ix), where they have been for most of the chapter.

In broader conclusion to this third, corroborative section in Paul's argument in Romans (4:1-25), it should be emphasized that a fair construal of the text does seem to supply a plausible scriptural attestation to Justification theory's main elements. In particular, vv. 1-8 endorse compactly almost all its critical motifs, only vi, viii, and x remaining unattested (God's justice, a specific reference to the gospel, and appropriate temporal references — which would be difficult given Abraham's historical location). From this point on, the subsections in the chapter's argument tend to endorse a more limited set of Justification motifs. Verses 9-12 primarily endorse the importance of faith (ii) in terms of scriptural witness (ix);

vv. 13-16a also perform this function, but with an attestation from v. 15 in an aside to works of law (v); and vv. 16b-22 again strongly endorse the element of faith (ii). Some of the subsections emphasize the associated motif of universality (within ii). The new motif of Abraham's ancestry — literally fatherhood — is strongly emphasized by Paul's argument in the second and third subsections, but arguably this emphasis functions in relation to faith and scriptural attestation as well, the former — "faith" — really redefining it. Verses 23-25 then emphasize righteousness, faith, atonement, and justification (i-iv, with scriptural attestation, ix, being implicit). And a cryptic allusion to the problem (v) is perhaps apparent in v. 25a, although not in articulated terms (viz., in terms of the failure of works of law). Hence, the witness of Romans 4 to the solution announced by Paul's thesis paragraphs is found primarily in vv. 1-8 and 23-25. The intervening material attests plausibly to important elements within it, notably to the motifs of faith and scriptural corroboration. Without the two bracketing sections, however, readers would be hard pressed to derive from that material a definition of the solution in its fullness.

And with our survey of the conventional approach to Romans 1–4 largely complete, it can now be seen that not all of the interpretative elements within it are of equal importance when we are weighing Paul's ultimate commitment to Justification theory.

§5. Some Implications

The analysis of Justification theory's key assumptions and metaphors that was supplied in chapter one can now be reintroduced usefully into our argument. There we saw that the definition of the problem is fundamental with the establishment of the theory's two root metaphors — a rational, reflective individual (I) becoming aware of a just God (II) — followed by the realization of wrongdoing or error (Ia). These elements must come first so that the entire theory works "forward." Metaphor I and the basis for metaphor II are both in place very early on in the conventional reading of Romans, being established by 1:18-20 (perhaps supplemented by 2:14-15). Metaphor II then emerges fully in relation to the introduction of Ia, human error, but the latter can be achieved by any of the subordinate subsections dealing with sinfulness: 1:21-23, perhaps with the addition of vv. 24-28 and/or vv. 29-31; or the hypocrisy articulated in 2:1-3 and again in 2:17-24; or the blanket scriptural condemnation in 3:10-18. Strictly speaking, only one of these subsections is even really necessary for the establishment of the key point. Similarly, an overt statement of the theory's principle of desert does not necessarily need to be made, and certainly not repeatedly: see 1:32 and 2:6 in context (i.e., extending to v. 10 or 11), and also 2:2. It is implicit in God's judgment of wrongdoing (II) that has already been noted, although doubtless it is helpful to have this important point spelled out.

With the all-important vestibule in place, the statement of the solution —

atonement in terms of some mechanism of satisfaction, and faith as the criterion of appropriation (IIa and Ib) — can be even briefer. In fact, the assertion of Christ's atoning death *is* brief, in 3:25. That of the appropriation of salvation through faith is also brief — perhaps only 3:22. If scriptural corroboration and elucidation is really necessary — as promised by 3:21 — then 4:1-8 certainly suffices at this point. It is hard to see what the rest of chapter 4 adds that is of vital theoretical significance (assuming for the sake of argument that the contribution of vv. 1-8 is), although the final christological focus in vv. 23-25 may be useful.

And this all adds up to a remarkably compact expression of Justification theory:

> 1:18-20, perhaps supplemented by 2:14-15;
> 1:21-23/24-28/29-31 or 2:1-3/17-24 or 3:10-18;
> 1:32 or 2:6[-10/11] or 2:2;
> 3:25;
> 3:22;
> plus possibly 3:21 and 4:1-8 and 4:23-25.

This is a total of just over fifty verses — counting generously — in a text of double that length. At minimum it could be as few as a dozen.[31] And a set of useful interpretative distinctions is now implicit in these realizations. In fact three zones of relative interpretative importance can now be identified.

We have already demarcated the first zone, which is concerned with the theoretical claims that are absolutely essential for corroborating the actual presence of Justification theory within Paul's text. There are not many such claims that have to be made, but at some point this minimal set must be explicitly endorsed by the text if Justification theory is actually to be affirmed. Moreover, if the presence of that theory within Paul's thought is going to be challenged, then the texts undergirding these particular claims will presumably play an especially strategic role in any such endeavor. This primary interpretative zone provides, in addition, a benchmark against which to measure other texts in Paul and the rest of the New Testament to see whether they launch the theory as well (although it is apparent almost straightaway that few, if any, do).

The second zone of interpretative importance concerns the claims necessary to establish the more general plausibility of the reading. We have just seen that the theory's essential claims are launched by a relatively small number of statements within the text. But they must be launched by a reading that can nevertheless supply a plausible account of the *entire* text. So a second zone of interpretative relevance comprises the more general exegetical claims that support its primary theoretical assertions. If this second zone is not defensible, then Justification theory will be vulnerable to a rereading that can supply an account of the text as a whole — and can accuse it, in effect, of theological cherry-picking.

But there is a zone of nuanced and subtle interpretative decision making beyond these two areas that does not affect *either* the activation of the theory *or* the basic plausibility of the exegesis on offer. So a third differentiation is possible, between the foregoing two categories and irrelevant, or adiaphoric, questions and claims (with this distinction probably existing more as a continuum than as a sharp dividing line).

Hence, not all exegetical decisions are of equal importance when our concern is ultimately to evaluate the plausibility of Justification theory as an account of Paul. Some decisions will not affect the presence or absence of the theory in Paul directly, but they remain important as part of a broadly plausible exegetical case. And other exegetical decisions will not be relevant to our concern at all. In short, we will not need to give a complete account of the text.[32]

With these interpretative distinctions in mind, we can turn to consider the conventional reading's remarkable dominance in secondary discussions of Paul.

§6. Survey

I suggest that we can rest in what follows on a high degree of interpretative consensus in relation to the foregoing description of a conventional reading of Romans 1:16–4:25. Although interpreters of this text in Paul differ over many points of detail, they tend to agree on fundamental exegetical judgments — on the text's broad argumentative function and objectives. Indeed, there is an astonishing degree of uniformity in terms of how to read this text at the most basic and important level.[33] So Robert Jewett speaks a little unhappily of "an Anglo-apologetic consensus," while A. J. M. Wedderburn characterizes the commentary at this point, even more unhappily, as "an ever-rolling stream."[34] Perhaps most importantly for my analysis, the reading dominates the key scholarly commentaries — with the partial exceptions of Dunn and Jewett — that work closely through the Greek text. It is not possible to undertake an exhaustive survey of the commentaries, although certainly we can note some of the most important.[35]

There is of course a long tradition of scholarly commentary on Romans from Germany, and the conventional reading seems apparent throughout. It is apparent in what is probably the preeminent current scholarly commentary in the German-speaking tradition, the magisterial multivolume treatment by Ulrich

Wilckens.[36] But the reading can be seen as well in the powerful account developed by Ernst Käsemann that is often presented as revisionist in apocalyptic terms — yet in relation to this reading, is not fundamentally different at all.[37] Similarly, the conventional reading is apparent in the famously explosive treatment by Karl Barth[38] and in the classic analysis by Adolf Schlatter.[39] (Schmithals's idiosyncratic work is admittedly a partial exception here, but it has generally received little support.)[40] Much the same reading is apparent in French-speaking scholarly commentary.[41] And the conventional reading is equally dominant in scholarly commentaries from the United Kingdom — so, for example, in the outstanding analysis by C. E. B. Cranfield,[42] the successor to the still significant work of W. Sanday and A. C. Headlam.[43] (J. D. G. Dunn and Robert Jewett's masterful analyses are also only partial exceptions to this claim; their revisionist aspects are treated in detail in chapter twelve.)[44] English commentary from other locations (principally, North America) also attests to this reading — for example, the essentially conservative but thorough readings offered by Douglas Moo[45] and Thomas Schreiner.[46] J. A. Fitzmyer's lucid and scholarly treatment also attests to the conventional reading of Romans 1–4.[47] Brendan Byrne's elegant and considered work is a further such Catholic attestation.[48] Philip F. Esler provides an especially indicative treatment — an explicitly sociological reading utilizing social identity theory that nevertheless recapitulates the conventional reading exactly.[49] A recent and utterly fascinating reading of Romans, deeply sensitive to rhetorical, contextual, and diatribal considerations, has been undertaken by Thomas Tobin. And it seems significant that his reading nevertheless essentially reproduces the conventional reading of Romans 1–4.[50] In a similar vein, Ben Witherington engages with rhetorical and sociological perspectives yet still arrives at the conventional reading and its conclusions.[51] And last but by no means least is Robert Jewett.[52]

I am not sure that any commentary will ever match the bibliographical depth and subtlety of this work — the culmination of a lifetime's labor on Romans.[53] And it is extremely fortunate for my analysis that it has recently appeared. Jewett traces and summarizes so much scholarly material that my own judgments in what follows can often rest to a large degree on his collations. Jewett is no mere collator, however, but a highly innovative reader of Paul, fully conversant with all the major fronts in his interpretation, and ultimately committed passionately to a socially constructive if not dynamic Pauline gospel — one rooted in a deep sensitivity to chronological, sociological, and historical issues.[54] That this benchmark analysis, then, both scholarly and probing, therefore still reproduces the conventional reading of Romans 1–4 in most particulars (with suitable qualifications),[55] is to my mind most indicative. In *this* respect — if only in this respect[56] — Jewett remains both conventional and representative of the interpretative status quo.

In sum, the tradition of advanced scholarly commentary on Romans — insofar as this sample of its leading representatives serves to indicate — *almost invariably produces the conventional reading of Romans 1–4.* The differences are only over questions of minutiae.[57]

Perhaps not surprisingly, the commentaries operating at a more popular and accessible level produce the conventional reading as well, and largely without exception. Indeed, the endorsement is sometimes rather clearer in their crisp and more streamlined analyses. It will not be necessary to annotate all the commentaries written in these terms; a representative sample should again suffice.

The endorsement of the conventional reading is especially clear in the work of C. H. Dodd,[58] but it is also apparent in comparable works.[59] Anders Nygren's lucid analysis is much consulted.[60] Most significantly, the overtly post-Sanders analysis by J. A. T. Ziesler *still* nevertheless affirms the conventional reading of Romans 1–4.[61] Similarly, the readings generated by innovative American interpreters Luke Timothy Johnson[62] and Paul Achtemeier[63] again essentially endorse the conventional approach in relation to Romans 1–4 (and this, in Johnson's case, despite affirming a subjective reading of the passage's various ambiguous πίστις Χριστοῦ genitives).[64] Leander Keck's recent contribution is highly significant because, rather like Jewett, he is a sophisticated and innovative reader of Paul, sensitive to many of the most important issues and difficulties in his interpretation; yet he still reproduces the conventional reading of the apostle's Justification material, thereby arguably generating many of those difficulties![65] An indicative set of contributions has also been made in this relation by Jean-Noël Aletti. His work, like Tobin's, is overtly sensitive to rhetorical and argumentative considerations, yet adumbrates the conventional reading of Romans 1–4 again![66]

There are, however, a few significant exceptions at this level that will have to be treated alongside the suggestions of other revisionists — short commentaries (of very different natures) by John O'Neill[67] and N. T. Wright (and Wright's assertions here are supplemented by numerous other short studies) — although, as usual, the conventional reading tends to linger within their analyses.[68] Contributions by Robert Morgan[69] and Brendan Byrne's preliminary study[70] will also require careful consideration, although ultimately, despite various probing suggestions, they are largely conventional as well. But this revisionist tradition is extremely small (and I will suggest in due course that its solutions are also not especially successful).

It should probably be granted by this point then that the conventional reading of Romans 1–4 does indeed dominate the bulk of its actual commentary, whether articulated at the most scholarly level or freighted in more popular terms. And the scholarly commentary will clearly be one of our most important dialogue partners in what follows, especially in terms of the conventional reading's justification and defense. But we will also engage with the legion of specialized studies that endorses various specific points within this consensus, as well as the accompanying auxiliary corps that attacks the revisionist criticisms and suggestions of interpreters like Sanders. It goes without saying that this great wave of studies assailing the "new perspective" also produces — and ardently defends — the conventional reading of Romans 1–4 and Justification theory.[71] (It should also be noted that German-speaking scholarship has generally responded to the new perspective only very recently, so its traditions of Pauline interpretation bear few if any marks from that debate and the issues it generates.[72]) And ecumenical discussions have also produced some trenchant defenses of Justification theory in relation to the conventional reading, as seen most clearly in the penetrating and scholarly work of John Reumann.[73]

Excursus: Additional Sources

My claim concerning the dominance of the conventional reading can be usefully corroborated by broadening the scope of our survey with some further soundings.

Systematic (or, at least, more systematic) treatments of Paul's thought almost invariably reproduce the conventional reading of Romans 1–4, parlaying that in turn into articulations of Justification theory.[74] So too broader treatments of New Testament theology are usually committed to Justification theory and its definitive articulation by Romans 1–4, when they turn to consider Paul. And treatments of Paul's thought in specific relation to Romans also tend to endorse the conventional reading.[75]

Bultmann is probably still the most important such representative; the elegance and intelligence of his analysis seem unmatched (although he is often opposed).[76] We have already noted in part two, chapter nine that he is a powerful advocate of the conventional reading. Other German theological treatments of Paul are comparable (in this respect!), if not so elegant or famous.[77] Of special note is Stuhlmacher, ostensibly a salvation-historical correction to Käsemann but also strongly affirmative of the conventional approach to Romans 1–4 and of Justification theory.[78] (Schnelle's major treatment swims against the tide for much of the time.[79]) A more conservative continental study that is nevertheless widely read in English-speaking circles — in translation — is Ridderbos.[80] And this affirms Justification theory in Paul emphatically, although alongside Reformed commitments.[81]

In English-speaking circles, J.-C. Beker has provided a powerful and much-discussed treatment of Paul's thought, and while this strongly affirms both apocalyptic and salvation-historical emphases, Justification theory remains apparent at times, and certainly in relation to Romans 1–4.[82] An older classic treatment treatment of Paul's thought, still influential, is by D. E. H. Whiteley, developed from his Oxford lectures.[83] The current standard treatment of Paul's thought in the English-speaking world, however, is by J. D. G. Dunn.[84] Dunn has his interpretative revisions and idiosyncracies, but *still* reproduces an essentially conventional reading of Paul that ultimately endorses the principles of Justification theory as the heart of his gospel. Since the appearance of this benchmark, a more conservative description has been offered by Thomas R. Schreiner[85] (and Gordon Fee's exegetical analysis of Paul's Christology should be included at this point[86]). The conventional reading of Romans 1–4, underwriting an overarching construal — at least at the key points — in terms of Justification, is discernible in all these studies.

Paul is of course also described within broader treatments of New Testament theology. However, these are rarer in English-speaking scholarship than they are on the Continent, those that exist are mostly rather dated, and they tend to adopt conservative — and hence, in the present relation, conventional — opinions: see, for example, the classic contribution by George Eldon Ladd, the posthumous work of George Caird, and recent treatments by Philip Esler, I. Howard Marshall, and Frank Thielman.[87]

In sum, all these studies, and indeed most of the theological descriptions of Paul currently on offer, tend to affirm both the conventional reading of Romans 1–4 and the construal of Paul's gospel, at least in part if not in whole, in terms of Justification theory.

(Moreover, it has already been noted how the admission of Justification theory at certain points then allows it to override other unconditional systems in effect: see part one, chapter three.) Cogent countervailing voices are rare.[88]

It is not surprising to find then that the conventional reading, linked closely with Justification theory, is widely apparent in introductory treatments of the apostle as well. It recurs in introductions specifically to Paul's thought, life, and writings;[89] in introductions to Paul in the context of broader introductions to the New Testament as a whole;[90] and throughout the standard reference works[91] — thereby dominating any initial approach to the subject by readers seeking an orientation to such questions.

This dominance extends — perhaps not surprisingly — to the highly influential introductions and comments supplied with study Bibles (at which point we begin to link hands with the soundings into popular conservative Christian culture made in part two, chapter nine — i.e., Billy Graham, the Four Spiritual Laws, the Roman Road, and so on).[92] I have consulted *The New Oxford Annotated Bible* (consulted in the NRSV translation)[93] and the *Life Application Study Bible* (consulted in the New Living Translation).[94] Many others could be mentioned in this regard.[95]

A final and possibly highly significant point of comparison is the set of avant-garde groups working on Romans at various scholarly colloquia — especially the annual meetings of the Society of Biblical Literature. An especially innovative group convened by Cristina Grenholm and Daniel Patte has nevertheless consistently reproduced the conventional approach to Romans 1–4 and the corresponding account of the gospel in terms of Justification theory.[96] Similarly, the earlier attempts of the Pauline Theology Group to address Romans with fresh eyes in the 1980s and 1990s resulted in a largely conventional reading (although Wright's contributions are a partial exception),[97] and this despite the exploration of a number of specific and highly revisionist interpretative proposals.[98] Reinterpretative pressure is also being exerted on the conventional approach indirectly from the newly politicized approaches to Paul that dialogue, in particular, with the imperial cult and its possible role within Paul's texts.[99] Many more such scholarly consultations could of course be noted.[100]

This concludes our preliminary description of the conventional reading of Romans 1:16–4:25, the construal that undergirds, and in effect unleashes, the operation of Justification theory in Paul. Many of the specific textual arguments that inform this reading will be revisited during the detailed exegesis that follows. But this account should suffice for us to begin our critical consideration of its cogency, which begins immediately, in chapter eleven. Although it is a plausible reading, we will see shortly that it is not a perfect one.

Feet of Clay

§1. Preamble

Three claims from the preceding argument set the stage for the following discussion, which now begins to turn again toward the critical task. First, we have seen at some length through part one, chapters one through six, that any commitment to Justification theory within the broader description of Paul's thought will lead to numerous difficulties at the theoretical level and in empirical terms. We have also seen how these difficulties underlie a great deal of modern Pauline debate. And, second, we have seen in chapter ten that the conventional reading of Romans 1:16–4:25 — a powerful and widespread reading — does indeed endorse Justification theory. It should follow immediately, then, that this reading will produce the difficulties that have already been noted in theoretical form.

Yet the difficulties generated by the conventional construal of Romans 1–4 are not widely recognized. Somewhat incredibly, the reading seems to enjoy a great weight of plausibility in any debate. And of course our discoveries in part two, chapters seven through nine, suggest why — and this is our third basic claim: Justification theory has developed a discourse that protects itself with a powerful hermeneutic of generosity, simultaneously directing a hermeneutic of suspicion against its critics and any exegetical alternatives, thereby smothering any putative difficulties.

Now, however, informed by clear understandings of what the theoretical level needs — not to mention, its destructive consequences — and how the discourse's broader superstructure could be insinuating itself illegitimately into interpretation, we are in a position to examine the relationship between the theory's textual base and its superstructure more closely. *Does the text of Romans 1–4 in fact support Justification theory as smoothly as it purports to?* In this chapter, we will discover numerous points where the text of Romans 1–4 does *not* deliver explicitly what Justification theory needs. These are, in effect, textual "sins of omission" —

what I have dubbed, in part two, chapter seven, *textual underdeterminations*. Further, we will find points where the text delivers overtly something that Justification theory does not need and at times is positively embarrassed by. These are, in effect, "sins of commission" — what I have dubbed *textual overdeterminations*.

Text overdeterminations (!) and underdeterminations[1] (?)

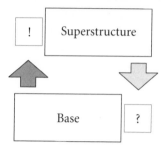

A detailed account of these textual under- and overdeterminations will contribute to a growing sense that the Justification reading of Romans 1–4 is vulnerable (and a total of thirty-five under- or overdeterminations will ultimately be suggested). Our investigation of the discourse's accumulating problems will then continue with a reprise of the theoretical problems that have already been noted through part one, although here in specific relation to Romans 1–4 — intrinsic, systematic, and empirical difficulties (while many of these also parlay at this point into difficulties at the proximate frame, i.e., the transition from chapters 1–4 to 5–8). Hence, by the end of this chapter, we will have compiled an agenda of problems that any advocate of both Justification theory and the conventional reading of Romans 1–4 — the theory's all-important textual base in Paul — simply must address.[2] Absent some effective response, the glittering edifice that is the Justification discourse, crowned by its famous theory, will turn out to have feet of clay.

§2. Textual Underdeterminations

Textual underdeterminations in the conventional reading of Romans 1–4 will be treated in what follows in terms of that reading's three main subsections as they are presently identified — 1:18–3:20; 1:16-17, 3:21-31; and 4:1-25.[3]

2.1. Textual Underdeterminations — Romans 1:18–3:20

There are four principal instances of textual underdetermination in 1:18–3:20, the first major phase in the conventional reading and its associated theory.

(1) *The Scene-Setting Strategy*

It is important to note that Paul never states in so many words that 1:18–3:20 is de-signed to fulfill the argumentative function that most interpreters hold it to fulfill (and reasonably obviously so). That is, he never states words to the effect, "1:18–3:20 will set the stage for the gospel," or "... will prepare for the gospel," or "... will first indict all humanity, so as to create a problem, to which 3:21-26 will announce the Christian solution." This critical assumption concerning the entire argumen-tative disposition of 1:18–3:20 is largely assumed to be operative without direct comment or supporting evidence from the text itself. It tends — as we have al-ready seen in chapter ten — to be simply asserted by modern readers.[4] Presum-ably, then, it is a retrospective judgment that this is the best or even the only co-herent way to construe the overarching argument, once that has been processed. So Paul's original auditors would not have made this decision initially but would have had to realize it in retrospect, after having reached at least 3:20, but more likely 4:25, and then looked back on the preceding discussion, presumably also having given some thought to the matter (and possibly assisted here by the letter bearer and reader). Two small pieces of localized evidence may have assisted this decision, but they both turn out to beg the question.

First, 1:18 is linked to the preceding verse and claims by γάρ, a word that of-ten carries causal force. Translated "because," this signifier could suggest that 1:18–3:20 is the rational explanation or cause of the claims in v. 17. The gospel is preached in vv. 16-17 "because" the problem has first been established, although its explication takes place beginning in v. 18. And certainly this is one possible reading of γάρ in 1:18, and a small but valid potential signal for the conventional reading's identification of Paul's argumentative strategy from here forward.[5] However, it is only fair to note that γάρ can take much looser meanings than this, sometimes connecting statements in a weaker sense better denoted by the En-glish "for." It can also merely clarify — "you see" — or denote inference — "so" or "then." It can even function pleonastically on occasion (i.e., as little more than a clearing of the throat, the equivalent of the English "um" or "ah"). *And Paul clearly uses it in these alternative, perhaps blander senses fairly frequently in the surrounding argumentation.* Indeed, on several occasions it is even nonsensical to supply a strong causal meaning to the marker in context, even in declarative sen-tences.[6] Hence, we need clear information from the surrounding text to help us to determine in what sense Paul is using γάρ in 1:18. γάρ is not an unambiguous sig-nal concerning Paul's argumentative strategy; rather, the strategy that we con-clude is operative from 1:18 onward will signal how we are to interpret γάρ in 1:18! And one *possible* reading of the connective γάρ is clearly insufficient reason to ground the claim that 1:18–3:20 is a particular rhetorical strategy that grounds Paul's entire theological program in turn! One reading of this marker can cer-tainly integrate with that proposal — that can be freely admitted — but it can hardly carry it.

The second possible snippet of evidence might come from Paul's brief discussion of his "gospel" just preceding 1:18 in 1:13-17 (see the verb's presence in v. 15, and a threefold reference to the noun in vv. 16-17). It might be argued that 1:18–3:20 is Paul's argumentative and theological preparation for the fuller explication of the gospel that begins in 3:21, because that is how Paul's gospel generally unfolds. But this suggestion begs the key question spectacularly and runs simultaneously into a set of awkward empirical and framing difficulties, some of which have already been noted and should suffice for the present moment (and some of which will be noted shortly, thereby reinforcing the strength of the argument's rejection here). We have already seen in part one, chapter five, how the meager evidence available to us in relation to these questions suggests that Paul did not evangelize primarily through formal preaching, as the conventional reading and its associated theory tend to assume. Nor — more importantly — did he apparently proclaim a gospel that was structured in this fashion, as a solution following a prior definition of a problem. Insofar as we can tell, his presentations were dramatic, narrative, christocentric, and pneumatological. So the external evidence, such as it is, suggests the *falsity* of the assumption that 1:18–3:20 prepares for the announcement of the gospel beginning in 3:21 by establishing a prior problem; this does not seem to be how Paul either spread the gospel or preached it. And in part four, chapter thirteen we will learn that essentially the same problems for this assertion recur at the letter's circumstantial frame (i.e., this is not why Paul generally wrote his letters, nor is it demonstrably why he seems to have written Romans; moreover, the only remotely plausible theories for the letter's composition do not support the claim that he began systematically to preach his gospel from the beginning of the letter body). Although the theoretical, paradigmatic, church-historical, and ideo-cultural locations of most modern readers of Romans incline them strongly toward the assumption that Paul must be working forward at this point, from plight to solution, part two has shown that these pressures are illegitimate and must, if necessary, be resisted. Such readers must not construct Paul in their own image. He must be allowed to speak and argue as an ancient, and possibly quite alien figure.

We conclude, then: the all-important assumption that 1:18–3:20 is an argument that prepares systematically, in an a priori fashion, for the later proclamation of the gospel is not stated by the text at any point. Moreover, good reasons exist for doubting that this is how Paul preached the gospel, and why he wrote Romans in any case. The basic case for the conventional reading here is largely circular: this is the best construal of the overarching argument; therefore, this is the strategy that we detect from 1:18 onward, and vice versa.[7]

(2) The Key Premises in Relation to Humanity and God

In like manner, the text never states that Paul himself is committed to the two underlying metaphors that drive both the conventional reading and Justification theory, concerning the natures of humanity and God (the former in terms of "philosophical man" and the latter in terms of retributive justice). The argument in 1:18–2:11 presupposes these root metaphors; however, Paul himself never explicitly declares his allegiance to them or to the argument in which they are embedded (as we have just seen).[8] And of course many difficulties are set in motion by the assumption that Paul is so committed, especially at the proximate and systematic frames. These difficulties will disappear if we relax this assumption, and nothing in the text stands overtly against this move, because Paul's personal commitments within this critical argument, like the strategy conventionally assumed to be operative, are unstated. And we come now to a more complex point.

(3) The Identification of the Hypocritical Judge in 2:1-5 as the Jew

It is universally acknowledged that the argument turns at 2:1 upon a particular figure (indeed, this is absolutely unavoidable). The conventional reading ends up identifying this figure with Judaism, and with Paul himself — momentous determinations. But in fact a combination of under- and overdeterminations is usually present in these claims. The text itself supplies a considerable amount of information concerning this figure but points the argumentative finger explicitly only at a Jewish Teacher. This encoded opponent is quite clear. However, the conventional reading's universalizing additions in terms of Jews per se, and then implicitly in terms of Paul himself, are never explicitly justified; they are vital to the developing argument and its associated theology, but they are underdetermined. Recognition of what data is present here then generates further embarrassments for the conventional reading in the form of an overdetermination that will be noted shortly. But we should begin our more detailed discussion by noting first what the text does explicitly and unavoidably encode — and then fails to specify.

The text turns in 2:1 on "a person who judges" — ὦ ἄνθρωπε πᾶς ὁ κρίνων. The arthrous nominative construction here continues the initial vocative, and Paul is now obviously apostrophizing — addressing some rhetorical construct in the second person singular. This figure who "judges" is then noted in vv. 1-3 no fewer than *five* times (four times in v. 1, once ironically, and once in v. 3; God's judgment, mentioned twice through vv. 2 and 3, seems ironically juxtaposed with this figure as well). But the figure is further identified as ἀναπολόγητος (2:1a), apparently because of the sinful things that he practices — τὰ [γὰρ] αὐτὰ πράσσεις ὁ κρίνων, a motif that is stated twice, as well as once more generically (see vv. 1, 2, 3). He has therefore justly earned the sobriquet "hypocrite," in both its ancient and modern senses: he is only "playacting," behaving inconsistently, specifically by teaching righteousness when he is in fact sinful (the ancient meaning), and as a result, he is also merely simulating virtue and masking turpitude (the Christian, and post-Christian and modern meaning).[9] And this is the obvious argumentative force of the text: a judger has sinned and so been found wanting by his[10] own standards; in condemning others, he has also rather foolishly condemned himself![11]

The commentators are largely unanimous in recognizing this basic dynamic, because it is so obvious.[12] But we must now tease out the further textual developments of this figure. Like the god Janus, he faces both ways.

In relation to what follows, Paul seems to encode this figure still more explicitly with a message of divine judgment on the basis of deeds — the program that the text articulates more fully in 2:6-8 (there utilizing scriptural language). And various explicit points confirm this content. In v. 2 the text draws the judge with a first person plural verb into broader agreement with the principle of judgment by works that has just been enunciated in Romans 1: οἴδαμεν δὲ ὅτι τὸ κρίμα τοῦ θεοῦ ἐστιν κατὰ ἀλήθειαν ἐπὶ τοὺς τὰ τοιαῦτα πράσσοντας. This figure is then taunted beginning in v. 3b with the prospect of resisting a patient and forbearing God who allows time for repentance before the day of judgment arrives. Paul's accusations in v. 5 that this figure is hard-hearted and impenitent are then completed by a direct assertion of God's judgment in accordance with deeds. That is, a figure just accused of hypocritically not practicing what he preaches about the expectations of a just God, is accused further of storing up judgment for himself. Consequently, this looks like a more specific characterization of the inconsistency in question — of actually preaching divine judgment on sin, and then sinning. Hence, this further determination by the text seems unavoidable: the judged judger makes his accusations *in terms of desert*. Desert is the actual content of his judging, and the reason for his hypocrisy.

A consideration of the paragraphs that precede the figure's explicit arrival in 2:1 reinforces this determination. The program of desert apparently endorsed by the judger — although not followed personally — *is an apt summary of the essential principles of 1:18-32,* and even echoes some of that subsection's concluding phraseology. Romans 1:18-32 is primarily an account of pagan ἀδικία, culminating in a crafted vice list that names twenty-one sins and emphasizes culpability; pagans are "without excuse" or ἀναπολογήτους (1:20). Thus, it is above all *a judgment* — a judgmental condemnation of the willfully culpable. Verse 32 concludes with the admission that the pagans know God's righteous judgment that those practicing such things are worthy of death (but they nevertheless brazenly approve of those who continue to do them . . .): οἵτινες τὸ δικαίωμα τοῦ θεοῦ ἐπιγνόντες ὅτι οἱ τὰ τοιαῦτα πράσσοντες ἄξιοι θανάτου εἰσίν κ.τ.λ. One of these phrases is then picked up exactly by what follows — twice (see 2:2 and 3) — and placed in the mouth of the hypocritical judger: λογίζῃ [δὲ] τοῦτο, ἄνθρωπε ὁ κρίνων τοὺς τὰ τοιαῦτα πράσσοντας [κ.τ.λ.], (and recall that this figure has also — to make matters still clearer — just been described himself as ἀναπολόγητος, 2:1). Hence, the figure in 2:1 is the mirror image of the discourse in 1:18-32 both substantively and dramatically (i.e., in terms of characterization). He has *spoken* the discourse of 1:18-32, at least in some sense, and the argument's bite after 2:1 consists of *this* figure's entrapment in his own aggressive program. This judge has been hoisted by his own petard. It seems, moreover, in the light of the entirely Jewish tenor of 1:18-32 that he is himself a Jewish figure in some sense. Certainly he is enunciating a recognizably Jewish discourse, while his hypocrisy only makes sense within a Jewish framework; he is resisting the need for repentance in relation to Jewish ethics — a program he himself espouses — and thereby risking condemnation by the one God on the future day of judgment. (Moreover, he possesses a degree of sophistication — almost certainly beyond basic literacy, involving eloquence and scriptural training. As we will see in more detail shortly, 1:18-32 is a witty, superior text replete with wordplays and graceful syntax. It also faithfully reproduces the Jewish propaganda literature in general, and the Wisdom of Solomon in particular. These markers of literacy, learning, elite status, and sophistication will be confirmed at every subsequent turn of the argument.)

And in fact the commentators — as we have already indicated — are largely unanimous in their recognition of most of these textual determinations; they are, after all, very clearly signaled. But what needs to be recognized further is that this encoded hypocritical judger runs consistently through the rest of this phase of the argument — as far as 3:19-20. Two principal streams of substantive and dramatic signals suggest this ongoing identification.

On the one hand, and as we have just seen, the judger is obviously committed in substantive terms to a program of divine judgment in accordance with desert, and this is the sustained position of one protagonist in the diatribe of 3:1-9a. As we will see in more detail in part four, chapter fourteen, the interlocutor in vv. 2, 4, 6, 8b and 9b merely reiterates the importance of divine action in strict accordance with the demands of retributive justice — even if every person is thereby condemned — thereby consistently repudiating any concessions to Jewish sinfulness. And this figure characteristically quotes Scripture in support of these rejections — Psalms 116:11 and 51:4 at least — as does 2:6. He consistently maintains the need for God "to judge the cosmos" (see 3:6). So this figure reproduces the theological posture of 2:1-6; they are the same in terms of content.

On the other hand, the judger in 2:1-6 should be identified with the figure who is apostrophized from 2:17 onward in terms of *dramatic characterization*. The precise identity of the "Jew" ('Ιουδαῖος) in 2:17-23 and the pericope's subsequent argumentative function have been a storm center in much recent interpretation. Revisionists have reacted strongly to the conventional identification of this figure with the Jew per se, and his subsequent treatment by Paul (and understandably so). Indeed, 2:17 has been an important wedge point for their countervailing readings (although I will argue in chapter twelve that these have generally proved unsuccessful in broader terms). But, setting aside for the moment the question of the figure's wider implications, the conventional reading has almost invariably identified the "Jew" of 2:17-24 with the figure under pressure after 2:1, and this identification *within the text's argument* seems correct.

Like that earlier figure, the person targeted from 2:17 onward is a Jew, a male, and a hypocrite — someone who does not practice what he preaches and hence is guilty of playacting and insincerity. Essentially the same charges are made of him in 2:21-23 as in 2:1-3. He is also a similarly judgmental figure, instructing, from a superior position informed by the law, a large category of inferiors: the "blind," "those in darkness," "the stupid," and "children." (The alpha-privative used here in ἀφρόνων is also reminiscent of the distinctive style of 1:18-32; see more on this just below.) And he is adept and literate, like that earlier figure — κατηχούμενος ἐκ τοῦ νόμου. He is, moreover, strongly identified with the earlier figure simply in dramatic and stylistic terms. In both 2:1 and 2:17 the discourse turns emphatically with similar vocative and nominative constructions to address this hypocrite in an unequivocal apostrophe; compare [Δ]ιὸ ἀναπολόγητος εἶ, ὦ ἄνθρωπε πᾶς ὁ κρίνων· ἐν ᾧ γὰρ κρίνεις τὸν ἕτερον, σεαυτὸν κατακρίνεις?, with [Ε]ἰ [δὲ] σὺ Ἰουδαῖος . . . ὁ . . . διδάσκων ἕτερον σεαυτὸν οὐ διδάσκεις? These are entirely distinctive, although analogous moments in Romans: "you . . . the one who judges another . . . do you judge yourself?" and "you . . . the one who teaches another . . . do you teach yourself?!" It is highly unlikely that Paul would inflict two different constructs on his Roman auditors within the space of seventeen verses without signaling that clearly. There are, however, no signals of a significant shift in identity, and those signals that we do have indicate continuity.

2:1-8:	2:17-24:
male	male
Jew	Jew
judger	judger
learned	learned
hypocrite (i.e., also sinful)	hypocrite (i.e., also sinful)
addressed in an apostrophe	addressed in an apostrophe

These correspondences are too strong to be plausibly denied.[13] But with this identification, a further set of correlations within the argument is suggested. This judger *is* almost certainly the stubborn interlocutor in 3:1-9a as well.

The judger of 2:1-3 was strongly committed to desert (but, according to Paul, failed that criterion himself). And that figure has just been identified with the hypocritical Teacher and judger of 2:17-24 on largely dramatic and stylistic grounds. The judger of 2:1-3 has also, however, been identified with the interlocutor in 3:1-9a on substantive grounds as well. Completing the triangle, it is now relatively easy to see the learned Teacher and judger of 2:17-24 *making* the series of defensive statements in 3:1-9a — statements made by a learned figure who quotes Scripture but adopts a posture of thoroughgoing judgment.[14] And this identification then seems to continue smoothly onward to the conclusion of this phase of the argument in 3:19-20. There Paul emphasizes that the law speaks to those ἐν τῷ νόμῳ as it condemns all to sin — a dramatic point that the learned judge probably needs to feel especially, but also a substantive statement that summarizes that figure's posture in the preceding argument (and thereby precisely fulfilling the expectations of 2:1). We can say, then, that a fairly overt network of dramatic, stylistic, and substantive signals systematically encodes the argument of 1:18–3:20 as a whole in terms of a particular figure. The figure on whom the argument turns in 2:1 is the figure on whom the argument focuses throughout. (It is also worth noting that, given the presence of this unfolding argument before the eyes and ears of the Roman Christians, this figure is probably a Christian as well — although Paul might not want to extend him that courtesy: see Gal. 2:4.)

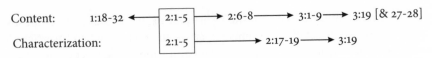

We come now to the critical point for the present discussion. It is clear that the text encodes *a* Jew as the target of Paul's argument in 1:18–3:20. However, the conventional reading identifies this figure as *the* Jew, not to mention as including Paul himself,[15] and this is absolutely critical for the function of the reading as the basis for Justification theory.[16] That theory must begin with a discussion of the generic condition of humanity as a whole; it begins with Everyman, who is also fundamentally Jewish. We can see now, however, that this vital identification in the text is underdetermined. *The text itself never takes this further momentous step unambiguously.* Although Paul does overtly attack *a* Jew in Romans 2:1–3:20, he never states in so many words that he is attacking his *own* definition of *Judaism* in general (a category that would presumably include him).[17] Neither does he introduce explicit biographical markers of inclusion (see 9:3; 11:1; Phil. 3:2-6). Extratextual considerations must be introduced in order to make this further connection, and these turn out on close examination to be rather dubious.[18]

In fact, it is surprisingly difficult to find explicit arguments in support of this claim, which is helpful further evidence of the paradigmatic nature of much of the discourse. The generic identification seems largely to be assumed.

One set of arguments that does seem to occur begins with the claim that Paul *must* "level the playing field" between pagans and Jews *before* he can preach the gospel. This establishes a fundamental equality between them before God and grounds the later claim that all are saved by faith.[19] However, while the recognition that Paul is leveling something is an accurate characterization of part of the argument in Romans 1:18–3:20, the further assumption that this is a necessary prior operation with respect to Judaism — the underdetermined move — is false on a number of counts.

(1) As we have already seen, Paul himself treats non-Christian Israel as privileged, not equal (a difficulty at the systematic frame). (2) Elsewhere in Paul any level playing field seems to arrive *in and with Christ* (see most famously Galatians 3:28; again, a difficulty at the systematic frame).[20] (3) The famous example of the grafted olive tree indicates the persistence of even a post-Christian degree of privilege for Jews (see Rom. 11:17-24); pagans are grafted into a fundamentally Jewish tree that remains Jewish (a third difficulty at the systematic frame). Added to this are two further implicit assumptions that beg the question (further instances of theoretical overdetermination). (4) It is simply not the case that Paul's critique of the law has to take place in the non-Christian vestibule as Justification theory dictates. The alternative schema drawn from Romans 5–8 indicates that Paul's argument for the law's ineffectiveness and abandonment could equally well be a post-Christian conclusion, and our analysis of Paul's biography even suggests that this was the case historically! Paul is perfectly entitled to abandon comprehensive law observance *after he has become a Christian!*, and so to ground that move christologically. Similarly, it might also be claimed (5) that only this prior demonstration of Judaism's failure establishes the later con-

clusion that all are justified equally, by faith alone. But the need for justification through faith alone must be established by the prior failure of works, not vice versa. Justification theory works forward, not backward.[21] (If this argument is accepted, a vicious circle of justification will be introduced into the heart of the discourse.)

On various counts, then, the critical hermeneutical move that identifies the Jew of 2:1–3:20 with a generic, universal Jew remains underdetermined. (And the situation is even more difficult than the conventional reader suspects. As revisionists point out, this identification is not only unwarranted; it seems to be contradicted by certain pieces of evidence, that is, by certain textual overdeterminations that will be noted in more detail shortly.)

In view of all this, it is difficult to avoid the conclusion that an absolutely critical assumption within the conventional reading is textually underdetermined; it is largely groundless (and even seems resisted by certain elements lying within and alongside the text noted momentarily). Paul never states explicitly in Romans 1:18–3:20 that he is criticizing Jews and Judaism per se, and thereby also himself, presumably in his former life. The text only ever criticizes *a* Jew — a learned, judgmental male. We turn now to the final instance of underdetermination in Romans 1:18–3:20.

(4) The Implicit Perfectionist Axiom

We saw earlier, in part one, chapter one, that Justification theory needs a "perfectionist axiom" to operate in the vestibule in relation to law observance, and so must also define Judaism in such terms. If perfect law observance is deemed initially necessary for salvation, then it is likely that all will fail to meet this requirement, thereby creating a universal constituency predisposed to become Christian. There will be *no exceptions,* and that is only appropriate. (We will discuss the main theoretical alternative to this configuration momentarily.) However, we also saw that this component in the theory raises acute difficulties at the systematic and empirical frames, because neither Paul nor Judaism more generally seems committed to perfectionism in quite this way.[22] And we can now note the further difficulty that the text never states it (raising the possibility that perfectionism is not in play).[23]

The characterization of the need for law observance is surprisingly brief and bland: the righteous judgment of God "will give to each person in accordance with his [or her] deeds" (2:5b-6). (Two sharply contrasting constituencies are then discussed, one very good and the other very bad, in 2:7-10; see more on this just below.) Further argumentative developments do not then seem to redress this apparent oversight. Paul's specific accusations of sin against a Jew in 2:21-22 are infamously crude (theft, adultery, and sacrilege; this issue is discussed further shortly) — hardly issues of perfectionism! And his final catena of condemnation in 3:10-18 functions in similarly crude terms, asserting that no one is righteous but all are corrupt in every bodily respect. Hence, these developments actually exacerbate the problem. The expectation of the argument seems at these later points to be of depravity, not the failure to perform perfectly. Thus the text of Romans 1:18–3:20 never states clearly that perfect law observance is necessary for all — but especially for Jews — and that guilt will follow on one infraction, however slight (as, e.g., The Westminster Confession does).

Perhaps, then, the actual argument of Romans 1:18–3:20 suggests the abandonment of the perfectionist position in Justification theory, however necessary it might be in theoretical terms, and the embrace of an alternative position that uses the notion of depravity. This modification might solve a number of problems. If humanity is deeply corrupt, then God need not expect perfect law observance; he could be satisfied with "reasonable" or even "minimal" law observance. But a corrupt humanity — including a corrupt Judaism — would be incapable even of this minimal level of acceptable behavior in reality and so would be condemned in any case. The universal condemnation of humanity would thereby be preserved, and God's apparent unreasonableness and harshness — expecting perfection and punishing harshly even the smallest shortfall — would seem to be mitigated. Most significantly of all, the position seems to have some purchase on the text, especially in the two sections just noted (2:21-22 and 3:10-18; perhaps supported by 1:19-32).[24]

However, these advantages are purchased for ultimately crippling costs. There are no fewer than five:

(i) The intrinsic difficulty already noted in Justification theory with respect to God's justice is mitigated only cosmetically by this reconfiguration of the theory. It still seems unjust for God to hold people accountable for not performing actions of which they are incapable. This basic conundrum is not eliminated by altering the terms of the problem — by shifting the apparent "quantities" involved. In the perfectionist variant, God expects 100 percent obedience from sinful people, and punishes them harshly — effectively executing them — if only 99 percent is forthcoming (or even only 99.9 percent!). In the depraved variant, God might expect only 51 percent obedience, but people are so deeply corrupt that they seem incapable of any effective obedience. Perhaps average obedience then lies between 1 and 10 percent. (So this situation is tantamount to expecting reasoned ethical behavior from small children, or even from animals.) Hence, the basic problem in relation to God's justice remains; it does not seem fundamentally fair to hold people accountable to a standard they cannot intrinsically attain.

(ii) The depraved variant greatly exacerbates the intrinsic problem of an incoherent anthropology. The corrupt facet within human nature has been deepened by this theoretical adjustment, so the question of how two different dimensions interrelate within the single human person is considerably complicated. The human mind now seems to be composed of the ontological equivalent of oil and water. And the deepening of the corrupt dimension within humanity leads to another possible complication.

(iii) With the corrupt side of humanity now so strong, it seems incoherent to ask a person so structured to negotiate the perceptive progressions that begin Justification theory — to make the necessary inferences about God and ethics from contemplation of the cosmos, and so on. It also seems pointless to expect this person to engage in extended ethical self-reflection, as the model unfolds. And by this stage, the conventional reading of Romans 1–4, and the entire prospective and voluntarist orientation of Justification theory, have effectively been curtailed. There is little point appealing to utterly depraved people for serious philosophical, theological, and/or ethical discernment. Hence, the addition of this strengthened caveat to the reading and theory undermines those dimensions of the discourse fairly directly.

(iv) But the empirical difficulties with respect to Judaism have also been exacerbated. Although now no longer necessarily accused of perfectionism and corruption, Judaism is necessarily accused of depravity! And it is even possible to conceive of an additional rejoinder from Judaism at this point. Whereas the external characterization of its concerns in terms of perfectionism could be rebutted as basically untrue, any characterization of its nature as inherently and obviously depraved could be rebutted not only with the same response in terms of inaccuracy but with a countervailing charge of Christian neurosis.[25] It seems positively unhealthy to see all of humanity, including all non-Christian Jews, as functioning in such a depraved way as a matter of course.

(v) Christian advocates of Justification theory might reply in turn that this is nevertheless a fundamental and essentially valid Christian insight — the deep truth of original sin. But this is a slightly deceptive deployment of an important Christian truth, and to invoke it at this non-Christian stage introduces fundamental epistemological inconsistencies into the heart of the Justification project. If this claim is to be valid, it cannot be inferred from the cosmos on an individual basis; it must be a revelation. (Only God really knows whether everyone is in fact fundamentally corrupt; a human being cannot know this definitively merely by observation, because his or her perceptions are not deep enough or the sample size wide enough; furthermore, humans cannot really know this, because they are indeed *corrupt*.) So Justification advocates, if they are to make a valid claim of depravity, must invoke a definitive particular disclosure, and one that is arguably also necessarily retrospective.[26] And in so doing, of course, they violate all the basic axioms and procedures in phase one of their model!

For all these reasons, the introduction of a depravity axiom will not save either the conventional reading of Romans 1–4 or the theory of Justification; the perfectionist axiom is probably better. And so the reading still contains an important underdetermination at this juncture. Paul never explicitly characterizes law observance in Romans 1:18–3:20 in terms of the need for perfect observance, although that axiom is critical to the successful function of the theory. Alternatively, if he does view humanity as depraved here — and this is arguably hinted at by the text — then his reading and its associated theory essentially collapse on a number of further problematic grounds and fronts. Most importantly, the theory's opening strategy becomes both pointless and self-contradictory.[27]

With these four underdeterminations identified in Romans 1:18–3:20, we turn to consider those points where Paul's thesis paragraphs arguably do not deliver what Justification advocates need.

2.2. Textual Underdeterminations — Romans 1:16-17 and 3:21-31

The key soteriological paragraphs in Romans 1–4 lend themselves to charges of underdetermination because they are so brief. I detect five principal instances of underdetermination.

(5) The Frequently Circular Analysis of the "Thesis" Paragraphs[28]

Two closely related issues are involved here. First, it is important to note that the *designation* of the so-called "thesis" paragraphs in Romans cannot be made in advance of the detailed construal of the rest of the letter.[29] (This would require Paul to mark them explicitly as thesis statements in a document unequivocally structured in terms of thesis statements, and I know of no definitive demonstration of these claims.) Certainly, this designation can emerge after the event as a fair characterization of the function of these subsections. So we can imagine the Roman Christians, after numerous rereadings and much discussion, observing that the small sections that we know now as 1:16-17 and 3:21-26 do in fact seem to summarize much that follows, and so operate as helpful theses. (And indeed, I will endorse this view myself in certain respects in due course.) However, the designation of these sections as theses cannot consequently be used to *control* the later interpretation of the letter (except insofar as the text being interpreted at that point falls outside the material already processed that led initially to the judgment that these are theses). This would be circular. In a similar sense, neither can the *content* of these subsections be imposed in advance, and used to dictate the content of the rest of the letter (or, at least, of its most important sections). The substance of the thesis paragraphs should emerge from the paragraphs themselves, and then their relationship with the rest of the argument be scrutinized.

I hope with these observations simply to forestall a vicious interpretative circle — that the main arguments of Romans are *x* because the thesis paragraphs deliver *x* in advance of the rest of the discussion; moreover, we know that they deliver *x* because the rest of the argument delivers *x*. (Or, alternatively, a false argumentative foundation — that *x* is in the thesis statements, essentially underdetermined, with *x* nevertheless used to structure the rest of the argument, *overriding* countervailing evidence there.)[30]

(6) The Strategic Function of δικαιοσύνη θεοῦ

In a similar vein to the foregoing, it is doubtful that the interpretation of the entire argument of Romans will turn significantly on the interpretation of δικαιοσύνη Θεοῦ alone. This phrase or its close equivalent is found only in 1:17; 3:5; 3:21-26 (4x); and 10:3 (2x), for a total of just eight instances. And while the strategic location of some of these instances might later legitimately emerge, the concentrations of the motif also suggest that a maximum of only four passages can be shifted by its reinterpretation (and other syntactical factors will of course have to be taken into account at these points as well). Thus, there is some work to be done before this phrase can announce the theme, or the heart, of the entire letter and redirect interpretation significantly (which is not to deny that it might be an important motif within any broader reinterpretation of the letter, but this is not quite the same thing). Certainly, such claims cannot just be asserted.[31]

(7) The Function of Paul's πιστ- Terminology as the Saving Criterion

Justification theory claims that "faith" is the means by which the individual appropriates salvation. And we have already supplied theoretical considerations that nuance this principle further in terms of "belief in Christ." This notion is sustained textually in Romans 1–4 principally by the noun πίστις. (The cognate verb πιστεύω is far less common, and so needs to be drawn into this orbit: see 1:16; 3:22; 4:3, 5, 11, 17, 18, 24 [excluding 3:2] — total, eight.) πίστις appears largely from 3:22 onward after a brief but concentrated anticipation in 1:16-17 — so in the thesis paragraphs (see 1:17 [3x]; 3:22, 25, 26, 27, 28, 30, 31; 4:5, 9, 11, 12, 13, 14, 16 [2x], 19, 20 — total, twenty). In chapter 4 it is of course bound up with the discussion of Abraham.

Many questions can be raised in relation to this important signifier and its conventional interpretation (and a critical cluster is investigated shortly as an instance of overdetermination). Here, however, we need only note that it is never stated overtly by the text that this word group denotes the means by which the individual *grasps* or *appropriates* salvation. The interpreter will search in vain for any brief statement to this effect. (In close relation to this, no statement is ever made that the discussion of Abraham, explicit in 4:1-23, is intended to provide an example of this criterion; we explore this further immediately below.)

To be sure, statements can be found that some process of "justification," which is usually bound up either with the verb δικαιόω or the famous noun phrase already noted, δικαιοσύνη Θεοῦ, is effected in relation to πίστις (see, e.g., 3:28). But such statements establish only that πιστ- terminology bears some relation to eschatological salvation. *And no alternative readings of these texts, or competing theories of salvation, deny this more general point and association.* Justification theory, however, requires the more specific claim to be established that faith is *an appropriative criterion* as against — for example — a sign of election, or a quality that Christians ought to evidence during the process of sanctification. It is something that the individual must exercise as a non-Christian in order to become a Christian in the first place (and this is then something that competing readings and theories deny, perhaps accusing this position of Arminianism). So the mere association of πιστ- terms with salvation is too vague. We must ask, then, how the conventional reader knows that such references contain the all-important notion of individual appropriation. And an interesting contention emerges at this juncture.

This role for πιστ- terminology in Paul's argument is usually explained by references to the preceding and ensuing phases of the argument — and the former in particular. That is, it would seem that for the conventional view of πίστις (etc.) in Paul to hold, the conventional construal of 1:18–3:20 must first be established. It is this prior discussion that seems to establish that the individual must do something in order to be saved — since such activity is a premise of the entire reading and its associated soteriological theory.[32] Moreover, this activity, in view of the failures of the first phase based on works, ought to be information-based, clear, manageable, and preferably also particular. (Of course, an important theoretical underdetermination has also already been noted at this point; beyond these delimitations, the theory leaves the content of the appropriating criterion unspecified. But that there must be such a criterion is indubitable.) And faith, freighted specifically by πιστ- terms, seems to fulfill this role in the texts that follow Paul's establishment of the need for salvation and its failure in relation to the more stringent criterion of works. Paul's πιστ- terminology seems to arrive at just the right point in the argument! Faith also falls within the necessary parameters, at least at first glance. Hence, interpreters seem to have assumed largely on this basis that faith in Paul is the all-important saving criterion that individuals exercise in order to appropriate salvation. Clearly, this assumption is not groundless.

The justification, however, is both more indirect and more distant than is often assumed. It depends almost entirely on the conventional reading of 1:18–3:20 (probably with a supporting role from Abraham's discussion in Romans 4 as well, but we will see shortly that this support is quite problematic). Hence, if this earlier reading of 1:18–3:20 falters, there will be little cause to read Paul's πιστ- terminology in Romans' thesis paragraphs as Justification theory both suggests and needs. The underdetermination of this pivotal principle in the thesis paragraphs will come back to haunt the conventional reading at this point, and the very legitimacy of Justification theory could be acutely threatened.[33]

(8) Argumentation Establishing Christ as the Definitive Atonement

Here we need only note that some critical theoretical lacunae noted in part one, chapter three, continue in concrete textual terms. In order to function coherently, Justification theory needs to explain both why the prevailing Jewish modes of atonement now prove inadequate and why Christ and Christ alone has to atone. A particular reading of Anselm seems the theory's best hope at these points (potentially killing these — and one or two other problematic birds —

with one stone). However, as was argued earlier, the metaphorical transitions made by this localized explanation prove ultimately unconvincing, and so the lacunae are judged to remain in theoretical terms. And here it needs to be emphasized that the text does not address them either. Nowhere in 1:16-17 or 3:21-31, or their settings, does Paul's text seem to provide a valid justification for Christ's displacement of various earlier Jewish means of atonement, and in particular of the temple cultus (as, e.g., Hebrews arguably does). And neither do these brief subsections explain why *Christ* had to perform this particular role. To *assert* that these things are the case — granting this for the moment — is not to justify them, and it is the justifications that are currently wanting. The text is simply silent in this relation. Unfortunately, given these lacunae, commentators can simply pass over the difficulties, leaving them unaddressed, because the text fails to raise them. But any such silences are not innocent. This leaves one of the vital transitions at the theory's heart underdetermined in both theoretical *and* textual terms — an invidiously weak position. (Alternatively, it leaves the conventional reading vulnerable to the accusation that the text is not addressing Justification theory.) Hence, the text seems to collude in the weaknesses of the theory at these closely related points.[34]

(9) The Function of Christ's Atonement in Propitiatory Terms

In a similar vein, it should be marked that the thesis paragraphs never state explicitly that Christ's atonement functions primarily to assuage the wrath of God. This notion is assumed to be present — especially in 3:21-26 — largely because of the conventional construal of Romans 1:18–3:20, although certainly it seems fair to assume the theme's presence in 3:21-26, given its salience in the immediate context. If Paul is addressing the just anger of God for much of 1:18–3:20, as the conventional construal avers, concluding that argument in 3:19-20, then it is reasonable to argue that he continues to bear this theme in mind as he progresses through 3:21-26.[35] However, this assumption is only as sound as that prior construal. If the conventional construal of Romans 1:18–3:20 falters significantly, then this view of the atonement in 3:21-26 will lose a principal line of reinforcement as well.[36]

2.3. Textual Underdeterminations — Romans 4:1-25

The two underdeterminations in relation to Romans 4 can be noted relatively quickly.

(10) Abraham's Exemplary Function in Romans 4

It is often claimed by conventional readers of Romans 1–4 that Paul presents Abraham in 4:1-25 as a programmatic example of his thesis that everyone is justified by faith; Abraham is the exemplum par excellence of salvation sola fide. So, for example, Dunn states that "the point of chap. 4's exposition is to demonstrate what 'justifying faith' is, to draw a parallel between Abraham's faith and the faith of all who believe in God's life-giving power...."[37] Dunn's comment is representative of a considerable amount of interpretative opinion.[38] It is worth noting, however, that Paul never says this in so many words. His closest comment to such a claim is probably 3:28: λογιζόμεθα γὰρ δικαιοῦσθαι πίστει ἄνθρωπον χωρὶς ἔργων νόμου. But although this comment doubtless has something to do with Paul's discussion of Abraham in 4:1-22, it follows hard on the heels of a christological paragraph (3:21-26), and it is separated from the explicit discussion of Abraham by three verses that contain a considerable amount of programmatic material that is less concerned with "justification by faith" than with other themes (and we are assuming here that we know exactly what justification by faith is by this point). This is also a monolithic claim; it implies that Romans 4 is concerned with one theme, and the argumentative realities are almost certainly more complex. Multiple questions may be in view. All of which is merely to suggest that claims like Dunn's concerning the argumentative function of Abraham in Romans 4 must be established and not merely asserted.[39] Admittedly, Romans 4 concludes by establishing an analogy between Abraham and later believers like Paul and his Roman Christian audience (see vv. 23-25), but — as we will see — the assertion of an analogy is not quite the same thing as the announcement of a programmatic paradigm. A paradigm is a definitive example of something and contains a degree of self-sufficiency; an analogy might apply to a situation in various ways that have yet to be completely understood and/or negotiated.[40]

(11) Abraham's Progression to Faith, and Initial Status as "Ungodly"

It has just been observed that Abraham is often said to be the definitive example of justifying faith. But as such he ought to progress from phase one of Justification theory to phase two, and so from attempted works of law and their repeated failure to justification by faith alone. And although a case can be made for Abraham's experience of "works" and sin prior to his moment of saving faith, the text does not directly support this reconstruction, and certain considerations stand against it.

The case for Abraham's progress from sin to salvation sola fide rests principally on two pieces of evidence.[41] First, 4:5 states that Abraham trusts in the one who "justifies the ungodly." Then, in 4:7-8, Psalm 32:1-2 speaks of the blessedness of the person to whom God does not credit transgressions or sins. But neither of these contentions proves that Paul's depiction of Abraham includes a prior phase of sinful striving. The predication of God in 4:5 carries no direct implications for Abraham's state. It could equally well be generic, and a similar claim in Romans 5:6 even suggests this (where Christ dies "on behalf of the ungodly"). Similarly, Psalm 32 is ascribed explicitly to David, not to Abraham — and David was a sinner.[42]

In addition to the delicacy of the text's implications concerning Abraham's possible sinful past, we should note the difficulty of asserting the existence of such a prior phase for him on other grounds. Presumably, if Abraham were to have tried to negotiate a prior phase of attempted justification by works, he would have had to do so as a pagan, attempting to obey the law of the cosmos and of conscience, and not as a Jew attempting to obey the law of Moses.[43] But Paul's text gives no indication of such a journey (see extensive instructions for this journey, however, in 1:18-32). There is, for example, no suggestion that prior to faith Abraham was an idolater or a sexual deviant in terms of Jewish gender codes. And neither do the contemporary Jewish sources make similar suggestions; they tend, rather, to interpret the patriarch generously.[44] (Even the faults apparent in the pentateuchal stories are overlooked, and his heroic qualities exaggerated and praised.) This depiction should then be the starting point for our construal of Paul's texts, since he was a Jewish exegete raised on these writings, unless other pieces of evidence denote a different reading. And that is precisely what we do not have in relation to this particular claim by Justification advocates. Moreover, it is difficult to assert that Abraham navigated through works prior to becoming a Christian saved by faith when the text goes on to overrule Jewish works like circumcision on *temporal* grounds. These two arguments, that are immediately juxtaposed, would be at obvious cross-purposes (and this difficulty will become clearer when some of the text's overdeterminations are considered momentarily).

Hence, the claim that Paul's depiction of Abraham in Romans 4 is a programmatic instance of the believer justified by faith is underdetermined in one further significant respect: the all-important vestibule that prepares for the Christian's acceptance of salvation sola fide through repeated failures in relation to works, which lead in turn to a consciousness of sin and despair, is not overtly present in Paul's text. Indeed, some good reasons seem present for denying this firmly. Abraham, as Paul presents him, does not seem to have had a significant experience of works prior to faith.

We turn now, in the next major subsection in this chapter, to the complementary question of textual overdeterminations.

§3. Textual Overdeterminations

Textual overdeterminations are possibly marginally more useful to our unfolding argument, because they are more difficult to deny. Underdeterminations are gaps in the text where we expect something to be present; one is consequently indicating an absence rather than something tangible — points where Justification theory should be supported by an explicit statement in Paul's text but does not seem to be. (So it is as if the piles are rotting away from beneath a wooden bridge. One can continue to walk on it, although one day the boards might give way.) Such hidden difficulties can be avoided by commentary — although they should not be — because the text does not explicitly raise them. The exposition of the text that is there can simply carry on regardless (and some examples of this have already been noted[45]). However, textual overdeterminations are sitting on the pages in black and white, so to speak, and are consequently more difficult to avoid. (They are more like vegetation that has fallen across a road.) They do occupy a spectrum in terms of difficulty. That is, certain aspects of the text are merely puzzling. The conventional reading cannot explain these features, although no one would construe this as fatal to its associated theory. Such stray branches simply make for a bumpy journey. Nevertheless, an alternative reading that could explain them — that could clear them away — would enjoy a slight advantage, so it is useful to note them. Some overdeterminations, however, seem profoundly embarrassing to Justification theory, and these are of course especially important. These are not branches but entire trees that have fallen across parts of the road. They must be cleared if the journey is even to continue.

The following account of textual overdeterminations in Romans 1–4 builds on the critical comments in a minority tradition of revisionist interpretation but is shaped here by the systematic framework and concerns of Justification theory (so perhaps a slightly more comprehensive account has resulted). Again, the various difficulties will be listed and described in relation to the three broad sections that have previously been identified in Romans 1–4 — 1:18-3:20; 1:16-17 and 3:21-31; and 4:1-25.

3.1. Textual Overdeterminations — Romans 1:18–3:20

I detect eleven instances of textual overdetermination in the conventional construal of Romans 1:18–3:20, although these vary in their degrees of acuteness.[46] They are listed here in the order in which they tend to be encountered, as readers work through the text.

(1) The Distinctive Style of 1:18-32

There are no fewer than five clusters of unusual stylistic indicators in Romans 1:18-32 that accumulate to create a significant distinctiveness for the passage's style. It seems, then, that this subsection is not composed in a typical Pauline mode at all. Indeed, it is entirely distinctive within his corpus. In view of this, several interpreters have gone so far as to argue that the passage is a later interpolation.[47] We will assess possible explanations for this curious stylistic difference at later points in our argument, in part three, chapter twelve, and part four, chapter fourteen (and I am not convinced by such interpolative theories). But irrespective of its explanation, this distinctive style remains a marked feature of this text.

(i) Romans 1:18-32 is a carefully constructed text in its own right. It begins with what amounts to a thesis statement in v. 18 and concludes with a definite summation in v. 32. Moreover, these boundaries are offset almost exactly in stylistic terms by an emphatic alliteration. Seven words beginning with alpha occur in v. 18 (ἀποκαλύπτεται . . . ἀπ’ . . . ἀσέβειαν . . . ἀδικίαν . . . ἀνθρώπων . . . ἀλήθειαν

... ἀδικία). These resonate strikingly with the five alpha-privatives that round off the subsection's concluding vice list in vv. 30b-31 (see more on these just below). So Romans 1:18-32 is marked off almost perfectly by an alpha-alliteration that is unparalleled elsewhere in Paul (whether in this passage, the letter as a whole, or the entire Pauline corpus).

Between these two boundaries that suggest a degree of self-sufficiency, much of the argument is structured with repeated phrases and cognates that are confined largely to this discourse as well. Three times we hear παρέδωκεν αὐτοὺς ὁ θεὸς . . . (in vv. 24, 26, and 28), followed by an enumeration of a particular category of sinfulness; and three times humanity foolishly "exchanges" God for idols (ἤλλαξαν in v. 23, and μετήλλαξαν in vv. 25 and 26). These phrases and repetitions are entirely distinctive to Romans 1:18-32.

(ii) Complementing these syntactical and phraseological markers is, as Harrison noted, an astonishing incidence of alpha-privatives.[48] No fewer than seventeen occur in this section of fifteen verses and some 36 lines. Romans — which runs for around 850 lines — contains only forty-eight in total. So just over one-third of all the alpha-privatives in Romans are in 1:18-32! (Verse 18 initiates this pattern with three instances within its broader alpha-alliteration — ἀσέβειαν and a twofold use of ἀδικία.)

(iii) Equally striking is the dense concentration of third person plurals, noted by Calvin Porter.[49] Third person plural verbs occur thirteen times (-σαν, -ξαν, or -σιν), and these are intensified a further thirteen times by plural forms of the pronoun αὐτός, along with one occurrence of the plural reflexive ἑαυτοῖς. Hence, the short passage sounds the note "they," "their," or "them" no fewer than twenty-seven times![50]

(iv) The passage contains numerous wordplays, some of them artfully reflecting the substantive principle that the punishment of certain pagan sins bears a recognizable — although ironic — relationship to the initial sin against God that catalyzed them.[51] In v. 23 the "glory" (δόξα) of the immortal God is exchanged for "a precise likeness" and an "image" (ὁμοίωμα; εἰκών), notions that overlap semantically within the broader Jewish discourse concerning idolatry (see Rom. 3:23; 8:29-30; 1 Cor. 15:35-49). At the same time — and a little more obviously — the "immortal God" (τοῦ ἀφθάρτου θεοῦ) is traded for "mortal humanity" (φθαρτοῦ ἀνθρώπου). In v. 25, having exchanged the truth for a lie, humanity worships and serves τῇ κτίσει παρὰ τὸν κτίσαντα. Similarly, in v. 28, since wicked people "did not consider it worthwhile understanding God" (ἐδοκίμασαν . . . ἐν ἐπιγνώσει), God handed them over to a "worthless mind," or understanding (εἰς ἀδόκιμον νοῦν). So the text deploys an entire series of antitheses that inflict various ironic reversals on humanity: that which is theologically hidden — the invisible God — is in fact apparent (vv. 19-20); ignoring this is apparently wise but is in fact stupid (vv. 21-22); the worship of something immortal is exchanged for the worship of mortal beings that are frail and corrupt (v. 23 — also the truth for a lie and the Creator for the created in v. 25); the failure to honor God leads to a failure to honor the body (vv. 24, 26-27); and finally, since they thought it not "worthwhile" to think correctly about God, God hands humanity over to thoughts that are indeed "worthless" (v. 28). These wordplays reach their culmination in the extraordinary vice list in vv. 29-31, characterized by numerous wordplays, which deserves separate, more detailed treatment.[52]

(v) In vv. 29-31, twenty-one separate vices are enumerated in a sequence that is both carefully constructed and highly distinctive. Paul uses vice lists from time to time.[53] And although all of these tend to have some common vices complemented by distinctive designations, the list in Romans 1:29-31 is the longest and most distinctive. Only seven[54] of the twenty-one vices articulated here are found in other vice lists in Paul (roughly half the normal proportion). This is also the most carefully constructed of Paul's vice lists, with *homeoteleuton* in v. 29 (repetition of an identical ending — here a dative singular), and *homeooptôton* throughout vv. 30-31 (the same case ending — here five genitive singulars, followed by twelve accusative plurals, which are in turn broken up into a group of six and a concluding group of four[55]). The last four words in the list also alliterate or use "head rhyme" (here repetition of a vowel at the start of each word — an alpha-privative).

In view of all these noteworthy features, it seems fair to conclude that Paul composed 1:18-32 in a quite deliberate style. Modern readers tend not to notice this; their competence in ancient Greek is usually not advanced enough to detect such stylistic shifts intuitively, so that the differences must be laboriously reconstructed. But the difference between this material and the rest of Paul's prose would probably have been as obvious to a competent ancient auditor as the difference between texts drawn (unidentified) from novels by Jane Austen and Stephen King would be to a modern one. Just why Paul did this of course — assuming that he wrote this subsection — remains to be seen.[56]

(2) *The Temporal Clash between 1:18 and 1:19-32*

The principal emphasis in 1:18-32 seems to be on pagan culpability, lending the text a judgmental tone throughout. Humanity deserves God's wrath, ". . . because the truth about God has been suppressed by them by means of their unrighteousness" (DC: . . . τῶν τὴν ἀλήθειαν ἐν ἀδικίᾳ κατεχόντων). In a sense, the explication of this claim will occupy the next fourteen verses, and this dire situation can then presumably serve as a springboard for other assertions, as those godless pagans who are listening, and are persuaded by the truth of the claims, are motivated to take some action to avoid a terrifying future. And this is all of course an important dynamic in the conventional approach. Such pagans will, in more colloquial terms, be prompted to turn to something in order to avoid being burned. But God's actual punishment of sinful activity — God's ὀργή — is mentioned again only briefly, in passing, in v. 32a: οἵτινες τὸ δικαίωμα τοῦ θεοῦ ἐπιγνόντες ὅτι οἱ τὰ τοιαῦτα πράσσοντες ἄξιοι θανάτου εἰσίν (κ.τ.λ.), and this seems to be future. Nor is there any signal within vv. 19-32 that the sinful activity being described *is* the wrath of God; on the contrary, it is this activity that *elicits* the wrath of God, as v. 32a makes clear. The basic thrust of the argument throughout is the claim that humanity willfully suppresses a correct understanding of and response to God, and thereby embraces a number of outrageous alternatives. Those actions, which all fall under the general rubric of willful disobedience, prompt in turn — and quite justly — the ultimate judgment of God. Thus, humanity is "without excuse" in the face of any judgment; they are ἀναπολόγητος.[57] And an interpretative difficulty is now generated.

The argument of 1:18-32 clearly reaches ahead to 2:5-10, where the wrath of God returns explicitly as one facet of God's just judgment in terms of desert. But that argument correctly denotes the judgment as future: God *will* give (2:6: ἀποδώσει[58]) "on that day" a judgment, including "wrath and distress" to everyone who has been persuaded by wickedness and disobeyed the truth (so v. 8). This future reference for God's punishment of wrongdoing accords with both the absence of any specific allusion to the present operation of wrath in 1:18-32 *and* the accompanying sense that God's wrath is pending (and this argument will, after all, generate most of the passage's rhetorical leverage). Romans 1:18-32 is concerned simply with the widespread evidence of willful pagan wrongdoing that establishes culpability in relation to this future punishment (and the idea is precisely *not* to experience it). But it follows from this that the *present* tense of the verb in v. 18, ἀποκαλύπτεται, *makes no sense in relation to the argument that immediately follows.* It seems, strictly speaking, to be a misleading and even a false claim. Any disclosure of God's wrathful action must and will be future. How then do we explain the present tense in 1:18? It can hardly be the announcement of the passage's thesis, because it does not correspond to it, and even as an announcement of the entire argumentative sweep through to 3:20 it is misleading.[59] In short, there is an easily overlooked but rather puzzling disjunction within the argument at the transition from 1:18 into 1:19-32. It would be nice to be able to explain it.[60]

(3) The Emphasis on Collective Decline and Fall in 1:18-32

A strictly just pagan scenario at the outset of Justification theory should involve unrestricted human capacity and an individual orientation; it should be constructed in terms of "philosophical man." Each person should be held accountable for any rejection of God and embrace of other sinful activities. If these parameters are constricted in any way, then the justness of the initial situation is compromised, and the justice of God's activity and character is called into question. In view of these theoretical criteria, Romans 1:18-32 contains troubling features.

The passage is essentially a collective, not an individual, address, being oriented consistently — as we have just seen — in terms of third person plural grammar. Even more importantly, after a foolish rejection of the single transcendent God, the disobedient pagans in the passage are rapidly overwhelmed by lusts (ἐπιθυμία τῶν καρδιῶν αὐτῶν εἰς ἀκαθαρσίαν in v. 24; in v. 26 πάθη ἀτιμίας), becoming so immersed in depraved behavior that they generate an entire culture of idolatry and sexual immorality (so vv. 23-27). The pagans are collectively trapped. Moreover, they even seem innately predisposed now to sinful acts because of the dishonorable lusts that are unleashed with their initial disobedience.[61] The level playing field has gone; philosophical man is nowhere in sight. Hence, it is difficult to imagine how subsequent generations can fairly be expected either to perceive a transcendent God or to act in accordance with that God's wishes. In short, these features of the scenario depicted in Romans 1:18-32 compromise the fundamental fairness of the whole situation irredeemably.[62]

(4) The Prominent Intertextual Relation with the Wisdom of Solomon

That the Wisdom of Solomon is playing some role in the early arguments of Romans, and especially in 1:18-32, is widely acknowledged.[63] But the full extent of this intertextual relationship is seldom appreciated. It is strikingly extensive. Moreover, the reason for the relationship, largely unparalleled in Paul, is seldom explored.[64] We will address first the question of extent in more detail.

It is possible in the first instance that the text of Romans 1 (etc.) resonates not with the Wisdom of Solomon per se but with a whole cluster of Jewish texts that uses arguments reasonably similar to those found in both these passages — the Jewish "propaganda literature"[65] (viz., the *Third Sibylline Oracle,* esp. vv. 8-45, 184-87, 594-600, and 764 [arguments concerning homosexuality]; Josephus, *Against Apion,* 2.145-286 [LCL, 350-407]; the *Letter of Aristeas,* 128-72; and *Ps-Phocylides,* esp. 190-92 [material on homosexuality] and 213-14 [discussion of long and short hair][66]). But a close consideration of these passages reveals a number of arguments and motifs that are shared by only Romans and Wisdom, supplemented by other points of contact that seem too precise and/or numerous to be coincidental. The principal resonances take place between Romans 1:18-32 and Wisdom 11–16, but the connections are by no means limited to these two stretches of text.

(i) The Wisdom of Solomon famously attacks pagan idolatry from 12:3 onward. Natural theology, and consequent pagan responsibility, are then emphasized at several points — in 13:1, 4, 5, and 9; also 15:11 (see Rom. 1:19-20). A progression to sexual immorality is then announced, as idolatry is equated with sexual immorality in 14:12, and this is made more explicit in 14:24. *A vice list then follows in 14:25 and 26!* These two argumentative progressions are unique to the Wisdom of Solomon and Romans 1. Josephus, *Against Apion,* 2.239-75, is the closest sequence otherwise, but is still different. There the progression is from natural theology, through aniconic monotheism, to questions of cultus, and then sexual relations. *Third Sibylline Oracle* has a brief instance of this sequence but interposes other concerns and has no concluding vice list. The latter instances are certainly sufficient to suggest that both Romans 1 and Wisdom are in touch with a

Jewish topos at this point. (But the affinity between Romans and Wisdom is also more than this.)

(ii) Israel is consistently given special treatment in Wisdom, being punished pedagogically and parentally, and not in accordance with strict justice as the pagans are. Precisely this distinction is also explored by Romans 1–3, although ironically; see Wis. 12:21-22 and esp. Rom. 3:1-9a.

(iii) Punishment is *equivalent* and *proportional* in Wisdom: see 11:16, 20b (see also 13:18-19). The pagans are punished by the consequences, or the inverse, of the sins that they have committed. Exactly this dynamic is also apparent in Romans 1 (and some of the evidence for this has already been considered in relation to our earlier description of the passage's style; this dynamic facilitates wordplays).

(iv) Nevertheless, time to repent is provided to Jews: see Wis. 11:23; 12:18b, 19b; 16:2 (which is why any punishment is only pedagogical or disciplinary for Jews). Romans speaks of precisely this opportunity as well — although ironically: see 2:1-5. (Pagans are also given the opportunity to repent in 12:10, 20, 26.)

(v) Those possessing the law in Wisdom are designated by various epithets over against the pagans that recur in Rom. 2:17-20: see Wis. 12:24 and 18:4. So Jews possess the law, are teachers of infants, and a light to those in darkness.

(vi) Romans 9:5-29 also resonates strongly with Wis. 12:2, 3-18; and 15:7; although — again — the Pauline usage is surprising and inverted.[67]

(vii) Both texts share a concern for the "righteous." Terminology of "the righteous" is prominent in Wisdom, especially from chapter 2, where it describes a lone righteous figure who is granted immortality after suffering and torture. This may resonate with "the righteous one" in Hab. 2:4. Note also the initial — and programmatic — claim in Rom. 3:10-18 that "there is not one righteous person, not even one."

(viii) I note fifteen other motifs that are common to the two texts, and possible textual echoes. They are not of course unique to these two texts, but their sheer number seems indicative: "abominations"/βδελυγμάτων/ὁ βδελυσσόμενος (Wisd. Sol. 12:23/Rom. 2:22); "worthy of death"/ἀξίαν θεοῦ κρίσιν (Wisd. Sol. 12:26; 16:1 [ἐκολάσθησαν ἀξίως]; 18:4 [ἄξιοι μὲν γὰρ ἐκεῖνοι στερηθῆναι φωτὸς . . .]/Rom. 1:32); "foolish *by nature*"/φύσει (Wisd. Sol. 13:1/Rom. 1:26-27; 2:14); "shame"/οὐκ αἰσχύνεται (Wisd. Sol. 13:17/Rom. 1:16?); "the immortal God"/τὸ δὲ φθαρτὸν θεὸς ὠνομάσθη (Wisd. Sol. 14:8/Rom. 1:23); "reptiles" — a "foolish" thought/ἀντὶ δὲ λογισμῶν ἀσυνέτων ἀδικίας αὐτῶν, ἐν οἷς πλανηθέντες ἐθρήσκευον ἄλογα ἑρπετὰ καὶ κνώδαλα εὐτελῆ κ.τ.λ. (Wisd. Sol. 11:15/Rom. 1:21, 23); "justice" (Wisd. Sol. 14:30-31/ see Rom. 2:6); δικαιοσύνη (Wis. 12:16; 14:7; 15:3/Rom. 1:17; 3:5; 3:21-26); "wrath" (Wis. 11:9; 16:5 [2x]; 18:20/Rom. 1:18); "transgressions" (Wis. 11:23; 12:19/Rom. 3:25; 4:25); the demonstration and vindication of God's justice at the judgment (Wis. 12:13/Rom. 3:4); a word play based on δικαιο- terminology — δίκαιος δὲ ὢν δικαίως τὰ πάντα διέπεις (Wisd. Sol. 12:15/see Rom. 3:26); νοησάτωσαν/νοούμενα (Wisd. Sol. 13:4/Rom. 1:20); Εἶτ' οὐκ ἤρκεσεν τὸ πλανᾶσθαι περὶ τὴν τοῦ θεοῦ γνῶσιν/οὐκ ἐδοκίμασαν τὸν Θεὸν ἔχειν ἐν ἐπιγνώσει . . . (Wisd. Sol. 14:22/see Rom. 1:28).

In view of all the thematic parallels, similar argumentative sequences, textual echoes, and common motifs apparent in these brief summaries, it is difficult to deny the existence of a fairly extensive relationship between the text of Romans — and especially its opening arguments — and the Wisdom of Solomon. Hence, the further question inevitably arises, why does this relationship exist (a query that is the more pressing once it is grasped that this relationship is at times mischievous, and even subversive)? Paul seems to undermine the theological program of the Wisdom of Solomon far more than he leans on it. Somewhat curiously, cogent explanations of *this* dynamic are rare.

Strictly speaking, the conventional reader does not need to worry about it because it is not a problem per se. Yet it remains curious. If Paul is setting out his gospel systematically, then he is arguing from first principles. There is no obvious reason at this point for him to engage *subversively* with other scriptural material.[68] He should merely deploy those texts that reinforce his developing argument (assuming a particular epistemology for the moment!). This extensive, and at times rather subtle, engagement with the Wisdom of Solomon therefore remains opaque — a widespread if gentle textual overdetermination that the conventional reader probably does not know quite what to do with. It is not fatal, but it is unusual, and therefore it remains a useful opportunity for alternative readings. Why is Paul engaging with the Wisdom of Solomon at every turn in Romans 1–3, and periodically through the rest of the letter, after an especially intense engagement in 1:18-32, and especially when he does not end up where that text does — with orthopractic Judaism? The conventional reader has no real answer to this query.

(5) The Function of the Argumentative "Turn" in 2:1

We resume here the discussion of an important underdetermination at the point at which it begins to spill over into an awkward overdetermination.

We observed in §2 how the text seems to encode a particular judgmental figure as the target of Paul's critique in Romans 1:18–3:20 — a figure that many commentators assume, largely without justification, is representative of Judaism in general.[69] The overdeterminative difficulty begins to emerge when we consider the rhetorical function of Paul's "turn" toward this figure in 2:1. Richard Hays states the matter with typically elegant concision:

> Romans 1:18-32 sets up a homiletical sting operation. The passage builds a crescendo of condemnation, declaring God's wrath upon human unrighteousness, using rhetoric characteristic of Jewish polemic against Gentile im-

morality. It whips the reader into a frenzy of indignation against others: those unbelievers, those idol-worshipers, those immoral enemies of God. But then, in Romans 2:1, the sting strikes: "Therefore you have no excuse, whoever you are, when you judge others; for in passing judgment on another you condemn yourself, because you, the judge, are doing the very same things." The reader who gleefully joins in the condemnation of the unrighteous is "without excuse" *(anapologētos)* before God (2:1), just as those who refuse to acknowledge God are *anapologētos* (1:20).[70]

Many interpreters concur with Hays's suggestion that Paul has been rhetorically skilled at this point, crafting an effective "sting."[71] The overdeterminative problem lies in explaining just why he does this, coupled with identifying whom exactly he is stinging.

As Hays notes, the most likely scenario is that Paul is stinging someone judgmental. But the exact nature of this judge must be grasped precisely. Paul — on the conventional reading — *agrees* with this judge in ultimate theological terms. Most importantly, both figures endorse the basicality of the retributive justice of God: "those who practice such [reprehensible] things deserve to die" (1:32a). So it must be this judger's *lack of self-awareness* with which Paul disagrees. It is in fact fine to think such things but not simply to direct them toward outsiders and leave things at that. One ought to be aware that one is in the same boat, so to speak; the judge is also a sinner and ought to acknowledge this. Hence, this turn is designed to jolt the figure into a healthier level of self-knowledge — one that might elicit repentance and salvation, rather than hard-heartedness and condemnation of others (see esp. 2:3-5).

It follows, however, that there is something inherently *stupid* about this figure. This judge does not practice what he preaches. He preaches desert, but does not achieve desert himself, and seems oblivious to this shortfall. He is, in short, a fool. Moreover, so fashioned, it follows as well that *this argumentative turn will catch only such stupid judgmental hypocrites.* Those who are *not* hypocritical in this sense will be immune. And this includes those who are judgmental of pagans, but combine this with the appropriate degree of self-awareness of transgression ("I too have sinned like you"), *and* those who simply do not indulge in such judgments of others — or, at least, not in these terms.[72] So the question arises, why is Paul doing this in contingent terms? What is the actual point of this rhetorical maneuver? Whom is he trying to sting? And there are only two real possibilities at this point. Paul either has a particular, localized constituency in view at Rome, or he is beginning a reasonably overt attack on Judaism, so this figure is not merely a Jew but *the* Jew.[73] But brief considerations of these alternatives suggest that both are implausible. We will consider the former, more contingent option first.

Are at least some of the Roman Christians passing judgment on one another harshly, and overlooking their own sins in the process, encouraging Paul to address this shortcoming adroitly at the outset of the letter's body? This suggestion might gain an initial plausibility in the light of Romans 14, where two groups are discernible, "the weak" and "the strong," the weak even being coded in terms of judgment (see 14:3b, 4a, 5 [in fact both groups here], 10, 13 [here seguing into sustained address of the strong], and 22b). However, a number of difficulties make this possibility unlikely, so that it is not to my knowledge advocated by many commentators.[74]

If certain Roman Christians are to recognize themselves in this judging figure in 2:1-5, then they ought to approximate its textual markers, which are male, Jewish, learned, and hypocritical. But these do not seem to be overly obvious markers for any Christian group at Rome, let alone the weak.[75] Perhaps more importantly, it is unnecessary if not inappropriate for Paul to address a question of Christian ethics at this point in his discussion. He is supposed to be laying the foundation for the gospel in Romans 1-3; he is articulating the pre-Christian situation. So he cannot coherently address Christians at this point in the argument, while to do so risks confusing that argument. Paul should address any issue of Christian intra-communal tension later — and in fact precisely where it becomes apparent, in Romans 14 (where the Christian markers are also explicit).

In addition, this reading delivers too much. If Paul is — rather clumsily — trying to modify the behavior of the judgmental weak at this point, he has provided far too much ammunition to the strong. This argument should utterly confound the weak for their judgmentalism. They are wrong and should repent immediately (2:5). That is, their position has no legitimacy at all, and self-evidently so, while nothing is said about the freedom of the strong (except perhaps that Paul denies it amounts to libertinism: see Rom. 3:8). Hence, construed in this fashion, Paul's approach to the two groups in 2:1-5 *contradicts* his later tactics in Romans 14 where, although apparently favoring the strong in theological terms, he takes pains to make extensive demands on *both* groups.[76] The weak are by no means to be confounded and rejected but treated with sensitivity and care. So these two strategies that ostensibly focus on the same contingent problem are actually working at cross-purposes.[77]

For all these reasons then, a contingent and localized identification of the judge in 2:1-5 in terms of "the weak" looks unlikely, and this leaves us with the majority reading's preference for his identification as "the Jew."[78] But this is not merely an implausible reading; it is positively odious.

If Paul is beginning to trap the Jews from 2:1 onward, then his argument works only if hypocrisy is *intrinsic* to the definition of Judaism! Otherwise, Jews simply reject his description and in effect walk away from his contentions — doubtless either puzzled or offended, and certainly unmoved. They would not identify with this figure. According to Paul then — and for the argument construed in these terms to work — Judaism is not merely contractual, conditional, perfectionist, monolithic, and ahistorical, *but innately judgmental and hypocritical!* It *necessarily* includes an internal insensitivity to sinfulness, combining this with a rigorously judgmental attitude to outsiders. In short, Jews are stupid as well as conditional. They promulgate a system that, to a man, they do not live up to themselves, but they nevertheless attack others on ethical grounds *and are unaware of their own ethical shortcomings.*

It seems then that the conventional reading of the sting in Romans 2:1 is premised on a latent unfairness toward Jews if it adopts this explanation. And clearly the empirical difficulty already present for Justification theory in this relation is enormously exacerbated by this decision (while Post-Holocaust concerns should also now be raised, along with other general problems of alterity). Do interpreters really want to suggest that the correct route to Christian salvation runs necessarily through an account of Judaism that includes an emphasis on its innate hypocritical judgmentalism? μὴ γένοιτο!

Perhaps this difficulty can be mitigated if interpreters back away from this identification, introducing Paul's critique of Judaism into the argument only at Romans 2:17. However, this expedient leaves this figure dangling unidentified. In the midst of a tightly integrated argument, Paul seems suddenly to deviate to catch a foolish judge; at 2:1 he springs a carefully crafted trap.[79] And conventional readers cannot tell us why (a lack of identification that essentially runs through 2:17, and will complicate analysis of the following argument).

Excursus: The Later Function of "the Stupid Judge"

The exegetical weaknesses of the construal resulting from the identification of "the foolish judge" in Romans 2:1-5 with Judaism raise the question why that reading still persists — often unquestioned — in the commentary. The following is not a definitive response but is a suggestion in this relation.

The judge so construed occupies a particular argumentative space that can then generate certain useful, essentially apologetic, inter-communal claims (and *not*, it should be noted, evangelistic advantages[80]). In the conventional reading the Jewish judge articulates the truth, Paul ultimately endorsing his premises firmly. Indeed, the entire thrust of the argument in Romans 1:18–3:20 derives from the truth of the judge's position vis-à-vis judgment. So Paul and the judger share their basic axioms with one another. Both appeal to the authority of Scripture as well, so their appreciation of preceding tradition is united. However, the judge *excludes himself from the further development of that tradition, refusing* to grasp the gospel, because he fails to recognize his *own* sinfulness and consequent need for that gospel. He therefore generates his exclusion from salvation and is morally culpable for doing so; he is ἀναπολόγητος. And I suggest that this characterization can perform a very useful function when a particular group is trying to explain its departure from a parent body — in more sociological parlance, a sect's explanation of its deviation and marginalization.[81] This also explains the palpably etic nature of this characterization.

The characterization allows a sect to affirm the truth of a previous tradition, which it shares (and on which much of its theology might be based). But it also explains why the members of that tradition have not gone on to share the new offer of salvation, and to do so in an entirely palatable way for the deviating group. It is of course the fault of the members of that tradition, not anything inherent in the sect itself; the traditionalists have proved sinful and stupidly refuse to acknowledge the reformed view of salvation currently being offered to them, which arises out of presuppositions that they themselves share. In short, this reading allows sects to narrate their illegitimacy plausibly. So it proves supremely useful when Christians are trying to explain the phenomenon of recalcitrant Jews, when Protestants are trying to explain recalcitrant Catholics, and so on — all situations that find aggressive etic definitions useful.

There is of course a vicious side to this rhetorical redeployment and etic function — the characterization of the parent group as stupid *and hence culpable* (i.e., to coercion and punishment). But this is implicit rather than explicit, and so need not be recognized straightaway. In fact it probably becomes apparent only when the deviating group becomes a social majority, and its antecedent tradition a minority, at which point the sinister implications become much clearer (because the resources of power can effect them). But this doesn't happen very often historically. Moreover, deviating minorities presumably find it hard to conceive of the social implications of their theological systems for majority and even Constantinian situations. (And such acts of theological imagination might even be foreclosed for theological reasons, i.e., the deviating groups expect to remain in the minority — perhaps as remnants — permanently.)

There seem to be good sociological reasons then for the persistence of the conventional reading of the foolish judge in Romans 2:1-5. However, those reasons are not especially accurate in exegetical terms, or palatable in terms of broader history. It is time for this reading to be superseded, if that is possible.

(6) The Premature Location of Repentance in 2:4b-5a

Strictly speaking, as we have already seen in part one, chapter one (and reinforced in chapter four), Justification theory requires perfect obedience in its first non-Christian phase. Only this requirement generates an initial result that admits no exceptions. All will prove to be sinful, at least in *some* respect, and so liable either to salvation through some easier requirement than perfect deeds, or to the appropriate condemnation at the end of the age. Moreover, if this strict requirement is relaxed then the consequences for the discourse's broader plausibility are severe. People saved by works apart from Christ and the gospel would then be allowed, which would generate insuperable framing tensions in turn (and so on). So there seem to be good reasons for requiring perfect obedience initially of all humanity, and then for expecting all to fall short of this stringent goal, at which point easier conditions for salvation can be offered through the gospel — principally belief in Christ, but often some combination of confession, contrition, and repentance as well. But in view of this it can now be seen that 2:4b-5a introduces a troubling overdetermination.[82]

In these verses Paul accuses the hypocritical judge of 2:4 of squandering the time and opportunity that God has kindly given him *to repent* (ἀγνοῶν ὅτι τὸ χρηστὸν τοῦ Θεοῦ εἰς μετάνοιάν σε ἄγει), thereby revealing an *unrepentant* heart (ἀμετανόητον καρδίαν) and so "storing up wrath for [him]self on the day of wrath, when God's righteous judgment will be revealed" (2:5). And the motif of repentance even contributes to the basic argumentative thrust of the text: the foolishness of the judger is more apparent because of his resistance to the obvious need for repentance, and to God's kindness in allowing him the opportunity to do so. As a result of this, a treasury of judgment, not reward, is compounding (θησαυρίζεις . . .). But it also seems, in view of these statements, *that Romans 2 views repentance as a possibility in the non-Christian phase,* and this is troubling.

If repentance is a possibility in the *first* phase of Justification theory, then the initial perfectionist calculus risks being undermined and the theory as a whole risks collapse. If those trying to do good deeds prior to Christ can sin and then *repent,* being forgiven those sins, then they may well arrive at the day of judgment effectively righteous. Given the appropriate contrition — which could presumably take place on their death beds if necessary[83] — such individuals would have been forgiven their sins and shortcomings and so be righteous. God would then have to declare them that and save them on the day of judgment, and they would then have been saved independently of Christ, the church, Christian preaching, and Paul! Moreover, given the emphasis in much Jewish literature *on* repentance, presumably many Jews could follow this route.[84] So Paul's introduction of the motif of repentance into the argument at this juncture in Romans — given its conventional construal — is the rhetorical and theological equivalent of shooting himself in the foot. *It is in the wrong place.* Such gentle conditions belong at the inauguration of the second, saving phase, and not the first. Located here, they undermine the apparent goal of his argument rather directly.

The presence of a motif and a resulting localized contention that seem to undermine the conventional construal of the overarching argument will become a familiar pattern as we work through this reading critically here (and see especially OD 10 noted just below). They suggest of course that the conventional construal is not the best construal *of* the overarching argument.[85]

(7) The Existence of Two Pristine Categories in 2:6-10 — the Righteous Saved and the Wicked Damned

It is deeply puzzling, once one thinks about it, that Paul seems so confident in 2:6-12 that all of humanity will fall neatly into two categories on the day of judgment in relation to desert — one characterized by a persistent seeking after eternal life, through good works, and the other by a consistent persuasion by wickedness (which is nevertheless constantly aware of the truthfulness of God, of his ethical demands, and of pending wrath!) and so disobedience to truth. It seems that individual humans will be, in terms of their own deeds, either *entirely* righteous or *entirely* wicked. And a moment's consideration suggests that this is unlikely to be the case. More likely is the opposite: no one will be monolithically good or bad in terms of deeds. Simply as an empirical claim about the future then, the existence of two discrete groups — one righteous and one evil — looks naïve and vulnerable (i.e., probably false).

This difficulty probably passes most conventional interpreters by because ultimately they hold the categories to be chimerical. There will be no occupants of the righteous alternative on the day of judgment. All will be condemned. But even if the categories are hypothetical, they still need to be valid possibilities for the overarching argument to work.

Their pristine quality could be maintained by emphases on a criterion of perfection and/or a universal ontological depravity on the part of humanity. Either of these would force all of humanity necessarily into one wicked category. But both these theoretical qualifications (which have already been noted to a degree) are problematic. The criterion of perfection is textually unstated and exacerbates the theory's problem of theodicy. The presence of depravity also exacerbates the issue of theodicy, and raises complementary difficulties of incoherence at the rhetorical and theoretical levels (*although it does explain this textual dynamic!*[86]).

Alternatively, it might be replied that Paul is simply echoing the exaggerated nature of much ancient ethical, religious, and polemical literature. The Bible itself frequently distributes Israel or humanity into two basic categories — the righteous and the wicked. Such generalizations are commonplace. However, this response does not really solve our difficulties, which derive from the inaccuracy of these characterizations. That Paul echoes other ancient inaccuracies — although some of those might be excusable in context — does not eliminate the fact of his own inaccuracy. Justification theory as a theory remains inaccurate at this point; it remains untrue. And a theory of salvation ought to be true.

Why, then, does Paul posit this inexplicably neat dichotomy in Romans 2? How does he justify it? (And if one category — the sinful one — contains everybody, but is defined by a failure to reach "perfection of way," why does he not say this, rather than presenting two ostensibly symmetrical groups?) These groups remain unaccountably "pure" in terms of their constitutions and resulting categorizations in relation to Justification theory — one further clue that Justification might not be the best explanation of Paul's developing argument.[87]

(8) Paul's Comment in 2:16b That Judgment through Christ Accords with "My" Gospel

The specification of the role of Christ in 2:16b as according with "my gospel," somewhat odd because it is so clearly redundant, becomes even more curious when combined with its contradictory substance. The implication is that the surrounding material is *not* "according to [Paul's] gospel."

In a little more detail: The brief reference to the day of judgment in v. 16a is qualified by certain criteria in v. 16b: κατὰ τὸ εὐαγγέλιόν μου διὰ Χριστοῦ Ἰησοῦ. This phrase contains two significant prepositional constructions — a κατά construction, followed by an instrumental διά construction. The κατά construction explicitly marks "the gospel" as "mine," that is, as Paul's. It also recalls the important κατά construction in v. 6 that announced the axiom of desert. Indeed, vv. 7-10 are little more than an articulation of the criterion of works — "according to" which, vv. 5-6 announce, God will judge the world on a day of wrath and just judgment. The criterion articulated in v. 16b, however, is now suddenly and explicitly — "according to [Paul's] gospel" — by means of Jesus Christ. And certain aspects of this cryptic statement, taken together, arguably create an embarrassment for the conventional reading.

We should note first that the criterion enunciated in 2:16b is "through Christ Jesus." But the criterion enunciated in 2:6 is completely different; there it is "according to works." Indeed, *Christ is entirely absent from the text's earlier construction of the day of judgment and its given criterion.* In fact, he is, somewhat notoriously, absent from the entirety of Romans 1:18–3:20 (save here), as well as from much of the following argument through 4:22.[88] Moreover, he *must* be absent from, and hence irrelevant to, that unfolding scenario as the text describes it. If the criterion for judgment is works, then Christ cannot interfere with this; he too has to show no partiality. He can only administer the appropriate responses, although presumably God is capable of this as well, as the text suggests. The scenario of judgment in accordance with works holds for all, irrespective of any knowledge of Christ; it precedes and surrounds any peculiar Christian judgments. Thus, any judgment "through Christ Jesus" must either be completely subordinate to the judgment scenario that has just been articulated in 2:6-11 (and hence its statement in 16b is redundant), or it must be contradictory to it, because it would alter its terms.

Complementing this cluster of difficulties is the redundancy of Paul's comment that "according to *my* gospel [judgment is] through Christ Jesus." The conventional reading holds Romans 1–4 to be nothing less than an extended articulation of Paul's gospel. He has been laying out systematically his all-important preparatory phase for salvation from 1:18 onward. We are deep in the middle of Paul's gospel. So for Paul suddenly and uniquely to mark this particular element as "his" is essentially redundant. The entire argument is "his," according to the conventional construal.

However, when this odd and apparently redundant claim is combined with the substantive difficulties that we have just noted, then this comment becomes more embarrassing than merely otiose. The one element that jars with the context — the intrusion of a christological element where there is no real room for one — is encoded as "Paul's" explicitly, apparently in contradistinction to the surrounding argument. So here Paul's voice intrudes into the text for the first time since the letter opening (1:1-15), and it marks an element at variance with the developing argument. The implication of this remark, of course, is that the surrounding argument is not Paul's gospel.

It might be objected to this claim that Christ does function in the judgment for Paul, as even Romans attests (see esp. 14:10b-12). And there is some force to this objection. But it is not entirely convincing.

We considered earlier on the possibility that God functions retributively in Paul (which amounts to the same issue), and found the evidence to be far from unequivocal (see esp. chapter three, §3.10 and the accompanying excursus). This is not to exclude that function from God automatically in Paul, but by the same token neither is it to include it automatically in any discussion of judgment, and especially when Christ is concerned. Not all judgment texts are soteriological (i.e. matters of life and death), some appearing to be merely evaluative (i.e. matters of limited accountability). Christ tends to appear in relation to the latter rather than the former situation. Moreover, even in the more punitive texts, it is possible to account for many of Paul's stronger claims in terms of a discourse of purity, as against one essentially rooted in freedom.[89] There are also countervailing statements of inclusion and universality in Paul, raising the further question whether his punitive statements are even consistent with his central evangelical convictions (see Rom. 8:28-39!).

But this evidence is not unequivocal, 2 Thessalonians 1:6-10 in particular ascribing a punitive eschatological action to Christ, using language that aligns neatly with analogous claims in undisputed Pauline letters (and evidence even from a later Pauline tradent cannot merely be ignored; see also Rom. 13:1-7 and 1 Thess. 2:13-16). So it remains *possible* that Christ functions punitively, and hence that Romans 2:16b is not especially inconsistent in context.[90] But how *likely* is this interpretation here? Two things in particular speak against it.

First, the Roman Christians did not have access to the Pauline corpus and so could not gain insight into Paul's comment here from 2 Thessalonians 1:6-10, as against 1 Corinthians 15:20-28 and Ephesians 1:9-10, 22-23 (and so on). They would therefore presumably have had to turn to the rest of the letter for clarification (assuming that any clarifications from the letter bearers are difficult to reconstruct decisively at this point). And Romans itself portrays Christ in a process of evaluation that seems explicitly oriented toward Christians and is non-soteriological (Rom. 14:4, 10b-12), while it also offers a great deal of information concerning his *salvific* roles (3:25; 5:6, 8; and so on). In short, Romans *itself* offers no way of integrating Christ coherently into the theses of 2:6-10, the question that v. 16b asks in terms of its parallel criterial κατά construction. So the contradiction evident here seems to remain, at least initially.[91]

Second, and most importantly, no Pauline evidence, whether internal to Romans or external, depicts Christ with a punitive future eschatological role *foundationally* — that is, in terms of a *preliminary* and *fundamental* theological claim made prior to the gospel's offer of salvation (and this stands to reason: it is difficult if not incoherent to preach Christ before the gospel). So, on the one hand, there is no Pauline evidence for Christ's punitive function *at this critical non-Christian point in the argument,* and, on the other hand, what evidence exists of Christological judging and punishment can now arguably be treated as a later vestige of Pauline thought occupying a secondary and derivative position, rather than a primary and non-negotiable axiom.[92] In essence, that Paul is prepared to appeal to Christ's future eschatological role in various exhortatory contexts vis-à-vis Christians does not entail that he appealed to his punitive eschatological role in his proclamation, according it foundational epistemological and theological roles as well (a non sequitur that is easily ignored if paradigmatic concerns are not recognized and neutralized — and here the discussion links up with part one, chapter five, §3.6, where Paul's preaching was briefly discussed).

In sum, it seems to me that, although some rebuttal by Justification advocates at this point is possible, the fragility of such protests ultimately renders them ineffective, and the basic overdeterminative difficulty remains.[93] Romans

2:16b is anomalous, generating awkward redundancy and contradiction within a conventional reading. If an alternative reading can integrate its claims more smoothly into its local setting, it will enjoy an advantage at this point.

(9) The Crudeness of the Attack on the Jew in 2:21-22

We have already noted how the identification of the figure that Paul criticizes from 2:17 onward is controversial. No one denies, however, that in 2:17-23 a learned Jewish figure in some sense is in view. But Paul's attack on this figure has been criticized — and rightly so.[94]

After the reintroduction of the theme of hypocrisy in 2:21a, three short conditionals occur in vv. 21b-23. These conditionals fling accusations of theft (v. 21b), adultery (v. 22a), and temple robbery (v. 22b: ἱεροσυλέω) at the learned Jew (see 2:17-21a). But it is (again) difficult to integrate these into any sensible reconstruction or critique of Judaism.

If Paul is crafting a broad accusation of sinfulness against Judaism in general, then the crudeness of these charges works directly against his supposed rhetorical objective. Presumably, few Jews would have had difficulty avoiding his specific charges here, so any critique of Judaism in these empirical terms would have been largely ineffective. A more effective strategy would have been the very converse of this tirade — to accuse Jews of subtle "internal" sins that are nearly universal and hence very difficult to deny, a strategy that Paul himself seems well aware of, and in Romans![95] Hence, Paul himself stands accused at this point of rhetorical incompetence (given the concerns of the conventional reading, of course).

Moreover, if the underdetermination that the text does not specifically encode Judaism at this point (noted in §2) is overridden, then the application of these charges to Judaism in broad empirical terms is also rather offensive. Paul is not just being incompetent, then; he is being nasty. (He is attributing serious ethical shortcomings to the Jews as a whole without foundation. And in view of this extraordinary implication, it is even stranger to find commentators happily affirming both the effectiveness of the critique and its accuracy — for its accuracy is implicit in any affirmation of its effectiveness.[96]) But is Paul *really* saying that the majority of Jews — if not all of them — are sacrilegious thieves and adulterers?! Unfortunately, when this basic difficulty is realized, attempts to circumvent it within the parameters of the conventional reading have inevitably proved lame.[97] Either Paul *is* attacking Jews here — as he should be, according to Justification theory — in order ultimately to establish the universal equality of all Christians by faith alone, or it is hard to say just what he is up to.

But our difficulties with this passage are not yet over. The asymmetry within the final charge has also proved troublesome — although this is not as dire a predicament as the preceding one.

Paul counterposes a charge of robbery to preaching against theft, and of adultery to preaching against the same. But it is difficult to explain why he counterposes a charge of temple robbery (ἱεροσυλέω) to preaching against idolatry. The expected sin here would be idolatry — "You that abhor idols, do you commit idolatry?!" So this charge disturbs the symmetry of the previous two challenges and seems rather odd in its own right. And those who notice the difficulty, again, do not seem to be able to explain it plausibly.[98]

In short, in Romans 2:21-22, the text seems suddenly to lurch in a profoundly unhelpful direction for the conventional reading. Given that reading, Paul himself now stands accused — with some reason — of opacity, disloyalty, harsh exaggeration, and argumentative incompetence (not to mention stylistic inconsistency). We turn now to another well-known difficulty in the argument as it is conventionally construed.

(10) The Presence of Righteous Pagans in Paul's Argument

The presence of certain mysterious figures in Paul's argumentation in Romans 2–3 has long been noted — people who seem to be pagan but law abiding and righteous, and therefore judged righteous by their deeds (if not also rightfully judging of others). After some initial suggestions in 2:13b-15, these figures surface unmistakably in 2:26-29. However, most interpreters simply do not know what to do with them, and certainly conventional readers are embarrassed by their appearance; they ought not to be in Paul's argument at all, as Justification theory understands that. (Non-Christians saved by works?!) Several explanations have been tried in the past, but all ultimately prove unconvincing. Consequently, these "righteous pagans" constitute a significant overdetermination by the text in relation both to the conventional reading and to Justification theory — a large tree across the path — while any alternative reading that could explain them satisfactorily would enjoy an obvious advantage at this point.

In a little more detail: The data usually mentioned in this relation occurs — at least at first glance — in two subsections of Paul's broader discussion: 2:13b-15 and 2:26-29. But it is important to realize that the origins of these figures lie much deeper in the text's argument. As early as 1:19-20, the text claims that pagans can recognize sufficient information about God and his ethical concerns from the cosmos to be culpable for ignoring it. So, in 2:6-10, the argument speaks of both Jews and Greeks being judged in accordance with deeds, and v. 13 goes on to affirm that "the doers of the law will be declared righteous," a constituency that clearly *could* — at least up to this point in the argument — include law-observant pagans. Verses 14 and 15 consequently seem to reiterate a premise that should not be in doubt: pagans *must* in some sense possess a law independently of the written law venerated and transmitted within Judaism. And both their righteous deeds (however occasional) and the debates of their consciences attest to their possession of this law "in their hearts" (v. 15a). Moreover, there seems little reason not to think at this point that at least some of them can keep it, which is what Paul's argument goes on to suggest.

These figures do recede somewhat from argumentative view until 2:26-29, where they reemerge in the assertion that someone "uncircumcised by nature but who keeps the law" will judge a circumcised but transgressing Jew, who as such is as good as uncircumcised. Moreover, this righteous pagan, in keeping the law, will be considered circumcised. Paul even goes so far as to say that such a figure redefines the nature of true Judaism and genuine circumcision; these are hidden matters of the heart, the text suggests, apparent only to God, and not necessarily to other people (so vv. 26b, 28-29) — rather brazen claims that we will consider in their own right shortly.

The conventional reading struggles to account for this constituency in Paul's argument (as in fact do all readings). Three principal explanations have been offered to identify and account for these figures.[99] But all must be judged interpretative failures.

(i) Should we perhaps not just accept that these figures are a significant feature of Paul's argument, and deliberately so? After all, they correspond to one of the possibilities repeatedly emphasized in the preceding discussion — salvation through good works (see 2:6-10). And at least this suggestion has the merit of treating the presence of these figures in the text with full seriousness — that is, as real.[100]

The problem is that their existence is directly contradicted by the argumentation of 3:9b-18 and the apparent conclusions of 3:19-20. In those later passages Paul seems concerned to state repeatedly that sin is universal, as is the divine judgment. Moreover, the conventional construal has good reasons for expecting this closure. Only those so convicted can become Christians, so if exceptions are admitted, then a doorway is being opened to non-Christian salvation. This seems rather shocking in and of itself, and it would contradict Paul's apparent rhetorical objective here, which is to convict humanity of sin *without exception*. If these figures are admitted in this sense, he has achieved only part of his aim, falsifying it in part himself, and apparently rather unnecessarily. It is also difficult to find evidence elsewhere in Paul for this occasional marginality of Christ, not to mention the unassisted ethical rectitude of non-Christians; the comparative evidence, especially at the systematic frame, seems to support the conventional reading's agenda here, foreclosing on this interpretative possibility. Hence, we seem forced to conclude that if these figures are real, Paul's argumentative incompetence has reached new heights; his rhetoric is fractured at a fundamental level. We may yet be left with this explanation; however, most do their utmost to avoid it — and so should we.

(ii) Are these figures hypothetical constructs then, and not real expectations? Perhaps they are projections of the argument and so do not really exist, being introduced to make only a limited polemical point.[101] This explanation has the merits of recognizing the linkage of these figures with the present argument's central principles, as well as the difficulties they pose to Paul's overarching coherence if they are real. However, in order for the argument to function at all where they appear — for the relevant polemical point to be made — *they have to be real!* A hypothetical that is ultimately a nonexistent eschatological scenario of mockery is hardly a deterrent. And neither does a hypothetical or nonexistent redefinition of the central identity of Judaism seem especially probative. Hence, usually this explanation too is rightly rejected.

(iii) A final significant possible interpretative option is that these figures are in fact Christians.[102] Of course, Christians ought to do good deeds at some point (although certain Christian traditions would want to define this very carefully), and Christians are obviously saved elsewhere in Paul. Moreover, this reading can appeal to Paul's brief opposition in 2:29a in probable terms of the Spirit (περιτομὴ καρδίας ἐν πνεύματι οὐ γράμματι).[103] Hence, this seems to be the best interpretative option we have yet considered, yet multiple contentions ultimately stand against its plausibility.

We should note first the degree to which these figures are integrated into the current argument's central principles (and this is a strength of the previous two options). As we have already seen, they are inseparable from several earlier claims in the text. Hence, whatever else they are, they are justified by works; they are fundamentally constituted and saved by desert. The text marks them explicitly in such terms twice (ἡ ἀκροβυστία τὰ δικαιώματα τοῦ νόμου φυλάσσῃ . . . ἡ ἐκ φύσεως ἀκροβυστία τὸν νόμον τελοῦσα . . .). Moreover, they access the relevant information about law observance from the cosmos and their hearts (see 1:19-20; 2:14-15). They are then "not merely hearers of the law but its doers," as a result of which God declares them "righteous," because that is what in fact they are.[104]

In view of all this, it seems difficult if not impossible to believe that these figures are Christians. If they are, then Christians have just been defined in a way that diametrically opposes the entire (ostensible) progression of the argument in terms of the need for justification through faith alone because of the universality of sin. Christians must now be defined in terms of perfect works as well.[105] Indeed, Christians have now ended up on both sides of Paul's argument in 1:18–3:20! And this seems patently absurd. These Christians can be saved without reference to Christ! They learn all that they need to know from heartfelt contemplation of the cosmos. (Are they saved by faith as well? This seems impossible, because those saved by faith have acknowledged internal sinfulness, and these figures have not sinned; they are saved by works. So do two completely different types of Christians now exist — those justified by faith and those by works?!)[106]

Probably enough has been said for most to concede the bankruptcy of this explanation too; however, its problems are not yet over. Just as the explanation's consistent application leads to absurdity with respect to the definition of Christians, the introduction of Christians at this point in the argument is inappropriate if not absurd as well. Paul is in the process here of setting the stage for the proclamation of the gospel; he is constructing a universal, non-Christian vestibule that all must traverse before hearing the Christian gospel that will save them. He cannot therefore define a key constituency within that vestibule in terms of Christianity; this would be to introduce the solution into the definition of the problem — to put the cart before the horse — at which point the assertion of the problem as an objective, universally accessible, non-Christian progression would be undermined. If this really is his strategy, then his argumentative incompetence is again apparent. (But is he really this dishonest, or this stupid?) In essence, any explicitly Christian contentions within a non-Christian progression must lack both appropriateness and cogency.

As if to reinforce these argumentative suspicions, we should now note the overt textual coding of these figures. Only the brief dative opposition in 2:29 could suggest that they are Christian, and alternative readings of this brief clause are possible (see part four, chapter fourteen). Otherwise, the immediate frames of their discussion (in 2:14-15 and 2:26-29) are universal and non-Christian, progressing in terms of generic Jews and Greeks. That is, all the textual markings of these figures, with one possible exception, indicate non-Christians. They are just what they seem to be initially: law-abiding, hence righteous pagans, who are justified by works. So it seems difficult ultimately to suppose that these figures are Christians. And added to this issue of interpretive economy is the difficulty of the implicit supersessionism if they are so identified.

To my knowledge, Paul *never* elsewhere in his writings defines a Christian — whom he would usually call a "brother" — as a "Jew," as v. 29 must suggest on a Christian reading of this figure. *This is unparalleled.* Nor, I would argue, can it be decisively proved that he ever *displaces* Israel with the church — a common misunderstanding.[107] When he uses broad ethnic distinctives like "Jew" and "Greek," he invariably respects this difference but overcomes it *in Christ,* applying *new* metaphors from that point onward — usually familial[108] (as Gal. 3:28 illustrates most famously[109]). Elsewhere, then, the pagan convert never becomes a "true" Jew. So the easy claim that this "true Jew" in Romans 2 is in fact a Christian makes an unparalleled supersessionist assertion — and one without much wider supporting evidence from the rest of Paul. It flies in the face of the overt textual coding of these figures, and it courts a charge of rather appalling salvation-historical insensitivity as well (although in so doing it may align with a pervasive weakness within Justification theory that is committed in a sense to this descriptive insensitivity toward Judaism). Hence, this option too should preferably be abandoned as implausible and insufficiently corroborated.

It is evident that the usual explanations of these mysterious righteous pagans who surface especially in Romans 2:14-15 and 2:26-29 are all problematic. Each seems to have a piece of the textual truth but to falter at some significant point. And we are left with an awkward textual conundrum — an enduring overdetermination. Romans 1:18–3:20, read conventionally, is studded with inexplicable figures that seem to make useful localized points but contradict utterly Paul's ostensible overarching objective. He seems to speak here — repeatedly — of law-abiding and hence righteous pagans, in a blatant contradiction of his soteriological theory and argumentative goals in Romans 1–3 as the Justification advocate construes them. Their recurring presence in the argument seems to suggest, then, either that Paul is confused and incompetent or that the conventional construal of Romans 1–3 has misunderstood his argument.

We turn now to consider a final difficulty that is closely related to this one.

(11) Paul's Redefinition of Circumcision and Judaism in 2:25-29

It is frequently noted that Paul's redefinitions of circumcision and the true Jew in vv. 26b, 28, and 29 are shocking; no Jewish literature attests to this sort of overruling, even when it strongly endorses the importance of ethics and desert (and Philo in particular will be discussed in more detail in due course).[110] In our parlance, however, this is an exacerbation of a difficulty at the reading's empirical frame: Paul does not seem to be describing Judaism fairly as Judaism represents itself, or indeed even as he himself describes it elsewhere.[111] But there is also an argumentative difficulty implicit in this move.

We observed earlier that Justification theory operates with two different epistemologies and laws and that this can cause various difficulties. Pagans seem to have a minimal law that is discerned naturally, while Jews are preoccupied with much more extensive and specific legislation that is revealed textually.[112] In relation to this theoretical disposition, it is worth noting that in 2:26-29 Paul's apparent redefinition of circumcision and the true Jew is consequently not strictly correct in argumentative terms.

It does not follow logically from the superior obedience of the pagan in terms of her own system, as opposed to the disobedience of the Jew in relation to his system, that the former state *displaces* and *redefines* the latter. This is a false deduction. The superior obedience of pagans to their minimal natural law in no way undermines the validity of the more extensive Jewish law, so Paul is wrong to make this move in the text, claiming that the observant pagan is a "true *Jew.*" Both ethical systems in the vestibule should retain their own integrity. A Jew, to be obedient, should still obey the entire law, including the command to be circumcised, and a law-observant pagan cannot displace that broader Jewish obedience (that is, unless a decision has been made in favor of the more minimal pagan system, but acute conundrums are raised by this decision, and it would, furthermore, need to be argued for; Justification advocates, writing from the later vantage point of postpagan Christianity, do of course often view the pagan system more generously, but that stance arguably remains awkward in theological terms).

We are left, then, with certain biting conundrums. First, Paul's redefinition, as the conventional reading construes it, simply seems wrong. Second, the argument presses in a direction that Justification theory ultimately cannot endorse — the abandonment of a broad Jewish ethic. (And the exacerbation of the empirical difficulty in terms of Judaism has also already been noted.) Thus, clearly a reading that can explain Paul's argument in a way that restores both its intrinsic validity and the coherence of its contribution to the overarching discussion will enjoy an advantage at this point as well.

3.2. *Textual Overdeterminations — Romans 1:16-17 and 3:21-31*

I detect two overdeterminations in Paul's so-called thesis paragraphs.[113] These are rather subtle, because the paragraphs are so compact. Nevertheless, they are ultimately very significant, so it is important to grasp them precisely.

(12) πίστις as Instrumental in Disclosure in 1:16-17 and 3:21-26

One of the first major textual enigmas we ordinarily encounter in commentary on the thesis paragraphs of Romans is the meaning of the prepositional series in 1:17. There Paul states that δικαιοσύνη [γὰρ] θεοῦ [ἐν αὐτῷ] ἀποκαλύπτεται ἐκ πίστεως εἰς πίστιν κ.τ.λ. Although numerous suggestions have been made in this relation (and they vary considerably in plausibility), the meaning of the series has greatly puzzled interpreters.[114] However, I am going to suggest almost immediately that this well-known difficulty unfolds into a less well-known problem in 3:21-22; consequently, two enigmatic textual features turn out on closer examination to denote precisely the same problematic argumentative dynamic — instrumentality within divine disclosure.

We will address the situation in 1:17 in more detail first (relying principally on an argument I first made in 1992 that still seems valid) and then turn to consider 3:21-22.[115] Four points in Romans 1:17 need to be noted and considered initially.

(i) Habakkuk 2:4 is quoted by Paul immediately after the problematic prepositional series in v. 17b and concludes the same sentence: δικαιοσύνη γὰρ θεοῦ ἐν αὐτῷ ἀποκαλύπτεται ἐκ πίστεως εἰς πίστιν καθὼς γέγραπται ὁ δίκαιος ἐκ πίστεως ζήσεται. In view of this, it is difficult to avoid the suggestion that Paul has quoted Habakkuk 2:4 — his first explicitly cited text in Romans — to resume, define, and affirm his use of its central phrase in the same sentence's preceding clause. Moreover, these two textual units must now be understood in parallel. It is implausible to supply a reading for ἐκ πίστεως in the prepositional series in 1:17a that Habakkuk 2:4 cannot accommodate in 1:17b. (This observation ultimately eliminates the elegant theocentric construal of the series; see more in this relation just below.)

(ii) A consideration of the broader distribution of these two datums in Paul's letters suggests strongly that the citation of Habakkuk 2:4 in Romans 1:17b does underlie Paul's use of the phrase ἐκ πίστεως in the series in Romans 1:17a (as well as, by direct implication, its uses everywhere else). Paul uses this phrase frequently in Romans and Galatians, where it occurs twenty-one times,[116] *but nowhere else* in his corpus. And so this distribution matches perfectly his quotation of Habakkuk 2:4, which he quotes only in Romans and Galatians. (Those two letters are also notably rich in scriptural quotations, and especially texts including πιστ- terminology.) This correlation is far too marked to be mere coincidence.

Hence, both localized and comparative evidence strongly support the interpretative claim that the meaning of the prepositional phrase ἐκ πίστεως and the citation of Habakkuk 2:4 are correlated.

(iii) In many passages Paul tends to juxtapose πιστ- terminology with slogans that speak of "works of law" and "doing" (ποιεῖν/ἔργων νόμου). So, for example, Galatians 2:16b states — rather famously — ἡμεῖς εἰς Χριστὸν ᾽Ιησοῦν ἐπιστεύσαμεν ἵνα δικαιωθῶμεν ἐκ πίστεως Χριστοῦ καὶ οὐκ ἐξ ἔργων νόμου. But Paul seems to employ a stylistic variation in some of these texts, using διά instead of ἐκ πίστεως. As Galatians 2:16a indicates, in a clause immediately preceding the statement just noted, οὐ δικαιοῦται ἄνθρωπος ἐξ ἔργων νόμου ἐὰν μὴ διὰ πίστεως ᾽Ιησοῦ Χριστοῦ (κ.τ.λ.). And it is really impossible to detect a significant shift in meaning between the prepositional variations used in these passages;[117] they seem mere stylistic flourishes supplied to avoid needless repetition, although as such they also supply important information about the function of ἐκ in the dominant phrase.[118] Paul's parallel use of διά in the genitive indicates that ἐκ is functioning *instrumentally;* the programmatic phrase ἐκ πίστεως therefore means "through . . ." or "by means of πίστις" (a meaning that is of course quite compatible with a reading of Hab. 2:4).[119]

(iv) This observation now opens up the relevant data still further. Other instrumental phrases can be seen functioning in further parallels to the statistically dominant phrase ἐκ πίστεως in certain passages — principally dative prepositions and phrases (and this reinforces our preceding judgment concerning the phrase's instrumental meaning).[120] Furthermore, the actual passages under discussion can be slightly broadened. Philippians 3:9 now seems relevant, although it does not use the key phrase from Habakkuk 2:4, but this is probably because that letter cites no Jewish Scripture overtly, since its pagan audience would not have recognized this.[121] However, the most important correlation for our present purposes is the powerful linkage that is established between Romans 1:16-17 and 3:21-26. These can now be recognized as sibling texts (if not as twins).

Both texts deploy δικαιοσύνη Θεοῦ in the position of subject, and then construct the predicate from a verb of revelation — ἀποκαλύπτω in 1:17 and φανερόω in 3:21. (These verbs overlap considerably in semantic terms as well.[122]) This sentence is then expanded with the addition of what we can now recognize as identical prepositional phrases in semantic terms — ἐκ πίστεως in 1:17 (echoed by 3:26) and διὰ πίστεως in 3:22 and 25. The characteristic purposive εἰς construction using πιστ- terms is also present in both texts (see 3:22). And the attestation of the Scriptures features prominently in both texts as well; note the actual citation of Habakkuk 2:4 in 1:17b, and the claim in 3:21 that the disclosure of δικαιοσύνη Θεοῦ is witnessed to by the Law and the Prophets. Indeed, this expansion is telling. As early as Romans 1:2 — before the formalities of the address have even been completed — Paul signals the importance of the promissory witness of "the prophets in the holy Scriptures," a motif resumed explicitly by 3:21 and concretely attested by 1:17, which cites his most important prophetic text. These are five points of explicit overlap developed in the main in terms of semantic identity. Clearly, then, the interpretations of Romans 1:17 (presumably alongside v. 16) and 3:21-26 belong together. They should be interpreted in parallel. But in reaching this judgment, we have also displaced the textual conundrum with which we began.

The meaning of the series ἐκ πίστεως εἰς πίστιν in Romans 1:17 is not a tightly localized or marginal issue; it runs to the heart of what Paul is trying to say in both these important subsections in Romans. He is speaking here, repeatedly, of some revelation or disclosure of the δικαιοσύνη Θεοῦ within which πίστις functions instrumentally: the δικαιοσύνη Θεοῦ is revealed *by means of* this πίστις. And at this stage our first significant textual overdetermination in the thesis paragraphs becomes apparent.

The conventional reading and its associated soteriology of Justification tend to attribute "faith" monolithically to the Christian; it is of course the act by which non-Christians grasp salvation, and as such, it occupies a critical role in the unfolding theory. The conventional reading is consequently happy to emphasize it at every possible turn textually, and will certainly need to find Paul speaking of it plainly at least once. Presumably, the reading has no difficulty attributing fidelity to God in some sense as well, if that is necessary. The generous provision of a gospel of salvation sola fide can be regarded as an act of loving fidelity to Israel (although the retributive character of God remains more fundamental; the fidelity of God is only operative relative to the fulfillment of certain conditions). Conventional readers therefore expect Paul to speak in his thesis paragraphs in Romans of salvation sola fide — in terms of the saving faith of the Christian.[123] He might also speak in this relation of divine fidelity, although this is not so necessary.[124] But what the conventional reading *cannot* explain is a "faith" that *discloses* or *reveals* the "righteousness of God" in instrumental terms (however we construe the meaning of this last important genitive phrase). "Faith" simply does not function as the means by which something moves from a position of invisibility to one of visibility, from the unknown to the known, and to affirm that it does is to make a basic semantic error — to assert something unmeaningful or ungrammatical.[125] "Faith" tends to affirm something *already known* as true, which is of course the way that it functions in Justification theory, in response to Christian preaching and the gospel. The gospel, when preached, makes God's saving act in Christ known. And "faith" then responds to that disclosure as an act of *affirmation,* not the act of *disclosure* itself.[126] Hence, to press it into the role of disclosure is simply to commit a semantic mistake; "faith" does not *mean* this, and so these texts, which speak explicitly and unavoidably of disclosure, cannot be read in this way. *Paul has to be talking about something else in these texts when he uses this phrase.*[127] (And this is of course not to exclude Christian faith from Paul's thinking more broadly; it is only to suggest that that is not what Paul is trying to articulate here. Paul's purposive εἰς constructions in 1:16b, 17a and 3:22 clearly denote Christian faith in some sense, presumably as the goal or end of this process of disclosure.)

An appeal could perhaps be made at this point to the divine fidelity: God's faithfulness could function in some sense as an instrument of the disclosure of the δικαιοσύνη Θεοῦ. This is perhaps a little awkward argumentatively and theologically, if not tautologous — the righteousness of God is being disclosed through the fidelity of God[128] — but it does not seem *semantically* impossible.

However, this appeal is excluded by the tight correlation that we have already noted between the programmatic phrase ἐκ πίστεως and the text of Habakkuk 2:4. Neither this text nor most of the other instances of the key phrase ἐκ πίστεως in Romans and Galatians can be read coherently in terms of God's faithfulness. (Paul's famous Christ genitives are especially problematic in this regard; see esp. Rom. 3:22, 26; Gal. 2:16; 3:22, 26; Phil. 3:9.) Again, this is not to exclude the notion of God's faithfulness from either Romans or Paul's thinking as a whole; clearly, it has a role to play there (see esp. Rom. 3:3). However, it is to point out that *that theme cannot be signified by these particular phrases and their associated texts!*

It would probably be conceded that the relevant overdetermination has been established. The conventional construal of Romans 1–4 cannot coherently construe the instrumental πίστις phrases that Paul uses repeatedly in his "thesis" paragraphs (see 1:17; 3:22). The reading is embarrassed by these statements — once they are read with due care — that lie at the heart of some of the texts that Justification theory relies on most heavily.

We turn now to consider a smaller but similarly awkward textual datum in Romans 3:25.

(13) The Syntactical Awkwardness of 3:25

Romans 3:23-26 is a notoriously difficult text in syntactical terms (and this text has attracted a degree of attention of late[129]). We will grapple with its dynamics in detail in part four, chapters fifteen through seventeen. For now it suffices to note certain issues in its central section:

24a. . . δικαιούμενοι δωρεὰν τῇ αὐτοῦ χάριτι
24bδιὰ τῆς ἀπολυτρώσεως τῆς ἐν Χριστῷ Ἰησοῦ·
25aὃν προέθετο ὁ θεὸς ἱλαστήριον
25bδιὰ τῆς[130] πίστεως
25cἐν τῷ αὐτοῦ αἵματι κ.τ.λ.

The particular difficulty that should be noted in the present relation is the phrase διὰ τῆς πίστεως, which is awkward in various possible ways.[131] If it denotes "faith" in a specified object supplied in context, then the notion of "faith in his [i.e., Christ Jesus'] blood" is both awkward and unparalleled for Paul. Nowhere else does Paul speak of believing in Christ's blood (or death), and any sense of trusting in it seems completely wrongheaded. However, if these two prepositional phrases are read independently of one another within the broader structure of the sentence — as coordinate — then this difficulty seems alleviated. The question now arises what it modifies from its broader setting, and this is the principal difficulty.

Conventional readers expect justification to be by means of faith, and Jesus' atoning death to be associated with any mention of blood — the two key elements in the second saving contract. So v. 25b should ideally be read as modifying 24a, and 25c read in relation to 25a. But the difficulties with these suggestions are obvious. Paul has begun a relative clause in 25a, so the suggestion that its second element (25b) should reach back into the preceding, semi-independent clause seems far-fetched. One phrase and one clause intervene between these two syntactical elements. Moreover, 25b itself intervenes between 25a and 25c. It might be suggested, then, that 25b is parenthetical. This would at least allow 25c to modify 25a reasonably directly. But 25b must still modify something, even if only implicitly; it must have *some* meaningful relationship with the sentence within which it appears and with the elements that immediately surround it even if it is a parenthesis. *And these are christological, not anthropological.* Hence, it makes little sense to read 25b even parenthetically in terms of the conventional reading and the preoccupations of Justification theory — in terms of some reference to human believing. And this suggestion returns us to the conundrum that the phrase reaches back to an earlier, semi-independent clause.[132]

Consequently, in my view it remains another small textual overdetermination for the conventional reading — one that is curiously similar in stylistic terms to the awkward instrumental πίστις phrases that were noted in the previous subsection. We do not know how this phrase fits into its present syntactical location, and what implicit object it is taking. But these two textual opacities seem to function in parallel.[133]

And with these observations a consideration of the final significant locus of overdetermination in Romans 1–4 is already upon us — Paul's discussion of Abraham.

3.3. Textual Overdeterminations — Romans 4:1-25

Although the discussion of Abraham in Romans 4:1-25 is widely regarded as a locus classicus for Justification theory,[134] a closer look at Paul's actual analysis reveals a veritable thicket of overdeterminative signals and conundrums. Far from being one of the theory's greatest strengths, the ostensibly definitive example of Abraham may turn out to be one of its weakest points of purchase on Paul's actual text. There are no fewer than eleven arguable overdeterminations in 4:1-25 — embarrassing errors of commission by the textual base against the theoretical superstructure. This passage cries out for a smoother interpretation.[135]

(14) The Scriptural Overruling of Boasting

We introduce here a difficulty that could have been addressed earlier in relation to 3:27 but seemed best left until the other relevant text had been brought into play, namely, 4:2-8. (We also link hands here with an underdetermination evident in that earlier subsection.)[136]

In 3:27 Paul states that "boasting has been precluded . . . διὰ τῆς πίστεως." (The ambiguities of this contentious last phrase do not need to be resolved for the overdetermination to emerge.) This statement is echoed by 4:2, where the text posits Abraham's right to boasting εἰ ... ἐξ ἔργων ἐδικαιώθη. But this possibility is denied immediately, and then confirmed by the citation of Genesis 15:6 in v. 3, which is explicated through v. 5 in terms of a gratuitous, undeserved crediting that Paul develops from the text's use of λογίζομαι over against a payment of wages calculated in some relation to desert. The citation of Psalm 32:1-2 in vv. 6-8 then corroborates this claim in terms of gracious crediting, by which stage the argument (at least on one level) seems clear. "Boasting" is overruled by the testimony of Scripture — here Genesis 15:6 and Psalm 32:1-2 — that demonstrates some righteous act by God directed toward Abraham in terms of gratuitous giving rather than obligated payment. Apparently, an equivalent act by God in relation to desert — here elaborated in terms of an explicit metaphor of currency and payment — would have legitimately allowed boasting (the boasting of the performance of the relevant acts that underpinned desert). However, that simply was not the case for Abraham, as Scripture suggests. God acted gratuitously, and so boasting did not take place *in fact*. But this textual demonstration is embarrassing for Justification theory.

Justification theory *expects* boasting to operate in the first, non-Christian phase of the overarching salvific progression, when justification is being attempted by the perfect performance of works of law. But such boasting is falsified there *essentially empirically and self-reflectively, through experience;* the attempted performance should fail because of transgression, this often being a repeated experience, although, strictly speaking, one transgression is sufficient. So the futility of boasting is an essentially psychological realization that precedes and prepares for the realization that if salvation is now to take place, then it must be by way of some easier criterion. (Of course, no boasting will be appropriate in relation to that criterion either, because it will not denote salvation for desert or through merit.) Indeed, if boasting takes place, then it can only denote a failure to grasp the objective ethical situation of the vestibule and thus will indicate the presence of a rationally and/or ethically deficient agent.[137]

It is at this point that the present overdetermination links hands with — and nicely complements — the underdetermination that we noted earlier in relation to this text (UD 11). Paul never overtly suggests that Abraham traversed a sinful first phase, learning through painful experience that works of law will not justify and that boasting is therefore inappropriate. This important element within Justification theory is missing. Moreover, when the text does state something overt, it supplies a different and essentially inappropriate argument. *The Scripture says* that the divine crediting of δικαιοσύνη to Abraham was based on his "faith." It is *this fact* that *overrules* boasting and attempted justification through works of law. And it is also this fact that embarrasses Justification theory. Justification by works and any attendant boasting cannot simply be overruled; it must fail.

Justification theory will not function without the internal collapse of attempted justification through works and its concomitant realizations. Without the establishment of the prior sinfulness of humanity, the need for salvation through the easier criterion of faith alone is not established. Hence, "faith" *never* simply *overrules* "works" in Justification theory; the legitimacy of the former depends entirely on the failed legitimacy of the latter, which is internal and empirical. (The scriptural overruling of the notion of attempted justification through works of law also exacerbates the epistemological tensions that were noted earlier; a revealed, particular truth should not overcome a position that has been established on generally recognizable, philosophical grounds — see ID 1 and SD 1, summarized below.) The supply by the text — not once but twice — of this argument from mere overruling on scriptural grounds is therefore an embarrassment to Justification theory's reasoned overthrow of attempted works and any related boasting. The overruling is for the wrong reason, and Justification theory cannot even really recognize it as right.[138]

Hence, the function of Abraham at this point is in fact profoundly embarrassing for the conventional reading. Paul's explication of Genesis 15:6 seems simply to falsify an account of justification in terms of works and boasting directly. *Two alternatives are juxtaposed: one legitimate, and the other illegitimate.*[139] A reading that can make sense of this argumentative antithesis will clearly enjoy an important advantage over the conventional reading.

(15) *The Temporal Overruling of Circumcision and Mosaic Law*

Another overdetermination in Romans 4 occurs in the arguments that run from v. 9 through v. 14, and — rather significantly — its dynamic is very similar to the difficulty just noted. Justification by works, and the work of circumcision in particular, is overruled again for the wrong reason, although here it is a different one. In this stretch of text Paul negates both the ritual of circumcision (vv. 9-12) and the Mosaic law (vv. 13-14; see also v. 16a) in favor of the principle of πίστις, and does so on *temporal* grounds (as against *scriptural* grounds, as in vv. 2-8). He argues here that the ordinance of circumcision and observance of the full Mosaic law occurred later in time than Abraham's experience of faith recounted in Genesis 15 and therefore cannot displace the principle that was established first. This would amount to an evacuation of that Scripture's content and hence would be unacceptable. Thus, it is the earliness of Genesis 15:6 and its attestation to πίστις that affords Paul his crucial argumentative leverage at these two points. And this is of course the wrong argument once more.

These are not the typical criticisms by Justification theory of law observance. Indeed, they are essentially invalid in terms of that schema, which has little concern with temporality. Attempted justification through works of law, which includes any dependence on the work of circumcision, is invalid *because the prescribed works cannot be performed perfectly.* Sin will interfere, leading ultimately to condemnation by a just God. It is this basic dynamic that clashes with Paul's arguments in terms of time in several respects.

First, a temporal argument is irrelevant. The occurrence of "faith" *first* does not overrule any later experience of works — far from it. Justification by works can lose its validity only if it fails *in fact*, as an experience. And this attempt can take place at any point in history, and in effect should, *in the life of every saved person!*

Second, faith will itself lack both legitimacy and recognizability if justification by works has not already been attempted. The individual will not know that she must be justified by faith alone, and neither will she yet feel her need for saving faith. So an argument from temporal priority is not merely invalid in terms of Justification theory; the prior placement of faith is incoherent in terms of that theory (or, alternatively, a strong commitment to the prior placement of faith directly undermines the structure and rationale of Justification theory).

In short, Paul's temporal arguments in 4:9-14 are both irrelevant and embarrassing. They prove nothing in terms of Justification theory but rather embarrass it significantly by assuming that they have done so and thereby undermining that theory's basic structure.[140]

Excursus: A Contextual Clarification — the Possible Meanings of πιστεύω and πίστις

This is a useful point at which to introduce two important semantic clarifications — technically, an input from the texts' general cultural frame. The first such clarification is very simple.

Without pretending to sort out all the semantic questions that surround the interpretation of Paul's πιστ- terminology at this point,[141] I merely want to emphasize an important semantic distinction that can be obscured by later Christian and post-Christian usage, a distinction elided or even erased in much discussion of Paul by the use of the substantive translation equivalent "faith." It is highlighted nicely, however, by the standard English options in relation to the verb πιστεύω, "believe" and "trust."[142]

As the use of those two verbs suggests, the English verbal equivalent to the originally Latin "faith" has been lost. Even more importantly, however, the two verbs preserve for us in English different possible connotations for ancient Greek πιστ- terms. On the one hand, those signifiers can denote matters of sheer rationality — the truth of certain statements, the credence given to those statements, and so on — matters, in short, of "believing" and "belief." On the other hand, they can denote that specialized subset of beliefs clustered around a certain sort of interpersonal relationship that modern English-language users would ordinarily denote with the word "trust." "Trust" is generally coded favorably,[143] denoting the belief that someone or something is "trustworthy," that is, reliable, if not benevolent. We then "trust" in such things. But these are additional and quite specific connotations within the broader realm of beliefs and believing. So there are many things that we believe but do not trust! Note, for example, the distinctions in the following sentences:

> "Andrew *believed* from a very young age that dinosaurs had once roamed the United States."
>
> "Andrew *believed* that a series of despotic tyrants had governed the Soviet Union since the end of World War II."
>
> "Andrew *trusted* that the piton he was hammering into the left face of the Eiger would hold his weight."

Koiné would probably use the same verb for each of these notions and yet clearly could mean rather different things (and the same applies to any equivalent use of the substantive). Issues of belief may have little or nothing to do with us interpersonally, are often value neutral, and do not necessarily connote something or someone reliable or benevolent. But issues of trust are generally regarded as more directly relevant interpersonally, and as essentially positive.

It turns out, then, that "trust" and "trusting" are a quite specific subset of the broader semantic field of "belief" and "believing." *The latter are clearly a necessary condition for the former* — trusting involves believing certain things — but "trusting" is by no means *reducible* to "believing." *They are not simply the same.*

A semantic map of belief and trust

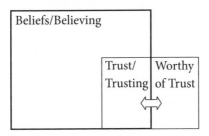

The danger in relation to the translation equivalent "faith" should by now be apparent (at least, in this specific relation[144]). It lacks precision. If we denote an action by Abraham in terms of "faith," it is not immediately apparent whether we mean an action of "belief" or one more specifically of "trust." "Faith" is such a broad designation that it covers both these senses immediately. (The same ambiguities may also then attend any related discussion of the verb.) Moreover, we might slide unwittingly from one connotation to the other without realizing it. Similar difficulties attend the notion of "faith in the gospel." Most would agree that for a Christian "to believe *x*" is potentially a significantly different thing than "to trust in *x*," and this is an especially important issue to clarify if salvation is dependent upon it. But we cannot tell in the first instance if "faith" is denoting only the first action or also the second.

We should now add one further important semantic clarification to this developing analysis — a second distinction. If someone trusts over time, and especially under duress, we would probably denote these additional elements in English by speaking of that person's "steadfastness," "endurance," "fidelity," or "faithfulness." The further notion is detachable from the notion of trust per se; it only overlaps with this semantic field. And the different English words used here again indicate that a semantic transition has taken place. We distinguish between acts of "belief," of "trust," and of "faithfulness." Consider again our last example in the previous list, and some possible extensions:

"Andrew *trusted* that Louise would not reveal his dark secrets to the rest of the church."

"In spite of her long absence, Andrew trusted that Louise would return from her missionary work in Guatemala."

"Louise served faithfully as a missionary in Guatemala for ten years."

The first example here is one of mere trust; the second segues into fidelity, however, because Andrew's trust endures both the passage of time and difficulty — here, absence.[145] The third sentence is also an instance of fidelity, in Louise; however, it demonstrates the point that fidelity may be unrelated to belief and trust per se. (Louise is not *trusting* faithfully but *serving* faithfully.) "Fidelity" seems to be predicable of many different actions and not merely of trusting. (It will of course involve certain beliefs.) "Trust" over time and through difficulty consequently can segue into "fidelity," or "faithfulness," but that category seems to exceed the boundaries of "belief" and "trust." And consequently both the postures of "trust" and "fidelity" should be distinguished, if necessary, from one merely of "belief."[146]

A semantic map of belief, trust and faithfulness

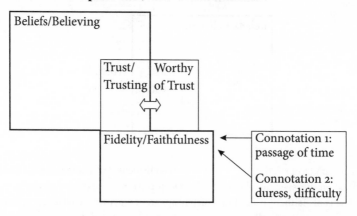

Armed with these useful distinctions, we can now return to consider Paul's analysis of Abraham in Romans 4, noting in particular several aspects of his "faith" that ultimately prove highly embarrassing to the conventional reading and Justification theory.

(16) The Personal Nature of Abraham's πίστις

We have already seen in part one, chapters one and three, that Justification theory has no cogent theoretical reason for shifting from the impersonal notion of saving "belief" to the more personal notion of "trust," or even of "fidelity," as the Christian dispensation arrives. Although most of the discourse's advocates have been uncomfortable with this and have argued in some sense for a personal dimension, Christian salvation, as dictated by Justification, is a response to information derived from the construction of the cosmos in the unsaved state. Hence, the theory provides no valid grounds for the exercise of relational qualities like "trust" as salvation is inaugurated. In light of these constraints, Abraham's explicitly personal trust in God in Romans 4 is an embarrassment to Justification theory — an overdetermination (although here it merely reproduces an overdetermination already widely conceded within the readings of even the discourse's advocates, which manifests especially as a difficulty at the systematic frame).

It is difficult to deny that Abraham's πίστις is personal through the argumentation of Romans 4. In this chapter Abraham does not merely believe certain things about God to be true, along with certain specific promises, although he does do this; he trusts God personally, as Genesis 15:6 itself suggests quite directly: ἐπίστευσεν [δὲ] Ἀβραὰμ τῷ Θεῷ κ.τ.λ. (see also . . . τῷ [δὲ] μὴ ἐργαζομένῳ πιστεύοντι δὲ ἐπὶ τὸν δικαιοῦντα τὸν ἀσεβῆ κ.τ.λ. in 4:5). The personal object in this programmatic scriptural citation draws Abraham's action immediately into the more specific semantic realm of "trust." Arguments would now have to be provided if Abraham's posture was to be interpreted here merely in terms of "belief." Like all who trust, he believes certain things to be true about the person trusted, but he is also involved in a direct personal relationship with that person (here divine) and views him as reliable. Genesis 15:6 is therefore best translated in the broader setting of Romans 4:1-25 as "Abraham trusted in God . . ." (and this is the connotation that it also carries in its original context).

Abraham is also described in vv. 18-21 as believing God's promise in Genesis 15 concerning an heir, in an unwavering fashion, through to the promises made in Genesis 17, concerning his fatherhood of many nations, and then beyond these until the birth of Isaac, which is recounted in chapter 21. The gap between the two sets of promises in the narrative is no less than fourteen years.[147] Now it could be argued that Abraham merely believed in these promises in the sense that they were propositions that would eventually come true, just as he was convinced concerning the proposition or information that God was powerful enough to effect the promises, despite the countervailing information concerning his and Sarah's infertility. But this seems a little odd (and is contradicted by the best reading of v. 17 as well). More likely is that Abraham trusted God personally to carry out his promises, and that it was this interpersonal relationship that underlay the surety of the promises, that is, the correctness of their information *and* their eventual fulfillment. The former reading makes the entire arrangement revolve around Abraham's own sense of mental certitude (indeed, it is positively Promethean). In the latter reading, Abraham trusts a trustworthy God, thereby shifting the emphasis from anthropology to theology, something that also seems more plausible in terms of the general tenor of Romans, of Paul's thought as a whole, and of Judaism in his day, all of which emphasized interpersonal piety and God. (That is, it seems dangerously anachronistic to Cartesianize this text ruthlessly, reducing everything to Abraham's mental state.)

In sum, the depiction of Abraham in Romans 4 seems to emphasize his personal relationship with God, which is specifically developed, in accordance with Genesis 15:6, in terms of unwavering trust over time, at which point it begins clearly to cross over into the sense of "faithfulness" as well. This unwavering trust involves a number of critical beliefs, and is even characterized by them (by, that is, precisely, an unwavering belief in God, etc.). But this deeply personal attitude is an embarrassment to the *propositional* criterion for salvation legitimized by Justification theory. The first phase of Justification theory cannot generate this sort of personal relationship with God. Hence, it seems almost incredible to observe that *the conventional reader of Romans 1–4 has no cogent grounds for affirming this central element within Paul's analysis of Abraham in Romans 4*, a text traditionally regarded as one of Justification's strongholds.[148]

(17) The Distinctive Epistemological Mode of Abraham's Attestation

We have already noted how Justification theory contains embarrassing shifts in epistemological mode. In the non-Christian state it juxtaposes a general, philosophical mode of knowledge rather awkwardly with a particular, historical, revealed mode central to Judaism — principally the Jewish Scriptures. Particularity then triumphs almost completely as the transition to Christianity is made. People become Christians by responding affirmatively to information that has been preached to them. Having heard about Christ, they believe in him. (So at least this later action maintains the emphasis of phase one, in both its epistemological modes, on information — provided we maintain theoretical consistency at this point; its particularity is more Jewish, however.) But Abraham, as Paul describes him in Romans 4, adds a further mode.

Although Paul does not elaborate on this point explicitly, the implicit prompt for Abraham's trust was the direct disclosure of God, which seems to have involved divine speech in particular; Abraham trusted in God via his words and promises (see esp. vv. 17-22). But these were not relayed to him by the book of Genesis (that is, through the way *we* generally learn of the situation, reading a text). He heard them *directly*, giving unwavering credence to them in view of his underlying trust in the one who spoke them — God (vv. 20-21a). This is a highly particular, historical, and revealed mode, which corresponds to the Jewish and Christian modes in these respects. But, as we have just noted, it is *personal*, thereby going beyond the theoretical emphasis on information, and *it is essentially unmediated as well*. It is in fact a *new* mode of theological knowledge from the foregoing, in which God speaks to people directly! And of course neither the conventional reading nor Justification theory emphasizes this mode in their ostensible programmatic figure (for largely obvious reasons[149]). Indeed, they fail to recognize it, and really cannot endorse it. Hence, it is another textual overdetermination. And a further, closely related overdetermination lurks within this activity.

(18) The Epistemological Incoherence of Abraham's Attestation

As we have just seen, Abraham is ostensibly an authoritative scriptural attestation to the claims of Justification theory. *We* learn that he is an authentic and valid witness to the cogency of this schema by reading about it in the relevant sacred texts. Moreover, the entire discourse is structured in this fashion — on the basis of authoritative exegetical corroboration. It is true ultimately "because the Bible says so." Yet, as we have seen, *Abraham did not himself learn anything from Scripture; Abraham responded to direct divine disclosure*. Hence, at this point the discourse is self-referentially incoherent.[150] *Its key example does not actually exemplify its key epistemological mode* (the mode that in fact underlies our supposed attention to Abraham *as* a key example in the first place!).[151] We read about the authoritative example of Abraham, who hears and responds to God directly, so his example does not validate our reading. The conventional reading consequently points authoritatively to the wrong epistemological mode, namely, fidelity in response to direct divine disclosure — a further overdeterminative embarrassment.

(19) The Strength of Abraham's πίστις

We have already spent some space in relation to the preceding issues remarking on Abraham's rather extraordinary behavior as recounted by vv. 18-21, and it is time to deepen that portrait. Paul describes Abraham's actions in a highly convoluted series of clauses that contains several important participles and prepositional phrases (see esp. vv. 18-21): Abraham trusted "from hope to hope" (18a); he did not "weaken in that trust" despite his and his wife's obvious infertility (19); neither did he "waver in distrust" but "waxed in trust," "giving glory to God" (20), being "completely convinced" that God was capable of doing (and presumably also willing to do) what had been promised (21; translations DC). We have also already noted that this attitude held for about fourteen years — a point that would have been obvious to any auditors familiar with the canonical narrative.

It is important now to consider carefully just what Abraham is said to have done. He undertook a fourteen-year journey of unwavering trust, flying in the face of overt biological realities, and this is described by Paul as being flawless, with no doubt, no wavering, and no anxiety. Abraham trusted, hoped, praised, and even grew stronger in those attitudes, throughout this period. Hence, there can be little doubt that Abraham's attitude here was positively superhuman. Of course, this portrayal accords with much of the Jewish hagiography surrounding the patriarch in Paul's time; Abraham was a famous ancestor whom we would expect to be lionized in this fashion.[152] But this poses another acute problem for Justification theory.

That schema views Abraham as an example of saving faith. Setting aside for the moment the various problems already noted above in his exemplification of the key criterion of "faith" — namely, its strangely personal quality, distinctive epistemological mode and incoherent attestation — we should now recall that it must also be manageable in order to fulfill the theoretical dictates of Justification theory. That schema hopes to save seriously incapacitated individuals who have already tried to observe the law but failed, and probably at numerous points. Law observance was too difficult because of human frailty and corruption, and God consequently had to provide a new saving contract that was rather easier. Its criterion must therefore be clear and understandable, information based, particular (in order to avoid obvious and acute framing difficulties), and *manageable*. But if Abraham illustrates the nature of saving faith here — and this subsection is the most detailed description of πίστις in the Pauline corpus, let alone the key Justification texts — the criterion looks extraordinarily difficult, if not impossible. *It looks more difficult than "works"!* Nobody faced with this criterion could contemplate salvation with any realistic hope of achieving it (except perhaps Jesus himself, viewed in orthodox terms) — a fourteen-year journey of doubt-free, unwavering trust in God and his promises, all perceptible realities to the contrary. It is too difficult because the portrait of Abraham here is in fact a typically exaggerated, hagiographical depiction of the patriarch in superhuman terms. We normally admire such portraits, and perhaps emulate them faintly. But to reproduce them completely is unrealistic (and is not their intention). We cannot all become saints — emulating hyperbolic narratives of their piety — in order to be saved.

Consequently, Justification theory is severely embarrassed at this juncture. If Abraham illustrates saving faith, in the light of vv. 18-21 one is tempted to ask, "Who then can be saved?" (Indeed, if Paul's occasional attestations to mental turmoil are taken into account, he might not even be saved himself!: see Rom. 2:15; 2 Cor. 11:29; Gal. 2:17-18; 5:17.) In short, the description of Abraham's πίστις in Romans 4:1-25, especially in vv. 17-22, constitutes an outstanding error of commission within the Justification discourse's textual citadel. For the conventional reader, this description late in the chapter is more a "text of terror" than a mighty fortress.[153] But our difficulties in this relation are not yet over.

(20) The Object of Abraham's πίστις

We should note now the difficulties caused for Justification theory by the object of Abraham's trust — God. As we have already seen, Justification requires an element of Christian particularity in its saving criterion, or the consequent difficulties — principally at the discourse's frames — are absurd and unsustainable. So we have spoken up to this point of "belief in Christ" fulfilling that necessity better than any other options. If this emphasis on particularity is relaxed at the theoretical level, then the entire soteriology ceases to be distinctively Christian and fades into mere monotheism. Immediately, it is difficult to exclude Jews, Muslims, and perhaps even Zoroastrians, from salvation. (And this position accords nicely with the absence of overtly Christian preaching from Paul's account of Abraham, which we have just noted. Such figures could be saved by God's direct intervention and speech, speaking to a perennial concern of some in relation to "the unreached.") But clearly, as an account of Paul, this explanatory option must be instantly rejected, however coherent it might be as a theory, and it does possess a measure of coherence. In Paul's thinking about salvation, as revealed both by his other texts and by his extensive missionary work, it is immediately demonstrable that Christian particularities are central (although, alternatively, his thinking at this juncture might simply be in a state of deep and inexplicable contradiction).

But it is precisely this extraordinary explanatory possibility — of what we might dub "radical fideistic monotheism" — that Paul's discussion of Abraham opens up. At the heart of the argument through Romans 4 is Genesis 15:6, which speaks of Abraham's trust "in God" — τῷ Θεῷ. Paul then goes on to allude to and to explicate this text extensively, yet never deviating from this particular aspect in its claims. He even builds this theocentric orientation into his summary formulae that link his discussions of the patriarch explicitly to the Roman Christian auditors: ἐγράφη . . . καὶ δι' ἡμᾶς . . . τοῖς πιστεύουσιν ἐπὶ τὸν ἐγείροντα Ἰησοῦν κ.τ.λ. In short, Paul's discussion of Abraham in Romans 4 is consistently in terms of a *theocentric* "faith."[154] And this emphasis is profoundly problematic for Justification theory, as we have just seen. If Justification theory accepts this particular (re)definition of its saving criterion, then it is immediately rendered absurd as an explanation of Paul by acute framing tensions (or, alternatively, Paul's thinking is immediately rendered absurdly contradictory). If it rejects this exegetical attestation, then one of its most important scriptural strong points has suddenly turned into a difficulty — an unenviable conundrum.[155]

(21) The Temporal Locus of Abraham's πίστις

The difficulties apparent in relation to Abraham's object of trust — God — are compounded by the recognition of the temporal location of that trust approximately two thousand years before the time of Christ. Just as the less-defined object of trust evacuated Abraham's example of Christian particularity (i.e., belief "in God"), so too the temporal distance between Abraham and Christ accomplishes the same problematic evacuation, although on different grounds. If Abraham is really saved, and is a programmatic example of salvation by faith as well, then it seems to follow inexorably that someone can be saved independently of any knowledge of Christ. And so the example of Abraham seems again to prove far too much. The Christian particularity of Justification theory — without which it instantly collapses into absurdity in view of its systematic and circumstantial difficulties — is undermined once again by this overdetermination. But in this particular relation, one of these difficulties appears as especially absurd.

By redefining the salvation of the progenitor of Israel in this fashion, the reading effectively eliminates Judaism as it appears in most of its history and sources as well. "True Judaism" consists only of those who, like Abraham, believed in God, and that is all — an absurd reduction of the complex development of the Jewish people, which parallels the similar reduction of the realities of the Christian church. It might be countered that Abraham's Judaism also consists of a preliminary engagement with "works of law," which at least restores a semblance of law observance to historical Israel. But this response is inadequate. If the example of Abraham is taken with full seriousness, then he provides no real support for this claim, at which point the underdetermination noted previously in terms of any demonstrable experience of works of law by the patriarch prior to "faith" (a negative experience in any case) comes back to haunt the conventional reading. No explicit data can be found in Paul's discussion of Abraham that suggest this phase within his development. On the contrary, several claims place law observance *after* his justification by faith, where he falsifies it temporally.

So it seems that the rather appalling implications of Abraham's programmatic status at this point stand; his earlier temporal location — if the programmatic status is taken seriously — reduces legitimate Judaism historically to a solitary fideism, thereby eliminating the bulk of its nature, development, and attestation in the Old Testament. And this is clearly an absurd implication.

The only way around this difficulty would seem to be the attribution to Abraham of Christian information proleptically: he alone had the Christian gospel of salvation proclaimed to him in an especially privileged fashion, and so was able to believe like a Christian "born untimely" (see 1 Cor. 15:8; see also perhaps Gal. 3:8). But this apologetic maneuver is eliminated by the needs of Justification theory, which has to find in Abraham (as Paul describes him here) an *independent* witness to its own construction of Christianity; Abraham is part of the all-important textual base. If he is being read in a Christian way at this point, then the theory is preceding the attestation and no longer being established by it. And there is precious little information in Romans 4 that codes Abraham in terms of the Christian *as Justification theory constructs that* in any case — that is, in terms of belief in Christ alone (etc.). Such data is simply missing. So this strategy seems confounded for the Justification advocate on two critical counts. And this temporal location, well before the time of Christ, remains an awkward overdetermination for Justification theory, paralleling the others that have just been enumerated.[156]

In short, if Abraham is taken with full seriousness, as a programmatic instance of fideistic salvation, then the consequences for Justification theory are problematic across a number of fronts. The theory is fractured by this "faith's" personal nature, its distinctive epistemological mode of direct revelation, its self-referential incoherence, its daunting strength, its more generalized object, and its temporal location — half a dozen (or so) distinguishable points of pressure. It would seem, then, that the figure of Abraham overshadows Justification theory not so much as a hero as a specter.

(22) Abraham's Literal Fatherhood

Abraham is described in Romans 4 as a father, especially in v. 1, vv. 11-12, and vv. 16-18. (It is mentioned directly seven times.) Justification theory tends to spiritualize this designation, interpreting it in an exemplary fashion. Abraham is a "forefather" in the sense that later Christians believe or trust as he did and so copy him. And this is one legitimate aspect within ancient conceptions of parenthood, which held that children ought to imitate their parents.[157] Moreover, Christians are clearly supposed to share the trust of Abraham himself; the text overtly designates them as similar in this respect (see esp. vv. 11-12 and vv. 23-25). However, the exemplary and merely imitative relationship that this explanation presupposes is, as we have already noted, underdetermined; the text never states that this is the case. And a number of explicit signals suggest that Paul is interested in Abraham's literal paternity in some sense — in his biological fatherhood (a conception that could ultimately encompass shared trust and fidelity as well, without being reducible to those). These suggestions match Paul's discussions of Abraham elsewhere, not to mention much contemporary Jewish treatment of the patriarch (thereby alleviating any framing difficulties in these relations). A full discussion of this point must wait until my rereading of this passage is undertaken in detail in part four, chapter eighteen; here we will note only the relevant overdetermination.

Paul's concern with Abraham's biological fatherhood emerges most explicitly as Romans 4 discusses the miraculous conception and birth of Isaac from v. 16b through v. 22. Although often unnoticed or underemphasized, Abraham's miraculous siring of Isaac is integral to the text's unfolding argument, although more as its presupposition than its focal point. We have already touched on this passage to a degree, but we must now investigate Paul's portrayal of Abraham's heroic πίστις here in a little more detail.

Paul quotes Abraham's covenantal response recorded in Genesis 15:6 through much of the argument of Romans 4, citing 15:5 in 4:18 as well, but in v. 17 he introduces a statement from Genesis 17 (which was foreshadowed in vv. 9-12) — the promise that Abraham would be "a father of many nations" (ὅτι Πατέρα πολλῶν ἐθνῶν τέθεικά σε; see vv. 17a and 18). As every Jew knew, this was the covenant associated with the renaming of Abram as Abraham and the promise of paternity of "many nations," and the covenantal "sign" in response of circumcision, a set of events that culminated in the birth of Isaac and so ultimately of the Jewish nation. But — ultimately quite significantly — Paul does not emphasize the practice of circumcision from this point. Instead, he develops a portrait of Abraham's fidelity in vv. 16b-22 in terms of a heroic trust in God concerning these two covenantal promises of fatherhood made in Genesis 15 and 17. Certain aspects of that trust should now be noted carefully.

First, one element in the heroic quality of Abraham's trust — as has already been noted — is its duration. This becomes evident when readers supply the rest of the narrative of Genesis to Paul's argument and realize that Abraham trusted in this fashion for fourteen years, from the age of eighty-six (or earlier), when he received the promises recorded in Genesis 15:6, to "around" the age of a hundred (ἑκατονταετής που ὑπάρχων; see 16:16; 17:1), when he received the promises of Genesis 17. Paul supplies the explicit temporal marker just noted, so readers are supposed to note this duration.

However, a second aspect of his trust deepens its heroic quality dramatically. During this time, Abraham was trusting in the promise of an heir, and he and his wife were both well past the age of realistic childbearing; the biological realities facing him were therefore insurmountable. Paul's text signals this aspect of the narrative explicitly as well. Abraham κατενόησεν τὸ ἑαυτοῦ σῶμα ἤδη νενεκρωμένον . . . καὶ τὴν νέκρωσιν τῆς μήτρας Σάρρας. (Note, the "death" of both his body and his wife's womb are meaningful contributions to the argument only if Abraham was trusting in these divine promises for literal offspring.) In this sense he had to believe "against hope in hope" — παρ' ἐλπίδα ἐπ' ἐλπίδι (v. 18a).

Paul now emphasizes that Abraham's trust at this time did not weaken or waver but, if anything, waxed in strength, overflowing in praise to God, continuing in complete certitude: μὴ ἀσθενήσας τῇ πίστει . . . εἰς δὲ τὴν ἐπαγγελίαν τοῦ

Θεοῦ οὐ διεκρίθη τῇ ἀπιστίᾳ ἀλλ᾿ ἐνεδυναμώθη τῇ πίστει, δοὺς δόξαν τῷ Θεῷ, καὶ πληροφορηθεὶς ὅτι ὃ ἐπήγγελται δυνατός ἐστιν καὶ ποιῆσαι (vv. 18, 19, 20-21a). Its nature was essentially flawless.

Paul's portrait of Abraham's "faith" is now largely complete, although we have yet to consider its broader argumentative function. It is clear, however, that this trust should be spoken of as "fidelity," or "faithfulness." Abraham's unwavering trust over time and under duress (notably in the face of the biological realities of his situation) segues semantically into the realm of steadfast endurance — of "faithfulness." Moreover, implicit in this fidelity is the unwavering expectation of an heir — of a biological child — who was of course Isaac, born the following year according to Genesis 21. *This expectation is the specific content of his fidelity, without which it makes little sense.* (Without it we would ask, "what was Abraham being faithful to?") But if any doubts remain in this relation, a number of corroborations confirm it decisively.

First, Paul describes God in this passage overtly in terms of resurrection. In v. 17 Abraham "trusts in the God who makes alive the dead and calls that which is not into existence" (. . . Θεοῦ τοῦ ζῳοποιοῦντος τοὺς νεκροὺς καὶ καλοῦντος τὰ μὴ ὄντα ὡς ὄντα), while in context this must be the calling into being of Isaac. Second, when Paul turns in v. 23 to apply Abraham in some sense to Christians, he speaks twice more of resurrection — τοῖς πιστεύουσιν ἐπὶ τὸν ἐγείραντα ᾿Ιησοῦν τὸν κύριον ἡμῶν ἐκ νεκρῶν ὅς . . . ἠγέρθη διὰ τὴν δικαίωσιν ἡμῶν (v. 24b, 25b). Both these emphases speak directly to the central problem facing Abraham that his body was "dead," along with the womb of his wife Sarah, so these are clearly not incidental details. Furthermore, some sort of resurrection would have to take place if the promise of an heir was to be fulfilled — some life-creating act by the God of life. Third, the promises themselves in Genesis speak consistently of an heir. Abraham's twofold complaint in Genesis 15:2-3 queried the validity of God's promises of protection and reward (made in v. 1) if he remained heirless. God responded with an explicit promise of an heir and countless offspring (noted in vv. 4-5), in which response Abraham famously trusted (v. 6). And essentially the same promises are made in Genesis 17 (see vv. 2, 4-8, 16-21). Fourth, when Paul returns to discuss Abraham in Romans 9, the patriarch is important principally as the father of Isaac, and the entire ensuing discussion of past Israel is in terms of literal (although also elected) descent (see 9:7 in the broader setting of vv. 6-17: οὐδ᾿ ὅτι εἰσὶν σπέρμα Ἀβραὰμ πάντες τέκνα . . .[158]). (This is then arguably confirmed by Paul's discussions of Abraham elsewhere; see esp. Gal. 3:29 in context.)

In view of these multiple corroborations, not to mention the fairly direct evidence of the argument itself, it seems difficult to deny that Abraham's biological fatherhood of Isaac is an integral part of Paul's unfolding discussion in Romans 4:16b-22. While it does not seem to be the rhetorical point of the argument, that point would make little sense without this premise — a premise that would be quite unremarkable for a first-century Jew to affirm (shifting the burden of proof thereby onto those who wish to deny it). And the relevant overdetermination is also by now apparent.

Paul does not treat Abraham in Romans 4, and especially in vv. 16b-22, as a *spiritual* father who exemplifies belief or trust. Abraham constitutes, among other things, an instance of superhuman fidelity, which revolves around his utterly miraculous but quite literal fatherhood of Isaac, through whom the nation of Israel came into being. Whatever role it plays in the broader analysis, then, Abraham's fatherhood in Romans 4 is entirely concrete; he is a "father" in the normal sense of that word. He is an *embodied biological* father. And of course Justification theory has no ability to account for this dimension in Abraham, because of its problematic and ultimately ahistorical treatment of Israel. Justification has no concern with biological descent or genealogy and so cannot explain this emphasis within Paul's text.[159] *Nobody* is born biologically in Justification theory, whether Jewish or Christian![160]

(23) The Saving Function of the Resurrection in 4:25

Paul rounds off his famous explication by turning the discussion back toward his Christian auditors. In vv. 23-25 he crafts an analogy (analyzed in detail in part four, chapter eighteen) that concludes with a resonant couplet. Christ, he announces, παρεδόθη διὰ τὰ παραπτώματα ἡμῶν καὶ ἠγέρθη διὰ τὴν δικαίωσιν ἡμῶν. The exact origins of this couplet's terms and structure — whether explicitly Old Testament and intertextual, perhaps in terms of Isaiah 53, or mediated by early church tradition — do not concern us at this point. Here it suffices to note that Paul in this text explicitly coordinates not merely Christ's death but his resurrection (ἠγέρθη) with the *salvation* of Christians (διὰ τὴν δικαίωσιν ἡμῶν).[161] The second member of this concluding couplet states clearly that the resurrection of Christ — which is prominent in the immediate context — is either "because of" or "for the sake of" the "vindication" or "acquittal" of those who echo the fidelity of Abraham before God.

This statement generates a difficulty for the conventional construal because Justification theory has, strictly speaking, no *saving* role for Christ's resurrection. Christ's death accomplishes all things necessary for salvation, perhaps assisted by his perfect righteousness if that is deemed necessary for Christians in some imputed sense. But sin is paid for completely by Christ's atoning death on the cross. Nothing more remains to be done. And although the resurrection seems to provide some surety to those Christians who lay hold of the atonement in terms of future salvation, arguably vindicating Christ's own innocence and saving effectiveness as well, there is no explicit coordination in the Justification schema between Christ's resurrection and the salvation of Christians. Hence, Paul's claim in 4:25 that Christ's resurrection effects the vindication of Christians directly is impossible to account for in terms of that theory; it is a textual overdetermination.[162]

It is worth noting in addition that 4:25 may be the thin end of the wedge. The saving efficacy and importance of Christ's resurrection — and the importance of the theme of resurrection as a whole — may have been significantly underestimated by the conventional reading under the impress of Justification theory, which has few soteriological expectations in this regard. Numerous subtle signals in the lexicography and argumentative developments of the text may have been narcotized by Justification's low expectations concerning resurrection. (The alternative soteriology, noted in part one, chapter three in relation to Romans 5–8, has strong saving expectations of resurrection, and this point will be emphasized again especially in part four, chapters sixteen and eighteen.) Romans 1–4 might be, in short, more concretely eschatological in a *soteriological* sense than its conventional readers allow.

But this is not the best place to pursue such suspicions in detail; they will emerge more clearly when my rereadings of the relevant texts are developed in part four, chapters fourteen through eighteen. For now it suffices to note that Romans 4:25 raises this issue explicitly in terms of its final clause, and by more subtle general implication for much of the rest of Paul's argument. If the resurrection of Christ in fact plays a vigorous soteriological role in Paul's thinking, and in the contingent argumentation of Romans, how does this alter our actual construal of his arguments in Romans 1–4, and how can Justification advocates account for this while keeping their own theory intact?

(24) Paul's Narrow and Aggressive Exegesis

One further difficulty can perhaps be added to this list. For Christians who root their soteriology in Justification theory, a great deal rests on the integrity of Paul's actual exegesis in relation to Abraham. If his arguments do not hold good at this point, then much of his law-free system seems to crumble. However, Paul derives all his positive argumentative leverage in Romans 4 from a resolute application of one verse from the Torah — Genesis 15:6. He uses this verse to override all other relevant verses in the story of Abraham (Genesis 12–25), at which point the disproportionate aspect in Paul's hermeneutic becomes apparent, and also the rather arbitrary selection *of* this verse. We know — and will see in more detail in part four, chapter eighteen — why Paul uses this verse so aggressively; it is the one verse that overlaps with key verses and words that he deploys elsewhere, and it allows him to make certain radical argumentative moves as well. So he was clever to recognize its possibilities and to exploit them. (It truly is an interpretative tour de force; demonstrating a law-free gospel from the Pentateuch is no easy matter!) However, it is one thing to prove skillful argumentatively and hermeneutically in the context of a debate with another exegete in the first century (or some similar contingent scenario); it is another to base salvation at all times and in all places on that exegesis. His selection and consequent ruthless application of this solitary verse are rather appallingly arbitrary if these processes themselves have no prior justification. As *mere exegesis* they are positively shocking. In short, the *rhetorical usefulness* of this verse to Paul in his original argumentative setting is not a sound justification for its *programmatic soteriological validity* — the grounding of certain claims universally through time and space. And to this arbitrary quality we must add the strained nature of Paul's interpretation.

The strangeness of Paul's exegesis is indicated by the way that previous, concurrent, and subsequent Jewish exegetes — while exploring numerous interpretative possibilities within this text — have never considered interpreting Genesis 15:6 in the radical, programmatic way that Paul does (i.e., essentially to override much of the rest of the Pentateuch). Only Christians already located in the position that Paul is basically affirming have found his exegesis persuasive (and they have very good reasons for doing so, although these are not necessarily exegetical). But it is likely as a result that his exegetical case is generally being construed overly generously. Certainly, Paul's reading does not conform to modern, historical-critical expectations. Nor am I convinced that it is the best demonstrably canonical reading of this text. And it is definitely not sensitive to the original context but tends rather to negate it (which is not to say that Paul's readings are not aware of the context in this relation; they seem acutely aware of the surrounding data, but they usually *override* it!). And all of these difficulties point to an underlying problem. If we use this exegesis *as* our base, then we encounter some serious difficulties; we rest, precisely, on its selective and puzzling if not aggressively arbitrary nature. But if we can reframe Paul's moves, setting them in a broader and more coherent paradigm, then there may be a possibility of affirming their validity in some respects.[163]

In sum, the selection and programmatic use of Genesis 15:6 are not a natural or secure foundation for Justification theory, undercutting its validity as a scriptural discourse (and especially over against other readings of Scripture in general, and of Genesis and Abraham in particular). It is even difficult to escape accusations of gross contextual insensitivity and arbitrariness at this point. So some superior, and less embarrassing explanation of his particular hermeneutical move on Paul's part is clearly desirable. And in summary of this subsection as a whole, it seems that eleven aspects in Paul's discussion of Abraham in Romans 4 appear to be embarrassments to Justification theory. Indeed, looking back, *it seems that almost the entire chapter of the letter is an embarrassment to Justification;* it is little more than an extended textual overdetermination! Far from being a strength underpinning Justification theory, Paul's analysis of Abraham in Romans 4:1-25 seems to call the relationship between that theory and its textual base into serious question.

§4. Summary and Implications

4.1. Summary of Textual Under- and Overdeterminations

It may be useful to summarize the problems of textual inconvenience for Justification theory we have now noted in the conventional reading of Romans 1-4. Thirty-five have been described: eleven underdeterminations, where the data does not supply what the theory needs; and twenty-four overdeterminations, where the data supplies something the theory does not need, and ranging from the mildly puzzling to the profoundly embarrassing.

Underdeterminations

Romans 1:18–3:20

UD 1: The scene-setting strategy

UD 2: The key premises in relation to humanity and God

UD 3: The identification of the hypocritical judge in 2:1-5 as the Jew

UD 4: The implicit perfectionist axiom

Romans 1:16-17 & 3:21-31

UD 5: The frequently circular analysis of the "thesis" paragraphs

UD 6: The strategic function of δικαιοσύνη Θεοῦ

UD 7: The function of Paul's πιστ- terminology as the saving criterion

UD 8: Argumentation establishing Christ as the definitive atonement

UD 9: The function of Christ's atonement in propitiatory terms

Romans 4:1-25

UD 10: Abraham's exemplary function in chapter 4

UD 11: Abraham's progression to faith from an initial status as "ungodly"

Overdeterminations

Romans 1:18–3:20

OD 1: The distinctive style of 1:18-32

OD 2: The temporal clash between 1:18 and 1:19-32

OD 3: The emphasis on collective decline and fall in 1:18-32

OD 4: The prominent intertextual relation with the Wisdom of Solomon

OD 5: The function of the argumentative "turn" in 2:1

OD 6: The premature location of repentance in 2:4b-5a

OD 7: The existence of two pristine categories in 2:6-10 — the righteous
     saved and the wicked damned

OD 8: Paul's comment in 2:16b that judgment through Christ accords with
     "my" gospel

OD 9: The crudeness of the attack on the Jew in 2:21-22

OD 10: The presence of righteous pagans in Paul's argument

OD 11: Paul's redefinition of circumcision and Judaism in 2:25-29

Romans 1:16-17 & 3:21-31

OD 12: πίστις as instrumental in disclosure in 1:16-17 and 3:21-26

OD 13: The syntactical awkwardness of 3:25

Romans 4:1-25

OD 14: The scriptural overruling of boasting

OD 15: The temporal overruling of circumcision and Mosaic law

OD 16: The personal nature of Abraham's πίστις

OD 17: The distinctive epistemological mode of Abraham's attestation

OD 18: The epistemological incoherence of Abraham's attestation

OD 19: The strength of Abraham's πίστις
OD 20: The object of Abraham's πίστις
OD 21: The temporal locus of Abraham's πίστις
OD 22: Abraham's literal fatherhood
OD 23: The saving function of the resurrection in 4:25
OD 24: Paul's narrow and aggressive exegesis

4.2. Intrinsic, Systematic, Empirical, and Proximate Difficulties Revisited

All the difficulties that have been noted previously in intrinsic, systematic, and empirical terms in relation to Justification theory — see part one, chapters two through five, summarized in six (§1) — can now be seen rising out of the conventional reading of Romans 1–4, although this is sometimes not acknowledged overtly. Furthermore, with the discourse's textual base clearly identified as Romans 1:16–4:25 (or –5:1-2), it can now be seen that many of these arise at that text's immediate *proximate* frame as well, notably the transition into Romans 5, at which point we can ask if Justification advocates have succeeded in explaining the difficulties when they arise at this textual juncture, or have left them generating a further set of problems for interpreters. So this is an important moment in my argument. If any exegetical anxieties still remain from the nature of my approach in part one, then they should be allayed by the following discussion, which demonstrates that the theory described in rather abstract terms in chapter one, and then traced through various problematic implications, settings, and debates, *is directly relevant to the exegesis of Romans 1–4 and its broader settings.*

Intrinsic Difficulties

All seven of the intrinsic problems noted in Justification theory in part one, chapter two resurface overtly in the actual text and argument of Romans 1–4 as it is conventionally construed, while some are also apparent in relation to Romans 5 and following. The first five difficulties are apparent especially in 1:18–3:20; the sixth and seventh in 1:16-17 and from 3:21 onward.

ID 1: *Epistemology.* The presence of two fundamentally incompatible epistemologies, one philosophical and rationalist and the other historical, revelatory, and personal — is apparent especially when 1:19-20 and 2:14-15 are juxtaposed with 2:17-20 and 3:10-19, although the tension is present whenever Scripture is cited in relation to a point originally established by 1:18-32. Throughout this section of argument, pagans, both sinful and righteous, discern God's nature and concerns from creation and their own consciences, while righteous Jews learn about God from Scripture, which is overtly rooted in their own history (see esp. 3:1-2!). This tension is then exacerbated by the argument of 4:1-25, signaled in advance by 3:21-22. The

Scriptures — a historical, revelatory mode — are understood to confirm Justification theory authoritatively in its saving phase, when that theory has begun with a universal, philosophical mode (although Abraham himself manifests a different mode again!). The particular revealed mode then takes over completely from Romans 5 onward.

ID 2: *Natural revelation*. An incoherent philosophical progression within a naturally revealed trajectory is implicit within the argument of 1:18-32. From 1:18 the text moves from the condemnation of atheism to the judgment of idolatry and polytheism, to sexual transgression, and then to a broader list of particular sins — murder, slander, disobedience, and so on (see 1:29-31). Although comprehensible in terms of Jewish polemic, this series admits of no necessary rational progression.

ID 3: *Law*. The assertion of two different sets of law is directly implicit in the brief juxtaposition of 2:12: "whosoever sins without the law will also be destroyed without the law; and whosoever sins through the law, through the law will be condemned" (DC). These are of course different laws, as indicated by the rather defensive verses that follow, in which Paul demonstrates again the pagan possession of some sort of law, here written on the heart and attested by the conscience (i.e., not possessed through the synagogue and the reading and explication of Jewish Scripture). This awkward disparity is also apparent in the righteous pagan of 2:26-29. According to these verses, an uncircumcised person keeps the law — which can hardly be the Mosaic law! — and so is "considered" "circumcised."[164] Both these types of figures, observing laws with different contents, are nevertheless said explicitly by 2:6-10 to be judged in accordance with deeds and desert. Clearly, different deeds are therefore meant, problematizing the operation of desert.

ID 4: *Anthropology*. An incoherent anthropology, presupposing capacity and incapacity simultaneously, runs through much of the argument of 1:18–3:20. That God will reward people in accordance with their deeds is stated most overtly in 2:6-10, and the argument betrays no pessimism about this possibility as far as 3:9a (even arguably supplying instances of pagan righteousness in 2:26-29). Equally emphatically, 1:18-32 recounts a generalized pagan sinfulness but in a way that repeatedly emphasizes pagans' culpability; they are "without excuse" because of an entire series of willfully wicked decisions. However, 3:9b-18 paints a gloomier picture of humankind, the scriptural catena asserting that not a single person is righteous but, rather, every aspect of humanity is corrupt. Similarly — although more subtly — 2:19-20 implies that the basic pagan condition is corrupt; it is "blind . . . in darkness . . . ignorant . . . [and] infantile." And this portrait of a fundamentally incapacitated humanity is massively reinforced by Romans 5 following, its narrative frame being introduced explicitly in 5:12-21, and a detailed analysis of (i.a.) human incapacity being offered in 7:7-25. So, in anthropological terms, the argument wants to have its cake and eat it too — a tension discernible within the textual base, and extending well beyond it.

ID 5: *Theodicy.* Corresponding to this difficulty is a question mark hovering over God's justice. If people, both Jew and Greek, are in fact incapable of good deeds, as the more pessimistic anthropological claims just noted suggest, then the fundamental fairness of the entire scenario that offers salvation in response to desert must be questioned; it seems chimerical. That scenario is stated most overtly in 2:6-8, and is contradicted most overtly in 3:19-20, where we learn that the entire cosmos is silenced and ought to be submissive to God. But this tension runs through almost the entire sweep of the argument in 1:18–3:20 as it is conventionally construed.

ID 6: *Christology and atonement.* Romans 1-4 supplies no cogent explanation for the displacement of traditional Jewish means of atonement, such as the temple cultus, and the introduction of Christ's death in that locus instead. In the compact statements concerning Christ's atoning death in 3:24-25, only three words seem overtly "atoning" — ἀπολύτρωσις, ἱλαστήριον, and αἷμα — along with one apparently related phrase — τὴν πάρεσιν τῶν προγεγονότων ἁμαρτημάτων. (This data will be revisited in much more detail shortly, in part four, chapter sixteen.) Romans 4:25 adds helpfully that Jesus has been handed over because of "our" transgressions, but the basic claim that Jesus atones in some sense is not what is in dispute. Rather, it is the precise rationale of that atonement that is uncertain, both as a displacement of Jewish means of atonement and as a functioning payment in its own right. And the text of Romans 1-4 does not immediately allay any concerns in this relation, principally because of its brevity.

ID 7: *Faith.* The problems identified in the notion of "saving faith" are likewise sustained in the text. While πιστ- terminology at first glance seems to function within the text at the right points for saving faith — notably, in the short summary paragraphs that precede and follow the extended account of "the problem" (see esp. 1:16-17; 3:21-26) — no information is provided that could either resolve the difficulties apparent in the Arminian variant (which stem primarily from belief voluntarism, but also from the material that ought to be believed) or elicit a more Calvinist reading. In the former relation, it should be queried how people can decide to believe that Jesus atoned for the transgressions of the world (4:25) and is now "Lord" (10:9-10) on the basis of preaching alone; how could such claims be verified? In the latter relation, it should be noted that no rationale is provided for the privileging of "faith," nor is the basic conundrum of a lack of coordination between those culpable (see 1:18-32) and those reached and saved unconditionally through preaching (see 1:16-17; 3:22) resolved. (An entire cluster of further difficulties is about to be noted in this relation as well: see esp. SDs 6 and 7.)

Systematic Difficulties

The account of Justification theory's systematic difficulties was generated in part one, chapter three largely with reference to Romans 5–8, which adds special force to the list at this point. Every systematic problem derived in chapter three now becomes a proximate problem as well that functions at the immediate frame of Romans 1–4 — double trouble. Most of the difficulties noted in this relation remain implicit in Paul's argument in Romans 1–4 as it is conventionally read, but some are arguably explicit.

SD 1: *Epistemology.* The tension already noted between general, philosophical knowledge and particular, revealed knowledge, and between prospective and retrospective theological reasoning, is plainly apparent in Romans 1–4 (and these two axes of tension are not necessarily coterminous). Both the pagan and the Jew seem to reason prospectively in Romans 1:18–3:20. But the pagan proceeds from a philosophical process in 1:19-20 to the requisite information for salvation, while the Jew proceeds from revealed Scripture (see esp. 2:12, 17-20; 3:2, 19). The forward progression of knowledge in both these figures contrasts with the retrospective configuration of knowledge in Romans 5–8 (which is consistent there with the depraved human mind: see esp. 7:24-25 and 8:6-8; and 12:2), and their respective modes of acquiring information contrast with one another as well. The pagan deduces key propositions about God from the cosmos and from conscience (see also 2:14-15), while the Jew learns about God from Judaism's traditions and history. The continued commitment of Romans 3:21–4:25 to revealed, scriptural knowledge then simply continues that particular axis of tension (see esp. 3:21 and 4:1).

SD 2: *Anthropology.* Linking up with both the foregoing difficulty and problem four above (anthropological incoherence), any emphasis within Romans 1–4 on human capacity is contradicted by Paul's depiction of humans elsewhere in terms of fundamental incapacity (see 5:14, 19-21; 7:5–8:10). The human condition seems capable of a great deal in 1:18–2:29 (aside from the hints of 2:19-20), and of *something* — that is, the fulfillment of a saving condition — in 3:22–4:25. Indeed, if humanity is not capable to some degree, then the entire argumentative sweep of Romans 1–4, and especially of 1:18–3:20, is wasted; it is pointless to appeal to people to undertake an action of which they are incapable. The basic rhetorical strategy of the conventional reading presupposes human capacity, and thereby clashes with any subsequent emphases by Paul on depravity. This conundrum is seen most succinctly in the famous slogan "God justifies the ungodly" (see 4:5). If those justified are *fundamentally* ungodly, then they *cannot* be justified by either the conventional reading or Justification theory, because they cannot undertake the necessary saving action that grasps such justification. Construed conventionally, God does *not* justify the ungodly (because of the contributions, however limited, that the ungodly must make to that process; the ungodly at the critical point justify themselves). Only a *fundamentally* elective God and soteriology will do so. (We revisit this slogan in part four, chapter seventeen, pressing some of these implications further.)

SD 3: *Theology.* The retributive justice of God is implicit throughout the conventional reading of Romans 1-4, and is explicit at certain points. Romans 1:32 notes that God's "righteous decree [is] that those practicing such [wicked] things are worthy of death," while 2:5b speaks of the δικαιοκρισία of God before enunciating the critical principle of judgment in accordance with desert in 2:6-8 (and this material amplifies 1:18). Similarly, the conventional reading coordinates the atonement terminology of 3:24-25 and 4:25 with the satisfaction of God's justice. Although benevolent attributes are mentioned at times as well (see esp. 2:4; 3:3, 5, 7, 26), *these are accommodated — at times overtly — to the more basic framework of retributive justice.* God is benevolent in these terms only when the demands of his justice have been satisfied — so, explicitly, 2:4, where God's kindness allows time for repentance prior to the execution of the demands of justice (i.e., it operates only within the broader framework of judgment)! This conception of God then inevitably clashes with any alternative conception of his fundamental character as Paul might discuss that elsewhere (see esp. 5:6-8; 8:31-39). It might be significant that Paul never denotes "God" as "Father" in Romans 1-4.[165]

SD 4: *Christology and atonement.* In close relation to the foregoing, and as has already been noted, Christ functions in the conventional reading principally to atone for sin in the sense of satisfying God's offended justice and "paying" for past transgressions, an interpretative burden carried largely by 3:24-25 and 4:25a. Indeed, the importance of this moment in Justification theory explains much of the emphasis accorded these very brief texts. This function contrasts with the emphases found elsewhere in Paul on a more liberating conception of the atonement and, correlatively, on the saving role of the resurrection of Christ (see esp. 4:25b; 6:1-11, 22-23; 7:1-6, 24; 8:2).

SD 5: *Soteriology.* The basic axioms of the model of salvation assumed by the conventional reading to be operating in Romans 1-4 are signaled relatively early on in the text (as indeed they must be within a prospective system; they then structure all that follows). Pagans are treated explicitly in terms of individual self-interest in 1:18-32, and Jews join this developing analysis overtly in 2:6. (They may be implicit in 2:1.) The principle of desert that is stated there, applying equally to both constituencies, presupposes individual, rational self-interest as the basis for salvation — the desire to achieve the reward of eternal life for good deeds and, presumably, the concomitant desire to avoid the "anguish and distress" of God's "wrath and fury" for bad deeds (2:7-9). The introduction of the principle of saving faith in 3:22 does not disturb this basic configuration (except inconsistently); people ought to choose to exercise faith, if only out of self-interest. That mode then remains explicitly individualist, as the rather solitary example of Abraham also suggests (4:1-25). And clearly this basic soteriological dynamic is in marked contrast to any elective, personal, participatory system as Paul describes salvation elsewhere (e.g., through much of Romans 5-8). An important connection with the anthropological conceptions and difficulties already noted is also apparent here. A deeply depraved humanity — a truly ungodly constituency — must be saved by an elective system, corresponding to Paul's alternative system as that is indicated by Romans 5-8 and parallels (and also perhaps by the very implications of this phrase, in 4:5 and 5:6).

SD 6: *Faith.* The salience and nature of "faith" in Justification theory are echoed directly by the conventional reading of Romans 1-4. And these emphases continue to clash with data from farther afield in Paul.[166]

In Romans 5-8, faith is strangely scarce (see only 5:1-2 and 6:8!). Verbal equivalents in chapter 8 then hint (correctly) that a common specific meaning for πιστ- terminology elsewhere in Paul is "steadfastness," "fidelity," or "faithfulness" (see esp. 8:24-25 and, slightly less obviously, endurance of the trials and powers of 8:35-39; see also the rather significant instance of Jesus' submission in 5:19). Alternatively, πιστ- terminology might simply denote correct beliefs about various aspects of the new Christian reality, although 6:8 signals clearly that this follows participation in Christ (see also 12:1-2). And in 12:3b Paul speaks explicitly of God gifting a "measure of faith" (and so also in 12:6b, prophecy should take place "in proportion to faith," prophecy being a gift given according to grace by the Spirit [so vv. 5-6a]). But the depiction of faith by the conventional reading of Romans 1-4 is at odds with this incidence and meaning.

The importance of faith in the conventional reading is signaled at the outset by four occurrences in 1:16-17. An intense concentration then begins in 3:22, continuing through to 4:25 (and in fact to 5:1 or 2[167]). And this corresponds exactly to the salience of the theme in Justification theory, where faith is the key criterion in the second, easier contract that saves people. Justification theory and Paul's opening argumentation in 1:18-32 also expect faith to consist primarily of correct beliefs (although, as we have just seen, Abraham seems to evidence belief — or, better, trust — *in* God, and not merely about him, one of many points of exegetical tension with the expectations of Justification theory).

The clashes between these two developments of faith in Romans 1-4 and 5-8 are therefore multiple, echoing the clashes at the systematic frame. In Romans 1-4 faith functions on the axis between damnation and salvation, under the control of humanity; it is primarily propositional and hence essentially belief; and it is central. In Romans 5-8 faith functions retrospectively, after the arrival of salvation; it is fundamentally personal, and often also carries the specific connotation of fidelity; and it is merely one of many virtues (and no less or more important than this). Indeed, it is much less salient. Consequently, it is hard to avoid the conclusion that faith plays two very different roles in these two passages.

SD 7: *Ethics.* The well-known difficulty that Justification theory has in generating wholehearted and even transformed ethical behavior from its converts is implicit in the conventional reading of Romans 1–4, although an appeal could be made to the many ethical chapters that follow (provided that the conventional readings of those later chapters could be harmonized with the construal of chapters 1–4). The convert in Romans 1–4 is characterized by faith, and really by faith only. No other ethical behavior is discernible through 4:25 (although it is discernible prior to salvation in 1:18–3:20; see esp. 1:19-32; 2:6-10, 25-29; and inversely in 3:10-18). So the relatively simple question arises, how can the theory generate a vigorous ethic from this point on (i.e., 3:22–4:25), with the convert saved emphatically by faith alone? There is no rationale evident in the conventional reading that covers for the corresponding ethical lacuna at the theoretical level.

Complementing this difficulty, we noted earlier that Justification theory fails to supply a cogent reason for abandoning a full Jewish ethic (and certainly for Jews). This generates an often-unnoticed but very important tension, since Paul clearly does not expect his pagan converts to follow a Jewish ethic in full (and he is greatly offended by this suggestion). Justification theory, although commonly deployed at this point, offers no explanation of it. And precisely this difficulty is raised by the argument of Romans 1–4, which negates law and "works" repeatedly from 3:20 onward through 4:25, although especially in 3:27-28 and 4:2-15.

SD 8: *Ecclesiology.* Exactly the same considerations apply to the contrasting conceptions of the church suggested by Justification theory, further informed by Romans 1–4, over against Romans 5–8. The convert saved by faith alone is a solitary and rational figure (or perhaps someone with a personal faith, although arguably inconsistently so), while Paul's conception of the church in Romans 5–8 and elsewhere is clearly a communal and vigorous phenomenon. Romans 1–4 suggests — we are told — that at the basis of Christianity is the heroic individual figure of Abraham, and presumably the church is composed of such figures; Romans 5–8, however, is emphatically corporate.

SD 9: *Judaism.* The differing conceptions of Judaism are much discussed and highly significant. And Romans 1–4 clearly delivers the conceptions underlying Justification theory — that Judaism is a "legalistic" religion conditional on perfect law observance but incapable of genuine and complete fulfillment. This configuration is both its real nature and the reason for its supersession by Christianity. It is consequently a universal, ahistorical, and monolithic religion (and is arguably even intrinsically hypocritical: see 2:1-5!). And this description is clearly delivered directly by 2:6-29 (although the argument here is premised upon 1:18-32), followed by 3:10-18 — a timeless, rationalistic analysis in its own right. There is no historical sensitivity present here, or a different conception of God. Paul even seems to deny explicitly and repeatedly in 3:1-9a various challenges from an interlocutor in terms of Jewish historical advantage and privilege (as the Justification advocate reads this text, with Paul rejecting such suggestions programmatically from v. 2 onward)!

Of course, this view contrasts strongly with Romans 5–8 and associated texts in Paul that suggest a rather different view of Judaism. It is not that Judaism is perfect or sinless. But its difficulties are apparent in retrospect. And before the arrival of the critical turning point in Christ, non-Christian Judaism was positive in many respects in and of itself. It was, moreover, a fundamentally *elective* entity — a result of grace. In short, it seems pointless to deny that the conventional reading of Romans 1–4, and especially of 2:6-29 in context, delivers the atemporal, legalistic, perfectionist construal of Judaism and the Mosaic law that causes such difficulty for Paul's description in this relation elsewhere (see esp. 9:4-5a), and in broader empirical terms.

SD 10: *Coercion and violence.* The endorsement elsewhere in Paul of the exercise of coercive violence against sin is debatable, but if it is granted for the moment that the theme is not especially prominent, then a degree of tension is apparent with one of the central dynamics of Romans 1:18–3:20, which asserts God's pending punishment of wrongdoing repeatedly. Romans 1:18 itself announces the point programmatically. Verse 32 then confirms that death will be meted out on pagan wrongdoing (justly of course), while all humanity, Jew and Greek, will be punished for wicked deeds according to 2:8-9 and 12, and as also suggested by 2:27 and 3:9 and 19. The conventional construal of Paul's atonement terms in 3:24-25 only reinforces this theme, thereby positioning it centrally within both major phases of the overarching argument. So this tension — insofar as it is present in Paul's thinking — is certainly activated, if not exacerbated, by the conventional reading of Romans 1–4. Arguably, however, although violence is discernible in Romans 5–8, it is the violence inflicted by the powers of Sin and Death on humanity that Christ conquers through submission and death (see esp. 5:14, 17, 21; 7:14, 23). And this conquest allows the Christian community to face those threats fearlessly (see esp. 8:18-39) — a conquest that does not employ violence, but accepts and thereby subverts it.

Excursus: Explanations of the Shift at the Proximate Frame

Once again, we will rely on a few representative soundings to establish a general interpretative problem.

Moo simply endorses the shift in perspective, apparently unaware of the problems in doing so. In fact, his summary of the argumentative issues in Romans 5–8 is right on target: ". . . Paul is continuing his defense of the gospel [in chapters 5–8]. His opponents (probably Jewish mainly) attacked his message as proclaiming no more than a legal fiction — a 'declaration' of a relationship that cannot be proved and which effects no change — and requires no change! — in this life and which offers no security for the day of judgment. Quite the contrary, Paul affirms, the person who has experienced the gospel as the justifying activity of God (see 1:17) is assured of finding that gospel to be truly 'God's power for salvation' (see 1:16) — power for dedicated Christian service in this life and for deliverance from all the forces of evil and judgment in the next" (*Romans*, 295). Moo's claims here that powerful eschatological and ethical contentions drive Romans 5–8 — and in a contested setting! — seem entirely correct. But there is no reason for Paul to respond to these as Moo suggests if Justification theory has already been established in Romans 1–4. Eschatological insecurity is now resolved by faith, not by actual deliverance. And ethical contentions ought to be left behind as a vestige of "works-righteousness." If they are to be addressed seriously, however — merely as ethics — then it is problematic to introduce an entirely new framework for that activity, and especially if its assumptions undermine key moves in Justification. In fact, Moo's analysis points directly toward the alternative schema sketched out in part one, chapter three — one that contradicts Justification at almost every turn. Change, (ethical) power, and deliverance are now to characterize Christian existence. He is exegetically correct then, but in so interpreting the text simply generates all the difficulties proximately that have previously been tabulated systematically.

Jewett is intriguing because, although writing from a very different perspective than Moo, he nevertheless recapitulates Moo's strategy fairly directly. He does not address this issue in detail in his commentary (see one programmatic remark in *Romans*, 346). But in his anticipatory study of Romans' rhetorical structure he suggests — in a graceful argument — that 1:18–4:25 is a *confirmatio* or basic thesis, and 5:1–8:39 an *exornatio* or elaboration, closely related to an *auxēsis* or amplification: "Following the Argument of Romans," in *The Romans Debate*, rev. ed., ed. K. P. Donfried (Peabody, Mass.: Hendrickson, 1991), 265-77. Understood in these terms, Romans 5–8 deals "with a series of objections raised against the doctrine of righteousness through faith [as established in Romans 1–4]" (271). The difficulty with this thesis is of course that it rephrases the basic difficulty without showing how Romans 5–8, with its different systematic conceptions, *can* be a *logical* response to *objections to another system* (and recall the argument of part one, chapter three). It is, precisely, an *illogical* response. It is as if a scholar has just laid out a reading of a particular classic text, and one of her auditors has objected strenuously to its fairness and implications. The teacher then responds, in defence, by appealing to a different reading!

Stuhlmacher simply follows the text — another common maneuver — as it begins to speak explicitly of salvation in transformational terms — although talk of "transfer" into another "sphere" helps! "[D]ie Gerechtfertigten in ein Gemeinschaftsverhältnis mit Gott *versetzt*, das zu ihrem Heil dient. . . . Der '*Raum*,' in den die Glaubenden durch Christus geführt werden, heisst 'Gnade'" (*Römer*, 74, 75, emphases added).

Cranfield states — in another common maneuver — that Romans 5–8 is "drawing out the meaning of justification . . . [that is] the life promised for the man who is righteous by faith . . . [specifically] being reconciled with God, being sanctified, being free from the law's condemnation, and being indwelt by God's Spirit" (*Romans I-VIII*, 254). The first three of these concrete results have already been achieved, however, *by* Justification, while the last assertion is unnecessary in terms of that theory. So the "drawing out" remains opaque.

Schreiner — to his credit — devotes some space to the question (*Romans*, 245-49). He suggests that "in chapters 5–8 Paul ties together righteousness by faith with future hope. . . . They [i.e., the new people of God] can look forward with confidence to a renewed creation in which they will fulfil the role of ruling over the world that Adam squandered when he sinned" (245).

This is a clever thesis that does, to my mind, succeed in correlating elements from Romans 1–4 and 5–8 together. The difficulty is that Schreiner relies on subsections from both those discussions — the "righteousness through faith" discussions in 3:22 and 3:27-4:25, emphasizing the promissory aspect (which only occurs in 3:21, 4:13-16 and 21), and the eschatological frame of Romans 5–8 in 5:1-11 and 8:14-39. Read in context, these localized discussions tend to be reoriented away from one another. In particular, Christian hope in Romans 8 turns out to be grounded on pneumatological participation in the crucified and resurrected one, and not on the individual's confession of faith that appropriates justification! Meanwhile, the rest of the broader discussions — including the bulk of Romans 5–8 — remain unexplained. Schreiner does not really succeed in explaining these marginalized units.

Like other commentators, he also segues smoothly into an affirmation of the ethics of Romans 5–8 in terms of "moral transformation" effected by the Spirit, without addressing the tensions that this new schema generates. His emphasis on Paul's Adamic explanation of sinfulness complements this new schema, raising tensions that we are already familiar with in terms of human (in)capacity and the explanation of sin.

He also speaks of consequences and implications: "The primary function of the δικ-words in Rom. 5–8 is not to explicate righteousness by faith, but to build on that justification and show what flows from it" (249). But the ethic in Romans 5–8 does *not* obviously flow from Justification! (Note, Schreiner does acknowledge here that Paul's use of δικ-terms shifts.)

Hence, although more insightful and candid than most interpreters, Schreiner does not resolve this set of problems.

Dunn also devotes some space to this question (*Romans 1–8*, 242-44). He attempts to avoid some of the difficulties by aligning 5:1-11 with 1:16–4:25 (although the former subsection is said to be oriented toward "the individual" and Romans 6–8). Following this, "the whole course of the argument so far is contained within 5:12-21. . . ." And after this, "each of the following sections can be said to function as an outworking of the gospel as thus expounded" (243).

Suffice it to say that Dunn's perceived correlations are overoptimistic; none of them really holds in detail. Most importantly, he just recapitulates the theory that Romans 5–8 (although here 6–8 in particular) "work out" Romans 5 and the material in the earlier part of the letter, thereby begging the question (see 243, 244). We are not told how these dramatically different discussions — framed in an entirely different way, in terms of Adam (see 5:12-21) — "work out" the earlier discussion. How can a discussion framed in terms of history, demonic powers, and human incapacity, flow as a coherent "consequence" or "outworking" from a discussion framed in terms of ahistorical, individual human capacity?!

Tobin gives a superb summary of the ethical challenge Paul addresses in Romans 5–7 in participatory and pneumatological terms (*Paul's Rhetoric*, 155-58) — it would be difficult to improve upon. But it bears no relation to the conventional reading of Romans 1–4 and Justification theory! And once he even seems to concede as much: "In these chapters [i.e., 5–7] Paul significantly rethinks and revises how he understands the relationship between Christian living and righteousness through faith apart from observance of the law" (157). Tobin's accuracy is commendable, but he leaves us with no explanation for the connection between these two discussions in Romans! He precisely states the very problem we are presently struggling with.

Keck orients this transition in terms of the "dual horizon" — the difference "between two events, between what God has already done and what God has yet to do, between 'the already' and 'the not yet'" (*Romans*, 134). And this is a fair characterization of much of the tenor of Romans 5–8 — especially at its frame — but, strictly speaking, Justification theory has no interest in further eschatological speculation. The key future issues have been settled ("freedom from the wrath of God"), and there are no remaining inaugurated issues; the individual is saved by faith, which is rooted in present creaturely existence and the here and now. So Keck's characterization of much of Romans 5–8 is fair, but fails to show how this transition is necessary or meaningful.

Probably enough has been said by this point to indicate how various sophisticated interpreters have nevertheless struggled to provide a coherent account of the transition between Romans 1–4 and 5–8. Consequently, the systematic contradictions that we have already tabulated in chapter three do seem to be explicitly activated in localized, textual terms by the argument of Romans (i.e., at the proximate frame of Paul's most important discussion of Justification), and they have yet to be adequately comprehended. By the end of Romans 5, and extending on through chapter 8, it is not merely the faithful individual, but the protests of Wrede and Räisänen (et al.) that have been justified. And a reading that can silence them — however different — must enjoy a significant advantage over any interpretative competitors.

Empirical Difficulties

ED 1: *Judaism.* It remains here largely only to repeat the observations of point nine above in a slightly different key. The "Judaism" established by 2:6-29 in the broader context of 1:18–3:20 clashes not only with Paul's own views elsewhere but with much broader evidence concerning the nature of Judaism in Paul's day. While a certain amount of the debate in this relation may have been misdirected in the past — concentrating at times on underlying psychological causalities and imprecise definitions — it is now apparent in the light of the particular dynamics of Justification theory that such a uniform, monolithic, and fundamentally perfectionist form of Judaism as Paul essentially explicates in Romans 2 did not exist in his day, and is certainly not a fair description of the bulk of late Second Temple Judaism. It is also of course a deeply contradictory construction, demanding perfectionism on the one hand, but expecting profound incapacity and sinfulness on the other. (And this should not surprise, because the description really derives from the premises underlying the critique of sinful pagans in 1:18-32 — premises that are not oriented toward Judaism in the first instance [a textual point taken up and explored in detail in part four, chapter fourteen].)

ED 2: *Conversion.* The entire sweep of the argument in Romans 1-4, understood in conventional terms, is an account of salvation and hence of
conversion; it is necessarily configured, moreover, in prospective, individualist, and rationalistic terms. Pagans and Jews ought to progress
from the relevant starting points in 1:18-32 and 2:1-29 and move through
to saving faith from 3:22 onward. It is foolish to resist this. And this account clearly clashes with a great deal of sociological investigation into
the actual manner of conversion. Certainly, this later literature must be
qualified because it does not pretend to supply a complete or uniform
account (although the latter point is in itself awkward for Justification
theory, which expects a single model), and much of it is modern. However, suitably nuanced, the considerable gap between the implications of
Romans 1-4 (conventionally construed), and the actual observations of
conversion remains.

ED 3: *Paul's conversion.* Similarly, Paul's "conversion" to "Christianity," insofar
as we can construct a picture of that pivotal journey, does not seem to be
corroborated by the conventional construal of Romans 1-4, or vice versa.
Paul's own ostensible progression from works and their failure (1:18–3:9a)
through the realization of sin (3:9b-18; perhaps also 2:21-22) to an embrace
of Jesus through faith alone (1:16-17; 3:21–4:25) is not mentioned in
Romans 1-4. There is *no* biographical material in this argument. The road
to Damascus should be implicit in 1:16-17 and from 3:22 onward, but Paul
gives no hints of this. Similarly, there are no corroborations for Justification theory in his biographical accounts found elsewhere.[168]

ED 4: *Paul's proclamation.* In line with the foregoing, the preaching template for conversion provided by Romans 1-4 is not evident in Paul's accounts of his actual preaching, where those are found elsewhere. Concomitantly, Paul does not commit himself overtly in Romans 1-4 to this
argument's fundamental evangelistic role for him. (He only seems to
complain at one point of his misrepresentation in terms of libertinism,
thereby pointing more to the discussions of chapter 6 as representative
of his approach; see 3:8 and 6:17.) So the cluster of difficulties evident
here in theoretical terms is implicitly activated again by the unfortunate
silences of Romans 1-4 (interpreted conventionally).[169]

4.3. Implications

This chapter has seen a significant expansion of the discourse's previous difficulties. To the twenty-one intrinsic, systematic, and empirical problems noted in
part one, we have added thirty-five specifically exegetical problems — that is, difficulties located in the relationship between the key Pauline text and its ostensible
theoretical superstructure. And the recognition of these additional problems now
generates several further important implications.

The new difficulties clearly reinforce the conclusions already achieved by the theoretical analysis of part one. In effect, the stakes of the discussion have been raised even further, since the Justification discourse now apparently contains a number of exegetical difficulties. Moreover, we have seen that all the intrinsic, systematic, and empirical difficulties noted in theoretical terms in part one are activated either implicitly or overtly by the conventional reading of Romans 1–4 in its broader setting; that is, strictly speaking, they are now *exegetical* difficulties as well (using that term in its broad, conventional sense). And any exegetical anxieties — that Justification theory was a straw man and/or had no textual relevance — should now have subsided. In short, the implications noted at the end of part one, chapter six have been significantly reinforced.

But perhaps most importantly, it is apparent that the conventional reading that underpins the discourse's superstructure is *vulnerable*. While it is both widespread and powerful — and its strengths must not be denied — it contains a significant number of problems, to put things mildly. And these suggest that it may not ultimately be the best construal of Paul's textual data. However, it is not enough simply to suggest this in hypothetical terms. The conventional reading can be displaced only by a reading that is demonstrably superior — by a reading that solves these difficulties and has fewer or no problems of its own.

Some scholars have of course attempted just that in relation to the relevant texts — a much smaller, minority tradition of "revisionist" interpretation in relation to Paul and Romans. But a cogent alternative reading has yet to appear in the critical literature (and Justification advocates are in my view entirely correct to point this out). The revisionist alternatives to the conventional construal can be shown to fail, and to do so in some cases at numerous points. Nevertheless, many clues concerning the eventual shape of a successful rereading become apparent as this alternative tradition's contours are critically traced. We turn, then, to a careful examination of the revisionist interpretative tradition. We will learn much from this consideration of alternative approaches to Romans 1–4, before attempting our own in part four.

CHAPTER TWELVE

Wide and Narrow Paths

§1. Preamble

I suggested at the end of the last chapter that those dissatisfied with the conventional construal of Romans 1–4 have not yet succeeded in displacing it, despite its many difficulties. Indeed, a wide path (or two) is discernible that would seem to promise resolution of our difficulties, but unfortunately, those traveling upon it seem to have arrived only at their own interpretative destruction. The real path to resolution turns out to be steep, narrow, and seldom traveled.

The debate concerning the reinterpretation of Paul in this general relation can seem overwhelmingly complex, but we can simplify it initially with two clarifications, the second introducing a basic methodological distinction.

First — as we have already noted — we are interested primarily in suggestions concerning Romans 1–4. Revisionist suggestions concerning other relevant texts in Paul are certainly significant and will be noted carefully in due course (i.e., in part five), but in all probability they cannot, for the reasons adduced in chapter ten (and reinforced in part five, chapters twenty and twenty-one), prove decisive. Romans 1–4 is the textual storm center for the entire debate, whether its participants recognize this or not, so we will focus on alternative approaches to this particular text in what follows.

Second, despite a superficial cacophony, all the revisionist suggestions concerning Romans 1–4 actually tend to operate in terms of two primary strategic approaches: *reframing* and *rereading*.

Many revisionists attempt to solve the difficulties with Paul at this point by *reframing*. That is, they supply a different account of the history of the text, whether in its original production or in subsequent transmission. Essentially, they offer a new narrative of what *generated* or *caused* the text — if pursued in relation to Paul himself, an account of the circumstantial frame. The solution they are pursuing, then, lies outside the actual process of reading that is at the heart of

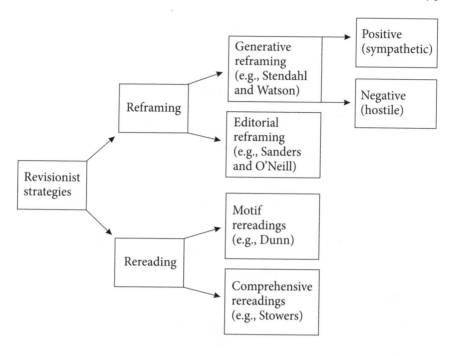

the discourse (often, perhaps, because they are not convinced that a different reading of the texts is possible).

Other revisionists refuse to make the basic exegetical concession here and attempt instead a *rereading* of Paul's texts, or at least some of their elements. These interpreters use a fundamentally different strategic option, challenging the actual meaning supplied by the conventional reading for specific units of text within Romans 1–4. Their treatments vary considerably in scope, from the reconstrual of comparatively small units of the text — mere words and phrases, or motifs — to more ambitious reconstruals of the entire argument.

Our more detailed analysis will be structured in terms of these two primary approaches, along with their main internal variations, although it is only fair to note that some revisionists craft complex positions that draw at times on both principal strategies and their variants. Revisionist proposals, if they are to be plausible, must be detailed; and accordingly, they merit a detailed critical evaluation. Indeed, this is vital if we are to learn anything of substance from them. Hence, I have chosen to proceed by way of detailed interaction with what I take to be the outstanding revisionists of the last thirty years or so — a small pantheon of truly brilliant rereaders: James Dunn, E. P. Sanders, Stanley Stowers, and Francis Watson. If the proposals of these stellar figures can be shown to fail, then it is unlikely that others will have succeeded.[1]

§2. Reframing

Reframers concede the basic correctness of the conventional reading of Romans 1–4 and place their reinterpretative pressure on various aspects of the circumstantial frame for that reading. They tend to point to one of two rather different loci as problematic in the long process of the text's production and transmission down to the present day. One tactic concentrates on the complex process that ostensibly lay behind the text's generation. This approach emphasizes the causality — especially within Paul himself — that led to the text's initial production, claiming that a deeper knowledge of the generative process removes, or at least mitigates, most of our interpretative difficulties. Consequently, this approach tends to invoke Paul's psychological state — or at least to open up the area of his intentionality. The other tactic attributes our difficulties to corruptions of Paul's original text, whether through interpolation or reediting or some similar process. Once these corruptions are identified and (if necessary) removed, then a clearer and more cogent Paul supposedly emerges.

We will deal first in a little more detail with the suggestion that takes place at the earliest point of composition, which is also the more popular strategic option. After this we will turn to consider reframing within the later process of textual transmission.

2.1. Generative Reframing

One of the first and most famous revisionist critiques was Krister Stendahl's, and its negative contentions have already been considered at length in part one, chapter six.[2] But Stendahl also models an attempted response to the difficulties he raised, and not merely criticism per se, and this is worth noting here in spite of its regrettable brevity. He challenged the prevailing readings of various key biographical and theological texts (see Romans 7 and Phil. 3:6). Most famously, however, he suggested that Paul's Justification discussions took place in defense of the law-free pagan mission, under the broader rubric of Paul's apostolic call to the pagans, and in the broader setting of the early church's vigorous discussion of that radical missionary movement. This approach also necessarily imparted, in his view, a stronger salvation-historical dimension to the argument of much of Romans. And this classic approach can exemplify nicely both the basic strategy and the intrinsic difficulties of any attempt to resolve the problems in the conventional construal by reframing the Justification texts psychologically and circumstantially, or generatively. First, we should consider how Stendahl's suggestions actually help us.

Stendahl's approach arguably results in several subtle new interpretative reorientations. The Justification texts are partly marginalized by a renewed emphasis on the salvation-historical analysis of Romans 9–11 and by their location within a highly politicized, at times even polemical, situation. In such a setting it seems possible that Paul might exaggerate, or make rash claims for temporary rhetorical advantage, or even make mistakes. He might also defend his positions wherever that proves necessary — where he is being pressed — rather than carefully and systematically setting out a given position. (That is, he might not be in control of the shape of the discussion.) Moreover, this renewed set of links with Paul's call, apostleship, and pagan mission separates the Justification texts from his "conversion" in terms of the Justification biography (and that front has also been weakened already by various textual claims). Several wedges are thereby cleverly driven into the Justification colossus — or into the "Lutheran" reading, as Stendahl unhelpfully referred to it. Moreover, a certain rhetorical force is detectable at this point in the argument. Stendahl's reframing encourages interpreters to think about Paul's texts in new ways — in terms of frameworks outside the traditional offerings of the Justification discourse. Hence, his argument may serve to liberate the interpretative imagination, and in that way may be a useful psychological preliminary to comprehensive reinterpretation. But just how damaging is his set of proposals in concrete methodological terms beyond the persuasive allure of imaginative reconceptualization?

We can recognize here what is essentially a reframing strategy functioning primarily in terms of the relevant texts' circumstantial settings. Stendahl has reframed the texts and implied as a result that they are less coherent and more contingent than Justification advocates aver; they are more creatures of the moment than statements of eternal evangelical truths. However, a number of problems are discernible if this is taken to be a definitive solution to all our difficulties.

First, Stendahl's recontextualization is asserted rather than demonstrated. And second, it is also prima facie false. The actual location of the relevant texts is a group of letters that Paul wrote to various congregations in Galatia, Rome, and Philippi, so the settings of the relevant arguments begin overtly with readings in the presence of those disparate communities. So if Stendahl's reframing strategy is to succeed, he must build some incontrovertible historical bridge from those epistolary settings to the polemics of Jerusalem, and he simply does not do so, nor does this look possible (see, for example, the difficulties of Jervell at this point, discussed in part four, chapter thirteen). A reframing strategy is only as good as the historical case that informs it, and in this case it rests on next to nothing.[3] Yet even if his colorful historical case proved successful — third — it contains an important interpretative non sequitur. Readings of texts are not reducible to their causalities (in its extreme form, this being the intentional fallacy, with the text reduced to the intention of its author).[4] Fourth, and most importantly, Stendahl's strategy *leaves the Justification construals intact*. The key texts remain largely in the hands of his opponents! Justification theory will still be launched, along with all its problems. And this is the crucial weakness of reframing strategies. They seek to marginalize the difficulties historically and biographically (or editorially) rather than actually removing them — the hermeneutical equivalent of taking a painkiller while a fatal disease continues its deadly progress.[5] Fifth, by leaving the conventional construal intact, Stendahl's strategy also weakens its case *for* a marginalization in terms of circumstance and strengthens the case of its opponents, who can appeal to their uncontested readings in support of their own reconstructions! That is, Justification advocates can simply appeal to their own biography, which integrates smoothly with their construals of Paul's texts. It is not a flawless position, but it is a powerful one, and it will certainly overwhelm unsupported assertions, which Stendahl tends to deploy.[6] Sixth, and finally, it is unclear how recontextualizing the Justification texts into the setting of early church debate fundamentally reinterprets them in any fundamental way; Justification advocates are presumably just as happy to debate the nature of Christian salvation in a church council at Jerusalem as at Galatia or Philippi. So it seems that Stendahl's circumstantial resetting does not deliver him the decisive marginalization that he wants.

The weakness of the generative reframing strategy is illustrated in certain respects by the difficulties its advocates encounter while settling the question of Paul's motivations even among themselves. Some reframers view Paul positively, trying to rescue his interpretation with this strategy. The apostle's reasons for apparently arguing badly are construed in a sympathetic light: he was in a heated polemical situation and so not at his best, and/or he was formulating temporary tactical considerations (so Stendahl); he merely wished to undercut Jewish ethnocentrism, and so was motivated fundamentally by generosity (so Bruce Longenecker); or some such. But other reframers view Paul in a very different light, suggesting, for example, that the apostle's problems are explicable because he was not capable of coherent thought (at least, certainly on these questions — so, i.a., Räisänen); or, alternatively, he was motivated by antipathy and even hatred toward his ancestral religion, Judaism (so Klausner and Maccoby); or he was a deeply conflicted person psychologically (so Dodd); or he was just making his argument up as he went along in order to get converts (so Watson in *PJ&G*); or he was trying to establish leadership over and coherence within certain social groups (Esler); and so on.[7]

Hence, the data is too scarce, and the methodological zone being debated too diaphanous, for any decisive explanatory leverage to result from the strategy of generative reframing. The very point where reframers try to make their case, once critically examined, is shown to be weak and contentious.[8] Moreover, even if their case here succeeds, it has not solved the crucial problem: the Justification readings remain intact.

Revisionists can at least learn from this strategy, however, that it is worth challenging Justification advocates on generative grounds, and that such challenges can open up new interpretive spaces within the debate: new explanatory narratives do seem possible. Certainly, the standard claims of the discourse in this relation do not seem as incontrovertible as they sometimes purport to be. Furthermore, the circumstantial frame should be reexamined, the claims of the Justification discourse at this point tested, and — if possible — a cogent new framing explanation sought. This concern for the historical particularities surrounding Paul's texts is a significant methodological insight and advance.[9] Such revisions could therefore *contribute* to a strategy that found its principal interpretative leverage elsewhere.

Excursus: Francis B. Watson's *Paul and the Hermeneutics of Faith*

I want to pause here to consider in detail the work of a more recent and complex reframing — Watson's *Paul and the Hermeneutics of Faith* (hereafter *P&HF*).[10] This is an exceptionally creative and learned treatment that nevertheless in my view courts the peculiar dangers of generative reframing, arguably without solving them (although it is also an idiosyncratic reframing strategy in certain respects). Its particular approach will be described first, then its strengths and strategic advances, after which point we will turn to critical evaluation.

Excursus §1: Watson's Position[11]

Watson is concerned in the first instance with the aspersions cast on Paul's manner of exegesis by (i.a.) Sanders and, before him, by Schweitzer — the much-repeated calumnies that the apostle's use of Scripture is ad hoc, careless and/or irresponsible, and hence secondary. He takes aim initially *at other revisionists*, apparently offended by their accusations in this relation. But Watson is also concerned with the questions surrounding Paul's descriptions of Judaism and the role of the law — one of the Justification theory's major difficulties at the empirical frame — and is sensitive to the possibility that these may even be "contradictory," a charge asserted most vociferously by Räisänen.[12] So he is clearly oriented by some of the basic difficulties generated by the Justification discourse and is appropriately considered here. Moreover, much of his analysis of Paul is involved with the construal of the discourse's basal texts. His suggested reading of Paul is quite ingenious.

In purely descriptive terms, Watson constructs a pyramid of interpretative theses about Paul. The foundational layer in *P&HF* is — as the book's title suggests — the claim that Paul occupies a hermeneutical space between a dogmatic, a priori, christological reading of Scripture[13] and an anachronistic, historical-critical posture, both of which are unacceptable. Paul, contends Watson, negotiates the narrow pass between the interpretative jaws of this Scylla and that Charybdis by reading Scripture essentially canonically, with due attention to questions of broader narrative and context.[14] He is above all a *careful* reader. Paul respects the text, in terms of both what it does and what it does not know. And he is particularly concerned with the Pentateuch. Paul's explicit citations from the Pentateuch are "representative" ("Scripture," 8). Watson means by this that quotations from the Jewish Bible's first five books function rather like icebergs that float visibly across the surface of the apostle's extant texts but are in fact positioned on a hidden substructure of much weightier exegesis — exegesis that Paul undertook earlier on, carefully, and essentially as a Jew. Paul learns certain key things from this prior reading.

The Jewish people are oriented toward "doing" the law, and this largely in the expectation of attaining "life," that is, eschatological life — an essentially conditional arrangement and a thoroughly reasonable one. This is the main import of Leviticus, as attested especially by 18:5. But the Pentateuch also attests to constant failures in relation to this program. The giving of the Law to Israel at Sinai — the central message of Exodus — only subsequently brought death, as seen especially in the episode of the golden calf (Exodus 32). The history of the Jews from Sinai onward is actually one of disobedience and rebellion, eliciting curse, punishment, and destruction — the central messages of Numbers and Deuteronomy, as attested in numerous places in Paul. Thus, through his exegesis of the unfolding Pentateuch, Paul detects a deep sinfulness within Israel (see especially Rom. 3:10-18, where prophetic texts speak as the law). The future, approached in such terms, is bleak, as Moses suggests in his last words to Israel recorded in Deuteronomy. Hence, the reasonable soteriological arrangement attested to by Leviticus led in fact, via continual rebellion, only to curse and death. Over against this stark antithesis, however, stands a third principle, namely, God's unconditional offer of eschatological salvation in relation to faith alone, the message of Genesis in 15:6 and also of Habakkuk 2:4 (around which the whole Book of the Twelve arguably pivots). This earlier (and later) message, couched in very different terms, shines like a beacon across the darkness of the intervening stories.

Paul, then, detects major tensions in the Pentateuch. This is simply what he finds as he reads it in its canonical form with due attention to what it says. Thus, Paul emerges as a rather Evangelical figure, not to mention one influenced strongly by interpretative principles we associate now with Brevard Childs.[15] But Watson is not content to rest here. Paul's soteriology, he claims, simply arises out of this patient exegetical work, and it is already reasonably familiar; it is basically Justification theory's construal of the gospel, which Watson characterizes as "righteousness by faith." This interpretation of the Pentateuch is "constitutive" and "generative" of Paul's soteriology, Watson suggests.[16]

It is useful to keep in mind that in certain key respects Watson's entire project is an antithesis. It reacts to a particular set of assertions by certain critics of Paul — hermeneutical accusations made by Schweitzer and revivified by Sanders, with an additional set of complaints from Räisänen playing a supportive role. The criticisms basically function as follows:

I. Paul's quotations of Scripture in his Justification texts are textually irresponsible and acontextual [hermeneutical features that are assumed to imply one another].

II. These quotations therefore underpin secondary claims in substantive terms, and it follows that the real Pauline gospel is found elsewhere.

[III. Presumably, that gospel is then *unsupported* by Scripture; that is, I denotes Paul's use of Scripture period.]

IV. Furthermore, Paul's characterizations of law observance and Judaism are contradictory: you can fulfill Judaism/you can't/God has provided another way in any case [perhaps leading again to II and III, or worse . . .].

Watson deals with proposition IV by relocating it from a contemporary empirical locus to a hermeneutical one (which still has contemporary and empirical force but is not fundamentally directed in those terms). However, he contradicts directly propositions I, II, and III, and this set of negations constitutes the heart of his book:

I. Paul's quotations of Scripture in his Justification texts are textually responsible and contextualized [hermeneutical features that are assumed to go together].
[Key qualifier: these quotations represent canonical readings of the Pentateuch.]

II. These quotations are therefore primary and "constitute" the real Pauline gospel.

[III. Substantive claims elsewhere are usually *unsupported* by canonical readings of the Pentateuch, further reinforcing II.]

IV. Paul's characterizations of the Pentateuch are admittedly contradictory: you can fulfill Judaism/you can't/God has provided another way in any case. But the Pentateuch *is* contradictory, further endorsing proposition I above!

With these clarifications in place, we should turn to consider just what strategy Watson is following, and what advantages his particular explanation has generated.

Excursus §2: Watson's Strategic Advances

During my own long consideration of Justification in relation to Paul, I have often wondered if its advocates should consider a defensive withdrawal to a thoroughgoing hermeneutical position, basing their gospel on exegesis alone and abandoning its conventional, rather generalized and philosophical, opening argumentation (and so on). My own judgment up to this point has been that, although certain advantages are immediately realized by this move — numerous criticisms are defused — certain fundamental problems are left unresolved, if not exacerbated. Hence, I have always thought that this tactical withdrawal would ultimately be unwise; it would be to choose the fire over the frying pan. However, Watson's masterful enactment of this tactic now allows me to see whether this evaluation is really sound, or whether the tactic is in fact a successful one.

In my view, Watson has very cleverly created a number of significant defensive advantages by his suggested hermeneutical reorientation of Paul. As we well know, Justification advocates ordinarily begin their account of the gospel with natural theology and the disclosure of certain undeniable axioms about God and individuals from within the cosmos — God's justice, human accountability for transgression, and so on (see Rom. 1:19-20). And this imparts a rationalistic dimension to the entire theory. It also generates a series of argumentative and theoretical tensions. Most acutely, an epistemological dualism is now operative within the theory — general, philosophical epistemology versus particular, revealed epistemology. Furthermore, some of these axioms go on to generate framing tensions in relation to other aspects of Paul's thought. The implicit models of Paul's "conversion" and conversion in general generate in turn strong tensions with both the evidence concerning Paul's actual call and the evidence of wider religious conversion (this last admittedly largely modern).[17]

But Watson has relocated the defensive perimeter of the Justification discourse to a new, thoroughgoing hermeneutical position, and this delivers him numerous immediate defensive benefits in terms of these problems. It eliminates most of Justification's essentially rationalistic apparatus at one blow, along with its various difficulties. Instead of self-interested, philosophical individuals, we have *Jewish readers* (and neither are the transitions from the one position to the other problematic any longer). This is a considerable step forward; certainly, it is the most comprehensive and significant such resolution that I can detect anywhere in the debate to date (with the possible exception of Stowers and those following his thesis).[18] Moreover, since Justification also draws on the particular Jewish scriptural tradition, Watson is in one sense merely reorienting that theory more consistently around a principle that it already accepts; indeed, he is taking Paul's treatment of Abraham with the utmost seriousness. We might say, then, that he has regrouped Justification on higher hermeneutical ground. The benefit he signals most overtly from this maneuver, however, is the new, highly defensible posture vis-à-vis criticisms of Paul in terms of Judaism — the nagging empirical difficulty that has already been much remarked upon.

Watson has jettisoned the very notion that Paul is describing contemporary Judaism at all. In this masterful side step, Watson argues that Paul's characterizations are merely readings of the Pentateuch. They do not necessarily refer to any contemporary soteriological or sociological realities or principles; any debate in such terms is therefore beside the point! Moreover, if the volley of further criticisms is still unleashed — as inevitably it will be — that these characterizations are nevertheless often at cross-purposes, Watson can reply plausibly that these contradictions are found in Paul's authoritative source material, the Pentateuch. Hence — in a supreme tactical triumph for his particular concerns —

Paul's attestation to these contradictions merely demonstrates his fidelity and responsibility as a reader! One set of critics' calumnies has thereby been turned on another.[19]

I can't help admiring Watson's adroit tactical maneuver here. It is quite simply one of the cleverest defensive moves that I have come across in the entire debate; moves within one debate are used to effect significant advantages in relation to another, and vice versa, while a great clarification and simplification of Justification itself seems to have taken place. We might say that its defensive front seems to have been significantly narrowed and strengthened. But we still need to note carefully where we end up.

After much thought I have positioned Watson's reading of Paul here as an instance of reframing (indeed, the most sophisticated one that I know of). Possibly not a great deal rests on this decision, but by it I suggest that he has essentially supplied us with a new and very extensive rereading of the *causality* of Paul's Justification texts. Lying *behind* these texts is a sophisticated hermeneutical operation — a responsible canonical reading of the Pentateuch — Watson avers, and one presumably undertaken (or, at least, inaugurated) much earlier on in Paul's life as a Jew. Indeed, Watson articulates a significant reconstrual of Paul's argument and theology at this level, but its explicit textual intersections are relatively slight (which is not to say that they are nonexistent). What Paul thinks about these matters, which is inextricably intertwined with how he exegetes the Pentateuch, hovers behind his contingent quotations and arguments. And this creates a peculiar dynamic in terms of our assessment of his plausibility. We can consider Watson's reconstrual of Paul's basic argumentative and hermeneutical position in terms of its argumentative and theological plausibility, but this is not an aspect of a broader *reading* of the key textual data; these considerations take place one step removed from the construal of data (although informing it, according to Watson). Clearly, this position delivers Watson certain advantages, but he purchases those for a price that he may not ultimately be able to pay. Suffice it for now to note that Watson's adroit hermeneutical withdrawal regroups the Justification discourse around the figure of Abraham and Paul's use of Genesis 15:6, relocating the apostle's consideration of Judaism at the same moment to a narrative reading of the Pentateuch. The emphasis in this explanation on a prior hermeneutic clearly suggests a reframing strategy, at least in the main, and its creativity suggests a revisionist position, at least at bottom. But Watson remains in some senses quite conventional, and he is explicitly opposed to many of the proposals of other revisionists. We should pause, then, to consider this intriguing dynamic.

The gospel that emerges from Watson's hermeneutical characterization of Paul is in some respects a fairly traditional construal — "righteousness by faith."[20] At the same time, various specific attacks on this position are beaten back — most notably, the specific revisionist proposals of Sanders, of the revivified Schweitzer, of Dunn, Wright, Hays,[21] Räisänen (to a degree), and Beker, along with their lesser-known comrades at arms. And Watson thus illustrates nicely two characteristic features (and shortcomings) of most revisionist proposals that either reframe or reread limited amounts of text.

First, most of the conventional reading, and hence also of Justification theory, tends to be left intact by these strategies, so it is no real surprise to see a position that is recognizably still a variant of Justification theory emerging from Watson's innovative proposals. Many revisionists, despite their best efforts, end up echoing the Justification discourse (something that we will also see momentarily in relation to Sanders and Dunn). Second, the frequent fragility of these proposals, operating as they do one step removed from the actual construal of the text, and hence within some reconstruction of the text's causality, entails a frequent lack of decisiveness. This lack of real purchase on the explicit evidence makes such proposals vulnerable to counterproposals. Consequently, revisionists tend to disagree with each other on these matters as much as they disagree with certain assertions by Justification advocates.[22] So what seems at first glance to be a slightly odd disposition by Watson vis-à-vis the rest of the debate turns out to be entirely understandable. Like many at this point, Watson is an ingenious and creative tactician who ultimately endorses a conservative strategy.[23]

Watson clearly intends to settle many of the major issues in the interpretation of Paul, even if he does not define them quite as I do here. The book is — despite its modest opening disclaimer (see ix) — a definitive word that reaches far beyond questions of intertextuality, and often in what are to my mind unquestionably brilliant terms. But has this skillful hermeneutical reorientation of the Justification discourse succeeded on all counts? Is that discourse now — suitably reformulated — problem free? We turn now to consider why this is unlikely.

Excursus §3: Watson's Problems

The most crucial question to ask of any reframing strategy is whether it is actually true. Reframers present Pauline interpreters with powerful explanations that hover just out of sight behind his actual texts — whether in terms of their original settings or later editing — supposedly mitigating the difficulties apparent in those texts. So the key question arises whether these explanations really existed or rather owe more to the ingenuity of the modern reframer than to Paul himself. Reframers must demonstrate the existence of their suggestions concretely at some point, in the extant evidence, exegetically. Conversely, the appearance of various sorts of problems at this interface casts doubt on the cogency of their proposals.[24] But Watson poses an interesting, more specific challenge for our analysis. He claims that an alternative textual base is evident in Paul — Galatians 3, rather than Romans 1–4. (The former is where he makes his case primarily, so it is in effect a new textual "citadel.")

(1) Paul's Ostensible Hermeneutic of Desire and Death concerning Exodus and Numbers

Presumably, few would deny that Genesis 15:6 is a definitive text related to salvation by faith for Paul, and that he holds the giving of the law to have taken place at Mount Sinai as Exodus recounts. I am also happy to grant — for now[25] — that Leviticus 18:5 is a useful and fair summary of "law observance" as a way to eschatological life, *and* that the curse of Deuteronomy applies in some programmatic way to Israel's subsequent history.[26] But in order for these texts to settle into a canonical hermeneutic of the Pentateuch, some of Watson's further claims need to hold good, namely, that the book of Exodus suggests the temporary and death-dealing aspects of the giving of the law, and that the book of Numbers underlies Paul's claim that the letter kills through desire. These claims, if successful, would then attribute significant contributions to Paul's gospel to each book in the Pentateuch, and would plausibly delimit the quotations from Leviticus and Deuteronomy already conceded to those particular books, as against more universally. Hence, a great deal depends on Watson's claims that narratives in Exodus and Numbers underlie Paul's statement that "the letter kills" in 2 Corinthians 3:6 (although see vv. 1-18 as a whole), and the apostle's more extended argument that the ministry of the law is a ministry of death in Romans 7:7-25 (*P&HF*, 281-98; 310-13; also 354-77). Is Paul's negative view of the law as expressed in this statement underpinned by a canonical hermeneutic? Watson also appeals to 1 Corinthians 10:1-11 in this relation, so his case rests largely on these three passages in Paul. The narrative of death from

Exodus that informs 2 Corinthians 3 is of course the famous story of the golden calf. And the motif of desire, so prominent in the Numbers narrative, is an important signal, according to Watson, that the narrative of rebellious Israel's wilderness wanderings is in play in Romans 7. Moreover, 1 Corinthians 10 overtly displays just such an abbreviated use of an extensive pentateuchal narrative by the apostle. This is an ingenious case, carefully and thoroughly argued. But it is also fragile. In response, I would suggest several points.

I am not convinced that Paul's use of the Numbers narrative in 1 Corinthians 10 supports Watson's case in relation to the law's death dealing (although I certainly concede that it provides evidence of the sort of narrative reading and allusory compression that Watson holds Paul to be undertaking frequently elsewhere). Several features of Paul's argument suggest that it is not doing quite what Watson needs it to do.[27]

Watson refers 2 Corinthians 3:6 ultimately to the story of the golden calf as well (i.e., Exodus 32). But the verse as a whole speaks of an antithesis between the old and new covenants, the latter being an explicitly pneumatological actualization of a prophetic text. A retrospective and more programmatic reading of the saying "the letter kills" is therefore clearly possible. (Perhaps significantly, the old covenant is also described as a ministry of condemnation — διακονία τῆς κατακρίσεως.) The key phrase — "the letter kills" — and these additional signals point fairly directly to the broader discussion of Romans 7:7-25 as critical background to Paul's use of the controversial phrase. And nothing else in 2 Corinthians 3 explicitly activates the Exodus narrative of the golden calf. So the possibility that a specific pentateuchal narrative underlies Paul's view of the law as a ministry that "kills" through the "letter" now rests largely on the interpretation of the important but much disputed passage in Romans.

The key issue for us here in relation to Romans 7 — a passage that we have already considered in part[28] — is Watson's claim that the argument there is informed by the narrative of Israel's wandering through the wilderness supplied by Numbers. That narrative emphasizes "desire." So is Romans 7 informed fundamentally by this story? Does Paul learn by reading the book of Numbers that desire, inflamed by the law, kills, and so write Romans 7 partly in the light of this? Clearly, this is possible. But a number of concerns need to be allayed before I can accede to this suggestion wholeheartedly.

The terminology of "desire" in Paul is highly significant and is not limited to Romans 7. It functions in an important relationship with the "flesh" and "the passions," both of which are key notions for Paul as attested by many other texts. The "thinking," "passions," and "desires" of the "flesh" — that is, of people insofar as they consist of their unredeemed Adamic ontology — are the principal protagonists that Christians face "within," and as such are susceptible to manipulation by evil forces from without. "The mind of the flesh is death," Paul utters famously, and not a little pessimistically, in Rom. 8:6 (see indeed, merely in Romans from this point, 8:1-15 passim; 12:2; and 13:13-14). Perhaps more significantly, Galatians 5 grounds its entire advocacy of pneumatological ethics on that state's superiority to a life lived in terms of the desires of the flesh: ". . . walk in the Spirit and you will not fulfill the desire of the flesh" (5:16, but see also vv. 17 and 24). Here the works of the flesh are extensive indeed and do not seem informed primarily by the narrative of the wilderness; they are a simple vice list (vv. 19-21).

Hence, "desire" functions for Paul within an entire discourse and cannot be analyzed simply with reference to Romans 7. Furthermore, when all its instances are explored, any suggestion that a narrative from Numbers is fundamental looks increasingly unlikely. This is an *eschatological* dualism between life in the present created order and life in the resurrected condition as effected by the Spirit (Gal. 6:14-15). The finger of the Spirit can re-create and resurrect, whereas the law, written in pen and ink with human hands, lacks this divine capacity to transform.[29]

We ought to note that it is largely uncontested that a particular scriptural template undergirds these views of Paul, at least in part — the story of Genesis 2–3, which is shaped by Paul to articulate the entry of the powers of Sin and Death into the human condition, or "flesh." The conclusion is largely unavoidable that Paul's understanding that "all die" is grounded in this text. Not only is this stated clearly in Romans (5:12-14), but the point recurs aphoristically in the very different setting of the Corinthian correspondence (see 1 Cor. 15:21-22; see also vv. 45-49). It would be risky to claim that Paul learned that people die purely by reading this story in the Pentateuch, but there can be little doubt that his explanation of the phenomenon is shaped fundamentally by this text. Moreover, that death was caused by the transgression of a divine commandment, as Paul avers in Romans 7. Thus, at bottom, according to Paul, people seem to die because of Adam, and Israel is of course in Adam (as evidenced presumably by the fact that most Jews in Paul's experience did eventually die). The post-Adamic condition, so to speak, seems one of "flesh," within which "desires" have been unleashed, along with the evil powers of Sin and Death.

Turning back specifically to Romans 7, we should now note certain important stylistic features. The argument is pursued relentlessly in the first person singular. Paul speaks repeatedly of "I." Moreover, the motif of desire is introduced explicitly into the argument in v. 7 by the quotation of the tenth commandment (and it does not appear frequently from this point onward in any case: see only v. 8). The argument is also developed from v. 14 by images of enslavement (see also esp. vv. 23-25). And this all adds up to a relatively simple interpretative suggestion.

Romans 7 is written from the perspective of a Jew in Adam. It suggests that the evil desires of the flesh can be further manipulated by Sin in relation to the law — the tenth commandment is intelligently chosen to illustrate this point. And the result is a constant exacerbation of evil activity and a consequent heightened appropriateness for Death. The very fact of constant transgression illustrates that this person is under the power of Sin and hence also under the power of Sin's immediate superior, Death. Hence, such a person is sinful, agonized, and helpless. He or she needs rescue. Moreover, although nothing in the law is technically to blame for this sorry situation, the law does exacerbate it as the plaything of Sin and Desire; it can be manipulated by these powers to deepen the situation's intrinsic difficulty. In this way it continues to produce Death. And only a dramatic transformation of human nature can resolve this scenario. (We could add further that the foregoing reading is a pentateuchal hermeneutic, although it is not a canonical one rooted in explicit citation; it is an instance of allusive and narrative intertextuality.)

With these preliminary and all too brief remarks we come to the critical question. Are there clear textual signals that prompt us to include the narrative of Numbers within this text? It seems best to answer this question in the negative. On the one hand, Romans 7 already seems sufficiently explained in other terms. On the other hand, there is no explicit citation of Numbers in Romans 7. The instance of 1 Corinthians 10 does not seem overly relevant, and the brief echo of similar phraseology in 2 Corinthians 3 requires determination itself from here rather than vice versa. Hence, I suspect that most interpreters of Romans 7 would demur at Watson's suggestion. But if it is not convincing at this point, then the more basic claim that Paul learned that the letter kills by reading Exodus and then Numbers begins to falter as well, at which point the entire thesis of an underlying canonical hermeneutic begins to unravel.[30]

(2) Paul's Ostensible Hermeneutic of Deuteronomy

A great deal now rests on Watson's account of Paul's quotations from the book of Deuteronomy. The apostle cites Deuteronomy 27:26 (see 28:58 and 30:10) in Galatians 3:10, and Deuteronomy 27:26/21:23 in 3:13. Did Paul learn from reading Deuteronomy as a whole that Israel would be cursed, summarizing that discovery in these two programmatic quotations? I have two principal lines of inquiry at this point.

First, it seems possible that the application of "curse" language to Israel by Paul here is partly motivated by contingent circumstances, that is, by superficial rather than fundamental considerations. The motif of curse occurs prominently at the beginning of Galatians, when Paul pronounces an anathema on anyone — including an angel — who proclaims a different gospel from his original one (1:8-9), as well as in 3:10 and 13. This curse is repeated. Against this prominence in Galatians, explicit curse language is conspicuously absent from the closely related letter to the Romans, and even where we perhaps might have expected it (see 16:17-20). However, Paul's other quotations and key words from the dense scriptural interaction in Galatians 3:10-14 all receive extensive amplification in Romans. Hence, it seems entirely possible that Paul is merely trying to neutralize the frightening curse language of his opponents in Galatia, who are themselves almost certainly appealing to a reading of Deuteronomy; they both ought to be cursed and are under a curse — for proclaiming a different gospel from Paul's and for advocating a return by Christians to law-observance. And this gathering suspicion is arguably reinforced when we turn to consider the overt conceptual underpinning for Paul's curse language in 3:10 and 13.

One of the key texts is clearly applied to Christ (Deut. 21:23 in Gal. 3:13), while both citations have been shaped to create a close parallelism. (They function opposite one another within a broader chiastic arrangement as well.) And the christological curse text is prefaced with a significant if brief explanatory gloss: "Christ *purchased* us from the curse of the law . . ." (ἐξηγόρασεν). This word is a critical motif in Paul's later argument in 4:1-10 — an argument some distance from here in a commentary, but a mere page of Greek away in terms of actual reading. That later argument explains in much more detail how Christ has saved humanity, including Israel. He has done so by entering a situation of confined, oppressed minority (v. 4) and liberating its occupants, thereby "purchasing" those "under law" (v. 5). And this claim brings to a climax Paul's central concern through much of chapter 3.[31] From 3:19 onward Paul has spoken of the law's irritating pedagogical function in relation to Israel and her transgressions. It has "locked up" Israel until Christ's arrival (both v. 22 and v. 23), presumably disciplining her lapses as a good pedagogue should (vv. 24 and 25), in which situation Jews, despite being heirs, are little better off than slaves (so 4:1-3; note, they are not actually dead).

Watson could easily chime in at this point that such a view of Israel's history can be derived from reading the Pentateuch, and he would be absolutely right. However, Paul states explicitly at the conclusion of this argument that its rationale and perspective are *retrospective*. "Now, knowing God — or, rather, being known by God — how can you turn again to weak and miserable principles . . . ?!" (4:9a). And this is a sustained theme throughout Galatians. The Galatians are not to lapse *back* from their *present* Christian state: "Christ freed us for freedom: stand firm, then, and do not again bear the yoke of slavery" (5:1, and so on). Hence, the difficulty inherent in Israel's situation that derives from her confined, immature, dominated position seems to be generated by way of explicit contrast to the free, adult, and liberated position of the Christian community. Israel here is indeed under a curse — confined under harsh tutelage, threatened with punishment if she sins, and beaten if she steps out of line. But this is all by way of comparison with life in Christ.[32]

In short, Paul's overt development of his curse language in Galatians 3:10 and 13 seems to suggest a *christologically grounded, retrospective* argument. Thus, the characterization of Israel as "cursed" is not necessarily — according to the text of Galatians — an intrinsic analysis of Judaism per se based on Deuteronomy but a comparative judgment concerning the nature of Judaism if Christians return to it. The curse's basis is actually life in Christ — a life of freedom, adulthood, inheritance, and the Spirit. In comparison with this life, Judaism under the law is confined, immature, harsh, and oppressed, and hence also cursed; it is the life from which Christians have been "purchased." The charge of "curse" is consequently not a canonical claim, although it is for him a true claim. He summarizes its logic pithily if a little offensively in Philippians 3:8: ἡγοῦμαι πάντα ζημίαν εἶναι διὰ τὸ ὑπερέχον τῆς γνώσεως Χριστοῦ Ἰησοῦ τοῦ κυρίου μου, δι᾽ ὃν τά πάντα ἐζημιώθην, καὶ ἡγοῦμαι σκύβαλα, ἵνα Χριστὸν κερδήσω κ.τ.λ.[33]

This retrospective christological rationale explains the incidence of the Deuteronomic curse texts in Paul nicely. That set of citations and argument are in one sense a contingent effort to defuse a powerful rhetoric of curse emanating from his opponents in Galatia. Hence, the motif of curse occurs explicitly only in Galatians, where that specific challenge is being faced (although it is ultimately rooted in deeper theological arguments that come to expression elsewhere). And with this more overt and economical explanation of Paul's Deuteronomic curse language lying to hand, there is little further evidence for the truth of Watson's complex and subterranean interpretative suggestion.

(3) The New Base — Galatians 3

It is apparent that Watson's new textual base is beginning to crumble. The allusions to Exodus and Numbers that Watson needs are not present here at all; "the letter" does not "kill" after the law's disclosure at Sinai (it "imprisons" and inflicts "pedagogy"), and neither is a wilderness narrative of desire and its deadly consequences developed. So two of the five books of the Pentateuch do not seem to be represented here at all. Moreover, the third — Watson's account of the Deuteronomic material — has just been challenged. So this only leaves Leviticus 18:5 and Habakkuk 2:4, the latter supported by Genesis 15:6.[34] But is Watson's construal of even these texts supported by Paul's broader argument? Watson's treatments of Paul's πιστ- texts here fall within the broader and highly complex debate that we have begun to note, but have yet to treat in detail. A sustained engagement is therefore best postponed for the appropriate points later on,[35] although enough has already been said to suggest that I will ultimately oppose his readings as insufficiently sensitive to the particular under- and overdeterminations in play, and will propose some rather different construals of the data.[36] And similar considerations apply to Leviticus 18:5. It is worth noting in passing, however, that Paul never really tells us here what this text refers to in detail. Paul's citation is — in both its instances — noticeably isolated, while its only overt justification is "catchword linkage" *(gezerah shawah),* a common Jewish exegetical technique, but one clearly not rooted in a comprehensive canonical hermeneutic. (Indeed, it contradicts that explanation directly; the text is quoted rather because it possesses the same *word* as its companion text, Hab. 2:4, namely, ζήσεται.)

In sum, it is difficult to see anything explicitly supportive of Watson's proposed hermeneutic in the notoriously concise citations of Galatians 3 and their broader context. I see only a contingent and retrospective use of curse language, a brief acknowledgement of the *event* of Sinai, a reference to Genesis that is developed rather differently from Watson's reading (that is, in terms of ancestry), and a vestigial reference to Leviticus that seems motivated more by rabbinic principles of exegesis than by a canonical hermeneutic. Narratives of death and desire are absent. Hence, it seems that Galatians 3 does not provide decisive evidence for Watson's proposed hermeneutic. (Of course, much more could be said at this point, but Galatians 3 will be treated in more detail later on.) It could be suggested then that Watson's depiction of Paul's ostensible hermeneutic is more asserted than actualized. The very virtuosity of his own hermeneutical performance, articulating Paul's supposed interaction with the Pentateuch in attendant implicit dialogues with similar Jewish texts, draws us into assent. But Watson arguably weaves expensive hermeneutical clothes for the apostle that do not actually exist.

(4) The Hermeneutical Constraints

The cogency of Watson's case in descriptive terms actually rests as much on what he excludes as on what he affirms. Watson claims that Paul's hermeneutic consists of explicit citations that summarize canonical readings of the Pentateuch; all other intertextual operations are therefore either secondary or nonexistent.[37] Accordingly, he does not emphasize allusions or echoes.[38] Nor does he privilege narrative per se; narrative is involved in Paul's hermeneutic, but only as it emerges from the reading of the Pentateuch where it is interwoven with other material — and it must be Watson's account *of* that narrative.[39] Watson also opposes — except where opposition is absolutely impossible — christological exegesis,[40] which is tantamount to practicing "dogmatic" exegesis.[41] His privileging of Paul's use of the Pentateuch assimilates key texts from the Prophets to agendas already established by that hermeneutic and rejects any independent use of the Prophets by Paul.[42] He also in effect excludes variation — the notion that Paul's use of the Pentateuch could shift significantly, either in terms of Paul's actual reading or in relation to the rhetorical situation surrounding his appeal to it.[43] At this point, then, he also basically excludes an overtly contingent dimension within Paul's intertextuality.[44] Finally, Watson's hermeneutical reconstruction presupposes a fairly high degree of competence within Paul's epistolary recipients.[45]

Thus, in asserting what Paul's hermeneutic *is*, Watson also asserts with equal force that it is by and large *not* acontextual, allusory, narrative (except in a canonical context), christological or dogmatic, careless or distorting,[46] derived from the Prophets, variable, contingent, or inaccessible. In so doing, Watson cuts a swath through much current debate over the nature of Paul's intertextuality, as he has to. But none of his exclusions here ultimately seem persuasive, and especially when they are viewed in this manner — in toto. The fundamental rigidity and constriction of Watson's hermeneutic seem implausible as an account of how Paul actually uses Scripture.

(5) Assumed Non Sequiturs

As we have already seen, in certain key respects, Watson's entire project is an antithesis. It reacts to a particular set of criticisms of Paul (ironically, by other revisionists). However, so conceived, it largely presupposes that the mere reversal of those criticisms both isolates the key issues and constitutes a coherent argument. And ultimately — and despite the tactical advantages of the conception — I am not sure that this is wise.[47] The reversal actually introduces an entire series of non sequiturs into the structure of Watson's case.

Acontextual exegesis by a first-century Jew is not necessarily disrespectful or irresponsible; it can be extremely respectful and grounded on a carefully worked out hermeneutic (as Watson's study of contemporary Jewish texts often shows). In terms of the hermeneutical discourse inhabited by Jews in the first century, it can also be entirely authoritative. The charge that such exegesis is poor is actually an anachronism — a dogmatic assertion of the superiority of modern, historical-critical exegesis!

Equally importantly, it simply does not follow from the fact that exegesis might be poor that it is also secondary. Poor exegesis can be (and often is!) primary, while, still more importantly both for Paul and for Watson, the converse is also the case. Excellent exegesis can be secondary. So both links in this argument fail to hold good.

Hence, the original charge that Paul exegetes badly in his Justification texts and therefore treats marginal matters founders on two counts: his interpretation is not necessarily bad simply because it is acontextual, and, in any case, it does not follow that such exegesis denotes a secondary matter. However, Watson's reversal of this position is equally invalid. Paul's exegesis is not necessarily superior or vindicated simply because it is contextually sensitive, and, still more importantly, neither does this elevated interpretation (conceding its correctness here for the sake of argument) necessarily indicate that his principal soteriological position is being discussed. There is no obvious reason why these particular stretches of exegesis should be primary just because Paul reads well in them.[48] Consequently, the central links in Watson's argument seem to part in strictly logical terms. If they were to hold good, he would have to demonstrate them in detail as a matter of fact, not logic, but he does not do so. The argument tends merely to be asserted.

(6) A Gospel of Salvation by Faith Alone and Law-Free?

Watson's account of faith in Paul is, as his book title suggests, very significant. He nuances the conventional approach to this theme in Paul, drawing on a suitably refined Bultmann.[49] Watson relies primarily on a suggested reading of Habakkuk 2:4 in Paul, supported by the apostle's use of Genesis 15:6. However, I have some significant reservations about this account.

In the first instance, we should note that Watson has significantly weakened his ability to make the traditional anthropocentric case for the meaning of salvation sola fide by abandoning many of the traditional resources underpinning that reading. In a more conventional account, Paul concludes that salvation is by faith alone in large measure because he has attempted already to be justified through works of law but has been thwarted by his endemic sinfulness. The prior approach, oriented by the law, has failed, so salvation *must* be by way of some other, easier condition. (The overarching tenor of the discussion also necessarily remains conditional.) Paul's texts then supply "faith" at the appropriate point. And this argumentative trajectory is then supposedly traceable through Paul's life as well, with the moment of faith arriving on the road to Damascus. Although it has weaknesses, this is a powerful and coherent account of just *why* Pauline Christianity looks so different from Judaism, and why Paul himself so vehemently opposes the suggestion that his pagan converts need to be circumcised. Watson, however, has dismissed this argumentative *and* biographical assistance. And this entails his abandonment of the traditional *rationale* for salvation sola fide. He claims that Paul simply realizes this principle by reading Habakkuk 2:4 and Genesis 15:6 in their canonical contexts. But I find these claims implausible, and for reasons that in large measure Watson himself provides.[50]

Without the relevant argumentation and biography, the πιστ- texts that Paul adduces simply do not suggest the principle of salvation *sola* fide; that vital part of their meaning is entirely unattested when they are read in their canonical contexts. That this is the case is affirmed by the parallel Jewish readings that Watson supplies, *none of which conclude that salvation is in fact sola fide*. All the other Jewish readers of these texts assume that this principle of faith — which they do not deny in and of itself — is still compatible with further extensive law observance (as do certain NT authors apparently as well: see James 2:17-26!). One should of course be faithful to God, but one should do everything else as well — love, hope, practice charity, pray, and so on. Of course, they conclude this because they are not operating in terms of Justification theory, which supplies a *prior* demonstration of the inadequacy of law observance. Without this theory, there is no contradiction between salvation by faith and law observance, and they read accordingly. And this only serves to confirm our suspicions that the principle of sola fide cannot in fact be established without this prior argumentation, and, consequently, that Watson, having abandoned that demonstration, has attributed it to the reading of these texts for anachronistic reasons.[51] He introduces it there himself, informed in part by the rich theological heritage of Protestantism (and he claims to be influenced especially by Bultmann). But this is not actually a fair canonical reading of these texts, and neither is it a cogent position in argumentative and theological terms. (This also fails to acknowledge the long heritage of foundationalist critiques of law-observance, whether those are directed against Jews, Catholics, or "religious man.") In affirming salvation sola fide but abandoning its conventional argumentative and biographical vestibule, not to mention failing to supply a cogent alternative, Watson has sawn off the branch on which he is sitting (and this is a recurrent problem for revisionists).[52] So Watson's program fails to deliver a convincing account of the motif that lies at the heart of that program — salvation sola fide. Moreover, he is caught up at this point in an acute problem of self-referential incoherence.[53]

Abraham, construed in terms of righteousness by faith, is a key figure in Watson's program. But as Watson describes Abraham's faith, and as the text of Genesis itself describes it, this normative moment of salvation did not derive in the fashion that Watson constantly asserts is the true basis for all such understanding — the reading of the Pentateuch. Abraham did not read the Scriptures and learn the truth about God. So the paradigmatic example of salvation and the program for salvation generally endorsed by Watson do not concur. Although we read about Abraham's salvation, we read that Abraham did *not* get saved by reading; God appeared and spoke to him directly. (Watson really needs a scriptural example of a sage at this point — a figure and moment more like Luther.) Insofar as Abraham attests authoritatively to Paul's underlying system, then, he attests to the wrong thing; insofar as that system remains in place, it finds no authorization in Abraham.[54]

(7) The Implications for Biography and Conversion

We have just noted that Watson has abandoned the conventional reliance on a particular biography of Paul along with its rather rationalistic model of conversion, and he clearly realizes a number of advantages in doing so. But it ought to be appreciated that by doing this Watson has substituted an alternative biography and mode of conversion for that problematic account. He has displaced the conventional journey from attempted law observance to faith with a hermeneutical voyage of discovery. Paul — and presumably other Christians as well — learns who God is and what he wants by reading the Pentateuch. Hence, as he grasps the correct readings, working through those five books in turn, he essentially becomes a Christian as against a Jew (although a Jewish Christian, because such reading is a central if not defining element of Judaism). And ultimately this suggestion seems absurd.

On the one hand, there is now nothing preventing Paul from discovering everything essential about his gospel *while he is still a Jew* (that is, *before* he encounters Christ on the Damascus road). Theoretically, Paul could have undertaken Watson's reading of the Pentateuch while he was persecuting Christians in Jerusalem! (Perhaps they were reading the Pentateuch incorrectly.)[55] On the other hand, we should see that Paul's biography did undergo major shifts, even if the precise details of those are not always apparent — from persecutor to apostle on the Damascus road, and from preacher of a law-observant gospel to preacher of a law-free gospel three years later in Antioch (as Watson well knows!). And these do not seem to have been generated hermeneutically. There is no extant evidence for this, and it simply seems implausible.[56] ("Revelation" seems a more likely candidate.)[57]

(8) Transpositions

We noted earlier on that Watson seems to sidestep neatly the empirical conundrum that Justification theory faces in relation to Judaism. Paul's descriptive jaundice and contradictions are relocated into the Pentateuch itself (and this act of relocation then further affirms Paul's integrity as a reader). But how effective is this crafty solution? In fact — and as we might have expected — it relocates but does not actually resolve our difficulties, while some are further exacerbated.

To draw an account about the nature of Israel in the wilderness from the Scriptures is in fact still to endorse that account as normative in Paul's day. (Either this, or Paul holds another account to be valid, but Watson does not introduce any such supplementary account; rather, he repeatedly affirms the normativity of the Pentateuch.) Hence, the empirical conundrum that many contemporary Jews did not describe Judaism in the fashion that Paul does seems to remain. That he did not *originate* that account does not entail that he does not *endorse* it; he must still be held accountable for its contradictions and difficulties. Moreover, although Paul no longer needs to accuse Jews of being irrational and/or obstinate legalists, he does still need to accuse them of being irrational or obstinate *readers*. So Watson's reformulation has not completely escaped the post-Holocaust strictures. Presumably, such recalcitrant readers can eventually be punished (etc.).[58]

Watson also retains the acute argumentative tension between the divine expectation that non-Christians fulfill some soteriological arrangement and the fact that their deeply sinful nature seems to render this impossible. (He eliminates most other internal argumentative tensions because he eliminates the argument!) This is both a contradictory anthropology and an apparent contradiction of God's justice. In Watson's reoriented system, such tensions are transposed to Israel and into the Pentateuch. However, this transposition does not alter the basic problem. God's treatment of Israel, in offering a conditional arrangement that they, being sinful, could not possibly fulfill (and then punishing them horribly), retains its contradictory and unjust qualities. Indeed, if anything, these seem strengthened, because they are written into the hermeneutical foundations of the faith (at which point one wonders how much progress has really been made).

(9) Various Epistemological Conundrums

We come now to an especially acute set of tensions. Watson's program contains a series of nasty epistemological conundrums.

In arguing for Paul's independent reading of the Pentateuch, Watson is necessarily committed to the claim that Paul is an a priori theologian, and hence fundamentally foundationalist. Such programs assert that a prior phase of understanding underlies and grounds the Christian gospel (as its "foundation"). They are committed to (i) the prior establishment of certain criteria of truth; (ii) the articulation of a specific case in terms of those criteria that is more successful than any alternatives *and* leads eventually to Christianity; and (iii) the prosecution of this case without recourse *to* Christianity.[59] Watson is not overly forthcoming on these issues, but he needs to be. The prior criteria that he urges for Paul are of course responsible readings of the Pentateuch. Watson is clear that the truth of Paul's gospel depends simply on his accurate construal of the Pentateuch, and only in this way, he asserts, can the Pentateuch witness to the Christ event. But we are now faced with several acute conundrums.

We should note first that Paul's reading, in order to be true, actually needs to be the best possible reading, which means that Watson must articulate the hermeneutical criteria that allow us (or Paul's fellow Jews) to evaluate his exegesis. But Watson is ambivalent about this question. He clearly holds that Paul's exegesis has integrity in the face of modern critics' charges, but he does not privilege Paul's readings over alternative construals by some of his Jewish contemporaries.[60] And this is quite extraordinary. If Paul's reading of the Pentateuch is not demonstrably superior to that of his fellow Jews, then the witness of the Scriptures to the Christ event is ambiguous and we have no way of knowing if it is true! Watson leaves us wondering whether Paul is actually right. When it comes to the critical point of assessment in relation to the Christ event, it is a toss-up between Paul and Philo! Hence — if Christianity is in fact to be true in terms of this foundation — Watson needs to articulate the criteria that allow the right decision here *and* show how Paul exercises those criteria, however embarrassing that demonstration might prove to be.

However, maybe he does this. We would doubtless be right to suspect that it is precisely Paul's reading of the Pentateuch in a canonically sensitive fashion that constitutes a "good" reading and that can thereby function responsibly as a witness to the Christ event. And Watson, if pressed, might well admit that he holds Paul's reading to be superior to those of his contemporaries. (If he does not, then the consequences are very dire.) But some further problems occur at this point.[61]

Watson is on uncertain ground in simply making this assertion. It could be denied that a canonical *and pentateuchal* hermeneutic *is* obviously foundational. (Why have the rest of the Scriptures been excluded?) Perhaps more importantly, even granting such a hermeneutic, it is difficult to see how it could ultimately attest to the Christ event in any case, which lies, Watson asserts, beyond its textual horizon. Those locked within the world of the text and reading it responsibly — that is, respecting the purview of its canonical authors — will almost certainly fail to recognize Christ as the arrival of God's definitive salvation, not to mention as God incarnate, *as the majority of Paul's Jewish contemporaries seem to have done.* Indeed, Watson's own parallel readings endorse this possibility! The basic problem here is that the text does not supply any information that would allow the recognition of this event, precisely because it is being read independently of it.[62] Hence, in pursuing a ruthlessly nonchristological and prior hermeneutic of the Pentateuch as an independent epistemological moment, Watson has in effect *eliminated the possibility of any attestation to the Christ event and to Christianity on both descriptive and epistemological grounds.* He cannot build on his foundation and reach Christ.[63] Thus, we end up — again — with an incoherent Paul.[64]

(10) The Case in Romans 1–4

Watson is more conscious than most of the difficulties posed for him by Romans 1–4, although his sustained treatment of this text is inaccessible.[65] However, it is perceptive and useful; in particular, Watson is sensitive here to the difficulties generated by the conventional reading (although he enumerates six, not fifty-six!). But his attempts to reread this text in terms of his particular hermeneutical reconstruction of Paul's basic program or, where this proves impossible, to marginalize it, are in my view unconvincing. He fails to resolve some of the problems that he begins by noting.[66] He tends to rely on causal assertions about Paul's argument and citation that rely in turn on concrete demonstrations elsewhere in Paul that we have already seen to be problematic. (That is, he presupposes the truth of his hermeneutical account of Paul, but this should not be conceded.) And — perhaps even more problematically — he is unable to explain the many features of Romans 1–4 that directly embarrass his program.[67] All these shortcomings leave this critical stretch of text in the hands of either conventional Justification advocates or their christological opponents, from which point it will be relatively easy to reassert its concerns over against Watson's program and the delicate signals of Galatians 3. It would seem, then, that the old citadel remains a critical tactical objective, and Watson has failed to capture it!

The difficulties of overthrowing the conventional reading and its associated theory of Justification, resolving all its problems in the process, are perhaps never more apparent than in Watson's treatment of Paul. In my view, the most creative, powerful, and successful reconstrual currently on offer, it nevertheless ultimately founders at numerous points. We might say that *Paul and the Hermeneutics of Faith* glimpses the new dawn but does not bring it, at which point one wonders if its arrival is even possible. But we should not despair before we at least consider some of the other strategies that are currently on offer. A proposal sharing the creativity and courage of Watson's, but addressing its shortcomings, may yet bring the new day.

2.2. *Editorial Reframing*

One interpretative trajectory of scholars has tried to explain some of the difficulties caused by the conventional reading of Romans 1–4 — whether in whole or in part — with a variation on the reframing strategy. It suggests that the key texts were originally more fragmentary and have only subsequently been combined into their present canonical form. And certainly such arguments can call on a long tradition of analysis of biblical texts that breaks them down into antecedent textual units. These explanations can run in different variations. Non-Pauline material might have been interpolated into Pauline texts at certain points, perhaps explaining especially acute contradictions.[68] Or antecedent Pauline texts written to deal with different situations might have been edited together into one composite, and hence also rather uneven, canonical letter. (Both these explanations can be present simultaneously.) But, while highlighting certain important facets within the evidence, this approach is even weaker than its immediate predecessor as a general explanation of our difficulties. Specifically:

(1) An important caveat on the editorial approach is introduced by our preceding analysis, namely, that the difficulties generated by the texts with which

we are currently concerned are coterminous with their ultimate endorsement of Justification theory. Hence, in the first instance, our difficulties
arise from the conventional construal of Romans 1:16–4:25. A successful editorial strategy would need decisive evidence from the textual tradition of
the appropriate seams — that is, breaks not within but at the borders of this
text — and this is not forthcoming (while the situation is even more difficult for the theory in Galatians).

(2) Moreover, in its interpolative variation, this strategy would need to craft
some plausible explanation of the non-Pauline provenance of all of Paul's
Justification texts, something even the discourse's critics would recognize
as absurd; consider a version of Romans that ran 1:1-15; 5:1–9:29; 11:1–16:27
(or thereabouts), attributing 1:16–4:25 and 9:30–10:21 to a non-Pauline
hand! It would not even really make sense (notably, in chapters 9–11).
Hence, this approach actually relies in part on a false delimitation of the
problem. Once the correct parameters of the difficulties generated by Justification theory and its associated construal are grasped, then the plausibility of any non-Pauline explanation tends to evaporate.[69]

(3) In the strategy's composite variation — that is, if the suggested antecedent
texts were assumed to be Pauline — some explanatory difficulties in the
foregoing could be ameliorated, notably, the non-Pauline provenance of
some of Paul's most characteristic terms and arguments. But the basic strategy's key advantages would also thereby be lost. All the contradictions and
tensions generated by the conventional construal would now remain. This
is because it really does not matter if the difficulties generated by Justification theory are produced by several antecedent letters now smoothed into
one or by one letter; the basic intrinsic, systematic, empirical, and
exegetical problems remain, *irrespective of their origin*. (And, in fact, they
are still currently produced by several different letters, namely, subsections
in Romans, Galatians, and Philippians — at which point we might ask why
these have not been smoothed together as well.) Hence, this explanation
solves none of our major difficulties.[70] They are merely narratively nuanced
(and so perhaps a semblance of a solution is created).

In summation of this section as a whole, it seems clear that reframing strategies in either of their two main variations — generative or editorial — are implausible as a comprehensive response to the problems generated by the conventional construal and its associated theory of Justification. Most importantly, they
tend to leave all those problems intact, courting their own additional weaknesses
in the process, and possessing few or none of the conventional construal's
strengths. Hence, in my view such strategies have rightly been judged ineffective
in the past by the discourse's advocates and rejected, and revisionists would be
best to abandon them as well as a global or complete explanation.

However, they might still play a more limited role within a broader solution
argued on different grounds, or in response to other problems in the interpreta-

tion of Romans, alerting interpreters especially to the presence of overt "seams" in Paul's texts and arguments; such observations might provide leverage for alternative readings and so will be assessed in due course. These strategies also serve to demonstrate, in their psychological variant, that the account of the relevant texts' frames offered by Justification advocates is not incontrovertible. If that explanatory locus is too fragile and indecisive to offer decisive revisionist purchase, it can certainly be called into question in the Justification discourse as well. Moreover, new explanations at this point can create an imaginative space within which revisionists can consider new readings — a psychological and rhetorical contribution to the solution of our difficulties rather than a comprehensive methodological one, which may nevertheless ultimately prove useful.

It seems then, in short, that reframing could prove to be a useful supplementary strategy but is too weak and indirect to be decisive in its own right. If some central resolution to our difficulties is to be found, it seems likely that at some point the Justification advocate's *reading* of the key texts will have to be challenged directly. A countervailing construal will have to be offered in relation to the data within the textual base — although it might be supplemented by a degree of reframing. So we turn now to consider those who have undertaken such challenges, although pausing en route to consider in more detail one of the most important revisionists — E. P. Sanders.

Excursus: E. P. Sanders's *Paul and Palestinian Judaism* and *Paul, the Law, and the Jewish People*

E. P. Sanders is perhaps the most perceptive critic of the difficulties caused for Paul's overarching description by the Justification discourse (although of course he does not phrase or frame things in these terms). But it remains to be seen whether the difficulties that he has isolated can be resolved by his own two key works on the subject — *Paul and Palestinian Judaism* (1977), and *Paul, the Law, and the Jewish People* (1983) (hereafter *P&PJ* and *PL&JP*).

Excursus §1: Sanders's Position

Sanders's solution, like those of many other brilliant revisionists, features a combination of strategies. But we address it at this point in the chapter because at a key moment it features an editorial suggestion. The following short summary will struggle to do justice to Sanders's sophisticated and complex account.

We should begin our more detailed description by recalling Sanders's analysis of much of the problem, which is largely unparalleled in depth. His is of course *the* name associated with the Jewish empirical conundrum (his concerns in this relation being considered carefully in part one, chapter four, where I argued that — suitably reformulated — they remain valid). But in *P&PJ* he also revivifies Schweitzer's criticisms that tend to function in terms of apocalyptic and participation (see 431-523), and so more at the systematic and proximate frames (reprised here esp. in part one, chapters three and six). That is, he articulates clearly the two distinguishable discourses in Paul of "participationist eschatology" and "righteousness by faith" (hereafter in this excursus PE and RF).[71] He then argues for the primacy of the former, *and* for *its retrospective structure*. When thinking in terms of participation and/or eschatology, Sanders argues, Paul "thinks backwards."[72] So, although eschewing all talk of "system," Sanders argues that the starting point for Paul's theology was christological,[73] whence the apostle derived his understanding of humanity's plight, the law, Judaism, and so on.[74] But this insightful treatment nevertheless leaves several important questions unanswered. So in *PL&JP* Sanders considers Paul's relationships with the law and with the Jewish people more directly (the discussion of the former being rather longer and concerning us more here[75]).

PL&JP employs multiple strategies as it navigates through the difficult question of Paul and the law. But principally it organizes the data in terms of the theory that different questions prompt diverse responses from the apostle. And Sanders has three principal questions in mind: (1) when Paul thinks of salvation, he argues that only faith is an entrance requirement over against works of law; (2) when he thinks of the law in relation to the purposes of God — as a good Jew ought to — he links it with sin (and in various specific ways); and (3) when he thinks of Christian ethics, he urges law-observance.[76]

Sanders finds Paul's reasoning in relation to each of these issues "coherent," although he discerns no overarching system, which might coordinate them all coherently (i.e., "systematically" or "logically"): "the different things which Paul said about the law depend on the question asked or the problem posed. Each answer has its own logic and springs from one of his central concerns; but the diverse answers, when set alongside one another, do not form a logical whole . . ." (4).[77] However, Sanders does not merely reorganize the data in this fashion. He suggests that the argument has often been misconstrued in each of these relations, and at this point an emphasis on retrospective thinking reemerges in various rereadings of Galatians 2–3, Romans 3:27–4:25, and 9:30–10:13 (*PL&JP*, 17-43).[78] Paul's thinking and arguing in these texts is consistently backward, not forward, Sanders suggests. (And he also utilizes Stendahl's account of the circumstantial frame in relation to issue one: when "faith" is opposed to "works of law" Paul is debating the entrance of pagans into the people of God, and nothing else.)

The relationship between the suggestions of *P&PJ* and *PL&JP* is not immediately apparent, and Sanders does not coordinate the two discussions in detail. However, it seems fair to suggest that the "righteousness by faith" discourse that Sanders articulates in *P&PJ* in a secondary position occurs in *PL&JP* largely in relation to issue one — how pagans become members of the people of God (and the one important textual exception to this correlation will be noted momentarily). The texts and concepts informing participationist eschatology tend to occur in Sanders's discussions of issues two and three (the purpose of the law and ethics). There are, however, no neat dividing lines. (I am assuming that Sanders's initial emphasis on the distinction between "getting in" and "staying in" in *PL&JP*, 4-10, corresponds largely to issues one and three, so it is fair to suggest that the terminology associated with righteousness by faith spills over occasionally into participatory texts and concerns, and vice versa.)

"Getting In"		"Staying In"
Issue One: Entrance	Issue Two: Law	Issue Three: Ethics
RF language predominant	(Some RF words)	(Some RF words)
(Some PE words)	PE language predominant	(Some PE words)

One further component in the argument of *PL&JP* must now be noted carefully. Sanders suggests on 123-35 that Romans 1:18–2:29 is "a synagogue sermon . . . , slashing and exaggerated, as many sermons are, . . . [with] no distinctively Pauline imprint . . . , [although] even if Paul did not compose the passage . . . , he did incorporate it" (129, 131). Thus he does not endorse an interpolative strategy per se at this critical point, but he does propose a synthesis of the preceding two reframing strategies — *Paul's* editorial inclusion in Romans 1–2 of material that he did not compose! And he provides several powerful arguments in support of this claim — principally, ODs 6, 9, and 10 (with a variation on 11). This suggestion serves to remove Romans 2 (as he calls it) from his broader description of Paul's thinking about the law in a more decisive way.

Excursus §2: Sanders's Strategic Advances

We have already noted two especially significant insights within Sanders's broad definition of "the problem" — the issue of fair Jewish description, and the phenomenon of disparate competing discourses within Paul. I suggest here that *P&PJ* and *PL&JP* make six more important contributions to our growing understanding of any effective solution to these difficulties.

(1) The Advantages of a Retrospective Dynamic

Sanders is well aware of how a retrospective dynamic in Paul's thinking — i.e., that he thought backward — eases the empirical conundrum with respect to Judaism. Given this dynamic, any of Paul's negative formulations regarding Jewish practices can be understood in terms of his own prior, distinctive, and overriding convictions, as a reflex of those convictions, and hence as views that non-Christian Jews would not be expected to share. Descriptions of Judaism by Paul and by Jews would then *necessarily* and *understandably* be different, and neither would Paul's negativity be absolute (i.e., "objective" and "universally accessible"; it would be a principally *relative* judgment). This mitigation of the Jewish question does not exhaust the theological advantages of a retrospective approach, but it is the key issue for Sanders.[79] It is a seminal insight.

(2) The Primacy of Participationist Eschatology

Sanders repeatedly establishes the dominance of participationist thinking through Paul over against "righteousness by faith," thereby sharpening the systematic and proximate tensions already noted here in part one, chapters three and six.[80] But this extension also implies that any reconstrual of Paul's Justification texts in terms of participationism will integrate smoothly at the systematic and proximate frames.

(3) Rereading the Relevant Texts

Where Justification advocates tend to find a progression between two states in many of Paul's Justification texts, from "works" to "faith," Sanders is sensitive to the possibilities that a directly antithetical argument is in fact being made, the Christian gospel *overruling* the opposing state and its Jewish markers — usually "works." (One of his favorite texts is Gal. 2:21b, which he suggests clearly implies a retrospective argument on Paul's part: ". . . if justification comes through the law, then Christ died for nothing.") So possible if not more likely construals work backward, not forward, thereby eliminating the Jewish empirical conundrum (and any analogous difficulties) from these texts.[81]

(4) Variations

Sanders unsettles the conventional interpretation by noting the shifts in meaning and rhetoric that can take place in relation to Paul's δικαιο- and πιστ- language and argumentation — observations pertinent to Romans 3:27–4:25, as well as to the secondary Justification texts. In Romans 3–4 he also detects argumentative problems — in our parlance, overdeterminations (and the relevant ones for the citadel have already largely been noted — see esp. ODs 14-16, 20-21, and 23).[82]

(5) Intertextuality

Sanders points to the critical role that various key biblical texts play in Paul's Justification arguments. Responsible accounts of their meaning, interrelationships, and argumentative roles, are a necessary part of any plausible account of the text as a whole. (This is especially apparent in his analysis of Galatians 2–3, but the observation holds for Romans 1–4, where most of the key intertexts recur: see *PL&JP*, 17-27, 32-36.)

(6) The Awkwardness of Romans 1–3

Most importantly, Sanders points to the anomalous nature of Romans 1:18–2:29 when it is viewed against the rest of Paul's thought — to its strange argumentation (given a conventional construal), puzzling lack of Christology, and so on. This discussion has the multiple virtues of demonstrating how difficult this text is for any reading, how central it is (nevertheless) to the conventional reading of Paul, and how critical its theoretical marginalization will be for any effective solution.

These are significant insights — so much so that any effective solution to our difficulties will bear their marks overtly; it is likely to be, more than anything else, a neo-Sanders construct. However, the conversation did not halt with Sanders, in part because his position seems to contain evident weaknesses as well as insights and advances.

Excursus §3: Sanders's Problems

We are interested here primarily in issues that affect Romans 1–4, the textual citadel that establishes and defends Justification theory, and consequently in the four following sets of concerns:[83]

(1) The alternative account of "faith" supplied largely by *PL&JP* strains coherence (at a *fundamental* level), and seems vulnerable to a Justification counterattack.

In the first instance, we should note that it doesn't really make sense. Sanders insists that faith is the appropriate criterion for membership in the (Christian) people of God, and not works undertaken in the light of the Jewish law. He contends that this makes Christian salvation universal in the sense that it is now clearly not dependent on Judaism, or on the people established by election. In so doing, he also insists that Paul's argument does not therefore progress from the inherent inadequacy of works to the notion of salvation through faith alone, so no external, objective critique of Jewish works is actually present. It is just that membership in Christianity is by faith.

But Sanders has arguably made a classic mistake at this point (and it recurs in the work of other revisionists: see especially the analysis of Dunn just below in §3.1). He has eliminated the conventional logic *for* the plausibility of a notion of salvation through faith alone, by eliminating the prior critique of works, and supplied an alternative rationale that is itself incoherent, and on several counts.

The need for salvation by faith alone makes sense if salvation through numerous works has just been attempted but failed. However, if the criterion of sola fide is stripped of this preamble, then it has no obvious validity. Simply nominating faith as the key principle for salvation is groundless and arbitrary — and especially when viewed against Jewish tradition (see Jas. 2:14-26!). That such faith is "universal" over against the "particularity" of Judaism is, moreover, a claim that Sanders himself denies at times, and correctly, despite appealing to it at other points in support of this emphasis.[84]

The Christianity that evolves from "faith" is quite particular, and the Judaism that does the law is sufficiently universal. (And the monotheism endorsed by Judaism is often held to imply universality quite directly.[85]) "Faith" is at bottom no more or less particular than "works."[86] In any case, the obvious response to any lack of universality on the part of law-observant Judaism is to encourage openness to converts, *not to change the criterion of entry to something else.* In addition, to suggest this change of criterion is to violate the principle of election that lies at the heart of Judaism and its Old Testament antecedents — to suppose that God has bumbled badly in salvation-historical terms. (We revisit these conundrums in more detail when discussing Dunn, who emphasizes this response more than Sanders.) In short, Sanders's alternative rationale at this point is problematic. And, given the weakness of his account of faith, Sanders's broader position is now vulnerable to an obvious countermove by Justification advocates.

They can supply an obvious and reasonably coherent explanation of salvation through faith alone by reintroducing "works of law" as the preliminary phase to that condition. Indeed, Sanders's continued commitment to the saving criterion of faith *invites* this supply (as it invites an ongoing conditional and contractual approach to salvation). And that reintroduction will only be strengthened by his own affirmation of Paul's desire to establish "equality" between Jew and pagan prior to salvation — an argument that works "forward." Sanders does not tell us how Paul achieves this argumentative goal, but it is one of Justification's strengths. (We also gain little idea from Sanders concerning how salvation through belief in Christ devolves ultimately into participationist eschatology, but see more on this just below.)

For all these reasons then, it seems that the alternative account of faith supplied in *PL&JP* founders. It is incoherent, and thereby opens the door to all sorts of awkward implications and reintroductions. If any solution to our difficulties is ultimately to be found by way of a plausible rereading, then a superior account of Paul's πιστ- language will have to be formulated.[87]

(2) The editorial marginalization of Romans 2, although understandable, is not plausible. In fact, we face a nasty explanatory dilemma at this point.

Sanders's explanation assumes a careless and even stupid integration, with arguments failing to match up with one another; the strange charges and arguments in Romans 2 must have slipped past Paul's editorial purview — and herein lie both their explanation and interpretive irrelevance. However, the rest of the letter is *extremely* well crafted. If Paul has integrated this material into Romans, then he has probably done so carefully and taken full responsibility for it. *But at this point the force of Sanders's explanation dissipates:* these arguments are present because Paul has introduced them into his text quite deliberately. In short, if it is not a stupid integration, the editorial suggestion is irrelevant; if it is stupid, then it is an implausible hypothesis.

We should note further that such an introduction does not explain all the argumentative problems in any case — note, e.g., the logical tangle of OD 11, which is as awkward in a synagogue sermon as it is here in Paul's discourse (and see also ODs 2, 3, and 7, which were not noted by Sanders). For these reasons, Sanders's proposal has not been widely endorsed. Nevertheless, it remains a fascinating suggestion, and for various reasons.

Sanders has felt the contradictions generated by Romans 1:18–2:29 deeply, and also noted the bizarre textual moments that occur in its conventional construal, along with the generally inadequate explanations of those. He has intuited that this text must somehow be eliminated from Paul's own theorizing — especially as that is apparent in other texts — *and* that it is actually pushing in a different argumentative direction from the function of universal indictment suggested by the conventional reading; it is seeking to catch a more limited prey, and functions well when it is reoriented in this way. But he has not of course supplied us with a plausible rereading that can deliver these intuitions. Instead, Romans 2 remains another vulnerability in his system. Conventionally read, it will simply reintroduce the worst features of the system that he is trying to displace — an a priori engagement with perfectionist legalism (from which point it could influence the interpretation of similar but ambiguous texts elsewhere, and also even justify coordinating issues one and two within Sanders's schema). Hence, we need some alternative approach to Romans 2 that achieves Sanders's overarching goals of reorientation and theoretical marginalization.

(3) Some further problems are also detectable in the overarching explanatory framework developed by *PL&JP* — that Paul's views concerning the law are coherently comprehended by the theory that he responds to different questions with different answers. The theory develops first in terms of the distinction made famous by *P&PJ* between "getting in" and "staying in." "Getting in" should correspond to issue one, concerning entrance requirements (*PL&JP*, 17-64), and "staying in" to issue three, concerning ethics (*PL&JP*, 93-122). But it is possible to discern within this schema the traditional distinction between justification and sanctification functioning in terms of new characterizations: individuals get saved through justification, thereby "getting in," or entering the people of God, and go on to live as Christians in terms of sanctification, thereby "staying in," and behaving ethically. Hence, in effect this schema just *renames* the systematic tensions that exist in Paul between his two primary soteriological discourses, which we already know well, *without resolving their fundamental contradictions* (and these also cause proximate tensions in Romans). Consequently, it is unlikely that analysis has moved forward very far. Renaming difficulties does not resolve them. But some further difficulties are also implicit here.

This schema affirms contractual categories at the heart of Paul's conceptualities as well, in relation to issue one, or questions of "entrance" and "membership." According to *P&PJ*, Jews in the late Second Temple period accounted for getting in through election — that is, through God's generous action establishing a covenant with Israel, which Sanders often speaks of in terms of "grace." Staying in was then a more anthropocentric and responsive activity informed by the law (which had just been given in the act of election). Paul, however, according to *PL&JP* in particular, expects his pagan converts to get in by faith, and then stay in through law-observance and the avoidance of heinous sins.[88] Consequently, *both* facets in the new Christian soteriological schema are anthropocentric, and conditionalism and contractualism are thereby unleashed at every point. And we have already seen at some length how negative the theological consequences of this can be, not to mention how the door will be opened again to Justification advocates, who are merely a contractual variant. Their rigorous exclusion will seem puzzling. (Acute tensions will also now be generated with Paul's alternative participationist discourse, if that is unconditional.) In short, Sanders's solution, with part of Justification theory mobilized in relation to the question of entrance by the affirmation of saving faith, intrinsically and permanently affirms the presence of conditional and contractual thinking in Paul's thought and thereby irreducibly disorders it (the lessons of part one, chapters two and three).

The actual coherence of this explanation of Paul must also be carefully considered. It is a coherent overarching explanation of Paul's thought, but not in substantive terms. *PL&JP* provides a coherent explanation of Paul's material in conceptual and psychological terms only (i.e., essentially in terms of generative reframing[89]); it can only endorse localized substantive coherences. Hence, the notion of "coherence" does double duty. But its overarching use cannot disguise the *lack* of coherence now operating at the substantive level, where Paul is still contradictory on various key questions. Different questions prompt different answers appropriately *when they concern different issues*, but different questions in relation to the same basic field of inquiry should prompt integrated answers! So it is as if Paul, according to *PL&JP*, is using Ptolemaic astronomy to account for the movement of the sun, and Copernican geometry to account for the movement of the moon. He is really deeply confused! And consequently (again) *PL&JP* has not resolved our difficulties. At the end of the day, the schema suggested by *PL&JP accepts* Paul's fundamental substantive incoherence and tries to come up with a plausible explanation *of* that incoherence, partly through appeals to generative reframing and partly by renaming it. As a result, it also remains vulnerable to a superior explanation if that can be offered by Justification advocates. And it must remain open to alternative readings that can generate a higher degree of coherence between the two main discourses in Paul and the different key questions. That is, we can still ask whether Paul was capable of coordinating his key convictions, having perceived their inherent tensions in relation to different — but related — questions, and if *we*, his later interpreters, are the problem, having misinterpreted his terminologies and arguments at certain critical points.

Indeed, at this point Sanders himself provides grounds for hope — although arguably in somewhat contradictory terms. Both *P&PJ* and *PL&JP* suggest that the terminologies that characterize the two main discourses in Paul cross over in relation to the key questions,[90] even though *PL&JP* goes on to insist that Paul's conceptual responses to these questions are tightly compartmentalized. But the terminological distribution might suggest not so much that Paul is separating his responses as that he is weaving together *complementary* discourses that respond to all these questions at different times with different emphases.[91] Certainly, if the same terminology is responding to the same questions, then prima facie it seems possible that the same answer is also being given (or, at least, an answer couched in the same basic terms)! Hence, complementary rather than contradictory interpretations are a legitimate option.

(4) One of Sanders's most important insights — that Paul reasons retrospectively — seems at cross-purposes with his schema coordinating different answers with different questions, although encouraging of alternative, more coherent explanations. If the trenchant demonstrations through *P&PJ* that Paul thinks backward are valid, then the apostle reasons from solution to plight. But the entire coherence of the later explanation of Paul's conceptuality in relation to questions of law and Judaism adumbrated principally in *PL&JP* depends on the apostle supplying different answers to different questions, so the thrust of this conceptuality is *from problem to solution* — in the opposite direction! — and this seems to be a major difficulty with the entire proposal. This is exacerbated by many of the ingenious rereadings in *PL&JP* that argue for retrospective localized arguments as well. To be sure, Sanders is at least partly aware of this difficulty, and he endeavors at times to show that Paul began with his solution, and then sometimes formulated prospective arguments.[92] But this is an extremely difficult hypothesis to sustain; the key contention must fly in the face of the thrust of the text, and is located itself in an uncertain domain (i.e., Paul's underlying rea-

soning and intentions). At the least, then, extensive arguments in favor of retrospectivism in both *P&PJ* and *PL&JP* raise the possibility that Paul basically thought everywhere in retrospective terms — in relation to all major questions. And if this proved to be the case, it would affirm a major element in Sanders's case, but necessarily override another. It seems that *Sanders* has given different answers to different (but related) questions!

Several other concerns could be mentioned,[93] but these should suffice for now to indicate that the solution anticipated by *P&PJ* and elaborated by *PL&JP* has flaws, and it must be set to one side while we explore alternatives. Indeed, it actually reifies our problems in a state of fundamental contradiction, so it should be accepted only as an explanation of last resort. However, although Sanders's theories in this relation are not finally satisfactory, they are both brilliant and prescient. He anticipates much of the solution that I will eventually propose here through parts four and five — a consistent *exegetical* demonstration through Paul's Justification texts of a *retrospective epistemological viewpoint* that then links up with his *participationist* discourse and language. Moreover, this exegesis must somehow make sense of Paul's intertextuality, discussions of "faith," and apparently prospective argumentation in Romans 1:18–3:20 (from which point the rereading of related texts outside Romans 1–4 should also be easier). These last features of Romans 1–4 can now be seen, especially in the light of Sanders's work, to be critical explanatory loci — strong points in Justification's textual citadel. Sanders never quite managed to wrest them away from the control of the Justification discourse, *P&PJ* and *PL&JP* affirming that discourse in certain important ways. But he certainly intuited that this was what needed to happen.

3. Rereading

The second main revisionist approach contains important internal variations like the first, but more by way of a spectrum than two clearly contrasting types. This is a spectrum of *reconstrual*, ranging from the reinterpretation of small units in the text to more comprehensive reinterpretations of the entire argument of Romans 1–4, or at least of significant sections within it (and beyond). Interpreters tend to cluster at the ends of the spectrum; hence, our analysis can safely proceed in terms of two general categories: more moderate rereadings of *motifs*, that is, small semantic units consisting of mere words or phrases; and more ambitious, *comprehensive* rereadings of large passages, if not the entire text in question (i.e., Romans 1–4). Each of these related but distinguishable strategies possesses peculiar strengths and weaknesses.

3.1. Motif Rereadings

Motif rereadings, as their name suggests, challenge the conventional construal of small semantic units within the text in the hope that reorientations of these motifs will resolve the main difficulties in Paul's conventional construal. The most important such proposals have focused on key and/or repeated motifs rather than peripheral material, because the former clearly have more leverage on the text to shift its interpretation.

Ernst Käsemann is a relatively early exemplar of this strategy, suggesting a new approach to the phrase δικαιοσύνη Θεοῦ (see Rom. 1:17; 3:5; 3:21, 22, 25, 26; 10:3). He was not the first to do so but has been a dominant figure in this relation. (He also stands as the high-water mark of German revisionism in such terms; the main subsequent revisionist proposals have come from the U.K. and North America.) We have already noted, in part one, chapter six, the concerns that led to Käsemann's passionate "apocalyptic" redefinitions on this front: δικαιοσύνη Θεοῦ is to be thought of as a power as much as a gift, which consequently lays a claim upon the cosmos and upon the church (and we will return to consider this proposal more carefully in part four, chapter seventeen). As such, the phrase is a subjective, more than an objective, genitive — although, as an act of God, it tends to break out of such categories. It denotes, as Romans 1:16 suggests, "God's saving power." Käsemann uses this meaning to press an "apocalyptic" interpretation of Romans through the rest of his commentary; the phrase is consequently the thin end of a thematic wedge that he drives through the rest of the letter.

More recently — that is, since the Sanders watershed within Pauline studies — much attention has been paid to the phrase ἔργα νόμου (see Rom. 3:20, 28; for "works" alone, see 2:6, 7, 15; 3:27; 4:2, 6; for "law," see 2:12, 13, 14, 15, 17, 18, 20, 23, 25, 26, 27; 3:19, 20, 21, 27, 28, 31; 4:13, 14, 15, 16). The names of J. D. G. Dunn and N. T. Wright are associated especially with the main revisionist approach to this phrase (as is the "new perspective," an interpretative trajectory already noted in chapter six).[94] Various nuanced differences notwithstanding, both these scholars basically view the phrase and its associated argument in sociological rather than strictly rationalist and soteriological terms. They suggest that it denotes a certain attitude toward the "boundary markers" of the Jewish covenant that were reified for Judaism especially by the exile and (or) the Maccabean crisis — dietary and temporal observances and the rite of circumcision (so a connection with soteriology is still apparent, but a historical, collective one). As such boundary markers, these practices function also as "badges" of covenant membership that distinguish the people of God from the surrounding pagan nations.

These scholars have proposed a concomitant reorientation of the meaning of δικαιοσύνη Θεοῦ. While not necessarily departing significantly from Käsemann's subjective and salvific emphases, Dunn, Wright, and those persuaded by them (also leaning here on earlier German work[95]), have layered God's saving action in this phrase with connotations of divine fidelity to the covenant. So, for example, the statements of Romans 3:3 and 3:5 are viewed as parallel substantively as well as argumentatively; God's "righteousness" and "faithfulness" are almost identical attributes and correlative actions, and both, moreover, are informed fundamentally by God's covenant with Israel. God's saving act in Christ is therefore to be understood primarily as an act of covenant faithfulness and restoration, and clearly this redefinition correlates with some of the covenantal connotations now asserted for the meaning of ἔργα νόμου as well.

A fierce debate is ongoing over the third main element within Paul's Justification arguments as well — his use of πίστις — although this debate tends to focus specifically on the word's presence in particular genitive combinations with Christ (Rom. 3:22, 26; for "faith" alone, 1:17 [3x]; 3:3, 25, 27, 28, 30 [2x], 31; 4:5, 9, 11, 12, 13, 14, 16 [2x], 19, 20; for such genitive constructions elsewhere, Gal. 2:16 [2x], 20; 3:22, possibly v. 26, if 𝔓⁴⁶ is followed; Phil. 3:9; see Eph. 3:12 and 4:13). Richard B. Hays is the most well known proponent of this view (although the view was discussed in Germany approximately one hundred years ago; however, it has not proved popular on the Continent since its rejection then). Hays and others suggest that Romans 3:22 and 26 should be construed in subjective, not objective, terms, generating the sense "the faithfulness *of* Christ" rather than any notion of "belief . . ." or "trust *in* Christ." Clearly, while this does not produce a widespread reorientation within Romans 1–4 (because it shifts meaning directly within only two phrases or so), it does reinterpret a key motif within the conventional construal and Justification theory — the definition of its saving criterion as it is spoken of by the letter's second, slightly longer thesis paragraph (3:21-26). Perhaps, then, it is the thin end of *another* interpretative wedge, and the suggestion has consequently been vigorously debated, not to mention — in some quarters — opposed.[96]

Other suggestions could be mentioned at this point,[97] but, for reasons that will become apparent shortly, only these three motifs need to be noted at present. We turn, then, to assess this strategy more critically.

It is important to appreciate first of all that there is no underlying coherence or unifying system present as various interpreters make revisionist moves in relation to one or more of these motifs within Romans 1–4. So, for example, Dunn shares the revisionist perspectives on δικαιοσύνη Θεοῦ and ἔργα νόμου with Wright and Hays but is a trenchant opponent of the revisionist reading of πίστις Χριστοῦ that they endorse (and instances of the reverse situation can also be documented[98]). Hence, motif rereaders do not necessarily occupy a coherent location as a whole; they have in common only this basic strategy, which can be applied quite diversely. With this judgment in place, we can turn to critically assess the strategy's ultimate effectiveness in relation to our overarching agenda, at which point various problematic tendencies in its basic nature can be seen to emerge. These are not necessarily insurmountable, but they do create certain conditions that the strategy must fulfill — or risk instant failure.

The limited nature of the changes usually suggested by motif rereadings issues in two interrelated problematic tendencies. On the one hand, we may lack any overt evidence from the immediate context that the different meaning being suggested for the traditional motif is actually right; that is, the rereading may be underdetermined at that point. (And this underdetermined quality may in turn force the interpreter to use rather dubious strategies to extend the implications and force of the rereading through the rest of Paul's argument — overdetermined lexical claims, for example. These are dubbed in what follows [dubious] strategies of extension.) On the other hand, the surrounding text, *still construed in essentially conventional terms,* may supply powerful countervailing arguments for the motif's traditional reading at that very point. The inherently limited nature of the strategy may then prove its downfall in basic exegetical terms.

But this is not invariably the case, *if* the suggested rereading is based upon textual evidence that has previously been narcotized — upon some textual overdetermination. And the surrounding conventional reading will not be able to reassert itself if *it* is based at the relevant points upon underdetermined material. We might say, then, that any such suggestions for rereading must pick their motifs wisely. And we have identified two conditions thus far necessary for success: a motif rereading *must arise from a textual overdetermination and a corresponding underdetermination in the conventional construal.* Put plainly, it must have positive, overt evidence in its immediate support and a lack of positive, overt evidence against it in the relevant context. Absent these conditions, it will probably fail.

However, a third problematic tendency now comes into view. Any significant reorientations of motifs within the conventional reading and its arrangement of the argument do shift those interpretative dimensions at certain points; such reorientations make some impact. Hence, without a compensating reorientation of the overall argument — which is not always possible — the result of such shifts is invariably a disordering of the reading being offered by the revisionist, *and especially in its argumentative dimension.* If a key component within the smoothly oiled machine of Justification theory is replaced with a foreign one, the inevitable result is that the machine begins to choke and sputter, if it works at all. *A critical premise cannot be changed within an integrated argument without disrupting that argument and rendering it incoherent.* A new argument must therefore be supplied. And if this new argument is disordered, then there are good grounds for continuing to prefer the conventional reading, which gives a robust account of Paul's contentions in Romans 1–4 as a whole. (It is, as we have earlier seen, not flawless, but it certainly has an impressive degree of coherence, along with numerous strengths.) Consequently, the suggested rereading of a motif can often be repudiated on sound exegetical grounds.

Hence, a third condition for the success of any such suggestion is now apparent: *it must be capable of integrating with a coherent construal of the text's surrounding argument.* Indeed, a revisionist suggestion concerning some motif in Romans 1–4 clearly cannot stand alone; it *must* be accompanied by some such broader reorientation. Any strategy resting upon the reorientation of a motif per se is almost bound to fail. And this leads to a fourth, closely related problematic tendency of motif rereadings.

Some suggested rereadings of motifs that survive the tests of determination and any argumentative pressures do so because they leave much of the broader argumentation intact. The price of such limited success, of course, is that they have not really solved our problems. And, perhaps somewhat surprisingly, some of the most well-known suggested rereadings of Paul's texts pay this price; *they do not change anything significant.* Most if not all of the difficulties generated by the conventional reading and its associated theory of Justification are still in place, at which point the value of any such reorientation in terms of our overarching concerns is undermined. A strategically useless semantic reorientation is still worth noting as an insight into the historical-critical reading of the text, but it is not an important step forward in terms of the broader analysis of Paul, and certainly not in terms of the concerns I am addressing here. Hence the fourth condition for success: a motif rereading *must be strategically effective*.

These last two conditions usually exist in a direct relation. If a revision is to be strategically effective, making a significant impact on our various problems, then it will significantly disorder the surrounding argument in Romans 1–4 as well, placing a high premium on a coherent reconstrual of that argument. It must generate a large or difficult condition in this relation if it is to be plausible. Conversely, a low impact revision strategically will not affect the argument much at all; hence, it will have low expectations (if any) of broader argumentative reconstrual. It will consequently be an easier suggestion to make, but a less important one. Suggestions promising high returns will court high contextual argumentative risks — but they are the only risks ultimately worth taking.

These important interpretive dynamics may be clearer if they are traced through in relation to a particular example.

Excursus: J. D. G. Dunn

One of the most important motif rereaders is J. D. G. Dunn. The achievements of Dunn should not be underestimated; he is one of the outstanding contributors to the entire debate. But he does turn out in my view to be an example of an unsuccessful strategy. It is not necessary to survey here all the texts in which Dunn has advocated his "new perspective" on Paul.[99] The information supplied by his key works should suffice.[100]

Excursus §1: Dunn's Position

The main lineaments of Dunn's revisionist position have already been sketched. Dunn suggests new semantic perspectives on the two motifs δικαιοσύνη Θεοῦ and ἔργα νόμου. The former is to be understood in terms of covenant faithfulness: "God is 'righteous' when he fulfills the obligations he took upon himself to be Israel's God, that is, to rescue Israel and punish Israel's enemies . . ." (*R1-8*, 41). The latter are defined — rather more distinctively — as "an identity factor, the social function of the law as marking out the people of the law in their distinctiveness (circumcision, food laws, etc.)," creating the Jews' "religious and national peculiarities" (159).[101] Dunn then presses these meanings through the text of Romans and related Pauline discussions. It is his suggestion concerning "works of law" that particularly concerns us here.[102]

Dunn's actual case for the reconstrual of "works of law" is — rather significantly — constructed in the main with framing explanations and texts drawn from Galatians. It has four subordinate components, although they can segue into one another: (i) a particular reconstruction of Judaism in Paul's day; (ii) associated reconstructions of Paul's biography and the development of the early church, especially as the latter struggled with the nature and implications of Paul's law-free mission to the pagans; and (iii) the tracing of these dynamics in explicit textual terms in relation to Galatians. (Dunn thereby effects an ingenious explanatory synthesis of Sanders, Wright, and Stendahl, salting their insights with various new emphases.) Dunn then (iv) extends this program through particular Pauline texts, using various additional strategies. Of all the revisionists engaging questions raised by the Justification discourse (although of course they do not define things in these terms), Dunn offers the most sustained and detailed exegetical support for his claims.[103]

(1) Judaism

Dunn initially orients himself explicitly in relation to Sanders's work on Judaism, but he nuances this in a certain direction.[104] He accepts the strong dichotomy that Sanders draws between "legalism" and "covenantal nomism," endorsing the latter as the correct description of late Second Temple Judaism as against the caricature that is the former (and arguably some difficulties are immediately implicit here; see part one, chapter four). So he concurs with Sanders that Judaism was "a religion of grace." But he qualifies Sanders's definition using Wright's emphasis on the sociological dimension in Judaism that was generated by certain epochal historical experiences — principally the exile and the Maccabean crisis (although the general experience of the Diaspora within a primarily Hellenistic culture should not be underemphasized). These experiences reified certain distinctive Jewish legal practices as "boundary markers" and special "badges" of covenant membership. Such practices denoted salvation but simultaneously generated sociological and cultural distinctions between the saved and the nonsaved — between Jew and pagan. As boundary markers and badges, they signified a privileged status for those who patrolled and/or possessed them; they set such people apart. These connotations are added to Sanders's emphasis on the keeping of the law as the means by which Jews stayed in their elected, saved constituency.

This broad understanding of Judaism is then denoted by a cluster of terms and phrases in various texts — "works of law," "Judaism," and "Judaizing" (for ἔργα νόμου, see esp. 1QS 5.21, 23; 6.18; 4QFlor 1.1-7; and 4QMMT; for Ἰουδαϊσμός, see 2 Macc. 2:21; 8:1; 14:38; for ἰουδαΐζειν, see Esth. 8:17 LXX; Jos. *War* 2.454, 462-63). These terms evoke a sociologically nuanced definition of late Second Temple Judaism in terms of "covenantal nomism" and its associated religious distinctives and demarcations.

(2) Paul's Biography

Dunn is also more aware than most of the biographical dimension within the debate — defined earlier in our terms as a contest of explanations at the circumstantial frame. Presumably alerted to these issues especially by Stendahl, Dunn is conscious that the biography customarily deployed in support of the conventional reading ought to be refuted, and he proceeds to do so (and we have already noted these contentions in part one, chapter five; his criticisms on this front remain sound in my view). But he also intends to generate positive support for his rereading from this locus, supplying a new biography of Paul, and then of the subsequent development of Paul's law-free mission, that corroborates his rereading of Judaism.

Dunn builds his initial biographical case principally from Galatians 1:13-14 and Philippians 3:3-6. He speaks of Paul's conversion from "covenant distinctiveness, *and . . .* a competitive practice within Judaism" (*TPA,* 350; emphasis added). Prior to this, Paul's infamous zeal "was directed against the Hellenistic Christians because they were seen to threaten Israel's distinctiveness and boundaries" (352). Moreover, "[t]he deduction is hard to avoid that this threat was constituted by the Hellenists taking the gospel of Messiah Jesus to the Gentiles" (352). Paul, then, converted — in a "clear implication" — to the position of those he had previously persecuted (353).[105] "[I]t now becomes more apparent how it was that justification through faith emerged in Paul's theology . . ." (353-54).

Dunn runs these parameters through the later Galatian conflict as well, claiming that the Jerusalem conference (2:1-10), the incident at Antioch (2:11-14), and the later Galatian controversy, to which the letter as a whole is addressed, all rotate around the same set of issues — Jewish covenantal nomism now mistakenly applied to the law-free mission to the pagans. The same reading is also endorsed at the appropriate points in Romans (although Dunn's detailed treatment of Romans actually preceded his exegetical work on Galatians).

(3) Connections in Galatians

However, Dunn needs to link his revisionist claims at some point with overt statements in Paul's texts, and he begins to create such connections in Galatians. There the argument moves at one stage from the discussion of what he takes to be key Jewish practices — boundary markers and badges of the covenant like circumcision and dietary observances — to the terminology that tends to structure the theoretical accounts of Paul's thought — "works of law" versus "faith" (this material pivoting through 2:14-15). And the surrounding argument consequently provides Dunn with his best exegetical opportunity. He claims that "when we turn to Paul's first use of the phrase ['works of law'], in Gal. 2.16, . . . Paul clearly uses the phrase to denote the attitudes he has opposed in the preceding verses (2.1-15)" — "circumcision (2.4) . . . [and] observance of various food laws (2:12)" (p. 359). The phrase next occurs in 3:2 and 5, where it is opposed by "hearing with faith" and the receipt of the Spirit. It then recurs in Galatians 3:10 alongside an Old Testament curse (Deut. 27:26), which Dunn explains as accruing to Israel because she has not obeyed the law's command to bless the nations (although his explanations at this point vary). This claim is supported by similar claims vis-à-vis the distinctive terms Ἰουδαϊσμός, used in Galatians 1:13-14 (see 2 Macc. 2:21; 8:1; 14:38), not to mention ἰουδαΐζειν, used in 2:14.

(4) Extension to Other Pauline Texts

Moreover, already "strategies of extension" are becoming apparent. Dunn speaks relatively frequently of hidden middle premises and unstated axioms (or even of "taken-for-granteds"!; see *JP&L*, 244), a technique that is even more pronounced when he analyzes Romans (see *R1-8*, 159 — see more in this relation momentarily).

Excursus §2: Dunn's Strategic Advances

A characterization of Dunn's strategy as a whole may make the most sense when approached from the Jewish end, so to speak. It is clear that Dunn is profoundly aware of the critique leveled by Sanders and others against the ostensible description of Judaism supplied by Paul in terms of "legalism" — the difficulty at Justification theory's empirical frame in this particular relation. His main revisionist move is the attempted removal of this definition of Judaism from the Pauline system by the insertion of the suitably nuanced definition of "covenantal nomism" instead (something that Sanders himself did not attempt). If Sanders's new definition of Judaism is both accurate and fair, then it follows that this strategy should solve any problems in Paul's supposedly jaundiced empirical description, if the new insertion proves plausible.[106] In effect, Dunn is suggesting that Paul's texts continue to deliver a theoretical account of salvation in the conventional manner, but incorporating a different definition of Judaism at the outset from the one supplied by conventional readers and Justification theory, one that removes the tension earlier detected by so many at the theory's empirical frame. So Sanders's "new perspective" on Judaism is the basis for Dunn's "new perspective" on Paul.

Given these assumptions, Dunn's broader explanation follows the Justification discourse's usual channels. Paul is still making programmatic claims about Judaism in these texts, in Dunn's view, so it follows that he himself experienced this Judaism, and these experiences must in some sense still lie behind the deliberations of the early church concerning the law-free gospel. Biographical and historical reorientations take place accordingly. With these adjustments in place, Dunn needs only to insert the new, empirically more palatable meaning into the relevant Pauline texts, which he proceeds to do, working primarily from the more favorable Galatians material. But there is a sense in which he does not need to work too hard exegetically, because few interpreters contest that Paul is discussing Judaism in these texts, and that the apostle's biography matches his arguments at these points. Hence, Dunn continues to rely on the broader structure of the Justification discourse at the key exegetical points.

Insofar as the force of the empirical difficulty with respect to Judaism is felt — and, to a lesser degree, the tendentiousness of certain aspects of the "Lutheran" biography of Paul — Dunn's case will seem more compelling than the conventional reading and Justification theory (at least to some degree). He seems to have generated a decisive advantage in relation to this important frame. He is also doubtless correct to emphasize the sociological dimension in many of Judaism's critical practices — one that could issue in attitudes unpalatable to modern liberal sensibilities, but presumably to be expected in an ancient (i.e., pre-modern, pre-liberal) context. These are healthy descriptive recoveries (although some require careful handling in a post-Holocaust setting). But our earlier analysis of this basic type of revisionist strategy — the rereading of a motif — leads us to suspect that Dunn's solution will encounter a number of acute difficulties as well.

Excursus §3: Dunn's Problems

Dunn's rereading faces difficulties on a number of fronts: problems of underdetermination (perhaps allied with illegitimate strategies of extension); of countervailing overdetermination from the surrounding text; of argumentative incoherence, resulting in reassertion of the motif's conventional reading; and of strategic ineffectiveness. (In this last respect, it is almost immediately apparent that Dunn's suggested reorientation of the meaning of "works of law" still ends up leaving almost all the difficulties of the conventional reading intact, if not exacerbated.) The conventional reading does not itself escape completely unscathed; Dunn's suggestions highlight usefully one of its particular weak points. However, Dunn's own position seems to collapse. We will now examine each of these problem areas in more detail.

(1) Textual Underdetermination, and Accompanying Strategies of Extension

We have already seen that Dunn's actual case relies primarily on (i) a particular description of Judaism, and then (ii) particular reconstructions of Paul's biography and of the debate in the early church over the law-free mission to the pagans. His overt Pauline evidence (iii) is supposedly found in Galatians, and rests heavily on an equation between the Antioch incident (construed in a certain fashion), recounted in 2:11-14, and the sudden arrival of the motif "works of law" in 2:16 (where it occurs three times). Dunn asserts that the phrase in 2:16 refers to the issue in 2:11-14, thereby drawing further occurrences of the phrase into that semantic orbit (see 3:2, 5, and 10). The resulting meaning must then in effect (iv) be transferred into the key occurrences of the same phrase in Romans (see 3:20, 27-28; but the notion is probably also implicit in 4:2, 6; 9:12, 32; and 11:6). But how plausible is this chain of claims, all of which must hold good for Dunn's case to stand firm overall?

It is interesting to note, first, that nowhere does Dunn claim that Paul supplies an explicit definition of "works of law" in the terms that he suggests. (Indeed, matters are even worse than this, as we will note momentarily.) His case rests entirely on reframing (i.e., the arguments that this is what Judaism was, and Paul is describing Judaism with this phrase). Moreover, each of his reframing suggestions is far from certain, and the connections between them are fragile. This all amounts to a weak position — to a chain constructed with brittle links, none of which seem necessarily to be joined.

The first two relevant frames — the first two links in the chain — have already been addressed in some detail, in part one, chapters four and five, so we can simply reintroduce the relevant conclusions from those earlier discussions here.

Like Justification theory, Dunn's case relies on a monolithic characterization of the nature of late Second Temple Judaism — although here emphasizing sociology — and we have already seen that such claims are almost certainly false. They impose a monochromatic explanation upon a phenomenon only partly known that was clearly diverse through time and space. Note, it is possible to accept the insights of Wright and Dunn in this relation — that certain features of law observance within the theological framework of a covenant with God had indubitable sociological consequences — without feeling the force of Dunn's further inference — that Jews must *necessarily* be involved with such questions when they convert to Christianity. Judaism was much richer than this narrow set of concerns implies. (Indeed, even the discussion of boundary issues supplied by Dunn is too narrow. Judaism was deeply concerned with sexual practices, drunkenness, and aniconic worship, concerns arguably even more deeply embedded in her boundary discussions than matters of dietary and temporal observance. We will return shortly to the implications of this important shortcoming.)

Dunn also tends to confuse rationale and effect in his analysis. As sociologists have long observed, the reasons that groups supply and then debate for certain distinctive practices are distinguishable from the sociological consequences of those practices, which are sometimes even unnoticed.[107] Ancient groups were not especially self-conscious in sociological terms. Accordingly, while some awareness of a basic boundary between Jew and pagan was doubtless present for many Jews, they seldom argued for their own practices *on the basis of an explicitly sociological rationale*. Practices with important sociological consequences were usually justified on traditional, scriptural, and/or theological grounds. This is a crucial distinction to grasp in the broader context of Dunn's case: it does not follow from the sociological function and consequences of certain Jewish practices that they were debated in such terms.

Similarly, although Dunn's critique of the Justification biography of Paul seems fair, its force applies to his own reconstruction as well. We lack the explicit evidence to confirm his claims concerning the nature of the early Christians that Paul persecuted (i.e., that they were law-free).[108] Indeed, some of the evidence that we do have seems to stand against this reconstruction. If that early movement was law-free, then the issue *must* have arisen when Paul visited Jerusalem three years after he had become a Christian (see Gal. 1:18-24) — if not before[109] — and not fourteen to seventeen years later. Hence, Dunn's claims in this relation push a critical transition within the early church that clearly involved Paul back behind Paul into an evidence-free zone. It is a regressive explanatory measure, while what evidence that we can glean stands against it (so chapter five).

What now of the further links in the chain — the tracing of these dynamics through Galatians and beyond — and their ostensible connections? Dunn argues — as he has to —

that part of the early church possessed the same basic attitude toward law-free pagan salvation as wider Judaism possessed toward Jewish apostasy, and consequently, this posture must lie behind the opposite side of the arguments in Jerusalem, Antioch, and Galatia, and can legitimately be imputed to it when Paul attacks it in the relevant texts (i.e., with the phrase "works of law"). We might say, then, that there was a reasonably direct correlation between the Maccabean crisis and the implications of Paul's pagan mission. Both were perceived as having the same destructive effect and so were opposed in the same theological terms. Dunn's argument at this point is then, in effect:

> Some Jews in late Second Temple Judaism were concerned about certain practices dictated by the law that established a "boundary" between Jews and pagans (viz., circumcision, distinctive diet, and Sabbath observance), and this boundary had to be policed and defended.

Therefore,

> when some early Jewish Christians opposed the law-free mission to the pagans by Paul, they did so because of just this rationale and no other (viz., it eroded that boundary conceived of in these terms).

Now this is a plausible *possible* argument. We can responsibly *imagine* early Jewish Christians feeling offended by Paul's proposals on these grounds. But it is dubiously suggested as *the* explanation of the Galatian crisis, because of that claim's implicit reductionism. This would impose a simple equation on what we suspect is a much more complex situation.[110] Moreover, it lacks attestation. We have no incontrovertible and direct evidence that this simple explanation was in fact the case. (It is not apparent in Gal. 2:1-14 or Acts 15:1, 5.) And there is certainly no logical force in Dunn's argument. (It is not a proper syllogism but only probabilistic.)[111] We even have some grounds for suspecting that the debate was in fact more complex than this. (It will emerge, especially from part four, chapter fourteen, that the Jewish Christian position that Paul is opposing is much more complex than this and is not oriented primarily in terms of sociology or boundaries, although they play some role in that system.) Most importantly, it confuses rationale and sociological effect. Even if boundary markers are in question, *those were likely to have been debated in different terms.* (Note, for example, how Paul describes his fierce defense of his heritage — a sociological practice — in terms of "zeal for the traditions of [his] ancestors"; Gal. 1:14b).[112]

So it seems that Dunn's reconstruction of the exact nature of the debate within the early church over the law-free pagan mission lacks probity. While it may be a partial explanation of that history, it is less likely to be the whole explanation. But do his exegetical claims concerning Galatians retrieve his case? Unfortunately, these too lack definitive force.

Dunn's case requires a perfect correlation between the issues in 2:1-10 and 2:11-14 and the terminology of 2:16. Boundary-defining practices must be at stake in all three of these pericopes, with part of the early church reproducing a typically Jewish concern to defend such practices first in Jerusalem, then at Antioch, and finally in Galatia. But although the practices at issue overlap — circumcision in Jerusalem (2:1-10); diet at Antioch (2:11-14); circumcision and temporal observances, at least, in Galatia (see 4:10; 5:2, 3) — there are no guarantees that their conceptualization and debate are precisely the same in all three of these settings.[113] That is, it seems more likely that different stages of the debate are in view, at which point we cannot assume that all the contentions are the same but ought, rather, to suspect that various developments have taken place.

Further, Paul *never explicitly links the phrase "works of law" with the boundary markers just mentioned.* Equally troublesome is his failure to oppose any of those boundary markers, when they occur earlier on, with some notion of πίστις. All the key terms of 2:15-21 in fact look "forward" in the letter, through chapter 3, where they occur, sometimes repeatedly; *none* resume material introduced in 2:1-14 explicitly. Neither do boundary markers surround the later occurrences of the phrase "works of law" in 3:2, 5, and 10, that is, later on where these notions are developed argumentatively. In short, nothing explicit makes Dunn's case in Galatians, whereas various implications within the text point in the opposite direction — that "works of law" do not summarize key boundary markers within Judaism like circumcision, dietary distinctions, and temporal observances, but represent a distinct set of contentions, related but possessing their own integrity.

The movement of the reading into Romans, and especially into Romans 1–4, is even more fragile. Dunn claims that the first instance of the phrase (in the plural), in 3:20, resumes 2:17-20, which was "[p]rominent in that indictment (1.18–3.20) . . . [and was] Paul's critique of the sense of privilege and distinctiveness expressed by the 'Jew'" (*TPA*, 362-63). Unfortunately, these arguments are stretched, if not overtly false. This subsection of four verses is hardly prominent (although it is present), so to assert that it dominates the summarizing function of 3:20 is patently tendentious. What of the remaining one hundred or so verses? And although 2:17-20 denotes the privilege and distinctiveness of the Jew in question, *Paul does not criticize this figure in these terms;* they merely *describe* him. Moreover, that description *is not in terms of generic boundary markers.* This figure possesses the law. Circumcision, diet, and Sabbath are not mentioned (although circumcision is introduced in v. 25.) His immediate development, furthermore, is in terms of hypocrisy in terms of theft, adultery, and temple robbery — sins that even the pagans would not approve of! (He is, in addition, not a generic Jew. He is a privileged Jewish male — privileged because he is literate and learned, although it could plausibly be suggested that such figures would be most likely to make objections in relation to boundary markers.) Hence Dunn's attempt to establish the programmatic summarizing force of 3:20 seems forced. Even where he asserts that a meaning in terms of sociological distinctives is operative in the preceding argument, it is not readily apparent. Indeed, somewhat dubious strategies of extension become apparent from this point, and these are indicative of Dunn's difficulties in Romans. He is forced largely to assert, *without any textual warrant,* the presence of the sociological dimension within Paul's phrase "works of law" in Romans 3:20,[114] 27-28,[115] and 9:32.[116]

In sum, Dunn's chain of claims, which ideally extends his suggested sociological rereading of "works of law" from Paul's Jewish background right through to his argument in Romans, is constructed from fragile links that are in turn only dubiously connected. Closer examination suggests that his basic claim is underdetermined at every point. But we have yet to consider much of the countervailing material.

(2) Textual Overdeterminations from the Surrounding Argument

Corresponding to a lack of overt positive evidence from the texts in favor of the reading, some evidence seems explicitly to contradict Dunn's claims by establishing a different meaning for the phrase "works of law." There are three principal areas of difficulty that reinforce one another.

(i) The phrase τὸ ἔργον τοῦ νόμου occurs in Romans 2:15, in the midst of a detailed discussion of evenhanded eschatological rewards from God apportioned in terms of desert — "in accordance with works" (2:6). The text even goes so far as to say "the doers of the law [i.e., not merely 'the hearers'] will be declared righteous (δικαιωθήσονται) . . . on that day" (2:13). It is difficult, then, to avoid the implication that the plural form of this phrase takes the same basic sense — denoting good works of all kinds that will be judged righteous by God on the future day of judgment (works by both Jews and pagans!).[117]

(ii) Chapter 4 of Romans provides a similarly embarrassing text. Dunn concedes that works of law are implicit in vv. 2-8, although the full phrase does not occur there. And v. 4 explicitly describes a worker (τῷ ἐργαζομένῳ), who receives wages in accordance with obligation (ὁ μισθὸς . . . λογίζεται . . . κατὰ ὀφείλημα) — that is, desert. This arrangement, furthermore, would clearly entitle any such person to boast, as v. 2 suggests. Hence, Paul explicitly encodes "works" and "workers" here with connotations of some notion of desert or appropriate earned reward, and it is difficult to integrate this material with Dunn's characterization of the phrase purely in terms of sociological boundary markers that establish mere distinction.

(iii) We should also note that the singular phrase in 2:15 follows instances of "doing" in vv. 13 and 14 (see οἱ ποιηταὶ νόμου in v. 13, and ἔθνη . . . τὰ τοῦ νόμου ποιῶσιν in v. 14), which it seems to reprise in some sense. "Doing" also recurs in the context of the other instances of "works of law" in Paul — arguably in Romans 9:32 (see esp. 10:5; see the more detailed discussion part five, chapter nineteen), and more definitely in Galatians 3:10 and 12 (so part five, chapter twenty). And this suggests some semantic similarity or overlap (something also explored in more detail in our later rereading; see esp. part four, chapter fourteen). But this returns us to the evidence first noted, drawn from Romans 2, where "doing" is elaborated in terms of righteous behavior per se, and placed in an explicitly eschatological framework.

This is not an overwhelming amount of evidence, but it is reasonably explicit. Where Paul seems to provide specific guidance concerning the interpretation of the phrase "works of law," it does not point in the direction of Dunn's proposal; rather, a fairly conventional reading seems to emerge — "works of law" as meritorious deeds of various types, that is, not explicit boundary markers (although doubtless some could function this way). And they are done in accordance with the instructions supplied by the law and are capable of being judged "righteous" by God on the future day of judgment. Hence, conventional readers are right to protest against Dunn's proposal (and any like his) on purely localized exegetical grounds. Insofar as Paul's texts speak about "works," they do not sound like Dunn. They speak conventionally.[118]

(3) Argumentative (In)coherence

We encounter now a particularly difficult problem for Dunn's case. Just as we have briefly considered the explicit exegetical material, we must also consider the broader construal of Paul's texts as an argument. This has traditionally been one of the conventional reading's strengths; its account of Paul's argument, although not without its own problems, is nevertheless reasonably compelling. But if we insert Dunn's suggested meaning for "works of law" into Paul's broader argument concerning salvation, the argument no longer makes much sense at all. Grasping this difficulty is complicated by the fact that Dunn's exact position seems to shift around (perhaps intuiting the problems here, if not betraying their presence). But even allowing for all the possible variations, every construal of Paul's argument in terms of Dunn's interpretation of "works of law" nevertheless seems to collapse at some point into incoherence.

We may pose four questions to the argument generated by Dunn's proposal, the first and third probably being the most serious: (i) what is the problem with Judaism? (ii) can converts from paganism simply ignore all Jewish boundary issues? (iii) why is Paul flexible in relation to boundary issues elsewhere? and (iv) what is the rationale for faith? In all these queries either countervailing evidence seems to prove that Paul did not think in the fashion that Dunn suggests, or the argument, construed in terms of Dunn's proposal, collapses into incoherence.

(i) What is the problem with Judaism?

The implications within this question run to the heart of Dunn's difficulties.

Like conventional Justification advocates, Dunn seems committed to a progression in Paul from plight to solution, the plight being defined in close relation to Judaism. (We will assume here for the sake of argument that Dunn is committed to a prospective reading of Paul.) Hence, although he eschews the traditional definition of the Jewish problem in terms of "legalism," he must still supply *some* definition of the problem, or the Jew will not become a Christian. (When one thinks forward, if Judaism is not a problem, then Christianity is not a solution.)

Dunn argues that Israel was set apart from the pagan nations, with their detestable practices, by the distinctive practices of the law (much as the Qumran community was set apart in turn from an unclean, apostate Israel by certain practices; see 4QMMT), leading to a "presumption of privilege" (R1–8, 157). The distinctiveness afforded by the law — presumably, a gift of the covenant extended to them by God — came nevertheless to function as a "blockage which prevented the gospel from reaching out beyond the boundaries of Israel marked out by the law" (364). It is the limiting function of this distinctiveness, generated somehow by an inappropriate understanding of covenantal nomism, that Dunn holds (Paul to hold) problematic.[119] But precisely what is behind the problem — its proximate cause — is rather more difficult to pin down. We will briefly explore what seem to be the two main possibilities.

Sometimes Dunn seems to suggest that the Jews are inappropriately proud of their heritage, "protecting Israel's privileged status and restricted prerogative" (*TPA*, 355). The Jews misunderstand something here, namely, that God really wishes to bless the pagans too. They "hoard" their covenantal privileges, refusing to share them with those who want them. This seems a fair criticism, if it is true. Certain evidence, however, suggests that it is not.[120] And even more importantly, this definition of the problem cannot possibly unpack into a solution in terms of either Christianity or salvation by faith alone. The appropriate solution to a miserly misunderstanding of the Jewish covenant and its halakhic response is simply to share those privileges with whoever wants them. Proselytes should be accepted, if not encouraged, and in this way the blessings of Judaism will indeed be shared with whichever pagans show an interest in them. (Problem solved, one is tempted to say.) So this does not seem a very coherent articulation of *Paul's* much more radical line of thought.[121] The appropriate solution to an inappropriately miserly Judaism is not salvation through faith alone, but Judaism's generous sharing of her law-observant practices with the nations — at which point we could hardly be further away from Paul!

The alternative conception, which Dunn seems to affirm at times as well, is that the problem is not an *inappropriate* sense of ethnic privilege but the Jews' ethnicity *per se.* Their very particularity, established by their covenantal response in terms of law, somehow hampered the universality of God's saving intentions, inscribing an irreducible particularity into history. God wanted to save the pagans, but covenantal nomism saved only Jews, by definition.[122] It *created* Jews. But there is something absurd if not rather appalling about this argument if Dunn intends it seriously. Covenantal nomism creates a distinction automatically, as God teaches his people the difference between right and wrong and so separates them from the surrounding nations. To turn around and view this distinction as problematic, then, is to abolish the distinction between right and wrong that the covenant enshrined, and also to attribute to God an utterly arbitrary experiment in human history with the Jewish people. Indeed, one wonders just how such a system could be wrong and God remain ethical himself.[123] (And, once again, faith alone is hardly the answer; faith is still particular — as is the church.)

It seems, then, that irrespective of its precise construction, Dunn's new articulation of the Jewish problem does not yield a coherent account of the Pauline gospel. Either the problem does not unpack into the necessary solution — "faith" — or the conception of the problem itself is not especially coherent. But Dunn's difficulties in this relation are not yet over.

(ii) Can pagan converts simply ignore all Jewish boundary issues?

It seems to follow from Dunn's account of Paul's system that all boundary markers can now be ignored in favor of salvation by faith alone. Such distinctions are problems that have been resolved — vestiges of sinful particularized Judaism that are now recognized and abandoned. However, Dunn's articulation of these distinctions is insufficient. Dunn speaks repeatedly of circumcision, dietary practices, and temporal observances. But the distinction between Jews and pagans was structured by many other critical practices, most notably, in Paul's day, by the observance of heterosexuality and the repudiation of idolatry — the very distinctions that concern Romans 1:18-32. It should follow from Dunn's reconstruction that pagan converts to Paul's gospel could dispense with any observance of these distinctions as well! But clearly they cannot, which suggests that Dunn has not really grasped Paul's argument (or, alternatively, that Paul is deeply inconsistent and his various recommendations on sustained versus abandoned Jewish practices lack all cogency).[124] Complementing this conundrum is a further anomaly.

(iii) Why is Paul flexible in relation to "boundary" issues elsewhere?

In both Romans 14 and 1 Corinthians 8 and 10 Paul seems to address two of the key boundary issues that Dunn holds to be underpinning the debate in Galatians and Romans 1-4 — dietary practices and temporal observances. If these create unacceptable distinctions between Jews and pagans, however, as Dunn avers, it is difficult to explain why Paul is so flexible about their observance in these other locations. In the alternative passages Paul seems happy to counsel complete flexibility on such matters in the greater interest of Christian unity; the "strong" are to bow to the concerns of the "weak." Yet observing such practices will erect the very distinctions that Dunn holds Paul to be stringently opposed to! The implication is that Paul is actually quite flexible in relation to boundary issues; hence, these issues are not in play in those texts where he is being inflexible, but different, and rather more serious, questions are probably in dispute.

(iv) What is the rationale for faith?

We return now to a difficulty we noted in question (i). There we explored two possible construals of Paul's argument in terms of Dunn's strategy — neither of which proved capable of leading coherently to a gospel of salvation through faith alone.

This is a conundrum that we have already encountered in Watson's suggested reconstruals (and it dogs many other revisionist proposals), and clearly, it is quite significant. Justification theory has its weaknesses, but at least it supplies a robust account of the law-free gospel and the need for salvation through faith alone. These conclusions allow some of its most significant interpretative successes in relation to Paul's texts and history. And, as we have seen, they are grounded in the dynamics of the first phase in Justification theory. There an experience of law, hampered by sin, leads to ethical failure (perhaps repeatedly) and to a sense of pending eschatological judgment. It seems to follow from this experience that salvation cannot be by means of the law but must, rather, be by the fulfillment of some more manageable criterion, and faith alone matches that requirement nicely (at least at first glance). So, in the conventional construal, a reasonable argument combines an account of the problem in Jewish terms with a solution that is both law-free and by faith alone.

It is of course a primary avenue of revision nevertheless to resist the definition of the Jewish problem in these terms. Although coherent, it also seems inaccurate and harsh. But if revisionists persist in a prospective interpretation of Romans 1–4 and of Paul's gospel (that is, an account that moves forward, from plight to solution), they must have some way of supplying the argumentative logic that cradles the distinctive claims of the second phase. If they displace the conventional description of Judaism, *they must find an alternate means of justifying a law-free gospel of salvation by faith alone.* Without such an equivalent argument, Paul's theory of salvation will simply fall apart (which is to say that the conventional construal will be able to reassert itself relatively easily). But revisionists generally overlook this critical condition, or fail if they do acknowledge it, and Dunn is a classic instance of this (as was Watson).[125] How plausible can an account of Paul's gospel be that cannot plausibly get from works of law, through their abandonment, to salvation through faith alone?!

In sum, just as Dunn's reconstruction of Paul's account of the Jewish problem (whatever its exact nuance) is incoherent, so too the broader progression of the reconstructed argument from plight to solution breaks down — a near crippling problem. But a fourth and final difficulty is evident in Dunn's proposal as well.

(4) Strategic (In)effectiveness

Dunn's proposed reconstruction deals with only three of the fifty-six problems we have previously noted. As we have already seen, he is self-consciously oriented in his rereading largely by Paul's ostensibly caricatured description of Judaism, the first of four difficulties that we have identified at Justification theory's empirical frame. He proceeds by inserting at this point the "new perspective" on Judaism, which he associates especially with Sanders. While doing so he also makes a bold attempt to reframe much of the discussion, perceiving that biographical issues are in play in support of the reading that he intends to displace — the second and third issues at the empirical frame. But — for the moment extending Dunn the benefit of the doubt — his proposed reconstruction leaves at least fifty-three problems unaddressed (some admittedly minor, but some also acute).[126] Clearly, then, Justification theory and the conventional reading have been left largely intact. And this is often evident in Dunn's other writings that defend major parts of the conventional construal and Justification theory.[127] Dunn's diagnosis of the Pauline interpretative community's illness seems strangely superficial. Moreover, it is arguable in any case to what degree he has solved the principal difficulty in the conventional reading that he *has* set himself to address — the empirical problem with respect to Judaism.

As we have seen, Dunn takes pains to avoid accusing Judaism in Paul's day of hypocrisy and legalism, but he does accuse Jews of something, thereby retaining the fundamentally a priori construction of Justification theory. They are accused of a certain inappropriate distinctiveness and sense of ethnic privilege as the specially chosen covenant people. But if this is the case, then Dunn seems to be accusing Judaism of what is currently known as "racism." And this seems to be an even more egregious sin than "legalism." Legalism is at least a fundamentally ethical system; it is based on desert. One gets what one deserves by working for it (whether good or bad). Indeed, numerous modern political movements — usually on the Right — regard its principles as positively virtuous. But far less can be said about racism — about the mere assertion of the superiority of some particular distinctive group on grounds intrinsic to that group's construction and not to merit per se. Hence — in something of an irony — Dunn's redefinition of the motif "works of law" in Paul, in an attempt to move beyond the legalistic caricature of Judaism implicit in the conventional reading of Romans 1–4, seems to have shifted the intrinsic difficulty within Judaism to the still more sinister plane of racial discrimination. (Either this, or his reading is being misunderstood in such terms, but any other understanding will yield equally acute difficulties: are the Jews really to be accused of being "ethnic"? This makes no sense.)

In sum, Dunn's suggested rereading of the motif "works of law" addresses three of the fifty-six problems identifiable in the conventional reading and its associated theory of Justification (although these are, admittedly, big problems). His principal concern is Paul's description of Judaism, but here, even allowing for a plausible case, he seems to embrace a still worse alternative. Hence, setting aside the question of veracity, his strategy is clearly defective by virtue of its very construction.

We can learn a great deal from the successes and failures of the revisionist strategy of motif rereading as exemplified by Dunn.[128] In the first instance, it is becoming apparent that past approaches of this type — even when a problem, and hence the need for a solution, is sensed or acknowledged — have tended to be superficial. Our problems are more widespread and deeply implicit in our reading strategies than many suspect, even in those of revisionists currently rereading motifs. This is probably because our difficulties are implicit in the conventional reading as a whole and its associated theory of salvation and not in a mere word or phrase; they reside in the very warp and woof of that interpretative construct. Moreover, the phrase "works of law" seems to be an especially difficult phrase to try to redefine; the explicit indications that Paul supplies seem to draw interpretation ineluctably toward a fairly conventional meaning. Certain further critical implications flow from this realization.

First, any solution that leaves the theory of Justification largely in place, presumably by way of the conventional reading, will not solve the majority of its problems. Piecemeal solutions, pursued through the redefinitions of words and motifs, are consequently not ultimately a viable solution to our difficulties. (And it is therefore important to look for the reemergence of Justification theory within any solutions offered by rereadings; this is generally a sign that an ineffective motif rereading is in play.) However, it seems to follow concomitantly that a more sweeping rereading that entirely displaces Justification theory *could* solve many if not all of our difficulties; a comprehensively nontheoretical solution *is* a viable ultimate solution in potential terms.

Such an approach would eliminate the argumentative, systematic, empirical, and proximate difficulties generated by the apostle's apparent commitment to Justification theory in Romans 1–4, and it would obviate the presence of textual underdeterminations. (Since Justification theory would no longer be present, a construal could no longer be faulted for failing to state clearly that it is there.) Only the problem of textual overdeterminations would remain, but clearly those could now be reassessed as well. Hence, we learn from the failures of motif rereadings, at bottom, that a *comprehensive, nontheoretical* approach is the *only* potentially effective solution to our difficulties, and it seems fair to dub such solutions "radical." Only a radical revisionist strategy can deal with the problems that we have detected within the Justification discourse.

However, as the countervailing exegetical challenges to the motif rereadings have made clear, any such solution will face the formidable conventional construal of Romans 1–4. So it follows in turn that any potentially effective nontheoretical solution will still have to satisfy the basic plausibility criteria operative in relation to claims made about the Pauline data in the base — the needs for exegetical "fit," for argumentative integrity, and for plausible explanations at the general cultural, proximate, and circumstantial frames. Any comprehensive solution will, in short, still have to win the exegetical battle — the struggle to be the best demonstrable reading of the texts in the Justification discourse's "mighty fortress," Romans 1–4. A radical rereading must possess integrity *as* a reading. Nevertheless, we have already compiled a formidable list of difficulties in the conventional reading. So there are grounds for hope. In particular, if an alternative construal can account for the text's overdeterminations, then it may well enjoy a decisive advantage.

But we have also learned something about the basic tenor of any such alternative reading from the struggles of the motif rereaders. On the one hand, it is clear that the construal of Romans 1–4 offered by Justification advocates will have to be challenged directly at some point (and, for example, not merely reframed). On the other hand, during that process of semantic challenge, motifs *and the surrounding argument* will have to be reconsidered in a more dynamic relation than has previously been the case (a point where the motif rereadings have tended to fail). The meaning of a given motif is intimately linked to the broader construal of the surrounding argument in Romans 1–4, and any failure to reconstrue that argument allows the conventional reading and its associated theory to reassert itself (if necessary, in spite of any reoriented motifs). The process of reconstrual must therefore extend to the reconstrual of the entire argument of Romans 1–4, and presumably the reconstrual of various motifs will be a part of that process. Indeed, we can safely predict that argumentatively strategic or crucial motifs will have to be reoriented if a comprehensive rereading is ultimately to prove successful.

It is arguably apparent in Dunn, and other related rereadings of motifs in Paul, that the question of Judaism in particular is fraught with hidden difficulties. It would seem to be next to impossible to resolve the empirical tensions in Justification theory related to Judaism by redefining Judaism in Paul's texts in some minor way but then continuing to pursue a prospective construction of the overall argument. Any such definition would alter a fundamental component within the unfolding coherence of Justification theory, disrupting it and discrediting the new reading. Moreover, it is unlikely that a healthy or acceptable definition of Judaism will be found that can *also* unfold into a law-free gospel of salvation through faith alone. (Certainly, the ingenious Dunn could not meet this challenge.) Indeed, these two conditions are really at cross-purposes — a positive description of Judaism that can nevertheless still function as the negative preparation for Christianity! It may well be, then, that *it is the claim that Paul is giving an account of Judaism itself that is at fault.* Only a reading that can dispense with this claim, and with any consequent unfolding of the argument into the Christian gospel (from problem to solution), offers any real hope of resolving the various acute difficulties that interpreters face in this relation. We must find some way of circumventing the empirical claims that the conventional reading makes in Romans 1–4, or embrace some form of caricature or argumentative failure.

In short, while appreciating the need for semantic challenge exemplified by the motif rereadings, along with some of the interpretative options that such challenges have created, we can see that those concerns must be integrated with a challenge to the conventional construal of Paul's *argument* in Romans 1–4 — and, in particular, at those points that are critical for the endorsement of Justification theory. Thus, even as we learn from motif rereadings, we also move beyond them. And as we do so, it is important to be aware of their potential to confuse debate. This unhealthy dynamic is usefully recognized and, if possible, rejected, before we move on to evaluate the radical revisionist proposals. Indeed, arguably in the past this false dynamic has obscured the very need to do so, that is, to pursue more radical solutions.

Although motif rereaders appreciate that some set of difficulties within the interpretation of Paul must be addressed — whether his description of Judaism, or his unhealthy introspection, or some such — we have just seen that their analyses of these problems, and the appropriate solutions that they consequently offer, lack the necessary depth and breadth. Moreover — and as a result — they continue to perpetuate much of the problem within their own purported solutions. One broader result of this unhelpful process can therefore be a false conception of the basic situation's parameters — an overly constrained interpretative playing field, the terms of which, if accepted, *preclude the discovery of any effective solution.* If the definition of the problem offered by motif rereadings is accepted,

The basic interpretative situation

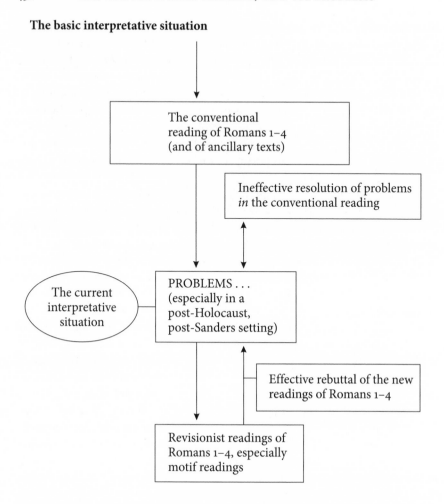

along with the strategy underlying its solution (i.e., the piecemeal reorientation of motifs), then the debate is doomed. There is no way forward, because if a solution exists, it must by definition be a comprehensive one that lies well beyond these parameters.

Corresponding to the fatal interpretative closure implicit in this dynamic is a set of hermeneutical temptations for advocates of Justification. Such advocates might be tempted to think that they have defended the conventional reading after they have repudiated the various exegetical suggestions of the motif rereadings. As we have just seen, however, repudiating these essentially incoherent solutions is not that difficult. (How hard is it to repudiate a solution to a false description of the problem that also, almost by definition, creates an incoherent argument?) But in so doing, Justification advocates might be tempted to overlook their own tendencies to fail to address major lacunae in their discourse — the need to fashion effective solutions to their own difficulties (and the list of those is quite extensive), *and* to provide some positive justification of their own particular reading of Romans 1–4.

We have already noted that Justification advocates tend to beg the question at these key points, and that if this is allowed to happen, further effective debate is stifled. Hence, the cheap successes achieved against motif rereadings may encourage Justification advocates to do just this. However — to put matters succinctly — pointing out the problems in an alternative reading is not the same thing as establishing the validity of one's own reading, or eliminating the problems still apparent in that reading. Justification advocates should not assume that the debate is over because motif rereaders have been seen off; the fight is really just beginning.

The consequences for broader debate that flow from any failure to grasp the shortcomings of the revisionist strategy of motif rereading are quite serious. Revisionists might be left operating within a constrained and ultimately incoherent and ineffective interpretative space, and Justification advocates might be further reinforced psychologically in their question-begging tendencies. The overall result is then an absence of resolution *and an inability to reach one* — interpretative gridlock.

Let us hope, then, that this situation is now clarifying to the point where revisionists and Justification advocates alike can move beyond it to address the critical issues. As we noted earlier, the interpretative playing field is rather broader at this point than many have previously suspected.

3.2. Comprehensive Rereadings

We know what we are looking for at this point in reasonably precise terms, thanks in large measure to the shortcomings of previous attempts to solve the difficulties evident within the Justification discourse through some strategy of reframing, or through the rereading of certain motifs in Paul's argument. We know now that we seek a radical solution — a comprehensive, nontheoretical reading — but one that also satisfies the basic plausibility criteria in the textual base better than the formidable conventional construal (i.e., in terms of exegetical fit, argumentative integrity, and at the relevant frames). We also need, ideally, an apostle who consistently thinks retrospectively in relation to the questions under consideration in Romans 1–4. If we know what we are looking for, then, has the debate yet supplied such an explanation? Obviously not, or this book would now end with a footnote (and as pleasant as that prospect seems in some respects). The need for a consistently nontheoretical reading has not been well appreciated, and what comprehensive rereadings the debate has provided have not been able to satisfy the basic plausibility requirements of the situation. But evaluating the struggles of these attempts will again prove instructive. Stanley K. Stowers's *A Rereading of Romans: Justice, Jews, and Gentiles* is in my view the most impressive example of this strategy to date.[129]

Excursus: Stanley K. Stowers's *A Rereading of Romans*

It is probably fair to accuse Stowers of being at times more passionate than clear. Insights from every conceivable interpretative angle tend to jostle together within his discussion. One result is that his *Rereading* dazzles so much that it can confuse. And this is a pity, because a more coherent reading arguably lurks within Stowers's prose than most of his critics either detect or aver, and many of his localized interpretative suggestions are positively inspired. Nevertheless, his overarching reading does contain troubling aspects, and consequently fails to convince.[130] Ultimately, in my view, his work deserves the judgment "so near and yet so far." It nicely illustrates many of the central methodological difficulties for radical rereaders: that localized shifts in meaning — however brilliant they seem at first — must be integrated within more broadly coherent exegetical, argumentative, and theoretical explanations if they are to succeed; that new readings cannot simply be suggested by way of reaction to old problems; and that the conventional reading is too formidable an opponent and too accurate a construal to be dismissed too quickly.

Excursus §1: Stowers's Position

Stowers's analysis begins with a rapid rehearsal of most of the insights that he will bring to bear on the text of Romans in detail — insights drawn from fields as diverse as reader response criticism, Greco-Roman philosophical and political discourses, and Jewish intertextual echoes (*RR*, 1-41).[131] He pays the most attention within this preliminary rehearsal, however, to an ancient discourse of "self-mastery" that he claims is especially important for Romans (see *RR*, 42-82). We will be particularly concerned in what follows with his rereading of Romans 1–4, and Stowers's book is in fact principally concerned with this section of text in the letter. He breaks Paul's text into fairly conventional subunits — 1:18-32, 2:1-16, 2:17–3:20, 3:21-26, and 3:27–4:25 (specifically 3:27–4:2 and 4:3ff.).[132] But he arranges these subunits and their internal arguments in an ingenious fashion.

Stowers begins his more detailed exegetical analysis by claiming that 1:18-32 echoes ancient "decline of civilization" narratives (which were both Greco-Roman and Jewish; the paradigmatic example of this was Hesiod). Romans 1:18-32 describes the decline of the pagans from a golden age through idolatry — although this is clearly a Jewish emphasis — into enslavement to corrupt and wicked desires. Disordered sexual and interpersonal relationships then follow.[133]

After this rather systematic and generalized opening, the text turns in 2:1 on a figure constructed in deliberate parallel to some of the text's audience, much as other ancient protreptics did. Romans 2:1-16 is consequently addressed initially to a pretentious pagan[134] who fails to recognize his practice of essentially the same wicked deeds as those detailed in 1:18-32 and his consequent eschatological peril. Stowers asserts that this figure is only ever coded as a pagan. This pagan "stores up wrath" for the day of judgment. However, repentance and the performance of good deeds will result in justification on that day — the pronouncement by God that he is righteous. This is God's strikingly impartial position: both Jews and Greeks (i.e., pagans) can be pronounced righteous and saved if they do good deeds.[135] Stowers goes on to claim that this pagan knows the law, as suggested by 2:12-15, not through natural theology (which was a far more flexible notion in ancient times than modern interpreters tend to appreciate), but through the Mosaic law (that is, through "cultural diffusion," which was a widely attested ancient notion as well).[136]

In 2:17, however, Paul "spots one of his competitors in the crowd, a Jew who has committed himself to teach gentiles about the Mosaic law. Paul knows that many gentiles in the audience have been attracted to such teachers and decides that he can best continue his missionary appeal by provoking a debate with the other Jewish teacher in front of his gentile audience (2:17–4:21)" (*RR*, 142). Hence, Stowers suggests that here "Paul censures the interlocutor for the disparity between his pretensions and his behavior" — a standard topos in ancient ethical discourse (*RR*, 148). In so doing, he "confronts another Jew who is also a teacher of gentiles" (149). This "dialogical fiction" then undergirds the argument through to the end of Romans 4.

The Jewish figure is censured for inconsistency in 2:21-24. The same approach is then pressed — although somewhat ambiguously — through vv. 25-29.[137] This pretentious and inconsistent Jewish Teacher is attacked by Paul for being a Jew in name only. He has also failed (along with others) "to responsibly witness [to the Gentiles] concerning God's promises" (*RR*, 192).

Stowers is an acknowledged expert on the diatribe, so his alternative account of 3:1-9 is especially interesting. In particular, he shifts Paul's commitments within the argument at v. 3 to place him on the other side of the discussion (*RR*, 165-66). That is, beginning in v. 3 Paul becomes the questioner, not the figure who answers throughout as the conventional reading assumes.[138] The Jewish Teacher remains in view. Moreover, 3:1-9 now speaks more consistently of the same issues that were raised from 2:17 and are articulated at length in Romans 9–11.

Stowers suggests that 3:9-20 employs rather exaggerated rhetoric that should not be overpressed. (When people use the word "all" they seldom mean this — "without exception"; numerous Jewish, Greco-Roman, and modern texts employ this sort of hyperbole.) He also notes briefly that "works of law" have never been part of God's plan to save the pagans in their ethical weakness. The phrase is consequently more limited in its application than most readers assume.

Stowers presses a subjective reading of δικαιοσύνη Θεοῦ in 3:21-26 and a christological emphasis within Paul's πιστ- terminology, these decisions allowing a more theo- and christocentric reading of this resonant passage. He also resists a heavily substitutionary and cultic reading of ἱλαστήριον in 3:25. Paul speaks here, rather, of a messianic "delay" complemented by Christ's "adaptability." Christ has adapted himself to the weak, allowing himself to be crucified as a messianic pretender, and delaying the full use of his powers and authority against those wicked powers, so that wicked Jews and pagans might be afforded time to repent before the day of judgment and God's wrath. God has, meanwhile, vindicated this humble decision by resurrecting Christ.

Stowers then argues for a stylistic continuity in 3:27–4:2. This is an integrated diatribe (and Stowers has a powerful case here). It also subtly distinguishes different modes of salvation for Jews and pagans, in his view. (Stowers draws on intriguing patristic evidence for Paul's use of different prepositions in 3:30, although ultimately — as already noted [in part three, chapter eleven, §3.2, n. 118] — I find this unpersuasive.) An emphasis on Abraham as a "founder of a blessed lineage, analogous to Christ rather than an example of saving faith" then informs his reading of the rest of chapter 4 (237).[139] Stowers argues that "God brings to pass his promises by founding lineages that incorporate whole peoples into the blessings made possible by the founding ancestors" (227). Abraham is the founding faithful ancestor of the Jews and establishes a people through his heroic faithfulness. Similarly, Christ is the founding faithful ancestor of pagans, allowing them to be incorporated into the original saved lineage of Jews. God adopted "whole peoples as his own by using the generative trust of Abraham and Jesus to work procreative miracles that founded new families" (229 — note that it is the Spirit who procreates pagans). Progressively briefer comments on the rest of Romans then follow.

This is an overly concise account of Stowers's argument, but it should suffice for our present purposes. We should note first its many strengths.

Excursus §2: Stowers's Strategic Advances

Stowers is more aware than most interpreters of Romans of the many problems that dog the conventional approach, so many of his revisionist suggestions are made specifically to circumvent those.

(1) His emphasis on a decline narrative in 1:18-32 circumvents the injustice implicit in this scenario if it is an account of individual failure and culpability. His rereading is able to explain the corporate perspective and singular decline that the argument seems to envisage.

(2) In 2:1-16 he carefully excludes Jews from Paul's critical analysis, noting the absence of explicit markers in the text to that effect. This move combines with a further suggestion to try to avoid a well-known problem in the conventional reading of chapter 2 (see immediately below).

(3) At 2:17 he orients the discussion toward a Jewish Teacher who is proselytizing pagans (badly, in Paul's opinion!). In combination with the previous move, this allows Stowers to avoid any blanket indictment of Jews in general by Paul's argument up to this point (in particular, the inconsistent and exaggerated charges in the traditional reading of hypocrisy, adultery, theft, and temple robbery).

(4) Stowers also avoids some of Paul's harsher and more inconsistent statements by repositioning him as the questioner within the diatribe of 3:1-9 at v. 3. The questioner seems far more consistent with Paul elsewhere than the interlocutor, and Stowers interprets accordingly over against the conventional construal. (The questioner, it should be recalled, complains about roles for God's fidelity and righteousness that seem to be overruled here by the interlocutor's consistent advocacy of judgment in accordance with desert.)

(5) These positive moves link up with Stowers's more general description of Judaism to explain the absence of any argument by Paul in Romans 1–4 against the atoning efficacy of the temple cult. (And Stowers tries to maintain this reading consistently even through 3:25.) The apostle is actually speaking only of pagan salvation in relation to Christ. The traditional Jewish modes remain intact, hence the absence of any argument against them, although some future combination of Jews and saved pagans (that nevertheless preserves their key distinctions) is envisaged.

(6) Stowers explains an underdetermination that has been noted previously principally in Romans 3:22 by referring much of Paul's πιστ- terminology to Christ himself, and not to the Christian. This resolves the question concerning the connection between instrumentality and divine disclosure (although he is not explicit about this argument).

(7) Likewise, he reads chapter 4 rather differently from the conventional reading, emphasizing Abraham's miraculous fatherhood of Isaac in particular, and thereby accounting for another obvious textual overdetermination (i.e., the textual emphasis upon the patriarch's literal paternity).

These are significant advances. (No other rereading, to my knowledge, makes such gains.)[140] Moreover, in making them, the discussion is packed with creative new approaches to various words, subsections, and arguments. However, Stowers illustrates some of the vulnerabilities of the rereading strategy at this point as well, as he tries to realize these gains. His suggestions cannot merely deal with localized difficulties, especially as those materialize at various empirical frames. They must combine localized exegetical plausibility with an overarching argumentative and (if necessary) theoretical coherence. If they do not, then despite their initial palatability, the conventional reading will be able to reassert itself by claiming superiority in terms of sheer construal. And Stowers's suggestions tend on closer scrutiny to unravel on all these interpretative levels. His virtuoso performance does not actually hold together, as that performance unfolds.

Excursus §3: Stowers's Problems

In the first instance, Stowers's reading lacks overarching coherence (and without this it is in fact very difficult to make a convincing localized exegetical case[141]). I see three principal points where Stowers's reading seems to break down.

(1) Stowers — following the conventional construal strangely closely — accepts that 1:18-32 is Paul's own position, and that the argument through 2:16 lays out common ground that both he and the Teacher accept. This argument builds from the natural revelation of God and his concerns to the impartial apportioning of salvation or judgment in accordance with desert. And although this material focuses on the pagan, Stowers concedes that it applies to the Jew as well. But this concession basically unleashes all the difficulties of Justification theory that are associated with its first phase — and they are numerous and severe. So, for example, God (accompanied by the returning Christ!) is violently angry with wrongdoers at the end of the age. Similarly, Stowers seems to have conceded the presence of natural theology in Paul. (He argues against this in relation to 2:14-15, but these arguments are unconvincing and do not in any case remove his earlier concession.) Moreover, God judges all finally in accordance with deeds and desert, and Stowers is not even able to deploy the conventional qualification of sola fide in relation to this scenario! Certain further difficulties are now generated for him.[142]

(2) Stowers is well aware that the role of Christ ought to be reoriented by any rereading, and posits an interesting combination of "adaptability" and "delay." But this causes further problems.

There is now an otiose quality to Christ's dispatch and death. His delay allows time for more pagans and Jews to repent. But if this was the case, he needed merely to wait, not to die. (Perhaps he was killed inadvertently, then, but Paul seems to emphasize this death unaccountably strongly.) Moreover, it was unaccountably harsh or stupid of God not to grasp this point before the coming of Christ. (And God does like it because he vindicates Christ after this generous delay by resurrecting him.) Furthermore, this action is at cross-purposes with God's and Christ's violent destruction of wrongdoers at the end of the age. Finally, it should be noted that Paul explicitly links Christ's death with some solution to the problem of human sins too frequently for this function to be unaccounted for. (One also wonders what the actual role of Christ's adaptability is in all this; it plays no role in his delay, which forbears the exercise of his messianic powers.)

In short, all the difficulties and inconsistencies in Justification theory that we have already noted at this point (i.e., in terms of the relationship between the Father and the Son, and in terms of God's fundamental character) are mobilized by Stowers's conception as well. But in certain respects they are deepened, because Stowers cannot point to the atoning function of Christ's death and its merciful implications. God operates inconsistently, at cross-purposes, and fundamentally violently, in Stowers's rereading. It is — in a supreme irony — a more vicious theological construct than Justification. (I am sure that this is inadvertent on his part.)

(3) Stowers's earlier concessions now problematize his introduction of a Jewish Teacher proselytizing pagans incorrectly (that is, in place of "the Jew," who is the conventional target of Paul's critique), along with his account of "works of law" in Paul, which the apostle plainly rejects. As with Dunn, Stowers has abandoned the conventional Justification argument that suggests rejecting "works of law," so he will have difficulty justifying Paul's strong rejection of these for pagans. In his case, however, given a two-track scenario, that task will be further complicated because he wants to retain works for Jews in any case. Why, then, are "works of law" so inappropriate for pagans, according to Stowers, to the point that Paul can roundly abuse a Jewish Teacher for stupidly suggesting this?

Apparently, this is simply because God has chosen to save Jews and pagans by similar but specifically different routes — incorporation into the lineage of a faithful ancestor. But two further problems emerge at this point. The Jewish Teacher is still entitled to promote law observance for pagans for ethical reasons (which may have been his only intention in the first place, and indeed would have been according to [one of] Stowers's description[s] of Judaism). Moreover, judgment will still take place in accordance with deeds informed by law, and Stowers has even gone so far as to argue specifically that the pagans have always been informed by the Jewish law. (Why the final judgment will be in accordance with deeds but salvation is through the lineage of a faithful one is never clearly resolved; one would have thought that these two things are basically different.) Paul's visceral opposition to this Teacher and his gospel of "works" is therefore completely opaque. And his critique of law observance is also puzzling.[143] In Stowers's terms, he does not really have one.[144]

These are serious problems. Once they have been identified, it is hard to avoid the impression that many of the difficulties of Justification theory have been retained (especially those generated by 1:18–2:16), while some of its key strengths have been traded away for a fundamentally incoherent argument. There are also numerous difficulties of straight textual under- or overdetermination — points where the text does not supply explicitly what Stowers says that it does, or where it supplies something different (although these need not detain us now in detail).[145] It is possible to push a little harder on Stowers's difficulties and discern some important underlying dynamics.

Arguably, Stowers makes *too many* revisionist moves. By doing so, he places enormous pressures on his reinterpretation, which seems to lapse frequently into contradiction. The conventional reading has its difficulties, but it is also an accurate reading in many respects. It seems, then, that some way must be found to stay closer to that reading, perhaps incorporating some of Stowers's revisionist insights at certain key points, but without generating the enormous interpretative challenges at the argumentative and theoretical levels that he does. Any suggested alternative to the conventional approach, if it is to be successful, will probably have to be more "surgical" than Stowers's reinterpretation, in the sense of excising and substituting carefully defined and specified motifs and issues, and then reconfiguring the argument accordingly. We will have to find a space somewhere between too little, and too much reinterpretation.

It becomes increasingly clear as his analysis unfolds that Stowers has not been sufficiently critical of his own conception of the problem, which relies heavily on Stendahl and hence tends to vilify an "Augustinian" approach to the text. Stowers fails to recognize the development in Augustine's thought, in terms of quite different systems, and thereby commits himself to eliminating *both* from Paul's text (something often pursued in relation to "guilt" and "introspection"). From this point, then, the baby has gone out with the bathwater — that is, the *entire* Western theological tradition, including its most important internal debates.[146] And this is ultimately implausible. (Indeed, a greater sensitivity to the distinction within Western theology between conditional and unconditional theology would have alerted Stowers to the difficulties he was creating by continuing to endorse Paul's commitments to 1:18-32 and 2:1-16.) As we have already seen, there is a deeply insightful dimension to Stendahl, but this coexists with a lack of coherence and accuracy, especially in relation to Augustine. And this combination of great intuitive insight and broader incoherence tends to characterize Stowers's analysis as well.

In sum, Stowers's rereading is simultaneously brilliant, insightful, polemical, and muddled. His difficulties should not be allowed to overshadow his positive contributions (perhaps damning them by association), but neither should they be overlooked. In the quest for a radical interpretative solution, Stowers's rereading of Romans is an important forerunner, but not the main event.[147]

As was the case with respect to the other basic strategies, we have learned a lot from the struggles of Stowers, who has pursued a more comprehensive solution to our difficulties. In the first instance it has become apparent that such a strategy is high risk. If specific attempts to construct a comprehensive rereading fail, then they tend to go down in flames; either they are right, or they are glaringly if not gloriously wrong. But precisely because such risk is intrinsic to the approach, past failures in this relation need not dissuade us. They should not prevent us from recognizing that this is the way ahead in methodological terms.

Moreover, radical revisionists must articulate more exactly just what is needed and where, and then craft a tighter construal (and, indeed, these specific questions have occupied much of my time since the appearance of Stowers's rereading in 1994). And it is becoming increasingly apparent that such attempts will need to stay much closer to the *exegesis* of the conventional reading — to its basic arrangement of Paul's sense units. The conventional reading is an accurate reading in terms of sheer construal. It is on the understanding of the *argument* that radical rereadings must probably place their principal reinterpretative pressure, guided by both the unsupported needs of Justification theory — which expose the conventional reading's key pressure points — and the construal's nagging overdeterminations. The latter texts are where any decisive exegetical edge might be found. In short, more precision and plausibility are required. A radical reconstrual *might* be possible, but only if it can fasten explicitly onto the conventional reading's key textual underdeterminations and, at the same time, resolve its nagging list of overdeterminations. It is also apparent that such rereadings should not mix strategies, dropping, for example, to motivational claims when the exegetical rereading seems to be going badly, and vice versa. This is both confusing and — more importantly — invalid. The pursuit of any comprehensive rereading must be consistent, accounting precisely for *all* the text, and supplying a convincing account of its causality to boot.

And in the light of these conclusions, we should pause briefly to consider where our overarching discussion has reached, and where it should now head.

4. Summary and Implications — the State of Play

It is important to appreciate what the exact state of play is at this point in our analysis. It is clear that at present no viable solution to the difficulties generated by the conventional construal of Romans 1-4, and its intrinsic endorsement of Justification theory, exists; no successful strategy is yet evident, only a wide path leading to hermeneutical destruction for all traveling upon it. But it is also clear what any such solution (if it exists) ought basically to look like. Its contours are apparent: it must be a comprehensive, nontheoretical, retrospective rereading that is also fundamentally plausible *as* a reading — an argumentatively radical but exegetically modest proposal. Only the actualization of this strategy offers any hope in terms of resolving our many difficulties. However, it does offer that hope concretely. A nontheoretical retrospective reading of Romans 1-4 — one that does not activate the theory of Justification — will immediately eliminate five of the six sets of problems that we have previously detected, and reframe the sixth.[148] So this is surely the steep and narrow path to our ultimate destination.

We should note further that the current state of play is somewhat deceptive. Although Justification advocates have been able to repudiate the many revisionist challenges to their key reading's cogency — usually on exegetical grounds (one of the main lessons of this chapter) — this has in no way eliminated the raft of difficulties apparent in the Justification reading itself (the lesson of part three, chapter eleven). The conventional reading remains deeply vulnerable. It is at present simply *the least worst alternative.* Consequently, if a superior alternative can be crafted, the conventional construal will face a formidable challenge, and on fronts that it is unaccustomed to defending; it will have to produce a stronger positive justification of its own reading *and* begin to resolve its extensive series of problems (and I am not convinced that these two tasks are ultimately possible).

We turn at this point, then, to articulate that reading in part four, a demonstration that unfolds in stages in chapters thirteen through eighteen. This demonstration will begin, for heuristic reasons, with some suggestions about reframing in chapter thirteen. As we have just seen, such discussions can free the interpretative imagination to consider new approaches to the text. We must open up a new perspective on why Paul might have written Romans, and this should allow in turn a fresh conceptualization of what he actually argues there, pursued in chapters fourteen through eighteen. So begins our journey up a steep and narrow — but promising — interpretative path.

PART FOUR

A Rhetorical and Apocalyptic Rereading

CHAPTER THIRTEEN

Rereading the Frame

§1. Preamble

We have just seen in part three (specifically, in chapter eleven) that the Justification discourse's textual base — the conventional reading of Romans 1–4 — contains upwards of fifty problems that are as yet unresolved, although among all the different approaches currently on offer in relation to this text, the conventional one remains the least worst alternative (this being one of the main lessons of chapter twelve). However, clearly some solution to all these difficulties is desirable. We have also learned from these different approaches to Romans 1–4 that any solution will have to take the form of a comprehensive, radical rereading that can also displace the conventional approach plausibly in terms of sheer construal. It would seem most obvious at this point, then, simply to attempt such a rereading. But the conventional approach still enjoys a high degree of confidence, especially among its advocates. Moreover, it is difficult for many interpreters to think in different ways about Romans 1–4, even if they want to, and so revisionists frequently reproduce much if not all of the conventional reading within their critical analyses. In view of these hermeneutical dynamics, it may be useful to preface our detailed reconstrual with a reframing discussion, that is, with an analysis of the circumstances that could have surrounded the composition and original reception of Romans 1–4. While not a decisive argument in its own right — because it addresses only the frame and not the text — such a discussion can, as we have already seen, open up new interpretative spaces (perhaps while simultaneously curtailing familiar but unreliable zones of hermeneutical operation); the imagination of the rereader might be liberated in certain respects. And such an explanation is, in any case, an important component of any broader historical-critical reading.[1] But any discussion of the circumstances surrounding the production of Romans 1–4 faces some peculiar difficulties of its own that will have to be navigated successfully before a framing explanation can make a useful contribution to our broader argument. Indeed, these are notoriously treacherous interpretative waters.

The difficulty apparent at this point was signaled as early on as the introduction. A complex and unresolved debate exists over just why Paul composed Romans — "the Romans debate."[2] Scholars have not agreed on a plausible explanation of why Paul composed Romans as he did and then dispatched this letter to Rome (and in the past this may have assisted the conventional construal of Romans 1–4 in certain respects[3]). It should be possible, nevertheless, to introduce some clarifications to this debate that will allow us to go on to grasp a single explanation of Romans' provenance and then to reframe the following detailed exegetical deliberations in chapters fourteen through nineteen (that is, the rest of part four and first chapter of part five) from an illuminating perspective, even if not all the tangles in the debate have thereby been resolved. These all-important clarifications will begin with a new consideration of the relevant data; any plausible explanation of Romans must account for sixteen different features of the data, satisfying any further issues that arise in the process — so §2. Following this, we will discuss through §3 the many explanations of that data that fail, isolating during the process some key interpretative dynamics. (There are ten main alternatives at this point.) In §4 we will turn to the one theory that does seem to be able to encompass the data without difficulty. We will also briefly consider some objections that might immediately be made to this theory, suggesting that — while such concerns are understandable — none actually derails our developing analysis. And with this entire discussion complete we will be able to approach the text of Romans 1–4 in chapter fourteen from a new interpretative angle — as a complex, carefully crafted debate with a powerful opposing position within which Paul competes for the assent and loyalties of the diverse Roman Christians.

§2. The Data

Any explanation of the original production of Romans must be able to account for all the data in that letter — its nature, structure, and so on. We seek to know why Paul wrote what he actually did (which is of course the point of this sort of explanation).[4] And Romans is quite peculiar in this regard. Some classic remarks by Kümmel provide a useful point of entry into this data: "Romans bears a double character: It is basically a dialogue of the Pauline gospel with Judaism. . . . And yet the Epistle contains expressions which definitely characterize the congregation as Gentile Christian."[5] In fact, we may speak more accurately of a *double* double character. The dialogue with Judaism noted by Kümmel is a slightly tendentious characterization of the letter body (1:16–15:13),[6] which consists of a series of discussions, at a fairly abstract, systematic level, of various issues and motifs that are fundamentally Jewish — the sinfulness of pagans because of their idolatry and gender deviance, law and law observance, a final judgment, Scripture, Abraham,

Adam, sin, creation, the election of the patriarchs, the present posture of Israel, and so on. Indeed, the point is obvious. Only at 12:1 does the text turn in any sustained fashion toward the letter's audience, and only from 14:1 onward are remotely practical local questions detectable, although even then Paul's treatment seems quite generalized (see 1 Corinthians 8 and 10). Romans' letter body consists, in short, of *abstract* — or apparently "coherent" — and *Jewish* material (which is not necessarily the same thing as a discussion of *Judaism*).

Most interpreters detect a fourfold division within this material — roughly in terms of chapters 1-4, 5-8, 9-11, and 12-15.[7] Different motifs and questions are treated in each of these subordinate units, and their manner of treatment can differ quite significantly, but they all tend to remain within a Jewish orbit. So, for example, the use of short scriptural quotations falls almost entirely into chapters 1-4 and 9-11, with smaller patches of citations in 12-14 and a climactic catena in 15:9-12. More than fifty explicit citations occur in these subsections, along with numerous softer textual echoes. But explicit citations occur only three times in all of chapters 5-8.[8] So the abstract Jewish letter body of Romans modulates significantly through at least four subordinate phases.

The letter frame of Romans (1:1-15; 15:14–16:23/24/27), however, seems to be practical and localized and is oriented, as Kümmel observed, primarily toward converted pagans.[9] Paul speaks in the frame of certain key motifs, especially of his apostolic call to the pagans, which seems to include the Roman Christians (1:1, 5-6, 11, 13-15; 15:15-22, 32). He also speaks of his desire to visit Rome, along with the reasons for its frustration until now (1:9-13; 15:23b-24), and of his plan to evangelize beyond Rome in Spain (15:24a, 28b), in the context of a "non-interference" clause (15:20) — that he wants to preach only where Christ is yet unknown. Paul makes a number of practical requests in the letter frame: for prayer support as he visits Jerusalem with the collection (15:25-28a, 30-31); for an appropriate reception at Rome for Phoebe, who is presumably the letter bearer (16:1-2); and for a process of mutual greeting at Rome (16:3-16). He also utters a warning concerning false teachers (16:17-20).[10] In short, Romans' letter frame, primarily oriented toward converts from paganism, is utterly practical or contingent. Quite concrete problems and actions are discussed.

Thus, Romans possesses a unique character within Paul's extant letters in terms of its interwoven complexity, structure, tone, and style. Moreover, it seems composed in terms of two principal complementary lines of tension — a practical letter frame oriented primarily toward converted pagans wrapped around a highly abstract, coherent letter body oriented apparently toward Jewish issues. And we now have the relevant data for our main set of explanatory criteria. Ideally, a plausible framing explanation of Romans ought to be able to comprehend this entire data set within its compass (a challenge, to be sure), and not merely one or two aspects of it; it must be able to explain Romans' double double character, along with all of the various further features apparent within that structure. These requirements can be summarized in the following enumeration.

Eight features of the letter frame (I-VIII) —

I: an address primarily to converts from paganism, both specifically and implicitly, in terms of Paul's authority (see II)

II: repeated emphases on Paul's apostleship (1:1, 5, 9, 13-15; 15:15-22) and gospel (see 1:1, 9, 16; 15:16, 19; see 16:25)

III: an elaboration of II in terms of a principle of "non-interference" (15:20) — Paul's desire, in accordance with Isaiah 52:15b, to preach Christ where he has not yet been named

IV: various nuances within Paul's generic expression of a desire to visit the Roman Christians — to strengthen and to harvest them, to be mutually encouraged, also to bring them a spiritual gift (1:11-13), and even perhaps to do signs and wonders among them (see 1:11; 15:19)

V: a desire to evangelize Spain, and a corresponding request for assistance (15:24, 28b)

VI: a forthcoming visit to Jerusalem and delivery of the collection, and a corresponding request for prayers for safety and acceptability (15:25-28a, 30-32a)

VII: a request that the Roman Christians greet one another (16:3-16a)

VIII: a warning against false teaching (16:17-20a)

Eight features of the letter body (IX-XVI) —

IX: a transition to the abstract level of discussion in the letter body (and back)

X: a transition to the Jewish concerns of the letter body (and back)

XI: a transition to Romans 1–4

XII: a transition to Romans 5–8

XIII: a transition to Romans 9–11[11]

XIV: admonitions against pagan Christian arrogance toward Jews (11:13-32)

XV: a transition to Romans 12–15

XVI: admonitions to the "weak" and "strong" (Romans 14)

Ideally, all these features need to be explained — I through XVI — if a plausible explanation of the character of Romans is to be supplied. And a set of critical explanatory dynamics is detectable in much of the debate, which develops in terms of two main interpretative trajectories.

Some of these features in the data are explicable in self-sufficient terms; they explain *themselves* in terms of their content sufficiently to warrant their inclusion within the letter without further justification. I would place within this category feature I, arguably also II, features IV through VI, VIII, and XIV-XVI. (I will elaborate on these claims momentarily.) But this leaves various features unexplained in self-sufficient terms — III, VII, and IX-XIII (some of which are very significant). And it is of course these unexplained features that create our difficulties with respect to Romans. The explanation of the provenance of Romans now reduces to two possible trajectories. A feature needs to be identified from among the self-sufficient ones that not only explains itself but can plausibly be extended to explain the unexplained features. Either this, or another explanation must be introduced that is not overtly attested in the letter but can nevertheless explain the outstanding features. Clearly, however, the second option also creates further difficulties for itself. Any such explanation must prove that it is actually relevant to Romans even though it is not directly attested (or, at least, not obviously so); the introduction of this further data must be plausible. The history of the Romans debate is in many respects just the exploration of these two main explanatory options.

Almost all of the self-sufficient features have been pressed at some point to see whether they can sustain the additional weight of the rest of Romans. Two are arguably too bland to offer much hope in these terms (I and IV). So basically this category includes explanations revolving around features II (and Klein includes III here), V, VI, VIII, XIV, and XVI (usually in combination with XV; XIV-XVI also go together well). I regard three of these explanations as especially plausible — VIII, XIV, and XVI, so they will be treated in the most detail in what follows. The rest seem to fail relatively overtly and quickly.

Complementing this broad explanatory trajectory, various external explanations have also been suggested from time to time, principally in relation to the unexplained features of Romans' letter body. These characteristically introduce further issues that need to be satisfied if their broader explanation is to hold good, and they tend to struggle at such points. Three types of explanation can be detected in this trajectory, bringing their own explanatory riders with them: the claim that Romans is an essentially coherent genre of text, such as a letter-essay or protreptic; the claim that it was a circular, sent originally to multiple destinations; and the claim that it is a composite.[12]

We should note finally that most explanations tend, to a greater or lesser degree, to embrace a multiple approach; they rely on more than one explanation to account for all the data in Romans. And this seems quite acceptable, except that it does introduce a further rider into the debate, namely, the various explanations must cohere. That is, it must be shown how these different questions arose for Paul at essentially the same time and place. Certainly, most of Paul's other letters were not occasioned by such multiple considerations, and for letters that were, this is both evident and plausible.[13] The difficulty of meeting this criterion will depend very much on the balance and nature of any broader, multiple explanation's subordinate underlying theories.

Key features in the data of Romans

Feature	Self-sufficient	Non-self-sufficient	Expandable
Letter frame			
I: address primarily to converts from paganism	•		
II: emphasis on Paul's apostleship and gospel	•		•
III: "non-interference" clause (15:20)		•	•
IV: expectations for the Romans (strengthening, etc.)	•		

Feature	Self-sufficient	Non-self-sufficient	Expandable
V: Spanish mission	•		•
VI: visit to Jerusalem with the collection	•		•
VII: mutual greeting at Rome		•	
VIII: warning against false teaching	•		•
Letter body			
IX: transition to abstract concerns		•	
X: transition to Jewish concerns		•	
XI: transition to 1–4		•	•
XII: transition to 5–8		•	
XIII: transition to 9–11		•	
XIV: warnings against pagan Christian arrogance toward Jews	•		•
XV: transition to 12–15	•		
XVI: admonitions to the "weak" and "strong" in 14	•		•

We can now evaluate these options in turn, although I will treat the explanation arising from feature VIII later (in §4), out of sequence, because it is in my view the most plausible and requires a more detailed evaluation.

§3. Various Explanations

It is entirely understandable that Paul would address the Roman Christians — and indeed be interested in them — primarily as converts from paganism (feature I; see 1:5-7, 13-15; 15:15-16, 18). This is the primary locus of his spiritual authority; however, any explanation of the letter in such terms clearly devolves into the closely related theme of Paul's apostleship to the pagans (feature II). Romans was not written simply *because* the Roman Christians were, in the main, converts from paganism.

Similarly, the desires for past visits that were frustrated and for future visits that would bring benefits are perfectly understandable; they were epistolary commonplaces. So Paul expresses numerous wishes in relation to the nature of his visit (feature IV) — for the Roman Christians' strengthening, perhaps primarily through the imparting of some spiritual gift (1:11), for mutual encouragement (1:12), for a further harvest among them (1:13b), for a blessing (15:29), and for refreshment (15:32b). But these expectations are too bland to explain the rest of the letter. Paul has not written Romans merely to express these wishes. His apostleship to the pagans, however, does seem potentially to explain much if not all of Romans, and various scholars have asserted as much.[14]

(1) *The Importance of Paul's Apostleship and Gospel*

The Roman Christians were — at least in the main — converted pagans; therefore, it makes perfect sense to suggest that Paul, the apostle to the pagans, would be concerned to establish his authority over them and his law-free gospel among them (that is, since he did not himself convert them). Indeed, this is one of the strengths of this theory; it ties together the emphases in the letter frame on Paul's apostleship and gospel with an apparent emphasis in the letter body on the gospel (that gospel usually being located in the conventional reading of Romans 1–4, thereby linking features II, IX, and XI as well).[15] Moreover, Romans' repeated emphasis on Paul's apostolic authority, while not as pronounced or overt as Galatians', is otherwise unparalleled among the highly formulaic openings and closings of Paul's letters. This can be seen especially in the almost liturgical affirmation and expansion of apostleship that Paul includes before reaching even the identification of the letter's addressees (see 1:1b-6) — a rather extraordinary interruption of ancient epistolary etiquette. He also returns to the theme in chapter 15 (see esp. vv. 15b-16, but vv. 17-29 and 32 significantly amplify and reinforce this theme as well[16]). Clearly, this is an important element of the letter that must feature in any plausible explanation of its provenance.[17] But can it sustain the explanatory burden of Romans as a whole? Could Romans be Paul's apostolic introduction to Rome, functioning simultaneously as an act of evangelical reinforcement and incorporation?[18] While this theory can explain most of the remaining features in the data, it struggles to account for certain key points — two in particular.

First, the suggestion that Romans is freighting Paul's gospel can account for only one of the three more abstract, Jewish units in the letter body — the unit chosen as Paul's gospel. From this point, interpreters tend to be thrown back on older and often rather problematic assertions — for example, that Romans 5–8 describes the process of sanctification after Romans 1–4 has described justification. Romans 9–11 then supposedly addresses "issues regarding Israel," but nowhere else in the Pauline corpus does a discussion of the gospel devolve into a further complex discussion of issues regarding Israel — neither in the otherwise rather similar Galatians, where much of the terminology of Romans 1–4 and 5–8 is discernible (although in a highly compressed form),[19] nor in briefer accounts of soteriological material in other letters. (Nor does anything in Paul's descriptions of his initial gospel presentation elsewhere suggest an *intrinsic* role for unbelieving Israel in that presentation.)[20] So this approach can theoretically account for one of the three argumentative units in Romans' letter body, and in abstract and Jewish terms, but much remains unexplained.

More awkward, second, is Paul's stated non-interference clause in Romans 15:20 (feature III). There Paul states boldly that his apostolic gift and duty, confirmed by signs and wonders (v. 19), involves preaching where Christ has not yet been named so that he does not build on "another foundation." And this also fulfils the Scripture that says "those to whom it has not been proclaimed concerning him will see, and those who have not heard will understand" (v. 21; see Isa.

52:15b). As Klein points out more clearly than most, Paul is contravening this stated principle if he is writing to Rome in an apostolic fashion. The problem could be mitigated if it is conceded that at this point Paul commits an egregious blunder. However, the emphasis in the letter closing on this dimension of Paul's missionary work is actually quite sustained (see at least vv. 20-22, rooted in vv. 15-19, and arguably related further to vv. 24 and 28b); it seems entirely deliberate.

Hence, Klein's own solution is superior, and we should pause for a moment to consider it. Klein suggests that Paul means by "foundation" an *apostolic* foundation. And, defined in these terms, the problem now inverts into part of the solution. Since the Roman Christians lack an apostolic foundation, Paul ought to write to correct that.[21] However, this ingenious solution falters in several ways and so should be discounted. Paul does not define the "foundation" in this apostolic fashion in 15:20; it is a matter merely of ignorance (see Isa. 52:15b!). Moreover, his development of "founder's rights" elsewhere never makes that claim in apostolic terms; it is simply a parental and generative metaphor and claim (see 1 Cor. 3:9-17; 4:14-16; see also 2 Cor. 10:13-17 and Gal. 4:19-20). Still more embarrassing, the Romans have apostles present with them already — Andronicus and Junia, whom Paul calls apostles (16:7). (Prisca and Aquila probably enjoyed this status as well, and if they did not, they could certainly act as apostolic proxies for Paul: see perhaps Col. 1:7.) So unfortunately, the incorporation of feature III into a theory based on II also falters. Paul's non-interference clause remains an embarrassment to the "apostolic" explanation of Romans.

The suggestions of Klein and those persuaded by him should not simply be dismissed; accounts of the data that he emphasizes are an essential part of any ultimately plausible explanation of Romans as a whole — the repeated developments of Paul's apostolicity, and the apparent contradictions caused by his expressed desire to preach "where Christ has not yet been named" (15:20) in combination with his obvious desires to influence and to visit Rome. But clearly these textual features and their resolution cannot carry this explanatory burden alone. We move, then, to consider the next possible explanation in terms of a self-sufficient datum with wider implications.

(2) Romans as a Request to Assist Paul's Mission to Spain

One of Paul's three overtly stated aims in Romans is a request for assistance as he travels onward to evangelize Spain (feature V; 15:24).[22] The verb προπέμπω that Paul uses here is significant, often denoting assistance to someone making a journey. When we "send people on their way" in the modern era, we generally mean by this — if we are speaking English — that we have also equipped them to some degree, perhaps having fed and accommodated them. They have been taken care of. And the connotations of the Greek are similar. Hence, as Robert Jewett and others have espied, Paul is in effect requesting assistance here from the Roman church for a mission to Spain, and this support could conceivably have been quite extensive.[23] Moreover, unity at Rome was a practical prerequisite for such support, perhaps explaining features XIV and XVI as well. And a request in advance of Paul's arrival in Rome would be prudent and so makes perfect sense. Other pieces of evidence that have already been noted can then arguably supplement this central concern. In particular, it is understandable why Paul would need to have his apostleship established. Moreover, it is even understandable why he would at some point supply a version of his gospel; the Roman Christians need to understand what they are supporting.[24] However, at this point, the theory arguably begins to break down.

It is not necessary for Paul to establish his entire gospel in advance of his arrival merely to solicit a request for prayer and missionary support. Paul requests a fairly ambitious favor from a figure he does not know personally in Philemon — as much as the release of his unhappy slave, Onesimus, to Christian service — and does little more than make a set of brief (albeit crafty) rhetorical appeals.[25] In fact, it would have been much easier simply to wait to establish both his apostolic credentials and his gospel in the usual fashion, in person and with some "demonstration of the Spirit and of power" (1 Cor. 2:4b; see Rom. 15:18-19a; 2 Cor. 12:12). It is difficult to imagine the Spanish mission itself being the especially urgent concern in relation to which not a moment could be lost in terms of theological exposition. And we run again into the same problems already encountered in relation to an emphasis on feature II (and to be encountered again shortly[26]) — that an emphasis on the proclamation of the gospel can only explain one of the three abstract argumentative units in the letter body. Hence, other theories would have to be mobilized, at which moment we have either abandoned this theory or subordinated it to another. Moreover, it must also be assumed that an emphasis at one point on the gospel can explain the text's preoccupation with diverse Jewish questions (feature X) — assuming in fact that the text is actually concerned with Judaism, and that the gospel is intrinsically concerned with Judaism as well, at which point, a key substantive question in relation to the Justification theory is clearly being begged. In short, while this feature of the data can arguably explain the urgency of Romans, many of the features of the letter frame, the paraenesis, and (arguably!) at least one section of the letter body that needs to be designated "Paul's gospel" (although none is overtly), it cannot explain the rest of the text's character. Furthermore, it tends to beg some critical questions at the vital point, and therefore must be judged deficient.

I would add that there is a danger of misunderstanding the immediate argumentative function of this datum as well. It is not an especially long or significant textual presence (see only 15:24, 28b), and its principal statement occurs after a much longer exposition concerning Paul's apostolic ministry and practice (vv. 15b-21). We may suspect, then, that the Spanish mission, although doubtless a genuine intention on Paul's part, has an important localized argumentative function. (This will be assessed in more detail in §4.) Suffice it to say for now that the theory of a Spanish mission is one more element that must be explained in the provenance of Romans and that it can open up surprisingly wide and constructive dimensions within the letter. But it clearly falls short of being a complete explanation.

(3) Romans as a Request to Assist Paul's Trip to Jerusalem

The second of Paul's overtly stated aims is a request for prayer that he might be "rescued from the disobedient in Judea" and his "mediation in Jerusalem be acceptable to the saints" (15:31; feature VI). It is clearly a strength in any explanation to be able to appeal to explicit requests by Paul in the text of the letter. However, equally clearly, it is difficult to understand why Paul would attach a letter body of some fifteen chapters to this request. A short letter framing this verse would suffice (and numerous papyri exemplify requests of this nature and length).[27] This explanation does have the virtue of explaining why the letter needs to be dispatched now. Obviously, the request for prayer support must be made before Paul goes to Jerusalem. But the character of the vast majority of the text is left unexplained. This datum needs to be involved, then, in any broader explanation of the letter, but it is too weak to sustain any plausible reading in its own right. But it is also the starting point for a powerful and influential suggestion by Jacob Jervell.

Jervell argued that Romans was really a rehearsal of the arguments that Paul felt that he would have to make on his arrival in Jerusalem: "The essential and primary content of Romans (1:18–11:36) is a reflection upon its major content, the 'collection speech,' or more precisely, the defense which Paul plans to give before the church in Jerusalem" (*RD*, 56[28]). We should pause to consider this famous theory more carefully.

Jervell makes his case in stages. He points to three instances in Romans of the verb παρακαλῶ, which frequently indicates significant matters in ancient letters (see 12:1; 15:30 and 16:17). Dismissing the relevance of 16:17 and, to a lesser extent, 12:1, he notes the position of 15:30 at the head of the request for intercession in relation to the forthcoming visit to Jerusalem. He then argues that Jerusalem's acceptance of Paul's mission is absolutely essential to its future and suggests further — probably quite fairly — that the church's receipt of the collection will imply that broader acceptance, although strong countervailing pressures seem to be at work, from both within and outside the church. Hence, vital issues are at stake, the risks are high, and Paul's request for prayer certainly seems fair. Moreover, the letter body of Romans has, he suggests, "the characteristics of a speech with marked apologetic, and to a lesser degree, polemic tendencies. In other words, we find here a presentation of Pauline preaching — yet always defensive and intent on clarifying possible misunderstanding" (*RD*, 61; Jervell points here especially to the many strategic questions in Romans, but also to its oversights in systematic terms). This allows the further important suggestion that the letter body of Romans is bound up with the situation in Jerusalem; it is both explanatory *and* defensive. Paul has sent these deliberations to Rome by letter as well so that the Roman Christians can understand precisely what is at stake and join with Paul in intercession for a safe and effective visit: "one thing is obvious: such prayer can only be said on the basis that one knows why and for what purpose one is praying, and that such prayer always takes place in unison" (*RD*, 62). Moreover, as a result, Paul is able to present himself in Jerusalem as a representative not only of the formerly pagan churches of the northeast but of the critical and prestigious church in the empire's capital — at the center.

This is a perceptive and provocative case. If true, it would resolve many if not all of the letter's explanatory challenges. But it stumbles at a critical point. Jervell struggles to explain the dispatch of arguments located in Jerusalem to Christians living in Rome. There are two difficulties here. First, not everyone will grant that the letter body of Romans is an account of what will take place rhetorically at Jerusalem. I find this a highly plausible suggestion, but there is no direct evidence for it. Certainly Paul never says as much.[29] And second, the claim that these arguments have been sent to Rome because the Roman Christians must understand exactly what they are involved with — the purpose of the requested prayers, and their necessary unanimity — seems weak if not overtly false. Paul's requests for intercession elsewhere never receive this sort of extended and detailed preamble.[30] Furthermore, Paul's account of prayer in Romans 8 specifically disavows the notion of complete understanding during prayer, undergirding this aspect of intercession with the work of the Holy Spirit in speechless petition! (Jervell also uses a dubious wordplay here. Clearly, there ought to be unison in prayer for Paul's safety and success — both Paul and the Roman Christians should obviously be praying for the same thing — however, it does not follow that Paul and the Roman Christians must also be unified *in every thought and theological position*, which would presumably make much Christian intercession difficult!)

There is still in my view much to learn from Jervell's provocative suggestion. But the theory itself must be judged deficient and rejected; a comprehensive explanation of Romans in terms of feature VI does not seem to work (although arguably it comes closer to working than many scholars realize).

Feature VII denotes the set of extensive mutual greetings that Paul includes in 16:3-16a (meaning by "mutual" Paul's instructions to the Roman Christians to greet each other). Only Colossians 4:10-18 is comparable in the rest of the Pauline corpus, and the relevance of that material is of course disputed. But even there we do not see the emphasis on *mutual* greeting in the manner of Romans 16. This distinctive feature of Romans consequently requires explanation.[31] However, lacking even self-sufficiency (that is, an obvious function of its own), it must be combined with some other theory if it is to explain the rest of Romans, so it will be considered further in §4 below. Suffice it for now to note that feature VII must be a part of any plausible account of Romans as a whole. Why does Paul spend so much time here setting up mutual relations within Roman Christianity?

Feature VIII emerges primarily in relation to certain pithy warnings against false teachers that Paul includes in 16:17-20. Such is this subsection's importance that I will consider it in detail in §4 below, filling out its relationship with the letter's other concerns. Clearly, it is self-sufficient; warnings against false teachers are frequent in Paul, as in much of the rest of the New Testament, and need no further justification. Its explanatory implications will need to be teased out shortly in detail.

With these qualifications and postponements in place, we have largely covered the features of Romans' letter frame, and only one has any real promise in terms of broader explanation. We turn, then, to the letter body, where features IX and X initially occupy our attention — the abstract and Jewish nature of Paul's discussion in this extended and complex text. Here our second main trajectory of explanations starts to become apparent. Certain interpreters have judged at the outset that Romans' letter body is not contingent at all but coherent — presumably in view of features IX and X — and so have sought to discover why Paul might have written a coherent text.[32] Two such theories are especially powerful (and a weaker version will be noted immediately as well).

(4) Romans as a Generalized Genre — Letter-Essay or Protreptic or Ambassadorial

One way of negotiating the treacherous path from contingency to coherence that is necessitated by this broad approach is to posit Paul's composition of an essentially coherent letter from the outset. Different variations of this basic approach are detectable in the literature, but all share the same underlying rationale. The letter body of Romans is abstract and generalized because Paul — uniquely — composed Romans in terms of some abstract and generalized genre, although presumably for quite concrete practical reasons. So, for example, Martin Stirewalt has suggested that Paul composed a "letter-essay"; David Aune, that he composed a "protreptic" letter; and Robert Jewett, that he sent an "ambassadorial" epistle (although Jewett's proposal links up cleverly with other important suggestions).[33] These scholars all face difficult explanatory riders, however. They must demonstrate the existence of the type of letter that they are suggesting Paul has written in Romans and then make a case for Paul actually writing it at this time to Rome for plausible practical reasons. And they tend at these later points to stumble and fall. The elegant suggestion that views Romans as a protreptic discourse serves to illustrate these difficulties.[34]

Aune and others have suggested that Romans is influenced by philosophical protreptic — a subcategory of the broader protreptic genre. Philosophical protreptics are basically propaganda on behalf of a particular philosophical position.[35] They seek to recruit converts to their own program, to refute competing programs and figures, and to strengthen those who are already loyal.[36] Their broad similarity to Romans's letter body is immediately evident — a concern with opponents, dialogues, exhortations, systematic refutation, comparison, proof, and so on. Although they are primarily Greco-Roman, Klaus Berger has also suggested some similarities with Jewish texts — specifically the Wisdom of Solomon 1-5 and the *Didache* 1-6 (especially in their emphases on "two ways"). Later Christian texts may also fall into this category — for example, Justin's *First Apology* — and Clement wrote a lengthy and overt instance.

Advocates of this viewpoint have spent much time establishing and delineating the philosophical protreptic genre and its occasional overlap with epistolary forms. I am happy to grant this level of the explanation; it is the further corollaries that concern me at the theory's all-important point of transition from coherence to contingency. I see a number of problems at this methodological juncture.

How do we know that in Romans Paul has actually crafted a protreptic letter? Do the two genres overlap sufficiently to make this identification certain? The evidence supplied at this point is not yet persuasive to me. (It is basically too generalized.[37]) That is, we do not have decisive evidence that Romans *is* a protreptic.[38] Conversely, if Romans is a protreptic, then arguably all of Paul's letters are! Moreover, it must be asked whether Paul could have composed a philosophical protreptic in any case. This seems unlikely, given the elite and specialized philosophical context of that genre and its representatives; Paul was a Pharisee and an artisan, not a Greek philosopher or a senator.[39]

Granting satisfactory responses here for the sake of argument, however, *would* Paul have composed a protreptic to Rome in order to convert and to exhort people there? All the available evidence stands against this. It is not — as we have already seen — how he normally presented his gospel in rhetorical terms, or how he sought to convert people; nor is it how he normally sought to strengthen and exhort people.[40] So at the critical point of transition from contingency to coherence, we lack any direct evidence that this is what happened, and the supporting evidence in terms of analogous activities by Paul tends to contradict this claim.

Moreover, it is difficult to account for various other elements in Romans that must ultimately be accounted for — and especially from the letter frame. The non-interference clause is especially opaque (III),[41] but so are the extended mutual greetings (VII). But I also query whether we have received much practical assistance in relation to the transitions that take place through the letter body. Simply specifying the abstract genre to which Romans belongs may explain features IX, X, and even XI, but it does not explain the awkward points of transition that occur later on (i.e., XII and XIII) any more effectively than previous theories do (although XVI is arguably more understandable as an exhortatory discussion typical of protreptic). A certain counterargument seems effective at this point as well.

It has long been observed that the letter body of Romans, although abstract, is not a comprehensive account of Paul's theology, because too many vital topics are left out — an account of the Eucharist, a full account of eschatology, and so on.[42] And that Paul would compose a protreptic (or a letter-essay or an ambassadorial letter), setting out his position systematically but omitting key topics from this gospel, seems incomprehensible. The letter body of Romans is abstract and often treats important questions, but it does not seem to be a balanced presentation of Paul's coherence — of his theology per se.

For all these reasons, then, the protreptic explanation must be judged an elegant failure, as must all analogous theories, which tend to stumble at just the same points. Granting the existence of some rather formal genre, the recognition of this genre in Paul's letter to Rome, along with his reasons for composing this sort of letter at this time, nevertheless remains unexplained and unjustified, as do several of his transitions and instructions (or lack of them!) within that text. The letter frame also remains opaque. However, another powerful explanation in coherent terms is available that courts fewer of these dangers.

(5) Romans as a Preserved Circular

One ingenious way to generate a coherent letter body was suggested by T. W. Manson, using the exciting new manuscript evidence available to him of $\mathfrak{P}^{46}$.[43] Manson suggested that the bulk of Romans was a circular, composed by Paul in deliberately general terms, and sent by way of multiple copies to different churches. Moreover, the textual confusion surrounding Romans 16, and the new evidence of a shorter version of Romans supplied by $\mathfrak{P}^{46}$, apparently confirmed this suggestion concerning multiple versions. Indeed, Manson supplied arguments for the original semi-independent status of Romans 16 and its address *to Ephesus.* He thereby isolated at least two original destinations within the canonical texts, thereby directly supporting his thesis of multiple destinations. And some manuscript traditions also omit specific references to Rome.

In my view, this is one of the most potentially effective contributions to the entire debate, and it deserves serious consideration. Manson has in fact solved most of our difficulties if he is right. Unfortunately, the evidence, when it is examined closely, proves either too weak to support such strong assertions,[44] or even subtly to contradict his claims. In particular, the manuscript evidence indicates a different textual history for Romans, in terms of later redactions, rather than an original existence in multiple forms. In addition, Romans 16 looks more integral to the letter than separate (at least, on text-critical grounds).[45] If an Ephesian address for Romans 16 is abandoned as unlikely, and that chapter attached firmly to the rest of the letter, then a single Roman destination looks unavoidable and Manson's contentions collapse. So this theory must be abandoned, which is a pity because it is one of the few theories that, if correct, could actually explain most if not all of our features. Like many theories, this one founders in relation to its explanatory riders; it cannot demonstrate the truth of the additional claims that need to hold good in order for its basic plausibility to be maintained.

We have already touched on a third theory in this general trajectory — the attribution of one of the letter body's subunits to the gospel (usually Romans 1–4) — and we ought now to consider it in a little more detail, since Romans has been read in this way for most of its interpretative history.

(6) Romans as Self-Expression — a Straightforward Statement of Paul's Gospel

Principally in view of features IX and X, and the assumed equation between the text following XI and Paul's gospel, Romans has been read for much of its interpretative history as a systematic theological statement. Melanchthon is often cited as a prime example of this view. He famously observed that Romans is a *christianae religionis compendium* and went on to write a lucid commentary in these terms, as well as a systematic theological treatise structured in the same way. We would now probably speak in Pauline circles of a coherent reading, using Beker's terminology; Romans is simply a statement of Paul's own theology and hence of his "coherence." Although modern historical-critical scholars have theoretically broken with this viewpoint, it remains strangely persistent. Commentators frequently approach Paul's text in this fashion, coherently. (Nygren and Moo are candid about doing so.[46] Many other interpreters, however, arguably treat the letter this way tacitly and/or in effect, assuming an equation between part of the letter body and Paul's gospel without any plausible explanation.[47]) Günther Bornkamm is often quoted in this relation, although a little unfairly.

Bornkamm spoke of Romans as "Paul's last will and testament" — "[a] great document, which summarizes and develops the most important themes and thoughts of the Pauline message and theology and which elevates his theology above the moment of definite situations and conflicts into the sphere of the eternally and universally valid . . ." (*RD*, 27-28). Bornkamm did not view the letter in these terms literally and took pains to say so; rather, he wrote that it has become this type of text *in effect,* and he is absolutely correct. Most interpreters treat Romans, and Romans 1–4 in particular, as a systematic statement of Paul's theological position — of his gospel — even when they disavow this approach elsewhere. However, this approach is supposedly no longer viable in the modern historical-critical period (at least, in terms of that particular language game).

It violates most of the canons of historicizing interpretation, ignoring both the contingency of Paul's letters and the role of the original audience, valorizing instead the later role of the church in an overtly anachronistic mode, and privileging — in a rather modern fashion — Paul's self-expression, and his supposed systematizing and reflective concerns. Hence, such an approach to the provenance of Romans ought to be dismissed from further consideration (that is, in a strictly historical-critical analysis), and interpretations in these terms held accountable. If Justification advocates rest ultimately on such views for their broader account of the letter, in this respect they will be vulnerable.

We should now consider one final approach to Romans' provenance in terms of coherence briefly, although it overlaps partly with contingent features. Indeed, it almost straddles our two main approaches, although it has already been treated critically in part three, chapter twelve and found wanting — the suggestion that canonical Romans is in fact a composite document.

(7) Romans as Composite

One alternative way of explaining the modulations within the letter body of Romans is to argue its composite nature. If canonical Romans was produced by the artificial conflation of previous shorter letters and texts, perhaps including non-Pauline materials on occasion, the noticeable modulations in the letter body would certainly be comprehensible — the strong transitions into Romans 1–4 (feature XI), and then to Romans 5–8, 9–11, and 12–15 in turn (features XII, XIII, and XV). And Romans 9–11 does arguably flow rather more smoothly in stylistic terms on from Romans 1–4, and Romans 12–15 from Romans 5–8. So this theory treats each element of Romans as contingent but explains the broader text's modulations in terms of a later editor (who may also have had more coherent concerns).

Unfortunately, however, this theory too fails to satisfy its explanatory riders. It needs evidence at the relevant text-critical seams and generally fails to find it, while supporting evidence for redaction and a redactor is absent as well.[48] So the suggestion of multiple preceding texts in Romans just does not seem to be true; it is a false characterization of the letter's origin. Moreover, this theory does not solve our problems in ultimate terms in any case. All the conceptual tensions within Paul's thought resulting from the clash of apparently different systems (and so on) remain. This should not necessarily undermine the plausibility of the theory as an explanation of Romans' circumstantial and proximate frames. Nevertheless, most of our difficulties — at the intrinsic, systematic, and empirical frames, and in terms of textual under- and overdeterminations — are only relocated in generative terms, not resolved.[49]

For all these reasons, explanations in terms of composite origin are best abandoned. They serve the useful purpose of highlighting our difficulties in these relations — the *facts* of overt modulations in the nature and direction of Paul's argument in Romans. However, as solutions to those difficulties they have rightly been found wanting. We will follow the majority opinion, then, and treat canonical Romans in what follows as an essentially unified document — one springing from a single situation and contingency.

We turn now to consider some further attempted explanations in rather more detail, because they raise important substantive points about key texts in Romans that ultimately will have to be integrated into any plausible theory of the letter's origin(s).

(8) Romans as Addressing Anti-Judaism at Rome

Many interpreters have suggested that Romans 11:17-24 in context (feature XIV) contains an important clue concerning the provenance of Romans as a whole. In 11:13 Paul turns to address a converted pagan audience explicitly: ὑμῖν δὲ λέγω τοῖς ἔθνεσιν.[50] An extended metaphorical argument then follows in vv. 17-24 in terms of natural and unnatural branches and their relationship to an olive tree.[51] Some of the natural branches in this tree — unbelieving Israel — have been broken off (although temporarily: see vv. 23b, 24b, 25-29), and the unnatural or wild branches that believe — pagan converts — have been grafted in.[52] But Paul goes on to encode the position of believing pagans vis-à-vis unbelieving Jews in various terms that relativize any superiority perceptible in this relationship: (1) the pagan converts should fear rather than exult, because the pagan engrafting could be terminated too (an argumentative redirection); (2) pagan converts remain in

God's kindness only by belief, which may contain an elective dimension (i.e., they do not deserve this privileged position, and neither does it depend fundamentally on their efforts: see 11:28-32); (3) outside of this belief, even more sternness awaits them than befell Jewish unbelievers, because they are wild, not natural branches (an argument a minori ad maius); (4) meanwhile, the natural branches can be grafted into the tree again, because God is able to do so; (5) indeed, this will be easier, because they are natural (a second argument a minori ad maius); and (6) it will in fact happen, something that has been revealed to Paul directly in a μυστήριον; so (7) the pagan converts' putative superiority is also only temporary, as well as being fragile and undeserved.

In view of the considerable argumentative development, it is clear that these admonitions on Paul's part are neither parenthetical nor minor. It also seems unlikely that they are merely generic. Although the diatribal style can be directed at abstract and indirectly relevant considerations, we will see in due course that the diatribe in Romans freights directly relevant concerns for Paul in relation to the Roman Christians; it manipulates quite practical issues. So we should grant that this argument potentially relates to a concrete issue in Rome — some form of Christian anti-Judaism among converts from paganism that Paul either knows of or is anticipating. And that such a dynamic would or could have been present in the Christian community there is entirely plausible. The Greco-Roman world was, by modern standards, endemically racist,[53] and marked anti-Judaism was widespread.[54] So Paul's anticipation of such an attitude among any Roman Christians converted from paganism (and perhaps even from Judaism in some cases: see 1 Thess. 2:14b-16!) requires no further justification; it is a self-sufficient datum.

It is no real surprise, then, to find many interpreters drawing attention to this element within the text as they attempt to explain Romans more broadly. Such concern on Paul's part is unique,[55] and it goes some way toward counterbalancing the harsh statements that he makes elsewhere about Jews.[56] But at least here he seems to express sentiments similar to the post-Holocaust concerns that inform so much recent Pauline scholarship (and this even if he stops short of fully endorsing "two-track" salvation). In this argument Paul momentarily seems to take the side of non-Christian Jews over against an arrogant pagan Christianity, a setting that fits much later Christian interpretation like a hand in a glove (and this even if the dynamics in the original situation were rather different). But in grasping this concern in 11:13-32, have we explained the rest of Romans — the crucial point in the present relation? Unfortunately, it is clear almost immediately that this feature cannot necessarily explain more than its own section of some twenty verses.

As we have just seen, Paul addresses the problem of pagan Christian arrogance toward unbelieving Jews in an illustration in which seven mutually reinforcing contentions reframe any such posture. He signals this concern with his previously pagan audience explicitly and admonishes them; however, problems arise if the concern is extended. Modern scholars expect rather more than such a brief treatment when they address this issue; they expect broader accounts of the nature of Israel and of Christianity, and of how those two histories relate to one another after the Christ event. These accounts then inform some position on the excruciating question of Jewish and Christian relations in a post-Auschwitz era — one that will often be complex and nuanced, to the degree that it is resolved at all. But it is difficult to argue that *Paul* had to supply such extended argumentation; such a claim begs the key question.

We have no evidence that Paul felt the need to justify this admonition in extended terms. Moreover, what evidence there is seems to stand against this assertion. The presuppositions for Paul's extended metaphorical admonition are all fairly obvious — salvation in relation to the kindness of God, Christ, belief of some sort, and the converse of this situation (i.e., unbelief), along with a preceding history of some special kind in relation to Israel (that is adequately acknowledged by Romans 9:4-5a). For the sake of argument, then, it could be granted initially that Romans 9–11 functioned to set out the presuppositions of the later admonition. Romans 9:1-3, 10:1, and 11:1b introduce Paul's personal concerns directly; 9:4-5 introduces Israel's privileges; 9:30–10:21 discusses the peculiar dynamic of πίστις in relation to Israel and the pagans; and 11:1a and vv. 2-12 then reinforce the contention of 11:15-16 and 30 that good ultimately comes out of this. Romans 9:6-29 can then be justified as an apology for the scandal of pagan inclusion in these blessings at all. But Paul does not need to include most of these broader arguments in order to make his basic case that converts from paganism should not be arrogant toward unbelieving Jews. The basis for Paul's admonition in 11:17-24 is fundamentally Christian (i.e., fear for *your* noninclusion, etc.). Moreover, some of Paul's broader arguments really *hinder* his later admonition, which depends secondarily on Jewish historical privilege in 11:13-17. (That privilege underlies the two contentions from minor to major considerations.) Romans 9:4-5a makes the case for Jewish privilege very compactly, but 9:6-29 turns on it, with considerable Jewish backing, while 9:30–10:21 seems to attribute Jewish noninclusion to Jewish recalcitrance. All of this accumulates to suggest the embarrassing conclusion that 11:13-32 functions to defuse any pagan Christian misunderstanding of Paul's previous argumentation, and not the reverse — i.e., that the more extended argumentation prepares for the later admonition. (This is how the passage is structured in any case in terms of both order and basic length.[57])

In support of our gathering suspicions, we should note that Paul's admonitions are not generally prepared for in this way — with extended salvation-historical preambles. It could be countered that since Paul is not writing in Romans to a congregation that knows him, he must supply extensive teaching here that could be presupposed in other situations, so it is not really surprising that we lack evidence of such preparation from those other texts. However, this appeal pushes debate into a realm where no verification or falsification is possible. We have no evidence that Paul prefaced his admonitions elsewhere in these terms, because we do not possess much evidence of Paul's original oral preaching and teaching. We are left with a category containing one possible instance, and it is the instance currently in dispute. Moreover, *it is assumed here that Paul's preparation for such an appeal is fundamentally salvation-historical.* And there is very little evidence of such argumentative preparation elsewhere in Paul at all.

Given the difficulties apparent in extending the explanatory force of the concern suggested by 11:13-32 as far as chapters 9–11, it is obvious what the main problems are with this datum as an explanation of Romans as a whole. There is no evidence that the explanatory force of this subsection should be so extended. Problems arise as it is so extended (because many of Paul's arguments do not seem to prepare properly for its concerns).[58] And the resulting argumentative structures within the subsection and the letter seem unbalanced if not inverted. (Basically, Romans does not obviously build toward 11:17-32, although this pericope is easily read as a correction to the overenthusiastic appropriation of 9:6–11:16.). Finally, we should mark that this explanation allows powerful modern hermeneutical concerns to be met, which surely must raise our historical-critical suspicions still further. Many interpreters would be comforted if Paul was functioning in this way, and so functioning rather like themselves, but this begs one of the most important questions in the whole realm of Pauline scholarship — whether the apostle was fundamentally a salvation-historical thinker, and one attuned, moreover, to post-Holocaust concerns.[59] Such assertions court obvious dangers of anachronism and so need to be proved more than most and not merely assumed.

In sum, then, an emphasis on either present or potential anti-Judaism among the Roman Christian converts from paganism — like almost all the other self-sufficient features — must play some role within any comprehensive explanation of the letter. However, it cannot itself deliver that comprehensive explanation. Romans is not just an elaborate preparation for Paul's admonition to such Christians to be sympathetic and not arrogant toward unbelieving Jews (however much we might like it to be). Paul does say this, and we may be grateful for it. But perhaps even this rather unusual statement on his part would benefit from a degree of further explanation.

(9) Romans as Contingent, Addressing the Weak and the Strong (or Some Such)

The most obvious feature in relation to which to seek some overtly contingent explanation of Romans is XVI — the presence of some potential conflict between the "weak" and another group as suggested by chapter 14. Indeed, this view seems to enjoy the most support currently of all the theories on offer and so can fairly be designated the "majority" position (and it will also consequently receive a more detailed treatment).[60] This approach exists in numerous subtle variants, often depending on the degree to which other features are incorporated into a particular account, but all are based at bottom on the situation broadly perceptible in Romans 14.[61]

There two types of Christians are treated who seem also to exist in a potentially problematic relation to one another — "the weak" and "the strong."[62] The former distinguish foods and days (see vv. 2 and 5; they possibly also make distinctions concerning wine: see v. 21); the latter do not. Paul exhorts the weak not to "judge" the strong, and the strong not to "despise" the weak, although he clearly sympathizes with the fundamental posture of the strong (see esp. v. 14a). But if the strong go on to despise the weak or — worse still — to cause them to stumble through their own uninhibited behavior, then Paul views this as a serious shortcoming.

However, the broader relevance of this extended admonition to a concrete situation at Rome has been challenged. Indeed, "the Romans debate" began in large measure because of Robert Karris's suggestion in 1973 that these instructions by Paul be treated in generalized terms, to which Karl Donfried replied emphatically in the negative. And Donfried was almost certainly correct to argue for a degree of specificity here.[63] Paul is not known personally to the Roman Christians and so has to tread rather softly in his admonitions, hence presumably the chapter's slightly blander tone. Moreover, the very fact that his advice in 1 Corinthians is so pointed counts against the suggestion that it is a generalized topos there, and only included in Romans for that reason; at Corinth Paul is clearly targeting a particular situation in that congregation caused by different postures toward certain Jewish practices, and ultimately by a complicated mission history. Confirming this contingency, the "topos" does not appear in any other noncontingent loci in Paul's letters where we might otherwise expect it in such terms — for example, in the paraenesis of Galatians, 1 Thessalonians, and Philippians.

But Karris's observations were not without force. Paul's treatment is significantly shorter and more generalized in Romans 14 than it is in 1 Corinthians 8–10, and this ultimately requires explanation. If a long and rather specific discussion in 1 Corinthians cannot explain the entirety of that letter and is, furthermore, not prefaced by extended theological discussions, why should we believe that a shorter, blander discussion so prefaced can explain Romans? We may concede, then, that the discussion in Romans 14 refers ultimately to an actual situation at Rome, but the extension of that feature to a comprehensive explanation has clearly been problematized by Karris's case. The problem seems less urgent at Rome than at Corinth, hence (in part) Paul's noticeably softer, briefer, and more generalized treatment.

Nevertheless, many scholars insist on making the attempt to explain Romans comprehensively in terms of the weak and the strong, and not without reason. It allows, among other things, for useful connections with some of the other important features in Romans that have already been noted. Links with features VII and XV are not too difficult to establish, supported by I, II, and IV. That is, Paul's unusual instructions in chapter 16 to the Roman Christians to greet one another are now comprehensible within a broader concern for the healing of divisions at Rome. A process of mutual greeting — involving travel, meeting, hospitality, and so on — is a strategy cleverly formulated to facilitate unity.[64] And chapters 12–15 are concerned frequently throughout with unity as well.[65] The same theme then reemerges with special force in this major subsection's conclusion (which is arguably the letter body's conclusion as well) — 15:1-13.[66] A prayer for an implicitly unified hope, joy, peace, and understanding, concludes the entire letter body in v. 13. So feature XVI can arguably be extended relatively easily to explain XV well. An acceptance of Paul's apostleship by the Roman Christians (II) — without which his exhortations would lack authority — and a concern on Paul's part for those pagan converts who seem to be experiencing disunity (I), are then clearly also explicable in this broader relation. Moreover, Paul's more generic desires to visit and to strengthen the Roman Christians (and so on) — feature IV — are also understandable in relation to this agenda. So feature XVI can encompass most of the motifs in the letter frame, along with the important data underlying feature XV in the letter body. Clearly, one important explanatory dimension within the provenance of Romans seems to have been grasped in all this.

But there is a great deal that remains unexplained. Moreover, once again, when this self-sufficient feature is pressed beyond certain obvious boundaries in the data to a more comprehensive function, its explanatory power seems to decline if not evaporate. I detect one principal set of difficulties here, and two further, more minor problems.[67]

The principal difficulty surrounding the elevation of feature XVI to a comprehensive level is that it does not seem able to explain the rest of the letter body in Romans — features IX through XIV. Why does Paul craft such a complex, modulated, abstract, and Jewish preamble, in largely unparalleled fashion, for his later exhortations, which are themselves noticeably blander than in 1 Corinthians? Indeed, 1 Corinthians is especially problematic in this relation. Paul clearly crafts a considerable amount of reinforcement there for his recommendations to the weak and the strong, constructing a chiastic discussion that pivots around an account of his own renunciations, flexibility, and discipline (1 Corinthians 9). So that evidence points both to a lower degree of urgency in the Roman situation (which is not to deny that the problem exists) *and* to Paul's evident lack of any need to provide an extensive abstract preamble of the sort just noted. It might be replied that the Corinthians already know Paul and his teaching and so do not require this additional material as the Romans do. But several considerations suggest that this objection is invalid.

The Corinthians have not necessarily yet been exposed to the language and argumentation of Justification. That claim depends on an approach to Pauline biography that has already been challenged (i.e., it is based on a naïve acceptance of the narrative sequence supplied by Acts and so ends up placing Galatians first in the sequence of extant Pauline letters). A good biographical case can be made that the Justification discourse evident at times in Paul's letters actually lies *later* than 1 Corinthians. So Paul has probably formulated this particular set of admonitions independently of the Justification discourse. More importantly, the discussion in 1 Corinthians 8 and 10 *nowhere references this underlying abstract theological material* (i.e., material similar to Romans 1–11). It actually tends to supply a different set of theological rationales from that material, where it does so, as we have already noted. *Nor does the discussion in Romans 14 reference this earlier ma-*

terial significantly (except in certain limited respects that will be discussed in more detail shortly).[68] And all of these indications point in the same direction: what evidence we have concerning Paul's practice suggests that he does not preface admonitions to congregational unity in terms of the weak and the strong with extensive, abstract, Jewish theological discussions that ostensibly ground those admonitions.[69] The only argumentation that Paul needs in order to address the congregational tensions apparent in Romans 14 *is* Romans 14 (perhaps supported by the rest of the paraenesis in Romans 12, 13, and 15).

Even if the foregoing case could be made, it could only explain one of the three preceding subunits — the theological preamble that grounded the later discussion. The reasons for Paul's inclusion of the other two units would remain opaque. So the all-important modulations within the letter body of Romans would remain unexplained in any case; two of the preceding three major subunits would still be undetermined.

The question of appropriateness arises here as well. Romans 14 is a tactful account that seeks to defuse possible recriminations between two groups with different evaluations of the importance of key Jewish practices — Sabbath and festal observances, and the consumption of properly prepared meat and wine.[70] Without conceding the theological position with respect to nonobservance, Paul seeks to fashion a flexible and sensitive posture for both parties. It needs to be asked, then — as a further criterion — if the conventional construal of the preceding subunits actually contributes constructively to these goals (a point already touched on in part three, chapter eleven).

If earlier subunits are explicable as the appropriate theological foundation for these later exhortations and postures, as advocates of the centrality of feature XVI urge, do they actually fulfill this function? In fact, Paul's widespread aggression in the earlier sections of the letter *against* the importance of many standard Jewish practices seems to cause problems in this regard. By the end of chapter 4 — according to its conventional construal — Paul has undermined the needs for law observance, for circumcision, and for direct (i.e., biological) descent from Abraham. Moreover, the Jewish Scriptures have been co-opted to support this program. Thus, Judaism, as it understood itself, has been almost totally undermined.[71] By the end of chapter 10, moreover, the bulk of Israel is not even saved (at least, currently)! And divine election for Israel has been redefined in relation to its prior history so that it now includes direct converts from the pagans!

A difficult rhetorical dynamic is now generated for this theory. Paul seems in Romans 14 to seek to mitigate any dismissive actions by the strong against the weak. The former are not to despise the latter because of their continued endorsement of certain Jewish practices. Similarly, the weak are not to judge the strong. If the preceding argumentative material is fundamentally explained by these admonitions, however, along with the situation that underlies them, then Paul has been clumsy. He has prepared for his later complementary and flexible admonitions by devastating the theological rationale underlying one party and massively reinforcing the position underlying the other. If Paul's preceding arguments hold good, the strong seem entitled to despise the weak, while the weak are simply foolish to judge the strong.[72] And these realizations point us in an intriguing direction.

As a systematic preamble to the admonitions in Romans 14, the letter's rhetoric is basically incompetent (if not completely implausible). However, if this relationship is *reversed*, then the letter's rhetoric instantly becomes comprehensible; Paul's earlier attacks on standard aspects of Judaism *could create* a situation of "strong aggression," and so Romans 14 might be added as a necessary constraint on that destructive result. (The earlier sections will of course require some independent explanation.) In short, Romans 14 seems to function better rhetorically as a constraint on preceding argumentation, mitigating its potentially harsh application, and not a climax to a preceding argumentative preparation — and just as we have seen Romans 11:17-32 functions best as well.

Our suspicion that feature XVI cannot plausibly be pressed to explain the entire letter is confirmed by two more minor sets of observations.

While it is plausible to suggest that some establishment of Paul's apostolic authority must take place for his admonitions to the strong and the weak at Rome to be effective (along with their ostensible theological preamble, which requires acceptance as well), a close reading of Paul's developments of his apostolicity suggests that this explanation is not entirely adequate. An explanation in terms of Romans 14 and feature XVI entails that Paul's apostleship is a necessary *presupposition* for the later discussion's effectiveness. However, Paul actually encodes his apostleship as — at least in part — the *cause* of his communication with the Roman Christians. This stronger, generative role is evident in both the letter's opening and its closing (and we have already noted some of the evidence for these assertions).

Paul begins to establish his apostleship from his initial declaration that he is the letter's sender — literally, from the letter's first word. He is the sole author of Romans, and he immediately expands this statement with genitive, participial, and prepositional phrases and clauses that articulate his apostleship and gospel in terms of scriptural legitimation and a christological focus. Verse 6 then includes the addressees, the Roman Christians, within this divine gift and call, along with any others "in Rome who love God and are called holy" (v. 7a). The gospel is reintroduced almost immediately at the outset of the thanksgiving paragraph to ground Paul's constant remembrance of and intercession for the Romans (v. 9). He wishes to visit them in order "to see" them, "to impart a spiritual gift" to them, and "to strengthen" them, all of which should be a mutual encouragement (vv. 11-12). His second reference to a desire to visit (in v. 13) is then expanded in terms of the desire to have a harvest among them as he has had among the rest of the pagans. Paul is "obligated" to this constituency — whether "Greek, barbarian, learned, or illiterate" (v. 14). Hence, both references by Paul in the proem to his desire to visit Rome are explicitly grounded in his service to the gospel, which is immediately to say as well — in terms of the information he has supplied in the letter's address — in his divine apostolic call to proclaim that gospel.

Exactly the same argumentative dynamic is evident in the letter closing. Paul begins to segue out of the letter body in 15:14, but in so doing he speaks immediately — albeit somewhat apologetically — of his divine gift and priestly duty to the pagans. Hence, this is what undergirds his actual writing of the letter in explicit terms: "I have written to you rather boldly at times so as to remind you of things because of the gift which has been given to me by God, namely, that I should be a sacred minister of Christ Jesus to the pagans with the holy duty of [his] divine proclamation . . ." (15:15-16a, DC). Paul's discussion of his apostleship continues — as we have already seen — through v. 23 and includes the troublesome claim that, in fulfillment of Isaiah 52:15, he proclaims Christ where he has not yet been seen or heard. The same apostolic theme then underlies 15:27, 29; 16:4, and 17, and arguably reemerges in 16:25-26 as one of the letter's final statements. Indeed, in 16:25 the text states that Paul's gospel and proclamation *strengthen* those pagans who submit to it, and who also believe and understand it.

So it seems clear that Paul's apostleship, which includes God's divine call to him to proclaim Christ to the pagans, seems in some sense to be a generative force for Romans. Both the letter opening and the closing place that apostleship at the basis of Paul's desires to visit and to write to the Roman Christians. It is consequently more than a mere presupposition for certain ethical admonitions. It is encoded in causal terms; it explains those desires in some sense. Hence, any explanation that can take account of this dynamic will benefit from the text's explicit encoding of Paul's motivations. And since a comprehensive explanation grounded in Romans 14 seeks, precisely, to generate the letter in relation to *that* situation in Rome, it must struggle in this relation.

We should note further that feature II — Paul's apostleship and gospel — is not merely somewhat redundant (i.e., as a causal factor) in a comprehensive explanation in terms of feature XVI, but its development in terms of the non-interference clause of 15:20 — feature III — is entirely opaque. Paul gains nothing argumentatively by including this development of his apostleship; indeed, he causes trouble for himself by inviting the obvious retort that he therefore has no business evangelizing or admonishing at Rome!

A final observation: a generative role for Romans 14 suggests that the entire letter is grounded in a serious deficiency at Rome, one serious enough to warrant a letter and complex enough to warrant a sophisticated and extended discussion. However, Paul's characterizations of the Roman Christians are generally positive. Although he clearly believes that a visit by him will be of benefit, he does not characterize the Roman Christians in fundamentally negative terms themselves. He praises the "worldwide" reporting of their fidelity, and in longing to see them and strengthen them concedes immediately that this will result in a mutual encouragement because of a shared fidelity (1:12). Indeed, precisely because his visits and writing are grounded in his own apostolic call, he does *not* ground the letter in Roman deficiencies. It is his obligation to preach that necessitates a visit and a harvest (vv. 13-15). His letter also consequently takes place in the mode of "reminding"; it is even "rather bold at times" (15:15).

Certain passing remarks in the letter body confirm this impression. As is well known, the Roman Christians "have become obedient from the heart to the form of teaching to which [they] were entrusted" (6:17b), thereby being "set free from sin" (6:18); they also "know the law" already (7:1). The letter frequently attests to a rich scriptural competence, at least on the part of some. Paul also has nothing but praise for the Christians that he names in Romans 16. In particular, Junia and Andronicus are "prominent among the apostles," have been in Christ longer than Paul, and have also been imprisoned like him — a key marker of Christian authenticity and dedication.

We may accept of course that epistolary flattery is both common and wise. Paul has no desire to alienate the Romans by criticizing them; they do not know him, so any aggression on his part would be foolish. Ancient etiquette also demanded compliments. He is trying to create a sympathetic hearing. However, there is no hint of deficiency or negativity in any of these remarks, and this is disquieting. On the one hand, there is now no direct evidence in the letter at all outside Romans 14 for its ostensible principal cause — the conflicts within that community. On the other hand, there is a level of flattery in relation to the Roman Christians that, if Romans 14 is causal, arguably approaches the untruthful. Indeed, it is worth noting that Paul can be reasonably blunt in his other letters when he feels that it is warranted! (One suspects that the absence of any such honesty from Romans cannot be *entirely* explained in terms of a lack of prior friendship; moreover, Paul does in fact already know some of the Christians at Rome quite well — certainly Prisca, Aquila, and Epaenetus.) At the least, it seems fair to suggest that an explanation that can account for the largely positive remarks by Paul about the Roman Christians (that is, arguably except in Romans 14) should be judged superior to one that cannot.[73]

It seems, then, that a comprehensive explanation of Romans in terms of feature XVI is in difficulties. Too many features of the data remain unaccounted for in relation to any such explanation, if they do not contradict it (whether gently or overtly) — II, III, IV, and probably most if not all of IX through XIV.[74] But this is not to say that one important element within the broader explanation of Romans has not been grasped. Feature XVI can account for its surrounding subunit in chapters 12–15 and much of the letter closing, which are important matters (i.e., features VII and XIV).[75] Hence, the sense is growing that another important subordinate element within the broader explanation of Romans has been identified — a sustained concern with congregational unity. (This should be added to Paul's evident concern with the possibility of Christian anti-Judaism, which also relates more broadly to the issue of unity.) However, the key explanatory dynamic for the letter still seems to lie beyond us. We turn, then, to consider one further attempt to grasp it. Could it lie in some combination of theories and features that we have already considered separately?

(10) A Multiple Explanation

The most popular such theory probably revolves around a combination of features XIV and XVI — anti-Judaism among converted pagans and possible conflict over Jewish issues between the weak and the strong. But any assessment of the validity of this combined position is complicated by the status of the historical reconstruction that is usually offered to support it.[76]

This explanation develops from an ostensible expulsion of the Jews from Rome by the emperor Claudius in 49 CE (see esp. Acts 18:2). An elegant, although rather complex, account of the development of Christianity at Rome can be supplied using the possible sociological consequences of this event that creates — largely simultaneously — a scenario of divided Jews and pagans at Rome, and of separate and alienated groups of Jewish and converted pagan Christians as well. This ostensibly generates features XIV and XVI *at the same time* — pagan Christian anti-Judaism, and tension between pagan and Jewish Christians. And this apparent explanatory coup in historical terms generates its own momentum in favor of the combined theory.[77]

A critical scrutiny, however, reveals numerous points of fragility, if not a dependence on claims that are either unfounded or overtly incorrect. In my view, this reconstruction is best abandoned. But this does not entail that the multiple explanation it supports needs to be abandoned as well (as I once thought). Both features XIV and XVI *are essentially self-sufficient;* they need no such external reconstruction in order to justify their presence in early Christian congregations, whether at Rome or elsewhere, and so be addressed by Paul in a letter as potentially problematic. The problem of weak versus strong arose at Corinth independently of any expulsion, and the existence of broader pagan anti-Judaism in any ancient city needs no justification. So the criterion of plausible simultaneity that must be satisfied — as for all multiple theories — is not failed if the usual narrative that undergirds this particular explanation is jettisoned. But this realization does render the issues surrounding that reconstruction something of a distraction, so it will not be treated in much detail here.[78]

In short, we should concede that it is quite possible in historical terms that a combination of issues underlay features XIV and XVI in Romans, and nothing more than this really needs to be said by way of broader historical reconstruction. But does this powerful multiple theory solve all our difficulties and supply the comprehensive explanation that we have been looking for in relation to the letter itself?

Unfortunately, it does not. The combination of these two theories explains more of Romans than one in isolation — hence, doubtless, its widespread endorsement — but large parts of the letter are *still* not covered — notably, features II through IV and IX through XII.[79] Essentially, a multiple theory — given a basic plausibility in terms of simultaneity — is only as good as the sum of its parts. And if the strengths of one of the component theories do not overlap perfectly with the weaknesses of another, and vice versa, thereby eliminating *all* the weaknesses, we must continue our search. Moreover, both these theories and their key subsections, when pressed, hinted that our expectations were possibly reversed (the tail wagging the dog, so to speak). When considered in the broader context of the entire letter, these subsections and their generative features — XIV in the context of

XIII, and XVI in the context of XV — worked better as rhetorical constraints and corrections to difficulties raised, rather than as climactic points to which every-thing else was building. And this may well prove a significant pointer to the one theory that ultimately does explain Romans.

Why is Paul so concerned in Romans to defuse possible anti-Judaism — and this repeatedly? He seems to bend over backward at times, creating multiple reasons and metaphors to try to ensure that his earlier arguments do not devolve into insensitive behavior toward either Jews (so 11:17-32) or Jewish Christians (so 14:1–15:13). Similarly, a sustained concern with unity is apparent, extending in particular through the letter's final quarter, and again with particular reference to Jewish practices. It is time to consider in detail the one theory that in my view can explain these emphases, along with the rest of Romans.

§4. A Successful Theory — Romans as an Attempt to Negate the Influence of Hostile Countermissionaries at Rome

At this point I simply want to suggest an explanation for Romans' circumstantial frame that, as far as I can tell, satisfies all the relevant criteria — the only theory that seems to be able to do so. This suggestion is not original (although perhaps I will press it further than has generally been the case, in terms of its implications). It has been made periodically since the inception of the modern historical-critical period, although as far as I can tell it has never enjoyed great salience.[80]

Fundamentally, Romans was written for the same reasons that Galatians was written — to defend Paul's gospel against the depredations of certain hostile countermissionaries. Moreover, the significant differences between these two let-ters are more apparent than real — the similarities are well known — and all are explicable in terms of the different relationship that Paul had with the Roman Christians, most of whom did not know him or his gospel (or this debate). He had of course founded and then probably also revisited the Galatian Christian congregations. (These contentions will be expanded shortly.) So this theory of Romans' origins builds primarily from feature VIII — Paul's caustic warnings in the letter closing against false teachers (16:17-20), the only feature in the data that seems self-sufficient or independently valid *and* capable of expansion in a way that can plausibly explain all the other issues.

An explanation of Romans as an engagement primarily with false teachers has probably been obscured in the past by many factors — perhaps in particular by the prevailing "systematic" reading of Romans as Paul's self-expression, abet-ted by a false reconstruction of Paul's biography. But Romans is best understood as an attempt by letter to forestall an attack on Paul's gospel in Rome, so it is a full-fledged engagement with "another gospel that is really no gospel at all" (see Gal. 1:6b-7a, DC) — a quite concrete circumstance. As such, the letter does contain an account of Paul's gospel, as conventional readers have always suspected, but it contains much more than this; it is frequently an offensive operation that attacks the opposing gospel, while it seeks as well — more defensively — to rebut the criticisms that the advocate of this opposing gospel has directed (at times quite ingeniously) at Paul's. In view of this fundamental dynamic, we can in large measure explain the letter's rather abstract argumentation, its concern with various Jewish questions, and its complexity. The letter is by turns aggressive, apologetic, and expository, because all of these rhetorical functions were a necessary part of any effective, persuasive advocacy of Paul's position in the highly contested setting of Roman Christianity, as he understood that situation to be developing.

In elaborating this theory, I will first point to the key pieces of evidence in the letter that underlie it. Then, second, I will show how this dynamic explains all the other previously opaque pieces of data (a discussion that also continues the process of attestation). It will become apparent that this explanation of Romans has the signal virtue of being able to appeal to evidence overtly in the text that is, moreover, capable of being expanded into a comprehensive explanation of the entirety of Romans in all its modulations and complexity — the only datum that can be successfully so expanded. Finally, third, I will consider possible objections to the theory, addressing certain methodological and text-critical concerns and investigating briefly the biographical and historical questions raised.

4.1. Internal Evidence

Paul tends to conclude his letters in almost as stereotypical a fashion as he begins them,[81] by running through several habitual speech acts:

- a peace benediction;
- a hortatory section (that can precede the peace wish);
- greetings, including more specifically
  - greetings,
  - a kiss greeting, and
  - an autograph greeting; and
- a grace benediction.
- Further optional elements are also often present, whether a doxology, an expression of joy, a letter of commendation, and/or a postscript.[82]

These final comments by Paul can contain especially significant information about the intended function of the letter that they conclude. So, although 16:17-20 occurs at the end of Romans, it is not for that reason marginal so much as located in a place of strategic importance.[83] It would in fact be the last piece of substantive instruction that the Roman Christians would hear from Paul. Following this, only greetings and a grace wish occur definitely (although the position of the latter is confused, and might also constitute a doublet[84]), along with a possible doxology. The short subsection also begins with an important verb, παρακαλῶ, which occurs here for the third time in this form (see 12:1 and 15:30[85]). While

Jervell exaggerates its importance, suggesting that its appearance in 15:30 is programmatic for the entire letter, its significance should not for this reason be underplayed. Paul follows customary ancient epistolary practice in using it to foreground significant matters for the letter's audience. It is a *strong* exhortation.

Following this verb — and ultimately in dependence on it — Paul exhorts the Roman Christians to be wary of certain troublemakers. He describes them very carefully. He first employs the verbs σκοπῶ and ἐκκλίνω ("watch out for" and "shun") and then crafts a complex phrase that characterizes these figures initially in schismatic terms; they cause factious dissensions (τοὺς τὰς διχοστασίας . . . ποιοῦντας; see 1 Cor. 3:3 v.l.; Gal. 5:20; see also 1 Clement 20:4; and Hermas, *Similitudes*, 8, 7, 2; 8, 7, 6; 8, 8, 5), and temptations or enticements (σκάνδαλα) "contrary to the teaching which you learned." Paul then deploys further elements from the ancient polemical discourse in relation to philosophical opponents (especially Epicureans), accusing these figures of pandering to their own appetites — literally, to their bellies or κοιλία — and of not serving Christ. Moreover, they "deceive the innocent in heart" (ἐξαπατῶσιν τὰς καρδίας τῶν ἀκάκων) "through smooth speech and false eloquence" (διὰ τῆς χρηστολογίας καὶ εὐλογίας).[86] The verb of deception recalls 7:11, which is in turn a probable echo of the work of the serpent as Eve describes it in Genesis 3:13 (and that Paul transposes into the work of Sin in Romans 7).[87] Paul then expresses his confidence that the famous submission of the Roman Christians, their ὑπακοή, will lead to their "wisdom concerning the good, but innocence concerning evil."[88] He concludes the subsection by stating that "the God of peace will shortly crush Satan under your feet" (20a),[89] following this assertion according to some manuscript traditions with his characteristic grace wish (although it may well be a little out of place here).

It is important to appreciate that this is not a generalized exhortation to avoid false teachers whoever they might be. Paul does not usually write *general* exhortations to avoid false teachers. And on the few occasions that he does, such warnings are clearly signaled as generic. So, for example, an exhortation to avoid "dissensions" (διχοστασίαι, and so not in fact false teachers per se) occurs in a vice list in Galatians 5:19b-21a; consequently, explicit signals are sent here to the Galatians that this list of behaviors is generalized. But Paul's numerous exhortations to avoid false teachers almost invariably have specific false teachers in view.[90] Furthermore, although scholars differ in the importance that they ascribe to it, all agree that false teachers are a major element within Paul's biography and consequently in the interpretation of much in his letters.[91] Hence — and perhaps most importantly — it seems significant that this subsection is *very* close in diction, syntax, substance, and tone to Paul's warnings to the Philippians to avoid false teachers, who in that setting seem clearly to be specific figures.[92] Added to this, we should now note that this subsection is carefully crafted; it provides a surprisingly detailed portrait of the teachers that Paul has in view. They are characterized by several key elements.[93]

Paul characterizes them initially as opposed to the teaching that the Roman Christians learned. We will explore this rather cunning characterization in more detail shortly. Suffice it for now to note that this marks these figures as overtly opposed to something important — if necessary, to the point of dispute and counteropposition. Not surprisingly, Paul impugns their motives and authenticity; they are not genuine servants of Christ but, rather, create temptations for genuine Christians through flattery (etc.), and the apostle ultimately implies that they are nothing more than servants of Satan. We gather from this that Paul himself is firmly opposed to these figures. Nevertheless, it is likely that they are Christians in some sense. Unless they lay claim to this identification, Paul's repeated warnings about their deceptive qualities, as well as his denial that they are servants of Christ, are pointless.[94]

We learn from this subsection, further, that they are *eloquent*. Paul describes them twice as possessing a manipulative eloquence; they have χρηστολογία *and* εὐλογία. It is this facility that creates in part their deceptive aspect that Paul emphasizes here so much. They create "temptations" or "traps" (v. 17) *and* "deceive" (see v. 18b). It is likely, then, that they are learned. Linguistic competence of this level probably denoted a rhetorical education or its equivalent. Moreover, they "serve their own bellies." This may simply be a piece of generalized ancient polemic; however, it opens up an important possibility. It may refer, slightly more specifically, to the presence of an underlying philosophical discourse of self-mastery. Various philosophers — sometimes echoed in turn by philosophical Jews[95] — offered liberation from the appetites or belly by adopting and practicing the appropriate techniques and systems. It was therefore an especially pointed retort to attribute to such ostensible masters a continued slavery to the appetites. This retort in Romans 16:18 *could* then indicate the presence in Romans of an underlying dispute over just this issue — how are evil passions mastered? — along with a dispute with someone opposed to Paul's system. It is by no means definitive proof that such an argument is present, *but it is entirely compatible with such a dispute* (and Paul makes exactly the same charge in Phil. 3:19). And this is of course an educated discourse — one circulating among essentially philosophical figures (i.e., including among sages). The educational status of the false teachers and their possible quasi-philosophical system seem to reinforce one another at this point. (Later indications from the text of Romans 1–4 will strongly confirm these indications.)[96]

We should now return to the point at which we began and note how Paul characterizes these figures. Although it is clear that this is a matter of deep concern to Paul, he characterizes the dissensions and temptations of the false teachers initially *in relation to the teaching that the Roman Christians themselves have learned* (an important point not often noted by the commentators). But those auditors bring certain identifications to this relationship from earlier in the letter that should then draw them to equate their opposition to these false teachers *with Paul's*. And at this point we begin to grasp one of the letter's central rhetorical strategies.

We have already seen how Paul frequently praises the Roman Christians for their many good qualities, and in fact he does so repeatedly here again, characterizing them as submissive, and hopefully also as wise and innocent, not to mention ultimately triumphant and peaceful. Moreover, he noted in passing in 6:17b that they "have become obedient from the heart to the form of teaching to which [they] were entrusted" (ὑπηκούσατε δὲ ἐκ καρδίας εἰς ὃν παρεδόθητε τύπον διδαχῆς). Similarly, in 15:14, as he makes his transition to the more practical concerns of the letter closing, Paul states that he is utterly convinced that the Roman Christians are full of goodness and knowledge and capable of instructing one another. But he goes on to describe the reason for his writing in this relation (in v. 15): he has written — and perhaps overly boldly — *to remind them* of this gospel, and his divine ratification can provide additional confirmation of its power and authenticity. According to this argument, Romans is little more than a reminder of what the Roman Christians already know independently of Paul; these two "texts" should be identified. And consequently, those who depart from what Paul says in Romans *depart automatically at the same moment from what the Romans already know and have been taught* — "the gospel they learned." Thus, Paul's opposition to the false teachers, which is described so caustically in 16:17-20, must now by definition include the opposition of the Roman Christians as well, and vice versa. And Paul has thereby drawn the Roman Christians, in terms of their loyalty to their original teaching, into *his* current opposition to the false teachers who are being vilified in 16:17-20, and in relation to whom the Roman Christians are so sharply warned. It may be helpful to present this argument in terms of its main propositions.

Paul begins with two separate situations, both of which are true:

(i) Paul opposes a certain false teacher and his teaching.
(ii) The Roman Christians have submitted to a form of the gospel.

But Paul wishes of course to introduce the subject of (ii) — the Roman Christians — into the action of (i) — opposition to the teacher and his teaching. This is his ultimate rhetorical objective both here and in the rest of Romans. So he argues:

(iii) The letter just written to the Romans is in direct continuity with the original Roman gospel (it is an act of "reminding" only).
(iv) The Roman Christians have submitted to this letter (and they are characterized by this praiseworthy virtue of submission).
(v) This letter and gospel oppose the false teacher and his teaching.
(vi) *Therefore,* the Roman Christians must oppose the false teacher and his teaching (and in the terms set out by the letter to the Romans). This action is now merely an extension of their original submission to the gospel, which is well known.

It is an artful move in rhetorical terms — both useful and diplomatic.[97] In the first instance we should note that a genuinely helpful interpretative strategy might now have been revealed in relation to other parts of the letter. If Paul is only "reminding" the Roman Christians of what they already know in much of Romans, we might expect him to build his case through the letter — when he is addressing them directly — from shared material, gradually adding his own distinctive commitments and claims to this original Roman gospel by degrees. In this way he would not merely pay lip service to the claim of remembrance but would actualize it. (It will be especially important to recall this possibility in part four, chapters fifteen through seventeen, when we address 1:16-17 and 3:21-26 in detail, but it is possibly even apparent in this pericope, as Paul arguably builds some of his exhortations from the wisdom tradition as that was shaped by Jesus.)

But this perception can also be seen to link up with an important element in the proem. That is, while Paul's real reason for writing Romans, along with the clever encoded strategy freighting that goal, is clear in the letter closing, we would expect some hint of this strategy to be present at the outset as well. And the motif of "strengthening" provides the appropriate point of contact. One of Paul's stated desires in the opening thanksgiving paragraph was to strengthen the Roman Christians; indeed, this was the point of giving them some spiritual gift, and would result in mutual encouragement through a shared fidelity: ἐπιποθῶ γὰρ ἰδεῖν ὑμᾶς ἵνα τι μεταδῶ χάρισμα ὑμῖν πνευματικὸν εἰς τὸ στηριχθῆναι ὑμᾶς. (Rather intriguingly, this motif then recurs in the letter's final disputed doxology at 16:25 as well.) And this notion of "strengthening" conforms exactly to the strategy Paul develops elsewhere in terms of supplementing something that the Roman Christians basically have already, but in relation to some future threat or trial. Hence, it is an entirely appropriate opening indication to the Roman Christians of how he intends his letter to function among them, since he cannot yet visit them.[98]

Further clues corroborate the presence of this concrete underlying concern in Romans with certain false teachers. In particular, 3:8 contains a pointed and revealing aside.[99] Paul speaks there — twice in fact — of being "slandered" by "some" "whose condemnation is deserved" (so his posture toward these figures is the same as it is in 16:17-20; they are enemies, fighting for the other side). Paul is apparently being accused by these figures of libertinism. And libertines in the ancient world were figures who could not control their own appetites; *they were slaves to their bellies!* Hence, this statement in 3:8 does not merely signal the presence of actual figures behind some of the charges that Paul is conscious of when he composes Romans; it overlaps fairly precisely with the figures described in 16:17-20. But it is also presumably no coincidence that just this issue — libertinism — is addressed at length in Romans 6 (see Gal. 2:17; 5:13; 6:7-9). Consequently, this small statement in 3:8 may provide us with a priceless insight into another of Romans' basic dynamics. Since 3:8 links a set of programmatic questions from elsewhere in Romans specifically with the charges of certain malevolent opponents, an explanation is thereby potentially generated for many of the other programmatic questions in Romans as well. They may derive from the debate unfolding between Paul and these hostile figures, who seem, like him, to be learned disputants. Paul cannot of course assume the specific contours of this debate before the Roman Christians (the original Romans debate); it must be presented more formally and intelligibly to them in terms of various issues and contentions, hence the text's many questions. Indeed, this is the appropriate point to turn and consider whether this expanding rhetorical dynamic can explain all the features that we have previously identified in the frame and the body of Romans, some of which have caused us such difficulties. If it can do so, then it will enjoy a distinct advantage over the other theories that we have previously considered, all of which stumbled badly at this point.

4.2. Explanatory Power

If Paul thought that teachers preaching a gospel opposed to many of his own most important concerns were approaching Rome, he would surely have seen this as a dire threat. Rome was the strategic location within the empire in any terms. Hence, such figures could not only turn any pagan converts in Rome from Paul's system but could block all further expansion through that strategic center, while presumably pursuing their own agenda from the empire's very heart. This would have been a nightmare scenario for Paul in evangelistic terms. It is therefore entirely understandable why the divinely appointed apostle to the pagans would want to prevent this situation from developing among any converts from paganism currently at Rome, thereby explaining features I and II in Romans. And given that the collection had to be taken from Corinth to Jerusalem by Paul first (feature VI), delaying his journey to Rome directly, the need for a letter to be sent to Rome must then have seemed doubly necessary. But we have also explained why Paul nuanced features I and II as he did. He is almost unremittingly positive in his characterizations of the Roman Christians, both so as not to offend them and to build from their competence to his in an act of reminding. His apostolic call to the pagans clearly *does* basically underlie his concern for the Romans; his authoritative understanding of the law-free gospel that saves them is about to be challenged in a crucial locus. Thus, his desire to strengthen them (feature IV) is explicable as well. But we can even explain the notoriously problematic motif of 15:20 at this point — Paul's "non-interference" clause (feature III) — although it will be helpful to introduce the Spanish mission at this juncture as well (feature V).

We have already seen that Paul seems to develop his apostleship in 15:15b-21 in a self-contradictory manner, asserting that he preaches where Christ has not yet been named in fulfillment of Isaiah 52:15b. He then immediately speaks of his desire to evangelize Spain, hopefully being sent on his way there by the Romans (see vv. 23-24). The questions consequently arise why Paul is either writing to the Romans and/or visiting them, given this caveat, or why he defines his apostleship in this unhelpful manner. But if we introduce the issue underlying feature VIII and the possible intrusion of false teachers at Rome, a clever rhetorical strategy can be detected.

We must first appreciate that Paul feels compelled to establish his particular gospel at Rome in the face of this opposition. Clearly, this is important. However, he does not know most of the Roman Christians and has not founded that congregation. So, as we have just seen, he fashions a rhetorical conceit in the letter opening and closing, suggesting that he is merely reminding the Romans of what they already know. Of course, he is doing rather more than this, but in explicit terms he would claim only to be strengthening that community; he is adding a spiritual gift to the many gifts they already possess, thereby participating in a process of mutual encouragement. The deliberate introductions of features III and V now both enhance this agenda and problematize any arrival by his opponents.

In defining his apostolic call as a scripturally corroborated orientation toward new constituencies, Paul is able to tempt the Roman Christians to listen to him and accord him due respect in view of his divinely ratified authority and capabilities — but also affirm that he is not actually imposing that authority on them. He is only *passing through Rome,* as his divine mandate dictates, *on the way to Spain,* a land not yet evangelized and so in keeping with his apostolic definition. (The two features fit together, then; they are part of a single rhetorical strategy.) The Roman Christians hear that Paul is a figure predicted in the Scriptures, no less, and are presented with the stunning way that God has acted through him in other missions among the pagans: signs, wonders, and miracles have been performed. And this both persuades them of his authority and makes them want him to visit so that they too may receive from him. But at no point do the terms of this visit spill over into an imposition of apostolic authority on the Romans by Paul himself. They are benefiting from him in passing, so to speak, in just the manner that they are currently benefiting from his reminding. Paul's angle of approach is thus entirely diplomatic. This apostle cares about the Roman Christians and has much to offer them, but he is not dominating them — and will not dominate them even in visiting, since this will be a mere transit.

But Paul's careful definition of his apostolic call does not just preserve the diplomatic terms in which he has couched his letter; it creates a set of conundrums for any rivals who might be arriving in Rome, and especially if they define themselves in apostolic terms, as seems likely (see Gal. 1:1, 6-9, 11-12).[100] If they seek to impose their own apostolic authority on the Roman Christians — perhaps trumping Paul's with "letters of recommendation" or some such[101] — then Paul's practices of gentle reminder and help in passing seem preferable; they dignify the Romans and present a more humble — but still clearly powerful — apostolic emissary. Moreover, if they seek to vilify Paul's typical arrogant power mongering,[102] then this polemic is instantly refuted. And any requests for money and support will seem selfish and dubious next to Paul's altruistic talk of a large gift for the poor in Jerusalem, requests for support for a mission to the Spanish (i.e., for others), and additional requests merely for hospitality for Phoebe and for prayer (Rom. 15:23–16:2). Finally, these opposing teachers can also be challenged in terms of their apostolicity: why are they too not fulfilling the Scriptures and preaching where Christ has not yet been named?! Why are they staying in Rome? True apostles do not act in such a fashion. (Do these figures even have a scriptural corroboration?!)

Thus, the entire apostolic strategy proves to be carefully constructed and rhetorically skillful (and this turns out to be an ongoing feature of the argument, as we will see in due course; most subsections are crafted to deliver more than one rhetorical advantage simultaneously). Moreover, features III and V can now be seen to function together within a diplomatic characterization of Paul's apostleship that is exactly congruent with Paul's basic letter-writing strategy in terms of remembrance.

It is not really necessary to explain why Paul mentions his forthcoming visit to Jerusalem — feature VI; as we noted earlier, it is this exigency that prevents him from traveling to Rome directly. Moreover, his solicitations of prayer are entirely understandable given the risks involved. However, it is worth noting that we have in fact validated a large part of Jervell's appealing explanation without relying on the more implausible aspects of that case, and recognizing this allows us to consider some of the features that lie just ahead of us — principally IX through XV. (The sole remaining unexplained feature of the letter frame — VII, mutual greeting — is best postponed until we consider XIV and XV, as we have already intimated.) It is worth noting, moreover, that these include the features that have generally proved impervious to attempted explanations.

Jervell's argument has an excellent feel for the shape and tenor of the letter body in Romans and, moreover, supplies a plausible setting for that material, even if Jervell is not able to prove the validity of that setting. Romans in his view possesses "the characteristics of a speech with marked apologetic, and to a lesser degree, polemic tendencies. In other words, we find here a presentation of Pauline preaching — yet always defensive and intent on clarifying possible misunderstanding." He adds that "[v]ery often questions mark the beginning of [its] discussions. . . . The abruptness and the structure of the letter are explained by the fact that Paul is on the defensive and must be apologetic" (*RD*, 61). We have summarized these aspects of the letter principally in terms of features IX through XIV — the abstract and Jewish nature of the letter body, with at least three significant internal argumentative modulations. Jervell notes that these features are all plausibly located in relation to Jerusalem, because "[t]he group around James probably never accepted Paul's teaching completely (Gal. 2:12; see also Acts 21:18)" (*RD*, 59).

In my view, Jervell's instincts are accurate at these points, but — like Stendahl — his case is slightly misdirected and falls short of definitive proof. He grasps correctly that the letter body is not a systematic exposition of Paul's teaching, as we have already seen; too many key notions in Paul's Christian thinking are omitted, and the flow of the argument in Romans is at times anything but obviously systematic. Hence, although *abstract*, it seems more *polemical*, responding to various agendas that are often prompted by difficult questions. Moreover, these questions resonate with what we can assume were queries being placed in Jerusalem, largely because they resonate with many of those either addressed by Galatians or implicit in Paul's position in that letter. And there were overt historical connections between the Galatian crisis and Jerusalem. Hence, Jervell is essentially pointing here *to the appropriateness of Romans to the earlier Judaizing crisis* — which, certain hints imply, is far from over. It is not implausible, then, to suggest the letter's orientation to Jerusalem, even if that suggestion is ultimately unprovable and also suffers from other weaknesses. But we can now see why Jervell's claims seem so intuitively appropriate.

It is not that Paul is going to face these questions primarily at Jerusalem (although he might); it is that *the previous debates in Jerusalem are about to arrive in Rome,* with the arrival of the false teachers there. *This* is the rhetorical dynamic that explains so much of Romans, and that Jervell's position resonates with (without quite grasping). But can Jervell's intuitions — suitably reformulated — be proved?

Part of the relatively simple argument that undergirds this thesis has already been supplied. We have noted that Romans seems to have been written to counteract the agenda of certain false teachers at Rome. We have observed, further, that they accuse Paul of libertinism — while he seems to accuse them of slavery to their appetites — and that this charge resonates with a set of questions that Paul explores more abstractly at a later point in the letter. But we can now add a further important layer to this description. The agenda of much of Romans is so similar to the agenda of much of Galatians that the identification of the groups of false teachers lying behind those two letters seems unavoidable — that is, the same group of contentious Jewish Christians is in view. This point does not need to be labored. It is widely recognized that Romans and Galatians overlap markedly in substantive terms.

The letters to the Galatians and the Romans share numerous motifs, questions, methods, terms, and arguments. They both emphasize apostleship (although Romans rather more subtly, as we have seen). Both speak of significant interactions with Jerusalem (although Galatians in retrospect, Romans in prospect). Both deploy a famous terminological antithesis between ἔργα νόμου and πίστις framed by δικαιο- terms, and this is a distinctive configuration among Paul's letters. But both also supplement this with a marked use of participatory terminology and argumentation (a less distinctive usage). Baptismal motifs figure centrally in this participatory material, as does the Spirit, and some terminology of "Father" and "Son." In these passages alone among Paul's letters, Christians cry "Abba, Father." The argument often proceeds by way of diatribal exchanges, and alternatively makes its case in relation to series of brief scriptural quotations. Abraham is a key figure in both letters, especially in relation to Genesis 15:6, but accompanying this text in both letters are Habakkuk 2:4 and Leviticus 18:5 (and these texts arguably supply much of the letters' key terminology). The end of the age is also prominent, and a strong eschatological dualism (i.e., the presence of both ages, often intersecting within the Christian). The letter body of both epistles concludes with a fairly generalized paraenetic section oriented toward the renewal of the Christian mind by the Spirit over against existence in the "flesh." Paul's exhortations then revolve at one point in both these subsections around the fulfillment of the law in the "love command" of Leviticus 19:18. Polemical comments about intruders and troublemakers are also apparent — comments that identify them as troublesome Jewish Christians.[103]

This is a not inconsiderable list of similarities, and it has prompted numerous interpreters to posit not merely substantive and contingent similarity but *temporal* proximity (thereby raising questions that will be addressed in more detail just below). Suffice it for now to state, however, that this extensive substantive overlap suggests that the same basic situation lies behind Romans and Galatians — false teachers promoting a certain teaching that Paul regards as deeply destructive.

That teaching and the teachers themselves are overtly identified together in Galatians. And in Romans we have identified certain false teachers, along with the agenda of the false teachers in Galatia — their teaching — in much of that letter's body. Equations between these two dimensions in Romans and then, beyond them, with the same situation in Galatia therefore seem highly likely. (Certainly, they seem more likely than any other explanation, once question-begging responses have been excluded.)[104] And this explains feature X — an explanation that will be strengthened momentarily as we move on to consider features XI through XIV. The Jewish agenda in Romans is explained by the Jewish commitments of the false teachers that Paul is opposing, which are complex and range across various questions. But this identification can now also be extended a little in historical terms.

Paul's heated excursus in Philippians 3 also fits this trajectory well (specifically, 3:2-19). The same terms, and the same vilification of ontologically enslaved opponents, are evident in this text as well as in Romans and Galatians — an essentially vicious characterization of that opposition (v. 2), a concern with circumcision that is allied with the Spirit over against rooted in the flesh (vv. 3-4a), an account of Paul's Jewish background (an overlap with Galatians; see vv. 5-6 and Gal. 1:13-14), the characteristic δικαιο- and πιστ- terms functioning in a strong opposition (vv. 6b, 9), and a powerful emphasis on participation in Christ (vv. 9a, 10-11). Just after this Paul's focus becomes eschatological, although this is interwoven with an ἀγῶν motif (an overlap with Romans; see vv. 12-16, Rom. 9:30–10:4), and he utters warnings again about false teachers who seem extraordinarily similar to the figures profiled in Romans 16 — ὧν τὸ τέλος ἀπώλεια, ὧν ὁ θεὸς ἡ κοιλία καὶ ἡ δόξα ἐν τῇ αἰσχύνῃ (as we have already seen; see also vv. 17-19; see Rom. 16:17-20; note, the emphasis on τέλος resonates also with Rom. 10:4, and on shame, with numerous other points in Romans — see i.a. 1:16; 9:33b; 10:11).

These overlaps are again remarkably comprehensive and suggest that the same situation probably lies behind this letter, at least in part.[105] But Philippians seems to look back on an earlier warning that was also presumably more comprehensive. It falls obviously, then — at least at first glance — into a sequence after Galatians, which looks like an earlier salvo within this trajectory. (Romans looks more considered and hence later; the respective positions of Romans and Philippians will be considered in more detail shortly, along with Romans' more "considered" character, which is a significant development.)

If Philippians pushes the trajectory of this strand of false teaching later, then Galatians denotes that certain events have also taken place earlier in other locations. Paul records two important incidents in Galatians that clearly precede that

letter and are closely connected with the same debate. Furthermore, those two incidents are linked. In Galatians 2:1-10 Paul recounts an important visit to Jerusalem, where Peter, John, and James recognize both his and Barnabas's apostleship to
the pagans. Galatians 2:11-14 then recounts briefly a confrontation between Peter
and Paul at Syrian Antioch — with Barnabas in the background, along with "some
from James." Whatever the specifics — and they are important and will be discussed shortly — these two incidents link the conflict in Galatia with a conflict in
Antioch instigated by certain figures originating with James in Jerusalem, and
with a meeting in Jerusalem itself, where Paul stands firm against figures he characterizes as "sneaking false brothers," "spies," and "enslavers" (2:4, DC).

A basic trajectory in the entire dispute is now discernible (and it explains
still further the appeal of Jervell's thesis). A particular group opposed to Paul's
missionary program is first observable in Jerusalem, although they do not necessarily originate there. They then travel to Syrian Antioch and Galatia. (The exact
order of these visits does not matter at this point; nor does the degree of their authorization by James — although they do seem to be so authorized in Antioch;
nor does a precise identification of Galatia.) Galatians presumably follows, a
communication with Philippi, and then Philippians 3. And it seems plausible to
locate Romans toward the final point in the trajectory as well. If we place these
events in a geographical arc — partly for simplicity's sake — then the following
broad trajectory for the overarching debate results:

Jerusalem → Syrian Antioch → Galatia → Philippi → Rome

It seems reasonable to conclude that the same basic problem is present and
debated in relation to all these locations in sequence, prompted by the operation
of the same group of opponents (with the important caveats to be noted shortly).
The development of the trajectory in historical terms is complicated by the fact
that the opponents and Paul might not themselves be physically present in a
given location as the debate arrives, hence the phenomena of various letters. But
the arrival of letters tends to follow or anticipate the arrival of people fairly
closely! Hence, it seems a broadly accurate sequence — a sweep of events rather
than a specific, point-by-point progression.

Paul's particular opponents here have of course usually been known in the
past as the "Judaizers," largely in dependence on the apostle's use of this verb in
close relation to them in Galatians 2:14 (. . . πῶς τὰ ἔθνη ἀναγκάζεις ἰουδαΐζειν;).
But this designation is not entirely appropriate.[106] It is better, then, to follow
Martyn's more neutral designation of these figures as the "Teachers,"[107] and I
will nuance this definition further here only in terms of singularity.[108] Paul will
turn out to focus much of Romans on a single Teacher — presumably, a particular figure who led the small group that was hostile to Paul. And it must be emphasized that he is a Jewish Christian, so the entire debate unfolds "in-house,"
between different Jewish Christian understandings of the pagan mission and its
implications. (Paul himself of course repeatedly characterizes this group as devi-

ant.) It is, in short, Paul's debate with the Teacher that explains much of Romans — and a great deal more in his life besides — the detailed explanation of which we can now undertake.

If the basic situation underlying the composition of Romans is similar to that underlying Galatians (and the rest of the trajectory), then it is time to address the evident differences that have been summarized previously in terms of features IX through XIV (although feature X has now been resolved, namely, the Jewish agenda in Romans; this can now be seen to derive from the particular Jewish concerns of the Teacher, who is himself a Jew, although in some Christian variant). Much of the letter body of Romans contains relatively abstract material debating Jewish questions and undergoing significant internal transitions. And this is explicable in terms of two important qualifications of the earlier arguments and discussions in Jerusalem, Antioch, Galatia, and perhaps also Philippi. The debate is now taking place in a very different setting, as it threatens to unfold at Rome. And the debate itself has moved on. Paul and the Teacher now know one another's strengths and weaknesses well, having in effect fought through several previous rounds. The discussion is much more informed. These two developments explain the differences between Romans and Galatians nicely, along with most of the remaining features of the Romans data.

The Roman Christians have not been privy to the actual debate that has previously unfolded in Galatia, Syria, and Jerusalem. It is possibly completely new to them (or, if it is not, perhaps it exists as little more than an uninformed rumor). Moreover, Paul cannot be sure whether his opposition will arrive in Rome before or after his missive, although presumably it is better for him if his letter reaches Rome first. So he cannot even presuppose the presence of the system that he is engaged with when his letter arrives. Hence, for both these reasons, he must present the key issues in this debate in a more formal way than he has previously. The Roman Christians must be able to understand what is at stake. (He must also resist appearing angry and dominant, because this would create further rhetorical vulnerabilities.[109]) This explains the abstract quality of the discussion, along with its progression primarily in terms of stated questions and issues — feature IX — but it does so without sacrificing contingency. Paul spells everything out in relatively neutral terms so that the Roman Christians can understand all the debate's dynamics and issues merely by studying the text of Romans — and so they will find no reason to be offended by his more polemical moments. This careful, expository composition nevertheless remains directed toward an entirely practical task with localized consequences — informing the Roman Christians of the issues at stake between Paul and the Teacher in a suitably slanted way.[110]

However, the debate has also moved on. Both Paul and the Teacher are well aware of each other's systems and have developed pointed criticisms in relation to one another, many of these linked to key scriptural texts. They have, moreover, almost certainly adapted their own positions to these unfolding criticisms, so a great deal of rebuttal is now part of the situation. And this evolving dynamic explains many of the substantive differences from the argumentation of Galatians, which is very similar but not identical to Romans. Material specifically relevant to the Galatian Christians has been dropped,[111] as has argumentation deemed weak or vulnerable or misdirected. Meanwhile, additional defensive discussions have been added, covering vulnerabilities and awkward implications. And a much more penetrating and informed attack on the Teacher's gospel can now be expected.

These similarities and differences create the basic contingency for Romans in the light of which the peculiarities of much of Romans' letter body can be explained in a new way (features XI through XIV). Romans contributes to an ongoing argument; it is consequently a rhetorical act shaped by a broader, quite specific debate unfolding before a largely uncommitted and uninformed audience. As such, it must respond to a complex rhetorical agenda that includes far more than a mere presentation of Paul's own position. For simplicity's sake, we can note three basic rhetorical tasks that Paul faces in the letter body: (a) he must certainly present his own position — the law-free gospel to the pagans (which is done as an act of reminder); but (b) he must respond to the most deadly criticisms that his opponents have made against this gospel, defending it and rebutting various pointed accusations; and (c) he should probably indulge in reciprocal activity himself, attacking the various inadequacies in the gospel of his opponents, trying to discredit it.[112] These potential rhetorical dynamics allow us — essentially for the first time — to provide a comprehensive, plausible explanation of features XI through XIV of the letter body of Romans.[113]

The shifts in Paul's discussion are potentially explicable as he shifts between these three tasks, expounding his own position, responding to assumed criticisms of that, and then going over onto the offensive, attacking various assertions by his opponent — tasks A, B, and C. The modulations between the first three major subunits in Romans — as well as, to a degree, within them — are therefore comprehensible as a function of the several goals and the resulting rhetorical dynamics of the text.

Detailed evidence must come later, and I will concentrate in what follows on one strand. Suffice it for now to note, then, that Paul's Justification texts have usually been read in the past as A statements — that is, as relatively systematic statements of his own position — because no other suitable approaches have been provided. But I suggest now that they are better read (i.e., they generate fewer problems) in terms of task C. That is, the arguments work best not primarily as expository but as critical; they attack an opposing gospel — quite brilliantly at times — only hinting in passing at the shape of Paul's position (although they are of course compatible with it ultimately). If a function in terms of C is mistaken for A (or indeed B for A) then the interpretative consequences are potentially disastrous. Paul is interpreted in terms of the image of his opponent! But we must now try to reverse this trend, considering the outline of an opponent in the various twists and turns that Paul lays with impressive detail before the Roman Christians in Romans 1–4 (and, later on, in relation to his other Justification discussions).

In Romans 5–8, however, we make a transition from certain key questions prompted by the Teacher to the exposition of Paul's own soteriological concerns. (After all, the Teacher's gospel lies in ruins by this point.) So a discussion in terms of task B segues into task A, as denoted by feature XII. I will suggest in due course that two particular questions generate this transition (see esp. chapter fifteen, §2, and chapter seventeen, §3). It must suffice for now to note that Paul seems concerned to address the interrelated questions of eschatological assurance and ethical effectiveness in this section of Romans. The Teacher's gospel links these two issues tightly together in a way that Paul finds theologically offensive. However, even if they can be prised apart and reset in more responsible theological locations, they remain important questions that go to the heart of Paul's own saving system as well. And so in Romans 5–8 he addresses them, essentially chiastically. The saving act of God in Christ through the Spirit guarantees the coming fullness of that salvation *and* overcomes any ethical incapacity on the part of an otherwise enslaved humanity (at least by way of inauguration) — as the *only* effective antidote to human sinfulness. So Paul can pivot at this point in terms of task A to address two important queries from his opponent — task B.

And what of Paul's concern in chapters 9–11 (generating feature XIII) to supply a detailed, scripturally corroborated account of the inclusion of the pagans within salvation, and to account simultaneously for the temporary exclusion of many Jews? This account is now understandable, as is, moreover, Paul's evident concern to prevent this inclusion of pagans spilling over into an arrogant condemnation of unbelieving Jews (feature XIV). Implicit in Paul's gospel is a potentially appalling distortion of salvation-history — one that, if true, could immediately discredit him. Many pagans are, according to his narrative, being included within Israel, although not in any recognizably Jewish form, while the majority of Israel are *not* so included. And this all adds up at first glance to a treasonous gospel by Paul; he has effectively turned his back on his own people. But it also seems palpably absurd — a massively counterintuitive deviation in the expected historical course of salvation. A resulting pagan Christian arrogance toward unbelieving Jews might then seem to be the last straw — a final absurd posture.

Romans 9–11, along with the specific concern with pagan Christian anti-Judaism in chapter 11, is therefore conceivable as a clever extended response to this cluster of interrelated charges — discussions again in terms of task B. These arguments attempt to justify pagan inclusion in salvation, Jewish exclusion (although a temporary one), and the need for ongoing pagan humility if they are so included. Moreover, they emphasize throughout Paul's passionate concern for his fellow Jews, as against disregard or treachery. Judgments of the validity of Paul's arguments have varied,[114] but they are at least fundamentally comprehensible in such terms as a contingent text at Rome; they respond fairly systematically to a salvation-historical critique of Paul's gospel, and therefore in terms again of task B (which is not to deny that they integrate well with his basic position).[115]

In sum, Paul's debate with the Teacher does seem able to explain much of Romans — especially features IX through XIV. Paul wrestles with the Teacher's sophisticated opposing Jewish Christian system through Romans 1–11, but before an audience that knows neither of them especially well, and certainly not much of this debate.[116] It is this peculiar contingency that explains most of the letter body's peculiar dynamics. But it explains more than this as well; it links up plausibly with the explanations that we have already noted probably underlie the remaining features in the data of Romans — XV, XVI, and VII.

A desire for the maximum degree of solidarity in the Roman Christian community is entirely understandable as a rhetorical objective on Paul's part, given the imminent arrival of the Teacher. Paul has been painfully aware since his difficulties at Corinth that any division within a Christian community provides an opportunity for an unscrupulous visiting teacher to exploit; it is a gift to any such interloper. Those dissatisfied with Paul are ready to form an alternative base of operations within the community, and the retrieval of such a divided situation could be very difficult indeed. Hence, Paul is rightly concerned that the Roman Christians present a united front to the Teacher. But the very geography of their situation seems to have created obstacles in this regard for the Roman Christians, along with their rather different missionary histories. There were potential fissures within the community at Rome that could be exploited. So in the text underlying features XV, XVI, and VII, Paul moves to address them, insofar as he can with a letter. He urges those with different attitudes toward certain Jewish practices, especially various dietary and temporal observances, to be sensitive to one another and not fractious, judgmental, or despising. These exhortations are not so pointed as to be rude and intrusive, but not so bland as to lack all specificity. Precisely this division (among others) had created strife at Corinth (one of the previous locations of Prisca and Aquila, it should be noted, and presumably of their particular Christian praxis as well, which may have been quite "strong"). They nestle, furthermore, in the midst of other exhortations designed to foster unity. Significantly, then, Paul also (probably)[117] counsels the Roman Christians to be obedient to the government, in effect avoiding involvement in civic protests. Such activity could presumably result in community divisions as well (on the protest's wisdom or appropriateness) and/or political repression, which might even culminate in the withdrawal of privileges and expulsion, thereby creating very difficult circumstances for Paul's missionary goals and accentuating divisive pressures on the Roman Christians. Rome had a history of such disturbances.

But Paul also urges mutual greetings — a process of visiting, hospitality, and so on — that could concretely foster greater solidarity in the Christian community at Rome, which seems to have been scattered in various tenements through the poorer suburbs of that vast and crowded city. The fulfillment of this wish would take some doing, but it would also contribute practically to the community's united front against any destructive interlopers. In sum, features XV, XVI, and VII in Romans seem entirely understandable as a set of practical subordinate rhetorical objectives within the broader ambit of Paul's desire to combat the arrival of the Teacher at Rome. The Teacher's system had to be opposed, Paul's promoted, and the Roman Christians prepared as best they could to resist his inroads. Unity was therefore an important goal within the overarching rhetoric of the letter.[118] And although this effectively introduces a multiple explanation, no difficulties in terms of simultaneity are evident. It is the basic exigency of the Teacher visiting Rome that creates Paul's persuasive needs in relation to two programs and the need for unity. Furthermore, the pending visit by Paul to Jerusalem with the collection (feature VI) — which overrules even the need to get to Rome — further explains the letter's dispatch at just this juncture.

And at this point it seems that all the features discernible in the data of Romans — I through XVI — have finally been explained. Moreover, in so doing, important new interpretative possibilities have been opened up vis-à-vis the text.

Romans 1–11 is a debate with the Teacher. We must therefore learn to ask different, rather more flexible, and — above all — *rhetorical* questions of this material: how does it work *as an argument* (rather than just as an exposition)?! Where is the position of the Teacher expounded — not entirely fairly, of course — as against the position of Paul? Where is Paul developing defensive and offensive rebuttal, hence second-order questions, as against his own most basic principles? What are the particular argumentative goals of each major and minor subsection, given that Paul is seeking to win the Roman Christians over to his views in competition with the opposing system of the Teacher? (and especially given that the Teacher may be the origin of the program denoted by "works of law"). In essence, the entire methodological apparatus of rhetoric and argumentation can now be deployed in relation to the analysis of Romans, and especially of chapters 1–11. This new appreciation of the provenance of Romans, in short, opens up possibilities for new detailed interpretative strategies as well (and I will lay out a specific strategy at the beginning of the next chapter). But before turning to these questions, some potential objections must be noted.

4.3. Possible Objections

I can imagine three initial objections that ought to be addressed briefly before we begin our detailed analysis of Romans 1–4 as an argumentative engagement with the Teacher and his gospel — certain methodological, interpolative, and biographical and historical concerns.[119]

(1) Objections in Methodological Terms

Certain protests have rightly been raised against appeals to opponents in explanation of much that Paul wrote. Perhaps most famously, John Barclay has detailed the difficulties that such "mirror-reading" can involve and has offered a set of useful controls on this process.[120] It is not sufficient, he points out, merely to reverse a particular Pauline assertion and claim that an opponent lies behind this mirror image, and it is even less acceptable to return and interpret large parts of the remaining text in the light of this ostensible reconstruction, perhaps overriding alternative readings in the process (a viciously circular interpretation).

Barclay does not repudiate the notion of opponents within Pauline interpretation (as he has sometimes been falsely represented as doing), but he certainly sounds a note of warranted caution, and he is not alone in doing so.[121] Will my reconstruction here fall foul of these strictures?

In fact, I would argue that a rhetorical reading of Romans in terms of an opponent offers just the controls that Barclay is looking for (thereby enhancing the slightly ad hoc list of imperatives that he originally supplied). Paul has deliberately formalized his opponent's teaching in Romans so that the Roman Christians can understand it. The shape of the argument therefore allows a highly controlled reconstruction of that opposing position. We need first simply to list the various conclusions that Paul repudiates with his different arguments in Romans and to ask whether they converge on a recognizable system — and in fact they do gather into a recognizable soteriology, with its own internal coherence. That program can then be further assessed in relation to various layers of sources — elsewhere in Paul's letters where the same opponent is probably in play, elsewhere in the New Testament (especially if writings can be found that represent this opposing point of view, or stem from it), and elsewhere in Judaism (although qualified here by the deviant Jewish Christian nature of the program), as well as Greco-Roman sources. The result of this process of five distinguishable assessments is a richly controlled portrait of an opposing system: (i) a convergence in terms of the different rhetorical targets in Romans; (ii) an assessment of the internal coherence of the system emerging from those combined targets; (iii) a comparison of that system with the same opponent's treatment elsewhere in Paul; (iv) the possible detection of further attestation to the system in the rest of the New Testament; and (v) the possible detection of Jewish and/or Greco-Roman texts that also articulate the system, or elements in it (perhaps extending here to direct involvement in that system as a known precursor text).

These five controls do not need to be applied seriatim every time that we interpret an argument in Romans. They tend to operate simultaneously in interpretative terms. (Their enumeration here is in terms of epistemological priority.) But they are all generally present, controlling the unfolding interpretation. Some further caveats should now be added to them.

First, this portrait should not be used to override difficult readings elsewhere that do not seem to fit it. It can adjudicate between equally well-attested readings but must not narcotize a superior reading. Such circularity must still be resisted. And, second, it must be appreciated that the resulting portrait is in the first instance only of an *encoded* opponent. Paul's depiction of his opponent in Romans is limited both by his rhetorical concern to present that opponent in an essentially biased way to the Roman Christians and by his own limited knowledge of that opponent (although we have noted earlier that those limitations have been receding for him). It is not therefore a portrait of the actual *empirical* opponent. Progress toward that descriptive goal can be made only if other sources more closely related to the opponent can be isolated, although this is possible at the fourth and fifth levels of our controls. Indeed, I would suggest that we do have documents from the hand of this opponent's leaders and later tradition in the New Testament; we also almost certainly possess Jewish texts that the opponent relied on heavily. But demonstrating these claims in detail lies outside the purview of this book. We must satisfy ourselves here largely with what Paul wanted the Roman Christians to think about the Teacher.

There are, however, rhetorical considerations that encourage the accuracy of this portrait (at least in ideal terms). If Paul paints an absurdly inaccurate portrait, he risks a loss of credibility and rhetorical effectiveness before his audience, and he thereby undermines his own ethos. The Roman Christians might see Paul as biased and venomous rather than the Teacher as foolish. Paul must consequently portray the Teacher with sufficient fairness so that the Roman Christians recognize this figure along with Paul's essentially accurate description of him. They must believe that he is making valid criticisms of a genuine position. Beyond these thresholds, Paul can manipulate that depiction. However, this is a surprisingly constrained and subtle interpretative space.[122]

In short, the position of an encoded opponent can almost certainly be recovered from Romans, which offers a richly controlled setting for that recovery. However, these controls will admittedly need to be employed regularly and carefully so as to avoid the pitfalls that can await much discussion of "opponents" in Paul's texts and their putative "gospels."

(2) Objections in Interpolative Terms

A potentially fatal objection to my suggested explanation of Romans is the thesis that 16:17-20 is interpolated — a claim that has been made not infrequently.[123] If it is correct, then my explanation's most overt piece of evidence is eliminated, and the broader account of Romans' provenance would struggle to establish itself. However, the evidence underlying this objection is really too weak to sustain it.

The main reason for excluding this subsection is — a little ironically — that scholars do not know how to interpret it in the broader context of the letter. They find it to be a shockingly abrasive intrusion that is out of step with the more moderate and ecumenical tone of most of Paul's previous argumentation. It is also opaque in its own right; it has no apparent function in its present locale. In view of this suddenness, incomprehensibility, and aggression, the text is excised. But closer examination suggests that this is a fragile set of contentions.

Excising a piece of text on the grounds that it does not fit a broader theory of a letter's provenance is clearly methodologically muddled. The data of the text should underlie the broader explanation, and not vice versa. Indeed, if this relationship is inverted, then most theories of provenance will ultimately be justifiable (because the data contradicting them can simply be excised!). And here the vicious consequences of this muddled procedure are especially apparent. On the grounds of a theory that is almost certainly implausible in ultimate terms (because all the explanations of Romans not ultimately revolving around 16:17-20 have demonstrable weaknesses), the critical piece of data underlying the only theory that *is* plausible in ultimate terms is being excluded and that theory thereby abandoned! Here, then, a false theory overrides the key piece of evidence in the only true one.

But we should also note that, with the development of the view that Romans responds to the gospel of the Teacher, a satisfactory role for 16:17-20 *has* been provided. It is therefore not "impossible to explain the extreme change of mood, [and] the angry tone of denunciation";[124] this is exactly how Paul characterizes the Teacher — who is the underlying problem in Romans — elsewhere. Indeed, the shift in tone is further explained as soon as it is grasped that Paul is warning the Roman Christians about a third party, whereas he has been engaging more directly with them throughout the rest of the letter (but see 3:8b). We have already noted the various considerations prompting Paul to conduct himself graciously vis-à-vis the Romans. But there are far fewer such constraints on his conduct toward his opponents (other than those just noted). And it is well attested elsewhere that Paul could be particularly cutting concerning his opposition (Gal. 5:12!), and could also make such remarks at the end of his letters, when pithy parting shots were called for (see 1 Cor. 16:22; Gal. 6:12).[125]

The most weighty evidence for interpolation derives from the section's ostensibly rare vocabulary and phraseology — and there is a certain initial plausibility about this contention. Jewett draws at this point especially on Ollrog's earlier case that seven hapax legomena or instances of unique usage are detectable in Romans 16:17-20.[126] Several other scholars also suggest that various elements in the style and phraseology of the subsection are unPauline.[127] And these are considerations that ought to feature in any theory of interpolation.

But they are fragile if they occur in isolation. Other explanations are often possible (and precisely as we will see shortly for 1:18-32 in the following chapter, and for 3:21-26 in chapters fifteen through seventeen, where equally marked shifts in vocabulary, tone, and style, are not ultimately indicators of interpolation). Moreover, the differences are not as marked as advocates of interpolation suggest. It is difficult to say with certainty that 16:17-20 is *that* distinctive for Paul, once the exaggerated claims concerning its composition have been laid to one side. (And the further suggestion, that a "plausible redactional rationale" can be offered for the subsection, is now hardly probative.)

Keck observes that Paul does not counsel the literal "avoidance" of false teachers anywhere else. But this too is understandable in Romans. Elsewhere, false teachers seem to be present with the community already, or fast approaching it; they should therefore be expelled or resisted. However, in Rome, given the scattered nature of its Christian community, the most practical course of action would be *to avoid going to any meeting arranged to meet the Teacher* (presumably in another, perhaps rather distant, tenement), thereby "avoiding" or "shunning" him.[128]

However, perhaps the most important difficulty for the interpolative case is the fact that, although the immediate setting has numerous text-critical seams, *no* such seams surround this pericope.[129] The pacific nature of the textual tradition must raise doubts about the suggestion that 16:17-20 should be excised.[130]

In short, when interpreters abandon the evidence of 16:17-20 as an interpolation, not only do they abandon the narrow path to interpretative accuracy, but they effectively close and bar that path to everyone else. In view of the weakness of the supporting evidence, it is really this suggestion that ought to be abandoned.

(3) Objections in Biographical and Historical Terms

It might be suggested that the scenario I offer to explain Romans — the pending arrival of the Teacher at Rome — is implausible in biographical and historical terms. The evidence actually falsifies it or, at least, renders it improbable; such opponents *cannot* lie behind Romans, if Paul's life is reconstructed correctly. This objection is essentially conservative, for reasons that will become apparent shortly. But there are several subordinate claims that must hold good if the basic retort is to prove valid.

First, this countervailing approach reconstructs Paul's life primarily in accordance with the information provided by the book of Acts. Acts must be deemed not merely episodically but *sequentially* accurate. All its information must be correct, whether concerning the incidents that involve Paul, their sequence, or their exact chronological disposition (and hence this approach is generally favored by more conservative interpreters, although it is not limited to such readers). Given this set of commitments, Acts provides a hard framework for the reconstruction of Paul's biography, into which the various letters can be inserted. And the consequences for the provenances of Galatians and Romans are significant (as we have already briefly seen, in part one, chapter six). These two letters must now be separated by a distance of some years and by many events.

Acts speaks of five visits by Paul as an apostle to Jerusalem, and two of these occur before he has undertaken missionary work beyond the southern part of the province of Galatia, which Paul and Barnabas reach during their "first missionary journey" (Acts 13–14). Galatians must therefore be positioned just after this period of activity but before the third visit to Jerusalem, which takes place in Acts 15 (and this visit also precedes any further missionary work by Paul to the west; Paul and Barnabas travel up to Jerusalem from Syrian Antioch on this third visit to the Jewish capital, because they seem to have been based there since the end of the first missionary journey). Galatians itself speaks clearly of two preceding visits to Jerusalem (see 1:18-20; 2:1-10), and of two only, so it *must* be located in this early position, and it does fit this locus well in certain respects. The inclusion of pagans in "the Way" law-free is certainly an issue at the time in Acts; indeed, just this issue seems to be debated in Jerusalem on Paul's third visit, at "the conference," which seems to take place just after Galatians has been written.

Romans, however, clearly looks toward Paul's final visit to Jerusalem, recounted in dramatic fashion beginning in Acts 19:21. It must therefore be composed much later in the story (and in fact close to most of Paul's other principal letters) when Paul is at Corinth, just prior to his departure for Jerusalem with a group of church leaders and the collection (see Acts 20:4; Rom. 16:21). Consequently, it must be written just before the fifth such visit noted by Acts.

And some time seems to have elapsed between these two visits. Acts itself supplies an interval of around three years that Paul must spend in Asia and Ephesus between these two points (see 19:8, 10, 22; 20:31). Moreover, he must undertake all the evangelism of the second missionary journey and the first half of the third before he returns to Jerusalem on his final visit — preaching in Macedonia, Achaia, and Asia, at the least (that is, the events of Acts 16–19).[131]

In addition, we should note that reasonably firm dates can be generated for these various visits by calculating their chronological distance from the main historical marker that the book of Acts supplies — Paul's trial before the governor Gallio in Corinth, recounted in Acts 18:12-17. This can be dated with reasonable precision by a fragmentary inscription from Delphi, and arguably cross-referenced as well with a possible dating of the expulsion of the Jews from Rome by Claudius, which seems to be mentioned in Acts 18:2 when Paul first arrives in Corinth, and the chronological interval of eighteen months that the text supplies for that mission in v. 11.[132] Ultimately, significant chronological pressures can be generated on other parts of Paul's story by this marker, but these can arguably be negotiated. And this yields a date of around 48 or 49 CE for the composition of Galatians, and around 56 CE for Romans. So these two letters now seem to be separated by some time and a great deal of activity. Two further elements must now be added to this developing picture.

This paradigm generally expects Galatians to address the issues raised by Paul's Jewish Christian opponents (often known as "Judaizers," although we prefer here the more neutral designation "Teachers") through a clear statement of the gospel, conceiving that generally in terms of Justification theory. That is, the Teachers ask Paul's pagan converts to assume full law observance in order to be saved (so they ask them "to judaize," or, to become Jews), a program epitomized above all in the acceptance by any converted pagan males of circumcision. Paul then repudiates this demand by deploying the gospel of Justification, which attacks Judaism per se. Such law observance is of course counterproductive, generating only the realization of sin and of the consequent need to be saved by faith alone. So this paradigm tends to argue that Paul responds to the Judaizing question by deploying Justification theory, since this is held to set out Paul's principal positions on Judaism and salvation. Galatians' use of the relevant terminology and argumentation is therefore identified as an especially coherent analysis, *catalyzed* by the Judaizing questions but *expositing* the gospel per se. And it follows from this early identification that any similar material in Romans is also evangelical — a statement of the gospel — now separated from the contingency that elicited it in Galatia. Paul can simply state the gospel as he understands it if he wants to; it does not need a Judaizing controversy to be called forth, since its opening categories apply to everyone, without exception. In short, this early location of Galatians identifies Paul's Justification texts with the gospel so that any later deployment by Paul of that material can be identified in such terms with no further justification.

A particular understanding of Paul's call is also usually invoked alongside this reconstruction of Paul's missionary work. Acts emphasizes Paul's "conversion" rather more than the apostle himself seems to, with three separate accounts (and we have already examined them in part one, chapter five). But Galatians certainly appeals to the conversion story in some sense as well (see esp. 1:12-16). Advocates of this broad approach to Paul therefore generally introduce a construction of the event in terms of Justification, deriving additional reinforcement for a reading of Galatians and its ostensible presentation of the gospel in such terms. A line is thereby drawn from Paul's conversion, through the Judaizing crisis at Galatia, and on to Paul's final, major and most systematic letter, Romans, in terms of Justification theory. This particular thread is held to be discernible at all these critical points (creating something of an alternative history to the arc of false teaching sketched in the previous major subsection).

The problems that arise from this biographical reconstruction for my earlier suggestion concerning the provenance of Romans perhaps now seem to be more psychological than necessary, but they are real. Galatians and Romans are separated here by perhaps as many as eight years and by much activity. They speak, moreover, of Paul's gospel; this is the material that they hold in common. Hence, the overlap in substance between Galatians and Romans that I have pointed to as an indicator that a common opponent is in view is explained, rather, by their common exposition of Justification, an essentially "coherent" explanation. The two different situations lying behind these letters — Paul's first and last — both elicit an account of the gospel from Paul, and an understanding of Paul's conversion in such terms reinforces these claims. The Teachers, furthermore, have presumably been dealt with since the apostolic council of Acts 15, at which point the early church came to a clear agreement about the key issues, and Acts even denotes these figures (in all probability) as operating "without authorization" (see οἷς οὐ διεστειλάμεθα in 15:24). From this point onward, the early church has been acting in perfect accord (while prior to this point it was functioning at cross-purposes, unawares). There is therefore no justification for introducing Jewish Christian Teachers into the explanation of any of Paul's letters other than Galatians, which were, after all, written at a much later point. In short, the Judaizing crisis is limited to Galatians, the commonalities between Galatians and Romans are explained coherently, as Paul's conversion also suggests, and the two letters are separated by the best part of a decade. The positing of the Teachers behind the composition of Romans is therefore simply not plausible.

It must suffice for now to note two sets of problems with the foregoing argument.

(i) As we have already seen in part one, chapter five, the entire scenario rests on a violation of the fundamental methodological principle operative in relation to any biographical accounts of Paul — the priority of the apostle's own letters over all other evidence, including Acts (because they are firsthand, not thirdhand, sources). The foregoing case works backward, although in this case unhealthily. If the letters are examined first, as is appropriate, then it seems more likely that Galatians and Romans were composed fairly close together (and Galatians is of course discussed in detail in part five, chapter twenty). Moreover, the series of five visits by Paul to Jerusalem recounted by Acts looks more literary than real; Paul's letters mention only three (see Gal. 1:18–2:10; Rom. 15:25-32). Meanwhile, various pieces of evidence suggest that even for Acts, the Judaizing crisis did not subside after the apostolic conference, recounted in Acts 15.[133] We have also already adduced numerous reasons for resisting any construal of Paul's conversion in terms of Justification theory; the available evidence just does not support this assertion, and various key pieces of evidence stand against it. (Acts never describes Paul's conversion in terms of Justification theory.) So much that the countervailing biographical case asserts seems fragile if not simply invalid, and the whole structure rests on a false principle. But these are not its only problems.

(ii) The case also rests on invalid argumentation. First, it does not follow that the Judaizing problem necessarily receded with the passage of time; this is a non sequitur. Hence, even granting the basic contours of this biography, it is still legitimate to suggest that the Judaizing problem returned later in Paul's ministry in relation to Rome as a phenomenon operating in more than one wave, so to speak. Nothing stands against this, and it is arguably also more realistic in historical terms. (Are *any* complicated problems solved completely after one major agreement?!) Even this biography concedes that Galatians was elicited by the Teachers, so there are no real difficulties suggesting that they lie behind Romans as well. Second, the assumption that the letter to the Galatians establishes Paul's gospel in terms of Justification against this threat — thereby drawing all similar material into that coherent definition — begs the key question rather baldly. As we will see in more detail in part five, chapter twenty, but have also already suggested, Galatians is, in and of itself, insufficiently detailed to establish Justification theory at all, let alone as Paul's primary mode of response to Judaizing questions. Moreover, the Teachers do not necessarily raise the question of Judaism directly; this is an assumption, not a necessity. We must then, in effect, wait and see what Paul argues vis-à-vis the Teachers in Romans in order to understand his earlier case in Galatians better. (This is not to minimize the importance or distinctiveness of Galatians in this relation, but it is to point to the considerable superiority that Romans possesses in terms of information and specificity.) So, once again, this particular case gets things the wrong way around.

Far from constituting a cogent objection to our unfolding scenario, this objection itself seems to be in need of revision. It turns out to be an ineffective rejoinder. And with its refutation, all the immediate objections to my developing suggestion seem to have been defused. We are free, then, to turn to its more detailed development in the chapters that follow, beginning with an overview of the specific interpretative strategy that it facilitates, and then applying that strategy in detail to the text of Romans 1–4.

CHAPTER FOURTEEN

Rereading Romans 1:18–3:20 — Indictment Reconsidered

§1. Preamble

In this preamble I want to take a big step and, in the light of where we have come from, set out a plan for the rest of our journey through Paul's texts. I will attempt to supply here an overview of the strategy that I suggest will solve all the difficulties we have amassed, rereading Paul's Justification texts with integrity but eliminating Justification theory en route — rereading them in effect *rhetorically* and, within that, *apocalyptically*.[1] But we must begin this overview by retracing some of our earlier steps.

We should recall first that at the heart of our current difficult situation lies a broad textual antithesis and its conventional interpretation (a cluster of terms and texts that has already been described in brief and will be set out in more detail in part five, chapter twenty). Suffice it for now to observe that in his Justification texts Paul often deploys an opposition between ἔργα νόμου and πιστ- terms, the relevant phrases and terms drawing the surrounding argumentation into their meaning. This opposition is enabled, moreover, by a common use of δικαιο-terminology. So, for example, δικαιοσύνη is revealed *not* by ἔργα νόμου but through πίστις in some sense (see Rom. 3:21-22). Key scriptural texts feature on both sides of this antithesis, and the figure of Abraham is also present, suitably interpreted. And Justification theory is constructed on top of this textual antithesis, supposedly as its best interpretation.

The basic antithesis

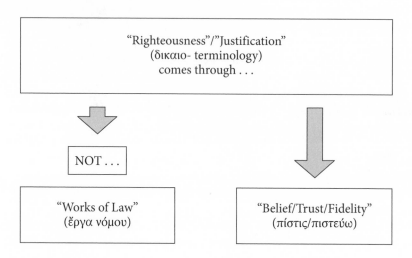

If we simplify this dynamic, we create two fundamentally different states — state A, characterized by "works of law," and state B, characterized by "belief."

Justification theory of course structures the antithesis in a highly distinctive way, and we must be careful to grasp all the assumptions that it brings to this act of interpretation. It assumes that Paul is speaking here — *throughout this entire antithesis* — of "the gospel," meaning by this the process of salvation as a whole. (How you get saved — and that you can be — is "the good news.") It is a soteriological construct. And this certainly seems a reasonable assumption in the first instance, because δικαιόω clearly has something to do with a process of salvific judgment. But Justification theory makes a series of further critical assumptions.

It structures these two states in strict relation to one another, *connecting them in a progression*. A full account of salvation therefore *begins* with state A and *progresses* to state B. This antithesis works *forward*.[2] Both states, and their interrelationship in just this manner — and only in this manner — constitute a complete account of salvation.

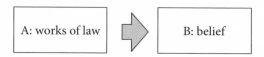

However, because the account of the gospel begins in state A, Justification theory is now committed to a *prospective* and *foundationalist* account of soteriology —

two very important features. Any prospective soteriological account — any account that is a priori, or moves or thinks "forward" — is necessarily foundationalist, and vice versa. Its account of the gospel, simply *because* it moves forward from A to B, *is dependent on the construction of A*. If A is not constructed correctly, then B cannot follow. Hence, A is the more basic, prior state. However, A is also the non- or pre-Christian state — here characterized specifically as "works of law." The gospel per se — state B — rests on this pre-Christian foundation, and depends on it. Certain additional assumptions are also set in play by this — namely, universality (versus particularity) and ahistoricality (also versus temporal particularity). The foundation for the gospel must necessarily apply to all people through time and space.

Justification theory is therefore a particular variant within the much larger category of prospective and foundationalist theologies. But because of its purchase here on Paul, it seems to have an especially powerful exegetical corroboration; it speaks as Paul speaks (although arguably we did not appreciate clearly that Paul spoke in quite this way until the 1500s CE). And we have already seen that Justification theory can meet both of the main challenges that lie here rather impressively. On the one hand, it can supply a plausible and coherent account of the way in which an individual first grasps the basic contours of state A and then learns that this state leads necessarily to B; it seems a coherent soteriological theory. On the other hand, it can supply a plausible account of some of Paul's texts that seem to say much the same thing; it is exegetically responsible. So a powerful theory is married to a powerful scriptural construal.

But we have also seen that this construal is by no means flawless. Numerous problems are unleashed within the broader interpretation of Paul when it is endorsed in relation to its chosen texts — problems at both the theoretical and the exegetical level — prompting the critical reevaluation of the entire discourse that we have undertaken in this book. Some sort of solution to all these difficulties seems to be highly desirable. Arguably, the difficulties of the discourse now outweigh its strengths and advantages. And one of the first steps toward a solution can be taken by placing this marriage of theory and exegesis firmly in its original historical context — an issue that can slip easily out of sight because of the programmatic quality of the things that Justification holds Paul to be asserting. It is difficult to think that the original historical situation is important in relation to the exposition of universal evangelical truths (and especially when those tend to override the specificities of local situations). But they are important.

No one disputes that the first extant statement of this theory in Paul — Galatians — was elicited by the arrival of figures in the Christian communities in Galatia who seem to have been hostile to Paul. Indeed, this is indisputable because Paul says it plainly.[3] Consequently, the original textual situation in the Justification discourse — its famous antithesis of "works" and "faith" — seems to have been caused in historical terms by the arrival of particular opponents — the Teachers.

But Paul also tells us plainly in Galatians that these Teachers presented a *gospel* to the Galatian Christians, that is, *an alternative soteriological program* (although he scornfully adds that it does not really merit this name: see esp. Gal. 1:6-9). Two gospels are therefore in play. And if my account of the production of Romans is correct, the same situation holds there as well: it is occasioned by the specter of the Teachers' arrival. Moreover, it is almost certain that Paul's emphatic and repeated negations in Galatians and Romans target this opposing (non-)gospel at some point. He is as opposed to the Teachers' *system* as he is opposed to them; the issues are not merely personal. Therefore, few interpreters have hesitated to attribute "righteousness" or "justification" "through works of law" in the first instance to the Teachers (at least in Galatians, but therefore also by implication in Romans). This harshly and repeatedly negated phrase seems to be a depiction by Paul of some feature of this opposing gospel. Certainly, this is the most obvious way to read the textual antithesis that we have already noted, given the basic situation that elicited it — false teachers and teachings. And we come here to a crucial point.

Although it is seldom noted, an interpretative fissure now opens up before us that the advocate of Justification theory must find some way to bridge (and so my rereading strategy for these texts will begin at precisely this problematic juncture, as we will see shortly). The Justification advocate must transform this initial antithesis of two different gospels into a connected progression that *together* constitutes *one* gospel (with state A leading to state B); this is the interpretative chasm that must be crossed. Certainly, such a progression is not immediately apparent in the texts. And so a number of key assumptions need to be introduced that must hold good if the Justification program is ultimately to be successful.

I. *Two* gospels: A versus B

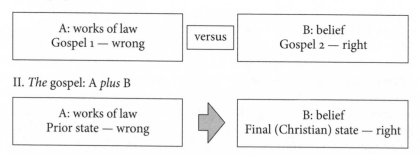

II. *The* gospel: A *plus* B

The assumptions that underlie this transformation need to be articulated clearly. In essence, both the Teachers and Paul *need to start their theological programs at the same point.* Both must begin with an account of state A, the state that non-Christians occupy — Judaism (the particular foundational variant that they both endorse). Thus, according to Justification theory, there is a paradoxically close relationship between the Teachers and Paul in substantive terms; they are quarreling theological siblings. But these shared assumptions also draw a third constituency into the conversation, namely, Judaism itself. Because both gospels begin with an analysis of the pre-Christian state, their correct progression should also encompass an objectively accurate and reasonable description of Judaism as Jews themselves supplied that — an obvious point at which the entire construction can be tested (so part one, chapter four).

Yet Paul must have some difficulty with this starting point and with his opponents, driving his progression beyond the first stage to the Christian gospel. And according to this theory, Paul's principal problem with the Teachers, as well as with other Jews, is that they have *not* analyzed *Judaism* correctly, thereby initiating the correct further progressions, first, to the collapse of Judaism as an independent and effective soteriology and, second, to the grasping of salvation through the easier mode of faith alone. This is why Paul supposedly negates state A in these texts. The Teachers, along with other unbelieving Jews, remain stuck in the first phase of the gospel, which is consequently not really a gospel at all. (And we know well by now that incorrect analyses of the character of God, his expectations, and/or individual sinfulness must underlie such intransigence.) Paul himself is able to move on to state B, thereby realizing the full Christian gospel, even as his opponents and fellow Jews remain muddled and lost in state A, which is by itself not good news.

If all these assumptions hold good, then any clash between Paul and the Teachers will probably elicit a systematic statement of the gospel as Justification understands it when the apostle confronts those opponents with letters. Since both parties begin at the same theological point and work forward — correctly or not as the case may be — then in order to correct a confused situation, Paul needs simply to begin where the Teachers begin and then lead them through the correct progressions to the gospel of salvation through faith alone. The antithesis *of* gospels in the text and its original settings can thereby become also a gospel *of* antithesis, with the failure of "works" leading on to "belief." *But without these assumptions,* Paul and the Teachers do *not* necessarily start at the same systematic point, *and we then have no way of knowing whether these two states should be connected.* Indeed, there is no reason *to* connect them; there are simply two gospels in play in the relevant texts — gospel A and gospel B. And this would of course be catastrophic for the generation of Justification theory. It would in effect fail to launch in textual terms. Some crucial corollaries now need to be noted.

In the first instance, these are such utterly basic assumptions — shaping the whole future direction of theological discussion as that is premised on Paul, not to mention the broader description of Paul himself — that they need to be proved. Once these texts are interpreted in terms of Justification theory, a retrospective theological approach (which many would argue is the only authentic one) has, for example, already been excluded, as have numerous other foundationalist approaches that launch from different prior starting points. The conventional interpretation locks these texts together into a single, progressive account of salvation and simultaneously locks many other interpretations out. So it is only appropriate to ask for proof at this point.

But, second, these assumptions need to be proved to a degree on historical grounds. That is, these further equations governing the relationship between Paul's gospel and the gospel of the Teachers do not *necessarily* follow, unless we have been given reasons for believing them to hold. We do not assume automatically, as a matter of course, that bitterly opposed parties at other times in history have shared the same underlying starting points and consequent theoretical structures. They *might* have, but such claims need to be demonstrated. We might be dealing with Mensheviks versus Bolsheviks or Emancipationists versus Abolitionists in the Galatian and Roman situations. But we might be dealing with fascists versus libertarians or with pacifists versus anarchists! How then do we know that the quarrel in Galatia is a bitter argument between people who are, in fundamental theological terms, like-minded?

We should note, third, that this reconstruction takes no account of the fact that the Teachers are Christians; it treats them throughout as quintessential Jews (*all* of whom are also rather self-deluded!). Paul clearly regards them as false Christians, but the indications are that this is a polemical ascription of "heresy" by Paul to a competing group that identified itself as a legitimate Christian variant (if not the only such variant!). The Teachers clearly have *some* distinctive Christian commitments. It is unlikely that they would be interested in Paul's pagan converts if they did not — or, indeed, that they would have been accorded a hearing by the Galatian and Roman congregations without them. And in fact they seem to have some connection with the mother church in Jerusalem (for example, attending the important meeting that took place there to discuss pagan salvation, as recounted in Gal. 2:1-10). But the preceding analysis in terms of Justification ignores this specific historical circumstance. It begins — crucially, as we have just seen — with the assumption that Paul and the Teachers start their accounts of the gospel with a description *of Judaism* (which is then shared with other Jews): state A articulates salvation as a Jew. Paul is therefore generally supposed to have held this position *before his conversion*, and the Teachers for some reason still hold it.

Now this is not necessarily a problem for the developing explanation of Paul himself; he is still recognizably Christian, because his description of Judaism develops rapidly in that direction after it degenerates to despair. The Christian gospel will arrive to save him as he reaches state B. However, this reading necessarily leaves the Teachers — Jewish Christians, in historical terms — in state A — Judaism — indefinitely. There is no essential difference between the Teachers and Jews, and, for the overarching construction to continue to work, *there cannot be any such difference.*[4]

The Justification discourse thus rests on a degree of circularity that can now be exposed. The best evidence for the foregoing *historical* claims is the construal of the relevant Justification texts in these terms argumentatively and theologically — as an account of the gospel that builds from a Jewish, pre-Christian state to a Christian state. *If this reading of Paul's argument is correct,* then we can work back from it in historical terms and reconstruct the identity of a group in early Christianity in these respects, following this — as we have to — with a much broader reconstruction of the entirety of contemporary Judaism in the same terms (and this is an increasingly embarrassing move). The success of the construal itself thereby underpins the necessary historical assumptions. Jews, Jewish Christians, and Paul, all start from the same place, because this is where the gospel starts. Clearly, however — and especially in a contested situation — the key questions are being begged spectacularly by all this. If we are worried about the cogency *of* Justification theory, there will be no corresponding need to grant the necessary accompanying historical scenario. Indeed, if we approach these texts again, there is now no historical need to read them in the way that Justification theory dictates, but quite the converse.

A construal in terms of Justification is actually quite a strange reading historically. It involves bridging an interpretative chasm by means of various historical and conceptual equations. And given the initial absence of any such equations, the success of the arrival on the other side is then claimed to undergird the soundness of the bridge that has just been crossed! What if there is no such bridge? (What if we have just jumped over the gap?!) The conventional construal seems to rest at this point on next to nothing — on its own theoretical assertiveness. We must consider, then, the consequences of remaining on the safe side of the chasm. We can do so by returning to the historical situation that is now appearing to be increasingly problematic.

We have already established that Galatians certainly, and Romans most probably, should be read as debates with the Teachers. And in my view — and this is perhaps the most crucial point in this entire discussion — a clear grasp of this basic historical setting will allow us to dispense with Justification as a reading of these texts (as was said at the beginning of this chapter), thereby solving all the problems that that reading generates.

There will be no need to introduce the additional set of assumptions necessary for the coherent development of a gospel from Paul's Justification texts in terms of Justification theory. Those texts can speak merely of two gospels or states — "works of law" in state A and "belief" in state B. And those states will not need to be linked into a *connected* progression, with state A *preparing for and founding* state B. They can simply be two different gospels *that have no inherent connection at all* (that is, other than the historical, circumstantial connection that their advocates were trying at certain times to convince the same groups of Christians to believe in their respective systems). And this simple interpretative move — which is really just the refusal to make a set of unjustified moves — will essentially eliminate Justification theory and all its associated difficulties from the description of Paul.

It is indeed, in the first instance, as simple as this; we should take Paul at his word and read his Justification texts as discussions of two gospels, along with all the assumed comparisons and contrasts that such a discussion implies. But as we contemplate this exciting interpretative prospect, two questions naturally arise. Is a plausible rereading of Paul's Justification texts in such terms possible, that is, in terms of a simple juxtaposition of two gospels, one good, the other bad? And can

Justification advocates construct a powerful enough case to override this reading and take us across the chasm to the far side in any case? Before we consider these questions, it is important to recall where the burden of proof now lies.

The main impediment to the pursuit of any alternative approach to Paul's Justification texts is of course psychological; it is very difficult to think differently about them, given their recent history and status. We are embedded in a powerful tradition of construal. We also are probably embedded in a set of prospective discourses — theological, paradigmatic, church-historical, and ideo-cultural. All these largely unrecognized interpretative templates encourage us to read Paul "forward," and hence to read these two states as one interconnected progression. (We have spent much of part two charting these unseen hermeneutical influences because of their importance at this exact point in our discussion.) But we need to think differently about these texts because of the considerable slate of difficulties that is generated by this conventional approach to their interpretation.

Clearly, both approaches — the conventional approach in terms of Justification and an alternative in terms of "two gospels" — must supply an exegetical case. Each must give a plausible account of the actual textual data. However, as we have just seen, the conventional approach needs to supply additional historical and exegetical material if it is to find Justification theory in these texts. Certain exegetical equations, undergirded by plausible historical explanations, must be supplied if that reading is ultimately to hold good — the linking of states A and B. In the absence of good reasons for doing so, we should not approach these texts with any presumption that they are structured in this way. We might say that there is nothing *obvious* about reading Paul's Justification texts in terms of one gospel of two progressive states, because they are structured initially merely in terms of two gospels. But certainly any alternative approach in terms of these two gospels will have to make its own case too. Does this look possible? I would suggest that it does.

It is important to note initially that such a reading is able to draw on various methodological reservoirs that Justification theory tends to bypass. Since the latter reads the relevant texts as statements of Paul's theological coherence, there has been little need to consider approaches that lie closer to the original occasions of Galatians and Romans — approaches closer to the surfaces of these two texts, so to speak. Paul has been held to be involved here primarily in self-expression. But a "two-gospel" approach is more sensitive to this interpretative level from the outset — indeed, it is enmeshed with it — and so can draw on the resources especially of rhetoric, argumentation, and performance (with the last two being subsets of the first, although not in popular parlance). These resources supply different expectations concerning Paul's argument. Instead of foundations, progression, and coherence, we can expect the dynamics of debate — statement, counterstatement, and critique (although this should still not lack coherence).

The remainder of this volume will develop a rereading of Paul's Justification texts in terms of "two gospels" that leans on these essentially rhetorical resources. The details will be demonstrated in all the chapters that follow, but it may be helpful to begin with a basic sketch of the rereading's approach and strengths.

One of the most natural ways to develop this solution is to trace first how it can resolve many of our former difficulties. We have already seen that most of the problems generated for the broader description of Paul by Justification derive more specifically from that discourse's prospective theoretical approach. Paul here seems to think "forward" and so establishes a prior theoretical phase with particular conceptions of humanity and God, which then control all the theory's later developments (the function of Christ, the nature of the church, and so on). Elsewhere, however, and especially in Romans 5–8, Paul develops a very different, retrospective approach, which Pauline scholars often designate as "apocalyptic" — an approach widely discernible in Galatians as well. Here the basic conceptions of humanity, God, Christ, and the church are significantly different from those underlying Justification theory. Furthermore, acute proximate as well as systematic tensions are discernible where these systems are juxtaposed — in terms of quite broad discussions in Romans, but often cheek by jowl in the more compact argumentation of Galatians!

With the abandonment of the necessary connection between state A and state B in these texts, the prospect is immediately raised that many of these tensions could be eliminated. If Paul's discussion of "works of law" characterizes a different gospel altogether, then that material can be stripped from any positive account of his own soteriology. The only material that must now be so included derives from the positive side of the Justification antithesis — the assertions revolving around πιστ- terms. It is *this* side of the comparison that presumably points to Paul's own position, and this side alone. Moreover, these assertions have now been liberated from any function within a prospective arrangement.

Clearly, the onus in any such reinterpretation lies more squarely on our construal of Paul's πιστ- terminology than has previously been the case, and in a subtly different sense; it can now be treated independently of the interpretation of the apostle's ἔργα νόμου material, *which has previously framed our approach to the later πιστ- terms with a set of basic and ultimately debilitating assumptions.* Paul's πιστ- terms can now be interpreted in a *nonprospective* setting.

Recent debate has rather fortuitously opened up the further possibility of an important *christological* premise in these texts, and of a *participatory* presupposition consequently informing Paul's arguments — an argument that could be extended and connected relatively easily with Paul's fuller apocalyptic discussions of the gospel, undertaken elsewhere, that tend to assume a participatory approach. The salience of "the fidelity of Christ," mirroring the fidelity of the Christian, suggests this possible broader interpretation quite neatly, the similarity of the two attributes pointing to a possible participatory causality underlying them (i.e., Christians are faithful because they are being molded by the Spirit into the likeness of the faithful Christ).

It seems, then, that a thoroughgoing apocalyptic interpretation of Paul is indeed possible. And if this sweeping reinterpretation can be achieved, we will not only reinforce what is arguably an orthodox and dynamic account of Paul's gospel, but with the very same stroke we will eliminate a massive set of contradictions and tensions from the apostle's thinking, thereby going some way toward restoring if not enhancing his theological integrity. The elimination of so many interpretative problems en route should serve as a strong validation. But we should now consider the nature of that reinterpretation in a little more detail.

We have already seen (in part three, chapter ten) that Justification theory must make its case primarily in Romans 1–4, and the same observation applies to any rereading of Paul's texts, although with slightly different consequences.

The compression of Paul's arguments in Galatians (as we will see) facilitates a relatively easier reconstrual of the key texts there in terms of a straightforward comparison of two different gospels, one of which is right, the other wrong.[5] And essentially the same can be said of the briefer texts found elsewhere in Paul that use Justification terms and moves — especially Philippians 3. These too can be read in terms of two gospels in a relatively straightforward fashion. The principal textual impediment to this interpretation is clearly Justification's "citadel," Romans 1–4.

I would suggest that Romans 1–4 is the only text in Paul where the apostle arguably sets out a theological program that is overtly prospective and foundationalist, and in a discussion that is extensive enough to launch Justification theory. It is here that the decisive exegetical battle must be fought. However, we are now able to approach this text in a rather new way. We know that a competing system is in play in some sense at Rome (whether in fact or by way of anticipation). Paul is about to engage with a false teaching, as well as promote his own. So it is now possible to posit a rather different, *nonprospective* construal of this argument, a possibility that we will pursue in detail for the rest of this chapter — perhaps the most important set of exegetical claims in this book. There is, at bottom, no immediate need to read this argument forward — once we have realized the fragility of this claim and its widespread destructive consequences. We should resist our inclinations at this point.

The argument in Romans 1:18–3:20 is, I would suggest, a tightly focused, contingent discussion, and not a sweeping, prospective, systematic discussion at all. It is essentially a reduction to absurdity of the alternative gospel of the Teacher, especially in terms of the Teacher's typical rhetorical opening with "fire and brimstone." Paul knows this alternative gospel well by the time he composes Romans. But in order to pick it apart — and he will — he must first reproduce its opening moves for his auditors, *who do not necessarily know it well themselves.* And Romans 1:18-32 fulfills this role.

Romans 1:18-32 reproduces compactly the opening rhetorical gambit of the Teacher — the way he usually seeks to introduce his gospel to a pagan audience, in standard Jewish fashion, with a critique of idolatry and sexual immorality (and this opening echoes parts of the Wisdom of Solomon as well, possibly quite significantly). So technically Romans 1:18-32 is an instance of προσωποποιία or "speech-in-character" — what we might call more colloquially a brief moment of "playacting" or "mimicry" or even "impersonation." Paul does not speak here in his own voice but in the voice of the Teacher. He mimics here that figure's fiery rhetorical entrance, which is lit — like that of so many preachers — by the flickering backdrop of hell.

Thus — in something of an irony — Paul reproduces in 1:18-32 the Teacher's initial definition of "the problem" and not his own, because ultimately he will drive several wedges between this definition and the Teacher's offer of "a solution." That is, at various points the Teacher's solution is not actually symmetrical to or consistent with his own definition of the problem, and Paul has cleverly spied out and isolated these weaknesses. So the argument in Romans 1–3 goes on to show, in three further steps from 2:1 through 3:20, how the implicit theological commitments of this first definition of "the problem" by the Teacher lead to the complete futility of his consequent "solution," or gospel! The result of the entire maneuver by Paul is to suggest that the Teacher's opening proclamation can be shown ultimately to save no one — *not even its proclaimer!* "[B]y means of works of Law, *no one* will be declared righteous . . ." (3:20a). Romans 1:18–3:20 thereby confounds the Teacher, *and largely in terms of the Teacher's own initial assumptions*. So the Teacher's gospel is not only an exercise in futility but *self-evidently* so — a double shortfall, and a double rhetorical victory for Paul. It seems that the Teacher's own system — properly understood — is self-defeating.

Viewed in this way, Romans 1:18–3:20 turns out to be an almost astonishingly penetrating argument; indeed, it is something of a rhetorical masterpiece.[6] Very little within this extended demonstration now represents the thinking of Paul directly. Consequently, all the problems generated by the conventional reading of Romans 1:18–3:20 and its endorsement of Justification theory basically evaporate. And this is the strongest evidence in my reconstrual's support.[7]

But it is best to begin the detailed exposition of this alternative reading by considering the objection that is often made against it around this point in its presentation. The complaint is frequently voiced that this understanding of 1:18-32 — as a reproduction of the Teacher's opening rhetoric and not Paul's — could not have been recognized as such by the Roman Christians (a bold claim to make in relation to audiences located in ancient Greco-Roman cities!). It is certainly true that later, predominantly Western readers have failed to recognize it as such for a long time, from which point it is difficult to consider my suggested alternative reading of the larger argument with any degree of empathy, and especially in view of some of its theological implications. Since this objection threatens to derail my entire approach at the outset, we need to pause here to consider carefully whether it is plausible — so §2, immediately following. However, after examining the methodological issues — and overruling this objection — we should be able to turn in §§3-7 to a more detailed presentation of my suggested rereading, tracing out the text's explicit and implicit encoding of a certain opposing Teacher and his initial preaching in Romans 1:18-32, and then pursuing this possible reading through the rest of its development, to 3:20, from which point its substantive advantages can also be appreciated.[8]

§2. Textual Voice Reconsidered

The principal objection that is usually made to my suggested reconstrual of Romans 1:18–3:20 corresponds exactly — if inversely — to the principal reason why interpreters have almost universally failed to detect a subversive argumentative strategy on Paul's part here and thereby avoid the conventional reading's difficulties in this section of Romans. This objection and that failure both relate to the practice of assigning the text a voice — an unavoidable hermeneutical judgment, it should be noted. My reading depends upon the original readers and auditors of Romans ultimately recognizing that Paul is not speaking in 1:18-32 in his own voice — that he is not articulating in this subsection his own position but is imitating the rhetoric of another person, the Teacher, who is essentially a Jewish Christian sage.[9] Paul recapitulates part of *his* teaching, I suggest, and in particular his opening rhetorical salvos, in Romans 1:18-32 (although it is important to appreciate that they do not need to achieve this recognition *straightaway*; many effective rhetorical strategies involving voice are delayed).

But would Paul's auditors have recognized his strategy in this passage, realizing eventually that a Jewish Teacher was speaking through 1:18-32 in condemnation of the pagans, rather than Paul himself? (And, indeed, could Paul even have intended such a strategy?) The inverse of this objection — the present-day auditor's failure to detect such an identification (assuming for the moment that it is present) — results in a false attribution of the text to Paul's *own* voice, the theological consequences of which are dire, as well as deeply ironic.[10]

It is my contention that the initial auditors of Romans could have detected such a strategy relatively easily through a plethora of nonverbal signals — the types of signals with which performed texts abound. And it must be emphasized that at this stage of our discussion it is necessary only to establish this identification as a possibility. Ultimately, my suggested rereading of Romans 1:18-32 will rely on evidence that emerges "downstream," so we will affirm this identification strongly only in retrospect. But it should be noted that this retrospective judgment is an accident of the text's canonical preservation, of the resulting loss of its original performed context, and also of some of our modern hermeneutical assumptions. We will realize belatedly what the Roman auditors could recognize relatively quickly, through the text's appropriate performance. For this reason, my auditors need for the moment only to be open to this reading of 1:18-32 as a possibility. Could the Roman Christians have detected a satirical textual operation here if it was indeed present?

Any objectors need something rather more decisive if they want to halt our investigation immediately. They need to prove that the detection of this strategy by the original Roman auditors was impossible (and/or that it was impossible for Paul as a technique). Anything less than a categorical exclusion leaves the question essentially open, allowing us to move forward.

But there is simply far too much evidence concerning the interpretative capabilities of ancient readers and auditors — not to mention of sophisticated polemical, comedic, and satirical texts in general — to sustain any such objection at the outset and in a priori terms. That the original audience of Roman Christians *could* have detected speech-in-character from 1:18 through v. 32, given a suitable performance of this passage with the correct nonverbal cues, seems an entirely plausible suggestion, although we must wait a little longer to see whether they probably did detect it. (I am of course confident that they did.) Six principal considerations support my basic interpretative contention here (and after introducing these I will supply some broader, supplementary arguments as well).

(1) The Nonverbal Dimension

Modern readers tend to norm the process of reading in terms of a silent, rather isolated engagement by a literate individual with a written text. But this is a relatively recent historical trajectory, brought about in part by the Reformation and subsequent Protestant emphases on Scripture, individualism, and even interiority, and in part by the advent of widespread literacy and the equally widespread availability of texts in an industrial age. For most people in the ancient world, reading was an aural and usually corporate experience. The people themselves were largely illiterate; their "reading" was an experience of *hearing* the text. Indeed, even private reading was usually done aloud. This fundamentally oral/aural world was the setting in which Paul's letters were composed and read — a setting that we must recover, as best we can, if we are to hear them as Paul's Roman Christian auditors probably did.

Paul's letters were read out loud by someone — presumably the letter bearer — to an audience. They were *performed*. In this sense, each letter exists for us rather like the script of an old play — but a script that often preserves only one actor's lines (although an important one). All the explicit stage directions, instructions from the playwright and director, not to mention the original coached performances, have been lost. And there would have been multiple performances. Romans, for example, probably involved repeated presentations to the small cells of Christians scattered through the suburbs of that large ancient city. A complete description of the preserved script's possible meanings, then, should take into account the broader range of effects that its full-blooded performance would have entailed within a communal setting.[11] It was an unfolding play busy with drama, insinuation, color, plot, and movement.[12] And like most plays, it probably had protagonists in some sort of conflict, whether in jest or in a more serious vein. In short, interpretation is best understood as the recovery of a set of performances by a letter bearer to an audience of listening Christians.

One result of any such recovery of the letters' original settings should be a greater sensitivity within interpretation to the nonverbal dimension operative within such communicative events. We must be prepared to posit the nonverbal cues that have since been lost — the cues that a good letter reader, like a good actor, would have given to assist the enjoyment and comprehension of the original auditors. I am not of course suggesting that these cues be made up. We need concrete confirmation from the preserved text in due course that our suggested performance of it is correct. And such cues should also be demonstrable as interpretative possibilities within the surrounding culture. But within these constraints we must as a matter of historical rigor remain open to the different interpretative possibilities that the orality, occasionality, and the performative settings of the letters could have imparted to the construals of their meaning supplied by their original audiences.

Recent research on nonverbal communication suggests that the amount of information transmitted by such nonverbal cues is considerable.[13] Arguably, the majority of "live" — in the sense of oral, performed — communication is nonverbal, consisting of the meaning transmitted by means of tone, timing, facial expression, gesture, posture, distance, movement, and even costume.[14] Certain written texts can even be given directly opposite meanings merely by a performance with different accompanying suites of nonverbal cues. It might be objected that such research generally takes place on modern subjects. However, there is little reason to think that the nature and importance of nonverbal communication differ fundamentally through history, although its precise cues and components will of course vary as much as the verbal languages with which it is interwoven. Nonverbal communication is still an essentially linguistic phenomenon — a language.[15] Moreover, there is good reason to think that Paul's original audiences were more sensitive to nonverbal cues than modern audiences are. A favored popular artistic entertainment in Rome was mime, *a completely nonverbal medium,* but clearly one that conveyed a great deal.[16] Paul's auditors otherwise inhabited a world dominated by performed oral texts. Consequently, their sensitivity to the nonverbal cues that accompanied texts probably greatly exceeded our own.

In view of all this, it would seem to be unhistorical and even unwise to refuse to consider the interpretative differences that can be generated by different performances of a Pauline text, taking into account in particular the range of meanings that can be generated by nonverbal cues. These must be entertained as formal interpretative possibilities. Hence, it seems fair to suggest that Romans 1:18-32 *could* have been performed as speech-in-character. (And had Paul composed this passage in this way, he presumably would have given Phoebe explicit instructions in how to perform it.) We must go on, then, to see whether the later evidence confirms the likelihood of this suggested performance.

(2) Προσωποποιία

My suspicion is that even if we could not identify the precise strategy that Paul was using in Romans 1:18-32 in terms of an attested ancient technique, we would still have to posit its presence there because of the superiority of the reading that it ultimately generates over against the conventional approach.[17] However, it certainly strengthens my case to be able to point to its overt attestation in Paul's day as the strategy of προσωποποιία or "speech-in-character." Stanley Stowers suggested in 1994 that Paul was using προσωποποιία in Romans 7:7-25.[18] We do not need to reach a decision concerning that suggestion here; it suffices to note Stowers's description of the technique and his subsequent defense of its general plausibility in relation to Paul.[19] Stowers points to the evidence in Quintilian and Cicero[20] and to the *Exercises* of Theon (2.115.10-11), and *Preliminary Exercises* of Hermogenes and Aphthonius (to which we can now add material from Nicolaus the Sophist, and excerpts from later commentators on Aphthonius, including fragments from Sopatros; note that Hermogenes, Aphthonius, Nicolaus, and Sopatros, all employ the term ἠθοποιία rather than προσωποποιία.[21]) Stowers appeals to Origen's later recognition and use of the technique in relation to both Celsus and Romans 7 as well (*RR*, 164-69) — and Origen's interaction with the technique is certainly instructive (to which we should add the evidence of Justin's *Dialogue with Trypho*[22]).

As Quintilian describes it:

> A bolder form of figure, which in Cicero's opinion demands greater effort, is *fictiones personarum,* or προσωποποιία. This is a device which lends wonderful variety and animation to oratory. By this means we display the inner thoughts of our adversaries as though they were talking with themselves. . . . Or without sacrifice of credibility we may introduce conversations between ourselves and others, or of others among themselves, and put words of advice, reproach, complaint, praise or pity into the mouths of appropriate persons. . . . It is also convenient at times to pretend that we have before our eyes the images of things, persona or utterances. . . . (9.2.30-33)

Significantly, Quintilian goes on to say that such "words may be inserted without the introduction of any speaker at all. . . . This [then] involves a mixture of figures, since added to προσωποποιία is ellipse, which here consists in omitting any indication of the one speaking" (9.2.37).[23] Equally significantly, the technique seems to be commonplace in Epictetus's *Discourses.*[24]

If both the existence and the possible appropriateness of this strategy are granted, then it remains only to note how it accords with a nearly ubiquitous feature of language and culture, namely, the human capacity to imitate someone else — enabling in turn a host of useful rhetorical goals such as mockery, refutation, satire, and so on. That some of the ancient practitioners named and described this strategy is certainly helpful, but its existence does not in fact depend on this. It would seem difficult to deny that people frequently speak in the voice of another. People act.[25] Nevertheless, it is encouraging to find that the ancient auditors of Romans would probably have called the literary strategy operative in Romans 1:18-32 — as I suggest it — προσωποποιία. But further evidence can be marshaled in support of this interpretative possibility.

(3) Διαφωνία

As Stowers points out, Greek readers were trained to detect shifts in authorial voice (διαφωνία) and to read accordingly.[26] And while such shifts could be signaled overtly, perhaps through a verb of speaking attributed to a particular character in a narrative, or by a description of a setting, sometimes the only signal of a shift in authorial voice might come from a significant change in style — instances of ἐναλλαγή or μεταβολή. Such changes are detectable in these texts only by a highly competent reader — and yet we do detect these subtle variations in our own language daily. In addition, in ancient texts these shifts would be crafted in terms of a consistent character encoded elsewhere in the text, and I will argue shortly that this is the case for Romans 1:18–3:20. But here it suffices to note that a detectable difference in style is often a critical signal that a change of voice should also take place during a text's performance (and possibly in terms of some previously encoded or stock character).

It might also be helpful to note that, in part because of the need to economize with precious paper, ancient readers were expected to supply far more information to their readings of texts than modern readers are; they contributed notions of phraseology and punctuation that we would expect overt markings to supply. Hence, in addition to being more oral/aural than modern readers, ancient readers were trained to be more active readers.

It is at precisely this juncture that the debate concerning the authenticity of Romans 1:18-32 becomes especially pointed. As we saw in part three, chapters eleven and twelve, several interpreters have argued that this text is a later interpolation largely on grounds of its distinctive style. The text-critical evidence (among other things) is too weak to sustain this radical hypothesis, and it has rightly been widely rejected; but the impressive evidence of an unusual style in Romans 1:18-32 that these scholars have collated has never been adequately explained otherwise. And I would suggest that this evidence is potentially very significant, although not as an indicator of later authorial insertion, as those scholars assumed, *so much as a change in authorial voice.* Indeed, it would constitute a classic signal for this function.

We noted in chapter eleven no fewer than five clusters of unusual stylistic indicators in Romans 1:18-32: (i) its self-contained structure, with an opening thesis statement, distinctive repeated phrases, and boundaries offset from the surrounding material by alliteration; (ii) an astonishing incidence of alpha-privatives — seventeen (and Romans contains only forty-eight in total); (iii) a dense concentration of third person plural verbs — thirteen — along with an equally dense incidence of third person pronouns; (iv) the presence of various puns or wordplays; and (v) a long and highly distinctive vice list. The combined force of these unusual stylistic features is simply too powerful to be ignored — although the supposition that this connotes an interpolation and non-Pauline authorship is misguided. This marked shift in style in Romans 1:18-32 is a carefully crafted signal from Paul that this passage is written in another voice and should be performed as such. Certainly, this text does not speak in the way that Paul normally speaks. Ancient auditors would have expected this different voice to speak in terms of a particular character, and the later argument in 2:1–3:20 will turn out to provide a consistent portrait of just the figure that we would expect to make this speech[27] — although by 3:19, he will have been temporarily silenced.[28]

(4) The Expectations of a Diatribal Discourse

We now need to consider the possible signals that are given with regard to genre, since these reinforce everything that has been said up to this point in terms of nonverbal cues, προσωποποιία, and stylistic shifts. My theses here are, first, that Romans is strongly reminiscent of the ancient Greco-Roman diatribe and, second, that when the conventions of the diatribe are fully grasped, it again becomes difficult to object in advance that 1:18-32 could not have been an instance of προσωποποιία.

Although Rudolf Bultmann supplied a classic earlier account of the diatribe, the modern discussion of this technique in Paul — and especially in Romans — is dominated by the work of Stanley Stowers.[29] It is uncontested that the subsections 3:1-9 and 3:27-31 are overtly diatribal. But Stowers points out that the diatribe was not limited to such abbreviated and easily recognizable dialogical exchanges, and a brief consideration of the relevant sources confirms this.

Ancient diatribe is essentially a distinctive mode of discourse built largely with apostrophe and speech-in-character. A constructed character is generally addressed by the discourse's central protagonist — who is a broadly Socratic figure — by means of the literary technique of apostrophe, so much of the discourse unfolds through the use of second person singular grammar. And that interlocutor then responds, whether in brief or at length, through the literary technique of speech-in-character, so here the author puts words in this character's mouth. The result is a dramatic discourse mimicking the to and fro of debate and conversation, although slipping where necessary into more extended speeches by one or the other party. (Epictetus's longest such speech is slightly longer than the text of Romans, which is itself roughly 5000 words in length.)

Once these features of the discourse are recognized, it becomes apparent that scholars have tended to categorize only the shorter, dialogical sections in Romans as diatribal, and this is an overly restrictive application of the genre. Longer speeches by the diatribe's protagonist — here Paul — and his interlocutor are also to be expected, but these nevertheless remain within the parameters of a fundamentally diatribal text.

The best source for the ancient diatribe is Epictetus, and his attestation is possibly quite significant for our current concerns.[30] Epictetus, a former slave who was brilliant enough to succeed as a philosopher with an international reputation, was a near contemporary of Paul's, living ca. 55-135 CE. His diatribes were collected, written down, and published by his pupil Arrian. The degree to which they were edited and reshaped during this process is both debated and difficult to determine, but it seems likely that, as a result of this process, they do retain a more occasional character than other self-consciously produced texts in antiquity. Certainly, the origins of these published discourses were Epictetus's live lectures and exchanges — his philosophical performances. And it seems quite significant that they are largely diatribal discourses that mimic direct exchanges between protagonists. There seem to be various reasons for this textual quality.

The diatribe originated — at least to some degree — in the earlier Socratic dialogue, and its form consequently contained certain previous epistemological assumptions. Plato's Socrates employed the dialogue in part because of his solution to the Meno paradox in terms of ἀνάμνεσις. He reasoned that investigation knew what it sought and could recognize it — thereby circumventing the paradox — because it was a rediscovery of previous knowledge that had been forgotten. Hence, good philosophers functioned as midwives, bringing truth to birth in their interlocutors from their own assumptions, teasing out a correct understanding by a process of cross-examination, *because the truth was already there.* (In particular, interlocutors could be confronted with the contradictions in their own positions and forced to abandon at least one half of such dilemmas, or they could be pressed to accept notions implicit within everyday analogies that they already affirmed, and so on.) One suspects, however, that the dialogical mode of much philosophical discourse simply reflected Hellenic cultural practices as well.

Oral performance in the Hellenistic world seems to have taken place in an essentially agonistic setting. Performers could be challenged by their audiences, and especially when they invited this through philosophical assertions and arguments. And those audiences could contain students, visitors, passersby, and rivals. (For these reasons it also seems wise to resist assigning diatribal discourses to any given social setting too strictly, as arguably Bultmann and Stowers both do — Bultmann to street preaching, and Stowers to the classroom;[31] this flexible discourse could function in numerous ancient social settings.) Hence, by the first century CE, the diatribe is advocated explicitly by Epictetus for pragmatic rhetorical reasons, not for epistemological ones. In *Upon the art of argumentation* (2.12.4-6), he says: ". . . the real guide, whenever he finds a person going astray, leads him back to the right road. . . . How did Socrates act? He used to force the man who was arguing with him to be his witness; . . . he used to make so clear the consequences which followed from the concepts, that absolutely everyone realized the contradiction involved and gave up the battle." This rather gentle procedure is contrasted here by Epictetus with amateurish confrontational argument, which is ineffective, ends up in abuse — in reviling and in being reviled — and may even result in blows! The dialogical strategy of the diatribe is a more effective way of engaging with opponents and then successfully refuting them — perhaps even to their own advantage — presupposing that such disagreements take place in an essentially agonistic setting. But dialogical discourses were also simply an entertaining and effective way of teaching (and, as any teacher knows, effective in part because they were entertaining).

So the suggestion that the letter body of Romans is predominantly diatribal is quite unexceptionable. An ancient letter was intended to be, at bottom, a substitute for the writer's presence; it was meant to mimic his or her speech in relatively straightforward terms. In an agonistic setting, then, the letter writer's speech may well have had a dialogical aspect, engaging with pupils or opponents — the broad setting that we also find reflected in the diatribe. Both genres were overtly oral and overlap directly.[32] Indeed, it even seems reasonable to suggest, as

Thomas Tobin does, that the letter body of Romans as a whole *is* effectively a diatribe (although probably this is taking matters too far).[33]

Four important results flow from these realizations for the interpretation of Romans 1:18-32 in the broader setting of Romans 1–4, as I have suggested reading that text here.

First, it is largely undeniable that Paul is making use of προσωποποιία in Romans at some point, because whenever he represents the position of other people directly — that is, as if they are speaking — he *must* do so using this technique; he has to place words in their mouths. No interpreters deny that Paul is doing this at least in the diatribal exchanges of 3:1-9 (and so on). And when Paul's interlocutor replies to one of the apostle's more shocking inferences with as little as μὴ γένοιτο, this too is an instance of προσωποποιία. So the key question cannot be whether Paul used προσωποποιία, because plainly he did so; it must be *whether he did so at this particular point* (and at such length).

Second, the partial indirection of diatribal discussion lends itself to a less confrontational and offensive analysis of an opposing point of view than direct polemic, and the author of the diatribe still retains a high degree of control over that discussion. An opposing construct is encoded by a diatribal discussion and then addressed before a text's audience. Particular people are therefore not named (or at least, not necessarily), and neither is the audience addressed aggressively, in a direct fashion. Moreover, even that construct is permitted the opportunity to speak. Indeed, it may even be addressed in large measure in terms of its own assumptions. According to Epictetus, this may well result in a more constructive exchange with an opposing interlocutor. (We will return to the further importance of these implications for Romans just below.)

Third, *a diatribal mode therefore prompts its auditors directly to identify the particular construct — the interlocutor — who is being enlightened within a particular text.* Just as the audience of a whodunit wonders actively throughout, "Who is the villain?" so the audience of a diatribe asks, "Who is it that is being enlightened?"[34] And an expectation of προσωποποιία would presumably also be operative, as the opposing figure would be expected to speak.

Moreover — and fourth — as often as not, that figure will be addressed and ultimately corrected *in terms of his or her own assumptions.* This technique is innate to the discourse's entire tradition, from its origins in the Socratic dialogue onward. So not only will a diatribal discourse's auditors be prompted to identify a figure who will ultimately be corrected, but they will expect that figure to receive instruction in relation to his or her own point of view, and so will either supply that point of view to the text — which is easy if the figure is a stereotype — or will be prompted explicitly by the text's encoding of that position. The audience will thus build up a picture of the interlocutor *and* of his or her position — although a skilful exponent of the diatribe will carefully control the exact nature of that portrait.[35]

It should be emphasized before moving on that not every diatribe employed all these conventions all the time, and neither is Romans a diatribe per se. But Romans is a letter that operates for much of the time in a way that seems to overlap directly with the agonistic and dialogical nature of the ancient diatribe — this is uncontested — and consequently, these particular expectations would be catalyzed within its auditors as possibilities. The Roman Christians, on hearing the first performances of this diatribally textured discourse, would have had various interpretative expectations instantly activated — that Paul might be engaging with an opposing interlocutor in terms of his own assumptions, some of which might even be explicitly signaled by the text when that interlocutor spoke in his own style and "voice." The actual performance of the text would then have confirmed or narcotized those expectations.

In view of the four broad considerations adduced thus far — the richness of nonverbal signals in a performed text that are often overlooked in a modern interpretative setting, the attested existence of an ancient technique of "speech-in-character," the marked shift in style in Romans 1:18-32, and the overlap between the technique of speech-in-character and the diatribal discourse that is widely conceded to be present in Romans — it does not seem overly plausible to deny the suggestion that a reading of Romans 1:18–3:20 in such terms is *possible* (and the stylistic evidence may even be positive evidence in its favor, since it is difficult to explain on other grounds). But some additional observations can be made in this possibility's support that derive more specifically from the circumstances surrounding the composition of Romans, and of Paul's letters in general.

(5) The Postponement of Specific Recognition as Diplomatic

The critical restraint facilitated by this technique could have achieved certain important rhetorical goals at Rome (and this observation dovetails with our earlier discussion of the letter's provenance in chapter thirteen). If Paul reproduces the position of an opposing Teacher in Romans 1:18-32, within the broader ambit of the persona and teaching of a stereotypical Jewish sage, and then proceeds to dissect that stance argumentatively in terms of its own assumptions, he is being both gradual in his criticisms and indirect. The target of his opposition emerges slowly, and any specific identification is both delayed and muted.[36] The result of these tactical choices is the fashioning of a detailed and ultimately firm opposition to someone *without actually engaging in either direct polemics or an aggressive frontal assault on that figure in person.* A position is attacked first — not a person, but a construct — and this incrementally and even with a degree of humor. Moreover, that construct is formed in large measure in stereotypical, not personal, terms. The specific ownership of the position is then treated very carefully and at a later point (not to mention in a decidedly muted fashion). And this is critical to the success of Paul's overarching strategy in Romans, given the particular social conventions that cradle the receipt of that letter. (It is here also that some of the critical differences with Galatians can be explained, as we have already seen in the previous chapter.) It was probably imperative that Paul *not* attack the Teacher aggressively and overtly in Romans, and for several reasons. Yet he still needed *to oppose him.* The delayed and indirect strategy that we can possibly observe operating at the outset of Romans is consequently part of Paul's literary solution to this tactical conundrum.

Only a handful of émigrés from Paul's Aegean churches actually know him at Rome — with certainty, Prisca, Aquila, and Epaenetus, and possibly also Rufus's mother (Rom. 16:3-5, 13). Most of the other Christians named or alluded to in Romans 16 seem, moreover, to meet in small separate conventicles — probably "tenement churches" — so that contact between the various addressees of the letter may have been minimal. Therefore, most of the Roman Christians do not know Paul, and do not have much contact with people who know Paul. Technically, then, they are not his "friends." And in view of this, in terms of the basic values of ancient Greco-Roman society, they owe him no loyalty, apart perhaps from a generalized Christian loyalty, but this will count for little if it has been sabotaged. Paul is, in essence, largely a stranger to them, if not someone who is currently viewed as dangerous. He cannot therefore attack another stranger and expect that strategy to be very successful. The Roman Christians have no reason to trust his judgment or to be loyal to him; he will come across as aggressive, meanspirited, and perhaps domineering in imposing his apostolic office. To make matters worse, he will then raise the matter of money.

Moreover, the Roman Christians may have heard rumors about Paul — that he is a renegade or an apostate, and someone who does not accept appropriate ecclesial authority but has a tendency to attribute authority to himself. (He even publicly insults the leaders of the early church on occasion — Gal. 2:11-14.) To be aggressive, then, would be apparently to confirm any such criticisms. Indeed, the rumormongers probably *want* Paul to write another Galatians, which might play directly into their hands.

For all these reasons, an indirect strategy, analogous to a rhetorical opening in terms of *insinuatio,* will be the best rhetorical approach, creating the impression that the Roman Christians are being allowed to make up their own minds. Paul will build cleverly from shared beliefs, while simultaneously suggesting that any rival teachings — not yet firmly coupled to particular Teachers — are self-contradictory. And all of this seems quite reasonable. Paul is not bullying, or even polemicizing. Perhaps even the rumors of his unreasonableness will then seem false.

Meanwhile, the fulsomeness of Paul's discussion will match the Roman Christians' lack of any previous teaching by him, and also probably their possible lack of textual resources over against the better equipped Teacher. (Paul probably cannot, for example, assume access by the Roman Christians to a copy of the Wisdom of Solomon.)

In sum, given the almost perfect match between the delicate rhetorical equations of the situation and an opening strategy of indirection, it seems unwise to deny Paul the option of beginning his detailed discussion in Romans with a rehearsal of an opposing position and not his own — a rehearsal that begins to unpack shortly and by degrees into a somewhat humiliating conclusion for that position's advocates. (And the inverse of this claim really holds as well, namely, that the conventional reading begins with a scathing attack on pagans, and then on Jews. Only committed Christians could find these sweeping condemnations remotely palatable.[37])

(6) Pauline Practice Elsewhere — Especially in 1 Corinthians

It is also worth noting that it is widely if not universally conceded that Paul behaves in essentially this fashion — quoting the positions of others, often unannounced — in the rest of his letters. To trace this phenomenon in detail would take us too far astray, but the point can be established by noting quickly certain uncontested instances in 1 Corinthians. These recitations of, and allusions to the positions of other people are quite abbreviated in 1 Corinthians but, like Galatians, such differences are explicable in terms of the different occasion of that letter. The Corinthians know Paul reasonably well, along with his teaching, and he knows their positions.[38] He is their founder — their "father." So no full rehearsal of the details of either system is necessary, but only brief citations and allusions. And most scholars detect a raft of such statements in 1 Corinthians, although their detailed reconstructions differ.[39] Intriguingly, the NRSV assists the reader in typical Western fashion by offsetting such remarks with the appropriate punctuation (a translation that of course reflects one set of choices concerning the reconstruction of these quotations): see 1:12; 3:4; 6:12-13; 7:1; 8:1, 4, 8; and 10:23; and possibly also 4:6b; 8:5a; 12:3; 15:12; and 15:35. But these quotations of Corinthian retorts suffice to make the point. In these texts Paul is not speaking in his own "voice"; he is reproducing the position of other people, which he then generally goes on to correct if not to criticize. (Occasionally, he builds from such quotations more constructively.) Performed with appropriate drama, these texts then all technically constitute instances of προσωποποιία:

1:12	"I belong to Paul" . . . "I belong to Apollos" . . . "I belong to Cephas" . . . "I belong to Christ"
3:4	"I belong to Paul" . . . "I belong to Apollos"
6:12-13	"All things are lawful for me" (2x) . . . "Food is meant for the stomach and the stomach for food" (although some argue strongly that the quotation continues through the next sentence — "and God will destroy both one and the other"[40])
7:1	"It is well for a man not to touch a woman"[41]
8:1	"all of us possess knowledge"[42]
8:4	"no idol in the world really exists" . . . "there is no God but one"[43]
8:8	"food will not bring us close to God" (while some include within this quotation ". . . We are no worse off if we do not eat, and no better off if we do")[44]
10:23	"all things are lawful"

And perhaps also:

4:6b	"Nothing beyond what is written"[45]
8:5a	"even though there may be so-called gods in heaven or on earth"[46]
12:3	"let Jesus be cursed"[47]
15:12	"there is no resurrection of the dead"
15:35	"How are the dead raised? With what kind of body do they come?"[48]

In sum, it seems that Paul does quote texts from others when composing his letters, and that he does not always signal those overtly with written cues; his letter bearers seem to have had sufficient instruction and ability to convey this information during their epistolary performances. The peculiar circumstances surrounding the composition of Romans seem to explain, beyond this, why Paul's quotation is so much more extensive in that letter (the Romans do not know him or his apostolic rival and probably also lack access to the necessary Jewish texts). Indeed, it seems fair to suggest that the apostle *could* have used the strategy of προσωποποιία when composing Romans 1:18-32, speaking for a time in the voice of another figure, and that his audience would have detected this while listening to Phoebe's delivery.

Excursus: Multiple Textual Voices and Hidden Transcripts[49]

I want to add two more general methodological observations here that, without pretending to be exhaustive accounts of the relevant debates, do complement one another and reinforce the preceding thesis.

We should note first that texts can abound in different "voices" (leading to a veritable interpretative industry in relation to certain texts and traditions). James Joyce's *Ulysses* is possibly the most famous current example of a text with multiple voices, but numerous other examples spring to mind — Gogol's Russian *Skaz,* Kierkegaard's pseudonyms, and so on.[50] Such changes are delivered through subtle shifts in the text's texture and are often also assisted with nonverbal, performative signals, where those are appropriate.[51] Once the ubiquity of this phenomenon is recognized — although New Testament interpreters are often not very sensitive to it — the claim that Romans speaks in more than one voice seems entirely unremarkable.

Second, it is important to realize that the explicit textual signals delivering different voices can often be muted or absent, especially in texts that are in some sense "hidden transcripts" (such as *Skaz*).[52] In such texts, the overt textual identification of a voice being subverted is *necessarily* avoided, because it would be dangerous if it fell into the wrong hands. Such texts therefore deliver their ironic and subversive potential *entirely performatively* (and are therefore also very much creatures of the moment; later reconstruction of the original semantic event is notoriously difficult). The Roman Christian auditors would be well used to such discourses, the majority of them (if not all) occupying the oppressed lower social strata where such discourses were both necessary and common.[53] (Moreover, much effective and humorous subversion deliberately postpones the moment of recognition.)[54]

§3. Romans 1:18-32 — the Teacher's Rhetorical Opening

If my suggested rereading of Romans 1:18-32 is admitted as a possibility, then how does it actually work in detail — remaining for the moment largely at the level of possibility? As has been suggested earlier at some length, Romans 1:18-32 can be read as an instance of προσωποποιία, or speech-in-character. A fuller characterization of the speaker of this material will emerge as the rest of Paul's argument unfolds — an important feature of the technique.[55] Suffice it for now to anticipate that the speaker is a recognizable "Teacher" of some sort, whose influence at Rome Paul is seeking to neutralize throughout Romans. And Romans 1:18-32 is in fact the fullest presentation of the Teacher's position that we receive from the hand of Paul. But it is not for this reason a completely fair or full presentation; it need only be sufficiently so to provide Paul with some rhetorical purchase (although ideally also without inviting an effective rejoinder in terms of caricature).[56] And it proceeds for now in rather general terms that are deliberately somewhat ambiguous. Paul does not yet wish to be too overt, although he will be pointed.

The apostle summarizes compactly in Romans 1:18-32 what he takes to be the Teacher's usual opening — his arresting προοίμιον, or *exordium*. Here Paul provides what we might call a cameo of this material. This short summary is full enough to provide the Roman Christians with everything they need in order to recognize this opening when they hear it elsewhere (if they have not already done so) *and* to be familiar, after study, with its main principles and moves. It is also distinctive enough to be recognizable against the broader backdrop of Paul's own material.[57] But, for critical argumentative reasons, Paul is interested at this point only in reproducing the Teacher's opening. He is going to exploit the underlying commitments of this opening in various ways through to 3:20, all of which are ultimately embarrassing. Indeed, Paul's entire argumentative strategy here is little more than the slow impalement of the Teacher on the dangerous implications of his own rhetorical prelude — in Theon's words, an instance of "contradiction" or "counterstatement" (ἀντίρρησις).[58] (So he will be "hoisted by his own [rhetorical] petard.") But before Paul can drive the Teacher onto his own initial assumptions, he must provide his auditors with the basis for that set of argumentative moves with a reproduction of the Teacher's typical opening tirade. And Paul has labored over this cameo. (He knows the topos well, perhaps even having used it previously himself.)

The Teacher's rhetorical prelude begins — as Paul presents it — with an important thesis: "the wrath of God is revealed from heaven against all [human] ungodliness and wickedness . . .": Ἀποκαλύπτεται . . . ὀργὴ θεοῦ ἀπ' οὐρανοῦ ἐπὶ πᾶσαν ἀσέβειαν καὶ ἀδικίαν ἀνθρώπων (v. 18a). As we noted earlier, however, in part three, chapter eleven, there is an initial awkwardness about this claim argumentatively if it is construed in conventional terms.

Verse 18 has clearly been constructed in part to correspond to the form of v. 17, where the present tense of the same verb is explicable in terms of the current disclosures mediated by the gospel. Paul seems to have intended to set these two programmatic statements in vv. 17 and 18 in parallel. But the awkward temporality of v. 18 is not entirely explained by this maneuver — the *present* disclosure of God's wrath, when all that follows builds toward its *future* revelation. A possible explanation for this often-unnoticed difficulty may lie in the way that God's wrath, which is pending in terms of its execution, is nevertheless revealed presently in terms of the human knowledge of that divine disposition that is introduced by its current proclamation. To reveal God's present displeasure with wrongdoing by speaking of this — by preaching it — is still to reveal it, even if its full disclosure, and God's definitive action of judgment, are not yet apparent, lying as they do in the future. So it is the teaching of 1:18-32 itself that arguably discloses the present anger of God with pagan wrongdoing, and we could thereby explain this difficulty in the conventional reading.[59]

However, I view this tempting option as less likely than the main alternative — that the present verb is really equivalent to a future (i.e., it is a rare "future present"). Paul does not resume the gospel's mediation of God's disclosure in the closely parallel 3:21-22, although the intervening argument has certainly emphasized the future disclosure of the wrath of God. It is difficult to make sense of the phrase ἀπ' οὐρανοῦ in a reading emphasizing present preaching, yet it integrates smoothly with an apocalyptic, future construal; Paul seems to be suggesting with this expression that the wrath of God is *itself* being revealed in some sense *from heaven against the cosmos*. And this is understandable in a future present construction — that it most certainly *will* be revealed shortly. Most importantly, the future present conveys a tone of "assurance" — "the wrath of God *is* to be revealed . . . ," and this fits the characterization of the Teacher exactly. Consequently, verse 18 is not merely construed in a neat parallelism to v. 17 but has a recognizably censorious tone.[60]

In short, Paul seems to be stating in v. 18 — in a suitably pompous manner — that the initial and hence essential content of the Teacher's position is a vision of the future wrath of God — of God as retributively just. And Paul does not think that this is the essential nature of the God of Jesus Christ. So he contrasts the Teacher's programmatic theological claim quite deliberately with the initial disclosure of his own position — his gospel — *which speaks of the saving intervention of God and hence of the divine compassion* (vv. 16-17). Paul is stating here compactly that *fundamentally different conceptions of God are at stake* in these two gospels. Moreover, it is immediately apparent that the Teacher's conception has no significant input from Christology. The stylistic parallel therefore denotes a deliberate contrast between two quite different theological programs.[61]

With these two sets of basic principles in place, Paul begins to explicate the Teacher's aggressive opening claims. Verses 19-32 set out in more detail (and in a quite distinctive fashion stylistically, as has already been noted) the chain of argument implicit within v. 18 — six steps to pagan culpability: (1) The truth about God is clear (vv. 19-20a and 21a). But (2) humanity has wickedly suppressed it (so vv. 21-22; see also 25a and 28a). In so doing, (3) pagans have embraced other wicked activities, and this in a strangely symmetrical fashion — an "exchange" of true, aniconic worship for false, iconic worship (vv. 23 and 25). Hence, (4) God "gives up" these pagans to desires that defile and dishonor their bodies in unnatural sexual acts (vv. 24 and 26-27). Moreover, (5) the pagans are abandoned to an impure mind, which issues in a flood of vices (vv. 28-31). Finally, (6) pagan culpability is emphasized by "approvers" (v. 32), and this scenario reiterates the opening claim of v. 18. Those who know God's concerns and final response to wickedness — a sentence of death — yet defy those divine opinions, practice wickedness, and even encourage others to do so, are clearly the worst of the worst. These steps warrant a slightly closer look.

(1) The fundamental premise within the argumentative chain that culminates in the Teacher's strident charge of pagan culpability is the universal and unimpeachable disclosure of the truth about God to all — a function of "general revelation," or "natural theology." The reality of this knowledge is asserted in vv. 19-20a. Although God is invisible and hence technically hidden (see τὰ ἀόρατα αὐτοῦ), the truth about God has been disclosed "through the things he has made" (τοῖς ποιήμασιν), a disclosure evident "since the creation of the world" (ἀπὸ κτίσεως κόσμου).[62] In this way the gap between invisibility and visibility is bridged. Creation somehow speaks unequivocally of the invisible but creator God's key attributes — of "his eternal power and divine nature."

(2) Humanity turns willfully away from these disclosures, neither honoring nor thanking this God, and the consequences are not a little ironic (vv. 21-22); humanity's apparent embrace of wisdom is in fact an embrace of stupidity — φάσκοντες εἶναι σοφοὶ ἐμωράνθησαν. Paul then presents the Teacher as reiterating this theme of culpability in v. 25 and v. 28. A foolish human decision lies at the heart of the problem. In this way, the human "suppression" of the truth about God first noted in the programmatic statement of v. 18 is both elaborated and emphasized — a suppression "by their wickedness" (. . . τῶν τὴν ἀλήθειαν ἐν ἀδικίᾳ κατεχόντων).

(3) The first result of this turn away from God — the first of three dire results — is idolatry, which the text repeatedly characterizes as an "exchange," and clearly a dubious one (so [μετ]ήλλαξαν in vv. 23 and 25; and this sin then overlaps with the descent into sexual immorality that is described as an exchange in v. 26). In elegant wordplays, the Teacher describes the displacement of worship of the glorious and immortal God by the worship of glorious images of mortal people, as well as various animals and even reptiles (v. 23) — ἤλλαξαν τὴν δόξαν τοῦ ἀφθάρτου θεοῦ ἐν ὁμοιώματι εἰκόνος φθαρτοῦ ἀνθρώπου κ.τ.λ.[63] The reference to animal images links the propaganda explicitly to Egyptian idolatry, which was notorious in Greco-Roman circles for this feature, and much of the Old Testament shares a similar opinion of it, although for somewhat different reasons. That Paul would be including such an emphasis in a letter to Rome, however, ultimately requires some explanation. I suggest that the Wisdom of Solomon is a key text for the Teacher, and this is perhaps the first point where that dependence becomes explicit. (Several gentler echoes could have been registered by the alert au-

ditor already.) Wisdom, being oriented toward Egyptian paganism, does engage overtly with animal idolatry. But it will be most useful to address this dimension within the Teacher's construction fully at a later point in the argument. For now it suffices to note that the Teacher is a literate person and hence also probably a learned exegete; it is likely, moreover, that he knows this book particularly well and depends on it, especially for his own opening rhetorical flourishes.

In his second wordplay on idolatry (v. 25), the Teacher states briefly that the pagans have ἐλάτρευσαν τῇ κτίσει παρὰ τὸν κτίσαντα, and even appends a short doxology to this statement.[64]

(4) The second result of the pagans' turn from God is their "surrender"[65] to various disgusting passions that contravene the natural order — εἰς πάθη ἀτιμίας (and note especially the double use of φυσική in vv. 26 and 27, where what is φυσική is "exchanged . . . for unnatural [sexual intercourse]" and "given up" [DC]). The Teacher states that not to honor God leads to the dishonoring of the body, here in contravention of natural heterosexuality by both males and females — the (in)famous claims of vv. 24 and 26-27: "women exchanged natural inter-course for unnatural, and in the same way also the men . . . were consumed with passion for one another." The final emphasis in this description is (as in v. 32) on the receipt of some "penalty" (ἀντιμισθία), although the notion is probably being used metaphorically here.[66]

(5) A further wordplay that we have already noted describes a third cluster of sins beginning in v. 28: καθὼς οὐκ ἐδοκίμασαν τὸν θεὸν ἔχειν ἐν ἐπιγνώσει, παρέδωκεν αὐτοὺς ὁ θεὸς εἰς ἀδόκιμον νοῦν.[67] This claim begins a short descrip-tion of a descent into "a debased mind," and a catalogue of consequent vices — a catalogue that has nevertheless been carefully chosen by Paul. Only murder is an explicit charge of wrongdoing. The other sins tend to revolve around generalized "attitudinal" problems of hatred, arrogance, schism, and wicked speech.[68]

Paul has thus placed a snare in this list, since he regards the Teacher as sub-versive and aggressive toward him. Jewish Christian sages who are bitterly op-posed to Paul's law-free gospel have probably tried to have him executed (see Rom. 15:31a; 16:4; Phil. 1:15-21; and perhaps 2 Cor. 1:8-10). Hence, in Paul's estima-tion they oppose God, and they are filled with all sorts of arrogant, envious mo-tives, schismatic ambitions, and vile speech. Probably the Teacher would not have used this exact vice list in his preaching, but he might well have approved of its contents before becoming aware of their pointed application! More importantly, the Roman Christians — who would not yet be aware of that application — would find this list of criticisms entirely plausible as well. Sinners of this nature ought to be condemned by a justly wrathful God, and the Teacher himself seems to have said this. The full enormity of the concessions made at this point will be-come apparent later.

(6) The obvious point concerning pagan culpability is finally driven home by the construction of "approvers" in v. 32, who knowingly practice these sins de-spite being aware of their wickedness (ὅιτινες . . . ἐπιγνόντες . . . ποιοῦσιν . . . καὶ συνευδοκοῦσιν . . .). This self-consciously sinful behavior by those who should

know better is reinforced by their explicit approval of those who practice such sins as well. Such figures *obviously* deserve God's sentence of death for wrongdoing; they are ἄξιοι θανάτου.[69]

Most readers are accustomed to agreeing with this argument. Paul is pronouncing the truth concerning a wicked humanity — a sinful humanity that stands over against the text's Christian auditors (and Christians do generally regard non-Christians as sinful). Even when later readers have wanted to disagree, they have generally still assumed that the text's voice and stance belong to Paul and hence that its main emphasis falls on the just condemnation of the sinful. But if we imagine the performance of this text in a slightly parodic fashion, we gain different impressions from its assertions.

First, we "hear" a certain style — elegant, crafted, but rather sonorous and heavy-handed. It enjoys negations and puns. So this speaker is well educated, but perhaps also rather pretentious. He seems happy to display his learning — to show off. We can detect certain key motifs: the wrath of God and a penchant for symmetries between initial sins and their consequences. Most importantly, however, we hear a voice that is relentlessly negative, intimidating, and perhaps not especially reasonable. It speaks in strongly condemning tones about others: "they have sinned and sinned and sinned again, . . . and I can assure you personally that God is angry with them" ("since he and I are on such good terms," one is tempted to add). Imagine, then, delivering this text with a ponderous, censorious tone and demeanor. Indeed, one should think of such a performance as roughly analogous to the frequent modern depiction of born-again Christians — and especially televangelists. Such figures are typically presented as humorless, strident, and hypocritical. They tend to judge others while being oblivious to their own deeper failings. There is generally nothing formally wrong with what they are saying for much of the time, so their scripts would read much as Paul's text does here. But the *performance* of those stereotypical ethical assertions denotes that they are people in glass houses throwing stones; in more biblical parlance, they point to specks of sawdust in their neighbors' eyes while overlooking the planks in their own.[70] In just this sense, the figure in Romans 1:18-32 has taken the ethical and rhetorical high ground in relation to the pagans, with a striking absence of self-knowledge. A superior Greek style pompously signals a superior attitude. In this speech, the wise condescends to the foolish and the righteous to the sinful, even as the Jew (in the sense of *this* Jew) condescends to the barbarian. The Teacher has launched a tirade from on high, pronouncing God's deserved judgment on the entire pagan world. He speaks for God, perhaps as something of a self-appointed representative; indeed, he discloses the future wrath of God now in his own preaching, thereby in part deploying it himself! But this figure has not included himself within this orbit of fallibility. He stands outside and above it. Hence, even if there are elements of truth in what he is saying, the tone of his judgment is potentially repugnant.

Suitably performed, the letter will alienate its auditors from this figure's program; indeed, those auditors will perhaps expect him to be upbraided and corrected by some learned Socratic interlocutor.[71] (They would have had as little trouble recognizing him as a modern TV watcher would have recognizing a speech containing the word[s] "hi-diddly-ho" as spoken by Ned Flanders.[72]) The standard way of achieving that goal would have been through a demonstration of this Teacher's hypocrisy, some inconsistency in his program that could be exposed and turned back upon his own head. And in fact the letter's auditors do not have to wait long for things to begin to turn in this direction. An argumentative whiplash begins in 2:1, culminating in the Teacher's complete rhetorical and theological humiliation in 3:19-20.

§4. Romans 2:1-8 — Paul's Universalization

Romans 2:1-8 is usefully viewed as the second step within Paul's overarching reduction of the Teacher to silence that takes place in four broad steps from 1:18 through 3:20:

> 1:18-32: "speech-in-character" — the Teacher's usual rhetorical opening
> 2:1-8: Paul's universalization of the opening's key premise
> 2:9-29: the awkward implications
> 3:1-20: the humiliating conclusion

Hence, in 2:1, after an instance of "speech-in-character," Paul finds his own voice, although it is worth emphasizing that he will still often reproduce the Teacher's program. From this point, such representation will usually be in the form of ironic quotation, not προσωποποιία (technically, παρῳδία — from which we derive our modern notion of "parody," although in ancient times it was not necessarily ironic, humorous, and/or biting).[73] Now the Teacher's commitments will begin to be flung back in his own face. (The Teacher begins to speak again directly only in 3:2.) The extended process of humiliation will proceed principally through the extraction of various concessions from the Teacher, and these are obtained initially by a clever argumentative maneuver — "universalization" — that takes place in 2:1-8. This move sets up an entire series of embarrassing implications that unfold through 2:9–3:18, entailing that the Teacher will be humiliated by 3:19-20 in terms of his own assumptions.

4.1. The Figure in Romans 2:1

It is universally conceded that the argument of Romans turns rather dramatically in 2:1, but, as we noted in part three, chapter eleven, the reference and broader rhetorical function of this turn are less widely agreed on. The text turns on a particular figure, identified by three explicit motifs that are repeated throughout this brief subsection (2:1-8) — a person who *judges* and condemns others for sinful practices that elicit the just condemnation of God, who *practices* the same sinful things himself, and who is therefore also *culpable*. But these motifs stud the discourse of Romans 1:18-32 as well, and they are explicitly foregrounded by its final statement in v. 32, which contains a double instance of πράσσω and an explicit articulation of the divine condemnation of sinful behavior — οἱ τὰ τοιαῦτα πράσσοντες ἄξιοι θανάτου εἰσίν. Hence — as the majority of commentators recognize — the figure on whom the argument turns in 2:1 *is* the figure who utters the condemning words *of* 1:18-32. This in fact could not be clearer: the text explicitly encodes the judger in 2:1 as uttering the words of 1:18-32, because some of those words are placed in his hypocritical mouth in 2:2-3. Moreover, 1:18-32 are no more than an extended judgment, a κατάκριμα, that condemns the pagans as "without excuse" in view of their catalogue of heinous sins, and this speech fits exactly the characterization supplied for the judger's words in 2:1-8.

The focus of interpretative disagreement is the suggestion frequently made by commentators that this encoded hypocrite is joined in the utterance of 1:18-32 by others — usually by Paul himself, and by Jews in general. But we have already noted many of the problems that accompany these additions, one of which is such momentous additions call for further evidence or justification, and it is difficult to see where that can come from in local terms. Indeed, the text itself neither needs nor explicitly supports them. (This addition is of course made by the conventional reading in order to make sense of the rest of the argument in terms of Justification's first phase of universal condemnation.) My suggested rereading, however, *does not require any such additions to make sense of Paul's developing contentions*, and this is one of its most important advantages; this turn by the text onto the utterer of the discourse of 1:18-32 is exactly what the alert auditor has been waiting for, and nothing more is necessary. So we do not need to insinuate legalistic Jews, or judgmental, moralizing Christians, or Paul himself, into the ongoing argument (thereby unleashing a raft of ultimately debilitating theoretical consequences). The arrogant and pretentious Teacher has now been identified and addressed explicitly, and his refutation will explain perfectly the rest of the discussion up to 3:20. In fact, here in 2:1-8 Paul has made the standard argumentative move against him of universalization. We must pause, then, to consider what this clever ploy involves.

4.2. Universalization

A universalization is an argumentative concession that can be forced onto the proponents of any position by insisting that the principles within that position — which are usually being directed against someone else at the outset of debate — be applied consistently to its proponents as well.[74]

This can be a surprisingly effective move, because discourses directed toward outsiders are so often informed by a hermeneutic of suspicion, and those toward insiders by a hermeneutic of generosity. These unequal criteria give rise to inequities, which is merely to say that double standards abound in ethical, social, and religious debate. A request for universalization can defuse some of these (or at least expose them) by forcing advocates to submit themselves to the harsher sets of principles that they customarily prescribe for others.

This move is of course often resisted, but one of the peculiar strengths of universalization is that the rhetorical costs paid for resistance are so immediate and so extensive. In essence, if a request for universalization is rejected, then the speaker involved is immediately shown to be inconsistent, hypocritical, and perhaps also opportunistic (if not simply stupid) — "he does not practice what he preaches," "his words are empty," and so on.[75] Hence, a failure to submit to universalization in any essentially neutral rhetorical situation is potentially catastrophic.[76] The credibility of the speaker is threatened with instant falsification, and without the audience's basic trust in the speaker, his ultimate cause is doomed.[77]

A skilful debater can extract considerable advantages from any acceptance of universalization (or, alternatively, from its refusal, but this situation is not apparent from Romans 2:1 because Paul is in control of the entire discussion and accepts the gambit for the Teacher). Certainly, Paul does so from Romans 2:1 onward. By turning the central principles of the discourse of Romans 1:18-32 onto the judger who utters them (and by extension onto any such judger), he is forcing a universalizing concession on that figure.

Universalization, once it is accepted, always involves *criteria,* which are *supplied by the opposing speaker.* This makes it an especially useful technique for Socratic and diatribal discussions, which often achieve their argumentative purchase in relation to the interlocutor's position. The precise nature of the criteria extracted in Romans 2:1-8 from the Teacher's opening discourse in Romans 1:18-32 is of course very important, because those criteria will provide the principal argumentative leverage throughout what follows.

4.3. The Criteria

Romans 1:18-32 asserts strenuously and at some length that God will judge the pagans both strictly and fairly for their sins. The pagans' knowledge of God, rejection of God, and willful turns to various prohibited and unnatural activities elicit the just response from God of angry condemnation and death (although this is fully actualized only on the day of judgment). Directly implicit in this discourse is the principle of *soteriological desert* — and nothing more. God acts here in relation to humanity in accordance with retributive justice. And so he sentences the sinful pagans to death for their indiscretions. The discourse underscores this presupposition by taking pains to point out repeatedly the pagans' *deliberate* turn from right to wrong behavior; *they* bear responsibility for their current plight, having known God initially but consistently refused to respond appropriately (see 1:19, 21-22, 25, 28). Fairly applied, however, this principle can play out in *two* directions. The consistent doers of bad deeds will of course be judged wicked and condemned to punishment and death, but the consistent doers of good deeds will be judged "righteous" and gifted with eschatological life, because they will deserve it. This premise of soteriological desert underlying the condemnations of 1:18-32 — which implicitly rests in turn on a basic human capacity and God's retributive justice — is spelled out explicitly by Paul in Romans 2:6-8: ἀποδώσει ἑκάστῳ κατὰ τὰ ἔργα αὐτοῦ. So [ἀποδώσει] τοῖς μὲν καθ᾽ ὑπομονὴν ἔργου ἀγαθοῦ δόξαν καὶ τιμὴν καὶ ἀφθαρσίαν ζητοῦσιν ζωὴν αἰώνιον, τοῖς δὲ ἐξ ἐριθείας καὶ ἀπειθοῦσι τῇ ἀληθείᾳ πειθομένοις δὲ τῇ ἀδικίᾳ ὀργὴ καὶ θυμός. Here, in v. 6, in scripturally resonant phraseology (see Ps. 62:12; Prov. 24:12; Sir. 16:14), Paul articulates the basic principle in all its fullness that is only implicit in 1:18-32. The criterion of desert in relation to which the divine decision takes place is denoted by κατά in the accusative and its attached conditions ("works," or "deeds"). Paul then notes in balanced, contrasting constructions in vv. 7-8 the two possible outcomes that can result from the principle's application: eternal life for those who do good deeds and God's wrath for those who do bad deeds. And by characterizing the wicked in terms of those who *reject* the truth and *disobey* it, being *persuaded* by wickedness[78] (τοῖς δὲ ἐξ ἐριθείας καὶ **ἀπειθοῦσι** τῇ ἀληθείᾳ **πειθομένοις** δὲ τῇ ἀδικίᾳ[79]), he subtly emphasizes human culpability. In short, the principle of soteriological desert — of divine eschatological action strictly in relation to deeds — is the implicit presupposition of 1:18-32, and it is made explicit by the universalization of the argument in relation to the Teacher beginning in 2:1. This principle must now be openly acknowledged and submitted to by all.

Paul has not turned on this figure's presuppositions, however, merely to make his assumptions explicit; the turn has rhetorical consequences that he intends to exploit. This process of argumentative exploitation unfolds in two further stages — 2:9-29 and 3:1-20.

§5. Romans 2:9-29 — the Awkward Implications

Romans 2:9-29 is the third major step within Paul's argumentative sweep from 1:18 through 3:20. Conventional readers, not to mention many revisionists, have often struggled with its function and implications, and not without reason. However, my suggested reading can offer a plausible account of what Paul is up to through all this material.

Conventional readers often assume that Paul is "leveling the playing field" between pagans and Jews here. Some process of redefinition is being applied, at times rather ruthlessly, to Judaism, resulting in a sense of fundamental equality (in sin) between pagans and Jews, and there does seem to be some sense of "leveling" in the text. But it is of course just this process that has appalled revisionists, who find the resulting portrait of Judaism inconsistent on numerous fronts (and the absence of any account of Judaism's remedial responses to sin inadequate as well). Arguably, my suggested rereading can affirm the insights of the conventional reading — that some process of strict leveling redefinition is going on —

while avoiding the scandalous implications noted by the revisionists — that Judaism is being treated unfairly.

I suggest that throughout this argumentative phase Paul is using the definition he has just extracted from the Teacher's rhetorical opening — the principle of desert — to override the Teacher's own suite of supposed Jewish advantages. Hence, Paul is using the Teacher's definition of "the problem" to override the Teacher's "solution"! If Paul manages to eliminate the saving set of Jewish advantages that the Teacher claims, then the Teacher's gospel will have been discredited as fundamentally ineffective — his proclamation of salvation will not save — *and* the Teacher himself will have been put in a vulnerable position, at which point Paul will be able to make a final, decisively humiliating argumentative move (and this takes place in 3:1-20). So two important rhetorical goals are implicit in the argument as it unfolds through 2:29.

It will also become apparent in the course of this discussion that Paul is exploiting a conceptual inconsistency in the Teacher's system — specifically, a difference in ontological commitments between the basic conceptuality presupposed by the definition of the problem and that assumed by the solution. These differences are not especially easy to detect and then to exploit, but once they have been identified, they certainly seem to exist (and similar tensions are observable in certain contemporary Jewish sources — perhaps most notably in the Wisdom of Solomon). Hence, Paul once again demonstrates a superb acuity in his argumentation. It is both penetrating and devastating. Of course, he would not be able to make his embarrassing extrapolations if the Teacher was not inconsistent in these respects — but apparently he is. (The Teacher is also not the last person to struggle with the strict implications of desert-based systems; Paul will exploit some notorious problems here.)

Paul's negation of the Teacher's gospel — the Teacher's solution — in the light of the Teacher's initial definition of the problem is usefully treated in two subordinate subsections — 2:9-16 and 2:17-29 — although it should be appreciated that some of these subsections attempt more than one argumentative goal. Paul's argumentative *strategy* throughout, however, is essentially simple. Having extracted a firm commitment from the Teacher to the principle of soteriological desert, he uses this principle to eliminate an entire set of supposed Jewish advantages — advantages as the Teacher defines them, that is. The Teacher *must submit to these eliminations or be exposed as inconsistent if not hopelessly self-contradictory.* Paul seems well aware, moreover, that the principle of desert, when it is strictly applied, *is peculiarly destructive to historical and elective concerns.* Its strict application can produce quite appalling results, if it is pressed.

5.1. Romans 2:9-16

This first subsection segues smoothly out of the establishment of the principle of desert in 2:1-8, pressing it in four important directions, the consequences of which the later subsections will drive home. The principle of desert is applied to Jews and then to sinful Jews, with the further clarification that judgment will not now be in terms of mere appearance. Moreover, pagans *must* possess some sort of internal law naturally, in the light of which they can be judged.

The principle of soteriological desert must deal strictly, and even rather harshly, with any ethnic or historical distinctiveness. It simply overrides all such considerations, at least insofar as eschatological salvation is concerned, because once it has been conceded that final, eschatological judgment will be in accordance with desert, then by definition *no other considerations are relevant*. So Paul can now deploy the classic antithesis of "Jew versus pagan" in relation to the principle of desert (in 2:9-10) and indicate how the latter overrides, and essentially vitiates the significance of, the former: [ἀποδώσει] θλῖψις καὶ στενοχωρία ἐπὶ πᾶσαν ψυχὴν ἀνθρώπου τοῦ κατεργαζομένου τὸ κακόν, Ἰουδαίου τε πρῶτον καὶ Ἕλληνος· δόξα δὲ καὶ τιμὴ καὶ εἰρήνη παντὶ τῷ ἐργαζομένῳ τὸ ἀγαθόν, Ἰουδαίῳ τε πρῶτον καὶ Ἕλληνι. The ubiquitous Jew versus pagan antithesis must now be redistributed within the more basic, overarching antithesis between the good and the wicked. Put slightly differently: both terms of the antithesis between the good and the bad now contain — at least potentially — Jews and pagans. Paul has not yet spelled out the full implications of this, but clearly they could prove embarrassing. He has two principal eschatological constituencies that he can now exploit: the bad Jew and the good pagan.

	Good (deeds)	*Bad (deeds)*
Jews	Good Jews (saved)	Bad Jews (not saved)
Pagans	Good pagans (saved)	Bad pagans (not saved)

The motif "first" in the statement "both Jew first and pagan" (see vv. 9 and 10) is revealed to be essentially meaningless by its broader setting here, so its uses by Paul at these points look fundamentally ironic (i.e., it is probably "parodic"). Any notion of Jewish priority is in fact being vitiated.

This overt flattening contributes to my broader suspicion that Paul is deploying the signifier πρῶτον within the antithesis "Jew-pagan" somewhat ironically and hence almost certainly drawing it from the Teacher's discourse. *It can have no effective or essential usefulness within the argument in literal or positive terms as Paul is developing it* (and this point holds whether my rereading is followed or not). Given that the principle of desert is presently overriding the ethnic difference between Jew and pagan, any notion of Jewish priority is either contradictory or simply useless. Meaning can be attributed to the word by suggesting that it refers here to a temporal priority during the process of judgment; Jews will be judged first by God, followed by the pagans. But this is a trivial point, and not attested to by Paul elsewhere. (The alternative — that it refers to some important eschatological priority — is contradicted by the rest of the argument, which is precisely that no one enjoys any eschatological priority other than in terms of desert.) And the temporal reading cannot satisfactorily explain Paul's use of the same phrase in 1:16b.[80] There, presumably, it would have to signify that the gospel was preached to Jews first and then to pagans. But this is not, strictly speaking, true. Certainly, the Judeans heard the gospel first in some sense, but other pagans are now hearing the gospel before many other Jews. (Roughly 85 percent of Jews lived outside Judaea in Paul's day.) The pagan auditors of Romans, for example, are hearing the gospel before all the Jewish inhabitants of the south and the west of the Roman Empire. Moreover, the claim remains rather trivial and hence opaque. Why would Paul insert this uncharacteristic phrase into a tightly crafted argument three times by 2:9 in order to make an otiose claim? To make matters worse, the key word is dropped as the same antithesis is overridden in 3:9b. Why would the constant assertion of temporal priority — if that is what Paul is suggesting — be deemed unimportant at this point?

To deal with these various difficulties, I experimented earlier with the possibility of emphasizing the conjunctive function of τε, thus allowing καί to function either pleonastically or additively and πρῶτον to modify what follows it rather than what precedes it, and in an adverbial sense. This yields the translation ". . . to the Jew and especially [or 'primarily'] also to the pagan." This translation had the virtue of sustaining through 1:16b the emphasis on Paul's mission to the pagans from the letter's introduction (and hence also a reading of Paul's discourse more in accordance with Stendahl's suggestion that the controversial law-free mission and inclusion of the pagans were often the points at issue in his polemical texts). The shocking statement that Paul seemed to be making with this slogan would then concern pagan inclusion, not Jewish priority. (This suggestion has sometimes been misinterpreted as asserting Paul's lack of interest in Jewish historical integrity or salvation [or some such],[81] but these countercharges are non sequiturs. There is plenty of evidence extant from elsewhere in Paul's writings that undergirds strong affirmations of the divine commitment to Israel. My point was, rather, that Paul's contingent emphases in Rom. 1:16b and 2:9-10 were on pagan inclusion within the divine saving initiative, rather than on Jews and Judaism.)

But this reading works better for 1:16b than for 2:9-10; the latter instances remain somewhat trivial. And I now suspect, in addition, that the τε . . . καί pattern almost certainly has the sense of "both . . . and" for Paul, which draws the reference of πρῶτον ineluctably back toward "the Jew." How then are we to make sense of this repeated phrase? My present rereading offers a better solution to this conundrum.

If Paul is once again quoting the discourse of the Teacher, his use of the phrase is polemical and hence quite understandable; he is embarrassing it. The Teacher almost certainly argued for Jewish priority in salvation (and we will see why shortly). Hence, in 1:16b the notion is overridden by God's salvation of "everyone who trusts." Then in 2:9-10 it is — still worse — overridden by the Teacher's own ostensible commitment to judgment in accordance with desert. So Paul deploys this phrase rather archly (and presumably its correct performance would have signaled this).

Lending support to this construal is the evident concern of chapters 9–11 with the same question of Jewish priority. The question is made explicit in the pointed diatribal queries of 9:30-33, which I take to indicate (again) the concerns of the Teacher (see esp. my suggested reading of Rom. 3:27–4:22 below in chapter eighteen): "What then are we to say? Gentiles, who did not strive for righteousness, have attained it, that is, righteousness through faith; but Israel, who did strive for the righteousness that is based on the law toward the law, did *not* attain to it?" [NRSV modified]. These complaints reproduce exactly the agenda summarized by the slogan that Paul quotes in 1:16b and 2:9-10 — and in the later discussion, Paul is at pains to explain the apparent reversals of these traditional expectations by what seems to have happened, providing multiple reasons why the conversion of the pagans seems to be preceding that of Israel. Furthermore, an ἀγών discourse seems to underlie this later material. Indeed (and as we will see in more detail later on), Paul is probably subverting an ἀγών discourse here. On the lips of the Teacher, then, Jews running in accordance with the law would have been coming in "first" and the pagans a distant second, if they were competing in the race at all. This perfect match with the concerns of chapters 9–11 underscores the plausibility of an ironic, polemical reading of the phrase. Paul *might* then be implying a temporal reading in his use of the phrase "first," because he is thereby trivializing an important element within the Teacher's discourse. This also seems to be a comparable function to the Jewish theologoumenon that Paul cites essentially aggressively in v. 11, which we discuss just below. A possible intertextual basis might also be detectable for this slogan (a question we will investigate in detail in chapters fifteen through seventeen, with the treatment of 1:16).

The first overtly embarrassing application toward which Paul presses the principle of soteriological desert does not concern Jews per se but sinful Jews. In 2:12b-13 he states: ὅσοι ἐν νόμῳ ἥμαρτον, διὰ νόμου κριθήσονται· οὐ γὰρ οἱ ἀκροαταὶ νόμου δίκαιοι παρὰ θεῷ, ἀλλ' οἱ ποιηταὶ νόμου δικαιωθήσονται, but merely resuming here the implicit threat of 2:9: [ἀποδώσει] θλῖψις καὶ στενοχωρία ἐπὶ πᾶσαν ψυχὴν ἀνθρώπου τοῦ κατεργαζομένου τὸ κακόν, Ἰουδαίου τε πρῶτον καὶ Ἕλληνος. And it is hard to avoid the detection in v. 13 of a slogan from the Teacher himself (if not from James) — the oft-repeated adage that the truly righteous must be "doers of the word, and not merely hearers who deceive themselves. For if any are hearers of the word and not doers, they are like those who look at themselves in a mirror; for they look at themselves and, on going away, immediately forget what they were like" (Jas. 1:22-24). It is also hard to imagine the Teacher objecting too strongly to the assertion that *some* Jews will be judged and condemned; especially wicked Jews would presumably suffer this fate, and rightly so. Nevertheless, Paul seems concerned to emphasize this explicit implication from the Teacher's own preaching. Jews will be judged and, if it proves necessary, condemned for wrongdoing, and their scrutiny will take place in relation to the Torah, ἐν ἡμέρᾳ ὅτε κρινεῖ ὁ θεὸς τὰ κρυπτὰ τῶν ἀνθρώπων (Rom. 2:16a).

A Jewish theologoumenon is quoted by Paul in 2:11 — οὐ γάρ ἐστιν προσωπολημψία παρὰ τῷ θεῷ — which is translated by the NRSV "[f]or God shows no partiality." Arguably the nuances of this type of translation are slightly wrong, and this might in turn obscure part of the development of Paul's argument later on. But the standard translation is not a significant distortion, nor does it significantly affect my broader rereading, so we will not get involved in an extensive discussion of an alternative at this point. Read in the standard way, as above, this saying seems once more to be a slogan used by the Teacher himself — and again unwisely — that reinforces Paul's argumentative reification from the Teacher's program of the ultimately rather embarrassing principle of desert. (The slogan is drawn from Deut. 10:17; see also 2 Chron. 19:7.) It is likely that this slogan was deployed in relation to different matters when the Teacher used it, as in James 2:1-4, where it functions as part of an authentic Christian ethic. Christian "synagogues" should not make overt distinctions, James asserts, between the rich and the poor, their members thereby showing partiality or favoritism and becoming "judges with evil thoughts" (v. 4b). However, redeployed in relation to God's future eschatological actions, this slogan reinforces Paul's emphasis on the implacable principle of desert that lies within the Teacher's initial program, overriding any distinction in *that* context between Jew and pagan and not merely between rich and poor. The Teacher is thereby again shown to corroborate Paul's account of his teaching in 2:1-16 and so seems to endorse the validity of Paul's subsequent account of its inherent shortcomings. (Certainly, any protests on his part against Paul's account — and especially in terms of its fairness — would seem further reduced in terms of their plausibility.)

I have long nursed slight suspicions about the usual translations and interpretations of this slogan. The debate has been dominated recently — and quite rightly — by Bassler's precise and thorough work.[82] I do not disagree with the bulk of her analysis. However, the assumptions of the conventional reading and of Justification theory, perhaps reinforced by deep-seated convictions concerning divine impassibility, play a significant role in support of the usual interpretation of the slogan in terms of divine *im*partiality. (And even if this role is not critical, the *reception* of this interpretation tends to be shaped by them.) A reconsideration of the Greek may add certain subtle emphases to the conventional interpretation that make good sense in relation to Paul's uses of the axiom both here and elsewhere.

The LXX translators did not necessarily supply a direct rendition of the Hebrew text with their use of προσωπολημψία or its equivalent, which draws on the Greek πρόσωπον and associates this with the verb λαμβάνω, whether within a phrase or a single signifier. As Lohse noted long ago, λαμβάνω cannot suggest the notion that might have been present in the underlying Hebrew of "lifting" the face (because this Greek verb simply does not suggest "lifting"), and hence the whole cultural coding of the slogan in those terms might have been obscured.[83] However, this possible shift between the MT and the LXX does not affect the meaning of the slogan in Paul's day. Our concern here is the Hellenistic reception of the LXX theologoumenon.

The Greek slogan seems to be suggesting that certain types of acceptance or receipt — so λαμβάνω — of "the face" are being prohibited. But πρόσωπον could denote not merely "face" but also "appearance," and even "mask," hence some sort of acting (see the modern equivalent use of "persona"). Greek culture seems to have spent much time considering the difference between appearance and reality, and some of the implications of this distinction for human relationships. So a Greek auditor could have detected a concern in the LXX slogan with a possible disparity between what is apparent and superficial in people — on the surface — and what is not so apparent — what is below the surface, or "deep." Greek auditors might therefore hear in this slogan an admonition, not merely against showing unjust partiality, but against doing so in situations where appearance and reputation — and hence also possible duplicity or insincerity or "playacting" — were concerned. Indeed, this seems to constitute a virtual topos by the time of the New Testament, with distinctive clusters of terminology. A translation of Romans 2:11 that evoked this topos might then be "God is not impressed by mere reputation [or 'by appearances']."

Complementing this point is the implicit counterclaim that God sees truly; God sees what is real, on the "inside," and consequently is not deceived by appearance, reputation, or insincere behavior. These are the additional senses that the Greek version of Deuteronomy 10:17 might convey.

I am confident that these additional nuances in terms of superficial appearance versus deeper reality — and common associated charges in terms of duplicitous playacting — are present in the slogan in Romans 2:11, because they seem apparent in Paul's deployment of the axiom elsewhere, especially in Galatians 2:1-14,[84] as well as in closely related discussions elsewhere in the New Testament (see i.a. Luke 20:20-26[85]; 1 Thess. 2:3-6[86]; and Jas. 2:1-4[87]). They also overlap with topoi widespread within the Greco-Roman world that treat (in)sincerity.[88] Furthermore, these nuances correlate *exactly* with some of Paul's later argumentative suggestions in Romans 2 (while this ironic usage of the slogan would correlate with his ironic deployment of other probable slogans from the Teacher in this manner[89]).

For all these reasons, I suggest translating the slogan in v. 11 in a way that activates these additional Hellenistic nuances — "God is not impressed by appearances," or some such. I do not view this suggestion as a significant departure from the standard reading and the research of Bassler (et al.); it is a small addition to work that remains in all essentials correct. However, to add these nuances will add further precision to our understanding of Paul's argument in Romans 2.

Just as Paul anticipates a later argument (to a degree) with his ironic quotation of one of the Teacher's theologoumena in 2:11 — here concerning superficial appearances versus deeper realities — so he prepares the way for the establishment of a later point (see esp. 2:25-29) by extending the full import of the principle of desert in vv. 14-15. These verses are something of an aside or parenthesis within the main flow of the argument.

Interpreters have often pondered the function and meaning of "nature" and "conscience" in Paul's claims in vv. 14-15. But I would suggest that different answers to these questions do not alter the basic sense of this small pericope significantly, which is in direct continuity with much of what has already been asserted. The emphasis in v. 14 on "doing" (τὰ τοῦ νόμου ποιῶσιν) seems overtly to resume an element within the preceding phrase in v. 13b, οἱ ποιηταὶ νόμου δικαιωθήσονται. And this "doing" is explicated further in v. 15 as demonstrating or proving (ἐνδείκνυνται) that the work of the law is therefore present within the pagan heart. Specifically, Paul claims in these verses that when pagans "do" those things prescribed by the law, this "demonstrates" that those good deeds, along with the law itself, are in some sense "written in their hearts," while the mental battle of conscience between accusing and defending thoughts further "attests to" the presence of this ethical knowledge. Hence, it matters little whether pagans possess a law "by nature," going on to do it, at least to some degree, or whether they "do" those good deeds "by nature" (φύσει functioning adverbially in both readings but in relation to different verbs). It also matters little whether the work of conscience is primarily good or simply an arena of cognitive ethical struggle (although the latter seems more likely in Paul's day). Paul's point is simply that such "doing" "demonstrates" prior pagan possession of an ethical code.

We must wait until 2:25-29 before this present insistence on pagan posses-sion of the essentials of the law "naturally" becomes fully comprehensible. At that point it will underpin an overt argumentative move. But its present emphasis should not occasion surprise. The claim that pagans possess this sort of innate knowledge is in direct continuity with one of the main claims of 1:18-32. It was stated repeatedly in that earlier "speech" that the pagans possess accurate knowl-edge about God. That they do so and fail to act on it is at the heart of their culpa-bility. In that earlier setting, it was their *theological* rebellion that was emphasized — their rejection of God — and so the knowledge that they possess but spurn was overtly said to include only information about God — "God's eternal power and divinity" (v. 20b). But interpersonal ethical knowledge was implicit throughout the rest of the Teacher's tirade. The pagans were condemned for sexual immoral-ity (vv. 24, 26-27), and then for all manner of sins against appropriate speech and attitudes toward others (vv. 29-31). So in 2:14-15 Paul is simply emphasizing overtly what has already been implied: *the Teacher's opening position concedes the presence of sufficient information about God and ethics within pagans independent of the actual possession of the Jewish law.* It is this fact that establishes their culpa-bility, and if it were denied, then the fundamental justice of the entire scenario would be undermined, and that would be an unacceptable extrapolation. The pa-gans *must*, in terms of the Teacher's most important presuppositions, possess in-nately some sort of sufficient ethical and theological "law." Hence, Paul's claim in 2:12 that they can be fairly judged ἀνόμως,[90] and his implicit claim in v. 13 — which is rather more controversial — that they could be declared righteous by ac-tually doing the law (and therefore with no expectation of Jewish missionary ac-tivity!), seem entirely valid. It remains only to note, then, that these remarks seem parenthetical. Paul is laying down an argumentative marker here; their full appli-cation is yet to come.

We have already noted that Paul's claims in vv. 14-15 arise from the notion of "doing" that was central to v. 13b — that present righteous "doing" will lead to a future declaration of "righteous." Such "doing" by pagans functions "to demon-strate" (ἐνδείκνυνται, a middle verb) their innate possession of the law, with their consciences functioning in parallel as a "witness" (συμμαρτυρούσης, a present participle within an extended genitive absolute construction). Those actions take place in the present, where the force of their demonstration is apparent. And this temporal location for the witness of conscience now creates an awkward shift as the text moves on in v. 16 to an overtly future reference with a dative of time and an explicit allusion to the day of judgment — ἐν ἡμέρᾳ ὅτε κρινεῖ ὁ θεὸς τὰ κρυπτὰ τῶν ἀνθρώπων κ.τ.λ.[91] However, the difficulty is solved once it is realized that vv. 14-15 are probably functioning parenthetically — as an aside prompted by the potentially controversial use of ποιέω in v. 13b in relation to pagan righteous-ness (and one that, moreover, sets up an ultimately polemical point). Paul's over-arching concern since Romans 2:5 has been the evenhanded eschatological judg-ment of God that is implicit in the Teacher's opening antipagan tirade, a judgment now beginning to accumulate various awkward implications. And I would suggest that v. 16a simply returns to this concern, supplying an explicit future temporal reference with a dative of time (which is almost identical to the construction in v. 5: θησαυρίζεις σεαυτῷ ὀργὴν ἐν ἡμέρᾳ ὀργῆς καὶ ἀποκαλύψεως δικαιοκρισίας τοῦ θεοῦ). Appropriate performance would have marked off vv. 14-15 as a parenthesis, with v. 16a resuming the principal argumentative claims of v. 13b: οἱ ποιηταὶ νόμου δικαιωθήσονται . . . ἐν ἡμέρᾳ ὅτε κρινεῖ ὁ θεὸς τὰ κρυπτὰ τῶν ἀνθρώπων.

In a similar vein, I suggest that v. 16b is a parenthesis as well, although rather shorter, and one that would have been in Paul's own voice (and this reading has already been discussed in part three, chapter eleven). Verses 14-15 continue to flesh out the difficulties inherent, although not necessarily immediately apparent, in the Teacher's opening rhetoric. So those statements are parenthetical but still in a Socratic mode; the discourse proceeds in terms of the Teacher's own assumptions. But every now and then within the broader sweep of Romans it seems that Paul cannot resist a small anticipation of his own positions that as yet lie principally ahead of his auditors — the technique of anticipation.[92] He has employed this technique overtly in the brief statements of 1:2-4 and 1:16-17, and he will elaborate further on some of this material — although still highly compactly — in 3:21-26. Paul does not begin to speak at length in terms of his own voice and assumptions until 4:24. Nevertheless, he finds it difficult to remain entirely silent! I suggest that v. 16b falls into this anticipatory category.

As we noted earlier, the suggestion of a brief shift to Paul's voice here is well supported by stylistic and substantive clues. The κατά construction in v. 16b recalls the similar construction in v. 6, which announced the criterion of judgment in the Teacher's gospel of desert. But in v. 16b that criterion is now — "according to my [i.e., Paul's] gospel" — by means of Jesus Christ, an incommensurable criterion, and Paul marks *this* canon explicitly as "his." But if it is a parenthesis, we have yet to consider the contribution it makes to the broader critique currently unfolding in relation to the Teacher's system.

One of the outstanding features of the Teacher's gospel — although the inattentive auditor may not yet have noticed it, and hence Paul's concern in v. 16b to make the point explicit — is its lack of Christology. Jesus Christ plays no overt or significant role within the entire construction. In particular, he has no function within the day of judgment as the Teacher's presuppositions shape that all-important event (and so he has no significant role within what is in effect the key moment in the Teacher's entire program). Indeed, he *cannot,* as the Teacher has set that event up. The criterion of desert necessarily overrides any significant contribution from Christ, and if the Teacher abandons that axiom, then his own rhetorical prelude is discarded, and his intellectual integrity as well — an unenviable conundrum. Consequently, Paul cannot resist noting parenthetically in v. 16b that (a) this lack of Christology is clearly a significant theological shortfall; and (b) "his" gospel will rectify this omission, emphasizing the role of Christ in the judgment, which (c) *will presumably substantially shift the tenor and criteria of that event.* This remark from Paul's own mouth and program indicates — very quickly in passing — that by omitting any role for Christ, the Teacher's account of the day of judgment is overtly deficient, not to mention his entire gospel. Conversely, Paul will shortly explicate Christ's central role within God's action toward and on behalf of the world in his gospel by means of a striking accumulation of instrumental clauses and phrases in 3:21-26, the most prominent of which are διά clauses in the genitive (thereby also resuming the prepositional constructions of 1:2-4 and 1:16-17). This is also probably why v. 16b ends with an emphatic διά Χριστοῦ Ἰησοῦ.[93]

In view of all this, I suggest punctuating the text of 2:12-16 as follows:[94]

> [12]*All who have sinned apart from the law will also perish apart from the law, and all who have sinned under the law* (ἐν νόμῳ) *will be judged by the law* (διά νόμου). [13]*For it is not the hearers of the law who* [will be] *righteous in God's sight, but the doers of the law who will be justified —* [14][for] [w]hen Gentiles, who do not possess the law, "do" instinctively what the law requires, these, though not having the law, are a law to themselves; [15][t]hey show that what the law requires is written on their hearts, to which their own conscience also bears witness; and their conflicting thoughts will accuse or perhaps excuse them — [16]*on the day when . . . God will judge the secret thoughts of all* (according to my gospel, through Jesus Christ!).

And with this detection of a probable parenthesis, we can move on to a more detailed discussion of the next subsection in the argument (still within our ongoing explication of step three, which unfolds in 2:9-29). In 2:17-29 the contours of the Teacher's "solution" — of his gospel — begin to emerge more clearly, as do the basic difficulties generated for it by Paul's argumentative strategy of holding this solution accountable to the Teacher's initial definition of the problem.

5.2. Romans 2:17-29

As we have seen in chapter eleven, the figure described overtly in 2:17-24 should be identified with the figure targeted in 2:1-8 — numerous signals in the text effect this linkage — and he seems to be Jewish in *some* sense, as the conventional reading asserts. But he does not seem to be a generic Jew — *the* Jew — or the consequences for Paul's powers of description and argument are dire, as revisionists point out. Squaring this particular interpretative circle has proved difficult in the past, but we are now in a position to make a suggestion that can avoid the problems of both conventional and revisionist readings in 2:17-24. We approach it by building from the text's most obvious features.

In 2:17-21a Paul challenges a "Jew" with a long string of questions that amount to an enormous protasis in an extended conditional challenge. Three shorter conditionals of the same basic nature then follow in vv. 21b-22 (and these will be considered momentarily).

^{17}[E]ὶ [δὲ] σὺ Ἰουδαῖος ἐπονομάζῃ
καὶ ἐπαναπαύῃ νόμῳ
καὶ καυχᾶσαι ἐν θεῷ
^{18}καὶ γινώσκεις τὸ θέλημα [θεοῦ]
καὶ δοκιμάζεις τὰ διαφέροντα
κατηχούμενος ἐκ τοῦ νόμου,
^{19}πέποιθάς τε σεαυτὸν
ὁδηγὸν εἶναι τυφλῶν,
φῶς τῶν ἐν σκότει,
^{20}παιδευτὴν ἀφρόνων,
διδάσκαλον νηπίων,
ἔχοντα τὴν μόρφωσιν τῆς γνώσεως καὶ τῆς ἀληθείας ἐν τῷ νόμῳ·
^{21}ὁ οὖν διδάσκων ἕτερον σεαυτὸν οὐ διδάσκεις;

Two constituencies are immediately recognizable, although we will add further details to their description in what follows. For now it suffices to register, on the one hand, a dominant Jewish figure who is clearly committed to the law, meaning here probably the Jewish Scriptures as a whole, although they were doubtless centered on the Pentateuch. He relies on the law and boasts that he knows God's will and can discern what really matters, being catechized by the law; he is consequently a guide, a light, a corrector, and a teacher. In the law he possesses "the embodiment of knowledge and truth." A strong distinction is made between this "insider" and "outsiders." Thus, we see, on the other hand, those lacking the law, who are "blind," "in darkness," "foolish," and "children." Not only are they separate from the realm of the law and its pedagogy, but these metaphors imply that such people lack any insight or capacity in their own right. The blind cannot see at all; those in darkness have no light; those who are ignorant require instruction; and children require either maturity or adult supervision. This non-Jewish constituency is of course part of "the problem," a sinful humanity separated from both God and the law — and so 2:19-20 resumes to a degree the judgments of 1:18-32. But the teacher of the law identified here bridges the gap between the helpless and depraved constituency and its salvation. This figure will bring the illumination, wisdom, and maturity of the law to those who currently lack it.

Hence, the hypocrite targeted beginning in 2:1 and then beginning in 2:17 is not a generic Jew representative of Judaism in general but a representative of an elite group of literate Jewish males who are learned in the law and various Jewish traditions, into which the Teacher falls. The figure in 2:17 *is* the figure of 2:1, and he is Jewish, but he is not *the* Jew — indeed, far from it. He is a teacher, implicit within which category in particular is the Teacher. (Paul does not wish to identify the Teacher with complete precision yet; this slightly broader identification will suffice for now.) However, we know that this figure is also ultimately Christian in some sense; he is engaging with Paul's pagan converts and can be contradicted with Christian teaching. Furthermore, he is either potentially or actually active in

Rome — a feature that emerges with particular clarity from a consideration of the next few verses in Paul's argument.

Paul reintroduces the theme of hypocrisy in 2:21a, charging the sage specifically — and, for conventional readers and revisionists alike (as we noted in chapter eleven), rather opaquely — with hypocrisy involving theft (v. 21b), adultery (v. 22a), and temple robbery (v. 22b: ἱεροσυλέω; this last associated, even more opaquely, with preaching against idolatry). The crudeness of these charges is difficult to integrate into any sensible reconstruction or critique of Judaism in general, and the asymmetry within the final charge is likewise vexing. However, if we recognize that Paul is ultimately concerned with discrediting a Jewish Christian Teacher at Rome, as my rereading suggests, these verses become transparent.

The three charges evoke the famous incident that, Josephus suggests, caused the expulsion of the Jewish community from the Roman capital by Tiberius in 19 CE.[95] Josephus recounts how certain Jewish figures, posing as sages, had cheated a prominent Roman noblewoman of a large donation to the Jerusalem temple. Presumably, they had talked her into the donation in the first place and then absconded with the money (so that the entire relationship may have been a deliberate confidence trick; or alternatively, genuinely learned figures had given in to greed). These ostensible sages had clearly robbed someone and simultaneously defrauded their own temple, and the association of this story with sexual immorality would have been stereotypical and widely believed — a weak-willed woman had been seduced both spiritually and physically (otherwise, why would she have given such a large sum of money to such a strange religion, and in the charge of such unethical men?). This incident was then associated with the trauma of the expulsion itself and was doubtless long remembered (and Paul's letter was written only thirty to thirty-five years after it).

This story explains Paul's inferences in Romans 2:21b-22 perfectly — how he can accuse a Jewish sage at Rome of hypocrisy involving theft, adultery, and temple robbery. These were the exact features of the infamous scam and the closely associated Jewish expulsion. The Jews presumably left Rome in 19 CE as dissidents and criminals. Hence, this scenario also fits nicely with Paul's charge in v. 24 that "as it is written, 'The name of God is blasphemed among the Gentiles because of you'" — apparently a prophetic prediction (Isa. 52:5) of the humiliation that was associated with the expulsion.

By reminding his auditors of the Roman catastrophe of 19 CE, Paul insinuates that the arrival of Jewish sages in Rome, proclaiming the virtues of the law, could have unintended and shocking consequences; the result of their preaching could actually be the *humiliation* of the Jews in the presence of the pagans, not their glorification.[96] The Roman Christian auditors are thus advised to beware any figures who match the profile of the charlatans of 19 CE. Not all Jewish teachers arriving in Rome and extolling the virtues of the law are what they claim to be. Such an appearance may mask more sinister motives, and the result of being fooled by such a performance in the past was disastrous and traumatic for the entire community. The Romans are to beware Jews bearing the law (and presumably especially if they are asking for money). This is not, however, Paul's principal objective within the pericope. He is building primarily toward another embarrassing argumentative implication that we have yet to note — one that both conventional and revisionist readers have again struggled with.[97]

I suggest that Paul strikes an important blow against the effectiveness of the law in the Teacher's gospel in this subsection, and this is his main reason for evoking the expulsion. In the Teacher's opinion, the possession of the law conveys some sort of significant advantage — it is a path for those who are blind, a light for those in darkness, and so on (and he is of course in touch with a recognizable Jewish discourse at this point). However, the story of these infamous Jewish charlatans shows unequivocally that the possession of the law, and even some expertise in it, can actually count for nothing. The most outrageous sins can still take place — and did! By merely recalling this incident, Paul has overtly and instantly falsified a key assumption within the Teacher's system. (He has also offered a concrete example of sinful Jews, the category created as a possibility in 2:6 and noted in 2:9-10.) And this conception of Paul's argumentative goal in 2:17-24 — the falsification of any "advantage" conferred *automatically* by mere possession of the law, as well as by learning in it — now links up with other clues from the pericope's setting to generate an important insight into the system of the Teacher that Paul is opposing throughout Romans 1:18–3:20.

It is now apparent (although it will become clearer by degrees through the arguments that follow) that the Teacher holds that the law provides a significant *ethical* advantage to its possessors, which in turn should provide a decisive *eschatological* advantage. Those outside the law's embrace, by contrast, seem mired in a sinful ontology, and so are doomed to damnation. There is no detailed anthropological elaboration of this assumption yet; that must wait for later discussions in Romans, coupled with analysis of the relevant Jewish and Greco-Roman sources. But the general point can be granted on the basis of what is already visible in Paul's argument here.

The Teacher's category of Jewish sages stands in Romans 2:17-21a over against an undesirable group characterized by ignorance of the will of God and of "what is best." Lacking the "embodiment of knowledge and truth" in the law, they live in blindness, darkness, foolishness, and immaturity. Clearly, this constituency that lacks the law — by definition, non-Jews — is *ontologically inferior*. They are sinful, and therefore eschatologically doomed, but they cannot help themselves. The blind must be led by someone who can see, those in darkness must be provided with light, those who are foolish must be taught, and children must be brought to maturity at the feet of their instructors and parents. And in this text it is of course the Teacher and those like him who fulfill this salvific role, introducing the law into an otherwise desperate situation. It therefore seems reasonable to impute this conviction to the Teacher's system: part of his solution to the problem of pagan sinfulness is the pedagogy of the law. Such pedagogy will illuminate, educate, and mature — and therefore also will save. This pedagogy will produce the good deeds that constitute "righteous activity" in general, resulting in a verdict from God of "righteous" on the day of judgment, at which point the convert will inherit the age to come and all its blessings. Because the eschaton is ethical, the ethical advantage conferred by the law on its followers is both eschatological and soteriological, although we have yet to consider in detail just how this ethical advantage takes place in relation to the sinful pagan condition.

This position's ability to resolve various problems dangling in the surrounding discourse adds to its plausibility, as does its integration with other Jewish texts that assert much the same thing. First, we should note that it makes good sense of Paul's argument in 2:17-24, while avoiding the difficulties already noted there in the conventional reading.

It has never seemed especially necessary for Paul to convict Jews explicitly of certain sins, as the conventional reading asserts that he does here, when an incontestable blanket condemnation is shortly to arrive in 3:10-18. (Alternatively, if this is important, then a more subtle accusation would be expected.) But there is nothing otiose about Paul's argument here if he is attacking the Teacher's convictions that the law provides decisive ethical and therefore eschatological advantages. The example of learned but deeply sinful Jewish sages serves to refute any *automatic* connotation in this set of convictions very effectively, while the lurid quality of their sins is very much to the point. Moreover, this account of the Teacher's system helps us with several nagging problems from the immediate setting of Romans 2:17-24. In particular, it explains why the two constituencies discussed in 2:6-10 are so pristine, and why the opening rhetorical proem concerning the sinfulness of the pagans contained a certain unhelpful collective dimension that was not, strictly speaking, fair (overdeterminations already noted in chapter eleven — ODs 7 and 3 respectively[98]).

If the Teacher is operating with the ontological dichotomy that we have just noted, then this pristine distribution is entirely understandable. In terms of his view of humanity, with the pagans enslaved to dark passions but the Jews ethically guided by the law and its observance, the day of judgment *will* know of only two, starkly different groups. And although the Teacher uses the principle of fairness for his rhetorical proem (and unwisely, as it turns out: see the elaboration of this point just below), he is not strongly committed to it; he is in fact more deeply convinced concerning the ontological depravity of pagans that only the pedagogy and illumination of the law can ultimately remedy. The sinful pagans need help — help they can get through the law.

A careful reexamination of 1:18-32 in the light of these concerns provides some further clues concerning the anthropological dynamic that seems to underlie the Teacher's convictions. The pagans there first abandon correct thinking about God (1:19-22), from which point their "thinking" becomes "futile" and "their senseless minds" become "darkened" (v. 21). God then abandons them to various impure and dishonorable lusts (vv. 24, 26), and they engage in sexual immorality and the dishonoring of the body's natural relations (vv. 26-27), followed by all manner of sins (vv. 29-31). Presumably, then, the correct sequence is the inverse of this decline, and a particular conception of the law integrates well with this. The law illuminates the mind concerning God and "his" aniconic worship, resulting in wise and enlightened thinking and the *control* of, not abandonment to, sinful passions, together with the observance of due order in relation to the body. Correct interpersonal relations then also follow. (Of course one must "do" and not merely "hear" the law.) The general result is then righteous behavior, and a final saving verdict from God on the day of judgment for "persistence in good works" (see 2:7). (Note, we will shortly add an important element to this discourse in the light of 2:25-29.)

Moreover, in all of this the Teacher is in touch with a recognizable Jewish discourse from Paul's day. Many Jewish texts contemporary to Paul speak proudly of the ethical assistance that the law can provide to sinful humanity by way of an essentially rationalistic anthropology. One of the best examples of this is 4 Maccabees, which is little more than an extended narrative affirmation of the conviction that the law provides pious Jews with the necessary virtues — that is, the goodness or rightness, wisdom, self-control, and courage — to conquer their own bodily appetites and passions even in the most extreme circumstances, here excruciating pain, fear, loss, and humiliation under torture (and this at the hands of dissolute passionate pagans, it should be noted!). But the same broad position is observable in many other Jewish sources as well (and it also bears a close resemblance to popular Platonic psychology).[99]

It seems significant that this developing understanding of the Teacher's "solution" makes excellent sense of the pericope that follows 2:17-24 as well — 2:25-29. Whereas Paul is concerned in 2:17-24 primarily with the law, he clearly turns his attention in vv. 25-29 to circumcision and the matter of "Jewish definition." And he attacks rival conceptions of these by juxtaposing two phenomena for which he has already carefully prepared the ground — sinful circumcised Jews and righteous uncircumcised pagans (see 2:11 and 2:9-10, 14-15).

Sinful Jews have been a *possibility* since 2:1. They were *asserted* explicitly in 2:9-10 and 12b on the basis of 2:6, and then *demonstrated* with a concrete historical instance in 2:21b-23 (the infamous Roman con artists of 19 CE). Such people, who do not "practice the law," will clearly not be "advantaged" at a final judgment based on desert, their circumcision notwithstanding: περιτομὴ [μὲν] γὰρ ὠφελεῖ ἐὰν νόμον πράσσῃς· ἐὰν δὲ παραβάτης νόμου ᾖς, ἡ περιτομή σου ἀκροβυστία γέγονεν. In this setting, their circumcision has in effect become uncircumcision; it will count for nothing (essentially because only comprehensive good deeds do count).[100] Hence, the mere existence of sinful Jews implies that circumcision is in and of itself ineffective. But Paul is not just interested in sinful Jews in this subsection.

The possibility of righteous pagans has been signaled clearly in advance as well. Paul asserted in 2:14-15 in passing — but unequivocally — that the presuppositions of the Teacher demand this option. Pagans must possess a law of sorts within themselves, as 1:18-32 asserted implicitly and at length, or God's implacable condemnation of pagan sinfulness would not be fair. (But it is, by definition, so they do.) As a result, the possibility must exist that some of the pagans could go on to keep this law that is written internally, perhaps in their nature, and certainly in their hearts, and so be saved. Paul mentions this possibility in 2:9-10 alongside the parallel possibility of sinful Jews — and this constituency has always been a thorn in the flesh for the conventional reading (or, for that matter, for any reading of Romans 1–3).

The existence of these two categories now creates an especially striking argumentative juxtaposition. It seems possible that a pagan who is righteous, keeping the law that exists within his or her heart, could condemn an unrighteous Jew on the day of judgment: "those who are physically uncircumcised but keep the law will condemn you that have the written code and circumcision but break the law" (2:27). So a further instance of Jewish humiliation seems possible, along with the more historical humiliation at Rome that was alluded to in 2:24. Moreover, circumcision per se has been marginalized. But the definition of "a true Jew" seems to have been shifted beyond all recognition by this juxtaposition as well. Paul's deployment here suggests that "a person is not a Jew who is one outwardly, nor is true circumcision something external and physical. Rather a person is a Jew who is one inwardly, and real circumcision is a matter of the heart. . . . Such a person receives praise not from others but from God" (2:28-29). This shocking redefinition is, however, a direct implication from the Teacher's premises in terms of desert; it is implicit within it. Paul is saying, in effect, "Surely, the righteous and the good are — *in terms of your presuppositions* — the true Jew?!" Here, then, Jewish identity is reduced to, and entirely defined by, desert — a shameful argumentative implication on the Teacher's part.

At this point, the letter's auditors might even have recognized belatedly that this dramatic reversal was artfully anticipated by Paul. Earlier, in 2:11, Paul cited the theologoumenon that God is not impressed by mere appearance or reputation — and this slogan is almost certainly one of the Teacher's own, although it was deployed by Paul in a very different setting in 2:11. Verses 25-29 now recapitulate a judgment scenario within which God does indeed judge truly, in accordance with what is really there in people, beneath their superficial appearances. The superficially impressive receive praise from other people, presumably now (and this group doubtless includes some Jewish teachers); but those who are truly righteous, in the secret places, receive praise from God. In this case, of course, this entails blessing the righteous uncircumcised pagan and condemning the circumcised and law-observant but unrighteous (i.e., insufficiently law-observant) Jewish Christian. Thus, one of the Teacher's own theologoumena turns out — suitably repositioned — to confirm Paul's contentions here. God will indeed look deep into people on the day of judgment, as the Teacher asserts, into their hearts, and so will not be fooled by a lack of correlation between physical indicia and deeper ethical corruption! The Teacher is — once again — hoisted by his own petard.

Of course, conventional readers and revisionists alike have struggled with the shocking implications of this argument by Paul. Although his conclusions seem formally correct, they also seem absurd; it is hardly acceptable to dismiss circumcision and the actual definition of Judaism in such terms merely in view of

this juxtaposition. Paul's arguments seem redundant, if not a little bizarre. However, the reintroduction of the Teacher's convictions allows us to explain these argumentative moves on Paul's part with relative ease.

Paul is refuting another component here within the Teacher's "solution" —
and in dramatic fashion! — namely, the Teacher's emphasis on the ethical "advantage" of circumcision. And Paul's response is (again) carefully crafted and effective. But in order to appreciate this response we must ask how circumcision could
have functioned in relation to the saving system that we have begun to uncover
within the Teacher — the salvation of the depraved pagans through the enlightenment of, and apprenticeship to, the law. What "advantage" could circumcision
confer in this relation? The information in certain Jewish sources is especially
helpful at this point.[101]

The trope of a circumcised heart — which Paul mentions explicitly in 2:29
— is attested in the Old Testament (see esp. Deut. 10:16; 30:6; Jer. 4:4; Ezek. 44:9
[see also 36:25-27]). But by Paul's day it could function within a broader, essentially ethical discourse that is well attested in Philo. In *On Special Laws* 1:1–11,[102]
Philo supplies a stereotypical apology — although with characteristic elegance —
for a rite that was widely mocked by Greeks and Romans, offering various reasons for its importance. It prevents disease (4), "secures the cleanliness of the
whole body" (5), makes "the part that is circumcised . . . ['resemble'] the heart" —
and both organs are, after all, concerned with generation, the heart of thoughts
and "the generative organ . . . of living beings" (6), and allows the seminal fluid to
proceed easily, making those nations practicing circumcision the most numerous
(7). Philo goes on to suggest, however, that these rationalizations are traditional
(8); he supplies two further arguments of a symbolic nature that are closely related to one another.

First, circumcision "is a symbol of the excision of all the pleasures which
delude the mind; for since, of all the delights which pleasure can afford, the association of man with woman is the most exquisite, it seemed good to the lawgivers
to mutilate the organ which ministers to such connections; by which rite they signified figuratively the excision of all superfluous and excessive pleasure, not, indeed, of one only, but of all others whatever, through that one which is the most
impervious of all" (9). Similarly, circumcision is a symbol of "discarding that terrible disease, the vain opinion of the soul" (10). Here, then, circumcision is symbolic of the excision of vice and of the achievement of a superior ethical state,
which Philo goes on to link immediately not merely with sound sexual ethics but
with the absence of idolatry. (This association between excision from the penis
and excision from the heart is also discernible in the third contention of his rehearsal of traditional rationales above.)

Similarly, in *Questions and Answers on Genesis*, 3,[103] Philo, in a more extended account, sees "a twofold circumcision" in the command of Genesis 17:10
— "that which is of the flesh . . . in the genitals, [and] that which is of the male
creature . . . in respect of his thoughts" (46), "[s]ince that which is, properly
speaking, masculine in us is the intellect, the superfluous shoots of which it is

necessary to prune away and to cast off, so that it, becoming clean and pure from all wickedness and vile, may worship God as his priest." Philo then goes on to link this explanation specifically with the Old Testament theme of the circumcision of the heart: "God says by an express law, 'Circumcise the hardness of your hearts,' that is to say, your hard and rebellious thoughts and ambition, which when they are cut away and removed from you, your most important part will be rendered free" (46).[104]

It is worth noting that there is also a concrete rationale for these claims by Philo; empirical and material signs symbolize *and often represent* spiritual realities: "in a wonderful resemblance, all things which are represented in appearance are yet in reality inanimate" (48). So a deeper comprehensive metaphysical system holds together the visible, physical, symbolic ritual and the invisible ethical surgery. (See also *On the Migration of Abraham*, 93.)

Philo reiterates this point when explaining the command of Genesis 17:12 that household slaves too should be circumcised: "each of these ['dispositions'] has its appropriate employment, and requires like a plant to be cleared and pruned in order that the good and fruitful parts may acquire constancy; . . . superfluities must be cut away; *but those who are taught by instructors cut away their ignorance*" (50, emphasis added). Philo's strongest statements on this subject are supplied, however, as he explains the command of Genesis 17:14 that a male infant not circumcised on the eighth day be "cut off from his people." He is aware of the apparent inhumanity of this injunction but is able to respond in terms of its "inward meaning," which he has already established: "the intellect which is not circumcised and cleared away from the flesh and the vices of the flesh is corrupt *and cannot be saved*" (52, emphasis added); it goes on to participate in a corruption from which all circumcised Israelites have now been removed.

The main thrust of Paul's argument in 2:25-29 now seems clear — although it emerges only as we add one more important principle to the Teacher's system. The Teacher seems to have argued that only the possession and fulfillment of the Jewish law, including circumcision, could constrain the sinful passions that rage in the hearts of all people — although especially in pagans — and thereby elicit the just wrath of God. Yet turning to the law *will* result in ethical rectitude, and so in final glory — the glory of a positive verdict from God on the day of judgment that can be boasted about, along with a subsequent entrance to glorious eternal life. The law saves. And acceptance of the law, signaled in the first instance by circumcision, *actually circumcises the heart as well as the body, and so allows the sinful passions to be tamed and controlled. Circumcision is an ethical and ontological surgery* in addition to being a mere anatomical excision. In this fashion, and *only* in this fashion, is ethical behavior possible, and thereby final salvation, which rewards those who are righteous in deed with eschatological life and blessedness.[105] Moreover, clearly this reward for that righteousness is extended only to "true Jews" — to those circumcised in body, heart, and mind — for only such people can act in the righteous fashion that leads ultimately to salvation. Indeed, such righteous figures will ultimately sit in judgment on the unrighteous, in an act of discernment and triumph.[106] Consequently, physical circumcision must correspond perfectly with ethical circumcision and with salvation; the true Jew is circumcised in both body and mind.[107]

This realization allows us to appreciate the importance — and the skill — of Paul's argument in 2:25-29 (not to mention in 2:17-24).

As we have just seen, for the Teacher — as for many Jews — circumcision conferred a significant and quite concrete soteriological "advantage" on its practitioners via its ethical impact. The correct sequence for the Teacher, then, was clear:

> depravity
> circumcision (physical and ethical)
> ongoing law observance
> consequent righteousness
> final verdict of "righteous" (a "true Jew")
> salvation[108]
> (along with, perhaps, judgment of the unrighteous)

However, Paul has already broken a critical link in this chain in 2:17-24. He has used an instance of Jewish depravity in certain famous sages to disprove the automatic association between law observance and righteous activity. And, armed with this concession, he has pressed the same point in 2:25-29 in relation to circumcision and Jewish definition. Those same sinful sages demonstrate that circumcision too may well be ineffective, and the righteous pagans compound this point (while they press the definition of the "true Jew" in another direction as well).[109] Hence, by 2:29 Paul has reversed most of the Teacher's saving sequence, beginning with a different premise, and thereby broken it:

> depravity — redeployed lower down the chain
> circumcision — falsified by depravity by the circumcised and good deeds by the uncircumcised
> law observance — falsified by depravity by the observant and good deeds by the unobservant
> righteousness — evident in good pagans, not in bad Jews
> verdict of "righteous" — appropriate on those pagans doing good deeds, and not on the sinful Jew
> salvation — associated with "true Jew" in the redefined sense of anyone doing good deeds, and hence circumcised or uncircumcised, Jew or pagan
> judgment — over unrighteous Jews by uncircumcised pagans!

After disrupting this sequence, none of the putative ethical and eschatological advantages of the Teacher in terms of circumcision and the law seem to hold good. By 2:29 *the Teacher actually has no saving solution to offer to the godless pagans* (or even to himself!); he has no real gospel. Circumcision and the possession and observance of the law do not actually count for anything — and may count for little in relation to the Teacher himself! But Paul has not merely falsified the Teacher's saving system; he has cleverly prepared the ground for a still more devastating argumentative move (although he will not unleash it just yet). But, as in 2:17-24, some further subtle inferences may be present here in addition to Paul's main points that should be noted before we move on.

First, the humiliation rather than the glorification of Judaism is again implicit within the Teacher's system (this will follow on any disobedience). An eschatological humiliation at the hands of the God who judges truly, without being misled by appearances, may follow on the historical humiliation that took place under Tiberius. And this is doubtless the opposite of the Teacher's announced intentions; his program promises glory to the righteous Jew, both historically (hopefully) and eschatologically (here more definitely).

Second, the proclamation of the law is now also implicitly otiose, although Paul does not make much of this overtly. But it does follow from this brief scenario, along with all its presuppositions, that the pagans do not apparently need either the teaching of the Jewish law or circumcision in order to act ethically and thereby be saved. They have their own internal law and seem to enjoy no significant advantage if they convert. The complete futility of the Judaizing aspect within the Teacher's mission is therefore glimpsed briefly within this subsection.

And third, Paul signals *very* briefly in v. 29 that ethical circumcision by means of the law is ultimately impossible in any case, when he states cryptically that circumcision of the heart is ἐν πνεύματι οὐ γράμματι.[110] In his view, only God's creative Spirit can alter the human condition. Hence, circumcision remains largely what it is within the Jewish propaganda literature — a symbol. And, as with all symbols, without the underlying reality — which must necessarily be grounded in divine action for Paul — it is empty. Consequently, Paul's cryptic criticism here is fundamentally realistic. The heart, as a metaphor for humanity's ethical condition, cannot be "circumcised" by any *literal* surgery (and presumably especially of the penis) or by literalism per se — by reading or some such. To change human nature and its ethical workings requires divine involvement through the Spirit of creation (or some equivalent ontological system and set of arguments, such as those supplied by Philo). This — like all of Paul's asides throughout this argument — is an important clue concerning both the future direction of his own recommendations and his deepest difficulties with the proposals of the Teacher.

At this point we can attempt preliminary answers to some intriguing questions. We can ask (1) what the Teacher's problems with Paul's gospel are; (2) what Paul's principal problem with the Teacher's gospel is; and (3) what Paul's basic argumentative strategy through Romans 1–3 consists of. Answers to all these questions are reasonably apparent.

(1) The Teacher's Problem with Paul

In the Teacher's view, Paul has left the pagans ethically defenseless (and so the apostle's teaching is deeply irresponsible). Although it may be true that the pagans have had their transgressions forgiven in Christ,[111] they have not been given control over their sinful passions, lacking the law and circumcision, and so presumably they continue to sin and sin again. They cannot do good deeds, lacking the illumination of the law and the pruning of the heart afforded by these traditional Jewish ordinances. But it is worse than this. They exist now in a state of false security. Paul has barred the way to heaven by rejecting law observance for pagans and has deployed defenses that make it still harder for these benighted pagans to hear the true gospel involving the law, to embrace it, and so actually to go on to be saved (by being declared righteous on the day of judgment on account of all their good deeds). Far from being saved, the Teacher asserts, all Paul's deceived pagan converts will be eschatologically humiliated. Wrath, not salvation, will be their final experience. And in all this, Christ's name is doubtless sullied as well. Paul advocates a shameful gospel that will ultimately issue only in shame for those who convert to it.

(2) Paul's Main Problem with the Teacher

Paul's main difficulty with the Teacher is actually similar to the Teacher's problem with him; he holds that the Teacher's rather traditional Jewish instructions in terms of circumcision and law observance are ethically inadequate. Paul holds that only participation in Christ's death and resurrection, through the divine Spirit, can change the sinful ontology of humanity — for both Jew and pagan. He views circumcision in a fairly literal manner, along with law observance; the former is a cutting away of a piece of skin by human hands, and the latter a book written by hand and mediated by human figures like Moses (which is not to deny divine causality or involvement). He views these ordinances as entirely inadequate for the task of human transformation, as he hints briefly in 2:29: circumcision of the heart must be done by God. Hence, the ethical inadequacy of the Teacher's gospel is for Paul grounded in its ontological incapacity, which is rooted in turn in an inadequate evaluation of the work of Christ and the Spirit in the Christian life. These concerns emerge ultimately in Romans 5–8, texts largely beyond our present purview, although we receive frequent cryptic hints. But Paul's current concerns are slightly different. He is trying to humiliate the Teacher on the Teacher's own terms. Paul's own fundamental convictions play a part in this argumentation, but they do not drive it in formal terms.

(3) Paul's Main Argumentative Strategy

We know by this point that the Teacher holds the pagans to be lost in a miasma of corrupt desires — a blind, dark, ignorant, infantile condition. The Jewish people, however, with circumcised bodies and hearts, are not so lost and enslaved. Indeed, in this state they are capable of near-perfect law-observance, the occasional transgression being wiped clean through Christ's atonement. Only the law has saved the latter, and it can create a bridge to salvation for the former. These are the Teacher's properly basic convictions, and they rest on the perception of a significant ontological difference between pagans and Jews, one created by circumcision and the law.

The Teacher's rhetorical prelude, however, is based on the principle of divine justice, as is his eschatology, the latter being strongly linked to his soteriology. And strict retributive justice presupposes human capacity and desert. These dual commitments are discernible at other points in Jewish literature of the time; however, strictly speaking, the two sets of convictions are not compatible. Considerations of pure fairness must clash at certain points with considerations based on substantial, material, or ontological differences. And while this might not ordinarily matter that much (for example, because a rhetorical strategy based on fairness is functioning in a clearly subordinate location), the Teacher now finds himself in a competitive, polemical situation opposed by a mind that has detected this set of anomalies. *Paul's unfolding strategies in Romans 1:18–3:20 are designed to exploit the tension in the Teacher's theology between contentions based on fairness and contentions based on ontology — that pagans and Jews are ontologically and ethically different.*

If the Teacher is strongly committed to a set of ontological convictions about Jews and pagans at some point (ontology bearing a close relation to ethics), *then his solution will not correspond to his initial account of the problem.* His problem will articulate issues of fairness, desert, and accountability, and his solution will address ontological matters. From this point, Paul can force the Teacher to maintain his commitment to his rhetorical opening or pay a number of acute rhetorical prices. On the one hand, if the Teacher abandons his opening, then he will look inconsistent and incompetent; he will look like a hypocritical fool (see Gal. 2:11-14!). But the assumption of fairness underlying those opening commitments, if he continues to affirm them, will — if pressed — *override* the Teacher's later solution, which addresses an ontological situation — an unenviable dilemma! The Teacher will thereby be confounded in terms of his own assumptions. This dynamic characterizes all of Romans 1:18–3:20, but it emerges with special clarity in 2:17-29, where Paul commits the Teacher to the painful route of consistency. The latter, a stretch of text that has usually proved very difficult to interpret, can now be seen to prosecute an economic and effective argumentative program.

§6. Romans 3:1-20 — the Taming of the Teacher

By Romans 2:29, the Teacher's missionary program to the pagans is in ruins, but he himself — along with many of his followers and potential converts — is not yet utterly forsaken. Up to this point in the argument, Paul has principally been exploit-

ing the commitment to desert that was implicit in the Teacher's opening discourse
— his definition of "the problem" (and this premise seems to have been endorsed
at other points in the Teacher's system as well[112]). This is a notoriously destructive
premise for religious and historical particularities, as other religious philosophers
have found out to their cost.[113] And once he has elicited admission to its centrality,
Paul has used it to override key elements within the Teacher's "solution," namely,
the ostensible ethical advantages of the law and circumcision. Conceivably, however, the Teacher himself is not yet in serious trouble. Presumably, he could simply
obey the law and try to achieve eschatological salvation. Nothing yet excludes this
possibility. But Paul suspects that if the ethical advantages offered by circumcision
and law observance fail, then the Teacher and his followers may not have resolved
the problem of the sinful passions in their own lives. They too may be sinners —
and doubtless their behavior toward Paul has either raised or reinforced this train
of thought for the apostle — at which point they will be condemned by the implacably just God that they proclaim. To demonstrate this would of course be the ultimate argumentative triumph for Paul; he would have shown that not only can the
Teacher's gospel not save pagans, but it cannot save the Teacher himself, its
preacher! However, in Romans 3:9a-20, Paul is still working with the Teacher's
own assumptions. So how is he going to demonstrate that the Teacher is mired in
sin and consequently damned in terms of his own system?

It is the Teacher's expertise in the law that will turn out to be his undoing. A
mass of quotations establishing Paul's basic charge will overwhelm the Teacher,
reducing his entire situation not merely to missionary irrelevance but to
soteriological damnation (and hence — in theological and argumentative terms
— to humiliated silence). Following this broadside in 3:9b-18, Paul will rapidly
make its pointed application in 3:19-20. The Teacher's gospel will not save even
the Teacher.

But Paul has a preliminary conclusion to establish before he can administer
this argumentative coup de grâce. He prepares for his definitive stroke with an
overtly dialogical subsection in 3:1-9a, where the Teacher's "voice" is heard directly once again. It will clarify his final argument if the Teacher has (rather stupidly) affirmed the rectitude of its basic claims in advance — that God will judge
all for their sinfulness on the basis of desert, and irrespective of any special privileges or pleading. If the Teacher himself proclaims this loudly and unequivocally,
Paul's final move will be that much more decisive.

6.1. Romans 3:1-9a

My suggested rereading of 3:1-9a, in the broader context of 1:18-3:20 as a whole,
has the particular virtue of placing Paul on the right side of the argument. The
overtly dialogical diatribe that Paul crafts at this point has two protagonists. We
will designate them for the moment simply A and B (and the following identifications of the actual exchanges are not controversial):[114]

A: ³:¹ What [then] is the advantage of the Jew? Or what is the benefit of circumcision?

B: ² Much in many respects! First, is it not that they have been entrusted with the very utterances of God?! (see Rom. 2:17-20)

A: ³ So what?! If some were untrustworthy, will not their untrustworthiness nullify the trust of God?

B: ⁴ Absolutely not! Let God be true though every person is false, just as it is written ". . . so that you might be judged righteous in your words, and blameless when you are judged." (Pss. 116:11; 51:4; see also Rom. 2:3b-11, 16)

A: ⁵ But if our inequity highlights God's equity,¹¹⁵ what then shall we say? Is it not unjust of God to pour out wrath on us? (I am of course speaking from a human perspective.)

B: ⁶ Absolutely not! Indeed, how will God judge the world [if that is the case]?

A: ⁷ But if by means of my falsehood the truthfulness of God overflows to God's glory, why then am I still condemned as a sinner? — ⁸and even as we are slandered, and as some report us as saying, should we not do evil so that good can come!?

B: . . . Whose judgment is positively deserved!

A: ⁹ What shall we say, then? Are we advantaged?¹¹⁶

B: Not in every respect.

It is significant that conventional interpreters (not to mention many revisionists) identify Paul in this dialogue with B, the respondent; they thereby correctly discern that speaker B is representative of the principle of desert that has been leveling Jewish privileges through the preceding passages of argument. Indeed, there is little choice in this matter; the text of Romans does not allow a different correlation. B is clearly endorsing the premise of strict soteriological desert throughout this exchange. (There are three explicit endorsements — the first supported by Scripture, the last rather brief.) And the conventional reading has committed Paul to this posture from 1:18. It views him as making this principle that is implicit in 1:18-32 explicit in 2:6, and then turning it on some pretentious figure, who is probably Jewish, throughout the rest of the argument. A is consequently a Jewish protestor who asks in 3:1 — rather understandably! — what the advantage of the Jew now actually consists of. B — assumed to be Paul — then simply insists (more and more tersely) that the principle of soteriological desert must hold. Thus, B also overrules any protests from A couched in terms of the possibility of divine leniency for sinners.

The difficulties with this reading, however, are numerous — in the main, the acute tensions that now develop at the reading's systematic and empirical frames. Paul, along with many of his Jewish contemporaries, seems committed elsewhere to the divine compassion that he seems here trenchantly to overrule. But it is one of the strengths of my suggested rereading of 1:18–3:20 to place

Paul on the other side of much of this argument, effectively eliminating these tensions.[117]

It is, I suggest, the Teacher's implicit commitment to desert that is being turned against him by Paul throughout this major subsection of Romans. The Teacher is of course the speaker of 1:18-32, and hence the figure committed to the principle of desert enunciated in 2:6; he is then the figure on whom the argument repeatedly turns. My rereading thus identifies Paul with A, not with B, and a far more contextually comfortable analysis of 3:1-9a results. It also positions Paul here in the role of the Socratic questioner, not the respondent (not to mention, as someone sensitive to Jewish privilege). With this reversal the many framing tensions generated by the conventional reading evaporate, a significant advantage in terms of the broader evidence for the plausibility of my suggested rereading. Read in this way, slightly different argumentative objectives and inferences are discernible within this set of exchanges, which should be considered now in more detail.

Romans 3:1-9a is a short clarificatory discussion that Paul deploys before introducing his clinching contentions beginning in 3:9b. Since 2:1 Paul has universalized the premise within the Teacher's first definition of "the problem" — soteriological desert — and then applied it to various key elements within the Teacher's "solution," stripping away any soteriological advantages that those might confer — the ostensible advantages of possessing the law, of being circumcised and therefore Jewish, et cetera (and all these were really based on underlying ontological distinctions). Hence, the perception of many interpreters that Paul has been "leveling the playing field" here is not inaccurate, although the broader argumentative function of this trajectory has tended to be misinterpreted. Paul is cornering the Teacher, not Judaism per se, *and in terms of the Teacher's assumptions,* not his own and/or Judaism's. By this point auditors attentive to the letter's original performance might even have sensed what Paul's final argumentative move was going to be; it was, after all, signaled in 2:1-5 (i.e., the Teacher too will probably prove to be a sinner, and so fall foul of his own system). However, Paul is not yet ready to make this final, definitive move. He wishes first to reintroduce the direct voice of the Teacher — which has been absent since 1:32 — and elicit from him a series of affirmations that these various argumentative moves are in fact fair and valid, both those preceding this conversation and the main move that is about to take place. (This is of course Paul's construction of the Teacher's response.) The Teacher ought to admit that Paul's stunning argumentative reductions of his gospel are fair, *along with their inevitable consequences for anyone who sins.* (These affirmations will also allow Paul to make a further important subordinate implication as well — and we have seen that an artful dual function is characteristic of Paul's carefully constructed exchanges in Romans 2.)

As we have already noted, Romans 3:1 makes explicit a question that Paul has been asking for some time, although it is important to appreciate that my suggested rereading nuances this issue differently from the conventional approach. The query is directly implicit in the powerful rehearsal of advantages attributed to the Jewish Teacher of the law in 2:17-20, and made explicit in v. 25 in relation to circumcision — "[c]ircumcision . . . is *of value* if you obey the law. . . ." But Paul has of course been leveling these ostensible advantages offered to pagan converts by the Teacher; they do *not* confer any *decisive* advantage in relation to the programmatic principle of final judgment by desert, because this would be unfair; neither do they offer any necessary ethical advantages, as certain celebrated instances of Jewish sinfulness denote. So he formulates a query to the Teacher directly in such terms: "What [then] is the advantage of the Jew? Or what is the benefit of circumcision?" (3:1).[118] One assumes that if the Teacher has grasped the preceding arguments correctly, he ought to reply, "None!" And this is presumably one of Paul's goals in this dialogue — to elicit the admission from the mouth of the Teacher that neither circumcision nor the law confers significant *ethical* and *eschatological* advantages. If a Jew sins then, according to the Teacher's gospel, he or she will be crushed by a just God at the final assize. However, the Teacher replies both enthusiastically and essentially stupidly: "Much in many respects! First, is it not that they have been entrusted with the very utterances of God?!" (3:2).[119]

Now this response by the interlocutor is of course rather misguided. Although the Jews do possess the definitive written edition of God's concerns, Paul's argument up to this point has shown that mere possession of the law, in tandem with a circumcision that is only physical, does *not* confer any decisive ethical advantage. And, because of this, it does not confer any decisive eschatological advantage either. The existence of various sinful Jews and righteous pagans is proof enough, and the argument's auditors know this well by now. But in this diatribe Paul will ultimately elicit the correct response from the interlocutor himself (which he does by 3:9a). In order to achieve this, however, he must shift the terms of the debate slightly. So the Pauline interrogator asks in 3:3, "So what?! If some were untrustworthy, will not their untrustworthiness nullify the trust of God?"

This change of argumentative direction is developed through a wordplay on the πιστ- stem,[120] and it can cause some interpretative confusion. But while it is a slightly new direction, Paul is in fact returning to a tension that he has been exploiting for some time. By reorienting the dialogue toward God, Paul is in effect asking his interlocutor, the Teacher, whether God's standards of judgment that have already been established are going to be relaxed in the face of Jewish transgressions. If a sinful Jew ultimately received any "advantage" in *this* relation, then the criterion of just judgment and the divine character so defined would somehow have been abandoned. So, in effect, Paul is inviting the Teacher to reaffirm here the eschatological scenario of 2:6-10 — which he duly does. And as a result of this it seems that any advantages will have to be realized by Jews *before* the final judgment in accordance with desert, at which point they will cease (although Paul has in fact already problematized them in those earlier locations as well). A circumcised and law-observant Jew will enjoy no decisive advantages when it counts, on the day of judgment — according to the Teacher's arrangement of problem and solution, of course.

Faced with this new perspective on matters, the interlocutor replies predictably, μὴ γένοιτο! Three sets of queries and responses unfold, in which Paul asks the interlocutor whether sinful behavior — even despite various advantages that such behavior might confer to God! — will either impugn the established character of God in terms of justice or alter God's judgment in accordance with that character.[121] The answer of course is that it will not; God's judgment will not bend in relation to sinful behavior, and those who suggest that it should are doubly condemned: "Let God be true though every person is false . . . (3:4a). Is it not unjust of God to pour out wrath on us? . . . (3:5b). Indeed, how will God judge the world [if that is the case]? (3:6). But if by means of my falsehood the truthfulness of God overflows to God's glory, why then am I still condemned as a sinner? . . . (3:7). . . . [the] judgment [of those saying this] is positively deserved!" (3:8b).

But the result of these serried negations is the interlocutor's rebuttal in 3:9a of his own counterassertion in v. 2. Paul asked originally in v. 1, "What [then] is the advantage of the Jew? Or what is the benefit of circumcision?" And he reprises this in v. 9a: "What shall we say, then? Are we advantaged?" To which the interlocutor replies now — presumably a little shamefacedly — "not in every respect." Hence, 3:1-9a turns out to be one more typically clever argumentative progression. Viewed from the perspective of the character of God, which is by now well established, the interlocutor is forced to admit — and even asserts vehemently — that no advantage exists *on the day of judgment*, and hence in fundamental salvific terms, for anyone in a sinful position. There are no valid grounds emanating from such a dubious situation that suggest God's modifying either his character or his behavior. (And Paul has already disposed of the immediate ethical advantages of circumcision and the law.) But why is Paul so concerned to rebut overtly, in this way, any lingering notions of Jewish "advantage" as the Teacher defines that? There are, in my view, two reasons.

First, Paul elicits in this manner from the mouth of the interlocutor — here doubtless representing the Teacher directly — the unequivocal condemnation of *anyone* who is sinful. No rejoinders or excuses are accepted by the Teacher in 3:1-9a, as he sternly defends the justice of God. There are no grounds for appeal. This set of apparent affirmations will greatly increase the effectiveness of the charge that Paul is about to make *to* the Teacher in 3:9b-18. In effect, Paul has eliminated any special pleading on the Teacher's part *and by the Teacher's own stringent affirmation*.

Second, by arranging the questions in this manner, Paul is able to segue from the question of Jewish "advantage" into a brief discussion of a particular charge made against him that is roughly symmetrical to the assertions that the Teacher is at present roundly rejecting.

The sinfulness of humans is being juxtaposed with the justice of God from 3:3 onward, and the former is not allowed to alter the latter. Any special pleading in this relation is therefore close to libertinism. The question, If my sinfulness accentuates God's glorious mercy, why should I still be judged? is asked here repeatedly, and it is refuted by the Teacher. This would compromise the retributive integrity of God. However, it is a very small step to the further contention, "shall we not do evil so that good can come!?" (in the sense that the divine mercy would thereby be further demonstrated). Of course, the Teacher condemns this overtly false position as well. But it is vital to note that Paul slips in an additional subject here — those slandering *him* in such terms. With this insertion, those who are slandering Paul for being a libertine *are included in the Teacher's judgment on libertinism in general,* and ὧν τὸ κρίμα ἔνδικόν ἐστιν. Hence, in condemning those who are saying this libertine thing — *and* those saying this about Paul — the Teacher has possibly just condemned himself.

It is likely that the Teacher views Paul's gospel as libertine.[122] In terms of the Teacher's own system, Paul's law-free ethic leaves any pagan converts uncircumcised in their hearts and so effectively defenseless against their evil passions. Moreover, since the law is rejected, its consequent illumination and ethical pedagogy are lost. Pagans are left to their own wicked devices, and their sinful behavior is therefore inevitable — although Paul insists all the while that they are nevertheless saved. Thus, Paul's gospel is *in effect* libertine (and the Teacher may even suspect Paul of having promoted it in such terms deliberately). Charges to this effect can be observed surfacing at strategic points within Romans and Galatians — especially here, in Romans 6:1 and 6:15, and in Galatians 2:17. So it may be that in Romans 3:1-9a Paul has not merely clarified the central commitment of the Teacher's system to an implacable process of judgment, in the face of which no protests — even from learned Jews — will be tolerated; he may also have elicited from the mouth of the Teacher a condemnation of one of the central charges that the Teacher makes against Paul! If this is the case, then once again a powerful primary assertion has been interwoven with a subtle but deadly ancillary insinuation.

We should pause here to note one further subtle inference from the diatribe in Romans 3:1-9a. Two different views of the fundamental character of God are in play, and Paul may also delicately imply that the harsh consequences flowing from the Teacher's conception and resulting system are unnecessary.

In vv. 3-4 and vv. 5-6 the Teacher assumes that the language used in Paul's characterizations of God is to be understood retributively. (Or, alternatively, he asserts that this language *should* be so interpreted.) The πίστις of God in v. 3 that is enduring the untrustworthiness of Israel should be understood as the unwavering ἀλήθεια of God's character in v. 4 — which is just. Hence, any cosmic lawsuit against God will be confounded, as Psalm 51:4 suggests, and even if every person ever born has been convicted on the other side of duplicity (as Ps. 116:11 might suggest). Similarly, the equity of God in v. 5, which the unrighteous person complains against ultimately as "unjust" in its wrathful aspect, must be maintained so that God can judge the cosmos. And the result of these affirmations turns out to be the exclusion of any notion of Jewish advantage (in the terms currently being discussed), whether that is conferred overtly, through possession of the law, or implicitly, by circumcision. Sinful deeds will still be treated as sinful deeds by God and punished. But a further point is implicit here.

The πίστις of God that endures Israel's ἀπιστία, and the δικαιοσύνη of God that endures ἀδικία, need *not* be understood in retributive terms. As the initial senses of these two statements imply, they can be understood in fundamentally benevolent terms (and in fact need to be: see vv. 3 and 5a). And such an understanding invites the interlocutor on two occasions to respond in a different way to Paul's queries. The infidelity of the Jew does not invalidate the fidelity of God, because God endures and then somehow overcomes that infidelity. Similarly, the righteousness of God, conceiving that as a benevolent, saving character, *is* highlighted by its endurance and then transformation of unrighteous people. Hence, if people sin, this does not in fact invalidate God's *compassionate* qualities; there is no need for God to respond to transgressions necessarily in terms of punishment. Indeed, a situation of sinfulness — regrettable as it is — *does* provide an opportunity to emphasize those qualities. "The greater the sin, the greater the grace" Paul will say shortly (paraphrasing a little: see Rom. 5:20b). Consequently, Paul's argumentative turn in v. 3 does not just succeed in revising the interlocutor's confident but false claim in v. 2; it indicates that the Teacher's fundamental conception of God is potentially limited, and his entire system flawed as a result. Again, Paul points ahead to a different conception of matters (as in 2:16b and 29b) — one to which the Teacher is stubbornly oblivious. Indeed, when Paul goes on to articulate the situation of unbelieving Israel in 9:27–11:36, it rapidly becomes apparent that the divine compassion is at the heart of both human history and any Jewish hope. So this implicit protest signals subtly that Paul's own position is very different — and we have also thereby eliminated some nagging systematic, proximate, and empirical framing difficulties.[123]

It would seem, then, that Paul's argument again operates on at least two levels.[124] The superficial and principal level is the eliciting of the admission from the Teacher that, given sin, Jews enjoy no "advantages," meaning in particular no eschatological advantages. To suggest as much would be to compromise God's basic character as the Teacher conceives it — the very foundations of the cosmos would be shaken. In close relation to this, the Teacher condemns those making libertine claims — along with those slanderously accusing Paul of such things! However, lurking below this progression is another set of theological and argumentative options that the Teacher passes over. Sin does not need to be dealt with retributively. The character of a compassionate God is not impugned by the endurance and transformation of wickedness; on the contrary, that character might be glorified by such behavior. However, to acknowledge this would be to acknowledge that the entire eschatological scenario by which the Teacher sets so much store is a misrepresentation — a possibility that can barely be contemplated. So these inferences remain unexplored by the diatribe and only return to prominence when Paul himself endorses this theological trajectory later on in the letter (and, again, in relation to both Jews and pagans: see esp. 9:6–11:36).

With these concessions from the Teacher's own mouth, and related barbs and insinuations, complete, Paul is ready to make his final and decisive argumentative move, which is inaugurated in 3:9b and concluded in vv. 19-20.

6.2. Romans 3:9b-18

My rereading does not construe the function of 3:10-18 significantly differently from the conventional reading. This catena functions in localized argumentative terms very much as it does in the usual approach — to falsify the figure who emerges from the argument at 3:9. The difference is that the figure emerging from my argument is the Teacher, whereas in the conventional reading it is a generic Jew representing a generic human being, so the implications of my rereading are rather more palatable. There is one potential difficulty with my suggestion — in 3:9b — which we will look at next. We will then turn to some intriguing possibilities raised by this rereading for the catena's composition; and will note (as usual) how the difficulties present within the conventional reading now tend to disappear. But these issues aside — and with the usual reorientation of the focus of the argument toward the Teacher introduced — the conventional reading's exegesis can be largely assumed at this point.

(1) A Potential Difficulty

Paul's further contentions are introduced in 3:9b with the claim that all — "Jews and Greeks" — are under sin (and it seems significant that the troublesome πρῶτον, which appeared in the three previous instances of this phrase — 1:16, 2:9, and 2:10 — has dropped from sight[125]). It is this claim of universal ethical depravity that will eliminate any further optimism on the part of the Teacher and those persuaded by him. However, my rereading does require a slightly different understanding of the main verb.

The conventional reader understands προητιασάμεθα as a reference to Paul's previous argumentative strategy, so he is the subject of this deponent aorist middle construction in the first person plural: ". . . we have already charged that all, both Jews and Greeks, are under the power of sin . . ." (3:9b). And the signifier ought to be construed in this general sense — that Paul has accused someone (here clearly "all Jews and Greeks" in the appropriate accusative) of something (here of being under sin, as suggested by the infinitive construction). However, my rereading certainly does not expect the further temporal and argumentative inferences in the conventional translation. Paul has *not* been charging "all" of being under sin *in the previous argument* — far from it. But if I cannot provide a plausible alternative construal of this verb, my broader interpretative suggestion will founder significantly on this lexical shoal.

However, there is in fact no need to allow the expectations of Justification theory to shape the specific translation of this verb that only appears here in extant Greek. This exceedingly rare signifier's frame should drive its interpretation. And it seems clear that Paul's reference is not to the argument that precedes 3:9b, but to the material that *follows,* in 3:10-18. Προητιασάμεθα appears in a sentence that goes on to explain its accusations with reference to Scripture, as the immediately following καθώς construction suggests; it is the serried mass of aggressive texts in vv. 10-18 that constitute Paul's accusation. The condemning function of *these texts* is then directly confirmed by v. 19: ". . . whatever the law says, it speaks . . . so that every mouth may be silenced, and the whole world may be held accountable to God." So we ought to construe the verb προαιτιάομαι in a way that makes sense of this following material.

If this verb refers to Paul's citation of Scripture in vv. 10-18, as seems likely, then the prefix προ- is more likely to be taking a spatial rather than a temporal meaning, suggesting that this accusation is public, rather than located in the past. Paul is proclaiming something to the Teacher in front of his Roman Christian audience with his massed citation of Scripture. This is a common enough reading of the prefix προ-, while we lack any extant evidence either way and must rely completely on the immediate context at this point. The first person plural "we" is therefore most likely an "apostolic" we, as it is in 1:5. An authoritative subject is making this charge. Paul, the apostle, is accusing his opponent of serious things with the words and attestation of holy writ. And further options are now created for the construal of the aorist. It is possible that this is an epistolary aorist, referring simply to Paul's public charge through the Scriptures prior to the actual receipt of the letter by the Romans, when the letter was composed (see also Phlm. 12, 21). Alternatively, as Stanley Porter has emphasized, it is not necessary to press the temporal force of the aorist, which is principally a statement of aspect rather than tense.[126] Porter's more general contentions fit 3:9b very well: Paul's public condemnation of the Teacher at Rome in scriptural terms is a completed act, a single event of accusation, and so a perfective notion. It is complete by v. 19. Hence he denotes it in 3:9b in its wholeness, and an aorist is the most appropriate verbal form for this suggestion.[127]

It is worth noting in further support of this reading that it circumvents a nasty conundrum in the conventional construal. The conventional approach views Paul as having attacked the Jew in empirical terms by this point in his argument. And while this critique arguably begins in 2:1, it is usually held to be present principally in the accusations of 2:17-24. But in overdetermination 9 we noted — building on the observations of other revisionists — that this critique was inadequate. In particular, it seemed crudely exaggerated and hence ineffective; it also seemed jaundiced and unfair — the charges that *all* Jews were sinful because of their hypocritical thieving (which is sometimes sacrilegious) and their adultery! (These problems raised the possibility that Romans 2 is not attacking a generic Jew at all.) So the assumption that the conventional reader brings to v. 9a is deeply vulnerable; that Paul *has* accused *everyone* of being under sin in his previous argumentation, especially the Jew, *seems untrue* (while to assume that he has done so is to accept the inadequate assertions of 2:17-24 and the accompanying empirical conundrum concerning the nature of Judaism in general). At best, he has only accused *some* Jews of sinfulness — precisely the thieving, adulterous, sacrilegious ones. And in fact only the catena of vv. 10-18 extends his critique to include all Jews within the ambit of sin. So the conventional reading of προῃτιασάμεθα in 3:9b — that Paul has previously charged all of sin — is not strictly speaking true. This would be a false characterization of the preceding argument, although one that Justification advocates are heavily invested in maintaining. However, if the word's interpretation is reoriented toward what follows rather than the conventional construal of what precedes, this set of difficulties is avoided nicely. Paul is no longer referring to the nature of his preceding argumentative strategy; he is referring quite correctly to his immediate argumentative move, against the Teacher, in charged scriptural terms.

In short, following the indications of the immediate context, and the overarching objectives of the argument (which are not of course oriented toward the humiliation of Jews in general), it seems apparent that in the claims of v. 9a Paul is not pointing backward, to the function of the preceding argument as a whole, so much as forward, to the rest of the sentence and the function of the catena at the close of his argument. While the Teacher has been promulgating a program of salvation that in some respects is essentially optimistic, he accuses that figure — along with any similarly persuaded — of comprehensive and deeply-rooted sinfulness, and he makes this public charge by reciting certain scriptural texts: "What then shall we say? Are we [Jews (as you define them)] advantaged? Apparently not in every respect. Indeed, we publicly accuse *everyone* — Jews as well as non-Jews — of being under sin, in accordance with what is written: 'There is *no one* righteous — *not even one'* . . ." (DC). The result of this charge is then, in v. 19, that "*every* mouth is silenced [including 'those in the law'] and the whole world made accountable to God" (DC), from which conclusion it follows further that "no one will be declared righteous by doing good deeds informed by the law" (i.e., by following the Teacher's gospel).

(2) The Catena's Composition

This approach to the catena in 3:10-18 raises some intriguing possibilities concerning its composition. The artfulness of the massed quotations has already been recognized by the conventional reading. A series of scriptural statements is linked, first by a repeated catchphrase, οὐκ ἔστιν, and then by a shared reference to sinful parts of the body. The final quotation then draws the two organizing motifs together within one statement — οὐκ ἔστιν φόβος θεοῦ ἀπέναντι τῶν ὀφθαλμῶν αὐτῶν. This has prompted consideration whether Paul has created this schema himself or drawn a preformed unit from early Christian tradition (or perhaps even from Jewish tradition). For our purposes, it does not matter which of these causal explanations is correct, although I have no difficulty with the notion of Paul carefully composing this orchestration over the winter months at Corinth; he was a skilful exegete and almost certainly had access there to Jewish Scriptures. More intriguing is a third possibility raised by my overarching construal — that Paul has drawn this set of citations from the Teacher and is now citing it against his system.

Interpreters have considered in the past not merely the origin of the quotations but their exegetical integrity. In particular, scholars have debated the extent to which Paul is being insensitive to the original contexts of these diverse scriptural claims, some seeing little sensitivity to the texts' original settings — so Paul is merely "proof-texting" — and others seeing a deliberate inclusion of contextual "echoes" that adds to the skill of the entire performance. (It is also an open question whether such judgments concerning contextual "[in]sensitivity" are, in phenomenological terms, [in]appropriate.)

The mobilization (or not) of the original settings of Paul's quotations and allusions is a delicate art. And my rereading approaches those settings with different concerns in mind. Rather than an accelerating strategy toward universal indictment, I see of course a barbed engagement with the Teacher's system. But these assumptions may assist us at this point.

It seems to me that *possibly* these were texts assembled and used by the Teacher, and certainly this would be an adroit argumentative maneuver by Paul. The Teacher's own scriptural virtuosity would then be turned decisively against him. In particular, Psalm 14/53 (13/52 LXX) seems to be directed universally and hence at least to include the pagan nations. The remaining texts in the catena are, in their original contexts, directed toward evildoers, another theme of the Teacher's: see Psalm 5:9; Psalm 140:3 (note, the wicked and greedy rich!); Psalm 10:7 (the rich again); Isaiah 59:7-8 (the violent and exploitative, especially in court; see also Prov. 1:16, although here generic sinners — γονεῦσιν ἀπειθεῖς!); and Psalm 36:1 (an inveterate, self-deceiving sinner).[128] And these emphases certainly fit the agenda of the Teacher. Was a fiery opening along the lines of 1:18-32 followed by the massed condemnation of 3:10-18?! (They do read nicely end-to-end.)

But all these texts also contain treatments of δικαιοσύνη θεοῦ in context (although in some cases implicitly).[129] This point has not yet been established, because it is treated in detail in chapter seventeen in relation to 1:16-17 and 3:21-26. Suffice it then for now to note that the root metaphor generally in view in relation to this important phrase — and hence arguably in these texts concerning God — is essentially compassionate and liberative, not retributive. And this may tilt the balance of opinion toward Pauline composition rather than the Teacher's. (He is also of course the default position for any attribution.)[130]

However, even this consideration is far from overwhelming. The original settings may not be significantly in play in relation to the quotations, and the Teacher may have been insensitive in any case to this "root" meaning, or he may even have been supplying his own alternative, and rather harsher, readings. Alternatively, both might be drawing on an early church discourse at this point. Hence, it seems to me that this question must be left essentially open as a suggestive possibility. Fortunately, it does not alter my overarching rereading; it merely nuances the sophistication and "bite" of the final move in the argument. Has Paul turned the Teacher's own quotations against him in 3:10-18? It seems quite possible — and would be an argumentative triumph — but more than this is hard to prove.

(3) Problems Solved

More important than the causality of the quotations is the set of difficulties that my rereading resolves.

We have noted earlier at some length how Justification theory contains two inherently contradictory epistemologies — an anthropocentric, universal, cognitive approach to knowledge, and a more particular approach developed principally in relation to Jewish history, revelation, and Scripture.[131] This tension becomes manifest within the conventional reading particularly acutely in 3:10-18, when this block of statements, grounded in a particular sacred written tradition and so deriving its legitimacy from that setting and within that setting only, overwhelms in argumentative terms a set of principles derived from the philosophical contemplation of the cosmos. Strictly speaking, this refutation is invalid. (Imagine citing the Bible in a philosophy seminar to disprove a theorem that seemed valid on general grounds!) The conventional reading, however, has no alternative but to embrace this contradiction wholeheartedly, attributing both epistemologies to Paul — and relying on the truth of both for the ultimate validity of the theory that he is supposedly articulating! It is, then, one of the great advantages of my rereading to be able to dispose of this tension.

This epistemological contradiction is part of the Teacher's system, not Paul's. It is the Teacher who foolishly begins his program in rhetorical terms on the basis of philosophical knowledge but switches throughout to endorsements that are drawn from the particularities of Jewish tradition (and that he probably views as basic). So in deploying a mass of Jewish scriptural quotations in order to refute the Teacher's program, Paul is not embracing a contradiction so much as exploiting one. The Teacher accepts this authority, as does Paul's audience, so its introduction is valid in argumentative terms. Its delay until this point in the argument, after some exploration of several of the internal difficulties caused by the Teacher's initial embrace of philosophical notions, is essentially for rhetorical effect. The Teacher's position has been broken down by degrees, and initially in terms of its own explicit assumptions. Now an external authority — which the Teacher nevertheless clearly acknowledges — is introduced to refute it definitively (if, that is, this block is not the Teacher's own exegetical work).

It is, quite simply, an enormous relief to be able to liberate Paul's conceptuality from the tensions caused by the apparent endorsement of two entirely different epistemological modes; this is the major difficulty resolved by my suggested rereading at this juncture. It remains only to note the argument's conclusion, in 3:19-20.

6.3. *Romans 3:19-20*

My rereading construes the application of Paul's famous assertions in 3:19-20 differently from the conventional interpretation, without significantly altering their meaning. These concluding comments have four components that can be usefully treated in turn.

(1) Οἴδαμεν δὲ ὅτι ὅσα ὁ νόμος λέγει τοῖς ἐν τῷ νόμῳ λαλεῖ

I am not sure that resolving the ambiguity in the function of the dative phrase here alters anything substantial. (Is this best translated as the object of the first or the second verb of speaking — "we know that whatsoever the law says to those in the law, it says so that . . . ," or "we know that whatsoever the law says, it says to those in the law, so that . . . "?)[132] Certainly, it does not affect my interpretation. The more important point is perhaps simply my explanation of exactly why Paul is emphasizing here that the law speaks to "those in the law." The conventional reading identifies these figures as "Jews," arguing for a universal application, however, by suggesting that "[a]ll the world can really be pronounced guilty if even the righteous is"[133] (or reasoning in some similar fashion). However, my rereading identifies these figures in relation to the Teacher, who is certainly "in the law," and in fact is clearly identified by the preceding argument as such (see esp. 2:17-20); indeed, his identification in these terms could not be clearer. So I suggest that the first component in Paul's conclusion includes the Teacher within the constituency addressed by the string of scriptural charges (i.e., without naming him directly; Paul wishes to perpetuate the illusion that he is speaking in somewhat generalized terms).

(2) ἵνα πᾶν στόμα φραγῇ καὶ ὑπόδικος γένηται πᾶς ὁ κόσμος τῷ θεῷ

This purpose clause then makes the appropriate application of the scriptural condemnation for Paul's present argumentative purposes. He has shown earlier how the Teacher's solution is effectively meaningless, the Teacher's claims in relation to circumcision, Jewish identity, and the law being overruled by the implacable operation on the day of judgment of the principle of desert. However, the scriptural charges have deepened the Teacher's woes. They assert with an undeniable massed testimony that *the Teacher himself, along with all his righteous followers, will be condemned* in terms of his opening assumptions and their subsequent development. No one will escape damnation, given the Teacher's characterization of the cosmos's basic situation before God. Hence, he himself is reduced to silence! (And this is the ideal goal in any diatribe — the reduction of a foolish interlocutor to silence, his protests stilled.[134]) The Teacher's preaching of a solution is ineffective, and his preaching of the problem ends up with the entire cosmos and himself being arraigned — some gospel! And the appropriate response to this devastating refutation — and largely in terms of the system's own assumptions — is silence.

In doing so, it is also worth noting that Paul has artfully brought his discussion almost full circle. The Teacher's proclamation to pagans begins by emphasizing their "lack of excuse" (ἀναπολόγητος), a conundrum that Paul promised to turn on the Teacher himself in 2:1. And by this point in this argument, clearly he has done so. With the Teacher's mouth stopped, he too is revealed to be "without excuse" or "accountable" — the probable meaning of the rare word ὑπόδικος that Paul uses in 3:19.[135]

(3) διότι ἐξ ἔργων νόμου οὐ δικαιωθήσεται πᾶσα σὰρξ ἐνώπιον αὐτοῦ

Paul now deploys one of his most important intertexts to articulate this conclusion clearly, and also to do so authoritatively, with scriptural backing.[136] He quotes Psalm 143:2b (142:2b LXX), suitably nuanced.[137] Significantly, this is only the second time that the phrase "works of law" has occurred in the entire argument (and the first instance was an uncharacteristic singular construction, in Rom. 2:15). But the most important data surrounding this important motif is yet to be considered. (It occurs later in Romans 10, and in Galatians.) May I suggest for the moment, then, that my rereading opens up a critical interpretative strategy as a possibility for this phrase and its attendant theological associations (which tend to be negative) — a strategy, sketched in outline in chapter thirteen, that we will revisit and corroborate further in due course (see esp. chapters eighteen, where an intertextual basis for this phrase is posited, and nineteen and twenty, discussing Romans 9–10 and Galatians respectively).

The motif "works of law" summarizes the Teacher's "gospel" to Paul's pagan converts; it denotes the Teacher's stern admonitions to observe the law, including circumcision of course, but, following the completion of that ritual, including everything else that is prescribed in the Torah as well. Paul's point, then, made by quoting Psalm 143:2b, is very simple — and not a little triumphant. In terms of that gospel's own assumptions, both philosophical and scriptural, it appears that no one can in fact be saved, because no one is righteous, and can be pronounced as such by God, through (mere) circumcision and law-observance. These activities cannot change sinful human nature (as Paul presumably knew well personally). And the Jewish Bible has even anticipated this sorry situation for Paul, predicting the system's futility. (Paul will in due course also provide his own theological nuancing of the verb here — δικαιόω — since his understandings of both the character of God and the final judgment are so different from the Teacher's.)[138] We turn, then, to Paul's final comment.

(4) διὰ γὰρ νόμου ἐπίγνωσις ἁμαρτίας

I suspect that this functions rather like the two parentheses we have already noted that principally point forward in the argument (see 2:16b and 2:29). However, it is also a fair comment on what has just taken place, making a brief but shrewd observation in relation to the Teacher's program, so it does not seem to be completely parenthetical in function.

In its immediate setting this comment affirms the argumentative move that Paul has just made in 3:10-18. The law — reading νόμος broadly at this point as

"Scripture" — does indeed seem only to offer a sustained statement of universal human sinfulness, which generates in turn the awkward problem for the Teacher that his gospel now saves no one. But this comment is also almost certainly a parting shot at the function of the law in the Teacher's entire system.

The Teacher promises life from this activity. The law is a path for the blind, a light for those in darkness, and so on (see 2:17-20). Doubtless, then, he holds out the law as a way to righteousness and life. Paul, however, pithily contradicts this. He holds that the law reveals not righteousness but sin, and not life but death — not God's benevolent and saving verdict of "righteous," but evidence of involvement in a kingdom of death. The statement that "through the law" comes only the recognition of sinfulness (3:20b) is therefore a negation of a key activity within the Teacher's gospel.

Now this claim may simply be an argumentative move on Paul's part — a refutation of a key part of the Teacher's program — and consequently a little arbitrary in hermeneutical terms. Indeed, we have not yet asked why Paul reads the law so pessimistically; why does he feel entitled to arrange a series of scriptural quotations that, in combination, speak only of human depravity?

It will emerge eventually in Romans that this compact claim is grounded in Paul's own convictions about human and Christian ontology (at which points he has fundamental theological disagreements with the Teacher). In the powerful alternative soteriology articulated by Romans 5–8 (and adumbrated here in part one, chapter three) it is apparent that, for Paul, all those without the Spirit of Christ are mired in Adam's narrative and being, where the forces of Sin and Death roam unchecked. Consequently, the law for Christians becomes a mere plaything of evil forces that entraps and executes. It generates sinful possibilities. It is this broader theological discussion that Paul may well be alluding to in 3:20b, in addition to making his more obvious and localized points.

"Sin" is the object of a verb of knowledge in Romans again only in 7:7, in which text — and context — the law is clearly involved as well!: . . . τὴν ἁμαρτίαν οὐκ ἔγνων εἰ μὴ διὰ νόμου. Indeed, this statement stands at the head of Paul's most extensive extant analysis of the law's relationship with Sin. It also follows another extended analysis of Sin, in Romans 6. So it seems fair to at least suggest that the short negation of 3:20b is pointing ahead to these detailed discussions that follow, in addition to making localized points (and see the discussion of 3:21-26 in chapters fifteen through seventeen for a similar function by that text). Certainly it coordinates the three motifs that those later discussions analyze in detail, *and in these basic terms*. We may well come at this point then to the nub of Paul's difficulties with the Teacher's gospel (which have already been noted in part): *it will not work*. That is, his purported solution to the problem of ongoing pagan sinfulness through circumcision and law is, in Paul's opinion, impotent. In terms of his own system then, any eschatological verdict is bound to be negative as well (and this is the most useful contingent emphasis for Paul, because it reduces the Teacher to silence). Note, however, that Paul's overt rejection of the Teacher's ethic also arguably calls the broader theological and eschatological settings of that ethic into question as well; if God is just and humanity — including Jews — deeply sinful, then no one can be saved. But if God *has* saved humanity, we must probably speak not just of a different ethic, but of a different divine nature as well. The Teacher's gospel is, in short, probably wrong in *every* respect.

§7. A Repunctuation of the NRSV — Romans 1:16–3:20

It might be helpful to supply a text at this point that is punctuated in accordance with my suggested rereading. In the rendering below, I have used the NRSV, altered only at critical points. It is important to appreciate, however, that there are two senses in which the voice of the Teacher can be detected in this material. There are certain instances where Paul attributes material to the Teacher directly, using the technique of προσωποποιία. In these texts the Teacher in effect speaks for himself (although suitably crafted by Paul, of course) — first in the opening of his usual conversion speech (1:18-32), and then later in dialogue with Paul (3:1-9). However, for much of the rest of the argument Paul is quoting the Teacher's teaching, and rather sarcastically, and this is entirely consistent with his main rhetorical goal throughout the section, which is to refute the Teacher in terms of his own gospel. In this second layer of material (mainly in chapter 2), Paul tends to redeploy the Teacher's teaching and use it against him. The Teacher's voice is still discernible, but it is not understood to be proceeding directly from his mouth, so to speak. In what follows, the Teacher's material is italicized, with his actual voice denoted by quotation marks as well.

> [1:16]For I am not ashamed of the gospel; it is the power of God for salvation to everyone who has faith, *to the Jew first and also to the Greek.* [17]For in it the righteousness of God is revealed through faith for faith; as it is written, "The one who is righteous will live by faith."
>
> [18]*"For the wrath of God is revealed from heaven against all ungodliness and wickedness of those who by their wickedness suppress the truth.*
>
> [19]*For what can be known about God is plain to them, because God has shown it to them.* [20]*Ever since the creation of the world his eternal power and divine nature, invisible though they are, have been understood and seen through the things he has made. So they are without excuse;*
>
> [21]*for though they knew God, they did not honor him as God or give thanks to him, but they became futile in their thinking, and their senseless minds were darkened.* [22]*Claiming to be wise, they became fools;* [23]*and they exchanged the glory of the immortal God for images resembling a mortal human being or birds or four-footed animals or reptiles.*
>
> [24]*Therefore God gave them up in the lusts of their hearts to impurity, to the degrading of their bodies among themselves,* [25]*because they exchanged the*

*truth about God for a lie and worshiped and served the creature rather
than the Creator, who is blessed forever! Amen.* [26]*For this reason God gave
them up to degrading passions. Their women exchanged natural inter-
course for unnatural,* [27]*and in the same way also the men, giving up natural intercourse with women, were consumed with passion for one another.
Men committed shameless acts with men and received in their own persons the due penalty for their error.*

[28]*And since they did not see fit to acknowledge God, God gave them up to
a debased mind and to things that should not be done.* [29]*They were filled
with every kind of*

wickedness, evil, covetousness, malice.
  Full of envy, murder, strife, deceit, craftiness,
    they are gossips, [30]*slanderers, God-haters, insolent, haughty,
      boastful,*
      inventors of evil, rebellious toward parents,
      [31]*foolish, faithless, heartless, ruthless.*

[32]*They know God's decree, that those who practice such things deserve to
die — yet they not only do them but even applaud others who practice
them."*

[2:1]Therefore you have no excuse . . .[139] when you judge others; for in passing
judgment on another you condemn yourself, because you, the judge, are
doing the very same things.[140] [2]You say, *we know that God's judgment on
those who do such things is in accordance with truth.* [3]*Do you imagine*[141] that
when you judge *those who do such things* and yet do them yourself, you *will
escape the judgment of God?* [4]*Or do you despise the riches of his kindness and
forbearance and patience? Do you not realize that God's kindness is meant to
lead you to repentance?* [5]*But by your hard and impenitent heart you are storing up wrath for yourself on the day of wrath, when God's righteous judgment
will be revealed.* [6]*For he will repay according to each one's deeds:* [7]*to those
who by patiently doing good seek for glory and honor and immortality, he will
give eternal life;* [8]*while for those who are self-seeking and who obey not the
truth but wickedness, there will be wrath and fury.* [9]*There will be anguish and
distress for everyone who does evil, the Jew first and also the Greek,*[142] [10]*but
glory and honor and peace for everyone who does good, the Jew first and also
the Greek.* [11]*For God does not respect mere appearance.*[143] [12]*All who have
sinned apart from the law* [literally "lawlessly"] *will also perish apart from
the law* ["lawlessly"], *and all who have sinned under the law will be judged by
the law.*[144] [13]*For it is not the hearers of the law who will be*[145] *righteous in
God's sight, but the doers of the law who will be justified . . .*[146] ([14][for] [w]hen
Gentiles, who do not possess the law, do instinctively what the law requires,
these, though not having the law, are a law to themselves; [15][t]hey show that
what the law requires is written on their hearts, to which their own con-

science also bears witness; and their conflicting thoughts will accuse or perhaps excuse them)[147] [16]. . . *on the day when . . . God will judge the secret thoughts of all* (according to my gospel, through Jesus Christ).[148]

[17]But if you call yourself a Jew and *rely on the law and boast of your relation to God* [18]*and know his will and determine what is best because you are instructed in the law,* [19]*and if you are sure that you are a guide to the blind, a light to those who are in darkness,* [20]*a corrector of the foolish, a teacher of children, having in the law the embodiment of knowledge and truth,* [21]you, then, that teach others, will you not teach yourself? While you preach against stealing, do you steal? [22]You that forbid adultery, do you commit adultery? You that abhor idols, do you rob temples? [23]You that boast in the law, do you dishonor God by breaking the law? [24]For, as it is written, "The name of God is blasphemed among the Gentiles because of you."

[25]*Circumcision indeed is of value* if you obey the law; but if you break the law, your circumcision has become uncircumcision. [26]So, if those who are uncircumcised keep the requirements of the law, will not their uncircumcision be regarded as circumcision? [27]Then those who are physically uncircumcised but keep the law will condemn you that have the written code and circumcision but break the law. [28]For a person is not *a Jew* who *is one outwardly,* nor is true circumcision something external and physical. [29]Rather, a person is *a Jew who is one inwardly, and real circumcision is a matter of the heart* ([and possible in fact only] by the Spirit, not the letter[149]). *Such a person receives praise not from others but from God.*[150]

[3:1]Then what advantage has the Jew? Or what is the value of circumcision?

[2]"*Much, in every way. For in the first place the Jews were entrusted with the oracles of God.*"

[3]What if some were unfaithful? Will their faithlessness nullify the faithfulness of God?

[4]"*By no means! Although everyone is a liar, let God be proved true, as it is written, 'So that you may be justified in your words, and prevail when you are being judged.'*"[151]

[5]But if our injustice serves to confirm the justice of God, what should we say? That God is unjust to inflict wrath on us? (I speak in a human way.)

[6]"*By no means! For then how could God judge the world?*"

[7]But if through my falsehood God's truthfulness abounds to his glory, why am I still being condemned as a sinner? [8]And why not say — as some people slander us by saying that we say — that we should do evil so that good may come?[152]

"*Their condemnation is deserved!*"

[9]What then? Are we any better off?

"*No, not in every respect.*"[153]

[Moreover] we have [together, by reading Scripture] charged all publicly, both Jews and Greeks, of being under the power of sin,[154] [10]as it is written:

> "There is no one who is righteous, not even one;
> [11]there is no one who has understanding, there is no one who seeks God.
> [12]All have turned aside, together they have become worthless;
> there is no one who shows kindness, there is not even one."[155]

> [13]"Their throats are opened graves;
> they use their tongues to deceive."
> "The venom of vipers is under their lips."
> [14]"Their mouths are full of cursing and bitterness."
> [15]"Their feet are swift to shed blood;
> [16]ruin and misery are in their paths,
> [17]and the way of peace they have not known."
> [18]"There is no fear of God before their eyes."

[19]Now we know that whatever the law says, it speaks to those who are under the law, *so that every mouth may be silenced, and the whole world may be held accountable to God.* [20]For "no human being will be justified in his sight" by deeds prescribed by the law, for through the law comes the knowledge of sin.[156]

§8. Summary of the Argument in Propositional Form

Note, I have summarized the argument in what follows more propositionally than rhetorically, to illuminate its inherent rationality and coherence rather than its dramatic and persuasive force when it is oriented toward the progressive humiliation of the Teacher's gospel before the Roman Christians.

The first phase (1:18-32) — the Teacher's rhetorical opening

1a. The impious and unrighteous pagans deservedly face the future wrathful judgment of God.
1b. They know the truth about God despite God being invisible. His nature and will are perceived by means of a noetic appreciation of the things that have been made — information clearly present since the world's creation.
1c. The pagans suppress this, however, and trade in the true Creator-God for falsehood deliberately.
1d. This renders them culpable — "without excuse."
1e. In view of this, God allows them to degenerate further, following their sinful desires into idolatry and sexual perversion, and ultimately into all manner of wickedness. They are now caught in their corrupt nature.

1f. Pagan culpability is especially well established since they encourage others to be wicked, despite knowing that God justly decrees that those doing such things deserve death.

The second phase (2:1-8) — Paul's universalization

2a. Anyone who censoriously proclaims this critique condemning sinful pagans will *also* not escape God's wrath on sinful acts if he or she commits them.

2b. (Implicitly) to deny this would be inconsistent and hypocritical.

2c. Apparently a time is granted before the judgment for repentance; here the kindness, patience, and forbearance of God operate temporarily, and it is essentially irrational to despise this opportunity to repent of transgression(s) — irrational on the part of sinful pagans *and* those who condemn them hypocritically!

2d. Informing all that has been said thus far under 1 (see 2a!) is the view that every person will eventually be judged by God justly (i.e., retributively or in terms of desert), and consequently in accordance with his or her works or deeds. (See 1a-f above.)

2e. Therefore, good deeds will be rewarded with honor and life. People persistently doing these deeds will be declared righteous by God at the judgment, and will inherit the age to come.

2f. Bad deeds will be recompensed with trouble and death. They will be declared unrighteous, and condemned. (See 1f.)

2g. The presence of sinful passions in the pagans, however, suggests that everyone will either be declared entirely bad, or entirely good (if, presumably, those passions have been neutralized).

The third phase (2:9-29) — the awkward implications
The possibilities of Jewish sinners and pagan saints

3a. But good deeds must therefore be rewarded with honor and life *irrespective of whether Jews or pagans do them*. So righteous pagans are a possibility under this system.

3b. And bad deeds must also be recompensed with trouble and death *irrespective of whether Jews or pagans do them*. So unrighteous Jews are a possibility under this system as well.

3c. Reinforcing this claim is the scriptural adage (quoted often by 2a) that "God is not concerned with mere appearances."

3d. It is invalid to object at this point that pagans cannot be declared righteous because they do not possess the law to inform their deeds. The argument has already conceded the existence of a law within the nature of pagans sufficient to establish culpability, *and hence also to underwrite righteousness*. (See 1b.)

3e. This claim of "innate possession" of the law is also verified by inner mental debate within the conscience — debate precisely over right and wrong.

3f. Note that this construal of the final judgment makes no reference to Christ (nor, strictly speaking, can it).

The dubious benefits of learning in the law

3g. A teacher can claim to have many benefits from learning in the law. Such learning is sufficient to instruct others in the way of good deeds.

3h. But it is of course still incumbent upon such a figure to practice what he preaches.

3i. Certain notorious Jewish teachers and charlatans previously operative in Rome — specifically through deceit, immorality, theft, and desecration — now demonstrate that possession of the law, and even learning in it, do not *automatically* protect from sin and the sinful passions. Such figures will not escape the appropriate final judgment; they will get what they deserve.

The problem with circumcision

3j. Clearly circumcision too only gives an advantage if the rest of the law is also kept.

3k. To fail at any point is effectively to become uncircumcised, especially in the sense of demonstrating the inability of that ritual alone to produce a perfectly obedient person.

3l. Correspondingly, the uncircumcised who do good deeds — i.e., the righteous pagans implicit in 2e and overtly established by 3a, c, d, and e — do not need literal bodily circumcision in order to cut off the sinful passions.

3m. Consequently, an uncircumcised but righteous pagan might end up condemning a sinful Jew, circumcised but wicked, on the day of judgment — a reversal of the traditional expectation that righteous, circumcised, law-observant Jews will condemn unrighteous pagans!

3n. Recall also that appearance is irrelevant. (See 3c.) A "true Jew" is now someone merely circumcised in the heart and *not* necessarily also in the body!

3o. (In fact, true circumcision of the heart in the sense of the sinful passions can only be effected by the divine Spirit, and not by anything merely human or hand-held.)

3p. Circumcision is clearly ineffective by itself for dealing comprehensively with humanity's sinful nature.

The fourth phase (3:1-20) — the taming of the Teacher

4a. Traditional Jewish advantages like circumcision and possession of the law are therefore not necessarily of any ultimate (i.e., eschatological) advantage. The principle of divine retribution will still apply to Jewish sinners.

4b. Divine leniency is impossible. The rule of divine judgment must be maintained at all costs.

4c. To suggest that a lenient God could be glorified as he helps sinners (i.e., for his benevolence and mercy) is also to come too close to the suggestion that one *ought* to sin so that God might be glorified — an overtly false libertine position.

4d. Those suggesting this — and those suggesting that Paul said this — ought to be condemned.

4e. Hence, a Jew defined in the foregoing terms has no real advantage in relation to the day of judgment, and can expect no leniency in relation to sinful behavior.

4f. The Scriptures state repeatedly and hence unavoidably and emphatically that *all* are sinful, and *comprehensively* so. *No one* is in fact righteous.

4g. The teacher accepts the authority of the Scriptures of course.

4h. It follows now that all — including any and all teachers of the law — will be held culpable and condemned on the day of judgment. No one will be declared righteous, and certainly not by doing deeds informed by the Jewish law.

4i. The Scriptures in fact predicted this situation.

Conclusion

By this point in Romans it is apparent that the Teacher's gospel is incoherent. Its opening — a definition of "the problem" facing all pagans (1) — leads to a set of contradictions in relation to its continuation (2 & 3) — its purported solution in terms of circumcision and law-observance — that ultimately overrule and undermine it (4). Properly understood, this gospel — understood in its own terms — saves no one, not even its proclaimer!

§9. Problems Solved

It is significant to note finally how many of the difficulties previously detected in the conventional reading of Romans 1–4 have now been solved — the principal argument in favor of this rereading's validity.

Underdeterminations

The four underdeterminations noted in relation to 1:18–3:20 have clearly been eliminated.

UD 1 Paul does not commit himself overtly here to a preaching strategy that "sets the scene" for the proclamation of the gospel because that is not what the argument in 1:18–3:20 is doing. Indeed, it is doing almost the converse; it is undermining an opposing gospel that begins by "setting the scene" — and rather foolishly, as it turns out, because its initial account of the problem does not match its later articulation of a solution. (But in adopting this rhetorical strategy, it is also easy to see why interpreters have mistakenly supposed that Paul is setting the scene — a mistake easily made once the text's original performative cues have been lost.)

UD 2 Similarly, Paul does not commit himself overtly to the basicality of humanity's essential rationality and capacity and God's retributive justice because those are not his positions but rather those underpinning the Teacher's rhetorical proem. He has no such evident commitments. (And neither probably does the Teacher; Paul is merely forcing him to be consistent with his opening premises, spying certain significant rhetorical advantages that flow from this.)

UD 3 The argumentative "turn" in 2:1 is also now fully explicable. Interpreters do not have to supply the additional premises that Paul is turning here on Judaism as a whole, including himself (at least in his previous life), because he is not. He is turning on the figure that he says he is turning on: a learned judger of others who also sins — someone ultimately unveiled as the Teacher.

UD 4 Finally, the troubling perfectionist axiom regarding law observance is not stated explicitly here because the argument is simply not functioning in these terms. Paul is not trying to drive everyone to Christianity, without exception, for which he needs a perfectionist axiom. The statement of desert can in fact be read just as it stands. It is implicit in just this sense (i.e., not in a perfectionist sense) in the Teacher's proem, and Paul exploits all the embarrassing possibilities that are latent in this concession. (Moreover — and somewhat ironically — the Teacher does seem committed to perfectionist law observance once the sinful nature has been circumcised, but Paul clearly does not share this optimism regarding either the efficacy of circumcision or the ethical capacity of unredeemed human nature.[157]) Perfectionism is not stated overtly, then, because it is not actually part of the unfolding argument. (It is possible, in the Teacher's opinion, once the sinful passions have been cut off by circumcision.)

Overdeterminations

We noted no fewer than eleven overdeterminations in relation to the conventional reading of 1:18–3:20; these too have all been eliminated by my suggested rereading.

OD 1 The distinctive style of 1:18-32 is now nicely explained as a sign that Paul is speaking in the voice of another — of the rather pompous and censorious Teacher.

OD 2 The strange programmatic function of 1:18 in the present rather than the future (where the disclosure of God's wrath with wrongdoing really lies) is now comprehensible as an indication that Paul is indeed introducing an alternative program (see 1:16-17), to which this statement stands as something of a thesis statement. Fundamentally different conceptions of God are at stake in the Teacher's and Paul's gospels, the Teacher's gospel beginning with a revelation of God's anger with pagan sinfulness that anticipates an angry eschaton — in colloquial terms, a "turn or burn" strategy. And 1:18 signals this in advance by way of its censorious future present construction.

OD 3 The rather unjust, collective analysis of 1:18-32 is now understandable as a brief intrusion of the Teacher's basic inconsistencies; he wishes to begin his preaching with a discourse of culpability but in fact holds (like many other Jewish exponents of this discourse) that humanity — and especially pagan humanity — is not fully capacitated but corrupted and enslaved to evil passions. So his opening includes this dimension as well, although it ultimately proves very problematic. Pagans have, in his view, declined en masse into depravity.

OD 4 The heavy and somewhat troublesome dependence of Romans 1–3 on the Wisdom of Solomon seems rooted in the Teacher's dependence on at least parts of that text. Paul therefore uses it to enhance his own presentation of the Teacher's position. This now seems both understandable and argumentatively and theologically appropriate.

OD 5 The further embarrassing implications of the argument's turn in 2:1 are also now perfectly explained. Most importantly, this is neither a nasty caricature of Judaism nor an inexplicable attack on hypocrisy among the Roman Christians but a turn on the Teacher himself, universalizing the commitments of his proem, from which maneuver the rest of the argument flows.

OD 6 It is also now comprehensible why repentance is introduced prematurely (in terms of the expectations of Justification theory) in 2:4b-5a, before the problem of universal sinfulness has been established, and appropriately contrite individuals are ready to turn to God in faith and be saved. This is where the motif functions in the Teacher's discourse; he summons godless and abandoned pagans to repentance at precisely this point — but in terms of circumcision and law-observance. (The former should enable the latter, and a resulting eschatological verdict of "righteous.") Paul of course now presses the Teacher himself in these terms, however. He asks archly if the Teacher is taking his own advice at this point (and, in view of the testimony of Scripture massed in 3:10-18, it seems that he is not).

OD 7 We also know why 2:6-9 (extending on through v. 12) contains such pristine categories of good and wicked people. The Teacher views humanity in these starkly antithetical terms, with one constituency enslaved to wicked desires but the other liberated by circumcision and controlled by the law and therefore perfectly righteous. These ontological distinctions entail quite discrete categories of humanity — one largely good (i.e., circumcised and law-observant Jews), the other largely bad (i.e., recalcitrant Jews and the pagans).

OD 8 Furthermore, Paul's brief parenthesis in 2:16b is entirely understandable. He is indeed briefly noting that "his" gospel contains an utterly divergent account of matters from that currently being expounded, interpreting Christ's implications and role in a fundamentally different way from the Teacher, even in relation to the judgment.

OD 9 It is of course a great relief to be able to link the Jewish figure of 2:17 with its textual antecedents but interpret him now as a singular instance rather than a representative of Judaism. Similarly, the crudeness *and* specificity of the attack on this figure in 2:21-22 is now comprehensible: Paul is alluding to the sordid events that were widely held to inform the Jewish expulsion by Tiberius in 19 CE, an apposite episode to recall as Jewish sages (whose motives he suspects) are again approaching Rome. Hence, this critique is entirely specific and in no way relevant to Jews universally (which would make it an exaggerated and incompetent argument). Here, rather, it simply makes the point that Jews learned in the law can still sin, as certain well-known examples indicate. Hence, it seems that mere possession of the law — although including here apparent learning in it — is no automatic guarantee of ethical behavior. And one of the most infamous problems in the conventional reading of Romans 1–3 has thereby been neatly resolved.

OD 10 A second infamous difficulty concerns the repeated appearance in Paul's argument of pagan figures justified by works (esp. in 2:14-15 and 26-29) — an awful embarrassment for Justification theory, however they are interpreted. But these too are now understandable precisely *as* embarrassing projections of the Teacher's opening assumptions (see 1:18-32; 2:6-8). They embarrass the Teacher's demand for circumcision and conversion, and his definition of "true Judaism," even mocking sinful Jews at the judgment; this is in fact their very intention. Indeed, these figures turn out to be one of the most sophisticated and telling argumentative developments in Paul's entire critique. They make a mockery of the Teacher's definition of Jews and Judaism.

OD 11 Similarly, the rather appalling abandonment of physical circumcision and redefinition of "true Judaism" that takes place as a result is now also explained as one further step within Paul's progressive embarrassment of the Teacher's gospel in relation to its inconsistencies. The implications of the Teacher's opening assumptions can be shown to vitiate some of his later important claims. Moreover, the argumentative shortfall implicit here in relation to Justification theory, is no longer a difficulty (i.e., the inappropriate overruling of the specific Jewish ethic by the more general pagan one). It is precisely Paul's intention to press such awkward implications. In short, the centuries of embarrassment suffered by exegetes at these points can now be safely redeposited in the lap of the Teacher, and Paul's clever exposure here of his inconsistencies.

So it can be seen that all of the puzzles and contradictions that have dogged previous conventional attempts to read Romans 1–3 — a formidable list! — have been explained by my suggested rereading. Not one remains. But what of the further twenty-one intrinsic, systematic, and empirical difficulties that were noted in relation to Justification theory, once the conventional reading of Romans 1–3 has been accepted and its ostensible theory of salvation identified as his gospel — that is, difficulties arising at the theoretical level in relation to the rest of Romans and Paul's thinking in general?

Intrinsic Difficulties

Five of the seven intrinsic argumentative difficulties (IDs 1-5) have been disposed of, and the resolution of a sixth (ID 6) — an important conundrum — is now apparent as well. Five of the ten systematic difficulties (SDs 1-3 and 9-10) have also been resolved, with significant contributions to the resolution of two more (SDs 4 and 7). And one of the four empirical difficulties has been eliminated — the well-known Jewish conundrum (ED 1) — with significant progress toward elimination of the remaining three (EDs 2-4).[158] Hence, well over half of our difficulties with the conventional reading through Romans 1–4 as a whole have been dealt with by this rereading of 1:18–3:20, whether explicitly or implicitly. So clearly we are well on our way to a complete solution to all our difficulties in this relation.

ID 1 At the argumentative level, as soon as the premises of 1:18-32 are relocated to the Teacher's gospel rather than Paul's, all the various contradictions that they generate are ameliorated. So the presence of two epistemologies in Paul is resolved as the general, philosophical approach is shifted to the Teacher's proem.

ID 2 The argumentative embarrassment that the series of naturally and universally revealed propositions in 1:18-32 is invalid is resolved in the same way. The Teacher is committed to the invalid progression, not Paul.

ID 3 The presence of two different sets of ethical codes of equal validity in the pre-Christian situation — a more minimal pagan system and an extensive Jewish system — can be dealt with in the same way. This is a projection of the Teacher's proem and has nothing to do with Paul's views on such matters.

ID 4/5 The incoherent anthropology, presupposing capacity and incapacity simultaneously, and the acute problem of theodicy that it generates are likewise revealed to be tensions that lie at the heart of the Teacher's system. Rather ironically, then, Paul has been blamed for a set of difficulties that he was entirely familiar with and was in fact trying to exploit for the benefit of the Roman Christians! (We will postpone consideration of ID 6 — the justification of Christ's atonement — for the next chapter, although part of the solution to that set of riddles is already apparent.[159])

Systematic Difficulties

SD 1/2/3 Some of the argumentative difficulties just noted have a dual role, arising again at the systematic frame as tensions in relation to the rest of

Paul's thought. So the contradiction between two different epistemological modes noted as ID 1 contains one mode — general and philosophical — that seems to be opposed by everything that Paul says elsewhere, generating SD 1. Similarly, the anthropological capacity that generates ID 4 in relation to the incapacity that Romans 3 ends by affirming also causes a systematic difficulty, because Paul elsewhere seems committed consistently to incapacity — SD 2. (There will also be a knock-on effect at this point for SD 7 — a coherent ethic.) Moreover, the basic conception of God operative from 1:18 in terms of retributive justice, so ID 5, seems contradicted by Paul's commitment elsewhere to a fundamentally compassionate God — SD 3. However, all these difficulties dissipate when it is realized that the principles causing them are located in the Teacher's proem rather than Paul himself (and, once again, Paul wants to exploit these tensions; he is profoundly aware of the issues at stake).

SD 9 Likewise, Paul's overarching depiction of Judaism is released from the need to accommodate a strangely ahistorical, monolithic, contractual definition, since that approach is rooted in both a misattribution of these premises to Paul and a misconstrual of the argument. Paul is not discussing Judaism per se in Romans 1–3. And it should be noted that even the Teacher's definition of Judaism is elicited from him by Paul here rather cunningly; that is, *the Teacher himself would probably not have endorsed the depiction of Judaism that he was presented with in Romans 1–3.*[160] (Whether he could have rejected it coherently is of course another matter.) Paul has cornered him in terms of some of unwise initial assumptions, on pain of embarrassing self-contradiction! So SD 9 is certainly ameliorated.

SD 10 Similarly, it is the Teacher's initial commitment to the wrath of God that generates any subsequent endorsement by the text of a coercive and violent response to wrongdoing and most of the consequent tension with Paul's commitments elsewhere to more forgiving and peaceful practices. So the tensions of SD 10 are mitigated as well. (And this will add to the probable contribution being made to the amelioration of SD 4 — the nature of the atonement.)

Empirical Difficulties

ED 1 Finally, the tensions caused by Paul's apparent description of Judaism in Romans 1–3 are now eliminated. This is not necessarily to suggest that *all* the descriptive problems raised by Paul's writings in relation to Judaism have been dealt with, but it is to claim that a significant number of them have been — and some of the most crude and awkward at that. As we have just seen with the equivalent systematic difficulty, the "definition" of Judaism that has previously been thought to operate in Romans 1–3 is actually an aggressive polemical derivation from the Teacher's rhetorical premises by Paul. So it no longer needs to play any role in a description of Paul's thinking at all. And in fact neither Paul nor the Teacher is making broader descriptive claims about Judaism in Romans 1–3; the stringently perfectionist legalistic construct *is a fundamentally argumentative entity* and is consequently best restricted to this particular exigency. The implications of this interpretative shift are potentially momentous and so worth noting in more detail.

First, the depiction of Judaism elsewhere in Paul can now basically stand on its own terms. It no longer needs to accommodate the especially embarrassing data set associated with Paul's Justification texts. The whole question of "Paul's relationship with Judaism" can therefore be asked again and answered in terms of a more limited, and potentially rather more coherent, data set. Second, and perhaps still more importantly, that relationship no longer needs to be construed in prospective terms. The description of Judaism can be *relocated* in Paul's thought as well, in a retrospective rather than a prospective position. And this liberates the interpreter from any need to construe Judaism in a fixed and fundamentally negative state (on which the gospel will build, as a solution to its problems). Paul's description need not even be empirical; it can be a normative relationship rooted in certain theological commitments and therefore cogent, if not comprehensible, only to "insiders." These are important steps forward in the interpretation of Paul. They remain largely potential at this point, *but they are made possible by this rereading of Romans 1:18–3:20.*

Moreover, although a full consideration of their solutions is best postponed until we have reread Paul's πιστ- passages, it can already be seen that Paul is not advocating in Romans 1–3 a particular rationalistic approach to conversion, to his own conversion, or to evangelism in general — the closely related EDs 2-4. This is a misunderstanding of the argument, and so there is now no need to attribute this construction to any aspect of conversion in Paul's broader thinking and experience. Not only can Paul's description be liberated from some of its most difficult claims about Judaism, but the rereading of Romans 1–3 raises the prospect of a similar liberation from some of the most coercive and unattractive forms of mission as well.

The suggested rereading's ability to resolve all these interpretative problems — no fewer than twenty-six — (with significant contributions to several more) seems a considerable advance on the conventional construal of Romans 1:18–3:20, which apparently cannot solve them. Hence, the evidence is mounting that as a problem-free interpretation, the suggested rereading is superior to that construal; it is the best reading currently available. With so many difficulties resolved, few good reasons seem to exist for resisting this conclusion, and they need of course to be supplied, if that option is still being urged.[161]

It is time, then, to see whether successful rereadings can also be offered for Paul's ostensible thesis paragraphs (1:16-17 and 3:21-31) and for his famous, but in fact highly problematic discussion of Abraham in Romans 4 — the concerns of chapters fifteen through eighteen. Such rereadings will now benefit from the new approach to Romans 1:18–3:20 that is already in place; new expectations will therefore be in play for these later subsections. And if their rereadings prove similarly successful, it seems that the conventional reading's days are numbered, as is the long hegemony of Justification theory over Romans 1-4.

CHAPTER FIFTEEN

Faith and Syntax in Romans 1:16-17 and 3:21-31

§1. Preamble

Paul's so-called "thesis paragraphs" — Romans 1:16-17 and 3:21-31 — have attracted a degree of interpretative attention that far outweighs their actual length; we are, after all, concerned here with subsections of only two and eleven verses respectively (and the latter will ultimately be reduced to six). However, several significant and difficult issues are raised by these texts, so we will have to navigate our way through them carefully. I propose treating them in a particular order, and addressing the key issues in a certain sequence as well, in order to maximize the clarity and probity of their unfolding interpretation.

I suggest first considering 1:17 in relation to 3:21-26. These are uncannily similar texts and should provide the most interpretative leverage early on for certain key questions (whose linkage has already been established in part three, chapter eleven). We will then begin our detailed analysis by addressing certain strategic syntactical issues and the meaning of Paul's πιστ- terminology,[1] a discussion that will spill over into a consideration of Paul's intertextuality (to a degree), since he quotes Habakkuk 2:4 in 1:17b. Once these important questions have been clarified, further progress can be made on the rest of the syntactical issues in the notoriously complex 3:23-26. Subsequent chapters will take up the remaining interpretative questions in the light of these initial advances.

Chapter sixteen will address the meaning of the resonant atonement words that Paul uses — ἀπολύτρωσις, ἱλαστήριον, αἷμα, and possibly also πάρεσις (3:24, 25) — from which point we will be able to interpret more precisely the verb δικαιόω (3:24, 26). We should then be equipped to double back, in effect, in chapter seventeen and consider the meaning of the key phrase δικαιοσύνη θεοῦ (1:17; 3:21, 22) and the closely related genitive phrase δικαιοσύνη αὐτοῦ (3:25, 26). And after these localized clarifications, we should be able to step back and consider the various roles that these two short paragraphs play in the broader argumentation of the letter. The meaning of 1:16 is also best considered at this relatively late point in our discussion, because certain formerly unnoticed emphases will — at least arguably — be evident by then.

What will become apparent overall is that Paul's "thesis paragraphs" are not always helpfully so designated. It is certainly fair to recognize their importance in this sense — and so I will use this designation from time to time — but they play more complex and nuanced rhetorical roles in Romans than this identification might suggest, and this needs to be borne constantly in mind even when speaking of "theses." Indeed, it seems that Paul uses them to effect a highly sophisticated rhetorical strategy vis-à-vis his auditors and the gospel of the Teacher.

These short texts seem to function as argumentative wedges. They begin by asserting traditional material that Paul and the Roman Christians share. However, by degrees, Paul supplements them with his own emphases, interpretations, and premises, eventually building quite extended arguments that stand over against the contentions of the Teacher and his alternative gospel. In this fashion, Paul is able to establish his own positions, in explicit opposition to the Teacher's, *but claim that they simply develop out of the Roman Christians' own theology* (a strategy already noted, of course, in chapter thirteen). These small sections, then, are indeed introductions of critical premises for the letter's later broader discussions and hence thesis statements in some sense. But the subtle rhetorical strategy informing these introductions — Paul's progressive supplementation of the traditional theology of his auditors, so that their initial commitments end up affirming his own principles — has generally been overlooked.

§2. First Things First — Basic Import and Argumentative Implications

Most interpreters of Romans 3:21-26, and its anticipation in 1:17, have arguably failed to see the forest for the trees. My suggestion in this subsection is that the basic import and argumentative implications of these closely related texts are reasonably obvious and indisputable and do not depend on a single controversial semantic or theological decision. We need merely to recognize the agency of God focused on the atoning function of Christ and his resulting catalysis of justification, together with the repeated sense of disclosure that is part of this process. These realizations will then allow us to grasp Paul's main points, along with the subsection's principal function in the broader argumentative setting of the letter as a whole, *irrespective of our decisions concerning more detailed and disputable matters.*

It has already been established that 1:17 and 3:21-26 are claims operating in a polemical, Jewish Christian setting. Their overtly intertextual constitution is consequently understood to suggest primarily that the Scriptures — suitably interpreted — support Paul's view of matters, that is, his gospel, and not the views of his opponent. They attest authoritatively to the truth of his claims about salvation and against the claims of the Teacher. However, in Romans 1–4 (as we will confirm in more detail) Paul's argumentation is primarily negative; it attacks the Teacher's gospel in the main and spends far less time elaborating on his own. The apostle's claims made in 1:16-17 and 3:21-22 in terms of πιστ- terminology will be developed shortly — beginning in 3:27 and 4:2 — largely as a set of further refutations of some of the Teacher's claims, using a particular exegesis of Genesis 15:6 to achieve those aims.[2] Paul's gospel will appear to a degree, because the argument in Romans 4 is a scriptural σύγκρισις, or comparison. But by 4:22 Paul will not yet have supplied a detailed account *of* his gospel, and in particular, of how it addresses the issues that he agrees with the Teacher should ultimately be addressed. He will therefore need at some point to turn argumentatively to those related but positive concerns — an account of the real gospel, as he understands it. And 3:23-26 begins to set up that rhetorical pivot by expanding in alternative language on the terms of 3:21-22 in such a way that those later, positive concerns are anticipated and framed in the most effective fashion. This important set of transitions needs to be sketched first in broad terms, then traced in more detail.

Romans 3:21-22 states that God is revealed (somehow) through the faithful Christ for those who are faithful (leaving the precise nuancing of this expression for discussion later), a set of claims that establishes the argument of 3:27–4:22. ("Faith" there, as it is attested in Gen. 15:6, will refute the gospel of "works" and "circumcision" once more.) This disclosure both fulfills Scripture and refutes "works of law." But Paul goes on to add in the following verses that this act of disclosure through Christ has a specific divine purpose: God's intention in Christ is to atone for *and* "to justify" humanity (specifically, "all who are faithful"). And a subjective reading of πίστις Χριστοῦ does not even have to be endorsed for this claim to be obvious; it is universally acknowledged that Paul is making these claims concerning God's justifying and atoning activity in Christ from v. 23 onward. We might say, then, that the disclosure of God's actions in Christ here reveals something quite particular — *a certain sort of saving action.* And this is all that Paul needs in order to launch his later positive argumentative agenda in Romans 5–8. But such is their importance that these claims need to be traced through 3:23-26 in a little more detail before we discuss their implications.

God's intentionality is implicit in the iterated subject and verb of vv. 21 and 22: "God's δικαιοσύνη has been made known . . . through the faithful Christ."[3] This is clearly a purposive action on God's part. (A sense of purpose is unavoidably implicit in a divine act of disclosure; it would be difficult to speak of a revelation by God that lacked a goal or an intention.) We encounter a slight ambiguity in the evidence in v. 25, where the verb προέθετο is very difficult to render precisely. However, the two main options either simply continue this implicit semantic trajectory or make it explicit. προέθετο could mean literally that "God set Christ before himself as a ἱλαστήριον," thereby continuing the sense of disclosure in the subsection's opening verb with its implicit purpose; rendered more functionally, it would suggest that "God displayed Christ publicly as a ἱλαστήριον."[4] But it could mean that "God intended Christ to be a ἱλαστήριον." (The Greek idiom denotes purpose as someone sets a plan "before him or herself.") I incline toward the latter meaning on three grounds: because (1) this is how Paul uses the verb elsewhere (Rom. 1:13); (2) it occurs in precisely this sense and relation in Ephesians 1:9, although this evidence is of course disputed (but not for that reason irrelevant);[5] moreover, (3) the substantive is also a key element in Paul's theological lexicon, and occurs in just this sense in other passages, both disputed and undisputed (thereby drawing important overlapping variations into play as well).[6] This decision will be further reinforced when we consider the meaning of ἱλαστήριον.

The evidence for and emphasis on divine purpose in this passage is then continued in the three principal prepositional clauses that structure its conclusion: εἰς ἔνδειξιν τῆς δικαιοσύνης αὐτοῦ . . . [26] πρὸς τὴν ἔνδειξιν τῆς δικαιοσύνης αὐτοῦ . . . and εἰς τὸ εἶναι αὐτὸν δίκαιον καὶ δικαιοῦντα τὸν ἐκ πίστεως Ἰησοῦ[ν]. It is widely — and rightly — acknowledged that these are purposive constructions.[7] God intended Christ to be a ἱλαστήριον (or set him forth publicly as one) *for* or *to be* a proof[8] of his δικαιοσύνη, something that functions in turn to show that he is δίκαιος even as he "justifies" the faithful.[9] Hence, 3:21-26 emphasizes divine intentionality either implicitly or explicitly no fewer than six times — in the two statements that begin the subsection, in its pivotal relative clause, and in the three main prepositional clauses that conclude it. But what is this divine agency accomplishing here, according to Paul? The answer to this question is reasonably obvious as well.

God is acting through Christ in terms of two overt trajectories: he is accomplishing some sort of atonement, and he is thereby liberating and "justifying" humanity in the form of all who are faithful. Both these trajectories combine to suggest strongly that God's activity in relation to humanity, mediated by Christ, is fundamentally soteriological. God's purpose is to save. But before drawing the relevant argumentative inferences from this evidence, these two trajectories through the text should be treated in more detail.

There is no need to specify the precise mechanics by which Christ atones for humanity in order to grasp the point from Romans 3:25 that Christ is somehow dealing with human sin definitively and so atoning for it in the broadest sense of that term. This verse states that he is functioning as a ἱλαστήριον, then that his blood has been shed; and he has clearly died in the fulfillment of this task. Whatever more particular meaning we then supply to the signifier ἱλαστήριον — whether a generalized act of atonement, an object, or the mercy seat itself (perhaps opened up in a final Yom Kippur), and whether functioning in an exemplary, expiatory, propitiatory, and/or participatory fashion — it must be held to denote some sort of atonement, and in indubitably final and definitive terms. (Paul never speaks of ἱλαστήριον additional to or after Christ.) Soon after this Paul speaks of how the Christ event has accomplished τὴν πάρεσιν τῶν προγεγονότων ἁμαρτημάτων — either release from, or the release or overlooking of, previously committed transgressions. So there are at least three incontestable references to Christ's atoning function. And there are two more if πίστις is consistently referred throughout this subsection to Christ; his faithfulness to the point of death, spoken of twice more (see vv. 25 and 26), clearly also denotes metonymically (on this reading) what the other atonement terms also reference.

It is vital to grasp that God is the acting subject in this trajectory; he intends Christ to function as a ἱλαστήριον (or displays him publicly as such), even as he reveals himself through the faithful Christ. In short, the agency of God that has already been noted — and that so dominates this subsection — must be correlated with Christ's atoning function.

This atoning function of Christ is complemented by a second semantic trajectory in the passage that attributes the free liberation and justification of humanity to this act. Christ's atonement effects ἀπολύτρωσις — some sort of "release," or "redemption"[10] — which is said emphatically to be gratuitous, or "free" (δωρεὰν τῇ αὐτοῦ χάριτι). This action is parallel to the iterated "justification" (see vv. 24 and 26) and symmetrically opposed to humanity's universal transgressions and "loss of the glory of God" (v. 23).[11] So four phrases in the subsection denote the broadly salvific consequences of Christ's atoning act (and this total could be increased to five if the atoning phrase noted at the end of the preceding paragraph is included here as well; clearly, Christ's atonement effects "release" in relation to humanity "of [or 'from'] transgressions").

It is now difficult to avoid the conclusion suggested by the subsection itself in 3:26. Romans 3:23-26 states — in explication of the intertextually resonant vv. 21-22 — that God's intention is to act through Christ to atone for the sins of humanity in order to save them. God's agency is emphasized six times, Christ's atoning function between three and five times, and the salvation of humanity four times. This set of three claims seems largely unavoidable on any reading of the passage. However, we must now add the final major semantic trajectory (which has already been partly noted). Paul speaks repeatedly through this subsection of disclosure or revelation.

The evidence for this assertion has already been noted in part in relation to the attestation of God's agency. That agency was said to be implicit in the two opening verbs of revelation (one of which is elided) — φανερόω in the perfect passive form πεφανέρωται. It is arguably present in the ambiguous verb προέθετο in v. 25a, and the theme certainly returns to prominence with the significant iterated clauses that follow, where Christ is said to be the ἔνδειξις of God's δικαιοσύνη. This yields four or perhaps five explicit references to disclosure in the subsection as a whole, with two significant clauses foregrounding the question of proof or demonstration in 3:23-26 (specifically, in vv. 25 and 26). We are now in a position to recognize Paul's principal argumentative claims in this subsection, and his broader strategic reasons for making them, at a basic and incontestable level.

Christ is the definitive disclosure of God — revealing here the divine δικαιοσύνη in some sense — and he is functioning to save humanity (a process described in various ways, both positive and negative), through some costly act of atonement during which he suffers and dies, an act that is, moreover, essentially free. *This* set of events reveals God's character *and* the locus of his solution to human sin. Hence, implicit in these repeated statements about a single sweeping event of salvation are the presuppositions for the two main arguments that Paul will make in Romans 5–8 (there responding almost certainly to two key issues in the Teacher's gospel).

The recognition that God is offering up his Son to save humanity in a costly act of atonement reveals God's fundamental posture toward humanity — one of utterly committed benevolence. And this recognition can now undergird a sense of complete eschatological assurance, irrespective of any apparent present realities or future threats — the argument of Romans 5:1-11 and 8:9-39. Moreover, God's act of atonement through Christ, the very act that reveals his compassion, contains implicitly his solution to the pressing problem of human sinfulness, and an effective ethic as well — the subject of Romans 5:12–8:8 (and 8:12-13). In short, implicit in the statement that God saves in Christ, which is made repeatedly in various ways in Romans 3:21-26, are both eschatological assurance and ethical efficacy.

The first critical argumentative trajectory in Romans 5–8 has long been recognized, thanks to a seminal study by Nils Dahl.[12] Dahl pointed out that Romans 5:1-11 anticipates in nuce all the main eschatological themes that begin to be elaborated from 8:9, flowing through to the triumphant conclusion of vv. 37-39: the work of the Spirit; the assurance of the love of God; and the recognition of the love of God in the offering up of his Son. These relationships then ground the assurance and hope of Christians if and when they suffer — which they ought to endure with perseverance and patience — and, in particular, any anxieties that they might be experiencing in the face of eschatological wrath and its associated apocalyptic forces. That God was prepared to offer up his son for a hostile humanity demonstrates that the fundamental posture of God toward humanity is one of love. And it follows from this that God is on humanity's side, whatever destructive forces are arrayed against it.

Between these two discussions — which function to enclose the intervening argument — Paul discusses at some length the ethical basis of Christianity as he understands it, the section's second critical argumentative trajectory. Such a discussion must inevitably contain an analysis of "the problem" in relation to which a "solution" is posited, so Paul begins in 5:12-21 by framing his entire argument in terms of the contrasting dispensations of Adam and Christ (the narrative of Adam arguably resurfacing in Romans 7, as I suggested in part one, chapter five). The detailed argument then proceeds first through a discussion of baptism that is oriented toward libertine challenges, couched in diatribal form: "Should we . . . sin in order that grace may abound?" (6:1b); and "Should we sin because we are not under law but under grace?" (6:15b). (The answer of course is "absolutely not!") A short allegory in 7:1-4 in terms of marriage, death, and adultery is then followed by Paul's well-known analysis of ethical incapacity in 7:7-25. And the discussion concludes in 8:1-9 and 12-14 with a countervailing description of life in the Spirit, a condition that apparently overcomes human incapacity, which can now be seen to be rooted in an Adamic ontology of flesh and enslaved to the forces of Sin and Death. The resurrected ethical condition in Christ, undergirded by the Spirit (and symbolized in baptism), is law-free in the sense of not taking its primary ethical orientation from God's written commands in Scripture (a posture that Paul accuses here of being deceptive and death dealing). Hence, whatever the specifics of this important set of arguments by Paul, it cannot be denied that he is laying out a distinctive ethical system informed by participation in Christ through the Spirit. It ostensibly offers a radical solution to the problem of sin — which Paul depicts as dwelling like an evil occupying force in human nature — effectively executing sin, and then assuming the inauguration of the resurrection of the Christian into a distinctively law-free praxis.

But it should now be apparent that these two critical argumentative trajectories through Romans 5–8 — concerning eschatological assurance and law-free ethical praxis — arise from presuppositions that Paul introduced in 3:23-26 by way of elaboration on vv. 21-22. It is precisely God's benevolent and loving act on our behalf in Christ that constitutes the ground for Paul's later argument in terms of eschatological assurance in 5:1-11 and 8:9-11 and 14-39. And the actual functions of God's act in Christ as an atonement for sin and redemption of humanity are the basis for Paul's later discussions of Christian liberation from sin as the Christian participates in the generic events of Christ's passion — 5:12–8:8, 12-13. God's act in Christ *is* the basis for Paul's later discussion of a superior and law-free Christian ethic. So it seems that 3:23-26, in elaborating on and clarifying vv. 21-22, also signal the later, more positive phases in Paul's argument that will unfold in chapters 5–8, while vv. 21-22 signal the immediately ensuing and rather polemical scriptural discussion in Romans 4.

Further confirming these suggestions concerning the rhetorical function of 3:23-26 is the symmetry that is perceptible between the two later argumentative developments that 3:23-26 anticipates and two of the principal points in the gospel of the Teacher that became apparent as Paul undermined that construct in 1:18–3:20.

We have already seen that a particular ethic and future eschatology play critical roles in the Teacher's gospel. The Teacher holds that a true and effective ethic is fundamentally Jewish. The circumcision of the body corresponds to the excision of the sinful passions from the heart, from which point law observance can guide and discipline the convert to truly and consistently righteous behavior. That behavior will result in a verdict from God at the end of the age of "righteous," and such a verdict will result in turn in entry into the blessings of the age to come. Outside of these practices, however, there is only a fearful expectation of wrath for wrongdoing, and this pending reality may consequently fulfill a useful rhetorical function, as an argumentative preamble that terrifies uncircumcised pagans and so encourages them to "turn (to the law) or burn."

It would seem, then, that in 3:23-26 we see Paul acknowledging that he must later address these particular issues in the Teacher's gospel in greater depth. The Teacher's concern with ethics is correct if not commendable, but his system is in Paul's view disastrously wrong; it overlooks the event that God has provided to resolve the situation — Christ! So Paul signals in 3:23-26 that the Christ event is the basis for the new *and much more effective* ethical reality that Christians now inhabit, and he will discuss this in greater depth shortly. (It must of course be correctly understood.) Only this divinely provided solution can effect real ethical change in humanity. Moreover, that same Christ event signals unequivocally that Christians need not fear the wrath of God at the end of the age — indeed, far from it. A God who is prepared to offer up his son to suffer and die in order to effect atonement for sinful humanity — *free* atonement no less! — is clearly utterly benevolent. This is a God of love, not a God of punishment. If anything, then, this God will defend the hapless Christian against accusations issuing from any other actor, whether human or superhuman! (And if God is on your side, who can really stand against you?) So here Paul in effect accepts the ethical and eschatological challenges of the Teacher but responds (essentially after a thorough critique) with what he holds are more accurate and christocentric answers.

These, then, are the principal implications of 3:23-26 in the broader setting of 3:21-26 and Romans 1–8; this is a set of compact anticipations of Paul's later eschatological and ethical assurances in chapters 5–8, assurances that unfold directly from the Christ event. And it is worth emphasizing that the basic theological premise undergirding all of Paul's reasoning here is the conviction that Christ is the definitive revelation of the activity and character of God. Moreover, these assurances seem to hold good irrespective of the nuanced decisions that scholars debate in relation to various subordinate issues within the passage, *and they are all that is necessary to sustain our broader rereading at this point.* In Romans 3:23-26 it seems that Paul is pointing ahead, clearly and consistently, to the apocalyptic characterization of his gospel that he will give at greater length in chapters 5–8.

We can now add further structural links to Dahl's important argument concerning the linkage between 5:1-11 and the second half of Romans 8. Just as 1:17 prepares for and is elaborated by 3:21-22 and 23-26, and 5:1-11 prepares for and is elaborated by 8:9-11 and 14-39, so too these two doublets can themselves be linked into a chain of cascading — and expanding — units of anticipation and elaboration stretching through the first half of Romans — indeed, stretching back even to 1:2-4, for reasons that will become increasingly clear in what follows.[13] (We will consider Paul's subtle rhetorical reasons for constructing this chain of argumentative anticipations at a later point — in chapter seventeen.) With these realizations in place, we can turn to consider the various more disputable matters that cluster thickly through 1:17 and 3:21-26, aware throughout that less rides on our decisions here than is usually thought to be the case. Nevertheless, any interpretative progress will be welcome, because it should result in an increasingly clear grip on Paul's argument.

**The strategic rhetorical functions of 3:21-26
in the argument from Romans 1–8**

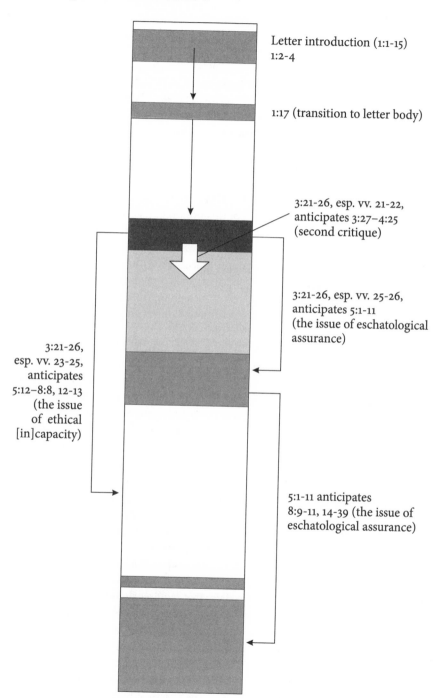

Letter introduction (1:1-15)
1:2-4

1:17 (transition to letter body)

3:21-26, esp. vv. 21-22,
anticipates 3:27–4:25
(second critique)

3:21-26, esp. vv. 25-26,
anticipates 5:1-11
(the issue of eschatological
assurance)

3:21-26,
esp. vv. 23-25,
anticipates
5:12–8:8, 12-13
(the issue
of ethical
[in]capacity)

5:1-11 anticipates
8:9-11, 14-39 (the issue of
eschatological assurance)

§3. Initial Syntactical Decisions and Paul's πιστ-
Terms in Romans 1:17 and 3:21-22

3.1. The Meaning of πίστις in Romans 1:17 and 3:22

We have already seen in part three, chapter eleven (§3.2) that the famously opaque prepositional series ἐκ πίστεως εἰς πίστιν in 1:17a devolved, via the underlying influence of Habakkuk 2:4, into an embarrassing textual overdetermination for the conventional reading at *both* 1:17a and 3:22 (OD 12). Whatever the precise meaning of δικαιοσύνη Θεοῦ in these two sentences, it is being revealed or disclosed *by means of* πίστις, and the conventional reading struggles to account for this. "Faith" appropriates salvation and the gospel in Justification theory, generally after preaching, so for conventional readers to speak of it "revealing" something seems semantically incoherent.[14] However, the quotation of Habakkuk 2:4 in 1:17b precludes any interpretation of this notion in terms of God's faithfulness in 1:17a (a reading that also seems rather tautologous, and it is impossible to reconcile with the appended Christ genitive in 3:22). But this overdetermination is eliminated immediately, not to mention gracefully, if the meaning of πίστις in these statements is related directly to Christ. Such a reading completes the exact sense of these Pauline statements nicely: "the δικαιοσύνη Θεοῦ is disclosed or revealed by means of the πίστις of Jesus Christ." And various further areas of evidence progressively corroborate this initial decision.[15]

We can remind ourselves initially of the lexicographical distinctions that were introduced in chapter eleven, where it was noted that πίστις can signify "belief," "trust," and "faithfulness," all of which are related but subtly different actions. Literature contemporary to Paul is replete with these distinctions (not to mention with shifts between them), and it is worth noting in particular that both Josephus and the LXX attest repeatedly to the notion of πίστις as "fidelity." Justification theory has little use for the meaning "fidelity," because it is too strong a condition for struggling non-Christians to fulfill in order to be saved; something more manageable is required as they journey through the pre-Christian state. Justification advocates can therefore have difficulty accepting a reading of πίστις in terms of "fidelity." However, when discussing Jesus, not the non-Christian, and in Koiné, the meaning "fidelity" is clearly quite reasonable here (as is a subjective construal of the genitive). It is also highly appropriate, as we will see.

We should also note that Paul frequently refers to a story of Christ's passion metonymically — that is to say, by mentioning only one element within it that serves to evoke the entire narrative, a claim that requires slightly longer discussion.

It is clear that Paul knows and uses a passion narrative.[16] He mentions the night of Jesus' last supper, establishment of the Eucharist, and betrayal, when he was "handed over" to his enemies. Paul also knows that Jesus submitted to the humiliation of an execution by crucifixion, endured that form of death, shed his blood, and died, the shedding of his blood serving both to atone for sin(s) in some sense and to fulfill the Scriptures. Jesus was then buried and, "on the third day," raised and enthroned, receiving at that point the acclamation of lordship.[17] Paul can of course emphasize one or another broad trajectory within this story as immediate circumstances demand. So he can allude at times to Jesus' suffering and atoning death, and at other times to Christ's resurrection and glorification — a broadly downward and/or upward movement. (The extent to which both of these narrative trajectories are in play in these particular texts is an important question that need not occupy us at the moment; it will be addressed shortly.)

But more often than not, Paul alludes to this story metonymically rather than by way of longer syntactical units and fuller descriptions, and doubtless because his early Christian audiences already knew it fairly well. So a single motif can denote the presence of the narrative — or of one of its broad trajectories — within the apostle's developing arguments: "obedience," "blood," "death," "cross/crucifixion," and so on. It is important to emphasize that none of these motifs are therefore functioning with strict literalness (although they may be assuming some contingent emphasis, but that is not the same thing). No one seriously suggests that when Paul refers to the blood of Christ he is referring *only* to the important liquid that ran in Christ's veins and then spilled out to a degree during his suffering and execution, thereby ignoring the rest of Christ himself and his actions. Similarly, any reference to Christ's death by Paul involves far more than a reference to the actual moment at which Christ expired. So the claim that the phrase "the fidelity of Christ" could denote Jesus' entire passion more broadly is quite consistent with Paul's usual practice as that is attested elsewhere.

Indeed, the notion of fidelity fits smoothly into the downward martyrological trajectory in the story of Jesus' passion. It is largely self-evident that fidelity is an ingredient within any essentially martyrological story. Martyrs faithfully endure suffering and death (if not a horrible execution); the story of martyrdom thus encodes its heroes with the quality of fidelity, even if only implicitly, in view of their endurance and steadfastness within those unfolding stories.[18] But numerous martyrologies mention fidelity explicitly as well (see 2 Macc. 7:40; *4 Macc.* 7:21-22; 15:24; 16:22; 17:2; see also 2 Macc. 6:30; *4 Macc.* 17:10).[19] So it seems entirely appropriate in terms of Paul's background to suggest that his account of Jesus' death — an essentially martyrological story — could include the element of faithfulness. Indeed, an examination of the lexical and narrative background would lead us almost to expect this narrative feature.

But it is worth noting further that overlaps with other similar and closely related narrative elements are frequently detectable in these texts as well — overlaps of faithfulness with patience, endurance, obedience, submission, trust, and so on. So it is clear that martyrs must in fact possess a marvelous steadfastness *of mind*. Those martyred for the sake of God need to believe certain things about God unshakably, trusting in him over time, under duress, in an unwavering fashion — usually for their resurrection — and thereby eliding into faithfulness. Martyrs, in short, run the full semantic gamut of πίστις: they believe, they trust, and they are faithful to the point of death.[20]

It seems especially significant, then, that ὑπακοή is used as a strategic summary of Christ's saving activity as the second Adam in Romans 5:19, where it functions opposite the first Adam's παρακοή. The context then develops these paradigmatic actions in terms of realizations of life and death (5:12-21). The cognate adjective ὑπήκοος is used in an identical position in Philippians 2:5-11 (see v. 8) — one of Paul's most explicit and profound accounts of the Christ event. In this more extended narrative Paul speaks of Christ humbling himself to death — death on a cross! And this is, moreover, a way of thinking that Paul urges on the Philippians — a mentality that "does not take advantage" but "empties" and "humbles" itself, ultimately becoming "submissive" to a humiliating execution (and so, ultimately, being glorified). Hence, it is apparent that Paul could denote Jesus' passion narrative metonymically by referring to one of the heroic personal attributes evident in that story — here obedience or submission (and on occasion several of the other elements in that underlying story are made explicit by these texts as well).

Finally, we should note that Paul even deploys the πιστ- and the ὑπακου- word groups together at times in what seem to be semantic overlaps, and there are good reasons for this in terms of Paul's social context. Inferiors — for example, clients — should be obedient in the fulfillment of their assigned tasks and duties. But this could be spoken of equally accurately as a faithful or trustworthy discharge of their duties. In this setting, *these qualities are largely interchangeable;* obedient clients *are* faithful, trustworthy, and even submissive clients, and vice versa. This consequently suggests that for Paul to speak of the ὑπακοή of Christ might be equivalent semantically to speaking of the πίστις of Christ, given certain settings for those statements. The question would be raised why Paul speaks of Christ's endurance in terms of πιστ- words in some texts and in terms of ὑπακου- words in others, but there is a plausible explanation, which we will address shortly.

Perhaps most indicative that this overlap is in fact present in Paul's texts is his interchangeable use of the cognate verbs in Romans 10 (a text that will be considered in more detail in part five, chapter nineteen). Paul speaks of believing in vv. 9, 10, 11, and 14 (2x) (in close relation to "confessing" and "calling"). A sequence of calling, believing, hearing, preaching, and sending or proclaiming is then enumerated from v. 14 onward, followed by the statement ἀλλ' οὐ πάντες ὑπήκουσαν τῷ εὐαγγελίῳ. And Paul then immediately quotes Isaiah 53:1, as if in explanation of the preceding claim: Κύριε, τίς ἐπίστευσεν τῇ ἀκοῇ ἡμῶν. So at two points in this subsection Paul seems to shift between πιστ- and ὑπακου- language seamlessly. The verb ὑπακούω negates an action in the preceding sequence denoted by πιστεύω. And this negation in terms of ὑπακούω is confirmed by a Septuagintal intertext that uses πιστεύω.[21] The same semantic interchangeability is also possibly evident in Philippians 2:12 and 17, and is definitely apparent in the more disputable evidence of 2 Thessalonians 1:8-10.[22]

In sum, several strands of evidence stand in favor of a christological interpretation of Romans 1:17 and 3:22, supporting our initial decision based on the immediate sense of the sentence: the reading is lexicographically and grammatically quite acceptable; it recalls the gospel narrative in Paul metonymically, like many of the apostle's other references to Easter; it makes a plausible equation between the story of Jesus' martyrdom and the quality of fidelity; and it is functionally equivalent to Paul's references to Christ's passion elsewhere with respect to ὑπακου- words, some of which even arguably overlap with πιστ- words in Paul directly. There is, in short, much to be said for it (and little to be said against it).[23] So the christological reading will be adopted here: *Christ's* fidelity, that Paul explicates elsewhere in particular relation to the story of his crucifixion, is functioning in 1:17 and 3:22 to reveal or disclose some righteous characteristic of, or action by, God.[24] And this is hardly a radical interpretative claim to make about Paul — that the death of Christ functions to disclose the purposes of God! An important corollary of this developing reading should now be noted.

3.2. *The Interpretation of Habakkuk 2:4 in Romans 1:17b*

We have already seen that Paul's use of ἐκ πίστεως in Romans 1:17a is correlated tightly with his citation of Habakkuk 2:4 in 1:17b, a text that uses the same phrase. This correlation explained the web of identical and similar prepositional expressions spread through Romans and Galatians (if not beyond), including 3:22; indeed, it was this broader correlation that established the instrumentality of the key phrase ἐκ πίστεως especially clearly (and that also largely explains the statistical dominance of πιστ- over ὑπακου- terms in these texts). But it remains to be seen whether the christological explanation that I have supplied for that instrumental function is now sustainable through 1:17b — a question that has not yet been answered. Can Paul's citation of Habakkuk 2:4 there be oriented christologically? Once again, it seems that good reasons may be added in support of this suggestion (and in due course we will see that no good reasons stand against it).[25]

We should note first that a christological orientation supplies a perfectly acceptable reading of Romans 1:17: "The δικαιοσύνη Θεοῦ is being revealed through it [the gospel] by means of fidelity and for fidelity, as it is written, 'The righteous one, by means of fidelity, will live.'" The righteous one spoken of here is plainly Christ, and this prophetic text, read in this fashion, suggests that by means of his faithfulness to the point of death he will live in the sense of being vindicated and resurrected.[26] So Habakkuk 2:4 now neatly predicts the passion of Jesus — his death and resurrection. It is a prophetic attestation to Paul's gospel, and to the disclosure of the δικαιοσύνη Θεοῦ it presupposes. There seem to be no immediate problems with this reading. But what can be said further in its favor?

(1) The use of a generalized arthrous construction to denote Christ — here employing the adjective δίκαιος — is entirely consistent with Pauline usage elsewhere. Merely in Romans itself, Paul seems to refer to Christ frequently in this way: see, for example, ὁ υἱός (1:3, 4, 9; 5:10; 8:3, 29, 32), ὁ Χριστός (9:3, 5; 14:18; 15:3, 7, 19; see 16:16), ὁ εἷς (5:15, 17, 18, 19), and probably also[27] ὁ ἀποθανών (6:7; 8:34).[28]

(2) δίκαιος is also a christological title recognizable from other parts of the New Testament.[29] The arthrous form is found in Acts 7:52 (an explicitly

martyrological setting) and 22:14 (here on the lips of Paul), and possibly also in James 5:6 and Matthew 27:19.[30] (We will consider Heb. 10:38 momentarily.) Also relevant are several anarthrous occurrences — Acts 3:14, 1 Peter 3:18, and 1 John 1:9; 2:1, 29; and 3:7. This is enough evidence — around ten instances — to establish the existence of the title clearly within early Christianity. The title is also, however, arguably apparent in certain Jewish sources as well.[31]

(3) The evidence in Hebrews is slight but consists of two considerations that seem to reinforce one another.

First, we should note that a messianic reading of the quotation of Habakkuk 2:3-4 in Hebrews 10:37-39 "is by no means an unreasonable one" since "the LXX translators produced a text that is readily susceptible to messianic interpretation."[32] Indeed, Hebrews 10:37 employs a text slightly different from the majority reading, deploying ὁ ἐρχόμενος in an overt parallelism to ὁ δίκαιος. This arthrous usage seems to point in a titular fashion, along with ὁ δίκαιος, to a particular significant figure, and is arguably messianic in its own right.[33] It seems reasonable to suggest, then, that the letter's early Christian auditors would have interpreted "the righteous" and "the coming one" here as Christ.

Second, in v. 39 the author exhorts his auditors to be "of faith," not "of shrinking back," and so have their souls redeemed (ἡμεῖς . . . ἐσμὲν . . . πίστεως εἰς περιποίησιν ψυχῆς). This could be an exhortation in an exemplary mode and so probably a characterizing genitive, but it is worth noting that only Jesus is described in the entire catalogue of heroes of faith that follows as having both a generative and a perfecting function for the faithfulness of others; in 12:2 the auditors are exhorted to "fix their eyes upon the *founder* (or 'originator') and *perfector* of πίστις, Jesus" (τὸν τῆς πίστεως ἀρχηγὸν καὶ τελειωτὴν Ἰησοῦν) whose own endurance and triumph are then briefly described. And since these two functions match perfectly the two outcomes spoken of in 10:39, a connection seems possible, in which case the genitive πίστεως there could be interpreted possessively or partitively. That is, Jesus could be the one who founds the auditors' fidelity, and the perfector who ultimately also redeems their souls, after it has run its course, and they are consequently exhorted as people who "belong to" or "are part of" the fidelity of the righteous one. Moreover, both these considerations point in the same interpretative direction within 10:37-39, further (albeit marginally) reinforcing this suggestion's probity.

(4) It is also worth noting that the Wisdom of Solomon speaks at some length of "a righteous man" who suffers and is then granted life by God (see esp. 2:12-20 and, a little less directly, 3:1-9; 4:7-16; 5:1, 15). And since the text in which this story is embedded is deeply implicated in the opening chapters of Romans, it seems likely that the letter's auditors would hear echoes of the righteous figure from that story when Paul cited Habakkuk 2:4 in Romans 1:17. The righteous person is not a messianic figure in the Wisdom of Solomon, but he is heroic, innocent, possessed of wisdom in his soul, and resurrected.[34] And if Habakkuk 2:4 was set against these particular narrative and intertextual expectations, it would have been read as a brief summary of the story of a righteous hero who suffered

and then received an eschatological vindication (and not as a story of how individual Christians are justified by faith). Christ was the central Christian hero, and the first righteous story cycle in the book would have been especially apposite because, like the figure portrayed there, Christ was a relatively young, innocent, crucified (not to mention resurrected) person. In short, the narratives in the Wisdom of Solomon concerning a righteous man — a δίκαιος — fit Christ better than they fit the generic Christian, especially in his heroic and resurrected features, and so the Christian readers of the Wisdom of Solomon and Romans would probably have interpreted Paul's first explicit intertext in the letter concerning "a righteous person" in a way that was related to their heroic messiah.[35]

(5) If Paul draws the key phrase ἐκ πίστεως from Habakkuk 2:4 in order to use it programmatically elsewhere (and we have noted its occurrences in Romans and Galatians another nineteen times), then this could explain the loss of the phrase's pronoun (μου[36]) from its scriptural antecedent. Paul cannot deploy the phrase in other sentences if it is encumbered by a pronoun, since in the new locations this word would have no antecedent (or, worse still, it would have the wrong one!). A christological reading can therefore explain this otherwise troubling omission.[37]

(6) A messianic reading of Habakkuk 2:4 directly fulfills the expectations that Paul set in motion in Romans 1:2-4. There he broke into his address — amounting to a breach of ancient epistolary etiquette — to affirm that his gospel concerned God's Son, who was descended from David and declared the Son of God by his resurrection in fulfillment of God's prophets in the Scriptures. Paul's explicit indications, then, would dispose the letter's auditors to read prophetic texts from the Scriptures in Romans as witnesses to the Son of God, Christ, and in particular to either his Davidic lineage or, probably more importantly, his resurrection. And a messianic construal of Habakkuk 2:4 conforms *precisely* to this announced agenda — a prophetic text attesting to the resurrected Son of God. This is, moreover, the first such text that is quoted in Romans. Hence, the Roman Christians would need to retain Paul's affirmations for a mere twelve verses, to the end of the epistolary introduction, in order to enact them there. In view of this, good reasons would need to be supplied for departing from such a reading.

(7) That Paul could deploy Scripture christocentrically should not be in dispute. He does not always do so, and may even evidence a slightly different central hermeneutical fulcrum in numeric terms[38] but that he frequently quotes Scripture in christocentric terms is undeniable. Moreover, he even articulates this interpretative principle explicitly on occasion (see especially 2 Cor. 1:20; 4:4-6). So there is no difficulty with the basic suggestion that Habakkuk 2:4 is functioning christocentrically for Paul.

These various positive considerations add up, in my view, to an increasingly compelling case for the christological construal of Habakkuk 2:4 in Romans 1:17. I do not view them as probative in their own right, but they function as supplementary contentions that increase by degrees our confidence in the initial judgment that Paul is speaking christologically in Romans 1:17, both a and b, as well as in 3:22.[39] The most constructive thing to do from this point in our developing analysis will therefore be to build on this insight, pressing on to answer the next set of localized interpretative questions,[40] the first of which is the prepositional completion of πίστις Χριστοῦ in Romans 3:22 with the phrase εἰς πάντας τοὺς πιστεύοντας.

3.3. The Meaning of εἰς πάντας τοὺς πιστεύοντας in Romans 3:22

Three interpretative issues arise in relation to this phrase — the implications of πᾶς, the sense of the participle and its underlying verb, and the implicit object (if that is relevant). The first issue is probably the most straightforward.

(1) The Implications of πᾶς

It is well known that πᾶς is a key word in Romans, occurring upward of seventy times.[41] But what does it actually mean, and especially now that this question has been detached from the strictures of Justification theory? There, it is usually taken to suggest that "everyone" who makes a decision of faith is saved, irrespective of other markers, especially "works of law." And clearly there is something to be said for this reading. However, it is no longer necessary to place the question of inclusion in a voluntarist setting, after a journey through a state characterized by "works of law." We will actually leave the detailed exposition of this motif until our discussion of Romans 10, because πᾶς receives an especially extensive and subtle treatment there. However, Paul does supply critical information here, in 3:22-24, that frames that later discussion, and this is worth considering now.

Paul's use of πᾶς in v. 22 is, in the first instance, apparently a counterclaim to the Teacher's gospel and its restriction of salvation to those Christian converts who had in effect become orthopractic Jews. Perhaps the Teacher even espoused a peculiarly restricted account of God's election, limiting that to Israel and those who had thoroughly proselytized (although that is hard to say, and especially at this point in our interpretation of the letter). But Paul clearly argues here that God's saving purpose has broken out from Israel in Christ and now encompasses pagans as well — whether "Greek or barbarian, educated or ignorant" (1:14, DC). And he asserts repeatedly that everyone who is marked by πίστις is a participant in this eschatological age — a marker that in fact applies also to "Jew (albeit first) as well as Greek" (1:16, DC)! So Paul's repeated assertion of "everyone who . . ." needs to be set in the first instance over against a more restrictive claim that is being made by the Teacher. Most importantly, the Roman Christians would probably fall outside that constituency as the Teacher defines it (because they are not fully law observant) but *inside* it as Paul marks it. And this is of course a critical rhetorical move on Paul's part. The Teacher is generating much of his ethical and rhetorical leverage by way of exclusion and consequent anxiety; the Roman Christians must do certain things in order to be saved at the final judgment —

things he recommends. However, by arguing that the appropriately marked Christians are saved *already,* Paul neutralizes this theological and rhetorical dynamic; he pulls the sting from this program (provided of course that his marker is deemed a plausible indicator *of* salvation).[42] And Paul seems to begin here to provide a theological rationale for this inclusiveness.

The abrogation of the traditional distinction between Jew and pagan rests, he suggests in 3:23, on their mutual participation in a deeper underlying problem — the human condition inherited from Adam. "All sinned and lack the glory of God" (v. 23); therefore, all benefit as well from participation in the solution to this problem that God has provided in Christ — a liberative solution that corresponds precisely to the inauguration of the age to come and is marked by πίστις. (So they are δικαιούμενοι δωρεὰν τῇ αὐτοῦ χάριτι, that is, "delivered freely by his grace," and this διὰ τῆς ἀπολυτρώσεως τῆς ἐν Χριστῷ 'Ιησοῦ, "through the deliverance that is through Christ Jesus.") The universality of the claim of "all" who have πίστις hence rests in Romans 3:23-24 on participation in the divine solution to the problem of an Adamic ontology that all also share — whether Jew or Greek.

Questions are of course immediately raised by this, especially, why God has in fact chosen to reach out beyond the traditional locus of salvation in Israel to include pagans directly in this new reality that overcomes the entire human dilemma. But these issues are addressed by Paul in Romans 9–11 and so best postponed until the detailed exegesis of that later discussion. For now it suffices to note what Paul does — and does not — say here, turning our attention to the remaining interpretative issues in v. 22b that revolve around his use of a πίστ- term to mark this broad, saved constituency, here in the form of a participle.

(2) *The Sense of the Participle and Its Underlying Verb*

Πίστις is clearly a marker of salvation for Paul in Romans, and rather scandalously, it marks both Jews and pagans. "All" who evidence it are destined for salvation, Paul asserts, over against the more restrictive definitions of the Teacher, who expects the saved to be marked by circumcision and perfect law observance. Its rationale is grounded, moreover, in a universal account of the human problem — an *Adamic* account. Because all share this plight, all who are incorporated in God's solution to that plight — in Christ — are saved. And this is an important shift in the explanation of universality and πίστις from Justification theory, which tends to ground this universality in human freedom to choose, and to locate it after a somewhat introspective journey on the part of the individual through law observance and its failures. Paul's definitions are ultimately more radical than this (and he does not share the optimism concerning human capacity).

But it is important to note that Paul does not yet tell us what the *mode* of πίστις is — that is, *how* these pagans and sympathetic Jews come to have it. He merely locates it several times as the *objective* of God's eschatological saving purpose effected through Christ; that purpose is being visibly worked out in relation to a constituency marked by πίστις. This point is made in 1:16b, 1:17a, and 3:22

(viz., . . . εἰς σωτηρίαν παντὶ τῷ πιστεύοντι; [. . . ἐκ πίστεως] εἰς πίστιν; and [. . . διὰ πίστεως Ἰησοῦ Χριστοῦ] εἰς πάντας τοὺς πιστεύοντας).

Romans 10 will have much more to say concerning mode, and about the intertextual plays that underlie this terminology as well. So, with the elimination of the relevance of 1:18–3:20 to this question, it is best to wait for that later, more detailed exposition to see how Paul's view of πίστις actually unfolds, although clearly quite different accounts of its causality and agency are now possible. But two further observations are possible at this point that can frame our later discussions: (i) the wordplay that unfolds through these texts based on πιστ- terms creates several important possibilities for the interpretation of "faith's" modality in Paul's thinking; and (ii) it seems clear that the interpretation of Paul's πιστ- language is bound up closely with intertextuality and must therefore itself be mediated by those dynamics. (We cannot simply read Paul's theology off a discussion that is conducted in deeply intertextual terms; his own expression might be constrained by the texts that he is utilizing.)

(i) It seems that Paul is punning on πιστ- terms in 1:17 and 3:22, and in fact reproducing much the same pun. In 1:16 he states that God's power ἐστιν εἰς σωτηρίαν παντὶ τῷ πιστεύοντι. And this purpose must inform the second member in the subsequent prepositional series that has proved so troublesome to commentators (not to mention to an exegesis informed by Justification theory), but that has been resolved here by attributing the central term to the faithful Christ: δικαιοσύνη Θεοῦ . . . ἀποκαλύπτεται ἐκ πίστεως εἰς πίστιν. We have suggested that the first member here anticipates the introduction of Habakkuk 2:4, which follows immediately, and references Christ as the innocent one who is faithful and then "lives." So Paul is stating in 1:17a that God's δικαιοσύνη is being disclosed *through* the faithful Christ *for* those who trust/believe/are faithful (literally, "through fidelity for fidelity"). And it is now apparent that this pun is reproduced — unsurprisingly! — in 3:22, when Paul shifts some of the key terms to synonyms but basically says the same thing: δικαιοσύνη δὲ Θεοῦ [πεφανέρωται] διὰ πίστεως Ἰησοῦ Χριστοῦ εἰς πάντας τοὺς πιστεύοντας. With the recognition of this wordplay, and the separation of these texts from Justification theory and its dominating interpretation of 1:18–3:20, different interpretations of the origin and actual nature of faith can now be recognized. Two main explanations seem possible.

The "faith" of the Christian (if we may call it that for the moment) echoes the fidelity of Christ himself in some sense; the two notions obviously overlap. Hence, we could develop this series, on the one hand, in an exemplary or strictly imitative mode: Christians are marked by "faith" because they copy the faithful Christ. However, this semantic overlap also creates the possibility, on the other hand, of a "participatory" interpretation: Christians possess "faith" because they participate in the faithful Christ, and this "faith" is therefore evidence of that participation — a mark in fact of a deeper shared character (only inaugurated, but nevertheless real for all that).[43] The arrival of this interpretative possibility is a pivotal moment within this developing rereading of Romans 1–4 as a whole.

It now seems possible to give an account of Paul's pervasive use of πιστ- terminology in Romans 1-4 and beyond that has exegetical and argumentative integrity (because it turns out to resolve the difficulties in the text better than the more conventional alternative) but also theological and rhetorical integrity. It can unfold directly into the participatory arguments that Paul will make in Romans 5-8 (the transition that has proved so difficult to make in the past), and it can in so doing affirm the fundamentally unconditional and "apocalyptic" account of Paul's gospel, thereby eliminating the raft of tensions and contradictions generated in substantive terms when that account is juxtaposed with Justification theory. The recognition of this simple πιστ- pun and its interpretative implications in Romans 1:16b-17a and 3:22 is a vital element in our unfolding argument (as indeed it was in Paul's). But it is often asked at this point, "why πίστις?" That is, why does Paul pun on, and elsewhere make such extensive use of, πιστ- terms? Why is "faith" *privileged* as the particular marker of inclusion in salvation in Romans (and Galatians, etc.) — a role that Justification theory at least supplied a vigorous answer to in terms of information, manageability, and so on, however problematic it turned out to be under closer scrutiny? The answer to this legitimate question lies in our second initial observation.

(ii) Paul's use of πιστ- terms is informed overtly and fundamentally by scriptural intertexts. We have already noted that his use of the substantive πίστις (at least, in many instances) and of the phrase ἐκ πίστεως is informed by Habakkuk 2:4, which is quoted in 1:17. But the second member in the pun is informed by scriptural texts that use πιστ- language as well. This dimension in 3:21-22 as a whole will be elaborated on shortly (and in relation to Romans 10), so here it suffices to note that in 9:30-10:21 Paul quotes Isaiah 28:16b twice — ὁ πιστεύων ἐπ' αὐτῷ οὐ καταισχυνθήσεται (in the second instance, following it rapidly with another πᾶς text, Joel 2:32, thereby resuming the language of 3:22 quite pointedly). And shortly after 3:21-26 Paul will of course discuss Genesis 15:6 extensively, which also contains the verb πιστεύω — ἐπίστευσεν δὲ Αβραὰμ τῷ θεῷ καὶ ἐλογίσθη αὐτῷ εἰς δικαιοσύνην. So Paul's πιστ- terms in 1:16b-17a and 3:22 are bound up deeply with intertextuality, and his participial phrase in the second member of this pun with certain texts in particular that use the verb — Genesis 15:6 and Isaiah 28:16b. It is for this reason that Paul can use a participle in the πιστ- series' second member, but never in the first.

(3) The Implicit Object

With these preliminary observations in place (which set up certain important later discussions and conclusions), we can turn to the third major interpretative issue in 3:22 that arises at this stage in our discussion and consider it from three angles. The intertextual, general, and syntactical evidence now point in the same direction in relation to the implicit object of the participle.

(i) In intertextual terms, it must suffice here to note that while Christ will certainly be one object of belief in Romans 9:30-10:21, both in 9:33 and as the risen κύριος in 10:9-13, God "the Father" is present there as the object of confession and belief in equal measure (and this is arguably Paul's specific point). More-over, God "the Father" is *always* the object of belief when Genesis 15:6 is dis-cussed, and that exegesis takes place almost immediately following 3:22 in Romans 4 (see esp. 4:23-25). This is of course not to exclude the importance of Christian beliefs about Christ; that is why Paul writes his letters in the first place. However, it is a matter of contingent emphasis. The intertextuality underpinning the apostle's use of the participle of πιστεύω in 3:22 — here almost certainly echo-ing the programmatic εἰς phrases in 1:16-17 — inclines fairly strongly toward the presence of God as the participle's implicit object. And bearing out this initial judgment are the comparative rareness of instances of Christ as an explicit object of πιστ- terminology in Paul, and the immediate syntactical implications. Who or what might we ordinarily expect to be the object of this "faith" in Romans 3:22?

In the undisputed letters, Christ is the object of knowledge and belief defi-nitely — excluding question-begging instances — only in Galatians 2:15-16. He is arguably the object in Philippians 1:29 — here more in the sense of trust — al-though it is very difficult to exclude the possibility of an elided εὐαγγέλιον in Philippians 1:29-30 in view of 1:27. Fidelity to Christ is then spoken of by the dis-puted Colossians 2:5 (see 2:7[44]). And while this sample does establish the possibil-ity of belief/trust/fidelity in/to Christ in Paul, it is clearly not an extensive sup-porting sample. Adding in the two quotations of Isaiah 28:16b that reference Christ at least partially in Romans 9–10, this gives totals of between three and some half dozen instances of Christ as the object of Christian belief or trust or fi-delity in Paul's extant corpus. Over against this sample we must now set the sig-nals that Romans itself supplies (and these would have been far more significant in any case for its original auditors).

(ii) Clearly, Christ himself is a significantly muted signal, occurring only twice as an object in Romans, much later on, and in a partial sense. It might be suggested, then, that "the gospel" is an appropriate object to supply for εἰς πάντας τοὺς πιστεύοντας in 3:22. However, this motif is not especially frequent in Romans either (noun 8-9x; cognate verb 3x) and is confined largely to the episto-lary frame. The last explicit mentions of the gospel prior to 3:22 were the preposi-tional phrase ἐν αὐτῷ in 1:17 and the aside of 2:16, which references the final judg-ment. Romans 1:17 is admittedly an anticipatory statement of 3:21-22, and it certainly includes the gospel; however, the motif receives absolutely no elabora-tion in 3:21-26, and is not used again until 10:16 (following the use of the cognate verb in Isa. 52:7, quoted in 10:15). Following this, only three further instances oc-cur, one disputed (15:16, 19; 16:25; see 1:1, 9, 16; and the verb in 1:15 and 15:20). Moreover, only in 10:16 is any notion of belief in the gospel discussed, although even there the point is made slightly indirectly; Paul speaks first of "*submitting* to the gospel," then he quotes Isaiah 53:1, which speaks of believing in a report (ἀκοή) — a pun in context that probably includes the gospel report. This scat-tered and rather scarce data must now be compared with the possibility that "God" is the implicit object of the participle.

Θεός occurs around one hundred fifty times in Romans[45] — forty-four times before we even reach 3:22 — and in a few instances even as the stated or directly implicit object of the verb πιστεύω (4:3, 17, 20; 10:9 [see also 10:2, 3]) — and this largely because "God" is the object of one of the key πιστεύω intertexts (i.e., Gen. 15:6; it is also directly implicit in the other — Isa. 28:16b). So it would seem that we have found our most likely implicit object on general grounds. Moreover, it is at this point that the syntactical implications become especially pointed.

(iii) It has already been suggested that . . . πίστεως Ἰησοῦ Χριστοῦ should be interpreted subjectively, as Jesus Christ's own fidelity. It is this fidelity, interpreted metonymically with reference to the rest of the story of the passion, that reveals God's δικαιοσύνη. But the implicit object of Jesus' fidelity is then clearly God — the God who raises him from the dead after his martyrological journey through suffering and death (see 4:23-25!). And in view of this evidence alone, the supply of "God" to the following phrase based on the cognate participle seems most likely. The object "God" is clearly stated in the context and directly implicit in the martyrological narrative of Christ just evoked in the immediately preceding phrase — not to mention foregrounded by the most relevant intertext and massively dominating the relevant spreads of lexical data. So this assumption on the part of Paul's auditors could hardly seem more obvious. ("The righteousness of God has been disclosed through the fidelity of Christ [in God] for those who trust [in God].") Moreover, if this is not the case, *then Paul has changed objects in adjacent πιστ- statements without supplying any explicit signal that he has done so,* and this surely asks too much of his auditors. ("The righteousness of God has been disclosed through the fidelity of Christ [in God] for those who trust [in Christ and/or the gospel]?!") Given that we have an obvious candidate for the unstated object of the participle, the reasons supplied to justify this unstated shift in focus would have to be very good.[46] (This reasoning and decision then seem to apply to related texts elsewhere in Paul; see esp. Rom. 1:16-17; Gal. 3:22.)

Determining the exact sense that the participle takes should probably await later elaboration; however, with an implicit object of "God," a personal rather than a merely cognitive orientation seems most appropriate — so "trust" rather than "belief" (and this choice will also align in due course with the cognates that Paul uses elsewhere of "submission" and "obedience"). This meaning, it should be recalled, does not exclude beliefs but suggests certain beliefs appropriate to a personal relationship. And with these clarifications in place, we can turn to address 3:23-26 — a compact, difficult, but highly significant text.

§4. Further Syntactical Decisions in Romans 3:23-26

We need now to press deeper into 3:21-26, from v. 23 onward. But as we do so, we will encounter some notorious problems. In particular, the syntax is distinctive and difficult to construe. Furthermore, certain rare but apparently significant atonement terms are embedded in this syntactical labyrinth, including two more ambiguous πιστ- statements (one of which rounds off the entire subsection). Pre-

cise analysis of those terms will depend on first clarifying their mutual relationships, as dictated by the syntactical context.

The syntactical difficulties seem to begin in v. 24. So it is probably most
useful to begin with what we do know, in vv. 21-22, and then to build from this
material. Verses 21-22 are readily understandable as a repristination of 1:17 with
an additional comment responding more to 1:18–3:20, where the Teacher's gospel
of works has just been negated.

> 1:17: Δικαιοσύνη γὰρ Θεοῦ ἐν αὐτῷ ἀποκαλύπτεται ἐκ πίστεως εἰς πίστιν
> κάθως γέγραπται κ.τ.λ.
> 3:21-22 Νυνὶ δὲ χωρὶς νόμου δικαιοσύνη Θεοῦ πεφανέρωται, μαρτυρουμένη
> ὑπὸ τοῦ νόμου καὶ τῶν προφητῶν, [22] δικαιοσύνη δὲ Θεοῦ [πεφα-
> νέρωται] διὰ πίστεως Ἰησοῦ Χριστοῦ, εἰς πάντας τοὺς πιστεύοντας·

But these sentences are in fact even closer than they seem at first glance. First, the
verbs ἀποκαλύπτω and φανερόω are for Paul often almost interchangeable. (We
should supply a second, elided instance of φανερόω in v. 22.) Second, the phrase
εἰς πίστιν in 1:17a is almost certainly a stylistically crafted reprise of the longer
phrase εἰς σωτηρίαν παντὶ τῷ πιστεύοντι based on the cognate participle in v. 16b,
creating a near identity with the same phrase in 3:22 (cf. εἰς σωτηρίαν παντὶ τῷ
πιστεύοντι in 1:16a with εἰς πάντας τοὺς πιστεύοντας in 3:22; πᾶς is of course a
crucial word for Paul in Romans). Third, we should probably supply an elided
ἔργων before νόμου in 3:21 (see 3:20, 27-28). Fourth, the semantic identity between διὰ πίστεως and ἐκ πίστεως has already been established. Hence, just as 3:21
speaks of the witness of the prophets, the διά phrase in 3:22 actually resonates
with the ἐκ phrase in Habakkuk 2:4 (see also Rom. 3:25 and 3:26; and we have already noted numerous grounds for reading 1:17 christocentrically, so Χριστοῦ is
in effect elided from ἐκ πίστεως there). In view of all these observations, we can
perceive a basic syntactical sequence of five components that underlies these two
sentences.

> (i)   Δικαιοσύνη Θεοῦ ἀποκαλύπτεται/πεφανέρωται
> (ii)   χωρὶς [ἔργων] νόμου
> (iii)   μαρτυρουμένη ὑπὸ τοῦ νόμου καὶ τῶν προφητῶν
> (iv)   ἐκ/διὰ πίστεως [Χριστοῦ/Ἰησοῦ]
> (v)   εἰς πάντας τοὺς πιστεύοντας/πίστιν

In fact, both sentences share four of these semantic components exactly, while
the fifth — element ii, which negates "works of law" — has clearly been added to
3:21 in view of the argument that intervenes in 1:18–3:20, where Paul has criticized the Teacher's gospel of works. Furthermore, element iii — scriptural, and
especially prophetic, witness — is *enacted* by 1:17, when it quotes Habakkuk 2:4,
and then both *stated* and *echoed* by 3:21-22. These observations should help us in
what follows.

At the end of v. 22, Paul comments on πᾶς in element v in what turns out to be a characteristic emphasis in Romans. (Almost exactly the same comment and expansion appear again in 10:12-13.) He asserts in v. 22 that "there is no difference," following this claim with a twofold characterization of "everyone" in vv. 23 and 24a. On the one hand, "all sinned and lack the glory of God," but on the other, they "are 'justified' freely by [God's] grace," a nicely balanced antithetical expansion and partial explanation of his initial claims in terms of πᾶς in v. 22:

> . . . εἰς πάντας τοὺς πιστεύοντας·
> οὐ γάρ ἐστιν διαστολή·
> ²³πάντες γὰρ ἥμαρτον καὶ ὑστεροῦνται τῆς δόξης τοῦ Θεοῦ,
> ²⁴δικαιούμενοι δωρεὰν τῇ αὐτοῦ χάριτι . . .

However, our syntactical difficulties in this section now begin in earnest. Ten short phrases and clauses follow that are grammatically dependent ultimately on this sentence (one begins with a relative pronoun, and the other nine are all prepositional).

> οὐ γὰρ ἐστιν διαστολή·
>
> ²³πάντες γὰρ ἥμαρτον
> καὶ ὑστεροῦνται τῆς δόξης τοῦ Θεοῦ,
> ²⁴δικαιούμενοι δωρεὰν τῇ αὐτοῦ χάριτι
>   διὰ τῆς ἀπολυτρώσεως τῆς ἐν Χριστῷ Ἰησοῦ·
>   ²⁵ὃν προέθετο ὁ Θεὸς ἱλαστήριον
>   διὰ [τῆς] πίστεως
>   ἐν τῷ αὐτοῦ αἵματι
>   εἰς ἔνδειξιν τῆς δικαιοσύνης αὐτοῦ
>   διὰ τὴν πάρεσιν τῶν προγεγονότων ἁμαρτημάτων
>   ἐν τῇ ἀνοχῇ τοῦ Θεοῦ
>   ²⁶πρός τὴν ἔνδειξιν τῆς δικαιοσύνης αὐτοῦ
>   ἐν τῷ νῦν καιρῷ
>   εἰς τὸ εἶναι αὐτὸν δίκαιον καὶ δικαιοῦντα τὸν ἐκ πίστεως Ἰησοῦ[ν].

So Paul has written a sentence here composed initially of two words and a connective particle, then connected another clause to this with a copula (so it uses a verb too) and added a participial construction that is dependent on his initial statement (by agreeing with the subject attributively). But he has followed this understandable arrangement with a further *ten* short modifying phrases, one of them initiating a relative clause. (Strictly speaking, that clause is dependent on the first prepositional expansion, and eight more then follow it.) Moreover, it is clear that much of the semantic material already deployed by Paul in vv. 21-22 is reprised by these later phrases, most notably, Ἰησοῦς [Χριστός] (which occurs here twice explicitly, with one further pronominal reference), Θεός (twice explicitly, with *three* further pronominal references), δικαιοσύνη (twice, but the cognate verb now appears twice as well), and πίστις (twice). Hence, a sentence that begins by expanding on one word within the subsection's initial statement — πᾶς — seems to continue for an inordinately long time and somehow gyrate enough semantically to incorporate a lot of other material from the previous statements within which that key word occurs (i.e., material from components i and iv, and not just v). Two important issues now arise: How is all this material to be comprehended and coordinated syntactically? And why is it so distinctive? Certainly, something unusual is going on in this text that warrants explanation (although we will not need to settle this question definitively). We will address the issue of syntactical coordination first, at which point the question can be sharpened.

4.1. Syntactical Coordination

Our principal difficulty seems to derive from the ambiguity of prepositional phrases' potential functions, which is compounded in this instance by their number. Each prepositional phrase could be functioning either adverbially or adjectivally. Moreover, each could be coordinate (or "parallel"), consecutive (or "sequential"), or parenthetical.

Paul is clearly using parallelism in this subsection, since it is attested overtly twice. And many of the prepositional phrases are anaphoric, beginning with the same preposition as preceding phrases (and others begin with a semantically equivalent preposition). So any given prepositional phrase could be arranged in parallel with another, both thereby modifying the same antecedent clause(s); at least two of them are certainly so arranged. A given phrase could also be arranged consecutively, in a subordinate sense, expanding on the meaning of a previous phrase or clause (and the same option applies necessarily to the relative clause). Or a phrase could function parenthetically, essentially out of sequence, to refer to something else not in the immediate syntactical context. We have already seen that Paul makes such parenthetical remarks not infrequently in the earlier argument of Romans. The number of phrases in Romans 3:23-26 greatly increases the difficulty of our initial decisions at these points, since almost all the phrases that Paul uses in this passage possess these initial ambiguities. Ambiguity compounds ambiguity. I will suggest a new solution to these difficulties, however, building initially from three realizations, one of which is already in place. I will try, moreover, to derive a clear sentence structure from what is more certain, reaching out from there to comprehend what is less immediately apparent.

We saw earlier that this subsection in Romans begins with a programmatic sentence and set of claims that resumes the agenda of 1:17 (that text being informed by 1:16, and 1:2-4 as well). It has five principal components: (i) the disclosure of the δικαιοσύνη Θεοῦ; (ii) independently of "works of law"; (iii) but as attested to by the Scriptures, here both Law and Prophets; (iv) *through* or by means of the fidelity of Christ; and (v) *for* everyone/all who believe(s). We can view this statement as a basic claim with three qualifications of its modality and a stated purpose. Component i drives the sentence grammatically (although we do not need to resolve its specifics just yet in order to address our difficulties here), and this process or event or action is ultimately on behalf of or "for" the constituency named in v, namely, "everyone who believes." Components ii, iii, and iv then describe the nature or mode of this process: it is not by means of works of law, is attested to by Scripture, and is by means of Christ. Moreover, two of these components develop a wordplay using πιστ- terms that has been deployed by Paul twice (i.e., in both 1:16-17 and 3:22; see also 3:25 and 26 and, later on, 9:30–10:17); some sort of similarity exists between the instrument of Christ and the goal of "all who believe," because both can be characterized by πιστ- terminology. This pun by Paul is theologically pregnant.

I want to anticipate now an argument that will be made in detail in chapter eighteen, when we turn to discuss Romans 4. It will become apparent at this later point that 3:27-31 belongs stylistically and substantively with Romans 4, seamlessly initiating an argumentative agenda that this later chapter will address systematically, in stages, through 4:22. Moreover, the entire discussion running from 3:27 through 4:22 — essentially a scriptural σύγκρισις, or comparison — is aptly comprehended by the statement that we have just noted in 3:21-22. In 3:21-22 Paul in effect announces the basic argumentative agenda that is then articulated by 3:27–4:1 in terms of four more specific, subordinate issues and then debated systematically in turn through 4:2-8, 9-12, 13-16a, and 16b-22.

The detailed evidence for this assertion will emerge later (and I am aware that the cogency of the argument I am making here rests in part on the plausibility of that later case). Suffice it for now to note that when Paul states in 3:21-22 that "the δικαιοσύνη Θεοῦ has been disclosed *not* through works of law but through the fidelity of Christ, extending to all who are faithful, *as witnessed by the Scriptures* — both Prophets *and Torah*," he is initiating the second major argumentative phase in his critical engagement with the Teacher's gospel in Romans 1–4. But in this phase, rather than confuting the Teacher in terms of his own assumptions as he did in 1:18–3:20, Paul will engage in a more direct, scriptural refutation. (The Teacher's assumptions will still be in play to a certain extent.) Moreover, he will do so in relation to the Torah. Paul has not yet made his case in relation to the Pentateuch, relying more up to now on Prophetic texts, but the Teacher doubtless did! So from this point Paul will introduce the Torah into the argument, as he really has to. Using a text from Genesis that his subsequent interpreters know well, Paul will try to show how, at several key points, this text refutes an element within the Teacher's gospel and affirms his own. The argument therefore proceeds in a very different manner from 1:18–3:20, but in the service of the same overarching rhetorical objective. Using a shared textual authority, an exegetical comparison will, on the one hand, refute the Teacher's program and, on the other, affirm Paul's.

If this set of claims can be granted temporarily for the sake of the argument and their detailed corroboration postponed until the subsequent chapter's discussions, then some further light is provisionally shed on the structure of 3:21-26. Paul has announced his principal argumentative agenda by the time he reaches the end of his second πιστ- claim in v. 22, and that argument begins in earnest at 3:27. So it seems that the intervening material — essentially vv. 23-26 — can be offset to a degree. We must introduce our third realization to discover why this might be the case. It will be helpful to enumerate Paul's strategic argumentative sequence once again:

   (i) δικαιοσύνη Θεοῦ ἀποκαλύπτεται/πεφανέρωται
  (ii) χωρὶς [ἔργων] νόμου
 (iii) μαρτυρουμένη ὑπὸ τοῦ νόμου καὶ τῶν προφητῶν
 (iv) ἐκ/διὰ πίστεως [Χριστοῦ/'Ιησοῦ]
  (v) εἰς πάντας τοὺς πιστεύοντας/πίστιν

Almost every element in this sequence is dependent on a scriptural intertext that supplies its principal terms (and in fact as element iii dictates, in continuity with 1:2). Romans 3:21-22 is nothing less than a pastiche of scriptural syntagms — with the exception of the claim that it should be this!

   (i) Psalm 98:2-3 (97:2-3 LXX)
  (ii) Psalm 143:1-2 (142:1-2 LXX); Leviticus 18:5
 (iii) a generic claim of scriptural attestation, actualized in the other components, and especially pointed toward 3:27–4:22
 (iv) Habakkuk 2:4
  (v) Genesis 15:6; Isaiah 28:16; Joel 2:32 (3:5 LXX)

> Psalm 98:2-3 (97:2-3 LXX): ἐγνώρισεν κύριος τὸ σωτήριον αὐτοῦ ἐναντίον τῶν ἐθνῶν. ἀπεκάλυψεν τὴν δικαιοσύνην αὐτοῦ. ἐμνήσθη τοῦ ἐλέους αὐτοῦ τῷ 'Ιακὼβ καὶ τῆς ἀληθείας αὐτοῦ τῷ οἴκῳ 'Ισραήλ. εἴδοσαν πάντα τὰ πέρατα τῆς γῆς τὸ σωτήριον τοῦ θεοῦ ἡμῶν.
>
> Psalm 143:1-2 (142:1-2 LXX): κύριε εἰσάκουσον τῆς προσευχῆς μου. ἐνώτισαι τὴν δέησίν μου ἐν τῇ ἀληθείᾳ σου. ἐπάκουσόν μου ἐν τῇ δικαιοσύνῃ σου. Καὶ μὴ εἰσέλθῃς εἰς κρίσιν μετὰ τοῦ δούλου σου ὅτι οὐ δικαιωθήσεται ἐνώπιόν σου πᾶς ζῶν.
>
> Leviticus 18:5: καὶ φυλάξεσθε πάντα τὰ προστάγματά μου καὶ πάντα τὰ κρίματά μου καὶ ποιήσετε αὐτά ἃ ποιήσας ἄνθρωπος ζήσεται ἐν αὐτοῖς. ἐγὼ κύριος ὁ θεὸς ὑμῶν.
>
> Habakkuk 2:4b: ὁ δὲ δίκαιος ἐκ πίστεώς μου ζήσεται.
>
> Genesis 15:6: καὶ ἐπίστευσεν Αβρὰμ τῷ θεῷ καὶ ἐλογίσθη αὐτῷ εἰς δικαιοσύνην.
>
> Isaiah 28:16: διὰ τοῦτο οὕτως λέγει κύριος ἰδοὺ ἐγὼ ἐμβαλῶ εἰς τὰ θεμέλια Σιὼν λίθον πολυτελῆ ἐκλεκτὸν ἀκρογωνιαῖον ἔντιμον εἰς τὰ θεμέλια αὐτῆς καὶ ὁ πιστεύων ἐπ' αὐτῷ οὐ μὴ καταισχυνθῇ.
>
> Joel 2:32 (3:5 LXX): καὶ ἔσται πᾶς ὃς ἂν ἐπικαλέσηται τὸ ὄνομα κυρίου

σωθήσεται ὅτι ἐν τῷ ὄρει Σιὼν καὶ ἐν Ἰερουσαλὴμ ἔσται ἀνασῳζόμενος
καθότι εἶπεν κύριος καὶ εὐαγγελιζόμενοι οὓς κύριος προσκέκληται.

Some of the supporting argumentation for these claims — that is, regarding the
relevance of Psalm 98:2-3, the only text here not explicitly cited by Paul at some
point elsewhere in Romans — must again be postponed until a later chapter. Leviticus 18:5, Isaiah 28:16, and Joel 2:32 are cited overtly by Paul in Romans 10 and
so are best discussed in part five, chapter twenty, but presumably few would want
to dispute their relevance. The relevance of Psalm 143:2, Habakkuk 2:4, and Genesis 15:6 needs no demonstration in the vicinity of Romans 3:21-22.

If this intertextuality in 3:21-22 can be granted for now for the sake of argument, the immediate interpretive consequences are again significant for our
present difficulties. (A further set of consequences will be noted shortly.) Such extensive quotation of Scripture comes at a price. Even as Paul is able to suggest that
his own position is deeply rooted in authoritative Jewish tradition, the precise articulation *of* that position is constrained by the terms and syntagms that he has appropriated from that Scripture's very different settings. He is clearly able to say
what he wants to say with these texts to some degree; otherwise, he would not use
them. However, certain limitations are to be expected. Hence, when Paul begins to
elaborate on these claims in more detail and no longer needs to emphasize his
scriptural authority quite so strongly (presumably because that point has already
been made), we might expect him to introduce paradigmatic lexical variations.[47]
This can avoid tedious terminological repetition and, in this setting, might also
enhance the clarity of his claims. By introducing such variations, Paul can speak
unconstrained, in his preferred terms — something that we have in fact already
seen happening in some of the subtle differences between 3:21-22 and 1:16-17.

Paul shifts the main verb between these two texts from ἀποκαλύπτω to
φανερόω (component i), and he shifts the key preposition that indicates the faithful Christ's instrumental role from ἐκ to διά (component iv). And it is hard to
avoid the conclusion that he has done so principally for the purpose of clarity.
The shift in the verb will not be completely clear until after the discussion of the
next subsection; however, the shift in the preposition makes the point nicely. Ἐκ
is a key marker for Paul, drawn from Habakkuk 2:4, that he uses repeatedly. But it
has already been demonstrated that ἐκ corresponds semantically to the less frequent διά (and it symmetrically opposes an equivalent paradigm of works that
are either ἐκ or διά νόμου). So why does Paul introduce this variation? Doubtless
partly to avoid tedium, but principally because διά conveys the instrumental
sense of the broader phrase slightly more clearly than ἐκ, which often functions in
Paul and the rest of Koiné to denote origin and not means. (Paul's parallel uses of
ἐν and the dative case then make the same point.) Paul thereby abandons a degree
of scriptural correlation in the interests of stylistic variation and clarity; as the
echo fades, the substantive point resonates more clearly.

We should now combine our three main realizations and suggest the beginnings of a resolution to the syntactical issues in 3:23-26.

Romans 3:23-26 is offset in part by the strategic rhetorical function of 3:21-22. Those opening verses signal Paul's argumentative strategy in 3:27–4:22, thereby slightly marginalizing the following four verses (a claim that will be detailed further in chapter sixteen). Moreover, 3:21-22 reproduces a key sequence from earlier in the letter (especially from 1:17), and so seems to be highly important in its own right — something apparently confirmed by its deeply scriptural constitution. Almost every word — except the statement of this principle — is drawn from a scriptural intertext. This prompts us to consider whether 3:23-26 might then be a restatement of that strictly scriptural language in slightly more straightforward terms, prior to the detailed argumentative enactment of its agenda; 3:23-26 could simply be an elaboration of 3:21-22. Of course Paul might also be able to insert additional anticipatory hints into this elaboration about arguments that will take place after 4:22, a question we will consider further in chapter seventeen. Can 3:23-26 be read essentially as a pointed elaboration on 3:21-22? In fact such a reading works well, once the components that Paul is elaborating on are clearly recognized. And our later stylistic observations will confirm this thesis still further.

I suggest that 3:23-26 expands in alternative terminology components i, iv, and v from 3:21-22 (and, earlier, from 1:17). Verses 23-26 work backward through the sequence that we have identified, elaborating first on "all" those who trust and are saved (component v), then on the instrumental function of Christ, by means of whom this salvation takes place (iv), returning finally to his demonstration thereby of the δικαιοσύνη of God (i). The subsection is therefore not concerned immediately with component iii — scriptural attestation — although hints of such a process can certainly be detected. That agenda will be taken up by Romans 4, and then by later sections of the letter. Moreover, it is in part the point of 3:23-26 *not* to echo Scripture so directly but to provide slightly clearer substantive equivalents for any such echoes. A sustained opposition to a gospel of "works of law" is an agenda reprised by 3:21 from 1:18–3:20, and resumed from 3:27 as well, so it is not necessary for 3:23-26 to address component ii either — an essentially negative point. Romans 3:23-26 is thus less scripturally constrained and more positive in its argumentative function than much of the surrounding material. Here we receive hints about some of Paul's own most significant convictions.

The thesis that in vv. 23-26 Paul is essentially explicating his key claims in vv. 21-22 allows us to navigate the rest of the subsection coherently in syntactical terms, although some difficult subordinate problems still have to be resolved en route!

We have already noted that vv. 23-24 elaborate on the πᾶς that occurs at the end of v. 22 in Paul's initial statement of component v — the salvation of "everyone who is faithful." We can now see, however, that v. 24b segues back to an elaboration of component iv, the instrumental role of the faithful Christ in this process, which was introduced in v. 22 with a διά phrase. Paul speaks in v. 24 initially of "the redemption" (τῆς ἀπολυτρώσεως), but it is "that" redemption "that is by means of Christ Jesus" (τῆς ἐν Χριστῷ Ἰησοῦ), and the entire phrase is connected to the preceding participle with a characteristic instrumental διά as well. Paul thereby neatly returns us to the mediation of Christ with an arthrous construction, but having signaled that intention with an anaphoric preposition as well. (ἀπολύτρωσις is grammatically connected by this preposition with the participle of δικαιόω): "justification . . . is *by means of* the redemption *that is by means of Christ Jesus.*" The way is now clear for Paul to elaborate on component iv, the mediation of Christ, which he proceeds to do by way of a relative clause (although component i is now reprised to a degree as well, since Christ is "set forth" as, or "intended" by "God" to be, a ἱλαστήριον). But two further prepositional phrases now occur that are both important and ambiguous. How is their function to be resolved?

> διὰ τῆς ἀπολυτρώσεως
> τῆς ἐν Χριστῷ Ἰησοῦ
> ²⁵ὃν προέθετο ὁ Θεὸς ἱλαστήριον
> διὰ [τῆς] πίστεως
> ἐν τῷ αὐτοῦ αἵματι

These statements are very difficult to arrange coherently. Are the two final prepositional phrases here coordinate, consecutive, or parenthetical? Moreover, are they a tightly integrated statement, like the preceding διά clause, or do they function independently of one another in relation to some earlier statement? It seems that the relative clause could be almost parenthetical, with the two subsequent instrumental clauses functioning in parallel to διὰ τῆς ἀπολυτρώσεως and hence in dependence ultimately on δικαιούμενοι.

> διὰ τῆς ἀπολυτρώσεως τῆς ἐν Χριστῷ Ἰησοῦ.
> ²⁵(ὃν προέθετο ὁ Θεὸς ἱλαστήριον)
> διὰ [τῆς] πίστεως ἐν τῷ αὐτοῦ αἵματι

Or the relative clause could be a significant syntactical element, with the two prepositional phrases elaborating upon it consecutively.

> διὰ τῆς ἀπολυτρώσεως
> τῆς ἐν Χριστῷ Ἰησοῦ
> ²⁵ὃν προέθετο ὁ Θεὸς ἱλαστήριον
> διὰ [τῆς] πίστεως ἐν τῷ αὐτοῦ αἵματι

Some scholars have also suggested a parenthetical function for the πίστις phrase here.[48]

> διὰ τῆς ἀπολυτρώσεως
> τῆς ἐν Χριστῷ Ἰησοῦ
> ²⁵ὃν προέθετο ὁ Θεὸς ἱλαστήριον

(διὰ [τῆς] πίστεως)
ἐν τῷ αὐτοῦ αἵματι

A considerable amount depends ultimately in substantive terms on our solutions to these conundrums. In particular, the relative clause contains a number of difficult but important atoning concepts, so the external leverage that can be applied to these will shift significantly depending upon which of the syntactical arrangements we endorse. But a decision concerning them does not seem possible in immediate terms. All these arrangements seem quite plausible initially (although perhaps the anaphoric reading seems marginally more plausible because of that). I suggest, however, that reasonably decisive evidence for a solution to these difficulties is provided by some of the material that follows in the subsection.

After these phrases, Paul supplies in v. 25b the statement εἰς ἔνδειξιν τῆς δικαιοσύνης αὐτοῦ. He then virtually repeats this claim in v. 26, merely varying the initial preposition to πρός and adding an article to ἔνδειξις. So these two phrases clearly function in parallel, in some coordinate way, and dominate the final meaning of the subsection. But the substance of the two phrases also clearly reprises components i and iv in the programmatic statements of 3:21-22 — God's disclosure of δικαιοσύνη through the faithful Christ. These simple and largely indisputable observations should provide enough material for us to construe the difficult preceding material in syntactical terms.

The earlier phrases must combine somehow to create a coherent statement through vv. 25b-26, which we have just seen is oriented by a repeated claim about the "demonstration of his [i.e., God's] δικαιοσύνη." However, *these later phrases assume in turn a prior claim regarding God,* to which the possessive pronouns refer. And if the relative clause in v. 25 is emphasized rather than subordinated, *then it structures just these later claims, because it speaks overtly of God in the position of subject as well.* Furthermore, it correlates Christ with the "proof" that Paul so emphasizes in these later phrases: ". . . whom God set forth as [or 'intended to be'] a ἱλαστήριον . . . to be a proof of his righteousness . . . ; to be the proof of his righteousness. . . ." Hence, a reading that emphasizes the relative clause provides just the prior emphases that we need for a smooth continuation of Paul's sense later on in the subsection in terms of both God and Christ. (Otherwise, the visible proof tends to be located in the process of justification, essentially reestablishing OD 12 — that is, this salvation of individuals does not in fact function to *reveal* something.) We should conclude, then, that when Paul crafts a relative clause in v. 25 centered on Christ, he is making an emphatic statement that will drive much of the rest of the subsection in semantic terms. The two prepositional phrases subsequent to it therefore function in a subordinate sense, elaborating on the content of this important relative clause — a useful result, because it will allow us to cross-reference all this material in substantive terms to achieve further insights into Paul's claims here about the atonement. (The question whether the πίστις phrase is arthrous or anarthrous is most appropriately considered when we discuss these further issues, along with the question of this phrase's parenthetical function.)

If we note quickly now that the two emphatic and repeated ἔνδειξις statements are almost certainly expanded by subordinate and (where appropriate) coordinate prepositional phrases as well — by two and one respectively — then a coherent and plausible sentence structure for 3:24-26 begins to emerge. (The first of these phrases contains a set of rare terms for Paul that will have to be considered carefully in due course. But the two dative prepositional phrases seem quite straightforward, the first being instrumental and the second temporal, although the exact sense of the ἀνοχή of God will depend on our construal of the phrase that precedes it.)

> ˙ δικαιούμενοι . . .
> διὰ τῆς ἀπολυτρώσεως
> τῆς ἐν Χριστῷ Ἰησοῦ·
> ²⁵ὃν προέθετο ὁ Θεὸς ἱλαστήριον
> διὰ [τῆς] πίστεως
> ἐν τῷ αὐτοῦ αἵματι
> εἰς ἔνδειξιν τῆς δικαιοσύνης αὐτοῦ
> διὰ τὴν πάρεσιν τῶν προγεγονότων ἁμαρτημάτων
> ἐν τῇ ἀνοχῇ τοῦ Θεοῦ
> ²⁶πρὸς τὴν ἔνδειξιν τῆς δικαιοσύνης αὐτοῦ
> ἐν τῷ νῦν καιρῷ . . .

It remains only to note that the entire subsection concludes with a resonant purposive clause that places God again in the position of subject (i.e., as in v. 25), at this point in a distinctive articular infinitive construction: εἰς τὸ εἶναι αὐτὸν δίκαιον καὶ δικαιοῦντα τὸν ἐκ πίστεως Ἰησοῦ. This clause seems to pun on the previous uses of δικαιο- terms in the subsection (the participle having occurred only once, in v. 24, and the adjective not at all, but the noun having been used four times), and it ends by reprising the πίστις Χριστοῦ phrase of v. 22 as well, although here with a stronger echo of that phrase's scriptural intertext, along with the rather unusual epithet Ἰησοῦ[ν]. (We will have to consider shortly whether the genitive is to be preferred here or the less well attested accusative.) And although this clause is dependent on the two parallel sets of phrases that precede it, it is still clearly an emphatic conclusion to the subsection as a whole, although its exact nuances have yet to be decided — i.e., does it summarize and emphasize components i and iv, or i, iv, and v?

At this point, then, the remaining questions notwithstanding, we have navigated most of the main syntactical issues in this difficult but important subsection. I have suggested construing it essentially as follows:

> ²¹Νυνὶ δὲ
> χωρὶς [ἔργων] νόμου
> ²²δικαιοσύνη Θεοῦ πεφανέρωται,
> μαρτυρουμένη ὑπὸ τοῦ νόμου καὶ τῶν προφητῶν,

δικαιοσύνη δὲ Θεοῦ [πεφανέρωται]
    διὰ πίστεως Ἰησοῦ Χριστοῦ,
        εἰς πάντας τοὺς πιστεύοντας·
        οὐ γάρ ἐστιν διαστολή·
        ²³πάντες γὰρ ἥμαρτον καὶ ὑστεροῦνται τῆς δόξης τοῦ Θεοῦ,
        ²⁴δικαιούμενοι δωρεὰν τῇ αὐτοῦ χάριτι
            διὰ τῆς ἀπολυτρώσεως
    τῆς ἐν Χριστῷ Ἰησοῦ·
²⁵ὃν προέθετο ὁ Θεὸς ἱλαστήριον
    διὰ [τῆς] πίστεως
    ἐν τῷ αὐτοῦ αἵματι
εἰς ἔνδειξιν τῆς δικαιοσύνης αὐτοῦ
    διὰ τὴν πάρεσιν τῶν προγεγονότων ἁμαρτημάτων
    ἐν τῇ ἀνοχῇ τοῦ Θεοῦ
²⁶πρὸς τὴν ἔνδειξιν τῆς δικαιοσύνης αὐτοῦ
    ἐν τῷ νῦν καιρῷ
εἰς τὸ εἶναι αὐτὸν δίκαιον καὶ δικαιοῦντα τὸν ἐκ πίστεως Ἰησοῦ[ν].

The text folds in on itself and out again, through an initial sequence of claims — i through v — and then back through the claims that remain relevant — v, iv, and i. So fundamentally, it has a chiastic structure, one of Paul's favorite compositional techniques. We should now be in a position to approach the remaining problems in the passage with a more precise grasp of its basic flow and sense. But before addressing them in detail, one final, more general syntactical issue must be addressed — the second major issue noted at the beginning of this subsection.

4.2. Syntactical Distinctiveness

As we have just seen, this subsection is constructed ordinarily enough in syntactical terms until v. 24. It begins with three relatively short sentences, the first two reprising a key sequence from 1:17 (etc.). Paul then starts to expand on the πᾶς that functions within component v in this sequence, initially by way of a short disclaimer — "for there is no difference." He begins another clarifying sentence in v. 23 that starts ordinarily enough with two independent clauses and an attributive participial construction, which, in substantive terms, continues to elaborate on his use of πᾶς in v. 22b. But *this* sentence ultimately continues through v. 26, journeying there — as we have seen — by way of ten further phrases and clauses, most of which are prepositional, although one is an important relative clause. This marked accumulation of such terms and syntagms is extremely unusual for Paul and demands explanation.

One popular theory has sought in the past to account for both the subsection's syntactical arrangement and its character by attributing this material — at least in part — to an earlier stratum in the church, from which Paul is quoting.

But I am unpersuaded by this theory in its pristine form. Most significantly, almost all of the terms in this passage are familiar from elsewhere in Paul, *and the actual structure of the syntagms is also quite Pauline;* it is merely their extended arrangement that is unusual, along with occasional words and phrases.[49] So it seems that Paul himself has composed the subunit deliberately in this distinctive fashion. What could account for this, preferably along with the incorporation of this more unusual terminology? Various pieces of data point toward a particular conclusion.

I suggest that Paul has composed this text in an overtly "ritual" manner,[50] and this would have been reflected in its appropriate performance during delivery — although a frustrating level of ambiguity must surround this suggestion. Nevertheless, this thesis enjoys a degree of wider support, and it explains our text neatly.[51]

We should first note that although the text is not perfectly symmetrical or balanced,[52] there is evidence of a striking degree of crafting in its ten phrases and clauses — two sets of symmetrical and slightly overlapping patterns of repeated phrases (and this would have assisted memorization and performance). After Paul's segue back to christological concerns in v. 24b, where the striking syntax and material begins, the syntagms are initiated as follows: διά . . . ἐν . . . ὃν . . . διά . . . ἐν . . . εἰς . . . διά . . . ἐν . . . πρός . . . ἐν . . . εἰς . . . (with a final ἐκ that does not seem so relevant). Only Paul's use of διά in v. 25b — and here, moreover, in a more unusual accusative construction — disturbs a composition in terms of two sets of five phrases and clauses, *although in so doing it reproduces a pattern from the previous set* (AB).

διά . . .	A
ἐν . . .	B
ὃν . . .	C
διά . . .	A
ἐν . . .	B
εἰς . . .	D
διά . . .	A
ἐν . . .	B
πρός . . .	E
ἐν . . .	B
εἰς . . .	D

This material is also extremely concentrated. A slower, more deliberate performance in ritual terms would have given auditors the time necessary to assimilate its information. Even more importantly, this distinctive presentation would simultaneously have signaled the text's argumentative distinctiveness and thereby have corresponded to the structure of the subsection that we noted earlier on. Paul reprises a critical argumentative sequence in 3:21-22 that indicates in particular how he will argue from 3:27 to 4:22, indicating other matters momentarily. So

3:23-26 is offset stylistically to correspond to this offset substantive role. If this text was performed in a distinctive style appropriate to its ritual patterning, this would have signaled its peculiar character to the letter's auditors, allowing the temporary cessation of the actual argument as it elaborated on the important but compact material in vv. 21-22, essentially hymning Christ and God's action through him.

In suggesting this, I have — somewhat ironically — returned to the old form-critical hypothesis, but only in part. That explanation's intuitions that this text is carefully and ritually composed seem to have been correct, but the approach I am suggesting here emphasizes Paul's rhetorical goals, his compositional freedom (thereby accounting for the inherently Pauline nature of the material), and the actualization of his goals by the text's appropriate performance. Viewed in these terms, the suggestion fits neatly into the flow of the letter's unfolding argument, which moves in direct substantive terms from 3:22 to 3:27 (as we will see shortly — although there are implications for other, later arguments in the letter as well).[53] Various pieces of evidence arguably support this suggestion, although they are not completely decisive. Nevertheless, the cumulative case seems indicative.

Romans is characterized by a number of doxologies (see 1:25b [although this probably ironic]; 6:17; 7:25; 9:5b; 11:33-36; and perhaps also 16:25-27; see also 1:23; 4:20; 5:2, 11; and 15:6, 7, 9-12) and prayers (1:8-10, 13; 8:26-27, 34b; 10:1; 15:13, 30-33; 16:20) — the patterned language of worship. And although none is as distinctive as 3:24b-26, there are several other subsections in Romans with an accumulation of prepositional phrases (1:3-4, 17; 4:25; and 11:36; with analogous discussions in 5:21 and 8:38-39; such material is usually christological). Romans 1:3-4 is especially important:

> Παῦλος δοῦλος Χριστοῦ ᾿Ιησοῦ
> κλητὸς ἀπόστολος
> ἀφωρισμένος εἰς εὐαγγέλιον θεοῦ
> ὃ προεπηγγείλατο
> διὰ τῶν προφητῶν αὐτοῦ
> ἐν γραφαῖς ἁγίαις
> περὶ τοῦ υἱοῦ αὐτοῦ
> τοῦ γενομένου
> ἐκ σπέρματος Δαυὶδ
> κατὰ σάρκα
> τοῦ ὁρισθέντος υἱοῦ θεοῦ
> ἐν δυνάμει
> κατὰ πνεῦμα ἁγιωσύνης
> ἐξ ἀναστάσεως νεκρῶν
> ᾿Ιησοῦ Χριστοῦ τοῦ κυρίου ἡμῶν κ.τ.λ.

Three features of this text are worth emphasizing initially. First, it is a complex periodic construction very similar to Romans 3:23-26. Here, as there, Paul uses a coordinating participle (1x; see 1x in 3:23-26), a relative clause (1x; see 1x), and arthrous infinitives (2x; see 1x) but leans primarily on prepositional phrases (8x; see 9x; but note also that *five* further prepositional phrases and clauses follow this material in 1:5-6, two incorporating relative pronouns but not being coordinated by way of those). Second, a chiastic pattern is again discernible governing some of these prepositions — here ἐκ . . . κατά . . . ἐν . . . κατά . . . ἐξ . . . in vv. 3b-4. (This sequence is then bracketed by a heavier use of instrumental prepositions, principally διά in the genitive and ἐν constructions — prepositions that are also central to 3:22-26.[54]) Third, scholars have long suggested that Paul is incorporating traditional material in these statements, and with good reason. An emphasis on Christ's Davidic lineage is unusual for Paul, and he seldom if ever describes Jesus' resurrection using the verb ὁρίζω or describes the Holy Spirit as the Spirit of holiness — πνεῦμα ἁγιωσύνης. The description of Christ here is, furthermore, wholly focused on Christ's messianic lineage, both historical and eschatological, and this is again uncommon for Paul.

However, all these considerations fall short of demonstrating that the entire subsection has been quoted from an early church tradition. Both the unusual terms used in v. 4 are familiar to Paul in other settings; they are part of his demonstrable lexicon.[55] It is merely their deployments here that are distinctive. Moreover, this syntax falls short of demonstrating direct quotation, as it does in 3:23-26 as well; these are all characteristically Pauline constructions, although their complexity and density here are unusual. The verb ὁρίζω is even part of a wordplay in the immediate context with ἀφωρισμένος in v. 1, a statement not likely to be part of any early church acclamation (and similar wordplays are apparent in 3:21-26 as well).

The most likely initial explanation of all these textual features is, rather, the supposition that Paul is echoing traditional theological positions that he thinks the Roman Christians endorse — a primitive messianic resurrection theology (and so this material is still a priceless insight into an early stratum of Christian thinking). The slightly unusual terms and emphases are oriented, then, by that shared theological tradition, and they are foregrounded here by their inclusion within a measured, crafted syntax *and* their placement in the middle of the epistolary address. Moreover, there are excellent rhetorical reasons for Paul to do this. He is thereby essentially affirming quite overtly his continuity with the gospel that the Roman Christians originally received (and he probably has quite a good understanding of that). This would be useful merely as a way of securing that audience's trust, but it will also allow the gradual pursuit of a more sophisticated and far-reaching rhetorical agenda, although the explication of that maneuver must wait for the moment. Here it suffices to note that Romans 1:2-4 is *very* similar to 3:21-26, and especially to vv. 24-26, in style and substance, Paul apparently crafting a complex set of statements that echoes more traditional theology and vocabulary.

The text ends with an overt affirmation of Jesus' lordship, this being a demonstrable feature of early Christian worship (see esp. Rom. 10:9-13; 1 Cor. 8:6;

12:3; Phil. 2:10-11). Scholars are rightly confident that the phrase "Jesus is Lord" — Κύριος Ἰησοῦς — was a central element in that setting and therefore constitutes an instance of ritualized language. But we should recall at this point that deliberately composed hymnic material was probably a feature of worship in the early church, as seen most clearly perhaps in 1 Corinthians 14:26 (ἕκαστος ψαλμὸν ἔχει κ.τ.λ.),[56] and Pliny's letter to Trajan, although doubtless this designated the use of traditional texts at times. So, although it becomes increasingly difficult to isolate such material clearly, the ritualized language of early Christian devotion and worship almost certainly included rather more than the two words just noted. And it is not necessary to demonstrate the actual patterns in use to suggest that such underlying ritualized language could explain Paul's use of relatively short, rhythmic syntagms with overt compositional patterns in Romans. Moreover, such material might have been performed in a certain way, although it is difficult to reconstruct this precisely. It *might* have been recited especially rhythmically and/or in a different tone than the surrounding material, or even chanted or sung (although this type of performance is partly driven by acoustic considerations in public worship, especially in large gatherings), which would have offset it from any surrounding material in the letter still more overtly. The question of ancient analogies is a vexed one.[57] But it seems possible to recognize here in Paul's text the ancient distinction also evident between "Du" and "Er" hymns — songs to a god, and so in the second person, as against about a god, and so in the third person. The doxologies and shorter prayers in Romans conform to the former, and the rich prepositional constructions including 3:24b-26 to the latter. Paul seems to praise God "the Father" directly in Romans, and to sing about Christ.

The possibility that Paul is echoing the ritualized language of early Christian worship inches toward probability in my view when other Pauline texts are introduced into the equation, although this is complicated by the occurrences of some of those passages in disputed letters. However, that phenomenon is not necessarily fatal to their implications.

It is well known that other Pauline texts contain material that is strikingly analogous to Romans 3:24b-26: Philippians 2 (vv. 5-11), Ephesians 1 (vv. 3-14), and Colossians 1 (vv. 15-20 — although vv. 12-14 here should also be noted; but see also shorter texts in 1 Corinthians 8:5-6, and perhaps also 1:30 and 6:11; and 2 Corinthians 1:3-7; see also 1 Peter 1:3-9/12). The most important such text is Ephesians 1, closely followed by Colossians 1 — letters whose authenticity is of course disputed. But before dismissing this evidence, we should consider three points. First, the letters may not be inauthentic. Second, even if they are, they provide evidence from the Pauline communal tradition of a certain distinctive sort of composition and performance that is therefore still highly suggestive. And third, it seems significant that the disputed texts are matched closely in stylistic terms by indisputably Pauline texts, especially Romans 1:2-4, 3:24-26, and Philippians 2:5-11. It would seem to follow that if Ephesians 1 turns out to be nearly identical to Romans 3:24-26 and its indisputably Pauline textual siblings, and can, moreover, be attributed with a degree of certainty to a ritual setting, then Romans 3:24-26 can plausibly be so attributed as well. Certainly, it seems more difficult to argue for any alternative explanation of the data.[58]

The similarities between the two extended sentences in Romans and Ephesians are quite striking (and are generally not noted). Most significantly, Ephesians 1:3-14 begins with a statement of divine "blessing" in v. 3 that echoes analogous invocations from Jewish ritual texts: Εὐλογητὸς ὁ θεὸς καὶ πατὴρ τοῦ κυρίου ἡμῶν Ἰησοῦ Χριστοῦ κ.τ.λ. (And here the lordship of Christ is invoked at the outset rather than at the conclusion of the text.) An arthrous substantive participial construction, however, coordinated with the object of blessing in v. 3, God, allows the text to shift principally to an Er form, in the third person, which continues through v. 12. A famously complex Greek sentence now ensues that unfolds with the help of conjunctions, participles, prepositional clauses and phrases, relative clauses, and infinitive constructions (both arthrous and anarthrous) — just the techniques that structure the comparable extended sentences in Romans 1:2-4, 3:23-26, and Philippians 2:5-11.[59] The similar prepositional phrases are especially noteworthy — various genitive διά, instrumental christological ἐν, and purposive εἰς constructions enfolding humanity (2x, 13x, and 9x respectively!).[60] But it is significant that the vocabulary of the Romans texts is discernible in the Ephesian passage as well. There are references both in Ephesians 1 and Romans 3 to Θεός, Ἰησοῦς Χριστός, χάρις, πιστεύω, ἀπολύτρωσις, αἷμα, and προέθετο, and similar probable references to δόξα, ἡ ἄφεσις τῶν παραπτωμάτων, and πᾶς/πάντα — an overlap of around ten words and motifs. The Spirit and the lordship of Christ are shared between Romans 1:2-4 and Ephesians 1:3-14, in addition to several of the words already mentioned. Indeed, in view of this evidence, irrespective of any other relationship, it seems that close stylistic and substantive similarities between Ephesians 1 and Romans 1 and 3 should be granted.

Various scholars have argued that the best explanation for this distinctive material in Ephesians 1 is its evocation of the patterned language of worship, whether public or private — worship influenced by Judaism but now centered on Christ. This passage seems to be a powerful opening to the letter body in resonant ritual terms.[61] Indeed, this is signaled at its outset overtly with the language of blessing (see Rom. 1:25; 9:5; 2 Cor. 1:3; 11:31; see elsewhere in the New Testament only Mark 14:61; Luke 1:68; 1 Pet. 1:3 [and only the Markan instance here is not an instance of worship]).[62] So Lincoln concludes — almost certainly correctly — that "[t]his opening passage with its outburst of praise has the form of an extended blessing or *berakah* . . ."; "the OT and Jewish worship provide the background for this form," which is "anchored firmly in Jewish worship" (*Ephesians,* 10, 11). This suggests by implication that Romans 3:24-26 echoes the ritualized language of prayer and blessing as well (as does Romans 1:2-4).[63] Moreover, this judgment dovetails exactly with the argumentative and intertextual indications already adduced that point to the slight offsetting of this material after the critical statements of 3:21-22. If Romans 3:24-26 was deliberately composed and performed to echo the more ritualized christological texts of early Christians (as well as to elaborate on the compact and possibly slightly opaque claims of v. 22), then that echo would cease after v. 26. And with this function further clarified, we can turn to consider some of the remaining interpretative issues in this subsection and its siblings — principally more detailed lexicographical questions, but ones laden with theological significance.

CHAPTER SIXTEEN

Atonement and "Justification" in Romans 3:21-26

§1. Preamble

Many agendas converge in Romans 3:21-26 and clash here; the very meaning of Christ's atoning death is often held to be at stake. However, Paul's immediate concerns in this subsection are not necessarily ours. This does not preclude us from mining this text for answers to our questions, but they will not necessarily be provided here by Paul with complete clarity. Indeed, I will argue shortly that this subsection has often been overinterpreted by modern readers. So we will pull back from some of the certainties of earlier debates and detect in their place something more akin to indications of later argumentative developments — a quite deliberate ploy on Paul's part, I would suggest.

It needs to be recalled that these texts and words have been liberated from their customary setting in relation to the first phase of Justification theory, which is usually held to have established a particular problem by this point in the letter. As we appreciate well by now, within that definition of the problem all the contours of its necessary Christian solution are implicit, so most scholars know exactly what they are looking for by the time they reach Romans 3:23. But we have already adduced numerous reasons for abandoning such expectations. Paul's initial critique of the Teacher's gospel has reached a largely self-sufficient conclusion in 3:20, so we can now approach the function and meaning of 3:21-26 with fresh eyes. The rereading of 1:18–3:20 that has earlier been suggested effectively frees this text to find its own place in Paul's argument. And as we began to explore its terminology and syntax in the preceding chapter, it became apparent that this text is in fact oriented largely by the pregnant intertextual claims of 3:21-22, which echo in turn 1:17 (and 1:16 and 1:2-4 a little more distantly); 3:23-26 then seems oriented most tightly and significantly toward the explication of the series of claims made in these apparently programmatic texts. With these important judgments in place — the orientation of 3:23-26 not toward 1:18–3:20 so much as toward 3:21-22 and, behind that, 1:17 — we will begin our more detailed analysis, beginning (as usual) with more obvious judgments, from which we will try to build to decisions concerning less obvious and often more controversial matters. We will be concerned in what follows especially with the meaning of Paul's atonement terms and statements in 3:23-25, then with the implied meaning of the verb δικαιόω in v. 24, followed by the meaning of a further atonement clause in 3:25b, and finally the subsection's conclusion in 3:26b.

§2. The Meaning of Romans 3:25a

An enormous amount of discussion has taken place over the interpretation of ἱλαστήριον in Romans 3:25 and over Paul's broader understanding of the atonement, which is presumably related to this rare but apparently important word. Moreover, there is a lack of clarity concerning the apostle's use of the signifier αἷμα, and the phrase διὰ [τῆς] πίστεως, which interposes between them, is troublesome as well. I am suggesting, however, that a christocentric approach to this last phrase — an approach with better exegetical support than any alternative — can resolve most of our difficulties in relation to the other two issues, leading in turn to a persuasive explanation of Paul's understanding of the atonement as a whole. There is indeed a key that unlocks these issues, and without it they remain virtually impenetrable.

2.1. The Christological Key

The critical textual material occurs at the beginning of v. 25:

> . . . ὃν προέθετο ὁ Θεὸς ἱλαστήριον
> διὰ [τῆς] πίστεως
> ἐν τῷ αὐτοῦ αἵματι . . .

Entire monographs, quite understandably, have been devoted to the analysis of ἱλαστήριον.[1] Studies debate whether this is an adjective or a substantive (which ultimately is probably not that important). They also debate the signifier's exact sense. It almost certainly carries some sort of functional connotation, and so might overlap semantically to a degree with the more common cognate verb, ἱλάσκεσθαι, but that function could be exemplary, expiatory, propitiatory, participatory, or some combination of these.[2] Or it could derive from some general theory of sacrifice based ultimately (and rather unwisely) on Freud or some primitivist or primordial conception.[3] The word could, moreover, refer specifically to the "mercy seat" (that is, to the gold lid of the ark of the covenant, on which the High Priest scattered atoning blood once a year during the festival of Yom Kippur), or more generally to costly atoning objects, or even — probably by way of analogy — to atoning events like the deaths of righteous martyrs.[4] And clearly circular hermeneutics tend to operate at this point between the meaning of the signifier, its reference, and broader conceptions of sacrifice and of atonement (which are themselves not the same thing). Those theories are informed, furthermore, by various broader cultural and religious antecedents, which usually look to the Old Testament[5] but sometimes include Greco-Roman material, as well as, or even in lieu of, Jewish precursors.[6] And the question of Jewish antecedents is not simple. Various preceding practices and/or narratives can be drawn on in supposed explanation of Paul's thinking about Christ and his use of this signifier (which was doubtless shaped by earlier Christian reflection as well) — generic Jewish understandings of sacrifice, the exodus, the possible construal of Isaiah 53, high priestly and other cultic conceptions, especially Yom Kippur, the sacrifice of Isaac in Genesis 22, more general Jewish martyrological conceptions, and so on.

These complex conversations then unfold, as we have already seen, in relation to a relatively scarce amount of specific data in a difficult syntactical location (although in relation to broader construals of the argument in Romans 1:18–3:20 that have usually seemed clear but have now been called into question). And to cap it all off, the absence of the article is hotly debated as well (although this is probably another false indicator).[7] The meaning of αἷμα is then swept up in these issues, although the range of possible semantic options here is much narrower. This could merely mean death in metonymic terms ("blood poured out . . .") or denote "life" in some sort of powerful, expiatory sense (see Lev. 17:10-16).[8] Its grammatical function in context is also debated.

Clearly, it is difficult to navigate all these swirling interpretive currents coherently and plausibly. Much has been suggested in the past, but arguably little has actually been resolved.

The phrase διὰ [τῆς] πίστεως, meanwhile, has seemed to interrupt these atoning concerns rather incomprehensibly, interposing as it does between ἱλαστήριον and αἷμα, and we must ask in addition whether πίστις is arthrous or anarthrous, and whether it is functioning with αἷμα as its object or modifying other material independently. Some of these difficulties have already been addressed in part three, chapter eleven. Indeed, we can assert now more strongly in the light of the syntactical analysis undertaken in chapter fifteen that these two short prepositional phrases seem to be functioning independently of one another in parallel, or coordinate, terms. It has already been established as well that the relative clause ὃν προέθετο ὁ Θεὸς ἱλαστήριον is functioning significantly, establishing certain claims that are then resumed by the key clauses at the end of the subsection — essentially, the revelatory and atoning purposes of God effected in Christ. The two short prepositional phrases that follow this important clause must consequently modify it in parallel. It makes no sense in any capacity to suggest that *God* intended *Christ* to function as a ἱλαστήριον (or to display him publicly) "*by means of* faith in his blood."[9] Neither God's faith, nor Christ's faith, nor human faith in Christ's bloody death can *instrumentally effect* the intention and action of God that Christ function as a ἱλαστήριον![10]

It seems even more unlikely now than it seemed in chapter eleven that διὰ [τῆς] πίστεως reaches back, essentially parenthetically, to earlier material. This phrase seems to function just where it is located, modifying the preceding relative clause in a deliberately patterned dyad of prepositional phrases. Adding more certainty to this suspicion is the fact that a plausible reading can be supplied for it in just this location. The phrase echoes διὰ πίστεως Ἰησοῦ Χριστοῦ in v. 22, which we have already determined is a christological statement denoting the fidelity of Jesus Christ. And the same reference in the later phrase διὰ [τῆς] πίστεως in v. 25 now makes perfect sense in context *and* recognizes this echo — not to mention the focus of the surrounding material on God's atoning act in Christ — resulting in an entirely acceptable reading: "God intended Christ to be a ἱλαστήριον by means of [his] fidelity, by means of his blood."[11] Both these phrases consequently gloss the atoning claim in v. 25a metonymically in terms of the narrative of Christ's passion. They also begin to fulfill Paul's basic goal in 3:23-26 of explication. Christ's "blood" glosses Christ's "fidelity," thereby pointing more clearly, unmediated by intertextual language derived ultimately from Habakkuk 2:4, to the exact reference of these claims: Christ's suffering and death on the cross (indicating overtly that this story of faithfulness culminated in that virtue's supreme test — death). *This* is where God's purpose to have Christ function as a ἱλαστήριον is effected; therefore, it is *by means of* this set of events and the narrative describing it that God's purpose of atonement is fulfilled (and this is hardly a surprising set of claims for Paul to be making).[12]

The presence or absence of the article is clearly of secondary importance in relation to this primary interpretative judgment — that πίστις here ought to be referred to Christ irrespective of whether the phrase is arthrous or anarthrous. However, this is an appropriate stage in our discussion at which to consider this entire contention, namely, whether the presence or absence of the article signifies a particular orientation in any following christological genitive. (διὰ [τῆς] πίστεως in Rom. 3:25 is not one of the infamous genitives, but it follows closely and echoes one; therefore, the interpretation of that construction and debate and this particular text are closely related.) Is *this* the key to the πίστις Χριστοῦ dispute and hence ultimately to the interpretation of 3:25 as well?

Both sides of the πίστις Χριστοῦ dispute have attempted grammatical solutions, which would have the virtue of economy. Advocates of the subjective reading of the genitive have suggested that an objective construal is ungrammatical, and rare if not entirely unattested. And advocates of the objective reading have suggested that the presence or absence of the article suggests definitively which type of genitive relation is in view — an objective one. But I am going to suggest that both these cases collapse and that the debate is consequently resolvable only in rather different terms — by considering the key texts and their probable causality in the broader settings of their arguments in Romans, Galatians, and elsewhere. A little ironically, however, the rather different function of the article *in Romans 3:25* does in my view ultimately cause difficulties for the objective reading.

Objective genitives involving πίστις are rare, but they are attested in

Koiné,[13] as are instances in relation to the cognate verb, πιστεύω. Perhaps most importantly, I will suggest shortly that Romans 4:17 — correctly understood — contains just such an instance in Paul himself (using the verb). An equivalent substantive phrase is, meanwhile, apparently attested in Mark 11:22 (although this instance is not in my view completely transparent).[14] But the invalidity of this basic contention by subjective genitive advocates is now being widely conceded and so need not detain us further.[15]

Advocates of an objective reading have, meanwhile, been more persistent in claiming that the article is a definitive marker of either the subjective or objective sense.[16] Specifically, they suggest that a subjective sense for the genitive would have been signaled by Paul with a fully arthrous construction, and so any other sort of construction — which we supposedly have invariably in all the disputed πίστις Χριστοῦ genitives — should be construed differently, and in all probability objectively (and they basically draw here on an ancient rule formulated by the grammarian Apollonius, although it is not applied precisely). But this is a curiously weak argument in practice.

There are three main difficulties with this case: (1) two indisputable instances in Paul — Romans 4:16 and Galatians 2:20 — falsify it directly; (2) the rule itself is clearly invalid as an explanation of Paul's use of the article, and especially in this relation; and (3) the presence of the article in certain manuscript variants of Romans 3:25 seems to cause difficulties for advocates of an objective construal in context.

(1) Direct Falsification

In Romans 4:16 Paul states that the promise will be established παντὶ τῷ σπέρματι, οὐ τῷ ἐκ τοῦ νόμου μόνον ἀλλὰ καὶ τῷ ἐκ πίστεως Ἀβραάμ (κ.τ.λ.). The rule of usage suggested by objective advocates would seem to suggest that the final genitive relation here is objective (i.e., denoting "faith *in* Abraham"), since its subjective meaning has not been signaled here, as it supposedly ought to have been, with a fully arthrous construction (viz., τῷ ἐκ τῆς πίστεως τοῦ Ἀβραάμ). However, no scholar suggests this reading, for it is patently absurd in context. It seems, then, that Paul can construct a subjective genitive phrase that is not fully arthrous (and in fact not arthrous at all). But this evidence is doubly significant for the issue in question.

In Romans 3:26 a precisely parallel expression occurs (and we will consider this carefully just below) — τὸν ἐκ πίστεως Ἰησοῦ.[17] Indeed, this is one of the half dozen or so explicitly disputed πίστις Χριστοῦ genitives in Paul. Hence, it necessarily follows from the existence of Romans 4:16 that this phrase in 3:26 *can* be construed subjectively, irrespective of any assertions about rules concerning articles by advocates of an objective reading. And if it can be so construed, v. 22 ought also to be so readable, because both phrases seem to be functioning clearly in parallel (and so on).[18]

Galatians 2:20 now adds to the difficulties of this contention, although from the opposite direction. There Paul states ὃ δὲ νῦν ζῶ ἐν σαρκί, ἐν πίστει ζῶ τῇ τοῦ υἱοῦ τοῦ Θεοῦ (κ.τ.λ.). The first definite article that we see Paul using here — τῇ — is significant; it signals that πίστις is functioning in apposition to the following phrase, "the son of God," but that Paul has pulled this signifier forward in the clause (presumably in an instance of hyperbaton, for the sake of emphasis). But read in its arthrously signaled location, so to speak, a fully arthrous construction results, which should of course, in accordance with the rule suggested by advocates of the objective construal of the genitive, be construed *subjectively*. (And the often-unnoticed Ephesians 4:13 provides an identical instance.) Two observations now increase the impact of this data still further.

First, Romans 5:15 provides an almost identical clause that is also overtly subjective, further reinforcing the plausibility of the subjective reading of Galatians 2:20: πολλῷ μᾶλλον ἡ χάρις τοῦ Θεοῦ καὶ ἡ δωρεὰ ἐν χάριτι τῇ τοῦ ἑνὸς ἀνθρώπου Ἰησοῦ Χριστοῦ εἰς τοὺς πολλοὺς ἐπερίσσευσεν. Second, the instance in Galatians 2:20 now threatens to draw the other instances of πίστις Χριστοῦ in context in Galatians into the same basic sense; otherwise, Paul seems to be shifting suddenly and inexplicably in his argument. And this clause follows shortly after one of the critical texts in the entire dispute, namely, Galatians 2:15-16, and precedes another important set of texts discussing πίστις, namely, 3:2-4 and 3:6-14. These all now seem susceptible to a subjective reading in terms of the rule established by objective advocates that seems to be functioning in 2:20.

The relationship between the two falsifications of the contention in terms of the presence or absence of the article now needs to be noted carefully. If the contention were true, then Galatians 2:20 would seem to prove the opposite of what the contention's advocates ultimately want, providing a definitive instance of a subjective construction (and further difficulties then follow from this in Galatians). But Romans 4:16 seems to suggest that the contention — in its inverse form — is false; Paul *can* provide a subjective phrase that is not fully arthrous. It does not follow, however, from this falsification that the first difficulty is now irrelevant. The fully arthrous construction might still signal a subjective construction (and this in fact seems likely).[19] It is just that the article's absence does not automatically denote the opposite — namely, a nonsubjective sense. So the objectivist contention concerning articles is falsified by the evidence in Paul, and also draws attention to perhaps the most difficult piece of evidence in the entire puzzle for the objective advocate! The worst of both worlds seems to have been achieved. And here the second major problem now seems to be emerging — namely, the objective camp does not seem to have given an accurate account of the function of the article in Paul (a point in the debate where Rom. 3:25 becomes directly relevant).

(2) Invalid "Rule" in Paul

Apollonius asserted that a subjective construction could be fully arthrous *or* fully anarthrous (article-substantive-article-substantive or A-S-A-S, or S-S). But most grammarians recognize the need to modify this canon immediately with the caveat that the governing noun may be anarthrous but not the governed (S-A-S). Further qualifying the canon, moreover, is the caveat that it does not apply to constructions involving *names,* at which point presumably A-S-S becomes possible as well![20] Hence, rather unhelpfully, all possible combinations of articles and their absence become compatible with a subjective construal of the disputed genitive constructions in Paul, because the governed substantive is almost always a name (i.e., presumably S-S, S-A-S, and A-S-S [if the latter is a name], could all signify a subjective construction consistent with this rule and its variations; and it goes without saying the A-S-A-S would as well).

But a more general consideration of the function of the article in Koiné might still assist us with πίστις phrases in the context of the disputed genitives (such as Rom. 3:25). Moule warns that the uses of the article are quite flexible. Consequently, he advises repeatedly against adjudicating important theological issues in relation to the presence or absence of the article (being particularly concerned himself with the interpretation of πνεῦμα and νόμος). And this note of caution must constantly be borne in mind. Of the handful of idioms he goes on to record, we should note in particular the idiom of "renewed mention," whereby writers insert an article when a thing mentioned is spoken of again.[21] We have now arguably explained all of the Pauline occurrences neatly in subjective terms — both the genitive constructions *and* instances of πίστις in context.

The governed substantive usually lacks the article in Paul's disputed πίστις Χριστοῦ genitives because it is almost always a name. The governing substantive usually lacks the article because it is an intertextual echo of an anarthrous phrase — διὰ πίστεως/ἐκ πίστεως. And the anarthrous state of the majority of the disputed πίστις Χριστοῦ genitives in Paul is thereby now completely explained. (Paul's phrases also now do not violate Apollonius's dictum, once it has been suitably modified to encompass Koiné.) Furthermore, these conclusions are confirmed — and the subjective position considerably strengthened — by Galatians 2:20, which is a unique construction.

"The Son of God" is not a name for Paul (and only Gal. 2:20 uses it). Moreover, the phrase in which this designation appears in Galatians, also uniquely, does not use an instrumental preposition in the genitive in relation to πίστις, thereby echoing Habakkuk 2:4. Thus, we might expect articles in relation to both the governing and the governed substantives if this phrase is subjective, *and this is of course exactly what we find.* It would seem, then, that the *basic* applicability of Apollonius's canon — suitably modified — holds for Paul, *and it indicates a subjective construal of the relevant genitive.* Where other related and disputed genitives occur, their peculiar construction invariably dictates the absence of the article, from both governing and governed substantives, for the reasons that have just been noted. But the one genitive construction not so constrained in the undisputed letters — by intertextuality and nomenclature — supplies an overtly subjective sense. The direct implication is that these other genitives are subjective as well, but any signals from the article are being masked by their differing construction. Galatians 2:20 is therefore an inordinately important text. But what of instances of πίστις in context?

Shorter instances of πίστις that occur in the immediate context of the genitives now seem to possess two basic possibilities. If they replicate the intertextual echo ἐκ πίστεως, then we would expect an anarthrous occurrence (and Paul seems happy to sustain this echo with διὰ πίστεως as well). However, if Paul is more concerned in these isolated phrases to signal the resumption of those genitives or their equivalent — that is, Christ himself — then an article is supplied. And this is clearly the case for the short possessive phrases. We almost always ask to whom a possessive pronoun and its governing substantive refer, at which point an article can provide invaluable assistance to the text's auditor(s). It coordinates by resuming a reference in context (and Rom. 4:16, just noted, is an excellent example of this practice). But does Romans 3:25 conform to this developing picture of Paul's usage? This text exists in different variants, the discussion of which will lead into the third major contention in this relation.

(3) Manuscript Evidence

I suggest that the manuscript variants actually do reflect these basic alternatives, to a degree, in Romans 3:25. A stronger manuscript tradition omits the article (so διὰ πίστεως),[22] but certain significant variants include it (so διὰ τῆς πίστεως).[23]

The former, majority, anarthrous variant is a more faithful echo of 3:22, and hence perhaps, more distantly, of 1:17 and Habakkuk 2:4 (which is then resumed still more strongly by 3:26). It is also, however, compatible with either a consistently subjective or objective construal of 3:22 and its implications by scribes.

The minority tradition seems to ask instead — quite reasonably — to what or whom this πίστις refers. The article, then, seems to resume the subject of Christ, like the following, arthrous phrase that functions in parallel to it — ἐν τῷ αὐτοῦ αἵματι. Both these phrases look back to ἱλαστήριον, and beyond this signifier to Christ, in v. 24, who is God's intended ἱλαστήριον (see also Eph. 3:12).[24] (There is no local mention of Christian faith to resume, unless the article reaches back to v. 22, but this looks unlikely; seven clauses, phrases, *and even sentences* are interposed between these two motifs, and moreover, it is *plural*.) Rhythmic considerations might also be worth factoring into this assessment, given the ritualized construction of Romans 3:23-26. An arthrous reading entails that both parallel phrases have three accents. It seems then that the minority tradition must presuppose a christological referent for πίστις in v. 25 and a subjective construal of v. 22; it is difficult to make much sense of the arthrous variant otherwise.

It seems likely on balance, moreover, that the minority, arthrous variant is original.[25] It seems probable that later scribes, having lost the christological reading of πίστις in Paul (which is essentially a Jewish Christian discourse), omitted the now puzzling article *and* brought the phrase in v. 24 into conformity with the preceding phrase in v. 22, thereby producing the majority reading, rather than that the converse modification took place. If the minority tradition is later, it would have had to insert an article that was rather opaque (participating in turn in an opaque phrase), thereby also drawing the phrase away from an otherwise identical preceding phrase. Perhaps reinforcing these observations is the fact that A omits the phrase entirely, apparently unsure what it means, thereby providing further evidence of attempts by later tradition to clarify the phrase once its christological reference had been lost. This case is admittedly not decisive, but it is indicative.

In short, it seems that the manuscript variants surrounding the presence or absence of the article in v. 25 do betray further subtle reinforcement for the christological reference of πίστις in Paul at this point. And the article was most likely in the original reading. Furthermore, these considerations based on grammar and the manuscript tradition add cumulatively to the case that has already been made on grounds of location and context, so that a reading of διὰ τῆς πίστεως in v. 25 in christological terms now seems almost surprisingly effective and obvious. The entire cluster of atoning claims is consequently best rendered (up to this point) as:

> . . . ὃν προέθετο Θεὸς ἱλαστήριον   . . . whom God intended to be a
>   ἱλαστήριον,
> διὰ τῆς πίστεως   by means of that faithfulness
> ἐν τῷ αὐτοῦ αἵματι . . .   by means of his blood [i.e., death]. . . .

And this translation decision, which seems reasonably firmly justified — especially on its two initial grounds — is, I suggest, the key that should unlock the rest of this controversial and important text.

2.2. The Underlying Martyrological Narrative

A christocentric reading of διὰ τῆς πίστεως resolves our interpretative difficulties in 3:25a by placing a *martyrological narrative* at the center of this text's atonement terminology and its significance.[26] Paul is alluding to the story of Christ's passion here metonymically — as is his usual practice — denoting this directly, twice, in terms of Christ's faithfulness and shed blood. Directly implicit here then is his execution as well — his death on a cross. But the Roman Christian auditors bring overt statements from earlier in the letter to this material, not to mention their own understanding of the passion. Romans 1:2-4 has foregrounded Christ's resurrection and heavenly enthronement, as has the messianic Scripture cited in Romans 1:17, Habakkuk 2:4, which spoke of Christ's innocence, faithfulness, and life (i.e., resurrection). And these emphases will be resumed strongly in 4:25 as well. So running underneath and beyond Paul's explicit statements here is the well-known story of Christ's suffering, shed blood, death on a cross, resurrection, and glorification, parts of which surface visibly at times to signal the presence of the rest of this seminal narrative. Paul does not of course mention the positive end of the story explicitly in 3:21-26, and reasons for this omission will be noted shortly. That it is implicit, however, seems undeniable.

The presence of an essentially martyrological story in this atoning material, encompassing the fidelity, blood, execution, and vindication of a heroic person, now points strongly to a particular initial judgment in relation to the many interpretative options that scholars have debated for the meaning of ἱλαστήριον and its broader implications. This cluster of terms and notions is found outside Romans in Greco-Roman and Jewish martyrological literature, and especially in 4 Maccabees.[27] Furthermore, this broad trajectory accounts for *all* of Paul's material in Romans 3:25, whereas any other option accounts for only part of it. The correlation with 4 Maccabees deserves particular consideration.

(1) Resonance with Fourth Maccabees

Fourth Maccabees — as we have already seen briefly in chapter fourteen — is couched as a funeral speech that spends much of its time extolling the virtues that are possible for a mind trained by the Jewish law in piety. Such a mind can be righteous, wise, self-controlled, and courageous. The stories of the Maccabean martyrs, as told also by 2 Maccabees 6 and 7, are then embellished to extraordinarily gruesome lengths to illustrate these claims (which probably had further rhetorical and political implications in their day). Eleazar and, after him, seven sons, one by one, are challenged, tortured, and executed, fearlessly enduring their torments and receiving the prize of immortality, both by reputation and by resurrection. Most importantly for the interpretation of Romans 3, however, their bravery and self-sacrifice also effect the liberation of their homeland, the forgiveness of the sin of the people, and the eventual demise of the tyrant presently oppressing them — ideas that the author seems to present almost in passing in 17:20-22:

> [20] καὶ οὗτοι οὖν ἁγιασθέντες διὰ Θεὸν τετίμηνται, οὐ μόνον ταύτῃ τῇ τιμῇ, ἀλλὰ καὶ τῷ δι᾽ αὐτοὺς τὸ ἔθνος ἡμῶν τοὺς πολεμίους μὴ ἐπικρατῆσαι [21] καὶ τὸν τύραννον τιμωρηθῆναι καὶ τὴν πατρίδα καθαρισθῆναι, ὥσπερ ἀντίψυχον γεγονότας τῆς τοῦ ἔθνους ἁμαρτίας· [22] καὶ διὰ τοῦ αἵματος τῶν εὐσεβῶν ἐκείνων καὶ τοῦ ἱλαστηρίου τοῦ θανάτου αὐτῶν ἡ θεία πρόνοια τὸν Ἰσραὴλ προκακωθέντα διέσωσεν.

This function and terminology bear a striking correspondence to Paul's description of Christ in Romans 3:25. The deaths of the martyrs are said in 4 Maccabees to be both cleansing[28] and atoning (τὴν πατρίδα καθαρισθῆναι, ὥσπερ ἀντίψυχον γεγονότας τῆς τοῦ ἔθνους ἁμαρτίας κ.τ.λ.). Their "blood," equated explicitly with death, also functions as a ἱλαστήριον by means of which Israel is saved, something that is especially significant. Only in these two texts — Romans 3:25 and 4 Maccabees 17:22 — is ἱλαστήριον identified directly with events as against objects, and in both texts the atoning deaths of heroic righteous figures are in view. But these explicit atoning claims are also bracketed by statements concerning the endurance and faithfulness of the martyrs, and their resurrection and immortality, and they are even described at times as "righteous ones."[29] Hence, some sort of relationship here simply has to be granted; there are too many overt and implicit correspondences to be denied: heroic, righteous figures being handed over to torture and death, enduring this fate faithfully, and being resurrected after it to glory, thereby also atoning for and cleansing the sins of the people, a set of events — not an object — that is described, moreover, as a ἱλαστήριον.[30] However, the exact nature of this relationship is a matter of some debate, and exaggerated claims at this point in the past may have obscured the basic relationship.

I suggest that a direct relationship between Romans and 4 Maccabees is unlikely.[31] The similarities between the two texts and documents are not precise enough to substantiate this stronger claim. There are, for example, no overlaps of entire phrases or sentences, but only more generalized narrative and terminological echoes (although these are numerous). The two texts share a particular general story, along with certain words that appear rather predictably within that story, but little else besides. And this judgment releases my claim concerning some relationship between the texts from the need to date *4 Maccabees* firmly to a pre-Pauline point (which would then allow Paul to be influenced by it directly), which is probably unlikely in any case.[32] Although *4 Maccabees* may well be later than Paul,[33] it seems to attest to an interpretative trajectory that predated him, and further evidence for this suspicion will be suggested shortly. So the causality in play is indirect, the mutual sharing of a common antecedent, rather than direct, from one text to the other.

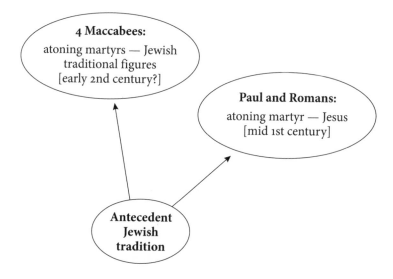

4 Maccabees:
atoning martyrs — Jewish traditional figures [early 2nd century?]

Paul and Romans:
atoning martyr — Jesus [mid 1st century]

Antecedent Jewish tradition

I suggest also that direct Greco-Roman antecedents are unnecessary to explain Paul's atonement theory.[34] Second Maccabees 6 and 7 are indisputably pre-Pauline and attest to the atoning efficacy of the deaths of martyrs (see 7:32-33, 37-38). Clearly, then, the influence of Greco-Roman martyrology on Judaism predates Paul by a considerable margin, and it was probably mediated to him through Jewish and early Jewish Christian traditions. After all, the data in Romans 3 still seems closer to 4 Maccabees than to any other source, even if the relationship is not direct.[35] (That Jewish martyrology in the late Second Temple period was influenced to a significant degree by Greco-Roman sources in general is not being denied.)[36] But this shared relationship with an antecedent tradition also contains indications of further important elements within that discourse.

First, we should note that 4 Maccabees seems to echo the feast of Yom Kippur, thereby resonating with a more general cultic echo that is detectable as a secondary layer in Romans. The author of 4 Maccabees, like Paul, uses ἱλαστήριον and αἷμα to describe the deaths of certain martyrs, which also thereby accomplish some forgiveness of or release from sins, accompanied by cleansing.[37] However, unlike Paul, he glosses those terms with ἀντίψυχος (in the accusative ἀντίψυχον) as against ἀπολύτρωσις. The author's first of two uses of this rare compound in 6:29 confirms its fixed associations with blood and atonement; just before he dies, Eleazar says: καθάρσιον αὐτῶν ποίησον τὸ ἐμὸν αἷμα καὶ ἀντίψυχον αὐτῶν λαβὲ τὴν ἐμὴν ψυχήν. The rare signifier ἀντίψυχος[38] is almost certainly here an adjectival compound constructed from a prepositional expression that occurs in the most significant biblical context for ἱλαστήριον, Leviticus 16 and 17. We must now turn to consider these terms in more detail.

Although the signifier ἱλαστήριον is used to denote parts of the altar that Ezekiel envisions in his new temple[39] — apparently, ledges that play a role in its atoning function — the principal reference for ἱλαστήριον in the LXX is the "mercy seat," that is, the cover of the ark of the covenant that stood in the holy of holies in Solomon's temple, after it had stood in preceding tabernacles[40] (although it should not be forgotten that there had not been an ark in the temple since the exile, so this symbolism was subsequently carried entirely by literary tradition — by Paul's day, a tradition approximately six hundred years long). The Greek term seems to be a characterization of this item's function, reproducing a Hebrew pun concerning the main ritual use of the ark's lid as the point where the high priest scattered atoning blood once a year during the festival of Yom Kippur, as described by Leviticus 16.[41] Leviticus 17 then contains one of the most extensive explanations of atonement in the Old Testament (if not the entire Bible), stating repeatedly that blood, which contains "life," has been given to the people and the priesthood in order to make atonement τὸ γὰρ αἷμα αὐτοῦ ἀντὶ ψυχῆς ἐξιλάσεται. It is this sacred function that — at least in part — underlies the strict dietary prohibition on its human consumption in the priestly codes. Hence, it seems that the author of 4 Maccabees is echoing Leviticus 16 and 17 and the feast of atonement, Yom Kippur, when he describes the atoning effect of the deaths of the martyrs; his repeated use of the distinctive term ἀντίψυχος in an atoning setting points unavoidably in this direction.[42] But a similar echo on Paul's part, although marginally more muted (because he does not use ἀντίψυχον), seems appropriate in view of the cultic material that echoes through Romans.

Scholars have long noted a cultic theme running through Romans. We have of course already grasped that Christ is probably being described in cultically resonant terms in *some* sense in 3:25 (i.e., in terms of ἱλαστήριον, αἷμα, and πάρεσις τῶν προγεγονότων ἁμαρτημάτων). But his blood is mentioned again in 5:9, and in 8:3 he "atones for sin" — περὶ ἁμαρτίας. In 8:34 he then intercedes from the right hand of God in a priestly fashion for those who have been justified, and in 15:8 he is described as a διάκονος, yielding a total of as many as seven cultic tropes. But such cultic (or potentially cultic) imagery is applied to Paul and the Christian community in other parts of Romans. In 15:16 Paul speaks quite distinctively of himself as a priestly figure entrusted with a sacred duty — εἰς τὸ εἶναί με λειτουργὸν Χριστοῦ Ἰησοῦ εἰς τὰ ἔθνη, ἱερουργοῦντα τὸ εὐαγγέλιον τοῦ Θεοῦ — with the ultimate goal of presenting the pagans as an acceptable offering to God — ἵνα γένηται ἡ προσφορὰ τῶν ἐθνῶν εὐπρόσδεκτος, ἡγιασμένη ἐν πνεύματι ἁγίῳ. This set of claims is heavily resonant with cultic imagery, both Paul and the community receiving a double characterization in such terms. The Spirit, moreover, is characterized in unusual terms in 1:4 as πνεῦμα ἁγιωσύνης, which seems to resonate with purity, and hence arguably also with cultic concerns. Meanwhile, the community is described elsewhere (rather famously) in cultic terms as well, in 12:1: παρακαλῶ οὖν ὑμᾶς ἀδελφοί . . . παραστῆσαι τὰ σώματα ὑμῶν θυσίαν ζῶσαν ἁγίαν εὐάρεστον τῷ Θεῷ, τὴν λογικὴν λατρείαν ὑμῶν. (And Epaenetus is the "first fruits" of Paul's labors in Asia, in 16:5.) All this material is just too pronounced to ignore. Christ, the Spirit, Paul himself, and the Christian community all receive overtly cultic coding at certain points in Romans, and — with the exception of the Spirit — this happens in each case more than once.

However, Paul's use of the material is also indicative. None of these claims plays a *fundamental* role within his deeper and more extended arguments.[43] Rather, the association seems to be automatic but secondary, capable of application to every aspect of the new Christian reality for nuancing and enriching points that have already been established on other grounds. That is, cultic language seems to fulfill a flexible and ornamental function, gracing Paul's prose with occasional Levitical flourishes.

What could explain this layer of cultic resonances within the martyrological tradition in both *4 Maccabees* and Paul that seems focused especially on Yom Kippur (especially in the case of *4 Maccabees*) but extends beyond it to encompass cultic references per se (at least in Paul's case), in a relatively fixed association, but without dominating the primary narrative? I know of only one explanation for these dynamics, although it is a plausible one: the underlying influence of the Jewish martyrological development of Genesis 22 that was later known as the Akedah, or "the binding of Isaac."

(2) Resonance with Genesis 22

Cultic resonances are intrinsic to the martyrological story of Genesis 22 for several reasons, but the dominant element within the tradition remains the fortitude of Abraham and the obedience of Isaac — that is, of the martyrological figures involved. This relationship would explain the dynamic that we have just observed in the atoning data in Paul and 4 Maccabees exactly — a story focused on heroic martyrs, who suffer and are resurrected, and in a fixed but secondary association with cultic material, and especially Yom Kippur.

The links between Genesis 22 and the temple, and especially with the holy of holies and so with Yom Kippur (the only day on which entry into the holy of holies was permitted), are established by the traditional location of the mountain on which Isaac was offered. The "high land" of the LXX (ἡ γῆ ἡ ὑψηλός) conceals a reference in the Hebrew to the land of Moriah (which seems to have been either incomprehensible or irrelevant to the LXX tradition). As early as the composition of 2 Chronicles 3:1, the mountain of the patriarchs' sacrifice was identified with the temple mount, an identification also well known to Josephus (see *Antiquities* 1.224, 26), and to the author of *Jubilees* (who states simply in 18:13 "It is Mount Zion"; *Jubilees* also links the story explicitly with the feast of Yom Kippur: see 17:15). Given that the angel of Lord speaks to Abraham as he is about to slay Isaac (Gen. 22:11), which is then interpreted as an appearance of God himself, it would have seemed appropriate to designate this location further as the site of the later holy of holies, where the ark would rest, and from which place God would speak to his people (see Abraham's reasoning in v. 14, σήμερον ἐν τῷ ὄρει κύριος ὤφθη; Exod. 25:22; also Lev. 16:2 — ἐν [γὰρ] νεφέλῃ ὀφθήσομαι ἐπὶ τοῦ ἱλαστηρίου). Isaac was offered to God at the temple's critical and most holy point, where God appeared and spoke. The substitution of a ram for Isaac creates obvious connections with the sacrificial system in general, while Isaac's role itself generates links with any sacrifices concerned with the firstborn (hence doubtless the later connotations in terms of the Passover and the exodus). Finally, the offering of Isaac on wood creates obvious connections with the later burnt offering, and these are noted by the text explicitly in vv. 2, 3, 6, 7, 8, and 13 (ὁλοκάρπωσις; Josephus also notes these explicitly in *Antiquities* 1.224, 25[44]). Thus, several features of the story link up with various aspects of Israel's later cultus.[45]

But the later designations of martyrs within Jewish tradition as ἱλαστήρια in particular are now entirely comprehensible. Their deaths were singularly spectacular, definitive, and atoning, so they presumably functioned like the ritual of Yom Kippur and the priestly approach on that day alone into the holy of holies to pour blood on the mercy seat. Hence, there is no need to distinguish too strongly between a reference by ἱλαστήριον in Romans 3:25 and 4 Maccabees 17:22 to the mercy seat per se, and to other costly objects of atonement and reconciliation. This is now a false antithesis. The particular narrative, practice, and symbolism associated with Yom Kippur are evoked by this signifier, but not to the exclusion of other atoning objects and events that overlap with this semantic field. Paul is not talking here about a new Yom Kippur per se but about a primordial martyrological event that is analogous to Yom Kippur, and in fact underlies it, and this is the crucial judgment for our interpretative purposes (at which point an important connection with what we might call "Homeric historiography" is apparent[46]). The basic resonance is with the story of Genesis 22, suitably interpreted. (Note also that by using a term that overlapped with wider Greek usage, even those auditors not immersed in Jewish tradition could have understood Paul's point, although those so immersed would have grasped the allusions here more richly and accurately.)

The importance of the binding of Isaac for the early church's account of the atonement has always had its advocates,[47] but it has also often been trenchantly opposed, and the principal line of attack fueling its rejection has usually been the claim that the fully developed tradition is too late to influence the New Testament.[48] A martyrological reading of Genesis 22 that includes the element of vicarious atonement, it is said, is best viewed as a compensation for the destruction of the temple in 70 CE, if not as a Jewish response to Christian claims about Christ's atonement. But a text from Qumran has begun to overturn this argument, which was really rather weak in any case.[49] (*Jubilees* associates the story palpably with Yom Kippur, and Josephus's account, which is unlikely to have been influenced by Christian reflections, is shot through with sacrificial language.) The text 4Q225, although fragmentary, supplies enough data to corroborate the presence in the second century BCE of a relatively well-developed form of the tradition, and with the elimination of this difficulty, interpreters are now free to follow the implications in the evidence if they lead in this direction.[50] Indeed, in my view, the rehabilitation of this evidence is now long overdue. The binding of Isaac supplies just the explanation that often seems lacking for New Testament scholars at the critical point — how the early Jewish Christians could have held the death of an innocent and pious figure like Jesus to have such powerful atoning value (rising again "on the third day"; see Gen. 22:4 and 1 Cor. 15:4), not to mention how they could have reached this conclusion so quickly, and seemingly found it so obvious, going on to celebrate it repeatedly with their ritual communal meal (see esp. 1 Cor. 11:23-25), and could apparently have been so willing, moreover, to endorse remarkable redefinitions of the Jewish temple cult in the light of it (see esp. Rom. 12:1; 1 Cor. 3:9-17; see also Eph. 2:19-22).[51]

In sum, this particular reading of ἱλαστήριον, rooted ultimately in the martyrological development of Genesis 22, is activated explicitly (1) by the repeated emphasis in context on Jesus's fidelity (see vv. 22, 25, and 26). (2) It utilizes the only other attestation to an analogy between ἱλαστήριον and a heroic person dying (which is the obvious focus of Romans 3:21-26). That is, it points to an event in a person's life rather than to a functional object per se. *None of the other instances extant in Greek does this.* (3) This allows Paul's talk of "blood" in v. 25b to integrate smoothly, not awkwardly, with his developing argument, "blood" denoting *the same event* of heroic martyrological death as ἱλαστήριον in a mere lexical variation. (4) The story also explains the multiple emphases here and in context on resurrection — emphases that explanations oriented strictly toward sacrifice and death (or toward an object) have more difficulty accounting for. (5) The presence of a broader discourse of cultic imagery in Romans is also now explained, and not merely noted. If Christ dies as the new Isaac, in a recapitulation of the Akedah, a recapitulation of the cultus is implicit. Moreover (6) it is now possible to see why this allusion is so delicate. Such a traditional, martyrological discourse only needed to be activated allusively for the Roman Christian auditors. (It is also not a shocking theological innovation on Paul's part, which would presumably need some explanation; it is part of his broader strategy of building from shared material. UD 8 is also now neatly addressed.)

These are weighty considerations in favor of the martyrological reading (which, it should be noted, does not depend on a Christological reading of πίστις in 3:22-26, although it is strengthened by it). Moreover, objections to this martyrological reading tend to be weak.[52] And the two main countervailing readings are weak as well — that is, construals of ἱλαστήριον as either "a sacrifice of atonement" (NRSV, NIV;[53] see the older translation "propitiation" AV[54]),[55] or "the mercy seat" (Young's Literal Translation, 21st Century King James Version, Darby Translation).[56] So we end up — a little ironically — rather close to the majority of modern translations. In Romans 3:25 Jesus's death is being described by Paul cryptically as "a singular atonement for sin"; it was appointed by God, and also seems to displace the existing cultus (and, as such, a secondary echo of Leviticus 16 is detectable). But Paul's use of the rare signifier ἱλαστήριον does not indicate a sacrifice as much as something singular in relation to the broader process of atonement and reconciliation — this atonement's extraordinary nature, like the annual ritual of Yom Kippur and the necessarily singular deaths of martyrs like Isaac, Eleazar, and the seven young men. It goes without saying that the expectations of Justification theory should *not* be imported into this translation, so this atonement need not be described either as a payment or in terms of propitiating an angry deity, although a connotation of sacrifice seems fair (as long as that is correctly nuanced). Paul's language and argumentation in Romans 3:25 and its immediate setting (i.e., 3:21-26) do not explicitly support either of the mercantile connotations that are so often attributed to them at this point.

Powerful corroborative evidence for the underlying role of Genesis 22 in its fully developed Jewish reading for Paul can be found in later parts of Romans, once interpreters have been sensitized to this possibility — although, once again, the case is largely narrative and therefore has perhaps been overlooked by interpreters using methodologies more sensitive to formulae, titles, quotations from earlier tradition, and so on. I have suggested elsewhere at some length that Paul's argument in Romans 8 presupposes the narrative deployment of Genesis 22, with God "the Father" fulfilling the role of Abraham (and hence his designation as father), and Jesus the role of Isaac, "the only beloved son."[57] I will not repeat those arguments here; it need only be noted that this encoding of the divine saving drama with the Genesis narrative achieves several crucial argumentative goals for Paul. Most importantly, the story now speaks fundamentally of God's

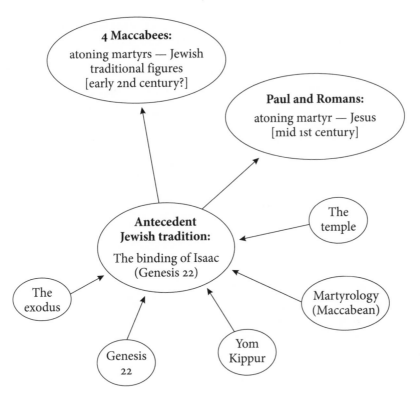

benevolence (and not his caprice, as seems apparent when he stands outside the story) as the beloved son is offered up to save a hostile humanity. The story also grounds the theological argument that Paul makes in Romans 8 — and in Romans 5:1-11 — for the unshakeable eschatological assurance of the Christian community; it informs these robust and important rhetorical phases in the letter. But it also speaks implicitly of God's act of atonement within this drama; God is somehow dealing with sin during this process as well — the claim that grounds Paul's ethical discussion in Romans 5–8, which unfolds between these eschatological concerns.

There is much more to be said on this point. But for now it must suffice to conclude that the story of Genesis 22, as developed martyrologically by later Jewish tradition, is detectable behind the terminology and substance of both Romans 3:25 and *4 Maccabees,* when those texts describe the deaths of their heroic protagonists as atoning. Their faithfulness and shed blood procure cleansing and forgiveness in a singularly definitive fashion, as did all ἱλαστήρια, but especially the central act of atonement performed on Yom Kippur that revolved around the mercy seat. However, that ritual is itself comprehensible now as an echo of the earlier climactic story of Abraham's near sacrifice of Isaac, a story of faithfulness, obedience, death, and resurrection, which is now seen by Paul to be fulfilled in Christ (and by the author of *4 Maccabees,* to be recapitulated in the deaths of his heroes Eleazar, the seven sons, and their mother). So in Romans 3:25 Paul states that God intended Christ to be "a singular act of atonement, through that fidelity, through his blood . . ." just as Isaac was on the temple mount, and as later acts of atonement by the high priest on the day of Yom Kippur in the holy of holies were as well. And a way finally seems to be opening for us into the complicated and contested area of Pauline atonement theory — a way opened by a largely unrecognized interpretative key. Before considering the precise mechanics of this atonement in more detail, however, we must address one further preliminary issue.

§3. A Liberative Analysis of "Justification" in Romans 3:23-24

We need now to consider the seam of material in Romans 3:23-26 that describes what Christ's atonement achieves for humanity — its results — although in the more overtly delimited sense of "for all those who believe" (3:22b). After this, we will be able to consider the question of its precise coordination with the atoning material that has just been noted. There are four pieces of textual evidence (at least initially, with a fifth to be considered in §4).

The first two pieces of evidence are related antithetically: v. 23 briefly describes the problem of the human condition — "all sinned" and "lack the glory of God"; and v. 24 begins to describe the solution — all who believe are δικαιούμενοι, usually translated of course as "justified."[58] The justification of believing humanity is immediately said, third, to be free — a claim essentially made twice, presumably for special emphasis; it is δωρεὰν τῇ αὐτοῦ χάριτι. And it is said, fourth, to be instrumentally caused by an ἀπολύτρωσις effected by Christ. In sum, we are considering the meaning of the following material:

> [23]πάντες γὰρ ἥμαρτον καὶ ὑστεροῦνται τῆς δόξης τοῦ Θεοῦ
> [24]δικαιούμενοι
> δωρεὰν τῇ αὐτοῦ χάριτι
> διὰ τῆς ἀπολυτρώσεως τῆς ἐν Χριστῷ Ἰησοῦ. . . .

Just as the important material considered in the preceding section turned out to possess an interpretative key — in the christological meaning of the phrase διὰ πίστεως — so too I suggest that a careful consideration of the meaning of ἀπολύτρωσις provides us with decisive semantic leverage in relation to this material. We will begin, then, with this term.

3.1. The Meaning of ἀπολύτρωσις in Romans 3:24

Interpreters often try to derive the meaning of the rare signifier ἀπολύτρωσις in Romans 3:24 from cognates, which are far more numerous, especially in the Old

Testament. This allows connections to be traced to monetary ransoms and ransom procedures (e.g., via λύτρον), which conventional readers expect this paragraph to supply in accordance with the expectations of Justification theory. Although this is a rare word in extant Greek, with only nineteen occurrences, fully seven of those are in the Pauline corpus (and three more in the New Testament), making Paul the dominant attested user of this signifier (possibly along with his later tradition) — and Paul never uses a cognate of this word group elsewhere, whether verb or noun. The only such arguable instance, in 1 Corinthians 1:30 and 6:11 (which we will discuss in more detail in due course), substitutes a homonym, with ἀπολούω appearing where we might have expected ἀπολυτρόω (although we might also have expected ἀπολύω). We should therefore resist the suggestion that something other than the implications of this specific data is meant when the signifier ἀπολύτρωσις occurs in 3:24. And there is sufficient data here to reach a judgment about the basic sense of this term.

ἀπολύτρωσις means "release," with the standard additional connotation of release from some enslavement or bondage, so it is appropriately translated "redemption" (in the sense of being set free) or — perhaps better — "release" or even "liberation."[59] Hence, it seems that the prefix ἀπο- is contributing a significant semantic component to this signifier; ἀπολύτρωσις is always release *from* something — almost invariably an unpleasant situation of constraint or imprisonment. It is consequently not surprising to find words denoting freedom frequently in its immediate context (see esp. Philo, *On the Preliminary Studies;* the inscription from Cos; and various New Testament instances, especially Eph. 1:7 and Col. 1:14). It is not necessary for this release to be effected by way of payment, although it might be. The context needs to supply this information, however. The signifier itself does not automatically suggest it.[60] If we take Paul at his word here, then, he is stating in v. 24 nothing more or less than that Christ has released believing humanity from some enslavement or bondage.

The immediate implications of this judgment are significant. The statement qualifies instrumentally a famous antithesis of problem and solution — of sins and justification — described in vv. 23b-24a. But ἀπολύτρωσις itself, correctly interpreted, describes a process of release from an enslaved condition. So in context the most obvious reading of this signifier views it as positioned *across* this antithesis, glossing the entire process with one word. It denotes that the movement from sin and a lack of glory (whatever that means specifically) to justification is a release from something enslaving or constraining. And it follows that the process of ἀπολύτρωσις and the notion of "justification" (which can most easily be referred to in what follows as δικαίωσις) are essentially the same; "justification," or δικαίωσις, is apparently a fundamentally liberative notion, denoting deliverance from some situation of constraint, and should be translated accordingly. Several further pieces of evidence seem to confirm this initial judgment (while any countervailing objections tend to be weak or invalid).

3.2. The Meaning of Romans 3:23

The interpretation of ἀπολύτρωσις as release seems also to yield the most likely reading of v. 23 — that Paul is defining "the problem" here in terms of a confined or enslaved condition. Previous interpreters have of course referred this compact statement *back* to 1:18–3:20, and consequently to a process presupposing human capacity and individual culpability (however contradictory that actually proves as Paul works the argument out). But our reading has been liberated from the need to correlate v. 23 with what precedes it in this fashion. The only potentially Pauline material in the preceding argument is the final phase's commitment to a universal and thoroughgoing sinfulness (see 3:9-18, 20) — a condition more akin to slavery than to capacity. We do not yet know that Paul is himself committed to this position, but it seems likely. That suspicion is reinforced, however, if the prospective function of v. 23 is now considered more closely — and it is becoming increasingly clear that 3:23-26 is anticipating, not summarizing (except, that is, in advance).

The phrase πάντες ἥμαρτον in v. 23a is in fact an exact anticipation of the final phrase in Paul's longer statement in 5:12 concerning the entry of Sin and Death into the world through Adam's transgression (. . . καὶ οὕτως εἰς πάντας ἀνθρώπους ὁ θάνατος διῆλθεν, ἐφ᾽ ᾧ πάντες ἥμαρτον), a sentence that initiates an important reframing of Paul's argument in terms of Genesis 2–3 and the narrative of Adam. And the following phrase in 3:23 concerning a lack of glory can now be seen to integrate smoothly with this implication; it seems to refer to humanity's loss of the glorious image of God that Adam and Eve possessed in the garden of Eden prior to their transgressions, but that the righteous hope to have restored in the world to come. (The notions of "glory" and "image" seem to be closely related for Paul, although v. 23 might simply refer to humanity's loss of that glory, which denoted then the presence of God.[61]) Moreover, there can be little doubt that Paul's later portrayal of Adamic humanity is in incapacitated terms, that is, at least in part, as a slavery (see esp. 7:14, 23, 25; see also Romans 6). And he goes on, beginning in Romans 7, to articulate humanity's recovery of glory — in company with the rest of creation — after its redemption in Christ (see esp. 8:18-23). In short, 3:23 does not merely contain an anticipatory echo of the beginning of Paul's later detailed discussion of sin in 5:12; it is an entirely appropriate summary of the extended argumentation that follows, indicating a condition enslaved by sin and deprived of glory. And this reading is of course just what we would expect given the implications of ἀπολύτρωσις, which speaks of release *from* slavery. Thus, the most likely reading of v. 23 can now be seen to integrate smoothly with the implications of ἀπολύτρωσις. The implications of these two contextual signals should now be applied to the interpretation of δικαίωσις (that is, of the cognate verb).

3.3. The Meaning of δικαιόω in Romans 3:24

Much of course has been written about δικαίωσις in Paul. The major surveys and analyses will be noted in chapter seventeen, when we address the meaning of δικαιοσύνη Θεοῦ. Here, however, we will establish some important background for that discussion, first considering its general semantic possibilities and then tracing the implications of its immediate context in Romans 3:24.

(1) Semantic Possibilities

Δικαιόω generally refers to the particular part of a judicial process when the presiding authority makes a critical decision, stating that someone is "in the right" (or not), that is, rendering a verdict. So a judge or judges may uphold a charge against a person or exonerate that person of the charge, and so on. Further implications about the *general* rectitude of the person, however, are not necessarily in view; someone could be pronounced in the right on a particular charge but not be especially righteous in other regards.[62] But in the broader context of Romans 3:24, the setting is eschatological, and the figure pronouncing the verdict is God. Hence, an important further element within this action needs to be noted carefully, although it is apparent in analogous human situations as well.

Judicial verdicts are *both* indicative *and* performative. They usually comment on a given state of affairs, recognizing something about those — that is, that someone is "in the right" or not — and so function indicatively, but in so doing they also *effect* a further state of affairs, and so function performatively. A person pronounced "in the right" by a human court may receive damages or be exonerated or perhaps be set free from prison. Thus, things happen as a direct result of this action and are in fact *enacted by* this verbal act.[63] And in an eschatological setting, these enacted consequences are especially important. In pronouncing his verdict, God actualizes either heaven or hell for those who have just been judged! To pronounce someone "righteous," or "in the right," in the final judgment qualifies and effects eternal life for that person — or the converse — as in fact Romans 2 clearly suggests.[64]

We should note first the repeated emphasis on the indicative aspect of this situation, God's evaluation of the ethical state of each person (underlined in the quotations below). As has already been noted in some detail, Romans 2 tends to use κατά constructions in the accusative initially to denote the criteria by which God will evaluate humanity. These criteria are then expanded in vv. 9-10 in terms of the equally appropriate (and rather significant) language of works. A chiastic arrangement is possibly discernible in this material, as Paul expands — at times rather archly — on the programmatic statement of v. 6.

> [6]ἀποδώσει ἑκάστῳ <u>κατὰ τὰ ἔργα αὐτοῦ</u>.
>> [7][ἀποδώσει] τοῖς μὲν <u>καθ' ὑπομονὴν ἔργου ἀγαθοῦ</u> δόξαν καὶ τιμὴν καὶ ἀφθαρσίαν <u>ζητοῦσιν</u> ζωὴν αἰώνιον,
>>> [8][ἀποδοθήσονται] τοῖς δὲ <u>ἐξ ἐριθείας καὶ ἀπειθοῦσι τῇ ἀληθείᾳ πειθομένοις δὲ τῇ ἀδικίᾳ</u> ὀργὴ καὶ θυμός.

⁹[ἀποδοθήσονται] θλῖψις καὶ στενοχωρία ἐπὶ πᾶσαν ψυχὴν
ἀνθρώπου <u>τοῦ κατεργαζομένου τὸ κακόν</u>, Ἰουδαίου τε
πρῶτον καὶ Ἕλληνος·
¹⁰[ἀποδοθήσονται] δόξα δὲ καὶ τιμὴ καὶ εἰρήνη παντὶ τῷ
<u>ἐργαζομένῳ τὸ ἀγαθόν</u>, Ἰουδαίῳ τε πρῶτον καὶ Ἕλληνι.
¹¹οὐ γάρ ἐστιν προσωπολημψία παρὰ τῷ θεῷ.

The Jewish theologoumenon cited in v. 11 in terms of God's lack of partiality also makes the indicative and evaluative point: God is, in this judgment, "no
respecter of persons." Hence, the indicative, evaluative aspect of the final judgment in this setting could hardly be clearer.

The second, performative dimension within this judgment is also plainly
apparent in these texts, interwoven inextricably with the former activity. Paul
notes, in balanced contrasting constructions in vv. 7-8, the two possible outcomes
that can result from the indicative evaluation — eternal life, for those who do
good deeds, and God's wrath, for those who do bad deeds. And exactly the same
outcomes are enacted by God as part of the process of judgment, in vv. 9-10, although here applied rather more provocatively to "Jew and Greek." Paul's polemical application should not obscure the important underlying fact, however, that
God is enacting outcomes for the two basic constituencies of righteous and sinner in these judgments; indeed, this is precisely what enables Paul's more shocking inferences. The divine act is denoted in this passage especially by the verb
ἀποδίδωμι, which is frequently elided by Paul but which probably governs this
entire series of sentences (a future, it should be noted).⁶⁵

⁶<u>ἀποδώσει</u> ἑκάστῳ κατὰ τὰ ἔργα αὐτοῦ.
   ⁷[ἀποδώσει] τοῖς μὲν καθ' ὑπομονὴν ἔργου ἀγαθοῦ δόξαν καὶ
   τιμὴν καὶ ἀφθαρσίαν ζητοῦσιν <u>ζωὴν αἰώνιον</u>,
      ⁸[ἀποδοθήσονται] τοῖς δὲ ἐξ ἐριθείας καὶ ἀπειθοῦσι τῇ
      ἀληθείᾳ πειθομένοις δὲ τῇ ἀδικίᾳ <u>ὀργὴ καὶ θυμός</u>.

   ⁹[ἀποδοθήσονται] θλῖψις καὶ στενοχωρία ἐπὶ πᾶσαν ψυχὴν
   ἀνθρώπου τοῦ κατεργαζομένου τὸ κακόν, Ἰουδαίου τε
   πρῶτον καὶ Ἕλληνος·
   ¹⁰[ἀποδοθήσονται] δόξα δὲ καὶ τιμὴ καὶ εἰρήνη παντὶ τῷ
   ἐργαζομένῳ τὸ ἀγαθόν, Ἰουδαίῳ τε πρῶτον καὶ Ἕλληνι.
   ¹¹οὐ γάρ ἐστιν προσωπολημψία παρὰ τῷ θεῷ.

It is easy to miss the extent to which God is actively allocating extraordinary outcomes in these texts, such are our usual preoccupations with Paul's polemical and evaluative material. But it is essentially incontestable that the forensic
language of decision here contains an important internal combination of indicative and performative functions — of the recognition of certain states of affairs,
combined with the enactment of further states of affairs as those seem appropri-

ately related to the foregoing — in an eschatological setting, life or death. A verdict recognizes *and* does something. We can dub this sort of situation "forensic-retributive," because the verdict in these usages is correlated with the perception of a particular just or unjust state of affairs. The result enacted is linked by the verdict to the prior state of affairs (as that has been discerned) appropriately, which usually means retributively. But we need now to introduce an important qualification to this observation.

The connection between a recognition based on justice and a further enacted consequence is not fixed or static. It needs first to be established that this relationship ought to be retributive, from which point the nature of the justice in question ought also to be debated. However, even where such questions have been settled, the relationship is hardly invariable. On a human level, in (for example) ancient Roman courts, verdicts were often (and even usually) *not* tied to matters of strict innocence or culpability but were heavily affected by status and wealth.[66] Hence, verdicts of "in the right" could frequently be pronounced in relation to figures that were not right (and vice versa); such "justice" could easily be bought, and frequently was. In such situations, the performative aspect of the verdict would be retained, but its distinctive indicative aspect would be lost — its recognition of a "right" state of affairs (or not) in some sense in the person being judged. It is worth emphasizing, moreover, that such forensic situations could possibly have been far more common in premodern societies.[67] It follows that forensic terminology could function — especially in the ancient world — simply in a performative manner, and in this capacity, probably most often in a fundamentally unjust manner, with the wealthy and guilty being acquitted for a bribe, and the powerless enemies of the wealthy imprisoned or executed for the same. Doubtless, individuals' social locations greatly influenced their perceptions and semantic construals in this regard. Those on the bottom or at the margins of society would presumably have frequent cause to dub such negative performative situations "forensic-oppressive" rather than "forensic-retributive."[68] The indicative and performative aspects of judgment would be viewed separately (or, at least, in some dubious relationship).

However, the detachment of the performative aspect of forensic procedures from the indicative — that is, from questions of strict justice, based on defendants' prior ethical and legal states — could also function positively. It was equally possible to enact judgments that would release or liberate people or constituencies with little or no obvious relation to previous rights or wrongs. Thus, it is not uncommon to find God acting in the Old Testament to liberate those who have been held captive *irrespective of whether they actually deserve that liberation,* in which case the criteria for so acting are not found in the merit or demerit of that constituency but in the character — the gracious "rightness" — of God himself. In these settings, God is effecting the release of his people from imprisonment by an act of "judgment," or some such — a forensic action — but one not correlated with prior merit (and the exodus of course springs to mind immediately, closely followed by the return from exile).[69] Any such positive performative judgments can be dubbed "forensic-liberative,"[70] and their sense is well captured by the terminology of *amnesty*.[71]

The frequency of this action by God and other actors in the Old Testament is increased — and also slightly complicated — by the premodern fusion between the executive and the judiciary. In modern societies that have separated the two, forensic terms tend to be limited to the judiciary, whereas in the ancient world, such language was often used for acts that we would describe now as executive, or political. Fortunately, modern societies have not lost this usage completely. An executive act of liberation might still be described in forensic-liberative terms, presumably drawing on some underlying notion of "rightness" (so, e.g., D-day, and the ensuing invasion and conquest of Nazi Germany, was often referred to as a "judgment"). But such language seems to have been much more frequent in the ancient world, in tribal and monarchical settings, where executive and judicial authority was ultimately concentrated in the same figure or figures.

In sum, various aspects within a "judgment" need to be distinguished if that act is to be interpreted sensitively. On the one hand, a forensic-retributive function is discernible when a performative judgment is correlated tightly with criteria concerning the rectitude, or not, of the figure(s) being judged. Here the enacted results of the judgment are meant to match the prior condition of the figure(s) precisely (although of course different cultures fill out the exact notion *of* "rightness" very differently; we have left this important question to one side for the moment[72]). On the other hand, however, in certain circumstances, this attention to prior criteria might be relaxed or absent, so that only the performative aspect of the judgment is still apparent, serving either a forensic-oppressive or a forensic-liberative function — in the latter case, an amnesty.

Performative forensic acts

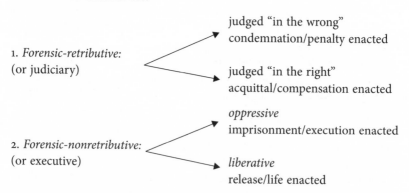

1. *Forensic-retributive:* (or judiciary)
- judged "in the wrong" condemnation/penalty enacted
- judged "in the right" acquittal/compensation enacted

2. *Forensic-nonretributive:* (or executive)
- *oppressive* imprisonment/execution enacted
- *liberative* release/life enacted

These general background observations should now help us grasp Paul's suggestions in Romans 3:24 more precisely, because they provide options that are more sensitive to the indications in context, as well as in terms of the broader debate that Paul finds himself in. (Conversely, Justification theory circumscribes these semantic options to the first category only, thereby arguably missing a great deal of what Paul is up to.)

(2) Contextual Implications

The immediate setting of δικαιόω in v. 24 suggests that the verb is operating there in a purely performative manner to denote a positive action by God that effects release from a previous situation, without conveying any judgment on the rectitude of that prior situation and/or the people who have been so released — a forensic-liberative action. We have already seen that the implications of 1:18–3:20 are irrelevant. So the retributive presuppositions of that argument no longer need to be assumed in the interpretation of 3:21-26, a significant lack of correlation that will be further elaborated shortly. For now, however, we can simply note that this frees the interpreter of 3:24 to pay closer attention to the immediate context, where the signals are consistently liberative.

Verse 23 indicates that the situation of humanity in Adam is *universally enslaved and trapped* (and this depiction is reinforced by v. 23's elaboration of the motif πᾶς, used in v. 22). Hence, there can be no thought of positive actions on its part or rectitude or consequent accountability; it needs to be rescued (see 7:24). That a rescue has taken place in Christ is affirmed by the use of ἀπολύτρωσις in 3:24b. So, caught between the incapacity of humanity in the definition of the problem in v. 23 and the liberative indications of the divine solution in v. 24b, δικαιόω in v. 24a now needs to be read in performative terms as a divine act — a judgment or declaration — that effects release for the captives; it is a command by God in Christ to set the prisoners free! This reading has the added virtues of corresponding to Paul's later usage in Romans 6 and 8, where only a performative reading in forensic-liberative terms is really possible — instances occurring in arguments that 3:23-26 is to a degree anticipating (and this will become more apparent shortly).

In Romans 6:7 Paul states: ὁ γὰρ ἀποθανὼν δεδικαίωται ἀπὸ τῆς ἁμαρτίας. The sense of this claim can be completed smoothly if it is read in a forensic-liberative sense: "the one who has died has been released from Sin" (and Scroggs has made a compelling case that this is in the first instance a reference to Christ in a study already noted in chapter fifteen[73]). The presence of ἀπό here is an especially strong indicator of Paul's fundamentally liberative meaning (and is an especially difficult problem for forensic-retributive readings). As the argument in Romans 6 goes on to make clear, death frees people from the rule and lordship of Sin and Death, so that in a resurrected state they are free to serve God: ἐλευθερωθέντες δὲ ἀπὸ τῆς ἁμαρτίας ἐδουλώθητε τῇ δικαιοσύνῃ (v. 18). And in v. 7 this event is denoted by the verb δικαιόω, which must therefore be construed in this fundamentally liberative sense — in forensic-liberative terms as "release," or some such.

Precisely the same forensic-liberative sense is apparent in Romans 8 as well — specifically, in vv. 30-34. There the verb first occurs in v. 30 in an elective chain that grounds the entire process of salvation in divine agency, following δικαίωσις with glorification. No reference to prior human merit here is either evident or possible. Verse 33 continues a vigorous diatribal exchange with the argument: τίς ἐγκαλέσει κατὰ ἐκλεκτῶν θεοῦ; θεὸς ὁ δικαιῶν. And it is again difficult if not impossible to render this claim in context in forensic-retributive terms, while forensic-liberative terms continue to make perfect sense. Considered in retributive terms, the identity of the condemner is irrelevant; what matters is the behavior of the person charged, which will result in the desired verdict — of being "in the right" — if he or she has in fact behaved rightly. In a purely performative setting, however, where the actual justice of the accused is irrelevant, then the power of the accuser versus the power of the defender becomes all-important (along with their advocacies) — the issue(s) at stake both here and in Paul's wider argument. With God on their side, people have nothing to fear from accusations by other powers or figures. But it follows that the action God is undertaking, described by δικαιῶν, is therefore not one of indicative declaration so much as one of advocacy. God is *delivering* humanity, as part of their trajectory from call to glorification. Other attempts to imprison them are consequently futile. And this reading integrates smoothly with the other liberative actions that are taking place in the context — the sacrifice of the only beloved son in vv. 31-32, and the resurrection of and intercession by that son in v. 34. It makes no sense to state that God's commitment to humanity is absolute and benevolent — as Paul says in vv. 31-32 — and then interpret the forensic action in v. 33 in retributive terms, which would imply an impartial decision on God's part in relation to humanity's ethical state. However, to construe there that God has released humanity from its Adamic slavery by an irreversible eschatological verdict of liberation makes excellent sense.[74]

Two further features of the immediate context in 3:24 now reinforce our developing interpretation of δικαιόω in forensic-liberative terms. The first concerns the final piece of textual evidence identified at the beginning of this section — Paul's apparent emphasis, with the words δωρεὰν τῇ αὐτοῦ χάριτι, on the gratuity of the process. A forensic-liberative interpretation of δικαιόω neatly explains this linguistic redundancy, which immediately follows the participle.

In v. 24 Paul qualifies the statement concerning release (δικαιούμενοι) with the words δωρεὰν τῇ αὐτοῦ χάριτι. And although the language of grace could be deployed in more broadly contractual contexts in the ancient world, here it is being deployed opposite an enslaved humanity (that is, enslaved by Sin and Death), to whom release has just been granted "freely, by God's grace." It would seem, then, that this particular release from slavery has *not* been obtained via a purchase price (that is, on the part of the enslaved).[75] Paul seems to want to make this immediately clear. And the implications are that, on the one hand, the release is indeed liberative and unconditional, granted freely, for humanity could do and "pay" nothing to obtain it. On the other hand, its gratuity denotes the limitless benevolence of the God who so offers it — just the point that Paul makes later in Romans 8, as we have just seen (and anticipates again in 5:1-11).

But this liberative construal of δικαιόω also speaks, second, to a pregnant gap in 3:21-26. This usage, as we have already seen, is linked to God's eschatological action, where a positive judgment results in eternal life and entry into the age to come. It follows, however, that Paul's use of δικαιο- terminology probably carries strong connotations of "life" and resurrection. The release that it speaks of is precisely the release from the oppressed Adamic age, ruled by Sin and Death, into the life of the world to come. And this explains the slightly puzzling absence of resurrection thematology and terminology in 3:21-26. The subsections that both precede this paragraph and follow it (as we will see in more detail shortly) all explicitly emphasize Christ's resurrection (see esp. 1:4, 17b; and 4:24b-25). Only the section 3:21-26 seems to pass over this theme in silence; Christ's life after death seems to slip here inexplicably from view. It can now be seen, however, that this subsection does not overlook Christ's resurrection or the centrality of this notion in general; resurrection is indeed present in Paul's liberative language as long as that is properly understood — in terms of a release from slavery and its confinement into a new, freed condition denoted by various δικαιο- terms. This *is* the language of life and resurrection, once its eschatological setting is appreciated, and its present status and past accomplishment point repeatedly to the centrality of the resurrected Christ himself to its actualization.

We are now in a position to grasp more firmly the broader rhetorical function of much of this material over against the gospel of the Teacher.

3.4. The Rhetorical Significance of Romans 3:23-24

The contours of the Teacher's gospel are apparent in much of Romans 1-3, and especially in Romans 2. And it is apparent there that the language of justification plays an important role in his gospel — one that Paul is concerned to undermine. The Teacher has a forensic-*retributive* understanding of δικαιο- terminology.

Excursus: Continuities with Contemporary Jewish Sources

Seifrid in particular has helpfully introduced the *Psalms of Solomon* into the broader construal of Paul at this point, but interprets their evidence monolithically.[76] Nevertheless it is true that evidence of a Jewish view of God's nature in fundamentally retributive terms can be found there. I suggest that the Teacher's gospel is in continuity with this material.

In a little more detail, in Psalms of Solomon 8 and 9 God's righteousness is "shown," "seen" (8:25) or "proven" most clearly (9:2; see also 8:7, and 2:10, 15, 16) in judgment according to desert — here rather harsh. However, the Psalmist(s) accepts it as fair, even inventing secret sins to account for this in some cases (see 8:9-13, which details incest, adultery, temple violation, and sacrifice in menstrual impurity!; see also the apparently fragmentary Psalm 1, and Psalm 2:8, 11-13). Redemption is then grounded in God's "mercy" (see 8:27, 28; 9:8, 11; also God's compassion and goodness: 8:27, 28; 9:6, 7, 8). But that compassion is accessed only after an acceptance of judgment, the showing of appropriate shame, and confession and repentance, and repeated requests for assistance and affirmations of God's goodness (see 8:29, 30-34; 9:6-11). So the basic framework remains contractual and the fundamental divine attribute retributive. The remaining relevant Psalms are briefer but still often indicative.

Psalm 2 overtly links retributive actions with God's kingship (vv. 30, 32): "the Lord's mercy is upon those who fear him, along with judgment. To separate between the righteous and the sinner; to repay sinners forever according to their actions" (vv. 33b-34). Psalm 3 does not mention righteousness, but seems highly retributive. Psalm 4 has expectations of harsh and thorough retribution on the wicked — judgments grounded finally in God's righteousness (v. 24), which is contrasted with mercy (v. 25). Psalm 6 emphasizes the rewards and safety of the pious and looks fundamentally retributive. Psalm 10 is ambiguous, but speaks of the importance of divine "discipline," as does Psalm 12, which expects those who are ultimately sinful to perish utterly (see v. 6). Psalm 15 is instructive because it is consistently retributive vis-à-vis outsiders and sinners, "for those who act lawlessly shall not escape the Lord's judgment" (v. 8b), but the Psalmist himself relies upon God's name and mercy (see vv. 1-4a; 13). In sum, Psalms 1, 2, 3, 4, 6, 8, 9, 15, and possibly also 10 and 12, evidence a retributive view of God in some sense, and sometimes link this with righteousness language explicitly.

However, a monarchical "distributive" activity is explicitly described in Psalms 17 and 18, while divine benevolence also arguably informs Psalms 5, 7, 10, 12, and 16.

Psalm 17 is, admittedly, retributively hostile to "a man alien to our race" who is usually identified as Pompey. Even his descendants are "hunted down" (see vv. 7, 9). However, the messianic king who delivers Jerusalem is supposed to rule with "righteousness" (see vv. 23, 26, 29, 37), and this includes "faithfully and righteously shepherding the Lord's flock, [so that] he will not let any of them stumble in their pasture." So all the possible meanings of right actions mingle in this psalm in relation to explicitly royal themes — forensic-retributive, forensic-oppressive, and forensic-liberative. Psalm 18 then elaborates quite consistently on the mercy of God and his messiah. That kingly figure will direct and discipline the people "in righteous acts, in the fear of God" (v. 8); however, this is not retributive punishment but affectionate pedagogy (see Psalms 10 and 12). And it is important to emphasize at this point that a pedagogical explanation of suffering as a learning experience is a different account of that experience from one rooted in punishment and the need for retribution. A pedagogical account of suffering is informed by a root metaphor and narrative of nurturing parenthood, as against a strict (i.e., retributive) metaphor and narrative.[77]

An emphasis on benevolent rule, and consequently on forensic-liberative notions, is also discernible in other Psalms. Psalm 5 gracefully hymns God's benevolent kingship, although it does not mention "righteousness" in this relation (it is a quality of the pious: see v. 17, 2x). This Psalm dallies ambiguously with retributive justice at one point (v. 4), but otherwise is consistently concerned with God's kindness and benevolence. "For you are good and merciful, the shelter of the poor. When I cry to you . . . you will not turn away from our prayer, for you are our God" (vv. 2, 5). In like manner, Psalm 7 is also confident about privilege and divine compassion being directed ultimately toward Israel. An alternative attitude might perhaps be discernible toward outsiders, because if even death was sent to Israel, it would have received "special instructions"! (v. 4). But the Psalm is preoccupied with the expectations of mercy, deliverance, compassion, and pedagogical instruction coming to Israel from God — all non-retributive actions.

In sum, then, a more distributive, compassionate nature and action seem to characterize God in Psalms 5, 7, and 18, are evident in Psalm 17, and arguably can be glimpsed in Psalms

10 and 12 as well (there in terms of pedagogy). Hence, the testimony of the Psalms of Solomon is not straightforward — although, as such, it is very useful. In effect, this corpus *debates* and *disagrees over* the divine character. And the Teacher seems to side with the slightly larger block of retributive material, while Paul seems closer to the distributive material.

Precisely the same tension is then discernible in *4 Ezra*. The angel Uriel consistently advocates a retributive view of God's activity (see 6:19-20; 7:17-25, 33-44, 60-61, 70-99, 102-5, 112-15, 127-31; 8:1-3, 37-40, 56-62; 9:7-13, 29-32; 10:17; 14:27-35; 15:4-27; 16:20, 48-50, 64-69, 76-77; note, this is a view that the later Christian prologue also seems to share — see 1:5–2:32), while Ezra complains about various unpleasant and harsh implications that flow from this, and pleads for a countervailing compassionate activity, arguing from the biblical examples of intercession and the compassionate names for God (see 5:23-30, 33, 40; 7:46-48, 62-69, 116-26, 132-40; 8:11-36, 44-45; 9:34-37). Of course, he submits to the wisdom of retributive justice eventually! Similarly, the Wisdom of Solomon expects God to behave compassionately toward Israel, even as the pagans are to be treated ultimately with dire retribution (see esp. 11:9-10, 23; 12:2, 10-11, 15, 19-27; 14:31; 16:2; 18:4; 19:13). That such a double standard exists indicates that the character of God was diverse, if not debated.

The evidence from Qumran is similar, although susceptible to different interpretation at certain key points.[78] There is a strong sense of God unconditionally initiating salvation for a corrupt and sinful humanity, perfecting the elect through the Spirit of Holiness and the law. The wicked are certainly destroyed; however, they were "predestined . . . for the day of annihilation . . . so they will be a sign and an omen . . . so that all will know your glory and your great might" (1QH^a 7.21, 24-25; see also 4Q280 [Brk^z]). So the judgment of the sinful is not generally framed in terms of culpability so much as in terms of predestination and (im)purity. Meanwhile, God makes known his mysteries and the paths of salvation to the elect, assists and sustains them on those paths, and eventually draws them into the heavenly community. And so God is hymned by the community for his compassion (see 1QH^a 7.8, 16-25; 8; see also 1QS 2.1-4; 9.3, 12-15). 4Q504 (Bt 3), is also especially clear: see esp. 2.7-17; 5.6–6.17; Fragment 4; and Fragment 7.10-13. For example, ". . . You have removed from us all our failings and have purified us ^{3}from our sin, for yourself. To you, to you, Lord, justice; for ^{4}you are the one who has done all this" (6.2-4 — and the appropriateness of the translation "justice" could of course be queried here). See also 4Q434 (SL71): "Bless, my soul, the Lord for all his marvels. . . . he did not kindle his anger against them [the needy and oppressed], nor did he destroy them ^{6}in his wrath, although all the wrath of his anger does not lessen, he did not judge them with the fire of his zeal. ^{Blank} ^{7}He judged them with much mercy. The judgments of his eyes are to test them" (Fragment 1, column 1.1, 5-7).

The Teacher threatens Paul's converts from paganism with a frightening future eschatological scenario, in which God will sternly judge all in terms of their deeds (i.e., retributively). Only those judged and pronounced "righteous" on that day will inherit eternal life, and only those circumcised and guided by the law will be capable of such righteousness. The rest will remain sunk in a typical pagan miasma of sin. Paul's law-free converts could well be intimidated by this prospect, and justifiably anxious about their salvation. They are frightened of what the future holds, browbeaten by the harsh condemnation of the Teacher, which merely anticipates in turn the still harsher and more penetrating judgment of God himself.

It seems clear, with the evidence of Romans 1–3 correctly correlated vis-à-vis 3:23-26, that Paul wants to make a number of interrelated points against this theological construct (although they are usually only being introduced at this stage in the letter, to be elaborated further later on). One of his principal rhetorical objectives is to defuse his auditors' sense of eschatological insecurity. But he also seems intent to correct the Teacher's serious theological failures in this regard. The Teacher's gospel effectively marginalizes the Christ event, which has already taken place inaugurating thereby a series of present realities for Christians. In this event — in Paul's view — the decisive aspects of the eschaton *have already taken place* and, accordingly, have disclosed just what the decisive aspects of the future judgment will be. So Paul has rhetorical and substantive reasons for opposing and undermining the Teacher's gospel.

The resources of Scripture and the semantic possibilities in the verb δικαιόω now allow Paul to achieve these objectives (at least in part) by wresting one of the Teacher's key terms away from him. The verb δικαιόω describes the goal of the Teacher's gospel neatly when it is deployed in its forensic-retributive sense. The circumcised and law-observant should strive to achieve this result on judgment day — the declaration that they are righteous (because they are) — at which point they will enter the blessings of the age to come. But by emphasizing its forensic-liberative possibilities, Paul is able to draw this signifier back into his own system: it denotes a decisive judgment by God, but as an act that releases captive humanity from the clutches of Sin and Death, an act that Paul holds to have taken place already through the Christ event, where that liberation was paradigmatically achieved and enacted. In the light of this past event, whose consequences are experienced in the present, Christ is taken with full seriousness *and* the eschaton *need hold no further fears for those so liberated.* That is, what God's act of judgment has actualized through Christ, God is committed to. And a God who has so acted — sacrificing his son for the ungodly — will continue to act benevolently on behalf of humanity. Hence, the future judgment is already in effect decided as well; the key decision has already been made. *There will in fact be no future retributive judgment;* there will be instead a triumphant realization for all of what the elect already know. So there is no need for the Roman Christians to feel intimidated by the threats emanating from the Teacher's rhetoric about their putative fate on the future day of judgment.

It is tempting to summarize these suggestions by pointing to Paul's slogan made famous by Lutheranism — that God justifies the ungodly (4:5; see also 5:6 and 8). This can now be viewed as a pointed refutation of the Teacher's gospel informed by the Christ event. And as such, it encapsulates perfectly just the terminological distinction and debate that is being suggested here. This slogan *specifically rejects the forensic-retributive interpretation of God and hence that interpretation of the verb* δικαιόω *as well.* The Teacher's God justifies *the godly;* God (according to the Teacher) declares righteous, on the day of judgment, those who are in fact righteous. That the uncircumcised and unobservant Roman Christians might not be declared righteous is then the rhetorical cudgel that the

Teacher can use to create a space for his own gospel among them — and much as "turn or burn" preachers still do today. However, Paul is convinced that God has acted in the Christ event to intervene in an ungodly situation — a scenario within which an enslaved and hostile humanity cannot help itself. It is this fundamentally benevolent action that reveals the deeply loving character of God: God "justifies" the *un*godly. His decisive forensic act — his judgment — is that they be released in Christ from their ontological prison; in Christ, he has set them free. God's "justification" is consequently a forensic-liberative act. Indeed, an emphatically Lutheran reading of Paul would seem to coincide neatly at this point with an apocalyptic one. Both speak correctly here of a critical polemical claim on Paul's part. Moreover, a correct grasp of this claim will lead to a corresponding imperviousness to the coercive threats of the Teacher and any like him.

One might ask why Paul would bother with this potentially confusing and difficult reclamation of terminology, but we have just seen that he had good reasons for doing so, both rhetorical and substantive. And it follows from this terminological struggle that interpreters must strive to be sensitive to whose system is in view at any given moment in a Pauline text. Two related but different senses of δικαιόω are frequently in play within Paul's arguments (and these may be seen immediately in the unavoidably different meanings apparent in 2:13 and 6:7). To be sure, this realization entails that we read Paul's arguments with particular care, but in so doing, we can at last explain these vexing semantic modulations.[79]

One of the added advantages of this interpretative realization is that the temporal shifts in 3:21-26, and especially in contradistinction to the surrounding material in Romans, become fully comprehensible in terms of the suggested rereading. As we have just seen, the Teacher's claims are rooted in an undisclosed and uncertain future (and this marginalizes Christ's role in that relation as well: see 2:16b). It is this locus that generates much of the intimidating force in his argument: "Will you be declared righteous on judgment day . . . ?!" Over against this, Paul emphasizes the decisiveness of the disclosure that has already taken place, in the recent past and now in the present. A God who is prepared to offer up his only son on behalf of an estranged, enslaved, and hostile humanity can be trusted completely to maintain that commitment through whatever the future might hold. Hence, Paul speaks at both the opening and the closing of Romans 3:21-26 of the disclosure of God's δικαιοσύνη "now" ([21]Νυνὶ δὲ . . . [26]. . . ἐν τῷ νῦν καιρῷ). Conventional readers, concerned to coordinate this evidence with the supposed prior establishment of humanity's culpability in 1:18–3:20, suggest that this contrast is a present one over against a past reality; the coming of Christ has brought the possibility of atonement and salvation now to the world. But this dramatically misreads Paul's meaning and overlooks certain key pieces of evidence. The detection of a temporal contrast is certainly valid, but the contrast being asserted is between the present *and the future*. Paul is claiming that the present evidence of the Christ event establishes certain guarantees in relation to the future, overruling the Teacher's alternative and rather aggressive scenario. And this is why so many of the forensic verbs in context contrast present (or past) and *future* tenses (and not, in the latter case, *past* tenses, as the conventional reading expects).

Present tenses dominate Paul's assertion of the gospel in 1:16-17, which is resumed with a *perfect* in 3:21-22. Present tenses are then present in vv. 24 and 26, as well as 27-28. However, *future* tenses dominate such assertions in Romans 2 and 3:1-20, where the Teacher's gospel is in view.

These begin specifically in 2:3 with ἐκφεύξῃ. The critical eschatological material in this chapter is then predominantly future, describing a day of "righteous judgment" when God ἀποδώσει ἑκάστῳ κατὰ τὰ ἔργα αὐτοῦ (this being a programmatic statement that governs vv. 6-10, as we have just seen). The future verbs continue in vv. 12-16 — κριθήσονται, δικαιωθήσονται, and (almost certainly) κρινεῖ — and resume in vv. 26-29 (see esp. λογισθήσεται in v. 26 and κρινεῖ in v. 27). Future eschatological scenarios are also endorsed in vv. 4 and 6 of the diatribe in 3:1-9, being resumed in 3:19, after which a future verb summarizes the entire argument: ἐξ ἔργων νόμου οὐ δικαιωθήσεται πᾶσα σὰρξ ἐνώπιον αὐτοῦ. (This sense then seems to be reprised in 3:30.)

Conventional readers can offer an explanation for this phenomenon, but that is not our concern just here; the important point, rather, is that the text explicitly supports a present-future temporal contrast, which is congruent in turn with my suggested rereading of 3:21-26. Paul is contrasting a decisive present (and past) act of God in Christ with a more uncertain and intimidating future eschatological scenario.

With these further interpretative realizations in place, we need to consider the meaning of Paul's second reference to the atonement, in 3:25b, and then, in §5, to consider the subsection's conclusion, in 3:26b. Following these discussions we will be able to address in chapter seventeen the sole remaining major issue of interpretation in 3:21-26 — the meaning of the phrase δικαιοσύνη Θεοῦ (or its close equivalent) — from which point the rhetorical function of the subsection in the letter as a whole (along with that of any related units) should be clear.

§4. The Meaning of Romans 3:25b

In v. 25b Paul states that Christ's proof of God's δικαιοσύνη is for the sake of τὴν πάρεσιν τῶν προγεγονότων ἁμαρτημάτων, a statement that bears some relation to ἡ ἀνοχὴ τοῦ Θεοῦ. What do these claims add to our developing picture of the atonement and "justification" in the sense of deliverance in 3:23-26?

The longer phrase has of course usually been interpreted in relation to the expectations of Justification theory, and so the extremely rare signifier πάρεσις has been held to refer — largely by way of analogy with the cognate verb παρίημι — to God's "passing over" sins that were previously committed by humanity, his thereby "patiently" waiting until Christ came and died, atoning for them (and in fact propitiating God's patiently withheld wrath, along with its dire consequences). These claims contribute smoothly to the conventional reading and its endorsement of Justification theory. But while πάρεσις *can* denote an overlooking or passing over — at least in one instance — this extremely rare word can also denote "release."[80] And with the interpretation of this clause released from the influence of Justification theory, the setting's immediate implications prompt the clause's interpretation in just these liberative terms.

We have already seen that the basic sense of the salvation obtained in Christ is one of release from slavery (see ἀπολύτρωσις in v. 24a) and, moreover, that the brief characterization in v. 23 of the plight from which humanity has been rescued points ahead to a deeply incapacitated situation, enslaved to Sin and Death in Adam. Largely in view of these indicators, it seemed best to interpret the verb δικαιόω in forensic-liberative terms, which accorded with the emphatic statement of gratuity that followed it immediately in v. 24, and Paul's later usage in Romans 6 and 8 as well. And it is now difficult to prize the interpretation of v. 25b away from these earlier indicators.

The clause speaks clearly of some solution to sin and so ought to be correlated with the implications of v. 23, which addresses the same subject. And its rare substantive πάρεσις overlaps significantly with the semantic field of ἀπολύτρωσις in v. 24. So the later statement in v. 25 is in effect triangulated by these words in its immediate context and should be interpreted accordingly. Christ's function as a singular atonement (at the behest of God) makes him a definitive proof of God's δικαιοσύνη, which must then function in turn "for the sake of the/that release from previously occurring transgressions." (Attributing a strong causal sense to διά and the accusative here makes little sense; the release from sins effected by Christ is not the *cause* of his demonstration of God's δικαιοσύνη but its effect — the same meaning as seems likely for this preposition again in 4:24-25 [3x!].) And with this decision, we need now to consider the meaning of God's ἀνοχή, which is coordinated with this release, and almost certainly in instrumental terms (a frequent meaning of ἐν phrases in Paul).

The conventional reading interprets this word as it also occurs in 2:4, to denote God's forbearance as he "holds back" his wrath until it is satisfied through the suffering and death of Christ on the cross. And ἀνοχή does refer literally to a "holding back" of something. But it is tempting, in the light of this earlier usage, and the entire context's rereading in relation to the Teacher's gospel, to detect another linguistic subversion in 3:25 on Paul's part. This act of holding back by God could refer instead to a more positive action, as it did in fact in various Greek statements in Paul's day (often with ἔχειν: see meaning 1, BDAG 86 — 1 Macc. 12:25;[81] Josephus, *War*, 1.173;[82] *Antiquities*, 6.72 [and 73];[83] Diodorus Siculus, *Fragments*, 11.36.4; *Oxyrhynchus Papyri* 1068; Hermas, *Similitudes*, 6.3.1;[84] see also Epictetus, *Discourses*, 1.29.62;[85] *First Enoch* 13:2;[86] *Papiri greci e latini: Pubblicazioni della Società Italiana* 632.13). In this alternative construal, God's ἀνοχή would refer to an act of respite within which God holds back something oppressive — here the enslaved human condition, which is decisively liberated in Christ. It would therefore refer to God's *merciful* intervention or clemency (see BDAG 86). Alternatively — and perhaps even better — it could refer to the respite that comes *from* God in Christ, in the form of the release effected by and in him from previously committed transgressions.[87] The liberative semantic connotations of these terms and phrases all now integrate smoothly.

In sum, the semantic possibilities that exist for the rare terms and phrases used in 3:25 conform nicely to the liberative thrust of the atonement that is well established in the subsection by now. Furthermore, there seem to be no good reasons for reading this material in a way that endorses the conventional reading rather than this developing view. Such an interpretation is arguably possible, but freed from any contextual assistance, it seems less likely than the liberative reading being suggested here, and the immediate context seems to stand consistently against it. Paul's analysis of the atonement in Romans 3:25 consequently remains fundamentally liberative, as it is throughout 3:23-25 — something with important implications for the subsection's famous final clause.

§5. The Meaning of Romans 3:26b

It is possible to draw two of the preceding argument's strands together now to interpret the final clause of 3:21-26 — εἰς τὸ εἶναι αὐτὸν δίκαιον καὶ δικαιοῦντα τὸν ἐκ πίστεως Ἰησοῦ[ν].

The participle here should be interpreted in parallel with its earlier occurrence in v. 24, and in accordance with all the surrounding contextual material as well, which nuances its meaning in a forensic-liberative direction. It denotes a divine speech-act that effects some sort of release from Adamic captivity into a glorious new freedom — a saving, eschatological meaning of "release," or "liberation," or "deliverance," ultimately in terms of resurrection. Similarly, the phrase ἐκ πίστεως Ἰησοῦ[ν] resumes the key intertext from 1:17 of Habakkuk 2:4, which ought to be interpreted messianically. It also echoes the preceding two references in the subsection to the faithful Christ, in relation to which fairly decisive evidence can be discerned locally, and so should be read accordingly as another reference to Christ, at least in some sense. That Paul refers here to "Jesus" alone in the vast majority of the manuscripts also seems to support this judgment. As Keck (i.a.) notes, such a single denotation in Paul invariably suggests that the earthly "historical" Jesus is in view for Paul, and faith *in* the earthly Jesus would be a strange suggestion from the apostle! The apostle's preferred confession concerns the heavenly enthroned Jesus' lordship.[88] Moreover, the subsection 3:21-26 now possesses a smoothly chiastic construction, returning at the end to the subject with which it began — the action of God through Christ (concerning which see more just below). Consequently, Paul seems to be speaking in 3:26b as he was at the beginning, in vv. 21-22 — of the eschatological release effected through the Christ event, and what this signifies. But we have yet to settle the *exact* nuances of this ringing conclusion.

These claims fill out a purposive construction that uses an articular infinitive to make the more basic claim that God is δίκαιος. This is an unusual suggestion on Paul's part in literal terms (although not for that reason unacceptable); however, Paul is almost certainly punning again, this time with the δικαιο- word group (see πιστ- terms in v. 22). This final clause seems to be stating that God is intentionally δίκαιος *as* and *in that* he acts through the faithful Jesus to liberate and to deliver (i.e., καὶ δικαιοῦντα τὸν ἐκ πίστεως Ἰησοῦ[ν]). This meaning integrates perfectly with the main themes that precede it, *and it returns God himself to the position of active subject,* where the subsection began (δικαιοσύνη Θεοῦ πεφανέρωται . . .) — component i in the five-component schema that was identified in chapter fifteen. Christ is not merely the definitive proof of God's δικαιοσύνη, then, as vv. 25b-26 suggest, but God himself *is* δικαιοσύνη (in some sense) *actively* as he liberates and delivers through that event, which doubles as a decisive demonstration of his δικαιοσύνη. And this seems to be the main import of the subsection's resonant conclusion: we end up where we began, with the self-disclosure of God in Christ.

Yet an often-unnoticed ambiguity is still present here. It is difficult to decide from this point whether the clause rounds off the subsection by emphasizing God's action in Christ alone or God's action *through* Christ on behalf of believers (see εἰς πάντας τοὺς πιστεύοντας in v. 22). Is he releasing Christ or believers *through* Christ (thereby emphasizing either components i and iv, or i, iv, and v in the five-component schema)? Both readings are completely unobjectionable in more general terms (and this should be noted), and both, furthermore, make excellent sense. Two further details in the text now come into play.

We should consider, first, the manuscript evidence concerning the subunit's final word, "Jesus," which is more difficult to resolve than is usually suggested, and, second, the feature in the evidence that may turn out (again!) to be the key to interpretation at this juncture — the presence of an article. D and sundry other witnesses (L, Ψ, 33, 614, 945, 1506, 1881, 2464, Clement) record an accusative Ἰησοῦν here rather than the more common genitive Ἰησοῦ (ℵ, A, B, C, 1739, vgst, sy^h, sa, bo^mss). Other important witnesses attest to early confusion at this point, either by omitting the name (F, G) or expanding it (629, it, vg^cl, sy^p, bo; 1984 has Ἰησοῦν Χριστόν). The main variants are finely balanced. It is possible to suppose that a scribe changed a genitive Ἰησοῦ (IY) to an accusative Ἰησοῦν (IN) deliberately — clearly being comfortable with a subjective construal or, alternatively, perhaps being unaware of it — in view of the accusative article that just precedes it (τὸν generating τὸν ἐκ πίστεως Ἰησοῦν). Less likely but still possible is a mistake transcribing *scripta continua,* with the eye being misled by the *nus* that either precede or follow (see αὐτὸν δίκαιον καὶ δικαιοῦντα in v. 26a and οὖν in v. 27). But equally likely is the supposition that a scribe deliberately changed the accusative to conform to the preceding genitive in 3:22, an accusative Ἰησοῦν following πίστις being unparalleled in Paul. And if an explanation in terms of scribal carelessness is sought, then the surrounding context is as studded with genitive endings (whether apparent or real) as it is with prompts for an accusative (see ποῦ οὖν . . . διὰ ποίου νόμου . . .). Most scholars pronounce definitively against the accusative reading, but once the prior influence of Justification theory is removed, there seem few good reasons for doing so. It is not in fact a difficulty that God would then be "justifying" Jesus himself here, because a forensic-liberative understanding of δικαιόω is consistent with Pauline statements about Jesus elsewhere, some of which have already been noted. Jesus is probably the subject of the verb in 6:7, and is certainly the subject of δικαίωμα in 5:18 (see also 4:25). Indeed, it can hardly be implausible to suggest that Paul speaks at times of God resurrecting Jesus! We should turn, then, to the immediate context for additional clues to resolve this conundrum.

One such clue might be the presence of the article in this expression. The entire disputed phrase is parallel to Paul's later statement in 4:16, τῷ ἐκ πίστεως Ἀβραάμ, which seems to establish the possibility (not the necessity) that the genitive in 3:26 be rendered subjectively. Most scholars assume that the article in 3:26 refers to Christians in general. However, as we have already had ample cause to note, articles often function resumptively in Paul; they point to another substantive in context signaling its renewed mention. Romans 4:16 illustrates this exactly, where τῷ ἐκ πίστεως Ἀβραάμ resumes παντί τῷ σπέρματι, which precedes it in the same sentence; there can be no doubt in this sentence about to whom τῷ refers. However, the article in 3:26 has no visible "antecedent." If it is referred to believers in general, it must reach back to "those justified" in v. 24, if not to "believers" in v. 22. Such a resumption would be taking place over some distance. Moreover, these are all *plural* categories, while the later article is singular; hence, such a reference would also be awkward. It is worth asking, then, in view of these difficulties, if the common assumption is in fact correct. A closer antecedent in context, which is singular, would be Christ himself. Several considerations — of varying strength — seem to support this suggestion.

First, the immediate context in vv. 25-26 is focused on Christ's disclosure of God, not God's justifying deliverance of Christians. (The latter notion, to reiterate, is not objectionable, but the material question here is what Paul is actually talking about in 3:26b.) The preceding series of five prepositional phrases and clauses has been oriented almost exclusively toward Christ as the visible evidence of God's δικαιοσύνη.[89] So a reading of the article in 3:26b in such terms simply completes these concerns smoothly, and in accordance with a common function of articles in Paul (and in this sense analogously to the function of the probable article in 3:25b). Instead of Christ functioning as the "proof" of God's δικαιοσύνη, we now hear that God is δίκαιος as he liberates Christ, *thereby himself creating that proof,* the article consequently resuming τὴν ἔνδειξιν from the important preceding phrase. Christ discloses God in vv. 25b-26a, and in v. 26b it seems to follow that God acts through Christ as that former disclosure's presupposition.

[25]ὃν προέθετο ὁ Θεὸς [εἶναι] ἱλαστήριον
    διὰ τῆς πίστεως
    ἐν τῷ αὐτοῦ αἵματι
εἰς ἔνδειξιν τῆς δικαιοσύνης αὐτοῦ

διὰ τὴν πάρεσιν τῶν προγεγονότων ἁμαρτημάτων
ἐν τῇ ἀνοχῇ τοῦ Θεοῦ,
²⁶πρὸς τὴν ἔνδειξιν τῆς δικαιοσύνης αὐτοῦ
ἐν τῷ νῦν καιρῷ
εἰς τὸ εἶναι αὐτὸν δίκαιον καὶ δικαιοῦντα τὸν ἐκ πίστεως Ἰησοῦ[ν].

Indeed, it could be suggested that reasons must be supplied to justify a departure in 3:26b from this christocentric concern and focus. On what grounds should another reference be introduced?

Second, 3:23-26 are composed in a consistent manner. We have already noted that these verses expand, in different terms, on three of the components in 3:21-22 — i, iv, and v. Moreover, they do so in reverse order, returning from a consideration of all who sin and are saved through trust in vv. 23-24a, to Christ's mediation of God's δικαιοσύνη in vv. 24b-25, to God's active disclosure in v. 26b (and 25a). With this reading of v. 26, no reintroduction of component v now interrupts this chiastic structure. The argument proceeds in terms of i — iv — v — v — iv — i.

Third, the phrase ἐκ πίστεως in 3:26b echoes Habakkuk 2:4, which was cited in 1:17b in a messianic fashion. Here, for the first time since 1:17, Paul resumes its terminology explicitly. Hence, it seems best to read the entire clause in a christocentric sense, and especially the article that precedes this programmatic phrase. For an auditor detecting the heroic protagonist of Habakkuk 2:4 from 1:17 — ὁ δίκαιος ἐκ πίστεως ζήσεται — the phrase τὸν ἐκ πίστεως in 3:26 would probably have evoked Christ rather than the Christian. There are explicit cues for the former, but not for the latter.

There is also no need to supply a participle at this point, as many commentators do in order to generate a smooth translation in English. Indeed, it is probably best not to do so, given the clause's contested meaning; any such supply would only beg the key questions. Paul seems to be stating here that God is "right in the very act of liberating that one by means of faithfulness."⁹⁰ But this observation takes us to the brink of an important realization concerning the clause's final word, Ἰησοῦ[ν].

Although the arthrous phrase seems to reach back plausibly to the phrases that just precede this final clause, where Jesus is identified as a ἱλαστήριον and then an ἔνδειξις, in accordance with God's purposes, it is still momentarily ambiguous in 3:26b just who the unnamed τὸν ἐκ πίστεως is — the figure whom God is liberating — and, perhaps even more precisely, whose fidelity it is. It seems that the final word in the sentence, Ἰησοῦ[ν], functions to clarify these ambiguities immediately in explanatory, or epexegetical, terms: "God is right in the very act of liberating that one by means of faithfulness — namely, Jesus." So the figure in question is definitely Jesus, and the fidelity his as well. (Significantly, αὐτοῦ would be an ambiguous clarification in view of its repeated uses in the preceding statements to refer to God "the Father.") Moreover, it is now possible to explain the difficulties in the textual tradition.

The majority tradition supplies an epexegetical Ἰησοῦ, which has the further virtue of harmonizing with the preceding genitive in v. 22, although it is not functioning subjectively here, as it does there. And this is most probably the original version. The minority western variants supply an appositional accusative, however, which generates essentially the same meaning. (The later western tradition, meanwhile, omits any clarifying name at all, perhaps since it is not, strictly speaking, necessary. Alternatively, it might be withdrawing from the textual puzzle that it no longer understands, or creating a possible reading in terms of general Christian faith, where both the accusative and genitive impede it, and I incline toward the latter possibility.)

For all these reasons then, what we might dub a thoroughgoing christocentric construal of 3:26 seems to make the most sense of the evidence both in 3:26b and in context. Not a great deal changes as a result of this. Presumably, few would want to deny either that God's nature is revealed through the Christ event for Paul, and especially through Jesus' resurrection, or that by means of this event God liberates humanity from its enslavement to Sin and Death. Nevertheless, further pointed inferences in the statement's immediate context will now be apparent. The nature of God, his δικαιοσύνη, seems to be revealed definitively in the Christ event, and especially in Christ's resurrection — an obvious but ultimately very significant claim.

CHAPTER SEVENTEEN

The Deliverance of God, and Its Rhetorical Implications

§1. Preamble

We have yet to determine the meaning of one of the key motifs in Romans 1:17 and 3:21-26 — δικαιοσύνη Θεοῦ. Only after we have decided what this phrase means will we be able to draw further conclusions about the subsections' rhetorical functions with a degree of confidence. But leaving this contentious debate until this point in our overall exegesis has been quite deliberate; this should allow us to do a methodological "end run," so to speak, around many of its pitfalls and ambiguities. Following our discoveries here, we will be able to address the subunits' argumentative roles within the rest of the letter — which are looking increasingly fascinating — and tidy up the remaining interpretative loose ends in these short but critical sections of text.

§2. The Meaning of δικαιοσύνη Θεοῦ

2.1. Preamble to the δικαιοσύνη Θεοῦ Debate

The debate concerning the meaning of δικαιοσύνη Θεοῦ in Paul is immense. One indicator of its size is the fact that many modern scholarly discussions' first annotations now need to reference surveys of the debate (if not surveys of surveys) rather than the primary data itself.[1] Key studies, meanwhile, date back over a hundred years.[2] This seems rather curious, however, when the primary data from Paul himself is assembled. The expression δικαιοσύνη Θεοῦ or its close equivalent occurs only eight times, in four places, in Romans, and Romans dominates its Pauline instances (see 1:17; 3:5, 21, 22, 25, 26; 10:3 [2x]). The phrase occurs once in 1 and in 2 Corinthians (1 Cor. 1:30; 2 Cor. 5:21), and probably twice in Philippians 3:9.[3] So an enormous debate seems to have been unfolding in relation to a relatively small number of phrases and texts. And partly in view of that size and complexity, together with this manageable number of primary texts, I propose reversing the usual flow of analysis.

I suggest that sufficient evidence exists in Paul himself to resolve the vast majority of questions surrounding the interpretation of this group of phrases. Moreover, these clarifications can be achieved reasonably quickly and incontestably. (It is difficult to overthrow a clear semantic judgment reached on primary grounds.) This resolution can then act as a control on the vast literature and rather overwhelming background analyses that otherwise threaten to smother context-sensitive interpretation. In the process, we will in fact end up largely confirming the main conclusions of a classic analysis of δικαιοσύνη Θεοῦ by Ernst Käsemann, first made in 1961, although by a different route; his definitions will essentially be endorsed.[4] So at bottom, nothing especially controversial will be suggested here — at least, in the first instance. (Admittedly, beyond this internal investigation and its results, matters will become more contentious.) But before addressing the internal evidence, we should first note some categories that must be firmly resisted as we begin to process it.

Even nonexhaustive soundings through the prior debate over the meaning of δικαιοσύνη Θεοῦ in Paul reveal problems that need to be addressed if any forward progress is ultimately to be achieved. Specifically, I suggest that three distinctions and three common methodological claims need to be resisted, since their dubiety can be recognized at the outset. Further, certain bland sets of semantic assumptions surrounding the key notions of "justice" and "rightness" need to be exposed (and they have already been uncovered in part), assumptions that overlap with translation problems that are usefully noted here as well. Grasping these difficulties at the outset and rejecting them where that is appropriate will greatly enhance the accuracy of the internal investigations that follow.

(1) Distinctions

It is not uncommon to encounter two common distinctions at the beginning of many investigations of the meaning of δικαιο- data in Paul. Interpreters often distinguish between broadly Protestant and Catholic interpretations. In close relation to this, some speak of a forensic and/or relational interpretation of this data as against a more ethical and/or substantive reading. The forensic and relational approach is of course supposedly more Protestant, and the ethical and/or substantive reading more Catholic.[5] But numerous difficulties are immediately apparent here.

Justification theory dictates that individuals are saved by faith alone, and so are still essentially sinful even after conversion. Moreover, they ought not to rely on good works for justification at all, even after salvation, since this might indicate a lapse back into the legalism of the model's first and futile phase. Justification advocates can thus recognize and account for ongoing difficulties in the lives of individuals and churches, but some adjustment to any straightforward, culturally analogous application of certain forensic actions by God is thereby also necessitated. The just God is satisfied by Christ's atoning payment for sins and agrees that individuals can be saved by faith alone. But his verdict of "rightness" concerning any such believing converts cannot now be taken with strict literality; the individuals standing before him who are saved by faith are not "right," and their entire approach to salvation necessitates that they stay sinful! Protestants consequently navigate Paul's apparent insistence on the use of δικαιόω to describe salvation by suggesting that God deliberately declares such figures right, thereby restoring them to a right relationship with him, but recognizing all the while that their innocence is effected vicariously. Something of a legal fiction holds, then, although a generous one.[6] God pronounces individuals "right" who are in fact *not* actually right in and of themselves — the converse of a good retributive court procedure. But in so doing, God "justifies the ungodly."

The ethical and substantive reading of this terminology, generally associated with Catholicism, tends to struggle with such claims, whether on theoretical or semantic grounds. Against the preceding emphases, it suggests that Paul's terminology implies, at least at times, an ethical transformation in individuals, which releases God from the need to enact a legal fiction. Such advocates often note that Paul expects his converts to behave righteously, at which point God can legitimately pronounce them righteous "in fact," and hence "ethically" and/or "substantively" (if a substantial ontology is being presupposed). And such interpreters can point to Paul's extensive ethical exhortations, as well as the difficulties that Justification advocates have navigating from salvation through faith alone to further ethical behavior, in support of these emphases. Forensic and relational advocates can nevertheless reply that Paul's converts all tend to remain overtly sinful, while his programmatic critique of salvation through works remains undisturbed. Moreover, too strong an emphasis on ethics may result in a blunting of the force of salvation through faith alone and its humble admission of sinfulness. (Presumably, it might also create unhealthy openings for various church monopolies.)

The tensions evident here, some of which have already been noted in specific relation to Justification theory, will not be resolved yet. It is important to grasp, rather, that these distinctions are themselves deeply problematic and ought to be largely abandoned; they tend to break down when they are examined more closely. This is not to suggest that they do not point to legitimate interpretive questions in Paul, but it *is* to suggest that those questions are not best treated by using these antitheses.

As we have already seen in part, the forensic and ethical dimensions tend to be correlated, but can be so in different modes — forensic-retributive and forensic-nonretributive (forensic-oppressive or forensic-liberative; in these, any verdictive acts take place in a more strictly performative fashion). So the relationship between the two dimensions is complex; they do not exist in a simple relationship of exclusivity (i.e., either-or).

It is even clearer that relational dimensions cannot be distinguished in kind from ethical actions. All ethical actions are relational (and so vice versa)! Is it even possible to conceive of a nonrelational ethical act or a nonethical relationship? It seems that we can always ask whether a given action or relationship is right or good. So this distinction seems to run the risk of sheer incoherence. Moreover, any treatment of ontology in terms of substances is increasingly problematic (on which see more below).

Thus, it seems that some of the basic analytic antitheses often operative in this debate are deeply flawed. Forensic and relational actions cannot be opposed to ethical actions, and substantive explanations of any such acts are quite problematic. It is more accurate to speak at the outset of forensic, relational, and ethical dimensions all operating at times in the same actions in Paul, although in different manners.

Given these burgeoning complexities, any neat correlations with broad ecclesial traditions look unlikely, and the more so when the internal complexities of those traditions are taken into account. Traditions are themselves seldom simple; they contain spectrums of opinion, if not trajectories of outright disagreement. Hence, the suggestion that the more analytic antitheses correlate neatly with Protestantism versus Catholicism is oversimplified in the order of several powers. We might find degrees of correlation at different points, but those would need to be established on a case-by-case basis.

These oversimplified and false antitheses — between forensic/relational and ethical/substantial, and between Protestant and Catholic — are readily identifiable in much previous debate over the meaning of Paul's δικαιο- terms and should be nuanced if not abandoned. However, another distinction that is possibly even more destructive in analytical terms is less often recognized.

Much debate in this relation seems to assume a strong distinction between being and act (see also action and activity), a staple assumption of much Western thought. Consequently, when analyzing Paul's δικαιο- terminology, interpreters working in terms of that static distinction (whether or not it is acknowledged) expect the verb δικαιόω used in relation to God to speak of a divine action, but the noun δικαιοσύνη and adjective δίκαιος to speak of God's being and hence be described best in terms of quite different ontological categories — perhaps attributes or substances or even essences. There are good reasons, however, for thinking that God's being and action are indistinguishable, and especially in relation to Christ; his being *is* activity (as is ours, much of the time). Furthermore, if Paul himself is not constricted by such distinctions (largely preceding them or, alternatively, being untrained in them), then any Western analysis of his use of δικαιο- terminology in these terms will struggle to comprehend its interrelated field of meaning. In particular, it may struggle to grasp the dynamic process suggested by the apostle's use of substantives,[7] often lapsing at such points into rather different notions underpinned by an alien metaphysical system. It will attribute different categories of being to notions that Paul thinks of more as activities (and that are therefore closer to the verb). We will have to see in what follows whether Paul's terminology and argumentation show evidence for or against a strong being-act distinction. If the latter — as seems likely for a pre- and/or non-Western thinker

— then other definitions of being will not need to be introduced, and more dynamic conceptions of the apostle's meaning can be pursued.[8]

(2) Methodological Claims

We need now to consider briefly some false methodological approaches — three in particular, although they tend to operate in concert.

Past studies of Paul's δικαιο- terminology often contain extensive surveys of the background data. And certainly such surveys must play a role in our deliberations at some point; they provide the range of semantic possibilities that the sign functions in question can activate at any given moment. But such surveys can be crafted and used erroneously. They may be oriented around a "core" or "essence" of meaning in a stem, a false claim and methodology generally known as *etymologism,* which we have already noted and rejected, in part one, chapter seven. But we have also already seen that this methodological tendency is especially pronounced when paradigmatic concerns are in play, as they are here, giving rise to *paradigmatic overinterpretation.* Signifiers regarded as fundamental tend to be not merely defined in a false, essentializing manner (i.e., in terms of etymologism) but overinterpreted in terms of an entire program. Mere words are said to necessarily signify meaning usually denoted by sentences (sentences often summarizing in turn books and strategic elements within theological systems). The result can be something of a linguistic masquerade ball; under the guise of an impartial, scientific assembly of the relevant linguistic data, a slanted narrative is in fact crafted in support of a given theological agenda. It is important, then, to treat such projects carefully. Moreover, the further, *question-begging assertion* is often implicit in these surveys that certain words are necessarily more important than other words for Paul; they are strategic and programmatic. Now, this may turn out to be the case, but it cannot be assumed at the outset! Such claims must be demonstrated. In short, we must be alert in what follows to any claims in the literature that are based on etymologism, paradigmatic overinterpretation, or question-begging strategic claims, as well as to any surveys constructed in these terms. We should consider now some more specific semantic complications.

(3) Semantic Claims

Notions of "justice" and "rightness" are often invoked by New Testament scholars in debates over the meaning of Paul's δικαιο- terms without due consideration for the underlying complexity of such claims.

It is assumed, for example, that "justice" has an obvious meaning, universally accepted, which is usually held, furthermore, to be a retributive one (although the literature often denotes this as "distributive," probably in dependence on the underlying Latin phrase *iustitia distributiva*). But these are shocking oversimplifications, as the ongoing debates within political philosophical circles over the very notion of "justice" indicate. The meaning of "justice" depends largely on complex underlying narratives and cultures that are anything but simple and universal. Very different definitions of "justice" can be supplied, a useful example being the relatively recent treatment in political philosophy, widely regarded as a classic, by John Rawls — *A Theory of Justice*. (Rawls's analysis begins with two self-evident definitions of justice, neither of which is remotely retributive.)[9]

Equally problematic are any assumptions that notions of "rightness" are straightforward. Like "justice," the meaning of "rightness" varies widely in terms of its specific ethical content as dictated by local differences in construals of the good (resting on different histories, cultures, narratives, metaphysics, and so on). What is "right" for one person is not necessarily "right" for another. We can, moreover, always ask whether a "right" action is truly "right" in a given situation (and so on).

It is important to note, further, that whether these are innate and/or universal categories is hotly debated. Moreover, "rightness" and "justice" themselves seem to be correlated in different ways. It cannot simply be assumed that the "right" thing to do is also the "just" thing, or that the best broad social and/or political arrangement is "just"; it may not necessarily be "right" to give priority in all arrangements *to* justice. "Rightness" and "justice" are not merely correlative notions.

Grasping the important differences at these semantic and ethical levels will actually allow us to grasp in turn the heart of much of the dispute between Paul and the Teacher in Romans — *the struggle caused by contrasting definitions of "rightness," especially as they relate to the actions of God in Christ.* But this complicated set of distinctions can be further obscured by translation difficulties, if they are not clearly recognized.

English struggles to supply appropriate translation equivalents for δικαιο-terms in Paul's Koiné that convey the similarity or overlap between the Greek cognates and any consequent semantic overlap or wordplay in his texts. (This is not of course to suggest that a word group based on a cognate necessarily possesses either a fixed common meaning or an essential notion conveyed by a stem; the semantic function of wordplay is different.) Whereas Paul can craft his discussions using a selection of similar sounding words δικαιοσύνη, δίκαιος, δικαίωμα, δικαίωσις, δίκη, δικαιοκρισία, and δικαιόω (and this list does not include alpha-privatives) — English has, for one reason or another, tended to lose the full range of cognate translation equivalents. Substantives based on the stem "right" ("righteous," "righteousness," etc., based on the Old English "riht") have no cognate verb in English that renders Paul's employment of δικαιόω accurately, the closest candidate being "rectify." (Compare the Old English "rihtwîs" [and Bultmann's translator actually chose to use this archaic term, although it has not been widely adopted]. It is perhaps worth noting as well that "right" in English can function as an adjective, a transitive verb, and a substantive! Scholars nevertheless generally hold that "to right" does not accurately convey the sense of Paul's use of δικαιόω.) So translators often make recourse to the "just" word group for Paul's verbal notions, using "justify," "justification" and so on — words based on the Latin *ius, iustus, iustificare,* and *iustitia* but influential on English primarily by way of French (see *justifier*). Such a decision, however, creates the awkward situation that a cognate word group in the Koiné is rendered in English by rather different-looking and -sounding equivalents — the Greek substantives by "right" words and the cognate verbs by "just" words. Any original wordplays and semantic overlaps are now obscured.[10] Equally significantly, any use of words in English based on the Latin stem *ius* almost automatically evokes connotations of "justice," and these are not necessarily appropriate for Koiné terms evoking "rightness." (The interrelated debates we have just noted are then automatically generated at these points.) These translation difficulties will have to be recognized and negotiated, as far as possible, in what follows.[11]

2.2. *The Meaning of* δικαιοσύνη Θεοῦ *in Paul, Especially in Romans 1:17 and 3:21-26*

One of the main reasons we have spent so much time interpreting 1:17 and 3:21-26 before turning to this programmatic issue is that it enables us to work backward toward a solution. It is clearly one of the central claims of 1:17 and 3:21-26 that the δικαιοσύνη Θεοῦ is disclosed by Christ definitively. One suspects that the principal rhetorical emphasis in this claim for the Roman Christians was the christological predicate; the long awaited δικαιοσύνη Θεοῦ is disclosed, even as it is actualized, *by him*. However, the difficult part of this proposition for modern Christian and post-Christian interpreters is the subject. We have not been able to agree on what it actually means (and often hold a lot to hang on it, thereby raising the stakes and complicating the issue). But we can gain definitive insight into it merely by reversing the equation that Paul is making here. We already know much of what Christ has achieved and therefore disclosed in 3:21-26 and related passages, thanks to the wealth of information that Paul supplies us with syntactically in these texts. *And this must be the content of* δικαιοσύνη Θεοῦ! Indeed, most of our queries are settled by this simple move; all we need is enough confidence to follow through its implications fully (that is, along with an exegetical strategy that interprets most of 3:21-26 before addressing this question[12]).

Seven subordinate semantic insights into the meaning of δικαιοσύνη Θεοῦ now unfold: (1) its content as an event or act; (2) its singularity; (3) its connotation as saving and, in this relation, (4) as liberating and (5) as life giving, and hence (6) eschatological, or resurrecting. Finally, (7) it is these aspects that allow Paul to pun on the genitive relation in the phrase, shifting between a genitive of subject and one of author or separation without a significant shift in meaning or reference, the δικαιοσύνη *of* God segueing into the δικαιοσύνη *from* God, which/ who is Christ. Following the discussion of these insights we will be able to press deeper into the contingent nuances of the phrase in Romans.

To reiterate the key methodological point: if Christ is the definitive disclosure of the δικαιοσύνη Θεοῦ, then if we know what Christ is, we can infer immediately the content of δικαιοσύνη Θεοῦ. In more formal terms, if A is revealed definitively by B, then to know B is also to know A. Moreover, that Christ *is* the definitive disclosure of God's δικαιοσύνη is well established in relation to Romans 1:17 and 3:21-26. We have already seen that this claim is made in those texts repeatedly, and is perhaps the least contestable element in them. (And largely the same claim in close or direct relation to this phrase is made or implied elsewhere in Paul as well; see Romans 10:3;[13] 1 Cor. 1:30;[14] 2 Cor. 5:21; and Phil. 3:9.[15])

(1) Event

If Christ is the definitive disclosure of δικαιοσύνη Θεοῦ, then this notion must have a fundamentally evental character;[16] it is an act by God and so also a process. Divine revelation is, among other things, an act. This is not of course to deny thereby that it is also God's being; but any significant being-act division needs to be firmly resisted. Moreover, as an act, this phenomenon will often be best expressed in terms of a narrative that recounts its evental process, at least from the perspective of those experiencing it. The phrase δικαιοσύνη Θεοῦ can consequently be elucidated by a story. And this aspect is perhaps most obvious in Romans 3:26, where Christ's definitive demonstration or proof of the δικαιοσύνη Θεοῦ is actually summarized in verbal terms — εἰς τὸ εἶναι αὐτὸν δίκαιον καὶ δικαιοῦντα τὸν ἐκ πίστεως Ἰησοῦ[ν] (but see also 1:17; 10:3; 1 Cor. 1:30; 2 Cor. 5:21; Phil. 3:9).

(2) Singular

This event must also be singular, focused on the singularity of the Christ event in particular and hence defined in terms of those specific space-time coordinates. The story framing this event therefore has a beginning, a middle, and an ending; there are a time and a space where the event has not taken place, after which everything changes (see esp. Gal. 3:15-26; but also Rom. 9:30–10:4; Phil. 3:8).[17]

(3) Saving

Most importantly, the event is saving, and this is an obvious but regrettably underemphasized aspect of δικαιοσύνη Θεοῦ. Paul emphasizes it repeatedly and indubitably. The interchangeability of δικαιοσύνη (Θεοῦ) and σωτηρία (Θεοῦ) is especially apparent in Romans 10, both in vv. 1-3 and in 9-10.

Paul prays in 10:1 for Israel's salvation and then states in v. 2 that she has a "zeal for God" but "not in accordance with understanding" or "recognition." He goes on to say in v. 3 that she "ignores" and "does not submit" to the δικαιοσύνη τοῦ Θεοῦ. It simply follows from these statements that recognizing and submitting to the δικαιοσύνη τοῦ Θεοῦ, and so having a knowledgeable zeal, ought to lead directly to salvation. Paul even apparently uses the distinctive teleological prepositional phrases εἰς σωτηρίαν and εἰς δικαιοσύνην interchangeably in 10:1 and 4 (see also v. 10). As if to confirm these suggestions, Paul uses the cognate verbs both in direct parallel *and* interchangeably as he explicates Deuteronomy 30:14 chiastically in vv. 9-10 (this text being cited in v. 8):

> ⁸... Ἐγγύς σου τὸ ῥῆμά ἐστιν
> ἐν τῷ στόματί σου
> καὶ ἐν τῷ καρδίᾳ σου . . .
> ⁹ὅτι ἐὰν ὁμολογήσῃς ἐν τῷ στόματί σου κύριον Ἰησοῦν
> καὶ πιστεύσῃς ἐν τῇ καρδίᾳ σου ὅτι Θεὸς αὐτὸν ἤγειρεν ἐκ νεκρῶν
> σωθήσῃ.
> ¹⁰καρδίᾳ γὰρ πιστεύεται εἰς δικαιοσύνην
> στόματι δὲ ὁμολογεῖται εἰς σωτηρίαν.

Here the two teleological prepositional phrases seem to function in an overt parallelism, both explicating a single salvific process denoted by the one verb σῴζω. It would be difficult to conceive of more explicit indicators of semantic overlap.

These explicit indications in Romans 10 now reinforce certain semantic hints supplied earlier in the letter. Paul prefaces his first use of the phrase δικαιοσύνη Θεοῦ in 1:17 with the claim in v. 16 that "the gospel δύναμις . . . Θεοῦ ἐστιν εἰς σωτηρίαν παντὶ τῷ πιστεύοντι." We will try to supply further precision here shortly; so suffice it for now to note that this close contextual parallelism can hardly be coincidental. Käsemann was right to draw the phrase in v. 16 into the definition of v. 17; the δικαιοσύνη Θεοῦ is in some sense "a saving power." Moreover, its saving aspect is again apparent in 3:5. There Paul asks hypothetically whether it is not "unjust" (ἄδικος) of God to pour out his wrath on wickedness (ἀδικία), since that wickedness "highlights his δικαιοσύνη." (The verb is συνίστημι.) But this argument works only if God's δικαιοσύνη is not strictly retributive but merciful or saving. The pouring out of wrath is identical with retributive δικαιοσύνη; endurance of wickedness, over against the outpouring of wrath — which is the premise of Paul's argument here — is identical with *saving* δικαιοσύνη. And these accumulating hints seem confirmed by texts in other letters.[18] We conclude, then — a little unremarkably — that δικαιοσύνη Θεοῦ has a significant saving connotation. Δικαιοσύνη Θεοῦ in relation to the Christ event as Paul deploys it must be *iustitia salutifera*.

(4) Liberating

Perhaps more innovatively, we can now see that this salvation should be nuanced in a decidedly liberative direction. Δικαιοσύνη Θεοῦ speaks of salvation *from* some prior, negative situation that is fundamentally enslaving and oppressive. It is in some central sense an act of liberation. Romans 3:23-25 provide numerous hints of this soteriological connotation that are then amply confirmed by Romans 5–8.

As we have already noted, 3:24 describes salvation in terms of ἀπολύτρωσις, a release from some enslaved condition (whether actual or metaphorical slavery) and v. 23 indicates that this situation is shaped by an Adamic narrative, in which

God's presence and glory have been forfeited. This information activates a probable forensic-liberative reading of the verb δικαιόω (see 6:6-8).

These brief hints then look forward to longer discussions in chapters 5–8 of two contrasting aeons, one ruled by Sin and Death and explicitly characterized by metaphors of slavery and military enslavement, and the other ruled by grace, life, and δικαιοσύνη (although this can also be spoken of in a certain sense as slavery[19]). In this connection we can also note Galatians 3:22-23, which speaks of the Scripture locking up or confining everything under sin, where those so confined wait, "guarded," until the disclosure of "the coming faithful one," who brings δικαιοσύνη — all explicit metaphors of constraint if not imprisonment (συνέκλεισεν . . . ἐφρουρούμεθα συγκλειόμενοι . . .).[20]

(5) Life Giving

This connotation of salvation as a liberation from a state that is negative and oppressive has a mirror image (which further confirms it, to some degree): salvation is taking place into a positive, life-giving state (implying in addition that the prior state involves death). That δικαιοσύνη Θεοῦ denotes life is evident in numerous texts, although perhaps most consistently in Romans 5–8, where the notion is stated repeatedly, with fourteen occurrences of ζάω and its cognates (see eleven elsewhere in Romans), and twelve of the cognate noun (see twice elsewhere in Romans; see also Gal. 2:19-21, where "life" or "living" occurs no fewer than *five* times). But this realization tends to lead immediately into the further insight that such life is fundamentally eschatological; Paul is speaking of *resurrection* life — of the life of the age to come.

(6) Eschatological/Resurrecting

That Paul is interested in resurrection life, and in Christ's in particular, is signaled in Romans before the end of the epistolary address in 1:4. In the light of this cue, it is difficult to interpret the citation of Habakkuk 2:4 in Romans 1:17 in any other sense; "the righteous one because of faithfulness will live" in the sense of ". . . be resurrected." This text thus foretells the passion, in both Jesus's descent through suffering — which is accepted and endured faithfully — to shameful death, and his ascent through resurrection to glorification as Lord. But eschatological life is implicit in the diatribe of 3:3-5 as well, and — as we will see in more detail shortly — in much of the argument of Romans 4. The δικαιοσύνη that God "credits" (or effectively "gifts") to Abraham is nothing less than the extraordinary conception and birth of Isaac, a miraculous act of conception from the God "who makes alive the dead" (see 4:19 and 17b; and similar interpretative possibilities exist for Gal. 3:6). An eschatological scenario is then apparent in 10:9-13 as well, where "everyone who calls on the name of the Lord will be saved" (see Isa. 28:16; Joel 2:32), a salvation linked explicitly and tightly to the confession of Christ's resurrection from the dead and ascended lordship (see also 11:15).

Various texts from other Pauline letters confirm these indications, although perhaps Galatians 3:21b is the most explicit, where a hypothetical conditional *equates* δικαιοσύνη and eschatological life: εἰ γὰρ ἐδόθη νόμος ὁ δυνάμενος ζῳοποιῆσαι, ὄντως ἐκ νόμου ἂν ἦν ἡ δικαιοσύνη (in the light of which 2:20-21 and 5:5-6 become especially pregnant, perhaps further illuminated by 6:14-15). Without this semantic equation, the conditional in 3:21b is not merely invalid but incoherent. But Philippians 3:9-11 also speaks powerfully of Paul's experience, dependent on the arrival of a δικαιοσύνην ἐκ Θεοῦ, of τὴν δύναμιν τῆς ἀναστάσεως αὐτοῦ . . . εἴ πως καταντήσω εἰς τὴν ἐξανάστασιν τὴν ἐκ νεκρῶν. This connotation matches the hints concerning liberation from enslavement and oppression that we have already noted. With δικαιοσύνη Θεοῦ Paul seems to be speaking of liberation from enslavement to the powers of Sin and Death in Adam, into the glorious life of the new age and the new creation.

(7) Genitive Flexibility

We have emphasized up to this point that δικαιοσύνη Θεοῦ is a way of describing the Christ event for Paul, inferring as a result that it denotes a singular, saving, liberating, life-giving, eschatological act of God. With this realization, the shifts in Paul's use of the genitive are now entirely comprehensible. Indeed, Paul can emphasize one or another aspect of this case as the context demands, without altering the basic notion in play. If Christ is the *act* of God, then he *both* discloses God as he truly is — a subjective sense, as the δικαιοσύνη *of* God — *and* he enters the cosmos, having been sent *by* God (and so distinguishable in a certain sense from God) as the δικαιοσύνη *from* God — a genitive of origin or separation. (We encounter similar flexibility in relation to other acts of God as well, which are both identifiable with God and distinguishable as acts; compare perhaps especially the speech or word of God.) Hence, a thoroughgoing christological interpretation of this phrase allows us to comprehend neatly Paul's apparent flexibility in relation to its internal genitive relation. This essentially Chalcedonian dynamic allows more than one semantic possibility grammatically, in effect spreading across them, and these can then be exploited as contingent need dictates. The immediate context, however, should tell us exactly how to nuance its interpretation in any given instance.

In Romans 3:21-26 it is reasonably clear that a disclosure *of* God by Christ is being discussed, so the subjective emphasis is to be preferred. The four similar δικαιοσύνη phrases (deployed in two nearly identical pairs) are best interpreted consistently, and the notion of Christ as the "demonstration" or "proof" of God is certainly best interpreted with reference to God's δικαιοσύνη. This reading is also then preferable in the parallel anticipation of 3:21-26 in 1:17. In 3:3-5 the Teacher's system is more in view than Paul's, and so a subjective sense is again preferable. Nevertheless, later in the letter I will suggest that Paul shifts to a more separative reading, speaking of Christ as the δικαιοσύνη from God in 10:3, the meaning that tends to dominate the phrase's rare occurrences in other Pauline letters. By this point — as we will see in more detail shortly — the definitive disclosure of the δικαιοσύνη *of* God, who thereby reveals to us the nature of God, has become the δικαιοσύνη *from* God, whom we must recognize and obey if we are to stay within God's desired purposes (and Paul is thinking here especially of Israel).

By an internal route, then, we have ended up largely confirming the famous definition of Käsemann. The δικαιοσύνη Θεοῦ is "God's sovereignty over the world revealing itself eschatologically in Jesus," leading to a saving gift with the characteristics also of a power (and clearly this last formulation is in part an attempt to overcome a being-act distinction; if Christ is an event, then he is automatically a dynamic gift as well).[21] With these judgments in place — which seem to settle the most important questions — we can turn to consider certain more nuanced matters.

2.3. A Possible Intertextual Relationship

Richard Hays suggested some time ago that Romans 1:17 is informed by Psalm 98:2-3 (97:2-3 LXX).[22] On first considering this claim, I rejected it as unlikely.[23] I have since, however, reversed that judgment and now hold the suggestion to be both probable and highly significant. To note the issue of significance briefly: if this intertext lies behind 1:17, then it may well nuance Paul's strategic first use of δικαιοσύνη Θεοῦ in Romans. But in order to generate this significance, the suggestion must of course first prove true, and our subsequent discussion will address this challenge in two stages.

First we must revisit the specific question of the echo itself that was posed initially by Hays: does Romans 1:17 demonstrably echo Psalm 98? Many have not detected this connection in the past. But if we conclude that it is likely, then we will have to explore the further semantic consequences of this realization — the broader echo chamber of the initial sounding, so to speak — since these have been largely overlooked. And I will suggest, in a move beyond Hays's initial work, that this echo generates a broad and rich resonance through Romans in terms of the ancient discourse of kingship. It is *this* particular chord that Paul is sounding with the strategic phrase δικαιοσύνη Θεοῦ, mediated by the text of Psalm 98, which is a psalm of divine kingship. δικαιοσύνη Θεοῦ denotes for Paul nothing less than the decisive saving act of deliverance by the divine King of his royal appointed representative — that is, the resurrection and enthronement of Jesus (the) Christ. The connotations of this royal discourse then underlie and color the more general semantic notions that we have already uncovered.

The first stage in this demonstration — the detection of the initial echo — can be dealt with relatively quickly. However, the second — its orchestration in terms of the discourse of kingship — is more complex and controversial and will take us a little longer.

(1) An Echo of Scripture in Romans 1:17

The detection of scriptural echoes is a delicate matter.[24] But an accumulation of various indicators suggests to me that Hays was absolutely right to assert that Paul is echoing the opening verses of Psalm 98 in Romans 1:16-17 — an echo that encloses the critical phrase in which we are currently interested. The Psalm reads (in the LXX):

ἐγνώρισεν κύριος τὸ σωτήριον αὐτοῦ
ἐναντίον τῶν ἐθνῶν· ἀπεκάλυψεν τὴν δικαιοσύνην αὐτοῦ.
³ἐμνήσθη τοῦ ἐλέους αὐτοῦ τῷ Ἰακώβ
καὶ τῆς ἀληθείας αὐτοῦ τῷ οἴκῳ Ἰσραήλ·
εἴδοσαν πάντα τὰ πέρατα τῆς γῆς τὸ σωτήριον τοῦ θεοῦ ἡμῶν.

Paul then writes in Romans 1:16-17:

δύναμις γὰρ Θεοῦ ἐστιν εἰς σωτηρίαν παντὶ τῷ πιστεύοντι,
Ἰουδαίῳ τε πρῶτον καὶ Ἕλληνι.
¹⁷δικαιοσύνη γὰρ Θεοῦ ἐν αὐτῷ ἀποκαλύπτεται
ἐκ πίστεως εἰς πίστιν καθὼς γέγραπται κ.τ.λ.

There are three distinguishable indicators that underpin this judgment: phraseological, lexicographical, and thematic. There is, first, an echo of a clause (i.e., of a potentially self-sufficient phrase) and not merely of isolated words here; compare δικαιοσύνη γὰρ Θεοῦ . . . ἀποκαλύπτεται in the target text with ἀπεκάλυψεν τὴν δικαιοσύνην αὐτοῦ from the source text. Although these syntagms are not precisely the same, they are essentially so — the same substantive, δικαιοσύνη, with a genitive denoting the same subject, God (Θεοῦ/αὐτοῦ), being developed by the same verb, ἀποκαλύπτω, although in different tenses and voices. It is worth noting, moreover, that this basic clause and association in the two texts *is unequalled in its proximity, whether elsewhere in Paul or in the LXX.*[25] Second, this essentially phraseological echo is accompanied in both texts by a parallel to δικαιοσύνη constructed with "salvation," the word σωτηρία occurring once in Romans 1:16, and its cognate twice in Psalm 98.[26] So a close lexical association seems to confirm the initial syntagmatic echo.[27] But, third, a series of broader thematic similarities is apparent as well. Both texts discuss an antithesis between Jews and pagans (Ἰουδαῖος καὶ Ἕλληνος/τὰ ἔθνή, Ἰακώβ and οἶκος Ἰσραήλ), in relation to which God is acting.[28] Moreover, in both texts God is acting to make something known, this point being made in Psalm 98 by further verbs of knowledge and of sight.[29] Finally, the aorist tenses in the psalm corroborate Paul's later temporal emphases in Romans 3:21-26 that the divine saving event has taken place "now," in the sense of the immediate past and the present, as against the future. God *has* acted. So the temporality of the two texts — which, as we have seen, is a crucial argumentative point in Romans for Paul — is identical as well.

In my view, this is an impressive accumulation of evidence, the force of which is difficult to deny. Phraseological, lexical, and three thematic echoes all reinforce one another in suggesting a connection, and more general considerations seem only to enhance these implications.[30] In view of all this evidence, some relationship between Psalm 98:2-3 and Romans 1:16-17 looks almost certain. Hays's initial perception was therefore, in my opinion, profoundly right. We will need to consider in due course why Paul does not mark this quotation explicitly, as he does his other key intertexts in Romans;[31] this particular scriptural usage is allusive rather than overt. But I will suggest an explanation for this reticence shortly. It is important for now to investigate the semantic implications of this intertextual linkage further — the moment at which previous exploration of this connection has tended to falter. And here we enter the second, more complex phase in our intertextual exploration.

(2) Paul and the Ancient Discourse of Kingship

Psalm 98 is a psalm of divine kingship,[32] and contains (as we will see in more detail shortly) terminology and thematology characteristic of that ancient Jewish discourse — a discourse that interwove in turn with broader conceptions of kingship, both divine and human, throughout the ancient Near East. The discourse of kingship had profoundly ancient roots but was also very much alive — sometimes in new variations — in Paul's day. And this raises the possibility that the phrase δικαιοσύνη Θεοῦ is operating within that broader discourse and is colored by its distinctive concerns. Our investigation of this possibility will unfold in an analysis of five subordinate questions:

(i)   the general contours of the ancient discourse of kingship
(ii) the meaning(s) of "right" actions by a king
(iii) the presence (or absence) of this discourse in Romans
(iv) the probable particular meaning of δικαιοσύνη Θεοῦ in Romans 1:17
(v)   the implications for the construal of δικαιοσύνη Θεοῦ in relation to the covenant

In navigating these last questions, we will be drawing upon certain recent scholarly advances in relation to Jesus' messiahship, resurrection, and lordship, some of which have recently been pressed through Romans, although in a fairly preliminary way.

(i) **The Ancient Discourse of Kingship**   Psalm 98 is part of a widespread ancient discourse concerning kingship and its particular ascription by pious Jews to their God.[33] (It is one of the classic expositions of this discourse as identified by Gunkel and Begrich in 1933. They pointed in particular to Psalms 47, 93, and 96–99,[34] texts that all name God explicitly at a certain point as "king," and so here in v. 6.) Psalm 98 is typically theocentric throughout, speaking primarily of acts by

God on his people's behalf in terms thought appropriate for the divine ruler — acts of salvation, deliverance, order, and judgment. These acts are accomplished by God's "right hand" or "holy arm." The people then respond with rejoicing and thanksgiving, and this response is typically hyperbolic; it is literally orchestrated, and other facets of creation join in as well (presumably because they are also ruled by God the King) — the sea and its contents, the world and all who dwell in it, the rivers, and the mountains. Significantly, because the scope of the divine King's rule is cosmic, these acts are visible to and indeed affect the pagan nations in addition to Israel.

Numerous other texts, both within and outside the Jewish scriptural tradition, freight this discourse in various ways.[35] But the complex data can be simplified (as is necessary here) by the recognition that much of it is characterized by a root metaphor concerning God — the metaphor precisely of God as a king.[36] The content of that image was generated largely by historical, human kingship, although presumably in the form of ideal types. God the King and the ideal human king were images that mutually interpreted one another, and this draws other illuminating texts into the elaboration of the discourse (especially Psalms 2, 45, 72, 89, and 110).[37]

We learn from these texts (supported by studies of ancient iconography, etc.) that ancient kings, and ancient gods conceived of as kings, had a fundamental duty of care in relation to their people.[38] This could unfold in two basic ways.

First, if a king's people were in some sort of difficulty, then it was the monarch's duty to resolve that difficulty. If they were oppressed or invaded, then the king was obliged to deliver or defend them. But this function was often narrated in the ancient Near East in cosmic terms (partly no doubt to underwrite the need for a king in the first place). Indeed, it was frequently in the first instance the divine king's duty to establish cosmic order, slaying or controlling the monsters of chaos that threatened the cosmos with instability or dissolution.[39] Alternatively, it was the chaotic waters bordering the world that needed to be controlled (and so on). Cosmic and more recognizably political activities thus intertwine throughout this discourse — and entirely deliberately. However, all of these actions, whether concretely political or more mythical and ritual, revolve around the basic notion of a ruler acting to save his people from disorder and oppression and to establish them in (relative) freedom and safety, whether that ruler is divine, human, or an alliance of the two.

Complementing this principal type of saving and ordering activity is the second broad duty incumbent on the divine and human monarchs, namely, sustaining a condition of peace and prosperity. Once order has been established, or reestablished, it is the duty of the divine monarch and/or the divinely appointed monarch to preserve it. It is worth noting that the "being" of kings, whether divine or human, consequently seems inseparable from their activity. Kings are what they do; character and activity are correlative notions in this relation.[40] We can now note some further common elements in this discourse that are relevant to our unfolding concerns.

As has already been intimated, an important alliance generally holds between the divine king and an appointed earthly representative, who is also a king, although in a derivative sense. Numerous variations on this basic dynamic are observable, including the strand in the Old Testament that rejects this relationship altogether ("no king for Israel but God"). Yet even in this radical variant, divine kingship is effected through appointed earthly agents or representatives who act with authority that they receive by way of delegation from the divine ruler, often as they are inspired by the divine Spirit. Usually, however, such figures are royal and part of a divinely ratified dynasty, "the Lord" establishing "the lord." (This alliance cries out for an ideological analysis, but this is not our present concern.) The earthly king, then, is usually involved in the fulfillment of his duties in both sacral and overtly political and military activities, although these interpenetrate in ancient societies. The establishment and preservation of cosmic and political order are his responsibility, so cultic and political capacities are developed to carry out his duties in those respective spheres. Accordingly, there is an important observable relationship between palace and temple (not to mention the military), one that influences much of the Old Testament.[41] David and Solomon dominate the kingly ideals as they are presented by the Old Testament, David acting overtly more as a deliverer of his people, the one who creates order, and Solomon as the establisher of a suitably impressive cultus over which he presides (see esp. 1 Kings 3:1-2; 5–6; 7:13-51; 8–9), thereby sustaining that order and prosperity. But he is also of course the archetypally wise ruler (see 1 Kings 2:6, 9; 3:9, 12, 16-28; 4:29-34; 5:7, 12; 10:23-24). The key symbols of scepter, crown, and throne — especially this last — are plainly evident in much of this material.[42]

(ii) "Right" Actions by a King   We must now ask the critical question in the present relation: what is a "right" action by a divine king or his appointed human representative? It can be seen almost immediately that the answer depends very much on the particular setting of a given action within the broader discourse. A "right" action may be a dramatic act of intervention that saves or reorders — a fundamentally liberative action, which presumably will have a corresponding oppressive effect on any opposing, hostile forces that are defeated. Alternatively, it may be an ongoing act that sustains peace and/or prosperity or an act that judges a given situation accurately in terms of the ethical rectitude of parties contending at law, thereby maintaining social order.[43]

Furthermore, because the ancient king combines in his person executive and judiciary functions, right actions can be described using terms drawn from either of these fields, although here the most important semantic crossover is probably the deployment of more strictly forensic terminology in relation to executive activity, the language of the law court being used to describe what a modern person would view as an executive political action. Hence, if a right action by a king is described using forensic terminology and imagery such as a "verdict" or "judgment," we might nevertheless be speaking of an essentially performative, oppressive or liberative event (and these two acts often go together), as against a more strictly retributive procedure (i.e., also performative but with an indicative dimension predicated on appropriate retribution). A military victory, a proclamation of the Jubilee, and an arbitration of a difficult civil case can all be described as "judgments" by the king, and certainly all of these ideally ought to be "right" as well, but they are "right" in very different senses.[44] (Such language is still detectable in modern political discourse, although not as frequently, so an election result might be characterized as a "judgment," not meaning by this a retributive action.) The immediate context must therefore tell us what kind of activity is in view at any given moment. The language of "rightness" is often deployed in the Old Testament, and in the specific setting of kingship, in all of these specific senses.

Excursus: The Relationship between Right Action and Kingship in the Psalter

The densest concentration of δικαιοσύνη terminology in the setting of kingship — most frequently, denoting a liberating act — is in the Psalter: see especially (LXX) Pss. 44:5, 8; 47:11; 49:6; 71:1, 2, 3, 7; 88:15, 17; 95:13; 96:2, 6; 97:2 (Paul's allusion in Romans 1:17), 9; 98:4; and 117:19. The liberative notion of δικαιοσύνη occurs in many other psalms as well, so this semantic field overlaps with the discourse of kingship but is not coterminous with it. For God's liberating righteousness, see in addition (LXX) Pss. 5:9; 7:18; 9:9; 21:32; 30:2; 34:24, 28; 35:7, 11; 39:10, 11; 50:16; 68:28; 70:2, 15, 16, 18, 24; 84:11, 12, 14; 87:13; 102:17; 110:3; 111:3, 9; 118:7, 40, 62, 75 [?], 106, 123, 138 [?], 142 [2x], 160, 164; 142:1 (this reference also being especially significant for Paul), 11; and 144:7. But this is hardly a problem for my case here. It simply suggests that this perception of the character of God was widespread (and maybe also that the discourse of divine kingship was more widespread than is often recognized — perhaps either tacitly or as a hidden transcript).

In sum, about 80 of the 336 instances of δικαιοσύνη in the LXX occur in the Psalter — around 25 percent. Approximately 50 of those 80 instances describe God, and then almost invariably in a liberative, salvific sense. Half a dozen of those instances, and several more important instances describing the human king in the same terms, also occur in texts that are indisputable enthronement psalms or texts denoting some other aspect of ancient kingship. This is where the lexical and thematological fields overlap especially clearly. Psalm 98 (97 LXX) operates within that intersection.

The correlation with various salvific terms is also worth noting, because it reinforces these claims. δικαιοσύνη occurs in close relation to salvific terms in the LXX almost entirely in the Psalter and Isaiah. See the strong connections between liberation, salvation, and δικαιοσύνη in Pss. (LXX) 16:1, 15; 39:10, 11, and 17 (see also vv. 14 and 18); 50:16 (a psalm traditionally linked to David and his repentance for his adultery with Bathsheba); 70:2, 15, 16, 18, and 24; 71:1-4 (a psalm of ideal human kingship); 84:8, 11-14 (a psalm oriented more toward the land); 97:1b-2, 9 (the psalm that launched this entire investigation; see also v. 3); 117:14, 19, and 21; and 118:40-41, 121-23, 169-76.

The links with both salvation and kingship are, however, perhaps even more overt in Isaiah: see (LXX) 39:8 (where King Hezekiah is grateful for δικαιοσύνη; the related thematology of "father" is also prominent in 63:7–64:11. But the *maintenance* of prosperity, in part through "due process," is apparent in 60:17 and 18, and intermingled with the liberative sense in 61:8 and 11 (and in this relation see also the closely related Amos 5:7, 24; see also 5:12, 15; 6:12).

Most importantly for our discussion here, δικαιοσύνη not infrequently denotes a liberating or delivering act — an action when it is "right" for either God the King or his appointed king to set someone free. Previously, some interpreters have referred to this particular subset of the data of δικαιοσύνη in the Old Testament as *iustitia salutifera,* because of the frequent occurrence of notions of salvation in context (and these have of course assisted our recognition of this usage as fundamentally liberative).[45] But possibly we now have a better explanation of just why the term functions in this way on occasion. It is "right" in certain circumstances for the king to act to deliver, especially if a client or his people are in some sort of difficulty. It is his duty to set them free — to save them. Similarly, God the King can act in such terms to deliver his appointed human king, provided that this king has done nothing heinously wrong (or, alternatively, that he has repented sufficiently of any such sins). Again, in these circumstances, it is "right" for God to act to save.[46]

It might be objected here that this ancient discourse is not especially significant for the New Testament — after all, by the first century CE Israel had not been ruled by one of her Davidic kings for a very long time. However, vigorous New Testament debates unfolding along various axes suggest that although the specifics of the discourse are far from clear, its presence is both significant and undeniable. The current discussions of the relevance of the Roman Imperial cult and Augustan ideology to the New Testament (especially to Paul), and the widespread data — especially in the Synoptic Gospels — concerning the "kingdom of God" (or its close equivalent), suggest this conclusion almost immediately.[47] This discourse was still very much in play — in all its subtle local variations — in the New Testament era.

With these broader observations in place, we can turn to consider an important contextual question in relation to Paul. Is a discourse of divine kingship operative in Romans?

(iii) Divine Kingship in Romans and the Early Church   This specific query touches on several important debates that are currently unfolding within New Testament studies.

Essentially since the seminal work of Wilhelm Bousset,[48] theological development in the early church has been viewed by many interpreters panoramically as a slow progression from limited, theologically primitive, Jewish, particular notions to a liberated, theologically mature, Hellenistic, universal gospel, perhaps best exemplified by John. And this famous paradigm has greatly influenced the reconstruction of almost every New Testament question, figure, and text, whether Jesus, the pre-Pauline church, Paul himself, or the figures that wrote after him like the authors of the Gospels. There have consequently been strong methodological tendencies to detach Paul's understanding of Jesus from "early," "low," and Jewish christological categories like Messiah and to interpret it instead in terms of "later," "higher" (although not necessarily "high/the highest"!), and Hellenistic categories, within which stratum the apostle's use of "Lord" is generally included. This is often combined with emphases on a spiritual rather than a bodily resurrection and a supposed disinterest in the teaching and life of the historical Jesus. (I would add that this agenda also integrates in certain useful ways with the individualism, the sense of liberation from the crabbed constraints of the law, and the view of the atoning death of Christ advocated by Justification theory.) All these concerns have of course influenced the interpretation of Paul's most discursive letter, Romans, leading to a certain myopia at key points that we must try briefly in what follows to redress.[49]

Various scholars have for some time been attempting to roll back the broad agenda of Bousset, and with some success.[50] To point to one particularly useful representative in the present relation, N. T. Wright has vigorously reemphasized the Jewishness and messiahship of Jesus, his bodily resurrection, and his exalted lordship (which ought to be understood, furthermore, in a thoroughly Jewish sense). He is in the process of pressing these emphases through the thought of Paul, the argument of Romans, and the general theological development of the early church.[51] It is of course not necessary to endorse all the details of Wright's various claims and arguments — which are numerous — in order to find these basic corrections to Bousset's paradigm plausible.[52] (Indeed, arguably they participate in a new paradigm that is gathering momentum within New Testament studies, at least in certain quarters.) But his principal corrections are of great moment for our present discussion.

If interpreters approach Paul and Romans with ears freshly attuned to the importance and integration of Jesus' messiahship, resurrection, and exaltation to lordship, then the textual surface of the letter begins to shift in some interesting new directions. Initially, it becomes apparent that these themes have simply been underemphasized by much previous interpretation. So, for example, resurrection is a much more prominent theme in Romans than most commentators seem to have realized, as is Jesus' Davidic descent. But following these realizations it rapidly begins to emerge that the various recovered motifs are not just isolated points of emphasis for Paul — spots where his authentic Jewishness is gratifyingly apparent, and/or his continuity with the thinking of the early church; rather, they are tightly integrated concerns that fulfill important argumentative and theological roles (and sensitivities to narrative and intertextuality are vital here, creating a direct link again with some of Hays's assertions). I would suggest, however, that while Wright and others have begun the resulting process of reinterpretation,[53] the addition of one or two more insights can bring still greater clarity and cogency to our reappropriation of the letter's argument.

I recommend that these recovered emphases be correlated in a significant interplay with the ancient discourse of kingship, which in Romans is now focused on — and in a real sense *realized by* — Jesus Christ. Indeed, an entire theological complex constructed in these terms is discernible within Romans, although subtly. This integrated program is signaled in nuce by Paul's famous opening statements in 1:1b-4 (a text we begin to recognize as programmatic for much of the rest of Romans):[54]

> Paul, a servant of Jesus Christ, called to be an apostle, set apart for the gospel of God, [2]which he promised beforehand through his prophets in the holy scriptures, [3]the gospel concerning his Son, who was descended from David according to the flesh [4]and was declared to be Son of God with power according to the Spirit of holiness by resurrection from the dead, Jesus Christ our Lord. (NRSV)

Christ's messiahship and lordship are here affirmed by his resurrection from the dead, which functions, furthermore, *as a heavenly enthronement.* This enthronement is effected by the Spirit of sanctification, who in the Old Testament sanctifies the cult and the people of God, and anoints the king. And, equally importantly, this event is widely attested by the Jewish Scriptures — both Torah and Prophets. Moreover, it is an explanation of Jesus' sonship. He is the Son of God because, as for any divinely appointed king, God has now become his Father. So he is the King of Israel not only by descent, as a "son of David," but by royal enthronement; his "coronation" has taken place. As a sanctifying act, this must somehow implicitly effect the broader reconciliation of God with creation and his people, presumably overcoming the oppressive and even chaotic forces that seek to disrupt that relationship. Order should be established and prosperity realized and preserved. So, entirely predictably, the appointed ambassadors of that reconciliation, like Paul, are sent out to establish the appropriate submission and fidelity to this ruler in the rest of the world by way of their delegation ("apostleship") and proclamation ("gospel") — so vv. 1b and 5-6.

This is an essentially narrative account — a story — rich with theological import that links Jesus' messiahship, resurrection, and lordship. And clearly, numerous Old Testament texts that speak of divine and human kingship will resonate with it. Scholars debate many further aspects within these broad assertions, but most of those debates do not concern us at this point.[55] What matters here is more limited — namely, the implicit evidence that this basic narrative is mobilized by Paul through a great deal of the rest of Romans. We can note five points of conspicuous emergence (followed by two further, supplementary pieces of evidence).

1. In Romans 5:1-11 God *reconciles* a hostile world to himself through the Christ event (see esp. vv. 10-11), Paul here describing the divine act in quite distinctive language that resonates with the language of diplomatic, political, and royal circles (and invariably so whenever a delegate is involved, as indicated by the presence of πρεσβευ- language).[56] There is, moreover, a complementary use of royal "access" language in v. 2, in relation to which this reconciliation takes place. Then, in 5:14, an emphatic use of the terminology of government begins, Paul speaking repeatedly of what are in effect two kingdoms, with two "rules," respective services, and even enslavements, and a military relationship of hostility and/or victory (these emphases continuing through subsequent chapters in the letter).[57]

2. In Romans 8 the thematology of heavenly enthronement and glorification of Christ signaled in 1:2-4 reemerges. In 8:15-17 those who cry "Abba Father"

receive "sonship" or "adoption" (υἱοθεσία), become "children of God," "and if children, also heirs — heirs of God and fellow heirs with Christ. . . ." Paul affirms here (and in Gal. 4:6) this cry's appropriateness for Christians, who participate in the "firstborn," namely, Jesus (see Rom. 8:29-30). His resurrection, understood also as a heavenly enthronement (see esp. 8:34: . . . ἐν δεξιᾷ τοῦ Θεοῦ), explains the access that Christians now have "in him" to the inheritance that he has received, their status as children of God, like him, and the consequent appropriateness of their cry to a God now characterized as "Father." And such father-son language and affirmations, in the context of adoption, inheritance, and glorification, seem best explained by texts like Psalm 89 and the broader discourse of divine kingship.[58] The preserved Aramaism in Romans 8:15 is meanwhile a marker of this christological tradition's antiquity within the early church. We seem to be in touch here, then, with an early explanation of the resurrection — as the heavenly enthronement and glorification of Jesus, and as his consequent affirmation as Messiah and Lord, who will rule the cosmos on behalf of his divine Father. Yet Paul, characteristically, interprets this tradition in Romans 8 in participatory terms.[59]

3. Kavin Rowe has pointed out that Paul's repeated affirmations of lordship in Romans 10:9-13 draw on important Old Testament intertexts and are rooted in the entirely Jewish monotheistic veneration of Yahweh as the only true God. Moreover, the affirmation of Jesus' lordship, which is included unavoidably here by Paul in this central Jewish confession, is confirmed by his resurrection — a connection illuminated best by the interpretation of the resurrection as the enthronement of the Messiah, Jesus, *as* Lord.[60] (Paul's unusual reference to "the Christ" in 9:5 is also now comprehensible in part as an anticipation of his later use of this narrative.)[61]

4. Although it is often overlooked, Romans 15:12 effects the closure of the main letter body by affirming Jesus' Davidic lineage through a citation of Isaiah 11:10 (see also [LXX] 42:4, which is closely accompanied by the divine King's δικαιοσύνη in v. 6). With this reference to "the root of Jesse," which resumes the Davidic claims of 1:3, Paul not only concludes his substantive discussion but fashions a messianic inclusio around most of the letter's discursive material.[62]

5. Although almost entirely unnoticed, Romans 16:20 — Θεὸς τῆς εἰρήνης συντρίψει τὸν σατανᾶν ὑπὸ τοὺς πόδας ὑμῶν ἐν τάχει — echoes both 1 Corinthians 15:25-27 and underlying messianic readings of Psalms 8 and 110 (8:6 and 110:1).

Both Psalms 8 and 110, when applied to Christ, speak of his messianic enthronement, implicitly through the resurrection, followed by a further process of subjugation in relation to all Christ's enemies, which will be consummated at his second coming "so that God might be all in all" (1 Cor. 15:28b; and this royal reading resumes the language of Gen. 3:15, along with the surrounding narrative[63]). Hence, not only does 16:20 echo the royal discourse, but it even seems to deploy that discourse — via Psalm 8 — opposite the Adamic thematology that is so important to Paul in much of Romans.[64]

These five texts all develop the clues that are supplied by Paul in Romans 1:2-4. We can see in each of these other places a narrative of Jesus' heavenly enthronement informing Paul's argument — a narrative that describes Jesus as Son, Christ, "firstborn," and Lord, because of his enthronement by the resurrection. At this point he has entered his inheritance (and in Paul's view this now also opens up that inheritance for all who indwell him, whether Jew or pagan). But this description of the Christ event rotates around the resurrection and interprets it in terms of the discourse of divine and human kingship.

If it is granted that these five texts are points of conspicuous emergence, where a robust narrative Christology developed in terms of ancient kingship protrudes into Paul's argument, it seems plausible to detect other points where such a discourse is operative in Romans, if not so overtly. At least two further texts are worth noting.

6. Paul cites Psalm 143:2 (LXX 142:2), suitably modified, rather pregnantly in 3:20a: διότι ἐξ ἔργων νόμου οὐ δικαιωθήσεται πᾶσα σὰρξ ἐνώπιον αὐτοῦ. This quotation is of course interesting in and of itself, but, as several scholars have noted, Psalm 143 speaks repeatedly of God's δικαιοσύνη (see esp. vv. 1 and 11), and this contextual material can hardly be coincidental when Paul is about to resume that motif emphatically in Romans 3:21, 22, 25, and 26.[65] It seems, then, that the rest of the psalm is implicit within Paul's allusion — at least, in some sense. Perhaps less obvious is the way the psalm echoes many of the key themes in the discourse of divine kingship. It does not itself function within that discourse, but it does articulate an element that functions within it, and this seems entirely deliberate.

Psalm 143 is a prayer for help grounded overtly in the goodness of God and his works that also specifically disavows help from God in response to the supplicant's piety. That is, this psalm *specifically repudiates retributive activity by God,* acknowledging that this would result in condemnation rather than assistance. So the psalmist observes (quite rightly in the view of much of the Christian tradition) that no one is entitled to help from God couched in such terms, because "no one living is righteous before you." The ground for any divine assistance must therefore be the divine character, which must in turn be compassionate and should result in liberative — and corresponding oppressive! (see vv. 3 and 12) — actions. Such behavior is directly compatible with either the divine or the human king rescuing one of his charges, as he ought to, merely by virtue of his own duty of care. This dyad of intertextual echoes in Romans 1–3 thereby reproduces the much broader pattern of such echoes in the Psalter itself. Both are informed by a basic perception concerning the goodness of God.

7. Finally, we should recall that in 1:17b a messianic reading of Habakkuk 2:4 foregrounds Christ's resurrection and eternal life in relation to the gospel as it is disclosed by the δικαιοσύνη of God: "the righteous one, through fidelity, will live." The letter's auditors are thereby prompted to find some connection between the gospel (i.e., the announcement of the divine King's good news through his appointed representative), Jesus' resurrection, and God's δικαιοσύνη.

(iv) The Meaning of δικαιοσύνη Θεοῦ in Romans 1:17, in relation to Psalm 98:2

We should recall now the insight that catalyzed this localized investigation — Richard Hays's observation that the phrase δικαιοσύνη Θεοῦ and its immediate development in Romans 1:17 echoes Psalm 98. If we supplement that insight by the additional observations that Psalm 98 is a psalm of divine kingship and that Romans itself develops the ancient discourse of kingship in relation to Christ explicitly from its outset, and repeatedly throughout its body (contra Bousset et al.), then the conclusion seems to follow ineluctably that the phrase δικαιοσύνη Θεοῦ is best interpreted in the light of that discourse as well. Such a reading fits Paul's local argument perfectly, resumes the opening concerns of 1:2-4 neatly, and integrates with the contextual hints we receive from the specific lexical data elsewhere in Paul.[66] And in the light of this broader frame, we can now invest this phrase with the meaning appropriate to its particular function within that broader discourse — here in relation to a decisive saving and delivering act of power by God, the divine King,[67] on behalf of his royal representative, Jesus. That is, Christ is not being judged by God here (or oppressed); he is being resurrected! So δικαιοσύνη Θεοῦ must mean in 1:17 "the deliverance of God," or something closely equivalent.[68] This is the specific content of the righteous act that God has just undertaken on behalf of his messianic agent, Christ — the act of resurrection, empowerment, and heavenly enthronement after his oppression and execution by evil opposing powers. It is "right" for God to act in this way on behalf of his chosen Son, who has been unfairly executed. It remains, then, only to ask why the psalm is present allusively rather than overtly.

I suggest that it is precisely the allusive activation of this broader discourse, and the critical enthronement narrative within it, that seems to underlie Paul's subtle use of the actual text of Psalm 98 in Romans 1:17. The words of Psalm 98:2-3 are *mediating* this construct — a discourse composed of scriptural texts, which now operates at one remove from those texts, as a distinguishable theological entity. Hence, the detection of this particular scriptural text plays no overt rhetorical role in the broader argument; the Roman Christian auditors are not supposed to be impressed by Paul's citation here of an authoritative Jewish text (as they are by his citation of Hab. 2:4 in 1:17b). They are merely meant to understand what he is talking about in more general terms, and they should be able to do so insofar as they inhabit this Jewish Christian discourse concerning Jesus' resurrection and kingship. Paul is merely using the words of Psalm 98:2-3 to say here what he wants to say (and presumably in a way that other Christians have already formulated and so can recognize) — that God the King has acted to save his messianic Son.[69]

An explanation of the similar reticence of Paul with respect to this discourse in the rest of Romans is hinted at here as well. As my detailed argumentative analysis of Romans continues to unfold, it will become apparent that the ancient discourse of kingship is not so much elaborated as presupposed. Paul does not seem intent to describe or to justify it so much as to interact with and exploit it in support of various contingent goals in relation to the Christians at Rome. It seems to be traditional theology that the Roman Christians share with both Paul and the Jerusalem church — an integrated, Jewish, and perhaps surprisingly "high" christological narrative that smoothly links Jesus' messiahship, sonship, resurrection, and exalted heavenly lordship. Paul then builds from this shared theology toward his more specific rhetorical points in Romans.

We turn now to consider the implications of this reading for the possible covenantal resonances of the phrase, because these have recently been proposed by many as the invariable central content of δικαιοσύνη Θεοῦ (not least by N. T. Wright and, as we have already seen in some detail in part three, chapter twelve, by J. D. G. Dunn). This phrase means for many nothing more nor less than "the covenant faithfulness of God."[70]

(v) The Relationship to the Covenant   If the phrase δικαιοσύνη Θεοῦ is located within the broader discourse of divine kingship, then covenantal associations are clearly not far away, and any such reading is not far from the truth. The earthly king was ratified at times by a particular covenant, and the divine King could structure his relationships with Israel directly in terms of a covenant, as the book of Deuteronomy perhaps most overtly attests.[71] It is certainly fair, then, to detect a covenantal strand within this discourse and hence possibly also in relation to this phrase, which operates within it. Indeed, there is something profoundly right about any such assertion, because it grasps and emphasizes that *God's fidelity is intrinsic to any act of salvation;* for God to save implies necessarily and immediately that God has, in that act, acted faithfully.[72] However, broader covenantal associations — that is, in terms of a more elaborate arrangement — are not always central and hence determinative or invariable. They may or may not be present in an act by a divine or human king in the Old Testament, which can take various more specific senses depending on its context, as we have seen, and are not always directly linked to a *covenant* (as in fact Psalm 98 demonstrated earlier). Covenantal connotations are consequently *possible* but not *necessary* semantic resonances of the phrase δικαιοσύνη Θεοῦ, and we would need contextual information to activate them in Paul.

That is, δικαιοσύνη Θεοῦ *might* denote a righteous act by the divine King in fidelity to his covenant with Israel — an act of covenant faithfulness (so perhaps an act that is πιστός or in terms of ἀλήθεια). However, it might denote a dramatically liberating act on behalf of Israel (σωτηρία/σωτήριον) that might — or might not — then be syntactically elaborated as — among other things — an act of covenant faithfulness. Or it might denote a saving act undertaken without reference to the covenant, or even in defiance of Israel's repeated violations of the covenant, and so be rooted merely in God's benevolence (ἔλεος). It might, moreover, denote an oppressive act against enemies — a righteous action — that has nothing to do with a covenant with them (a κρίμα). Alternatively, it might denote a retributive act that has nothing to do with a covenant but is oriented by the perception of an innocent person or group being accused or the guilty being acquitted (again a κρίμα, although here of a different sort). And so on.[73]

It is not surprising, then, that the phrase δικαιοσύνη Θεοῦ or its close equivalent is sometimes found in the same textual locations as covenantal notions in the Old Testament (and the same considerations apply to links with creation). Both are elements within the discourse of divine kingship,[74] and so the phrase may possess legitimate covenantal resonances. In any later usage, however, these have to be established explicitly and not merely assumed. The covenant was not a central, standard, or invariable element in the discourse of divine kingship and hence in the phrase δικαιοσύνη Θεοῦ. We must let Romans itself tell us how this complex discourse is being activated.

In the immediate location of 1:16-17, and its particular allusion to Psalm 98, I see nothing that activates such specific resonances explicitly. The phrase seems there, rather, to be oriented in a fundamentally *christocentric* direction. It speaks not of the covenant with Israel — although it has implications for that! — so much as of the inauguration of the age to come by way of Christ's enthroning resurrection. It therefore speaks of a liberating act that has implications for all of humanity (Israel of course included). Romans 3:21-22 and 23-26 confirm these suspicions rather strongly, as the claims of those later, related texts point ahead to universal arguments in Romans 4–8. The "right" act of God in relation to Christ, resurrecting him from the dead and enthroning him on high, has implications for all of creation — something that Israel is implicit in without exhausting its implications. (And indeed here we perhaps need to emphasize precisely the *eschatological* nature of this "right" act, again in continuity with Ernst Käsemann's classic study;[75] a new creation has been inaugurated.)

Somewhat ironically, the psalm that Paul echoes in 1:17 makes this point nicely. While in v. 2 Psalm 98 speaks of the saving deliverance that is being effected by God in plain view of the pagan nations, in v. 3 it goes on to articulate in a syntactical development that this action is an act of fidelity to the house of Israel. And just the same considerations seem to apply to the phrase δικαιοσύνη Θεοῦ when Paul deploys it later in Romans with specific reference to Christ. Christians suggest of course that the resurrection of Christ is ultimately also an act of fidelity toward Israel and so is the supreme expression of covenant loyalty and fulfillment by God. But these claims are not implicit in the semantic content of the phrase itself; they are further related theological claims that must therefore be argued for (and of course in certain respects they are by no means obvious). So Paul himself goes on to attempt to make, in Romans 9–11, an extensive case that his christological claims *should* be so understood (see also 15:8)! And as his argumentative maneuvers unfold there, it becomes increasingly obvious that these implications are far from uncontested. Hence, to claim that he is merely semantically unpacking δικαιοσύνη Θεοῦ in so doing is to overstrain his language (as well as to ignore what he does syntactically and argumentatively).

It needs to be emphasized that this reading does not exclude Israel from the Christ event for Paul — far from it. We have merely reached a semantic judgment that when Paul deploys the phrase δικαιοσύνη Θεοῦ, and especially in the early argumentative stages of Romans, he is not speaking of something overtly and fundamentally covenantal and hence rooted in the past and in a certain conception of history. He is discussing a liberative and eschatological act of God in Christ — a fundamentally present and future event rooted in the resurrecting God (which therefore arguably introduces a reconceptualization of history). In sum, it seems that — on internal grounds — δικαιοσύνη Θεοῦ in Paul denotes a singular, saving, liberating, life-giving, eschatological act of God in Christ. The intertextual echo of Psalm 98:2 (LXX 97:2) detected in Romans 1:16-17 — in combination with other clues — then nuances this act in terms of the rich and powerful ancient Near Eastern discourse of divine kingship. And it connotes here in particular Christ's heavenly enthronement by God after his faithful death at the hands of his enemies — one of which was Death — as God's appointed messianic agent and the cosmos's κύριος (which is clearly a singular, saving, liberating, life-giving, eschatological act by God). In undertaking this act in Christ, God is operating as the divine King ought to, delivering his captive creation from its bondage; he is therefore doing the "right" thing, acting as his character and role demand. And δικαιοσύνη Θεοῦ is, as a result and in essence, the deliverance of God. These realizations afford an important new perspective on 1:16 and its possible anticipation of later argumentative developments in the letter, especially in Romans 10.

2.4. Romans 1:16 and the Discourse of Divine Kingship

In Romans 10, and perhaps even more explicitly in 1 Corinthians 1:30, the δικαιοσύνη Θεοῦ — that is, the right and saving act of God, the divine King, in resurrecting Christ, his appointed royal representative — evokes connotations of divine wisdom. And the realization in the foregoing discussion that this phrase participates in a discourse of divine kingship now makes that association entirely understandable. The discourse of divine wisdom was intimately linked with the discourse of divine kingship. It was by wisdom that both divine and human kings ruled, an association evident in the ancient Egyptian precursors of the Jewish discourse (where rulers ruled by *ma'at*), and extending in its Jewish development from obvious Jewish precursors to texts roughly contemporary to Paul. Indeed, it can hardly be coincidental that one of the fullest developments of this association was in the Wisdom of Solomon, a text that is heavily implicated in Paul's argument in Romans. We will note this subordinate discourse's utilization by Paul in Romans 10 in more detail shortly. Here it will suffice to consider whether it is mobilized in Romans 1–4. And the text that suddenly seems illuminated by this possibility is 1:16:

[(15) οὕτως τὸ κατ' ἐμὲ πρόθυμον καὶ ὑμῖν τοῖς ἐν Ῥώμῃ εὐαγγελίσασθαι.] (16) Οὐ γὰρ ἐπαισχύνομαι τὸ εὐαγγέλιον. δύναμις γὰρ Θεοῦ ἐστιν εἰς σωτηρίαν παντὶ τῷ πιστεύοντι, Ἰουδαίῳ τε πρῶτον καὶ Ἕλληνι.

Interpreters have invariably translated v. 16 with the gospel as the unstated subject of the second sentence, placing the "power of God" in the predicate as a consequent description of the gospel: "For I am not ashamed of the gospel; it is the power of God for salvation to everyone who has faith, to the Jew first and also to the Greek" (NRSV).[76] But although this decision is not without justification, its grounds are not especially strong. Some considerations seem to stand against it. And more numerous and stronger considerations seem to point instead to δύναμις Θεοῦ as the subject, thereby producing a statement more evocative of the discourses of divine wisdom and kingship that Paul is mobilizing through this short section, in resumption of 1:2-4 and in anticipation of 3:21-26 and beyond.

Verse 16 *can* be construed legitimately in the conventional fashion in grammatical terms, with the object of the preceding sentence being assumed as the subject of the verb ἐστιν and the nominative phrase δύναμις Θεοῦ read in the predicate. That Paul is continuing to discuss the gospel in some sense is, moreover, confirmed by the short phrase ἐν αὐτῷ that occurs in v. 17. This pronoun really must point back to "the gospel" in v. 16a. Paul has spoken of the gospel at some length in his epistolary introduction, whether implicitly or directly (see esp. vv. 1-4, 8, 9, 13-15). And 1 Corinthians 1:18 even seems to provide a directly equivalent instance (ὁ λόγος . . . ὁ τοῦ σταυροῦ . . . τοῖς . . . σῳζομένοις ἡμῖν δύναμις Θεοῦ ἐστιν). Of course, the conventional reading tends to assume that Romans is centrally concerned with the gospel itself, explicating it systematically from this point in terms of Justification theory. That theory privileges preaching and the acquisition of right information by attentive individuals, so its advocates expect Paul to speak of such matters in any early, programmatic statement. God's salvation is indeed — according to Justification theory — centrally oriented by its representatives and what they say (at which point the individualist and rationalist dimensions of the theory become evident again, not to mention its preoccupation with information). However, it hardly needs to be said at this point that such considerations are no longer automatically relevant to our developing reading. The privileging of any notion of the gospel by Justification theory should be scrutinized and not assumed. We need, rather, to be sensitive to different possible roles for τὸ εὐαγγέλιον in Paul's thinking and argument.

Against the conventional reading we can note immediately that it overrides the syntactical signal Paul has sent concerning the interpretation of δύναμις Θεοῦ by means of its placement. This noun phrase precedes the verb and therefore is best construed in the first instance as that verb's subject. Moreover, in so preceding, it parallels exactly the following sentence, which has a similar substantive phrase concerning God in the first position — a phrase that is invariably read as the sentence's subject. If δύναμις Θεοῦ is read in the predicate, then both these apparent signals are being ignored. Such a reading is not impossible, but it would need supporting reasons, and it is difficult to know what they might be (that is, other than a priori ones). At first glance it seems that the δύναμις Θεοῦ and the δικαιοσύνη Θεοῦ in vv. 16b-17a are parallel acts of God. Indeed, 1:18 *also* foregrounds an act of God — there his wrath — in the position of subject, although not in the sentence's first position.

In support of any initial leaning toward an alternative reading of δύναμις Θεοῦ as the subject of v. 16b on grounds of syntax and local parallels is the broader comparative evidence. Where δύναμις is qualified by Θεοῦ elsewhere in Paul (whether directly or implicitly), *it invariably denotes an act by God,*[77] and *usually within a discourse informed by divine wisdom.* This evidence is both striking and consistent. In fact, 1 Corinthians 1:18 in context is a clear demonstration, inaugurating an argument where both Christ and the Spirit are linked tightly with δύναμις Θεοῦ (see esp. 1:24 and 2:4-5 — an argument that also discusses revelation[78]).[79] Hence, the deployment of this evidence in support of a predicative reading of δύναμις Θεοῦ in v. 16 is actually misleading. Moreover, these are precisely the expectations that are activated by the recognition that 1:3-4 refers to an act of messianic enthronement (the divine King's establishment of his agent's authority); and the phrase δικαιοσύνη Θεοῦ ἀποκαλύπτεται (κ.τ.λ.), used in 1:17a, resonates with a psalm of divine kingship (Psalm 98 [LXX 97]), and with that discourse more broadly. *And 1:16 even partly resumes the earlier kingship text,* where it is precisely the δύναμις Θεοῦ — in 1:2-4, associated with the Spirit of sanctification — who effects this enthronement by raising Jesus from the dead (see v. 4: . . . τοῦ γενομένου ἐκ σπέρματος Δαυὶδ κατὰ σάρκα τοῦ ὁρισθέντος υἱοῦ θεοῦ ἐν δυνάμει κατὰ πνεῦμα ἁγιωσύνης ἐξ ἀναστάσεως νεκρῶν). All these gathering hints will only be confirmed by the later discussion of Romans 10, where "the word of God" acts through much of that argument in terms of divine wisdom. So it seems reasonable to conclude tentatively that δύναμις Θεοῦ is best read as the subject of its sentence, and both 1:16 and 1:17 now seem to speak primarily of acts of God.[80]

And with these clarifications, we can turn to reconsider the rhetorical functions of the first two subunits where the famous phrase δικαιοσύνη Θεοῦ occurs, namely, 1:17 and 3:21-26 — fascinating and sophisticated argumentative roles that are becoming increasingly apparent.

§3. The Rhetorical Function of Romans 1:17 and 3:21-26

The main rhetorical contributions of 1:17 and 3:21-26 to Romans have already been discussed in chapter fifteen, and our subsequent semantic and interpretative decisions have only enhanced those initial judgments. There it was suggested that 1:17 anticipates 3:21-22, which sets out a particular series of critical claims that are freighted in deeply intertextual language. The complete series has five principal components: (i) the disclosure of the δικαιοσύνη Θεοῦ; (ii) *independently* of "works of law"; (iii) but as *attested* to by the Scriptures, here both Law and Prophets; (iv) *through* or by means of the fidelity of Christ; and (v) *for* everyone/all who believe(s):

(i)   δικαιοσύνη Θεοῦ ἀποκαλύπτεται/πεφανέρωται (see Ps. 98:2 [LXX 97:2])
(ii) χωρὶς [ἔργων] νόμου (see Rom. 1:18–3:20; Ps. 143:2b [LXX 142:2b]; Lev. 18:5)
(iii) μαρτυρουμένη ὑπὸ τοῦ νόμου καὶ τῶν προφητῶν (see Rom. 1:17; 3:17–4:22)
(iv) ἐκ/διὰ πίστεως [Χριστοῦ/'Ιησοῦ] (see Hab. 2:4)
(v)   εἰς πάντας τοὺς πιστεύοντας/πίστιν (see Gen. 15:6; Isa. 28:16; Joel 2:32 [LXX 3:5])

Romans 3:23-26 can then be seen to expand on the critical positive contentions here further, especially components i, iv, and v, effectively crafting a compact chiastic discussion through v. 26 that is probably also characterized by ritual patterning and presentation. These expansions, along with the initial statements of 3:21-22 themselves, introduce the major argumentative moves that structure the rest of the argument in Romans 4-8.

As we will see in the next chapter, the claim that God's right act of eschatological salvation in Christ (i.e., the δικαιοσύνη of the divine King effected through his earthly representative) is attested by the νόμος, or Torah, and not merely by the Prophets is the basis for Paul's discussion in Romans 4. There Genesis 15:6, the most important pentateuchal quotation in Romans, will be explicated in a number of ways in opposition to the Teacher's gospel of "works" and circumcision. So 3:21-22 indicates the inauguration of this second aggressive phase in Paul's argument — a scriptural σύγκρισις.

But Paul intends to respond to some of the issues in the Teacher's position with countervailing positive explications and not merely with refutation. Paul will address specifically the issues of eschatological assurance and ethical efficacy — points at which it is not the Teacher's concerns that are wrong so much as his particular solutions. The Teacher links these issues in his opening rhetorical salvos and throughout his system, as we have already seen in 1:18–3:20, where it is evident that he follows a classic "turn or burn" strategy. Future eschatological consequences should empower present ethical activity for the Teacher — although informed of course by circumcision and the law. But Paul has his own, very different answers to these important questions, solutions that derive from a more radical and consistent consideration of the Christ event and its implications. His positive elaborations unfold in Romans 5-8 in moves that he signals in 3:23-26. (The issue of eschatological assurance brackets the longer treatment of ethical efficacy, 5:1-11 and 8:9-29 enclosing 5:12–8:8.)[81] God's benevolent act in Christ on our behalf is implicit in 3:21-22 and is then elaborated in liberative terms, and as an overt proof of benevolence, in 3:23-26. So these verses point ahead quite specifically to the concerns of Romans 5-8. (These basic assumptions then also underlie Romans 9–11 — especially 9:30–10:21 — and the more contingent ethical exhortations of Romans 12–14 as well.)

It is now possible, in the light of our discussion since these points were first presented, to supply more precision and to recognize certain deeper qualities in Paul's argumentation. Two implications in particular are now apparent.

(1) Paul's Juxtaposition of Two Irreconcilable Conceptions of God and the Christ Event

Now that we have determined the meaning of δικαιοσύνη Θεοῦ, the subject and predicate of 1:16-17 and 3:21-26 become much clearer, as does the theological wellspring of Paul's opposition to the Teacher's countervailing gospel. δικαιοσύνη Θεοῦ speaks of God's liberating act in Christ, through which a captive and helpless humanity — and ultimately a screaming creation as well — are delivered. And because the content of this divine act is supplied by the Christ event, and because of its utterly saving character, Paul characterizes God consistently as a deliverer — a divine king who is acting with a right action and a "judgment" that does nothing other than save and save gratuitously. In short, for Paul, God, as revealed by Christ, is benevolent. He acts for us and can be relied on to do so consistently in the future, as he has just done in the past and is doing in the present. He can, moreover, be relied on to act in such a way as to resolve our difficulties (which are significantly ethical). There is no other character of God behind this acting God; this is God as he truly is — the God who delivers through Jesus Christ. Paul's root metaphor of God, then, is benevolent, or merciful. *There is no retributive character to the God revealed to Paul by Christ.* (This is not of course to suggest that Paul's benevolent God does not care about sin — quite the converse; he cares enough to send his only son to deal with it by dying shamefully, and Paul himself is consistently so concerned as well, but the level at which this concern operates is crucial.) *And this is what lies at the heart of Paul's dispute with the Teacher.* The Teacher has not taken Christ's disclosure of God's benevolence with full seriousness; that disclosure has been subordinated and assimilated to some prior conception of God that is retributive. In this sense, then, the Teacher's conception of God is Christianized but not Christian; it is not revised by the Christ event at a fundamental level. In more modern parlance we might say that the Teacher is a theological foundationalist — a non-Christian foundationalist. Paul, moreover, can object that there is no legitimate ground for actually knowing that God is retributive (and certainly no legitimate Christian ground); how do we conceive of God apart from the disclosure of his character in Christ?! Hence, *fundamentally different conceptions of God are at stake at Rome.*

Paul signals this by juxtaposing a brief statement of his position, in 1:16-17 — which also anticipates the key series of argumentative moves against the Teacher's gospel in the letter — with a statement of the theological axiom that lies at the heart of the Teacher's gospel, in 1:18. Paul's gospel, oriented entirely by Christ, speaks of a fundamentally saving and benevolent God — of a compassionate divine King whose sole concern is to act to save a wretched humanity (i.e., to rescue the ungodly). His gospel is rooted in a δικαιοσύνη Θεοῦ. The Teacher's gospel is rooted, however, in an ὀργὴ Θεοῦ — an "anger" that responds to all actions retributively, and to sinful actions punitively. *These two basal conceptions of God could not, in this sense, be more different.* And only one is thoroughly rooted in the implications of the Christ event.[82]

We come at this point, then, to the heart not merely of Paul's difficulty with the Teacher but of the interpretative history of Romans that has subsequently so tangled the apostle's interpretation. It is becoming apparent that Justification theory *mistakes the presuppositions of the Teacher for the presuppositions of Paul, thereby assimilating Paul's gospel to the parameters of the Teacher!* A more ironic interpretative outcome is hard to imagine. The theory fails to grasp the exact nuances of the apostle's phrase δικαιοσύνη Θεοῦ (indeed overlooking its christological content) and goes on to assume that the wrath of God is directly correlative (not antithetical) and that the subsequent "turn or burn" argument is Paul's own. We do not end up with the Teacher's gospel exactly, because of the actual movement of the text and its various appeals to some notion of "faith," but we end up with a conditional Christian system constructed in the Teacher's conditional and retributive image, within which "faith" replaces circumcision and "works" as the critical appropriation of salvation, and the work of Christ, equated in large measure with his death, is subordinated to a harshly just God. That is, we end up with just the theological shortcomings of the Teacher, now writ large in Justification theory and transposed into a slightly more Christian and pagan key. The initial leveling of the Teacher's gospel in its own terms by Paul, then, becomes Paul's prior leveling of Judaism and the rest of humanity — the necessarily aggressive and constricted preamble to any proclamation and appropriation of the gospel, with all its unrealistic, anti-Jewish consequences. Surely, few such semantic and argumentative mistakes in history can have led to such ironic, significant, painful, and protracted misinterpretation! Equally surely, it must be time to correct them.[83]

In sum, we can now see more clearly that the juxtaposition of divine attributes in Romans 1:17 and 18 (then restated in 3:21-22) — the δικαιοσύνη Θεοῦ over against the ὀργὴ Θεοῦ — is not a compatible juxtaposition, the second axiom existing as a possible development of the first (i.e., God's δικαιοσύνη functioning in its innate punitive aspect against wrongdoing). As Paul's specific semantic allusions and later argumentative developments make clear, this is a fundamentally *incompatible* juxtaposition denoting two irreconcilable gospels and interpretations of the Christ event.[84] In this opposition reside two fundamentally different theses about the nature of God.

(2) Paul's Rhetorical Reframing of the Atonement

If the preceding clarification concerns presuppositions, this one concerns Paul's rhetorical treatment of the atonement (although these concerns are at bottom intimately related). We have already seen that Romans 3:23-26 anticipates Romans 5–8, part of which discusses the question of ethical efficacy (5:12–8:8/12-13) — an issue raised by the Teacher's gospel. I would now suggest that Paul effects a sophisticated rhetorical maneuver in 3:23-26 on the way to that later, more extended discussion. Not only does he anticipate his later treatment of a subject raised by the Teacher's gospel, but he introduces it in such a way that he can segue out of the atonement theology probably shared by the Roman Christians into his own later, more radical conception, *thereby implying that he is only restating in Romans 5–8 what his auditors have already heard and submitted to.* It is a subtle maneuver that many conventional readers have missed, but it is consistent with the overarching rhetorical strategy that we have already detected is framing the letter (see chapter thirteen). Nevertheless I only make this suggestion here tentatively, because the principal text is so abbreviated, and a full corroboration of my claim would require consideration of much of the rest of Romans, and then, beyond this, of the NT as a whole — lengthy tasks that should not be attempted here.

Christ's death is presented by Paul in 3:23-26 with great care. Christ faithfully atones for sin as a ἱλαστήριον and sheds his blood, and his death is then said to be "for the sake of that release from previously committed transgressions" (διὰ τὴν πάρεσιν τῶν προγεγονότων ἁμαρτημάτων). It seems likely that the specific claims concerning Christ's atonement here echo traditional early church theology that Paul holds his Roman auditors to share.

This collocation of atonement terms is rare if not unparalleled for Paul (although it occurs again in Hebrews 9). But it resonates with the martyrological reading of Habakkuk 2:4 in Romans 1:17 that we already suspect is traditional. Moreover, it explains the metaphorization of the cultus that Paul mobilizes repeatedly in Romans without ever using in a fundamental way.[85] As noted by Martyn, a plural reference to sins (or their close equivalent) by Paul in any atoning claim, as is made here, seems generally to denote an affirmation of traditional atonement theology.[86] *Paul never develops such instances argumentatively or theologically,* and the rareness of the terms used reinforces these suspicions.[87] Paul's preferred theological analysis of sin, which becomes apparent in Romans shortly, treats it in the singular as a power. The apostle nevertheless explicitly links such plural language for sin to prior early church tradition in 1 Corinthians 15:1-4: Χριστὸς ἀπέθανεν ὑπὲρ τῶν ἁμαρτιῶν ἡμῶν κατὰ τὰς γραφὰς καὶ . . . ἐτάφη καὶ . . . ἐγήγερται τῇ ἡμέρᾳ τῇ τρίτῃ κατὰ τὰς γραφάς. This material is καὶ παρέλαβον. And these accumulating considerations all point in one direction: Paul's account of the atonement in Romans 3:23-26 is meant to echo his auditors' traditional position at Rome — as are his earlier account of Christ's resurrection and heavenly enthronement as Lord, in 1:2-4, and his use of a recognizable christological proof text, in 1:17. He has echoed this traditional material in a peculiarly artful fashion, although in order to recover this artistry we must consider where he is heading.

One of Paul's main concerns in Romans 5–8 is to provide an alternative account of Christian ethics (as we have already seen in part one, chapter three). He holds this to be an authentic and effective account, rooted in Christ, whereas the Teacher's, mired in the structures of the present world, is not. Moreover, his account is — largely in correlative terms — also a liberated, law-free system. Paul generates it principally by way of participation in Christ's death and resurrection, effected by the Holy Spirit. That participation accomplishes both the execution of the evil desires unleashed since Adam in human flesh and the re-creation of a mind concerned with the things of God and the Spirit. Thus, in this account, the problem is defined in large measure in terms of the oppression and enslavement of humanity by the evil power of sin (so, perhaps better, Sin), from which liberation must be effected — and is ("thanks be to God"), by way of participation in Christ's execution *and resurrection.* As a result of all this, Paul's ethic is characterized by fundamental commitments to the notion of sin in singular terms as an evil, oppressive power; to the consequent liberative nature of any "atonement" (i.e., from that power); and to the critical atoning or saving role of Christ's *resurrection,* as well as his death. In the light of these later commitments, it is possible to see that Paul is preparing the way in Romans 3:23-26 for the claim that they arise out of the Roman Christians' own, more traditional theology (an ambitious rhetorical maneuver, because in fact they don't).

The Roman Christians (and the Teacher!), as we have seen, do not seem to attribute saving or atoning efficacy to Christ's resurrection, which functions to affirm his lordship (see Rom. 1:2-4). It is most likely that they view any atonement as having been accomplished through his death (so 3:25) and, moreover, that they connect that event with their own eschatological vindication and resurrection *sequentially.* Christ's death cleanses them from sins, and so they are enabled to behave righteously and receive a final verdict from God of "righteous," thereby inheriting life in the age to come. (And this is indeed a fundamentally martyrological account of Christ's passion.) In this system, however, not only are their cleansing and final acquittal held apart, but Christ's story has only limited contact with their own. In particular, his resurrection has no strong relation to their own. Christ's death functions more as an apparent replacement of the temple cultus, which cleanses or wipes various individual transgressions from the relevant worshipers and their consciences (see Heb. 9:11-14, 24-28). Hence, there is no further atoning role for the resurrection to play.

Paul's understanding of the implications of the passion is, of course, far more radical than this, not to mention more integrated. He holds all these things together. Atonement is effected for Christians, in his view, as they participate in Christ's death *and* resurrection; this effects a much deeper liberation from the very power of Sin, not merely cleansing from sins. Christians are not merely enabled to live, purified, in the present world, but their very being is transformed and they enter a new world. How then is Paul to bridge the gaps between these notions in the thinking of the Roman Christians — bridging operations that are necessary if his later claims are to make any sense and/or to possess any legitimacy?

He does not do so explicitly in 3:23-26, but he creates certain rhetorical pressures in this direction that prepare the way for his later, more explicit claims. Basically, in this preparatory text, he repeatedly juxtaposes his distinctive notions with the more traditional conceptions of the Roman Christians, thereby creating several points at which those auditors can "slide" across to his more radical views.

What does it really mean to say that "all sinned and lack the glory/glorious image of God"? This alludes in an unexceptionable way to a story that can be developed in terms either of human capacity or incapacity (and Paul, beginning in 5:12, builds from the latter). The notion of δικαιόω that occurs twice is similarly ambiguous. It could denote a forensic-retributive process, following some earlier trajectory of cleansing and righteous living, but it could denote a forensic-liberative process, setting an imprisoned figure free from captivity. Everything depends on how these narratives and terms are framed and then later developed.

The notion of freedom operative here is especially important. If the early church conceived of atonement in terms of cleansing from sins, then it already contained a particular notion of negative liberty; the individual who is cleansed has in a certain sense been released from his or her sins and their consequences much as a figure who has had a bath is clean and so freed from all previously accumulated muck and grime (so sins are being understood here in terms primarily of purity). But it is precisely this connotation of freedom "from sins" that allows a notional transition to a more radical conception of the atonement that utilizes a liberative, atoning resurrection. The resurrection can of course be described repeatedly in liberative terms, because it is itself also a liberative event.

> Cleansing and hence freedom from sins [leads to] the freedom of resurrection.
> Cleansing and hence freedom from Sin [*is the*] freedom of resurrection.

Here the two notions of liberation operative within two different accounts of the atonement are juxtaposed. And this allows their auditors to blend them together and thereby accept subtly the legitimacy of the second, more radical conception. This is just a hint in 3:25-26, but it paves the way — if only subliminally — for Paul's later argument. Freedom from sins is becoming freedom from Sin (see esp. 5:12-21).

This semantic and theological transfer is reinforced by the developing implication that Christians participate in Christ's story. He is faithful and dies, effecting "deliverance" and being himself "released" from death. And any participation in this story by Christians now tends to pull the resurrection and some of its consequences into the present. Christ has experienced his resurrection, so it makes sense to suggest that if Christians are participating in Christ, then this resurrection can also be tasted by them now, so to speak. In this way, a liberative event postponed into the future by the Teacher (and many others!) is drawn, by way of pneumatological participation, into the present. But the liberative connotations of the resurrection can also be deployed at the point in the story, where some freedom is already being experienced by Christians — in relation to transgressions! The experience of Christ's liberating resurrection in the present therefore presses the interpretation of the atonement in relation to sins in a similar direction; Christians have been liberated from sins, and liberated from the very structures of Sin.

> Christ is faithful, atones, and has been resurrected and liberated.
> Christians are trusting, receive atonement, and are [*in him*] resurrected and liberated (experiencing this in an inaugurated fashion).
> Therefore, the atonement *itself* seems to be liberating, functioning in some relation to the resurrection.

Hence, there are good theological grounds for Paul's subtle theological segue. His argument does not rest on the juxtaposition of similar semantic resonances alone.

In short, the tight and repeated juxtaposition in Romans 3:23-26 of notions stated in deliberately ambiguous and hence analogous terms encourages their integration and not merely their sequencing (and the notion of negative liberty is especially significant). Moreover, the repeated juxtaposition of the story of Christ next to the story of Christians in general (something underwritten by participation) reinforces any such integration. None of this is explicated at length or more than hinted at in 3:23-26. It is a subtle strategy (although I would suggest not overly so). Nevertheless, after carefully attending this text, the letter's auditors were probably predisposed to hear the subsequent account of salvation in participatory and liberative terms in Romans 5–8 as something that built recognizably on their own presuppositions. Paul is therefore only "reminding them" at these later points of what they already know — of the form of the gospel that was originally entrusted to them (see 6:17; 15:15), although it turns out of course that the repristinated form in Romans, properly understood, entails a trenchant opposition to the suggestions of the Teacher and a comprehensive commitment to Paul's radical gospel!

§4. Problems Solved

Like the rereading of Romans 1:18–3:20, the reconstruals of 1:16-17 and 3:21-26 suggested here resolve the long list of difficulties that was previously noted in relation to the conventional reading of these pericopes, and this is the principal factor in their favor. Basically, I have suggested reconstruing 1:16-17 and 3:21-26 more christocentrically, thereby facilitating a more participatory and apocalyptic approach to Paul's soteriology in general. And this in turn allows these short but powerful sections to anticipate smoothly Paul's more extended discussions of salvation later in Romans, especially in chapters 5–8, thereby eliminating the primary tensions perceived between these major blocks of material and their implicit theological systems — one of the enduring conundrums in modern Pauline interpretation. But numerous other, more minor tensions have been softened as well. In short, fifteen problems are either partly or fully alleviated by my suggested rereadings of Romans 1:16-17 and 3:21-26.

Underdeterminations
UD 5: It can be stated somewhat arbitrarily that these subsections are "thesis paragraphs," laying out Paul's key propositions in Romans, which then turn out, a little unsurprisingly, to be the key axioms in Justification theory. It seems, after their detailed exegesis, that there is some truth in this claim; however, these paragraphs are not thesis paragraphs per se so much as compact initiations and anticipations of later argumentative strategies. Their claims therefore correspond directly to Paul's major argumentative thrusts, but not necessarily directly to his deepest theological convictions. The route from argumentative contingency to

theological coherence must still be traced. So it is illegitimate to lift propositions from these units and without further ado claim that they speak of Paul's central concerns theologically.

UD 6: The overarching strategic function of δικαιοσύνη θεοῦ must likewise be nuanced. This is clearly not *the* leitmotif for the letter as a whole, although it is important. This phrase contributes, in an intertextually mediated fashion, to a broader proposition, itself also intertextually mediated, which speaks of God's decisive saving act through Christ on behalf of all who trust. (Further insight into this phrase's argumentative role will be generated in part five, chapter nineteen, when Romans 10 is discussed in more detail.)

UD 7: It is crucial to note that Paul's πιστ- terminology is never said explicitly to function as the criterion for Christian salvation — because it is not functioning in that way (i.e., as Justification theory defines it). Certainly, πίστις *marks* those who are currently being saved by virtue of their incorporation into Christ, but it is not necessarily functioning beyond this as the key action that individuals must exercise in order to *appropriate* salvation. This entire interpretative dimension is exegetically, argumentatively, and theologically unnecessary. It is not stated explicitly by Paul (creating UD 7), because it is not actually part of his argument. (Again, our later investigation of Romans 10 in part five, chapter nineteen will shed further light on this motif's actual rhetorical function — an interesting one.)

UD 8: Argumentation establishing Christ as the definitive atonement over against other systems, especially the extensive Jewish apparatus, is absent because, once again, Paul is not making a broader argument in these terms. Intriguingly, Christ's displacement of the temple's atoning function seems to be assumed by both protagonists in this dispute — by both Paul and the Teacher. So an argument at this point does not arise, whether between Paul and the Teacher or between Judaism and Christianity. This raises interesting questions (e.g., what underlies this shared and radical displacement in the early church), but they are not germane to the present discussion (although strong hints concerning the rationale at this point have already been supplied by chapter sixteen, when we discussed the traditional atonement language that Paul uses in 3:25-26). These textual and argumentative absences in relation to Justification theory, but not in relation to the suggested rereading, are telling.

UD 9: In close relation to the foregoing, not only does Justification theory require some justification for Christ's displacement of alternative modes of atonement, but it needs a clear statement that his atonement is propitiatory, satisfying the just wrath of God with human sins. This notion is inherently problematic in terms of its underlying coherence — specifically, in terms of the atonement as some sort of payment — but if we grant its conceptual possibility for the sake of argument, it must still receive some overt mention in Paul's text at some point, and it does not. My rereading explains this by suggesting that Paul is not committed to such a propitiatory view and hence does not need to state it. He is committed, rather, to a much more subtle set of transitions, from an essentially expiatory and liberative view of the atonement shared with the early church to a more radically liberative conception that he will explicate in more detail in Romans 5–8.

Overdeterminations

OD 12: We noted the important textual embarrassment that πίστις seems to be functioning as a means or instrument in some process of disclosure in 1:16-17, 3:21-22, and elsewhere. Justification theory's anthropocentric account of "faith" cannot account for this; it simply seems confused in semantic terms to expect human faith to disclose something, functioning to bring an unknown entity to a state of knowability. However, a christological reference copes with this textual feature with ease. The faithful Christ reveals the saving will and act of God (and even *is* that act).

OD 13: Similarly, the syntactical awkwardness of Paul's reference to πίστις in 3:25 is resolved by referring it to Christ (a reference that resolves in turn many of the difficulties clustered around Paul's atonement terms in 3:25-26).

Intrinsic Difficulties

ID 6: This difficulty, and its resolution by my rereading, has already been noted in relation to OD 8 above. A cogent explanation for Christ's singular atonement is never supplied because Paul does not need to; he is not laying out an argument that requires it.

ID 7: We saw earlier how an anthropocentric account of "faith" in Paul runs into acute conceptual difficulties. Faith cannot simply be exercised as an act of the will (we cannot make ourselves believe that something is true simply by wanting to), but if it is instead a gift, its privileging is unaccounted for, along with its gifting only to a privileged few (and not to all those who have negotiated phase one successfully). However, by centering Paul's account of "faith" on Christ, these problems are potentially avoided, although the detailed discussion of this is best postponed until after both Romans 4 and Romans 10 have been considered in more detail. The rereading of 1:16-17 and 3:21-26, with its emphasis on the faithful Christ, nevertheless opens up the possibility for this less problematic, alternative understanding.

Systematic Difficulties

SD 4: With its emphases on an unconditional, participatory, and liberative soteriology centered on Christ, my rereading also offers the possibility of a smooth integration with the explication of soteriology elsewhere, especially in Romans 5-8, rather than a dramatic set of tensions — an important advantage for this rereading. The role of Jesus Christ in the atonement is no longer different elsewhere from the model that seems presupposed by 3:24-26 (i.e., when that text is read in conventional terms).

SD 5: In just the same terms, the nature of salvation, including the basis and depth of Christian assurance, now potentially integrates with Paul's understanding stated elsewhere, rather than generating a set of jarring differences.

SD 6: The nature and role of "faith" are also more integrative, although a decisive consideration of this motif is being postponed until after consideration of Romans 4 and 10.

SD 7: The conception of ethics is drawn into an integrative alignment with the other advantages of the suggested rereading. This construal's emphasis on Christ, and the possibility of participation in him, now grounds ethics both more effectively and more consistently.

SD 8: The nature of the church can be realigned as well. My rereading potentially delivers a far more intimate, committed, and robust Christian polity than Justification theory can, because of its implicit commitment to participation in the divine communion, and to an inherently relational personhood.

SD 10: The suggested rereading also no longer generates any endorsement of coercion and violence in the divine activity; violence is done *to* God, in Christ, but not also *by* him. At this point, we link hands with one of the most important advantages of my rereading of Romans 1:18–3:20. The Teacher endorses the wrath of God and its punitive outworking. It turns out that Paul has the profoundest difficulties with that system as a whole, and with its basic conception of the character of God in such terms. My rereading reveals that the basic character of God for Paul is one of unconditional benevolence.[88]

This is a formidable slate of interpretative successes — many of which either continue advances made in relation to 1:18–3:20 or anticipate further advances in relation to 3:27–4:25. The resolution of all these problems, along with their implicit theological implications that otherwise furrow Paul's interpretation at such depth, seems to be an important step forward in the apostle's interpretation. With these realizations in place, we are ready to consider the last major block of material in Romans 1–4, specifically, 3:27–4:25. I suggest that Paul undertakes here a second extended argumentative engagement with the Teacher's false gospel. It is as thorough and effective as his first, although its angle of approach is different. Paul now debates Scripture with particular reference to the supremely authoritative Torah, and hence the significance of the great patriarch Abraham.

CHAPTER EIGHTEEN

Rereading Romans 3:27–4:25 —
Our Forefather Reconsidered

§1. Preamble

Romans 4 is beginning now to come clearly into view. Paul's discussion of Abraham here has traditionally been regarded as a stronghold for Justification theory — a fortified tower in its ring of defenses — but earlier on, in part three, chapter eleven, a whole slate of difficult interpretative problems and implications was identified in that position. In this chapter we will consider whether a rereading along the lines we have been exploring can resolve this slate. In the process, however, we must also consider the short subsection that precedes Romans 4, namely, 3:27-31. This pericope has often proved extremely troublesome to interpreters, whether conventional or revisionist. But I will suggest here that it is precisely the expectations and reading generated by Justification theory that have made it so opaque. Approached from a new, less constrained direction, this subsection can be seen to integrate smoothly into Paul's unfolding critique of the Teacher; it is, in fact, a critical set of markers within his carefully crafted attack. Consequently, we will find that an integrated rereading of Romans 3:27–4:25 can resolve all the difficulties generated by the conventional construal of this text, simultaneously undercutting any endorsement of Justification theory — and that fairly decisively. Far from being one of the theory's strongholds, Romans 4 will turn out to be one of its vulnerabilities — a tower vulnerable to total collapse, along with the citadel that it defends.

§2. Romans 3:27–4:1 as a Follow-on

We will address the basic structure of this subsection and try to articulate its most obvious implications before considering some of the infamous interpretative problems that it raises. Most importantly, we should recall that we are freed at this point from the expectations of Justification theory, here specifically that Paul will begin an authoritative scriptural illustration in 4:1 of his thesis of "justification by faith (not by works of law)," as stated in 3:21-26. Those expectations have tended to marginalize 3:27-31, as we noted earlier in part three, chapters ten and eleven; it is left dangling between these two important passages with no obvious function. But we are free now, rather, to follow the immediate suggestions of the text. And the break at 3:27 is certainly marked.

Prior to this point Paul has crafted a text that seems to echo early Christian and Jewish ritual language. In 3:27, however, he begins a diatribe, a clear stylistic signal for an interpretative shift. Unfortunately, absent the array of performative signals (verbal and nonverbal) that would originally have cued the Roman Christian auditors, precise assignments of roles and exchanges within the following dialogue are more difficult for us (although fortunately not a great deal turns on the exact reconstructions that are supplied here). I suggest arranging the exchanges as follows, with a degree of tentativeness. But a more critical point now arises, namely, that the expectations of Justification theory *and* the probable psychological influence of a chapter break at 4:1 seem to have ended this diatribal section prematurely for most interpreters. As Stowers notes, the diatribal style inaugurated in 3:27 in fact continues directly and indeed seamlessly into Romans 4.[1] Our diatribal reconstruction should reflect this (although, for reasons to be noted momentarily, we will halt our interpretation here temporarily after 4:2.)

A^1: ^{27}Ποῦ οὖν ἡ καύχησις;

B^1:   ἐξεκλείσθη.

A^2:   διὰ ποίου νόμου; τῶν ἔργον;

B^2:   οὐχί,[2] ἀλλὰ διὰ νόμου πίστεως.
           ^{28}λογιζόμεθα γὰρ δικαιοῦσθαι πίστει ἄνθρωπον χωρὶς ἔργων νόμου.

A^3: ^{29}ἢ[3] Ἰουδαίων ὁ θεὸς μόνον.

B^3:   οὐχὶ[4] καὶ ἐθνῶν;

A^4:   ναὶ καὶ ἐθνῶν.

B^4: ^{30}εἴπερ[5] εἷς ὁ θεὸς ὃς δικαιώσει περιτομὴν ἐκ πίστεως καὶ
           ἀκροβυστίαν διὰ τῆς πίστεως.

A^5: ^{31}νόμον οὖν καταργοῦμεν διὰ τῆς πίστεως;

B^5:   μὴ γένοιτο· ἀλλὰ νόμον ἱστάνομεν.

A^6:   4^{1}τί οὖν ἐροῦμεν εὑρηκέναι Ἀβραὰμ τὸν προπάτορα ἡμῶν κατὰ
           σάρκα; ^{2}εἰ γὰρ Ἀβραὰμ ἐξ ἔργων ἐδικαιώθη, ἔχει καύχημα.

B^6:   ἀλλ' οὐ πρὸς Θεόν. ^{3}τί γὰρ ἡ γραφὴ λέγει; κ.τ.λ.

Paul has stated some of his key presuppositions in 3:21-26, there resuming and elaborating the earlier, more allusive claims of 1:2-4 and 1:16-17. In 1:16-17 he has stated that God is saving humanity by means of a progression of πίστις, and in 3:21-26 he has supplied further details. God has acted in the present — "now" — through the faithful Christ, liberating, resurrecting and enthroning him (here recalling information from 1:2-4). And he now reaches out through those events to include all those who trust in him, whether Jew or pagan, thereby reestablishing his sovereignty over a humanity that has been wrested from him. This set of positive statements follows an extensive critique of the Teacher's gospel on internal grounds, one that has reduced the Teacher himself to a pained silence in 3:19. But further questions now arise.

At this point in the letter, at 3:27, both gospels are on the table, so to speak, and comparative questions that have not yet been asked are consequently generated automatically. How does the Teacher's gospel fare when compared with Paul's basic assumptions (as against simply on its own terms)? Certainly, several things need to be said here. An interlocutor — represented as "A" in the quotation above — therefore places a set of interrelated, comparative queries to Paul in this short diatribe. And the concerns of the Teacher, already evident in 1:18–3:20, are discernible in each of these queries, suggesting that figure A is meant to represent the Teacher.[6] Figure A asks about the one who glories or boasts in his works, about what has happened to a teaching of "works of law," about the Jewish preferences of what is, after all, the Jewish God (whom the Teacher claims to represent), and about the possibility that Paul's key principle, πίστις, will eviscerate the Pentateuch. And these concerns are all easily recognizable as key features of the Teacher's gospel; they restate the Teacher's central concerns over against the new set of principles that Paul himself has just introduced and elaborated. Paul then seems to respond to each of these claims, as figure B, with a brief counterassertion based on his own position as that has just been stated in 3:21-26, especially 3:21-22. With this basic structure in mind, we can consider the exchange in a little more detail.

The Teacher asks first, in v. 27, where "the boaster" is. This figure has been negatively coded by Justification theory and Reformational and post-Reformational polemics; however, he is not necessarily to be conceived of pejoratively.[7] (Paul himself deploys this notion positively in 5:2-3.) It can refer to what someone rejoices or glories in. And the Teacher, like all merit-based thinkers, regards a degree of self-congratulation as perfectly legitimate if not positive, provided that the conditions for that rejoicing have been met. Truly righteous people who have performed the prescriptions of the law scrupulously and faithfully are entitled to glory in their accomplishments when God pronounces them "righteous" on the day of judgment. (People should be allowed to enjoy the fruits of their efforts.) But what has become of these figures — the crowning point of the Teacher's system — in the light of Paul's gospel of πίστις? How can a person who is ostensibly judged on the basis of πίστις alone boast at all, since no meritorious works are now in view?! This concern seems to underlie the Teacher's question in A[1].

Paul replies — although here rather cryptically — that this figure and posture has now been excluded, to which rejection the Teacher responds immediately, "Through what sort of teaching — a teaching of works of law?!" In one sense this is an understandable rejoinder, one that also serves to emphasize the key points at issue. The Teacher's gospel of works, which is based on following the scriptural commands in the Pentateuch, is precisely what can lead to boasting, and it seems to have been excluded, if Paul's terse rejoinder is to be believed. And Paul duly confirms this rejection in B². It is the disclosure of πίστις, by means of which a person is ultimately delivered, that overrules the Teacher's gospel in relation to "works of law." But the Teacher is also raising the question of authority here, and especially in relation to Scripture. He is still not sure why Paul's strange gospel of πίστις is more relevant than his own, which lays claim to extensive backing from the Torah. Several points within this critical exchange now need to be noted carefully, since they underlie some of the most difficult interpretative issues raised by this subsection.

Paul refutes the Teacher's claims in B² with one of the most compact statements of his countervailing system that he ever supplies; indeed, it is so compact that interpretative reductionism has arguably resulted. When Paul states that δικαιοῦσθαι πίστει ἄνθρωπον, the Roman auditors should recognize, however, a conflation of the two narratives that Paul has previously placed in a progression — the progress of God's eschatological salvation *through* the faithful Christ and his resurrection *to* those who trust and will therefore be resurrected, allowing in turn the statement that God "delivers a person by means of fidelity." Romans 3:28 conflates these earlier distinguishable narratives into one principle in the interests of brevity and repartee (although their similarity allows such conflation if the argument dictates a need for it; indeed, a useful rhetorical reason for this move will become apparent shortly). But that this claim includes a christological dimension and is, moreover, christologically grounded is likely.

It follows very shortly after a strong affirmation of God's self-disclosure through the faithful Christ's resurrection in 3:26, that statement echoing in turn two such previous claims (in 3:22 and 25). Added to this, Paul tends to speak of Christians in general by way of the verb and the participle, not the substantive (because different intertexts are operative), but here he uses the substantive, which tends more to underlie a primary christological reference. Indeed, Paul's subsequent πίστις language here will continue to resonate primarily with his own earlier christological statements, with its distinctive echo of Habakkuk 2:4 and related arthrous constructions (see esp. vv. 30 and 31a). But in addition, it is important to appreciate that the cogency of Paul's counterclaim and argument in fact rests here on a christological position as well.

In an embarrassment for Justification theory, Paul simply *overrules* the Teacher's gospel of works in 3:28.[8] And he does so because he now knows that "deliverance" is "by fidelity" and *therefore* the gospel of works must be repudiated — or so he says rather cryptically in v. 28/B². But how does he know this, especially given that the δικαιο- language that he uses here is eschatological, and so usually functions in the future?

Romans 3:21-26 has just provided the answer to this question. The resurrection of Christ has signified the arrival of God's decisive eschatological activity in both the immediate past and the present (hence the use of the present passive infinitive of δικαιόω here, δικαιοῦσθαι — an act that reaches out to include others but is grounded in Christ himself). It is this event that overrules any alternative soteriology.

It is difficult to translate δικαιοῦσθαι appropriately, because a wordplay is now operative. In the light of the Christ event, Paul is denying here not just the basis and the temporal location of the divine verdict in the Teacher's gospel *but its nature*. Given the present tense, δικαιοῦσθαι seems to be operating in a primarily Pauline sense and so without connotations of a divine evaluation of human rectitude, which is being specifically denied in context. The Teacher's use of this verb is future and refers to a future event. Hence it seems to be retaining here connotations of the divine decision that sets people free (a meaning shared by Paul and the Teacher), prompting my use of "delivered" above. Paul is deploying this verb, then, in a primarily christocentric way. Moreover, the entire claim is christocentric, as against christological alone, or anthropocentric.

We turn now to the final puzzle in this difficult text — the interpretation of νόμος.[9] We will be helped here by our growing recognition of Paul's extensive use of wordplays as he engages with the Teacher, and further, by our growing realization of what Paul is basically getting at. Indeed, the introduction of the Teacher into the interpretation of Paul's argument points to a very satisfactory account of this signifier.

While I have been speaking up to now of the argument between Paul and the Teacher in terms of two different systems or programs or "gospels" (and it should not be doubted that the two protagonists used this last term themselves), Paul and the Teacher may well have spoken of "teaching(s)" as well — in Hebrew, of *torah(s)*. And *torah* was translated — a little unhappily — by the Greek signifier νόμος. Moreover, a larger discourse was activated by any such reference.[10] We may note immediately, on the one hand, that such teaching often carried the connotation of divine revelation or disclosure. And this was because, on the other hand, it was rooted *in* the Torah, meaning here both the Scriptures more broadly and the Pentateuch more narrowly. Jewish teaching was authoritative because it was rooted in the Scripture that God had revealed to Israel (etc.). Notions of "walking," that is, of *halakah*, were then often closely associated with these references as well. And it seems almost certain that the Teacher would have spoken of his teaching as a torah, which in Greek would have been signified by νόμος; he was a learned Jewish exegete who seems to have grounded his claims extensively in Scripture (see 2:17-20). Romans 3:27-28 now seems to indicate fairly clearly that Paul opposed the Teacher's torah with one of his own — one based on Christ and inclusion in him. So two νόμοι clash here — a torah, or teaching, of works versus a torah of fidelity.[11]

But Paul introduces this designation at this specific point for a further reason: it will allow him to slip into a related argument introduced in v. 31 (and how many times have we had cause to note how carefully composed Romans is?!). Before discussing this, however, we must address vv. 29-30 and steps A³-B⁴.

I suggest that the Teacher replies with a fairly obvious challenge in A³ to Paul's dismissive claim in B² that God "delivers [i.e., resurrects] a person by means of fidelity, apart from works of law." As has already been noted repeatedly, the Teacher correlates salvation tightly with circumcised and law-observant Judaism, while Paul keeps pressing outside those boundaries with his gospel, abandoning much distinctive law observance in the process. Hence, the Teacher marks in A[3] that Paul's emphasis on faith, by abandoning works of law, has apparently led to a strange redefinition of the people of God in relation to God himself. The Jews worshiped the one true God and observed the commands that he had given to them. Therefore, the Teacher says pointedly, "Or is [not] God the God of the Jews only?!" (English speakers would prompt an affirmation here — somewhat paradoxically — by using the word "not," but Koiné does not require this; indeed, to supply this would prompt the opposite answer to the one intended!)

The expectations of Justification theory can obscure the point of the diatribe at this juncture, as can the conventional reading. If we imagine that *Paul* is asking a question here, the obvious answer that we expect is "no — of course not!" The following phrase is then read as a repetition of the same point: "Is he not also [God] of the pagan nations?" But it is equally possible to read the expectations of the initial statement here as being positive, because they are the expectations of the Teacher, and the subsequent question as a counterassertion by Paul. "Or is [not] God the God of the Jews only?!" the Teacher replies (not unreasonably), to which he expects the response "yes — of course he is!" But Paul *counters* this challenge with the question, "Is he not also the God of the pagan nations?" And the Teacher can only respond to this query with "yes" (presumably reluctantly): "yes . . . [he is] also [God] of the pagan nations." Of course, Paul's rejoinder to the Teacher's query is not quite to the point, but things are being stated here very briefly and will be discussed in more detail in due course.[12] And Paul does at least establish the principle that the sovereign God can act as he pleases. In corroboration of this translation suggestion is its exact resumption by v. 30. (In further partial corroboration is the observation that this explains the absence of any marker from A[3] that anticipates a negative response, thereby aligning the two statements; see especially the absence of μή or μέν.)

After the Teacher's concession that God is the God of all the pagan nations, Paul makes his second programmatic claim, although its grammar has often defied interpreters. But a smooth reading can be generated if we continue to trace the trajectory through that is suggested by the unfolding argumentative concerns already noted.

εἴπερ is an emphatic marker that should initiate a conditional statement in support of the counterclaim that Paul has just made. So a protasis and apodosis should at some point become apparent. But the sentence lacks a main verb, with the only verb supplied overtly operating in a relative clause. We can make some interpretative progress by assuming an ellipse of the same verb in the subsequent clause (δικαιώσει), at which point we must consider the words εἰς ὁ θεός, which must have *something* to do with the sentence's subject. It is possible to construe the rest of the sentence reading εἷς ὁ θεὸς simply as the sentence's subject, as an arthrous substantive construction, "one" functioning adjectivally — "the one

God." This produces the following reading: "If indeed the one God, who will deliver the circumcision 'through fidelity,' will also deliver the uncircumcision through that fidelity . . ." (DC). But this is an awkward construal. The deliverance of the Jews, spoken of in the relative clause, seems almost parenthetical, and the sentence as a whole does not respond very satisfactorily to the claim that Paul has just made concerning God's concern for the pagans as well as for Jews. It is not an impossible reading, because it does respond in some sense, but it is weak and redundant. "If God does in fact deliver the pagans 'through fidelity' [i.e., through Christ] then he is indeed the God of the pagan nations as well as the God of the Jews." Indeed, a complete conditional statement is never supplied, Paul's wording trailing off in what amounts to an extended protasis that seems to frame the preceding statement as the apodosis!

However, if an elided ἐστιν is supplied to the initial monotheistic claim then the entire sentence makes perfect sense, as a full-blooded conditional, and functions smoothly in its argumentative context.

εἴπερ εἷς [ἐστὶν] ὁ θεὸς
ὃς δικαιώσει περιτομὴν ἐκ πίστεως
καὶ [δικαιώσει] ἀκροβυστίαν διὰ τῆς πίστεως.

The actual argument rests on two initial predications of God that then justify the final claim that the uncircumcised will "also" be delivered διὰ τῆς πίστεως (and this seems clearly to be an additive use of καί; see v. 29 *twice* just previously, i.e., B[3] and A[4]). *If* God is one, or unified — the God, that is, who will deliver the circumcised "through fidelity" — *then* it follows in a certain sense that he will also deliver the uncircumcised "through that fidelity." Indeed, the point seems neatly made, and good reasons would have to be supplied for departing from this reading.[13] If God is unified, then, on one level, we would expect consistent, unified action from him, and so he could act consistently to save both Jews and converted pagans in the same basic manner. A satisfactory account of this difficult statement does consequently seem possible.

It remains only to note that Paul's use of πίστις here echoes Habakkuk 2:4 and so seems to continue a probable christocentric argument. Paul believes that the pagans are being delivered, as well as the Jews, because of the Christ event and its consequences.[14] The subsequent use of an arthrous πίστις phrase then accords perfectly with our earlier observations about the function of the article made in relation to 3:25; it resumes the earlier πίστις phrase, which is itself anarthrous, because it is reproducing an anarthrous scriptural text (i.e., ἐκ πίστεως). Paul's christocentric signals here are entirely consistent.

Paul seems, then, by the end of v. 30, to have briefly repudiated the Teacher's assertion in A[3] that salvation by the Jewish God should be limited to Jews. The criticism of the implication in Paul's teaching that non-Jews can now be saved in some independence from Jews and Judaism is not surprising. But Paul basically asserts that the Christ event has simply accomplished as much, and that the one God is allowed to act in this way if he chooses (i.e., as sovereign) — claims that are elaborated on much more fully in Romans 9. So the Teacher moves quickly on to another issue, although it is related.

Paul's gospel of πίστις seems to undercut his own extensive emphasis on the Torah and its prescriptions (resuming here the concern intimated in v. 27 and A²). It seems, in short, to invalidate Torah. Moreover, again this seems a fair retort. A central emphasis on the Christ event and the process of fidelity does displace the Torah from that position. But Paul responds vigorously that his teaching of πίστις upholds or establishes Torah.

In fact, Paul has exploited an ambiguity at this point once again. The Teacher's concern is that Paul's gospel of πίστις completely undercuts law observance (see 3:27), and in this sense the Scripture as a whole that attests to it, both these things being "laws." Paul does not deny this (because he can't), but he does claim that his gospel of "πίστις" in fact upholds the Torah. It does not uphold it in the same sense as the Teacher does, but it does uphold it in a particular way. And with this judgment we come to 4:1.

Most interpreters introduce a significant break in the argument here, but stylistically there is no need to, as Stowers has pointed out. Doubtless the original Roman Christian auditors simply continued to be swept along in the diatribe's heated exchanges. Moreover, it is the Teacher's turn to speak again, and he does not seem entirely convinced by Paul's terse rejections that have just taken place. Indeed, he seems to appeal here to an authoritative witness from the Torah in support of his claims over against those of Paul — to Abraham, "our forefather according to the flesh." We ought to infer, then, that the questions of law observance versus fidelity (vv. 27-28), pagan exclusion or inclusion (vv. 29-30), and evisceration versus support of the Torah (v. 31) are about to be explored again, presumably to be settled decisively by this appeal to Abraham.

It seems likely that the Teacher would appeal to Abraham (and doubtless with a degree of confidence). Abraham was the pagan proselyte par excellence — as well as the father of Judaism — and therefore established from the Torah itself just what was and was not acceptable. It is consequently hard to imagine a Jewish Christian evangelist like the Teacher, who promoted circumcision and law observance to pagans, overlooking this figure. Abraham, especially as narrated by contemporary Jewish exegetes, supported his position.[15] Paul, of course, would not be advantaged by any such appeal, and so he does not seem to make much of it outside his debates with the Teacher. However, he does not duck this fight here, trying to wrest the interpretation of Abraham over to his side of the debate, even as he has fought to bring over other key terms from the Teacher's gospel.[16] If he does not do so, he will concede a powerful example to his opponent and will also admit that the witness of Torah itself does not support his position — a potentially fatal admission if his auditors venerate the Torah. But if he can win this particular exchange, he will reverse a key strength in the Teacher's argument and also lay claim to a positive witness from the Pentateuch to his own position. He has of course chosen his ground very carefully in order to try to make his stand, because the terrain is not generally favorable to him.[17] However, the false expectations of Justification theory can again interpose an interpretative stumbling block at this point.

Conventional readers and advocates of Justification theory expect Paul to attest positively here to his gospel of salvation through faith alone, a salvation understood, moreover, largely in individualist, rationalistic, and introspective terms. Abraham is supposedly the quintessential believer and corresponds not merely to Paul but to the interpreter. It is his journey — to a degree — that the trajectory through works of law to faith in Romans 1–4 has been tracing out, because this is the generic journey that we must all undertake. Hence, it is generally assumed that Paul's question in 4:1 (because it is of course assumed to be Paul who is speaking throughout Romans) asks what Abraham himself "discovered" (NIV) or "gained" (NRSV). These are the obvious orientation and sense to supply at this point, and they do no violence to Paul's grammar, which can be understood in this fashion (i.e., with the accusative "Abraham" understood as the subject of the infinitive, and the following material understood merely to be qualifying him adjectively — τί οὖν ἐροῦμεν εὑρηκέναι Ἀβραὰμ τὸν προπάτορα ἡμῶν κατὰ σάρκα).

But we are presently approaching this text with significantly different assumptions, expecting — along with the Roman auditors — the Teacher to be making some rejoinder to Paul. (Paul could be supporting his bold assertion in v. 31 here with a slightly longer statement, as he does in vv. B² and B⁴, but the short query that initiates 4:1, τί οὖν ἐροῦμεν, suggests, in typical diatribal fashion, a change in direction. And this change also supplies the best sense for what follows.) The Teacher has just been encoded, *twice,* as an advocate of Torah. An appeal *to* Torah, then, is almost to be expected. Moreover, that attestation will presumably not be restricted to the principle of πίστις alone but will range across at least the three related but distinguishable concerns that the Teacher has just reintroduced in 3:27-31 — the teaching of the Pentateuch concerning works as against πίστις and the consequent right to boasting or glorying, the exclusion or not of the uncircumcised from the Jewish God's concern, and the witness of the Pentateuch (i.e., whether Paul's appeals to the Torah are legitimate, either eviscerating or affirming it). And given these diverse concerns, the witness of Abraham cannot be limited to his own introspective journey — his trajectory to faith. This would be to read him as relating to only one of these issues, the first. It is best, then, not to read 4:1 as indicating Abraham's personal journey, which would so limit his relevance (although in accordance with the concerns of Justification theory), but to read it in the contested setting of Rome as indicating what "we" find out about the authoritative witness of Abraham in relation to all these issues, meaning in particular the Roman Christian audience as tutored by both Paul and the Teacher.

In short, the absence of illegitimate pressure from Justification theory, the continuation of the immediate concerns of the diatribe (which began in 3:27), and the introduction into the text of the dramatic exchanges currently taking place between Paul and the Teacher all point toward the basic rectitude of Richard Hays's elegant reconstrual of Romans 4:1, which we might paraphrase, "What then shall we say that *we* have found out[18] in relation to Abraham, 'our forefather according to the flesh'?"[19] (In Greek, with the proposed ellipses resupplied, the text reads, τί οὖν ἐροῦμεν ἡμᾶς εὑρηκέναι Ἀβραὰμ τὸν προπάτορα ἡμῶν κατὰ σάρκα; the helpful first person plural pronoun was probably omitted both in the interest of stylistic brevity — because of the diatribe — and to eliminate a clumsy redundancy in the sentence's subject.) A probable explanation of the curious infinitive construction also now lies just to hand.

Paul is constructing a dialogue in 3:27–4:1 but drops at this point into indirect discourse.[20] Normally, this would be signaled in both Paul and the rest of the New Testament by a ὅτι construction; however, participles and infinitives[21] — which harked back to more classical usage — could also be used, and this seems to be the case here[22] (hence my supply of a translation just above in terms of indirect discourse, using an English "that").[23] And it is worth recalling that Paul makes exactly the same shift into indirect discourse in the diatribe of 3:1-9a toward its end, at 3:8 (although he uses a ὅτι construction there).

In sum, 4:1 introduces Abraham as a star witness from the Pentateuch in relation to the three issues just enumerated by the Teacher over against Paul's gospel as that was proclaimed summarily in 3:21-26 (and I will suggest shortly that a fourth issue has also been stealthily insinuated here). Furthermore, in the programmatic claims that began that earlier pericope, Paul did state that this was just what he intended to do in more general argumentative terms; the disclosure of God's righteous saving act in the faithful Christ is "apart from (works of) law" — and hence from the Torah construed in that sense — but "attested to by *the Law and the Prophets*" (see 3:21-22). And it is of course this particular block of Jewish Scripture that poses the deepest challenge to Paul's account. He has already marshaled plenty of prophetic support for his gospel by the time he reaches 3:21, and even more will be forthcoming through the rest of the letter — at times a veritable flood. But a witness from the Pentateuch itself is a different matter. Hence, only here, in Romans 4, does Paul try to deploy a pentateuchal text positively, in direct support of his own gospel, in broader engagement with the Teacher. (Leviticus 18:5 will be introduced later, as a negative characterization of the Teacher's gospel; texts from Deuteronomy will also be alluded to then, although heavily reinterpreted.) So Paul's unusual appeal in 3:21 to the witness of Torah seems entirely deliberate; it anticipates the agenda that begins to unfold explicitly in 4:1.

But it is important to appreciate as well that it is the Teacher's voice that introduces this challenge in 4:1: "What then shall we say that we have found in relation to Abraham . . . ?" We have already seen that there are good reasons for thinking that the Teacher appealed to the figure of Abraham in his own system. So Paul cleverly seems to let the Teacher bring this ostensible key witness forward himself. And it will of course turn out to be a characteristically foolish gambit; the Teacher, by 4:16, will be hoisted by his own scriptural petard. But this ascription of voice in the text draws v. 2a into the Teacher's side of the argument as well, thereby resolving another nagging difficulty in the unfolding text — the odd shift in direction that takes place in v. 2.

Verse 2a makes the Teacher's claim on behalf of Abraham, a figure attested to by Torah: "For if Abraham was declared righteous by [his] works, then he had a boast" — and the Teacher's claims of 3:27 would then be vindicated. This statement consequently deploys Abraham on the opponent's side of the argument, introducing him in explicit illustration of the first set of protests that were made in 3:27-28 — that an eschatological declaration of "righteous" is based on merit and deeds, thereby facilitating boasting. However, Paul contradicts this claim with a counterassertion and then immediately appeals to a reading of Genesis 15:6, his chosen text in relation to Abraham: "But not before God! For what does the scripture say . . . ?" With this appeal to the text, a much longer, discursive discussion begins. And it is important to grasp a moment of outstanding stylistic craft from just this point in the letter.

It turns out that Romans 4:2b-22 corresponds *directly* to the three issues that have just been articulated by 3:27-31, with the final phase in the argument pivoting (in v. 16b) to include an integrated discussion of a fourth, related issue that was hinted at in 4:1.[24] So beginning in 4:2b Paul takes up seriatim the three concerns just introduced and systematically refutes them in relation to Abraham (although only as the patriarch is described by Genesis 15:6!). And each discrete refutation is marked off from its neighbors by the resumption of just the terms that the Teacher and Paul have already used, assisted by their absence from the surrounding material. Thus, the diatribe of 3:27–4:1 turns out to be not merely juxtaposing rapidly the Teacher's main concerns with Paul's — the Teacher's having been introduced in 1:18–3:20 and Paul's more briefly in 1:16-17 and 3:21-26 — but introducing an agenda for a detailed comparative evaluation with respect to the Pentateuch and the authoritative figure of Abraham. Furthermore, Paul now speaks continuously, explicating the text to refute the various contentions of the Teacher decisively.

§3. The Structure of Romans 3:27–4:16a

I am suggesting that 4:2b-22 resumes explicitly a fourfold argumentative agenda introduced diatribally by Paul in 3:27–4:1, an agenda identified principally by the marked resumptions and cessations in Paul's use of various distinctive terms. In the present section and the next, we will examine the first three argumentative subunits: 4:2-8, which resumes the concerns of 3:27-28; 4:9-12, which resumes 3:29-30; and 4:13-16a, which resumes 3:31. (The fourth phase is something of a special case and so will receive its own detailed treatment later, in §5.) It will be clearest to note first the evidence for these overarching correlations; after this, in §4, we will discuss them individually and in more detail.

Two motifs are present throughout the entire discussion, namely, πιστ- and δικαιο- terms (there are twenty-one occurrences of πιστ- terms — fifteen of the noun and six of the verb — and thirteen occurrences of δικαιο- terms — eight of the noun, four of the verb, and one of the rare δικαίωσις). And this should not be surprising. Paul addresses all the issues that have been raised here in terms of Abraham and Genesis 15:6, a text that basically supplies this terminology (and that also shares cognates with other key texts like Habakkuk 2:4).[25] Hence, the most important evidence concerning our suggested correlations derives from identifying the more distinctive motifs involved in each specific phase of discussion — the motifs supplied by the Teacher. Once they are foregrounded, these distinctive thematic and terminological correlations and their subtle expansions are quite striking.

3 [27]Ποῦ οὖν **ἡ καύχησις**; ἐξεκλείσθη. διὰ ποίου
νόμου; **τῶν ἔργων**; οὐχί, ἀλλὰ διὰ *νόμου* πίστεως.
[28]λογιζόμεθα γὰρ δικαιοῦσθαι πίστει ἄνθρωπον
χωρὶς **ἔργων νόμου**.

4 [2]εἰ γὰρ Ἀβραὰμ **ἐξ ἔργων** ἐδικαιώθη, ἔχει **καύχημα**, ἀλλ᾽ οὐ πρὸς θεόν. [3]τί γὰρ *ἡ γραφὴ λέγει; ἐπίστευσεν δὲ Ἀβραὰμ τῷ θεῷ καὶ ἐλογίσθη αὐτῷ εἰς δικαιοσύνην*. [4]*τῷ* δὲ **ἐργαζομένῳ** ὁ μισθὸς οὐ λογίζεται κατὰ χάριν ἀλλὰ κατὰ ὀφείλημα, [5]*τῷ* δὲ μὴ **ἐργαζομένῳ** πιστεύοντι δὲ ἐπὶ τὸν δικαιοῦντα τὸν ἀσεβῆ λογίζεται ἡ πίστις αὐτοῦ εἰς δικαιοσύνην· [6]καθάπερ καὶ *Δαυὶδ λέγει* τὸν μακαρισμὸν τοῦ ἀνθρώπου ᾧ ὁ θεὸς λογίζεται δικαιοσύνην **χωρὶς ἔργων**· [7]*μακάριοι ὧν ἀφέθησαν αἱ ἀνομίαι καὶ ὧν ἐπεκαλύφθησαν αἱ ἁμαρτίαι· [8]μακάριος ἀνὴρ οὗ οὐ μὴ λογίσηται κύριος ἁμαρτίαν*.

3 [29]ἢ Ἰουδαίων ὁ θεὸς μόνον; οὐχὶ καὶ ἐθνῶν; ναὶ
καὶ ἐθνῶν, [30]εἴπερ εἷς ὁ θεὸς ὃς δικαιώσει
περιτομὴν ἐκ πίστεως καὶ *ἀκροβυστίαν* διὰ τῆς
πίστεως.

4 [9]Ὁ μακαρισμὸς οὖν οὗτος ἐπὶ *τὴν περιτομὴν* ἢ καὶ ἐπὶ *τὴν ἀκροβυστίαν*; λέγομεν γὰρ ἐλογίσθη τῷ Ἀβραὰμ ἡ πίστις εἰς δικαιοσύνην. [10]πῶς οὖν ἐλογίσθη; ἐν *περιτομῇ* ὄντι ἢ ἐν *ἀκροβυστίᾳ*; οὐκ ἐν *περιτομῇ* ἀλλ᾽ ἐν *ἀκροβυστίᾳ*· [11]καὶ σημεῖον ἔλαβεν *περιτομῆς* σφραγῖδα τῆς δικαιοσύνης τῆς πίστεως τῆς ἐν τῇ *ἀκροβυστίᾳ*, εἰς τὸ εἶναι αὐτὸν πατέρα πάντων τῶν πιστευόντων δι᾽ *ἀκροβυστίας*, εἰς τὸ λογισθῆναι [καὶ] αὐτοῖς [τὴν] δικαιοσύνην, [12]καὶ πατέρα *περιτομῆς* τοῖς οὐκ ἐκ περιτομῆς μόνον ἀλλὰ καὶ τοῖς στοιχοῦσιν τοῖς ἴχνεσιν τῆς ἐν *ἀκροβυστίᾳ* πίστεως τοῦ πατρὸς ἡμῶν Ἀβραάμ.

3 [31]νόμον οὖν **καταργοῦμεν** διὰ τῆς πίστεως; μὴ
γένοιτο· ἀλλὰ νόμον **ἱστάνομεν**.

4^{13}Οὐ γὰρ διὰ νόμου ἡ ἐπαγγελία τῷ Ἀβραὰμ ἢ τῷ σπέρματι αὐτοῦ, τὸ κληρονόμον αὐτὸν εἶναι κόσμου, ἀλλὰ διὰ δικαιοσύνης πίστεως. ^{14}εἰ γὰρ οἱ ἐκ νόμου κληρονόμοι, **κεκένωται** ἡ πίστις καὶ **κατήργηται** ἡ ἐπαγγελία· ^{15}ὁ γὰρ νόμος ὀργὴν κατεργάζεται· οὗ δὲ οὐκ ἔστιν νόμος οὐδὲ παράβασις. ^{16}διὰ τοῦτο ἐκ πίστεως, ἵνα κατὰ χάριν, **εἰς τὸ εἶναι βεβαίαν** τὴν ἐπαγγελίαν παντὶ τῷ σπέρματι, οὐ τῷ ἐκ τοῦ νόμου μόνον ἀλλὰ καὶ τῷ ἐκ πίστεως Ἀβραάμ ὅς ἐστιν πατὴρ πάντων ἡμῶν, κ.τ.λ.

3.1. Romans 3:27-28 and 4:2-8

There are no fewer than three motifs peculiar to 3:27-28 and 4:2-8 — boasting, works, and a mutually applicable notion of νόμος (that is, a notion applicable *both* to works and to πίστις; see, in addition to 3:31, other unusual but different senses in 13:8 and 10, and Gal. 5:14, also Gal. 6:2).[26] Boasting is introduced in 3:27 and reprised in 4:2, a verse that also resumes the motif of works, which is introduced in 3:27 and 28 and not elsewhere in the diatribe. (These two notions are closely linked within the Teacher's system: see 2:17-24.) So 4:2a signals the uptake of these two motifs from 3:27-28 quite clearly, grounding both on the verb used in 3:28, δικαιόω. And works turn out to be the central concern of the subsection, being referred to three more times, and elaborated in some detail in v. 4. Indeed, in juxtaposition to πίστις and under the overarching consideration of scriptural texts, it dominates the short discussion. Significantly, however, boasting and works disappear completely after this point; they occur nowhere else in Romans 4 or prior to it in 3:29–4:1.

The uptake of the third specific motif — νόμος as applied both to works and to πίστις — is much debated, but I have already suggested that Paul means by this unusual wordplay in 3:27 the testimony or teaching of Torah; this meaning could apply equally to "works" and πίστις.[27] The signifier νόμος has been used earlier in this sense in Romans (see especially 2:17-23), and *torah* is doubtless part of the Teacher's system. Hence, it seems significant that just this sense of νόμος is taken up by 4:2-8, specifically by 4:3 *and* 4:7-8, where the testimony of Scripture in the sense of an authoritative teaching is introduced explicitly as Paul states, τί γὰρ ἡ γραφὴ λέγει and, later, καὶ Δαυὶδ λέγει, following these formulae with scriptural quotations (Gen. 15:6 and Ps. 32:1-2). In fact, nowhere else in Romans 4 does Paul either signal the introduction of Scripture so prominently or combine two scriptural texts in this positive fashion, in full, to address a single point.[28] Thus, it seems likely that 4:2-8 also resumes the third unique motif in 3:27-28 — νόμος — understanding it as some authoritative teaching of Jewish Scripture. The subsection's argument confirms these stylistic hints. But doubtless many would grant this correlation between 3:27-28 and 4:2-8 in any case, because v. 28 is widely believed to be the programmatic announcement of Justification theory,[29] and 4:2-8 its definitive elaboration. These linkages are well known. The key point, then, is to observe that although certain motifs are retained, this particular argument and set of concerns do not in fact continue past 4:8. Another set takes its place that does not so much follow on from this initial cluster of issues as activate a related but distinguishable component within the Teacher's system — circumcision.[30]

3.2. Romans 3:29-30 and 4:9-12

The only motifs continued in 4:9-12 from vv. 2-8 are δικαιοσύνη (and the closely associated μακαρισμός, with three and one instance(s) respectively; δικαιόω is not used), and πίστις (with three instances in addition to one cognate participle), accompanied by a repeated use of λογίζομαι (three instances also) — all terms essentially supplied by Genesis 15:6 itself, which is cited here slightly differently. And just as the contrasting motifs of boasting, "works," and competing scriptural attestation have faded, two new motifs in another antinomy suddenly dominate the argument, *both of which were specifically signaled by 3:29-30.* That earlier subsection spoke of "Jew and pagan" and περιτομή καὶ ἀκροβυστία. There is no discussion of "Jew and pagan" in 4:9-12, but both terms of the second antinomy, περιτομή καὶ ἀκροβυστία occur no fewer than six times each in this subsection — and nowhere else in Romans 4 (and of course nowhere in 3:27-31 outside v. 30). Thus, the stylistic signals here seem unmistakable.

Corresponding to the stylistic shift is an argumentative shift. We are no longer considering whether Abraham boasted before God because of a meritocratic accumulation of works (to which Paul has already answered negatively in favor of a looser system of transfer), but the discussion now focuses on the precise temporal point at which Abraham was gifted δικαιοσύνη by God. Moreover, as in 4:2-8 with its details concerning works, the concerns of the subsection are signaled not merely by the high statistical profile of certain new motifs but also by their syntactical elaboration and the presence of rarer terms in relation to them. So Paul says here καὶ σημεῖον ἔλαβεν περιτομῆς σφραγίδα τῆς δικαιοσύνης τῆς πίστεως (κ.τ.λ.); circumcision is a "sign" and "seal" of a state already existent.[31] Hence, the key principle Paul wishes to negate, present within the subsection in a statistically prominent way, is also characterized in terms of a more unusual (and subordinating) motif. The demarcations in the argument are again very clear. And this clarity continues as a third phase begins, corresponding to a third issue raised in the preceding diatribe by the Teacher.

3.3. Romans 3:31 and 4:13-16a

Romans 3:31 asked whether πίστις negated Torah (continuing here the reading of νόμος that the argument seems to have suggested). And the motif of abolition, suggested by the verb καταργέω in 3:31, is reprised exactly once in the corresponding section of Romans 4, and nowhere else, while the similar κενόω is used there once as well, and nowhere else. Moreover, probably corresponding to ἱστάνομεν, the countervailing verb of establishment used in 3:31, is the closely related phrase . . . εἰς τὸ εἶναι βεβαίαν in 4:16 (again, its only occurrence in Romans 4; see elsewhere in Romans only 15:8). These instances are admittedly not as statistically dense as the key motifs in the preceding two phases of the argument — perhaps because this subsection is considerably shorter — but they are present and they are as distinctive in terms of the adjacent discussion. And once again, the subsection possesses other related but distinctive motifs as well.

The motif of promise, ἡ ἐπαγγελία, is confined largely to this particular subsection. There are no instances of ἡ ἐπαγγελία up to v. 13, but then it occurs in vv. 13, 14, and 16. (It recurs again within the chapter only in v. 20, the cognate verb occurring in v. 21, although in different syntactical combinations.) This distribution is echoed by that of ὁ κληρονόμος, which occurs in this subsection twice in a clear and close relation to "promise," but nowhere else in Romans 4. So once again small, unique details seem to assist the main point of the subsection, thereby marking it off from its surroundings. Indeed, this subsection and its anticipatory announcement seem to continue exactly the structural and argumentative dynamics that we have already observed for 3:27-28 in relation to 4:2-8 and 3:29-30 in relation to 4:9-12. We will merely have to consider in due course whether those dynamics extend through 4:22, or whether additional concerns have been introduced prior to that point.[32]

§4. Substantive Engagement in Romans 3:27–4:16a

It is now possible to recognize Romans 4:2-16a as an engagement by Paul with three different aspects of the Teacher's gospel. Contrary to his strategy in 1:18–3:20, however, Paul's approach here is scriptural and comparative — a σύγκρισις. There he attacked the Teacher's gospel in terms of its own assumptions (entailing a statement of those assumptions at the outset — helpful and perhaps necessary for his Roman Christian auditors, but potentially confusing for later readers, once the original performative signals have been lost). In Romans 4 he refutes it with Scripture, seeking at the same time to establish his own position by way of contrast. Precisely the same issues are evident here as there; they are just being attacked from a slightly different angle.

It is worth recalling that this attack has been cleverly framed in terms that partly resume that earlier strategy. In a dialogue beginning in 3:27 the Teacher himself has reintroduced some of his own soteriological principles, apparently by way of protest against Paul's axiom stated in 3:21-26 of salvation through πίστις. And now he has appealed to the witness of Torah, and specifically to the witness of Abraham, in 4:1 (he is, after all, a Jewish Teacher). So Paul in effect takes up this challenge that is internal to the Teacher's system and proceeds to turn it upon him by exploiting the possibilities provided by Genesis 15:6. The Teacher's specific stated concerns are all recognizable elements within his own program. He has queried (doubtless sharply) why a meritorious observance of deeds prescribed by the law, along with any appropriate associated boasting, has been "excluded." He has also challenged Paul to explain how the God of the Jews is now saving pagans, apparently having thereby abrogated the boundary between them of circumcision (presumably along with much that that boundary implies). Paul's continued affirmation that this is indeed the case has prompted the understandable rejoinder that this new system of πίστις effectively eviscerates Torah — an implication that Paul has strenuously denied. So at this point the Teacher has appealed to Abraham, presumably confident that works and the associated boasting, together with the need for circumcision, can be attested by the patriarch authoritatively in Torah, and he begins by recalling the issue of works in 4:2a. (He also possibly makes this appeal in a rather pregnant fashion, describing Abraham as "our forefather according to the flesh.") Paul accepts this challenge in 4:2b, framing the discussion immediately in terms of Genesis 15:6. And he will now work through these three issues in turn, in phases that are neatly demarcated by both stylistic and substantive signals.

4.1. Romans 3:27-28 and 4:2-8

I do not disagree with the conventional reading of 4:2-8, although I will resist some of its overstatements, and will also attempt to show how an approach to this argument with a debate between Paul and the Teacher in mind does clarify some of the apostle's statements still further. The conventional reading of this text is in my view basically accurate (as indeed is its construal of the text itself of most of Romans 1-4; it is the overarching argumentative arrangement of that material that is in my view less plausible).

A more precise grasp of Paul's argument in 4:2-8 will be attainable only if λογίζομαι, which occurs in Genesis 15:6b, is interpreted correctly (LXX: ἐπίστευσεν καὶ Ἀβρὰμ τῷ θεῷ καὶ ἐλογίσθη αὐτῷ εἰς δικαιοσύνην). Although this verb could suggest a process of "viewing," and Paul himself tends to use it in this sense outside this pericope,[33] there can be no doubt that he is interpreting it in its more concrete, commercial sense here — the sense of "credit."[34] That notion of crediting should, moreover, be understood in terms of an ancient, not a modern, economy.

Credit in a modern economy suggests a payment of money whose use is in effect rented from the lender. At some point it must be paid back. Most importantly, credit in a modern banking system, once granted, is paid almost instantaneously. By contrast, credit in an ancient economy — as Paul's subsequent argument makes clear — is more akin to the modern notion of a check (non-U.S. English "cheque"), which is in effect little more than a "letter of credit." Money is promised to the recipient of the check and is now *in effect* his or hers, but the money itself *has not yet been paid.*[35] This basic type of commercial usage for the notion of "credit" holds the possibility of a nonmeritocratic deployment as well. A check is *ordinarily* paid to someone who has earned the money that it promises. But it need not be. A check can also be a gift — the promise of money paid gratuitously (perhaps to a penurious son or daughter). And it is this semantic possibility that the text of Genesis 15:6 allows Paul to exploit.

We should note first that Paul is quite explicit in 4:3-8 that λογίζομαι suggests some notion of credit; he is using it in its specific mercantile sense. In v. 4 he defines someone who works, earning his[36] wages and therefore receiving them in accordance with "obligation," not "grace" (τῷ δὲ ἐγραζομένῳ ὁ μισθὸς οὐ λογίζεται κατὰ χάριν ἀλλὰ κατὰ ὀφείλημα). The actual verb used to denote this process of payment is of course λογίζομαι, and it *must* take the sense here of "credit." (Workers do not have their wages "viewed" in accordance with obligation.) This commercial sense is then reinforced by Paul's quotation of Psalm 32:1-2a (LXX 31:1-2a) in vv. 7-8, which speak of the blessing of the person "to whom the Lord will not credit sin" (μακάριος ἀνὴρ οὗ οὐ μὴ λογίσηται κύριος ἁμαρτίαν).[37] It is difficult if not impossible to account for the accusative ἁμαρτίαν here if the verb is read as "viewed" (and this reading would also have to override the implications of v. 7 [Ps. 32:1], where various transgressions and sins have been "released" and "covered"). So Paul is clearly using a broadly commercial reading of the verb (and even if that violates the Jewish scriptural antecedents). However, the Teacher is unlikely to protest against this reading, because he shares it; his system is fundamentally meritocratic, and he certainly expects God to "repay" the righteous for their deeds on the day of judgment with glory and eternal life. It is in precisely this sense that they will earn it, by working for it. Paul's telling argumentative move comes not from the meaning of this verb but from the first clause in Genesis 15:6 that effectively qualifies its operation: ἐπίστευσεν δὲ Ἀβραὰμ τῷ θεῷ.

It is this correlation that allows Paul to claim — at this point rather obviously — that God is *not* apparently behaving in a meritocratic way toward Abraham but is "paying" him something in response merely to "trust." As Paul goes on to point out in vv. 4-5, "workers" are not paid simply because they trust in the payer! This is an absurd notion. But God, according to Genesis 15:6, does pay someone here who merely "trusts" and has not yet "earned" or "worked." And such a God can therefore pay things to the outright ungodly as well. Abraham, and then David's psalm, attest to just this behavior by the divine sovereign — some sort of gift or payment that is clearly not in response to merit. These texts specifically disavow the notion of merit as the basis of God's action — which would create a forensic-retributive relationship — correlating that act, rather, with "trust" (at least in the case of Genesis 15:6).

We will postpone a detailed consideration of the meaning of δικαιοσύνη in Paul's localized argument until we address 4:16a-22, where this motif is dramatically embellished. Suffice it for now to note that it makes perfect sense for Paul to claim here that some righteous saving act by God, the divine King, is being spoken of.[38] It is very important to appreciate in addition, however, that Paul is not suggesting in this argument that God "views" either Abraham or the blessed person of Psalm 32 (31 LXX) *as* righteous because that nature has somehow been "credited" or transferred to them (which would involve an unjustified reading of the verb, and a *double usage* in context). This is to confuse Paul's argument unnecessarily, introducing a notion that is not there. The verb is consistently taking the sense of "credit" in this pericope, so something is being given (or promised) concretely to these trusting figures for the future — something presumably effected in and by God's resurrecting act of δικαιοσύνη. So the all-important text of Genesis 15:6 is best translated, "Abraham trusted in God, and it [i.e., his trust[39]] was credited to his advantage[40] *with* δικαιοσύνη." The expression εἰς δικαιοσύνην is consequently a Semitism that overlies a simple accusative, as BDAG points out, and Paul even uses that simpler equivalent construction in v. 6 to denote the thing that is being credited: καθάπερ καὶ Δαυὶδ λέγει τὸν μακαρισμὸν τοῦ ἀνθρώπου ᾧ ὁ θεὸς λογίζεται δικαιοσύνην. (Consequently, the NRSV and NIV lead their readers astray by translating this phrase consistently ". . . as righteousness." It is, furthermore, difficult for εἰς δικαιοσύνην actually to mean this, i.e., for εἰς to mean "as."[41])

And this is the appropriate point at which to revisit a puzzling set of underdeterminations noted in part three, chapter eleven, arguably to resolve them. It has always been embarrassing for the advocate of Justification that Abraham does not recapitulate any journey from works, and the consequent realization of sin, to faith, as that theory demands. The purchase that Romans 4:2-8 ostensibly supplies for that progression turns out to evaporate on closer examination, leaving the theory painfully underdetermined by the text at this point (and a key text at that!). But we can now see why these putative absences characterize the text. In the context of a debate between the Teacher and Paul there is only a simple opposition — two colliding opinions of what Abraham signifies, one of which is right and the other wrong. Moreover, Abraham is basically virtuous, heroic, and authoritative for both camps, so there is no need to establish any prior journey through works to sinfulness (and indeed this would be counterproductive). The "absences" from Paul's argument exist because Paul was not in fact arguing in terms of Justification theory (in support of which the text falls short). When the debate between the Teacher and Paul is recognized, the text says exactly what we would expect it to.[42]

In sum, Paul interprets the Genesis text, not entirely unfairly, to suggest that in view of Abraham's trust God promised to do something for him in the future; a divine check was written to the patriarch that in this case had clearly not been worked for or earned.[43] Something was merely promised to him. And this is a devastating blow to the Teacher's system, provided that we accept the hermeneutical rules that facilitate it — and almost certainly Paul, the Teacher, and many Roman Christian auditors did. This text from the Torah suggests that God does not act salvifically in relation to merit created by works and so supports Paul's earlier exclusion of meritorious achievement and boasting, along with his counterassertion of the relevance of "trust" (see 3:27). With this refutation effected, Paul turns to the next point that the Teacher raised — the question of circumcision.

4.2. *Romans 3:29-30 and 4:9-12*

The covenant of circumcision is traced by pious Jews back to Abraham himself, as described by Genesis 17. Abraham received a reiterated set of divine promises and blessings at that time for him and all his descendents. His biological ancestry is then attested overtly and ritually through the circumcision of all Jewish-born males on the eighth day after their birth. Hence, it seems inappropriate in several fundamental respects to suggest, as Paul does, that God is delivering those promised blessings to people who are not involved in this ancestry and marked in this way (in the case of the men).

But Paul thinks that he can wriggle out of this challenge that was made explicit in 3:29-30. In Romans 4:9-12 he makes the simple argument that δικαιοσύνη was promised by God to Abraham in relation to his trust, as attested by Genesis 15:6, and that this short narrative unfolded well in advance of the covenant of circumcision, which was established later, in Genesis 17. And to deny this point is difficult, since it would undermine both the efficacy of God's promise and the validity of Abraham's "salvation" from 15:6 onward, if not from the point of his call in Genesis 12.[44] This, then, has the fortunate result of allowing Abraham to prefigure both uncircumcised and circumcised trusters who will be gifted with δικαιοσύνη. It also facilitates the controversial redefinition of the "sign" of circumcision in terms of a mere "seal."

The former term seems to have been prompted — rather significantly — by the account of the covenant of circumcision given in Genesis 17 (see LXX v. 11: . . . καὶ ἔσται ἐν σημείῳ διαθήκης κ.τ.λ.).[45] Circumcision is a definite sign of involvement in the covenant people — the people of Abrahamic descent and divine blessing. But Paul qualifies this signifier in Romans 4:9-12 as a "seal" or "stamp."[46] A seal or stamp marked overtly on an item (or even a person) a state of ownership, possession, or identification, *confirming something that was already established on other grounds* (and this was effected usually by the prior exchange of money, but in the case of a letter, by composition). The "sign" of the covenant, then, according to Paul, has become instead a "stamp" signifying the presence of a prior and more fundamental state (that is, of a transaction or event that has already taken place), which Paul suggests is associated with πίστις on the grounds of the earlier situation of promise narrated by Genesis 15:6. Moreover, something need not necessarily *bear* a stamp to be owned or possessed by someone; the stamp, strictly speaking, is optional. So, in effect, trusting Jews bear their stamp of divine ownership overtly, while trusting pagans do not — something of a reversal of traditional Jewish expectations, but another legitimate argument in terms of the rules of the Jewish scriptural game current in Paul's day.[47] Hence, a smooth reading of this pericope seems entirely possible once it is located within the unfolding debate between Paul and the Teacher. And this reading simultaneously accounts for the embarrassing overdetermination that this text has previously generated for Justification advocates.

In part three, chapter eleven, it was noted that Romans 4:9-12 creates an argumentative anomaly for Justification theory by supplying a narrative, historical, and fundamentally temporal argument for the superiority of πίστις over works, when any such contention was actually invalid in terms of that theory (because it is irrelevant). Moreover, the correct argument is not hereby supplied — namely, that circumcision participates in a broader project of "works" that is doomed to implode soteriologically because of repeated transgression by sinful humans (and this was, technically, an underdetermination). But once again, the rereading being suggested here does not raise these expectations and so is not disappointed when they are not met. It gives a meaningful account of Paul's need to make this particular argument in this text: he is specifically refuting the Teacher's contention in relation to circumcision, and nothing more or less. A temporal refutation therefore works quite adequately. The boundary line distinguishing the saved from the unsaved must be redrawn around those who trust, as against around those who are circumcised (although Paul has yet to tell us in detail in Romans how such people come to trust; he can assume at this point that his audience does — see 1:5-8, 12; 6:17; 15:14).[48] And with this conclusion, Paul turns to the challenge of 3:31 that his principle of πίστις eviscerates Torah while, implicitly, the Teacher's torah of salvation through works affirms it.

4.3. Romans 3:31 and 4:13-16a

Paul deals with the Teacher's assertion about his system of πίστις negating Torah — at least in the first instance — very briefly. His case is made in vv. 13-14 and 16a, and it depends on connections that have already been established. (I will suggest that v. 15 is a parenthesis just below.) If it is indeed the case that God's δικαιοσύνη has been credited to Abraham in relation to his trust, as a ruthlessly consistent reading of Genesis 15:6 suggests, then it simply follows that any alternative mode of crediting would "negate" the initial arrangement and effectively "empty" that promise and text and activity. So, strictly speaking, an alternative arrangement — for example, based on law observance — would eviscerate the promise, and the maintenance of the arrangement serves to affirm or "establish" this text in the Torah. It is as simple as that, and so Paul himself does not labor the point.[49]

The simplicity and directness of this argument are what in part create the suspicion that v. 15 is a parenthesis. It does not seem to contribute directly to this contention but makes an alternative point that seems to have been noted already in parenthetic and cryptic terms (see 3:20b, 23) and will be discussed at much greater length later on (5:14, 20; 7:7–8.1). Paul makes an extensive argument in due course suggesting that law observance per se creates a situation that the power of Sin cannot but exploit, leading to the awakening of desire, and then to transgression, to God's displeasure, and ultimately to Death. In view of that later argument, this short set of statements can now *reverse* a number of propositions that the Teacher holds dear. The law itself thus *works* wrath (meaning presumably the wrath of God); it does not avoid it. Indeed, only in a situation where the law and its futile observance by human flesh have been eliminated do we find an absence of transgression, which should be set against the Teacher's claim that only where law observance *exists* do we find works and the absence of transgression. The realities, Paul cryptically avers, are just the converse.

And this all amounts to an additional and rather deeper reason for insisting that πίστις fulfills the law, whereas observance through "works" eviscerates it. Obedience is possible in Paul's view only in the new reality inaugurated by Christ and marked by πίστις. This fulfills the law's larger promise of life and indeed allows humanity to fulfill the commands of God (see 1 Cor. 7:19). Ongoing existence in present reality, however, which is implicit in the Teacher's system of "works," eviscerates the law by failing to address the powers that make obedience to it impossible. The results of this system can only be domination by Sin and Death generating sins, curse, and wrath in turn. And Paul alludes to this complex set of negative results rather cryptically by saying that "the law works wrath, . . . so only where there is no law is there no transgression." This verse is a neat anticipation of Paul's later argumentative contention in relation to Christian ethics. Moreover, we receive here a hint that the state characterized by πίστις is far more complex and powerful than an emphasis simply on πίστις itself might suggest if it is read in terms of an individual's decision! It somehow denotes a new reality — and presumably through involvement in the narrative of Christ.

And with this observation, one further, fascinating aspect of Romans 4:13-16a begins to emerge. This subsection supplies us with a series of further dramatic insights into the nature of God's act in terms of δικαιοσύνη. However, those insights are best considered in tandem with the evidence that becomes apparent in vv. 16b-22, so we will consider the argumentative function of those verses first and then return to this important semantic issue.

§5. Romans 4:16b-22

This subsection of Romans 4 has generally been neglected by the interpretative tradition, and understandably so. It is impossible to integrate with Justification theory; its account of trust in God as an extraordinarily difficult if not superhuman action looks extremely unrealistic as a manageable criterion for sinful humanity to exercise. To pass this text by, however, is to overlook the most extensive account of the nature of "faith" that can be found in the Pauline corpus! Doubtless, it should be a part of the discussion. But the argumentative function of 4:16b-22 is not immediately clear.

Why does Paul continue a sentence that he began in v. 16 (in response to the challenge of 3:31) with a tangled accumulation of clauses and phrases through v. 22? This is not a text with ritual echoes, like 3:24-26. Moreover, he seems to have responded appropriately to the three challenges of the Teacher already, as those were expressed by 3:27-31 and 4:1. So why does he include this extended and rather convoluted text? A consideration of the Teacher's broader position should help us detect a satisfactory — and rather interesting — answer to this question.

Paul is possibly arguing once again on two levels. On one level, 4:17-21 is nothing more than an extended account of the trust of Abraham. And it is described in heroic terms. Abraham does not waver in doubt but is fully convinced that God can do the impossible things that have been promised — bring life to Abraham's sterile, aged loins and to Sarah's equally sterile and aged womb. Indeed, Abraham is said to wax in trust, giving glory to God![50] In the light of this, it seems fair for Paul to imply that such πίστις does indeed establish and fulfill the law. Surely, this heroic narrative is the pinnacle of law observance. And if this were denied, would not a central narrative and virtue have been stripped from the Torah — a narrative of miraculous life?!

But there is something unsatisfying about this account. It is not unfair or irrelevant so much as inadequate. Paul has crafted a powerful, extended description of Abraham, one unparalleled in his writings, and Romans is not carelessly constructed. Construed merely in this fashion, his prose seems suddenly to veer toward rhetorical overkill. He seems to be hammering home a point repeatedly and even unnecessarily. Surely there is something else going on here.

Paul is suggesting what has just been outlined, but he is doing more than this. He is simultaneously anticipating and countering a potentially devastating rejoinder to the set of argumentative moves he has made in Romans 4:2-16a. Paul moves to block that rejoinder in vv. 16b-22. But in order to appreciate Paul's skill and his argumentative point, we must first recover certain features from this text that have usually been overlooked.

An important relative clause ends v. 16 and begins the long text that we are concerned with here, and it overtly reemphasizes Abraham's paternity: . . . Ἀβραάμ, ὅς ἐστιν πατὴρ πάντων ἡμῶν, thereby recalling both 4:1 and 4:11-12. I suggest that two aspects of Abraham's fatherhood are important for a complete understanding of Paul's argument. First, this fatherhood, like most fatherhood, is biological, and by extension, generative of kinship; hence, in Abraham's case fatherhood is focused on the conception of Isaac, a miraculous conception by means of which the family and nation of Israel subsequently came into being in fulfillment of God's original promises to the patriarch. And, second, the question of Abraham's fatherhood of Isaac, and thereby of Israel, is linked by the book of Genesis with the rite of circumcision, a connection established especially by Genesis 17. This link is quite problematic for Paul, as we will see shortly. But is Abraham's paternity in specific relation to Isaac's conception and birth actually a factor in Romans 4? Certainly, much commentary does not seem to emphasize it.[51] Put slightly differently, is Abraham's paternity — an explicit motif — being considered here in fundamentally realistic terms by Paul, as it was by many of his contemporaries?

The motif of fatherhood is admittedly not limited to this final argumentative phase in Romans 4. It occurs three times in the chapter's second subsection, in vv. 11 and 12 (2x), in addition to three times in the present subsection, in vv.

16b-18 (but not, it should be noted, in the third subsection). In all these cases it is Abraham's fatherhood "of us" that is important, that is, Paul is clearly concerned to extend the illustrious Jewish patriarch's paternity over his pagan converts in some sense (and the exact method of that extension should not be prematurely assumed). But while vv. 11-12 claim the paternity of Abraham over the uncircumcised and circumcised alike on the basis of Genesis 15:6, that section does not elaborate or prove the claim of fatherhood itself — merely, as we have seen, the legitimacy of God's δικαιοσύνη being given to someone in an uncircumcised state characterized only by πίστις. The motif receives no syntactical development there. Hence, I suspect that the motif's occurrences in vv. 11 and 12 only reiterate the claim laid to Abraham's appropriate "fatherhood" of pagans made by 4:1, although that Paul mentions this in the context of circumcision will ultimately prove significant. Verses 16b-22, however, grapple directly with the issue of Abraham's paternity ultimately of "us" pagan converts, and it is at this point that its concrete definition begins to become apparent.

As the well-known contexts of Genesis 15:6 and 17:5 suggest, Abraham's paternity was effected there through the miraculous conception and birth of Isaac to Sarah, events recounted in Genesis 21. This was the specific fulfillment of the earlier divine promises of blessing to him that were overtly connected, in typical tribal fashion, to progeny and thereby to multiple descendants, and to their inheritance of that staple of existence, land. (Abraham's promises in Genesis 12 and complaints in Genesis 15 were similarly oriented.) In the original Old Testament account, Isaac was therefore the first link in a biological and familial chain of paternity that would lead, through Jacob, to the nation of Israel, and beyond that somehow to the many nations. His conception and birth were the critical events that enabled the fulfillment of the promises made in Genesis 15:1-5 and 17:1-5 (as well as elsewhere). And the bulk of later Jewish consideration of Abraham — although often emphasizing different details in his story — assumes this pragmatic notion of fatherhood. He was the father of the nation in a literal sense. In view of this essentially invariable background material, I would suggest that the same traditional expectation of Abraham in Genesis that a son and heir would be born in accordance with God's promises in order to facilitate the blessing of many descendants — an expectation maintained by Abraham's later descendants, the Jews — is imprinted across Paul's narrative in Romans 4 as well (and after all, he assumes as much in Rom. 9:6-13!). Furthermore, good reasons would have to be supplied to depart from it. But the text indicates reasonably clearly that Paul continues to work within this traditional narrative.

In v. 17 Paul speaks of a God who can give life to the dead and who calls things that are not as though they are — ἐπίστευσεν θεοῦ τοῦ ζωοποιοῦντος τοὺς νεκροὺς καὶ καλοῦντος τὰ μὴ ὄντα . . . ὡς ὄντα. And this predication corresponds directly to the statements of v. 19 that Abraham's loins and Sarah's womb were dead, something bound up, clearly problematically, with the promises: κατενόησεν τὸ ἑαυτοῦ σῶμα [ἤδη] νενεκρωμένον, ἑκατονταετής που ὑπάρχων, καὶ τὴν νέκρωσιν τῆς μήτρας Σάρρας. The problem was of course that the old couple was impossibly past *childbearing,* and that God therefore in effect had to create life from the dead in order to fulfill his promises, an action then realized in the conception and birth of Isaac. Hence, Isaac is the unstated but necessary focus of v. 17b *and* vv. 19-21. If he is not supplied to this situation, then Abraham's concerns as stated in v. 19 make no sense; but if he is, then they make perfect sense.

Verses 24-25 confirm these implications by briefly supplying an analogy between Christians and Abraham. Christians will be given δικαιοσύνη, as Abraham was, because they trust in the God who raises Jesus from the dead, and v. 25 adds that Jesus himself was handed over to death and raised to life. For this analogy to hold fully, however, Abraham must trust God *concerning Isaac,* a son conceived in the face of death and thereby in a sense also resurrected (and later on, in Genesis 22, he will again in effect be received back from the dead).[52] That is, Christians trust God "the Father" concerning "his Son," dead and raised, just as Abraham trusted God concerning *his* son, conceived from the dead and thereby brought to life (and also later raised "on the third day"). If we drop Isaac from this comparison, then all the christological information supplied by Paul in vv. 24b-25 becomes otiose, and the entire analogy is made weaker and less apposite.[53]

In support of these two direct textual implications we may note that Genesis 15:5 is quoted in Romans 4:18b — "thus will be your seed" (οὕτως ἔσται τὸ σπέρμα σου) — a text appropriately read in its contexts (i.e., originally in Genesis, elsewhere in Paul, in Galatians 3, and here in Romans) as a singular reference to Isaac, a phrase anticipated by the singular statement in 4:13: Οὐ γὰρ διὰ νόμου ἡ ἐπαγγελία τῷ Ἀβραὰμ ἢ τῷ σπέρματι αὐτοῦ, τὸ κληρονόμον αὐτὸν εἶναι κόσμου. This is not to deny the plural application of this promised inheritance eventually (see 4:16a, παντὶ τῷ σπέρματι), but it seems to be mediated here by a single seed and figure distinguishable from Abraham — Isaac (and see also Rom. 9:7-9, esp. the quotation of Gen. 21:12 in v. 7b: ἐν Ἰσαὰκ κληθήσεταί σου σπέρμα). Finally, Paul alludes to Genesis 21:5 in v. 19,[54] a verse drawn from the chapter, and actual pericope, that recount Isaac's miraculous conception and birth.[55]

Consequently, it seems reasonably well attested — once we are attuned to look for it — that behind Abraham's paternity of "the many nations" in fulfillment of Genesis 15:5 and 17:5 (etc.) in Romans 4 is the miraculous birth of Isaac, the son through whom the promises are initially continued in order later to be fully realized. And with this realization we come now to the acute problem that this narrative potentially poses for Paul's previous argumentation in Romans 4:2-16a.

The problem is signaled almost immediately in this subsection with the citation of Genesis 17:5 in Romans 4:17, the text that explicitly states Abraham's future fatherhood of the pagans: πατέρα πολλῶν ἐθνῶν τέθεικά σε. This text occurs twice in the subsection, providing two of the three instances of πατήρ there (it is cited again in v. 18). And I suspect that the presence of this particular text at this point in Paul's argument is very important. Intriguingly, Paul did not cite Genesis 17:5 in Galatians, although he employs Abrahamic traditions there extensively.[56] Neither does Paul cite Genesis 17:5 anywhere else in Romans,[57] *and for obvious reasons.* Genesis 17 links Abraham's fatherhood of many pagan nations explicitly with the covenant of circumcision (which, it also says, will be *"a sign"* of "an everlasting covenant"). Abraham even receives that promise as his name in the context of undergoing the ritual surgery.[58] And it is a short step from here to another argumentative antinomy that aligns nicely with the other challenges from the Teacher that Paul has been attempting to resolve in context.

Genesis 17:5 introduces circumcision in the context of Abraham's fatherhood, not in relation to the generic convert, and so does not consider the ritual as an isolated observance.[59] Moreover, as we know by now, the original story as recounted in Genesis assumes the fulfillment of that fatherhood in a rather concrete fashion in the conception and birth of Isaac, the child of promise.[60] As we have just seen, Abraham became the father of Israel, and then somehow of "many nations," specifically through Isaac, a succession denoted in much Jewish literature merely by the phrase "the/our fathers" or its equivalent.[61] And this critical event, which fulfilled Abraham's divine promises of fatherhood and blessing, now creates a difficulty for Paul *because it occurred well after the events of Genesis 15:6, while the covenant of circumcision, established in chapter 17, now stands between them.* So a powerful possible counterargument to Paul's contentions in Romans 4:2b-16a becomes apparent — that Abraham's paternity of Isaac, and through him his paternity ultimately of "many nations," while perhaps promised before circumcision, in Genesis 12 and 15, nevertheless in fact occurred only *after* the covenant of circumcision was established and accepted in Genesis 17, *and hence the latter ritual is still a critical precondition for the realization of the former promises.* In short, the link between Abraham's later paternity of and through Isaac (recounted in Genesis 21) and circumcision, a link effectively established by Genesis 17:5 but also assumed by much Judaism of the time, is what seems to create a potential problem for Paul, given his present emphasis on 15:6 (and not the link between salvation and circumcision per se, which is addressed in 4:9-12). Crucially, Genesis 17:5 seems to suggest that acceptance of the covenant of circumcision was a critical intermediate step on the way to this famous and miraculous fulfillment of the promises.

If we grant that this challenge lies behind Romans 4:16b-22, a challenge freighted by Genesis 17:5 in relation to Abraham's paternity of Isaac and the intervening step of circumcision, then we can grasp that it constitutes rather a peculiar argumentative difficulty for Paul and will consequently require a slightly different response from his preceding ones in Romans 4. Much of Paul's argumentative leverage in 4:2-16a against the challenges raised by the Teacher in 3:27-31 derived from the early placement of Genesis 15:6 in the overall story of the patriarch. This text was able to trump the matters of meritorious law observance and circumcision largely because it occurred earlier than and hence independently of those events, as well as being itself a clear scriptural assertion, and a rather minimalist one.[62] However, Genesis 15:6 is now limited in its argumentative usefulness, since Isaac's birth took place much later, in chapter 21. Any easy temporal trumping or equivalent direct refutation is now precluded. So how does Paul make his case?

In fact, Paul seems to follow the same basic strategy. That is, he again uses

Genesis 15:6 to disrupt the rejoinder from the Teacher, in this case the ostensible connection between Abraham's paternity of Isaac and circumcision. But he has to broaden the apparent relevance of his key text rather than merely introducing it in its own right, so several new premises must be supplied to make his case plausible. And a rather cunning piece of argumentation ensues. Specifically, Paul brackets Genesis 17:5 with statements that speak of another story, a story extrapolated from Genesis 15:6, thereby essentially assimilating the problematic later text in narrative terms. The two key narrative dynamics are, on the one hand, (of course) Abraham's πίστις and, on the other, the resurrecting God who gifts salvation. These dynamics are so emphasized that they rather overwhelm the specific contributions of Genesis 17:5. Any protests against this unfolding story, as Paul tells it, will ultimately look unnecessary, and perhaps even impious, even though the distinctive concerns of Genesis 17:5 in its own context will actually thereby have been marginalized! In all this the interplay between Genesis 15 and 17 — along with one or two other snippets from Genesis — is little remarked on, but very significant. Paul plaits these texts together throughout his argument; this technique lies at the base of his strategy.

> . . . Ἀβραάμ
> ¹⁷ὅς ἐστιν **πατὴρ πάντων ἡμῶν**⁶³
>   καθὼς γέγραπται ὅτι **Πατέρα πολλῶν ἐθνῶν τέθεικά σε,**
>   κατέναντι οὗ⁶⁴ ἐπίστευσεν θεοῦ
>   τοῦ ζῳοποιοῦντος τοὺς νεκροὺς
>   ¹⁸καὶ καλοῦντος τὰ μὴ ὄντα ὡς ὄντα.
> ὅς παρ' ἐλπίδα ἐπ' ἐλπίδι ἐπίστευσεν εἰς τὸ γενέσθαι αὐτὸν **πατέρα πολλῶν ἐθνῶν** κατὰ τὸ εἰρημένον, ¹⁹Οὕτως ἔσται τὸ σπέρμα σου,⁶⁵
> καὶ μὴ ἀσθενήσας τῇ πίστει
> κατενόησεν τὸ ἑαυτοῦ σῶμα [ἤδη] νενεκρωμένον, ἑκατονταετής που ὑπάρχων,⁶⁶
> ²⁰καὶ [κατενόησεν] τὴν νέκρωσιν τῆς μήτρας Σάρρας,
> εἰς δὲ τὴν ἐπαγγελίαν τοῦ θεοῦ οὐ διεκρίθη τῇ ἀπιστίᾳ
> ἀλλ' ἐνεδυναμώθη τῇ πίστει,
> ²¹δοὺς δόξαν τῷ θεῷ,
> καὶ πληροφορηθεὶς ὅτι ὃ ἐπήγγελται δυνατός ἐστιν καὶ ποιῆσαι.
> ²²διὸ [καὶ] ἐλογίσθη αὐτῷ εἰς δικαιοσύνην.

The Greek of vv. 16b-22 is complex. In fact, one sentence runs from v. 16 to v. 21, constructed with a series of subordinate clauses using relative pronouns, participles, conjunctions, and parentheses (see, to a degree, 3:21-26). The point of transition into the distinctive concerns of this fourth argumentative subsection seems to be marked by the relative pronoun that coordinates "the fatherhood of all of us" with Abraham (and note the resonance with 4:1), thereby introducing a different subject from that in 4:13-16a, which was concerned with the negation versus the fulfillment of Mosaic torah. Three stages of semantic layering and argumentation are apparent from this point: Paul characterizes Genesis 17:5 in a particular fashion in v. 17; he relates it directly to Genesis 15:6 in v. 18; and he embellishes that depiction dramatically through a distinctive accumulation of clauses in vv. 19-21. The result is that *Genesis 17:5 ends up reading like Genesis 15:6.*

(1) Stage One

The first stage, v. 17, quotes Genesis 17:5 and attaches a qualifying clause with the phrase κατέναντι οὗ. This raises some complex questions. However, for the detailed reasons adduced just below, I suggest the following construal of this clause: "... the faithful Abraham, who is the father of us all, [17]just as it is written, 'the father of many nations I have made you,' in the presence of which [i.e., that declaration], *he trusted* the God who makes alive the dead and calls the nonexistent existent." In further support of this reading — as we will see shortly — v. 18 makes exactly the same point.

Excursus: The Syntax and Construal of Romans 4:17

BDF suggests (§294, esp. [2]) that a switch in word order has taken place here after the attraction of the relative pronoun to its antecedent (which, after the switch and so as things stand in the text, now follows the relative). That is, Paul intends to say κατέναντι [τοῦ] θεοῦ ᾧ ἐπίστευσεν, but ends up saying κατέναντι οὗ ἐπίστευσεν θεοῦ — "in the sight of God, in whom he trusted" as against "in the sight of [something], he trusted God" (see also 2 Cor. 1:4 and Eph. 1:6). I hesitate to dispute with BDF, but on this occasion I suspect that its recommendations are wrong.

The clause so construed does not integrate easily into its context: "*in the sight of God,* the one who makes alive the dead and calls the nonexistent existent, *in whom he trusted.*" This statement supposedly follows the citation of Genesis 17:5 and precedes a new line of thought introduced by a relative pronoun that points back to "Abraham" in v. 16a, so it must be relatively self-contained. It can only work, in fact, if the two clauses concerning fatherhood that intervene between τῷ ἐκ πίστεως Ἀβραάμ in v. 16a and κατέναντι in v. 17b are themselves marginalized parenthetically (or some such) and the emphasis of the prior phrase on Abraham's πίστις is assumed to be central. Even then, however, it does not make a great deal of sense: "in the presence of God, Abraham trusted in God." This seems an odd, if not completely redundant, assertion. Paul does not speak of "trust" in these terms anywhere else. BDF's suggestion also requires the relative pronoun *both* to have switched its correct place with the substantive θεός *and* to have been attracted to its case, a twofold assumption.

The immediate context (i.e., v. 18 and following) suggests, rather, that the matter of Abraham's paternity is *central* (not marginal) to the following discussion, so to suggest a parenthetical function in vv. 16b-17a looks incorrect. The relative pronoun is also already in the right case opposite κατέναντι (i.e., the genitive), so there is no need, at least initially, to assume its attraction and relocation. The crucial question, then, is what other possible antecedents are present, apart from θεός, that could take the appropriate sense of κατέναντι. We must start by considering the semantic range of κατέναντι itself.

The relevant comparative semantic sample for κατέναντι used in this figurative sense is small: 2 Cor. 2:17; 12:19; also Sir. 28:26; and Jdt. 12:15, 19. In these texts the improper preposition, always taking a genitive, means basically "in view of" or "in the presence of" (hence in this sense also "before") — and so it is understandable that BDF sought to place God here as its object. Paul speaks in Christ and in the presence of (or "before," or "in view of") God; Sirach warns against an unguarded tongue allowing exploitation because of statements made in the presence of others; and Judith has her maidservant lay down lamb-skins for her to sit on, and then eats and drinks her prepared food, in the presence of Holofernes.

But can Abraham stand "in the presence of" the only other possible antecedent in context, namely, *the saying itself* (i.e., Gen. 17:5: see τὸ εἰρημένον in v. 18 and τὴν ἐπαγγελίαν in v. 20a), and then go on to trust in God?[67] In fact, the ensuing context states twice that Abraham *does* orient himself vis-à-vis God's statements (see vv. 18 and 20, cited above). Indeed, all of Romans 4 presupposes the argumentative implications of Abraham's trusting God's promises — in context, usually the statements of Genesis 15:1-5. That Abraham would stand "in the presence of" or "opposite" or "before" God's statement of Genesis 17:5, and then go on *to trust* God himself concerning the outcome of that statement, makes excellent sense within our broader construal of the subsection. I would suggest further that it is Paul's exact intention here to link *the statement* of Genesis 17:5 with *the action* of Genesis 15:6 in terms of trust, hence his mention of that action immediately following the citation of the other text. This also seems possible in the broader context of much Old Testament piety. Moreover, *no displacement or attraction of the relative pronoun now needs to be posited.*[68]

In this first stage of the subsection's argument, God is embellished by Paul distinctively. He "makes the dead alive" and "calls the nonexistent existent" (the Greek is plural). It seems fair in general terms for Paul to state in v. 17 that God is these things in relation to Genesis 17:5; many Jews believed in a resurrecting God.[69] But the suggestion is even more appropriate given the specific context of Paul's claim. In vv. 19-21 (as we have noted) it becomes clear that these attributes pertain specifically to the conception of Isaac, and the birth of Isaac will clearly be an especially life-creating event given the state of his parents. Hence, Paul foregrounds here in v. 17 the twin elements of Abraham's trust (. . . κατέναντι οὗ ἐπίστευσεν . . .) and God's life-creating power that is soon to be focused in Isaac *in relation to Genesis 17:5,* while any concomitants are allowed to slip unmarked into the background.

(2) Stage Two

Verse 18, reaching back to the antecedent of Abraham in v. 16b with a second relative pronoun, now links Genesis 17:5 to Genesis 15:5 explicitly and adds further important qualifying material to the verb πιστεύω, which has just been used in v. 17. And so the second component in the narrative dynamic Paul wishes to establish is now elaborated. Abraham is said specifically to trust literally "from hope to hope" (ὃς παρ᾽ ἐλπίδα ἐπ᾽ ἐλπίδι). And this again, as a positive claim in context, seems fair. Of course Abraham hoped that God would grant him an heir.

Verse 18 also notes, however, that this particular attitude and hope had already been established by Genesis 15:5, because that text promised Abraham "seed," that is, both texts spoke of promises and were ultimately focused on Isaac, the heir. Abraham "trusted, from hope to hope, that he would be 'father of many nations' [Gen. 17:5] according to the saying 'so numerous shall your descendants be' [Gen. 15:5]." In effect, then, this similarity and linkage push Abraham's attitude of hopeful trust in God's promise back thirteen years. By the time God speaks in Genesis 17:5, Abraham has been trusting in hope for well over a decade. The implication is that he will continue to do so as Genesis 17:5 is spoken to him, that promise merely adding the further information that he will thereby be the father "of many nations" (although this was something already apparent to the careful reader of Genesis in 12:3). So Abraham's trust is thereby extended over time *and* a symmetry between Genesis 17:5 and 15:6 is further enhanced.

Paul has introduced the twin elements of the resurrecting, life-creating God and Abraham's ongoing hopeful trust in him into the context of Genesis 17:5 on the basis of their general narrative plausibility there, and an apparent continuity with Genesis 15:6 has thereby been established. Their later presence seems entirely natural given the surrounding story of Isaac's promised conception and Abraham's trust in God concerning this. But the fact that they are the only elements that Paul is specifying at this stage also ineluctably highlights them as *the* interpretative keys to Genesis 17. The next argumentative stage now dramatizes this suggestion considerably (that is, Paul doesn't want us to miss the point).

(3) Stage Three

Verses 19-21 use three conjunctions to add three further verbs and their clauses, along with three participial clauses, to this unfolding picture (and this is clearly the most complex of the semantic layers Paul crafts in the subsection). These clauses link more tightly the two narrative motifs we have already noted, although the focus remains on Abraham's attribute of trust as in v. 18. In v. 19 Abraham does not merely trust in God and his promises hopefully and over time; he trusts specifically in spite of "the death" of his loins and "the death" of Sarah's womb (i.e., their death in procreative terms). And God's life-giving attribute, noted in v. 17, now corresponds precisely to this particular problem, something that is entirely appropriate in narrative terms since the production of a son remains Abraham's central concern. That is, it is narratively plausible for Paul to emphasize once more that Abraham's trust that is being spoken of in relation to Genesis 17:5 existed in the context of a struggle between his death in procreative terms and God's promise of an heir. Genesis 17:5 must presuppose this ongoing fidelity that was spoken of in Genesis 15:6.

The more elaborate text here states, furthermore, that Abraham is not weak or wavering in the face of this knowledge but, rather, his trust waxes in strength and he even glorifies God because of his deep conviction that God is able to do what has been promised (and indeed will do it). That is, the principle of πίστις is massively reified in this subsection — embellished in glowing, heroic terms — and is also connected directly with the story's central concern — God's miraculous creation of Isaac. After this breathless accumulation of clauses dramatizing Abraham's trust, it seems entirely plausible for Paul to state that "*therefore* (διό) δικαιοσύνη was given to him" (this being another echo of Genesis 15:6). Who would deny the appropriateness of God's response to Abraham here in the light of this heroic contest in terms of trust? At the end of a steadfast battle with biological realities extending over fourteen years, Abraham's belief in God's cryptic promises seems to have been vindicated. But what has Paul achieved in argumentative terms with this series of dramatic narrative selections and embellishments?

As has already been suggested, the argument is not formal in the sense that it has been in Paul's three previous subsections; Paul at this point cannot use Genesis 15:6 to simply knock out the opposing contention. Hence, he has used a mixture of bombast, pathos, and narrative suggestion, so that at the end of the subsection we perceive Paul's point as a generally plausible impression more than grasp it as a clear logical victory.[70] Primarily on overarching narrative grounds, Paul has claimed that the promise to Abraham of fatherhood in the context of circumcision in Genesis 17:5 is best understood in terms of the two crucial dynamics set in motion by Genesis 15:6, namely, Abraham's unbending trust in God's promise of an heir and God's later life-creating response in terms of Isaac's miraculous conception. That trust is now elaborated in heroic terms, evoking our admiration and sympathy as well as our judgment of general narrative plausibility. During this brief but powerful dramatization *Paul simply does not mention the attendant issue of circumcision raised by Genesis 17. But we tend not to notice this omission;* our attention is otherwise engaged! God seems to gift Abraham his paternity in response to his extraordinary fidelity, and Genesis 17:5 has thereby been subsumed within an elaborated Genesis 15:6. Moreover, to add anything to this short story of extraordinary trust and its reward — if we do notice its oversimplifications — now seems somewhat gauche. This would detract from Abraham's heroism, to which God responds graciously as he promised.[71]

While Paul's case so construed in vv. 16b-22 is not overly plausible in formal terms (and indeed, I suspect that it will persuade only those already convinced), it does nevertheless seem a plausible construal of his argument in context. This reading makes sense of his troublesome and unusual deployment of Genesis 17:5, which otherwise is the intertextual equivalent of shooting himself in the foot. It also explains the question concerning Abraham's fatherhood "of us" in terms of kinship (i.e., through actual descent, hence in Abraham's specific case, through Isaac: see also 9:6-13 and Gal. 4:21-31), and this in the broadly antithetical terms that characterized the other three issues discussed in context. We can even see why Paul's argument at this point is uncharacteristically labored. His favored proof text, Genesis 15:6, cannot deal so effectively with this particular challenge, and he must resort to more indirect techniques — to drama, narrative insinuation, and even bombast. But even if his case is not so deadly in formal terms, there is still a real effectiveness in the subsection in rhetorical terms.

If this reading of vv. 16b-22 is granted, we can now see how Paul has skillfully set it up in 4:1, thereby providing an anticipatory announcement — albeit a subtle one — in addition to the three more overt signals of the Teacher's challenges in 3:27-31, which Paul treated in 4:2b-16a. The Teacher introduces Abraham in 4:1 — foolishly, as it turns out — as his leading witness concerning circumcised and law-observant conversion to Judaism, which thereby fulfills, rather than eviscerates, the Torah. He asks, "What have we discovered in relation to Abraham . . . ?" — going on to characterize the patriarch as "our forefather according to the flesh" (τὸν προπάτορα ἡμῶν κατὰ σάρκα), and this now seems to be a clever wordplay on Paul's part. Abraham is certainly being introduced in the first instance as the ancestor of the saved in merely concrete, historical terms, an authoritative witness in relation to the difficult questions just raised. However, the phrase κατὰ σάρκα also echoes Genesis 17, where "the flesh" is a repeated motif (see vv. 11, 13, 14, 24, 25), and the complete adjectival phrase evokes that narrative nicely, since Abraham's paternity is tightly associated there with circumcision of the flesh — the very association that Paul introduces and overrides in Romans 4:16b-22. The question, "What then shall we say that we have found out in relation to Abraham, 'our forefather according to the flesh'?" therefore does double duty as a rhetorical marker. It introduces the figure of Abraham in general, but it also points ahead to the one issue that is not explicitly announced in 3:27-31 but is nevertheless discussed in detail in Romans 4 after the analysis of the explicit questions — namely, whether Abraham's paternity of Isaac is indissolubly linked to his circumcision — and this is something that the Teacher has almost certainly suggested, and hence a title that he seems indubitably to have used.

However, perhaps we may detect in Paul's subtlety here a concession that this issue is also the most difficult for him to deal with, to the extent that a critical scrutiny of his argument might even find it wanting. Possibly, then, he wanted the issue to be addressed *only if it had already been explicitly raised*. Otherwise, it could pass by the letter's auditors in a less emphatic role as an elaboration of the issue raised by 3:31 of Torah fulfillment (although perhaps a rather long and passionate one). Paul's argument emerges into full clarity *only once the text and argument of Genesis 17 are known* and their implications considered in relation to Paul's use of 15:6 and the fulfillment of both Genesis 15 and Genesis 17 later in Genesis 21 (at which point the linkage and problems seem obvious). Romans 4:16b-22, correctly understood, may consequently operate rather like a "sleeper agent," embedded in a particular situation for a long time but activated only by certain particular circumstances, at which point it springs to life. Hence, Paul's text seems, once again, to be carefully crafted — so much so that different argumentative levels are again discernible within it. And with this realization we can turn to consider the chapter's resonant final verses.

§6. Romans 4:23-25

In vv. 23-24 Paul suggests that Genesis 15:6 was not written for Abraham alone, specifically concerning the gifting of δικαιοσύνη, but for "us" — those to whom it is *about* to be gifted (οἷς μέλλει λογίζεσθαι). Paul then characterizes these beneficiaries as τοῖς πιστεύουσιν ἐπὶ τὸν ἐγείραντα Ἰησοῦν τὸν κύριον ἡμῶν ἐκ νεκρῶν, [25]ὃς παρεδόθη διὰ τὰ παραπτώματα ἡμῶν καὶ ἠγέρθη διὰ τὴν δικαίωσιν ἡμῶν. And it seems likely that this final crafted and balanced couplet in v. 25, which speaks of Christ, echoes Isaiah 53:6 and 12, at least in its first clause: παρέδωκεν αὐτὸν ταῖς ἁμαρτίαις ἡμῶν . . . διὰ τὰς ἁμαρτίας αὐτῶν παρεδόθη (see also Isa. 53:5; 64:6).[72] In view of this, a prospective rather than a strongly causal reading of the four accusative instances of διά in vv. 23-25 seems most likely (i.e., "for the sake of" rather than "because of"). This seems unavoidable in the second and fourth instances and unexceptionable in the other two. So Christ was ". . . handed over for the sake of our transgressions, and raised for the sake of our deliverance." Paul seems to be signaling several things with this compact but powerful set of claims.

We should note first that the Roman Christians are characterized overtly as analogous in their πίστις to Abraham. The definition of their πίστις is therefore now drawn into the narrative characterization of Abraham that has just taken place in Romans 4, and especially in the verses that immediately precede vv. 22-24, where Paul has described the character of Abraham's πίστις most explicitly. This analogy confirms strongly our earlier judgment that the principal object of this πίστις is God, who is, moreover, not merely someone about whom certain things should be believed — although this is clearly implicit — but someone who is trusted in, and that faithfully, if necessary under extreme duress, and over time (see 4:18-21). Steadfast endurance, trust, and belief are *all* therefore discernible in the definition of Christian faith that Paul supplies for his auditors — a challenging portrait! God is also, however, implicitly characterized as a "father," like Abraham, since he raises his Son from the dead (see esp. 5:10; the ensuing argument in the letter will also make this quite clear, esp. Romans 8). But just as the Roman Christian auditors have had their definition as "trusters" filled out (see esp. Rom. 1:8, 16, 17; 3:22), Paul has also inserted a christological premise into the situation, and a number of implications flowing from this qualification now need to be noted carefully.

Both substantively and stylistically, Romans 4:25 seems also to resume 3:21-26 and, before that, 1:16-17 and 1:2-4; it reaches back overtly to these earlier christological sections. The carefully measured parallelism and balance in 4:25 evoke the crafted phraseology of 3:23-26. And this stylistic signal is matched by the substantive resumption of the twofold narrative of πίστις that has earlier been spoken of (and that is in fact only here resumed explicitly; Christ has not been mentioned overtly by Paul since 3:31). God's right and saving act in Christ was said earlier to extend to all who trust, and this constituency has just been noted carefully in 4:23-24. But this act is effected through the faithful one, Christ himself. And 4:25 can now be seen to evoke his martyrological narrative neatly. The trajectory of descent — of humiliation, suffering, and death — is evoked by Christ being "handed over for the sake of our transgressions," and the trajectory of ascent — of resurrection, glorification, and heavenly enthronement — is evoked by the fact that God "raised him for the sake of our deliverance." Romans 4:25 thereby elaborates precisely on the two facets of Habakkuk 2:4, read christologically, that have spoken earlier of Christ's "fidelity" and "life," and links them in turn to certain "trusters," who trust here on analogy with Abraham, the second member in the πίστις progression that has appeared earlier on. Two further points now ensue.

Paul's own use of δικαιο- terminology, conditioned by the Christ event, continues in this passage to function liberatively. There is no avoiding the correlation here between "resurrection" and δικαίωσις. The situation Christ saves "us" from is one characterized by death, while the realm he gives access to is characterized by life (see 5:18). Meanwhile, any relevance of forensic-retributive procedures to Abraham has just been strenuously denied (see esp. 4:2-8)! Consequently, a forensic-liberative reading seems unavoidable. The trusters are being acquitted in the sense that they are being delivered or released from jail; God has liberated them through the Christ event.

It is vital to grasp here, moreover, that Paul is deploying Christ's resurrection in a soteriological capacity; it plays a critical role in his conception of salvation — in the deliverance of humanity from a realm characterized by transgressions and death. Such a deployment poses an acute problem for Justification theory, as a textual overdetermination, but integrates smoothly into the rereading that I am developing. An emphasis on Christ's death and life as a saving narrative (in which God "the Father" is also deeply involved) is just the soteriological schema that unfolds in Romans 5–8 (as we saw in part one, chapter three). Paul consequently seems to be pointing forward quite consistently to this later material in 4:25. Indeed, it is possible to detect now what Paul is probably trying to achieve with 4:23-25.

The Teacher has taken a second battering in 3:27–4:22. His gospel was attacked on its own terms in 1:18–3:20 and shown to be seriously deficient. The Teacher then appeared to take a more scriptural and comparative stance from 3:27, introducing an authoritative example that would supposedly prove decisive over against Paul's key Scriptures and claims — the patriarch Abraham. However, that too was revealed by closer examination (principally of Gen. 15:6) to prove embarrassing for his position, knocking back his key concerns again at almost every turn (see esp. 4:2-16a, with a possible objection anticipated and countered in 4:16b-22). But Paul's critiques of the Teacher have largely run their course by the end of 4:22. The Teacher's system lies in ruins (at least for the attentive auditor!). It is time, then, for Paul to begin to respond in his own terms to the Teacher's key criticisms of his gospel — responses signaled briefly in 3:23-26, which also set the stage for the development of his own primary positions. There we learned that the Christ event will speak both to the eschatological threats that the Teacher makes to Paul's pagan converts and to a law-free ethic. Paul thus begins to pivot toward these discussions in 4:23-25. He shifts from the figure of Abraham to his analogous contemporary believing audience at Rome and then reintroduces the all-important Christ event — a story of death and resurrection — as the content of their belief and the ground for their trust (and this fills out the analogy further). Like Abraham, Christians trust in a God who raises a son from the dead, but in their case a son who was handed over to death and then raised for the sake of both cleansing from transgressions and liberation from the entire realm of Death. And with these transitions, the way is clear for Paul to discuss the key eschatological and ethical issues at length precisely on the basis of this act of God in Christ (and in what is arguably the most important theological discussion that he ever penned). Hence, 4:23-25 is a rhetorical pivot back to the christocentric concerns of 1:16-17 and 3:23-26, opening up the way for several major new argumentative discussions in Romans 5–8.

Two final observations should be made concerning 4:23-25 before we turn to consider the many advantages of its reconstrual in these terms over against the difficulties faced by its conventional reading.

(1) A Messianic Discourse

In echoing Isaiah 53, as well as resuming the distinctively crafted and intertextual language of 3:21-26, Romans 4:24-25 seems to add further reinforcement to the hypothesis that Paul might be presupposing at times a messianic discourse in the early church, which is crafted from an anthology of key texts from the Old Testament linked together by key motifs and themes. Lying at the heart of that anthology seems to be the story of a son who is also "the righteous one," that is, a person who dies an atoning death and is subsequently raised and enthroned on high. The same narrative cue seems detectable behind Paul's citation of Habakkuk 2:4 and Isaiah 53:6/12 in relation to Christ *without fanfare,* a cue also detectable in the Wisdom of Solomon, which is implicit in so much of Paul's argument in Romans, as well as in the system of the Teacher. (The cue is also present in Daniel, but Paul does not seem to exhibit as much interest in that text as other New Testament authors.)

That the early church explained the death of the innocent and pious Jesus in terms of certain key texts, linked together through shared words, phrases, and stories, seems plausible.[73] (Many reasons for this would have existed — apologetic, theological, didactic, ritual, evangelistic, and so on.) Precise specifications of the texts are of course much more difficult, but it seems plausible to suggest that they included Habakkuk 2:4, selections from Isaiah 53, and probably also selections from the Wisdom of Solomon (2:12-20 at least, but perhaps also 5:1-2, 7). Daniel[74] may have been represented there, and some selections from the Psalter seem likely (2, 89, 110, etc.). I suspect strongly that elements from Genesis 22 were also involved (see 1 Cor. 15:4; also v. 3).[75] One key link between these texts, facilitating both their grouping and their memorization, seems to have been the motif ὁ δίκαιος or its close equivalent, although not all the texts needed to be coordinated by the same motif.[76] That Paul can merely echo Isaiah 53 in relation to Jesus in Romans 4:25 and expect his auditors to catch this phraseology, thereby also resuming earlier and highly distinctive texts in the letter that did much the same thing in relation to other echoes (i.e., crafted ritual texts), suggests to me that this hypothesis rests on a reasonable amount of evidence. This is by no means to preclude other forms of intertextuality in Paul's argumentation; clearly, he uses Jewish narratives quite radically and originally at times to articulate his theological claims, while at other moments he proof-texts overtly and aggressively. But his subtle, crafted, christological texts seem to occupy a hermeneutical space of their own within the broader texture of his argument, a space that they in turn seem to share with other New Testament witnesses.[77] That is, this phenomenon of a messianic discourse seems to be multiply attested.

(2) The Meaning of δικαιοσύνη

This rereading of Romans 4, and especially of Paul's concerns in 4:16b-22, provides fairly decisive reinforcement for the reading of δικαιοσύνη Θεοῦ that was developed in chapter seventeen. It is now apparent that the righteous saving act that Paul sees God promising to Abraham in Genesis 15:6 — εἰς δικαιοσύνην — is the miraculous conception and birth of Isaac, that is, a life-creating event by the resurrecting God. But not only is this theological connection and narrative explication apparent in Romans 4 as a whole; some of Paul's specific statements in terms of δικαιοσύνη seem comprehensible *only* in such terms.

Paul states in 4:13 that it is by way of a particular seed that the promise to Abraham that he would inherit the cosmos is fulfilled, that is, διὰ δικαιοσύνης πίστεως. The discussion of Abraham's miraculous and faithful paternity of Isaac follows shortly, in vv. 16 through 21. The motif of promise is then resumed in v. 21, where Abraham is "fully convinced that [God] was capable of doing what had been promised" (πληροφορηθεὶς ὅτι ὃ ἐπήγγελται δυνατός ἐστιν καὶ ποιῆσαι). And Paul concludes the argument in v. 22 with the important statement, διὸ [καὶ] ἐλογίσθη αὐτῷ εἰς δικαιοσύνην — a statement relating to Paul's previous emphasis on Abraham's unwavering trust. And these statements all point in the same direction.

Abraham is convinced that God is capable of giving him an heir. And if God does so, then the further promises are enabled — more offspring, land, and even the inheritance of the cosmos. Moreover, when God does so, Abraham's longstanding trust in God is finally rewarded. Hence, it seems hard to avoid the conclusion that Isaac *is* God's righteous and saving act — his act of grace toward Abraham. Isaac is the δικαιοσύνη that God gifts to Abraham, having promised him earlier on. And this realization explains the final orientation of Romans 4 toward resurrection. Christians are to trust in the God who raised Jesus from the dead, just as Abraham trusted in a resurrecting God who conceived Isaac from sterile parents.[78]

It is rewarding to see the clarity and authority of Paul's argument in much of Romans 4 emerging when the meaning of δικαιοσύνη throughout the discussion is held to be a righteous act by God whose specific content is the birth of Isaac. This meaning, moreover, confirms the sense that emerged from our earlier investigations (i.e., δικαιοσύνη as a singular, saving, liberating, life-giving, eschatological act by God, who in so acting is behaving as the divine ruler of the cosmos can and should). Paul's position is fundamentally apocalyptic. A god of revelation has acted dramatically to deliver one of his famous, archetypal servants — an interpretative realization grounded in turn for Paul in the great act of deliverance effected in Christ. And these emphases open up the way for a smoothly continuous reading of his argument through Romans 5–8 and the rest of the letter; the eschatological reassurance and ethical transformation wrought by this event in the lives of those who trust will be discussed there in satisfying detail. We turn from this point, then, to consider the advantages of this apocalyptic rereading of 4:23-25, and of Romans 4 as a whole, over against the conventional reading and Justification theory.

§7. Problems Solved

We are now prepared to grasp how this rereading has solved the various problems identified in part three, chapter eleven that bedevil Justification theory in relation to Romans 4 (along with those theoretical difficulties noted in part one). Those problems are raised in particular by the chapter's final two verses, so our considerations can begin there, moving on to assess the advantages of the rereading of Romans 4 (i.e., Rom. 3:27–4:25) as a whole. We will then draw together the benefits of this new approach to Romans 1–4 in its entirety, bringing the discussion of part four to a close.

7.1. Problems Solved in Romans 4:23-25

Romans 4:24b-25 raises the question of how Christ relates both to the analogy that just precedes his mention in 4:25 and to the broader argumentation centered on Abraham that stretches back to 4:1 — isometric concerns as it turns out. The correct answer to this twofold query should resolve a cluster of difficulties that dogs the conventional reading at this point.

As we have just seen, 4:23-25 creates an analogy between Abraham and Christians. But in so doing this equation also implicitly encodes much of the preceding argumentation as well; how Christians relate to Abraham in 4:23-25 will probably correspond to how they relate to the different aspects of his history that were recounted favorably by Paul in 4:2b-22. So the entire discussion of 4:1-25 is swept up into the terms of Paul's comparison in 4:23-25. And the majority of interpreters read this analogy in what we might call a "thin" sense.

They see two basic members in the analogical comparison, and the comparison is legitimized by the earliest member in historical terms — by Abraham.

Abraham trusts God to create life from the dead for him (here specifically in the form of Isaac), and therefore Christians trust God to create life from the dead for them (eventually in terms of their own resurrection). It is Abraham's behavior in this sense that overrides "works of law," meritorious activity, and boasting (4:2-8), the need for circumcision (4:9-12), the need for full Mosaic law observance (4:13-16a), and so on. Indeed, his example provides converts from paganism with their principal rationale for a Christian ethic that ignores several of Judaism's key practices. Moreover, the terms of this "thin" analogy dictate that Christians must essentially *copy* him. Abraham is consequently often spoken of as an "example," if not a paradigm of faith.[79] There is no organic relationship between Abraham and later Christians, however, so his "fatherhood," spoken of in vv. 1, 16b, 17, and 18, is a symbolic and metaphorical one. This is the view of "faith" that basically underlies many of the claims of Justification theory. Christians ought to be saved by believing like Abraham — presumably if necessary choosing to do so. And they should of course maintain that choice over time.

The thin reading of the analogy between Abraham and Christians

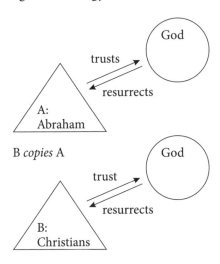

But the conventional reading faces numerous acute problems in this relation. I have chosen to deal with these mainly in terms of textual under- and overdeterminations rather than theoretical difficulties, but this is to some extent a judgment call. If the example of Abraham is incorporated within the very theory of Justification, then the difficulties that he raises become internal argumentative, theoretical, and framing contradictions rather than points of tension between the textual base and the theoretical superstructure. It is arguably more generous to the theory to treat Paul's "example" of Abraham as a textual aberration; however, not much rests on this judgment. These problems exist either way.

The thick reading of the analogy between Abraham and Christians

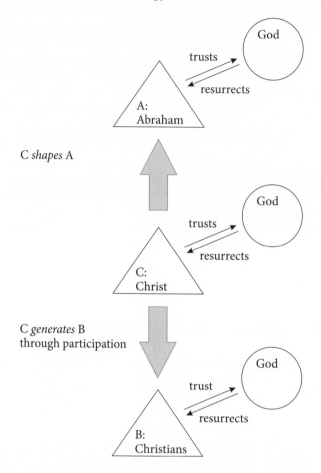

If the example and analogy of Abraham are taken seriously, an entire spread of debilitating difficulties is generated. These are not often noted, because Abraham in Romans 4 is treated so charitably by his interpreters, who are, after all, generally expounding the absolute heart of Justification theory and its scriptural attestation at this point. However, a minority tradition of interpreters has been a little more penetrating. And so, assisted by those critical studies, we compiled in chapter eleven a list of two underdeterminations — UDs 10 and 11 — and nine overdeterminations — ODs 16 through 24 — that are raised by this particular set of claims — a truly formidable list. And these should be added to the various theoretically-related difficulties already noted through part one (especially chapters two, three, and six) — intrinsic, systematic, proximate, and empirical difficulties. (The thin account of faith in view here either generates these difficulties directly, or contributes significantly to them.)

Hence, it is rather astonishing to realize that all our problems in this relation are resolved if we take a cue from the christocentric material that brackets Paul's exegesis of Abraham, in 3:27-31 (esp. 3:27b-28/B² and 3:30-31/B⁴) and 4:24b-25, not to mention 3:21-22. Our developing rereading foregrounds this dimension in Paul's position much more strongly than the conventional reading does. The figure and narrative of Christ stand both before and after Paul's analysis of Abraham — phenomena oriented themselves, moreover, around πίστις. If we consequently insert a mediating christological dimension between Abraham's fidelity and later Christian fidelity, thickening the nature and terms of Paul's analogy, *then we solve all of our difficulties.* Indeed, it is quite satisfying to see our formidable list of problems fading away as this adjustment is made to Paul's argument. The analogy — now consisting of three members — functions entirely smoothly. We should observe first that the various exegetical difficulties noted in this relation in chapter eleven have all been dealt with.

Underdeterminations

UD 10: Abraham's paradigmatic exemplification of saving faith is never clearly stated because Abraham is not functioning as an example of that principle, so much as a type of Christ (see 5:14b) — *the* example of πίστις.

UD 11: Abraham does not progress to "faith" from an ungodly state characterized by "works of law" because he is not an example of salvation by the progressions of Justification; he foreshadows the sinless Christ and so needs no such prior sinful phase in his narrative.

Overdeterminations

OD 16: Abraham's πίστις is personal, involving "trust" — not merely "belief," based on information — just as Christ's was and the Christian's ought to be. This analogical disjunction present in Justification theory consequently disappears.

OD 17: That Abraham's πίστις is prompted by a direct word from God seems appropriate in an apocalyptic account of the gospel (i.e., one resting on direct, unconditional disclosure; see Gal. 1:15-16). So this second analogical disjunction also disappears. (This is not to exclude the mediation of the word of God; see Rom. 9:6.)

OD 18: Abraham's example is no longer self-referentially incoherent — a scriptural corroboration of a philosophical journey that is itself revelatory. Instead, his story, as Paul depicts it, correlates strongly with the underlying Christ narrative (see OD 17 just above). We read a scriptural attestation to a figure who corresponds to the figure of Christ; the latter therefore grounds and illuminates the former.[80]

OD 19: Abraham's πίστις is impossibly strong and enduring — unwavering in the face of unbelievable promises over many years — because Paul's portrayal is affected by an underlying narrative of Christ. It is not something to be emulated — a hopeless prospect! — but rather to be participated in. The analogical disjunction at this point is thus removed. The impossible quality in Paul's actual narrative *of* Abraham is also explained; it is driven by his christological framing of that story.

OD 20: Abraham believes in God ("the Father"), as do Christ and subsequent Christians, and so the absence of the object required by Justification theory — the gospel and/or Christ — is no longer problematic. Neither does any awkward multiplication of objects need to be suggested. The awkward analogical disjunction at this point, too, is therefore eliminated (i.e., that Christians should copy Abraham's belief in God by believing in the gospel, or some such).

OD 21: Abraham's defining activity of πίστις takes place many centuries before the coming of Christ, anticipating him typologically. It does not, then, *establish* Christian salvation; fulfillment of this powerful reality is premised directly on the coming of Christ himself, the Faithful One par excellence (although presumably this does not exclude prior participation in Christ by pious Jews, etc.). The debilitating potential analogical disjunction at this point is thereby eliminated as well.

OD 22: The text emphasizes Abraham's literal biological fatherhood of Isaac, an event with no relevance for Justification theory, but one that does indeed lead to the subsequent existence of Israel, into which tradition and ancestry the Messiah is born and later pagan converts are grafted (see Rom. 9:5, 6-13; 11:17-24). Paul now argues completely consistently in this relation. And Abraham's paternity does not need to be spiritualized, in defiance of the text's suggestions.

OD 23: The saving function of the resurrection in 4:25 — effectively impossible to account for in Justification theory — is now entirely legitimate; an eschatological event is now clearly saving for Abraham, for Christ, and for subsequent Christians. And this emphasis points ahead smoothly to Paul's extended discussions of salvation in Romans 5–8 (esp. ch. 6).

OD 24: Paul's narrow and aggressive exegesis that revolves largely around Genesis 15:6 is now arguably more understandable and responsible; he is simply scanning the Pentateuch and then reading an appropriate verse, along with its implicit narrative, in the light of the Christ event. Those who share this presupposition will presumably find his reading plausible if not helpful; those who do not would not, and neither can they be blamed for not doing so. They are simply reading in relation to a different conversation and different presuppositions. But *the Teacher* and the Roman Christians are meant to be reading within the same circle of expectations, so this exegesis is not unfair or distorted for them.

If the extensive set of difficulties set in motion by the conventional reading of Romans 4:23-25 has now been dealt with by our alternative rhetorical and apocalyptic approach, then what of the remaining problems that were noted earlier in the conventional construal of Romans 4 as a whole?

7.2. Problems Solved in Romans 3:27–4:25

There are two further textual difficulties specific to the broader interpretation of Romans 3:27–4:25 in conventional terms, both overdeterminations, and they seem to have been eliminated smoothly as well.

> OD 14: Strictly speaking, it is not appropriate in Justification theory merely to overrule justification by works and any consequent boasting before God in relation to meritorious behavior simply in favor of some principle of πίστις. The collapse of justification by works should be internal, so 3:27-28 is quite an embarrassment. However, given our apocalyptic rereading, which is merely contrasting different gospels from 3:27 onward, the direct overruling of one of those alternatives, corroborated by Scripture, is exactly what we would expect — Paul's gospel (assisted by the appropriate use of Scripture) overruling the Teacher's countervailing assertions. This argumentative anomaly therefore disappears.
>
> OD 15: In like manner, the temporal overruling of circumcision and Mosaic law that Paul effects in Romans 4:9-16a is embarrassing for Justification theory, which again relies on a different argument in relation to Judaism and fails concomitantly to recognize the validity of any temporal argument. But these maneuvers are hardly problematic for our developing rereading in terms of two different gospels. Paul (again) simply overrules one gospel (a false one) in favor of the other (his true one).

As a result of this, it can now be seen that *all* the exegetical difficulties detected in the conventional reading of Romans 1–4 — principally through the analysis of part three, chapter eleven — have been dealt with. Moreover, with the inclusion of the insights of the exegetical analysis of this chapter — especially that "the Abraham analogy" of Romans 4 should be understood in a thick, christocentric sense — the eleven under- and twenty-four overdeterminations generated by the conventional reading at this point (which, among other things, reads this analogy in thin, mimetic sense) have all been resolved as well. And this is an apposite point to note just how extraordinary the set of advantages delivered to the interpreter by the rereading of Romans 4 in the foregoing terms is.

Paul's discussion of Abraham in Romans 4 has generally been regarded as one of Justification's trump cards — as a definitive proof that he does indeed hold and endorse the concerns articulated by that theory. This material has consequently been deployed aggressively against various other readings of Paul, supposedly to refute them decisively (and it is an effective rejoinder against certain counterproposals[81]). But we have now seen that a reading of Abraham in Romans 4 in terms of Justification is deeply flawed; that reading is riven with difficulties. However, my alternative account of this data, characterized by a broader sensitivity to the rhetoric of the letter (which is of course basically a debate between Paul and the Teacher), and a heightened awareness of Paul's apocalyptic and

christocentric argumentation within one pole of that unfolding rhetoric, eliminates all those difficulties. Not one remains standing. The alternative reading
therefore seems to be decisively superior to the conventional account. And, far
from being a strong point in the case for understanding Paul in terms of Justification, Romans 4 now seems to be one of its deepest vulnerabilities — a stretch of
text and argumentation where that reading's and theory's difficulties are most
clearly exposed. In the absence of any effective rebuttal in this relation, then, to
speak of Abraham in Romans 4 is now to point to some of the gravest inadequacies of the conventional approach. Conversely, to read Abraham in Romans 4
with a constant awareness of the underlying template of the faithful Christ is to
eliminate those inadequacies and to read this text well.

But the conventional reading of Romans 4 also unleashes far more than a
slate of strictly exegetical difficulties (however extensive that seems in its own
right); it launches Justification theory as part of Paul's broader thinking as well.
Hence, part one documented the numerous difficulties generated by this theoretical level in the discussion — seven intrinsic, ten systematic, and four empirical
difficulties, many of which also resurface at the proximate frame of Romans 1–4
(namely, the transition into the argumentation of Romans 5–8). And it can now
be seen that the remaining problems in *this* slate of difficulties have *also* been resolved by the alternative construal of faith developed in this chapter in relation to
Romans 4. But in order to appreciate this clearly, we should first summarize the
new account of faith that has been developed.

The notion of "faith" emerging from my rereading of Romans 1–4 is essentially participatory. That is, "Christian faith," which seems to embrace several related aspects ranging from right beliefs about God, through trust, to steadfast fidelity over time, is isomorphic with Christ's own "faith." Moreover, Christ's "faith"
is a metonymic motif that evokes the broader phenomenon of his passion, and in
particular the downward trajectory of his martyrdom — that he was "obedient to
the point of death — even death on a cross" (Phil. 2:8b). So the motif of "faith" is
best located in a set of key narratives; Christian faith, like Christ's faith, functions
within a story (a story, it should be recalled, attempting to narrate a reality that
grips both Christ and the Christian). But given that these stories follow a trajectory through suffering, death, and resurrection, it ultimately makes little sense to
speak of a comprehensive mimetic relationship (i.e., of a thin analogy between
Christ and the Christian). More likely is a participatory relationship, the Christian being caught up into Christ's story in the deeper sense of being caught up
into Christ himself, presumably by the work of the Spirit, thereby being drawn
into the new creation of the age to come. These are stories of divine transformation — eschatological stories. A human appropriation would therefore be faintly
ludicrous, if not pitiful (see 1 Cor. 15:13-19). The term "apocalyptic" emphasizes
the dramatic, reconstitutive, and fundamentally unconditional nature of the acts
of which these narratives speak — and in a permanent protest against their reduction to a merely human level! In sum, then, in Paul's language of "faith" we actually glimpse potentially, if not necessarily, a dramatic underlying set of claims

about the transformation of the Christian through the death and resurrection of Christ — the claims of much of Romans 5–8, as we have already seen in part one, chapter three. And at this point it remains only to ask why Paul privileges the language of faith so strongly in Romans 1–4 (i.e., at certain points). Surely all of this could have been expressed rather more clearly — as indeed it seems to be in Romans 5–8, not to mention elsewhere. The answer to this question is bound up with the contingent argumentation that we have been uncovering in Romans 1–4 — the text's rhetorical dimension.

I have suggested that Romans 1–4 is a subtle but penetrating engagement by Paul with the gospel of the Teacher; such a reading is the most coherent in terms of the letter's probable contingency, and also solves all the exegetical difficulties apparent in its conventional construal. But one of the Teacher's strengths is his exegetical skill; he is precisely a *teacher,* learned in the Jewish scriptures! Paul nevertheless clearly feels equal to this challenge, being a trained exegete himself, so here, in Romans 1–4, he crafts his opposition to the Teacher's claims in fundamentally scriptural terms. Using various key texts (most of which we know by now, although one or two more will be uncovered in chapter nineteen when we consider Romans 9–10) he voices his initial opposition to the Teacher's constructions in phrases and terms that both the Teacher and his audience will find authoritative — the language of Scripture. In fact, he carefully constructs a network of interrelated texts that falsifies the teacher's gospel, and corroborates his own. And one of the key links within that network is πιστ- terminology (along with δικαιο- terminology of course). Through Romans 1–4 (and his other Justification texts), Paul manipulates his selected faith texts skillfully to counteract various claims and criticisms by the Teacher. These manipulations are not reducible to a single argument, neither do they lead us *directly* to the heart of Paul's own gospel — although they are premised on it, as I have already indicated; the implicit rationale for their deployment is participatory and apocalyptic. But this rationale must be recovered from their rhetorical function, which is polemical, antithetical, and scriptural.

We have of course already recovered their principal argumentative implications and deployments in Romans 1–4 — which occur largely in 3:21–4:25, with a brief anticipation in 1:16-17. (Their deployments in Romans 10, Galatians, and beyond, will be considered in detail in part five.) Paul states his reliance on these πιστ- texts in 3:21-22 (having anticipated this claim in 1:17), emphasizing, in an obvious allusion to Romans 4, that at least part of his scriptural witness is from the Torah — Genesis 15:6. In this way he sets up a scriptural comparison, in 4:2-22, which is intended to refute the Teacher's various claims about Abraham, articulated in 3:27-31. But in 3:23-26 and 4:23-25 the underlying participatory rationale of Paul's πιστ- claims comes into view more clearly — their evocation of Christian participation in Christ's death and resurrection — anticipating the ethical and eschatological challenges addressed by Paul in detail in Romans 5–8 (although in this material he drops his point-for-point, scriptural engagement with the Teacher's gospel, and πιστ- terms per se largely fade from view). These deployments by no means exhaust Paul's use of πιστ- texts against the Teacher's position; more interesting exchanges will be traced through subsequent chapters here. But enough is apparent by this point for us to address the theoretical issues.

We saw in part one that the account of faith suggested by Justification theory generated a number of difficulties in its own terms, and contributed to a spread of further problems within Paul's broader interpretation. But I suggest that all these difficulties are now resolved by the alternative account of faith that emerges from my rhetorical and apocalyptic rereading — that is, by the essentially participatory account summarized briefly here.

Intrinsic Difficulties

ID 4: Justification theory presupposes a fundamental capacity and incapacity in humanity. Moreover, that capacity relates to two important sets of actions. Humanity is held accountable for falling short of ethical perfection in the non-Christian state (where capacity should be extensive) — a problem resolved by the argumentative reorientation of Romans 1:18–3:20 in chapter fourteen. But humanity is also expected to have the capacity to choose to believe and so be saved, thereby entering phase two — the easier criterion of faith acknowledging a reduced capacity, but still presupposing *a degree* of capacity that is arguably challenging (and especially if the example of Abraham, as elucidated by Rom. 4:17-22, is taken seriously). With the removal of a voluntarist construal of faith from Romans 3–4, and the introduction instead of a participatory account, the problems associated with human capacity have been resolved. (Human incapacity can be graciously transformed in Christ, faith being one aspect of that transformation.)

ID 7: The account of faith suggested by Justification theory raised various serious difficulties in its own right — whether in the voluntarist A, or the involuntary (more elective) C variant. But the participatory account of faith avoids both these conundrums. The genesis of faith is no longer problematic, as it is for the A variant; it is generated through participation. And the baffling and/or arbitrary nature of faith in the C variant is also resolved; faith is now tightly connected to God's act in Christ, and derives directly from it.

Systematic and Proximate Difficulties

SD 1: A participatory account of faith aligns as a phenomenon with the depiction of theological understanding apparent elsewhere in Paul, which is retrospective and unconditional (or, in a word, apocalyptic).

SD 2: The anthropological implication of a participatory account of faith is now also consistent — that humanity needs rescue.

SD 3: The basal conception of God, as benevolent, is congruent with a participatory account of faith.

SD 4: A participatory account of faith opens directly onto a fuller and consistent account of the atonement — a saving narrative that progresses from obedience, through death, to resurrected life.

SD 5: A participatory account of faith is entirely consistent with the nature of salvation, including the basis and depth of Christian assurance, apparent elsewhere in Paul — which is of course participatory! This is especially important because these soteriological tensions generate the principal proximate tensions as well, as the letter's argument moves from chapters 1–4 to 5–8.

SD 6: The nature and role of "faith" apparent elsewhere in Paul now align smoothly with the account of faith supplied by Romans 1–4. It is gifted to the Christian, in community, and then seems to be one aspect of ongoing Christian existence.

SD 7/8: A vigorous and coherent ethic and ecclesiology are implicit in a participatory, christocentric and pneumatological account of faith.

SD 9: The problem of Jewish description has already been largely resolved by the arguments of chapter fourteen, but it is worth recalling that the conventional depiction of Abraham is offensive and problematic in descriptive terms in relation to Judaism as well, exacerbating this difficulty (see OD 21 — and OD 22 is also troublesome). Reducing Judaism to "salvation through faith alone" on the basis of an uncompromising reading of Genesis 15:6, and then excluding all "works," i.e., all additional Jewish praxis — even that dictated by the OT — seemed odd, and especially when Paul himself seemed to supply alternative descriptions elsewhere (and see more on this shortly, in chapter nineteen). The christocentric account of Paul's hermeneutic is consequently a welcome rejoinder to this difficulty. That is, Paul is not making claims about Judaism, or Jewish exegesis, but supplying a Christian account of Abraham and the Abrahamic Scriptures applicable only to that constituency.

Empirical Difficulties

ED 1: As we have just seen in relation to SD 9, Paul is not now supplying an account of Judaism (i.e., in terms of "faith alone") that must tally exactly with the available self-descriptions of Judaism in Paul's day but rather a Christian reading of part of the Pentateuch and of Jewish tradition. Some continuity ought to be discernible in this relation — and arguably it is — but the basis for this reading is Christianity, not Judaism, and the portrayal of Abraham that results is intended primarily for Christians (including Jewish Christians), not Jews.

ED 2/3/4: Justification's accounts of conversion in general, of Paul's conversion, and of the nature of Paul's missionary preaching were all found to be deficient. However, the fundamentally rhetorical and comparative account that I have supplied of Romans 1–4, including its apocalyptic description of Paul's side of the argument, liberates the interpretation of Romans 1–4 from the need to describe conversion at all (even as it provides a corresponding liberation from the need to describe Judaism in prior terms). The "faith" spoken of repeatedly here by Paul is not the individual's saving faith whereby he or she converts, but evidence of a participation in the faithful Christ that has already been effected. Romans 1–4 is not a programmatic account of salvation and its progressions, or by implication of Paul's own journey, or by implication of Paul's missionary preaching. All the tensions apparent here in relation to the Justification discourse consequently evaporate. Implicit only is the elective and participatory nature of salvation, and of conversion understood within that framework. That Paul is describing conversion in any sense in Romans 1–4 directly, however, now seems unlikely.

It is of course Paul's opponent, the Teacher, who is committed to a more programmatic notion of conversion similar to the set of positions generally ascribed by Justification advocates to Paul, because he shares a foundationalist approach to salvation with Justification theory. The two systems are not identical, because the Teacher does not endorse salvation through faith alone. However, the underlying similarities are more important than the superficial differences. Any prospective, rationalistic, anthropocentric understanding of salvation *must* coordinate preaching, argumentation, and conversion (however unhappily in ultimate sociological and theological terms). Such advocates hold that individuals essentially think their way to salvation, from which conviction all these other deleterious associations inevitably follow. What a bitter irony it is to have construed Paul's brilliant attack *on* foundationalism *as* a foundationalist discourse for so long! In fact, Paul's participatory account of "faith" directly contradicts this entire conception; the apocalyptic faith that he speaks of and presupposes is revealed and unconditional.

And with these important realizations, it remains only to consider where the debate as a whole, and my unfolding argument in this book, now stand.

7.3. A Problem-Free Reading

I would suggest that the textual citadel for Justification theory in relation to which all else essentially stands or falls — that is, the conventional construal of Romans 1–4 — has been taken. A vast array of difficulties and problems is apparent in its conventional reading, while the rereading offered here, as far as I can tell, resolves *all* of those problems, raising no further difficulties of its own. And this creates a new interpretative state of play. Justification theory must, if it is to recapture this critical ground and survive as a plausible historical construction in relation to Paul, carry out three tasks, at least to some degree.

First, it must supply a positive justification for its own construal, and not merely assert its truth by reputation or default (that is, by begging the question). Second, it must resolve the difficulties now apparent in that construal, of which there are upward of fifty (although admittedly these vary in severity). And, third, it must find difficulties of equal or greater weight in the suggested rereading. (I am not yet aware of any, although these could be problems of either justification or implication, just as I have suggested exist for the conventional construal.) These are clearly considerable tasks. Furthermore, in view of their severity as well as their necessity, it is no longer enough simply to say, "I do not believe" (viz., in this alternative reading). Things have now moved beyond any defense in terms of mere denial. A great weight of tradition and commentary is no remedy for absent justifications, crumbling defenses, and undamaged alternatives. Still, the suggested rereading faces further tasks of its own. We must now introduce the remaining texts of relevance into our discussion — the task of part five. Is the new rhetorical and apocalyptic rereading sustainable outside Romans 1–4?

PART FIVE

Rereading the Heartland

CHAPTER NINETEEN

Rereading the Rest of Romans

§1. Preamble

We have now reached an important juncture in the unfolding argument of this book — in fact, the final one. By this point the conventional reading of Romans 1–4 has been displaced by an alternative interpretation that is, more broadly, a rhetorical reading, and more narrowly, an apocalyptic account of Paul's gospel. This alternative interpretation is able to avoid the multitude of problems that the conventional construal generates — partly because it does not raise many of them by inaugurating Justification theory — and seems in addition to raise few if any of its own, so it ought to be judged the best reading of Romans 1–4 that is currently available. With the success of this alternative construal, the main exegetical support for Justification theory as an account of Paul's gospel has been eliminated (which is *not* to say that Paul's *gospel* has been eliminated!). Romans 1–4 can now be seen to point in another direction. It remains only to see whether this localized victory can be maintained through the rest of Paul's texts usually held to endorse Justification theory — various well-known pericopes from Romans and elsewhere that have already been noted in part and now need to be articulated in more detail. It is this further, more extended analysis that is the subject of the fifth and final part in my overarching argument. But as we turn to assess these texts, it is important to appreciate that the interpretative tables have been subtly turned. Different interpretative dynamics are now in place, and these should allow us to treat these texts more rapidly than we did Romans 1–4.

These dynamics derive in the first instance from the nature of the texts. While they share obvious points of similarity with Romans 1–4, they are invariably rather briefer than that extended discussion, and in some instances they are extremely vestigial and allusive. Previously, it has not been that difficult for advocates of Justification to maintain the central claims of their discourse through these briefer texts; they have been able to presuppose the presence of the discourse largely unopposed, given its power and overt demonstration in Romans 1–4[1] — until now, that is. In the light of the present argument, any such interpretative maneuvers must now be deemed inappropriate (because that reading of Romans 1–4 has been eliminated) and ought to be resisted. So when we approach these texts in what follows, with ears attuned to both the problems of Justification theory and the advantages of a more rhetorical and apocalyptic approach, new interpretative dynamics will become apparent.

On the one hand, it will be increasingly evident that Justification theory cannot rise again from these texts. Without the detailed moves of Romans 1–4, they are invariably too brief and vestigial to launch this complex theory (i.e., Justification theory is textually underdetermined by them). Although much of the commentary seems oblivious to this problem, it is not difficult to demonstrate that the exegesis of all the relevant texts outside Romans 1–4 invariably steps back *into* that key text at some point or points to find direct corroboration and explication of most if not all of its key claims. With Romans 1–4 removed from the equation, however, this underlying dependency — and consequent vulnerability — becomes apparent. So we will confirm here in fact what earlier seemed likely on prima facie grounds. Without the help of the conventional reading of Romans 1–4 — whether overt or subliminal — the generation of Justification theory from these additional texts proves difficult if not impossible. It is for these reasons that we can speak of Romans 1–4 as the Justification discourse's "citadel," and these related, ancillary texts as its "heartland."[2] Exegetical control of the citadel is determinative of the surrounding discourse's viability — much as political and military control of Jerusalem was inevitably determinative of Judea's fate.

On the other hand, more rhetorical and apocalyptic rereadings of these texts do seem entirely sustainable and indeed "smooth" — the vital result if my rereading of Paul's Justification texts is to be maintained more broadly. By this I mean that these alternative readings seem to give an entirely satisfactory account of all the available textual data, and nothing obvious stands against them (i.e., in the manner of the textual overdeterminations that continue to arise in relation to Justification theory). But the relative balance between these two sets of exegesis should also be noted carefully, since it is this asymmetry that allows the following treatments to be rather shorter than was previously the case.

If Justification theory is to recover, at least in part, it needs a decisive victory in these texts. If it could be shown that another text in Paul outside Romans 1–4 articulated Justification theory quite plainly, then the theory would have to be admitted as a fair description of at least part of Paul's thought (precisely on these grounds). Moreover, an overwhelmingly obvious exegetical victory would probably force us to reevaluate our construal of Romans 1–4. The discourse as a whole might then be set on the road to recovery. However, my rereading does not need another such victory in exegetical terms; in my view, that has already been achieved. (Roman 1–4 *must* be interpreted in an alternative way.) So all that is needed for the apocalyptic rereader is *sustainability* — the military equivalent of a series of draws or standoffs. If the rereading developed in relation to Romans 1–4 can be maintained, largely problem free, through all the other related texts in Paul, then the demise of Justification theory seems assured, *and even if it too can offer a sustainable reading of some of Paul's other Justification texts* (which I think it can[3]).

That is, for a given text, in the absence of any clear indications from elsewhere in Paul in favor of Justification theory — and the presence of clear indications concerning a different, rhetorical and apocalyptic approach in Romans 1–4 — the interpretative balance must tilt decisively in favor of the latter rereading. We now simply lack any good reasons for supposing that Justification theory *is* functioning in Paul, unless these ancillary texts directly supply it. We already know that Paul thinks and argues in apocalyptic terms, both in relation to Romans 1–4 and in other extensive discussions. So we are entitled to endorse further interpretations in terms of the latter, but at present we have no good reasons for asserting the validity of the former (and this is why the struggle for Romans 1–4 is so strategically important).

In short, an appropriate exegetical suggestion in relation to all these texts on behalf of my rereading will be enough to guarantee the success of my overarching project (although it is important to note that included within the definition of "appropriate" here is the absence of any overt countervailing data). Justification advocates, however, will need at least one decisive victory at some point — a text where their reading *must* be right, and overtly and demonstrably so.

As we work through the relevant texts, some of the difficulties already uncovered by a hard-nosed scrutiny of the relationship between Romans 1–4 and Justification theory will be reinforced as they arise again. But additional difficulties will also be exposed — new points where Paul's texts and arguments seem unavoidably to embarrass Justification. So which texts are we actually concerned with? It is time to consider this question in a little more detail.[4]

§2. Identifying the "Heartland" Texts

In striking lexical and phraseological similarities, a number of passages echo the argumentation of Romans 1–4. And although at first glance they do not seem to articulate it in sufficient detail to establish Justification theory in their own right, in view of their close family resemblance to the key text in Romans, the Justification schema may legitimately be transferred into, and assumed within, their argumentation (provided of course that it has been established elsewhere). It is fair for a citadel to extend its control over a surrounding χώρα. We can dub this set of ancillary texts the discourse's "heartland."[5]

In identifying these texts, we may be guided in the first instance by the distinctive lexical correlations in the citadel. Paul's argument in Romans 1–4 deploys δικαιο- terms at strategic points using both the noun and the cognate verb. The phrase δικαιοσύνη Θεοῦ (or its equivalent) also occurs in sudden densities in distinctive locations. The argument then deploys πίστις instrumentally in relation to these terms, less frequently using the verb πιστεύω, this last often in the form of a participle. Most importantly, it sets πίστις (or πιστεύω) over against ἔργα νόμου (or an obviously analogous participle), in a famous antithesis. Hence, the discourse's summarizing rubric is almost invariably "justification by faith" complemented by ". . . not [justification] by works of law." In essence, the citadel sets up a fourfold correlation, using two sets of words with the distinctive stems δικαιο- and πιστ-, and then νόμος in relation to ἔργα or to ποιέω, arranging this last motif antithetically against πίστις within a broader frame established by the δικαιο- terms. Thus, more significant than the mere incidence of any of these words alone in the Pauline corpus will be their occurrence in this distinctive fourfold correlation, or in some recognizable sequence drawn from the fuller arrangement.

δικαιοσύνη/δικαιοῦν   οὐ δικαιοσύνη/δικαιοῦν
ἐκ πίστεως/πιστεύειν   ἐξ ἔργα/ποιεῖν νόμου

And in fact we find this pattern in a number of other, shorter Pauline passages alongside Romans 1–4.

The first set of terms to cross-reference is νόμος in relation to some notion of "working" or "doing." Ἔργα νόμου (or its equivalent) occurs in Romans 2:12 (2x), 13 (2x), 14 (4x), 15, 17, 18, 20, 23 (2x), 25 (2x), 26, 27; 3:19, 20 (2x: v. 20a/Ps. 143:2), 21 (2x), 27 (2x), 28, 31 (2x); 4:2, 4, 5; 9:31 (2x); 10:4, 5; Galatians 2:16 (3x: v. 16c/Ps 143:2); 3:2, 5, 10 (2x: v. 10b; Deut. 27:26), 11, 12 — that is, in Romans 2:12–4:5 and 9:31–10:5, and in Galatians 2:16 and 3:2-12.

In conjunction with δικαιο- terms it occurs as follows: in Romans, with δικαιοσύνη, in 3:21; 9:31-32; 10:5; with δικαιόω in 2:13; 3:20, 28; 4:2; and with δίκαιος in 2:13; in Galatians, with the verb only, in 2:16 and 3:11-12. (For Philippians compare 3:2, 6, 9.) Hence, *wherever it occurs, the phrase ἔργα νόμου (or its close equivalent) tends to appear in conjunction with δικαιο- terminology.*

But *overlaps between πιστ- terms and ἔργα νόμου also occur in these texts:* in Romans in 3:20-22, 27-31; 4:11-17; 9:30-33; 10:4-6; and in Galatians in 2:16; (3:2, noun only); and 3:5-11 — that is, *in essentially the same texts* (see again Phil. 3:2, 9).

And it completes this set of correlations to observe that πιστ- and δικαιο- terms *also* tend to coincide distinctively in these texts, although the pattern is more complex because of the greater number of these cognates. In Romans πίστις coincides with δικαιοσύνη in 1:17; 3:3-5, 22, 25, 26; 4:3/5, 9, 11, 13, 20/22; 9:30-33; 10:3-6?; (14:17/22-23?); and πιστεύω coincides with δικαιοσύνη in 1:16/17; (3:2/5?); 3:22; 4:3, 5, 11, (17, 18, 24?); 9:33; 10:4, 9, 10, 11. Similarly, in Galatians, the verb πιστεύω correlates exactly (in Gen 15:6!) in 3:6, and closely in 3:21/22, and not otherwise; it is in any case very rare (four or five instances). The substantive πίστις also has a very strong correlation: 2:20/21; 3:5/6/7, 21/22/23; 5:5. Philippians 3:9 is also a perfect — and somewhat typical — correlation.

The pattern with respect to the verb δικαιόω is similar. In Romans, πίστις occurs close to δικαιόω in 3:3/4, 22-26, 28, 30; 4:5; 5:1; and πιστεύω occurs in context in 3:2/3/4, 20/22/24/26; 4:2/3, 5; 6:7/8. In Galatians, the noun πίστις correlates perfectly with δικαιόω when the latter occurs: see 2:16/17; 3:8, 11, 24; 5:4/5, and the uncommon πιστεύω also correlates strongly, except in 2:7: see 2:16; 3:6/8, 22/24. The rare adjective πιστός is close as well: see 3:8/9/11.

It is also worth noting that the correlation is almost perfect for δικαιοσύνη Θεοῦ: see Romans 1:17; 3:5, 21, 22, 25, 26; 10:3 (2x); 1 Corinthians 1:30; 2 Corinthians 5:21; and Philippians 3:9b. (See also possible implicit instances in Romans 9:30, 31; 10:4, 6; Galatians 2:21; 3:21; 5:5).

To draw a long statistical story short, where νόμος is cross-referenced with some sense of "working," the resulting group of references *also* tends to coincide with a significant incidence of δικαιο- *and* πιστ- terms. So there is a distinctive four-way correlation in certain texts. This is highly significant: while all the word groups we have investigated are found not infrequently outside these particular texts (and, indeed, outside the three or four letters where these texts occur), the fourfold correlation is *not* found outside these texts. Even a twofold correlation is difficult to detect. Hence, these texts almost certainly constitute the further territorial heartland of the Justification schema in Paul. To go beyond these texts will prove very difficult to argue. To go as far as them, however, will be relatively easy to maintain.

Several passages emerge as possessing the same lexical pattern as the citadel text: Romans 5:1-11 (esp. vv. 1-2 and 9),[6] perhaps 6:7-8,[7] and certainly 9:30–10:21 (although the terminology fades as chapter 10 progresses, with the last instance of this correlation occurring in v. 17); Galatians 2:15–3:29 (although it is both more precise and perhaps also more significant to point specifically to 2:16; 3:1-5, 3:6-14, and 3:21-25 or 26); and Galatians 5:5-6 (possibly also with a backward glance at v. 4, and one forward to 6:14-15). Philippians echoes this pattern a little more distantly in 3:9, especially in the light of 3:2 and 6 (as does Ephesians 2:8-10, perhaps still more distantly).[8] This set of heartland texts consequently amounts — at most — to a total of about sixty verses, a mere 60 percent of the length of the key Romans text itself (which is just over one hundred verses long). Inevitably, then, the argumentation in these ancillary texts will be less detailed than that of the citadel.[9]

In support of the foregoing we should note four further correlations in the citadel and heartland texts:

1. the antithetical motifs of περιτομή and ἀκροβυστία;[10]
2. the similarly antithetical coordination of boasting and shame — καύχησις (verb καυχάομαι) and ἐπαισχύνομαι/καταισχύνω;[11]
3. the detailed discussion of Abraham;[12] and
4. in the context of discussions of Abraham, the tendency to quote short scriptural texts (texts containing all of our key signifiers and phrases or their close equivalents).[13]

None of these further observations are *entirely* limited to the Justification heartland, but they are reasonably distinctive and may function as supporting considerations with respect to this cluster of texts; they correspond very closely to the group of texts already isolated and so confirm our earlier preliminary judgments. Their causality is not perfect, but it certainly seems significant.

The heartland texts

The basic antithesis of four correlated terms, which identifies a particular set of texts, with supporting considerations

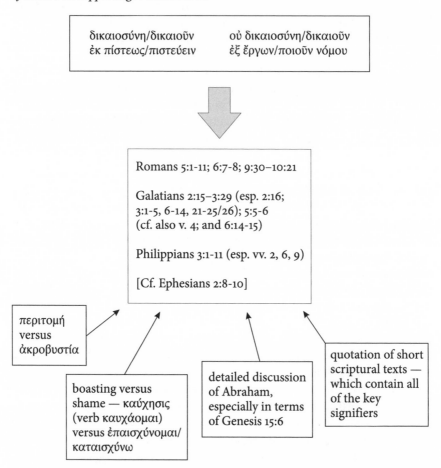

With this lexical identification of the discourse's heartland in place, we are prepared to venture beyond the citadel to test the exegetical sustainability of both the Justification reading and the suggested rhetorical and apocalyptic rereading of Paul's Justification texts.

§3. The Argumentative Dynamic of Romans 9–11

The obvious point at which to begin this investigation of exegetical sustainability is with the rest of Romans, where our main focus will be chapter 10 (specifically, 9:30–10:21).[14] This notoriously difficult passage contains the densest accumulation of key Justification terms and motifs found anywhere in the letter other than the citadel text (Romans 1–4). Furthermore, it provides several of the most explicit challenges in all of Paul to my suggested rereading of his Justification texts, especially in its account of Israel's deficiencies in terms of "works of law" (see esp. 9:31-32), its characterization of Christ as the τέλος of the law (in 10:4), its quotation of Leviticus 18:5 in 10:5 apparently to describe Jewish activity again in terms of "works" (here literally "doing"), and its account of saving "faith" (see esp. 10:9-10). It will consequently be vital to the overarching cogency of my project to show how an alternative, apocalyptic rereading of this text is possible — one that can deal fairly with the challenges just noted.

Interpreters have struggled to grasp how Romans 9–11 functions consistently both within itself and in relation to the letter as a whole. (Solutions offered to resolve this last question range across a full spectrum, from Dodd's suggestion essentially to excise it as a poorly integrated, preexisting unit to Baur's suggestion that it is the climax of the entire letter! In the disparity between these theories the difficulty of the passage is immediately apparent.[15]) However, I suggest that these difficulties can be resolved in large measure if we consider this text as part of an ongoing debate with the Teacher, who is, it should be recalled, a learned Jewish Christian still committed in some sense to circumcision and law observance by any converts to Christ. As I have already suggested (in chapter thirteen), Romans 9–11 makes excellent sense in this particular setting as a cluster of arguments of type B, that is, defensive arguments mounted by Paul to rebut serious criticisms of his own position.[16] And those criticisms are now not especially difficult to detect.

In essence, the Teacher seems to have asked whether the anomalous salvation history generated in part by Paul himself calls Paul's version of the gospel into question and discredits it. An absurd salvation history implies, after all, an absurd gospel (along with an absurd, not to mention treacherous, apostle).[17] There are, moreover, multiple absurdities evident at this point, namely, saved pagans, those reprobates being saved — still worse — law-free (i.e., without circumcision, etc.), and unsaved Jews, this all being advocated by a former Jewish teacher! Romans 9–11 is consequently viewed usefully as an attempt by Paul both to articulate these issues for his Roman Christian auditors and to rebut them satisfactorily. And there is something highly plausible about this overarching interpretative suggestion.

The Teacher is making an astute set of observations; they are, after all, frequently echoed even today. While exact numbers and percentages are lacking, it seems probable that the majority of Jews rejected the implications that the early church ascribed to Jesus. Moreover, various missions seem to have succeeded in attracting converts from paganism to him (and still do), and Paul's mission did not insist on circumcision or law observance in this relation (in fact insisting, rather, that these practices not be enacted, and this is still largely the case today). These two countervailing conversion trends create an excruciatingly anomalous position for the gospel, and especially for Paul's version of it. The ancestral people of God, prepared for salvation for millennia, have turned their backs on this ostensible salvation when it has arrived, despite possessing sacred texts that tutor them concerning its nature and meaning. Meanwhile, those unprepared and traditionally unresponsive to God seem to have begun to convert, and they are not even being asked to adopt the key ancestral practices — the true markers of holiness and righteousness (etc.). In the light of these realities, the claim that the God of Israel has saved the world climactically in Jesus does seem absurd. The right people have not recognized this, and the wrong people have. It seems more likely that the gospel underlying this bizarre dynamic is simply wrong, and the man who proclaims it, a liar or a fool.[18]

It is worth noting that the Teacher himself is also probably in a difficult position in relation to these trends. He too must deal with the fact that the majority of Israel has rejected his Messiah. But it seems to be a particular point of contention between him and Paul that the latter's law-free mission is greatly exacerbating a difficulty that is already acute enough. By insisting on an apparently profligate mission to pagans, Paul further discredits the Christian movement as an authentically Jewish phenomenon. At least the Teacher insists on full pagan conversion to Judaism; pagan converts join the traditional house and lineage of Israel as Jewish proselytes. And possibly the Teacher even continues to believe that not all unbelieving Israel is lost. So perhaps such converts from paganism join with the rest of the saved remnant, to preserve Israel as a whole until widespread conversion takes place (a fascinating possibility that will be noted further momentarily). But Paul's law-free mission enrages the very constituency that the Teacher is trying to appeal to and further discredits a position that is already sufficiently deviant (i.e., acceptance of Jesus of Nazareth as Messiah). We sense at this point, then, that from the Teacher's point of view, Paul is a loose cannon; he takes a gravely difficult situation and greatly inflames it.

It seems quite indicative that Paul articulates, with reasonable clarity, the two basic issues — pagan conversion to Christ, scandalously law-free in the Pauline missions, and the rejection of Christ by the majority of Israel — in Romans 9:30-31.

> [30]Τί οὖν ἐροῦμεν;
> ὅτι ἔθνη τὰ μὴ διώκοντα δικαιοσύνην κατέλαβεν δικαιοσύνην,
> δικαιοσύνην δὲ τὴν ἐκ πίστεως,
> [31]Ἰσραὴλ δὲ διώκων νόμον δικαιοσύνης εἰς νόμον οὐκ ἔφθασεν;

The perception that this agenda underlies Romans 9–11 seems to offer a reasonable explanation of its overarching coordination with the rest of the letter. These conundrums are clearly grave, but they are not central; indeed, they must presuppose certain still more basic phenomena even to constitute a problem. The apparently anomalous conversion trends unfolding since the Christ event assume that conversion to Christ is important and achieves something. The *implications* of the gospel are being used here to discredit the gospel *itself*.[19] (And as we press deeper into the section's arguments, we will find Paul appealing to more fundamental claims as he crafts his response.) Hence, it seems at first glance that Romans 9–11 contains arguments of type B (defense), not type A. However, they are still *important* arguments. Paul regards these criticisms as serious enough to warrant an extensive engagement. That is, some objections can be trivial or foolish, allowing responses of dismissal, ridicule, and so on. But here, Paul struggles through a long discussion to provide serious answers. He respects these particular problems — as he ought to — and it is clear as a result that significant issues are being raised. (And we may be grateful that Paul felt prompted to address them so thoroughly; Romans 9–11 is one of the most sophisticated engagements with these issues in the New Testament.) But before moving on to consider how this basic approach plays out through the texts in detail, either supporting our ongoing program of rhetorical and apocalyptic rereading or undermining it, it is worth noting one more subordinate item within this agenda that can explain a further feature of these texts.

In view of these broad missionary dynamics, Paul's advocacy of a law-free mission to the pagans makes him vulnerable to the criticism that he is a traitor to his own people, abandoning them and their heritage, and advocating the same to whoever will listen to him. To all intents and purposes, then, he has turned his back on authentic Judaism, endorsing some strange pagan variant that is really no Judaism at all, and he seems not to care that his compatriots are almost all condemned (at least in his view[20]). He of course encourages other Jews to join in with his mad scheme. He is consequently that most despicable of all people — a quisling.

This further subordinate argumentative dynamic explains, in my view, the unprecedented presence of Paul himself in the argumentation of Romans 9–11. Paul inserts biographical fragments into this discussion no fewer than three times — in 9:1-3; 10:1; and 11:1b. His first such insertion is characterized by very strong truth claims — the assertion of truthfulness, the repudiation of lying, the witness of conscience, *and* the attestation of the Holy Spirit. And what he asserts is his deep and constant grief over his fellow Jews, almost certainly because of their lack of response to Christ (see 10:1-3). Such is his concern that he says he is even prepared — in an echo of Moses' similarly heroic offer — to sacrifice himself for them (9:3; see Exod. 32:30-32). And 10:1 makes a similar point. Paul asserts that his heart's desire and prayer to God is for their salvation. In 11:1 Paul appears again, in argumentative terms to attest to God's salvation of at least *some*. God has not completely abandoned Israel, because a few Jews, like Paul himself, are saved. Moreover, in making this assertion, Paul introduces his own Jewish pedigree for the first time in Romans, reciting that he is an "Israelite, of the seed of Abraham, of the tribe of Benjamin." He thereby affirms his own authentic Jewish identity *and* implies that he values it; certainly, it is positive enough for him to claim publicly in this way. (The rehearsal of Jewish privileges in 9:4 makes much the same point in more general terms.)

These three assertions by Paul can be treated uncritically by interpreters — especially those concerned to find the appropriate post-Holocaust sensitivities anticipated in Paul himself, who elsewhere views Israel rather harshly. It can be claimed that here we catch a glimpse of what Paul really thinks and feels.[21] More important in the first instance than any judgment of sincerity, however, is a consideration of these comments' rhetorical function(s). They operate to create a particular impression of Paul in the minds of his auditors — of a person who cares profoundly about the plight of unbelieving Jews, being rooted firmly in that tradition himself. And it is a short step to the probable reason for this deliberate self-portrait (one that we have already noted).

Paul has been accused of abandoning his Jewish heritage and not caring about the fate of unbelieving Jews; hence, he asserts just the contrary in these passages. Admittedly, this is a mirror-reading, but it is controlled in context by the perfect integration between these charges and the rest of the argument, not to mention the developing portrait of the Teacher's gospel. It is consistent with the Teacher's program and the present argumentative agenda that Paul would have been accused of these things. Paul's mission to the pagans is itself a direct turning away from the Jewish mission, which does not seem to be going very well, and it further complicates that outreach because of its scandalous nature. His law-free gospel seems, moreover, to imply his own abandonment of his Jewish identity. Paul seems himself, then, in view of these broader trends, neither to be authentically Jewish nor to care for the Jews and their conversion. It appears that the Teacher has rather cleverly exploited some ad hominem possibilities (and Paul will frequently reply in kind, when he can).

With these observations on Paul's initial comments and probable overarching argumentative strategy in Romans 9–11, we can turn to consider the argument in more detail, beginning with Romans 9.

§4. Romans 9:6-29

While it might not be apparent at first, Paul's argument in Romans 9 (specifically, vv. 6-29) is important for this project in several respects. In particular, it confirms strongly two of my earlier claims — the importance of the Wisdom of Solomon (not to mention divine wisdom itself) for the broader debate, and Paul's use of rhetorical "traps" fashioned out of the Teacher's own material. I suggest that these dynamics reemerge as Romans 9 addresses the first aspect in the broad salvation-historical conundrum that Paul is now grappling with in his unfolding debate with the Teacher at Rome — the scandalous inclusion of the pagans in Israel's salvation.[22] I suggest, moreover, that Paul has dealt with this issue to his own satisfaction by v. 26, from which point the discussion turns to the much more difficult issue of Israel's apparent unbelief, a subject that will occupy Paul through 11:36.

(So Romans 10 functions in the context of that particular question, and the present discussion of Romans 9 serves in part to establish it.) For most of Romans 9, then, Paul is responding to the question, Can the pagans plausibly be included by the God of the Jews within the salvation promised to the Jews (see 3:29)? And he argues here that the Teacher *must* accept this inclusion on pain of acute self-contradiction. Indeed, Romans 9 turns out to be another masterful argumentative stroke on Paul's part.

I suggest that the Teacher — and many other Jews at the time — would find nothing disagreeable in Paul's argument from v. 6 through v. 24a. In fact, they would probably warmly endorse it — and this is exactly Paul's design. If this argument is endorsed, then God *must* be allowed to include pagans in salvation in principle. Moreover, the rapid citation of Scripture that ensues suggests that God does in fact wish to do this, having announced it beforehand to those who have ears to hear.

More specifically, Paul exploits here the principle of "election" that is implicit in Israel's patriarchal origins, in the exodus, and in the repeated scriptural motif of God as the potter and humanity (or Israel) as his lump of clay. No Jew would dispute the legitimacy of these three stories, because Israel's very identity is bound up with them (especially the first two). They all revolve around God's election, which tends of course to be warmly endorsed by Jews when it is directed toward a Jewish constituency. However, by conceding this material, the Teacher and all those like him have unwittingly exposed themselves to Paul's reversal, effected from v. 24b, which merely plays out the practice of divine election in relation to pagans and then deploys some scriptural support for that unexpected action.[23]

It is a clever and essentially unanswerable argument. But it has probably been obscured in the past by a fundamentally non-Jewish posture that has facilitated the construal of these stories with a latent hostility to Judaism — or at least an attitude of indifference (an approach that has then created its own problems[24]). Nevertheless, it is vital to grasp that Paul and his interlocutor, along with their Roman auditors, would almost certainly have read these stories *generously*, as true accounts of the origins of Israel — of *their* origin. Their sympathies would have lain with the Jewish protagonists throughout, and it is this expectation that facilitates the implicit concession that Paul then turns into a stunning argumentative reversal. Without this initial preference, the argument functions differently, and rather less effectively.

The first step of Paul's argument, in vv. 6b-13, recounts rapidly the patriarchal origin of Israel, which was of course highly selective. In vv. 7-9 we are reminded that Sarah gave birth to Isaac because of God's promise — a story that the Roman Christian auditors know well by now! (i.e., from Rom. 4:16b-22). And implicit is the exclusion of Ishmael, who was *not* the child that was promised and then miraculously conceived. "Not only this" (v. 10a), but Rebecca, the wife of Isaac, also had two sons, Esau and Jacob, but God intentionally called only one, Jacob. The principal causality in both these births and preferences was therefore divine. No "works" were involved, Paul observes in vv. 11-12, because God announced these destinies before any could be done. It was fully appreciated, it should be stressed, that the origins of Israel involved the divine preference of Isaac over Ishmael and of Jacob over Esau. Israel as a nation was descended from Abraham, Isaac, and Jacob; these figures, and these alone, were "the fathers."[25] But from a Jewish point of view, *this is hardly shocking or even problematic.* It is simply the way God has constituted them in order to bless them!

The same divine activity is discernible in the second great event that lay at the origin of the nation of Israel, namely, the Exodus, to which Paul alludes briefly in vv. 14-18. Is this unfair? Of course not, the pious Jew replies. God showed mercy to Israel, delivering her from bondage in Egypt, and displayed his patience and wrath at the same time in relation to Pharaoh, who was an evil tyrant. (Expecting a Jew to feel sympathy for Pharaoh is a little like expecting modern Europeans to feel sympathy for Adolf Hitler.) Once again, God acted both sovereignly and rightly. What Jew would deny that the Exodus was an act of God, and a wholly legitimate one, because it involved a preference for Jews?!

This dynamic is apparent for the third time in the familiar story of the potter and the clay, which Paul reprises in vv. 19-23 (see Isa. 29:16; 45:9[-11]; Wis. 15:7; see also Wis. 12:12). Potters are allowed to make what they want to out of their clay, whether special, honorable, and glorious vessels, or mundane, ordinary, and even inglorious ones. However, it is vital to grasp that any Jewish sympathizers will continue to read this story positively. *Israel* is the special, honorable, and glorious vessel shaped by the divine craftsman, while only despicable pagans are shaped for ordinary or even destructive use. The preceding two stories have both just made this point, so it seems obvious that the same sympathies should be deployed in relation to this third antithesis (and the divine predications affirm this as well; God's mercy and glory have been consistently directed since v. 6 toward Israel, so the vessels of mercy and glory made by the potter should continue to be identified with Israel — that is, unless clear signals to the contrary are supplied, but they are not).

Hence, by v. 23 Paul has probably elicited a confident "amen" from the mouths of any Jewish auditors or sympathizers. Given that they are positioned within the group being repeatedly privileged through history by God, it is unlikely that they would object. Indeed, to do so would involve protests against some of the core elements in their identity — their descent from Abraham, Isaac, and Jacob (one of the things, it should be noted, to which Paul is currently being accused of disloyalty; but see 11:1!). More likely is their continued endorsement of this privilege's rectitude, and their corresponding repudiation of any objections to it, here in the form of a plaintive interlocutor who queries the rightness of this activity in vv. 14 and 19, although ineffectively. Such interlocutors take their stand with the boorish Ishmael and Esau, whose descendants were later enemies of Israel, and with the great oppressor of Israel, Pharaoh. Paul is drawing, then, on the prevailing hermeneutic of generosity among Jews toward the key accounts of their origins, and the corresponding hermeneutic of suspicion toward any outsiders to that history, as well as any concomitant protests against it in terms of its ethical propriety. However, the operation of these hermeneutics leads to the unwitting endorsement of a principle that can then be used against some of the prejudices embedded within them and their narrative and historical privileging of Jews.

Indeed, with these realizations, we are in a position to grasp the force of Paul's argumentative trap that springs in v. 24. It arrives at the end of a long, seemingly ungrammatical sentence in vv. 22-23 that discusses the activity of the divine potter in relation to honorable and dishonorable vessels. Nevertheless, by v. 23b it is apparent that certain "vessels of mercy" have been "prepared for glory," and these either comprise or include "us, whom he also called, *not only from the Jews but from the pagans . . .*" (v. 24). And it is with this last statement that Paul's argument finally bites.

Jews or Jewish sympathizers now have no grounds on which to challenge the divine right to include pagan converts within the saved people of God. Insofar as they have endorsed the previous account of the constitution of Israel through history, they *must* allow God to make this selection too, should he choose to do so. It is an identical action in terms of divine election or call. So it can be denied only if the preceding history of Israel in these terms is also denied. However, the brilliance of Paul's preparation becomes especially apparent at this point. Not only has God's electing activity been introduced and endorsed in a sympathetic setting, but any objections to this mode of activity have been carefully dismissed en route as well. Are Jewish objectors really going to take their stand at this point, then, with the long pedigree of Israel's enemies — with Ishmael, Esau, and Pharaoh?! Is the clay suddenly going to have its right of protest against the potter upheld?! This seems unlikely. More acceptable — and certainly so in rhetorical terms — will be an acquiescence, however reluctant, to the claim that Paul is making here, namely, that the people of God now can legitimately include pagans should God wish to call them.

Scriptural citation confirms this possibility immediately as Paul quotes Hosea 2:23 (25 LXX) and 1:10 (2:1 LXX) in 9:25-26 in explication of just this point: "Those who were not my people I *will* call 'my people,' and her who was not beloved I *will* call 'beloved.' And in the very place where it was said to them, 'You are not my people,' there they *shall* be called children of the living God [υἱοὶ θεοῦ ζῶντος]" (NRSV). Pagan inclusion in the saved people of God, then, seems to be not merely a possibility latent in the divine action of calling but a reality prophetically foretold.

This is a regrettably brief account of a rhetorical approach to Romans 9 that holds the views and concerns of the Teacher in view; however, it is apparent, even at this early stage of discussion, that it makes excellent sense of the text. Seven features in this reading should be emphasized quickly, in preparation for our more detailed engagement with the next phase of Paul's argument.

(1) Wisdom of Solomon

It seems very likely that the Wisdom of Solomon is again implicitly involved in much of the argument. That text undertakes an extended rehearsal of Israel's early history in chapters 10–19,[26] and this is echoed — and greatly compressed —

by Romans 9:7-18. Patriarchal and exodus material is prominent in this rehearsal (especially the exodus), as it is in Paul's brief reprise. Furthermore, the Wisdom account includes both the characteristic objection noted in Romans 9:14 and 19 (see Wis. 12:12[27]) *and* the motif of the potter and the clay. And even though the extended metaphor of potter and clay in Romans is recognizable as a conflation of the texts of Isaiah 29:16 and 45:9, *only Wisdom discusses the potter in terms of two vessels, one for "clean" and one for "contrary" use* (see 15:7[28]). We must then either follow the implications of Romans 1-4 and continue to see Paul exploiting various appeals by the Teacher to the Wisdom of Solomon, or we must ascribe all these echoes and their mutual relationships to coincidence. It seems best to affirm our earlier judgment that the text of the Wisdom of Solomon is in play in this debate, Paul constantly seeking to subvert the Teacher's use of it.

(2) Argumentative Entrapment

It seems highly significant that one of the same argumentative strategies posited in my rereading of Romans 1-4 is apparent at this point as well. As in Romans 1-3, Paul seems to be manipulating certain commitments of the Teacher in order to extract important concessions from him under the threat of self-contradiction. In Romans 1-3, the initial rhetorical commitments of the Teacher (which were especially close to Wisdom 12-14) were manipulated to undermine his particular solution to the problem there, which included circumcision and law observance. Those practices were eliminated as demonstrably unhelpful and self-contradictory. And the threat of self-contradiction is used in Romans 9 once again, beginning with a summary of the Teacher's own presuppositions, although the point in this argument is not to destroy the Teacher's own position (which may no longer require such treatment). Rather, Paul is extracting the admission that the divine inclusion of pagans within the salvation promised to Israel is acceptable in terms of the Teacher's own account of Israel (which is in turn found in the Wisdom of Solomon, especially in chapters 10-19). The Teacher's criticism of Paul in this sense, then, ought to be abandoned. And this second deployment of essentially the same argumentative move should greatly increase our confidence that Paul made just such an argument in Romans 1-3 as well. The use of the Teacher's presuppositions against him — those presuppositions being informed explicitly by the Wisdom of Solomon — seems to be a repeated tactic in Romans (and Paul himself presumably has little fondness for much of that text).

We should turn now to consider the subtle introduction of two motifs in Romans 9 that will prove to be increasingly important as the rest of Paul's argument unfolds in this subsection (i.e., through 11:36).

(3) Divine Wisdom

It should not be surprising to find the motif of divine wisdom in play in Romans 9. The numerous allusions to the Wisdom of Solomon certainly raise this further possibility (see esp. Wis. 6:12-16; 7:22–8:8). And I suggest that some of Paul's characterizations in Romans 9 also point in this direction, although they remain at this stage little more than hints. In 9:6a Paul states, as the NRSV puts it, "It is not as though *the word of God* had failed" (Οὐχ οἷον δὲ ὅτι ἐκπέπτωκεν ὁ λόγος τοῦ θεοῦ, a text to which we will return momentarily). This λόγος then reappears in v. 9, as the promise that at a certain time God will come again and Sarah will miraculously conceive a child (which we know from Romans 4 is a creative event, in which something that "is" will come from something that "is not," since she must conceive in a "dead" or infertile womb). Paul rarely speaks of "the word of God."[29] Nevertheless, the divine activity in relation to the patriarchs is spoken of shortly again as ἡ κατ᾽ ἐκλογὴν πρόθεσις τοῦ θεοῦ, which is operative once again through creative and effective *words*: ἐρρέθη αὐτῇ ὅτι ὁ μείζων δουλεύσει τῷ ἐλάσσονι. In accordance with this theme, God's "call" echoes through much of this chapter, and parts of chapter 10 as well, resulting in eight of a total of twelve such references in Romans (counting instances of καλέω and ἐπικαλέω in this total: see 9:7, 12, 24, 25, 26; 10:12, 13, 14; note also that three of the other four appear conspicuously in 8:30 (2x) and 33; see elsewhere only — highly significantly — 4:17!). It seems fair, then, to detect the subtle operation of divine wisdom in this cluster of terms and motifs. The creative word of God, coterminous in many texts with God's hidden, eternal purpose, both calls and acts to bring life to those of God's choosing. It is not necessary to insist upon the obvious presence and role of this discourse in Romans 9, but later argumentative moves by Paul will strongly confirm our gathering suspicions in this regard.

(4) ἀγών

In like manner, Paul introduces an ἀγών discourse at this point, but so lightly that commentators have not generally known what to do with it. Nevertheless, its presence is unmistakable. In 9:16 Paul states that God's preference for Jacob over Esau did not depend on human "willing or *running*" (τρέχοντος; see 1 Cor. 9:24, 26; Gal. 2:2; 5:7; Phil. 2:16; see also 2 Thess. 3:1). When exactly were Jacob or Esau "running," one wonders.[30] (The answer to this question will become apparent shortly.)

(5) ἐκπίπτω

It is worth noting, in the light of the foregoing discoveries, that the opening claim in this discussion (9:6a) seems not infrequently to have been misinterpreted. This statement is almost invariably translated, as we have just seen, in terms of *failure* — hence the NRSV: "It is not as though the word of God had failed." To be sure, "failure" is a possible sense for the verb ἐκπίπτω. But this translation arguably obscures Paul's actual argument (and it also tends to legitimize a host of dubious claims about the broader argument of Romans 9–11[31]). Paul's rhetorical mechanics in this passage have now been clarified, along with the issue presently at stake

— that of the scandalous inclusion of pagans in the people of God, a constituency that was traditionally coterminous with the Jews. Furthermore, we have observed how Paul traces the origins of Judaism back to the patriarchs, where God's word created some of those ancestors (notably Isaac) and excluded others (notably Ishmael and Esau). It seems far more likely, then, that the verb ἐκπίπτω used in 9:6a takes meaning two, as BDAG presents that — namely, "to drift off course" (which also facilitates the sense "run aground"; see 307-8; see also Acts 27:17, 26, 29, and possibly also 32). This sense fits the present argument and its focal issue like a hand in a glove: (to modify the NRSV) "It is not as though the word of God *deviated* [or *drifted off course*]," that is, *to include pagans as well as Jews* (and perhaps even to the exclusion of the latter). There is no explicit claim, either in this localized argument or more broadly, that *God's* purpose has ever failed, although it might have been thwarted temporarily;[32] this is a conundrum that interpreters must supply to the text (and are perhaps assisted in doing by modern apologetic concerns).[33] Neither Paul nor the Teacher, I suggest, doubts either the reality or the ultimate fidelity of God. There is, however, an overt and sustained instance of apparent deviation — namely, pagan inclusion in salvation. We can virtually hear the Teacher accusing Paul in such terms: "Has the creative and saving word of God drifted off course?! Your gospel seems to suggest that it has, dragging pagans into the people of God! Indeed, it seems destined for shipwreck . . ." (And so on.)

(6) A Historical, Collective, Elective Judaism

It is important to note that Paul conducts this entire argument within fundamentally historical and collective parameters. He also artfully introduces and develops the principle of divine election.[34] These emphases run through the center of the entire discussion; they are both obvious and unavoidable. But in so characterizing Israel's past, the text presents a fundamental challenge to Justification theory, which, as we have seen in some detail, characterizes the pre-Christian phase in a timeless, ahistorical, individualistic, and contractual fashion. And these two portraits of Judaism are — quite simply — incompatible. So the emphases apparent in Romans 9 are a further — and massive — overdetermination in relation to that theory and reading.

(7) The Argumentative Turn (9:27-29)

It seems, moreover, that the argument in Romans 9–11 begins its most significant turn in 9:27. In 9:27-29 Paul introduces some sobering texts from Isaiah that are oriented explicitly toward Israel (see esp. Isa. 10:22; 1:9). These speak dialectically of Jewish salvation and rejection, thereby raising the second question in the basic salvation-historical conundrum that Paul is battling through Romans 9–11 — the apparent unsaved state of most Jews (although, with typical craft, the chosen texts point as well to part of Paul's positive response to that issue by speaking of a remnant). This issue will dominate the rest of the discussion, and 9:27–11:36 should consequently be read as a sustained engagement with the question of Jewish salvation in relation to Christ (barring explicit indications of pagan address, of course; see esp. 11:17-24) — a very difficult question that will elicit some of Paul's most ingenious argumentative moves. With this realization we have achieved a further interpretative advance; scholars have struggled to account for the shape and orientation of Paul's argument from this point. But it seems entirely plausible to view Romans 9:27–11:36 as a discussion of the profound dialectic currently operative in relation to Jewish salvation — a discussion that will try to account for that situation in terms that will answer for Paul's Roman Christian auditors the pointed charge in this regard from the Teacher (who is himself of course a Jewish Christian, and quite possibly also a somewhat agonized one).

§5. Romans 9:27-10:5

This subsection and the next (Romans 10:6-21) are potentially "texts of terror" for my apocalyptic rereading, and on at least four counts.

First, Paul states explicitly in 9:31-32 that one factor preventing Israel from receiving the saving righteousness available in Christ is her pursuit of God in the light of the Torah and "by means of works [of law]." And this statement clearly creates the possibility that Israel's *prior* pursuit of "works" impeded her receipt of Christ.[35] If this reading proves correct, then Paul will have imputed to the history of Israel just the system that Justification theorists expect to find there (and however unfairly in general descriptive terms). Hence, this text opens the door to an a priori, prospective construction of the relationship between Judaism and Christianity in Paul, overthrowing at the same moment any retrospective construction of that relationship — the construction being pursued through this project in unconditional, apocalyptic, and hence retrospective terms. Romans 9:31-32 may, in short, be the rock upon which the apocalyptic construal stumbles and falls. But our potential problems in this text are not yet over.

Second, Paul states in 10:4 (in all probability) that "Christ is the τέλος of the law," thereby perhaps reinforcing the earlier hint of prospectivism. Most previous debate of this famous claim has concentrated on whether τέλος means "end" or "goal." However, I suggest that more important issues are at stake. Can this statement be construed, on *either* reading, retrospectively and hence apocalyptically? — because at first glance a reading in terms of end *or* goal seems to point ineluctably toward a prospective process. Israel either fails to grasp that Christ has ended her relationship — at least in certain major respects — with the law (and so does not abandon it, moving on to faith), or, in a similar but not identical fashion, she fails to grasp that Christ has fulfilled the law for her (and so does not take hold of that fulfillment in faith).[36] In like manner, third, Paul seems to describe illegitimate Jewish activity in Romans 10:5 in terms of Leviticus 18:5 — "the person who does these things will live by them," thereby raising the possibility once more that a legalistic description of Judaism prior to Christ might be in view.

As if these three challenges were not serious enough, fourth, Romans 10:6-10 is widely cited as a quintessential statement of Paul's notion of saving "faith." Paul's discussion seems both straightforwardly anthropocentric and conditional: *if* a person believes in Christ, both resurrected and as Lord — information that lies near to hand, because of missionaries and preachers — *then* that person will be saved (vv. 6-10; see also vv. 14-17). And this applies to "everyone" who does so, generating the important, universal dimension in Christian salvation as Justification theory constructs it (vv. 11-13). The offer of faith is open to all. This argument seems to be unavoidably voluntarist, implying that faith is a choice or decision that can just be made (note especially the third-class conditional construction used in v. 9). So it seems that Romans 10 affirms strongly the principle of salvation that lies at the heart of Justification theory.

The apocalyptic rereading of Paul faces perhaps its most difficult challenges in this stretch of text.[37] However, rereaders need not lack hope altogether. It is widely acknowledged that Paul's Greek here is abbreviated and difficult, so his statements may well turn out on closer investigation to be more susceptible to an apocalyptic reading than they first appear, especially given certain key interpretative possibilities that we are familiar with by now — a christological emphasis within Paul's πίστις language, which influences in turn a more christocentric and dynamic interpretation of δικαιοσύνη. These two critical semantic insights can then be linked profitably with Paul's subversion of the athletic imagery functioning in this passage (the ἀγών topos). And this all opens up the possibility of a more sustained apocalyptic understanding of Paul's argument as a whole. We will begin our more detailed analysis, however, by considering the text that actually frames Paul's entire argument, both here and beyond — namely, 9:27-29. Following that analysis, the difficult and contested argument in Romans 9:30–10:21 will be considered in two stages — in terms of 9:30–10:5, and then 10:6-21 (specific Justification terminology fading in fact from v. 17).

As has already been noted, Paul quotes Isaiah 10:22 and 1:9 in 9:27-29, after having cited Hosea 2:23 and 1:10 in 9:25-26. The Hosea quotations function as the capstone to his opening argument in vv. 6-24, justifying pagan inclusion within the saved — traditionally Jewish — people of God. The Isaianic quotations that follow these texts then speak of the complementary salvation-historical issue of Jewish recalcitrance and exclusion: "If the Lord of hosts had not left survivors to us, we would have fared like Sodom . . ." (etc.: 9:29a, NRSV). Paul signals this reorientation toward Israel explicitly as he frames his citations: Ἠσαΐας δὲ κράζει ὑπὲρ τοῦ Ἰσραήλ. . . . He has not addressed this question directly since 9:1-5. So this citation formula and set of quotations seems to serve an important rhetorical function; it moves this issue back into argumentative centrality (see 1 Cor. 1:19). His engagement with the question of Jewish salvation in Romans 9–11 ought therefore to be recognized as beginning in 9:27, after which point we will need clear signals to turn away from it (see 11:17; 12:1).[38]

But as we turn to consider 9:30 following, we encounter a notoriously dense thicket of exegetical problems. So interpretative progress will be rather slow and irregular for a while. We can generate a degree of insight concerning 9:30 itself by reintroducing some of the lexical decisions that were made in Romans 1–4. But after this we will have to abandon any sense of linear analysis momentarily in order to work our way through this text from its clearest claims onward.

5.1. Semantic Considerations

(1) Romans 9:30 — πίστις and δικαιοσύνη

Translated literally, Romans 9:30 states: "What then shall we say?! The pagans who do not pursue righteousness have grasped righteousness — a righteousness 'through fidelity.'" Paul has made a final distinction here in some sense, and it is very important — the appositional statement δικαιοσύνην δὲ τὴν ἐκ πίστεως. I would suggest that by this stage in the letter the signifier πίστις (see 9:30, 32; 10:6, 8) would have been understood by the letter's auditors with reference to Christ when it is present in the phrase ἐκ πίστεως (or in parallel to this phrase in context; see 9:30, 32; 10:6). As we have already seen, lying behind this key qualifier is Paul's messianic use of Habakkuk 2:4, a text Paul reads as "the righteous one through fidelity will live." Ἐκ πίστεως, and πίστις in context, therefore denote allusively a key part of Jesus' life, namely, Good Friday, which was an event of faithfulness to the point of death, followed by resurrected life and heavenly enthronement on Easter Sunday, as the scriptural prophecy goes on to say. I hasten to add that the cognate verb πιστεύω (often present in the form of a participle) tends to refer to Christian actions, largely on analogy to Genesis 15:6 supported by Isaiah 28:16, so human trust in God is not excluded by this suggestion. (This last text is quoted twice by Paul in the broader argument here — see 9:33b and 10:11 — and human trust is referred to again in 10:4, followed by 10:9, 10, 14, 16, and 17.) But the δικαιοσύνη ἐκ πίστεως, gifted here to the pagans despite their lack of pursuit of it, is operative through the Christ event. And this allows us to confirm our earlier suggestions for another critical term more precisely.

This "righteousness" actualized in Christ is for Paul clearly divine in origin; it is an act, in some sense, of God.[39] And it is a singular act — the Christ event. It is, furthermore, obviously a saving act; Christ saves. Indeed, Paul prays in 10:1-3 for Israel's salvation, and he states twice at the same time that she ought to recognize the δικαιοσύνη τοῦ θεοῦ. (He also uses the phrases εἰς σωτηρίαν and εἰς δικαιοσύνην interchangeably in this chapter; see 10:1, 4, 10.) But "saving" in what sense? The Habakkuk quotation speaks of "life" — "the righteous one through fidelity *will live*" (ζήσεται) — and there is good reason to think that this denotes eschatological life, the life of resurrection. In the first instance, this is the best way to read the Habakkuk citation (assuming a messianic reading), which suggests that Jesus was resurrected and glorified after his faithful death on the cross. But various hints from the context confirm these implications.[40] So the δικαιοσύνη ἐκ πίστεως is a divine irruption of new life into a setting dominated by death (and this is very important, because it underlies all of Paul's theological reasoning in this subsection, as we will see shortly). Furthermore, it seems that divine being is inseparable from divine activity in all this. "Righteousness" cannot here be a static property or attribute of God, perhaps transferable to humanity in a quasi-substantial way; it is a divine action — an event. Ontology is therefore inseparable from ethics, and vice versa, and our translations have been right to try to reflect this. "Righteousness" is really "righteous activity" or, as here, a "righteous act" or ". . . event"[41] (at which point some of Paul's odd grammatical shifts also become comprehensible; see more on this just below).[42]

In short, we can confirm from 9:30 and its immediate setting that the δικαιοσύνη ἐκ πίστεως is an equivalent phrase to the δικαιοσύνη Θεοῦ and is, furthermore (and consequently), a singular, saving, and resurrecting act by God, right in this context and so "righteous," and effected through Christ. So we can translate this verse more explicitly as "the pagans, who are not pursuing righteousness, have [nevertheless] grasped righteousness — the righteous [saving] act of God, effected 'through fidelity' [in the sense of 'through the faithful Christ']."[43] Paul states here, then, that the Christ event has saved the pagans even though they were not expecting it. And he has argued at length immediately before this claim, in 9:6-26, that the electing God is allowed to do precisely this.

With 9:31, however, our problems begin. A difficult, abbreviated section ensues, yet one fraught with momentous theological consequences. Verse 31 is parallel to v. 30 in some but not all (or even the expected) ways. In this verse it seems that Israel pursues a νόμος of righteousness — a strange phrase — in contrast to the pagans, who do not pursue righteousness at all. She is then characterized as not doing something; however, the verb in question, φθάνω, is both rare and ambiguous. It could mean here "preceded" (see 1 Thess. 4:15), "arrived," "overtaken" (see 1 Thess. 2:16), or merely "attained" (see Phil. 3:16),[44] and Paul himself uses it in at least three of these senses elsewhere. It is clearly not the same verb as καταλαμβάνω, and the usual prepositional phrase denoting an object, which could help us, is not supplied — unless it is εἰς νόμον, but this can be read in relation to διώκω as well (see Phil. 3:14). Finally, where we expect δικαιοσύνη — after οὐκ ἔφθασεν at the least — it is not supplied! To make matters worse, the verse that follows, 32a, is a difficult verbless clause, a mere juxtaposition of programmatic prepositional phrases — literally, "because not through fidelity but as through works" (ὅτι οὐκ ἐκ πίστεως ἀλλ' ὡς ἐξ ἔργων). We *must* supply elided material in order to make sense of this statement — at least a verb or participle — but any such addition assumes that we know exactly what Paul is saying in v. 31, and we don't.

At this point, then, the normal technique of exegesis seriatim simply seems to fail us; Paul does not provide sufficient information in his actual claims here or their immediately preceding statements to guide the modern reader through all these ambiguities.[45] So I suggest that we jump forward to a clearer set of statements and then try to develop a consistent interpretation of the passage as a whole from there. Fortunately, just such a lucid entry point seems to be provided by 10:1-3, which resumes the term that we have just been engaging — δικαιοσύνη.

*(2) Romans 10:1-3 — God's Righteous Act in Christ
and Israel's Twofold Response*

In the first three verses of Romans 10 Paul seems for the moment to speak plainly. This is the second of three biographical intrusions that take place through chapters 9–11 — one at the beginning of each chapter (see 9:1-3; 10:1; 11:1b). Paul says here in v. 1 that the desire of his heart and his prayer to God on behalf of Israel is for her salvation (so clearly she is not, in his view, currently saved[46]). In v. 2 he notes Israel's zeal but immediately qualifies this as lacking in "recognition" or "acknowledgment" (ἐπίγνωσις; see 1:28; 3:20; Phil. 1:9; Phlm. 6). The motif of misguided ignorance is then emphasized in the participial construction that begins v. 3, and probably also in the main verb that concludes it: so "being ignorant of the righteousness that comes from God . . . they [i.e., Paul's Jewish compatriots] have not submitted to[47] God's righteousness" (NRSV). Significantly, complementing this refusal to acknowledge the δικαιοσύνη τοῦ θεοῦ is a "seeking to establish their own [righteousness][48] . . ." (which could be interpreted as an elaboration of Israel's zeal that was noted in v. 2). We learn four important things from these claims.

(i) It seems difficult — if not impossible — to avoid an identification between the δικαιοσύνη τοῦ θεοῦ that Paul speaks of twice here in v. 3 and the δικαιοσύνη ἐκ πίστεως that he has just spoken of in 9:30 (and implicitly in 9:31);[49] both these expressions denote the Christ event. And with this realization, Paul's strange case shifts in 10:3 are revealed to be genitives of separation or origin — "the righteous saving act *from* God," that is, Christ.[50]

(ii) But it can be seen now that *two* types of "righteousness" are involved in Paul's argument, and one is an aspect of Israel's "misstep."[51] On the one hand is the righteous saving act of God in Christ. On the other hand, opposing it, is some establishment of their own righteousness that certain Jews now seek — a "righteous activity" that is neither from nor endorsed by God.

(iii) This alternative, competing "righteous activity" is one aspect of a twofold misstep by Israel. Not only is she apparently involved in a righteous project that lacks divine authorization, but she is ignoring the Christ event, and this is Paul's main emphasis. (Including two instances from 9:32 on, he alludes to this rejection of Christ five times; the false competing righteous activity is spoken of three times — thus far — although it will fade dramatically from view as Romans 10 unfolds; see later only 11:6.)

(iv) If God has set forth a way to salvation in the Christ event — God's way — then it follows fairly directly that this alternative Jewish activity is also a form of salvation — one elected by Israel herself. It might be more than this, but it is at least this. To have rejected God's way to salvation implies that Israel has some alternative up her sleeve.

The argument in Romans 10:1-3

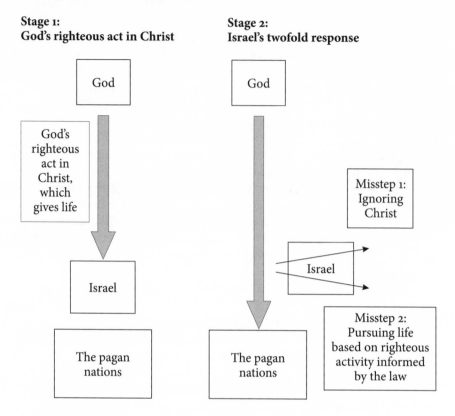

Stage 1:
God's righteous act in Christ

Stage 2:
Israel's twofold response

God

God's
righteous
act in
Christ,
which
gives life

Israel

The pagan
nations

God

Misstep 1:
Ignoring
Christ

Israel

Misstep 2:
Pursuing life
based on righteous
activity informed
by the law

The pagan
nations

(3) Romans 10:5 — Israel's Righteous Activity ἐκ νόμου

This is an appropriate point at which to introduce 10:5 into our discussion — a quotation of Leviticus 18:5: "Moses writes concerning the righteousness that comes from the law, that 'the person who does these things will live by them'" ('Ο ποιήσας αὐτὰ ἄνθρωπος ζήσεται ἐν αὐτοῖς).[52] The evidence is accumulating that this statement reprises the competing righteous activity of Israel; it encapsulates her alternative saving system. Not all the evidence for this assertion is yet apparent, but perhaps the decisive pieces are.

The case for this judgment begins by noting that Leviticus 18:5 must corroborate one of the two types of righteousness that we have just noted. Moreover, as the quotation explicitly attests, this righteousness concerns a way to life, here meaning a way to resurrection, the subject of all the other instances of δικαιοσύνη in the subsection. It is difficult to see how the phrase "the person who does these things . . ." reprises anything significant that Paul has said previously about the righteous saving act of God in Christ. Paul has linked his description with the instrumental phrase from Habakkuk 2:4 — "through fidelity." This is the space where phraseology from Leviticus 18:5 would have to function, if it were to corroborate God's δικαιοσύνη as well. And in fact Paul never speaks of Christ "doing" something — that is, using the verb ποιεῖν — in the manner that he repeatedly denotes Christ acting ἐκ πίστεως. However, the Levitical text works nicely as an account of the righteous activity that Israel seeks to establish in opposition to God's. Israel does indeed seem to be "doing" something here, and thereby seeking to live. And Paul even marks it explicitly as something effected ἐκ [τοῦ] νόμου, or "through law."

In view of this, the ἔργα νόμου, or "works of law," Paul mentions in 9:32 are probably an echo of Leviticus 18:5 and so summarize one aspect of Israel's misstep. Ἔργα seems to be Paul's deliberate allusion to the participle ποιήσας in Leviticus 18:5. (He probably doesn't use the cognate substantive for ποιέω, ποίημα, because this was rare in Koiné.)[53] The basis for Paul's important phrase "works of law" finally seems clear! And underlying this echo is a broader intertextual situation that should now be made explicit.

Leviticus 18:5 resonates with Habakkuk 2:4. Paul does not cite Habakkuk 2:4 near Romans 10:5, but he echoes its key phrase three times in the immediate context and speaks repeatedly of its subject matter — the act of God in Christ that gifts life to the world (i.e., δικαιοσύνη θεοῦ). He does juxtapose these texts explicitly in Galatians 3:11-12, where he has sculpted them into a parallel stylistic form (an arthrous substantive, an identical verb, and a key instrumental prepositional phrase). And that juxtaposition is antithetical.[54] Moreover, Paul negates a scriptural endorsement of "doing the law" in Galatians 3 not once but twice (and this total does not include his other negations of "works of law").[55]

These considerations point to an important exegetical judgment. The citation of Leviticus 18:5 in Romans 10:5 is a programmatic summary of Israel's own righteousness that she "seeks to establish" over against the righteous saving act by God in Christ. Leviticus 18:5 suggests that certain Jews seek life on the basis of their fulfillment of the Mosaic law, and this suggestion resonates both stylistically and theologically in counterpoint to Habakkuk 2:4. The righteous activity affirmed by the Leviticus text will ostensibly lead to resurrection, probably through a declaration by God on the day of judgment that such people are in fact righteous and so deserve eternal life. Hence, we can recognize immediately in this system — derived here largely independently — the conditional, essentially Arminian (if not Pelagian!) system of the Teacher (but applied here in some sense to Judaism).[56] Perfect fulfillment of the positive demands of the law is still apparently necessary if the stated axiom of Moses is to be fulfilled; however, this accords with what we discovered earlier as well.[57] But it is important to note that the full theological rationale underlying this polemical summary, along with its exact salvation-historical location, has yet to be determined in the present context. (The reading must also remain somewhat tentative until we have interpreted 10:4.) Nevertheless, with these realizations we are in a strong position to go back and resolve the ambiguities of 9:31-32a and then to grasp the full contingent force of 9:30-32a.

(4) Romans 9:31-32a — Israel's Torah of Righteous Activity

We have learned from the rest of the subsection that Israel's twofold misstep is, on the one hand, to fail to acknowledge Christ and, on the other, to engage in a false appraisal and use of the law — a righteous activity ἐκ νόμου. Furthermore, as long as she persists in this activity, God's righteous saving action in Christ is not experienced; these two righteous modes are incompatible. And these claims now result in a good reading of vv. 31-32 with a minimum of elided material.

We can first resolve the elided verb in v. 32a that drives the juxtaposition of Paul's well-known prepositional phrases, [ὅτι] οὐκ ἐκ πίστεως ἀλλ᾽ ὡς ἐξ ἔργων. It is now apparent that these are the two aspects of Israel's misstep — ignorance of the faithful Christ and a preoccupation with the law. Hence, "pursuit" or "pursuing" seems the most likely ellipse.[58] This short set of comments seems to function as a pivot in the broader discussion: ignoring the faithful Christ is picked up by the rest of this verse and the verse that follows (v. 33), while "works of law" seem to have been the concern of the preceding verse (v. 31).

Turning to v. 31, we can now recognize in its truncated statements the two types of righteous activity that were spoken of in 10:1-3 and 5, along with one aspect of Israel's misstep (i.e., the false form of righteous activity). Israel has clearly not "attained" to the righteous saving act of God in Christ, the righteousness "through fidelity" that the pagans received in 9:30 and that she ignores through 10:3. The elided δικαιοσύνην can now be recognized at the end of v. 31.[59] And one aspect of her mistake, in terms of "works of law," is now recognizable through v. 31 in terms of the alternative program of self-appointed righteous activity and salvation. In view of the scriptural text quoted in 10:5 — Leviticus 18:5 — this is accurately described as a torah, or teaching, concerning righteousness — a νόμος δικαιοσύνης — although a false teaching. (This then echoes perfectly with analogous torahs, or teachings, in 3:27, where a teaching concerning πίστις excluded a teaching concerning "works.") Moreover, by "seeking to establish her own righteousness," thus following a particular "teaching concerning righteousness," Israel is clearly not focused on the Christ event but on her own ethical performance informed by torah. Any race that she is running is in terms of the law, and so in effect she pursues the law, hence Paul's phrase εἰς νόμον. To insist on a torah of righteousness, a νόμος δικαιοσύνης, is also to run in some sense toward the law, and so εἰς νόμον.

> [30]Τί οὖν ἐροῦμεν;
> ὅτι ἔθνη τὰ μὴ διώκοντα δικαιοσύνην
> κατέλαβεν δικαιοσύνην, δικαιοσύνην δὲ τὴν ἐκ πίστεως
> [31]Ἰσραὴλ δὲ διώκων νόμον δικαιοσύνης εἰς νόμον
> οὐκ ἔφθασεν [δικαιοσύνην].
> [32]διὰ τί; ὅτι [διώκων] οὐκ ἐκ πίστεως ἀλλ᾽ ὡς ἐξ ἔργων· προσέκοψαν κ.τ.λ.

This is the ideal point at which to reach out for Paul's contingent meaning in these verses. That is, much of what has been said up to this point is a clarification for modern interpreters of what would have been fairly obvious to Paul and his original auditors. Now, having grasped the semantic building blocks that Paul and his audience could assume, we can consider the argument itself that the apostle was constructing.

The voice of the Teacher seems to be recognizable once again in the complaints of 9:30-31, which also serve the purpose of foregrounding the two main issues under discussion.[60] As we have already seen, Paul has quoted a set of important scriptural texts in vv. 27-29 to round off his argument concerning pagan inclusion in salvation (9:6-26) and to inaugurate his engagement with the second and rather more difficult question of Jewish salvation (9:30–11:36). The quotations he uses are shockingly negative. Israel is as scattered as the sand, and that suddenly. Furthermore, but for the Lord's preservation of a small remnant, she would be as Sodom and Gomorrah! So these scriptural texts serve to establish the absurd missionary dynamics that Paul is currently struggling with — pagan inclusion and Jewish exclusion. It seems most likely, then, that the voice that *queries* this set of dynamics in vv. 30-31 is that of the Teacher: "What then are we to say!? Gentiles, who did not strive for righteousness, have attained it . . . ?! [B]ut Israel, who did strive for . . . righteousness . . . did *not* succeed?!" (NRSV, emphasis added). (Τί οὖν ἐροῦμεν; ὅτι ἔθνη τὰ μὴ διώκοντα δικαιοσύνην κατέλαβεν δικαιοσύνην . . . [31] Ἰσραὴλ δὲ διώκων νόμον δικαιοσύνης εἰς νόμον οὐκ ἔφθασεν [δικαιοσύνην].) It is then *Paul* who qualifies the correct sense in which the pagans have received "righteousness" (a δικαιοσύνην [δὲ] ἐκ πίστεως, of course; this also explains its parenthetical character in syntactical terms). And he responds in v. 32 with a brief characterization of the two problems to which he attributes this anomalous situation for Israel: διὰ τί; ὅτι [διώκων] οὐκ ἐκ πίστεως ἀλλ᾽ [διώκων] ὡς ἐξ ἔργων προσέκοψαν κ.τ.λ. Thus, the full exchange in 9:30-32 (DC):[61]

> Teacher: What are we to say then? *Pagans* not pursuing righteous activity have received a righteous act [from God]?!
>
> Paul: The righteous act [of God] "through faithfulness."
>
> Teacher: But *Israel*, pursuing a torah of righteous activity toward that Torah, have *not*?!
>
> Paul: Why? Because they did not strive for it "through faithfulness" but "through works." They have stumbled over the stumbling stone. . . .

The following argument simply elaborates on these two basic claims. But it seems that in the process Paul also subverts a standard Greco-Roman and derivatively Jewish topos known to modern readers as the ἀγών motif. Indeed, this is a vital insight, which will enable us ultimately to understand 10:4.[62]

5.2. Paul's Subversion of the ἀγών Motif

The ἀγών topos involves the use of metaphors associated with Hellenistic athletics, although these overlap significantly with military imagery as well.[63] Common is the metaphor of a stringent race, as seen most famously in the New Testament perhaps in Hebrews 12:1-4. Paul uses such ἀγών imagery quite frequently, emphasizing one or another aspect of the broader discourse as his contingent concerns dictate.[64] Various clues in both Romans 9:30–10:5 and its broader setting suggest that athletic imagery is indeed in play in this text. But Paul is not endorsing the ἀγών in a straightforward fashion here as he does elsewhere, and as those commentators who note the motif's presence tend to assume;[65] he is twisting the normally heroic discourse into a farce.

First, the evidence that the ἀγών is present: Paul speaks four times in 9:30-32 explicitly or implicitly of "pursuit" (διώκω), at the end of which a "grasping" and "attaining" (or not) take place — the terminology associated with winning and gaining a prize. This process is then interrupted by a stumble. So clearly a race of some sort is involved, although a somewhat unfortunate one. There are *eight* such references here (including the supplied ellipses). Prior to this pericope, moreover, as we noted earlier, Paul stated in 9:16 — to the near universal bafflement of commentators — that God's preference for Jacob over Esau did not depend on human willing or *running* (τρέχοντος). In 11:11 Paul resumes the metaphor, asking whether Israel has stumbled so seriously that she has fallen and suffered "defeat."[66] These references seem too frequent and sustained to be mere metaphorical flourishes on Paul's part (and his comic manipulation of the topos will also later speak against this). But how exactly does Paul subvert the discourse? In the course of 9:30–10:5 he twists the topos in three essentially absurd directions.

(1) Romans 9:30 — Those Not Competing Have Won the Prize

In 9:30 Paul states that the pagans are not running anywhere; they are not even in the ἀγών, striving for "righteousness" and so for a prized crown on the future day of glorious reward. "Righteousness," in the sense of God's righteous action that saves them, drops into their lap, and they grasp it. So their race is over and the prize won before they have even begun to compete (see Matt. 20:1-16). It is as if the spoils have gone not to the athletes but to the spectators. This is the first move in the parody — those not competing have won the prize.

(2) Romans 9:31-32a — Israel's Race Is Misguided

Israel, however, is self-consciously competing in a religious race. In 9:31-32a Paul describes this as her pursuit of a teaching concerning righteous activity and so toward the law, and we have no reason to doubt the discipline and sincerity of this race (see the zeal of 10:2). But Israel has ignored the granting of the prize to those who are not competing — the pagan nations. Hence — in Paul's second subversive move — she has overlooked the fact that the real race is over and she is now running onward in a race of her own making.

It is not difficult to find an explanation for Paul's concern to undermine the motif in Romans so thoroughly, especially when he otherwise endorses it. The ἀγών motif would have lent itself readily to the teaching of his opponents, as much as it did to Paul's own exhortations elsewhere. The righteous are engaged in a strenuous contest for perfection; they must train their bodies and minds by constant practice and effort, guided in particular *by the law and its teachers.* After long, disciplined application, struggle, and competition, they will eventually win the coveted prize made available on the day of judgment — the victory wreath of salvation and divine approval![67] It seems likely, then, that an ἀγών motif was a part of the Teacher's gospel;[68] hence, it is understandable that Paul would be subverting it here.[69]

(3) Romans 10:4 — the Christ Event as the τέλος — the End of the Race

A particular construal of Paul's famous statement in Romans 10:4 — τέλος [γὰρ] νόμου Χριστὸς εἰς δικαιοσύνην παντὶ τῷ πιστεύοντι[70] — integrates nicely with this farcical Jewish ἀγών.[71] If τέλος is understood here to be the end of a race or contest — a meaning apparent in ancient literature[72] — then we activate connotations of *both* "end" *and* "goal" (thereby perhaps moving beyond that debate), *yet do so in a way that is not theologically debilitating.*[73]

Such a reading is certainly consistent with the comic manipulation of the ἀγών motif that we have just noted in 9:30-32a, where those not competing win and those competing seem to be doing so in a misguided race. But we appreciate now still more clearly that it is misdirected, because the real competition is already finished. If the Christ event is the end of the race for the law, in the sense almost of being the finish line, then the key point is that the race is over (see Phil. 3:2-16). Any subsequent racing on the part of Jews is therefore misdirected if not ludicrous.[74] The advantage of this reading is that it can integrate the strong contextual signals that τέλος in 10:4 suggests some sort of goal[75] with the equally strong signals that something is being terminated, or ended.[76] But the mistake of Israel — from Paul's point of view — is also interpreted in an a posteriori rather than an a priori fashion; Israel makes her mistake *after* the end of the race has arrived, not on the way *to* that goal. So she can be held responsible primarily for not responding appropriately to Christ, and for treating the law inappropriately from that point on, rather than for stupidly and/or unethically failing to understand her own law, Scriptures, and history[77] prior to Christ's arrival.[78] Consequently, this reading draws the theological sting from the motif — from an apocalyptic point of view — while respecting its semantic content.

But we have yet to consider 9:32b-33 — the final piece in this pericope's intriguing puzzle. Paul's metaphorical enthusiasm, not to mention aggression, leads to a slight complication here.

(4) Romans 9:32b-33 — the Christ Event as a Stumbling Stone

In v. 33 Paul introduces a set of scriptural texts that intensifies his subversion of the ἀγών discourse — his third such move. The Christ event is, according to Isaiah 8:14 (and probably by way of a Hebrew stone/son wordplay[79]), a stone laid in Zion, a stone that offends and trips, although the one who believes in it will not be ashamed (so the appended Isa. 28:16). Israel has not believed, so she stumbles, and this clearly undermines further any sense that Jews are involved successfully in a religious race. If they are, then they have fallen flat on their faces according to Paul's use of Isaiah.[80]

The stumbling motif is a significant one for Paul, because he returns to it in 11:11 to ask whether it is irrecoverable, asserting there that it is not. However, this notion operates awkwardly in relation to the subversion that he has developed in 9:30-32a and 10:4. There the race is over before it starts; Israel races off into the distance on an absurd race of her own making. Here, however, she is racing along but trips and falls. Now technically, she can't do both these things at once — race off in a competition that is over *and* fall while competing.[81]

However, I am not sure that this matters very much. Paul is subverting a metaphorical discourse within a broader polemic on his part. It is not fatal, or perhaps even surprising, if he mixes his own metaphors in the process. The letter's auditors probably got the basic point. Any suggestion that the Christian life is a race run in accordance with the law is not an inspiring appeal so much as a ludicrous illustration. Such runners race off in the wrong direction, or they trip and fall. But it might be worth noting in addition that Paul's two comic subversions here also correspond reasonably well to the two aspects of Israel's misstep. Insofar as she pursues salvation through righteous activity oriented by the law — through "works" — she runs a race of her own making, ignoring the fact that the real race is actually over. Insofar as she rejects the Christ event as God's appointed route to salvation, she trips up and falls over something important that is lying at her very feet; she overlooks a vital point. So Paul's mixed metaphors are arguably caused in part by his desire to illustrate the two aspects of Israel's basic difficulty, and to do so while subverting an ἀγών discourse, with one eye at the same time on a useful prophetic text. (Small wonder that not everything correlates perfectly!) And with these interpretative judgments in place, we are now in a position to consider the important underlying implications.

5.3. Implications

It is clear that Romans 9:30–10:5 contains a juxtaposition of religious modes — ἔργα νόμου and πίστις — and this creates a critical set of interpretative options. We could construe the antithesis in a prospective manner, as the majority of interpreters do; the concern of the Jews with their own righteousness *leads to* the rejection of the later righteous act by God in Christ.[82] A prospective construal would ultimately endorse Justification theory, or some similar reconstruction of Paul's thinking, both here and elsewhere. But this interpretative decision is, as far as I can tell, invariably assumed rather than established. Nothing decisive is ever cited from the text in its support. And indeed, as far as I can tell, *there is nothing in the text that stands against the opposite possibility* — that anthropocentric, Jewish righteousness is a post-Christian phenomenon. On this reading, the Jews' *ignoring* of the Christ event — the righteous act of salvation proceeding from God — results in the *subsequent* establishment of a false, alternative righteous activity, *and arguably even does so necessarily*. "Works of law," then, do not precede faith, but follow it.

I want to consider this important question "semi-independently" at first, since this can provide stronger corroboration for the rereading that was developed earlier (semi-independent because a particular approach to Paul's use of πιστ- terminology must still be imported from that earlier point, the immediate evidence here being insufficient to decide this question either way). And there are in fact two closely related but distinguishable questions to be addressed. What is the order of these two states, and what is Paul's theological rationale for so arranging them? — questions, we might say, of narrative and of explanation. The question of narrative should be addressed first, because if a retrospective plot-line can be established, so to speak, then the theological rationale follows from that automatically — i.e., an essentially retrospective, apocalyptic rationale that we are already quite familiar with. Conversely, a prospective plot-line opens up the possibility of less constructive, non-apocalyptic rationales.[83]

What, then, is the narrative priority of these two basic states? Does Israel's establishment of her own righteous activity precede her repudiation of the faithful Christ in Paul's discussion, or does her repudiation of the faithful Christ result somehow in her establishment of her own righteous activity? Do "works of law" as a religious program (so to speak) go before or follow the Christ event, as Paul articulates these events here? Much rests on the answer that we give to this basic question. And the available evidence seems to indicate that "works of law" by Jews *follow* the Christ event for Paul, and do not precede it.

(1) Paul seems constantly to treat this antithesis as a perfect correlation and real alternative: it is *either* "works of law" *or* πίστις, as in 9:32a (and, in effect, 10:3). However, if "works" refers to a pre-Christian, preparatory state, there is not a perfect correlation. For all those practicing "works of law" who are not reached by preaching — and this group includes significant numbers of pagans, as well as Jews living before ca. 30 CE — there is *only* "works of law." Πίστις is not an option. But, as far as I can tell, Paul never explicitly suggests or affirms this scenario — a statement of the principle of "works of law alone." Rather "works of law" versus πίστις always seems to be a live option; it is one or the other. If "works of law" follow the Christ event, then Paul's antithesis stands, but not vice versa.

(2) In close relation to this, it is not surprising to find that the immediately preceding context for Romans 9:30–10:5, namely, 9:6-26, which contains Paul's most extensive treatment of the nature of pre-Christian Israel, never characterizes that situation in terms of "works of law" — far from it. Paul characterizes pre-Christian Israel, as we have seen, in terms of gifts, privileges, and election. (This corresponds with his analysis of pre-Christian Israel elsewhere as well, notably, in Galatians 3:15-25; see also Phil. 3:2-6.) Indeed, that the divine election of the patri-

archs is based on works *is explicitly denied in 9:12!* (οὐκ ἐξ ἔργων ἀλλ᾿ ἐκ τοῦ καλοῦντος . . .). This is not to deny that pre-Christian Israel possesses a certain freedom, not to mention a certain sinfulness, and is engaged to some degree in law-regulated activity. But Paul never articulates that situation in terms of "works of law" — as righteous legal activity directed ultimately toward salvation in a contractual or conditional fashion (except arguably here, and hence this text's importance). "Works of law" arrive in 9:32, *just after Christ does.* (The divine call to the pagans in Christ is spoken of using prophetic intertexts from 9:24 onward.[84])

(3) The disobedience of Israel that Paul goes on to emphasize strongly in context, in Romans 10:6-21, is almost completely oriented by the rejection of Christ. Indeed, "works of law" now drop completely from view. (See only 11:6, which is another denial, and almost certainly inferential, not temporal.) But they should not if "works" characterize a preceding generic state, without the traversing of which recognition and acceptance of Christ are impossible. In that role they should continue to be an ongoing part of Israel's problem. That they are not suggests that they do not fulfill this preparatory role for Paul.

(4) Paul's account of why "works of law" are wrong in this passage is inadequate; it is too "flat." As we have already seen at some length, most accounts of "works" suggest that they are not wrong in and of themselves; technically, they should be salvific, but humans are too sinful to perform them. It is the realization of human sinfulness through their repeated attempted performance and failure that prepares for the arrival of the gospel and the exercise of "faith" — a deeper, richer account of their theological function.[85] But Paul never articulates this deeper internal psychological dynamic here. He simply denotes that any pursuit of salvation through "works of law" is misguided in and of itself as a practice, *irrespective of any theological lessons learned.*[86] It is wrong *as a way to life.* And this again points to a responsive, rather than a preparatory function.

(5) Paul's subversion of the ἀγών motif in relation to Israel places the bulk of Israel's activity after the arrival of Christ; this is what makes the subversion effective. She races off after the race is over. Paul thus characterizes "works" as a false preoccupation after Christ's arrival.[87]

Hence, I conclude that there is little or no evidence from the immediate context of Romans 9:30–10:5 to support the conventional, prospective arrangement of "works of law" and πίστις in this text, but quite a bit to be said in favor of the opposite view — that "works of law" follow Christ here.[88] And with this judgment, our second important question can be answered — namely, that a retrospective theological analysis of "works" and "faith" is probably also in play. This rationale will be detailed in due course — after a scrutiny of Paul's argument in 10:6-21 (see esp. §8.1) — so it can suffice to say at present that the first three challenges issued by Romans 9:30–10:5 to an apocalyptic rereading of Paul seem to have been defused — this text's apparent generic endorsement of the law in terms of "works," its characterization of Christ as some sort of τέλος in relation to the law, and its citation of Leviticus 18:5. All of these motifs can and arguably should be read within a retrospective, apocalyptic schema — conclusions apparent even on a semi-independent reading. And with these judgments we can turn to examine the fourth challenge in detail — the theme of "faith" that is so prominent in the rest of Romans 10 (specifically, vv. 6-17, although the relevant arguments extend through v. 21).

§6. Romans 10:6-21

Somewhat incredibly, we hear little of "works" in Romans 9–11 after 10:5 — or before 9:31-32. There is the briefest of repudiations in 11:6, corresponding to an equally brief dismissal in 9:12. But there is an extensive discussion of "faith," extending through both famously resonant and infamously obscure (or even unfair) claims by the apostle — the fourth interpretative challenge that the apocalyptic rereader faces in this text. Are we forced to endorse a more anthropocentric and conditional construal of the function of faith here, or is an alternative, christocentric reading sustainable — or even preferable?!

6.1. Romans 10:6-8

The subsection's obscure statements seem to arrive first, in vv. 6-8:

> ⁶ἡ [δὲ] ἐκ πίστεως δικαιοσύνη οὕτως λέγει·
> μὴ εἴπῃς ἐν τῇ καρδίᾳ σου·
> τίς ἀναβήσεται εἰς τὸν οὐρανόν;
> τοῦτ᾽ ἔστιν Χριστὸν καταγαγεῖν·
> ⁷ἤ, τίς καταβήσεται εἰς τὴν ἄβυσσον;
> τοῦτ᾽ ἔστιν Χριστὸν ἐκ νεκρῶν ἀναγαγεῖν.
> ⁸ἀλλὰ τί λέγει;
> ἐγγύς σου τὸ ῥῆμά ἐστιν
> ἐν τῷ στόματί σου καὶ ἐν τῇ καρδίᾳ σου,
> τοῦτ᾽ ἔστιν τὸ ῥῆμα τῆς πίστεως ὃ κηρύσσομεν.

A number of questions have puzzled interpreters at this point, in particular, the identity of the speaker in v. 6-8, whom Paul identifies only as ἡ [δὲ] ἐκ πίστεως δικαιοσύνη, and the rationale — if any — that underlies Paul's astonishing reinterpretation of Deuteronomy 30:12-14 in a christocentric and rather "oral" fashion. Beyond these issues (and building on them), interpreters ask why Paul has actually done all this — that is, quoted Deuteronomy 30:12-14 in this slanted way at this point in his discussion. What is the rhetorical purpose of this somewhat outlandish maneuver? I will need to find plausible answers to these questions if I am to claim subsequently that my rhetorical and apocalyptic reading is sustainable through this material. However, some reasonable answers do arguably become apparent if we interpret this text in continuity with the rereading that has

been developed up to this point in the letter. Three elements within that rereading are now especially helpful: (1) the reference of much of Paul's πιστ- language,
especially by way of the substantive πίστις and the phrase ἐκ πίστεως, to Christ;
(2) the emerging connection between Christ and wisdom (see esp. 1:16 and 9:6-
26); and (3) the invariable rhetorical backdrop to Paul's assertions of the Teacher's
opposing gospel, which probably used this Deuteronomic text for its own, more
conventionally Jewish purposes (i.e., to urge the observance of the law upon any
prospective converts). When these three insights are integrated into the discussion, Paul's difficult text comes into focus more clearly; it seems much more responsible, in both intertextual and rhetorical terms, than we might previously
have been led to believe, from which point we can also build toward a plausible
interpretation of the broader discussion.

(1) The Reference of Paul's πιστ- Language to Christ

Our first step toward greater clarity takes place as we attribute the two instances
of πίστις used here by Paul to Christ himself. The first such attribution, in v. 6,
merely follows the intertextual cue that has been so significant throughout the
letter (i.e., ἐκ πίστεως) and has been used already in context in 9:30 and 32. These
instances should be interpreted consistently. Moreover, the phrase ἡ [δὲ] ἐκ
πίστεως δικαιοσύνη clearly resumes Paul's earlier, concentrated use of δικαιοσύνη
in vv. 30, 31, and 10:3, with an almost identical phrase occurring in 9:30 —
δικαιοσύνην δὲ τὴν ἐκ πίστεως. We have good reason already for interpreting this
material with respect to Christ. But this decision in relation to v. 6 is reinforced
by the overt twofold reference of the Deuteronomic text to Christ himself in vv.
6b and 7; Paul states explicitly that *Christ* is the one who does not need to be
sought either in heaven or in the abyss. These decisions have the further virtue of
allowing the phrase τὸ ῥῆμα τῆς πίστεως in v. 8 to be referred to Christ as well.
And once this is done, a satisfying unity is imparted to the voice's recommendations, as against a somewhat puzzling divergence of reference. The word that is
near to the mouth and heart of the listener is identical with Christ, who does not
need to be brought nearer by retrieval from either heaven or the abyss. Paul
speaks throughout this set of verses of Christ and Christ alone. This identification does not resolve all our interpretative difficulties, but at least we can now
recognize that Paul is talking consistently in some sense about Christ in vv. 6-8.
(And — to recall an earlier caveat — this is not to exclude the role of belief on the
part of the recipient of Christ; that activity will become more prominent in Paul's
argument momentarily.)

Most interpreters hold that the christological reinterpretations of the
Deuteronomic text that are taking place through vv. 6-8 are clarifications by Paul,
analogous to other *pesher* interpretations in his day.[89] It is reasonably obvious that
the clauses τοῦτ᾽ ἔστιν Χριστὸν καταγαγεῖν, τοῦτ᾽ ἔστιν Χριστὸν ἐκ νεκρῶν
ἀναγαγεῖν, and τοῦτ᾽ ἔστιν τὸ ῥῆμα τῆς πίστεως ὃ κηρύσσομεν, are not being spoken by the "voice" of vv. 6 and 8. All three comments are introduced by the overt

interpretative signal τοῦτ' ἔστιν, while the third must refer to Paul and his fellow missionaries (see esp. vv. 15-17), drawing him explicitly into these statements (". . . the word concerning the faithful one that *we* proclaim"). So Paul is clarifying things here for his auditors. But it is not these clarifications that have occasioned discussion in the past, so much as their rationale (or apparent lack of one).

(2) Paul's Rationale — a Christianized Wisdom Discourse

Running through the center of this argument is, of course, a Deuteronomic text that applies in its own context quite unequivocally to the law. Moreover, it was delivered (in canonical terms) by Moses from the east side of the Jordan to the assembled Israelites in an important reaffirmation of the earlier covenantal event of Horeb. So Paul's bald ascription of this text to Christ simply seems exegetically appalling — a groundless and even interpretatively violent reappropriation of one of Judaism's most precious moments. However, this ascriptive violence is palliated — at least to some degree — by the observation of M. Jack Suggs and Elizabeth Johnson (i.a.) that Judaism had *itself* already reread this text with reference to wisdom, and this reorientation probably underlies its further reappropriation by Paul in Romans 10 in relation to Christ.[90] These scholars point to the rereading of this Deuteronomic tradition in Baruch 3:29-30: "Who has gone up into heaven, and taken her [i.e., wisdom], and brought her down from the clouds? Who has gone over the sea, and found her, and will buy her for pure gold?" (NRSV). It is clear that Christ is the wisdom of God for Paul;[91] hence, if Judaism was already reascribing the words of Deuteronomy 30:12-14 to wisdom, it hardly seems so offensive for the apostle to articulate that identification here further in terms of Christ. Moreover, that Paul is manipulating wisdom traditions in Romans, and in the context of Romans 10 in particular, is already apparent, reinforcing the likelihood of this identification still further.

A subtle allusion to wisdom has already been noted in 1:16 in close association with the terminology of δικαιοσύνη, along with the emergence of a wisdom thematology in Romans 9:6-25. However, resonances with wisdom are also detectable in Romans 10 in various ways. First, Paul has switched the term "sea" in the original Deuteronomy text (which also recurs in its rereading in Baruch) for the far less common "abyss" (ἄβυσσος), a term found principally in wisdom literature.[92] Second, Paul speaks in v. 12 of the Lord "*enriching* everyone who calls him" (πλουτῶν εἰς πάντας τοὺς ἐπικαλουμένους αὐτόν). This is most unusual terminology in this relation for Paul (if not in the rest of the New Testament),[93] but it resonates directly with the common trope in wisdom discourses that praises the value of wisdom as far in excess of gold and other treasure.[94] It may then be no coincidence that, third, Paul quotes a wisdom text at the conclusion of this particular argument in v. 18b — Psalm 19:4 (and see esp. 19:10!). Fourth, the repeated language of calling, words, and summons that sounds through Romans 9–11 seems to echo with those interwoven tropes in wisdom discourses. (See more on this material momentarily.) Fifth, and finally, this link will integrate perfectly with the probable reconstruction of the Teacher's gospel at this point — a recon-struction that Paul is almost certainly trying to counter at this stage in his argu-ment. (See more on this aspect of the discussion momentarily as well.) Hence, it seems fair to suggest that Paul is using a wisdom discourse in Romans 10 here in relation to the Deuteronomic text that he is manipulating christologically.

But this realization that a wisdom discourse is operative in Romans 9–11 may also allow us to resolve a further puzzle in this passage, namely, the identity of the speaker in vv. 6-8 — ἡ δικαιοσύνη ἐκ πίστεως. It now seems likely that this voice is simply God's as he speaks to his people about his special child, wisdom, who is now identified more specifically as Christ. Indeed, even more specifically, God seems to be *calling* his people to recognition of this vital fact, summoning them to acknowledge and receive Christ even as wisdom frequently calls to the wise and to Israel in her texts. This identification builds on the strangely active and "oral" activity of God in Romans 9–11. (And, again, it integrates exactly with Paul's probable argumentative strategy here, as we will see shortly.) Significations of speech and speaking are heavily concentrated in Romans 9–11, and several strategically critical instances are linked directly to God himself.

The verb λέγω, admittedly common in the New Testament, is nevertheless densely deployed here, with no fewer than twenty-five instances. It complements the occurrence that is rather less usual in Paul of λόγος, which has three of its seven occurrences in Romans in chapter 9. More indicative than mere statistical instances, however, is the grammatical coordination of several of these instances with God. As we have already seen, "the word of God" is one of the driving forces in the account of Israel's ancestral history in Romans 9 — see especially 9:6 and 9. But rarer words of speech are also clustered in this text.

Paul uses the alternative designation of "word," ῥῆμα, much more infre-quently than he does λόγος, and it tends to be prompted by its occurrence in scriptural intertexts. Of its six occurrences in his undisputed letters, four are in Romans 10 (see Rom. 10:8 [2x, the first instance — of course — Deut. 30:14], 17, 18 [Ps. 19:4]; 2 Cor. 12:4 [a pun]; 13:1 [a quotation of Deut. 19:15]; see Eph. 5:26; 6:17 [this last a reference to the Spirit]). καλέω, meanwhile, occurs eleven times in Romans, eight of those being in Romans 9–10 (and two in 8:30)! Even more sig-nificantly, God is the subject of *all* the "calls" in chapter 9 (see 9:7, 12, 24, 25, 26; he is also the subject of the calls in 4:17 and 8:30 [2x]).

When this repeated emphasis on speech, and in particular the speech of God in Romans 9–11, is combined with the repeated allusions to wisdom and its emphases on calling and summons, it seems likely that the voice speaking the Deuteronomic words in vv. 6-8 is the voice of God, discoursing about his child, wisdom, who is now arriving in and as Christ. The righteous act of God through the faithful Christ entails that Christ has come down from heaven, and up from the abyss, and in that act God himself is speaking to his people. The two divine acts fuse. But if Paul's strange use of Deuteronomy 30:12-14 is now more compre-hensible in broader interpretative terms — as part of a Christianized wisdom dis-course — we have yet to find out why he is deploying this complex textual interplay at this point in Romans. However, an answer to *that* question now lies near to hand.

(3) Paul's Rhetorical Purpose — Israel's Accountability for Her Rejection of Christ

I suggest that there are two rhetorical aspects to Paul's rescripting of Deuteronomy 30:12-14 in accordance with divine wisdom in Romans 10 — one negative and one positive (and, as we have seen, this double rhetorical function is characteristic of much of Paul's carefully crafted argument in Romans).

First, negatively, it seems highly likely that the Teacher was also using Deuteronomy 30:12-14 in his gospel presentation, so Paul's careful reorientation of this text in Romans 10 toward Christ counters and even subverts any such deployment by the Teacher. As he has done for so many of the Teacher's key terms and motifs, Paul attempts here to wrest material away from that competing system, although in this case an entire text! Several observations undergird this judgment.

Deuteronomy 30:12-14 is reasonably well attested in Jewish literature in Paul's day, and sometimes even in programmatic locations.[95] Moreover, it is easy to understand why the Teacher would have used it. The link between the law and wisdom — well established in Judaism by now — opens up a host of powerful rhetorical opportunities. Acceptance of the law understood in this sense would involve access to a superior personal ethic, as wisdom indwells the soul of the righteous person; but it would also supply access to the secrets of just government and the cosmos and guarantee the tutelage and care of God's providence. The treasures of the universe are contained in it! At the same time, the countervailing theme of the inaccessibility of wisdom would have allowed the purveyors of wisdom mantic roles of considerable influence; they alone could provide access to this wisdom through their texts and teachings. The wisdom discourse can consequently underwrite rhetorics of status and power by their proclaimers.

That the Teacher endorsed this Jewish discourse is almost certain. In Romans 2:17-20 Paul reproduces the Teacher's privileges (in order to undermine them, of course), and their principal component is learning in the law. But Paul goes on to describe the law in relation to the Teacher as "the embodiment of knowledge and of truth" (... τὴν μόρφωσιν τῆς γνώσεως καὶ τῆς ἀληθείας ...) — wisdom language! Moreover, the Teacher's deep involvement with the Wisdom of Solomon is well attested by now, suggesting his familiarity with this discourse.[96] So Paul almost certainly had good reason to reorient Deuteronomy 30:12-14 away from the law and from wisdom, and toward Christ. In so doing, he was attempting to defuse one of the Teacher's main scriptural texts, along with one of his key sets of claims. Perhaps a discussion of Deuteronomy 30:12-14 was meant to follow the initial establishment of the problem by the Teacher in terms analogous to Romans 1:18-32. In this relation, it is worth recalling that the immediate frame for this Old Testament text is "[c]hoose life that you might live" (Deut. 30:19); it is a *decision* text (and even seems to be attested as such by other roughly contemporaneous Jewish texts).[97] But now when the Teacher quoted Deuteronomy 30 and invoked his listeners to choose life that they might live, the Roman auditors, having heard Romans 10, would think immediately of God's wisdom incarnate in Christ — which was presumably a choice, and a life, that they already had made and grasped — and not of law, where the Teacher hoped to direct their enthusiasm.

Yet while this hypothesis for the negative aspect of Paul's rhetorical strategy seems basically plausible, it does not explain completely why Paul undertakes this delicate textual reorientation precisely here in his unfolding argument. In order to address this explanatory shortfall, we must turn to consider a possible positive aspect in Paul's argument.

It is important to recall the broader issue that Paul is addressing in Romans 10 — the failure of the majority of Israel to respond positively to Christ, a failure that seems in turn to discredit Paul's "Jewish" gospel and his own Jewish loyalties (and especially if he views unbelieving Jews as condemned). In the light of this overarching agenda, Paul's manipulation of Deuteronomy 30:12-14 can arguably be seen to function within a particular rhetorical trajectory that is unfolding through Romans 9–11 in response to these challenges. Paul has initiated this line of argument already, in 9:33a, and he seems to continue it after 10:6-8 as well, especially in 10:14-17, so our full discussion of this dynamic should be postponed until those later verses have been addressed. However, we can certainly note enough information at this point to respond to our current dilemma.

In 9:33a Paul quoted Isaiah 8:14, which states that God has laid a "stone of stumbling and rock of offense in Zion." Certainly, this text predicts trouble in relation to any Jewish response to the designated stone; it is prophetically foretold that this rock will trip and offend. However, it is important to appreciate that this text suggests as well that *God himself has placed this stone in Zion.* The all-important stone, trust in which will deliver from eschatological humiliation, has been set by God in Jerusalem. In other words, God seems to have stooped down and come near to his people, placing the key to their life and salvation in their very midst. And Paul's reorientation of Deuteronomy 30:12-14 corresponds exactly to this earlier sentiment. It suggests that God has spoken to his people directly, bringing Christ down (or up) to them, so that no travel either to heaven or into the abyss is necessary in order to find him. This wisdom is not inaccessible, then, but could not be more accessible (a striking reversal of certain aspects of the wisdom discourse as well).[98] Indeed, God has placed the critical word(s) in their very mouths and hearts.

Paul has thus responded to the conundrum of Jewish rejection of Christ by suggesting quite simply that God has come all the way to Israel, presenting her with the easiest of responses, so that as she refuses, her accountability for that response is plain and unavoidable. She is, one might say, ἀναπολόγητος. God has done everything that he can to present her with this option; he has come near in Christ — as near as the mouth and the heart (and we will address the theological ground that underlies Paul's rather shocking confidence in this regard shortly).

So it seems to be a simple but effective rebuttal. Moreover, in this way he has also subverted one of the Teacher's key decision texts, turning it against him. That text now functions in an apologetic account explaining the *unbelief* of Israel, not the belief of pagan converts!

In short, in response to the challenge that the majority of Israel has not responded to Christ, Paul seems to be replying in Romans 10:6-8 that Israel is nevertheless accountable for this turn away from God's action in Christ, not God or anyone (or anything) else.[99] It is her fault. He has much more to say on this question; however, this is the relevant element here, because it explains what he is doing in Romans 10:6-8. And we can now see that this argumentative trajectory continues through the verses that follow (and that continue to concern us) — vv. 9-10, 11-13, and 14-21.

6.2. *Romans 10:9-10*

We come now to Paul's famous statements in vv. 9 and 10:

> [8]. . . Ἐγγύς σου τὸ ῥῆμά ἐστιν
> ἐν τῷ στόματί σου
> καὶ ἐν τῇ καρδίᾳ σου,
> τοῦτ' ἔστιν τὸ ῥῆμα τῆς πίστεως ὃ κηρύσσομεν.
> [9]ὅτι ἐὰν ὁμολογήσῃς ἐν τῷ στόματί σου κύριον Ἰησοῦν
> καὶ πιστεύσῃς ἐν τῇ καρδίᾳ σου ὅτι ὁ Θεὸς αὐτὸν ἤγειρεν ἐκ νεκρῶν
> σωθήσῃ.
> [10]καρδίᾳ γὰρ πιστεύεται εἰς δικαιοσύνην
> στόματι δὲ ὁμολογεῖται εἰς σωτηρίαν.

The first thing to note is the way that Paul has crafted this material as a further explication of the texts he has been citing since v. 6; these verses are actually all of a piece. So on one level, he extends the mouth-heart antithesis of Deuteronomy 30:14 with an artful chiasm (mouth's confession — heart's trust — heart's trust — mouth's confession). But the *content* of these two complementary activities also resumes, at least in its first chiastic wing, the signals of Deuteronomy 30:12-13, where another, complementary antithesis was deployed, although there in relation to Christ — heavenly life and death in the abyss. In v. 9 the mouth confesses Jesus' lordship, which the confessors have not had to ascend to heaven to ascertain, and the heart trusts in Christ's resurrection, which the trusters have not had to descend into the abyss to effect or ascertain. Hence, the entire discussion is integrated as an explication of Deuteronomy 30:12-14. But we must not lose Paul's principal rhetorical point in the details of his intertextual craft.

The overarching impression generated by this exquisitely constructed textual interplay is that the speaker of Deuteronomy 30:12-14 — God — has done everything to bring Christ to the very threshold of his people's being — to their mouths and their hearts (and even "in" them, as the text suggests). Everything has been accomplished, except for the responses of confession and trust and call (and these will be glossed momentarily by Paul in terms of submission as well: see v. 16). God has come near to his people in Christ and asked only for them to confess the resurrection, heavenly enthronement, and lordship of his Christ — the very confession in fact that the Roman Christians have been affirming since vv. 2-4 of the letter. If these responses are present, then they are indeed saved. (Unfortunately, however, we know already that they are not.)

A number of details in this dramatic offer are worth noting before we consider the verses that follow.

(1) These verses strongly confirm the saving and eschatological nuances that were previously detected in Paul's use of δικαιοσύνη (see chapter seventeen). Saving language functions interchangeably with δικαιο- language in these verses, and it completes a process focused on the resurrection and heavenly enthronement of Christ.

(2) The progression in Paul's use of πιστ- language apparent earlier in the letter is evident here as well, although in a slightly more articulated fashion. Paul's rereading of Deuteronomy 30:12-14 in Romans 10:6-10 begins by focusing on a narrative of Christ — his death, resurrection, and heavenly enthronement — which is recounted briefly in vv. 6-7 and 8b and then continues as Christians believe in and confess that narrative, as suggested by vv. 8a and 9-10. So God's saving act proceeds "through faith" — the faithful Christ — "to faith" — in the belief and confession of Christians.

(3) The conditional structure of v. 9 should not be overinterpreted. Here Paul states that "if you confess with your lips that Jesus is Lord and believe in your heart that God raised him from the dead, [then] you will be saved" (NRSV). Strictly speaking, the conditional relationship expressed in this sentence relates the content of the protasis to the apodosis and nothing more; those who confess and believe in this fashion will be saved. We might say more baldly that if A is present, then so is B; A is the condition that, if present, results in the further correlation of B. (Consider the statement, If someone is born in the United Kingdom, then he or she is a British citizen. It does not of course follow from this that he or she *chose* to be born in the UK.) So this sentence by Paul in v. 9 does not speak directly to the *causality* of A in conditional terms, as it is often assumed to — in this case, that the saving belief and confession of the Christian is itself a condition that can be undertaken voluntarily. This would be a false extension of the sentence's grammatical conditionality. Paul's surrounding argument — both locally and more broadly — will have to fill out his exact understanding of its agency. We learn primarily from this conditional claim that belief in and confession of Christ is correlated for Paul with salvation. If this is present in Israel, then she is saved (but in the main it is not). And it is perhaps worth pointing out that belief in and confession of her Lord is not meant to be something new for Israel, although the orientation of that confession and belief has been expanded — but these observations prompt us to consider the important material that follows.

6.3. Romans 10:11-13

In v. 11 Paul reprises one of his scriptural texts (from 9:33) — an unusual act for him — and modifies it. In 10:11 he suggests that πᾶς ὁ πιστεύων ἐπ' αὐτῷ οὐ καταισχυνθήσεται (Isa. 28:16). As in 3:22-23, the use of πᾶς seems to stimulate here an immediate discussion of ethnicity and difference, although it culminates in 10:13 in a citation of Joel 2:32 (3:5 LXX) — πᾶς [γὰρ] ὃς ἂν ἐπικαλέσηται τὸ ὄνομα κυρίου σωθήσεται. And this last citation suggests that the preceding elaboration is anything but coincidental.

Twice in the immediate context of Joel 2:32 the prophet has spoken of the removal of the people's shame (2:26 and 27), and the occurrence in 2:27 seems especially important: καὶ ἐπιγνώσεσθε ὅτι ἐν μέσῳ τοῦ Ἰσραὴλ ἐγώ εἰμι, καὶ ἐγὼ κύριος ὁ Θεὸς ὑμῶν, καὶ οὐκ ἔστιν ἔτι πλὴν ἐμοῦ, καὶ οὐ μὴ καταισχυνθῶσιν οὐκέτι πᾶς ὁ λαός μου εἰς τὸν αἰῶνα. There are simply too many resonances between this text and Paul's discussion in Romans 10:10-13 to ignore (i.e., as mere coincidence) — the presence of God, the κύριος, or *Lord,* with *all* his people, who will never again *be put to shame.* Indeed, it is almost certainly this association that legitimizes Paul's modification of Isaiah 28:16 in v. 11 with the addition of πᾶς (at which point it can be asked whether the citation in v. 11 is better viewed as a conflation of Joel 2:32 and Isaiah 28:16 rather than merely a modification of the latter text). So Paul's two textual citations here, and the intervening discussion, seem entirely deliberate.

Moreover, in the light of these two texts, drawn from explicitly Jewish contexts and set here in an overarching argument oriented toward Jews, it seems that the dismissal of any significant difference between Jew and Greek that takes place in v. 12 is oriented in this setting primarily toward Jews as well. The Jew who believes is also included in the salvation already extended toward believing pagans (see 9:25-30); believing pagans and Jews can *all* be saved by the same Lord. (And Paul's emphasis at this point on "all" — a feature of the text drawn from Joel — anticipates his important concluding statement in 11:26 that "all Israel will be saved"; this is, moreover, the text's emphasis in its original context.) So it can be seen that Paul's artful intertextual weaving in Romans 10 continues from vv. 6-10 through v. 13, coming to a climactic point in the affirmation of Jesus' lordship. Moreover, he has reversed the probable thrust of the Teacher's discourse at this point as well. Whereas the Teacher probably begins with Israel and then asks whether pagans can be included within that privileged constituency — answering that they can be only on the condition of full law observance, including circumcision — Paul here suggests that Israel can be included within the privileged constituency of the saved (as she certainly ought to be) provided that she evidences belief and confession in the resurrected Lord.

In an important study, Kavin Rowe has shown how the immediate setting of lordship in these verses ascribes deity to Christ rather directly (i.e., the term "lord" is functioning in its full Old Testament sense as a title for God), although without identifying him with divinity exclusively. In a sense, then, the Christian (re)definition of God peeps through the intertextually constituted tensions in this text.[100] I would only want to add that this is quite consistent with the broader apologetic that we have seen Paul developing through this chapter of Romans. His point is that *God has come to Israel in person,* so any rejection of this gracious drawing-near is the more incomprehensible. Paul's broader apologetic agenda in context leads to this particular theological emphasis. But this also explains why Christ is so overtly specified as the object of Christian belief at this point, which is an unusual emphasis for Paul (elsewhere see only Gal. 2:15-16; possibly Phil. 1:27-28; see Eph. 1:15; Col. 1:4; 2:5). Ordinarily, he speaks of belief in the gospel or of trust in God "the Father." However, here Christ has been "placed in Zion"; God has come right to his people, so there is even less excuse (if indeed any) for failing to believe in this event.[101] This is an unusual situation and consequent emphasis for Paul that are then hardly programmatic for the determination of the object of some of his other πιστ- statements. We might say that Christ functions explicitly as the object of saving belief for Paul where an apology vis-à-vis Jewish unbelief is also evident, and hence where Isaiah 28:16 is cited (perhaps supported by Joel 2:32, which emphasizes Christ's lordship).

Numerous other powerful theological questions and answers are set in motion by this material; however, before considering those relevant to our current investigation in more detail, we should briefly note the consequent function of vv. 14-21.

6.4. Romans 10:14-21

Although the opening verses of this material are almost invariably read as an explication of Paul's mission to the pagans (and I would not dispute this in broader terms, either in Paul's life or in his theology), our developing rereading suggests that the climax deployed by vv. 14-15a may in fact continue to address Jews as well, just as the preceding material in vv. 11-13 has. Indeed, a plausible reading of this entire section is possible in just these terms.

On the heels of Paul's claim of the ease of salvation for all Israelites merely in relation to the confession of Christ's lordship, it is easy to imagine an objection (and one still made not infrequently today). It amounts to the typical complaint concerning those who have *not* heard, although here it is made on behalf of Jews. Indeed, it is possible that the querulous interlocutor of 9:30-31 has returned once again, asking at this point how Paul's claims in vv. 9-13 can possibly be true without some sort of presentation to the Jews of all this critical information about Christ (at which point the resonance of this text with certain central concerns of Justification theory is apparent). It seems unfair to hold Jews accountable for rejecting Christ when they do not actually know the key pieces of information about him, and it is perhaps easiest to imagine that Diaspora Jews are especially in view at this point; Christ has, it seems, already come to Zion (see 9:33). So the Teacher duly challenges Paul with these counterquestions (the following being my translation throughout).

¹⁴But[102] how can they "call" [as you assert with Joel 2:32] on the one in whom they have not believed?

And how can they "believe" [as you assert with Isa. 28:16] in the one of whom they have not heard?

And how can they hear apart from preaching [of some sort]?

¹⁵And how can they preach unless they are sent [to preach]?! . . ."

¹⁶ᵃ". . . but not everyone submitted to the good news . . ."

¹⁸ᵃ". . . but I ask,[103] surely they did not hear . . ."

¹⁹ᵃ". . . but I ask (again), surely Israel did not understand (or, more literally, 'know')?!"

Verse 14 can be seen to inaugurate a series of essentially hostile questions to Paul's suggestion that Israel is accountable to God's act through Christ in terms of some response of belief and submission — questions that continue in vv. 18 and 19a as well. The Teacher places the essentially practical objection here to Paul that Jews everywhere will need to be told about Christ if they are to believe in and call on him, as Paul suggests they ought to. But as is usually the case with the Teacher's provocative intrusions — which are, after all, shaped by Paul — these ultimately serve only to strengthen the apostle's position. And here he duly knocks back each challenge with a blunt citation of Scripture — an especially effective rejoinder in the present situation because these texts are addressed to Israel, and are well known to her. The result of this interchange is *a deepened sense of Israel's accountability*, Paul's main point in context. All her excuses prove groundless, and are even scripturally attested as such.

Thus, Paul replies in v. 15b to the Teacher's complaint that the Jews must be told about Christ with the statement from Isaiah, "How beautiful are the feet of those proclaiming good news" (Isa. 52:7). This text implies the arrival in Israel of just the messengers that the Teacher asserts must be present for Paul's claims to hold good. They have arrived and announced their message because the prophet speaks of the beauty of their feet. However, the Teacher retorts in v. 16a, "But not everyone submitted to the good news. . . ."

Now this is not technically an objection to Paul's basic challenge to Israel in Romans 10 in terms of unbelief, but it is an embarrassment. The majority of the Jews have not believed in this good news. However, even this embarrassment has been foretold in Scripture, lessening its scandalous nature: "Isaiah says, 'Lord, who has believed in the things heard from us?'" Moreover, Paul parlays this text into a further, probably parenthetical rejoinder to the previous challenge that the Jews need to hear something before they can trust and be saved. Isaiah's text establishes the reality of this sequence as well; the prophet asks who has believed in things that *have been heard*. And hence Paul is able to state here: "So, then, belief is through that which is heard [which Isaiah spoke of] — and that which is heard through the word concerning Christ."[104]

However, the Teacher is not yet finished in terms of this line of argument. He complains next, "But I ask, surely they did not hear?" (The emphatic double negative in the Koiné used here expects a negative answer to this query — "no"; see ἀλλὰ λέγω, μὴ οὐκ ἤκουσαν.) But Paul contradicts this implication (again) — μενοῦνγε — and quotes a useful Scripture once more in v. 18b: "Their voice has gone out into all the land, and their words to the edges of the empire." This is a quotation from Psalm 19:4, although it does not need to be recognized as such for Paul's counterargument to work. In context, it seems likely to be predicting the work of missionaries like Paul who have been sent to the Jewish people scattered through the known world (see Gal. 2:7-9), although we have already noted that this is a wisdom text, thereby raising the possibility that this is again the voice of God. Whatever the identity of the tongues and voice, this text affirms that Israel everywhere in the world has heard.

After the counterassertion of v. 18b, the Teacher has one last protest to make in this vein: "But I ask [again], surely Israel did not understand [or, more literally, 'know']?!" However, Paul once more refuses to supply the expected negation, and he begins to round off this subordinate discussion concerning Jewish culpability with a set of important scriptural quotations.

He quotes first from Moses — specifically, Deuteronomy 32:21 — in v. 19, and then twice from Isaiah — specifically, 65:1 and 2 — in vv. 20 and 21. The Deuteronomic text begins an argumentative turn toward the next stage in his argument, articulated through most of Romans 11, where he finds various positive aspects within the basic tragedy of Israel's failure to respond to Christ. Here in 10:19 he anticipates the suggestion elaborated later that pagan conversion will make the Jews jealous, goading them into a correct response. However, implicit in this "jealousy" is knowledge. (One must have knowledge of certain things even to become jealous.) The Isaianic texts in vv. 20-21 then speak more bluntly of where Paul's argument has presently ended up.

Recapitulating the paradoxical salvation-historical scenario that was stated clearly in 9:30-31, and has been implicit all along, Paul states that the pagans, who were not interested in God, have nevertheless somehow received him. "I have been found by those who did not seek me; I have shown myself to those who did not ask for me" (NRSV). But Israel has not only *not* received God in Christ; as Paul has shown in 10:1-18, she has *rejected* Christ. God has come near in Christ and his other appointed representatives, but Israel has pushed them away. So she has not acted in ignorance (as vv. 14-15a, 18a, and 19a suggest) but deliberately, and has in effect chosen to establish her own route to salvation and to life rather willfully (as vv. 3, 5, and 16a assert). So Paul can cite the apparent prophetic prediction of this in closing that "[a]ll day long I have held out my hands to a *disobedient* and *contrary* people" (NRSV). And this citation concludes his initial apologetic response to the charge from the Teacher that the majority of Israel has not believed, thereby discrediting his gospel. Paul has responded through much of Romans 10 that the fault for this salvation-historical absurdity is Israel's, not God's, and certain parts of Scripture can be read in support of this claim.

In view of all this, it is not surprising to find at the end of this discussion the further, refreshingly direct query of the Teacher, who seems by now to have grasped the import of the argument: "I ask then, has God not simply abandoned his people [as, in view of the foregoing, he has a right to]?!" But Paul himself, while holding Israel responsible for rejecting Christ, will not of course allow this to be the end of the matter. Just as God's election triumphed over pagan ignorance in 9:6-26 and 30, so too it will triumph over Jewish disobedience — and in many subtle ways! Israel's rejection of God in Christ is by no means the last word. But it is not necessary for the present investigation to probe these important suggestions by Paul in Romans 11 in more detail here. Justification language and theory fade during the course of Romans 10, especially from v. 17, and it is necessary to ask in the present relation only whether we have succeeded in rereading this material both plausibly and apocalyptically. We should be able to answer this question shortly in a more definitive way, once some of the deeper theological implications of Romans 9:27–10:21 have been teased out a little further.

§7. A Repunctuation of the NRSV[105] — Romans 9:27–10:21

PAUL: [9:27]And Isaiah cries out concerning Israel,

"Though the number of the children of Israel were like the sand of the sea,
only a remnant of them will be saved;
[28]for the Lord will execute his sentence on the earth quickly and decisively."

[29]And as Isaiah predicted,

"If the Lord of hosts had not left survivors to us,
we would have fared like Sodom and been made like Gomorrah."

TEACHER: [30]What are we to say then? Pagans not pursuing righteous activity have received a righteous act [from God]?!

PAUL: The righteous act [of God] "through faithfulness."

TEACHER: [31]But Israel, pursuing a torah of righteous activity toward that Torah, have not?!

PAUL: [32]Why? Because they did not strive for it "through faithfulness" but "through works." They have stumbled over "the stumbling stone," [33]as it is written,

"See, I am laying in Zion a stone that will make people stumble,
a rock that will make them fall,
and whoever believes in him will not be put to shame."

[10:1]Brothers, my heart's desire and prayer to God for them is that they may be saved. [2]I can testify that they have a zeal for God, but it is not enlightened. [3]For, being ignorant of the righteous act from God, and seeking to establish their own, they have not submitted to the righteous act from God. [4]For Christ is the finish line for the

Torah, with the result of righteousness for everyone who believes. [5]Moses writes concerning the righteous activity that is through the Torah, that

> *"the person who does these things will live by them."*[106]

[6]But the righteous act that takes place "through faithfulness" says,

> *"Do not say in your heart, 'Who will ascend into heaven?'"*
> (that is, to bring Christ down) [7]or
> *"Who will descend into the abyss?"*
> (that is, to bring Christ up from the dead).
> [8]But what does it say?
> *"The word is near you, on your lips and in your heart"*
> (that is, the word of the faithful one that we proclaim);

[9]because if you confess with your lips that Jesus is Lord
and believe in your heart that God raised him from the dead,
you will be saved.
[10]For one believes with the heart and so is delivered,
and one confesses with the mouth and so is saved.
[11]The scripture says,

> "All who believe in him will not be put to shame."

[12]For there is no distinction between Jew and Greek; the same Lord is Lord of all and enriches all who call on him. [13]For,

> "All who call on the name of the Lord shall be saved."

TEACHER: [14]But how can they "call" on one in whom they have not believed? And how can they "believe" in the one of whom they have not heard? And how can they hear apart from preaching? [15]And how can they preach unless they are sent?

PAUL: As it is written,

> "How beautiful are the feet of those who bring good news!"

TEACHER: [16]But not everyone submitted to the good news.

PAUL: [And] for this reason, Isaiah says,

> "Lord, who has believed our proclamation?"

[17]So then, belief comes from what is heard, and what is heard comes through the word of Christ.

TEACHER: [18]But I ask, surely they did not hear?

PAUL: Indeed they have; for

> "Their voice has gone out to all the earth,
> and their words to the ends of the empire."

TEACHER: [19]But I ask, surely Israel did not understand?

PAUL: First Moses says,

> "I will make you jealous of those who are not a nation;
>   with a foolish nation I will make you angry."

[20]Then Isaiah is so bold as to say,

> "I have been found by those who did not seek me;
> I have shown myself to those who did not ask for me."

[21]But of Israel he says,

> "All day long I have held out my hands to a disobedient and contrary people."

TEACHER: [11:1]I ask, then, surely God has not abandoned his people?

PAUL: Of course not! I am an Israelite. . . .

§8. The Theological Implications

We began this chapter, and §5 in particular, by noting that Romans 9:27–10:21 contains four serious explicit challenges to my suggested rereading of Paul — two remarks concerning Israel and "works" (9:31-32; 10:5) that could be construed with reference to a pre-Christian activity, one remark implying that Christ was an "end" or a "goal" (10:4), but that on either reading could suggest some prospective process, and a long account of "faith" in Romans 10 that could be construed conditionally in relation to salvation (see esp. 10:9-10), again thereby unleashing a broader contractual and prospective structure within Paul's thinking. So at four points Justification theory could potentially be activated, and this would then contradict the unconditional, apocalyptic, and retrospective process I derived from Romans 1–4 in part four, and would also unleash all the pernicious consequences generated by Justification theory that my apocalyptic rereading is designed to avoid. In every case, however, I have suggested that these statements and their localized contexts — if approached without prospective and conditional precommitments — can (and even should) be read retrospectively (see esp. §§5 and 6 above). And the prospective challenges present within these texts are therefore — at least arguably — repudiated. However, we have yet to explore my exegetical suggestions' implications in these texts at a deeper level. If they hold good, and Paul's thinking turns out to be satisfyingly retrospective, then what are the implications for that thinking? Romans 9–10 does not merely parrot (or contradict), but *deepens* the account of Paul's thought derived already from Romans 1–4 and 5–8 in several important ways. We gain further insight into the precise nature and dynamic of the apostle's retrospective argumentation, explored here in §8.1; we grasp more precisely the reasons for the profoundly intertextual nature of his discussion, as well as the closely-related reasons for the resonances between Romans 1:16-17, 3:21-26, and 9:30–10:17 (although I have suggested that the argument here spans 9:27–10:21), articulated here in §8.2; and we learn more about his notion of Christian faith, analyzed here in §8.3.

8.1. The Retrospective Ground of Paul's Argument

The validity of Paul's contention from Romans 9:27 onward depends entirely on the validity of his claim that God *has* acted in Christ definitively to "deliver" both pagan and Jew. In the light of this claim, Paul holds all other salvific claims to be relativized, including any associated use of the law. Only given the overt truth of this prior claim — that God *has* brought salvation and life to Israel in Christ — are Paul's other negations remotely acceptable. But given this premise, they do make sense. Obviously, Paul is convinced of the claim's truth. So the crucial question is, what is the exact basis of Paul's confidence and its ensuing relativizations? The repeated implication from Romans 9:30–10:21 is that Christ's eschatological life has provided the critical disclosure of God's salvation for Paul, together with the consequent dislocation of all alternative modes of salvation.[107] Hence, it seems that Christ's resurrection from the dead and ascension to lordship are the new, definitive revelation of salvation, of life, and of God's "deliverance."[108] Moreover, those who merely evidence trust in this set of events, and in the God who acts through them, seem to be guaranteed a future share in the events themselves.

The importance of Habakkuk 2:4 for Paul is apparent here. That citation speaks of Jesus' "life," that is, his resurrection and existence in glory: "the righteous one through fidelity will live." This is in pointed (implicit) contrast to Leviticus 18:5, cited in Romans 10:5, which speaks of life through law observance. (The contrast is explicit in Gal. 3:11-12.) "Life" in both these texts is almost certainly a reference to eschatological life.[109] If one "lives" in relation to Christ's resurrection, then self- or human-centered salvific activities are displaced and excluded.[110] It is *this* set of facts that automatically marginalizes all other possible routes to eschatological salvation, including any reliance on Moses, other than as a testimony to the Christ event.[111] To rely on any other activity, in Paul's view, is clearly *not* to live on the basis of the life available in relation to Jesus Christ himself,[112] who has been sent by God.

Hence, Paul's overall posture now seems clear — the basis of his conviction and his relativizations. On the ground of Christ's resurrection, who is assumed to be the definitive eschatological action for others by God, Paul reasons retrospectively and exclusively with regard to any other, Jewish type of activity (and he would doubtless extend this exclusion to any human activity that was competitive with the Christ event). Whatever that activity may be in precise terms — and precise terms no longer need to be given![113] — it is now redundant, and any reliance on it will lead inevitably to a missing of the actual route to salvation established by God. Moreover, if that route — God's definitive act in his Son — is repudiated, then for Paul, *by definition,* an alternative and essentially human route to resurrection has been adopted instead, any protestations notwithstanding. Consequently, Paul speaks in 10:3 of Israel "seeking to establish her own righteous activity."

We should note now that this repudiation can be effected by as little as *adding* something to the Christ event. So in fact two categories of unwise "doers" are discernible in Paul: Jews who repudiate Christ in the name of the law, and Jewish Christian Teachers who advocate law observance as mandatory for converts from paganism to Christianity, in addition to their loyalty to Christ. Paul regards both categories as equally misguided, and indeed *both make the same fundamental error:* they deny the complete saving efficacy of the righteous act of God in Christ, choosing to supplement this with certain instances of mandatory human activity. Moreover, in a sense, to follow the Teacher's gospel is also to *exacerbate* the current difficulty of unbelieving Israel, rather than to resolve it — at least, this is the artful inference that lies submerged in Paul's developing position — because it would encourage Jews to add mandatory, law-informed practices to the saving act of God in Christ (or at least affirm that posture). And so the Teacher's calumnies have, once again, been turned back on his own head. Paul is not the one with an excruciating difficulty in relation to unbelieving Israel, so much as the Teacher, whose Arminian (if not Pelagian) gospel endorses their unbelief.

There are other categories of "doers," however, that seem quite acceptable. Jewish law observance that does not impinge on the eschatological sufficiency of the Christ event seems unexceptionable — so 1 Corinthians 9:20 (although clearly, this is quite flexible). Indeed, one suspects that "messianic Jews" are not just acceptable but normative for Paul — so 1 Corinthians 7:17-24. Righteous activity informed by the law prior to Christ is unexceptionable as well, although it now seems largely irrelevant — so Philippians 3:3-6.[114] But Paul's opposition to the unacceptable categories can hardly be understated.

He regards such programs as futile and misguided, but also ultimately as dangerous — in large measure, because they lack fundamental ethical efficacy. God's appointed route to eschatological life, the Christ event, addresses the enslavement of human nature by evil forces in the death of Christ and then offers a resurrection. However partial its present experience, Paul holds that death in Christ is the only effective basis for righteous activity by humans — whether Jews or Greeks — because only participation in Christ's execution terminates humanity's sinful condition and reconstitutes it in a more effective ethical state, ultimately to resurrect it — something Paul can describe as a "real" circumcision that has cut the sinful nature off from the human heart.[115] Any reliance on human activity for eschatological vindication without the ethical surgery that God provides in Christ, however zealous its pursuit, will result only in humiliation. *And* it ignores the gracious and effective system lying just to hand that God has actually provided![116]

8.2. *Paul's Intertextuality*

We are in a position now to answer our second important question in this relation — why the characteristic terminology of Romans 1:16-17 and 3:21-26 recurs
so overtly and intensively in Romans 9:27–10:17 — a question bound up with
Paul's intertextuality in these passages.

It seems that when Paul wishes to engage directly some of the Teacher's
central claims, asserting his own emphasis on Christ's centrality in response, he
turns consistently to a cluster of important scriptural texts. The Teacher's claims
about salvation through law observance are freighted and supported by certain
key scriptural texts as well; hence, as Paul narrates the confrontation for his auditors, he is presenting them with a clash between two "torahs," and not merely one
torah over against a more innovative and recent gospel (i.e., Paul's).

In Romans 1:16-17 and 3:21-26 Paul is signaling briefly the presuppositions
in his gospel that contradict the Teacher's opening and fundamental claims about
God and ground his own later counterarguments in chapters 5–8. Over against a
God of retributive justice (who thereby effectively marginalizes the disclosure
and work of Christ), introduced — and criticized! — in 1:18–3:20, Paul wishes to
signal the definitive disclosure and action of God *through* Christ *on behalf of* a
very different, more inclusive constituency (thereby also revealing a fundamentally different God as well — a God of deliverance, not punishment). So, as we
have seen, he deploys, against Leviticus 18:5 (etc.), a compilation of phrases and
words drawn from Psalm 98:2, Habakkuk 2:4, Genesis 15:6, Isaiah 28:16, and Joel
2:32. Similarly, in Romans 9:27 Paul turns again to speak of the climactic moment
within the history of Israel that is the Christ event — the arrival of the divine wisdom in the midst of her people. So once again he makes recourse to his key Scriptures and their terms, although supplementing those at this point with Isaiah 8:14
and Deuteronomy 30:12-14 (and introducing Joel 2:32 explicitly), supporting
those with other useful texts as well (among which Isa. 52:7 is probably especially
programmatic). In short, when Paul needs to speak of God acting definitively
through Christ to save, in direct confrontation with the Teacher's claims, he uses
language infused with key scriptural texts in order to lend those claims legitimacy
and authority. And those moments arrive in Romans in 1:16, 3:21, and 9:27. It
seems, moreover, that we can now discern the origins of this ingenious
intertextual interplay — and this will also further emphasize our earlier resolution of the third significant challenge in Romans 10 to our developing, retrospective rereading.

That challenge was found in 10:5, where Paul quotes Leviticus 18:5: "the person who does these things will live by them." I have already suggested that this
text is best read in context as a reference in some sense to law-observant behavior
by Israel after the coming of Christ. So it seems unlikely that Paul is quoting this
text as a programmatic characterization of historical Israel — just the interpretation I am trying to avoid. But if this is not the quotation's function, what is it? At
this point two further possibilities open up for us.

Has Paul drawn this text from Moses in order to describe the gospel of his opponent, in order ultimately to refute it? This option seems fraught with difficulties (although they are not as serious as the preceding option). To start, it would seem to be tendentious — ascribing a purely Mosaic text to the Teacher — and it is also prone to misunderstanding, that is, in just the terms that we previously noted, as a description of Mosaic religion per se. Furthermore, the phrase does not ever seem to be explicitly qualified as such by Paul. It is also possibly unfair; the Teacher might reasonably reject Paul's tendentious description of his gospel in these terms. (Alternatively, he would be allowed a fortuitous comeback; Paul would have thereby conceded the *legitimacy* of the Teacher's account of Moses.)

But these problems are all avoided if the text's original citation and deployment are attributed to the Teacher himself. And on reflection it seems quite likely that Leviticus 18:5 (possibly supported by phraseology found in Ps. 62:12, Prov. 24:12, and Sir. 16:14, viz., "he will give to each according to his works") was a key text of the Teacher's. It speaks of "life," in the sense of eschatological life, through "doing," which translates directly into "works," persistent good works resulting in a righteous state and the verdict from God on the day of judgment of "righteous" and hence "saved" and "blessed" (at which point a little boasting might even be in order; this righteous behavior is of course made possible after circumcision of the sinful passions). Leviticus 18:5 is therefore an accurate summary of just the gospel that Paul attacks in Romans 1–4 — the gospel of the Teacher, a gospel of "justification" (in the full ethical and indicative sense of that word).[117] So it seems likely that the Teacher himself introduced the terminology of "works" and "doing" into the debate, rooting these — entirely characteristically — in key scriptural texts. And this realization allows us to avoid falling back into any prospective theological trap on Paul's part. But this also, simultaneously, points to the linguistic origin of this entire cluster of key texts in Romans. *Paul has crafted his own countervailing set of texts specifically to refute, word by word, the key scriptural claims of the Teacher.* (Rather indicatively, the baldest disposition of these texts is then in Gal. 3:6-11, a passage that we will consider shortly in chapter twenty.)

The core of the textual engagement is the juxtaposition of Habakkuk 2:4 over against Leviticus 18:5. As Romans 2:6 also indicates, however, when an instrumental, substantive phrase is drawn from Leviticus 18:5, both Paul and the Teacher prefer the more idiomatic construction "works" (ἔργα) over "doings" (ποίημα or some such). Paul then negates these, affirming salvation or "life" ἐκ πίστεως instead — through Christ.

ὁ ποιήσας αὐτὰ ἄνθρωπος ζήσεται ἐν αὐτοῖς [see Rom. 10:5; Gal. 3:12]
[ἀποδώσει ἑκάστῳ κατὰ τὰ ἔργα αὐτοῦ] [see Rom. 2:6-10]
ὁ δίκαιος ἐκ πίστεως ζήσεται [see Rom. 1:17; Gal. 3:11]

It is worth emphasizing, moreover, that the heart of Paul's position is christological and retrospective. He knows that a person is not ultimately saved through works because he knows that a person is ultimately saved by way of some connection to Christ, who has already been resurrected and hence saved. It is by being grafted into this life that others achieve life themselves — a grafting that God must of course effect. Moreover, that grafting has in Paul's experience stretched out to include some who are non–law observant (i.e., pagans). And a set of texts is used to express these important facts as well — Isaiah 28:16 and Joel 2:32. "Everybody" or "all" who reflect this engrafting by reflecting the character of Christ are guaranteed the same life and resurrection, so Paul freights this implication by building from πιστ- terms, using the contextual overlap in Joel to effect a further important set of qualifications in terms of universality — "all" — and confession of Christ's lordship.

> ὁ πιστεύων ἐπ᾽ αὐτῷ οὐ καταισχυνθήσεται [see Rom. 10:11]
> πᾶς [γὰρ] ὃς ἂν ἐπικαλέσηται τὸ ὄνομα κυρίου σωθήσεται [see Rom. 9:33; 10:13]

Furthermore, Paul is confident enough to suggest that this salvific dynamic is discernible in the Old Testament as well, and especially in the patriarchal narratives. In Romans he makes this argument most famously by leaning on the key πιστ- stem again and explicating Genesis 15:6. (The Teacher leans more on Genesis 17, but those texts do not need to be included here.)

> Ἐπίστευσεν [δὲ] Ἀβραὰμ τῷ Θεῷ καὶ ἐλογίσθη αὐτῷ εἰς δικαιοσύνην [see Rom. 4:3; Gal. 3:6]

Paul is also concerned, however, to refute another set of key items in the Teacher's gospel with Scripture. The Teacher almost certainly emphasizes God's declaration of the law observant as "righteous" (and hence saved) on the day of judgment — a use of the verb δικαιόω. And so Paul attacks this claim with a text as well — Psalm 143:2. This text affirms Paul's conviction that no one will be declared righteous in this fashion, for numerous compelling reasons. He also attacks the Teacher's slogan at this point that "God declares righteous the righteous" with his own, rather shocking claim that "God declares righteous (in the sense of delivering) the unrighteous" (usually translated "ungodly").

> ἐξ ἔργων νόμου οὐ δικαιωθήσεται πᾶσα σάρξ ἐνώπιον αὐτὸν[118] [see Rom. 3:20; Gal. 2:16]
> [Θεὸς δικαιοῖ τὸν ἀσεβῆ, οὐ τὸν δίκαιον] [see Rom. 4:5; see 5:6]

But the Teacher almost certainly makes further use of righteousness language; he probably enjoins righteousness on his converts in the sense of persistent righteous activity informed by the Mosaic law. He also threatens his converts with dire consequences if this activity is not undertaken; such people will experience the wrath, not the blessing, of God. His righteous, retributive justice will condemn them to hell on the day of judgment, instead of blessing them. They will be shamed.

Paul's textual response is at its most artful at this point. He deploys a "swing" text — one that can refute two claims here within the Teacher's system simultaneously. Against *both* the righteous activity of the convert *and* the punitive wrath of God he speaks, rather, of God's right act of saving deliverance, echoing in particular Psalm 98:2 (but also drawing on broader notions of divine kingship) — a wordplay that is impossible to reproduce in translation. This text suggests in nuce that Paul does not depend on his *own* righteous activity but on *God's*. Moreover, the God that Paul knows in Christ is characterized fundamentally *by salvation,* not by wrath. So entirely different conceptions of God are at stake as well. The echo of Psalm 98:2 makes both these points whenever it is used.

[δικαιοσύνη μου . . .] [see Rom. 10:3; Phil. 3:6-8]

δικαιοσύνη Θεοῦ ἀποκαλύπτεται . . . [see Rom. 1:17; 3:5; 3:21-22; 10:3; also
   perhaps Gal. 2:21; 3:21; 5:5]

[ὀργὴ Θεοῦ . . .] [see Rom. 1:18; 2:5-9]

And he attacks the suggestion as well that his law-free converts will be shamed on this future day of judgment (with a useful text that has already been deployed in support of another point).

[πᾶς] ὁ πιστεύων ἐπ' αὐτῷ οὐ καταισχυνθήσεται [see Rom. 9:33; 10:11]

It is worth stepping back for a moment to evaluate what Paul has achieved in and through this textual engagement.

First, we should note the techniques that he seems to have used. The main principle undergirding all of his textual deployments seems to be *gezerah shawah,* or "catchword linkage" (although it seems that a cognate will suffice to establish a connection). Only three of his quotations echo their original contexts, at least to the extent of some surrounding verses — Psalms 98:2 and 143:2, and Joel 2:32.[119] But at some point all the texts seem to say explicitly what Paul needs them to say argumentatively, in the form of either a clause or a complete sentence; they seem invariably to contradict something that the Teacher has been claiming directly (his claims often being couched in terms of Scripture as well). Hence, we do not need to detect the echoes to understand the rhetorical function of these quotations, although they help us understand those functions more precisely at times (including the theological positions that sometimes lie behind them). (So, e.g., the linkage between Isa. 28:16 and Joel 2:32 is difficult to detect without grasping the contextual echoes.)

Second, we can consider what Paul is doing here, at least to a degree. Opinions of his skill have of course varied enormously. Some charge him with gross exegetical distortions. Others detect underlying canonical frameworks of considerable sophistication (and so on). This question is not especially relevant to our developing argument; we are more interested in what Paul is actually doing rather than its value or skill. However, it might be worth suggesting that judgments that

Paul's quotations are somehow "inadequate" tend to presuppose anachronism. In terms of the contemporary rules of the exegetical game, Paul was perfectly entitled to quote small snippets of Scripture out of context (etc.), if he wanted to, and as he has done here. Certainly, his exegesis is not modern and historicizing, but why would it be? Similarly, it is difficult and probably also unnecessary to detect deep underlying hermeneutical configurations that drive these superficial quotations, much as tectonic plates drive superficial shifts in the earth and seabed. These texts function argumentatively very much as they appear. And it is seldom necessary to move beyond them to understand Paul's rhetorical points (although the presence of certain echoes looks both likely and helpful). And having said all this, there does seem to be something remarkably skillful in what Paul has done.

Paul has not chosen this scriptural ground; the Teacher has. And yet Paul seems to have constructed an entire network of mutually supporting texts, some of which even make multiple points, all connected with one another or with the Teacher's gospel by key words or stems, in order to undercut that opposing gospel at all its key points. Each of these texts must fulfill a double function; it must refute a component in the Teacher's system *and* integrate either with that system or with Paul's developing system through the possession of a shared cognate. (So Paul's set of texts is a bit like a complex crossword puzzle.) And Paul has constructed this system without modern aids and even a single Bible that he can flip through and consult (i.e., much of it is almost certainly dependent on his memorization of Scripture). In terms of his own scriptural game, then, this seems to be a masterful performance. Clearly, he knows the Jewish Scriptures intimately.

It is also important to appreciate that this type of quotation by Paul is highly contingent; he argues in this way only when he is opposing the Teacher and his gospel. So it is an important false inference to extrapolate from this type of exegetical activity to Paul's "own" approach to Scripture. This is *not Paul's* use of Scripture, in the deepest sense of that phrase. It is often little more than a rhetorical tit-for-tat. We must seek Paul's own, perhaps constitutive use of the Jewish Scripture beyond this contingency, and elsewhere (where I would suggest that narrative trajectories are very important[120]).

Finally, it needs to be emphasized that we should not press this material directly into theological service. As we have already seen (especially in part four, chapter fifteen), this scriptural interplay both expresses and constrains Paul's communication. He seems frequently to restate — in slightly different, presumably clearer language — what he has said elsewhere by way of quotation. It is dangerous, then, simply to reconstruct Paul's contingency directly in terms of language drawn from his polemically deployed proof texts without additional controls on any such reconstructions. And this methodological caveat leads to our final programmatic comment concerning Romans 10 (which is probably the most important).

8.3. The Nature of Faith

Romans 9:27–10:21 does not just pose problems for a thoroughgoing apocalyptic rereading of Paul's view of Judaism, with its references to "works," Christ as the τέλος of the law, and its quotation of Leviticus 18:5 (all of which could be interpreted in terms of a prospective analysis by Paul, with Judaism's inadequacies leading to and hence establishing salvation by faith). It speaks constantly of "faith" as well, and has consequently been read as one of the clearest statements in Paul of faith as *the* criterion for salvation. Paul's words in 10:8-10 seem to suggest this especially directly: "'The word is near you, on your lips and in your heart' (that is, the word of faith that we proclaim); because if you confess with your lips that Jesus is Lord and believe in your heart that God raised him from the dead, you will be saved. For one believes with the heart and so is justified, and one confesses with the mouth and so is saved" (NRSV). The realization that this material is oriented toward Israel (see §6 above) does not alter this implication very significantly; if this — and this alone — is what Israel must do in order to be saved, then by implication that principle still applies to everyone (as Paul even seems to admit in passing, in v. 12). Should "faith" and "believing" in this text, then, be read in the way that Justification theory expects and so falsify my developing apocalyptic reconstrual of Paul? Does Paul commit himself clearly here to a condition for salvation, and to this one alone?

I freely admit that if this text is read in isolation from its setting, it can be construed in a way that integrates with Justification theory. However, I also contend that if the expectations of Justification theory in relation to this text are resisted and if certain key insights from our developing rereading of the surrounding discussion are held in view, then it can be construed in an apocalyptic sense as well. Once again we face a conundrum like that noted in chapter eighteen concerning the interpretation of the believing Abraham and his analogical relation with later Christians. That analogy could legitimately be read in its immediate setting in either a "thin" or a "thick" sense. The "thin" reading supported Justification theory, while the "thick" reading was more christocentric and apocalyptic, and either reading seemed initially acceptable. But various considerations from the text's broader setting suggested — rather strongly — that the "thick" reading was ultimately the correct one (or, at least, the better one). So the analogy ended up vindicating, not undermining, the broader apocalyptic reading of Paul. *And similar considerations apply, I suggest, to Paul's discussion of "belief" in Romans 10.*

It is not that what Paul is saying here should be denied; he is saying that if Israel only confesses and believes in Christ, then she will be saved (and this applies to everyone else as well, as v. 12 states). However, the causality underlying this process is more complex and profound than first meets the eye, as a result of which such "belief" ends up functioning more as a *marker* of salvation than a solitary *condition*; it is a marker of participation in the faithful and resurrected Christ, which thereby implicitly *guarantees* for the believer a future participation in the resurrection that Christ has already achieved. It is this underlying reality, I suggest, that Israel has been called to in Romans 10 but has rejected (and, in a sense, her rejection is the more scandalous in view of this; that is, she has pushed away a confession already operating within her).

A thin reading views belief in Romans 10 as essentially propositional. Apostles, missionaries, or preachers present individuals with the essential facts about Christ — that he has been resurrected by God and is now "Lord" — and those individuals ought then to believe this information and to confess their belief. If they do so, then they are officially saved. Nothing more is mentioned, so nothing more, strictly speaking, needs to be done.[121] However, although this is a possible reading of Romans 10:8-10, as we have already seen in the much more extensive conventional construal of Romans 1–4, various difficulties emerging downstream suggest that this thin account of the text may not be the best one.

First, we should note that several of the textual difficulties observed in relation to the conventional construal of Romans 1–4 will recur if we follow this thin approach. The emphasis from Romans 9:30 onward on Christ's fidelity now becomes otiose, and the emphasis on Christ's resurrection arbitrary. These two features of Christ resonate against similar features in the lives of believers — they seem to have been selected for these reasons deliberately. However, there is no substantive reason for these similarities on the thin reading of the text. Nothing meaningful connects them. Strictly speaking, individuals do not even need to believe in Christ himself in order to be saved; God could have specified *any* item as the object of belief in order to grant salvation. And if he wanted to maintain some special reference to Christian realities and the church, there is no obvious need to single out Christ's resurrection and lordship as the key items. Just how to negotiate the conundrums of belief voluntarism (or, alternatively, of elected belief) is unspecified as well. So certain aspects of a thin reading of this text remain puzzling.

Second, many of the acute conceptual tensions noted in relation to Justification theory and the conventional construal of Romans 1–4 now surge back into prominence — tensions apparent as other claims in Romans are juxtaposed with the thin reading of these claims in Romans 10.

We are again puzzled by how an enslaved and depraved person, as evidenced especially by Romans 7, could exercise such belief; "the mind that is set on the flesh is hostile to God; it does not submit to God's law — indeed it cannot, and those who are in the flesh cannot please God" (8:7-8 NRSV). God seems once again to be unreasonable and unjust. There are, moreover, no good reasons for believing that Christ *is* both resurrected and Lord. How do individuals know this? (They cannot travel up to heaven to view the enthroned Christ, nor travel into the abyss of death to see if he is still there!) And if they do not verify these things, then how can they believe them? (While, if they do not believe them, how can they choose to do so?!)

Furthermore, the role of the Spirit is once again opaque. Previously it simply seemed unnecessary, but in the light of Paul's intervening discussion, especially in Romans 8, a contradiction is now generated. Paul has now attributed a key role in salvation to the work of the Spirit, who pours out the love of God into the hearts of the delivered (5:5) and liberates the mind of flesh from Sin and Death (8:2). This contradiction is perhaps seen most acutely in the ethics and ecclesiology that are elaborated in more detail beginning in 12:1. There Paul clearly speaks of a transformed mind, and of a pneumatologically called and ordered community (vv. 2-8). Faith is even specifically mentioned in v. 3 as *a gift* (φρονεῖν εἰς τὸ σωφρωνεῖν, ἑκάστῳ ὡς ὁ Θεὸς ἐμέρισεν μέτρον πίστεως). That is, the Spirit's transformation of the person seems here to undergird the new ethic of the Christian, and a communal existence of power and intimacy. This is not the minimal action of faith and the consequent contractual association of believing individuals implicit within salvation through faith alone.

Added to these gathering problems (and the foregoing is a mere sample) is the material from elsewhere in Paul's extant writings that suggests confession is itself a pneumatologically inspired event. In relation to the Corinthians, Paul recounts at length how his preaching is mediated, authenticated, and understood by the work of the Spirit (1 Corinthians 2): ἡμῖν δὲ ἀπεκάλυψεν ὁ Θεὸς διὰ τοῦ πνεύματος. . . . ὁ πνευματικὸς ἀνακρίνει [τὰ] πάντα (2:10, 15). Hence, later on he argues with complete consistency that οὐδεὶς δύναται εἰπεῖν, Κύριος Ἰησοῦς, εἰ μὴ ἐν πνεύματι ἁγίῳ (12:3). First Thessalonians seems to speak of this modality more compactly: εὐχαριστοῦμεν τῷ Θεῷ ἀδιαλείπτως, ὅτι παραλαβόντες λόγον ἀκοῆς παρ' ἡμῶν τοῦ Θεοῦ ἐδέξασθε οὐ λόγον ἀνθρώπων ἀλλὰ καθώς ἐστιν ἀληθῶς λόγον Θεοῦ, ὃς καὶ ἐνεργεῖται ἐν ὑμῖν τοῖς πιστεύουσιν (2:13).

The proliferating tensions apparent here are eliminated, however, and a superior reading of Romans 10 realized, if the cues in these confessional texts are followed. Belief and confession in the risen Lord are effected for Paul by the work of God, by both the Spirit and the word. Messengers and their message consequently *mediate* this process, but they do not *cause* it or *exhaust* it. Moreover, Romans 10 itself seems to point gently toward this "thick" rather than "thin" reading.

We have already noted that Romans 10 subtly invokes a wisdom discourse, in so doing resuming some reasonably strong cues from Romans 9. It seems entirely likely, then, that "the word of God" is again active in Romans 10. Indeed, here God "the Father" speaks certain important words to Israel concerning his wisdom, now incarnate as Christ. Paul's text then notes that missionaries like Paul bear "the word" to their constituencies, so that they might believe, confess, and be saved. But this "word" is also originally spoken by the divine voice, who uses words from Deuteronomy 30:12-14 in vv. 6-10 — "the word is near you. . . ." Moreover, that word, spoken by the divine voice, and carried and proclaimed by missionaries, is *in the very mouths and hearts* of its recipients — a place where only the Spirit of God can go. Hence, it seems likely that the voice and words of Psalm 19:4, quoted in Romans 10:18, refer not just to missionaries by themselves but to a broader process in which missionaries participate but that rests fundamentally on the voice and words of God. After all, only God's voice reaches out immediately and literally into every land and to the ends of the earth, as the original Psalm also suggests.

These cues are subtle, but they seem to confirm the thick reading that is almost forced upon us by the jarring theoretical contradictions that it immediately resolves. If Romans 10 speaks of a process of mediated belief, in which God, the divine word, and the Spirit are actively at work (not to mention various called emissaries), then it fits smoothly into Paul's broader discourse in Romans and accords with many of his confessional texts that occur elsewhere as well.

Most importantly, this reading allows us to correlate meaningfully the fidelity and resurrection of Christ and those of the Christian. I suggest that these symmetrical features in the text are not arbitrary or coincidental; they subtly convey the point that belief, confession, fidelity, and eventual resurrection in the Christian are undergirded by a theology of participation. Faith is not the mere fulfillment of a condition, to which God responds with a promised future resurrection — the connection between these two events being conditional and arbitrary (and their presence in Christ opaque). Faith in a Christian stems from participation in the faithful one and indicates that resurrection is therefore guaranteed; resurrection is simply the further part of the story of Christ that the Christian has yet to experience. But Christ has been resurrected and enthroned, so this hope is certain. Hence, faith is functioning in this reading as evidence that the Christian is in fact and indeed presently a part of this programmatic unfolding story. *It is a marker of divine involvement, not the fulfillment of a contractual condition.*[122] And, as such, it *must* be mediated by divine involvement, at which point all of Paul's claims elsewhere about the role of the Spirit become more comprehensible. (His repeated suggestion that God has come in person to Israel also becomes more comprehensible.) In short, only this participatory account of Paul's argument explains fully the symmetry between the faithful and resurrected Christ and the believing Christian who will hopefully be resurrected in the future. Yet once it is mobilized, it does so neatly and powerfully, simultaneously eliminating all the contextual and theoretical tensions that the thin reading of this data in terms of Justification generates.

There seem to be few or no good reasons for opposing a "thick," apocalyptic reading of Romans 10 emphasizing its christocentric account of faith, and many for endorsing it. It should not, however, merely be assimilated within our broader apocalyptic construal. Romans 10 adds its own subtle emphases to our overall construal of Paul's argument and thinking. Four in particular are worth noting here briefly as the discussion of this subsection comes to a close.

(1) This text affirms the role of human freedom within the broader process of salvation; to emphasize the priority of God's call and election is clearly not, for Paul, to remove human freedom in any decisive sense. It seems important, then, to resist the customary application of an "either-or" choice upon Paul's thinking at this point. Salvation is still "free," but any further specification of that notion requires careful — and theological — elucidation.

(2) Similarly, Romans 10 emphasizes that at the heart of the Christian response to God is belief and confession, because these are the appropriate responses to the Christ event. To be caught up in the new Christian reality is inevi-

tably to be committed to certain key speech acts that attempt to describe that reality's most basic features; Christians ought to believe in and speak of the coming to them of Christ. Theological articulation — not to mention reflection — therefore lies at the very center of this new reality. (And that articulation is facilitated by the language of Scripture.)

(3) The exact nature of Israel's "unbelief" needs to be defined very carefully. It is not so much that Jews have received a certain piece of information and then decided "no" (another "thin" reading of the data). It is that they have repudiated the coming of God — the opportunity to participate in the very being of God, the life of God. This would be easy to accept on their part, because God has in effect come the whole way to them; God has come to his people again. And this is what has been repudiated (in part, in favor of some law-oriented life). Moreover, this belief in Christ's lordship is continuous in certain important respects with what they already do — namely, confess God as the Lord. Certainly, Paul is asking Jews to submit to a new clarification of that identity, but it is not a *new* identity! So in a sense, the majority of the Jewish people turn their backs at this point on the Shema. They are asked to continue to believe in the Lord but refuse to do so in the new, Christian definition of that Lord's identity (which is nevertheless — from the Christian point of view — the correct, and the original one).

(4) It is important to recall that the Roman Christian auditors would process this analysis of "belief" in terms of assurance, not appropriation. They do not need to undertake the appropriate acts of belief and confession in order to be saved; they enact them already (see esp. 1:2-4; 6:17; 15:14-15). So Paul's account of saving belief in Romans 10 affirms them in their current saved location rather than presenting them with a condition that they need to fulfill in order to be saved. As *evidence* of salvation, not its appropriation, belief in the Lord Jesus Christ is therefore a *necessary* criterion, but not necessarily a *sufficient* criterion. So the way is cleared for Paul to make much more extensive ethical requests of his converts. (That is, we are no longer committed to the constricting sola that is often associated with fides.)

§9. Loose Ends in Romans

We ought now to address briefly the other points in Romans where the key terms associated with Justification theory occur. Five texts are worth noting: Romans 5:1-2; 6:7-8; 12:1-8; 11:20-23; and chapter 14 (esp. vv. 1, 2, 22 and 23).[123] All of these texts either pose problems at first glance for my apocalyptic rereading but can be shown on closer examination to support it — or at least to be compatible with it — or they pose acute problems for a conventional construal in terms of Justification theory but prove immediately and overtly compatible with an apocalyptic reading.

9.1. Romans 5:1-2

We noted in chapter fifteen that Paul makes a significant set of transitions in 5:1-11 to address certain critical issues raised by the Teacher that nevertheless run to the heart of his own program — his christological response to the problems of sin and ethics in the life of the saved, and the issue of eschatological assurance. I endorsed there Nils Dahl's claim that 5:1-11 anticipates the longer discussion of Romans 8, before 5:12-21 reframes that discussion in relation to a narrative of Adam. Paul's initial transition into this new discussion uses distinctive Justification terminology — which then fades from view almost completely (see only 6:7-8, treated just below). And this poses challenges for both Justification advocates and my apocalyptic rereading. The former may argue that this material is signaling that the following discussion is based on this opening terminology and its implicit soteriology, but they still need to explain its sudden and almost complete disappearance and the apparent shifts in the actual categories that Paul is using from Romans 5 onward. Rhetorical and apocalyptic rereaders need to show, conversely, how this language can be read in terms of their system and can integrate with the following discussion (rather than framing it in terms of a different system), perhaps explaining its puzzling absence from most of Romans 5–8, at which point they arguably begin to enjoy an interpretative advantage over Justification advocates.

Paul's initial use of key Justification terms in v. 1 is uncontested: Δικαιωθέντες οὖν ἐκ πίστεως εἰρήνην ἔχωμεν πρὸς τὸν Θεὸν διὰ τοῦ κυρίου ἡμῶν Ἰησοῦ Χριστοῦ κ.τ.λ. But a text-critical problem arises in v. 2 over a possible second instance of πίστις· δι' οὗ καὶ τὴν προσαγωγὴν ἐσχήκαμεν τῇ πίστει εἰς τὴν χάριν ταύτην ἐν ᾗ ἐστήκαμεν κ.τ.λ.[124]

Alexandrinus includes the preposition ἐν just before the disputed dative πίστις (to which a first hand has also corrected ℵ). However, this is easily explicable as a reproduction of the preceding verb ending prompted in addition by the dative case of πίστις. Nothing substantial changes on either of these readings in any case. More significant is the relatively equal division in significant early witnesses between the inclusion and the omission of the entire construction. (Among the key minuscules, B, D, F, and G exclude; A in its modified form, and ℵ, C, and Ψ include.) I incline rather strongly, however, to the phrase's inclusion on several grounds.

I find it hard to explain the scribal addition of the phrase to v. 2, and in a different form from the preceding phrase that presumably prompted it in v. 1 (ἐκ πίστεως becoming τῇ πίστει), although it seems plausible to explain the omission of the phrase through sheer puzzlement (see the decision of A in 3:25). If πίστις is understood with reference solely to the Christian, as the act that appropriates salvation, then its inclusion in v. 2 seems to be a theological mistake more than a mere redundancy. ("Access" presumably follows on "justification," which has already been achieved by "faith," as the aorist participle indicates, so the further exercise of faith at this later point seems unnecessary.) But this linguistic pattern accords exactly with Paul's authentic usage elsewhere; the first instance is an explicit echo of Habakkuk 2:4, and the second instance reverts to the slightly clearer instrumental dative construction, but indicates its resumption of the first phrase with the article (see 3:22 and 25, and 3:30). Furthermore, including the phrase results in a chiastically balanced set of statements in 5:1-2a:

A: Δικαιωθέντες οὖν
  B: ἐκ πίστεως
    C: εἰρήνην ἔχωμεν πρὸς τὸν Θεὸν
      D: διὰ τοῦ κυρίου ἡμῶν Ἰησοῦ Χριστοῦ
      D′: ²δι' οὗ καὶ
    C′: τὴν προσαγωγὴν ἐσχήκαμεν
  B′: τῇ πίστει
A′: εἰς τὴν χάριν ταύτην ἐν ᾗ ἐστήκαμεν . . .

Only the A clauses lack an explicit signal of correlation — that is, the use of the same word in both clauses (πίστις . . . ἔχω . . . διά . . .). And it seems better to preserve this symmetry through the retention of the disputed phrase τῇ πίστει than to disrupt it. Added to this are the more substantial reasons that follow, as we begin to probe these statements' sense.

Justification advocates would of course understand these instances of πίστις as appropriative actions by the individual believer, and the participle δικαιωθέντες as a reference to some sort of imputed, forensic-retributive procedure and status that is effected by those acts. They achieve peace with God, because the wrath of the retributively just God — appropriately aroused by sins — has been satisfied by the sacrifice of Christ, and the terms of the new, saving contract have been correctly fulfilled. So the Justification advocate can supply a fair reading of this material (although the subjunctive ἔχωμεν does seem a little puzzling; the indicative is better).

However, this reading does not seem to smooth the way in broader substantial terms for Paul's discussions of ethics and eschatology that follow in 5:2b–8:39. It remains puzzling why Paul's key terms drop from view (except in 6:7-8, although their deployment there is awkward for Justification advocates, as we will see momentarily) and why the important issues raised are now analyzed in such different terms from those supplied by Justification theory. And certain direct hints from the context might even suggest that another reading of these verses is better (as we will see just below).

Rhetorical and apocalyptic rereaders have no difficulty construing Paul's statements here in terms of their own, more liberative and christocentric construal: "Being delivered 'through faithfulness' [i.e., the faithfulness of the righteous one], we will have peace with God through our Lord Jesus Christ, through whom we *also* have access [now] by means of that fidelity into this favor, by means of which we stand. . . ." Several considerations commend this reading as a good one.

(1) It speaks directly to the issue that Paul is anticipating here — eschatological assurance — *and* to the strategy that he will deploy to settle it (see esp. 8:18-39). The present action of God in Christ, which saves an enslaved and undeserving humanity, *guarantees* future salvation from a wrathful God, because it displays a fundamentally benevolent God. Hence, in the future there will be peace, not punishment. This action also concretely effects access, in participatory terms, into God's presence. Moreover, in making these claims Paul is clearly trying to defuse one of the Teacher's principal rhetorical strategies and theological axioms — the intimidation generated by a retributive God. Romans 5:1-2a inaugurates his detailed response to this program.

(2) I suggest that this is a better reading of the participle δικαιωθέντες. In 4:25, the preceding verse, Paul has invoked the saving activity of Christ with reference to both Good Friday and Easter Sunday — the context strongly emphasizing the Sunday — describing the resurrection as effective διὰ τὴν δικαίωσιν ἡμῶν. And this local indication aligns directly with the liberative connotations in Paul's δικαιο- terminology that have already been suggested by its earlier usage (see esp. 3:21-26). These indications now combine to suggest — rather strongly — that the participle δικαιωθέντες in 5:1 ought to refer in some liberative sense to resurrection. Indeed, good reasons need to be supplied for *not* so reading it. Otherwise, a dramatic shift in meaning is necessary between 4:25 and 5:1. But the rhetorical and apocalyptic rereading I am suggesting here, including its liberative understanding of the verb δικαιόω, supplies just this sense. It *is* a reference in the first instance to Christ's resurrection that effects the deliverance of all those participating in him — ἡμῶν.

(3) The better-attested subjunctive ἔχωμεν now also makes sense. The liberating resurrection indicated by the participle is effected *by Christ* (as 4:24-25 has just said), and Paul introduces this axiom immediately with a characteristic metonymy — an echo of the prophetic text that he uses to refer to the Christ event, namely, Habakkuk 2:4. As we have already seen at some length, the phrase ἐκ πίστεως evokes that narrative and set of underlying events. And the subjunctive that follows now makes excellent sense — although probably more as a future indication than a simple exhortation.[125] "We will have peace with God" *because* of our present liberation in Christ; the latter guarantees the former. That is, the christocentric emphasis in this interpretation of v. 1 allows the decisive saving events to be located and inaugurated in the immediate past by him, but with implications for wider humanity now and in the future. And this reading has the additional virtue of correlating with the many future tenses in the immediate context — see especially v. 9, but also v. 10.

(4) Verse 1 can now be seen to make exactly the same point as vv. 9-10, and the parallels *and* variations between these two sets of statements to be neatly explained. In v. 9 Paul makes his a fortiori argument explicit, πολλῷ οὖν μᾶλλον δικαιωθέντες νῦν ἐν τῷ αἵματι αὐτοῦ σωθησόμεθα δι' αὐτοῦ ἀπὸ τῆς ὀργῆς, spelling out the exact grounds for this confidence in v. 10: εἰ γὰρ ἐχθροὶ ὄντες κατηλλάγημεν τῷ θεῷ διὰ τοῦ θανάτου τοῦ υἱοῦ αὐτοῦ, πολλῷ μᾶλλον

καταλλαγέντες σωθησόμεθα ἐν τῇ ζωῇ αὐτοῦ. (The characteristic additional emphasis on the present reconciled situation of the Christian then follows in v. 11; see earlier v. 2a). This argument not only replicates the sense of our reading of v. 1; its christocentrism is exactly parallel as well, ἐν τῷ αἵματι αὐτοῦ in v. 9 reproducing the messianic echo in v. 1 of ἐκ πίστεως. Δικαιωθέντες [νῦν] ἐν τῷ αἵματι αὐτοῦ and δικαιωθέντες [οὖν] ἐκ πίστεως are *directly* parallel statements by Paul that speak of liberation through Christ (see also Rom 3:25!).

(5) This reading continues to resolve the significant tensions generated by a reading in terms of Justification theory vis-à-vis the ensuing context, at both a terminological and a substantive level. We now know why Paul shifts into different terms at 5:2; he is moving beyond his intertextual signaling to equivalent terms that convey his meaning a little more directly — a pattern discernible in 3:21-26 as well. The substance of the discussion has not changed at all, only its surface modality. Nevertheless, when those distinctive, intertextual terms recur, as they do in 6:7-8, they still integrate into the participatory argument that Paul is currently laying out in full, because the apocalyptic construal of his intertexts and intertextual terminology devolves into that broader soteriology quite directly.

In sum, a rhetorical and apocalyptic rereading of 5:1-2a seems very much to support our broader unfolding interpretation. Interpretative momentum seems to be building. But can it be sustained through the next important pericope that must be considered — 6:7-8 — as I have just claimed?

9.2. Romans 6:7-8

I suggest that the rhetorical and apocalyptic rereader enjoys a decisive advantage in this brief but significant text. It quite explicitly delivers *exactly* the meanings for the key Justification terms that the apocalyptic rereading has been suggesting that they in fact take all along. Indeed, Justification advocates are consistently embarrassed by this text, and so have to find various ways of marginalizing it. But there is now no need to do this; it fits smoothly into our unfolding alternative construal. Romans 6:7-8 is highly christocentric, uses an explicitly liberative instance of the verb δικαιόω, connects that verb directly to the resurrection, grounds the entire process in participation in Christ, and deploys πιστ- terminology in relation to the Christian in a secondary and constituted, rather than a prior and constitutive, role. All these implications embarrass Justification theory directly but strongly affirm our developing apocalyptic approach.

Paul writes in 6:7-8: ὁ γὰρ ἀποθανὼν δεδικαίωται ἀπὸ τῆς ἁμαρτίας. [8] εἰ δὲ ἀπεθάνομεν σὺν Χριστῷ, πιστεύομεν ὅτι καὶ συζήσομεν αὐτῷ. . . . The identity of the figure in v. 7 who dies — ὁ ἀποθανών — has been debated: is this a generic figure or Christ? I am persuaded by Scroggs's case that a christological reference is more plausible than a generic reference; however, not a great deal rides on that judgment in relation to our particular concerns here (although it will add clarity to Paul's argument if we follow it).[126] More important is the explicitly liberative sense of δικαιόω, which clearly denotes release from the power of Sin — a forensic-liberative usage. Sin is functioning here as an oppressive power that constrains and confines Christ and humanity (see 5:12-21; 7:7-25), and in leaving its clutches Christ is therefore experiencing something analogous to a liberation from jail. The verb thus conveys an explicitly apocalyptic notion and meaning, and the function of the preposition ἀπό here could hardly make this clearer. Concomitantly, the supply of any of the meanings advocated by Justification theory simply makes no sense; Christ cannot die, leave the dominance of Sin behind, and so be "acquitted" or "justified" or even "vindicated." (How could he be ". . . vindicated *from* Sin"? He can only be vindicated *in relation to* or *over against* Sin, which are not the prepositions that Paul uses!)

The grounding of this liberation in the resurrection is then explicit, and repeatedly so in the immediate context. This event is equivalent to "living," to "being raised," and to "death no longer ruling." So the apocalyptic reading of the verb δικαιόω in terms of "liberation" or "deliverance" is both reinforced in context *and* grounded in the resurrection of Christ. Moreover, just so (and in context), the entire tenor of the discussion is participatory. "If *we* die with Christ, *we* believe that *we* will also *live in him*" (6:8). So Paul goes on to say, "Consider [or, more strongly, 'understand . . .'] yourselves, on the one hand, to be dead to Sin, but, on the other, to be living to God *in Christ Jesus*" (v. 11; DC).

It remains only to note that in keeping with this participatory process, Christians have had their mental landscape altered dramatically as well. "Believing" here refers to the process wherein new beliefs characterize the Christian condition — beliefs that are mapping the dramatic process that is taking place. Christians ought to understand that as people immersed in Christ they are no longer ruled by Sin and Death, but by God. They should believe, moreover, that they will therefore "live in him." And this is an accurate state of affairs. Christians *ought* to believe these things and will, moreover, be characterized by those beliefs. Furthermore, the converse also ought to hold: those who are characterized by this christologically transformed self-understanding *are therefore presently and necessarily participating in this process.* Such beliefs are an accurate marker of authentic Christian involvement and salvation (much as circumcision was viewed by some as a badge of involvement in Judaism — not a condition of this, but a sign). And this is of course a rather different account of the nature and role of "faith" in the life of the Christian from the one supplied by Justification theory.

In a sense, "faith" here is tantamount to the basic theological posture of the Christian in Christ. It attempts to describe truthfully and accurately the broad outlines and implications of that location, *yet it clearly presupposes being in that location in order to understand it.* It is therefore a retrospective and conditioned action, contrasting strongly with the prospective action undertaken by the convert in Justification theory, which is necessarily under the control of that individual and exists prior to contact with Christ (precisely in order to effect that). Suffice it to say, then, that Romans 6:7-8 strongly endorses the apocalyptic reading of Paul's πιστ- terms over against any construal in terms of Justification (for which it causes acute problems). It will be helpful now to jump forward and note a text from the latter half of Romans that integrates with this developing, apocalyptic view of Christian faith.

9.3. Romans 12:1-8

Just the understanding of Christian "faith" sketched out in relation to 6:7-8 is found, stated in a programmatic form, in 12:2. Although πιστ- terms are not used in the statement itself, they do return in the following verse, v. 3, and then again in v. 6.

In v. 2 Paul exhorts his Roman Christian auditors "not [to] be conformed to this age, but [to] be transformed by the renewing of your minds, so that you might discern what is the will of God. . . ." And this powerful charge can be viewed as the basis for all that follows, even as far as 15:13. Most significantly for our concerns here, Paul follows the statement of this principle immediately in vv. 3-8 with a set of exhortations encouraging sober and humble thinking despite the presence of different roles and gifts within the church. This material echoes more extensive exhortations in 1 Corinthians (and Ephesians) and deploys the well-known metaphor of a body to undergird a sense of ecclesial diversity within a more fundamental unity. Within this material the signifier πίστις occurs twice, and in rather suggestive settings.

In v. 3 Paul exhorts his auditors "through the grace that has been given to me" to think of themselves not arrogantly but humbly, ἑκάστῳ ὡς ὁ θεὸς ἐμέρισεν μέτρον πίστεως. Then in v. 6 Paul begins to enumerate seven ecclesial roles on the basis of different gifts of grace, naming prophecy first, which ought to be practiced κατὰ τὴν ἀναλογίαν τῆς πίστεως[127] (the only gift and role to be coordinated specifically with πίστις). It is not possible to unravel all the intricacies of this discussion here; certain salient points, however, should be noted.

(1) It seems clear that the entire subsection is undergirded by a sense of giftedness and grace (see vv. 3, 6 [2x]); roles in the church have been distributed by the Spirit freely, and so no invidious comparisons are necessary. This would be as foolish as comparing different members within one body; all are necessary to the body's health. But the signifier πίστις therefore participates directly in this broader discourse of giftedness — a sense that its specific deployment corroborates. πίστις, like everything else in context, *is a gift.*

(2) It seems likely that the two clauses using πίστις are largely equivalent. Both seem to use a metaphor of measurement (μέτρον/ἀναλογία), which accords with the overall thrust of the discussion. Hence, Paul seems to be suggesting that the Spirit has gifted, in gracious freedom, a particular amount — or even type — of understanding to each person, thereby in part creating the differentiation that is mapped metaphorically by the notion of a body's different members. The beliefs shaping the minds of individuated Christians differ, although this does not detract from the fundamental unity of their corporate existence.

(3) There is a strong emphasis throughout this subsection (and before and after it as well) on the thinking of the Christian; Paul is speaking of how Christians should think as Christians, and so is continuing the sense of "faith" that was apparent in 6:7-8, where a theological journey seemed implicit. The basic sense of πίστις here seems, then, to be "belief" or "understanding." This sense accords with both the gift of such understanding to every Christian, spoken of in v. 3, and the more specialized gift of particular understanding gifted to prophets, spoken of in v. 6. The basic meaning of the signifier in both these verses is therefore the same — belief — although its precise depth and actual content clearly differ — that is, in terms of various beliefs. (Moreover, the other six roles and gifts enumerated require a certain sort of understanding as well — a particular set of beliefs.)

In sum, this text seems to confirm the developing apocalyptic account of πίστις that I am suggesting is present throughout Romans, especially its fundamental giftedness. It also helpfully points to the sense in which Paul can emphasize this notion as it takes shape in the church and in Christians — the sense of a renewed and also diverse understanding or set of beliefs (which then extends even to a differentiation of roles). But it is important not to lose sight of the fact that earlier in the letter Paul grounds this process explicitly in the mind of Christ (see esp. 8:5b, 6b, 9-10, and 12-16), which then seems to be appropriated diversely by the work of the Spirit.[128] This is a powerful and sophisticated account of faith, one that seems fundamentally incompatible with the account supplied (and needed) by Justification theory. With these realizations in place, we can turn to consider some potentially more problematic texts — 11:20-23 and 14:1-2 and 22-23.

9.4. Romans 11:20-23

In 11:20, in the midst of his celebrated horticultural portrayal of ancient Jewish and pagan relations — that is, in terms of grafting and pruning olive trees — Paul observes that the natural, Jewish branches have been broken off because of ἀπιστία, while the unnatural, pagan branches stand by means of πίστις (σὺ δὲ τῇ πίστει ἕστηκας). He goes on to counsel certain pagan converts, as a result of this, not to think arrogantly but to fear. Then in v. 23 he asserts, concerning the pruned Jewish branches, that ἐὰν μὴ ἐπιμένωσιν τῇ ἀπιστίᾳ, ἐγκεντρισθήσονται. Do these statements open the door to the Justification model's account of "faith," as the all-important, voluntarist decision by which Christians stand or fall?

I concede that such a reading of this data is possible, but I would deny that, read appropriately in context, these statements are *necessarily* so construed; an apocalyptic account of Paul's statements here is also possible. Furthermore, I will suggest that certain hints in the text might even affirm this alternative approach. Indeed, we basically return at this juncture to the same conundrum that we encountered on a much larger scale in Romans 9 and 10.

Paul is quite happy to involve human agency in the form of unbelief or belief in a broader account of divine election. But this involvement should not be construed overeagerly, symmetrically, or in any modern sense. "Belief" remains largely the product of divine agency (although not to the exclusion of human freedom), and "unbelief" remains the sinful human rejection of any such divine agency. So a linguistic symmetry overlies a theological *a*symmetry. And this basic set of equations explains 11:20-23 in context as adequately as it comprehends Romans 9 and 10 as a whole. The Jewish unbelief that is spoken of here in vv. 20 and 23 corresponds to the repudiation of Christ by the majority of Jews that was articulated earlier in 9:31–11:10 (although especially in 9:31–10:5). And the belief by means of which the grafted pagan branches live is the appropriate mediated response to the Christ event as illustrated by 9:30, 33, and 10:6-13. Certain more specific points are now worth noting carefully.

Although Paul observes that many Jews have been broken off from the tree of life by means of their unbelief (and this accords with his earlier discussion), he does not state explicitly that the unnatural branches converted from paganism have been grafted in specifically *by means of* their belief; to the contrary, they *stand* by means of that belief. So directly implicit in this claim is the fact that they have *already* been grafted in (presumably by the gardener, and in an act that is repeatedly characterized in terms of "kindness"). And this is consistent with both the wider argumentative context and the account of πίστις that Paul supplies elsewhere. Πίστις is a sign of inclusion or participation, but the embrace of sinful ἀπιστία effects separation (resulting in "sternness"). In context, this belief is the recognition that God has acted on the converts' behalf and through them in Christ. Moreover, if this is repudiated — as by certain Jews — then Paul is entirely consistent to suggest that it will result in a further breaking off — and of unnatural branches too, if that is appropriate (which are presumably easier to break off and harder to graft back in again, Paul avers). Therefore, any pagan converts should indeed fear rather than boast; that is, they should focus on the fragility of their own contribution to their position rather than on the lot of others, who have done nothing worse than fall into the state from which they themselves originally came!

In short, it is vital to appreciate that the sinful repudiation of God's act in Christ through unbelief and its consequences does not entail that any initial participation in that event is effected by the opposite action — far from it. Paul's discussions in 11:20-23, and more broadly in 11:11-24 and chapters 9–11, seem quite consistent in denying this simple symmetry and working with a more subtle set of equations in which — to put matters slightly too simply — divine election *effects* belief (through "grafting"), and then *responds* to unbelief (through "pruning" or "breaking off"), without apparently overriding the basic meaningfulness of either of those human activities. Hence, 11:20-23, in the broader context of 11:11-24, turns out to be a consistent discussion that aligns neatly with Paul's broader apocalyptic argument. Carefully read, it also arguably presents more of a challenge to Justification theory than an endorsement.

9.5. Romans 14 (esp. vv. 1, 2, 22, and 23)

Paul's use of πιστ- terminology in Romans 14 — specifically, in vv. 1, 2, 22, and 23 — might raise another difficulty for the apocalyptic rereading of Justification discussions throughout Romans. Paul is clearly speaking in these texts of certain "beliefs" — the beliefs, in particular, of "the strong" (see 14:2a; 15:1) over against "the weak" (see 14:1, 2b). The strong believe that they can eat anything, and they regard all days as alike (i.e., none as especially sacred). The weak, conversely, are offended by the consumption of certain meats and wines and hold certain days to be sacred. (And Jewish scruples are likely here, although the position has been contested and is not completely certain.)[129] Paul seems to be trying to defuse any recriminations that might be dividing the Roman Christian community as a result of these different convictions and practices — judgment of the strong by the weak (i.e., condemnatory judgment), and contempt of the weak by the strong (a scenario and rhetorical strategy that we explored briefly in chapter thirteen). Moreover, Paul goes so far as to say, in 14:23, that "the one who doubts if he eats has been condemned, because this is not ἐκ πίστεως. And everything which is not ἐκ πίστεως is sin."

At first glance, these claims seem to pose a challenge to my developing rereading. What I have earlier suggested is that an important intertextually motivated echo of christological material — and usually, moreover, of fidelity — namely, ἐκ πίστεως, seems to be deployed here in overt relation to beliefs and an individuated Christian. But I would suggest that any difficulties evaporate as the broader context of the argument is taken into consideration, and 15:1-6 in particular. First we should note, however, that in Romans 14 Paul cleverly reframes the locations of the two quarreling groups.

Initially, the apostle reminds them of their orientation toward God, as his servants (see esp. vv. 4-12) — a frame with a strongly future orientation. The accountability of each Christian to his or her own master, God, obviates — and positively precludes — the need for Christians to judge and condemn one another. But then Paul goes on to affirm their present location, where they participate by way of the Spirit in an inaugurated kingdom of God that lies now beyond matters of food and drink (see esp. vv. 14, 17). And these two discernible reframing strategies arguably target the two groups at Rome in turn, although they are superficially applicable to both. The weak are not to judge the servants of another for their ostensibly irreverent behavior — and God's servants at that! And the strong are not to cause the weak to stumble through such behavior, when that action is now simply unnecessary (i.e., not part of the new spiritual kingdom of God). This is not acting in love toward someone who is "the work of God" (v. 20). Paul's comments about beliefs and action ἐκ πίστεως occur as this second strategy is being pressed beyond its initial primary reference to the strong, from v. 22.

At this point Paul exhorts the strong to keep their convictions to themselves and before God alone. "Blessed is the person who does not condemn himself through what he [correctly] approves," he asserts (perhaps a little ironically).

He is saying that such approval can result in eating and drinking that offends someone else, dear to God as well, thereby causing that person to "stumble," and so provoking God's displeasure by this careless and insensitive behavior. The sinful stumble could be, presumably, a countervailing act of sinful judgment (which is both inappropriate and incorrect), but it is more likely that person's consumption of the same things as the strong person without the same degree of confidence, leading to doubt and resulting sin. And this is certainly the suggestion of v. 23. There Paul notes that the one who doubts and eats has been condemned, because such eating did not take place ἐκ πίστεως. We should now pause to note the implications of this material for our current question.

The three occurrences of πίστις correlate with convictions grounded in the realities of the kingdom of God — the "deliverance and peace and joy [imparted] by means of the Holy Spirit" (14:17, DC). These dictate that "everything is indeed clean" (v. 20). Any food is therefore bad only if its consumption causes offense to someone else (v. 20b), *or* if someone does not possess the requisite belief that it is irrelevant and so doubts, but still eats (v. 23a). This is sinful. Indeed, "everything that is not of faith [ἐκ πίστεως] is sin" (v. 23b) — perhaps a dangerously strong statement on Paul's part.

On one level, this assertion merely clarifies the exact nature of the failure in the previous sentence: all eating that does not proceed from the convictions of the strong, grounded in the new life of the kingdom of God that is beyond dietary matters, is wrong. If it is not so grounded, then eaters have broken a taboo that they still take seriously. They have done something that they think offends God. So "everything that does not spring from [accurate strong dietary] conviction is sin." But it remains rather hyperbolic to suggest that *everything* that does not spring from that source is sin. Everything *dietary* that does not so spring from conviction is presumably sinful, so perhaps we are merely supposed to understand this caveat. But perhaps this saying also operates on another level.

These subtle maneuvers might be clarified if some of the information supplied by 15:1-6 is introduced. There the strong are addressed again — in fact for the first time by that actual designation — and exhorted to bear the frailties of the weak and to please neighbors rather than themselves, in order to emulate Christ (vv. 1-3a). Having quoted the Scriptures (Ps. 69:9 [68:10 LXX]), Paul prays in v. 5 that "the God of perseverance and encouragement might give to you *the same thinking among one another that accords with Christ Jesus . . .*" (DC; Gk τὸ αὐτὸ φρονεῖν ἐν ἀλλήλοις κατὰ Χριστὸν Ἰησοῦν). This strategic appeal by Paul to participation in the thinking of Christ arguably undergirds the remainder of the letter body's closing, which appeals repeatedly to united thinking and praise (see esp. vv. 6, 7, 11, 13). But this statement also clarifies some of the preceding argument's presuppositions.

The life of the kingdom, imparted by the Spirit, and beyond matters of food and drink, is a participation in the thinking of the self-sacrificing Christ (as Rom. 12:1-2 also suggests), who did not please himself but others. To be shaped by this mind is therefore to be *both* beyond the scruples of food and drink and also committed to sensitive self-sacrifice on behalf of others. Indeed, it can be seen now that v. 23b is probably another pun on Paul's part, pointing in more than one direction: "everything that is not 'of belief' is sin."

We learn immediately that the "belief" or "conviction" spoken of in 14:23b is grounded in the mind of Christ (15:3, 5), mediated by the Spirit (14:17). So the beliefs involved are rather wider than mere dietary confidence; they extend to concern for others, not self, and so on. Moreover, it is indeed now true and not exaggerated for Paul to suggest that "everything that is not of belief [in the sense of 'not *of Christ*'] is sin," because it is necessarily "of Adam," where Sin still reigns (5:12-21; 7:7-25). Specifically such an unbelieving mind might either condemn another for something passé (on eschatological grounds), or insensitively cause another to stumble through guilty actions or unfair judgments. The adage is neatly formed, then, and points in both relevant directions. Indeed, only if the belief in question here is a reference to the mind of Christ is Paul's exaggerated claim correct; not to be of Christ *is* to be in the realm of Sin automatically and — at times — quite specifically!

Hence, arguably Paul has again effectively drawn his language of faith into the orbit of Christ, in a way that is consistent with its fundamentally apocalyptic function elsewhere in the letter. Correct beliefs, possessed by the strong, are a function of participation in Christ and are mediated by the Spirit. For Paul, they are gifted, or revealed, and reflect accurately the nature of Christian existence in a retrospective fashion. They should then lead to freedom with respect to dietary matters (at least in relation to oneself), but also to self-sacrifice on behalf of others, so as not to cause offense and guilt; and if necessary they should encompass trust and fidelity. So I would suggest, in essence, that Paul's scattered use of πιστ-terms in Romans 14 continues to corroborate our broader rhetorical and apocalyptic rereading, and to pose concomitant problems for any account in terms of Justification.[130]

With this final realization concerning Romans — at which point our texts of terror are all resolved, and many of the remaining Justification texts are shown to be strongly supportive of the apocalyptic rereading, and hence texts of terror more for Justification advocates — we can turn to consider the relevant discussions in Paul's other letters in a similar vein. Are they compatible with the suggestions that have been made up to this point in terms of Romans? Do they pose insuperable problems for that construal? Or, carefully read, do they continue in fact to pose problems for Justification advocates? These questions will occupy our final chapters.

CHAPTER TWENTY

Rereading the Heartland — Galatians

§1. Preamble

In the final two chapters we investigate whether the rhetorical and apocalyptic re-reading strategy developed for Romans also fits the Justification texts that appear elsewhere in the Pauline corpus. Those texts have already been identified in chapter nineteen and lie principally in Galatians 2:15–3:26, with a short, passionate treatment in Philippians 3. Otherwise, only small — but intriguing — snippets of Justification material are identifiable. The Galatians material will be the focus of the present chapter, and the remaining texts will be dealt with in chapter twenty-one.

It seems likely that these texts can be treated more summarily than Romans 1–4. They are almost certainly too brief to present us with a comprehensive and decisive restatement of Justification theory — although we must remain open to this possibility (and an important caveat will be noted here shortly). Such a restatement would, strictly speaking, be an overdetermination in relation to *my* rereading; however, we are far more likely to find here a pervasive underdetermination in relation to Justification theory — a failure to deliver that theory in sufficient detail to make its presence in the thinking of Paul and his auditors plausible. Hence, I have allocated these texts an ancillary function in our broader discussion and dubbed them "heartland" texts that surround a "citadel" (and that decisive stronghold has in my view already fallen). If this underdetermination in the ancillary texts continues to be the case, these texts should also integrate quickly and smoothly with the alternative construal that has been developed in relation to Romans 1–4 and then the rest of Romans — a broadly rhetorical rereading that construes these texts as a debate with the Teacher and his followers and finds a set of apocalyptic commitments in Paul at the heart of his side of the argument. They should offer little resistance to this strategy.

But while weighing these two main countervailing interpretative trajectories — textual underdetermination in relation to Justification theory and sustainability in relation to my suggested apocalyptic rereading — we will continue to search for overdeterminations as well, that is, for instances where these texts overtly embarrass Justification theory. Any such instances should increase our confidence in the developing alternative construal by providing yet more evidence that the conventional approach does not ultimately provide the smoothest account of Paul's texts. Reread with critical and hence refreshed eyes and ears, these texts will devolve into rather simpler and more constructive discussions than has often been thought to be the case. It will be helpful to summarize here at the outset just what textual arguments and motifs the debate of such possibilities tends to cluster around in these ancillary texts.

No scholars seriously assert that any Pauline texts outside Romans deliver Justification theory in full. So the structure that was detailed in part one, chapter one, if it is present at all, would have to be delivered essentially in metonymic terms (and hence rather as Paul alludes to Christ's passion); that is, the presence of an explicit motif from within that structure would need to be taken as evidence that the entire structure was being mobilized. And this would not be an unfair claim in relation to Paul's undisputed correspondence outside Romans. In all these letters he is writing to congregations that already know him and his teaching well — perhaps having benefited from a further visit after the founding mission, or perhaps from visits from Paul's coworkers (and so on) — and so the apostle need only summarize and allude to material that they have already heard and memorized. Consequently, the mere presence of certain key motifs might be evidence in favor of the presence of Justification theory in these texts over against the operation of the rhetorical and apocalyptic argumentation that I am advocating.

In particular, any explicit commitment to a retributive view of God and a correlative view of the atonement; to a prospective theological program, with an explicit vestibule that the individual must negotiate prior to conversion; to the operation of the law in that vestibule; or to the appropriation of salvation by exercising the condition of "faith" would mobilize the rest of Justification theory and serve to overthrow my suggested alternative construal (or, at least, to begin to overthrow it). Paul tends to use — according to Justification advocates — δικαιο-terminology to deliver his retributive conceptions; arguments related to the law and its "works" to speak of any navigation by a prospective convert through a vestibule prior to Christian salvation; and πιστ- language to denote the condition in the second, more generous contract that must be exercised for salvation to be grasped. So texts using words based on these stems and phrases and perhaps disposing them in ways evocative of Justification theory will be the focus of our analyses that follow.

However, it might be helpful to note — to anticipate the basic shape of this analysis — that all the relevant texts will prove in my view to be fundamentally ambiguous for Justification interpreters, or worse. That is, while Justification advocates can offer a *possible* reading of most of these texts and terms, it is *always* equally possible to offer an alternative rhetorical and apocalyptic reading of them as well; there is never anything *decisive* that permits one to prefer a Justification construal to my alternative approach (and this is perhaps not entirely surprising, given the relative brevity of these discussions). Moreover, at times decisive evidence *does* seem to point toward the rectitude of the apocalyptic construal, once interpretation is aware of all the hermeneutical pressures disguising and distorting these dynamics. In essence, I suggest that a rhetorical and apocalyptic approach can make sense of all of the relevant texts outside Romans in Paul; and for certain texts, it is the only construal that makes sense (or it is, at least, demonstrably superior to a conventional construal). These basic interpretative trends — invariable ambiguity supplemented by occasional decisive evidence in favor of an apocalyptic approach — will be apparent in all the detailed textual explorations that follow.

§2. Galatians — Preliminary Issues

Galatians raises a host of complex and contentious biographical issues in relation to the broader reconstruction of Paul's life and letter sequence. Fortunately, however, many of those are not strictly relevant to my developing argument, and of those that are, the most complex have already been treated. It is necessary, then, only to reaffirm what amount to certain scholarly givens in the methodological preamble to our more detailed consideration.

It is essentially incontestable that Galatians was occasioned in large measure by certain opponents who seem to have disrupted Paul's communities of converted pagans in Galatia, subverting Paul's work among them. This, at any rate, is Paul's view of matters, which is all that we presently need — the perception on his part that a group of preachers opposing him is circulating through Galatia. Too much evidence in the letter points directly to this agenda for it to be gainsaid.[1]

It has been customary in the past to encode these opponents rather negatively, but more recent scholarship has tried to draw back from such judgments, at least initially. So, as we have already seen, J. Louis (Lou) Martyn characterizes these opponents courteously as "the Teachers," although that designation is narrowed by Romans to a single figure, "the Teacher." However, almost certainly this figure had an entourage, and possibly the clarification concerning the leadership of a single figure lay beyond Paul when he wrote Galatians, so we may as well retain the plural form in this chapter. (Alternatively, Romans could be focused more on an ideal type than the empirical situation; Paul does switch to plural designations in Rom. 3:8 and 16:17-18.) And I suggest that it is not necessary to press much beyond this basic judgment at this stage in my argument.[2]

The presence of these figures in the background of Galatians allows us to approach this text much as we approached Romans earlier on — rhetorically, as an argument or one component within an unfolding debate. As Donaldson puts it, "[i]n Galatians a Jewish Christian author debates an opposing Jewish Christian position for the benefit of his Gentile Christian readers."[3] Hence, the presence of an opposing position, or "gospel," is now to be expected at some point in Paul's analysis, while any localized arguments might now perform one of the broader rhetorical functions that have already been identified: they might be expository (arguments of type A), defensive (type B), or aggressive (type C), whether expounding Paul's own position, defending it from the countervailing criticisms of the Teachers, or attacking the Teachers' assertions.[4] These possibilities are now automatically opened up for us merely by the recognition that some opposing third party possessing some learning and a perceived countervailing agenda is involved in the Galatian situation. But we do not need any further details at this point concerning their precise identity or agenda, or the accuracy of Paul's presentation; those details can simply emerge in what follows.

Thus — significantly — the specifics of the underlying historical situation beyond this do not affect my developing rereading in any material way. It does not really matter for our present purposes whether this unfolding argument is being conducted in terms of a single historical wave of conflict, washing over Paul's churches perhaps in roughly a calendar year, or a series of successive delegations and subversions extending over several years.[5] Conflicts do, after all, come in both these forms, and many more besides. Whatever the particularities of the historical situation, the basic soteriological debate can still be the same, and this is all that my rereading needs here.[6]

There are many reasons for anticipating that Galatians will be a far less full account of matters than Romans. It is, on almost every conceivable reconstruction, earlier than Romans, whether by several months or several years (so this, strictly speaking, is a second useful point of unanimity in the broader discussion). It does not name its sources or bearer, suggesting some defensiveness on Paul's part concerning the legitimacy of those, or perhaps even an absence of direct and hence accurate information from the congregations themselves. Certainly, we cannot verify the accuracy of Paul's sources. Moreover, Paul personally founded the Galatian communities, so they have had prolonged exposure to his teaching, as the Roman Christians have not; he can therefore presuppose a great deal of information as he admonishes them now by letter. He has also almost certainly revisited them (see esp. 4:13b — δι᾽ ἀσθένειαν τῆς σαρκὸς εὐηγγελισάμην ὑμῖν τὸ πρότερον), providing the first century equivalent of a refresher course, not to mention an updating, so this process of abbreviated allusion in the letter can be even more concise.[7] Moreover, Paul seems to have written in anger and/or in haste. Galatians is clearly an urgent letter (even if the horse may already have bolted, so to speak), and it seems likely that Paul has not had the chance to reflect on these issues for very long.[8] So Galatians may lack some of the focus that Romans possesses. And all these observations confirm any initial suspicions that Justification material in Galatians will probably be far more abbreviated than in Romans, so that the ultimate lines of interpretative causality will probably run from the more explicit Romans to Galatians (which is how things have usually unfolded). Justification advocates will, in short, be facing an uphill battle in Galatians, if that is the text from which their broader discourse is to be launched independently from Romans and, if necessary, over against it. Prima facie, the rhetorical and apocalyptic rereader should have a much easier time of it. This is not to override the independent contributions of Galatians to broader reconstructions of Paul but merely to note that, for multiple reasons, it is a much briefer and more allusive letter.

We should recall here our careful examination in part one, chapter five of Paul's "conversion," much of the information for that probe coming from Galatians. Whether in Galatians or elsewhere, Paul's journey to conversion dictated by the Justification model was not borne out by the evidence in Paul's own case. And it follows from this lack of connection that little or no support for a conventional construal of the Justification texts in Galatians, which start principally in 2:15, should be garnered from his deployment of biographical material in 1:11–2:14; no straightforward relationship of corroboration or support exists here on biographical grounds as Justification theory conceives that, so none will be assumed in what follows.[9]

Finally, it might be helpful to observe that a "conventional reading" of the relevant texts that seems to be structured fundamentally by Justification theory is less apparent in relation to Galatians than it was in relation to Romans, and especially in Romans 1–4 (see part three, chapter ten). This observation immediately both confirms part of my preceding argument and enhances the probability of my overall thesis.

That is, the conventional reading of Paul's Justification texts in Galatians that are characterized by certain distinctive terminologies and correlations is certainly apparent in both the tradition of commentary and the broader secondary literature.[10] But a countervailing revisionist trajectory is also much more clearly apparent for this material than it was for Romans (although this dynamic is slightly muddied by the presence of much discussion of Galatians from the "new perspective" — that is, as I termed it earlier, in terms of motif rereading, and especially of the phrase "works of law"[11]). In particular, perhaps no scholar is more sensitive to the epistemological issues involved than J. Louis (Lou) Martyn, who has supplied the Pauline interpreter with what is arguably one of the finest commentaries on Paul ever penned, on Galatians, *and* a compendium of essays detailing many of the most important issues in the underlying debate.[12] However, Martyn is ably supported by numerous other commentators who trace — to a greater or lesser degree — much the same trajectory (most notable among whom is probably Richard Hays).[13] So I can appeal to stronger support from the secondary discussions for alternative exegetical suggestions in Galatians than I could in Romans, *and this is no coincidence.*

Those scholars already unhappy with one or more of Justification's implications tend to find more interpretative room to explore in Galatians, since that text does not deliver Justification theory at any point explicitly and comprehensively; there is no stretch of text there directly equivalent to Romans 1:18–3:20 that locks interpretation into the conventional reading.[14] Thus, it is entirely predictable that some of the more successful revisionist moves in recent years have taken place in relation to Galatians, not Romans. Of course, this cannot prove ultimately decisive for the broader interpretation of Paul. The entire conundrum can only be resolved by a successful rereading of Romans, and especially Romans 1–4, *that also proves transferable to Galatians*. I suggest that we are now in that second, easier position.

And with these preliminary observations, we can turn to consider the relevant texts in Galatians in more detail. They are reasonably easy to identify. The key terms in the Justification discourse occur in discrete distributions through Galatians, as has already been noted — essentially in 2:15–3:26 and 5:5-6. We will basically follow this sequence in our investigation. The argumentative modulations that occur through 2:15–3:26 will be illuminated, however, by treating 2:15–3:5; 3:6-14; and 3:21-26 separately (although this last subsection invokes its surrounding context vitally as well). The critical discussions will focus, moreover, on the interpretation of πίστις. All the other key terms from the Justification discourse — "works of law," "righteousness," "justification," and so on — are far less frequently deployed in Galatians. Galatians — and my revisionist analysis that follows — turns out to be all about "faith."[15]

§3. Galatians 2:15-21

My main contention in relation to most of the relevant material in Galatians 2:15–3:5 is that it is fundamentally ambiguous, and, frustrating as it feels here, this has important consequences for our overarching argument. Essentially, this text affords no grounds on which the Justification advocate can reassert the incontestable presence of that theory in Paul — indeed, quite the converse. Any such presence is contestable on every level. It *might* be present here in Paul, but it might not. And this conclusion opens the door to the elucidation of this passage's ambiguous epigrams by material drawn from elsewhere in Paul (and presumably, in the first instance, from the rest of Galatians).[16]

However, I will suggest in due course that one motif is present in this material that does arguably deliver a more decisive interpretation — namely, Paul's statement in 2:20b. There is one especially likely way to construe his claims here. And so it might be suggested, further, that this material tilts its neighboring statements in the direction of a rhetorical and apocalyptic reading — a tilt that is arguably strengthened by the analyses that follow and that integrates perfectly with and is immeasurably strengthened by the introduction of material from Romans. So this sentence from the mouth of Paul in 2:20 is like the first domino in a complex line; as it tips over, a set of decisions is delivered in a clattering sequence through the rest of the surrounding material. But we will consider the ambiguities in this subsection first; that is, we will set up the dominos end to end before we try to tip one over.

Πιστ- terminology has not been especially frequent up to this point in Galatians, with only one instance of the noun in 1:23 and one explicit instance of the verb in 2:7 (a second probably being presupposed).[17] But in 2:15–3:5 Paul uses the substantive five times and the verb once, inaugurating a much more concentrated use of this terminology that continues through 3:26. In fact, the verb remains rare in Galatians, occurring again, besides the early instances just noted, *only* in 2:16; 3:6, and 22. However, the noun is frequent, occurring *twenty-two times:* see 1:23, then 2:16 (2x), 20; 3:2 and 5; then, in a chain of twelve instances, in the following material — 3:7, 8, 9, 11, 12, 14, 22, 23 (2x), 24, 25, 26, fading after this sequence until more isolated occurrences in 5:5, 6, 22, and 6:10.

Δικαιο- terminology also moves into prominence in 2:15. Four of the seven instances of the verb occur here (see 2:16 [3x] and 2:17; see 3:8, 11, and 24), and one of the four instances of the noun (see 2:21; see 3:6, 21; 5:5). Moreover, the phrase "works of law" now features prominently as well, with five of its six occurrences in Galatians here (see 2:16 [3x]; 3:2, 5; see elsewhere only in 3:10; the word "works" occurs in isolation — probably deliberately — in 5:19 and 6:4). All of this data points, on the one hand, to the virtual if not complete absence of these terms and phrases — and so presumably of their associated concepts and axioms — from the biographical arguments in Galatians 1:11–2:14 (much to the embarrassment of the Justification biography), and, on the other hand, to a dense concentration of this material in 2:15–3:5 and then on through much of Galatians 3, beginning with the densest concentration of such terms together *in the entire letter* in the sentence that begins in 2:15. This to my mind corroborates rather strongly Betz's important thesis that 2:15 and its immediately following material introduce compact epigrams that are to be elaborated by what *follows* and not by what precedes — a judgment reinforced as the cogency of a reading guided by this suggestion unfolds.[18] Hence, we should consider 2:15-16 carefully.

3.1. Galatians 2:15-16

᾽Ημεῖς φύσει ᾽Ιουδαῖοι καὶ οὐκ ἐξ ἐθνῶν ἁμαρτωλοί· [16]εἰδότες[19] ὅτι οὐ δικαιοῦται ἄνθρωπος ἐξ ἔργων νόμου ἐὰν μὴ διὰ πίστεως ᾽Ιησοῦ Χριστοῦ, καὶ ἡμεῖς εἰς Χριστὸν ᾽Ιησοῦν ἐπιστεύσαμεν, ἵνα δικαιωθῶμεν ἐκ πίστεως Χριστοῦ καὶ οὐκ ἐξ ἔργων νόμου, ὅτι ἐξ ἔργων νόμου οὐ δικαιωθήσεται πᾶσα σάρξ.

Interpreters debate many important questions in this sentence, among them the meaning of the key terms just noted, the syntax, and Paul's possible allusion to Psalm 143:2 (142:2 LXX) in the final clause. I would suggest that too much ambiguity surrounds these questions for us to reach any decisive conclusions yet. The syntax seems to offer the promise of at least one resolution for Justification advocates, but I will suggest that this implication dissolves on closer analysis. And in view of these interrelated opacities, it seems unwise to make any programmatic claims for this material — that it establishes shared confessional material, for example.

It might be suggested that at least the contentious πίστις Χριστοῦ genitives here — of which Paul uses two — are resolved by the apostle's apparent supply of a construction with the cognate verb, which also thereby points to the appropriative and conditional function of faith in some process of Justification (and the latter seems to unfold, furthermore, in the present, at least to some degree, since the first instance of the verb δικαιόω here is a present passive). These would be vital conclusions if they could be sustained. Such interpreters suggest that the clause ἡμεῖς εἰς Χριστὸν Ἰησοῦν ἐπιστεύσαμεν ἵνα δικαιωθῶμεν ἐκ πίστεως Χριστοῦ be rendered "we believed in Christ Jesus *so that* we might be justified through faith in Christ" — a purposive construal of the conjunction ἵνα (see BDAG 475-76, meaning 1; alternatively, this could be a substitute for an infinitive of result — a "consecutive" or "ecbatic" reading; see BDAG 477, meaning 3).[20] And this is certainly a fair possible construal of the clause. It might be pointed out that this construal of the following πίστις genitive in objective terms is rare in Hellenistic Greek, but it is not impossible (and this data has already been noted in part four, chapter sixteen). Moreover, there is a slight awkwardness about the present nature of justification in this clause and its decidedly future orientation in the sentence's final clause. But these observations are hardly fatal. The main difficulty, however, is that there seems to be no decisive reason (or any reason at all) for preferring this construal that accords with the expectations of Justification theory over an alternative construal that interprets the clause in terms of an apocalyptic understanding of Paul, and so differently at all the critical points.

A rereader fresh from my alternative approach to Romans might suggest the following construal of 2:16 instead: ἡμεῖς εἰς Χριστὸν Ἰησοῦν ἐπιστεύσαμεν ἵνα δικαιωθῶμεν ἐκ πίστεως Χριστοῦ could be rendered ". . . we believed *concerning* [or *about* or *with respect to*] Christ Jesus *that* we are delivered through the faithfulness of Christ" — an essentially explanatory construal of the conjunction ἵνα that is not uncommon in the New Testament (see BDAG 476-77, meaning 2, the text noting helpfully that "[v]ery oft. the final mng. is greatly weakened or disappears altogether," ἵνα here substituting for an infinitive that supplements the verb[21]). And this reading also interprets the accusative prepositional construction here as it usually functions in both Paul and the rest of Koiné, to denote the thing about which certain beliefs are held.[22] Encouraging this construal is its repetition of an earlier clause in the sentence, effecting a neat parallelism: ἡμεῖς φύσει Ἰουδαῖοι . . . εἰδότες ὅτι . . . anticipates the similar construction . . . καὶ ἡμεῖς εἰς Χριστὸν Ἰησοῦν ἐπιστεύσαμεν ἵνα. . . . Here the first person plural pronouns echo one another directly, this subject then being further elaborated by some particular knowledge signaled by a verb of perception or understanding (. . . εἰδότες . . . ἐπιστεύσαμεν . . .) and an explanatory conjunction (. . . ὅτι . . . ἵνα . . .) that introduces the further, more specific information that is in fact known — the superiority of "justification" through the faithful Christ as against through "works of law." (This reading is then arguably further corroborated by the probable explicative meaning of ὅτι in 2:16c — see more on this just below; and a neat series of explanatory conjunctions now runs through the sentence: ὅτι . . . ἵνα . . . ὅτι.) This judgment creates in turn another neat parallelism between "works informed by law" and "the faithful Christ."[23]

Ἡμεῖς φύσει Ἰουδαῖοι καὶ οὐκ ἐξ ἐθνῶν ἁμαρτωλοί·
¹⁶εἰδότες ὅτι
οὐ δικαιοῦται ἄνθρωπος ἐξ ἔργων νόμου ἐὰν μὴ διὰ πίστεως Ἰησοῦ
Χριστοῦ,
καὶ ἡμεῖς εἰς Χριστὸν Ἰησοῦν
ἐπιστεύσαμεν ἵνα
δικαιωθῶμεν ἐκ πίστεως Χριστοῦ καὶ οὐκ ἐξ ἔργων νόμου,
ὅτι ἐξ ἔργων νόμου οὐ δικαιωθήσεται πᾶσα σάρξ.

Given this approach to the pivotal clause — pivotal, that is, for our present interpretative questions — the entire sentence can now be construed smoothly in terms of the rhetorical and apocalyptic rereading that has already been established in Romans. Paul is stating here that "we, born Jews and not sinners from the pagans, perceiving that a person is not delivered [i.e., resurrected] through 'works of law' but also through the faithful Christ, *we also* believed concerning Christ Jesus that we would be delivered through the faithful Christ and not through 'works of law.' . . ." So here Paul simply counterposes his own gospel, based on the Christ event and mediated through intertextual terms that are already familiar to us, to the assertions of the Teachers, which are grounded in his view on a false, ultimately nonchristological analysis of resurrection but which also draw on scriptural texts (Lev. 18:5 in particular; see more on this question in Galatians just below). The "belief" spoken of by the alternative apocalyptic reading of the verb is consequently a retrospective Christian understanding — here, in a rather interesting emphasis, on the part of Jewish Christians — concerning the significance of Christ. Indeed, they *have* to look back on *this* information! And it should be recalled that the entire Christ event, grounding the Christian's resurrection, is implicit in Paul's repeated reference to the faithful Christ.²⁴

Some of the advantages of our earlier construal of Romans 1–4 now emerge. All the key terms in this sentence, which receive no definition here, can nevertheless be integrated with a coherent argument drawn from elsewhere that uses just these terms but explains them much more fully. The conventional meaning enjoys no such luxury of interpretation. It must remain fundamentally opaque. We do not know what the key phrases and terms here actually mean if we are following the suggestions of Justification advocates, because Paul supplies us with no telling expansions at this point; the text is just too compact. So how is one to translate δικαιόω and ἔργων νόμου, and even πίστις, all of which have multiple possible meanings, if all that we have to guide us *is* 2:15-16?! The developing reading of the Justification interpreter seems at this point to wander like a sheep without a shepherd.²⁵

Enough has probably been said by now to suggest that an alternative reading of this material that offers no support to Justification theory but that corroborates directly the rhetorical and apocalyptic reading I am presently advocating seems entirely possible. I do not think that it can yet be decisively proved as the best reading, in its own immediate terms; however, it certainly seems equally plausible to the conventional construal. And in the light of this fundamental ambiguity, certain other claims not infrequently made for this text ought to be held in abeyance as well.

Some interpreters assert the creedal nature of this text, going on to suggest that Paul speaks here of material held in common by the early church and so shared between him and the other leaders mentioned in context. And this might be a supremely useful point, if it proved true. Paul and the Jerusalem leadership might now agree on all the essentials of Justification theory — a Protestant triumph in terms of catholicity, one is tempted to observe — although it is slightly disconcerting to note that essentially the same argument has been used to support quite different construals of this material from both "new" and "apocalyptic" perspectives![26]

But the evidence supporting such assertions is thin. It derives from (1) Paul's assertion of mutual belief in Christ; (2) the putative function of this material in 2:15-16 as a propositio (or, alternatively, a partitio); and/or (3) Dunn's perceptive argument concerning the presence of the "exceptive" ἐὰν μή in 2:16a. A quick examination of these supports suggests that these overarching — and very important — claims are fragile, if not groundless, and so will not affect the judgments that I have just made. Indeed, pressing on this evidence will only tilt us further toward the cogency of my suggested apocalyptic reading.[27]

(1) Paul's Assertion of Mutual Belief in Christ

Paul's appeal to a shared understanding concerning Christ *might* denote officially recognized, common material; however, it might also denote material that he thinks the Jerusalem leadership, along with all other Jewish Christians, *ought* to share with him! That is, this could be a rhetorical strategy, not a creedal affirmation. He could be saying, "*properly understood,* the Christ event, *to which you are already in some sense committed,* leads to my current conclusions and not to those of my opponents." This appeal to a putative shared basis for progress is a common argumentative move. And it is precisely the point of such a strategy to move its target audience from an authentically shared position to a desirable but perhaps new position by virtue of an appeal to the notion that it *is* shared! This is what makes the move more palatable. So such arguments basically say, "you already believe this, but you just don't know it yet," and they are of course ubiquitous.[28] Modern interpreters do not really know that this is what Paul is doing in 2:15-16, as against affirming shared creedal material, but it seems entirely possible in the context of the heated polemic unfolding at Galatia, and perhaps marginally in its favor is the observation that Paul never actually states that he is making a catholic claim here as he does in 1 Corinthians when he makes such a claim in a heated situation (see 1 Cor. 11:2, 16, 23a; 15:1, 3a). Here Paul literally argues for a correct understanding on the part of Jewish Christians about Christ, a broad category that could as easily include his current Jewish colleagues at the point of the letter's writing (see 1:2a) and/or the Jerusalem leadership as the Teachers. Further ostensible support for the catholic claim has been derived, however, from rhetorical sources.

(2) The Putative Function of 2:15-16 as a Propositio or a Partitio

Some ancient rhetors state in their handbooks that propositios can proceed from shared to contentious matters, and so a few scholars have argued that 2:15-16 is precisely such shared material — claims held in common by all sides in this dispute — before the contentious matters are introduced. But there are several problems with this argument. It must first be established that 2:15-16 functions in or as a rhetorical propositio. And while analogous relationships with rhetorical structures seem possible, the hypothesis that Paul is writing the direct equivalent of a forensic speech in his letter to the Galatians has been widely, and rightly, rejected.[29] Hence, recommendations concerning propositios cannot be applied directly to Paul's text without further justification. Even more importantly, the advice that ancient rhetors gave concerning the structure and function of the propositio varied considerably. Only on certain occasions, and in particular theorists, is the movement from shared to contested material evident. In other advice, very different structures and strategies are urged.[30] So the claim that 2:15-16, as part of a propositio, *must* begin with shared material, begs the key questions quite spectacularly. If 2:15-16 is a propositio — which in fact it isn't — we still don't know whether it is this *type* of propositio. We turn at this point, then, to what is probably the most cogent argument.[31]

(3) The "Exceptive" ἐὰν μή in 2:16a

Paul uses the construction ἐὰν μή in 2:16a, which means literally "if not" and therefore in English "unless" or "except." And so Dunn, Martyn, and de Boer — not always in concert — have argued perceptively that this denotes an underlying confessional tradition.[32] This expression is *always* exceptive elsewhere in Paul (see Rom. 10:15; 11:23; 1 Cor. 8:8; 9:16; 14:6-7, 9, 11, 28; 15:36), despite the desire of both commentators and translators to read it differently (supplying "but" or some such, thereby shifting Paul's meaning subtly into an outright opposition, which is what most interpreters expect at this point). Correctly translated exceptively, however (at least in the first instance), this qualification supposedly yields a sentence that Paul would not have asserted himself: "a person is not declared righteous through works of law except [also] through the fidelity of Jesus Christ. . . ." That is, saving faith in (or of) Christ is directed here to a constituency who all practice "works of law" already and might even view "faith in/of Christ" as an *additional* criterion. And Paul wishes to modify this, pushing the potentially complementary antithesis of instrumental terms into a mutually exclusive one in the following clauses: ". . . we believed in Christ [so] that we might be declared righteous through [the] faith in/of Christ *and not* [καὶ οὐκ] through works of law. . . ."

I grant the initial semantic observation here — and hold it ultimately to be quite important — but deny the inference that confessional material is therefore in view. The "except" that Paul supplies here is an entirely understandable qualification in relation to Jewish Christians, the subject of the sentence (see v. 15), who are all of course law observant already, and presumably did not cease being so on conversion. Moreover, that the following antithesis is then positioned in tension with this initial statement seems to me to misunderstand the broader sentence's actual structure. It is possible to give an entirely straightforward account of the brief argument in 2:15-16 — although at this point the evidence begins to tilt toward the plausibility of its apocalyptic construal.

Paul's argument is perhaps deceptively simple. He seems to be suggesting, first, that the Jewish constituency of v. 15 (presumably including Peter and him) was law-observant when it was transformed through the Christ event (i.e., Christ's death and resurrection).[33] But that law-observance was revealed to be secondary if not irrelevant *to* this transformation by this event precisely because that transformation took place through Christ. The result of this dramatic event was therefore the complete dependence of the Jewish Christians for transformation on the Christ event, *and* the necessary and automatic relativization of the law (and therefore also in terms of any future version of that transformational event — a point to be discussed shortly). This implication is not immediately apparent, but it is implicit in what has happened (so 2:15-16a), and this is consequently what Paul spells out (in 2:16b and c).

Note that Paul's argument assumes that this transformation is mutually exclusive with respect to the law and Christ, but this exclusivity should probably be granted. That is, the Teacher could presumably object to Paul's reasoning that law-observance is at least a necessary condition for transformation, even if it is not a sufficient one. But these are very different processes, *as vv. 17-21 go on to make clear immediately.* Something decisive is meant to have happened with respect to sin on the arrival of Christ, leading to the possibility of a scandal if sin is still overtly present in the lives of Christians (so vv. 17-18). And once this implicit exclusivity in modes is grasped, Paul's argument in vv. 15-16 appears to be reasonably straightforward. Hence, it is as if he is saying, "We [Jewish Christians] had A, and then T came through B. So we might say that T came through A and also B. But precisely because T came through B, it is clear to us that it does not really come through A at all, and neither *will* it come through A. In fact, T comes through B *and not* through A."

In short, by acknowledging the crucified and resurrected Christ, and relying on him for deliverance — a deliverance that is already in some sense inaugurated (so vv. 17-20) — Paul observes that Jewish Christians *have automatically displaced law observance from a critical saving and transformational role.*[34] Consequently Paul is building here on a shared experience of the death and resurrection of Christ (and this is the truth of the "confessional" reading of this material). These Jewish Christians have all, in effect, now banked on this event precisely *as* Christian Jews — and even if they do not yet realize that clearly!

Paul then seems to press this point at the sentence's conclusion with a coordinate construction that aligns ὅτι in 2:16c with the sentence's previous instances of ὅτι and ἵνα both syntactically and semantically (i.e., in terms of ". . . that . . . ," thereby supplying a better construal than a causal reading in terms of ". . . because . . .").[35] So the sentence concludes: ". . . even *we* believed concerning Christ Jesus that . . . through works of law all flesh will not be declared righteous." The declaration of righteousness through law observance at the future day of judgment has therefore been excluded by Christ's resurrection for *anybody*, even as it has been excluded for present saved Jewish Christians, so Paul broadens the implications of Christ's resurrection here still further. Paul might be suggesting with this final clause that the resurrection of the faithful Christ, by excluding law observance as a possible mode of salvation for Jews, also does so for *all flesh* — that is, for pagans, Paul's particular mission constituency. Alternatively, he might be implying that it is the flesh — σάρξ — that is the principal ontological difficulty underlying the failure of the law to deliver and resurrect (see Gal. 3:21), an insight made plain to him "in Christ" (see Rom. 3:20; 7:7-25; and Phil. 3:2-7, treated in chapter twenty-one). He might also be implying that a future judgment in terms of works has been implicitly excluded. Fortunately, not much turns on a definitive judgment on this question, so it will not be pursued further here.[36] It should be noted, however, that this developing apocalyptic construal of 2:15-16 has the added advantage of making sense of the shifts in tense in Paul's three uses of δικαιόω in 2:15-16, the first two instances being present but the third future.

The first two instances apply to Christ and his implications for others committed to him, and hence to the present, liberative connotation of the verb linked to God's forensic-liberative act of deliverance that was Christ's resurrection. That event is in the past for Christ, where it was recognized by the Jewish Christians (thus the present verb in 2:16a coordinated with an act of knowledge in the past conveyed by the participle εἰδότες, and the discussion of past events in vv. 17-20), and is now inaugurated for them too, although awaiting a future consummation (so, in part, the subjunctive in 2:16b, although this is necessary in any case following ἵνα). But in the light of this, the alternative system of the Teacher, which is oriented toward a future, forensic-retributive act by God, is falsified as well (thus the denial of 2:16c in the future tense). Indeed, as the echoed context of Psalm 143:2 [LXX 142:2] in v. 16c suggests, a decisive saving act *by God*, responding to a hapless humanity, has relativized any forensic-retributive process. Most importantly, it can now be seen that this construal arguably enjoys a slight advantage over a reading in terms of Justification theory.

Paul's argument against "works of law" at this point now does not actually function in terms of Justification theory, but embarrasses that construct, just as we have already seen for several points in Romans as well (esp. 3:27-28; 4:9-14). Whereas Justification theory expects a progression from works to faith, that progression being powered by the inherently negative experience of life under the law, Paul here in 2:15-16 runs the argument *in exactly the opposite direction!* The Christ event, spoken of through vv. 15-16 in intertextually motivated terms of faithfulness, *overrules* and *displaces* works of law. *Because* transformation comes through the Christ event, works of law have been negated (at least in relation *to* transformation), along with any subsequent construction of their importance. "While doing A (i.e., works), B arrived and effected transformation, *therefore* transformation is effected — and we trust and believe it — in relation to B *and not* A." And so Paul's awkward connective construction in v. 16, itself overruled for so long, can now be seen to say exactly what we would expect it to — on a retrospective and apocalyptic reading of course! Arguably, then, careful attention to the grammar of 2:15-16 tilts us once again toward the cogency of a rhetorical and apocalyptic reading of Paul's arguments.[37] It might be helpful at this point to note the slight divergence between my "apocalyptic" construal, and that of figures like Martyn and de Boer.

We still stand within a fundamentally similar trajectory, insisting that the unconditional disclosure of salvation by God through the Christ event is at the center of Paul's life, mission, and gospel, along with his argumentation in Galatians. So our broad strategic goals remain identical.[38] However, there is a discernible divergence in tactics at this point. Martyn, and those influenced by him, tend to root their exegetical claims concerning the subjective reading of the disputed πίστις Χριστοῦ genitives, and Paul's key points of pressure in relation to the Teachers (especially in relation to law observance), in form-critical arguments. However, I regard such argumentation as overly fragile in terms of the evidence, and as incorrect in more ultimate causal and historical terms.[39]

As we have already learned in relation to Romans (especially in part four, chapters fifteen and seventeen), Paul's terminology and argumentation in his Justification texts must first be traced through his own intertextuality (at which point I am clearly more influenced by Longenecker and Hays). Paul's quotations bear some relation ultimately to early church discourses, *but at one remove;* it is therefore distorting to infer directly from his intertextuality *to* those earlier contexts. That is, given that much of Paul's intertextuality — although intentionally *comprehensible* in terms of early church discourses — is derived simply to oppose the Teacher's system, we must press through it in order to discern the real ground of his objections, and their historical locus. Paul's radical posture toward law observance in soteriological terms is in my view informed by a profoundly coherent theological position (and I hope this is already clear from the preceding analysis of Romans); however, to assume that this position *emerged from* the earlier texts, being mediated by them directly, is — rather ironically — to assume the truth of Justification theory — that is, its claim that these texts and their arguments are ex definitione central and coherent for Paul (an error that we saw played out on a grand scale in Watson's brilliant reconceptualizations as well, in part three, chapter twelve). Although such assumptions are deeply entrenched in our interpretative traditions, we are well past them by now. Paul's argumentation here is in fact rather simpler. He is engaging with another false gospel, as his prescript suggests (see Gal. 1:1, 6-9, 11-12). And this is the level on which we should treat his argumentation, unless strong evidence exists to the contrary; it is also, in the first instance, where we should mobilize his intertextuality. Anything beyond this requires further justification.

By this point in our analysis, then, it seems that all the evidence offered in support of the creedal origin of 2:15-16 — by various interpretative trajectories — is fragile, and so the claim itself should be abandoned. It also ought to be concluded that appeals to the programmatic function of 2:15-16 (especially in particular terms) are unwise — at least in advance of investigating the rest of the letter's argument. It seems that we will have to read on in the letter to find further evidence that might tilt the interpretative balance of this contested sentence one way or the other, *and* to try to determine its overall orientation and function. But this is of course highly significant: the Justification advocate needs a decisive victory here yet does not get one; the apocalyptic rereader needs only sustainability and has little difficulty generating it, seeming even to find some advantages in the evidence. (There is a big difference between possibility and probability when analyzing an ancient text!) However, arguably a more decisive text does exist in this textual neighborhood — 2:20.

3.2. *Galatians 2:20*

The key statement in Galatians 2:20 is ὃ δὲ νῦν ζῶ ἐν σαρκί, ἐν πίστει ζῶ τῇ τοῦ υἱοῦ τοῦ Θεοῦ τοῦ ἀγαπήσαντός με καὶ παραδόντος ἑαυτὸν ὑπὲρ ἐμοῦ. We have already noted the singularity and significance of this construction in an earlier discussion of the πίστις Χριστοῦ debate.[40] At this point, then, we need only recall that the repeated articles that Paul uses here — supplying no fewer than four — ask auditors in the first instance to coordinate πίστις with "the Son of God" in an appositional construction that fulfills all the grammatical expectations in Koiné of a subjective relationship (i.e., it is a fully arthrous arrangement). Good reasons would need to be supplied from the immediate context for auditors to resist this construal — because it is not *invariably* subjective[41] — but none seem forthcoming. The context *encourages* this reading.

First, we should note that the following arthrous participial clauses, coordinated with this phrase, function well as an elucidation of the precise sense of the expression πίστις υἱοῦ Θεοῦ; the phrase "the faithfulness of the Son of God" denotes Christ's love and self-sacrifice on behalf of humanity — that is, the story of the cross.[42] (This observation then integrates nicely in turn with our earlier observation that Paul frequently mobilizes the passion metonymically, by referencing just one element within its narrative, and πίστις is one such metonymic reference for him, albeit a particularly important one.)

Confirming these initial judgments, second, is the overtly participatory tenor of the preceding discussion. Participatory concerns dominate the text from v. 17, some sort of inclusive claim being made by Paul from that point through v. 20b no fewer than three times. He first posits an awkward question about those who are seeking to be delivered "in Christ" (v. 17) — the existence of transgressions. Having laid the blame for this at the feet of those so transgressing, in v. 18 (παραβάτην ἐμαυτὸν συνιστάνω), he goes on in v. 19 to assert that he has died to law so that he might live for God;[43] indeed, he has been crucified together with Christ (Χριστῷ συνεσταύρωμαι). He then states famously in v. 20 that "I myself live no longer, but Christ lives in me." That is, since v. 17 Paul has been speaking of the execution of his own identity, and his immersion in Christ's. He is still distinguishable as a person within this process (see ". . . the life that *I* live in the flesh . . ."). But the overarching process of participation and identification enfolds that distinction so that any characterization of his external, prior, and independent rational agency would be false; indeed, this would be the antithesis of what he is actually asserting here, namely, his *death, co-crucifixion, and present life in Christ*.[44] "Paul's *egō* has been decisively transformed."[45]

A subjective reading of the christological πίστις construction integrates exactly with this localized emphasis, and especially when it is grasped that πίστις Χριστοῦ metaleptically or metonymically denotes his loving self-sacrifice for humanity on the cross, as v. 20 goes on to make clear. Construed in these terms, the subjective reading simply continues the subsection's emphasis on Paul's participation in Christ's crucifixion — the transformational event that lies at the heart of his gospel. He lives by means of the faithfulness of the Son of God, that is, by means of *his* loving self-sacrifice. It is an entirely integrated interpretation, and so seems increasingly favored by commentators.[46] An objective reading, however, now has a hard row to hoe.

In the first instance, it has to override the grammatical signals sent by the repeated articles. It could do so if the context suggested that this ought to be done. However, the context does not, as we have just seen. The objective construal is itself, rather, a *contra*-contextual reading. It must introduce a shift in the basic mental landscape of the passage, opposing the sustained implications of the context that we have just noted — a shift that is positively jarring. Such a reading asserts that in v. 20b Paul shifts from participatory concerns to speak of "faith," a condition that an individual must fulfill in order to appropriate the benefits of Christ's death. Hence, the passage suddenly presupposes a relationship between the individual and Christ that depends on that individual's external agency; an individual must act, and continue to act, in an unconstrained and independent way that is distinguishable from Christ (i.e., as the decision of faith is made and maintained). *And this set of basal assumptions is exactly what the preceding three verses seem to have been denying.* It is here, in fact, that we encounter some of the most overt examples of the presuppositional pressures that so influence the interpretation of Paul's Justification texts, along with the dramatically altered dynamics of their current interpretation. Many interpreters nevertheless suggest that Paul does shift to an anthropocentric posture in 2:20b; they read πίστις there in terms of human faith *in* the Son of God, and they do so on the grounds that this is a resumption of the claims of 2:15-16, and of the broader theological system of Justification that is widely supposed to be an important feature of Paul's thought.[47]

But the very existence of that broader system has been called into question by my analysis (at least, in relation to Paul himself); it can no longer be presupposed. And an alternative reading of 2:15-16 has been offered that reduces the implications of that text to ambiguity (and this, at the least). Consequently, the interpretative relationship between these two texts has now been *reversed,* and the subjective reading of the πίστις construction looks fairly certain. In the light of this interpretative fulcrum, we can turn to consider the meaning of the other key terms for the Justification system that Paul uses in context.

It is possible to infer — albeit subtly — that "works of law" are located in another realm, a realm of death, by 2:19-20. Paul's "death" and subsequent existence as "Christ lives in [him]" is what separates him from law observance. However, this inference need not yet be pressed. It is also possible to observe that Paul seems to coordinate "life" in parallel with the verb δικαιόω in 2:16, which is to say that this forensic verb is bound up with "life," at least in relation to Christ, suggesting an *eschatological* and potentially forensic-liberative construal. However, little more can be said at this point beyond the detection of these pregnant implications. We should turn, then, to consider the last remaining puzzle in 2:15-21 — E. P. Sanders's repeated suggestion that 2:21 uses an overtly retrospective argument against law observance, implying that Paul's posture vis-à-vis this practice and/or system is dictated by his Christian existence and not vice versa, as Justification advocates expect.[48] If he is right, then 2:21 would be an important overdetermination from this subsection, and we would be foolish to set it aside. Does 2:21 continue the christocentric perspective that has been established by 2:17-20?

3.3. Galatians 2:21

Galatians 2:21 states:

οὐκ ἀθετῶ τὴν χάριν τοῦ Θεοῦ·
εἰ γὰρ διὰ νόμου δικαιοσύνη,
ἄρα Χριστὸς δωρεὰν ἀπέθανεν.

Paul's argument here can appear initially baffling, because he seems to be eliding some of its vital elements and also reordering it away from the most obvious logical progression for rhetorical purposes. It is, after all, only a brief, staccato rejoinder. Closer analysis reveals, however, a clever rhetorical stratagem.

Paul is forcing a mutually exclusive choice on his auditors by this arrangement. Moreover, he is linking one option in the choice with an emotionally and theologically shocking action — the nullification of God's act in Christ! He therefore speaks in the first person of recoiling *himself* from any neutralization of God and Christ — "I do not set aside God's gracious act" (see 3:15) — and then speaks of how any endorsement of δικαιοσύνη by means of law effectively does this; it makes God's act in Christ gratuitous![49] In effect, he is asking his auditors to join him in the repudiation of the law in this relation, but he is actualizing this through the emotional shock of contemplating an abandonment of Christ, and this not once but twice. Paul's Galatian auditors are thereby being led to repudiate δικαιοσύνη διὰ νόμου, but by recoiling in the first instance from any shocking repudiation of *Christ*. And now that this cunning contingent effect has been recovered and explained, we can turn to consider the actual logic of the case.

In fact, there seem to be two important unstated premises implicit here, without which the argument does not strictly follow: (1) that both of these two "modes" can be oriented toward δικαιοσύνη (which seems a reasonable enough inference in context[50]), and (2) that they are mutually exclusive. Moreover, Paul places a statement ahead of its explanation. If these two premises are supplied, and the argument slightly reordered, then it seems to work coherently. It is basically structured as follows:

> (Unstated) X and Y are oriented toward the same thing (say Z).
> (Unstated) XZ and YZ are mutually exclusive.
> To endorse YZ is (therefore) not to endorse X[Z]! (Gal. 2:21b)
> I endorse X! (Gal. 2:21a) Of course!
> (So also, implicitly, I do not endorse YZ!)

It seems, then, that Paul does not supply all his premises, and he states his conclusion first. Things would be rather clearer if he said: "Both the law and Christ are avenues to δικαιοσύνη. They are also mutually exclusive. Hence, if I pursue the avenue of law to δικαιοσύνη, I necessarily do not pursue the avenue of Christ. I therefore, in effect, nullify it. In fact, I set it to one side — the act of God. So I will not! (And neither should you!) Set aside instead the avenue of law." Paul does not articulate the argument this clearly in Galatians 2:21, but this must be his implicit reasoning if it is going to make much sense. And we are now in a position to answer the key question in this relation, namely, Sanders's claim that Paul's epistemological stance here is retrospective.

We need to be careful here. In fact, Paul has actually provided us only with an argument based on *mutual exclusivity* combined with *preference*.[51] He endorses Christ as the way to δικαιοσύνη, and this apparently excludes using the law to that end as well. This is, moreover, a gracious act of God, and the possibility of evacuating that of its efficacy and meaning seems horrifying. But strictly speaking, Paul's argument is not *explicitly and necessarily retrospective*. It is — as we have just seen — simply mutually exclusive, and implicitly oriented toward the superiority of Christ (as an act of God's grace), although these implications alone remain embarrassing for Justification advocates. In Justification theory, the law and Christ are not really two mutually exclusive options, one from God and one not; the law is a *failed* option, leaving Christ as the only remaining one (although within the framework that the law has supplied), and both these options come from God.

It seems clear, then, that we must nuance Sanders's certainties a little. His actual reconstructions of Paul's argument and implicit progressions at this point have been plausible, but also slightly inaccurate. Basically, Sanders just reverses the final statement in v. 21b and then the order of the conditional, bouncing out of Paul's explicit claims into their converse and generating the following implicit construct that in effect follows Paul's text in v. 21 elliptically: "Christ did *not* die gratuitously; *therefore,* δικαιοσύνη is not through law." And this is basically right, although it is not really Paul's rhetorical emphasis ("I do not set aside the gracious act of God in Christ"). The difficulty is that this is a logical statement based on mutual exclusivity (which is all that we can say with certainty in Gal. 2:21); it is therefore not a statement of *causality* or *biography* as well. Yet it is so easy to slide from one relationship here to the next, because all are potentially conveyed within the useful word "therefore"; and Sanders repeatedly does so.[52] However, careful attention to what Paul argues — and to the entirety of v. 21 — forbids adding unstated causal or biographical contentions, which is what we need to do in order to make Paul's argument explicitly retrospective. (Another way of exposing this would be to point out that Justification advocates could retort fairly in this relation that further premises must be added in order to make sense of Paul's "therefore," and these could quite legitimately be drawn from Justification theory; nothing excludes this procedure here. So, e.g., "δικαιοσύνη is through Christ and not through law because the law cannot actually deliver δικαιοσύνη; therefore God has provided the gracious gift of δικαιοσύνη through Christ [and so on]." This might be awkward for the two reasons noted earlier, but it is by no means impossible.) Hence — perhaps a little unfortunately for apocalyptic advocates — Galatians 2:21 is not the decisive blow that Sanders suggests. It is awkward, but no more than this; certainly, it seems surmountable. And we must wait a little longer to find evidence in Galatians that Paul's thinking is explicitly retrospective (specifically, until 3:11-12). However, by the same token, we have not encountered anything that stands against a rhetorical and apocalyptic reading of 2:21 or its broader setting, which brings us to a more general contention that is worth noting.

Perhaps the point is nowhere as clear as it is in Albert Schweitzer's famous observations that Paul's texts often manifest a tension between different systems or discourses. These tensions, writ large on the well-organized Romans, occur in Galatians *within* 2:15-21, where they jostle cheek by jowl — and the very different circumstances of the two letters largely explain this. (The tensions have been enumerated in argumentative, systematic, empirical, and contextual terms in part one, chapters two through six — a considerable list.) However — and this is the critical point — *if* we endorse a consistently apocalyptic approach throughout (here through 2:15-21), *then they disappear.* Conversely, if we continue to introduce Justification theory into the terms and sentences conventionally associated with that theory, *then we continue to generate these tensions.* So, on the one hand, a persistent endorsement of Justification theory generates frequent and widespread tensions, and, on the other, a consistent endorsement of a rhetorical and apocalyptic reading does not. Hence, our future interpretative posture seems clear.

There is just no need to assert any more — continuing the point of view of Schweitzer momentarily — that Paul shifts to his principal system from v. 17 after an initial flirtation with Justification conceptuality in vv. 15-16, thereby moving from the "subsidiary crater" to the "main crater," or from the "fragment" back to the "more comprehensive mystical redemption-doctrine" from which faith has been "broken off and polished to give [Paul] the particular refraction which he requires."[53] There is no need to mobilize Justification conceptuality here *at all* — that is, to posit the *existence* of the subsidiary crater "within the rim of the main crater" (225). Paul's thinking is all of one piece — one smoothly rounded crater.

And this has been achieved by construing the opening antitheses in 2:15-16 rhetorically, one gospel opposing another, and then apocalyptically, Paul's half of this antithesis incorporating a subjective construal of the πίστις Χριστοῦ genitives and an eschatological use of δικαιο- terminology. He speaks of resurrection and deliverance through the faithful one, Christ, rather than of any alternative — here, attempted salvation through law observance, which is the gospel of the Teachers. These interpretative realizations allow this text to unpack smoothly and directly into the participatory concerns that Paul goes on to deploy overtly from v. 17, and with particular clarity in vv. 19-20; this argument is apocalyptic throughout. Moreover, Paul is suggesting throughout much of this material only that "deliverance" (or "release" or "liberation") in the sense of a forensic-liberative act of resurrection by God, is effected through the "fidelity" of Christ, which is to say, through his loving death and resurrection. In essence, Paul is maintaining nothing more than that "our" resurrection comes through Christ's resurrection and "our" transformation through Christ's transformation. Salvation then comes as people participate in the prototypical events associated with Christ — a salvation that it is foolish to ignore (see 2:21; 3:1-5) *and that overrides any alternatives!* Hence, the whole subsection — and by implication, the rest of Paul's Justification texts — now read in a unified manner. In short, a simpler Paul now seems possible, although there has been no reduction in his theological dynamism; indeed, arguably he now speaks even more clearly of Christian existence in the crucified and resurrected Son of God, the one who was faithful in that sense on behalf of others, thereby making access to this existence possible.

Furthermore, in the light of the reasonably decisive evidence surrounding the interpretation of 2:20b, we can see that the ambiguities evident in 2:15-16 and 2:21 *should* arguably be resolved in those texts in favor of the christological interpretation (and this accords with the delicate hints in this direction already apparent). There is no reason for Paul to change his mind about the meaning of πίστις anywhere in this short stretch of text, and a consistently christological reading makes perfect sense throughout, while in 2:20b it seems positively necessary. So 2:20b now overrides the ambiguities in those other texts in context, and not vice versa. We can return, then, to affirm the apocalyptic construal of 2:15-16, since Paul is not likely to have changed his argument fundamentally in the space of three verses (and we were tilting in this direction in any case), similar considerations applying to 2:21.

With all these realizations in place, we can turn now to consider the enigmatic assertions contained in 3:1-5.

§4. Galatians 3:1-5

This material has already been considered briefly in part one, chapter five, where Paul's actual preaching was analyzed, so suffice it here to note that the exact meaning of the key repeated antithesis seems initially opaque. When Paul opposes [ἡ] ἀκοὴ πίστεως to ἔργα νόμου, he might be speaking at first glance of at least four things (although possibly of even more)!

The meaning of ἀκοή: The meaning of πίστις:	The thing heard — "report"	The act of hearing
Christocentric	Something heard (i.e., a report) about the faithful one	Hearing about the faithful one
Anthropocentric	Something heard (i.e., a report) about faith	Hearing that is faith, or perhaps from faith

It is hard to tell, in the first instance, which one of these four options should be heard — or whether more than one is supposed to resonate simultaneously. Each of these possible meanings can be inserted with equal facility into Paul's cryptic antithetical challenges. However, some clues from the context are worth noting, and these may ultimately unpack into a more decisive interpretative decision.

This whole question has been much discussed.[54] We can simplify things initially, however, by speaking from this point onward of ἀκοή as a "report" or "proclamation" (i.e., "the thing heard") rather than the act of "hearing," although nothing decisive turns on this yet. The meaning "proclamation" opens up the same semantic possibilities as the meaning "hearing," and more besides. Two considerations suggest this judgment: (1) the letter's strong and sustained emphasis on an apostolic comparison (see esp. 1:1, 6-12), which suggests that the question of the particular announcements of rival missionaries is a primary rhetorical concern for Paul, and not the Galatians' "hearing," *which is never mentioned again in the letter;*[55] and (2) Paul's use of the verb προγράφω in 3:1, along with his emphasis there on the moment of "prior depiction" to the Galatians' *eyes,* not to their ears (. . . οἷς κατ᾽ ὀφθαλμοὺς Ἰησοῦς Χριστὸς προεγράφη ἐσταυρωμένος). This points to their reception of a report that was metaphorically *seen* rather than *heard.* (A "report" can be "placarded publicly" or "published" in the sense of being inscribed on a plinth, or some such.)[56] "Hearing" remains a formal possibility for ἀκοή, as Romans 10:13-18 demonstrates, but it seems unlikely given this explicit context.[57] This decision reduces the interpretative alternatives before us to the critical ones, which are established in a sense by Romans 10:13-18 as well.

In that illuminating — but also difficult — parallel passage, both preaching and hearing *precede* any activity of believing or trusting and therefore seem to be critical preconditions for eliciting it; the sequence of actions there is ἀποστέλλω . . . κηρύσσω/ἀκοή/ῥῆμα . . . ἀκούω . . . πιστεύω/ὑπακούω . . . [καὶ] ἐπικαλέω. So, in a sense, belief can arise from hearing or the thing heard or be "in" the thing heard, but not vice versa. That is, as Paul describes this sequence, neither hearing nor the report can arise from belief, and neither can hearing really be "in" a belief in the way that belief can be placed in something heard. (If something is believed, then in some sense it has *already* been heard.)

(sent → preaching →) thing heard → hearing → belief (→ calling)

And it can be seen, in the light of this, that Justification advocates would have little difficulty construing a reversed genitive in 3:2 and 3:5 — namely, ἐκ πίστεως ἀκοῆς. *This* phrase could denote either the belief that comes from the report (a genitive of source), or belief *in* the report (an objective genitive; and note that "hearing" does not work so well for this construction). *And this is in fact how the majority of commentators construe it.*[58] However, we are of course confronted with the *opposite* construction — ἀκοὴ πίστεως. So it seems that a conventional construal has three rather more difficult options,[59] namely, to argue:

(i)   that the genitive is reversed, so that πίστις is the governing noun here and ἀκοή the governed (thereby allowing one of the preceding options); or
(ii) that πίστις legitimately denotes the *content* of Paul's proclamation in some sense — although not in terms of Christ, which would be to concede the argument to the christocentric advocates; so πίστις here must correspond somehow to the preaching that occurs *earlier* in the chain of activities described in Romans 10:13-18 — the ἀκοή/ῥῆμα/κήρυγμα — and not to the faith of Christians, which occurs *after* hearing (thereby allowing a construal of the genitive in terms of content — "proclamation of the faith");[60] or
(iii) for some unusual causal or generative genitive relationship that effectively reverses the genitive of source (so the "proclamation" that *elicits* or *causes* "belief").[61]

But difficulties attend each of these options. They are not immediately and obviously fatal — hence my characterization of this entire case as suggestive rather than decisive — but they certainly exist and so seem to tilt interpretation in a christocentric direction ineluctably, since that approach has no difficulties at all, as we will see shortly.

(i)   *A reversed genitive.* In this anarthrous and repeated construction, we would need some signal from Paul that the governing and governed words are out of their usual order (which is very unusual for him); in the absence of such explicit signals, the average auditor would read the words' sequence *as* that critical signal, and of course there are no such apparent countervailing markers here — articles and the like. Moreover, it is difficult to find evidence from elsewhere in Paul of πιστ- terms functioning *in* the governed position, or its equivalent, *in this sense;* this seems unattested[62] (although see further just below). So this option looks unlikely.

(ii) *A genitive of content — in a sense other than Christ.* Interpreters invariably beg the question at this point by citing evidence from outside Paul and hence later than him (by which point certain theological concretions are arguably probable in terms of creeds, "the faith," and so on), or evidence from elsewhere in his corpus that is ambiguous at best or contradictory at worst. Most important in this relation are Galatians 1:23; 3:23-25; and 6:10.[63] I will address these constructions in detail shortly, so suffice it to say here that 3:23-25 should emphatically *not* be construed in this sense, and no evidence from elsewhere in Galatians or Paul suggests construing 1:23 or 6:10 in this sense, while certain local considerations stand against those decisions as well. The result of these appeals is then a circle of question-begging evidence, with no decisive evidence at any point — hardly a strong case. That is, there is no clear evidence that Paul *ever* deploys the notion of believing or belief as the *content* of his preaching, or *the thing in which* Christians have to believe (but there is of course much evidence of *Christ* as the content of that preaching; see, e.g., Gal. 3:1). It goes without saying that Christians need to believe certain things, *but apparently not in belief itself.*

(iii) *An unusual causal genitive.* It has to be said that such a construction is *extremely* rare for Paul, and while I am reluctant to exclude any semantic possibilities for the flexible genitive relation in Paul, this suggestion does seem to be pressing that semantic envelope to its limit. (Does Paul *ever* speak in such terms elsewhere?) Moreover, we must ask what considerations encourage us to read the genitive in this sense in any case, when the contextual clues — to which we now turn — stand against it.

We have already noted how two localized considerations encourage a construal of ἀκοή in terms of "proclamation" (i.e., "the thing heard") rather than "(the act of) hearing": (1) Paul's opposition to another "gospel" throughout Galatians, with no further mention in the letter of the Galatians' "hearing"; and (2) in 3:1, Paul's "writing" something obvious "in front of the Galatians' very eyes — *Christ crucified.*"[64] It now merely needs to be noted that these considerations also stand against option (iii) above, not to mention options (i) and (ii). That is, the broader and the localized contexts point strongly toward construing the disputed phrase ἀκοὴ πίστεως in similar terms if that is possible, and of course it is; ἀκοὴ πίστεως can speak directly of Paul's depiction of Christ if it is construed as "the proclamation of the faithful one" (that is, a genitive of content, and this particular content for the gospel is well attested elsewhere in Galatians and in Paul; a more literal translation would be "proclamation of fidelity," with an implicit reference to the text, "the righteous one through fidelity will live"). There seems to be nothing objectionable about such a construal, while, as we have just seen, all the other more conventional suggestions are problematic in certain respects.

In sum, it seems that the ambiguous phrase ἀκοὴ πίστεως in 3:2 and 3:5 should be resolved, on closer analysis, in favor of a christological reading — one that ultimately unpacks into the rhetorical and apocalyptic reading that I am suggesting for Galatians more generally. The phrase denotes "the proclamation of fidelity" (in the sense of the righteous and faithful one), thus characterizing the arrival of Paul's gospel in Galatia *without reference to human response* but merely in terms of a graphic depiction in relation to Christ and the outpouring of the Spirit — that is, of revelational events (see Gal. 1:12, 15-16).[65] Clearly, this does not exclude human involvement or activity (so 1:17–2:14; 4:12-20; 5:13–6:10), but it is primarily a declaration of the principal agency and causality involved in Paul's gospel — a declaration that Paul's original opponents and Justification advocates alike seem to have found shocking and unacceptable, and so resisted. The indications are nevertheless that this is what he meant and what his original Galatian auditors heard — or, still better, "saw."

§5. Galatians 3:6-14

I suggest at this point in my broader argument that Galatians 3:6-14 — not unlike some of 2:15–3:5 — is rather less decisive than many interpreters suspect. Certainly, it falls far short of incontestably demonstrating the presence of Justification theory in Paul's argument. This is not to suggest that the text is incompatible with Justification theory; Justification can supply a plausible possible reading of this material. But a rhetorical and apocalyptic construal is equally possible, and one or two hints — although they remain little more than this — in my view even suggest it. The result of this ambiguity is then, in effect, to continue the successful onward march of my alternative, apocalyptic reading. Justification theory finds itself once again with no good reasons for asserting its existence as a plausible construction of Paul's thinking.

The main reason for this indecision in Galatians 3:6-14 is the extreme concision of Paul's text at this point; it consists of little more than a string of scriptural quotations with the barest of expansions. And the result of this concision is an unsurprising compatibility with a range of more detailed interpretations. Various complex interpretive schemes can simply be inserted into the many gaps within this text's explication. And as long as they do not obviously violate the arrangement of and brief commentaries on Paul's quotations, they can then lay claim to a degree of plausibility. It is just that we lack any criteria for arbitrating between these various readings decisively. We should probably favor the reading that appeals the least to any such unstated material. But this is not necessarily a decisive criterion, especially given the concision that we have already noted is a signal feature of Galatians' construction. Paul's corroborations found elsewhere — or lack of them — will ultimately prove more important.

Some interpreters have also detected a chiastic arrangement here.[66] I concur that some such pattern seems unavoidable, with discussions revolving around Abraham (vv. 6-9 and 14) flanking statements about curse (vv. 10 and 13), that flank in turn contrasting, symmetrical quotations concerning life (vv. 11-12). This much seems difficult to deny. But the precise limits of the inclusio have proved difficult to determine, although they probably do not need to be determined exactly. As things stand, the first member (A) is rather longer than its counterpart (A′), and if material addressing the Spirit is drawn into A from 3:1-5, then this imbalance becomes even more pronounced. Fortunately, this question does not need to be resolved here for the relevant interpretative implications for my argument to emerge.

[³˙⁵ὁ οὖν ἐπιχορηγῶν ὑμῖν τὸ πνεῦμα καὶ ἐνεργῶν δυνάμεις ἐν ὑμῖν, ἐξ ἔργων νόμου ἢ ἐξ ἀκοῆς πίστεως;⁶⁷]

A
⁶καθὼς Ἀβραὰμ ἐπίστευσεν τῷ Θεῷ, καὶ ἐλογίσθη αὐτῷ εἰς δικαιοσύνην·
⁷γινώσκετε ἄρα ὅτι οἱ ἐκ πίστεως, οὗτοι υἱοί εἰσιν Ἀβραάμ.
⁸προϊδοῦσα δὲ ἡ γραφὴ ὅτι ἐκ πίστεως δικαιοῖ τὰ ἔθνη ὁ θεός, προευηγγελίσατο τῷ Ἀβραὰμ ὅτι ἐνευλογηθήσονται ἐν σοὶ πάντα τὰ ἔθνη·
⁹ὥστε οἱ ἐκ πίστεως εὐλογοῦνται σὺν τῷ πιστῷ Ἀβραάμ.

    B
    ¹⁰ὅσοι γὰρ ἐξ ἔργων νόμου εἰσίν, ὑπὸ κατάραν εἰσίν· γέγραπται γὰρ ὅτι ἐπικατάρατος πᾶς ὃς οὐκ ἐμμένει πᾶσιν τοῖς γεγραμμένοις ἐν τῷ βιβλίῳ τοῦ νόμου τοῦ ποιῆσαι αὐτά.

        Γ/Γ′
        ¹¹ὅτι δὲ ἐν νόμῳ οὐδεὶς δικαιοῦται παρὰ τῷ θεῷ δῆλον ὅτι ὁ δίκαιος ἐκ πίστεως ζήσεται·
        ¹²ὁ δὲ νόμος οὐκ ἔστιν ἐκ πίστεως, ἀλλ᾽ ὁ ποιήσας αὐτὰ ζήσεται ἐν αὐτοῖς.

    B′
    ¹³Χριστὸς ἡμᾶς ἐξηγόρασεν ἐκ τῆς κατάρας τοῦ νόμου γενόμενος ὑπὲρ ἡμῶν κατάρα, ὅτι γέγραπται· ἐπικατάρατος πᾶς ὁ κρεμάμενος ἐπὶ ξύλου,

A′
¹⁴ἵνα εἰς τὰ ἔθνη ἡ εὐλογία τοῦ Ἀβραὰμ γένηται ἐν Χριστῷ Ἰησοῦ, ἵνα τὴν ἐπαγγελίαν⁶⁸ τοῦ πνεύματος λάβωμεν διὰ τῆς πίστεως.

That Paul's Galatian auditors would have detected the six scriptural quotations here (highlighted for convenience) is in my view likely. Each one is emphasized with an introductory marker: καθὼς . . . ὅτι . . . γέγραπται [γὰρ] ὅτι . . . ὅτι . . . ἀλλὰ . . . ὅτι γέγραπται. . . . Three of these six signals are admittedly abbreviated. But that they ought to function as introductory signals seems indicated by vv. 10 and 13, where ὅτι is expanded with γέγραπται, implying its unspoken presence in at least some of the other instances.⁶⁹ (Καθὼς γέγραπται is in fact Paul's usual citation formula.)⁷⁰ Verse 8 also suggests helpfully that "the Scripture preached the gospel to Abraham in advance . . . that . . ." (προευηγγελίσατο . . .

ὅτι). Paul's brevity is comprehensible — both in this specific respect and more generally in this subsection — if his Galatian auditors are only being reminded here of important material that he has already presented to them on his previous visit (see esp. 4:13).[71] That some of these texts are used by Paul for fixed pedagogical purposes in this debate seems confirmed by their repetition in Romans (notably, Gen. 15:6; Hab. 2:4; and Lev. 18:5). But I would suggest that very little decisive interpretative material is supplied here by Paul outside of his quotations of these key texts, along with the terms and phrases that they supply, and these do not necessarily tell us a great deal yet. Indeed, I suggest something of a thought experiment at this point. If we restrict ourselves to what Paul either says here or directly implies for the sake of argument, and do not appeal outside this subsection for any elucidation, then the reading that results is surprisingly minimal.

Abraham trusts in God — and so can be characterized as either trusting or trustworthy (v. 9) — and is "viewed" as righteous. Or, alternatively, he has some righteous activity or act "credited" to him, and this is presumably a blessing either way. (Rather unhelpfully, the verb λογίζομαι does not occur again in Galatians.) Through him, however — as Scripture says — all the pagan nations will be blessed as well, thereby receiving the epithet "sons of Abraham" — an important feature of Paul's argument in Galatians 3 in more general terms (see esp. v. 29).[72] This blessing takes place in some relation to πίστις, literally, ἐκ πίστεως, a phrase that seems to be supplied by Habakkuk 2:4 in v. 12. *It is repeated independently of this text four more times in this subsection, with a fifth possible echo in v. 14b.* Verse 12 also indicates that this blessing can be characterized as "life." The final verse in the chiasm (v. 14) then points toward some sort of promise (see perhaps v. 8), and the involvement of the Spirit, although whether the latter is the content of the former or its source (or something else) is difficult to say. Certainly, any explicit link between the Spirit and the content of a promise is not obvious, and especially in relation to the promises that Paul discusses here (i.e., the Abrahamic covenants).[73]

This state of πίστις, blessing, life, promise, and Spirit, in which Abraham seems to participate, and in relation to which later pagan converts can be named descendants of Abraham, seems to have been achieved by a process of purchase or redemption (v. 13), from a realm that can in some sense be characterized as cursed. Rather surprisingly for devout Jews, law observance also seems implicit in that realm, especially if it is not perfect; "everything in the book of the law must be done" or the law's curse is activated — an intriguing reorientation of a verse that seems in the first instance to curse those *not* observing the law in any sense, that is, non-Jews. But Christ has effected release from this situation for those marked by πίστις by means of some process of identification; he has become a curse, and this has somehow effected the release or purchase of others, including pagans, from that cursed state, which seems moreover to be a countervailing "life" characterized by "works" (or not).

And this is really all that we can say at this point with any confidence in broad terms.[74] However, eight elements in this subsection are worth exploring further to see whether a little more information can be scratched from Paul's cryptic remarks.

(1) Leviticus 18:5 and "Works of Law"

The key phrase "works of law" does seem to be undergirded by Leviticus 18:5, although supported here by Deuteronomy 27:26. "Works" seems to be a substantive expression that refers to the notion of "doing" that is mentioned in both the scriptural intertexts. And this effectively confirms our suspicions expressed in chapter nineteen in relation to Romans 10. The famous substantive phrase "works of law"/ἔργα νόμου in Paul seems to echo deliberately the infinitive that is supplied by Paul in these quotations — ποιῆσαι. The meaning of these two sets of data is therefore intimately connected, although we have yet to determine exactly what this means either here or in Galatians as a whole up to this point, because Paul has not told us.

(2) Habakkuk 2:4 and "Faith"

In like measure, Paul's "faith" terminology seems to be dominated by the citation of Habakkuk 2:4. Three times pagan converts are directly characterized in the subsection by the substantive πίστις, *on each occasion in the form ἐκ πίστεως*, thereby echoing Habakkuk 2:4 directly. The verb in Genesis 15:6, however, is *never* resumed; it is applied only to Abraham, who later on is not even described himself in terms of the verb or participle, but by the adjective. (So the designation οἱ ἐκ πίστεως was almost certainly not formed in deliberate opposition to the phrase οἱ ἐκ περιτομῆς that was used in 2:12.[75])

(3) The Critical Antithesis

These two texts — Leviticus 18:5 and Habakkuk 2:4 — thus seem to constitute the critical antithesis for Paul. Not only is their terminology dominant throughout the subsection, but they are positioned at the heart of the chiasm *and* shaped phraseologically to form a neat, symmetrical contrast — three factors pointing toward their importance:[76]

ὁ δίκαιος ἐκ πίστεως ζήσεται·
ὁ ποιήσας αὐτὰ ζήσεται ἐν αὐτοῖς.

(4) The Equation of "Justification" and "Life"

As an antithesis, Leviticus 18:5 and Habakkuk 2:4 contrast two different types of "life," one characterized by "works," or "doing" (i.e., the doing of all the things written in the book of the Law), and one by πίστις. But this "life" must be paralleled in context — at least loosely — by the notions of blessing, sonship, promise, and Spirit — and, most significantly, "justification." (Note also some role in this relation for δικαιοσύνη.) Habakkuk 2:4 states that the one ἐκ πίστεως "will live" — clearly, a central claim for the entire subsection. And those pagans converted to Christ, and characterized as ἐκ πίστεως, will be blessed (and this is mentioned three times), will become "sons" of Abraham, will receive some sort of promise, and will have some relationship to the Spirit. These things seem basically correlative.

Moreover, it is also this statement (namely, Hab. 2:4) — as we will see momentarily — that seems to imply that no one is "justified" by means of law observance. So these two notions are actually equated here in semantic terms. If someone is not "justified" by works of law but *is* made alive by πίστις, then the two verbs are implicitly correlative (as are any cognate nouns).

(5) The Eschatological Signifiers

Arguably, the curse texts used in context now tilt the interpreter toward interpreting this Saussurean paradigm of signifiers in *eschatological* terms. The curse inflicted by the law according to the citation of Deuteronomy 27:26 in 3:10 at least includes the curse of death.[77] Moreover, when 3:13 speaks, through Deuteronomy 21:23, of Christ "purchasing" those under a curse "by becoming a curse for them," a reference to the crucifixion is almost certain, along with a confirmation of that realm as one characterized by death. Christ identifies here with the cursed condition, and dies in it. And after this of course he is raised to eschatological life. So the only moment of transition that the subsection speaks of is a journey through identification with curse and death to eschatological life. And in view of this, it seems fair to at least suggest that the other positive signifiers in the subsection all carry the same eschatological reference; certainly, no problems for such a reading seem apparent. So the "justification," "life," "blessing," "sonship," "promise," and "righteousness," that Paul is speaking of in this passage — things coupled, furthermore, with the Spirit — could well be different ways of speaking of the inclusion of Paul's pagan converts in the age to come.

(6) Christ's Identification with Curse

The means by which Christ effects this salvation should also be noted carefully. He does so by *identifying* with a condition of curse. Even as some have failed to do all the things written in the book of the Law and so incurred a curse, presumably along with death, Christ *becomes* a curse, as he is laid on wood in the accursed death of public execution on a gallows and thereby "purchases" those under the curse.[78] And this emphasis on identification is arguably a further overdetermination in relation to the theory of the atonement that Justification theory provides.

As we have already seen at some length, especially in part one, chapter two, Justification theory struggles to account for Christ's involvement in the atonement at all — especially the needs for him to be God incarnate and to displace

Jewish modes of atonement. And we should recall now that the dominant metaphor in this relation — assuming for the sake of argument that it is even cogent — is one of *payment*. Christ's sinlessness pays an appropriate price for the sins of humanity. However, this metaphor depends fundamentally for its cogency on an absolute differentiation between Christ and sinful humans. It is his sinlessness, despite his incarnation, that creates the appropriate fund of merit. (The incarnation is, strictly speaking, unnecessary!) An exchange then takes place, Christ's merit in effect paying the penalty due for humanity's sins (as that payment is activated on an individual basis by the act of faith). The only element of identification present within the theory, then, is an initial identification by Christ with humanity per se. But this identification is thinly justified and, even more importantly, it is vital that any further identification, with *sinful* humanity, be resisted. If Christ is too deeply involved in sin, perhaps even sinning himself, then — to put matters crudely — the purity of his sacrifice is polluted and the all-important payment cannot be made. So Justification theory actually has good reasons for *resisting* any comprehensive identification by Christ with humanity in its sinful depths. And Galatians 3:13 seems to assert something that reaches beyond these constraints, thereby generating an overdetermination.

Christ identifies here, it suggests, with a cursed constituency *by becoming a curse.*[79] Moreover, that process of identification *seems to be constitutive to his resolution of the situation.* It is *because* he becomes a curse that he can somehow free those who are cursed. His solution to their problem — his atonement — therefore rests precisely on a complete identification with the problem. Some sort of transfer therefore seems to have taken place, but a *direct* transfer, and not one *mediated by the equivalent of a payment of money.*

Money is in fact little more than the guarantee of something equivalent, usually labor; it is not the actual provision of the same good or service. But Christ here has not paid money of equivalent value to a particular problem; he has not worked hard and then paid for the medicine that will cure someone's disease. Christ *has assumed that disease himself* and thereby — miraculously — taken it from the sufferer. Consequently, it is as if Justification advocates have said that Christ has actually *become* the transgressions of the world in order to deal with them, which is the very thing that they cannot say![80]

It seems, then — at the least — that Justification theory cannot account for this passage. This Pauline claim does not make sense within that framework; hence, it points in another direction altogether. Paul's conception of the atonement, as indicated by Galatians 3:13, seems more radically participatory than Justification theory suggests.

(7) The Perfectionist Requirement

It is worth noting briefly that the argument seems to suggest at first glance that the realm of life that unfolds under the law — a realm that is ultimately cursed — ought to be characterized by perfect observance. People are cursed who do not do *everything* — πᾶσιν — that is written in the book of the Law. And while support can arguably be garnered from other parts of the letter for this implication (notably 5:3 — μαρτύρομαι [δὲ] πάλιν παντὶ ἀνθρώπῳ περιτεμνομένῳ ὅτι ὀφειλέτης ἐστὶν ὅλον τὸν νόμον ποιῆσαι), it does seem outlandish in broader empirical terms, thereby reinforcing that particular difficulty. Judaism did not make this demand without providing extensive means of support and restoration. (Alternatively — with supreme realism — it did not make it, or, at least, did not expect strict enforcement.) But Paul mentions none of those caveats here. It seems that one must either be perfect or be cursed. And consequently, a text exhorting people to take up the law has become a text that attacks those observing the law, and arguably rather unreasonably. It is this premise that generates the shocking reapplication of this legal exhortation here by Paul.[81] We come now to our final and perhaps most important observation, so we will spend a little more time on it.

(8) Paul's Rhetorical and Apocalyptic Argument

In this chiasm's central element, a retrospective argumentative pressure may again be detectable. Paul's chiastic arrangement, which offsets these four statements, should assist our reconsideration of this material.

> [11]ὅτι δὲ ἐν νόμῳ οὐδεὶς δικαιοῦται παρὰ τῷ θεῷ δῆλον,
> ὅτι ὁ δίκαιος ἐκ πίστεως ζήσεται·
> [12]ὁ δὲ νόμος οὐκ ἔστιν ἐκ πίστεως,
> ἀλλ' ὁ ποιήσας αὐτὰ ζήσεται ἐν αὐτοῖς.

It seems most likely, reviewing these statements alongside one another, that Paul has introduced a set of logical deductions here, the information for his initial premises being supplied by his key scriptural texts. He then draws the appropriate and in fact necessary conclusion, although this is actually his *first* statement in the sense unit. And so perhaps it has been placed here for emphasis (hyperbaton), although it also balances things stylistically (see 2:21).

He begins with a statement that delays its subject: "that nobody is declared righteous before God by means of law is clear."[82] However, this bold claim as yet lacks a rationale. Hence, it is most indicative that Paul now quotes Habakkuk 2:4 and not some text oriented toward the law. Moreover, he quotes a text that speaks not of eschatological declaration directly (at least, in forensic-retributive terms) but simply of "life": "the righteous person will live by means of fidelity." Two statements now follow that serve to link this claim to the judgment that was first made. Paul points out that "the law is *not* 'through fidelity,'" corroborating this claim with the statement that "the one who *does these things* will live *by means of them*" (a quotation of course of Lev. 18:5). And it can now be seen that he has constructed a legitimate argument, although — again — its rhetorical deployment does not match its internal connections. This is how the argument works in logical terms.

A. The righteous person will live by "faith."
B. This is "clear."
C. Existence in relation to law is characterized by "doing these things."
D. This also is oriented toward "life."
E. A does not equal C, which is to say that A and C are not commensurate but incompatible modes of attaining life. Clearly, then, they are different (i.e., you cannot travel to San Francisco by train and by plane at the same time).
F. Implicit assumption: there is only one way *to* life.
G. *Because* life comes about through A and B, it does *not* therefore come about through C and D — through "works of law" (here using the term δικαιόω).

This is a reasonably coherent argument, at which point several further observations are in order.

First, the argument seems to require the equation of "life" and "justification" (i.e., of δικαιοῦται and ζήσεται). Without this equation, it does not make any sense. Most importantly, the conclusion does not then correspond to the rest of the argument. (Perhaps the only way forward from this point would be to split v. 11a away from the rest of the sense unit and read it as the conclusion to what precedes it in v. 10, but this would disrupt the signals that seem to be sent by the overarching chiastic arrangement of the passage.) However, with this semantic equation, the statement fits smoothly into its context; the "life" being spoken of is the eschatological life of the age to come — and in fact we have noted this equation throughout my broader analysis.

Second, it is difficult to supply any profundity or even coherence to Paul's claims concerning life ἐκ πίστεως here without linking that phrase to Christ, at which point the entire argument makes perfect sense. If this phrase is referred to human decision making, then it is not obvious *why* this mode of life *overrules* law observance — *and especially in an eschatological sense*. As things stand, there is no rationale for the claim of salvation sola fide. It would merely be baldly — and rather unconvincingly — asserted. ("It is clear that Justification is not through law *because* it is by faith . . ."?) So Justification advocates feel the loss of any explicit attestation by Paul to their preparatory vestibule under law here especially acutely (although at least this masks the tensions generated for their account of faith when it is correlated tightly with Abraham, as it is here: see 3:6-9). And it is worth recalling that Räisänen raised this difficulty from another angle when he pointed out that Paul seems merely to overrule the law from the point of view of faith, which is not of course what full-fledged Justification theory suggests (and, as I emphasize, without which that move lacks any coherent rationale).[83]

However, if this phrase refers primarily to Christ's death and resurrection, then the entire argument makes perfect sense *precisely as it is stated, and this reading even supplies the missing premise. Because* eschatological life has now been provided by God through Christ, notably through his resurrection (so premise F), all other modes of attaining life have necessarily been displaced, including any system that emphasizes law observance, as the Teachers' does (an emphasis that pushes "life" into an uncertain future). These two modes of attaining resurrection and the blessedness and glory of life in the age to come are simply incommensurate. So this seems the likeliest interpretative option.[84]

Third, in the light of this, it can now be seen that Paul's argument operates retrospectively. *Because of* the achievement of life by Christ's πίστις — and especially his resurrection — and the incompatibility of that way to life with one oriented by "works," the way of "works" is excluded (and the way Paul's argument works in terms of sheer "overruling" is also now understandable). We can therefore resurrect Sanders's contention at this point concerning the retrospective orientation of Paul's argument, which faltered in relation to 2:21. Galatians 3:11-13 *does* seem to presuppose this distinctive purview, suggesting that 2:21 *and* 2:15-16 are effecting the same maneuver as well.[85] The entire subunit, then, seems to be developing into an overdetermination for Justification theory, which works forward and cannot work backward or view things retrospectively. This text resists such an arrangement.

We should now note, fourth, that this compact subsection seems to be explicable in part as a detailed and aggressive response to a distinct countervailing agenda that appeals to Jewish Scripture. The cogency of this claim rests on the recognition that a great deal of Paul's material here is highly distinctive if not unique to this passage, not to mention quite difficult for him to deal with. (So why would he raise it himself?)[86]

(i) Paul's citation of Genesis 12:3, which plays a significant role in his ensuing argument here (see more on this just below), is never cited again elsewhere.

(ii) The phrase υἱοὶ Ἀβραάμ is unique to 3:7.

(iii) Paul's emphasis on "curse," and his use of the two curse texts Deuteronomy 27:26 and 21:23, is unique to 3:10 and 13.

(iv) Paul's use of ἐξαγοράζω in 3:13 is paralleled elsewhere only by Galatians 4:5.[87]

(v) Paul's use of blessing — εὐλογέω/εὐλογία — which is anticipated by 3:8 and stated overtly in 3:9 and 14, is his only use of this motif. (It is, however, a widely recognizable Jewish theme with respect to Abraham.)[88]

(vi) The word προευαγγελίζομαι, used in 3:8, is unique to Paul here, and in fact the entire Bible.

(vii) The construction ὑπὸ [τινα] — "to be under the power of something" — is rare elsewhere in Paul but studs his argument through the central part of Galatians, being introduced here in 3:10 (see also 3:22, 23, 25; 4:2, 3, 4, 5, 21; 5:18[89]).

(viii) The very construction and arrangement of this passage is unique in Paul — a chiastic configuration oriented around six scriptural texts with cryptic accompanying expositions. This concentration of texts is rare (see elsewhere only perhaps Rom. 3:10-18; 9:25-29; 10:18-21; 15:9-12; perhaps 2 Cor. 6:16-18), and in this antithetical and briefly annotated form, unique.

This cluster of distinctive if not unparalleled motifs and techniques has convinced many interpreters that a countervailing agenda is discernible in relation to this passage. And, if it is true, then this reinforces my broader suggestion that Paul's Justification texts function within a rhetorical crucible, and ought to be interpreted as such. We do not of course need to mirror-read this material simplistically, reversing it and claiming to have thereby recovered Paul's opponents. However, we can press through Paul's serried claims for correlations with the description of the Teachers' gospel that has been emerging elsewhere — a system that Paul's moves here fit very well.[90]

In sum, it seems that some of the implications in Galatians 3:6-14 point the letter's auditors subtly toward a rhetorical and apocalyptic construal of this material (while, conversely, Justification theory tends to run into various problems). A retrospective argument from the sufficiency of life through Christ against "works" and the presence of a strong perfectionist strand in the Teacher's gospel are just what we expect to find Paul discussing in debate with that figure, along with much debate of the implications of Abraham, the father of the Jewish nation and also the model proselyte. Moreover, the argument between the Teacher and Paul is overtly eschatological throughout; the "life" in question is ultimately the life of the age to come, thereby fulfilling those implications as well. (They simply differ strongly on the best way to access that.) Furthermore, we expect an apocalyptic Paul to speak of Christ's resolution of humanity's depressing, cursed situation by way of a radical identification with it, this act enabling a participatory way out of that oppression — just the sense of 3:13. And this developing apocalyptic reading has the added virtue of aligning this material with the important clue supplied earlier in relation to 2:15–3:5 from 2:20, where a single but reasonably overt christological reference for Paul's πίστις terminology was apparent (being assisted there by various other clues in context). Paul's own position seems, then, to be smoothly and consistently apocalyptic as it develops through these subsections in Galatians.

Beyond these subtle adjustments, I concede that this subsection can *perhaps* be construed in terms of Justification theory — or in terms of "the new perspective," as Dunn suggests, or with a stronger connection with salvation history, as Wright suggests, or in "canonical hermeneutical" terms, as Watson suggests.[91] However, all of these scholars must import a considerable amount of explanatory material into the gaps in this text in order to read it in the fashion that they recommend, and such unstated material is hardly a decisive challenge to the apocalyptic approach being urged here. Moreover, they tend to override the delicate textual signals against such readings that we have already noted. In addition, the interpretative virtue of economy arguably becomes relevant at this point, because an argumentative and apocalyptic rereading does not need to import anything — only terminological and phraseological clarifications.[92]

However, I suggest that in the end the most decisive evidence for or against any reading of 2:15–3:14 will come not from within these arguments but from what follows this material in Galatians, especially in 3:15-26. We need, then, to examine which reading is most successful at negotiating this difficult, convoluted, and famously impassioned text. In my view, a decisive advantage for the apocalyptic reading becomes apparent through this material. So perhaps the key to the construal of 3:6-14, at least in terms of Justification issues, is to posit a reading that can flow smoothly on through the rest of chapter 3 — a task we now turn to pursue in more detail.

§6. Galatians 3:21-26 in Its Broader Context

6.1. Preliminary Considerations

Delimiting the scope of our discussion at this point is difficult. Although the inauguration of Paul's particular argument in this relation is clear, in 3:15, the key terms for the Justification discourse enter the argument only in v. 21 and then fade as it unfolds. The last relevant signifier — πίστις — occurs in 3:26. But the argument itself continues unabated through at least the end of the chapter (i.e., v. 29), and probably on to 4:10 or thereabouts — a further thirteen verses, or the same length of discussion again.[93] Added to this strange distribution (at least, for Justification theory), among all these terms, only πίστις has a real presence in the argument, occurring six times in vv. 22-26, once in each of those verses although twice in v. 23. Δικαιοσύνη occurs only once overall, in 3:21, δικαιόω once, in 3:24, and ἔργα not at all (its last instance being in 3:10, although "doing" and "work" do occur later in the letter[94]).

Given this distribution, the discussion of πίστις will clearly preoccupy us in what follows, and especially given that the key implications for Paul's sparse use of δικαιο- terminology here have already been largely supplied — concerning δικαιοσύνη in part four, chapter seventeen, and — perhaps a little more by implication — concerning δικαιόω in chapter sixteen. So those results need only to be summarized briefly before we address Paul's multiple use of πίστις in 3:15-26.

Paul's use of δικαιοσύνη in 3:21 has already been adduced as important evidence of the deliverative and eschatological sense of this signifier in the context of his debate with the Teacher's gospel. Indeed, this verse attests particularly clearly to its possible life-giving connotation in that broader discussion.[95] Such a connotation is really unavoidable in Galatians 3:21, where Paul crafts a conditional argument: εἰ γὰρ ἐδόθη νόμος ὁ δυνάμενος ζῳοποιῆσαι, ὄντως ἐκ νόμου ἂν ἦν ἡ δικαιοσύνη. Although it is not Paul's contingent emphasis in context, the two terms ζῳοποιῆσαι and δικαιοσύνη *must* denote the same thing here *or the argument does not work*[96] (i.e., it is not fundamentally coherent; and it is worth recalling that we have just found exactly the same argumentative coordination in 3:11-12). This realization draws the three other instances of δικαιοσύνη in Galatians — in 2:21, 3:6 (here Gen. 15:6), and 5:5 — into this semantic orbit, since the contextual signals in those texts are so similar, that is, apocalyptic and eschatological.[97]

Paul's use of the verb δικαιόω in 3:24 also confirms nicely the sense already indicated by Romans 3:24 and 26. Not only can it take a forensic-liberative meaning at this point, but the context affirms this quite strongly. Paul deploys metaphors of imprisonment in the context of v. 24b. In v. 23 he speaks of being "locked up" and "confined" before the revelation of the coming πίστις (see ὑπὸ νόμον ἐφρουρούμεθα συγκλειόμενοι . . .). Indeed, he makes this point three times by speaking of confinement in v. 22 as well. Then in v. 24a he defines the law's role in this situation as that of a παιδαγωγός. We will discuss this well-known metaphor further just below, so suffice it for now to observe that the metaphors of imprisonment just noted in vv. 22-23 code this metaphor rather negatively as well; the pedagogue here is therefore most probably a confining and harsh figure, as he could be in the ancient world (i.e., even bullying and beating his young charges on occasion, because such methods of child rearing were widely regarded as appropriate). Verse 25 then affirms this metaphor, although more positively, proclaiming that any involved in Christ are no longer under this pedagogue. And in this context, surrounded by metaphors of constraint and discipline, the signifier δικαιόω clearly *ought* now to take a forensic-liberative meaning of "release" or "deliverance" in the more specific sense of release and deliverance *from* this confinement. Paul seems to be using that verb here to state that ἐκ πίστεως (which is to say ultimately through the fidelity of Christ) "we are delivered (from our harsh confinement)." Christ's identification, death, and resurrection have set us free.

In short, Paul's two uses of δικαιο- terms in Galatians 3:15-26 not only integrate seamlessly with the apocalyptic senses that we have already detected for these terms from the evidence in Romans, but they positively affirm those earlier judgments. And with these conclusions strengthened, we can turn to consider the major interpretative issue raised by this text: the most likely construal of its πιστ- terminology.

6.2. A Christological Construal of *πίστις* in Galatians 3:15-29

We will not solve all the notorious difficulties of Galatians 3 here.[98] But I do suggest that a strictly context-sensitive reading of Paul's argument tilts us strongly toward a christological reading of the disputed πίστις Χριστοῦ genitive in 3:22, and of the rest of Paul's πιστ- language in context, and will also greatly simplify Paul's argument throughout the subsection as a whole, opening up its revelatory and participatory dimensions. Indeed, many of our interpretative difficulties at this point will turn out to have been self-inflicted, as we have sought to introduce Justification concerns into a text that comprehensively resists them. So, I suggest, Galatians 3:22-26 in its broader context will turn out to offer fairly decisive evidence in favor of the rhetorical and apocalyptic reading that I am advocating in relation to Paul's Justification texts more generally, and will, in addition, lend further confidence to our judgments reached earlier in relation to the more ambiguous texts in this letter. The case for an explicitly apocalyptic reading from 3:15 onward begins with the observation that Paul uses a string of πίστις statements in the latter half of Galatians 3 — tightly integrated material that is not often given the attention it deserves:[99]

> v. 22:   ἡ ἐπαγγελία **ἐκ πίστεως** Ἰησοῦ Χριστοῦ δοθῇ **τοῖς πιστεύουσιν**
> v. 23a: πρὸ τοῦ [δὲ] ἐλθεῖν **τὴν πίστιν** . . .
> v. 23b: . . . εἰς **τὴν** μέλλουσαν **πίστιν** ἀποκαλυφθῆναι
> v. 24:   . . . ἵνα **ἐκ πίστεως** δικαιωθῶμεν
> v. 25:   ἐλθούσης [δὲ] **τῆς πίστεως** . . .
> v. 26:   διὰ **τῆς πίστεως** [ἐν Χριστοῦ Ἰησοῦ][100]

We should note at this point that the sequence of five singular instances of πίστις in vv. 23-26 is introduced by a fuller genitive construction in v. 22, one of our well-known disputed πίστις Χριστοῦ genitives, and it is also associated there with a cognate participle. Several observations now become important to our developing argument. We should consider, first, that it would have been difficult for an auditor to construe the string of single instances of πίστις in vv. 23-26 in isolation from the first signal given here by the genitive construction in v. 22. These interpretative questions are in fact bound up tightly with one another. So we must attempt to give a unified interpretation to this set of terms, or provide good reasons why they might vary in meaning.[101] However, we will consider the actual construction in v. 26, and the contribution of the participial phrase in v. 22b, to Paul's overall argument shortly. For now we will concentrate on the five substantives in the singular. And here we can see, second, that an obvious clue to their unified reference is provided by the repeated motif of "coming," which is associated with πίστις in this series no fewer than three times (twice using ἔρχομαι and once μέλλω).

> v. 22:   ἡ ἐπαγγελία ἐκ πίστεως Ἰησοῦ Χριστοῦ δοθῇ τοῖς πιστεύουσιν
> v. 23a: πρὸ **τοῦ** [δὲ] **ἐλθεῖν τὴν πίστιν** . . .
> v. 23b: . . . εἰς **τὴν μέλλουσαν πίστιν** ἀποκαλυφθῆναι
> v. 24:   . . . ἵνα ἐκ πίστεως δικαιωθῶμεν
> v. 25:   **ἐλθούσης** [δὲ] **τῆς πίστεως** . . .
> v. 26:   διὰ τῆς πίστεως [ἐν Χριστοῦ Ἰησοῦ]

Indeed, since three of the five singular instances of πίστις are explicitly stated to be "coming" we cannot really miss the point, even on one reading. But this immediately sets up a further important link in Paul's argument — our third observation. Before this πίστις series begins in v. 22, Paul has been occupied, among other things, with "the seed" (v. 16 [3x] and v. 19; see also v. 29). At this slightly earlier stage in the letter he has been interpreting a text from Genesis in a direction that modern interpreters often find rather shocking but that is nevertheless an entirely possible, if literal, construal of the scriptural text καὶ τῷ σπέρματί σου.[102] It is this text that introduces "the seed" into his discussion. And in v. 19 he states, in a temporal clarification to the first half of that verse, ἄχρις ἂν ἔλθη τὸ σπέρμα ᾧ ἐπήγγελται (σεε ΝΡΣ , "... υντιλ τηε οφφσπριγ ωουλδ *come* to whom the promise had been made" — emphasis added). It seems, then, that the seed in v. 16 and following who comes should probably be identified with the πίστις ωηο ορ ωηιφη ιν ςς. ⁱⁱα, ⁱⁱβ, ανδ ⁿ⁵ αλσο φομεσ. Ειτηερ τηισ, ορ σομε στατεδ ρεδεπλοψμεντ οφ τηε νοτιον οφ φομιγγ ωουλδ νεεδ το βε συππλιεδ βψ Παυλ, βυτ νο συφη εξπλιφιτ ρεοριεντατιον ισ αππαρεντ ιν τηε τεξτ. Τηε σεεδ ανδ τηε πίστις βοτη "φομε" ανδ σο βοτη σεεμ το βε τηε σαμε τηιγγ.

v. 16: τῷ δὲ Ἀβραὰμ ἐρρέθησαν αἱ ἐπαγγελίαι καὶ **τῷ σπέρματι** αὐτοῦ. οὐ λέγει· καὶ τοῖς σπέρμασιν, ὡς ἐπὶ πολλῶν ἀλλ' ὡς ἐφ' ἑνός· καὶ **τῷ σπέρματί** σου, ὅς ἐστιν Χριστός.

v. 19: . . . ἄχρις οὗ **ἔλθῃ τὸ σπέρμα** ᾧ **ἐπήγγελται**

v. 22: ἡ ἐπαγγελία **ἐκ πίστεως** Ἰησοῦ Χριστοῦ δοθῇ τοῖς πιστεύουσιν

v. 23a: πρὸ **τοῦ** [δὲ] **ἐλθεῖν τὴν πίστιν** . . .

v. 23b: . . . **εἰς τὴν μέλλουσαν πίστιν** ἀποκαλυφθῆναι

v. 24: . . . ἵνα **ἐκ πίστεως** δικαιωθῶμεν

v. 25: **ἐλθούσης** [δὲ] **τῆς πίστεως** . . .

v. 26: **διὰ τῆς πίστεως** [ἐν Χριστοῦ Ἰησοῦ]

v. 29: εἰ δὲ ὑμεῖς Χριστοῦ, ἄρα τοῦ Ἀβραὰμ **σπέρμα** ἐστέ, κατ' ἐπαγγελίαν κληρονόμοι.

We can also observe, however, fourth, that the seed and the πίστις are correlated by *another* motif that is repeated throughout this discussion, namely, ἡ ἐπαγγελία. In v. 19, as we have just noted, the coming seed is characterized as ᾧ ἐπήγγελται.[103] And, in a direct parallel to this, Paul states in v. 22 that the purpose of the Scripture imprisoning all things under sin is ἵνα ἡ ἐπαγγελία ἐκ πίστεως Ἰησοῦ Χριστοῦ δοθῇ τοῖς πιστεύουσιν. The first association here then returns in v. 29 where Paul states — in an important concluding conditional claim — εἰ δὲ ὑμεῖς Χριστοῦ, ἄρα τοῦ Ἀβραὰμ σπέρμα ἐστέ, κατ' ἐπαγγελίαν κληρονόμοι. So the seed and the πίστις share the motif of coming *and* the motif of promise.

v. 16: τῷ δὲ Ἀβραὰμ ἐρρέθησαν **αἱ ἐπαγγελίαι** καὶ **τῷ σπέρματι** αὐτοῦ. οὐ λέγει, καὶ τοῖς σπέρμασιν, ὡς ἐπὶ πολλῶν ἀλλ' ὡς ἐφ' ἑνός· καὶ **τῷ σπέρματί** σου, ὅς ἐστιν Χριστός.

v. 19: . . . ἄχρις οὗ **ἔλθῃ τὸ σπέρμα** ᾧ **ἐπήγγελται**

v. 22: **ἡ ἐπαγγελία ἐκ πίστεως** Ἰησοῦ Χριστοῦ δοθῇ τοῖς πιστεύουσιν

v. 23a: πρὸ **τοῦ** [δὲ] **ἐλθεῖν τὴν πίστιν** . . .

v. 23b: . . . εἰς **τὴν μέλλουσαν πίστιν** ἀποκαλυφθῆναι

v. 24: . . . ἵνα **ἐκ πίστεως** δικαιωθῶμεν

v. 25: **ἐλθούσης** [δὲ] **τῆς πίστεως** . . .

v. 26: **διὰ τῆς πίστεως** [ἐν Χριστοῦ Ἰησοῦ]

v. 29: εἰ δὲ ὑμεῖς Χριστοῦ, ἄρα τοῦ Ἀβραὰμ **σπέρμα** ἐστέ, **κατ'** ἐπαγγελίαν κληρονόμοι.

The σπέρμα spoken of in vv. 16 (2x) and 19 operates in some significant relation to a promise, and comes, while the πίστις spoken of in vv. 22-26 (5-6x) also operates in some significant relation to a promise, and comes. Paul seems, then, to have deliberately crosshatched all these motifs through the argument of 3:15-29 to tie them together. But added to this — fifth — there is a basic set of symmetries between the two motifs in any case. Both the seed and the πίστις are singular entities. And both are involved with singular events as well — a coming or arrival — which is worth grasping, since these points can be conflated. Multiple entities can be involved in a singular event, and a singular actor can make multiple arrivals, but Paul seems to be speaking here of a singular entity making a single arrival. Hence, even if we cannot unravel all the details of Paul's argument in this subsection, we are still strongly justified in making an initial identification between "the coming seed" and "the coming πίστις," both of whom are also related to "promise" — the first initial conclusion in our argument here concerning Galatians 3. The text signals this identification quite clearly.

As a result, a steel chain of references, ten links long, now stretches through Paul's argument in Galatians 3 from v. 16 to v. 29, since the seed enters Paul's discussion explicitly in v. 16 and the relevant motifs fade after v. 29. And we can be confident of the strength of this chain — of its inner connection — even as it passes occasionally through murky argumentative waters, because of the constant reprise of the associated motifs of coming and promise (each with four occurrences). We should also recall that the fourth link in this chain is one of the famous disputed πίστις Χριστοῦ genitives, but the rest of the links are simple motifs in the singular, whether the seed or the πίστις, and these motifs all undertake the strikingly singular action of coming or arriving.

v. 16: τῷ δὲ Ἀβραὰμ ἐρρέθησαν αἱ ἐπαγγελίαι καὶ **τῷ σπέρματι αὐτοῦ**. οὐ λέγει, καὶ τοῖς σπέρμασιν, ὡς ἐπὶ πολλῶν ἀλλ' ὡς ἐφ' ἑνός· καὶ **τῷ σπέρματί σου**, ὅς ἐστιν Χριστός.

v. 19: . . . ἄχρις οὗ ἔλθῃ **τὸ σπέρμα** ᾧ ἐπήγγελται

v. 22: ἡ ἐπαγγελία **ἐκ πίστεως** Ἰησοῦ Χριστοῦ δοθῇ τοῖς πιστεύουσιν

v. 23a: πρὸ τοῦ [δὲ] ἐλθεῖν **τὴν πίστιν** . . .

v. 23b: . . . εἰς **τὴν** μέλλουσαν **πίστιν** ἀποκαλυφθῆναι

v. 24: . . . ἵνα **ἐκ πίστεως** δικαιωθῶμεν

v. 25: ἐλθούσης [δὲ] **τῆς πίστεως** . . .

v. 26: **διὰ τῆς πίστεως** [ἐν Χριστοῦ Ἰησοῦ]

v. 29: εἰ δὲ ὑμεῖς Χριστοῦ, ἄρα **τοῦ Ἀβραὰμ σπέρμα** ἐστέ, κατ' ἐπαγγελίαν κληρονόμοι.

In view of this data, I now want to suggest five sets of reasons why the chain of singular references here ought to be interpreted with reference to Christ, only the final link, in v. 29, broadening out its applications to include all those who belong to Christ by way of participation in him (as vv. 26b-28 famously suggest; note the important Χριστοῦ of v. 29).

(1) The Initial Identification of the Chain of Motifs with Christ

Paul begins this chain of references with a statement about "the seed" in v. 16 that is made, as we have just seen, with terminology drawn from the Septuagintal account of Abraham. Certain promises have been made to Abraham "and to his seed." And immediately after this allusion Paul makes the claim much lamented by critical scholars that the seed referred to here is not many seeds (see καὶ τοῖς σπέρμασιν) but one, singular seed (see καὶ τῷ σπέρματί σου, ὅς ἐστιν Χριστός).[104] Irrespective of the hermeneutical fairness of this claim, Paul tells us here quite explicitly to whom this chain refers by overtly identifying its first link with Christ. If this chain exists — and there seem to be numerous good reasons for thinking it does — then "the seed," "the coming one," "the promised one," and "the πίστις" are all merely different references by Paul to Jesus Christ. Moreover, there is no obvious need to vary the reference of the subsequent links once the first has been explicitly identified — thereby presumably breaking the chain — although further pieces of evidence will also point toward the chain's christological unity.[105]

But perhaps 3:22 *does* point in another direction. The ambiguous πίστις Χριστοῦ genitive in this verse could be construed in isolation as denoting belief in Christ rather than his belief (or his trust or fidelity). So this verse could potentially break the chain that we have just constructed. But should it be interpreted in this fashion? I suggest that the evidence, once again, points toward Christ.[106]

(2) The Likely Analogy in 3:22 with Abraham

As we turn to consider 3:22b in more detail, we should note initially that there is no comparable progression of πιστ- words in Galatians outside 3:22.[107] As we have already seen, the verb πιστεύω is surprisingly rare in Galatians. There are two innocuous instances in 2:7 (one of which is elided) that can be discounted in the present relation immediately. Then, outside 3:22 itself, there are only two other potentially relevant instances in the entire letter, namely, 2:16 and 3:6, the last of these being a quotation of Genesis 15:6. Moreover, nowhere outside 3:22 does Paul in Galatians actually call Christians "believers" or "trusters." So where are the auditors of Galatians to turn, if they seek help for the interpretation of this compressed and ambiguous clause? It seems that they have only two choices. So do they turn to 2:15-16 or to 3:6 and Genesis 15:6 for help? (It seems likely that *some* connection with an earlier instance of the verb is operative.)

The former text, 2:15-16, might suggest supplying Christ as an implicit object. Christians are then being described in 3:22, by implicit extension, as those who believe in Christ or who trust in him (and probably the former, given the most likely construal of the verb in 2:16, where it is used in parallel to a participle of knowing; this is of course to concede the conventional construal of 2:15-16 merely for the sake of argument). Alternatively, 3:6 and Genesis 15:6 supply God as the object of trust or belief on analogy to Abraham. Several considerations prompt us to read 3:22 more in alignment with this latter text rather than with 2:16 — which is ambiguous in any case.[108]

Galatians 3:6 is a bit nearer to 3:22 than is 2:15-16, so it asks less of an audience to recall 3:6 than it does for them to reach back to 2:16 — although it still asks a certain amount. Rather more importantly, a strong set of allusions to Abrahamic material in 3:22 and its immediate setting assists this recall, and no strong signals in terms of the verbal construction in 2:16 are apparent, where Jewish Christians are discussing their commitments to Christ. This is not to suggest that such considerations are completely absent; my point is just that they are not being mobilized very explicitly in the context of 3:22, as Abrahamic motifs are. The two πίστις Χριστοῦ constructions used in 2:16 would of course be of some help, but these are the only potential links. Meanwhile, Abraham is mentioned by name as late as v. 18 and has been central to Paul's discussion from v. 14 up to that point, having been introduced in v. 6. He is also clearly relevant to Paul's ongoing argument through at least v. 29, that is, well after the phrase we are considering now in v. 22. So repeated and overt references to Abraham surround the text we are currently considering.

But it is also in specific relation to him that the motif of "promise" is initially introduced into the discussion, then being repeated, as we have just seen, with no fewer than nine occurrences (see vv. 14, 16, 17, 18 [2x], 19, 21, 22, 29). Most importantly, v. 22 states specifically that the πίστις Ἰησοῦ Χριστοῦ *enables "the promise" to be given to those who trust or believe.* Hence, it seems that the "promise" motif in v. 22b explicitly refers the auditor back to the Abrahamic material that Paul has deployed from 3:6 onward, which has discussed promises repeatedly. And if this is the case, then I suggest that the initial πίστις Χριστοῦ genitive should be construed subjectively, and the implicit object of "God" supplied for the participle πιστεύοντας as well. A set of interrelated considerations prompts these judgments.

First, it seems clear that some sort of analogy with Abraham and his narrative is being suggested by 3:22 (see Rom. 4:23-25). Both the verb and the motif of promise point to the relevance of this earlier material, so this earlier reference is, in effect, triangulated by the signals that Paul supplies from 3:22. And Abraham trusted *in God,* as Genesis 15:6 says, receiving both promises and — to a certain extent — their realization (for him, principally through the miraculous conception of Isaac, which was of course a resurrecting act; see part four, chapter eighteen). Hence, the Galatian auditors should construe the πίστις Χριστοῦ genitive here in the same terms, as denoting Christ's faith in God; that is, he functions here like Abraham, as a paradigmatic and faithful figure.[109] Furthermore, the unstated object of the participle should be the same, and this creates an entirely smooth reading, because the same object of trust or belief is now supplied for all the relevant parties — for Abraham (who, as we have just seen, is implicit in Paul's comparisons), for Christ, and for the Christians named at the end of the clause. There are no awkward shifts in the focus of their trust or belief.

The subjective construal of v. 22:	Abraham	trusts	God
	Christ	trusts	God
	Christians	trust	God

In short, this reading follows the local evidence in relation to Abraham, where both the promise and the verb are relevant markers. And most importantly — and as we will see momentarily — *it generates no immediate contextual or broader temporal difficulties;* it is a smooth reading. Indeed, if we follow this localized decision in v. 22b, then 3:22 can now be seen to confirm rather than overthrow our earlier identification of the links in the chain stretching through Galatians 3:15-29 with Christ.

(3) The Motif's Singularity

It ought also to be recalled now, however, that the first nine links of the chain, prior to its final expansion, are singular in grammatical terms (τῷ σπέρματι αὐτοῦ... ἐφ' ἑνός· καὶ τῷ σπέρματί σου... τὸ σπέρμα... ἐκ πίστεως... τὴν πίστιν ... τὴν μέλλουσαν πίστιν... ἐκ πίστεως... τῆς πίστεως... διὰ τῆς πίστεως). Paul then seems to mark any applications of this figure's achievements to his many followers with explicitly plural constructions, as we have just seen in vv. 22, 24, and 29 (²²δοθῇ τοῖς πιστεύουσιν... ²⁴δικαιωθῶμεν... ²⁹εἰ δὲ ὑμεῖς Χριστοῦ, ἄρα τοῦ Ἀβραὰμ σπέρμα ἐστέ, κατ' ἐπαγγελίαν κληρονόμοι). Consequently, we would need reasons to read this figure generically, as a reference in fact to numerous believers. It seems better to understand the singular seed who comes, effecting the promise somehow via faith, as the single figure of Christ, and these references as participating in Paul's usual practice of referring to the Christ event metaleptically, any applications to a pluralized constituency then being signaled by Paul with plural constructions. But a more important singularity should now be noted — one bound up with the way that the singular seed and πίστις "come" to the enslaved cosmos.

(4) The Motif's Singular Arrival

We have already observed how Paul explicitly marks the motifs of the seed and the πίστις as "coming" four times, thereby in part indicating their identity (see ¹⁹... ἄχρις οὗ ἔλθῃ τὸ σπέρμα ᾧ ἐπήγγελται; ²³ᵃπρὸ τοῦ [δὲ] ἐλθεῖν τὴν πίστιν...; ²³ᵇ... εἰς τὴν μέλλουσαν πίστιν ἀποκαλυφθῆναι; ²⁵ἐλθούσης [δὲ] τῆς πίστεως...). It now needs to be noted carefully that this temporal event is also a singular one; some point in time between the time of Abraham and the present time — that is, the time in which the Galatian converts are being incorporated into the lineage of Abraham through Christ — is being denoted here. Indeed, it is the arrival of this time that allows such an incorporation, and the consequent passage of these converts from imprisonment, slavery, and infancy into liberation, freedom, and adulthood (this being an important argumentative contention in the letter that we will take up in more detail shortly). A decisive καιρός seems to have just arrived! And the temporal singularity — the event — that inaugurates this καιρός is best interpreted as a *singular* incursion into the cosmos *by Christ*, since he presumably entered the cosmos at some point in order to deliver it (hence this is also a singular *incursion*). In short, a christological identification of the πίστις accounts nicely for the singular *event* of arrival and liberation that the text speaks of, in addition to the singular *subject*. This event seems to fulfill the programmatic promises made to Abraham that spoke of the inauguration of this new age.[110]

(5) The Motif's Synonymous Parallelisms in Context

Finally, we should note briefly the parallelism between the two temporal εἰς constructions in 3:23 and 24 (to which v. 25 could be added as well).[111] This observation overlaps with my previous contention that πίστις "comes," but it is still worth noting in its own right.

Verse 23 is explicitly temporal, essentially crafting a redundancy: πρὸ τοῦ δὲ ἐλθεῖν τὴν πίστιν ὑπὸ νόμον ἐφρουρούμεθα συγκλειόμενοι εἰς τὴν μέλλουσαν πίστιν ἀποκαλυφθῆναι. The first half of the verse states that "before the coming of the πίστις we were guarded under the law." The second half then elaborates on this notion, reversing it by way of an attributive participial construction, to create a final emphasis on the revealed πίστις: ". . . confined until the coming πίστις should be revealed." It can be seen at a glance, then, that temporal notions are involved, some period of constraint under the power of the law preceding the coming and disclosure of the πίστις, while the εἰς construction in v. 23b is clearly part of this periodized statement by Paul; it must be temporal, and no one seriously disputes that it is.

Verse 24, however, continues just the same narrative: ὥστε ὁ νόμος παιδαγωγὸς ἡμῶν γέγονεν εἰς Χριστόν, ἵνα ἐκ πίστεως δικαιωθῶμεν. This verse adds the detail that in so functioning, the law acted like a pedagogue (on which see more just below). And a second detail emerges: that the arrival of πίστις will lead to the deliverance of those previously confined (so δικαιόω in v. 24b). But the critical point in this relation builds from the almost elementary observation that εἰς τὴν μέλλουσαν πίστιν in v. 23 and εἰς Χριστὸν in v. 24 *must* both be functioning in the same temporal sense, while the two markers πίστις and Χριστός seem as a result to interchange here synonymously. Indeed, they *have* to.

If they do not function synonymously, then Paul's narrative — in consecutive statements, using the same terms otherwise — is marking its turning point in relation to two *different* things! It is as if he has said, "We Americans were in bondage to the English until the arrival of George Washington, waiting for him to come. And with the coming of Abraham Lincoln, liberation duly took place." To put matters simply, Paul's argument is rendered incoherent unless these two terms are held constant. And yet of course there is no reason *not* to hold them constant. If πίστις is merely an alternative locution for Christ, then Paul says here exactly what he seems to want to say; there was an awkward period of time under the law before Christ (otherwise known as "the faithful one") and a liberation from that period effected precisely by the arrival of Christ.[112]

Hence, these two temporal εἰς constructions in vv. 23-24 merely suggest in detail what has already been noted more broadly — that a strong temporal contrast runs through the center of Paul's argument in 3:15-29, pivoting around the coming of Christ, but this is tantamount repeatedly in context to the arrival of (that) πίστις. At this critical point the bondage of the law ceases and a promised liberation is realized. And it is really impossible, in view of this, to construe the πίστις as anything or anyone other than Christ himself; to do so makes a complete mess of Paul's argument, while this identification creates a clear and sustained narrative, so that Paul's contentions flow smoothly through v. 25 as well, where the same issues arise.

Ἐλθούσης [δὲ] τῆς πίστεως οὐκέτι ὑπὸ παιδαγωγόν. Here Paul uses a temporal participial construction, not an εἰς construction, but his point is the same, and the pressure of the text is once again toward the identification of Christ (denoted directly in v. 24) with the πίστις. Only this identification continues Paul's argument coherently, and there seem to be no good reasons for opposing it.[113]

In sum, then, these five considerations — the initial identification of the chain of motifs with Christ, the most likely reading of 3:22 on analogy with Abraham, the motif's singularity, its singular arrival, and its synonymous parallelisms in context — all seem to point toward the identification of this chain of motifs and phrases through Galatians 3:15-29 with Christ, and hence to imply the identification of Christ with the motif of πίστις throughout as well. But we should turn now to consider the other side of the argument — that is, the possible rebuttal of my developing apocalyptic approach.

6.3. The Implications of Galatians 3:26 and 𝔓[46]

Can Justification advocates overthrow the five contentions just adduced here in favor of a christological construal of Paul's πίστις terminology through Galatians 3:15-26, and establish their own, more conventional, anthropocentric reading? I would suggest that they tend to run into difficulties here — two in particular.

First, their criticisms of the Christocentric reading that I have just suggested tend to lack penetration. Simultaneously, when they turn to establish their own reading in positive terms — as they have to — they can point to no explicit evidence in its favor.[114] But, second, that reading raises numerous additional problems, and these are often acute. Galatians 3:15-26 turns out to *resist* a construal in terms of Justification, and at several points; hence, not only does a reading in terms of Justification lack overt supporting evidence (alongside cogent reasons for dismissing my developing apocalyptic reading), but there seem to be good reasons for *not* adopting it (i.e., a large number of overdeterminations). We will now trace these two distinguishable sets of difficulties through in more detail.

I know of only one further point where Justification advocates can cogently challenge a christocentric account of the data in Galatians 3:15-29, suggesting that Paul's text contradicts such a construal directly — the πίστις construction in 3:26. (The other possible rejoinder in terms of 3:22b has already been dealt with.) But I suggest that closer consideration will find only fundamental ambiguities in this phrase, and by this point it is clear that Justification advocates need rather more than this; they need a decisive semantic and argumentative victory, which is just what they do not get (see 2:15-16). But certainly the apocalyptic approach's one remaining potential weak point deserves some attention.

We can begin by admitting that in some respects 3:26 is a complex text. However, at least the relevant elements within the sentence begin in a way that seems familiar — with διὰ τῆς πίστεως. The majority text continues with a dative construction, ἐν Χριστῷ Ἰησοῦ, yielding the statement — translating literally — "through the faith[fulness] in Christ Jesus." But before we can consider whether this statement falsifies our previous claims by supplying an overt instance of "faith *in* Christ," we must address the important manuscript variant supplied by 𝔓⁴⁶.

This very early manuscript lacks the article and the dative preposition ἐν, supplying a genitive construction instead that is similar to 2:16 and the other disputed genitives in Paul — διὰ πίστεως Χριστοῦ Ἰησοῦ. This reading is supported by a few other traditions: 1739 and 1881, which are important minuscules for Paul that arguably denote their own family of variants; the Peshitta; and the Sahidic variant of the Coptic (which often agrees with B and 𝔓⁴⁶); and these are not unimpressive witnesses. Even if it is not original, this variant — as Barry Matlock has pointed out — contributes information to the broader debate that needs to be assessed.[115] But we will consider the question of originality first.

Most commentators suggest that this reading is probably a harmonization of v. 26 to the other πίστις Χριστοῦ genitives in Galatians, especially to 3:22. And many of the other suggestions of 𝔓⁴⁶ in Galatians do not look overly convincing. This scribe seems to have made numerous mistakes, most of which were not detected by later correctors. However, against these contentions it *could* be argued that the majority reading is an attempt to make sense of an awkward genitive in terms of a traditional understanding of faith. Later Christian readers tended to construe Paul's faith statements anthropocentrically, and there is evidence of manuscripts performing similar alterations in relation to other awkward faith statements in Paul, most notably, Alexandrinus (A), which drops a difficult instance of πίστις in Romans 3:25, and F and Boernarianus (G), which drop the awkward πίστις genitive altogether from Romans 3:26. At this point, then, we should consider the exact variations:

διὰ τῆς πίστεως ἐν Χριστῷ Ἰησοῦ
διὰ πίστεως Χριστοῦ Ἰησοῦ

But in their original scribal abbreviations, these texts looked more like the following:

ΔΙΑΤΗΣΠΙΣΤΕΩΣΕΝΧΡΩΙΗΥ
ΔΙΑΠΙΣΤΕΩ ΣΧΡΥΙΗΥ

It does seem more likely from this viewpoint that 𝔓⁴⁶ is secondary. The article has been dropped and a christological construction supplied that the text supports earlier, in 3:22 (although in reverse, and spelled slightly differently — see ΙΗΥΧΥ in 3:22), as well as later, in v. 28b. And these are conceivable as straightforward omissions and mistakes, born of haste and/or fatigue.

The text surrounding 3:26 then seems to corroborate this reading. It contains several errors and possible word substitutions. Συγκλειόμενοι is misspelled in v. 23 (as συνκλειόμενοι), and παιδαγωγός in v. 24 (as παιδαγογός; the second instance, in 25, is spelled correctly). Οὐκέτι is supplied for οὐκ ἔνι in v. 28, probably in all three instances, although only two are visible.[116] Ἐγένετο is supplied (as in B) for γέγονεν in v. 24. So it seems possible that the scribe may not have known Greek very well.[117] Perhaps most importantly, however, a genitive Χριστοῦ is supplied for the dative Χριστῷ in v. 28b as well (here accompanied by A). Indeed, the reading of v. 28b is especially truncated — πάντες ὑμεῖς ἐστε Χριστοῦ. The movement from a prepositional construction in the dative to a genitive without the preposition therefore seems like a tendenz for the scribe, who is either making a mistake at these points or is thinking in terms of some notion of Christian "belonging" as connoted by the genitive. However, he manifests no difficulties with dative constructions earlier — namely, in 2:19-20 — so the former possibility here seems the more likely. Possibly, then, some combination of imprecision, speed, incompetence, and fatigue is leading to a misreading of ΧΡΩΙΗΥ as ΧΡΥΙΗΥ.

If the movement from the majority reading to 𝔓⁴⁶ is comprehensible, however, it is more difficult to explain the expanded majority text assuming movement in the reverse direction. Presumably very early on — to explain the variant's distribution — a scribe would need to introduce both an article and a preposition, altering the case of Χριστοῦ accordingly to Χριστῷ. This last alteration would then have to be replicated in v. 28b, at which point a neat inclusio would be formed with vv. 26-28. But the sense of that verse would have to be altered quite significantly as well in order to accommodate this genitive, the widely attested εἰς being resupplied, at which point the basic sense of the text would be considerably disrupted. Hence, this whole process looks unlikely.

But even if it is judged secondary, we should still consider whether this reading sheds light on our broader debate. Matlock has suggested — rather ingeniously — that 𝔓⁴⁶ reproduces an overtly objective construction in the majority text, thereby supplying evidence from an early Greek reader of the capacity of the genitive construction to convey an objective sense in relation to πίστις. However, I am not convinced that this scribe is an adept Greek reader. Moreover, his alterations do not seem driven by broader issues of sense so much as by weariness or haste (i.e., he is just making mistakes). The same alteration two verses later has nothing to do with πίστις constructions! So from this point we will follow the majority text tradition and will dismiss this possible evidence of intentional grammatical shifts. Unfortunately, 𝔓⁴⁶ tells us nothing in this relation.[118]

At first glance, the phrase πάντες γὰρ υἱοὶ Θεοὶ ἐστε διὰ τῆς πίστεως ἐν Χριστῷ Ἰησοῦ seems a straightforward statement concerning belief "in" Jesus Christ and hence a definitive vindication of Justification theory; exercising this "faith" seems to deliver divine sonship to "all" who so believe. But certain features of Paul's statement give us pause. Most important is the striking parallelism between 3:26 and 3:28b — πάντες γὰρ ὑμεῖς εἷς ἐστε ἐν Χριστῷ Ἰησοῦ. In this nearly identical statement the phrase "in Christ Jesus" modifies the subject adjectivally, the verb affirming here the "oneness" of such participants; the prepositional construction gives further information about just whom Paul is addressing, so that his auditors understand that "all of you *who are in Christ Jesus* are one and the same" (as corroborated by numerous contextual indicators[119]). And this opens up the possibility that the same phrase is functioning in this way in v. 26 as well — adjectivally, as it does in vv. 27-29 that follow, to modify πάντες.[120] However, the phrase διὰ τῆς πίστεως would function instrumentally and adverbially, as all the preceding instances of πίστις have in 3:22-25, to modify the verb ἐστε (and it is an identical arthrous phrase to vv. 23 [2x] and 25). The entire sentence, read in this way, would then state: "all of you who are in Christ Jesus are sons of God by means of that faithful one." It might also be noteworthy, in immediate support of this possible construal, that the appearance of Christ as an object of faith following the dative preposition ἐν elsewhere in Paul is rare if not unparalleled.[121]

As a result of this syntactical possibility, the evidence of 3:26 turns out to be — at the least — ambiguous. And if the evidence of the broader context is taken into account, where several explicit signals encourage the reference of διὰ τῆς πίστεως to Christ, then I suggest that the coordinate reading becomes the most likely one. It smoothly continues the argument of the preceding four verses, which is concluded around 3:26, and so the πίστις construction drops out of the otherwise parallel 28b. This reading is arguably facilitated in addition by the chiastic arrangement made possible in vv. 26-28 by way of an adjectival reading of ἐν Χριστῷ Ἰησοῦ.[122] So the case for Justification at this point seems to rest — once again — on a possible reading (and this at best). And at this stage in our argument, possibilities are not good enough.

Beyond this putative evidence, I know of no other cogent refutations of the christocentric reading of Galatians 3:15-29 — that is, in terms of textual overdeterminations, where data in the text causes explicit difficulties. It seems to be an entirely smooth account of that data, and several pieces of evidence already noted seem to support it. Conversely, I know of no explicit evidence *for* a Justification construal, but only of possible readings at certain points. However, significantly, there does seem to be evidence that explicitly resists such a reading, which we should now consider.

6.4. The Difficulties of an Anthropological
Construal of πίστις in Galatians 3:15-29

We should note first the difficulties caused for Justification advocates by the sin-gularities in Paul's argument — the singularity of the central actor, accompanied by the singularity of his arrival to set an imprisoned cosmos free (features of the text that the apocalyptic reading has no difficulty explaining, but positively en-dorses). However, in order to appreciate the implicit difficulties here, we should recall briefly the nature and role of "faith" in Justification theory.

According to Justification advocates, "faith" is the means by which individ-uals are saved, and it occurs in response to the proclamation of the good news concerning Jesus Christ. Every Christian has exercised faith at some point, and continues to exercise it. Hence, faith is as spread out through time and space as Christians are; *it is a massively pluralized phenomenon.* But, as we have seen, Galatians 3:15-29 speaks repeatedly of a single event of "coming" or "revelation" (see v. 23) in relation to a single subject. It seems, then, that this theory and that text are simply talking about different things. If the "faith" in Galatians 3:15-29 is singular in nature *and* arrival, then it *cannot* be the faith that Justification theory describes. However, Justification advocates have long noted this set of difficulties and they tend to respond with a further qualification, the cogency of which should now be carefully assessed.[123]

Justification advocates generally assert that Paul is speaking in these singu-lar temporal statements not of the phenomenon of faith itself, which must be plu-ralized, but of the arrival of its *possibility* with Christ and the good news concern-ing him.[124] And there is an initial plausibility about this claim in general terms. Trust in Christ does not seem to be possible before the coming of Christ himself. So the opportunity to trust in him arrives only as he does, and then presumably as the message about him is spread. But numerous difficulties are implicit with this counterproposal.

In the first instance, this suggestion requires the introduction of a series of partly and completely elided motifs into the chain that we earlier analyzed. Ini-tially, either "faith" must be introduced in relation to the "seed," or the seed in re-lation to faith, throughout (because Paul must be speaking at these points of "faith in the seed," and not merely of "the faith" or "the seed" alone).[125] Moreover, the notion of "possibility" (or perhaps, alternatively, "ground") must also now be introduced at every point in relation to the motif of "coming" or "arrival." And this is a lot of elided material, even allowing for the fact that Paul does elide re-peated material frequently and so might be expected to here, in such a repetitive passage.

> (v. 16: the seed is Christ)
> v. 19: . . . until [the possibility of faith in] the seed comes
> v. 22: through [the possibility of] faith in Jesus Christ . . . to those who believe [in him]

v. 23a: . . . before [the possibility of] faith [in the seed] comes

v. 23b: . . . until the [the possibility of] coming faith [in the seed] is
         revealed

v. 24:   . . . that we might be justified through [the possibility of] faith
         [in the seed]

v. 25:   [the possibility of] faith [in the seed] has come . . .

v. 26:   through [the possibility of] faith in Christ Jesus . . .

Moreover, whereas the introduction of elided material concerning faith can
at least be justified provisionally from the more explicit evidence of 3:22 and 3:26,
suitably construed — or, conversely, the idea of "faith in the seed" inferred from
explicit data — Paul *nowhere explicitly mentions the notion of "possibility" and its
arrival at all* (which also seems an anachronistic emphasis for the interpretation
of a Jewish Christian missionary in the first century CE[126]). The entire tenor of
Paul's argument has been qualified by these unstated caveats, and yet one key element in that qualification — the motif of possibility — *can point to no warrant in
the text at all!* The issue of underdetermination thus reaches an acute level here.
But this set of qualifications encounters further difficulties.

It must be asked in what sense a possibility of faith *can* "come" or "arrive,"
and especially as Paul develops that notion here. Repeatedly in 3:15-29 he speaks
of πίστις breaking into a confined and enslaved situation, in order to effect deliverance from it — of "God's invasive act of liberation."[127] So there is a literal connotation in the sense of arrival; πίστις comes from somewhere "outside" and enters the oppressed human cosmos, just as those involved in this event are meant
to move out of their imprisonment. In short, πίστις actually "arrives" and does
something. Consequently, Paul can also speak of this event as a "revelation" in
v. 23, a word that Paul ordinarily associates with dramatic interventions by
God.[128] But "possibilities" do not, strictly speaking, arrive from anywhere; they
are merely latent potentialities in actors and therefore not located somewhere
prior to their actualization by those actors. (Where is a word before it is spoken?)
It makes little sense, then, to speak of the dramatic arrival and disclosure of the
possibility of saving faith in the seed, who is Christ, unless perhaps by this is
meant the arrival of *the good news* concerning this possibility, or some such.

But at this point we have inserted an incredible *fourth* element into all the
links in Paul's argumentative chain, each link usually now eliding *three* of those
elements! And while no one would dispute that Paul could arrive with a gospel
concerning salvation, the gospel is not mentioned in Galatians after 2:14, and is
never itself spoken of in terms of possibility — or, for that matter, of "coming" or
"arrival." (The verb recurs in 4:13.) This would seem then to be an illegitimate insertion of material into a context that does not call for it directly, to try to rescue a
reading that otherwise seems to lack both support and coherence.[129] It is better
simply to discard this entire teetering construction of qualifications and ellipses.

As if in confirmation of these gathering suspicions, we should observe that
Paul does not ever describe this complex construction in his text. He speaks re-

peatedly of πίστις *itself* entering the cosmos — not its possibility or its representative or its proclamation; πίστις itself comes! So to assert the more complex reading actually *changes* what Paul has stated in the text into a more palatable interpretation. Something other than πίστις then comes, which is not of course what he said, and did so repeatedly. But beyond its inherent fragility and subtle displacement of Paul's stated meaning, there is one more good reason for challenging this construction.

If these complex qualifications are granted for the sake of further argument — the possibility of faith in the seed, Christ, arriving, as Paul comes with the gospel — then this construct immediately runs foul of Paul's emphasis on Abraham in 3:6-9 as someone who heard the gospel previously and was apparently saved — an explicit overdetermination.

As we have already seen many times, and noted in relation to Romans 4 as well (in part four, chapter eighteen), Abraham trusted God, and he did so before the arrival of the faith that Paul now seems to be discussing. So not only is his object different from the one that Justification advocates assert is now operative — that is, God, not Christ — but he is temporally out of sequence. Indeed, the figure of Abraham simply cannot support an argument that revolves around the possibility of faith in Christ arriving with Christ himself and the gospel. He must contradict this claim in both these respects — in terms of its timing *and* its object.[130] Paul's use of the patriarch in Galatians 3:6-9 must therefore now constitute *a counterexample* to the Justification advocate's suggested construal of 3:15-29. Far from supporting it, as is often claimed, he falsifies it. The christological advocate, however, will quickly point to the way that he integrates perfectly with that alternative approach; just as Christ was steadfastly faithful to God, so too Abraham was, and we should be as well — although these are difficult examples to follow. So the careful qualifications piled up by Justification advocates to avoid one set of overdeterminations — the text's senses of singularity and arrival — are now contradicted by another aspect of the text — its emphasis on the trusting Abraham (and I am granting here that those qualifications are convincing in and of themselves). Another feature of the text therefore contradicts the careful defensive operation that Justification advocates must mount in order to deal with the difficulties in that data at this difficult point — defenses that are not in any case overly plausible. One overdetermination therefore confounds the attempt to defuse another.

In short, a careful reading of 3:22-26 in context, with its repeated commitment to πίστις arriving in the cosmos and its claims concerning the earlier attestation of "the trusting Abraham" to this arrival (see 3:6-9), seems to contradict the claims of Justification theory in several respects: that theory views πίστις as a decision of faith (i.e., not something that "arrives" or "comes"), possible only after the coming of the gospel (i.e., centuries after the time of Abraham), in the content of the gospel, Christ (i.e., not in Abraham's object of belief, God), and therefore dispersed through time and space (i.e., not singular). Meanwhile, 3:22 and 3:26 have proved unstable supports as well. We have already noted how the figure of

Abraham also encourages the interpretation of the genitive in 3:22 in a christocentric direction, supplying the object of "God" to Christ and the Christians being spoken of there, essentially eliminating this piece of potential support for a Justification reading. Hence, it is apparent that the text of Galatians 3:15-26 fractures the theory of Justification in several ways. Or — put the other way around — as an interpretative template, Justification just does not seem to fit what Paul is talking about here very well at all.

It seems that a christocentric, apocalyptic reading offers a far simpler account of the text, with the added benefits of resting on several points of explicit attestation while raising no obvious instances of falsification. I conclude, then, that the christocentric, apocalyptic approach to Galatians 3:15-29 is *demonstrably superior* to any construal suggested by Justification advocates. And this is the best point at which to draw an important conclusion that is now clear to us, Paul's modern interpreters, at 3:29 — but that was probably apparent to Paul's original Galatian auditors from at least 2:16.

This data is the strongest confirmation yet that Paul's πίστις language in any debate with the Teacher is underpinned ultimately and primarily by his citation of Habakkuk 2:4. Most importantly, however, it is now clear that this critical text is for Paul also a *messianic* text that speaks of Christ achieving resurrection and eschatological life through the cross. He deploys this text to affirm his own account of the centrality of the Christ event in soteriological and eschatological terms, and also to contradict any system, putatively justified by Scripture, that nevertheless locates the achievement of eschatological life in relation to something else, like law observance (whether this is alternative or merely additional to Christ). These judgments apply particularly to any use of the phrase ἐκ πίστεως, the closely allied phrase διὰ πίστεως (which might then also use a resumptive article in context, so διὰ τῆς πίστεως or some such), and any singular instances of πίστις in the immediate context — just the data that we find in Galatians 3:22-26, and in fact throughout Galatians. These phrases all echo Habakkuk 2:4, which was cited in 3:11. And these critical conclusions confirm the suspicions that have been building since 2:15 — although with some confidence in relation to 2:20 there. Paul's repeated allusions to the Christ event through the language of πίστις that was apparent in 2:20 in the broader setting of 2:15-21 (and applying there especially to the double instance of ἐκ πίστεως in 2:16), in 3:2 and 5, and in 3:6-14, where the hints from 3:11-12 seemed especially indicative, are now confirmed by 3:22-26 in the broader setting of 3:15-29. And this set of insights shifts the entire argument of the letter decisively in an apocalyptic direction. In all these texts Paul is speaking of the coming of Christ, the faithful one. This is the decisive event from God that has redefined salvation, and the one it is so perilous to ignore.

With these dramatic realizations, we should note one final implication before turning to consider the last decisive passage in the letter, namely, 5:5-6.

6.5. The Meaning of the Metaphor of the Law as a "Pedagogue" (Gal. 3:24, 25)

A last point of potential recrimination is still available to Justification advocates in Galatians 3 — the famous metaphor operative here, already noted briefly, that views the law's function as a pedagogue. That is, although the motif "works of law" drops from sight after 3:10-12, Justification advocates have often appealed to the motif of "pedagogue" that Paul deploys twice in 3:24-25 in support of the presence of their theory in Paul's argument in its later stages.[131]

If it is framed by Justification theory, then this metaphor can speak of its central concerns quite directly. Operating in the first phase of that theory's salvific progression (where prospective converts are struggling to fulfill the demands of the initial salvific contract of perfect law observance), such a metaphor seems to describe precisely how such converts ought to learn from their transgressions in the light of the law about their sinfulness and their probable future destiny, and so be ready to grasp the offer of salvation by faith (if it should be made to them) — the *usus legis didacticus*. So the law does indeed seem to function at this point like a pedagogue in the ancient world — that is, a guardian and tutor who prepares the child for adulthood, if in a rather confined and at times even harsh and unpleasant way. The ultimate intentions of this pedagogue are good, even if his manner is occasionally rough.[132] But there are two principal difficulties with this assertion by Justification advocates on the basis of Galatians 3:24-25, a text that otherwise seems to fulfill their theoretical concerns so neatly. First, this is not how Paul uses the motif in his argument; it operates there — as I will demonstrate momentarily — in an explicitly *retrospective,* not *prospective,* manner. Moreover, it is addressed overtly in context *only to Israel,* and *not* to pagans in general. In view of these problems, then, any deployment of the metaphor by Justification advocates in terms of their own prospective, generic concerns is contradicted by the text and therefore illegitimate; it constitutes another instance of textual overdetermination in relation to that theory from Galatians 3 (i.e., as one more textual motif that supports that text's broadly retrospective, not prospective construal).[133]

We have already marked how the immediate context codes Paul's deployment of the motif of παιδαγωγός in a negative direction, supplying particular connotations of an unpleasant confinement.[134] Paul speaks in v. 22 of everything being "locked up together" by the Scripture (συνέκλεισεν ἡ γραφὴ τὰ πάντα ὑπὸ ἁμαρτίαν), and twice in v. 23 of being "imprisoned."[135] He then introduces the motif of pedagogue with the statement, ὥστε ὁ νόμος παιδαγωγὸς ἡμῶν γέγονεν εἰς Χριστὸν ἵνα ἐκ πίστεως δικαιωθῶμεν. (Given the expression of purpose and/or result by the final clause in this statement, a construal of ὥστε in independent rather than dependent terms seems marginally better, although a coordinate construction seems possible as well; however, not much turns on this.) Here, the imprisonment effected by ἡ γραφή (vv. 22-23) clearly facilitates the function of the law as a pedagogue (v. 24a), until the disclosure of Christ, who liberates those so constrained (Christ being "the faithful one" spoken of here, it should be recalled). Paul then goes on essentially to repeat this statement in v. 25, asserting — arguably, a little obviously — that "after the faithful one has come, we are no longer under the pedagogue" (see ἐλθούσης δὲ τῆς πίστεως οὐκέτι ὑπὸ παιδαγωγόν ἐσμεν). And from this point the apostle speaks in the rest of the chapter of the sonship of those who are in Christ, and who have thereby been transformed, but who also exist in some continuity with Abraham. As a result, these "sons" can anticipate the fulfillment of the dramatic eschatological promises made originally to the patriarch. Hence, in this setting, the negative coding of the motif of pedagogue seems clear. It operates alongside metaphors of confinement and imprisonment, and it contrasts with a state of full sonship and inheritance (i.e., adulthood).[136] But arguably, its retrospective function is equally explicit.

It is important to recall that Paul locates his auditors in the time *after* the pedagogue, in Christ, the faithful one — indeed, in the time established by that faithful one's arrival (and he goes on to emphasize this location strongly in context; see esp. 3:26, 28, and 29). He is writing to converts. Moreover, the time of the law and its function as a pedagogue is referenced unavoidably to the time *after* the giving of the law through Moses, "four hundred thirty years after" the promises were spoken to Abraham (see 3:17, 19, 21), but *until* the coming of "the seed" and the πίστις, "who is Christ." And this is of course the time prior to that of Paul's present auditors, whoever they might be specifically. So his argument here must be functioning backward to suggest, "why go back to unpleasant infancy?" and not, "why not go forward from unpleasant infancy to adulthood?" Thus, Paul states in v. 25 that "*after* the faithful one has come" — and it does not even matter for this argument whether such faith is construed christologically or anthropocentrically — "we are *no longer* under the pedagogue."

Reinforcing this basic but significant insight is the correlative realization that Paul locates this awkward confinement in explicit relation to Israel and her existence under the law between the time of Moses and the time of Christ, as we have just seen. Hence, this is the period of time and the constituency in which the law functions as a pedagogue — a time that is now over, Paul emphasizes, because Christ has come. So the metaphor of the pedagogue functions here as part of a broader salvation-historical argument oriented by a new historical vantage point in Christ. *Jewish* Christians should not sensibly choose to return to Jewish life under the law (i.e., in a way ultimately exclusive of Christ), because this would be to choose infancy over the present experience of adulthood.

That Paul is arguing in this fashion seems to be corroborated by his virtual repetition of the same argumentative dynamic in 4:1-10, 4:7-9 making his retrospective purview most explicit. In this subsection he speaks first of a son and heir, who is, Paul suggests, little different from a slave in his supervision by "stewards and managers" until the prior determination of his father comes into effect. Paul then universalizes the metaphor, saying, "so also we, when we were children, were enslaved under the principles of the cosmos" (v. 3). But God, at the appointed time, sends his Son to liberate those so enslaved, who are both "from women" *and* "from law," effecting sonship and inheritance over against their slavery and confinement. And it is at this point that Paul's retrospective argument becomes quite explicit.

He states first, ὥστε οὐκέτι εἶ δοῦλος ἀλλὰ υἱός, and this claim again locates his auditors in a generic sonship, in Christ, that lies beyond the slavery just spoken of. Then — after a brief remark about the Galatians' prior pagan location in servitude to "those that are by nature not gods" — he goes on to say, νῦν δὲ γνόντες θεόν . . . πῶς ἐπιστρέφετε πάλιν ἐπὶ τὰ ἀσθενῆ καὶ πτωχὰ στοιχεῖα, adding, οἷς πάλιν ἄνωθεν δουλεύειν θέλετε (that is, ". . . whom, once more, *again* you wish to serve [as slaves]?!"). The incredulous question is asked no fewer than three times, "Do you want to go back?!" And I suggest that Paul's statements here are a useful confirmation of his central argumentative strategy since at least 3:19 that has been unfolding in primarily retrospective terms.

The Galatian Christians have been liberated by their incorporation into the Christ event, which inaugurates a new, free, and mature reality. Hence, *any* prior location — Jewish or Greek — is an immature confinement now by way of comparison. Paul's point in sketching all this out — somewhat repetitively — is consequently to make the anguished claim, "Given where you are now, in Christ, free and adult, *why go back to servitude, constraint, and infancy?!*" (And as he develops it here, the argument applies to both Jews and pagans — and hence, perhaps, its repetitions.) He is therefore speaking to those who are presently Christians, exhorting them not to lapse back into their non-Christian, enslaved condition; he is *not* writing to *non*-Christians exhorting them — somewhat self-contradictorily — to move forward and leave their servitude behind.

As a result, these later statements seem to confirm strongly the function of the metaphor of the pedagogue as it was earlier described. It operates within Paul's accumulating depiction of the negative state into which he is urging the Galatian Christians not to fall back — a condition of imprisonment or confinement, (unpleasant) discipline, minority, and servitude. Furthermore, in this broader setting, it has such a negative meaning only viewed retrospectively from the free, adult position that the Galatians and Paul now occupy (Paul perhaps more firmly than the Galatians); it therefore possesses *relative,* not *absolute,* negativity. That is, the entire basis of the argument is a relative one premised upon the positive nature of the present Christian state — one of sonship, inheritance, promise, the Spirit, and so on — *in the light of which* any prior existence in the cosmos is coded negatively, with corresponding metaphors of confinement and immaturity. It follows, however, that this prior state cannot necessarily be perceived in these negative terms until the later, more positive state has been entered; *this negativity is visible only in retrospect.* And although reasons could be suggested for this necessarily being the case, it suffices to observe that Paul's arguments here offer no explicit opening for the opposite viewpoint, namely, that this prior state *ought* to be experienced negatively prior to entering into the Christian condition. Paul says nothing about that here; his argument offers no support for such a claim.

Perhaps in marginal reinforcement of this point, it can be recalled that the metaphor of the pedagogue is applied specifically in context only to those Jews in Israel who have lived "under law" until the coming of Christ. In the light of his arrival, they now ought to look back on the law as a pedagogue in their prior history, who guided and constrained them until Christ brought full adulthood, autonomy, and inheritance. "After he has come" — and presumably *only* after — "are we no longer under the pedagogue" (see 3:25). Moreover, this realization is possible only for those Jewish Christians who are contemplating some displacement of the centrality of Christ within their Christian life in favor of some central role for the law (i.e., presumably the Teachers). That would be, in Paul's view (to update the metaphor a little), like wanting to return from a modern, academic teaching career to study in middle school — a fundamentally laughable prospect. This is not to deny the appropriateness of law observance — on analogy here to middle school — in its proper place, but to reframe its significance. (Paul is of course happy for Jewish Christians to observe the law, provided that this is not, in effect, compulsory either for them or for pagan converts; it is an activity framed by freedom; see esp. 1 Cor. 9:19-22.)

Thus, we can see that even the metaphor of the law functioning as a pedagogue, which has so frequently been deployed to support Justification theory — and then to reinforce a construal of the argument of Galatians 3 in those terms — is, properly understood, a problem for that theory rather than a solution. It participates in an explicitly retrospective argument — and a powerful one — that more resembles the alternative soteriology sketched out in part one, chapter three on the basis of Romans 5–8 than Justification theory. Moreover, it is contextualized historically and specifically only in relation to pre-Christian Israel. Carefully read in context, it is just one more overdetermination that embarrasses rather than confirms the paradigm of Justification. And with these clarifications, we are free to turn and consider the compact but significant summary statements that occur later on in the letter, in 5:5-6.

§7. Galatians 5:5-6

Hung-Sik Choi notes fairly that "Pauline scholars have either overlooked or undervalued the importance of Gal 5:5-6 for the debate [on] the meaning of πίστις Χριστοῦ."[137] His 2005 study seems — somewhat surprisingly — to be the first attempt to argue in detail for a thoroughgoing christological interpretation of the two instances of πίστις that occur in Galatians 5:5-6. While I will not reproduce his arguments here exactly, his contribution has shaped my own views of this text in certain helpful ways. I concur with Choi that 5:6 seems to have more evidence relevant to our current question; hence, I will treat it first in what follows, not second. And there are, I would suggest, two clusters of interrelated contentions that incline interpretation of this verse toward a christological construal of Paul's πίστις terms, and to a more rhetorical and apocalyptic reading of this statement as a whole.

(1) The Capacity and Synonymity of Existence "in Christ/πίστις" with Love

Paul states in 5:6, ἐν γὰρ Χριστῷ ['Ιησοῦ] οὔτε περιτομή τι ἰσχύει οὔτε ἀκροβυστία ἀλλὰ πίστις δι' ἀγάπης ἐνεργουμένη. As Choi and many other commentators have noted, the language of power is prominent here, being contributed largely by the verbs ἰσχύω and ἐνεργέω (the latter being present of course in participial form). But what is less often noted is the way this language problematizes the interpretation of the statement in terms of Justification theory, inclining it, rather, toward an emphasis on Christ.

It is likely in the first instance that the participle ἐνεργουμένη is in the middle voice. It is usually translated as an active. But such expedients should no longer be necessary, that is, the overriding of the text's explicit grammar. This participle should be interpreted initially as a middle or a passive if that is possible (or a case must be made for a deponent reading, which looks very improbable in terms of the verb's wider usage and the context), and I incline toward the middle reading.[138]

Paul seems to be using it to describe faithful Christians in Christ here, in parallel to 5:5, and as the initial phrase ἐν Χριστῷ suggests. He is contrasting their activity, which is effective (ἐνεργουμένη), with the powerlessness and lack of effect of any location in terms of *either* "circumcision" or "uncircumcision" (τι ἰσχύει οὔτε). A passive reading of the participle locates the effective activity of "faith" in *its* production by love — "faith *being* effected by love." Those characterized by faith are not actually effecting anything themselves, in this reading, in a positive contrast to the ineffective binary opposition that Paul has just dismissed. And this looks unlikely if not incoherent. A middle construal, however, allows the faith in question to be active in relation to itself — putting itself into effect — here of course by means of "love." Hence, a middle reading makes sense initially of what Paul seems to be intimating — that the Christian state "in Christ" is superior in its effectiveness to either "the circumcised" or "the uncircumcised." And it is at this point that we reach the first interpretative rub in relation to Justification theory — in fact, a series of interrelated difficulties.

Faith does not "put itself into effect" through love in Justification theory. It has no need to do so, and neither can it. That is, it makes no sense to suggest, in terms of that theory, that the state of faith is a more effective *ethical* state, in the sense of being more "powerful" than either circumcision or uncircumcision. Justification theory is not initially concerned with ethical capacity per se, and it ultimately makes little contribution to the Christian's capacity, as we have already seen at some length; it is ethically anemic. The decision of faith merely escapes the *consequences* of the ethical incapacity of the individual that flow from God's just recompense, so that considerations like those just adduced by Paul — which state is "stronger" or "more effective" — are otiose. This is to discuss the wrong question. (And a genuine passive reading makes even less sense; faith is not effected by love, but by desperation, as attempted justification by works fails!) Justification itself cannot, then, account for Paul's unavoidably ethical use of language here — in terms of capacity and generation, here most specifically of love. Hence, we seem to be facing another awkward textual overdetermination. Adding to this discomfort, however, is the observation that Paul also seems to equate the state of being "in Christ" *with* "faith" in 5:6.

Faith, for Justification advocates, is the condition by which converts are saved. It integrates very awkwardly with any notion of being "in Christ," because it does not include — and even resists — any sense that the Christian's ontology is changed by conversion. Thus, it is often difficult to make sense of a juxtaposition of the two notions. But in 5:6 they seem to refer to the same situation; they are *synonymous* (that is, if the phrase is to be understood as a metaphorical locative modifying πίστις adjectivally, as seems likely[139]). Justification theory simply cannot account for this, as a result of which the text yields a second overdetermination. A participatory or apocalyptic construal, however, makes perfect sense of this provocative claim and Paul's emphasis in context on ethical capacity in the sense of faith's causality in relation to love.

For anyone rooted in Christ, the preeminently faithful one, a new state *has* been inaugurated that *ought* to issue out of that locus characterized by fidelity in terms primarily of love. Such "faith," which is really to say "Christ," should put itself into effect "through love," just as Christ's act of fidelity in relation to the cross was a supreme expression of his love for humanity (see Gal. 2:20). Faith and love are closely linked in the apocalyptic construal of the Christ event, and so any participation in Christ by Christians subsequently ought to result in a similar intertwining of those two virtues (see also 5:22). Moreover, if this really is God's solution to the sinful bondage of humanity, it ought to be more effective than any location in terms of either Jew or Greek, or, more pointedly, in terms of either Judaism's or paganism's antidotes to Sin. Indeed, Paul is confident of this. So the capacity *and* synonymity of existence in πίστις (that is, with love), as those are implied by 5:6, point ineluctably toward an underlying christological rationale for the all-important πίστις expression that is used there. But there is more yet to be said in this relation — the second of our basic contentions.

(2) The Argumentative Pattern of Antitheses

The antithetical arrangement of the argument in 5:6 is problematic for Justification advocates in several respects. On the one hand, all the evidence in context points to an overtly christological construal of the πίστις clause (that is, in terms of some new ontological location facilitated by and centered in Christ). On the other hand, it does not fit the expectations of Justification theory.

Paul, it should be recalled, negates the relevance of one antithesis in 5:6 in the interests of another, broader and more fundamental one. He pronounces neither the circumcised state nor the uncircumcised state to be "capable of something" (τι ἰσχύει); rather, only "(are we capable) in Christ Jesus . . . faith putting itself into effect through love" (ἐν [γὰρ] Χριστῷ ['Ιησοῦ] . . . πίστις δι' ἀγάπης ἐνεργουμένη). The underlying pattern of antitheses is therefore "*neither* A *nor* B *but C.*" And A and B effectively become one term in another antithesis — the term transcended — so that Paul is essentially arguing in two stages: "A + B = D" and "not D but C." (Alternatively, if the first equation here has already been made, he can skip stage one and simply state stage two.) Indeed, this is a pronounced feature of the argumentation throughout Galatians.

Choi points to 5:2-4 and 5:11 in context. In those texts Paul opposes circumcision and law observance to Christ and grace (5:2-4), and circumcision to the cross (5:11). But Choi also points quite rightly to 6:11-14, where flesh, circumcision, the law, and the cosmos are all opposed to the cross.[140] To these we should add the even more overt instances of 3:28 (and 26 in context) and 6:15, where the distinctive pattern of 5:6 is recapitulated exactly — an initial antithesis (or series of such) is pronounced irrelevant, both such terms (or sets of terms) being abolished by a broader antithesis.[141] So in 6:15 Paul states, in a close linguistic, as well as thematic and argumentative, parallel to 5:6: οὔτε γὰρ περιτομή τί ἐστιν οὔτε ἀκροβυστία ἀλλὰ καινὴ κτίσις. Choi's argument — strengthened by this additional evidence — is that *everywhere else in Galatians the opposing, positive term is Christ, and not something human* (whether in terms of human faith or anything else); it is this second christological term, and this reality, that transcends and partly abolishes the opposing terms, which might include many other traditionally significant oppositions, but in the light of this new juxtaposition of realities no longer do so. Hence, 5:6 ought to be interpreted in this way as well, as indeed its initial phrase suggests, namely, ἐν Χριστῷ ['Ιησοῦ] — that is, unless good evidence is provided to the contrary. But no such evidence is yet apparent. Consequently πίστις ought to be referred here to Christ, as it functions in the superior term of the antithesis.

This useful argument from both the immediate and the broader settings of Paul's statement in 5:6 may be marginally reinforced by the observation that Justification theory struggles to make sense of this fundamental argumentative pattern in any case. The antithetical abolitions that we have just been noting clearly function retrospectively. In the light of the new reality found in Christ, previously significant distinctions seem to have been relativized. And this retrospective exhortation is the basis for much of what Paul argues through Galatians, and understandably so; he is trying to forestall a return to law observance by his pagan converts in Galatia, which in his view would effectively reinstate the significance of these distinctions while falsifying the principal one created by Christ. Hence, it is worth noting as well that Justification theory would not arrange these antitheses in this fashion, or negate them in this way (i.e., it does not argue eschatologically).

The distinction between Jew and pagan is not simply irrelevant (although it is problematic for the theory, as we saw in part one, chapter two, especially where two different laws had to be spoken of). Justification advocates are concerned that everyone, Jew and pagan, attempts to be justified through law observance. So there is a sense in which every pagan must become a diluted Jew, although Justification advocates might not put things this way; they might simply define "authentic paganism" in terms of Judaism. More importantly, this initial antithesis is revealed to be futile, and *then* Christ comes, along with faith, as its solution. So the initial antithesis is not overruled but taken with the utmost seriousness. It then implodes on itself, thereby creating a situation that the second, saving state addresses. Yet, understood in this way, it still remains in effect.

In short, Justification advocates cannot simply eliminate the first phase in their theory, or the entire structure collapses. That theory needs Paul to say, "the pagan acts like a Jew, and the Jew realizes that Judaism *itself* is futile, so s/he *then* needs to be justified by faith." And the actual argumentative pattern of antitheses that Paul deploys in 5:6 — echoing in this text a multiple pattern throughout the immediate context and the letter — is in tension with these expectations. In 5:6 Paul simply overrules an antithesis of equal partners in the name of a superior Christian state, and a Justification reading cannot really account for this pattern, and so the text constitutes a further textual overdetermination for it.[142]

I view these two distinguishable clusters of contentions as fairly decisive (although perhaps the first more so than the second). Even though 5:6 is a brief text, then, it embarrasses Justification in several respects. But all these embarrassments are avoided if 5:6 is rendered in christocentric terms. An apocalyptic construal of Paul's basic posture makes perfect sense of the antithetical patterns that we have just noted. The inauguration of a new eschatological reality by Christ's resurrection, his death having terminated everything that was evil or in-adequate in the old age, is just what it expects Paul to say. Moreover, this state-ment nicely conveys the sense in which Christians access that new reality by in-dwelling Christ's own journey. So an apocalyptic construal of 5:6 suggests that the fidelity of Christ's passion, indwelled by the Christian, does indeed transcend the old distinction between Jew and pagan (at least, in certain critical respects). In addition, it affects the basic capacities of any such participants; they are now "ef-fective," and Christ's story figures forth in their lives in terms of love (or it ought to). So "faith," in the sense of Christ's fidelity, which stretches out to include his entire trajectory of self-sacrifice, ought to simultaneously be recognizable in love toward others emanating from those who indwell him, as Galatians 5:13b-14 and 6:2 later suggest. Indeed, interpreted in these terms, "faith" and "love" are closely synonymous, and Galatians 2:20 says as much.

It remains, then, only to draw 5:5 into this developing interpretative trajec-tory: ἡμεῖς γὰρ πνεύματι ἐκ πίστεως ἐλπίδα δικαιοσύνης ἀπεκδεχόμεθα. Although I know of no decisive arguments in the text of 5:5 that establish a christocentric construal, it must be interpreted in close relation to what precedes and what fol-lows, and so its reference to πίστις is now coded christocentrically by the more decisive considerations evident in 5:6. And this conforms to the christocentrism of 5:1-4. Moreover, all of this accords with the hint delivered by the phrase ἐκ πίστεως, which echoes Habakkuk 2:4, quoted in 3:11, and has since been coded overtly in christological terms by the argument especially of 3:22-26 in the broader setting of 3:15-29 (although here probably only making clear for modern readers what Paul's original Galatian auditors already knew). Paul's exhortation in 5:5 is inclusive, but it remains christologically grounded; "we by the spirit and 'through fidelity' await the hope of [God's] deliverance." That is, the exhortation to wait faithfully is here linked to the work of the Spirit, and so — characteristically for Paul — also to Christ. And Paul is subtly signaling in this charge that those who so wait are participating in a faithful journey that has already taken place and resulted in a resurrection and heavenly glorification (hence the importance of the Spirit, who effects participation and reconstitution in that new personal reality). Consequently, 5:5 is not merely an exhortation to the Galatians to have faith and hope in terms of their own pious resources; rather, it reminds them to live in the unshakeable and irresistible faith and hope *that Christ has already established for them* — a much stronger suggestion. The Galatians' faith is resourced from elsewhere, and its end, in the glories of life at the eschaton, is already certain, as long as they do not forcefully abandon this location.

In closing our discussion of this brief but dramatic text, it will perhaps be helpful to indicate how this developing apocalyptic sense integrates Paul's argument with a debate with the Teachers.

As we have already seen at length in Romans, eschatological and ethical issues are prominent in Paul's clash with the Teacher and his followers, both of these missionaries having comprehensive but very different accounts of how these loci ought to fit together. I suggest that 5:5 and 5:6 respond to the Teacher's positions with pithy rejoinders in terms of Paul's countervailing system, 5:5 speaking to the eschatological issue that was raised by 5:4, and 5:6 following up that rejoinder with a further counterstatement concerning the related ethical question.

It should be recalled that the Teacher probably intimidates his prospective converts at times with a "turn or burn" scenario that is generated ethically but oriented ultimately in eschatological terms. Those who do not do good deeds will eventually face the ire of God, being sentenced at a great assize to death. And they will also then doubtless experience intense and indelible shame. Those who have circumcised the passions, however, and tutored and disciplined themselves with the law, will produce the requisite good deeds, be judged righteous, and enter into life and glory on that day — even legitimately boasting of their achievements, and perhaps even reviling those who have rightfully been humiliated! So there seem to be good reasons for embracing the alternative of circumcision and law observance, at the encouragement of the Teacher and his colleagues.

Paul, however, holds this entire construction to be flawed on numerous levels. It is incoherent and insufficiently Christian, to name only two major difficulties. And in 5:5-6 he supplies some pithy rejoinders to this system, after his main substantive efforts in Galatians have finished. Here he continues to appeal to his Galatian converts in an essentially personal phase of argument, just prior to directing his attention toward the Teacher in direct and fairly aggressive terms. Galatians 5:5 then supplements more positively his negative remarks of 5:2-4.

In those prefatory verses, Paul suggests that any acceptance of the Teacher's system of law observance entails a loss of the reality found in Christ. The entire law must be kept (the troublesome perfectionist feature of Paul's discussion that we have now explained in terms of the Teacher's rather optimistic ethical perfection-ism). But in Paul's view, those who are to be "declared righteous through the law" have fallen away from the offer available in Christ, which is a gracious one. And I suggest that this reference to the eschatological judgment, by way of the verb δικαιοῦσθε in 5:4 (which seems to reflect the Teacher's system at this point more than Paul's), now prompts Paul's remark in 5:5. Having raised the question of es-chatological judgment and hence security, he asserts that his converts who remain in Christ simply await God's deliverance in hope and fidelity, completely assured of that event as the Spirit involves them in *Christ's* fidelity. Their resurrection is therefore guaranteed, and this is Paul's main point. No judgment per se will take place (i.e., no forensic-retributive verdict) — only God's forensic-liberative action of deliverance (which has, moreover, already begun). His converts do not need to "work" (that is, in insecurity and anxiety) but only to "wait." However, the Teacher's converts remain in a position of fundamental insecurity, and especially if God does indeed judge them finally in the terms that they expect.[143]

But, in addition, Paul is convinced that the sinful passions presently at large in the flesh cannot be dealt with by the law, and so any such converts to law ob-servance will fail to reach the necessary standards for salvation in any case — a double bind. However, Paul is confident that his alternative system *does* mediate an effective solution to sinful passions, as they are crucified with Christ, from which point the ethical qualities of Christ are evident. And this is his basic point in 5:6, which follows immediately. The Teacher's reliance on circumcision to pro-vide ethical capacity is misguided; no essential ethical difference is evident be-tween the circumcised and the uncircumcised. Both these categories of people are largely powerless to act correctly because they remain slaves of the powers of Sin and Death; both categories sin, and both die. However, for those located in Christ, the virtues of Christ himself can figure forth effectively — here fidelity, followed by the closely related love — a set of concerns that Paul will address in Galatians in more detail shortly, beginning in 5:13 (see Rom. 5:12–8:8, 12–13).

In short, the Teachers' system receives a pithy combined rejoinder in Galatians 5:5-6. Against their suggestions, only Paul's gospel provides real escha-tological security, in Christ and the Spirit — so 5:5 — and real ethical efficacy, from the same sources — so 5:6. And it seems that an apocalyptic understanding of Paul's statements here, mediated by a christocentric construal of his πίστις ter-minology, consequently facilitates a broader rhetorical reading in context that fits the letter's developing arguments like a hand in a glove.

With these realizations, only two further clauses in Galatians require our attention — in 1:23 and 6:10.

§8. Galatians 1:23 and 6:10

The relevant issues in these two verses can be settled reasonably quickly. In both 1:23 and 6:10 Paul uses πίστις constructions in a way that has generally consternated his conventional interpreters — that is, where the difficulties have been recognized. But alternative approaches have no such difficulties at these points, and certain subtle indicators are arguably present in 6:10 that point toward the cogency of an apocalyptic approach to that claim.

In 1:23 and its immediate setting Paul is relating to the Galatians how he was unknown in appearance to the Judean Christians (v. 22), but they nevertheless heard that he, their former persecutor, was now preaching what he had previously been destroying (v. 23), as a result of which they glorified God because of him (v. 24). However, in relaying this information Paul characterizes it uniquely, writing that εὐαγγελίζεται τὴν πίστιν. Later interpreters have often had little difficulty translating this much as the NRSV puts it — "proclaiming the faith" — since this usage accords with so much later Christian practice. As we have already seen — especially in part two, chapter nine — the term "the faith" has become very common throughout Christendom (and especially in certain circles) as a characterization of Christianity. But serious problems are implicit in this decision in historical-critical terms.

Such a reading presupposes that early Christianity in Paul's day had already developed to the point that a relatively fixed body of doctrine had emerged with a fundamentally creedal form, to which the name could then be supplied — by way of transfer — "the faith" in the sense of "that which we Christians believe." Christians located within a creedal tradition can certainly suggest that they believe in the things that ought to be believed, and so designate Christianity as "the faith." However, such creedal formation postdates Paul by a considerable margin. And while hints concerning such a formulation can arguably be detected in other parts of the New Testament, these all postdate Paul as well, and possibly by quite some time. Meanwhile, there is no overt evidence from elsewhere in Paul *himself* that he *ever* placed a πιστ- term in the position of object in this way, let alone used this meaning, allowing such a reading here. For him, belief — or something similar — is an activity by Christians or Christ or even God directed principally toward God or the gospel or perhaps to a wayward Israel or humanity. (Occasionally, Paul positions Christ unambiguously as an object here as well.) "Faith" in this sense operates only in relation to the subject, as an activity. To put matters plainly, Paul never to my knowledge speaks of believing in belief (or of something similar) — πιστεύομεν εἰς τὴν πίστιν. And, indeed, where he is most likely to have done so, in 1 Corinthians 15:1-11, he betrays no consciousness of such linguistic possibilities. Conversely, he speaks repeatedly and emphatically of "proclaiming" or "the gospel" (i.e., εὐαγγελίζω or εὐαγγέλιον), *the content of which is invariably either God or Jesus Christ*[144] (and here we link hands with our earlier discussion of 3:2 and 5).[145]

In view of these absences, it is difficult to know what grounds exist for interpreting 1:23 confidently in such terms. This seems a blatant anachronism. Not only is it assumed that Paul can speak of Christianity or the gospel as "the faith" when there is no evidence for this, but it privileges one of the main issues that is later disputed through the subsequent interpretation of the rest of Galatians by assuming that Paul's gospel *should* be characterized centrally by such "faith" — namely, the need to have faith in order to be saved, which is the central concern of Justification theory but not other approaches to Paul's gospel and theology. When we do not yet know whether Paul's gospel should be interpreted with respect to Justification theory at all, it seems unwise largely to assume that he characterizes it as such, in terms of Justification's central principle, in 1:23. And it seems equally unlikely that he is proclaiming the importance of "believing." But in view of our later construal of πίστις in Galatians, there are no obvious difficulties with a construal of 1:23 in christological terms: "he preaches the faithful one, whom then he was destroying. . . ." If the Galatians were already aware of Paul's messianic proof texts, as seems likely, then this usage poses no difficulties in terms of recognition, and it seems fair to include Paul's persecution of Jesus himself (as Acts suggests in 9:4-5//22:7-8//26:14-15) within his persecution of the church (see 1:13; note also that the ἐκκλησία cannot be spoken of as the content of Paul's gospel, or as τὴν πίστιν). Indeed, there seem to be few reasonable alternatives to such a reading, which itself seems unexceptionable.[146]

The interpretation of 6:10 seems even more decisive. As the letter closes, Paul exhorts his auditors — in what may well be his final dictated remark, before he takes up the pen himself in v. 11 — to "do good to everyone, as the opportunity presents itself . . ." μάλιστα δὲ πρὸς τοὺς οἰκείους τῆς πίστεως.[147] Interpreters have tended to translate this πίστις phrase with the same unsound assumption that underlies the usual approach to 1:23, supposing that Paul can speak of "the faith," objectifying either the act of belief or its content into a description of the heart of the gospel, as a result of which he speaks here of "the family of faith" (or some such; why the NRSV adopts a singular "family" here is unclear). But such a translation is as flawed here as it was in 1:23.

As we turn to consider a better reading, *a singular object seems necessary,* because Paul has provided *a genitive,* not an adjectival construction in the plural. (Perhaps this could be an adjectival genitive, but in that case we might expect agreement, although this may not necessarily be the case given the apparent general preference in Koiné for the singular of πίστις.) However, a christological construal again makes perfect sense: ". . . as we have the opportunity, work the good to everyone, but especially to the households belonging to the faithful one (i.e., Christ)" — a reading that now aligns with the previous twenty-one instances of πίστις in the letter.[148]

Perhaps in marginal support of this suggestion we should note that when Paul uses the cognate signifier οἶκος elsewhere (7x; for the rarer οἰκεῖος see only here in Gal. 6:10, and the disputed Eph. 2:19), he almost invariably qualifies it immediately in terms of its owner — the understandable exception being 1 Corinthians 11:34 — usually using a genitive construction to convey this information (see also *Rom. 16:5;* 1 Cor. 1:16; 11:34; 14:35; *16:19; Phlm. 2;* see also *Col. 4:15* [the genitive constructions are italicized]; and the use of οἰκεῖος in Eph. 2:19 conforms to this pattern as well). Indeed, it seems possible that Paul is participating in a widely recognized ancient discourse of familial and household relations at this point and therefore *ought* to characterize these householders in terms of their primary figure and consequent ground of mutual relationship — here, most naturally, Christ.[149] So the christological reading seems a reasonable one, and even the only plausible one.

In sum, what evidence is apparent in relation to Paul's πίστις statements in Galatians 1:23 and 6:10 seems to suggest that not only do these texts *not* constitute overtly difficult statements for our developing apocalyptic reading of Paul's Justification material, but they seem marginally to confirm it, since a christological construal is plausible in the first instance and likely in the second.

It can now be seen that Galatians itself seems to offer nothing to gainsay and much to affirm my developing rhetorical and apocalyptic rereading of Paul's Justification material.[150] We leave the evidence of this letter, then, with increased confidence in the cogency of that entire approach, while its conventional detractors leave with still more textual difficulties to resolve. And with these judgments in place,[151] we can turn to the sole letter that remains in the Pauline corpus with an overt subsection of Justification material that has not yet been discussed in detail — Philippians, and its brief but important Justification claims in 3:6 and 9.

CHAPTER TWENTY-ONE

Rereading the Heartland — Philippians and Beyond

§1. Preamble

We continue in this final chapter to assess the feasibility of my suggested reread-ing of Paul's Justification texts in more rhetorical and ultimately apocalyptic terms. These "ancillary" or supporting texts are, however, getting ever shorter. We must consider Philippians 3:1-11 first, then still briefer texts from Paul's other un-disputed authentic letters (viz., 1 Cor. 1:30 and 2 Cor. 5:21; 2 Cor. 4:13 in context; 1 Thess. 1:9b-10; and then the motifs of "belief in Christ" and "the wrath of God" drawn from several of these). We will cast a few glances in the direction of the disputed letters in passing, since some of that evidence is indicative, but any de-tailed consideration of that material is best left for another day.[1] Our attention here will focus on texts in Philippians, 1 and 2 Corinthians, and 1 Thessalonians. We will of course consider both those texts that seem to support my rereading and those often cited as problematic for it (whether directly or because they are held to attest overtly to Justification theory).

The key question is usually Paul's use of πίστις — whether this denotes the condition whereby individuals are saved, which would imply the existence of an underlying prospective soteriology like Justification theory, or whether it denotes Christ's passion metonymically and can thereby be read in participatory terms that unfold in turn into an unconditional, apocalyptic account of his gospel. Other important motifs will of course be considered where they arise — for ex-ample, δικαιοσύνη θεοῦ in 2 Corinthians 5:21 — but my rereading's feasibility tends to stand or fall in the main in relation to the meaning of "faith," so close readings of that data will dominate what follows. If we understand the causality and epistemological location of "faith" in Paul correctly, then most of the other is-sues seem to fall into place.

§2. Philippians 3

Philippians 3 contains several instances of δικαιοσύνη in vv. 6 and 9 (v. 9 has two explicit and one possible further elided instance), two of πίστις (both in v. 9), and a certain amount of biographical material (esp. in vv. 5-7), within which perhaps we can include the "evil workers" of v. 2. So, at first glance, Philippians 3 may well seem to contain one of the most important affirmations of Justification theory in the Pauline corpus, despite the brevity of its actual claims in and around vv. 6 and 9. Finally, a text seems to tie Paul's biography and his gospel together.

But closer examination suggests that this text's support for the Justification paradigm is deceptive. That theory turns out to be significantly underdetermined by Paul's statements here, if not contradicted by them at several points. Indeed, we could hardly ask for a crisper statement from Paul than Philippians 3 of just the concerns that I am suggesting actually characterized his arguments in this relation — a vibrant, participatory, and apocalyptic understanding of the Christ event, deployed in an overt antithesis to the claims of the Teacher (i.e., rhetorically), and in an explicitly retrospective fashion. This text is really the jewel in the revisionist crown.[2]

2.1. Preliminary Issues

Again, most matters of provenance will not be relevant. We are concerned at this point only with the light that Philippians 3 sheds on Justification theory over against my suggested rereading. Hence, whether this material is functioning within a more broadly integrated letter or is a product of a later editorial decision alters little in relation to these questions. In terms of the more traditional questions of provenance, I am not in fact persuaded that the letter is a composite, although this is not the place to argue that case in detail.[3] Philippians almost certainly follows Galatians in the broader sequence of Paul's letters, although its placement vis-à-vis Romans is debated, as is its distance in time from Galatians. Unfortunately, the letter's claims are too brief to discover evidence of decisive development in thematic terms, although the evidence is fairly clear that Paul's eschatological views have shifted to his "late" position, with the expectation that those who die go directly to be with Christ (see Phil. 1:20-23), rather than falling asleep and waiting until his return to be resurrected (see 1 Cor. 15:51; 1 Thess. 4:15-16). However, this observation does not help us resolve the question of possible editorial conflation, since most scholars place Philippians either contemporaneously to 2 Corinthians (or at least part of it) or some time after it.

A conventional explanation of the letter's provenance would place it rather later than Romans — in fact, in a Roman imprisonment.[4] However, again, I am not convinced by this theory, holding that certain quite practical considerations stand against it. An imprisonment in Caesarea is an even more unlikely location. The evidence of the letter itself suggests Paul's imprisonment in a provincial capital reasonably close to Philippi (see 1:13; 4:22), or even in a de facto capital, where the governor retained an official residence (i.e., Ephesus). But again, this does not really matter for our present purposes. The important point is the incontestable one — that Philippians 3, especially vv. 1-11, addresses opposition to Paul that he views as threatening the Philippian community. So he responds to this perceived threat, possibly not for the first time (see v. 1),[5] with one of the most aggressive and revealing passages extant from his writings, and this allows a fundamentally rhetorical and ultimately apocalyptic exegesis. Somewhat curiously, apocalyptic concerns do not seem to be especially well represented in the literature — curious because this text seems finally to read so decisively in their favor.

2.2. Substantive Points of Interest

Six sets of contentions apparent within the outburst of Philippians 3:1-11 and its immediate developments in vv. 12-21 are worth noting carefully.

(1) The Opponents' Identification

The opponents are clearly Jewish, and almost certainly characterize themselves as Christian as well, although Paul would probably not extend that courtesy to them. Thus, they are similar to if not identical with the group Paul describes earlier in the letter, who preach Christ but in so doing cause difficulties for his imprisonment. There seems to be deep mutual hostility between Paul and these figures — hostility extending as far as abuse, if not judicially assisted homicide (see 1:14-15, 17)! In 3:2 he calls them τοὺς κύνας, τοὺς κακοὺς ἐργάτας, and τὴν κατατομήν. He then counterposes to these three negative descriptors claims of "circumcision," "spiritual worship," and "glorying in Christ Jesus as against having confidence in the flesh." It is clear that Paul views these opponents as involved with a false doctrine of circumcision, to which he opposes his own, true version, and as insufficiently christological and pneumatological, relying instead on the "flesh." Moreover, in this setting it seems possible that Paul has reversed onto their heads a common Jewish description of pagans as "dogs" (see Matt. 7:6; 15:26-28; 2 Pet. 2:22; Rev. 22:15; see also 1 Sam. 17:43; 24:14; 2 Sam. 9:8; 16:9; 2 Kings 8:13), so these opponents may well be talking to and about "pagan dogs," presumably including Paul's converts from paganism at Philippi.[6] And in view of these indications, it is hard not to detect an emphasis on "works" in their teaching as well, since Paul accuses them of "evil works."[7] In short, it seems that we have here a group of Jewish Christians advocating circumcision and good works informed by the law to pagans, who without these retain their traditional status as dogs (presumably "without God and without hope in the world"; see Eph. 2:12). Like Romans and Galatians, then, Philippians 3 seems to address the Teachers, viewing them as a real threat and allowing us to approach this text rhetorically.[8]

However, as if this evidence were not enough, it is worth noting that Paul's *later* description of these figures, in vv. 17-19, also aligns with this hypothesis (and this speaks in favor of the unity of Philippians 3). As we have seen already in part four, chapter thirteen, when discussing the provenance of Romans, this later polemical material echoes Paul's characterizations of certain dangerous figures in Romans 16:17-20 — figures enslaved to their appetites and hostile to his gospel (which is spoken of in Philippians 3 as the cross). So a triangle of evidence is completed at this point: the opponents in Romans seem to be the same as those in view in Philippians 3, even as the opponents in both these letters seem similar to the opponents in Galatians. The Teachers are once again in view.

(2) Paul's Irreproachable Jewish Piety

Apparently cued by his reference to "the flesh" in v. 4a, Paul goes on to supply a short biographical résumé intended to exceed the "fleshly" qualifications of his opponents. Εἴ τις δοκεῖ ἄλλος πεποιθέναι ἐν σαρκί, ἐγὼ μᾶλλον, he states confidently in v. 4b. He then lists an impressive set of activities: his perfect Jewish pedigree involving correct circumcision and descent, extending apparently to an Aramaic-speaking upbringing; his learning, evidenced by his Pharisaism; and his zeal, demonstrated by his attacks on the early Christians. These qualifications culminate in a claim of being "blameless" in his righteous activity informed by the law (κατὰ δικαιοσύνην τὴν ἐν νόμῳ γενόμενος ἄμεμπτος). We have already discussed this claim at some length in part one, chapter five, so here it suffices to recall that this is probably not an assertion of complete mental perfection but one of flawless "external" performance, if we may be permitted to use that inadequate metaphor. Nevertheless, Paul is still making an impressive claim. Certainly, no guilt or neurosis is evident in such a comment, although a consciousness of sin may not for that reason necessarily be absent. From the point of view of any outsiders, however, Paul seems to view his piety as irreproachable, which is the relevant implication. (And Dunn is quite right to suggest that Paul's account of his pre-Christian Judaism at this point seems close to if not identical with "covenantal nomism."[9]) Then, in v. 7, he effects a stunning argumentative reversal.

(3) The Reversal

In vv. 7-8 Paul states and elaborates with extraordinary passion and clarity that his viewpoint is now completely changed "because of (the knowledge of) the Christ."[10] This "superior knowledge" has led to a complete reversal of his previous estimations — of all that was "gain" into "loss."[11] All that was previously considered good, praiseworthy, and even outstanding, is now "loss" if not "filth" or even "excrement" in comparison with "being found in Christ" and "gaining" him. Hence, Paul's retrospective move here could not be clearer: ἅτινα ἦν μοι κέρδη, ταῦτα ἥγημαι διὰ τὸν Χριστὸν ζημίαν. Nor could this reversal be stronger, reducing his previous privileges to σκύβαλα, that is, to something odious and filthy that evokes pollution, dissmell, and disgust, good only to be disposed of as garbage.[12]

And this explicit inversion now generates two complementary sets of implications for our broader questions. On the one hand, this account causes serious difficulties for Justification theory, and in a number of ways. On the other hand, it confirms exactly the christological, pneumatological, and participatory reading that I have been urging (since chapter thirteen) is the correct way to interpret Paul's Justification passages, and (since chapter five) to interpret his biography. We will concentrate for the moment here on the difficulties raised for Justification theory, turning to consider the positive contributions of this material to an apocalyptic reading under the next heading.

As was noted at the outset of our analysis of Philippians, this short passage seems to offer the initial promise to Justification advocates of an integration of biography with the appropriate theological terminologies and structure, only to snatch that away. And this is the point at which all sorts of problems start to become apparent for that theory.

We can begin by noting that the biography is too optimistic. Paul is entirely positive about his pre-Christian life as a Jew here. His privileges and activities are all things that he gloried in, and could glory in still if he were continuing to be oriented by the flesh. Indeed, they are only now to be evaluated negatively, after his encounter with Christ. And this is not an appropriate characterization of the journey through law observance to despair that Justification both expects and needs. (One wonders whether it is possible to be judged unrighteous on the day of Judgment with no "external" transgressions at all.)

Moreover, Paul details here a number of privileges that could not actually be "worked for" or earned as Justification theory dictates — notably, his Jewish descent, specifically from the tribe of Benjamin, and his possible descent from Aramaic speakers as well. These are not potentially meritorious actions, because they lie outside an agent's direct control. So his picture of Judaism does not accord with the schema of "works" and their attempted performance. It is actually more collective and ethnic than this — "*something given* him with his birth. . . ."[13]

One of these works is also difficult to reconcile with the expectations of Justification theory in the vestibule, namely, his persecution of the early church, concerning which Paul boasts that it demonstrates his zeal. This "work" seems to be included in part because of its ironic implications and its capacity to be reversed; it was of course implicitly — and completely — misguided. So it sets up Paul's narrative turn, both here and in Galatians, to Christ. However, this particular demonstration of zeal can only with difficulty be viewed as a good work prescribed by the law on the journey to despair.[14] Do Justification advocates seriously expect those experiencing the dictates of the law prior to conversion to persecute the church, as they attempt to observe it?!

We should grasp now that the specific depiction of the law in Paul's life by this material is very difficult to reconcile with Justification theory — see especially v. 6b. At no point is it coordinated with "works" — the all-important criterion in Justification theory's account of the pre-Christian situation, by which everyone will supposedly be judged, if only in principle. Indeed, works are mentioned — if at all — merely as an abusive characterization of Paul's opponents (v. 2), which deepens this difficulty, locating that practice with their probable gospel and not in the universal description of Judaism that Paul himself is (ostensibly) supplying here. Complementing this critical soteriological lacuna, Paul proclaims that his righteous activity under the law was "blameless" (v. 6b). Moreover, his entire argument informs the straightforward accuracy of this judgment. He has just claimed that whatever the essentially historical claims to privilege and competence of his Jewish Christian opposition, he can exceed them (v. 4), and so we expect the characterization of his law observance to conform to this argumentative objective. And it does. It is Pharisaic in its learning and rigor, and essentially unfaultable. There are no openings in the text for a negative coding of this experience as Justification theory demands — in terms of the loop of despair — or even for suspicions of this nature. The stated argumentative objective of the text in fact pushes interpretation in the opposite direction. In a competition of competences, Paul introduces his law observance as one of his greatest achievements — as demonstrably superior to everyone else's. So he is clearly not learning the right things about law observance at this point, according to Justification theory.[15]

In view of these emphases in the text, the addition of key elements from Justification theory by advocates of that reading of Paul is evidence merely of that discourse's paradigmatic dimension and inappropriate resulting pressures (i.e., of theoretical overdeterminations). So O'Brien asserts that Paul's δικαιοσύνη is "nothing other than self-righteousness," that is, "his moral achievement, gained by obeying the law . . . and intended to establish a claim upon God" (*Philippians*, 395, 94). He then quotes Bruce's even more astonishing remark with approval that Paul "had attained full marks in competing for legal *righteousness*. . . . [And] what good had [it] . . . done him after all?"[16] So Sanders is wrong, O'Brien asserts: "the expression ἐμὴν δικαιοσύνην τὴν ἐκ νόμου *is* about 'attitudinal self-righteousness' . . . [and] individual performance" (395-96, emphasis added). Gundry too argues that this text incorporates "an autobiographical as well as a dispensational shift."[17] And Williams speaks of δικαιοσύνη ἐκ νόμου as "self-attained righteousness," intermingling this with talk of "achievement."[18]

It need hardly be said that these statements are all additions to what Paul actually says, and, moreover, they tend to *override* what he says — that what was previously *gain* for him is now loss in comparison with Christ, and *only* therefore in comparison with Christ. The word ἄμεμπτος (see v. 6) alone speaks of Paul's basic mental posture in the pre-Christian situation, and while it is too brief to offer definitive insights, it is incompatible with all the judgments just offered by various modern interpreters in relation to that period in Paul's life.

Adding to these gathering tensions, we should note that Paul's account of Judaism and his transition to Christ does not end where it ought to according to Justification advocates, namely, with his conversion, an experience that ought to be linked, moreover, with the language of faith. Although faith terminology does appear in the subsection shortly, in v. 9, it does not appear at the relevant point, namely, the transition between Judaism and Christianity, *which takes place from v. 7 onward.* Furthermore, Paul does not characterize that transition as he ought to, as a set of realizations and a conversion. Indeed, *there is no mention of his actual conversion at all.* He simply shifts *perspectives* to his present location "in Christ." In other words, the preceding biographical material is not functioning as a description of a journey *to* Christ; it is a more straightforward juxtaposition of pre-Christian Jewish life with his present life as a Jewish Christian in Christ, and this is not the basic contrast that characterizes Justification theory. But we turn now to perhaps the most important point.

Paul is quite explicit from v. 7 onward that he is supplying an account of Judaism that is written from two perspectives. The first perspective is located within pre-Christian Judaism, where he regards his privileges and activities as something to be proud of (v. 4a) and a gain (v. 7). In any competition with other Jews, he even feels confident enough to claim that he exceeds the quality of their pedigrees. However, his second perspective is located in (the) Christ, and from this vantage point he looks back on his previous "gains" and counts them as "loss" if not "filth." He states quite explicitly that the superiority of the knowledge of Christ leads to this retrospective devaluation of his former Jewish privileges. In relation to this new situation, they are of no account, if not odious. And this shift in perspectives, along with its explicit reevaluation of Judaism, contradicts the structure and progression of Justification theory at its most basic level.

Justification theory, as we know well by now, expects its converts to experience Judaism *first,* to undergo a *negative* experience there (i.e., in *absolute* terms), and to progress *from* that negative experience *to* the relief of salvation by faith, at which point the convert's opinion of Judaism cannot change but must remain constant (because conversion in terms of faith alone builds on that account directly). And Paul's discussion in Philippians 3:2-8 could hardly be more difficult to reconcile with this. Philippians 3 betrays *no negative prior* experience of Judaism, but quite the opposite; it is positive! Moreover, *no* progression from conclusions reached there to Christianity is apparent, but again the opposite; the convert looks back from the new vantage point of being in Christ and so *reevaluates* the positive prior experience there now in (relatively) negative terms! The two accounts are therefore *diametrically opposed at every major point* (viz. — to enumerate these critical contrasts in series — a prior experience of Judaism as positive versus negative; no progression versus a progression; and a retrospective change in valuation versus a prior constant valuation: "gain//Christ → loss" versus "loss → Christ").

In sum, considered in biographical terms, Philippians 3:2-8 is a tissue of overdeterminations in relation to the explanations of Justification — a constant and overt contradiction. From an apocalyptic perspective, however, it is exactly what we expect. We should turn, then, to consider the participatory tenor of the passage in more detail.

(4) Apocalyptic Correlates

An "apocalyptic" approach to Paul emphasizes the revelatory and hence unconditional nature of his soteriology. In contrast to Justification, it consequently
works backward, not forward. Converts are, in effect, shifted into the new,
Christian state in an event of grace — the apocalyptic moment of revelation —
and so look back on the problems from which they have been rescued, reaching
new definitions of them. A more objective understanding is now possible with
the mind freed from the deceptions and constraints of Sin. So it is gratifying to
find Philippians 3:2-8 confirming these expectations, generated originally by
Romans 5–8 (as we saw in part one, chapter three), in precise terms. This point
need not be labored because it is already apparent in much that has been said in
relation to the biographical difficulties of Justification theory with this text. Suffice it to say that Philippians 3:2-8 affirms explicitly and repeatedly that Paul's
epistemological stance is retrospective, being grounded in the Christ event,
which he indwells in an ongoing fashion. From this vantage point he looks back
on his Jewish past and reevaluates it. So what was previously advantageous and a
possible ground for self-congratulation (i.e., in a positive sense) is now considered nothing, if not contemptible (although these judgments are also strictly relative and comparative, not absolute[19]). And this retrospective perspective, accompanied by its characteristic shift in evaluation of the past — from
advantageous to relatively negative — accords precisely with the broader explanatory framework derived from Romans 5–8. In contrast to the numerous difficulties of Justification theory then, an alternative, apocalyptic reading of Paul
encounters only smooth confirmations in biographical terms from Philippians
3:2-8. But this passage supplies more than just biographical affirmations for our
developing, alternative approach.

It is important to recall that the alternative soteriological theory found in
Romans 5–8 and elsewhere is not merely an epistemological construct, important
though that aspect of it is. Implicit in any gracious shift to a new location in
Christ, along with its revolutionized understanding of both the past and the present, is a set of *ontological correlates* — of changes in being. This change is, first of
all, a change of the mind, and a concrete one (hence the change in understanding). And such changes can be effected only by an act of God. So implicit in any
reconstitution of the person's mind in Christ is the work of God, which is almost
certainly effected by the Spirit, who is characteristically at work in an act of creation, although that unfolds here of course in principal relation to Christ. Hence,
any "apocalyptic" account of Paul's argumentation — that is, presupposing that
an apocalyptic understanding underlies his own soteriological position within
the broader contingent argument — will almost certainly have pneumatological
and participatory correlates, in addition to distinctive epistemological shifts. And
these, as we have just seen, should also be unconditional and retrospective. And
again, this is exactly what we find in Philippians 3. (In fact, such correlates extend
well beyond the Justification texts that we are currently exploring, through the

rest of that letter, but it will not be necessary to introduce all this available evidence; Paul's participatory emphases in the immediate context will suffice.)

Paul's affirmation of his Christian location "in Christ" is sustained right through this brief passage, but his first signal of the all-important divine actors who effect this relocation is one of his most important, because it encompasses the pneumatological dimension. In v. 3, while reviling his opponents — that is, the Teachers — he claims that he and his Christian converts are those "who worship by means of the Spirit of God, thereby glorying in Christ Jesus" (οἱ πνεύματι θεοῦ[20] λατρεύοντες καὶ καυχώμενοι ἐν Χριστῷ Ἰησοῦ), a state that is opposed to life in "the flesh," the flesh functioning here as a programmatic designation of being that is rooted in the old creation and so outmoded (see Rom. 3:20; Gal. 2:16c). Consequently, it can be seen that at the outset of his brief polemic Paul reaches for a critical ontological distinction that underlies his entire argument; his vantage point is in Christ mediated by the Spirit, while his opponents' location is fleshly.

Paul then speaks — as we have already seen — of the centrality of this new location in epistemological terms. In vv. 7 and 8 he refers three times to what he now thinks of as his past privileges and achievements, counting previous gains loss "for the sake of (the superiority of the knowledge of) the Christ." Then, at the end of v. 8, he grounds his most shocking reevaluative statement in a desire for deeper participation; because he so wishes to "gain" Christ and "be found in him" (v. 9), he considers everything else "filth"; . . . ἡγοῦμαι σκύβαλα ἵνα Χριστὸν κερδήσω [9]καὶ εὑρεθῶ ἐν αὐτῷ κ.τ.λ. It is precisely his desire for this state that leads to his outrageous devaluations of everything else, including his outstanding Jewish pedigree.

Justification terminology — which we will consider in more detail momentarily — then occurs in v. 9, but syntactically it is difficult to avoid the implication that the cryptic expression of being found in Christ (along with what intervenes) is further interpreted by the arthrous genitive infinitive construction that begins in vv. 10-11 and seems either purposive or epexegetical. (Fortunately, little turns on a decision at this point.) The pronoun referring to Christ in v. 10 — τοῦ γνῶναι αὐτόν — seems to echo deliberately the programmatic participatory statement at the beginning of v. 9 — εὑρεθῶ ἐν αὐτῷ.[21] The intervening material is oriented in its own terms by a participial construction. And the nominative participle συμμορφιζόμενος in v. 10b then reaches back in grammatical terms to modify the subject of the verb εὑρεθῶ. It seems here then that Paul introduces a fundamentally explanatory statement — τοῦ γνῶναι αὐτόν — and articulates it in a fairly complex fashion with a double antithesis.[22] This opposition is arranged, to a degree, chiastically, and expresses the two main aspects experienced in Christ, death and resurrection — also, as Tannehill observes, encompassing the dialectic of realization versus fulfillment that often characterizes such participatory material.[23] It is a carefully constructed statement:[24]

καὶ εὑρεθῶ ἐν αὐτῷ . . .
τοῦ γνῶναι αὐτόν

καὶ τὴν δύναμιν τῆς ἀναστάσεως αὐτοῦ
   καὶ [τὴν] κοινωνίαν [τῶν] παθημάτων αὐτοῦ,
   ¹¹συμμορφιζόμενος τῷ θανάτῳ αὐτοῦ,
εἴ πως καταντήσω εἰς τὴν ἐξανάστασιν τὴν ἐκ νεκρῶν.

It seems that to know Christ's death is also to attain at some point knowledge of his resurrected life. And this is the great "prize" (see 3:14) in relation to which Paul counts all other things as loss if not repugnant. Moreover, it is worth emphasizing that the apostle's account of life in Christ oscillates constantly throughout this argument as it develops (i.e., in 3:12-21) between present realization and future fulfillment, and between divine and human agency. Paul emphasizes strongly in what follows the human agent's striving for this goal (thereby also denoting its future aspect), in one of his most concentrated deployments of ἀγών material — imagery that emphasizes human agency emphatically. But he also qualifies this account in v. 12b with an assertion of God's agency within the contest as well (and in a way that disrupts his deployment of the athletic imagery) — διώκω δὲ εἰ καὶ καταλάβω, ἐφ' ᾧ καὶ κατελήμφθην ὑπὸ Χριστοῦ (and see 1:3-6; 2:12-13). He takes pains to point to its present partial realization (see esp. 3:3, 8, 16). Most important for our present purposes, however, is the powerful statement of participation in vv. 10-11.

To be in Christ is to be "conformed" to his death, and therefore "participating in his sufferings," which guarantees a conforming to his glorious resurrection body as well (see 3:21). These resonant claims and promises, made in double measure for emphasis, conclude the very sentence in which the majority of the Justification terms occurring in Philippians 3 are embedded. It is impossible, then, to prise these discourses apart and try to interpret these terms in isolation from the surrounding argument — a context that is, as we have already seen, thick with participatory claims and images. And, in the light of all this, just how should those key terms now be interpreted? It is precisely here where earlier analyses have either failed to apply the implications from the setting or have explicitly overridden them.

(5) The "Righteous Act" of God

As was noted earlier, Paul contrasts two instances of δικαιοσύνη in Philippians 3:9 in an antithesis, expanding the second, positive instance — which is "from God" and not "his" (literally "mine") — with two instances of πίστις. The first, negative instance of δικαιοσύνη is correlated, rather, with νόμος:

⁹καὶ εὑρεθῶ ἐν αὐτῷ
μὴ ἔχων ἐμὴν δικαιοσύνην τὴν ἐκ νόμου
ἀλλὰ τὴν διὰ πίστεως Χριστοῦ,
τὴν ἐκ θεοῦ δικαιοσύνην ἐπὶ τῇ πίστει,
¹⁰τοῦ γνῶναι αὐτὸν κ.τ.λ.

It needs to be appreciated first that there is nothing standing in the way of a thoroughly apocalyptic construal of these statements. It is fair to suggest that Paul is stating here that he desires to be "found in Christ," not possessing any righteous activity generated by a life lived in the flesh in relation to the Jewish law — and so "from law," and irreducibly human in origin and orientation, and therefore also "his." Paul's reevaluation of such activity has been a significant part of his previous argument in vv. 5-8. In the light of Christ, he has absolutely no desire to return to it. He desperately desires, rather, to have the righteous act of God, which comes "from" God and is effected "on the basis of the faithful one [i.e., Christ]" — ". . . that I might be found in him, not having my righteous activity that is by means of law, but that which is by means of the faithful Christ — the righteous act that comes from God on the basis of that faithful one — ¹⁰knowing him . . ." (DC).²⁵ And by this "righteous act" Paul is speaking essentially of the *life-giving* act of God made available in Christ, and so, in other words, of the resurrection and of subsequent life in glory — *of the very experiences that he goes on to point toward in the rest of the sentence in vv. 10-11,* as well as in vv. 12-21. It is of course not an anthropocentric conception of salvation at all but a gift of God in a radical sense, and hence the contrast that Paul is presently generating.

Such a reading is by now quite familiar to us, and it links up with similar statements made by Justification texts in other Pauline letters — perhaps especially with Christ as the righteous act from God in Romans 10:3, and with the faithful one's mediation of resurrection and life through his loving self-sacrifice and death spoken of by Galatians 2:20.²⁶ But it is also easy to misunderstand Paul's argument at this point, and especially if categories from Justification theory are applied carelessly.

Here in Philippians, Paul is addressing his converts from paganism more directly than he often is in his other Justification arguments, where extensive interaction with the Teachers' system tends to take place as well. In those other locations, his pagan converts often overhear a debate between Paul and the Teacher, doubtless in part to gain familiarity with it and ultimately to judge it. But that phase is probably past in relation to the Philippians (see 3:1b: τὰ αὐτὰ γράφειν . . . ἐμοί . . .). Here in 3:2-11 Paul is briefly reiterating the main issues to them directly in order to "safeguard" them further (see 3:1). Thus, he exhorts the Philippians themselves to continue to run a race toward a glorious goal — the transformation of their bodies and inheritance of a glorious heavenly citizenship. They ought to ignore those running another, foolish race (whose goal is actually destruction) and leave any such entanglements and impediments behind, stretching on toward what lies ahead (and doubtless this also includes abandoning any intracongregational conflicts; see 2:2-5; 4:2). Moreover, in so doing *they are emulating Paul himself,* who has done just this.

Although outstanding in his Jewish credentials — hence winning that particular race — Paul himself is now oriented by another goal, a far higher one, namely, Christ himself. In the light of *this* goal, he has abandoned everything else as "loss" if not "filth." And this includes any law observance that he might have undertaken in his previous life in the flesh, when he was perhaps running another race. In the light of this new race, any such activities, good in and of themselves originally, are mere impediments to be cast off. Moreover, in running this new race — and somewhat paradoxically — Paul is operating in terms of a life that has come from God, as against a life that is lived out in a primarily human (and hence currently enslaved) realm. In striving to take hold of Christ, then, Paul is being taken hold of by God (see v. 12b). Hence, with these modifications of his central image, Paul betrays the theological ground of his extended metaphor's legitimacy. This new race is actually a new reality inaugurated by God through the Christ event. To ignore it and try to run another race is therefore to turn one's back on the intervention of God, and to try to live a life grounded in the frailties and enslavements of created but fallen human capacity — a foolish life to try to lead, and to encourage others to lead (see Rom. 1:32).

It seems clear by this point that the comparison Paul has crafted here between a righteous activity informed by the law and so based on human action and a righteous act proceeding from God to anyone in Christ is congruent with the fundamentally apocalyptic construal of his thought that I have been promoting elsewhere in Paul's Justification discussions — retrospective, unconditional, life-giving or eschatological, and participatory throughout. Moreover, the context strongly supports this reading. Phrased slightly differently, it can be suggested that this reading of v. 9 integrates exactly with its broader context, while nothing obvious stands against such a reading.[27] And — putting matters at their plainest — it can be said that the surrounding emphases on an act of God operating through Christ, over against any human activity located in and oriented by the flesh — a divine act that renders that human activity in comparative terms as the equivalent of excrement (if not *as* excrement) — incline us strongly to read the "righteous act[ivity]" and "fidelity" of v. 9 precisely *as* the act of God in Christ over against any nomistic activity of the flesh (that is, rooted in the capacities of the created and sinful human person). That act through the faithful Christ is explicated directly, in the same sentence, in participatory terms, as a sharing in his suffering and death en route to a sharing in his glorious resurrection. The entire argument is therefore smoothly continuous.[28]

It remains only to note, then, that Paul is probably punning here on the meaning of δικαιοσύνη in v. 9. When used in relation to law observance by those located in the flesh, this word denotes "righteous activity" — a meaning also apparent in v. 6. Furthermore, the Teachers seem to suggest that in the light of such activity — assuming that it is flawless — God will ultimately apportion life in the age to come. "Righteous activity" *for them* is the fulfillment of the necessary conditions for eschatological salvation. But when used by Paul in relation to life in Christ, δικαιοσύνη means something a little different in practical terms. It is still a "right action." However, it is for Paul an act of God that is focused in Christ, so it can be spoken of as both "of" and "from" God. In addition, it is singular, as the Christ event is singular — "the right[eous] *act*" of God. Moreover, it *is* the eschatological event. The "right act" of God in Christ — that is, of God the divine ruler, acting through Christ, his royal appointed representative — is to deliver his people, along with any receptive pagans, from their enslavement to hostile powers. So *God's* "righteous act" *effects* resurrection, while "righteous activity" by the law observant (ostensibly) fulfills the necessary prior conditions *for* resurrection. These specific divergences underlie Paul's use of the same signifier in 3:6 and 9. Nothing essential changes in semantic terms as a result of these realizations — a righteous act or activity is being spoken of in both instances — but the subtly divergent connotations of this signifier in context are worth noting for the sake of interpretative and theological precision. With this final clarification in place, we can turn to consider the suitability of Justification theory to Philippians 3:9.

We should first recall the critical material.

⁹καὶ εὑρεθῶ ἐν αὐτῷ
μὴ ἔχων ἐμὴν δικαιοσύνην τὴν ἐκ νόμου
ἀλλὰ τὴν διὰ πίστεως Χριστοῦ,
τὴν ἐκ Θεοῦ δικαιοσύνην ἐπὶ τῇ πίστει,
¹⁰τοῦ γνῶναι αὐτόν (κ.τ.λ.)

I suggest at this juncture that Justification advocates can supply an entirely fair construal of this verse and its terminology in terms of their own theory. Paul might be speaking here initially of an abandonment of attempted justification in relation to the law as denoted by phase one of that theory — μὴ ἔχων ἐμὴν δικαιοσύνην τὴν ἐκ νόμου — followed by an appropriation of the new righteousness available from God through or by means of faith in Christ — ἀλλὰ τὴν διὰ πίστεως Χριστοῦ. And this point is so important that Paul might well repeat it for emphasis with an appositional parenthetical clarification — τὴν ἐκ Θεοῦ δικαιοσύνην ἐπὶ τῇ πίστει (see Rom. 9:30). The evident arrival of this righteousness "from" God might then add further support to the suggestion (derived presumably from Romans 4:2-8 originally) that God imputes righteousness to believers positively, even as believers' transgressions are no longer reckoned to their account because of Christ's atonement (that is, if an essentially "substantial" sense can be maintained for δικαιοσύνη more broadly). This reading seems quite fair. But we return at this point to two familiar conundrums.

First, there is no way of deciding in immediate terms whether this reading of v. 9 or the apocalyptic one is correct. Both seem entirely possible — and they are very different! That is, we touch here again on the nagging problem for Justification advocates of interpretative ambiguity. Their readings never seem able to lay claim to a demonstrably superior construal of any Pauline data; an apocalyptic construal is always, at the least, equally plausible. But, second, as we move to consider the surrounding context of 3:9, everything begins to protest against the construal in terms of Justification and corroborates instead a reading in terms of apocalyptic concerns. That is, the construal of v. 9 offered by Justification advocates relies on notions *that the surrounding argument explicitly contradicts.*

The biographical claims implicit in the Justification construal of v. 9 are not supported by the context (i.e., the need for a negative prior experience of Judaism, and in terms of works, etc.; this is not visible in the surrounding biography); the supposed journey through the flesh informed by works of law is unsubstantiated (i.e., there is *no* direct evidence that the failure of justification through works is being spoken of here); the surrounding argumentation is heavily participatory (which always grates on Justification theory at any points of transition, but is actually *coordinated* here with the Justification terms, as an apparent description of the same state — see Gal. 5:5-6); and the entire orientation of the surrounding argument is epistemologically retrospective (i.e., not prospective). So things could hardly be worse for Justification advocates than they are here. It would seem that the Justification construal of v. 9 is sustainable only if this verse is read in complete isolation. Hence, in the light especially of the context, Philippians 3 appears to be a powerful overdetermination for Justification theorists, and on numerous counts. Conversely, the apocalyptic construal comprehends this text with ease, smoothly continuing the exact sense of the context, and it should therefore be the preferred construal.[29] It remains, then, only to note some important implications flowing from this judgment.

(6) Implications

First, it is worth emphasizing that Paul's treatment of Judaism here is nuanced, and it largely confirms the delicate strategy that we have seen operating in Romans 9–10 (see chapter nineteen), over against the potentially harsh posture created by Justification theory.

Because Paul's evaluation of his Jewish heritage is retrospective, being informed explicitly by his new location in Christ, it does not apply in independent terms to any prior occupants of Judaism (including himself, which is one of his claims in context). There is consequently no need to characterize Judaism in and of itself and apart from Christ negatively. Only with the arrival of the superior knowledge of Christ is there any need to enter into such judgments. Furthermore, these are only relatively, not absolutely, negative. *In comparison with Christ* Paul views other aspects of Judaism negatively, and not in other terms. His negative posture is therefore an entirely Christian phenomenon. Indeed, strictly speaking, such judgments are not even available to those positioned outside Christ, because they lack the knowledge that makes them possible or even apparent.[30]

Moreover, Paul's characterization of his Jewish heritage lacks any orientation in terms of "works." Nor does he describe any negative or tortured mental state. His brief characterization of law observance as a pre-Christian Jew lacks all meritocratic and negative emotional elements (apart, that is, from his persecuting zeal, which was probably an angry activity). This law observance is, furthermore, embedded in the description of various inherited ancestral qualities — circumcision, tribal descent, linguistic heritage, and so on. And perhaps most importantly, he never orients his account of Judaism toward a question of salvation, nor is his law observance so oriented (see also Gal. 1:14). So Judaism is not necessarily self-interested or even preoccupied with soteriological issues in this description, as Justification advocates tend to portray it. All of which is to observe that Paul's account of Judaism in this passage is clearly commensurate with the description that emerges from many of the extant Jewish sources contemporary to him, thereby easing if not erasing for the apocalyptic reader the empirical difficulty that Justification theory faces in this relation (see part one, chapter four). Furthermore, there is also no need to engage in negative theological or emotional descriptions of Judaism, since these are explicitly relative, christocentric judgments and not external, "empirical" evaluations. According to the apocalyptic reading of Philippians 3, non-Christian Jews are not self-evidently immoral and/or irrational and hence also justly subject to the retributive wrath of God, if not of governments.

We should now note, second, that Paul's use of δικαιοσύνη in 3:6 and 9 can set up a dangerous false equation with Romans 10:3 if that relationship is not grasped precisely. In both these texts, "two types of righteousness" are apparent, but I would suggest that they are not the *same* contrasting couplet.[31]

In Philippians 3, as we have just seen, Paul is contrasting his former righteous activity as a pre- and non-Christian Jew with a righteous act that he receives from God in Christ, characterizing the relationship between the two types of activity in terms of a retrospective reversal of valuation. Prior to Christ, he gloried in his Jewish righteousness, but in the light of the superior knowledge now found in Christ, he rejects that activity as excrement by comparison. So it would of course be foolish in his view to go back to it. *This* is the basic point that he is making for his Philippian auditors, who are possibly being exhorted to adopt the law. They ought to imitate Paul and stretch out toward what lies ahead — the resurrection of Christ — and continue to abandon those things that lie behind in the past and are good but redundant — Jewish law observance (see Gal. 4:12).

In Romans 10:3 and context, however, I suggest that the situation is subtly but significantly different. There — as we have already seen in more detail in chapter nineteen — Paul also contrasts two types of righteousness, and the positive term is once again the righteous act from God in Christ. However, the other, contrasting δικαιοσύνη is the righteous activity of Israel, who is apparently *continuing* to observe the law and thereby to undertake a certain sort of righteous activity *after Christ has already come,* hence more in the manner of the Teachers and not of the pre-Christian Paul. Indeed, the reorientation of the ἀγών discourse in Romans 9–10 makes this point nicely. Whereas in Philippians 3 Paul is urging the abandonment of what lies behind in order to run forward effectively toward what lies ahead, in Romans 9–10 Paul accuses Israel of something different; she is continuing to run on — rather ludicrously — *after the race is over.* Of course, Christ is the goal of the race in both deployments. So while one of the terms in these two righteousness couplets is being held constant — the goal of the race, who is Christ — the different positions of the other terms reflect the different contingent argumentation (although the broader situation is basically the same) and the different constituencies who are the targets of that argumentation. And it is also apparent that *three* different types of righteousness are being spoken of.

There is, first — to proceed in chronological order — the righteous activity of Jews prior to Christ, informed by the law, although Paul does not attribute "works" or a soteriological orientation to this activity. Second, there is the righteous act from God in Christ — the decisive right act that brings the preceding righteous activity to an end, much as the light of the rising sun tends to overwhelm the paler light of stars. Then, third, there is the righteous activity reflected in Romans 10 and context undertaken by certain law-observant Jews (but not necessarily limited to them), who ignore and resist the second righteous act of God in Christ and continue to undertake righteous activity after it has arrived. This third type of righteous activity — the only illegitimate form — is described by Paul as an activity of "works" oriented toward "life," and rooted in fundamentally human concerns and capacities (i.e., "the flesh"). And this is entirely consistent on his part. If God's right act that establishes life is ignored, then it follows by definition that the alternative mode being endorsed is a competing right act, oriented toward life as well (because God's way has been rejected), but rooted in human convictions and aspirations. This is the locus that Paul holds the Teachers to occupy.[32]

But this dynamic is not in play in Philippians 3 in quite the same way, because whereas in Romans 9–10 Paul is addressing the Teachers' position and situation fairly directly — not to mention Israel's — in Philippians he is exhorting his converted pagan auditors to follow his *own* example (see esp. 3:17). The result of these exhortations should still be the same — the rejection of the law observance recommended by the Teachers — but the route to that end is different. In Romans 10 the second and third types of righteousness are directly in view, and Paul is confronting advocates of the third type with accountability for their rejection of the second. That they have endorsed the third demonstrates that they have at least some responsibility for rejecting Christ (one of Paul's main problems in context). In Philippians 3, the first and second types are in view, because Paul is exhorting the Philippians to copy *his* progression, from comprehensive law observance to its radical reevaluation in the light of Christ (see 3:17), along with, if necessary, its abandonment. *If the Philippians grasp Paul's reasoning in relation to the first type of righteousness from the nature of the second, then they will not follow the Teachers into the third.* Ultimately, I would suggest that the distinction between the two righteousness couplets found in Philippians 3 and Romans 10 is as simple as the distinctions present in these different contingent arguments — distinctions that preserve some critically important theological implications, and that Paul was well aware of.

And with these final clarifications, we have completed our rapid survey of the main Justification passages in Paul, finding that an apocalyptic construal is everywhere sustainable, if not demonstrably superior to a reading in terms of Justification theory. It remains, then, only to address some final, dangling textual loose ends from other parts of the Pauline corpus, before our detailed exegetical analysis is concluded.

§3. Loose Ends

A few brief comments on Pauline texts drawn from outside Romans, Galatians, and Philippians — the letters widely acknowledged to contain Paul's principal Justification discussions — should prove helpful in closing.

3.1. 1 Corinthians 1:30 and 2 Corinthians 5:21

I argued earlier (in part four, chapter seventeen) that the internal evidence indicated — fairly unequivocally — that the phrase δικαιοσύνη Θεοῦ denoted a singular, saving, liberating, life-giving, and eschatological event, in which being is inseparable from action. Moreover, the subtle evocation of the ancient discourse of kingship, especially by way of the language of Psalm 98 (97 LXX) in Romans 1:16-17, suggested nuancing this sense further in terms of "the right act" of God, the divine monarch, on behalf of his appointed royal representative, Jesus. And this took place concretely in God's resurrection, heavenly enthronement, and glorification of Jesus as the Christ. But one further advantage of this position is now worth noting.

Instances of this phrase that occur outside Romans, Galatians, and Philippians — notably, in 1 Corinthians 1:30 and 2 Corinthians 5:21 — have already been integrated into this developing position in part, because their evidence contributed to our initial investigation of the phrase's basic sense. I want to note now, however, that these texts also integrate with the more specific, monarchical reading of this material that I subsequently suggested. Both these texts from the Corinthian correspondence occur in contexts characterized by numerous other images that either directly evoke the ancient discourse of kingship or are compatible with it.

1 Corinthians 1:30 speaks of how Christ, the Lord, has come to the Corinthians from God and therefore brought "wisdom" (σοφία) to them, along with "deliverance and cleansing and release" (δικαιοσύνη τε καὶ ἁγιασμὸς καὶ ἀπολύτρωσις; and see later especially 6:11). We have already seen from Romans 1:16-17 that Paul seems well aware of the explicit coordination of a dynamic or powerful wisdom with kingship (see also in context 1 Cor. 1:18, 24-25). But the other associations here are also standard features of ancient kingship — acts of deliverance, cultic purification, and liberation from unjust enslavement or oppression, by a people's lord. So at the least 1 Corinthians 1:30 seems compatible with this phrase's connotation of ancient kingship.

I would suggest that 2 Corinthians 5:21 is similarly resonant in context with royal themes, although drawn from different parts of the ancient discourse. In the immediate setting of this text, God, the cosmic ruler, is graciously making a diplomatic overture to an estranged cosmos to be reconciled to him (see 5:18-19). He has even gone so far as to (at least arguably) provide a scapegoat for the relevant offences himself (5:21). But he is also now extending this offer through his appointed ambassadors (although they are marked in a distinctively undignified way!; see 5:18-20, 6:4-10); they have been entrusted with this embassy — an offer that promises nothing less than a new creation (5:17). Indeed, these ambassadors make truthful speeches, are supported by God's power, and even possess weaponry, although it is metaphorical — "through the weaponry of righteous activity in the right hand and the left" (6:7, DC). So the discourse of ancient kingship, both divine and human, is plainly evident.

These observations allow the further claim that my suggested interpretation of δικαιοσύνη Θεοῦ can now be held constant through *all* its occurrences in Paul's extant writings. The only significant variation is the one already noted, namely, the emphases of given deployments either on the cause of this act, best rendered as the right act *of* God in Christ (as possibly in 2 Cor. 5:21), or on its arrival, best rendered as the right act *from* God in Christ (as in 1 Cor. 1:30). But both these emphases, which activate different grammatical possibilities in the genitive, lie within exactly the same underlying semantic field of action, here divine. This unified interpretation of the phrase δικαιοσύνη Θεοῦ through Paul seems to me to be a small advantage over more dislocated positions and so worth noting, however briefly.

We turn now to a more extended discussion of a brief but especially pregnant text.

3.2. 2 Corinthians 4:13

My interest in this text stems initially from its bearing on the πίστις Χριστοῦ debate. Second, 2 Corinthians 4:13 has not often been discussed in this relation in any detail, usually being mentioned briefly in passing, if at all,[33] by the debate's protagonists. On one level this is understandable; the ambiguous constructions in 2 Corinthians 4:13 are not πίστις Χριστοῦ genitives. But it is unfortunate, because this verse may offer clear evidence not merely of Jesus acting faithfully but of him doing so in relation to the verb. As we have already seen, it is a common complaint by opponents of "the faithfulness of Christ" motif in Paul being urged throughout this book that Christ is never the subject of πιστεύω in a Pauline text, from which observation it supposedly follows that Paul could not therefore be suggesting Christ's own faithfulness when he uses the cognate substantive in a genitive construction like διὰ πίστεως Χριστοῦ.[34] If he had intended this meaning, the objection runs, then he would have supplied us with at least one instance of Christ as the subject of the verb πιστεύω — so Χριστὸς ἐπίστευσεν or some such.[35] Hence the potential relevance of 2 Corinthians 4:13, where Christ might be, and I will argue *is*, the *directly implicit* subject of πιστεύω (and not once, but twice, also then drawing the cognate substantive explicitly into this meaning). This seems a useful conclusion to reach, if it can be established. However, before analyzing the text in detail, a caveat is necessary.

This exchange of contentions could generate some broader argumentative distortions that we must guard against. In reality, the objection by opponents of the subjective genitive reading in terms of Christ being or not being the subject of the cognate verb in Paul ought to be ignored on logical, methodological, and broader evidentiary grounds.[36] It is, in short, a bad objection. A detailed engagement with 2 Corinthians 4:13 as putative counterevidence runs the risk of affirming its cogency, when it does not really deserve such respect. However, it would presumably be an even greater shame if a dubious objection hindered the consideration of a text that can ultimately yield important insights into Paul's thinking. So we will proceed to analyze 2 Corinthians 4:13 in what follows, with this caveat in mind. And we will do so in two main phases.

First, we will consider 2 Corinthians 4:13 itself, which is a subtle and complex text. Then, second, we will turn to consider its contexts in a series of widening circles — the immediately following v. 14, which is actually part of the same sentence by way of a participial construction, then the preceding context, especially 2 Corinthians 4, then the following context, especially 2 Corinthians 5.

By the end of these various discussions an apocalyptic and participatory reading of 2 Corinthians 4:13 should be emerging into plain view — that is, a reading emphasizing Paul's identification with Christ by way of the Spirit, with Christ as the original subject of the verb πιστεύω, a conclusion with implications not only for the πίστις Χριστοῦ debate but for how we understand the activity of "faith" in Paul in general. Hence, this text will turn out to be fundamentally supportive of the broader rereading of Paul's Justification texts that I am urging through parts four and five of this book; 2 Corinthians 4:13, properly understood, aligns with the apocalyptic rereading precisely.

(1) 2 Corinthians 4:13

We begin our more detailed analysis by noting that interpreters and commentators alike have not really known what to do with 2 Corinthians 4:13.[37] Certainly, it does not play a prominent role in most explications of Paul's argument. But I suspect that this is in part because the verse operates a bit like Rubik's Cube. One senses that there is a coherent disposition in Paul's statements — a point at which all the relevant but presently muddled colors align — however, twisting and repositioning the components of his argument into that intelligible arrangement is strangely difficult. There are in fact three rather unusual subordinate elements that we must try to construe intelligibly, both in their own right and in relation to one another. We must: (i) discern the meaning of the phrase τὸ αὐτὸ πνεῦμα τῆς πίστεως [κατὰ τὸ γεγραμμένον κ.τ.λ.] — "the same spirit of faith [that is in accordance with scripture . . .]" (NRSV); (ii) account for Paul's citation of the three words from Psalm 115:1 LXX (116:10 MT & Eng.)[38] ἐπίστευσα διὸ ἐλάλησα — "I believed, and so I spoke" (NRSV);[39] and (iii) explain the underlying causal relationship between believing and speaking denoted by the inferential conjunction διό. Indeed, Paul seems to be emphasizing the notion conveyed by διό at this point in his broader argument by repeating it and applying it to himself in the plural — καὶ ἡμεῖς πιστεύομεν, διὸ καὶ λαλοῦμεν (rendered by the NRSV rather weakly as "and so"; this should really be "therefore" or "for this reason").[40] Resolving these semantic components in relation to one another is a tricky interpretative puzzle. I suggest, however, that the best way to work initially toward a coherent reading of these disparate elements is to grasp the narrative dimension that is implicit in Paul's argument.

Somewhat characteristically, Paul has not supplied the easiest argumentative sequence of claims for his auditors, having apparently reordered them away from their most obvious substantive unfolding for rhetorical effect. However, his reasoning must be as follows:

A: It is written, "I believed; therefore I spoke."
B: We have the same "spirit" of belief [for a reason as yet undisclosed].
C: Therefore, we too "believe and speak."

Paul has supplied this argument to the Corinthians in the form B-A-C; however, it works logically in this way (at least, up to a point: on this see more shortly). We might simplify the reasoning a bit further by saying:

Person I undertakes X and, for this reason, Y.
Person II has X in common with Person I.
Person II therefore undertakes X (already) and also, for this reason, Y.

It should be emphasized that Paul has stressed the inferential connection between X and Y, or believing and speaking, with a double usage of a Greek "therefore," which grounds his speaking, like the psalmist's, on a prior activity of believing, and probably causally: "I believed; *therefore* [διό] I spoke." And this claim has troubled interpreters in the past (where they have noticed it). The sequence and possible causality is, strictly speaking, invalid *unless the entire narrative of the suffering and vindicated psalmist is also in play,* because Paul claims in v. 13a only to have the same spirit of faith as the psalmist. It does not follow from this shared *fidelity* that the psalmist's ensuing *speech* should *also* figure forth necessarily in Paul's life as well; they share only their faith. Hence, Paul's shared spirit of fidelity cannot ground the "therefore" in Psalm 115:1 when it applies to his own life, unless the rest of the psalm's narrative, which links faith and speech, is somehow invoked as well. And neither can it support the plausibility of the basic sequence of "believing" and then "speaking" that he affirms. (I suspect that it is in large measure the cognitive dissonance generated — perhaps subliminally — by this difficulty that has hampered convincing interpretation of the verse in the past.)[41]

So it seems that the entire narrative of the psalm is in play in Paul's life or his argument at this point is simply invalid; his quotation is off the mark.[42] And we must now add an important unstated premise to our earlier sequence of claims.

A: It is written, "I believed; therefore I spoke."

B: We have the same "spirit" of belief [for a reason as yet undisclosed].

B': That shared "spirit" denotes a sharing of the writer's entire narrative of believing and speaking (etc.).

C: Therefore, we too "believe and speak."

When it is taken into consideration, the echo is plausible, not to mention richly informative. Psalm 115 (LXX) speaks of the vindication of a righteous sufferer (discussed in German scholarship — although usually of a previous generation — as *der leidende Gerechte*[43]).

The psalmist has maintained his faithfulness and has spoken with integrity, even though he has suffered greatly (v. 1b LXX). And he has done so in part because he knows that the death of the Lord's holy ones and servants is precious in God's sight (vv. 6-7). Therefore, the Lord has gifted him life and salvation (vv. 3, 4a, 7c), freeing him from his bondage (v. 7c), and he is now able to thank God in the presence of his people, quite evidently alive, in the courts of Jerusalem (vv. 3, 8-10). His speech in the first part of the psalm is therefore an optimistic proclamation — among other things, of the fact that "all people are liars" (v. 2)! And he speaks despite his present suffering because of the underlying confidence — hence the ongoing belief and trust — that God will ultimately vindicate him, and if necessary through and beyond death (which leads at this point to further speech). As we will see shortly, this reading makes excellent sense in context, although our principal concern at present is its cluster of implications for 2 Corinthians 4:13 itself.

It seems clear, then, that Paul is assuming a resonance between his ministry and the figure described in this psalm; *his argument requires this broader implicit narrative dimension* (and so Hays was quite right to point to it). But with this clarification, we must turn to consider the relationship that probably underpins it — a relationship that Paul characterizes as "having the same spirit of belief" (ἔχοντες δὲ τὸ αὐτὸ πνεῦμα τῆς πίστεως).[44] Why is Paul echoing the psalmist, and with "the same spirit of belief"? And what warrant does this echo bring to his present claims to the Corinthians concerning belief and speech?[45]

There are essentially only three possibilities at this point, although one can be dismissed almost immediately. Paul might be speaking in rather literal terms of some transmigration of souls, a possibility that need not be dwelled on further.[46] Alternatively, Paul might be speaking of an imitation of the psalmist's struggles and response, so that the apostle's claim to share the same spirit of belief as the psalmist is just a metaphor for the emotional resonances between that narrative and Paul's life — the sort of identification that happens every day between a reader and a figure in a gripping text. ("I shared the rage that Romeo experienced on hearing of the death of his best friend, Mercutio.")[47] Or Paul might be speaking of a still stronger, participatory identification with a prophetic anticipation in this psalm of Christ's passion.

But as we seek to decide between our two main alternatives of mimesis or participation, we must also connect them with the two main interpretative options for Paul's actual statement of similarity, just noted, which is made in pneumatic terms. Is the "shared spirit of belief" a metaphor for a shared attribute or a reference to the work of the divine Spirit? Two interpretative forks, then, lie before us. Nevertheless, it seems likely that any solutions to these two sets of alternatives align with one another, and this will surely help us. If Paul's language of "spirit" is metaphorical, then the merely imitative reading looks more plausible. But if Paul's language of "spirit" is fully pneumatological (i.e., a reference to God's Spirit), then a messianic and ultimately christological reading looks more plausible. Once it has been conceded that the Holy Spirit is identifying Paul with another person, it will be difficult to resist the further implication that this must be Christ; the Spirit is, after all, for Paul the Spirit *of* Christ![48] So complementary sets of contentions can now be brought to bear in support of the same exegetical solution — hints that suggest that this "spirit" is not a spirit of imitation but is *the* Spirit, and that this is not the language of imitation in the thin sense of mere copying but of participation. And although I do not think that a completely decisive judgment results, a strong balance of probabilities certainly seems apparent.

On the one hand, we should note that this verse is unlikely to contain a merely mimetic or imitative set of claims because: (1) this is not Paul's language of mimesis (and the usual examples cited in this relation are dubious — so Bultmann, etc.);[49] (2) Paul's conception of mimesis is arguably participatory in any case, so this "thin" reading of imitation is just not present elsewhere in Paul;[50] (3) such an identification — at this intimate biographical level with an ancient psalmist — would be unparalleled in Paul (i.e., not even Abraham is indwelled in this way by the apostle); (4) Paul does not ever claim explicitly that he is identifying fully with the life of the psalmist (this is only implicit in his argument, which we have yet to construe fully; the only explicit claim of identification concerns believing by itself); (5) this position ultimately yields quite a weak broader argument and set of claims — "I believe and speak because I identify or resonate with an Old Testament figure who believed and spoke too"; and (6) as Fee pertinently observes, the language of "spirit" is then redundant.[51] None of these difficulties is fatal to the reading, but they are all problems (and those problems are added to as we progress into the context).

On the other hand, we should note that this verse *is* likely to contain a participatory rationale because: (1) this is Paul's usual language for the work of the Spirit (i.e., the use of the signifier πνεῦμα in a suitable setting); (2) such a reading explains the implicit presence of the rest of the psalmist's narrative in Paul's life — that is, of other aspects of Christ's passion figuring forth; this would not need to be specified if the passage's rationale is participatory throughout (i.e., it could just be assumed); (3) there are numerous parallels from Paul elsewhere that suggest his intimate identification with Christ;[52] and (4) a stronger argument results from such an identification (as we will see in more detail shortly; this will also be strongly confirmed by the context).

It might be objected that it is problematic to claim that Paul is identifying with a psalm, which is identified in turn with Christ's passion. But in fact it is not. Paul does this demonstrably elsewhere on occasion, as Richard Hays has shown — particularly in Romans 15 — and this reading strategy seems to be rooted in still-earlier church practice (because it is unexplained in Paul, and attested in other New Testament texts).[53] And at this point we should appreciate that the assumption that Paul is identifying with a prophetic anticipation of Christ in Psalm 115 (LXX) generates a surprisingly satisfying reading of 2 Corinthians 4:13.

If the psalmist is a prefiguration of Christ, then the Spirit can identify Paul and his coworkers with Christ as Christ speaks prophetically through that text of his own suffering and resurrection — the additional move that commentators in the past have either overlooked or resisted.[54] And Psalm 115 (LXX) reads beautifully as a text that speaks of Christ's vindication after a period of rejection and suffering in relation to his faithful ministry. Almost every line can be construed to evoke some aspect of the passion or its consequences. Hence, if Paul is assuming an early Christian reading of this psalm with reference in the first instance to Christ himself, then it speaks of Christ's ministry, his fidelity, his suffering, his death, his subsequent resurrection, and his testimony to his community assembled in Jerusalem; in short, it fits that narrative very nicely indeed. And the same narrative can then undergird Paul's claims concerning trusting and speaking in turn in his own apostolic ministry. Because Paul participates in Christ's story, where speech in the midst of faithful suffering is eventually vindicated, he too as an apostle can speak in similar terms, despite any present shame or suffering, and with the certain expectation of eventual vindication — the set of connected points that he is basically making here to his Corinthian auditors (and these will be elaborated on momentarily when we turn to consider the context).

It seems, then, that we can explain the three distinguishable elements in v. 13 in a tidy and mutually coherent fashion; we can solve this textual Rubik's Cube. However, *only* this participatory approach — with its rich implicit Christology and vigorous pneumatology — can explain it convincingly. A more conventional approach, in largely mimetic terms, leaves us with various problems — a weak argument, a puzzling identification, linguistic gaps and redundancies, and so on — while no such difficulties are apparent in a participatory construal. But can we say more than this? In fact, another distinguishable and rather important stream of evidence converges on just this judgment — evidence from the surrounding context.

(2) The Contexts of 2 Corinthians 4:13

The implications of the surrounding context of 2 Corinthians 4:13 become apparent at several levels: immediately in v. 14; more broadly in the preceding context, in chapter 4; and more broadly again, in the material that follows vv. 13-14, in the first half of chapter 5. We will briefly discuss these widening contextual circles in turn.

(i) The Immediate Context — Verse 14 All the material in verse 14 is coordinated by way of a participle with Paul's claims in v. 13: Ἔχοντες δὲ τὸ αὐτὸ πνεῦμα τῆς πίστεως κατὰ τὸ γεγραμμένον· ἐπίστευσα, διὸ ἐλάλησα, καὶ ἡμεῖς πιστεύομεν, διὸ καὶ λαλοῦμεν, [14]εἰδότες ὅτι ὁ ἐγείρας τὸν [κύριον[55]] Ἰησοῦν καὶ ἡμᾶς σὺν[56] Ἰησοῦ ἐγερεῖ καὶ παραστήσει σὺν ὑμῖν. We must try to give *some* account of how Paul's claims in v. 14 relate to those of v. 13, since they are part of the same sentence.[57] And at this point a participatory construal seems to enjoy a significant advantage over any alternatives. It can supply an account of this entire sentence that poses no difficulties (and integrates easily with the broader context), whereas a more conventional, anthropocentric approach presupposing mere copying struggles to do so.

According to the participatory reading, Paul is supplying further information in v. 14 about the knowledge that he and his auditors are said to share in v. 13 with the psalmist, who is in a sense also speaking as Christ. All these figures believe in the midst of suffering, speak, and are eventually vindicated. Hence, this dynamic is ultimately underpinned by the paradigmatic narrative of Christ's passion, Good Friday being followed inexorably by Easter Sunday. It makes perfect sense, then, for Paul to go on to suggest in v. 14 that the knowledge in question in the case of himself and his auditors is grounded in that explicit narrative. Because Christ has spoken, and has been resurrected and glorified, those who participate in his fidelity and his speech now are guaranteed that resurrection in the future, and this should fill them with hope. The one who resurrected Christ will resurrect both Paul and his auditors (and this is of course God).[58] The participatory reading already suggested by a detailed consideration of v. 13 in isolation consequently continues directly on through v. 14, while any alternative construal clearly does not.

An imitative reading has no way of explaining the transitions from the relationship between the past and the present in v. 13 into the relationship between the present and the future in v. 14, and from an identification with an ancient psalmist in v. 13 to a communion with the risen Christ in v. 14. It also lacks any specific markers *of* imitation in this clause. Indeed, if v. 14 were separated from v. 13 — perhaps being relocated to another page by some bemused copyist — then no one would dream of interpreting it in imitative categories oriented toward the Psalter.

Consequently, v. 14 seems to offer fairly decisive evidence that the participatory construal of v. 13 is on the right track. But can our developing interpretation integrate with its broader settings in 2 Corinthians?

(ii) The Preceding Context — 4:1-15

[10]. . . πάντοτε τὴν νέκρωσιν τοῦ Ἰησοῦ ἐν τῷ σώματι ἡμῶν περιφέροντες,
ἵνα καὶ ἡ ζωὴ τοῦ Ἰησοῦ ἐν τῷ σώματι ἡμῶν φανερωθῇ.
[11]ἀεὶ γὰρ ἡμεῖς οἱ ζῶντες εἰς θάνατον παραδιδόμεθα διὰ Ἰησοῦν,
ἵνα καὶ ἡ ζωὴ τοῦ Ἰησοῦ φανερωθῇ ἐν τῇ θνητῇ σαρκὶ ἡμῶν.
[12]ὥστε ὁ θάνατος ἐν ἡμῖν ἐνεργεῖται, ἡ δὲ ζωὴ ἐν ὑμῖν.

¹³Ἔχοντες δὲ τὸ αὐτὸ πνεῦμα τῆς πίστεως κατὰ τὸ γεγραμμένον·
ἐπίστευσα, διὸ ἐλάλησα,
καὶ ἡμεῖς πιστεύομεν, διὸ καὶ λαλοῦμεν,

¹⁴εἰδότες ὅτι ὁ ἐγείρας τὸν [κύριον] Ἰησοῦν
καὶ ἡμᾶς σὺν Ἰησοῦ ἐγερεῖ καὶ παραστήσει σὺν ὑμῖν.

A quick reprise of 2 Corinthians 4 — especially vv. 10-12 — indicates that the verses leading up to v. 13 are explicitly participatory and christocentric, in emphases that smoothly continue Paul's overarching rhetorical objectives in 2 Corinthians 4 as a whole. Since v. 1 the apostle has been concerned to stress both the integrity and the glory of his apostolic ministry. He brings to the Corinthians nothing less than the glory of God that shone in creation and is now revealed more explicitly in his apostolic proclamation of the glory of Christ. However, Paul is also concerned to emphasize the concealment of this glorious ministry in "vessels of clay" (4:7). And the concealment is ostensibly designed to show that this divine power is indeed from God, and not from any human source (see 1 Cor. 2:5). The struggles that Paul faces — "afflicted," "perplexed," "persecuted," and "struck down" (see vv. 8-9) — are therefore merely evidence of this basic dynamic. Moreover, as vv. 10-11 go on to assert, these difficulties are all informed by a christological sequence — already very familiar to us — within which resurrection follows suffering and death. In addition, Paul's emphasis upon the actual life and death of Christ is signaled in this passage by his unparalleled use of the simple designation "Jesus" (v. 10 [2x], v. 11 [2x], v. 14 [(probably) 2x]), which is generally an indicator for him of a focus on — as modern scholars put it — "the historical Jesus."[59] In being given over to death, then, God's divine and resurrecting power is evident in him, as it was for Jesus himself paradigmatically, although this is something that clearly benefits the Corinthians ultimately as well. Because of this narratively shaped participation, *Paul's* sufferings are evidence of *their* eventual glorification. As v. 12 puts it — perhaps a little opaquely at first glance — ". . . death is at work *in us,* but life *in you.*" And we have just seen that v. 14 makes essentially the same point, explaining it marginally more clearly: ". . . we know that the one who raised the Lord Jesus will raise us also with Jesus, and will bring us with you into his presence."

Thus, it seems clear that the basic argument that Paul is developing from 4:1 onward, and more specifically from 4:7, continues through v. 14 (being applied to an even wider constituency in v. 15). Paul's sufferings are evidence of the fundamental dynamic of Christ being played out in his life and the lives of his communities, thereby guaranteeing at some future time the glory of resurrection.[60] Moreover, this dynamic informs his ministry — his proclamation of this glorious if temporarily hidden reality in a "vessel of clay." These are good reasons for affirming that ministry's integrity and truthfulness, as against deriding or abandoning it in favor of some presentation and apostle who is superficially more glorious and attractive but is not thereby evidencing any participation in the crucified and resurrected Lord. A period of faithful speech and witness, which seems inevitably to incur suffering if not execution, is followed nevertheless by divine vindication. And it can now be seen that a christological reading of the psalm quotation in v. 13, along with Paul's participation in that prophetic anticipation of Christ's passion, confirms this broader argument exactly. Moreover, the emphasis in context on Paul's *speech* is also now readily comprehensible.

The speaking that Paul offers by way of participation in the faithful speaking of the suffering Christ is both an affirmation that this resurrection will come and a scripturally foretold element in the initial christological dynamic of suffering. Hence, Paul is really suggesting, through the use of this particular text, that true Christian speech is faithful speech in the midst of suffering that is oriented even so toward life and hope. It is speech that therefore corresponds to an apostle whose glorious ministry is presently concealed in an earthen vessel of suffering (as against an apostle who is not so constrained but is vastly more impressive in appearance and apparent success — one of the main contingent problems that Paul faces at Corinth).

It might seem that enough has been said by now to suggest the probity of a reading of 2 Corinthians 4:13 in participatory terms, but we have one more area of evidence to consider.

(iii) The Following Context — 4:16–5:7   We have just seen that because Christ has spoken and has been resurrected and glorified, those who participate in his fidelity and his speech now are promised that resurrection in the future (see especially v. 14). The one who resurrected Christ will resurrect both Paul and his auditors (and this is of course God). And the following context in 2 Corinthians now confirms that this is not just an imitative and narrative argument. That is, such hope rests on more than the fidelity of God, who will kindly do to Christians what has already been done to Christ. Because these auditors possess the Spirit of Christ, the resurrected one — the implications of v. 13 — they share *directly* in his life. Consequently, the experiences of his fidelity, suffering, and speech are now a *guarantee* that the resurrection is coming. *Those experiences are the concrete manifestation of involvement in that same trajectory, thereby guaranteeing its end point in resurrection and glorification* (and we can see this dynamic at work in numerous other Pauline texts, once they are correctly understood). Indeed, it is at this point that we begin to grasp the participatory definition that 2 Corinthians 4:13 supplies for the whole notion of "faith" in Paul. "Faith" as suggested by this text is not an appropriation of salvation that was not previously present but a marker of salvation in those who have been appropriated by God, assuring the faithful that this salvation is already present, despite any appearances to the contrary, such as suffering. Against all appearances, it will result in glory.

This argument is already familiar to Pauline interpreters, since it is made at some length in Romans 8. But it needs to be pointed out that just the same set of contentions is recapitulated briefly — yet strongly — in the sentences that follow 4:14 in 2 Corinthians. The one working in the lives of suffering Christians (2 Cor.

5:5a), who groan (5:2, 4) awaiting their heavenly dwellings (5:1-4), is God, the one who has also given the down payment of the Spirit (5:5b). Christian life, then, is not lived in terms of what is "seen" (4:18; 5:7) but "by means of fidelity." That these various coordinated motifs, all echoing Romans 8, appear in immediate explication of 4:13-14 in 2 Corinthians seems highly significant. In the first instance, it serves to draw the fourth occurrence of πιστ- language in this textual neighborhood — in 5:7 — into the interpretation of 4:13-14, where the other three πιστ-terms in context occur. (See more on this just below.) But even more importantly, it points again to the basis of the argument that has been emerging here — in terms of a pneumatologically effected participation. This seems to be a powerful argument for present fidelity, speech, and hope in Christian leaders and their communities.

(3) Implications

With the participatory reading of 2 Corinthians 4:13-14 now strongly established, we should turn to consider a few of this reading's implications. There are four in particular.

(i) **The "Objectivist" Objection**   Although the foregoing is a complex case, it is not for that reason in my view an uncertain one. A number of contentions, drawn from several overlapping areas of evidence, suggest quite strongly that Christ is implicit in Paul's citation of Psalm 115:1 (LXX), a text the apostle is reading messianically, and hence the Messiah is the original subject of the verb πιστεύω when it is used there. It is Paul's participation, through the Spirit, in Christ, who is anticipated by this prophetic text, that grounds his actual assertions in 2 Corinthians 4:13 vis-à-vis the Corinthians. He believes and therefore speaks to them in the steadfast hope of future vindication and resurrection, appearances notwithstanding. This is an entirely intelligible and contextually integrated reading. By contrast, any alternative construal struggles to deliver basic validity and intelligibility to these statements by Paul, let alone contextual illumination. For these reasons I view 2 Corinthians 4:13 as fairly decisive evidence for — among other things — the rejection of the claim that Christ is never the subject of the verb πιστεύω in Paul. He is, and such claims should now cease. But these realizations concerning 2 Corinthians 4:13 do more than merely falsify a dubious objection within the πίστις Χριστοῦ debate; they move our broader agenda forward positively as well.

(ii) **A Participatory Purview**   This reading is intelligible only — yet also completely — when it is pursued in participatory, which is also to say apocalyptic, terms; and we can now grasp even more clearly the basic constituents of that paradigm, which is now explicitly attested in 2 Corinthians 4, in radical contradistinction to the main alternative paradigm of Justification. The participatory model of the Pauline gospel understands the person — best *not* viewed in individualistic terms — to be saved as she is grafted onto the journey of Christ, sharing both his downward trajectory through suffering and execution and his upward trajectory through resurrection and glorification. That journey must be represented linguistically in narrative terms, with major emphases on both crucifixion — a martyrological story — and resurrection — an eschatological story.[61] Moreover, the process of personal participation must be understood pneumatologically; indeed, it makes little sense without the constitutive work of the Spirit. Participation ought to be understood in this "thick" sense, and each one of these elements is either explicit or directly implicit in 2 Corinthians 4:13 and its context — a pneumatological participation in Christ, both in his martyrdom and in his eschatological resurrection and glory.[62] But where does such a discourse position the activity of "faith"?

(iii) The Function of "Faith"   It can now be seen still more clearly that "faith" is a post- rather than pre-Christian phenomenon, facilitated by participation in the faithful Christ's journey. So a Christ-Christian resonance in this activity is to be expected, not resisted; it will serve to confirm the validity of the entire process. This entails that "faith" is a marker of participation in the salvation announced by the gospel; it functions in terms not of appropriation but of assurance (and hence rather like circumcision: see Rom. 4:11-12). It is sometimes doubtless an important question to ask what marks Christians — that is, what marks them for resurrection and a share in the life of the age to come. (This question is prompted especially by any challenges from the Teacher[s].) And one scripturally attested and repeated answer in Paul is "faith" — usually meaning, more specifically, steadfast belief in God (and this in spite of suffering), and/or trust, and/or trust over time under duress, which could equally be characterized at such points as "faithfulness" or "fidelity." (There is probably no harm in characterizing these different but overlapping actions with the umbrella term "faith" at this point, provided that this is all that is being claimed.)

(iv) The Involvement of Intertextuality   "Faith" language is not especially common in 2 Corinthians as a whole, with only eleven occurrences of πιστ- terms throughout.[63] (There are also three adjectival alpha-privatives — ἄπιστος.) And this makes the sudden cluster of πιστ- signifiers in and around 4:13 all the more significant; it contains four of the total eleven instances of πιστ- terminology in 2 Corinthians (including 5:7 in that total), or just over 36 percent. And this data seems to confirm the hypothesis introduced earlier[64] that "faith" discussions in Paul are often prompted by the citation of Old Testament texts that use "faith" terms, so there is always an important intertextual relationship in play. This means that the meaning of "faith" for Paul and his use of these antecedent texts are questions that stand and fall together; any explanations of his contingent rhetorical emphases on "faith" must relate directly and plausibly to his contingent reasons for citing the relevant Scriptures as well. And it follows from this that scholars cannot simply pass directly from instances of faith language and argumentation to Paul's coherent core or gospel, as advocates of Justification tend to do. The hurdle of contingent intertextuality must first be negotiated.

In the light of all these judgments, it may be clearer to translate 2 Corinthians 4:13-14 as follows, with certain substantive ellipses supplied:

> Having the same Spirit of belief [as Christ] in accordance with what was written [that he spoke] — "I believed; therefore I spoke" — so also we believed, and therefore we also spoke [to you], knowing that the one who raised the Lord Jesus will also raise us with Jesus and will present us together with you.

So construed, this text can now be seen to provide an instance of the verb πιστεύω being used with Christ as its subject, with an application of his ongoing trust to the Christian by way of the Spirit specified in context — just the arrangement that apocalyptic readers tend to advocate (see esp. 5:5). Christian fidelity also then functions where those advocates suggest — confirming Christians in their new location until the eschaton (see 5:6-7). This text is thus an important corroboration of my rereading as a whole, and a difficulty for those who oppose it. Furthermore, it ought to be recognized more widely as an important contribution to the πίστις Χριστοῦ debate, if not a reasonably decisive one. The textual clues consistently seem to point toward this christocentric and ultimately apocalyptic reading of 2 Corinthians 4:13 being the correct one.

3.3. 1 Thessalonians 1:9b-10

We should now consider a potentially more difficult text for my project — 1 Thessalonians 1:9b-10:

> [9]... ἀπαγγέλλουσιν . . . πῶς ἐπεστρέψατε πρὸς τὸν Θεὸν ἀπὸ τῶν εἰδώλων δουλεύειν Θεῷ ζῶντι καὶ ἀληθινῷ [10]καὶ ἀναμένειν τὸν υἱὸν αὐτοῦ ἐκ τῶν οὐρανῶν, ὃν ἤγειρεν ἐκ [τῶν] νεκρῶν, Ἰησοῦν τὸν ῥυόμενον ἡμᾶς ἐκ τῆς ὀργῆς τῆς ἐρχομένης.

It is sometimes claimed by Justification advocates that this text summarizes in nuce just the reading that they suggest is writ large in Romans 1:18–3:20, thereby confirming its correctness.[65] Paul seems to recapitulate here a discourse that exhorts the abandonment of idolatry because of the wrath of God, and then patient endurance by those so persuaded (see τοῖς πιστεύουσιν in v. 7), in faith (see v. 3 and ἡ πίστις ὑμῶν ἡ πρὸς τὸν Θεὸν in v. 8), until the arrival of the resurrected Christ (here also called God's "Son"), who will effect an escape from divine judgment. But I am not convinced by this suggestion, for several reasons.

First, Paul is not directly referencing his own preaching at this point. He is recounting reports that he has received from others in Macedonia, Achaia, and beyond of how the Thessalonians *responded* to his initial arrival so positively (and he is thereby flattering those auditors). Such reports supposedly make it unnecessary for Paul to preach in such places, he suggests, in a fairly overt *captatio benevolentiae;* it is as if the key work has already been done by the piety of the Thessalonians themselves. But the crucial point to note is that this report details *the behavior of the Thessalonian Christians,* and *not the argumentative strategy of Paul's initial preaching.* As a result of his preaching, they (1) turned from idols and now (2) serve the living, true God, (3) evidence loyalty to the resurrected Jesus,[66] and (4) wait for his return, at which point they will (5) escape from divine wrath.

We should note, second, that there is nothing atypical or remarkable about this particular narrative of a Pauline community. All of Paul's communities follow roughly this trajectory after his preaching, as far as we can tell, so it seems entirely generic. Paul does not countenance the worship of idols in any of his churches; indeed, only in relation to the Corinthians are boundary issues in relation to idolatry even discussed in detail (i.e., εἰδωλόθυτον). It seems to follow, then, that Paul's teaching included a strict prohibition on idolatry; in all of his other communities this simply seems to be a given. We do not know how this prohibition was argued strategically or rhetorically, although we can guess its probable theological basis (see 1 Cor. 8:5-6). We only know that Paul taught his communities not to practice idolatry.

Similarly, all of Paul's communities are supposed to wait patiently and faithfully for Jesus to return, even as they are supposed to believe in the content of his initial preaching, along with all the other things that he subsequently teaches them — "whether in person or by letter" (see 2 Thess. 2:2). And, in the interim, they are supposed to worship the "living and true God" and "his Son" (and presumably no one else, except perhaps the divine Spirit).

Third, we have already seen (in part one, chapter three) that Paul himself is ambivalent concerning the judgment of God; different texts seem to send different signals concerning this topos. However, it is certainly fair to point on occasion to the possibility in his writings of divine wrath against sinful people. Where sin is present, Paul does seem not infrequently to expect the eventual operation of God's righteous anger against it. (And it is also worth pointing out that Paul does not explicitly coordinate God's wrath here with idolatry; that anger is something that arrives eschatologically and that the faithful Thessalonian believers now avoid through Christ's deliverance.)

Thus, it seems to me that the case made by Justification advocates rests again on ambiguity, here involving also some non sequiturs. We have already noted that the narrative briefly recounted by 1 Thessalonians 1:9-10 is by no means restricted to Romans 1:18–3:20. Certainly, it overlaps with the concerns of that text, but it overlaps with the subsequent behavior of all of Paul's communities as well. Hence, although the basic posture of this narrative and of the conventional reading of 1:18–3:20 is the same — their aniconic goals, so to speak — the tactical issues of how to achieve those goals, and how and when to argue the case against idolatry, and this in relation to the wrath of God — that is, the critical matters — *are never addressed here.* We simply do not know whether 1 Thessalonians 1:9-10 details the actual content of Paul's preaching as well as its broader results, thereby creating a parallel to the conventional construal of Romans 1:18–3:20. Nowhere does Paul give us an unequivocal statement that these things are all commensurate.

To this it could be added that the community at Thessalonica — as probably elsewhere — is not the result of Paul's preaching only, but of his other strenuous missionary work and teaching there as well (see 1 Thess. 2:7-12). To equate his initial *preaching* with the *results* of that preaching for the community's development is to make just the equation that Justification theory expects, but one that our earlier work in part one, chapter five, on the nature of conversion called radically into question. The development of an early Christian community doubtless took place in relation to a host of different factors, only one of which was the apostle's initial speech to its potential members (if, indeed, he even made one).

In addition to the foregoing ambiguities, however, we can note that — read carefully — this text contains certain embarrassments for Justification theory as well. It emphasizes the resurrected Jesus, who returns here alive to rescue the Thessalonians from the coming wrath. Moreover, he is designated as God's Son. And although these are familiar elements within Paul's teaching elsewhere, we have already seen that they are problematic in relation to Justification theory.

First, Christians do not need to be rescued from anything, in the strict sense of that term, according to Justification theory (i.e., in the sense of being delivered from aggressive forces too powerful for them). And they certainly do not need a powerful Lord to save them from a global apocalypse of God's wrath. Jesus' principal contribution to salvation has long been accomplished (and, a little strangely, that is not mentioned here). If the Thessalonians grasp the gospel by faith, then it follows that God himself will not judge them harshly at the end of the age. So the liberative connotations of salvation here are awkward for the theory; 1 Thessalonians 1:9-10 reads more like a discourse of divine rescue from anger — doubtless occasioned in part by idolatry — accomplished by a resurrected and powerful Savior, than a forensic-retributive schema revolving around culpability, law observance, and judgment. Second, there is no place in Justification theory for a strong emphasis on the resurrection of Christ. As we have earlier seen at some length, the theory struggles to assign a meaningful role to this event (see esp. part one, chapter three). However, in this brief narrative it appears to be playing a key role in the final eschatological drama of salvation — the role precisely of rescue. And, third, Justification theory cannot adequately explain the Sonship of Jesus, the title he is accorded by this narrative.

These three awkward overdeterminations for Justification theory, which have already been explored elsewhere, thus return here to embarrass that theory once again. They combine to suggest that in 1 Thessalonians 1:9-10 Paul is not in fact arguing in terms best captured by that theory; something more liberative and resurrecting is probably implied. It seems, then, that on all fronts, this countertext in favor of Justification concerns is a weak one. Its critical evidence is ambiguous, while certain features of this evidence subtly contradict its supposed attestations.

3.4. Belief in Christ

Some further clarifications of the role of "faith" in the life of the Christian can usefully be introduced at this point, although we ought first to recall an important feature of an apocalyptic approach to Paul.

This construal of Paul's gospel is still strongly committed to Christians believing certain things, as indeed Paul himself seems to be. Furthermore, the evidence for this claim is not limited to the occurrence of words using the stem πιστ-. Every sense unit that Paul composes in a letter is an attempt to modify the beliefs or *thinking* of its Christian recipients, so clearly he is deeply committed to this process, as are his later tradents (i.e., the authors of arguably pseudonymous letters in the Pauline tradition). Hence, the *existence* of belief — not to mention specifically *Christian* belief — in the life of the church is not at issue in this broader debate. The *causality* and the *location* of these acts are the critical issues being currently debated. Justification theory tends to place belief in the hands of the individual, and to locate its critical moves prior to the proclamation of the gospel. Apocalyptic advocates, however, regard these judgments as textually unsupported, theologically dangerous and incoherent, and politically sinister (at least potentially). Conversely, they place Christian thinking under the ultimate control of divine intervention, locating its critical developments *after* the Christ event (that is, after the irruption of grace into the life of Christians), the signifier "apocalyptic" really just emphasizing this epistemological stance, that is, the fundamentally "revealed" nature of Christian knowledge. From this point on, such advocates are more than happy to talk about Christian beliefs, and are in fact *necessarily committed to this process;* such reoriented beliefs are, indeed, evidence of this revelation's reality. They are markers of the arrival of the eschaton in Christ, however partially. So beliefs or thinking as such is not in dispute between Justification and apocalyptic advocates; the points of contention are their causality and epistemological location.

We should note in addition, however, that the apocalyptic reader understands the causality of Christian thinking in a participatory fashion. That is, the information revealed to Christians is not relayed to them independently of their incorporation into a broader relationship; it is one facet of their introduction into what is essentially the divine communion, much as some might know things about their spouses because they are married to them and live with them. Information is not separable from relationality. And, accordingly, the process by which Christians acquire this information reflects in a significant way their incorporation *into* Christ by the Spirit — an act of divine re-creation, in which Christ is the template for the new humanity and the new creation (see esp. Rom. 8:29). So Christians understand things as they take on the mind of Christ (which is effected through the Spirit of Christ). Hence, Paul himself can go so far as to say that any failure to possess the Spirit of Christ is not to belong to Christ (see Rom. 8:9). However, those who do have the Spirit — which is also to say whom the Spirit has — "walk according to the Spirit," no longer oppose God, and "think the things of the Spirit," among which are "life and peace" (see Rom. 8:4b, 5b, and 6b). They possess a "transformed" and "re-created understanding" (or "mind"; see Rom. 12:2) which is, of course, the mind of Christ (see 1 Cor. 2:16b). All of which is to say that the beliefs of Christians in the church ought in some sense — if an apocalyptic understanding of Paul is correct — to reflect the mind of Christ himself. This correlation is to be *expected*.

From this vantage point, we can now address two recurring criticisms of the apocalyptic reading of Paul. (And it is sobering to consider that even his later tradents arguably evidence a firm grasp of the underlying issues — in particular, the author of Ephesians.)

First, it is not a difficulty for apocalyptic readers when Paul or his tradents speak of Christian belief, whether in God or in the gospel (or even in Christ), as is evident in Ephesians 1:13 and 19 (where understanding specifically of the gospel is denoted). This is entirely to be expected. It would be problematic if an explicitly causal role was assigned to certain beliefs, salvation being granted on the condition of their fulfillment, or if that fulfillment was also placed in the hands of the individual Christian. But that is not demonstrably the case in these or any other Pauline texts, and much evidence arguably stands against it.[67] Moreover, the existence of such belief per se is neither unexpected nor especially problematic as part of the broader process of salvation; beliefs are an automatic concomitant of involvement in Christian salvation, and as such they can function as a marker of authentic Christian existence. They indicate that the mind of the Christian has begun to be transformed, and can even on occasion be used as a name for Christians (although this is not Paul's preferred designation — which is "brothers").

Second, it is entirely predictable to find Paul exhorting his Christian auditors either to continue in or even to manifest some of the key virtues of Christ himself, among which are "trustworthiness" and "loyalty," at which point we tend to move beyond the semantic realm of "belief" alone. Trustworthiness is a standard component of generally virtuous behavior, especially in relation to a patron or superior; in such settings it is tantamount to submission and obedience, which are also important Christian virtues and were demonstrated supremely by Christ's passion (see Rom. 5:19; Phil. 2:8). Christians ought then to be trustworthy, especially leaders.[68] And this situation seems to be reflected in both Paul's and later tradition's uses of the adjective, at least on occasion (see 1 Cor. 4:2, 17; 7:25; see also Gal. 3:9; see also Col. 1:7, 4:7, 9).

Furthermore, this meaning can develop into the slightly stronger, more active sense of "fidelity," or "faithfulness." A trustworthy person tends to be trusted in relation to some task or issue, the implication being that trust can be placed in that person by someone else; a faithful person, however, often endures in a relationship under duress, whether that derives from the passage of time or more extreme pressure, and there may be no specific task in view or person desiring to place trust in him or her. Such people are simply faithful in and of themselves. And just as Christ was faithful to God, and God faithful to Christ, to a dead humanity, and to Israel within that, Christians ought to be faithful to God, to Christ, and to one another. This is simply one aspect of sound, virtuous behavior — of healthy relationality, as the Christ event supposedly constitutes that. And just this usage is arguably evident throughout the Pauline corpus on occasion as well.

Of special note here is the loyalty or faithfulness toward Christ that Paul speaks of in Philemon 5 and 6.[69] First Thessalonians 1:3 is possibly also relevant at this point.[70] (Closely parallel phrases oriented toward God seem to occur elsewhere as well; see 1 Thess. 1:8.) In the disputed letters, Colossians 1:4 and 2:5[71] and Ephesians 1:15 seem similar. I certainly concede that these instances create the possibility that Paul's important πίστις Χριστοῦ genitives occurring elsewhere *could* be construed in terms of loyalty toward Christ. But I have already suggested that this is unlikely, given the relevant contextual signals in the settings of those phrases, not to mention their probable intertextual basis. Here, then, it merely needs to be emphasized that an apocalyptic reading is not troubled by the notion of loyalty toward Christ per se, as one feature of the church that the faithful Christ has constituted. The relationships within this community *ought* to be characterized by loyalty toward *all* the relevant parties — to God, Christ, the Spirit, other Christians, to the Jewish people, and to other relevant groups (if not, ultimately, toward humanity and creation as a whole). Paul wants to include himself and his coworkers within this circle of loyalty not infrequently as well! It is just that this notion does not seem to exhaust his use of πιστ- language, which is strongly informed by particular scriptural texts and argumentative functions when he confronts the Teachers.

3.5. The Wrath of God

It remains at this point, then, only to address briefly the motif of the wrath of God, which is clearly evident in 1 Thessalonians 1:10, and perhaps in 2:16 as well (see also 5:3, 9); it is also apparent in various texts in Ephesians (2:1-3), Colossians (3:6), and 2 Thessalonians (1:6-10; cf. also 2:2-12). It might be argued by Justification advocates that these texts evidence a clear commitment by both Paul and subsequent Pauline tradition to God's punitive judgment. But, as we have already seen earlier in this chapter in relation to 1 Thessalonians 1:10, and in part one, chapter six, in relation to the themes of judgment and punishment in Paul in general, it does not follow from the fact that Paul occasionally endorses an aggressive process of divine action, usually by way of forensic metaphors of judgment (which must of course be interpreted carefully in relation to executive and monarchical themes as well), that this process is functioning *in a theologically foundational location within his thinking.* And this is the critical point. An apocalyptic account of God's wrath in these texts can be provided as well — that is, in terms of a loving God's anger directed against any situation that is evil. Anger can be the reflex of benevolence or love just as much as it can spring from concerns with desert. And, as such, it can be a response to a prior initiative and its repudiation, and hence function in a secondary position, just as much as it can be the first action undertaken, functioning in a primary location. At this point, then, it needs to be noted that none of these texts explicitly places the wrath of God in a prior location; all are comprehensible as God's reaction against a sinful situation and hence conceivably understandable as part of an account of divine benevolence. Nor do any of these texts attribute this activity to God in a fundamental fashion.[72]

So, for example, Ephesians seems to note carefully in 2:1-3 that the situation under the "anger" of God is one characterized by a hostile, evil ruler — "the ruler of the authority of the air" — along with the practice of sinful, fleshly desires, to which humanity seems enslaved. It is this situation that is apparently godless and hopeless (see v. 12), *except* of course that God is rich in mercy and love, and so intervenes to make those who are "dead" in this situation "alive in Christ" (so vv. 4-10, 13-22). Hence, as the letter's prologue makes clear (1:3-14), God's *first* word to humanity is spoken in Christ, "before the foundation of the world," and speaks of grace, mercy, and love, not of anger. Moreover, the situation underlying God's displeasure is one for which humanity is not held fully (i.e., "strongly") accountable (although neither is humanity without accountability). The letter's perspective seems, in short, to remain thoroughly and consistently apocalyptic, and this consistency extends to all the other pieces of evidence in this relation as well. Hence, I suggest that for Paul or one of his later tradents to speak of God's wrath is by no means to establish that this attribute is foundational in the sense that Justification theory claims and needs.

Conclusions

One will not necessarily win a footrace just because one's entangled shoelaces have been unknotted, but one will certainly *not* win if they remain entangled. This book is an attempt to unknot the shoelaces of the modern Pauline reader so that an important race can continue.

It is of course not uncommon these days to read that Pauline interpretation faces acute challenges. Especially since E. P. Sanders's monumental *Paul and Palestinian Judaism,* most scholars have known that Paul's description is problematic in important respects, although such concerns predate 1977 by well over a century. And other important figures — often cited at the inception of the "new perspective on Paul" — have named different problems from those articulated by Sanders, who was principally occupied with Paul's relationship to Jewish description. So Heikki Räisänen has pointed to the possible existence of acute contradiction in Paul's conceptualizations of Judaism and the law — of outright incoherence — and Krister Stendahl has complained about several problems, including an overly introspective emphasis in Paul's description, the anachronistic intrusion of later church-historical preoccupations (i.e., introspection) into interpretation, a misunderstanding of the precise settings within which many of the apostle's key Justification statements were first made, and so on. (Such concerns built upon the complaints made by earlier generations of scholars, principally from within the German tradition.)

However, this study is different from preceding studies in the way it views "the problem." I have argued that the problem is rather more extensive and complex than most previous analyses have suspected — even the classic treatments just mentioned; that it spreads across several dimensions, including the process of interpretation itself; but that it possesses a recognizable inner coherence that — if grasped accurately — offers the possibility of comprehensive resolution. In short, in my view, previous characterizations of the problem, along with their corresponding attempted solutions, have tended to lack depth, along with — pre-

931

dictably — any concomitant reinterpretative success. A knot or two might have been identified and loosened, but the shoelaces of the Pauline interpreter have remained perplexingly tangled (and perhaps at times another knot has been added!). I contend here of course that these shoelaces can be untangled, but the process of doing so is long and complex; they form a veritable Gordian knot! So what exactly is the tangle that current Pauline interpreters find themselves caught up in?

At the heart of this project, and of much of the current, modern interpretation of Paul, is a multidimensional interpretative construct or discourse — a *destructive, alien,* and *viciously circular* one (in exegetical terms), that possesses distinctively modern, in the sense of post-European commitments to *foundationalism* and *contractualism* (theological foundationalism leading invariably to sinister ethical and political self-ratifications, and in this instance, to characteristically modern ones). Previous accounts of the problem in Paul have tended to describe only parts of it, much as the blind scholars of "Indostan" described only parts of an elephant. But the entire construct needs to be removed (if of course it can be) because of the breadth and depth of its destructive consequences — the destructive consequences precisely of foundationalism and contractualism. It should be removable, because it is alien; but its removal is extremely difficult, because of its powerful circle of interpretative self-legitimation — and hence, to a large degree, the length and complexity of my preceding treatment. How does one break down and supplant a powerful self-legitimizing interpretative discourse in relation to an ancient figure's texts? It might be clearest at this concluding point to work backward, as I have argued consistently that Paul does.

Clearly, if any resolution to our difficulties in relation to Paul is ultimately to be found, an alternative reading of the key texts must be offered — one that avoids or resolves their problematic implications. It must, moreover, be pursued in detail and with exegetical integrity; it must offer a plausible account of the texts in their entirety, through every twist and turn, and in plausible reconstructions of their original settings. This has been offered in parts four and five of this volume, in chapters thirteen through twenty-one.

But such a demonstration cannot be offered in a vacuum. The integrity of an alternative reading must be assessed in relation to the prevailing reading that is generating the problems, and this is simply the situation in any case; the interpretation of the relevant texts is hotly contested. So some account of that competing reading must also be given, along with an account of the exegetical difficulties that the new alternative purports to resolve, thereby demonstrating its superiority *as* a reading. Other rereadings should of course be part of this conversation as well. And these accounts have been offered in part three, chapters ten through twelve.

Such a set of exegetical accounts, however, can hardly be attempted straightaway. Not knowing precisely what the key texts are, we might read the wrong ones and/or miss the main ones; not knowing what key problems we are seeking to avoid, we might resolve some but endorse others. And even more basically, we might not be aware of any illicit influences on our interpretation. We might be caught up in a vicious interpretative circle without even realizing it, thereby foreclosing on constructive interpretative alternatives.

Clearly, then, some prior scrutiny of our interpretative method and categories is necessary, to alert us to possible interpretative dangers. And, following the initial lead of Stendahl, it should look not merely at how we tend to read texts, emphasizing the detection and elimination of blind spots within that process, but also at how unnoticed church-historical commitments might be influencing our interpretation. Moreover, it should not be limited to church history; our modern political, ideological, and cultural commitments need to be scrutinized in like measure. This has been the focus of part two, chapters seven through nine.

It remains, then, to identify precisely the problems that we are dealing with, along with the key texts that consequently need to be discussed — the issues behind parts three through five. We must also identify the specific influences on interpretation that might be operating illicitly through church-historical and ideocultural means — the issues behind much of part two. Some prior analysis of the problem as a whole is therefore necessary. But it must be attempted *without detailed recourse to the construal of the texts, since that is taking place later,* so here analysis seems to run straight into the difficulties of the Meno paradox. We need to know what we are searching for so that we can search for it. To resolve this paradox, as in all explanations — following Polanyi — there seems to be no realistic alternative to simply taking some inspired jump into the explanatory quagmire that aims at landing on a piece of firm ground, although it should be apparent, on landing, that it *is* firm ground (or not). I have suggested that this initial ground is an erroneous account of Paul's soteriology in largely theoretical terms — an account that emphasizes its foundationalist, conditional, and contractual character as "Justification."

From this starting point a large number of difficulties in Paul's analysis are illuminated. They are not of course at this point resolved, but it is apparent that they are implicated in the discussion — debates usually kept apart in Pauline discourse but that need to be brought together, such as the discussion of Paul's account of Judaism, of his conversion, of his commitment to natural theology (or not), and his conceptions of ethics and the church (et cetera). This was the concern of part one, chapters one through six. And the surprisingly cogent explanation of the problem that resulted — at a theoretical level — served as a useful preliminary check on the cogency of this starting point. It also served the useful rhetorical purpose of shaking interpretative confidence in any discourse that centered around this construct, thereby creating a corresponding openness to an account of the construct's exegetical problems (so part three), and to alternative ways of reading its key corroborative texts (so parts four and five). It became apparent what prior categories were being brought to the construal of the texts, perhaps reinforced by church-historical or ideocultural commitments (so part two). And an important argumentative objective could also now be achieved. We became aware of what texts we actually needed to discuss, and to what level of detail, since not all the texts proved equally important. The theory dictated what those texts were — the texts that ostensibly freighted the soteriological construct of Justification in Paul (principally Romans 1:16–4:25, treated in part four; supported by Romans 9:30–10:21 and various other short passages; Galatians 2:15–3:26; 5:5-6; and Philippians 3:1-11; treated in part five).

In short, the unusual staggering of the account of the problem here, and the unusual length, breadth, and complexity of the discussion, seem justified when the project is viewed in retrospect. A plausible analysis of the problem, yielding an effective and sustainable solution, simply demanded this treatment, even if at first it seemed counterintuitive. And I suggest now, in conclusion, that although this book is not a definitive rereading of Paul's soteriology per se, a great deal has nevertheless been achieved.

In a sense, I hope to have made that important project possible where previously it has been constrained and distorted by a complex and largely unacknowledged problem — that is, the intrusion of an alien discourse. The way is now clear for us to reappropriate a more coherent ancient figure. We will be able to stop tripping over our own feet, laces entangled, as arguably we have been doing for a very long time, and to race after the real quarry — namely, the responsible and constructive description of Paul's thought. And if this overarching goal is now clearly appreciated, it should be helpful to note in closing what other things have, and have not, been achieved.

It is very important to appreciate that this analysis is consequently not an attack on *the* gospel but an attack on *a version of* the gospel, and *one that I maintain Paul himself would view as false.* It is therefore a thoroughly evangelical discussion in both method and purpose. Moreover, the solution that I am aiming toward is deeply Protestant if not Lutheran. To put things at their simplest, only if my rereading is true is it possible to affirm coherently Paul's slogan that "God justifies the ungodly," since he means by this that God delivers the wicked from their enslavement to Sin, when they cannot deliver themselves, and thereby demonstrates his unconditional grace and love. Alternative construals of this slogan are caught by irreconcilable contradictions and theological conundrums — issues of theodicy, capacity, and so on. But in affirming the slogan in this sense we are of course being loyal to some of the central insights of Protestantism and of Luther. Furthermore, only now is it possible to affirm coherently Paul's construal of "sanctification," which he seems to discuss with such profundity in Romans 5–8, elevating this material now to its rightful status. Paul's account of sanctification *is* the gospel. His description of deliverance and cleansing "in Christ," through the work of the Spirit, at the behest of the Father, the entire process being symbolized by baptism, *is* the good news. It requires no supplementation by other systems.

But my summary comments up to this point — like much of the debate in general — have tended to reference various aspects of Protestantism. And it ought to be appreciated that Catholicism is deeply implicit in both the problem and the solution as well. The problematic prospective and conditional reading of Paul that has so obscured descriptions of the apostle's thinking in the past has roots deep in the Western Christian tradition (although the distinctive variant of Justification is Reformational). But the countervailing gospel of sanctification, ethical efficacy, and ecclesial community is also richly resourced by elements within Catholicism. All of which is to suggest that such denominational distinctions are now best abandoned as necessary and obvious analytic categories in any sense (at least, in this relation). In essence, my argument is meant to be an important moment in the advance to ecclesial and scholarly triumph of the participatory and apocalyptic gospel, which is also really to say, of the Trinitarian gospel — an ecumenical gospel that both Protestants and Catholics can presumably affirm (obviously in accord with both the Orthodox and most modern post-Protestant traditions), a gospel both old and new. This book is an important step in the recovery of the authentic and orthodox Pauline gospel.

If this seems surprising, then it ought also to be recalled that the ostensibly evangelical construct I am criticizing throughout the book is in reality a contractual and liberal construction (although "liberal" of course in the political sense) and so is a characteristically *modern* gospel. And so Paul is often currently being read under its impress in a way that is in effect uncritically North American. Certain modern readers — curiously unassisted at this point by postmodernity — are constructing Paul in their own image. And it can hardly be wrong in Christian terms to reject *this* construct!

Having made these negative observations, however, I would emphasize that — just as was the case for Protestantism and Catholicism — the way forward in interpretative terms now seems largely North American as well, in that the necessary exegetical and biographical moves are practiced primarily within its academic traditions (with important German and British antecedents, to be sure, but these traditions seem to have rejected most such moves in more recent times). I do not believe that these have yet been properly integrated — that is, until this point — but all the pieces of the Pauline puzzle, so to speak, have been on the table in front of interpreters in North America for some time. It is just that they have not been brought together cogently. There is something characteristically North American, then, about both the problem and the solution.

In closing it must be emphasized that the situation vis-à-vis Paul's Justification texts has now changed irrevocably, and this whether it is acknowledged by Justification advocates or not. Hence, any question-begging responses — which have so bedeviled previous debate — should be carefully noted and rejected. The conventional reading, and especially of Romans 1-4, needs now to justify itself positively and not merely assume its superiority. And it needs to deal with its numerous problems, of which over fifty have been enumerated. It also needs to refute my rereading positively in the same ways, undermining its positive supports and/or finding problems in its account of the text or implications (and I am as yet unaware of any). In the absence of these, any simple retort to my rereading of "I am unconvinced" must immediately itself be judged unconvincing. Things have moved well past the stage of mere dismissal. The conventional construal of Paul's Justification texts has been only the least worst alternative, and with a new, superior alternative now present, it has much work to do beyond the hermeneutics (and politics) of assertion. Justification must adapt to a brave new world — or quietly expire.

Moreover, we can all now also be more presuppositionally self-aware, and our conversation more hermeneutically sophisticated, confident in the realization that this does not entail interpretative relativism. We must be more honest at times about what we are bringing to the text — our hopes and fears. But we also need to trust the text to resist any false impositions (and our interpretative traditions and communities will of course assist us at this point). A broader and more complex interpretative conversation should ensue, involving theology, hermeneutics, church history, and modern philosophical and political history, in addition to the standard New Testament discussions of provenance and meaning. And the latter should also be a more integrated conversation. Reading Romans involves more than mere exegesis; it must include distinguishable issues of argumentation, theological coherence, and presuppositional influence as well. Only when these are included does our interpretative process hold out the prospects of genuine insight and progress.

We may also need to be bolder than we have been, pressing deeper into the issues, refusing to be satisfied by incomplete answers. It is not enough to speak of new perspectives. These are ultimately superficial analyses of both the problems and the solutions that leave us enmeshed in our difficulties, and irretrievably so — which is not to say that they lack value or were not helpful insights in their day. But "Lutheranism versus the new perspective" is now a false antithesis that should be abandoned; we must move well beyond these terms of debate. It is a regrettably clichéd notion, but we need *a new paradigm*. And we must be both brave and clear-sighted enough to grasp it.

Dramatic new opportunities for the reconstrual of Paul will open up for us if we do so. In those famous words, a kinder and gentler Paul will become visible. But, equally importantly, he will be simpler and more coherent. He will also be less like his modern Western readers, and so ultimately more able to help them. Hence, modernity may yet benefit from the abandonment of an essentially modern reading of Paul. It seems that beyond our European conceits, the real Paul awaits us.

Notes

Note to the Preface

1. Chapter thirteen reframes that discussion with an analysis of the provenance of Romans.

Notes to the Introduction

1. The use of the term "Lutheran" will be addressed shortly.

2. A full description of this soteriological system will be offered momentarily, in part one, chapter one. I generally refer to it in what follows as "Justification."

3. There is an important relationship between this line of interpretation and the *Religionsgeschichtliche Schule,* that included figures like Reitzenstein, Heitmüller, and Boussett. This is discussed in more detail in part one, chapter six; some more problematic contributions from this tradition of scholarship will also be noted later, esp. in part four, chapter seventeen.

4. I use this term to denote all those scholars who seriously challenge the interpretative status quo, and hence it functions in what follows essentially negatively — i.e., *against* that status quo. Consequently, revisionists may share little in common except the target of their criticisms. The status quo itself is defined especially in part one, chapter one, and part three, chapter ten.

5. More detailed accounts of all these claims are given in part one, chapter six.

6. Philadelphia: Fortress.

7. We will discuss the different lines of argument initiated by Sanders in more detail in part one, chapter four, including an assessment of the precise force and cogency of this descriptive claim. It is worth noting at this point, however, that he also reintroduced forcefully the issue just noted, especially by way of an appeal to Schweitzer — that is, the apparent tension in Paul's thinking between forensic and participatory categories, a move implicit in part one, chapter three, and discussed more explicitly in part one, chapter six.

8. This unresolved quality is still apparent in the important revised and expanded edition, *The Romans Debate,* ed. K. P. Donfried (Peabody, Mass.: Hendrickson, 1991 [1977]), discussed in detail in part four, chapter thirteen.

9. The six wise men, in John Godfrey Saxe's wonderful poetic version of the Buddhist tale, successively pronounce the elephant to be a wall, spear, snake, tree, fan, and a rope, having successively grasped its side, tusk, trunk, knee, ear, and tail ("The Blind Men and the Elephant"; see *The Udana: In-*

spired Utterances of the Buddha, trans. from the Pali by John D. Ireland [Kandy: Buddhist Publication Society, 1997], 6.4; see *Udana* 68-69).

10. Its theoretical structure is described in detail in part one, chapter one, its hermeneutical dynamics in part two, chapter seven, and its primary textual locus in Paul — Romans 1–4 — in part three, chapter ten (and these are the first chapters in each of these three parts).

11. "Rational" in fact in the sense of being rationalis*tic,* which I take to be a particular, highly reductive account of human rationality tantamount to "philosophical" or "economic" man. The following analysis maintains a commitment to rationality per se, but defines and locates that activity differently from the "Lutheran" model. (See in this relation esp. part two, chapter seven.)

12. See esp. part one, chapter three.

13. See esp. part one, chapters three through six.

14. This is the infamous double character of Romans, described neatly by Kümmel (see part one, chapter thirteen). In fact, however, as just stated, Romans possesses a *double* double character: a Gentile or pagan/specific vs. Jew/general tension between the letter frame and its body. This is discussed in more detail in part four, chapter thirteen.

15. From this point on I will also prefer "pagan" (etc.) to the more common "Gentile" to refer to Paul's Christian converts from non-Jewish ethnicities. Objections have been raised to this nomenclature on the grounds that its original reference in Latin as *paganus* was significantly different from "non-Christian," being rather "country-dwellers": see Robin Lane Fox, *Pagans and Christians* (New York: Random House, 1987). The term only subsequently became attached to non-Christians because rural populations seem to have remained non-Christian for several centuries after the Greco-Roman cities converted to Christianity. However, as a modern translation equivalent, this connotation has long since been lost (i.e., this is an invalid etymological objection to its usage here). Moreover, it preserves for modern readers the frequently offensive connotation that Jews could attach to non-Jewish ethnicity (see "dogs," discussed briefly in relation to Phil. 3:2 in part five, chapter twenty-one), thereby emphasizing the fundamentally scandalous nature of Paul's mission, especially insofar as he left various pagan practices intact after conversion. Concomitantly, "Gentile" has been effectively domesticated by its long usage in biblical translation, and might even retain a *positive* connotation, in relation to the signifier's predominantly Gentile readership.

It should also be appreciated that references to "pagans" are not to pagans per se unless this is clearly specified, but to "converts *from* paganism *to* Paul's Christian movement," meaning by this that such converts come from some specific ethnic variation within Greco-Roman paganism in the Principate, "paganism" being an accepted umbrella term for those. And they also convert to a type of early Christianity that was still, in some respects, recognizably pagan as against Jewish. But it is clearly too cumbersome to use this explanation at every appropriate point, so I generally just use "pagan(s)" in what follows.

16. To a degree a figure of speech: ". . . or the Roman Christians perceived none." Hermeneutical questions are addressed in more detail in part two, chapter seven.

17. This complex and fascinating history is charted in more detail in part two, chapter nine — although still regrettably programmatically.

Notes to Chapter One

1. As Foucault once remarked, "I wish I could have slipped surreptitiously into this discourse which I must present today. . . . I should have preferred to be enveloped by speech, and carried away well beyond all possible beginnings, rather than to have to begin it myself. I should have preferred to become aware that a nameless voice was already speaking long before me, so that I should only have needed to join in, to continue the sentence it had started and lodge myself, without really being noticed, in its interstices . . ." ("The Order of Discourse," in *Language and Politics,* ed. Michael Shapiro [New York: New York University Press, 1984 (1970)], 108). Just so, finding the best entry point into this discussion has been a vexed issue. Its difficulty is caused largely by the fact that the interpretative situ-

ation is both circular and multidimensional. So any starting point tends to end up presupposing material functioning earlier on in the circle and/or in relation to some other dimension affecting the current point; it needs that material in order to be established, but also ends up affecting and shaping it later on! (This circularity and these various dimensions will become especially apparent from part two, chapter seven onward.) However, an entry into the entire situation by way of its theoretically induced problems does ultimately seem to be the clearest point of access. The main concession made by this rhetorical choice is to postpone any textual analysis, perhaps thereby creating "exegetical anxiety" in a reader. I address this concern briefly in §1.1 below, and in detail in part three.

2. It is in fact this double relationship that creates much of the complexity within the discussion. *Both* criteria must be satisfied simultaneously, and one should not, strictly speaking, be played off against the other or, worse still, shifted at will to suit the defensive needs of discussion.

3. These are introduced in detail in part three. Readers who cannot wait until then to find out what they are are welcome to jump to that material now. In the meantime though it is worth noting that I would have little to gain from knocking down a theoretical straw man if the texts turned out ultimately not to relate to it!

4. See George Lakoff's account of the two main current American political positions, utilizing a methodology that is also helpful in this relation: *Moral Politics: How Liberals and Conservatives Think,* 2nd ed. (London & Chicago: University of Chicago Press, 2001 [1996]). Some of Lakoff's insights will be pressed later in this chapter: see §5.

5. More skeptical objectors may not be satisfied by this. I might still be accused of setting up a caricature. For such criticisms to hold, however, it must be shown just where my account is unfair or deficient (and in a way that ultimately satisfies the theory's various complex requirements for explanatory integrity: see part two, chapter seven). In other words, the charge that my account is deficient cannot merely be made; it must be demonstrated *and* a more coherent theoretical alternative offered.

6. By "absence of rigor" is meant a lack of system or coherence — in other words, the presence of confusion and contradiction. And it is perhaps worth noting at this point in addition that one cannot insist on a universal lack of coherence without making a universal coherent claim that is then contradicted by its own assertion! One is then in violation of one's own claim.

7. Ironically, a straw man may lie behind *this* argument, namely, an image of a later systematic theologian writing extensive, closely argued scholastic treatises — for example, Thomas Aquinas. But no one seriously suggests that Paul was like Aquinas. Even more importantly, it does not follow from this difference that Paul and Aquinas did not share similar basic activities; it does not follow from the fact that someone does not think like Thomas Aquinas that he or she does not think at all. (For some preliminary observations along these lines, see my *Quest for Paul's Gospel: A Suggested Strategy* [London: T&T Clark International (Continuum), 2005], 29-34.)

8. As we will see in more detail later on, an entire series of difficulties is implicit here. If objectors abandon rationality, then (1) they will be vulnerable to any readings of equal exegetical cogency but superior coherence, and (2) they will have difficulty deploying rational considerations in support of interpretative points that they care about. (3) One also wonders how persuasive a reading that lacks argumentative integrity will prove over against one that possesses it merely as a reading; argumentative considerations *are* exegetical. Perhaps even more pointedly, (4) such objectors have effectively abandoned the theological construal of Paul in any sense: Paul can no longer offer an account of the gospel. (Theology is an attempt to give a coherent account of God's actions toward us in Christ; as such, it is inherently rational in a certain sense.) And finally, (5) this clearly does not represent what Paul himself thinks that he is doing.

9. As Karl Barth once noted: "[F]rom the standpoint of a strict Christian theology there is no such thing as 'Calvinism,' just as there ought never to have been any such thing as 'Lutheranism'" (*CD* II.2, 36 [§32, s. 2.1]).

10. See esp. James B. Torrance, "Covenant and Contract, a Study of the Theological Background of Worship in Seventeenth-Century Scotland," *Scottish Journal of Theology* 23 (1970): 51-76; "The Contribution of McLeod Campbell to Scottish Theology," *Scottish Journal of Theology* 26 (1973): 295-311; and "Preface," in John McLeod Campbell, *The Nature of the Atonement* (Edinburgh: Handsel,

1996 [1856]), 1-16 — essays of exemplary grace and insight, although regrettably little known. Also valuable are "The Covenant Concept in Scottish Theology and Politics and Its Legacy," *Scottish Journal of Theology* 34 (1981): 225-43; "The Incarnation and Limited Atonement," *Evangelical Quarterly* 55 (1983): 83-94; and "The Concept of Federal Theology — Was Calvin a Federal Theologian?" in *Calvinus Sacrae Scripturae Professor: Calvin as Confessor of Holy Scripture,* ed. Wilhelm H. Neuser (Grand Rapids, Mich.: Eerdmans, 1994), 15-40. The following leans primarily on this material. I also owe a debt to Alan J. Torrance, however, who introduced me to this material but supplied his own insightful perspectives as well, especially concerning theological foundationalism and the important associated question of a priori versus a posteriori (or prospective versus retrospective) theological epistemology: see *Persons in Communion: An Essay on Trinitarian Description and Human Participation with Special Reference to Volume One of Karl Barth's Church Dogmatics* (Edinburgh: T&T Clark, 1996); "Creation Ex Nihilo and the Spatio-Temporal Dimensions," in *The Doctrine of Creation,* ed. C. E. Gunton (Edinburgh: T&T Clark, 1997), 83-103; "The Trinity," in *The Cambridge Companion to Barth,* ed. John Webster (London: Continuum, 2000), 72-91; "Jesus in Christian Doctrine," in *The Cambridge Companion to Jesus,* ed. Markus Bockmuehl (Edinburgh & New York: Cambridge University Press, 2001), 200-19; and *"Auditus Fidei:* Where and How Does God Speak? Faith, Reason, and the Question of Criteria," in *Reason and the Reasons of Faith,* ed. Paul J. Griffiths and Reinhard Hütter (New York & London: T&T Clark [Continuum], 2005), 27-52.

11. Note that we are drawing principally on James Torrance's theological observations; his historical account of Scottish Presbyterianism does not have to be correct in all its particulars for his theological insights to hold good (although I suspect that he is reasonably accurate).

12. It is important to appreciate that no questions of translation are being conceded here. I use these terms because they are conventional, not because they are necessarily the best modern English equivalents for certain signifiers occurring in Paul's texts. These issues are revisited in parts four and five.

13. We touch here on an ancient and complex intellectual debate, namely, the nature of justice, which will be considered further in relation to this key premise in due course. Note also that I have opted to use these particular characterizations of the types of "justice" involved in the interests of clarity. In older discussions what I call "retributive" is often known as "distributive." However, in my view this nomenclature can cause confusion with end-state conceptions of justice that are overtly (re)distributive.

14. Quite specific instances of this theological trajectory are discussed later in relation to the christological interpretation of key OT texts — especially lament Psalms revolving around a righteous sufferer: see part five, chapter twenty-one, §3.2. This eschatological concern clearly runs directly through all of Paul's Justification texts — perhaps most especially, Romans 2 (Paul's own, alternative view arguably becoming more visible in Romans 4 and 10).

15. Some problems in these designations will, however, be noted shortly, especially in part one, chapter four.

16. Desert-based systems are usually associated with the modern political Right.

17. The analogy with something quantitative is very important and will be discussed further shortly.

18. See, e.g., *Jubilees* 30:22: "But if they transgress and act in all the ways of defilement, they will be recorded in the heavenly tablets as enemies. And they will be blotted out of the book of life, and written in the book of those who will be destroyed and with those who will be rooted out from the land."

19. The phenomenon of atonement can complicate things if it is introduced here; however, it will be clearest to treat this issue at a later stage in our discussion.

20. It is important to emphasize that this is introspection of a particular variety, as we will note further later on in part one, chapter six. There are actually *three* decisive components here, namely, the introspective activity itself, its parameters, and the discovery, in the light of these, of persistent sinfulness. For Stendahl's original claims, see Krister Stendahl, "The Apostle Paul and the Introspective Conscience of the West," *Harvard Theological Review* 56 (1963): 199-215.

21. *Luther's Works,* 55 vols. (Minneapolis, Minn.: Fortress & St. Louis, Missouri: Concordia, 1957-86), 27:13, emphasis added; see also 26:387-88, 404-6.

22. Indeed, it *has* to be: see more on this important implication in chapter two immediately following.

23. See more in this relation in part two, chapter eight.

24. For example, assessing Aristotle too extensively; see *The Heidelberg Disputation,* thesis 6 and its explanation (*Luther's Works* 31:39-58 [vol. 31, ed. Harold J. Grimm and Helmut T. Lehmann, 1957]).

25. A question we will consider in detail from chapter two onward.

26. Some of the key variations on Justification depart from this point, although I will suggest, ultimately incoherently; they are assessed from chapter two onward.

27. See esp. George Lakoff, *Moral Politics,* this study being a contemporary development and application of the more programmatic earlier study (with Mark Johnson) *Metaphors We Live By,* 2nd ed. (Chicago, Ill.: University of Chicago Press, 2003 [1980]). I know of little use of his work in any substantial way in NT studies. John L. White has made a beginning in this relation, applying the notion of "root metaphors" to some aspects of Paul's thought in *The Apostle of God: Paul and the Promise of Abraham* (Peabody, Mass.: Hendrickson, 1999), esp. 3-19. Richard Hays also notes Lakoff in passing: see *The Faith of Jesus Christ: The Narrative Substructure of Galatians 3:1–4:11,* 2nd ed. (Grand Rapids, Mich.: Eerdmans, 2002 [1983]), 290, n. 46 (remarks originally made at SBL in 1991). Some further interesting engagements with Lakoff's methodology include James W. Underhill, "Meaning, Language, and Mind: An Interview with Mark Turner," *Style* 36.4 (Winter 2002): 700-717; and Nora Miller, "Calling Out the Symbol Rules: Thinking Inside the Frame," *Et Cetera* 62.2 (April 2005): 202-6; less flattering is Jim Swan, "'Life without Parole': Metaphor and Discursive Commitment," *Style* 36.3 (Fall 2002): 446-65 (although this is not in my opinion an especially convincing critique).

The importance of Lakoff's emphasis on root metaphors, and of the present study's emphasis on the root metaphor of retributive justice in God (i.e., Lakoff's "strict parent" model), has been recently corroborated significantly to my mind by The Baylor Survey of Religion (BSR) of images of God in America.

Four basic images of God were tabulated — authoritarian (31.4%-43% in the South!), benevolent (23%-28.7% in the Midwest!), critical (16%-21.3% in the East), and distant (24.4%-30.3% in the East). These results suggest that the authoritarian God is characterized basically by retributive justice, as is the critical God, although that image is not viewed as so closely involved in human affairs (i.e., a slide toward Deism has taken place). The benevolent God, however, is *fundamentally* different, but for a minority of the population (as are certain forms of the distant God — a more pantheist notion at times). So this survey suggests, first, that different root metaphors concerning God are indeed present in modern American religiosity. Second, however, and most importantly, these root metaphors proved to be *extremely* powerful predictors of other social and moral behaviors, correlating with attitudes toward the nature of government, ethical questions (such as abortion), and so on.

The survey was formulated by the Baylor Institute for Studies of Religion [ISR], Baylor University, Waco, Texas, funded by The John M. Templeton Foundation, and conducted by the Gallup Organization in Fall 2005. Its principal investigators were Christopher D. Bader, Kevin Dougherty, Paul Froese, Byron Johnson, F. Carson Mencken, Jerry Z. Park, and Rodney Stark. Follow-up surveys took place over the next two years. Preliminary findings were published in a research report, "American Piety in the 21st Century: New Insights to the Depths and Complexity of Religion in the US" (Baylor ISR, Baylor University, September 2006: www.baylor.edu/content/services/document.php/33304.pdf). The survey's results were sufficiently interesting to elicit widespread press coverage, for example, Cathy Lynn Grossmann, "View of God Can Predict Values, Politics," *USA Today,* September 12th, 2006.

28. Images and metaphors, being complex entities, may offer large numbers of potential relationships that can then be argumentatively elaborated with more clarity. Indeed, it is often the positing of startling metaphors in an attempt to explain old problems that creates new explanatory purchase and progress, something then articulated through argumentation — a principal element in

Michael Polanyi's view of epistemology: see *Personal Knowledge: Towards a Post-Critical Philosophy* (London: Routledge & Kegan Paul, 1958); see also T. S. Kuhn, *The Structure of Scientific Revolutions*, 3rd ed. (London & Chicago: University of Chicago Press, 1996 [1962]). I am particularly impressed at present by the capacity of musical and sonic metaphors to reconceive difficult theological issues helpfully (often exposing simultaneously a spatial bias in previous attempts to understand them): see, in particular, Jeremy S. Begbie, *Theology, Music, and Time* (Cambridge: Cambridge University Press, 2000); and *Resounding Truth: Christian Wisdom in the World of Music* (Grand Rapids, Mich.: Baker Academic, 2007).

29. There are of course endless subtle variations on exactly how this takes place, but these need not concern us here.

30. It is worth noting that this knowledge often includes ruling ideas or concepts, that is, notions that are inferred to structure the world in some fundamental way, a point at which many philosophical traditions diverge.

31. Like the overlapping notion of "economic man," this should in my view be gendered deliberately, because it has tended through its history to be tacitly coded in terms of elite male stereotypes, and has often tended to presuppose their underlying social and historical locations.

32. The analogy is rather less frequently female (hence the use of the masculine pronouns).

33. However, at this point the model has become overtly "Christian," because the generic individuals are responding to specifically Christian information when they believe (or at least are usually said to be; merely "theistic" variants are possible at this point). And so secondary metaphorical layers relating to the dissemination of Christian information can now easily be introduced to reinforce the model, for example, accounts of evangelism, preaching, missionary activity, and so on — and these are important aspects within Christianity, no matter how their role and dynamic are conceived.

Notes to Chapter Two

1. I tend to use the term "frame" rather than the more familiar "context" to indicate — in ultimate dependence on some suggestions from Derrida — that interpretative acts are involved in their construction as well as in the reading(s) that they surround. "Context" (et cetera) can suggest an inappropriately neutral activity. This point and notion are discussed in more detail in part two, chapter seven, where hermeneutical issues are treated extensively.

2. We will not consider explicitly textual issues at this point, because they are not yet introduced appropriately. Here we are considering only theoretical difficulties: does Justification work coherently and responsibly simply as a theory of salvation? All the textual difficulties are best considered later on once various problems within the process of textual interpretation have been identified and controlled by part two.

3. Such apologetic dynamics actually tend to become salient at the exegetical, rather than the theoretical level, so they are addressed from chapter eleven onward.

4. And it is important to recall at this point that these problems cannot always be defused by simply modifying the theory. There are important textual constraints on this process that must constantly be borne in mind; the theory must not lose contact with its textual base. (This last claim is established principally by part three, chapter ten.)

5. We could also try to reverse this strategy, giving a particularized account of the first phase in the model and somehow eliminating its philosophical epistemology. But this would take us well beyond Justification theory and so would fall into the category of "radical" or "revisionist solutions," which are considered in part three, chapter twelve.

6. That is, a case could presumably be made that these two modes can coexist within certain systems. However, Justification theory asserts not merely their coexistence but their *integration*. It is the latter point that makes things so difficult. Justification claims that individuals start their progress to Christian knowledge in the one mode but finish in the other.

7. Monogamy is not in fact an obvious inference from 1:18-32, but this tends to be overlooked and then assumed. Paul does not characterize polygamy in this text as a heinous and obvious sin.

8. The model is supposed to be universally and objectively true, and hence presumably so in all times and places.

9. The classic figures are Anselm, Aquinas, Berkeley, Kant, and Hume. An excellent genealogy of this particular tradition is provided by Stanley Hauerwas in "God and the Gifford Lectures," ch. one in *With the Grain of the Universe: The Church's Witness and Natural Theology, Being the Gifford Lectures Delivered at the University of St. Andrews in 2001* (London: SCM, 2002), 15-41. Jill Payton Walsh discusses many of these issues in a charming narrative format in *Knowledge of Angels* (Boston: Houghton Mifflin, 1994). A recent and nuanced counterattack on my endorsement at this point of post-Enlightenment philosophical skepticism is Denys Turner, *Faith, Reason, and the Existence of God* (Cambridge: Cambridge University Press, 2004). Also relevant is A. J. Torrance, *Persons in Communion: An Essay on Trinitarian Description and Human Participation with Special Reference to Volume One of Karl Barth's Church Dogmatics* (Edinburgh: T&T Clark, 1996); "Is Love the Essence of God?" in *Nothing Greater, Nothing Better: Theological Essays on the Love of God*, ed. Kevin J. Vanhoozer (Grand Rapids, Mich.: Eerdmans, 2001), 114-37; and *"Auditus Fidei:* Where and How Does God Speak? Faith, Reason, and the Question of Criteria," in *Reason and the Reasons of Faith*, ed. Paul J. Griffiths and Reinhard Hütter (New York & London: T&T Clark [Continuum], 2005), 27-52 (this entire volume being relevant to this issue).

10. There are some further interesting implications from this initial point. If the model fails to establish the initial phase of its opening argumentation, then the consequent argument will fail. But the presuppositions themselves will also fail, that is, the existence and particular vision of God, and the nature of God's demands. We will not know God and, moreover, will have apparently good reasons for ignoring him. This model creates, in short, the very situation it seeks to deny: a self-confident atheism. And that possibility will be further reinforced if the model continues to deny the validity of alternative models. Clearly, then, as a theological method, the consequences of this approach are self-defeating, and ultimately disastrous. This dynamic is expounded brilliantly by Michael Buckley, *At the Origins of Modern Atheism* (London & New Haven: Yale University Press, 1987).

11. This is an important caveat. Strictly speaking, the charge of injustice holds only if there is an expectation of perfect obedience.

12. It would be hard to argue that two very different sets of criteria were nevertheless precisely equivalent in terms of rigor and reward.

13. Calvin's difficulties at this point are noteworthy: see his more detailed treatment in part two, chapter eight.

14. Note that I am not hereby excluding the possible later construction of a Christian ethic that ends up positioned in similar terms to a ceremonial- or ritual-moral distinction. But that would be an explicitly a posteriori and christological undertaking. Justification requires — of course — an explicitly a priori distinction in these terms, and I find this unconvincing. Heikki Räisänen discusses this problem extensively, pointing out both the dubious way that this distinction is often made (viz., while maintaining either the unity of the law/Old Testament or its abolition), and the strangeness of this distinction for Jews: see *Paul and the Law*, WUNT 29 (Tübingen: J. C. B. Mohr [Paul Siebeck], 1983), 23-41 (hereafter *P&L*). (He refutes in detail a learned but delicate attempted case here by K. Berger in *Die Gesetzesauslegung Jesu* [Neukirchen: Vluyn, 1972], esp. 1, 38-55.)

15. Räisänen makes a similar argument (*P&L*, 23-28).

16. Underlying this problem is the apparent fact that capacity and incapacity seem to be judgments of quality about the selfsame thing — a reality disguised by an uncritical use of spatial categories. But as we have seen, the latter collapse in any strict sense when we note their metaphorical function. We attribute either fundamental healthiness and wholeness *or* a degree of unhealthiness and depravity (perhaps quite extensive) to our ethical reasoning and activity. But we cannot attribute both judgments to them simultaneously! This would be the equivalent of claiming that an individual is at the same time entirely (that is, monochromatically) red and blue.

17. And this will limit in turn the ability of the theory to maneuver out of the difficulties associ-

ated with its "perfectionism" by relaxing its ethical demands. Any such affirmation exacerbates the problem we are discussing here of incoherence, and also preserves the problem of theodicy, which we will address in the next section.

18. This interpretative strategy is assessed in more detail in chapter three following, and also documented in more detail in part three, chapters ten and twelve.

19. Still other objections could be raised. It could be queried, for example, what the actual basis for this realization of depravity is. Here one faces again the problem that a deeply corrupt mind will struggle to formulate accurate thoughts about its own condition before God; one would expect, in fact, the formulation of inaccurate and evasive thoughts! Hence, an assertion of deep human depravity really makes sense only as a retrospective claim undergirded by revelation (at which point, arguably, it makes perfect sense). Conversely, Justification advocates have no basis for making this claim coherently; *they* are working *prospectively.* How then do they *know* at this point that humanity is depraved? This could only be a revelation, which would be inconsistent with the present epistemological construction and function of the model. (And if recourse was made to revelation in any case, then one would want to know why such an axiom was granted primacy at this point; a fragile or even arbitrary prior decision would then almost certainly be revealed.) In sum, the a priori assertion of human depravity is a risky venture that tends to break down the more it is examined; the doctrine is best left within a retrospective framework.

20. Are toddlers punished for throwing a tantrum?

21. It could arguably be relaxed and the model's rhetorical and theological objectives achieved if a strong emphasis were placed on human depravity; utterly sinful people would not fulfill even a relatively easy law. But again, this recalibration of the model would not solve the basic problem of God's unjust demands, along with the incoherence just noted of expecting people so constructed to process them rationally. And it contains further epistemological difficulties (see the preceding note).

22. That is, it could be countered immediately that God should have been generous from the start of the model. He should not have introduced this quality suddenly at a later stage in relation to only a privileged few. This seems capricious.

23. "By what logic or necessity did God become man, and by his death, as we believe and profess, restore life to the world, when he could have done this through the agency of some other person, angelic or human, or simply by willing it?" See *The Major Works: Anselm of Canterbury,* ed. and intro. Brian Davies and G. R. Evans (Oxford & New York: Oxford University Press, 1998), 265. *Cur Deus Homo,* translated in this edition as *Why God Became Man,* is on 250-356 (original ca. 1100 CE).

24. Note, our concern here is simply whether this argument works at the theoretical level, thereby saving the broader theory. The question whether Paul himself ever actually makes or alludes to this case will be considered later (although if the theory is not worth alluding to, then this subsequent question is clearly not so important).

25. Karl Barth engaged in a celebrated rereading of Anselm, suggesting that he had been greatly misunderstood, although not so much in his theory of the atonement as in his proof for God's existence (and this claim has also been contested): *Anselm: Fides Quaerens Intellectum: Anselm's Proof of the Existence of God in the Context of His Theological Scheme* (London: Pickwick Publications, 1975 [1931]). It is Anselm's "misunderstood" reading that is most useful here — that is, his reading in foundationalist terms. See also in this relation D. Bentley Hart, "A Gift Exceeding Every Debt: An Eastern Orthodox Appreciation of Anselm's *Cur Deus Homo,*" *Pro Ecclesia* 7 (1998): 333-49; and Robert W. Jenson, "On the Doctrine of the Atonement," *CTI Reflections* 9 (2007): 2-13 (*CTI* referring here to the Center of Theological Inquiry, Princeton, New Jersey).

26. The "fact" of human sin is also established prior to, and independently of any discussion of Christ's atonement, leading to the redefinitions of God's mercy and generosity already noted in Justification theory, *and* to a rationalistic appeal to the unbeliever to convert out of self-interest! See *Why God Became Man,* Bk 1, §§24-25, 312-3. This establishment of "the problem" in Book 1 is, moreover, characteristically longer than the discussion of the solution, in Book 2 (although Anselm complains in his Preface that the work was released prematurely, and Book 2 arguably shows signs of being less polished than Book 1). See *Why God Became Man,* Book 1, 250-315; and Book 2, 315-56.

27. And Anselm repeatedly asserts — essentially apodictically — that punishment or recompense for sin must be made in view of God's justice. So merciful acts of forgiveness and restoration — which Boso not infrequently suggests — are simply ruled out: see, i.a., *Why God Became Man,* Bk 1, §11, 283; §12, 284-6; §14, 287; §15, 289; §20, 303-5; §21, 306-7; §23, 308-9; §24, 311. It is therefore not that surprising Boso when eventually says, "I see that one has to look for some other 'mercy of God' than the 'mercy' to which you are referring" (§24, 312). Note also that Book 2 is then concerned for some time with the mechanics of the God-Man, or, the incarnation: see esp. §§7-9, 320-5.

28. See *Why God Became Man,* Bk 2, §6, 319-20.

29. See analogous criticisms of the sinister roles played by the currency trope/discourse/narrative in contemporary globalization's inequalities and colonializations by Romand Coles, "Contesting Cosmopolitan Currency: The Nepantilist Rose in the Cross(ing) of the Present," *Nepantla* 4.1 (2003): 5-40.

30. Quantitative notions enter the argument clearly and metaphorically from Book 1, §11, 283, onward. There Anselm suggests that "[i]f an angel or a man were always to render to God what he owes, he would never sin. . . . This is the debt which an angel, and likewise a man, owes to God. . . . Someone who does not render to God this honour due to him is taking away from God what is his, and dishonouring God, and this is what it is to sin. As long as he does not repay what he has taken away, he remains in a state of guilt." The standard retributive axioms of Justification theory are also stated clearly in Bk 1, §12, 284: "if no satisfaction is given, the way to regulate sin correctly is none other than to punish it. . . . Therefore, it is not fitting for God to forgive a sin without punishment. . . . Everyone knows that the righteousness of mankind is subject to a law whereby it is rewarded by God with a recompense proportional to its magnitude" (et cetera); and the Constantinian endorsement follows on p. 285 — "it belongs to no one to take vengeance, except to him who is Lord of all. I should explain that when earthly powers take action in this way in accordance with right, it is the Lord himself, by whom they have been appointed for the task, who is acting." So the NT teaches forgiveness so that Christians "should not presume to do something that belongs to God alone"! See also a recap of the same point in Bk 2, §19, 348-9.

31. George Lakoff points out that ethical systems based on strictness appeal heavily to quantitative metaphors within their systems of ethical accounting: see *Moral Politics: How Liberals and Conservatives Think,* 2nd ed. (London & Chicago: University of Chicago, 2001 [1996]), 44-107.

32. See A. C. Thiselton, *The First Epistle to the Corinthians: A Commentary on the Greek Text,* NIGTC (Grand Rapids, Mich., Cambridge, & Carlisle: Eerdmans & Paternoster, 2000), 475-79, esp.: "Cost in some form remains implicit in the use of price, although the imagery does not require that speculations are encouraged about *to* whom a price might be paid. The imagery stresses primarily the new ownership, and secondly a costly act on the part of the new owner" (477). In this general relation it is also worth noting that the entire discourse of slavery in the NT must be treated in a nuanced fashion: see Dale B. Martin, *Slavery as Salvation: The Metaphor of Slavery in Pauline Christianity* (New Haven, Conn., & London: Yale University Press, 1990); and I. A. H. Combes, *The Metaphor of Slavery in the Writings of the Early Church,* JSNTSup 156 (Sheffield: Sheffield Academic Press, 1998).

33. Admittedly, God is worshipped; however, "he" is invisible, cannot be imaged, and hence is known only indirectly, through the cosmos. He is also known through natural law, that is, in terms of a list of ethical propositions (continuing to assume for the sake of argument that the individuals are acquiring this information correctly). So God will be experienced directly only in the future at the last judgment, over which he presides. The various relations in this phase do not amount to a personal relationship; they could easily be effected by a book or a computer.

34. And Anselm's classic discussion illustrates this dilemma nicely. When Anselm and Boso turn to discuss who will benefit from the reward that God ought to give to Christ's payment, the conditional appropriation of that reward is clear, but its criteria are not: "B. . . . [I]t seems to me that God rejects no member of the human race who approaches him on this authority. A. So it is, *if* he makes the approach in the way that he should. Moreover, how one should approach the state of sharing in this grace . . . is something which Holy Scripture teaches . . ." (Bk 2, §19, 353; see also §20, 354).

35. This of course raises the possibility that "faith" in Paul's texts is *not* actually functioning as a

condition for salvation at all, which raises the further possibility that another, tighter explanation of its function could be supplied. If so, this might explain in addition the puzzling ambiguity that often surrounds discussions of faith. Despite its theoretical importance, interpreters often struggle to supply a precise description of the exact content of saving faith: is it faith in God, in Christ, in the gospel, or in all three? Ought it to be accompanied by repentance and/or contrition and/or confession? And what role do the sacraments play in relation to it? We will take up these difficulties when we address the appropriate texts in detail, from part three onward.

36. Although it is common for interpreters of Paul to use the signifier "faith" at this point, that translation can cause several possible confusions. First, "faith" is a substantive, not a verb, and it seems important, at least initially, to use an appropriate verb to emphasize the action undertaken by the individual in exercising the criterion. Second, "faith" (unlike "belief" or "believing") does not point clearly to the essentially cognitive relationship at the heart of the model. And third, the broader use of "the Faith" to refer to the gospel provides no indication of what is believed; at first glance it might seem again that one merely had to believe in the importance of believing, an absurd position as we have already noted. But the saving criterion "believing in Christ" is clear, information-based, apparently manageable, and appropriately particular.

37. See James W. McClendon and James M. Smith, *Convictions: Defusing Religious Relativism*, rev. ed. (Valley Forge, Pa.: Trinity Press International, 1994 [1975]). The point is also very familiar to students of Ludwig Wittgenstein.

38. I say "arguably" because this may be too much of a concession. It could be suggested that any nonempirical or nondeducible claims are inadmissible at this point because they cannot be verified by individuals who are operating in terms of the epistemology of phase one. Individuals *must* be able to evaluate the propositions being presented to them, and in phase one the only way they can do so is through some judgment of rational inference or deduction. In a sense, almost no proposition offered in relation to Christ would fall within this purview — certainly not the resurrection (see 1 Cor. 15:4). It is also worth noting that, strictly speaking, nothing *new* can be said about God in relation to Christ, because the axioms lying at the heart of the first phase cannot be overruled. (Acute framing tensions may be generated by accommodation here as well.)

39. It is no coincidence that a large apparatus of Evangelical apologetics exists at just this juncture. For example, many Christian students working within this paradigm rely heavily on Josh McDowell, *Evidence That Demands a Verdict,* rev. ed. (San Bernardino, Calif.: Here's Life Publishers, 1979), or one of his numerous other apologetic books (see www.josh.org).

40. I am aware that these terms are not being used with historical precision; however, a broad analogy should still hold, which suffices for the present discussion: see Richard A. Muller, "Arminius and Arminianism," in *The Dictionary of Historical Theology,* ed. Trevor A. Hart (Grand Rapids, Mich.: Eerdmans, 2000), 33-36; and Carl R. Trueman, "Calvinism," in *The Dictionary of Historical Theology,* 103-6.

41. In some respects this is a classic Lutheran move, both by Luther and within much subsequent Lutheranism and Protestantism — suggesting yet again the inappropriateness of calling Justification theory simply "Lutheran." Rather significantly, this position also enjoys the direct support of certain Pauline texts (as we will note in more detail shortly). This move also avoids the common criticism of the Arminian variant that faith is still a "work." I am not so concerned about avoiding that criticism, however, because "works," as far I can tell, are not wrong in and of themselves; they are wrong as a comprehensive soteriological system. And phase one in Justification theory, far from condemning a basic activity in terms of voluntarism, actually expects this.

42. I do not for one moment deny the importance of faith in the life of the Christian. What is at issue is not its presence but the point at which it begins, and then by whose agency. That Paul eventually speaks extensively of faith does not entail that he is speaking of it as a condition for the appropriation of salvation. It may be a result of salvation. So any appeal to the mere presence of "faith" within Paul's texts settles nothing. The key question remains what the point of privileging it here is (along with how such privileging can be explained separately from Christ; see just below).

43. And we might also be puzzled at this point by the determined separation between this gift

of faith and Christ, especially if the Spirit is held to generate faith in converts. Presumably any other key Christian virtues are mediated through Christ.

44. Alternatively, phase one is not a condition, at which point the entire theory of Justification has actually been abandoned, and new readings must be supplied for the relevant texts in Paul!

45. The decision of faith in the Arminian variant can at least explain why the church is grounded in particularity: faith responds to a certain message carried by specific people and presented at a given time and place. Furthermore, only some choose to respond in this way. But the Arminian variant can supply a robust explanation of this too: only certain individuals have traversed the preceding argumentative progressions, thereby becoming predisposed to accept the solution. However, the Calvinist variant has eliminated this notion of acceptance (not to mention problematized its mode in terms of faith), and in so doing either imperiled the particularity of the Christian condition or imposed it arbitrarily and incoherently. Once again, it would seem that the price being paid for apology is too high.

46. Strictly speaking, this arrangement is not unjust, although advocates of the Arminian variant might claim that for God to save individuals unconditionally, without their consent, is unjust. In my view, however, this claim derives from a characteristically modern Liberal political viewpoint and so is only arguably in touch with a more universal definition of justice. This debate is discussed further in part two, chapter nine.

Notes to Chapter Three

1. This exercise will also prove useful when we consider Justification theory's textual base and its "proximate" frames, beginning in part three, chapter ten (that is, the immediate contexts of its key textual sections in Paul's letters). The question could also be raised at this point why I did not approach Justification in this way as well, in the preceding discussion — inductively.

This would have been possible. But it might also have been disadvantageous in certain respects. I have structured the overarching argument in a theory-driven way to prepare the reader for an especially self-conscious approach to Romans 1–4 — one aware of the theological issues in play, along with all their difficult consequences. I will also challenge the way this text has been conventionally construed, suggesting a fundamentally different approach. These are in fact my principal goals in what follows. Placing a brief synopsis of my target text and its customary reading at the beginning of my analysis would therefore risk a tacit, if not overt conferral of legitimacy on it — the very thing I want to avoid! (It would also be necessary to return to a much more detailed presentation of this reading just prior to its critique — the task here of chapter ten. So quite significant repetition would be necessary as well.)

But I have no such qualms about Romans 5–8. It is not a target of revisionist analysis or a principal concern in what follows (although it is my ultimate concern); it is at this point merely a foil to my focus on Romans 1–4 and related texts, introducing a particular set of problems. So a brief inductive approach to its concerns seems unobjectionable. Hence, the structure and focus of my overarching project do not necessitate methodological symmetry at this point.

2. That is, in addition to the broader project that we are currently engaged with, if it is still being viewed hypothetically vis-à-vis Paul.

3. This method has a scholarly pedigree in the deliberations of the Pauline Theology Group of the Society of Biblical Literature through the 1980s: see Jouette M. Bassler, ed., *Pauline Theology*, vol. 1, *Thessalonians, Philippians, Galatians, Philemon* (Minneapolis: Fortress, 1991); David M. Hay, ed., *Pauline Theology*, vol. 2, *1 & 2 Corinthians* (Minneapolis: Fortress, 1993); David M. Hay and E. Elizabeth Johnson, eds., *Pauline Theology*, vol. 3, *Romans* (Minneapolis: Fortress, 1995); and David M. Hay and E. Elizabeth Johnson, eds., *Pauline Theology*, vol. 4, *Looking Back, Pressing On* (Atlanta: Scholars, 1997).

4. See my study *The Quest for Paul's Gospel: A Suggested Strategy* (London: T&T Clark International [Continuum], 2005) for some similar articulations, esp. chapters three through five, 56-111.

5. Implicit in this characterization of God and God's actions through Christ and the Spirit — and considerably reinforced by the characterization of Adamic humanity that we will take up momentarily — is a powerful explanation of mission and hence also of Paul's apostolic calling to the pagans.

6. And it is hard to avoid the impression that he enters this condition from *outside*, thereby *assuming* it: see *Quest*, 89-90.

7. It is well known that this is not an entirely lucid analogy.

8. See his *Two Concepts of Liberty* (Oxford: Clarendon, 1958).

9. We will revisit this issue in more detail in chapter five when we discuss Paul's conversion.

10. See esp. 4:19b; 9:9-10. And in my view this opens up the possibility of a narrative, rather than a strictly gendered reading of the male markers that Paul uses here: see *Quest*, 69-94.

11. Nevertheless, we should probably infer with some confidence that a God so acting in the past and present will act consistently, and therefore not do violence to humanity, or necessarily engage with some future punishment of people. But this is not necessarily to suggest that some sort of exclusion or even elimination is not possible. It is of course tempting to appeal to Romans 11 at this point, specifically to v. 26, "and so all Israel will be saved," and vv. 29-32, "for the gifts and the calling of God are irrevocable. . . . For God has imprisoned all in disobedience so that he may be merciful to all." But various other Pauline texts could also be cited, and on both sides of the issue. We will discuss Rom. 9–11 in more detail in part five, chapter nineteen; the issue of judgment is addressed in more detail momentarily.

12. It is also articulated briefly in *Quest*, esp. 57-62, 101-4, 113-17.

13. See Rom. 1:16-17; 3:21-22; 5:5; 8:27; 11:25; 12:1-2, 3; 16:25 (if genuine); 1 Cor. 1:18–2:16; 7:10, 12; 13:12; 15:3-8, 51; 2 Cor. 3:2-3, 17-18; 4:5-6; Gal. 1:1, 11-12, 15-17; 2:2; 4:9; Phil. 3:8-11, 12, 20-21; 1 Thess. 1:5; 2:4, 13; 4:15-17; see also Eph. 1:4-5, 17-23; 3:3, 8-10, 18-19; 4:13-16; Col. 1:11-13, 26-27; 2:2-4; 3:4; 2 Thess. 1:7, 2:7-8, 13-14.

The evidence from 1 Cor. 1–2 is especially important in this relation. This argument simply seems to rule out "natural theology" or "general revelation" in its general attack on "the wise, the literate, and the debater of this age" (1:20 DC).

A case can be made that Paul's argument here presupposes the failure of some prior phase of natural theology in 1:21: see ἐπειδὴ . . . οὐκ ἔγνω ὁ κόσμος διὰ τῆς σοφίας τὸν Θεὸν. . . . But the force of ἐπειδὴ should fall on ἐν τῇ σοφίᾳ τοῦ Θεοῦ here rather than the clause οὐκ ἔγνω ὁ κόσμος διὰ τῆς σοφίας τὸν Θεὸν. Moreover, in its contingent situation, I am not convinced that this is the correct way to read this data in any case. Much of Paul's argumentative and theological impetus here seems to come from Isa. 29:14, quoted in 1:19, where God decides to shame the wise and powerful through the foolish preaching of the cross. So the frustration of the wise is grounded in God's agency, and not the failure of natural theology. Furthermore, their wisdom in context seems linked primarily to sophisticated argumentation and speech, not to natural theology (see 1:17b, 20; 2:1-5) — things Paul has good reason to criticize at Corinth! Against them, the preaching of the cross by Paul mediates a hidden, mysterious Wisdom revealed by the Spirit. So there is in my view no need to assume the prior failure of some project in terms of natural theology here. A brief treatment of this passage especially sensitive to its intertextual dimensions is given by Richard B. Hays, *First Corinthians* (Louisville, Kentucky: John Knox Press, 1997), 26-47. A. C. Thiselton's treatment is typically comprehensive and insightful: *The First Epistle to the Corinthians: A Commentary on the Greek Text,* NIGTC (Grand Rapids, Michigan & Cambridge & Carlisle: Eerdmans & Paternoster, 2000), 147-286.

It might be replied that Acts 17:22-31 — Paul's speech to the Areopagus — at least provides evidence of Paul's occasional endorsement of "natural theology" in his preaching. But there are several difficulties with this case: (1) even if it does attest to Paul's preaching, its introduction does not remove the fundamental epistemological contradiction already apparent at *this* point; however, (2) it is difficult to argue directly from this speech to Paul's generalized practice given the function of speeches within Hellenistic historiography in general, and in Acts in particular (i.e., where they carry the plot and expound the narrative as much as represent a historical speech-act); (3) Paul's argument here should be viewed in any case as a clever strategy designed to avoid certain serious charges (see 17:18), and hence in part a concession to difficult circumstances; (4) there are irreconcilable differences between the arguments of Acts 17:22-31 and Rom. 1:18-32, so its introduction creates as many difficulties as it arguably removes (people ought to infer from God's creative powers that he therefore does not live in shrines and cannot be "served by human hands" [v. 25]; moreover, their *own* semi-divine constitution indicates that God cannot be imaged [vv. 28-29; cf. Rom. 1:23!]; but this "ignorance" has until now been "overlooked" [rather than generating sexual depravity and other appalling vices as in Rom. 1:24-32, thereby earning the sentence of death]); and (5) it is doubtful that this speech does explicitly endorse natural theology and general revelation in the *foundational* manner that Justification theory needs it; i.e., Paul does not build here on generally revealed premises that undergird both the problem and the solution, but makes a discontinuous epistemological transition in vv. 30-31 with the command to repent in relation to the preaching of the resurrected Christ and the coming day of Judgment. Consequently, there is no explicit *epistemological* relation between his final Christian exhortations and the initial claims made by Paul in the speech, although a *rhetorical* relationship is discernible. "True knowledge and application of Greek philosophy should not endorse idolatry," Paul suggests, so such thinkers should repent at the proclamation of Christ and the promise of judgment, rather than accusing and condemning Paul of advocating unacceptable foreign gods in Athens.

This speech is much discussed, but not always sensitively in relation to the theological and epistemological issues. However, Barth is of course alert to them (see *CD* II.1, 119-23 — although his tactical treatment of Rom. 1 is different from mine), as is my colleague, C. Kavin Rowe. (I am grateful for his expertise and references in relation to this text, which inform much of this note.) More representative of the generally blander NT approaches is C. K. Barrett, *A Critical and Exegetical Commentary on the Acts of the Apostles,* vol. 1, *Preliminary Introduction and Commentary on Acts I–XIV,* ICC (London: T&T Clark [Continuum], 1998), 834-54; see also Martin Dibelius's classic study, "Paul on the Areopagus," ch. 2 in *Studies in the Acts of the Apostles,* ed. H. Greeven, tr. M. Ling (London: SCM, 1956 [1951]), 26-77; T. D. Barnes, "An Apostle on Trial," *Journal of Theological Studies* 20 (1969): 407-19; and, more recently, N. Clayton Croy, "Hellenistic Philosophies and the Preaching of the Resurrection (Acts 17:18, 32)," *Novum Testamentum* 39 (1997): 21-39.

14. Formerly "under sin": see Rom. 5:12-21; 6:6-7, 10-23; 7:7-8, 11, 13, 20, 23; 8:5-8; 11:30-32; 1 Cor. 3:1-4; 5:11-13; 6:9-11; 15:22, 54-56; 2 Cor. 5:16-17, 21; 6:14–7:1 (arguably); Gal. 1:4; 3:13, 22-24; 4:2-9; 1 Thess. 1:9; 4:3-7; 5:6-10; see also Eph. 2:1-2, 11-12; 4:17-19, 22; Col. 1:13-14; 2:13; 3:5, 8-9; 2 Thess. 2:10-12; 3:2, 3.

15. See the more detailed discussion of this debated question in part four, chapter eighteen.

16. For the "Father" in Paul, see Rom. 1:7; 6:4; 8:15; 15:6; 1 Cor. 1:3; 8:6; 15:24; 2 Cor. 1:2; 6:18; 11:31; Gal. 1:1, 3-4; 4:2, 6; Phil. 1:2; 2:11, 4:20; 1 Thess. 1:1, 3; 2:11; 3:11, 13; Phlm. 3; see also Eph. 1:2, 17; 2:18; 3:14; 4:6; 5:20, 31; 6:23; Col. 1:2, 12; 3:17; 2 Thess. 1:1; 2:16.

For the Son, see Rom. 1:3, 9; 5:10; 8:3, 29, 32; 9:9; 1 Cor. 1:9; 15:28; 2 Cor. 1:19; Gal. 1:16; 2:20; 4:4, 6; Phil. 2:22; 1 Thess. 1:10; see also Eph. 4:13; Col. 1:13; 2 Thess. 2:3.

For the Spirit, see Rom. 1:4, 9; 5:5; 7:6; 8:2, 4, 11, 13, 23, 26; 9:1; 12:11; 14:17; 15:13, 16, 19, 30; 1 Cor. 2:4, 10-14; 3:16; 6:17, 19; 7:34, 40; 12:3, 7, 11, 13; 2 Cor. 1:22; 3:3, 6, 8, 17; 5:5; 6:6; 12:18; 13:13; Gal. 3:2, 5, 14; 4:6, 29; 5:5, 22, 25; Phil. 1:19; 2:1; 3:3; 1 Thess. 1:5; 4:8; 5:19, 23; see also Eph. 1:13, 17; 2:2, 18, 22; 3:5, 16; 4:3-4; 5:18; 6:17; Col. 1:8; 2 Thess. 2:13.

17. So the two contrasting systems will create quite different expectations vis-à-vis any judgment texts in Paul. And consequently it is important to avoid begging the question when these texts are discussed exegetically. Any process of judgment in Paul is not *automatically* or even *necessarily* retributive and/or soteriological (i.e., one on which salvation rests). This important question is resumed when Paul's attitude to coercion and violence is discussed in §3.10 just below. (Further options for these texts will also be created when the ancient discourse of kingship is considered in part four, chapter seventeen.)

18. If perfect righteousness needs to be imputed to the Christian, then this would justify his sinless life. However, the exegetical basis for this function will be examined carefully in due course and, in my view, found wanting.

19. In view of his death's representative and generally atoning function, it is understandable why sacrificial metaphors would sometimes be used to explain it. But we should not assume automati-

cally that these denote a satisfactory function — a question arising again, and so addressed in detail, in part four, chapter seventeen. Cultic imagery in Paul is also used rather more widely than this: see Rom. 5:2 ("procession" to the Father; see also Eph. 2:18; 3:12); 12:1 (sacrifice of "Christian" bodies); 15:16 (sacrifice of the pagans); 2 Cor. 2:14 (knowledge of Christ as odor of a sacrifice), 2:15 (Christians as odor of a sacrifice), 2:16 (sacrificial odor of death and of life); Phil. 2:17 (Paul's possible death as sacrifice); and 4:18 (monetary gift as sacrifice).

20. This resonates with the principal point of departure for McLeod Campbell's important reflections on soteriology. He perceived that conditional systems inevitably generate a high level of anxiety, because any converts, in ultimate terms, are necessarily dependent for their salvation upon an action under their own control and may consequently doubt their ability to fulfill that action consistently. In addition, unconditional but unbenevolent soteriologies generate insecurity within Christians in equal measure. An unconditional and benevolent system, however — which McLeod Campbell argued was the essence of Calvin — should produce a contrasting disposition of security and assurance: see J. McLeod Campbell, *The Nature of the Atonement* (Edinburgh: Handsel, 1996 [1856]).

21. See most obviously Rom. 6:1-10 and 1 Cor. 10:16-22.

22. The phrase "in Christ" or its equivalent, which denotes — at least in some instances — this close relationship, is ubiquitous in Paul: see (i.a.) Rom. 3:24; 6:11, 23; 8:1-2, 39; 9:1; 12:5; 15:17; 16:3, 7, 9-10; 1 Cor. 1:2, 4, 30; 3:1; 4:10, 15, 17; 15:18-19, 22, 31; 16:24; 2 Cor. 1:21; 2:14, 17; 5:17, 19; 12:2, 19; Gal. 2:4, 16-17; 3:14, 26, 28; 5:6; Phil. 1:1, 26; 2:1, 5; 3:3, 9, 14; 4:7, 19, 21; 1 Thess. 2:14; 4:16; 5:18; Phlm. 6, 8, 20, 23; see also Eph. 1:1, 3, 9, 12, 20; 2:6-7, 10, 13; 3:6, 11, 21; 4:32; Col. 1:2, 4, 28; 2:5; and 2 Thess. 1:1, 12; 3:4, 12.

23. That is, Paul's impassioned evangelism and pedagogy of pagans is so obvious that it is easy to forget its strangeness. But here we find a plausible explanation of just this dynamic.

24. See Heb. 12:2 (DC). It has been asserted that Jesus' possession of beliefs is Arian: see P. F. Esler, *Conflict and Identity in Romans: The Social Setting of Paul's Letter* (Minneapolis, Minn.: Fortress, 2003), 158-59. But it is a fully Chalcedonian position to endorse Jesus' humanity, and without beliefs Jesus would clearly not be human. Esler surmises that it is a "residual legacy of liberal Christianity [in North America], stronger than Karl Barth's influence could budge" (159), within which Jesus is — presumably merely — an example, "our 'buddy.'" But it is futile to deny the presence of an exemplary strand in Paul's thinking. The challenge, rather, is to interpret that strand constructively. If Jesus' role is interpreted in terms of participation, then Esler's fears would presumably be allayed. Meanwhile, it is ironic to note Esler's deployment of Barth on the other side of this issue. Barth was the probable origin of the christocentric view's appearance in English-speaking scholarship in the 1950s in the work of G. Hebert and T. F. Torrance, and in France in 1960 in the work of P. Vallotton. Barth himself also provides rich resources for understanding all aspects of Paul's thinking in relation to "the faithfulness of Christ" — and not in Arian or (theologically) liberal terms.

25. Compare 1 Cor. 15:1-11 and probably also vv. 14 and 17 with Phil. 1:27; 2:17; and 1 Thess. 1:3, 8; 3:2, 5.

26. See Rom. 4:24-25; 10:9-10 (treated in more detail in part four, chapter eighteen, and part five, chapter nineteen).

27. See Rom. 4:17b-22.

28. Gal. 5:22-23.

29. As signaled especially strongly, of course, by 1 Cor. 13.

30. See esp. Gal. 5:6, and arguably also 2:20 (treated in more detail in part five, chapter twenty).

31. Notably Galatians 3. We will treat this text more carefully in due course (see part five, chapter twenty); see also *Quest*, 208-32.

32. These texts are discussed in detail in the sustained exegetical treatment of the issues that begins in part four (see esp. chapters sixteen through nineteen); the issue is also noted in chapter six.

33. No gender-specific reference is intended by the use of this pronoun. Unfortunately, English lacks a nongendered pronoun that in ordinary usage references a person. A personal reference *is* intended.

34. We link hands at this point with the well-known debate over "the third use of the law," but I am going to press it harder in this relation (because it would be inconsistent not to).

35. Räisänen presses Cranfield on this point: see *Paul and the Law*, WUNT 29 (Tübingen: J. C. B. Mohr [Paul Siebeck], 1983), 42-50. Cranfield is well aware that the law "correctly understood" ought to remain in force and so attempts to show that all Paul's abolitionist statements in relation to the law — Gal. 3:15-20; 2 Cor. 3; Rom. 7:1-6 and 6:14 (to which Räisänen adds Gal. 2:18; Rom. 14:14, 20; 1 Cor. 10:23; and 6:12) — concern a "misunderstanding" of the law in terms of "legalism" et cetera ("St Paul and the Law," *Scottish Journal of Theology* 17 [1964]: 43-68). But Räisänen correctly shows how this special pleading is ultimately rather unconvincing. Paul did (at least in these texts) clearly assert the abolition of the Torah itself — the very words of Moses! A so-called misunderstanding is never criticized, while the correct solution to such a problem in any case would clearly be a corrected understanding and not the death of Christ (see Rom. 7:1-6). And this then generates the difficulty that we note above: Justification has — as Cranfield intuited — no good grounds for abolishing the law, and yet — as Räisänen shows — Paul does so. But the problem is also broader and deeper than this. Paul's letters and life as a whole clearly do *not* expect complete observance by his pagan converts of the Jewish law. What, indeed, were the Jerusalem conference, the incident at Antioch, *and* the Galatian controversy, about (Gal. 2:1-10, 11-14; Acts 15; Galatians, passim)? In my terminology, this amounts to an acute tension at the systematic frame.

36. In terms of evidence, it is difficult to find material in Paul's letters that is *not* in some sense ethical, while clearly none is based on the need for full law-observance. Even descriptive statements concerning the movements of Paul and his co-workers usually contain ethical implications. Liturgical acts of doxology and prayer implicitly urge imitation as well.

37. The assembly of saved individuals (that is, the church) will probably emphasize the purity of its information, since this lies at the heart of its self-definition. And that information must include both a correct account of the pre-Christian condition, including its journey to despair, and a correct definition of the saving criterion — according to our earlier analysis, "faith," or belief in Christ. Correct confession in the sense of the affirmation of the same vital pieces of information will probably then characterize any assembly arising out of this model. Not to grasp or to affirm the correct information is not to be saved. So the community *must* consist, at bottom, of the like-minded. Paradoxically, the potential for endless schism is implicit in this arrangement as the contours of the pre-Christian journey, and the nature of the ensuing saving criteria, are nuanced (and here presumably at times through a multiplication of criteria designed to deal with embarrassing ethical shortfalls).

38. We have already noted the epistemological tensions implicit here. It is intriguing to ask, however, if the presence of this principle within the theory implies the existence of some guild of biblical scholars who are able to interpret the Scriptures appropriately. This would involve trained scriptural interpretation and exposition, which are quite skilled operations, especially in a contested setting. Hence, an entire subculture of critical biblical exposition may actually undergird the model in its ecclesial setting.

39. And this is also not to deny that institutionalization in some sense may be necessary.

40. This point is too obvious to need extensive documentation; however, see Rom. 12:3-8; 14; 15:1-7, 26-27; 16:3-16; 1 Cor. 10:16-17; 12:4-27; 13; 14; 2 Cor. 6:16 (arguably); 8:13-15; Gal. 1:2; 3:26-29; 6:1-6; Phil. 1:27-28; 2:1-5; 3:20; 4:2-3, 15-16; 1 Thess. 1:3-10; 4:9-10; 5:14-15 (i.e., Paul's various statements about the church as Christ's body or a new temple; the claims underlying much of his discussion of the collection for Jerusalem; the constant command that Christians greet one another; and so on — and note, this is not to invoke his extensive familial and household discourses). See also Eph. 1:10; 2:14-22; 4:4-16, 25; Col. 1:18; 2:19; 3:12-14; 2 Thess. 1:3.

41. Paul's emphases in many texts upon the patriarchal blessing and upon promise should also be noted: regarding promise, see Rom. 9:6-29; 11:5-10, 25-32; esp. 9:8, 9; also 15:8; 2 Cor. 1:20; 7:1; and Gal. 3:14, 17, 21, 22, 29; 4:23, 28; and regarding blessing, in addition to the foregoing, see Gal. 3:8, 9, 14.

42. Calvin is committed to it at times: see a more detailed treatment of this issue in part two, chapter eight.

43. Both also attach considerable importance to the Scriptures. However, Justification does so,

as we have already seen, rather inconsistently in epistemological terms. The alternative theory does so consistently, because it endorses a particular, revelatory epistemology throughout.

44. It is important to note that the roles of the law are rather different in these two different schemas. As is already well known, the law serves a critical preparatory function in Justification theory. It also returns after conversion in some "third" capacity (the other role being its underwriting of government). The alternative schema does not need to assign a soteriological role to the law in the pre-Christian situation at all, and argues for its transcendence in the new, Christian dispensation in view of the centrality of Christ and the Spirit — the new Torah, so to speak.

45. These references *must*, however, be correctly interpreted; many are framed by a distinctive, post-Christian setting that adds certain critical theological dynamics. Some of these are articulated in part five, chapter nineteen following, when Rom. 9–10 are discussed; some are also touched on in part five, chapter twenty, in relation to Gal. 3 and the famous metaphor used there of the law as a pedagogue; see also, for a programmatic outline of pitfalls as against more promising methodologies, chapter seven, "Paul's Gospel, Judaism, and the Law," *Quest*, 132-45. For discussions of Israel elsewhere in Paul (i.e., outside Romans), see 1 Cor. 10:18; 2 Cor. 3:7-15; 11:22; Gal. 6:16; Phil. 3:5; see also Eph. 2:12; for references to Ἰουδαῖοι, see 1 Cor. 1:22; 9:20; 10:32; 12:13; 2 Cor. 11:24; Gal. 2:13; 3:28; 1 Thess. 2:14; see also Col. 3:11.

46. I am making a strictly theoretical set of points at this stage in my argument, so it is entirely possible for advocates of Justification nevertheless *not* to endorse these implications, and church history provides numerous examples of this. However, I would still want to ask what grounds such figures provide for resisting these implications in terms of the theory itself — as against in terms of the alternative theory evident in Paul, or a different root metaphor concerning God, or by appealing to other biblical passages. I am, in short, principally concerned with whether Justification theory can resource different approaches to punishment and related notions of government, or is intrinsically committed to punitive practices.

47. This fuses participatory and ethical concerns; for a detailed analysis of this text, see part five, chapter twenty-one.

48. "Their destruction" is admittedly present here; this and analogous texts are addressed shortly.

49. Note that I am presupposing here Susan Eastman's reading of Gal. 4:30: "'Cast Out the Slave Woman and Her Son': The Dynamics of Exclusion and Inclusion in Galatians 4.30," *Journal for the Study of the New Testament* 28 (2006): 309-36.

50. On this verse, and the action in view through vv. 1-13, see Thiselton, *The First Epistle to the Corinthians*, 382-418. Thiselton argues — persuasively in my view — that the action decreed in v. 5 is not a death sentence, as many have thought, but a speech-act effecting the expulsion of the outrageously unethical offender from the Spirit-filled world of the community into the fleshly world outside the church. It seems intended to produce repentance, thereby destroying the flesh and saving the spirit (see 2 Cor. 7:8-12). It also seems oriented primarily in terms of table fellowship (so v. 11). Hence, this is not a punishment so much as a fundamentally pedagogical action.

51. This point is made especially clearly in the disputed Eph. 6:10-18. The Christian is armed there against the devil, the rulers, the authorities, "the cosmic powers of this present darkness, [and] the spiritual forces of evil in the heavenly places" with truth, righteousness, the gospel of peace, fidelity, salvation, and the Spirit, the latter being especially present in prayer. A more slender illustration of essentially the same point is provided by the undisputed 1 Thess. 5:8, where the Christian's breastplate consists of faith and love and her helmet the hope of salvation. (See also Isa. 59:17.)

52. I mean here by this controversial term simply that the visible world is understood to be dominated by superhuman forces: see J. Louis Martyn, *Theological Issues in the Letters of Paul* (Nashville: Abingdon, 1997), 111-40. This term and its implications are further defined in much of what follows — especially part one, chapters five and six, part four, chapter thirteen, and part five, chapter twenty. Related to this discourse is the notion of "powers" or spiritual forces: see G. B. Caird, *Principalities and Powers: A Study in Pauline Theology* (Oxford: Clarendon Press, 1956); Walter Wink, *Naming the Powers: The Language of Power in the New Testament* (Philadelphia: Fortress 1984); Wesley

Carr, *Angels and Principalities: The Background, Meaning, and Development of the Pauline Phrase hai archai kai hai exousiai*, SNTSMS 42 (Cambridge: Cambridge University Press, 1981); and Peter W. Macky, *St. Paul's Cosmic War Myth: A Military Version of the Gospel* (New York: P. Lang, 1998).

53. My inclination is to include 2 Cor. 5:10 under this rubric of Christian accountability as a dim echo of the threats of 1 Corinthians 3. The language is consistently first person plural, that is, inclusive of Paul and his audience.

54. To speak κατὰ ἄνθρωπον, it is more like a job appraisal than a job interview.

55. We will discuss the dating of Romans in more detail in part four, chapter thirteen. Suffice it to say here that a conventional date would suggest that the early years of Nero's reign are in view, and an earlier, more radical date, the last years of the emperor Claudius. So on either view the particular government in question was reasonably good.

56. D*, F, and G omit the prepositional phrase. Note also the cognate for ἐκδίκησις in 2 Thess. 1:8.

57. This text is much discussed, but I am assuming a conventional attribution of its positions to Paul at this point. An excellent treatment is Jan Botha, *Subject to Whose Authority? Multiple Readings of Romans 13* (Atlanta: Scholars Press, 1994); Robert Jewett's treatment is also exemplary, with fulsome annotation in *Romans,* Hermeneia (Minneapolis, Minn.: Fortress, 2007), 780-803; and Richard B. Hays's treatment is nuanced and significant in *The Moral Vision of the New Testament* (New York: HarperCollins, 1996), 5, 174, 185 (n. 15), 187-88, 190, 230-53, 330-31, 467. I deny, however, that this material is overtly presuppositional for Paul, and hence potentially operative in the "state of nature," as a generic datum obvious to any right-thinking person (i.e., that it is part of phase one in Justification theory). The God who establishes the governing authorities in 13:1-2 has just been identified as the God of Jewish and Christian confession in 12:19, whose actions are also illuminated by Scriptures peculiar to that historical tradition (i.e., Deut. 32:35 and Prov. 25:21, quoted in vv. 19 and 20 respectively). Paul's conceptual locus at this point must therefore be sought in the complex Jewish and Hellenistic discourse concerning government.

58. See Jewett, *Romans,* 777-78.

59. I do not find the arguments against its authenticity, and in favor of its interpolation, convincing — as convenient as that would be! They are sagely scrutinized by Robert Jewett in *The Thessalonian Correspondence: Pauline Rhetoric and Millenarian Piety* (Philadelphia: Fortress, 1986), 36-41.

60. See the elegant suggestions of Martinus C. de Boer, "Pauline Apocalypticism," in *The Encyclopedia of Apocalypticism*, vol. 1, *The Origins of Apocalypticism in Judaism and Christianity,* ed. Bernard McGinn, John J. Collins, Stephen J. Stein (London: Continuum, 2000 [1998]), 345-83.

61. Related discussions of violence, Christian pacifism, etc., are noted in chapter six. Insightful overviews of the Pauline data informed by a pacifist tradition may be found in Hays, *The Moral Vision of the New Testament,* esp. 16-59 (and see also 60-72), 317-46; and Willard M. Swartley, *Covenant of Peace: The Missing Peace in New Testament Theology and Ethics* (Grand Rapids, Mich.: Eerdmans, 2006), esp. 189-253.

62. In particular, this will allow us to address E. P. Sanders's ingenious attempted solution to these systematic tensions after we have first considered his magisterial account of "the Jewish problem" — addressed here following, in chapter four, in my terms, as an empirical difficulty generated at Justification's frame by its claims concerning Paul's Jewish background. And this also follows the order in which Sanders himself addressed these issues in his major publications on Paul — *Paul and Palestinian Judaism* (Philadelphia: Fortress, 1977), and *Paul, the Law, and the Jewish People* (Philadelphia: Fortress, 1983).

Notes to Chapter Four

1. See esp. part two, chapter nine.

2. Because of these objective initial claims, Justification theory automatically "acquires" individuals irrespective of their own locations and self-understandings. The theory's account of their situ-

ation is correct as against their own. Moreover, once acquired, because of the axioms the theory brings to bear, those individuals *must* be driven to the point of despair that constitutes the ideal context for the proclamation of the gospel; either that, or they are justly condemned. So the entire theory has a "seek-and-destroy" quality. It acquires its targets and then reduces them inevitably to a particular negative disposition that is meant to lead on to salvation. It just needs to be let loose to do its work, at any time and in any place. Its advocates of course tend to view the theory's simple objectivity and sheer inevitability as strengths.

3. Everyone has access to this information and *ought* to follow these progressions. Hence, those who refuse to do so are culpable; they incur judgments of irrationality and/or willful disobedience, and ultimately "their condemnation is deserved" (Rom. 3:8).

4. Although this also requires preaching. More accurately, then, we might say that everyone who grasps the truth about reality will be ready to become a Christian.

5. It should be noted in addition that we have already dealt with a third cluster of difficulties — the derivation of the model's basic axioms about God from the contemplation of the cosmos — as an intrinsic problem. Those criticisms could be deployed at this point as well but seemed best treated as a theoretical and argumentative, rather than a strictly empirical question.

6. Philadephia: Fortress. Hereafter *P&PJ*.

7. See (i.a.) Solomon Schechter, *Some Aspects of Rabbinic Judaism* (New York: Schocken, 1961 [1909]); C. G. Montefiore, *Judaism and St. Paul: Two Essays* (London: Max Goschen, 1914); see also H. Loewe and C. G. Montefiore, eds., *A Rabbinic Anthology* (New York: Schocken, 1974 [1938]); George Foot Moore, "Christian Writers on Judaism," *Harvard Theological Review* 14 (1921): 197-254; and *Judaism in the First Centuries of the Christian Era — The Age of the Tannaim*, 3 vols. (Cambridge: Harvard University Press, 1927-1930); W. D. Davies, *Paul and Rabbinic Judaism: Some Rabbinic Elements in Pauline Theology*, 4th ed. (London: SPCK, 1980 [1948]); E. R. Goodenough, *Jewish Symbols in the Greco-Roman Period*, 13 vols. (New York: Pantheon, 1953-1968); David Daube, *The New Testament and Rabbinic Judaism* (London: Athlone, 1956); Samuel Sandmel, *Judaism and Christian Beginnings* (Oxford: Oxford University Press, 1978); also *The Genius of Paul*, 3rd ed. (Philadelphia: Fortress, 1979 [1958]); James Parkes, "Jews and Christians in the Constantinian Empire," in *Studies in Church History*, ed. C. W. Dugmore and C. Duggan (London: Thomas Nelson, 1964), 69-79; also *The Conflict of the Church and the Synagogue: A Study in the Origins of Antisemitism* (New York: Athenaeum, 1974); H. J. Schoeps, *Paul: The Theology of the Apostle in the Light of Jewish Religious History*, trans. Harold Knight (London & Philadelphia: Lutterworth Press & Westminster, 1961); Richard N. Longenecker, *Paul, Apostle of Liberty* (New York: Harper & Row, 1964).

8. This "narrative of the problem" echoes — in its earliest phases — Moore's account, which traces an inadequate Christian historiography of Judaism in detail through Weber, Bousset, and Schürer ("Christian Writers on Judaism," 228-48), although Moore also includes a brief notation on a dependent English analysis by Oesterley and Box (248-50). Moore grounds Weber's work in careful accounts of his academic context (228), and previous Christian analyses of Judaism through the centuries (198-221). In other words, Weber is not the *origin* of the false analysis, but a particular systematization of it, with additional false elements. Ironically, Weber ignores a responsible contemporary account of Judaism by Gfroerer because — Moore opines — the latter was a pupil of F. C. Baur's at Tübingen *and* a convert to Catholicism (231)! One of Weber's most important innovations was, however, to present Judaism as the antithesis of (Protestant) Christianity, whereas the Reformers had generally sought to present the older Jewish views in parallel with their own over against Catholicism (which is not to say that they were not critical of Jews). So Weber repositioned Judaism emphatically on the side of "the problem" in Paul. He also embodied a modern trend toward a deistic description of Judaism in terms of an "abstract," "transcendent" God (251-52). Moore attributes this to the influence of individualistic pietism, which sought an antithesis to the intimate piety distinctive of Jesus in the Judaism of his time (252).

9. According to Sanders, it is not a "system" in the conventional sense of that term, nor is it a highly articulated and fundamentally future-oriented soteriology, but it does possess a basic coher-

ence and all-pervasiveness, and it speaks to concerns of "getting in" and "staying in." His distinctions in this relation are revisited in part three, chapter twelve.

10. See the classic studies by (i.a.) James H. Cone, *A Black Theology of Liberation* (Philadelphia: J. P. Lippencott, 1970); Gustavo Gutiérrez, *A Theology of Liberation*, 15th anniversary ed. (Maryknoll, N.Y.: Orbis, 1988 [1973]); Rosemary Radford Ruether, *Faith and Fratricide: The Theological Roots of Anti-Semitism* (New York: Seabury, 1974); and E. Schüssler Fiorenza, *In Memory of Her: A Feminist Theological Reconstruction of Christian Origins* (New York & London: Crossroad & SCM, 1983).

11. We revisit the most important contributions to this revision of Jewish description in §5 below; the relevant revisions of Paul are treated in part three, chapter twelve.

12. See (i.a.) Robert Gundry, "Grace, Works, and Staying Saved in Paul," *Biblica* 66 (1985): 1-38; Mark A. Seifrid, *Justification by Faith: The Origin and Development of a Central Pauline Theme* (Leiden: Brill, 1992); also *Christ, Our Righteousness: Paul's Theology of Justification* (Downers Grove, Ill.: InterVarsity Press, 2000); Colin Kruse, *Paul, the Law, and Justification* (Peabody, Mass.: Hendrickson, 1997); C. E. B. Cranfield, *On Romans, and Other New Testament Essays* (Edinburgh: T&T Clark, 1998); Kent L. Yinger, *Paul, Judaism, and Judgment According to Deeds* (Cambridge: Cambridge University Press, 1999); Mark Adam Elliott, *The Survivors of Israel: A Reconsideration of the Theology of Pre-Christian Judaism* (Grand Rapids, Mich.: Eerdmans, 2000); Gary W. Burnett, *Paul and the Salvation of the Individual* (Leiden: Brill, 2001); D. A. Carson, ed., *Justification and Variegated Nomism*, vol. 1, *A Fresh Appraisal of Paul and Second Temple Judaism* (Grand Rapids, Mich. & Tübingen: Baker Academic & Mohr-Siebeck, 2001); D. A. Carson, Peter T. O'Brien, and Mark A. Seifrid, eds., *Justification and Variegated Nomism*, vol. 2, *The Paradoxes of Paul* (Grand Rapids, Mich. & Tübingen: Baker Academic & Mohr Siebeck, 2004); Peter Stuhlmacher, *Revisiting Paul's Doctrine of Justification: A Challenge to the New Perspective* (Downers Grove, Ill.: InterVarsity, 2001); A. Andrew Das, *Paul, the Law, and the Covenant* (Peabody, Mass.: Hendrickson, 2001); Maureen W. Yeung, *Faith in Jesus and Paul* (Tübingen: Mohr-Siebeck, 2002); Simon J. Gathercole, *Where Is Boasting? Early Jewish Soteriology and Paul's Response in Romans 1-5* (Grand Rapids, Mich.: Eerdmans, 2002); Seyoon Kim, *Paul and the New Perspective: Second Thoughts on the Origin of Paul's Gospel* (Grand Rapids, Mich.: Eerdmans, 2002); Steven Westerholm, *Perspectives Old and New on Paul: The Lutheran Paul and His Critics* (Grand Rapids, Mich.: Eerdmans, 2004), who is guarded but fundamentally critical (hereafter *PO&NP*); see also his essay "The 'New Perspective' at Twenty-Five," in *Justification and Variegated Nomism II*, 1-38; and Chris VanLandingham, *Judgment and Justification in Early Judaism and the Apostle Paul* (Peabody, Mass.: Hendrickson, 2006); and many of the relatively recent commentaries on Romans, esp. Douglas Moo, *The Epistle to the Romans*, NICNT (Grand Rapids, Mich.: Eerdmans, 1996) (a commentary on Rom. 1-8 appearing in 1991); and Thomas R. Schreiner, *Romans*, BECNT (Grand Rapids, Mich.: Baker, 1998). An earlier variant here is Glenn N. Davies, *Faith and Obedience in Romans: A Study in Romans 1-4*, JSNTSup 39 (Sheffield: JSOT, 1990). The views of Martin Hengel should also be introduced at this point, esp. *Between Jesus and Paul*, trans. John Bowden (London & Philadelphia: SCM & Trinity, 1983); with Anna Maria Schwemer, *Paul between Damascus and Antioch: The Unknown Years*, trans. J. Bowden (London: SCM, 1997); and with Roland Deines, *The Pre-Christian Paul*, trans. John Bowden (London & Philadelphia: SCM & Trinity, 1991).

13. My concerns here are similar to those apparent in Westerholm's important study, but we are operating with quite different terminological templates. Consequently, our "clarifications" of Sanders are rather different: *PO&NP*, 341-51.

14. The meaning of "grace" and grace-related terminology within the New Testament is debated. To be sure, it can function within conditional situations. My concern here is not to make arbitrary semantic claims about that evidence but to designate a particular theological use of "grace" in the interest of theoretical clarity. Ultimately, it does not matter what we call an unconditional model in order to distinguish it from a conditional one as long as that distinction is appreciated. The unconditional model being suggested here is grounded in a free, or elected, benevolence. "Grace" therefore seems as good a term as any to describe it at this point; it signifies that God's concrete benefaction of humanity in Christ — a gracious deed — is unelicited and unconditional. Reciprocity in response to

this gift is appropriate but not necessary. So my use of "grace" is not a semantic claim vis-à-vis Paul's context, but an explicitly theoretical and theological distinction. (See BDAG 1079-81.)

15. In fact, the terminology of "response" in Sanders's description tends to be deployed less to establish soteriological conditions (or their absence) than to underline the different motivations that can inform Jewish activity. Sanders is concerned to counteract mercantile or purely self-interested characterizations of that activity, and we will address this entire area in more detail shortly, when we consider the relationship between theoretical (i.e., soteriological) and psychological dimensions within Jewish description.

16. This was one of the seven or so standard negative European Christian stereotypes of Jews. Others included the charges that they desecrated the host and other sacred Christian items such as crosses and altars, in the former instance effectively resacrificing or remurdering Christ and thereby also recommitting the sin of deicide; that they sacrificed small boys to obtain blood that was then used for sinister purposes (e.g., making Passover matzohs) — the "blood-libel cult"; that they poisoned wells (this especially in relation to the bubonic plague, beginning in 1347); and that they were thieves disguised as wandering beggars. See Jacob Marcus, *The Jew in the Medieval World: A Sourcebook, 315-1791* (New York: Jewish Publication Society, 1938); also Parkes, *Conflict of the Church and the Synagogue*, passim.

17. So, for example, a cobbler might contend that he is "owed" one hundred denarii for the completion of a pair of boots in terms of a preceding contract and its agreed amount and thus "deserves" to be paid. But it would not be immediately clear whether this sum was deserved simply because the buyer had contracted to pay it or because one hundred denarii was in fact a "just" recompense for the materials and labor involved with the making of the boots. Under the market conditions of the day, perhaps only sixty denarii would be considered just, in which case the cobbler would be insisting — arguably quite fairly — that he had nevertheless "earned" one hundred because that was the contracted amount. His buyer, however, might be arguing — understandably — that he did not *deserve* this because it was not the accepted fair price of the day for such work.

18. That is, a priori. I would of course suggest that contractual theological structures are ultimately deeply problematic, and ought not even to be freely attributed to Judaism if that is avoidable. Jewish tradition arguably contains resources affirmative of unconditional soteriologies.

19. These are not *absolutely* necessary — the benefits could be for others and the actions therefore altruistic. Nor do such motivations necessarily exclude other motivations; one could be simultaneously self-interested and grateful.

20. This means that a degree of uncertainty must characterize them as well. The fulfillment of the requisite conditions cannot be predicted in advance by the individuals concerned.

21. Which is also to say that if self-interested behavior on the part of individuals is necessarily negative in theological terms, then another, entirely different, unconditional soteriology would need to be endorsed eventually.

22. Sanders seems to use the term "grace" to emphasize this, arguably a little unhappily. However, his substantive emphasis here is entirely appropriate. Most Jews do not initially accept this contract in the manner that Christian converts do; they are born into it collectively and automatically. So this dimension within Judaism is unconditional and non-contractual (although some Jewish traditions interpret the initial giving of the covenant at Sinai as a contractual moment!; his *Paul and Palestinian Judaism* [Philadelphia: Fortress, 1977], 87-98 [hereafter *P&PJ*], supplies numerous references to rabbinic sources). However, Jews do ultimately need to "respond" to this generosity and at that point seem to occupy a conditional relationship, although also a reasonable one.

23. An earlier, Deuteronomistic understanding would expect the appropriate rewards and punishments to be meted out during the life of the individual and the people, and a later, eschatological understanding would emphasize some great future recompense. It is important to emphasize in addition that the future scrutiny may not necessarily be soteriological — the proverbial job appraisal rather than a job interview already noted as an important possible distinction for Paul in chapter three.

24. Hence, although Sanders pejoratively attaches "uncertainty" to "legalism," the conditional

dimension in covenantal nomism unavoidably entails that it too will be characterized by a degree of uncertainty.

25. This interpretative emphasis is explored in more detail in part three, chapters ten through twelve.

26. Although in his view Sanders's account of Paul is not much better: the apostle is "idiosyncratic . . . arbitrary and irrational"; see James D. G. Dunn, *Jesus, Paul and the Law: Studies in Mark and Galatians* (London & Louisville, Ky.: SPCK & Westminster/John Knox, 1990), 185, 187, emphasis original.

27. James D. G. Dunn, "The Justice of God: A Renewed Perspective on Justification by Faith," *Journal of Theological Studies* 43 (1992): 6-7, emphases original.

28. There is an important point of contact here with a methodological problem widely known in literary circles since the rise of New Criticism as the "intentional" fallacy. That fallacy assumes the reduction of a text to its psychological antecedents — a *false* reduction, in fact, since a text is qualitatively distinct from those antecedents, and is also far more accessible to analysis. Reconstructing the psychological state of an author that putatively lies behind a text's genesis is clearly a fragile interpretative operation. We have no direct access to that state of mind and few or no controls on our reconstructions! Moreover, a great deal of interpretation can still be offered for a text for which authorship is unknown and hence any analysis of prior psychological states in effect impossible — in the NT (at the least), the Gospels (which are technically anonymous), Acts, and Hebrews (although presumably pseudonymous texts are appropriately included at this point as well). I do not want to exclude this dimension from interpretation altogether, but it must be carefully defined and controlled, something I attempt in part two, chapter seven. But this does not seem to be the case in much discussion of late Second Temple Judaism in relation to Paul. The classic analysis of the intentional fallacy is W. K. Wimsatt, "The Intentional Fallacy," in *The Verbal Icon: Studies in the Meaning of Poetry* (Lexington, Ky.: University of Kentucky Press, 1954), 3-18; see also R. Wellek and A. Warren, *A Theory of Literature* (New York: Harcourt Brace, 1956 [1949]). New Criticism was doubtless excessive in its repudiation of "psychologism" and "intentionality," but arguably something of value still remains in these warnings.

29. For Dunn's views, see nn. 26 and 27; for Alexander's views see esp. "Torah and Salvation in Tannaitic Literature," in *Justification and Variegated Nomism I*, 261-301.

30. I would accept the modified claim here that the description is *dominant* through time and space as against *universal*. Strictly speaking, as an objective derivative from the cosmos (et cetera) the view of Judaism ought to be universal, or easily demonstrable as such; however, I could allow that not everyone is intelligent or honest enough to grasp it (although I am not sure that this caveat is ultimately very wise). We will address this issue momentarily in §5.

31. The rejoinder could be made that a "two-track" soteriological schema would still work (the suggestion of Gaston, Gager, Stowers, and others). We will assess this strategy's plausibility in more detail in chapter twelve (although there, admittedly, principally in exegetical terms and in relation to Stowers). Suffice it here to note that its exegetical plausibility is low (although not without some strong features), and it will also run into acute difficulties of justice if the world's pagan inhabitants are still confronted with a harsh, perfectionist contract, but Jews are not. Ethical ambiguities will also recur (et cetera).

32. Sanders offers a useful list in *P&PJ*, 157-80.

33. Further objections could be raised were that necessary. Such an arrangement is difficult to attest from the relevant Jewish sources. One also wonders how the assertions that everyone sins profoundly and all the time could be established in terms of the opening premises of the Justification model (at which point the entire system would become self-referentially incoherent). We really have no way of knowing whether an assertion of total depravity is true without certain prior revelations, which breaks with the model's construction.

34. The angel Uriel's position in *4 Ezra* is the extant Jewish instance perhaps closest to this view, but of course he is trenchantly opposed by Ezra! For the somewhat special case of Qumran, see §5.

35. Somewhat incredibly, certain scholars have actually tried to argue this case — e.g., Moo, *Romans*, esp. 211-17; and Das, *Paul, the Law, and the Covenant*, 12-69.

36. Justification theory will also not be saved at this point by appeals to synergistic descriptions of Judaism — that it gets one part of an irreducibly confused picture correct. Justification theory does not itself give a confused account and so needs to find a correspondingly unconfused description in the relevant sources.

37. The experiences of parts of the Western church have also played an important role in this development: see part two, chapters eight and nine.

38. There is also a textual dimension involved here, but it is actually slight enough to ignore at this point, given our other present concerns. The hermeneutical issues are addressed in part two, chapter seven.

39. The former point is implicit in the latter, but that is not necessarily the case vice versa. That is, a soteriological description of all of Judaism is necessarily monolithic, but a monolithic description is not necessarily soteriological.

40. See *P&PJ*, 7, 9-18. Sanders is especially critical of Davies in relation to the detection of "motifs."

41. See esp. *On Religion: Speeches to Its Cultured Despisers,* tr. John Oman (Louisville, Kent.: Westminster John Knox, 1994 [1799]).

42. Indeed, one suspects that this assertion is far from being necessarily true for all religions throughout history, while the very category "religion" is problematic.

43. Still, it is important to take Sanders's suggestion to heart that most religions will at some point evidence a pattern or patterns, and these will often bear an important relationship to soteriology. These reduced claims seem to my mind to be both fair and useful.

44. See 1QS 1.8, 5.24, 8.1, 8.10, 8.18, 9.6, 9.19, 10.20, 11.2, 11.10-11; CD 2.14-16; 1QH 1.36; 7.17 (see also Sanders, *P&PJ*, 287-98).

45. A relationship articulated nicely by Joel Marcus in two important but little known studies, "The Evil Inclination in the Epistle of James," *Catholic Biblical Quarterly* 44 (1982): 606-21, esp. 611-13; and "The Evil Inclination in the Letters of Paul," *Irish Biblical Studies* 8 (1986): 8-21. (As we will see in part five, chapter twenty, J. Louis Martyn utilizes Marcus's work.) W. D. Davies also points to the importance of this discourse for Paul, emphasizing rabbinic sources in support, in "The Old Enemy: The Flesh and Sin," ch. 2 in *Paul and Rabbinic Judaism: Some Rabbinic Elements in Pauline Theology,* 4th ed. (Philadelphia: Fortress, 1980 [1946]), 17-35.

46. See Bockmuehl's comment: "The community combined a strong sense of the sinfulness of all humanity with a belief in divine grace to the believer as the only means of salvation" ("1QS and Salvation at Qumran," in *Justification and Variegated Nomism I,* 413).

47. See 1QH [Thanksgiving Hymns[a]] 3.21; 4.36-37; 6.6-8; 7:26-31; 11.10; 14.24; 1QS [Rule of the Community] 11.11 (see Sanders, *P&PJ*, 272-98).

48. 4Q394-99[a-f] [4QMMT or the Halakhic letter]. This text is much discussed. But it should be clear by this point that it does not deliver the information that Justification theory really needs.

49. Martin Hengel, *Judaism and Hellenism: Studies in Palestine During the Early Hellenistic Period,* ed. John Bowden, 2nd ed., 2 vols. (London: SCM, 1974); see also Hengel, *The 'Hellenization' of Judaea in the First Century after Christ,* trans. John Bowden (London & Philadelphia: SCM & Trinity, 1989).

50. As (i.a.) Hengel notes, much of the elite in late Second Temple Judaism was organized in terms of sages or teachers, sacred texts, and school settings, and discussed issues that included eschatology, angels, and resurrection. The elite in earlier, OT Judaism was not an essentially philosophical group, and neither did it discuss — or even know about — these issues.

51. John M. G. Barclay, *Jews in the Mediterranean Diaspora from Alexander to Trajan (323 BCE–117 CE)* (Edinburgh: T&T Clark, 1996). Many more studies of Diaspora Judaism could be mentioned: see (i.a.) J. Lieu, J. North, and T. Rajak, eds., *The Jews among Pagans and Christians in the Roman Empire* (London & New York: Routledge, 1992); Paul Trebilco, *Jewish Communities in Asia Minor* (Cambridge: University Press, 1991); Judith Lieu, *Image and Reality: The Jews in the World of the Christians*

in the Second Century (Edinburgh: T&T Clark, 1996); and John M. G. Barclay, "The Politics of Contempt: Judeans and Egyptians in Josephus' *Against Apion*," in *Negotiating Diaspora Jewish Strategies in the Roman Empire*, ed. John M. G. Barclay (London: T&T Clark, 2004), 109-27. The classic early study is E. R. Goodenough, *Jewish Symbols in the Greco-Roman Period*, 12 vols. (New York: Bollingen Series, 1953-65).

52. Jacob Neusner, W. S. Green, and E. S. Frerichs, eds., *Judaisms and Their Messiahs at the Turn of the Christian Era* (Cambridge: Cambridge University Press, 1987).

53. T. Engberg-Pedersen's edited volume then pushes the point still further: *Beyond the Judaism/Hellenism Divide* (Philadelphia: Westminster/John Knox, 2001).

54. Jacob Neusner, *The Rabbinic Traditions about the Pharisees before 70*, 3 vols. (Leiden: E. J. Brill, 1971); also *The Transformation of Judaism: From Philosophy to Religion* (Champaign: University of Illinois Press, 1991). The following is also interesting in the present context: "Mr. Sanders' Pharisees and Mine: A Response to E. P. Sanders, *Jewish Law from Jesus to the Mishnah*," *Scottish Journal of Theology* 44 (1991): 73-95.

55. Many challenges to Sanders's description of the rabbis are less radical than Neusner's (who at times nevertheless concedes that Sanders's account is "obvious"): see Friedrich Avemarie's frequently cited study, *Tora und Leben: Untersuchungen zur Heilsbedeutung der Tora in der frühen rabbinischen Literatur* (Tübingen: J. C. B. Mohr [Siebeck], 1996). Avemarie — contrary to many of his citations — is basically supportive of Sanders's description. He does, however, tend to nuance it: see his essay "The Tension between God's Command and Israel's Obedience as Reflected in the Early Rabbinic Literature," in *Divine and Human Agency in Paul and His Cultural Environment*, ed. John M. G. Barclay and Simon J. Gathercole (London: T&T Clark International [Continuum], 2006), 50-70.

56. "Torah and Salvation in Tannaitic Literature," in *Justification and Variegated Nomism I*, 261-301.

57. Imagine reducing the policy of a modern political party — even a small one — to a single unified opinion shared happily by all its members. That we are discussing an accumulating *legal code* — that is, a system that reacts over time to complex local and practical situations that were often unforeseen by earlier lawmakers — makes the project still more unlikely.

58. The suggestion of Dunn (and N. T. Wright, who is discussed more in part three, chapter twelve) that "works of law" functioned as distinctively Jewish sociological boundary markers can be usefully introduced into the debate at this point. Sabbath observance, the food laws, circumcision — and presumably also endogamy! — served to demarcate Jews from their non-elect pagan neighbors. Dunn and Wright tend to link this broad function with a soteriological theory; however, this is not necessary. This position — along with the question whether it is also a comprehensive solution to the difficulties of Justification theory in the relevant Pauline texts — is considered in detail in part three, chapter twelve.

59. See "Predestination and Free Will in the Theology of the Dead Sea Scrolls" (paper presented at "Divine and Human Agency in Paul in His Cultural Environment," a conference held at the University of Aberdeen, August 18-21, 2004: see www.abdn.ac.uk/divinity/Gathercole/paper-alexander.htm). Much the same case is made by Markus Bockmuehl, "1QS and Salvation at Qumran," in *Justification and Variegated Nomism I*, 381-414. However, he emphasizes the synergistic dimension to Qumran at this point more than Alexander does: "Membership in the covenant of God was characterized both by a sustained individual voluntarism and by an all-embracing doctrine of divine predestination" (413). Bockmuehl never stoops to calling the covenanters "confused," but this is arguably one implication of his analysis.

60. Sanders denies that any Jewish traditions were strictly unconditional: see *P&PJ*, 87-101, 257-70, 361-64.

61. (Ed. with T. Rajak) *Jews among Pagans and Christians;* and *Image and Reality;* also *Neither Jew Nor Greek? Constructing Early Christianity* (London: T&T Clark International [Continuum], 2005).

62. Earlier grid and group conceptuality is nicely exemplified by the work of Mary Douglas,

Purity and Danger: An Analysis of the Concepts of Pollution and Taboo (London: Routledge and Kegan Paul, 1970). But theory has progressed a long way since her day! A more modern, and exemplary analysis of interlocking theoretical models is provided — in relation to "the Mediterranean" — by Peregrine Horden and Nicholas Purcell, *The Corrupting Sea: A Study of Mediterranean History* (Oxford: Blackwell, 2000).

63. This challenge of course raises further questions. No value-free or theory-free descriptive work is ever really possible. However, I would still want to suggest that certain values and theories allow objective realities to emerge with more clarity. This is one of Michael Polanyi's basic claims (as we will see further in part two, chapter seven). Theory-laden description does not entail empirical relativity. Moreover (and probably unlike Lieu), I am quite happy for normative descriptions of entities like "Christianity" and "Judaism" to be supplied, provided that they are both transparent and retrospective in their claims. Such descriptions can also be relatively uniform. Indeed, any sense of uniformity within a description of either "Judaism" or "Christianity" is almost invariably a sign that some normative set of criteria *is* operative. This does not in my view render such descriptions invalid automatically (except as "pure" descriptions). But it should lead directly to a discussion of the theological criteria in use. These can and should be debated. We could put this slightly differently and suggest that *any uniform description of late Second Temple Judaism is almost certainly a fundamentally normative and hence theological construct as against a descriptive one.* And it should be responded to in the appropriate terms. Justification theory, of course, requires a descriptive construct, however — or at least ought not to be falsified by that; although its account is in fact theological. A theological stance vulnerable to empirical falsification is an invidious position to defend.

64. See E. P. Sanders, *Judaism: Practice and Belief: 63 BCE–66 CE* (London & Philadelphia: SCM & Trinity Press International, 1992). On the broader methodological issues implicit in this point see esp. James C. Scott, *Domination and the Arts of Resistance: Hidden Transcripts* (London & New Haven, Conn.: Yale University Press, 1990).

65. See Anthony Giddens, *Sociology,* 5th revised & updated ed. (Cambridge: Polity Press, 2006); the classic work is Max Weber, *Economy and Society* (Berkeley and Los Angeles: University of California Press, 1968 [1956]); also instructive is John Ralston Saul, *Voltaire's Bastards: The Dictatorship of Reason in the West* (New York: The Free Press [Macmillan], 1992).

66. Certainly, the suggestion that any core or defining essence of Judaism can be detected within these varieties must be abandoned. The most that could be argued for is the presence of a "family resemblance," to borrow Wittgenstein's useful notion, although this suggestion does seem plausible: Ludwig Wittgenstein, *Philosophical Investigations,* ed. G. E. M. Anscombe and R. Rhees, trans. G. E. M. Anscombe (Oxford: Blackwell, 1953), esp. §67, p. 32^e; §77, 36^e; §108, 46^e-47^e; §164, 66^e; §179, 72^e-73^e. However, one of the points of an explanation in terms of a family resemblance is precisely to relate the phenomenon of recognition or broad perceived similarity with the actual presence of a host of individual detailed variations that function in turn across different axes. Shaye D. Cohen's remarks are apposite at this point as well, namely, that the different locations and concerns of modern scholars tend to shape their interpretations of the data as well, injecting yet more diversity into the broader situation (a hermeneutical phenomenon explored in more detail in part two, chapter seven — although not in relation to the historiography of ancient Judaism): see "The Modern Study of Ancient Judaism," in *The State of Jewish Studies,* ed. Shaye J. D. Cohen and Edward L. Greenstein (Detroit, Mich.: Wayne State University Press, 1990), 55-73.

67. I have not emphasized here the important overarching constraint of extreme limitations on our knowledge.

68. And arguably, this is just what we see in a lot of the discussion of Justification — the puzzlement of Jews and their sympathizers.

69. At which point it is also worth asking, even if they did, how they could then be saved in any case before the coming of Christ and the gospel.

Notes to Chapter Five

1. We will continue to use the contested term "conversion" for the moment until the appropriate point arrives for its critical reconsideration at the end of this chapter.

2. I am not supplying a complete account here of the negative consequences of endorsing Justification theory, a large subject that is taken up in the main in chapter six, but this particular problem is appropriately noted in the present context.

3. I will privilege sociology and empirical studies over psychology and its more introspective and individual analysis in the following, in part for obvious reasons (i.e., to privilege the latter would risk committing precisely the anachronism that Stendahl criticizes). But there are also further considerations, which are addressed just below.

4. We will see shortly that his church-historical claims concerning Augustine and Luther are also imprecise (see part two, chapter eight). But Stendahl — as usual — certainly grasped something both important and vulnerable at this point, as the anguished response to him by various Justification advocates indicates.

5. Grant Wacker and Lamin Sanneh supply an interesting overview of major recent historians of cross-cultural issues in relation to conversion: "(Review Essay) Christianity Appropriated: Conversion and Intercultural Process," *Church History* (1999): 954-61. For the conversation with anthropology, see Andrew Buckser and Stephen D. Glazier, eds., *The Anthropology of Religious Conversion* (Lanham, Maryland: Rowman & Littlefield, 2003). See also Karl F. Morrison, *Understanding Conversion* (Charlottesville, Va.: University of Virginia Press, 1992); and *Conversion and Text: The Cases of Augustine of Hippo, Herman-Judah and Constantine Tsatsos* (Charlottesville, Va.: University of Virginia Press, 1992).

My general impression is that the best of this more narrative, historical work tends to confirm the main findings of sociological conversion theory, especially in relation to the importance of concrete interpersonal networks. A persistent emphasis on the experience of "seekers" is also evident.

Not surprisingly, more attention is now being paid to Islam: see Lewis R. Rambo, "Theories of Conversion: Understanding and Interpreting Religious Change," *Social Compass* 46 (1999): 259-71.

6. See esp. the classic study by William James, *The Varieties of Religious Experience: A Study in Human Nature* (New York: Mentor, 1958 [1902]); and A. D. Nock's learned analysis of the ancient phenomenon in similar terms: *Conversion: The Old and New in Religion from Alexander the Great to Augustine of Hippo* (Oxford: Oxford University Press, 1972 [1933]). Intriguingly, many of the recent studies of Paul's conversion emphasize the retrospective and constructed aspects in Paul's conversion: see more in §3 just below.

7. See Stanley Hauerwas's arguments in "The Faith of William James" and "God and William James," chapters two and three in *With the Grain of the Universe: The Church's Witness and Natural Theology, Being the Gifford Lectures Delivered at the University of St. Andrews in 2001* (London: SCM, 2002), 43-86.

8. As my colleague, C. Kavin Rowe, recently reminded me. And I am more than happy to concede this point. I am here, in fact, committed to an "interactionist" model of social behavior (as I suspect all theological explanations of human behavior are), trying to integrate rationality into a broader "embodied" process. On the one hand, I want therefore to resist a reductionist analysis that ignores human rationality and thought altogether, and, on the other hand, an overly psychological approach that tends to privilege rationality as the key overriding factor, if not the only one of importance — the temptation fostered by an over-dependence on James.

9. I am aware that Lofland, Stark, et al., arguably represent a distinctively American approach to social science and sociology, especially in their emphases on rationality and choice. I do not mean to suggest that their approach is to be identified with social science per se. It is merely one distinctive and powerful school (with frequent internal subdivisions!). An interesting exchange within Pauline studies that reflects these methodological differences (to a degree) is David Horrell, "Models and Methods in Social-Scientific Interpretation: A Response to Philip Esler," *Journal for the Study of the New Testament* 78 (2000): 83-105; and Philip F. Esler, "Models in New Testament Interpretation: A Re-

ply to David Horrell," *Journal for the Study of the New Testament* 78 (2000): 107-13. See also Zeba A. Crook, "Reflections on Culture and Social-Scientific Models," *Journal of Biblical Literature* 124 (2005): 515-32. Horrell stands more within the Continental tradition, which emphasizes certain key metatheories and close narrative work. He also depends primarily on Giddens and structuration theory, which can be seen as attempting to bridge this gap. Esler often uses models and approaches rooted more in the rationalism and empiricism of North American sociology (although by no means exclusively).

10. See esp. John Lofland and Rodney Stark, "Becoming a World-Saver: A Theory of Conversion from a Deviant Perspective," *American Sociological Review* 30 (1965): 862-75; and Lofland, "Becoming a World-Saver Revisited," *American Behavioral Scientist* 20 (1977): 805-18.

An excellent introduction to the theory is William Sims Bainbridge, "The Sociology of Conversion," in *Handbook of Religious Conversion,* ed. H. Newton Malony and Samuel Southard (Birmingham, Ala.: Religious Education Press, 1992), 178-91; a further brief summary and excellent survey of the model's development is Lorne L. Dawson, "Who Joins New Religious Movements and Why: Twenty Years of Research and What Have We Learned?" in *Cults and New Religious Movements: A Reader,* ed. Lorne L. Dawson (Oxford: Blackwell, 2003), 116-30. The theory is summarized and applied to early Christianity in the brilliant study by Rodney Stark, *The Rise of Christianity: A Sociologist Reconsiders History* (Princeton, N.J.: Princeton University Press, 1996), which now should be supplemented by *Cities of God: The Real Story of How Christianity Became an Urban Movement and Conquered Rome* (San Francisco: Harper, 2006).

Further elaboration can be found in Rodney Stark and Williams Sims Bainbridge, "Networks of Faith: Interpersonal Bonds and Recruitment to Cults and Sects," *The American Journal of Sociology* 85 (1980): 1376-95; David A. Snow, Louis A. Zurcher Jr., and Sheldon Eckland-Olson, "Social Networks and Social Movements: A Microstructural Approach to Differential Recruitment," *American Sociological Review* 45 (1980): 787-801; Lewis R. Rambo, "Current Research on Religious Conversion," *Religious Studies Review* 8 (1982): 146-59; and Lorne L. Dawson, *Comprehending Cults: The Sociology of New Religious Movements* (Toronto: Oxford University Press, 1998).

11. David A. Snow and Cynthia Phillips, "The Lofland-Stark Conversion Model: A Critical Reassessment," *Social Problems* 27 (1980): 430-47. However, as Dawson notes ("Who Joins New Religious Movements and Why," 118-19), the findings of Snow and Phillips vindicate two of the most important aspects of the Lofland-Stark model explicitly, at least as those were developed by Eileen Barker, *The Making of a Moonie: Choice or Brainwashing?* (Oxford: Blackwell, 1984).

12. So Dawson, "Who Joins New Religious Movements and Why," 118.

13. Dawson, "Who Joins New Religious Movements and Why," 118.

14. See esp. Rodney Stark and Williams Sims Bainbridge, *Religion, Deviance, and Social Control* (London: Routledge, 1996); also Rodney Stark, with William Sims Bainbridge, *A Theory of Religion* (New York: Peter Lang, 1987).

15. Stark has gone on to be a dominant if controversial figure in the field. I find all his work highly suggestive, but the following are probably especially relevant to the following discussion: on the spread of Christianity in the US, with Roger Finke, *The Churching of America, 1776-2005: Winners and Losers in Our Religious Economy,* 2nd ed. (Piscataway, New Jersey: Rutgers University Press, 2005); on the important analogy of Mormonism, *The Rise of Mormonism,* ed. Reid Larkin Neilson (New York: Columbia University Press, 2005); on the critical possible impact of monotheism on the nature and growth of Christianity, *One True God: Historical Consequences of Monotheism* (Princeton: Princeton University Press, 2001); *For the Glory of God: How Monotheism Led to Reformations, Science, Witch-Hunts, and the End of Slavery* (Princeton: Princeton University Press, 2003); and *The Victory of Reason: How Christianity Led to Freedom, Capitalism, and Western Success* (New York: Random House, 2005).

Stark is not without his critics: see (i.a.) Steve Bruce, *Choice and Religion: A Critique of Rational Choice Theory* (Oxford: Oxford University Press, 2000); and Pippa Norris and Ronald Inglehart, *Sacred and Secular: Religion and Politics Worldwide* (Cambridge: Cambridge University Press, 2004).

To reduce the role of rational choice in his explanations in response to such critics is by no means to eliminate all his explanations, however. Moreover, these critics can of course themselves be criticized.

16. Stark, *Rise of Christianity*, 18.

17. Dawson, "Who Joins New Religious Movements and Why," 119.

18. Various examples of this spring to mind — for example, teenage religious adherence in the US in general: see (i.a.) the now definitive evidence of Christian Smith, with Melinda Lundquist Denton, *Soul Searching: The Religious and Spiritual Lives of American Teenagers* (Oxford: Oxford University Press, 2005). Carol E. Lytch comments accurately in her review of this study: "We have known for years that parents are key influences on teens' religious lives. Despite the tendency of parents to say they are helpless in this area, three out of four religious teens consider their own beliefs somewhat or very similar to those of their parents. . . . In choosing friends, teens tend to surround themselves with people who reinforce the shaping influence (religious or nonreligious) of their parents. . . . [Thus, although] peers may be important to teens, . . . parents are still primary when it comes to religion": "A Survey on Youth and Religion: What Teens Believe," *Christian Century*, September 6 (2005): 20. See also Ronald K. Crandall, *The Contagious Witness: Exploring Christian Conversion* (Nashville, Tenn.: Abingdon, 1999); this book is underpinned at certain points by extensive empirical research and at others by explicitly normative agendas. See also Stephen R. Warner, *New Wine in Old Wineskins: Evangelicals and Liberals in a Small-Town Church* (Berkeley & Los Angeles: University of California Press, 1988); and Callum G. Brown, *The Death of Christian Britain* (London: Routledge, 2001).

19. Stark, *The Rise of Christianity*, 18. I have substituted here a more accurate account of the beginnings of the Jesus movement than Stark himself supplies.

20. The origins of Buddhism — not noted by Stark, who is a theorist in the main of Western contexts — lay in the four ascetic friends of the Gautama whom he famously converted under a plane tree after his enlightenment: see Huston Smith, *The World's Religions*, rev. & updated ed. (San Francisco: HarperCollins, 1991 [1958]), 82-153; Masao Abe, "Buddhism," in *Our Religions*, ed. Arvind Sharma (San Francisco: HarperCollins, 1993), 69-138.

21. This stands to reason; presumably people have been networking through friends and families since the dawn of society. However, methodological circumspection is certainly still in order! Note that, strictly speaking, I am not using the modern social scientific analysis of conversion to make assertions about ancient society here, although I consider that possibility worth considering. Justification theory ought to be true universally, so a comparison grounded in the modern period is apposite. But *if* this theory is applied to ancient conversion, then any of its suggestions rooted in the middle class within the modern period would have to be carefully screened.

22. This creates some of the central tensions of network growth. Unattached people are easier to convert but less advantageous, because they bring few further opportunities for growth. In order to grow in a sustained fashion, religious movements need to convert people living within reasonably effective networks, which may mean accessing new types of networks periodically. However, extremely tight networks — like committed Jewish communities — will probably prove impervious to penetration and conversion. So the right types of networks need to be accessed if ongoing growth is to take place.

23. Stark, *The Rise of Christianity*, 16.

24. The basic correctness of Stark's observation here can certainly be granted. However, it is not necessary to analyze deviance in entirely rationalistic terms, nor is it necessary to interpret all conversion as a response to shifting continua of perceived deviance. So, for example, another way of putting this is to suggest that these new interpersonal loyalties enable a perceived barrier of social stigma reinforced by emotions of shame and/or disgust to be crossed into a religious group perceived as deviant, where individuals now nevertheless enjoy more significant attachments or relationships. One suspects that social relationships and their shifts are a bit more complex; hence, this further theoretical development of network theory will not be pressed in what follows.

25. See Stark, *The Rise of Christianity*, 174-79.

26. See Curtis W. Freeman's fascinating observations on certain traditions of conversion and conversion narration within Baptist circles in the American South. He notes that "[n]o one could en-

ter when 'a door of the church was opened' for membership without a satisfactory testimony of a conversion experience": "Conversion Work: The Growth and Identity of Baptists in the South 1755-1801,"
paper presented to *The American Society for Church History* annual conference, Seattle, 2005, 3.

27. The two perspectives are also by no means incompatible. Cognitive realizations are often
an important part of the journey through conversion to a religious movement and community, and
tend to stand out in retrospect. There is a tendency therefore to narrate that journey by privileging
those moments. Such a narration also conforms to widely accepted narrative principles (i.e., the telling of a story that moves from a problem through a climactic resolution to some solution); may accord
with the learning of the community's conversion narrations (which may themselves accord with widespread plots); emphasizes the individual's agency; and overlooks — characteristically — the host of
accompanying factors that only trained sociologists generally detect (things like networks). So to emphasize such moments is not in itself necessarily untrue; however, the sociologist suspects merely that
they are part of a much more complex story in reality. (I am grateful to Christian Smith for his insights
in this regard.) An important connection is in effect created by this bundle of perspectives with the
"seeking" component in conversion as will be noted shortly.

28. Stark's explanatory dependence on rationality should not be caricatured. He adopts a
nuanced account of human rationality — "subjective rationality." It is not mere maximization of benefits: see esp. "A New Look at Old Issues," in *Acts of Faith*, ed. Rodney Stark and Roger Finke (Berkeley:
University of California Press, 2000), 27-41, esp. 35-41; also "Rationality and the 'Religious Mind,'" in
Acts of Faith, 42-56.

29. So, for example, it is useful to cross-reference Stark's work with the more discipline-specific
work of (i.a.) Ramsey MacMullen, *Roman Social Relations* (London & New Haven: Yale University
Press, 1974); *Paganism in the Roman Empire* (London & New Haven: Yale University Press, 1981); and
Christianizing the Roman Empire (A.D. 100-400) (London & New Haven: Yale University Press, 1984).
Stark responds to some of MacMullen's different perspectives in *Cities of God*, suggesting on the basis
of a statistical model that conversions did take place in ancient urban centers — especially in ports
and larger cities (i.e., with populations over 75,000, Stark suggesting that eight cities in the Principate
had or exceeded this size): see *Cities of God*, 81. Jack T. Sanders adopts an explanatory position between these two poles in *Charisma, Converts, Competitors: Societal and Sociological Factors in the Success of Early Christianity* (London: SCM, 2000).

30. It is important to recall that "religions" in the ancient world were not necessarily coterminous or symmetrical with modern ones, or with each other. Religion is arguably an essentially modern category (see more in this relation in part two, chapter nine).

31. For evaluations of this approach, and broader overarching model, see Lawrence A. Young,
ed., *Rational Choice Theory and Religion: Summary and Assessment* (London: Routledge, 1997); and
the critics of Stark noted earlier — Bruce, *Choice and Religion*; and Norris and Inglehart, *Sacred and
Secular*.

32. His work has been further developed by other theorists. James T. Richardson makes a plea
for a more "active," "meaning-seeking" subject: see "The Active vs. Passive Convert: Paradigm Conflict in Conversion/Recruitment Research," *Journal for the Scientific Study of Religion* 24 (1985): 163-79.
This development of the Lofland-Stark model counteracts the hostile and rather inaccurate portrayal
of conversion to cults in terms of "brainwashing." These converts, it turns out, are often actively seeking such a conversion in general terms.

Dawson then emphasizes the notion of religious conversion as "role-play." Many such converts
are not in fact "fully" converted but are simply trying out the new group and will leave within two
years. This further reinforces the picture of converts as active but also reinforces the picture of conversion more generally as gradual rather than climactic. See Lorne L. Dawson, "Self-Affirmation, Freedom, and Rationality: Theoretically Elaborating 'Active' Conversions," *Journal for the Scientific Study
of Religion* 29 (1990): 141-63.

33. That is, with the "Willow Creek" model of church growth, associated with Bill Hybels, that
is often oriented around "seeker services": see Bill Hybels and Lynne Hybels, *Rediscovering Church:
The Story and Vision of Willow Creek Community Church* (Grand Rapids, Mich.: Zondervan, 1995).

34. This then raises important methodological questions in relation to the potential explanatory contributions of psychology and social psychology. The possible existence of "personality types" is also implicit here.

35. The latter observation is well attested empirically, although susceptible to different explanations. Higher education is a process that often isolates individuals, separating them from their traditional past attachments as they relocate in order to study for several years, so perhaps this factor is further evidence of the importance of networks — or their absence — in conversion. (This phenomenon in modern societies could then be compared to the frequent conversions of merchants and soldiers in the Principate to foreign cults; such figures were significantly dislocated and isolated in that context. But extreme care should be taken here.) Converts to NRMs also tend to be disproportionately young, so the link with education might be more apparent than real. (That is, young people are often being educated.) Still, such conversions often require the assimilation of new texts and ideas, something well-educated people are presumably less intimidated by and more adept at. So higher educational levels may be a factor within the more rational aspect of the process (although — again — this factor *could* be explained affectively in terms of networks, as students are trained to gather around teachers and may, in cults, simply be gathering around the relevant new "guru"!). Clearly, more research needs to be done assessing the possible role of this factor in conversion.

36. Dawson, "Who Joins New Religious Movements and Why," 120.

37. Stark nuances his basic model in relation to the growth of early Christianity in a number of quite fascinating ways in *The Rise of Christianity* and *Cities of God*. He goes on to argue, for example, that significant growth by religions (i.e., around 3.42% per annum or 40% per decade) occurs as they access networks that are not sufficiently powerful to provide effective alternatives to the religious groups themselves. Such a growth rate would have enabled the early Christians to become the majority population of the Roman empire by 350 CE. The argument has not been unopposed but still seems basically plausible.

38. I hope to rectify this lacuna shortly, although the basic appropriateness of this methodological approach also needs to be carefully considered.

39. For some of the most important sociological work on Paul, see Gerd Theissen, *The Social Setting of Pauline Christianity* (Philadelphia: Fortress, 1982); Wayne A. Meeks, *The First Urban Christians: The Social World of the Apostle Paul* (New Haven: Yale University Press, 1983); Francis Watson, *Paul, Judaism and the Gentiles: A Sociological Approach* (Cambridge: Cambridge University Press, 1986); Margaret Y. MacDonald, *The Pauline Churches: A Socio-Historical Study of Institutionalization in the Pauline and Deutero-Pauline Writings*, SNTSMS 60 (Cambridge: Cambridge University Press, 1988); P. F. Esler, *The First Christians in Their Social World: Social Scientific Approaches to New Testament Interpretation* (London & New York: Routledge, 1994), 37-69; also *Galatians* (London & New York: Routledge, 1998); also *Conflict and Identity in Romans: The Social Setting of Paul's Letter* (Minneapolis, Minn.: Fortress, 2003); and David Horrell, *The Social Ethos of the Corinthian Correspondence: Interests and Ideology from 1 Corinthians to 1 Clement* (Edinburgh: T&T Clark, 1996).

Much of the relevant Pauline work has taken place in relation to Corinth, because the data there is — relatively speaking — more extensive. Abraham Malherbe offers some salutary cautions in *Social Aspects of Early Christianity* (Baton Rouge, La.: Louisiana State University Press, 1977). And we have already noted J. T. Sanders's lively study of conversion in relation to the New Testament and its ancient setting (encompassing a broader purview): *Charisma, Converts, Competitors*. There are significant differences of opinion even within this relatively small sample over just what constitutes good social scientific analysis of Paul.

John M. G. Barclay is — quite rightly — much cited and broadens the conversation to include Thessalonica in "Thessalonica and Corinth: Social Contrasts in Pauline Christianity," *Journal for the Study of the New Testament* 47 (1992): 49-74. Robert Jewett has also written a perceptive study on the Thessalonians that incorporates sociological insights: *The Thessalonian Correspondence: Pauline Rhetoric and Millenarian Piety* (Philadelphia: Fortress, 1986).

Andrew Walker offers a highly informative study of the development of small charismatic movements in the United Kingdom that is extremely suggestive in relation to New Testament questions: *Restoring the Kingdom* (London: Hodder & Stoughton, 1985). Much of this work resonates with the classic proposals of Ferdinand Christian Baur, *Paul, the Apostle of Jesus Christ, His Life and Works, His Epistles and Teachings: A Contribution to a Critical History of Primitive Christianity,* tr. and rev. A. Menzies and E. Zeller, 2 vols. (London: Williams & Norgate, 1873-1875 [1845]).

40. Some of the key works on Paul's conversion in sociological terms, and on conversion within his communities are Alan F. Segal, *Paul the Convert: The Apostolate and Apostasy of Saul the Pharisee* (New Haven, Conn.: Yale University Press, 1990); Terence L. Donaldson, *Paul and the Gentiles: Remapping the Apostle's Convictional World* (Minneapolis, Minn.: Fortress, 1997); and Stephen Chester, *Conversion at Corinth* (London: T&T Clark [Continuum], 2003); of more general — but considerable — importance is Zeba A. Crook, *Reconceptualising Conversion: Patronage, Loyalty, and Conversion in the Religions of the Ancient Mediterranean,* BZNW 130 (Berlin & New York: Walter de Gruyter, 2004) — Paul is treated in "Chapter Four: The Rhetoric of Patronage and Benefaction in Paul's Conversion Passages," 151-97. Segal, in particular, supplies an excellent brief appendix documenting psychological and sociological work on conversion (*Paul,* 285-300), although the theoretical matters are left rather unresolved and the literature cited is now rather dated.

41. We have already noted the main studies of sociological relevance above, as well as some grounds for being less enthusiastic about more psychologically oriented analyses (see §2 above). Hence, not all of the classic studies of Paul's conversion prove strictly relevant to the following discussion's concerns with Justification theory. In fact, many of the more recent studies sound notes of caution concerning the use of ancient material for "empirical" work on conversion, thereby reinforcing some of the most basic insights of network theory — that conversion accounts are narratives learned after conversion and hence shaped by normative agendas, and that their self-conscious deployment in literature is often even more highly rhetorical and hence less biographically reliable. A classic study making this point is Paula Fredriksen, "Paul and Augustine: Conversion Narratives, Orthodox Traditions, and the Retrospective Self," *Journal of Theological Studies* 37 (1986): 3-34. (Fredriksen's approach to Augustine here has been challenged by John Riches, although the results of this clash do not significantly affect my argument at this point; see the further discussion of Augustine, however, in part two, chapter eight.) See also the seminal analysis, Beverly Roberts Gaventa, "Conversion in the Letters of Paul," in *From Darkness to Light: Aspects of Conversion in the New Testament* (Philadelphia: Fortress, 1986), 17-51. That the critical analysis of ancient and New Testament texts has generated these parallel suspicions is to my mind something of a methodological triumph.

See also G. Lohfink, *The Conversion of St. Paul: Narrative and History in Acts* (Chicago: Franciscan Herald, 1976); Carey Newman, *Paul's Glory-Christology: Tradition and Rhetoric,* NovTSup 69 (Leiden: E. J. Brill, 1992); J. M. Everts, "Conversion and the Call of Paul," in *DP&L,* 156-63; and Larry W. Hurtado, "Convert, Apostate, or Apostle to the Nations: The 'Conversion' of Paul in Recent Scholarship," *Studies in Religion/Sciences Religieuses* 22 (1993): 273-84.

42. Here following Knox's important methodological insight: see John Knox, *Chapters in a Life of Paul,* ed. D. Hare, rev. ed. (London: SCM, 1987 [1950]).

43. Gaventa speaks correctly of "slender" evidence comprising no more than "a fragment" of his letters: "Conversion," *ABD* 1:1132 (broader discussion 1132-33, bibliography 1133).

44. At this point Mark 1:11 and 9:2-7 are interesting potential echoes.

45. Paul contrasts this commission directly with instruction derived from the other apostles, describing it in terms drawn from the Old Testament prophetic call narratives. Hence, it seems reasonably clear that it had linguistic content and that this apostolic call — which Paul constantly and explicitly attributes to God — was rooted in verbal instruction from God to be in effect a missionary to the pagans. This instruction, however, should be carefully distinguished from the delicate question of its practical and ethical *mode.* The remaining evidence points, in my view, to a development in Paul's missionary techniques, including in relation to pagan converts' adoption of the Jewish law. (See more on this just below.)

46. See also possible influences from Isa. 42:6 and 52:7.

47. The correspondence with scriptural figures and missions legitimizes Paul's similar activity.

48. The debate is nicely presented and argued by Richard N. Longenecker, *Paul, Apostle of Lib-*

erty (New York: Harper & Row, 1964), 86-97, 109-16; see also Werner G. Kümmel, *Man in the New Testament,* trans. J. J. Vincent (London: Epworth, 1963 [1929]). Much-cited of late is P. W. Meyer, "The Worm at the Core of the Apple," in *The Conversation Continues: Studies in Paul and John,* ed. R. T. Fortna and B. R. Gaventa (Nashville: Abingdon, 1990), 62-84 (although I am unpersuaded!). An interesting reappraisal of Kümmel is undertaken by L. Thuren, *Derhetorizing Paul: A Dynamic Perspective on Pauline Theology and Law* (Tübingen: Mohr [Siebeck], 2000); see also his "Romans 7 Derhetorized," in *Rhetorical Criticism and the Bible: Essays from the 1998 Florence Conference,* ed. S. E. Porter and D. L. Stamps (Sheffield: JSOT, 2002), 420-40. L. Ann Jervis has written an intriguing study that anticipates many of my own later emphases here: "'The Commandment Which Is for Life' (Romans 7.10): Sin's Use of the Obedience of Faith," *Journal for the Study of the New Testament* 27 (2004): 193-216. Emma Wasserman's developing contributions in this relation are also important: see esp. "The Death of the Soul in Romans 7: Sin, Death, and the Law in the Light of Hellenistic Moral Psychology" (PhD dissertation; Yale University, 2005).

49. Justification theory also does not match this description at other ostensibly crucial points: 7:7-25 is oriented by the tenth commandment, found in the revealed Torah, and not by natural theology; there is no apparent elaboration in terms of either idolatry or sinfulness; and it is clearly unjust to require ethical perfection of the sort of incapacitated person depicted here — and perhaps also unrealistic to require certain philosophical realizations and progressions as well. This description of the basic problem facing humanity is one of bondage, not of God's just judgment.

50. This last point is emphasized by Stanley K. Stowers, *A Rereading of Romans: Justice, Jews, and Gentiles* (London & New Haven, Conn.: Yale University Press, 1994), 260-64. However, he also points to the importance of Wasserman's study in this relation: "The Death of the Soul in Romans 7."

51. And this view also integrates nicely with a particular contingent reading of this material's argumentative function, although that is best discussed in detail from part three, chapter thirteen.

52. Richard N. Longenecker adds that this appearance was "on a par with" all of Jesus' other postresurrection appearances (see 1 Cor. 15:3b-7); distinguishes Jesus as "content" from Jesus as "agent" (arguably a little awkwardly: see Gal. 1:12, 16b); and also emphasizes the "revolutionary effect" on Paul's life (see Phil. 3:7-11). This is largely a difference of enumeration, however. See his "Realized Hope, New Commitment, and Developed Proclamation," in *The Road from Damascus: The Impact of Paul's Conversion on His Life, Thought, and Ministry,* ed. R. N. Longenecker (Grand Rapids, Mich.: Eerdmans, 1997), 25.

53. Just what he learned is a matter of considerable debate.

54. See Rom. 16:25, although this text is admittedly also disputed. But the same notion occurs undisputedly in a different relation in 11:25; also more certain are 1 Cor. 2:1, 7; and 4:1; see also 13:2; 14:2; 15:51.

55. The proposal most notably of Seyoon Kim, *The Origin of Paul's Gospel,* WUNT 4 (Tübingen: J. C. B. Mohr [Paul Siebeck], 1981); see also his *Paul and the New Perspective: Second Thoughts on the Origin of Paul's Gospel* (Grand Rapids, Mich.: Eerdmans, 2002). This claim is assessed in more detail in my engagement below with the "Lutheran" account of Paul's conversion. Fortunately, not all aspects of the debate concern us here. If Paul received vital christological information at this point, that does not help Justification theory. Indeed, in a way it hinders the theory still further.

56. I am not sure that the exclusion of 2 Cor. 12:1-4 really needs to be argued for as well. Simply on chronological grounds, any application of this classic apocalyptic experience to Paul's conversion looks impossible.

57. Nevertheless, this and related proposals receive more detailed treatment shortly.

58. "Saul, Saul, why are you persecuting me? . . . I am Jesus of Nazareth whom you are persecuting. . . . Get up and go to Damascus; there you will be told everything that has been assigned to you to do."

59. See . . . ἀκούοντες μὲν τῆς φωνῆς μηδένα δὲ θεωροῦτες (9:7), and τὸ μὲν φῶς ἐθεάσαντο τὴν δὲ φωνὴν οὐκ ἤκουσαν τοῦ λαλοῦντός μοι . . . (22:9).

60. It would be unwise to understand this as a precise reference to Paul's psychological state. First, it is present only in this expanded version of Paul's conversion and so is arguably merely

redactional. Second, it fulfills an obvious role within the narrative, elucidating the nature of Paul's previous activity for a partly pagan audience, here represented by Festus. Third, and most important, it contains an obvious reference to Paul's persecution of the church. This action, which is overtly signaled by the text (not to mention by Paul's own statements), fulfills the semantic expectations of the saying in terms of a hard struggle that is diametrically opposed to God's will. Hence, we would need overt justification to go beyond this reference and include some other aspect of Paul's internal psychological state.

61. It is difficult to determine whether Acts has dramatized and compressed Paul's conversion, narrating it on the road to Damascus. Perhaps Paul had already arrived and was busily engaged in further persecutions. Either way, significant contact after his call with the Christians in Damascus seems likely.

62. Here, perhaps significantly, the third account in Acts seems closest to Paul's own account, because it alone contains a direct apostolic commission by God. However, does Paul's own account in Galatians omit this human mediation of the divine command for obvious rhetorical reasons?

63. Acts exaggerates the nature of Paul's reception in Jerusalem at this time, claiming that he met "the apostles" (which in Acts denotes meeting the Twelve; see 9:27; also 1:21-26). Paul himself swears before God that he only met Cephas and James! (Gal. 1:18-20).

64. We could perhaps further specify the identity of one of Paul's early catechists as Ananias. This seems inoffensive, but it ultimately adds very little to our developing biography (although perhaps it illuminates 1 Cor. 15:3-6). Acts adds other narrative details that are also difficult to corroborate, but seem inoffensive. Paul's conversion took place specifically on the road *to* Damascus, rather than merely in its vicinity. Paul was of course just coming from the persecution of the Stephen circle in Jerusalem, and the killing of Stephen himself.

65. If the composition of Philemon is placed in a late Roman imprisonment, the two markers could perhaps be reconciled, since thirty years might have passed between Paul's persecution of Stephen and the composition of that letter (i.e., between the early 30s and early 60s CE). However, I regard this late provenance as dubious. More likely is an elapse of around twenty years, if that, and I am not convinced that a man of forty is appropriately denoted as a πρεσβύτης! Philo calls Hippocrates a πρεσβύτης at the age of fifty to fifty-six (*On the Creation*, 105), although Dio Chrysostom 74.10 has the term following μειράκιον νεανίσκος (BDAG 863). If Paul was using it simply as the equivalent of ἀνήρ, however, it is difficult to know what rhetorical force it could have in his letter. It is also worth noting that an iticizing tendency in pronunciation would favor confusion and transferability between the signifiers, but a plosive pronunciation of the diphthong in question would not.

66. There are other factors that are marginally in favor of this emendation and hence in favor of Paul's relative youth as a convert as suggested by Acts. Paul's capacity to endure suffering — repeated travel, lashings, beatings, and shipwrecks — seems more compatible with youth than with advanced age. His relative youth *might* explain his early marginalization by Jerusalem as well. After fourteen more years, at the age of thirty-five or forty, he would have carried rather more weight at a plenary conference, although presumably the Jerusalem leadership would have been justified in failing to trust even an older person making the radical proposals that Paul was!

67. Douglas Harink expresses the matter succinctly: "If the point of the gospel . . . was 'faith in Jesus Christ' rather than in human effort, Paul missed the perfect opportunity to say that is exactly what he learned from his own experience as a Jew": *Paul among the Postliberals: Pauline Theology beyond Christendom and Modernity* (Grand Rapids: Brazos, 2003), 32, n. 15. To this we could add the observation that Paul seems to miss this opportunity repeatedly.

68. Πίστις occurs in 1:23. The construal of this signifier in context is addressed in detail in part five, chapter twenty. However, we can note even at this early point that this solitary occurrence is well past the point of conversion for Paul, and is linked somehow to proclamation rather than to his own new posture of "belief" or "faith."

69. Romans 11:2 fails to develop the promising beginning of 11:1, supported by 9:1-3 and 10:1.

70. It may also be significant that Eph. 2:8-10 contains the only occurrence of Justification ter-

minology in that letter, and these claims are some distance from the extended account of "Paul's" apostolic office (which is in turn not especially biographical; see 3:2-13).

71. Potentially, then, the key terms "faith" (πίστις) and "righteousness" (δικαιοσύνη), which do occur here, are dominated semantically by the text's immediate concerns. Consequently, they arguably have a christological content, not an anthropological one. That is, precisely in view of all the difficulties for Justification theory in the immediate frame, along with an almost total absence of overt support for it in context, we should ask whether the terms "faith" (πίστις) and "righteousness" (δικαιοσύνη) *do* in fact attest to its presence and so warrant a rendering in a sense that suits it. These considerations are pursued further in part five, chapter twenty-one.

72. Wilckens, "Die Bekehrung des Paulus als religionsgeschichtliches Problem," in *Rechtfertigung als Freiheit: Paulusstudien* (Neukirchen-Vluyn: Neukirchener Verlag, 1974), 11-32, esp. 15, 18, 23-25; Stuhlmacher, "'Das Ende des Gesetzes': Über Ursprung und Ansatz der paulinischen Theologie," in *Versöhnung, Gesetz und Gerechtigkeit: Aufsätze zur biblischen Theologie* (Göttingen: Vandenhoeck & Ruprecht, 1981), 166-91; Kim, *The Origin of Paul's Gospel*; also *Paul and the New Perspective*; C. Dietzfelbinger, *Die Berufung des Paulus als Ursprung seiner Theologie*, WMANT 58 (Neukirchen-Vluyn: Neukirchener Verlag, 1985); brief treatment and references in Rainer Riesner, *Paul's Early Period: Chronology, Mission Strategy, Theology*, trans. D. Stott (Grand Rapids, Mich.: Eerdmans, 1998 [1991]), 235-37; see also Ch. Burchard, *Die Dreizehnte Zeuge: Traditions- und Kompositionsgeschichtliche Untersuchungen zu Lukas' Darstellung der Frühzeit des Paulus*, FRLANT 103 (Göttingen: Vandenhoeck & Ruprecht, 1970). The most well-known and extensive contributions in English-speaking circles probably come from Martin Hengel: see esp. *Between Jesus and Paul*, trans. John Bowden (London & Philadelphia: SCM & Trinity, 1983); with Roland Deines, *The Pre-Christian Paul*, trans. John Bowden (London & Philadelphia: SCM & Trinity, 1991); see also, to a lesser extent, with Anna Maria Schwemer, *Paul between Damascus and Antioch: The Unknown Years*, trans. J. Bowden (London: SCM, 1997).

The largely German tradition is also arguably the most trenchant representation of the view. But see also J. Dupont-Sommer, "The Conversion of Paul, and Its Influence on His Understanding of Salvation by Faith," in *Apostolic History and the Gospel: FS F. F. Bruce*, ed. W. W. Gasque and R. P. Martin (Exeter: Paternoster, 1970), 176-94.

An interesting and highly accessible survey of Paul's conversion is R. N. Longenecker, ed., *The Road from Damascus*.

73. Bruce Corley notes ("Interpreting Paul's Conversion — Then and Now," in Longenecker [ed.], *The Road from Damascus*, 1-17) that a "preparationist" model similar to the a priori Lutheran view is found in some of the Puritans, and then in the psychological reductions of the post-Enlightenment period, and not so much — if at all — in Medieval piety or the Reformation. Corley points especially to Bullinger as an advocate of the preparationist view, then to figures like John Bunyan (*Grace Abounding to the Chief of Sinners*, published in 1666). But Hooker and Preston cautioned against this reading. The view continued in aspects of Wesley and Whitefield and the Evangelical awakenings. Medieval and Reformation traditions, however, tend to treat Paul's conversion as an instance of unconditional and unexpected grace, with God breaking into a violent and hostile person's life. In the West this was symbolized as Paul was struck down from his horse — a proud rider, like the high status knight, being humbled. See also Norman Pettit, *The Heart Prepared* (New Haven, Conn.: Yale University Press, 1966).

74. The suggestion associated esp. with C. H. Dodd that Paul was psychologically tormented by the law, as revealed in particular by his statement — in Acts 26:14 — that he was "kicking against the goads," has already been addressed, and is self-evidently fragile in any case: see esp. "The Mind of Paul," in *New Testament Studies* (New York: Scribners, 1952), 67-128.

75. See esp. "'A Light to the Gentiles,' or, 'The End of the Law?' The Significance of the Damascus Road Christophany for Paul," in James D. G. Dunn, *Jesus, Paul and the Law: Studies in Mark and Galatians* (London & Louisville, Kent.: SPCK & Westminster/John Knox, 1990), 89-107; see also "Works of the Law and the Curse of the Law (Gal. 3.10-14)," in *Jesus, Paul and the Law*, 215-41. Dunn is especially sensitive to this dimension within the debate, in part because he has developed a distinctive

conception of Paul's biography, although not in a strong dialogue with sociological theory (and this despite an emphasis on interpreting "works of law" in Paul in "sociological" terms). His own positive suggestions are evaluated esp. in part three, chapter twelve as part of a potential solution to our difficulties. His pertinent criticisms of "Lutheran" biographers are usefully noted here, however (and they are generally right on target). See also H. Räisänen, "Paul's Call Experience and His Later View of the Law," in *The Torah and Christ: Essays in German and English on the Problem of the Law in Early Christianity* (Helsinki: Finnish Exegetical Society, 1986), 55-92; "Paul's Conversion and the Development of His View of the Law," *New Testament Studies* 33 (1987): 404-19; *Paul and the Law,* 2nd ed., WUNT 29 (Tübingen: J. C. B. Mohr [Paul Siebeck], 1987 [1983]), 229-63, esp. 249-51 and (on the Stephen circle) 251-56 (hereafter *P&L*). Räisänen is alert to question begging in many of the "Justification" arguments at these points.

76. Even granting the initial hypothesis that the Stephen circle was law-free, we still lack any data describing how Paul integrated with it after his conversion, or even that he did. It is blithely asserted that he converted to the movement that he was persecuting, but we do not actually know that he converted to this particular variant within the early Jewish Christian spectrum of possibilities. Put slightly differently: how do we know that Ananias was a member of the Stephen circle, and hence presumably law-free himself?

77. Räisänen makes this point nicely: *P&L,* 59-61, 249-51. He notes that the view was expressed by Schweitzer and observes further that Paul never attributes Jesus' crucifixion to the law in any sense — far from it! Paul attributes Jesus' crucifixion to evil powers: see 1 Cor. 2:8. Philippians 2:8 even suggests that it was a fate voluntarily accepted by Christ in accordance with God's will! Moreover, no one ever suggested that the law was invalid because it punished innocent sacrificial victims like the scapegoat. "If there was a connection between Paul's exegesis of Deut. 21:23 and his critique of the law, he never spells it out" (250). To this I would add the points that 1 Cor. 2:8 and Gal. 3:13 are rather dubiously linked in any case; neither text overtly references the other and yet this link is very important for the developing argument.

78. See more detail in this relation in part five, chapter twenty.

79. Räisänen again makes this point: *P&L,* 59.

80. See, i.a., Rom. 1:1-4, 9-16; 12:4-8; 15:15-22 (and possibly also 16:25-27).

81. I suspect that the main value of Stendahl's classic remarks about "call" versus "conversion" lies in these observations. It does not really matter whether Paul describes his conversion as a call within his writings so long as this call functions in terms of Justification theory. Thus, it seems to me that Stendahl's initial criticism is weak. However, as Stendahl (and others) point repeatedly to the analogies with prophetic calls, the *implicit unconditionality* of Paul's conversion emerges, along with its *particularity.* And we have just seen that these aspects of his conversion — which are nonnegotiable in terms of the sources — then cause difficulties for Justification theory.

82. Numerous possible locations for this transition have been explored by Pauline scholars in the past: in Paul's Jewish background; at his call; from some contemporary Jewish position; from some Old Testament text; from Jesus' teaching; from earlier converts — presumably the "Hellenists"; from general missionary experience; or during the Judaizing crisis (see Räisänen, *P&L,* 229-64). But only the scenario that will be urged here enjoys any ultimate plausibility, in my view (and it falls within category seven above, although in a distinct way). The others all suffer from a lack of direct corroborative evidence, and the last in fact overrides what evidence there is and also fails to explain Paul's earlier advocacy of the view on his founding missions.

83. I am aware that I have argued earlier (in chapter three) that this is a false implication of the theory. But I am not addressing the theory in its pure form here so much as the theory as characterized by the "Lutheran" biographers, who are strongly committed to Paul's gospel becoming "law free" from the point of his conversion. They know that this dynamic is crucial to the later intelligibility and plausibility of their schema. If, in response to the awkward theoretical point that we have already noted in chapter three, they are happy to relinquish the claim that Paul's gospel *was* law free, then I am happy to abandon this line of argument here. However, I suggest that Justification advocates will (again) have leaped from the frying pan into the fire. They now cannot explain why Paul's gospel *was*

later law-free (because they have abandoned their only explanation for this, which for Justification is strictly correlated with Paul's conversion)! And this generates such an acute framing tension that their entire paradigm is instantly rendered absurd. For these reasons then, Justification advocates have generally tried to establish Paul's law-free gospel on the road to Damascus, ignoring some of the strict implications of their theory — an unenviable conundrum for them to negotiate.

84. Donaldson's work is a forerunner of my analysis at this point (although not in all respects): see *Paul and the Gentiles: Remapping the Apostle's Convictional World.*

85. The account in Acts that is most probably parallel, 15:1-29, basically concurs with Paul's description.

86. So correctly — and perceptively — Markus Bockmuehl, "James, Israel, and Antioch," in *Jewish Law in Gentile Church: Halakhah and the Beginning of Christian Public Ethics* (Edinburgh: T&T Clark, 2000), 56-61, 71-73 (thesis one).

87. See part five, chapter twenty, for a more precise analysis of this text.

88. This then allows him to make a related point in the second half of the verse that is not entirely lucid. The inference seems to be that if Paul were continuing to preach a gospel of circumcision (presumably elsewhere!), then the offense of the cross would also have been removed. Presumably, Paul means to imply by this that the cross, which is itself an offensive event, has in fact offensively abolished any need for the circumcision of pagan converts. Any reversal or neutralization of this offense is therefore self-evidently false, again disproving the claim that he still preaches circumcision. The cross is *inherently* offensive. Hence, this brief argument both reinforces one of his basic claims in the Galatian setting and emphasizes his refutation of the charge that elsewhere he "still preaches circumcision." Strictly speaking, Paul's claim here rests on a cunning transfer of the notion of "offense" from the cross itself to its implications in his gospel for circumcision; he plays on the similar connotation of offense in both these scenarios. And his opponents could have disputed this transfer as illegitimate: "We accept that the cross is offensive, but not your particular development of that offense, which is quite different." But such inconsistencies were not likely to be detected within one clause in a raging presentation. In short, Paul supplies in this verse two apodoses for one protasis that contains a false charge in an attempt to refute or to discredit it. (See 1 Cor. 15:18 for a similar use of ἄρα continuing an apodosis; BDAG suggests, 2a, an expression of result — "then, as a result," with "suggestion of emphasis" [127]. See also 1 Cor. 15:14; 2 Cor. 5:14; Gal. 2:21; 3:29; 5:11.)

89. T. D. Donaldson is one of the few scholars alert to the importance of this evidence: see *Paul and the Gentiles: Remapping the Apostle's Convictional World;* summarized in "Israelite, Convert, Apostle to the Gentiles: The Origin of Paul's Gentile Mission," in Longenecker (ed.), *The Road from Damascus,* 62-84. However, ultimately he develops a case very different from mine. For an earlier position of his — eschatological pilgrimage — see "The 'Curse of the Law' and the Inclusion of the Gentiles: Galatians 3.13-14," *New Testament Studies* 32 (1986): 94-112.

J. Louis (Lou) Martyn notes that ἔτι may have an additive meaning — "in addition to" — yielding the meaning "*from time to time* Paul *adds* as part of his gospel message the demand of circumcision" (*Galatians,* AB 33A [London & New York: Doubleday, 1997], 477). (This is probably the correct reading in 1:10.) But, he points out, this draws ἔτι away from the overt meaning of "still" in 5:11 that it takes in the apodosis. It also places an explanatory burden on interpreters so arguing; they must construct the rather curious scenario that underlies this putative charge by Paul's opponents (although Acts 16:1-3 might help). Martyn correctly notes this difficulty, even though he endorses the reading (and here he is candid: "We do not know," 477). In the absence of such explanation, given the presence of a cogent historical alternative scenario for the charge (of which Martyn is unaware: see 476), and given the double usage, this interpretative alternative is best abandoned. Most importantly, the additive reading does not seem to make sense simply *as* an argument: "If I were on occasion advocating circumcision of Gentile converts, the persecution of me . . . would cease" (477). Clearly, if this advocacy were only on occasion, the persecution would *not* necessarily cease! The occasions on which circumcision was not advocated would engender persecution! However, the temporal argument makes perfect sense: "If I were still advocating circumcision of Gentile converts, the persecution of me . . . would cease" (to paraphrase Martyn's statement of matters).

P. Borgen's ingenious suggestion that Paul is endorsing some spiritual and hence nonliteral circumcision is also best abandoned: see "Paul Preaches Circumcision and Pleases Men," in *Paul and Paulinism: Essays in Honour of C. K. Barrett*, ed. Morna Hooker and S. G. Wilson (London: SPCK, 1982), 37-46. Such an approach should cause no difficulty for Paul's opponents in Galatia. Furthermore, the protasis really requires a condition that Paul wants to reject, and it is difficult to conceive of why Paul would abandon such preaching. Moreover, there is no real offensive dimension to such preaching, as v. 11b demands. And, in view of all this, scholars are right to reject Borgen's suggestions (so Martyn, *Galatians,* 476, n. 30, supported there by Dunn and Barclay).

90. Jewish designations were primarily geographical — "Nazoraeans" and perhaps also "Galileans"; see Hengel and Schwemer, *Paul between Damascus and Antioch,* 225-30.

91. "The ending *-ianus* is Latin," notes C. K. Barrett, suggesting that this was probably not a self-designation by the early Christians: see *A Critical and Exegetical Commentary on the Acts of the Apostles*, vol. 1, *Preliminary Introduction and Commentary on Acts I–XIV,* ICC (London: T&T Clark [Continuum], 1998), 556. Latin was the language of high-level provincial administration in the east, although parts of the army may have spoken it as well. Hence, it seems unlikely that this name was coined by the movement itself — by "insiders." It is therefore an etic rather than an emic designation. (Moreover, it is difficult if not impossible to decide this question in relation to the verb used in Acts. χρηματίσαι — for what it is worth — is ambiguous in terms of voice in this relation, as Barrett notes, and the evidence is further compromised by confusion in the text.) Hengel and Schwemer note that this is a civic, familial, and political designation analogous to the Herodiani. As such, it supplies priceless information about this early Christian community. "Christ" is already a name, not an appellative or title. He is widely perceived by outsiders to be "alive" (see Suetonius, *Life of Claudius* 25.4). And his followers are perceived to be a discrete group of family members and clients of this leader. This last perception could be based on the familial self-designation of the group (Christians are "brothers," et cetera), or on their perceived loyalty to "Christ," their leader, or on both these factors. (If this loyalty were overtly political, then we might expect a higher degree of hostility from the authorities, but they seem to have been named and left alone and hence presumably were perceived as relatively harmless; this may tell against the view that the early Christians were an overt alternative to imperial ideology.) Note that the name "Christ" would have no special meaning to Roman outsiders. Roman writers do change it not infrequently to the slave name "Chrestus" — if this is not simply a misunderstanding based on similar pronunciation: see Suetonius, *Life of Claudius* 25.4; Tacitus, *Annals* 15.44.2-4; see also Phlm. 11! Fitzmyer discusses recognition by early Christian authors of the same phenomenon — Tertullian, *Apology* 3.5 (CSEL 69.10); *To the Nations* 1.3 (CSEL 20.63); Lactantius, *Divine Institutions* 4.7 (CSEL 19.293-94); while a similar pun can be found in Justin Martyr, *First Apology* 4.5 (see A. W. F. Blunt, ed., *The Apologies of Justin Martyr* [Eugene, Ore.: Wipf & Stock, 2006 (1911)], 6) — discussed briefly by Joseph A. Fitzmyer, *Romans: A New Translation with Introduction and Commentary,* AB 33 (New York: Doubleday, 1993), 31.

92. Circumcision was a clear marker of Jewish identity for pagans: see Martial *Epigrams* 7.35, 82; Horace, *Sermons* 1.9.60-78; Suetonius, *Life of Domitian* 12.2; Petronius, *Satyricon* 102.14; Tacitus, *Histories* 5.5.2: see John M. G. Barclay, *Jews in the Mediterranean Diaspora from Alexander to Trajan (323 BCE–117 CE)* (Edinburgh: T&T Clark, 1996), 438-39. And perhaps it is significant that Roman perceptions here were especially acute. Only in exceptional circumstances — if then — could this requirement be relaxed for proselytes. It was also a reasonably obvious marker in the Greco-Roman world, where nudity was not that uncommon, most notably in the public toilets, the baths, and during athletics and exercise.

However, I am mindful that rather gentle missionary work among pagans seems to have been occurring in other places, most notably in Rome, *without resulting in a new name in those locations* (see Romans 16). So perhaps a slightly stronger differentiation from standard perceived Jewish practice than the mere abrogation of circumcision is implicit at Antioch, while out-and-out pagans have not yet been embraced, as seems to have happened with Sergius Paulus and the rest of the Sergii (see Acts 13:13a). This points to an abrogation of the dietary laws, which would have resulted in different dining practices, without necessarily extending to the occupation of new and scandalous eating spaces (see perhaps 1 Corinthians 8 and 10). And marginal confirmation for this scenario is supplied by Cephas's embrace at some point of non-Jewish eating practices at Antioch, which is multiply attested (Gal. 2:14; Acts 10:9-16).

93. See J. Murphy O'Connor, *Paul: A Critical Life* (Oxford: Clarendon, 1996), 101-2.

94. Clearly, this raises a host of fascinating questions, but perhaps in particular concerning the possible social setting(s) for such a transition. The most likely in my view was ecclesial, liturgical, and charismatic, not individualist and rationalist (and this is another blow to Justification theory). For some brief considerations concerning such a scenario, see compact treatments in S. G. Wilson, *The Gentiles and the Gentile Mission in Luke-Acts*, SNTSMS 23 (Cambridge: Cambridge University Press, 1973), 138-53; S. Brown, "The Matthaean Community and the Gentile Mission," *Novum Testamentum* 22 (1980): 193-221; and Heikki Räisänen, *P&L*, 255, esp. notes 139 and 144. There are also some preliminary explorations in my *Quest*, chapter five, 95-111, esp. 109-11. I hope to address this question in more detail shortly in a separate publication, treating the implicit — and very important — theological issues at the same time.

95. The secondary discussion is rather sparse and scattered. For brief introductions and bibliographies, see Fred B. Craddock, "Preaching," in *ABD* 5:451-54; and R. H. Mounce, "Preaching, Kerygma," in *DP&L*, 735-37. Gerhard Friedrich is an earlier and richer analysis: "κῆρυξ, (ἱεροκῆρυξ), κηρύσσω, κήρυγμα, προκηρύσσω," in *TDNT* 3:683-718. C. H. Dodd's study is seminal, *The Apostolic Preaching and Its Developments* (London: Hodder & Stoughton, 1936). Bultmann has also cast a long shadow over this particular discussion: he is discussed in more detail in part two, chapter nine. Duane Litfin discusses Paul's most extensive analysis of preaching, which is implicit in much of 1 Corinthians 1–2 in *St. Paul's Theology of Proclamation: 1 Corinthians 1–4 and Greco-Roman Rhetoric*, SNTSMS 79 (Cambridge: Cambridge University Press, 1994). See also various typically insightful contributions by Martyn, *Galatians*, ##1 (92-95), 3 (97-105), 4 (105-6), 5 (116-17), 7 (127-36), 8 (145-46), 9 (146-48) and 31 (286-89). E. P. Sanders makes some typically crisp remarks: see *Paul and Palestinian Judaism* (Philadelphia: Fortress, 1977), 444-47 (citing Bornkamm and Munck).

96. Evidence from the disputed letters also complements this data: see Eph. 1:13-14; 3:2-12; 6:15, 19-20; Col. 1:5-8, 23, 25-29; 2:1-5; and 2 Thess. 1:3-12; 2:4, 9-12 (here, inversely), 13-15.

97. The following discussion anticipates at numerous points the results of my later detailed exegesis (and it is clearly noted where this is the case).

98. So the evidence in my view strongly endorses the push past Bultmann's minimal reconstruction of the kerygma (which was embarrassed by the historical Jesus) to the more extended, narrative content associated with the post-war Yale school of interpretation — namely, Brevard Childs, George Lindbeck, and Hans Frei; see also, still more recently, Richard B. Hays, esp. *The Faith of Jesus Christ: The Narrative Substructure of Galatians 3:1–4:11*, 2nd ed. (Grand Rapids, Mich.: Eerdmans, 2002 [1987]).

99. Although an important question in Paul's broader theological discussion, it does not affect our current analysis. So it is best to leave its controversies temporarily to one side. It is discussed a little more fully in my *Quest*, 69-94.

100. We return to this material more fully in part four, chapter fifteen.

101. John Howard Yoder puts it nicely: "The *keryx* or herald announces an event. The event is announced as true, of course, and in fact as very important for the hearers, especially for those who have not heard it before. If it were not true the herald would not be raising his or her voice. Yet, no one is forced to believe. What the herald reports is not permanent, timeless, logical insights but contingent, particular events. . . . The truth claim of the herald or witness must remain thus non-coercive if it is to be valid. You never *have* to believe it." See "The Disavowal of Constantine: An Alternative Perspective on Interfaith Dialogue," in *The Royal Priesthood: Essays Ecclesiological and Ecumenical* (Grand Rapids, Mich.: Eerdmans, 1994), 256.

102. Beverly Gaventa has rightly emphasized this discourse: see esp. *Our Mother Saint Paul* (Louisville, Ky. & London: Westminster John Knox, 2007).

103. In the merely communicative, rhetorical situation, Paul's announcement of the solution might respond to problems perceived already by his audience and articulated by him. But the solution

in no way *builds upon truths revealed while the problem is established* that thereby ground the truth as well as the intelligibility of the solution, as is the case in Justification theory. This issue has already been treated — to a degree — in chapter three: see esp. the discussion in §3.1 for a more detailed treatment of the primary texts, and the relevant secondary literature; the broader theological and epistemological issues are treated again in chapter six, in §3.1.

104. These distinctions should speak to Chester's main concerns as expressed in his *Conversion at Corinth,* passim.

Notes to Chapter Six

1. See the Introduction.

2. Hence Justification theory tends to be defended by its advocates in different ways, at different points in the discussion, as we will see in due course — principally in part three, chapters ten and twelve.

3. Ironic of course because this difficulty is usually attributed to Paul himself and not to those modern interpreters with whom the fault can now arguably be seen to lie.

4. The much-used descriptor "the new perspective" is drawn from an important article by J. D. G. Dunn, "The New Perspective on Paul" (originally the Manson Memorial Lecture in 1982 and first published under this name in *Bulletin of the John Rylands Library* 65 [1983], 95-122; republished in *Jesus, Paul and the Law* [London: SPCK, 1990], 183-206 with an Additional Note on 206-14). I do not regard the new perspective to be a particularly helpful notion; it encompasses too much critical and methodological diversity. Really this rather loose aggregation of views is allied only in their general orientation against a contractual reading of Paul. For these reasons, I do not treat it monolithically but rather consider the contributions of its main advocates — principally, Stendahl, Sanders, and Dunn — separately, where they arise most appropriately in the course of this study. Stendahl focuses on a number of potential difficulties: the apostle's introspection, conversion, anachronistic construal, and so on. Sanders is concerned primarily with Paul's description of Judaism, but also — like Schweitzer — with the tensions in Paul's thought between forensic and participatory categories. So these thinkers are all treated in what follows here immediately, although under separate heads — Stendahl in §2.1; and Sanders in §§2.2, 2.4, and 2.5. Dunn, however, essentially accepts these concerns; he adds little if anything to the definition of "the problem." Rather, his proposals attempt to respond to them by reinterpreting Paul's problematic texts, thereby hopefully taking Paul's actual gospel beyond their range. So Dunn's work is best treated as we consider solutions to our difficulties later on. (His type of solution is considered specifically in part three, chapter twelve, and at this point Sanders reappears briefly as well, advocating another type of solution.) Similar considerations apply to other figures that might be grouped within the new perspective as well — N. T. Wright, and so on. Ultimately, my argument here seeks to supply an alternative approach that is more powerful than the new perspective in explanatory terms — one that places the questions of theory and theology centrally, and so is able to offer a more systematic account of our difficulties. Moreover, in doing so, it becomes apparent that our problems are far deeper and more serious than most advocates of the new perspective realize, and the necessary solution rather more radical, not to mention different in shape to their usual suggestions. In these senses then we try to move here beyond both the old perspective of "Lutheranism," and the "new" perspective as well.

5. A "concern" is a difficulty within Paul's construal perceived by the person, group, or tradition.

6. We also ought to regroup our criticisms of the "Lutheran" reading of Paul accordingly, while any grouping that fails to grasp this underlying causality deriving from Justification theory will almost certainly falter at various points.

7. Krister Stendahl, "The Apostle Paul and the Introspective Conscience of the West," *Harvard Theological Review* 56 (1963): 199-215; repr. in *Paul among Jews and Gentiles, and Other Essays* (Philadelphia: Fortress, 1976), 78-96 (page references in what follows to the latter). This should be supplemented by "Paul among Jews and Gentiles" (*Paul*, 1-77), which also originated in 1963 within a lecture

series. His later lectures do not alter things substantially: *Final Account: Paul's Letter to the Romans* (Minneapolis: Fortress, 1995).

8. He points out — quite correctly — that Bultmann's interpretation, although radical in some respects, arose from this same essential distortion (*Paul,* 87-88); this will be apparent in more detail in part two, chapter nine.

9. This strategy will be treated in more detail in part two, chapter seven (as a generic strategy), and part three, chapter twelve (in terms of specific famous examples). Suffice it for now to note that it is a particular type of interpretative strategy concerned primarily with a given text's causality rather than its explicit sense.

10. Stendahl is not alert to the important potential differences in function between prospective and retrospective moments of introversion (et cetera).

11. And reverting here to Stendahl's terminology momentarily.

12. So he posits here three from the lists of problems that have been described earlier in more formal terms, and he also recognizes the contractual, hermeneutical, and church-historical difficulties — the greatest spread of relevant issues noted to my knowledge by any revisionist. Not all are of equal penetration, but this is to be expected.

13. He does not pursue the point in quite the manner that I do here, but see E. P. Sanders, *Paul and Palestinian Judaism* (Philadelphia: Fortress, 1977) (hereafter *P&PJ*); *Paul, the Law, and the Jewish People* (Philadelphia: Fortress, 1983) (hereafter *PL&JP*); and *Paul* (Oxford: Oxford University Press, 1991). One of the best accounts of "participationist" soteriology in existence is supplied by *P&PJ,* 447-74. Its main flaw is arguably the uncritical inclusion in *this* discourse of "believing" as "expressing the *transfer* to being Christian" (463; see also 446-48; 473). Sanders then struggles with the competing Justification discourse that works forward, in *P&PJ,* 481-95. Much the same situation is also evident in Jouette Bassler's recent study, where the two discourses jostle throughout: see *Navigating Paul: An Introduction to Key Theological Concepts* (Louisville, Ky., & London: Westminster John Knox, 2007).

14. Albert Schweitzer's own account of the tradition — which is not completely trustworthy — notes H. Lüdemann (whose work appeared in 1872), O. Pfleiderer (1873), R. Kabisch (1893), W. Wrede (1903), and A. Deissmann (1911; ET 1912; 2nd ed. 1929); see *Paul and His Interpreters,* trans. W. Montgomery (New York: Schocken, 1964 [1912]). Schweitzer's work appeared in a rather interrupted fashion because of his unusual life. He was clearly formulating and endorsing this viewpoint as early as 1906; however, his own systematic treatment of Paul appeared only in 1929, well after German scholarship had largely dismissed the approach: see *The Mysticism of Paul the Apostle,* trans. W. Montgomery (New York: Seabury, 1968 [1931]). Schweitzer's concern was to wrest the mystical reading of Paul away from its usual deployment in relation to the Greco-Roman or Hellenistic construal of the apostle that cut Paul off from his Jewish roots by explaining him in terms of the mystery religions (then currently voguish): see (i.a.) R. Reitzenstein (1909) and W. Bousset (1913): see, in particular, Bousset's influential *Kyrios Christos: A History of the Belief in Christ from the Beginnings of Christianity to Irenaeus,* trans. (from the 4th ed.) J. E. Steely (Nashville, Tenn.: Abingdon, 1970 [1st ed. 1913; 4th ed. 1965]). Schweitzer felt that this created a great dislocation within the early church between the eschatological Jesus and subsequent developments, not mention that it supplied an ultimately false account of Paul. He tried to deal with the problem by rereading Paul's mysticism *eschatologically,* thereby killing two birds with one stone: Paul remained Jewish and continuous with the eschatological Jesus, but also mystical — suitably defined — and not forensic.

Dunn gives a succinct and informative account of this trajectory. He attributes the main original impetus here to Deissmann and Bousset, observing that the view has since "faded" and "become fragmented" if not "a back number": see *The Theology of Paul the Apostle* (Edinburgh & Grand Rapids: T&T Clark & Eerdmans, 1998), 390-95 (hereafter *TPA*). A recent revisitation to this entire question, listing more current scholarship, is Robert C. Tannehill, "Participation in Christ: A Central Theme in Pauline Soteriology," in *The Shape of the Gospel: New Testament Essays* (Eugene, Oregon: Cascade [Wipf & Stock], 2007), 223-37.

15. James Stewart, *A Man in Christ: The Vital Elements of St. Paul's Religion* (London: Hodder & Stoughton, 1935).

16. It has never *disappeared* from German interpretation, as the important recent statement of Paul's gospel in essentially participatory and transformational terms by Udo Schnelle makes clear: see *Apostle Paul: His Life and Theology,* trans. M. Eugene Boring (Grand Rapids, Mich.: Baker, 2005 [2003]), 410-505. It is a moot point to what extent Schnelle represents the previous fifty years of Pauline interpretation in Germany, or even how he reflects current readings.

17. See (i.a.) C. F. D. Moule's accounts of Paul in *The Phenomenon of the New Testament: An Inquiry into the Implications of Certain Features of the New Testament* (London: SCM, 1967), 22-29, 39-42; and *The Origin of Christology* (Cambridge: Cambridge University Press, 1977), 47-96; and Morna Hooker's notion of "interchange" in Paul's thought: see *Pauline Pieces* (London: Epworth, 1979), 36-52; and *From Adam to Christ: Essays on Paul* (Cambridge: Cambridge University Press, 1990), 13-69.

18. So I learned of the approach from my Doktorvater, Richard N. Longenecker, who taught then at Wycliffe College in Toronto, Canada, and had previously taught in the United States.

19. This was effected principally by *P&PJ.* The Mystery Religions hypothesis has also been revivified by some, although unwisely: see Hyam Maccoby, *The Mythmaker: Paul and the Invention of Christianity* (New York: Harper & Row, 1986); and *Paul and Hellenism* (London: SCM, 1991); see also the widely read novel by A. N. Wilson, *Paul: The Mind of the Apostle* (London & New York: W. W. Norton, 1997). A degree of overlap is discernible here with Räisänen's criticisms of Paul's coherence, but he tends not to juxtapose systems, being convinced that Paul has none, and is not so interested in the question of ancient cultural backgrounds either. Räisänen is discussed just below in §2.4.

20. See T. Engberg-Pedersen, *Paul and the Stoics* (Edinburgh: T&T Clark, 2000), 296-97.

21. These difficulties manifest as tensions or contradictions that extend through the two systems' epistemologies, anthropologies, theologies (in the specific sense of their differing fundamental definitions of God's nature), conceptions of the atonement (here linking up with different basic christological commitments), understandings of soteriology (including different basic conceptions of the role of the Spirit) and assurance, of faith, of ethics, of the church, of Judaism (including the roles attributed to the law), and of the proper role (if any) of coercion and violence. It can be seen at a glance then that underlying most of the tradition's specific concerns is the set of tensions generated by the construal of Paul at certain points in terms of Justification but at other points in terms of an alternative soteriological system — one with a fundamentally participatory and transformational understanding of salvation.

22. W. Wrede, *Paul,* trans. E. Lummis (London: Green & Hull, Elsom, 1907 [1904]), esp. 74-154.

23. Wrede cavils at this point a bit: Paul for him lacks the idea of a personality in the sense of human individuality, so he thinks that Paul could not conceive of Christ as a real man. It is also unthinkable for us "that a being in substance divine should enter into a true union with humanity" (90). So Wrede does not always fully endorse the incarnation. At other points, however, he concedes that the logic of the system necessitates a full identification.

24. Wrede later returns to baptism, in his discussion of the sacraments. Through baptism "into the death of Christ," the believer "becomes incorporate with Christ, so that he forms, so to say, one person with him." Baptism, then, "in conjunction with belief, in a perfectly real if undefinable way, bestows redemption on the individual, and makes him a member of the body of Christ" (*Paul,* 122).

25. We have already noted this strategy's use by Stendahl as well just above; it is a common recourse by critics of Justification, but limited in its effectiveness, as part three, chapter twelve will suggest.

26. He also notes — almost incredibly — that Paul's account of Judaism at this point is not entirely fair: "Some slight element of caricature enters into this conception of the Jewish religion; for it was not ignorant of grace; it even laid stress on grace" (*Paul,* 127).

27. Wrede remains an excellent example of the alternative theory, especially through his emphases on Christ's solidarity with an oppressed human condition and on human participation within his death and resurrection assisted by the work of the Spirit. It is these emphases — and the transformational realities to which they point — that combine into a saving system as people pass through Christ's death and on into his resurrection (although this process is only inaugurated). Wrede diverges from our earlier account only — and arguably a little inconsistently — by allowing at one point that belief in Christ "effects" this saving participation. A view of faith more consistent with the

alternative theory is implicit in the central section of Romans, and some German scholars were aware of this. (In this respect, Deissmann can be viewed as more advanced than Wrede.) Furthermore, that central part of Romans attributes soteriological causality — as Wrede himself in fact frequently does — to the unconditional work of God effected by the Spirit. Hence, this process is best symbolized if not also effected by the sacrament of baptism. These accents are found in Wrede. (Indeed, Wrede may emphasize the role of the Spirit in this relation more than much subsequent Pauline analysis.) But it must be allowed that Wrede is also not untypical of many members of this interpretative trajectory in attempting to integrate a soteriological condition based on faith with the more unconditional and ontological emphases of "Christ mysticism" or participation, however awkward this turns out to be in theoretical terms. Wrede also frequently emphasizes the more vigorous ground for ethics in Paul's participatory system, here opposing the typically liberal emphasis of his day on individual ethical effort that is also principally cognitive or mental and rooted in a merely imitative or exemplary Christology — the long shadow of Kant.

28. His advocates are not helped because, on the one hand, they have to defend a contradictory description of Paul's thinking against its detractors — an essentially untenable position. So critics of Paul, such as Räisänen, are essentially vindicated. This battle will be lost. On the other hand, it is also difficult to *teach* Paul, because his conceptions are so confused. Even if it is not acknowledged as such, my experience is that students nevertheless struggle to appreciate Paul's thinking, because in large measure they are grappling subliminally with his multiple contradictions. They are *confused — and understandably so!*

29. Quoted appositely by Douglas Moo, *The Epistle to the Romans,* NICNT (Grand Rapids, Mich.: Eerdmans, 1996), 350 — who does not question the arguably contradictory nature of this explanation. Dunn phrases things in more contemporary terms: "'Salvation' properly speaking is the climax or end result of a process. The process has a decisive beginning, but it is also a lifelong process. . . . In terms of Paul's theology of justification, the decisive beginning has to be worked out until and in the final verdict of acquittal" (*TPA,* 493).

30. See esp. Rom. 6:19, 22; 1 Cor. 1:30; 6:11. And we will also see in part four, chapter thirteen, how Paul places the language of purity and sanctification at the very center of his apostolic mission.

31. Hence, these realizations do have the further virtue of affirming that any responsible account of a process of "sanctification" in Paul is likely to be a fair account of his soteriology per se. So most conservative scholars, who otherwise endorse Justification, nevertheless also tend to describe Paul's actual soteriology accurately.

32. Unfortunately, such problems have not prevented this explanation from being remobilized, although under a different banner. That is, essentially the same explanation — in terms of a justification-sanctification distinction — can still be offered in serious explanation of the tensions noted in this relation in Paul, but articulated in slightly different, less traditional terms. Sanders is an excellent example of this approach (although he also utilizes other modern explanatory categories). He is assessed in more detail in part three, chapter twelve.

33. See his *New Testament Questions of Today,* trans. W. J. Montague (London: SCM, 1969 [1965]), 168-82. This debate is discussed in more detail, in the broader context of a detailed analysis of the meaning of δικαιοσύνη Θεοῦ, in part four, chapter seventeen.

34. See my *The Rhetoric of Righteousness in Romans 3:21-26,* JSNTSup 65 (Sheffield: JSOT Press, 1992), 144-47.

35. My account of the grounds of Ernst Käsemann's protests here arises also from a more general consideration of his work on Paul — especially his famous essays. Tragic personal circumstances prevented Käsemann from ever producing a more comprehensive treatment of Paul beyond these essays and his commentary on Romans (this last based primarily on his famous lectures on Romans at the University of Tübingen). See *New Testament Questions of Today; Perspectives on Paul,* trans. M. Kohl (London: SCM, 1971); *Commentary on Romans,* trans. Geoffrey W. Bromiley, 4th ed. (Grand Rapids, Mich.: Eerdmans, 1980 [1975]). An excellent treatment of Käsemann's thought is D. Way, *The Lordship of Christ: Ernst Käsemann's Interpretation of Paul's Theology* (Oxford: Clarendon, 1991).

Käsemann has also influenced Charles Cousar's important study, *A Theology of the Cross: The Death of Jesus in the Pauline Letters* (Minneapolis, Minn.: Fortress, 1990).

36. Beker wrote one of the dominant texts on Pauline theology in the last decades of the twentieth century: J.-Christiaan Beker, *Paul the Apostle: The Triumph of God in Life and Thought* (Philadelphia: Fortress, 1984 [1980]). Beker stressed future eschatology a little awkwardly, and Martyn justly accused him in addition of flirting inconsistently with salvation history (thereby reprising an earlier exchange between Käsemann and Stendahl): see J. Louis Martyn, "Review of Beker's *Paul the Apostle*," in *Word and World* 2 (1982): 194-98. Nevertheless, the imprint of Käsemann's protests against the prevailing reading of Paul is evident in the warp and woof of this powerful treatment.

Leander Keck has not produced a major study of Paul; however, he has consistently and intelligently pressed Käsemann's agenda — suitably modified — in a series of important articles: see esp. "Paul and Apocalyptic Theology," *Interpretation* 38 (1984): 229-41; "Toward the Renewal of New Testament Christology," *New Testament Studies* 32 (1986): 362-77; "Jesus in Romans," *Journal of Biblical Literature* 108 (1989): 443-60; "Paul as Thinker," *Interpretation* 47 (1993): 27-38; "What Makes Romans Tick?" in David M. Hay and E. Elizabeth Johnson, eds., *Pauline Theology*, vol. 3, *Romans* (Minneapolis: Fortress, 1995), 3-29; "Rethinking New Testament Ethics," *Journal of Biblical Literature* 115 (1996): 3-16; and "Searchable Judgments and Scrutable Ways," in David M. Hay and E. Elizabeth Johnson, eds., *Pauline Theology*, vol. 4, *Looking Back, Pressing On* (Atlanta: Scholars, 1997), 22-32. An outline of his concerns is evident in *Paul and His Letters*, rev. ed. (Minneapolis: Fortress, 1988). Many of these concerns are also drawn together in his recent commentary *Romans*, ANTC (Nashville, Tenn.: Abingdon Press, 2005). (The suggestions of this elegant treatment will be considered carefully in due course.)

Other figures — now reaching a third generation of such apocalyptic interpreters — could easily be included here: see (i.a.) Martinus de Boer, Alexandra Brown, Charles Cousar, Michael Gorman, Beverly Gaventa, and Ann Jervis (while much that Richard Hays argues also belongs in this tradition, although his interpretative work is not reducible to this trajectory). Many of their specific contributions to the apocalyptic reconstrual of Paul are noted through parts four and five below.

37. Martyn's most important contributions are now gathered in the main within two volumes: his commentary on *Galatians*, AB 33A (London & New York: Doubleday, 1997) and a collection of essays, *Theological Issues in the Letters of Paul* (Edinburgh & Nashville, Tenn.: T&T Clark & Abingdon, 1997). He is discussed in particular in part four, chapter thirteen, and part five, chapter twenty.

38. See, i.a., *P&PJ*, 442-44, 481-85, 497-502, 508-11.

39. And this observation — along with similar commitments by Wrede and the participatory trajectory — creates further continuities with those interpreters of Paul previously mentioned who emphasize the role of "the powers" in his thought, e.g., Walter Wink, *Naming the Powers: The Language of Power in the New Testament* (Philadelphia: Fortress, 1984); *Unmasking the Powers: The Invisible Forces That Determine Human Existence* (Philadelphia: Fortress, 1986); and *Engaging the Powers: Discernment and Resistance in a World of Domination* (Philadelphia: Fortress, 1992) (a tension already noted in part one, chapter three, §3.10).

40. Martyn tends to define Paul's δικαιο- language in liberative terms and his πιστ- language christocentrically. He attributes much of the material usually associated with Justification in Paul's writings to the apostle's opponents, "the Teachers" (yielding the interpretative irony that Paul has been construed for a great deal of his history — at least in part — in the image of his opposition). Much of what follows here is explicable largely as an attempt to take Martyn's perspective with complete seriousness, especially in relation to those parts of Romans that do not seem to integrate with it easily in the first instance. We will return to his more detailed consideration especially in part five, chapter twenty, when we interpret the relevant parts of Galatians in detail, while his particular contribution to my overarching exegetical strategy here is sketched in part four, chapter thirteen.

41. These remarks echo a slightly longer discussion of the same issue in *Quest*, 56-57, esp. note 3. (There I suggest that the acronym PPME will ultimately help interpreters to treat each important feature within a fundamentally participatory account of Paul's gospel appropriately — "pneumatologically participatory martyrological eschatology." This acronym need not be taken too seriously; it is

merely a heuristic suggestion.) R. B. Matlock's study is *Unveiling the Apocalyptic Paul: Paul's Inter-preters and the Rhetoric of Criticism,* JSNTSup 127 (Sheffield: Sheffield Academic Press, 1996). Also useful at this point is Martinus C. de Boer, "Paul and Jewish Apocalyptic Eschatology," in *Apocalyptic and the New Testament: Essays in Honor of J. Louis Martyn,* ed. J. Marcus and M. Soards (Sheffield: JSOT Press, 1989), 169-90. De Boer highlights the divergent commitments of ancient apocalypses in relation to questions of human capacity and incapacity, thereby demonstrating that any appeal merely to "apocalyptic" cannot settle this critical issue. Käsemann, Beker, Keck, and Martyn would probably all want to characterize Paul more narrowly than this, as committed to an unconditional soteriology. A standard discussion of the thorny question of genre is John J. Collins, *Apocalypse: The Morphology of a Genre,* vol. 14, *Semeia* (Missoula, Mont.: Scholars, 1979); see also *The Apocalyptic Imagination: An Introduction to Jewish Apocalyptic Literature,* 2nd ed. (Grand Rapids: Eerdmans, 1998 [1984]).

42. *Paul and the Law,* 2nd ed., WUNT 29 (Tübingen: J. C. B. Mohr [Paul Siebeck], 1987 [1983]), 11, emphases original — hereafter *P&L.*

43. See John W. Drane, *Libertine or Legalist? A Study in the Theology of the Major Pauline Epis-tles* (London: SPCK, 1975); Hans Hübner, *Law in Paul's Thought,* ed. John Riches, trans. James C. G. Grieg (Edinburgh: T&T Clark, 1984) (2nd ed. Tübingen: J. C. B. Mohr [Paul Siebeck], 1987); and Sanders, *PL&JP.* Stephen Westerholm surveys the three chosen advocates of inconsistency in *Perspec-tives Old and New on Paul: The Lutheran Paul and His Critics* (Grand Rapids, Mich.: Eerdmans, 2004), 164-77 — hereafter *PO&NP.* He points out that Räisänen's charges of inconsistency in Paul with re-spect to Romans 9–11 are made primarily in "Römer 9–11: Analyse eines geistigen Ringens," *Aufstieg und Niedergang der römischen Welt: Geschichte und Kultur Roms im Spiegel der neueren Forschung* II, 25, 4 (1987): 2891-939; and "Paul, God, and Israel: Romans 9–11 in Recent Research," in *The Social World of Formative Christianity and Judaism,* ed. P. Borgen, J. Neusner, E. S. Frerichs, and R. Horsley (Philadelphia: Fortress, 1988), 178-206. Räisänen himself points in addition to the earlier suggestions of contradiction made by H. J. Schoeps, *Paul: The Theology of the Apostle in the Light of Jewish Reli-gious History,* trans. Harold Knight (London & Philadelphia: Lutterworth Press & Westminster, 1961); see also *The Jewish-Christian Argument* (London: Faber & Faber, 1965); and notes briefly the similar comments of other scholars like Percy Gardner and James Parkes, not to mention Wrede (*P&L,* 11-12). Negative judgments of Paul's abilities to argue and reason are also tabulated by Räisänen from Montefiore, Sandmel, Wernle, and Loisy (*P&L,* 13).

44. Certainly George Foot Moore's principal difficulties are removed. His brilliantly incisive statement is worth quoting at length: "Paul's argument rests on two premises equally alien to Jewish thought and repugnant to its spirit: *First,* as we have seen, that the righteousness which is under the Law the condition of salvation in us is nothing less than perfect conformity to the law, see, e.g., Gal. 3, 10-12. *Second,* that God, in his righteousness, cannot freely forgive the penitent sinner and bestow upon him a salvation that is of grace, not of desert. This second assumption is less explicitly developed than the first; on it rests, however, the whole necessity of the expiatory death of Christ; see, e.g., Rom. 3, 25. It is to be noted that Paul shifts the whole problem from forgiveness to 'justification'" (*Judaism in the First Centuries of the Christian Era: The Age of the Tannaim,* 3 vols. [Cambridge, Mass.: Harvard University Press, 1927, 30], 3:150; emphases original).

45. Some of Räisänen's struggles with an implicit distinction between an abolished "ceremo-nial" or "ritual" law, and the moral law, still in force, in Paul, fall into this category. These concerns ought to be addressed in part exegetically, and in part by the exploration of a retrospective theological agenda operating in terms of the soteriological schema apparent in Romans 5–8 (as against prospec-tive agendas utilized by approaches in terms of either Justification or salvation-history). Räisänen does not generally seem sensitive to the important distinction potentially operative here, and its im-plications: see *Quest,* 132-45.

46. The scholars cited here also tend to deploy different explanations for these contradictions. Räisänen is relatively cynical, viewing Paul as inherently confused if not opportunistic. He can infer no more coherent explanation of the difficulties than this. Drane and Hübner adopt developmental strate-gies: Paul changes his mind over time as he encounters different circumstances, they assert, so they rely heavily on explanations of the circumstantial frame (an explanation Räisänen rejects — and with some

cause: see esp. *P&L*, 7-10). While, as we have already seen, Sanders suggests that Paul deploys different systems in order to answer different questions (which would also fall technically within the category of explanations in terms of the circumstantial frame). But here we are not interested in their explanations — most of which we will assess later — so much as in the mere fact of contradiction.

47. Arguably his detection of "oscillation" is also relevant, but Räisänen grounds this at the crucial points on a particular exegesis of Gal. 3:13-14 and 23-26 (*P&L*, 18-23). After this he certainly affirms that Paul abolishes the Law.

48. And some of his contributions here have already been noted: see the Excursus "The 'Lutheran' Biography of Paul," in chapter five, §3.4.

49. *P&L*, v; see also Schoeps, *Paul: The Theology of the Apostle in the Light of Jewish Religious History.*

50. I will offer different readings, e.g., of Gal. 3:13-14 and 3:23-26 in part five, chapter twenty, that will not yield the contradictions that he asserts are present here. (In his view Paul speaks in these texts in an "oscillating" fashion of, i.a., *pagans* being under the curse and the pedagogy of the Law, whereas elsewhere they are not: see *P&L*, 19-20; in my view, these texts do more likely refer simply to Jews and Jewish Christians.)

51. It seems to be no coincidence that all the advocates of the view of Paul's Damascus event as a paradigmatic conversion previously noted in chapter five also tend to advocate the following additional biographical positions — see esp. Hengel and Riesner. To this list we can add F. F. Bruce, *Paul, Apostle of the Heart Set Free* (Grand Rapids, Mich.: Eerdmans, 1977); also *The Book of the Acts*, rev. ed., NICNT (Grand Rapids, Mich.: Eerdmans, 1988); and a "Tyndale House" tradition of scholarship represented by Andrew D. Clarke and Bruce W. Winter, eds., *The Book of Acts in Its Ancient Literary Setting*, vol. 1, *The Book of Acts in Its First Century Setting* (Grand Rapids, Mich.: Eerdmans, 1994); David W. J. Gill and Conrad Gempf, eds., *The Book of Acts in Its Graeco-Roman Setting*, vol. 2, *The Book of Acts in Its First Century Setting* (Carlisle and Grand Rapids, Mich.: Paternoster and Eerdmans, 1994); Brian Rapske, *Paul in Roman Custody*, vol. 3, *The Book of Acts in Its First Century Setting* (Grand Rapids, Mich.: Eerdmans, 1995); Richard Bauckham, ed., *The Book of Acts in Its Palestinian Setting*, vol. 4, *The Book of Acts in Its First Century Setting* (Grand Rapids, Mich.: Eerdmans, 1995); Irina Levinskaya, *The Book of Acts in Its Diaspora Setting*, vol. 5, *The Book of Acts in Its First Century Setting* (Grand Rapids, Mich.: Eerdmans, 1996); and Colin Hemer, *The Book of Acts in the Setting of Hellenistic History*, ed. Conrad H. Gempf, repr. ed. (Winona Lake, Ind.: Eisenbrauns, 1990). See also my Doktorvater, Richard N. Longenecker, "The Acts of the Apostles," in *The Expositor's Bible Commentary*, ed. Frank E. Gaebelein (Grand Rapids, Mich.: Zondervan, 1981), 207-573; and (ed.) *The Road from Damascus: The Impact of Paul's Conversion on His Life, Thought, and Ministry* (Grand Rapids, Mich.: Eerdmans, 1997). But such advocacy is by no means limited to more conservative scholars. Many interpreters of Paul follow an essentially Acts-based schema, perhaps unaware of all the theological and theoretical implications of doing so.

52. A good example of how this rather credulous reconstruction of Paul's missionary praxis can influence even an avowedly revisionist analysis is Mark Nanos, *The Mystery of Romans* (Minneapolis: Fortress, 1996). (This is not to impugn this study's positive contributions.)

53. One such challenge might be, given a different use of Acts and a different biography, that the first extant letter by Paul is 1 Thessalonians and that this letter contains little evidence of Justification theory (although some would dispute this challenge too: see, i.a., Westerholm, *PO&NP*, 353-61; the most difficult aspects of this text are treated in part five, chapter twenty-one).

54. Acts 24:27; 28:30.

55. So Käsemann's charge of "early catholicism": see *New Testament Questions of Today*, 236-51. It is worth recalling here that the well-known German Protestant New Testament scholar Heinrich Schlier — a student of Bultmann's — converted to Catholicism in 1953, in part prompted by exegetical work on Ephesians: see *Der Brief an die Epheser* (Düsseldorf: Patmos, 1957); see also his more popular explanations offered in *We Are Now Catholics*, ed. Karl Hardt (Westminster, Maryland: Newman Press, 1959), 193-214.

56. A dynamic if superficial presentation of the case can be found in Charles H. Buck and

Greer Taylor, *Saint Paul: A Study of the Development of His Thought* (New York: Scribner's, 1969). C. Wanamaker makes a good case for the reversal of the canonical order of 1 and 2 Thessalonians: *Commentary on 1 & 2 Thessalonians*, NIGTC (Grand Rapids: Eerdmans, 1990), esp. 37-63.

57. This is not the only scenario that can be elaborated in relation to an authentic 2 Thessalonians, but it is the most troublesome one for Justification advocates.

58. The classic account of these concerns is John Knox, *Chapters in a Life of Paul*, ed. & intro. D. Hare, rev. ed. (London: SCM, 1987 [1950]). They are presented especially acutely by John C. Hurd, *The Origin of I Corinthians*, new ed. (Macon, Georgia: Mercer University Press, 1983 [1965]). See also Gerd Luedemann's early work: *Paul, Apostle to the Gentiles: Studies in Chronology*, trans. F. S. Jones (Philadelphia: Fortress, 1984 [1980]); *Opposition to Paul in Jewish Christianity*, trans. M. E. Boring (Minneapolis: Fortress, 1989 [1983]); and *Early Christianity according to the Traditions in Acts* (Minneapolis: Fortress, 1989). Karl P. Donfried makes much the same point accessibly in "Chronology — New Testament," *ABD* 1:1011-22. It is interesting also to consider Luke's redaction of Mark, which is clearly not rigorously sequential in historical terms: see J. A. Fitzmyer, *The Gospel According to Luke I–IX*, AB 28 (Garden City, New York: Doubleday, 1982), 66-72; and C. F. Evans, *Saint Luke* (Philadelphia: Trinity Press, 1990), 17-21, 30-34, 37-40.

59. The classic statement of this opinion is Lightfoot's. The suggestion is often made in tandem with the claim that Galatians is addressed to the central and northern part of that province and hence to ethnic and not merely provincial Galatians (i.e., the inhabitants of the cities visited by Paul on his "first missionary journey" — Pisidian Antioch, Iconium, Lystra, and Derbe); for a learned overview of the debate see Martyn, *Galatians*, 15-20, 180-86, 222-28. However, the same critical concern is quite compatible with the acceptance of a southern provenance. These debates are addressed in more detail in part four, chapter thirteen, and part five, chapter twenty.

60. Hurd is a good example of a critical biographer's recovery of confidence in Pauline authorship of these disputed letters: see John C. Hurd, "Introduction," in *Colloquy on New Testament Studies: A Time for Reappraisal and Fresh Approaches*, ed. Bruce C. Corley (Macon, Georgia: Mercer University Press, 1983), 265-70; as is Knox himself: see "On the Pauline Chronology: Buck-Taylor-Hurd Revisited," in *The Conversation Continues: Studies in Paul and John in Honor of J. Louis Martyn*, ed. B. R. Gaventa and R. T. Fortna (Nashville, Tenn.: Abingdon, 1990), 258-74; see also D. W. Riddle, *Paul, Man of Conflict: A Modern Biographical Sketch* (Nashville, Tenn.: Cokesbury, 1940), who follows an epistolary methodology, and so firmly endorses the authenticity of Colossians; and Buck and Taylor, *Saint Paul*.

More conservative scholars are arguably caught between different sensibilities at such points. Their explanations of the differences between all these letters should be scrutinized carefully: see, e.g., Donald Guthrie, *New Testament Introduction* (Downers Grove, Ill.: Apollos [InterVarsity Press], 1990 [1961-65]), esp. 403-667, 1001-28.

61. The debate has been especially prominent — particularly in North American New Testament circles — since the publication of Hays's important doctoral thesis in 1983 (reprinted in 2002 with a new extended introduction): see *The Faith of Jesus Christ: The Narrative Substructure of Galatians 3:1–4:11*, 2nd ed. (Grand Rapids, Mich.: Eerdmans, 2002 [1983]). I learned about this debate from my Doktorvater, Richard N. Longenecker, who participated within an earlier round of discussion that overlapped more with British scholars, and he has also published some helpful contributions to it: see "The Obedience of Christ in the Theology of the Early Church," in *Reconciliation and Hope: FS Leon Morris*, ed. Robert Banks (Grand Rapids, Mich.: Eerdmans, 1974), 142-52; "The Faith of Abraham Theme in Paul, James, and Hebrews: A Study in the Circumstantial Nature of New Testament Teaching," *Journal of the Evangelical Theological Society* 20 (1977): 203-12; and *Galatians*, WBC 41 (Dallas: Word, 1990), esp. 87-88, 93-94. The literature and debates are canvassed thoroughly in the exegetical discussions that follow — see esp. part four, chapter fifteen, and part five, chapters nineteen through twenty-one.

62. This issue and appropriate further discussions have already been noted in chapter two, §2.2. The early Barth's position on natural theology — in debate with Emil Brunner — is famous: see Karl Barth, "No!," in *Natural Theology* (London: Centenary Press, 1946), 65-128. Some of Barth's later

views are found in *CD* I.2, 304-7; and II.1, 118-23; also *Shorter Commentary on Romans* (Richmond, Va.: John Knox, 1959), 24, this last arguably being a better point of comparison than his famous earlier commentary. His comments to Carl Zuckmeyer are also interesting, made in May 1968: "I would gladly concede that *nature* does objectively offer a proof of God, though the human being overlooks or misunderstands it. Yet I would not venture to say the same of natural *science,* whether ancient or modern." See Karl Barth, *A Late Friendship: The Letters of Karl Barth and Carl Zuckmayer,* ed. G. Bromiley (Grand Rapids, Mich.: Eerdmans, 1982), 42, as noted also by Eugene Rogers, *Thomas Aquinas and Karl Barth: Sacred Doctrine and the Natural Knowledge of God* (London & Notre Dame: University of Notre Dame Press, 1995), 7, 206.

It is also worth noting that Thomas Aquinas cites Rom. 1:20 as the warrant for his Five Ways in Question 2 of the *Summa Theologiae.* He also supplies philosophical proofs when explicating Rom. 1:19-21 in his Romans commentary (at this point only three). However, an intriguing argument is now made by Eugene Rogers, in favor of reducing the distance between Aquinas and Barth on grounds of the importance of Question 1. Less ambiguous are the statements of Leo XIII and Vatican I in *Aeterni Patris* (see Rogers, *Aquinas and Barth,* 205-13).

Michael Buckley makes this point about atheism most explicitly in *At the Origins of Modern Atheism* (London & New Haven: Yale University Press, 1987). Buckley suggests that Leonard Lessius (or Leys) of Louvain and Marin Mersenne of Paris were especially important figures in arranging the Western marriage of theology with prevailing philosophical systems.

63. See Alan J. Torrance, "Forgiveness: The Essential Socio-Political Structure of Personal Being," *Journal of Theology for Southern Africa* 56 (1986): 47-59; "The Theology of Liberation in Latin America," in *Different Gospels: Christian Orthodoxy and Modern Heresies,* ed. Andrew Walker (London: Hodder & Stoughton, 1988), 183-205; and, with Hilary Regan and Antony Wood, eds., *Christ and Context: The Confrontation between Gospel and Culture* (Edinburgh: T&T Clark, 1993). These concerns are also central to much of Hauerwas's work. He articulates them clearly in relation to Barth in chapter six, "The Witness That Was Karl Barth," in *With the Grain of the Universe: The Church's Witness and Natural Theology, Being the Gifford Lectures Delivered at the University of St. Andrews in 2001* (London: SCM, 2002), 141-71.

64. And this is an important qualification. Barth ultimately allows various limited roles for natural theology, but not a *foundational* one. Justification theory, however, along with the usual construal of Rom. 1:19-20, underwrites the latter.

65. Irving Greenberg provides the yardstick for this perspective with his famous adage that nothing should be said except that which can be spoken in the presence of the burning children: "Cloud of Smoke, Pillar of Fire: Judaism, Christianity and Modernity after the Holocaust," in *Auschwitz: Beginning of a New Era?* ed. Eva Fleischner (New York: Ktav, 1977), 7-55; also "Religious Values after the Holocaust: A Jewish View," in *Jews and Christians after the Holocaust,* ed. Abraham Peck (Philadelphia: Fortress, 1982), 63-86. The classic account of post-Holocaust concerns in NT scholarship is Rosemary Radford Ruether, *Faith and Fratricide: The Theological Roots of Anti-Semitism* (New York: Seabury, 1974). More recent is Paula Frederiksen and Adele Reinhartz, eds., *Jesus, Judaism, and Christian Anti-Judaism: Reading the New Testament after the Holocaust* (Louisville: Westminster John Knox, 2002). A powerful exploration of some of the broader issues is also provided by Joel Marcus in *Jesus and the Holocaust: Reflections on Suffering and Hope* (New York: Doubleday, 1997). Rereading strategies pursued in relation to Paul by scholars persuaded by the urgency and cogency of this particular issue are assessed — where relevant to issues raised by Justification, of which we have just noted some — in part three, chapter twelve (see there in particular suggestions by Lloyd Gaston, John Gager, and Stanley Stowers), and my own is sketched in part four, chapter thirteen.

There is an important overlap here with the issue of alterity, which runs through a great deal of current analysis (but is difficult to pin down). The question of alterity arises again in relation to definitions of sexuality and gender that are noted just below, and then by implication for questions of race and ethnicity — so the standard analysis by Simone de Beauvoir, *The Second Sex,* trans. H. M. Parshley (New York: Vintage, 1952 [1949]); also Edward W. Said, *Orientalism* (New York: Pantheon Books [Random House], 1978). More recent is the insightful analysis of Elaine L. Graham, *Making the*

Difference: Gender, Personhood, and Theology (London: Mowbray [Cassell], 1995). See also Romand Coles, *Self/Power/Others: Political Theory and Dialogical Ethics* (London & Ithaca, New York: Cornell University Press, 1992). Foucault can be introduced usefully at this point as well. An insightful introduction to some applicable elements of his thought — along with their inevitable reworking — is David Toole, *Waiting for Godot in Sarajevo: Theological Reflections on Nihilism, Tragedy, and Apocalypse* (Boulder, Colorado: Westview, 1998), 129-204.

66. See Charles Marsh's powerful discussion, "Douglas Hudgins: Theologian of the Closed Society," *God's Long Summer: Stories of Faith and Civil Rights* (Princeton, New Jersey: Princeton University Press, 1997), 82-115. Hudgins was minister of First Baptist Church in Jackson, Mississippi, in the 1950s and 60s — the premier church in the state, which also included its most prominent and powerful segregationists. Marsh notes that Hudgins's theology and preaching were so pietistic and individualized that no comment was or could be offered in relation to racism or other appalling actions — even when the home of a Jewish friend, Rabbi Perry Nussbaum, was bombed. "He articulated in his sermons, Bible studies, and occasional writings, and embodied in his church leadership, an austere piety that remained impervious to the sufferings of black people, as well as to the repressive tactics of the guardians of orthodoxy. In Hudgins's view, the important matters of faith were discovered in the interior dimensions of the soul's journey to perfection" (90). (Note, this familiar discourse also interweaves unhealthily with a discourse of purity: see esp. 91-92, 106; at which point it is intriguing to note that Anselm made a similar connection, speaking of a rich man and his pearl that fell in the mud and was not cleaned before being placed in his treasure chest: see *The Major Works: Anselm of Canterbury*, ed. and introduced by Brian Davies and G. R. Evans [Oxford and New York: Oxford University Press, 1998], §19, 301-2. Needless to say, a punitive atonement cleans the pearl appropriately.) It is also fascinating to see the consensual basis of the congregation being used by Hudgins in 1954 to avoid the Southern Baptist Convention's resolution that year in support of *Brown vs. Board of Education* (99-100): "every Baptist congregation in the world . . . is a democratic entity, and is responsible to no other body or individual. . . . [So the decisions of convention reports etc. are] actions of subjective cooperation. They are not authoritarian nor disciplinary." Marsh traces Hudgins's theological posture primarily to the influence of Baptist theologian E. Y. Mullins, whose "landmark book" *The Axioms of Religion* is clearly oriented around Justification, individualization, and ecclesiastical contractualism: "faith's chief concern is 'the soul's competency before God' " (106-7). The result in this instance is then cultural capture, not merely to anti-Jewish stereotypes, but to "the Southern Way of Life," coupled with political and ethical impotence. (My thanks to Curtis Freeman for this reference.)

67. My colleague Mary McClintock Fulkerson drew my attention to the appropriateness of speaking of "Queer" theory at this point so as to incorporate gay, lesbian, bisexual, and transsexual perspectives: see also Laurel C. Schneider, "Queer Theory," in *Handbook of Postmodern Biblical Interpretation,* ed. A. K. M. Adam (St. Louis: Chalice, 2000), 206-12.

68. A classic contribution to this debate is Richard B. Hays, *The Moral Vision of the New Testament* (San Francisco: HarperCollins, 1996), 379-80, 391-94; see also Dale Martin, *Sex and the Single Savior: Gender and Sexuality in Biblical Interpretation* (Louisville, Ky.: Westminster John Knox, 2006); and Deryn Guest, Robert Goss, Mona West, and Thomas Bohache, eds., *The Queer Bible Commentary* (London: SCM, 2006). On the broader theological issues, see esp. Eugene Rogers, *Sexuality and the Christian Body: Their Way into the Triune God* (Oxford: Blackwell, 1999). For some preliminary remarks on the Pauline interpretive questions, see "The Witness to Paul's Gospel of Galatians 3.28," chapter five in *Quest,* 95-111; the specific issue of gay — and by extension Queer — ordination is treated in "A Brief Case Study in the Ethical Aspect of Paul's Gospel: Gay Ordination," chapter six in *Quest,* 112-31.

69. So, for example, in the United States, a constitutional amendment forbidding homosexual marriage would be entirely consistent with this theological stance. A corresponding amendment that defined marriage as between a man and a woman (mooted by the GOP in 2004-6) would be similarly consistent, while both would illustrate that such a theological axiom is supposed to apply indiscriminately to Christians and non-Christians alike, and can if necessary be supported coercively by the state.

70. See John Howard Yoder, *The Politics of Jesus: Vicit Agnus Noster* (Grand Rapids, Mich.: Eerdmans, 1994 [1972]) — which, unbeknownst to many, is concerned for much of its length with the interpretation of Paul (as Harink notes: see more just below). See also Yoder, "Constantinian Sources of Western Social Ethics," in *The Priestly Kingdom: Social Ethics as Gospel* (Notre Dame, Indiana: University of Notre Dame Press, 1984), 135-47; *Christian Attitudes to War, Peace, and Revolution: A Companion to Bainton* (Elkhart, Indiana: Peace Resource Center, 1983), 5-54; "The Disavowal of Constantine: An Alternative Perspective on Interfaith Dialogue," in *The Royal Priesthood: Essays Ecclesiological and Ecumenical* (Grand Rapids, Mich.: Eerdmans, 1994), 242-61; and "Christ, the Hope of the World," in *The Original Revolution: Essays on Christian Pacifism* (Scottdale, Pa.: Herald, 1971), 203-7. See further Stanley Hauerwas, "Epilogue: A Pacifist Response to the Bishops," in *Speak Up for Just War or Pacifism: A Critique of the United Methodist Bishops' Pastoral Letter "In Defense of Creation,"* ed. Paul Ramsey (University Park, Pa., & London: The Pennsylvania State University Press, 1988), 149-82; also *After Christendom? How the Church Is to Behave if Freedom, Justice, and a Christian Nation Are Bad Ideas,* new ed. (Nashville, Tenn.: Abingdon, 1999 [1991]). See also Douglas Harink, *Paul among the Postliberals: Pauline Theology beyond Christendom and Modernity* (Grand Rapids: Brazos, 2003), esp. 105-49.

The possible tacit and rather sinister alliance between Justification theory and the modern liberal state that is noted here at various points is discussed in detail in part two, chapter nine. To endorse the modern liberal nation-state project is necessarily also to have endorsed Constantinianism in some redefined form.

71. Paul raises issues of hierarchy, power, and coercion, outside his Justification texts, as seen esp. in an analysis such as Neil Elliott, *Liberating Paul: The Justice of God and the Politics of the Apostle* (Maryknoll, New York: Orbis, 1994); see also the studies listed under §3.5 below. I advocate an approach to *these* issues in terms of Sachkritik. It is sketched out in tentative terms — as already noted — in my study, *The Quest for Paul's Gospel: A Suggested Strategy* (London: T&T Clark International [Continuum], 2005), chapters five and six, 95-131. (*Quest* anticipates — in part — the rereading strategy pursued here in detail in relation to the Justification texts, esp. there in chapters nine through eleven, 178-261.)

72. The pursuit of "justice," retributively conceived, can proliferate conflict: see Abraham Rotstein, "The Apocalyptic Tradition: Luther and Marx," in *Political Theology in the Canadian Context,* ed. Benjamin G. Smillie (Waterloo: Wilfrid Laurier, 1978), 147-208; also "The World Upside Down," *Canadian Journal of Political and Social Theory/Revue Canadienne de théorie politique et sociale* 2 (1978): 5-30; see also Hauerwas, chapter two, "The Politics of Justice: Why Justice Is a Bad Idea for Christians," in *After Christendom?,* 45-68.

73. This thesis has of course been overstated, generating a baby-with-the-bathwater conundrum: see Chris Hedges, *American Fascists: The Christian Right and the War on America* (New York: Free Press, 2007), which includes an intriguing short analysis by Umberto Eco, "Eternal Fascism: Fourteen Ways of Looking at a Blackshirt" (6 pp., not paginated). Hedges's analysis is frequently problematic, but nevertheless pushes in the right general direction. Yoder comments appositely, however — specifically addressing the broad post-Constantinian mentality — that "[o]ur world [then] has a divinely imparted duty to destroy or to rule over their world" ("Constantinian Sources of Western Social Ethics," 138). Perhaps one might say then that Fascism is really just a state that is being honest.

An interesting relationship with the phenomenon of Christian manliness is also discernible at this point. On the one hand, the affirmation of Jesus' masculinity in the US in the first half of the twentieth century was, in part, a reaction *against* the distant and wrathful father associated with Justification theory (as well as with Calvinism, etc.). On the other hand, this affirmation endorses the foundational gender constructions in the theory *and* any association between authority, power, and coercion, thereby legitimizing the theory's root metaphor concerning God: see Stephen Prothero, "Manly Redeemer," in *American Jesus: How the Son of God Became a National Icon* (New York: Farrar, Straus, and Giroux, 2003), 87-123.

74. Arguably an overlap is apparent at this point with the current debate concerning Paul's relationship with the imperial cult. Certainly some of the same issues seem to be implicit. However, a

considerable amount of redefinition and reorientation would be necessary before those could be introduced coherently with this project, so it seems best to leave that relationship in this loosely specified state. See Richard A. Horsley, ed., *Paul and Empire* (Harrisburg, Pa.: Trinity Press International, 1997); also (ed.), *Paul and Politics: Ekklesia, Israel, Imperium, Interpretation* (Harrisburg, Pa.: Trinity Press International, 2000); also (ed.), *Paul and the Roman Imperial Order* (London & Harrisburg, Pa.: Trinity Press International [Continuum], 2004). An exceptionally mature and nuanced exploration of the issue that can be applied indirectly to the interpretation of Paul is C. Kavin Rowe, "Luke-Acts and the Imperial Cult: A Way through the Conundrum?" *Journal for the Study of the New Testament* 27 (2005): 279-300.

75. Well-known postmodern readings of Paul include Dale B. Martin, *Slavery as Salvation. The Metaphor of Slavery in Pauline Christianity* (New Haven, Conn., & London: Yale University Press, 1990); also *The Corinthian Body* (New Haven, Conn., & London: Yale University Press, 1995); also *Sex and the Single Savior*; E. Castelli, *Imitating Paul: A Discourse of Power* (Louisville, Ky.: Westminster John Knox, 1991); and Daniel Boyarin, *A Radical Jew: Paul and the Politics of Identity* (London, Berkeley & Los Angeles: University of California Press, 1994).

76. Moreover, an overlap of concerns is apparent again at this point with various interpreters concerned with gender and sexuality, and race and ethnicity, although arguably an overlap also exists with what we might simply dub "good science" — where presuppositions and associated theoretical concepts model a complex reality accurately in an appropriately sensitive feedback loop.

77. Jean-François Lyotard, *The Postmodern Condition: A Report on Knowledge* (Paris: Minuit, 1979), xxiv.

78. One of Boyarin's most potent points against certain interpretations of Paul, if not against Paul himself: see *A Radical Jew*.

79. See esp. the concerns voiced by "the doctor of particularity," Colin Gunton, in *The One, the Three, and the Many: God, Creation, and the Culture of Modernity* (Cambridge: Cambridge University Press, 1993).

80. For relevant literature see chapter five, esp. §2.

81. This concern links up with anxieties over a Justification notion and definition of personhood over against a Cappadocian definition: see esp. John D. Zizioulas, *Being as Communion* (New York: SVS Press, 1985); A. J. Torrance, *Persons in Communion: An Essay on Trinitarian Description and Human Participation with Special Reference to Volume One of Karl Barth's Church Dogmatics* (Edinburgh: T&T Clark, 1996); also J. Moltmann, *The Trinity and the Kingdom of God,* ed. Margaret Kohl (London: SCM, 1981); and Leonardo Boff, *Trinity and Society,* trans. Paul Burns, new paperback ed. (Eugene, Oregon: Wipf & Stock, 2005 [1988]). Epistemological concerns should also be mentioned in this relation: see esp. A. I. C. Heron, "Homoousios with the Father," in *The Incarnation: Ecumenical Studies in the Nicene-Constantinopolitan Creed A.D. 381,* ed. T. F. Torrance (Edinburgh: Handsel, 1981), 58-87; see also Alan J. Torrance, "The Trinity," in *The Cambridge Companion to Barth,* ed. John Webster (London: Continuum, 2000), 72-91. Many of these issues are canvassed briefly and more accessibly by T. F. Torrance, in *The Mediation of Christ* (Colorado Springs, Col.: Helmers & Howard, 1992 [1983]).

82. Most important in the present relation are James Torrance's brief remarks on how contractualism — and hence Justification — fatally fracture a Trinitarian understanding of the atonement at several points: see "Covenant and Contract, a Study of the Theological Background of Worship in Seventeenth-Century Scotland," *Scottish Journal of Theology* 23 (1970): 68-69, 73-77; "The Contribution of McLeod Campbell to Scottish Theology," *Scottish Journal of Theology* 26 (1973): 298, 301, 303-11; "The Incarnation and Limited Atonement," *Evangelical Quarterly* 55 (1983): 92-94; and "Introduction," in John McLeod Campbell, *The Nature of the Atonement* (Edinburgh: Handsel, 1996 [1856]), 4-16.

The atonement tends to be a locus of perennial debate for Pauline interpreters, although naturally such discussion fluctuates; it is often structured — at least to a significant degree — by categories either contributed by Justification theory or in opposition to it. The literature on it is legion, but see most recently the arguments of Stephen Finlan, *The Background and Content of Paul's Cultic Atone-*

ment Metaphors (Atlanta: Society of Biblical Literature, 2004); also *Problems with Atonement: The Origins of, and Controversy about, the Atonement Doctrine* (Collegeville, Minn.: Liturgical Press [Michael Glazier], 2005). (I sympathize with many of Finlan's strategic concerns, but argue ultimately that different framing and localized exegetical solutions are necessary.) A useful theological overview of atonement issues is C. G. Gunton, *The Actuality of the Atonement: A Study of Metaphor, Rationality, and the Christian Tradition* (Edinburgh: T&T Clark, 1998). Often cited is the early classic Gustaf Aulén, *Christus Victor* (London: SPCK, 1953), although it is now necessary to move well beyond Aulén's categories and evidence. More conservative views are usefully canvassed by Frank A. James III and Charles E. Hill, eds., *The Glory of the Atonement: Biblical, Historical, and Practical Perspectives: Essays in Honor of Roger Nicole* (Downers Grove, Ill.: InterVarsity, 2004). J. Denny Weaver's is a well-known case for an alternative "non-violent" understanding of the atonement; he usefully introduces ethnic and gender concerns: *The Nonviolent Atonement* (Grand Rapids, Mich.: Eerdmans, 2001) (and, again, I sympathize with many of his strategic goals, but the same qualifications apply to his work as to Finlan's). Also relevant at this point is Christopher D. Marshall's important work, *Beyond Retribution: A New Testament Vision for Justice, Crime, and Punishment* (Grand Rapids, Mich.: Eerdmans, 2001); and, in a similar vein, Timothy Gorringe's *God's Just Vengeance: Crime, Violence, and the Rhetoric of Salvation* (Cambridge: Cambridge University Press, 1996). Joel B. Green and Mark D. Baker also probe new directions pertinently in *Recovering the Scandal of the Cross: Atonement in New Testament and Contemporary Contexts* (Downers Grove, Ill.: InterVarsity, 2000). Girard's views are often introduced in this relation (although ultimately, in my view, largely unhelpfully): the classic discussion of these in relation to Paul is Robert G. Hamerton-Kelly, *Sacred Violence: Paul's Hermeneutic of the Cross* (Minneapolis: Fortress, 1992). Provocative and insightful — as usual! — is Stanley Hauerwas, *Cross-Shattered Christ: Meditations on the Seven Last Words* (Grand Rapids, Mich.: Brazos, 2004). An important and subtle exploration of many of these questions is Hans Boersma, *Violence, Hospitality, and the Cross: Reappropriating the Atonement Tradition* (Grand Rapids, Mich.: Baker Academic, 2004). Similarly insightful and significant is Justyn Charles Terry, *The Justifying Judgement of God: A Reassessment of the Place of Judgement in the Saving Work of Christ*, Paternoster Theological Monographs (Milton Keynes: Paternoster, 2007) — originally a Ph.D. thesis from King's College London supervised by the late Colin Gunton. (Ultimately I don't see Paul pushing in *quite* the same direction as Boersma and Terry advocate, but there is much of value in these treatments.) Numerous studies could of course be added to this list.

83. Work on the Spirit in Paul has been strangely limited. Gordon D. Fee's treatment is now definitive, *God's Empowering Presence: The Holy Spirit in the Letters of Paul* (Peabody, Mass.: Hendrickson, 1994). But I suggest that even he fails to integrate this sustained emphasis and treatment with Justification questions in Paul: see esp. chapter sixteen, "Christ and the Spirit: Paul as a Proto-Trinitarian," in his *Pauline Christology: An Exegetical-Theological Study* (Peabody, Mass.: Hendrickson, 2007), 586-93.

On pneumatology in more general, theological terms, see esp. Alasdair I. C. Heron, *The Holy Spirit: The Holy Spirit in the Bible, in the History of Christian Thought and in Recent Theology* (London: Marshall, Morgan & Scott, 1983); Thomas A. Smail, *The Giving Gift: The Holy Spirit in Person* (London: Hodder & Stoughton, 1988); and Eugene Rogers, *After the Spirit: A Constructive Pneumatology from Resources Outside the Modern West* (Grand Rapids, Mich.: Eerdmans, 2005).

In this relation, however, I am particularly interested in Revivalist, Pentecostal, and African-American treatments: see, i.a., Tom Smail, Andrew Walker and Nigel Wright, *Charismatic Renewal: The Search for a Theology* (London: SPCK, 1995); and Andrew Walker and Kristin Aune, eds., *On Revival: A Critical Examination*, paperback ed. (Carlisle: Paternoster, 2003).

The debate over "speaking in tongues" *(glossolalia)* overlaps significantly with the question whether this is evidence of the fulfillment of some of the necessary conditions for salvation, a condition itself, a phenomenon to be rejected altogether as authentically Christian because it is an unintelligible condition, or something else altogether!: see esp. Grant Wacker, *Heaven Below: Early Pentecostals and American Culture* (Cambridge, Mass.: Harvard University Press, 2001); also Walter Hollenweger, *The Pentecostals: The Charismatic Movement in the Churches* (Minneapolis, Minn.: Augsburg, 1972);

Robert Mapes Anderson, *Vision of the Disinherited: The Making of American Pentecostalism* (Oxford: Oxford University Press, 1979); also *Pentecostalism: Origins and Developments Worldwide* (Peabody, Mass.: Hendrickson, 1997); and Mark J. Cartledge, ed., *Speaking in Tongues: Multi-Disciplinary Perspectives* (Carlisle: Paternoster, 2006).

84. See esp. James B. Torrance, "The Priesthood of Jesus. A Study in the Doctrine of the Atonement," in *Essays in Christology for Karl Barth*, ed. T. H. L. Parker (London: Lutterworth, 1956), 155-73; "The Vicarious Humanity and Priesthood of Christ in the Theology of John Calvin," in *Calvinus Ecclesiae Doctor*, ed. Wilhelm H. Neuser (Kampen: J. H. Kok B.V., 1978), 69-84; "The Vicarious Humanity of Christ," in *The Incarnation: Ecumenical Studies in the Nicene-Constantinopolitan Creed A.D. 381*, 127-47; "The Concept of Federal Theology — Was Calvin a Federal Theologian?," in *Calvinus Sacrae Scripturae: Professor Calvin as Confessor of Holy Scripture*, ed. Wilhelm H. Neuser (Grand Rapids, Mich.: Eerdmans, 1994), 15-40; and *Worship, Community, and the Triune God of Grace* (Carlisle: Paternoster, 1996). Also significant in this relation are T. F. Torrance, chapter four, "The Mind of Christ in Worship: The Problem of Apollinarianism in the Liturgy," in *Theology in Reconciliation: Essays Towards Evangelical and Catholic Unity in East and West* (London: Geoffrey Chapman Publishers [Macmillan], 1975), 139-214; and R. T. Kendall, *Calvin and English Calvinism to 1649*, new ed. (Carlisle: Paternoster, 1997 [1981]), and the debate it both continued and provoked. Calvin's specific contributions to these and related questions are considered in more detail in part two, chapter eight.

85. And this arguably makes those endorsing this paradigm peculiarly vulnerable to Docetism. In order to protect Christ's sinless state, his full engagement with the human condition can be denied. It serves no useful theological function within the model in any case. Even granting Anselm's justification of Christ's divinity, we still do not really know why Christ had to become *human!* (Much of the extraordinary reaction to Martin Scorsese's production *The Last Temptation of Christ* [1988, funded and produced by Universal Studios, Paramount Pictures having abandoned the project in 1983], by largely conservative American Christian groups, is explicable in terms of this dynamic.) Of course, any tacit endorsement of Docetism creates further acute tensions in relation to the alternative schema that we have noted in Paul, and it also makes the wholehearted endorsement of Christian Orthodoxy difficult, if not impossible.

86. There is admittedly much discussion within certain traditions — notably certain strands of Presbyterianism — concerning the need for Christ's righteousness to be imputed to the believer, and not merely the sin of the believer imputed to Christ. However, irrespective of the exegetical basis and theological cogency of this claim (and the former is examined in part four, chapter eighteen), it is still difficult to derive any *active* notion of Christ's obedience from this commitment. He must still in effect remain sinless so that his perfect righteousness can avail for sinners. But believers are certainly not incorporated within him and thereby gathered up toward God; the relationship between the believer and God remains one of imputation (and hence perilously close to a legal fiction) and is undergirded by the demands of retributive justice, not ontological identity.

87. See again esp. the studies by Torrance listed under §§4.1-3 above, although all the studies listed in these preceding subsections are relevant again to this concern.

88. Douglas Hudgins, the radically individualistic and hence passively racist theologian already noted in §3.2 as discussed by Charles Marsh, consequently refused to speak of sacraments at all but only of the two "ordinances" of baptism and "the memorial supper" ("Douglas Hudgins: Theologian of the Closed Society," 107-8).

89. See T. F. Torrance, chapter two, "The One Baptism Common to Christ and His Church," and chapter three, "The Paschal Mystery of Christ and the Eucharist," in *Theology in Reconciliation: Essays Towards Evangelical and Catholic Unity in East and West*, 82-138; James B. Torrance, chapter three, "Baptism and the Lord's Supper — The Way of Communion," in *Worship, Community, and the Triune God of Grace*, 58-83. Zizioulas makes stronger assertions — as one might expect from a representative of Orthodoxy — in *Being as Communion*, passim.

90. Yoder is of course a nice instance of such concerns, as are Hays and Hauerwas: see the

studies already noted under §§3.3 and 3.4 above; but the Trinitarian advocates noted in §3.1 also belong here — i.a., Barth and the Torrances.

91. That is, the Wesleys and the Methodist tradition are both indicative and important resources at this point: see esp. Richard P. Heitzenrater, *Wesley and the People Called Methodists* (Nashville, Tenn.: Abingdon, 1996); and Randy L. Maddox, *Responsible Grace: John Wesley's Practical Theology* (Nashville, Tenn.: Kingswood Books [Abingdon], 1994).

92. Indeed, many of the difficulties arising from most of the traditions noted so far in this list are underwritten by a common concern for the vitality of the church. It is difficult if not impossible to separate concerns for stringent ethical behavior and discipleship, for holiness, and even for properly rich conceptions of the Trinity, pneumatology, and the sacraments, from a conception of the church that is profoundly real and deeply committed. There should, in short, be correlative emphases on ethics and ecclesiology in most of the critics of Justification just mentioned — and whether those critics are explicitly targeting Justification, or merely by implication.

93. The Lutheran World Federation and The Roman Catholic Church, *Joint Declaration on the Doctrine of Justification* (Cambridge & Grand Rapids, Mich.: Eerdmans, 2000 [1999]), 1 (9) — hereafter *JD*.

94. II, 1 (see *The Book of Concord,* 292); trans. William R. Russell (Minneapolis: Fortress, 1995), 5-6.

95. There have been different reactions to the *JD* subsequently, and (of course) different evaluations of the future of ecumenism: for a sample of opinions from various perspectives, see Geoffrey Wainwright, *Is the Reformation Over? Catholics and Protestants at the Turn of the Millennia* (Milwaukee: Marquette University Press, 2000); E. Jüngel, *Justification: The Heart of the Christian Faith: A Theological Study with an Ecumenical Purpose,* trans. J. F. Cayzer, from the 3rd German ed. (Edinburgh & New York: T&T Clark, 2001 [1999]); Anthony N. S. Lane, *Justification by Faith in Catholic-Protestant Dialogue: An Evangelical Assessment* (London: T&T Clark [Continuum], 2002); and Mark Husbands and Daniel J. Treier, eds., *Justification: What's at Stake in the Current Debates* (Leicester & Downers Grove, Ill.: Apollos & InterVarsity, 2004). Related studies testifying to the current difficulties scholars face interpreting Justification include Bruce L. McCormack, ed., *Justification in Perspective: Historical Developments and Contemporary Challenges* (Grand Rapids, Mich.: Baker Academic, 2006); David E. Aune, ed., *Rereading Paul Together: Protestant and Catholic Perspectives on Justification* (Grand Rapids, Mich.: Baker Academic, 2006); and Wayne C. Stumme, ed., *The Gospel of Justification in Christ: Where Does the Church Stand Today?* (Grand Rapids, Mich.: Eerdmans, 2006). I do not engage in a detailed dialogue with these and related works; ultimately — although sharing most of their major concerns — I will challenge the construal of Paul that underlies most of their deliberations. My main suggestion here is that many of the basic interpretative boundaries shaping these debates need to change.

An earlier ecumenical collection particularly significant for Pauline studies is J. Reumann, *"Righteousness" in the New Testament. "Justification" in the United States Lutheran–Roman Catholic Dialogue, with Responses by Joseph A. Fitzmyer, Jerome D. Quinn* (Philadelphia, Pa., & New York & Ramsey, New Jersey: Fortress & Paulist, 1982). Intriguingly, this dialogue seems to have led Fitzmyer's interpretation of Paul in quite a classically Protestant direction, as we will see in more detail in part three, chapter ten. Reumann's own position remains strongly committed to the centrality of Justification as well. He argues that Paul's conception of Justification is the center of the NT, and then by implication of the entire canon: see his *Variety and Unity in New Testament Thought* (Oxford: Oxford University Press, 1991).

96. Arguably more relevant Pauline debates could — suitably qualified — be added — notably, over Paul's conceptions of the atonement, pneumatology, the nature and function of the sacraments, ecclesiology, and over his attitude (whether explicit or implicit) to the imperial cult. Moreover — and as we will note again momentarily — the *exegetical* difficulties implicit here have not yet been tabulated.

97. See esp. *Quest,* 29-33, 46-48.

98. Attempted rebuttals and rejoinders will be considered further in part three, chapter eleven. However, this judgment really follows necessarily from the theory-driven nature of the argument up

to this point; any difficulties within the theory could be eliminated only by an alternative, superior construal. But I know of no such superior construal and, furthermore, there are tight constraints on any such alternative (principally exegetical). This theory cannot be altered willy-nilly to deal with its problems. It is also worth emphasizing in this connection how fundamental these problems are. Hence, eliminating them will really require a different theory, which is what I will ultimately offer.

99. There are various exegetical issues that we have yet to enumerate exhaustively. And we have yet to consider in detail the church-historical stakes — although for important methodological reasons. These tend to operate within the broader discussion in a fundamentally different way from the problematic implications we have been considering thus far — that is, hermeneutically. Their involvement has also tended to be, in pointed contrast to the foregoing, exaggerated by much past discussion. I will suggest that *not as much* is at stake church-historically as has often been suggested (in part because the church-historical stakes are so much more complex than has previously been appreciated by Pauline scholars).

100. It should be emphasized at this point that fundamentally synergistic explanations of Paul do not constitute an effective solution. A synergist Paul is really just a confused and contradictory Paul; these are but different names for the same thing. Moreover, such an approach is an explanation of last resort as a matter of methodological necessity. All coherent options must be exhausted before an incoherent option is embraced. If incoherence is endorsed as a methodological principle, then *all* coherent argumentation and description is thereby undermined — both within Paul and of him!

101. It is also already to have grasped why so many other attempted solutions are bound to fail. In particular, it seems unlikely that the redefinition of mere motifs within Paul's Justification texts and arguments will suffice to overturn the theory as a whole; such revisions will probably succeed merely in further disordering the argument internally without actually displacing or significantly reconfiguring it — a conundrum explored in more detail in part three, chapter twelve.

102. A strategy also known as *petitio principii.* Such claims are frustrating on the one hand but encouraging on the other. They are frustrating because they make an effective dialogue difficult if not impossible. A certain point of view can be asserted, no real reasons supplied for its truth, and no engagement with any opposing point of view even thought necessary! (If engagement actually takes place, any evidence can be dismissed as "weak" despite the absence of any standard for making such a judgment.) But such claims are also encouraging, because they attest to the reality of a distorting hermeneutical situation that we must spend a certain amount of time trying to address; they are consequently a vindication of the real need for part two within my overarching argument. They also attest to the truth of one of my most important claims — that a "paradigmatic" situation is present (and this is explained further in part two, chapters seven and nine).

Notes to Chapter Seven

1. The story of much of chapter twelve.

2. The following is (of course!) not a comprehensive account of reading per se; it is specifically oriented by certain concerns and texts in Paul. But some of my hermeneutical suggestions should be transferable.

3. My principal methodological indebtedness in much of what follows is to Michael Polanyi, *Personal Knowledge: Towards a Post-Critical Philosophy* (London: Routledge & Kegan Paul, 1958); but see also *The Tacit Dimension* (New York: Doubleday, 1966); and (with Harry Prosch), *Meaning,* new ed. (Chicago: University of Chicago Press, 1977). (Polanyi's work was introduced to me by Alan J. Torrance.) Polanyi shapes my thinking about epistemology, and hence also about methodology and hermeneutics, fundamentally. He allows me to accord a significant interpretative role to readers and their presuppositions (thereby opening up a link with Eco's work: see just below) without losing the sense that some readings of particular data are better than others. Furthermore, he makes it possible to understand a clash between different readings more constructively, helpfully informed by his notion of the tacit dimension. We are not, it seems, always aware of the mechanics and commitments of

our readings, because reading is such a complex task, and human analysis is inherently focal. Put slightly differently, Polanyi, in combination with other more directly related hermeneutical theorists, allows me to break out of the false presuppositional/subjective versus nonpresuppositional/objective dichotomy, crafting instead an account of reading as both inherently presuppositional *and* objective — although, in some cases, also wrong. See also D. Bruce Hamill, *Doing Ethics Theologically: A Study of the Conceptual Possibilities Offered by Polanyi's Epistemology for Barth's Ethic of the Divine Command* (Ph.D. thesis, University of Otago, Dunedin, New Zealand, January 1995).

I acknowledge more distant influences from Kuhn, whom I take nevertheless to be usefully corrected by Polanyi: see esp. T. S. Kuhn, *The Structure of Scientific Revolutions,* 3rd ed. (Chicago & London: University of Chicago Press, 1996 [1962]). Kuhn and Polanyi point to the embedded nature of explanations — "paradigms" in Kuhn's terminology. Their advocates *must* be personally committed to them, which complicates, although it does not eliminate, the possibility of their critical evaluation. (A link with Tomkins's work is also established by this — namely, the origin of all human activity in the activation of some affect, here "interest-excitement": see just below.) I also use, to a degree, some of the work of Plantinga in this relation, most notably the idea of "basicality"; the phrase "properly basic" is his: see Alvin Plantinga, *Warrant and Proper Function* (Oxford: Oxford University Press, 1993); and *Warrant: the Current Debate* (Oxford: Oxford University Press, 1993). These notions are summarized and applied theologically in Alan J. Torrance, "*Auditus Fidei:* Where and How Does God Speak? Faith, Reason, and the Question of Criteria," in *Reason and the Reasons of Faith,* ed. Paul J. Griffiths and Reinhardt Hütter (New York & London: T&T Clark [Continuum], 2005), 44-50, esp. n. 67 (44).

I am informed fundamentally on language and reading by F. de Saussure, *Course in General Linguistics,* ed. C. Bally, A. Sechehaye, and A. Riedlinger, trans. W. Baskin (New York: McGraw-Hill, 1959 [1915]); my appropriation here was helpfully assisted by J. Culler, *Saussure* (London: Fontana, 1976). Semiotics, principally via Eco, has also been a significant influence on my understanding of language: see Umberto Eco, *A Theory of Semiotics* (Bloomington, Ind.: Indiana University Press, 1976); *The Role of the Reader* (Bloomington, Ind.: Indiana University Press, 1979); *Semiotics and the Philosophy of Language* (Bloomington, Ind.: Indiana University Press, 1983); and Stefan Collini, ed., *Interpretation and Overinterpretation: Umberto Eco with Richard Rorty, Jonathan Culler, Christine Brooke-Rose* (Cambridge: Cambridge University Press, 1992). But Eco's well-known emphasis on the role of the reader and his terminology of "encyclopedias" are helpful as well. I take Eco and Polanyi to be constructively informed by one another here.

There are more distant and limited influences from Derrida, specifically on the issue of context/framing/setting (Derrida's discussion being mediated to me personally by Pieter Botha), and from Foucault, specifically on the notion of a discourse, although I do not develop this notion as comprehensively as he does: see esp. Barbara Johnson, "The Frame of Reference: Poe, Lacan, Derrida," in *The Critical Difference: Essays in the Contemporary Rhetoric of Reading* (Baltimore & London: The Johns Hopkins University Press, 1980 [1978]), 110-46, 152-54; and Michel Foucault, "The Order of Discourse," in Michael Shapiro, ed., *Language and Politics* (tr. Ian McLeod; New York: New York University Press, 1984 [1970]), 108-37. I draw occasionally on themes from Wittgenstein; his notion of a "family resemblance" is often useful in what follows (and has already been used in chapter four in relation to the description of Judaism), as are his concerns about "private language": see *Philosophical Investigations,* ed. G. E. M. Anscombe and R. Rhees, trans. G. E. M. Anscombe (Oxford: Blackwell, 1953), esp. § 67, p. 32^e; § 77, 36^e; § 108, 46^e-47^e; § 164, 66^e; § 179, 72^e-73^e.

There are, in addition, some broad methodological influences from complexity theory, profitably introduced by M. Waldrop, *Complexity: The Emerging Science at the Edge of Order and Chaos* (London: Penguin, 1992); from Silvan Tomkins's pioneering work on social psychology in terms of affects and script theory, this last helpfully introduced by Donald L. Nathanson, *Shame and Pride: Affect, Sex, and the Birth of the Self* (New York: W. W. Norton, 1992); and D. B. Moore and J. M. McDonald, *Transforming Conflict in Workplaces and Communities* (Maryborough, Victoria: Australian Print Group, 2000); and from cognitive theory, i.e., Lakoff. Of course, I have already made use of the notions of root metaphors, radial systems, and "quantitative" morality to describe Justification theory in chapters one and two: see esp. George Lakoff, *Moral Politics: How Liberals and Conservatives Think,*

2nd ed. (London & Chicago: University of Chicago Press, 2001 [1996]); and, with Mark Johnson, *Metaphors We Live By,* 2nd ed. (Chicago, Ill.: University of Chicago Press, 2003 [1980]).

For my understanding of gender issues I am particularly indebted to Mary McLintock-Fulkerson (see esp. chapter six): see esp. "Feminist Theology," in *Postmodern Theology,* ed. Kevin J. Vanhoozer (Cambridge: Cambridge University Press, 2003), 109-25. (This methodological dimension — along with the race/ethnicity dimension — is of course important for any broader account of Paul's thought: for some preliminary remarks on the appropriate approach see chapters five and six in my book *The Quest for Paul's Gospel: A Suggested Strategy* [London: T&T Clark International (Continuum)], 95-131.) Scott's important insights will also prove useful later on, esp. in part four, chapter fourteen: see James C. Scott, *Domination and the Arts of Resistance: Hidden Transcripts* (New Haven, Conn., & London: Yale University Press, 1990).

Finally, I borrow "base-superstructure" conceptuality — fairly obviously — from Karl Marx. His most important texts are usefully collected in David McLellan, ed., *Karl Marx: Selected Writings* (Oxford: Oxford University Press, 1977).

4. See esp. *A Theory of Semiotics,* passim.

5. See Alan Torrance, *"Auditus Fidei,"* 37-38, who also leans here on Murray Rae's superb analysis of Christian epistemology in relation to Kierkegaard: *Kierkegaard's Vision of the Incarnation: By Faith Transformed* (Oxford: Clarendon, 1997).

6. This concern for interpretative transparency is similar to that expressed by Cristina Grenholm and Daniel Patte, eds. (somewhat coincidentally, also in relation to Romans), in *Reading Israel in Romans: Legitimacy and Plausibility of Divergent Interpretations,* Romans through History and Cultures Series (Harrisburg, Pa.: Trinity Press International, 2000), see esp. 1-54.

7. These dimensions will fall into the two more specific categories of "levels," and "settings" or "frames." A "level" is a distinguishable aspect *within* a reading; a "setting" or "frame" is a broader interpretative context within which a given reading is situated — essentially, another reading that surrounds the reading on which we are presently focusing.

8. Similar methodological concerns are also evident in some of Robbins's suggestions. My hermeneutical model is shaped and denoted differently from his program because of its particular relationship with Paul and Justification theory: see V. K. Robbins, *Exploring the Texture of Texts: A Guide to Socio-Rhetorical Interpretation* (Valley Forge, Pa.: Trinity Press International, 1996); and *The Tapestry of Early Christian Discourse: Rhetoric, Society and Ideology* (London: Routledge, 1996).

9. It will not be necessary to unravel here the important but complex epistemological disputes over the nature of argumentation and, in particular, over enthymematic or abductive reasoning and its relation to logic. The argumentative cases made later by various readings with respect to Paul's Justification texts will not require such subtlety. Further guidance may be given by L. Gregory Bloomquist, "A Possible Direction for Providing Programmatic Correlation of Textures in Socio-Rhetorical Analysis," and Arthur Gibson, "Relations between Rhetoric and Philosophical Logic," in S. Porter and D. Stamps, eds., *Rhetorical Criticism and the Bible: Essays from the 1998 Florence Conference* (Sheffield: Sheffield Academic Press/Continuum, 2002), 61-96 and 97-128 respectively.

10. So, in a sense, we could formulate this as +/+ > +/- > -/+ > -/-. To reduce the situation to +/- versus -/+ is therefore a false alternative, *which also marginalizes argumentative considerations in a good reading* (i.e., +/+).

11. This issue has already been touched on in chapter one, § 1.2. See also a brief treatment in *Quest,* 30-31.

12. Data tends to exist in more continuous fields than much modern analysis, with its tendency toward atomism, sometimes realizes. Hence, disputes over exactly where one theme or argument stops and another begins are sometimes misconceived.

13. Interpreters are in any case usually forced to articulate distinctions like these in order to facilitate further, more focused analysis; we generally cannot examine all the interconnected data of a field simultaneously.

14. As noted earlier, I am influenced here especially by Derrida, mediated to me by Botha: see n. 3.

15. Eco speaks helpfully at this point of a text's given "encyclopedia" or "social treasury": see esp. *Interpretation and Overinterpretation*, 67-68. I would suggest further that the relevant encyclopedia is *the author's*. The text is created initially with reference to this structure, although not necessarily consciously. Much composition is intuitive and tacit. Stefan Alkier makes some further useful analytical distinctions in this relation (in conversation with other scholars): see, with Richard B. Hays, eds., *Die Bibel im Dialog der Schriften: Konzepte intertextueller Bibellektüre* (Tübingen & Basel: Francke, 2005). We would then speak here of the "encoded" and "generative" encyclopedia as against the "empirical" or "received" encyclopedia.

16. They may of course figure in a history of interpretation.

17. And Pauline scholars tend to rely in this relation on an axiom and terminology introduced by J. Christiaan Beker — the distinction between "contingency" and "coherence": see *Paul the Apostle: The Triumph of God in Life and Thought*, paperback ed. (Philadelphia: Fortress, 1984 [1980]), xiii-xx, 11-16, 23-36; see also "Recasting Pauline Theology: The Coherence-Contingency Scheme as Interpretative Model," in *Pauline Theology*, vol. 1, *Thessalonians, Philippians, Galatians, Philemon*, ed. Jouette M. Bassler (Minneapolis: Fortress, 1991), 15-24. Beker observes that any discussions of Paul's coherent thought — which other scholars refer to in terms of "system" or something similar — *must* proceed through a responsible consideration of his texts' circumstantial orientations and designs — their contingency — simply because all of his texts were so oriented. To jump straight to coherence when interpreting a Pauline text risks confusing circumstantial and perhaps even intentionally partial, temporary material, with more constant and committed positions. (Note that his basic case must be nuanced: see *Quest*, 18-20.) This material will be reintroduced (briefly) in part three, chapter twelve; part four, chapter thirteen (discussing the provenance of Romans), and part five, chapter twenty (discussing Galatians).

18. Proximate and circumstantial accounts will often overlap to a degree, since adjacent texts will presumably often carry important information about the circumstances surrounding a letter's composition. Such overlap is in fact helpful, offering further evidence (or not) of interpretative validity. That is, framing accounts ought to fit reasonably with one another, just as they ought to fit reasonably with the account of the textual data that is our primary focus.

19. A classic introduction to the intentional fallacy is given by W. K. Wimsatt, "The Intentional Fallacy," in *The Verbal Icon: Studies in the Meaning of Poetry* (Lexington, Ky.: University of Kentucky Press, 1954), 3-18. C. S. Lewis gives a famously readable description of the problem in passing (which he offers as a series of "bleats"), in "Modern Theology and Biblical Criticism," in *Christian Reflections* (Grand Rapids, Mich.: Eerdmans, 1994 [1967]), 152-66. But he is here merely making accessible something observed by many.

20. Admittedly, we might conceivably end up with a family of different but equally plausible framing accounts, and this would be quite acceptable. But if, conversely, a given reading did not seem compatible with *any* plausible framing account in relation to these questions, then we would have grounds for questioning the adequacy of the reading itself, and especially if other plausibly framed readings were currently sitting on the table. As was noted in the Introduction, New Testament interpreters have in fact struggled to explain Romans in this relation, as well as, to a lesser extent (and in a slightly different respect) Galatians, so it seems more likely that cogent circumstantial framing accounts will be in short, rather than over-, supply.

21. So, especially clearly, T. F. Torrance. The theme is ubiquitous in his writings, but see, e.g., "The Church in the New Era of Scientific and Cosmological Change," in *Theology in Reconciliation: Essays Towards Evangelical and Catholic Unity in East and West* (London: Geoffrey Chapman, 1975), 267-93.

22. To be explanatorily powerful in this sense is not necessarily also to be ethical, as the immensely powerful explanations associated with nuclear fission most famously demonstrate.

23. So exegetical "fit," that is, fit between data and its construal, clearly differs from this explanatory "fit," when a reading is functioning as an explanation of something else. Texts are of course objects and their construal therefore explanatory in that sense. Here, however, I am pointing to an inter-

pretative distinction between an account of a text *as* an object and an account of a text that in turn is an account of some *other* object.

24. Some philosophers even speak of a theory's aesthetic qualities at this point.

25. We have of course already suggested at length in chapter two that Justification theory, while impressive in certain respects, is not especially coherent internally; it does not fit together *that* well if it is subjected to critical scrutiny.

26. The European intellectual tradition expects its explanations to be argued, unlike other traditions in which explanations can be established on the basis of authority, custom, revelation, and so on. It is a moot point, however, whether even European models can argue their cases in their entirety (i.e., this may be a prejudiced narrative of the actual situation). European models use warrants in addition to argumentation, and non-European systems still argue — although sometimes in different terms. Moreover, *every* system seems to a degree to be foundationalist, because every system has basic presuppositions from which subsequent argumentation departs; we begin with properly basic axioms, to use Plantinga's terms, which are not themselves argued but in the light of which everything else is argued. They are, however, still "warranted" and "justified," which is " 'not identical with being able to justify a belief' ": see esp. Alan Torrance, *"Auditus Fidei,"* 44-46, quoting here from C. Stephen Evans, *The Historical Christ and the Jesus of Faith* (New York: Oxford University Press, 1996), 216. It also partly follows that argumentation *reflects* explanation, *especially in the matter of verification. The nature of an object,* comprehended by a theory, or explanation, *dictates where we look for confirmation.* Hence, we should not necessarily expect all arguments ultimately to depart from the same universal plane of ideas and concepts, however attractive that prospect might be. We must often supply socially embedded explanations of premises: see esp. Polanyi, *Personal Knowledge,* passim; and T. F. Torrance, "The Church in the New Era of Scientific and Cosmological Change."

27. The word "systematic" need and should not be interpreted anachronistically: see *Quest,* 30-33.

28. Chapter three has of course already addressed this question.

29. Issues explored already in chapters four and five in terms of Judaism and conversion respectively — the two main sets of referential claims made by Justification theory.

30. It is important to appreciate this implication precisely. The theoretical reading is not in this case immediately disqualified *as a reading;* however, if that reading supports a flawed theory, then we can expect that the reading's internal argumentation may in fact be disordered as well. And both these inaccuracies may then create vulnerabilities in relation to readings that do not present these difficulties. The falsified theoretical reading is now in effect a +/- construal (if not approaching a -/-!) that will be vulnerable to a +/+ account.

31. As we have already noted, Plantinga speaks of things that are "properly basic" at this point: see *Warrant and Proper Function,* passim; and *Warrant: The Current Debate,* passim. Kuhn also describes a similar phenomenon (although the term "paradigm" is not being used here precisely as it is in his classic analysis): *The Structure of Scientific Revolutions,* passim.

32. Although, arguably, it is also now superseded, at least in part.

33. This is *not* to accord legitimacy to some notion of time as a constant, but is a merely phenomenological claim in relation to a particular history of interpretation: see Alan J. Torrance, "Creation Ex Nihilo and the Spatio-Temporal Dimensions," in *The Doctrine of Creation,* ed. C. E. Gunton (Edinburgh: T&T Clark, 1997), 83-103.

34. Stendahl is famous for already having made such critically edged inquiries (pushing them back far further than the Reformation), but, somewhat typically, he failed to integrate them into an accurate account overall. Nevertheless, he was almost certainly right to point to their importance. So the question remains how best to deal with them. They are analyzed in detail in chapter eight.

35. A connection here might also occasionally be detected with affect theory as developed by Silvan Tomkins, and summarized (i.a.) by Donald Nathanson, and D. B. Moore and J. M. McDonald. The affects are always orchestrated culturally, Tomkins using "script theory" to explain this. And a parental root metaphor, as Lakoff develops it, *is* a script. (For detailed references consult n. 3 above.)

36. That is, the notion is not being used here strictly as it is in Foucault but in a weaker, re-

duced sense. This usage should also be distinguished clearly from the more limited and technical sense of the term in relation to "discourse analysis."

37. And *not* of the *Lutheran* discourse, for reasons that by now should be increasingly obvious, although the full case for this disclaimer is only complete after chapter eight.

38. It might be suggested that a class or sectional dimension should have been included in my account. However, I prefer to view this — and its many permutations — as in possible and often rather complex alliances with the factors already identified. Like the broader family of desert-based systems, the Justification discourse can *in fact* legitimize the material and social privileges of those advocating the model and hence promote or frustrate various class or sectional interests. I do not exclude such functions, but neither do I view them as a *necessary* element in the discourse. Any such function would be a more complex — albeit very interesting — question requiring specific historical treatment, and hence lies outside my current concern.

39. That is, in addition to the question whether there are good reasons why the sacred text being read ought to be viewed as true.

40. Strictly speaking, the theoretical dimension is a level within the process of reading, although it arises out of the other dimensions within reading and is *detachable* from them. The arguments in certain texts are held to combine into a theory, at which point that theory can be restated, separated from its underlying texts, and promulgated in its own right. It then automatically generates its own peculiar framing requirements — systematic and empirical. Beyond this point in the discourse, we can then speak of further *settings* as this theoretical reading begins to operate in different contexts in diachronic terms. We can ask how it is used in relation to other theories and issues — perhaps paradigmatically. We can investigate how it operates in relation to important Christian figures in history, and in the setting of church traditions more generally. And we can examine how it resonates with surrounding ideological and cultural settings. But the value of tracing these further settings, essentially diachronically, is not the integrative necessity that they impose on the original reading in historical-critical terms; it is the potential influence that they can exert on that reading illegitimately later on.

41. And here my argument intersects with standard historical-critical concerns. The historical critic wishes to recover — or, perhaps better, to attempt to reconstruct rigorously — the original readings that lie behind later interpretative ventures and consequences. He or she crafts plausible readings in terms of the text's original "encyclopedia" and its receptions. And although the problems inherent in this methodology need to be acknowledged, it will nevertheless suffice for our present purposes. All the participants in the debate with whom I hope to communicate share these commitments and will find shifts in such readings probative.

Misgivings about the historical-critical approach are succinctly expressed by David C. Steinmetz, "The Superiority of Pre-Critical Exegesis," *Theology Today* 37 (1980): 27-38; and, at more length (although in relation to a specific modern US context), by Stanley Hauerwas, *Unleashing the Scripture: Freeing the Bible from Captivity to America* (Nashville, Tenn.: Abingdon, 1993).

42. That is, if the alternative reading is both more successful and non-theoretical.

43. And especially for those readers influenced by the prevailing post-Enlightenment account of "science" and "rational inquiry."

44. Needless to say, this manifests not infrequently as the "science versus religion" debate. In the light of the discourse's construction, summarized in point one above, one would expect the discourse's advocates to continue to favor scriptural verification, and hence verification through reading, over any countervailing signals from various objects. But this situation, if it arises, can still prove profoundly awkward. Hence, one would also expect vigorous attempts to reconcile any conflicting judgments, perhaps both through interpretative strategies (that is, modifying what the texts supposedly say, if that is possible — and given the semantic plasticity of many texts, especially of ancient ones, this is usually an option) and in some relation to the "external" empirical evidence. The validity of that evidence might be challenged in various ways, and given that much "scientific" evidence also exists in narratives and paradigms, such countervailing criticisms are often possible. (Of course dissonance at

the empirical frame might also contribute ultimately to the realization that an alternative reading of the key texts that generates no such dissonance is possible.)

45. Perhaps the discourse could also affirm itself by knocking down carefully selected straw men.

46. An ideology of objective or presuppositionless exegesis may be enormously helpful to the superstructure's illegitimate influence here as well. This amounts to the a priori denial that any such illegitimate influence takes place or is even possible. And such a posture then does not allow this question even to be raised!

47. Couched in formulaic terms (useful for heuristic or mnemonic purposes): A, R, and R/R.

48. See James Barr, *The Semantics of Biblical Language* (Oxford: Oxford University Press, 1961). But this concern is also informed more generally by the view of language developed (i.a.) by de Saussure and Eco (see n. 3 for further details).

49. They will be pressed, however, in what follows. Note also that Barr's own analysis left something to be desired as well, as Francis Watson points out: see his *Text and Truth: Redefining Biblical Theology* (Edinburgh: T&T Clark, 1997), 18-26, 29.

50. I also refer to this as "lexical overinterpretation."

51. Intriguingly, here the usual diachronic flow in etymologism is reversed: later meaning is retrojected into the early reading of signifiers that have only subsequently been designated as critical, instead of earlier meaning being assumed to have remained attached to their stems over time (although these two agendas can be mutually reinforcing).

52. We would be close at this point to Wittgenstein's fallacious "private language," as referenced already in n. 3.

53. Presumably because of the operation of different underlying paradigms. That is, not many New Testament scholars are so deeply rooted in a Chalcedonian paradigm that they find it hard to step outside it, but they generally are rooted in *some* paradigm — and often enough, in the Justification discourse.

54. Paradigms can attempt to justify a properly basic function by illuminating reality in a broad way through the application of other derivative and more limited explanations. But this procedure is difficult to apply to Paul's Justification texts, which are based on a reading.

55. As we have already noted, there is an acceptable question-begging quality to very basic explanations in all systems. The fundamental assumptions in such explanations are "properly basic," in Plantinga's terminology. However, the Justification paradigm remains vulnerable to questioning here because of its scriptural claims, namely, that the witness of the Scriptures to the nature of salvation is more basic than any model ostensibly erected on that basis. Indeed, arguably, this paradigm has usurped a properly basic function from the Scriptures themselves at this point.

56. Indicators that a question-begging defense is in operation are statements like "surely it is unthinkable that . . ." or "I don't have to justify X . . ." or "obviously. . . ."

57. And it can be very difficult to get scholars to recognize when a paradigm they indwell is being criticized and hence that its mere reassertion is not sufficient to carry the day; there is a universal and understandable reluctance to reinvestigate questions of paradigmatic truth. It is time consuming and possibly also psychologically threatening. It is vital, however, if effective debate is to take place in relation to important matters.

58. If this rationale is accepted, the paradigm never actually has to prove that it is right. Moreover, if it is well entrenched psychologically, any countervailing evidence will also have to escape the deadening clutches of narcotization even to make the point that there are problems that need to be addressed (and these can then in turn be simply ignored or denied in an instance of direct question begging). The entire complex thereby turns out to be circular and self-sustaining. It is also thoroughly vicious: a paradigm's self-confidence has translated into an unassailable position in relation to almost any evidence. But clearly the superstructure is here sustaining the base and not vice versa. If the relevant texts did not support the superstructure at this point, we would have little chance even of knowing it!

59. Those begging the question are not helping themselves: they cannot know whether their *own* position is true.

Notes to Chapter Eight

1. James D. G. Dunn quotes Patrick Collinson appositely: "What was the gospel of Christ, according to Luther and all subsequent Protestants?" "That man enjoys that acceptance with God called 'justification,' the beginning and end of salvation, not through his own moral effort even in the smallest and slightest degree but entirely and only through the loving mercy of God made available in the merits of Christ and of his saving death of the Cross. This was not a process of gradual ethical improvement but an instantaneous transaction, somewhat like a marriage, in which Christ the bridegroom takes to himself an impoverished and wretched harlot and confers upon her all the riches which are his. The key to this transaction was faith, defined as a total and trustful commitment of the self to God, and in itself not a human achievement but the pure gift of God": see Dunn, *The Theology of Paul the Apostle* (Edinburgh & Grand Rapids: T&T Clark & Eerdmans, 1998), 335-36; quoting Collinson, "The Late Medieval Church and Its Reformation," in *The Oxford Illustrated History of Christianity*, ed. J. McManners (New York: Oxford, 1990), 258-59. Stephen Westerholm is less strident and oversimplified, but nevertheless illustrates the same basic *tendenz* by dedicating the first part of *Perspectives Old and New on Paul: The "Lutheran" Paul and His Critics* (Grand Rapids, Mich.: Eerdmans, 2004) to analyses of Augustine (3-21), Luther (22-41), Calvin (42-63), and Wesley (64-87), following these with an integrated summary of this basic theological trajectory in terms of seven theses (88-97) (hereafter *PO&NP*). Theses one through five summarize Justification theory, while theses six and seven raise problems (concerning the presence of sin in the lives of Christians, and the possibility of irresistible grace, respectively). Westerholm's perception that these figures are in play is commendable. My summaries of their thinking here do differ from his a little, however (as does my earlier presentation of Justification theory and its difficulties in part one). We need to push deeper into a complicated situation (which is not to suggest that the following is definitive!).

2. Luther's exegetical observations naturally remain important — as do those of many other powerful exegetes within church history — but these can be fed into the exegetical process and considered alongside all the other exegetical considerations that have been suggested in the modern period.

3. There is the further conundrum that original exegesis would then be effectively impossible. If readings that lie beyond those of an authoritative exemplar are not recognized, then that exemplar has in effect foreclosed on the process of reading. Mere variations from this point onward will be possible.

4. Moreover, the relationship in their thinking between exegesis and theology — and subsequent church organization and practice — is by no means straightforward, although I will not elaborate on these complex issues here.

5. It should also be emphasized that "Lutherans" and "Lutheran readings" are of course not reducible to Luther.

6. That is, pointing to Luther's endorsement of non-Justification material in Paul does not tell us what to do with the Justification material that remains in him.

7. I am not therefore offering a complete account of any of these figures, but attempting the far more modest goal of articulating how their thinking exceeds the oversimplified ways in which it has previously been portrayed. Once this complexity has been grasped, my main goal in this chapter will have been achieved. I then happily leave more definitive pronouncements to the relevant specialists.

8. The following is not intended as a definitive or exhaustive analysis; it is not a specialized contribution to Luther studies. The standard introductions to Luther are Paul Althaus, *The Theology of Martin Luther*, trans. Robert C. Shultz (Philadelphia, Pa.: Fortress, 1966); also *The Ethics of Martin Luther*, trans. Robert C. Shultz (Philadelphia, Pa.: Fortress, 1972); and Gerhard Ebeling, *Luther: An Introduction to His Thought*, trans. R. A. Wilson (Philadelphia, Pa.: Fortress, 1970). An excellent introduction to Luther in terms of intellectual history is David C. Steinmetz, *Luther in Context*, 2nd ed. (Grand Rapids, Mich.: Baker, 2002 [1995]). A highly readable account of Luther from an earlier gener-

ation of scholarship is Roland Bainton, *Here I Stand: A Life of Martin Luther* (New York: Abingdon & Cokesbury, 1950). It is possible that the following is a significant misreading of Luther; I am open to this alternative. However, irrespective of its fairness to Luther himself, there seems little doubt that this appropriation of Luther has greatly influenced the subsequent construal of Paul, and this is our primary concern in what follows. A useful introductory anthology of Luther's writings is Timothy F. Lull, and William R. Russell, ed., *Martin Luther's Basic Theological Writings,* 2nd ed. (Minneapolis, Minn.: Fortress, 2005). Widely read on this specific question is Alister E. McGrath, *Iustitia Dei: A History of the Christian Doctrine of Justification,* 3rd ed. (Cambridge: University Press, 2005), 208-41.

9. Much later, in 1545, Luther composed a preface to the first volume of his collected Latin works that were then being published. There he seems to suggest that his famous insight concerning God's relationship with humanity, rooted in a new reading of Rom. 1:17, occurred only in 1519, well after this early exegetical period and the advent of controversy in late 1517. He states that it took place in the year preceding the Diet of Worms, which itself took place in 1520. He also speaks of turning to the Psalms *again.* However, other clues suggest that Luther — looking back after about thirty years and perhaps in haste — has made a mistake here. He states in this preface that Augustine's *On the Spirit and the Letter* assisted him in his breakthrough, and that treatise, as well as the distinctive insights he links with Rom. 1:17 in his 1545 account, are reasonably apparent in his lectures on Romans that date from 1515. So it is probably best to begin our survey with a consideration of that commentary, on the assumption that Luther's spiritual breakthrough has already occurred. By 1545 he is remembering the past through the lens of his present — a ubiquitous human problem.

10. All references in what follows are to Wilhelm Pauck, ed., *Luther: Lectures on Romans,* LCC 15 (London: SCM, 1961), hereafter *LLR.*

11. Luther cites Augustine in support at this point: "The Apostle Paul 'contends with the proud and arrogant and with those who are presumptuous on account of their works . . . ; moreover, in the letter to the Romans, this theme is almost his sole concern and he discusses it so persistently and with such complexity as to weary the reader's attention, yet it is a useful and wholesome wearying'" (*LLR,* 3, citing *Spirit and Letter* 7, 12).

12. Luther makes further comments on the genitive on 15-16, 18, 19, 117.

13. Viz., 1:1–5:2 (1-156) and 9:30–10:21 (278-304).

14. The system is stated on 3, 4, 10, 16, 17, 42, 54, 55, 57, 66-72, 99, 107, 111-12, 118, 120-21, 135-38, 141, 288-89, 298-99, 302-3 (this is not an exhaustive enumeration).

15. The principle of faith is also stated overtly on 17-18, 19, 34, 45, 62-65, 70-71, 74-79, 81, 89-90, 98, 101-7, 109-10, 134, 137-38, 154, 155, 279, 281-85, 288-90, 293, 294, 296, 301, 304 (this is not an exhaustive enumeration).

16. For example, Luther is much preoccupied throughout with corrupt leadership, both secular and ecclesial. Hence, a reforming tendency is clearly in evidence, although it is never specifically focused on indulgences.

17. See *Luther's Works,* 55 vols. (St. Louis: Concordia Publishing House, & Philadelphia: Fortress Press, 1957-), 31:25-26 — hereafter *LW.*

18. Note especially thesis 7 and the end of thesis 14; *LW* 31:98-107, 124-25. Also noteworthy is a terrible description of despair in thesis 15 (129), immediately following extensive citation of the Psalms, usually laments, and also of Tauler.

19. "Through faith in Christ, . . . Christ's righteousness becomes our righteousness and all that he has becomes ours; rather, he himself becomes ours" (*LW* 31:298), this last comment also indicating the participatory dimension in Luther's thinking.

20. Luther's publications in 1519 were primarily preoccupied with Eck, his *Asterisks* responding in March to Eck's *Obelisks,* published the previous year. Theses also passed between them, Luther later publishing the *Disputations* as well. They debated in person on July 4-14. But much of this material is not highly relevant to the Justification model of salvation.

21. "To preach Christ means to . . . set [the soul] free, . . . provided it believes the preaching. Faith alone is the saving and efficacious use of the Word of God" (346).

22. I also use the following translation: Martin Luther, *A Commentary on St. Paul's Epistle to the Galatians,* trans. Theodor Graebner, 2nd ed. (Grand Rapids, Mich.: Zondervan, n.d.).

23. In context, it has another use, as a civil instrument.

24. Quoted from Graebner's considerably abridged translation: *Commentary, 67.* On the theme of faith, see up to this point 9, 12, 20-21, 30, 41, 43-49, 52-53, 55, 58-60, 62-63, 65-66. After this point the theme occurs passim to 126, and then on 131, 140, 142-49, 151, 153, 157, 158, 160, 163-65, 167, 169, 171, 181, 183-85, 188-89, 192-93, 195-97, 202-10, 213-14, 217-21, 225, 227, 229-30, 232, 237-39, 246, 250 and 252 — a fairly pronounced emphasis, one would have to grant.

25. This was supposed to be at Mantua in 1537; it finally convened at Trent in 1545.

26. Martin Luther, *The Smalcald Articles,* trans. William R. Russell (Minneapolis: Fortress, 1995), 5-6 — hereafter *SA.*

27. A criticism applicable (i.a.) to Thomas C. Oden, *The Justification Reader* (Grand Rapids, Mich.: Eerdmans, 2002). (Note, this criticism should not overshadow the many useful features of this treatment.)

28. Psalm 51:4 in particular is a repeated refrain: "Against thee, thee only, have I sinned."

29. We are primarily interested in the modern consequences of the reading and not its precise point of origin. Hence, if the reading did not originate with Luther, this is not overly important in terms of our present analysis. It was certainly Luther who popularized it and effectively anointed it with paradigmatic status for much of Protestantism, both then and subsequently (a result of his own fame and influence, his contacts with other Reformers, the popularization of his work effected by the printing press and mass publication, and so on). So the attribution remains essentially valid.

30. The following uses F. Kramer's translation: Melanchthon, *Commentary on Romans* (St. Louis: Concordia, 1992) — hereafter *MCR.*

31. Romans 1:1–5:2 is treated on 59-124; 9:30–10:15 on 193-203. The model is outlined, or at least a significant element within it explicated, on 59-61, 64, 69-75, 81, 85, 87-88, 90, 93, 95-123, and 193-203.

32. See article 6 (which cites Ambrose).

33. Also: "For it is necessary that the doctrine of Christian liberty be preserved in the churches, namely, that the bondage of the Law is not necessary to justification, as it is written in the Epistle to the Galatians: 'Be not entangled again with the yoke of bondage' (Gal. 5:1). It is necessary that the chief article of the Gospel be preserved, to wit, that we obtain grace freely by faith in Christ, and not for certain observances or acts of worship devised by men" (article 28).

Paul is cited in support of each of the articles directed toward perceived church abuses: article 22, an undivided sacrament; 23, the marriage of priests; 24, teaching in the vernacular and not saying private masses for a fee; 25, confession; 26, meats; 27, monasticism; and 28, ecclesiastical power.

34. There is ambiguity in Melanchthon. (Prof. Christoph Schwöbel suggested to me in conversation that it develops in a distinctive direction in relation to sacramentalism and Melanchthon's reception of Aristoteleanism.) Steinmetz provides a useful overview in *Reformers in the Wings: From Geiler von Kaysersberg to Theodore Beza,* 2nd ed. (Oxford: Oxford University Press, 2001), 49-63.

35. Page references throughout are to Henry Beveridge's translation: John Calvin, *Institutes of the Christian Religion,* 2 vols. (Grand Rapids, Mich.: Eerdmans, 1989) — hereafter *CI;* references use both traditional divisions, and volume and page numbers in the Beveridge ed. I am not entirely convinced by the suggestion that the later Calvin was less, if not completely, unconditional. James B. Torrance suggests that the 1559 *Institutes* differ significantly from the 1536 edition, following Paul in Galatians 3 more at the beginning of chapter seven (book two). "In the 1536 first edition of the *Institutes,* Calvin had followed the pattern of Luther's *Short Catechism,* treating first law and then gospel. . . . But in the light of Galatians 3, Calvin abandons that order and argues for the priority of grace over law": "The Concept of Federal Theology — Was Calvin a Federal Theologian?" in *Calvinus Sacrae Scripturae: Professor Calvin as Confessor of Holy Scripture,* ed. Wilhelm H. Neuser (Grand Rapids, Mich.: Eerdmans, 1994), 31. See also I. John Hesselink, "Luther and Calvin on Law and Gospel in Their Galatian Commentaries," *Reformed Review* 37 (1984): 69-82; and "Law and Gospel or Gospel and Law? Calvin's Understanding of the Relationship," in *Calviniana: Ideas and Influence of Jean Calvin,* ed. Robert V. Schnucker (St. Louis, Mo.: Sixteenth Century Essays and Studies, 1988), 13-32. An el-

egant introduction to Calvin is David C. Steinmetz, *Calvin in Context* (New York: Oxford University Press, 1995).

36. Steinmetz summarizes Osiander in *Reformers in the Wings*, 64-69.

37. E.g., *CI* 3.16.1 (2:98-99); *CI* 3.17.8 (2:111). Here, as in much that follows, numerous more references could be added. However, only a few representative examples seem necessary.

38. E.g., *CI* 3.11.11 (2:47); *CI* 3.16.1 (2:99).

39. For example: "the wrath of God lies upon all men so long as they continue sinners" (*CI* 3.11.21 [2:57]).

40. See also *CI* 3.17.1 (2:105); *CI* 3.17.13 (2:116).

41. E.g., *CI* 3.11.11 (2:48-49); *CI* 3.12.3 (2:62-63), and Calvin quotes Bernard in this connection; *CI* 3.13.3 (2:70).

42. E.g., *CI* 3.17.11 (2:114 — see also 3.17.12; 2:115); see *CI* 3.18.8 (2:127).

43. E.g., *CI* 3.17.8 (2:111).

44. E.g., *CI* 3.11.19 (2:55-56).

45. There are also frequent glimmerings of other positions through this account that will be noted shortly.

46. An alternative schema is also discernible at times — not Luther's simple, stark antithesis of promise and commandment but a more covenantal and historical schema: "Moses was not appointed as a Law-giver, to do away with the blessing promised to the race of Abraham; nay, we see that he is constantly reminding the Jews of the free covenant which had been made with their fathers, and of which they were heirs; as if he had been sent for the purpose of renewing it" (*CI* 2.7.1; 1:300), this last being, more specifically, "the covenant of free adoption" (*CI* 2.7.2; 1:302).

47. In chapter 9 Calvin argues that the Jews knew Christ as well, although rather more dimly (*CI* 2.9; 1:363-67).

48. The Sabbath, of all the commandments, is superseded. No especially good reasons are given for this in terms of the surrounding schema, however (*CI* 2.8.28-34; 1:339-44). The Sabbath is a "mystery of perpetual resting from our works" (*CI* 2.8.31; 1:341). It is superseded because Christ, the truth and the body, has come, banishing "the ceremonial" and "the shadows" — citing here Rom. 6:4 and Col. 2:16, 17, somewhat opaquely. The Sabbath is also practical, suggesting a weekly gathering, and it reminds us not to oppress those subject to us.

49. Many of the Protestant Reformation's lesser lights also arguably follow the two leading Reformers in their endorsement of this theory. Zwingli simply accepts Luther's early work (up to 1519) and so can be safely viewed as endorsing Justification as well. Bullinger is highly conditional, although he does not articulate the full Federal schema: see J. Wayne Baker, *Heinrich Bullinger and the Covenant: The Other Reformed Tradition* (Athens, Ohio: Ohio University Press, 1980). Bullinger asserted the conditionality of the covenant in an unpublished treatise on baptism as early as 1525; however, he maintained the existence of only one covenant, in contradistinction to the Federalists (etc.). Weir suggests that Calvin and the Geneva theologians were less conditional than Zwingli, Bullinger, and the Rhineland theologians as a whole: see David A. Weir, *The Origins of the Federal Theology in Sixteenth-Century Reformation Thought* (Oxford: Clarendon, 1990); see also Steinmetz, *Reformers in the Wings*, 93-99, esp. 94-97.

50. The school is usefully introduced by Carl E. Braaten and Robert W. Jenson, eds., *Union with Christ: The New Finnish Interpretation of Luther* (Cambridge & Grand Rapids, Mich.: Eerdmans, 1998); see also Tuomo Mannermaa, *Christ Present in Faith: Luther's View of Justification*, ed. Kirsi Stjerna (Minneapolis, Minn.: Fortress, 2005 [1979]).

51. The complementary problem of theodicy is also generated.

52. There is doubtless an important connection here with the Augustinian and Thomist emphases on grace's work within the soul: see Gordon Rupp, *The Righteousness of God* (London: Hodder & Stoughton, 1953), 118.

53. Luther also cites the highly ethical comment of Augustine at this point: "What else are the laws of God that are divinely written in our hearts than the very presence of the Holy Spirit who is the

finger of God? By his presence, love is shed abroad in our hearts and this is the fulfillment of the law and the end of the commandment" (*Spirit and Letter,* 21.36). Augustine wrote this in 412 CE.

54. Arguably, Luther presupposes the operation of the entire contractual model at this point with its specific progressions, but it is simpler to read this thesis as a somewhat contradictory endorsement of election and the fundamental role of God, as against humanity, in salvation, along with a corresponding foregrounding of the fundamental divine attribute of love, as against retributive justice (statements probably prompted by certain biblical texts).

55. *LW* 26:34.

56. Trans. William R. Russell (Minneapolis: Fortress, 1995) — hereafter *SA.*

57. Luther is partly conscious of guarding against "the enthusiasts": see 3.8.3; *SA,* 29.

58. This is further evidence that the claim by the Finnish school that Luther's understanding of faith is inherently participatory is often along the right lines.

59. The similarity at this point to the material just quoted from *The Smalcald Articles* is striking.

60. In this precise relation Luther means primarily John and Paul, the latter testifying in his view especially clearly to human incapacity in Romans 7 and Galatians 5 (see *LW* 33:288).

61. Melanchthon has much more muted ambiguities, which were therefore noted in passing in the previous subsection.

62. So see, e.g., "free will does not enable any man to perform good works, unless he is assisted by grace; indeed, the special grace which the elect alone receive through regeneration" (*CI* 2.2.6; 1:228).

63. Calvin cites Rom. 5:12 following and 1 Cor. 15:22 repeatedly through book 2, chapter 1; he also appeals to Eph. 2:3.

64. It is interesting to note Calvin's emphasis toward the end of this discussion — partly in dependence on Augustine — on the motif of perseverance: "by means of the same grace, the heart being impressed with a feeling of delight, is trained to persevere, and strengthened with invincible fortitude" (*CI* 2.3.14; 1:264), an interesting allusion to a possible role for faithfulness within an elective soteriology.

65. Obvious difficulties here are partly obviated by repeated arguments from typology and its fulfillment and hence supersession; this allows "ceremonial" ordinances to be abandoned (so, to a degree, Calvin's treatment of the Sabbath within his extended analysis of the Ten Commandments in chapter 8). Calvin asserts consistently that the Jews knew Christ in these typological prefigurations, although of course more dimly, and that the two testaments are in this fashion fundamentally united (*CI* 2.6-7; 1:292-313; and 2.9-11; 1:363-99). So typology functions at two significant points in Calvin's affirmation of Justification, although he seems to have an uneasy conscience about its overt application at times in Paul (see his treatment of Col. 2:13-14 and Eph. 2:14 in *CI* 2.7.17; 1:312-13).

66. (I.a.) Jer. 31:18; Isa. 6:9-10.

67. For hints of regeneration see *CI* 2.1.6 (1:215); 2.2.5 (1:227); 2.2.6 (1:228); 2.3.1 (1:249); and 2.3.6-7 (1:255-56).

68. Hence, as we noted at the outset of this subsection, this unconditional and transformational understanding of salvation must — as Calvin seems quite aware at this point — redefine the Justification discourse. It is an essentially different approach to salvation, one grounded in pneumatology. And Calvin thereby places pressure on that soteriology from both ends: its account of pre-Christian humanity is too optimistic, and its account of the movement to salvation is therefore too anthropological, neglecting the necessary transformational role of God by means of the Spirit that continues into the ethical construction of the Christian, an involvement corroborated by the motif of election.

69. It is interesting to note that Luther suggests in a letter written in 1518 that a similar view of *poenitentia* was taught by Staupitz: "[Y]ou said that *poenitentia* is genuine only if it begins with love for justice and for God and that what they consider to be the final stage and completion is in reality rather the very beginning of *poenitentia.*" Luther continues: "Your word pierced me like the sharp arrow of the Mighty [Ps. 120:4]. . . . [W]hile formerly almost no word in the whole Scripture was more

bitter to me than *poenitentia* . . . , now no word sounds sweeter or more pleasant (*LW* 48:65-66; see Rupp, *Righteousness of God*, 118-19).

70. An important historical application of this argument then follows in relation to indulgences in chapter 5; these receive short shrift. However, it is interesting to note the location of these criteria vis-à-vis the former actions in Calvin's account of a system he dislikes and opposes. As one falls short of fulfilling the requisite demands of faith, repentance, and penitence — the relevance of both the atonement and baptism having already been circumscribed — a large space is created for *further* satisfaction to be made to God, something exacted in purgatory if it is not dealt with beforehand. But the requisite payment can of course also be made from the treasury of merits accumulated by the saints, martyrs, and office-holders of the church, in return for a literal payment to the church (an adroit fund-raising maneuver, it must be conceded). It is important to note that it is here that Calvin emphasizes the completeness or sufficiency of Christ's atonement. No additional "payment" needs to be sought outside the singular event of Christ's death, he claims, a point especially emphasized by texts from Hebrews (here attributed to Paul).

71. Indeed, the opposite is more likely to be the case; see, e.g., Richard B. Gaffin, Jr., "Biblical Theology and the Westminster Standards," *Westminster Theological Journal* 65 (2003): 165-79. Gaffin states at one point, "in the Westminster Standards the heart of the application of salvation, underlying all further consideration of *ordo salutis* questions, is being united to Christ by Spirit-worked faith, a union providing for multiple other benefits without one benefit either being confused with or existing separately from the others. This is essentially Calvin's 'ordo salutis,' though not as clearly elaborated as one might wish" ("Biblical Theology," 175). Gaffin's comments here are cited by Douglas J. Green in an unpublished paper "N. T. Wright — a Westminster Seminary Perspective," 5, n. 14 (available at www.ntwrightpage.com/Green_Westminster_Seminary_Perspective.pdf; consulted 10/27/2007).

72. *Reformers in the Wings*, 4 — in full: "It is the polychromatic character of the Reformation that this book attempts to stress and which, I think, may be its primary contribution" (and I am not sure that this contribution has yet been decisively refuted).

73. Debates over regeneration through pneumatology, and in relation to conditionality or contractualism per se, do not seem to have been so immediately apparent. Hence, arguably, something of a foundationalist mind-set still pervaded much Protestant thinking, emphases on election and depravity being compatible with a prospective theological construct — although a radically different one from Justification theory. The perception that a *retrospective* theological construct was still more appropriate for Christian theology is arguably present in Calvin (and also, to a degree, in Luther), but was articulated most clearly subsequently in minority traditions, one of which underpins much of this study — i.e., the Marrowmen and John McLeod Campbell in Scottish Presbyterianism, discussed by James B. Torrance's important essays, "Covenant and Contract, a Study of the Theological Background of Worship in Seventeenth-Century Scotland," *Scottish Journal of Theology* 23 (1970): 51-76; "The Contribution of McLeod Campbell to Scottish Theology," *Scottish Journal of Theology* 26 (1973): 295-311; and "Preface," in John McLeod Campbell, *The Nature of the Atonement* (Edinburgh: Handsel, 1996 [1856]), 1-16.

74. By the Westminster tradition I mean in particular The Thirty-Nine Articles (1563/71), The Westminster Confession of Faith (1646), The Westminster Shorter Catechism (1647) and The Westminster Larger Catechism (1647): see comments by the Torrance brothers: James B. Torrance, "Strengths and Weaknesses of the Westminster Theology," in *The Westminster Confession in the Church Today*, ed. A. I. C. Heron (Edinburgh: St Andrew's Press, 1982), 40-54; and T. F. Torrance, "The Westminster Tradition," in *Scottish Theology: From John Knox to John McLeod Campbell* (Edinburgh: T&T Clark, 1996), 125-55.

75. Emphases on prospective, or a priori, epistemology, coupled with a confidence about natural theology, a rationalist anthropology, and a God of retributive justice are the main constituents of Justification, as against mere introspection. Correspondingly, introspection can take many forms that lie beyond the bounds of Justification theory. Thus, Stendahl's claim about introspection is potentially deceptive and requires careful deployment, as we will see shortly.

76. Although of course since part one, chapter five, this notion must be defined flexibly: see more on the question of "conversion" just below.

77. The classic biography of Augustine's life is Peter R. L. Brown, *Augustine of Hippo: A Biography,* new ed. with an epilogue (Berkeley, Calif.: University of California Press, 2000 [1967]). A recent challenge to Brown's magisterial account is James J. O'Donnell, *Augustine: Confessions,* 3 vols. (Oxford: Oxford University Press, 1992); see also *Augustine: A New Biography* (New York: HarperCollins, 2005). McGrath provides a useful summary of Augustine's views of Justification — whom he describes as "the fountainhead" — in *Iustitia Dei,* 38-54. The period between Augustine and the Reformation is then charted in 55-207.

78. A classic account of this watershed is John M. Rist, "Augustine on Free Will and Predestination," *Journal of Theological Studies* 20 (1969): 420-47; see also William S. Babcock, "Augustine's Interpretation of Romans (A.D. 394-396)," *Augustinian Studies* 10 (1979): 55-74; and Brown, *Augustine,* 146-57. McGrath endorses this biography: *Iustitia Dei,* 39.

79. Some have argued that the shift began earlier on, following Augustine's ordination. It is arguably detectable in various parts of *Free Will:* see, e.g., Rowan Greer, "Augustine's Transformation of the Free Will Defense," *Faith and Philosophy* 13 (1996): 471-86. While Book 1 of *Free Will* was written in 387, while Augustine was at Cassiciacum and before his baptism, Books 2 and 3 were written four years later, in 391, after his ordination. In books 2 and 3, which were also written before his letter to Simplician, Augustine describes humanity's incapacity to know and to will the good apart from grace. For instance, he writes, "man cannot rise of his own free will as he fell by his own will spontaneously." All people can do in a state of sin is "hold with steadfast faith to the right hand of God stretched out to us from above, even our Lord Jesus Christ" (2.20.54: see *Augustine: Earlier Writings,* trans. J. H. S. Burleigh, LCC [Philadelphia: Westminster Press, 1953], 169). (My thanks to Warren Smith for his insights at this point.)

80. The "watershed" biography of Augustine is almost certainly a narrative oversimplification — as we have just seen — but it is serviceable in this relation; certainly it is better than any undifferentiated analysis (see Westerholm, *PO&NP,* 3-21).

81. References in what follows are to the translations in Paula Fredriksen Landes, *Augustine on Romans* (Chico, Calif.: Scholars, 1982).

82. See 1.1: "justification of faith" *(iustificatio fidei)* and "justified through belief" *(iustificati credendo);* 8.6, "sins . . . remitted through faith" ([*peccata*] *remissis per fidem*); 10.13, "peace . . . through faith" *(pacem . . . per fidem);* also 3.2 (54-55) — "the Gospel, in which believers are justified by faith" *(. . . fide credentes iustificantur).*

83. So Babcock, "Augustine's Interpretation of Romans," 55-74; see also Eugene Teselle, *Augustine the Theologian* (New York: Herder & Herder, 1970). But it is also interesting to chart some of his other exegetical work during this period. Augustine wrote on Galatians: *Expositio in epistulam ad Galatas;* compare his *Eighty-three Different Questions,* nos. 66-74. His other biblical works from the period 391 (the date of his ordination) through 396 AD were *Enarrations on the Psalms* (on the first thirty-two psalms) and *On Genesis Literally Interpreted,* a commentary on Genesis. He also wrote on the Sermon on the Mount. Prior to his ordination he had written only one biblical commentary: *On Genesis against the Manicheans* (388/389 CE).

84. The citation of Pauline material predominates in this argument. Augustine quotes Romans 1:25; 5:3, 4, 5; 8:20, 28, 29, 30, 35, 36, 38, 39; 11:36; 12:2; 13:10; 14:2-21; 1 Corinthians 1:23-25; 5:6; 6:11-20, 12, 13; 7:1-7, 14, 31; 8:8; 11:19; 15:22, 47-49, 54, 55, 56; 2 Corinthians 4:16, 18; Galatians 1:10; Colossians 2:8; 3:9, 10; and Ephesians 3:7, 14-19. However, he is here primarily "proof-texting" in support of an essentially neo-Platonic argument against Manicheanism. (Texts available at www.ccel.org/ccel/schaff/npnf104.toc.html.)

85. Some widely read studies have asserted the stronger claim at this point — that the theory began with Paul and then simply continued relatively smoothly through church history in a discernible trajectory (although it received particular clarification and impetus during the Reformation and from modern Evangelicals!): see (i.a.), at a more popular level, Oden, *The Justification Reader.* These

claims arguably rest in part on certain basic errors that were discussed in chapter seven, §4 (i.e., theological and lexical overdeterminations).

86. See Theodore de Bruyn, *Pelagius's Commentary on St Paul's Epistle to the Romans* (Oxford: Clarendon, 1993); and Kathy L. Gaca and L. L. Welborn, eds., *Early Patristic Readings of Romans*, Romans through History and Cultures (London & New York: T&T Clark International [Continuum], 2005).

87. Augustine arguably employs the "faith as gift" reading that was also adopted by many later interpreters — that God requires faith of the individual for justification and salvation, but elects who will receive that faith as a gift. However, I am not convinced that Augustine, when endorsing this or a similar schema, has navigated successfully around the problems pointed out in it by part one, chapter two, §2.7. Furthermore, at these points he is not advocating Justification theory as defined in chapter one, and exegetically derived from Paul in chapter ten.

88. Much of this debate — although generally failing to make some of the important distinctions, and thereby arguably attesting to their importance — is apparent in the fascinating collection Daniel Patte and Eugene Teselle, eds., *Engaging Augustine on Romans: Self, Context, and Theology in Interpretation,* Romans through History and Cultures (Harrisburg, Pa.: Trinity Press International, 2003). I find the blanket suggestion that Augustine in effect *created* the introspective Western mind unconvincing.

89. We have already noted the important study of Augustine in relation to Paul and conversion by Paula Fredriksen, "Paul and Augustine: Conversion Narratives, Orthodox Traditions, and the Retrospective Self," *Journal of Theological Studies* 37 (1980): 3-34 (in part one, chapter five, §3.1), although Fredriksen's conclusions have been criticized: see John K. Riches, "Readings of Augustine on Paul: Their Impact on Critical Studies of Paul," in Patte and Teselle, eds., *Engaging Augustine,* 173-98.

90. These exegetical reflections have greatly puzzled scholars who have assumed that Augustine was simply providing an account of his conversion. They articulate in scriptural terms an unconditional view of divine action in relation to humanity — thereby fulfilling exactly the theological agenda of a reconception of the nature of divine action.

91. So Westerholm sensibly notes Wesley: *PO&NP,* 64-87. I am more interested here, however, in the Reformational claims made by Justification advocates explicitly on behalf of their discourse, and then in the broader, often unstated support of modernity. So Wesley — who might well straddle both these sets of influences — is best considered on another occasion. (Some important studies in this relation have already been noted in part one, chapter six, §4.6; and Wesley is relevant again, in a broader historical context, as noted by chapter nine.)

Notes to Chapter Nine

1. So I will rely here to a degree on the ability and desire of modern readers to take a personal inventory in this relation, perhaps assisted by the key intellectual and historical markers supplied in this chapter. A useful tool in this relation is Norman K. Gottwald, "Framing Biblical Interpretation at New York Theological Seminary: A Student Self-Inventory on Biblical Hermeneutics," in *Reading from This Place,* vol. 1, *Social Location and Biblical Interpretation in the United States,* ed. Fernando F. Segovia and Mary Ann Tolbert (Minneapolis, Minn.: Augsburg Fortress, 1995), 251-61.

2. See the insightful perspectives in this relation of Amy Laura Hall, *Conceiving Parenthood: The Protestant Spirit of Biotechnological Reproduction* (Grand Rapids, Mich.: Eerdmans, 2007). Some amusing and insightful material can also be found in the shorter and less rigorous analysis by Bridget Booher, "Helicopter Parents," *Duke Magazine* 93 (2007): 1-3.

3. So, e.g., Luther quotes Matt. 23:2-5, which denounces the scribes and the Pharisees, in relation to Rom. 2:21 and 29 — "you that teach another, do you not teach yourself?" — and so on: see Wilhelm Pauck, ed., *Luther: Lectures on Romans,* LCC 15 (London: SCM, 1961), 54-56, 59 — hereafter *LLR;* see also Matt. 9:12; Luke 4:18 and 15:4 (*LLR,* 70).

4. That is, a characteristic post-Enlightenment, Liberal pretension to universality of discourse

and understanding is detectable here — a false, and ultimately also rather imperialistic understanding. Criticizing this tendency underlies much of Stanley Hauerwas, *After Christendom? How the Church Is to Behave If Freedom, Justice, and a Christian Nation Are Bad Ideas*, new ed. with a new introduction (Nashville, Tenn.: Abingdon, 1999 [1991]).

5. The historical connections are traced in more detail on occasion — see esp. the widely acclaimed study, Nathan O. Hatch, *The Democratization of American Christianity* (New Haven & London: Yale University Press, 1989); also George M. Thomas, *Revivalism and Cultural Change: Christianity, Nation Building, and the Market in the Nineteenth-Century United States* (Chicago: The University of Chicago Press, 1989). Mark A. Noll also provides some useful historical information (sometimes in passing) oriented toward the North American situation in *The Scandal of the Evangelical Mind* (Grand Rapids, Mich.: Eerdmans, 1994); *America's God: From Jonathan Edwards to Abraham Lincoln* (Oxford: Oxford University Press, 2002); and *The Old Religion in a New World: The History of North American Christianity* (Grand Rapids, Mich.: Eerdmans, 2002). More detailed analysis of the Wesleys, Whitefield, and Jonathan Edwards could also be usefully introduced at this point. This last figure has received a magisterial description by George M. Marsden's *Jonathan Edwards: A Life* (New Haven, Conn. & London: Yale University Press, 2003). I suggest that the dynamics of Justification — especially the wrathful God and question of conversion — are clearly discernible in Edwards's life and thought, although in an interesting interaction with Calvinism.

6. In *Scandal* Noll states that "[i]n one of the most useful definitions of the phenomenon, the British historian David Bebbington has identified the key ingredients of evangelicalism as conversionism (an emphasis on the 'new birth' as a life-changing religious experience), Biblicism (a reliance on the Bible as ultimate religious authority), activism (a concern for sharing the faith), and crucicentrism (a focus on Christ's redeeming work on the cross)" (8, quoting David Bebbington, *Evangelicalism in Modern Britain: A History from the 1730s to the 1980s* [London: Unwin Hyman, 1989], 2-19). Hence, Bebbington's and Noll's analyses of modern British and American evangelicalism overlap rather neatly with points 1, 5, 9, and 11 (and arguably also 10), noted previously in §2 as strengths of Justification theory, apparently confirming its penetration. The widespread popular distribution of this notion is perhaps affirmed most strongly, however, by the recent US survey results noted in part one, chapter one, §5 (i.e., The Baylor Survey of Religion) in relation to the importance of certain root metaphors concerning God — principally the retributive metaphors.

7. Moreover, because "gospel" is a bisyllabic word with an unstressed ending a more emphatic monosyllabic alternative is potentially especially useful. Similarly, "Christian" is not a particularly prominent signifier in the New Testament, so a more scripturally resonant signifier for this is helpful.

8. Arguably, there are other New Testament texts that attest to this meaning, but we are concerned here with Paul; the key Pauline texts in this relation are addressed in part five, chapter twenty.

9. Acts 11:26; 26:28; 1 Pet. 4:16.

10. The raw figures are altered by canonical commitments and a few text-critical decisions, but not the basic ratios. In a ten-letter canon the ratio is 127:42:23 ("brother"/"saint"/"believer"); that is, "brother" is almost *six times* as frequent as "believer," and "saint" almost *twice* as frequent. To prefer the name "believer" for the description of Christians when giving an account of Paul's theology is consequently to have made a highly motivated decision.

11. Graham founded the Billy Graham Evangelistic Association (BGEA), through which he conducts his ministry, in 1950. Projects of the BGEA include *Decision* magazine, its official publication (available in English, German, and Braille, with a circulation of more than 600,000); the My Answer newspaper column; the weekly *Hour of Decision* radio program, broadcast around the world for more than fifty years; frequent prime-time crusade television specials; and World Wide Pictures, which has produced and distributed more than 125 films translated into thirty-eight languages and viewed by more than 250 million people. In addition, Graham has written twenty-five books, many of which have become top sellers. *How to Be Born Again* (London: Hodder & Stoughton, 1977) had the largest first printing in publishing history with 800,000 copies. Of his other books, *Approaching Hoofbeats: The Four Horsemen of the Apocalypse* (Waco, Texas: Word, 1983) was listed for several weeks on *The New York Times* best seller list; *Angels: God's Secret Agents*, new ed. (London: Hodder &

Stoughton, [1995] 1975), sold one million copies within ninety days; and *The Jesus Generation* (Grand Rapids, Mich.: Zondervan, 1971) sold 200,000 copies in the first two weeks. Graham is one of the best-known figures in recent Western history. Clearly, his influence is enormous. (This information was retrieved from www.billygraham.org.)

12. See also Billy Graham, *Peace with God,* rev. ed. (Waco, Texas: Word, [1984] 1953). *Peace With God,* like *How to Be Born Again,* is structured in three parts — "Assessing the Situation," "Advancing the Solution," and "Applying the Antidote." There is much more than Justification theory operating through these major argumentative divisions, but the fundamentally foundationalist agenda endorsed by Justification is immediately apparent in the "forward" thinking of the book, and is apparent more specifically throughout.

The Statement of Faith on the BGEA website also contains the following: "The Billy Graham Evangelistic Association believes. . . . That all men everywhere are lost and face the judgment of God, and need to come to a saving knowledge of Jesus Christ through His shed blood on the cross" (www.billygraham.org/StatementOfFaith.asp). This is probably an assertion of the truth of Justification theory. However, the Statement also contains emphases on Christ's resurrection, and on Christian holiness and social concern — key elements in the alternative soteriology sketched earlier in chapter three. Just how all these elements integrate together is not specified.

13. There are many other telling statements in this book, e.g., "Crime requires punishment and sin has a penalty" (72); and "In order to guard His holiness, God must exercise justice. Since all sin is an offence to God, the principle of God's justice is vital to an orderly universe, just as a nation must have certain laws and codes. But unlike human government, which uses justice in ways that are suitable to the rulers or heads of government, God's justice is pure; no mistake is ever made" (85). The following anecdote is especially indicative:

> My friend and associate, Cliff Barrows, told me this story about bearing punishment. He recalled the time when he took the punishment for his children when they disobeyed. "They had done something I had forbidden them to do. I told them if they did the same thing again I would have to discipline them. When I returned from work and found that they hadn't minded me, the heart went out of me. I just couldn't discipline them." Any loving father can understand Cliff's dilemma. Most of us have been in the same position. He continued with the story: "Bobby and Bettie Ruth were very small. I called them into my room, took off my belt and my shirt, and with a bare back, knelt down at the bed. I made them both strap me with the belt ten times each. You should have heard the crying! From them, I mean! They didn't want to do it. But I told them the penalty had to be paid and so through their sobs and tears they did what I told them." Cliff smiled when he remembered the incident. "I must admit I wasn't much of a hero. It hurt. I haven't offered to do that again, but I never had to spank them again either, because they got the point. We kissed each other when it was over and prayed together." In that infinite way that staggers our hearts and minds, we know that Christ paid the penalty for our sins, past, present, and future. That is why He died on the Cross. (*How to Be Born Again,* 99)

14. I am using (in the main) www.crusade.org/fourlaws/law4.html (see also www.crusade.org/downloads/article/resources/4SpiritualLaws.pdf); supplemented by the pdf version from the Campus Crusade Web site (Orlando: New Life, 2002: http://www.greatcom.org/laws/english/pda/the-files/4laws-foldout.pdf). All added information has been drawn from Campus Crusade for Christ International's NEWSROOM: http://www.demossnewspond.com/ccci/ (the "Newsroom" link under "About Us" on the CCCI site); note also the Press Kit sublinks there. (My thanks for Carol Shoun for the additional links used here.)

15. Some versions of the Laws include the following claim under Law Four: "When We Receive Christ, We Experience a New Birth," citing John 3:1-8 (see www.godlovestheworld.com/ or www.gospeloutreach.net/law_four.html). But others do not, eliminating this statement and scriptural text (see the versions cited previously). Hence, in certain recensions, an *increase* in the system's contractualism seems to have recently taken place, at the expense of a transformational understand-

ing of salvation — and one supported directly by a scriptural text! (My thanks to Carol Shoun for pointing this out to me.)

16. "Receiving Christ involves turning to God from self (repentance) and trusting Christ to come into our lives to forgive our sins and to make us what He wants us to be. Just to agree intellectually that Jesus Christ is the Son of God and that He died on the cross for our sins is not enough. Nor is it enough to have an emotional experience. We receive Jesus Christ by faith, as an act of the will" (www.crusade.org/fourlaws/law4.html). One could ask immediately of course how an act of the will could conceivably lead directly to a complete displacement of the will-governed self, as well as how the individual could believe that Jesus is divine and died on the cross in atonement and somehow also "trust" these things without the prior revelation that they are true and trustworthy.

17. These soundings could also easily be added to. The widely-popular Alpha Course, run by Holy Trinity Brompton in London, UK, although differing from the foregoing in certain important respects, tends to lean on Justification in its account of the atonement. Even more clearly, The Roman Road, a popular concatenation of texts from Romans ostensibly outlining salvation, is structured — at times outrageously out of context — in terms of Justification theory: see Rom. 3:23; 6:23; 5:8; 10:9-10, and 13. (Some versions add 1:20-21; 2:4; 3:10-18; 5:1, 12; 6:3-7; 8:1, 38-39; 10:11; and 11:36; at different points: see, i.a., www.westarkchurchofchrist.org/library/romansmap.htm; www.gotquestions.org/Romans-road-salvation.html; www.new-testament-christian.com/roman-road-to-salvation.html; and www.fishthe.net/digitracts/roman.htm; consulted 12/11/2007.) Further soundings into the more intellectual quarters of these traditions only confirm this impression — see the studies esp. by Mark Noll already cited in this subsection: *Scandal, America's God,* and *The Old Religion in a New World.* Many of the conservative trajectory's key modern exegetical representatives are noted when Paul's Justification texts are treated in detail from part three, chapter ten onward.

18. Rudolf Bultmann, *Theology of the New Testament,* trans. K. Grobel, 2 vols. (New York: Scribners, 1951, 1955).

19. "*God's demand* encounters man concretely in the *nomos, the Law of the Old Testament,* the purpose of which is no other than to lead man to life" (*Theology of the New Testament,* 1:259, emphasis original); while "[t]he presupposition for understanding the proposition that not works lead to 'righteousness,' but only faith, is the acknowledgement that the Law's demand is just, *that God is the Judge who demands good deeds of man*" (1:262, emphasis original; Rom. 1:18–3:20 is cited here). Moreover, "[t]he reason why man's situation under the Law is so desperate is not that the Law as an inferior revelation mediates a limited or even false knowledge of God. . . . The reason why man under the Law does not achieve 'rightwising' and life is that he is a transgressor of the Law, that he is guilty before God" (1:262-63). Bultmann goes on to point out that "[i]t is the insight which Paul has achieved into the nature of sin that determines his teaching on the Law" (1:264). So "by this process the Law leads man to God as the Creator who bestows life and from whom alone life can be given to man" (1:267).

20. "[T]his is what his [Paul's] conversion meant: In it he surrendered his previous understanding of himself; i.e. he surrendered what had till then been the norm and meaning of his life, he sacrificed what had hitherto been his pride and joy (Phil. 3:4-7). His conversion was not the result of an inner moral collapse. . . . It was not rescue from the despair into which the cleavage between willing and doing had allegedly driven him. His was not a conversion of repentance; neither, of course, was it one of emancipating enlightenment. Rather, it was obedient submission to the judgment of God, made known in the cross of Christ, upon all human accomplishment and boasting. It is as such that his conversion is reflected in his theology" (*Theology of the New Testament,* 1:188).

21. Otherwise it is just mythology, although it does, additionally, speak of the prior/prevenient love and grace of God (*Theology of the New Testament,* 1:304-5).

22. Treated in chapter 3 (*Theology of the New Testament,* §§9-15; 1:63-183); Jesus is treated in chapter 1 (§§1-4; 1:3-32), and "the kerygma of the earliest church" in chapter 2 (§§5-8; 1:33-62).

23. Note, in particular: "one perceives *the deep relatedness in substance that exists between John and Paul* in spite of all their differences in mode of thought and terminology" (*Theology of the New Testament,* 2:9, emphasis original; see further 2:6-14).

24. Although somewhat ambiguously, given the indebtedness Bultmann sees in John to Gnosticism.

25. See, e.g., more recently, T. Engberg-Pedersen, *Paul and the Stoics* (Edinburgh: T&T Clark, 2000).

I am also confident that the position apparent in Bultmann's *Theology* is borne out by the rest of his writings (although, to reiterate, those writings are not reducible to his particular account of Justification): see (i.a.), *Jesus Christ and Mythology* (New York: Charles Scribner's Sons, 1958), 36, 40-43, 53-59, 62-73, 76-85.

26. Many reasons can be adduced for this — the inherent unreliability of the contingent, historical realm; the lack of freedom there (because it is viewed as a closed causal nexus); and so on.

27. In this relation I lean in particular on the analyses of Karl Barth, *Protestant Theology in the Nineteenth Century: Its Background and History*, trans. B. Cozens and J. Bowden (London: SCM, 1972); and *CD* I.1; C. E. Gunton, *Enlightenment and Alienation* (Basingstoke: Marshall, Morgan & Scott, 1985); and, with C. Schwöbel, ed., *Persons Divine and Human: King's College Essays in Theological Anthropology* (Edinburgh: T&T Clark, 1991); H. Thielicke, *The Evangelical Faith*, vol. 1, *Prolegomena*, trans. Geoffrey W. Bromiley (Edinburgh: T&T Clark, 1974 [1968]); T. F. Torrance, "The Church in the New Era of Scientific and Cosmological Change," in *Theology in Reconciliation: Essays Towards Evangelical and Catholic Unity in East and West* (London: Geoffrey Chapman, 1975), 267-93; Alan J. Torrance, *Persons in Communion: An Essay on Trinitarian Description and Human Participation with Special Reference to Volume One of Karl Barth's Church Dogmatics* (Edinburgh: T&T Clark, 1996); "*Auditus Fidei*: Where and How Does God Speak? Faith, Reason, and the Question of Criteria," in *Reason and the Reasons of Faith*, ed. Paul J. Griffiths and Reinhardt Hütter (New York & London: T&T Clark [Continuum], 2005), 27-52; Stanley Hauerwas, *Sanctify Them in the Truth Holiness Exemplified* (Edinburgh and Nashville, Tenn.: T&T Clark and Abingdon, 1998); and *With the Grain of the Universe: The Church's Witness and Natural Theology, Being the Gifford Lectures Delivered at the University of St. Andrews in 2001* (London: SCM, 2002). While not being explicitly theological, the following studies were also especially useful: E. Gellner, *Plough, Sword, and Book: The Structure of Human History* (Chicago: University of Chicago Press, 1988); Charles Taylor, *Sources of the Self: The Making of the Modern Identity* (Cambridge: Cambridge University Press, 1989); and R. Poole, *Morality and Modernity* (London & New York: Routledge, 1991). My understanding of science depends, as usual, primarily on Michael Polanyi, supplemented at certain points by T. Kuhn and a general notion of complexity theory: see chapter seven, §1. Many other thinkers and studies could of course be cited at this point.

28. See G. E. Lessing, "On the Proof of the Spirit and of Power," in *Lessing's Theological Writings*, ed. H. B. Nisbet (Cambridge: Cambridge University Press, 2005 [1777]), 83-8.

29. This principle is then easily transferable to other apparently religious discourses — of course defining them highly reductively in the process! Hence, Schleiermacher is often regarded as the father of religious studies. Indeed, through him we introduce the further very indicative equation that "a religion" equals "a faith" and vice versa.

30. Friedrich Schleiermacher, *The Christian Faith*, ed. D. M. Baillie, H. R. MacKintosh, and J. S. Stewart, 2nd ed. (Edinburgh: T&T Clark, 1999 [1830]). Note also that important continuities are then detectable between Scheiermacher's introspective spiritual individualism and James's epochal work: William James, *The Varieties of Religious Experience: A Study in Human Nature* (New York: Mentor Books, 1958 [1902]); meaning, in turn, that both arguably perpetuate certain fundamental modern errors in relation to theological truth: see Hauerwas, *With the Grain of the Universe*, 43-86.

31. Thielicke, discussing the program's antecedents, points to Spener (1688) and then notes the analogous concerns of Lessing and Schleiermacher. Theodor Hermann and Albrecht Ritschl are also important figures in this program, in his view. See *The Evangelical Faith*, vol. 1, *Prolegomena*.

32. See also "the alternative to lay hold of one's true existence or to miss it is synonymous with the alternative to acknowledge God as the Creator or to deny him" (*Theology of the New Testament*, §22; 1:232).

33. Probably an anti-neo-Kantian and "ethical" caveat in favor of a sharper, more existentialist, and also more classically Lutheran approach.

34. This draws on a useful distinction made by Luther in relation to preaching and the spoken word between a *Thettel-Wort* or Deed-Word and a *Heissel-Wort* or (just) a Naming-Word. A sermon ought to be the former; it "does not merely call existing things by their correct names, like Adam naming all the beasts in Paradise; it calls new things into existence, like God on the first day of creation.... God is not distant but present in, with, and under the material elements of human language": see David C. Steinmetz, *Luther in Context,* 2nd ed. (Grand Rapids, Mich.: Baker, 2002 [1995]), 135 (with a brief explication of the broader issues on 132-35). In a sense, Luther is also anticipating with this distinction some of the insights of Speech-Act theory that will be utilized later on, esp. in part four, chapter sixteen.

35. M. J. Buckley is a masterful account: see *At the Origins of Modern Atheism* (London and New Haven: Yale University Press, 1987).

36. "The myth of scientific progress" is classically narrated and exposed by Kuhn, *The Structure of Scientific Revolutions;* but see also MacIntyre, "Epistemological Crises, Dramatic Narrative and the Philosophy of Science," in *The Tasks of Philosophy: Selected Essays* (Cambridge: Cambridge University Press, 2006 [1977]), 3-23.

37. See some of the studies cited both earlier and later, in §§3 and 6 respectively.

38. Gilbert Ryle, *The Concept of Mind* (Chicago: The University of Chicago Press, 1949). It should be emphasized that he views any such strong dualism, ultimately deriving from Descartes, critically.

39. I have found the following especially important in this relation: James B. Torrance, "Covenant and Contract, a Study of the Theological Background of Worship in Seventeenth-Century Scotland," *Scottish Journal of Theology* 23 (1970): 51-76; "The Contribution of McLeod Campbell to Scottish Theology," *Scottish Journal of Theology* 26 (1973): 295-311; "The Covenant Concept in Scottish Theology and Politics and Its Legacy," *Scottish Journal of Theology* 34 (1981): 225-43; Joan Lockwood O'Donovan, "Historical Prolegomena to a Theological Review of 'Human Rights," *Studies in Christian Ethics* 9 (1996): 52-65; "Christian Platonism and Non-Proprietary Community," in, with Oliver O'Donovan, *Bonds of Imperfection: Christian Politics, Past and Present* (Grand Rapids, Mich.: Eerdmans, 2004), 73-96; Stanley Hauerwas, "The Church and Liberal Democracy: The Moral Limits of a Secular Polity," in *A Community of Character toward a Constructive Christian Social Ethic* (Notre Dame, Ind.: University of Notre Dame Press, 1981), 72-96; *After Christendom? How the Church Is to Behave If Freedom, Justice, and a Christian Nation Are Bad Ideas;* "Knowing How to Go On When You Do Not Know Where You Are: A Response to John Cobb," "History as Fate: How Justification by Faith Became Anthropology (and History) in America," and (with Michael Broadway) "The Irony of Reinhold Niebuhr: The Ideological Character of Christian Realism," in *Wilderness Wanderings: Probing Twentieth-Century Theology and Philosophy* (London: SCM, 1997), 25-61.

To these seminal studies can be added B. Tierney, *The Foundations of Conciliar Theory* (Cambridge: Cambridge University Press, 1968); David A. Weir, *The Origins of the Federal Theology in Sixteenth-Century Reformation Thought* (Oxford: Clarendon, 1990); C. B. MacPherson, *The Political Theory of Possessive Individualism: Hobbes to Locke* (Oxford: Oxford University Press, 1962); Poole, *Morality and Modernity;* and esp. Anthony Giddens, *Power, Property, and the State: Volume One of a Contemporary Critique of Historical Materialism* (Berkeley & Los Angeles: University of California Press, 1982); and *The Nation-State and Violence: Volume Two of a Contemporary Critique of Historical Materialism* (Berkeley & Los Angeles: University of California Press, 1987).

Later rights theorists are also worth consulting: some classic treatments are John Rawls, *A Theory of Justice* (Oxford: Oxford University Press, 1971); and Robert Nozick, *Anarchy, State, and Utopia* (New York: Basic Books, 1974); an earlier classic is Isaiah Berlin, *Two Concepts of Liberty* (Oxford: Clarendon, 1958).

Economic issues are important in this relation as well: a seminal account of the rise of capitalism is Karl Polanyi, *The Great Transformation: The Political and Economic Origins of Our Time* (Boston: Beacon Press, 1957 [1944]); see, more recently, Bob Goudzwaard, *Capitalism and Progress: A Diagnosis of Western Society,* trans. J. van Nuis Zylstra, 2nd rev. ed. (Grand Rapids, Mich.: Eerdmans, 1979 [1978]).

40. Accessible in the following editions: *A Letter Concerning Toleration,* introd. P. Romanell (New York: The Liberal Arts Press, 1950); *Two Treatises of Government,* ed. Ian Shapiro (New Haven: Yale University Press, 2003); *An Essay Concerning Human Understanding* (London: Aldine, 1961); *Some Thoughts Concerning Education and Of the Conduct of the Understanding,* ed. R. W. Grant and N. Tarcov (Indianapolis, Ind.: Hackett, 1996); and *The Reasonableness of Christianity: As Delivered in the Scriptures,* ed. John C. Higgins-Biddle (Oxford: Oxford University Press [Clarendon], 1999).

41. MacPherson, *The Political Theory of Possessive Individualism,* passim.

42. As Romand Coles puts it, "conceptions of currency-based fairness make the exchange of equivalents the central paradigm for human cooperation" (see his "Contesting Cosmopolitan Currency: The Nepantilist Rose in the Cross(ing) of the Present," *Nepantla* 4 [2003]: 17). And this generates in turn an "obvious" discourse for understanding the atonement — an entirely human and historically specific one! Coles goes on to point out that one dangerous consequence of the extended and uncritical application of a currency trope or narrative is an overriding of critical *qualitative* differences — precisely the theological difficulty at this point.

43. That is, it would be extremely easy to move from a weak position over against private property to a strong endorsement of private property by arguing from the "state of nature" in its favor, as traditional rights theorists did.

44. Various quite general pieces of evidence reinforce our claim concerning the dominance of political liberalism. We should note in particular the centrality of a discourse of "decision" — especially in much commercial parlance and in politics. That discourse dictates that rationalizing individuals will come, as a result of their deliberations, to certain conclusions, which will then result in certain actions that ought therefore to be deemed rational, and may even be predictable on that basis. Often implicit in this account is a thought-act dichotomy. Undergirding the initiation of the act we often find the faculty of "will," a notion with an ancient pedigree, especially in Stoicism, although difficult both to find and to define in real terms. Setting aside the problems implicit here, the result is that a notion of "decision" arises directly out of the tradition's central concerns. And this can also be seen to permeate several important areas within liberal society.

Marketing and sales often describe the process that they are trying to effect — however inaccurately — in terms of "reaching a decision." (It goes without saying that much evangelistic discourse is also structured in these terms, and often with a quite deliberate borrowing of commercial sales language.) Likewise, democracies are understandably preoccupied with electoral decisions, which are the focus of sustained political efforts. Even military ventures can be rendered in such terms, the point of decision being a "decisive" battle. (Note the frustration of Western military analysts with opponents who do not play by these rules, avoiding such battles and relying instead on general attrition; this is sometimes described as an "Asian" mentality, which is sometimes denoted further as barbaric and perhaps even unmanly: see John Keegan, *A History of Warfare* [London: Hutchinson, 1993].) And it is not surprising to see this distinctive aspect of liberal ideology pervading adjacent social areas such as education, psychology, and even much of the culture of popular entertainment. In short, the "vertical" dissemination of this ideology throughout many modern societies is nothing short of staggering. However, it is important to appreciate that its influence is not limited to the European social order.

A discourse of decision has already been carefully considered in part one, chapter five — there specifically in relation to conversion. Some important critics of this entire approach to the explanation of human behaviour were also noted there in §2. This study is generally in favor of both rational explanations and a rational component within human behaviour, but not of any overextension and overemphasis on these — what was earlier dubbed and criticized as rationalistic.

45. A relatively recent competitor to this tradition is the attempt to adopt Islamic law as constitutional in some form. The attempt by Iran to combine Western liberal democratic principles with strict Islamic law observance is especially interesting, as is the newly inaugurated Iraqi experiment. Pakistan in particular has been struggling with this issue for some time. Turkey resolved it almost a century ago by explicitly secularizing in dictatorial fashion (a model that later failed in Iran).

46. Perhaps this strength is best explained (at least in part) in terms of a transfer of traditionally very strong ties to locale and local people to a redefined entity that retained sufficiently numerous

ties with the old loyalties to make such a transition possible. Social identity theory may be relevant at this point; it is briefly considered (in relation to Paul's Justification texts) in part three, chapter twelve.

47. The classic account is Max Weber, *Economy and Society* (Berkeley and Los Angeles: University of California Press, 1968 [1956]); see more lately John Ralston Saul, *Voltaire's Bastards. The Dictatorship of Reason in the West* (New York: The Free Press [Macmillan], 1992).

48. A useful overview of this history in the U.K. can be found in Asa Briggs, *A Social History of England,* 2nd ed. (Harmondsworth: Penguin, 1987), 216-65. Debates over the exact nature and extent of "globalization" remain unresolved, but the more general points are doubtless relevant here.

49. The classic account is Max Weber, *The Protestant Ethic and the Spirit of Capitalism,* trans. Talcott Parsons and Anthony Giddens (London & Boston: Unwin Hyman, 1930 [1904-5]); followed by R. H. Tawney, *Religion and the Rise of Capitalism* (London & New Brunswick: Transaction, 1998 [1926]). Giddens also revisits this question in *Capitalism and Modern Social Theory: An Analysis of the Writings of Marx, Durkheim, and Max Weber* (Cambridge: Cambridge University Press, 1971).

50. If greed is one of the most powerful and enduring factors in human history, then a material account of that history retains in like measure an enduring plausibility (while intellectual superiority may contribute to a strange neglect of this visceral causality). Moreover, as Marx observed, this account is specifically observable not just in the technological dimension of societies but also — and perhaps more so — in the legal and conventional structuring of the way technology's benefits are distributed. Ideologies and philosophies — if not theologies — then tend to map those underlying developments to a rather astonishing degree. Is this the case for modern philosophical individualism? Arguably, very much so. A more positive account that overlaps with some of these concerns could presumably be supplied, however, in terms of bodiliness.

51. Note also that I am not sketching the basic relationship between modern philosophical and political individualism and Justification merely to make blanket charges of hermeneutical projection; I will suggest ultimately — especially in part four, chapter fourteen — that readers positioned unselfconsciously within these powerful traditions tend to bring particular assumptions to Paul's Justification texts at certain critical points, leading to concrete, particular, and self-legitimizing decisions and readings. That is, quite specific connections are apparent at this interface, once we have been alerted to their possibility. It is this danger — shared by both liberal and conservative, who share it precisely because both are fundamentally modern postures — that ultimately I want to expose and to counter in this project.

Notes to Chapter Ten

1. Paul's ostensible articulation of Justification theory in Romans 1:16–4:25 takes 103 verses, or around 190 lines of Greek text (in the N-A²⁷). This chunk of material is about the same length as, if not slightly longer than, Paul's letters to the Philippians and to the Thessalonians *in their entirety* (meaning here 1 Thessalonians; 2 Thessalonians is much shorter, as is Philemon; Colossians is about the same length again). Incidentally, the closest competitor (possibly quite significantly) is probably The Wisdom of Solomon, but that text does not of course lead to Justification through the atoning work of Christ and individuals' faith.

2. And nothing is really lost by proceeding in this manner. If other texts in Paul turn out to be determinative for Justification theory, then this will simply emerge at the later points when they are discussed. So no harm is done by addressing Romans 1–4 first. If it emerges that Justification theory is not actually endorsed by Romans 1–4, then it would be inappropriate to allow such an approach to Romans 1–4 to influence the exegesis of those other texts in any case.

3. The pericope beginning most probably in 5:1 is arguably still integrally related to what has just been discussed; however, not much turns on its inclusion or exclusion at this point, so it is discussed in more detail later on — in part five, chapter nineteen, §9. Justification theory is well and truly launched by this point irrespective of whether Paul continues to speak of it in Romans 5.

4. See Karl Barth, *The Epistle to the Romans,* trans. E. C. Hoskyns, 6th ed. (London: Oxford

University Press, 1933), 42-91 — "By the law they [i.e., men/Jews] are placed under indictment, and are pronounced to be sinners in God's sight; . . . When this occurs, men hear the decision of the law, and understand themselves in the peculiarity of their experience and of their piety. Then it is that they hear the final truth, the truth of redemption and atonement" (90); Ernst Käsemann, *Commentary on Romans,* trans. Geoffrey W. Bromiley, 4th ed. (Grand Rapids, Mich.: Eerdmans, 1980 [1975]), 35-90 — "to bring out its world-embracing reality [i.e., salvation's], the apostle first proclaims its necessity. . . . The righteousness of God in its universal character can be grasped only when the world before and apart from Christ is seen under the wrath of God . . ." (35-36); Käsemann adds insightfully that ". . . missionary preaching should not and must not make God's wrath its starting point," but there are no reasons on the basis of what he has just said *not* to do this! See also Douglas Moo, *The Epistle to the Romans,* NICNT (Grand Rapids, Mich.: Eerdmans, 1996), 92-93.

5. This objective is also arguably stated earlier, in 3:9b, perhaps anticipated in 1:32, and its basis reiterated in 3:20: "'no human being will be justified in his sight' by deeds prescribed by the law."

6. A possible citation of Ps. 62:12/Prov. 24:12 (and perhaps Sir. 16:14); note also the immediate elaboration in vv. 7-8 and the statement that "the doers of the law . . . will be justified" in v. 13b.

7. It is difficult to locate the precise end of this subordinate stage of Paul's argument, a problem compounded by the rareness and ambiguity of the verb προεχόμεθα, in v. 9a. It is clear, however, that an argumentative transition takes place somewhere around v. 9.

8. The NRSV also provides an alternative here: "The one who is righteous through faith will live."

9. I have omitted a couple of others that are arguably apparent because they do not affect our analysis at this point.

10. Here following the NIV, "righteousness from God," which construes this important phrase's genitive in terms of authorship, as did Luther: see 1:17a; 3:21, 22. The NRSV supplies a subjective genitive, "righteousness of God," and so assimilates this motif to either vi or vii (depending on the exact connotation supplied for "righteousness"). Similarly, the NRSV speaks of "reckoning righteousness" in Romans 4, and the NIV of "crediting" it — different renderings of the verb λογίζομαι. The exact suitability of these different translation preferences will be assessed in detail in due course (see especially part four, chapters seventeen and eighteen).

11. This might also be related to *boasting:* see esp. 3:27; 4:2.

12. Again, different translation decisions would make this more or less explicit. It is a necessary inference from the construal of "the problem" as it is described in 1:18–3:20 that God's justice must be satisfied. δικαιοσύνη in 3:25-26 *may* then articulate this overtly, if it denotes God's "justice." The NIV is convinced of this; the NRSV, however, remains with "righteousness," indicating a reading more in terms of motif vii.

13. Although the verb in 3:21 is in the perfect tense (πεφανέρωται), the verb of revelation in 1:17 is in the present (as is the same verb in 1:18 — ἀποκαλύπτεται). Some temporal contrast therefore clearly seems intended, and most interpreters construe this as being in relation to the past and its problems, a theme just noted by Paul at some length. (See also the "sins previously committed" mentioned in 3:25.)

14. There is less unanimity among interpreters over the reckoning or crediting of Christ's perfect righteousness to the sinner. Certainly, most agree that the punishment due the sinner is dealt with by Christ's death; the sinner's penalty is thus credited to Christ. However, some Reformers urged that the crediting must also run in the opposite direction, "clothing" the sinner in Christ's perfection. This would make Christians not merely sinless but perfect in the eyes of God. It is not necessary to resolve the dispute at this point in our analysis. It need only be noted here that the dispute turns in these texts largely on the construal of the genitive in Paul's important phrase δικαιοσύνη Θεοῦ. This may be rendered in the first instance, as we have already indicated, as either "*of* God" or "*from* God." This question then links up with the discussion of Abraham in Rom. 4:1-8, and the significance of the verb λογίζομαι in Paul's argument (see §4 following). These texts will be interpreted in detail in part four, chapters seventeen and eighteen.

15. This notion departs specifically from the verb δικαιόω, which is present in participial form

in 3:24 and 26. The verb also occurs as a passive infinitive in 3:28 and as a future in 3:30 (which possibly also elides a second instance), giving a total of four (or five) instances in the immediate context. Romans 4:25 supplies an interesting possible variation on this, stating that Christ was "raised for our justification" (ἠγέρθη διὰ τὴν δικαίωσιν ἡμῶν), this last a rare cognate noun found only twice in Paul — or, for that matter, in the New Testament — the other instance being Rom. 5:18.

16. Arguably implicit here is the sense of mission in Paul's life that reaches out beyond traditional Jewish boundaries and through the world in spatial terms: "I am a debtor both to Greeks and to barbarians, both to the wise and to the foolish — hence my eagerness to proclaim the gospel to you also who are in Rome" (1:14-15 NRSV).

17. The NIV's translation is clearer in relation to these commitments if motif vi is present; the NRSV nuances the text more in the direction of vii, as we have already noted.

18. That is, the element of atonement is assumed to be addressed by a brief cluster of atonement terms present in 3:24-25 — "redemption," "sacrifice of atonement," and "blood," along with the clause "he had passed over the sins previously committed" (3:25c). Lying behind these translation decisions are the Greek terms ἀπολύτρωσις, ἱλαστήριον, αἷμα (although this is indubitably translated in the first instance as "blood"), and πάρεσις. And clearly much will eventually turn on their exact interpretation. Romans 4:25 speaks of Christ being "handed over to death for our trespasses." Support for this characterization of Christ's death elsewhere in Romans is comparatively rare: in 5:9, following two general references to Christ's death in vv. 6 and 8, his "blood" is spoken of again, and in 8:3 his death is described as atoning or as a sin offering — the Greek περὶ ἁμαρτίας can take either of these senses. See part four, chapter sixteen, for a more detailed analysis of these terms and phrases.

19. Translation decisions affect the emphases that Paul apparently places on different aspects of the process in these texts, but to my knowledge none of the conventional translation decisions can actually eliminate one of the identified motifs. As we have already noted, much turns on the rendering of δικαιοσύνη Θεοῦ. If this phrase is interpreted subjectively, then repeated references to God are involved as against an emphasis on imputed righteousness. If δικαιοσύνη is interpreted in retributive terms, then God's justice is being affirmed (vi); if it is nuanced more benevolently or salvifically, then that aspect of the process is being stressed (vii).

20. The gospel (and, by implication, Paul's apostolate) is mentioned in 1:16a, picking up the rarer cognate verb that functions centrally in the preceding verse. Elsewhere in Paul the gospel is supposedly often the object — even if only implicitly — of the verb "to believe" (see 1:16b and 3:22b; also 4:24-25). Intriguingly, Paul states at the beginning of v. 16 specifically that he is "not ashamed" of it. A popular way of integrating this last statement into the surrounding material is to view it as litotes; hence, in effect Paul is stating that he is proud of the gospel, and glories in it (see 5:2, 3, 5; 10:11; 15:17; see also 2:17; 11:13).

21. Numerous other allusions to scriptural texts and themes are arguably detectable, although the verification of such echoes remains a delicate matter. It is widely, although not universally, conceded that the *Shema* is alluded to in 3:30. There is a possible reference to Leviticus 16 in Paul's use of ἱλαστήριον in 3:25. Other echoes are arguable, for example, from Isa. 28:16b in relation to 1:16 (see Rom. 9:30 and 10:11; see also Isa. 45:15-17) and from Ps. 97:2-3 (LXX) in relation to the phrase δικαιοσύνη Θεοῦ (or its close equivalent). Adamic material, especially in its later Jewish development, could also be implicit in 3:23. And some detect Isaianic allusions in 4:25 (see Isa. 53:5-6). (This last verse of course follows directly on an extended discussion of Gen. 15:6.) These possible echoes do not need to be determined decisively here (the foregoing list contains seven); they suffice, in combination with the direct citation of and claims to scriptural warrant already noted, to establish the basic point that the thesis paragraphs in the Justification reading lay claim to the testimony of the Jewish Scriptures (ix). For a more detailed analysis, see part five, chapter nineteen.

22. The element of crediting righteousness to Christians is negotiable. And those of scriptural attestation, the gospel and Paul's apostolicity, and the temporality of this disclosure (as taking place "now"), are quite particular. The awkwardness of their integration with the universal assumptions of phase one in Justification theory has already been noted in chapter two.

23. Verses 13-22 are convoluted and tend to figure less centrally in most expositions. They are

generally read as a more detailed illustration of the nature of saving faith, although, for reasons that will become especially clear later on, that depiction should not be pressed too hard. Their role is generally subordinate to what precedes, as (i.a.) Dunn's account of "faith" in Paul at this point suggests: "... it is here [in 4:20] that Paul brings out most clearly the character of Abraham's faith. Gen 15:5-6 shows that Abraham's faith was nothing other and nothing more than trust in God's promise; it was not faithfulness; it was not covenant loyalty. The strength of Abraham's faith was precisely that it was unsupported by anything else; it was not something which Abraham could do. It was trust, simple trust, nothing but trust" (see James D. G. Dunn, *Romans 1-8*, WBC 38A [Dallas, Texas: Word, 1988], 225-41, esp. 236-39, quoting from 238). This is not really an accurate account of 4:13-22, which seems to emphasize that Abraham is doing something rather extraordinary; moreover, it cannot be spoken of either in simple terms or merely as "trust." Dunn also describes Abraham's trust as "helpless" (238) and "naked" (239, see v. 22). But these are not elements drawn from Paul's text.

24. Τί οὖν ἐροῦμεν εὑρηκέναι Ἀβραὰμ τὸν προπάτορα ἡμῶν κατὰ σάρκα.

25. Following here the NIV momentarily; the NRSV supplies a possible but less likely translation alternative: "What . . . are we to say was gained by Abraham . . . ?"

26. I will again follow the NIV in discussing vv. 1-8, because its use of "credit" to translate λογίζομαι is clearer than the NRSV's choice of the slightly archaic "reckon."

27. Reverting to the NRSV from this point.

28. So the NIV supplies — here probably wisely — "[those] who also walk in the footsteps of the faith that our father Abraham had before he was circumcised."

29. Paul has not spoken of "promise" explicitly since 1:2 and hence has not introduced it at all before now in the actual citadel text, Rom. 1:16–4:25. But it may be implicit in motif ix, scriptural attestation.

30. We do not yet need to decide whether this text draws on Isaianic material and/or is drawn from early church tradition.

31. And these judgments now qualify my opening remarks in this chapter concerning the complexity of Justification and the corresponding need for its articulation by a significant stretch of Scripture; as long as it is crystal-clear, the theory's scriptural articulation can be short.

32. And arguably, this would be impossible in any case.

33. The relatively few studies that offer alternative perspectives are considered in detail in chapter twelve.

34. See Robert Jewett, "Major Impulses in the Theological Interpretation of Romans since Barth," *Interpretation* 36 (1980): 17-31; A. J. M. Wedderburn, "'Like an Ever-Rolling Stream': Some Recent Commentaries on Romans," *Scottish Journal of Theology* 44 (1991): 367-80.

35. Joseph A. Fitzmyer accurately cites the most important up to ca. 1992: see *Romans: A New Translation with Introduction and Commentary,* AB 33 (New York: Doubleday, 1993), 191-214; to which some further important studies can now be added. A briefer survey is supplied by Ben Witherington III, with Darlene Hyatt, *Paul's Letter to the Romans: A Socio-Rhetorical Commentary* (Grand Rapids, Mich.: Eerdmans, 2004), xvi-xix.

36. Ulrich Wilckens, *Der Brief an die Römer,* vol. 1, *Römer 1-5,* 3 vols. (Zürich, Einsiedeln, Köln, & Neukirchen-Vluyn: Benziger & Neukirchener, 1978).

37. Käsemann's innovative suggestions are considered through part three, chapters eleven and twelve.

38. Karl Barth, *The Epistle to the Romans;* see also *Shorter Commentary on Romans* (Richmond, Va.: John Knox, 1959 [1956]). Barth's first major commentary is of course unusual. It pushes against the conventional reading in a number of ways, and yet also at times affirms it; so, for example, its characterization of the argument's structure is reasonably conventional (1:16-17 theme; 1:18-32 the Night; 2:1-29 the Righteousness of Men; 3:1-30 the Righteousness of God; 3:31–4:25 the voice of History [although this last is an especially creative suggestion]). The plight that humanity finds itself in at the end of this argument is also little more than an eloquent statement of the loop of despair — of "man who is terrified and hopes" (41): "We stand here before an irresistible and all-embracing dissolu-

tion of the world of time and things and men, before a penetrating and ultimate *krisis,* before the supremacy of a negation by which all existence is rolled up" (91).

39. Adolf Schlatter, *Romans: The Righteousness of God,* trans. Siegfried S. Schatzmann (Peabody, Mass.: Hendrickson, 1991 [1935]).

40. Walter Schmithals, *Der Römerbrief als historisches Problem* (Gütersloh: Mohn, 1975); *Der Römerbrief: Ein Kommentar* (Gütersloh: Mohn, 1988). See responses by A. J. M. Wedderburn, "Purpose and Occasion of Romans Again," in *The Romans Debate,* ed. K. P. Donfried (Peabody, Mass.: Hendrickson, 1991), 195-202; Neil Elliott, *The Rhetoric of Romans: Argumentative Constraint and Strategy and Paul's Dialogue with Judaism,* JSNTSup 45 (Sheffield: JSOT, 1990), 29-32; and Leander Keck, "What Makes Romans Tick?" in *Pauline Theology,* vol. 3, *Romans,* ed. David M. Hay & E. Elizabeth Johnson (Minneapolis, Minn.: Fortress, 1995), esp. 6-16.

41. See, i.a., Franz J. Leenhardt, *The Epistle to the Romans: A Commentary,* trans. Harold Knight (London: Lutterworth, 1961 [1957]).

42. C. E. B. Cranfield, *A Critical and Exegetical Commentary on the Epistle to the Romans,* vol. 1, *Introduction and Commentary on Romans I-VIII,* ICC, 2 vols. (Edinburgh: T&T Clark, 2004 [1975]); see also his *Romans: A Shorter Commentary* (Grand Rapids, Mich.: Eerdmans, 1985). Cranfield explicates the conventional reading quite thoroughly; Romans 3:21-26 is "the centre and heart of the whole of Rom. 1.16b–15.13" (*Shorter,* 68). His explication of Abraham in particular emphasizes the motif of boasting.

43. William Sanday and Arthur C. Headlam, *A Critical and Exegetical Commentary on the Epistle to the Romans,* ICC, 2nd ed. (Edinburgh: T&T Clark, 1902 [1st ed. 1896]).

44. James D. G. Dunn, *Romans 1-8;* and *Romans 9-16,* WBC 38B (Dallas, Texas: Word, 1988).

45. *The Epistle to the Romans;* anticipated by *Romans 1-8* (Chicago: Moody, 1991).

46. Thomas R. Schreiner, *Romans,* BECNT (Grand Rapids, Mich.: Baker, 1998). Schreiner is in dialogue with transformational and salvation-historical perspectives, but he endorses the conventional reading of Romans 1–4 and its endorsement in turn of Justification theory. Arguably, the latter approach tends to subordinate the former ones throughout.

47. Fitzmyer, *Romans.* Fitzmyer pushes against various commitments within the conventional reading at certain points: he denies that Paul is strictly committed to natural theology; he argues for an active and salvific understanding of God's "righteousness"; and he emphasizes the role of Christ's resurrection whenever Paul speaks of the Gospel. However, his division and basic construal of the overall argument by Paul is nevertheless conventional.

48. Brendan Byrne, *Romans,* Sacra Pagina 6 (Collegeville, Minn.: Michael Glazier [Liturgical Press], 1996).

49. *Conflict and Identity in Romans: The Social Setting of Paul's Letter* (Minneapolis, Minn.: Fortress, 2003).

50. Thomas H. Tobin, *Paul's Rhetoric in Its Contexts: The Argument of Romans* (Peabody, Mass.: Hendrickson, 2004).

51. *Romans.* Some interesting nuances are certainly apparent in Witherington's reading. Unfortunately, however, although he often points to more innovative work in the footnotes, he never introduces this material into either the main text or his basic exegetical exposition.

52. Robert Jewett, with Roy D. Kotansky, *Romans: A Commentary,* Hermeneia (Minneapolis, Minn.: Fortress, 2007).

53. As scholarly literature continues to proliferate and also move into digital form, it seems likely that the comprehensive commentary will fade. So this most comprehensive of all the commentaries on Romans may well remain the definitive example of this genre for the foreseeable future. See Dale Martin, "Lecture 2: Scripture as Sanctuary, Commentary as Hypertext," in *The Gustafson Lectures in Biblical Studies* (United Theological Seminary of the Twin Cities, Minnesota, Oct 18-19, 2004).

54. See especially — in relation to historical critical work on Paul — (and i.a.) Robert Jewett, *Paul's Anthropological Terms* (Leiden: Brill, 1971); *A Chronology of Paul's Life* (Philadelphia: Fortress, 1979); *The Thessalonian Correspondence: Pauline Rhetoric and Millenarian Piety* (Philadelphia: Fortress, 1986); "Tenement Churches and Communal Meals in the Early Church: The Implications of a

Form-Critical Analysis of 2 Thessalonians 3:10," *Biblical Research* 38 (1993): 23-43; and "Tenement Churches and Pauline Love Feasts," *Quarterly Review* 14 (1994): 43-58. And in dialogue with modern, principally North American culture: *Christian Tolerance: Paul's Message to the Modern Church* (Philadelphia: Westminster, 1982); *The Captain America Complex: The Dilemma of Zealous Nationalism,* 2nd ed. (Santa Fe, New Mexico: Bear & Company, 1984 [1973]); with John Shelton Lawrence, *The American Monomyth,* 2nd ed. (Lanham, Maryland: University Press of America, 1988 [1977]); *Saint Paul at the Movies: The Apostle's Dialogue with American Culture* (Louisville, Ky.: Westminster John Knox, 1993); *Saint Paul Returns to the Movies: Triumph over Shame* (Grand Rapids, Mich.: Eerdmans, 1999); with John Shelton Lawrence, *Captain America and the Crusade against Evil: The Dilemma of Zealous Nationalism* (Grand Rapids, Mich.: Eerdmans, 2003); and *Paul the Apostle to America: Cultural Trends and Pauline Scholarship* (Louisville, Ky.: Westminster John Knox, 2004).

55. Jewett is influenced by Dunn as he interprets Paul's Justification texts — especially where "works of law" and related attitudes by a Jew are addressed. Otherwise many of the difficulties that I see in the conventional interpretation of Paul's Justification texts remain unremarked on, and hence also unrebutted. Insofar as Jewett nuances Dunn's rereading strategy, he generates the same difficulties that Dunn does (and, as has already been noted, these are described in chapter twelve).

56. That is, I agree with many of Jewett's overarching theological and interpretative goals, and hold that the rereadings suggested here deliver those better than the conventional readings that he endorses in relation to Paul's Justification texts. Moreover, in my view these rereadings also integrate smoothly with most of his other interpretative suggestions concerning Romans and Paul — i.e., where the apostle's Justification texts are not being addressed. Perhaps they can be seen, then, as supplementing his broader commentary work at these points. (These suggestions are expanded in a paper presented at the Symposium, "The 2007 Hermeneia Commentary on Romans in the context of New Zealand Culture," at the International meeting of SBL in Auckland, New Zealand; July 6-10, 2008.)

57. Supporters of the reading might retort that this is because there is only one plausible reading; however, in view of the many problems the reading activates, such confidence seems misplaced (see esp. chapter eleven). It is also worth noting that the situation is very different when we turn to consider the scholarly work on Galatians, which offers numerous revisionist readings in learned commentaries, and yet presumably shares many motifs and arguments with Romans. This phenomenon is documented in more detail in part five, chapter twenty.

58. *The Epistle of Paul to the Romans* (London: Collins [Fontana], 1959 [1932]). Dodd reproduces the conventional reading very concisely, although he is certainly aware of some of its weak points — see especially his comment that the argument in 3:1-8 is "feeble" (46)!

59. See, i.a., J. A. T. Robinson, *Wrestling with Romans* (London: SCM, 1979) (both these scholars being attestations from an earlier generation of British scholarship).

60. *Commentary on Romans,* trans. C. C. Rasmussen (Philadelphia: Muhlenberg, 1949 [1944]).

61. John Ziesler, *Paul's Letter to the Romans* (London & Philadelphia: Trinity Press International, 1989).

62. Luke T. Johnson, *Reading Romans: A Literary and Theological Commentary* (New York: Crossroad, 1997).

63. *Romans: A Bible Commentary for Teaching and Preaching* (Louisville, Ky.: John Knox, 1985). Achtemeier also pushes against the conventional reading, however, suggesting that Paul's initial exposition begins in v. 14, vv. 14-23 being a long series of dependent clauses. He also emphasizes notions of covenant and gift and argues that the lordship of God in Jesus Christ is the theme of the letter more than 1:16-17 and "righteousness by faith" (the influence of Käsemann here, obviously). But his argumentative divisions are still in terms of the conventional reading; and conventional emphases on the universality of sin and judgment, on God's impartiality, and on the wrath of God are still evident.

64. To these endorsements of the conventional reading can be added other essentially conventional treatments: e.g., Charles H. Talbert, *Romans* (Macon, Ga.: Smyth & Helwys, 2002). Talbert is well aware of many of the pitfalls of Justification theory and a complementary approach to the interpretation of Romans 1-4, but he is unable to fight his way clear of all these implications in his actual exegesis.

65. Leander E. Keck, *Romans*, ANTC (Nashville, Tenn.: Abingdon Press, 2005).

66. Aletti has written a short commentary: see "Romans" in *The International Bible Commentary*, ed. William R. Farmer (Collegeville, Minn.: Liturgical, 1998), 1553-1600. He has also crafted a number of shorter, more specialized studies, along with one more extended treatment; of particular relevance in this relation are "Rm 1,18–3,20. Incohérence ou cohérence de l'argumentation paulinienne?" *Biblica* 69 (1988): 47-62; *Comment Dieu est-il juste? Clefs pour interpreter l'épître aux Romains* (Paris: Éditions du Seuil, 1990); "La présence d'un modèle rhétorique en Romains. Son role et son importance," *Biblica* 70 (1990): 1-24; "La dispositio rhétorique dans les Épîtres Pauliniennes," *New Testament Studies* 38 (1992): 385-401; "Comment Paul voit la justice de Dieu en Rom. Enjeux d'une absence de definition," *Biblica* 73 (1992): 359-75; "Romains 2. Sa cohérence et sa fonction," *Biblica* 77 (1996): 155-77; and *Israël et la Loi dans la lettre aux Romains* (Paris: Cerf, 1998).

67. *Paul's Letter to the Romans* (London: Penguin, 1975).

68. "The Letter to the Romans: Introduction, Commentary, and Reflections," in *The New Interpreter's Bible*, ed. L. Keck, 13 vols. (Nashville, Tenn.: Abingdon, 2002), 10:393-700. Wright acknowledges much of the conventional reading in Romans 1–4 but tends to *layer* this reading's endorsement of Justification theory with additional apocalyptic and salvation-historical perspectives. (We might say that for Wright it is seldom "one-or-the-other" in interpretative terms; it is usually "both-and.") He also shifts several key motifs semantically. Wright's work is thus an important example of a revisionist rereading of Romans 1–4. The success of this highly innovative reading is assessed in chapter twelve, although principally in relation to Dunn, whose key revisionist move he prompted.

69. Robert Morgan is strongly influenced by Käsemann, and hence his partial endorsements of the conventional reading and of Justification theory are the more significant; see *Romans*, New Testament Guide (Sheffield: Sheffield Academic Press, 1995).

70. Brendan Byrne, *Reckoning with Romans: A Contemporary Reading of Paul's Gospel* (Wilmington, Del.: Michael Glazier, 1986).

71. This interpretative trajectory has already been discussed in part one, chapters four and six, and is noted again in chapters twelve and thirteen. Especially important in this relation is D. A. Carson, Peter T. O'Brien, and Mark A. Seifrid, eds., *Justification and Variegated Nomism*, vol. 2, *The Paradoxes of Paul*, WUNT 181 (Tübingen & Grand Rapids, Mich.: Mohr Siebeck & Baker Academic, 2004) — a sustained instance of the conventional reading and Justification theory, with fulsome annotation. Richard H. Bell's treatment of 1:18–3:20 aligns with this trajectory as well: *No One Seeks for God: An Exegetical and Theological Study of Romans 1.18–3.20*, WUNT 106 (Tübingen: Mohr [Siebeck], 1998); it provides a wealth of information on this stretch of text.

72. Räisänen was, to a certain extent, an early representative on the Continent of Sanders: see *Paul and the Law*, 2nd ed., WUNT 29 (Tübingen: J. C. B. Mohr [Paul Siebeck], 1987 [1983]). And his protests have continued!: see *The Torah and Christ: Essays in German and English on the Problem of the Law in Early Christianity* (Helsinki: Finnish Exegetical Society, 1986); *Jesus, Paul and Torah: Collected Essays*, trans. D. E. Orton, JSNTSup 43 (Sheffield: JSOT, 1992). He elicited many responses, but was largely rejected; see esp. Hans Hübner, *Law in Paul's Thought*, ed. John Riches, trans. James C. G. Grieg (Edinburgh: T&T Clark, 1984). The new perspective, associated more with the suggestions of Dunn, has been discussed recently in German circles, but the debate is still in its infancy compared with the English-speaking analysis: see Michael Bachmann, ed., *Lutherische und Neue Paulusperspektive: Beiträge zu einem Schlüsselproblem der gegenwärtigen exegetischen Diskussion*, WUNT 182 (Tübingen: Mohr [Siebeck], 2005); see also J. D. G. Dunn, "Philippians 3.2-14 and the New Perspective on Paul," in *The New Perspective on Paul: Collected Essays* (Tübingen: Mohr Siebeck, 2005). This is apparent in the failure of most recent German theological treatments of Paul to respond to new perspective issues, as noted just below.

73. See esp. J. Reumann, with responses by Joseph A. Fitzmyer (and) Jerome D. Quinn, *"Righteousness" in the New Testament: "Justification" in the United States Lutheran–Roman Catholic Dialogue* (Philadelphia, Penn., New York, & Ramsey, New Jersey: Fortress & Paulist, 1982); see also his *Variety and Unity in New Testament Thought* (Oxford: Oxford University Press, 1991). Fitzmyer was the principal Catholic respondent and seems to have been largely persuaded by Reumann. A significant

shift toward conventional Justification readings and theory is evident from this point on in Fitzmyer's work.

74. J. Louis (Lou) Martyn is a significant exception: *Theological Issues in the Letters of Paul* (Edinburgh & Nashville: T&T Clark & Abingdon, 1997). His important commentary on Galatians is noted just below.

75. See esp. William S. Campbell, *Paul's Gospel in an Intercultural Context: Jew and Gentile in the Letter to the Romans* (New York, Bern, Frankfurt am Main, & Paris: Peter Lang, 1991). William Campbell is no friend of Justification theory but does not always avoid its endorsement. See also Arland J. Hultgren, *Paul's Gospel and Mission: The Outlook from His Letter to the Romans* (Philadelphia: Fortress, 1985); also *Christ and His Benefits: Christology and Redemption in the New Testament* (Philadelphia: Fortress, 1988) — emphatic endorsements of the conventional reading and Justification theory.

76. Rudolf Bultmann, *Theology of the New Testament,* trans. K. Grobel, 2 vols. (New York: Scribners, 1951, 1955).

77. See, i.a., Klaus Berger, *Theologiegeschichte des Urchristentums: Theologie des Neuen Testaments* (Tübingen: Francke, 1994); Ferdinand Hahn, *Theologie des Neuen Testaments,* 2 vols., 2nd ed. (Tübingen: Mohr Siebeck, 2001, 2005 [1st ed. 2002]); Hans Hübner, *Biblische Theologie des Neuen Testaments,* 3 vols. (Göttingen: Vandenhoeck & Ruprecht, 1990-93); Ulrich Wilckens, *Theologie des Neuen Testaments,* 4 vols. (Neukirchener-Vluyn: Neukirchener Verlag, 2002-5); Georg Strecker, *Theology of the New Testament,* trans. E. Boring (Louisville, Ky.: Westminster John Knox, 2000 [1996]); Joachim Gnilka, *Theologie des Neuen Testaments,* HTKNTSup 5 (Freiburg: Herder, 1994); and François Vouga, *Une théologie du nouveau testament* (Geneva: Labor et Fides, 2001).

In this relation, Rowe notes appositely that the German-speaking treatments, learned as they are, respond either minimally or not at all to new perspective questions and related issues in North American scholarship, like narrative: C. Kavin Rowe, "New Testament Theology: The Revival of a Discipline. A Review of Recent Contributions to the Field," *Journal of Biblical Literature* 125 (2006): 408-9. However, he does trace opposition to Bultmann's program through the work of Hahn, Wilckens, and Stuhlmacher.

78. Peter Stuhlmacher, *Biblische Theologie des Neuen Testaments,* vol. 1, *Grundlegung: Von Jesus zu Paulus,* 2 vols. (Göttingen: Vandenhoeck & Ruprecht, 1991); Paul is treated on 221-392.

79. Udo Schnelle, *Apostle Paul: His Life and Theology,* trans. M. Eugene Boring (Grand Rapids, Mich.: Baker, 2005 [2003]).

80. H. Ridderbos, *Paul: An Outline of His Theology,* trans. J. R. de Witt (Grand Rapids, Mich., & London: Eerdmans & SPCK, 1997 [1966]).

81. T. Engberg-Pedersen has already been noted (in part two, chapter nine), and is unusual in the degree to which he is conversant and interacts with North American scholarship. He is of course supportive of a basic approach to Paul in terms of Justification: see *Paul and the Stoics* (Edinburgh: T&T Clark, 2000).

82. J.-Christiaan Beker, *Paul the Apostle: The Triumph of God in Life and Thought* (Philadelphia: Fortress, 1984 [1980]).

83. D. E. H. Whiteley, *The Theology of St. Paul,* 2nd ed. (Oxford: Oxford University Press, 1974 [1964]).

84. *The Theology of Paul the Apostle* (Edinburgh & Grand Rapids, Mich.: T&T Clark & Eerdmans, 1998).

85. Thomas R. Schreiner, *Paul, Apostle of God's Glory in Christ: A Pauline Theology* (Downers Grove, Ill. & Leicester: InterVarsity Academic & Apollos, 2001); see esp. chs. 5-9, 103-249.

86. Gordon D. Fee, *Pauline Christology: An Exegetical-Theological Study* (Peabody, Mass.: Hendrickson, 2007).

87. See George Eldon Ladd, *A Theology of the New Testament,* ed. D. Hagner, rev. ed. (Grand Rapids, Mich.: Eerdmans, 1993 [1974]); G. B. Caird, *New Testament Theology,* ed. L. D. Hurst (Oxford: Clarendon, 1994); I. Howard Marshall, *New Testament Theology: Many Witnesses, One Gospel* (Downers Grove, Ill.: InterVarsity, 2004); Philip F. Esler, *New Testament Theology: Communion and*

Community (Minneapolis, Minn.: Fortress, 2005); and Frank Thielman, *Theology of the New Testa-ment: A Canonical and Synthetic Approach* (Grand Rapids, Mich.: Zondervan, 2005). These studies are canvassed insightfully by Rowe, "New Testament Theology," 402-5, 409; who also rightly includes Brevard S. Childs in the conversation: see *Biblical Theology of the Old and New Testaments: Theologi-cal Reflection on the Christian Bible* (Minneapolis, Minn.: Fortress, 1992). Childs endorses Justification in relation to Paul at points, although reluctantly: see esp. ch. five, "Reconciliation with God," 485-529.

88. Michael J. Gorman's recent revisionist suggestions should not be overlooked; he is pushing in important new directions that are generally compatible with my analysis: see *Cruciformity: Paul's Narrative Spirituality of the Cross* (Grand Rapids, Mich.: Eerdmans, 2001); *Apostle of the Crucified Lord: A Theological Introduction to Paul and His Letters* (Grand Rapids, Mich.: Eerdmans, 2004), 115-45; and esp. "Justification by Crucifixion: The Logic of Paul's Soteriology" (paper presented to the Pauline Soteriology Group, SBL Annual Meeting, Washington, D.C., 21st Nov., 2007). Neil Elliott is rather different in his approach as well, but tends to use marginalizing strategies based on causal or generative factors (see more in this relation in chapter twelve): see *Liberating Paul: The Justice of God and the Politics of the Apostle* (Maryknoll, New York: Orbis, 1994).

89. See (i.a.) Marion Soards, *The Apostle Paul: An Introduction to His Writings and Teachings* (New York: Paulist, 1987); Leander Keck, *Paul and His Letters*, rev. ed. (Minneapolis: Fortress, 1988); Joseph A. Fitzmyer, *Pauline Theology: A Brief Sketch*, 2nd ed. (Englewood Cliffs, New Jersey: Prentice Hall, 1989); John Ziesler, *Pauline Christianity*, rev. ed. (Oxford & New York: Oxford University Press, 1990); E. P. Sanders, *Paul*, Past Masters (Oxford: Oxford University Press, 1991); Charles B. Cousar, *The Letters of Paul* (Nashville, Tenn.: Abingdon, 1996); and David Horrell, *An Introduction to the Study of Paul* (London & New York: Continuum, 2000).

90. See (i.a.) Robert A. Spivey and D. Moody Smith, *Anatomy of the New Testament: A Guide to Its Structure and Meaning*, 5th ed. (Upper Saddle River, New Jersey: Prentice Hall, 1995 [1969]); Ray-mond E. Brown, *An Introduction to the New Testament* (New York: Doubleday, 1997); Luke Timothy Johnson, assisted by Todd C. Penner, *The Writings of the New Testament: An Interpretation*, rev. ed. (Minneapolis, Minn.: Fortress, 1999); Delbert Burkett, *An Introduction to the New Testament and the Origins of Christianity* (Cambridge: Cambridge University Press, 2002); and Bruce M. Metzger, *The New Testament: Its Background, Growth, and Content*, 3rd rev. ed. (Nashville, Tenn.: Abingdon, 2003 [1965]).

91. See (i.a.) Hans Dieter Betz, "Paul," *ABD* 5:186-201, esp. 196-97; Alister E. McGrath, "Justifi-cation," *DP&L*, 517-23; (indicatively) J. D. G. Dunn, "Romans, Letter to the," *DP&L*, 838-50, esp. 844-46; and G. L. Borchert, "Wrath, Destruction," *DP&L*, 991-93.

92. And this survey could of course be extended much further, to examples of preaching, pop-ular teaching and teaching aids, popular books, and programs. The history and church-historical ex-tent of this reading has already been considered in chapter nine.

93. The NRSV in *The New Oxford Annotated Bible* (New York: Oxford University Press, 1991) introduces Romans (NT, 208) in the following way: "The gospel as God's power for salvation to all who believe is the theme of Romans (see 1.16-17 n.). It is expressed especially in terms of God's saving righteousness, or justification by faith (see 3.24 n.), and with a universal concern for both Jew and Gentile (note the frequent use of 'all' and 'every' 1.16; 3.9, 19, 23-24; 4.11, 16; 5.12, 18)." The note on 1.16-17 (NT, 209) states the theme of the letter thus: "In Christ God has acted powerfully to save *Jew* and *Gentile*, offering righteousness and life, to be received in faith. 17: *The righteousness of God* originates in the divine nature (3.5) acting to effect pardon or acceptance with God, a relationship that is not a human achievement but God's gift. *Through faith for faith*, faith is the sole condition of salvation" (emphasis original). The *New Oxford Annotated Bible* is nuanced, and by no means a conservative study edition, but it still makes overt concessions here to the dominance of Justification theory.

94. Wheaton, Ill.: Tyndale House Publishers, 1996 (1988). The *Life Application Study Bible* de-scribes Justification theory, articulated by the opening five chapters of Romans, as the "foundation" of the gospel (a repeated characterization of the reading and theory), beginning with "an airtight case for the lostness of humanity and the necessity for God's intervention (1:18–3:20)," after which "Paul pre-sents the Good News" (1763). This edition also sets out five "Megathemes" for the letter, the first two

of which — Sin and Salvation — adumbrate Justification theory in relation to Romans 1–4, and the second two of which — Growth and Sovereignty — are explicitly subordinated to the first two through the addition of conditions. In relation to Growth and the message of chapters 5–8, "By trusting in the Holy Spirit and allowing him to help us, we can overcome sin and temptation," and, in relation to Sovereignty and the message of chapters 9–11, "Because of God's mercy, both Jews and Gentiles can be saved. We all must respond to his mercy and accept his gracious offer of forgiveness" (1764). (Intriguingly, on 1767, despite a continued emphasis on faith, a synergist solution is urged strongly as well: faith is a gift given by God, the notes advise in relation to 1:16-17.)

95. *The HarperCollins Study Bible,* which also uses the NRSV, is a partial exception (New York: Harper Collins, 1993). The introductory comments to Romans — by Leander E. Keck — are nuanced and balanced.

96. In the Romans Through History and Cultures series, see esp. Daniel Patte and Cristina Grenholm, eds., *Reading Israel in Romans: Legitimacy and Plausibility of Divergent Interpretations* (Harrisburg, Pa.: Trinity Press International, 2000); Daniel Patte and Eugene Teselle, eds., *Engaging Augustine on Romans: Self, Context, and Theology in Interpretation* (Harrisburg, Pa.: Trinity Press International, 2003); Yeo Khiok-khng (K. K.), ed., *Navigating Romans through Cultures: Challenging Readings by Charting a New Course* (London: T&T Clark International [Continuum], 2004); Daniel Patte and Cristina Grenholm, eds., *Gender, Tradition and Romans: Shared Ground, Uncertain Borders* (London: T&T Clark International [Continuum], 2005); and Kathy L. Gaca and L. L. Welborn, eds., *Early Patristic Readings of Romans* (London & New York: T&T Clark International [Continuum], 2005). This group has other agendas; it is in large measure struggling against monovalent and historical-critical readings. Despite some shortcomings in relation to Romans 1–4, many of the hermeneutical assertions of the group are important and will be echoed in what follows.

97. David M. Hay and E. Elizabeth Johnson, eds., *Pauline Theology,* vol. 3, *Romans* (Minneapolis: Fortress, 1995). In chapter six, "From Wrath to Justification: Tradition, Gospel, and Audience in the Theology of Romans 1:18–4:25," Andrew Lincoln strongly reasserts the conventional reading of Romans 1–4 and its link with Justification theory (130-59). Douglas Moo, in chapter eleven, "The Theology of Romans 9–11: A Response to E. Elizabeth Johnson," does the same in relation to Romans 9–11 (240-58). Lincoln's piece is an excellent compressed articulation of just the issues that I am targeting throughout this chapter and book.

98. David M. Hay and E. Elizabeth Johnson, eds., *Pauline Theology,* vol. 4, *Looking Back, Pressing On* (Atlanta, Georgia: Scholars Press, 1997). This volume principally explores, in specific terms, the "faith of Christ" debate, a suggestion we will address at length at the appropriate time (primarily, part four, chapters fifteen and sixteen, although some of the key pieces of evidence are introduced from chapter eleven on, and the debate itself has already been noted in chapter six; and part five, chapters twenty and twenty-one). It also collects various opinions about the shape and nature of Paul's theology, within which Dunn's advocacy — in large measure — of Justification theory is notable: "In Quest of Paul's Theology: Retrospect and Prospect" (*Pauline Theology,* 95-115).

99. Much of the impetus for this reinterpretative trajectory was catalyzed by the work of classicists on the imperial cult: see, i.a., S. R. F. Price, *Rituals and Power: The Roman Imperial Cult in Asia Minor* (Cambridge: Cambridge University Press, 1984). Richard A. Horsley then championed the approach in Pauline circles, although he has been supported by many other scholars: see ed., *Paul and Empire* (Harrisburg, Pa.: Trinity Press International, 1997); ed., *Paul and Politics: Ekklesia, Israel, Imperium, Interpretation* (Harrisburg, Pa.: Trinity Press International, 2000); and ed., *Paul and the Roman Imperial Order* (London & Harrisburg, Pa.: Trinity Press International [Continuum], 2004).

100. Volumes that coordinate collections of studies on Romans are highly indicative as well. The dominance of the conventional reading — although admittedly in varying degree — is apparent in (i.a.) L. Ann Jervis and Peter Richardson, eds., *Gospel in Paul: Studies on Corinthians, Galatians and Romans for Richard N. Longenecker,* JSNTSup 108 (Sheffield: JSOT, 1994); Sven K. Soderlund and N. T. Wright, eds., *Romans and the People of God: Essays in Honor of Gordon D. Fee on the Occasion of His 65th Birthday* (Grand Rapids, Mich.: Eerdmans, 1999); and Sheila E. McGinn, ed., *Celebrating Romans: Template for Pauline Theology: Essays in Honor of Robert Jewett* (Grand Rapids, Mich.:

Eerdmans, 2004). Most important, however, is Karl Donfried, ed., *The Romans Debate,* rev. ed. (Peabody, Mass.: Hendrickson, 1991 [1977]). This famous volume, as its title suggests, embodies the Romans debate. However, even in this collection it is possible to discern much defense of the conventional reading and of Justification theory, along with a rather scattered set of alternatives that often seem at cross-purposes. We will frequently revisit the agenda of this volume in what follows, in relation to its theological, structural, and historical concerns.

Notes to Chapter Eleven

1. Recalling that a textual underdetermination will usually correspond to a theoretical overdetermination, because if the scriptural text does not explicitly suggest something that the theory needs, the theory will nevertheless usually assert that this has been suggested, perhaps even arguing that this is obvious.

2. Textual under- and overdeterminations from Justification texts outside the textual citadel will be noted in due course, in part five, chapters nineteen to twenty-one. Possible circumstantial difficulties will be discussed in part four, chapter thirteen.

3. It will be simplest to treat 4:23-25 as part of Romans 4 for the moment. In due course we will assess its textual relationships more precisely — primarily in part four, chapter eighteen. In what follows I will lean primarily on the following commentaries and studies in commentary form.

In my experience, the relatively recent, weighty conservative commentaries tend to state the issues especially clearly; they are attuned closely to both the text and the theological issues, and engage vigorously with revisionist suggestions. So they will be emphasized in what follows — notably, Douglas Moo, *The Epistle to the Romans,* NICNT (Grand Rapids, Mich.: Eerdmans, 1996); and Thomas R. Schreiner, *Romans,* BECNT (Grand Rapids, Mich.: Baker, 1998). As was noted in the Introduction, Robert Jewett's analysis is especially rich in documentation and insight: (with Roy D. Kotansky), *Romans: A Commentary,* Hermeneia (Minneapolis, Minn.: Fortress, 2007). C. E. B. Cranfield remains largely unsurpassed in his articulation of alternatives and reasoned assessments (although they are sometimes a little brief!). And his recent essays are often important: see *A Critical and Exegetical Commentary on the Epistle to the Romans,* vol. 1, *Introduction and Commentary on Romans I–VIII,* ICC (London: T&T Clark International [Continuum], 2004 [1975]); and *On Romans, and Other New Testament Essays* (Edinburgh: T&T Clark, 1998). James D. G. Dunn is a well-known exponent of a revisionist perspective on "works of law," but also often reproduces conventional viewpoints: see *Romans 1–8,* WBC 38A (Dallas, Texas: Word, 1988). Thomas H. Tobin is sensitive to diatribal issues — a vital interpretative dimension in Romans: see *Paul's Rhetoric in Its Contexts: The Argument of Romans* (Peabody, Mass.: Hendrickson, 2004), esp. 104-54. Leander E. Keck is especially sensitive to questions of apocalyptic — also a vital dimension: see *Romans,* Abingdon New Testament Commentaries (Nashville, Tenn.: Abingdon Press, 2005). Other commentaries and studies will of course be utilized when it is appropriate.

4. As Moo puts it: "We must consider 1:18–3:20 as a preparation for . . . the gospel of God's righteousness . . . a necessary preparation if what Paul wants to emphasize about this righteousness is to be accepted by the Romans. For only if sin is seen to be the dominating, ruling force that Paul presents it to be in this section . . . will it become clear why God's righteousness can be experienced only by humbly receiving it as a gift — in a word, by faith. . . . And only if Jews as much as Gentiles are understood to be subject to this imprisoning effect of sin will it become clear that all people need to experience this righteousness of God" (*Romans,* 92; see also 176-77). The questions begged by this explanation will be further clarified shortly.

5. Antoinette Clark Wire elaborates this point precisely: "In questions, answers and wishes *gar* may have the adverbial sense of 'in fact', 'indeed', but when appearing as the second word in declarative sentences it is a causal coordinating conjunction that offers a reason for or an explanation of a preceding statement": see "'Since God Is One': Rhetoric as Theology and History in Paul's Romans," in *The New Literary Criticism and the New Testament,* ed. Elizabeth Struthers Malbon and Edgar V.

McKnight, JSNTSup 109 (Sheffield: Sheffield Academic Press, 1994), 210-27 (quoting here from 212). However, these claims are an object lesson in the dangers of applying grammatical rules too rigorously. Paul's actual usage does not conform *precisely* to these norms, although it conforms *in large measure*. And for the argument from the presence of the particle to hold — that it denotes an explanation if not a cause in a declarative setting — it must *always* function predictably. (I will suggest an alternative reading here in chapter fourteen.)

6. γάρ can just be clarifying (BDAG, mng 2, 189-90) — "for," "you see." The emphatic sense of "certainly," "by all means," "indeed," or with an allied connotation of inference — "so" or "then" — is usually in conclusions, exclamations, questions, etc., where the point is obvious. (Intriguingly, the NIV treats it as pleonastic; the NRSV uses "for.") There is plenty of evidence from the rest of the immediate argument that demonstrates that Paul can use γάρ in a minimal and/or non-inferential fashion. For blander uses, see Rom. 1:9; probably 1:16 (because the explanation or ground for Paul's desire to preach the gospel in Rome as expressed in vv. 13 and 15 is v. 14, as the initial οὕτως of v. 15 confirms; it therefore probably does not spring from the absence of shame denoted by v. 16, which seems to have an alternative explanation in Romans in any case); 1:17 (because the saving power of God is probably not *caused* by God's "righteousness," but is a parallel or even the same action); probably 2:11 (because it is unlikely that God's impartiality *grounds* the preceding discussing of the eschaton in terms of desert), and 2:14 (because the evidence of natural knowledge of the law in pagans does not *ground* their judgment by desert); certainly 2:12, 24, 25, and 28 (probably clarifying); 3:3; possibly 3:9b (where it indicates a slightly new line of argument rather than grounding the brief preceding conclusion to the diatribal dialogue); and possibly 3:20b (which could clarify or denote inference).

Cranfield also makes an important suggestion — that an adversative γάρ signals an unexpressed "no" in a dialogical text (*Romans I-VIII*, 106), citing the support of Lagrange, Moffatt, and Dodd; see also LSJ, mng Id (338) — and this could be a particularly apposite reading.

7. The detection of this strategy also seems to have been a particular concern of the later church, Melanchthon being a nice example: see part two, chapter eight. More recently, Mark Seifrid has argued for a slightly different characterization of the text at this point, intending thereby to blunt a plight-to-solution characterization along with its problems. He speaks of Paul *proclaiming* the solution and the plight, the latter being an acknowledgment implicit in the former: "Unrighteous by Faith: Apostolic Proclamation in Romans 1:18–3:20," in *Justification and Variegated Nomism*, vol. 2, *The Paradoxes of Paul*, ed. D. A. Carson, P. T. O'Brien, and Mark A. Seifrid (Tübingen: Mohr Siebeck, 2004), 105-45, drawing here esp. from 105-7. And on one level this is exactly right; an apocalyptic construal of Paul's gospel does recognize a plight in the light of the solution. But Seifrid does not succeed in integrating his programmatic claims with a plausible rereading of the text. He lapses back frequently into the conventional construal (see, e.g., 120, 121, 124, 127, 132), which *must* be construed as a preparatory argument, thereby imparting a contradictory aspect to his recommendations. See, e.g., his early claim that Paul's "opening announcement of the gospel . . . is not *comprehensible* apart from his *subsequent* diagnosis of the human condition" (105, emphases added). It is hard to tell in the first instance what "subsequent" here means. If it denotes the mere order of discussion in Romans, then Seifrid has just endorsed the conventional reading, which he immediately denies doing. But if — more likely — it denotes the epistemological place of this diagnosis, subsequent to the announcement of the gospel and implicit in it, then the claim that the gospel is incomprehensible without it does not seem valid. Some of Seifrid's ensuing sentences then do not clarify matters. He goes on to claim that the announcement of the gospel "implicitly urges the acknowledgement of the human state which he (Paul) subsequently describes" — a retrospective, apocalyptic, and in my view, correct claim. But in the preceding sentence Seifrid states that Paul's "proclamation [of the gospel] *presupposes* the human 'plight' which it addresses" (105, emphasis added), which seems to be the opposite claim. Is Paul's analysis of the plight of humankind a presupposition of the gospel, or its consequence? It cannot be both at once. Moreover, if it is the former, then this is the conventional reading, with all its problems. If it is the latter, then Seifrid must show us how to read Paul's argument in this unconventional way, and not merely suggest that it means this in general terms. Having said this, to his credit, Seifrid insightfully identifies the main target of Paul's attack — a Hellenistic wisdom discourse (128-30, 36, 42-43). Unfortunately, he

tends to develop this directly into the conventional reading and Justification theory without solving the further problems thereby raised — in particular, the textual underdeterminations, and the theoretical and empirical difficulties caused by this universalization. Hence, there is much to learn from his intriguing analysis, but it falls short of being a coherent overarching interpretation.

8. Especially important of course is the fundamental divine nature in view — retributive or benevolent — because it will prove determinative for all that follows. See, e.g., Moo, *Romans*, 99, 101, 111, 276.

9. See Ulrich Wilckens, "ὑποκρίνομαι κ.τ.λ.," in *TDNT* 8:559-71.

10. Respecting the grammar of the text here and following.

11. Stowers observes that any diatribal expectations would usually encode this figure with foolish qualities: "Boasting forms the hallmark of the *alazôn* in the Hellenistic ethological tradition": *Rereading Romans: Justice, Jews, and Gentiles* (New Haven: Yale University Press, 1994), 101: see also 100-9 — hereafter *RR*.

12. Tobin identifies here a "discrepancy between the addressee's claim to have a higher morality and the reality of the addressee's practice . . . [i.e.] hypocrisy": *Paul's Rhetoric*, 111. There are important dissident voices, however: Francis Watson notes the advocacy of an indefinite identification by Barrett, Leenhardt, Franzmann, Pregeant, Wright (to a degree), and Dahl: see *Paul, Judaism, and the Gentiles*, rev. ed. (Grand Rapids, Mich.: Eerdmans, 2007), 197, n. 11 — hereafter *PJ&G²*. And quite different, more generalizing interpretations are apparent in some of the church fathers: see Gerald Bray, and Thomas C. Oden, ed., *Ancient Christian Commentary on Scripture: New Testament VI: Romans* (Downers Grove, Ill.: InterVarsity, 1998), 50-54. Chrysostom applies the rhetorical turn to "rulers," and Pelagius to "judges and princes" (50). However, these readings are difficult to sustain in exegetical terms.

To these figures we could add the brilliant advocacy of a Stoic identification by Diana Swancutt, developing the earlier views of Elliott and Stowers: see "Sexy Stoics and the Rereading of Romans 1.18–2.16," in *A Feminist Companion to Paul*, ed. A.-J. Levine, Feminist Companion to the New Testament and Early Christian Writings (Cleveland, Ohio: Pilgrim, 2004), 42-73; Neil Elliott, *The Rhetoric of Romans: Argumentative Constraint and Strategy and Paul's Dialogue with Judaism*, JSNTSup 45 (Sheffield: JSOT, 1990), 119-27; Stowers, *RR*, 100-42. I argue in what follows (and in part four, chapter fourteen) that they are right to resist the negative implications concerning Judaism *and* to point to the weaknesses of the conventional reading, but wrong to deny the similarities between the two figures.

13. I am not convinced that those who deny this correlation, have responded adequately to this evidence — viz., Swancutt, et al. Keck's response is intriguing. He correctly denies that Paul is targeting a Jew from 2:1 onward, but then reasons incorrectly that this figure must therefore be someone else — in fact, a continuation, presumably, of the indicted pagans of 1:18-32 in some sense, a "judger": "To regard this judge as a Jew who finds Gentile immorality repugnant, as is often claimed, is to miss a significant part of the argument . . ." (*Romans*, 75).

14. The sustainability of both this set of identifications and this construal of the argument will be detailed in part four, chapter fourteen. But the conventional reading largely assumes them as well.

15. See part one, chapters four and five; part three, chapter ten; and part four, chapter fourteen.

16. This claim should also be largely self-evident by now, but to recapitulate the case briefly: Justification theory requires Judaism to channel everyone to Christianity (the failure of Judaism *creating the very need for Christianity and its offer of salvation through faith alone*), but to collapse itself in the process (thereby explaining the relationship between the two dispensations, the two testaments, the law-free mission, and so on). Hence, it is committed to a necessary prior construction of Judaism that is inherently valid, takes a certain shape, but is also unstable and unsustainable. It follows necessarily that Paul himself is part of this dynamic. He describes it theologically and experienced it biographically. See part one, esp. chapters one, four, and five.

17. A struggle with the nature and definition of Judaism becomes apparent in 2:28–3:1, when Paul speaks of a Jew praised by God for secret virtue rather than mere appearance, and then of the advantage or benefit of the Jew and of circumcision. But by this point in the argument, with the interloc-

utor involved either querulously (if he is speaking 3:1) or combatively and defensively (if he is responding in 3:2), it is difficult to tell if Paul is engaging with the interlocutor's characterization of Judaism rather than his own. Certainly that position is strongly manipulated in 2:25-3:9a! And some rather shocking claims are made by Paul, if he is in fact articulating his own definition of Judaism (see more just below, esp. OD 11). It is also unwise simply to identify the marker "circumcision" with a discussion of "Judaism." Although the ritual could function metonymically in this fashion, it could also denote many other things as well (see esp. part four, chapter fourteen).

18. Moo suggests the Jewish identity of this figure is "clear": *Romans*, 126. Gathercole states simply ". . . most scholars note, the interlocutor is not an isolated individual, but a representative of the nation, or the Jew *qua* Jew. . . . [He is] a Jewish compatriot . . . [identified with] the whole Jewish nation . . . [i.e.] 'stiff-necked'": "Justified by Faith, Justified by His Blood: The Evidence of Romans 3:21-4:25," in *Variegated Nomism*, vol. 2, *The Paradoxes of Paul*, ed. D. A. Carson, P. T. O'Brien, and Mark A. Seifrid (Tübingen: Mohr Siebeck, 2004), 147-84, quoting from 149. He also cites Dunn to this effect: "[He is] the typical Jew . . . that is, the Jew per se": *Romans 1-8*, 109. Gathercole then later asserts, in relation to 4:1-8, "It is vital to recognize that here Paul in Romans 4 is not directly addressing the concerns of 'Judaizers.' Rather, he is expressing his position in relation to Second Temple Judaism" (160). Andrew Lincoln concurs: "the attitudes depicted [in 2:1-5, 17-23, 25, 27] . . . are characteristic of Judaism": "From Wrath to Justification: Tradition, Gospel, and Audience in the Theology of Romans 1:18-4:25," in David M. Hay and E. Elizabeth Johnson, eds., *Pauline Theology*, vol. 3, *Romans* (Minneapolis: Fortress, 1995), 130-68, quoting from 133. Cranfield pushes the Jewish identity of Paul's target into 1:18-32!: *Romans I-VIII*, 105-6; see also 138-39.

19. Gordon D. Fee gives a pithy explication of this view, oblivious to its problems, while building toward his reading of the Spirit in 2:29: see *God's Empowering Presence: The Holy Spirit in the Letters of Paul* (Peabody, Mass.: Hendrickson, 1994), 492. See also Moo, *Romans*, 127, 151, 206.

20. The conviction that Paul treats pagans and Jews with a basic similarity and equality in relation to Christ — repudiated only by non-Christian Jews and advocates of a dual covenant schema — is probably correct; however, it begs the question to assert that such soteriological equality must be established *prior* to Christ (i.e., in the individual pagan and Jewish journey to salvation, as supposedly discussed by 1:18-3:20). In fact, the alternative soteriology of Romans 5-8 provides extensive indicators that the solidarity of pagan and Jew is explained, for Paul, by a narrative based on Adam (see 5:12-21; 7:7-25; 11:32) and hence is located elsewhere, both textually and theologically. Most importantly, the discernment of this equality seems to be retrospective, in direct contradiction to any assertion of its a priori, prospective location.

21. It might be replied that this is an exegetical claim; the later exegesis of Rom. 3:21-4:25 establishes that justification and salvation are obviously "through faith alone," and this reading then implies a construal of the earlier argument in preparatory and universal terms. But the problem with this rejoinder will turn out to be the fragility of this set of claims once the conventional reading of Romans 1-3 has been called into question. The conventional construal of Romans 3-4 will turn out to be even more dependent on the prior conventional construal of Romans 1-3 than vice versa.

22. Some Jewish texts speak of perfection, or of complete law observance, but this is invariably counterbalanced by compensatory mechanisms — means of atonement and restoration, and also direct ethical assistance toward perfection. At Qumran, the covenanters — at least in some texts — were elected to salvation, and assisted in perfect law observance by the Spirit of Light, thereby overcoming the evil inclination. It is precisely the absence of such mechanisms, making a very harsh initial requirement, that creates the difficulties for Justification theory. See part one, chapter four.

23. We have already shown, in part one, chapter four, how few commentators make this key Justification axiom explicit. And it can be seen now — compounding the problem — that the textual justifications for this introduction are slight indeed. Moo emphasizes it, although in tandem with other explanations — ". . . only a *perfect* doing of the law would suffice to justify a person before God" (*Romans*, 156, emphasis original; see also 156-57, 158, 168, 217). Cranfield spends much time denying that "works" need to be perfect (*Romans I-VIII*, 147, 73), but then affirms the point (198)!

24. Moo clearly advocates this position (as well!): see *Romans*, 155, 215; see also Schreiner, *Romans*, esp. 164-69.

25. A charge that Stendahl and those persuaded by him would presumably echo enthusiastically: see part one, chapter six.

26. To make a valid claim about the corruption of the human mind in advance of its transformation — i.e., *with* a corrupt mind — is clearly incoherent. This claim can certainly be made in retrospect, however — and in terms of Christian orthodoxy, probably ought to be ("I was blind, but now I see"). See esp. Alan J. Torrance's insights noted already in part one, chapter one, §1.4, n. 10 (ultimately derived from Karl Barth, esp. *CD* I.1).

27. The other alternative is to relax law observance to a reasonable level; however, this destroys the basic function of the argument, which is to prepare everyone to become a Christian. If accepted, there will be numerous exceptions to the theory's basic dynamic — those who are confident that they have fulfilled the reasonable demands of the law and so do not feel the argument's pinch by 3:19-20. By the theory's own admission, then, many Jews and pagans will not need to embrace Christ through faith. But however attractive this reformulation might be on some grounds (some of which can even arguably be found in the text), the systematic framing difficulties in Paul are immediately acute, to mention only one serious problem. Paul never really suggests or implies that Christ is optional — although see OD 10.

28. Moo couldn't be clearer: see *Romans*, 64. Cranfield speaks of "the centre and heart of the whole of Romans 1:16b–15:13": *Romans I–VIII*, 199; see also 87, 108. Stuhlmacher characterizes 3:21-26 simply as the "Definition seines Evangeliums" and hence the "Herzstück des Römerbrief" (*Römer*, 54).

29. So, correctly, D. Moody Smith: "The broader context . . . cannot be determinative for exegesis unless one has already decided that vss. 16f., and especially the Habakkuk quotation, constitute a distinct and intentionally programmatic as well as a thematic statement — a conclusion we have found reason to question": see "'Ο ΔΕ ΔΙΚΑΙΟΣ ΕΚ ΠΙΣΤΕΩΣ ΖΗΣΕΤΑΙ," in *Studies in the History and Text of the New Testament in Honor of Kenneth Willis Clark*, Boyd L. Daniels and M. Jack Suggs eds. (Salt Lake City, Utah: University of Utah, 1967), 13-25, quoting from 17. Smith also sensibly integrates 1:16-17 into the letter's thanksgiving (i.e., 1:8-15).

30. I am not excluding temporary, provisional, and psychological circles of interpretation at this point; my concerns here are ultimately methodological and exegetical.

31. The phrase, and its complex surrounding debate, is discussed in more detail in part three, chapter twelve, and part four, chapter seventeen. Its reinterpretation is an avenue explored more by revisionists, who are discussed in the following chapter, and I offer my own views in relation to my detailed rereading of the thesis paragraphs in chapter seventeen. Moo (again) couldn't be clearer: see *Romans*, 70. A classic statement of this reading is Adolf Schlatter, *Romans: The Righteousness of God*, trans. S. Schatzmann (Peabody, Mass.: Hendrickson, 1995 [1935]), esp. 19-24.

Ulrich Wilckens is an important commentator fully aware of the difficulties inherent in a retributive reading of the phrase. His subtle exegetical solutions ultimately fail to convince — largely because he feels forced to reproduce the bulk of the conventional reading of Romans 1–4. But in strategic terms he is prescient: see *Der Brief an die Römer*, vol. 1, *Röm 1–5* (Zürich, Einsiedeln, Köln, & Neukirchen-Vluyn: Benziger & Neukirchener, 1978), esp. 82-92, 101, 127-31, 195-96 — see, i.a., ". . . δικαιοσύνη θεοῦ als forensischer iustitia distributiva. Dieses Missverständnis rührt her von einem juristischen Sühneverständnis, das von Anselm v. Canterbury grundgelegt worden ist als Verstehenhorizont . . ." (195).

32. Moo, *Romans*, 218, 20, 24. Cranfield disavows the conditionality of faith explicitly (90), citing Barth (*CD* IV.1 608-42, 740-49), but then interprets it conditionally!: see *Romans I–VIII*, 98, 100, 203 (". . . received by means of faith . . ."), 210, 214. Schlatter offers a more sophisticated explanation than most, but ends up attributing a quasi-apocalyptic quality to the gospel in 1:16-17, in close relation to faith: "Faith has this causal power because it arises from the message proclaiming God's salvation . . .": *Romans*, 23. He is also alert to the syntactical issues in Rom. 3:22, trying to resolve them by reading the instrumental prepositional phrase attributivally, and then supplying a further appropriate

implicit verbal notion. Indeed, he concedes that if the phrase is read adverbially, then it must refer to Christ's fidelity! However, he views this reading as unlikely *because of his conventional construal of the preceding argument*: "the urgent question is what kind of behavior is able to bring the individual into that relationship intended by God . . . how the individual may obtain God's pleasure" (*Romans*, 94; see also 93-95).

33. An alternative justification from the foregoing is to suggest that God simply establishes the saving criterion of faith with no reference to the preceding argument — what we might dub "the Abraham caveat." But this is highly unsatisfactory for several reasons that will be noted just below. (Abraham in Romans 4 is discussed extensively in part four, chapter eighteen.) So this suggestion is best dismissed from further consideration. (An important variation will be discussed in chapter twelve, when Francis Watson's revisionist proposals are considered in detail.)

34. Why are earlier modes displaced? Why is Christ that displacement? — as Sanders frequently points out, esp. in *Paul, the Law, and the Jewish People* (Philadelphia: Fortress, 1983), *passim* — hereafter *PL&JP*. Moo overlooks the issue when it ought to be discussed: see *Romans*, 126; but he does invoke Anselm's famous theory on 242. Generally, I find no comment on this critical issue, and Moo representative of any response on atonement that does exist.

35. Gathercole emphasizes this aspect of Rom. 3:21-26 entirely on the basis of a conventional construal of the prior argument: see "Justified by Faith, Justified by His Blood," 168-83, esp. 181: "The divine verdict upon humanity in Romans 1:32 and the fate of Jesus in Romans 3:25 are identical. . . ." Moo invokes this relationship frequently: see *Romans*, 219, 221, 231, 235, 236, 237, 238. (Christ's function as a "ransom payment" is also asserted on 229-30.) Cranfield is reticent but concedes the point eventually: *Romans I–VIII*, 216, n. 2. Note that the putative lexicographical basis for the presence of this emphasis in 3:25 will be discussed in detail in part four, chapter sixteen.

36. An additional possible line of reinforcement might come from the construal of δικαιοσύνη θεοῦ in terms of retributive justice. This would import the satisfaction of God's just nature into the thesis paragraph itself (and repeatedly: see 3:21, 22, 25, 26; Paul's concluding phrase here would also probably be construed in relation to retributive concerns — εἰς τὸ εἶναι αὐτὸν δίκαιον καὶ δικαιοῦντα τὸν ἐκ πίστεως Ἰησοῦ[ν]). However, few if any scholars still endorse this construal, and we will see in part four, chapter seventeen that there are good reasons for preferring a very different reading of the phrase. It might also be suggested that Paul's atonement *terms* suggest this, but in due course I will deny that this is the case as well: see esp. part four, chapter sixteen.

37. James D. G. Dunn, "Once More, ΠΙΣΤΙΣ ΧΡΙΣΤΟΥ," in *Pauline Theology*, vol. 4, *Looking Back, Pressing On*, ed. Hays and Johnson (Atlanta, Georgia: Scholars Press, 1997), 76 (61-81; orig. publ. 1991; also repr. in Richard B. Hays, *The Faith of Jesus Christ*, rev. ed. [Grand Rapids, Mich.: Eerdmans, 2002 (1983)], 249-71).

38. Moo makes this claim clearly: see *Romans*, 243, 257; as does Tobin: *Paul's Rhetoric* — "Abraham is not only an example from the past but also a paradigm for the present" (125; see also 143-44). See also Stuhlmacher: "Grundmodel" (*Römer*, 68), and "das geschichtlich massgebende Urbild des Glaubens an den Gott" (70).

39. So it must be demonstrated that 3:28 makes a programmatic statement, and concerning Romans 4, and that it also somehow overrides 3:29, 30, and 31. It must be shown, moreover, how 4:1 sets up the same issue (or at least does not contradict it). And so on.

40. The exegetical implications of this are explored in part four, chapter eighteen.

41. I have not included here the suggestion that v. 2 denotes Abraham as "working" at some point. It is a first-class conditional that Paul goes on to negate and is clearly hypothetical. Even the most ardent advocate of Justification would not allow Abraham to "work" and then *legitimately* boast! At this point, then, a concrete reference to Abraham's behavior is unacceptable to both advocate and revisionist.

42. Gathercole places Abraham fairly firmly in the broader category of the ungodly, and largely on a priori grounds: "Justified by Faith, Justified by His Blood," 156-60. Lincoln implies the same (citing Wilckens and Dunn in support): "From Wrath to Justification," 151, esp. n. 35. Stuhlmacher does so

implicitly: ". . . Gott hat sich schon Abraham gegenüber erwiesen als der Gott, der den Gottlosen (Frevler) rechtfertigt, und zwar durch Christus (vgl. 4,25; 5,6)" (*Römer*, 68).

43. So a different strategy must be in play from the one attested by *Jubilees* (for example), where Abraham was ostensibly law observant in an extensive way. That Paul is thinking in such terms here is disqualified by what he goes on to say.

44. *Jubilees* does of course narrate Abraham as a pre-Mosaic, law-observant figure, but only *after* his call and circumcision. See more in this relation below in relation to ODs 14-22.

45. This is arguably a real interpretative peril associated with "vertical" commentary on an argumentative text (see Preface).

46. Problems one and four are relatively mild in their implications, but a reading that could explain these features of the text would be desirable. Problems two and eight are tiny textual signals that something else may be going on beneath the assurances of the conventional reading. The remaining seven problems, however — numbers three, five through seven, and nine through eleven — are more serious argumentative fissures within the conventional construal (i.e., small to large trees). These problems also vary in the degree to which previous revisionist interpretation has noted them. They range from the well known to the previously unrecognized.

47. See (i.a.) P. N. Harrison, *Paulines and Pastorals* (London: Villers, 1964); John C. O'Neill, *Paul's Letter to the Romans* (London: Penguin, 1975); Sanders, *PL&JP*, esp. 123-35; Calvin Porter, "Romans 1.18-32: Its Role in the Developing Argument," *New Testament Studies* 40 (1994): 210-23; William O. Walker, "Romans 1.18-2.29: A Non-Pauline Interpolation?" *New Testament Studies* 45 (1999): 533-52; and also *Interpolations in the Pauline Letters*, JSNTSup 213 (Sheffield: Sheffield Academic Press, 2001). Of course, they have not always limited this suggestion to Rom. 1:18-32: see John C. O'Neill, *The Recovery of Paul's Letter to the Galatians* (London: SPCK, 1972). We revisit some of these hypotheses in more detail in part three, chapter twelve, when revisionist reading strategies for Romans 1–4 are assessed.

48. Harrison, *Paulines and Pastorals*, 83 (and noted by Walker, "Romans 1.18-2.29," 538, n. 33).

49. Porter, "Romans 1.18-32," 218-19.

50. As a further point of comparison, the NRSV translates this subsection with thirteen sentences. So each sentence in effect contains a third person plural verb and a further third person plural emphasis with a pronoun. This style is then marked off quite distinctively against the second person grammar that characterizes much of Romans 2 and 3.

51. Intriguingly though, as Moo notes (*Romans*, 96), the word "pagans" never occurs in 1:18-32.

52. Verse 18 emphasizes ἀδικία and might play on it as well, since it functions in two slightly different locations. In combination with ἀσέβεια, it elicits the wrath of God, and then it is named as the cause of the suppression of the truth that ultimately leads to the broader ἀδικία of humanity (i.e., which ultimately elicits the wrath of God); it is therefore both an initial means and a final state (see also 1:29).

53. See Rom. 13:13; 1 Cor. 5:10-11; 6:9-10; 2 Cor. 12:20-21; Gal. 5:19-21; see also Eph. 5:3-5; Col. 3:5, 8; 1 Tim. 1:9-10; 6:4-5; 2 Tim. 3:2-4; Tit. 1:7; 3:3; 1 Pet. 2:1; 4:3, 15; Mark 7:21-22; Rev. 22:15. Also important are the later vice lists from *1 Clement* 35:5-6 (which is heavily dependent on Rom. 1:29-31); *Didache* 5:1b-2; and *Barnabas* 19-20. The "two ways" are especially obvious in these last two texts (which also exhibit a high degree of dependence). See also Wis. 14:25-26; 4 Macc. 1:26-27; 2:15; the *Testament of Reuben* 3:3-6; the *Testament of Levi* 17:11; *1QS* 4:9-11; *2 Enoch* 10:4-5; *3 Apocalypse of Baruch* 8:5; 13:4; and Philo, *On the Sacrifices of Cain and Abel*, 32 (which has over 140 items!). This material is discussed briefly by Dunn, *Romans 1–8*, 67-68.

54. ἀδικία, πλεονεξία, κακία, φθόνος, ἔρις, ψιθυριστάς, and καταλάλους (and I am generously counting the occurrence of cognates as an instance of overlap).

55. These groups have two-word phrases interposed between them in v. 30b — ἐφευρετὰς κακῶν, γονεῦσιν ἀπειθεῖς — but this shift from single words to short phrases, usually of two words, is apparent in other vice lists: see esp. Wis. 14:25-26; *Didache* 5:1b-2; and *Barnabas* 19-20.

56. Jewett notes the unusual style repeatedly, but offers no real explanation for it: *Romans*, 148-50, 165, and this seems characteristic.

57. It is this textual material in particular that proves fatal to the "immanentist" conception of God's judgment espoused by C. H. Dodd and Ulrich Wilckens — that God's judging action against sin takes the form of an inevitable outworking of sin *itself* in various distorted and painful consequences. As Wilckens puts it: "ein fester Folge-Zusammenhang alles menschlichen Tuns mit entsprechendem Ergehen": *Röm 1-5*, 128. Gathercole notes the view (tracing its German-speaking variant back through OT scholars Klaus Koch, Hartmut Gese, K. Hr. Fahlgren, and Johannes Pedersen) and correctly observes that the text of Romans 1-2 does not allow this interpretation: "Justified by Faith, Justified by His Blood," 169-75. This is not of course to deny its broader applicability to Paul's thinking, once Romans 1-4 have been construed more constructively! It is a theologically palatable if not responsible reading, but lacks exegetical accuracy.

58. See also 2:12 and 13, corroborated by v. 16a — ἀπολοῦνται, κριθήσονται, δικαιωθήσονται . . . ἐν ἡμέρᾳ ὅτε κρίνει ὁ θεὸς τὰ κρυπτὰ τῶν ἀνθρώπων.

59. I will suggest an interpretation in due course that explains its function: see part four, chapter fourteen.

60. Moo notes this debate: see *Romans*, 100, 134. Jewett provides an extensive and nuanced discussion: *Romans*, 150-53.

61. There were arguably no such evil passions in the constitution of Adam and Eve in the garden of Eden (although Jewish opinions on this topic varied).

62. This feature of the argument consequently contributes to Stowers's rereading of the paragraph in terms of a Jewish "decline-of-civilization narrative," on analogy to Hesiod's well-known account (see *RR*, 83-125). I will suggest in chapter twelve that this is not ultimately a plausible solution (although it overlaps with one); however, at least Stowers recognizes the problem. Conversely, Moo endorses the depravity of humanity at this point, without apparently grasping the problematic implications of this: ". . . the sinfulness of human beings [entails] . . . without grace [they] are unable to respond appropriately to whatever knowledge of God they may possess" (*Romans*, 124). If this is the case, then his reading of Paul's argument is meaningless and/or incoherent.

63. John M. G. Barclay introduces this text concisely in *Jews in the Mediterranean Diaspora from Alexander to Trajan (323 BCE-117 CE)* (Edinburgh: T&T Clark, 1996), 181-92. The link with Romans is discussed by K. Romaniuk, "La Livre de la Sagesse dans le Nouveau Testament," *New Testament Studies* 14 (1966-1967): 67-68, 498-514; and noted (i.a.) by Wright, "Letter to the Romans," 429, 432, 433, 438; and T. Laato, *Paul and Judaism: An Anthropological Approach,* trans. T. McElwain, South Florida Studies in the History of Judaism 115 (Atlanta: Scholars, 1995), 85-89, 94-95. A little ironically, Samuel Sandmel's famous attack on "parallelomania" departs from this ostensible relationship. I agree with Sandmel's general contention, but not in this relation!: see "Parallelomania," *Journal of Biblical Literature* 81 (1962): 1-13. The relationship is often noted: e.g., Moo speaks of it repeatedly: see *Romans*, 97, 113, 125, 128, 133.

64. Less well known is a possible relationship between parts of 1 Corinthians and the Wisdom of Solomon. On this, see Rodrigo Morales, "The Spirit, the Righteous Sufferer, and the Mysteries of God: Echoes of Wisdom in 1 Corinthians?" (paper presented to the New Testament and Judaic Studies Colloquium at Duke University, Durham, North Carolina, January 2005). This is a rather different substantive relationship, however — if it exists — and so does not alter my claims here significantly.

65. See John J. Collins, "A Symbol of Otherness: Circumcision and Salvation in the First Century," in *"To See Ourselves as Others See Us": Christians, Jews, "Others" in Late Antiquity,* ed. Jacob Neusner and Ernest S. Frerichs (Chico, Calif.: Scholars, 1985), 163-86; but originally the phrase of Gottlieb Klein, *Der älteste christliche Katechismus und die jüdische Propaganda-Literatur* (Berlin: G. Reimer, 1909), the function of this literature being much debated since then. See esp. V. Tcherikover, "Jewish Apologetic Literature Reconsidered," *Eos* 48 (1956): 19-93; and Collins, *Between Athens and Jerusalem: Jewish Identity in the Hellenistic Diaspora* (New York: Crossroad, 1983), esp. 8-10.

66. Dunn, drawing on other interpreters, lists further possible intertexts, but their specific content, while not irrelevant, is still further away from our concerns here: see *Jubilees* 3:28-32; *Adam and Eve; 4 Ezra* 4:30; *Second Baruch* 54:17-19/22 (suggested by Schulz); the Letter of Jeremiah, the *Tes-*

tament of Naphtali 3:2-4 (suggested by Jeremias); *1 Enoch* 91:4ff; 99ff; and the *Testament of Moses* 1:13. Also Philo, *On Rewards and Punishments,* 43; Ps-Aristotle, *De Mundo,* 399ab; Epictetus, *Discourses,* 1.6.19.

67. See Tobin, *Paul's Rhetoric,* 335. This dynamic is explored in more detail in part five, chapter nineteen.

68. The full extent of this subversion depends on the way we ultimately construe Paul's argument; I will suggest in due course, in part four, chapter fourteen, and part five, chapter nineteen, that it is even more extensive than the conventional reading suspects.

69. These signals are so sustained and explicit that ultimately a Jewish identification could not plausibly be denied. However, we also saw that the conventional construal has to go well beyond this restricted target. It broadens Paul's attack to encompass Judaism as a whole, representative here also of humanity as a whole, and this state necessarily includes an accurate account of Paul's own non-Christian life as well. The underderterminative problem is that the text never explicitly endorses this massively expanded target — one that sets so many sinister implications in motion.

70. *The Moral Vision of the New Testament* (San Francisco: Harper Collins, 1996), 389. Käsemann tries to avoid the strict implications of Paul's argumentative turn here, freighted by διό, by describing v. 1 as an early marginal gloss, originally drawing a conclusion from v. 3 but now wrongly inserted at the beginning! (*Romans,* 54)

71. See also N. T. Wright: "This paragraph . . . appears to be addressed to anyone who, faced with the vices mentioned in chap. 1, tries to adopt a superior posture . . . , but . . . Paul here has in mind not only pagan moralists but also Jews. . . . [B]ehind the screen of 'whoever you are' in v. 1, Paul envisages as his hypothetical listener not just a pagan moralist but a moralizing Jew" ("Letter to the Romans: Introduction, Commentary, and Reflections," in *New Interpreter's Bible,* 12 vols., ed. L. Keck et al. (Nashville, Tenn.: Abingdon, 2002), 10:437-48). Tobin is similar, as already noted; he suggests that this address in 2:1-11 "gives Paul . . . the rhetorical foundation he needs to speak explicitly in 2:17-29 about Jewish conduct in the same way that he has been speaking about the conduct of this anonymous addressee": *Paul's Rhetoric,* 112. But this is not entirely persuasive: Paul needs no such preliminary, anonymous condemnation of hypocrisy to condemn it more explicitly a few verses later; moreover, this reading activates the Jewish empirical conundrum directly.

72. So, for example, Fundamentalist preachers are not liable to capture by Paul's argument at this point because, although often judgmental of others, they tend to accompany this with long confessions of personal sinfulness as well. Billy Graham's milder material evidences the same dynamic: see *Peace with God,* rev. ed. (Waco, Texas: Word, [1984] 1953). He is certainly judgmental, and frequently upholds a retributive view of God, but also has a charming confessional dimension.

73. The critique could be usefully directed later on by Christians against Jewish Christians, Protestants against Catholics (and so on) — see more just below.

74. See P. S. Minear, *The Obedience of Faith: The Purposes of Paul in the Epistle to the Romans* (London: SCM, 1971); and Jewett, *Romans,* 197-203.

75. We link hands here with the underdetermination already noted at this point.

76. There is also a puzzling absence of any christological argumentation in Romans 2 (perhaps except 2:16b, but see more on this just below).

77. Jewett partly responds to my concerns here by viewing this pericope as a rhetorical trap. The judgment of the Roman Christians is first elicited against a bigoted outsider, and only later do some of them realize that this judgment must now be applied to themselves. This is an ingenious reading — and a great improvement on the conventional approach. However, in my view it still does not deal effectively with the difficulties already noted.

The nature of Paul's characterization of the judge in Romans 2 allows the Christian judger of Romans 14 an easy escape route. It would, e.g., be a relatively easy matter for the weak to make confession of their own faults, and then go on to uphold their critique, as many modern evangelists do. And the judgment scenarios seem, moreover, to be decisively different. Adding to these concerns, no linguistic markers resume this earlier trap, in effect springing it. And the characterization of the judge in 2:1-5 does not correspond closely enough to the strong in Romans 14 for this recognition to take place automatically. We also remain unsure why Paul undertakes this elaborate maneuver in Romans 2, in his characterization of the pre-Christian situation, only to unleash it in Romans 14 (and effectively unannounced) in his development of Christian ethics. In this relation, even the basis of his appeals later on is different — the nature of life "in Christ." Christology seems by this point in the letter to have replaced a foundational notion of desert as the basis for ethics, making any overarching rhetorical link ineffective as well as unlikely. So it seems to me that Jewett's suggestion is a big interpretative step forward, but also ultimately inadequate.

78. See (i.a.) Moo, *Romans*, 126, 128; Cranfield, *Romans I–VIII*, 138-39, 142. Käsemann states that "Paul's argumentation [from 2:1 onward] sees Jewish reality as exemplary for humanity as a whole" (*Romans*, 54).

79. And note that this seems a better reading than the view that he is *baiting* a trap that he *springs* only in Romans 14.

80. Useful evidence in support of this observation is the general absence of this turn in the argument from other paradigmatic evangelistic reproductions of it. That is, Justification evangelists do not generally use this "turn." They use some combination of 1:18-32 and 3:10-20 to set the stage, so they simply endorse fully the initial premises of the argument *(on which Paul turns at 2:1!)*. The entire middle section of argument in Romans 1–3 is usually absent, because it is rhetorically redundant in almost all circumstances. See esp. the evangelistic systems noted in part two, chapter nine of the BGEA, the Four Spiritual Laws, and the Roman Road.

81. This suggestion overlaps with Francis Watson's important thesis in *PJ&G*[2]. He views Paul himself as justifying the sect of law-free Pauline communities over against the parent body of Judaism, and doing so in typically exaggerated and contradictory terms — thereby explaining those exaggerations and contradictions. I view Justification as a relatively coherent explanation (although contradictory in its broader settings). But it is a misreading of Paul partly prompted *by* this *later* sociological function in church history. Many of the contradictions that Watson detects in the text are therefore indications for me that there is another more original and coherent reading underlying this blatantly sociological one, but the power of that later function has overridden those delicate historical signals (which is not to say that the original construal I detect is not also sociological; but it is not in my view participating in a parent body-sect dynamic, which is arguably anachronistic for the 50s CE). Nevertheless, many of Watson's insights are directly transferable at this point. His proposals are discussed in more detail in chapter twelve.

82. This was drawn to my attention initially by a student in one of my Romans classes, Sanford Groff, and I am grateful for it (NEWTEST 117B, held at The Divinity School, Duke University, in Spring 2007). Sanders astutely notes the anomaly in passing, but does not analyze it with depth or precision: "Paul's statement about repentance (2:4) has no true parallel and is at best atypical" (*PL&JP*, 125).

83. See Gen. 27:1-40; 48:9-49:33; 2 Kgs. 20:1-6; Isa. 38 (esp. v. 17b); and The Prayer of Manasseh.

84. So one of George Foot Moore's key complaints has special bite at this point: see "Christian Writers on Judaism," *Harvard Theological Review* 14 (1921): 197-254; see also *Judaism in the First Centuries of the Christian Era — the Age of the Tannaim*, 3 vols. (Cambridge: Harvard University Press, 1927, 1930), 1:117-8, 498, 500-34; see also Solomon Schechter, *Some Aspects of Rabbinic Judaism* (New York: Schocken, 1961 [1909]), 313-43; Sanders, *Paul and Palestinian Judaism* (Philadelphia: Fortress, 1977), 174-80, 500-1; and Laato, *Paul and Judaism*, 163-66.

85. That is, unless Justification advocates can give an account of this motif that integrates it into their concerns, which seems unlikely. This problem is seldom recognized. Laato (i.a.) is oblivious; *Paul and Judaism*, 165; as is Moo, *Romans*, 133-34; and Cranfield, *Romans I–VIII*, 144-45. Stuhlmacher charitably views Paul as ascribing this possibility of repentance to "the Jew" (in "correction" of 1 Thess. 2:16!), without apparent recognition of the disruption this could cause to his argument and gospel (that is, as Justification advocates present it): *Römer*, 39. On this reading, any Jew could, strictly speaking, repent and be saved, with no reference to the gospel of faith. Note, Stuhlmacher also opens the door to my suggested rereading, with his statement "Bei seiner Anklage gegen 'den' Juden . . . hat Paulus jene Judenchristen im Blick, die seine Verkündigung bis hinein nach Rom kritisieren" (42).

Unfortunately, Stuhlmacher views Paul's own endorsement of the first, judgmental phase of Justification theory as an appropriate response to the Teacher — as a demonstration, presumably, of the fact that he, the apostle to the pagans, is not "soft on sin" (see also Gal. 1:10; 2:17)!

86. If humanity is depraved, then it falls entirely within the sinful category; however, those miraculously liberated and transformed by an act of God should fall entirely within the good category. So *ontological* categories and *transformational* views of salvation seem to underlie the text at this point.

87. I do not know of any recognition of this problem by commentators.

88. The conventional reading would view him as the object of faith in 3:22, 25, and 26; as providing "redemption" in 3:24b; and as providing atonement in 3:25, and thereby "proving" God's righteousness (a point repeated by v. 26). So he is present before 4:2 only in 3:22-26 (and perhaps then alluded to by 3:27-28), and is himself "active" only in 3:24b-25.

89. That is, in terms of fundamentally corrupt and hence impure and sinful people being finally excluded if not destroyed, as against fundamentally capable people sinning and being punished legitimately for their transgressions.

90. So Sanders's observations oversimplify a more complex and nuanced situation, but are basically on target: "Rom. 2:13 is entirely unlike Rom. 14:10, 2 Cor. 5:10, and other passages in which Paul mentions judgment according to deeds, for the other passages refer to Christians; Rom. 2:13 refers to *all humanity*" (*PL&JP*, 126). 2 Thess. 1:6-10 refers to non-Christians. Sanders would doubtless counter that this is pseudonymous material, but its links with authentic material must then be explained away, and I am not confident that this can be done decisively. More importantly, there is occasional evidence of retributive acts by God or Christ in Paul, and these could apply by extension to non-Christians in eschatological terms.

91. The argument in Rom. 13:1-7 is of course not christological.

92. So this debate would need to be settled decisively in favor of the latter position by a Justification advocate before such a claim could be made in relation to Rom. 2:16. And I know of no such successful case.

93. Moo concedes that this is "awkward" (*Romans*, 153; see also 153-55). Cranfield also equivocates: *Romans I–VIII*, 63 ("not immediately clear . . ."; "[He meant] probably . . . the gospel which he preached together with other Christian preachers"). As Jewett notes — concerning "the unending controversy" surrounding this statement — one expedient is to characterize either the offending statement or the entire verse as a gloss, although it lacks evidence. (Jewett subsumes the issue within his broader rhetorical treatment of 2:1-15, which I have already queried.) See *Romans*, 217-18.

94. Sanders states the problem exactly (as usual): "the description of Jewish behavior in 2:17-24 is unparalleled" (*PL&JP*, 124); also, "Paul's case for universal sinfulness . . . rests on gross exaggeration" (125). Moo notes the problem, but suggests — rather unconvincingly — that this strategy is "exemplary"; *Romans*, 158, 164, 165. Most commentators echo this evasion (where they feel the need for evasion). Cranfield seems to feel no such qualms (*Romans I–VIII*, 163-71): "The phenomenon of the teacher who teaches others but not himself is . . . apparently regarded by Paul as characteristic of Jewish life" (168)!

95. An excellent candidate is "covetousness": who has not coveted *something* wrongly at some point? It is one of the ten commandments as well, and so arguably functions as part of the universal ethical law apparent in the cosmos and conscience: see Exod. 20:17; Deut. 5:21. That Paul is aware of this possible example and strategy in Romans is evident in 7:7-25. See Billy Graham's observations that "Iniquity has to do with our inner motivations, the very things that we so often try to keep hidden from the eyes of men and God . . . [an] inner corruptness. . . ." He adds that "sin [is] *missing the mark*, falling short of the goal that has been set. God's goal is Christ. . . . He came to show us what it is possible for man to achieve here on earth; and when we fail to follow His example, we miss the mark and fall short of the divine standard" (*Peace with God*, 54-55, emphasis original). It would be difficult indeed to have perfect inner motivations and/or to live exactly as Christ did.

96. Sanders notes the enthusiastic affirmations of Mussner, Ridderbos, and Beker in this relation (*PL&JP*, 124-25). Many still more recent interpreters could be added to this list, e.g., Cranfield

seems comfortable with the critique, citing Matt. 5:21-32, 48: *Romans I–VIII*, 168-70. Schreiner states of 2:17-29 that "[t]he implicit object of Paul's attack in verses 1-16, the Jews, is now explicitly named in verse 17. . . . In verses 17-29 Paul ensures that the Jews cannot evade the implications of his previous argument. . . . Mere possession of the law and circumcision will not shield them from God's judging righteousness" (*Romans*, 127). (There is of course quite a lot of activity that falls between "mere possession of the law" and adultery and sacrilegious theft!) Schreiner, to his credit, is alert to the polemical difficulties but wishes to defend the conventional reading. Eventually, he suggests that these sins exemplify graphically a principle: "Paul uses particularly blatant and shocking examples (like any good preacher) to illustrate the principle that Jews violated the law that they possessed" (134). But Paul is not "illustrating" a "principle" at this point in his argument, and neither does the text ever articulate this concern explicitly. Paul is supposed to be *proving* an *empirical* point — that Jews sin. And his argument, so construed, only succeeds in catching sacrilegious Jewish adulterers. Hence, Schreiner is a nice example of a theoretical overdetermination, the needs of Justification theory explicitly overriding the text — and both when the text says what it ought not to (at which point it is redefined or ignored — narcotized), and when it does not say what the theory needs for it to (at which point that material is introduced as an unstated supposition). Moo's strategies and difficulties are almost identical (*Romans*, 157-66). Laato suggests that Räisänen has exaggerated Paul's argument that all Jews are condemned — an "empirical" claim. Laato notes — quite rightly — that the text does not support this universal accusation (and he is supported by Thurén, Schlier, and Watson at this point): Laato, 78-79, 91-93. But he never goes on to specify a plausible alternative reading. Neither does he show how an "indictment" of all Jews — which he does view as taking place in Romans 1–3 — can be effective when it is not "empirically" accurate (an indictment without fact?!).

97. As we have already noted, the suggestion that this is just ancient polemic overlooks the fact that Paul's statements here need to be true for Justification theory to function properly (see Byrne, *Romans*, 98). Moreover, if Paul is wrong, albeit only through negative exaggeration, then the Jews are not convicted of wrongdoing and they do not need to be saved by faith alone (etc.). That is, the rhetorical strategy does not work.

98. Cranfield (*Romans I–VIII*, 169-70), Fitzmyer (*Romans*, 318), and D. B. Garlington, "'ΙΕΡΟΣΥΛΕΙΝ and the Idolatry of Israel (Romans 2.22)," *New Testament Studies* 36, no. 1 (1990): 142-51, view the sin of "temple robbery" "metaphorically." But, as Byrne notes, this is not plausible in view of the concrete nature of the two preceding sins in the list (*Romans*, 100). He suggests that the reference is to the pilfering and sale of sacred objects from pagan temples "on the pretext that . . . pagan deities have no reality (see 1 Cor. 8:4)" (100) — a suggestion with an ancient pedigree (Moo notes its advocacy by Chrysostom: *Romans*, 164, n 35). But no specific examples of this practice are cited, nor does this suggestion deal with the difficulties specified here. A more generalized meaning for the sin is unlikely lexicographically. It also undercuts any sense that Paul is criticizing the performance of the Decalogue (in addition to the obvious problem that if he is criticizing fulfillment of the Ten Commandments, then he really ought either to state that or to cite all ten). Two of the three sins occur in the Decalogue, it is true, but this does not seem especially relevant to the interpretation of Paul's argument. That some reference to Israel's exile is meant, drawing on the broader context of Isa. 52:5, cited in 2:24, is also implausible. Nothing overt signals the presence of the exile; nothing even signals a salvation-historical perspective and/or the subject of Israel and her history. And the exact sins in question are again problematic. The Old Testament attributes the exile primarily to idolatry, disloyalty, and social injustice. See also J. Duncan M. Derrett, "You Abominate False Gods; but Do You Rob Shrines?" (Rom 2.22b)," *New Testament Studies* 40 (1994): 558-71.

99. Other explanations that could be explored are even less plausible than these. Sanders notes some in addition to the main approaches in *PL&JP*, 125-26. Moo canvasses several options; *Romans*, 140. Cranfield cites and dismisses the possibility that Paul is just inconsistent (his option i): *Romans I–VIII*, 151.

100. So this explanation links up — although it is not normally noted — with certain well-known studies arguing for the possibility of justification through works of law in Paul, largely on the basis of Romans 2: see esp. Karl Donfried, "Justification and Last Judgment in Paul," *Zeitschrift für die*

neutestamentliche Wissenschaft und die Kunde der älteren Kirche 67 (1976): 90-110; and Klyne Snodgrass, "Justification by Faith — to the Doers: An Analysis of the Place of Romans 2 in the Theology of Paul," *New Testament Studies* 32 (1986): 72-93. Their suggestions are equivalent to options 1, and 2a-b in Moo (*Romans*, 140), i.e., these figures are real.

101. Options 2d and e for Moo (which he basically endorses; *Romans*, 140-41); option ii for Cranfield (of ten!): *Romans I–VIII*, 151.

102. Options 2c and 3 for Moo (*Romans*, 141); options iii-vi for Cranfield (*Romans I–VIII*, 151) — options that they basically prefer. Bray and Oden note the support for this reading of Ambrosiaster, Pseudo-Constantius, Pelagius, and Origen: see *Ancient Christian Commentary on Scripture: New Testament VI: Romans*, 63-66.

103. It would ease my argument to adopt an adjectival reading (see NRSV's "spiritual and not literal"). But the Spirit-letter opposition is a leitmotif for Paul: see esp. Rom. 7:6b; also 2 Cor. 3:7; see also Col. 2:11. The Old Testament intertexts that Paul is invoking here also never actually speak of a circumcision of the heart by *the Spirit*. (If they did, then Paul's language could be attributed to a text and a source rather than to the Spirit per se, lessening the likelihood of a direct Christian reference; see elsewhere Jer. 31:31-34 [LXX 38:31-34] and Ezek. 11:19; 36:26-27; 37:1-14.) Although not sharing my overarching argumentative concerns, Fee nevertheless endorses my essentially parenthetical reading at this point: "[a] kind of proleptic (foreshadowing) usage is most likely what lies behind this mention of the Spirit. . . . What is said here will receive its reaffirmation and explication in the argument of 7:1-6, especially in vv. 5-6. . . . [T]his little theological insertion is full of theological grist that will be milled for all it's worth later in this letter": *God's Empowering Presence*, 489, 493. It is also indicative that Fee notes the explicitly covenantal and transformational dimensions implicit in this statement, which are really quite different from Justification. (He also cogently rejects the NRSV's suggestion dominated by notions of "inner" and "outer": 491-92.)

104. We will see in more detail in part four, chapter fourteen the extent to which these figures are woven into the warp and woof of the entire argument. They cannot therefore be lightly dismissed as a marginal textual issue; neither can they be interpreted outside of this integration and definition.

105. It is highly significant that Christianity is now experiencing all the argumentative dynamics that normally fall upon Judaism within the argument; its particularity is being stripped away by the remorseless operation of the principle of desert.

106. It is curious that many Protestant commentators endorse this reading (or something worse) in an effort to save the conventional construal. However, in so doing they embrace a stance on Christian "works" that they bitterly oppose when they encounter it in most other contexts. So, for example, the Council of Trent offered a version of "works" far more nuanced than this and yet was roundly rejected by Protestantism.

107. I dispute strongly a supersessionist reading of Gal. 6:16. Certainly, it is unnecessary. Paul does apply Jewish metaphors to the church, but this is not the same thing as *replacing* Judaism with the church as the new Israel. Invariably, a melding of new and old is in view, rather as his famous grafting illustration in Rom. 11:17-24 suggests. The church does arguably displace the temple for Paul, but this should not be extrapolated into a broader and complete displacement of the entire nation. Once, in an undisputed letter, Paul speaks of the church as "the circumcision" (Phil. 3:3), a claim echoed by Eph. 2:11 and Col. 2:11, 13. Neither of these texts then presses the point to a redefinition of historical Judaism in toto, however. For a more consistent and constructive reading of these discussions of circumcision see part four, chapter fourteen, and part five, chapters twenty and twenty-one; an alternative account of this motif's function in Paul's argument is also provided there.

108. The metaphor of immersion then reinforces the extent to which both the old ethnic identities are washed away and creatively renewed. Stripping off and reclothing make the same point; see esp. Gal. 3:27.

109. But see also Rom. 1:14-15; 1 Cor. 12:13; also Col. 3:11; and, in a larger horizon, Eph. 2:13-22. (If anything, in Eph. 2:19 the church is absorbed in Israel!) Note, the same point is also discernible in Paul's frequent deployments of other standard antitheses in relation to ancient constructions of gen-

der and class, a dynamic discussed briefly in my study *The Quest for Paul's Gospel: A Suggested Strategy* (London: T&T Clark International [Continuum], 2005), chapters five and six (95-131).

110. To his credit, Stuhlmacher recognizes how Paul's position "geht selbst *über* die radikalisten jüdischen Gerichtstexte wie 4Esr 7,33ff.; syrBar 85,12ff. hinaus . . ." (*Römer,* 47, emphasis added). For further discussion of Philo, see part four, chapter fourteen.

111. See esp. part one, chapter three, §§2 & 3.9.

112. And these differences cause certain theoretical problems that derive principally from the two systems' essential incommensurability. However, the theory does try to endorse the validity of both systems, problems notwithstanding. To fail to do this would generate textual and theoretical mayhem — an instant collapse of the discourse.

113. A third could arguably be mentioned at this point — namely, the way the unity of God is apparently used to undergird the salvation of both Jews and pagans through belief (see 3:30). This is not, strictly speaking, a valid argument in terms of Justification theory, which relies on the universal failures and difficulties of the non-Christian phase to establish both the universality and nature of the Christian scenario. But this does not seem to be a sufficiently obvious problem to justify working through the thicket of interpretative difficulties that 3:30 raises at this point in our broader discussion. Alternative readings of this enigmatic verse could be offered that avoid this implication. So it seems best not to add it to our lists of difficulties in the conventional reading at this stage, and to postpone the detailed analysis of 3:29-30 until part four, chapter eighteen.

114. Most recently, see the suggestions of Charles Quarles, "From Faith to Faith: A Fresh Examination of the Prepositional Series in Romans 1:17," *Novum Testamentum* 45 (2003): 1-21; and John W. Taylor, "From Faith to Faith: Romans 1.17 in the Light of Greek Idiom," *New Testament Studies* 50 (2004): 337-48. Moo notes the difficulties: see *Romans,* 76; as does Cranfield, *Romans I-VIII,* 98-100. R. Barry Matlock's latest contribution to the πίστις Χριστοῦ debate unfortunately overlooks this important contention entirely (being preoccupied with arguments in terms of redundancy): "The Rhetoric of πίστις in Paul: Galatians 2.16, 3.22, Romans 3.22, and Philippians 3.9," *Journal for the Study of the New Testament* 30 (2007): 173-203; see esp. 184-87.

115. If this argument is correct, then it immediately falsifies a great deal of the recent discussion (i.e., Quarles, Taylor et al.). To my knowledge, no cogent rejoinders or refutations have yet been made to it. See my studies, "The Meaning of ΠΙΣΤΙΣ and ΝΟΜΟΣ in Paul: A Linguistic and Structural Investigation," *Journal of Biblical Literature* 111 (1992): 85-97; and "Romans 1:17 — a *Crux Interpretum* for the ΠΙΣΤΙΣ ΧΡΙΣΤΟΥ Dispute," *Journal of Biblical Literature* 113 (1994): 265-85.

116. Including the citations of Hab. 2:4 in this total. More specifically, it occurs in Romans twelve times, Galatians nine times, and elsewhere in the New Testament only in Heb. 10:37-38, which cites Hab. 2:3-4, and James 2:24. The first study to notice this strange set of correlations was, to my knowledge, Bruno Corsani, "ΕΚ ΠΙΣΤΕΩΣ in the Letters of Paul," in *The New Testament Age: Essays in Honor of Bo Reicke,* ed. W. C. Weinrich (Macon, Ga.: Mercer University Press, 1984), 87-93.

117. Which is also to suggest that a shift would have to be demonstrated. Stowers has made the most perceptive and plausible such attempt in relation to Rom. 3:30, but no one has attempted this in relation to Gal. 2:16 (i.e., in terms of this phrase alone), which undermines the case in Romans. And Stowers's case has other problems: see "Ἐκ πίστεως and διὰ τῆς πίστεως in Romans 3.30," *Journal of Biblical Literature* 108 (1989): 665-74.

118. The parallelism and stylistic variation are apparent compactly and immediately in Rom. 3:30-31 and Gal. 2:16, but are also apparent, in a slightly more diffuse way, in Rom. 3:21-26; 4:13-16; (arguably) 5:1-2; Gal. 3:7-14; and 3:21-26.

119. See BDAG, mngs 3 and 4, 224-25 (here, in due course, 4, i.e., agency); and see esp., in Paul, Rom. 1:8; 2:16; 7:25; 1 Cor. 8:6; Gal. 1:1; 3:19; see also Col. 1:16, 20; 3:17. Meaning 1 — "through" — looks unlikely at this point as well, partly on the grounds of parallels in context (esp. the dative constructions: see just below), and partly on grounds of contradiction. If an essentially spatial notion of passing "through" is intended, then faith functions *simultaneously* as both a way station and a goal on that journey — an obvious contradiction. Paul is not asserting with these series the theological equivalent of the statement, "I passed through Durham on the way to Durham." For the overlap with ἐκ see

BDAG, mngs 3d-f, 296-97 — to denote effective cause, so "by, because of" (2 Cor. 7:9); reason, so "by reason of, as a result of, because of" (Rom. 3:20, 30; 4:2; 11:6; 12:18 [?]; 2 Cor. 13:4; Gal. 2:16; 3:2, 5, 24); or means in relation to a definite purpose, so "with, by means of" (Lk 16:9).

120. See, e.g., Rom. 3:28; 5:2 (perhaps extending to vv. 9-11); possibly Gal. 3:11 and 14 in context; arguably 3:26; and Phil. 3:9b.

121. Eph. 2:8-10 can also now be seen to resonate with these texts as well, along with 3:12 and 17.

122. See further in part four, chapters fifteen through seventeen.

123. We have already seen, in n. 32, the affirmations of Moo, Cranfield, and Schlatter (who may be taken as representative); see also Gathercole, "Justified by Faith, Justified by Blood," 151-52.

124. This is not infrequently suggested as the meaning of ἐκ πίστεως in Rom. 1:17a, and rather less frequently suggested in relation to διὰ [τῆς] πίστεως in 3:25; it is, however, an impossible reading of πίστις in 3:22 and 26. It is also impossible in 1:17a if an intertextual link is affirmed there (as it really must be). This reading of 3:25 is discussed in more detail just below, and later on, in part four, chapter sixteen.

125. That is, unless it is being used in the sense of "proof." This was not an uncommon usage in Paul's day, and is Philo's most common use. But it is difficult if not impossible to argue that in Romans' "thesis" paragraphs πίστις generally means "proof." David M. Hay has attempted this case but was forced to combine two distinguishable meanings of πίστις into one signifier! (He suggested that πίστις meant "ground for faith.") See "*Pistis* as Ground for Faith in Hellenized Judaism and Paul," *Journal of Biblical Literature* 18 (1989): 461-76. The case has been made more generally by James L. Kinneavy, *The Greek Rhetorical Origins of Christian Faith* (Oxford & New York: Oxford University Press, 1987). In fact, Paul tends to use ἔνδειξις when he wants to speak of a "proof." Even more importantly, it is impossibly awkward to construe Hab. 2:4 in these terms — the text that sources these broader instances in Paul.

126. So, for example, an act of belief cannot disclose to me what is hidden inside a box. I can have beliefs about what is hidden, but these may be right or wrong; they will not *reveal* what is hidden, which can only be done by opening the box and scrutinizing what is inside (or some such), at which point I might then find my beliefs confirmed or disconfirmed.

127. Moo is especially indicative: "Paul highlights [in 3:22a, resuming a "key theme" from 1:17] faith as the means by which God's justifying work becomes applicable to individuals" (*Romans*, 224). Of course, Paul doesn't actually *say* this. Verse 22 does not contain the verb δικαιόω, the motif of "applicability," or an individual (except arguably as an implication of "faith in Christ"; the second reference to faith is plural — πάντας τοὺς πιστεύοντας). The apostle speaks here of faith as the "means by which" God's righteousness is disclosed — rather a different thing. Similarly, Gathercole omits the verb that Paul uses, contrasting two ways by which God's righteousness "is received" or "comes" — verbs that avoid this problem but that Paul does not use: "In 3:20-21, Paul's contrast is between two ways of receiving the righteousness of God, one real and one imagined. . . . God's saving act of righteousness in Christ does not come through the Law, but comes independently of it. It is not received on the basis of obedience to the Torah. By contrast, how is it to be received? The answer to this lies in seeing the crucial parallelism between 3:21 and 3:22:

3:21:   the righteousness of God independently of the Law
        χωρὶς νόμου δικαιοσύνη θεοῦ
3:22:   the righteousness of God through faith in Jesus Christ
        δικαιοσύνη δὲ θεοῦ διὰ πίστεως Ἰησοῦ Χριστοῦ

. . . Negatively, the righteousness of God comes independently of the Law, 'not through' the Law. Positively, it comes 'through' faith in Christ" ("Justified by Faith, Justified by His Blood," 151-52). The omission of the actual verb, φανερόω, and the substitution of different, more palatable verbs into the exposition here, are quite striking.

Stuhlmacher, commenting on 1:16, states ". . . das Evangelium von der Gottesgerechtigkeit in Christus, die *auf Grund* von Glauben *erfahrren wird* . . ." (*Römer*, 30; emphasis added to the words here that Stuhlmacher adds to Paul's Greek); and earlier he notes how Christ is "received" on the basis of faith *(empfangen)*, adding "Einzig und allein im Glauben wird Gottes Greechtigkeit rettend erfahrren" (30).

128. Presumably, the Jewish Kabbalistic tradition would not have a difficulty at this point.

129. Bruce W. Longenecker built strongly on some suggestions in my doctoral work in his short study "ΠΙΣΤΙΣ in Rom 3.25: Neglected Evidence for the Faithfulness of Christ?" *New Testament Studies* 39 (1993): 478-80. R. Barry Matlock has since objected to his arguments vociferously in the context of one of his studies of Paul's πίστις Χριστοῦ constructions, although ultimately not cogently: "Πίστις in Galatians 3:26: Neglected Evidence for 'Faith in Christ,'" *New Testament Studies* 49 (2003): 433-39. (This debate is assessed in part four, chapter sixteen, and is also touched on in part five, chapter twenty.)

130. We will subsequently consider the article's presence or absence carefully in part four, chapter sixteen.

131. Moo suggests that "'through faith' is not likely to modify 'set forth,' since faith was not the instrument through which God 'set forth' Christ as *hilastêrion*. Rather the phrase modifies *hilastêrion* and indicates the means by which individuals appropriate the benefits of the sacrifice" (*Romans*, 236). Moo's initial observation here is basically correct, given his view of faith, but his interpretative suggestion adds a great deal to the text, and he could solve his difficulties by modifying his initial reading of faith.

132. Alfons Pluta has suggested in view of this that the phrase refers to the fidelity of God: see *Gottes Bundestreue: Ein Schlüsselbegriff in Röm 3,25a* (Stuttgart: Katholisches Bibelwerk, 1969). But, although this is superior to an anthropological interpretation, 25b still intervenes awkwardly between 25a and 25c, and the theme of God's fidelity is unattested in the immediate context; we must reach back to 3:3 for its explicit mention (that is, unless this connotation can be associated tightly with δικαιοσύνη Θεοῦ, but see the next comment in this relation). Even more importantly, the instrumental function of the phrase is awkward; in an analogous difficulty to the one noted in the previous subsection, how does God's fidelity function as *the means by which* Jesus is either set forth or intended to atone? Finally, this suggestion cannot comply with the parallelism that runs through the section in relation to πίστις, although this point will be explicated in detail only in part four, chapters sixteen and seventeen. For all these reasons, then, although it is a useful and elegant suggestion — and is certainly superior to an anthropological and/or parenthetical reading — I regard Pluta's reading of 24b as unlikely.

133. That is, when interpreters seek the implicit defining relationship for πίστις in v. 25 from the context, the construal of v. 22 is likely to be determinative (provided it is also sustainable for v. 26). So the problem of disclosure and instrumentality already noted with respect to v. 22 will ultimately affect the interpretation of v. 25 decisively as well.

134. See §2.3, UD 10.

135. Critical studies of the conventional reading of Abraham in Romans 4 are rare, but I have been assisted in this relation esp. by Lloyd Gaston, *Paul and the Torah* (Vancouver: University of British Columbia Press, 1987), 45-63, 202-8; and T. L. Donaldson, "Abraham's Gentile Offspring: Contratextuality and Conviction in Romans 4," paper presented to the Society of Biblical Literature Annual Meeting (San Francisco: 1992), available at http://listserv.lehigh.edu/lists/ioudaios-l/Articles.html, tdrom_4; see also some briefer remarks in *Paul and the Gentiles: Remapping the Apostle's Convictional World* (Minneapolis: Fortress, 1997), 103-4, 122-28. An earlier generation of scholars was also greatly stimulated by the studies of G. Klein in this relation: see *Rekonstruktion und Interpretation* (Munich: Kaiser, 1969) (specifically "Römer 4 und die Idee der Heilsgeschichte" [orig. 1963], 145-69; "Individualgeschichte und Weltgeschichte bei Paulus" [orig. 1964], 180-224; and "Exegetische Probleme in Römer 3,21-4,25" [orig. 1964], 170-79). So, e.g., Käsemann engages frequently with Klein's sharp contentions.

136. My own realization of the difficulties implicit here was first catalyzed by Räisänen, although I develop the issue in a slightly different way: see *Paul and the Law,* 2nd ed., WUNT 29 (Tübingen: J. C. B. Mohr [Paul Siebeck], 1987 [1983]), esp. 51-52, 170-71. Moo certainly asserts this ar-

gument from "overruling," without acknowledging the problematic implications: see *Romans*, 246-47, 249.

137. Moo asserts this, without signaling the implicit difficulties. In effect, he introduces the argument of 1:18–3:20 into the text — specifically at 3:27 — when the text *itself* does not really say or allow this: see *Romans*, 250.

138. It cannot on epistemological grounds that have already been noted (i.e., it is impossible for a philosophical position to recognize the validity of a countervailing claim from revelation). But, even allowing some such recognition for the sake of argument, one wonders whether this can be allowed on argumentative grounds in any case. If the first phase of the theory has not been traversed correctly, then the entire theory fails to function or to hold any validity. It is therefore entirely self-defeating for advocates of Justification theory to concede any avoidance of the necessary salvific and psychological journey through the vestibule on any grounds. In short, if phase one is not established and experienced, then the theory as a whole *does not work*.

139. It could also be suggested that the evident linkage between boasting and the boaster and Judaism in some sense — see 2:17, 23; 3:27; 4:2 — is also curious; boasting is supposedly intrinsic to the loop of foolishness and hence to *everyone* who is stupidly attempting justification through works. So foolish working pagans are presumably as prone to boasting as foolish working Jews. It might be answered, however, (i.e., by the Justification advocate) that Jews represent such foolish boasting par excellence. Of course the empirical difficulty in this relation is sharpened again by this response, but given how many concessions have already been made on this front, one further negative qualification hardly seems fatal. For these reasons I have not included this potential problem in my principal list of overdeterminations, although it *could* arguably be added there.

140. This difficulty seems to be universally overlooked by the commentators.

141. These will be investigated further in part four, chapter sixteen.

142. Existing surveys of the Koiné data can be misleading, as Matlock points out: "Detheologizing the ΠΙΣΤΙΣ ΧΡΙΣΤΟΥ Debate: Cautionary Remarks from a Lexical Semantic Perspective," *Novum Testamentum* 42 (2000): 1-23. The actual data is well summarized in *TDNT*, although Bultmann's conclusions are of course deeply slanted: see (with Artur Weiser), "πιστεύω [κ.τ.λ.]," in *TDNT* 6:174-228. The divisions within BDAG must be treated with caution (818-20). I make some recommendations concerning more accurate categories in *Quest*, chapter nine, esp. 178-88, arguing there principally in relation to Philo, Josephus, and Paul.

143. It can be coded negatively in a broader setting of gullibility — e.g., "the American electorate is trusting" in the sense of trusting too much what politicians say and promise, perhaps rather stupidly — but this subtle negative meaning is clearly parasitic on the positive sense.

144. We will note a further danger later (especially in part five, chapter twenty, when Galatians is discussed in detail) — translation of πιστ- terms in Paul as "the Faith." I will suggest that this is anachronistic for Paul, despite the assurances of BDAG (see mng 3, 820).

145. This might suggest that only a single connotation is necessary — difficulty — within which broader category the passage of time may fall, since this is widely assumed to cause problems in a relationship. However, little of material significance is gained by such a generalization, so we will remain for the moment with two connotations.

146. Koiné also used πίστις to designate the notion of "fidelity," and it is the most common usage in both the LXX and Josephus, although these distinctions do not exhaust the possible meanings of πίστις in Greek. Like English, however, Koiné does not seem to have used a cognate verb at this point; there is no verb for the notion "to be faithful" or some such, possibly because it is not a discrete action but a general disposition and hence best described adjectivally. Meanwhile, the Greek verb πιστεύω seems to have operated primarily in relation to the two meanings that were noted here first, namely, "to believe" and "to trust." One important consequence of this is that verbal or participial equivalents could be expected in relation to uses of the substantive in these first two senses — "belief/believe" and "trust/trust" — but would not necessarily be expected in relation to uses in the third sense, in terms of "faithfulness."

147. A point taken up in more detail when ODs 21 and 22 are documented shortly.

148. Commentators frequently *assert* that Christian salvation has a personal as well as a propositional dimension, but they seldom *explain* or *justify* this qualitative shift in the relationship at the heart of the process. (The text allows this shift to be asserted here because, as we have just seen, it seems likely in Romans 4 that Abraham trusted God in a personal way — a nice example of the dangers of vertical as against horizontal commentary.) Dunn's endorsement of this understanding of Abraham has already been noted (see n. 37; see also n. 162), but see also Moo, *Romans,* 67.

149. Viz., it seems theologically dangerous, and would also undermine the model that they are trying to develop, which relies ultimately on the reading of Scripture.

150. Some Jewish readings partly mitigate this problem by viewing Abraham as a natural philosopher, who discerned divine truths from the created order, both external and internal (see below).

151. I was introduced to the pervasive problem of — and phrase — "self-referential incoherence" by Alvin Plantinga: see (i.a.) "Reason and Belief in God," in *Faith and Rationality,* ed. Alvin Plantinga & Nicholas Wolterstoff (Notre Dame, Ind.: University of Notre Dame Press, 1984), 16-93.

152. Richard Longenecker provides a useful introductory list of texts along with a brief discussion: see "Excursus: Abraham's Faith and Faithfulness in Jewish Writings and Paul," *Galatians,* WBC 41 (Waco, Texas: Word, 1990), 110-12. He cites Sir. 44:19-21; *Jub.* 23:10; 1 Macc. 2:52; *Cant. R.* 1.13; *m. 'Abot* 1.10-12; *Exod. R.* 44.4 (on Exod. 32:13); and *Lev. R.* 2.10 (on Lev. 1:12). This portrayal is not always in accordance with Abraham's πίστις, although Philo emphasizes this attribute and related text (see *Who Is the Heir?* 90-94; *On the Life of Abraham,* 262-75). Watson provides a more extensive discussion of fewer Jewish texts than Longenecker in "Genesis (2)," *Paul and the Hermeneutics of Faith* (London: T&T Clark International [Continuum], 2004), 220-69 — hereafter *P&HF.*

153. And really in two senses. If it is taken seriously, it jeopardizes the viability of salvation by faith for anyone; but if it is realized that its stringency is problematic, then it calls Justification theory into question for its advocates. Indeed, such is its acuity that most conventional readers seem to deal with it by ignoring it; a definition of "faith" is generally supplied in advance of any detailed exegesis of 4:17-22 that is consequently far removed from Paul's actual discussion of the subject. But any definition of faith in Paul that does not incorporate this material should be judged deficient. Indeed, it is intriguing to catalogue the extent to which definitions of saving faith Paul offered on the basis of Romans 4 *ignore* and *contradict* the extended evidence of vv. 17-21. Moo emphasizes the strength of Abraham's faith, although with a caveat: "When Paul says that Abraham did not 'doubt . . . because of unbelief,' he means not that Abraham never had momentary hesitations, but that he avoided a deep-seated and permanent attitude of distrust and inconsistency in relationship to God and his promises. . . . [He] maintained a single-minded trust in the fulfillment of God's promise": see *Romans,* 284-85. Of course, the text does not really say this. (And his oscillation between different objects of faith here is also noteworthy; this should prompt complementary shifts in the faith involved since faith in God is personal, and trust in a promise less so.) Gathercole is more strongly committed to the powerful nature of Abraham's faith, but provides no suggestions about how to achieve it: "Justified by Faith, Justified by His Blood," 162-63.

154. It might be replied that Paul does at least identify God here as the one who raised Jesus from the dead. However, he does not state that this predication is a necessary part of saving faith, while his preceding scriptural analysis of Abraham corroborates this. Abraham is never said to have known the God of Jesus Christ, but always trusted in God alone — the one who resurrected in general. Hence, no way of navigating in a coherent fashion through to an explicitly Christian predication and confession is provided by Romans 4. So it seems to me that the difficulty remains.

155. The rather deceptive elision of saving objects supplied by commentators is again worth noting: see, i.a., Moo, *Romans,* 67, 78, 282. Moo even acknowledges this: "While, therefore, the locus of faith has shifted as the course of salvation history has filled out and made ever more clear the specific content of the promise, the ultimate object of faith has always been the same" (288). However, if the object of faith is in any overt sense christological, then this is patently not the case. This is a shift in specific content! (Does God lie behind Christ as some deeper, more definitive content — an instance of Sabellianism?)

Gathercole similarly repudiates a mediating analogy in terms of Christ, but redescribes saving

faith as oriented toward God and "resurrecting." He also admits that construing "the relationship between Abrahamic faith and (Pauline) Christian faith . . . is certainly not easy": "Justified by Faith, Justified by his Blood," 164. Strangely, these further specifications on the basis of Romans 4 do not affect
his earlier or later characterizations of saving faith as faith or trust in Christ: see, e.g., 152, 61, 83.

156. I am building here on Klein's original complaint that if this reading of Abraham is maintained, then Israel's development is "radikal entheiligt und paganisiert" ("Römer 4," 158; note, this is
translated incorrectly when quoted in the English trans. of Käsemann's commentary as "radically
desecularized and paganized"; this should be "radically *desecrated* . . ."; *Romans,* 117, emphasis added).
Käsemann's retorts to Klein are unsatisfactory: see his *Romans,* 116-17; also "The Faith of Abraham in
Romans 4," in *Perspectives on Paul,* trans. M. Kohl (London: SCM, 1971 [1969]), 79-101. He charges in
his commentary (1) that if Klein is correct on this point, then *any* appeal to the OT is rendered questionable; (2) limiting Abraham's example to an isolated pre-Christian role makes "both the exclusive-
ness and the choice of Abraham . . . absurd . . ." (i.e., Paul's exegesis here looks either foolish or tendentious [or both]; *Romans,* 117); and (3) it would lead us to Marcionism. However, objection 1 is a fairly
blatant non sequitur. Klein is only objecting to *this,* peculiarly destructive scriptural example. Other
attestations — e.g., messianic — are still quite acceptable. Objection 2 is easily countered if Abraham
is principally an example of the Teacher's, as seems likely (see more on this in part four, chapter eighteen); if it is not, then it is difficult to avoid the stupidity of Paul's selection (but at least Käsemann acknowledges this; certainly this is not *Klein's* fault!). And it is still entirely possible to affirm the role
and historical precedence of Israel from an apocalyptic perspective, thereby countering objection 3;
indeed, this is rather healthier than any a priori insistence on Israel's priority (which also seems a curious thing for Käsemann to be emphasizing!; in this relation see *Quest,* 63-68).

Outside explicit debate, many commentators generate this difficulty, and often without acknowledging it; so, e.g., Moo: ". . . the OT itself teaches not 'covenantal nomism' but 'promissory
pistism' — that a *saving* relationship with God comes, as it did for Abraham, through human response
to God's grace expressed in his promise and not through the Mosaic covenant [i.e., through faith]"
(*Romans,* 126-27, emphasis original; see also 215). But historical Israel is effectively erased by this
claim, as is the law, which is an extraordinary omission from the OT simply on *exegetical* grounds.
Moreover, monotheists are now *included.* Moo never considers if it is problematic to extend Christian
salvation automatically to Muslims. (And so on.)

Tobin is aware of the difficulty, but attributes it to Galatians, suggesting that the rather different treatment of Abraham in Romans 4 is palliative. However, it is difficult to see exactly how the argument in Romans — conventionally construed — removes the challenges of Galatians (and, in fact,
of Romans itself): see *Paul's Rhetoric,* 127-30, 43-45.

157. As Simon J. Gathercole rightly points out: see *Where Is Boasting? Early Jewish Soteriology
and Paul's Response in Romans 1–5* (Grand Rapids, Mich.: Eerdmans, 2002), 233.

158. Note, the statement that "not all Abraham's seed are children [of Abraham]" does not suggest in context any nonliteral, spiritual descendants of Abraham but rather the opposite point — *that
not all his literal descendants are part of Israel.* Those descendants counted — and in fact chosen — for
Israel are still his literal descendants. But the nation of Israel descends through Isaac and Jacob, not
through his other literal descendants Ishmael and Esau. Some of his literal descendants have been excluded. See further on this in part five, chapter nineteen.

159. This strictly individual, meritocratic system is contradicted by the notion that a key figure
could do something that would directly affect all of his or her descendants.

160. Once again, recognition of this difficulty by the commentators is disappointing. Moo describes Abraham's fatherhood spiritually: ". . . Abraham is the 'father of us all' — the spiritual forefather of all of 'us' who are believers"; *Romans,* 279, commenting on 4:16b: see also 280. Dunn states:
". . . Gentile Christians would call Abraham 'father' . . . but 'father' in terms of faith, not in terms of
physical descent. But the slightly pejorative note in the phrase 'according to the flesh' further implies
that to understand that inheritance from Abraham in merely fleshly, ethnic terms is inadequate. . . .
Abraham's paternity extends beyond the realm of the physical and visible (cf. 2:28-29). . . . God's cove-

nant righteousness extends to believing Gentile as well as to Jew without regard to national identity as determined by the law" (*Romans 1–8*, 226-27).

161. Paul uses δικαίωσις only in Romans, here and in 5:18. There it appears in a genitive construction with ζωή, and functions opposite κατάκριμα.

162. Some commentators try to avoid this by shifting the terms of the salvation in play, and in effect moving to a transformational and participatory model when the text has not yet introduced that (according to the conventional reading) — a good example of this is Moo: see *Romans*, 289. Alternatively, semantic slippage takes place within rather sweeping and rhetorical exposition to blur the conceptual difficulty. Dunn is an excellent example of these tactics and so worth quoting at length: ". . . the link between justification and Jesus' resurrection was not merely prompted by the preceding exposition, but also further underscores its point — that the justifying grace of God is all of a piece with his creative, life-giving power. Abraham's trust would have been wholly vain if in the event God had not given him and Sarah seed after all. Just so, Christian faith would be vain unless God actually raised Jesus. Had Jesus' death not been followed by his resurrection, any understanding of his death as sacrifice would only have become part of Israel's martyr theology, without power of itself to provide the eschatological breakthrough which his resurrection demonstrated. Jesus' resurrection is proof positive that the same life-giving power which wrought for Abraham and Sarah is still at work in this new stage of God's dealing with humankind and at work in eschatological strength. Faith knows it is accepted precisely because its acceptance is the same effective power which raised Jesus and which will also give life to these mortal bodies (8:11) in the final reckoning" (*Romans 1–8*, 241). Every statement here seems fair in relation to Paul generally (except perhaps the last, which is ambiguous), *but none are to the point*. Furthermore, all talk of eschatology is a move into the alternative soteriology (see Romans 5–8 and part one, chapter three). Nevertheless by the end of this exposition "faith" has been juxtaposed plausibly and repeatedly with resurrection, so the uncritical reader will probably not detect a problem here. Yet one exists, and it has not been resolved. Earlier Dunn is a little more candid, describing the link between δικαίωσις and resurrection as "somewhat surprising" (although this comment may apply to the presence of this particular word: see elsewhere in Paul only Rom. 5:18). He then states that 4:25b "does at least . . . underscore the soteriological significance of Jesus' resurrection and prevent its being regarded solely in terms of Jesus' vindication." This is correct, but, again, it does not *resolve* the problem of just *how* the resurrection functions soteriologically in broader relation to Justification (225). Such claims beg the question.

Schreiner states more succinctly that Jesus was raised because "his resurrection authenticates and confirms that our justification has been secured. . . . The resurrection of Christ constitutes evidence that his work on our behalf has been completed. The death and resurrection of Christ [also] fulfill the promise of universal blessing made to Abraham . . ." (*Romans*, 244). If this is the case then (1) it is curious that the authenticating role of the resurrection is not stated explicitly in 1:2-7 by Paul when it is first discussed, and (2) that the resurrection is not then also introduced in 3:21-26, where Christ's atonement is discussed programmatically; (3) it is also unnecessary to resurrect Christians, because *their* sacrifices are not being authenticated (and ultimately this will drive a wedge between the function of Christ's resurrection and the general resurrection); and (4) it seems strange that Paul never explains *how* a resurrection authenticates a universal sacrifice. This is important because no sacrifices seem to have been resurrected previously in the Jewish sacrificial tradition, yet their efficacy was not thereby questioned; this explanatory link is not obvious. It should also be noted (5) that this is not what Paul actually *says:* the resurrection does not "authenticate" or "confirm" a prior act or status of justification in 4:25; it *effects* that act or status. Furthermore, that the death and resurrection speak to Abraham's legacy of universal blessing is irrelevant as well as potentially embarrassing, because this contention is grounded in historical particularities foreign to Justification's ahistorical categories. (It is a fair claim concerning Paul in and of itself, but it does not resolve the problem that we are grappling with here.) So it seems to me that Schreiner's attempted explanations all founder.

163. Watson makes the best case that I know of for the importance of this verse, emphasizing it courageously (*P&HF*, 169-219; see also *PJ&G²*, 260-69). But he leaves many of these problems essentially unresolved. I evaluate his proposals in detail in chapter twelve.

164. This distinction is pressed incoherently when circumcision is overruled entirely by 2:25-29 — OD 11. Tobin is alert to this dimension in the text, and — not unfairly — mobilizes traditional Hellenistic Jewish arguments to explain it (see esp. his use of Philo: *Paul's Rhetoric*, 115). But these explanations do not *explain* the distinction! In claiming that natural laws "find their highest and clearest expression in the Mosaic law" the problem is merely restated (whether by Philo or Tobin), and not recognized and resolved (i.e., how God can judge with strict justice in relation to two *different* ethical codes).

165. A note of caution is present here because ancient conceptions of fatherhood should not be sentimentalized; they could be quite "retributive," if not overtly tyrannical. However, I would want to argue that the conception of divine fatherhood as Paul specifically develops that — especially in Romans 5–8 — is emphatically and fundamentally benevolent. In my view, he uses a particular scriptural narrative to make this point: see my essay, "The Story of Jesus in Romans and Galatians," in *Narrative Dynamics in Paul: A Critical Assessment*, ed. B. W. Longenecker (Louisville, Ky.: Westminster John Knox, 2002), 97-124 (repr. in *Quest*, ch. 4, 69-94).

166. This tension links up with the debate over the meaning of Paul's half dozen or so πίστις Χριστοῦ genitives.

167. The point where faith disappears depends to a degree on disputed text-critical questions. These are addressed in part five, chapter nineteen.

168. Phil. 3:1-11 is assessed carefully in part five, chapter twenty-one. And I suggest there that its best construal aligns with this judgment.

169. Again, part five, chapter twenty-one, addresses some of the key texts.

Notes to Chapter Twelve

1. We will of course note the contributions of many other figures in passing. Hence, there is a briefer treatment of Krister Stendahl, the magnitude of whose contributions to this debate should already be apparent. However, he seldom offers either detailed exegesis or comprehensive solutions, as these figures do, and so does not feature so centrally in this chapter.

It is also probably becoming apparent why I have avoided structuring my discussion in terms of the "new perspective." As will become even clearer shortly, its key representatives are often exercising fundamentally different strategic options as they try to resolve certain problems in the Justification discourse, and their accounts *of* those problems often differ fundamentally as well. At bottom, the new perspective combines perceptions and strategies that ought to be distinguished. We need to move well beyond its categories and debates — and the following discussion tries to do so. (I made these claims earlier on in part one, chapter six, §1, n. 4, and document them in more detail in this chapter, assuming that the diversity of the criticisms emanating from the new perspective is already apparent from part three, chapter eleven).

2. See §2.1, esp. n. 7.

3. It is important to keep asking how Stendahl knows the things that he says he knows. It is also worth noting that this set of difficulties dogs the reconstruction offered in Francis Watson, *Paul, Judaism, and the Gentiles*, first ed. (Cambridge: Cambridge University Press, 1989), and rev. ed. (Grand Rapids, Mich.: Eerdmans, 2007) — hereafter *PJ&G*[1] and *PJ&G*[2] respectively. While interpreting Paul's letters — intra-*ecclesial* documents — Watson keeps relocating their concerns within an early *missiological* dynamic — an *external* context — largely assuming that the two are coterminous.

4. This fallacy has already been noted in part one, chapter four, in §4. My account of the text's circumstantial frame in part two, chapter seven, §2.4, tried to integrate intentionality into the broader interpretative process coherently. So suffice it for now to note that a text's generation is qualitatively different and hence distinguishable from its content, even if these dimensions are connected. See also this illuminating statement: "Interpretive problems in Romans 2 are mitigated considerably when one asks what Paul is here seeking to *do* in this chapter. . . . [T]he answer is that he is seeking to reinforce the barrier separating the church from the synagogue. Denunciation of the iniquity of leading repre-

sentatives of the Jewish community is part of that strategy. What matters is not whether the charges can be substantiated, but whether Paul's readers are disposed to find them plausible" (Watson, *PJ&G²*, 97, emphasis original). In other words, only the rhetorical function of the texts is relevant; their *truth* is subordinate to that goal!

5. Watson's reconstruction in *PJ&G¹* and *PJ&G²* then arguably *reinforces* them, by locking Paul's Justification texts into a social situation that preserves some of the worst dynamics in those texts. Whereas it is true that Paul no longer converts in an individualistic — and ultimately unrealistic — fashion from law-observant Judaism, which he characterizes negatively, to law-free Christianity, on the Damascus road, nevertheless he still polemicizes against his former "parent" religion, as he justifies the emergence of his law-free communities. Hence, the relocation of these texts to a later missiological and communal setting in no way disrupts the fundamentally negative relationship between law-observant Judaism and Christianity that their conventional reading supplies, still constructing that relationship in the conventional a priori way, from which point all the pernicious implications of Justification theory are unleashed. *Relocating* this argumentative and theological dynamic does not *remove* it. Certainly, *something* has changed in the interpretation of these texts, perhaps creating the impression of significant change, *but it is not the essential thing!* (Moreover, its ongoing existence might even have been disguised by this maneuver.)

6. Watson's reconstruction in *PJ&G²* is not as vulnerable to this problem as Stendahl's because of the extensive historical scenario he offers there — and he is to be commended both for recognizing the need to do this and offering such a creative and probing account. I engage with the details of this reconstruction especially in part one, chapter five, and part four, chapter thirteen.

7. Bruce W. Longenecker, *Eschatology and the Covenant: A Comparison of 4 Ezra and Romans 1-11*, JSNTSup 57 (Sheffield: JSOT, 1991); see also *The Triumph of Abraham's God: The Transformation of Identity in Galatians* (Edinburgh: T&T Clark, 1998); and "Sharing in Their Spiritual Blessings? The Stories of Israel in Galatians and Romans," in *Narrative Dynamics in Paul: A Critical Assessment,* ed. Bruce W. Longenecker (Louisville, Ky.: Westminster John Knox, 2002), 58-84; Heikki Räisänen, *Paul and the Law,* 2nd ed., WUNT 29 (Tübingen: J. C. B. Mohr [Paul Siebeck], 1987 [1983]) — hereafter *P&L;* J. Klausner, *From Jesus to Paul* (Boston: Beacon, 1939); Hyam Maccoby, *The Mythmaker: Paul and the Invention of Christianity* (New York: Harper & Row, 1986); and *Paul and Hellenism* (London: SCM, 1991); C. H. Dodd, "The Mind of Paul," in *New Testament Studies* (New York: Scribners, 1952), 67-128; P. F. Esler, *Conflict and Identity in Romans: The Social Setting of Paul's Letter* (Minneapolis, Minn.: Fortress, 2003). Watson's work is treated in more detail just below.

8. Stowers observes appropriately (specifically in relation to the suggestions of Sanders and Räisänen) that such "psychological speculation is a jump out of the quagmire into the quicksand": *A Rereading of Romans: Justice, Jews, and Gentiles* (New Haven: Yale University Press, 1994), 6 — hereafter *RR.*

9. It is impossible to improve upon Watson's formulation at this point: "It is *a priori* plausible that Paul's Gentile mission and his radical relativizing of the Torah developed in conjunction with each other, and that his statements about the Torah thus have a social correlate.... To make this point is *not* to assign to 'social reality' a priority and a determining role in relation to 'theology' — as though theology did not already belong to social reality. It is simply to say that we should expect to find correlations between the two" (*PJ&G²*, 60). *PJ&G²* is not always faithful to this imperative, but certainly Watson is aware of it.

10. London: T&T Clark International (Continuum), 2004. This principal study is usefully supplemented by "Constructing a Hermeneutic: A Rereading of Romans 1-4" (paper presented to the New Testament Doctoral Seminar, the Divinity School, Duke University: November, 2004); and "Scripture in Pauline Theology: How Far Down Does It Go?" (paper presented to the Pauline Soteriology Group, Society of Biblical Literature Annual Meeting, San Antonio, Tex.: November 2004) (both available at http://andygoodliff.typepad.com/my_weblog/pauls_letters/index.html and http://www.abdn.ac.uk/divinity/staff/details.php?id=f.b.watson). "Not the New Perspective" was something of a forerunner to these analyses; it has subsequently been withdrawn by the author but still contains some useful indications of future directions: Francis Watson, "Not the New Perspective"

(paper presented to the BNTS annual conference, Manchester: 2001) (consulted at www.abdn.ac.uk/ divinity/staff/watsonart.shtml on 9/27/2004). Also important in this relation is Watson's first book, *PJ&G* — also a brilliant argument. (Some material from the papers just cited is worked into the latest edition.) However, the relationship between *PJ&G* (whether 1 or 2, because the earlier argument is not substantially withdrawn or reformulated) and *P&HF* generates some intriguing questions.

PJ&G² is principally a clarification of Watson's "ambivalent relationship with the New Perspective on Paul" (xii), although clarifications with respect to *P&HF* do of course also arise. But the latter relationship seems awkward if not at cross-purposes because two fundamentally different views of Paul's *textuality* seem to be promoted by these two books (although both are generative). The main claim of *PJ&G* (whether 1 or 2) is that a tight, retrievable, and critical relationship exists between what Paul says — especially in the Justification texts that concern us here — and his social context in a flowering law-free mission to pagans (a commendable thesis, even if problematic in points of detail). And at times Watson teeters on the brink of overt reductionism in this relation. As we will see shortly, however, the main thesis of *P&HF* is that Paul writes many of his texts — and especially his Justification arguments — under the impress of an independent, recognizable, and responsible consideration of the Pentateuch. He writes because he reads Scripture well, largely as a Jew, and *not* because he is evangelizing pagans and legitimizing their law-free status. Thus, if pressed, these two causalities are simply irreducible; quite different explanations are provided for the origins of Paul's Justification texts. But if one is not pressed in the interests of explanatory harmonization, then the thesis in that book is undermined; it has been reduced to the other. (That is, both are comprehensive explanations; they are not couched in complementary or subordinate terms.)

I will concentrate on *P&HF* in what follows here, partly because I agree with the methodology of *PJ&G*, but disagree with some of the details in its reconstructions. (And some further clarifications will be suggested concerning *PJ&G* at the relevant stages of the following argument: see esp. part four, chapter thirteen, and part five, chapter twenty; some issues have already been noted in part one, chapters four and five.)

11. Some of my comments here have been anticipated by "An Evangelical Paul: A Response to Francis Watson's *Paul and the Hermeneutics of Faith*," *Journal for the Study of the New Testament* 28 (2006): 337-51. However, the following is a more detailed and extensive engagement, and is also oriented slightly differently, given the specialized terminology that has been introduced throughout this investigation. Richard B. Hays's engagement is also well worth noting: see "Paul's Hermeneutics and the Question of Truth," *Pro Ecclesia* 16 (2007): 126-33. Watson has responded to Hays: "Response to Richard Hays," *Pro Ecclesia* 16 (2007): 134-40; and to me: "Paul the Reader: An Authorial Apologia," *Journal for the Study of the New Testament* 28 (2006): 363-73. However, his characteristically eloquent replies in my view remain inadequate in substantive terms in relation to the concerns that we have raised.

12. See *P&HF*, 6-29, 33-40, 274-75.

13. Also called "alien," "nonnegotiable" (*P&HF*, ix-x, 183), "unilateral"/"unilaterally imposed," determinative (*P&HF*, 16, 516), "arbitrary" (*P&HF*, 517), "a dogmatic positivism" ("Scripture," 7), "positivistic christology" ("Scripture," 8), etc.

14. Watson argues that only in this way can Scripture function as a genuine witness to Christ, with a degree of independence from him. It is important to note in addition that the presence of this interpretative space between the relatively independent appropriation of the Pentateuch by Paul and the Christ event allows a genuine dialogue to unfold in relation to other contemporary Jewish readings of the same texts. Watson argues that all these readings occupy the same hermeneutically constituted field and represent reasonable actualizations of the semantic potential of its shared texts; hence, all these readers are fundamentally "Jewish." Paul himself does not of course recognize the validity of alternative readings, and other Jews have differences with one another. Indeed, Paul's fellow readers are inadequate in large measure because they fail to detect the contradictions within the text that he does. However, Watson himself is nervous about privileging one of these Jewish readings over another. Each is to a degree a different hermeneutic and he argues that there is no objective Archimedean point lying outside this debate on which basis to judge it. And this allows Watson to emphasize

Paul's shared Jewishness *and* his distinctiveness in a mutually enriching rather than a bluntly antithetical manner. For Watson, to be Jewish is primarily to be interpreting the Jewish canon and therefore necessarily to be involved in interpretative divergence. Such differences are a constitutive part of that identity. Watson's study, then, is not simply about Paul, although I will concentrate on his reading of Paul here. Indeed, it is a distinctive feature of the book that Watson's exploration of Paul's readings takes place — in a rather fascinating way — within an ongoing dialogue with other Jewish readings of the same material by Philo, Josephus, and the authors of texts like Baruch, *4 Ezra*, and the Wisdom of Solomon.

15. My use of these terms is emphatically not pejorative, merely descriptive.

16. See *P&HF*, 16-17. Watson's use of the term "constitutive" in this relation is to my mind rather unfortunate (see also 43). See his statements in "Scripture": "the Pauline Christ is intertextually constituted" (8); and — still more alarmingly — "[W]hen, in the fullness of time, God sends forth God's son, born of a woman, the particular form that this event takes is determined not by Mary alone but also by scripture and its apostolic reception. For Paul, scripture — *interpreted* scripture — is the comprehensive medium within which Jesus comes to be who he is" (9). I can only assume that this theological madness is hyperbole deployed in support of a thesis. As far as I can tell, Watson really means by all this that Scripture is constitutive of *the language* and *discourse* used to proclaim Christ, and not constitutive of the event itself or the person himself. I am not entirely sure why this has to be emphasized so much. It simply seems to be the case that the language used to proclaim the Christ event was scriptural — or, at least, significantly so. Thus, there seems to be little point in opposing an impossible hypothetical, viz., that Christ was *not* proclaimed by scripturally influenced language: see also 529-30. This clarification is perhaps more obvious in Watson's paper "Scripture": ". . . an ongoing dialogue with scripture is one of the generative principles of his theology . . ." (1); "[it is] a fundamental element of Pauline theological discourse. Scripture does not float on the surface, it goes all the way down" (2). These claims seem more sober and plausible.

17. The axiomatic commitments to natural theology and to a retributively just God also clash with Paul's countervailing commitments evident elsewhere. And arguably a tendency within the model to endorse violence in a number of respects grates with Paul's commitment to nonviolent mission (and so on).

18. In terms of the earlier enumeration of theory-related difficulties, he has eliminated or mitigated intrinsic difficulties (IDs) 1, 2, and 3, and *possibly* also 4, 5, 6, and 7 (one of the benefits of moving to a more consistent internal system); he has eliminated systematic difficulties (SDs) 1, and possibly 2 and 3 (I am not convinced that difficulties 4-10 have been negotiated); and empirical difficulties (EDs) 1, and possibly 2 through 4. We will postpone for the moment a consideration of the possible mitigation of exegetical under- and overdeterminations in Romans 1-4, although I think that this is actually the main weakness in Watson's proposal.

19. Watson has also in so doing laid down a significant marker within the broader debate over the nature of Paul's intertextuality. We have not been so concerned about this debate here as yet, but Watson and others certainly hold it to be important. We will pass over for the moment the question whether he has characterized that intertextuality entirely accurately. More important at this stage is the recognition that Watson's case is both highly sophisticated and "maximalist." (Watson means by this both that Paul quotes or alludes to Scripture a lot *and* that this process plays a critical role in his thinking.) He supplies — at length — a model of Paul's scriptural engagement that is undeniably powerful, extensive, and cogent. Hence, from this point onward easy dismissals of Paul's hermeneutic have been permanently foreclosed. (Carefully argued redefinitions and redeployments remain possible.)

20. By his own account, Watson did not intend to reach this position as one of "Lutheranism's" many apologists; he states that this is simply where he ended up (see *P&HF*, 28-29). It is in part this end point, along with the implicit soteriology, that prompted me to characterize him as — still! — Lutheran in "An Evangelical Paul." But Watson has protested strongly against this (see *PJ&G*², 25, n. 42), and in certain respects this complaint seems fair.

Watson has always been a creative and insightful critic of certain key aspects of the orthodox Lutheran construal of Paul — its neglected sociological setting (so much of *PJ&G*), Paul's use of scrip-

ture (so much of *P&HF*), and so on. So my charge must be explained and reoriented. When I characterize Watson as "Lutheran" I mean only that his version of Paul's gospel still *overlaps fundamentally*
with the version of the gospel offered by Luther (see part two, chapter eight), and the relevant post-
Luther interpretative tradition, because both are committed to salvation "by faith alone," and this was
a distinctive interpretative insight in relation to Paul made by Luther. Moreover, it is cradled — as we
have seen — by certain arguments, and hence by certain construals of other Pauline texts; this motif
has irreducible soteriological concomitants that Watson must share with Luther, or lapse into complete incoherence (e.g., the conviction that in Romans 1–4 Paul reasons "forward"). So there is a reasonably extensive degree of overlap between them at a very important point. This then entails that
Watson has, at the critical point of the construction of the gospel, not moved beyond the basic interpretative paradigm that Luther also occupies, and in part defines. However, in this sense, Watson is
certainly not "Lutheran" in terms of a strict descriptive homology — far from it. But, if the arguments
of this book are correct, he remains an occupant of the broad Lutheran paradigm of Justification, so *a
family resemblance is discernible* between Watson and Luther. Hence, it is only in this last, weakened
sense that I make the charge that Watson is "Lutheran" (using that term because this is how the majority of NT scholars characterize what I designate the JF model in *Quest,* and the Justification discourse
here). Indeed, I am happy to withdraw it if it causes offense and/or confusion, and substitute the
charge that Watson remains at bottom an occupant of the Justification paradigm in his construal of
Paul's gospel, like Luther — although he is one of its most creative and self-critical representatives.

21. Watson claims to support the basic epistemological reconstruction of J. L. Martyn in relation to Paul, although not Martyn's account of Paul's exegesis in Galatians. (Certainly he shares
Martyn's nervousness with all forms of linearity, including any narrative linearity.) He also supports
much of Hays's work on Paul's intertextuality, although he repudiates Hays's reading of some of Paul's
πίστις language with reference to Christ, and turns out to pursue quite a different account of
intertextuality in Paul.

22. I suspect in addition that Watson simply shares certain features of the British debate — the
skepticism of many British New Testament scholars of his generation with all things "new perspective." These scholars have generally failed to be convinced by the most significant local representatives
of various revisionist readings (and with some justification) — J. D. G. Dunn and N. T. Wright. The
opinions of Morna Hooker and Bruce Longenecker concerning Paul's use of πίστις have not made
much headway either (nor my own efforts 1996-2003!).

23. It is probably only fair to note in addition that Watson is — like many — offended by crude
critical assertions concerning Paul's hermeneutics. This issue is the explicit starting point for his book,
much of which is an extended apology for the apostle's integrity in this regard, so Watson places himself specifically at odds with certain tactics by other revisionists. He is also discernibly starting to embrace a "post-post-Sanders" perspective on Judaism, being sensitive to some of the difficulties within
Sanders's original critique of Weber et al. (We have already teased out some of these issues in part one,
chapter four.) Even as Sanders accused scholars of previous generations of caricaturing Judaism, he
tended himself at times to caricature the situation in an opposite direction, and Watson rightly reacts
to this tendency. Whether in so doing Watson has resolved the underlying, and appropriately redefined, empirical conundrum is, however, another matter.

24. A further common problem for reframers is the persistence, in spite of their reframing, of
the various problems of the Justification discourse that the reframing leaves intact in the underlying
conventional reading. But Watson is playing something of a double game, and so is less susceptible to
this line of criticism, at least in the first instance. His reframing explanation is also a reconstrual of
Paul's thought. Paul is operating with a canonical hermeneutic of the Pentateuch, he argues, that results in a primary emphasis in his gospel on salvation and "righteousness by faith." And even though it
does not arise directly out of Paul's texts and contingent arguments, this hermeneutic nevertheless operates for Paul at the equivalent level to Justification theory (of which it is a fairly significant modification), from which point it arguably does solve a number of difficulties apparent in the conventional
reading and its attendant theory of Justification.

25. Many would not grant this point, but the debate is enormously complex and is best consid-

ered later, especially in relation to the exegesis of Romans 9:30–10:5 (see part five, chapters nineteen and twenty).

26. The meaning of the "curse" quotations is addressed momentarily.

27. Paul's use of that narrative here does not respect the purview of the canon, because it is explicitly Christianized in vv. 1-4 (see also v. 11). Then in v. 6 Paul states explicitly that these stories are "types" illustrating that "we" should not desire evil things. Specific references to idolatry, sexual immorality, provocation of God, and grumbling follow. Finally, everything is focused on care with respect to what one eats now, meaning of course meat sacrificed to idols. "Therefore, my beloved ones, flee from idolatry" Paul admonishes sternly in v. 14. And this argument is not to my mind directly supportive of the view that the law has created these sinful instances in Israel by first prohibiting them, from which point death is inflicted on disobedience.

It is true that the law prohibits most of them, but this is because they are evil and obviously so. The children of Israel did not commit idolatry simply because the law told them not to; it was wrong to be disloyal to God. (Moreover, strictly speaking, they had not received the law when they ran off after the golden calf.) And Paul locates the problem here simply in evil desires, not in the law. The law certainly exposes the problem of evil desires, but there is no sense in this passage that it *creates* that problem, and therefore that Paul learned of its death-dealing qualities in relation to desire by reading the original pentateuchal stories. (Paul's conflation of these narratives is problematic for Watson's thesis as well, although not necessarily fatal to it.) In short, Watson has to add the key premise to this argument in Paul that sin and its consequences were generated by the giving of the law; the law thereby created the opportunity for sin, punishment, and death, a possibility that Israel duly enacted. But the text itself reads as a fairly straightforward indictment of characteristically pagan behavior by people who should have known better but who gave in to their evil desires. It is a critique of idolatry *tout court*. (Watson is very hard elsewhere on scholars who introduce important principles into Paul's arguments that are not directly supported by the text.)

28. In part one, chapter five.

29. Alternatively, as Watson articulates at times, the Spirit in the new covenant writes in the lives of human beings, "on their hearts," changing them, whereas in the old covenant the Spirit's finger wrote words on tablets of stone.

30. Watson also claims that when Paul speaks of the giving of the law in 2 Corinthians 3, the veil covers Moses' face to conceal the fading of his glory and therefore indicates something deceptive about the law (see Exod. 34:34-35); the law cannot disclose its own fallibility (etc.). Hence, a subtle canonical hermeneutic underlies Paul's argument at this point as well. Moreover, this incident is indicative of the entire status of the law — glorious but deceptively transient. And this reading might restore our faith in Watson's proposed hermeneutic (although, strictly speaking, it is not a canonical hermeneutic). But Watson's reading is dependent on the rendering of the key verb καταργέω, used in vv. 7, 11, 13, and 14, in terms of "fading." And this translation has recently been definitvely refuted by Richard Hays (who favors "nullify") in "A Letter from Christ," *The Conversion of the Imagination: Paul as Interpreter of Israel's Scripture* (Grand Rapids, Mich.: Eerdmans, 2005), 122-53, esp. 133-36.

31. This text too will be treated in more detail later on, in part five, chapter nineteen.

32. These exegetical claims are argued in more detail in part five, chapter twenty.

33. This text is explicated more fully in part five, chapter twenty-one.

34. Watson's reading of this text can also be challenged immediately in context. The principal burden of the apostle's appeal to the patriarch is clearly *ancestry,* meaning a connection by later Christians with him in terms of concrete biological kinship and not "faith." Genesis 15:6 plays almost no overt role in the developing argument, while the "promise[s]" and "blessing" related to "the seed" are clearly salient. In 3:29 this contention culminates in Paul's declaration that everyone who belongs to Christ — the promised single seed — is a descendant of Abraham and an heir. As Watson notes, this trajectory from Abraham and Genesis precedes the giving of the law at Sinai, thereby dominating it in theological terms (although one could demur at this point), but Paul's purview then simply seems to extend to the apostle's time, including Israel from Sinai to the arrival of Christ within an ongoing and deeply onerous pedagogy — one stretching without interruption through the further pentateuchal,

historical, *and* prophetic narratives. Nothing here looks like a canonical hermeneutic of the Pentateuch that culminates in the principle of "righteousness by faith."

35. See especially part four, chapters fifteen through seventeen (1:16-17; 3:21-26), eighteen (4:1-25), and part five, chapter nineteen (9:30–10:5 in its broader context).

36. We will note momentarily a further difficulty within Watson's program that overlaps with this set of issues — his circumscription of Paul's intertextuality.

37. Paul's citation of Lev. 19:18 is especially problematic (see Rom. 13:8-10 and Gal. 5:14 in context). Furthermore, Paul's claims in relation to this text simply seem false — unless it is defined christologically. The apostle states baldly in both these passages that the entire law is fulfilled by Lev. 19:18 but then in Romans lists only the interpersonal commandments from the Decalogue. What has happened to God, not to mention the first five commandments (explicitly in Romans and by implication in Galatians; the Sabbath is also swept out of sight)? Watson argues skillfully that Paul, like Philo, is referring here only to the second table of the Decalogue, and few would dispute that Lev. 19:18 is an effective summary of this material. However, Paul never actually says this, and neither is it likely — especially in the context of Galatia! (Watson's Philonic reading would leave the first table of the Decalogue in force in its own right; but see Gal. 4:9-11!) Paul seems to mean what he says, namely, that the *entire* law is fulfilled in Lev. 19:18 (ὁ . . . πᾶς νόμος in Gal. 5:14). Hence, Watson is forced to fall back on mere assertion. He states that some texts "are more fundamental . . . than others. Removal of Leviticus 18.5 would affect its whole structure [i.e., Paul's basic reading of the Torah in Watson's terms], whereas removal of Leviticus 19.18 would not" (*P&HF,* 521). However, this reasoning clearly begs the question. Leviticus 19:18 simply falsifies his proposed hermeneutic. And it is not an isolated instance. (Paul also uses the "divine impartiality" theologoumenon repeatedly, and this is hard to reconcile with Watson's overarching schema: see Deut. 10:17 in Rom. 2:11 and Gal. 2:6b; see also Sir. 35:15.)

38. Watson allows in principle for their involvement; however, any contributions of this nature have to be controlled by the canonical and pentateuchal hermeneutic.

39. Paul, Watson asserts, does not build on scriptural *stories* but on *books,* and these may or may not contain stories. However, in light of this concession, it is difficult to account for Watson's exclusions of allusive narrative analyses, even when these are pentateuchal. We have already seen that he does not ascribe the story of Adam, introduced in Rom. 5:12, a great deal of significance in Romans 7, despite its arguable centrality there. (Watson holds that readings of Exodus and Numbers underpin Romans 7.) Similarly, he ignores the possibility that the story of Abraham's near sacrifice of Isaac, rooted in Genesis 22, may be implicit in Romans 8, informing the relationship between God the Father and his only Son, as first indicated in 5:6 and 8. He notes in passing that an exodus narrative might also be in play in Romans 8 (as suggested by Keesmaat) but fails to develop the point: see S. Keesmaat, *Paul and His Story: (Re)Interpreting the Exodus Tradition,* JSNTSup 181 (Sheffield: Sheffield Academic Press, 1999). An even more overt instance of such narratives in Paul is Gal. 4:21-31, where the stories of Sarah and Isaac, and of Hagar and Ishmael, intertwine — both the conceptions of the two sons of Abraham, and their later fates (with a contingent application in Galatia; the Galatians are to stand firm, are not to accept the yoke of the law through circumcision and its attendant slavery, and are thereby to hold on to their inheritance as prefigured in Isaac). It is not difficult to explain Watson's lack of emphasis at these points. The application of these narratives by Paul is localized, typological, retrospective, and unashamedly contemporary (i.e., the stories are applied to Christians and/or to non-Christians in general terms); hence, they contradict Watson's proposed Pauline hermeneutic, which is generalized, historical, prospective, and canonical in purview.

40. Let it suffice to note for now that running through Galatians 3 is a shockingly christological hermeneutic. Paul states in 3:16, to the endless chagrin of critical scholars, that the singular seed in respect to whom the promises were made — presumably in Gen. 13:15 and/or 17:8 and/or 24:7 (ἐρρέθησαν αἱ ἐπαγγελίαι . . . καὶ τῷ σπέρματί σου) — is Christ. This claim seems to undergird Paul's earlier statement in v. 8 that the gospel was proclaimed beforehand to Abraham. The seed, who is Christ, then provides the salvation-historical pivot around which all the blessings and promises offered to Abraham are finally fulfilled (see 3:19–4:7).

41. That is, christological intertextuality is excluded because it is dogmatic, presupposed, de-

terminative (*P&HF,* 16), imposed, overwhelming (17), etc., and therefore unacceptable. But several problems lurk here. It does not follow from Watson's dislike of such exegesis that Paul does not practice it (as we have already seen). Moreover, Watson is strongly committed to theological exegesis. Is it to be suggested seriously that theological exegesis is permitted but christological exegesis is not? Furthermore, this is a strange deployment of the post-Enlightenment critique of religion in a hermeneutical context that has long been repudiated as essentially untrue. Recalling some of the arguments of part two, chapter seven, it can be emphasized here that all explanation, including hermeneutical explanation, is presuppositional and involves the "imposition" of explanatory categories on given fields of data. The reader, like the scientist, is active; texts do not read themselves. Consequently, all explanation, including hermeneutical explanation, is to a significant degree dogmatic. Hence, Watson's critique here is not grounded in the reality of either his own procedures or investigation generally. But, furthermore, it seems doubly strange to fault *Christology* for its dogmatic status. Is Watson really suggesting that christological commitments, usually viewed as essential by the church, should be fundamentally *negotiable?* Should Christology actually *lack* dogmatic status? Christology is a dogma and appropriately so on all sorts of grounds, but it does not follow from this that its hermeneutical involvement with the interpretation of Paul is inevitably inappropriate.

42. Watson recognizes the importance of Hab. 2:4 for Paul in Romans but subordinates its meaning to a conventional approach rooted primarily in Gen. 15:6. Yet Hab. 2:4 is Paul's opening scriptural corroboration in Romans, cited explicitly in 1:17, and we must wait until 4:2 for Paul's analysis of Gen. 15:6. So should these roles not be reversed? (although more on this shortly). Similarly, when Paul deploys a carefully crafted catena of prophetic texts in Rom. 3:10-18, Watson simply ascribes this testimony to the law. Paul certainly allows that it is the voice of ὁ νόμος, but this is not necessarily the same thing as an ascription to the Pentateuch. "Torah" could mean, for Jews, the voice of *Scripture.* Watson's thesis demands these reorientations; however, there seems little overt evidence for them. The entire catena is from prophetic texts (assuming the canonical view that David was a prophet who composed the Psalms: see 4:6-8 and 11:9-10 [etc.]). Perhaps even more telling is Watson's inattention to prophetic texts that seem to inform Paul's call and apostolic self-understanding significantly. Paul himself, in Rom. 1:2, goes so far as to speak of the gospel's being promised beforehand in the Prophets (i.e., in those texts alone). Indeed, it is hard to imagine how the Pentateuch could attest either to Jesus' Davidic lineage or to his resurrection from the dead in the power of the sanctifying Spirit (vv. 3-4), as Paul outlines things briefly here! Later, in an important analysis of his proclamation, Paul cites Isa. 52:7 — "how beautiful are the feet of those proclaiming good things" (i.e., literally, "gospeling" — εὐαγγελιζομένων). It seems highly likely that this verse underpins Paul's designation of his message as "the gospel," at least to some degree, especially in view of the constant benedictions of peace that begin and end every letter, as this prophetic text continues to suggest. Moreover, when describing his call in Gal. 1:15-16, Paul draws on Isa. 49:1 and Jer. 1:5. Much more could be said at this point, but perhaps these hints are sufficient to illustrate the deep interweaving of Paul's self-understanding and activity with prophetic texts. This important dimension of Paul's texts is largely missing from Watson's account, and it is a rather astonishing lacuna. An essentially intertextual thesis seems to override the intertexts supplied explicitly to elucidate the nature of the implied author.

43. Paul's analysis of Abraham arguably changes between Romans and Galatians. Whereas the apostle develops an important argument in Galatians 3 by referring "the seed" in various versions of the Abrahamic covenant ostensibly to Christ, in Romans *he arguably refers the same text simply to Jewish Christians (if not to Christians per se)* — note the casual phrase in 4:16, "to every seed, not to the one of the law only but to the one also of the fidelity of Abraham . . . ," as well as v. 18's citation of Gen. 15:5. (Genesis 15:6 receives much more prominence in Roman 4 as well.) This raises the potential problem that Paul seems to shift in his analysis of pentateuchal material from letter to letter. (We return to consider this intriguing text in part four, chapter eighteen.)

44. Watson largely overrides the protest that Paul might cite texts at times merely circumstantially — that intertextuality might arise out of the needs of a given ecclesial moment and not out of his theologically fundamental reading of the Pentateuch. And this exclusion seems to ignore the practical realities of much scriptural debate, not to mention the methodological axiom within Pauline studies

of contingency. Controversy often elicits debate over the meaning of Scripture. But the specific biblical texts debated may or may not reflect the most important texts in theological terms for the protagonists themselves. One might say that one seldom fights on scriptural grounds of one's own choosing.
Without a detailed reconstruction of the circumstances of the apostle's letters, however, Watson cannot really control his case in relation to this possibility within Paul's citations. This axiom is associated
especially with J. Chr. Beker; it has already been addressed briefly in part two, chapter seven, in terms
of circumstantial framing requirements; and is reintroduced in the discussion of part four, chapter
thirteen (§1), when the provenance — or "contingency" — of Romans is discussed in detail. (Note, I
am certainly not suggesting that Watson is unaware of the debates over the letter's contingency; he
contributes to these intelligently: see esp. *PJ&G²*, 163-91. I am questioning the degree to which these
contributions are coordinated with his claims concerning Paul's hermeneutics. Arguably these discussions at times work at cross purposes.)

    45. That is, if Paul was a reasonably skilled communicator, he would have anticipated and pre-
sumably not overtaxed his recipients' competence. Hence, there would have been little point investing
his letters with subtle canonical summaries that his auditors would almost certainly have overlooked.
(Note also that in taking this stance Watson is in effect reemphasizing the role of the author.) Arguably, Paul's original recipients were not especially competent. Perhaps only a very small percentage of
early Christians could read, and of those who could, few (if any) were Jews and therefore trained in
the Jewish texts and/or had access to scrolls of Jewish Scripture (which did not themselves yet exist in
a definitive collection or text) — the complaint (i.a.) of Christopher Stanley, *Paul and the Language of
Scripture: Citation Technique in the Pauline Epistles and Contemporary Literature*, SNTSMS 74 (Cambridge: Cambridge University Press, 1992); "The Rhetoric of Quotations: An Essay on Method," in
Early Christian Interpretation of the Scriptures of Israel: Investigation and Proposals, ed. Craig A. Evans
and James A. Sanders (Sheffield: Sheffield Academic Press, 1997), 44-58; "Pearls before Swine: Did
Paul's Audiences Understand His Biblical Quotations?," *Novum Testamentum* 41 (1999): 124-44; and
Arguing with Scripture: The Rhetoric of Quotation in the Letters of Paul (London & New York: T&T
Clark International [Continuum], 2004).

    46. These two issues will be discussed in more detail shortly.

    47. With a simple reversal of the argument, Paul practices theology as a good Evangelical
should, while Watson never really has to establish the point. That is, Paul begins with his Bible (here
circumscribed to the Pentateuch for important tactical reasons), reads it responsibly and carefully,
that is, *in context* (which Watson skillfully defines canonically), and learns from this process everything significant that he needs to know about God and salvation. Only in this relatively independent
way, asserts Watson, can Scripture function *as* Scripture over against the Christ event, thereby witnessing to it. Hence, at bottom, Watson seeks, from an initial negative position in relation to certain
criticisms of Paul's intertextual integrity, to construct a scripturally foundationalist apostle — an
"Evangelical" Paul (whether consciously or not). This agenda explains Watson's failure to blow the
whistle on the argument's non sequiturs *and* to deal with the intertextual accusations more economically. Watson wants to rebound from his repudiations into a positive description — and to take as
many of Schweitzer's and Sanders's enemies with him as he can. In this fashion the critics of the critics
become, perhaps in part unwittingly, the supporters of his positive project. If Schweitzer and Sanders
(at this point) are wrong, then it seems obvious that Watson is right — but does this follow?

    48. Watson also flirts with some other dangerous assumptions at this point — that contingent
or pastoral exegesis is inferior to deep, systematic, reflective interpretation, and that the overtness of a
citation is directly proportional to its theological importance. (He rightly repudiates the claim that
quantity of citation is necessarily directly proportional to importance.)

    49. In his detailed exegesis concerning the point (*P&HF*, 33-77, 127-63), Watson claims that
Paul learns from Hab. 2:4 that "all human life is to be lived in the light of God's final, comprehensive
act of salvation, . . . [i.e.] the radical priority of divine saving action even over the human action en-
joined in the law itself. God's eschatological act of salvation is to be the foundation, origin and goal of
all human living and acting. The term 'faith' speaks of the human recognition and acknowledgment of
God as 'the God of my salvation,' elicited by the divine word of the gospel . . ." (162). Note, it is never-

theless difficult to determine if Watson intends us to understand "faith" conditionally or unconditionally — as something that Abraham still ought to do in order to be saved, or as an appropriate but in one sense irrelevant response to the divine saving action that took place without ground.

50. This problem is in fact shared by *P&HF* and *PJ&G*, although the latter argument removes the prior critique of the law for sociological reasons: "the two things [i.e., Christ/faith and law-observance/circumcision] are incompatible because he [Paul] says they are . . . [the] Pauline antithesis *asserts* the separation of church from synagogue, but does not *explain* theologically why such separation is necessary" (*PJ&G*[2], 131, emphases original). Such claims are of course vulnerable to readings of Paul's antitheses that can find cogent arguments there. Watson might reply that he can detect their rationale in Paul's interpretations of the Pentateuch, but we are presently finding cause to be suspicious of this.

51. Watson might reply that Paul learns about the inadequacy of the law by reading on further in the Pentateuch, through Exodus, Leviticus, Numbers, and Deuteronomy, where he finds a story of awakened desire, curse, and death. And there is some merit in this claim. However, it is not canonically sensitive to introduce that material into the earlier story of Abraham. To do so would violate the integrity of Genesis (and presumably also the integrity of Habakkuk, which is not especially concerned with law observance). Abraham had no access to these lessons. Perhaps, then, it is simply that the law, in the full Mosaic sense, has not yet arrived. Abraham consequently lives by faith alone. However, he is still asked to undertake circumcision, to continue to resist idolatry, and to practice endogamy. So the difficulties remain in any assertion of salvation sola fide on the basis of canonical reading alone.

52. And I have not entered deeply here into his problematic reasons for excluding a christological approach to Paul's πιστ- texts. Watson argues that the authors of these texts did not know Christ and "Paul respects the fact that these pre-Christian texts cannot explicitly refer to Christ" (*P&HF*, 38). Hence, his hermeneutic has "a degree of reticence" about Christology (39). "Reticence" is the language of an important judgment on Paul's intertextuality made by Richard Hays in 1989, but Watson has deployed it here in a way that Hays has explicitly nuanced if not withdrawn: see Hays, *The Faith of Jesus Christ: The Narrative Substructure of Galatians 3:1–4:11,* 2nd ed. (Grand Rapids, Mich.: Eerdmans, 2002 [1983]), xxxviii. But this is a problematic argument on numerous counts. In the first instance — as we have already seen in part — it is not true; Paul *does* undertake christological readings on occasion, and arguably even of pentateuchal texts. Moreover, if Watson is to affirm a complete christological reticence in Paul's treatment of the Pentateuch, he creates a very awkward conundrum that we note momentarily. Watson supports the foregoing exclusion by stating that when Paul wishes to apply a text to Christ (in some sense), he alters its mode of citation in accordance with a discussion like Rom. 10:6-8. But it doesn't follow necessarily from an alteration in one instance that all such instances must be so altered (a false inference from the particular to the general). And this observation also undercuts his original claim that Paul is reticent about Christology in the pentateuchal texts!

53. Plantinga's insight, already utilized in part three, chapter eleven: see §3.3, problem (OD) 18.

54. In fact, we run here into an important set of unresolved problems in Watson's account. Although he does succeed in dispensing with a large number of difficulties in the conventional reading, he does not dispense with all of them. And those that remain, clustering around his key texts, now become especially acute. These are not merely embarrassing textual overdeterminations but direct falsifications of the heart of his system. Note especially underdetermination (UD) 10 (the claim that Abraham is a paradigmatic instance of salvation) and overdeterminations (ODs) 15-19, and 22.

55. Indeed, it is better for Watson's thesis if this *is* the case, because if Paul came to this particular hermeneutic as a Christian, perhaps after some especially powerful revelatory experience, then we would immediately suspect that christological presuppositions were in fact in play dogmatically within his hermeneutic.

56. This is one point then where *PJ&G*[2] (esp. 59-99) arguably causes problems directly for the central thesis of *P&HF*.

57. Neither does the evidence confirm Watson's claim that Jewishness is defined significantly if not *principally* in terms of exegesis. Paul defines his own Jewish life in terms that overlap with but do

not precisely match these claims. First, his concern for "Judaism" included great enthusiasm for learning "the traditions of my fathers" (Gal. 1:14). We cannot reconstruct these traditions with complete precision, but while they were focused on the Torah, they included extra-pentateuchal texts and positions as well, most notably, strong commitments to eschatology and the resurrection from the dead. Second, there was a schooled dimension to this learning. Paul learned to read Torah in a community with teachers and traditions. Third, he was characterized by violent zeal for God. This places nonexegetical action at the heart of his Judaism, and this in devoted obedience to God. Judaism was for Paul fundamentally concerned with obeying the will of God. Judaism is therefore personal and ethical. Fourth, Paul's Jewish ancestry was very important — his direct Jewish descent from Semitic forebears ultimately within the tribe of Benjamin and denoted by the distinguishing mark of circumcision. In view of this evidence, Watson's claims about Paul seem reductionist. Paul is much more than a reader and almost certainly was shaped by more than mere reading. This is of course not to deny reading — and even creative, intelligent individual reading — a *role* in his thinking and development. But it is a far cry from *reducing* Paul's thought and his Jewish identity to such a process.

58. And this difficulty retains a corresponding systematic framing tension as well. Just as the conventional view of Jews seems to be contradicted by Paul's descriptions elsewhere of Jewish disobedience in terms drawn partly from unconditionality (i.e., in terms of election) — the empirical conundrum — so too this accusatory account of Jewish hermeneutics seems at odds with Paul's descriptions elsewhere in unconditional terms. Jewish readers of Moses have been blinded by the God of this age (2 Cor. 4:4). The blinding veil is removed if, like Moses, they turn to the Lord, the Spirit, and to the attendant freedom (3:14-17), but this movement is also described in the passive and in terms of divine sovereignty (3:18; 4:6). So Watson's attribution of hermeneutical accountability to them seems puzzling. If he does not do this, however, his program faces even worse difficulties.

59. Any such prior appeals to Christianity would be circular; one cannot independently establish the truth of Christianity by way of, at least in part, appealing *to* Christianity, without making such appeals false and absurd.

60. See, e.g., "it will not normally be our place to adjudicate between the various readings," here meaning "the scriptural text [in] its Pauline and non-Pauline realizations" (*P&HF*, 4); "similarity and difference are relative and not absolute concepts" (527; also 528, 523-33).

61. One of these has already been noted — that Jews who do not read appropriately should be held responsible for this. In Watson's account, Paul is now entitled to call these obstinate contemporaries stupid readers — as are we (although of course he calls them "blind," and christologically so!: see 2 Cor. 4:4, 6).

62. Moreover, with these excisions, *Watson has removed the traditional supports for the doctrine of the atonement* — the claims that Christ's death achieved something, namely, some divine response to human sinfulness. And this is a rather ironic reversal of the conventional conundrum. Justification theory explains the atonement — in punitive terms — but there is no obvious connection with the resurrection and ascension. Watson affirms the resurrection — rather inconsistently, on the basis of his key texts' assertions of "life" (or its close equivalent) — but those texts fail to establish any role for Christ's death.

63. Watson could retort that I am being extreme and that the process actually operative in Paul is more circular than this. There is a prior revelation of Christ assisting us at times (see *P&HF*, 190-91). However, this is to jump from the a priori frying pan into the epistemological fire. (It would also be to undermine most of his exegetical arguments against christological readings.) It is fine to speak of a hermeneutical circularity in psychological terms; indeed, this seems realistic. But it is not acceptable to endorse an *epistemological* circularity (and Paul's hermeneutic here is functioning epistemologically according to Watson; it establishes what is true). Either one fundamental set of truth criteria is ultimately endorsed and in play, or a thinker is in a state of hopeless confusion and contradiction. (This point is elaborated in my earlier analysis of Watson, "An Evangelical Paul.")

64. Because Paul clearly does need Christ, and so — if Watson's account of his underlying reasoning is correct — does so incoherently.

65. His position on Romans 1–4 is quite scattered in *P&HF* and must essentially be recon-

structed. The argument of *P&HF* follows a canonical Old Testament template. Watson has, however, partly addressed these shortcomings in his paper: "Constructing a Hermeneutic: A Rereading of Romans 1–4" — hereafter *CAH*.

66. Watson concedes that 1:18-32 contributes a radically different epistemology and foundation for the premise of universal sinfulness from the one supplied by the testimony of Scripture (*CAH*, 10). However, he makes no attempt to reconcile the acute tensions that result. Moreover, his suggestion concerning the problematic sinful Jewish Teacher in 2:17-24 that "sin turns out to be remarkably prevalent even within the bastions of respectability" (*CAH*, 11) is insufficient. Paul should have demonstrated this scripturally, if he was following Watson's program — not introspectively and argumentatively. In addition, there seems little point to this paragraph so construed (and the argument in Romans 1–4 is nothing if not tightly woven). Watson knows that this is a standard interpretative problem in Romans, but he does not help us solve it. Finally, he correctly notes that the problematic "obedient Gentiles" in chapter 2 "illustrate the logic of impartial divine judgment" (*CAH*, 11); this is exactly correct. But how this illustration functions in relation to the preceding and following claims, not to mention his own hermeneutic, is not elucidated. Like the vulgar condemnation of the Jewish Teacher, their argumentative function is pointless. We do not even know why Paul so emphasizes divine impartiality, "fundamental to the whole chapter" (*CAH*, 11). In short, while Watson recognizes some of the key conundrums, he does not resolve them, and this is particularly embarrassing for his own case. Not one of these difficulties derives from a canonical reading of the Pentateuch. So if Watson cannot explain them, then his own rereading does not help us, and the evidence of the text in the very form of these problems stands against its validity.

67. I will set aside for the moment his treatment of Paul's πιστ- texts and his exclusion of christological readings in this relation. We can note briefly here four other problems: (1) Watson fails to recognize that the argument Paul builds from 1:18-32 leads directly to *Jewish* culpability in Romans 2. This then contradicts his overarching hermeneutical thesis vis-à-vis Paul's hermeneutical discovery and analysis of Jewish sinfulness. In Romans 2 Jewish sinfulness is a self-reflective process developed in relation to attempted works of law. But Watson asserts that Paul obtained this knowledge by reading the Pentateuch, and especially Exodus, Numbers, and Deuteronomy. (2) The texts that Paul cites before Romans 4 are almost all drawn from the Psalms and the Prophets. Not one of the key pentateuchal texts that Watson relies on elsewhere to support his claim that Paul learns about sin by reading about Israel in the Pentateuch is used in this discussion by Paul — an acute embarrassment for his thesis. (3) The citations crafted by Paul into a catena in 3:10-18 do not function "canonically," as Watson avers Paul usually quotes Scripture. Indeed, we are now arguably at two removes from his account of Paul's hermeneutic — reading isolated quotations of nonpentateuchal texts. (See more on this text in part four, chapter fourteen.) (4) The claim that Romans 1–2 is "not premised on scripture" (*CAH*, 7) is plainly false. Of course it is (or, at least, Scripture is heavily involved in the unfolding argument). The key principle stated in 2:6 is a text attested in the Psalms, Proverbs. and Sirach. Isaiah 52:5 is cited overtly in 2:24. And the Wisdom of Solomon is used in numerous ways from 1:19 onward, *as Watson well knows*. Indeed, apart from Paul's discussion of Gen. 15:6 (and related verses) in chapter 4, *chapter 2 uses the only citations from the Pentateuch in the entire subsection!* (Deuteronomy 10:17 lies directly behind Rom. 2:11; and Deut. 30:6 might be echoed by 2:29.)

In short, Watson does not really know what to do with Rom. 1:18–2:29. He begins by marginalizing its importance on a priori grounds but never supplies a convincing account of its overall contribution to Paul's argument, or indeed of what its key component parts — often so difficult in their own ways — are doing. And yet it is clearly connected quite powerfully to Paul's ongoing argument in the letter as that develops through Romans 3. It is a sustained textual embarrassment for his program, both argumentatively and hermeneutically.

68. Most famously perhaps John C. O'Neill, *Paul's Letter to the Romans* (London: Penguin, 1975), esp. 40-56; and for his similar views concerning Galatians see *The Recovery of Paul's Letter to the Galatians* (London: SPCK, 1972). William O. Walker's essay lists the main studies: "Romans 1.18–2.29: A Non-Pauline Interpolation?" *New Testament Studies* 45 (1999): 533-34 — studies principally by A. F. Loisy, P.-L. Couchoud, R. M. Hawkins, P. N. Harrison, and W. Munroe; see also Walker, *Interpolations*

in the Pauline Letters, JSNTSup 213 (Sheffield: Sheffield Academic Press, 2001). But broader theories than those limited interpolations noted by Walker in relation particularly to Rom. 1:18–2:29 are also potentially significant at this point: see esp. Robin Scroggs, "Paul as Rhetorician: Two Homilies in Romans 1–11," in *Jews, Greeks and Christians: Essays in Honor of William David Davies,* ed. R. Hamerton-Kelly and R. Scroggs (Leiden: Brill, 1976), 271-98. C. H. Dodd famously suggested that Romans 9–11 was an interpolated sermon on "the Jewish question" "incorporated here wholesale to save a busy man's time and trouble in writing on the subject afresh": see *The Epistle of Paul to the Romans* (London: Collins [Fontana Books], 1959 [1932]), 161-64. And Sanders uses the same explanation for Rom. 1:18–2:29!: see *Paul, the Law, and the Jewish People* (Philadelphia: Fortress, 1983), 123-35 — hereafter *PL&JP.* (He is discussed in more detail momentarily.) See also Jurji Kinoshita, "Romans — Two Writings Combined: A New Interpretation of the Body of Romans," *Novum Testamentum 7* (1965): 258-77. An especially detailed, radical, and comprehensive theory by Schmithals has already been noted in part three, chapter ten, §6. It has enjoyed little success (as critical responses noted there by Wedderburn, Elliott, and Keck indicate). Leander Keck is more attuned to this line of explanation than most modern interpreters, and also judicious in his rejection of it: see "What Makes Romans Tick?" in *Pauline Theology,* vol. 3, *Romans,* ed. David M. Hay & E. Elizabeth Johnson (Minneapolis, Minn.: Fortress, 1995); also *Romans* (Nashville, Tenn.: Abingdon Press, 2005). (He does accept, like many, that 16:17-20 is an interpolation — a judgment that will be vigorously scrutinized in part four, chapter thirteen.)

69. Scroggs's brilliant analysis comes closest to this suggestion ("Paul as Rhetorician: Two Homilies in Romans 1–11"); however, he attributes all the antecedent units to Paul, thereby running afoul of the next difficulty with the strategy.

70. Proximate tensions would be eased, but this is not a decisive interpretative advance. Paul would now change his mind *between,* rather than (also) *within* letters!

71. "Righteousness by faith" is treated largely on 481-95, and "participationist eschatology" throughout (i.e., 431-523).

72. Sanders uses various expressions to denote this dynamic, and he often states it in reverse — that is, by suggesting that other, prospective analyses of Paul's thought have things the wrong way around, or "backwards." (He is dependent here in part on Schweitzer.) See *Paul and Palestinian Judaism* (Philadelphia: Fortress, 1977), 434-35, 438-40, 442, 474-85.

73. In fact, he supplies a cluster of key propositions here, set forth as two "primary convictions" that governed Paul's theology: "(1) that Jesus Christ is Lord, that in him God has provided for the salvation of all who believe (in the general sense of 'be converted'), and that he will soon return to bring all things to an end; (2) that he, Paul, was called to be the apostle to the Gentiles" (*P&PJ,* 441-42).

74. "Paul's logic seems to run like this: in Christ God has acted to save the world; therefore the world is in need of salvation; but God also gave the law; if Christ is given for salvation, it must follow that the law could not have been; is the law then against the purpose of God which has been revealed in Christ? No, it has the function of consigning everyone to sin *so that* everyone could be saved by God's grace in Christ. It seems to me completely impossible to make the argument run the other way, beginning with an anthropological analysis which shows in advance that humans are bound over to sin because of the desire to save themselves. . . . [T]he analysis of the human plight . . . fails as the *starting point* for Paul's theology. Although it would be expected in advance that the conception of the plight should precede the conception of the solution, Paul's thought seems to have run the other way" (*P&PJ,* 475, emphases original).

75. Paul's views of the law are treated on 17-167, and Paul's relationship with the Jewish people on 171-206 — one hundred fifty versus thirty-five pages.

76. Sanders notes also a fourth, having to do with the notion of old and new dispensations, but these three dominate his analysis: see *PL&JP,* 10, 137-41.

77. See also "[Paul's] answers to questions of behavior have a logic of their own. There is no systematic explanation . . ." (*PL&JP,* 114; see also 147-48).

78. Of these texts, only Romans 3:27–4:25 lies in "the citadel" and so concerns us directly here.

79. A retrospective dynamic is more epistemologically and ethically coherent as a whole, the

advantageous position with respect to Judaism being transferable to any other features of the non-Christian vestibule (see part one, chapter three, and, to a degree, in inverse relation, chapter six — that is, the difficulties caused by a prospective account).

80. He uses different arguments to make this case at different points, but their accumulated effect is impressive: see, e.g., *P&PJ*, 482-84. Galatians has no analysis of a preceding plight; argues retrospectively in Gal. 2:21 (one of Sanders's favorite texts; it is analyzed carefully in part five, chapter twenty); appeals to the Spirit (3:1-5); and supplies a "dogmatic" argument in Gal. 3:6-29 (i.e., it simply *overrules* justification by "works"). Similarly, 2 Cor. 3:7-18 and Philippians 3 do not depict the human plight but reason retrospectively (484-85). Likewise, 502-4 suggest that: (1) participatory statements are more "typical," "frequent," and lead to analyses of the sacraments and paraenesis (503); (2) the discourse associated with Paul's juristic language — "repentance," "forgiveness," "guilt" — is rare or absent (and the argument of Rom. 1:18–3:20 ends up with all "under Sin"); (3) discussion of exclusion from the kingdom of God through transgression is developed in terms of "unions" (see 1 Cor. 6:12-20); and (4) "Paul's 'juristic' language is sometimes pressed into the service of 'participationist' categories, but never vice versa" (503): see esp. Rom. 6:7; 1 Cor. 6:9-11; Gal. 3:21, 25-29; Phil. 3:4-12 (503-8). Sanders is building here self-consciously on Schweitzer's brief but perceptive case, which "despite over-simplifications and errors in detail . . . [is] convincing; and [has] . . . never been effectively countered" (440).

81. These alternative readings will be particularly useful to us in part five, when we turn to consider the briefer Justification texts in Paul that lie outside the Justification discourse's "textual citadel" — principally Rom. 9:30–10:21; Galatians 2–3; and Philippians 3.

82. See *P&PJ*, 489-91; *PL&JP*, 32-36.

83. If we were discussing Paul's thought as a whole, I would mention several more issues — the use of essentialist and spatial categories in relation to ontology; the strong separation between the work of Christ and the Spirit; and the absence of any plausible explanations for the relationships between forgiveness of transgressions and release from the power of Sin, between present, participationist, and future eschatology, and between death and resurrection in the ontology of the Christian, in both its present and its future dimensions. I would also query the oversight of the political dimension in Paul's reconciliation terminology, and suggest that a stronger introduction of ancient kingship material might explain this and hold together several other elements that are currently separated (and so on). But in many respects, these are simply requests for further clarifications of issues that Sanders has already recognized and articulated.

84. Leaning here on an important analysis by Nils A. Dahl cited in *PL&JP*, 160 and 166, n. 45: "The One God of Jews and Gentiles (Romans 3:29-30)," in *Studies in Paul: Theology for the Early Christian Mission* (Minneapolis: Augsburg, 1977), 178-91. See now also Denise K. Buell, *Why This New Race? Ethnic Reasoning in Early Christianity* (New York: Columbia University Press, 2005).

85. Commentators often affirm this when analyzing Rom. 3:30. This implication of monotheism, while not uncontroversial, is the basis of much of Rodney Stark's sociological and historical work: see *One True God: Historical Consequences of Monotheism* (Princeton: Princeton University Press, 2001); and *For the Glory of God: How Monotheism Led to Reformations, Science, Witch-Hunts, and the End of Slavery* (Princeton: Princeton University Press, 2003). This major thrust in much current sociological work *and* historiography of the late Second Temple period is a constant falsification of the suggestion that Christian "faith" is inherently more universal than Judaism.

86. And without a plausible explanation of faith independently of works as a saving criterion, Stendahl's reframing of the discussion in terms of pagan membership of the people of God does not help. Justification advocates will simply reply that the discussion of membership revolves around the collapse of works followed by the affirmation of faith alone. These are not two simultaneous alternatives, if Sanders cannot explain just how that situation arose and coherently unfolds in different terms.

87. In my view, a more christological approach to Paul's πιστ- language would have helped Sanders enormously but he resists this — presumably because he is unconvinced by the case. At one point he endorses Bultmann's "admirable summary" of πιστ- language in the New Testament: see *P&PJ*, 441 n. 54. It is intriguing to note that in this and several other respects, Sanders reproduces the

standard conservative commitments of the Justification discourse — a pervasive contractualism (abetted where necessary by synergism), an emphasis on faith in relation to a conditional notion of entrance and membership, a justification-sanctification distinction (on which see more below), and an emphasis on a final punitive judgment. We noted earlier in part one, chapter four, Philip Alexander's suspicions that a liberal Protestant tendenz informs Sanders's work on Judaism at times, and these observations tend to reinforce that suspicion: see "Torah and Salvation in Tannaitic Literature," in *Justification and Variegated Nomism: A Fresh Appraisal of Paul and Second Temple Judaism*, ed. D. A. Carson, Peter T. O'Brien, and Mark A. Seifrid (Tübingen and Grand Rapids: Mohr Siebeck and Baker Academic, 2001), 271-73.

88. And this problem links up with the set of issues discussed above under point 1. The constant commitment to entrance, or salvation, by faith, along with the understanding of that faith in conventional, individual terms, generates this contractual dimension: see "'Faith' alone, in a way, *is* a prerequisite, since it signifies conversion and being Christian: the Spirit is received by believing the gospel message" (*P&PJ*, 492, emphasis original).

89. And these are *very* difficult to verify.

90. "The juridical and participatory statements are not in fact kept in water-tight compartments, as we have seen also to be the case in such passages as Phil. 3.8-11 and Gal. 3.24-29" (*P&PJ*, 487). In *P&PJ*, Sanders goes so far as to say that "righteousness by faith and participation in Christ ultimately amount to the same thing" (506); hence, Schweitzer is faulted because he "did not see the *internal connection* between the righteousness by faith terminology and the terminology about life in the Spirit, being in Christ and the like . . . a connection which exists in Paul's own letters" (440: in this relation, *P&PJ* cites Rom. 14:23; Gal. 3:1-5; and 5:6). Similarly, "Paul did not have a bifurcated mind, in one part of which he thought in terms of transgression and expiation, while in the other part thinking of sin as dominion and freedom as participation with Christ. . . . Paul could readily hold together the 'juristic' and the 'participatory' (or lordship) categories" (*P&PJ*, 501).

91. And we link hands at this point with a related difficulty in Sanders's approach to these Pauline texts — that he is insufficiently sensitive to their contingency. It is significant that he endorses an essentially systematic approach to Romans, affirming the views of Bornkamm and Manson (see *P&PJ*, 487-88; *PL&JP*, 30-31): "I am on the whole persuaded by those who . . . view Romans as primarily coming out of Paul's own situation. . . . It seems best . . . to view Romans as being Paul's reflection on the problem of Jew and Gentile in the light of his past difficulty in Galatia and the coming encounter in Jerusalem" (*PL&JP*, 31). This view of Romans will be criticized in part three, chapter thirteen. While acknowledging the importance of John Knox's approach to chronological issues at one point (*P&PJ*, 432), Sanders also never develops a Pauline biography or connects this methodology with the critical related question of contingency advocated by Beker — that variations in Paul's texts must be investigated (and certainly in the first instance) in relation to the specific circumstances that elicited them. This seems doubly odd when the important role of questions is apparent in Sanders's theory; most Pauline scholars would want to ask at this point immediately what caused or elicited those questions (and who) in relation to these particular communications. (Beker's work was available to Sanders only after *P&PJ* but before *PL&JP* and is cited by the latter — see esp. 58-59, nn. 70 and 75.)

92. *P&PJ*, 488-99: "Paul actually came to the view that all men are under the lordship of sin as a reflex of his soteriology: Christ came to provide a new lordship for those who participate in his death and resurrection. Having come to this conclusion about the power of sin, Paul could then *argue* from the common observation that everybody transgresses — an observation which would not be in dispute — to *prove* that everyone is under the lordship of sin. But this is only *an argument to prove a point*, not the way he actually reached his assessment of the plight of man" (499, emphases original).

93. Notably, (and in addition to those broader concerns already noted above) a strangely anemic case against circumcision results (that is, a "voluntary" circumcision should not be problematic, according to the reconstruction suggested by *PL&JP*, allowing Paul's opponents at Galatia — and perhaps also in Jerusalem — an obvious and easy rebuttal of his law-free gospel); Paul's charges of perfectionism in relation to law observance still seem puzzling (see Gal. 3:10 and 5:3; see part four, chapter fourteen, and part five, chapter twenty, for an explanation of these texts and Paul's probable meaning);

and the evidence seems very thin for Christian law observance. (The case rests here largely on Rom. 8:4; 12:2; 13:8-10; 1 Cor. 7:19; 9:21; Gal. 5:14, 22; 6:2; and Phil. 1:11; see *PL&JP*, 94, and for the broader arguments, 93-135.)

94. However, we have not yet noted that Wright was really the first to formulate the position and articulate it in his 1980 Oxford D.Phil. thesis on Romans, unfortunately unpublished. Dunn won the race into print, producing a detailed Romans commentary using this rereading in 1988, and he supported this work with numerous shorter studies, some of them now very well known. He has also written an encyclopedic study of Paul's theology. (The thesis did shift slightly in the process.) Wright has produced numerous short studies and a relatively short Romans commentary, but we still await his detailed treatments of Paul and of Romans. Perhaps at this point, then, Dunn is Engels to Wright's Marx (although these two scholars' generalized descriptions of Paul's thought are ultimately more different than this analogy suggests). Further details are supplied in the Excursus just below.

95. Most probably Walter Eichrodt's influential thesis concerning Old Testament theology: see *Theology of the Old Testament*, trans. J. A. Baker, 6th ed., 2 vols. (Philadelphia: Westminster, 1961, 1967).

96. It receives detailed assessment in due course, esp. in part four, chapters fifteen and sixteen, and part five, chapters twenty and twenty-one; it has also been introduced already in part two, chapter six, and part three, chapter eleven.

97. Notably, "boasting," recently discussed in a significant study by Simon Gathercole (*Where Is Boasting? Early Jewish Soteriology and Paul's Response in Romans 1-5* [Grand Rapids, Mich.: Eerdmans, 2002]); and various debates over the meaning of Paul's atonement terms used in 3:24-26, especially ἱλαστήριον.

98. Most notably, J. L. Martyn endorses the christological reading of πίστις Χριστοῦ but trenchantly opposes any strong covenantal nuances in Paul's δικαιο- terminology (attributing these to his opponents in Galatia!), and he does not press any sociological dimension in Paul's language of "works."

99. The use of the key term "new perspective" can be confusing and so needs careful definition. Dunn introduced it into the debate originally to describe Sanders's "new perspective on Judaism." In Dunn's own early work, then, it applied to what we have defined here as the empirical challenge to Justification theory in terms of Judaism. More recently, however, the reference of the term has shifted to denote primarily Dunn's own solution to this difficulty — his motif rereading *of Paul*. It is thus possible to endorse the "new perspective" in one sense — its observations about Judaism, suitably mitigated — but to reject it in another — its strategic response to this problem in Paul in terms of motif rereading and the accompanying exegetical suggestion that "works of law" mean, at least in part, a Jewish sociological boundary marker. One "new perspective" can be right — although it is arguably incomplete — but another substantially mistaken.

100. Namely, *Romans 1-8*, WBC 38A (Dallas, Texas: Word, 1988) — hereafter *R1-8*; *Romans 9-16*, WBC 38B (Dallas, Texas: Word, 1988) — hereafter *R9-16*; "The New Perspective on Paul," in *Jesus, Paul and the Law* (London: SPCK, 1990 [1982, 1983]), 183-206 (also 89-182 and 215-64) — hereafter *JP&L*; "The Justice of God. A Renewed Perspective on Justification by Faith," *Journal of Theological Studies* 43 (1992): 1-22; *The Theology of Paul's Letter to the Galatians* (Cambridge: Cambridge University Press, 1993); *The Epistle to the Galatians*, BNTC (London: A&C Black, 1993); "Once More, ΠΙΣΤΙΣ ΧΡΙΣΤΟΥ," in *Pauline Theology*, vol. 1, *Looking Back, Pressing On*, ed. D. M. Hay and E. E. Johnson (Atlanta, Georgia: Scholars Press, 1997), 61-81; and *The Theology of Paul the Apostle* (Edinburgh & Grand Rapids, Mich.: T&T Clark & Eerdmans, 1998), esp. 334-89 — hereafter *TPA*. (This debate has already been noted in a preliminary way in part one, chapter six, §1.)

101. Dunn also states that "a natural and more or less inevitable converse of this sense of distinctiveness was the sense of *privilege*, precisely in being the nation specially chosen by the one God and favored by gift of covenant and law": *R1-8*, lxx, emphasis original; see also lxxi-ii.

102. The meaning of δικαιοσύνη Θεοῦ is best considered when we address Rom. 1:16-17 and 3:21-26 in detail, in part four, chapters fifteen through seventeen. (And Dunn does not, in any case,

make a great deal out of this particular rereading, nor does he add significantly to the claims of other interpreters in this relation.)

103. Watson and Wright offer some detailed exegetical nuggets, and a great deal of slightly more programmatic exegesis. Stowers's treatment of Romans is also programmatic. (Wright and Stowers essentially both supply a possible rereading of Romans 1–4.) Sanders is acutely insightful at times, but he never supplies a comprehensive exegetical treatment. Only Dunn offers detailed conventional commentaries on both Romans and Galatians that engage, verse by verse, with the Greek text, ostensibly generating his rereading in the process over against alternative construals.

104. See esp. "The New Perspective on Paul" and "The Justice of God."

105. Dunn also makes these intriguing claims in this relation: "The psychology of the conversion experience is easily recognizable and cannot be easily discounted" (*TPA*, 353).

106. Dunn notes that Sanders despaired of this particular type of solution: "Sanders himself did not offer much help here, since in the light of the new perspective on Second Temple Judaism he could only see an incoherent and inconsistent Paul" (*TPA*, 339). It might be more accurate to say that Sanders's solution emphasized reframing but was less aggressive semantically than Dunn's (although Dunn does rely on reframing as well). Sanders does argue vociferously for a certain sort of coherence in Paul's thinking.

107. Rodney Stark's work on the rise of early Christianity, noted already in part one, chapter five, often illustrates this nicely: see esp. *The Rise of Christianity: A Sociologist Reconsiders History* (Princeton, New Jersey: Princeton University Press, 1996); and *Cities of God: The Real Story of How Christianity Became an Urban Movement and Conquered Rome* (San Francisco: Harper, 2006).

108. The further claim that Paul converted to the theological position of the group that he had been persecuting seems reasonable, given what we know of converts, but a figure as well-educated and assertive as Paul could also possibly have shifted the theological material that he inherited.

109. Indeed, a still stronger claim could arguably be made. In Gal. 1:22-23 Judean Christians who do not know Paul "by sight" nevertheless state that he had previously been persecuting them (literally, "us"). So the offensive theological position of that movement was located in Judea before Paul's first visit back to the Jewish capital. Yet clearly, no discussion of a law-free praxis has taken place.

110. That is, even as we can imagine this rationale being part of the debate, we can imagine many other plausible explanations as well that may have combined with it or displaced it, either of which outcomes is fatal for Dunn's argument. So, for example, it seems problematic to assume that certain early Christians opposed the law-free mission to Judaism in entirely traditional Jewish terms — qua generic Jews. And we have already seen that it is problematic to reduce Judaism to the question of sociological boundary markers. Moreover, presumably some elements of the discussion were distinctively Christian (i.e., deviant in terms of majority Judaism). In addition, it is problematic to assume that this resistance by part of the early church to the law-free mission must necessarily be reducible to "boundary issues." They may have been concerned about other matters, e.g., final eschatological salvation, rather than current matters of religious definition. And even if boundary issues were involved, these may not have been conceived of in terms of those parameters; they may have been unintended sociological consequences of practices discussed in fundamentally theological terms (e.g., "doing this is the will of God, as laid down by Moses," or some such). And this last objection is especially difficult for Dunn. He needs the debate to be prosecuted with the explicit *content* of boundary markers, not merely this *effect*.

111. It might also be queried if the Pauline mission is recruiting into a newly defined form of Judaism. (If it is not then presumably orthopractic Jews could simply ignore this strange deviant tradition: see Acts 5:35-39.) Evidence in support of the claim that Paul's communities do not displace Israel has been noted already in part one, chapter three, and will become apparent further in part five, chapters nineteen and twenty.

112. Hence, one cannot help feeling that Dunn basically begs the question. It is obvious that some Jewish Christians in the early church rejected Paul's law-free mission to the pagans, favoring instead a full proselytism to Judaism. But this apparent fact is not the explanation of, or rationale for, this opposition. It does not explain *why* such people opposed Paul. Indeed, at this point Dunn risks being

merely tautologous: certain Jewish Christians resisted including pagans in the people of God law free because they wanted to resist including the pagans in the people of God without law observance.

113. Indeed, it is difficult to imagine why diet is even being debated at Antioch (assuming that incident's later placement) if the issue of circumcision has already been discussed in Jerusalem, and the same consideration applies to the Galatian controversy itself.

114. "There is, we might say, . . . a hidden middle term in 3:20 between 'works of the law' and 'shall be justified' — a middle term which Reformation exegesis largely missed. . . . The connection of thought in 3:20 does not run directly from 'works of the law' to 'shall be justified' and is not aimed directly at works of the law *as a means to achieving* righteousness and acquittal. The connection of thought is more indirect, of works of the law *as a way of identifying the individual with* the people whom God has chosen and will vindicate and of *maintaining his status within* that people. In a word, the hidden middle term is the function of the law as an identity factor, the social function of the law as marking out the people of the law in their distinctiveness (circumcision, food laws, etc.). It is 'hidden' at 3:20 simply because it could be taken for granted in the Roman world of this period when talking about the Jews with their religious and national peculiarities; 'hidden' too simply because it was clear enough already in 2:1–3:8 and need not complicate the final summary statement beyond the sufficiently clear phrase 'works of the law'" (*R1–8*, 159, emphases original).

115. See *R1–8*, 185-94. "The key to exegesis [in 3:27b, τῶν ἔργων] is the *axiomatic* three-way association in Jewish thought between the national pride of the covenant people, the law as the particular focus and reason for that pride, and works of the law as the expression of Jewish devotion to their God and his law particularly through those obligations which marked them out in their distinctiveness as his people, the people of the law. . . . [T]he typical Jew of Paul's time could not think of the law other than in its distinctiveness . . ." (*R1–8*, 186, emphasis added). Indeed, the similarity between Rom. 3:28 and Gal. 2:16 indicates that "here as there Paul is able to appeal to what was a basic and agreed statement of the gospel common to all the earliest Christians, loyal Jews as well as Gentiles" (192). This seems to go beyond what Paul states overtly, and beyond the possibility that in Romans Paul has merely remembered his key claims from Galatians. Furthermore, it is hard to understand the repeated negation of this phrase by Paul if the point is agreed upon and now positively creedal. (Creeds tend to affirm things; hence, an argument is really needed to show how a creed's affirmations depend on prior negations.) More likely is the possibility that someone is urging "works of law" in some sense, and Paul disagrees.

116. *R1–8*, 582-83, 593: "Paul reverts once again to the contrast which has been fundamental to his own apologetic. . . . Israel's mistake was to understand righteousness as something peculiarly theirs . . . [hence] the negative note against 'works' *is* clearly struck and is clearly intended to evoke the indictment of Israel summed up in 3:20" (582-83, emphasis original). Dunn does not justify these assertions on the basis of local evidence.

117. Dunn denies this on the grounds that this initial occurrence is a singular, not a plural, and it denotes something commendable, not negative, which is exceptional (*R1–8*, 100). But these do not seem especially powerful objections. He holds the later plural phrase in 3:20 to summarize the earlier stretch of argument, which seems to undermine his first objection. And the later turn in the argument clearly sweeps up a considerable amount of material that was initially considered relatively positively — traditional Judaism, no less. Dunn also begs the question. The phrase in 2:15 refers to an inward matter of the heart, he suggests, and hence cannot refer to the content of the later plural phrase, which is "something outward, lacking in depth." It could be replied of course that this is overt evidence that Dunn's later reading is wrong!

118. And this judgment will not in fact be opposed in anything that follows. That is, after the collapse of Dunn's revisionist case in relation to this motif, it is apparent that the conventional reading supplies the best account of Paul's phrase "works of law." Any plausible rereading will need to find its purchase on Paul's conventional construal at some other point or points.

119. They are also accused of failing to understand the true purpose of the law, that is, to make them "conscious of sin, aware of being under the power of sin even as members of the covenant people," which is tantamount to being "more aware of their *continuing* need of God's grace" (160, empha-

sis original). Of course, here the standard concerns of Justification theory are recognizable — the inability of Jews, whether immorally or ignorantly, to understand their own parlous condition as purportedly law observant but sinful that was earlier described as "the loop of foolishness" (see *TPA*, 128-61; and part one, chapter one).

120. Some Jews at least seem to have been quite open to proselytes. The book of Ruth is an important canonical example; also especially apposite is *Joseph and Aseneth*.

121. Similar difficulties hamper the ostensibly more benign suggestion that the Jews were characterized by an inappropriate nationalism and religious pride. On the one hand, some of their texts do not bear this accusation out (i.e., those texts that evidence a deep awareness of frailty and sinfulness). On the other hand, the appropriate responses to this are repentance and humility, neither of which develops obviously into a law-free mission to the pagans and salvation sola fide.

122. For example: "Paul was concerned about . . . the fact that covenant promise and law had become too inextricably identified with ethnic Israel as such, with the Jewish people marked out in their national distinctiveness by the practices of circumcision, food laws, and sabbath in particular (Wright appropriately coins the phrase 'national righteousness'). . . . [W]hat Paul was endeavoring to do was to free both promise and law for a wider range of recipients, freed from the ethnic constraints which he saw to be narrowing the grace of God and diverting the saving purpose of God out of its main channel — Christ" (*R1-8*, lxxi-lxxii).

123. Hence, this is a construction of Judaism far more sinister than the one supplied by Justification theory. In the conventional reading Judaism has value and formal goodness; it is simply not capable of fulfillment, because of human sin. In this reading of Dunn, however, Judaism has no intrinsic value whatsoever. It is inadequate by virtue of its very construction.

124. Dunn is probably benefiting here from the tacit force of an old hermeneutical distinction much used by Christians but largely rejected by academic interpretation — the distinction between the ritual and the moral law. The former has widely been abrogated by the church and so is regarded as unimportant (and esp. when accompanied by anti-Catholic sentiments); the latter, however, is regarded as very much in force. When Dunn suggests, then, that Paul is dispensing with matters of Jewish definition that fall largely under the rubric of the ritual law, Christian and post-Christian interpreters tacitly agree with his conclusion (and so are less likely to disagree with his argument). However, if the same conclusion is applied to elements of the moral law, then the difficulties in his position are more likely to be felt.

125. One further explanatory possibility already noted in relation to Watson, and endorsed by Dunn at times, is to assert the notion of salvation by faith alone on a priori, prospective grounds, and principally in relation to the example of Abraham as interpreted by Gen. 15:6. But a host of difficulties in relation to the example of Abraham must be negotiated before this suggestion is plausible. It is, in addition, difficult to make this case in the face of a christological reading of πίστις, when the Justification arguments in phase one have been abandoned. Moreover, it is deeply inconsistent to revert suddenly, under pressure, to a retrospective posture. This ought to involve — as we well know — a radical reinterpretation of Romans 1–4, which is generally not in evidence.

126. The problems most likely to be recognized and dealt with by him in addition are ODs 8-11, 13, and 23, which much of the commentary on Romans 1–4 recognizes as problematic in any case — i.e., OD 8 (2:16b); 9 (the crudeness of the attack on the Jew in 2:21-22); 10 (the righteous pagans in 2:14-15 and 26-29); 11 (the redefinition of circumcision in 2:25-29); 13 (the syntactical awkwardness of 3:25); and 23 (the saving function of the resurrection in 4:25). However, Dunn's particular rereading does not actually help him at any of these points, and he generally fails in his detailed exegetical work either to recognize them or to solve them very satisfactorily when he does so: see *R1-8*, esp. 98-128, 172-73, 181, 224-25, 240-41.

127. Dunn's vigorous defense of the conventional approach to "faith" demonstrates this especially clearly: see especially his counter to Hays in "Once More, ΠΙΣΤΙΣ ΧΡΙΣΤΟΥ." But his endorsement of a gospel of "justification by faith" in continuity with the Reformation is widespread: see *TPA*, §§6, 14 (128-61, 334-89). So Dunn — not unlike Watson — seems to want to be a revisionist and at the

same time a recognizably traditional advocate of the "Reformational" approach to Paul's gospel in terms of faith alone.

128. The suggestions of other motif rereaders are arguably caught up with Dunn's strategies and difficulties: see, in particular, N. T. Wright, although he develops his suggestions in a heavier dependence on δικαιοσύνη Θεοῦ, and we do not yet have a detailed treatment of Romans from him (although the one that we do have is interesting and provocative). Wright is also more concerned than Dunn to articulate coherent argumentative and theoretical levels in Paul.

129. New Haven & London: Yale University Press, 1994 — hereafter *RR*. There are other important rereadings as well — principally Neil Elliott, *The Rhetoric of Romans: Argumentative Constraint and Strategy and Paul's Dialogue with Judaism*, JSNTSup 45 (Sheffield: JSOT, 1990); John Gager, *Reinventing Paul* (Oxford & New York: Oxford University Press, 2000); and Diana Swancutt, "Sexy Stoics and the Rereading of Romans 1.18–2.16," in *A Feminist Companion to Paul*, ed. A.-J. Levine, Feminist Companion to the New Testament and Early Christian Writings (Cleveland, Ohio: Pilgrim, 2004), 42-73. See also, to a lesser extent, Glenn N. Davies, *Faith and Obedience in Romans: A Study in Romans 1-4*, JSNTSup 39 (Sheffield: JSOT, 1990); John D. Moores, *Wrestling with Rationality in Paul: Romans 1-8 in a New Perspective*, SNTSMS 82 (Cambridge: Cambridge University Press, 1995); and Wendy Dabourne, *Purpose and Cause in Pauline Exegesis: Romans 1.16–4.25 and a New Approach to the Letters*, SNTSMS 104 (Cambridge: Cambridge University Press, 1999). (Note that the principal comprehensive rereadings tend to be the work of more mature scholars; doctoral dissertations often focus on motifs and so only produce localized rereadings.) Jonathan Draper and Robert Jewett would include Colenso's classic commentary within this category, although I am not convinced that it is an overt rereading (and certainly not in relation to Romans 1–4): see John William Colenso, *Commentary on Romans*, ed. Jonathan Draper (Pietermaritzburg, South Africa: Cluster, 2003 [1861]), originally entitled *St. Paul's Epistle to the Romans: Newly Translated and Explained from a Missionary Point of View*; see also Jonathan Draper, "A 'Frontier' Reading of Romans: The Case of Bishop John William Colenso (1814-1883)," in *Navigating Romans through Cultures: Challenging Readings by Charting a New Course*, ed. (K. K.) Yeo Khiok-khng, Romans through History and Cultures Series (London: T&T Clark International [Continuum], 2004), 57-72.

130. He also arguably tends to fight unnecessary battles, urging innovations that are occasionally implausible or that fail to advance his agenda significantly. This can create an unnecessarily provocative quality in his work.

131. Leaning especially on the work of O'Neill, Sanders, and Räisänen, he grasps the interpretative tradition critical of the conventional reading, and is especially sensitive to the post-Holocaust agenda; he is sensitive to the role of the reader, to the related importance of punctuation decisions regarding the Greek, and to the role of later interpretative history; he is sensitive to the various dimensions of intertextuality — quotations, allusions, topoi, and discourses; he notes the relevance of canonical decisions and the MSS tradition; he is sensitive to numerous Greco-Roman motifs, especially the diatribe, speech-in-character, figures, types of transition, ring compositions, ancient constructions of otherness, the discourse of self-mastery (on which see more just below), decline narratives, ancient psychology, ancient athletic and gender codes, and the theme of adaptation; he notes possible differences in authorial voice and related questions of audience; and he emphasizes various issues in relation to Judaism — the relevance of the temple cult, of purity and pollution issues, and so on. This is a veritable methodological smorgasbord! It also illustrates how methodologically and substantively comprehensive any plausible rereading of Romans 1–4 needs to be.

132. The refusal to break significantly at 4:1, however, is innovative and important. (Note also that — somewhat curiously — Stowers's analyses of these textual subunits do not correspond to his chapter divisions.)

133. Stowers strongly repudiates any echoes of either the fall and Genesis 1–3, or later Israelite texts or allusions such as Psalm 106 and/or the incident of the golden calf.

134. Stowers's preferred usage is "gentile."

135. Stowers leans here on Bassler's seminal early work on divine impartiality, endorsing her perception of something approaching a ring composition in Rom. 1:18–2:16, as well as a thematic con-

stant in these terms: see Jouette M. Bassler, *Divine Impartiality: Paul and a Theological Axiom*, SBLDS 59 (Chico, CA: Scholars, 1982); and "Divine Impartiality in Paul's Letter to the Romans," *Novum Testamentum* 26 (1984): 43-58.

136. Stowers's endorsement of an atypical translation of ἀνόμως in 2:12 as "lawless," not "outside the law," is a necessary rider on this broader set of claims.

137. Stowers struggles with 2:25-29, presumably because two figures are present in Paul's argument — a pretentious, inconsistent Jew ("in name only") whom the text criticizes, and a criticizing pagan *who redefines Judaism*. Stowers's argument accounts for the former but struggles to account for the latter. Indeed, that figure contradicts it. There is no need for Paul to be so aggressive in definitional terms if Jews can maintain their own independent mode of salvation, as Stowers asserts, and if Paul's difficulty at this point is only with an inauthentic Jew. (As for Dunn's reading, the appropriate response to inauthentic Judaism is authentic Judaism.) Stowers introduces five different contentions to explain the pericope, but none explain away this central difficulty.

138. Stowers goes on to suggest that the diatribe affirms that God will bring good from the disobedience of some within Israel to bear God's oracles to the world — the message, presumably, of God's impartial salvation of gentiles as well as Jews. Hence, he reads the dialogue in relation to his later analysis of Romans 9-11, and also in heavy dependence on S. K. Williams's rendering of δικαιοσύνη Θεοῦ in terms of God's faithfulness to his promise to Abraham: see Williams, "The Righteousness of God in Romans," *Journal of Biblical Literature* 99 (1980): 241-90.

139. Stowers's exegetical treatments are getting briefer by this point in the book.

140. That is, without a signal dependence on Stowers. However, Swancutt is similarly impressive, although her essay halts at 2:16; she arguably provides a closer — i.e., blow-by-blow — reading of Paul's Greek in the subsection 1:18-2:16 than Stowers.

141. It is still arguably possible in certain cases, but then little is actually gained.

142. For one thing, Stowers thereby fails to avoid the Jewish empirical conundrum; he is still committed (at least here) to a description of Judaism in terms of "justification by works." (How this squares with his claims elsewhere that Judaism is a temple cult and a discourse concerned with self-mastery are further difficult questions.)

143. Perhaps Stowers would reply that such law observance is too weak to respond to the depraved condition of the pagans, who have had their desires unleashed. But this seems a strange claim. Surely a reintegrated pagan would benefit from law observance? Moreover, if it is too weak for pagans, a case can be made that it is also too weak for Jews. Stowers periodically affirms the basic equality of these two communities, and he notes one of Paul's accounts of unleashed desire in 5:12-21 that encompasses Jews. (See also Gal. 3:22.)

144. He also creates an overt textual underdetermination at this point, repeatedly introducing a distinction within the law between those practices incumbent on all Jews and those reduced practices expected of pagan proselytes. Paul never makes this distinction in the text, and certain statements even stand against it. We have already noted the many problems that flow from the presence of two different versions of the law. Stowers again, then, exacerbates, rather than resolves some of our most pressing difficulties.

145. So, for example, the faith of believers is an awkward motif for Stowers, who barely mentions it (see esp. 1:16, 17; 3:22; 4:23-24). Even granting that the texts are primarily concerned with Christ's fidelity, they are not *solely* concerned with it. Stowers argues at one point that later followers reflect the faithfulness of their founders, but this seems to apply only to later pagan followers of Jesus, not to Jewish followers of Abraham, and by this reasoning both Jews and pagans ought to be characterized by such fidelity. Moreover, it is not apparent what function this belief has. What does it do?

146. That is, Romans 5-8 and any associated soteriology has really been jettisoned, along with Romans 1-4! This is probably too much to excise, and certainly creates enormous interpretative challenges. In doing this, Stowers has really opened up a second front in addition to the challenges that I am facing here (at this last point, alongside him).

147. Prior to the appearance of Stowers's study in 1994, I was working with a number of the revisionist moves that Stowers then made in print. My doctoral work and early publications indicate the

parallels in many of those interpretative developments: a subjective reading of the πίστις Χριστοῦ genitives (which I learned from my doctoral supervisor, Richard Longenecker); a revisionist approach to Rom. 3:21-26 and its atonement theology, leading to a position closer to that of S. K. Williams; a reorientation of much of Paul's argument in 2:17–3:9a away from a generic Jewish figure and toward the encoded Teacher; a revisionist approach to Paul's analysis of Abraham in Romans 4 emphasizing his role as a primordial ancestor; and a repositioning of Paul on the other side of the diatribe in 3:1-9a. Since that time, however, I have learned several further important if not vital things from Stowers directly. Those intellectual debts are signaled clearly in what follows.

148. That is, eliminate the intrinsic, systematic, empirical, and underdeterminative difficulties, along with — presumably — the proximate tensions in Romans itself, and offer the hope of resolving the textual overdeterminations as well.

Notes to Chapter Thirteen

1. This aspect of the text's explanation was introduced in part two, chapter seven in relation to the need for explanations at a text's circumstantial frame (see §2.4). It is most economically analyzed in terms of J. Christiaan Beker's framework of contingency versus coherence — the occasional or particular dimension of a text versus the abiding and normative: see esp. *Paul the Apostle: The Triumph of God in Life and Thought,* paperback ed. with new intro. (Philadelphia: Fortress, 1984 [1980]), xiii-xx, 11-16, 23-36.

2. The scholarly community is well served in this regard by an outstanding edited collection of essays, now in a revised and expanded form: Karl P. Donfried (ed.), *The Romans Debate* (Peabody, Mass.: Hendrickson, 1991 [1977]) — hereafter *RD.* But see also esp. A. J. M. Wedderburn, *The Reasons for Romans,* SNTW (Edinburgh: T&T Clark, 1988); A. Andrew Das, *Solving the Romans Debate* (Minneapolis: Fortress, 2007); Francis Watson's updated discussion in *Paul, Judaism, and the Gentiles,* rev. ed. (Grand Rapids, Mich.: Eerdmans, 2007), 163-91 — hereafter *PJ&G²*; and Jewett's magisterial discussion, with Roy D. Kotansky, *Romans: A Commentary,* Hermeneia (Minneapolis, Minn.: Fortress, 2007), 1-91.

3. The conventional construal often proceeds in terms of straight coherence, which is unparalleled in Paul's extant texts. (It reads Romans 1–4 as a direct account of Paul's gospel; no circumstances at Rome are directly in view — see §3 option 6 below.) However, the strangeness of this approach is partly obscured by the lack of consensus over Romans' contingency. In strictly argumentative terms, the lack of a particular explanation of Romans' contingency is not probative for a claim that Romans can simply be read coherently — but in psychological terms it is probably useful. It is difficult to challenge the conventional reading's lack of contingency without a demonstrably plausible explanation of Romans' contingency to hand.

4. The other questions that are usually involved with the broad issue of provenance are not generally in dispute for Romans — who wrote it, when, from where, and to where. It is largely undisputed that Paul wrote Romans to the Roman Christians from Corinth at the end of his missionary work in the Aegean (this can be dated slightly differently, but variations here will not affect our discussion), assisted by the scribe Tertius (16:22). Questions concerning the letter's integrity generally tend to be settled conservatively as well (as we have seen already — to a degree — in part three, chapter twelve; and see more on this below in relation to key subsections like 16:17-20).

5. Werner G. Kümmel, *Introduction to the New Testament,* trans. (from the 14th rev. ed., 1965) A. J. Mattill (London: SCM Press, 1966), 218. Kümmel goes on to reason that "the announcement of his visit, the explanation of his intentions, and the wooing of understanding and help from the Christians in Rome in respect to the goal of his mission, which he is pursuing, explain only the external occasion and the immediate purpose of the Epistle. The broad, theological discussion and the controversy with the Jews which permeates the book must have other, more deeply lying foundations" (220). But this is of course, in a certain sense, exactly the wrong way to approach the entire problem. J. A.

Fitzmyer is also especially sensitive to this data: see *Romans: A New Translation with Introduction and Commentary,* AB 33 (New York: Doubleday, 1993), 69-73.

6. Tendentious because it assumes, along with Justification theory, that Paul's engagement with Jewish motifs and questions is an engagement with Judaism per se.

7. Precise delineations of these subsections do not matter at this point. However, more exact specifications will emerge later on, in tandem with detailed exegetical work. Robin Scroggs has provided a classic analysis of these units in "Paul as Rhetorician: Two Homilies in Romans 1–11," in *Jews, Greeks and Christians: Essays in Honor of William David Davies,* ed. R. Hamerton-Kelly and R. Scroggs (Leiden: Brill, 1976), 271-98.

8. See Exod. 20:17/Deut. 5:21 in 7:7; and Ps. 44:22 in 8:36; probably along with Gen. 22:12 and 16 in 8:32. Admittedly, certain key Jewish narrative echoes are discernible in these chapters as well, but their treatment is arguably distinctive.

9. There has been a great deal of discussion of the audience of Romans — whether it is pagan, Jewish, or some mixture of the two. Paul's detailed greetings in Romans 16 identify three Jews explicitly in his Christian audience (Andronicus, Junia, and Herodion: see vv. 7 and 11), and Acts asserts the same identity for Aquila, and presumably for Prisca by marriage and conversion (v. 3; see Acts 18:2). (Romans 4:1, 7:1, and 9:10 point to Jews less decisively.) Beyond this evidence, the encoded audience seems originally pagan, although the possible presence of God-fearers complicates this matter still further. However, ultimately I am not convinced that the detailed resolution of this issue — if it *is* resolvable — will solve the broader question of purpose. Paul does not elsewhere address Jewish questions at length, abstractly, just because his audience contains Jewish Christians (see 1 and 2 Corinthians). And to suggest that he does so in Romans because the Roman Christians do not know him begs the key questions. (Ephesians, however, is an intriguing counter-example at this point.) Conversely, to suggest that he cannot address Judaism because his audience is entirely pagan is a weak contention (as the legion of scholars converted from modern secular paganism and now fervently addressing Jewish questions in relation to Paul perhaps attests). We ought of course to pursue the identification of Paul's empirical audience, but also to balance this construct against constructions of the implied and the encoded audiences, and integrate these theories in turn with a broader hypothesis concerning the letter's purpose and design.

10. I will assume the inclusion of Romans 16 with the rest of the letter in what follows, as the majority of interpreters do. I will address the integrity of vv. 17-20 shortly — although, again, only a small minority suggests its excision.

11. Strictly speaking, more relationships exist between the four main subunits in the letter body than the three mentioned here; however, for simplicity's sake they are arguably reducible to these three main transitions. Plausible explanations at these points — at the proximate frames — should encompass plausible explanations of the other implicit substantive relationships as well.

12. I will not engage here with some of the older and overtly false theories that are touched on from time to time by *RD* — for example, the German claim in a previous generation that Paul needed to visit the capital of the empire in order to crown his missionary achievements (that is, by way of comparison with a mission to the German Reich that failed to evangelize Berlin), or that Paul was dealing with antinomians (Lütgert's view, in which relation one might also usefully consider Luther's attitude to the enthusiasts), and so on.

13. The most likely candidates for multiple causation are 1 Corinthians and Philippians. Subsidiary goals may also exist for 2 Corinthians, if it is not a composite. First Corinthians is perhaps the most complex occasional letter in the Pauline corpus and hence susceptible to a multiple explanation. But most of that letter is explicable in terms of a letter from Corinth to Paul (responding to an earlier letter from Paul) and an oral report, both of which contained complex internal agendas. It is not implausible, moreover, to suggest that these different sources of information arrived simultaneously in Ephesus, and they may even have coinhered in the same vehicle — the Corinthian letter bearers. There is overt evidence within the letter for all these dynamics; thus, in this case, the theory of multiple causation has little difficulty justifying its multiplicity (and is not in any case as multiple as it first appears).

14. Günter Klein, "Paul's Purpose in Writing the Epistle to the Romans," *RD*, 29-43. See also the perceptive treatment by L. Ann Jervis: *The Purpose of Romans: A Comparative Letter-Structure Investigation*, JSNTSup 55 (Sheffield: JSOT, 1991).

15. Paul's apostleship and gospel are so closely intertwined that in other letters the two notions can sometimes interchange almost seamlessly (see esp. Gal. 1:6-9, 11-12, 15-17; 2:2, 5, 7-9). A close reading of parts of Romans suggests the same conclusion.

16. So Klein observes correctly that "it is exactly the theme of the gospel and Paul's responsibility for carrying it out in Rome which connect the letter's opening, body, and closing" (*RD*, 34, n. 22 — although this is not the *only* such connection!).

17. So Klein notes correctly again: "every hypothesis concerned with the intention of the Epistle to the Romans must submit to another criterion: whether it can succeed in relating the purpose and content of the letter as closely as both the text and the projected apostolic activity in Rome call for" (*RD*, 34-35).

18. An intriguing comparison is thereby set up with Ephesians. If authentic, this letter was most likely sent to Laodicea as the companion letter to Colossians and Philemon. And as such it seems to have functioned in very much these senses — an introduction of Paul's apostolic office and a description of his soteriology and ethic. This would explain, among other things, its smoother, more complex and abstract style, which is much like Romans.

19. One reading of Gal. 6:16b limits these issues largely to one clause of eight words!

20. It should be emphasized that these observations in no way exclude accounts of Israel from broader descriptions of Paul's thought; however, the case needs to be made here that an account of the gospel raises such issues in detail almost automatically, so that an attribution of Romans 1–4 to the gospel can explain simultaneously the presence of Romans 9–11 in the same letter.

21. "Paul can consider an apostolic effort in Rome because he does not regard the local Christian community there as having an apostolic foundation" (*RD*, 39). And it is a short step from this realization to the further claim that Paul must therefore in effect preach the gospel to Roman Christians, supplying them with "a theological treatise" (*RD*, 42). Klein adds that this is why Paul never refers to the Roman Christians as an ἐκκλησία (although, as Watson notes, the Philippians are not accorded that title either; see Phil 1.1 [however, see also 4:15]; *PJ&G²*, 189). (A more practical explanation for this fact also arguably exists; see the further discussions of feature VII below.)

22. Talbert notes his desire to impart some spiritual gift to strengthen the Roman Christians (1:11-12; 15:15-16; feature IV); his request for prayer (15:30-31; part of feature VI — see theory 3 just below); and this request for assistance in a mission to Spain (15:24: feature V); see *Romans* (Macon, Georgia: Smith & Helwys, 2002), 12.

23. See "Following the Argument of Romans," *RD*, 265-77; Robert Jewett, "Ecumenical Theology for the Sake of Mission: Romans 1.1-17 + 15.14–16.24," *Pauline Theology*, vol. 3, *Romans*, ed. David M. Hay and E. Elizabeth Johnson (Minneapolis, Minn.: Augsburg Fortress, 1995), 89-108; and *Romans*, 80-91. (Klein also notes the endorsement of this feature's importance — at least in part — by Kümmel, Friedrich, Dodd, Feine-Behm, Zahn, Jülicher-Fascher, and Georgi: see *RD*, 32, n. 16; 33, n. 18.)

24. Paul could indeed want to strengthen the Roman Christians (IV), so that their assistance would be facilitated. His solicitation of their prayer support for Jerusalem (VI) also further involves them emotionally and spiritually in his work (as well as providing prayer support for a difficult situation). And so on.

25. The addition of Ephesians and/or Colossians to this communication might partly offset this contention, however.

26. See options 3, 4, 5, and 6.

27. See John L. White, *Light from Ancient Letters* (Philadelphia: Fortress, 1986), examples 11, 71, 77-79, and 115a (10-11, 70-71, 117-19, 182-83).

28. Fitzmyer discusses the parallel views of Fuchs and Suggs at this point: *Romans*, 75.

29. I find it significant that we run into the same difficulty here that dogged Stendahl's famous reframing suggestion. Both Stendahl and Jervell reposition the arguments of Romans in a defensive

frame ultimately concerned with Paul's radical law-free mission to the pagans. There is something inherently plausible about this suggestion, fundamentally because it locates Romans within the Judaizing crisis apparent elsewhere in Paul's letters — notably Galatians and Philippians 3. Material in those letters is similar to Romans. Moreover, scholars do tend to assume that many of the arguments Paul was forced to make there would also have been made in Jerusalem (see Gal. 2:1-10; also Acts 15). In emphasizing the defensive quality of the argument in Romans, along with its Jewish concerns, both Stendahl and Jervell (the latter probably more effectively) create space for an explanation of its content and modulations through the letter body — features IX through XIII. But they fail to make the specifics of their case, which is not without foundation but is clearly fragile. Important elements of this case will be incorporated in the explanation of Romans' provenance later on (see §4).

30. "The request for solidarity in their intercessory prayers can *only* be made at the end of the letter after Paul has finished his *detailed* account" (*RD*, 62; emphases mine).

31. A point made originally by T. Mullins, and frequently overlooked since: see "Greeting as a New Testament Form," *Journal of Biblical Literature* 87 (1968): 418-26.

32. Reintroducing Beker's important terminology and methodological distinction at this point. The scholars noted below propose a directly coherent content for the letter body of Romans but argue that certain circumstances elicited this (in effect thereby avoiding Beker's strictures).

33. Stirewalt's and Aune's proposals are represented in *RD*, 147-71 and 278-96 respectively. Jewett's proposal was first stated in "Romans as an Ambassadorial Letter," *Interpretation* 36 (1982): 5-20; although this should be supplemented by the material noted earlier in relation to feature V, the Spanish mission. More of his suggestions will also be introduced later. So Jewett's richly considered views are not reducible to this particular theory.

34. Klaus Berger was the first to make this connection — briefly — in 1984; see his *Formgeschichte des Neuen Testament* (Heidelberg: Quelle & Meyer, 1984), 217; and "Hellenistische Gattungen im Neuen Testament," in *ANRW* II, 25/2 (Berlin: de Gruyter, 1984), 1140. Aune is a well-known representative of the view, partly because of his elegant presentation, and partly because of his inclusion in *RD*. The theory has since been argued at length by Anthony Guerra in *Romans and the Apologetic Tradition*, SNTSMS 81 (Cambridge: University, 1995).

35. The most famous examples are Aristotle's *Protrepticus* (which has been lost but preserved in part in the writings of Iamblichus), and Cicero's *Hortensius*. But the reconstruction of the genre can be assisted by fragments and indirect comments in ancient texts as well — see, e.g., Plato, *Euthydemus*, 278E-82D (esp. τὸ [δὲ] δὴ . . . ἐπιδείξατον προτρέποντε τὸ μειράκιον ὅπως χρὴ σοφίας τε καὶ ἀρετῆς ἐπιμεληθῆναι; "What you have . . . to do is to give us a display of exhorting this youth as to how he should devote himself to wisdom and virtue": *Plato IV*, LCL; trans. W. R. M. Lamb [London: Heinemann, 1924], 402-3); and Isocrates, *Against the Sophists*. See also Justin Martyr, *Dialogue with Trypho*, 1-9, esp. 1.4-1.5 and 2.3-6.2.

36. Advocates of this theory balance these objectives slightly differently at times, but I find that their reasons for doing so are often overly delicate. It is difficult to prove that a text could be intended and received only by "insiders" as against "outsiders," or vice versa (as Aune asserts). A text is not susceptible to this sort of control once it has been published and released to its readerships.

37. Advocates of this theory need to demonstrate that the text of Romans contains explicit markers of a protreptic discourse that are sufficient to elicit that recognition from competent auditors — and to make *this* identification rather than any other. These markers must consequently be stronger than all other possible identifications, and be sufficiently specific. And I am not convinced that these cases have actually been made. The claims are usually couched in terms of generalities; opponents, exhortations, diatribe, refutation, two ways, etc., are said to characterize that discourse and this text. But these motifs can be found in most of Paul's other letters as well, none of which are identified as protreptic. Much of the case seems to rest, then, on the generally soteriological tenor of philosophical protreptics — that this way of life should be embraced because it leads to life. But see more on this claim just below.

38. John of Sardis, in his *Preliminary Exercises*, suggests that "protreptic speeches are deliberative, yes, but on agreed upon subjects," indicating that their orientation is quite rigid and formal (al-

though his discussion in context is complex): see George A. Kennedy (ed.), *Progymnasmata: Greek Textbooks of Prose Composition and Rhetoric* (Leiden & Boston: Brill, 2003), §11, 216.

39. And we do not know of any other Pharisees and artisans composing protreptics. Paul did not write texts remotely similar to Aristotle's or Cicero's. Wisdom of Solomon 1–4 and *Didache* 1–6 are not convincing parallels to the genre.

40. Most importantly, and as we have already seen, the evidence from elsewhere in Paul — such as it is — does not suggest a carefully crafted and polished rhetorical presentation of the gospel. Nor does it support the "speech-based" model of evangelism (which tends to presuppose the rationalistic emphases of Justification theory). Paul's conversions seem to have taken place through networks and in relation to informal speech. This does not preclude his formal speaking on occasion, but the evidence concerning the nature of those performances is limited. Similarly, when Paul exhorts elsewhere in his letters — which he does frequently — he never employs a protreptic discourse.

41. Indeed, this is doubly problematic. It is incomprehensible why Paul would insert this unhelpful principle into the conclusion of a protreptic. But, even more importantly, it provides a completely different account of what motivates Paul and why he proclaims his gospel — it is a divinely revealed and authorized event, attested ultimately by the work of the Spirit. Insofar as Romans participates in this program, then, it is not a protreptic at all.

42. So (i.a.) Kümmel: "The old view that Romans is a systematic, doctrinal presentation of Christian belief . . . is untenable, for important elements of Pauline teaching, such as Christology and eschatology, do not receive full attention, and some, such as the Lord's Supper and church polity, are not touched upon at all" (*Introduction,* 220-21).

43. He is not the sole representative of this basic theory. Donfried notes the support of Bultmann, Bornkamm, Marxsen, Knox, and Suggs (*RD,* 44, n. 1), although Marxsen is also an important advocate of explanation 9, noted below. In terms of the history of scholarship, the detachment of Romans 16 is now an "older" view, currently not much suggested, if at all.

44. His contentions about the Ephesian address of Romans 16 are indecisive. It is true that Prisca and Aquila were last noted in Ephesus (see 1 Cor. 16:19), but this couple moved around, and Acts documents their origin in Rome (18:2). Similarly, in relation to Epaenetus, it is quite plausible that a convert from Asia would migrate to Rome. His close association with Prisca and Aquila might even indicate this, because he may well be part of their household. (We also have no evidence that Paul's first convert in Asia was Ephesian.) These observations are not without weight altogether; they *might* indicate an Ephesian address. But they can be plausibly explained in different terms. And important prosopographical counterevidence points more directly to Rome, most notably, the households of Aristobulus and Narcissus: see esp. Peter Lampe, *From Paul to Valentinus: Christians at Rome in the First Two Centuries* (trans. M. Steinhauser; Minneapolis, Minn.: Fortress, 2003 [1989]), esp. 124, 164-65, 183, 359, 378.

45. Like most, I am relying here on H. Gamble's detailed work: *The Textual History of the Letter to the Romans,* Studies and Documents 42 (Grand Rapids, Mich.: Eerdmans, 1977); although this should be complemented, if not corrected, by P. Lampe, "Zur Textgeschichte des Römerbriefes," *Novum Testamentum* 27 (1985): 273-77. Jewett provides a judicious summary of text-critical issues (*Romans,* 4-18) — although he is strongly committed to the excision of 16:17-20; see more on this just below. This reinforces Donfried's desideratum that "[a]ny study of Romans should proceed on the assumption that Rom. 16 is an integral part of the original letter" (*RD,* 104).

46. So Nygren simply states at the outset of his (part) commentary, "What the gospel is, what the content of the Christian faith is, one learns to know in the Epistle to the Romans as in no other place in the New Testament. Romans gives us the gospel in its wide context. It gives us the right perspective and the standard by which we should comprehend all the constituent parts of the Gospels, to arrive at the true, intended picture": *Commentary on Romans,* trans. C. C. Rasmussen (Philadelphia: Muhlenberg, 1949 [1944]), 3 — although Nygren goes on to emphasize Rom. 5:12-21 especially strongly in this relation, which is not a conventional reading (see esp. 19-28).

Moo states that "the major part of the body of Romans, chaps. 1–11, develops by its own internal logic: Paul's focus is on the gospel and its meaning rather than on the Romans and their needs. . . .

[P]ast battles . . . forced Paul to write a letter in which he carefully rehearsed his understanding of the gospel, especially as it related to the salvation-historical questions of Jew and Gentile and the continuity of the plan of salvation" (*The Epistle to the Romans* [Grand Rapids, Mich.: Eerdmans, 1996], 20-21). Moo goes on to summarize: "We moderns must beware the tendency to overhistoricize: to focus so much on specific local and personal situations that we miss the larger theological and philosophical concerns of the biblical authors. That Paul was dealing in Romans with immediate concerns in the early church we do not doubt. But, especially in Romans, these issues are ultimately those of the church — and the world — of all ages: the continuity of God's plan of salvation, the sin and need of human beings, God's provision for our sin problem in Christ, the means to a life of holiness, and security in the face of suffering and death" (22). And it is worth noting that of the five "ultimate" issues named here, at least two and probably three are rooted in a conventional reading of Romans 1–4 (although perhaps including 5:1-11), while the others arguably raise acute systematic difficulties.

W. Sanday and A. C. Headlam are not dissimilar: "the most powerful of all the influences which have shaped the contents of the Epistle is the experience of the writer. . . . [T]he Apostle has made up his mind on the whole series of questions at issue [i.e., "the controversy relating to Jewish and Gentile"]; and he takes the opportunity of writing to the Romans at the very centre of the empire, to lay down calmly and deliberately the conclusions to which he has come" (*A Romansitical and Exegetical Commentary on the Epistle to the Romans* [Edinburgh: T&T Clark, 1896], xlii, xliii).

47. Less overtly, T. Schreiner rejects a purely coherent approach (*Romans*, BECNT [Grand Rapids, Mich.: Baker, 1998], 15-16), but lapses back into it at all the key points: see "[h]e must satisfy both Jewish and Gentile Christians that his stance on the Mosaic law, circumcision, and the place of Israel accords with the OT Scriptures. . . . Paul's intention is to show [the Gentile wing in the church] that his gospel constitutes the true fulfillment of what the OT Scriptures teach about the Mosaic law, circumcision, and the role of Israel (and Gentiles) in salvation history" (21); and "[h]uman beings will reflect on the wisdom of [God's] plan and honor him. Paul ultimately wrote Romans . . . to honor his Lord" — actions not necessarily to be denied in a broader sense, but that seem to be very odd explanations for the composition and dispatch of a letter by Paul to Rome in the 50s CE (23). Principally in relation to the evident concern of Romans 12–15 with unity (i.e., features XV and XVI), Schreiner argues that "Paul wrote to unify the church so that they [i.e., Jews and Gentiles in Rome] would function harmoniously. Such unity could only be obtained by a thorough explication of Paul's gospel, for Paul's advice would be heeded only if the Romans were persuaded that his understanding of the gospel was on target, especially in relationship to the Mosaic law and the place of Israel in salvation-history" (22). But several questions are begged by this additional reasoning.

As we will see in more detail shortly, Paul does not elsewhere preface exhortations to unity — and even in the specific sense of between "weak" and strong" — with accounts of the gospel, nor does he link these two types of discussion together in abbreviated form. His authority does not necessarily rest on this process of evaluation by the Roman Christians, nor does he define his authority in this fashion in Romans. He is appointed an apostle by God!, who affirms this through signs and wonders if necessary. In addition, his reliability is more likely to have been evaluated in terms of his relationship with tradition: see 1 Cor. 15:1-7! Finally, that his understanding of the gospel that underpins his exhortations to unity would necessarily include some "relationship to the Mosaic law" *assumes* that the gospel *is* Justification (although Schreiner immediately introduces an awkward salvation historical dimension as well), and ignores the difficulties of that gospel generating ethical exhortations. It also ignores the controversial answers that Paul supplies to many of the Jewish questions — answers that would probably have elicited hostility and rejection from Christians with Jewish loyalties, as against acceptance and acquiescence. (Romans, when read conventionally, does not in my experience function especially well in modern ecumenical discussions between Jews and Christians. Aspects of this problem have of course been touched on already in part one, chapter four.)

For all these reasons, then, Schreiner's attempts to link coherence and contingency together seem unsatisfactory, and his lapses into coherent explanation consequently lack probity. And in this he is representative of many other commentators.

Kathy Grieb courts this danger by way of a narrative emphasis: "Romans is a sustained argument for the righteousness of God that is identified with and demonstrated by the faithfulness of Jesus Christ, understood primarily as his willing obedience to suffer death on the cross. . . . Paul's argument in [Romans] . . . is constructed on a series of stories nested within the one great story of what God has done for Israel and for the Gentiles in Jesus Christ" (*The Story of Romans* [London & Louisville: Westminster-John Knox, 2002], ix). She is of course alert to it (see xiii).

N. T. Wright interprets similarly: ". . . to understand why Paul wanted to say just this at just this moment to these people, the most important thing to do is to grasp the main theme of the letter and to see why it was important to first-century Jews in general, to Paul in particular, and to him in this setting most specifically . . . [namely] God and God's covenant faithfulness and justice, rather than . . . 'justification.' . . . Paul's aim, it seems, is to explain to the Roman church what God has been up to and where they might belong on the map of these purposes" ("The Letter to the Romans. Introduction, Commentary, and Reflections," in *The New Interpreter's Bible,* ed. L. Keck [Nashville, Tenn.: Abingdon, 2002], 10:397, 403, 404).

Talbert is more dialectical, but still emphasizes coherence: "[Three stated aims] functioned as catalysts for Paul's letter. The argument of Romans, however, was determined by the logic of the gospel as Paul had thought it out during his Aegean mission. In this sense, Romans is a summary of Paul's mature thought insofar as it applied to the Roman occasion" (*Romans,* 12). He also invokes feature XVI, which will be assessed shortly: "[t]he *function* of Paul's gospel [in Romans] was to unify Jewish and Gentile Christians in Rome" (19, emphasis original).

Brendan Byrne is a rhetorical variation, viewing Romans as "a genuine 'preaching of the gospel' — not as an instrument of initial conversion but, in epideictic mode, as a 'celebration' of values held in common, to increase adherence to those values and further detachment from rival values [i.e., the Jewish law!] that could threaten them" (*Romans,* Sacra Pagina [Collegeville, Minn.: Glazier, Liturgical Press, 1996], 18). However, just why Paul undertakes this epistolary "celebration" at Rome is not entirely clear.

Fitzmyer lapses into this view as well (partly by way of Stirewalt's advocacy of Romans as a "letter-essay": see more on this theory just below): "[Paul] writes the essay-letter to introduce himself to the Roman Christians, who are mostly unknown to him personally, and sets forth in it his view of the gospel, which he has been preaching in the east, and his reflections upon it, hoping that it will aid the lives of Roman Christians as well . . ." (*Romans,* 79). Ultimately Fitzmyer draws together several views of Romans' provenance — as many as eight! — in a "multiple" explanation that strains credulity.

48. See part three, chapter twelve, §2.2.

49. We would still have to speak, then, of multiple contradictions or developments in Paul's thinking.

50. It seems possible at first in context that this is a dative of respect and hence not an explicit marker concerning a pagan audience, since Paul goes on to speak of his ministry *to* pagans that might arouse some of *his kindred* to jealousy and salvation ("I speak to you with respect to pagans," i.e., concerning pagans). However, Paul explicitly marks converted pagans as his audience again in v. 17 (σὺ . . . ἀγριέλαιος ὢν . . .), so the concerns of vv. 13b-14 seem parenthetical and should probably be punctuated and delivered as such.

51. This illustration is grounded in basic horticultural practice in Paul's day (and it is still widely evident): see John Ziesler and A. G. Baxter, "Paul and Aboriculture: Romans 11:17-24," *Journal for the Study of the New Testament* 24 (1985): 24-32.

52. Most interpreters hold the tree trunk and root to be historical Israel, but a minority argues that it is Christ: see N. Walter, "Zur Interpretation von Römer 9–11," *Zeitschrift für Theologie und Kirche* 81 (1984): 172-95. This rather fascinating question does not need to be settled here.

53. Not meaning by this characterization that the ancient world defined its discriminatory categories in the same terms that modern racists do. I refer here to pervasive attitudes of hostility, suspicion, and denigration, directed in the ancient world toward ethnic groups different from one's own. See Paul Cartledge, *The Greeks: A Portrait of Self and Others* (Oxford: Oxford University Press, 1993); and Denise K. Buell, *Why This New Race? Ethnic Reasoning in Early Christianity* (New York: Columbia University Press, 2005); a useful introduction to ethnicity more generally is John Hutchinson, and

Anthony D. Smith, ed., *Ethnicity* (Oxford & New York: Oxford University Press, 1996). Rodney Stark notes that, "taking a realistic view of ethnic relations, the king [i.e., Seleucus I] had the two [original founding] sections [of Syrian Antioch] walled off from one another": *The Rise of Christianity: A Sociologist Reconsiders History* (Princeton, New Jersey: Princeton University Press, 1996), 157. Philip F. Esler links notions of ethnicity more tightly to Paul and Romans in *Conflict and Identity in Romans: The Social Setting of Paul's Letter* (Minneapolis, Minn.: Fortress, 2003).

54. Judaism was also of course admired by some. However, this was almost certainly a minority position. Anti-Jewishness seems to have been widespread: see M. Stern, *Greek and Latin Authors on Jews and Judaism,* 3 vols. (Jerusalem: The Israel Academy of Sciences and Humanities, 1974), 81, 84.

55. So some contingent explanation of this emphasis remains desirable. Alternatively, perhaps the oddity is that this problem is not more apparent in any of his other letters.

56. Most notably, 1 Thess. 2:14-16, that has just been cited, but many other Pauline statements have also been judged harsh. See also, e.g., Gal. 2:14 in context, and perhaps 6:16. And Rom. 15:31 should perhaps also be given due consideration, not to mention 16:20a in context.

57. If 11:13-32 are included in Paul's admonition concerning anti-Judaism — twenty verses and around thirty-seven lines of Greek — then seventy verses and around 131 lines of Greek precede and follow this subsection. If 11:13-32 is pressed as an explanation for this entire section of argument, one wonders whether the tail is wagging the dog.

58. A difficulty that is especially important if interpreters want to link this feature with XI more strongly. Moreover, a further explanatory tension can be generated that is noted just below. It is very difficult to satisfy features XI, XIII, and XIV, within the same basic appeal: see C. H. Cosgrove, "The Justification of the Other: An Interpretation of Rom 1:18–4:25," *Society of Biblical Literature 1992 Seminar Papers* (ed. Eugene H. Lovering; Atlanta: Scholars, 1992), 613-34.

59. The qualification here in terms of Paul thinking *fundamentally* in salvation-historical terms should be noted. It is not being denied that his thinking has salvation-historical dimensions; indeed, I would argue that this is necessary. At issue, rather, is the question whether his most basic, controlling notions are salvation-historical. See my comments in chs. 3 and 7 in *The Quest for Paul's Gospel: A Suggested Strategy* (London: T&T Clark International [Continuum], 2005), 56-68, 132-45.

60. "Majority" being used here in a relative, not an absolute, sense.

61. Klein notes the earlier support of H. Preisker, H. W. Bartsch, and W. Marxsen ("Paul's Purpose," *RD,* 35). To these representatives we should add the rather maximalist account of Paul S. Minear (*The Obedience of Faith: The Purposes of Paul in the Epistle to the Romans* [London: SCM, 1971]); the classic version by Wolfgang Wiefel (see "The Jewish Community in Ancient Rome and the Origins of Roman Christianity," *RD,* 85-101); and the more recent advocacy of the view by James Dunn (*Romans 1-8* [Dallas, Tex.: Word, 1988], esp. xliv-liv); N. T. Wright ("The Letter to the Romans," 406-8); A. J. M. Wedderburn (*The Reasons for Romans;* see also "Purpose and Occasion of Romans Again," *RD,* 195-202); Fitzmyer, *Romans,* esp. 76-78 (although he also endorses other theories); and Esler *(Conflict and Identity in Romans).* (Many more figures could be named here.)

Watson also advocates this position — see *PJ&G²,* 163-91; see also "The Two Roman Congregations: Romans 14:1–15:13," *RD,* 203-15.

But he nuances it distinctively. Watson argues in *PJ&G²* that the *intra*-Christian tensions evident in Romans are directly related to *external* relations between the law-free church emerging at Rome — a sect — and the synagogues — the parent body. But there is no direct evidence of this vital additional dynamic. It also ignores the probable arrival of law-free Christianity in Rome in some close association with Paul and his coworkers. The claim that this radical form of early Christianity has been in Rome for some time independently of the radical Pauline mission — the crucial point for Watson's thesis to work — needs justification, and none is forthcoming. (These issues have already been briefly addressed in part three, chapter twelve, §2.1.)

62. "The strong" are not so designated until 15:1 — a point worth noting but not overemphasizing.

63. Robert J. Karris, "Romans 14:1–15:13 and the Occasion of Romans," *RD,* 65-84; Karl P. Donfried, "False Presuppositions in the Study of Romans," *RD,* 102-24.

64. Watson grasps this often overlooked point especially clearly: "The Two Roman Congregations: Romans 14:1–15:13," in *RD*, 203-15, esp. 211; see also *PJ&G*², 186. And this realization should be supplemented by the important work done more recently on the sociology of the Roman Christians — see esp. Jewett, "Tenement Churches and Pauline Love Feasts," *Quarterly Review: A Journal of Theological Resources for Ministry* 14 (1994): 43-58; and Peter Lampe, *From Paul to Valentinus*.

65. Paul emphasizes a unified service and discernment in 12:1-2, and then urges a humble, not arrogant, appreciation of giftedness in the broader context of the single body of Christ in vv. 3-8. Verses 9-16 are a set of generalized but essentially harmonious exhortations probably organized around the central virtue of love (v. 9a).

66. The strong are to follow Christ's example and please not themselves but the weak, and to receive one another as Christ received them. Moreover, Christ served the Jews in order to fulfill that tradition *and* to extend God's mercy to the pagans (and this in fulfillment of numerous scriptural sayings).

67. Although I also do *not* detect a problem where many other scholars do. That is, it does not seem necessary to identify these parties precisely for the broader explanation to hold good. For Paul to write a letter oriented in these terms, he needs only to know of a destructive relationship between two groups who are separated by their posture in relation to standard Jewish practices. He then encodes these groups into the letter's admonitions. Hence, we do not need to grasp the empirical situation in Rome precisely in order to understand the letter as a rhetorical composition and event.

68. In one sense we are raising here an additional criterion incumbent on this type of explanation. It seems reasonable to ask for subunits that are ostensibly dependent on other subunits for their theological rationale to provide some linguistic and argumentative evidence of that dependence; Paul should at points explicitly flag up the argumentative relationship through linguistic markers and/or theological and argumentative summaries. In the absence of any such connections, it is fair to query whether a conceptual relationship exists. What secondary, dependent discussion takes place in Paul that does not at some point mark that dependence overtly?

69. It could be replied that precisely because the Romans are not like the Corinthians, who know Paul well, they require the extensive theoretical preamble that underlies Paul's later practical arguments. However, there is no strong evidence that Paul tutored the Corinthians with Justification arguments. Nor do his discussions in 1 Corinthians or in Romans reference that material directly.

70. It could be argued on the basis of Romans 14 alone that non-Jewish practices might also explain the underlying situation, most notably, Pythagorean temporal and dietary instructions. However, given the broader concern of Romans with Jewish questions, the most likely explanation of its provenance (which we consider shortly), the most probable origins of the Roman Christian house churches, and their explicit marking in Romans 16, a Jewish explanation does seem the more likely one.

71. So we return here to a point already noted in relation to Romans 9–11, and apparent in Cosgrove's study, "The Justification of the Other."

72. There is also a difficulty with the way these arguments and later constituencies have been coded. The opening arguments of Romans devastate a law-observant and arrogant judger. This is not quite the depiction of "the weak," however, that Paul later supplies. They are not a group of confident, learned pedagogues who base their actions on instruction and Scripture, but a group afflicted by the pangs of conscience. This lack of correlation further complicates any claim that Romans 1–3 prepares for the discussions of ch. 14.

73. Feature XIV could also be introduced here — pagan Christian anti-Judaism. And I concede the presence of this in some sense at Rome, but would not yet concede that it concretely characterizes Roman Christians per se. Still, it is certainly possible counterevidence and should be noted. Its relevance is discussed immediately below.

74. It might be argued that a statement of the gospel should precede the admonitions of Romans 14 to ground them theologically, but I have suggested that this is implausible. However, a concession in terms of Paul's rhetorical incompetence can partly rescue this position. A multiple theory might also mitigate this shortfall partly as well; see more on this immediately.

75. It might also prove the best explanation for Klein's observation that Paul seems, rather unusually, to avoid calling the Roman Christians an ἐκκλησία, which would have implied their unity.

76. See esp. the accounts of Wiefel, Dunn, and Wright, already noted in relation to hypothesis 9 above.

77. The theory posits that Claudius expelled all the Jewish Christians from Rome, along with the Jews, in 49 CE. The converted pagan Christians remained behind, not being subject to the edict. Claudius's edict supposedly lapsed upon his death in 54 CE, at which point the Jewish Christians returned. But they were now a somewhat alienated minority within the Roman church — one with different traditions. And they were also viewed with still more suspicion by the surrounding pagan populace than they had been prior to their expulsion. The pagan Christians may have even been tempted to ratify this broader pagan view, being converts from paganism themselves, with no local Jewish Christian correctives.

78. Further details in this relation can be found in Dixon Slingerland, *Claudian Policymaking and the Early Imperial Repression of Judaism at Rome,* South Florida Studies in the History of Judaism 160 (Atlanta: Scholars, 1997).

79. Feature II concerns Paul's apostleship, which remains unexplained as a causal factor by any emphases on anti-Judaism at Rome. The non-interference clause (III) also remains opaque. Moreover, the lack of any widespread signals from Paul of overt deficiencies among the Roman Christians further problematizes this theory — evidence related to feature IV. (Emphases on features XIV and XVI can beg the question at this point.) Similarly, the multiple abstract and Jewish units in the letter body preceding chapters 9–11 have not been explained either — features IX through XII and chapters 1–8. Clearly, these are serious deficiencies. It seems, then, that we cannot simply multiply our way out of our difficulties.

80. I note the earlier advocacy of this hypothesis by F. C. Baur and C. Weizäcker in "Determining the Gospel through Rhetorical Analysis in Paul's Letter to the Roman Christians," in *Gospel in Paul: Studies on Corinthians, Galatians and Romans for Richard N. Longenecker,* ed. G. P. Richardson and L. Ann Jervis, JSNTSup 108 (Sheffield: JSOT Press, 1994), 327-49. More recently, this approach has been argued at length in James C. Miller, *The Obedience of Faith, the Eschatological People of God, and the Purpose of Romans,* SBLDS 177 (Atlanta: SBL, 2000). J. Louis Martyn pursues it in his important commentary on Galatians: see *Galatians: A New Translation with Introduction and Commentary,* AB 33A (New York: Doubleday, 1997), 13-20, 28-29, 117-26 (#6), 217-19 (#21), 236-40 (#25), 302-6 (#33), 447-57 (#45), 457-66 (#46). Among the Romans commentators, F. Godet, *Commentary on St. Paul's Epistle to the Romans,* tr. A. Cusin (Edinburgh: T&T Clark, 1886), 496; Sanday and Headlam, *Romans,* 429 ("evil teachers probably of a Jewish character . . . whose advent to Rome he dreads"); Peter Stuhlmacher, *Der Brief an die Römer* (Göttingen: Vandenhoeck & Ruprecht, 1989), 222-23; and Ulrich Wilckens, *Der Brief an die Römer,* 3 vols. (Zürich, Einsiedeln, Köln, and Neukirchen-Vluyn: Benziger & Neukirchener, 1978), 3:141, 144-45; all note the presence of false Jewish Christian teachers in relation to 16:17-20, but do little to press the interpretative implications further. Andrew Lincoln concedes that "it cannot be denied that in terms of the rhetorical situation in the letter, the addressees for whom this dialogue with a Jew [in Romans 2] would have particular force are Jewish Christians, for whom belief in Jesus as Messiah has been added to earlier beliefs about Israel's privileged covenant status and the necessity of observing the law and who object to the far more radical version of the gospel Paul is preaching in his ministry to the Gentiles": "From Wrath to Justification: Tradition, Gospel, and Audience in the Theology of Romans 1:18–4:25," in Hay and Johnson, eds., *Pauline Theology,* vol. 3, *Romans,* 130-68, quoting from 133.

Das objects to this reconstruction — that he calls "apologetic" — on several grounds (*Solving the Romans Debate,* 43-49): (1) it cannot account for the "climactic place of Rom 9–11" (i.e., feature XIII); (2) it also cannot explain the maintenance of Israel's position in that discussion over against Gentile arrogance (XIV); (3) Paul's paraenesis in Romans 12:1–15:13 is not comprehensible in this relation either (XV and XVI); and (4) Paul does not provide "any indication that the Romans had objections to his message or harbored suspicions about him because of a supposed reputation for controversy in the East" (42: see VIII). Later he also argues (5) that the figures addressed in Rom. 16:17-18 —

who "serve . . . their own appetites" — are not plausibly identified with the Teacher(s), who advocated Jewish law-observance (see VIII again). (Unfortunately, this issue is slightly misrepresented. I do not equate the Teacher(s) with "the weak" of Romans 14: see *Solving*, 44-45.) All these concerns are addressed in detail in what follows.

81. See esp. Jervis for a detailed account of the letter openings and thanksgiving paragraphs: *The Purpose of Romans*. The openings contain: (1) a sender formula including (a) the name of the sender (and co-sender/s), (b) title/s (apostle/servant), and (c) a short descriptive phrase indicating the source of the title/s; (2) a recipient formula including (a) an identification of the recipient (usually using ἐκκλησία), and (b) a short phrase positively describing the recipients' relationship to God; and (3) a greeting formula including (a) a greeting (grace and peace), (b) a recipient (to you), and (c) a divine source (from God our Father and the Lord Jesus Christ).

82. More detailed accounts are supplied by Jeffrey A. D. Weima, *Neglected Endings: The Significance of the Pauline Letter Closings*, JSNTSup 101 (Sheffield: JSOT, 1994); and, specifically for Romans, in "'Preaching the Gospel at Rome: A Study of the Epistolary Framework of Romans," in Richardson and Jervis (eds.), *Gospel in Paul*, 337-66.

83. It has been queried whether this subsection was originally a part of Romans. This issue is considered briefly in §4.3 below — "Possible objections."

84. The text-critical evidence is complex. The Western tradition (principally D, F, G) tends to place a similar grace wish after v. 23 instead (and some MSS place the wish after v. 27). Gamble and Jervis suggest that a doublet was present (and I am inclined to agree with them): see Gamble, *Textual History*; and Jervis, *Purpose*.

85. It occurs absolutely in 12:8. See also 1 Cor. 1:10; 4:16; 14:31; 16:15; 2 Cor. 2:8; 5:20; 6:1; 8:6; 10:1; 12:8; Phil. 4:2; 1 Thess. 2:12; 4:1; 5:11, 14; see also Eph. 4:1; 2 Thess. 3:12; see BDAG, 764-65.

86. See also χρηστολόγον in Julius Capitolinus, *Pertinax* 13 — "a smooth talker" (cited in BDAG, 1089-90; see also εὐλογία, 408-9).

87. And this raises the possibility in turn that Rom. 16:20 echoes Gen. 3:15 — the crushing of Satan under the feet of the Romans recalling Eve's crushing of the serpent's head. See more on this just below.

88. Some scholars detect a wisdom discourse here and at other points in the pericope (esp. in Paul's use of ἐκκλίνω, ἄκακος, and σόφος: see Dunn, *Romans 1-8*, 900-907; Dunn could also have pointed to the apocalyptic tenor of "Satan"). They may be correct, but I am not sure of its overt interpretative significance. *If* an echo of Matt. 10:16 is detectable (where ἀκέραιος occurs as well: see v. 19), then this *could* constitute a rather wicked instance of subversion — the Teacher's proverb perhaps being turned against him (see chapter fourteen). But Paul thematizes wisdom in relation to the gospel in Romans in any case, so such echoes may be no more than this (although see also part five, chapter nineteen, where a wisdom discourse is linked to the Teacher fairly directly by way of Romans 10). An entirely practical and local reading is also possible — that the Roman Christians should be wise enough to recognize the goodness of Paul and his letter, but innocent and pure of the evil practiced by the dissenters.

89. There are no direct linguistic signals of a connection between 16:20 and Gen. 3:15; hence, the echo, if it exists, must be fundamentally narrative. Nevertheless, Dunn suggests that Gen. 3:15 was a staple of Jewish hope, citing Ps. 91:13; *Testament of Simeon* 6:6; *Testament of Levi* 18:12 (to which we should add *Testament of Zebulon* 9:8); and Luke 10:18-19 (a text that includes a note of joy, like Rom. 16:19-20) (and to which we should also add 1 Cor. 15:25 and 27, citing Ps. 8:6b — a further element within the theme); and supported by *TDNT* 5:81, Michel, Käsemann, and Stuhlmacher (who notes the foregoing: see *Römer*, 223), and Cranfield (*Romans 9-16*, 905). Apart from Ps. 91:13, this seems to be a Jewish *Christian* discourse, however, that does not affect the claim being explored here. It seems that Paul is alluding to an earlier Jewish Christian tradition concerning Christ, which counterposed Psalm 8 to the garden of Eden (reading that Psalm messianically of course).

90. See 2 Cor. 10:12–12:13; Gal. 4:17; 5:7-12; 6:12; Phil. 3:1-19; 1 Thess. 2:1-12; see Col. 2:4, 8, 16-19; 2 Thess. 2:1-12.

91. An insight whose origins go back to Ferdinand Christian Baur: see *Paul, the Apostle of Jesus*

Christ, His Life and Works, His Epistles and Teachings, 2nd ed., ed. and rev. A. Menzies and E. Zeller; 2 vols. (London: Williams & Norgate, 1873-1875). More recently, see also Dieter Georgi, *The Opponents of Paul in Second Corinthians* (Philadelphia: Fortress, 1986); Jerry L. Sumney, *Identifying Paul's Opponents: The Question of Method in 2 Corinthians*, JSNTSup 40 (Sheffield: JSOT, 1990); Karl Olaf Sandnes, *Belly and Body in the Pauline Epistles*, SNTSMS 120 (Cambridge: Cambridge University Press, 2002); Stanley Porter, ed., *Paul and His Opponents* (Leiden & Boston: Brill, 2005); see also Thomas J. Sappington, *Revelation and Redemption at Colossae*, JSNTSup 53 (Sheffield: JSOT, 1992). Martyn's reading of Galatians is of course oriented significantly by this perception (see, in detail, the discussion of part five, chapter twenty). Note also that Porter's contribution to his edited volume overlooks important pieces of evidence, and so comes to an unduly pessimistic conclusion about the possible presence of opponents of Paul's at Rome: see "Did Paul Have Opponents in Rome and What Were They Opposing?" *Paul and His Opponents*, 149-68.

92. See Phil. 3:17-19; see also 1:15, 17; 3:2. This connection is explored in detail in Sandnes's graceful study, *Belly and Body*. Philippians 3 is examined in detail — and this agonistic reading justified — in part five, chapter twenty-one. The suggestion by Das that the figures attacked in Phil. 3:17-19 are generic is ultimately unconvincing. None of the other figures criticized in Philippians are! (*Solving the Romans Debate*, 47, n. 194.)

93. Keck would add that Paul's consistent use of articles in v. 17, and the correlative adjective τοιοῦτος in v. 18 — "those who . . ." — is a further indication that specific teachers and teaching are in view (*Romans*, ANTC [Nashville, Tenn.: Abingdon, 2005], 375; echoing an earlier endorsement by H. W. Schmidt). Michel argued that this was simply a part of the style of such exhortations; however, I am not sure that this is accurate (as noted by Dunn, *Romans 9–16*, 904). Certainly, these indicators are consistent with the presence of specific teachers and teachings.

94. Non-Christian figures, moreover, would enjoy no initial legitimacy among the Roman Christians. That Paul perceives them as a threat to the Christians in Rome implies directly that they are themselves Christians. Keck concurs (*Romans*, 376).

95. See *Testament of Moses* 7:4-7 (which is directed to gluttony per se); *3 Macc.* 7:11 (a generic reference to transgressors); and Philo, *On the Virtues*, 182 (which encompasses both senses) (Dunn, *Romans 9–16*, 903).

96. It is also possibly significant that Paul links them with "Satan," literally, "the accuser" (he uses the article). If it retains its literal force, this characterization may denote the rather aggressive, judgmental tone that will emerge as a central feature of the Teacher's discourse: see chapter fourteen. The Teacher browbeats, threatens, and judges his auditors, so this reference by Paul to the primary accuser seems entirely apposite.

97. And it is therefore unnecessary to endorse Wilckens's far-fetched explanation that Paul includes the warning against false teachers at this late point because he has only just heard about them (*Römer*, 3:143)! Any connection with the weak and the strong is also unlikely. Schreiner observes correctly that "[i]n that text [i.e., Romans 14] tensions between strong and weak believers in the Roman churches are adjudicated. Here [in 16:17-20] a menace from outside the community is anticipated" (*Romans*, 801). Mark Nanos makes a similarly unlikely suggestion — that Paul is urging continued submission to the Apostolic Decree: see *The Mystery of Romans* (Minneapolis: Fortress, 1996), 216-17. Setting aside the fragility of the biography that underpins this claim, it ignores the rhetorical strategy that Paul encodes in the letter overtly. (Nanos does, however, perceptively note the relevance of 6:17.) Byrne notes this rhetorical move on Paul's part briefly (*Romans*, 18-19).

98. Romans 15:15-19 also arguably supplies an extended definition of Paul's gift of priestly service to the pagans in relation to Christ, mediated and corroborated by the Spirit; this material illuminates nicely the short phrase χάρισμα πνευματικόν that he uses in 1:11.

99. Stuhlmacher is essentially alone among the commentators in noting the significance of this verse and connection (*Römer*, 222-23). Dunn (*Romans 1–8*, 137), endorsed by Das (*Solving the Romans Debate*, 48), has opposed this reading, arguing that the issue of libertinism is characterized too vaguely to denote a concrete opposing position. But the vagueness of the allusion is part of a deliberate rhetorical strategy on Paul's part that is not yet fully apparent in the letter (see more on this just be-

low). The further charge that libertinism is a corollary of Paul's own exposition, and therefore does not arise from an opponent, is problematic on a number of counts. It is *not*, strictly speaking, a *corollary* of Paul's exposition; this is why he opposes it so vehemently! Hence, not surprisingly, it does not occur wherever Paul is involved in exposition of his gospel (see, e.g., 1 Cor. 15:1-8), but only where that gospel is being contested by orthopractic Jewish Christians, i.e., in Galatians. Moreover, even if it is a possible misunderstanding, nothing prevents that misunderstanding from being used against Paul by those who oppose him. In other words, Dunn's claim here is a non sequitur; where he needs a necessary and exclusive causal connection, he has only a possible one (and then only arguably so), so the counter-argument collapses.

100. See Martyn, *Galatians*, 93-94, who argues that "[t]he Teachers themselves do not claim to be apostles (contrast Paul's opponents in 2 Cor 11:13), but they do claim to represent the apostles in the Jerusalem church . . ." (94).

101. See 2 Cor. 3:1b.

102. See, e.g., 1 Cor. 4:19-21.

103. We return to this claim in part five, chapter twenty. Suffice it for now to note the documentation of E. P. Sanders, *Paul, the Law, and the Jewish People* (Philadelphia: Fortress, 1983), 42-43, 45-48, 148-49.

104. These important inferences speak to Das's concerns that neither 16:17-20 nor Romans as a whole addresses Jewish Christian Teachers overtly — concerns 4 and 5. The important rhetorical reasons for Paul's subtlety and indirection in Romans have also already been supplied.

105. A case needs to be made, largely in view of this material's distinctive nature and function, that it is an integral part of canonical Philippians — although the current tide of scholarly opinion is flowing quite strongly in favor of that case; for further details see part five, chapter twenty-one.

106. The difficulties are discussed in part five, chapter twenty-one.

107. Martyn, *Galatians, passim*.

108. Later, with the added material from parts of Romans reread, we will be able to deepen Martyn's portrait of this figure and his soteriology.

109. That is, his relationship with the Roman Christians must be delicately nuanced, so he cannot proceed too personally. We might say that the polemics of the debate's previous rounds have created vulnerabilities before a more distant and impartial audience.

110. These exigencies should be added to the need already noted that Paul not appear dominant or overbearing, and especially to Christian groups who do not know him and have not been founded either by him or one of his coworkers. Ben Witherington III is sensitive to this dynamic: "The art of persuasion had to be pursued differently in a letter written to those who were not Paul's converts and thus not inherently under his authority, compared to letters written to those who were Paul's converts and who recognized that they were. . . . [Hence] [i]t will not do to judge Romans and its rhetoric in the same sort of way one would judge Galatians or 1 Corinthians. While this letter is partially an attempt to establish rapport with and authority over the Roman Gentile Christians, it is not an example of exercise of the authority we would see where Paul already had a power relationship" ([with Darla Hyatt] *Paul's Letter to the Romans: A Socio-Rhetorical Commentary* [Grand Rapids, Mich.: Eerdmans, 2004], 2).

111. For example, imagery rooted in an upper-class household and/or in local Galatian Cybele cults.

112. There are ultimately dialogical and circular dimensions operating to blur the precise application of these dynamics. Note also that these dynamics explain why Romans is not a systematic presentation of Paul's theology, with many supposedly vital topics treated superficially, if at all — the Eucharist, Christology, ecclesiology, eschatology, and so on. Only certain aspects of Paul's gospel, and the Teacher's, are at issue.

113. As such, it will *not* be merely an account of Paul's self-expression. The voice of the Teacher will appear in Romans reasonably frequently, lest the Roman Christians be unprepared to repudiate it when it arrives in person. Hence, we will have to mirror-read Romans, at least to some degree (and the methodological issues here will be addressed shortly).

114. A careful comparison between these arguments and Galatians might even suggest that Paul has crafted these particular positions in response to the criticisms of the Teacher since an earlier round of the discussion. It is unlikely that Paul's posture toward unbelieving Israel is completely unconsidered, but there is nothing like controversy to sharpen consideration! Other Pauline texts also suggest that he could be much harsher toward Israel, when the contingent need required. Hence, Romans 9–11 seems, to a significant degree, contingently formed as well. See more in this relation in part five, chapter nineteen.

115. So my suggested reading actually provides an excellent explanation of Romans 9–11, along with its short exhortation in terms of possible pagan Christian arrogance, thereby speaking to Das's first two critical concerns.

116. The methodological issues raised by this approach are addressed in the following section — §4.3.

117. The voice of the Teacher is arguably discernible in this paraenesis at certain points.

118. And the need for this strategy also defuses Das's final critical concern (i.e., 3) — that Paul's paraenesis is inexplicable in an apologetic reading. It is, on the contrary, entirely comprehensible in such a situation.

119. Criticisms of the actual mechanics of the explanation — largely by Das — have already been addressed in passing. That is, it should be apparent by now that this explanation appeals to solid readings of certain texts, and also satisfactorily explains all the other features of the text. Moreover, no cogent problems are discernible in the theory's workings. So at this point only the more programmatic methodological objections remain.

120. John M. G. Barclay, "Mirror-Reading a Polemical Letter: Galatians as a Test Case," *Journal for the Study of the New Testament* 31 (1987): 73-93.

121. See esp. Sumney, *Identifying Paul's Opponents*. Others have moved beyond warnings to outright repudiation, asserting instead that Paul's texts be interpreted without reference to opposition. However, this is simply unhistorical.

122. Much ancient polemic did not take place in a relatively neutral arena, and so did not need to observe such parameters. Biased arenas allow unfair and intensely hostile portraits of opponents.

123. Most recently, Jewett has added his impressive voice to this position (*Romans*, 985-96, esp. 986-88; see also "Ecumenical Theology for the Sake of Mission," 105-6), noting in addition the advocacy of Baur, Erbes, Knox, Schmithals, Ollrog, O'Neill, Byrne, Brändle and Stegemann, and Boismard (*Romans*, 986, n. 5). Keck should now be added to this line of interpretation as well (*Romans*, 375-79).

124. Jewett, *Romans*, 986.

125. As Dunn notes correctly, Paul "was by no means averse to a final polemical thrust . . ." (*Romans 9–16*, 901). So the suggestion that this subsection is inappropriate in its immediate context is not really correct; it misunderstands the nature of Paul's letter endings, and overlooks the important evidence from other letters of similar activity.

126. Jewett summarizes Ollrog's list — ἐκκλίνειν, χρηστολογία, ἄκακος, ἀφίκεσθαι, συντρίβειν, ἐν τάχει, and εὐλογία ("Ecumenical Theology for the Sake of Mission," 106, n. 69; see *Romans*, 987). ἐκκλίνειν occurs, however, in Rom. 3:12 when Ps. 14 is cited. And although Ollrog and Jewett contend that εὐλογία is used in a nonPauline way to mean "well-chosen words," the assertion that it is therefore unPauline is hardly probative (see Rom. 15:29; 1 Cor. 10:16; 2 Cor. 9:5, 6; Gal. 3:14; see Eph. 1:3). Similarly, denying Paul the alpha-privative form of κακός is hardly convincing (see in Romans alone 1:30; 2:9; 3:8; 7:19, 21; 12:17, 21; 13:3, 4, 10; 14:20). ἀφίκεσθαι, συντρίβειν, and the expression ἐν τάχει (not to mention ἄκακος), are all well-attested in the LXX. Hence, that 16:17-20 is *distinctive* may certainly be granted, but that it is for this reason necessarily unPauline is to stretch the evidence too far.

127. The use of διδαχή to denote a body of teaching, and σκάνδαλον in the plural, are supposedly atypical, as is the phrase "serve our Lord Christ" (τῷ κυρίῳ ἡμῶν Χριστῷ [οὐ] δουλεύουσιν). Συντρίψει is future, whereas Pauline blessings generally use the optative. "Obedience" is ostensibly used in an unparalleled way, "because it is unconnected with either faith or the gospel" ("Ecumenical Theology," 106, n. 70). And the expression "the God of peace" is used in a way inconsistent with the use of peace in Rom. 5:1; 14:17; and 15:33.

But these arguments are forced as well. It is part of Paul's strategy in Romans to connect his gospel with the body of teaching — the διδαχή — that the Romans have received (see 6:17). Paul can hardly be refused a plural form, and knows and uses the signifier σκάνδαλον widely (see merely in Romans, 9:33; 11:9; and 14:13). The unusual phrase "serve our Lord Christ" occurs almost verbatim in Col. 3:24, which is at least an attested part of Pauline tradition, but may constitute evidence from Paul himself. That any combination of words should be excluded from Paul's highly flexible uses of Christ's titles looks dubious in any case. The verb συντρίψει occurs in an assertion, not a final blessing, and so need not be in the optative (and in koiné, the future indicative and the more uncertain moods were often interchanged in any case: see Rom. 5:1). "Obedience" is not always directly connected with either faith or the gospel in Paul, and is, in any case, a leitmotif in Romans: see 1:5; 5:19; 6:16 (twice, occurring along with the cognate verb, and at no point in direct relationship to either faith or the gospel); 15:18; see also 16:26. And finally, while the action of the "God of peace" in 16:20 crushing Satan underfoot is arguably inconsistent with some of Paul's central theological tenets (as noted esp. in chapter three, §3.10 and the Excursus there), it is by no means incompatible with some of his more aggressive eschatological statements (see elsewhere only in Romans, 12:18-21; 13:1-7). In this connection, the establishment of "peace" can be anticipated in terms of an aggressive military victory by God over his enemies: see 1 Cor. 15:25, 28, 54-55, 57. (Whether it *ought* to be is another question.)

128. Keck adds that the final unique assertion of v. 20a that Satan will soon be crushed under the Roman Christians' feet is difficult to integrate "into the thought of the rest of the letter, which never mentions Satan, [and] requires too much exegetical dexterity to be convincing" (*Romans*, 378). But the saying has a clear argumentative rationale where it is located. The false teachers are deceptive servants of Satan, allied with Sin, as the echoes of Gen. 3:13 and Rom. 7:11 in v. 18a suggest. And this sentiment is entirely Pauline: see 2 Cor. 11:13-14.

129. See the text-critical situation regarding 16:25-27, which is overtly confused; yet the subsection *still* has its defenders in terms of authenticity.

130. Positive evidence of authenticity also includes Paul's use of δέ in v. 17. And the use of ὑπακοή in v. 19, as has already been noted, echoes a theme throughout the letter.

131. Acts notes missions on these journeys (at least) in the cities of Philippi, Thessalonica, Berea, Athens, Corinth, and Ephesus. And a mission in Troas should also be assumed, although not necessarily by Paul (see Acts 20:5-12; 2 Cor. 2:12-13 [the parallel text being Acts 20:1-2!]).

132. The fragmentary inscription from Delphi that mentions Gallio — see (i.a.) *Sylloge inscriptionum graecarum* 2, no. 801 D, or *Fouilles de Delphes*, III, *Epigraphie*, 4:286, l. 6 — is referenced chronologically in l. 2 by the 26th acclamation of Claudius as imperator (κϛ'). (His tribunician year — the twelfth — is reconstructed.) The dates of the 24th and 27th are known independently, suggesting that this inscription was erected at some point between mid-51 and mid-52 CE, although probably in the latter half of this year (see the concise discussion by Robert Jewett, *A Chronology of Paul's Life* [Philadelphia: Fortress, 1979], 36-38, 126-29). Gallio may consequently have been proconsul of Achaia either in 51-52 or 52-53 CE. (It is not impossible but rather unusual to hold a post in a senatorial province for more than one year. Gallio also seems to have fallen ill and left his post early, attributing his sickness to the place and not his own health: see Seneca, *Letters,* 104.1.) The conservative case requires the former option — 51-52. An expulsion of the Jews from Rome is mentioned by Acts and Suetonius but dated only by Orosius (ca. 385-420 CE). This notoriously unreliable historian places that event in Claudius's "ninth year," or January 25, 49 through January 24, 50 CE (*Historiarum Adversus Paganos,* 7.6.15-16): [15] Anno eiusdem nono expulsos per Claudium urbe Iudaeos Iosephus refert. Sed me magis Suetonius movet, qui ait hoc modo: "Claudius Iudaeos inpulsore Christo adsidue tumultuantes Roma expulit" (adding [16] quod, utrum contra Christum tumultuantes Iudaeos coherceri et conprimi iusserit, an etiam Christianos simul velut cognatae religionis homines voluerit expelli, nequaquam discernitur). But Orosius attributes this information to Josephus falsely and claims to prefer the account of Suetonius, which is actually undated. (Orosius is therefore most probably confusing Josephus's account of the earlier *Tiberian* expulsion with this supposed expulsion under Claudius — a similar mistake perhaps to that of Suetonius himself. The Tiberian expulsion, which is well attested, took place in 19 CE.)

133. Most significantly, Acts is silent concerning any reception of the collection by the early church in Jerusalem, although it knows of alms given by Paul to the temple (see 24:17). It is also silent about support from the early church during Paul's two years of imprisonment in Caesarea (24:27). Some of the book's final comments also seem pointed (28:21-22). The implication, then, is that Paul's radical gospel was not accepted at this point even by early church leaders in Jerusalem — presumably James. Paul himself attests to the dangers of his forthcoming visit to Jerusalem in Rom. 15:31. He asks for prayer not only for rescue from those in Judaea who do not believe, but that ἡ διακονία μου ἡ εἰς Ἰερουσαλὴμ εὐπρόσδεκτος τοῖς ἁγίοις γένηται κ.τ.λ.

Notes to Chapter Fourteen

1. An important term defined earlier on in part one, chapter six, §2.3.

2. To reiterate, this was Sanders's seminal insight, although he does not develop it in the way that I do here (i.e., linking the prospective model with epistemological foundationalism and contractualism, and so on).

3. It does not matter for the present point whether the same genesis is endorsed for Romans, although I have argued in chapter thirteen that this is the most plausible account of its origins as well.

4. If the Teachers provide an inaccurate account of Judaism, then the universal starting point of the gospel of Justification is a *false* starting point — an embarrassing if not crippling inference.

5. Indeed, I would suggest that most of the work in Galatians has already been done, largely by J. Louis (Lou) Martyn. When we finally consider the relevant material in Galatians, we will therefore be able to rest to a significant extent on his work, but also of course on the work of the like-minded in this regard — e.g., (i.a.) Martinus C. de Boer, Alexandra Brown, Charles Cousar, Beverly Gaventa, Richard Hays, Ann Jervis, and Frank Matera.

6. It could be queried whether Paul is not, in so arguing, creating the possibility of a dangerous misunderstanding. However, he was *not* writing for the later church, or with an awareness of many of its theological presuppositions (on which see more shortly). He actually had a quite specific problem in mind.

7. My reading in what follows operates principally at the argumentative, as against the exegetical, level (that is, as I have defined these earlier; see especially part two, chapter seven). I do not dispute the conventional reading's detailed rendering of Paul's Greek into basic units of sense — the construal of words, clauses, and sentences (although I will make some suggestions at this level). My main proposal, rather, is that the various subunits of this extended and complex argument have been significantly misunderstood *as* an argument.

8. And this figure has been emerging into view already in some of the discussions of part three, where especially close attention to the details of the text required his presence — see esp. chapters eleven and twelve.

9. The grammar of the text encodes a single male. I suspect that more than one person was actually involved, but this doesn't affect our argument. We will simply respect the grammar of the text in what follows.

10. Ironic in fact in two senses: much of the gospel of Paul's opponents is attributed to him, and most if not all of the difficulties experienced by modern interpreters at this point are self-inflicted.

11. African hermeneutics is also a partial corrective at this point: see Teresa Okure, "'I Will Open My Mouth in Parables' (Matt 13.35): A Case for a Gospel-Based Biblical Hermeneutic," *New Testament Studies* 46 (2000): 445-63; Grant LeMarquand, "African Biblical Interpretation," in *Dictionary for Theological Interpretation of the Bible*, ed. K. J. Vanhoozer (Grand Rapids, Mich.: Baker & SPCK, 2005), 31-34 — "[t]he dialogue is . . . not so much between the *reader* and text as between community and text" (32).

12. Stanley K. Stowers, *A Rereading of Romans: Justice, Jews and Gentiles* (New Haven: Yale University Press, 1994), 6-33 — hereafter *RR*; "Apostrophe, Προσωποποιία and Paul's Rhetorical Education," in *Early Christianity and Classical Culture: Comparative Studies in Honor of Abraham J.*

Malherbe, ed. T. H. Olbricht, J. T. Fitzgerald, and L. Michael White (Leiden and Boston, Mass.: Brill, 2003), 351-69; Paul Saenger, *Space between Words: The Origins of Silent Reading* (Stanford, Calif.: Stanford University Press, 1997).

13. Useful introductions to nonverbal communication include Laura K. Guerrero, Joseph A. Devito and Michael L. Hecht, eds., *The Nonverbal Communication Reader: Classic and Contemporary Readings,* 2nd ed. (Prospect Heights, Ill.: Waveland Press, 1999); and Valerie Manusov and Mike L. Patterson, eds., *The Sage Handbook of Nonverbal Communication* (London: Sage, 2006). (A significant connection is discernible here with Affect theory: see studies listed in part two, chapter seven, §1, n. 3.)

14. J. K. Burgoon suggests that around 60-65% of social meaning is generated by nonverbal cues: "Nonverbal Signals," in *Handbook of Interpersonal Communication,* M. L. Knapp and G. R. Miller, eds., 2nd ed. (Thousand Oaks, Calif.: Sage, 1994), 229-85 (cited in *The Nonverbal Communication Reader,* 4). The percentage of information conveyed by nonverbal cues varies in relation to type of communication. In a persuasive and complex text like Romans, the role of nonverbal communication would be reduced — i.e., probably not dominant. The codes with which nonverbal meaning is communicated can be organized in terms of (1) kinesics (bodily cues, eye behavior sometimes being denoted by a separate category — oculesics), (2) physical appearance, (3) olfactics (codes of smell like perfume), (4) vocalics (changes in voice — tone, rhythm, et cetera), (5) proxemics (i.e., codes of space and proximity), (6) haptics (i.e., codes of touch), (7) chronemics (i.e., codes of time), and (8) environmental features (whether given or contrived; for the latter consider a play's staging): see *Handbook of Interpersonal Communication,* 43-45, and, more generally, 43-263.

15. See, e.g., the reconstruction of ancient codes of gesturing: Gregory Aldrete, *Gestures and Acclamations in Ancient Rome* (Baltimore, Maryland: Johns Hopkins University, 1999); Alan L. Boegehold, *When a Gesture Was Expected: Selected Examples from Archaic and Classical Greek Literature* (Princeton, New Jersey: Princeton University Press, 1961); Fritz Graf, "Gestures and Conventions: The Gestures of Roman Actors and Orators," in *A Cultural History of Gesture,* ed. Jan Bremmer and Herman Roodenburg (Ithaca, New York: Cornell University, 1992), 3-58; and W. S. Shiell, *Reading Acts: The Lector and the Early Christian Audience* (Leiden & Boston: Brill, 2004), esp. ch. 3, "Conventions of Greco-Roman Delivery," 34-101. Shiell organizes his analysis principally in terms of gestures, facial expressions, and vocal inflections, remarking that "[t]hese elements were combined when an orator imitated another character using the conventions of προσωποποιία'" (100).

16. An awareness of this is only breaking recently on Pauline scholars: see esp. L. L. Welborn, *Paul, the Fool of Christ: A Study of 1 Corinthians 1-4 in the Comic-Philosophic Tradition* (London & New York: T & T Clark [Continuum], 2005).

17. The argumentative consequences of this point should be appreciated. In order to overthrow my suggested rereading of Rom. 1:18–3:20, it will be necessary first and foremost to deal with the conventional reading's many difficulties *and* to find some overt difficulties in my rereading. Complaints in terms of putative genre and/or technique — that they could not hold in this fashion — will not be enough, given the remaining evidence.

18. See esp. *RR,* 16-21, 36-39, 44, 100-107, 127-29, 142-58, 175, 232-33, 252, 264-84, 309. When I first identified a plausible alternative reading of Romans 1:16–3:20 as a whole, I did not identify my suggested construal of 1:18-32 as προσωποποιία; that further identification took many years, in part because I was not persuaded by much of what Stowers was suggesting in *RR* (although I was always impressed by his virtuosity). In particular, I was not convinced that Romans 7:7-25 was an instance of προσωποποιία, failing to see how this identification could integrate with a reading of that text in some relation to an Adam narrative. (Emma Wasserman's work now speaks to some of these difficulties: see "The Death of the Soul in Romans 7: Sin, Death, and the Law in the Light of Hellenistic Moral Psychology," Ph.D. diss., Yale University, 2005). I considered many other possible interpretative strategies for 1:18-32 — most notably irony, parody, protreptic (perhaps specifically in the sense of ἔλεγχος), and *refutatio* — before finally being convinced that προσωποποιία was the technique being used. I am happy to acknowledge this as a point in my present argument where I am indebted significantly to Stowers. (Indeed, I have since come to appreciate more deeply many of his earlier suggestions, as the

discussion in part three, chapter twelve indicates.) Stowers derived the useful name "speech-in-character" from James R. Butts, *The Progymnasmata of Theon: A New Text with Translation and Commentary* (Ph.D. diss., The Claremont Graduate School, 1986).

19. In addition to *RR*, note his "Romans 7.7-25 as a Speech-in-Character (Προσωποποιία)," in *Paul in His Hellenistic Context*, ed. Troels Engberg-Pedersen (Minneapolis: Fortress, 1995), 180-202; and "Apostrophe, προσωποποιία and Paul's Rhetorical Education." Stowers is particularly concerned with the objections of R. Dean Anderson, *Ancient Rhetorical Theory and Paul* (Kampen: Pharos, 1996). In my view, precise terminology is not critical here — and may have eluded some of the ancient theorists themselves, as Quintilian's slightly muddled account implies. Whether the technique should instead be called ἠθοποιία, *sermocinatio* (dialogue), *interrogatio*/ἐπερώτησις, or even *exclamatio*, matters little for our present purposes. A comprehensive compilation of the primary sources, categorized conveniently, can be found in H. Lausberg, *Handbook of Literary Rhetoric: A Foundation for Literary Study*, ed. David E. Orton and R. Dean Anderson, trans. Matthew T. Bliss, Annemiek Jansen, and David E. Orton (Leiden: Brill, 1998).

20. See *Institutes* 1.8.3; 6.1.25-26; 9.2.20, 30-37; see also the *Rhetoric to Herennius*, 4.53.66.

21. See George A. Kennedy, ed., *Progymnasmata: Greek Textbooks of Prose Composition and Rhetoric* (Leiden & Boston: Brill, 2003).

22. See Justin Martyr, *Dialogue with Trypho*, ed. Michael Slussner and Thomas P. Halton, trans. Thomas B. Falls (Washington, D.C.: The Catholic University of America Press, 2003); Justin Martyr, *Dialogue avec Tryphon*, vol. 1, *Introduction, Texte grec, Traduction*, ed. Philippe Bobichon (Fribourg: Academic Press Fribourg, 2003).

23. Stowers notes a similar discussion of introductory signals in the fifth century CE orator Emporius ("Romans 7.7-25," 187-88). For Emporius, who discusses classic narrative instances of *ethopoeia* (i.e., not occasional texts such as letters and classroom exchanges), (i) the setting could be stated, (ii) the famous character could be addressed by authorial apostrophe, or (iii) the character could simply begin speaking in the first person, which amounts to an absence of overt introduction (*RR*, 20).

24. See 1.4.28-29; 1.9.12-16; 1.26.5-7, 10, 20-22, 26-49; 3.24.68-70, 97-102 (passages noted by Thomas H. Tobin, *Paul's Rhetoric in Its Contexts: The Argument of Romans* [Peabody, Mass.: Hendrickson, 2004], 93).

25. The close connections between προσωποποιία, acting, and comedy are indicated by one of Quintilian's other remarks on the technique: "Neither is it good, like some teachers, to indicate speech-in-character (προσωποποιία) in the manner of a comic actor, even though one ought to make use of some modulation of voice [when reading] in order to distinguish speech-in-character from where the poet is speaking in his own person *(persona)*" (*Institutes* 1.7.3).

26. *RR*, 19; see also Saenger, *Space between Words;* see also Theon's instructions on reading aloud in his *Exercises:* "Above all, we shall accustom the student to fit voice and gestures to the subject of the speech. It is this that actualizes the art of the speech. We shall present and imagine with the greatest care all that concerns an orator: his actions, credibility, age, and status; the place where the speech was delivered, the subject it treats, and everything that contributes to the feeling that the speech actually concerns us as we read it aloud. This is how the actor Polos interpreted his roles, so well, they say, that he shed real tears on stage" (Kennedy [ed.], *Progymnasmata*, 102P-103P).

27. Note the Jewish "propaganda" topos found in texts like Wisdom of Solomon 11-19; *Third Sibylline Oracle;* Josephus, *Against Apion;* and *Letter of Aristeas;* see also Justin, *Dialogue with Trypho,* 93.1-2; 95.1. This material is discussed more in what follows.

28. A subtle clue to this character's identity is also possibly buried in the specifics of the vice list. I will argue later that this (a) effects a useful argumentative move from 2:1; and (b) also subtly identifies his opponent.

29. See Rudolf Bultmann, *Der Stil der paulinische Predigt und die kynisch-stoische Diatribe* (Göttingen: Vandenhoeck & Ruprecht, 1910); Stowers, *The Diatribe and Paul's Letter to the Romans,* SBLDS 57 (Chico, Calif.: Scholars, 1981); also Stowers, "Paul's Dialogue with a Fellow Jew in Rom. 3.1-9," *Catholic Biblical Quarterly* 46 (1984): 707-22. And I am not sure that earlier work overshadows his

research, or that later work on Paul in this relation has really added to it: see George L. Kustas, *Diatribe in Ancient Rhetorical Theory* (Berkeley, Calif.: Center for Hermeneutical Studies, 1976); Thomas Schmeller, *Paulus and die "Diatribe": Eine vergleichende Stilinterpretation* (Münster: Aschendorff, 1987); Runar M. Thorsteinsson, *Paul's Interlocutor in Romans 2: Function and Identity in the Context of Ancient Epistolography* (Stockholm: Almqvist & Wiksell, 2003). A brief introduction to this textual mode can be found in Tobin, *Paul's Rhetoric*, 87-98. (Tobin presses the technique more than other commentators.)

30. Among other ancient authors who use it, Philo (ca. 10 BCE–40 CE plus) is of course particularly significant. But see also the discourses of Teles (ca. 235 BCE), Musonius Rufus (ca. 30-100 CE), and some of the discourses of Dio of Prusa (ca. 45-112 CE), Plutarch of Chaeronea (ca. 50-120 CE), Seneca the Younger (ca. 2 BCE–CE 65), and Maximus of Tyre (second century CE). In the Christian era — as has already been noted — Justin and Origen are outstanding examples: see Origen, "Against Celsus," in *Ante-Nicene Fathers*, trans. F. Crombie (Grand Rapids, Mich.: Eerdmans, 1979), 4: 395-669. It seems that controversial engagements were often treated in this dialogical fashion; this was a deeply rooted textual expectation.

31. Stowers, "Social Stature, Public Speaking and Private Teaching."

32. See the Cynic Heraclitus's letters 4, 7, and 9: see Abraham J. Malherbe, ed., *The Cynic Epistles* (Missoula, Mont.: Scholars, 1977), 190-93, 200-7, 210-15. These are, however, published philosophical letters.

33. We probably lose nothing and gain much by incorporating this suggestion into our broader interpretative strategy, but for the sake of methodological purity, it is probably safer to resist such an identification. Romans is a letter.

34. This is not *always* the case, but that it is often the case is enough. Epictetus's *Discourses* are sometimes more essay-like presentations of his own views in a nondialogical manner: see *Of Providence* (*Discourses*, trans. W. A. Oldfather, LCL [Cambridge, Mass.: Harvard University Press, 1925], 1.6, pp. 39-44).

35. It is not — and is not intended to be — "fair"; it is a biased argumentative construct. But it would detract from the plausibility of the overall refutation if it were only a caricature, so skillful philosophers had to craft portraits that in effect navigated effectively between these two extremes. The portraits of their opponent(s) needed to be recognizable and plausible, but ultimately also overtly fallible, and preferably slightly ludicrous or comic as well.

36. A direct overlap is detectable here with the "ironic" style as described by pseudo-Libanius: εἰρωνικὴ δι' ἧς ἐπαινοῦμέν τινα ἐν ὑποκρίσει περὶ τὴν ἀρχήν, ἐπὶ τέλει δὲ τὸν ἑαυτῶν σκοπὸν ἐμφαίνομεν, ὡς τὰ ῥηθέντα καθ' ὑπόκρισιν εἰρήκαμεν. Note in particular the repeated terminology of "acting" — ὑπόκρισις: see A. Malherbe, *Ancient Epistolary Theorists*, SBLSBS 19 (Atlanta: Scholars, 1988), 68, 17-19. This is *exactly* the strategy of Romans 1:18–3:20, as I analyze it here. (My thanks to Alicia Myers for bringing this reference to my attention.)

Theon's *Exercises* also link προσωποποιία to letter writing (and to epicheiremes) (see Kennedy, ed., *Progymnasmata*, §8, 47 [2.115-18]), as do Nicolaus the Sophist's *Preliminary Exercises*: "it [ἠθοποιία] seems also to exercise us in the style of letter writing, since in that there is need of foreseeing the character of those sending letters and those to whom they are sent" (§10, 166); and John of Sardis (§11, 214). The latter makes an especially noteworthy remark at the end of his consideration of this technique: "Practice in ethopoeia is most useful everywhere; for it does not contribute to only one species of rhetoric, but to all. Everywhere, as it happens, we form characters and attribute speeches to persons. . . . [W]e shall have need of it in any speech" (§11, 217).

37. One of C. H. Cosgrove's points in an intriguing article: "The Justification of the Other: An Interpretation of Rom 1:18–4:25," in *SBLSP*, ed. Eugene H. Lovering (Atlanta: Scholars, 1992), 613-34.

38. In part this is also a result of numerous visits by messengers and intermediaries, from whom a wealth of information would presumably have been extracted orally and informally (see, e.g., Paul's knowledge of the situation at Corinth, derived from "those of Chloe," Stephanas, Fortunatus, and Achaiacus: see 1 Cor. 1:11 [divisions]; 5:1-2 [incest], 6 [pride over the incest]; 6:1-8 [lawsuits within

the congregation]; 11:4-5 [women praying with an uncovered head]; 11:17-21 [divisions during the Eucharist]; 15:12, 35 [mockery of the notion of a resurrected body]).

39. So, e.g., A. C. Thiselton states in relation to 6:12: "There can be no question that the initial clause of v. 12 represents a quotation used as a maxim by some or by many at Corinth. . . . The overwhelming majority of modern scholars adopt this view . . ."; see *The First Epistle to the Corinthians: A Commentary on the Greek Text*, NIGTC (Grand Rapids, Mich. & Cambridge & Carlisle: Eerdmans & Paternoster, 2000), 460-61, esp. n. 192.

40. So Thiselton, *Epistle*, 462-63.

41. This is contested, but the evidence seems to be tilting reasonably firmly toward the theory of allusion or quotation: see Thiselton, *Epistle*, 498-500.

42. The inclusion of "we know" (οἴδαμεν) within the quotation is disputed: see Thiselton, *Epistle*, 620-21. John C. Hurd argues that this statement is a Corinthian retort to Paul in terms of the apostle's original teaching: see *The Origin of I Corinthians*, new ed. (Macon, Georgia: Mercer University Press, 1983 [1965]), 68, 279.

43. Again, the exact extent of the quotation is debated, but most scholars see *some* such quotation as present: see Thiselton, *Epistle*, 628-31. Thiselton endorses v. 5 as a quotation from the Corinthians as well.

44. See Thiselton, *Epistle*, 644-49, esp. 647-48. Translation decisions affect whether both parts of the verse are rightly designated as Corinthian, or merely v. 8a.

45. See Thiselton, *Epistle*, 351-56. Some have argued, conversely, that this is a later insertion — a result of several small mistakes by copyists.

46. So — cautiously — Thiselton, *Epistle*, 631-35. Verse 6 is also much discussed, whether as a possible early church confession or some other confessional fragment (635-38). As such, it is not necessarily the reproduction by Paul of a Corinthian position but may be a different form of intertextuality — a shared authoritative text — and hence not one that Paul will himself correct, but one that nevertheless is meant to correct the Corinthians.

47. Thiselton lists no fewer than twelve possible interpretations of this statement: *Epistle*, 918-24. Most of the options listed, however, refer the cry to the Corinthians in some sense.

48. See Thiselton, *Epistle*, 1172-76, 1216, 1261-63. Major variations exist concerning just *why* the Corinthians had difficulties on this point, but no one doubts that it was the Corinthians who had these difficulties and that these statements consequently reflect Corinthian theology, at least to some degree. (Thiselton notes the theories that some Corinthians could not evidently believe in postmortem existence; that the resurrection had already in some sense occurred, perhaps "spiritually"; that the resurrection of *the body* was the key difficulty; and that different groups at Corinth had different problems.)

49. I am especially grateful to T. J. Lang for his assistance with the following material.

50. The phenomenon of *Skaz* has been discussed by Mikhail Bakhtin. His notion of heteroglossia is especially relevant here, as is the closely related notion of polyphony. See "Discourse in the Novel," in *The Dialogic Imagination: Four Essays*, ed. Michael Holquist, trans. Caryl Emerson, and Michael Holquist (Austin, Tex.: University of Texas Press, 1981), 259-422.

51. A useful illustration is Marie Jones's play *Stones in His Pockets* (New York: Applause, 2001 [2000]). This is a two-actor play, but with fifteen characters (on a film set in a poor rural village in Ireland), and is performed largely without props. Hence, the only signals for shifts from one role to another are supplied nonverbally by the actors — through posture, expression, and voice (i.e., through acting!).

52. As James C. Scott has famously — and plausibly — argued, disempowered groups that are involved directly in patronage relations often use temporary, nonidentifiable discourses to express their anger, hope, contempt, etc.; see especially his *Domination and the Arts of Resistance: Hidden Transcripts* (New Haven, Conn., & London: Yale University Press, 1990). For certain important reasons, these subtleties tend to be overlooked by later historical reconstruction. As Scott observes: "even close readings of historical and archival evidence tend to favor a hegemonic account of power relations" (xii). That seems to be the case here as well. The original readers of Romans may have detected

a disguised transcript, whereas later readers have identified with the powerful figure — powerful here principally because he is educated — who is in fact being mocked and undermined. Scott's work has received a preliminary assessment in relation to the interpretation of Paul, but could, in my view, be applied much more rigorously, broadly, and imaginatively: see Richard A. Horsley, ed., *Hidden Transcripts and the Arts of Resistance: Applying the Work of James C. Scott to Jesus and Paul,* Semeia Studies 48 (Leiden: Brill, 2005).

53. That the phenomenon of shifting textual voice is widespread within various oral and written traditions creates an awkward problem for any a priori criticism of my proposal concerning Romans 1:18-32. It is clear that language contains the possibility of mimicry intrinsically, and that various authors have used this possibility on numerous occasions — with subtle variations — historically. It is also clear that these possibilities are especially important in overtly oral settings that are themselves emphasized by illiteracy. To deny Paul's texts this interpretative option, then, in advance of their examination, entails that he be denied any access to such literary or linguistic creativity. And this denial naturally seems implausible, both on general grounds — as an unsustainable claim concerning an individual figure and his linguistic competence given his general milieu — and in the specific sense that we are dealing with a creative and intelligent figure, who wrote at a point of theological and hence linguistic foment (and in an oral setting). Denying Paul the use of this textual strategy would be a little like denying that a Renaissance artist from Florence could use perspective. We must simply see if the apostle did use it.

54. Having been alerted to the importance of nonverbal signals in performed texts, I have been studying local instances of satire and mockery carefully and have noticed an interesting phenomenon. In an occasional setting, almost invariably those actors who have embarked on an essentially humorous instance of playacting — usually ridiculing some political figure or celebrity — *do not signal the object of their ridicule at any point overtly.* In fact, *to do so would detract greatly from the effectiveness of their ridicule.* One of the key elements within a performance of this nature seems to be the audience's recognition, otherwise unassisted, of the figure being satirized. Indeed, it is this moment that seems to generate much of the humor and enjoyment within the performance. The actor seems commended for his or her skill, and the audience can congratulate themselves for being clever enough to detect the person in question. It is as if the actor and the audience share a conspiracy against the figure in question. And these moments of recognition can be almost exquisitely enjoyable, as the particular foibles of a certain well-known person are presented, recognized, but also exaggerated, and mocked — and, needless to say, the better the comedian, the better the caricature and the humor. Conversely, to signal the figure in question overtly creates an impression of clumsiness, and much of the situation's enjoyment is dissipated.

55. See some of Origen's complaints about Celsus's inaccurate and inconsistent characterizations of "the Jew" in *Against Celsus,* e.g., Bk 1, §28 (408): ". . . he does not maintain, throughout the discussion, the consistency due to the character of a Jew"; see also §§43 (414), 44 (415), 48 (417), 49 (417-18).

56. We will see shortly just how fair it is.

57. It might be objected that this is too long to be a convincing instance of προσωποποιία, but Paul needs to set out the position of the Teacher in sufficient detail for it to be recognizable and to inform. It is in fact a masterful summary. A comparable discussion of much the same material is *much* longer: see Wisdom of Solomon 11–19.

58. At least arguably: ". . . discourse that attacks the credibility of another discourse . . . [showing] that the other discourse is . . . inadequate in thought or expression . . . confused . . . contradictory . . . or that the speaker spoke as much against as for himself — what some call turning his argument against himself . . ." (Kennedy [ed.], *Progymnasmata,* 111P-112P).

59. Ulrich Wilckens supplies an explicitly apocalyptic analysis, noted by Robert Jewett: "the word 'reveal' . . . describe(s) the disclosure of future events that the seer conveys to his contemporary hearers: 'In this sense the revelation of the wrath of God occurs in present proclamation'": *Der Brief an Die Römer,* 3 vols. (Zürich, Einsiedeln, Köln, and Neukirchen-Vluyn: Benziger & Neukirchener,

1978), 1:102; also noted by Jewett, *Romans*, Hermeneia (Minneapolis, Minn.: Fortress, 2007), 150-51, n. 19. (Other advocates of this basic approach are also noted by Jewett ad loc.)

60. See C. F. D. Moule, *An Idiom Book of New Testament Greek*, 2nd ed. (Cambridge: Cambridge University Press, 1959), 7, citing Matt 26:18; Mark 9:31; Luke 13:32; 1 Cor 15:32; see also H. W. Smyth, *Greek Grammar*, rev. ed., ed. G. M. Messing (Cambridge, Mass.: Harvard University Press, 1956), §1879, 421-22.

61. Hence, as noted in part three, chapter eleven, the γάρ in v. 18 is not strongly inferential or causal but a muted link, if it is not pleonastic, although a clarifying or emphatic reading is also possible — "you see," or "certainly." I am not yet suggesting that this interpretation is either self-evident or immediately necessary. It is simply the interpretation that fits my broader rereading. The evidence for that rereading, and so for this interpretation of γάρ in v. 18, will emerge shortly. Note also that the shift in the texture of Paul's argument at this point, into the Teacher's voice, would probably have been signaled by an appropriate voice and gesture as well.

62. It does not matter for our purposes whether this is a redundancy or a temporal clause, as the NRSV cited here decides; I incline toward the latter simply to avoid the redundancy, but this is clearly not a decisive argument.

63. Paul has definitely borrowed this language from certain Old Testament texts, but I am not convinced that intertextuality plays any broader role in the argument at this point. Certainly, I cannot see where any such implications are explicitly activated. See Psalm 105 [LXX], esp. v. 20: καὶ ἠλλάξαντο τὴν δόξαν αὐτῶν ἐν ὁμοιώματι μόσχου ἔσθοντος χόρτον; Jer. 2:11: εἰ ἀλλάξονται ἔθνη θεοὺς αὐτῶν, καὶ οὗτοι οὐκ εἰσιν θεοί. Ὁ δὲ λαός μου ἠλλάξατο τὴν δόξαν αὐτοῦ, ἐξ ἧς οὐκ ὠφεληθήσονται; see also Deut. 4:15-19. Dunn also suggests that Isa. 44:9-20 is relevant: *Romans 1–8*, WBC 38A (Dallas, Tex.: Word, 1988), 61; see esp. vv. 9-11, 19-20.

It is frequently suggested that a strong echo of the Adam narrative can be detected here as well. But Dunn's claim that Adam and the Genesis narrative is "obviously" in v. 22 is especially puzzling, given the continuation of the sentence in v. 23 in relation to Egyptian idolatry (*Romans 1–8*, 60-61). See also Morna Hooker, "Adam in Romans I," *New Testament Studies* 6 (1959-1960): 297-306. If the reading had already been established that Rom. 1:18–3:20 was a universal indictment by Paul of humanity for sin, then this partly submerged allusion to Adam would be useful; certainly it would be more consistent with Paul's account of sin later on in Romans explicitly in terms of Adam. But without this establishment, the suggestion tends to beg the question.

64. This could be performed as an instance of disingenuous piety or as a parenthetical Pauline insertion that reminds us of the apostle's genuine piety. Perhaps we would not expect an "amen" from the letter's initial auditors at Corinth if the former was the case, but perhaps the insertion of this word took place later. I incline toward the former explanation. The Teacher indwells the doxological language of the synagogue, and it is unlikely that Paul questions his piety. Perhaps, indeed, this was one of his characteristic mannerisms. (And so perhaps Paul's desire to subvert it explains in part the many other doxologies in Romans.)

65. The repeated use of a surrender formula is a noticeable stylistic feature of the argument: see vv. 24, 26, 28 (see also Ps. 81:12 [80:13 LXX]: καὶ ἐξαπέστειλα αὐτοὺς κατὰ τὰ ἐπιτηδεύματα τῶν καρδιῶν αὐτῶν, πορεύσονται ἐν τοῖς ἐπιτηδεύμασιν αὐτῶν).

66. A motif that has puzzled the conventional reading. An emphasis on penalty, however, certainly integrates with the broader sense of the Teacher's reading that my interpretation develops. Jewett provides a brilliantly contextualized reading at this point; see *Romans*, 178-79.

67. A chiastic pattern is also arguably detectable here.

68. That is — rather unusually for Paul — this list does *not* resume the earlier concerns of Rom. 1:18-32 with *porneia* and idolatry — sins characteristic of all of Paul's other vice lists. Typical concerns elsewhere with stereotypical gross pagan sins such as theft, drunkenness, witchcraft and magic, vulgar speech, and anger, are also absent from it. The many sins enumerated in Rom. 1:29-31 are in fact generally quite subtle, attitudinal sins, or sins against proper speech ethics, although, again, not in terms of pagan vulgarity or blasphemy; Paul enumerates here δόλος, κακοήθεια, ψιθυριστής, and κατάλαλος. The only gross and overt sin is φόνος, "murder."

69. If the Teacher is implicit within the vice list of vv. 29-31, then this picture applies directly to him (as well as, presumably, to any of his supporters); he just does not yet realize it.

70. George Bernard Shaw's *Major Barbara* contains a nice early example of such satire of Christians — Snobby Price. Some of this dynamic is also apparent at a more scholarly level: see, e.g., Sam Reimer's sociological study of Evangelicals that frequently contrasts perceptions and realities: *Evangelicals and the Continental Divide: The Conservative Protestant Subculture in Canada and the United States* (Montreal and Kingston: McGill-Queen's University Press, 2003). Stowers's comment on 2:17-29 is apposite here: "Today people who have never seen the inside of a church instantly recognize the comedian's parody of a fundamentalist preacher" (*RR,* 145).

71. Tobin correctly notes the rhetorical value of this turn: "Paul obviously expects his Roman Christian audience to react with indignation and to condemn this discrepancy, this hypocrisy [exposed from 2:1 onward]. Indignation, that is, grief over someone else's *undeserved* good fortune, was one of the main emotions that an orator often wanted to arouse in his audience": *Paul's Rhetoric,* 111.

72. Nedward "Ned" Flanders of *The Simpsons* is a well-known lampoon of Evangelical Christians; he is said on one occasion by Homer Simpson to be "even holier than Jesus." Having said this, the depiction of Ned is often partly sympathetic, so he is not directly analogous to Paul's parody in Romans 1:18-32, which is ultimately unsympathetic. (*The Simpsons* is an animated sitcom produced by Matt Groening for Fox Network since 1989 — the longest-running American animation.)

73. See Quintilian, *Institutes,* 6.3.97 and 9.2.34 (this last reference describing παρῳδία, when words or writings are made up ad imitationem alterius scripturae; my thanks to Kathy Dawson for alerting me to this dimension of the text).

74. It is therefore not quite the same thing as a particular argument in modern philosophical ethics that originated with Kant's first formulation of the categorical imperative, that was then developed in a certain form especially by R. M. Hare. "Universalizability" as I am using it here refers more simply to consistency between prescription and behavior, inconsistency creating certain rhetorical vulnerabilities. We ought to act and do as we exhort others to act and do — see 2 Sam. 12:1-9! (This also indicates that the origins of this argument are much earlier than Kant; note also that the biblical instance makes a clever application that elicits an admission from David himself of his wrongdoing.) I recently came across a compact formulation in a blog that is difficult to improve upon: "[Note] this two-step logical train: (1) Standard X is dishonest and corrupt. (2) Those who advocate and apply Standard X to others ought to have that standard applied to them." (Glen Greenwald, "Michelle Malkin's hate sites," www.salon.com; posted 7/25/2007, consulted 7/28/2007. Greenwald's specific concern was that Michelle Malkin was being inconsistent by attacking "liberal" websites for hate-filled posts, when her own contained many as well, some of which he documented. Greenwald's post is also a nice illustration of the fact that such inconsistency is only damaging for an uninvolved audience; audiences who are already partisan tend to overlook any such inconsistencies — in this context, apparently, Malkin's readers.)

75. Following here the grammar of the Romans text to suggest what the rhetorical consequences for the Teacher would be of failing to submit to Paul's universalization.

76. "Neutral" must be emphasized here. As has just been noted, the technique — like most techniques — is ineffective in a partisan situation, where loyalty is already guaranteed.

77. Political events in the United States provide an almost embarrassingly large number of recent examples of the effectiveness of argumentative universalizations — usually when traditionally conservative and frequently moralizing Republican candidates are caught in sexual indiscretions, or similar inconsistencies (see Arnold Schwarzenegger; Scooter Libby; Mark Foley; David Vitter; Larry Craig; and so on).

78. This last signifier links the characterization of the condemned here explicitly to the overarching characterization of pagan sinfulness in 1:18-32, where ἀδικία was a *leitmotif* (see v. 18, 2x; and the head of the vice list in v. 29).

79. It is worth noting that ἐκ here seems instrumental, and it functions in parallel to an instrumental dative construction.

80. Mark Nanos suggests at some length that this saying summarizes compactly Paul's mis-

sionary methods, especially as the latter is attested by Acts; the apostle goes to the Jews first and then, when they reject him (and only *if* they reject him?), to the pagans: *The Mystery of Romans* (Minneapolis: Fortress, 1996), esp. 21-40. But while this reading seems initially to explain 1:16b (although not without courting some dangers — notably, in the uncritical use of Acts to reconstruct the Pauline mission), it is difficult to see how it can explain 2:9-10. It is not so much that this reading is utterly nonsensical, because presumably Paul could go to the Jewish synagogues first and preach judgment as well as the gospel of salvation through faith. It is more that this program is nowhere to be seen in 2:9-10 or its immediate vicinity. The slogan there must, rather, be linked somehow to God's eschatological action in terms of desert (because this is what the text says). Moreover, Paul seems to attest quite explicitly in Gal. 2:6-10 that his only real prerogative is to preach to pagans, not to Jews (although 1 Cor. 9:19-20 could arguably be cited against this — but see also Gal. 5:11, which was discussed earlier).

81. See Rikki E. Watts, "'For I Am Not Ashamed of the Gospel': Romans 1:16-17 and Habakkuk 2:4," in *Romans and the People of God*, ed. Sven K. Soderlund and N. T. Wright (Grand Rapids, Mich., and Cambridge: Eerdmans, 1999), 3-25, esp. 20, n. 81.

82. Jouette M. Bassler, *Divine Impartiality: Paul and a Theological Axiom*, SBLDS 59 (Chico, Calif.: Scholars, 1982); and "Divine Impartiality in Paul's Letter to the Romans," *Novum Testamentum* 26 (1984): 43-58.

83. Eduard Lohse suggests that the Hebrew injunction is rooted in ANE protocols: see "πρόσωπον, κ.τ.λ.," *TDNT* 6:768-80. Supplicants greeted superiors by lying face down on the ground, thus "dropping," or averting, their faces (see Gen. 32:20; 33:3-11). Acceptance of their presence and/or petitions was indicated when the relevant superior(s) lifted them up, thereby "lifting" their faces. Consequently, to lift the face of only one party within a dispute without just warrant or because of bribery was to show favoritism or partiality to that party (and in the case of bribery, presumably to the rich). The Hebrew slogan asserts that God does not show such corrupt partiality and therefore neither should the Israelites in relation to marginal and disempowered groups within their community (whether in a judicial setting or not). Any translation of the slogan that reproduces the basic sense that God does not show corrupt or unjust partiality, then, is a fundamentally adequate rendering. However, the LXX translators may have supplied a cultural equivalent rather than a direct translation, perhaps obscuring the ANE sense of "face-lifting," if that was a typical original connotation, but adding different connotations that are coded as often as not by dramatic metaphors.

84. Galatians 2:1-14 touches on numerous aspects of this topos (and really warrants its own separate study in this relation). In 2:1-10 Paul states that the apostolic leaders in Jerusalem — James, Peter, and John — added nothing essential to his revealed gospel. Moreover, in this he was duly unimpressed by those who "seemed" to be something and hence fulfilled the demands of the theologoumenon, introduced in v. 6, not to be impressed by mere reputation. In fact, the apostles "seemed to be pillars" but were not (see vv. 2, 6 and esp. v. 9: οἱ δοκοῦντες στῦλοι εἶναι), as Peter's wobbling at Antioch later suggests, so Paul was right not to be impressed. Peter's inconsistent actions with respect to diet are described in 2:11-14 in terms of a lexicon of dramatic inconsistency: he was motivated by "fear" (v. 12b), he "acted" (v. 13, 2x), and so did not "walk in a straight fashion" (v. 14, DC). These accumulating connotations might then suggest translating κατὰ πρόσωπον in v. 11 as an accusation of Peter by Paul "concerning appearance" or even "concerning playacting," rather than the usual rendering in terms of some public confrontation in which Paul accuses Peter to his face (which seems a little otiose); on this last suggestion see also 2 Cor. 10:1-11, especially vv. 1 and 7.

85. Luke 20:20-26 reproduces essentially the same lexicon of insincerity and playacting as Gal. 2:1-14 (and it is interesting that this thematology is especially clear in Luke, as against in the parallel passages in Mark [12:13-17] and Matthew [22:15-22]). Certain figures, who are "masquerading as righteous" (ὑποκρινομένους ἑαυτοὺς δικαίους εἶναι), "lie in wait" for Jesus so that they can arrest him. Their public questions are overtly insincere; they praise Jesus himself for "speaking straightly" and for not "accepting appearance" (i.e., being swayed by reputation): Διδάσκαλε, οἴδαμεν ὅτι ὀρθῶς λέγεις καὶ διδάσκεις καὶ οὐ λαμβάνεις πρόσωπον. . . . Jesus, conversely, "understands their duplicity" (κατανοήσας [δὲ] αὐτῶν τὴν πανουργίαν) and reduces them to amazement and silence (θαυμάσαντες . . . ἐσίγησαν).

86. 1 Thessalonians 2:3-6 (which is usefully compared to 2 Cor. 10:1-11) also seems heavily indebted to the terminology of duplicity as against sincerity — λαλοῦμεν οὐχ ὡς ἀνθρώποις ἀρέσκοντες ἀλλὰ θεῷ. . . . ⁵οὔτε γάρ ποτε ἐν λόγῳ κολακείας ἐγενήθημεν, καθὼς οἴδατε, οὔτε ἐν προφάσει πλεονεξίας . . . ⁶οὔτε ζητοῦντες ἐξ ἀνθρώπων δόξαν οὔτε ἀφ' ὑμῶν οὔτε ἀπ' ἄλλων; it seems especially close to Gal. 1:10: Ἄρτι γὰρ ἀνθρώπους πείθω ἢ τὸν θεόν; ἢ ζητῶ ἀνθρώποις ἀρέσκειν?

87. It seems especially significant that the slogan, operating more as a topos, is prominent in Jas. 2:1-9. Here the author begins an important subsection with the injunction that "the faith of our glorious Lord Jesus Christ" (DC) not be "held onto" (ἔχετε) ἐν προσωπολημψίαις. The motif is then reiterated in v. 9 (and it is interwoven there, intriguingly, with "the royal law," Lev. 19:18: see Rom. 13:8; Gal. 5:14). An extensive description of biased treatment of the rich over against the poor during the community's gathering takes place between these two references — and it is roundly condemned as "evil" (v. 4).

88. Both rhetors and philosophers had to contend with charges in terms of playacting: see (i.a.) Duane Litfin, *St. Paul's Theology of Proclamation: 1 Corinthians 1-4 and Greco-Roman Rhetoric*, SNTSMS 79 (Cambridge: Cambridge University Press, 1994); and Ronald F. Hock, *The Social Context of Paul's Ministry: Tentmaking and Apostleship* (Philadelphia: Fortress, 1980). Different philosophical traditions debated the roles of payment and money in this relation especially intensely. Rhetors could be accused of supplying crowds with what they wanted to hear and hence of acting at times in a cowardly fashion. Inconsistency was a hallmark of such odious behaviors, and this could be denoted by spatial imagery in terms of deviation as well as by accusations rooted in the dramatic tradition of acting. Sincere teachers, by contrast, were not swayed by money or cowed by public disapproval and were consequently consistent. Spatial imagery of "trueness" or "straightness" was therefore an appropriate description, since their underlying character and positions were consistent with their public personas.

89. See, e.g., Rom. 1:16b and 2:9-10, which we have just noted, along with the especially resonant text from James.

90. This has usually been translated in principal dependence on 1 Cor. 9:19-22, and so somewhat tamely, as "outside the law." Stowers makes the typically creative suggestion that other lexicographical evidence points toward a more aggressive sense in the alpha-privative — "against the law," "lawlessly," or some such (*RR*, 134-38). It is difficult to make sense of the signifier's second occurrence in Rom. 2:12a with this suggestion, however (not to mention of 1 Cor. 9:19-22); ἀνόμως καὶ ἀπολοῦνται can hardly mean that God is (also) destroying the sinful pagans lawlessly! Nevertheless, it is possible to accept Stowers's additional evidence to some degree by recognizing here a further possible ironic use of terminology by Paul against the Teacher, who seems to have had a great fondness for alpha-privatives and doubtless used them in relation to pagans in a thoroughly pejorative sense (see esp. 1:18-32). Paul's point here, then, would be that a typically "lawless" pagan must be judged "outside the law" as well, and hence by implication actually possess some law — a fact that will ultimately embarrass the Teacher's program. Hence, the invective of ἀνόμως is used *against* the Teacher through wordplay and extension. An "outlaw" and in this sense "lawless" pagan, if he is judged fairly by God — which he is — is not a law*less* pagan in the sense of a figure lacking an ethical compass altogether, and could, moreover, be judged (righteous) "outside the [Jewish] law." So Stowers's lexicographical perceptiveness at this point possibly uncovers a further subtle dimension in the unfolding debate between Paul and the Teacher.

91. This verb is probably better punctuated as a future, not a present.

92. See later, esp. chapters fifteen through seventeen (and also, to a degree, the treatment of 3:27–4:1 in chapter eighteen, and of 9:30-31 in part five, chapter nineteen).

93. It might be objected that I am failing to do justice to Paul's accounts of the day of judgment elsewhere. However, it is important to grasp that I am not denying an account of that "day" in Paul, or indeed even an evaluative aspect to it. We need look no further than Rom. 14:4b-12 to see that Paul retains an important role for this event, and foresees a significant sense of assessment then: ἕκαστος ἡμῶν περὶ ἑαυτοῦ λόγον δώσει. However, *all of Paul's other accounts of the day of judgment are in some sense quite christocentric*, and it is precisely my point that Rom. 2:5-13 has *no* necessary role for Christ at all, nor is he mentioned at any point except in v. 16b. Moreover — as we have already discussed in

part one, chapter three — no other account of the judgment in Paul suggests that for the Christian, salvation itself is at stake, and some discussions seem explicitly to deny this. However, in Rom. 2:5-13, 16a, salvation is overtly and necessarily at issue, and entirely in relation to the criterion of "works."

94. Following the NRSV except where indicated; the Teacher's probable words and slogans are in italics. A text (based on the NRSV) of the entire argument in Rom. 1:16–3:20, punctuated in accordance with my suggestions, is supplied in §7.

95. *Jewish Antiquities* 18.81-84. It does not matter for our purposes whether Josephus is actually right in his analysis of Roman domestic policy; that he reproduces the story indicates its probable widespread currency as an explanation of what actually happened. It transfers any responsibility for that expulsion from the Roman Jews as a whole to a small group of scoundrels who are unrepresentative of the broader group. Francis Watson notes the probable influence of this incident in *Paul, Judaism and the Gentiles: A Sociological Approach*, SNTSMS 56 (Cambridge; New York: Cambridge University Press, 1986), 114, hereafter *PJ&G*[1] (rev. ed., 203-5 — hereafter *PJ&G*[2]).

96. The prophetic text quoted also signals that this is a programmatic possibility. There is a history at Rome of such reversed expectations. Paul of course holds that the Teacher's system is ultimately futile and so may well result in such an anomaly, as its protagonists are demonstrated to be hypocrites and sinners.

97. Conventional readers have struggled with the redundancy and clumsiness of the subsection. (And if the redundancy is countered by way of an appeal to some sort of learning experience, the empirical difficulty in relation to Judaism is sharpened.) Revisionists have sometimes reoriented the discussion toward an exemplary and rather vulgar figure but have struggled to explain Paul's reasons for doing this.

98. See §3.1. Other pieces of evidence that reinforce this construal of the Teacher's system, especially from further afield in Romans, will be noted shortly. For example, this reading is particularly helpful for understanding Paul's argumentative objectives in Rom. 7:7-25.

99. Stowers is especially sensitive to this dimension in the argument of Romans — which he tends to call "an ethic of self-mastery" (see *RR*, esp. 42-82, 144-53). He traces its links through Greco-Roman philosophy, Julio-Claudian political propaganda, various branches of Judaism, and Paul's specific networks at Rome. His astute discussion tends to be assertive in methodological terms, but my exegetical findings support most of his claims in this relation. A rereading shaped in part by his concerns and insights regarding "self-mastery" does demonstrably eliminate many of the problems apparent in the conventional construal of Romans 1–3. See also (of course!) Philo: i.a., *On the Preliminary Studies*, 85-87.

100. And is this also an impish use of an alpha-privative by Paul?!

101. E. P. Sanders and Peder Borgen emphasize *Questions and Answers on Exodus*, 2.2; and *On the Migration of Abraham*, 92: see Sanders, *Paul, the Law, and the Jewish People* (Philadelphia: Fortress, 1983), 131, 135; and Borgen, "Observations on the Theme 'Paul and Philo,'" in *Die Paulinische Literatur und Theologie*, ed. S. Pedersen (Aarhus: Forlaget Aros, 1980), 85-102; and "Paul Preaches Circumcision and Pleases Men," in *Paul and Paulinism: Essays in Honour of C. K. Barrett*, ed. Morna Hooker and S. G. Wilson (London: SPCK, 1982), 37-46. Watson adds the further Philonic material considered here: see *PJ&G*[2], 74-79. Tobin also notes the point briefly: *Paul's Rhetoric*, 116-17. Our discussion overlaps at this point with the lively and ongoing debate over the need for circumcision in relation to Judaizing in Paul's day (which has already been touched on in part one, chapter five). Fortunately, all the disputants agree that circumcision for Philo symbolizes the excision of the pleasures; they disagree over whether his texts suggest that bodily circumcision must always follow for proselytes. Incidentally, the argument of Romans suggests that the Teacher did regard bodily circumcision as mandatory, with further corroborations from Galatians and Philippians 3. On the broader debate (in addition to the studies already noted) see Neil J. McEleney, "Conversion, Circumcision, and the Law," *New Testament Studies* 20 (1974): 319-40; John Nolland, "Uncircumcised Proselytes?" *Journal for the Study of Judaism* 1 (1981): 173-94; and James Carleton Paget, "Jewish Proselytism at the Time of Christian Origins: Chimera or Reality?" *Journal for the Study of the New Testament* 62 (1996): 65-103. Three of Joel Marcus's studies are also esp. important: "The Evil Inclination in the Epistle of James,"

Catholic Biblical Quarterly 44 (1982): 606-21, esp. 611-13; "The Evil Inclination in the Letters of Paul," *Irish Biblical Studies* 8 (1986): 8-21; and "The Circumcision and Uncircumcision in Rome," *New Testament Studies* 35 (1989): 67-81. The first two of these essays, in particular, serve to broaden the Jewish reference of the debate through the theme of the law's taming of the evil inclination, after its spiritual circumcision.

102. Using here the translation by Yonge and pagination by Hendrickson — Philo, *The Works of Philo,* new updated ed., trans. C. D. Yonge (Peabody, Mass.: Hendrickson, 1993).

103. Yonge, ed., 857-60.

104. Philo briefly returns to this theme of the circumcised (male) mind after justifying Jewish circumcision of males only over against Egyptian circumcision of both genders: "the intellect in us is endued with the power of sight, therefore it is necessary to cut away its superfluous shoots. And these superfluous shoots are empty opinions, and all the actions which are done in accordance with them. So that the intellect after circumcision may only bear about with itself what is necessary and useful; and . . . whatever causes pride to increase may be cut away" (47). Following these observations Philo rehearses at greater length the traditional pragmatic rationales that we have already noted, returning briefly to the claim that circumcision excises the wicked desires of the human intellect and heart. As a lack of physical circumcision causes diseases for the body, a lack of spiritual circumcision allows ethical diseases to infect both body and soul (48). "[God in Gen. 17:12] warns us to cut away not only all the superfluous desires, but also pride, as being a great wickedness and an associate of wickedness" (48).

105. Marcus's studies of the evil inclination have the dual virtues of demonstrating the widespread nature of this set of conceptions within Judaism in Paul's day *and* showing how it is embedded in Paul's texts, esp. Galatians, and the discourse of his opponents, namely, James: see "The Evil Inclination in the Epistle of James," and "The Evil Inclination in the Letters of Paul."

106. See Wis. 3:8; *1 Enoch* 91:12; 98:12; *Apocalypse of Abraham* 29:19; 1QM [+ 1Q33] [War Scroll]; also 1 Cor. 6:2; see also Douglas Moo, *The Epistle to the Romans,* NICNT (Grand Rapids, Mich.: Eerdmans, 1996), 171-72. In my view this motif should be added to the gospel of the Teacher(s). (This anticipated role also foreshadows our discussion of right "kingly" actions in chapter seventeen, interweaving forensic and executive actions.)

107. Thus, in essence, the Teacher preaches — presumably for the best of motives — "turn (to circumcision and the Jewish law) or burn; only circumcision of the body and the heart will allow you to act righteously and so obtain a final verdict from God of rectitude that leads to salvation. Otherwise, your typical pagan sins, running riot in an untamed pagan nature, will overwhelm you and elicit a final verdict of wickedness that leads to damnation. (You are, after all, apart from the law's illumination and therefore blind, groping in darkness, foolish, and mere children.) Embrace the Jewish advantage that is both ethical and soteriological — the law — and symbolize this acceptance by being circumcised, and your underlying lusts will be pruned as well."

108. It is worth emphasizing how the motif "works of law" functions in an essentially conventional way in this schema *in immediate semantic terms;* it denotes various righteous or good acts undertaken in the light of the Jewish law, and the person who does them constantly will consequently be pronounced "righteous" by God on the day of judgment. However, the broader soteriology within which this motif is embedded is significantly different from the conventional account of nonChristian reality offered by Justification theory, because it involves important ontological assumptions as well. Justification theory overlooks these additional assumptions that inform Paul's argument, and thereby generates many of its exegetical and argumentative difficulties in Romans 1–4.

109. We have already noted that the definition of what "a true Jew" is seems to have been shifted beyond all recognition by Paul's juxtaposition — and perhaps absurdly so. This redefinition is a direct implication of the Teacher's premises in terms of desert — it is implicit within it. But Paul is of course undermining the probable ancillary claim here on the part of the Teacher that physical circumcision defines a Jew, both physically and ethically. If someone wants to become a true Jew — and "salvation is only from the Jews" — then, according to the Teacher, it is necessary to be circumcised. Only this action, accompanied by diligent law observance, can save. Paul, however, has cleverly shown that

the assumption undergirding the Teacher's opening rhetoric — desert — leads not only to a radically different definition of Judaism but to an evacuation of the Teacher's actual demands in such terms. *In terms of his own assumptions, the Teacher's definition of "the true Jew" is wrong.* (And the deployment of his own theologoumenon in terms of appearance versus deeper reality affirms this judgment.)

110. I am not convinced that this is merely an adjectival antithesis, as the NRSV suggests (presumably under the influence of the immediately preceding verse) — "it [i.e., circumcision, as a matter of the heart] is spiritual and not literal." It is too similar to important summary phrases that Paul uses elsewhere, most notably ἐν καινότητι πνεύματος καὶ οὐ παλαιότητι γράμματος in Rom. 7:6b (also 2 Cor. 3:6). Moreover, although Isaiah 59 sees the Spirit as critical in placing God's words permanently in the mouth of Israel, the prophetic anticipations of the transformation of the human heart tend not to invoke the agency of the divine Spirit directly: see also Jer. 31:31-34. It should be apparent by now that the righteous pagan that appears here is inextricably rooted in the presuppositions of the argument; he is nothing more nor less than a projection of the principle of desert. And we have already seen how "Christian" and "hypothetical" interpretations are deeply problematic for this figure. This short phrase, then, is best interpreted parenthetically, as an anticipation of an important set of claims occurring later in the letter (i.e., not as a qualification of a Christian figure). Paul has already crafted anticipations overtly in 1:2-4 and 1:16-17, and briefly — *in just this manner and argumentative location* — in 2:16b. Gordon Fee concurs, although his reasoning rests heavily on the passage's conventional construal!; alternative arguments for the same judgment are nevertheless still possible: see *God's Empowering Presence: The Holy Spirit in the Letters of Paul* (Peabody, Mass.: Hendrickson, 1994), 489-93 — a "proleptic (foreshadowing) usage . . . full of theological grist that will be milled for all it's worth later in this letter" (489).

111. A point that will become clearer during the discussion of Rom. 3:24-26.

112. It is apparent in the emphasis on "works" and "doing," which may also be attested in the Teacher's companion texts; and of course it is central to his final eschatological scenario.

113. That is, the Mu'tazilites, the first philosophical school in Islam. See J. A. Nawas, "A Reexamination of Three Current Explanations for al-Ma'mun's Introduction of the Mihna," *International Journal of Middle East Studies* 26 (1994): 615-629; "The Mihna of 218 A.H./833 A.D. Revisited: An Empirical Study," *Journal of the American Oriental Society* 16 (1996): 698-708; Michael Cooperson, *Al-Ma'mun* (Oxford: Oneworld, 2005).

114. My own translation throughout. Note also that it is not always necessary to insist on the particulars of the various assignations of speakers and roles; often minor adjustments are possible that do not affect the overarching course of the argument. I am entirely open to such adjustments.

115. Following this translation of δικαιο- terminology for the moment.

116. This is a notoriously difficult translation decision. The verb is, strictly speaking, either a middle or a passive, but is usually translated in deponent terms as an active. I am not sure that it alters my contentions a great deal if any one of these three alternatives is favored. Neither the middle translation, as elaborated elegantly by Nils Dahl ("what can we hold before us as a defence?"), nor the passive, as argued vigorously by Stowers ("are we disadvantaged?"), is without merit: see Dahl, "Romans 3.9: Text and Meaning," in *Paul and Paulinism: Essays in Honour of C. K. Barrett*, ed. Morna Hooker and S. G. Wilson (London: SPCK, 1982), 15-29; and Stowers, *RR*, 173-74. However, both those readings require the translation "nothing at all" of the phrase οὐ πάντως, which follows immediately. (Granting Stowers's broader rereading avoids this difficulty for him, but we have already adduced reasons for resisting that construal: see part three, chapter twelve.) A more literal rendering ("not altogether/in every respect"), which is quite compatible with Paul's uses of this phrase elsewhere (see 1 Cor. 5:10; 16:12), follows meaningfully only on a deponent reading: "Are we advantaged? Not in every respect it seems. . . ." And this also completes the opening claims of the diatribe neatly, not only resuming the question in v. 1 but *correcting* the rejoinder in v. 2. Hence, I prefer the deponent rendering. (D and G* also seem to assume an active meaning: προκατέχομεν περισσόν; also Ψ: προεχόμεθα περισσόν; along with the Syriac and old Italian MSS, and several of the church fathers.)

117. Neil Elliott has already argued for this reorientation, following a partial redeployment by Stowers: see *The Rhetoric of Romans: Argumentative Constraint and Strategy and Paul's Dialogue with*

Judaism, JSNTSup 45 (Sheffield: JSOT Press, 1990), 132-141, 200-3; Stowers, *RR*, 159-75; see also Richard B. Hays, "Psalm 143 and the Logic of Romans 3," *Journal of Biblical Literature* 99 (1980): 107-15; W. S. Campbell, "Romans III as a Key to the Structure and Thought of the Letter," *Novum Testamentum* 23 (1981): 22-40; and Stowers, "Paul's Dialogue with a Fellow Jew in Romans 3.1-9," *Catholic Biblical Quarterly* 46 (1984): 707-22. Clearly I agree with these interpretative objectives informing this debate, and the basic shape of Elliott's reading. However, my suggested rereading is framed and grounded differently from his (and hopefully a little more securely).

118. It must be emphasized that Paul is addressing here the Teacher's definition of a Jew and the value of circumcision — "according to your system, what is the value of Judaism?" Paul's broader point is that the Teacher has in fact undermined his own Jewish construction; his Jewishness is incoherent. Paul himself, meanwhile, constructs Judaism and circumcision very differently.

119. μέν can be read as a marker of contrast without express correlation, continuing the contradictory assertion of v. 2a in response to the query of v. 1. It could also denote the first of a series that is never finished (that would presumably include circumcision here). I am not sure that much rests on a judgment in relation to these options.

120. Πρῶτον μὲν [γὰρ] ὅτι ἐπιστεύθησαν τὰ λόγια τοῦ θεοῦ. Τί γάρ, εἰ ἠπίστησάν τινες, μὴ ἡ ἀπιστία αὐτῶν τὴν πίστιν τοῦ θεοῦ καταργήσει;

121. These inquiries continue to use wordplays. The second uses the stem δικαιο-, and the third returns to the theme of truth that was introduced by 3:3. The particular "benefits" that might be introduced by sinful behavior are that God's πίστις, δικαιοσύνη and ἀλήθεια might be highlighted even more clearly and so the whole process lead to his glory.

122. And this has already been noted in chapter thirteen.

123. SD 3 (the character of God), and SD 9 (Judaism), which have corresponding proximate difficulties in Romans, and ED 1 (Judaism), which overlaps with SD 9.

124. And this understandably causes difficulties for the passage's interpretation. The two lines of argument need to be distinguished. Without this, the argument often seems slightly confusing.

125. This supports the suggestion that its earlier use is ironic; if it is innate to Paul's thinking and present discourse, then its omission here is difficult to explain.

126. Porter has written much on this issue: see, i.a., *Verbal Aspect in the Greek of the New Testament, with Reference to Tense and Mood* (New York: Peter Lang, 1989).

127. It is possible that a middle deponent meaning is present — that this is really a passive (see also Rom. 10:3). It is true that Koiné often confused the middle and the passive. But Paul does not seem to include himself explicitly in this charge. He would not of course exclude himself on general grounds (see esp. 11:32), but his present argumentative focus is the Teacher. Verse 19 also seems to stand against this reading because of its specific concern with "those in the law." Alternatively, the verb could be a dramatic aorist — a statement with present force, at a critical point (and Rom. 3:9b is a critical point), as in John 13:31. This possibility cannot be excluded. Γάρ, in this setting, probably takes clarifying ("you see") or — more likely — emphatic ("indeed"), rather than inferential or causal force ("for," "because"): see the discussion of 1:18 in chapter fourteen.

A further interpretative possibility that I do not want to exclude completely takes Paul to be cunningly including the Teacher's previous citation of Scripture in his own downfall here. Both Paul and the Teacher are learned exegetes, who have cited these Scriptures at some point in the past. So, in effect, both have *already* accused *themselves* of complete and utter sinfulness. "Indeed, we have already accused everyone — Jew as well as Greek — of being under sin [since we have already read these texts out and affirmed them in the past], as it is written. . . ." So "whatever the law says [through our public recitation] it speaks to those in the law [i.e., to those reciting it — you and I] so that the whole world might be accountable [i.e., you] . . ." (DC). It was one of Paul's most pointed criticisms in 2:17-24 that the learned exegete does not practice what he teaches. This reading consequently expects "the one who teaches others to teach himself" (see 2:21a) — here in the specific sense that the one who condemns others also condemns himself. Fortunately, not much turns on a final decision at this point, so I will leave these options essentially unresolved. (I am grateful to Carol Shoun for pressing me in relation to this text, and for making some key interpretative suggestions.)

128. The LXX references are, respectively, Pss. 5:10; 139:4; 9:28; and 35:2.

129. See Isaiah 59 (δικαιοσύνη occurs in vv. 9, 14, 17); and Psalms 5 [LXX] (a psalm of overt divine kingship; δικαιοσύνη occurs in v. 8), 9 [LXX] (a psalm also of divine kingship; δικαιοσύνη is not mentioned, although it is arguably implicit in vv. 12, 14-18); 13/52 (both themes are arguably only implicit; see also Rom. 11:28); and 35 (δικαιοσύνη θεοῦ is treated in vv. 5 and 11; divine kingship is not overt).

130. A further possible piece of evidence is the "tone" of 3:19b, which follows. If Paul is held to be echoing the rhetoric of the Teacher here, this might in turn marginally reinforce a parodic use of the Teacher's catena in 3:10-18; however, a "straight-faced" Pauline idiom in 3:19b would provide no such support. The eschatological thrust of the verse and its slight argumentative redundancy incline me (just) toward the possibility that Paul is again being parodic. But this judgment remains a delicate one.

131. The universality and objectivity of philosophical epistemology should not of course be overstated; in fact, this too is a particular tradition of knowledge. However, the critical point is not the putative contrast between universality and particularity but the contrast between two fundamentally different traditions and modes. Modern readers are arguably especially sensitive to the importance of the "philosophical" mode, and perhaps also thereby especially prone to exaggerating its importance, because it has been so central to post-European culture since the Enlightenment.

132. Elliott discusses this issue perceptively in *The Rhetoric of Romans*, 142-46.

133. Ernst Käsemann, *Commentary on Romans*, 4th ed., trans. Geoffrey W. Bromiley (Grand Rapids, Mich.: Eerdmans, 1980 [1975]), 85 (also cited by Elliott, *The Rhetoric of Romans*, 143, n. 1).

134. See also Mark 12:34b.

135. I was alerted to this possibility by Moo's discussion, although of course he does not follow it himself; see *Romans*, 205.

136. Its importance is indicated certainly by its quotation also in Gal. 2:16 (addressed in part five, chapter twenty), and possibly also by the extensive use of the verb that Paul makes throughout Romans and Galatians (a question we will consider in more detail in chapter sixteen).

137. Verse 2 reads, καὶ μὴ εἰσέλθῃς εἰς κρίσιν μετὰ τοῦ δούλου σου, ὅτι οὐ δικαιωθήσεται ἐνώπιον σου πᾶς ζῶν. Clearly, Paul has added the phrase "works of law" to his quotation.

138. My suggested interpretation of these short concluding comments is admittedly not demonstrably superior to the conventional reading. Both readings seem quite possible. These comments are only brief summaries, and it is difficult to obtain a decisive purchase in such a brief arena. But all I need to be able to do at this point is to indicate how a fair possible reading of 3:19-20 accords with my previous construction of the argument. The validity of one or the other reading then depends on the validity of those previous readings of a considerable amount of material, and I am confident that my approach offers some advantages.

139. Excising "whoever you are."

140. The terminology of culpability and practice (ἀναπολόγητος, πράσσω) used here by Paul is probably drawn from the Teacher's discourse as well (see 1:20, 32), as I argued earlier on in this chapter (see §4). The NRSV obscures this, but it would be overly clumsy to italicize it.

141. Again omitting "whoever you are."

142. The presence of this important phrase is slightly deceptive. It is, I would suggest, part of the Teacher's system, but it has been redeployed here in an embarrassing new setting by Paul.

143. A better translation of this theologoumenon in context, I would suggest. See Jas. 2:1-7, 9.

144. I incline toward including even this sentence within Paul's subversive disposition of the Teacher's system. Again, he has redeployed existing elements in an embarrassing new juxtaposition.

145. A more consistent and appropriate rendering in the future tense than the present used by the NRSV.

146. See Jas. 1:22 (and vv. 23-25).

147. My suggested parenthetical reading.

148. Retaining the translation with a syntactical, parenthetical rearrangement.

149. Rejecting the NRSV's adjectival and contextual rendering here as unlikely.

150. These are, again, the Teacher's views, but he would not split them apart as Paul does. A true Jew ought to possess inward circumcision, of the body (literally "heart"), and so should ultimately receive praise not from men but from God, but that will also — in the Teacher's system — correspond directly with outward, physical circumcision. Paul, however, has cleverly driven a wedge between these two dimensions.

151. Following the alternative translation that respects the passive infinitive more.

152. Respecting the shift in the Greek to indirect speech. Technically, this is an instance of the Teacher's speech as well. But it is not part of his gospel; rather, it is a criticism of Paul's.

153. A more accurate rendering of the Greek οὐ πάντως.

154. A suggested alternative that supplies a clearer sense of Paul's argument. The charge is made in part by the voice of Scripture itself, as v. 19 indicates, where the law "says" and "speaks" — here a plural voice drawn from Psalms and Prophets.

155. These quotations could be derived originally from the Teacher, but this is difficult to prove beyond reasonable doubt. The assertion of universal and absolute depravity perhaps marginally inclines me to think that they are Paul's construction; the Teacher does not view Jews this way — although he does view pagans this way!

156. See 2:16b and 29.

157. We return to this point again briefly in part five, chapter twenty, when discussing Gal. 3:10.

158. In sum, 5-6 of 7 IDs; 5-7 of 10 SDs; 1-4 of 4 EDs; 11-17/21 in total.

159. That is, the atonement per se in not in dispute, since both Paul and the Teacher probably accepted basic Christian claims; furthermore, Paul is not now working "forward," so he does not need to ground his account of Christ's atonement on an account of the inadequacies of Judaism's modes of atonement; and so on.

160. And positive evidence in support of this claim may well emerge as we consider the argumentative dynamics of Romans 9–10 in more detail, in part five, chapter nineteen.

161. And this is an important point to emphasize in passing. It is no longer sufficient simply to reject my alternate reading out of hand. Reasons must be supplied in support of this rejection, because the conventional reading that this rejection usually presupposes is now in such jeopardy.

Notes to Chapter Fifteen

1. Paul uses the substantive πίστις three times in 1:17 and then in 3:22, 25, and 26; he uses the cognate participle in 1:16 and 3:22; Hab. 2:4 is quoted in 1:17b.

2. Those arguments will in the first instance simply humiliate further the gospel of the Teacher, but they will also defend Paul's against certain related criticisms.

3. Πεφανέρωται is clearly elided from v. 21 and ought to be supplied. Bailey suggests that ἐστιν has been elided: Daniel P. Bailey, "Narrative Soteriology in Romans 3:21–26: Maccabean Martyr Theology or the Biblical Exodus–New Sanctuary Tradition?" paper presented at SBL Annual Meeting, Pauline Epistles Section (San Antonio, Tex., 11/22/2004). But although this is the most frequently elided verb in Paul, such an omission is unlikely here. First, such a claim is unparalleled elsewhere in Paul (i.e., that "the righteousness of God is . . ."); second, it ignores the parallel subject and broadly parallel set of prepositional modifiers in v. 21 that ask the Greek reader for a similar construal; and — most importantly — third, it ignores the parallelism between 3:22 and 1:17 that confirms the need for a verb of disclosure. (Arguably, as we will see shortly, this suggestion overlooks the important intertext in play at this point as well.)

4. BDAG asserts that the middle could convey a sense of disclosure — "display publicly, make available publicly" (889): see Appian, *The Civil Wars,* 3.26.101; Justin Martyr, *Dialogue with Trypho,* 65.3. BDAG suggests the same for the cognate substantive in Matt. 12:4; Mark 2:26; Luke 6:4 (1 Sam. 21:6 [1 Kgdms. 21:7 LXX]); Heb. 9:2; however, these limit the case for "set forth," since all are references to the "showbread" (869). But see Gal. 3:1 for a text where Paul speaks firmly of God "placarding" Christ's cross. (See also "offer," attested in inscriptions and papyri according to BDAG, 889 — mng 2.)

5. Ἐν ᾧ ἔχομεν τὴν ἀπολύτρωσιν διὰ τοῦ αἵματος αὐτοῦ, τὴν ἄφεσιν τῶν παραπτωμάτων, κατὰ τὸ πλοῦτος τῆς χάριτος αὐτοῦ, ἧς ἐπερίσσευσεν εἰς ἡμᾶς, ἐν πάσῃ σοφίᾳ καὶ φρονήσει, γνωρίσας ἡμῖν τὸ μυστήριον τοῦ θελήματος αὐτοῦ, κατὰ τὴν εὐδοκίαν αὐτοῦ ἣν προέθετο ἐν αὐτῷ κ.τ.λ.

6. See esp. Eph. 1:11; but also Rom. 8:28; 9:11; see Eph. 3:11; and see also 2 Tim. 1:9. In Ephesians 1 the substantive (v. 11) and the verb (v. 9) also occur in close proximity to [προ]ορίζω (v. 11), the verb and its cognate also appearing in Rom. 1:2, 3.

7. This is the only meaning of εἰς that really fits. Clearly, movement in time, space, or state, is not being spoken of, nor are most of the more idiomatic possibilities (see BDAG, 288-91); similar considerations apply to πρός (see BDAG, 873-75). That this is a purpose and not a result may also be affirmed with a degree of confidence because of the parallelism with the final clause and its articular infinitive construction, and perhaps also the probable purposive signal of the verb in v. 25. It seems best, moreover, to suppose that Christ's function as a proof was intended by God, and not merely a result of another divine action. Indeed, this connotation cannot be avoided in view of the claims of vv. 21-22, where God disclosed his δικαιοσύνη through Christ. Not much rests on this distinction in any case.

8. The meaning of ἔνδειξις as "proof" seems both unremarkable and incontestable. It denotes for Paul concrete evidence of something invisible in a contested setting in relation to which it gives tangible evidence of that thing decisively: see 2 Cor. 8:24 and Phil. 1:28. W. G. Kümmel has written an elegant and perceptive study on the question that is hard to improve upon: "Πάρεσις und ἔνδειξις: Ein Beitrag zum Verständnis der paulinischen Rechtfertigungslehre," in *Heilgeschehen und Geschichte: Gesammelte Aufsätze, 1933-64* (Marburg: N. G. Elwert, 1965 [1952]), 260-70. He argues, however, that the translation "demonstration" (Erweis) ought to be favored over "proof" (Beweis), because the latter implies that God is having to prove himself to someone, and this is theologically unacceptable. But it is not necessary to endorse a connotation of divine necessity in this act of proof while accepting the allied connotation of overt demonstration in relation to someone who ought to know better (i.e., who is having something proved to him or her). Paul's use of this signifier is invariably in contested settings. And here he is opposing another gospel with a fundamentally different conception of God. This evidence in Christ therefore functions as "proof" to the Roman Christians over against the countervailing gospel of the Teacher. We might say, then, that *God* is not proving something here, but *Paul's* appeal to Christ as the definitive disclosure of God is! (The issue of how this motif influences a possible reading of πίστις as proof is considered just below.)

9. The explicative reading of καί is clearly the preferable one here. If God's δικαιοσύνη is revealed through the Christ event (see vv. 21-22), and that event functions in turn to justify (δικαιοῦν) all the faithful (see v. 24), then it simply follows that God's δικαιοσύνη is also revealed by that further justification as well. If this syllogism is to be resisted, then these events would have to be split apart, but this seems to fly in the face of what the text has already established. (In fact, even an "Anselmian" reading of the text does not need to deny this; the justification of the sinner by the atoning death of Christ does still reveal the [distributive] justice of God.)

10. See more on the translation of this signifier just below.

11. On which, again, see more just below.

12. See "Appendix I: A Synopsis of Romans 5:1-11 and 8:1-39," in *Studies in Paul: Theology for the Early Christian Mission* (Minneapolis: Augsburg, 1977), 88-90.

13. It is worth considering whether 6:1-11 functions within this chain of ascending discussions as well; however, this claim does not need to be established here for the broader suggestion to hold, along with its implications.

14. It could I suppose be argued that an individual's possession of certain accurate beliefs about a situation is a necessary (but not sufficient) condition for an act of communication to take place, so that act could theoretically be attributed in part, in instrumental terms, to the possession of those correct beliefs. Without them, the communication could not take place, so an instrumental role is implicit in them. However, it is unlikely that Paul is arguing in these terms in Romans. If he is making this subtle argument, we would expect him to say so, and he never articulates anything approaching this situation. Furthermore, there seems to be little or no obvious rhetorical *or* theological leverage in so doing. His emphasis on the role of beliefs in these terms would also be inexplicable; what about all

the other necessary conditions that are less subtle and more practical? Moreover, in order to do so, he would probably need to articulate many of the overtly post-Cartesian concerns and assumptions that undergird it! For these reasons, an instrumental role for human beliefs in this sense need not be seriously entertained as an interpretative option. (The corroborative contentions noted just below also stand against it.)

15. This reading also accounts for the perfect tense of the verbs in 3:21-22 (one of which is elided) better than the conventional alternative, although I do not regard this as a decisive contention. It could be argued in reliance on Galatians 3 that the possibility of "faith" arrived decisively with Christ has an ongoing effect. This is not in my view a very satisfactory reading of Galatians 3, but it will serve to delay any decisive advantage being generated by Paul's use of the perfect tense in Romans 3:21-22.

The argument in terms of redundancy ought to be abandoned completely (i.e., that there is something problematic about the redundant reading that advocates of an objective construal produce). An emphatic redundancy emphasizing "all" also speaks to the possible objection that "faith" ought not to function as both a means and an end, as the prepositional series ἐκ . . . εἰς . . . might suggest. The accusative construction — it might be replied — denotes extension rather than purpose, and is included for rhetorical emphasis: "righteousness has been disclosed by means of faith, extending to *all* who have such faith." A counterobjection to this defence is conceivable — namely, that purposive constructions are prominent in the context of 3:22, and constructions of mere reference or extension absent (although see παντὶ τῷ πιστεύοντι in 1:16b). However, this evidence seems too fragile to be emphasized strongly (although it does seem worth noting). (As already noted in chapter eleven, R. Barry Matlock has correctly advocated abandoning any argument in terms of redundancy as well: "The Rhetoric of Paul: Galatians 2.16, 3.22, Romans 3.22, and Philippians 3.9," *Journal for the Study of the New Testament* 30 [2007]: 173-203. But his preoccupation with this weak contention seems to lead him to overlook the strongest arguments in favor of the subjective reading in relation to this text, which consequently remain unrebutted by his work: see esp. 184-87.)

16. See Richard B. Hays, *The Faith of Jesus Christ: The Narrative Substructure of Galatians 3:1–4:11*, 2nd ed. (Grand Rapids, Mich.: Eerdmans, 2002); and Douglas A. Campbell, "The Story of Jesus in Romans and Galatians," in *Narrative Dynamics in Paul: A Critical Assessment*, ed. B. W. Longenecker (Louisville, Ky.: Westminster John Knox, 2002), 97-124; repr. in *The Quest for Paul's Gospel: A Suggested Strategy* (London: T&T Clark International, 2005), 69-94.

17. This is a truncated account of the story, which could be extended in each direction. However, it will suffice for the present discussion.

18. This quality is discernible in both militantly violent and pacifist narratives of martyrdom: see Daniel; Wisdom of Solomon; 2 Maccabees 6 and 7; 3 and 4 *Maccabees;* but pagan and Christian martyrologies make this point as well: they are collected in H. A. Musurillo, ed., *The Acts of the Pagan Martyrs* (Oxford: Acta Alexandrinorum, 1954); and *The Acts of the Christian Martyrs* (Oxford: Acta Alexandrinorum, 1972). Jan W. van Henten articulates this point esp. clearly (in relation specifically to 2 and 4 *Maccabees*): "The author of 4 Maccabees frequently presents εὐσέβεια ("piety") as the motive underlying the behaviour of the martyrs, but sometimes he uses instead phrases with πίστις or πιστεύω, which again corresponds to the image of the suffering righteous": *The Maccabean Martyrs as Saviours of the Jewish People: A Study of 2 and 4 Maccabees* (Leiden: Brill, 1997), 298; see also 125-35, 184.

19. See also 1 Macc. 2:52 (the cognate adjective), 59 (cognate verb); 2 Macc. 1:2 (adjective); and 4 *Macc.* 7:19, 21 (verbs).

20. And this of course raises the possibility that πίστις Χριστοῦ could denote the "belief" (i.e., conviction) or "trust" rather than the "faithfulness" of Christ and/or be developed argumentatively in such terms if the rhetorical need required.

21. The preaching and sending mentioned in vv. 14-15 are not negated but affirmed as taking place, as corroborated by Isa. 52:7; the hearing is taken up by vv. 17-18; and the calling of v. 14a is not resumed by the subsection's argument but seems rooted rather in vv. 12-13 that precede it.

22. Several more disparate parallelisms are arguably apparent elsewhere as well. In Romans —

as we have already seen in chapter thirteen — Paul speaks repeatedly of the "obedience" of the Roman Christians to the gospel: see especially 6:17; 15:18; and 16:19; 10:2-3 seem to resonate here as well; and 10:16 has just been noted. (Somewhat curiously, although they are described at times as "believers" — 1:16[?]; 4:23-24[?]; 6:8[?]; 13:11 — and commended for their fidelity — 1:5, 8, 12; 5:1[?]; 14:22[?] — their belief in the gospel is never explicitly noted as such.) However, when Paul speaks of responding to the gospel in other letters, he often uses πιστ- terminology in the same location — to denote the appropriate human response to it: see 1 Cor. 15:1, 2; 2 Cor. 11:4 (receive); Phil. 1:29; 1 Thess. 1:5; see also Eph. 1:13 (believe); and Col. 1:5, 23. A similar interchangeability is then at least arguably apparent when Paul links πίστις and ὑπακοή together in Romans 1:5 (and the same phrase occurs in 16:26). The meaning of this genitive relation is disputed, but a martyrological reading that effectively equates them epexegetically is clearly possible, and all the considerations that have just been adduced function in support of such an interpretation. An extended treatment of this phrase is Donald Garlington, 'The Obedience of Faith': A Pauline Phrase in Historical Context, WUNT 38 (Tübingen: J. C. B. Mohr [Siebeck], 1990).

23. Two further, rather strong corroborations will emerge shortly when we consider the meaning of 3:25 in relation to OD 13, and then the meaning of Abraham in Romans 4 and the various ODs clustering around his conventional construal (principally 19 and 20; these issues are all discussed in chapters seventeen and eighteen). And a third reason could arguably be added here as well, but it depends on the fulfillment of a large prior task — the determination of the meaning of δικαιοσύνη Θεοῦ.

If it can be shown prior to any analysis of these verses that this phrase has a cosmic, eschatological, and "apocalyptic" meaning, then the disclosure of this essentially divine action could hardly be *conditional on a human action* — faith. This would be absurd; it would be to take a divine, worldwide, and singular event and break it up in relation to each individual act of faith. (A theocentric instrumentality seems similarly flawed.) However, I prefer to try to determine the meaning of δικαιοσύνη Θεοῦ after the πίστις questions have been settled, using evidence from the latter material to help determine the former. So this additional argument is not available to me.

A fourth but more minor contention will also be noted periodically with respect to the construal of "believers" (see Rom. 1:16b, 17a; 3:22; etc.). Things are more difficult in this data for conventional readers than they perhaps suspect.

24. This also opens up the possibility of a reading of πίστις as "proof"; see more on this below.

25. The suggestion is not especially new, but it is not usually linked with the πίστις Χριστοῦ debate. However, Hays certainly made this connection (although he has not pressed it as hard as I do). Earlier advocates of the messianic construal of Hab. 2:4 in Rom. 1:17 include A. T. Hanson (etc.): see *Studies in Paul's Technique and Theology* (Grand Rapids, Mich.: Eerdmans, 1974), 39-45; and see further references in Douglas A. Campbell, *The Rhetoric of Righteousness in Romans 3:21-26*, JSNTSup 65 (Sheffield: JSOT Press, 1992), 211, n. 1 — hereafter *RRR*. The connection is now also firmly advocated by Francis Watson: see *Paul and the Hermeneutics of Faith* (London; New York: T&T Clark, 2004), 42-77.

26. A christological reading of Hab. 2:4 automatically settles the earlier debate over whether the phrase ἐκ πίστεως modifies the subject or the verb. Paul could hardly be suggesting here that Jesus is the one who is righteous by faith! However, it seemed most likely in any case that the phrase's function is adverbial. D. Moody Smith's case is definitive: see "Ὁ ΔΕ ΔΙΚΑΙΟΣ ΕΚ ΠΙΣΤΕΩΣ ΖΗΣΕΤΑΙ," in *Studies in the History and Text of the New Testament in Honor of Kenneth Willis Clark*, ed. Boyd L. Daniels and M. Jack Suggs (Salt Lake City, Utah: University of Utah Press, 1967), 13-25. Smith assembles seven contentions, the combined weight of which is overwhelming: (1) all attested Jewish antecedent texts read the phrase adverbially (see MT; LXX [in both main variants]; Targum Jonathan; 1QpHab; see also Heb. 10:38), so an adjectival function would be a Pauline innovation; (2) Paul could then have modified the subject and its associated phrase into a clearer, attributive form (i.e., ὁ δὲ δίκαιος ὁ ἐκ πίστεως or ὁ δὲ ἐκ πίστεως δίκαιος), given that he almost certainly modified the text in any case by dropping the pronoun μου; (3) the verse functions in the letter's thanksgiving, where the fidelity of the Roman Christians is a particular emphasis, i.e., the way they are living (see 1:5, 8, 12); (4) in 1:17a the same phrase functions adverbially; (5) Hab. 2:4 functions in parallel to Lev. 18:5 in Gal. 3:11-12 and the phrase ἐκ πίστεως must be adverbial there (see further in part five, chapter twenty);

(6) the main argument in favor of an adjectival function is a poor one — the suggestion that, construed in this way, the text anticipates the structure of Romans 1–8 (see, i.a., Nygren, Feuillet, and Cambier) — although, if this is true, then the text is a poor anticipation of the rest of Romans, leaving both 9–11 and 12–14 out of account; and (7) elsewhere, Paul speaks frequently of living as Christians in relation to πίστις (see Rom. 12:3; 14:23; 15:13; 1 Cor. 16:13; 2 Cor. 1:24; 4:13; 5:7; Gal. 2:20; 3:11, 23, 25; 5:5), but never of someone who is righteous ἐκ πίστεως, so the latter construal of Rom. 1:17b is hardly more Pauline.

27. R. Scroggs's important study is to my mind convincing: "Rom. 6.7: ὁ γὰρ ἀποθανὼν δεδικαίωται ἀπὸ τῆς ἁμαρτίας," *New Testament Studies* 10 (1963): 104-8; see also Rom. 8:34; 14:9.

28. Paul might also be referring to Christ in Rom. 5:7 where τοῦ ἀγαθοῦ resumes δικαίου. In Paul's other letters it is of course important not to overlook ὁ κύριος.

29. As noted some time ago by Richard Longenecker: see *The Christology of Early Jewish Christianity* (London: SCM, 1970), and canvassed recently by Larry Hurtado, *Lord Jesus Christ: Devotion to Jesus in Earliest Christianity* (Grand Rapids, Mich.: Eerdmans, 2003), 189-90.

30. The accusative construction in James could be merely generic; however, it is arthrous, is couched in the singular, in the past (using two aorists initially), and the text of James resonates with much of Romans' early argument. A reference here to Christ cannot therefore confidently be excluded (and an economic explanation of his execution opens up intriguing possibilities).

In the Matthean text, the origins of the title are more probably discernible than an overtly messianic usage. Here the phrase certainly denotes an innocent person who is being accused. (This verse notes the advice of Pilate's wife to him on the day of Jesus' trial: "Have nothing to do with that innocent man. . . .") Martyrs were of course accused, perhaps tortured, and then executed, despite their innocence of any charges and their piety, so the name "righteous" was well suited to them; see also its application to Lot in 2 Pet. 2:8. However, it is possible that Matthew is engaging in a subtle wordplay, rather as Mark does with the title "son of God" in 15:39b.

31. See Isa. 3:10; 53:11; 57:1; and various motifs in the Similitudes of *1 Enoch* — 38:2; 53:6, and also possibly 47:1 and 4; also *The Letter to Diognetus*, 9:2, 5 (the first of these references echoing 1 Pet. 3:18); Justin, *Dialogue with Trypho*, 13.7 (Isa. 53:8); 16.4 (Isa. 57:1; see Jas. 5:6), 5 (Isa. 57:1); 17.1-3 (57:1; 53:5; 51:4); 86.4 (2x — once here citing Ps. 91:13 LXX, which is then the basis for a related messianic introduction of Ps. 1:3 LXX); 119.3; 133.2 (Isa. 3:10); 136.2 (Isa. 57:1); see also 110.6 (citing 1 Pet. 1:19 and Isa. 53:9; 53:8; 57:1). See Hays, "'The Righteous One' as Eschatological Deliverer: A Case Study in Paul's Apocalyptic Hermeneutics," in *Apocalyptic and the New Testament: Essays in Honour of J. Louis Martyn*, ed. J. Marcus and M. Soards (Sheffield: JSOT Press, 1988), 191-215; repr. as "Apocalyptic Hermeneutics: Habakkuk Proclaims 'The Righteous One,'" in *The Conversion of the Imagination: Paul as Interpreter of Israel's Scripture* (Grand Rapids, Mich.: Eerdmans, 2005), 119-42; see also James C. Vanderkam, "Righteous One, Messiah, Chosen One, and Son of Man in 1 Enoch 37–71," in *The Messiah: Developments in Earliest Judaism and Christianity*, ed. James H. Charlesworth (Minneapolis, Minn.: Fortress, 1992), 169-91. Daniel Bailey discusses the relationship between Isaiah 53 and Justin's *Dialogue* more generally in "'Our Suffering and Crucified Messiah' (*Dial.* 111.2): Justin Martyr's Allusions to Isaiah 53 and His *Dialogue with Trypho* with Special Reference to the New Edition of M. Marcovich," in *The Suffering Servant: Isaiah 53 in Jewish and Christian Sources*, ed. Bernd Janowski and Peter Stuhlmacher (Grand Rapids, Mich.: Eerdmans, 2004), 324-417. Morna Hooker does not consider the force of the corroborative evidence, especially from 1 Pet. 3:18 and Justin's *Dialogue*; her dismissals are therefore unconvincing: see *Jesus and the Servant: The Influence of the Servant Concept of Deutero-Isaiah in the New Testament* (London: SPCK, 1959), 111-12.

32. Hays, *Faith*, 135-36.

33. Hays points to the importance of this motif and title in Luke in particular (see esp. 7:18-23; 19:38; he also discusses the possible resonance with Isa. 35:5); see "Reading the Bible with Eyes of Faith: The Practice of Theological Exegesis," *Journal of Theological Interpretation* 1 (2007): 5-21, esp. 16-21. It is also a prominent Johannine motif: see John 6:14; 11:27; 12:13 (see Ps. 118:25-26 [117:25-26 LXX]; see also John 12:15, citing Zech. 9:9); with further possible echoes in 1:9; 3:31 (2x); and 4:25. Josephus may also attest to this motif (inadvertently) in *War* 5.272, when he describes how watchers in the towers of

the besieged Jerusalem cried out warnings concerning incoming artillery stones in the form "a/the son is coming/comes" (i.e., in the form of a joke) — ὁ υἱὸς ἔρχεται. This intriguing text will be noted again in part five, chapter nineteen (including the probable basis for the joke).

34. This text's heroes are invariably masculine, although wisdom is portrayed as feminine.

35. We link hands at this point with a fascinating debate and possibility — that Isaiah 53 (esp. v. 11) lies behind the short narrative of the oppressed righteous man in the Wisdom of Solomon. If so, then this text could also inform the early Christian appropriation of Hab. 2:4. (That Isaiah 53 is informing Paul more generally on the atonement is almost certain; see the discussion of Rom. 4:24-25 below.) See esp. Suggs, "Wisdom 2:10-5: A Homily Based on the Fourth Servant Song," *Journal of Biblical Literature* 76 (1957): 26-53; see also Hooker, *Jesus and the Servant*, esp. 103-33 — at the skeptical end of the interpretative spectrum (which she largely established), and rather too much so; Donald H. Juel, *Messianic Exegesis: Christological Interpretation in the Old Testament and Early Christianity*, new ed. (Minneapolis, Minn.: Augsburg Fortress, 1998 [1988]), 119-33; Joel Marcus, *The Way of the Lord: Christological Exegesis of the Old Testament in the Gospel of Mark* (Louisville, Ky.: Westminster John Knox, 1992), esp. 186-96; Richard Bauckham, *God Crucified. Monotheism and Christology in the New Testament* (Carlisle: Paternoster, 1998), 45-79, esp. 51-53, 56-61; also "The Worship of Jesus in Philippians 2:9-11," in *Where Christology Began: Essays on Philippians 2*, ed. R. P. Martin and B. J. Dodd (Louisville, Ky.: Westminster John Knox, 1998), 128-39; and Bernd Janowski and Peter Stuhlmacher, eds., *The Suffering Servant: Isaiah 53 in Jewish and Christian Sources* (Grand Rapids, Mich.: Eerdmans, 2004 [1996]). This hypothesis is considered briefly again in chapter eighteen, esp. §6. The importance of the "psalms of the righteous sufferer" in this connection should also not be overlooked: a useful summary (oriented of course toward Mark) is given by Marcus, *The Way of the Lord*, 172-86. That is, the underlying intertextuality could be more complex (and almost certainly was), involving the interpretation of various Psalms as well. Marcus speaks appropriately of a "genetic closeness" between these texts (186).

36. Its location also varies — whether ὁ [δὲ] δίκαιός μου ἐκ πίστεως ζήσεται (A, C, Heb. 10:38) or ὁ [δὲ] δίκαιος ἐκ πίστεώς μου ζήσεται (ℵ, W). The shift apparent in the LXX from ὁ MT, from a third to a first person pronoun, *might* be explicable in terms of Hebrew pronominal forms and either the deliberate substitution or misreading of a yodh for a vav (ʾ/ʾ). The MT — if it was prior — should have generated αὐτοῦ in the LXX.

37. This factor also contributes significantly to an explanation of Paul's use (or not) of the article in these phrases.

38. In a classic discussion, Hays suggests that Paul's main tendency is "ecclesiocentric" interpretation: *Echoes of Scripture in the Letters of Paul* (New Haven: Yale University Press, 1989). More recently, Watson has suggested that Paul uses a canonical reading of the Pentateuch (*P&HF*, discussed in detail in §2.1, part three, chapter twelve). Both these scholars, however, concede the presence of numerous christological citations in Paul. And Hays of course argues vigorously for such a reading here, having also moved away somewhat from his earlier claim, which needs to be appreciated carefully in its context: see "On the Rebound: A Response to Critiques of *Echoes of Scripture in the Letters of Paul*," in *Conversion of the Imagination*, 163-89, esp. 186-87.

39. The discussion in chapter seventeen will supplement these claims with a further important explanation related to another intertextual dimension in 1:17.

40. So I am treating the πίστις Χριστοῦ debate in a rather oblique way, but my different angle of approach is arguably more sensitive to the actual shape of the data (and certainly as far as Romans 1–4 is concerned). In this I am taking seriously the suggestion of (i.a.) Hays, that progress in the πίστις Χριστοῦ debate can be made only as the larger shape of Paul's argument is simultaneously introduced and assessed: see "Πίστις and Pauline Christology: What Is at Stake?" in *Pauline Theology*, vol. 4, *Looking Back, Pressing On*, ed. David M. Hay and E. Elizabeth Johnson (Atlanta, Georgia: Scholars, 1997), 38-39; *Faith*, xxiv. An excellent and more recent treatment of just this question is David L. Stubbs, "The Shape of Soteriology and the *pistis Christou* Debate," *Scottish Journal of Theology* 61, no. 2 (2008): 137-57. Later on we will consider the argumentative implications of this reading, along with various possible objections to its various claims. But the latter are best treated when the former task is

complete, since objections are often couched in terms of the broader implications. And those cannot be grasped without further progress first taking place through some of the specific interpretative questions that remain (especially in 3:23-26). More specific, grammatical objections in terms of the article are best treated when v. 25 is discussed in chapter sixteen.

41. 71x in undisputed material, and also in 16:26.

42. Few things can be more deflating to a "turn or burn" theologian than the quiet claim that someone is saved already, provided that he or she is confident enough to make and to sustain that claim under pressure.

43. And such a participatory account should also include the imitative and exemplary language in Paul: see esp. Susan G. Eastman, *Recovering Paul's Mother Tongue: Language and Theology in Galatians* (Grand Rapids, Mich.: Eerdmans, 2007).

44. Colossians 1:4 is arguably a participatory statement; see also, at this point, Eph. 1:15.

45. 151x excluding 16:25-27; 153x including those verses.

46. It is only fair to note that an objective reading of πίστις Ἰησοῦ Χριστοῦ partly alleviates the difficulties of an unstated and changed object for the following participle if that too is referred to Christ, but it *still* creates a baffling line of argument, because the key intertext ostensibly supporting this claim *now supplies a different object (i.e., God)!* The paucity of this object elsewhere in Romans (and Paul) is also a problem. And this object has certainly not been signaled clearly in the anticipation of 3:22 in 1:16b-17 (see OD 20).

47. Using "paradigm" here in the Saussurean sense.

48. This suggestion is addressed in more detail in chapter sixteen.

49. The theory is canvassed reasonably fully in *RRR*, ch. 2. A powerful critique from a slightly different angle is offered by Stephen Fowl, *The Story of Christ in the Ethics of Paul: An Analysis of the Function of the Hymnic Material in the Pauline Corpus*, JSNTSup 36 (Sheffield: JSOT Press, 1990). Without withdrawing my criticisms of the full-fledged "quotation hypothesis," I do think that I left the actual textual data unexplained as a result. It is this shortfall that I try to address here, and in a way that respects Fowl's appropriate concerns with earlier form-critical work.

50. Meaning by this that the text draws on linguistic patterns used by Jews and Christians in various worshipful locations — prayer, etc. This pattern would have been denoted by an earlier generation of New Testament scholars as "liturgical," a designation probably based in part on the panliturgical convictions then attributed mistakenly if not anachronistically to the early church. Scholars of liturgy, however, now reserve this term for ritual public language, and there is no firm evidence that the linguistic pattern I am attributing to Paul here could have overlapped with ritual public language or liturgy in his day. More likely is the supposition that the language of private prayer was patterned at times in this manner.

51. It is important to note that this is not a full-fledged "quotation hypothesis"; Paul wrote this material, but he did so in a particular, distinctive style drawn overtly from the early church's language of worship.

52. Arguably, such expectations are inappropriate culturally in any case.

53. There is also consequently no necessary exclusion of the narrative dimension in Paul's Christology, a legitimate concern of Fowl's in *The Story of Christ in the Ethics of Paul.*

54. I cannot detect a pattern in this material, merely a tendency.

55. For ὁρίζω see Rom. 8:29, 30; 1 Cor. 2:7; 2 Cor. 6:17 (however, here quoting Isa. 52:11 in a disputed text); Gal. 1:15; 2:12; see Eph. 1:5, 11. In the New Testament the term is otherwise primarily Lukan, with ten occurrences. For the rarer ἁγιωσύνη, both other New Testament occurrences are Pauline, although one instance — somewhat curiously — falls into the same disputable passage as ὁρίζω: see 2 Cor. 7:1; and the indubitable 1 Thess. 3:13.

56. A. C. Thiselton is less confident than Fee, Barrett, and Hays that this statement denotes — at least in part — free Christian composition (and appeals to Lietzmann, Conzelmann, and Wolff). While it can be granted that the context is not especially explicit and so this possibly refers to Christian use of the Psalms, to restrict it to such use in the context of Corinth seems unwarranted, because much of that church was previously pagan — and as Thiselton concedes: see *The First Epistle to the*

Corinthians: A Commentary on the Greek Text, NIGTC (Grand Rapids, Mich., Cambridge & Carlisle: Eerdmans & Paternoster, 2000), 1134-35, esp. 1135.

57. We do not know a great deal about the Jewish liturgy at this time; nor is much more known about Greco-Roman forms, especially in the Mysteries.

58. It would have to be argued that the later tradition reset these earlier authentic texts in a ritualized setting. But it would have to be asked why these particular texts were consistently selected, and not others (i.e., in Colossians 1 and Ephesians 1). It seems simpler to suppose that these texts were selected because they were already ritually resonant.

59. Other techniques could also be emphasized here — an unusually high number of genitive constructions, use of cognates and resulting word plays, and parallelism: Andrew Lincoln, *Ephesians*, WBC 42 (Dallas, Tex.: Word, 1990), 12.

60. Ephesians 1 also uses relative clauses to direct subordinate sets of clauses and phrases at subordinate figures in the liturgy — Christ in v. 7 and the Spirit in vv. 13b-14.

61. See the discussion in Lincoln, *Ephesians*, 8-44, esp. 10-19. K. G. Kuhn's observations here should be noted in particular — that this syntax is similar to the liturgical texts at Qumran: see "The Epistle to the Ephesians in the Light of the Qumran Texts," in *Paul and Qumran*, ed. J. Murphy-O'Connor (London: Chapman, 1968), 115-31; see esp. 1QS 11.15; 1QH 13.20-22a [5.20-22a]; 18.14-19 [10.14-19]; 19.27-34 [11:27-34] (*berakah* in 27b, 29, 33); 18.14-15 [16.8] (citations changed to conform to the arrangement in Florentino García Martinez, ed., *The Dead Sea Scrolls Translated*, trans. W. G. E. Watson [Leiden: Brill, 1994]; original references supplied in brackets).

62. The purposive phrase εἰς ἔπαινον [τῆς] δόξης [τῆς χάριτος] αὐτοῦ, repeated three times in vv. 6, 12, and 14, should also be noted especially in this relation.

63. The possible associations of the text with baptism are also potentially important. Lincoln notes the claims made in this relation for Ephesians 1 (*Ephesians*, 18), and the most relevant primary texts (Acts 2:38; Col. 1:14). Possible resonances with wisdom might ultimately prove significant here as well, a linkage especially evident in the Qumran blessings, but evident also in Wis. 7:22 in the broader context of 6:9–11:8.

Notes to Chapter Sixteen

1. Notably Wolfgang Kraus, *Der Tod Jesu als Heiligtumsweihe: Eine Untersuchung zum Umfeld der Sühnevorstellung in Römer 3,25-26a*, WMANT 66 (Neukirchen-Vluyn: Neukirchener Verlag, 1991); see also Daniel P. Bailey, "Jesus as the Mercy Seat: The Semantics and Theology of Paul's Use of *Hilasterion* in Romans 3:25" (Ph.D. thesis, University of Cambridge, 1999). These two studies both suggest alternative narrative routes through Rom. 3:21-26 that will be assessed momentarily.

2. Useful surveys and arguments can be found in Stephen Finlan, *The Background and Content of Paul's Cultic Atonement Metaphors* (Atlanta: Society of Biblical Literature, 2004), 123-62, 200-4; and Robert Jewett, *Romans*, Hermeneia (Minneapolis, Minn.: Fortress, 2007), 284-88. See also my earlier work, although I do not stand by all its arguments and conclusions, as the following analysis shows: see *The Rhetoric of Righteousness in Romans 3:21-26*, JSNTSup 65 (Sheffield: JSOT Press, 1992), esp. 107-13, 130-37 — hereafter *RRR*. Colin Gunton analyzes the theological issues crisply in *The Actuality of the Atonement: A Study of Metaphor, Rationality, and the Christian Tradition* (Edinburgh: T&T Clark, 1998). A classic early discussion that established many of the debate's terms in the English-speaking world is C. H. Dodd, *The Bible and the Greeks* (London: Hodder & Stoughton, 1935). (Dodd prefers "expiation" [etc.] to "propitiation," the former suggesting a process of cleansing, and the latter the placating of an angry deity.) A subtle participatory view is championed especially by scholars from Tübingen and is unjustly neglected in English-speaking circles: it originated in the work of Hartmut Gese: see *Essays on Biblical Theology* (Minneapolis, Minn.: Augsburg Fortress, 1981). More directly relevant to the analysis of Paul are Peter Stuhlmacher's studies, *Reconciliation, Law, and Righteousness: Essays in Biblical Theology*, trans. E. Kalin (Philadelphia: Fortress, 1986 [1975]), esp. "Recent Exegesis on Romans 3.24-26," 94-109; *Der Brief an die Römer* (Göttingen & Zürich: Vandenhoeck & Ruprecht,

1989); and *Biblische Theologie des Neuen Testaments*, vol. 1, *Grundlegung: Von Jesus zu Paulus* (Göttingen: Vandenhoeck & Ruprecht, 1991). This interpretative trajectory is also evident at many points in Bernd Janowski, and Peter Stuhlmacher, eds., *The Suffering Servant: Isaiah 53 in Jewish and Christian Sources* (Grand Rapids, Mich.: Eerdmans, 2004 [1996]). Brevard Childs provides a judicious summary in "Reconciliation with God," *Biblical Theology of the Old and New Testaments* (London: SCM, 1992), 485-529.

3. That is, a universal conception of sacrifice rooted ultimately in Freud (although in dialogue with anthropologists as well), and mediated to Christian scholarship more recently by René Girard: see esp. Robert G. Hamerton-Kelly, *Sacred Violence: Paul's Hermeneutic of the Cross* (Minneapolis: Fortress, 1991). Finlan provides a useful survey: *The Background and Content of Paul's Cultic Atonement Metaphors*, 12-27. See also Jonathan Klawans, *Purity, Sacrifice, and the Temple: Symbolism and Supersessionism in the Study of Ancient Judaism* (New York: Oxford University Press, 2005).

4. Bailey denies that it *ever* denotes an act in the extant evidence, but only objects: see, i.a., *Jesus as the Mercy Seat*, 268. This claim is important, and is almost correct. However, 4 Macc. 17:22 stands against this — an inordinately important text in the present relation. See more on this just below.

5. A complex area, of course, in its own right, as the studies previously listed generally note.

6. See, i.a., David Seeley, *The Noble Death: Graeco-Roman Martyrology and Paul's Concept of Salvation* (Sheffield: JSOT Press, 1990). A classic early work is Walter Burkert, *Homo Necans: The Anthropology of Ancient Greek Sacrificial Ritual and Myth*, trans. Peter Bing (Berkeley & Los Angeles: University of California Press, 1983 [1972]). Martin Hengel provides a crisp summary of the Greco-Roman data in *The Atonement: A Study of the Origins of the Doctrine in the New Testament* (London: SCM, 1981), 1-32.

7. See Bailey, at length: *Jesus as the Mercy Seat*, 145-76; more briefly, see also *RRR*, 109, 111. Bailey's case is definitive — that the absence of the article from a predicate accusative is grammatically not merely innocuous but *necessary*. Hence, the oft-made objection to a reference by the anarthrous ἱλαστήριον in Romans 3:25 to the invariably arthrous mercy seat in the LXX is invalid.

8. See *RRR*, 113-15; S. David Sperling, "Blood," *ABD* 1:761-63.

9. R. Barry Matlock suggests that "it is possible *in principle* to adopt such a reading (with Calvin and others)": see "ΠΙΣΤΙΣ in Galatians 3:26: Neglected Evidence for 'Faith in Christ'?" *New Testament Studies* 49 (2003): 433-39, emphasis original. But presumably he means by this that such a reading is possible if it pays no attention at all to the phrase's immediate settings. My observations here rule this reading out, and Matlock seems to concur with this localized judgment in any case.

10. It *might* be responded that God's faith in Christ's blood could function as a means by which he fulfills his purpose to have Christ's death operate as a ἱλαστήριον, but this is clearly rather odd: "God intended Christ to be a ἱλαστήριον, by means of God's faith in Christ's blood." It needs to be asked just what role God's faith would be playing within this process; it seems both redundant and unparalleled. Similarly, that Christ would have faith in his own blood is a strange instrument assisting God's intention to have him function as a ἱλαστήριον: "God intended Christ to be a ἱλαστήριον, by means of Christ's faith in his blood." Why would Christ's attitude toward his own blood or death be a critical instrument in the purpose of God, one wonders. That this phrase could denote human faith in Christ's blood functioning instrumentally in the purpose of God is, however, simply untenable (and recapitulates the overdetermination already noted at length in relation to 3:22): "God intended Christ to be a ἱλαστήριον, by means of individual faith in his blood." Inserting human faith in Christ's death *instrumentally* (and hence conditionally!) into the purposes of God unfolding between the Father and the atonement of the Son is clearly incoherent. This notion can be accommodated only if further theological material is supplied — for example, some notion of application or appropriation — at which point the statement could arguably make sense. However, such ellipses would need to be justified, and I know of no good arguments that do so. To make matters worse for this reading, a superior reading of the material lies just to hand.

11. Bruce Longenecker's short study (resuming a still briefer suggestion in *RRR*, 64-65) notes the smoothness of this reading in context, and its immediate contextual signals; he does not appeal to the echo of v. 22, because he is approaching the entire debate by way of this text rather than another

point of entry: see "ΠΙΣΤΙΣ in Rom 3.25: Neglected Evidence for the Faithfulness of Christ?" *New Testament Studies* 39 (1993): 478-80. Matlock attempts to provide a partial rejoinder to Longenecker's suggestion, arguing that (1) "we still have three separate elements, with some sense that the second interrupts the other two" ("ΠΙΣΤΙΣ in Galatians 3:26?" 434); and (2) if 𝔓⁴⁶ is secondary to the majority reading of Gal. 3:26, then this is evidence of a (probable!) Greek reader construing that text objectively, and presumably without difficulty (434-39). And this then provides evidence of an objective construal of the genitive, and of a more broadly "objective" understanding of a πίστις ἐν construction. But almost all of Matlock's contentions in this relation are invalid.

His first claim, of an "interruption," is simply wrong, as my analysis shows momentarily. The two phrases, like most of the surrounding hypotactic constructions in 3:21-26, modify preceding notions carefully, in a way that is deliberately enriching in semantic terms. They are informed, moreover, by metonymic and ritual dynamics. Matlock's difficulties on this front should be alleviated if he introduces these insights into his exegesis of Rom. 3:25.

However, his second, primary claim is also problematic. Most seriously, he begs the key question, assuming that the majority text form of Gal. 3:26 is supplying an objective notion of faith. If this were the case, then his further observations would follow. But good reasons can be provided in support of a subjective reference for πίστις throughout most of Galatians 3 (see, i.a., Douglas A. Campbell, *The Quest for Paul's Gospel: A Suggested Strategy* [London: T&T Clark International, 2005], 208-32) at which point his argument collapses (or, at least, devolves to another level). That is, the scribe penning 𝔓⁴⁶ might have read a subjective construction in Gal. 3:26 and reshaped it in accordance with the smoother subjective construction already supplied in 3:22 and, still earlier, in 2:16. It is rather astounding to my mind that Matlock never considers this possibility. The objective sense of the majority text form of Gal. 3:26 is simply asserted by him (437). (These questions are all investigated in detail in part five, chapter twenty.)

But even setting aside these difficulties in his building argument, nothing of real significance seems to follow for Longenecker's case concerning Rom. 3:25 if Matlock is right about Gal. 3:26. One difficulty in the Romans text, much noted, consists not so much in the possible presence of an objective πίστις ἐν construction (which the variants in Gal. 3:26 affirm in Matlock's view) as in the object of that construction being "blood," an unparalleled construction in Paul that Gal. 3:26 does not explain. (Matlock is aware of this issue.) Even this difficulty is arguably not insurmountable. However, the principal difficulties for an objective reading of διὰ [τῆς] πίστεως in Rom. 3:25 derive from what surrounds this statement in Romans. As Longenecker correctly points out, it simply seems best to link "blood" with ἱλαστήριον, and especially in view of the alternative reading's rareness in Paul.

As far as I can tell, Matlock's study leaves all these issues unaddressed, and hence Longenecker's reading intact. It is difficult, then, to detect in what sense Matlock's appeal to Gal. 3:26 "cast[s]" that evidence [i.e., Rom. 3:25] in a different light," as he claims (439; or, indeed, to see how he has in fact provided "neglected semantic evidence for the objective genitive reading of πίστις Χριστοῦ"; 439). Perhaps Matlock's principal point is really that Gal. 3:26 needs to be read consistently with the other instances of πίστις in its context, which certainly seems a fair suggestion. And I will endeavor ultimately to do just this — although the results of such consistency cause difficulties for the objective construal of the genitive, rather than the subjective (see chapter twenty, §6)!

Bailey also criticizes Longenecker's christological reading: see Appendix U, "Πίστις Χριστοῦ and the Syntax of διὰ πίστεως," *Jesus as the Mercy Seat*, 267-68. He suggests that (1) it does not make sense. And in order to make sense (2) a linking participle "accomplished" needs to be added, which cannot "achieve" a ἱλαστήριον, which is an object, not an act like a sacrifice.

An appreciation of the metonymic and narrative function of a christological construal of πίστις speaks to the first objection, however (i.e., such a reading makes excellent sense), at which point the second objection also becomes redundant. This objection also overlooks, in any case, the function of ἱλαστήριον as an event in *4 Macc.* 17:22; the different interpretative possibilities generated by a construal of προέθετο as "purposed"; the possibility that a different participle could be added;

and the parallel function in context of the semantically equivalent ἐν τῷ αὐτοῦ αἵματι. For all these reasons, Bailey's rejection of Longenecker's suggestion for this text should be discounted.

12. The economy, focus, and echoes in this reading therefore mitigate against a reading in terms of God's fidelity, as noted by Alfons Pluta in a widely overlooked but highly cogent study: *Gottes Bundestreue: Ein Schlüsselbegriff in Röm 3,25a* (Stuttgart: Katholisches Bibelwerk, 1969) — Jewett is alert to its importance though: see *Romans*, 270, 283, 284, 287, 288. Longenecker also observes that this would "disrupt the flow [of thought in the text], ἱλαστήριον referring to Christ, πίστις referring to God, and ἐν τῷ αὐτοῦ αἵματι referring again to Christ" ("ΠΙΣΤΙΣ in Romans 3:25?" 479).

13. See Philo, *On the Life of Moses*, 1.90; Josephus, *War*, 1.485; *Antiquities*, 2.272, 283; 10.268; and possibly also 17.327. Matlock is right to correct my suggestion that extant Greek outside Paul contains only half a dozen instances; I ought to have said of course that extant *Jewish* Greek outside Paul supplies that number of instances, having surveyed Philo, Josephus, and the LXX. (And there may be some instances in other Jewish sources outside this principal sample that I have yet to discover.) Matlock then expands my sample by adding examples from Hellenistic sources — from Polybius, Strabo, and Plutarch. See "Detheologizing the ΠΙΣΤΙΣ ΧΡΙΣΤΟΥ Debate: Cautionary Remarks from a Lexical Semantic Perspective," *Novum Testamentum* 42 (2000): 1-23, adding Polybius, *History*, 2.4.8.1 [LCL 2.4.7]; Strabo, 1.3.17; and Plutarch, *Lives*, 5.5.1 [5.4] *(Fabius Maximus)*; 26.6.1 [26.4] *(Pelopidas)*; 43.9.2 [43.5] *(Caius Marius)*; 1.6.3 [1.3] *(Phocion)*; 43.10.2 [43.6]; 55.1.4 [55.1] *(Cato the Younger)*; 47.5.3 [47.3] *(Cicero)*; 29.4.2 [29.3] *(Brutus)*. However, seven of these ten instances are contestable — notably, Polybius (a very doubtful objective genitive: see "[the queen] . . . undertook the details of administration through the trustworthiness of friends" — LCL is rather paraphrastic); Strabo (arguably not: see ". . . to furnish fully a strong proof concerning the works of nature . . ."); Plutarch, 26.4 (probably not, contra LCL: see "the fidelity [or trustworthiness] *of* its justice"); 43.5 (probably not: see ". . . even a pledge of hospitality and/or friendship had no firmness against fate"); 1.3 (probably not: see ". . . making the proof of virtue still weaker"); 55.5 (difficult to say because the second member of the antithesis may be dominating the case of the governed substantive — φόβον τοῦ ἀνδρός); 29.3 (almost certainly not, contra LCL; in context ". . . the trustworthiness/fidelity of his [Brutus's] purpose"). A little ironically, Matlock sometimes proves insensitive here to lexical semantic considerations, overlooking plausible readings based on possible meanings of πίστις that are attested infrequently in the Bible but frequently in Philo, Josephus, et cetera (like "pledge" and "proof": see *Quest*, 178-82). Nevertheless some of these references are certainly correct (i.e., at least three) and ought to be added to the growing sample of attested objective genitive constructions with πίστις. (I would add, further, Justin, *Dialogue with Trypho*, 52.4.) That this sample is now approaching a dozen instances, however, does not seem to suggest that it was a common or even a predictable construction. That this construal of the genitive was possible may certainly be granted, *but it remains extremely rare*. Hence, Paul is still held by the objective reading's advocates to use this construction far more than any other extant contemporary author, with at least six constructions in three letters. (If Plutarch uses it roughly the same number of times, his corpus is nevertheless much more extensive than Paul's.) A Greek auditor would therefore not bring objective expectations initially to this construction, but would need that reading to be suggested *by explicit contextual indicators*. Alternatively, we must posit a private Christian language that used this construction repeatedly — in effect, the position of C. E. B. Cranfield and those arguing like him: "On the Πίστις Χριστοῦ Question," in *On Romans, and Other New Testament Essays* (Edinburgh: T&T Clark, 1998), 81-107. So both these suggested interpretations require explicit evidence in their favor at some point. Consequently this argument from (in)frequency is not in my view decisive, but it ought to be appreciated. It affects the burden of proof.

14. See also 2 Thess. 2:13 (πίστει ἀληθείας/[NRSV] "belief in the truth"), noted (i.a.) by Gordon D. Fee, *Pauline Christology: An Exegetical-Theological Study* (Peabody, Mass.: Hendrickson, 2007), 225; and Phil. 3:8-9 (τῆς γνώσεως Χριστοῦ Ἰησοῦ/"knowing Christ Jesus my Lord"); Rom. 10:2 (ζῆλον Θεοῦ/"zeal for God"); and Acts 3:16 (ἐπὶ τῇ πίστει τοῦ ὀνόματος αὐτοῦ/"faith in his name"), noted by James D. G. Dunn, "Once More, Πίστις Χριστοῦ," in *Pauline Theology*, vol. 4, *Looking Back, Pressing On*, ed. D. M. Hay and E. E. Johnson (Atlanta, Georgia: Scholars Press, 1997), 63 (who notes 2 Thess. 2:13 as well on 64). I am, incidentally, not convinced that Acts 3:16 does supply an objective

genitive construction, but suggest rendering its two instances of πίστις in terms of "proof," and the genitive consequently more as one of content — the proof of God's saving activity in Christ that is supplied by the miraculously healed cripple. However, I concede the other three. Cranfield adds the evidence of Jas. 2:1, Rev. 2:13, and 14:12: "On the Πίστις Χριστοῦ Question," 81-107, here 84-85; however, these instances are all contestable. Nevertheless, most concede that Mark 11:22 is an objective construction, although Ian Wallis demurs, stating — not unfairly — "it is possible that a genitive of origin should be preferred" because often in Judaism "faith was conceived of as an eschatological gift from God" (referring here esp. to *1 Enoch* 108:13; *Third Sibylline Oracles* 584-85; *Testament of Isaac*, 1:8): see *The Faith of Jesus Christ in Early Christian Traditions*, SNTSMS 84 (Cambridge: Cambridge University Press, 1995), 53-54; on this logion in its broader setting, see 24-64. Certainly Wallis succeeds in showing how the interpretation of Mark 11:22 is bound up with much broader and more complex discussions of the portrayal of Jesus and his miracles in the Gospels. Whether this entails a non-objective reading of the genitive construction here is harder to say.

15. See, e.g., Richard B. Hays, *The Faith of Jesus Christ: The Narrative Substructure of Galatians 3:1-4:11*, 2nd ed. (Grand Rapids, Mich.: Eerdmans, 2002), 276-77.

16. See Arland J. Hultgren, "The *Pistis Christou* Formulations in Paul," *Novum Testamentum* 22 (1980): 248-63; Dunn, "Once More," 61-81, esp. 64-66; and Gordon Fee, *Pauline Christology*, 224-25 — formidable scholars ordinarily!

17. Assuming for the moment the correctness of the genitive variant.

18. I am therefore not suggesting here, as do some, that for this reason they *are* functioning in a precise parallel. But this *must* be a possibility, and in the grammatical terms established by 4:16.

19. The context might still overrule a fully arthrous construction in favor of some alternative construal — perhaps objective. But this ought to be signaled incontestably, as it is in Justin, *Dialogue with Trypho*, 52:4.

20. See C. F. D. Moule, *An Idiom Book of New Testament Greek*, 2nd ed. (Cambridge: Cambridge University Press, 1959), 114-15.

21. *Idiom Book*, 117 (leaning here on Middleton). He also notes the occasional demonstrative or deictic function of articles (*Idiom Book*, 111), and the frequent absences of articles in predicate nouns that precede the verb and in similarly positioned names (leaning here on a study by Colwell; *Idiom Book*, 115).

22. א, C*, D*, F, G, 0219^vid, 365, 1505, 1506, 1739, 1881. Note also that Alexandrinus seems so puzzled by the use of πίστις in this paragraph that this entire phrase is omitted from this clause! (see www.csntm.org/Manuscripts/GA%2002/GA02_089a.jpg, consulted 7/18/2007; the scribe also emends [or transcribes] v. 22 to διὰ πίστεως ἐν Χριστῷ Ἰησοῦ!).

23. 𝔓^40vid, B, C³, D², Ψ, 33, 𝔐.

24. And this function suggests a metonymic rather than a titular reading as well. It does not really make sense for Paul to say here that "God intended Christ to be a ἱλαστήριον, by means of the faithful one. . . ." However, a more attributive reading works well: "God intended Christ to be a ἱλαστήριον, by means of that fidelity [i.e., the fidelity evident there, or that enabled it], by means of his blood. . . ."

25. It is implicit in this hypothesis that C³ and D² are correcting their MS in the light of alternative MSS, but this is not improbable.

26. Most notable among the few who have grasped this is Jan W. van Henten: see "The Tradition-Historical Background of Romans 3:25: A Search for Pagan and Jewish Parallels," in *From Jesus to John: Essays on John and New Testament Christology in Honour of Marinus De Jonge*, ed. Martinus C. de Boer (Sheffield: JSOT Press, 1993), 101-28; see also, in this relation, "Zum Einfluss Jüdischer Martyrien auf die Literatur des frühen Christentums, II. Die Apostolischen Väter," in *ANRW* II.27.1 (1993): 700-23; and *The Maccabean Martyrs as Saviours of the Jewish People: A Study of 2 and 4 Maccabees*, JSJSup 57 (Leiden: Brill, 1997), and see esp. 135-63. Among the commentators, Brendan Byrne affirmed this reading in his short preparatory study of Romans, but withdrew it in his later expanded treatment: see *Reckoning with Romans: A Contemporary Reading of Paul's Gospel* (Wilmington, Del.: Michael Glazier, 1986), 81-85; cf. *Romans*, Sacra Pagina (Collegeville, Minn.: Gla-

zier, Liturgical Press, 1996), 126-27, 32-33. The related hypothesis of Sam K. Williams — that Paul is dependent here on *4 Maccabees* — is considered shortly. A useful introductory resource in this relation is Jan van Henten and Friedrich Avemarie, eds., *Martyrdom and Noble Death: Selected Texts from Graeco-Roman, Jewish and Christian Antiquity* (London & New York: Routledge, 2002).

27. In addition to the discourse's occurrence in 2 and *4 Maccabees*, see the Prayer of Azariah, esp. Dan. 3:39-40 LXX. Van Henten also surveys a number of intriguing pagan texts — esp. an inscription from Sardinia describing the sacrificial death of Atilia L. Pomptilla for her ill husband as like Alcestis, if not surpassing that mythical event (and he recovered!): see *Corpus Inscriptionum Latinarum* 10.7577; noted in *The Maccabean Martyrs as Saviours,* 140-63.

28. See also 1:11.

29. See esp. 16:21; 18:15. A connection with the well-known OT discourse of the "righteous sufferer" is apparent here — and this doubtless underlies 2 Cor. 4:13, discussed in detail in part five, chapter twenty-one. Unlike such sufferers, however, the later martyrs are rewarded *posthumously,* with resurrection, as van Henten emphasizes: *The Maccabean Martyrs as Saviours,* 298.

30. It is this set of multiple narrative resonances that overwhelms the far more delicate, alternative narrative suggestions of Kraus and Bailey: respectively, that Jesus is being presented as a new sanctified temple cultus (see *Jubilees* 1:27-29; 4:24-26; 11Q19 [*Temple Scroll*] 29.8-10; and Ezek. 43 — Finlan adds *Targum Isaiah* 53:5 [*Paul's Atonement Metaphors,* 149]), or in accordance with the Song of Moses in Exod. 15:1-18, which speaks of both a new exodus and a new sanctuary. Bailey is drawing here on a suggestion by William Horbury: see "Land, Sanctuary and Worship," in *Early Christian Thought in Its Jewish Context,* ed. John M. G. Barclay, and John Sweet (Cambridge: University Press, 1996), 207-24; "Septuagintal and New Testament Conceptions of the Church," in *A Vision for the Church: Studies in Early Christian Ecclesiology in Honour of J. P. M. Sweet,* ed. Markus Bockmuehl and Michael B. Thompson (Edinburgh: T&T Clark, 1997), 1-17; and "Messianism in the Old Testament Apocrypha and Pseudepigrapha," in *King and Messiah in Israel and the Ancient Near East: Proceedings of the Oxford Old Testament Seminar,* ed. John Day (Sheffield: Sheffield Academic Press, 1998), 402-33. But Kraus's suggestion relies almost entirely on an explicit reference by ἱλαστήριον to the temple, which begs the key questions at this point — that this signifier *only* denotes the Jerusalem cult as against another atoning object or a martyr's death. He also assumes that Paul's language denotes cult establishment and *cleansing* or *sanctification* — notions not explicitly stated. This is not in my view an unfair detection of cultic resonances, for reasons to be noted shortly; however, these fall far short of an extended cultic narrative. And Bailey exaggerates the proximity of the Song of Moses to Rom. 3:21-26 by claiming that, uniquely for the OT, it links "God's saving righteousness and his activity of redeeming people (λυτρόω)" (*Jesus as the Mercy Seat,* 194-95). But Paul *never* uses the verb λυτρόω, let alone in Romans 3:21-26, so this link is dubious. In addition, the scriptural attestation spoken of in v. 21 is explained sufficiently by the analysis of Gen. 15:6 in 4:1-25, which is initiated in relation to Hab. 2:4 in v. 22, and the echo of Ps. 97:2 (LXX) in 3:21-22, which seems corroborated by the echo of Ps. 142:2b (LXX) in 3:20. (These are discussed in detail shortly, principally in chapter seventeen.) Consequently, this creative application of Horbury's elegant suggestion to Rom. 3:21-26 by Bailey seems far-fetched. Both Kraus and Bailey, in short, suffer from overinterpretation. However, both also point fairly to the need for explanations of these key signifiers in any more broadly persuasive interpretation of Rom. 3:21-26 — of the unusual signifier ἱλαστήριον, which probably has *some* cultic resonance, and of the repeated phraseology using δικαιοσύνη, that seems underwritten in some sense by Jewish Scripture.

31. The suggestion most notably of Sam K. Williams, *Jesus' Death as Saving Event: The Background and Origin of a Concept,* HDR 2 (Missoula, Mont.: Scholars, 1975).

32. I suggest that it is probably this stumbling block more than any other that underpins a widespread lack of endorsement for Williams' important thesis (although for interpreters within certain traditions, the dependence of Paul at this critical point on a non- or dubiously canonical text might also be a psychological impediment).

33. I would now go a little further than I did in my earlier work ("Appendix 3: The Date of *4 Maccabees,*" *RRR,* 219-28) and suggest that it is Trajanic or early Hadrianic, rather than later (having thought long and hard about a Gaian provenance as well; I continue to regard E. Bickerman's argu-

ments for a date mid-first century CE as brilliant but ambiguous: "The Date of IV Maccabees," in *Studies in Jewish and Christian History: Part One* (Leiden: Brill, 1976), 275-81). There are indications in 17:23-24 and 18:5 of "Antiochus's" military prowess, especially in siege warfare, *and* a campaign against Persia. In the final years of Trajan's reign a massive campaign against Persia was launched that included the capture of the Persian capital, Ctesiphon (114-16 CE). This coincided with the persecution of Jews when they rose up — a primarily Diaspora phenomenon. Roman repression was severe in Cyprus, Egypt, and Cyrene. Trajan died soon after these events, in August 117 CE (see 18:5, 22), so the dynamics of this period lingered through the first years of Hadrian's reign, when 4 *Maccabees* may actually have been written. A brief summary of these events may be found in Emil Schürer, *The History of the Jewish People in the Age of Jesus Christ*, ed. Geza Vermes, Fergus Millar, and Matthew Black, new rev. English version ed., 3 vols. (Edinburgh: T&T Clark, 1973 [1901-9]), 1:529-34. These events correlate well with the various dynamics apparent in the text, which would then derive from ca. 115-20 CE — some sixty-five years later than Romans — and most likely from Alexandria (although certainty on this last point is both impossible and unnecessary). Schürer (rev.) opines that *The Acts of the Pagan Martyrs* were also written at this time (1:533).

34. See (i.a.) Seeley, *The Noble Death*.

35. Hengel (i.a.) notes that a brief text in Lucan's "Pharsalia" or *Civil War* (composed ca. 55-65 CE) seems close to the language of Paul and 4 *Maccabees* (*The Atonement*, trans. John Bowden [London: SCM, 1981], 23, 24, 88). He refers to Cato's speech to Brutus: "let the pitiless gods have in full Rome's sacrifice of expiation, let us defraud the fighting of no blood. O if only this head, condemned by heaven's gods and Erebus', could be exposed to every punishment! When Decius offered his life, enemy squadrons overwhelmed him: let me be pierced by twin battle-lines, let Rhine's barbarous hordes aim its weapons at me, let me, exposed to all the spears, standing in the midst, receive the wounds of all the war. Let this my blood preserve the people, let this my death atone for all the penalties deserved by Roman morals": see *Lucan: Civil War*, trans. Susan H. Braund (Oxford: Clarendon, 1992), book 2, ll. 304-13 (30) (Hengel quotes the Latin). In fact this is a fragment from another discourse that overlapped with and probably informed Jewish Christian martyrological discussions — the Roman discourse of *devotio*, in which a general deliberately sacrificed himself to turn the wrath of the gods away from Roman forces and their defeat and toward the enemy, or, in the case of Lucan during the civil war, to turn the force of the destructive internecine conflict entirely upon himself. Van Henten points toward P. Decius Mundus and Menoiceius as instances of the former type (and Lucan's Cato refers to the example of Decius): *The Maccabean Martyrs as Saviours of the Jewish People: A Study of 2 and 4 Maccabees* (Leiden: Brill, 1997), 140-63 (and Hengel is alert to this discourse as well). Roman *devotio* was itself a part of a broader discourse of patriotic military martyrdom.

36. It is most likely that this influence began simply with the Hellenization of Judaism in the Second Temple period but was greatly accelerated by the Maccabean crisis, when the deaths of large numbers of pious Jews demanded explanation outside the traditional Deuteronomistic categories. Greco-Roman martyrology provided the appropriate categories — suitably fused with eschatological material! This concern is evident in (i.a.) Daniel, the Greek expansions to Daniel, and 1 and 2 Maccabees (continuing also through 3 *Maccabees*).

37. Paul does not use cleansing language in Romans 3, but that claim is made extensively in Romans 6.

38. LSJ notes elsewhere only Lucian, *Lexiphanes*, 10; Dio Cassius, *Histories*, 59.6; and an instance in Hesychius's lexicography. Van Henten gives a full discussion of the signifier, noting instances also in Ignatius, *Letter to the Ephesians* 21:1; *Letter to the Smyrnaeans* 10:2; *Polycarp*, 2:3 and 6:1; see *The Maccabean Martyrs as Saviours*, 151.

39. 43:14 (3x), 17, 20.

40. LXX: Exod. 25:17, 18, 19, 20 (2x), 21, 22; 31:7; 35:12; 38:5, 7 (2x), 8 (overlooking 26:34; 30:6; 37:6, 7, 8, 9 (2x); 39:35; 40:20, and also 1 Chron. 28:11); Lev. 16:2 (2x), 13, 14 (2x), 15 (2x); Num. 7:89; also Amos 9:1.

41. The term does not seem therefore to evoke the revelatory function of the place, as suggested by Exod. 25:22 and Num. 7:89.

42. See elsewhere only *4 Macc.* 6:29. The phrase ἀντὶ ψυχῆς occurs elsewhere only in Exod. 21:23; Lev. 24:18; and Deut. 19:21.

43. The one arguable exception is the material presently under discussion; however, we are already developing a satisfactory explanation here in other terms, and will consider further arguments shortly that suggest resisting overinterpretation in additional directions (that is, at a fundamental level).

44. More generalized martyrological references in terms of ὁλοκαύτωμα can be found in the Prayer of Azariah (Dan. 3:39 LXX/Theodotion), and the *Martyrdom of Polycarp* 14:1.

45. Arguably, the death of the martyr Isaac, who could be known, like other martyrs, as "a/the righteous one" (i.e., innocent), also creates possible linkages with other texts that discuss "a/the righteous one," the most famous being Isaiah 53 — a possibility already noted in chapter fifteen. Note also that in 4Q225 (psJbᶜ), noted in more detail momentarily, a discussion of Gen. 15:6 segues immediately into a discussion of the birth of Isaac, followed by an account of his near-sacrifice (see also Jas. 2:21-23)!

46. That is, the well-known historiographical trait in the post-Homeric, Hellenistic period that sought to ground and justify many cultic sites and practices in relation to primordial heroes and narratives — often fugitives from Troy: see most famously *The Aeneid*.

47. In a judicious and well-annotated survey, Jewett traces the influence on Pauline analysis — esp. of Romans 8:32 — to a 1946 study by H. J. Schoeps, although broader treatments of the discourse predate this, one of the first exponents in the modern period being Abraham Geiger in "Erbsünde und Versöhnungstod: Deren Versuch in das Judenthums einzudringen," *Jüdische Zeitschrift für Wissenschaft und Leben* 10 (1872): 166-71; see Jewett, *Romans*, 537-38; Schoeps, "The Sacrifice of Isaac in Paul's Theology," *Journal of Biblical Literature* 65 (1946): 385-92, reprised in *Paul: The Theology of the Apostle in the Light of Jewish Religious History*, trans. Harold Knight (London & Philadelphia: Lutterworth Press & Westminster, 1961), 141-49. James D. G. Dunn also supplies a useful overview in *The Theology of Paul the Apostle* (Edinburgh & Grand Rapids: T & T Clark & Eerdmans, 1998), 224-25. More recently, the view is especially associated with Geza Vermes, "Redemption and Genesis XXII: The Binding of Isaac and the Sacrifice of Jesus," in *Scripture and Tradition in Judaism* (Leiden: Brill, 1961 [1973]), 193-227. But see also perceptive studies by Nils Dahl, "The Atonement — an Adequate Reward for the Akedah?" in *Neotestamentica et Semitica: Studies in Honour of Matthew Black*, ed. E. Earle Ellis and Max Wilcox (Edinburgh: T&T Clark, 1969), 15-29; Alan F. Segal, "He Who Did Not Spare His Own Son . . . Jesus, Paul and the Akedah," in *From Jesus to Paul: Studies in Honour of Francis Wright Beare*, ed. John C. Hurd and P. Richardson (Waterloo, Ont.: Wilfrid Laurier University, 1984), 169-84; C. T. Robert Hayward, "The Present State of Research into the Targumic Account of the Sacrifice of Isaac," *Journal of Jewish Studies* 32 (1981): 127-50; "The Sacrifice of Isaac and Jewish Polemic against Christianity," *Catholic Biblical Quarterly* 52 (1990): 292-306; Jon D. Levenson, *The Death and Resurrection of the Beloved Son: The Transformation of Child Sacrifice in Judaism* (London & New Haven: Yale University Press, 1993); Romano Penna, "The Motif of the ʿAqedah against the Background of Romans 8:32," in *Paul the Apostle*, vol. 1, *Jew and Greek Alike* (Collegeville, Minn: Liturgical/Glazier, 1996), 142-68 (and the dominance of Jewish scholars in this interpretative tradition is noteworthy); James C. Vanderkam, "The Aqedah, Jubilees, and Pseudo-Jubilees," in *The Quest for Context and Meaning: Studies in Biblical Intertextuality in Honor of James A. Sanders*, ed. C. A. Evans and S. Talmon, Biblical Interpretation Series 28 (Leiden: Brill, 1997), 241-61; and Bruce N. Fisk, "Offering Isaac Again and Again: Pseudo-Philo's Use of the Aqedah as Intertext," *Catholic Biblical Quarterly* 62 (2000): 481-507. The story's importance for Matthew has recently been argued at length by Leroy Huizenga, "The Akedah in Matthew" (Ph.D. thesis, Duke University, 2006).

48. Most notably in B. Chilton and P. Davies, "The Aqedah: A Revised Tradition History," *Catholic Biblical Quarterly* 40 (1978): 514-46; see also W. D. Davies, "Passover and the Dating of the Aqedah," *Journal of Jewish Studies* 30 (1979): 59-67. J. F. Fitzmyer also expresses his skepticism in a learned discussion: "The Sacrifice of Isaac in Qumran Literature," *Biblica* 83 (2002): 211-29.

49. A less extreme form can certainly be granted — that the destruction of Jerusalem probably further emphasized the Akedah, along with other alternative modes of atonement.

50. Geza Vermes, "New Light on the Sacrifice of Isaac from 4Q225," *Journal of Jewish Studies* 47 (1996): 140-46.

51. This "correlative" evidence provides important additional support for the entire explanation. There are too many overlaps for the Jewish and early Christian discourses to be in a coincidental relationship; and influence from the Christian to the Jewish tradition at this point is highly unlikely. (Certainly there is no evidence of this.) Prima facie then a Jewish influence on the early Christian tradition — if not on Jesus himself — looks likely.

52. Bailey supports the more traditional rendering in terms of "the mercy seat," and a primary echo of Leviticus 16, and so is well aware that he must marginalize the evidence of 4 Maccabees 17:22. He suggests that the author of 4 Maccabees probably drew the term ἱλαστήριον from its normal Hellenistic sense of a "propitiatory votive offering" (*Jesus as the Mercy Seat*, 142; see also 93-142). He then posits two completely separate semantic developments for *4 Maccabees* 17:22 and Rom. 3:25. Both authors end up with the same signifier coincidentally, but mean very different things by them, and they derived them, moreover, in utterly independent ways. This argument clears the way for a reading of ἱλαστήριον in terms of "the mercy seat." But there are four significant problems with this case: (1) Bailey asserts that *4 Maccabees* 17:22 is an overtly different usage from Romans 3:25, and so excludes it, *before* he has considered the meaning of Romans 3:25! This reveals the presence of a rigid underlying agenda in his study — a commitment to the reading "mercy seat" prior to his consideration of key pieces of evidence. (2) The ostensible Hellenistic sense of ἱλαστήριον as an object with a propitiatory votive function seems to be smoothly applicable to the Levitical usage, not different from it, as Bailey claims. This "Hellenistic" construal suggests merely that the lid of the ark of the covenant — or some key part of Ezekiel's future altar — *is* the divinely-appointed atoning object — an unexceptionable reading. The main disagreement in the relevant sources is therefore not *lexical*, over the meaning of terms, but *theological*, over which object is legitimately and singularly atoning! (3) It is clear that the author of *4 Maccabees* knew Jewish tradition, and the texts underlying Yom Kippur in particular. He even alludes to these directly, as we have already seen! So it seems certain that the signifier ἱλαστήριον in *4 Maccabees* 17:22 is being informed by Judaism, and is not a monolithically "Hellenistic" development (the latter claim being an outmoded one in any case — that Judaism was somehow sealed off from Hellenistic culture, and so such independent lexicographical developments could confidently be supposed to have taken place; this false assumption has already been noted in part one, chapter four). (4) The two deployments of the signifier are actually very similar — in the narrative settings of heroic, faithful martyrs dying horrible deaths, and hoping to achieve something vicariously atoning by way of this. They also die in the firm expectation of resurrection. In the light of these parallels — which far outweigh the parallels between Romans 3:25, and the cultus and Yom Kippur — the claim that the two authors derived and applied the signifier ἱλαστήριον to their stories *completely independently of one another* is implausible. Indeed, the converse is clearly the case; both authors are using the same signifier for much the same reasons — reasons that do not exclude the cultus and Yom Kippur, but stretch beyond that single denotation, as many of the other extant Greek instances indicate (see esp. Josephus, *Antiquities,* 16.182).

53. Today's NIV references "the atonement cover on the ark of the covenant" and Lev. 16:15, 16, thereby having its cake and eating it in lexical terms.

54. See also a translation that inserts the expectations of Justification theory into the text still more markedly — "a sacrifice to pay for sins" (New International Reader's Version).

55. The translation of ἱλαστήριον as "a sacrifice of atonement" or some similar sense is probably the preferred modern rendering, translating the more archaic notion of "propitiation," which nevertheless has the virtue of emphasizing the placating of an angry deity. The modern translation is especially sensitive to the emphasis in context on "blood," and assumes that Paul *ought* to be speaking at this point of some sort of sacrificial payment for the sins of the world, which have just been exposed in 1:18–3:20. However, it strains the largely invariable sense of the signifier when it is used elsewhere in Koiné. Bailey's observation is broadly correct: "in Greek, a ἱλαστήριον is never an act of 'sacrifice'" (268); it is always — with the important partial exception of *4 Macc.* 17:22 — an object or a thing. So this entire approach to translation is lexically dubious (that is, unless other arguments are supplied).

This is not to exclude an atoning or reconciling function from the object, or part of an object, so designated, but the signifier points primarily to a concrete reference and must include that.

56. The translation of ἱλαστήριον as "[the] mercy seat" is better than the previous option. It can draw on the thread of cultic imagery running through Romans that has already been noted. But there are several problems. We should note first the issue of sheer recognizability. The mercy seat had ample textual attestation in the OT (principally in Leviticus and Ezekiel), but was lost along with the rest of the ark of the covenant in any real or concrete sense since the Babylonian invasion in the sixth century BCE, and so does not seem to have been viewed as a necessary cultic item after that; Philo, Josephus, and the Mishnah consequently do not mention it at all in their detailed descriptions of the temple and Yom Kippur (see Philo, *On the Special Laws*, 1.72, 188; Josephus, *Jewish Antiquities*, 8.63-98; *m. Yoma*, 5.1-3). Hence, the motif is only later recovered *in literary terms* by those both able and motivated enough to do so (see Philo, *On the Cherubim*, 25; *On Flight and Finding*, 100; *On the Life of Moses*, 2.95, and 97; *4 Macc.* 17:22; Heb. 9:5). Presumably Paul was adept enough to do this if he wanted to, but such a recovery needs to be clearly signaled, and without this (or even with it) his auditors might have been taxed! And in Rom. 3:25 any such recovery is being activated by the signifier itself, which begs the key question (perhaps with assistance ultimately from the phrase περὶ ἁμαρτίας in Rom. 8:3; see Lev. 16:3, 5, 6, 9, 11 [2x], 15, 16, 21, 25, 27 [2x], 30, 34). The argument that Paul's claim of attestation from the Pentateuch in v. 21 affirms this reading is not convincing; in context this must point initially to Gen. 15:6. And the motif of "blood" is too generalized to denote either the temple or Yom Kippur automatically. It is therefore a highly abbreviated, even cryptic reading. (Note, by way of contrast, how much detail Hebrews 9 supplies in order to make the comparison explicit.) And this reading still does not explain Paul's subtle utilization of a cultic discourse throughout Romans. It *participates* in that discourse comfortably, but does not *explain* it. It must also be an explicitly metaphorical reading, to accommodate Paul's later expansion ἐν τῷ αὐτοῦ αἵματι (which refers to an atoning event). And this is unparalleled in extant Greek instances, except for *4 Macc.* 17:22. It seems then — in sum — that a reading of ἱλαστήριον in Romans 3:25 in terms of "mercy seat" is an overly delicate reading. Arguably it remains possible, but it is cryptic, thinly justified, complex, and somewhat unsatisfactory. Conversely, a reading in terms of *4 Macc.* 17:22, and the underlying Akedah tradition, as we have just seen above, seems well attested, rather simpler, also rather more obvious, and satisfying in explanatory terms. It seems, in short, to be decisively superior.

57. Douglas A. Campbell, "The Story of Jesus in Romans and Galatians," in *Narrative Dynamics in Paul: A Critical Assessment*, ed. B. W. Longenecker (Louisville, Ky.: Westminster John Knox, 2002), 97-124 (repr. *Quest*, 69-94).

58. Other less popular attempts to render its exact sense more precisely in English include "to set right," "to rectify," and "to rightwise." For some general introductory remarks to "the Righteousness Debate" see my *RRR*, 138-56. But the following material updates my broad remarks and the specific analysis of δικαιόω offered on 166-76. Much of the voluminous literature on this question is unhelpful: (1) it is oriented toward the meaning of Paul's supposed key phrase δικαιοσύνη Θεοῦ, so that debate and evidence overwhelm the specific contributions of the verb (it is also best noted when I discuss the noun phrase in detail in chapter seventeen); (2) it addresses the construct "Justification" in Paul, thereby drawing on a great deal of material beyond the evidence of the verb (see my analysis of Justification theory in part one, chapter one); and (3) it fails to make certain critical linguistic distinctions in terms of performative speech-acts, thereby skewing the presentation of the lexical data (see BDAG, 249). The following discussion of the cognate verb deliberately precedes analysis of the noun phrase, focuses on the immediate evidence, utilizes the key methodological distinctions, and is meant to stand independently of any later discussions (at least in the first instance).

59. The *Letter of Aristeas* contains a charming account of the release of large numbers of Jews enslaved ostensibly by Ptolemy, son of Lagos (13). ἀπολύτρωσις is used in vv. 12 and 33 to denote their release. This story, and word use, is then reproduced by Josephus (*Antiquities* 12.27). Philo produces an analogous story of a young enslaved Spartan, who despairs of ἀπολύτρωσις and commits suicide (*That Every Good Person Is Free*, 114). But Philo also provides a more generalized, metaphorical usage, although a complex one. He speaks here of Abraham interceding literally for

Sodom but figuratively for God's mercy to fall on the barren and blinded soul, freeing it to return to him (*On the Preliminary Studies*, 109). There is no mention of a payment in this story; the release is effected by God's mercy and Abraham's intercession (or, alternatively, by humility). Plutarch's account of Pompey includes a brief allusion to those taken captive by the pirate scourge that Pompey eliminated (*Life of Pompey*, 24.5). An inscription from Cos likewise uses ἀπολύτρωσις as part of the technical regulation of a process of manumission (*Inscriptions from Cos*, ed. Paton and Hicks, no. 29; it can be viewed in the original at www.csad.ox.ac.uk/Kos/PH29). The word is linked specifically with (probably) "the magistrate's registration of release" (see lines 6-7: τὰν ἀναγραφὰν] [τὰν δαμοσίαν τ]ᾶς ἀπολυτρώσιος). In view of this evidence, it is entirely understandable that the signifier could be applied to the exodus, as it is by Justin (*Dialogue with Trypho*, 86.1). Intriguingly, the only LXX occurrence — Dan. 4:34 [G LXX] — is more metaphorical, but consistent with this developing picture; the setting is Nebuchadnezzar's "day of release" from his seven years of madness and sinfulness. No ransom is present, only a humble intercession (see Philo, *On the Preliminary Studies*, 107-9).

The instance in Diodorus Siculus is indecisive, although generally informative (see *Fragments*, 37.5.3). The signifier occurs in the broader setting of an account of the famously efficient and fair governorship of Asia in 97 CE by Quintus Mucius Scaevola (37.5.1-6 [omitting §5a]). Its narrower setting is Scaevola's rapid crucifixion of the leading extortionate local "publican," after his conviction, but before his bribes and deals with the authorities could effect his "liberation" or "freedom." So it is impossible to tell if ἀπολύτρωσις correlates in this story only with the corrupt official's freedom from trial, imprisonment, and pending death — so "release" — or also with the promised gifts of money and favours — so "ransom." Either reading is possible, although the former seems more likely (because the governor himself, who caused the trial, could not be bribed). This instance *does* demonstrate clearly, however, that the signifier is closely correlated — irrespective of any monetary associations — with release from confinement or bondage, which is here imposed in an explicitly judicial fashion. This slave sought "release" if not "liberation from" his charges and closely related imprisonment.

The New Testament evidence is consistent with this, most notably in Rom. 8:23 and Heb. 11:35, which overtly denote release from bondage. Otherwise, the New Testament evidence is significantly eschatological, especially Rom. 8:23; Eph. 1:14; 4:30; and Luke 21:28. It is of course difficult to introduce a ransom payment into the *future* redemption of Christians, but the basic notion of release from the bondage of the present age remains appropriate. The occurrences in Rom. 3:24; Eph. 1:7; Col. 1:14; and Heb. 9:15 are oriented toward transgressions.

60. BDAG therefore arguably errs in making this notion part of the signifier's "original" meaning, which is rooted in the concrete situation of "'buying back' a slave or captive, i.e., 'making free' by payment of a ransom," thereby perhaps implying its ongoing relevance (117). This builds a lot on one attested instance (i.e., the inscription from Cos). Nevertheless, read carefully, BDAG correctly suggests that the other, metaphorical uses of the signifier need carry no necessary connotation of ransom or payment but denote release from either a painful interrogation or a captive condition (and presumably the former presupposed the latter).

61. Rom. 1:23 also indicates this connection when a foolish humanity exchanges τὴν δόξαν τοῦ ἀφθάρτου θεοῦ for ὁμοιώματι εἰκόνος κ.τ.λ.; see also *Apocalypse of Moses* 20:2; 21:6; 39:2-3; 1QS 4.23; 4Q504 (DibHamᵃ, Bt 3) Fragment 8.4, 7. More broadly, see W. D. Davies, *Paul and Rabbinic Judaism: Some Rabbinic Elements in Pauline Theology*, 4th ed. (London: SPCK, 1980 [1948]), 36-57; Robin Scroggs, *The Last Adam: A Study in Pauline Anthropology* (Philadelphia: Fortress, 1966); and Dunn, *The Theology of Paul the Apostle*, 79-101, esp. 93-94 (Dunn affirming this echo and pressing it rather further than I do); see also *Romans 1-8*, WBC 38A (Dallas, Tex.: Word, 1988), 167-68. Jewett concurs, but sees an honor-shame dynamic suggested by Paul's use here of the verb ὑστερέω, which often meant "failure to reach a goal, *to be inferior to someone*, to fail, to come short of something" (*Romans*, 280, emphasis added). This is an important potential insight, but I am unsure whether it is valid here; the verb is seldom used in this sense elsewhere in Paul (see 1 Cor. 1:7; 8:8; 12:24; 2 Cor. 11:9; Phil. 4:12), and when it is, a comparison is clearly signaled (see 2 Cor. 11:5; 12:11).

62. This explains the puzzling equation between the poor and the righteous that occurs fre-

quently in the Old Testament. They are "innocent" and hence "in the right" in terms of their economic oppression.

63. Drawing here on J. L. Austin and J. Searle, whose insights are often neglected by New Testament interpreters. (I was first introduced to this material by Alan Torrance.) But see A. C. Thiselton's fascinating analyses in *1 Corinthians: The First Epistle to the Corinthians: A Commentary on the Greek Text*, NIGTC (Grand Rapids, Mich. & Cambridge & Carlisle: Eerdmans & Paternoster, 2000), with uses indexed on 1372, 76, and 91; see esp. 456-58; and A. Brown, *The Cross and Human Transformation* (Minneapolis: Fortress, 1995). Mark Seifrid makes use of this material in this relation as well, having being introduced to it by Oswald Bayer: "The Narrative of Scripture and Justification by Faith: A Still Fresher Reading of Paul," paper presented to a *Symposium on Exegetical Theology* (Concordia Theological Seminary, Fort Wayne, Ind.: 2006), 20, n. 61. Francis Watson also makes occasional use of this material: see (i.a.) *Text and Truth: Redefining Biblical Theology* (Edinburgh: T&T Clark, 1997), 98-103, 124.

Thiselton's applications are perhaps the most sophisticated. He skillfully reinterprets the enduring conundrum in Justification theory caused by God's declaration of the ungodly righteous in what amounts to a legal fiction. He suggests that this is an anticipatory statement of who "counts" as righteous on the last day — a linguistic phenomenon widely grounded in everyday language. I concede the plausibility of this explanation, but argue in chapter fourteen and here that this is not in fact what Paul is doing with this language, as he engages with the claims of the Teacher. (Thiselton is still working within the basic parameters of Justification theory, assuming that God is engaged with some sort of factually [in]accurate, eschatological judgment — the claim, in my view, of the Teacher.) Paul's point is rather simpler: God has declared humanity free in Christ, and therefore begun to effect this (i.e., it is a performative speech-act). Moreover, this act sets free those who could not set themselves free, and did not deserve to be set free (i.e., the ungodly). Nevertheless the God of grace, as revealed definitively by Christ, has done this.

64. Seifrid points out that this is a constative utterance ("Narrative of Scripture," 21) — one that makes a claim about a situation that can then be evaluated as either correct or incorrect. Note, however, that this is a peculiarly difficult constative utterance, which only God can make — a judgment concerning the ethical condition of every person.

65. Verses 7 and 8 could be coordinated through apposition, but nothing changes whichever coordination is asserted. I incline toward supplying an elided verb because of the shift in number and the complexity of the sentences that would otherwise have to be coordinated. Moreover, an elided verb *has* to be supplied to vv. 9-10, and these sentences seem to be arranged with vv. 8-9 chiastically.

66. We have already encountered a good example of this when investigating the meaning of ἀπολύτρωσις — the account in Diodorus Siculus of the just governorship of Asia in 97 CE by Quintus Mucius Scaevola (*Fragments*, 37.5.1-6 [omitting §5a]), which was famous and exemplary because it was just! An important link with patronage is also evident here: see, i.a., Richard A. Horsley, ed., *Paul and Empire* (Harrisburg, Pa.: Trinity Press International, 1997), 88-137. Material collated in relation to Paul's trials is also indicative: see H. W. Tajra, *The Trial of St. Paul*, WUNT 2:35 (Tübingen: J. C. B. Mohr [Siebeck], 1989); and Brian Rapske, *The Book of Acts in Its First Century Setting*, vol. 3, *Paul in Roman Custody* (Carlisle & Grand Rapids, Mich.: Paternoster & Eerdmans, 1994).

67. Which is not to claim that modern Western courts are perfect; in a North American setting, the era of Jim Crow legislation is relatively recent, being dismantled (in part) only after 1955 and 1965. There is nevertheless a far stronger commitment to impartiality now than was generally the case in premodern times (a partly positive legacy of Constantinianism?).

68. An insight further assisted by James C. Scott's insights: see esp. *Domination and the Arts of Resistance: Hidden Transcripts* (New Haven, Conn., & London: Yale University Press, 1990).

69. Examples of such generally magnanimous acts are not limited to God. The *Letter of Aristeas* describes a similar magnanimous act by the ruler of Egypt, as a hundred thousand Jewish slaves are released and paid for principally as a gesture of goodwill (12, 14-27). See (probably) Sir. 26:29; and (possibly) *Testament of Simeon* 6:1.

70. These generally require a dynamic functional translation. I know of no way to convey the

correct meaning with a traditional stem that then conveys the wordplays in the underlying Greek as well — some variation on "right" or "just."

71. This is therefore a particularly important insight in the work of Elsa Tamez: see *The Amnesty of Grace: Justification by Faith from a Latin American Perspective,* trans. S. H. Ringe (Nashville, Tenn.: Abingdon, 1993); and "Justification as Good News for Women: A Re-Reading of Romans 1–8," in *Celebrating Romans: Template for Pauline Theology, Essays in Honor of Robert Jewett,* ed. Sheila E. McGinn (Grand Rapids, Mich.: Eerdmans, 2004), 177-89. And see also in this relation esp. Miroslav Volf, *Free of Charge: Giving and Forgiving in a Culture Stripped of Grace* (Grand Rapids, Mich.: Zondervan, 2005).

Note that "vindication" is a better translation option than "justification," but still not ideal, because it maintains a connotation of "rightness" in the figure who is being vindicated, and therefore cannot denote a purely performative act (see BDAG 249).

72. With these distinctions in place, a reading of Paul's Justification material becomes possible that can move around the vexed question of the nature of justice in any case. *Whatever* the exact content of "justice" in the Teacher's gospel — and it looks fundamentally retributive — Paul rejects it, preferring a fundamentally different definition of the divine character (i.e., one best not characterized by justice at all, in any sense). On the question of the nature or content of "justice" see chapter seventeen.

73. "Rom. 6.7: ὁ γὰρ ἀποθανὼν δεδικαίωται ἀπὸ τῆς ἁμαρτίας," *New Testament Studies* 10 (1963): 104-8.

74. It is worth noting that Paul uses the signifier ἀπολύτρωσις close by these claims, in 8:23. It is not so much the presence of this distinctive signifier but its operation in a broader argument presupposing slavery that reinforces still further the liberative connotations of Paul's δικαιο- terminology, when he begins to use that in v. 30. Note also that 1 Cor. 6:11 conforms exactly to this usage as well. (I would not include 1 Tim. 3:16 here, however.)

75. Paul is of course aware that the metaphor of slavery could be developed in relation to Christians by way of a price: see 1 Cor. 6:19b-20a; 7:23. However, that argument is rare, rather vestigial, and is never used in Romans. It is also, in any case, arguably compatible with the contingent emphases that Paul is developing in Rom. 3:24. The Christ event costs God a great deal; therefore, Paul urges an appropriate *response* to that "payment" in 1 Corinthians, when Christians are involved in serious ethical lapses. However, that costly salvation is still offered to Christians freely, the point Paul wishes to make here in Romans. Dietrich Bonhoeffer captured the distinction perfectly with his aphorism that grace is free but not cheap: see *The Cost of Discipleship* (London: SCM, 1959 [1937]; reprint, Touchstone 1995).

76. See Mark Seifrid, *Justification by Faith: The Origin and Development of a Central Pauline Theme,* NovTSup 68 (Leiden: Brill, 1992). The following translations are by R. B. Wright from *The Old Testament Pseudepigrapha,* vol. 2, *Expansions of the "Old Testament" and Legends, Wisdom and Philosophical Literature, Prayers, Psalms, and Odes, Fragments of Lost Judeo-Hellenistic Works,* ed. James H. Charlesworth (New York: Doubleday, 1985), 651-70.

77. See the application of George Lakoff's explanations to Justification theory in part one, chapter one, esp. §5: see *Moral Politics: How Liberals and Conservatives Think,* 2nd ed. (London & Chicago: University of Chicago, 2001 [1996]).

78. E. P. Sanders provides an insightful survey in *Paul, the Law, and the Jewish People* (Philadelphia: Fortress Press, 1983), 305-12. Philip Alexander's views of Qumran piety have already been noted in part one, chapter four, where the community's emphasis on "perfection of way" was also emphasized. Translations from Florentino García Martinez, ed., *The Dead Sea Scrolls Translated,* trans. W. G. E. Watson (Leiden: Brill, 1994).

79. We will have frequent cause in what follows to note other important juxtapositions and reclamations on Paul's part of terms and axioms from the Teacher's system.

80. See my *RRR,* 31-32, 45-51; see also esp. Dio Chrysostom, *Thirtieth Discourse: Charidemus,* 30.19 (almost certainly "release from . . ."); Dionysius of Halicarnassus, *The Roman Antiquities,* 7.37.2 ("release" or "forgiveness," in the broader setting of the trial of Coriolanus); and Appian, *Basilica,* 13.1 ("overlook"/"pass over"). The occurrences of ἄφεσις and ἀπολύω frequently in the immediate settings

of these instances is to my mind highly significant, given the liberative connotations that are detectable throughout Rom. 3:21-26. Most commentators and BDAG (116) are influenced by possible readings of the cognate verb, which Paul never uses, along with the conventional reading of Romans 1–3 of course. (The verb occurs in the New Testament in this sense only in Luke 11:42.) Thomas Tobin comes to a similar conclusion as I do here — "remission" — but in the light primarily of the evidence in Phalaris, *Epistle* 81.1: *Paul's Rhetoric in Context: The Argument of Romans* (Peabody, Mass.: Hendrickson, 2004), 135, n. 18.

It is worth noting that the noun and cognate verb often mean "weak" and hence "paralysis/paralyzed" (see Heb. 12:12). This meaning works surprisingly well in 3:25, where it would point to the problem more than the solution; however, the entire statement seems to be echoed by other New Testament statements in terms of ἀπολύτρωσις and ἄφεσις τῶν ἁμαρτίων (see esp. Eph. 1:7; Col. 1:14). This repeated, even patterned usage points to a formulaic and hence liberative sense (see also — rather importantly — Heb. 9:15 and its immediate setting).

81. Here Jonathan takes the initiative against his enemy and does not offer him "the opportunity" (NRSV), or "respite," to attack him.

82. Another military setting: Aristobulus hopes for some "respite," so that he can raise another army to fight the Romans. But they wait only two days before attacking him in Machaerus and capturing him.

83. Very much the same as the two preceding instances, although here involving "Galadenians." They hope for seven days of respite to summon reinforcements.

84. Sheep tangled in a valley in thorns and thistles, miserable and beaten, who are in a "wretched plight" and "receive no *rest.*"

85. Here in a possible contrast with ἀπολύω!

86. The setting is explicitly enslaved — "They will put you in bonds, and you will not have (an opportunity for) rest and supplication, because you have taught injustice. . . ."

87. I don't know of an English adjective that specifically suggests the introduction of some sort of respite, as the Greek here really demands. So a genitive of separation is perhaps a better reading.

88. See Leander Keck, "Jesus in Romans," *Journal of Biblical Literature* 108 (1989): 443-60. That the phrase, read in this way, anticipates Rom. 4:16 (τῷ ἐκ πίστεως Ἀβραάμ) is *not* to my mind an argument in favor of reading the πίστις construction in 3:26 subjectively, as some have suggested. This later text merely demonstrates the christocentric *possibility* for 3:26, although this is really obvious in any case.

89. One phrase speaks of "the release from previously occurring sins" effected by the Christ event, but it functions hypotactically. The emphasis of the most significant repeated phrases is on Christ's definitive disclosure of God.

90. It is tempting to supply "lives" here, in view of the preceding argumentative consideration concerning Hab. 2:4; see . . . εἰς τὸ εἶναι αὐτὸν δίκαιον καὶ δικαιοῦντα τὸν ζόντα ἐκ πίστεως or "the one who lives by faithfulness. . . ." (And this temptation is especially difficult to resist given that interpreters are so used to supplying a participle at this point). But this is also unnecessary. The text is too controversial and important to analyze in terms of ellipses if a plausible reading can be supplied that does not need to make appeals to such notions. An alternative, rather plausible suggestion is the supply of "justified," which could be elided on grounds of overt stylistic redundancy — εἰς τὸ εἶναι αὐτὸν δίκαιον καὶ δικαιοῦντα τὸν δικαιούμενον ἐκ πίστεως Ἰησοῦ[ν]. But, again, this temptation should probably be resisted.

Notes to Chapter Seventeen

1. Among the commentators, see esp. C. E. B. Cranfield, *A Critical and Exegetical Commentary on the Epistle to the Romans*, vol. 1, *Introduction and Commentary on Romans I-VIII*, ICC (London: T&T Clark International [Continuum], 2004 [1975]), 92-99; *A Critical and Exegetical Commentary on the Epistle to the Romans*, vol. 2, *Commentary on Romans I-XVI and Essays*, ICC (London: T&T Clark

International [Continuum], 2004 [1979]), 824-33; James D. G. Dunn, *Romans 1–8*, WBC 38A (Dallas, Tex.: Word, 1988), 40-42; *The Theology of Paul the Apostle* (Edinburgh & Grand Rapids: T&T Clark & Eerdmans, 1998), 334-89, esp. 340-46; Peter Stuhlmacher, *Der Brief an die Römer* (Göttingen & Zürich: Vandenhoeck & Ruprecht, 1989), 30-33; Joseph A. Fitzmyer, *Romans: A New Translation with Introduction and Commentary*, AB 33 (New York: Doubleday, 1993), 257-63; Douglas Moo, *The Epistle to the Romans*, NICNT (Grand Rapids, Mich.: Eerdmans, 1996), 70-75; Brendan Byrne, *Romans*, Sacra Pagina (Collegeville, Minn.: Glazier, Liturgical Press, 1996), 52-54, 57-60; Thomas R. Schreiner, *Romans*, BECNT (Grand Rapids, Mich.: Baker, 1998), 63-71; N. Thomas Wright, "The Letter to the Romans: Introduction, Commentary, and Reflections," in *New Interpreter's Bible*, 12 vols., ed. L. Keck (Nashville, Tenn.: Abingdon, 2002), 10:397-406; Ben Witherington III, with Darlene Hyatt, *Paul's Letter to the Romans: A Socio-Rhetorical Commentary* (Grand Rapids, Mich.: Eerdmans, 2004), 52-54.

For surveys and discussions see Manfred T. Brauch, "Perspectives on 'God's Righteousness' in Recent German Discussion," in E. P. Sanders, *Paul and Palestinian Judaism* (Philadelphia: Fortress, 1977), 523-42; see also Sanders's more detailed discussions in 2-4, 9, 304-12, 470-511; also in *Paul, the Law and the Jewish People* (Philadelphia: Fortress, 1983), *passim*; and in *Paul, Past Masters* (Oxford: Oxford University Press, 1991), 44-76; see my *The Rhetoric of Righteousness in Romans 3:21-26*, JSNTSup 65 (Sheffield: JSOT Press, 1992), 138-56 — hereafter *RRR*; see also Richard B. Hays, "Justification," in *ABD* 3:1129-33; and J. Reumann, "Righteousness (Early Judaism/Greco-Roman World/ NT)," *ABD* 5:736-73. Reumann's other discussions are also exemplary: (with responses by Joseph A. Fitzmyer and Jerome D. Quinn), *"Righteousness" in the New Testament: "Justification" in the United States Lutheran-Roman Catholic Dialogue* (Philadelphia, Pa., New York & Ramsey, N.J.: Fortress & Paulist, 1982); and *Variety and Unity in New Testament Thought* (Oxford: Oxford University Press, 1991), where he argues for a central canonical role for this motif; see also K. L. Onesti and M. T. Brauch, "Righteousness, Righteousness of God," in *DP&L*, ed. Gerald F. Hawthorne and Ralph P. Martin (Leicester & Downers Grove, Ill.: InterVarsity), 827-37; Alister E. McGrath, "Justification," in *DP&L*, 517-23; see also his well-known church-historical study *Iustitia Dei: A History of the Christian Doctrine of Justification*, 3rd ed. (Cambridge: University Press, 2005), already noted in part two, chapter eight; see also Jouette M. Bassler, "The Righteousness of God," in *Navigating Paul: An Introduction to Key Theological Concepts* (London & Louisville, Ky.: Westminster John Knox, 2007), 49-69. Bruno Blumenfeld provides an intriguing, politically-charged analysis of righteousness in Paul in *The Political Paul: Justice, Democracy and Kingship in a Hellenistic Framework*, JSNTSup 210 (Sheffield: Sheffield Academic Press, 2001), 415-50. Especially influential in conservative circles (although not uncontested, even there) are Mark Seifrid's many studies: see, i.a., *Justification by Faith: The Origin and Development of a Central Pauline Theme*, NovTSup 68 (Leiden: Brill, 1992); *Christ, Our Righteousness: Paul's Theology of Justification*, New Studies in Biblical Theology 9 (Downers Grove, Ill.: InterVarsity Press, 2000); and "The Narrative of Scripture and Justification by Faith: A Still Fresher Reading of Paul" (paper presented at the Symposium on Exegetical Theology, Concordia Theological Seminary, Fort Wayne, Ind., January 2006); see also numerous relevant studies — including several more by Seifrid — in D. A. Carson, Peter T. O'Brien, and Mark A. Seifrid, eds., *Justification and Variegated Nomism*, vol. 1, *A Fresh Appraisal of Paul and Second Temple Judaism*, WUNT 2/140 (Tübingen: Mohr-Siebeck, 2001); and D. A. Carson, Peter T. O'Brien, and Mark A. Seifrid, eds., *Justification and Variegated Nomism*, vol. 2, *The Paradoxes of Paul*, WUNT 2/181 (Tübingen: Mohr Siebeck, 2004). These volumes are supposedly a trenchant critique of "the new perspective." But in fact (and as has already been noted in part one, chapter four) Volume 1 contains much nuanced descriptive material concerning Paul's Jewish background. Volume 2 is, however, a detailed endorsement by various conservative scholars of Justification theory in Paul, and its associated conventional readings, including in relation to Paul's righteousness terminology. An insight into another aspect of German debate can be found in Udo Schnelle, *Apostle Paul: His Life and Theology*, trans. M. Eugene Boring (Grand Rapids, Mich.: Baker, 2005 [2003]), 454-72. As noted in part one, chapter six, the recent "Joint Declaration on the Doctrine of Justification" has prompted its own stream of theological and church-historical reflection, some key contributions being noted there in §4.7.

2. See esp. H. Cremer, *Die paulinische Rechtfertigungslehre im Zusammenhange ihrer*

geschichtlichen Voraussetzungen, 2nd ed. (Gütersloh: Bertelsmann, 1900); Ernst Käsemann, "The Righteousness of God in Paul," in *New Testament Questions of Today* (London: SCM, 1969 [1965]), 168-93; Rudolf Bultmann, *Theology of the New Testament*, trans. K. Grobel, 2 vols. (New York: Scribners, 1951/55), 1:270-85; and "Δικαιοσύνη Θεοῦ," *Journal of Biblical Literature* 83 (1964): 12-16; Peter Stuhlmacher, *Gerechtigkeit Gottes bei Paulus* (Göttingen: Vandenhoeck & Ruprecht, 1966); see also "The Apostle Paul's View of Righteousness," in *Reconciliation, Law, and Righteousness: Essays in Biblical Theology*, trans. E. Kalin (Philadelphia: Fortress, 1986), 68-93; and Peter Stuhlmacher and Donald Hagner, *Revisiting Paul's Doctrine of Justification: A Challenge to the New Perspective* (Downers Grove, Ill.: InterVarsity, 2001); Sam K. Williams, "The Righteousness of God in Romans," *Journal of Biblical Literature* 99 (1980): 241-90; John Ziesler, *The Meaning of Righteousness in Paul* (Cambridge: Cambridge University Press, 1972); and "Justification by Faith in the Light of the New Perspective on Paul," *Theology* 94 (1991): 188-94. Also extremely influential in this relation — as already frequently noted! — is Krister Stendahl, "The Apostle Paul and the Introspective Conscience of the West," *Harvard Theological Review* 56 (1963): 199-215; *Paul among Jews and Gentiles, and Other Essays* (Philadelphia: Fortress, 1976), 78-96; see also his *Final Account: Paul's Letter to the Romans* (Fortress: Minneapolis, 1995).

3. I will suggest later that Galatians 2:21, 3:21, and 5:5 should join this conversation, but this is to broaden the data field unusually; other solitary instances of δικαιοσύνη in context in Romans will also be important in due course.

4. Käsemann, "The Righteousness of God in Paul."

5. See, i.a., Ziesler, *The Meaning of Righteousness in Paul*; Reumann, *'Righteousness' in the New Testament*; Cranfield, *Romans 1-8*, 95.

6. A. C. Thiselton sensibly emphasizes the performative dimension here, as was seen in chapter sixteen: see *The First Epistle to the Corinthians: A Commentary on the Greek Text*, NIGTC (Grand Rapids, Mich. & Cambridge & Carlisle: Eerdmans & Paternoster, 2000), 456-58. It seems reasonable for God and the church to "count" individuals as "righteous," in the specific sense of gaining entry into the age to come (although I have disputed that this is what Paul actually means in Romans 2 and elsewhere).

7. This being a highly indicative grammatical category!

8. See John D. Zizioulas, *Being as Communion* (New York: St. Vladimir's Seminary Press, 1985); Eberhard Jüngel, *God's Being Is in Becoming: The Trinitarian Being of God in the Theology of Karl Barth: A Paraphrase*, trans. John Webster, 4th ed. (Grand Rapids, Mich.: Eerdmans, 2001); Colin E. Gunton, *Act and Being: Towards a Theology of the Divine Attributes* (London: SCM, 2002); also David Burrell, *Aquinas: God and Action* (Notre Dame, Ind.: University of Notre Dame Press, 1979).

Some scholars have detected the way in which Paul's terminology and argumentation seem to resist a strong being-act distinction but have understood this instead in terms of a programmatic distinction between the "Greek" and the "Hebraic": see, i.a., T. Boman, *Hebrew Thought Compared with Greek*, trans. J. L. Moreau (New York: Norton, 1970 [1954]); (partly endorsed in this relation by Dunn, *Romans 1-8*, 40-41). The Greek-Hebraic distinction, however, like the other antitheses just considered, has long proved oversimplified and unsustainable. Judaism in all its forms was deeply interpenetrated by Hellenistic categories by the late Second Temple period, even as those categories were no longer purely Hellenic. Nevertheless, insofar as this distinction grasps the invalid being-act antithesis and rejects it, any approach that uses it may result in valid analyses, although couched in terms of a false explanatory framework. There is consequently often something recoverable in assertions that Paul is doing something "Hebraic" — that is, apart from this claim itself! Such observations should be recast in terms of a (false) being-act distinction, and its rejection.

9. A classic analysis of different notions of justice (δικαιοσύνη) is Plato's *Republic*; a little more recently, see Alasdair MacIntyre, *Whose Justice? Which Rationality?* (Notre Dame, Ind.: University of Notre Dame Press, 1988). Also useful — as just noted — is John Rawls, *A Theory of Justice* (Oxford: Oxford University Press, 1971), who illustrates how far modern notions of justice have moved away from retributive conceptions. A famous libertarian study complementing Rawls's more redistributive views is Robert Nozick, *Anarchy, State, and Utopia* (New York: Basic Books, 1974), which makes much

the same point (i.e., defines justice non-retributively — although also rather differently from Rawls!). Moving away from a foundational analytic role for justice in any sense (as I am suggesting that Paul is), is Stanley Hauerwas, *After Christendom? How the Church Is to Behave If Freedom, Justice, and a Christian Nation Are Bad Ideas,* new ed. (Nashville, Tenn.: Abingdon, 1999 [1991]), see esp. "The Politics of Justice: Why Justice Is a Bad Idea for Christians," 45-68.

10. Some of these problems could be avoided if δικαιοσύνη Θεοῦ were rendered "the justice of God," but the majority of scholars hold that this is an inappropriate translation.

11. An excellent introductory account of these problems is supplied by Sanders's *Paul,* 45-47.

12. The usual practice is the reverse. However, we then lose the semantic indications and controls that the later material contributes. Stuhlmacher makes this point: see "The Apostle Paul's View of Righteousness," 83.

13. Here Israel does not have zeal for God κατ' ἐπίγνωσιν, but ἀγνοοῦντες . . . τὴν τοῦ Θεοῦ δικαιοσύνην.

14. Christ ἐγενήθη σοφία ἡμῖν ἀπὸ Θεοῦ.

15. Of particular importance is the way Paul expands on the phrase τὴν ἐκ Θεοῦ δικαιοσύνην in v. 9b with an arthrous genitive infinitive in v. 10a — τοῦ γνῶναι — which is in my view an epexegetical construction.

16. Alain Badiou's useful term. "For me, Paul is a poet-thinker of the event. . . . He brings forth the entirely human connection, whose destiny fascinates me, between the general idea of a rupture, an overturning, and that of a thought-practice that is this rupture's subjective materiality": *Saint Paul: The Foundation of Universalism,* trans. Ray Brassier (Stanford, Calif.: Stanford University Press, 2003), 2. (I would of course demur at Badiou's affirmation here of "an entirely human connection," as would Paul, but the remainder of his characterization here is insightful.)

17. Ultimately, however, we might get into theological and interpretive difficulties if we treat time as a constant: see A. J. Torrance, "*Creatio ex Nihilo* and the Spatio-Temporal Dimensions," in *The Doctrine of Creation,* ed. C. E. Gunton (Edinburgh: T&T Clark, 1997), 83-103.

18. Notably, 2 Cor. 5:21 in the broader setting of 5:11–6:3, an argument steeped in the language of reconciliation and salvation. The reconciling act of God, the content of which is pithily described in 5:21, is urged upon the Corinthians, and Paul then cites Isa. 49:8 and characterizes the present as that "day of salvation."

Also interesting in this relation are the parallels between 1 Thess. 5:8 and Isa. 59:17/Wis. 5:18. In 1 Thess. 5:8 the breastplate of righteousness in Isaiah and Wisdom of Solomon is transmuted into one of faith and love, with the helmet of salvation retained, but with the insertion of "hope." See also Gal. 5:5-6 and Eph. 6:14 in context.

19. See 6:16-22.

20. The same notion is conveyed by imagery of a pedagogue (see vv. 24-25) and, still later, by imagery of minority (see 4:1-6) (both motifs being discussed further in part five, chapter twenty). This connotation is arguably reinforced still further by 1 Cor. 1:30 (especially in conjunction with 6:11), and 2 Cor. 3:9.

21. Käsemann, "The Righteousness of God in Paul," 180.

22. Richard B. Hays, *Echoes of Scripture in the Letters of Paul* (New Haven: Yale University Press, 1989), 36-37. Others have since noted some sort of connection, apparently independently of Hays: see Cranfield, *Romans I–VIII,* 96 (parenthetically and without further comment); Robert Jewett, *Romans,* Hermeneia (Minneapolis, Minn.: Fortress, 2007), 143; who cites Klaus Haacker, *Der Brief des Paulus an die Römer,* THKNT 6 (Leipzig: Evangelische Verlagsanstalt, 1999), 41; also Robert Morgan, *Romans,* New Testament Guide (Sheffield: Sheffield Academic Press, 1995), 20-21, who has influenced A. Katherine Grieb, *The Story of Romans. A Narrative Defense of God's Righteousness* (London & Louisville: Westminster-John Knox, 2002), 11. Seifrid cites this text as central to the broader debate but never connects it with Rom. 1:16-17 (*Christ, Our Righteousness,* 38-40). However, none of these interpreters develops the observation very extensively.

23. One of the mistakes in my *RRR:* see 165.

24. Hays's own initial treatment of the methodological issues in *Echoes* (esp. 29-32) is difficult

to better; his criteria for detecting an echo are presented again and revised in his "'Who Has Believed Our Message?' Paul's Reading of Isaiah," *The Conversion of the Imagination: Paul as Interpreter of Israel's Scripture* (Grand Rapids, Mich.: Eerdmans, 2005), 25-49. Some helpful recent refinements are undertaken by Leroy Huizenga, in dialogue in particular with the semiotic theories of Umberto Eco and Stefan Alkier: see esp. "Chapter 1: Dictionaries, Encyclopedias, and the Model Reader," in "The Akedah in Matthew" (Ph.D. diss., Duke University, 2006), 43-101.

25. Intriguingly, the Hebrew texts Isa. 56:1 and CD 20:20 are close to this clause, as Haacker notes (*An die Römer*, 41), but the LXX blunts the echo of Isaiah in the Greek, translating *tsedeqah* with ἔλεος, and Paul's reproduction of a clause from Qumran directly is of course unlikely. Romans 3:21-22 is also a partial exception to this claim, although there, as we have already seen, the verb has changed to a synonym — φανερόω.

26. Strictly speaking, the LXX uses the neuter adjective τὸ σωτήριον at this point.

27. This correlation is very significant because it limits the relevant background texts to those that speak of *iustitia salutifera*. Moreover, this particular action occurs (as Morgan points out in *Romans*, 20-21) primarily in the Psalter, although Isaiah supplies a significant cluster of such instances as well.

28. This emphasis is apparent in the context preceding Rom. 1:16-17 as well, where Paul has been speaking of his apostolic commission (to) Ἕλλησίν τε καὶ βαρβάροις, σοφοῖς τε καὶ ἀνοήτοις.

29. And there is even a hint of priority of action toward Judaism in Psalm 98, as God is said to have remembered his mercy and fidelity to Israel, something the pagan nations there "see." This arguably echoes the overt statement of Jewish priority in Romans 1:16b — Ἰουδαίῳ τε πρῶτον καὶ Ἕλληνι — although I would not want to press this point. (See more in this relation when Romans 10 is treated in more detail in part five, chapter nineteen.)

30. It is widely conceded that Paul quotes and alludes to Scripture repeatedly through Romans. Within this practice, it is also evident that he makes extensive use of texts from the Psalms (see especially 3:10-18 and 20a in the immediate setting). And the later 3:21-22, which is so closely constructed to 1:17, is little more than a pastiche of scriptural texts — except, that is, at *this* point, where the disclosure of the δικαιοσύνη Θεοῦ is stated, so the lacuna has now been addressed. Admittedly, this last argument may be a little opaque in the present setting, but it is, I would suggest, ultimately quite significant. If 3:21-22 is elsewhere demonstrably a pastiche of intertexts, then we might expect some intertext to emerge here as well, as indeed Ps. 98:2-3 does.

31. That is, with a quotation formula — usually γέγραπται.

32. Hays does not develop this point, referring rather to lament and exile (which are not to be excluded from the interpretation either of Paul or of Romans but do not seem so directly relevant here); see *Echoes*, 38. Seifrid is sensitive to this connotation but, as noted above, does not connect it directly to the key texts and phrases in Romans; see *Christ, Our Righteousness*, 39.

33. Keith W. Whitelam provides an excellent summary and bibliography in "King and Kingship," *ABD* 4:40-48; see also J. H. Eaton, *Kingship and the Psalms* (London: SCM, 1976); James Luther Mays, *The Lord Reigns: A Theological Handbook to the Psalms* (Louisville, Ky.: Westminster John Knox, 1994); and J. Richard Middleton, *The Liberating Image: The* Imago Dei *in Genesis 1* (Grand Rapids, Mich.: Brazos, 2005). A brief account more directly relevant to our concerns here is Richard Bauckham, *God Crucified: Monotheism and Christology in the New Testament* (Carlisle: Paternoster, 1998), 9-13.

34. Denoting them "Enthronement Psalms" (as noted by Whitelam, "King and Kingship," 43). Significantly, S. Mowinckel had earlier worked with a much more extensive range of texts, so the Enthronement Psalms provide a very minimalist data pool. Mowinckel includes Psalms 8; 15; 24; 29; 33; 46; 48; 50; 66a; 75; 76; 81; 82; 84; 87; 114; 118; 132; 149; and Exod. 15:1-18; and the data can arguably be broadened still further.

35. And the Hellenistic and Roman data should not be ignored: see esp. Aristotle, *Politics*, 3.14-18; 5.10-11; Seneca, *De Clementia*; and Dio Chrysostom, *Discourses* 1–4 (see also *Discourse* 62); see E. R. Goodenough, "The Political Philosophy of Hellenistic Kingship," *Yale Classical Studies* 1 (1928): 55-102; and Blumenfeld, *The Political Paul*.

36. Drawing here again on the term and method of George Lakoff: see esp. *Moral Politics: How Liberals and Conservatives Think,* 2nd ed. (London & Chicago: University of Chicago, 2001 [1996]); see also his earlier classic study George Lakoff and Mark Johnson, *Metaphors We Live By,* 2nd ed. (Chicago, Ill.: University of Chicago, 2003 [1980]). His work has already been introduced and discussed earlier in part one, chapter one, and part two, chapter seven.

37. Strong boundaries in the evidence should not be drawn between Jewish, ancient Near Eastern, and more recent Hellenistic and Roman discourses.

38. See the later medieval and aristocratic notions of both *royaume* and *noblesse oblige;* see also, most importantly, Psalm 72, where this duty is often spelled out explicitly. Whitelam states more discursively (in relation specifically to human kingship) that "[t]he justification of kingship with its centralized social structure was based upon a guarantee of order, security, prosperity, fertility, etc., in return for loyalty and subservience" ("King and Kingship," 42).

39. The need to control the forces of chaos was widespread in the ancient Near East, although in different local forms: see, e.g., the Egyptian ideology of the pharaoh as the Lord of *ma'at,* as against the Babylonian epic *Enuma Elish,* where Marduk establishes a right to rule by defeating the sea monster Tiamat. Ugaritic material evidences similar notions as well. (For references, see Whitelam, "King and Kingship," 45.)

40. A deliberately sustained methodological emphasis in this chapter.

41. The celebration of the human king as the "son of God" at an annual enthronement festival in ancient Israel has been much debated. Fortunately, this question does not have to be decided here.

42. See Whitelam, "King and Kingship," 42, although arguably he overlooks the emphatically gender-coded symbolism of multiple beautiful wives and concubines as well: see esp. 2 Sam. 16:20-22 and 1 Kings 2:13-25.

43. All of these actions are widely attested, in relation to both God and human kings, in the Old Testament.

44. These are distinguished in more detail in chapter sixteen. In forensic-nonretributive actions, the rectitude of the parties being judged is irrelevant; the action is usually grounded in the right action — and hence character — of the primary actor — God or the king. In forensic-retributive actions, the rectitude of those being judged is relevant and needs to be assessed accurately by God or the king, so that the resulting judgment rightly reflects that prior ethical calculus.

45. This data was emphasized by Cremer, *Die paulinische Rechtfertigungslehre.* A useful brief overview is supplied by J. J. Scullion, "God's *sedeq-sedaqa:* Saving Action" in "Righteousness (OT)," *ABD* 5:731-34.

46. The conviction seems to be widespread in the Old Testament that God "cares" and hence can be appealed to directly for help in all sorts of difficult circumstances, irrespective of any claim on that help that might be generated by the appellant's ethical state. Sometimes that putative basis for a claim is introduced, but often it is not, and at times it is even directly disavowed in a repentant mode.

47. Many other debates could be added to these two — for example, the stilling of the storm pericopes, which arguably present Jesus as the Divine Warrior; the triumphal entry; and so on. Wright gives an especially vigorous account of the presence of royal thematology in Jesus' life: N. T. Wright, *Jesus and the Victory of God* (Minneapolis: Fortress, 1996), esp. chs. 6–13 (198-653); the relevant data is listed in an appendix, "'Kingdom of God' in Early Christian Literature," 663-70. An interesting application to a Pauline text of thematology especially associated with the Divine Warrior is Timothy G. Gombis, "Ephesians 2 as a Narrative of Divine Warfare," *Journal for the Study of the New Testament* 26 (2004): 403-18. Further important material on kingship, its development by the early church, and its relationship with key scriptural texts — although specifically in relation to Mark — is given by Joel Marcus, *The Way of the Lord: Christological Exegesis of the Old Testament in the Gospel of Mark* (Louisville, Ky.: Westminster John Knox, 1992), esp. 130-52.

48. W. Bousset, *Kyrios Christos: A History of the Belief in Christ from the Beginnings of Christianity to Irenaeus,* trans. [from the 4th German ed.] J. E. Steely (Nashville, Tenn.: Abingdon, 1970 [1st edn. 1913; 4th 1965]).

49. An accessible overview of this and related trends can be found in Larry W. Hurtado, *Lord*

Jesus Christ: Devotion to Jesus in Earliest Christianity (Grand Rapids, MI: Eerdmans, 2003), 1-26. For more detailed engagements see the following note.

50. Among others in this relation, see esp. Bauckham, *God Crucified;* J. A. Fitzmyer, "The Semitic Background of the New Testament Kyrios-Title," in *The Semitic Background of the New Testament* (Grand Rapids, Mich.: Eerdmans, 1997), 115-42; "New Testament Kyrios and Maranatha and Their Aramaic Background," in *To Advance the Gospel: New Testament Studies*, 2nd ed. (Grand Rapids, Mich.: Eerdmans, 1998 [1981]), 218-35; Martin Hengel, "Christological Titles in Early Christianity," in *The Messiah: Developments in Earliest Judaism and Christianity*, ed. James H. Charlesworth (Minneapolis, Minn.: Fortress, 1992), 425-48; "'Sit at My Right Hand!' the Enthronement of Christ at the Right Hand of God and Psalm 110:1," in *Studies in Early Christology* (Edinburgh: T&T Clark, 1995), 119-225; Larry W. Hurtado, *One God, One Lord: Early Christian Devotion and Ancient Jewish Monotheism*, 2nd ed. (London: T&T Clark International [Continuum], 1998 [1988]); *Lord Jesus Christ;* and C. Kavin Rowe, "Romans 10:13: What Is the Name of the Lord?" *Horizons in Biblical Theology* 22 (2000): 135-73. (For N. T. Wright see the following note.)

51. Wright's principal treatments are *The Climax of the Covenant: Christ and Law in Pauline Theology* (Edinburgh: T&T Clark, 1991); *The New Testament and the People of God* (London: SPCK, 1992); *Jesus and the Victory of God;* "The Letter to the Romans"; and, *The Resurrection of the Son of God* (Minneapolis, Minn.: Fortress, 2003). He references numerous shorter studies, many on Romans, in these major works.

52. Arguably, there are insensitivities in certain aspects of his work, not to mention occasional gaps; for a slightly different account of the resurrection, for example, see Dale C. Allison, *Resurrecting Jesus: The Earliest Christian Tradition and Its Interpreters* (London & New York: T&T Clark International [Continuum], 2005). I am assuming here, however, that his basic claims are plausible.

53. The work of Daniel Kirk is also of significance in this relation: *Unlocking Romans: Resurrection and the Justification of God* (Grand Rapids, Mich.: Eerdmans, 2008).

54. Wright makes this point clearly: "The Christology of 1:3-4 is by no means an isolated statement attached loosely to the front of the letter but not relevant to its contents. It is the careful, weighted, programmatic statement of what will turn out to be Paul's subtext throughout the whole epistle (see also 9:5; and 15:12, the final scriptural quotation of the main body of the letter)"; later he also points to 5:12-21 and "all the elements of chaps. 6-8 that follow from it" ("The Letter to the Romans," 10:413, 415-19, quoting from 417 and 418). Robert Jewett provides a nuanced analysis in full dialogue with the extensive secondary discussion (*Romans*, 96-98, 103-8).

55. It is not, for example, immediately apparent how "high" this Christology is. Paul's use of "lord" here could be divine, entirely human, or roaming somewhere in between. But this question is best addressed in relation to Romans 10:9-13 (see part five, chapter nineteen, and see esp. Rowe, "What Is the Name of the Lord?"). And it ought to asked in due course whether this material represents Paul's thought exhaustively, or is presupposed by him in relation to his auditors.

56. Jewett surveys the "reconciliation debate" in Paul in *Romans*, 364-66, noting that detailed studies by F. Hahn, M. Hengel, and C. Breytenbach support the reading being suggested here. Jewett also discusses "access" on 347-50, although without linking the two debates.

57. So, for example, Paul uses the verb [συμ]βασιλεύω a total of only ten times, but six of those are in this section of Romans: see 5:14, 17 [2x], 21 [2x]; 6:12 (also 1 Cor. 4:8 [3x] and 15:25, where the royal connotations of this term are explicit). In Rom. 8:15 and 21 he uses δουλεία, and elsewhere only in (the closely similar) Gal. 4:24 and 5:1. In 8:37 he speaks of ὑπερνικάω, a hapax legomenon. And so on.

58. αὐτὸς ἐπικαλέσεταί με Πατήρ μου εἶ σύ, θεός μου καὶ ἀντιλήπτωρ τῆς σωτηρίας μου· κἀγὼ πρωτότοκον θήσομαι αὐτὸν, ὑψηλὸν παρὰ τοῖς βασιλεῦσιν τῆς γῆς (Psalm 89:26-27 [LXX 88:27-28]). Note also the use of δικαιοσύνη to describe benevolent and salvific acts of God in vv. 14 and 16 (LXX 15 and 17), in parallel with κρίμα, ἔλεος, εὐδοκία, καύχημα and ἀλήθεια. It may also be legitimate to detect an influence from Ps. 110 at this point in the reference to God's right hand — another royal enthronement psalm of course, and one much used by the early church: see Donald H. Juel, *Messianic Exegesis: Christological Interpretation of the Old Testament in Early Christianity*, new ed. (Minneapolis, Minn.: Augsburg Fortress, 1998 [1988]), 135-50; see also Joel Marcus, *The Way of the Lord: Christo-*

logical Exegesis of the Old Testament in the Gospel of Mark (Louisville, Ky.: Westminster John Knox, 1992), 130-45. (Marcus indicates how expectations of kingship changed significantly after 70 CE — a point that needs to be borne in mind: see 145-51.)

59. See Douglas A. Campbell, "The Story of Jesus in Romans and Galatians," in *Narrative Perspectives on the Pauline Gospel*, ed. B. W. Longenecker (Louisville, Ky.: Westminster John Knox, 2002), repr. *The Quest for Paul's Gospel: A Suggested Strategy* (London: T&T Clark International, 2005), 69-94.

60. Rowe, "What Is the Name of the Lord?"

61. Indeed, this subsection of Romans is arguably replete with various messianic and royal connotations, and most notably perhaps of wisdom. For more details see part five, chapter nineteen.

62. The discourse's connotations are arguably detectable to an even more significant degree if the contexts of the three other texts quoted are explored — Ps. 18:49 (certainly) and Deut. 32:43 (a book that generally assumes the kingship of God). Psalm 117:1 seems too brief to set up any such resonances. For some elaboration of these claims see Hays, *Echoes*, 70-73; see also "Christ Prays the Psalms: Paul's Use of an Early Christian Exegetical Convention," in *The Future of Christology: Essays in Honor of Leander E. Keck*, ed. A. J. Malherbe and W. A. Meeks (Minneapolis: Fortress, 1993), 122-36, esp. 134-35; and Wright, "The Letter to the Romans," 733, and 744-49, esp. 748.

63. There are no direct linguistic signals of a connection between Rom. 16:20 and Gen. 3:15; hence, the echo, if it exists, must be fundamentally narrative. Nevertheless, Dunn suggests that Gen. 3:15 was a staple of Jewish hope, citing Ps. 91:13; *Testament of Simeon* 6:6; *Testament of Levi* 18:12 [to which we should add *Testament of Zebulon* 9:8]; and Luke 10:18-19 (a text that includes a note of joy, like Rom. 16:19-20); and supported by *TDNT* 5:81, Michel, Käsemann, Stuhlmacher (*Römer*, 223), and Cranfield. See Dunn, *Romans 9-16*, WBC 33B (Dallas, Tex.: Word, 1988), 905-7.

64. Wright, like Dunn, points rather to Ps. 91:13, which is actually a markedly less apposite intertext. (In particular, there is no connection with 1 Cor. 15:25-27.) Somewhat curiously, he nevertheless detects the Adamic allusion, routing that through Luke 10:17-19 (see Rev. 12:10-11). The strongest intertextual echo in this subsection for Wright is the evocation of the Jesus saying recorded in Matt. 10:16 by 16:19b, which does not disturb the set of resonances being suggested in v. 20 ("The Letter to the Romans," 10:764-65). These connections are all clearer in 1 Cor. 15:25-27, and are further affirmed and explained by Eph. 1:20-22 and Heb. 1-2 (see esp. 1:13; 2:6-8a). See A. C. Thiselton, *The First Epistle to the Corinthians: A Commentary on the Greek Text*, NIGTC (Grand Rapids, Mich., Cambridge & Carlisle: Eerdmans & Paternoster, 2000), 1230-36. Hays also puts these points succinctly, introducing Mark 12:35-37 into the mix for good measure!: *First Corinthians*, Interpretation (Louisville, Kentucky: John Knox Press, 1997), 265-66. The future tense of the verb inclines me to suspect that Psalm 110 is to the fore in the echo in v. 20, but probably only marginally. Moreover, Satan is presumably one of the enemies who will eventually be placed under the feet of God.

65. Classic studies are Hays, "Psalm 143 and the Logic of Romans 3," *Journal of Biblical Literature* 99 (1980): 107-15; and William S. Campbell, "Romans III as a Key to the Structure and Thought of the Letter," *Novum Testamentum* 23 (1981): 22-40.

66. See especially the discussion of the preceding subsection.

67. And this sets up another resonance with 1:4, which also speaks of δύναμις.

68. That is, "the salvation of God" or "the redemption of God." At this point my recommendations overlap with an insightful study, Peter Leithart, "Justification as Verdict and Deliverance: A Biblical Perspective," *Pro Ecclesia* 16 (2007): 56-72.

69. This rhetorical qualification should serve to meet some of Christopher Stanley's concerns with Hays's methodology as expressed in *Arguing with Scripture: The Rhetoric of Quotations in the Letters of Paul* (London & New York: T&T Clark International [Continuum], 2004).

70. Wright, esp. "The Letter to the Romans," 397-406, 413, 464-78. Hays himself endorses this reading at times as well — see, e.g., "Justification," *ABD* 3:1129-33, although he tends to speak of Christ's death and resurrection in the same breath, which links up with my recommendations here. Somewhat curiously, J. D. G. Dunn, although on the opposite side of many questions from Wright and

Hays, concurs on this issue; see his *Romans 1-8,* 40-42 (and this point is discussed in more detail in part three, chapter twelve).

71. Moshe Weinfeld suggests that it is modeled on an Assyrian suzerainty treaty and hence fundamentally covenantal: see *Deuteronomy 1-11* (New York: Doubleday, 1991). So construed, it is also arguably generous, although it remains conditional. (The royal covenant evident elsewhere in the Old Testament looks unconditional.) This potential concession to contractual theology in certain covenantal forms is further cause for caution with the interpretation of δικαιοσύνη Θεοῦ in this sense; the dangers lying here have already been noted carefully in part one.

72. The order of this set of predications must be noted carefully. *We know that God is faithful because* he has acted to save. Hence, we do not *ground* that act of salvation *on* his faithfulness, as if these two dispositions could be prioritized, humanly speaking, and the latter made the basis of the former. Rather, we grasp two complementary aspects of God's personhood, which is now disclosed definitively in Christ. Some of the important salvation-historical implications implicit here are sketched in *Quest,* 63-68.

73. That is, many further semantic variations are conceivable. The phrase might denote a right but wrathful action by God against Israel. Or it might denote a judgment or a posture within a trial between God and Israel — a more retributive scenario.

74. And similar observations apply to any resonances with Roman imperial ideology.

75. "The Righteousness of God in Paul," 168-82. Hence, my suggestion here should be viewed as an attempt to build on Käsemann's central insights and not to overthrow or deny them.

76. So, e.g., the exemplary Cranfield does not even consider another syntactical possibility (*Romans I-VIII,* 86-89).

77. See Rom. 1:4, 20; 9:17; 15:13, 19 [2x] (otherwise only 8:38); 1 Cor. 1:18, 24; 2:4, 5; 4:19, 20; 5:4; 6:14; 15:43 (otherwise only 12:10, 28, 29; 14:11; 15:24, 56); 2 Cor. 4:7; 6:7; 12:9 [2x, the second instance being "power of Christ"]; 13:4 [2x] (elsewhere only 1:8; 8:3 [2x]; 12:12); Gal. 3:5 (probably); Phil. 3:10 (the power of the resurrection); and 1 Thess. 1:5 (an especially important parallel to 1 Corinthians and here: τὸ εὐαγγέλιον ἡμῶν οὐκ ἐγενήθη εἰς ὑμᾶς ἐν λόγῳ μόνον ἀλλὰ καὶ ἐν δυνάμει καὶ ἐν πνεύματι ἁγίῳ καὶ [ἐν] πληροφορίᾳ πολλῇ); see also Eph. 1:19; 3:7, 16, 20 (elsewhere only 1:21); Col. 1:11, 29; and 2 Thess. 1:7 (Jesus and his angels, a slightly ambiguous phrase), 1:11 (see elsewhere 2:9). So 25 of 36 follow this usage in the undisputed Pauline letters, and 33 of 46 instances in a ten-letter canon.

78. See esp. 2:10: ἡμῖν δὲ ἀπεκάλυψεν ὁ Θεὸς διὰ τοῦ πνεύματος.

79. δύναμις Θεοῦ cannot be identified merely with Paul's proclamation or gospel in this argument; his gospel *mediates* the δύναμις Θεοῦ, which is elsewhere identified with Christ and the Spirit. It follows that "the word" in 1:18 is not a reference merely to the gospel but to the divine Word, who acts through the gospel. Δύναμις is also equated here very directly with wisdom; see 1:24: Χριστὸν Θεοῦ δύναμιν καὶ Θεοῦ σοφίαν (not to mention the continuation of this statement in v. 25: τὸ μωρὸν τοῦ Θεοῦ σοφώτερον τῶν ἀνθρώπων ἐστὶν καὶ τὸ ἀσθενὲς τοῦ Θεοῦ ἰσχυρότερον τῶν ἀνθρώπων).

80. It might be objected that the construal of . . . ἐστιν εἰς . . . in this reading is now forced. But this construction probably occurs elsewhere in Paul — in some MSS in Rom. 10:2, and it is presupposed by 10:4. So the preposition denotes here, typically, the relationship between God's active power or act and salvation — it is, precisely, a "saving power" (see BDAG 288-91, esp. meaning 4 — "marker of goals involving affective/abstract/suitability aspects, *into, to*" [290-91]). This sense then seems to be resumed by a dative of advantage in v. 16b.

81. As I noted earlier, the second transition is not especially sharp, ethical concerns resurfacing in 8:12-13.

82. We link hands here with our earlier suspicion that Paul is wresting the verb δικαιόω back from the Teacher's system, redeploying it in his offensive slogan "God justifies the ungodly." The two polemical antitheses thus conform closely to one another. There will be occasion to note several more, one in particular that likewise departs from "the deliverance of God." That is, Paul will not just contrast the righteousness of God, in the sense of God's liberative purpose disclosed in Christ, with a conception that emphasizes "the wrath of God," or retribution; he will also contrast the delivering righteousness *of God* with the righteous activity *of people* — and here, presumably, of law-observant

Jewish Christians. Paul will ask, in effect, Which of these two righteous acts/activities do you want to rely on? (This contrast will be discussed in relation to Rom. 10:3 and Philippians 3.)

83. We also come at this point to an important qualification of the detailed discussions of Jewish literature that tend to operate in these debates. As far as I can tell, the two conceptions of God just noted were debated by Jews contemporary to Paul (doubtless along with others), as illustrated especially clearly by the *Psalms of Solomon* and *4 Ezra*. Some Jews regarded God as fundamentally benevolent, while others regarded him as fundamentally retributive, and only conditionally benevolent. Some, moreover, seem to have understood the divine character to be fundamentally elective (see Qumran), while doubtless many figures and texts managed to combine different, essentially incompatible notions (arguably also Qumran). Paul can therefore be seen — to a certain extent — to be participating in this broader contemporary Jewish debate. But he brings a critical qualification to it. His view of God has been *decisively* qualified by the Christ event, to the point that any previous views seem to have been — if necessary — fundamentally renegotiated. Contemporary Jews outside the church were not doing this; this is not the theological discourse within which they were participating. Hence, any direct application of material from Jewish background texts to the construal of Paul — here of δικαιοσύνη Θεοῦ — must be heavily qualified. Paul has correlated the Christ event tightly with his basal understanding of God; this is, more or less, what he says compactly and repeatedly in Romans 3:21-26, anticipating these claims in 1:16-17 and, still earlier, in 1:2-4, and elaborating them at more length beginning in 4:23. Hence, in a sense it is the Teacher's inability to move out of the broader Jewish debate and qualify some of its resources more decisively in the light of the Christ event that Paul is objecting to so strenuously.

84. One final insight into his developing rhetoric is now visible, although this is a point that will become clearer when we discuss Romans 10 and Philippians 3. It is apparent that Paul, like Martin Luther, is discussing two types of righteousness. Just as he opposes δικαιοσύνη Θεοῦ to ὀργὴ Θεοῦ in 1:17-18, Paul's choice of terminology also seems influenced by the desire to contrast the δικαιοσύνη Θεοῦ to a δικαιοσύνη ἐμοῦ/αὐτοῦ on the part of the Teacher and his followers — a saving act by God, which can also be characterized as a right act, to righteous and hopefully saving activity *by people themselves.*

85. Both of these links are of course generated by an underlying commitment to Jewish martyrological thinking, and especially the specific story of Abraham's sacrifice of Isaac on the temple mount, which is now being applied to Christ.

86. J. Louis Martyn gives a masterful account of this point in relation to the equally important Gal. 1:4: *Galatians: A New Translation with Introduction and Commentary,* AB 33A (New York: Doubleday, 1997), 88-91; see also 263-75; he points as well to Gal. 2:20; Rom. 4:25; 8:32; and Eph. 5:2, 25; see 1 Tim. 2:6; Tit. 2:14.

87. As Martyn notes, "While Paul uses the word 'sin' in the singular rather frequently, the plural form emerges only four times in the genuine letters. Of these four instances one is in a sentence Paul explicitly identifies as an early Christian confession (1 Cor 15:3); a second stands in the broad context of that confession (1 Cor 15:17); the third functions in effect as a plural adjective modifying a plural noun (Rom 7:5, "sinful passions"); and the fourth emerges in the present verse [Gal. 1:4]. Only when he is quoting traditional formulas does Paul speak of Jesus as having died for our *sins* (Gal 1:4; 1 Cor 15:3)" (*Galatians,* 89). Martyn then points his readers presciently to Rom. 3:25 and a possible influence from *4 Maccabees* (89-90).

88. And this raises the possibility in turn that if Paul is not consistently committed to nonpunitive and nonviolent divine and ecclesial action elsewhere, *then he ought to have been!*

Notes to Chapter Eighteen

1. Stanley K. Stowers, *A Rereading of Romans: Justice, Jews and Gentiles* (New Haven: Yale University Press, 1994), esp. 231-42 — hereafter *RR.*

2. BDAG, 249, meaning 2, emphatically negative — "no, by no means" — with ἀλλά (742).

3. As Simon Gathercole notes, "ἤ is not identical to a γάρ, so that 3:28-29 does not necessarily form a logical progression. Rather, Paul often uses ἤ with questions to get to the answer he wants to explore": "Justified by Faith, Justified by His Blood: The Evidence of Romans 3:21–4:25," in *Variegated Nomism*, vol. 2, *The Paradoxes of Paul*, ed. D. A. Carson, P. T. O'Brien, and Mark A. Seifrid (Tübingen: Mohr Siebeck, 2004), 147-84, quoting from 155.

4. BDAG meaning 3, an interrogative sense expecting an affirmative answer — "not?" (742).

5. BDAG meaning 6 l, "if indeed . . . since" (279).

6. The interrogator in a diatribe was not always the author in the guise of a heroic Socratic questioner, although he usually was; this role varied.

7. Gathercole's study is instructive on this point: *Where Is Boasting? Early Jewish Soteriology and Paul's Response in Romans 1–5* (Grand Rapids, Mich.: Eerdmans, 2002).

8. As noted in part three, chapter eleven, in dependence originally on Heikki Räisänen, *Paul and the Law*, WUNT 29 (Tübingen: J. C. B. Mohr, 1983), esp. 51-52, 170-71.

9. This issue is much discussed, although in my view often with insufficient attention to both the broader theoretical issues and the wider argumentative context: an especially precise study is Michael Winger, *By What Law? The Meaning of Νόμος in the Letters of Paul*, SBLDS 128 (Atlanta: Scholars, 1992).

10. See esp. W. D. Davies, "Law in First-Century Judaism," in *Jewish and Pauline Studies* (London: SPCK, 1984), 3-26.

11. And the much-discussed genitive also takes a reasonable meaning at this point as well; it is really a genitive of content. The content of the Teacher's teaching is a system of "works," while the content of Paul's gospel is a narrative of πίστις. (A similar case could be made for a characterizing genitive, and there is little to choose between this option and the preceding one; fortunately, not much rests on a decision here in any case.)

12. Paul's rejoinder to the implications of the Teacher here actually depends on an ambiguity in the predications being used of God. When the Teacher asserts that "God is the God of the Jews only," he implies that a particular arrangement has been established by God with that people, which is oriented by the law. So the sense of the claim that "God is the God of the Jews alone" is that he cares about them primarily and saves them only precisely because they are his people. Paul's response simply depends on the sovereignty of God over the created cosmos and all of humanity. In this sense God is the God of all, but it does not necessarily follow from this predication that God also cares for those parts of humanity not in covenant with him (supposing that they have repudiated that covenant).

13. Certainly there seems no reason to abandon it for a *less* grammatical reading, and neither is any a priori assertion of the importance of Justification theory probative.

14. And it might even be possible to detect a more profound theological point here (which is, in turn, possibly taken up by Romans 10): God is to non-Jews as he is to Jews because in both actions he is acting in Christ and this reveals him as he truly is. This disclosure does not change, and therefore supplies content to the notion of the divine unity.

15. See esp. Jas. 2:21-24; see also Watson's interesting reflections in *Paul and the Hermeneutics of Faith* (London; New York: T&T Clark, 2004), 172-82, 220-69 — hereafter *P&HF* (considering principally *Jubilees*, Philo, and Josephus); and Nancy Calvert-Koyzis, *Paul, Monotheism and the People of God: The Significance of Abraham Traditions for Early Judaism and Christianity*, JSNTSup 273 (London: T&T Clark International [Continuum], 2004). Other Jewish analyses of Abraham are referenced below.

16. Most notably the predications of God in terms of unity and "righteousness"; the sense of God's performative judgment; and the witness of Scripture more generally.

17. He does not seem equally confident about the interpretation of Moses and so seems to use different interpretive strategies: see Rom. 5:20; 2 Cor. 3:6-18.

18. Paul usually deploys this verb in the sense "to find": see Rom. 7:10, 21; 10:20 [Isa. 65:1]; 1 Cor. 4:2; 15:15; 2 Cor. 2:13; 5:3; 9:4; 11:12; 12:20; Gal. 2:17; Phil. 2:8; 3.9; see also LNSM, 325-26, 29, §§27.1, 27. It may mean "to obtain" (or "to attain"): see esp. Matt. 11:29; Acts 7:46; Heb. 9:12; also Josephus, *Antiquities*, 5.41 (where "obtain" seems better than "find," but the latter is not impossible); see also LNSM

151, 807-8, §§13.17 & 90.70. But the former meaning looks more likely once it has been determined that "we" are the subject of the sentence.

19. See Richard B. Hays, "'Have We Found Abraham to Be Our Forefather According to the Flesh?' A Reconsideration of Romans 4:1," *Novum Testamentum* 27 (1985): 76-98. I engage with this proposal first in "Towards a New, Rhetorically Assisted Reading of Romans 3.27-4.25," in *Rhetorical Criticism and the Bible: Essays from the 1998 Florence Conference*, ed. S. E. Porter and D. L. Stamps (Sheffield: JSOT Press, 2002), 355-402. The following is a modification of those earlier opinions. In the reading suggested here, ultimately in dependence on Hays although not following his suggested translation word-for-word, the accusative "Abraham" is functioning as an accusative of respect.

20. This reading was suggested to me by Stanley Porter (at the fifth conference on Rhetoric and Scriptural Interpretation, Florence, 27-30 July 1998). Any errors in the brief outworking of that approach here should be attributed to me.

21. The perfect tense of the infinitive is appropriate because it has present force for the notion of the paternity of the nations, but that acquisition was rooted in a past event.

22. Paul uses the more typical New Testament construction in 3:8. The participle is an alternative. BDF cites 2 Cor. 5:19 (which uses a participle; see also v. 20); 11:21 (a perfect verb; see v. 17); and the possibly useful 2 Thess. 2:2 (a perfect verb); see also 3:11 (noted by Benjamin Chapman and Gary Steven Shogren, *Greek New Testament Insert* [Sterling & Herndon, Va.: Stylus Publishing, 1994]).

23. Indirect discourse has largely disappeared from the New Testament in favor of direct discourse. "Indirect discourse with (acc. and) infinitive, so strongly developed in classical Greek, is almost entirely wanting in the NT; Luke is probably the only one who retains it to any considerable degree, and even he quickly slides over into the direct form (s. A 25:4f . . .)" (BDF 203, §396). And where it does appear, distinctive particles tend to signal its presence, namely, ὅτι and/or ὡς. See C. F. D. Moule, *An Idiom Book of New Testament Greek*, 2nd ed. (Cambridge: Cambridge University Press, 1959), 153-54, esp. his examples of Luke 24:23; Acts 25:4, 28:6. Moule also points to Rom. 2:18 (see also vv. 17 and 19).

24. The three phases of argument here have been noted by some scholars, but the fourth, more subtle correlation has generally been overlooked. See, e.g., Halvor Moxnes, *Theology in Conflict: Studies in Paul's Understanding of God in Romans* (Leiden: Brill, 1980). Thomas Tobin uses a four-fold division, but does not interpret Paul's argument as I do here: see *Paul's Rhetoric in Its Contexts: The Argument of Romans* (Peabody, Mass.: Hendrickson, 2004), 125-26.

25. The verb λογίζομαι, supplied by Genesis 15:6, also occurs frequently.

26. The two motifs common to the entire discussion occur in this announcement and its correlative subsection with the presence of πιστ- terminology (one substantive in 4:5 echoing the wording of 3:27-28, assisted by two participles) and the corresponding event or process denoted by δικαιο- terms (twice the wording of 3:28 is reproduced with the verb and three times the cognate substantive appears, doubtless influenced in the immediate context by Genesis 15:6). The signifier λογίζομαι also recurs in both texts, but it is used in a different sense in 4:3-7 (and elsewhere in chapter 4) from 3:28; hence, it might signal the linkage between these two sections merely lexically, and not substantively (it also occurs in vv. 9-10, there also largely under the influence of Genesis 15:6, which has just been cited again, and it occurs again in vv. 22-24 within the entire discussion's conclusion).

27. See esp. Davies, "Law in First-Century Judaism" — this point holds well in retrospect.

28. Romans 4:9 is a partial exception, but it does not use the distinctive introductory formulae found in 4:3 and 4:6 and quotes only half of the key text (suitably rearranged).

29. An opinion shared, to a degree, by Luther, who frequently amended the text in v. 28 to *sola fide* or "alleyn/alleine durch den Glauben" — although in doing so, he was merely following a rather long interpretative tradition! Fitzmyer notes, in addition to Luther, Origen, Hilary, Basil, Ambrosiaster, John Chrysostom, Cyril of Alexandria, Bernard, Theophylact, Theodoret, Aquinas, Theodore of Mopsuestia, Marius Victorinus, and Augustine: see Joseph A. Fitzmyer, *Romans: A New Translation with Introduction and Commentary*, AB 33 (New York: Doubleday, 1993), 360-61.

30. This sudden shift in terminology and argumentation has supplied a principal point of pressure for various revisionists: see, e.g., Hays, "'Have We Found Abraham to Be Our Forefather Accord-

ing to the Flesh?'"; T. L. Donaldson, "Abraham's Gentile Offspring: Contratextuality and Conviction in Romans 4," paper presented at Society of Biblical Literature Annual Meeting, San Francisco, Nov. 1992), 9 (available at http://listserv.lehigh.edu/lists/ioudaios-l/Articles.html or ftp://ftp.lehigh.edu/pub/listserv/ioudaios-l/Articles/tdrom_4); N. Thomas Wright, *The Climax of the Covenant: Christ and Law in Pauline Theology* (Edinburgh: T&T Clark, 1991), 36, 167-68; "Romans and the Theology of Paul," in *Pauline Theology*, vol. 3, *Romans*, ed. David M. Hay and E. Elizabeth Johnson (Minneapolis, Minn.: Augsburg Fortress, 1995), 30-67, esp. 39-42; and "The Letter to the Romans: Introduction, Commentary, and Reflections," in *New Interpreter's Bible*, ed. L. Keck (Nashville, Tenn.: Abingdon, 2002), 487-507; and Stowers, *RR*, 221-50. Against the conventional reading, these interpreters, perceiving — correctly — the importance of circumcision and promise in what follows, tend to assert more salvation-historical construals of Paul's argument at this point. Such approaches, however, still need to deal with the presence of the conventional reading in vv. 1-8 *and* with the subsequent modulations in the terminology of circumcision and promise, motifs that do not occur in juxtaposition, and both of which *also* drop out of sight well before the end of Romans 4!

31. See more on this development just below.

32. Paul's ability to anticipate a later, extended argument with an agenda of short theses should not occasion surprise. Most arguments in fact contain a set of interrelated questions, and certainly the Teacher's program elicits engagements on a number of different fronts. Good arguers simply argue in this way; they address all the issues (that is, if they can do so effectively). Indeed, numerous cultural analogies for just this sort of enumeration exist from Paul's day. Rhetorical training based on the handbooks attests to particular sections within the ideal speech that performed such enumerations — the προκατασκευή, προέκθεσις, μερισμός, or partitio. These laid out in advance the key points that the proofs (πίστεις, probatio) would subsequently address. The thesis paragraph — the (προ)θέσις or propositio — also summarized the main point at issue in advance of the rest of the speech. The Hellenistic rhetorical tradition that looked to Hermagoras of Temnos also specialized in the formulation of a compact statement of the key issue — στάσις, status, or constitutio — and in its subsequent manipulation. My earlier study elaborates on these claims: "Towards a new, rhetorically assisted reading of Romans 3.27–4.25," esp. 394-98. Evidence of the practice from elsewhere in Paul is noted on 391-94. See also Troy Martin's useful inquiry into the use of stasis theory in Galatians: "Apostasy to Paganism: The Rhetorical Stasis of the Galatian Controversy," *Journal of Biblical Literature* 114 (1995): 437-61. (I don't find his suggestion ultimately probative for Galatians, but his analysis of stasis theory is exemplary.) Robert Jewett is especially alert to rhetorical considerations in Romans generally: see *Romans: A Commentary*, Hermeneia (Minneapolis, Minn.: Fortress, 2007), *passim;* summarized and anticipated by "Following the Argument of Romans," in *The Romans Debate*, ed. K. P. Donfried, rev. ed. (Peabody, Mass.: Hendrickson, 1991 [1973]), 265-77.

33. Of thirty-three instances total in Paul, excluding here the eleven instances in Romans 4, perhaps only Rom. 2:26 (possibly); 1 Cor. 13:5, 11 (possibly); 2 Cor. 5:19; and Gal. 3:6 (which quotes Genesis 15:6) take the sense of "credit" or "impute." Romans 2:3; 3:28; 6:11; 8:18, 36; 9:8; 14:14; 1 Cor. 4:1; 13:11; 2 Cor. 3:5; 10:2 (2x), 7, 11; 11:5; 12:6; Phil. 3:13; and 4:8 suggest "view."

34. For the two overlapping but comparable meanings in Koiné, see BDAG, 597-98. These distinguishable meanings can sometimes be obscured by the English translation "reckon" (as is used by the NRSV), which spans both senses. The more archaic verb "impute" possesses similar ambiguities and has, moreover, been heavily coded by subsequent theological discussions and so is probably best avoided. "Credit" is used by the NIV. On the precise construal of λογίζομαι, as well as the timing of the "crediting" of δικαιοσύνη, see Lloyd Gaston, "Abraham and the Righteousness of God," in *Paul and the Torah* (Vancouver: University of British Columbia Press, 1987), 50-52, citing esp. *Mek.* 4 (on Exod. 4.31).

35. In ancient business that was often for reasons of practicality. It was impractical and indeed dangerous for merchants to travel with large sums of money, so letters of credit between trustworthy parties in different markets would have been preferred.

36. The text is coded grammatically in terms of a single male, presumably because Abraham is in mind.

37. In terms of Hillel's traditional seven rules of *middoth*, this claim and connection is based on principle two, *gezerah shawah* (i.e., verbal analogy based on a similarity of words, or "catchword linkage"). It is more difficult to identify Paul's following moves in terms of these traditional principles. A good introductory treatment to this and related Jewish exegetical questions is Richard N. Longenecker, *Biblical Exegesis in the Apostolic Period* (Grand Rapids, Mich.: Eerdmans, 1975), which should be supplemented by Richard B. Hays, *Echoes of Scripture in the Letters of Paul* (New Haven: Yale University Press, 1989); Donald H. Juel, *Messianic Exegesis: Christological Interpretation in the Old Testament and Early Christianity*, new ed. (Minneapolis, Minn.: Augsburg Fortress, 1998 [1988]); and Joel Marcus, *The Way of the Lord: Christological Exegesis of the Old Testament in the Gospel of Mark* (Louisville, Ky.: Westminster John Knox, 1992).

38. The suggestion of chapter seventeen.

39. Both previous Jewish textual tradition and Paul's later discussion (esp. in v. 9b) clearly identify πίστις as the subject of the passive verb ἐλογίσθη. So, somewhat unusually, the action of the verb in the first independent clause becomes the subject of the verb in the second independent clause, rather than either of the figures present in that first clause (i.e., God or Abraham).

40. αὐτῷ is best read as a dative of advantage; God's gift of δικαιοσύνη *is* an advantage!

41. Admittedly, Romans 9:8 may provide a possible instance of this, but only as the verb is translated in the sense of "view" or "consider," a meaning that *must* be excluded here.

42. Put a little more technically, I would suggest that in order to create the progressions of Justification theory out of a simple opposition between two views of Abraham, one of which argues in terms of "works" and merit and the other in terms of trust, certain additional pieces of information are required. Abraham needs to evidence both these states clearly himself; moreover, in the state of works he needs to realize sinfulness. If these additional qualifications can be found in the text, then the interpreter is justified in placing the two states in a broader narrative progression through the patriarch's life. But it is precisely these additional critical pieces of information that are not in the text. And this suggests in turn that Justification theory is not actually giving a good account of the text's argument. Paul seems to be working with a simple "compare and contrast," which is explained by a debate between him and the Teacher.

43. Paul neglects to make a temporal argument in support of his basic contention, which is argued in relation to the verbs. This text is drawn from the beginning of Abraham's life (although he has arrived in Canaan), by which point he has not yet completed most of his most impressive works in any case, and especially as Jewish texts narrated him. Certainly, the binding of Isaac lies well ahead of him (see Genesis 22).

44. Scholars evaluate the success of Paul's argument here diversely, with opinions ranging from C. H. Dodd's "a palpable hit" (*The Epistle of Paul to the Romans* [London: Collins (Fontana Books), 1959 (1932)], 91) to Donaldson's judgment that it is "contratextual" (that is, distinctly dubious: see "Abraham's Gentile Offspring").

45. For "sign," see elsewhere in Romans only 15:19, and elsewhere in Paul largely generic usage in 1 Cor. 1:22; 14:22; 2 Cor. 12:12 (2x); see also 2 Thess. 2:9 and 3:17.

46. See elsewhere in Paul only 1 Cor. 9:2. The possibly related σφραγίζω is used in Rom. 15:28; 2 Cor. 1:22; see also Eph. 1:13 and 4:30.

47. Paul's syntax is a little unusual at this point, possibly creating *three* distinguishable groups of Abrahamic descendants — the uncircumcised faithful (v. 11), the circumcised (v. 12a), and the circumcised faithful (v. 12b); see Ulrich Wilckens, *Der Brief an die Römer*, vol. 1, *Röm 1-5* (Zürich, Einsiedeln, Köln, and Neukirchen-Vluyn: Benziger & Neukirchener, 1978), 264-67; Douglas Moo, *The Epistle to the Romans*, NICNT (Grand Rapids, Mich.: Eerdmans, 1996), 270-71.

It is *very* difficult to resolve the ambiguity present in Paul's phraseology in v. 12. He states that "Abraham is the ancestor of the circumcision — of those who are not only of the circumcision but also those who walk in his faithful footsteps . . . (τοῖς οὐκ ἐκ περιτομῆς μόνον ἀλλὰ καὶ τοῖς στοιχοῦσιν κ.τ.λ.)" (DC). Much of the secondary discussion focuses on Paul's ostensibly clumsy, repeated articles (the second of which is not, strictly speaking, necessary, and is even confusing), but a determination in this respect does not actually resolve the difficulty, as far as I can see. (I incline toward a clumsy resumption.) The principal problem is the difficulty determining if the specified limitation — ". . . not only . . . but also . . ." — is an absolute negation of the category of "circumcision," or a qualification merely in terms of addition. If it is the former — i.e., absolute — then Abraham's paternity is being *limited* to believing Jews, and *denied* by Paul to unbelieving Jews. If it is the latter — additive — then it is being *extended* to believing Jews, and not denied to the rest of Judaism. And I incline toward the latter option, although admittedly on delicate grounds.

Abraham's paternity of unbelieving Jews simply cannot be denied to Paul elsewhere; see esp. Rom. 9:5, 7-8; 11:28. (As Wilckens observes: "Dass er die Heiden vor den Juden nennt, bedeutet keine Destruktion der jüdischen Heilsgeschichte": *Römer 1-5*, 266.) Moreover, it is unlikely that pre-Christian Israel should be "Protestantized," and characterized exclusively or primarily in terms of faith; there is no evidence in Paul for this. Indeed, this is one of the more appalling projections of Justification theory (see esp. part one, chapter four, §6). Paul's "additive" insistence here is understandable if the Teacher is querying the legitimacy of certain Christian Jews, suggesting that they have abrogated their Abraham ancestry, probably by advocating abandonment of the law by pagan converts. ("Those who deny the need for circumcision are no better *than* the uncircumcised, and so have in effect turned their backs on their forefather Abraham; they are not *true Jews*" — see 2:25-29.) This seems to be an attested polemical move in intra-Jewish debate (see Luke 3:8; John 8:37-48!). And this possibility excuses the main objection to the "additive" reading, which is its point — or lack of it — in context. It has previously been difficult to understand why Paul would want to extend Abrahamic paternity from unbelieving Israel to Christian Judaism. But the possible presence of a painful accusation by the Teacher makes such a move on Paul's part quite understandable. (I am grateful to Joel Marcus for awakening me to the issues involved here.)

48. An interesting ethical question is also implicit in this claim, because the Teacher holds circumcision to deliver decisive ethical advantages. Hence, it is important to recall that when Paul elaborated his saving πίστις narrative from 3:21-22 in 3:23-26, he indicated that it ultimately implies an effective ethical solution.

49. The more obvious reading for a traditional orthopractic Jew would of course be to take things the other way around, with law observance fulfilling Torah and Paul's abandonment of that in view of πίστις alone appearing to neutralize or evacuate a large portion of Scripture. But an utterly consistent application of Genesis 15:6 overrides those expectations. The key question is then whether that application is fair or justified in broader terms, as against whether the argument actually works formally.

50. A link has plausibly been detected at this point with Rom. 1:21, although I interpret this as another sly subversion on Paul's part; the great convert *from* idolatry and its false images *to* the correct glorification and worship of God (the one who cannot be imaged), is now oriented by πίστις, not circumcision and law-observance, as the Teacher probably argued. See E. Adams, "Abraham's Faith and Gentile Disobedience: Textual Links between Romans 1 and 4," *Journal for the Study of the New Testament* 65 (1997): 47-66; Calvert-Koyzis, *Paul, Monotheism, and the People of God*, 129; noted by Jewett, *Romans*, 157.

51. For example, Ernst Käsemann's magnificent discussion passes over it in silence; "The Faith of Abraham in Romans 4," in *Perspectives on Paul* (London: SCM, 1971 [1969]), 79-101. Lloyd Gaston is a partial exception, noting — intriguingly — the point briefly in his consideration of Gen. 15:6 in its original Hebrew context: see "Abraham and the Righteousness of God," *Horizons in Biblical Theology* 2 (1980): 41. The presuppositions and eventual direction of this study are very different from Gaston's, but his sensitivity to Jewish understandings of Abraham, and thereby to previously overlooked nuances in Paul's discussion, is exemplary. Similar considerations apply to Stowers, *RR*, esp. 225, 229; and to Donaldson, "Abraham's Gentile Offspring"; and *Paul and the Gentiles: Remapping the Apostle's Convictional World* (Minneapolis: Fortress, 1997).

52. Jesus of course is also a son: see 1:3, 9 (see 1:4); 5:10; and 8:3, 29, 32 (Gen. 22:12/16!).

53. Christians, like Abraham, trust in a God who resurrects from the dead (see 4:17) — a "flatter" reading with no christological rationale or distinctive Christian content; see more on the resurrecting God just below.

54. Verse 19b states that Abraham is "approximately a hundred years old" (ἑκατονταετής που ὑπάρχων), a statement informed by Gen. 21:5, and 17:1, 17, and 24. In Gen. 17:1 and 24 he is "ninety-nine years old," ἐτῶν ἐνενήκοντα ἐννέα, and in Gen. 21:5 (and 17:17) "a hundred years old," ἑκατὸν ἐτῶν. Paul's approximate terminology here is therefore deliberate. Isaac has not yet been born, but the promise in Gen. 17:5 has already been given. So according to the text he is *almost* a hundred years old. Paul's chronological accuracy in terms of the text is also apparent in Galatians (see esp. 3:17).

55. And note that the citation of a fragment of Gen. 15:6 in Rom. 4:22 following the statement that "God was able to do what had been promised" is almost certainly also taking its meaning from this divine conception. The giving of δικαιοσύνη to Abraham is indeed the gift of a salvific eschatological event or action that is, furthermore, in context, the giving of a miraculous son born of, in procreative terms, dead parents. It is a life-giving, resurrecting, eschatological action, as v. 17 has already hinted.

56. He deployed a mixture of Genesis 12:3 and 22:18 (and 26:4; see also Sir. 44:21) in 3:8: ἐνευλογηθήσονται ἐν σοὶ πάντα τὰ ἔθνη. The verbs are identical in both texts, and the dative phrases very similar — ἐν σοί in 12:3 and ἐν τῷ σπέρματί σου in 22:18 and 26:4. The subjects are also close: πᾶσαι αἱ φυλαὶ τῆς γῆς in 12:3 and πάντα τὰ ἔθνη τῆς γῆς in 22:18. So either the dative phrase from 12:3 (i.e., ἐν σοί) has been slipped into 22:18, or the subject of 22:18 has been substituted for that of 12:3. In the context of Galatians, one suspects the former (seed will be a prominent motif in Paul's later argument as will — arguably — the story of Genesis 22). Gen 18:18 is also very close, using ἐν αὐτῷ instead of ἐν σοί.

Paul also cites Genesis 15:6 in Gal. 3:6, and a phrase found specifically in Genesis 12:7, 13:15, 17:7-8, 9, and 24:7, in Gal. 3:16 — καὶ τῷ σπέρματί σου (see also Genesis 22:18, a dative, and vv. 17 and 18a for accusative instances, τὸ σπέρμα σου; only καί is missing from these texts). He also uses the stories of Hagar and Ishmael and Sarah and Isaac as recounted in Genesis 16 and 21 in 4:21-31, citing Gen. 21:10 explicitly in Gal. 4:30.

57. In fact, this is the text's sole occurrence in the New Testament. Acts 7:5 cites Gen. 17:8, a reference made to the land in Stephen's speech.

58. This link with circumcision can also explain Paul's undeveloped use of "father" in the chapter's second subsection, a section also concerned with circumcision. The two motifs are probably linked in his mind by their connection within their original context in Genesis, although they were in any case a standard Jewish association: see *Jubilees* 15:9-34; Sir. 44:19-21 (esp. v. 20b: ἐν σαρκὶ αὐτοῦ ἔστησεν διαθήκην); 1QS 16.1, 5-6 (see *m. Ned.* 3.11 and *Genesis R.* 46.1: "Great is circumcision, for despite all the religious duties which Abraham our father fulfilled, he was not called perfect until he was circumcised"; see also *Genesis R.* 2.3, 42.8 and 44.4). I owe the insight that Paul is grappling with circumcision and the awkward implications of Genesis 17 in Romans 4 originally to Donaldson ("Abraham's Gentile Offspring"), although he would probably disapprove of the way I have developed this notion here. I think that Donaldson is profoundly correct in his claim that Paul is struggling here (at times) with an opposing reading of Abraham based on Genesis 17, although in my view this does not explain *all* the argumentation in Romans 4 — merely that particular announcement and consequent subsection.

This problem for Paul *might* be reinforced by a contemporary Jewish view that truth comes in two forms, elemental then developed — in this context, then, Gen. 15:6 *then* 17:5: see David Daube, *The New Testament and Rabbinic Judaism* (London: Athlone Press, 1956), 141-50; taken up by Richard N. Longenecker in the context of Galatians; *Galatians*, WBC 41 (Dallas, Tex.: Word, 1990), 111. This would be entirely appropriate here, but I see no explicit evidence that the view is in play.

59. See *y. Bikk.* 1.4, *Tanh. B.* 32a, and *Pesiq. R.* 108a!; collected in G. Walter Hansen, *Abraham in Galatians: Epistolary and Rhetorical Contexts*, JSNTSup 29 (Sheffield: JSOT Press, 1989), 197.

60. A point that, if true, draws Paul's discussion of Abraham here much closer to some of his discussion of Abraham in Galatians. Pagans enjoy Abraham's fatherhood only when they are grafted into his illustrious son, someone descended from Isaac and also corresponding to him — that is (of course), Jesus, the miraculously conceived, crucified, and, "on the third day" (see Gen. 22:4), resurrected One.

61. So we ought to resist spiritualizing the text at this point. I would suggest that it is Abraham's biological fatherhood that is under discussion; see esp. Sir. 44:22 following vv. 19-21; *Jubilees* 16:12, 16b (see 19:16-29, where Abraham also recognizes that God will bless the seed of Jacob rather than Esau, seed meaning descendants); also Isa. 51:2, 2 *Bar.* 57.1; see also — in more general terms — Daniel Boyarin, *A Radical Jew: Paul and the Politics of Identity* (London, Berkeley & Los Angeles: University of California Press, 1994); see also Stowers, *RR,* 221-50. Much modern non-Jewish exegesis passes too easily over the substantial intermediate steps between Abraham, his fatherhood, and "us," which to a Jewish mind were probably entirely normal and necessary. Abraham's fatherhood of Jews is one of kinship and descent. Conversely, an exemplary spiritualized "fatherhood" looks suspiciously like a later Christian contribution to the reading of Abraham. So Stowers's pointed observation: "later Christian readings, with their categories of sin and salvation, have obscured the issues of ethnic lineage and inheritance that would have appeared central to Paul's ancient readers. Paul writes about gentiles who . . . [are] outside of the fleshly lineage of Abraham and its sonship . . ." (*RR,* 221). Of course, the spiritualized reading might ultimately prove correct, but it would have to be established in the face of the general exegetical trend contemporary to Paul, which we must assume, at least at first, that he shared. Indeed, we would need to find reasonably unambiguous textual indications in support of such a phenomenologically revisionist reading.

62. Its temporal location is irrelevant to its effectiveness in relation to questions of fulfillment versus negation of the Torah.

63. Direct quotations and echoes of Gen. 17:5 in bold and Gen. 15:6 underlined.

64. See Gen. 17:1, 18 (LXX).

65. Gen. 15:5b.

66. Gen. 17:17.

67. LNSM demonstrates that the preposition can take an impersonal object, citing Matt. 21:2 (a village opposite), Mark 13:3 (the Mount of Olives), and 15:39. This last reference is dubious, since a personal reference to Christ seems likely; however, the broader point is certainly fair (see 718, §83.42).

68. It is worth noting in passing that this is now a clear instance of the verb πιστεύω taking a genitive as its "object."

69. Some scholars suggest a scriptural echo, most likely of Isa. 48:13, but this statement looks more like a variation on a Jewish theologoumenon. As Ch. Burchard comments, "[a]round the beginning of our era 'He who gives life to the dead' had become all but a definition of God in Judaism": "Joseph and Aseneth: A New Translation and Introduction," in *The Old Testament Pseudepigrapha,* vol. 2, ed. James H. Charlesworth (New York: Doubleday, 1985), 234. See also Otfried Hofius, *Paulusstudien* (Tübingen: Mohr [Siebeck], 1989), 121, n. 1, who cites in comparison with "the one who makes alive . . ." 2 Cor. 1:9, *Joseph and Aseneth,* 8:9 and 20:7, the second of the eighteen benedictions, and *b. Ket.* 8b; and in relation to "the one who calls . . ." 2 Macc. 7:28 (an important text: see also vv. 22-23), 2 *Baruch* 21:4 and 48:8b, Philo, *On the Special Laws,* 4.187 (also *On the Creation,* 81); see 2 *Clement* 1:8 and *Apostolic Constitutions* 8.12.7. See also the contextually related notion of giving glory to God, so Matt. 5:16 and 1 Pet. 2:12; also, more generally, John 5:21.

70. I do not detect either enthymemic or abductive reasoning here.

71. One can imagine Paul retorting, "Are you really suggesting that the poor man has not done enough yet?! Or that this superhuman contest is in some way inadequate?!" (arguments alternatively in terms of pathos and logos). This is tantamount to saying that a martyr, having just been executed for his confession of the one God, will be saved only if he also kept the Sabbath correctly throughout his life, a not invalid point but an insensitive one in context, and possibly asking too much. Such a suggestion here also belittles the piety of the great patriarch (and this allows, in turn, a subtle redirection of any potential criticism; it could be presented as an attack on Abraham, the patriarch, rather than on a particular — rather tendentious — *portrayal of* Abraham, the great patriarch). I suspect that Paul was well aware of these fallback positions. Furthermore, such a contention integrates with a widespread view in Paul's time of Abraham in heroic terms and as supremely faithful to God more in the manner of a martyr (see 1 Macc. 2:52) than of someone perfectly law observant (as in *Jubilees, pass.,* T. *Levi* 9:1-14, 2 *Bar.* 57:1-3, 1QS 3.2-4, and *m. Kidd.* 4:14, *Lev. R.* 2.10 [on Lev. 1:12]), a view generated

primarily but not exclusively by Abraham's behavior in Genesis 22. (Note also the Jewish tradition of Abraham's faithfulness through ten trials, the last and most important of which was the Akedah.) Paul does not introduce the Akedah here explicitly (unless perhaps it is implied by vv. 24-25), but the general heroic view of Abraham certainly seems operative: see Samuel Sandmel, *Philo's Place in Judaism: A Study of Conceptions of Abraham in Jewish Literature* (New York: Ktav, 1971); Hansen, *Abraham in Galatians*, 175-99; Longenecker, *Galatians*, 110-12; Watson, *P&HF*, 220-69.

72. Δικαίωσις may in part be Paul's echo of δικαιῶσαι δίκαιον εὖ δουλεύοντα πολλοῖς κ.τ.λ. in Isa 53:11b LXX. Hooker denies the link but overlooks the way that the unusual accusative διά and the notion of some atonement for sins — and both are distinctive claims for Paul — corroborate the direct echo of verbs: see *Jesus and the Servant* (London: SPCK, 1959), 122, 38.

73. This theory is sometimes rooted in a specific florilegium. It was frequently suggested by an earlier generation of scholars, and we now possess rather more evidence of the existence of such collections, within both Jewish and non-Jewish traditions. An excellent survey of the evidence and theory is supplied by Stanley Porter, "Paul and His Bible: His Education and Access to the Scriptures of Israel" (paper presented to the Paul and Scripture Seminar, Society of Biblical Literature Annual Meeting, Washington, November 2006), available at www.westmont.edu/~fisk/paulandscripture/Porter.html. I am not suggesting a principal role for a florilegium here, however, as much as a central role for a discourse woven out of key texts.

74. See 12:2-3.

75. Possibly also elements from Job: see Phil. 1:18-20 and Job 13:13-16; 14:13-16; 19:25-27; 42:10, 12-13, 16-17 (as noted by James P. Ware, "Paul and Job in Philippians 1:19," paper presented in Pauline Epistles Section, Society of Biblical Literature Annual Meeting, Washington, November 2006).

76. See Gal. 3:10-13, discussed further in part five, chapter twenty.

77. See in particular the New Testament texts noted earlier that speak of δίκαιος in some respect.

78. Clearly, Christ himself was also faithful unto death, receiving resurrection and enthronement after his submission (see Phil. 2:5-11).

79. See chapter ten, §4; and chapter eleven, §2.3 (UD 10).

80. It could be suggested at this point that a degree of incoherence still remains, because Paul is undertaking a scriptural attestation to an apocalyptic and revelatory system. But he is doing so (1) because both his opponent, the Teacher, and his audience, the Roman Christians, accept the authoritative role of Scripture, so it is — if nothing else — a useful pragmatic rhetorical argument; and (2) his underlying hermeneutic is itself grounded in the revelatory event to which he directs it — something apparent from its christological shape. It is therefore not witnessing in full independence from that event, which would set up embarrassing epistemological disjunctions, but mediating it.

81. For example, Paul's discussion of Abraham in 4:2-8 is problematic for the rereading of "works of law" suggested by advocates of the new perspective like Dunn and Wright (see part three, chapter twelve).

Notes to Chapter Nineteen

1. The paradigmatic overdetermination of lexicography has been a particularly important technique to identify — see esp. part two, chapters seven and nine.

2. And within this citadel, or fortified city, we have seen that certain strongpoints proved especially critical to its defense.

3. This is because Justification readings can benefit from these texts' frequent brevity and consequent ambiguity, which allow the theory to be read into the semantic gaps.

4. A beginning has already been made in part four, chapter fourteen.

5. Perhaps controversially, then, it would follow that the Justification arguments and texts in Galatians remain fundamentally ambiguous without a controlling influence from the more detailed discussion in Romans 1-4 — and indeed Luther himself commented on Galatians in detail only hav-

ing already spent much time lecturing on Romans. Furthermore, even subsequent Justification discussions in Romans itself require the earlier detailed elaboration in order to make their case fully.

6. Romans 5:1-11 begins with a reasonably distinctive reprise of two of the schema's key terms, namely, δικαιόω and πίστις (the latter occurring twice, in vv. 1 and 2, assuming the cogency of the text-critical case for the second instance's inclusion), and δικαιόω recurs in v. 9. But beyond this point the key terms are not in evidence and indeed largely drop out of the letter's argument until much later. In and of themselves, then, these instances look somewhat vestigial and are perhaps merely retrospective (see Gal. 3:26). However, there is a strong emphasis on Christ and his instrumentality throughout this text; his death is explicitly mentioned four times (vv. 6, 8, 9, 10), and this is especially redolent of 3:21-26. Wrath is mentioned as well (in v. 9; see the programmatic 1:18), and the motifs of shame and boasting are prominent (boasting in vv. 2, 3, 11; shame in v. 5 — καταισχύνει, translated rather unhelpfully by the NRSV and NIV as "disappoint"; Robert Jewett provides an accurate account: *Romans*, Hermeneia [Minneapolis, Minn.: Fortress, 2007], 355-56; see also his programmatic remarks about honor and shame on 46-59). None of these last are decisive, but together they do constitute accumulating counterevidence. On balance, it seems best to concede that 5:1-11 should receive *some* consideration with respect to the Justification schema, but not as a direct summary, because it seems to be freighting distinctive emphases (and thus may open up new interpretative angles).

7. Romans 6:7-8 deploys two key verbs in a compact and most illuminating statement (δικαιόω, in the perfect, and πιστεύω). The broader setting also speaks of moving beyond the law (see esp. 6:15 in relation to 6:1; also 7:1-4). I am inclined therefore to include it in the heartland, although again in a somewhat indirect way (i.e., as marginal, and even disputed, territory).

8. The Corinthian instances of δικαιοσύνη Θεοῦ in 1 Cor. 1:30 and 2 Cor. 5:21 seem even more distantly related, in that *none* of the other key terms occur in their context, and similarly 1 Cor. 6:11, where δικαιόω occurs in a baptismal setting (elsewhere in this letter, see only 4:4). It would seem, then, that these texts can assist our lexical and phraseological semantic decisions but ought not contribute to important explanatory decisions; they are probably in any case too brief to do so. (However, the baptismal setting similar to Rom. 6:7-8 is certainly worth noting.) Much the same limitation applies to the πιστ- and νόμος language that occurs in these letters, including the provocative statement in 1 Cor. 7:19 concerning God's commandments. Only with great difficulty can these texts be assumed to deploy Justification theory overtly, but they can still aid our evaluation of that schema in a more distant semantic sense.

9. And if the Galatians material is not monolithically committed to the schema, then this ratio is even less impressive, with fewer than fifty verses of ancillary discussion, or less than 50 percent of the citadel text!

10. Circumcision (περιτομή) occurs in Rom. 2:25 (2x), 26, 27, 28, 29; 3:1, 30; 4:9, 10 (2x), 11, 12 (2x); 15:8; so fourteen of fifteen Romans instances in the textual citadel; also in Gal. 2:7, 8, 9, 12; 5:6, 11; 6:15 (5:6 is part of the heartland, but clearly the distribution here does not correlate with the Justification schema as closely as it does in Romans, probably because of contingent differences). In addition, the signifier occurs in 1 Cor. 7:19, Phil. 3:3, 5, Eph. 2:11, and Col. 2:11 (2x), 3:11, and 4:11 — largely innocuous instances for our present purposes, although the Philippians instances may well also belong to the heartland. The antithetical ἀκροβυστία occurs in Rom. 2:25, 26 (2x), 27; 3:30; 4:9, 10 (2x), 11 (2x), 12; so all eleven instances are in the citadel; also in Gal. 2:7; 5:6; 6:15 (and we have just affirmed that 5:6 is part of the heartland). It occurs elsewhere in the Pauline corpus in 1 Cor. 7:18 and 19, in Col. 2:13 and 3:11, and in Eph. 2:11; again, largely innocuous instances.

11. The motif of boasting often functions ostensibly in the "loop of foolishness," and where this word group occurs in Romans, it is distributed largely in the textual citadel: see καύχημα in 4:2; καύχησις in 3:27; 15:17; and καυχάομαι in 2:17, 23; 5:2, 3, 11. See also καύχημα in Gal. 6:4; Phil. 1:26; 2:16; καύχησις in 1 Thess. 2:19; and καυχάομαι in Gal. 6:13, 14; Eph. 2:9; Phil. 3:3; (Jas. 1:9; 4:16).

But these words are especially common in the Corinthian correspondence (for καύχημα, see 1 Cor. 5:6; 9:15, 16; 2 Cor. 1:14; 5:12; 9:3; for καύχησις, 1 Cor. 15:31; 2 Cor. 1:12; 7:4, 14; 8:24; 11:10, 17; for καυχάομαι, 1 Cor. 1:29, *31* [Jer 9:23]; 3:21; 4:7; 13:3; 2 Cor. 5:12; 7:14; 9:2; 10:8, 13, 15, 16, 17; 11:12, 16, 18, 30

[2x]; 12:1, 5 [2x], 6, 9). So, clearly, this word group is not *necessarily* distinctive to the Justification schema (or some equivalent).

The motif *is* correlated when it is juxtaposed with semantically antithetical verbs of shame, ἐπαισχύνομαι (Rom. 1:16; 6:21) and καταισχύνω (Rom. 5:5; 9:33; 10:11 [Isa. 28:16]; elsewhere in Paul only in the Corinthian correspondence, but there quite extensively: see 1 Cor. 1:27 [2x]; 11:4, 5, 22; 2 Cor. 7:14; 9:4).

12. Abraham is discussed in detail in Rom. 4:1-22 and mentioned more briefly in 9:7 and 11:1. (A reference in 2 Cor. 11:22 is incidental.) He is also discussed in detail in Gal. 3:6-18, 29, and is significant in 4:21-31. So, once again, although not a perfect correlation, the deployment of Abraham fits the Justification schema to a significant degree. Notably, where Gen. 15:6 is in play, the correlation is perfect.

13. Scripture is quoted in these passages with peculiar frequency. The statistics in *The Greek New Testament*, ed. M. Black et al., third corrected ed. (Stuttgart: United Bible Societies, 1983) may be taken as indicative. Of sixty-four listed references to the Old Testament in Romans (899), sixteen are in the citadel and a further thirteen in 9:30–10:21 — that is, almost half! This density of quotation is matched only by the closely related chapters 9 (vv. 1-29, ten references) and 11 (eight references), and the letter's probable argumentative conclusion, which contains a catena (15:9-12, five references). By way of contrast, chapters 5–8 contain only three (or four, including a reference to Gen. 22:12/16 in 8:32, which this tabulation omits).

Similar considerations apply to Galatians (900). Aside from the quotation of Lev. 19:18 in 5:14, the other eleven citations occur between 3:6 and 4:30, with nine of these occurring between 3:6 and 3:16! (I would add an allusion to Ps. 143:2 in 2:16.) This density is almost squarely in our heartland.

14. Following a detailed investigation of this text in its broader setting, we will return in the chapter's final section to treat the much shorter, related texts in Romans — elements in chapters 5, 6, 12, 11, and 14.

15. See C. H. Dodd, *The Epistle of Paul to the Romans* (London: Collins [Fontana Books], 1959 [1932]), 161-63; Ferdinand Christian Baur, *Paul, the Apostle of Jesus Christ, His Life and Works, His Epistles and Teachings: A Contribution to a Critical History of Primitive Christianity*, trans. A. Menzies and E. Zeller, 2nd ed., 2 vols. (London: Williams & Norgate, 1873-1875), 326-32 — Romans 9–11 forming "the centre and pith of the whole, to which everything else is only an addition" (327). I will also rely in the following — in addition to the main commentaries already used for Romans — on J. Ross Wagner's important and elegant study (although it is concerned primarily with different questions): *Heralds of the Good News: Isaiah and Paul in Concert in the Letter to the Romans* (Leiden: Brill, 2002).

16. As set out in part four, chapter thirteen, A arguments present Paul's own gospel; B arguments defend this gospel from criticisms; and C arguments attack the gospel of the Teacher. Rhetoric cannot of course be reduced to these basic argumentative functions; the categories, however, are useful if blunt tools for organizing Romans.

17. Emphasizing the faithfulness of God over against the unbelief of Israel as the "two questions [that] dominate these three chapters," *the latter calling the former into question:* so N. Thomas Wright, "The Letter to the Romans: Introduction, Commentary, and Reflections," in *The New Interpreter's Bible*, ed. L. Keck (Nashville, Tenn.: Abingdon, 2002), 621, slightly misstates both the attribute of God in play and the orientation of these two important notions theologically in Paul's broader thinking. God is "elective," which includes rather more than mere "fidelity." Such a God initiates, freely, hence the legitimacy of pagan salvation independently of complete law observance. Nevertheless, the responsibility for Israel's unbelief *rests on Israel*. Unbelief, when God has come to Israel in Christ, is wrong. Yet as these two vast processes collide, the unbelief of Israel *cannot overthrow that divine election*. God's election will triumph. So Wright has these principles the wrong way around. (If he is correct, it is also very difficult to explain the question of 11:1 — "has God abandoned his people, then?" This challenge presupposes that God is in the right, his people in the wrong. It is not God's fidelity that is in question; it is *Israel's!*)

18. And so it is apparent that the discussion cannot be designated salvation history per se. Certain specific episodes within salvation history are in view as potential problems for the legitimacy of

Paul's gospel. But this is not quite the same thing as presenting a salvation history. Moreover, the discussion's principal orientation is present and future.

19. They are also creating the vulnerability of encouraging pagan anti-Jewishness, which was presumably almost always a latent possibility within Paul's congregations — hence 11:17-24. And this issue may have connected unhelpfully in turn with any friction between more and less law-observant groups — the weak and the strong: see Romans 14. So further sound, essentially pastoral reasons existed for Paul to take this set of criticisms seriously.

20. It is possible that this is a criticism and argumentative dynamic merely extrapolated from Paul's position — that *Paul* holds Israel not to be saved outside Christ, but the Teacher does not share this opinion. The accusation of being a traitor then holds only in terms of Paul's side of the argument: "If what you say and believe is true, then you are a traitor, because you hold your fellow Jews to be damned." And, after some vacillation, I currently incline toward the cogency of this reconstruction, as against the reconstruction that both Paul and the Teacher view Israel as condemned outside Christ; see Matthew and Revelation. If the Teacher did not view Israel as saved, then it is difficult to explain why Paul would be spending so much time arguing that despite Israel's current rejection God will triumph and save them all eventually. This would be a position that they share, and therefore it would not be embarrassing to Paul in the present context. Concomitantly, it would not make sense for the Teacher to criticize Paul's gospel for implying absurdly that the Jews are damned, because he would share this view. He could only point to the absurdity of including pagans in the saved constituency, and the discussion of Romans 9–11 could then in effect stop at 9:26. But of course it does not, suggesting that an element within the early church endorsed something of a Sonderweg. There may indeed have been an ongoing debate about the status of unresponsive Jews — whether or not they were saved. (Presumably, the destruction of Jerusalem later made a powerful impact on this debate.) And this posture on the part of the Teacher accords with his soteriology, which bases salvation on law observance. There is nothing to prevent the temple from fulfilling the atoning functions that he ascribes to Christ. Christ is for him, in effect, a more convenient cultus (the advantages of which should not be downplayed). Alternatively, the early church might fulfill a vicarious atoning role on behalf of the rest of Israel (see, to a degree, Qumran).

21. Stowers is sophisticated, but still ends up privileging these assertions as special insights into Paul's "core" and "ultimate commitment [to the Jewish people]": see *Rereading Romans: Justice, Jews, and Gentiles* (New Haven & London: Yale University Press, 1994), 289-93, quoting from 293 — hereafter *RR*.

22. I am not convinced that their law-free ethic is currently at issue, because Paul has just addressed this question at length in Romans 5–8. The orientation of Israel toward the law, however, continues to be debated.

23. Presumably, Paul's apostleship to the pagans alerted him to the previously undiscovered resources in these accounts, and in the Scriptures in this relation.

24. That is, in terms of "double predestination."

25. See Gen. 35:10-12; Exod. 3:15; Deut. 29:13.

26. This treatment is interwoven with other discussions, e.g., of the origin of pagan idolatry, etc.

27. Two of the same verbs are used in Rom. 9:19 and Wis. 12:12: see τίς γὰρ ἐρεῖ Τί ἐποίησας; ἢ τίς ἀντιστήσεται τῷ κρίματί σου; in Wis., with Ἐρεῖς μοι οὖν· τί ἔτι μέμφεται; τῷ γὰρ βουλήματι αὐτοῦ τίς ἀνθέστηκεν in Romans.

28. . . . κεραμεὺς . . . ἐκ τοῦ αὐτοῦ πηλοῦ ἀνεπλάσατο τά τε τῶν καθαρῶν ἔργων δοῦλα σκεύη τά τε ἐναντία, πάντα ὁμοίως· τούτων δὲ ἑτέρου τίς ἑκάστου ἐστὶν ἡ χρῆσις, κριτὴς ὁ πηλουργός.

29. See 1 Cor. 14:36; 2 Cor. 2:17, 4:2; 1 Thess. 2:13; see Col. 1:25.

30. Hence, the commentators seem largely to pass over this motif and its significance in 9:16, viewing it as a metaphor for "works" in some sense — so "activity": see C. E. B. Cranfield, *A Critical and Exegetical Commentary on the Epistle to the Romans*, vol. 2, *Commentary on Romans IX–XVI and Essays* (London: T&T Clark International [Continuum], 2004 [1979]), 485; "doing": James D. G. Dunn, *Romans 9–16*, WBC 38 (Dallas, Tex.: Word, 1988), 552-53; "human effort generally": Thomas R.

Schreiner, *Romans*, BECNT (Grand Rapids, Mich.: Baker, 1998), 508; "achieving": Brendan Byrne, *Romans*, Sacra Pagina (Collegeville, Minn.: Glazier, Liturgical Press, 1996), 296; and Thomas H. Tobin, *Paul's Rhetoric in Its Contexts: The Argument of Romans* (Peabody, Mass.: Hendrickson, 2004), 330; "exertion": Leander E. Keck, *Romans*, ANTC (Nashville, Tenn.: Abingdon Press, 2005), 233. This intuition is true to a degree, but it fails to catch Paul's inauguration of a discourse that is later developed in very significant ways. It will ultimately become apparent that this topos is present in the Teacher's system as well, hence why Paul is beginning to subvert it here. The NRSV masks this signal by *translating* τρέχοντος as "exertion," as does the NIV, which prefers "effort"!

31. This can now be oriented in a theologically apologetic direction rather than a salvation-historically apologetic one (i.e., Has God failed? or some such). Of course, this is an important question, and it certainly worries many modern interpreters. However, I am not convinced that the integrity of God is at stake between Paul and the Teacher; both endorse it strongly, as far as I can see, *but hold radically different opinions of its outworking.*

32. That is, apart from a possible reading of this verb in 9:6a. But this is precisely the issue in dispute.

33. And some candidly admit as much, e.g., Wright: "Two questions dominate these three chapters: the question of unbelieving Israel, and the question of God's faithfulness. The two are, of course, intimately connected: the latter is raised by the former. Israel's refusal (as a whole) to believe the gospel of Jesus raises in its sharpest form the question of whether God has in fact been faithful to his promises. It is somewhat paradoxical that Paul does not spell out these questions themselves; they are, it seems, too huge and obvious" ("The Letter to the Romans," 621).

34. Significantly, the suggested rereading frees Paul's notion of election from a strong sense of double predestination, because the key statements establishing that dynamic are primarily argumentative entrapments more reflective of the views of Paul's opponent, the Teacher, rather than his own position. The roots of the apostle's view of election must now be sought elsewhere, and probably most clearly in the strongly elective statements of Romans 8, where what we might dub a thoroughgoing christocentric election is apparent. That position might then also be resumed by what follows after Romans 9, at which point the consistency that a rigorously apocalyptic rereading imparts to Paul will be still more apparent. At the least, Paul's commitment to election can now be redescribed.

35. Paul's statements in Rom. 9:11 and 11:5-6 are indecisive because they are negations. (οὐκέτι should be read in 11:5-6 as a marker of inferential, not temporal, negation: see BDAG 736, meaning 2.) Elsewhere in Paul the phrase "works of law" occurs in the context of debates with other Jewish Christians, or in contexts that are arguably characterized as such: see Rom. 2:6-7, 15; 3:20, 27-28; 4:2-8; Gal. 2:16; 3:2, 5, 10; see also Eph. 2:9-10. (The Romans texts, as we have already seen, address only "a Jew" or "Jews," hence not necessarily Israel as a whole.)

36. Justification theorists tend to prefer the reading "end," because Christ "fulfills" the negative, prior experience of law observance only indirectly, satisfying the wrath of God unleashed there against sin and functioning in an analogous, contractual fashion to save those who exercise the appropriate criterion for salvation, which is now the easier condition of faith. Advocates of more salvation-historical and/or "scriptural" readings of Paul find the sense "goal" more palatable; the Scriptures point to Christ, as any right-thinking exegete should realize. The meaning "goal," however, if attested, can still assist the Justification advocate over against the apocalyptic rereader, because at least Paul still seems to be thinking prospectively, however opaquely. In either of these readings, the potentially harsh consequences for Israel of such "prospectivism" are apparent as well; in both cases Israel fails to grasp something obvious and can be accused of stupidity, resulting in a strong accountability if she continues to reject Christ (i.e., one appropriately met with punishment): see my study, *The Quest for Paul's Gospel: A Suggested Strategy* (London: T&T Clark [Continuum], 2005), ch. 7, 132-45.

37. It should be noted that this text's challenges are by no means limited to those made in relation to an apocalyptic reading. For example, all readings struggle to explain Paul's use of Deut. 30:12-14 in 10:6-8.

38. This possibility passes largely unnoticed by the commentators, who generally assume that Paul's scriptural citations in vv. 25-29 function in a single subsection and also serve an essentially sec-

ondary, corroborative argumentative function: see, i.a., Joseph A. Fitzmyer, *Romans: A New Translation with Introduction and Commentary*, AB 33 (New York: Doubleday, 1993), 571-75.

39. See Rom. 3:5, 25 and 26; and hence also, almost certainly, 1:17, 3:21 and 22.

40. First, the (repeated) quotation of Isa. 28:16/8:14: shame and glory are important themes in Romans rooted in the eschaton: see, i.a., Rom. 5:2-5; and Ernst Käsemann, *Commentary on Romans*, trans. Geoffrey W. Bromiley, 4th ed. (Grand Rapids, Mich.: Eerdmans, 1980 [1975]), 279; second, belief, trust, salvation, and resurrection are intimately connected in 10:9-13; and, third, the suggestions of various other parts of the letter, in particular, chapter 8, where life is clearly resurrected, eschatological life. "Life" is an important theme in Romans, as noted in a classic analysis by Robin Scroggs, "Paul as Rhetorician: Two Homilies in Romans 1–11," in *Jews, Greeks and Christians: Essays in Honor of William David Davies*, ed. R. Hamerton-Kelly and R. Scroggs (Leiden: Brill, 1976), 271-98.

41. Note, in addition to Käsemann's classic reading, Keck's apposite remark: "God's righteousness is not simply an attribute . . . but God's saving action in Christ" (*Romans*, 248); see also the earlier discussion in part four, chapter seventeen.

42. It is important to emphasize that the exact *content* of righteous acts is heavily context dependent. In chapter seventeen it was suggested that this content in Romans is influenced by the discourse of divine kingship.

43. Paul's pun here is impossible to capture in translation. He slides from the "righteous activity" espoused by the Teacher to the "righteous act" of God, both of these practices being describable in Greek by δικαιοσύνη.

44. BDAG 1053.

45. I am possibly exaggerating our difficulties here; some purchase on this text is perhaps possible. But no precise *temporal* decisions are possible, and this is the critical point at issue in our present discussion.

46. Hence, this speaks immediately against dual covenant construals of Paul: see John Gager, *Reinventing Paul* (Oxford & New York: Oxford University Press, 2000); Lloyd Gaston, *Paul and the Torah* (Vancouver: University of British Columbia Press, 1987); and Stowers, *RR*. The difficulties of this overarching reconstruction will deepen as we consider Romans 10 in more detail.

47. A passive, usually translated here in precise terms with a middle sense. Douglas Moo suggests that Koiné not uncommonly confused these voices: *The Epistle to the Romans*, NICNT (Grand Rapids, Mich.: Eerdmans, 1996), 633, n. 18.

48. The text-critical decision is not especially significant because if the word was not originally present, it had to be presupposed (i.e., it was elided); see Moo (*Romans*, 630, n. 2).

49. If they are not the same, then Paul would have changed subjects dramatically! The righteous act of God that the pagans received in 9:30 and that Israel did not attain to in 9:31, the act that leads to the reverse of eschatological shame (i.e., to glory) in 9:33b, would now *not* be the content of Paul's prayer for salvation in relation to Israel in 10:1 or the object of her ignorance in 10:2-3! In 10:4 the two notions are married explicitly, with the statement that Christ leads to δικαιοσύνη[ν] for everyone who trusts.

50. Note the differentiated cases in 10:3 — τὴν τοῦ θεοῦ δικαιοσύνην and τῇ δικαιοσύνῃ τοῦ θεοῦ. These are unique in Romans, and in Paul's entire corpus. There is little or no need for such differentiation if Paul wishes to speak simply of God's own righteous activity, as he has done before (see esp. Rom. 3:5). Explicit christological genitives in such terms are also apparent elsewhere in Paul, that is, with prepositions supplied: see 1 Cor. 1:30 and Phil. 3:9. I suspect that 2 Cor. 5:21 ought to be read in this sense as well.

51. Gaston's useful characterization, drawn from Rom. 11:11 (see *Paul and the Torah*, 116-50).

52. The checkered textual history of this verse suggests that it greatly puzzled the early church as well. However, the variant found in 𝔓⁴⁶, B, part of the Western tradition (the second corrector of ℵ, D, and G), and the majority text fits my developing interpretation perfectly. (Moo gives a full discussion in *Romans*, 643, n. 2.)

53. It occurs only twice in the New Testament, in Rom. 1:20 and Eph. 2:10. By way of contrast, ποιέω occurs 568x, and ἔργα 169x. These connections are articulated nicely by Simon J. Gathercole,

Where Is Boasting? Early Jewish Soteriology and Paul's Response in Romans 1–5 (Grand Rapids, Mich.: Eerdmans, 2002), 92-96; and Francis Watson, *Paul and the Hermeneutics of Faith* (London: T&T Clark International [Continuum], 2004), 315-35 — hereafter *P&HF.*

54. See also Gal. 3:10, which includes the key phrase ποιῆσαι αὐτά.

55. So has Paul changed his mind when he writes Romans, and this despite his continued negation of the "catch phrase" drawn from this text?!

56. See also my final remarks on the church-historical pedigree of Justification theory in part two, chapter eight; see also the analysis of "faith" in Justification theory in part one, chapter two.

57. See part four, chapter fourteen; and see further in chapter twenty. Indeed, this is why Paul characterizes this opposing gospel in terms of perfectionism: see esp. Gal. 5:3; 6:13a; see also Jas. 2:10. However, probably only perfection in the "active" sense is meant by this — that is, the positive doing of good deeds; see Rom. 2:6-10. Jesus still presumably provides atonement for transgressions; see Rom. 3:24-25; 1 Cor. 15:3; 2 Cor. 5:19; Gal. 1:4.

58. As Cranfield urges (*Romans IX–XVI*, 508-9), although probably in the form of the appropriate participle (a form that he dismisses without comment): ὅτι [διώκοντες] οὐκ ἐκ πίστεως ἀλλ' ὡς ἐξ ἔργων κ.τ.λ.

59. And it is supported by the parallelism between vv. 30 and 31. Here Paul contrasts pagans not pursuing something but getting it — "righteousness" — and Israel pursuing something but not getting it — that is, most obviously, righteousness. If Paul shifts the goal of this pursuit, then the point of the contrast in activities is lost.

60. Pelagius was alert to these interpretative possibilities in relation to voice: "If this is spoken in the person of the apostle. . . . But if the whole of the above thought belongs to the objectors, the apostle here is replying and summarizing the issue by saying: 'What shall I say to these objections . . . ?'": noted in Gerald Bray and Thomas C. Oden, eds., *Ancient Christian Commentary on Scripture: New Testament VI: Romans* (Downers Grove, Ill.: InterVarsity, 1998), 259. Some of his comments on preceding material in Romans also indicate that he is participating in much broader debate at this point: "Those who think that that this is not Paul talking [in 9:26] but the Jews interpret it to mean . . ." (257; see also 258).

61. It should be reiterated that the basic cogency of my rereading does not usually depend on absolutely precise assignations of voice; some latitude is often possible in relation to such decisions, which are intriguing as against vital.

62. This largely because of the standard study of the topos in Paul by V. Pfitzner, *Paul and the Agon Motif: Athletic Imagery in the Pauline Literature* (Leiden: Brill, 1967). More recently, see Nigel J. Spivey, *The Ancient Olympics* (Oxford & New York: Oxford University Press, 2004).

63. It is clearly a "masculinist" discourse.

64. See 1 Cor. 9:24-27; Phil. 3:12-16; 1 Thess. 2:2; and Gal. 2:2b; 5:7 (and 1:14?); see also Col. 2:1; 1 Tim. 6:12; and 2 Tim. 4:7.

65. Fitzmyer represents well the view that relates this discourse primarily to Judaism (*Romans*, 567, 576-81) and Old Testament texts; see also Moo (*Romans*, 593); and Dunn (*Romans 9–16*, esp. 580-81). But while some influence — especially at the stylistic level — may be granted, a strong Old Testament causality is unlikely. The texts that Fitzmyer and others cite cannot actually explain Paul's argument, and they do not encompass even half of Paul's athletic vocabulary, which includes here τρέχω, διώκω, καταλαμβάνω, φθάνω, τέλος, and an implicit prize — βραβεῖον (and the lexicon in the closely related Phil. 3:12-16 is still more extensive). Indeed, these observations reverse the causality suggested by Fitzmyer et al. The ubiquitous ancient imagery of pursuit, competition, and struggle that is deployed self-consciously by the ἀγών topos and used here in turn by Paul *also* informs numerous Old Testament texts. Some commentators at least acknowledge the presence of the athletic imagery (e.g., Käsemann, *Romans*; Dunn, *Romans 9–16*; Fitzmyer, *Romans*; Byrne, *Romans*; and Moo, *Romans*). However, they generally do little with it argumentatively. Largely alone, Stowers grasps the subversive aspect to Paul's use of the topos, although he interprets Paul's argument rather differently from what is being suggested here (*RR*, 303-6, 312-16). Keck also notes that it is an "anomaly" (*Romans*, 242).

66. Stowers again is alert to the cluster of athletic motifs here — πταίω, πίπτω, παράπτωμα, and ἥττημα (*RR*, 312-16).

67. See perhaps most obviously 1 Cor. 9:24-27; Phil. 2:16; 3:12-14; 4:1.

68. See J. Louis Martyn, *Theological Issues in the Letters of Paul* (Edinburgh & Nashville, Tenn.: T&T Clark & Abingdon, 1997), esp. 12-24; see also 25-45.

69. And his subversions do not of course begin here. He undermined a probable agonistic slogan, "the Jew first, *then* the pagan," in Rom. 1:16; 2:9-10; and 3:9 (see part four, chapter fourteen).

70. It is suggested by some interpreters that the phrase εἰς δικαιοσύνην be read adnominally here in relation to the law and not "everyone who trusts." But this is unlikely. Result and purpose clauses using εἰς are a characteristic feature of Paul's argument in Romans. Paul's movement between the language of "righteousness" and "salvation" in Romans is also frequent. Hence, it seems most likely that this phrase merely reprises εἰς σωτηρίαν in 10:1 and anticipates the juxtaposition of the two phrases in v. 10. (Moo gives useful additional reasons for rejecting the adnominal alternative: *Romans*, 636-38.)

71. As even Schreiner concedes *(Romans)*, athletic imagery pervades 9:30-33, and all the other key motifs from those verses are (as we have seen) still being discussed in 10:1-4 — namely, Christ, false law observance, the righteous but misguided behavior of Israel, and the righteous act of God in Christ. Moreover, 10:5 continues the discussion of these motifs. This all suggests that the athletic imagery evident from 9:30 onward might certainly still be in play in 10:4.

72. General references can be found in Robert Badenas, *Christ the End of the Law: Romans 10.4 in Pauline Perspective*, JSNTSup 10 (Sheffield: JSOT, 1985); see also BDAG 998-99. In general, see Plutarch, *Moralia*, 511F. This particular meaning is also apparent in many of the references suggested by LSJ 1774, meaning III, 2 ("winning-post, goal in a race").

73. That is, the long debate whether τέλος means "end" or "goal" is arguably a false storm center. Both attitudes to the law are well attested in Paul: he speaks clearly elsewhere of the law's termination in some sense, as well as its fulfillment (see most obviously Rom. 3:21 — which combines both notions — but also Rom. 1:2-4; 15:4; 2 Cor. 1:20; 4:13; etc.). And both meanings are not infrequently present in this signifier's use; certainly both are present in its construal as "the end [of a race]." To his credit — and largely alone among the commentators — Dunn argues for deemphasizing this question and endorsing a "both-and" reading (although in fact he emphasizes the notion of "end"): *Romans 9-16*, 589. However, neither alternative resolves the more important underlying question whether Paul is arguing retrospectively or prospectively at this point, since both "end" *and* "goal" are compatible with prospective characterizations of his gospel.

74. And it is not difficult to find further support in this realization for my earlier suggestion that 9:6a be rendered in terms of "deviating" or "drifting off course."

75. The strength of which is seen in Badenas's study *(Christ)*. He is well aware of the use of τέλος to denote the end of a race in the sense of its finish line. Keck points to this specific connection as well (*Romans*, 249).

76. It should not be controversial to suggest that for Paul the arrival of Christ terminates the law in some sense: see Rom. 7:6; 8:2; Gal. 3:23-25; 4:4-5; 5:1-4; Phil. 3:7-11. It is important to grasp in addition that the use of the law prior to Christ does not necessarily correlate with its later use by particular Jews or Jewish Christians: see Phil. 3:3-6. The clearest law-related terminations in context are the abandonment of "works of law," which are mentioned in 9:32, along with pursuit of God's righteous action by way of a νόμος δικαιοσύνης εἰς νόμον (9:31). Israel is also described as "zealous" but "ignorant" in 10:2, and involved in 10:3 in some attempted establishment of her own righteous activity, which is wrong. Presumably, all these things should cease.

77. There is also no need to assert a fixed, negative description of Judaism in the period prior to the coming of Christ, on which the gospel account will build — one of the enduring conundrums of Justification theory. See part one, chapters one, four and six; also *Quest*, 132-45.

78. In other words, the metaphor of a "goal" is being subverted by Paul in 10:4, so that motif does not need to imply that Israel was involved prior to Christ in goal-oriented activity as well, a read-

ing that potentially endorses a prospective theological program. Paul is not necessarily endorsing the discourse *and* subverting it at the same time.

79. See אָבֶן and בֵּן; see also Richard N. Longenecker, *The Christology of Early Jewish Christianity* (London: SCM, 1970), 50-53; also *Biblical Exegesis in the Apostolic Period* (Grand Rapids, Mich.: Eerdmans, 1975), 202-4; and the nuanced account of Wagner, *Heralds of the Good News,* 126-42; see also Josephus, *Antiquities,* 10:210 (where he is evasive concerning the meaning of the stone spoken of in Dan. 2:34); and *War,* 5.272. The latter text recounts a fascinating practice that took place during the siege of Jerusalem, and has already been noted in part in chapter fifteen.

80. A minority has suggested identifications for the stone other than Christ (e.g., Meyer, Gaston, Davis, and Meeks, surveyed by Keck, *Romans,* 245). However, this seems unlikely in view of the act of belief in it, echoed by 10:4 and 10:9-13, which points both implicitly and explicitly to Christ: so correctly A. Katherine Grieb, *The Story of Romans: A Narrative Defense of God's Righteousness* (London & Louisville, Ky.: Westminster-John Knox, 2002), 98. Indeed, in the insistence that Israel has stumbled over a stone consisting of her own misreading of the law, we encounter — probably unwittingly — the apogee of the anti-Jewish, prospective reading (which does not make the reading wrong, but it does encourage us to explore alternatives).

81. The commentators generally overlook this distinction, but it is unavoidable in the text. The pagans, Paul states in 9:30, are *not* involved in a race at all, hence the irony of the receipt of a prize. This activity then contrasts with the racing Israelites who do not attain to that prize because of some form of misdirection in relation to the law; they are racing in the wrong direction, εἰς νόμον, after the finish line has already been passed by. So there is no actual race unfolding *between* pagan and Jew. Neither is this apparent in 11:11-12. When Paul does return to comparison between the two he uses the metaphor of a tree, not of a competition (see 11:17-24), the terms of the discussion being shifted overtly in 11:15-16. Consequently, 9:33 *must* add a further layer to a set of subversions rather than fill out a single, consistent analogy.

82. Commentators are in broad agreement on this point. That the antithesis could be completely nonprospective does not seem to occur as a possibility. Some commentators do stretch to a "mixed" approach: see Stowers, *RR;* and Keck, *Romans,* 242-48; Tobin, *Paul's Rhetoric,* 341. But I am not sure that this is ultimately helpful. If Paul is held to be reasoning theologically in opposed directions simultaneously — both prospectively and retrospectively in relation to "works of law" — then the consequences for our interpretation of his thinking are dire (so *Quest,* 33, 46-48).

83. This approach will preserve the relative independence of our analysis of Romans 9:30–10:5. Once the order has been determined, we can infer Paul's rationale here with a reasonable degree of certainty. Without the judgment in terms of narrative priority that he did proceed in this manner, however, there seems to be no basis for proving or disproving that this was in fact his underlying theological program.

84. And perhaps corresponding to this puzzling absence, the pagans in 9:30 are said by Paul explicitly *not* to be pursuing "works of law" when they receive the δικαιοσύνη ἐκ πίστεως (although perhaps — the Teacher might reply — this is because they are not listening and have completely rejected this mode of salvation, or its equivalent — Rom. 1:18-32!).

85. A point made famous of course by Stendahl's accusation of "introspection" (see part one, chapter six); for a precise theological account see chapter one (in largely theoretical terms), but also in part two, chapter eight, and part three, chapter ten (i.e., in church historical and exegetical terms).

86. The absence of any description of the appropriate corresponding function for Christ — as an atoning sacrifice paying for those sins committed while pursuing works of law — is also embarrassing.

87. This observation must be tempered, however, by the third move in the subversion — the stumble — which seems to occur part of the way through a race. In response, it can be suggested that the ludicrous ἀγών (as against the failed ἀγών) is more prominent in context, being negated three times. But this is not a decisive contention.

88. The more historicized approach urged by Dunn and Wright — with "works of law" denoting selfish Jewish attitudes to the badges of the covenant such as circumcision, diet, and Sabbath observance — admittedly avoids some of these problems. However, other, even more serious problems

arguably attend this explanation, as we have seen already in part three, chapter twelve. Moreover, it is worth noting that nothing *in* Romans 9:30–10:5 or its context actually supports this suggested, sociological interpretation of the phrase! So, e.g., Dunn's commentary simply introduces the notion repeatedly, without explicit justification (*Romans 9–16*, 576-77, 581-83, 586-88, 593, 595-96).

89. See Christopher Stanley, *Paul and the Language of Scripture: Citation Technique in the Pauline Epistles and Contemporary Literature*, SNTSMS 74 (Cambridge: Cambridge University Press, 1992); Watson, *P&HF*, 336-41 (see also 415-513). Timothy H. Lim correctly notes that it is not *entirely* accurate to call Paul's technique here a *pesher*; see *Holy Scripture in the Qumran Commentaries and Pauline Letters* (Oxford: Clarendon, 1997), 124-39; and "Midrash Pesher in the Pauline Letters," in *The Scrolls and the Scriptures: Qumran Fifty Years After*, ed. Stanley E. Porter, and Craig A. Evans (Sheffield: JSOT, 1997), 280-92.

90. M. J. Suggs, "'The Word Is near You': Romans 10:6-10 within the Purpose of the Letter," in *Christian History and Interpretation*, ed. W. R. Farmer et al. (Cambridge: University Press, 1967), 289-312; R. B. Hays, *Echoes of Scripture in the Letters of Paul* (New Haven: Yale University Press, 1989), 73-83; E. Elizabeth Johnson, *The Function of Apocalyptic and Wisdom Traditions in Romans 9–11*, SBLDS 109 (Atlanta, Georgia: Scholars, 1989); Edith M. Humphrey, "Why Bring the Word Down? The Rhetoric of Demonstration and Disclosure in Romans 9:30–10:21," in *Romans and the People of God*, ed. Sven K. Soderlund and N. T. Wright (Grand Rapids, Mich.: Eerdmans, 1999), 129-48; Wright, "The Letter to the Romans," 658-66; Wagner, *Heralds of the Good News*, 159-68.

91. See most obviously 1 Cor. 1:30. I would add, however, that the two notions are not coterminous for Paul; he identifies wisdom with the Spirit as well.

92. It occurs around 50x in the LXX (including four instances in the Odes in this total), principally in wisdom literature. It is very rare in the New Testament, occurring outside Revelation only here (Rom. 10:7) and in Luke 8:31 (when the legion occupying the demoniac begs not to be sent into the abyss). In Revelation the word is more common, occurring in 9:1, 2, 11; 11:7; 17:8; 20:1, 3.

93. There are only twelve occurrences in the New Testament, and three in Paul; see elsewhere only a literal use in 1 Cor. 4:8, and the most intriguing 2 Cor. 8:9, which may well also participate in a wisdom discourse, although this does not always seem to be noted. The commentators are preoccupied with refuting James D. G. Dunn's thesis that Christ is not pre-existent in Paul: see *Christology in the Making: A New Testament Inquiry into the Origins of the Doctrine of the Incarnation* (London: SCM, 1980); the parallel with Phil. 2:5-11; and the possibility that genuine economic poverty is meant in some sense: see Victor P. Furnish, *II Corinthians: A New Translation with Introduction and Commentary*, AB 32A (New York: Doubleday, 1984), 404-5, 417-18; Ralph P. Martin, *2 Corinthians*, WBC 40 (Waco, Tex.: Word, 1986), 262-64; Margaret E. Thrall, *A Critical and Exegetical Commentary on the Second Epistle to the Corinthians*, vol. 2, *Commentary on II Corinthians VIII–XIII* (London: T&T Clark International [Continuum], 2004 [2000]), 532-34.

94. See classically Prov. 2:1-4; 3:13-16; 8:18-19, 21 (here promising wealth as well as exceeding it).

95. In addition to Baruch 3:29-30, see esp. Philo, *On the Posterity of Cain*, 84; *On the Change of Names*, 237; *On the Virtues*, 183; and *That Every Good Person Is Free*, 68. The relevance of *4 Ezra* is noted just below.

96. See esp. Wis. 6:12-19; 7:1–8:21.

97. See esp. *4 Ezra* 7:129; see also 8:56, noted by Richard Bauckham, "Apocalypses," in *Justification and Variegated Nomism*, vol. 1, *The Complexities of Second Temple Judaism*, ed. D. A. Carson, Peter T. O'Brien, and Mark A. Seifrid (Tübingen: Mohr [Siebeck], 2001), 171. Bauckham detects the use of Deut. 30:19-20 in *4 Ezra* 14:30 as well. Wright also notes a "proverbial" use in *4 Ezra* 4:7-8 ("The Letter to the Romans," 661).

98. In this sense, moreover, Paul is being faithful to both the original Deuteronomic text and its later reinterpretation in terms of wisdom. Both those texts essentially predicate a certain approach to God — a stooping down to bring what is necessary for Israel near (in Deuteronomy, the law, and in Baruch, wisdom identified with the law).

99. I hasten to add that this notion of "accountability" must be framed very carefully indeed. Paul hedges it with various qualifications (see esp. 11:32), and it should certainly *not* be located in any a

priori, prospective schema, as in Justification theory. Paul places it, rather, in this qualified and a posteriori position. It is best, then, to speak of a "soft" rather than a "hard" accountability in Paul. Moreover, it is vital to resist reading this situation in an essentially modern, "Kantian" way, in which "ought implies can." For Paul, this does not necessarily seem to have been the case. Israel ought to have responded to Christ, although he holds elsewhere that she could not respond to him.

100. Kavin Rowe, "Romans 10:13: What Is the Name of the Lord?" *Horizons in Biblical Theology* 22 (2000): 135-73.

101. This also reinforces the suggestion that 9:5 be read as a full-fledged reference to Christ as divine; again, although unusual, this is one of Paul's key apologetic points in context. Romans 9:5, read in this fashion, correctly anticipates Paul's later argument: God has come to Israel in Christ.

102. And this probably also suggests an adversative use of οὖν: BDAG 737, meaning 4.

103. BDAG 589-90, meaning 2a, although 2d is also possible, namely, "assert," or even 2e, "maintain."

104. This last quotation is therefore a resumption of the reinterpretative moves that we have already seen taking place in relation to Deuteronomy 30:12-14 in vv. 6-10; indeed, all of Paul's quotations in this passage are christocentric and are probably justified by an underlying connection with divine wisdom, as Paul's distinctive phrase here [διὰ] ῥήματος Χριστοῦ suggests. His use of ῥῆμα here resumes the use of that word in Deut. 30:14, quoted in v. 8 and echoed in the following phrase, τὸ ῥῆμα τῆς πίστεως, and it anticipates the same word in the quotation of Ps. 19:4 in 10:18.

105. With the appropriate modifications at certain points.

106. Instances here and through v. 8 (italicized) of ancient parody, Paul quoting the Teacher's own favored text and words, although after this quotation, in a radically different sense.

107. Christ's resurrection is spoken of twice overtly (10:7, 9b). His lordship, meaning his heavenly enthronement and glorification, is spoken of at least once but perhaps twice (10:9a, and perhaps 6). And it has already been noted that this terminology is set in overt parallels to Paul's uses of δικαιο- and σωτερ- language, drawing those signifiers too into an eschatological orbit of meaning. Finally, the repeated "shame" texts refer as well to the eschatological event of the final judgment (see Isa. 28:16 [2x], in 9:33 and 10:11; and Joel 2:32 in 10:13).

108. Of course, this is hardly a new assertion for the argument of Romans; see Rom. 5:17-19, 21.

109. As we have already seen, esp. in part four, chapters fifteen through eighteen, and will further confirm in chapter twenty.

110. This implication is perhaps clearest in Phil. 3:7-11, as we will see in chapter twenty-one.

111. See Rom. 1:2-4; 3:21; and perhaps also 16:26. (And it is not surprising to find that Paul, a former Pharisee, is deeply sensitive to such concerns; see Acts 23:6-7.)

112. See Gal. 2:21; 3:21b.

113. This is an important point, and especially if the argument in this text is to contribute to broader articulations of Paul's views of Judaism and of the law. If Paul's view is retrospective — "thinking backward" — then he need not have formulated detailed criticisms of Judaism in its own terms. Thus, E. P. Sanders's famous aphorism is basically correct: see *Paul and Palestinian Judaism* (Philadelphia: Fortress, 1977), 434-35, 438-40, 442, 474-85; see also part three, chapter twelve, §2.2, for further references and a more detailed discussion. However, it can now also be phrased more precisely: What Paul found wrong with Judaism was not so much that it was not Christianity (or anything in its own terms per se) but that it was not based on the resurrected Christ. Furthermore, we could add that insofar as it was, then presumably it was not wrong.

114. However, note as well that this is automatically a redundant question in any discussion involving at least one Christian participant. (Law-observance is also *never* said explicitly by Paul to be saving; as we have just seen, his account of Israel in Rom. 9:6-23 is elective.)

115. A point already discussed in part four, chapter fourteen, in relation to Rom. 2:25-29: see Deut. 10:16; 30:6; Jer. 4:4; Ezek. 44:9 (see also 36:25-27); see also Col. 2:11; and Philo, *On the Special Laws* 1.1–11; *Questions and Answers on Genesis* 3.46-52; *Questions and Answers on Exodus* 2.2; and *On the Migration of Abraham*, 92.

116. I make this suggestion in part to point out that an apocalyptic system still contains a vigor-

ous critique of "works." Indeed, arguably its critique of any such system is more radical than the repudiation effected by Justification theory. In the latter, "works" remain valid in a certain sense, and necessary to the function of the entire system, although they should be left behind in its first, pre-Christian phase. A legitimate space within Paul's thought must therefore be maintained for them. The transition to Christianity must also be accomplished by some work — the work, of course, of faith. In an "apocalyptic" gospel, however, "works" are simply and completely wrong; unconditional grace implicitly judges all human-centered activity as superfluous, if not also as sinful. Yet this repudiation does not generate in turn a repudiation of ethics. Paul expects a rigorous ethical commitment from his communities.

117. It also seems significant that similar if not identical "gospels" to this one can be detected in other parts of the NT, further corroborating its probable existence. The construct even seems multiply attested!: see Jas. 1:22-25; 2:12, 14-26; Matt. 5:19-20.

118. The allusion in Rom. 3:20 includes the phrase ἐνώπιον αὐτόν, which echoes ἐνώπιόν σου in the LXX (although in a different position); Gal. 2:16 omits this. The phrase ἐξ ἔργων νόμου has been added in both instances.

119. This is admittedly a minimalist account of the echoes possibly present. However, I do not want to base any substantive conclusions here on disputed textual resonances, as far as that is possible. More may well be present, but they will not affect my main conclusions.

120. See *Quest*, 69-94.

121. See, e.g., Moo, *Romans*, 643-70; Schreiner, *Romans*, 550-76, esp. 550-51, 564; and Watson's remarks: *Paul, Judaism, and the Gentiles*, second ed. (Grand Rapids, Mich.: Eerdmans, 2007), 243.

122. Advocates of the new perspective — esp. Wright — emphasize this aspect of the text helpfully, although it must also sometimes be extricated from other considerations! Wright states accurately: "Genuine heart-level belief can only come about, Paul believed, through the action of the Spirit in the gospel. This faith is the sure sign that the gospel has done its work" ("The Letter to the Romans," 664).

123. 1:5 and 16:26 are not decisively problematic texts for my rereadings, and so do not require detailed treatment here. Their construal can simply be integrated with the conclusions already established. They have also already been addressed briefly in passing in part four, chapter fifteen.

124. A notorious text-critical debate also exists in relation to the mood of the verb ἔχω in v. 1. The subjunctive is immeasurably better supported by the external witnesses, but many interpreters nevertheless prefer the indicative. A clearer example of the unwarranted hermeneutical intrusion of Justification theory could hardly be wished for than this debate. The grounds used to overrule the better-attested subjunctive are strongly correlated with the conviction that Paul is mobilizing some form of Justification theory here *and so could not possibly be indicating an uncertain or future situation at 5:1*; see, e.g., Moo, *Romans*, 295-96, n. 17: "Most modern translations and commentators . . . adopt the indicative . . . (because) the context strongly favors a statement about what we have rather than an exhortation to enjoy what we have." Moo even goes on to identify this reading with "Pauline usage and context"! If Justification theory is held in abeyance, however, then no such considerations exist and a future or exhortative reading is entirely possible. Furthermore, exegetical considerations to be explored shortly seem to support this.

125. C. F. D. Moule notes how the subjunctive often has a future sense in Koiné: *An Idiom Book of New Testament Greek,* 2nd ed. (Cambridge: Cambridge University Press, 1959), 21-23.

126. See R. Scroggs, "Rom. 6.7: ὁ γὰρ ἀποθανὼν δεδικαίωται ἀπὸ τῆς ἁμαρτίας," *New Testament Studies* 10 (1963-64): 104-8. I canvass the debate briefly in *RRR*, 210-11, n. 6.

127. Ἀναλογία probably takes the meaning "proportion" here, the whole phrase reading ". . . in accordance with the proportion of πίστις" (see BDAG 67). It is also worth asking, however, whether this expression has been elided from the six roles that follow.

128. Hence, 15:13 should be noted at this point as well, where the work of the Spirit in fashioning the mind of the Christian is elegantly linked to several key Christian attitudes — hope, joy, peace, and understanding or believing. (This *might* also be an implicitly trinitarian formulation; see 2 Cor. 13:13.)

129. The debate concerning this material is voluminous but fortunately need not detain us here. The classic study of this material is Mark Reasoner, *The Strong and the Weak: Romans 14.1–15.13 in Context*, SNTSMS 103 (Cambridge: Cambridge University Press, 1999); a full account of both primary and secondary sources is supplied by Jewett, *Romans*, 829-73. This debate has also already been assessed — to a degree — in part four, chapter thirteen.

130. The text also echoes Paul's earlier characterization of Abraham in Romans 4 (see a similar use of "full conviction" in 4:19 and 14:5; the motif of "doubt" in 4:20a and 14:23; and of "strength," in 4:20b and 15:1), suggesting that his narrative portraits of πίστις can be developed argumentatively in the subordinate sense of mental certitude or conviction; the latter attitude is a necessary condition for the former activity, allowing its argumentative use in this fashion should the need arise. (An analogous situation exists for the attitude of "trust.") Andrew Lincoln notes this link: see "From Wrath to Justification: Tradition, Gospel, and Audience in the Theology of Romans 1:18–4:25," in David M. Hay and E. Elizabeth Johnson, eds., *Pauline Theology*, vol. 3, *Romans* (Minneapolis: Fortress, 1995), 130-68, this point being made on 153.

Notes to Chapter Twenty

1. This evidence has been much rehearsed and so need only be noted here: Paul interrupts his letter opening with a rather defensive assertion of his divinely ratified apostleship (see 1:1), and this seems clearly connected with the presence of "some who are intimidating you and wanting to pervert the gospel of Christ" (v. 7 — translations in this note DC). The salience of this issue for Galatia is further emphasized by Paul's double anathema on alternative versions of the gospel that follows (vv. 8-9), and his repudiation of disingenuous rhetoric (i.e., presentation) in v. 10. The assertion of his own apostolic legitimacy is reiterated in vv. 11-12, and a narrative of its recognition by the Jerusalem leadership recounted in 2:1-10. He then confronts Peter, Barnabas, the Jewish Christians, and "some from James," in 2:11-14 — alternative loci of leadership and authority. Personal considerations return overtly in 4:11, and Paul goes on to speak of some "who are zealous in relation to you, [which is] not good . . ." (v. 17). In 5:7-12 he portrays the same figures as "cutting in on the Galatians" (a metaphor of unsporting behavior in athletics), "not persuading in truth" or from the God who calls them (v. 8), as "yeast" (v. 9 — traditionally a negative image in Judaism), and — resuming the statement of 1:7 — as "troublers" or "intimidators" (v. 10). Further warnings are uttered in 6:12 concerning the dubious motives of "those wanting [the Galatian Christians] to be circumcised." And this is only to note the relatively direct evidence concerning certain perceived interlopers who are challenging Paul's apostleship! Note that we do not need to press beyond the implied opponents to any empirical opponents, since we are interested in interpreting Paul's argumentation within this situation.

2. Richard B. Hays supplies a crisp account of the main options: "The Letter to the Galatians: Introduction, Commentary, and Reflections," *The New Interpreter's Bible* (Nashville, Tenn.: Abingdon, 2000), 181-348, quoting from 184-85; he also considers "agitators" (see 1:7; 5:10, 12), "Judaizers" (see 2:14), and "missionaries" (as suggested by Dunn), endorsing this last designation. A more detailed account is supplied by Richard N. Longenecker, *Galatians*, WBC 41 (Dallas, Tex.: Word, 1990), lxxxviii-xcvi. Incidentally, why it is necessary to refrain from the designation "Judaizers" strikes me as puzzling. It is true that the verb usually refers to its subjects, who are adopting Jewish customs. But nothing *semantic* prevents the *grammatical* and *syntactical* use of this verb with respect to third parties, and as in fact it is being used in Gal. 2:14! Here Peter is accused by Paul of "compelling pagans to adopt Jewish customs," the verb being used as a complementary infinitive. Moreover, there is nothing inherently pejorative about it. It is the context that delivers the negative valence (which is of course quite deliberate on Paul's part). So it seems entirely fair to suggest that the Teachers are also Judaizers, wanting — like Peter, as described in 2:14 — the Antiochene converts from paganism to adopt Jewish customs.

3. See T. D. Donaldson, "The 'Curse of the Law' and the Inclusion of the Gentiles: Galatians 3.13-14," *New Testament Studies* 32 (1986): 94-112, quoting from 97.

4. Longenecker makes a similar set of distinctions (*Galatians*, lxxxix), in terms of (1) exposi-

tion (my type A); (2) polemic (or "aggressive explication"); and (3) apology (my type B). I am not sure whether his category of polemic/aggressive explication is my type C — i.e., critique — or a variation on type A. Irrespective of this, he points out entirely correctly that any reconstruction of the opponents' gospel can only proceed in relation to the appropriate arguments — for him, 2 and 3, and for me, principally C, perhaps supplemented by B. (And this observation makes me suspect that his argument type 2 *is* the equivalent of my type C.)

5. That is, in terms of a more radical, epistolary biography that builds directly from the letters, or a more traditional biography based on a literal and sequential reading of Acts; the former is preferable, but we do not need to enter into this debate here. I have engaged earlier with aspects of Paul's biography in more detail — see part one, chapter five, and part four, chapter thirteen. I am, however, largely assuming that Dunn's hypothesis has been left behind — viz., in terms of Antioch, the food laws, etc. I have, admittedly, rejected this schema largely on grounds of argumentative incoherence. However, I also see little to recommend it biographically. In my view, it misreads the argument of 2:11-14, its broader rhetorical function in the letter, and its consequent biographical and theological implications. I hope to elaborate on these claims in more detail in my own biographical treatment of Paul that has been under development in parallel to this project on Justification. The "incident at Antioch" is notoriously complex and debated, and merits much more than a superficial treatment. The interaction between Sanders and Esler is a useful starting point for those so interested: E. P. Sanders, "Jewish Association with Gentiles and Galatians 2.11-14," in *The Conversation Continues: Studies in Paul and John in Honor of J. Louis Martyn*, Beverly Roberts Gaventa and R. T. Fortna, eds. (Nashville, Tenn.: Abingdon, 1990), 64-69; Philip F. Esler, *Community and Gospel in Luke-Acts* (Cambridge: University, 1987), 71-109; and "The Problem with Mixed Table-Fellowship," in *Galatians* (London & New York: Routledge, 1998), 93-116; to which I would add Markus Bockmuehl, "James, Israel and Antioch," in *Jewish Law in Gentile Churches: Halakhah and the Beginning of Christian Public Ethics* (Edinburgh: T&T Clark, 2000), 49-83. For Dunn's position, see "The Incident at Antioch (Gal. 2.11-18)," in *Jesus, Paul and the Law: Studies in Mark and Galatians* (London & Louisville, Ky.: SPCK & Westminster John Knox, 1990), 129-82 (first published in 1983) — hereafter *JP&L*. An initial counterproposal can be found in Gerd Luedemann, *Paul, Apostle to the Gentiles: Studies in Chronology*, trans. F. S. Jones (Philadelphia: Fortress, 1984 [1980]), esp. 57-59, 75-77.

6. Indeed, the most important and contested aspect of this reconstruction has already been decided in part four, chapter thirteen — that *Romans* was written to counteract the work of an opposing Teacher as well. Once Romans is being read like Galatians, it is not difficult to make Galatians align with Romans!

7. This observation, although much impugned, still seems sound to me. Even if the key word (i.e., πρῶτος) is the equivalent in Koiné to "first," it still seems to indicate a second visit, because otherwise it is redundant. That is, if Paul has visited the Galatians only once, when obviously he preached the gospel to them, then he does not need to qualify his statement that he preached the gospel to them "because of an illness" further by saying "first." This would have been obvious. Furthermore, even advocates of a Pauline biography based on a literal and sequential reading of Acts agree that Paul has been through the southern part of Galatia at least twice (see Acts 15:36–16:6), and those favoring an epistolary approach must send Paul back to Syrian Antioch at some point from the Aegean, and then presumably return him to Asia (see Gal. 2:11-14), at which point a traverse through Galatia is entirely possible. Longenecker is not persuaded by this (*Galatians*, 190); neither is J. Louis (Lou) Martyn (*Galatians: A New Translation with Introduction and Commentary*, AB 33A [London & New York: Doubleday, 1997], 420), but I am not sure on what grounds. Andrew Wakefield has suggested to me in conversation that "first" might modify the preaching of the gospel in a temporal sense, implying that Paul preached the gospel to the Galatians *initially* because of an illness but then continued to preach after he was well again. However, it is difficult to read this arthrous phrase adverbially, and especially in its final location. Moreover, Paul's presentation of the gospel tends to be more punctiliar than this (insofar as we can reconstruct this!: see part one, chapter five). He sets it out, and then he continues to teach his communities if they accept it (although this is admittedly more a tendency than a hard and fast rule): see 1 Thess. 2:1-12, esp. vv. 9 and 12. This reading also does not deliver the same rhetorical

impact as the alternative; it seems otiose for Paul to state that he preached initially because of "a weakness of the flesh," although it is meaningful for him to distinguish between an initial mission that was oriented by illness and another, later visit that was not.

8. There is even evidence of a degree of confusion in Galatians with problems at Corinth addressed in 1 and 2 Corinthians, problems eliminated from the fuller statement of matters in the later Romans. See the following brief enumeration (which is concerned primarily with 2 Corinthians): a concern with persuasion and flattery (see Gal 1:10; 2:11-14; 5:8; compared with 2 Cor. 10:10 — hereafter Gal./2 Cor., unless otherwise enumerated; see also 1 Cor. 2:1-16); with the irrelevance of appearance (2:2, 6, 9/10:1, 7); with angels, possibly as dispensers of wisdom (1:8; 3:19; 4:14/11:14; see also 1 Cor. 6:3; 11:10; 13:1); with a parental ethos (4:19-20/12:13-15); with weakness (4:13/10:10; and see 1 Cor. 4:9-13); with shame and the cross (2:19-20; 3:1; 5:11, 24; 6:12, 14/13:4; see 1 Cor. 1:13-31; 2:2, 8); marks on the body (6:17/12:7); the presence of the Spirit, especially as attested by signs and wonders (3:5/12:12); the absence of "wronging" or "offending" (probably Paul: 4:12b/2:5-11; 7:12; 12:13); the presence of "another gospel" (1:6-9/11:4); the language of ministry, extending as far as official terminology (2:17/11:13-15); Jewish credentials (1:13-14/11:22); covenantal language (3:15-18; 4:21-31/3:1-18); the mention of "yeast" (5:9/1 Cor. 5:6-8) and of "seed" (6:7-9/9:6-10); the presence of certain anxieties on Paul's part about the congregation — specifically, over schism (5:15, 20, 26/12:20-21, etc.), licentiousness and immorality (5:19-21; and perhaps also 6:1/13:2), intracongregational aggression (5:15/1 Cor. passim); and concerns with food (2:11-14/1 Corinthians 8 and 10); the collection (2:10/8–9; and 1 Cor. 16:1-4); and the use of allegory (4:21-31/3:1-18; also 1 Cor. 10). Even allowing for motifs shared with other letters, this is an impressive degree of correspondence. See in this relation Udo Borse, *Der Standort des Galaterbriefes* (Bonn: Hanover, 1972).

9. We observed, in addition, that the absences of Justification terminology and argumentation from Paul's conversion, and of his conversion from his later Justification material are embarrassing. If these two narratives are as tightly coordinated as Justification theory suggests, then we would expect to find a more intertwined discussion of them in Galatians, but we do not. They are in fact clearly distinguished and separated, suggesting that they do *not* belong together. However Paul was converted, it did not apparently have anything to do with the issues in relation to which he deploys Justification material. But this is *not* to foreclose on the use of biographical material in support of an apocalyptic construal of his theology, if that seems appropriate. In addition, if the texts overtly deliver strong interrelationships — and in terms of Justification — this will of course be noted.

10. E.g., (i.a.) Hans Dieter Betz, *Galatians* (Philadelphia, Pa.: Fortress, 1979); also "Galatians, Epistle to The," *ABD* 2:872-75; Ernest de Witt Burton, "ΝΟΜΟΣ," "ΔΙΚΑΙΟΣΥΝΗ," and "ΠΙΣΤΙΣ," in *A Critical and Exegetical Commentary on the Epistle to the Galatians* (Edinburgh: T&T Clark, 1921), 119-21, 443-85; D. Hans Lietzmann, *An die Galater*, 3rd ed. (Tübingen: J. C. B. Mohr [Paul Siebeck], 1932); Dieter Lührmann, *Galatians: A Continental Commentary* (Minneapolis, Minn.: Fortress, 1992); and Franz Mussner, *Der Galaterbrief*, HTKNT 9 (Freiburg, Basel, Vienna: Herder, 1974). William J. Dalton gives a crisp survey of these: *Galatians Without Tears* (Collegeville, Minn.: The Liturgical Press, 1992), 11-22.

Intriguingly, even James D. G. Dunn falls into this camp to a significant extent, innovating in relation to the interpretation of "works of law" but maintaining an essentially conventional approach to both δικαιο- terminology and faith (and especially the latter): see esp. his *The Epistle to the Galatians*, BNTC (London: A&C Black, 1993); *The Theology of Paul's Letter to the Galatians*, New Testament Theology (Cambridge: Cambridge University Press, 1993); "Once More, Πίστις Χριστοῦ," in *Pauline Theology*, vol. 4, *Looking Back, Pressing On*, ed. D. M. Hay and E. E. Johnson (Atlanta, Ga.: Scholars Press, 1997), 61-81.

Numerous secondary studies also basically share this trajectory — see esp. now Francis Watson, who ends up largely endorsing the conventional reconstruction of Paul's gospel in Galatians (and elsewhere), although on innovative grounds: see part three, chapter twelve: *Paul and the Hermeneutics of Faith* (London: T&T Clark International [Continuum], 2004); see also *Paul, Judaism, and the Gentiles*, 2nd ed. (Grand Rapids, Mich.: Eerdmans, 2007), esp. 100-135. Similarly — and rather earlier on — Heikki Räisänen (*Paul and the Law*, 2nd ed., WUNT 29 [Tübingen: J. C. B. Mohr (Paul Siebeck),

1987 (1983)] — hereafter *P&L*), and E. P. Sanders (*Paul, the Law, and the Jewish People* [Philadelphia: Fortress, 1983] — hereafter *PL&JP*) tend to endorse the conventional reading of Paul's Justification texts, including those in Galatians, while criticizing their consequences — see esp. part one, chapter six. And Hans Hübner ought also to be noted at this point: *Law in Paul's Thought*, ed. John Riches, trans. James C. G. Grieg (Edinburgh: T&T Clark, 1984). Even Robin Scroggs — no conservative — essentially reproduces the conventional reading in his contribution to the deliberations of the Pauline Theology Seminar at SBL, a forum that allowed free play to alternatives: "Salvation History: The Theological Structure of Paul's Thought (1 Thessalonians, Philippians, and Galatians)," in *Pauline Theology*, vol. 1, *Thessalonians, Philippians, Galatians, Philemon*, ed. Jouette M. Bassler (Minneapolis, Minn.: Fortress, 1991), 212-26.

Moreover, even as many revisionists struggle to break free from the conventional construal but seem to fail to do so, numerous studies continue to affirm that approach vigorously and deliberately, especially those analyses from the essentially conservative counterattack to the new perspective: see (i.a.) Stephen Westerholm, *Perspectives Old and New on Paul* (Grand Rapids, Mich.: Eerdmans, 2004), 366-84; G. Walter Hansen, *Abraham in Galatians: Epistolary and Rhetorical Contexts*, JSNTSup 29 (Sheffield: JSOT, 1989); and Moisés Silva, "Faith Versus Works of Law in Galatians," in *Justification and Variegated Nomism*, vol. 2, *The Paradoxes of Paul*, ed. D. A. Carson, Peter T. O'Brien, and Mark A. Seifrid (Tübingen & Grand Rapids, Mich.: Mohr [Siebeck] & Baker Academic, 2004), 217-48.

11. Notably Dunn (see preceding note); but see also (i.a.) N. Thomas Wright, "Curse and Covenant: Galatians 3.10-14," and "The Seed and the Mediator: Galatians 3.1-20," in *The Climax of the Covenant: Christ and the Law in Pauline Theology* (Edinburgh and Minneapolis, Minn.: T&T Clark & Fortress, 1992), 137-56, 157-74.

12. J. Louis Martyn, *Galatians*; and *Theological Issues in the Letters of Paul* (Edinburgh & Nashville, Tenn.: T&T Clark & Abingdon, 1997).

13. Hays, "The Letter to the Galatians," 181-348; but see also Frank J. Matera, *Galatians*, Sacra Pagina 9 (Collegeville, Minn.: The Liturgical Press [Michael Glazier], 1992); S. K. Williams, *Galatians* (Nashville: Abingdon, 1997); and L. Ann Jervis, *Galatians* (Carlisle & Peabody, Mass.: Paternoster & Hendrikson, 1999).

See also numerous fine secondary studies informed by this perspective: see esp. Beverly Roberts Gaventa, "The Singularity of the Gospel," in Jouette M. Bassler, ed., *Pauline Theology*, vol. 1, *Thessalonians, Philippians, Galatians, Philemon* (Minneapolis: Fortress, 1991), 147-59. Various, at times rather idiosyncratic studies by Sam K. Williams are also worth noting — "Again *Pistis Christou*," *Catholic Biblical Quarterly* 49 (1987): 431-447; "Justification and the Spirit in Galatians," *Journal for the Study of the New Testament* 29 (1987): 91-100; and "Promise in Galatians: A Reading of Paul's Reading of Scripture," *Journal of Biblical Literature* 107 (1988): 709-20. An earlier but still penetrating analysis is Nils Dahl's "Contradictions in Scripture," in *Studies in Paul: Theology for the Early Christian Mission* (Minneapolis, Minn.: Augsburg, 1977), 159-77 (which has influenced Martyn's work on Galatians 3 significantly; see more on this just below).

Other works by Hays on Galatians are also significant; especially important in this relation are *Echoes of Scripture in the Letters of Paul* (New Haven: Yale University Press, 1989); and *The Faith of Jesus Christ: The Narrative Substructure of Galatians 3:1-4:11*, 2nd ed. (Grand Rapids, Mich.: Eerdmans, 2002). But the following may also be usefully consulted: "Christology and Ethics in Galatians: The Law of Christ," *Catholic Biblical Quarterly* 49 (1987): 268-90; "Crucified with Christ: A Synthesis of the Theology of 1 and 2 Thessalonians, Philemon, Philippians, and Galatians," in Jouette M. Bassler, ed., *Pauline Theology*, vol. 1, *Thessalonians, Philippians, Galatians, Philemon* (Minneapolis: Fortress, 1991), 227-46; and *The Moral Vision of the New Testament* (San Francisco: Harper Collins, 1996).

It should be noted as well that the fine commentary by Longenecker *(Galatians)* is a partial exception to all these categorizations, because it tends to combine both highly traditional and quite innovative interpretive suggestions alongside one another, usually denying that they are in tension. And numerous secondary studies arguably share this approach, combining old and new in their interpretations: see esp. (and not surprisingly) the elegant analysis of Bruce W. Longenecker, *The Triumph of Abraham's God: The Transformation of Identity in Galatians* (Edinburgh: T&T Clark, 1998); and

Charles H. Cosgrove, *The Cross and the Spirit: A Study in the Argument and Theology of Galatians* (Macon, Georgia: Mercer University Press, 1988). From my point of view, of course, these denials of tension are not ultimately wise; however, such treatments still contain much of value.

14. As we have already seen at some length, the contractual argumentative structure of Justification theory is delivered by Paul explicitly only in Romans 1–4 — especially its all-important preamble in terms of natural theology and attempted justification by works, a construct articulated by the conventional reading of 1:18–3:20. Without this preamble, the entire theory cannot be generated. But few if any interpreters have come up with a dramatically new way of reading Romans 1–3, so revisionists have turned instead to Galatians.

15. Justification discussions in Galatians are abbreviated and deeply intertwined with apocalyptic material, generating at numerous locations throughout Paul's argument in Galatians 2–3 the tensions that were detected en masse between Romans 1–4 and 5–8 at that single point of transition. Under- and overdeterminations will consequently tend to occur throughout this text, while proximate issues will not be so neatly distributed.

16. As Hays (*Faith*, 122) and Betz (*Galatians*) basically suggest. Hence, I am going to resist making programmatic claims for any of the statements in this pericope in advance of undertaking exegesis of the rest of the relevant argument.

17. It will be easiest to consider the isolated first occurrence in relation to one of Paul's parting shots, 6:10 — the task of §8.

18. The basic position of Betz, who has certainly persuaded Longenecker (*Galatians*, 80-83). I do not, however, endorse Betz's suggestion for the programmatic rhetorical reasons he supplies, which are more dubious (i.e., that Galatians is equivalent to the forensic apologetic speech); *stasis* theory may well be more apposite, as has already been noted in relation to Romans (in part four, chapter eighteen, §3). But simply as a set of basic argumentative and exegetical suggestions, his view seems to be accurate. Moreover, if Betz is broadly correct, then my earlier rejection of any significant correlation with 2:11-14 seems further corroborated. The Antioch incident recounted there certainly casts something of a dramatic shadow over what follows, portraying Paul as a solitary and heroic protagonist fearlessly opposing vacillating and somewhat untrustworthy leaders from Jerusalem. Doubtless, the letter's auditors are meant to carry these basic impressions on into the letter's abstract argumentation. But to draw stronger connections between these pericopes seems doubtful. Galatians 2:15-21 and following bears no characteristics of either direct or indirect discourse (which would suggest a continuation of Paul's ostensible "speech" to Peter). And the terminology is sharply distinguished, as we have just seen. More likely is that different issues are now under discussion (see 1:10-12 with 2:15–3:5).

19. The δὲ supplied by many MSS here is omitted by some witnesses — 𝔓⁴⁶, A, D², Ψ, etc. It *might* have been prompted by a desire to distance the material in 2:16 from the Jewish identifications of 2:15, which can be read as a separate sentence. But, then again, it might refer originally to a Christian (or Messianic) qualification of the broadly Jewish subjects of 2:15. Fortunately, not much turns on this decision.

20. Purposive and ecbatic usages are notoriously difficult to distinguish, but fortunately they seldom need to be, as here. The genitive construction is of course being rendered "objectively," with Christ as the object of the faith in question. Silva is rightly dubious of such categorizations, and I will use them in what follows simply for convenience ("Galatians," 218-20).

21. See, i.a., Jn 6:29; 15:12; 17:3 (taking "the place of the explanatory inf. after a demonstrative" according to BDAG 476 — "a favorite usage" [of John's]); but note also 15:13; and 4:47 and 17:15 (supplementing a request or demand).

22. The construal of "Christ Jesus" as the object of the verb πιστεύω in this sense should occasion no comment. This is exactly what we would expect from his supply after the accusative preposition εἰς, which denotes the content of the thing believed: see variations on this construction elsewhere in Paul such as Rom. 4:5 (τῷ δὲ μὴ ἐργαζομένῳ πιστεύοντι δὲ ἐπὶ τὸν δικαιοῦντα τὸν ἀσεβῆ), 18 (ἐπίστευσεν εἰς τὸ γενέσθαι αὐτὸν πατέρα πολλῶν ἐθνῶν κατὰ τὸ εἰρημένον), 24 (τοῖς πιστεύουσιν ἐπὶ τὸν ἐγείραντα Ἰησοῦν τὸν κύριον ἡμῶν ἐκ νεκρῶν); 6:8 (εἰ δὲ ἀπεθάνομεν σὺν Χριστῷ, πιστεύομεν ὅτι καὶ συζήσομεν αὐτῷ); 10:9 (πιστεύσῃς ἐν τῇ καρδίᾳ σου ὅτι ὁ Θεὸς αὐτὸν ἤγειρεν ἐκ νεκρῶν); 9:33/

10:11 [Isa. 28:16 LXX] (πᾶς ὁ πιστεύων ἐπ᾽ αὐτῷ οὐ καταισχυνθήσεται); 10:14 (Πῶς οὖν ἐπικαλέσωνται εἰς ὃν οὐκ ἐπίστευσαν); Phil. 1:29 (τὸ εἰς αὐτὸν πιστεύειν . . .); and 1 Thess. 4:14 (πιστεύομεν ὅτι Ἰησοῦς ἀπέθανεν . . .).

The evidence in relation to the cognate noun is also worth noting: 1 Thess. 1:8 (ἡ πίστις ὑμῶν ἡ πρὸς τὸν Θεὸν); Philem. 5 (σου τὴν ἀγάπην καὶ τὴν πίστιν, ἣν ἔχεις πρὸς τὸν κύριον Ἰησοῦν); see perhaps also Col. 1:4 (τὴν πίστιν ὑμῶν ἐν Χριστῷ Ἰησοῦ καὶ τὴν ἀγάπην ἣν ἔχετε εἰς πάντας τοὺς ἁγίους); more probably 2:5 (τὴν τάξιν καὶ τὸ στερέωμα τῆς εἰς Χριστὸν πίστεως ὑμῶν); and perhaps also Eph. 1:15 (τὴν καθ᾽ ὑμᾶς πίστιν ἐν τῷ κυρίῳ Ἰησοῦ καὶ τὴν ἀγάπην τὴν εἰς πάντας τοὺς ἁγίους).

Genitive and arthrous possibilities in this sense will be noted below.

This reading also assumes that a genitive is not necessarily a direct reproduction of a verbal construction using the accusative. (The verbal construction in Paul using πιστεύω and Christ as this verb's object in the accusative is also rare — Rom. 10:14 and Phil. 1:29.) Williams suggests a more "metaphysical" reading of 2:15-16 on analogy to 3:27, but this is not necessary, and neither are these two texts commensurate ("Again *Pistis Christou*," 441-42).

Romans 3:25 and 15:13 use the same construction, but not to denote an object.

23. This signal is noted by Longenecker (*Galatians*, 88); see also a similar emphatic construction in 2:17, καὶ αὐτοὶ ἁμαρτωλοί (89). Silva overlooks this possible construal of 2:15-16 without offering a detailed syntactical analysis of his more conventional construal *or* any justification of the rectitude of that construal over against others. Instead, he merely asserts that "Paul in effect exegetes the construction [πίστις Χριστοῦ] by saying εἰς Χριστὸν Ἰησοῦν ἐπιστεύσαμεν . . ." ("Faith Versus Works of Law," 232). But clearly other interpretative possibilities exist. Somewhat disconcertingly, Silva also cites 3:6 and 3:22 as making it "undeniably true that the human act of believing in Christ is both present in Paul's argument . . . and vital to it" (233-34). But the second claim here does not follow from the first, and it is the important one for his conventional case; those emphasizing a christological reading of some of Paul's πιστ- constructions do not exclude Christian believing. Moreover, not even the first claim is accurate. Galatians 3:6 is a citation of Gen. 15:6, where Abraham believes *in God*. And 3:22 — Silva presumably referring to the second participial πιστ- construction in that verse — *specifies no object at all*. (The implications of the first πιστ- construction here are of course disputed.) In fact, only 2:16 itself supplies Christ as an explicit object of "faith" in Galatians. And while this certainly makes "belief in Christ" possible and meaningful for Paul in some sense — and nobody really wants to deny this — there is some distance to travel before it becomes a "vital" component in his argument that must be presupposed on all other occasions.

24. The "faithful Christ" is an intertextually motivated, metonymic allusion to that story. So the christological grounding of the "deliverance" or "liberation" of Christians is entirely understandable, although the "fidelity" or obedience of Christ unto death is what is mentioned specifically, since this is the emphasis supplied by Paul's underlying intertext — Hab. 2:4. (See part four, chapter fifteen.) The adjectival translation "[the] faithful Christ" is used here merely for convenience; it is not a strictly literal translation of Paul's intertextually motivated phrase ἐκ πίστεως — "through fidelity" — but rendering the latter literally on all occasions is clumsy.

25. Unfortunately, question-begging claims are rife in the literature at this point. A clear example is Silva's analysis ("Faith Versus Works of Law"), but he is not alone in these difficulties (and even resists question-begging moves in relation to "works of law" better than most — which makes his use of the same in relation to Paul's πίστις Χριστοῦ constructions the more puzzling).

R. Barry Matlock — to his credit — has offered some arguments at this point. He argues in terms of a combination of symmetry and explication, and also relies on a negative argument: see "The Rhetoric of πίστις in Paul: Galatians 2.16, 3.22, Romans 3.22, and Philippians 3.9," *Journal for the Study of the New Testament* 30 (2007): 173-203. The positive considerations should be addressed first (and are more important).

Matlock rightly repudiates the artful literary analyses of 2:16 by other scholars (that rely largely on chiasm and/or symmetry, but excise offending material), offering his own instead. He suggests that Paul has deployed two antitheses of "works versus faith," and explicated the final phrase of each antithesis with a further amplifying, explanatory clause — an explanatory faith clause being supplied first (. . . καὶ ἡμεῖς εἰς Χριστὸν Ἰησοῦν ἐπιστεύσαμεν ἵνα κ.τ.λ.), followed by a clause explanatory of works of law (. . . ὅτι ἐξ ἔργων νόμου οὐ δικαιωθήσεται πᾶσα σάρξ). Since the explanatory faith clause must be referred to Christians, Matlock concludes that the preceding faith genitive does as well, along with the following one, thereby resolving the πίστις Χριστοῦ ambiguity. But several problems undermine this proposal:

(1) Matlock leaves out 2:15! Including this material disrupts the symmetry of his own solution, and alters the sense of the sentence, as we will see shortly.

(2) The claim that 2:16 is symmetrical is problematic; it might not be (and, I would argue, is not — although *some* evidence of balance is present). Furthermore, this feature of the text in and of itself has no direct semantic or interpretative implications.

(3) The all-important claim concerning the explanatory clauses is unsustainable for the final law-oriented "explanation." As I show in more detail shortly, the sentence's final ὅτι clause is best interpreted explicatively, not explanatorily or causally, because the latter reading supplies two different grounds for the same set of claims within one sentence — an incoherent reading!

(4) The collapse of the explanatory function of the final clause undermines the claim that the earlier explanatory clause is so functioning as well, within Matlock's balanced symmetrical account.

(5) The verbal clause ought not to be read in this way in any case, because it is syntactically coordinated with the second law-faith antithesis, not the first. Syntactically and semantically it simply *must* be a causal, ecbatic, or explicative statement with respect to the second antithesis because of its coordination with that material by a ἵνα construction (. . . καὶ ἡμεῖς εἰς Χριστὸν Ἰησοῦν ἐπιστεύσαμεν ἵνα δικαιωθῶμεν ἐκ πίστεως Χριστοῦ καὶ οὐκ ἐξ ἔργων νόμου . . .), at which point we do not know if it is explanatory or not. (To claim that it is begs the key question.) The first antithesis is actually coordinated by a participle with the phrase in 2:15 that supplies a rather complex subject for the entire sentence. So Matlock's "explanatory" suggestion breaks down on closer analysis at every point; it does not give an accurate account of the Greek. The key clauses are not in fact explanations in the sense he suggests.

(6) Matlock's observation that the conjunctions are all functioning in parallel (. . . ὅτι . . . ἵνα . . . ὅτι . . .) further undermines his broader explanatory contention, supporting my apocalyptic reading instead! The first of these constructions *must* be a mere explication, following the participle εἰδότες. We have just noted that the third is also most probably explicative as well (see point 3). And these two observations and the parallelism now converge to confirm the same function for the all-important ἵνα clause! An anthropocentric reading of Paul's faith statements here *must* have a causal or ecbatic reading at this point — "we believed in Christ Jesus *so that* we might be justified through [that] belief in Christ. . . ." But this reading now seems unlikely; this connection looks merely explicative — "we believed in Christ Jesus *that* we would be delivered through the fidelity of Christ. . . ." Indeed, Matlock's contentions are at cross-purposes here, and his stronger claim in terms of the evidence undermines his overarching anthropocentric reading.

So it seems to me that Matlock's attempt to establish a traditional, anthropocentric reading of Gal. 2:16 founders — although he is to be commended for at least making the attempt, and doing so with some sophistication. In these respects he is in advance of most of his peers in the debate.

Matlock also relies upon a negative claim — an extensive repudiation of an argument from redundancy in ostensible support of the Christological reading. However, I endorse his repudiation of this contention (not having made it publicly since 1992, and having withdrawn it explicitly in 2005: see *The Quest for Paul's Gospel: A Suggested Strategy* [London: T&T Clark International (Continuum), 2005], 221-22, n. 19). This is a weak argument and ought to be abandoned. However, if Matlock places too much emphasis on this critique, he is at risk of savaging a straw man; there are other, far stronger contentions in favor of christocentric construals of the relevant passages that need to be addressed (and presumably he will do so in further publications; this article does not really address any further important arguments by christocentric advocates in detail beyond redundancy).

26. See, e.g., on the one hand, Betz (*Galatians*, 114-19); and Dunn (*Galatians*, 132-40, 157, 268); on the other, Martyn (*Galatians*, 246-52, 263-77); Longenecker (*Galatians*, 83); and the fine study by Martinus C. de Boer, "Paul's Use and Interpretation of a Justification Tradition in Galatians 2.15-21," *Journal for the Study of the New Testament* 28 (2005): 189-216.

27. I emphasize "my" at this point, because it will differ slightly in its rationale and some of its connotations from the "apocalyptic" approach advocated by Martyn and de Boer in ways to be detailed shortly.

28. See perhaps esp. §73, "The Group and Its Members," in L. Olbrechts-Tyteca and C. Perelman, *The New Rhetoric: A Treatise on Argumentation*, trans. J. Wilkinson and P. Weaver (Notre Dame, Ind.: University of Notre Dame Press, 1969 [1958]), 321-27, although Perelman is interested primarily in other manipulations of the group-individual relationship — for example, the effect of group prestige on the reception of the suggestions of one of its perceived members, or the converse, namely, the discrediting of a group by focusing on the shortcomings of one of its members (and vice versa). Nevertheless, Paul is arguably running a recognizable variation on this basic relationship and its argumentative possibilities in Gal. 2:15-16. Perelman also talks in this section about the related issues of exclusion — usefully applied to Paul's opponents — and restraint.

29. Longenecker's interaction with Betz is instructive (*Galatians*, cix-xiii); see also my *The Rhetoric of Righteousness in Romans 3:21-26*, JSNTSup 65 (Sheffield: JSOT, 1992), 73-74 — hereafter *RRR;* and David Aune, "Review of H. D. Betz's *Galatians,*" *Religious Studies Review* 7 (1981): 323-28. Betz's hypothesis has been widely imitated and also defended: see esp. Margaret M. Mitchell, *Paul and the Rhetoric of Reconciliation* (Tübingen: Mohr, 1992); and Frank W. Hughes, *Early Christian Rhetoric and 2 Thessalonians*, JSNTSup 30 (Sheffield: JSOT, 1989). But it is hampered by (1) the smallness and formality of Betz's supporting examples (viz., Plato's *Epistle* 7; Isocrates' *Antidosis*; Demosthenes' *De Corona;* Cicero's *Brutus;* and Libanius's *Orator* 1); (2) their status as high literature (i.e., as polished, published documents, not practical, direct communications); and (3) his frequent appeal to rhetorical handbooks, whose instructions were not generally followed closely, especially by professional rhetors. (In this relation, one might think of academics composing their scholarly papers in accordance with written instructions on writing papers that they received while in high school.) Hence, even rhetorical enthusiasts such as George Kennedy have significantly nuanced Betz's thesis, asserting, e.g., that Galatians is deliberative, not forensic, rhetoric, etc.; see George Kennedy, *New Testament Interpretation through Rhetorical Criticism* (Chapel Hill, North Carolina: University of North Carolina Press, 1984). The evidence of the epistolary manuals is also not especially supportive, while being more directly relevant: see Abraham Malherbe, *Ancient Epistolary Theorists*, SBL Sources 19 (Atlanta: Scholars, 1988). The result of these accumulating difficulties is a possible charge against Betz of "parallelomania": see Samuel Sandmel, "Parallelomania," *Journal of Biblical Literature* 81 (1962): 1-13.

30. See esp. *Rhetoric to Herennius*, 1.10.17; Cicero, *On Invention*, 1.22.31-32; Quintilian, *Institutes*, 4.5.26-28. Several types of argumentative composition are apparent in the advice of these learned theorists. See also H. Lausberg, *Handbook of Literary Rhetoric: A Foundation for Literary Study*, ed. David E. Orton and R. Dean Anderson, trans. Matthew T. Bliss, Annemiek Jansen, and David E. Orton (Leiden: Brill, 1998), 160, §§346, 47.

31. I am tempted to add that it is also a rather suspect construal of the broader argument; the suggestion that the antithesis between faith and works is *in its entirety* shared material in the Galatian debate seems to override the fact that it is, precisely, an antithesis and is frequently deployed and disputed as such in what follows. The argument that follows in Galatians 3 consistently marginalizes law and law observance in favor of πίστις. The latter everywhere negates the former. Martyn might reply that Paul is drawing out the implications of a shared position that the Teachers, and even the Jerusalem leadership, do not yet appreciate. I am not ultimately convinced, however, that this is the best explanation of Paul's terminology — an issue treated in more detail just below.

32. Dunn was apparently the first to make this observation in his famous Manson Memorial lecture, "The New Perspective on Paul" (University of Manchester, 4 November 1982); the text is reprinted in *JP&L*, 183-206 (with later, additional notes on 206-14); Gal. 2:16 is discussed on 188-200. This observation was subsequently taken up — although developed in rather different directions — by (i.a.) Martyn and de Boer (see above). De Boer supplies other arguments in support of the confessional hypothesis (a-d), but none are convincing; this remains the best piece of evidence. Convincing reinforcement for the exceptive reading of ἐὰν μή is supplied by A. Andrew Das, "Another Look at ἐὰν μή in Galatians 2:16," *Journal of Biblical Literature* 119 (2000): 529-39. Longenecker endorses Burton's

suggestion that the phrase is only exceptive of the main clause (*Galatians*, 84; Burton, *Galatians*, 120-21). However, both general and Pauline usage stand against this expedient. Debbie Hunn has recently argued that ἐὰν μή does not *have* to be exceptive, on the evidence of wider Greek literature — a fair claim: "ἐὰν μή in Galatians 2:16: A Look at Greek Literature," *Novum Testamentum* 49 (2007): 281-90. However, Das's study has established that ἐὰν μή is *always* exceptive *in Paul*, so arguments from the context need to be adduced for an alternative reading, and I know of none that avoid begging the question (i.e., "Paul simply *cannot* have meant something exceptive [because we know already that he is thinking and arguing here antithetically, in terms of Justification theory] . . ."). The creation of a plausible possible reading using the exceptive reading is therefore fatal to the alternative, purely antithetical possibility, as we will see shortly.

33. It will clarify Paul's argument if I supply temporarily the word "transform" for the verb δικαιόω here. That present and immediately past transformation *is* in view is reasonably clear; the verb is in the present tense in its first instance in v. 16a, and is resumed in this exact form by v. 17, which speaks of present transformation, as do vv. 18-21.

34. Which is not to say that it had this role originally in any case. But after the coming of Christ this can be effected inadvertently, so to speak, as we saw earlier in relation to Romans 10 in chapter nineteen.

35. This following statement supplies no real cause or ground for what precedes — which would be suggested by a reading of ὅτι in terms of "because" — but merely asserts something that has already been established by 2:16a. So this clause follows on well as a further explication of what has just been realized and believed, in a parallel coordination. An implicit γέγραπται and act of quotation faces similar problems of causality at this point and so should also be discounted. That is, Paul is not supplying *two* different reasons here for his central claims — one from each end of the same sentence!

36. After much thought, I am leaning away from an *explicit* activation of Ps. 143:2 (142:2 LXX) at this point by Paul; the syntagm reproduced is very abbreviated — ὅτι οὐ δικαιωθήσεται . . . πᾶς . . . — and there are certain syntactical difficulties that have just been noted. Further, there are few if any echoes of Psalm 143 in the immediate context. However, this is not to deny the influence of this psalm on Paul's own thinking more broadly, and in relation to Rom. 3:20, where more echoes *are* discernible. That is, he may well have drawn this clause primarily from Psalm 143:2, but it does not seem to be doing any argumentative work here as such (i.e., as a scriptural quotation); it seems, rather, to be part of his own linguistic discourse in this relation, which is clearly informed by scriptural texts (see the echo of Psalm 97:2 [LXX] in Rom. 1:16-17) — many of them, rather intriguingly, oriented by δικαιο- terminology. It may then be operating as part of the early church's discourse of realized divine kingship, as I have suggested in part four, chapter seventeen. *This* connotation is in my view recognizable and active.

37. My argument here clearly depends primarily on the exceptive meaning of ἐὰν μή, which is a delicate consideration. However, I am not as yet aware of decisive reasons for ignoring it, as we have already seen earlier in n. 32. Furthermore, the broader difficulty is not *solely* generated by an exceptive reading. Paul does seem here to basically *overrule* "works of law" *because of* πίστις Χριστοῦ (something the exceptive reading makes especially clear), and *this* is the major difficulty for Justification advocates. Human faith does not overrule works in any comprehensible fashion, although the coming of Christ presumably could.

38. Can the main issue be put better than this? "Here, too [in Gal. 3:15-18], in some recent strains of interpretation a theological motif is being given to Paul, whereas in fact it belongs to the Teachers. When one identifies as the subject of Galatians 'the condition on which Gentiles *enter* the people of God,' one presupposes that Paul is concerned with the specific line of movement along which it is now possible for Gentiles to transfer from their sinful state to the blessedness of those who are descendants of Abraham. This possible movement is their own, and the goal of their movement is that of getting into the people of God. The question is how they can get in. To a large extent, as we have seen earlier, this formulation describes the theology of the Teachers, the theology against which Paul wrote the letter to the Galatians! In Paul's theology the fundamental and determining line of movement is God's. . . . He [Paul] speaks, that is, not of the *possibility* of human movement into the family of Abraham, but rather of the *power* of God's already-executed movement into the cosmos in

the singular seed of Abraham, Christ. In a word, Galatians is a particularly clear witness to one of Paul's basic convictions: the gospel is about the divine invasion of the cosmos (theology), not about human movement into blessedness (religion). The difference between the two is the major reason for Paul's writing the letter at all" (Martyn, *Galatians*, 348-49; see also 413)!

39. These scholars are less "thoroughgoing" or even aggressive than I am in their christocentric construal of Paul's πίστις terminology. They might view my sustained emphasis here as excessive. But I view their restraint as unnecessary and unwise; amongst other things, it creates a weakened defensive perimeter.

40. The reasons for the singular syntactical clarity of this arrangement — to us — became clear in part four, chapter sixteen. Here, and only here, Paul has temporarily abandoned his usual terms in the disputed πίστις Χριστοῦ expressions, which are constrained by intertextuality and the peculiarities of nomenclature. Πίστις in the debated genitive phrases is elsewhere embedded in a phrase that echoes Habakkuk 2:4, whether as ἐκ πίστεως or its direct equivalent, διὰ πίστεως. So Paul does not supply an article at this point, which is absent from his source text and would blur this resonance. (However, he will do so occasionally to indicate the phrase's resumption of an earlier christological statement when there is no governed genitive to make that clear.) And the governed genitive is usually a reference to Christ by way of his *names* — "Jesus" and/or "Christ" (which functions here as a name) — which also do not take the article in genitive constructions. So elsewhere we invariably lack the double arthrous construction. Only here, in Galatians 2:20, has Paul moved away from *both* an intertextual echo — probably because he has just made that echo twice in v. 16 — and a reference to Christ in terms of names. He chooses here instead one of his titles, "the Son of God," which can take the article in a subjective. Consequently a fully arthrous construction results.

41. Romans 5:15b is an identical construction in grammatical terms and is subjective (so Hays, *Faith*, 153-55); see also Eph. 4:13 — less often noticed but in my view subjective as well. However, 1 Thess. 1:3 is similar again, but probably objective.

42. Hays rightly takes pains to distance this love from sentimentality: "The two participles in v. 20b . . . [point] to the singular past event of the cross as the locus of Jesus' love and self-donation. In other words, the love of which Paul speaks here is not Jesus' warm feeling of affection toward humanity; rather, it is an *enacted* love, a love that was made manifest in action and in suffering. Precisely that action gives content to the expression 'the faith of the Son of God'" ("The Letter to the Galatians," 244, emphasis original).

43. To nominate one of a number of possible readings of this dative phrase; this issue does not need to be resolved here.

44. Nicely brought out by Longenecker, *Galatians*, 92-93.

45. Williams, "Again *Pistis Christou*," 445.

46. So Hays, *Faith*, 153-55, 291 (a reprint of "What Is at Stake"); "The Letter to the Galatians," 244; Martyn, *Galatians*, 259; Matera, *Galatians*, 96, 101. I press the context a little more strongly than these interpreters, and I challenge Justification advocates to provide reasons for *not* construing this construction subjectively. In fact, Silva fails to mention this text in his apology for the conventional construal of faith through Galatians 2–3 ("Faith Versus Works of Law")! It should be noted that the MSS variations shed no light on these questions.

47. Longenecker betrays no cognizance of the signals supplied by the serried articles, providing a surprisingly conventional reading (*Galatians*, 94). Betz is similarly conventional (*Galatians*, 124-26). He pays little attention to this statement, stating that "[t]his faith is of course faith in Jesus Christ," citing 2:16 in support. However, he opens the door to a more christocentric analysis by saying immediately that "[t]he full interpretation of this 'thesis' is to be found in the entire *probatio* section (3:1–4:31) and in the *exhortatio* section (5:1–6:10)." I endorse this suggestion wholeheartedly, although contend that it may lead in a different direction than the one Betz ultimately asserts. Dunn is similarly apodictic, citing 2:16 as determinative as well, although he concedes that 2:20 "is more cumbersome than usual" (*Galatians*, 146). (Dunn's important observations concerning ἐὰν μή in 2:16 in fact undermine his case there against the christological construal, as we have already seen!)

48. *Paul and Palestinian Judaism* (Philadelphia: Fortress, 1977), 443 (and 442-47 more gener-

ally); 481-82 (appealing here also to similar arguments by Pfleiderer and van Dülmen); and 484; also *Paul, the Law, and the Jewish People* (Philadelphia: Fortress, 1983), 27, 152, 159, 165 (n. 34), 208.

49. Lloyd Gaston makes an ingenious but implausible case with respect to the meaning of δωρεάν here and the immediate context: *Paul and the Torah* (Vancouver: University of British Columbia Press, 1987), 66-67, 72. Gaston accepts that some sort of conditional statement is being made but does not translate accordingly; his own rendition is difficult to make much sense of: "I do not set at nought the grace of God; for since through law is [the] righteousness [of God], consequently Christ has died as a free gift" (66). Hays's comments are on target: "Paul's formulation in v. 21 contains a deft wordplay . . . : 'If rectification comes through the Law, then Christ died *gratuitously*'" ("The Letter to the Galatians," 245, emphasis original). See Jn 15:25 for a similarly negative use of δωρεάν (citing Pss 34:19/68:5 LXX).

50. Although unfortunately, we cannot press further here to discern what this signifier means in this context; the indications are too brief. Galatians 3:21 is rather more decisive.

51. So, correctly, Longenecker: "To affirm one is to deny the other, and vice versa" (*Galatians*, 95).

52. "The reasoning apparently is that Christ did not die in vain; he died and lived again 'that he might be Lord both of the dead and the living' (Rom. 14.9) and so that 'whether we wake or sleep we might live with him' (I Thess. 5.10). If his death was *necessary* for man's salvation, it follows that salvation cannot come in any other way and consequently that all were, prior to the death and resurrection, in need of a saviour. There is no reason to think that Paul felt the need of a universal saviour prior to his conviction that Jesus was such" (*P&PJ*, 443, emphasis original). Sanders has moved quickly here to other Pauline texts — not even in Galatians — and has ignored Paul's preceding statement in 2:21, which is part of his argument in context. He has also shifted — not uncharacteristically — from an argumentative point to an argumentative assumption *and* a psychological (i.e., generative) explanation.

53. See Albert Schweitzer, *The Mysticism of Paul the Apostle,* trans. W. Montgomery (New York: Seabury, 1968 [1931]), 225 and 220; although all of chapter ten, "Mysticism and Righteousness by Faith," is especially important in this relation (205-26).

54. This data is discussed by (i.a.) Luke T. Johnson, "Rom 3:21-26 and the Faith of Jesus," *Catholic Biblical Quarterly* 44 (1982): 77-90. Sam K. Williams, "The Hearing of Faith: ΑΚΟΗ ΠΙΣΤΕΩΣ in Galatians 3," *New Testament Studies* 35 (1989): 82-93; Hays, *Faith*, 124-32; Martyn, *Galatians*, 284-89.

55. Something noted perceptively by Martyn (*Galatians*, 287).

56. Meaning 2 in BDAG (867), as against meaning 1, "to write in advance/beforehand." This is not to suggest that the Galatians did not hear something! I am merely pointing out that Paul's discourse at present is favoring an ocular image, and this mental mapping should incline us to the more ocular understanding of ἀκοή. His rhetorical point is doubtless his gospel's obviousness. However, this "prior publication" *might*, in addition, be an artful play on the presence of the Sergii name in Pisidian Antioch on numerous inscriptions, some of which have been preserved (although arguably not as many from the first century as was previously thought). Just as this family's name has been published there repeatedly for all to see — "before everyone's very eyes" — thereby affirming its importance, so too, with equal obviousness, the crucified and resurrected Christ has been published to the city's inhabitants by Paul. To ignore this would therefore be as obstinate and "ignorant" as overlooking or forgetting the powerful inscriptional evidence in Pisidian Antioch concerning the Sergii. See Michel Christol and Th. Drew-Bear, "Les Sergii Paulli et Antioche," in *Actes du 1er Congrès International sur Antioche de Pisidie,* ed. Thomas Drew-Bear, Taslialan Mehmet, and Christine M. Thomas, Collection Archéologie et Histoire de l'Antiquité 5 (Lyon: Université Lumière-Lyon, 2002), 177-91; briefer pertinent background information can be found in Stephen Mitchell and Marc Waelkens, *Pisidian Antioch: The Site and Its Monuments* (London: Gerald Duckworth with The Classical Press of Wales, 1998); and Barbara Levick, *Roman Colonies in Southern Asia Minor* (Oxford: Clarendon, 1968).

57. Hays (*Faith*, 128-32) is more confident than I am about the implications of the evidence elsewhere in Paul — principally Rom. 10:13-18; 1 Cor. 12:17; and 1 Thess. 2:13. First Corinthians 12:17 seems irrelevant, speaking of "the faculty of hearing." And the other two instances look essentially ambiguous. We have already addressed the salient points from the Romans evidence (see chapter nine-

teen). The contribution of 1 Thess. 2:13 is similarly difficult to gauge. I incline toward a reading in terms of "report" in this text, but not on decisive grounds. Abraham Malherbe suggests that the active sense of "hearing" "agrees with the dynamic nature of God's word described in this verse" (*The Letters to the Thessalonians*, AB 32B [New York: Doubleday, 2000], 166), but this is hardly probative. There is no *need* for these two things to correlate, nor does Paul say here that they do. Malherbe also cites John 12:38 and Heb. 4:2 in this relation, although hardly decisively (166). In fact, his claim here seems to rest — at least in part — on his prior commitment to the essentials of Justification theory: "Fundamental to Paul's understanding is that the word is heard and faith engendered by it (Rom. 10:14-18)" (166). But Rom. 10:14-18 emphasizes the word itself, in addition to hearing, calling it "the thing heard." It seems, in short, that this external evidence is slight and ambiguous.

58. See Longenecker, "believing what you heard" (*Galatians*, 102-3). This is either the reversed Greek phrase, assuming a genitive of object, or option i below (although not identified as such).

59. A fourth might be suggested, namely, "hearing characterized by belief or trust" (i.e., a characterizing genitive). But this seems slightly confused. Hearing and believing are two complementary actions that should go together in relation to the preaching of the gospel; so, strictly speaking, believing cannot *characterize* hearing *itself* as an attribute of hearing. This is a figure of speech. A person hears the gospel message, and then also (one hopes) believes in it, so, as always, hearing precedes such believing. It might be retorted, then, that this expression merely associates these two activities loosely — "hearing accompanied by believing" — and there may well be something in this suggestion. However, the context supplies little encouragement for it, and neither does the wider Pauline evidence (i.e., where else does he speak in these terms?). But see more on this just below.

60. A popular choice: Williams notes the support of Hays (as one option), Betz, Meyer, Schlier, Oepke, Mussner, Ebeling, and Kittel ("The Hearing of Faith," 82, n. 2). If πίστις *is* still referred to Christian believing, then a case needs to be made that this is at times the central content of Paul's gospel and not merely part of an appropriate response to it.

61. Martyn's reading — "the faith-eliciting gospel" (*Galatians*, 281-94; also #31, 286-89), citing BDF §166. Presumably, in the absence of a christological construal, it is the best option for a determinedly apocalyptic reader. However, arguably, it is no longer necessary.

62. Πιστ- language does occur in the governed position, but never in any obviously comparable sense. Williams notes Rom. 1:5 (see 16:26); 3:27, 31; 4:11, 13; 4:12; 12:3; 12:6; 2 Cor. 4:13; Gal. 6:10; and Phil. 1:25 ("The Hearing of Faith," 83, n. 1). These texts have already been treated in earlier chapters, or will be here shortly, so I will not discuss them in detail at this point.

63. Both Hays (*Faith*, 124-32; "The Letter to the Galatians," 252-53) and Silva ("Faith Versus Works of Law," 235-36) adduce these texts in this way.

64. Hays adds a third argument that I find highly attractive but ultimately indecisive (*Faith*, 124-32; "The Letter to the Galatians," 252-53). He observes that 3:5 queries whether God's outpouring of the Spirit is ἐξ ἔργων νόμου ἢ ἐξ ἀκοῆς πίστεως and then suggests that this event can hardly be coordinated instrumentally with a reading of ἐξ ἀκοῆς πίστεως in terms of some human act of belief (and see esp. Gal. 4:6). God's sending of the Spirit is not *conditioned* by human activities in Paul (or, for that matter, elsewhere in the Bible). But the difficulty with this entirely accurate observation is that the divine outpouring here can hardly be coordinated instrumentally with Paul's proclamation of Christ either, at which point we must read the prepositions as speaking of *mediation* rather than some more involved role. And at this point both proclamation and belief seem plausible readings — that is, as possible mediations of God's pneumatological activity in the lives of the Galatian converts.

Silva seems to err in the opposite direction, claiming that the phrase ἐναρξάμενοι πνεύματι (3:3) *must* be understood as "a human activity" ("Faith Versus Works of Law," 235-36). This is to underemphasize the importance of the Spirit here, who is presumably the principal agent, and also to overlook the possible ironic argumentative contrast that Paul is suggesting between, precisely, a beginning through the action of God and a continuation through self-oriented activity. (Silva bases his contentions here on his reading of 3:6, 7, and 9, which he holds can be decisively oriented toward human faith [234-36]; but see the section that follows in relation to such overconfident claims.)

65. This reading avoids a nasty potential systematic tension in terms of pneumatology, namely,

the relegation of the Spirit's arrival to a time after the fulfillment of a prior condition by the convert. The Spirit can now arrive *with* the proclamation of the crucified Christ, partly no doubt to authenticate and facilitate his recognition. And this realization speaks in turn to Hays's concern with the appropriate pneumatological signals being sent by this material ("The Letter to the Galatians," 253-54).

66. J. Bligh was an early advocate of chiasms in Galatians but found so many that his credibility was damaged: *Galatians in Greek: A Structural Analysis of St Paul's Epistle to the Galatians with Notes on the Greek* (Detroit: University of Detroit Press, 1966); Hansen supplies a useful brief survey in *Abraham in Galatians*, 73-79; postdating Hansen is I. H. Thomson, *Chiasmus in the Pauline Letters*, JSNTSup 111 (Sheffield: JSOT, 1995) — a rather more persuasive analysis in many respects; see more generally Hays, *Faith*, 132-41; and I supply a brief overview in *RRR*, 72, esp. n. 3.

67. I suggest construing this awkward sentence as follows: "Is then the one who pours out the Spirit also working miracles among you 'through works of law' or 'through fidelity'?" In other words, I supply an elided ἐστίν, and understand ὁ . . . ἐπιχορηγῶν ὑμῖν τὸ πνεῦμα to be the sentence's subject — God — interpreting the καί additively (BDAG 495-96, meaning 2).

68. Some MSS supply εὐλογίαν — 𝔓⁴⁶, pc, b, vgᵐˢ, D*·ᶜ, F, G, Marcion, and Ambrosiaster — an impressive tradition. However, this is probably a Marcionite variant encouraged by a vertical dittographical prompt.

69. And G, vgᶜˡ, and Ambrosiaster supply it!

70. And this inclines me toward marking off v. 6 from v. 5 as the beginning of a new subsection — although drawing the motif of the Spirit through from 3:1-5. Martyn notes the concurrence of Meyer, Klumbies, and Stanley (*Galatians*, 296-97, n. 39). The unique disclosure formula Paul uses in v. 7 — although evident in the papyri — seems to apply the force of Gen. 15:6 (a point emphasized by Longenecker, *Galatians*, 108, 112).

71. Silva observes, in relation to the phrase ἔργων νόμου: "that Paul makes no effort to define the phrase . . . seems to [imply] . . . that his readers will have little difficulty understanding it" ("Faith Versus Works of Law," 222). The same insight applies to all the motifs that Paul uses here, including "faith" and "justification."

72. Martyn observes that the precise expression υἱοὶ Ἀβραάμ nevertheless never recurs in Paul, let alone Galatians, and so probably draws on the vocabulary of the Teachers (*Galatians*, 299).

73. Hays ingeniously suggests the subtle influence of Isa. 44:3, a nicely apposite text (*Faith*, 181-83; "The Letter to the Galatians," 261-62). Longenecker points to the content of the promise in 3:18 as inheritance (*Galatians*, 134), and the salience of that discourse through much of the rest of Galatians, "the idea [of inheritance] being prominent in the illustration of 4:1-7 [as well], the allegory of 4:21-31, and the blessing of 6:16." Although this last reference might be pressing things, word occurrences enhance the basic claim: κληρονομία occurs in 3:18; κληρονόμος in 3:29; 4:1, 7; and κληρονομέω in 4:30; 5:21. Most interpreters fail to consider the possibility of a genitive of source 3:14, which is puzzling when Paul seems happy to use it elsewhere for divine acts (see esp. Rom. 10:3 and Phil. 3:9).

74. Many interpreters nevertheless assert that we can say much more — and especially about Abraham — but I deny this. Abraham is conspicuously underdeveloped as an argument here (see Rom. 4:2-25). And his significance *can* be developed in several different ways — as a prototype of Christian faith parallel to the faithful protagonist of Hab. 2:4 (i.e., the conventional reading); as a prototype of Christ; as the original recipient of a promise made ultimately with respect *to* Christ (see Gal. 3:16, 18, 19); and so on. We simply have to read on in Galatians to find out how to interpret this figure further — and he does reappear several times (see 3:15-19, 29; 4:21-31). However, the literature tends to pay lip service to this methodology and then ignore it.

So, e.g., Silva just begs the question when he states that "Abraham's true children . . . must surely mean *those who believe,* following the pattern of Abraham" ("Faith Versus Works of Law," 223, 227). There is no "surely" in Gal. 3:6-14, one is tempted to respond, but only a "possibly." (Furthermore, if we follow the cue that Silva supplies — οἱ ἐκ πίστεως — we are led to Hab. 2:4, not directly to Abraham at all, as we will see momentarily.) But Dunn is even more obvious. He makes the following statement concerning 3:6-7 and its citation of Gen. 15:6: "The inference which Paul draws [in v. 7] is that those who believe like Abraham are equally acceptable to God. The crucial claim, however, is that *such faith constitutes the believer as a child of Abraham*. It is a thematic statement, of course, and will have to be unpacked — a task to which Paul devotes the next two chapters. But the outline and issues are already clear enough" (162, emphasis added). However, although this text correlates "believing" with Abraham in some sense, it does not explain δικαιοσύνη as "acceptability"; we have *no* explanation of this term yet in Galatians. Nor do we know how to correlate Hab. 2:4 with this complex — the text from which the phrase under discussion is actually drawn. Even more importantly, Paul *never* states *explicitly* that "such faith *constitutes the believer as a child of Abraham*." This is simply not clear, and to suggest that it is begs the key question. I will suggest shortly that Galatians 3 provides an entirely different account of these relationships, as vv. 28-29 almost immediately suggest: "it is no longer possible to be a Jew or a Greek . . . *in Christ Jesus*. [29]And if you belong to Christ, *then* you are seed of Abraham. . . ." We understand the thematic statements in Galatians *in the light of* their later unpacking; to do otherwise is to risk controlling that later exegesis with unwarranted and tendentious claims — here, of course, Justification theory.

75. As Hays ("The Letter to the Galatians," 256) following Dunn (*Galatians*, 163), and at times even Martyn (*Galatians*, 299), affirm, although arguably unwisely at this point.

76. The subject of the sentence that Paul quotes from Lev. 18:5, ἃ ποιήσας ἄνθρωπος, has been sculpted by Paul into an arthrous participial construction, ὁ ποιήσας, that consequently contrasts very neatly with the arthrous adjectival construction that is the subject of Hab. 2:4, ὁ δίκαιος. This has also been done of course to create a self-sufficient statement — a sentence — since Paul could hardly have begun his quotation here with a relative pronoun. However, a suitable subject lay just to hand in the Levitical text — ἄνθρωπος — presumably suggesting ὁ ποιήσας ἄνθρωπος as the subject of his quotation. He actually eliminates this, supplying a pronoun instead (which is perhaps influenced by the preceding phrase in 18:5 — καὶ φυλάξεσθε πάντα τὰ προστάγματά μου καὶ πάντα τὰ κρίματά μου καὶ ποιήσετε αὐτά . . .). But the result of these modifications and selections is a pair of closely parallel quotations. Further details can be found in Martyn, *Galatians*, 311-16; Christopher Stanley, *Paul and the Language of Scripture: Citation Technique in the Pauline Epistles and Contemporary Literature*, SNTSMS 74 (Cambridge: Cambridge University Press, 1992), 245.

77. Hooker, citing a conversation with Christopher Stanley, suggests that the curse is not necessarily *enacted* in 3:10, since Paul avoids using ἐπικατάρατος of those observing the law, characterizing them only as ὑπὸ κατάραν: Morna Hooker, "ΠΙΣΤΙΣ ΧΡΙΣΤΟΥ," *New Testament Studies* 35 (1989): 327, n. 1.

78. See Dunn, *Galatians*, 178, who notes earlier Jewish references in these terms to execution in 4Q169 (4QpNah) 1.7-8, and 11Q20 (The Temple Scroll) 64.7-13. The former reference views it compassionately — i.e., as an "atrocity" (and this was presumably the atrocious mass execution by Alexander Jannaeus) — but the latter, retributively — i.e., as deserved, for anyone spying on Israel or cursing the land while abroad. I have already cast doubt on the view that Paul reached his view of the law by way of this verse; see part one, chapter five.

Martyn notes the possible presence of the Binding of Isaac (*Galatians*, 317, n. 105), a view suggested by Dahl ("Contradictions in Scripture," 171). I am ordinarily a strong advocate of that discourse's importance in Paul (see esp. part four, chapter sixteen, discussing Rom. 3:25), but I view the establishment of those implications here as a complex and fragile argument — although not for this reason impossible. The other curse language in Galatians — the citation of Deut. 27:26 in 3:10 — is probably contingent (see 1:8-9; 3:10), functioning to counter the probable use of Deuteronomic curse language by the Teachers. And this judgment seems to be reinforced by the only other use of the verb ἐξαγοράζω in Paul later, in Gal. 4:5, where it operates neatly within Paul's developing argument in relation to the law. So a comprehensive explanation of the function of the citation of Deut. 21:23 in 3:13 is possible in purely contingent terms; we do not need to go beyond this explanation.

However, it would certainly enhance Paul's counterclaim if this text came from an early church tradition. ("Texts you yourselves use refute your own contention at this point!") Nevertheless, if it did, it is unlikely that it was operating there opposite Deut. 21:23, since the early Jewish Christians were all law observant and seem to have found Paul's push beyond the law difficult (see 2:1-14). We would need, then, to reconstruct a plausible and hopefully also attested context within which Christ purchased his early followers from a curse.

Suggestions are not wanting at this point. Wright, for example, would point immediately to the purchase of the community from the Deuteronomic curses associated with the exile, which were held to be in force still, as indeed was the exile to some degree, since many of the Jews were scattered among the pagan nations and Judea itself was ruled by "foreign oppressors." Some evidence from Jewish sources attests to this mentality. So the initial plausibility of Wright's suggestion is not problematic. (He is followed here, i.a., by Dunn and Hays.) But is there any evidence for the existence of this discourse in the early church and Paul?

Paul himself never associates these key notions elsewhere in explicit terms, nor does he introduce or allude to this text in any other appropriate places in these terms (although this might be because he himself is not that interested in this discourse). Nor do the relevant Jewish sources, to my knowledge, use Deut. 21:23 in this way. (They are far more direct, as we have just seen.) It is worth noting that an Adam discourse could also perhaps explain the "curse" language, but Paul does not use Deut. 21:23 in this relation again *either*.

Hence, at the least Hays's caution seems warranted: "Whether Paul is the author of that tradition or whether vv. 13-14 are his citation of a tradition is impossible to determine with confidence" ("The Letter to the Galatians," 261). And it could be added that it is likewise impossible to determine with confidence *the nature of* that tradition — in terms of the Binding of Isaac, exile, or anything else.

79. Obvious comparative texts in Paul are 2 Cor. 5:21 and 8:9; Martyn also notes 1 Cor. 1:30, although arguably that text is related to Gal. 3:13 a little more obliquely (*Galatians*, 318).

80. Interpreters have offered much more complex accounts of this atoning process, but this is as far as the local evidence takes us explicitly. Martyn's discussion is nuanced (*Galatians*, 309, 318, esp. n. 110, 319-21, 324-28). Stephen Finlan offers a judicious account of the key discussions of this notion in terms of scapegoat rituals (etc.): *The Background and Content of Paul's Cultic Atonement Metaphors* (Atlanta: Society of Biblical Literature, 2004), esp. 101-10. My observation would be that discussion of ἐξαγοράζω in 4:5 and its context is never mentioned in explication of Paul's terse remark in 3:13 by either him or his interlocutors (with the exception of Daniel R. Schwartz's intriguing study, which links the verb ἐξαποστέλλω in 4:4 and 6 with Lev. 14 and 16:10, 21: "Two Pauline Allusions to the Redemptive Mechanism of the Crucifixion," *Journal of Biblical Literature* 102 [1983]: 259-68; I fear, however, that this is little more than coincidence, the prefix ἐξ- in 4:4 being suggested by the same prefix in the parallel 4:6, which is rooted in the metaphor of purchase "from" slavery). And particularly problematic of course is the retrospective orientation of that later discussion (i.e., the definition of the problem in the light of the solution, and not vice versa; this must sharply limit the relevance of background analysis for the determination of Paul's meaning); see more on this just below. Of course, Hooker emphasizes the implicit "interchanges" here: see "ΠΙΣΤΙΣ ΧΡΙΣΤΟΥ," 332 and 338, esp. n. 1.

81. This emphasis is also apparent in Rom. 2:6-8. So (i.a.) Martyn resists this reading as unreasonable (*Galatians*, 310-11), and it *is* an unreasonable construal of Judaism, as noted in part one, chapter four. However, as a component of the Teachers' gospel, it is entirely understandable; they expect perfect law-observance from their circumcised converts, who have been separated from their sinful passions. (Part four, chapter fourteen elaborates this point; see also UD 4, discussed in part three, chapter eleven.) Paul's troublesome "perfectionist" statements concerning law-observance can now be neatly explained, in an additional confirmation of our developing rereading.

82. Andrew H. Wakefield (endorsed by Hays, "The Letter to the Galatians," 259, esp. n. 150) suggests perceptively — and fairly — that δῆλον belongs with the following sentence in the phrase δῆλον ὅτι and not in this first claim, as the majority of commentators have assumed: *Where to Live: The Hermeneutical Significance of Paul's Citations from Scripture in Galatians 3:1–14* (Atlanta: Society of Biblical Literature, 2003). (Wright makes the same observation, crediting his student Christopher Palmer with the observation: see "Curse and Covenant," 149, n. 2.) And this would accord with the almost invariable usage of this phrase in Koiné. (BDAG includes comprehensive data corroborating this claim; see 222.) I am strongly tempted by this insightful proposal yet demur for the following reasons:

(1) It seems possible if not likely that Paul has elided γέγραπται from just after ὅτι, so that this

conjunction is not functioning within the Koiné phrase δῆλον ὅτι at all. This would not be enough in and of itself to reject the suggestion; however, any suspicions here seem confirmed by a second observation.

(2) If we follow Wakefield, positioning δῆλον ὅτι at the beginning of the second sentence, the *first* ὅτι in v. 11 becomes essentially incomprehensible. It cannot now be construed explicatively — as "that" — and neither does it function meaningfully in a stronger causal or explanatory sense — "because." (Both its location and its content forbid linking it causally to v. 10, which precedes it.)

Advocates of this reading might then respond that it *can* be treated meaningfully: "Now because no one is rectified by the law, it is clear that 'the righteous one will live by faith. . . .'" Hence, the first clause now provides the warrant for the second — a clear assertion of Justification theory! (See Hays, "The Letter to the Galatians," 259.)

However, this translation renders the *following* two clauses meaningless! Paul now has no need to explain that the law is not ἐκ πίστεως, because its redundancy is self-evident and established on other grounds. Hence, these two later statements become irrelevant, which seems unlikely.

So — after some heart searching — I have returned to the majority reading, which remains a little deceptive in terms of the Greek but is partly palliated if an elided γέγραπται is assumed.

83. Discussed in more detail in part one, chapter six, and part four, chapter eighteen, not to mention previously in this chapter, in relation to Gal. 2:15-16 and 2:21.

84. This reading is of course resisted in the literature, but never, as far as I can tell, for a good reason. Even Martyn demurs, viewing it as "unlikely" (*Galatians*, 313). However, he arguably supplies a still more unlikely reading — essentially a "both-and" position: "Paul can use the single word 'faith' to speak simultaneously of Christ's faith and of the faith it kindles, referring in fact to the coming of this faith into the world as the eschatological event that is also the coming of Christ (3:23-25). In the promise of Hab 2:4 he hears, then, a reference to this hypostasized faith. This is a point that must be consistently borne in mind when one uses the expression 'rectification by faith'" (314). This suggestion is argumentatively confusing (because it operates on two distinguishable levels that are not identified as such in the text) and exegetically unnecessary (because a simpler reading lies to hand), and so inherently improbable. Perhaps most puzzling, however, is its lack of any coherent explanation for Paul's emphasis here on human faith, which is retained even in Martyn's attempt to read this text apocalyptically. Paul ends up repeatedly asserting that the law curses and that rectification is only through faith, *but he never explains why.* And some of the most perceptive complaints of the Teachers are thereby left unanswered. Hays's timidity is also puzzling at this point ("The Letter to the Galatians," 259-60). His *Faith* promised an interpretative eschaton for this subsection in Galatians, but he later states that Paul's "argument can be understood nonmessianically, as an assertion that Hab 2:4 provides the key to understanding how God has chosen to bring about rectification and life: through faith, not through the Law" (259). If Hab. 2:4 is not interpreted messianically, then its assertion of sola fide is arbitrary. (Not even Habakkuk himself would have suggested this!) Fidelity is important as one component of appropriate piety, but that it should be both isolated and privileged as many modern Christian interpreters of Paul seem to assume is a shocking redefinition that requires extensive justification — precisely the lacuna evident here if Hab. 2:4 is not interpreted with reference to Christ. But then, as soon as it is, that lacuna disappears. (Besides, not even Paul reduces Christian piety to faith; he is principally concerned in ethical terms with love: see Gal. 5:6; 1 Corinthians 13.)

85. Sanders himself overlooks the possibility of his particular attestation because he does not read πίστις with reference to Christ. As a result of this decision, he also supplies a far more convoluted account of Paul's argument in 3:6-14! See *PL&JP*, esp. 17-27.

86. The following list has been produced in the main from the observations of Longenecker (*Galatians*, 107-25) and Martyn (*Galatians*, 294-336), who tend to emphasize different markers; see also the classic study by C. K. Barrett, "The Allegory of Abraham, Sarah, and Hagar in the Argument of Galatians," in *Rechtfertigung: Festschrift für Ernst Käsemann zum 70. Geburtstag*, ed. J. Friedrich et al. (Tübingen: Mohr [Siebeck], 1976), 1-16.

87. ἀγοράζω is also rare elsewhere: see only 1 Cor. 6:20; 7:23, 30. It occurs in participial form in Eph. 5:16 and Col. 4:5.

88. See Gen. 12:3; 18:18; 22:18; 26:4; 28:14; Ps. 72:17 (71:17 LXX); Sir. 44:21.

89. See elsewhere in this sense Rom. 3:9; 6:14, 15; 7:14; 16:20 — very similar passages — and 1 Cor. 9:20 (4x!); and 15:25, 27; see also Eph. 1:22. (Rom. 3:13 and 1 Cor. 10:1 assume location; see also Col. 1:23.) On this motif see the, to my mind, definitive treatment by Joel Marcus: "'Under the Law': The Background of a Pauline Expression," *Catholic Biblical Quarterly* 63 (2001): 72-83. Marcus's analysis again contributes helpfully to the developing picture of the Teacher's system.

90. And Martyn's reconstruction is — as usual — difficult to better: *Galatians*, 302-6, 324-25. Martyn integrates the Ishmael-Isaac contrast confidently into his reconstruction of the Teachers' sermon (see Gal. 4:21-31), and also emphasizes the "Two Ways." I am not entirely convinced of these two incorporations, although I certainly endorse the emphasis by the Teachers on the Evil Impulse: see part four, chapter fourteen, and the studies, in particular, by Joel Marcus: "The Evil Inclination in the Epistle of James," *Catholic Biblical Quarterly* 44 (1982): 606-21, esp. 611-13; and "The Evil Inclination in the Letters of Paul," *Irish Biblical Studies* 8 (1986): 8-21. Moreover, in the light especially of Romans 2, this sermon ought also in my opinion to have a slightly more aggressive, future, eschatological orientation, but such an element fits well with what Martyn has already reconstructed. I would also introduce the motif "under the power of" into the Teachers' sermon at some point (see point vii above and 3:10) — presumably, "under the power of Sin/the Evil Impulse" and hence also "of curse." (On this point, see another study by Marcus, just noted: "'Under the Law': The Background of a Pauline Expression.") Martyn goes on to give a powerful account of the way the law curses (326-28). I would prefer to refrain from supplying such details, however, prior to considering the argumentative and theological contribution of 4:1-7.

An important question is whether the Teachers emphasized Gen. 12:3 initially or Paul did, because this text certainly seems to have allowed him an alternative reconstruction of Jewish history leading up to the Christ event and the mission to the pagans (so 3:15–4:7). However, Martyn observes correctly that blessing opposes curse in the Deuteronomic material that the Teachers seem to be using (324), and this observation is usefully supplemented by Longenecker's emphasis on the Jewish discourse attesting to the Abrahamic blessing (see point v above). The terminology surrounding this motif's introduction is also quite distinctive. So I am inclined to agree with Martyn again. The absence of the argument from Romans (esp. from Romans 4) also seems to confirm this judgment. If it was Paul's own creation and he maintained its integrity, it is hard to understand why it would not be redeployed there. If it was only a contingent counterargument, though, then we can readily understand why Paul would not appeal to it again — presumably the Teachers have dropped *their* appeal to Gen. 12:3 (etc.) by this point. (However, it is also interesting to consider that he did do this — that is, move on from some of the famously peculiar argumentation of Galatians 3.)

91. And more possibilities could of course be added. So Longenecker notes sagely: "vv 6-14 have been the focus of a great deal of study, with widely divergent interpretations common" (*Galatians*, 124). Hays leans heavily on Wright at this point; see "The Letter to the Galatians," 257-62; and Wright, "Curse and Covenant," 137-56. Longenecker himself presses form-critical claims strongly, which are difficult in my view to sustain in an interpretatively contested setting (*Galatians*, 108-9, 121-23). Martyn's analysis is subtle and complex, as we have just seen; I am close to his reconstruction (*Galatians*, 294-336). Dunn suggests at one point that vv. 10-14 are "a midrash on Deuteronomy's three-stage schema of salvation-history" — namely, covenant, exile, and restoration (*Galatians*, esp. 180), and in doing so is not far from Hays and Wright. But *not one of these notions is explicitly marked in the text.* Moreover, this analysis presupposes that Paul is engaging here with *Judaism* and not with a Jewish Christian variant, the latter being the explicit concern in Galatians. So Dunn exposes his underlying endorsement of Justification theory, despite the famous variations that he introduces into that schema, which expects of course to engage with Judaism as the necessarily preliminary stage for salvation through faith — just the sort of false assumption that I am interested in exposing in this chapter. Francis Watson emphasizes this text strongly in *P&HF*, finding his principal attestation here to Paul's canonical hermeneutic of the Pentateuch (canvassed in detail in part three, chapter twelve,

§2.1). Other noteworthy studies in this relation include C. D. Stanley, "'Under a Curse': A Fresh Reading of Galatians 3.10-14," *New Testament Studies* 36 (1990): 481-511; and Donaldson, "The 'Curse of the Law,'" 94-112, who argues for a revision of Jewish eschatological expectations here — "the inclusion of the Gentiles is seen as a consequence of the eschatological redemption of Israel" (100). However, he overlooks the retrospective nature of Paul's argument (on which see more just below), and the probable chiastic arrangement of Paul's claims, which entails that their argumentative function is not necessarily linear.

92. Although this is a delicate consideration, as has already been noted, because of the letter's particular contingency.

93. Most of the key Justification terms then resurface suddenly in a compact and important set of statements in 5:5-6, which will be considered in its own right momentarily (i.e., in §7 just below), but they are otherwise largely absent from the rest of the letter. The exception again is πίστις, which recurs in 5:22 and 6:10.

94. See "works" in 5:19 and 6:4 (singular here); and "doing" occurs in two Scripture citations in Galatians 3, namely, Deut. 27:26 in 3:10, and Lev. 18:5 in 3:12; this notion then recurs in 5:3, 17; and 6:9.

95. This point tends in fact to be quite widely conceded: see Martyn, *Galatians,* 314-15; Longenecker, *Galatians,* 143-44 (who terms them "cognate expressions"); Williams, "Justification and the Spirit," 97; Silva, "Faith Versus Works of Law," 224, n. 19 ("parallelism"). Silva also points helpfully to the way that this equation corresponds to the evident parallelism between δικαιοῦται and ζήσεται in 3:11. My point here is that this equation tends not to be applied more broadly in Paul's usage, which is puzzling when we struggle so much with the interpretation of this signifier. Furthermore, to apply *this* particular meaning more broadly works so well.

96. Somewhat unusually, Paul is defending the law — specifically, repudiating the charge here that it is *opposed to* the divine promises. He attempts to do this with the conditional claim just noted, namely, that if a law had been given to Israel that was able to create life, then certainly such a "righteous act" would have been effected through law. Paul's contention seems slightly weakened by the hypothetical nature of his argument (i.e., how do we know this, if it isn't the case?). But if we overlook this difficulty for the moment, his basic claim in context is that the law could have served God's promises directly, realizing them, if it was capable of doing so. So it is clearly congruent with them in a basic sense, and not opposed to them, and this justifies his repudiation of that hostile suggestion in v. 21a. However, in order for the argument to make any sense at all — i.e., to follow on the most basic level — the two "process" terms in the respective clauses must be held equivalent. "If Y was actually possible through the law, then surely Y would have come through the law." If the two terms are not equivalent, then it is difficult to supply any sense to Paul's argument, and critical ellipses are necessary even to approach it (ellipses that turn out to beg the question, of course). The only way forward if the two terms are not equivalent would be to suggest that the events in the protasis are functioning as preconditions for the situation asserted in the apodosis — if one must be made alive through the law, then "righteousness" is possible. However, this makes little sense in and of itself as a conditional construction (why is the giving of life a precondition for "righteousness"?; ordinarily, this would be the other way around), and even less sense as an ostensible repudiation of the charge just noted in v. 21a.

97. It also implies that Paul might be speaking in these texts of δικαιοσύνη θεοῦ, but has elided the genitive — and rather unhelpfully for his later interpreters! But if a key scriptural text or set of texts underlies this usage on his part, his Galatian auditors would already have been attuned to that, and especially if Gen. 15:6 was part of this complex, as seems likely, this being a text that Paul does cite explicitly in the argument of Galatians at 3:6. (See part four, chapter eighteen.)

98. Viz., the full application of the legal metaphor from v. 15; the mention of angels and a mediator in relation to the Mosaic Torah in vv. 19b-20a; the syntax in v. 19; and so on.

99. One reason for this oversight seems to be the fact that commentary tends to have made its mind up about these issues before it reaches this point in the letter, thereby anesthetizing the independent contribution of 3:15-29. A nice example of this is Silva: "This means that faith in Christ *must* be part of what Paul has in mind [in 3:23-26]," a statement he makes well before he supplies an exegesis of that material ("Faith Versus Works of Law," 240, emphasis supplied), on the basis of earlier faith

constructions (principally in 3:2-11). Rather curiously, he has also just said that "Paul's language regarding 'the coming of the faith' is unique to this passage and altogether remarkable" (240). Surely,
then, we should consider this material *in its own right* and *then* return to try to integrate our findings
with other πιστ- constructions in the letter.

A second possible reason for overlooking the importance of this material is that other difficult
questions do tend to preoccupy interpreters at this point — especially the analysis of 3:19b-20, which
raises a thicket of difficulties; see Longenecker, *Galatians*, 136-43.

Important exceptions to this general oversight are, however, (i.a.) Hays, *Faith, passim*; Hung-
Sik Choi, "ΠΙΣΤΙΣ in Galatians 5:5-6: Neglected Evidence for the Faithfulness of Christ," *Journal of
Biblical Literature* 124 (2005): 467-90; also, in briefer treatments, Williams, "Again *Pistis Christou*,"
437-38, 443, 444-45; Hooker, "ΠΙΣΤΙΣ ΧΡΙΣΤΟΥ," 328-30; and Robert C. Tannehill, "Participation in
Christ: A Central Theme in Pauline Soteriology," in *The Shape of the Gospel: New Testament Essays*
(Eugene, Oregon: Cascade [Wipf & Stock], 2007), 223-37, esp. 231-32. I have analyzed this evidence in
"The Coming of Faith in Paul's Gospel: Galatians 3," ch. 10 in my *Quest*, 208-32 — however, the follow-
ing supersedes that analysis.

Apart from these, I know of few if any other studies that use this evidence. One important but
idiosyncratic exception is Greer Taylor, "The Function of ΠΙΣΤΙΣ ΧΡΙΣΤΟΥ in Galatians," *Journal of
Biblical Literature* 85 (1966): 58-76 — one of the most brilliant analyses of this text ever penned, but
unfortunately not for that reason valid. Hays supplies a useful critique (*Faith*, 184-89). He also rebuts
the "rabbinic logic" introduced by Dahl and much used by Martyn (*Faith*, 189-92), and Betz's "rhetorical logic" (which has already been noted in relation to 2:15-16, in §3 above), supplying his own "narrative logic" instead (*Faith*, 194-207). I will use this last "logic" extensively in what follows.

Matlock's latest article offers a *possible* anthropocentric construal of *some* of the relevant data
in Galatians 3 ("The Rhetoric of πίστις in Paul," 187-93); but his reading needs a decisive interpretative
victory at this point in our discussion, and in terms of all of the data. His reconstruction also ought to
align more smoothly with Justification, or he will run into trouble in other Pauline texts (i.e., he pursues the "Abraham-first" strategy here, without any apparent realization of its awkward implications;
Watson's analysis is far more circumspect at this point: see part three, chapter twelve). Indeed, Matlock's reading of Gal. 3 contradicts the reconstruction of Paul's broader argumentation finally supplied
by "Detheologizing the ΠΙΣΤΙΣ ΧΡΙΣΤΟΥ Debate: Cautionary Remarks from a Lexical Semantic Perspective," *Novum Testamentum* 42 (2000): 1-23 — there the traditional, prospective, works-faith progression. Significantly, I detect no cogent rebuttal in this essay of the problems in the anthropocentric
construal of Galatians 3, or, more importantly, of any of the positive contentions in favor of a
christocentric reading. These were sketched out in *Quest*, 208-32, and are tightened up in this chapter.
(Matlock does not refer to *Quest*.) He does, however, make a tell-tale concession: "At several points in
Gal. 3, Paul extends his πίστις/νόμος contrast with ἐκ phrases that are on anyone's view somewhat
awkward, but for which Paul has particular contextual and intertextual reasons . . ." (193, n. 23). Of
course, these phrases are actually only awkward for Matlock's traditional, anthropocentric reading!
My rereading, building on the work of Hays and Martyn, negotiates these "difficulties" smoothly, supplying just the contextual and intertextual reasons that elude the anthropocentric interpreter. It seems
then that this analysis by Matlock of Gal. 3:22 in context is redundant. We need fresh arguments from
him in relation to this text if the objective reading is to regain any plausibility.

100. 𝔓⁴⁶ supplies an important variation here that we will consider shortly.

101. I emphasize that if compelling reasons are supplied, then I have no difficulty ascribing different senses to these serried signifiers, but those reasons do need to be supplied; in their absence, it
seems prima facie that the *same* notion is being discussed throughout. Without such signals of variance, why would we think that something different was being discussed? Hence, I find the concessions to variation made at this point *without apparent reason* by important commentators unwise.
Longenecker notes — rather cryptically — that these interpretative questions are tightly related to one
another but nevertheless goes on to break the series up: ". . . it [i.e., πίστις in v. 26] is not the same as
τὴν πίστιν or τῆς πίστεως found in the immediately preceding vv 23 and 25 that have the content of the
Christian gospel in view, though it is like διὰ τῆς πίστεως of 3:14 earlier. The article here may specify

the human response of trust and commitment that Paul spoke about throughout 3:1-14" (*Galatians*, 151-52). This just looks like contextually insensitive, a priori, and hence bad exegesis. But Hays makes a similar concession, that 3:23-25 refer metonymically to "the gospel" (*Faith*, 296). Appeals in this relation to Gal. 1:23 and/or 6:10 will be noted shortly.

102. This expression occurs exactly in Gen. 13:15, 17:8 and 24:7 (LXX), but close variations on it — σπέρμα plus a possessive pronoun — occur throughout the narrative, with approximately eighteen instances in Genesis 12–25 (excluding 24:60). However, Genesis 17 enjoys seven of these, the highest such concentration in one chapter. Genesis 17 also of course describes the *covenant* of circumcision. And διαθήκη occurs sixteen times in the same stretch of text, but *thirteen* times in chapter 17 (see elsewhere only 15:18; 21:27, 32; see also verbs denoting divine speech in 17:3, 22, 23). It is most likely, then, on grounds of concentration and — more importantly — contextual appropriateness, that 17:8 is in view here in Gal. 3:16.

103. A difficult statement to translate exactly, but the basic correlation seems clear. I incline toward construing this as a dative of means (see 3:22b), but a dative of respect also seems plausible.

104. Some have argued for an unstated Jewish intertextual basis for this correlation (that might, at least, reinforce it), esp. 2 Sam. 7:12-14 (see 4Q174 [4QFlorilegium] 1.10-11). Martyn is cautiously affirmative, noting the support of Dahl, Dulling, Juel, and Hays (*Galatians*, 340, n. 161). This hypothesis is unnecessary, however, if Paul is trying to subvert a claim by the Teachers — presumably that only full proselytes to Judaism can be "seed," not to mention "sons of Abraham."

105. See Hays, *Faith*, 136-38, 172-77.

106. See Hays, *Faith*, 141-53.

107. It is already evident, however, on the basis of Romans (esp. 1:17 and 3:21-26), that this progression is a significant one for Paul; see esp. part four, chapter fifteen.

108. That is, there are reasons for thinking that the Galatian auditors may have already been aware of the subjective denotation of Paul's πίστις Χριστοῦ constructions, knowing the messianic proof text that underlay them (Hab. 2:4). And such auditors would therefore have read 2:15-16 in the nuanced fashion already suggested — as indicating their understanding of resurrection by means of the faithful one, along with some of its key implications. Needless to say, the same approach would have then been applied to 3:22.

109. It is a little bizarre that some interpreters object to the notion that Christ believed in God. To do so would seem to suggest that Christ had no beliefs or concepts, i.e., no mind. This objection also runs into difficulties with the extensive evidence elsewhere in the New Testament that Christ did in fact communicate with other people, often by way of a body of teaching. Such things are difficult without a mind, along with its associated beliefs (many of them about God), its capacity for language, and so on. That Paul held Christ to believe certain things is also clear by the way he — for example — uses his words on occasion. It is not necessary to find an instance when Christ is the subject of the cognate verb, then, to establish this point. One could add the extensive evidence from Paul's writings urging "having the mind of Christ," or something similar (see Phil. 2:5). I will in any case suggest shortly (in chapter twenty-one) that Christ is implicitly but overtly the subject of the verb πιστεύω in Paul once.

110. See Hays, *Faith*, 288-89 (originally "Πίστις and Pauline Christology: What Is at Stake?").

111. Noted by Hays, "The Letter to the Galatians," 270. Longenecker also emphasizes that "in context, . . . only the temporal sense is possible [for εἰς Χριστὸν in v. 24]," but he does not apply the implications to the interpretation of πίστις in context (*Galatians*, 148-49).

112. The interpretative expedient adopted by most interpreters is of course to identify the coming of Christ and the coming of the gospel and/or "the faith." This dubious suggestion is addressed in detail below.

113. And in fact Martyn's nuanced reading is *very* close to my recommendations here; I am simply a little more overtly monological (*Galatians*, 362).

114. And these problems tend to be related in Galatians 3. Any evidence contradicting my apocalyptic reading should do so by establishing the Justification approach, so its absence generates

both this lack of critical penetration and that embarrassing underdetermination in relation to Justification contentions.

115. Note that Matlock's contentions in this relation have already been considered in some detail in part four, chapter seventeen (and found to be astute but ultimately irrelevant): see R. Barry Matlock, "ΠΙΣΤΙΣ in Galatians 3:26: Neglected Evidence for 'Faith in Christ'," *New Testament Studies* 49 (2003): 433-39.

116. Although admittedly there is something attractive about this particular variant!

117. He does not know what to make of συνεσταύρωμαι in 2:19, supplying a marked variant CYNECTPAI, and some spacing, clearly intending to return to correct it.

118. And we have already noted the principal problem for Matlock's argument in part four, chapter sixteen — that the underlying construction is probably not an "objective" construction in any case, but coordinate or parallel. This claim is important enough to be addressed again here.

119. This is suggested by several detailed comments in context, but most notably by the way the state of being "in Christ" is opposed to the states of "Jew-Greek," "slave-free," and "male-female" (v. 28a) and is also entered by way of immersion "into Christ" and reclothing in him (v. 27). Belonging to Christ is then the way in which the promises to Abraham are accessed as well, according to v. 29. All of these indicators suggest that the phrase "in Christ" denotes here a state of being in Paul's argument.

120. And — a little ironically — 𝔓⁴⁶ *may* turn out to assist us at *this* point, the scribe clearly construing these two statements in parallel (i.e., vv. 26 and 28b), if not deliberately modifying them in this way together!

121. Note elsewhere only Col. 1:4 and Eph. 1:15 (and the evidence collated in n. 22 is instructive in this relation).

122. Hays speaks here of a "virtually universal critical agreement," which includes the Revised Standard Version; see *Faith,* 155; see also 119-56 on this question more broadly.

123. Silva is worth quoting at length in this relation, because he illustrates the interpretative dynamics that can be encountered here so clearly ("Faith Versus Works of Law," 240-41):

> It is . . . evident . . . that a simple identification here between πίστις and the "generic" act of believing will not work, since Abraham . . . had earlier been described as having exercised faith. Moreover, one can make little sense out of the notion that the act of believing "has come."
>
> The use of the verb ἐλθεῖν, in fact, suggests strongly that Paul must be referring to Christ, an identification that is confirmed by the immediate context (3:19, ἄχρις οὗ ἔλθῃ τὸ σπέρμα, compared with v. 16; note also v. 24, γέγονεν εἰς Χριστὸν). If so, we should probably understand this use of πίστις as a simple metonymy whereby the word stands for the object of faith. Whatever the precise nuance of this use, Paul's main point is clear enough: the faith that is distinctively connected with Christ (ἡ πίστις Ἰησοῦ Χριστοῦ) made its appearance subsequent to the epoch of the law and in fact marks the end of the latter. Lightfoot is therefore quite right in paraphrasing ἡ πίστις in this passage as "the dispensation of faith."
>
> We should not minimize the boldness of Paul's expression, however. Remarkably, the apostle uses language that suggests, at first blush, the absence of faith prior to the coming of Christ, as well as the absence of law subsequent to it. Neither of those two elements is true in a literal, absolute sense. . . . But Paul is willing to take the risk of being misunderstood in order to draw the eschatological contrast as sharply as possible. The Galatians' most fundamental error was precisely their blurring the distinction between the time of law, of curse, of flesh, . . . and the time . . . of the Spirit, of sonship, of freedom.

There are several problems here. We should note first that Silva accurately notes four of the pieces of evidence extensively discussed in this chapter that point toward an identification of Paul's use of πίστις in this argument with Christ. He then infers correctly that this all "suggests *strongly* that Paul must be referring to Christ" (emphasis added). But he nevertheless goes on to identify, *without grounds,* πίστις *in terms of something else* — a metonymy for the object of faith! (He also cites

Lightfoot's suggestion with approval that Paul is speaking here of "the dispensation of faith," a reading different from his suggestion and never explicitly stated in the text.) So the exegetical evidence here is ignored, and an interpretive claim made without exegetical justification — one that also disorders Paul's argument, as Silva seems quite aware (see "[w]hatever the precise nuance of this use, Paul's main point is clear enough . . .").

Adding insult to injury, Silva goes on to suggest that what Paul states here is not really true! But his reasons for excluding Paul's statements about the end of the epoch of law and the arrival of the epoch of πίστις — a sense in the text that he concedes is "clear enough" — are mere overrulings of these claims in the name of Justification theory justified in turn by solitary verses drawn from other settings (and here, it should be recalled, we are discussing an extended argument) — citations that tend to beg the question concerning just what *those* verses actually mean and/or imply (see Gal. 3:6; Rom. 4:3-9; see Heb. 11 [?!]; Rom. 8:4; 1 Cor. 7:19; Gal. 5:14).

But, as if this were not serious enough, he goes on to excuse Paul's "boldness" — presumably in pronouncing at length certain things that are not true — as risking misunderstanding so that an eschatological contrast can be drawn for the Galatians "as sharply as possible," because the failure to draw that contrast is their "most fundamental error." One wonders just how the Galatians will be usefully assisted and corrected by the drawing of a contrast that is not, strictly speaking, true. Moreover, if it is not true for Paul, why is it *their* most fundamental error to fail to draw it? As Silva constructs this picture, it is apparently wrong for the Galatians to fail to draw a distinction that is itself nevertheless wrong!

At this point, then, Paul's basic theological argument, his rhetorical strategy, and the position of the Galatians have all been reduced to incoherence. Moreover, this has been achieved by ignoring the clues supplied by the text and substituting a reading that has no attestation (and that also clearly disorders the argument). Yet an apocalyptic construal of the argument — which Silva in fact concedes is the obvious one — gives a simple, coherent account of the text, and also accounts for Paul's rhetorical strategy and the Galatian problem perfectly, *and in just the terms that Silva supplies for them!* It reinstates the eschatological distinction effected by the coming of Christ that has become blurred for the Galatians.

It is worth noting that the proposals Silva cites with approval as supports or alternatives offer no advances in cogency — viz., (in addition to Lightfoot's) Burton (*Galatians,* 198), Mussner (*Galaterbrief,* 256), and Axel von Dobbeler, "Metaphernkonflikt und Missionsstrategie: Beobachtungen zur personfizierenden Rede vom Glauben in Gal 3,23-25," *Theologische Zeitschrift* 54 (1998): 14-35 (arguing πίστις is an adaptation of the metaphor of the family).

124. For further variations and representatives additional to those in the preceding note, see Hays, *Faith,* 200-204. He follows Schlier's nuanced suggestion in this text, which is essentially bipolar: "Der Glaube ist das Mittel (als solche auch das Prinzip) des Heils, Christus aber sein Grund. Mit dem Offenbarwerden des Heilsgrundes ist aber auch das Heilsmittel da. Christus Jesus setzt mit seinem Kommen objectiv den Glauben als den neuen Zugang zu Gott" (*Faith,* 203, citing Schlier, *Galatians,* 167). But while this reading has a certain theological profundity — the coming of "the ground of faith," along with its means — it needs to be pointed out that Paul never says this, or supplies a construction close to this in Galatians 3, with the possible exception of 3:22 if that is read in a christocentric fashion. However, we have already seen that such a construal is unlikely. (The closest such possibility might then be the two instances of πίστις in Phil. 3:9, the second of which uses ἐπί in the dative — ἐπὶ τῇ πίστει.) Moreover, this approach *still* panders to Justification theory, thereby begging the key questions. It is tantamount to a reading of Christ as the "object" of faith. It could perhaps be drawn closer to the Greek with a rhetorical reading in terms of "proof"; see James L. Kinneavy, *The Greek Rhetorical Origins of Christian Faith* (Oxford & New York: Oxford University Press, 1987); and David M. Hay, "*Pistis* as 'Ground for Faith' in Hellenized Judaism and Paul," *Journal of Biblical Literature* 18 (1989): 461-76. However, at this point we are really speaking of Christ himself; we are therefore essentially endorsing an apocalyptic approach. Hays himself does this in his commentary, published in 2000 ("The Letter to the Galatians," 268-71), noting that ". . . problems are avoided if we adopt the straightforward translation . . . 'so that what was promised might be given through the faithfulness of Jesus Christ to

those who believe'" (269). He goes on to add that "'the faith' [in vv. 23-25] cannot possibly refer to human subjective believing, because it is something that comes by revelation, and Paul has insisted from the beginning of the letter that revelation is not a matter of human possibility; rather, it is a matter of divine action and divine disclosure (see, e.g., 1:11-12)" (269-70).

125. Recall that according to Justification theory, πίστις is an action that people undertake in order to become, and then to remain, saved. As such, it must contain at least two components — the acting subject, who exercises belief or trust, and the object believed or trusted in, here presumably Christ, as suggested by Gal. 2:16 and 3:22. So it is a fundamentally bipolar notion. (The christological reading, although it does assume an object for Christ's fidelity, namely, God the Father, is not so concerned that Paul actually specify this. The emphasis within this reading is on Christ himself and on his faithfulness to the point of death, in fulfillment of Scripture.) The first problem facing Justification advocates, then, is how to prove that this bipolar understanding of faith is actually present in Paul's argument in Gal. 3:21-29, when the text seems to speak in the main of a singular entity. It follows that a series of elisions must be posited in Paul's central argumentative chain (and if this is not done, it ought to be).

126. Although the notions of the possibility of actions and their importance to the individual sit comfortably with certain modern branches of philosophy and theology, it must be questioned whether these emphatically anthropocentric commitments can be projected responsibly into the context of the first century CE. I suspect that an entire phase of post-Cartesian philosophy is really required in order to make this interpretative option plausible — something of an anachronism for Paul and his audience of course. Put slightly differently, we must ask whether Bultmann's program — which leaned so heavily on Marburg neo-Kantianism — is right, for without his support, the case for Justification is severely weakened at this point. It all looks suspiciously modern.

Rudolf Bultmann is of course — as we have already seen at some length in part two, chapter nine — a classic representative of a theology of appropriation and its possibility for the individual, *but he explicitly acknowledges that this is an accommodation to the concerns and mind of the modern person!* This program has also not been without its critics: see, e.g., the detailed evaluation of H. Thielicke, *The Evangelical Faith*, vol. 1, *Prolegomena*, trans. Geoffrey W. Bromiley (Edinburgh: T&T Clark, 1974 [1968]). Regarding our current theme, Thielicke notes: "Perhaps one might say first and generally that Theology A [i.e., Cartesian theology as represented by Bultmann] is marked by a dominant interest in the addressee of the message, the one to whom it is directed and who is to appropriate it. . . . [T]his is a lawful interest . . . integral to almost all vital theologies since the Enlightenment. Nevertheless, one may question whether a theological system ought to *begin* with this question of the addressee. The orientation or first step might control all further developments. . . . *[The] primary concern [of the Cartesian approach] is the process of appropriation, or, more radically, the possibility of this process*" (38; emphases added). The continuity between Bultmann's approach and nineteenth-century philosophical and theological thinkers is also apparent in Karl Barth's classic analysis, which demonstrates quite clearly the Enlightenment origins of the entire project; see *Protestant Theology in the Nineteenth Century: Its Background and History*, trans. B. Cozens and J. Bowden (London: SCM, 1972). Bultmann also of course had many "sons," although their relationship to his original program is complex: see, e.g., Dieter Lührmann, *Glaube im frühen Christentum* (Gütersloh: G. Mohn, 1976); "Faith (New Testament)," in *ABD* 2:749-58; and *Galatians: A Continental Commentary*.

127. Martyn, *Galatians*, 361.

128. See Gal. 1:16, with the cognate being used in 1:12; see also Rom. 1:17, 18; 8:18; 1 Cor. 2:10; 3:13; 14:30; Phil. 3:15; see also 2 Thess. 2:3, 6, 8 — although this evidence should not be overpressed.

129. See 1 Thess. 1:5, 9; 2:1-13 — although neither ἔρχομαι nor μέλλω are mentioned. Paul also prefers the motif of "sending," which we might expect to see in context: see Rom. 10:14-18. Galatians, meanwhile, seems to more emphasize "call"; see 1:6, 15; 5:8, 13.

130. It is perhaps possible to respond to one of these difficulties by suggesting that the gospel was preached in advance to Abraham, as Paul states clearly in 3:8, so he is really a Christian born out of sequence. But this does not alter the fact that it is not, strictly speaking, true for Paul to claim later — and repeatedly — that faith arrives or comes with the Christian dispensation. Even if it has only

been anticipated earlier in Abraham, it has still already arrived there. Moreover, it could presumably also arrive in relation to many other pious pre-Christian Jews as well. That is, this suggestion generates acute salvation-historical tensions with respect to Judaism and Jewish history. There is also the problem emphasized frequently during the preceding argument that Abraham is said to believe in *God* (i.e., in God "the Father").

131. This motif is much discussed; see Hays, "The Letter to the Galatians," 269-70; Williams, *Galatians,* 102-3; Martyn, *Galatians,* 363, esp. n. 225; Longenecker, *Galatians,* 146-50; Matera, *Galatians,* 139-40. Important, more detailed studies include D. Lull, "'The Law Was Our Pedagogue': A Study of Gal 3:19-25," *Journal of Biblical Literature* 105 (1986): 481-98; and N. H. Young, "Paidagogos: The Social Setting of a Pauline Metaphor," *Novum Testamentum* 29 (1987): 150-76. Longenecker discusses various informative texts drawn from the classical Greek corpus, although these must be used with caution when explicating a metaphor in the first century CE: see Plato, *Republic,* 373C and 467D; *Lysis,* 208C; *Laws,* 7.808D-E; Aristotle, *Ethics,* 3.12.8; Xenophon, *Constitution of Lacedaemon,* 3.1. Matera points to certain Jewish texts that attribute a pedagogical function — although not the metaphor itself — to the law as well (140): see Josephus, *Against Apion,* 3.173-74; *Letter of Aristeas,* 142. These raise the intriguing possibility that Paul is subverting a favored metaphor in the Teachers' discourse at this point, even as he develops his own argument. Given the Teachers' fondness for the ἀγών discourse, this seems entirely possible.

132. And the law can return in a similar role after conversion, to guide the convert ethically — the "third" use of the law. A tension at this point in Justification theory has already been noted — that all the law, strictly speaking, seems to remain in force (see part one, chapter three; the "two laws" conundrum implicit here is noted in chapter two as well).

133. This is the principal difficulty in Donaldson's otherwise astute analysis. He grasps the argumentative dynamic here between Israel and the pagans more clearly than most, but not the retrospective thrust of Paul's overarching argument. So he states: "Christ redeemed Israel *so that* the Gentiles might be blessed . . . [indeed] as the *precondition* of the blessing of the Gentiles . . ." ("The 'Curse of the Law,'" 98, emphases added). Paul never says this, and for him to do so would contradict his central argument in Galatians 3. Donaldson's failure to grasp this point is the more strange given that he grasps the rhetorical dynamics in play in Galatians (as we have already seen) *and* the importance of Sanders's famous dictum concerning Paul's retrospective thinking — a slogan with which he closes (107).

134. So, as Hays puts it: "Nowhere in Galatians, or in any of his other letters, does Paul argue for a progressive educative function of the Law; its purpose, according to these verses, is *protective custody*" ("The Letter to the Galatians," 270, emphasis added).

135. And perhaps the emphasis on a written text here recalls the issue of mediation that Paul has been concerned to stress in 3:19-20, over against the direct, spoken will of God in 3:15-16.

136. So Martyn, observing that six of the ten times that Paul refers in Galatians 2-4 to being "under the power of" something (i.e., ὑπό plus accusative), that entity is the law. Hence, "he is using the term *paidagôgos* in the sense of a distinctly unfriendly and confining custodian, different in no significant way from an imprisoning jailer" (*Galatians,* 363).

137. Choi, "ΠΙΣΤΙΣ in Galatians 5:5-6," 470. I am indebted to Choi's study for drawing my attention to several lines of argument and pieces of evidence in favor of a christological reading of 5:5-6 but do not find all his contentions equally persuasive. In what follows I have tried to remedy a few gaps in his argument, combining what I take to be his strongest contentions and adding new material at certain points. Of course, I share his judgment that the evidence for the christological reference of πίστις in 5:5-6 from 3:23-26 is "decisive" (472), although one result of this line of argument is the reduction of the importance of 5:5-6 from a "crux" to a "corroboration." I am not convinced that its considerations are strong enough to stand alone in the broader debate — although perhaps they are. Note that the neglect of these verses in relation to this particular question does not mean that they have been neglected more generally; many commentators emphasize their importance — e.g., Longenecker, *Galatians,* 222, 229, 235; Burton, *Galatians,* 279; Betz, *Galatians,* 262.

138. Martyn concurs (*Galatians,* 474), following Mussner (*Galaterbrief,* 354). He rejects K. W.

Clark's advocacy of the passive: "The Meaning of *Energeo* and *Katargeo* in the New Testament," *Journal of Biblical Literature* 54 (1935): 93-101; see also A. L. Mulka, "Fides quae per Caritatem Operatur," *Catholic Biblical Quarterly* 28 (1966): 174-88. However, Martyn also tends to translate and discuss this phrase in context as an active — see "Paul declares . . . the newly arriving existence of another [world], characterized by faith active in mutual love" (473) — although this is certainly christologically grounded. His later statement is perhaps more accurate: ". . . gospel-elicited faith expresses itself in love of the neighbor" (474); see also Hays, "Christology and Ethics in Galatians: The Law of Christ," 268-90.

139. See especially the next cluster of arguments in support of this judgment. However, even an instrumental reading is awkward. Faith should not be caused by Christ Jesus according to Justification theory. One better alternative might be to refer the initial construction to the final participle as an adverbial modifier, so "faith puts itself into effect through love by means of Christ Jesus," thereby enlisting Christ's agency to overcome some of the difficulties just noted. There is now, however, a slight clash of causalities — faith acts on behalf of itself, but then also because of Christ. And this instrumental reading seems rather less likely in any case.

140. Choi, "ΠΙΣΤΙΣ in Galatians 5:5-6," 485.

141. See Martyn, *Galatians,* 473, pointing in particular to Gal. 5:6; 6:15; and 1 Cor. 7:19.

142. It also makes little sense in terms of Justification theory to assert that the uncircumcised are not capable of anything. This is obvious; it is the law-observant Jew that constitutes a more difficult case.

143. The concerns of Rom. 5:1-11 and 8:9-11, 14-39, raised by the scenario implicit in 1:18–3:20.

144. The verb is much rarer than the noun in Paul and only once suggests its content or an object, more usually designating a constituency to whom the gospel has been proclaimed. *However, that solitary instance is Gal. 1:16,* where Paul is charged by God to preach "him," i.e., "his Son," Christ, among the pagan nations. Galatians 1:23 of course occurs soon after this instance. When the noun occurs with a genitive of content (and, note, not a possessive: see, i.a., 1 Thess. 1:5), the noun *invariably* is either (1) "God," as in Rom. 1:1; 15:16; 2 Cor. 11:7; 1 Thess. 2:2, 8, 9; or (2) some variant on Christ, whether "his Son," as in Rom. 1:9; or "Christ," as in Rom. 15:19; 1 Cor. 9:12; 2 Cor. 2:12; 4:4 ("the glory of Christ"); 9:13; 10:14; Gal. 1:7; Phil. 1:27; and 1 Thess. 3:2. (See also "the gospel of your salvation" and "of peace" in Eph. 1:13 and 6:15; and "of our Lord Jesus" in 2 Thess. 1:8.) The one apparent exception to these trends is Gal. 2:7, τὸ εὐαγγέλιον τῆς ἀκροβυστίας; however, this is a genitive oriented toward a constituency rather than strictly in terms of content. So the NRSV correctly translates this as "the gospel for the uncircumcised." That is, no one seriously suggests that Paul is describing the content of his preaching *here* in terms of "uncircumcision," although it does ultimately include this stance.

145. BDAG asserts that Rom. 1:5, "perhaps" Gal. 3:23-25, and, for "many," Rom. 12:6 take the substantivized, creedal meaning (meaning 3: see 820). But all these suggestions are distinctly dubious. Jude 3 and 20 are also listed, and then only material from the Pastorals — 1 Tim. 1:19; 4:1, 6; 6:10 (see 21); 2 Tim. 2:18; 4:7. And most of this later evidence is debatable as well, whether in terms of sense and/or date. Galatians 3:2 and 5 are in fact arguably some of the only such instances from Paul himself; however, as we have already seen, it is difficult to argue that πίστις is functioning indubitably here as the object of hearing. We should also ask at this point what Paul normally proclaims, and is in fact the divinely appointed envoy of — the gospel. The evidence of Galatians itself firmly corroborates this: see 1:11, 12, 16. On the issue of creeds, a useful introduction is J. N. D. Kelly, *Early Christian Doctrines,* rev. 5th ed. (New York: Harper & Row, 1978).

146. One cogent alternate might be to render πίστις in terms of "loyalty" — a common enough meaning in Koiné. So Paul would be saying, "The one persecuting us then now proclaims that loyalty which then he was destroying. . . ." This is not especially frequent for Paul but makes perfect sense in context, and has the added virtue of aligning the two objects of persecution — namely, "us" and "that πίστις which he then was destroying" — more exactly together in the same entity, the Christian community. Given this alternative, the Christological reading of 1:23 should not be insisted on.

147. Longenecker notes the inclusio that this creates in Paul's "ethical" material with 5:13 (*Galatians,* 282).

148. In a somewhat bizarre turn, some interpreters object to my developing interpretation here (and similar readings) that the resulting emphasis on Christ "is in danger of overkill" (see Dunn, "Once More, ΠΙΣΤΙΣ ΧΡΙΣΤΟΥ," repr. in Hays, *Faith*, 249-71, with this point being made on 257-59). It is hard to conceive of what grounds exist for plausibly denying the suggestion that Paul is being thoroughly christocentric — and in Galatians (2:18-20)! If pressed, however, it is worth noting that an insidious false metaphor can operate within such an objection — a metaphor of quantity (see our earlier discussion of the atonement in part one, chapter two).

If interpretations can be placed on a spectrum, the sober and moderate exegete should presumably prefer the "middle" way between the "radical" and "extreme" interpretations operating on the edges of the putative standard distribution of readings. But this metaphor is problematic on every level: first, it is not a true account of the disposition of readings; second, Paul was radical; and third, a more accurate construal of the situation should contrast *paradigms*. That is, we are concerned with the different explanatory frameworks that are being offered to explain data, and these are not assessed relative to one another in terms of an integrated population that could then be analyzed statistically. Some explanations are simply better than others. So, for example, there was a significant shift some time ago to the endorsement of the explanation of the earth's basic shape as round, as against flat. If the metaphor of quantity and distribution just noted is applied to this shift, note what happens: those endorsing the round theory are being "radical" and "extreme." More sober interpreters would prefer a middle way between the two alternatives of round and flat — presumably the view that the earth's shape is oval or perhaps hexagonal. Clearly we should orient ourselves to the data under discussion, and not to a putative standard distribution of readings and its false analogical appeals to moderation.

149. See BDAG for numerous such references (694). The role of the Sergii in the Galatian Christian communities — which is to my mind likely — also speaks in favor of this reading.

150. It might be helpful to note how I regard this evidence in dialogue with Hays, the other scholar who treats it most extensively from christological and apocalyptic viewpoints. I see the following texts as decisively in that interpretative paradigm's favor: 2:20; 3:22-26 in their broader context (i.e., 3:15-29/4:9); and 5:6. I regard all the rest of the relevant texts as "probably" apocalyptic, and in varying degrees of strength — some quite strong: 1:23; 2:15-16; 3:2 and 5; 3:6-14 (esp. vv. 11-12); 5:5; and 6:10. In all these texts at least *some* evidence seems to point toward the correctness of the christological emphasis, and this can be quite extensive, while a conventional construal faces difficulties. (I am constantly tempted to move 1:23, 3:2 and 5, 3:11-12, and 6:10, over into the "decisive" category.) Hays, in his landmark *Faith* (originally published in 1983) presses hard on 2:20 as well, and quite hard on 3:2 and 5. He is less aggressive with 3:6-14 and 3:21-26 than I am, conceding some of the evidence in this last passage to alternative readings. His later commentary ("The Letter to the Galatians," published in 2000) is more consistently christological in 3:21-26, but given its format, this case is not argued for in any detail. In that later work he also places little emphasis on 5:5-6 (313-14), and makes some arguably dangerous concessions vis-à-vis 3:11-12. In both works he tends to concede 1:23 (see "The Letter to the Galatians," 217) and 6:10 (see "The Letter to the Galatians," 337-38) to the conventional reading. I suppose, then, that one person's inconsistency is another person's nuancing (and one scholar's consistency is another's monochromatic semantic insensitivity!). It can be seen, in short, that I push the christological envelope in Galatians as far as it will go, but see no reasons for not doing this, and suggest further that the resulting interpretation is actually stronger, because it involves no concessions to competing alternatives. Paul is both more consistent and more christocentric — surely good things.

151. I have omitted an extensive treatment of Gal. 3:10 and 3:13 here because enough has already been said about these texts and their citations of Deuteronomic material in my evaluation of Francis Watson's ingenious revisionist proposal in part three, chapter twelve. (They were also discussed briefly in part one, chapter five.) I conclude there that the available evidence points toward their marked contingency — that is, they operate only in this early phase of the debate between Paul and the Teacher, in relation to a very specific question of passing moment, and so do not point to especially deep matters in the apostle's theology. Conversely, Lev. 18:5, Hab. 2:4, and Gen. 15:6 do recur in Romans, and in positions of some prominence, to which I would want to add the echoes of Ps. 98:2

and Ps. 143:2. Furthermore, certain "universal" texts have been added by that point as well — principally Isa. 8:14, 28:16, and Joel 2:32 (3:5 LXX), not to mention the Isaianic material that reflects more directly on Paul himself. (The evaluation of their status in relation to Paul's coherence is a fascinating question that will not be attempted here, although some indications have been given.)

Notes to Chapter Twenty-One

1. Ephesians 2:8-10 in particular raises important but complex questions, so it is best considered in its own right on another occasion. For a promising beginning in relation to Eph. 3:12 see Paul Foster, "The First Contribution to the Πίστις Χριστοῦ Debate: A Study of Ephesians 3:12," *Journal for the Study of the New Testament* 85 (2002): 75-96.

2. I will lean in what follows in the first instance on Peter T. O'Brien, *The Epistle to the Philippians: A Commentary on the Greek Text* (Grand Rapids, Mich.: Eerdmans, 1991), esp. 346-417; Gordon D. Fee, *Paul's Letter to the Philippians* (Grand Rapids, Mich.: Eerdmans, 1995), 285-337; Markus Bockmuehl, *The Epistle to the Philippians* (Peabody, Mass.: Hendrickson, 1998); and Stephen E. Fowl, *Philippians*, The Two Horizons New Testament Commentary (Grand Rapids, Mich.: Eerdmans, 2005), esp. 143-58.

Elements in the following monographs have also proved useful: Gregory L. Bloomquist, *The Function of Suffering in Philippians*, JSNTSup 78 (Sheffield: Sheffield Academic Press, 1993); Peter Oakes, *Philippians: From People to Letter*, SNTSMS 110 (Cambridge: Cambridge University Press, 2001), esp. 103-28; and Demetrius K. Williams, *Enemies of the Cross of Christ: The Terminology of the Cross and Conflict in Philippians*, JSNTSup 223 (Sheffield: Sheffield Academic Press, 2002), esp. 148-93.

The additional secondary literature can be poorly focused in this relation: Morna Hooker makes some brief remarks: see "ΠΙΣΤΙΣ ΧΡΙΣΤΟΥ," *New Testament Studies* 35 (1989): 321-42, esp. 324, 331-33. Similarly — and more recently — Robert C. Tannehill notes the importance of this text briefly: "Participation in Christ: A Central Theme in Pauline Soteriology," in *The Shape of the Gospel: New Testament Essays* (Eugene, Oregon: Cascade [Wipf & Stock], 2007), 223-37, esp. 233-35. Veronica Koperski has contributed one of the few detailed studies of the πίστις issues, arguing from a conventional perspective: "The Meaning of *Pistis Christou* in Philippians 3:9," *Louvain Studies* 18 (1993): 198-216. (The cogency of this study will be assessed shortly.) James D. G. Dunn has also written a useful short essay on Philippians 3, from his distinctive perspective, of course: "Philippians 3.2-14 and the New Perspective on Paul," in *The New Perspective on Paul: Collected Essays* (Tübingen: Mohr Siebeck, 2005), 463-84; this was prompted in part by a study by D. Marguerat: "Paul et la Loi: le retournement (Philippiens 3,2–4,1)," in *Paul, une théologie en construction*, ed. A. Dettwiler, et al. (Genève: Labor et Fides, 2004), 271-75. So Dunn notes appositely "Phil. 3 [has] been too much neglected in the current debate on Paul and the law and . . . it [is] a major resource for moving the debate beyond the impasse in which the debate [is] in danger of becoming stuck" (463); it could be added that this "major resource" may also enable us to move past a number of important, interrelated and deadlocked debates, and not merely questions surrounding the law (see here esp. part one). Sanders makes a series of typically pithy observations in *Paul, the Law, and the Jewish People* (Philadelphia: Fortress, 1983), 43-45, 139-41. And R. Barry Matlock's latest study addresses Phil. 3:9: "The Rhetoric of πίστις in Paul: Galatians 2.16, 3.22, Romans 3.22, and Philippians 3.9," *Journal for the Study of the New Testament* 30 (2007): 173-203.

3. It might matter more if *part* of chapter 3 was an addition; however, I regard this hypothesis as rather unlikely. Some useful evidence against it will emerge in what follows — namely, the way an athletic *topos* functions across any ostensible seam around vv. 11 and 12, apparently within the same basic argument; the presence of opponents in both subsections also seems to point to the unity of this material. The tide is running strongly against partition theories of Philippians in any case (and perhaps in even more general terms, with respect to Paul's corpus as a whole). On questions of partition see David Garland, "The Composition and Unity of Philippians: Some Neglected Literary Factors," *Novum Testamentum* 27 (1985): 141-73; Duane F. Watson, "A Rhetorical Analysis of Philippians and Its

Implications for the Unity Question," *Novum Testamentum* 30 (1988): 57-88; Loveday C. A. Alexander, "Hellenistic Letter-Forms and the Structure of Philippians," *Journal for the Study of the New Testament* 37 (1989): 87-101; and J. T. Reed, *A Discourse Analysis of Philippians*, JSNTSup 136 (Sheffield: Sheffield Academic Press, 1997).

4. So, in a sense, as Paul writes Philippians he is experiencing a local church situation that ought to have been significantly formed by that earlier letter.

5. Fowl (*Philippians*, 143-44), following Reed (*Discourse Analysis*, 231-38), tends to read v. 1a as a "hesitation formula" attested in the epistolary papyri and related to the repetition of the "rejoice" exhortation (see 2:17, 18), and not to what follows; v. 1b is then an exhortation to remain "steadfast." So v. 1 is arguably not part of Paul's address to the Teachers. If this argument holds, then nonverbal cues would be signaling the letter's change of direction from v. 2. I am not entirely convinced by this; talk of repetition and "safety" seems to make more sense in relation to a possible repetition of stern anti-Teacher material than the brief "rejoice" formula — which occurs again at 4:4 without apology. Fortunately, not much turns on a definitive decision here.

6. O'Brien (*Philippians*, 354), Fee (*Philippians*, 295), and Dunn ("Philippians 3," 464) concur. Fowl is correct, however, to let the third derogatory term here — κατατομή — have decisive force for this question, in view of the polysemy of the first two designations (*Philippians*, 145-46).

7. So Gerald Hawthorne, *Philippians* (Dallas: Word, 1989), 125; Bockmuehl, *Philippians*, 187-89; and Dunn, "Philippians 3," 465, Dunn pointing to the immediate occurrence of "boasting" in v. 2 in further corroboration of this claim. This is a common association in the Teachers' discourse, as we have already seen. Dunn goes on to invoke Rom. 2:28-29 repeatedly as explaining this opposition (466-67), although this is less wise; certainly, nothing explicit in the text *demands* the introduction of that material, and Dunn's explication tends to be merely assertive. Different interpretations can therefore be supplied (see of course part four, chapter fourteen).

8. Dunn concurs with this judgment: "Philippians 3," 463-64. Not all conclude that they are a present threat; they might be deployed here in an exemplary fashion (see, i.a., Fowl, *Philippians*, 145-47) — although Paul's engagement here is hardly irenic! The wordplay on circumcision tends to elicit comparison with Rom. 2:26 (see, e.g., Fowl, *Philippians*, 147-48), but my rereading of that material allows an alternative emphasis at this point; in speaking of genuine "circumcision" among Christians as against mere "mutilation," Paul is not necessarily talking about "entry requirements" and "true membership of the people of Israel" but is indicating, rather, *their superior ethical condition* over against the system urged by the Teachers, in particular through their victory over the evil inclination. This is why Paul goes on immediately to emphasize the role of the Spirit over against the credentials of the flesh.

9. "Philippians 3," 468 — and see more in this relation just below. Dunn is also right to observe that "works" and "merit" do not enter this description (468-69).

10. There is probably little to choose between the two essentially causal translations that are possible for an accusative διά — "because of" and "for the sake of" — although the argument can be nuanced in *slightly* different directions by this distinction. Paul uses this construction three times in rapid succession in vv. 7 and 8 (twice in v. 8), almost certainly in a similar way.

The provision of an article for "Christ" in v. 7 allows a more titular translation of that signifier as "the Messiah." If this is correct, then Paul is not merely saying that Christ Jesus has reversed his valuation of all his previous Jewish privileges and advantages but that the crowning point *of* those Jewish privileges — the Messiah — has effected that reversal (see Rom. 9:4-5, 33), and this seems an entirely possible emphasis in context.

11. It is frequently noted that this language is redolent of accounting; see, i.a., Williams, *Enemies*, 174-75. Less often observed is that such language overlaps with the language of "advantage" (ὠφέλεια) discussed earlier in relation to Romans 2 (see esp. Rom. 3:1; see part four, chapter fourteen); so Dionysius of Halicarnassus, *The Roman Antiquities* 8.44.2 (cited originally by Margaret M. Mitchell, *Paul and the Rhetoric of Reconciliation* [Tübingen: Mohr, 1992], 203-6, n. 57). Probably, then, another strand within the Teachers' discourse is detectable at this point.

12. Indeed, arguably this motif participates in a subtle but consistent inversion of Jewish purity regulations that is taking place throughout this text. Those who are traditionally viewed as clean and

pure — law-observant Jews — are in fact dogs and mutilators (an unclean category and practice). Their good works are evil. Those traditionally regarded as unclean, however — the pagan "dogs" — are those who serve God in his presence by his Spirit. Then, in v. 8, all Paul's privileges, including his zealous pursuit of nomistic purity as a Pharisee, are viewed as unclean or filthy compared with knowing Christ (a knowledge that involves, moreover, a participation in a dangerously polluting execution: see Gal. 3:13 and Deut. 21:23). Paul consequently stating here that Christ has inverted traditional purity categories: those previously clean are dirty (if they do not recognize him), and those previously dirty are clean (in him). Is this also then a subtle jab at the opponents' *Pharisaic* identity (see Acts 15:5)?

13. Dunn, "Philippians 3," 469, emphasis original. Dunn also has little difficulty repudiating the extraordinary recharacterizations of Paul's concerns at this point in more conventional categories — e.g., "das Selbstvertrauen des Menschen" or "das Sich-Rühmen der Selbstgerechtigkeit" (see esp. 469, n. 28, citing T. Laato, *Paulus und das Judentum: Anthropologische Erwägungen* [Helsinki: Abo, 1991], 259, 63). Dunn goes on to assert, however, that Paul is objecting here to *"confidence in ethnic identity."* But he isn't. He is listing his own grounds for security or confidence in his status as a Jew over against those who can list similar qualifications. He is then going to abandon these qualifications in a dramatic argumentative move. He is not objecting to anything yet, and when he does, he will object simply that such things are not Christ. Dunn is right here, then, in what he repudiates, but mistaken in what he affirms.

14. Consequently, it tends to be narrated by some interpreters as a product of guilt and anger that demonstrates, rather, that the law is doing its work and Paul is sinking into a pit of frustrated performance and guilt, which leads in turn to outbursts of cruelty and anger like his persecuting activity. It may also reflect his deep-seated admiration for Christians. (The classic analysis in these terms [as we saw in part one, chapter five] was supplied by C. H. Dodd: see "The Mind of Paul," in *New Testament Studies* [New York: Scribners, 1952], 67-128.) However, at least two difficulties with this approach are evident. First, Paul attaches no negative emotions or coding to any of his discussions of this activity. (The potential contribution of Acts 26:14 was discussed briefly in part one, chapter five; it is not relevant.) There is consequently no evidence that he did feel negative about this activity as he was undertaking it. Second, Justification theory can hardly code the Jewish situation in the vestibule with this type of work *necessarily*, asserting that vicious persecution of nonconformists is intrinsic to the journey through law observance. This is unlikely on empirical grounds, and politically and ethically unthinkable. Dunn asserts that it was "motivated by . . . concern to maintain and protect Israel's holiness against incursions from 'Gentile sinners'" (472). This seems more plausible in broader cultural terms, but we have no evidence that this *was* actually Paul's motivation. Moreover, that he was motivated against "gentile sinners" entering the church in the early 30s CE strikes me as highly unlikely; it was largely Paul himself who later created this problem! Unfortunately, Paul only tells us the "what" here and not the "why."

15. He could arguably be in the "loop of foolishness," but this is not coded in the text with the key qualities of hypocrisy, stubbornness or recalcitrance, ignorance, etc.

16. *Philippians,* 393 (citing Bruce, *Philippians,* 90).

17. Robert Gundry, "Grace, Works, and Staying Saved in Paul," *Biblica* 66 (1985): 1-38, citing from 13. Note that in one sense this is right, because the shift in ages is being experienced by Paul himself. However, Gundry is also emphasizing some *prior* autobiographical journey by Paul, which cannot be found in this text.

18. *Enemies,* 182; also 180.

19. See point 6 for more on this.

20. The supply of Θεῷ here by some MSS is probably explicable in terms of attraction. The word's omission by 𝔓⁴⁶ seems idiosyncratic, although little turns on this if it is the original reading.

21. O'Brien canvasses the grammatical options succinctly: *Philippians,* 400, esp. n. 107. This phrase reaches back in turn to the statements at the end of v. 8: ἡγοῦμαι σκύβαλα ἵνα Χριστὸν κερδήσω.

22. Nothing flows from the nature of the genitive.

23. This last observation might incline interpretation toward a purposive construal of the genitive arthrous infinitive. However, if purpose is stressed too strongly, then Paul's argument becomes decidedly future in orientation, and this overlooks the various emphases in context on a *present* sharing in Christ's sufferings (see, e.g., 3:12-16).

24. Tannehill, "Participation in Christ," 233-34. These statements are especially evocative of Gal. 2:19b-20.

25. Construing ἐπί in the dative here in v. 9b in terms of meaning 6 (BDAG 364-65). And this decision seems to point in turn — although not decisively — toward a christological reference. If a sense of extension toward believers is in view here, then we would expect the accusative (see meaning 16, "for": BDAG 366). But of course we do not get this, and neither does anything in the context indicate such a concern here on Paul's part. We could note further that this process of extension in a πιστ- series in Paul elsewhere *always* moves through a single reference to one marked as plural, whether explicitly, in its own right (see Rom. 3:22; Gal. 3:22), or in context (see Rom. 1:16-17; 10:9-13).

26. It has enjoyed some support in the commentary. O'Brien favors a christological reference for the first instance of πίστις in v. 9 (*Philippians*, 398-400), as do Bockmuehl (*Philippians*, 211), and Fowl (*Philippians*, 154). But having granted its probability in the first πιστ- statement, it is difficult to see what grounds exist for denying its relevance in the second instance, *which seems positioned in a deliberately repeated phrase:* τὴν διὰ πίστεως Χριστοῦ elides δικαιοσύνην, and so reads in full τὴν δικαιοσύνην τὴν διὰ πίστεως Χριστοῦ. That is, the second πιστ- phrase seems to be an appositional expansion inserted to emphasize that *this* righteous activity comes from God, not humanity (see ἐμήν). It repeats the important preceding phrase with a small stylistic abbreviation and variation — τὴν ἐκ Θεοῦ δικαιοσύνην ἐπὶ τῇ πίστει. These two statements therefore need to be interpreted in parallel, not in a series, as Fee realizes. However, he opts for the conventional reading, which is poorly supported in context (*Philippians*, 324-34, esp. n. 44). R. Barry Matlock's latest study affirms Fee's analysis in more detail — that the two instances of πίστις ought to be interpreted in parallel: "The Rhetoric of πίστις in Paul: Galatians 2.16, 3.22, Romans 3.22, and Philippians 3.9," *Journal for the Study of the New Testament* 30 (2007): 173-203, esp. 178-82. I agree completely with Matlock's initial syntactical analysis of this sentence. The employment of ἐπί in the dative — which is unique for Paul in this relation — seems to emphasize that the basis for all Christian experience of God's righteous action is the Christ event (and not, precisely, "their" activity), *and this has of course been Paul's sustained and explicit concern throughout this subsection.*

Dunn also recognizes that Paul is repeating himself here, pointing perceptively to the frequent repetitions in the argument elsewhere (i.e., "beware," 3x; "confidence in the flesh," 3x; "loss," 3x; "on account of . . . Christ," 3x; and "attain," 3x), and this supports a consistent reading of the πιστ- data. (Hooker also makes this observation: "ΠΙΣΤΙΣ ΧΡΙΣΤΟΥ," 331.) However, he offers little in favor of his conventional construal, stating simply that "the second 'faith' is certainly that of the believer" ("Philippians 3," 476, n. 53), and going on to insist that the two instances be interpreted in the same way. This is a useful way to wedge the conventional reading of πίστις into the "double-minded" interpretations just noted that interpret the two instances divergently, but it has little to say to an interpretation that interprets both instances consistently with respect to Christ. Dunn also fails to address just how his reading of "faith" responds coherently to the issue of ethnic privilege that he sees operating through the argument just prior to this (my main concern in Douglas A. Campbell, "The ΔΙΑΘΗΚΗ from Durham: Prof. Dunn's *The Theology of Paul the Apostle*," *Journal for the Study of the New Testament* 72 [1998]: 91-111; see also part three, chapter twelve) or, indeed, how "faith" can be "the righteousness which is 'from God'" (476). And he fails to address the familiar conundrum (by now) that this faith tends to be explicated as faith in God — and needs to be in order to skirt certain difficulties — while the text supplies faith *in Christ*. "Paul's point is . . . that faith alone is the basis for an effectively right relationship with God — the trust in God and the reliance on God which Abraham had so exemplified in regard to the promise of an heir (Rom. 4:16-21) as the medium through which, on the basis of which, out of which life should be lived (Rom. 14:23)" (476). The divine decision to privilege faith is simply arbitrary in Dunn's reading; so Paul's "fundamental religious insight" (477) bears no coherent relation to an account of Judaism in terms of the "covenantal nomism" that he has just so carefully argued for in

Paul's thinking. Introducing the example of Abraham also points either to an incoherent argument or to the fidelity of Christ, because the object in question is God. And the strong emphasis on Abraham's exemplification makes Dunn's reluctance to cede such a role to Christ puzzling.

This reluctance is even more puzzling when Dunn goes on to describe accurately and in some detail Paul's expectations in vv. 10-11 of Christian participation in Christ's death: "Christ's sufferings still had to be shared. Paul had yet to be fully conformed to Christ's death. . . . The full saving effect of Christ's death was its effect in transforming the believer to share ever more fully in that death, that is, what Paul refers to elsewhere as the dying off/wasting away of 'our outward man' . . . (2 Cor. 4:16)" (480-81, 484). This looks like participation in Christ's "fidelity" to me.

27. Koperski provides the most thorough attempted refutation in "The Meaning of *Pistis Christou* in Philippians 3.9." (Matlock's latest analysis is treated just below; it is also not as extensive as Koperski's concerning Phil. 3:9.) But, although her treatment is detailed and makes some valid observations (e.g., concerning the indecisiveness of arguments in terms of redundancy), the argumentation is dated and misdirected — if not at times a bit confused — and so ultimately fails to gain any effective purchase on the data in the face of a reading that is already well established. Concomitantly, it fails to offer anything decisive in favor of her own, conventional approach.

There are the usual invalid arguments in terms of what Paul *doesn't* do (i.e., which he would have done if he had intended a subjective or christological sense), when we must of course address what he *does* do. She correctly notes how Phil. 3:9 suggests initially a contrast between righteousness from a human source as against from God — but she overrides this implication because of a conventional reading of Gal. 2:16 (213)! She then argues that a subjective construal is unclear: "Does the obedience/faithfulness of Christ come from God?" (214; this challenge has of course already been answered both here and elsewhere in ample measure; see also Hooker's useful explication: "ΠΙΣΤΙΣ ΧΡΙΣΤΟΥ," 331-32). She asserts that 3:9 is also "a restatement of Phil 1:28-29" without justifying this claim, or supplying an interpretation of that difficult text (214). She also points to the contrast in Phil. 3:7-11 between relying on the flesh and glorying in Christ Jesus, going on to claim — rather incredibly — that this text therefore contrasts two human attitudes (214)! (Yet this is then called a gift of God.) She claims that it is "generally accepted" that the second instance of πίστις in 3:9 is to Christian faith. (Of course, I do not accept this, and I think that certain considerations stand against it, e.g., the meaning of ἐπί in the dative.) This also presumably connects the text with Rom. 10:9-10 (although the key text driving Christ's function in that text — Isa 28:16 — is not cited in Philippians 3). Her presuppositions then become quite clear: although making an argument in terms of Christology (214-15), she is actually committed to a conventional anthropological approach: "our righteousness does not come about *automatically* through the obedience of Christ; it is also necessary for those who would be righteous to *appropriate* the gift of belief in Christ that is offered by God" (215, emphasis added). But Paul never actually says this, and there are several good reasons for thinking that he is not concerned with human appropriation in Phil. 3:1-11, but with the implications of a retrospective Christian purview for law observance. Koperski also seems nervous about the christological reading of 3:9, asserting that "the obedience of Christ is . . . in a totally different category than the obedience of Abraham or any other holy person" (215 — which seems to flirt with Docetism; a reference to Christ's πίστις is really just incarnational, and focused in particular on the atonement). However, it turns out that she is in fact worried about subordinationism (216), asserting — a little strangely — that "if Paul does not consider Christ to be divine [in 3:10], then Paul must be considered guilty of blasphemy" (216). In sum, Koperski never actually supplies a close reading of 3:1-11 but supplies various ad hoc claims derived from other Pauline texts (usually read conventionally without explanation) and from various theological postures and their ostensible implications (not always coherent), prefaced with attacks on various straw men (i.e., caricatures of the positions of Johnson, Williams, and Hooker), to *override* Paul's contextual implications in 3:9, all the while claiming that the subjective reading is not clear. In my view, this all amounts ultimately to an insignificant challenge to that reading, which also lacks a degree of self-awareness.

28. Matlock briefly offers three "clear contextual indications" in favor of an objective reading: (1) 1:29, where — in the only explicit instance in the letter — a πιστ- term and Christ are coordinated,

and in an objective fashion; (2) Paul's use of πεποίθησις in 3:4 (and the cognate verb is used in v. 3); and (3) the motif of the knowledge of Christ, which has just been discussed extensively here: see "The Rhetoric of πίστις in Paul: Galatians 2.16, 3.22, Romans 3.22, and Philippians 3.9," *Journal for the Study of the New Testament* 30 (2007): 173-203, esp. 182-84. But, on closer examination, these arguments prove fragile.

(1) 1:29 refers to the fidelity of a Christian community to both Christ and the gospel (see vv. 27-28) in the face of opposition. Indeed, such heroism is a proof of the authenticity of the Christian reality. This fidelity is therefore an *explicitly post*-Christian activity. It is not really possible then to claim that it is also the condition for becoming a Christian, as Matlock's objective reading of 3:9 suggests. Fidelity is also, in the later location, a means to divine δικαιοσύνη — hardly the subject of the discussion in 1:29! It is true that suffering is present in both locations, but suffering is present throughout Philippians 1–3. And this prompts us to ask a more programmatic question: how are suffering and fidelity treated by Paul in this text?, at which point we arrive at Matlock's second and third arguments. However, the motif of "confidence" that Matlock points to in 3:3 and 3:4 as "indication" (2), is clearly part of the broader discourse of knowledge running through this text that he points to as his third contention, so this contention collapses into that final, third claim.

(3) Matlock is quite right to point to the discourse of knowing Christ in this text. But *he completely misunderstands its emphatic participatory qualification throughout*, thereby misunderstanding the critical implications for this debate as well — that everything Paul possesses as a Christian, and urges the Philippians to indwell as well, is mediated by indwelling the crucified and resurrected Christ. (The context of 1:29 is thick with participatory language as well, that he overlooks: see esp. 2:1-5!) So all talk of Christian "knowledge" in this text is obtained directly from Christ's own narrative and ontology, and this knowledge — "from God" — is utterly distinct from any knowledge rooted in the flesh — "of his/'my' own." Understood in the light of this basic argumentative and theological contrast, Christian fidelity must — like all Christian virtues — be obtained by indwelling the faithful Christ. To miss this point is simply to misunderstand Paul's entire argument. It is also to misconstrue the basic features of Christian knowing, as Paul describes that process here. Matlock does grasp that the "direction" of "knowing" Christ and the interpretation of πίστις in v. 9 must be correlated (183). But his brief remarks do not grasp or articulate this "direction" correctly — one, at the very least, that contains a critical turn against the passage's initial, anthropocentric "direction," but that he never describes. (Admittedly, Matlock's remarks here are very brief; he may well correct these shortcomings given more space to address this text at length. This having been said, his analyses generally do not attend to the overarching argumentative and theological questions — levels in the debate that require careful attention if localized suggestions are ultimately to have any plausibility. [His few remarks on this front have already been noted in chapter twenty — a brief, uncritical insertion of Justification theory.] My broader characterizations are of course supplied by part one, chapters one and three, corroborated particularly by part three, chapter ten.)

29. Dunn notes the apposite comments of several commentators — including himself — who recognize the fusion between "forensic" and "mystical" or "participatory" thinking here; these two strands "interlock," or some such ("Philippians 3," 479). But simply making this assertion does not resolve the massive underlying clash of conceptualities if Justification theory is affirmed. An apocalyptic reading of v. 9, however, *does* resolve this clash. And at this point Dunn's judgment becomes applicable to his own reading: "His righteousness from God and his being in Christ were two sides of the same coin, fully integrated in his own understanding of God's saving righteousness. Any attempt to play off one against another or to play up one over the other would almost certainly have been sharply contested by Paul himself" (484).

Williams tries to deal with this issue by comprehensively denying all participatory claims in context as reducible to imitation (see *Enemies*, 178-93) — hardly a convincing account of most of what Paul is saying here!

30. These relative judgments are still true, and in fact more true than the supposedly "objective" judgments. (I mean by "objective" *not* that these claims are true but that they are derived independently of the Christ event, in some prior epistemological location.)

31. Numerous commentators make this move: Fowl canvasses them (*Philippians*, 154, esp. n. 36).

32. It might also be worth emphasizing at this point that continuation in righteousness type one, after the arrival of righteousness type two, entails that type one transmutes into type three; the arrival of type two changes everything. And this is not unusual. Note how the arrival of the musket changed the role and implications of swordplay in human society. The activity itself was of course unchanged, but instead of remaining an important aspect of weapons training it became an aristocratic conceit, and then something confined largely to specialized athletics and fiction. To continue with swordplay after the arrival of the firearm was therefore actually to make a *new* statement and to undertake an activity with a different broader meaning. The changed setting necessitated this shift, despite the activity itself being held constant.

33. Richard B. Hays has consistently noted its importance, without ever undertaking a detailed analysis: see "Postscript: Further Reflections on Galatians 3," in *Conflict and Context: Hermeneutics in the Americas*, ed. Mark Lau Branson and C. René Padilla (Grand Rapids, Mich.: Eerdmans, 1986), 274-80; and "Christ Prays the Psalms: Paul's Use of an Early Christian Exegetical Convention," in *The Future of Christology: Essays in Honor of Leander E. Keck*, ed. A. J. Malherbe and W. A. Meeks (Minneapolis: Fortress, 1993), 122-36, reprinted with revisions as "Christ Prays the Psalms: Israel's Psalter as Matrix of Early Christology," in *The Conversion of the Imagination: Paul as Interpreter of Israel's Scripture* (Grand Rapids, Mich.: Eerdmans, 2005), 101-18.

Hooker pays some attention to this text, "ΠΙΣΤΙΣ ΧΡΙΣΤΟΥ," 335 (and she notes 2 Cor. 1:17-22 as well in a convoluted but suggestive analysis on 334-35). Koperski also notes its significance briefly: "The Meaning of *Pistis Christou*," 209; as does Dunn, "Once More, ΠΙΣΤΙΣ ΧΡΙΣΤΟΥ," in Hays, *Faith*, 259, n. 44.

Silva notes the possible importance of this text and makes an interesting concession on its basis ("Faith Versus Works of Law in Galatians"). He states first in the body of his essay that ". . . we cannot find even one *unambiguous* reference to the πίστις that belongs to Christ. To put it differently but more concretely, Paul never uses πιστεύω with Χριστός as its subject . . ." (231). This claim is part of one of his five principal arguments against the christological reading of πίστις Χριστοῦ (etc.; see 228-34). But he admits in n. 38 (232) that 2 Cor. 4:13 is such a possibility if Ps. 116:10 is understood messianically by Paul (introducing 2 Tim. 2:13 as well). Hence, this contention weakens the claim that "such language is not *typical* of Paul" (232). And this is an important concession, amounting in fact to a different, rather weaker argument (i.e., such usage is "untypical" as against "unattested"). Moreover, Justification advocates face their own challenges in relation to issues of typicality, since — as we have had frequent cause to note — Paul seldom uses Christ as an object of the verb πιστεύω.

A small minority of earlier readers of 2 Corinthians has also urged this reading: see H. L. Goudge, *The Second Epistle to the Corinthians* (London: Methuen, 1927), 41-42; and A. T. Hanson, *The Paradox of the Cross in the Thought of St Paul* (Sheffield: JSOT, 1987), 51-53.

34. See esp. Rom. 3:22; Gal. 2:16 (2x), 20; 3:22; and Phil. 3:9 — all treated earlier.

35. See (i.a.) Koperski, "The Meaning of *Pistis Christou*," 209 and 210 (noting on 209, n. 68, also Silva, Lambrecht, and Hay — a list that could be greatly lengthened).

36. The argument involves a hypothetical and ultimately untrue conditional claim: *if* Christ is faithful in Paul, *then* he would be the subject of the verb — but he isn't, so he isn't. Hence, *by virtue of the very structure of the argument*, the protasis cannot be supported; there can be no evidence for the truth of a conditional claim that leads to a counterfactual conclusion — evidence for a claim that is untrue or without content. Moreover, in methodological terms, it is clearly false to demand that all readings of substantive constructions in Paul have a corresponding verbal cognate, especially given the limited data that we have firsthand from Paul. Indeed, many of those making the demand here do not themselves apply it to other notions and readings elsewhere. Does Paul ever say that Christ "bled," thereby allowing us to speak of the blood of Christ? Is Christ ever the subject of the verb "to atone" (ἱλάσκεσθαι)? (And so on.) There is the added difficulty that this argument involves tacitly endorsing Justification theory when it equates the substantive construction with the putative notion of "believing in God/Christ" — the very construct being questioned. And this endorsement leads to an ignor-

ing of the wider semantic spread of the noun than its cognate verb (which means that a substantive phrase might very reasonably not correspond to a verbal one). It also means ignoring the reading that subjective advocates suggest is in play, thereby ignoring the parallel constructions that *are* offered to the disputed genitives, which are not cognate constructions but are nevertheless still legitimately introduced as parallels! So numerous good reasons exist for rejecting this contention, in addition to the possibility explored here that it is not in fact true.

37. Among the commentators, I have relied in what follows esp. on Victor P. Furnish, *II Corinthians: A New Translation with Introduction and Commentary,* AB 32A (New York: Doubleday, 1984), 252, 257-59, 285-87; Ralph P. Martin, *2 Corinthians,* WBC 40 (Waco, Texas: Word, 1986), 81-84, 89-90, 94-95; and Margaret E. Thrall, *A Critical and Exegetical Commentary on the Second Epistle to the Corinthians,* vol. 1, *Introduction and Commentary on II Corinthians I-VII* (London: T&T Clark International [Continuum], 2004 [1994]), 337-44 (this last an especially impressive and integrated account of this verse, but one that nevertheless stops short of the reading being urged here — and arguably a little inexplicably).

38. Several questions arise at this point that are also difficult to answer, but fortunately they do not affect my unfolding argument very much. Paul is, as usual, citing the LXX. But, beyond this, it is difficult to say whether he is conscious of the alternative versification and division found in the MT, and what significance this might have. To avoid unnecessary difficulties, then, the following argument will concentrate on the LXX version (i.e., MT/NRSV 116:10-19).

39. Paul also uses a unique citation formula — an arthrous participial construction (see τò γεγραμμένον above).

40. See BDAG 250; also Rom. 1:24; 2:1; 4:22; 13:5; 15:22; 2 Cor. 1:20; 5:9; Phil. 2:9 — a contraction of δι' ὅ hence essentially an accusative διά; see also BDF §§442, 12; 451, 5.

41. Such confusions seem to have led to various rather weak interpretative suggestions that need not detain us further. Furnish notes how Paul frequently correlates believing with *apostolic* proclamation (at least arguably) — see Rom. 10:14-17; Gal. 3:2, 5; 1 Thess. 2:2, etc. (*II Corinthians,* 258). However, most of this evidence *reverses* the causality that Paul seems to be endorsing in 2 Cor. 4:13-14, where believing leads *to* speaking; these alternative texts speak of apostolic preaching leading *to* believing. So this evidence actually exacerbates the difficulty! He goes on to note correctly that Paul is referring here, as in 1 Thess. 2:2, to "[c]ourage to speak out despite adversity" (285), but he has not provided interpretations of "believing" and the quotation of Ps. 115:1 that actually deliver this notion.

Thrall explores a range of solutions. She considers first whether this text simply "provides scriptural warrant for Paul's assertion that because he believes the gospel he proclaims it," in which case "the identity of the speaker in the psalm is of no interest" (*II Corinthians,* 340). However, the identity of the speaker *is* foregrounded, because Paul shares "the same spirit of fidelity" with him (2 Cor. 4:13). This explanation leaves us puzzled over the role of the psalm and the psalmist in Paul's argument. It is also a largely unheralded and unattested claim in context. In addition, it supplies unstated qualifications for the notion of belief — specifically, that this "belief" *is* belief in the apostolic gospel. And Paul himself never articulates this notion in these terms elsewhere. His apostolic "belief" is a "call" to the "gospel." Presumably, he then speaks, but "belief" language occurs through and at the end of this process, not at its inception: see esp. 1 Cor. 15:1-11; Gal. 1:10-24; 2:7-9.

Ultimately, Thrall is "compelled to the conclusion that . . . Psalm 115 (LXX) . . . was in Paul's mind as a significant exposition of the suffering righteous man, and so as relevant to his own situation . . ." (341). Thus, she ends up with the fuller narrative reading that I am advocating here.

But to halt interpretation at *this* point does not explain why the righteous sufferer is relevant to Paul, grounding the assertions and connections that he makes to the Corinthians in turn; it is also not sensitive to the further clues supplied by the context of 2 Cor. 4:13, which are so strongly christocentric; and no cogent reason is thereby provided for denying a further identification — as Hanson suggested — of the righteous sufferer with Christ. (Perhaps Thrall opens the door — with the utmost caution and delicacy — to this possibility, conceding that the speaker of the psalm might be "representative of the righteous sufferer," and "[i]n this case the psalmist would prefigure, as well as predict, the sufferings of Christ" [340]. She seems nervous, however, about explicitly conceding the actual presence of Christ in relation to the psalm.)

These difficulties probably explain why various other commentators begin new subsections at this point, or speak of "loose connections" or traditional material or some such. So Furnish notes — and dismisses — Windisch's suggestion in these terms, which is clearly a counsel of despair (*II Corinthians*, 285).

Martin also makes much of traditional formulations in v. 14, but this does not solve any difficulties in v. 13.

There he also posits "the opening of a new section" (*2 Corinthians*, 89-90), but a christological reading again makes this unnecessary, facilitating a reading in direct continuity with vv. 12 and 13 and the rest of the text's context.

42. It could be objected at this point that this is not unusual for Paul, and so we should not press on to any deeper level of putative coherence. However, any such assertion here is invalid, on two principal grounds. First, Paul is often accused of citing texts unfairly, perhaps because he is insensitive to their original context, or shifts their wording, or some such. But he invariably (at least arguably) uses them coherently in his own contingent settings. Sustaining this objection then requires Paul to go to the trouble of citing a *meaningless* quotation, which is *not* his usual practice. To be sure, this possibility cannot be excluded at the outset, but, second, if a meaning*ful* account of this citation can be given, then this objection is falsified *in fact*. And it would be incoherent to assert that a quotation is incoherent and ought to be treated as such when a coherent — albeit alternative — construal has been presented. This is consequently an explanation of last resort and we will not need to use it.

43. As noted among the commentators especially by Thrall, *II Corinthians*, 329-31, 340-41. Useful background information on this topos (oriented toward Mark) is given by Joel Marcus in *The Way of the Lord: Christological Exegesis of the Old Testament in the Gospel of Mark* (Louisville, Ky.: Westminster John Knox, 1992), 172-86. As L. Ruppert originally noted, the this-worldly expectations of vindication by the protagonist of the "psalms of the righteous sufferer" have transmuted here typically into eschatological expectations: see Wis. 2:12-20; 5:1-7; *4 Ezra*; *2 Baruch* (cited by Marcus, *The Way of the Lord*, 177, in dependence on Ruppert, *Jesus als der leidende Gerechte? Der Weg Jesu im Lichte eines alt- und zwischentestamentlichen Motivs* [Stuttgart: Katholisches Bibelwerk, 1972], esp. 42-43).

44. As I have pointed out earlier in this book and elsewhere (principally in *The Quest for Paul's Gospel: A Suggested Strategy* [London: T&T Clark International (Continuum), 2005], 189-90), use of the translation equivalent "faith" is dangerous for all sorts of reasons. So, if it is possible, use of an alternative is usually better. Moreover, "belief/believing" is certainly appropriate here, especially in view of the participle of knowledge that coordinates v. 14 with v. 13. However, a case could also be made for "trust." That the psalmist believes in God's personal care for him despite present adversity suggests that the particular beliefs in question amount to "trust." But since "trust" automatically involves various beliefs (as attested in fact by v. 14), the broader point of this investigation remains valid irrespective of which translation equivalent we ultimately endorse — that Christ "trusts" entails directly and automatically that he also "believes."

45. Martin asks appositely: "What has led Paul to join his witness to that of the psalmist?" (*2 Corinthians*, 89).

46. It is not a ludicrous suggestion, but it is unlikely given what we know of Paul's anthropology from elsewhere, not to mention how he actually distinguishes between his identity and the psalmist's clearly in this text. Paul is not characterizing himself here as an Elijah redivivus, on analogy to Mark 8:28 (i.e., "I *am* the psalmist . . .")! See Christine E. Joynes, "The Returned Elijah? John the Baptist's Angelic Identity in the Gospel of Mark," *Scottish Journal of Theology* 58 (2005): 455-67.

47. It needs to be emphasized that I am using the notion of "imitation" in a "thin" sense here, with no theological overtones, to denote a mere copying of someone else.

48. Although some interpreters do seem — rather remarkably — to resist this implication and correlation: see (i.a.) Gordon D. Fee, *God's Empowering Presence: The Holy Spirit in the Letters of Paul* (Peabody, Mass.: Hendrickson, 1994), esp. 323-24; also *Pauline Christology: An Exegetical-Theological*

Study (Peabody, Mass.: Hendrickson, 2007), esp. 223-26 (the latter discussing the Πίστις Ἰησοῦ Χριστοῦ phrase and issue in relation specifically to Gal. 2:16 and 20, but by extension with reference to 2 Cor. 4:13, where Fee does not detect Christology; he discusses 2 Corinthians in 160-206).

49. Furnish notes this opinion by Hughes and Bultmann, who cite 1 Cor. 4:21 and Gal. 6:1 (*II Corinthians*, 258), and Thrall toys with it as well (*II Corinthians*, 338-39). These last two texts are intriguing. Both speak of "a/the spirit of gentleness" (πνεύματι [τε] πραΰτητος) and hence arguably supply a generic meaning for "spirit" in terms of "disposition" or some such. However, these texts are not decisive for 2 Cor. 4:13. They do not function in the broader setting of a parallel scriptural figure and narrative, linking Paul with those. Moreover, both these exhortations are arguably grounded in the Spirit of Christ in any case, strengthening that identification here: see Gal. 5:22-23!; and Fee, *God's Empowering Presence*, 118-21 (1 Cor. 4:18-21), 458-64 (Gal. 6:1-3). (Fee sees Gal. 6:1 as decisive for 1 Cor. 4:21, and the contextual indications as especially strong for the former text since it occurs in "a context where πνεῦμα has always and only referred to the Holy Spirit" [462].) So Furnish is also right to reject this essentially insipid suggestion, affirming the presence of the Spirit in 2 Cor. 4:13 and commenting correctly that this "is in accord with what Paul has written earlier about the Spirit's work (3:3, 6, 8, 17, 18), and with what he will shortly reiterate about the Spirit's presence (5:5; see 1:22)" (*II Corinthians*, 286). (See more on this contextual argument below in relation to Fee.)

For mimetic texts and language elsewhere in Paul, see μιμητής in 1 Cor. 4:16; 11:1; Phil. 3:17; 1 Thess. 1:6; 2:14; see also Eph. 5:1, and elsewhere in the New Testament only Heb. 6:12; see also ὑπόκρισις and πρόσωπον in Gal. 2:11-14.

50. See esp. Susan G. Eastman, *Recovering Paul's Mother Tongue: Language and Theology in Galatians* (Grand Rapids, Mich.: Eerdmans, 2007). Eastman is a significant correction of the important but rather neglected analysis of E. Castelli, *Imitating Paul: A Discourse of Power* (Louisville, Ky.: Westminster John Knox, 1991), which is perceptive but presuppositionally straitened.

51. Fee supplies four arguments, the first two of which seem especially cogent (*God's Empowering Presence*, 323-24). He observes (1) that the participle ἔχοντες has been a repeated and important feature of Paul's text from 3:4, occurring also in 3:12, 4:1, and 4:7. In each case it denotes a continuation, and so 4:13 should probably be read in the same way, pointing thereby to Paul's extensive earlier emphases on pneumatology (see esp. 3:3, 6, 8, 17 [2x], 18), and his immediate earlier emphasis on participation in the death and life of Christ. Given these preceding emphases "it is difficult to imagine that the word should now occur in some lesser sense as 'attitude' or 'disposition,' since the Spirit has been the crucial matter right along" (323). Moreover, (2) he points out — in the argument I note here in the text — that the addition of the word "spirit" to the phrase is redundant if all Paul intended was to speak of having the same "faith" as the psalmist; he seems to intend, rather, to speak precisely of some sharing of the same *spirit* of faithfulness (323). These arguments are also strengthened by our earlier suspicions of the contention that the phrase "a spirit of X . . ." in Paul denotes a mere disposition. Pneumatology is elsewhere almost certainly in view in this phrase, viz., in 1 Cor. 4:21 and Gal. 6:1.

52. See (i.a.) Romans 6; Phil. 3:7-17.

53. See "Christ Prays the Psalms."

54. As already noted, Hanson has urged this reading, although not in detail (see *Paradox*, 51-53; and so Thrall is well aware of it; *II Corinthians*, 340); Hanson also cites Goudge, *Second Corinthians*, 41-42.

55. Some important witnesses omit this — principally 𝔓⁴⁶ and B — which would accord with usage throughout the chapter (see vv. 10, 11, and 14b), so I incline toward its correctness. However, not much turns on this.

56. Less impressive witnesses supply διά with the genitive here instead of σύν — principally ℵ², D¹, and Ψ. The minority reading disturbs the apparent sense of Paul's argument, which is christologically inclusive rather than instrumental at this point (not that instrumentality is absent from inclusion). It also represents a shift from less attested usage to something recognizably Pauline. So this variant looks secondary.

57. It is not easy to say exactly how the critical participle εἰδότες in v. 14 is functioning in grammatical terms, but it seems best to view ἔχοντες and εἰδότες as parallel, and both consequently seem to

be adverbial and essentially causal. That is, they both supply reasons for the main actions of the sentence — for believing certain things, and so speaking. Thrall suggests that ἔχοντες in v. 13 is causal, following Plummer and Furnish (*II Corinthians*, 338).

58. In doing so, as Thrall notes (*II Corinthians*, 343-44), God also ends up presenting his resurrected Son, Jesus, Paul, and the converted Corinthians to himself, but this is not *that* awkward for Paul; see 1 Cor. 15:24-28, where a slightly different although equally complex process is in view; see also Eph. 5:26-27, where Christ presents his bride to himself.

59. This point has already been noted in relation to Rom. 3:26 in part four, chapter sixteen: see esp. Leander Keck, "Jesus in Romans," *Journal of Biblical Literature* 108 (1989): 443-60.

60. Not all commentators have emphasized the eschatological sense of v. 14 and the verb παραστήσει, but this seems difficult to deny given the double instance of resurrection language that precedes it, supported by its future tense and its emphatic σύν language; see also 1 Thess. 4:14, 17. These questions are well canvassed by Thrall, *II Corinthians*, 343-44.

61. Given more space, the Jewish constituents of these stories that have been reconfigured by the Christ event could be discussed further, but this is not the place for that analysis; for some beginnings see *Quest*, 57-62, 69-94; and *one* narrative element here has already received some attention — the story of kingly enthronement: see esp. part four, chapter seventeen.

62. And this soteriology is of course especially apparent in the alternative system of salvation sketched in part one, chapter three, on the basis largely of Romans 5-8.

63. See also further instances of the noun in 1:24 (2x); 8:7; 10:15; and 13:5 (that is, in addition to 4:13 and 5:7; note that the verb does not occur outside 4:13); and the adjective in 1:18 and 6:15; the alpha-privative in 4:4; 6:14 and 15.

64. See esp. part four, chapter seventeen, and part five, chapter twenty.

65. See, e.g., Stephen Westerholm, *Perspectives Old and New on Paul* (Grand Rapids, Mich.: Eerdmans 2004), 353-61.

66. It is of course at this point that the narrative departs from standard Jewish lines. On Jewish and Christian discourses concerning idolatry, see John M. G. Barclay, "The Politics of Contempt: Judeans and Egyptians in Josephus' *Against Apion*," in *Negotiating Diaspora: Jewish Strategies in the Roman Empire*, ed. John M. G. Barclay (London: T&T Clark, 2004), 109-27; also Joel Marcus's perceptive study, "Idolatry in the New Testament," *Interpretation* 60 (2006): 152-64. A subtle exploration of the navigation of idolatry by Paul in Corinth is David Horrell, *The Social Ethos of the Corinthian Correspondence: Interests and Ideology from 1 Corinthians to 1 Clement* (Edinburgh: T&T Clark, 1996).

67. There are no grounds for preferring a conditional or causal reading of the participle in 1:13 over other readings, whether in terms of attendant circumstance or mediation. The designation of Christians as τοὺς πιστεύοντας in 1:19 is also quite isolated and hence indeterminable.

68. The alpha-privative is also an apparent designation for non-Christians: see 1 Cor. 6:6; 7:12, 13, 14 (2x), 15; 10:27; 14:22 (2x), 23, 24; 2 Cor. 4:4; 6:14, 15 (where it can oppose the cognate participle: see 1 Cor. 14:22). God is of course trustworthy as well: see 1 Cor. 1:9; 10:13; 2 Cor. 1:18; 1 Thess. 5:24.

69. And perhaps it is echoed by Philippians 1:29 that uses the cognate verb. However, arguably here Paul is eliding one part of a twofold construction in vv. 27-29 — namely, τὸ εὐαγγέλιον τοῦ Χριστοῦ. He elides "Christ" in v. 27b and "gospel" in v. 29, the pronoun being attracted to the gender of the stated antecedent. Admittedly, a reference to Christ is probably easier, but the alternative ought at least to be considered.

70. The fidelity of the Thessalonians is an important theme in that letter, and is one of, if not *the* cause for Paul's thankfulness and original inquiries: see esp. 1 Thess. 3:2, 5, 6, 7, 10; 5:8; see also 2 Thess. 1:3, 4, 11. First Thessalonians 1:3 is, however, arguably a fully arthrous, *objective* genitive construction! See μνημονεύοντες ὑμῶν τοῦ ἔργου τῆς πίστεως καὶ τοῦ κόπου τῆς ἀγάπης καὶ ὑπομονῆς τῆς ἐλπίδος τοῦ κυρίου ἡμῶν Ἰησοῦ Χριστοῦ ἔμπροσθεν τοῦ θεοῦ καὶ πατρὸς ἡμῶν.

71. The evidence in Colossians is intriguing. The noun also occurs in 1:23 and 2:7 and 12, while the cognate verb does not occur at all. Colossians 2:12 seems to be a reference to the fidelity of God resurrecting Christ, although this phrase echoes the christologically oriented phrases in Rom. 3:25, Gal. 3:23-26, and Phil. 3:9. The solitary arthrous instances in Col. 1:23 and 2:7 are characterized by

metaphors of construction, immovability, and rootedness, as is 2:5. Hence, a participatory explanation of this material (excepting 2:12) certainly seems possible. And 2:7 may even require this; it is difficult for human faith *to establish* the Colossian Christians in context, which is the sense required by the passive perfect participle βεβαιούμενοι. Conversely, they could be established by means of or in the faithful one, Christ — a reading that also continues the implications of the preceding clause. Whether this is probable over against other construals, however, would take much more detailed inquiry to decide — something that is not really necessary at this point.

72. And we have not considered the possibility that Paul's thinking may not be entirely consistent; certainly, some things could be said here, but that is not really necessary at this point in our discussion.

Index of Authors

Index of Scripture and Other Ancient Literature